The Western Perspective

A History of Civilization in the West

SEPTENTRIO
AMERICÆ PARS Estotilād
Laboratoris terra
DROGEO
FRETUM DAVIS
GROENLANDIÆ PARS
Serelingers
MARE CONGE
Ponit hoc loco Gerardus Mercator ut & alij terram Polarem uti vocat; at nos qui ex nostratum navigationibus certi sumus, hic nullam esse terram, siquidem ultra 81. gradum navigarunt. Anno 95. et 1596.
Frislandt
ISLAND
HYPERBOREUS OCEANUS
Circulus Arcticus
DEUCALEDONIUS OCEANUS
Farræ insulæ
Hitland al. Schotland
Hebrides Insl. 43.
HIBERNIA
SCOTIA
OCEANUS GERMANICUS
OCCIDENS
ATLANTICUS OCEANUS
OOST ZEE SVEVICUM
Finnicus sinus
Bodicus Sinus
Polonia
Hungaria
Bavaria
CANTABRICUS OCEANUS
HISPANIA
Galicia
Castilia
Arragonia
Valentia
Andaluzia
Estremadura
Mare Gallicum
Balearides ins.
Mare Ibericum
MARE
Mare Tyrrhenum et Inferum
Golfo di Venetia, olim Adriaticum et Superum mare
Sicilia
Canariæ I.
BARBARIA
AFRICÆ PARS
Miliaria Germanica. Duytsche Mylen.
10 20 30 40 50 60 70 80 90 100 110 120
MEDI
MERI

Philip V. Cannistraro
Queens College, The City University of New York

John J. Reich
Syracuse University in Florence, Italy

The Western Perspective

A History of Civilization in the West

Harcourt Brace College Publishers

Fort Worth Philadelphia San Diego New York Orlando Austin San Antonio
Toronto Montreal London Sydney Tokyo

Publisher Earl McPeek
Acquisitions Editor David Tatom
Product Manager Steve Drummond
Project Editor Laura J. Hanna
Art Director Garry Harman
Production Manager Kathleen Ferguson

Cover Credit *King and Queen* by Henry Moore (shown here with Florence, Italy, in the background). The Henry Moore Foundation.

Address for Orders: Harcourt Brace College Publishers, 6277 Sea Harbor Drive, Orlando, FL 32887-6777. 1-800-782-4479

Address for Editorial Correspondence: Harcourt Brace College Publishers, 301 Commerce Street, Suite 3700, Fort Worth, TX 76102

Web site address: http://www.hbcollege.com

Harcourt Brace College Publishers will provide complimentary supplements or supplement packages to those adopters qualified under our adoption policy. Please contact your sales representative to learn how you qualify. If as an adopter or potential user you receive supplements you do not need, please return them to your sales representative or send them to: Attn: Returns Department, Troy Warehouse, 465 South Lincoln Drive, Troy, MO 63379.

ISBN: 0-03-045643-6

Library of Congress Catalog Card Number: 98-72301

Printed in the United States of America

9 0 1 2 3 4 5 6 7 048 9 8 7 6 5 4 3 2

Dedicated to our Students

Formats

To accommodate teachers at institutions with different versions of Western Civilization courses, this book has been produced in seven different formats.

A complete, one-volume edition containing the entire text

Volume I: To 1715

Volume II: Since 1500

Volume A: To 1500

Volume B: 1300–1815

Volume C: 1789–Present

Alternate Volume: Since the Renaissance

About the Authors

PHILIP V. CANNISTRARO. Born in New York City, Philip V. Cannistraro is an authority on modern Italian history and the Italian American experience. He studied in both the undergraduate and graduate programs at New York University and is now Distinguished Professor at Queens College and at the Graduate School, the City University of New York. Professor Cannistraro serves on the boards of several journals and is editor of *The Italian American Review.* He has written or edited a number of books, including *Civilizations of the World* (with R. Greaves, R. Murphey, and R. Zaller, 3rd ed., 1997), *La fabbrica del consenso: Fascismo e mass media* (1975), *Fascismo, Chiesa e Emigrazione* (with G. Rosoli, 1979), *Historical Dictionary of Fascist Italy* (1981), and *Il Duce's Other Woman,* a biography of Margherita Sarfatti (with B. Sullivan, 1993).

JOHN J. REICH. A native of England, John Reich was trained as a classical archaeologist and did both his undergraduate and graduate work at the University of Manchester. He is an authority on Minoan civilization, pre-Roman Italy, and music. Professor Reich is associated with the Syracuse University study program in Florence, Italy. Reich lectures frequently in Europe and the United States on history, art, and the humanities and is the author of many scholarly articles and several books, including *Italy Before Rome* (1979) and the widely acclaimed *Culture and Values* (with Lawrence S. Cunningham, Harcourt Brace, 4th ed., 1998). He lives in a Medieval castle in the hilltop town of Panzano in Chianti in Italy.

Table of Contents

PART V The Early Modern World 488

Documents on History

Perspectives on History

Public Figures/Private Lives

Tables and Graphs

Maps

Acknowledgments

This project began what seems like centuries ago, when Ted Buchholz, now President of Harcourt Brace College Publishers, asked us to write what has evolved into *The Western Perspective*. Since then he exhibited unfailing faith in our ability to carry this project to conclusion and gave us the full support of Harcourt Brace's extensive publishing resources. Immediately after we agreed to undertake the book, we had the good fortune of working under the close direction of David Tatom, senior editor for history, who over many years worked with us on the planning and development of the book, bolstered our spirits, and encouraged our work at every turn. Over the last several years, Kristie L. Kelly has been our developmental editor, in which capacity she has helped to put the manuscript into final form and skillfully managed the details of what became an increasingly complex undertaking. Laura Hanna moved the book through the last stages of creation as senior project editor; Kathy Ferguson and Garry Harman served as production manager and art director. Elsa Peterson was the photo researcher.

A number of friends and colleagues have contributed to this book in many important ways, and we wish especially to thank the following individuals: Eric D. Brose, Robert S. Browning, H. James Burgwyn, Elisheva Carlebach, Peter Carravetta, Jennifer Cook, Patricia A. Cooper, Alexander DeGrand, Spencer DiScala, Karen Dubno, Monte Finkelstein, Elisabeth Giansiracusa, Charles L. Killinger, Julie Mostov, David Nasaw, Nunzio Pernicone, Ben Reich, Cecil O. Smith, Donald F. Stevens, David Syrett, Elena Frangakis-Syrett, Frank Warren, and M. Hratch Zadoian.

In addition, we are indebted to our colleagues who generously shared with us their wealth of experience and knowledge. Our sincere thanks to the following instructors:

Phillip Adler, East Carolina State University
Gerald Anderson, North Dakota State University
Jay P. Anglin, University of Southern Mississippi
Martin Arbagi, Wright State
Patrick Armstrong, Jefferson State Community College
Frank Baglione, Tallahassee Community College
Carol Bargeron, Louisiana State University
Ed Beemon, Middle Tennessee State University
Alan Beyerden, Ohio State University
Lawrence Blacklund, Montgomery County Community College
Stephen Blumm, Montgomery County Community College
Melissa Bokovoy, University of New Mexico
Paul Bookbinder, University of Massachusetts at Boston
Darwin Bostick, Old Dominion University
James Brink, Texas Tech University
Daniel P. Brown, Moorpark College
Tom Bryan, Alvin Community College
Gary Burbridge, Grand Rapids Community College
Thomas Burns, Emory University
Elizabeth Carney, Clemson University
Lamar Cecil, University of North Carolina at Chapel Hill
Thomas Christofferson, California State University at Northridge
Orazio Ciccarelli, University of Southern Mississippi
Franz Coetzee, Yale University
Fred Colvin, Middle Tennessee State University
William Connell, Rutgers University
John Contreni, Purdue University
Jessica Coope, University of Nebraska
Marc Cooper, Southwest Missouri State University

Frederick M. Crawford, Middle Tennessee State University
Gary Cross, Pennsylvania State University
Paige Cubbison, Miami Dade Community College
Nancy Curtin, Fordham University
Maribel Dietz, Louisiana State University
Michael Doyle, Ocean Community College
Charles Endress, Angelo State
Thomas Fabiano, Monroe Community College
Gary Ferngren, Oregon State
Monte Finkelstein, Tallahassee Community College
Edward W. Fox, Cornell University
Carl Frasure, University of Alaska
Elizabeth Furdell, University of North Florida
Alan Galpern, University of Pittsburgh
Richard Golden, Clemson University
Seella Gomezdelcampo, Roane State Community College
Karen Gould
David Gross, University of Colorado at Boulder
Alan Grubb, Clemson University
James D. Hardy, Louisiana State University
Jeanne Harrie, California State University at Bakersfield
Stephen Hauser, Marquette University
Peter Hayes, Northwestern University
Neil Hayman, San Diego State University
Robert Houston, University of the South
Bill Hughes, Essex Community College
Susan Hult, Houston Community College
Laura Hunt, University of Dayton
Frances Kelleher, Grand Valley State University
George Kelner, Rhode Island College
Susan Kent, University of Colorado at Boulder
Charles Killinger III, Valencia Community College
Lloyd Kramer, University of North Carolina at Chapel Hill
Thomas Kselman, University of Notre Dame
David Large, Montana State University
Frederick Lauritsen, Eastern Washington University
Ron Lesko, Suffolk Community College
Mary Ann Lizondo, Northern Virginia Community College
Paul Lockhart, Wright State
Gary Long, Methodist College
Leo Loubere, SUNY at Buffalo
Gladys Luster, John C. Calhoun College
David MacDonald, Illinois State University
Paul Maier, Western Michigan University
James Martin, Campbell University
William Mathews, Ohio State University
John Matzko, Bob Jones University
John McFarland, Sierra College
James Mini, Montgomery County Community College
Thomas Mockaitis, DePaul
Marjorie Morgan, Southern Illinois University
Rex Morrow, Trident Technical College
Pierce Mullens, Missouri State University
Francis J. Murphy, Boston College
Martha Newman, University of Texas at Austin
Bill Olsen, Marist College
Fred Olsen, Northern Virginia Community College
Thomas Ott, University of North Alabama
Neil Pease, University of Wisconsin at Milwaukee
Jack Pesda, Camden County Community College
John Pesda, Camden County College
Donald Pryce, University of South Dakota
Herman Rebel, University of Arizona
Marlette Rebhorn, Austin Community College - Rio Grande Campus
Larry Rotge, Slippery Rock University
John Rothney, Ohio State University
Jose Sanches, St. Louis University
Lura Scales, Hinds Community College
Robert G. Schafer, University of Michigan at Flint

Ezel Kural Shaw, California State University at Northridge

Susan Shoemaker, University of Delaware

Ronald Smith, Arizona State University

Eileen Soldwedel, Edmonds Community College

William Stiebing, University of New Orleans

David Tait, Oklahoma State University

Maxine Taylor, Northwestern State University

Janet TeBrake, University of Maine

David Tengwall, Anne Arundel Community College

Jack Thacker, Western Kentucky University

Richard Todd, Wichita State University

Spenser Tucker, Texas Christian University

Thomas Turley, Santa Clara University

Jeffry von Arx, Georgetown University

L. J. Worley, University of Washington

Finally, the authors would like to thank each other: their long friendship over many years not only survived the close and constant working together on this project, but actually strengthened. All collaborations should be this good.

Preface

To vary a cliche, each generation rewrites the history textbooks. As a result, there are today about a dozen books on the market that are suitable for use as texts in college-level Western Civilization courses.

Why, then, still another one?

We have each taught Western Civilization or similar courses at large universities for more than 25 years and, like countless colleagues, have wished for a book that we felt met the needs of our students as well as our own requirements as teachers. Existing books run the full range, from traditional works that emphasize political, diplomatic, and military history and look at developments largely from the point of view of leaders and élites, to more recent books that emphasize one approach, particularly social history, and try to present historical change as experienced by ordinary people.

Traditional treatments reinforce the views of earlier generations but do not stress the trends in more recent scholarship, while the new texts can leave students confused about how history changes and civilizations evolve. Another characteristic in recent textbook writing has been the tendency to underrate students and to "unclutter" the picture by omitting the kind of detail that is the guts of history. The stress on analysis and pattern, rather than on facts, of necessity emphasizes broad economic and social forces to the exclusion of human agency and, yes, even of historical accident.

We believe the best approach is one that conveys the full range of human experience and that considers both the material processes and spiritual values of historical development. We have sought to achieve a genuine balance between narrative and analysis. The writing of history at its best has always been the ability to tell a story—by which we mean a narrative of the record of human struggle and achievement, of conflict and community, of cultural diversity and social change. It is not always an easy or pleasant story to relate, but it should be told as much as possible as it unfolded rather than as we would have wanted it to. Moreover, history without detail may leave students bored and deprive them of the kind of vivid images that give life and breath to the story. Abstract analysis, while important to critical thinking, is not a substitute for factual knowledge. Both are necessary to our understanding of history and vital to navigating the ever more complex world in which we live.

Our Structural Design. A textbook is a learning and a teaching tool and should reflect the realities of the classroom. It occurred to us early on that our text should correspond to the needs and interests of today's teachers. A major case in point is the fact that the 30 to 35 chapters into which most books are divided do not conform to the number of class sessions usually available to the instructor. As teachers we must constantly think about how to break up and present material in topics that can be handled in one class period and that students can digest. This means, inevitably, dividing the conventional, large textbook chapters into smaller units.

To correct this longstanding pedagogical problem, we have given our book a unique—although not a startlingly different—structure by arranging the story of Western Civilization in 95 smaller "Topics," corresponding to the approximate number of class sessions in an academic year. Most of our Topics are appropriate for a single class period.

At first glance instructors might assume that this structural design artificially separates material that should be presented in an "integrated" manner. But a closer look will reveal that we have simply divided the overly large chapters of conventional texts into logical, teachable units. The result provides the instructor with a great deal more flexibility in terms of assigning student reading, syllabus design, and in-class analysis. We have also taken pains to provide students with ways to connect these smaller topics in the larger stream of historical narrative as well as with methods to focus on important themes. Furthermore, we grouped the 95 topics into eight broad chronological "Parts," corresponding to the traditional divisions of Western history. Each Part is introduced by an essay discussing the broad trends and patterns that characterize the period.

Our approach has been to provide full coverage of all major aspects of historical experience. In addition to the political, diplomatic, and military events of the more traditional texts, each Part contains Topics that deal individually with social, economic, cultural, and intellectual history. Our treatment of cultural history is unusually rich, including a full discussion of art and music. We have also written Topics that deal fully with regions that are generally neglected or given only brief mention, such as eastern and southern Europe, and we have included topics that examine economic and technological developments in depth. Our discussion of social trends seeks to offer students an understanding of daily life and the broad patterns of social change, as well as of the status of slaves, Jews, and other ethnic, religious, or sexual minorities. We have, of course, tried to incorporate the most recent findings from the burgeoning world of women's history into our narrative.

The title of our book, *The Western Perspective*, reflects the fact that while our focus is the Western experience, we believe it is important to place that experience in the wider context of world history. We therefore discuss developments in Africa, Asia, the Americas, and the Pacific when they had an impact on, or were affected by, Western history.

Special Features. In addition to the overall structure of our book, we have designed a number of innovative special features that we believe lend both deeper insight and immediacy to the narrative.

Each Part contains a number of essays called "Perspectives on History," written especially for this book by leading experts in the field. These essays furnish students with a sense of the clash of scholarly opinion about particular subjects, such as the French Revolution and Fascism, or shed special light on a particularly interesting and unusual aspect of historical experience, such as the status of women in ancient Mesopotamia or the earliest Africans in Europe.

Each Part also contains sections entitled "Public Figures and Private Lives." These consist of portraits of the private and public lives of couples in which one or both partners played an influential part in culture, society, or politics. Such sketches serve a number of useful purposes: by relating larger trends to individuals, they give students immediate and easily understandable insight into an important era or development; they provide specific examples of the different roles of, and the interaction between, men and women in various historical periods, and suggest the impact of gender on social and private lives.

Most texts print short quotations from primary sources to add flavor to the narrative. Our "Documents on History" sections are designed with a specific pedagogical purpose in mind. Each one of these document sections consists of several pages that provide a variety of readings from primary sources on a selected issue. In this way students are able to gain a serious, in-depth insight into historical method, to analyze conflicting documents, and to engage in genuine class discussion.

Each of our 95 Topics begins with an overview, which provides a brief look at the major themes and subjects to be discussed. Where appropriate, the Topics contain one or more boxes of "Significant Dates" of principal events. Each Topic ends with a conclusion, set off from the text, a series of questions for further study, and an up-to-date bibliography.

To make this book a vivid visual experience, it has been designed as a full color production, with hundreds of illustrations and maps, as well as charts and tables.

Test Manual to accompany *The Western Perspective* Marlette Rebhorn Austin Community College

This test bank provides the instructor with a variety of question styles. In addition to multiple choice questions, there are identification questions, essay questions, and book report questions. Free to instructors.

Computerized Test Banks Available in four formats
IBM® 5.25″ IBM® 3.50″ Macintosh® MS Windows®

Study Guide to accompany *The Western Perspective* Gerald Anderson North Dakota State University

This student guide includes a brief overview of each Topic, as well as identifications, geographical identifications, map exercises, timeline questions, short-answer exercises, and essay questions.

Computerized Study Guide This new student supplement is designed specifically to accompany *The Western Perspective*. It offers students, at an affordable price, a variety of interactive exercises tied to the chapter organization of the text. Free preview for instructors. Available in Windows® format from Educational Software Concepts, Inc. To order, or for more information, call toll free 1-800-748-7734.

Instructor's Manual to accompany *The Western Perspective* This manual includes a summary of chapter topics, lecture notes, suggested readings, and discussion questions which will spark debate among your students.

Overhead Transparency Package A comprehensive collection of 183 full color acetates including 128 maps, 35 transparencies of major works of art, tables, and charts.

Western Civilization Videos/Films for the Humanities Choose from a wide variety of videos from the extensive Films for the Humanities history catalog. Contact your local Harcourt Brace sales representative for a complete listing of available videos. Adoption requirements apply.

Arts & Entertainment History Videos Many outstanding selections are available from the Arts & Entertainment video library which include selections from A & E's extensive *Biography* collection. Contact your local Harcourt Brace sales representative for a complete listing of available videos. Adoption requirements apply.

PBS Video Series Several outstanding videos are available from the PBS video series written and narrated by David Macauley. Contact your local Harcourt Brace sales representative for a complete listing of available videos. Adoption requirements apply.

The Western Civilization Videodisc This disc provides the instructor with a wide-ranging resource, organized in a unique, flexible format, which makes it easy to prepare illustrated lectures and tailor-made presentations. Adoption requirements apply.

Harcourt Brace's *The Western Perspective Web Site* This Web Site provides access to many online resources for instructors and students.

Students have access to topic summaries, primary sources, annotated Internet links relevant to each topic, links to topic-relevant search engines, Web-based exercises, online practice quizzes, and a bulletin board that allows students taking the course to communicate with each other.

Instructors have access to all student material plus overhead transparencies, answers to the Web-based exercises, a downloadable computerized test bank with answer key, lecture outlines, and a mail list for instructors using *The Western Perspective* to correspond with each other.

Start your tour with our home page at www.hbcollege.com.

The Western Perspective

A History of Civilization in the West

PART I

THE ANCIENT WORLD

The long, slow evolution of modern humans began some 4 million years ago. It took until around 35 thousand years ago for our common ancestor, *Homo sapiens sapiens*, to appear. The first human groups lived on the move, by hunting and gathering, and only with the discovery of farming techniques around 8000 B.C. did the first settled communities begin to develop.

The people of this Neolithic Age invented weaving and the manufacture of pottery. They built houses and lived together in towns. Toward the end of the Neolithic period, around 3500 B.C., the Sumerians of Mesopotamia discovered how to smelt and work with metal, and—a giant step forward in the development of civilization—devised a system of writing. The ability to preserve human thought in permanent form marks the real beginning of recorded history.

River valleys provided the setting for the first flourishing civilizations. Shortly after the Sumerians' inventions, writing and metalworking appeared in the cultures of the Yellow River valley in China and the Indus valley in India. The new skills also spread to Egypt, where the most enduring of all ancient civilizations was developing in the valley of the River Nile.

Mesopotamia, the region between the rivers Tigris and Euphrates, saw the rise and fall of successive peoples, among them the Sumerians, the Babylonians, and the Assyrians. The most important cities had their own governors and priests, who divided between them control of the running of the city and worship of its deities. Law codes began to appear, as the ruling classes sought to establish acceptable patterns of human behavior and regulate human relationships.

In Egypt, the pharaohs (or kings) ruled over a more unified society, combining their role as living god with their political and military duties. Over time the authority of the central goverment slowly eroded, and the stability of the Old Kingdom—the Age of the Pyramids—gave way to the growing disturbances of the First Intermediate Period and the Middle Kingdom. In the New Kingdom, periods of imperialist aggression alternated with waves of anarchy.

Throughout the many centuries of Egyptian history, religion remained the most powerful unifying force in Egyptian society.

Elsewhere in the ancient Near East, other peoples developed their own cultures. The Phoenicians were commercial leaders, trading widely in the Mediterranean world, while the rise of Persia saw the formation of a multiethnic, multicultural empire. Among those ruled for a time by the Persians were the Hebrews (the Jews), over whose long history there developed the belief in a single, universal god.

For all the peoples of the Ancient World, religion was fundamental to their societies, and the conflict between sacred and secular authority became a crucial issue. The arts served as a means of expressing universal human feelings, which ranged from the triumphant grandeur of the New Kingdom temples built for Ramses the Great to the hopeless pessimism of the Mesopotamian poem, the *Epic of Gilgamesh*. At the same time, the ruling classes sought solutions to political, economic, and social problems which continued to trouble most subsequent human societies.

I

Topic 1

People Before History

The earliest stages in the evolution of the human species go back millions of years. Over millennia a succession of species of hominids (the forerunners of modern humans) appeared, slowly developing the use of their forelimbs and walking on their backlimbs. Around a million years ago a creature we call *Homo erectus* walked much like modern humans. As brain capacity grew, the species learned to survive by hunting and gathering food, and began to make stone tools—the period from the first use of stone implements to the introduction of farming some 10 thousand years ago is known as the Paleolithic, or Old Stone, Age. It was then that the earliest forms of family and social group began to develop. Some 80 thousand years ago Neanderthal people invented a system for producing new types of stone tools such as blades and flints. They were also the first living beings to bury their dead.

The species to which we humans all belong, *Homo sapiens*, has been in existence for only about 35 thousand years. For the first 25 thousand years of their history, *Homo sapiens* continued to live by scavenging for food and using new and more complex forms of stone tools. They have left us the first works of art in existence, in the form of paintings on the inside walls of caves and small stone sculptures.

Beginning about 10 thousand years ago, humans began to find two fundamental new ways of maintaining their communities: by cultivating crops and domesticating animals. The period which saw the beginnings of farming is called the Neolithic, or New Stone, Age. This revolutionary break occurred over a prolonged period of time, and was conditioned by major changes in climate and environment. Agricultural techniques probably developed independently in various parts of the world, rather than being diffused by a single group of people.

The shift to agriculture brought many important changes in the patterns of human life. Rather than wandering in search of food, people could settle down in stable villages, where they learned to produce pottery and other manufactured objects. Freed from the need constantly to search for food, they had time for thinking and experimenting. Communities became diversified, as different individuals performed specific functions. Neolithic people developed elaborate cults of the dead and produced works of art that were stylized rather than realistic, as Paleolithic art had been. Economic and social distinctions appeared, as a small minority in each community grew to possess most of the productive land, and thus a greater wealth and authority.

These agricultural villages remained small and self-sufficient. They formed the basis for the growth of city life, which began to develop at the end of the Neolithic Age.

THE PLANET EARTH: LIFE AND THE ENVIRONMENT

The solar system, of which our planet earth forms a part, came into being around four and a half billion years ago. As far as we know, earth is the only one of the nine planets in the system to support life: scientists have yet failed to find any trace of living things on Mars or Venus, the other two planets whose atmospheres are theoretically capable of maintaining living organisms. Yet our world may not be the only one in existence. Astronomers believe that our galaxy, the Milky Way, composed of about 100 billion stars, contains a billion planets where life could exist. Modern telescopes, furthermore, have identified some 100 million other galaxies. The human perspective, therefore, is inevitably a very narrow one. It is not impossible that other worlds have their own histories of civilization.

The Earliest Forms of Life

Life began to develop on earth sometime in its first billion and a half years of existence. A thin layer of gases on the planet's surface contained the chemical elements necessary for living organisms. Electrical energy caused by the lightning accompanying violent rainstorms, high-energy particles and ultraviolet rays from the sun, and other forms of energy, created the kinds of complex molecules which were to form living things.

The earliest cell-like organisms, fossils of which have been found in rock that solidified over 3 billion years ago, gradually evolved into photosynthetic cells—with the ability, that is, to convert solar energy into chemical energy. Living off the sun, they produced oxygen, a gas without which higher forms of life could not exist.

These early stages of life occurred in the warm waters that covered much of the earth's surface: the water protected the cells from the sun's ultraviolet rays, which would otherwise have destroyed them. As the oxygen layer around the earth began to build up, it too formed a protective barrier against the sun's dangerous rays, and forms of life began to evolve which were capable of existing on the earth's land surface.

In our own time, scientists and ecologists are increasingly preoccupied with the destruction of this protective layer by what is called the "Greenhouse Effect," the devastating impact of human pollution on the ozone around our planet (ozone is a condensed form of oxygen). From the time of the first photosynthetic cells, living things have changed the natural environment. Modern humans, however, run the risk of destroying the environment and making all life insupportable.

From the Dinosaurs to the First Mammals

From the earliest water-dwelling organisms there developed the first vertebrates, animals with a central nervous system and an internal skeleton which increases in size along with the animal over time. The earliest of these were fish, and over millions of years some fish species began to evolve with simple forms of lungs. This in turn led to the appearance of amphibians—modern examples include toads and frogs—which could survive both in water and on land. Some 300 million years ago, a new step in the process saw the appearance of the first reptiles, creatures which reproduced by the internal fertilization of an egg, and which could spend their whole lives on land. For the next 200 million years, reptiles were the dominant form of life on earth. These dinosaurs (the word comes from Greek, meaning "terrible lizard") varied in size from that of a small chicken to the gigantic *Diplodocus*, 90 feet long and weighing 30 tons, with a tiny head and long neck and tail. Creatures such as this roamed the surface of the earth, living on the abundant plant life available, although some dinosaurs, including the giant *Tyrannosaurus rex*, were meat eaters. During the same millennia the layers of fossil fuels—coal and oil—slowly formed that were one day to make possible the industrial revolution and help to shape the modern world.

At the height of the dinosaurs' domination of the earth, the first mammals, warm-blooded and meat eating, began to appear. Birds also evolved around the same time. The earliest mammals were probably a form of shrew: small mouse-like creatures that lived on worms and insects. By comparison with the massive dinosaurs, these tiny creatures—probably nocturnal animals with poor eyesight—must have seemed insignificant. Yet, as in the case of the birds, their warm-bloodedness made them capable of a high level of physical activity and a greater sense of mental alertness.

After coexisting with these early mammals, the dinosaurs disappeared around 65 million years ago. No completely satisfactory explanation has been found to account for the sudden extinction—sudden in geological terms, at least—of the giant reptiles, whose period of domination of the planet for millions of years emphasizes the brevity of our own history. Among the causes that have been suggested were changes of climate and environment, to which the dinosaurs could not adapt. These changes may have been produced by the impact of a giant meteor on the earth.

The First Stages of Human Evolution

The theory of human evolution first popularized by the English scientist Charles Darwin in *The Descent of Man* (1871) did not claim, as many of his opponents accused him of doing, that humans are descended from monkeys. Instead, Darwin argued that modern humans and the other primates (the most developed order of mammals, which includes humans, monkeys, and lemurs) share a common ancestral form. About 14 million years ago the evolution of this form split in two directions: one path led to the gorillas and chimpanzees, the other eventually to our own species.

The evidence for the process of human evolution is fragmentary, and new finds provoke constant reinterpretation of earlier discoveries. Nevertheless, in spite of the many uncertainties and controversies, it is possible to establish some general idea of the process.

The creatures whose gradual evolution led over millions of years to the human species are called hominids. The earliest species of hominid, *Ramapithecus*, is known from fossil fragments discovered in Kenya (east Africa) and in northern India; they date to about 8–14 million years ago. Both sets of fossils consist of teeth and part of a jawbone. Unlike the apes, these creatures do not seem to have used their teeth for stripping and tearing up leaves and other vegetation. They probably used their front limbs for this purpose, perhaps moving around on their back limbs.

The next hominid of which we have evidence is *Australopithecus*, in the form of fossil fragments from sites in eastern and southern Africa. The oldest dates to about 4 million years ago. These creatures, between four and five feet tall, had broad thumbs and the ability to use their hands to grip; also, they walked upright.

MR. BERGH TO THE RESCUE.

THE DEFRAUDED GORILLA. "That *Man* wants to claim my Pedigree. He says he is one of my Descendants."

MR. BERGH. "Now, Mr. DARWIN, how could you insult him so?"

A cartoon by one of Darwin's contemporaries, Thomas Nast, ridiculing his ideas.

Significant Dates

Chief Developments of Prehistoric Humans (all dates B.C.)

Before 8,000,000	Ramapithecus
4,000,000	Australopithecus
1,000,000	Homo erectus
500,000	Use of cave shelters
80,000	Homo neanderthalis
35,000	Homo sapiens sapiens
25,000	Earliest prehistoric art

The species *Homo erectus*, which appeared around a million years ago, is far closer to our own species, but there may well have been other forms of hominid between *Australopithecus* and the development of *Homo erectus*. British and American anthropologists working in Africa have discovered skeletal remains dating to 3 million years ago which show resemblances to modern humans. These finds, along with fossil discoveries in China, are beginning to provide a more complex picture of the course of human evolution, which may have occurred over a longer period of time than was hitherto believed.

Homo erectus had a skeleton and walk closely resembling our own, and a brain capacity about half that of ours. The species, which spread from Africa into Europe and Asia, was the first to use fire and invented the earliest tools, made of stone chips. Over time it evolved into *Homo sapiens*, from which our own subspecies, *Homo sapiens sapiens*, developed.

Homo Neanderthalis

Another variant of *Homo sapiens* is known as *Homo neanderthalis*, the earliest found in Europe. The first examples were discovered in the Neander valley of the river Rhine near Düsseldorf (Germany) in 1856. Since then Neanderthal specimens have been found in many parts of Europe, in the Middle East, and in north Africa. Neanderthal people flourished from about 40 thousand to 80 thousand years ago. They were muscular and heavy, with a thick skull and a low forehead. Reconstructions based on an early find, the skeleton of an arthritic, did much to shape the popular modern notion of "primitive man," but Neanderthals had brains the same size as modern humans, and their period marks a major development in the history of human thought. Neanderthal people were the first living creatures to bury their dead carefully and place funerary offerings in the graves—the earliest indication of the existence of religious beliefs.

The Paleolithic burial of a woman aged about 25–30 years. She was buried in the crouched position under a small stone monument.

Around 35 thousand years ago, the Neanderthalers became extinct at the same time as our own subspecies, *Homo sapiens sapiens*, appeared (*Homo sapiens sapiens* is sometimes called Cro-Magnon, after the site in France where remains of the subspecies were first discovered). Skeletal fragments from sites in Europe seem to show large numbers of violent deaths among the last Neanderthal people, who were perhaps attacked and destroyed by the new subspecies. Alternatively, *Homo sapiens sapiens* may have been resistant to a disease which wiped out their predecessors. Whatever the circumstances, with the appearance of *Homo sapiens sapiens* all other forms of hominid died out, and the newcomers began to spread throughout the world. It is to this subspecies that all peoples today, including Europeans, Africans, Amerindians, and Asians, belong.

THE FIRST PEOPLE

Along with physical changes, the immensely long period of human evolution saw the slow growth of social patterns of behavior. Like the other primates, early hominids lived in groups which were organized according to a system of social hierarchy. Judging from the size of their living areas, bands of *Homo erectus* consisted of around 30 adults and their young. At some sites there is evidence of the butchering and dividing up of food among the various group members, a form of cooperation that distinguished them from other primates. This ability to coexist and collaborate with one another played an important part in the early development of human society.

The First Families

Alone among the primates, humans developed societies that were based upon the nuclear family, together with the formation of permanent male-female bonds. Some scholars argue that in Paleolithic times women were the dominant force in society, although this theory has not been proven by the evidence. Individual males had exclusive sexual rights to one or more females, and the two sexes worked together to care for and provide for the young. Most groups lived on plants and small game. Men hunted larger animals, while women probably combined childbearing and raising with food gathering. In this way, the group's survival depended equally on both sexes.

It is not clear whether individual family units combined to form groups, or whether preexisting bands divided up into families. In any case, two important principles soon came into play. The first was that incest became taboo, since interbreeding would have disrupted the formation of nuclear family units (early people did not, of course, realize the genetic dangers of incest). The second increasingly common practice was exogamy, or marriage outside the group. With group membership so small, parents could not always find eligible mates for their offspring. By promoting unions between members of neighboring bands, early humans could "settle" their dependents when they wished, and also establish friendly relations with their neighbors. Thus they reduced the risk of intergroup fighting, while at the same time extending their hunting territory. The use of "arranged marriages" of this kind remains common in many parts of the world.

Living Conditions and Technology

Although, like the other primates, early hominids lived on the move, they developed an important difference in living patterns. Many groups formed permanent or semipermanent base camps that were used over several years. The hunters would move out from these, leaving behind the children, and return bringing game. The earliest communities, those of the *Australopithecines*, were probably in the open; the sites in southeast Africa are often located near lakes or rivers, useful both for their water and for the animals they would have attracted.

The earliest evidence of the use of caves as habitations dates to about half a million years ago—among the first examples are the Choukoutien caves near Beijing. The move to natural shelters became possible because of a major breakthrough in human development: the discovery of fire. Hearths dating to around 500,000 years ago have been found both in China and in Hungary. With the protection offered by fire, cave settlers could keep out the bears and other large mammals that also lived in shelters. It also became possible to cook food. Meat was more digestible when cooked, and boiled or roasted grains and seeds—which the human alimentary system cannot digest raw—helped to enrich the diet.

According to evidence found in late *Australopithecine* sites in east Africa and early *Homo erectus* sites in China and southeast Asia, tools seem to have first been used about a million years ago. Known as pebble tools, these implements were smooth stones with flakes split off at the end. Both the pebble and the flake served for chopping, scraping, or cutting.

Over hundreds of thousands of years, successive generations of *Homo erectus* gradually developed a new kind of tool, the so-called hand ax, which was probably an all-purpose instrument. Although hand axes were used throughout Europe, Africa, and western Asia, they never appeared in China and southeast Asia, where people continued to use pebble tools. The spread of hand axes—often similar in design—within specific geographical areas, and their absence from other regions, is an early example of cultural diffusion. The technological advances made possible in the areas where the axes were employed were the result of the communication and exchange of ideas, and not due to physical evolution. This ability of humans to acquire and spread information was a crucial factor in their development.

Neanderthal people continued to use hand axes, but also devised a new and far more efficient form of

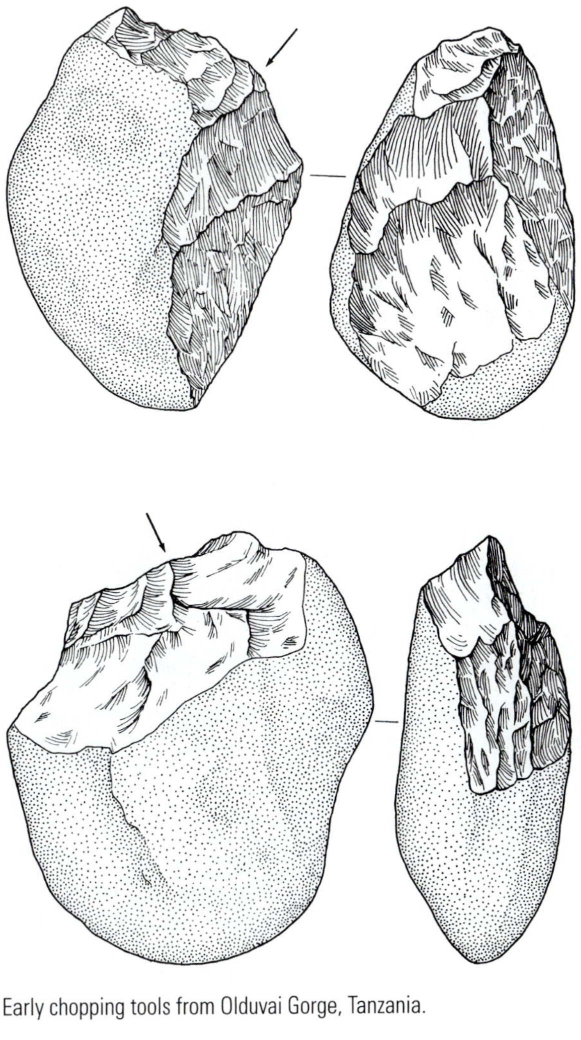

Early chopping tools from Olduvai Gorge, Tanzania.

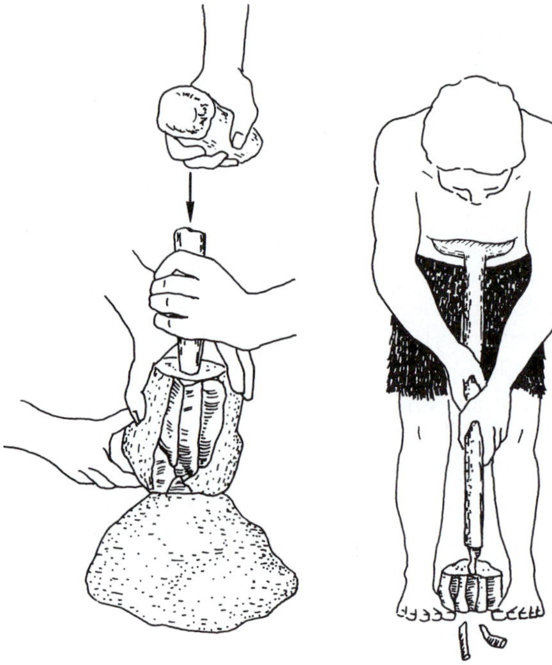

Two methods of making tools by using a punch.

instrument, consisting of sharp flakes of stone struck off from a precut disk. These flints and disks, so characteristic of Neanderthal culture, were in use from 70 thousand years ago to about 32 thousand years ago. The flints would have served to scrape animal hides for the manufacture of simple clothing, another important development that occurred along with organized burial during Neanderthal times.

The tools which *Homo sapiens sapiens* began to produce around 35 thousand years ago were far more refined. At first they still consisted of stone, but the blades were shaped by the use of other stones—a tool to make a tool—into a wide variety of shapes. A tool kit might include instruments for scraping and piercing, chisels, knives, and burins (engraving tools). Our ancestors used these to work materials such as ivory and bone into various kinds of sharp points: barbed tips for spears, fishhooks, and needles for domestic use. This in turn led to another vast step forward, the use of decoration on some of the instruments themselves and the use of other tools to carve stones and paint on cave walls. Humans had invented art.

One of the largest of the painted caves at Lascaux: The Hall of the Bulls.

EUROPE IN THE STONE AGE: HUNTERS AND ARTISTS

The earliest awareness of aspects of life other than mere survival emerges from a number of the Neanderthal cemeteries. These first examples of careful disposal of bodies imply that Neanderthal people developed more complex ideas about the nature of life and death. Some of the dead in the graves were buried with weapons and food—in one case a joint of meat. In another case, the body had been covered over with spring flowers. Many bodies in Neanderthal graves were colored with a pigment produced from red earth before being buried.

The *Homo sapiens sapiens* people of the late Paleolithic period left even more elaborate offerings with some of their dead, including necklaces and headdresses. A grave in the former Czechoslovakia, at Vestonice, contained the body of a woman of around 40. She had been painted with red coloring, and was protected by two mammoth bones, one of which has lines carved on it. One of her hands held the tail and paws of an Arctic fox, and the other the fox's teeth (in later times the fox was famous for its speed and cunning). The grave also contained stone tools.

Cave Painting

Finds such as these reveal dawning interest in appearance, and, more significantly, the use of images as symbols. Even if we cannot really decipher the meaning of the contents of the grave in Czechoslovakia, those who buried the woman intended them to convey a specific message—whether in this world or in an afterlife. About 20 thousand years ago, this fascination with images suddenly inspired the creation of the first surviving works of art in human history.

Perhaps the most compelling example of prehistoric art is the painted caves of France and Spain. The scenes of animals depicted there still startle the modern viewer with their keen observation and lifelike vividness. The cave artists incised the outer lines of each image, often making use of the natural irregularities of the stone surface to suggest, say, the hump of a bull. Then they filled the outline with charcoal and paints made from ground minerals.

From the time of their rediscovery—Lascaux in France, one of the most famous examples, came to light only in 1940—the cave paintings have raised intriguing questions. Why were they created? Are the animals intended as magic symbols for hunting rituals? But if so, why are the scenes always located in the most remote and inaccessible parts of the caves, far from any source of natural light? A magical function, furthermore, would not explain the paintings' most striking characteristic, their realism, since rituals require only symbolic representation. Some modern observers believe that the herds of animals represent seasonal migrations, while still others have suggested that the various animals were the totems (emblems) of families or clans (human figures appear only very rarely in the paintings, and are always represented as simple stick figures). What remains certain is that with great care, and under difficult conditions, the cave artists sought to reproduce the animal world they saw around them as vividly as they could.

The First Sculptors

Other artists of the late Paleolithic period turned to bone, horn, and stone. Some of the carvings are of animals, including a magnificent bison from southwestern France, carved out of reindeer horn. As in the paintings, human subjects were shown in a more stylized way. The tiny *Venus of Willendorf* has a featureless face, covered with what look like curls. Clutching her huge breasts, she looks down toward her pregnant belly. The emphasis on sexual characteristics in this and other female figures may tell us something about prehistoric attitudes to gender. Perhaps women's practical role as source of birth and life became symbolic of a more

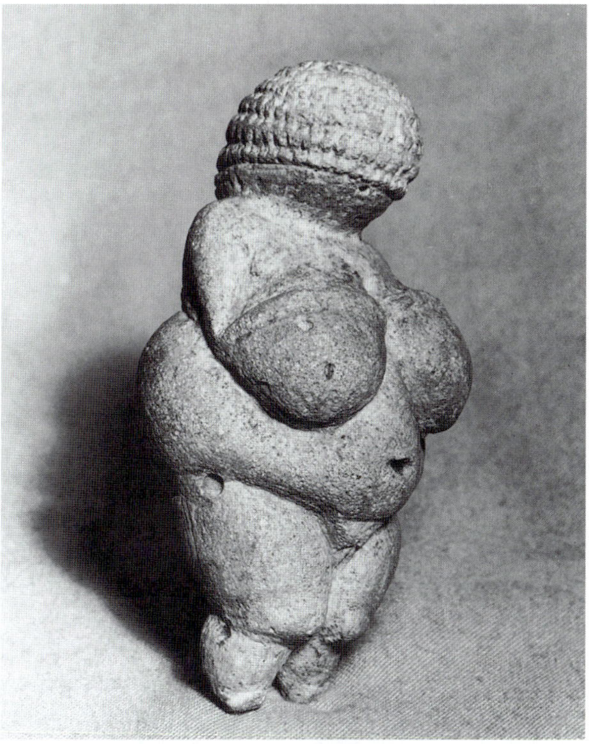

The *Venus of Willendorf* (c. 30,000–25,000 B.C.), a tiny Paleolithic limestone figurine.

profound feminine life force that sustained the masculine world of the hunt.

THE NEOLITHIC REVOLUTION: FARMING AND TECHNOLOGY

The term *Neolithic* (New Stone Age) was originally coined by 19th-century archeologists to describe the period at the end of the Stone Age when settled and stable human communities had learned to survive by cultivating crops and domesticating animals, but had not discovered metals and still used stone tools and weapons. More recent discoveries tend to show that the development of both agriculture and metalworking took place over a long period of time, and at a different rate in various regions of the world. In some areas people used advanced farming methods along with stone tools, while elsewhere metalworking was combined with less developed agriculture. It is probably best, therefore, to use "Neolithic" to describe the gradual appearance of food production over the period between 7000 and 4000 B.C.

In any case, the gradual discovery of systems of agriculture by Paleolithic people did not in itself immediately lead to a more settled form of living and the appearance of stable communities. There is evidence from excavations in Egypt's Nile Valley that for thousands of years before the Neolithic period nomadic peoples had planted barley and wheat in the silt left by the river Nile when its floods subsided, without ever settling down as farmers. It is probable that elsewhere, too, hunters and gatherers learned to grow crops which served as part of their food supply. The creation of permanent communities came at a relatively late stage in the development of agriculture.

Neolithic Farmers

The first Neolithic farming communities all began to form around 9 thousand years ago in four parts of the world: the Near East, western Africa, northeastern China, and Central and South America. Scholars used to believe that farming techniques were invented in the first of these regions (the Near East), and subsequently spread elsewhere. It now seems more likely that various peoples made the same discoveries at around the same time. The reasons remain uncertain, but are perhaps related to the climatic conditions left by the last Ice Age, which ended about 9 thousand years ago.

In northeastern China, a culture known as Yangshao appeared along the middle course of the Yellow River. Its people kept herds of pigs and grew millet, and gradually learned to make pottery. Farmers in western Africa domesticated a wide variety of plants, including yams and sorghum. At a slightly later date, Central and South American Indians raised corn, squash, and beans.

The largest Neolithic centers developed in the Near East. Between 8000 and 7000 B.C. at Jericho, in Palestine, a population of some 3000 lived in round houses made of mud brick set on sturdy stone foundations—the earliest houses in history to have survived. Ancient Jericho contained a large columned structure, perhaps a temple, in which archeologists found models of humans and animals. Together with the impressive defense wall surrounding the settlement, this structure justifies the description of Jericho as the first city in history.

The inhabitants of sites excavated in Iran, Iraq, and Turkey kept herds of sheep and cultivated vegetables including lentils and peas, and barley and wheat. They located their villages near water, and as the communities prospered they began to expand. The site of Çatal Hüyük in modern Turkey developed between 6400 and 5600 B.C., and eventually covered 32 acres.

European civilization developed more slowly than in the Near East, yet by 3300 B.C. it had clearly

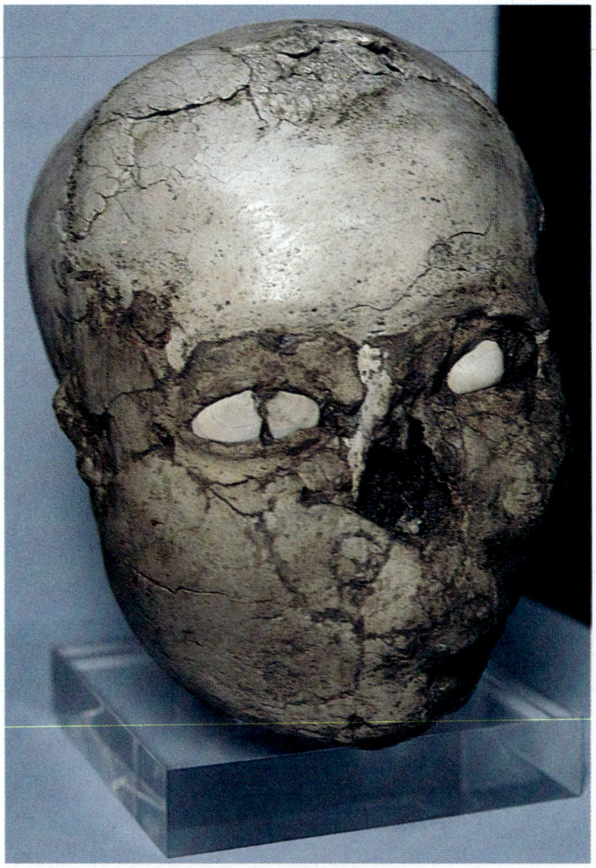

Neolithic plastered skull from Jericho, c. 7000 B.C.

begun the transition to the late Neolithic era. In 1991, the virtually intact body of a man was discovered in a melting Alpine glacier on the border between Austria and Italy. This remarkably preserved "Iceman," or *Homo tyrolensis*, who died some 5300 years ago, was perhaps a herdsman, between 25 and 35 years old. In addition to a cap and leather shoes, he wore a woven grass cape over a fur robe. In his fur quiver were found arrows with flint points and feathers, which show that the bearer was familiar with ballistic principles. Also found along with the body were a wooden-handled flint dagger and a copper ax blade. The one decorative object he carried, perhaps a talisman, consisted of a donut-shaped stone disk with a tassel of string.

Neolithic Society

Once the nomadic ways of hunting and gathering of the Paleolithic period had given way to farming and settled human communities, the way lay open for the growth of civilization. A major factor was the rise in population size and density. Earlier hunting groups, which had a high rate of natural mortality, had probably limited their numbers still further by abortion and infanticide. Neolithic communities probably tended to expand to the limits of available food resources, as most modern ones do—farmers can feed a much larger number of people from cultivated land than hunters can from a similar area. The consequence was bigger settlements which were often within reach of one another. Their residents had the opportunity to develop some precious new concepts, among which were leisure and comfort.

Within these communities, individual responsibilities became far more varied. Food production was now in the hands of only a few, and others could develop their own specialized skills, including the making of pottery (which first appeared in the ancient Near East in Iran around 6500 B.C.), and the carving of stone figurines.

Differences in occupation in turn led to differing economic status. Unlike their predecessors, Neolithic people could accumulate material possessions and own land. Furthermore the production of goods created possibilities for trade, and some large settlements may have served as much for trading as for food production. Around 6000 B.C., the invention of simple forms of transport such as rafts further encouraged the exchange of goods. In the process, the relative equality of earlier times slowly gave way to far more complex distinctions between various members of the communities. Thus the social divisions which form part of the history of civilization have their roots in the growing stratification of Neolithic life.

The long, slow material and technological progress of the Neolithic period was to lead to the eventual discovery of metals, the invention of writing, and the growth of cities—all important events in the rise of civilization chronicled in the following pages. The period between the earliest Neolithic villages and the first real Sumerian cities, which are discussed in the next Topic, spanned some 6 thousand years; during this time, humans learned to dominate and control their environment, and to put other creatures at their service.

Along with the material advances, many of the basic social and cultural characteristics that were to mark civilized life began to appear. (Historically, the term "civilization" is purely descriptive in its significance, with neither positive nor negative connotations.) The importance of commerce, the development of a class system, and the central role

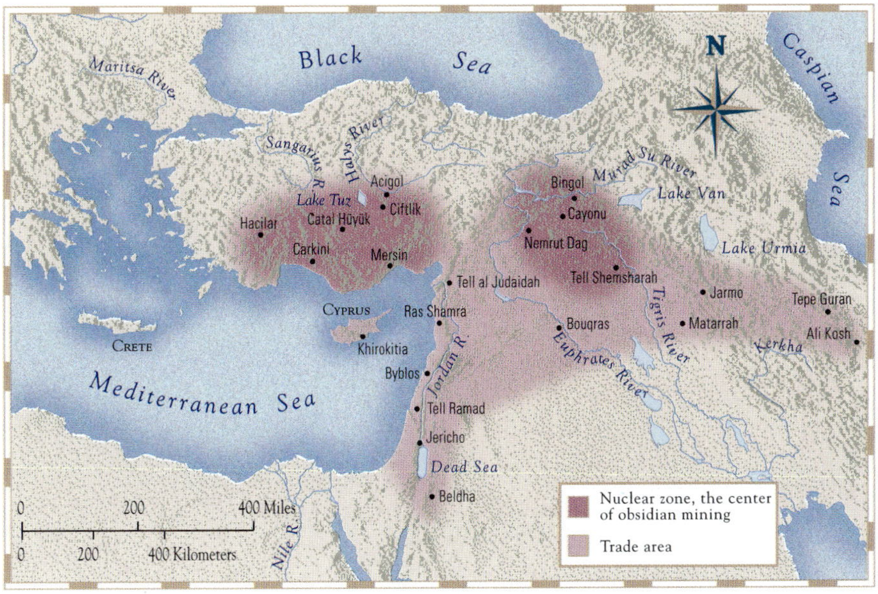

Map 1.1 Near Eastern Obsidian Trade Routes in the Neolithic Period

played by organized religion all seem to have had their origins in Neolithic communities.

The same may be true of the gender distinctions which characterized Neolithic society. Among earlier hunting and gathering groups, all members played a significant role and enjoyed relative independence. The division of labor which a sedentary existence made possible for the first time may have resulted in women being limited to activities and occupations performed at home. The chief of these were related to child raising, and the practical management of family life, although they probably also included cottage industries such as the manufacture of pottery.

As a result, the rise of civilization saw the appearance of gender inequality. As political and religious structures began to develop within individual communities, creating the need for leaders and organizers, men assumed the chief positions in public life, either excluding women or confining them to private life. This became reinforced when conflict of interest between various communities led to war (another mark of civilization as it developed), since men once again played a dominant role.

To judge from surviving works of art, the worship of a female fertility deity continued. Women remained associated with the natural world, and the Earth Mother—or Mistress of the Animals—who appears in the religions of the early civilizations seems descended from a Neolithic prototype. Neolithic artists developed a new style. In contrast to the realistic and exuberant depictions of Paleolithic art, Neolithic decoration is often linear, even abstract. Many of the female figurines are geometric, without the overt sexuality of the earlier period.

The Neolithic Age did more than make possible the rise of civilization by providing stable conditions. For all its apparent remoteness, it established basic patterns of human organization and behavior which were to endure for millennia.

Questions for Further Study

1. What kinds of evidence can historians draw on in the study of prehistory? How do they differ from the information used for studying later periods?
2. What do prehistoric works of art tell us about the people who made them? How far can we use them to reconstruct their ways of thinking?
3. Compare the importance of toolmaking and farming in the early development of human civilization.

Suggestions for Further Reading

Barker, G. *Prehistoric Farming in Europe*. Cambridge, 1985.

Champion, T., Gamble, C., Shennan, S., and Whittle, A. *Prehistoric Europe*. London, 1984.

Cohen, M. N. *The Food Crisis in Prehistory*. New Haven, CT, 1977.

Gowlett, J. *Ascent to Civilization: The Archaeology of Early Man*. New York, 1984.

Johnson, D., and Edey, M. *Lucy: The Beginnings of Humankind*. New York, 1981.

Leakey, R. *The Origin of Humankind*. New York, 1994.

Lerner, G. *The Creation of Patriarchy*. New York, 1986.

Sheratt, A., ed. *The Cambridge Encyclopedia of Archaeology*. Cambridge, 1980.

Wenke, R. J. *Patterns in Prehistory: Humankind's First Three Million Years*, 3rd Ed. Oxford, 1990.

1

Topic 2

Mesopotamia and Its Cities

Mesopotamia (the land between the rivers Tigris and Euphrates), where urban life first developed, is a flat region of the Middle East stretching from eastern Asia Minor to the Persian Gulf. In order to farm successfully, its inhabitants needed to build dikes to reduce flooding during the rainy season, and dig channels to distribute water throughout the rest of the year. Early settlers discovered that they could more easily construct large-scale projects by combining resources and merging their villages.

By around 3500 B.C., the dominating people in southern Mesopotamia were the Sumerians, who built towns with simple temples. Over the next two millennia, some of these urban centers became larger and more complex as the Sumerians developed many of the innovations which made civilization possible. Among them was writing, used to keep records of expanding Sumerian trade.

About 3000 B.C., cities such as Ur and Uruk—each of them the center of a small city-state—became the bases from which the Sumerians expanded to control the rest of Mesopotamia. In spite of internal conflicts between individual Sumerian cities, Sumerian influence over the Semitic peoples of northern Mesopotamia lasted from 2900 to 2331 B.C. (The term "Semitic" originally applied to the language group that included the Hebrews and many of the peoples of the Arabian peninsula.) This period also marked the zenith of Sumerian culture, including the construction of impressive temples and the production of lavish jewelry and gold treasures, together with an amazing sophistication in mathematics.

For the next millennium, a succession of invasions disrupted the entire region. Sumerian rule was ended in 2331 B.C. by Sargon, chieftain of the Akkadians, one of the northern Semitic peoples. After conquering Sumer, Sargon pushed west to the Mediterranean. The Akkadians maintained Mesopotamia united under their control from 2331 to 2150 B.C. Borrowing many features of Sumerian civilization, including irrigation methods and writing, they used them for large-scale trade and agricultural projects.

When Akkadian rule came to an abrupt and violent end with a severe climate change, accompanied by the invasion of tribes from Iran, the cities of southern Mesopotamia saw a revival of Sumerian culture. About 2000 B.C., this too was overthrown, and the whole of Mesopotamia fell into a state of disunity.

A reunited Mesopotamia finally emerged again under the Babylonians, whose most famous king, Hammurabi, ruled from 1792 to 1750 B.C. Equally skilled at warfare and diplomacy, Hammurabi's most lasting achievement was the code of laws he devised. His capital city, Babylon, became a center for the arts and for mathematicians and astronomers.

Around 1530 B.C., new invasions from the east ended Babylonian rule. The Kassites ruled over the former territories of Sumer and Akkad until c. 1200, after which the Assyrians eventually emerged as the ruling power in Mesopotamia. Militant empire builders, they led expeditions of conquest to the north and west, and by 1100 B.C. Assyrian forces had spread as far as the Black Sea and the Mediterranean. After a period of military decline, Assyria rose to new power under a series of warrior kings, notable for the harshness with which they treated the peoples they conquered.

The Assyrian capital, Nineveh, became one of the most magnificent cities of its age, and the clay tablets from its library provide the basis of our knowledge of Mesopotamian literature. In 612 B.C., however, Nineveh fell to an alliance led by the Babylonians and the Medes. Mesopotamia eventually became a province in the Persian Empire, ending its 2500-year-old independent history.

THE TIGRIS AND EUPHRATES: RIVERS AND CIVILIZATION

All four of the world's first centers of civilization—the Middle East, Egypt, northern China, and northwest India—lie in river valleys, whose abundant water and fertile land attracted early settlers. In the Middle East, the rivers Tigris and Euphrates both have their sources in the rocky peaks of Armenia. [In this account, the term "Middle East" is used to refer to the geographical area. The ancient civilizations in this and subsequent topics are described as those of the Near East.] Flowing southeast, they leave behind the mountains, to cross first barren, flat desert land, and then a 6000-square-mile expanse of marshes and mudflats. Finally, the two rivers join and enter the Persian Gulf.

In Mesopotamia, the land between these two rivers—often known as the Fertile Crescent—the first civilizations in western Eurasia began to develop. Neolithic societies had formed stable communities, and improved tools and farming methods. The production of manufactured goods led to the beginnings of trade. The transition from these settlements to cities, with organized government, economy and religion, occurred in the years between 5000 and 3000 B.C.

The Birth of Civilization

The key factor in the rise of civilization was improved farming methods. By growing more food and rearing more animals, communities could enlarge and prosper. Early settlers learned first to irrigate land close to the river, and then to divert water by canals to more distant fields. The river waters, with their rich mud, provided a fertile basis for growing crops. At the same time, the rivers not only supplied the developing cities with mud, reeds, and clay for building and pottery making, but also contained fish, which played an important part in the Mesopotamian diet.

These great rivers were not always benevolent to those living beside them. In the rainy spring season, unpredictable floods often devastated entire cities as torrents of water poured down from the mountains across the flat desert and marshlands. The biblical story of Noah and the Ark is a reminder of the destructive power unleashed by floodwaters, as is one of the three Sumerian epic accounts of a disastrous flood. (For a discussion of the account of the flood in the *Epic of Gilgamesh*, see Part I, Topic 5.) The waters tended to produce a buildup of salt in the soil, while also often creating social havoc.

To avert the danger, the river dwellers sought the protection of their gods. Both the flood described in Genesis and that of the Sumerian tradition were believed to have been sent as divine retribution for human behavior, and the power of the priesthood that developed in the early cities no doubt depended on its role as intercessor. More practically, communities joined forces to plan and build networks of canals to distribute water, and control—or at least reduce—the force of the flooding. Such planning required effective organization and administration, from which there grew the centralized authority necessary for urban life.

THE SUMERIANS AND THE RISE OF CITIES

The land of Sumer lies in the southern part of Mesopotamia, in the fertile valleys separating the

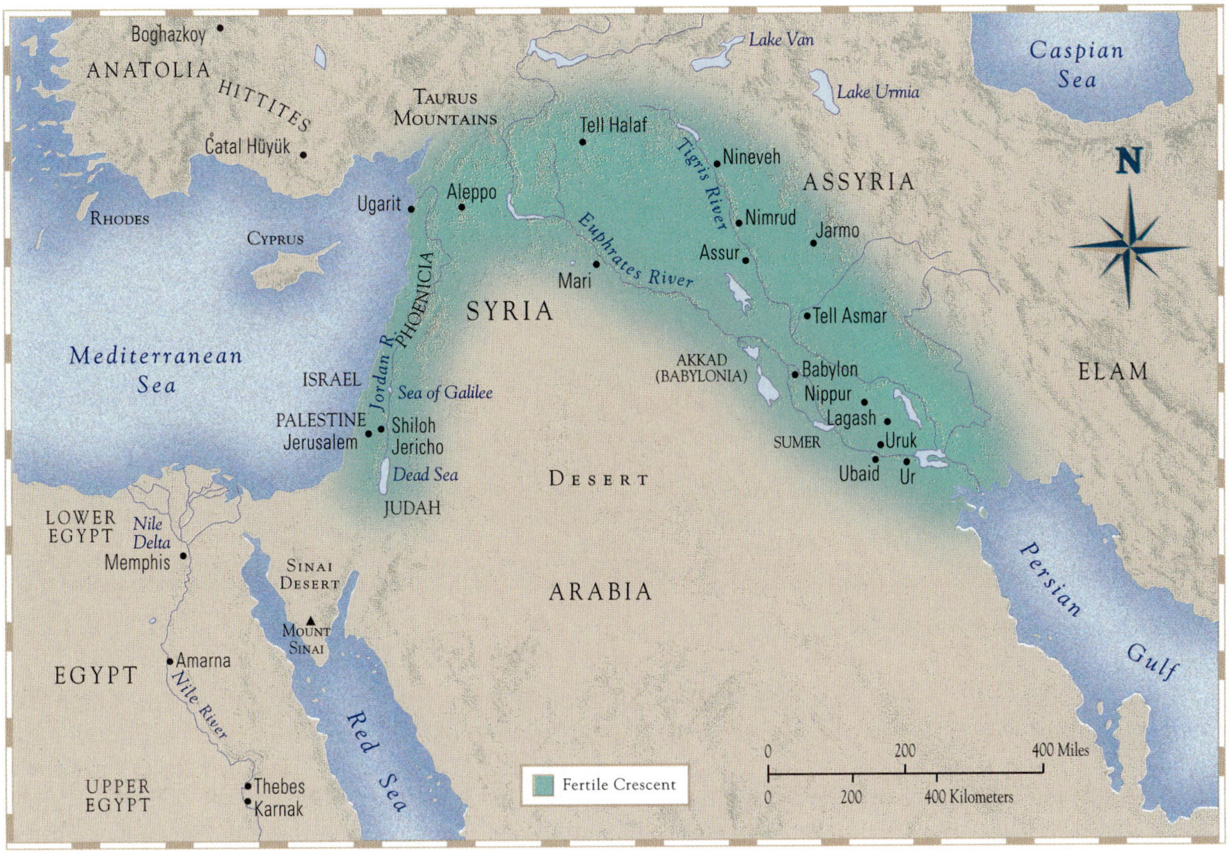

Map 2.1 The Ancient Near East

desert from the Persian Gulf. By 3000 B.C., its inhabitants had developed political stability and sufficient food supplies to maintain large-scale communities. Cities such as Uruk and Lagash supported populations as large as 20 thousand. In its heyday, Ur and its surrounding region—the largest Sumerian settlement—perhaps had as many as 400,000 inhabitants.

Each of these cities, numbering about twenty, ruled over its own state. Sharing a common language and religion, the communities nonetheless maintained their autonomy. Conflicts between neighboring cities over land and water rights led to the development of rival alliances and effectively prevented the establishment of a single leading power. The Sumerians managed to achieve their astonishing series of discoveries and inventions in the context of virtually constant warfare against one another. Only around 2400 B.C. did the ruler of Umma briefly unite most of the Sumerian cities under his control. Fifty years later the Sumerians were conquered by the Akkadians.

The Temple and the Palace

The responsibility for governing each of these city-states fell on two authorities: the priests and the civil governor. At the center of each city stood the chief shrine to the gods; in later Sumerian history this was often placed atop a *ziggurat*, a rectangular, stepped mound. The priests who oversaw the design and construction of the temples, and performed the divine rituals in them, lived off the land set aside for them by the community. They divided some of the produce between themselves and their staff, used some as offerings for the gods, and sold off the rest to pay for building and maintenance.

Although the priesthood was central to Sumerian life, the priests did not, as scholars used to believe, own all the land and govern the cities by controlling their economies. It is now thought that one third of the land in each state was owned by the priests, one third under royal control, and the remaining third in private hands.

The chief political authority in each state was a king or governor, who probably achieved power by military prowess. Over time, as the kingship became hereditary, a class of nobles developed. The king and the nobles owned most of the rest of the land. The workers on their estates were either free citizens, who received in return a small piece of land with which to support themselves, or slaves. The Sumerians were among the earliest people to institutionalize slave labor,

The Neo-Sumerian mountain shrine, or ziggurat, at Ur (c. 2100-2000 B.C.).

using prisoners of war and captured foreigners, mainly women.

The land not controlled by the priests or the nobles belonged to other free citizens, whose families had their own estates. Although they were clearly subordinate to the two powerful ruling classes, these commoners remained independent, and played some part in their community's political life.

Technology and Trade

Shortly after 3000 B.C., the Sumerians discovered how to combine copper and tin to make bronze, and used the new material to cast weapons and tools. They also worked in gold and silver and learned how to solder and rivet. They were the first people to use a wheel for the manufacture of pottery. At the same time, they devised new methods of transport, inventing the wagon wheel and building sailboats. (One of the Sumerians' minor contributions to civilization was their discovery that by fermenting grain they could produce alcoholic beer.)

Mesopotamia had little in the way of natural resources. Wood, stone, and metal had to be imported from outside the region, and the Sumerians were thus driven to developing an extended trading network. They sent out expeditions and set up overseas trading centers throughout the area from Asia Minor to India; tin came from Asia Minor and Syria, shells from India, lapis lazuli from Afghanistan, and cedar and pinewood from the forests of Syria and Iran.

The trade was not always peaceful: where necessary, the Sumerians obtained their goods by military campaigns, helped by the superiority of their weapons. In the process, their influence spread over a wide area, while they in turn learned from the peoples with whom they came into contact. Among the outside ideas imported into Mesopotamia was the animal-drawn metal plow.

Ram in a thicket (offering stand) from Ur, c. 2600 B.C.

The Invention of Writing

As patterns of trade and administration became ever more complex, the Sumerians found the need for new systems of organization and control. In seeking to create these, they invented writing, one of the most crucial tools of civilization. It now seems that around 5000 B.C. earlier peoples of the ancient Near East had devised simple methods of using token signs to record on stone or clay tablets for trade transactions, but the Sumerian cuneiform script was the first fully developed writing system in history. Its signs were based on the shapes of the earlier token signs.

The script's name, cuneiform, comes from two Latin words, *cuneus* (wedge) and *forma* (shape). The earliest Sumerian inscriptions used signs that took the form of simplified pictures representing a group of

These inscriptions show the evolution of writing. The upper tablets show early picture writing. In the middle is an Egyptian hieroglyphic inscription. Below is an example of Babylonian cuneiform.

related meanings. A leg, for instance, meant not only the leg itself but also the idea of walking. The scribes drew or impressed the signs on soft clay tablets, which were then baked hard. Over time, as the production and circulation of tablets increased, the Sumerians simplified the pictures by using a split reed to press wedge-shaped marks into the wet clay—hence the name cuneiform.

The cuneiform script remained in use for the next three millennia in western Asia, as the Akkadians, Babylonians, Assyrians, and many other peoples adapted versions of the Sumerian system to their own languages. For them, as for the Sumerians themselves, writing proved an essential political and economic tool. It also made possible two other turning points in human culture: the appearance of literature and the setting up of schools. The first schools served as training centers for scribes, but they soon attracted scientists and scholars. Among the subjects taught were mathematics, spelling, and literature. The staff member responsible for discipline was known as "the man in charge of the whip."

For all their creativity and high cultural achievement, the Sumerians' inability to coexist peacefully with one another proved their downfall. When the Akkadians attacked them in 2331 B.C., they were too weak to resist, and Sumerian domination of Mesopotamia came to an end.

THE AKKADIAN CONQUEST AND ITS AFTERMATH

The Akkadian conquest and unification of Mesopotamia formed the cornerstone in the creation of the world's first empire. Sargon (c. 2371–2316 B.C.), who overthrew his overlord to become chieftain of this Semitic-speaking people of central Mesopotamia, was to boast that his power and influence stretched "from the lower sea to the upper sea"—from the Persian Gulf to the Mediterranean.

Sargon's success was due to his combination of military strength with the technology he had learned from his southern neighbors. Akkad, the capital city he founded for his people in 2370 B.C., served as the base for the newly united Mesopotamia. For the first time, the idea of a territorial state replaced that of the city-state, and led to a period of imperial expansion: for 150 years, Sargon and his successors dominated the entire area from Syria in the north, to the Persian Gulf in the southeast, to Egypt in the west.

Significant Dates

Civilizations in Mesopotamia (all dates B.C.)

c. 3000–c. 2350	The Sumerians
c. 2350–c. 2200	The Akkadians
c. 2100–c. 2000	The Third Dynasty of Ur
c. 1800–c. 1600	The Babylonians
c. 1600–c. 1200	The Kassites
c. 2000–c. 850	The rise of the Assyrians
c. 850–612	The Assyrian Empire

The Akkadians and Sumerian Culture

The culture and technology which the Akkadians spread throughout this wide region were basically Sumerian. The chief Akkadian contribution was to use Sumerian ideas and techniques in a broader, more organized way. Irrigation projects no longer fell under the control of the priests, but were administered by secular officials. Thus knowledge of agricultural construction methods, which the Sumerian priests had jealously guarded, circulated more widely and made possible large-scale public works programs.

Like the Sumerians, the Akkadians needed to import raw materials for their constructions, and were even more inclined than their predecessors to mount military campaigns for the purpose. One of Sargon's most ferocious attacks was on the timber-yielding mountains of the Lebanon. The Akkadians' chief rivals in the pursuit of materials were the Egyptians, but there is no evidence of any marked contact between the two peoples. There were tenuous links between Mesopotamia and ancient India, with Indian ivory being exchanged for Mesopotamian oil and textiles.

Only in the past few years have archeologists been discovering the extent to which the Akkadians spread Mesopotamian culture. At the site of Ebla, in northern Syria, excavations have revealed thousands of clay tablets with inscriptions in a version of the Mesopotamian script developed under Sumerian influence, and the works of art produced in Ebla show strong Sumerian influence. The city of Ebla passed under Akkadian rule when it was conquered by Sargon. Other Syrian cities in turn picked up the new culture and spread it further afield. Akkadian imperialism may have been inspired by the drive for conquest, but its lasting effects were to provide a common culture for much of the ancient Near East.

The Fall of Akkad and the Sumerian Renaissance

The unity which the Akkadians had imposed on Mesopotamia came to a sudden and violent end around

Portrait of Gudea, the governor of Lagash, standing in an attitude of devotion before the gods.

2150 B.C. Recent discoveries suggest that at that period there occurred a major climatic shift, marked by severe drought. When this was accompanied by a wave of invading tribes from the upper valley of the Tigris destroying the Akkadians' central authority, Mesopotamia once again divided into a series of separate kingdoms.

The collapse of the Akkadian empire brought a rebirth of civilization and art in Sumer which lasted for almost a century. Gudea (c. 2144–2124 B.C.), the ruler of Lagash, was a patron of the arts and commissioned important temple complexes. A number of statues of Gudea have survived, showing him in humble and devout prayer. His impact was sufficient for later generations to worship him as a god.

After Gudea's death, Ur replaced Lagash as the principal Sumerian city. Its best-known ruler was Ur-Nammu (c. 2112–2095 B.C.), who introduced a series of laws governing various aspects of society—one of his provisions established a set fine for anyone who raped a virgin female slave without the permission of her owner. Although Ur-Nammu's laws touched on only a select number of issues and did not form a complete law code, they marked the first time in history that a ruler tried to provide his people with some basis of legal order.

Attacks from east and west put an end to Ur's renaissance around 1950 B.C. For the next century and a half, Mesopotamia lost its importance as a cultural center, but the Sumerians had laid the foundations not only for ancient Near Eastern society but for much of the later development of Western civilization. Meanwhile, power passed elsewhere as a new people, the Amorites, began to play an increasingly aggressive role in the Fertile Crescent. The third great period in Mesopotamian history began with its conquest shortly after 1800 B.C. by the Amorites' most famous king, Hammurabi of Babylon.

THE BABYLONIANS: THE RULE OF LAW

The Amorites were a Semitic people who migrated from the desert fringes of Arabia about 2000 B.C. Soon after settling in Mesopotamia, they adopted Mesopotamian culture. Their chief city was Babylon, located between Sumerian and Akkadian territory, and thus able to control trade in both directions. Babylon and its inhabitants gradually extended their power throughout Mesopotamia, and at the same time began to establish links further west, with the peoples of Asia Minor. By the time of their definitive conquest of Mesopotamia, their commercial contacts reached as far west as the Mediterranean, while under the dominance of the city of Babylon the trade routes in the region had shifted from the south to the north.

Hammurabi and the Unity of Mesopotamia

Babylonian power reached its peak in the reign of Hammurabi (c. 1792–1750 B.C.). Using an adroit blend of diplomacy and aggression, Hammurabi united the whole of Mesopotamia under his rule, and made Babylon the region's capital. Among the techniques he used to encourage unity was religious propaganda: the combined deities of Mesopotamia, he claimed, had elected Marduk—the principal Babylonian god—as their king. As a result, Babylon became Mesopotamia's most important religious center.

The city itself boasted splendid temples decorated with elaborate sculptures, and the annual New Year festival held there attracted crowds of worshipers. Hammurabi used Babylon's religious prestige to reinforce his own authority, claiming that the gods appointed "me, Hammurabi, the obedient god-fearing prince to cause righteousness to appear in the land, to destroy the evil and the wicked, that the strong harm not the weak."

The Law Code

In order to accomplish these aims, Hammurabi drew up a law code, the first complete one in history to survive. It established procedures for the courts of law, laid down property rights, codified the duties and responsibilities for family members, and fixed penalties for crimes. The system of justice it records was in all probability based on basic legal principles and precedents established by earlier cases. The laws were carved on an 8-foot-high pillar, with Hammurabi himself shown at the top in the presence of the sun god Shamash. The king described himself as the sun god's "favorite shepherd." (For a more detailed discussion of the social implications of the law code, see Part I, Topic 6.)

Many of Hammurabi's letters and orders have survived, and they provide a vivid picture of an active administrator, who took pride in describing himself at the end of the law code as "the efficient king." Among the issues he deals with in his correspondence are reform of the calendar, the punishment of officials for bribery, and the clearing of a blockage in the Euphrates which was holding up traffic. In one letter he orders the delaying of a legal hearing to let one of the participants, the temple baker, organize the catering for a religious feast at Ur.

The Stele of Hammurabi, showing the seated sun god dictating the law to the king (c. 1780 B.C.).

The End of the Babylonian Empire

Hammurabi's empire did not long survive his death. Once again Mesopotamia began to fragment, and in c. 1530 B.C. a Hittite army raided Babylon. (For a discussion of the Hittites, see Part I, Topic 4.) The resulting confusion left Babylonia wide open to an invasion of Kassites. A nomadic mountain people from the upland region to the northeast of the Mesopotamian plain, the Kassites were able to conquer the region because of their mastery of chariot warfare. They occupied Babylon for some four centuries. The period seems to have been one of relative stagnation, and little has survived from this period. Mesopotamia rose to prominence again only when it came under Assyrian rule around 1150 B.C., when the last great era of Mesopotamian culture began.

THE ASSYRIANS AND THE THIRST FOR EMPIRE

The centuries of Kassite rule at Babylon saw the gradual rise to power of their northern neighbors, the Assyrians. This Semitic-speaking people occupied the unprotected plains of the upper valley of the river Tigris, where their most important city was Assur, co-capital together with Nimrud. Forced to defend themselves both from the Babylonians to the south and the fierce nomadic tribes to their north, the Assyrians evolved into one of the most aggressive and grimly militarized societies in history.

With the fall of the Hittites, their chief rivals in western Asia, around 1200 B.C., the Assyrians began to expand rapidly. King Tiglath-Pileser I (c. 1115–1077) grandiloquently took as his title "King of the World, king of Assyria, king of all the four rims of the earth." His boast may have been exaggerated, but his empire building was considerable: he took over much of the Hittite territory to the northwest of Assyria, conquered northern Syria, pushed as far as the Mediterranean coast, and defeated Babylon.

His immediate successors lost some of these gains, but by the time of their period of greatest success, 883–612 B.C., the Assyrians ruled over a mighty empire, stretching at its widest from the river Nile almost to the Caspian Sea, and from northern Syria to the Persian Gulf, and containing virtually all the earlier centers of power in the ancient Near East.

The Assyrian Military Machine

In order to gain and hold their empire, the Assyrians developed a formidable military force at home and built a reputation as ferocious and bloodthirsty terrorists abroad. All fit Assyrian males were required to serve in their army, the first fighting force to be fully equipped with iron weapons. Assyrian siege artillery was capable of demolishing the city walls of those who were unwise enough to hold out against them.

After the conquest of a city came a campaign of terror. Torture, mass executions, destruction, and plunder were often followed by the uprooting of the surviving inhabitants of a captured town. Assyrian rulers boasted proudly of their deeds: "Their boys and girls I burnt up in flame . . . pillars of skulls I erected before their town . . . I dyed the mountains with their blood like red wool." Tiglath-Pileser III (744–727 B.C.) proclaimed the forcible transportation of 30,300 people at a time.

The Assyrians undoubtedly encouraged the spread of their reputation for savage cruelty as a means of discouraging resistance and revolt. At the same time, however, their rule brought benefits to their victims. The imperial administration was the most sophisticated and organized in the history of Mesopotamia. Provincial governors, with their own bureaucracies of scribes and advisers, could collect taxes, decide legal disputes on the basis of a written law code, and raise local armies. They could keep in touch with developments elsewhere thanks to the construction of a road network which linked the chief centers of the empire, and to the existence of an efficient postal system.

More important, perhaps, the use of Aramaic as a common language and the wholesale population movements—both of soldiers on duty and civilians—led to the formation of a multinational empire sharing central rule and a common culture, the forerunner of later empires in the ancient Near East: those of the Persians, of Alexander, and eventually the Romans.

Assyrian Culture

For all their aggressive political domination, the Assyrians remained under the cultural influence of the Babylonians. Tiglath-Pileser III implicitly acknowledged this when he added to his title that of "ruler of Babylonia" around 725 B.C. The great library of Asurbanipal (c. 669–630 B.C.) at Nineveh contained a vast collection of Sumerian and Babylonian literature; some 25 thousand tablets from that collection are now to be found in the British Museum.

The huge palaces constructed at Nimrud and Nineveh were decorated with intricately carved scenes. Many of them are of war episodes, showing fierce fighting and battlefields littered with the bodies of dead and dying soldiers. The carvings which most clearly evidence an independent Assyrian character are those showing hunting scenes. From as far back as the great Tiglath-Pileser I, Assyrian kings had prided themselves on their hunting prowess, yet surprisingly enough the most striking feature of many of the hunting reliefs is the careful depiction of the animals, together with a sympathetic identification with their suffering.

The End of the Assyrian Empire

The very size of the Assyrian Empire proved in the end to be its undoing. The army, overextended and increasingly dependent on foreign mercenaries, could in the end no longer crush internal revolts or foreign attacks. In 612 B.C. two tribes, the Medes and the Babylonians,

Relief from the Palace of Asurbanipal at Nineveh.

joined forces to sack Nineveh, and Assyrian domination was over. By the following century, Mesopotamia had become part of the Persian Empire. The verdict of the Old Testament prophet Nahum was probably heartily echoed by most of his contemporaries: "Nineveh is laid waste; who will bemoan her?"

The Neo-Babylonian Empire

For less than a century following the fall of Nineveh, a part of Babylonia enjoyed a brilliant revival. Chaldean tribes, who had resisted Assyrian rule, set up their kingdom with Babylon itself as its capital. Under King Nebuchadnezzar (ruled c. 605–562 B.C.), the city became one of the wonders of the ancient world, with its palaces and temples, and the spectacular Hanging Gardens.

In 586 B.C., Nebuchadnezzar's forces crushed the kingdom of Judah, destroyed Jerusalem, and took the Jews back to Babylon in captivity (see Part I, Topic 4). An internal power struggle after his death left the Neo-Babylonian Empire fatally weakened, and in 539 B.C. Cyrus the Great, king of the Medes and Persians, captured Babylon and made Babylonia a province of the Persian Empire.

The earliest settlers of the land between the two rivers, the Sumerians, failed to achieve lasting political or military dominance, but their cultural contribution to Mesopotamian history, and to the growth of civilization, was enormous. All subsequent ruling powers there profited from Sumerian discoveries and advances. The urban skills they developed made possible the ordered society of Hammurabi and the centralized empire of the Assyrians. Sumerian religion and literature continued to influence the ancient Near East for more than a thousand years after their age. Babylonians and Assyrians developed scientific and astronomical research first undertaken by Sumerians.

Yet without the administrative abilities of the Akkadians, and then of the Babylonians and Assyrians, Sumerian ideas would never have had the wide circulation that they were to achieve. Each successive conquering power borrowed the culture and, to some extent at least, the religion of its predecessors, and spread them increasingly widely throughout western Asia.

With the absorption of Mesopotamia into the Persian Empire, the direct transmission of accumulated Mesopotamian tradition came to an end. When Alexander the Great conquered Persia, however, Greek scientists inherited from their Mesopotamian predecessors the astrological zodiac and the gleanings of hundreds of years of astronomy. Furthermore, Greeks in Asia Minor had earlier borrowed the Mesopotamian system of time divisions: 24 hours in a day, 60 minutes in an hour, 60 seconds in a minute. Greek art and architecture for a while adopted Mesopotamian and Egyptian styles, but the Greeks were quick to find their own characteristic approach to art.

If anything, the longterm legacy of the history of Mesopotamia, and of the Sumerians in particular, was to implant in the Near East a tradition of small, independent states, capable of surviving the rise and fall of empires. The strong sense of regional diversity outlasted the rise and fall of the Roman Empire, and the rise of Islam, and still dominates the political, religious, and cultural world of the Middle East today.

Questions for Further Study

1. What were the main cultural and political similarities and differences between the Sumerians, Babylonians, and Assyrians? How did these differences affect their history?
2. What part did trade play in the development of Mesopotamia?
3. Among the legacies of the peoples of the ancient Near East were writing and law codes. In what other ways did Mesopotamian culture affect later times?
4. What were the effects of climate and geography on the growth of the first cities? How relevant are these factors to urban life today?

Suggestions for Further Reading

Chiera, E. *They Wrote on Clay: The Babylonian Tablets Speak Today*. Chicago, 1966.

Nagle, D. B. *The Ancient World: A Social and Cultural History*. Englewood Cliffs, NJ, 1979.

Nissen, Hans J. *The Early History of the Ancient Near East*. Chicago, 1988.

Oates, J. *Babylon*. New York, 1986.

Oppenheim, A. L. *Ancient Mesopotamia: Portrait of a Dead Civilization*. Chicago, 1977.

Roaf, M. *Cultural Atlas of Mesopotamia and the Ancient Near East*. New York, 1990.

Roux, Georges. *Ancient Iraq*. Baltimore, 1980.

Saggs, H. W. F. *The Greatness That Was Babylon*. New York, 1962.

Saggs, H. W. F. *Civilization Before Greece and Rome*. New Haven, CT, 1989.

Schmandt-Besserat, D. *Before Writing*, 2 vols. Austin, TX, 1992.

Seton Lloyd, H. *Archaeology of Mesopotamia*. London, 1978.

Silver, Morris. *Economic Structures of the Ancient Near East*. New York, 1985.

I

Topic 3

Egypt of the Pharaohs

The geography of ancient Egypt played a determining role in the formation of its culture. Lower Egypt lay at the delta of the river Nile, and its access to the Mediterranean facilitated contacts with neighboring peoples. Upper Egypt to the south, on the other hand, was far more isolated. Because the climate has always been very dry, farmers depended on the river's waters, especially those accumulated in the annual summer flooding.

Egyptian history is divided into four main periods, which were separated from one another by times of upheaval: the Old Kingdom (beginning c. 2700 B.C.), the Middle Kingdom (beginning c. 2050 B.C.), the New Kingdom (beginning c. 1570 B.C.), and the Late Period (beginning c. 1070 B.C.), which ended with Egypt's incorporation into the Persian Empire around 500 B.C.

The unification of Upper and Lower Egypt preceded the Old Kingdom by just over a century. Throughout the Old Kingdom a series of powerful *pharaohs*—the word later used by the ancient Egyptians for their kings—ruled over the country. The pharaoh provided strong central government and headed the state religion. He was regarded as a living god, and wielded absolute power, although over the centuries the official bureaucracy tended to increase its influence. The grandiose temples and tombs of the Old Kingdom (which include the pyramids) reflect the stability and prosperity of the age.

Around 2185 B.C. political and religious disputes began to undermine the authority of the pharaoh. Order was restored only a century and a half later in 2050 B.C. with the Middle Kingdom. During the first part of this period, Egypt flourished, as improved systems of irrigation raised food production and living standards. The Egyptians began to establish trading contacts abroad and protect their southern borders by military campaigns. By c. 1640 B.C., however, internal rivalries and weakness made it possible for a foreign people, the Hyksos, to invade and conquer the country.

Within less than a century, hatred of their foreign rulers united the Egyptians behind a new dynasty of pharaohs who drove out the Hyksos and established the New Kingdom. For the first time, Egyptian rulers began to wage aggressive empire-building campaigns abroad. Thutmose III even crossed the Euphrates into Mesopotamia. Religion continued to follow the centuries-old traditions. Only the pharaoh Akhenaton rejected much of traditional polytheism and encouraged the worship of the god Aton. After his death, the priests branded Akhenaton a heretic, and overthrew his reforms.

Toward the end of the New Kingdom, Hittites, Libyans, and others began to make raids on Egypt, and even the mighty Ramses II (1304–1237 B.C.) was forced to conclude a peace treaty. Not long after his reign, Egypt fell increasingly under foreign control, eventually being conquered first by Assyria and then by Persia.

THE NILE AND ITS VALLEY

Egypt's life is inextricably linked to the Nile. At the beginning of Egyptian history, the earliest Neolithic communities settled in the river's valley, and from then on the Nile inspired and controlled Egypt's political, religious, economic, and social life.

The river divided Egypt into two parts. Lower Egypt consisted of the northern region of the delta, broad marshy lowlands extending from the modern city of Cairo to the Mediterranean. Upper Egypt was a long, very narrow strip of immensely fertile land stretching some 600 miles along the river, surrounded on both sides by barren desert alternating with cliffs. The area around the valley had originally been a grassy plain, which became desert around 6000 B.C., when there was a shift in the patterns of Atlantic rains. Farmers were thus virtually dependent on the river waters, augmented by the summer rains and the water of the Nile's six cataracts, for the production of their crops.

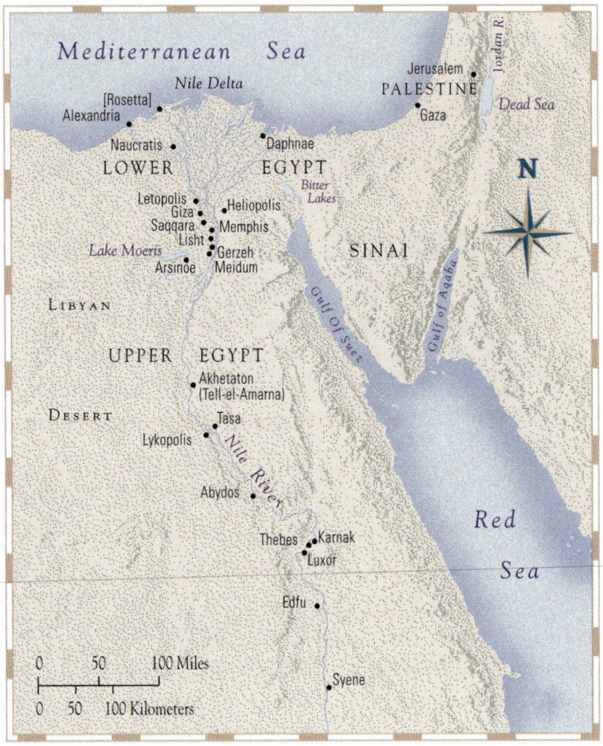

Map 3.1 Ancient Egypt

The Unification of Egypt

Although the earliest settlements along the Nile go back to Neolithic times, at first their scattered locations, strung out along the river valley, discouraged them from pooling their resources and joining together. With time, however, communication and commercial exchanges along the river broke the barriers, and the various small communities united to form two states: the kingdoms of Upper and Lower Egypt.

According to tradition, the first ruler to unify the two kingdoms was Menes (ruled c. 3100 B.C.), who also founded the new nation's capital at Memphis and inaugurated the first dynasty of Egyptian pharaohs. Throughout its 3000-year history, ancient Egypt maintained the tradition of its origins as two states: the official title of the pharaoh was "Lord of the Two Lands."

Menes' original name is lost to us, although most Egyptologists use the name Narmer. The form in which it survived is Greek, and comes from the history of Egypt written in Greek by an Egyptian high priest, Manetho (c. 280 B.C.). Manetho's account is also responsible for the traditional division of Egyptian rulers into groups known as dynasties. The period of Egyptian history before Menes is called Predynastic, and from the time of Menes to that of the mid-4th century B.C. there were 30 dynasties.

The Early Dynastic Period (c. 3100–2700 B.C.)

Little is known of Menes and his successors. The royal tombs of the period are known as *mastabas*, and were built of mud brick. In the 3rd Dynasty the Egyptians turned for the first time to stone, the material that was to characterize their architecture for the rest of Egyptian history. King Zoser (c. 2668–c. 2649 B.C.) commissioned the construction at Saqqara, near Memphis, of a magnificent funeral complex. Its architect was Imhotep (flourished 2630 B.C.), the first known example of a great creative genius. Renowned in his day not only for his buildings, but also as astronomer, priest, and minister to Zoser, Imhotep was revered by later generations for his skills in medicine and worshiped as a god.

Zoser's actual tomb took the form of a step pyramid, a shape that many of his Old Kingdom successors would modify into true pyramidal form. His reign thus began the tradition of building grandiose funerary monuments to guarantee the immortality of their occupants. Since Egyptian religion taught that physical preservation of the body was necessary for the survival of the soul, the Egyptians developed the art of mummification. Using a complex mixture of oils and spices, they embalmed the corpse and placed it, wrapped in fabric and contained in a series of cases, one within the other, at the center of the funerary monument.

The Traditions of Egyptian Religion

The formation of traditional Egyptian religious beliefs and structures also goes back to the Predynastic Period. The pharaoh's role as head of state drew additional strength from his status as living god. Beneath him were the priests, jealous guardians of tradition. The idea of divine ruler served to underline the Egyptian view of creation. From the time of Zoser, the chief Egyptian deity was the sun god Re, who had created the world by bringing order from the primeval chaos of the universe. His representative, the pharaoh, similarly ordered the real world.

By the time of the Middle Kingdom, Egyptian religion was based on the belief in life after death. All Egyptians, not only the rich or powerful, could hope for survival in the next world as the reward for a good life. Elaborate funeral rituals recounted the ceremony of the judgment of the dead, who were then pronounced worthy to pass on to the next life. The ruler of the Underworld and judge of the dead was Osiris, who came to symbolize resurrection. Over time, Osiris—together with his wife Isis and son, the falcon god Horus—became the symbol of spiritual, rather than merely material, survival.

In addition to the central cults, Egyptians worshiped an almost infinite number of other deities. The mythology and ritual that developed around these figures came to dominate the daily life of every Egyptian. The sky goddess Nut often appears stretched out on the ceilings of the tombs, swallowing the sun and creating night. Each morning, she would give birth to the sun again. The jackal-headed Anubis was the god of embalming and of the dead.

Painted relief of Osiris conversing with Thoth, the ibis-headed god of writing.

THE RISE AND FALL OF THE OLD KINGDOM

The 3rd Dynasty inaugurated the Old Kingdom, which lasted from 2700 until 2200 B.C. Three of the 4th Dynasty pharaohs, Cheops, Chefren, and Mycerinus, were responsible for the famous group of pyramids at Giza, while Chefren also commissioned perhaps the most familiar of all Egyptian images, the colossal human-headed lion known as the Sphinx, which guards his tomb.

The Age of Stability

We know practically nothing about the rulers of the 4th and 5th dynasties, apart from their monuments. Later ages recalled Chefren as a good king, and Cheops as a tyrant. Certainly the extraordinary size and mathematical precision of Cheops' Great Pyramid suggest a powerfully controlled state, capable of organizing an imposing workforce. Most laborers on the pyramids were peasants working on construction projects when the Nile flooded. The concentration of thousands of slaves and workers in a single place would have required strong security forces, a constant flow of supplies and food, and massive coordination.

The imposing monuments, together with the superb offerings they contained, mark this period as one of the high points in Egyptian history. The relief carvings of 5th Dynasty tombs provide a detailed description of daily life in pharaonic Egypt, with scenes of goldsmiths, farmers, sandal makers, boat builders, and many others at their work. In general, the animals, workers, and craftsmen appear more naturalistic than

A view of the Pyramids at Giza, with the Sphinx in the center.

the dead princes and high officials whose tombs the scenes decorate; the deceased are shown in a limited number of formal poses.

All indications suggest that the age was one of stability, in which centralized and efficient government ruled a rigidly stratified society. Contacts with the outside world were limited. There is evidence of some trade with western Asia. Egyptian artifacts of the period have come to light at sites in modern Turkey and Syria. On the whole, however, the 4th and 5th dynasties were a period of internal consolidation.

The End of the Old Kingdom

The tombs of the 6th Dynasty (c. 2350–c. 2200 B.C.) are far less ambitious than earlier ones, a sign of the diminishing power of the pharaohs. The nobles and high officials in the huge bureaucracies, which ran religious and economic affairs, increasingly challenged the central authority. Meanwhile, a number of small local principalities sprang up in Egypt whose rulers feuded with one another and ignored the orders of the pharaoh.

With the decline of the Old Kingdom, there began a century of violence, exacerbated by the major droughts and climate shifts in the region, which elsewhere contributed to the end of Akkadian domination in Mesopotamia (see Part I, Topic 2). One significant factor was the extremely low levels of Nile flooding. Excavation of contemporary cemeteries shows a sharp rise in death rates. With the end of central power and endless fighting between the local rulers or *nomarchs*, uncertainty replaced the granite solidity of the earlier age.

THE MIDDLE KINGDOM: THE WANING OF STABILITY

The civil wars finally came to an end when Mentuhotep (c. 2061–c. 2010 B.C.) reestablished a central authority and once again united Upper and Lower Egypt. He moved the capital south to Thebes (modern Luxor), which—apart from one brief pe-

Significant Dates

Chief Stages in Egyptian History (all dates B.C.)

c. 6000	Neolithic and Predynastic Periods
c. 3100	Early Dynastic Period
c. 2700	Old Kingdom
c. 2185	First Intermediate Period
c. 2050	Middle Kingdom
c. 1800	Second Intermediate Period
c. 1570	New Kingdom
c. 1070	Late Dynastic Period (Third Intermediate Period)
c. 525	Persian Conquest

riod—remained the seat of religious influence for the rest of Egypt's independent history. The patron god of Thebes, Amen (whose name means Hidden One), who had earlier been a relatively minor figure, became a dominant force in Egyptian religion.

The Middle Kingdom lasted from c. 2050 until c. 1780 B.C., about two and a half centuries. It began, like the Old Kingdom, with political order, economic stability, and a wave of artistic achievement. Rulers commissioned the building of monuments throughout Egypt, while lavish temples began to adorn the city of Thebes.

Earlier pharaohs were satisfied to protect Egypt's borders against invasion, the greatest threat having come from hostile Nubians to the south. (Most of ancient Nubia lay in what is now called Sudan; its people continued to play a role in later Egyptian history, which has been the subject of much recent attention.) In the Middle Kingdom, the Egyptians went on the offensive. The powerful pharaoh Sesostris III (c. 1878–c. 1844 B.C.) instructed his son: "A valiant man must attack. To retreat is cowardly. Consequently any son of mine who strengthens the frontier which My Majesty has created is truly my son." Sesostris lived up to his words by leading troops against the Nubians on their own territory. He then constructed fortresses along the new border he had created. Other pharaohs preferred to extend Egyptian influence by building trade contacts, and Palestine and the sea ports of the Lebanon became outposts for the Egyptian economy.

The Hyksos Invasion

For all the prosperity of the Middle Kingdom, the warning signs of regional squabbles began to appear at the beginning of the 13th Dynasty (c. 1780 B.C.). The rift between Upper and Lower Egypt reopened, and each half further split into warring states.

At this moment of weakness (about 1700 B.C.) Egypt suffered the first invasion in its history. The newcomers were the Hyksos, a group of Semitic immigrants from Palestine. Dominating the Nile Valley, they exacted tribute from the Egyptian rulers of Thebes whom they allowed to retain nominal power. In fact, the Hyksos kept the native kings weak by encouraging several rival claimants to the throne at the same time. One of the reasons for the Hyksos' military successes was their mastery of chariot warfare: prior to the arrival of the Hyksos, the Egyptians did not use wheeled vehicles.

Although Egyptians of later ages remembered the Hyksos with hatred and fear, their arrival in Egypt brought a host of technological and cultural benefits. Cut off by geography and natural disposition from any real contact with other peoples, the Egyptians had failed to benefit from new ideas and techniques developed in western Asia and by Mediterranean Bronze Age peoples. Under Hyksos influence, they learned to replace their copper tools with bronze ones, which were sharper and lasted longer. Horse-drawn chariots, bronze armor and weapons, and more efficient bows all revolutionized Egyptian warfare. The Hyksos also introduced new kinds of trees and plants, perhaps including the olive and the pomegranate.

After a century of Hyksos influence, Egyptian resentment toward the foreigners drove them to unite behind Ahmose (c. 1570–c. 1546 B.C.). The pharaoh routed the Hyksos in 1550 B.C. and drove them from power. The unified state that he went on to create, with its first capital at Thebes, became during the New Kingdom one of the great international powers of the late Bronze Age.

EMPIRE AND GRANDEUR: THE NEW KINGDOM

For half a millennium, a succession of New Kingdom pharaohs ruled over a powerful and prosperous state. They were absolute monarchs, warrior kings who were also responsible for some of the most enormous buildings ever constructed. The grandeur of their cities and the richness of their treasures were stupefying. The tomb of Tutankhamen, one of the least important pharaohs of the period, was packed with priceless masterpieces of art.

Foreign Policy in the New Kingdom

The military and political climate in which these rulers operated was a new one. Before the Hyksos invasion, Egypt's geographical location had protected it from attack. While Mesopotamia endured wave after wave of violence, Egypt was vulnerable only at its borders, in particular that to the south where the

The first view of the treasures of Tutankhamen.

Nubians continued to threaten. Even aggressive Middle Kingdom pharaohs like Sesostris, chiefly concerned with security at home, were not interested in empire building or the military occupation of other countries.

In the New Kingdom, however, the Egyptians began to play a far more active role in international affairs. Relying on a powerful army, made up in large measure of mercenaries, the pharaohs used a combination of force and diplomacy to dominate the eastern Mediterranean. Thutmose III (c. 1504–c. 1450 B.C.) waged no less than 17 military campaigns, in the course of which he conquered Palestine and Syria, and pushed as far east as the river Euphrates. Local governors ruled the occupied territories, and the Egyptians shipped forced laborers back home to work on the monuments and buildings erected to commemorate Egyptian victories.

The policy of empire building continued under Thutmose's successors, his son Amenhotep II (c. 1453–c. 1419 B.C.) and grandson Amenhotep III (c. 1386–c. 1350 B.C.). The latter was one of the few pharaohs to marry a commoner, queen Tiy. The daughter of the commander of the chariotry, she exerted considerable influence during her husband's reign.

Amenhotep led a successful expedition into Nubia, and maintained Egyptian prestige high in western Asia. Under his patronage, the capital city of Thebes became the site of magnificent temples, including that of Luxor. Yet within a few years of his death, the capital was moved elsewhere, and centuries of Egyptian traditions were swept away. The old ways were soon to return, but for a brief time the son of Amenhotep and Tiy, whose official title was Amenhotep IV, single-handedly attempted totally to reform Egyptian religious and political life. He is better known to posterity by the name he assumed, Akhenaton.

AKHENATON AND THE SUN GOD: THE REVOLUTION THAT FAILED

The reign of Akhenaton (c. 1350–c. 1334 B.C.) was a brief and dazzling break in the centuries of Egyptian tradition. Rejecting many of the deities of conventional Egyptian religion, Akhenaton promoted the worship of a deity, the *Aton* (the disk of the sun),

PUBLIC FIGURES AND PRIVATE LIVES

HATSHEPSUT AND THUTMOSE III

The New Kingdom ruler Queen Hatshepsut (c. 1498–1483 B.C.) was probably the first woman in Egyptian history to become pharaoh. The daughter of Thutmose I, she married his son and heir, her half-brother Thutmose II, and became co-ruler with him—hence, one of her official titles was "Pharaoh's wife and daughter." The royal couple had no male children, and on the death of her husband, the next in line for the throne was Thutmose III, the son of Thutmose II by one of his concubines. Hatshepsut refused to step down, however, and continued to act as regent for the young pharaoh. So far her actions were not unprecedented, for on two earlier occasions queens had reigned for brief periods.

In 1498 B.C. the ambitious Hatshepsut declared herself pharaoh and assumed full power, sending off Thutmose III—by now come of age—to expand Egypt's foreign conquests. In this way she simultaneously disposed of her chief opponents—her resentful stepson and the army which backed him. The queen was astute enough to win over the priesthood, still the most influential force in Egyptian society, by claiming divine birth and maintaining traditional customs.

Many of Hatshepsut's official portraits show her with the royal beard that was a sign of kingship. Indeed, in some of them she appears as a man, while in others is clearly portrayed as a woman. The male depictions and the use of the pharaonic beard were probably a means of reassuring the priests that she did not intend to break with religious conventions.

Among the leading figures at her court was the great architect Senmut, who designed her funerary temple at Deir el-Bahri. Some scholars have explained Senmut's preeminence by speculating that he and Hatshepsut were lovers. While there is no direct evidence of this, the presence of carved figures of Senmut in a small chapel in the queen's temple complex is highly unusual.

When Hatshepsut died in 1483 B.C., Thutmose became sole pharaoh. During the next 28 years, while he ruled over a period of great prosperity, many of the monuments erected by Hatshepsut were systematically defaced—presumably by royal command. Appearances of

continued next page

Funerary Temple of Hatshepsut, Deir el-Bahri.

Hatshepsut's name in inscriptions were obliterated or covered over, even those in the inner shrines of temples visible only to a handful of priests. In addition, statues and images representing her were destroyed. Even in her funerary temple at Deir el-Bahri, where for once the queen was portrayed alongside her official coruler, Thutmose III himself, the vengeful pharaoh hacked out Hatshepsut and cut away most of the statues of Senmut, leaving only his own image. At the great temple complex of Karnak, Hatshepsut's 97-foot-high obelisk had a wall built around it.

The careers of Hatshepsut and Thutmose reveal a well-documented power struggle, in which the formidable queen used all the means at her disposal—family, access to power, skill in manipulation—to score a remarkable triumph over a man who was himself one of the most powerful and determined figures in Egyptian history. She was helped by the fact that according to Egyptian law women and men were equal, and gender discrimination was far less prevalent in Egyptian society than in other cultures of the period. (For a more detailed discussion of the role of women in the ancient world, see Part I, Topic 6.) Indeed, viewed from the perspective of the past three and a half millennia, the fact that Hatshepsut was a woman seems to have played a surprisingly small role in her official life.

which symbolized the divine essence; Akhenaton, the name he assumed, means "the servant of Aton." Throughout Egypt, he had the name of Amen, the chief deity of Thebes, erased from inscriptions in temples.

Abandoning the sites which had been sacred for centuries, Akhenaton built a new capital, Akhetaton, two hundred miles north of Thebes (the location is generally known by its Arab name, Tel el-Amarna). From time immemorial, the Egyptians had buried their dead on the west bank of the Nile, the direction of the setting sun. Akhenaton reversed the process, having tombs constructed on the east bank.

The motives for this wholesale revolution in Egyptian religion may have been in large measure political, as a means of freeing the pharaoh from the powerful and entrenched priests of Amen. The previous 40 years had seen a struggle between the priests of Amen and those of the rival cult of Re, god of the sun. The attempts of the priests of Amen to deemphasize the sun cult led to the rise of the worship of Aton which

Akhenaton promoted. His preoccupation with religious reform dominated his reign, which saw the collapse of Egypt's empire in Asia. At the same time, a new style of art developed at his capital, which proved equally revolutionary.

The "Amarna" Style

Traditional Egyptian art made use of weighty, massive scale to portray its subjects in an idealized form. For the first time in Egyptian history, the artists of Akhenaton's reign produced naturalistic works, showing Akhenaton and his family in relaxed and even humorous mood. In portraits such as that of his wife, Nefertiti, grace and elegance replace the official solemnity of earlier ages. Depictions of Akhenaton himself suggest that the pharaoh was physically deformed in some way, and some statues show him with female breasts. The meaning of these strange works remains mysterious, although they may be intended to combine male and female elements as symbolic of Akhenaton's unique creative force—in imitation of the creator god Aton.

Akhenaton's revolution barely survived him. After his death, the priests reintroduced the worship of Amen, and Thebes once again became Egypt's capital. Tel el-Amarna was abandoned, and remained uninhabited desert for almost 3000 years. Many of Akhenaton's statues and buildings were destroyed, and others were thrown down and buried. Later pharaohs branded him a heretic, and cut his name out of the monuments of his reign that survived the destruction. References to him in later Egyptian history invariably call him "the criminal Akhenaton."

The End of the New Kingdom

It is uncertain whether Akhenaton's successor, Tutankhamen (c. 1334–1325 B.C.), was his son or half-brother. His reign, which marked a transitional stage between the worship of Aton and traditional religion, is best known for the treasures of his tomb—the only Egyptian royal grave to have survived intact. Tutankhamen himself made little impact on Egyptian art or history, but later rulers, including the mighty Ramses II (c. 1279–c. 1212 B.C.), built some of the most massive of all Egyptian temples while waging war in Asia. The following century, however, Egypt's power began to decline. The central authority of the pharaoh started to crumble as the priests assumed more and more secular control.

Akhenaton, Nefertiti, and three of their children.

THE DECLINE OF EGYPT

By the end of the New Kingdom, a series of powers in Mesopotamia began to chip away Egypt's conquests in Asia, and pushed the Egyptians back within their frontiers. Innately conservative, the Egyptians paid the price for their unwillingness to adapt to new ways; they were slow to change from bronze to the newly discovered material, iron, which their Mesopotamian enemies used for weapons.

As central authority declined, petty kings, high priests, and usurpers fought for power. In the ensuing chaos, Libyan mercenary soldiers were able to gain the throne. There was little new building, and the three centuries following 1000 B.C. were marked by stagnation. Only with the reign of the Nubian pharaoh, Shebaka (712–698 B.C.), was Egypt once again unified. The last century of Egyptian independence saw a revival of the arts, in which artists and architects returned to Old Kingdom models, in some cases making actual copies of works from almost 2000 years earlier.

By the time of Shebaka, Egypt had lost any claim to be a major power. For most of the next two centuries following his rule, the Egyptians maintained a precarious independence by a constantly changing series of alliances with the various warring Mesopotamian states. After being invaded by the Assyrians in 667 and 664 B.C., they finally succumbed to the Persians, who invaded Egypt in 525 B.C. The ruthless Persian king, Cambyses (c. 530–522 B.C.) crowned himself king of Egypt and rampaged through the country in a wave of pillaging and destruction. (For a discussion of the Persian Empire, see Part I, Topic 4.)

Few cultures in human history have preserved their traditional ways as determinedly as the Egyptians. The majestic certainties of the Old Kingdom, with its serene statues and religious ceremonies, remained an inspiration to later Egyptians for almost 3000 years. Lacking the aggressiveness of their Babylonian or Assyrian contemporaries, and the intellectual restlessness of the Greeks, the ancient Egyptians dedicated themselves to an unchanging vision of eternity—

Perhaps the most grandiose of all New Kingdom buildings: the Temple of Ramses the Great at Abu Simbel.

the anomaly of the reign of Akhenaton serves only to highlight the astonishing consistency of Egyptian culture.

During the New Kingdom, commercial expansion combined with increasing involvement in international affairs to place Egypt on a larger stage. Yet for most pharaohs the conquest of an empire remained secondary to the preservation of the traditions of Egypt itself; unlike the Akkadians, Babylonians, or Assyrians, the Egyptians were rarely driven by naked territorial expansion.

The Egyptian attitude was partly created by the country's geography. The Nile provided a means of unification and communication, whereas in Mesopotamia, by contrast, the Tigris and Euphrates, with their numberless tributaries, divided up the land into isolated areas whose inhabitants were prone to feuding. In addition, the amazing fertility of the Nile Valley meant that Egypt was virtually self-sufficient—not for nothing did the Greek historian and traveler Herodotus call Egypt "the gift of the Nile." Raw materials were abundant, notably the stone used for the temples and statues that commemorated Egyptian traditions.

To the south, the Nubian Desert protected Egypt from invasion; to the north lay the Mediterranean, a barrier for would-be immigrants. Even when foreigners did succeed in penetrating Egypt's defenses, as in the case of the Hyksos, they left little permanent impression. Thus, unlike the various peoples of Mesopotamia, the Egyptians had centuries of undisturbed peace in which to develop their civilization. Once they had formed their culture, they remained faithful to it for 3000 years.

Questions for Further Study

1. What was the relationship between Egyptian religion and Egyptian political and social development?
2. How did the Egyptians' strong emphasis on tradition affect their history? How does it contrast with their contemporaries?
3. What were the main features of Akhenaton's revolution?

Suggestions for Further Reading

Aldred, C. *Akhenaton, King of Egypt*. New York, 1988.
Clayton, P. A. *Chronicle of the Pharaohs*. New York, 1994.
Gardiner, A. *Egypt of the Pharaohs*. London, 1978.
Knapp, A. B. *The History and Culture of Ancient West Asia and Egypt*. Chicago, 1988.
Johnson, R. *The Civilization of Ancient Egypt*. London, 1978.
Redford, D. B. *Akhenaton, the Heretic King*. Princeton, NJ, 1984.
Smith, W. S., revised by W. K. Simpson. *The Art and Architecture of Ancient Egypt*. Baltimore, 1981.
Trigger, B. B. G. et al. *Ancient Egypt: A Social History*. Cambridge, 1983.

I

Topic 4

Other Peoples of the Ancient Near East

The valley peoples of Mesopotamia and Egypt were the earliest to develop urban civilizations in the ancient Near East, but from around 2000 B.C. the gradual rise of other cultures in the deserts and mountains of the region created new forces which often came into conflict with the older powers.

Newcomers who spoke an Indo-European language arrived in western Asia (modern Turkey) shortly after 2000 B.C., and combined with the preexisting population to found the Hittite kingdom. By 1600 B.C., the Hittites were strong enough to attempt the conquest of Syria and Babylon. Their empire reached its height in the reign of Suppiluliumas (1375–1335 B.C.), only to fall victim around 1200 B.C., like the Egyptian New Kingdom, to the migratory "Peoples of the Sea." Hittite society and culture owed much to Mesopotamian influences, but also had their own original aspects. Women achieved a higher social and religious status than in other contemporary societies, while the Hittites made contributions to fields as diverse as architecture and law.

To the south of the land of the Hittites lay Phoenicia (modern Lebanon), where the vital trade routes between Hittite territory, Egypt, and Mesopotamia all intersected. The first important culture to develop there was that of the Canaanites, a collection of petty city-states and kingdoms. The southern part of their territory fell to the Philistines around 1200 B.C.; to the north the surviving Canaanites, now known as the Phoenicians, became the leading traders and seafarers of the Mediterranean world. Among their lasting contributions to civilization was the further development of an alphabet which was copied by the Greeks, and became the script, as well as the means of transmission, of most of Western culture. Their navy also played a crucial role in military and commercial dealings between Assyrians, Neo-Babylonians, Persians, and Greeks.

The high plateau of ancient Persia (modern Iran) was the home of several important peoples. Both the Medes and the Persians probably migrated there before 1000 B.C. Nomadic tribes, they were famous for their horse breeding and riding exploits. With the vacuum left by the collapse of Egypt and Mesopotamia, their unified forces began the conquest of much of the ancient Near East: Nineveh (the Assyrian capital) in 612 B.C., Babylon in 539 B.C., all Egypt by 525 B.C.

Among the peoples living in the Persian Empire were the Jews. Originally a nomadic people in Mesopotamia, according to the Old Testament account the Hebrews migrated to Egypt. After the "Exodus" they settled in Palestine, where Saul established the first monarchy shortly before 1000 B.C. The kingdom eventually split into two: Israel to the north, and Judah to the south. The northern half was conquered by the Assyrians in 722 B.C., and its population dispersed; the southern kingdom of Judah fell to Babylon in 586 B.C. When Babylon itself fell to the Persians a few years later, the Persian ruler Cyrus the Great encouraged the reconstruction of Jerusalem.

THE KINGDOM OF THE HITTITES: IRON, WAR, BUREAUCRACY

Before the 20th century, the Hittites were an obscure, little understood people, chiefly known from biblical references. Now, after a century of archaeological excavation and research, it is clear that they were one of the most powerful and influential forces in the ancient Near East. Furthermore, they played an important role in passing on to their western neighbors, the predecessors of the Greeks, many of Mesopotamia's cultural achievements.

The Indo-Europeans

Unlike the Semitic-speaking peoples of Mesopotamia or the Egyptians, the Hittites spoke and wrote a language belonging to the Indo-European family. The original speakers of this group of languages probably came from the steppes of Central Asia and may have begun to migrate to Europe, the Near East, Iran, and India around 2000 B.C. As a result, nearly all modern European languages and Sanskrit, the sacred tongue of India, are related.

Recent estimates suggest that almost half the population of the planet at the end of the 20th century speaks—and thinks in—a language derived from Indo-European. To take a random example, the English word "three" shares its origins with the Russian *tri*, the Italian *tre*, the Bengali *tri*, and the Welsh *tri*. Yet the origins of the first speakers of Indo-European are remote and confused. As one recent scholar has written, "The Indo-Europeans did not burst into history; they straggled in over a period of 3,500 years."[1] Other experts prefer not even to use the term "Indo-European" for an actual people, but reserve it for a family of languages.

In any case, the appearance of the Hittites in the central Turkish region of Anatolia marks the earliest recorded appearance in history of an Indo-European language—recorded on over 25 thousand clay tablets discovered at their capital, Hattusas (modern Boğhazkōy), where the palace archives span the period from 1650 B.C. to 1200 B.C. Since most of their neighbors spoke a Semitic language—or else, like the Egyptians, one that was non-Indo-European—the earliest Hittites to settle in Anatolia probably migrated there, perhaps from north of the Black Sea. The first wave of arrivals probably occurred around 2300–2200 B.C. and the newcomers blended in with the preexisting population.

The Hittite Old Kingdom (c. 1750–1450 B.C.)

By 1750, a strong centralized state had emerged, with a king who appointed royal governors for the individual cities. Society was essentially feudal and consisted of three classes: land-owning warrior nobles, artisans, and peasants. Much of the strength of the Hittite Old Kingdom was based on trade. The Hittites mined large quantities of silver, copper, and lead. They also discovered how to smelt iron, but jealously guarded the new technology. The technique of iron-working remained their secret until the collapse of the Hittite Empire in 1200.

Hittite scribes developed two writing systems, one based on the Mesopotamian cuneiform and the other their own form of hieroglyphic (picture) script. The hieroglyphic inscriptions remained undeciphered until the first discovery of a bilingual text—in hieroglyphic Hittite and Phoenician—in the mid-20th century. Using these scripts, the Hittite government officials of Hattusas and other centers organized elaborate and thorough archives which contained copies of a wide variety of documents: trade records, diplomatic negotiations and treaties, official histories. Surviving literary works retell creation and flood legends, mostly based on traditional Mesopotamian myths.

Although Hittite legal documents were also influenced by Mesopotamian models, they show their own characteristics. The Hittites were clearly enthusiastic bureaucrats who sought to order their society with a seemingly endless series of regulations. The state fixed the prices for manufactured goods, food, and clothing, and there was an official tariff for services. Land grants were made in return for military service and strict conditions governed how the land should be farmed.

[1] J. P. Mallory, *In Search of the Indo-Europeans* (Thames and Hudson, 1989).

By contrast with many of their bloodthirsty neighbors, Hittite rulers favored relatively mild punishments. Even premeditated murder received only a financial penalty, and there is no mention of such sentences as impalement or castration, both of which were routinely inflicted by Assyrian law. One of the few crimes to earn the death penalty was stealing property from the royal palace; even a Hittite ruler's clemency had its limits.

The Hittite Empire (c. 1450 B.C.–1200 B.C.)

For the most part, Old Kingdom rulers concentrated on internal consolidation. Around 1600, Mursilis I overran northern Syria and pushed on as far as Babylon, but almost immediately lost his conquests.

About 1450, the Hittites felt secure enough to enlarge their borders. By the reign of Suppiluliumas I (c. 1352–c. 1322 B.C.), they had built up a state that stretched from Anatolia to northern Syria and included parts of Phoenicia and Palestine. The Hittites had to deal with the "great power" in the region, Egypt, and the next decades saw an alternation of diplomatic negotiations and skirmishing between the new imperialists and the Egyptians.

The rivalry culminated in 1276 with a pitched battle at Kadesh, in Syria, at which even the mighty pharaoh Ramses II failed to defeat his opponents. The Hittite forces, according to a contemporary inscription, included 2500 chariots and "the troops of sixteen nations," a formidable coalition. Both Ramses and Muwatallis, the Hittite king, claimed victory. More to the point, the two leaders negotiated a treaty, preserved in an Egyptian hieroglyphic inscription still visible at Karnak in Upper Egypt, which established friendlier relations between the two states.

Within three generations, the Hittite Empire was gone, perhaps swept away by large-scale climatic changes, coupled with the vast migrations of a group of peoples across Anatolia. These wanderers were called by Egyptian scribes the "Peoples of the Sea," whose origins remain obscure. Around 1200, they made a determined effort to settle in Egypt and were only beaten off by massive Egyptian resistance. The result was the weakening and collapse of Egypt's New Kingdom. (See Part II, Topic 1, for further discussion of the mysterious "Peoples of the Sea.)"

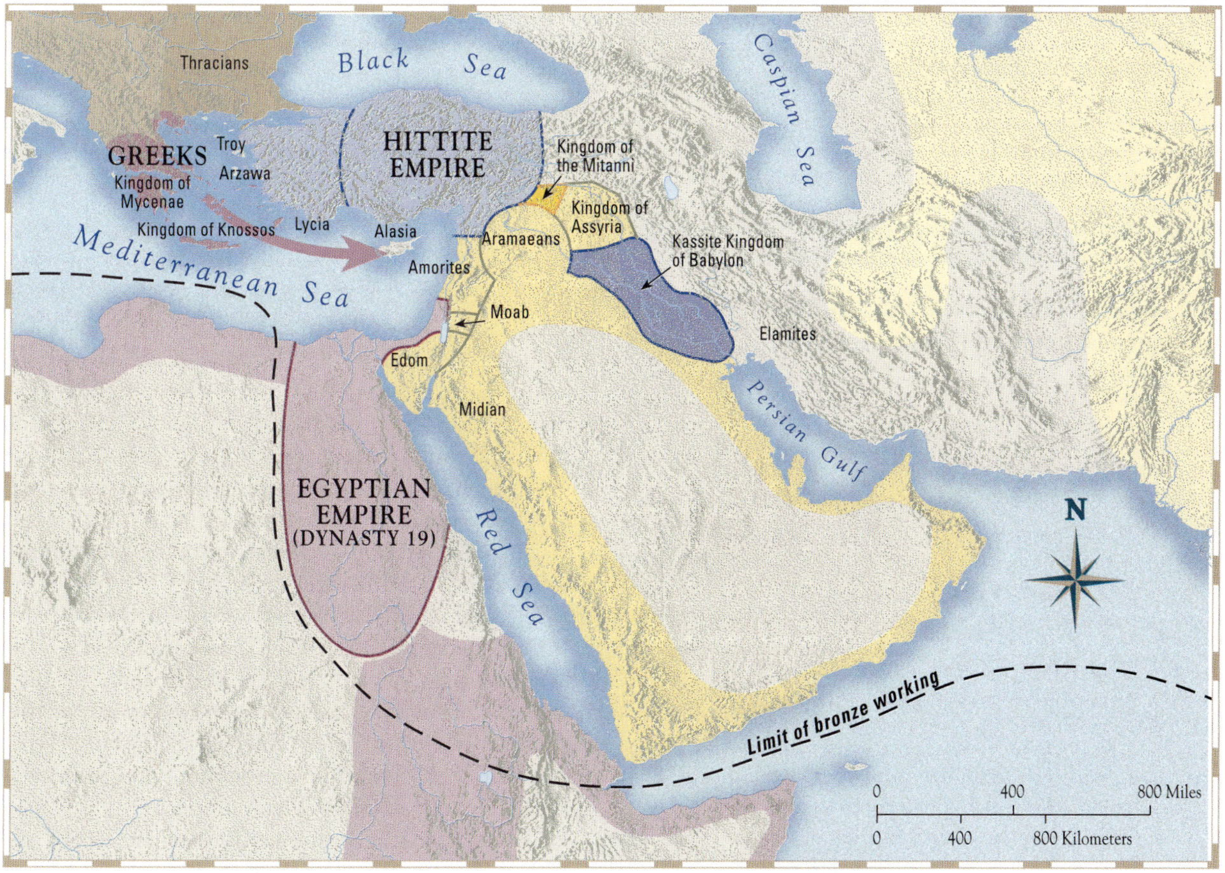

Map 4.1 Egypt and the Ancient Near East, c. 1300 B.C.

Hittite king and queen worshipping a bull, Alaja Hüyük.

For the Hittites, the turmoil of the times brought the collapse of centralized authority: the long military struggle with Egypt had left the state too weak to resist the new invaders. Some individual Hittite cities in north Syria continued to prosper, but by the end of the 8th century they were annexed by the Assyrians.

Significant Dates

Rise and Fall of Empires in the Ancient Near East (all dates B.C.)

c. 1750–1450	Hittite Old Kingdom
c. 1450–1200	Hittite Empire
c. 1400–1200	Canaanites flourish
Between 1300 and 1200	Hebrew exodus from Egypt
c. 1200	Migrations of Peoples of the Sea
c. 1200–1000	Rise of Phoenicians
c. 1020–1000	Reign of Saul, first Hebrew king
c. 1000–971	Reign of King David
c. 971–931	Reign of King Solomon
c. 800	Foundation of Phoenician colony of Carthage

THE PHOENICIANS: TRADERS AND SAILORS

Among the Semitic peoples to settle on the Mediterranean coast were the Canaanites, one of whose leading cities, Ugarit, flourished between 1400 B.C. and 1200 B.C. The city's location, together with its splendid natural harbor, made it a center for international trade: its archives have been found, and reveal commercial links with Egypt, the Hittites, and the Mycenaeans of mainland Greece (for a discussion of the Mycenaeans see Part II, Topic 1).

Like the rest of the Near East, the Canaanites were submerged in the chaos brought by the Peoples of the Sea around 1200. Shortly thereafter, the southern half of Canaanite territory was settled by the Philistines, one of the Peoples of the Sea. To the north, the Canaanite survivors—now known as the Phoenicians—rebuilt their chief cities, Byblos, Tyre, and Sidon, and soon became prominent and successful traders and seafarers in the Mediterranean.

The Phoenicians explored the ancient world, established important colonies, and developed technological innovations in metalworking and shipbuilding. Furthermore, their alphabet was imitated (with some

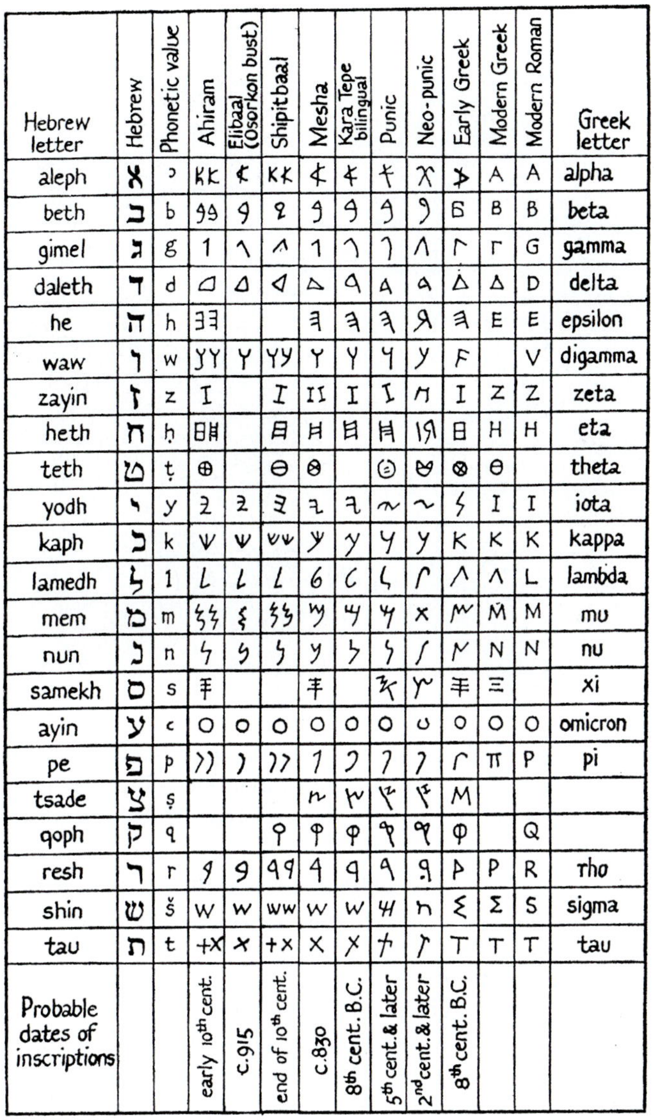

The development of the modern alphabet.

modifications) by the Greeks, and became the system of communication for virtually all Western civilization. Despite these achievements, they are generally not thought of as central to the history of the ancient world.

The reason for the relative neglect of the Phoenicians by later historians lies probably in the fact that they fell foul of the two peoples to whom we owe most of our information about them, the Greeks and the Romans. The Greeks saw them as their implacable—and often superior—rivals in the quest for colonies. The Romans feared their power in the western Mediterranean; after two ruthless and bloody wars, Roman troops systematically razed the Phoenician colony of Carthage. The general feelings of classical antiquity about the Phoenicians were summed up by the Greek historian Plutarch: "A people full of bitterness and surly, submissive to rulers, tyrannical to those they rule, abject in fear, fierce when provoked, unshakable in resolve, and so strict as to dislike all humor and kindness."

It must be admitted that we have little material evidence to offset this unflattering picture. Phoenicia itself was conquered first by the Assyrians and then by Persia, while the Romans either destroyed or resettled Phoenician centers in the west. As a result, little Phoenician art and practically no Phoenician literature has survived. We have no way of knowing what the Phoenicians thought of the Greeks or Romans, although it is not difficult to guess. Yet discoveries at colonies and trading sites throughout the Mediterranean are beginning to provide a more favorable impression of the nature of Phoenician culture, and correct ancient prejudices.

Phoenician Traders

The Phoenicians were above all traders and travelers. Phoenician ships transported goods found or made at

Carving depicting Phoenician trading ships carrying logs—perhaps cedars of Lebanon.

home, including wine, glass, wood—cedars of Lebanon were used in the construction of Solomon's temple at Jerusalem—and the purple dye for which they were famous. The trading vessels also served as international carriers, shipping products between the eastern and western Mediterranean.

As early as the first works of Greek literature, Homer's *Iliad* and *Odyssey*, we meet the figure of a Phoenician trader. In the *Odyssey*, Odysseus describes how he was abducted by a man "practiced in deceit, a greedy rogue who had already done much mischief," who first took him back to Phoenicia and then shipped him off on a cargo boat bound for Libya. The vagueness of the invective is striking, as is also the fact that Odysseus himself has just invented the whole story to fool his questioners.

To facilitate their trading, the Phoenicians established a series of bases throughout the Mediterranean. Moving westward, they founded colonies on the islands of Cyprus, Malta, Sicily, and Sardinia, and in mainland Spain. The traditional date of the foundation of their first North African settlement, Utica, was as early as 1100 B.C. By far the most important of the Phoenician colonies in North Africa was Carthage, founded in 814 B.C. When Phoenicia itself fell under Assyrian domination, and eventually under Persian rule, Carthage remained the center of Phoenician power and commerce in the west. (For an account of Rome's Punic—i.e. Phoenician—Wars with the Carthaginians, see Part II, Topic 7.)

These bases served both as trading posts and for exploration. One Phoenician sailor, Himilco, sailed north by the Atlantic coast of Spain and France to Britain, while the Greek historian Herodotus describes others as having circumnavigated Africa. Overland routes established trade relations with the interior of the Sahara, and perhaps even with Nigeria. These Phoenician caravan routes remained in use throughout Roman times, providing gold, ivory, wild beasts, and above all slaves.

In the absence of much written documentation, it is difficult to gain any real impression of Phoenician politics or society. Although Tyre and Sidon were the richest cities, other communities seem to have maintained a relative degree of independence. The Phoenicians apparently lacked the sense of national identity and taste for empire of the Hittites or the Romans; their various foreign settlements, with the notable exception of Carthage, were commercial bases rather than real towns—another reason we know so little about how they lived.

The names of Phoenician kings are recorded in the Bible and in Assyrian documents, but the system of hereditary monarchy seems to have died out, to be replaced by a council of elders and (according to Aristotle) an assembly of the people. The choice of magistrates and membership of the council depended on wealth rather than birth—an unusual social tolerance in the hierarchical world of the ancient Near East. The same openness applied to their attitude to their neighbors. Fierce to defend their own self-interests, they seem to have lived peaceably alongside a wide range of other peoples. They shared Sicily with the Greeks for over 500 years, and only deliberate Roman provocation brought them into open conflict with their eventual conquerors.

PERSIA: THE TOLERANT EMPIRE

Assyrian inscriptions of the 9th century B.C. provide us with the earliest reference to the Medes and Persians. Both peoples spoke Indo-European languages. They probably arrived in what is now Iran as a result of the same extended process of Indo-European migration which had brought the Hittites to Anatolia a thousand years earlier.

The region in which they first settled, to the southeast of the Caspian Sea, is largely composed of arid upland plateau, unsuitable for intensive farming. The Medes and Persians, originally nomadic peoples, devoted their energies to horse breeding, and they soon became famous for the quality of their animals and for their own prowess in riding.

At the beginning of the 7th century, the Medes gathered together their loose confederation of clans to form a settled society ruled by a king. The Persians followed their example, establishing themselves to the south of the Medes. By the end of the century, the Medes had established themselves as the stronger of the two peoples and made the Persians subject to them. The Persians retained their own king, who was, however, subordinate to the Median ruler. In 612 B.C., the Medes were sufficiently powerful to join with the Babylonians in destroying Nineveh, the capital of the hated Assyrians. The Median Empire they established, the first in Iran, lasted until the charismatic leadership of the Persian king Cyrus the Great enabled Persia to conquer the Medes and turn Media into the first satrapy (province) of the Persian Empire.

Cyrus the Great (559–530 B.C.)

Cyrus is one of the few imperial conquerors in history to have been respected, even revered, by the people he governed. The Greeks and the Jews, two peoples who fiercely disagreed about virtually everything else, both regarded him as a model ruler. Much of his popularity was due to his openness and tolerance: from the beginning he seems to have wanted to create a genuine "world empire," composed of different peoples living side by side while maintaining their own traditions and religions.

After coming to power in 559, Cyrus conquered Media in 550 and moved west. First Anatolia and then the Asia Minor kingdom of Lydia fell to the Persians. The latter conquest brought with it a string of Greek colonies which had been founded the previous century on the coast of Asia Minor. The inhabitants of these Greek towns were thus the first Europeans to become part of a Near Eastern empire.

Leaving part of his army as a garrison, Cyrus moved east to gain control of a vast swathe of land that stretched as far as the Indus Valley in western India. With his eastern borders now secure, and with his army swelled by recruits from the conquered territories, he moved south into Mesopotamia. In 539, Babylon was captured and Babylonia became a Persian province.

Cyrus spent the rest of his life—he was killed in battle in 530—organizing and administrating the empire he had built. He encouraged its various peoples to maintain their own religious and cultural traditions by restoring and rebuilding temples. He made it possible for the Jews, brought in captivity to Babylon 50 years

Darius and Xerxes giving audience.

Significant Dates

The Hebrew Kingdoms and the Persian Empire (all dates B.C.)

722	Kingdom of Israel destroyed by Assyrians
700–600	Unification of Persians under Achaemenid Dynasty
612	Nineveh destroyed by Medes and Babylonians
586	Fall of Jerusalem and kingdom of Judah; Hebrew exile in Babylon
550	Persians win control over Medes
539	Persian conquest of Babylon
538	Return of Hebrew exiles to Jerusalem
530	Death of Cyrus the Great
521–486	Reign of Persian King Darius

earlier, to return to Jerusalem and rebuild their own temple there. Locals were appointed to government positions in their own states, and Medes served as military commanders alongside Persians.

The Persian Empire Under Darius

Cyrus was succeeded as Great King of the Persians by his son Cambyses (530–522 B.C.), whose chief achievement was to conquer and add to the empire the only Near Eastern state which was still independent, Egypt. In 525 B.C., with help from Phoenician ships, Cambyses defeated the Egyptians and had himself declared pharaoh.

The long reign of Cambyses' successor Darius (521–486 B.C.), which included a minor conflict with the Greeks (for the viewpoint of the Greeks, who saw the Persian Wars as a crucial turning point in their history, see Part II, Topic 2), marked the definitive ordering of their now vast empire. Darius divided it into twenty satrapies, based on local customs, language, and religion. Each province's administration was in the hands of a satrap, a word literally meaning "protector of the Kingdom." The satraps were responsible for both civil and military affairs, and also for collecting taxes. To discourage these local governors from abusing their considerable power, royal inspectors traveled throughout the empire, reporting any irregularities to the central administration in the chief Persian capital, Susa. The inspectors were mockingly dubbed by the Greeks "the eyes and ears of the Great King."

Crucial to the working of the empire was a quick and efficient communication network. The pride of the Persian road system was the Royal Road, more than 1600 miles long, which led from Sardis in Asia Minor to Susa, with connecting roads to the empire's chief cities. Another of Darius' innovations which helped promote unity was the introduction of a standardized coinage, an idea first invented by the Lydians before their conquest by Cyrus. It is not certain whether Darius himself personally introduced Zoroastrianism, the empire's most widespread religion; he certainly favored its spread, without, however, discouraging other religions. (On Zoroastrianism, see Part I, Topic 5.)

THE HEBREWS: THE PEOPLE OF THE BOOK

The ancestors of the Jews of Cyrus' kingdom were a Semitic people, the Hebrews. The term "Hebrews" describes the 12 original Hebrew tribes; the Jews were two of those tribes, citizens of the kingdom of Judah, who survived the Babylonian conquest. The Hebrews were the first people in history to record their own origins and story in a consecutive written account covering many centuries. That narrative is contained in the Old Testament, where it is interspersed with other kinds of writing—poems (the Psalms), proverbs (the Book of Proverbs), and stories (Ruth).

Many parts of the story were written down only centuries after they occurred. Many experts agree that the earliest sections date to about 850 B.C., and the contents and arrangement of the work we call the Old Testament were established only in the 2nd century B.C. How reliable is this account, then, in describing the early history of a nomadic people with a tradition of grazing flocks and herds rather than settled farming and urban life?

For some 2000 years, many Jewish and Christian readers accepted the Bible (the word means "book" in Greek) as the inspired word of God. In the 19th and early 20th centuries, however, many Old Testament scholars came to treat it as a collection of folk tales and legends, valuable for its unconscious revelations about the source of the Judeo-Christian tradition rather than for serious historical accuracy.

Individual readers will evaluate the Old Testament's spiritual and moral dimensions in their own ways. For scholars, it is probably safest to regard the historical parts as essentially reflecting, if oversimplifying, the events they describe.

The Centuries of Migration

According to tradition, the Hebrews were the descendants of the patriarch Abraham, who was born in Mesopotamia, perhaps around 1800 B.C. Abraham and his people migrated westward to the land of Canaan, later settled by the Philistines around 1200. At some time after 1600, driven perhaps by famine, the Hebrews migrated to Egypt and settled down peacefully there. The dates approximately correspond with the Hyksos occupation of Egypt (see Part I, Topic 3). The Hyksos, a Semitic people, might well have been sympathetic to the Hebrew settlers.

Later Egyptian rulers—presumably after the expulsion of the Hyksos—enslaved the Hebrews. Around 1300 B.C., the charismatic figure Moses defied the pharaoh, whom some scholars identify as Ramses II, freed the Hebrews from bondage, and perhaps led the "Exodus" toward the Promised Land. On the Sinai peninsula, Moses may have forged what had been so far only a loose collection of tribes into a more united confederation.

For almost three centuries, the Hebrews battled first the Canaanites and then the Philistines to win territory in Palestine. Their division into 12 separate tribes, ruled by "judges" who were religious rather than military leaders, proved a serious handicap to organizing coordinated action. It was only when Saul (c. 1025–c. 1000 B.C.) welded the tribes into a single united monarchy that the foundations of a settled kingdom were laid.

The Monarchy and the Two Kingdoms

Saul himself seems an enigmatic figure. Although he achieved some military success against the Philistines, he was eventually driven to suicide by a defeat. His successor—and former rival—David (c. 1000–c. 971 B.C.) scored a series of overwhelming victories, driving the Philistines into a narrow strip of land in the western coastlands.

David's reign marked the Hebrews' final transition from a nomadic life to a settled urban community. Jerusalem became the capital, where David's son Solomon (c. 971–c. 931 B.C.) began an elaborate and expensive building program. At the heart of Solomon's new temple stood the Ark of the Covenant, the chest handed over by Moses as supreme symbol of the Invisible God.

Solomon's love of splendor, and his attempts to imitate the power and luxury of other Near Eastern monarchs, proved in the end unpopular and divisive. At his death, the 10 tribes in the north established a separate kingdom of Israel, while the remaining two retained Jerusalem as the capital of the kingdom of Judah. The northern kingdom soon fell prey to the Assyrians, who imposed the payment of tribute. Finally in 722 B.C. Assyrian forces destroyed the kingdom and Samaria, its capital. The conquerors deported the Hebrew population to various parts of their empire, where over time they disappeared, absorbed by the local population—they are often known as the "ten lost tribes."

The kingdom of Judah managed to survive for another century, helped by the fact that Assyrian power was declining. It was the Babylonians, who had finally defeated the Assyrians a few years earlier, who conquered Judah in 586 B.C. Under their king, Nebuchadnezzar, they plundered and burned Jerusalem and carried off its leading citizens to captivity in Babylon. Babylon itself fell in turn to the Persians in 538 B.C., and Cyrus encouraged the Jews—the population of the kingdom of Judah—to return to Jerusalem and reestablish the kingdom of Judah as part of the Persian Empire. It remained under Persian control until it was taken by Alexander the Great in 331 B.C. In 63 B.C. the Romans absorbed the kingdom into their empire.

The Jews remained politically subject to imperial powers for centuries, and their gradual spread

A reconstruction drawing of Solomon's Temple.

A depiction of the spoils from the sack of Jerusalem by the Romans.

throughout many parts of the world, a process known as the "diaspora," began early: the first Jewish community at Rome was founded in 139 B.C. Yet unlike the Hebrews of the "ten lost tribes," they never lost their sense of identity. Through the Babylonian captivity, they came to transform the notion of nationhood as linked with a specific place (or kingdom) into the sense of a community bound together by shared experience and, above all, religious observance.

God, the Covenant, and the Law

The survival of the Jews, together with the special role they played in the Western tradition, is not due to conquest or to political domination, but to the unique character of their religion. In terms of numbers and material power, in fact, they were overshadowed by many other ancient Near Eastern peoples. Their legacy consisted not of monumental sculptures or imperial palaces, but of a concept of God. This belief evolved over the early centuries of Hebrew history, until by the 6th century B.C. the Jewish concept of monotheism was fully established.

According to the Hebrew prophets of the 8th and 7th centuries B.C., there was only one God for all peoples, in all times and places. Immortal and invisible, his name, Yahweh, means "he causes to be." Ruler of the world, God stands outside the natural world he created: thus, to worship the sun or stars, as many ancient Near Eastern peoples did, was as idolatrous as to worship statues. A loving father, "slow to anger and rich in love," God would nevertheless punish those who persisted in breaking the ethical principles of divine law.

According to the Hebrew tradition, God first revealed the divine ideals of behavior immediately after the "Exodus." Through the mediation of Moses, God and the tribes of Israel entered into a covenant, whereby the Hebrews promised obedience to God's law as expressed in the Ten Commandments. In return, they became taken under divine protection as the "chosen people."

Thus, at the very heart of Hebrew monotheism lay the notion of the law of God, which established universal ethical principles by which to live. Many other ancient peoples also ordered their societies by devising law codes. These, however, served mostly to maintain a rigid class structure and to protect the power of the rulers. Since the God of the Old Testament was good and loving, his law was one of ethical provisions which apply to all humans: you—that, is, everyone—shall not kill, steal, commit adultery. The moral standards applied to all, rich and poor, rulers and ruled, and subsequent Hebrew laws made a point of protecting the weak—widows, orphans, slaves—from the excesses of the powerful.

The Prophets

Moses' encounter with God on Mount Sinai produced the basis for Hebrew law, which subsequently became expanded and extended by the teaching and preaching of the prophets. Many of these figures served as unofficial (and often unwanted) advisers to rulers of the two kingdoms in the times when Assyrian or Babylonian conquest loomed. They drew their authority from the fact that they claimed to speak with God's authority. Rather than try to foresee the future, they sought to call their people back to observance of the covenant, and warned of the dire consequences of breaking it.

Prophets such as Amos and Isaiah also concerned themselves with the ethical nature of social justice. Worship in the temple on its own was not enough; it had to be combined with an active life of fairness, generosity, and compassion toward all, especially those most in need of help. The prophets bitterly denounced extravagance and arrogance, and the mistreatment of the weak. Furthermore, they taught that the Hebrews had been chosen by God to transmit this spirit of universal social justice to the world. Someday they would lead in building a universal human community, bound in peace by its worship of the one true God. In this way, the prophets transformed the separateness of the original covenant into a vision of human unity and the end of war: "Nation will not take up sword against nation, nor will they train for war anymore."

Their warnings and gloomy predictions were generally ignored. The consequences, they claimed, were the Assyrian and Babylonian conquests of the two kingdoms, whose citizens were punished in this way for ignoring God's law and breaking the covenant. Their ideal vision of a world united one day in universal peace seems as remote at the end of the 20th century as it did to the prophets themselves two and a half thousand years ago. Yet the vision survived the disasters of the times, and passed on to become one of the most powerful inspirations of Western culture.

The first half of the first millennium B.C. *saw the final decline of the founders of western civilization 2000 years earlier. Egypt became reduced to a province in the Persian Empire, and the long series of dominant Mesopotamian peoples ended with the Persian victories over the Assyrians and the Babylonians. The Hittites, relative newcomers to the imperial scene, disappeared into obscurity. The Phoenicians lost their homeland in the course of the struggle between the leading powers, although Carthage—their western colony—survived long enough to present a serious challenge to the most successful of all imperialists, the Romans.*

All of these cultures developed complex societies and produced significant works of art, described and analyzed in the next two Topics. Yet their people are long since gone, swallowed up in the course of history. The only survivors from the ancient Near East are the Jews, whose tiny kingdoms, established with difficulty, were conquered by Assyrians, Babylonians, Persians, Alexander's Macedonians, and eventually by Rome. The people who gave Western civilization the source of one of its two great traditions—the Judeo-Christian and the Classical—maintained their own traditions throughout the centuries of the diaspora.

Questions for Further Study

1. How did culture spread in the ancient world? Consider the relative importance of writing, colonization, trade, and technology.
2. What were the chief differences between the Persian Empire and other earlier imperial powers? What were their results?
3. Hebrew culture was, from the beginning, patriarchal. How did this affect its later developments and eventual contribution to Western civilization?

Suggestions for Further Reading

Anderson, B. W. *Understanding the Old Testament*. Englewood Cliffs, NJ, 1986.
Bright, John. *A History of Israel*. Louisville, KY, 1981.
Cook, J. M. *The Persian Empire*. New York, 1983.
Dothan, T., and M. Dothan. *People of the Sea: The Search for the Philistines*. New York, 1992.
Drews, R. *The End of the Bronze Age: Change in War and the Catastrophe ca. 1200* B.C. Princeton, NJ, 1993.
Finkelstein, I. *The Archaeology of the Israelite Settlement*. Jerusalem, 1988.
Grant, M. *The History of Ancient Israel*. New York, 1984.
Gurney, O. R. *The Hittites*. Baltimore, 1981.
Harden, D. *The Phoenicians*. Baltimore, 1980.
Macqueen, J. *The Hittites and Their Contemporaries in Asia Minor*. Boulder, CO, 1975.
Miller, J. M., and J. H. Miller. *A History of Ancient Israel and Judah*. Philadelphia, 1986.
Sandars, N. K. *The Sea Peoples: Warriors of the Ancient Mediterranean*. London, 1978.
Shanks, H., ed. *Ancient Israel: A Short History from Abraham to the Roman Destruction of the Temple*. Washington, DC, 1988.
Stiebing, Jr., W. *Out of the Desert? Archaeology and the Exodus/Conquest Narratives*. Buffalo, NY, 1989.

I

Topic 5

Art and Belief in the Ancient World

For all their enormous chronological and geographical range and variety, many of the civilizations of the ancient world shared certain common attitudes to religion and art. The only important exceptions were the Hebrews.

The chief deities of most cultures were inspired by the natural world. The sun god of the Egyptians, the Hittite weather god, and Enlil, the Mesopotamian god of wind, are all examples of forces that could be both life-giving and destructive. The earth itself was often symbolized as a mother goddess.

The priests in charge of the worship of the various deities frequently achieved wealth and political power. In Sumerian city-states, the temple formed the center of the community, and the priests played a major role in the city's economic life. The Egyptian priests of Amen and Re at Thebes became the country's richest landowners. In some cultures, the priests jealously guarded the traditional rites and beliefs: in the whole of Egyptian history, only one pharaoh ever sought to make fundamental changes in the established religion. Other peoples were more open to change, which was often inspired by outside influences. The Hittites' religion combined Egyptian and Mesopotamian elements with their own Indo-European gods.

The political leaders of virtually all ancient societies depended for their authority on the goodwill of the priestly class. In some cases—the Egyptian pharaohs, for example—these rulers were worshiped as divinities. Babylonian kings such as Hammurabi, by contrast, thought of themselves as the servants of the gods on earth. The most independent rulers were the Assyrian kings. Although officially the vice-regents of the god Ashur, they acted as absolute monarchs with unlimited powers.

Both political and religious leaders turned to artists to express the beliefs and policies of the state. The great temple constructions of the Nile Valley combined architecture and sculpture to proclaim the immortality of their builders. Tombs themselves provided another opportunity to architects, while among the noteworthy palace complexes are the Hittite palace at Boğhazkōy, and the Assyrian royal palace at Nineveh.

When free from the constraints of official control, and working on a smaller scale, ancient artists often used precious materials to produce works combining realistic elements with a fine sense of design. Many examples of Mesopotamian carved seals, Egyptian jewelry, and Phoenician ivories seem at least in part to have been made to give pure visual pleasure.

Apart from archives and letters, the writings of the ancient world are generally sacred in inspiration. They range in mood from the weary pessimism of the Sumerian *Epic of Gilgamesh* to the lyric passion of the *Song of Solomon* in the Old Testament: the Old Testament was the Hebrews' major contribution to the cultural achievement of the ancient world.

GODS, PRIESTS, AND WORSHIPERS: VARIETIES OF RELIGIOUS EXPERIENCE

The leading cultures of the ancient world left a rich religious and artistic legacy, much of it still worthy of our attention. The daily life of Westerners at the end of the 20th century may seem to have nothing in common with that of the people of Mesopotamia or the wandering Hebrews. Yet many of the overriding issues faced by past civilizations are still valid. Do our lives have a meaning, and do they continue in some form after death? Is there a spiritual level of existence, watched over by some form of divinity? On a more mundane level, how should religious issues relate to the secular life of the state?

Perhaps the most powerful link of all between the ancient world and the late 20th century is our shared concern with the world of nature. As we face the ecological crises of the next millennium, the respect of the ancients for the earth—wind and weather, rivers, animals, and vegetation—seems especially relevant. When we can see this sympathy for nature expressed in the form of works of art, the essential unity of human experience becomes even clearer.

Facing such universal problems, it is not surprising that many ancient cultures arrived at similar solutions. Behind the seemingly endless variety of deities and their depictions, and political and social systems of organization, there are often common responses. One people, however, formed an important exception to this tendency: the Hebrews. The belief which they evolved of a single transcendent universal deity has no parallel elsewhere, even in the monotheism of Egyptian religion under Akhenaton or in Zoroastrianism, the religion of ancient Persia. As for the visual arts, the Hebrew ban on depicting religious images prevented the development of any significant tradition in painting or sculpture, while the relative poverty of their small kingdoms left little in the way of architecture: the

A limestone relief showing cattle fording a canal.

only Hebrew building to achieve fame, Solomon's temple, was essentially designed and built by Phoenicians. By contrast, the only surviving Hebrew work of literature, the Old Testament, was a key element in the formation of the Western tradition.

The Egyptians and the Divine Forces of Nature

For the Egyptians, the entire world, human and natural, was subject to divine forces. The source of life was the sun, and the sun god Re had created the world by bringing order out of primeval chaos. The human equivalent of the sun was the Egyptian ruler, the pharaoh, whose title proclaimed him the "Son of Re."

Egypt's survival depended on the annual flood of the Nile, whose waters kept the land fertile, and the river and land deities Isis and Osiris played a central role in Egyptian religion. The god Osiris was killed by his evil brother and then reborn, thanks to the devotion of his wife Isis. His resurrection symbolized the annual rebirth of the earth at flood time.

Over time, the cult of Isis, Osiris, and their son, the falcon god Horus came to represent the Egyptian belief in human resurrection after death. Osiris presided over elaborate funeral rituals, at which the dead had to account for their lives; the god then judged whether they were deserving of a happy afterlife. These ceremonies were originally reserved for the ruling class, but by the Middle Kingdom Egyptian religion extended the possibility of life after death to all those Egyptians who could afford a tomb, mummification, and proper burial rites—in practice, the upper and middle classes.

Other deities, in the form of animals, symbolized forces of nature. The hawk god Seker was god of the night sun; the cow goddess Hathor symbolized pleasure and love, and was also associated with one of the creation myths. Certain animals, notably the bull and the cat, also had sacred properties. Bastet, the elegant cat goddess, was worshiped at Bubastis; her temple there was begun in the 4th dynasty, and later pharaohs continued to enrich it over the following 17 centuries. Recent exploration at Bubastis has uncovered a cemetery, whose underground galleries contained thousands of mummified cats. The tales and rituals that developed around these deities, subdeities, and nature spirits formed a bewilderingly rich accumulation of belief, jealously preserved by the priests.

The Mesopotamian Universe

Like the Egyptians, the Sumerians and later Mesopotamian peoples were at the mercy of their environment. The Egyptians could count on the Nile's regular flooding, but the climate of the land between the two rivers (Tigris and Euphrates) was much less stable, so that springtime melting of winter snows often produced raging and uncontrollable floods.

Female head from Uruk; the original hair was probably gold leaf.

The deities symbolizing these forces were thus seen as both creative and destructive, with the power to wreak havoc in human lives. Unlike the Egyptians, with their strong sense of order in the universe, the Mesopotamians felt helpless in the face of the inscrutable forces of nature. Their gods were capable of both good and evil, and in any case were themselves unable to control the world. Nor could the Sumerians hope for a happier life after death: they believed that beyond the troubles of this world lay only the dim prospect of eternal gloom.

The three chief gods represented the sky, the earth, and the wind. As sky god and father of the gods, Ana ruled over all, and Sumerian kings served as his agent on earth. Enki, god of the earth, had charge of rivers and canals, which were vital to the irrigation systems of Mesopotamia. The wind god Enlil symbolized force and energy, sometimes positive and creative characteristics, sometimes the cause of violent destruction.

The chief goddess was Ninhursaga, a more beneficent power. Her early connection with mountains and plants gradually changed emphasis, and she became thought of as a mother goddess figure. The other deities included a goddess of the morning and evening star, Inanna, and gods of the sun and moon, Utu and Nanna.

The Hittite weather god, armed with thunder (a hammer) and lightning.

The Weather Gods of the Hittites

The mountainous territory of the Hittites was a region of clouds and storms, with an ever-changing climate. Not surprisingly, the chief Hittite god was the weather god Taru. On one relief carving he stands threateningly brandishing what seems to be forked lightning. Unlike the Egyptians and Mesopotamians, the Hittites worshiped a female sun deity, whose name was Wurusemu. The sun goddess became the supreme head of the Hittite state, and the king always turned to her first for help in battle or in time of national emergency: "Queen of the land of Hatti, Queen of Heaven and Earth, mistress of the kings and queens of the land of Hatti!" The son of Taru and Wurusemu was the god of agriculture, of whom his father says: "This son of mine is mighty, he harrows and ploughs and makes the crops grow."

As the Hittites came into contact with neighboring cultures, they began to incorporate other religious practices into their own. The Mesopotamian gods Ana and Enlil appear in Hittite texts, and the Hittites followed the Babylonian custom of organizing a great New Year festival to mark the triumph of spring over winter—life over death or good over evil. The Hittites themselves may, in turn, have influenced the Greeks. The burial rituals described by Homer in his account of the funeral of Patroclus (*Iliad*, Book XXIII) are remarkably similar to those referred to in a series of inscribed Hittite tablets.

Rituals, Sacrifices, and Divination

Each ancient culture devised its own form of ritual for honoring its deities, but as we have seen in the case of the New Year festival, the holidays and ceremonies of different peoples often resembled one another. The seasons of the year, the consecration of a new temple, a victory over an enemy, all these were marked by processions and sacrifices. Most sacrificial rites involved food, and many included the slaughter of animals. Human sacrifice was rare, but not unknown. After a military defeat, the Hittites sacrificed a man in a ritual of purification, and abundant evidence has come to light of the Phoenician sacrifice of infants, thus confirming the Old Testament account. Some Early Dynastic Egyptian kings had their servants buried in buildings alongside their own tombs. The practice was soon abandoned, and later pharaohs' servants and companions were represented symbolically. (The Sumerians also buried servants alongside their masters, as demonstrated by the finds in the tombs of the first dynasty at Ur, c. 2500 B.C.)

In addition to the official state cults, the events in the life of an individual were marked by the appropriate ceremonies. The most obvious example is the funeral ritual. Virtually all the peoples described in these Topics inhumed dead bodies (that is, buried them intact). The Hittites sometimes inhumed their dead and sometimes cremated them. The Egyptians were unique in their preservation of the body by an elaborate mummification process, and also in the complexity of their tombs.

Magic played a large part in much ancient religion. The Babylonians and Assyrians, in particular, developed a wide variety of techniques for trying to read the future by communicating with their gods. The inspection of animal organs, the throwing of dice, a reading of the movements of the stars, were all ways to foretell divine intentions. Appropriate prayers could then try to change those intentions if they were undesirable.

DOCUMENTS ON HISTORY

Aspects of the Divine in the Ancient World

One of the functions of religious literature in the ancient world was to explain how the world came into being, and creation myths can be found in many different ancient cultures, often bearing striking similarities. At the same time, since rulers claimed their authority to govern from divine patronage, it was in their interest to emphasize the omnipotence of the gods who had entrusted them with earthly rule.

For ordinary subjects, however, faced with the uncertainties of their daily routine and the mysteries of human existence, the granite certainties of official pronouncements were not always convincing. Documents from both Mesopotamian and Egyptian sources bear witness to a vein of pessimism and scepticism underlying attitudes to sacred and secular authority.

One of the continuing appeals of religion is the performance of public ceremonies and rituals. For the most part, the ancient versions of these are lost to us, but a fascinating Hittite text offers a detailed and vivid account of a "Royal Ritual."

THE CREATION OF THE WORLD

Many of the creation myths which circulated in the ancient world have points in common. They emphasize the emergence of order from chaos, the separation of land and sea, the division between heaven and earth, and the creation of humankind in the image of the divine. The first extract below describes the Egyptian creator-god Re-Atum, who existed before the creation of the world. The "primeval hillock" in Hermopolis was one of the "creation mounds" where, the Egyptians believed, the world began. Its shape probably inspired the use of the pyramid as the site of the burial—and subsequent rebirth—of the pharaoh.

The next two passages give first the Sumerian and then the Babylonian version of creation. The benevolent Sumerian god Enlil, "Lord Air," separated the earth from the sky. Marduk, the Babylonian equivalent, is an altogether more ferocious spirit. Clad in "an armour of terror, a turban of fearsome halo," and riding his storm chariot, his victory over chaos reflected the Babylonians' own violent conquest of their Sumerian predecessors.

Re-Atum

I am Atum when I was alone in Nun (the primordial waters); I am Re in his first appearance, when he began to rule that which he had made. What does that mean? This "Re when he began to rule that which he had made" means that Re began to appear as a king, as one who had existed before the air god Shu had even lifted heaven from earth, when he, Re, was on the primeval hillock which was in Hermopolis.

From H. and H. A. Frankfort, *Before Philosophy.* Copyright © 1949. The University of Chicago Press.

The Sumerian View

Without Enlil, the Great Mountain,
No city would be built, no settlement founded,
No stalls would be built, no sheepfolds established,
No king would be raised, no high priest born. . . .
The rivers—their floodwaters would not bring
overflow,
The fish in the sea would not lay eggs in the canebrake,

The birds of heaven would not build nests on the wild earth,
In heaven the drifting clouds would not yield their moisture,
Plants and herbs, the glory of the plain, would fail to grow,
In field and meadows the rich grain would fail to flower,
The trees planted in the mountain-forest would not yield their fruit. . . .

From S. N. Kramer, *History Begins at Sumer.* Copyright © 1959, pp. 93–94. Reprinted with permission of Mrs. Samuel Kramer.

The Babylonian View

All lands were sea
Then there was a movement on the midst of the sea;
At that time Eridu was made. . . .
Marduk laid a reed on the face of the waters,
He formed dust and poured it out beside the reed
That he might cause the gods to dwell in the dwelling of their hearts' desire.
He formed mankind
With him the goddess Aruru created the seed of mankind.
The beasts of the field and living things in the field he formed
The Tigris and Euphrates he created and established them in their place:
Their name he proclaimed in goodly manner
The grass, the rush of the marsh, the reed and the forest he created,
The lands, the marshes and the swamps;
The wild cow and her young, the lamb of the fold,
Orchards and forests;
The he-goat and the mountain-goat. . . .
The Lord Marduk built a dam beside the sea. . . .
Reeds he formed, trees he created;
Bricks he laid, buildings he erected;
Houses he made, cities he built. . . .

From *Ancient Civilizations,* by N. F. Cantor and M. S. Werthman, p. 26. Copyright © 1972 Harlan Davidson, Inc. Reprinted by permission.

DIFFERING HUMAN ATTITUDES TO THE DIVINE

The four following extracts convey a wide range of responses to traditional religious beliefs. In the first, Hammurabi, the proud king of Babylon, proclaims his achievements, accomplished under divine patronage. The second comes from a letter written by a simple Babylonian citizen, Apiladad, who feels neglected by the god who should be protecting his interests, and writes to the deity in protest. Apiladad implies that the gods have need of faithful worshipers. He politely hints that his devotion will continue only if his protector solves his problem (perhaps by asking Marduk, lord of the gods, to cure an illness).

The other two documents are far more somber. In the first, an anonymous Babylonian, echoing the mood of the Sumerian Epic of Gilgamesh, *meditates on the brevity and uncertainty of life. The other, the* Song of the Harper, *dates to Middle-Kingdom Egypt. Like the Mesopotamian writer of the previous passage, its author describes the transitory nature of human achievement, but in the end draws comfort from the idea of living for present pleasure.*

Hammurabi's Achievements

(Hammurabi speaks)
I rooted out the enemy above and below;
I made an end of war;

continued next page

I promoted the welfare of the land;
I made the people rest in friendly habitations;
I did not let them have anyone to terrorize them.
The great gods called me,
So I became the beneficent shepherd whose sceptre is righteous;

My benign shadow is spread over my city.
In my bosom I carried the people of the land of Sumer and Akkad;
They prospered under my protection;
I have governed them in peace;
I have sheltered them in my strength.

From Pritchard, J. B., *Ancient Near Eastern Texts Relating to the Old Testament.* Copyright © 1995 by Princeton University Press. Reprinted by permission of Princeton University Press.

A Babylonian Citizen

To the god my father speak; thus says Apiladad, thy servant:
"Why have you neglected me so?
Who is going to give you one who can take my place?
Write to the god Marduk, who is fond of you,
That he may break my bondage;
Then I shall see your face and kiss your feet!
Consider also my family, grown-ups and little ones;
Have mercy on me for their sake, and let your help reach me!"

From H. and H. A. Frankfort, op. cit., p. 221.

The Uncertainty of Life

Who came to life yesterday, died today.
In but a moment man is cast into gloom, suddenly crushed.
One moment he will sing for joy,
And in an instant he will wail—a mourner.
Between morning and nightfall men's mood may change:
When they are hungry they become like corpses,
When they are full they will rival their god,
When things go well they will prate of rising up to heaven
And when in trouble, rant about descending into hell.

From Stephen Langdon, *Babylonian Wisdom.* Copyright © 1923, pp. 35–66.

Song of the Harper

One generation passes away
And others remain in its place
Since the time of the ancestors.
The gods that were aforetime
Rest in their pyramids.
They that built houses,
Their places are no more;
What has been done with them?
I have heard the sayings of Imhotep and Djedefhor,
With whose words men still speak so much;
What are their places?
Their walls have crumbled,
Their places are no more,
As if they had never been.
None cometh from thence
That he might tell their circumstances,
That he might tell their needs
And content our heart
Until we have reached the place
Whither they have gone.
May thy heart be cheerful
To permit the heart to forget
The making of funerary services for thee.
Follow thy desire while thou livest!
Put myrrh upon thy head,

Clothe thyself in fine linen,
Anoint thee with the genuine wonders
Which are the god's own.
Increase yet more thy happiness,
And let not thy heart languish;
Follow thy desire and thy good,
Fashion thine affairs on earth
After the command of thy heart.
That day of lamentation will come to thee,
When the Still of Heart does not hear their lamentation,
And mourning does not deliver a man from the netherworld.
Make holiday!
Do not weary thereof!
Lo, none is allowed to take his goods with him,
Lo, none that has gone has come back!

From Miriam Lichtheim, "The Song of the Harper," *Journal of Near Eastern Studies*, IV, The University of Chicago Press. Copyright © 1945, pp. 192–193.

RELIGION AND RITUAL

Ancient sculptures and paintings often depict official ceremonials involving rulers and priests. They include the burial rites shown in the Egyptian Book of the Dead, *Assyrian scenes of sacrifice, and depictions of Hittite rulers in prayer. In many of these rituals divine figures appear alongside the humans.*

In the case of Hittite ceremonies, we have a chance to observe the enacting of a ritual moment by moment, as it is described in the "stage directions" which have survived on inscribed tablets. The following instructions relate to a major Hittite festival, perhaps the Spring Festival in honour of the weather gods which—like the Babylonian New Year ritual—celebrated the return of spring and the triumph of good over evil. They provided the participants with a detailed account of how to carry out the ceremony.

The king and queen come out of the house. Two palace-servants and one member of the bodyguard walk in front of the king, but the lords, the rest of the palace-servants, and the bodyguard walk behind the king.

The king and queen go into the temple of Zababa. They kneel once before the spear; the statue worshipper speaks, the herald calls. . . .

The king and queen sit down on the throne. Two palace-servants bring the king and queen water from a jar of gold. The king and queen wash their hands. The chief of the palace-servants gives them a cloth and they wipe their hands.

Two palace-servants place a knee-cloth for the king and queen.

The verger walking in front, the "table-men" step forward.

The verger walks in front and shows the king's sons to their seats.

The verger goes outside and walks in front of the chief cooks, and the chief cooks step forward. . . .

The Master of Ceremonies goes inside and announces to the king. They bring forth the "Ishtar" instruments—the king says, "let them bring them forth!"

The Master of Ceremonies goes outside to the courtyard and says to the verger, "They are ready, they are ready!" The verger goes out to the gate and says to the singers, "They are ready, they are ready!" The singers pick up the "Ishtar" instruments. The verger walking in front, the singers bring the "Ishtar" instruments in, and take up their position.

The cooks place ready dishes of water and meat; they divide the lean from the fat.

[At this point there follows a ceremonial meal, eaten to the accompaniment of music, and the ritual ends with sacrifices.]

From O. R. Gurney, *The Hittites*. Copyright © 1954, pp. 153–155.

Portrait of the Old Kingdom pharaoh Chefren, builder of one of the pyramids.

One of the regular duties of a Mesopotamian ruler was to spend a night in his state's chief temple, sacrificing, praying, and finally sleeping. The god would then appear to him in his dreams and give him his orders. On one recorded occasion, when the river Tigris failed to rise, Gudea of Lagash went to sleep in the temple to find out the meaning of the drought.

RELIGION, POWER, AND THE STATE

The vast mass of religious materials—prayers, spells, rituals, the interpretation of signs—were all firmly under the control of the priests, who thus wielded power over rulers and ruled alike. The notion of a separation between state and religion would have been unthinkable for any ancient people, but the actual system of government varied from culture to culture.

Egyptian Theocracy: The Rule of God

The Egyptians did not distinguish between the power of the state and that of the gods: they were one and the same. The pharaoh was the link, recreating on earth the role of the sun god in the heaven and bringing order out of anarchy and chaos. The gods had sent him to tend humankind, but he himself was not human, standing as he did between his subjects and the gods. One Middle Kingdom ruler wearily advised his son and successor: "Do not approach your subordinates in your loneliness. Fill not your heart with a brother, know not a friend, nor create for yourself intimates."

The pharaoh's duties included the performing of specific rituals which were signals to the gods that Egypt was attentive to their needs. In theory, only the pharaoh had access to the cult statue of the god in the Holy of Holies, the innermost sanctum of the temple. Furthermore, according to state law the king was the sole priest for all the gods throughout Egypt.

Beneath the ruler were various ranks of priests, some serving state cults, some in the service of local deities, whom the pharaoh appointed as his deputies. By the end of the Old Kingdom, these religious officials had devised a series of rituals and ceremonies which remained consistent throughout Egyptian history. In religion, as in everything else, the Egyptian fidelity to tradition is one of their most consistent characteristics. The early rituals prescribe certain kinds and quantities of offerings to the gods. The Egyptians followed the prescriptions, virtually unchanged, for almost 2000 years.

For all the nominal authority of the pharaoh, so strong a tradition reinforced the power of the priesthood, and over time the Egyptian theocracy depended as much on their rule as on the pharaoh's. Akhenaton, the only ruler to defy the forces of religion and undermine the entrenched position of the priests, was a unique exception, and his reforms collapsed with his death (for a discussion of his reign, see Part I, Topic 3). The reaction of succeeding rulers and priests was predictably violent.

By the New Kingdom, the chief religious centers of Egypt had accumulated riches and landholdings, and the power of their priests tended to increase. The priests of Amen and Re at Thebes owned even more capital and land than the pharaoh. One of the results of their wealth is a temple whose size is staggering even by Egyptian standards. Legal texts record a number of cases in which the priests of Thebes, and also those of the god Ptah at Memphis, abused their powers.

Thus the "Rule of God" was really the rule of religion. The priesthood demanded blind obedience to a system which gave the temples power and control, while the very remoteness which gave the pharaoh his divine authority eliminated any possibility of change. Every aspect of Egyptian culture worked to maintain its "eternal" character.

Kings and Priests in Mesopotamia

Government in each of the cities of Mesopotamia was in the hands of a civic ruler, who acted in the name of the community's divine protectors. Unlike in Egypt, a Mesopotamian king's subjects did not automatically consider him a god or make him the focus of a cult, although certain rulers became thought of as divine. Instead, acting as the servant of the gods, the king's function was to protect and improve the lives of his citizens by overseeing government projects. Among his responsibilities were economic planning, construction

Abu, the god of vegetation, and the mother goddess, with priests and worshippers.

of civic and religious building projects, and the maintenance of the laws.

All official business was conducted in the name of the gods. Thus, the Babylonian king Hammurabi claimed to rule the land and publish his law code—with its concern for family relationships and the rights of wives—with the authoritative approval of the sun god (see Part I, Topic 6).

Only the Assyrian rulers, toward the end of the history of an independent Mesopotamia, managed to achieve a consistent degree of secular independence and governed as absolute monarchs sustained by brute force. The militaristic and aggressive nature of Assyrian society meant that successful military leaders could win great power and wealth. Sargon II (721–705 B.C.) probably became king as the result of a military coup. Throughout his reign, his control of the efficient and ruthless Assyrian army enabled him to crush a constant series of rebellions and fend off all challenges to his power.

The Assyrians' almost constant state of warfare meant that their warrior kings were able to maintain their superiority over rival religious leaders. Nor could the temple authorities take control of other areas of civic life: the lack of a stable peace caused trade and commerce to decline. In any case, the Assyrian ruling class seemed to regard these peacetime occupations as unworthy of fighting men. Thus the only area in which the priests could maintain their influence was that of agriculture, since over the preceding centuries the temples had inherited most of the best farmlands.

ANCIENT ARTISTS AND THEIR WORLDS

In societies so dominated by the ruling classes and by religion, in general the visual arts served to reinforce the official state ideology. The most lasting memorials of ancient culture are temples, tombs, and palaces, and public architecture played a major role in expressing each society's self-image. It is no coincidence that the earliest creative artist whose name is known to history was the Egyptian Imhotep, who worked around 2630 B.C. as the architect and adviser to the pharaoh Zoser.

Temples, Tombs, and Cities

For the Egyptians, a temple was inhabited by the deities to whom it was consecrated, and represented a model of the universe seen from the gods' point of view. Around the outside of the buildings making up a temple complex ran a wall of mud brick, isolating the temple's sacred space from the outside world. This protective barrier symbolized the first stage of creation, the primeval mud produced by uniting heaven and earth. The outer walls of the actual temple showed carved scenes of the pharaoh fighting and winning battles against the forces of darkness, human and divine. Ordinary Egyptians could not pass beyond this point, for only ritually purified priests entered the temple proper.

The colossal temples to Amen, the wind god, at the ancient city of Thebes are the result of successive periods of building extending over hundreds of years. The earliest parts of the temple complex of Karnak date to shortly after 2000 B.C., while the outer gate, begun around 350 B.C., was never finished. At the heart of the constructions at Karnak lies the gigantic Hall of the Columns, begun in 1307 B.C. by Ramses I (1307–1306 B.C.) and finished by his grandson Ramses II (1290–1224 B.C.), the most prodigious of all builders in the New Kingdom. The Hall contains hundreds of columns (the highest 79 ft. [24.4 m.] high) symbolizing a thicket of papyrus plants, springing from the primeval swamp of creation. Outside, the walls bear battle scenes, while the inside surfaces show creation myths.

Relief slab from Nimrod showing Ashurnasirpal II hunting lions.

The total space inside the hall is large enough to contain the entire cathedral of Notre Dame, Paris.

Across the Nile from the temple of Karnak, in the Valley of the Kings on the West Bank, are the tombs of successive generations of rulers and high officials. Perhaps the most famous is that of Queen Hatshepsut (1473–1458 B.C.). Its architect, Senmut—a commoner by birth and reputed to be the queen's lover—integrated the tomb's façade into its natural setting, placing it against an immense cliff face towering to a height of 1000 feet above it. Nothing in Mesopotamia or the ancient Near East matches the grandeur of Egypt's monuments. The existence in Egypt of vast quantities of high-quality granite and other extra-hard stone provided a natural source of construction material that both inspired architects and enabled their buildings to survive the ravages of time. The mud brick structures of the Sumerians proved less durable.

Toward the end of Mesopotamian history, Assyrian builders created more permanent works by importing stone from the mountains to the north of the rivers Tigris and Euphrates. At the palace at Nineveh built for Asurbanipal (668–626 B.C.), the brick walls and gateways have stone slabs lining them, on which are carved scenes of war and the hunt. The battles show the victorious Assyrians demolishing cities, plundering, and taking away prisoners. In the hunting episodes, the artists seem to depict the suffering of the dying animals with greater sympathy than that of the human victims in the scenes of warfare.

The Hittite capital at Boğhazköy illustrates an earlier tradition of palace sculpture and architecture. The city spread out over 300 acres, within a massive defensive wall of stone and mud brick. Monumental stone lions and sphinxes flank the gateways, and inside there are four temples, each with its own courtyard. In a nearby rock sanctuary, stylized processions of warriors and deities show none of the vitality and action of the later Assyrian relief carvings.

Art in Miniature

If most artists and craftsmen spent their time on official state projects, others produced jewelry, small sculptures in ivory or other semiprecious materials, and carved sealstones. This last category varied in style from people to people. The Egyptians used engraved seals in the form of a beetle (a symbol of the sun), known as scarabs. Set into finger rings or worn on a chain round the neck, the stones supposedly brought good luck. The ancient Mesopotamians produced vast numbers of cylinder seals, carved with a design or an inscription, which they rolled along on soft clay or wax to make a repeated pattern.

Many of the most skilled ivory carvers in the ancient world at this time were Phoenician, in part because the Phoenician colony of Carthage in North Africa had its own elephant farms (elephants seem to have become extinct in Mesopotamia during the time of the Assyrians). The animals may have served as fighting beasts in the Carthaginian Army, while their tusks provided the material for Phoenician artists. Phoenician traders sold ivory statuettes, combs, hairpins, and small wooden boxes inlaid with ivory, as well as larger pieces of furniture, throughout the ancient world. The Assyrian rulers were good customers, and their palaces and tombs contained thousands of ivory objects either sold by Phoenician businessmen or paid as tribute. In the west, the Etruscans of Central Italy bought Phoenician ivories, and some pieces even reached Spain.

FAITH, HOPE, AND DESPAIR IN ANCIENT LITERATURE

Much of our understanding of the daily life of the peoples of the ancient world comes from their written records. These range from the trading records of the Babylonians to recipes for love potions found in Egypt, from instructions on how to conduct a Hittite funeral to the law codes of the Mesopotamian states. Little of this material, however, was meant primarily to be read as literature.

Religious texts provide a more universal category of ancient writings, setting out ideas which are often expressed in the form of poetry. Most of them contain the official teachings of the ruling classes, while at the same time they reflect the differences between the various cultures of the ancient world. The Egyptian *Book of the Dead,* for example, is a sort of guidebook to the underworld. Its illustrated text describes the judgment of the soul after death and offers to those Egyptians able to afford the appropriate rituals the chance of a happy life in the next world if their lives satisfy the gods. This essentially positive view of death is also borne out in more informal, popular songs:

> Death stands before me today
> Like the fragrance of myrrh,
> Like sitting under the shade on a breezy day.

The Epic of Gilgamesh

The Mesopotamian religious texts convey a very different idea of death and the next life. Beset by the awesome forces of scorching winds and torrential rains, the Mesopotamians viewed existence as a fleeting and harsh struggle against nature, ending in the bleak darkness of death:

> He who came to life yesterday, died today.
> In but a moment man is cast into gloom,
> suddenly crushed.

By far the most impressive Mesopotamian work, perhaps the first in our past that truly can be called literature, is the *Epic of Gilgamesh*. This Akkadian work was first composed around the beginning of the 2nd millennium B.C., although its roots are probably Sumerian. It tells the story of Gilgamesh, ruler of the city of Uruk in southern Babylonia, who is driven by the death of his beloved friend Enkidu to set out on a quest in search of the meaning of life. If death is an evil—the supreme punishment—why are we punished if we have committed no wrong? What role can justice have in a universe where all must die?

Gilgamesh wanders to the mountains of the setting sun and follows it into the darkness of night, despairing of ever seeing light again. All those he meets tell him that the search for meaning is hopeless, and advise him to try to make the best of his life: "When the gods created humans, they let death be their share, and withheld life in their own hands. Gilgamesh, fill your belly and wear fresh clothes. Look at the child who is holding your hand, and let your wife delight in your embrace. These things alone are the concern of men."

Yet Gilgamesh refuses to accept his destiny and struggles on. He even crosses the waters of death in search of the plant which can, so he hears, rejuvenate those who eat it. When he finds the sacred plant he sets off back home in triumph. But exhausted by the heat, he pauses to swim in a cool lake, and a serpent steals the plant: "Then Gilgamesh sat down and wept, tears streaming down his cheeks." The end of the *Epic* sees no hope in sight, no answers to the questions. The weary king returns home and dies.

The Old Testament

The writings described so far help to bring remote civilizations to life, but the Bible has been central to the development of our own culture. Whatever our individual beliefs may be, our societies, languages, laws, and systems of values have been shaped by the books of the Old and New Testaments, which together make up what is often called simply The Book. The standard form of the Hebrew Scriptures, called the Tanach and established in A.D. 90, contains 24 books. The Catholic and Orthodox Old Testaments have 46, while the Protestant Old Testament contains 39.

The three traditional divisions of the Hebrew Scriptures are known as the Law, the Prophets, and the Writings. Although the Bible's Hebrew authors occasionally echo themes and ideas which occur elsewhere in ancient religious writings—the Flood found in the book of Genesis has a parallel in the *Epic of Gilgamesh*—its general spirit is profoundly original.

The first five books of the Old Testament are probably compilations of documents going back to the 9th century B.C. The present form of the Old Testament was established by an assembly of rabbis in A.D. 90, although the discovery of the Dead Sea Scrolls, which include large portions of the Hebrew text of the Old Testament, proves that it already existed centuries earlier: the community which produced the Scrolls, a Jewish sect known as the Essenes, flourished around 200 B.C.

In contrast to the many gods of other religions, Judaism evolved into a monotheistic religion. Its one God is transcendent and cannot be depicted, a fact

Painting from the synagogue of Dura-Europos showing The Crossing of the Red Sea.

which explains the absence of a tradition of visual art in Jewish culture. Pure Being, he existed before the world, which he created out of a chaotic ocean—"tehom," "the Deep." Having created the world with humans as the highest form of living creature, God is involved in the ongoing course of human history as a positive force for good—not, like the gods of many other religions, an impersonal force of nature.

The first part of the Bible sets out the moral code by which, according to its authors, God expects us to live, and describes the "covenant." This is a relationship with the people of Israel, whereby they will spread knowledge of the word of God throughout the world. In the second part, Jewish leaders of the 8th and 7th centuries B.C.—called prophets, although they were concerned with their contemporaries rather than the future—laid great stress on social justice. By contrast with the law codes of the Mesopotamians, or the royal decrees of Egypt, their teachings are based not on power but on compassion, not on the orders of the state but on a personal code of ethics.

In the Writings of the third part, these ideas are illustrated in a series of stories and poems. Figures such as Job and Daniel, Esther and Ruth, illustrate the consequences of human behavior and divine action. This part also contains the Psalms, 150 songs many of which were traditionally ascribed to King David, which deal with varieties of religious experience. The book known as the Song of Solomon, or the Song of Songs, on the other hand, is made up of a series of passionate love songs; both traditional Jewish and Christian commentators have interpreted these as symbolic of God's love for his people.

The teachings of the Old Testament serve to underline the separateness of Jewish culture from their contemporaries, a gulf emphasized by the idea of the Covenant. Elsewhere in the ancient world, artists used images and buildings to express the beliefs and attitudes to life of their societies. The individual was subordinate to society as a whole, which in turn accepted the rule of its dominant upper class, often perilously split between sacred and secular authorities. The overwhelming importance of religion in all aspects of life gave the priests a distinct advantage in maintaining their power.

Yet in spite of the often impersonal character of ancient art, the visual artists of the times created works that transcend the remoteness of their cultures. Their sensitivity to the world of Nature, which many ancient peoples believed even more sacred than their gods, provides a link with our own experience. The writings of the period also continue to be relevant. Few thoughtful persons will be unfamiliar with the kind of questions posed by Gilgamesh in the Epic, *while the Old Testament provides the basis for a religious tradition which still influences the lives of millions of Jews and Christians.*

Questions for Further Study

1. How did the character of the Egyptians' society affect their art? What were the chief subjects depicted by Egyptian artists and why?
2. What was the relationship between state and religion in the ancient Near East, and how did it differ from culture to culture?
3. What are the main features of epic poetry? How many of these can be found in the *Epic of Gilgamesh?*
4. In what ways did Hebrew religion and culture differ from those of their neighbors? What were the long-term consequences of these differences?

Suggestions for Further Reading

Alter, Robert. *The World of Biblical Narrative.* New York, 1992.
Frankfort, H. *The Art and Architecture of the Ancient Orient.* Baltimore, 1970.
Friedman, R. E. *Who Wrote the Bible?* New York, 1987.
Jacobsen, T. *The Treasures of Darkness: A History of Mesopotamian Religion.* New Haven, CT, 1976.
Kramer, S. N., ed. *Mythologies of the Ancient World.* Garden City, NY, 1961.
Lichtheim, M. *Ancient Egyptian Literature* (3 vols.). Berkeley, 1973–80.
Morenz, S. *Egyptian Religion.* London, 1973.
Nicholson, E. W. *God and His People: Covenant and Theology in the Old Testament.* Oxford, 1986.
Pritchard, J. B. *Ancient Near Eastern Texts Relating to the Old Testament.* Princeton, 1969.
Smith, M. S. *The Early History of God: Yahweh and the Other Deities in Ancient Israel.* San Francisco, 1987.
Spencer, A. *Death in Ancient Egypt.* Baltimore, 1982.
Strouhal, N. *Life of the Ancient Egyptians.* Norman, OK, 1992.

I

Topic 6

The Structure and Economic Life of Ancient Society

Given the conservative nature of most ancient societies, social mobility was rare. A small ruling class dominated large numbers of workers, peasants, and slaves, whose status was fixed. The most rigid social system of all operated in Egypt. In cultures where trade and commerce were important, such as those of the Sumerians or the Phoenicians, an artisan and trader class developed, offering limited possibility for social advancement.

Laws and traditional patterns of behavior reinforced the family as the basis of society. Mesopotamian law codes illustrate women's rights in their private life and in relation to their family duties. Few women achieved any status in public life, although there were exceptions: the Egyptian queen Hatshepsut and the Hittite queen Puduhepa both played a crucial role in their countries' affairs. The Old Testament also provides examples of influential female figures, who often serve as role models.

Agriculture provided the chief source of wealth and work. The ruling classes jealously guarded their possession of the land; laws regulated complicated systems of land tenure and transfer. Fertility in the great estates of Egypt depended on the annual flood of the Nile. Mesopotamian farmers had to deal with a much less predictable climate and learned to develop elaborate irrigation systems and produce abundant crops.

Once communities were self-sufficient in food supplies, they could trade surpluses with neighbors. At the same time, new technologies led to increased manufacture of goods, many of them made for barter or sale abroad. By around 1500 B.C. traders had created a wide network of commercial relations throughout the Mediterranean and the Near East. Each culture had its special products: Egypt was famous for stone dishes and wooden furniture (the wood itself often imported from the Phoenicians) while the Babylonians produced high-quality woolen textiles.

In most ancient societies, cities served originally as religious and administrative centers for the ruling classes. The vast majority of the population lived and worked on the land. Over time, more complex patterns of urban life began to appear in Mesopotamia, reflected in the laws: Hammurabi's Code requires the execution of a builder responsible for a house which collapses and kills the owner.

In each society an individual possessed specific rights and obligations, whether as ruler, farmer, woman, son, or builder. In the rigid hierarchy of ancient life, even slaves had certain established rights, which structured the relationship between them and their owners. In Egypt, these rights were minimal, while elsewhere, as in some periods of Mesopotamian history or among the Hittites, the law provided some variation in the harshness of slavery.

CLASS, STATUS, AND FAMILY

Only with the rise of urban civilization in Egypt and the Near East did there develop a rigid class structure that governed all aspects of life. At the top was the ruling class, drawn from a small number of families. This select group, born to power, controlled the economy, state religion, and the armed forces.

Aristocracy in Egypt and Mesopotamia

In the most extreme form of aristocracy, that of Egypt in the Old Kingdom, a single figure was in supreme command of the state. The pharaoh was god-king, head of the state religion, military commander, and owner of all his country's land, large tracts of which he rented out. Powerful and successful pharaohs sought to maintain their family's rule by founding a dynasty which might last for a hundred years or more.

Limestone figure of a seated scribe, an important occupation in pharaonic Egypt.

The three main classes of Egyptian society reinforced this hierarchical pattern. In the first, immediately below the pharaoh, the nobles and priests formed the upper classes and ran the government. Three subgroups made up the middle classes: scribes, merchants, and artisans. Day-to-day administration was in the hands of the scribes, who combined the functions of civil servant, lawyer, and tax collector; popular tales often described them as crooked, greedy, and opportunistic. The merchants organized trade and barter, both internal and international. The artisans produced works of art to decorate the royal palaces, to accompany the upper classes to the next life, and for commercial use.

The overwhelming number of Egyptians belonged to the lowest class. While most worked the land, some labored on building projects or served in the army or as domestic servants.

Over the centuries this rigid system underwent some change. During the Middle Kingdom, as the economy expanded, the nobles unwillingly made concessions to the middle-class businessmen and manufacturers, while generally retaining most of their privileges. The New Kingdom, with its constant military campaigns and conquests, brought more substantial change. A class of professional soldiers occupied a position below the nobles but above the middle classes. At the very bottom were now the slaves, captured in the wars abroad; their large numbers made possible the grandiose building projects of the 18th and 19th dynasties.

Mesopotamian society was also based on birth, with the same three general divisions into nobility, middle-class commoners, and workers. It lacked a single supreme ruler, however, corresponding to the Egyptian pharaoh. The resultant conflict between civil and religious authorities and the gradual rise in importance of those engaged in trade and manufacturing meant that traditional social patterns needed some form of codification to set out the official dogma. The Mesopotamian law codes, of which Hammurabi's is the most complete, establish the principle of "an eye for an eye," but at the same time depict a society in which each individual's rights depended on class: "If a nobleman knocks out the tooth of one of the same rank, one of his shall be knocked out. If he knocks out a commoner's tooth, he shall pay a fine." Yet the laws

A hunting expedition along the Nile, with overseer and slaves.

punished nobles more severely than lower-class citizens for some crimes, and guaranteed certain rights for the lowest classes.

In both Egyptian and Mesopotamian society, the social rules of public life had their counterpart in private. Like the state, family life was authoritarian, ruled from the top down. Mesopotamians were constantly reminded: "Listen to the word of your mother as to your god; revere your older brother; do not anger the heart of your older sister." An Egyptian father, advising his son on how to behave to his aging mother, urges him "to carry her as she carried you."

There is some evidence for a less rigid class structure elsewhere in the ancient world. A Hittite royal document, summoning an assembly to advise the king, lists its members as "fighting men, servants, and nobles." Early Phoenician communities were ruled by hereditary kings, but over time, with the growth of a rich merchant class, these were replaced by "councils of elders," whose members owed their status to their success in business rather than to their birth.

WOMEN, POWER, AND SUBJUGATION

The position of women in the ancient world emerges most clearly in the evidence we have about family life. On the whole, ancient society was patriarchal, with men exerting the dominant role, but some traditional patterns were unexpectedly enlightened for so early a period in the history of relations between the sexes.

Women in Ancient Egypt

On the whole, Egyptian women enjoyed better conditions than most of their counterparts elsewhere in the ancient world. In Egypt most men had only one wife, although they could take another if the first was childless. Even the pharaoh, with his royal harem, distinguished between his Great Wife, the senior one, and the others. Although Egyptian married women were generally subordinate to their husband's authority, they retained control of their own property, with the right to

Limestone portrait of Nefertiti, wife of Akhenaton.

inherit it and pass it on. They, as well as their husbands, could initiate divorce proceedings. Some collections of popular wisdom suggest that they also had emotional rights which were recognized. One such book advises a husband to "make your wife's heart glad as long as you live."

Women confined most of their activities to the home, where they took charge of domestic arrangements and the education of children. Some, however, operated businesses, and upper-class women could serve as priestesses. Other areas in which women were employed included music and dance, while countless Egyptian peasant women toiled in the fields. Apart from the very last period of Egyptian history, under the Ptolemies, women played no part officially in the affairs of state. The only exception, an important one, was Queen Hatshepsut (for a discussion of this remarkable figure, see Part I, Topic 3).

Women and the Law: The Hittites

Clearly the legal status of women was not uniform throughout the ancient world. Indeed, even in the Near East, legal differences existed. On the whole, Hittite custom seems to have resembled that of the Babylonians. In some respects, however, Hittite women had greater rights. Thus Hittite laws allowed the mother as well as the father to participate in choosing a husband for their daughter, and laid down conditions under which a mother could disinherit her son. Married couples generally lived together, but in some cases a woman had the possibility of continuing to live with her father. This custom also existed among the Assyrians, and presumably applied when a marriage served purely political or financial ends.

A special law governed the welfare of Hittite widows. The nearest male relative on the dead husband's side was obliged to take care of the widow by marrying her and giving any children of this second union the name and inheritance of the dead man. A similar tradition appears in the Old Testament, to preserve the family of the first husband, "that his name be not blotted out of Israel."

The less restrictive conditions of Hittite women may reflect the earliest origins of Hittite society, which were probably matriarchal. By contrast, the Mesopotamian tradition was patriarchal. One result was that a Hittite queen had a much more independent position than her Egyptian or Babylonian counterparts. On the death of a king, his widow became queen mother; the new king's wife had no right to the title of queen until the queen mother's own death. The widow of the great warrior King Suppiluliumas (1380–1346 B.C.) caused so much ill-feeling at the court of the new king, their son Mursilis II (1345–1315 B.C.), that in exasperation he expelled her from the palace.

The most famous of all Hittite queens was Puduhepa, wife of Hattusilis (1289–1265 B.C.). She played an important role in state affairs and her name appears alongside her husband's in state documents. She even conducted her own correspondence with the Egyptian court: a treaty with Egypt bears a seal impression showing her in the embrace of the sun goddess.

The Women of Ancient Israel and Judah

The Old Testament reflects the patriarchal tradition of the first Hebrews. As early as the story of Eden in the book of Genesis, it is Eve who is made responsible for listening to the serpent and convincing Adam to eat with her the apple of the tree of knowledge of good and evil—in contravention of God's orders. God decrees that all future women will suffer the consequences of her disobedience: "I will greatly multiply your pain in childbearing."

In the early books of the Old Testament, several patriarchs have two wives or a wife and a concubine—Jacob has two concubines as well as two wives. Women

PERSPECTIVES ON HISTORY

The Status of Women In Ancient Mesopotamia

JoAnn Scurlock
Elmhurst College

It might be supposed that, being more ancient than ancient Greece, Mesopotamian society was comparatively backward in its treatment of women. However, although Mesopotamian women were hardly well-off by modern standards, they managed to exercise more rights and to enjoy more freedoms than their Athenian counterparts.

For most Mesopotamian women, marriage and childbearing were an expected (and desired) part of growing up. Marriages were arranged by parents, or by the prospective groom and the adolescent bride's family. Marriages were considered family alliances; if an Assyrian bride or groom died without children, the widow(er) might find him/herself married to one of the late spouse's siblings. This did not invariably result in a young girl being saddled with an old husband. In such marriages, a new husband might be considerably younger than his wife (though at least 10 years old).

Neither was it the case that a woman never had the right to choose. There was a way, if somewhat risky, that "true love" could prevail. Unlike their Athenian counterparts, respectable Mesopotamian girls could be seen in the city streets or out in the countryside, and could attend religious festivals with only female friends for company. If a girl allowed a man to deflower her, and if she had clearly done so with marriage in mind, he could legally be forced to marry her. This was also true if she had been flirting with him and he got carried away. "Playing around" was not, however, an option—a nonvirginal bride was damaged goods, facing not only her father's anger but sharply diminished marriage prospects. Girls whose virginity was questioned were cleared by gynecological examination.

A girl who disliked her new husband—if she avoided giving the impression that she had other irons in the fire—could get local authorities to dissolve the marriage. A widow or divorcee with children was free to make her own marital arrangements using her dowry as bait. In Assyria, she could even become a common-law wife, although she lost her property if she moved in with her lover. If, on the other hand, she could persuade him to move in with her, she became owner of his property.

As in ancient Greece, a woman entered marriage with a dowry which was supposed to keep her fed and clothed in the style to which she was accustomed. Unlike the situation in ancient Greece, the Mesopotamian husband was expected to pay her father a bride price for the right to her labor, her undivided sexual attentions, and her children. This was because Mesopotamian wives were not "useless mouths" but essential contributors to the family economy, whether by laboring in the fields or weaving on the family loom. Old Assyrian merchants expected their wives to run the family textile business in Assur while they were off in Anatolia selling cloth and tin. Nuzian husbands gave their wives the right to act as "father and mother" of the household after they died, as long as the widow did not remarry. Even Neo-Babylonian dowry inventories pay silent testimony to a wife's contribution to the family's income: they contain, besides jewelry and household furniture, items of manufacture such as brewing equipment.

Male professions open to women included, in addition to weaver, miller, and musician, not only prophet and pharmacist but also smith and scribe. Some all-female professions also allowed women to live without male support. These ranged from the barely respectable tavern keeper, bathing attendant, and prostitute to midwife, wet nurse, and governess and, on the upper end of the social scale, virgin priestesses such as the Old Babylonian *naditu* (cloistered nun), the Middle Assyrian *qadistu* (who performed magical rituals to assist women in childbirth and tended the souls of stillborn children) and the *entu* (often a king's daughter thought of as the secondary wife of a city's chief god and maidservant to his divine consort).

Old Babylonian virgin priestesses, whether cloistered or allowed to engage in childless marriages, were particularly independent economically, being entitled by the laws of Hammurabi to up to a third of their father's property as their dowry, none of which fell under control of the man they married. Conventional wisdom warned prospective husbands: "In your trouble she will not support you; in your quarrel she will mock you. There is no reverence or obedience in her. The man who marries her will not be able to oppose [her]."

In contrast to the situation in ancient Greece, women were legal persons. Not only could they serve as witnesses or sue and be sued in court but they could also make contracts, inherit, own, or dispose of property without the consent of a husband, male relative, or appointed guardian. The custom of guardianship for women was introduced by the Greeks, who, after Alexander the Great's conquest of the Persian Empire, imposed their notions of women's status on Egypt, Palestine, and Mesopotamia. Also foreign to ancient Mesopotamia was the Athenian custom forcing women whose fathers had died without male heirs to marry their cousins or even their uncles (although Solon thoughtfully guaranteed them intercourse three times a month).

A wife was personally liable for her husband's debts, raising the dismal prospect of grinding grain, spinning wool, or performing manual labor in a stranger's house, although the laws of Hammurabi protected her from mistreatment and required her release after three years. Nothing prevented a husband from helping himself to slave concubines or prostitutes, and he could kill his wife if he caught her with another man. A woman whose behavior occasioned wagging tongues but who was not caught in adultery could clear herself by river ordeal; if she proved her innocence by floating, the false accuser was punished with a stiff fine or flogging. If a married woman was raped in a public place or in someone else's house, resisted her attacker or at least complained immediately, she could get him executed. If, however, she invited the alleged rapist in or led him on, she herself became liable to the penalty for adultery. In Assyria, married women had to be careful about running away from husbands or even traveling without them—unless they traveled or took refuge with male relatives, they risked losing their ears.

There were laws protecting women from assault, particularly when pregnant. An Assyrian man could lose a lip for kissing an unwilling victim, and a finger for spanking her. Even husbands were not allowed, when chastising wives, to go beyond beating, hair pulling, and ear boxing or ear piercing. Not that Assyrian women were helpless—stiff penalties were envisaged for women who caused bodily injury to men (crushing their testicles was a particularly dreaded method of assault). Old Babylonian tavern keepers, typically women, were expected to police their male customers vigorously; according to Hammurabi's laws, criminals gathering in their establishments were to be seized and taken to the authorities on pain of death.

A Mesopotamian woman's husband was responsible for *her* debts and, despite the dowry, she was entitled to support throughout the marriage (and after his death unless she remarried). If a virgin priestess or other childless woman wished to choose a second wife for her husband, and if she paid the bride price, the husband could not take a second wife of his own choosing and the second wife (often the first wife's younger sister) could be required by contract to side with the first wife and act as her maidservant. Any children produced from such a marriage belonged to the first wife. A woman who felt neglected could get an injunction forbidding her husband from visiting his prostitute mistress. If a husband chose to divorce his wife without her fault, she was entitled to a substantial payment, especially if she had children. Even if the children were adopted, she could keep them upon divorce provided that she, not he, had paid the adoption payment.

continued next page

If, then, the legal status of Mesopotamian women was low by modern American standards, it was still much higher than in ancient Greece, due to a difference in attitudes toward women. According to ancient Greek thinkers, a woman made no positive contribution to a man's baby. Apart from killing it, the most she might do was to overpower his good seed and deal him a daughter in place of the desired son. For ancient Mesopotamians, the baby's mother was not just the oven that baked the father's loaves, and stillborn children were not the product of a woman's trying to have a baby without male assistance, as ancient Greek philosophers would have it; rather the Mesopotamian woman was understood as the steerswoman of a boat formed inside her by the man's semen. It was her duty (and a dangerous one which Assyrian poets compared to men's duty to fight in battle at the risk of their own lives) to float this boat on her amniotic fluid across to the netherworld, where it could receive not merely its sexual characteristics but also its soul. Women gave birth in the home, surrounded by female relatives, tended by a midwife aiding the delivery by massage and medicines, and protected from supernatural harm by a female magical expert. Only in the most difficult deliveries was it necessary to summon a male doctor.

Ancient Mesopotamians associated civilized culture with the coming together of men and women, and untamed nature with either sex attempting to act alone. While they would certainly have agreed that a man should be master in his household, the ultra-masculine man without women in the Greek style is presented as at best an "Amorite" and at worst no better than an animal. When the hero Gilgamesh faces the problem of a wild man Enkidu running amuck in the back country of Uruk, he turns him into a civilized human being by sending a prostitute out to seduce him. Similarly, women without men untamed by marriage were regarded as savage, wild, and dangerous.

If a member of either sex died before this civilizing coming together could occur, he or she became a demon doomed to prowl the streets looking for the fulfillment that a cruel fate had denied him/her: "Young girl not fated to be married; young woman who was never impregnated like a woman; young woman who was never deflowered like a woman; young girl who never experienced sexual pleasure in her husband's lap." "Young man who always sits, silent and alone, in the street; young man who cries bitterly in the grip of his death-demon; young man who never married a wife, never raised a child; young man who never experienced sexual pleasure in his wife's lap." For ancient Mesopotamians, it was not rape, but dying without enjoying sexual pleasure in the arms of a man who "loved her like a wife" that was, for a woman, a fate literally worse than death.

had to be sexually faithful but not men. Husbands could divorce their wives for a series of reasons ranging from forging keys to adultery, but wives could not divorce their husbands. Even the normal processes of menstruation and childbirth were thought to make women ritually "unclean." The birth of a son made a woman "impure" for seven days, whereas after the birth of a daughter, the mother was "impure" for fourteen days.

In contrast to the mainly restrictive picture of women's rights which emerges from the Hebrew tradition, the Old Testament describes several outstanding women who illustrate a wide variety of virtues, and the description of their exploits was clearly intended as inspiration to others. Deborah, a wife and mother, is also a prophet and judge. Together with another woman, Jael, she rallies her people against their enemies. Jael even kills the enemy general by hammering a nail into his head. Judith, a pious widow, performs a similar heroic act by decapitating the Assyrian general Holofernes and bringing back his head in a "food bag" to inspire the Hebrew Army.

Other Hebrew women symbolized less violent heroism. Queen Esther, wife of the Persian king, showed loyalty to her people by preventing the massacre of all Persian Jews. The story of Ruth is an example of steadfastness and loyalty on a more personal level. Widowed during a famine, she followed her mother-in-law Naomi to Bethlehem, where she survived by gleaning barley from the fields.

An early Renaissance depiction of the Expulsion from Paradise; the painting is by Masaccio (1425–1428).

THE AGRICULTURAL ECONOMY: FOOD PRODUCTION AND CONSUMPTION

In one important way all ancient societies except the Hebrews and the Persians (both monotheistic) shared a common attitude toward the feminine: they worshiped the earth and the world of nature in the form of a mother goddess. The Egyptian "Great Goddess," the Semitic Ishtar, the Hittite sun goddess Arinna, the Phoenician Astarte or Tanit, all represented the cycle of life and growth which annually renewed itself.

Agriculture had first made possible the birth of civilization, and it remained the economic basis of all ancient societies. Even the Assyrians, with their contempt for trade and business, recognized the need for adequate food production and distribution.

Phoenician ivory carving showing Isis.

Farming in the Ancient World

After marriage and the family, the next most common area which ancient law codes sought to control was land ownership. Early in Egyptian history there had been free farmers, owning their own land, but by the end of the Old Kingdom the pharaoh owned all the farmland and granted or rented estates to the nobles and the religious centers.

In Mesopotamia the laws specified the terms under which tenant farmers could work the land and pay their rent in the form of crops. Another matter of great concern was irrigation, vital in a region where the weather was unpredictable. Both owners and tenants were responsible for keeping the water channels in good repair and the water flow efficient. Since one system of irrigation often served several adjoining farms, the failure of one farmer could cause damage to his neighbors. Those whose carelessness caused the destruction of others' crops, and who could not pay for the damage, were liable to be sold into slavery.

Hittite records document similar farming problems, including the danger of fire and stray animals or the theft of a swarm of bees. One land deed also provides a description of the estate of a smallholder called Tiwataparas. It included one acre of meadow as pasture for his six oxen, and three and a half acres of vineyard which also contained 40 apple trees and 42 pomegranate trees. His 22 sheep and 18 goats probably grazed in the hills around. With this property, the farmer could support himself, his wife, a son, and two daughters.

Food and Drink

The Sumerians of Ur used ox-drawn plows to cultivate a wide variety of grains and vegetables: barley, millet, lentils and beans, onions, leeks and garlic, lettuce and cucumbers. Among their dishes was a round, flat pancake made of ground barley dough garnished with onions and greens, which they baked on a heated stone—a kind of Ur-pizza.

Because most of the beef came from cattle which were old or sick and were of little food value, the ruler of Ur had it distributed to his dogs. The Sumerians bred sheep and goat for their meat, while the domestic pig was introduced into the Near East before 2000 B.C. from Central Asia. Freshwater fish provided another source of protein, and vendors circulated in the streets of cities such as Ur and Lagash with slices of fish fried in sesame oil, along with grilled vegetables and drinks sweetened with honey or dates.

Grapes were cultivated in Mesopotamia as early as 3000 B.C., but by far the most popular alcoholic drink was beer and half of each year's grain crop was used for brewing. There were at least 19 different types of beer, produced from various combinations of grain. Workers received a daily supply: a liter to each common laborer, five liters to a supervisor—the abstemious could use their allowance as the equivalent of money to barter for other products.

The Egyptian diet was even richer and included fish from the river and the sea, game from the hunt (including deer and antelope), geese, ducks and pigeons, and a wide range of fruits. Among the grains was semolina, known in modern Arabic as "couscous" and still popular in North Africa today. A more simple ancient Egyptian dish consisted of a puree of beans flavored with ground coriander and garnished with almonds.

As in Mesopotamia, food served for bartering. In the time of Ramses III (1186–1155 B.C.), a laborer received four sacks of grain a month, while his overseer's wage was seven and a half sacks. More than a millennium earlier, even the humble workers employed to build the pyramids could expect a daily allowance of grain, dried fish, garlic, and onion. No wonder that as

Sumerian seal impression showing peasants farming with their cattle.

the Hebrews crossed the Sinai Desert on the way to the Promised Land, they looked back nostalgically to the diet of their exile in Egypt: fish, lamb, eggs, melons, cucumbers, onions, garlic. Many of these play a part in the ritual meal, the Seder, with which pious Jews still commemorate the Passover, the departure from Egypt. At the Seder the bread eaten is unleavened, made without the use of yeast.

ARTISANS AND TRADERS: THE RISE OF COMMERCE

Once the cultures of the ancient world could count on self-sufficiency in food production, they could move toward the next stage of economic development, manufacturing and trade. The making of works of art and craft began very early, generally to satisfy the wishes of the ruling class. The miniature ivories of Ur and the monumental sculptures of the Old Kingdom are just two contrasting examples of works commissioned for official use. The artisans who made these acquired the technical proficiency to produce increasing numbers of pieces, and over time merchants began to organize the manufacture and sale of objects.

Raw Materials

In some cases traders used goods to exchange for raw materials lacking in their state, which were then used for the production of other objects for export. Thus the Sumerians learned to capitalize on the advantages of their land, and remedy its deficiencies. The river valleys of Mesopotamia were poor in metal deposits and hard wood suitable for furniture. At the same time, sheep farming was common there and grain production high. As a result, the Sumerians made and exported woolen fabric and grain, bartering it for commodities such as copper and tin. Their craftsmen used the imported metals to produce works of art which served for a further round of trading.

The Egyptians also traded in raw materials, exchanging gold mined in Sudan and high-quality

Map 6.1 Ancient Trade Routes, c. 1300 B.C.

Map 6.2 Ancient Trade Routes, c. 825 B.C.

ceramics for silver and ivory. Among their trading partners were merchants from Phoenicia and Syria.

Some peoples managed to maintain a monopoly on a particular commodity. The Phoenicians, for example, were famous for a rich and highly prized purple dye made from a shellfish called murex, large quantities of which swam in the waters off their coast. Phoenician traders imported plain woolen cloth from Mesopotamia and cotton textiles from Egypt, dyed them, and exported the finished product in exchange for grain and livestock, in which Phoenicia was deficient.

The great mountain masses of the Hittites' land were rich in minerals, and Hittite merchants traded in copper and silver. Hittite craftsmen even discovered how to smelt iron—a process requiring a very high temperature—and work it. Iron was a metal harder than any other known at the time, and iron objects fetched a good price. The Hittite kings were careful, however, to keep the smelting technique secret and to limit the export of iron products. In one letter to a Mesopotamian ruler (perhaps Assyrian), the Hittite king Hattusilis III refuses a request for "good iron," which, he says, is not available: "I tell you that this is a bad time for producing iron." This may be an early example of an official embargo on vital military supplies, expressed in the language of diplomacy.

Patterns of Urban Life

As manufacturing and trade became increasingly important sectors of the economy, the function of the cities began to change. Urban centers had originally served as bases for administration and important state religious cults. Both nobles and peasants lived on the great land estates, the former in luxurious villas and the latter in mud brick hovels.

By 2000 B.C. settlements like Ur, Uruk, and Lagash had many of the features of metropolitan life, as excavations at Ur have vividly revealed. Through narrow doors in blank, windowless walls, the visitor could enter the cool central courtyard of a town house. The

A model of a street in Ur, c. 2000 B.C.

main floor contained the workshop and storeroom, bathroom, and a large oblong room for receiving guests and providing them with a bed for the night. The servant quarters were also downstairs. The owner and his family lived on the floor above.

Elsewhere along the streets were small shops, either grouped together to form a bazaar or set among the houses. Each shop had a showroom opening on to the street and a small backroom for storing the merchandise, which might be food, spices, rugs, perfumes, or pots. The dark workshops of the metalworkers, lit with a furnace, alternated with restaurants serving fried fish, cucumbers, and onions. Here and there were little chapels with clay statuettes decorating their façades.

The objects and inscribed tablets found in these buildings make it clear that their residents were neither particularly wealthy nor powerful. Gimil-Sin was the headmaster of a small private school, where he taught writing, mathematics, history, and religion. The bronzesmith's factory contained a Sumerian-Akkadian grammar text, while records found in the copper merchant's house reveal that an unlucky business deal had forced him to sell part of his house to a neighbor. All these were modest middle-class citizens living in a town which was but one of a number of similar communities in the area.

SLAVERY, HUMAN RIGHTS, AND THE LAW

The various law codes of the ancient world sought to define the rights and obligations of individual citizens to the overlapping larger groups to which they belonged: their family, their fellow-professionals, their city, the state. This complex web of interdependence was the chief means whereby all citizens felt themselves members of a single and united community.

The one class that remained relatively uninvolved in this sense of participation was that of the slaves. Even in their case, however, many ancient peoples had laws which tried to regularize the status of slaves and in some cases provide certain basic rights. In Egypt these were minimal. The slaves and land serfs of the Old and Middle Kingdoms had the same possibility of judgment and reward after death as other Egyptians. In life their fate remained grim. The thousands of foreigners captured in the wars of the New Kingdom and sold into slavery worked in the mines and quarries or on building projects. Over time they were allowed to serve as conscripts in the army and could gradually improve their status.

Slavery and the Law

The Mesopotamian law codes made a careful attempt to define the relationship between slaves and their owners. In part this was because not all slaves were born as such or captured in foreign wars: full citizens guilty of certain crimes were punished by being sold into slavery. The offenses included striking an elder brother or kicking one's mother, or defaulting on a loan. Mesopotamian slaves were thus legally entitled to continue to hold property and engage in business, to marry free citizens (their children were free), and to buy their own freedom. Such concessions were clearly for the benefit of citizen slaves and of little consolation to those born or sold into slavery, or taken prisoner.

Hebrew law also permitted the enslavement of citizens who could not repay a debt or make good a

Copper statuette of Sumerian slave carrying a basket of bricks to a building site. A Mesopotamian votive figure from the third millennium B.C.

theft, but only for a period of six years: "in the seventh year he is to go free, without paying anything." Other Hebrew laws encouraged favorable treatment of slaves and punished their abuse: a slave who had been physically injured was set free. On the other hand, a freed slave's wife and children remained the property of his owner. Domestic slaves seem to have been regarded as members of the family with whom they lived. There are cases of slaves even marrying into the family or inheriting its property. Those employed in the mines or on building programs such as Solomon's reconstruction of Jerusalem probably endured far harsher lives; many of them were prisoners of war or purchased abroad.

Several Hittite documents serve as a reminder that it is difficult to evaluate the real nature of human relations from law codes which tried to provide objective "guidelines" for rulers and slaves. Common sense suggests that those living under the same roof must have tried to establish some form of mutual respect. One Hittite text tells us that "if a servant is in any way in trouble, he goes to his master, and his master hears him and is kindly disposed to him, and puts right what was troubling him." Yet the same writer continues: "If ever a servant vexes his master, either they kill him, or they injure his nose, his eyes, or his ears. And if he dies, he does not die alone, but his family is included with him. After all, if anyone vexes the feelings of a god, does the god punish him alone for it? Does he not punish the man's wife and children, his family, his cattle and his harvest?"

The birth of civilization in the ancient world saw the emergence of order in the form of urban communities. The regular production of food supplies, the development of large-scale architecture and engineering skills, the growth of manufacturing and trade together with improvements in travel, and the organization of effective systems of government and administration: all these areas of human experience provided challenges which many ancient societies managed to overcome. In the process, they laid the foundations of later developments.

At the same time the rise of city life created a whole new series of more subtle and complex problems, as people began the often painful process of learning to live together. As the great French historian Fernand Braudel noted of a later age, towns are like electric transformers: "They increase tension, accelerate the rhythm of exchange, and ceaselessly stir up men's lives." All the ancient cultures examined in these Topics tried to deal with and to control issues of human relations in their communities by decree from above, often in the name of the gods. The edicts of Egyptian pharaohs or the law codes of Mesopotamian rulers were the earliest means we have of knowing how people tried to understand themselves and their relations with others. In many cases—the treatment of women, the exploitation of la-

bor—the solutions may seem harsh and arbitrary, even contradictory.

Yet modern observers at the dawn of the third millennium can hardly fail to notice how many of the issues which these earliest civilizations tried to face and resolve remain with us still. If the art of the remote past—the monuments of Egypt or the Epic of Gilgamesh*—illustrates our shared cultural heritage, the daily problems faced by those past civilizations, and their often faltering solutions, remind us of our own common humanity.*

Questions for Further Study

1. What evidence is there for the role of women in the cultures discussed in this chapter? How does it differ in the various societies, and what features remain the same?
2. What was the role of slavery in the ancient world?
3. To what extent did trade and commerce affect political developments in the ancient Near East?
4. What are our main sources of evidence about life in the ancient world? How does their character affect the nature of our impressions of ancient society?

Suggestions for Further Reading

Baron, B. W. *A Social and Religious History of the Jews* (17 vols.). New York, 1952–1983.
Cameron, A., and Kuhrt, A., eds. *Images of Women in Antiquity*. Detroit, 1983.
Gobineau, J. A. de. *The World of the Persians*. Geneva, 1971.
James, T. G. H. *Pharaoh's People: Scenes from Life in Imperial Egypt*. London, 1984.
Saggs, H. W. F. *Everyday Life in Babylonia and Assyria*. New York, 1965.
Silver, M. *Prophets and Markets: The Political Economy of Ancient Israel*. Boston, 1983.
Trigger, B. J. et al. *Ancient Egypt: A Social History*. Cambridge, MA, 1983.
Vaux, R. *Ancient Israel*. New York, 1965.
White, J. *Everyday Life in Ancient Egypt*. London, 1963.

PART II

The World of Classical Antiquity

If the developments of the ancient world laid the bases for the growth of civilization, the specific forms which Western culture have taken owe their existence to the two chief peoples of Classical Antiquity, the Greeks and the Romans.

The Greeks themselves, for all the originality of their contribution, did not exist in a void, and many of the ideas which they developed and which became fundamental to Western civilization perhaps originated elsewhere in the Mediterranean world. In particular, scholars have begun to explore the role which Egypt—and perhaps other African cultures—may have played in the formation of the Greek tradition.

Civilization began to develop in the eastern Mediterranean as early as 3000 B.C., and the first two important cultures to appear were the Minoans of Bronze Age Crete, and the Mycenae-

ans of mainland Greece. The Bronze Age came to an end around 1100 B.C., and the links between the Greeks of the early Iron Age, around 1000 B.C., and their Bronze Age predecessors are still not clear.

The early stages of the development of Greek civilization saw a pattern that was maintained throughout Greek history: the formation of small, independent city-states. During the three centuries from 1000 B.C. to around 700 B.C., the Greeks laid the foundations of later cultural developments. This period of internal growth led to a century of expansion abroad, throughout the Mediterranean world, during which Greek city-states established colonies from Italy to Egypt to Asia Minor.

The result was contact with other cultures, in particular those of Egypt and western Asia, which revolutionized the economy and intellectual life of the Greek city-states. During this period, in many of them, individual strong leaders (known as tyrants) replaced the former aristocratic ruling class. By the time Greece was faced with the threat of invasion by the mighty Persian Empire, shortly after 500 B.C., the two leading cities in the Greek world were Sparta, a conservative military oligarchy, and Athens, which had moved from aristocratic rule to a form of democracy.

With the Persians finally repulsed, the 5th century B.C. saw the high point of Classical culture, while at the same time the Athenians and Spartans, together with their respective allies, prepared for confrontation. By the end of the century, the Peloponnesian War was over, leaving Athens defeated, and over the following decades the various city-states fought for leadership before unity finally came, imposed by rule under Philip of Macedon. The brief if spectacular reign of Philip's son, Alexander the Great, carried Greek culture throughout the territories in Asia that he conquered. In the succeeding Hellenistic period, Alexander's conquests fell into three separate kingdoms: Ptolemaic Egypt, Seleucid Asia, and Macedon itself.

The Greeks, for all their intellectual achievements, never managed to create political unity. The Romans, their eventual conquerors and successors in the Classical world, built an empire which spread the culture of Classical Antiquity throughout much of Europe and North Africa, and large parts of Asia. Founded in the mid-8th century B.C., Rome fell under the domination of the Etruscans, before emerging as an independent republic around 500 B.C. After a period of consolidation, during which the aristocratic patricians and the mass of the population—the plebeians—hammered out a series of political compromises, the Romans began to expand outside Italy.

Their first conquests were in the western Mediterranean, where they faced off against the Carthaginians. Roman power subsequently spread east, absorbing Greece, Egypt, and much of western Asia. External expansion, adding to internal strains, eventually led to the collapse of republican political institutions and to civil war.

After a century of political violence, rule by the leading families and personalities of the republic would be replaced by a system of monarchy. Octavian, the adopted son of Julius Caesar, became the first Roman emperor under the name Augustus. The last five centuries of Roman domination brought a renewed period of consolidation, followed by a long, slow decline. By the time Roman power disappeared in the West, a new set of religious and philosophical beliefs had become established: Christianity. The eastern part of the Roman world continued to exist in the form of the Byzantine Empire.

The Greek contribution to the Western tradition laid the foundations for how we think—and talk—about many of the issues that continue to dominate our lives: politics, human relations, the economy, the arts and sciences. First under Alexander, and then for centuries under the Romans, Greek ideas circulated on three continents. The Romans themselves created a multiethnic empire which brought extended periods of peace to the Mediterranean world, while devising a legal system which remained one of their most durable achievements, and, with the acceptance and spread of Christianity, established the other great tradition of Western culture. From the Western perspective, the world of Classical Antiquity is fundamental in understanding our past.

II

Topic 1

The Emergence of Greece: From Bronze to Iron

Throughout the ancient world of the Mediterranean, the period around 1000 B.C. saw a major change in ways of life. Iron replaced bronze as the chief material for the manufacture of tools and weapons, and the new technology revolutionized societies at many different levels. In a small corner of southeastern Europe, the mainland and islands of Greece, the break with the past had special significance for the future of Western history.

In the preceding Bronze Age, the Minoans on the island of Crete and the Mycenaeans of mainland Greece had developed rich and sophisticated cultures and established commercial contacts in many parts of the Mediterranean. With the violent disturbances which brought the Bronze Age to an end around 1000 B.C., their cultures disappeared, only to be rediscovered by archeologists in the 19th and 20th centuries.

Thus, the first Greek communities of the Iron Age began afresh to organize their societies and establish an artistic tradition. The development of independent settlements, each known as a "polis," or city-state, determined the competitive and often hostile nature of the Greeks' relations with one another.

The first great cultural achievements in the Western tradition–the *Iliad* and the *Odyssey*, two epic poems attributed to Homer and set in the Bronze Age—also date to the beginnings of Greek history and even reflect the earlier Mycenaean period.

The initial growth of Greek culture took place on home territory. By 700 B.C., however, the Greeks were on the move. Greek traders had discovered the rich markets of western Asia and Egypt, and settlers were beginning to establish colonies throughout the Mediterranean. In the process, they spread their ideas and artistic styles and, equally importantly, absorbed the influences of the peoples with whom they came into contact. At the same time, attitudes to religion and philosophy began to evolve as the Greeks became the first people in the ancient world to ask theoretical questions about the nature of the universe and human existence.

This first period of widespread artistic production and trade saw the development of a style known as Orientalizing, as Greek artists adopted Eastern ideas in their painting and sculpture—and later in their architecture. By the beginning of the following Archaic Age, they had used what they had learned to create a specifically Greek approach to art and ideas that borrowed from other cultures to form the foundation of Western style.

BRONZE AGE CULTURE IN THE AEGEAN: THE MINOANS AND MYCENAEANS

The earliest centers of Bronze Age culture in southeastern Europe were on the Cyclades, a group of islands in the Aegean Sea about halfway between the Greek mainland and the largest Greek island, Crete. Shortly after 3000 B.C., small towns began to develop on the Cyclades, whose inhabitants knew how to work stone and metal. Cycladic merchants traded with the peasant communities beginning to grow in mainland Greece and Crete, and even went farther afield to sell their pottery and bronze jewelry: Cycladic objects have turned up as far west as Spain.

The most famous and beautiful Cycladic products are the elongated marble statues, or idols, which were made in large numbers and often buried in graves along with the dead. The vast majority of the statues are female, and are perhaps related to the Mesopotamian cult of the mother goddess. Certainly a similar reverence for the Earth Mother was central to the people who dominated the following centuries in the eastern Mediterranean, the Minoans of Crete.

Idol from the Cyclades, made of fine local marble (c. 2500 B.C.).

The First Civilization of Europe: The Minoans

Greek myths of the later Iron Age told of the rich and powerful Cretan kingdom of King Minos, who ruled from his palace at Knossos. According to the tales, Knossos was one of many centers on the island. In the *Odyssey*, Homer speaks of "Crete of a hundred cities." Yet the Greeks who retold the story of Minos and the monstrous Minotaur—the creature half human and half bull kept imprisoned in the labyrinth at Knossos—knew the Crete of their day as only an impoverished backwater. Throughout the Iron Age the island played no part in Greek history, and neither the Classical Greeks nor any later people on the island tried to see if there was any basis for the legends.

In 1894 the English archeologist Arthur Evans first went to the Cretan village of Knossos, to see if anything could be found of the mythical civilization. He returned in 1900, armed with a permit to excavate a small hill to the side of the village. On March 23, his workers "drove a desolate donkey from the hill's slope, and digging began." As Evans' account describes, the donkey had been standing above the site of the throne room of the vast, five-story palace complex he discovered buried in the hill.

Excavation of the Palace of Knossos continued for three decades under Evans' direction, and work is still in progress there. Within the first few weeks Evans and his team had already found enough pottery, frescoes, jewelry, and inscribed tablets to demonstrate the existence of an urban center of great sophistication and technical refinement. More importantly, he had uncovered an entire culture, which he named Minoan, dividing its history into three main phases: Early Minoan (c. 2500–1950 B.C.), Middle Minoan (c. 1950–1550 B.C.), and Late Minoan (c. 1550–1100 B.C.). These di-

The Throne Room of the Palace of Minos at Knossos; the throne itself is visible on the right.

visions formed the basis for most subsequent study of Minoan civilization, as other towns and palaces came to light. Scholars have disputed the details of Evans' chronology, but as new excavations continue to produce finds, they confirm his description of the main sequence of events.

The Early Minoan period saw the appearance of small towns in southern and eastern Crete, whose inhabitants began to trade with Egypt and Mesopotamia. After a long, slow growth, this phase came to an abrupt end shortly after 2000 B.C. Abandoning the scattered communities, the Minoans gathered in large urban centers, such as the one at Knossos. We call these Middle Minoan structures palaces, but in addition to providing homes for the ruling classes they also fulfilled a wide variety of other functions. They were centers of manufacture, trading, and administration, and also contained important religious shrines. Many of these activities required some form of written documentation. Minoan scribes first used a hieroglyphic system of writing, and then a simpler script known as Linear A. Neither of these has been deciphered.

Throughout the Middle Minoan period, palace artists produced a wide range of works: superb gold jewelry, decorated stone and ceramic vessels, and the brilliant frescoes which decorated the buildings. Unlike their contemporaries in Egypt and Mesopotamia, they preferred the small, even miniature, to the monumental scale. In depicting nature—dolphins, plants, a cat stalking a bird—Minoan artists aimed for realism and what sometimes seems like humor. The recent excavation of a Minoan colony on the Cycladic island of Thera has uncovered some wonderfully fresh depictions of the Minoan world. They range from an elaborate naval scene to the "springtime" room, with its walls showing bright flowers and soaring birds.

These works document another original aspect of Minoan culture, the importance of women. To judge from the character of Minoan art in the palaces, the aristocratic world gave prominent status to women and men. Scenes in the frescoes and on exquisitely carved sealstones show both sexes in elaborate costumes which leave much of the body naked, taking part in palace ceremonies and entertainments. Girls and boys (perhaps slaves who will die in the ritual) share in the various activities, including the ritual "game" of bull-leaping—which may have been at the root of the later legend of the Minotaur.

Bulls played an important part in Minoan religion, but the central figure in Minoan worship was a

Snake Goddess, from the Temple Repository, the palace at Knossos.

goddess figure. Sometimes accompanied by animals, sometimes surrounded by vegetation, depictions of a goddess occur throughout Minoan history. The most famous of all, the terracotta statuette known as the *Snake Goddess*, shows her grasping a snake in each hand, and a miniature lion sits on the crown of her hat—the figurine, like many of the other similar ones found, may in fact represent a priestess.

By the Late Minoan period, Minoan power was on the wane, and around 1450 B.C. invaders attacked Knossos and occupied it. Among the changes they introduced was a revision of the Minoan writing system in the form of a new script known as Linear B. The Linear B tablets contain an early form of Greek, and the invading force probably came from mainland Greece. In any case, shortly after their arrival there is evidence of widespread destruction throughout Crete. Palace life came to an abrupt end sometime after 1400 B.C., with the few survivors retreating to the remote and rugged mountains in the center of the island.

What caused the collapse of Minoan civilization? An internal revolt against the new rulers of Knossos followed by massive reprisals? A further invasion from outside? Natural causes? A massive volcanic eruption had occurred earlier on the island of Thera, around 1625 B.C., which may have created some ecological disaster. The mystery remains unsolved, but one important factor may well have been the rise of a rival power on the mainland, perhaps responsible for the invasion of 1450 B.C.: the Mycenaeans.

Mycenae, Rich in Gold

The Mycenaeans, the Minoans' successors as dominant power in the eastern Mediterranean, take their name from their most powerful Bronze Age center in mainland Greece, Mycenae. The Homeric epics speak of "Mycenae, rich in gold," and from the first days of his excavations there in 1876, the German archeologist Heinrich Schliemann discovered the truth of Homer's words. Prior to his explorations, scholars regarded the story of the Mycenaeans and Troy as a fantasy: the wealthy Schliemann believed that the Homeric epics were founded on historical reality, and he had the financial means to prove it by excavation. In the Royal Grave Circle, just inside the palace walls, his team uncovered the tombs of Mycenaean rulers dating to around 1600 B.C., filled with stupendous quantities of gold treasures. In addition to jewelry, weapons, diadems, and goblets, the finds included gold death masks, which allow us to look upon the faces of some of the first rulers in Western history.

Schliemann's whole career was driven by his urge to prove the historical accuracy of Homer's epic poems, which describe a war between the Mycenaeans and the city of Troy. Although the detailed results of his exca-

The so-called "Mask of Agamemnon" from Mycenae.

vations have become challenged in recent years—he may have set up some of his "findings" by placing together objects from a variety of sources—the general lines of the picture he described seem accurate enough.

His first major campaign took him in 1870 to the site of Troy itself on the northwest coast of modern Turkey. After uncovering the walls and gate of Homer's city and numerous treasures, he moved to Greece to complete his task by finding the conquerors of Troy, the Mycenaeans. Schliemann was always convinced that the royal family buried in the Grave Circle at Mycenae was that of Agamemnon, the leader of the expedition against the Trojans described in Homer's *Iliad*. Subsequent excavations have revealed that his finds dated to a period toward the beginning of Mycenaean history, long before the Homeric Trojan War.

The earliest stages of construction at Mycenae took place just before 1600 B.C., and Schliemann's discoveries revealed that from its foundation, Mycenaean culture was rich and sophisticated. For their first two centuries, the Mycenaeans were strongly influenced by the leading Aegean power of the time, the Minoans. With the fall of Knossos around 1400 B.C., the Mycenaeans asserted their independence and became the dominant force in the region.

Their control lasted for some 200 years, from 1400 to 1200 B.C. During that time, Mycenaean traders traveled east and south to the Near East and Egypt, and westward to Italy, selling their goods and importing raw materials. The successful Mycenaean campaign against Troy, which occurred around 1250 B.C., may well have been the result of a trading dispute or commercial rivalry. Their victory over the Trojans seems to have been complete, yet only a few years later, around 1200 B.C., the Mycenaean territory was in ruins, its chief cities destroyed, and most of them abandoned. As in the case of the fall of Knossos, the cause remains mysterious. Later Greek stories, describing the violent events which followed Agamemnon's triumphant return to Mycenae after the Trojan War, may be based on memories of internal strife caused by dynastic rivalry. Other possibilities include external invasion or natural disaster.

Whatever the causes, the Mycenaeans' political and economic domination of the Mediterranean came to an abrupt end. A few inhabitants who had fled returned to their homes, and some Mycenaeans moved eastward to form settlements on the islands of Rhodes and Cyprus. A burst of renewed violence around 1100 B.C. cut short their brief recovery, and the Greek Bronze Age ended suddenly.

The century from 1100 B.C. to 1000 B.C. is known, with good reason, as that of the "Dark Ages." Invading forces, some of them Greek-speaking, passed through former Mycenaean territories. Some Mycenaean cultural traditions survived, particularly in Crete and at Athens, but on the whole, when life began to develop again in Greek lands around 1000 B.C., the break with the past was profound. The Greeks of the Iron Age had to discover for themselves the skills of civilization (including writing), how to build, and forms of social and political organization.

Yet despite the gulf that lay between the splendors of the Bronze Age and the simple beginnings of Greek culture proper, some links remained. Many later Greek myths have their roots in Minoan and Mycenaean times, as do the earliest Greek works of literature, the Homeric poems. Perhaps most significant of all, throughout the history of later Greek religion, the cult of the mother goddess—and female creative power in general—echoed Minoan and Mycenaean worship of the Earth Mother, and served in the Classical period as a powerful counterbalance to the dominance of Father Zeus. Shrines to the Greek goddesses Hera, Artemis, and others, depictions on vase paintings, and the nature of many myths all attest to the continuity of Bronze Age religious traditions.

THE GREEKS OF THE EARLY IRON AGE: THE BIRTH OF THE CITY-STATE

For the first two and a half centuries of their history, from around 1000 until 750 B.C., the early Iron Age Greeks remained relatively isolated from the outside world. Under the Mycenaeans, the Aegean world had been in close contact with other parts of the Mediterranean, but their Greek successors did not begin to make contact with their neighbors until the beginning of the 8th century B.C. Thus, the Greeks' cultural development, at this crucial stage in their history, was slow.

The Significance of the "Polis"

Within Greece, the early Iron Age saw the development of a series of separate and independent regions. The mountain ranges of the Greek mainland served as natural dividers, creating geographical areas that were often isolated from one another. Within each zone, an urban community began to develop that served as a base for the farming of the surrounding countryside. In a similar way, each individual Greek island formed its own urban administrative center. Thus the cities of Athens, Thebes, and Sparta became the dominant forces in, respectively, the mainland regions of Attica, Boeotia, and Laconia, while the capitals of Naxos, Samos, and other islands controlled their island territory.

Map 1.1 Ancient Greece

The name given by later Greeks to these centralized urban communities, originally formed as military fortifications for defense, was "polis," a Greek word generally translated as "city-state." As the chief form of social and political organization from the beginnings of Greek culture, the polis played a vital role in Greek history, both for good and bad. Each individual city-state generated its own political, social, religious, and artistic developments. The ties of loyalty and obligation which bound its citizens were far more important than any sense of shared identity with the members of other Greek communities. The sense of competition between the various cities stimulated an astonishing growth in intellectual and cultural achievement, the results of which laid the foundations of Western civilization. At the same time, however, increasingly bitter rivalries led to a constant series of quarrels between cities that developed on occasion into outright war.

Government in the City-States

In the early days of the city-states, the ruling class consisted of the richest, or the "best," people. The Greek word for the "best," the *aristoi*, gives us the term for the system under which they governed: an aristocracy based on birth and inherited land and wealth. These powerful families owned most of the good land, located near enough to the city walls to be easily defended against outside raiders, and could afford the horses and armor necessary to protect the community. In some cities, poorer farmers and workers lived in villages on the outskirts of the polis.

The ruling body in most early city-states was a Council of the "Best Men," or "Elders." This Council elected executive officers to carry out its decisions, which were reported to the community at town meetings. The aristocrats also had charge of the chief religious cult of their city. This generally focused around a temple dedicated to the state's patron deity, located in a position of prominence. Thus the Acropolis ("high part of the city") at Athens was crowned by the Temple to Athena.

Eventually, as populations grew, popular dissatisfaction with the restricted political system of these early city-states led to important changes in Greek life. Around 800 B.C., increasing numbers of resentful citizens abandoned their communities to form new cities, known as colonies, often on the fringes of the Greek world or even outside it. In other cases, rulers themselves founded colonies and sent members of their families to run them. The Greek "colonizers" of the 8th and 7th centuries B.C. played a vital role in broadening Greek perceptions of the world around them.

The Athenian Acropolis.

Meanwhile, back at home, toward the end of the 7th century B.C. broad popular frustration with the conservative rule of the "Best Men," which concentrated power in the hands of a few, produced a wave of revolutions leading to the replacement of aristocratic government by "tyranny"—the rule of a single individual whom the lower classes viewed as a social benefactor.

The early political development of the city-states permitted the slow evolution of the first Greek experiments in the visual arts, the growth of religious speculation, and—most astonishingly—the creation of the first, and still among the greatest, of Western literary masterpieces, the *Iliad* and *Odyssey*.

Significant Dates

From Bronze to Iron in the Greek World (all dates B.C.)

3000–2500	Culture flourishes in the Cyclades
2500–1950	Early Minoan Period
1950–1550	Middle Minoan Period
1625	Earthquake on Thera
1600	First settlement at Mycenae
1450	Knossos attacked and occupied
1400–1200	Mycenaean power at its height
1250 (??)	Mycenaean campaign against Troy
1200–1100	Destruction and partial reoccupation of Mycenae
1000–750	Early Iron Age in Greece
800	Beginnings of Greek colonization
800–700	Greeks begin to use alphabet

GODS, GODDESSES, AND THE WORLD OF HOMER

Most of the vast body of Greek religious myth goes back to the time of the early city-states—or, in some cases, even earlier, to the Bronze Age. Later Greeks embellished the stories and sometimes tried to reconcile contradictory versions, but the original character of the Greek attitude to religion remained consistent.

The Nature of Greek Religion

Despite the enormous influence of Greek culture on our own heritage, Greek religion had little in common with Judaism or Christianity, the chief religious faiths of the Western tradition. In the first place, the Greeks had no single, divinely inspired text providing a central body of teaching of the kind offered by the Bible to Jews and Christians or the Koran to Muslims. Then, far from seeking to record a series of objective historical events, Greek myths are often tales that illustrate aspects of human behavior.

Father Zeus, the dispenser of lightning and justice, comes as close as any figure in the Greek pantheon to the Almighty God of the Judeo-Christian tradition, and often presides over the triumph of right over wrong. Yet the same majestic cloud gatherer became involved in a series of erotic affairs which sometimes degenerate into downright rape (sexual violence is common in Greek myth). The consequences, frequently involving a showdown with his wife Hera, are undignified and sometimes comic.

The explanation of these characteristics is that, unlike Western religions, Greek beliefs tried to understand and illustrate human nature rather than the divine. The Greek gods serve not to illuminate the supernatural, but to symbolize recognizable aspects of human behavior. The goddess Aphrodite epitomizes erotic love; Artemis, the moon goddess, is the guardian of chastity; and Ares is the god of war. No Greek deity represents supreme good, and there is similarly no equivalent of the Christian Satan, or supreme evil. For the Greeks, moral issues could be solved by humans only on an individual basis, without reference to a divinely inspired code of morality.

The various Greek gods reflected the fact that human nature in each of us is often contradictory. Thus the deities Apollo and Dionysus illustrated the duality of reason and emotion. Apollo, the god of light and music, represented order and reason, the power of the mind. Dionysus, god of wine and the theater, represented the casting aside of inhibitions, the power of the emotions. The Greeks, recognizing the duality of human behavior, acknowledged both forces and tried to find a middle way between the two extremes: the "golden mean." One of the few universal statements of Greek religion expresses this search for a prudent balance in the phrase, "Nothing in excess."

Greek writers and artists based their plays, poems, and statues on mythical subjects because the tales illustrated characteristics of practical human experience, albeit often in extreme form. At the same time, the epic plots provided their audiences with the exciting stories that appealed so profoundly to the Greek imagination.

The Homeric Epics

At the beginning of the Western literary tradition stand two works, the epic poems we know as the *Iliad* and the *Odyssey*. Subsequent ages have regarded their author, Homer, as one of the towering figures of our cultural history. Yet many aspects of his life and achievements still remain mysterious, as indeed they were for the Greeks themselves.

According to later myth, Homer was a blind traveling poet. He seems to have lived toward the end of the five centuries between the late Mycenaean period and the 8th century B.C., when the Homeric works as we know them were in existence. The poems themselves are in any case probably not simply the creation of a single mind, but a combination of various folktales, evolving over centuries into their final form.

There are many indications that the process was not an accidental one. The style and language are consistent throughout, and the poems are carefully structured, in spite of the long time it took for them to crystallize. The earliest versions probably go back to the late Mycenaean period, perhaps describing a Mycenaean raid exaggerated by memory and nostalgia, and then passed down by word of mouth among the traveling professional storytellers of early Greece. They first took written form shortly before 500 B.C., when they were put into order and used for the Panathenaic festival at Athens. The works as we have them are in an edition made by a scribe at Alexandria in the 2nd century B.C.

At some stage in this long process, the accumulated mass of material received its definitive form by passing through the imaginative genius of the person we call Homer. Some readers, struck by the different moods of the *Iliad*—grim and violent—and the more romantic, leisurely *Odyssey*, have even suggested that a separate creator was responsible for each. The 19th-century writer Samuel Butler was the first—but by no means the last—to suggest that the author of the *Odyssey* was a woman.

The theme of the *Iliad* is the significance of personal responsibility: we must accept the consequences of our actions, even when they cause harm both for ourselves and for others. Against the background of the bloody conflict between Greeks and Trojans, Homer sets the personal tragedy of Achilles, proudest and most valiant of Greek heroes. Offended by the behavior of Agamemnon, his commanding officer, Achilles decides to deprive the Greeks of his strength and withdraws from the fighting. Even when Greek casualties mount, and Agamemnon seeks to make amends, the resentful Achilles stubbornly refuses to return to the action. It takes the violent death of his dearest friend, Patroclus, at the hands of the Trojan hero Hector, to drive Achilles out of his tent and back to the battlefield. In raging anger he kills Hector and then, driven by guilt at having allowed Patroclus to go to his death, mutilates his opponent's corpse. Only when the dead Trojan's father, Priam, comes to beg for the body of his son does Achilles finally break down and recognize the tragic consequences of his behavior. (Later accounts describe how, doomed to an early death, Achilles was killed by a poisoned arrow fired into his heel, the only vulnerable part of his body. His mother Thetis had held him by the heel when dipping him into the river Styx to protect the rest of him.)

Although the gods make numerous appearances in the *Iliad*, and frequently play an important—often crucial—role in determining the actions of the work's characters, the humans themselves decide and think, and hold themselves, and not just the gods, responsible for their fates. Achilles and the others must bear the full weight of their conduct. Nor is Achilles guilty of

A scene from *The Odyssey:* Odysseus and his companion blind the one-eyed giant Polyphemus.

breaking some divine commandment in his refusal to soften his anger. He chooses freely, and he himself, his slaughtered friend, and the other dead Greeks must bear the consequences. Thus, from the earliest times, the central element in the Greek view of life is not divine order or justice, but individual human conduct. In the eyes of the Greeks, we are all at least partly in control of our destiny: if we cannot completely control the time when we die, we can—and should—control the way we live.

The world of the *Odyssey* is more relaxed and discursive. It describes the long wanderings of the Greek warrior Odysseus as he makes his way home to Greece after the Trojan War. His adventures bring him into contact with a one-eyed giant, a beautiful if dangerous enchantress, a romantic young princess, and other varied distractions, before he finally returns to the arms of his ever-faithful wife, Penelope.

The period in which the Homeric stories take place purports to be that of late Mycenaean times. Historically, however, the actual conditions described by the poet are a mixture of those of the late Mycenaean period, the Dark Ages, and the very early Archaic period, during which the poems came into existence. The political structures of Homer's world, the councils of elders, resemble those of the early city-states. Even at a more mundane level, the details reveal Homer's daily life. At the funeral games to mark the burial of Patroclus, one of the valuable prizes offered in an athletic competition is a lump of iron: valuable, that is, for Homer's contemporaries, nonexistent for Achilles and his fellow Mycenaeans of the Bronze Age.

THE GREEKS ABROAD: COLONIES AND MARKETS

For the first two centuries of the Iron Age, the city-states grew in prosperity under their aristocratic rulers. By the early 8th century B.C., there began to develop a series of intercity sacred festivals that saw the rival communities in peaceful athletic competition. The most famous and venerable of these was at Olympia, a sanctuary sacred to Zeus, where every four years the Olympic Games took place. The first games were held, according to tradition, in 776 B.C., and the last of ancient times over a thousand years later in A.D. 394, after which the Byzantine Emperor Theodosius abolished them because of widespread cheating.

As the Greek cities developed, they began increasingly to trade with their neighbors. By 700 B.C., Greek traders had established themselves in markets to the east in Asia Minor and as far north as the Black Sea. To the south in Egypt, Greek merchants sold wine and oil in exchange for grain, and bartered Greek pottery for Egyptian jewels and carved seals. Both Asia Minor and Egypt had recovered from the disturbances of the end of the Bronze Age, and their economic resurgence helped to stimulate the expanding Greek economy. Most importantly, other Greeks moved west to Italy, first as traders and increasingly as colonizers; they founded a number of cities in southern Italy and Sicily.

The Age of Colonization

The motives for the wave of colonization that saw the Greeks establish overseas communities from the southern coast of Russia to the western Mediterranean were twofold. In part they were a result of economic frustration at home, leading to trading abroad: business contacts with the local populations led to permanent settlements. Food shortages in Greece after 800 B.C. also stimulated overseas migration. At the same time, however, Greek colonizers often left home to escape from political frustration. In spite of the growing prosperity of their cities—or in some cases because of it—the entrenched aristocratic rulers continued to retain power. Ambitious citizens either went abroad to find freedom and fortune, or, if they seemed to present a threat to the rulers, were sometimes sent abroad.

An Archaic-style temple built by Greeks at Paestum, a colony in southern Italy.

Around 700 B.C., the Spartan leaders eliminated the threat posed by a revolutionary political movement by packing its members off to southern Italy. The exiles founded their new home at Taranto, which grew to become one of the wealthiest of Greek colonies in Italy. Two important new developments helped to facilitate the burst of Greek activity after centuries of relative calm. The first, which occurred sometime between 800 and 700 B.C., was that the Greeks began to use an alphabet. They borrowed a system of writing from one of their main trading rivals, the Phoenicians, and adapted it to their own language. The ability to write provided immediate benefits in conducting long-distance business affairs, which was probably the reason for the Greeks' eagerness to become literate. At the same time, it had vast consequences for the development of our culture as well as theirs: the letters in modern Western alphabets are the Roman adaptations of the Etruscan form of the Greek alphabet.

The other significant event was the invention of metal coinage around 700 B.C. in Asia Minor. The Greeks' contacts with the peoples of this region led them to take up the new aid to commerce, and by 600 B.C. most Greek cities, both in the homeland and in abroad, minted their own coinage. In this way, the Greeks simplified their trading and reinforced the identity of their individual cities, since each community's currency bore its own individual emblem: the owl of Athens, symbol of the goddess Athene; the head of Dionysus for Naxos, symbolizing the island's chief export, wine. The increasing complexity of financial transactions was to produce less happy results over the next century (see Part II, Topic 3).

GREEK IDEAS AND EASTERN ART

The introduction of writing and coinage were only two of the benefits the Greeks derived from their broader contacts. At a more subtle level, their exposure to new ideas radically influenced their intellectual and artistic progress.

Geometric Art

In the absence of writing, it is difficult to have much notion of Greek thinkers before the Age of Colonization, but in the case of their art, some of the earliest works have survived. They take the form of clay pots painted with a wide range of geometric designs. It may seem strange that a people who relished the exciting narratives of Homer should have limited their visual range to abstract decorations, but the complexity of many of the Geometric vases produced between 900 and 700 B.C. is evidence of the Greek obsession with order and balance. If we are inclined to think of later Greek art as supremely realistic, it is important to remember that Greek artists were always concerned with mathematical relationships. That concern with intellectual clarity is visible even in these earliest pieces.

Geometric vase from the Dipylon cemetery, Athens.

The Orientalizing Style

First contacts with the long artistic traditions of the Egyptians and the Near Eastern peoples came when the resurgence of the older economies began to stimulate Greek economic growth and trade. The result was a revolution in Greek art. The new style, actually a mixture of various stylistic elements, is known as the Orientalizing, from the strongly eastern influences (although Egypt is in North Africa, the style of its art during the 1st millennium B.C. had much in common with that of the ancient Near East). In place of the Geometric designs, artists began to decorate their pots with a wide range of motifs borrowed from their eastern neighbors: sphinxes, papyrus and palm foliage, winged humans and monsters. Bold colors replaced the black and red of earlier Geometric art. Most importantly, many painters—especially those working at Athens—began to use their works to tell a story. The narrative tradition in Western art was born in Greece shortly after 700 B.C.

Contacts with Egypt inspired the Greeks' first attempts at stone sculptures. The earliest examples, dating like the narrative paintings to the years following 700 B.C., are stiff and tense, but already they show the beginnings of Greek interest in how human bodies actually work, and in proportion. Just as the artists of the Geometric period repeated a few basic designs over and over to perfect them, so the Orientalizing sculptors produced statue after statue of young women (clothed) and young men (nude) to work out the depiction of the human form.

The Greeks of the 7th century B.C. also based their first steps in stone architecture on Egyptian

Nikandre's Kore (c. 650 B.C.), the earliest surviving stone female figure in Greek (i.e. Western) art.

The New York Kouros (c. 615 B.C.), one of the earliest and tallest of standing male figures.

models. Little of the early buildings has survived, but the first stone temples in Greece—those at Corinth and Olympia—made use of the post and lintel structure of monumental Egyptian architecture. By 600 B.C., Greek architects had evolved the earliest of their own styles, that known as Doric. With the foundations of painting, sculpture, and architecture established, Greek art was ready for the extraordinary developments of the succeeding Archaic Age.

The collapse of Bronze Age culture in Greece saw the disappearance of almost 2000 years' achievements. The Greeks of the early Iron Age, limited to their own rocky terrain, and cut off from the outside world, had to begin to construct a civilization anew. With the momentum of their colonizing movement, driven by economic and social pressures, the Greeks were ready to build on outside influences to create their own unique intellectual and artistic achievement. If the isolation of the first two and a half centuries of their history seems a slow beginning for so dynamic a culture, the speed with which they absorbed a bewildering assortment of outside ideas and influences is equally striking. The 100 years from 700 to 600 B.C. were sufficient for the Greeks to find their own identity.

The following centuries carried Greek political and intellectual experiments and developments further and further from their early Iron Age beginnings. Yet in one respect, at least, they retained a link with their origins and with their Bronze Age predecessors. From childhood, Greeks of later times read and learned by heart the Iliad *and the* Odyssey*. Through all the hectic and often violent events of their later history, the Greeks never lost their reverence for Homer and his world.*

Questions for Further Study

1. What are the differences between the creation of the Homeric epics and other great works of literature? What effect do they have on the character of the *Iliad* and *Odyssey*?
2. What role has archeology played in the discovery and study of Minoan and Mycenaean civilization? How does its importance—and the absence of other kinds of evidence (literary and others)—influence the picture we have of Bronze Age culture?
3. What evidence is there for the role of women in the Bronze Age?

Suggestions for Further Reading

Boardman, J. *The Greeks Overseas*. New York, 1982.
Burkert, W. *Greek Religion*. Cambridge, MA, 1985.
Finley, M. I. *Early Greece: The Bronze and Archaic Ages*. New York, 1982.
Graham, A. J. *Colony and Mother City in Ancient Greece*. Chicago, 1983.
Krzyskowska, O., and L. Nixon, eds. *Minoan Society*. Bristol, 1983.
Vermeule, E. *Aspects of Death in Early Greek Art and Poetry*. Berkeley, CA, 1981.

II

Topic 2

The Greeks in the Archaic Era

The Archaic period (600–480 B.C.) was a period of political, economic, and cultural development which saw the collapse of the old aristocratic order in most of the Greek city-states. Many of the new rulers were disgruntled or ambitious aristocrats and rose to power by playing on the unrest of the middle classes: they were known as "tyrants."

At Athens, programs of social and political reform at the beginning and end of the 6th century B.C., introduced respectively by Solon and Cleisthenes, broadened the base of government. In the period between them, midcentury Athens was ruled by the benign tyrant Pisistratus, under whom the city flourished economically and culturally.

By the latter part of the 6th century B.C., the Athenians' chief rivals in the Greek world were the Spartans, who enforced their rigid political conservatism with austere military discipline. Sparta's conquest of the surrounding territory, and enslavement of many of the local inhabitants, enriched the city's citizens, or "Spartiates." By the early 5th century B.C., Sparta had become the symbol of conservativism in Greece and the natural opponent of the progressive Athenians and their allies.

At the end of the Archaic period, in 490 B.C., the threat of open hostility between the two camps temporarily subsided in the face of external danger from the leading power of the day, the mighty Persian Empire. The Persians first came into contact with the Greek cities of the eastern Mediterranean as Persian imperial conquests spread westward in the 6th century B.C. Persian governors absorbed the Greeks into their empire, took over the rule of the Greek cities, and imposed taxes on their citizens.

In 499 B.C. these Greek cities revolted against their Persian overlords. The Persians crushed the rebellion, but not before the Athenians had sent help to their fellow Greeks. Darius, the Persian king, launched an expedition against mainland Greece in 490 B.C. The decisive victory of the Athenians at the Battle of Marathon drove the Persian forces from Greece, and at the same time reinforced Athenian prestige as the leading city of Greece.

Ten years later, Athens and Sparta inflicted an even more crushing defeat on the vast military expedition assembled and led by Xerxes, Darius' son and successor. With the end of the Persian threat, and the appearance—at least—of unity among the leading Greek city-states, the following years of the 5th century B.C. inaugurated the high point of Greek culture, the Classical Age.

CITY-STATES IN TRANSITION: ARISTOCRACY, TYRANNY, AND THE PEOPLE

By around the middle of the 7th century B.C., citizens of most Greek city-states fell into one of three distinct levels of social category. At the top were the aristocrats, whose claim to rule depended on both birth and money. The descendants of the original aristocratic founders of their states, they alone controlled political power. They were also the only citizens who could afford the military equipment and horses on which their cities relied for defense, and thereby controlled state security.

At the lower end of the class system were the peasants and land workers, disenfranchised and at the mercy of the upper-class rulers. As the cities grew, an increasing population of urban poor added to the numbers of this lower class. Some of its members chose to escape the helplessness of their position in their home city by emigrating and founding colonies abroad (see Part II, Topic 1). For others, however, the growth of urban life and commerce brought the possibility of economic betterment and social progress. A middle class of merchants, craftsmen, and successful farmers began to emerge as the Greeks increased their manufacturing and trading activities throughout the Mediterranean world.

Around 650 B.C., an important military development gave these middle-rank citizens a way to exert their influence: many cities began to use foot soldiers in close formation to supplement the traditional cavalry battalions. The new infantry formation which developed, consisting of rows of eight men, each heavily armed, was known as a *phalanx*. Unlike mounted fighters, who needed to provide their own valuable equipment and horses, foot soldiers could serve at little cost to their families, and sons of middle-income merchant and farming families could now play a role in their city-state's military forces. The demand for a say in political affairs was bound to follow.

Funerary marker of Aristion, a Greek foot soldier.

The Rise of the Tyrants

The evolution of the middle class was only one of the factors that destabilized the established aristocratic regimes. In many cities, disputes within the ruling families led to the formation of rival aristocratic clans. Their leaders competed for middle-class support, and also claimed to champion the interests of the discontented lower classes. Many of the poorest of these had fallen victim to one of the consequences of economic instability, crushing debt. The result of all this unrest was a rash of political revolutions in the chief trading cities.

The popular leaders who rode to power on the wave of revolt were called tyrants. (For the ancient

Greeks, the word did not have the modern negative sense, and was equivalent to our "boss" or "chief.") Few of the tyrants ruled for more than a few years. Theagenes of Megara (a city near Athens) came to power in 640 B.C. He won the support of poor farmers by ordering the slaughter of cattle straying on to their land, and pleased urban housewives by building an aqueduct to bring running water into town. By 620 B.C., however, he had lost the support of his people, who drove him into exile.

Elsewhere, tyrants managed to pass on rule to their descendants. Cypselus of Corinth (c. 657–627 B.C.) was succeeded by his son Periander (c. 627–586 B.C.), whose efficient ruthlessness increased Corinth's prosperity but alienated its citizens. They overthrew his successor shortly after Periander's death. As the example of Corinth demonstrates, the duration of a tyranny depended on the degree to which a ruler could satisfy often conflicting demands. Only a few tyrants tried to hold on to power by deliberate cruelty. The most notorious of these was Phalaris (570–554 B.C.), the tyrant of Akragas—modern Agrigento in Sicily—who roasted his opponents alive inside a hollow bronze bull over open flames. Even so, Phalaris' subjects eventually overthrew him and executed him by his own method.

For all the abuses of a Phalaris, on the whole the tyrants served a useful purpose in the development of their city-states. They liberated them from an outdated and inadequate aristocratic system, ended the frequently bloody squabbles of contending aristocratic factions, and provided a period of internal peace. Furthermore, their public works programs—constructions such as Theagenes' aqueduct—stimulated economic growth. At Athens, the ruling tyrant Pisistratus brought even greater benefits to his city, where the 6th century B.C. saw a series of extraordinary political developments.

REFORM AT ATHENS: THE DEMOCRATIC EXPERIMENT

In one important respect, the early history of Athens differs from that of the other chief Greek city-states: the Athenians established no colonies abroad. Political development was slow at Athens, and tyrants—the promoters of colonies in other states—appeared there only relatively late in the Archaic period. Furthermore, although poor in quality, Athenian territory was large enough for its farmers to be able to make a living without going overseas to seek their fortune. Athenian law, however, was extremely harsh, and favored the rich and powerful. It took written form around 620 B.C. under the supervision of Draco, whose name is still synonymous with severity; a later Athenian described the Draconian law code as "written in blood."

In the rest of Greece, tyrants came to power during the late 7th century B.C. to remedy ancient injustices. The Athenians chose a different method of changing the political system. Instead of waiting for someone to seize power, they agreed on a reformer who could command the respect and trust of all classes of citizens: the unusually cooperative spirit which led to this procedure was to lead over time to the growth of democracy. Their choice was Solon (c. 630–560 B.C.). Solon was of aristocratic birth, but a merchant of no particular wealth. His chief claim to fame at Athens lay in his poetry, much of it openly patriotic. In 594 B.C. Solon took office as reforming magistrate, with full authority to introduce economic and constitutional changes.

The Reforms of Solon

When popular support brought Solon to power, many Athenians were suffering from a severe economic crisis. With the increasing circulation of money, and the growing custom of interest-bearing loans, poorer citizens fell into debt. Farmers forfeited their land when they were unable to repay their debts, while creditors seized other insolvent debtors and their families as slaves, even selling them abroad.

Those poorer citizens who expected Solon to redistribute landholdings on a fairer basis were disappointed, but his fellow aristocrats would hardly have agreed to his appointment if he had been likely to do so. He did, however, outlaw the enslaving of any Athenian for debt, launched a scheme for finding and buying back those who had been sold abroad, and cancelled all existing agricultural debts. Further, he forbade the export of food products (except for olive oil, of which there was a surplus). Wealthy farmers could no longer make profits abroad while poorer Athenians went hungry at home. Other reforms standardized the coinage and introduced a more humane law code.

Solon's constitutional reorganization was equally far-reaching. When he took office, the traditional rulers of Athens were the aristocratic members of a Council of the "Best Men." Before the executive magistrates, the archons, carried out the Council's decisions, an Assembly of the people confirmed them, but this Assembly had no prestige and could take no initiative. Thus the Council of the Best Men, known as the Areopagus (the name of the place in Athens where they met), effectively ran the city.

Under Solon's reforms, the Assembly of the people became central to the government of Athens. All free Athenian males became automatic members, whatever their financial status. Magistrates had to report to this popular Assembly and account for their actions. Solon left the members of the Areopagus with all their ancient prestige as elder statesmen, although wealth rather than birth now served as the qualification for their election. He may have also added a new council, the Boule (the Greek word for council) to take over the Areopagus' role of preparing business for submission to the Assembly of the people. Participation in the Boule was open to all middle-income citizens. Its 400 members, 100 from each of Athens' four chief ethnic groups, or Tribes, were chosen at random by lot in order to give all citizens a chance to serve.

By contrast with the rest of the Greek world, Solon's reforms introduced strong elements of democracy into Athens, and in the process—like many reformers since—he left all sides unhappy. He claimed to have given the people "power enough," and complained at their ingratitude when they accused him of having done too little. The wealthy resented their loss of privileges and the cancellation of the debts owed to them. The weary and disgruntled reformer, tormented "like a wolf among many dogs," left the city in disgust to travel abroad.

If many of his contemporaries bitterly criticized his decisions, later Athenians revered Solon's memory as great poet and the wisest of all statesmen. Among the remarks attributed to him was his reply to Croesus, the fabulously wealthy king of Lydia, when Croesus asked the sage who was the happiest of all men: "Call no man happy until he is dead." Before Solon's own death, he saw Athens finally under the rule of its first tyrant, but the democratic nature of his reforms was to leave a permanent mark on Athenian history.

Athens after Solon: The Pistratids

The immediate result of Solon's departure from Athens after 594 B.C. was renewed political instability. By giving new rights to the lower classes, his reforms drew the poorer citizens' attention to their previous mistreatment. The resulting class struggles, combined with rivalries within the aristocratic clans, produced fierce conflict.

The figure to emerge victorious from the confusion was Pisistratus (605?–527 B.C.), a nobleman and successful general, who became Athens' first tyrant in 546 B.C. Pisistratus was no democrat, making sure that his supporters held the chief positions of power in the state. He left Solon's constitution intact, however, and the stability of his rule made economic recovery possible: one of the contributing factors was his redistribution to the small farmers of the land of aristocrats who had fled to other states. A significant indication of the Athenians' new peace of mind under Pisistratus was the widespread increase in the planting of olive trees in the first years of his tyranny, encouraged by state subsidies: olive trees, which produce little fruit for the first 30 years, are a long-term investment.

A more general sign of confidence at Athens was the outburst of artistic activity there. Later Greek historians credited Pisistratus with commissioning the first written versions of the Homeric epics, and with instituting the dramatic festivals in honor of the god Dionysus, at which Greek tragic drama was born (see Part II, Topic 4). The large-scale production of fine painted pottery led to the development of an important style, the red figure, and Athenian merchants enriched the home economy by exporting red figure vases throughout the Mediterranean. With Pisistratus' encouragement, architects changed the ap-

Scene of olive harvesting on an Athenian black-figure vase.

The Death of Sarpedon, on a red-figure vase.

pearance of Athens, erecting imposing temples and aqueducts.

When Pisistratus died in 527 B.C., rule passed peacefully to his sons, Hippias and Hipparchus. Lacking their father's tact and skill, their government became increasingly repressive and unpopular. In 514 B.C. two young Athenians, Harmodius and Aristogiton, assassinated Hipparchus in an attempt to end their rule (Hippias escaped), and in 511 B.C. Spartan troops took advantage of the increasing unrest at Athens to drive Hippias out, a rare case of interference by a city-state in another city's internal affairs—the Spartan intervention was allegedly in response to the oracle at Delphi, which ordered them to "liberate Athens." (Later Athenians naturally preferred to regard the two tyrannicides, not the Spartans, as the agents of Athenian democracy.) Hippias fled to Persia, seeking refuge at the court of the Persian king.

Cleisthenes and Athenian Democracy

It is a sign of the Athenians' newfound political maturity that Hippias' exile did not plunge the city into a fresh burst of political turmoil. At the first sign of aristocratic rivalry, the popular democratic forces united under Cleisthenes—himself a member of one of Athens' noblest families—to implement Solon's reforms. The anger of the wealthy landowners induced the Spartans to interfere once again and briefly drive out Cleisthenes, but by 507 B.C. he was back in power.

The new political organization which Cleisthenes devised and put into effect at Athens at the end of the 6th century B.C. continued the growth of participatory democracy in Greece which Solon had initiated. His system aimed to eliminate the basic problem in the Athenian political system, the continued influence of a few wealthy and aristocratic families within the traditional Tribes. In order to dismantle the power of the old guard, he invented a new, purely artificial set of Tribes based on location rather than family.

Each of his ten new Tribes included some citizens from all three of the geographical regions into which he divided Athenian territory: the city itself, the coast, and the farmland of the interior. In this way, the members of any one Tribe would be of varied origins, so that sailors would vote alongside farmers and traders and craftsmen from the city. The system seems artificial and improbable, but it worked: it cut through generations of family influence and self-interests, and persuaded individual citizens to think of the good of the community as a whole, rather than try to promote their own narrow concerns. It also appealed to the Greek sense of order and balance.

In other reforms, Cleisthenes revised Solon's constitution. The Assembly of the people became the sole legislative body, and magistrates were entirely responsible to it. The Council, or Boule, enlarged from 400 to 500 members, prepared business to present to the Assembly. The 500, each of whom served for a year, were still chosen by Solon's system of random lot drawing, and no man could be on the Boule more than twice in a lifetime. As a result, at any one time in Classical Athens not only were all adult male citizens members of the Assembly of the people, but many thousands of them had served as Boule members, with the experience of participating in the detailed work of government administration.

To reinforce the importance of the democratic Boule and Assembly of the people, the ancient Council of the "Best Men," the Areopagus, lost virtually all effective power, becoming little more than symbolic. Beginning in the generation after Cleisthenes, even the archons—originally chosen by the "Best Men" from among their own number—were selected by lot and had only ceremonial duties.

Cleisthenes' reforms built on those of Solon to eliminate past inequities and prejudices. They created a forward-looking state, modernized and efficient, where the arts could thrive—and did—and in which all voting citizens could feel that they played an active part in running their government. By the end of the Persian Wars, Athens was renowned throughout the Greek world for its political evolution. Those suspicious of popular democracy looked elsewhere for inspiration and leadership: to Sparta.

THE SPARTAN ALTERNATIVE: CONSERVATISM AND THE MILITARY IDEAL

Sparta, the leading city in southern Greece—a region known as the Peloponnese—developed a system of government unique in the Greek world: a military aristocracy. The early growth of population there had led the Spartans, like many other Greek cities, to send out colonizers, including those who founded Taranto in southern Italy. In their urge for more territory closer to home, however, toward the end of the 8th century B.C. the Spartans made the highly unusual move of conquering land in their own region, that of their western neighbors, the Messenians. They enslaved the local population, and from then on, alone of the Greek city-states, maintained a permanent army to put down revolts by their subject peoples.

By the Archaic period, Spartan society was rigidly stratified. At the top were the aristocratic Spartiates (Spartan warriors), the only true citizens. Beneath them came the *perioikoi,* or "dwellers around," consisting of conquered neighboring peoples who vastly outnumbered the Spartiates and had no political rights. At the bottom were the "helots," or serfs, also acquired from Spartan conquests. These were not bought and sold as slaves of individual Spartiates, but belonged to the state, and mostly worked the land. The threat that a possible helot uprising posed to state security was a constant preoccupation for the Spartiates.

Spartiate Training

The way of life of the ruling upper class was intended to maintain this social system: a dominant minority holding down and exploiting a huge population of potentially dangerous subjects. At a time when revolutions elsewhere in Greece—and Solon at Athens—were bringing new rights to the lower classes, the Spartans continually reinforced their conservative military discipline.

The Spartans claimed that their system was the invention of a lawgiver called Lycurgus, who, they believed, had lived in the 9th century B.C. (the later historian Plutarch dated Lycurgus to the period following 669 B.C.). It seems more probable that it evolved over time, as Spartan domination over their captives required increasing severity. The revolt of the Messenians, around 630 B.C., which took the Spartans some 30 years to suppress, seems to have been the final factor in the creation of a state dependent on an efficient fighting machine always ready to swing into action.

Those Spartan babies which appeared weakly were left out to die (infanticide was also practiced in other Greek states, generally as a means of birth control, while the Spartans used it primarily to strengthen the physical condition of their citizens). At the age of seven, male children left their mothers to live and train in camps, where they received scanty clothing and insufficient food. Their elders expected them to survive by stealing from nearby farms, and beat them if they were caught, not for dishonesty, but for their clumsiness in being found out. At twenty, the young men stood for election to one of a series of military messes or "clubs." Failure to win unanimous election by the club's members meant utter social disgrace. The young Spartiate warriors were expected to marry by the age of thirty, but even then they continued to eat and sleep at their club residence and serve in the military. Spartan men could not farm, trade, or do professional work, all of which fell to the perioikoi.

Spartan girls remained with their mothers, living under a regime to promote their physical fitness and prepare them for their chief role in life: motherhood. Domestic activities such as housecleaning and sewing, elsewhere in Greece the normal duties of women of all classes, fell to women of inferior status, and Spartiate young women concentrated on gymnastics, music—an important aspect of education—and studying domestic management and childrearing.

One of the effects of the military system was to emphasize the importance of women to the state, and in general the rest of Greece saw Spartan women as outspoken and immoral. When the Spartan army was abroad for an extended period, the state seems to have encouraged the wives left behind to have relations with young and healthy helots, in order to rebuild the population as an insurance against heavy military losses. Even within Spartiate society, according to Athenian writers, wife-sharing was tolerated: the more Spartiates born, the better.

Politics at Sparta

Young Spartans of both sexes learned to denounce potential troublemakers to the state's ruthless secret police, and the Spartan political constitution betrayed a similar distrust of its citizens. There were two kings. As a further safety measure, the kings themselves fell under the supervision of five *Ephors*, or "Overseers." Chosen by lot, these served for a year. A Council of Elders, the Gerousia, served as the chief executive body. The Spartiate Assembly approved or rejected the executive's proposals, but it could not debate and—to the amused bewilderment of other Greeks—it expressed its opinion not by voting but by shouting: the loudest side won. If the Assembly reached no clear-cut decision, the kings and Ephors could order it suspended.

The same rigidity marked Spartan relations with the rest of the Greek world. The prosperity of the aristocratic upper class depended on agriculture, since Sparta discouraged commercial activities and trade with other states. Even though the Athenians and others had developed a controlled currency and banking system which made possible commerce abroad, the Spartans continued to use antiquated and clumsy iron currency. The very presence of foreigners in Sparta, with their new and unwelcome ideas, was subject to strict control, and from time to time the state would expel those who had managed to obtain admittance.

Painted plate from Sparta showing King Arcesilas presiding over the weighing of silphium for export.

The cruelty and brutality of many aspects of Spartiate life were clear to their Greek contemporaries. If the Spartans kept their subject peoples under the most ruthless control, their own lives were just as grim and austere. One visitor from Greek Italy remarked, after a dinner in an army mess: "Now I understand why the Spartans do not fear death!"

Yet if many Greeks made fun of the Spartans' stubborn conservatism, they were not blind to what they saw as Spartan virtues. They admired the Spartan sense of *eunomia*, of "law and order," and civic discipline. A later writer, Plutarch, tells of an incident at the Olympic games. A feeble old man was wandering round in search of a seat, to the jeers of the crowd. When he came to the Spartan stands, all the young men, and many of the older ones, sprang to their feet to offer him a place. As the old man gratefully sank down, he sighed: "All Greeks *know* what is right, but only the Spartans *do* it."

The Spartan sacrifice of comfort and self-interest in the interests of the state represented an ideal that gave individual lives a meaning and purpose. Developing its characteristic political system before the Athenians had established theirs, Sparta provided a model for other Greek states throughout the 6th century B.C. By the beginning of the 5th century B.C., with the growing threat from Persia, the Greeks' mighty eastern neighbor, the Spartan lifestyle and discipline exerted an increasingly powerful appeal.

Significant Dates

The Archaic Age (all dates B.C.)

650–620	Messenian revolt against Sparta
620	Law code of Draco introduced at Athens
594	Reforms of Solon
546	Pisistratus becomes tyrant of Athens
514	Assassination of Hipparchus
507	Reforms of Cleisthenes
499	Ionians revolt against Persians
490	Darius defeated at Battle of Marathon
480	Xerxes defeated at Battle of Salamis
479	Greek victory at Plataea ends Persian Wars in Greece

THE PERSIAN CHALLENGE AND THE VICTORY OF THE GREEKS

While the Greeks were working out their internal political problems and refashioning their states, the peoples to their east in Western and Central Asia fell with relative ease under the rule of the Persians (see Part I, Topic 4). By the middle of the 6th century B.C., the Persian king Cyrus the Great had conquered Babylon and moved westward to capture the territory of the Lydians. The Lydian empire included the Greek colonies of Western Asia (the Greek region along the coast there was known as Ionia), which were under the benevolent rule of the Lydian king Croesus, who a generation earlier had asked Solon to name the happiest of men. With Cyrus' victory over the Lydians in 546 B.C., these Greek cities now became part of the Persian Empire, along with the rest of Lydia.

Thus from the mid-6th century B.C., with the Persians established in Greek Ionia, the mainland Greeks had to face an alarming possibility: a future Persian king might decide to move further west to add their own territory to his empire. The best hope of opposing any future Persian aggression lay in a defensive military alliance led by Sparta, the most powerful state in late 6th-century B.C. Greece, but continued squabbling between the various Greek cities made this an unlikely prospect.

From the Ionian Revolt to Marathon

In 499 B.C., after half a century of Persian rule, the Ionian Greeks revolted. Burdened with high taxes and the rule of old-fashioned tyrants imposed by the Persians, they looked with enthusiasm to mainland Greece for help.

The Ionian rebels sent messengers to the leading Greek cities to ask for help. Sparta, involved in a local war in the Peloponnese, refused. At Athens there was fierce debate between those in favor of sending aid to their fellow Greeks in Western Asia, and the pro-peace party who thought resistance to the Persians useless. As so often happens, compromise won and the Athenians sent a small contingent of 20 ships, which they withdrew a few months later.

It took the Persians six years to beat down the Ionian revolt. A few years after they had finally succeeded, in 490 B.C., Darius—the Persian king (ruled 522–486 B.C.)—led an expedition intended to punish the Athenians for their interference in internal Persian affairs and to discourage any future Greek meddling. He took the former Athenian tyrant Hippias with him, to install as pro-Persian dictator after the Persians had conquered Athens. The Persian force was relatively small, consisting of some 20,000 men: Darius seems to have counted on internal feuding among Athenian politicians to weaken the city's resistance and place Hippias back in power.

Against all expectations, virtually unaided, the Athenians managed to defeat the Persians at the Battle of Marathon. An urgent plea for assistance had gone out to Sparta, but the Spartans, cautious of fighting alongside their Athenian rivals, refused to send help immediately. Because of a religious festival, they claimed, troops could not march before the next full moon (Spartan forces arrived, in fact, after the battle was over). In the battle on the plain of Marathon, some 25 miles north of Athens, an Athenian force of about half the size of the Persian Army left some 6400 Persians dead, at the cost of 192 Athenian lives. A further Athenian casualty was the long-distance runner Pheidippides. After running to Athens nonstop to report the Athenian victory, and prevent the garrison there from surrendering prematurely, Pheidippides collapsed and died.

The Invasion of Xerxes

Few in the Greek world doubted that the Persians would seek a crushing revenge for their humiliating defeat. Fortunately for the Greeks, a revolt in Egypt and the death of Darius created a temporary distraction. Nonetheless the new Persian king, Darius' son Xerxes (ruled 486–465 B.C.), hastened to settle matters in Egypt and began preparations for a massive onslaught on Greece.

For once the Athenians managed to compose their differences and think ahead. In the ten years between their defeat of Darius at Marathon and Xerxes' invasion of 480 B.C., Athenian miners struck a rich vein of silver in the hills of Attica's hinterland. Following the advice of the statesman Themistocles (c. 525–c. 460 B.C.), the Athenian Assembly voted to spend the money on strengthening the city's fortifications and building up their navy. In the three years before the Persian invasion, the Athenian shipyards constructed 200 massive new warships. Their naval strength, which made Athens the greatest maritime power in the Greek world by the end of the Persian Wars, served both for maintaining Athenian domination at sea in their own region, and as insurance against possible foreign attack. At the same time, it increased the spread of democracy by empowering the poor who formed the crews of the powerful new warships known as "triremes." Each ship had a crew of 200 men, arranged in three tiers.

Athenian preparations paled, however, in the face of Xerxes' plans. His generals ordered huge cables

Map 2.1 The Persian Wars

for building two bridges of boats across the dangerous straits of the Hellespont, which separate Europe from Asia. To avoid the dangerous waters around the cape below Mount Athos, thousands of Persian workers dug a canal through the promontory. In May 480 B.C., after the spring rains, the Persian expedition set out. It took seven days and nights for all the troops, horses, mules, camels, and wagons to cross the bridge over the Hellespont and begin the journey south toward Greece.

Long before Xerxes began the march, the Greeks had realized what was in store for them. A congress met at Corinth, under the presidency of Sparta, at which a number of Greek city-states tried to settle on some plan of concerted response, but arguments over who should command any joint forces they might succeed in putting together led to a stalemate. Many of the smaller Greek city-states preferred defeat at the hands of a remote enemy to burying generations of rancor and cooperating with one another. In the end, with the threat of Persian invasion becoming a reality, Athens managed to forge an alliance with the Spartans and their allies. Themistocles even persuaded the Athenians to place their navy under a Spartan admiral.

In the early summer of 480 B.C., the Persian troops moved into northern Greece, and Xerxes sent envoys ahead to demand the surrender of the Greek cities on their route south. Terrified and awed, most complied. When the Persian ambassadors arrived in Sparta and issued their king's orders, the Spartans had the envoys killed. Now there was no possibility of truce or negotiation.

As the Athenians and Spartans awaited the wave of Persian invasion, Athens sent to Delphi to ask the advice of the oracle of Apollo. The mysterious message

Portrait of the Athenian general and statesman Themistocles.

came back that the Athenians should put their trust in their wooden walls. Themistocles, convinced that the Greeks would have to defeat the Persians at sea—their numbers on land were too unequal—persuaded the Assembly that the wooden walls referred to by the oracle were those of the Athenian ships. The Athenian Assembly passed a decree mobilizing the fleet, evacuating women and children, and moving the government and army to the island of Salamis, in the bay to the west of Athens.

Greek strategy was to lure the Persians south to face their naval forces, and to hold the land front as best they could. The first major confrontation came at the narrow pass of Thermopylae. In August 480 B.C., a small force of the finest Spartan soldiers and about 1000 other Greeks, under the command of the Spartan king Leonidas, held at bay the vast Persian army—recent estimates put the Persian numbers at around 200,000 men, with around 70,000 horses, mules, and camels. In the fighting the Spartans perished to a man, but their stand had bought time, and their courage became legendary.

The most detailed account of the Persian invasion is that of Herodotus (see Part II, Topic 4), who describes the Greeks' growing despair as the Persians continued their inexorable advance south, burning and pillaging. The Athenians evacuated all remaining residents from the city, leaving a volunteer garrison on the Acropolis. Within days, Xerxes reached Athens, captured and burned down the buildings on the Acropolis, and massacred its guards. As the summer ended, Xerxes sent home the news of his "victory."

He still needed to take the Peloponnese, however, and crush the Spartans on their own territory, if possible before winter conditions made feeding his huge expedition problematical. To put an end to the Athenians, meanwhile, the Persian fleet had to defeat the Athenian navy guarding the island of Salamis and put to the sword the Athenian population evacuated there. Themistocles decided to provoke the Persians into risking a decisive confrontation at sea. He smuggled a message to Xerxes, saying that the Athenian fleet, hopeless and demoralized, was about to break up and flee, and that he himself wanted to defect to the Persian side. The Persians struck—and Themistocles had the naval battle he had hoped for and planned for a decade.

Trapped in the narrow straits between Salamis and the coast, and facing the experienced Greek crews fighting in their home waters, the Persians were routed. Their ships rammed into one another as the Greeks skillfully encircled them and struck them down one by one, snapping off their oars: "You could not see the water for blood and wreckage" (Herodotus). When night fell, the Athenians still did not realize the completeness of their victory, but at daylight the next morning it became clear that Xerxes had ordered what was left of his fleet to retreat: not an enemy ship was in sight.

The danger was not yet over since the Persian land forces still presented a threat. The Persians no longer seemed unstoppable, however. The Greeks had the winter to reorganize themselves while Xerxes sent

Greek troops march out to battle, accompanied by a musician playing the double oboe.

Part of a stone slab honoring Athenian soldiers killed in battle.

many of his troops home, leaving a moderately sized force in the neighborhood of Thebes to hold what had already been conquered. In the spring of 479 B.C., in the greatest land battle of Greek history, an army led by the Spartans won a shattering victory at Plataea, and the invasion was over. As the remnants of the Persian Army limped home, it remained only for the victorious allies to liberate the Greek cities of Ionia, and to ensure that never again would free Greeks have to face the threat of interference from the Great King of Persia.

As the Greeks well knew, the relative unity with which they had withstood the Persians was the result of the extreme danger the invaders represented. Even then, the unity was incomplete: among the bravest contingents fighting at Plataea was that sent by the Greek city of Thebes, but the Thebans fought for, not against, the Persians.

By the end of the wars, it was clear that only the desperately forged alliance between Athens and Sparta had guaranteed success. As a result of the hostilities, both cities had built up their armaments and troop numbers, Sparta on land and Athens at sea. Both Athens and Sparta could claim vastly increased prestige in the Greek world and the right to exercise moral leadership. Could they put aside past hostilities and resentments and coexist peacefully? In the immediate celebration of their victories and the outburst of creative ferment at Athens, everything seemed possible, and the optimism of the Greeks' triumph inspired the achievements of the succeeding Classical Age. Yet less than 50 years later, Athens and Sparta were locked in mortal combat, and within a century the conflict between the warring Greek city-states was so violent that the Great King of the Persians was able to step in and impose a peace of his own devising, without fighting a single battle.

Questions for Further Discussion

1. How and why did the political systems developed at Athens differ from those of Sparta? What effect did the differences have on society in the two city-states?
2. What were the strengths and weaknesses of democracy at Athens?
3. What were the main factors in the Greeks' success in the Persian Wars? What were the political consequences of their victory?

Suggestions for Further Reading

Burn, A. R. *Persia and the Greeks: The Defense of the West c. 546–478 B.C.* Stanford, 1984.
Grant, M. *The Rise of the Greeks*. New York, 1987.
Hanson, V. D. *The Western Way of War: Infantry Battle in Classical Greece*. New York, 1989.
Hooker, J. T. *The Ancient Spartans*. London, 1980.
Manville, P. B. *The Origin of Citizenship in Ancient Athens*. Princeton, NJ, 1990.
Sainte-Croix, G. E. M. de. *The Class Struggle in the Ancient Greek World*. Ithaca, NY, 1982.
Starr, C. G. *The Birth of Athenian Democracy*. New York, 1990.

II

Topic 3

The Greek World in Conflict: The Peloponnesian War and Its Aftermath

With the defeat of the Persians in 479 B.C., the victorious alliance between Athens and Sparta began to crumble and the Greek world returned to its divisive ways. While the Spartans withdrew again into isolation, the Athenians remained diplomatically active. Their arguments convinced a number of Greek city-states to join with them in a league to defend Greece from any future threat of aggression by Persia. By 454 B.C., when the Athenians moved the league's treasury from its original neutral location on the island of Delos to Athens itself, the free association of independent city-states had turned into an Athenian Empire.

Over the following two decades, under the leadership of their most famous statesman, Pericles, the Athenians reinforced their domination of the Greek world. The sight of the growing power of Athens, made visible in the city's magnificent new buildings, awoke old suspicions and rancors. Fear of Athenian imperialistic designs drove those cities not yet under her control to form an alliance led by Sparta. Outright war, setting the Spartans and their new allies against the Athenian Empire, seemed increasingly inevitable.

It came in 431 B.C. The Peloponnesian War dragged on until 404 B.C., when it ended with the ignominious defeat of Athens. One of the main causes of Athens' eventual collapse was a disastrous campaign the Athenians waged against the Greek city-states of Sicily between 415 and 413 B.C., during a lull in the main fighting. Its utter failure left Athens weakened and demoralized, although the remaining ten years of war saw some further Athenian victories.

In the generation following the end of the war, the Spartans maintained a brutal if uncertain control over Greek affairs, under the watchful eye of the Great King of Persia. In 371 B.C. Thebes briefly succeeded in challenging Spartan supremacy, but rivalry between Thebes, Sparta, and Athens continued to destabilize the Greek world.

In the end, the ruler of Macedon, a kingdom to the north of Greece, stepped in to fill the vacuum. Philip of Macedon, who became king in 359 B.C., first cajoled and then used open force to take control of Greek affairs. By the time of his death in 336 B.C., he had defeated a combined Theban and Athenian army and united the chief Greek city-states in the League of Corinth. Only the Spartans stubbornly held out.

Alexander, his son and successor, paused only long enough to enforce Macedonian domination in Greece before launching a triumphant campaign eastward against Persia. With their political independence gone, the Greeks became absorbed into the multinational Macedonian Empire that Alexander built. In the process, however, Greek culture and ideas became increasingly influential in the Mediterranean world, as Alexander's conquests spread them abroad.

PERICLES AND THE PRIMACY OF ATHENS

The Persian threat had finally managed to unite the Greeks, but with the wars over and the Persians defeated, the chief Greek city-states reverted to their traditional behavior. The Spartans withdrew into isolation. They had no intention of helping in the future protection of the Greek cities of Ionia, or of defending the Aegean against another Persian attack. As long as no immediate danger threatened the Peloponnese, the Spartans—a land power—were content to stay home, where they could protect their agricultural economy and guard against the possibility of a helot uprising.

The Delian League

In 478 B.C., the Athenians, by now the greatest naval power in Greece, willingly took on the role of organizing a defensive association to be ready for any future emergency. To this end, they organized a league, whose members consisted of the chief maritime city-states of the Aegean region. Each member-state could contribute ships, men, or money. The Athenian general, Aristides the Just, assessed the financial payments, which were collected in a treasury on the island of Delos; the association became known as the Delian League.

Delos, a small island in the central Aegean, was the home of the great panhellenic shrine of Apollo—Greek alliances always had a religious basis—and its choice as headquarters was intended to demonstrate the League's neutrality. From the outset, however, it was clear to all the participants—not to mention outside observers such as the Spartans—that Athens was the League's dominating force. Quite apart from the Athenians' enormous political prestige, the 200 ships they contributed to the joint forces gave them an overwhelming military superiority. Many of the other members provided only one or two vessels, and most of the smaller city-states preferred to pay a money contribution instead.

The Athenians' willingness to exert their dominance became clear in 469 B.C., when one of the members, Naxos, announced its decision to withdraw from the League. The Athenians blockaded Naxos and forced the islanders to surrender, then compelled them to reenroll. Over the next few years other states wishing to resign their membership received the same treatment, and some of those who had never been members were forced to join.

The transformation of an association of independent partners into an Athenian Empire became plain to all in 454 B.C., when the Athenians moved the headquarters and treasury of the League from Delos to Athens. At the same time, they insisted that all legal disputes between members should be settled in the Athenian courts. The justification for these actions was "administrative convenience," but the effect was to confirm the suspicions of Athens' enemies that the Athenians were aggressively building an empire. Furthermore, the use of the League's funds to underwrite Pericles' public works projects in Athens alienated many of the Athenians' allies.

Athens under Pericles

Throughout this crucial period, which was to culminate in 431 B.C. in the outbreak of the Peloponnesian War, the leading political figure at Athens was Pericles (c. 495–429 B.C.). The policy of the dominating politician of the previous generation, the aristocratic Cimon, had been to build up Greek defenses against another Persian attack, while keeping on friendly terms with Sparta. In 461 B.C., however, the popular forces at Athens drove Cimon from power, and Pericles, a moderate, replaced him. From then until his death in 429 B.C., Pericles was by far the most influential and popular politician in the Assembly. Although elected frequently to public office, his chief political role was as speaker at Assembly meetings.

In theory, as Pericles himself pointed out, the humblest Athenian citizen had as much right as he to express opinions on the complex and vital questions of the day, before the Assembly then democratically decided on Athenian policy. In practice, the power of Pericles' oratory and the success of his recommendations when they were followed left him as unchallenged leader for some 30 years.

Certain points remained constant in Pericles' political program. He reversed Cimon's priorities by making peace with Persia and accepting the inevitability of bad feelings between Athens and Sparta. After further skirmishes, the Athenians finally came to an agreement with the Persians and the two sides reluctantly signed a peace treaty in 449 B.C. Neither party was very proud of the terms, which included unpopular concessions, and at the time the treaty received little publicity.

As for Sparta, the best Athens could do—according to Pericles—was to become so powerful that no other Greek state or alliance would dare to attack her with impunity. The support of the Delian League and the financial contributions of its members were a vital element in this military buildup. In 445 B.C. Sparta and Athens made a halfhearted attempt to block the drift toward war by opening negotiations. Each side yielded a series of relatively minor concessions and signed the Thirty Years Peace. Few were optimistic, however, about the probability of its lasting as long. Pericles observed later: "What I bought was not peace but time." The Athenian and Spartan worldviews, as represented by their political systems, had been different for so long and to such a degree that conflict was likely. The two sides chose not to avoid it, and within 14 years the uneasy peace was over.

Pericles used the time he had won not only to build up military forces, but at the same time to provide Athens with a visible splendor that would proclaim the city's cultural supremacy. Ever since, later generations have looked to the artistic achievements of this High Classical period as a golden age.

As the clouds of war began to gather, on the hill of the Acropolis thousands of workers finally cleared the debris of the buildings destroyed by the Persians in 480 B.C. In their place arose the temples still visible there. The crowning glory was the Parthenon, constructed under the supervision of Phidias, the greatest sculptor of his day and a personal friend of Pericles (see Part II, Topic 4). Work began on the Parthenon in 447 B.C., and the final stone sculptures were in place by 432 B.C., on the eve of the outbreak of war. The Athenians built it in honor of Athene, their patron goddess, but its real purpose was to provide a monument for all time to the glory of Periclean Athens.

The years of construction on the Acropolis also saw the performance in the Theater of Dionysus, below

Plan of Athens.

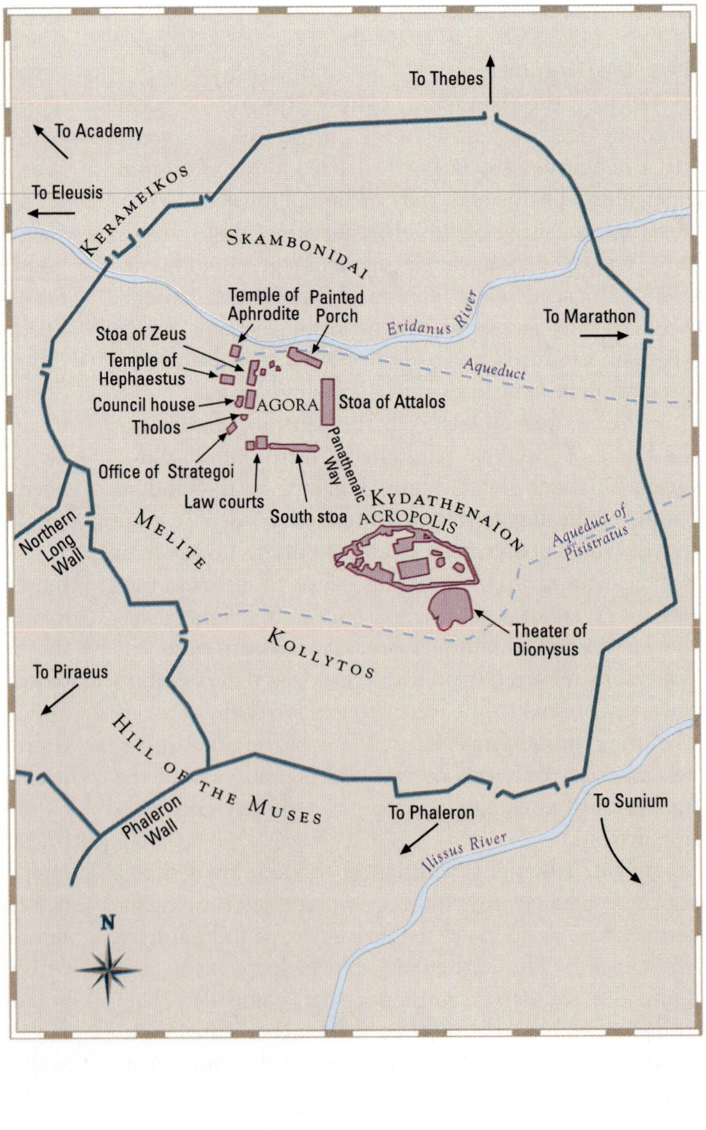

the Acropolis, of the tragic dramas of Sophocles and others, many of them still ranking among the masterpieces of Western literature. Two other momentous developments occurred in this same period. Herodotus arrived in Athens from one of the Greek cities of Ionia, to continue work on his *Histories*. The earliest surviving Greek historical work written in prose, it has won Herodotus the nickname, "the Father of History." Meanwhile, Socrates, a stonemason (he may even have worked on the Parthenon), began to debate with those Athenians who would stop and listen to him. Socrates himself never wrote down his ideas, but a generation later Plato, one of his pupils, wrote dialogues featuring Socrates and in so doing laid down the foundations of Western philosophy. (For the cultural developments of the period see Part II, Topic 4.)

THE GREEK WORLD DIVIDED: THE PELOPONNESIAN WAR

By the outbreak of the Peloponnesian War in 431 B.C. Greece was openly divided. Each of the two sides claimed to be on the side of freedom, although neither really practiced what it preached. The Athenians encouraged, even insisted on, their allies maintaining democratic systems of government in their states, but prevented those states from acting contrary to Athenian wishes—by force, if necessary. The Spartans and their allies accused Athens of ruling its empire as a tyranny, while their own states were antidemocratic oligarchies, in which most residents had no rights. The irony of Athens' or Sparta's claim to be the champion of Greek freedom was not lost on many observers.

The First Ten Years

In the end, war came not because of a fight about political theory, but over a matter of money and trade. The Spartans had little interest in business, and Athens' main commercial rival was Corinth. When the Athenians began to interfere in relations between Corinth and the Corinthian colonies in western Greece, the Corinthians persuaded the Spartans that Athens had imperialistic designs on the whole of trade with the western Greeks. If the Spartans and their allies did not act now, it would soon be too late: the Athenians would add the western Mediterranean to their empire. Thus when war finally came, it was the result of Corinthian reaction to Athenian pressure, rather than as a conscious step on the part of Sparta or Athens.

Gravestone of Crito and Timarista, c. 420 B.C.

Although hostilities in the Peloponnesian War dragged on for 27 years, from 431 to 404 B.C., they were not continuous. The first ten years' campaigns led to a stalemate and a temporary peace treaty. Neither side scored a decisive victory. The Spartan Army marched overland to lay waste the countryside around Athens, while Athenian naval forces raided the Peloponnesian coast. The greatest blow to Athens in the early stages of war came, in fact, not from the Spartans but from the terrible plague of 430–427 B.C. In addition to the loss of life and consequent psychological damage caused by the disease, the death of Pericles left the Athenians bereft of firm leadership at the worst possible time.

PUBLIC FIGURES AND PRIVATE LIVES

ASPASIA AND PERICLES

Pericles' influence and authority at Athens depended on his popularity. The democratic support which sustained him faltered only once. In 430 B.C., the second year of the war, with Athens overcrowded with refugees, a plague hit the city. In the blazing summer heat it spread rapidly and raged for months: perhaps as much as a quarter of the population died. In the ensuing panic, the Assembly suspended Pericles from office, ordered the inspection of his financial accounts, and fined him when the inspectors found them in confusion. Pericles bitterly remarked that "the plague was the one thing I did not foresee." The next year the popular mood changed, and the Athenians voted Pericles back into office.

With Pericles' public status came the glare of popular attention. Not only did he oversee Athenian domestic and foreign policy, he also played an active part in plans for the building program on the Acropolis and other cultural affairs. No wonder his fellow-Athenians noted that "Pericles never had time to go to parties."

Yet in his private life he kept in touch with the intellectual ideas of the day. Among his close friends was Anaxagoras—the first foreign philosopher to take up residence in Athens and teach there—whom Pericles personally provided with financial support for many years. At the height of Pericles' political activity, he found time to pursue his musical interests, by standing for election in 442 B.C. to the committee organizing a new music festival.

Pericles married early in life. His wife, as often happened in aristocratic families, was a distant relative. She bore him two sons before the couple divorced, apparently by mutual consent. The austere statesman now devoted all his time to public life. The Athenians nicknamed him "Zeus" and called his speeches to the Assembly "the divine thunder."

In 445 B.C., shortly after negotiating the Thirty Years Peace, Pericles—then around 50 years old—began a relationship with a young woman that lasted until his death, and provided Athenian writers and gossips with a never-ending source of material. Aspasia was born around 465 B.C. at Miletus, a Greek town in Ionia. She came to Athens to earn her living as a *hetaira*, a "companion to men." These women, generally freed slaves or non-Athenians, were self-employed prostitutes. The state required them to register and levied a special tax on them. The highest-paid, in addition to their physical beauty, were often educated and cultured women who could provide their customers with a level of intellectual companionship beyond the reach of most sheltered Athenian housewives (for the social status of the *hetairai* see Part II, Topic 5).

As all Athens knew, Pericles and Aspasia set up house together. Observers recounted, with a mixture of amusement and disbelief, that "Pericles would kiss her warmly when he left the house for work and when he came home again." The couple had a son, but since Aspasia was not an Athenian citizen, their child was not entitled to citizenship. A few weeks before the great statesman's death in 429 B.C., the Assembly—perhaps guilty at its fickle treatment of their leader—voted to confer citizenship on his and Aspasia's son.

Public opinion was not always so favorably disposed toward the couple. The comic playwright Aristophanes jokingly accused Pericles of starting the Peloponnesian War through Aspasia's influence, and other writers openly called her a whore. These attacks became more serious the year before the war, when Pericles' political enemies launched an attack on Aspasia as a means of undermining Pericles' own position. They brought her to trial for "impiety," and witnesses at the hearings claimed that, as a foreigner, she was a "security risk." The fact that she was known to be well-educated and politically astute—Socrates often visited her, bringing his pupils—was held against her. Her detractors claimed that she played too strong a part in Pericles' political decisions. With war looming and political tension at its height, Pericles himself appeared in court at her trial to plead for her. He broke down and wept, and the jury acquitted her.

At a time when respectable Athenian males, especially those in the public eye, rigorously maintained the social rules, Aspasia and Pericles—the most visible of all couples—openly flouted all conventional standards of behavior. It says much for their prestige at Athens that the Athenians continued to reelect Pericles as first citizen, and that—for all the gossip—Aspasia retained their respect. After Pericles' death, Aspasia married a democratic politician and continued to live quietly at Athens.

The events of these years form the subject of the *History of the Peloponnesian War*, written by the Athenian Thucydides (c. 455–c. 399 B.C.). He based his incomparably lucid account on his own experiences, serving in the fighting as a general at one point. The *History* breaks off with the winter of 411–410 B.C., but not before its author provides a dramatic and on the whole impartial description of the war's course to that point (see Part II, Topic 4).

Thucydides' Athenian birth and admiration for the achievements of Pericles did not blind him to the growing violence with which Athens waged war after Pericles' death. By the time the weary combatants paused for breath in 421 B.C., the Athenians, upholders of democracy, were as guilty of atrocities as their opponents. When in 422 B.C. their erstwhile ally Skione revolted, the Athenians starved out its citizens, executed all male adolescents and adults, and sold the women and children into slavery. With the signing of the Peace of Nicias (named after Athens' leading general and negotiator) in 421 B.C., neither side could easily assert its moral superiority.

The Sicilian Disaster

In the aftermath of the peace negotiations, Nicias (c. 470–413 B.C.) reinforced his position as spokesman for the political moderates at Athens. The leader of his more radical opponents was Alcibiades (c. 450–404 B.C.), one of the most complex and contradictory figures to emerge in these tumultuous years. Handsome, charming, extravagantly flamboyant, Alcibiades seemed determined to outrage his fellow aristocrats by supporting the radical democrats in the Assembly. Yet he became one of the closest intimates of Socrates, alongside whom he had served as a young soldier. Plato assigns Alcibiades an important role in the dinner party attended by Socrates which he describes in *The Symposium*.

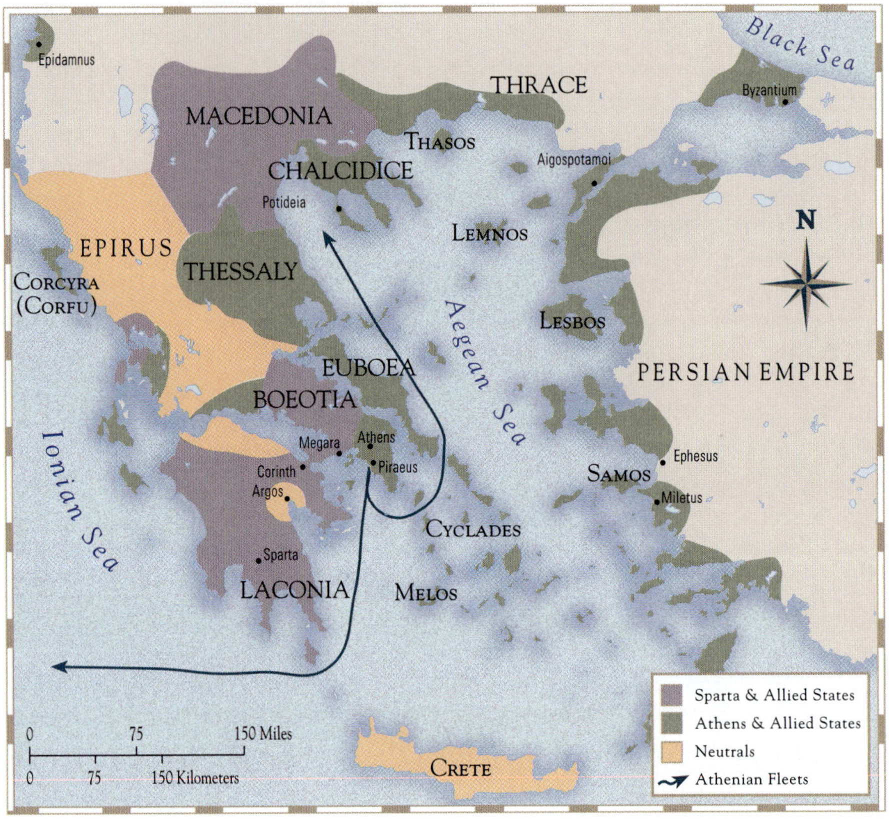

Map 3.1 Greece During the Peloponnesian War

As the relief at the coming of peace gave way to planning for the inevitable resumption of war, Alcibiades threw his support behind a foolhardy and dangerous scheme, the conquest and pillage of Sicily. The rich cities of Greek Sicily were centers of trade and prosperity, famous for their cultural and intellectual achievements—the remains of their spectacular buildings are still visible today. The greatest dramatic poet of the mid-5th century B.C., Aeschylus of Athens, visited Syracuse and wrote plays for the theater there. The Syracusans, like many other Sicilian Greeks, lived in a democratic state, with a constitution modeled after the one invented by Cleisthenes for Athens in the late 6th century B.C.

The capture of all this wealth, Alcibiades urged, could fund Athens' renewed war effort and lay the basis for an Athenian Empire in the west. At the same time, Sicily was a major grain producer whose crops supplied many of Sparta's allies. By gaining control of the island the Athenians could starve out their enemies. The threefold appeal of money, strategic advantage, and military glory proved irresistible, and in 415 B.C. the Athenians prepared their Sicilian Expedition to sail westward. Nicias argued in vain that Athens should concentrate on reconstruction at home rather than taking such an immense leap into the unknown. The members of the Assembly overruled him, although, as Thucydides caustically observes, "most of them had no idea of the size of the island or of its population, or that they were embarking on a war as serious as that against the Peloponnesians."

When it was clear to Nicias that no considerations of caution—to say nothing of morality—would overcome the Athenians' eagerness for conquest, he successfully urged them at least to send the largest possible force. In the spring of 415 B.C., the huge naval and land force prepared to set out under the joint command of Alcibiades, Nicias, and the general Lamachus.

During the night preceding the expedition's departure, unknown vandals mutilated sacred statues in Athens. The incident caused panic, and was taken as the worst of omens for the coming campaign. The culprits were never identified. Alcibiades' enemies accused him of being responsible, and pointed to his notorious lack of reverence and love of creating outrage, but it was too late to halt the fleet. It sailed with the hostility between the two chief commanders, already implacable political opponents, further inflamed by the suspicions falling on Alcibiades.

In the event Alcibiades played little part in the Sicilian debacle. Shortly after the troops arrived in Sicily, the Athenians recalled him to Athens for questioning about his possible involvement in the mutilations. Whether or not he was guilty, Alcibiades had no intention of going home and submitting to investigation. He gave his guards the slip and fled to Sparta. In his absence, the Athenians found their former commander guilty and sentenced him to death.

In the meantime Nicias and Lamachus embarked on the siege of Syracuse. Lamachus fell in the initial skirmishes, leaving Nicias, by now fatally ill, the sole commander of an expedition he had always opposed. When news came that the Spartans, taking the advice of their new friend Alcibiades, were sending troops to help the Syracusans, Nicias' colleagues begged him to order a retreat. The dying commander, fearing the wrath of the Athenians at home, refused.

The result was disaster. The Syracusans blocked the Athenian ships in the bay of Syracuse. The desperate troops on board disembarked to take refuge on land, where the Spartan troops picked them off. The Spartan commander, Gylippus, received Nicias' surrender and reluctantly handed him over to the Syracusans for execution: Gylippus would have preferred to send the defeated Athenian back to Sparta to be put on display there.

White ground lekythos showing warrior by his tomb.

Significant Dates

Greece in the Classical and Late Classical Periods (all dates B.C.)

478	Formation of Delian League
454	Treasury of Delian League moved to Athens
431–404	Peloponnesian War
430–427	Plague in Athens
429	Death of Pericles
421	Peace of Nicias
415–413	Sicilian Expedition
404	Fall of Athens; rule of "The Thirty"
399	Trial of Socrates
387	The King's Peace
359	Philip becomes king of Macedon
338	Battle of Chaeronea
336	Assassination of Philip and accession of Alexander

The few Athenian survivors were herded into the quarries outside Syracuse, where a few months of winter cold and damp and below-starvation rations soon finished most of them off. Far from enriching Athenian coffers, the calamitous Sicilian Expedition fatally weakened the Athenians' morale and fighting capacity. When fighting in Greece resumed in 412 B.C., the end was only a matter of time.

The End of the Peloponnesian War

The last phase of the war began under conditions not very different from those a hundred years earlier, with Athens torn by political rivalry, and the Persians preparing to interfere in Greek affairs.

The failure of the Sicilian Expedition helped the conservatives at Athens to discredit the democratic leaders responsible for it. In 411 B.C. a group of oligarchs calling themselves the Council of Four Hundred staged a coup to oust the democratic Boule and seize power. Their plan was to replace the Assembly with a carefully selected Council of Five Thousand, made up of their supporters, and to try to make peace with Sparta.

The scheme was foiled by the reappearance on the scene of Alcibiades. He had outstayed his welcome in Sparta and, living under Persian protection, he urged the Athenians not to give in but to continue to fight the Spartans. With the restoration of democracy at Athens in 410 B.C., the Athenian fleet once again went on the offensive with Alcibiades returning triumphantly as its commander.

Yet the longer the war dragged on, the more hopeless became the Athenians' chances. When Cyrus, the Persian king, decided to intervene and sent help to the Spartans, even Alcibiades' charisma was of no avail. The Athenians called him back to Athens once more. Again he fled into exile, leaving the Athenian navy to face ignominious defeat in 405 B.C. at the Battle of Aigospotamoi. Of the 180 Athenian ships present, only nine escaped. The Spartans executed 4000 prisoners in cold blood, as reprisal for similar atrocities committed by the Athenians.

Back at Athens, refugees poured into the city. Somehow or other, under siege and with people dying in the streets, the Athenians made it through the winter. By spring 404 B.C., they could take no more. The fight was over. The Athenians offered unconditional surrender.

THE DEFEAT OF ATHENS AND ITS CONSEQUENCES

When the victors convened at Sparta to fix the terms of Athenian surrender, Thebes and Corinth urged that the city should be put to the sword. The Spartans, however, cautious as ever, refused to destroy a city "which had done good service" in the defense of Greece against the Persians. The Athenians could keep twelve ships, but lost control of their foreign policy to Sparta and had to demolish the defensive long walls which connected the city to the harbor of Piraeus. The Spartan fleet sailed to Athens to enforce the terms, and "the walls were demolished by eager hands, while the flute girls played, and men thought that day marked the beginning of freedom for Greece." Events were soon to prove them wrong.

Revolution in Postwar Athens

For many Athenian voters, the democratic party was responsible for Athens' present lamentable state. The democrats had, under Pericles' leadership, got Athens involved in the war in the first place and had consistently refused to negotiate an end to the fighting with Sparta. To make matters worse, their leaders were implicated in the acts of wanton violence—the killing of hostages and innocent civilians—which had made Athens so hated by her conquerors.

In the weeks following the city's surrender, a group of archconservatives seized power. "The Thirty," as they were styled, acted with the full approval and protection of the Spartan general in command of the garrison still occupying Athens. It soon became clear that rule by The Thirty was becoming a reign of terror, in which any conceivable opponent faced summary arrest and execution. As the number of innocent victims mounted, the democrats summoned the courage and the popular support to fight back.

They banded together during the winter in the hills around Athens, and early in 403 B.C. open opposition to The Thirty, by now dubbed The Thirty Tyrants, broke out in Athens. A burst of violent street fighting at Athens' harbor, Piraeus, left the ringleaders of the oligarchy dead, and within a short time the brutal tyranny was over. Once again, Spartan intervention played a part in Athenian internal politics, but this time on the side of democracy: the Spartan king forbade his general to protect the conservatives or to move against the democrats.

The Death of Socrates

The most controversial event in the early years of renewed democratic government at Athens occurred in 399 B.C.: the trial of Socrates on charges of impiety and corrupting the youth of Athens, and his execution. The conduct of the trial itself, Socrates' subsequent time in prison, and the actual scene of his death are all immortalized in the accounts written by his pupil Plato. Under the influence of Plato's poignant and dramatic descriptions, posterity has accepted his verdict that the death of Socrates was the end of "the noblest and wisest and most just of men." Plato went on to use Socrates as the mouthpiece for much of his own philosophy (see Part II, Topic 4), thereby increasing our sense of outrage at the execution of Socrates by a supposedly democratic regime, especially on charges that even at the time seemed flimsy.

The real reasons for Socrates' trial have far more to do with the psychological state of postwar Athens than with Socrates' religious beliefs. Years of preparation and almost 30 years of brutal war had ended in utter humiliation and the bloodthirsty tyranny of The Thirty. Throughout the whole period, Socrates made it his business publicly to question traditional Athenian standards of belief and morality, and point out the defects of democracy. Among the young Athenians who flocked to hear and take part in Socrates' discussions, none was better known or more hated by the average Athenian than Alcibiades. To make matters even worse, the chief instigator of The Thirty's reign of terror, Critias, was also Socrates' pupil and friend.

Portrait of the philosopher Socrates, teacher of Plato.

Socrates himself had always been loyal to Athens, but popular opinion held that Alcibiades had learned his treachery and Critias his ruthlessness from their teacher.

In the circumstances, the trial produced a verdict of guilty by a majority of 281 votes to 220. The prosecutors claimed the death penalty, and Socrates had the right to propose an alternative; the jury would then decide between the two. After saying that if it were up to him, he would choose to be maintained for life as a public benefactor, Socrates gave way to the pressure of his friends and proposed a fine. The jury, offended, voted for the death penalty by a larger majority than had found him guilty. Socrates himself could have agreed to face exile rather than execution. Once imprisoned and awaiting death he could have escaped from jail as his judges encouraged him to do, in order to avoid having to carry out the sentence. Yet Socrates died, as he had lived, according to his principle of consistency and obedience to the laws: "No evil can come to a good man, either living or dead."

Sparta versus Thebes

The war finally behind them, the Athenians began the long, painful process of adjusting to their new, reduced position in the Greek world. With their military strength gone, and their status as political and moral leaders of Greece a thing of the past, the Athenians could only watch helplessly as the other Greek city-states fought for supremacy.

Of the two chief contenders, Sparta and Thebes, the Spartans were the first to establish themselves as the dominant power in Greece. They had, after all, led the coalition responsible for breaking up the Athenian Empire. Whatever goodwill they may have gained in the eyes of the Greeks, however, they soon lost by their behavior as victors. The boards of military governors which they set up proved to be arrogant and rapacious, and speedily alienated the local populations under their jurisdiction.

The result was an extended period of skirmishing between the Spartans and a coalition of other states, led by Thebes, during which the Persians quietly stirred up as much rancor as possible between the various parties. Finally, in 387 B.C., the Persian king dictated the terms of the King's Peace, by which all Greek city-states were to regain their independence: less than a century after their humiliating defeat, the Persians were openly interfering in Greek affairs.

The Persian intervention was a failure. Even the Great King himself could not stem the tide of Greek violence, much of it due to a resurgent Athens, and the Spartans once again went on the attack. Their leadership came to a violent end in 372 B.C., when the Thebans and Spartans clashed head-on in the Battle of Leuctra. To the astonishment of all of Greece, the Thebans won. In a move typical of the confusion of the times, the Athenians, who had been enthusiastic backers of Thebes, immediately switched sides, and transferred their loyalty to the defeated Spartans.

The last hopes of the Greeks ever setting aside their destructive rivalries came in 362 B.C. at the Battle of Mantinea, where Spartans and Athenians fought side by side against the Thebans. The result was a draw. The historian Xenophon (c. 430–c. 354 B.C.), whose son died on the battlefield, comments: "There was even more chaos and confusion after the battle than there ever had been before in Greece."

PHILIP OF MACEDON AND THE END OF GREEK INDEPENDENCE

For the better part of a century, first the Athenians, then the Spartans, and finally the Thebans had tried to establish their supremacy over the rest of Greece. In the end, it took an outsider to impose unity, and the result was the loss of independence for all the Greek states.

Painting from a Macedonian royal tomb, perhaps that of Philip himself.

To the north of mainland Greece was the kingdom of Macedon, rich in farmland, horses, and timber and, in the eyes of the Greeks, populated by barbarians (a term used by the Greeks to describe all foreigners). The Macedonians spoke a rough dialect of Greek, to be sure, but their language was the subject of jokes at Athens. Furthermore, unlike the sophisticated Greeks to the south, the Macedonians were still ruled by kings, under a system of government reminiscent of the primitive world of Homer.

In 359 B.C., rule of Macedon passed to a new king, Philip (ruled 359–336 B.C.). Twenty-two at the time, in his youth Philip had been a hostage in Thebes, and was thus educated in Greek culture. Now he was quick to see the possibilities presented by the chaos in Greece, and launched a plan of expansion aimed at uniting the Greeks under his rule. The first task was to improve his armed forces. The Macedonians already had fine cavalry troops, and Philip added to them infantry brigades trained and disciplined in the Greek way.

Demosthenes, Athenian politician and fiery opponent of Philip of Macedon.

Demosthenes and the Failure of Athens

Over the next 20 years, Philip negotiated, bribed, and when necessary fought his way to controlling most of north and central Greece. The chief obstacle blocking his way to complete conquest was the passionate campaign waged against him—not on the battlefield but before the Athenian Assembly—by the greatest of Greek orators, Demosthenes (384–322 B.C.).

Demosthenes was one of the first in Greece to realize that Philip's growing involvement in Greek affairs represented a dangerous threat. The only way the Greeks could maintain their independence was to form a panhellenic coalition, led by Athens and Thebes—and helped, if possible, by Persia. In the years from 351 to 338 B.C., Demosthenes delivered a series of powerful and increasingly desperate orations against Philip, known as the *Philippics*.

By the time Demosthenes had succeeded in convincing the Thebans to fight alongside Athens, it was too late. At the Battle of Chaeronea in 338 B.C., Thebans and Athenians stood together for Greek freedom. They went down fighting, but the battle was lost. The following year Philip assembled a league at Corinth. When the Spartans contemptuously refused to participate, the Macedonians confiscated some of their territory in reprisal. The function of the league, which operated under Macedonian supervision, was to end external and internal war among the Greeks, protect the seas, and form a joint army.

The supreme commander of this force was Philip himself. At the age of 45, and at the height of his powers, Philip's next goal was to lead his army into Asia and defeat the Persian Empire. In 336 B.C., a young assassin stabbed and killed the king while he was walking in a triumphal procession. Philip himself never fulfilled his dream of conquering Asia, which fell instead to his son and successor, Alexander (see Part II, Topic 6).

The political, economic, and social divisions that beset ancient Greece came to a head in the war between Athens and Sparta. The resulting defeat of Athens was the first step in a process that led to the disintegration of an autonomous Greek civilization at the hands of the Macedonians.

By the end of Philip's reign, the history of an independent Greece was at an end. The Greeks first became subordinate allies of the kingdom of Macedon, and then became part of the vast Macedonian Empire which Alexander built in the few years before he died. In the course of time, Greece took its place as one of the provinces of the Macedonians' eventual successors, the Romans (see Part II, Part 7). The Greeks never regained complete control over their own affairs or political destiny, yet in one way their influence increased with their defeat. The impact of the Greek intellectual and cultural achievement became diffused throughout the territories of its conquerors, to form the foundation of Western civilization.

Questions for Further Study

1. What were the chief causes of the Peloponnesian War? How—if at all—could collision between Athens and Sparta have been avoided?
2. What effect did the Sicilian Expedition have on the outcome of the war? What role did Alcibiades play in the Sicilian Expedition itself and in the following decade?
3. What were the underlying factors leading to the trial of Socrates? In what ways did his defense and ultimate execution illustrate his philosophical principles?
4. What were the main stages in Macedon's rise to power? When and how could the Greeks have blocked Philip's advance?

Suggestions for Further Reading

Borza, E. N. *In the Shadow of Olympus: The Emergence of Macedon*. Princeton, NJ, 1990.

Fine, J. V. A. *The Ancient Greeks: A Critical History*. Cambridge, MA, 1983.

Grant, M. *The Classical Greeks*. New York, 1989.

Hornblower, S. *The Greek World, 479–323 B.C.* New York, 1983.

Ober, J. *Mass and Elite in Democratic Athens: Rhetoric, Ideology, and the Power of the People*. Princeton, NJ, 1989.

Rhodes, P. J. *The Athenian Empire*. Oxford, 1985.

Roberts, J. W. *City of Sokrates: An Introduction to Classical Athens*. London, 1984.

II

Topic 4

The Classical Vision

Alongside the political upheavals of the 5th and 4th centuries B.C., there occurred in Greece a series of artistic and intellectual developments which permanently shaped Western culture. The Greeks' striving for order and balance left its mark on literature and the visual arts, and their pursuit of self-knowledge opened up new ways of thinking about human existence, among them history and philosophy.

At the theater festivals of Athens, tragic dramatists produced cycles of plays that used myths to explore human behavior, both individual and collective. Meanwhile, comic playwrights wrote satires, often bitter ones, on contemporary events, including the Peloponnesian War.

Greek painters and sculptors continued to explore ways of depicting the human form realistically, working along lines already laid out in the preceding Archaic period. By the High Classical period, artists were able to achieve a balance between realism and idealism that has remained "classic" ever since. In the Late Classical 4th century B.C., the heroic calm of High Classical art gave way to a greater interest in the emotional states of individuals.

Pericles' plans to make Athens the cultural center of the Greek world included an ambitious building program to reconstruct the temples on the Athenian Acropolis, which the Persians had destroyed in 480 B.C. The structures built there during the second half of the 5th century include the Parthenon, and represent the high point of Greek architectural achievement, and one of the supreme moments in the history of Western art.

Writers and thinkers of the Classical Age laid the foundations for three areas of intellectual inquiry: history, science, and philosophy. The historians Herodotus and Thucydides, in their very different ways, chronicled the chief events of their own age. Even before the 5th century B.C. and the time of Socrates, thinkers had begun to study the physical nature of the world. In doing so, they asked questions that anticipated the inquiries of modern science.

The teachings of Socrates, which he expounded at Athens in the late 5th century B.C., formed the inspiration for the works written by Plato in the 4th century B.C. Plato's dialogues attempted to achieve imaginative insights into the general nature of the universe. Plato's successor, Aristotle, sought not so much to speculate about universals as to order and classify the visible world. Between them, Plato and Aristotle laid the foundations of Western philosophy.

FATE AND THE HUMAN CONDITION: THE THEATER AT ATHENS

The tragic dramas written and performed at Athens during the 5th century B.C. represent some of the most enduring of all Classical masterpieces. The first works in the history of the Western theater, many of them still retain the power to grip and move audiences today, some two and a half thousand years after their creation.

The Dramatic Festivals of Dionysus

The origins of drama go back to the 6th century B.C., in the form of choral hymns in praise of the god Dionysus. For the Greeks the theater retained its connection with worship, and audiences at the performances of the Classical era regarded them as religious rituals. All the surviving plays were written for one of the two annual festivals of drama dedicated to Dionysus, the god of the theater and of wine.

Each author competing in the festival—competition always played an important part in the Greek attitude to life—composed four plays, to be performed on a single day. The first three dramas were tragedies, sometimes forming a *trilogy*—three episodes in a single story—and sometimes three different stories with a common theme. The last work in each author's offering was a more lighthearted "satyr" play. The plots of the tragedies were generally based on myths, with which the spectators would already be familiar. Writers could thus employ "dramatic irony," whereby the audience was in possession of information still hidden from the characters.

Sophocles and *Oedipus the King*

The dramatist Sophocles (496–406 B.C.) made especially powerful use of this device in *Oedipus the King*. The fact that at the beginning of the play we, the onlookers, already know the terrible secret of Oedipus' birth—how he was fated to kill his father and marry his mother—only increases the tension as the other characters gradually realize what the proud king himself refuses to see. When Oedipus finally faces the truth and learns who he is, he blinds himself in horror.

Oedipus the King, like many of the Classical tragedies, deals with the nature of suffering and human destiny. Sophocles seems to be pointing out that we cannot avoid our fate, even if we seem to have done nothing to deserve it. For all the glorious possibilities of human achievement, there are aspects of existence beyond our understanding and control. As the play ends and the wretched figure of Oedipus, self-blinded, leaves Thebes to go into exile, the new king of Thebes, Creon, sends him on his way with the warning: "Do not seek to be in control of all things, for what you control will not follow you through life." Yet by

The ancient theater at Epidaurus prior to a modern performance.

blinding himself, Oedipus has regained control and responsibility for his own life: the individual asserts his independence in the face of fate and divine will.

Sophocles was a young man when the Greeks triumphantly defeated the Persians, yet he lived long enough to see the glories of Periclean Athens shattered by the disastrous Peloponnesian War. The inevitability of the tragic events in many of his plays seems to some degree to reflect the collapse of Athenian glory.

Aeschylus and Euripides

If Sophocles seems to epitomize the contradictions of the Golden Age of Athens, the other two dominant figures of 5th-century drama, Sophocles' predecessor Aeschylus (525–456 B.C.) and his successor Euripides (c. 484–406 B.C.), illustrate the spirit of their own times. Aeschylus was old enough to have fought with the victorious Greek troops at the Battle of Marathon, and died when Athens' prestige was at its height. For all the grim violence of his works, they emphasize that although human suffering is inevitable, in the end justice will guarantee the triumph of right—as the Greek victories in the Persian Wars seemed to demonstrate.

The fullest statement of this principle comes in the *Oresteia,* the only complete trilogy by any Classical author to have survived. Aeschylus uses the myth of Agamemnon, king of Argos, and his family to illustrate the passage from primitive society, based on *vendetta*—blood for blood—to civilization and the rule of law. The violence and despair of the first two plays, in which Agamemnon's wife, Clytemnestra, murders her husband only to be murdered in turn by her son Orestes, give way at the end of the trilogy to the victory of reason and moderation. An Athenian court tries Orestes. When the jury is evenly divided, Athene makes her casting vote in favor of Orestes and brings to an end the cycle of violence.

Vase painting showing a scene that also occurs in Aeschylus' *Oresteia,* the murder of Agamemnon.

By contrast, Euripides' plays, written at the end of the 5th century B.C., express the sense of frustration and disillusionment caused by the disasters of war. Many of his works, including *The Suppliant Women,* are openly antiwar statements, describing the senseless miseries that humans inflict on one another. He drew the stories from traditional mythology, but the situations would have had a terrible relevance for the Athenian audiences of the late 5th century B.C., with news of the calamitous Sicilian Expedition ringing in their ears.

Euripides also broke new ground in his sympathetic understanding of the problems of women in a world dominated by men. Characters such as Medea and Phaedra, depicted with vivid psychological realism, struggle against the conventions of a society that tries to make them conform. This concern with the personality and choices of individuals, rather than broad general principles, foreshadows the spirit of 4th-century B.C. philosophy and art. Nor does Euripides have any belief in divine justice. If the gods exist, they are as cruel and irrational as humans.

Greek Comedy

Aristophanes (c. 450–385 B.C.), the greatest of Greek comic playwrights, used satire and ridicule, rather than blood and violence, to hammer home an antiwar message similar to that of Euripides.

One of his best-known plays, *Lysistrata,* was written in 411 B.C., the year in which fighting resumed in the Peloponnesian War. Its chief character, Lysistrata, persuades the women of Athens to seize the Acropolis and refuse to make love with their husbands until the men agree to negotiate a peace settlement. Driven by their frustrations, the husbands give in and summon ambassadors from Sparta. As the play ends, Athenians and Spartans dance together in joy at the return of peace. In the real world, seven years were to pass before—far from negotiating—Athens was reduced to abject surrender.

PERFECTION AND REALISM: CLASSICAL PAINTING AND SCULPTURE

By the mid-5th century B.C., artists were producing works that tried to find a perfect compromise between

Roman copy of the *Spearbearer* by Polyclitus.

realism and idealism. The notion of perfection of form in the human body became expressed by a canon of proportion, a series of mathematical formulas which represented ideal beauty of form. The famous Classical sculptor Polyclitus (active mid-5th century B.C.) even wrote a book, *The Canon*, which described the perfect male body. The book is lost, as is the statue of the *Spearbearer* which he made in bronze to illustrate his text. Many marble copies of his statue have survived, however, which give us a good impression of Classical notions of ideal beauty.

The Parthenon Sculptures

For the most part, sculpture was public art, intended for display, and the works of the Athenian High Classical period generally aimed to reinforce the pride and self-confidence of Periclean Athens. The finest examples of this spirit are the sculptural decorations of the Parthenon, produced between 448 and 432 B.C. under the general supervision of Phidias (c. 500–c. 430 B.C.).

The Parthenon has three distinct parts decorated with sculpture. In each place the subject and even the technique is different, but the three themes all illustrate the glory of Athens. The frieze running around the entire building, carved in low relief, shows the Great Panathenaic Festival, a religious celebration held every four years. We see crowds of Athenians walking, riding, and leading sacrificial animals in procession, to attend the ceremony. The gods themselves are present at the center of events, sitting and chatting quietly amongst themselves—they have come in order to do honor to the Athenians.

The statues decorating the scenes on the east and west pediments are freestanding. Both scenes commemorate Athene, the city's patron and protector. The east end shows her birth, while on the west end she persuades the citizens to accept her patronage by presenting them with the olive tree. By implication, it is the city which honors Athene, rather than the reverse. Her losing rival for the Athenians' favor, Poseidon, falls back in dismay.

The scenes on the *metopes*, stone slabs around the outside wall of the building, are carved in high relief. They, too, although mythological in subject, relate to Athenian greatness. Most of them show episodes from the battle between the Lapiths, a people in central Greece, and the Centaurs (half men, half

One of the carved metopes from the Parthenon, showing a fight between a Lapith and a Centaur.

horses). This story, which the Greeks used frequently in the years following the Persian Wars, became symbolic of the Greek victory over the Persians: the human Lapiths represent civilization and therefore the Greeks, while the monstrous Centaurs stand for barbarism, in this case that of the Persians. For the Athenians, the Lapith victory was a reminder of their finest hour in the past and, at the same time, a message for the future, as they prepared to defend civilization in the Greek world.

By the end of the 5th century B.C., with the war news ever grimmer, and the demand for gravestones and funerary art increasing, we observe a change in mood. The grave markers remain quiet and calm in feeling, but now there is no doubting the intensity of grief. Painted vases from the same period echo the same personal sense of loss. The emotion remains under control, but the serenity of the Periclean years is gone.

Pothos (Desire), copy of a statue by Scopas.

Late Classical Art

By the Late Classical period, artists used realism to depict emotion. One of the very rare examples of Greek wall painting to have survived the ravages of time dates to this period, a scene showing the rape of Persephone by Pluto.

Sculptors, too, developed new themes. Praxiteles (active c. 370–330 B.C.) was famous for his statue of Aphrodite nude, one of the first attempts in Western art to depict the sensuality of the female body. The original is lost, but some 50 copies have survived. Another new area for exploration was that of the portrait. Our impressions of Alexander the Great owe much to the works of his official portraitist, Lysippus (active mid-4th century B.C.), known to us through copies.

Perhaps the most renowned of all Late Classical statues, again surviving only in copies, was by Scopas (active mid-4th century B.C.). It was called *Pothos*, or *Desire*, and its intense, yearning pose is in the strongest contrast with the sturdy, stocky *Spearbearer* of a century earlier. The statue dramatically illustrates the Late Classical concern with individual emotional states.

ARCHITECTURE AND THE TRIUMPH OF ORDER

The Greeks' concern with order and proportion emerges in its most complete form in their architecture. The origins of the Greek architectural orders go back to the period around 650 B.C., when Greek colonizers established their earliest links with Egypt and became familiar with the stone temples there. By 600 B.C., two main styles of Greek temple architecture had developed, the Doric, popular in mainland Greece, and the Ionic, which was widely used in the Asian Greek cities of Ionia.

The Parthenon

The Doric order is the simpler and grander of the two. Austere and dignified, with little in the way of superfluous decoration, it reached its climax in the Parthenon. This, the crowning monument of Periclean Athens and the largest Doric temple in Greece, stands on the highest point of the Acropolis. Its architects were Ictinus and Callicrates. Work on the building took from 447 to 438 B.C., and the sculptural decoration was all in place by 432 B.C.

The design of the building incorporates a number of refinements, which give the Parthenon its unique

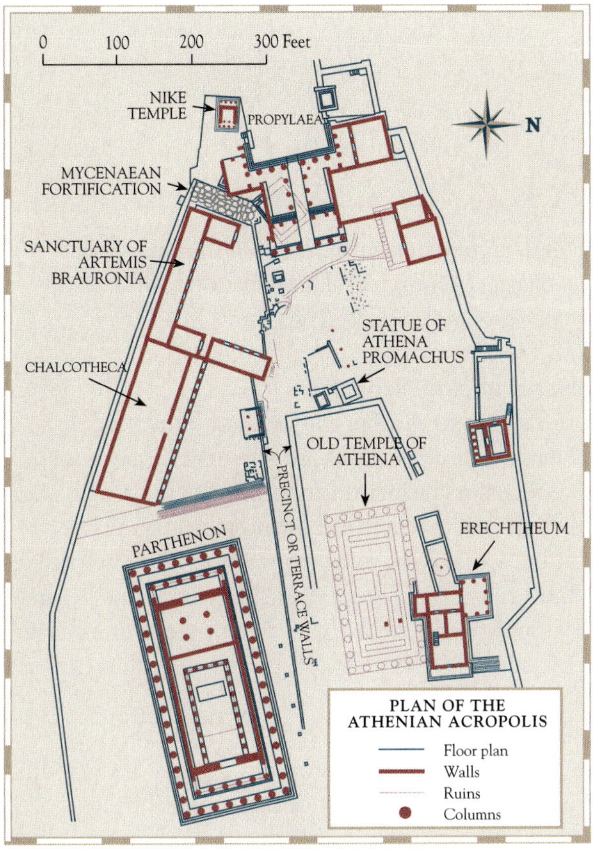

Map 4.1 Plan of the Athenian Acropolis.

sense of richness. The columns, whose thickest point is not at their base but about a third of the way up, taper inward. If extended upwards, their tops would meet at a single point about two miles above the top of the building. The corner columns are thicker than the others, and closer together. The floor, which appears flat, is in fact convex. All of these features correct optical distortions, and required the most careful and precise mathematical calculations. Their perfect execution represents the Classical concern with order and control in its most complete form.

The Ionic Order: The Erechtheum

The other chief style of Greek architecture, the Ionic, is more decorative and graceful. Unlike the simple, massive Doric columns, Ionic columns are slender and rise from an elaborate base. The ornate carving which decorates an Ionic temple conveys a sense of lightness, by contrast with its more weighty Doric counterpart.

The most important Ionic structure on the Acropolis is the temple known as the Erechtheum, the last building to be completed there. Begun in 421 B.C., after the signing of the Peace of Nicias, it was finished only in 406 B.C., on the eve of Athens' defeat. It commemorates a number of important religious events in the history of Athens, and was the center of the celebration of the Great Panathenaic Festival, illustrated in the sculptures of the Parthenon frieze.

In the South Porch of the Erechtheum, the Ionic love of ornateness reaches its most complete form: the roof rests not on columns but on statues of young women, the famous *caryatids*. They stand quietly with one knee bent, supporting the weight of the building. Above and below them are decorative bands of carving, emphasizing the delicate figures. The Erechtheum, which combines architecture and sculpture, structure and decoration, rejects traditional attitudes and raises new possibilities in a way similar to Euripides' questioning of conventional religious and moral beliefs.

Later Greek architects increasingly preferred the elaborate Ionic order to the more traditional Doric. The greatest building project of the Late Classical Age was the Ionic Temple of Artemis at Ephesus. An earlier 6th-century B.C. Ionic temple on the same site, built under the Lydian king Croesus, was destroyed by fire in the early years of the 4th century B.C. Work on its reconstruction, one of the Seven Wonders of the Ancient World, began in 356 B.C., the year in which Alexander the Great was born. Worship of the statue of Artemis which stood in the temple was still going strong in the 1st century A.D., when St. Paul visited Ephesus.

The Porch of the Maidens (caryatids) on the Athenian Acropolis.

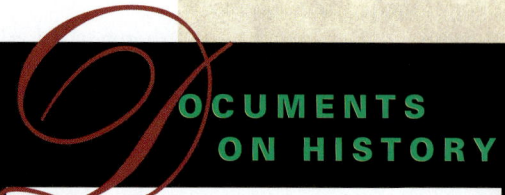

DOCUMENTS ON HISTORY

Classical Attitudes to Historical Methods

Most of the Greek historians writing before the 5th century B.C. are only names to us, although some fragments of their works have survived. The later historian Dionysius of Halicarnassus (fl. 30–8 B.C.) describes their methods. The most important was probably Hecataeus (fl. c. 500 B.C.), the first Western author to write on history and geography in prose rather than verse.

Hecataeus' works were among those used by Herodotus in preparing his *History of the Persian Wars.* At various points in his narrative, Herodotus refers to the ideas of his predecessors, sometimes with approval, and sometimes to dismiss them. Apart from a general statement of his theme, he sets forth no specific attitude to history, although he makes clear the large amount of "fieldwork" his research involved: the long digression on Egypt in Book II is based on his own travels there.

Thucydides, by contrast, sets out his philosophical approach to the writing of history. For later Greek writers such as Polybius, Thucydides' work marked a watershed between mere chronicles and serious historical writing, while the satirist Lucian makes fun of a wide assortment of "approaches to history."

DIONYSIUS OF HALICARNASSUS

The best account of early Greek historians comes from the collected writings of Dionysius of Halicarnassus, a Greek scholar of the late 1st century B.C.

Dionysius of Halicarnassus

Before I begin to discuss the work of Thucydides, I want to say a few words about the other historians, his predecessors and contemporaries, which will throw light on the method of the man, thanks to which he was able to excel those who went before him, and his genius. Now of earlier historians before the Peloponnesian War there were a great number in a great many different places. [A list of earlier historians follows.]

These men all adopted a similar method as regards the choice of themes and in talents did not differ very widely from one another, some of them writing Hellenic histories (as they called them), others barbarian histories; but instead of coordinating their accounts with each other, they treated of individual peoples and cities separately and brought out separate accounts of them; they all had the one same object, to bring to the general knowledge of the public the written records that they found preserved in temples or in secular buildings in the form in which they found them, neither adding nor taking away anything; among these records were to be found legends hallowed by the passage of time and melodramatic adventure stories, which to the modern reader seem very naive indeed; the language which they used was for the most part similar (as many of them adopted the same dialect of Greek), clear, simple, unaffected, and concise, appropriate to the subject-matter, and not revealing any elaborate art in composition; there is nevertheless a certain charm and grace which runs through their writings, to a greater degree in some than in others, thanks to which their works still survive.

Dionysius of Halicarnassus, *Thucydides,* 5, trans. L. Pearson, in *Early Ionian Historians,* Oxford University Press, U.K. Copyright © 1939.

HERODOTUS AND HIS SOURCES

After briefly announcing his subject at the opening of the first book of his History of the Persian Wars, *Herodotus provides a leisurely survey of events in the Mediterranean region and the Near East since the time of the Trojan War. He only reaches the Ionian Revolt, which eventually led to the Persian Wars, in the fifth of his nine books. At various points along the way, we learn how he acquired his material.*

Why Herodotus Wrote History

In this book, the result of my inquiries into history, I hope to do two things: to preserve the memory of the past by putting on record the astonishing achievements both of our own and of the Asiatic peoples; secondly, and more particularly, to show how the two races came into conflict.

Herodotus, *History,* Book I, 1, trans. A. de Selincourt. Penguin Books Ltd. Copyright © 1954; all translations of Herodotus below are from this source.

On Flooding in the Nile Delta

I have observed for myself that Egypt at the Nile Delta projects into the sea beyond the coast on either side; I have seen shells on the hills, and noticed how salt exudes from the soil to such an extent that it affects even the pyramids; I have noticed, too, that the only hill where there is sand is the hill above Memphis, and—a further point—that the soil of Egypt does not resemble that of the neighboring country of Arabia, or of Libya, or even of Syria, but is black and friable as one would expect of an alluvial soil formed of the silt brought down the river from Ethiopia. The soil of Libya is, as we know, reddish and sandy. . . . I had from the priests another striking piece of evidence about the origin of the country: namely that in the reign of Moeris the whole area below Memphis used to be flooded when the river rose only twelve feet.

Herodotus, *History,* Book II, 12.

In the Footsteps of Hecataeus in Egypt

When the historian Hecataeus was in Thebes, the priests of Zeus, after listening to the attempt he made to trace his family back to a god in the sixteenth generation, did to him precisely what they did to me—although, unlike Hecataeus, I kept clear of personal genealogies. They took me into the great hall of the temple, and showed me the wooden statues there, which they counted; and the number was just what I have said, for each high priest has a statue of himself erected there before he dies. As they showed them to me, and counted them up, beginning with the statue of the high priest who had just died, and going on from him right through the whole number, they assured me that each had been the son of the one who preceded him.

Herodotus, *History,* Book II, 143.

THUCYDIDES AND HISTORICAL METHOD

Unlike most of his fellow historians, Thucydides was personally involved in many of the events he described in his History of the Peloponnesian War. He served as a general with the Athenian forces, and in 424 B.C. *lost the town of Amphipolis to Spartan troops. As a result, "For twenty years I was banished from my country, and associating with both sides, with the Peloponnesians quite as much as*

continued next page

with the Athenians, because of my exile, I was thus enabled quietly to watch the course of events."

As the following passage makes clear, Thucydides places high importance on his sense of detached objectivity. He explains his attitude in reporting the many speeches included in the History, *few of which he personally heard delivered, and then goes on to describe his general approach to his material.*

Thucydides' Historical Method

As to the speeches which were made either before or during the war, it was hard for me, and for others who reported them to me, to recollect the exact words. I have therefore put into the mouth of each speaker the sentiments proper to the occasion, expressed as I thought he would be likely to express them, while at the same time I endeavored, as nearly as I could, to give the general purport of what was actually said.

Of the events of the war I have not ventured to speak from any chance information, nor according to any notion of my own; I have described nothing but what I either saw myself, or learned from others of whom I made the most careful and particular enquiry. The task was a laborious one, because eyewitnesses of the same occurrences gave different accounts of them, as they remembered or were interested in the actions of one side or the other. And very likely the strictly historical character of my narrative may be disappointing to the ear. But if he who desires to have before his eyes a true picture of the events which have happened, and of the like events which may be expected to happen hereafter in the order of human things, shall pronounce what I have written to be useful, then I shall be satisfied. My history is an everlasting possession, not a prize composition which is heard and forgotten.

Thucydides, *History,* Book I, 21, trans. Benjamin Jowett.

POLYBIUS ON THE WRITING OF HISTORY

By the time of Polybius (c. 203?–c. 120 B.C.*), author of a* History of the Mediterranean World, *many historians had abandoned the objective approach of Thucydides in favor of a more dramatic and emotional style, which would appeal to a broader readership. In condemning one of his contemporary colleagues, Phylarchus, for his overexcited descriptions, Polybius sought a return to Thucydidean objectivity.*

Polybius' Approach to the Writing of History

In his eagerness to arouse the pity and attention of his readers Phylarchus treats us to a picture of clinging women with their hair disheveled and their breasts bare, or again of crowds of both sexes together with their children and aged parents weeping and lamenting as they are led away to slavery. This sort of thing he keeps up throughout his history, always trying to bring horrors vividly before our eyes. Leaving aside the ignoble and womanish character of such a treatment of his subject, let us consider how far it is proper or serviceable to history. A historical author should not try to thrill his readers by such exaggerated pictures, nor should he, like a tragic poet, try to imagine the probable utterances of his characters or reckon up all the consequences probably incidental to the occurrences with which he deals, but simply record what really happened and what really was said, however commonplace. For the object of tragedy is not the same as that of history, but quite the opposite. The tragic poet should thrill and charm his audience for the moment by the verisimilitude of the words he puts into his characters' mouths, but it is the task of the historian to instruct and convince for all time serious students by the truth of the facts and the speeches he narrates, since in the one case it is the probable that takes precedence, even if it be untrue, the purpose being to create illusion in spectators, in the other it is the truth, the purpose being to confer benefit on learners.

Polybius, *History,* Book II, 56, trans. Moses Hadas, in *Ancilla to Classical Reading,* Columbia University Press. Copyright © 1954.

HOW NOT TO WRITE HISTORY, ACCORDING TO LUCIAN

*The Greek writer Lucian (*A.D. *c. 115?–c. 180) earned his living as an administrator and public speaker. His books include* A True History, *which begins with the words: "Every word of this is a lie, and my readers should put no trust in it at all." One of his most lively works is an essay on* How to Write History, *although, as the following passages reveal, most of Lucian's energy is devoted to telling historians how not to write.*

Lucian on Bad Historians

Here is a serious fault to begin with. It is a fashion to neglect the examination of facts, and give the space gained to eulogies of generals and commanders; those on their own side they exalt to the skies, the other side they disparage intemperately. History has only one concern and aim, and that is the useful; which again has only one source, and that is truth.

One writer is a keen emulator of Thucydides, and by way of close approximation to his model starts with his own name—most graceful of beginnings, redolent of Attic thyme! Look at it: "Crepereius Calpurnianus of Pompeiopolis wrote the history of the war between Parthia and Rome, how they warred one upon the other, beginning with the commencement of the war." After that exordium what need to describe the rest—harangues, plague, and so forth.

Another puts down a bald list of events, as prosy and commonplace as a private's or a carpenter's diary. However, there is more sense in this poor man's performance; he flies his true colors from the first; he has cleared the ground for some educated person who knows how to deal with history.

Then there is another distinguished artist in words—rather more Thucydidean than Thucydides—who gives, according to his own idea, the clearest, most convincing descriptions of every town, mountain, plain, or river. I wish my bitterest foe no fate worse than the reading of them. It is helplessness about the real essentials, or ignorance of what should be given, that makes them take refuge in word painting. Well, the man I spoke of gives the most unconvincing wounds and singular deaths: someone has his big toe injured, and dies on the spot; the general Priscus calls out, and seven-and-twenty of the enemy fall dead. As to the numbers killed, he actually falsifies despatches; at Europus he slaughters 70,236 of the enemy, while the Romans lose two and have seven wounded!

My perfect historian must start with two indispensable qualifications: the one is political insight, the other the faculty of expression. Let him be a man of independent spirit, with nothing to fear or hope from anybody. The historian's task is to tell the thing as it happened; he must sacrifice to no god but Truth; he must neglect all else.

From Lucian, *How to Write History,* trans. Moses Hadas, in *Ancilla to Classical Reading,* Columbia University Press. Copyright © 1954.

HISTORY AND PHILOSOPHY: THE GREEK MIND

The Greeks' interest in understanding themselves and their world led them to ask questions that opened up whole areas of human existence for the first time. In fields as diverse as town planning and medicine, government and mathematics, Greek thinkers laid the foundations for later achievements.

The First Historian

One of the many results of the Greek victories in the Persian Wars was to inspire the first surviving work of historical writing in the Western tradition. Herodotus of Halicarnassus (484–420 B.C.) migrated from his home in Greek Ionia to Athens during the time of Pericles. His *History* has as its main subject the Greek victory over the Persians. Herodotus interspersed this with frequent digressions, including a fascinating account of the Egypt of his times. One tale in the Egyptian section, that of Rhampsinitus and the thief, is the first detective story in our literature.

Like any good scholarly author, Herodotus traveled in order to research his subject; among the places he visited were Babylon, North Africa, and Egypt itself. Wherever he went, he consulted local archives and questioned experts, and set down in his *History* a faithful record of the information he collected. In cases where his research came up with contradictory explanations, Herodotus did his best to evaluate the relative value of his sources, often including explanations which he himself did not believe, so that later readers could decide for themselves.

Herodotus' achievement won him the nickname of the "Father of History," but his work was not scientific history in the modern sense. His grasp of military strategy was uncertain, and his geographical information often confused. He paid little attention to underlying political or economic issues, and preferred to interpret events on the basis of personal character. His portrayal of the mad Xerxes is a case in point, with its unforgettable description of the obsessed despot ordering the sea, guilty of wrecking the Persian fleet, to be lashed with chains.

Yet his virtues far outweigh his weaknesses. The *History* dealt with a conflict between Greeks and foreigners, and was written, moreover, at a time of intense national pride, but Herodotus' account always remains impartial and free from racial prejudice. It constantly reveals its author's curiosity about the world around him and the people he meets in it, brought to life by his acute powers of observation. Above all, Herodotus triumphantly vindicates the role of historian as storyteller. His dramatic grasp of the narrative keeps the reader constantly gripped, as the tale reaches its climax in the Greeks' final victories.

Thucydides, the Analytical Historian

The lives of Herodotus and his great successor, Thucydides (c. 460–c. 399 B.C.), overlapped, and both are famous for their accounts of a war. Thucydides' work was his *History of the Peloponnesian War.* Both of them were concerned to establish the accuracy of their accounts, and Thucydides states in his introduction that he conducted careful investigations and questioned eyewitnesses. Furthermore, both writers manage to rise above partisanship and give an impartial account of their subjects.

Yet the spirit of their writings is very different. In part this is the result of the differences between the Persian and Peloponnesian Wars. Herodotus' account emphasizes the belief that the Persians lost because they were morally in the wrong; the Greeks owed their victory to the triumph of right over might. The war which Thucydides described was one in which both sides quickly forfeited any claim to moral ascendancy. Thucydides, though an Athenian and an enthusiastic supporter of Pericles, had no illusions about the corrupting effects of power upon his city. His condemnation of the atrocities committed by Athenian forces is unqualified, and he leaves no doubt about the criminal folly of the Sicilian Expedition.

While Herodotus seemed chiefly motivated by the love of a good story, Thucydides' intentions were more complex. In keeping with the intellectual drive of his times, he used his material to understand human behavior. By analyzing the motives and reactions of those involved in it, he hoped to provide a lesson to posterity based on the behavior and mistakes of his contemporaries. Like the tragic dramatists, and Classical artists, Thucydides sought to demonstrate universal principles of human nature.

The First Philosophers: The Presocratics

The Western tradition of philosophy was born in the Greek world in the 6th century B.C. For the first time in history, thinkers began to use the power of reason, rather than religion, to ask questions about the universe and human existence. A variety of different schools of thought began to form, which would be known as the "Presocratics." The name refers to the fact that they lived in the century before Socrates, who, together with his pupil Plato, was the first major Western philosopher. The thinkers so described did not belong to a single school of philosophy.

The various Presocratic thinkers are often difficult to understand, in large measure because their ideas

Gravestone of Hegeso, a wealthy woman of the 4th century B.C.

have survived only in fragmentary form. Many of the problems they tried to solve seem scientific, rather than philosophical. How did the world come into being? What is it made of? How does it work? Their answers are varied, but all rejected traditional belief in the gods, especially those in human guise. After all, as Xenophanes of Colophon (c. 570–c. 460 B.C.) caustically remarked, "If horses and cattle had hands and could draw, they would draw the gods like horses and cattle."

The ideas of Thales of Miletus (active c. 585 B.C.) were typical of the Materialist school. Thales believed that water is the basic substance of which the universe is made. A later Materialist, Empedocles (active c. 495 B.C.), had a more complicated explanation. There are four basic elements, fire, earth, water, and air. These combine through love and separate through strife and war, causing the natural process of birth, growth, decay, and death. Even if the theories of Thales and Empedocles may seem far-fetched or absurd, the importance of the Materialists is that they were the first people to consider the possibility that the world evolved naturally, rather than having been divinely created.

The most influential Presocratic philosopher was Pythagoras (active c. 550 B.C.), who came from Greek Ionia and settled in southern Italy, where he founded a community. Unlike the Materialists, Pythagoras concerned himself with moral questions. The members of his "commune" had to lead pure and chaste lives, in the spirit of order and harmony for the common good. Basing his theories on the numerical relationship of musical harmonies, Pythagoras claimed that mathematics represented the underlying principle of the universe and of morality—the "harmony of the spheres."

The generation before Socrates saw the last important Presocratic school, that of the Atomists, led by Democritus (active c. 460 B.C.). They believed that the ultimate, unchangeable reality consisted of atoms (tiny invisible particles) and the void, or nothingness. The study—and eventual rejection—of their astonishing insights was to inspire the work of the German physicist Werner Heisenberg in the 1920s on quantum mechanics.

The Sophists

Another approach to philosophical investigation developed during the 5th century B.C., that of the Sophists—the "wise men." These were itinerant teachers, who debated the skills of rhetoric and the qualities needed for success in political life. Both Socrates and Plato attacked them for taking fees; teaching skepticism about law, morality, and knowledge; and concentrating on how to win arguments regardless of truth—hence the modern use of "sophistry."

Socrates and Plato

Toward the end of the 5th century B.C., as the Greek world plunged deeper into war, the search for universal truths took a new direction. At Athens, the teachings of Socrates (c. 469–399 B.C.) questioned traditional values and sought to understand the fate of the individual, rather than the community as a whole. When Socrates was executed in 399 B.C. (see Part II, Topic 3), his pupil Plato (428–347 B.C.) preserved his memory by writing dialogues in which Socrates appeared as the principal character.

Socrates himself is a difficult figure to evaluate. He wrote nothing, yet the influence of his teaching and the example of his life are central to Western philosophy. In the difficult years following the death of Pericles, he went around Athens, to public markets and private parties, testing the ideas of anyone who would debate with him—as he put it, "following the argument wherever it led."

Among the enthusiastic band of his youthful disciples was Plato. Sickened by Socrates' death at the hands of the restored Athenian democracy, Plato left Athens in 399 B.C. and devoted the rest of his life to

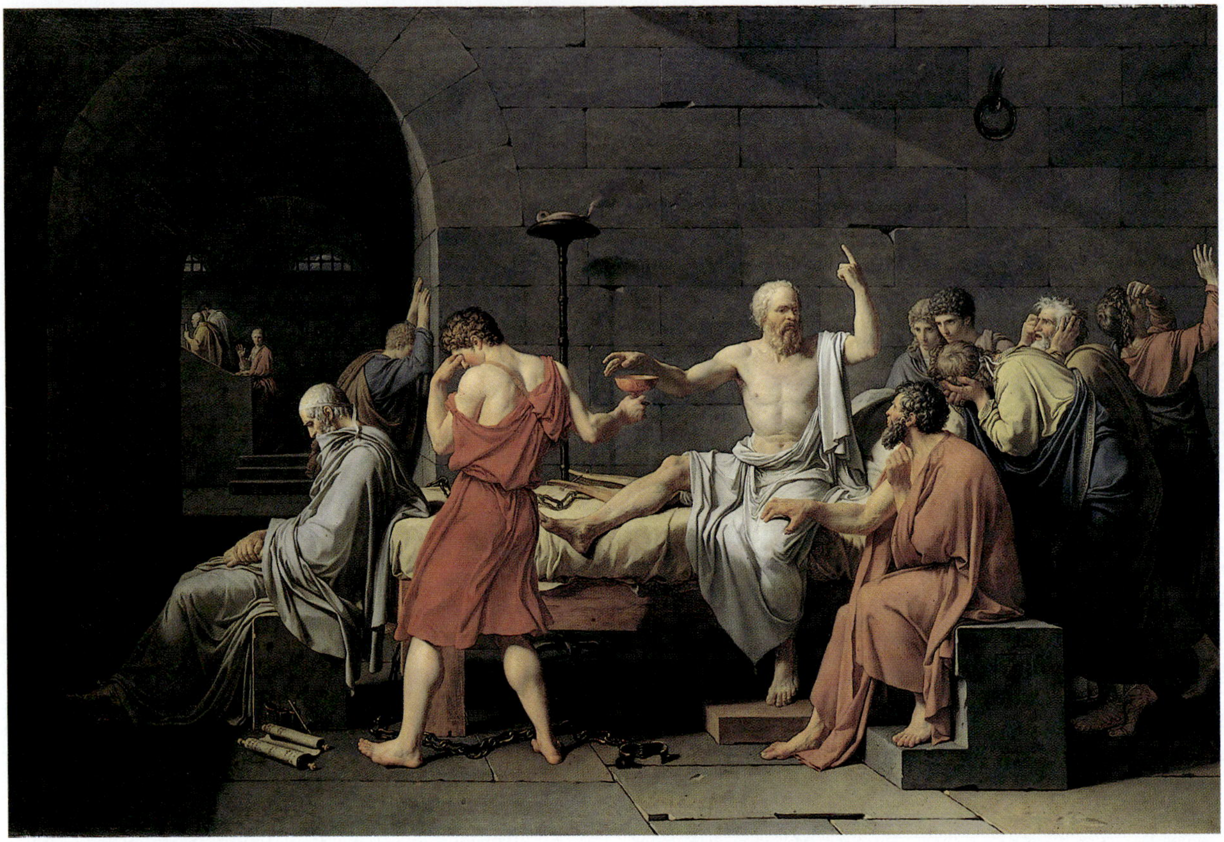

Posterity's view of the death of Socrates: Jacques-Louis David's painting dates to the late 18th century.

perpetuating the memory of his master. Socrates appears in virtually all of Plato's works, which take the form of dialogues between Socrates and a wide variety of other figures. Whether these dialogues literally reproduce Socrates' ideas or are mainly Plato's own inventions has been the subject of endless debate. Modern opinion generally holds that Plato's early works, such as the *Apology*, which purports to be Socrates' defense speech at his trial, probably reflect Socrates' teachings fairly closely. In his later writings, including the *Republic*, Plato used the figure of Socrates to express his own ideas.

When Plato returned to Athens in 387 B.C., he founded the Academy, forerunner of the modern university, where he spent much of his intellectual life studying the relationship between education, political theory, and government—subjects dealt with in the *Republic* and the *Laws*. In 368 B.C. he had a chance to put his theories into practice, when the young king of Syracuse, Dionysius II, invited the great philosopher to Sicily to create an ideal state. The result was a complete failure, and Plato was soon back teaching in Athens.

The notion of ideals lay behind his most famous idea, the Theory of Forms. According to Plato, in a dimension of existence higher than our own there are perfect Forms. The objects and phenomena which we perceive in the world around us are pale shadows of the ideal Forms. Thus our notion of justice or beauty reflects the Form of ideal Justice or Beauty. When we recognize these qualities in a person or an action, we are dimly aware of the ideal Form.

Aristotle: Philosopher and Scientist

Aristotle (384–322 B.C.), Plato's most gifted pupil, was less interested than his teacher in abstract speculation. He broke with Plato in 335 B.C., and founded a rival institution, the Lyceum. Full-time students came from other parts of Greece to attend Aristotle's morning lecture courses, spending their afternoons doing research in the library, museum, and map collection which formed part of the Lyceum's facilities. Aristotle himself gave afternoon lectures to the general public, and occasionally took on a private pupil. Among his rare failures was a spell as tutor to the young Alexander the Great: little of Aristotle's intellectual subtlety seems to have left its mark on the future world conqueror.

In a vast range of works, Aristotle aimed to systematize and classify just about every aspect of human knowledge. In studying the history of animals and describing their parts, he laid the foundation of modern biology, while *De Anima (On the Soul)*, which deals with sensation, thought, and imagination, is the first definitive work on psychology. His analyses of literature include the *Rhetoric*, on oratory, and the *Poetics*, the surviving part of which discusses epic and tragedy. The *Physics* is concerned with the elements that compose the universe, and the laws by which they operate.

Aristotle laid out his theological ideas in the *Metaphysics*, where he defines God as "thought thinking of itself," and "the Unmoved Mover." He considered the most important human sciences to be ethics and politics. On the latter, he observed: "People came together to live in cities for the sake of life; they continue to do so for the sake of the good life."

The influence of Aristotle's works on later ages was immense. Widely read in Roman times, they were translated into Latin in the Middle Ages, and became the basis of Christian theology. St Thomas' synthesis of Aristotelian philosophy and Christian teachings is still the official philosophical position of the Roman Catholic Church. For much of Western intellectual history, Aristotle has stood, in the words of Dante, as "the master of those who know."

To some extent the greatness of Classical Greek thinkers and artists lies in the fact that they were often the first in their fields—the first to write history, create naturalistic statues, invent tragedy and comedy. Yet the Greeks were no mere pioneers, discovering ideas that later figures would perfect. Greek dramas are revived in the modern theater and on television because they provide experiences as intense as any later works in the Western theatrical tradition. The style of Greek architecture continues to influence architects at the end of the 20th century, in the Post-Modern movement. Furthermore, a resurgence of interest in Classical art—in the form of Neoclassical revivals—has recurred constantly in the history of Western culture, from the Augustan era of 1st-century B.C. *Rome, to the 19th century in Paris.*

The reason for the perpetual appeal of Greek art and ideas is not difficult to understand. The Greeks of the Classical period consciously set out to create works that would transcend the limitations of their own time and make universal statements. Pericles' building plan for the Acropolis, like Thucydides' History, *was deliberately intended to be a "possession for future generations." It is some measure of the degree to which the Greeks achieved their goal that, two and a half thousand years later, their works continue to inspire admiration and awe.*

Questions for Further Study

1. What contributions did Plato and Aristotle make to the development of philosophy? How did they differ in their approach to the questions they considered?
2. How was sculpture used to decorate the buildings on the Athenian Acropolis? What was the significance of the myths used?
3. How did the works of the chief tragic dramatists reflect the times in which they lived?
4. What were the attitudes of Greek historians to their subject? In which ways—if any—did they differ from those of modern historians?

Suggestions for Further Reading

Barnes, J. *Aristotle*. Oxford, 1982.
Boardman, J. *Greek Art*. New York, 1985.
Finley, M. I., ed. *The Legacy of Greece: A New Appraisal*. Oxford, 1981.
Goldhill, S. *Reading Greek Tragedy*. New York, 1986.
Herington, J. *Aeschylus*. New Haven, CT, 1986.
Lloyd, G. E. R. *Early Greek Science: Thales to Aristotle*. New York, 1974.

II

Topic 5

The Life and Commerce of Classical Greece

For all the urban character of their civilization, the Greek city-states depended for their prosperity on agricultural production. The possession of land was a mark of social status, and farmers learned to cultivate crops suitable for the extremes of summer heat and winter cold. They planted wheat and barley on the plains, and cultivated olives and vines on the hillsides.

Although the colonizers of the 8th and 7th centuries B.C. did not leave home with the intention of setting up trading centers, by the time of the Classical period Greek colonies throughout the Mediterranean served as the basis for a complex commercial network. As production increased in mainland Greece, and individual cities began to compete for business at home and abroad, trade rivalry provoked disputes between the leading commercial powers. The long-standing financial competition between Athens and Corinth was the immediate cause of the Peloponnesian War.

In the rich world of Greek mythology and religion, male and female figures—both human and divine—play an equal role. The reality of life in Classical Greece, however, was very different. At Athens, the primary duty of a woman was to marry and produce future citizens. Only men could vote, serve on juries, or hold public office. Women whose family income allowed them the possession of slaves spent most of their lives at home, where they had their own part of the house. Poorer women, who needed to go out to do their shopping or washing, were more likely to spend time socializing with other women as they performed their chores.

Slavery was common at Athens, although only rich citizens owned large numbers, using them as labor in factories and mines. The average Athenian family had a domestic servant, or perhaps an assistant for workshop or farm. Slaves sometimes rose to become managers of businesses. They were able to acquire personal savings, and could win liberation for loyal service. Some who did so had their own slaves, whom in turn they set free.

LAND, FARMING, AND FOOD

Greece is a mountainous country, with little in the way of flat land suitable for farming. Where there are plains, however, as in the region of Thessaly, they are generally very fertile: the limestone folds of rock allow rainwater to seep slowly down the mountainsides and irrigate the flatlands. Each plain of any size contained a city. As Greece emerged from the Bronze Age, most of the good land around these cities was in the hands of the leading families, and its possession distinguished the "best men" from other citizens.

With the revolutions of the Archaic period, ownership of land became more diffused, and by the time of Solon relatively humble Athenians had their own plots. In a bad year they often had to sell or mortgage their holdings, enabling the newly rich who were not of noble birth to buy them out and build estates for themselves. Solon's reforms were in part an attempt to redress the confusion of debt which had built up (see Part II, Topic 2).

By the Classical period the larger cities had developed suburbs, and farmers lived in the country and worked on the land they owned. Thanks to Cleisthenes' constitution (see Part II, Topic 2), the Athenian farmers living outside the city could participate fully in the government of their polis.

With the exception of Sparta, where the aristocratic Spartiates used their helot serfs to labor on the great estates, most Greeks considered farming an honorable profession, and in many parts of Greece farmers regarded it as their duty to work their own land. As late as the 3rd century B.C., the eminent general and statesman Philopoemen (253–182 B.C.), in spite of his public responsibilities, insisted on taking part in the harvest on his property. Wealthy Athenian owners of large estates employed slaves or freedmen, while smallholders worked their holdings together with their families and perhaps one or two slaves.

Most cities viewed agriculture and its products as of the highest importance to the whole community. Athenian young men, at the age of 18, swore an oath to protect their city's grain, vines, figs, and olives, as well as obey its laws. Furthermore, none but full citizens could own land. Even the richest foreigners and freedmen were not allowed to purchase Athenian farmland.

The Farming Life

The blazing Greek summers made a winter cycle of cultivation more practical than a summer one. The agricultural year began just before the heavy fall rains. Oxen pulled a wooden plow tipped with iron to break the thin topsoil, while one of the farmer's family or a slave walked behind to break up the clods, and another worker scattered seed (generally wheat or barley) and covered it with earth.

Throughout the winter and spring farmworkers weeded the fields by hand. The amount of land that one family could cultivate was around two and a half acres. Harvest time came in May, and all hands labored to gather the grain and carry it to the stone threshing "circles" where oxen were driven round to tread it and separate the wheat from the chaff. The grain harvested had to last until the same time the following year.

Olive trees and vines, with their long roots, could survive the long dry summer, and so farmers planted them on the hillsides surrounding the plains. The time for harvesting the fruit was the early fall, and wine made at that time was ready for drinking by the late spring harvesttime. Many farm residents cultivated small plots of beans and peas by their houses, and grew fig, apple, and nut trees. Honey, together with figs, provided the most common source of sweetness.

Olive trees on the island of Crete.

Greek farmers working in the fields.

The Greek Diet

In general, the average Greek's diet was simple, based chiefly on cereals—a recent study estimates that Greeks of the Classical Age got some 70 percent of their daily caloric intake from barley, wheat, and millet. In his description of an ideal state, the *Republic,* Plato recommends the "preparation of bread from toasted barley, served on clean vine-leaves." Bread of this kind was unleavened, and often had various herbs and flavorings—thyme, rosemary, olives—mixed in the dough. Sweet loaves contained raisins and dried figs. According to one ancient gourmet, Athenaeus (late 2nd century A.D.?), citizens of Periclean Athens could choose from 72 different kinds of bread.

With starch as the basic filler, the Greeks added a wide variety of accompaniments: beans and lentils (often cooked with pork fat), olives, onions, cheese, the latter generally of goat milk. Poorer Greeks probably lived mainly on this simple diet, together with anchovies and sardines, washing it all down with water ("the best drink of all," says the poet Pindar), or with *melikraton.* This was a mixture of honey and water which, when left to ferment, became highly alcoholic.

Prosperous diners had a greater range of possibilities. Athens was famous for its olive oil, which was exported throughout the Mediterranean, while Athenian fruit was known as the sweetest in Greece. Game such as hare and pheasant was popular, but on the whole meat remained a rarity even for the wealthy. Homer's heroic banquets, at which warriors slaughtered whole oxen and roasted them over coals, represented only a dream for most of his audience. Domestic animals were too valuable a part of a farmer's capital to provide more than the occasional treat. Fish was more common. The Greeks caught fresh tuna in their own waters and imported dried tuna from the Black Sea region. Squid, shrimp, and freshwater eels were for special occasions.

The Greeks always drank their wine diluted, and often added honey and spices. (The Macedonians did not dilute their wine, which may explain why both Philip and Alexander apparently had problems with alcohol.) They exported it in jars made waterproof by spreading a layer of pine resin on the inside—the origin of the *retsina* (resinated wine) still drunk in Greece today. The chief time to drink wine was at the end of a meal, with the dessert course. The drinking session, or "symposium," often involved singers and musicians, although the most famous of all after-dinner sessions, recorded in Plato's *Symposium,* deals with complex intellectual matters.

A small Corinthian perfume flask (c. 625 B.C.).

MANUFACTURING AND TRADE IN THE GREEK WORLD

Throughout Greek history, cities depended on agriculture to provide the economic basis for their prosperity. Among the most commonly traded commodities in the Greek world were high-quality food products, whose reputation sometimes spread even further afield. In the 3rd century B.C. an Indian king wrote to Athens asking for "some syrup of grapes, some figs, and a philosopher." The Athenians sent the first two items but not the third, on the grounds that "it is illegal to trade in philosophers."

Trade in manufactured goods increased over time, although it never outweighed the importance of farming. By the Archaic period, individual cities were becoming famous for their products and styles. The Corinthians, for example, manufactured scented oils which they sold in elegant little flasks. The characteristic decoration and ease of transport of Corinthian perfume flasks made them popular among the Greeks and other neighboring peoples.

By the early 5th century B.C., Athens, Corinth's chief business rival, had captured the market for fine quality painted pottery, and was selling vases and other works of art throughout the Mediterranean. Corinthian resentment at the growing success of Athenian sales in foreign markets, especially those in Italy, was one of the factors that led to the outbreak of the Peloponnesian War in 431 B.C.

Not even the Athenians ever developed any large-scale industry. The two chief categories of goods

Greek plate showing cobbler at work.

manufactured for export were pottery and weapons, produced in small numbers by individual craftsmen in their workshops. Assisted by one or two slaves, they filled orders tailored to the requirements of individual customers. The largest production facility we know of in Periclean Athens was a shield factory owned by a resident alien, where the workforce consisted of 120 slaves.

Overseas Trade

The Greek city-states organized their business dealings by setting up trading posts abroad, competing with one another in the foreign market. Excavators digging at Al Mina, a Greek settlement in northern Syria, have uncovered residential quarters and warehouses. Most of the pottery stored there for sale in the 6th century B.C. consisted of exports from Corinth and the Greek cities of Ionia. The traders of Al Mina enlarged their settlement around the time of the Greek victories in the Persian Wars, and the bulk of the vases stored in the new warehouses of the 5th century B.C. came from Athens.

The same picture emerges in the western Mediterranean. The Greek cities founded in Italy by the colonists of the 8th and 7th centuries B.C. owed their origins for the most part to overcrowding and political disputes in the home communities. By the Classical period, however, the Greek colonies of southern Italy and Sicily formed a complex network of commercial bases. Goods produced in mainland Greece and the islands were exported to these colonies and sold both to the western Greeks and to other peoples in Italy.

Among the Greeks' most enthusiastic customers in Italy were the prosperous Etruscans (see Part II, Topic 7). Indeed, according to the Roman writer Pliny the Elder, a Corinthian aristocrat called Demaratus actually settled in the Etruscan city of Tarquinia shortly before 600 B.C., bringing with him a painter and three clay modelers. Demaratus married a local woman and opened a business, thereby introducing the technique of clay sculpture to central Italy.

The sale of Greek art in Etruria continued to grow in volume in the Classical period. At the time of the Persian Wars, many Greeks fled from the troubles in the Ionian cities of Asia Minor to seek refuge in the West. Some opened shops in the Etruscan cities to supply a market which had learned to appreciate the quality of imported Greek pottery. Others began to trade in reverse, buying raw materials such as iron and minerals from the Etruscans, and even the occasional Etruscan work of art, and taking them back to Greece for sale there. Etruscan bronzes have been found at Olympia and Lindos (Rhodes), and even on the Acropolis at Athens.

Mining

The only economic activity requiring large numbers of workers was mining. The silver mines of Laurion, to the southeast of Athens, were under state ownership. Small operators leased sections from the state and worked them with slave labor, paying royalties on their finds to the Athenian treasury. Several thousand slaves worked ten-hour shifts underground—the time has been calculated from the capacity of their oil lamps.

The mines were a major factor in the Athenian economy. The discovery in 483 B.C. of an extremely rich vein of silver helped to fund Themistocles' program to build up the Athenian navy, and thereby defeat the Persians a few years later. Toward the end of the 5th century B.C., as the Peloponnesian War reached its final stages, the slaves of the silver mines took advantage of the desperate conditions at Athens to escape. With their silver supply cut off, the Athenians had to melt down bronze and even gold statues to make coins.

SEXUALITY AND FAMILY LIFE IN CLASSICAL ATHENS

Our picture of private life in Classical times is chiefly based on the evidence from Athens. The aim of the Athenian laws and customs relating to the marriage of Athenian citizens was the production of future citizens. Marriages were the responsibility of the guardian of the bride, who was her nearest male relative (usually her father), and the groom. Women often married two or three times, and a dying husband would sometimes select his soon-to-be widow's next partner.

The Basis of Marriage and Divorce

A responsible father began the search for a suitable husband for his daughter at her birth. If there seemed

PERSPECTIVES ON HISTORY

Marriage in Classical Athens

Louis Cohn-Haft
Smith College

Scholars generally agree on these basic facts: Athenians (and Greeks in general) were monogamous. Marriage was between a man and a woman of citizen family. Normally, but not necessarily, marriage was celebrated by a wedding, with family in attendance, with religious ritual, and with feasting and ceremony. Normally a dowry, in the form of a substantial sum of money or of property, accompanied the bride, to be administered by the bridegroom but remaining always the wife's property, eventually to be inherited by her children.

The bride was usually quite young, 14 to 17 years of age, whereas the bridegroom seems generally to have been a man of mature years, from 30 to 35, often considerably older. Marriage was arranged, a contractual agreement between two men, the bridegroom and the father of the bride. The marital couple may not even have laid eyes on each other prior to their wedding day.

But marriage was viewed as not only setting up a new family and home but also as cementing or creating a relationship between families. Marriage between members of families closely related by friendship or by blood was common. Marriage between first cousins, between uncle and niece, even between half-siblings was not merely permitted but often enough occurred. Perhaps therefore the depiction of a marriage between strangers may be softened, since a prior acquaintance of the couple at family gatherings must not have been unusual.

But what was an Athenian marriage really like? What was the personal relationship between spouses? The privacy of an Athenian home was carefully guarded, so that we know very little about the daily life that went on behind closed doors, and that little is biased, fragmentary, and often ambiguous.

The scholarly effort to understand the reality of Athenian marital relations is guided by two items, one a fact, the other an attitude. The fact is that wives are after all a particular category of women, and the subordination of women to men in Athenian society is solidly established beyond question. The attitude is that of the modern historian, and is a combination of ideology and prejudice and the play of imaginative hunches.

The position of women in Classical Athens is an affront to the modern Western mind. Not only was a woman barred from participation in public life; worse, her legal status was permanently that of a minor, that is, she was all her life under the guardianship of a man—first her father, then a husband, finally often enough a son. She was overprotected to the degree that, in theory at least, she was not able to leave her home unescorted. Her guardian (the Greek word is *kyrios*, literally "lord and master") had legally complete control over her every action. A woman could be accused of crime, tried by a court, found guilty and punished, but she could not defend herself or testify in person in the court.

For some modern historians, these facts settle the matter. For them, the Athenian home is a patriarchal tyranny, in which wife, children, and servants are all heaped together under the absolute rule of a being who regards himself as innately superior. The wife's lot is to be bullied and humiliated, treated with contempt by a worldly, experienced older man who can find no basis for a personal relationship with an ignorant, inexperienced, childish female. The husband can barely bring himself to perform the duty of breeding children with this inferior creature, whom he despises. He spends most of his time with his male friends. He seeks sexual pleasure with prostitutes trained to give pleasure and to be witty and amusing in the bargain, or with young boys. Some historians go so far as to find misogyny, the hatred of women, a fundamental aspect of Athenian male ideology. This is, to be sure, an extreme view, but it is influential. One is probably correct in saying that the general run of current historical opinion is that the daily life of the Athenian wife was empty and miserable, worse even than that of most wives in most societies through the centuries of history, in almost all of which women have been regarded as inferior to men.

This writer believes that the true picture is significantly more complex. Such contemporary evidence that has come down to us is found mainly in two very different forms of literature, drama and courtroom oratory. In drama, in tragedy and also in comedy, women are depicted as accepting their statutory inferiority with something less than passive acquiescence. There are despairing, cruelly used, weeping women, but there are also women of strong character who act independently and vigorously—although not always with success. Scholars have for generations used these fictional characters to arrive at very diverse conclusions as to what they tell us about actual Athenian women. Indeed, the very fact that the patron deity of Athens, from whom the city took its name, was a female, the goddess Athene, has served as testimony to support entirely opposing views as to what that tells us about the treatment of Athenian women by their men.

The trial orations, which rank far below dramatic poetry as a literary form, have received—perhaps for that reason—less attention by historians, many of whom are content, if they cite them at all, to observe that women are spoken about but can never speak for themselves. But women, wives too, are spoken about occasionally, and even quoted in the orations. It is noteworthy that if they are women of citizen family they are regularly alluded to with respect, now and then with affection. They are sometimes depicted as competently engaged with their husbands in business and financial matters; occasionally widows ran their own affairs. They are sometimes referred to, even directly quoted, playing a forceful, dynamic role in family affairs.

There are few such references, alongside the greater number which take it for granted that women are passive and obedient, protected denizens of the home. These bits of positive evidence, few though they are, have a special value as testimony to the reality of Athenian domestic life. They have that value because the peculiarities of the Athenian judicial system mean that they can be trusted in a way that no fictional evidence, however carefully analyzed, can match.

In an Athenian trial, there were no lawyers, nor was there a district attorney to represent the state. A trial was a contest between two individuals. Both plaintiff and the defendant had to present their own cases, calling and questioning witnesses, and making speeches to the jury. The jury consisted of a large number: 101 (always an odd number, thereby guaranteeing a decision, which was by simple majority vote) or more of the contestants' fellow citizens, ordinary Athenian men. Despite being under oath, a pleader might, of course, lie or at least twist the facts to make a good impression. Therefore the accuracy of what was claimed in court cannot be relied upon. More important, however, is the certainty that the speaker would want to persuade his hearers, who were not instructed by a professional judge but made their decisions entirely on their own. The speaker is therefore practically guaranteed not to have made an assertion that would sound ridiculous to those ordinary men of the jury. Thus when a man in court speaks of his wife as having full knowledge and competence in business matters, he may or may not be speaking truthfully, but it is certain that he is not claiming something that the jurymen would automatically disbelieve. Similarly, when he speaks of his wife with affection and respect, he is sure that his hearers will not break into jeering laughter. As already noted, references of this sort are few—not surprising, given the reticence of Athenians regarding their private lives—but they are reliable.

One striking example is illustrative of the sort of information we can get from the orations. In a defendant's speech in a murder trial, a certain Euphiletos describes an apparently normal evening meal in his home, at which he and his wife were served by a slave girl. The scene, which happens to be the single most nearly intimate insight into Athenian domestic life we have, can

continued next page

best be characterized as cozy. Alas, this homey relationship was not what it appeared on the surface, for Euphiletos' point in describing it is to show himself a trusting fellow. He was on trial for the murder of his wife's lover, whom he had caught in bed with her in his home. He had killed the lover on the spot. From this rare and not very heartwarming glimpse, we can at least know that Athenian domestic life could include a warm relationship between spouses and that an Athenian wife was not necessarily without initiative and boldness—altogether a situation not all that unfamiliar in our own world.

In the context of male authority one may ask how male superiority was expressed. Did an Athenian husband use physical force on his wife? Given what we know of battered wives in many societies, this is not an idle question. Oddly, there is not a shred of evidence, not so much as a hint, that any Athenian husband ever struck his wife. Obviously, absence of data cannot prove anything, and one recent historian has confidently explained this curious negative fact as a "cover-up."

It may, however, reflect Athenian attitudes toward violence in general. Civic status was of utmost importance in Athens. There were three main categories: citizen, free noncitizen, and slave. A slave was a piece of property; a free individual who was not a citizen had some rights (but would be prudent not to assert them in conflict with a citizen); a citizen was inviolate in his person. There are several known cases in which the claim is made that a citizen had been assaulted by a fellow citizen. The punishment in such cases was severe. Even the death penalty might be invoked. That Athenians felt strongly about physical assault on a citizen—and even verbal insult—is amply attested by their laws, their actions, and their words. Women and children, thought of as helpless creatures, were in the most protected category in this respect.

A most interesting illustration of this attitude occurs in an oration, not in a trial, but in a political debate. The celebrated orator and politician, Demosthenes, accused his rival, Aeschines, while on a diplomatic mission during a war, of having at a drunken party laid indecent hands on a captive woman, a citizen of the enemy city. The speech that Aeschines made in reply happens also to have come down to us. Aeschines says that if even one person among his hearers believed that even drunk he could have done such a thing to a free person or indeed to any human creature, he would not think his life worth living. A grand rhetorical exaggeration, to be sure, but certainly Aeschines did not expect his listeners, who were his male fellow citizens, to laugh at him; he was expressing an attitude that he expected would win their approval and respect.

The probability, then, is that however lacking an Athenian wife was in active rights, and however lordly and masterful her husband may have been in his dealings with her, she may have been at least immune from physical abuse.

To sum up, marriage in Classical Athens appears on balance to have been surely no worse, and in some respects probably less burdensome, for the wife than in most of the male-dominated societies that history records.

no prospect of contracting a marriage, a female baby would sometimes be left to die. The natural rate of infant mortality meant that this was generally achieved by neglect, rather than a deliberate act. Some infant females were reared to become slaves, while on occasion prostitutes would bring up girls and train them in their own profession.

The principal factor in arranging a marriage was economic, and the father or other male relative had to provide the groom with a dowry that could guarantee his future wife's maintenance. Poor men often turned to wealthy relatives for help. In certain cases the state provided dowries to the daughters of men in public service. Management of the dowry itself passed directly to the groom on marriage, who used the interest on the money, usually calculated at 18 percent, to maintain his wife. If he died, or the couple divorced, the money returned to the woman's guardian, to be used for any future remarriage.

Divorce was common and easily attained by men, and lacked any social stigma for them, as the termination of Pericles' marriage proves (see Part II, Topic 3).

Clay plaque with husband and wife; their children are shown (in miniature) in front of them.

Pericles and his wife divorced by mutual consent, but in theory the law permitted either party to initiate court proceedings. In practice, however, divorce was much more difficult for women, and brought greater stigma, as Euripides' play *Medea* suggests. A man divorcing his wife returned her to her male guardian. Women wanting to divorce their husbands needed a male citizen (generally their father) to bring the case before the courts.

Children born to Athenian couples were the property of their father. When a marriage ended—either in divorce or in the death of the husband—any children remained in the father's house, leaving the woman free to remarry and produce children for her new husband. The evidence of skeletal remains suggests that the average Athenian woman gave birth to 4.6 infants, with an infant mortality rate of 1.6, leaving 3 survivors per female. Abortion was one of the means used to limit the birthrate: Aristotle distinguished between abortions performed before the fetus felt sensation, which were acceptable, and those performed later in a pregnancy, of which he did not approve.

Sexuality in Periclean Athens

The laws regulating sexual behavior in Athens went back to the time of Solon. Since the aim of marriage was to produce legitimate Athenian children, both adultery and rape were held to be crimes against the state, as well as against the father and husband. The husband of a woman who had either been convicted of adultery or raped was required by law to divorce her. The woman could not speak in her own defense, but had to persuade her male guardian to represent her. Few women divorced on these grounds had any chance of remarriage. A man responsible for raping another man's wife received a fine, while the punishment for adultery was more severe. The husband was acquitted if he killed his wife's seducer in passion.

Custom required citizen couples to have sexual relations on average no more than three times a month, presumably to maintain a low birthrate. Few women were likely to run the risks inherent in adultery; they were closely watched. There is no evidence for female homosexuality at Athens, although contemporary societies at Sparta and in Mytilene, a town on the island of Lesbos, did not discourage it: hence the term "lesbian."

Since Athenian men generally did not marry before the age of 30, young Athenian males' sexual activity involved prostitutes and slaves. Married men also made use of prostitutes, and their female slaves were available either for their own use or that of their friends. Greek culture assumed that most men practiced both heterosexual and homosexual relations as a normal aspect of their sexuality. Excess in either was discouraged, but no moral stigma attached to homosexuality.

PRIESTESSES, WIVES, AND PROSTITUTES: THE ROLES OF GREEK WOMEN

Archeological evidence from Greece in the Bronze Age suggests that the religion of that period may have centered on a mother goddess, whose chief votaries were priestesses. The myths of later times confirm the importance of female deities in Greek religious beliefs.

The Feminine and the Divine

The mother goddess of Minoan Crete (see Part II, Topic 1) was probably the ancestor of the Greek earth deities Ge—the name means "earth"—Hera, and Demeter. (Some scholars have disputed the connection between Bronze Age and Classical religion, or even the existence of a prehistoric mother goddess cult, and the question remains open.) All three Greek goddesses symbolized aspects of agricultural fertility, and Hera and Demeter are among the "Twelve Olympians," the chief deities of Greek (and later Roman) religion.

Hera, the wife of Zeus, father of gods and men, was the protectress of marriage, and thus constantly tried by her own husband's infidelity. Zeus, like other gods and heroes, had both heterosexual and homosexual

A sculpted stone slab containing a decree in honor of the goddesses Hera and Athene, seen above.

affairs. For all her rank and power, Hera followed conventional Greek custom by remaining faithful to her promiscuous mate. Aphrodite, the only other Olympian goddess to marry, represents a very different attitude to male-female relations. As the goddess of beauty and sexual passion, Aphrodite seduced a chain of gods and mortals, including no less a figure than Ares, god of war. Her importance as symbol of sexuality in all its forms made her both sacred to prostitutes and, especially in Hellenistic times, a goddess of marriage.

The other two major female deities are the virgin goddesses Athene and Artemis. Athene is a complex figure, born uniquely from the head of Zeus, and combining aspects of male and female. She is the patroness of weaving and other domestic crafts, and her gift of the olive—fertility symbol—to Athens won her the city's name. At the same time, she is a warrior goddess, often portrayed fully armed, and famous for her wisdom. As commentators have noted, Athene represents the woman who finds fulfillment in a man's world by sublimating her femininity and acting like a man, and she even appears in some myths in male disguise. Her chastity is thus the denial of her sexuality. Artemis, by contrast, symbolizes purity. At the same time she watches over women's physical welfare, helping them in the moments of shared female experience such as menstruation and childbirth.

Women and Worship

The worship of these and other deities was practically the only aspect of public life in which women of Classical times could take part. The cults of Athene and Demeter, in particular, had priestesses as their leading figures, and women commonly participated in religious festivals.

The chief priestess of the patron goddess of Athens held one of the city's most prestigious offices. On a number of occasions, chief priestesses played an important political role in Athenian affairs, as when in 480 B.C. the chief priestess of the day endorsed Themistocles' proposal to evacuate Athens before the Battle of Salamis.

The chief religious festival of the Athenian calendar was the Panathenaea, celebrated annually on Athene's birthday. Every fourth year the Greater Panathenaea saw the replacement of the sacred robe draped around a statue of Athene in the Erechtheum. The task of weaving this robe fell to a group of four young girls known as the *Arrephorai*. Aged between seven and eleven, they were chosen annually from noble families to live and work in the temple of Athene. Other young women carried the "sacred baskets" in the annual processions, as depicted in the sculptured frieze of the Parthenon.

The most important center for the worship of Demeter was at Eleusis, outside Athens, where celebration of the Eleusinian Mysteries drew women, men, children, and Greek-speaking slaves from all parts of the Greek world. The secret nature of the ceremonies—participants had to swear not to "reveal the mysteries"—means that we know little about them. They seem to have involved a fertility cult based on the annual death and rebirth of the crops, with an ear of grain as their central symbol. This illustrated the myth of Demeter's daughter, Persephone, who died every winter, only to be reborn in the spring. At the head of the cult was the chief priestess of Demeter, and women performed many of the most sacred rituals, including dances and a dramatic enactment of Demeter's separation from her daughter, followed by their blissful reunion.

Private Lives

With the exception of their participation in religious events, women had no role in public life at Athens. They could not vote, take part in debates, hold office, or sit on juries. Respectable women of the upper and middle classes did not appear in public, and spent most of their time at home. Even there, they were confined to the women's quarters, generally located on an upper floor and away from the street (female slaves lived alongside their mistresses). The only men whom they could meet were close relatives. Any man who broke this custom by coming into the presence of a free Athenian woman in the house of another man was tried as a criminal. No women, even upper-class Athenians, could inherit or own property. It was attached to them and ultimately went to their children. Although in general young males had a better chance of receiving an education, some women were educated and many men were illiterate.

Wealthy women supervised the performance of domestic work at home, while most Athenian housewives ran their own homes. Cooking, cleaning, the care of children, and the nursing of the sick occupied most of their daily lives. The fetching of water was a female task, but since visits to the fountain might lead to casual encounters and gossip, upper- and middle-class women normally sent their female slaves. Poorer women went themselves. The only domestic activity performed by men was shopping, so that women could avoid public markets and strange shopkeepers. Athenian female citizens did not work unless they had no economic choice, and the jobs working women performed were generally extensions of their activities at home, such as washing, spinning, selling food, and nursing.

Athenian males came of age at 18. In legal terms, Athenian females always remained minors. Although women in Classical Athens could inherit property or receive it by gift, all control of their financial affairs was in the hands of their husbands or male guardians. (In Sparta, by contrast, noble Spartiate women managed their own estates.) The gap between Athenian husbands and wives was made even more acute by the lack of female education. When an Athenian male wanted to enjoy the companionship—intellectual, social, or erotic—of a sophisticated, cultured woman, he turned to a prostitute.

Woman at home putting away clothes in a chest.

Companions to Men

By the Archaic period prostitution was already established as an institution at Athens, with state-run brothels staffed by female slaves. In Classical Athens prostitution was by no means confined to slaves, and large numbers of noncitizen women and freed slaves earned a living in this way. Some of them, women whose physical beauty was accompanied by intellectual and artistic gifts, became known as *hetairai,* "companions to men." The most famous of these was Aspasia, Pericles' companion (see Part II, Topic 3), and a number of other hetairai had more freedom and greater influence than the wives of Athenian citizens—itself a commentary on the status of freeborn Athenian women.

In some cases, Athenian men developed long-term relationships with noncitizen women, and couples lived together. The law offered such unions the same protection as regular marriages. Rape or seduction of a female partner brought the same penalties as similar acts committed against a legitimate wife. By the time of Pericles, however, children born to unmarried couples did not have the right to Athenian citizenship.

Successful prostitutes were the only women in Athens who could maintain their financial independence and control their own income, and they could choose whom they met. Furthermore they were more likely to raise girl children than boys, and save the unwanted infant females of others. They trained these children in their own trade, to support them when they themselves could no longer attract customers. Some of the hetairai became famous in their own right. Phryne, one of the most beautiful 4th-century B.C. prostitutes, was the lover of the sculptor Praxiteles and, it was said, inspired his great statue of Aphrodite. She also posed for his friend, the painter Apelles. On the other hand, the lives of many of the prostitutes and courtesans were generally miserable and often brutal.

FREEDOM AND SLAVERY IN GREEK SOCIETY

In the mid-5th century B.C., as the Greeks prepared themselves for war, the overall population of Athens stood at around 250,000. Of these, some 125,000 were citizens—60,000 men and their wives—and 125,000 slaves (all figures are rough estimates). Slightly over half the slaves, some 65,000, were engaged in domestic labor. Of the rest, 50,000 worked in shops and factories, and the remaining 10,000 in the mines. The remainder of the population consisted of resident aliens.

The treatment of the mineworkers was brutal, but in general the other slaves in domestic employment at Athens shared the living conditions of their employers. The Spartans, whose treatment of their serfs was even more inhumane, scoffed that in the streets of Athens you could not tell a slave from a citizen. Male domestic slaves accompanied their masters on the daily trip to the market, while female slaves lived in the women's quarters of the house. By comparison with the grim conditions of ancient Egypt, or the work camps and farm estates of the Roman Empire, or the cotton plantations of the 19th-century American Deep South, even the slaves engaged in agricultural labor seem to have worked alongside their employers and shared their lifestyles.

Yet there still remained a vast difference between the lives of even the poorest citizens and slaves. Employers were under no obligation to treat their slaves humanely. Beating, chaining, and starvation were common ways used to control them. In the mines, many slaves were literally worked to death. If a slave's evidence was required in a law court, it had by law to be given under torture. Nor did slaves have any sexual rights, while the owners of both male and female slaves could make sexual use of their "property" or make them available to others.

Like all ancient cultures—and many modern ones—Greek society in general, and Athenian in particular, was hierarchical. The only residents who enjoyed all the benefits of life at Athens were male citizens. Foreign residents, who were numerous, were given the same legal protection as citizens, and shared the same obligations to pay taxes and do military service. They could not own land or houses, however, but had to rent them. Foreign women often led freer lives than their Athenian counterparts.

The fate of slaves at Athens depended on that of their employers. For many poor citizens, life must have seemed not much more free than for the slaves in domestic employment alongside whom they worked. The only entire category of Athenian resident to suffer from serious underprivilege—and, of course, it was a vast one—was that of female citizens.

Socrates praised the democratic nature of public life at Athens, with its Assembly made up of "laundrymen, shoemakers, carpenters, smiths, peasants, and shopkeepers." When Socrates' wife, Xanthippe, came to visit him in prison before his execution, to see him for the last time, the philosopher told his friends to take her away, before settling down to spend his last hours surrounded by his male friends. The gulf between husband and wife was far greater than that between the aristocratic Pericles and the laundrymen and peasants, sitting and debating together in the Assembly.

Questions for Further Study

1. What were the attitudes in Classical Greece to gender, marriage, and the status of women? How did they affect Greek society?
2. What role did agriculture play in the development of Greek life?
3. How important was trade in the economies of the Greek city-states? What political impact did it have on political relations between them?

Suggestions for Further Reading

du Bois, P. *Sowing the Body: Psychoanalysis and Ancient Representations of Women*. Chicago, 1988.

Frost, F. *Greek Society*, 5th Ed. Lexington, MA, 1997.

Garlan, Y. *Slavery in Ancient Greece*. Ithaca, NY, 1988.

Just, R. *Women in Athenian Law and Life*. London, 1990.

Keuls, E. C. *The Reign of the Phallus: Sexual Politics in Ancient Athens*. New York, 1985.

Lacey, W. K. *The Family in Classical Greece*. Ithaca, NY, 1984.

Manville, P. B. *The Origin of Citizenship in Ancient Athens*. Princeton, NJ, 1990.

Pomeroy, S. *Goddesses, Whores, Wives, and Slaves: Women in Classical Antiquity*. New York, 1976.

Wood, E. *Peasant-Citizen and Slave: The Foundations of Athenian Democracy*. London, 1988.

II

Topic 6

Alexander and the Hellenistic Age

The century following the accession of Alexander in 336 B.C. marked one of the major turning points in Western history. Within a hectic few years, the young Macedonian king invaded Asia, conquered the most powerful empire of the ancient world, that of the Persians, and put together a kingdom stretching from Greece to India.

With Alexander's premature death, his conquests split into a series of warring successor states, whose rulers—Alexander's former generals—struggled for power. Three ruling dynasties emerged from the conflict: the European Antigonids, the Asian Seleucids, and the Ptolemies of Egypt.

The foundation of the culture that developed in these states, known as Hellenistic, was Greek. Yet although it shared a common language, Greek, and a single basic intellectual tradition, that of 5th-century B.C. Athens, the Hellenistic world was truly international. It was strongly influenced by Achaemenian (Persian) and Egyptian culture, and provided the basis for the growth of the Roman Empire in western Asia and the eventual spread of Christianity.

The economic and social basis of the Hellenistic kingdoms remained agriculture, but the city, modeled on the Greek city-state, became of increasing importance. (The term "Hellenistic" is used to refer to the history and culture of the peoples "Hellenized," that is, brought under Greek influence, by Alexander's conquests.) The growth of urban centers such as Alexandria and Antioch reinforced, in fact, the importance of agriculture and food production while spreading the Greek concept of civilization. At the same time, trade and industry flourished, particularly in Asia.

The impact of non-Greek religious ideas from western Asia and Egypt on traditional Classical patterns of thought stimulated new forms of religious experience. Some of these, like the worship of state rulers, arose for political reasons. Others represented a wide range of philosophical responses to a changing world. Two schools of philosophy, the Stoic and the Epicurean, found different solutions to the significance of the divine in human affairs. Other people turned instead to "mystery cults," which promised secret revelations.

The wealthy capitals of the Hellenistic kingdoms—Alexandria, Pergamum, and others—became centers of research in the pure and applied sciences. There were major breakthroughs in astronomy, medicine, and mathematics, while the search for more efficient weapons and defense systems led to progress in engineering.

In all these respects, the Hellenistic Age marked the diffusion on three continents of the cultural legacy of Classical Greece, a process that was to continue with the rise of Rome.

ALEXANDER THE GREAT AND HIS EMPIRE

When Alexander succeeded his father Philip as king of Macedon in 336 B.C., his first challenge came from the Greek city-states that Philip had conquered. Taking advantage, as they thought, of the young and inexperienced new ruler—Alexander was 20 at the time of his accession—the Greeks rose in revolt. Alexander's response was immediate. Macedonian troops poured south and stormed Thebes, and Alexander gave orders for the ancient city to be razed to the ground. Only the temples and the house of the 6th-century B.C. poet Pindar were to be spared. The other Greek cities, horrified, abandoned any further notion of opposition.

Alexander Builds an Empire

With Greece secured, Alexander turned his attention east, and in 334 B.C. launched a massive invasion of Asia. By 331 B.C. his forces had crushed the Persian army, driven Darius, the Great King, into flight, and occupied the royal cities of Babylon and Persepolis. The most powerful empire of the ancient world was now in Macedonian hands.

For the next five years Alexander continued his drive east, simultaneously conquering new territory and fighting to hold on to land already won. Finally, in 326 B.C., after barely winning a ferocious combat in the Punjab, the weary army refused to go any farther. Alexander's men had been badly scared by the Indians' secret weapon, a herd of 200 trained elephants. Even Alexander's combined glamour and ruthlessness could not drive them on, and the expedition returned to Persia.

Alexander set up his court in Babylon. In 327 B.C., to celebrate his "marriage of East and West" Alexander himself married Roxana, daughter of a Persian noble. Three years later, in 324 B.C., he assigned noble Persian brides to his officers: some 9000 weddings took place on a single day at Susa, as Greek

Mosaic from Pompeii showing Alexander's victory over the Persians at the Battle of the Issus.

priests and Persian magi prayed together. Only Alexander's death of a fever in 323 B.C. prevented the addition of yet another territory, for he spent his last months planning the conquest of Arabia.

Alexander's empire stretched from western Greece to India, from the Caucasus to the Sahara. He seems to have had no particular plan for its future, except to add more conquests, and never planned how to organize so vast an assortment of peoples and cultures. Long before his death, his Greek and Macedonian followers came to resent the influence of the old Persian aristocracy, many of whom Alexander left in their former positions of power. Nor did they relish the pomp and splendor of court life at Babylon, with Alexander encouraging his subjects to worship him as a god. The last years there saw a succession of intrigues and political trials, and the liquidation of potential opponents to the regime.

News of Alexander's death stunned his contemporaries. One Athenian refused to believe it, remarking bitterly that if it were true the stench would fill the world. Alexander had administered his conquests by improvising as circumstances evolved. The only members of his family left—a mentally limited half-brother and a son born a month or so after his death—were incapable of continuing his work, and it is a measure of his grip on the imagination and the loyalty of his subjects that the overwhelming majority of them remained obedient to his successors.

A vividly carved portrait head of Alexander the Great.

THE SUCCESSOR STATES: CHALLENGE AND COMPETITION

Any chance of a united Macedonian Empire surviving its founder soon disappeared, as Alexander's generals killed off his surviving family and began to battle amongst themselves for supremacy. The first two to split off their own territory were Ptolemy (ruled 323–285 B.C.), Alexander's intelligence officer, who won Egypt, and Seleucus (ruled 306–281 B.C.), commander of the footguards, who seized the former Persian possessions in Asia. A succession of generals struggled for control of Macedon, which fell in the end to Antigonus Gonatas (ruled 276–239 B.C.). A generation after Alexander's death, his empire no longer existed.

Ptolemaic Egypt

Ptolemaic Egypt was the most durable of the Hellenistic kingdoms. Under the pharaohs, Egypt had long been ruled by absolute monarchs, and Ptolemy took advantage of the tradition. He established a highly organized bureaucracy at his capital, Alexandria. Alexander himself had founded the city in 332 B.C., and Ptolemy reinforced his claim to the succession by hijacking the royal body on its journey back to Macedon and had Alexander buried in Alexandria. The lavish tomb which Ptolemy constructed for his late master has never been found.

Ptolemy's other great building project at Alexandria was the "Temple of the Muses," or "Museum," which included the famous library containing copies of everything of note ever written in Greek that had survived. A famous center for research, the library attracted scholars and students from the entire Hellenistic world.

Other foreigners—traders, soldiers, technicians—flocked to Egypt as Ptolemy's efficient administration produced growing prosperity. A complex tax system was in the hands of traveling officials, who were encouraged to be fair in the exaction of revenue. One "memo" to junior bureaucrats tells them, "As you travel about, try to go from one person to another and speak words of encouragement and make them all more cheerful."

All agricultural land remained in the hands of the king, who leased it to private farmers. The abundant supply of wheat grown in the Nile Valley increased as the result of new irrigation systems and new strains of food plants introduced by visiting experts, mainly Greek. Some commodities, including oil, were royal monopolies which only the state could produce and sell. Imported goods carried a heavy duty payable to the king.

Map 6.1 The Hellenistic World

Within a generation Ptolemy managed to combine a backward country of poor farming peasants with a small all-powerful aristocracy. The peasants continued to live in miserable conditions, excluded as they were from many of the benefits of Hellenization. Alexandria remained the only real center of political and cultural life: of all the successor states, Ptolemaic Egypt was the least urbanized. Some of the Greek men who emigrated there married local women, and their children combined the language of their fathers with the religious practices of their mothers. Greek was the official language. The only Ptolemaic ruler ever to speak Egyptian was the last, Cleopatra (ruled 51–30 B.C.; see Part II, Topic 9). Nonetheless, native Egyptians could rise in the civil service and, from the late 3rd century B.C., serve alongside Greeks in the army.

Asia under the Seleucids

Ptolemy's task in Egypt was made easier by the inherent nature of his kingdom, relatively small and with a single native ethnic people. The Asiatic parts of Alexander's empire were vast and sprawling, encompassing many different races, while the enormous wealth of many of its regions attracted a succession of rival kings and generals. Largest of all the Hellenistic kingdoms at the death of Alexander, Seleucid Asia shrank during most of its history as the outlying provinces fell to invaders. Furthermore, the Greeks who emigrated and settled there were never able to impose a cultural or even a linguistic unity. Greek was the official language, but a wide variety of local languages

Hellenistic coin with portrait of Seleucus.

continued to flourish and Seleucid rulers had to make many concessions to differing local traditions.

Its first ruler, Seleucus, died in 280 B.C., assassinated by one of Ptolemy's sons, after founding a new capital at Antioch, named after his son and successor, Antiochus (ruled 280–261 B.C.). Antiochus spent most of his reign embroiled in an interminable series of wars, first against Gallic invaders from northern Europe and later against his fellow Asian monarch, Eumenes of Pergamum. Even these heroic efforts failed to halt the erosion of his empire, and only the brilliant military and diplomatic career of Antiochus the Great (ruled 223–187 B.C.) brought a temporary restoration of Seleucid authority.

Successive rulers tried to construct an artificial sense of unity. As their losses increased, Seleucid kings increased the lavishness of their court, to impress their subjects and enemies alike, and claimed divine status for themselves. In the end, later Seleucid monarchs became trapped in the elaborate ritual and ceremony, buried beneath the masses of attendants and gold ornaments. Symbolically they represented the "living law of the land." In practice, the various regions of their empire increasingly went their own way. By the time the Romans unified Asia under their rule, little was left of the former Seleucid Empire except Syria.

Macedon after Alexander

The end of its royal family plunged Macedon, the third of the Hellenistic kingdoms, into immediate chaos, from which it eventually emerged under the efficient and organized rule of Antigonus Gonatas. Antigonus resisted the temptation to follow the example of the Seleucids and introduce a cult of king worship. He replied to a poet who obsequiously praised his divinity: "The man who carries my chamber-pot knows better."

Unlike the other Hellenistic kings, Antigonus and his successors made little attempt to expand their territory. They even left the Greeks free to resume the fratricidal intercity feuding that Philip had managed to stop a century earlier. The only area in which Macedonian rulers enforced their authority was control of the Aegean sea routes, which involved facing up to and defeating the Ptolemies of Egypt. By around 200 B.C., Macedon, together with the rest of Greece, began to fall into the orbit of Rome.

Significant Dates

Alexander and the Hellenistic Kingdoms (all dates B.C.)

336	Accession of Alexander
332	Foundation of Alexandria in Egypt
331	Alexander defeats Persians
326	Alexander reaches India
323	Death of Alexander; Ptolemy becomes ruler in Egypt
306	Seleucus becomes ruler of Seleucid kingdom
276	Antigonus becomes king of Macedon
250	Publication of Septuagint
223–187	Reign of Antiochus the Great

SOCIETY AND ECONOMY IN THE HELLENISTIC WORLD

Although Alexander's legacy of Greek language and culture helped to unify the Hellenistic world, there still remained an important social gap between the new Greek cities established in Asia and Egypt and the resident local populations. The new urban centers followed the model of the old Greek city-states, with the citizen-immigrants owning their land and farming it with the help of slave labor. These communities became sophisticated islands of culture surrounded by the great estates of the kings, where peasants continued to live in villages and work the land as they had for centuries.

City Life

The first three Seleucid kings founded a chain of Greek-style cities running from the Aegean as far east as the Hindu Kush. Many of them were laid out on a rectilinear grid pattern and used the latest engineering techniques to provide public water supplies and toilet facilities. The majority of the inhabitants were a mixture of colonists from Greece and Asia Minor and retired veteran soldiers, pensioned off to populate the new settlements.

The political and social organization of these communities followed the model of a Greek polis. Thus a form of government invented in the city-states of Archaic Greece over three centuries earlier became transplanted to Central Asia and the borders of India. Each city had its own council and popular assembly, magistrates, and code of law. Many acted as if they were free and independent states, although they paid taxes to the king and were subject to his control. In turn the king maintained the political illusion that he "assured the autonomy and democracy of the people."

Unlike the Seleucids, the Ptolemies did not encourage the growth of numerous cities, but concentrated

Reconstruction model of the Hellenistic city of Pergamum.

their resources in Alexandria. The city's population, made up of Greeks, Macedonians, Jews, and Egyptians, was far more cosmopolitan than the Asian Greek communities. Some lower-class Greeks married Egyptians, but on the whole the Greeks did not mix socially with the other groups. Their centers were the *gymnasia*, clubs where young Greek men went to study literature and mathematics, practice sporting activities, and maintain their "Greekness."

There was more contact in the neighboring countryside, where surviving papyrus records describe racial tension. A camel driver, probably Arab, ascribes the nonpayment of his fees to the fact that "I am a barbarian, and do not know how to behave like a Greek." On other occasions Greeks complain of being discriminated against because of their race.

Ptolemaic Egypt was the scene of the earliest documented anti-Semitic riots. Many Jewish residents adopted Greek ways, speaking Greek rather than Hebrew. One of the results was the earliest translation of the Hebrew Bible into Greek, a work known as the *Septuagint* from the over 70 scholars who worked on it over a period of some hundred years. The Septuagint was published around 250 B.C. at Alexandria under the patronage of Ptolemy's son, Ptolemy II. The book of Ecclesiastes, written about the same time, shows the impact of Greek ideas on traditional Jewish beliefs. Not all Jews accepted this Hellenization of their faith, and the book of Ecclesiasticus, composed in Hebrew in 197 B.C. and translated into Greek in 132 B.C., represents an attack on Greek influences. Both the Jewish and Protestant Bibles place the book of Ecclesiasticus in the Apocrypha.

The Hellenistic Economy

The cultural contrast between the sophisticated lifestyle of the cities and the peasant life of the countryside had significant economic consequences. City dwellers of Greek origin were accustomed to using metal coinage, and one of Alexander's most important economic innovations was the introduction of a standard system of money. In the years following his death, large numbers of silver coins bearing his portrait circulated throughout the Hellenistic kingdoms. Both the Antigonids of Macedon and the Seleucids imposed a fixed weight on the money, which became the basis for the first international coinage in Western history.

Local populations living in the villages, on the other hand, were accustomed to an economic system that relied on barter and payment in goods. Bad harvests and grain shortages remained a constant fear, alleviated to some extent by improvements in agricultural methods. A greater use was made of iron plows, and new forms of dam building and construction of canals helped improve irrigation.

Both in Egypt and in Seleucid Asia, the rulers needed to transfer the huge quantities of agricultural produce coming from their estates into cash for the purchase of other materials and the payment of services. The cities, with their more sophisticated economies, fulfilled the role of middleman. Their residents bought the grain and paid the government in

Hellenistic coin with portrait of Alexander.

ready money, which the state could then use for the purchase of manufactured goods.

Some cities built highly successful economies based on this trade and industry, and used their prosperity to introduce social legislation to protect the less-well-off of their citizens. The Greek writer Strabo (64 or 63 B.C.–after A.D. 21) describes the city of Rhodes, whose rulers "wish to look after their multitude of poor. Accordingly, they supply them with corn, and following an ancient custom the well-to-do support the poor."

Specific cities became famous for their industrial production, Tyre for its dye-works, Tarsus for its linen. Most Hellenistic rulers encouraged the process of industrialization. Antiochus IV (ruled 175–164 B.C.) was famous for escaping from the suffocating life of court ritual to visit the silversmiths and goldsmiths in their workshops, to discuss the technicalities of production with them. As in Classical Greece, the production remained small-scale, with most businesses consisting of the owner and one or two slaves.

MYSTICS, STOICS, AND EPICUREANS: THE CONFLICTS OF RELIGION AND PHILOSOPHY

Belief in the traditional gods was already on the wane in Classical Greece. Socrates and other thinkers had encouraged their contemporaries to take a fresh look at old ideas, and many people continued to perform ancient rituals out of habit rather than conviction. The Hellenistic world brought the Greeks into contact with a whole range of non-Greek peoples and faiths, and the result was a wide variety of new forms of religious experience.

New Aspects of Ancient Beliefs

Some aspects of Hellenistic religion were the direct result of political pressures from the ruling class. All of Alexander's successors came to power by force, and therefore felt that they needed some form of justification for their own rule and that of their descendants. The most common was for kings to claim descent from the gods, and require their subjects to worship them and their families. They also claimed worship on the basis of their own accomplishments, as had been the case with Alexander himself.

The ancestor of the Antigonids of Macedon, the royal family asserted, was Hercules, and Macedonian coins bore Hercules' symbol, the club. This convenient fiction served a double purpose: it provided the ruling family with divine origins, and at the same time linked them with the family of Alexander and his father Philip, who also claimed to be descended from Hercules. Seleucus went even further, since the king was reputedly no less than the son of Apollo—a fact demonstrated by a birthmark on his thigh in the shape of an anchor, Apollo's symbol. In honor of the Seleucids' divinity, many cities in their kingdom celebrated special festivals every four years, dedicated to music and athletics, pursuits sacred to Apollo.

In strong contrast to the official cults were the ways in which ordinary people sought to deal with changing attitudes and new social conditions. One of them was the increase of interest in mystery religions. Many of these cults, like the Eleusinian Mysteries, went back to much earlier days (see Part II, Topic 5). They offered secret initiation ceremonies and individual salvation, and emphasized irrational emotions. One of the most popular was the worship of Asclepius, the god of healing, at the Greek sanctuary of Epidaurus. Pilgrims claimed miraculous cures after spending a night in the temple, as the offerings and inscriptions left there throughout the Hellenistic period demonstrate.

The mystery cults emphasized that the lives of their members had an essential meaning and purpose. Many people, however, faced with the tumultuous events around them, preferred to turn to a very different form of worship. No deity received more attention in the Hellenistic world than Tyche, goddess of Fortune. The power of Tyche was ambiguous, wavering between good and bad, sometimes random and sometimes under the control of a higher force, which itself operated in an ambiguous manner. Many cities tried to

The Apollo Belvedere (Roman copy of a Greek original), a typical work of the Hellenistic period.

win the favor of Fortune by portraying her on their coinage, accompanied by a symbol of abundance, while the historian Polybius (c. 203–120 B.C.) claimed that Fortune played an important role in people's lives—for better or worse—and could not be ignored.

Still other worshipers turned to the greater certainties provided by the ancient gods of Eastern religion. Shrines to the Egyptian resurrection goddess Isis sprang up throughout the Hellenistic world and remained centers of pilgrimage for centuries. Cybele, the mother goddess of Anatolia, the Assyrian Atargatis, and many others had temples built to them in Greece and the Near East. Some of their followers saw them all as incarnations of a single deity, different forms of one god. This process of assimilation, known as syncretism, helped to pave the way for the spread of Christianity.

Stoics and Epicureans

Athens remained the center of philosophy during Hellenistic times, chiefly because of the prestige of the schools founded there by Plato and Aristotle, the Academy and the Lyceum. The two main systems of philosophical belief to develop after Alexander were Stoicism and Epicureanism. They attracted those in search of intellectually satisfying explanations of life, rather than systems of faith that appealed to the emotions.

The Stoics took their name from the building in which their school was located: the Stoa Poikile, or Painted Hall. The movement's founder, Zeno (335–263 B.C.), taught that the force governing the world was Reason. Through the power of Reason it was possible to learn virtue, which was the supreme good. Those who lived virtuously were under the protection of Divine Providence, which would never allow them to suffer evil.

The other main system, Epicureanism, was based on the teachings and writings of Epicurus (341–271 B.C.), whose aim was to free humans from the threat of divine retribution or the fear of the unknown. According to Epicurus, even if the gods exist, they play no part in the world or in human affairs. We are free to live our lives according to principles of moderation and prudence in the pursuit of pleasure. The Epicureans believed that the universe consisted of small particles of matter, or atoms, moving at random in empty space. At death, the atoms separate, and no part of us survives. As a result we should not fear to die, since it involves only the complete ending of any sensation.

Both these schools, first developed at Athens, spread during the Hellenistic period and also flourished at Rome (see Part II, Topic 8). Another popular movement, that of the Cynics, had a much less intellectual foundation. Its originator, Diogenes (c. 400–c. 325 B.C.), taught that life should be lived with a minimum of material comfort, complete freedom of speech, and shamelessness of action. His behavior won him the nickname of "the Cynic," which in Greek means "the Dog," a label later applied to his followers.

THE NATURE OF THE UNIVERSE: SCIENCE, MEDICINE, AND TECHNOLOGY

While the traditional pursuit of philosophy continued at Athens, the great centers of scientific progress in the Hellenistic world were the new royal capitals, cities like Alexandria and Pergamum, whose monarchs subsidized research projects. The protected life of the scholars working in the museum and library at Alexandria drew the scorn of one contemporary, who described the scientists of his day as "well-propped pedants who quarrel without end in the Muses' bird-cage."

Astronomy and Medicine

The conquests of Alexander had expanded the horizons of immense numbers of people. Perhaps as a conse-

Drawing of the lighthouse at Alexandria, one of the Seven Wonders of the Ancient World.

quence, astronomers began to explore new ideas about the world and its place in the cosmos. Aristarchus of Samos (active c. 270 B.C.) was the first person in history to maintain that the earth rotates on its own axis and revolves around the sun. Hipparchus (active c. 146 B.C.) astonished his contemporaries by compiling a catalogue of stars. Two centuries later, the Roman scholar Pliny the Elder observed: "Hipparchus dared to do something that would be rash even for a god. He numbered the stars for his successors and checked off the constellations by name."

Experiments conducted by astronomers in taking measurements led to important geometrical discoveries. Apollonius (c. 262–190 B.C.), known to his age as the "Great Geometer," introduced concepts such as the ellipse and the parabola, and worked on conic sections. Eratosthenes (275–194 B.C.), the chief librarian at Alexandria in the time of Ptolemy III, managed to measure the circumference of the earth, arriving at a figure within 4 percent of the actual one. Eratosthenes also wrote on geology and literary criticism, showing a versatility that led his envious fellow scholars to nickname him "Beta"—"Second-rater"—because there was no single field in which he was first.

While astronomers studied the place of humans in the universe, Alexandria's medical researchers studied humans themselves. Herophilus (c. 335–c. 280 B.C.) founded an institute of anatomy in Ptolemy's capital. One of the first to study the workings of the body by conducting postmortem examinations, Herophilus was able to describe the liver, the genitals, and the ventricles of the brain, to explain the function of the nerves, and to time the pulse.

Advances in Technology

By around 300 B.C. many important technical devices were already in use, including the lever, pulley, wedge, and windlass. The greatest of all Hellenistic scientists, Archimedes (c. 287–212 B.C.), refined the use of levers, boasting "give me a place to stand and I will move the earth." He also invented another device, a "screw" used for raising water.

After studying in Alexandria, Archimedes returned to his native Syracuse in Sicily, where he became scientific adviser to King Hiero II. Like many of his fellow researchers, he spent much of his time working on projects related to warfare. Hellenistic kings were constantly trying to improve the capability of their weaponry, while strengthening their defense capacities. Among the works designed by Archimedes for Hiero were catapults and grapnels to help in the defense of Syracuse under siege. The grapnel hooks served to tear down mobile siege towers which formed part of the equipment of a Hellenistic army on the attack.

Toward the end of the Hellenistic period, the drive to invent new technologies began to flag. Nonetheless, Hellenistic scientists and engineers on the whole amply demonstrated two vital methods of research: the use of mathematics to investigate natural phenomena, and the importance of practical experiment to discover the truth.

Alexander dreamed of the "unity of empire." Far from becoming unified, the lands and peoples he conquered spent the century after his death in a state of constant tension and rivalry. Hellenistic kings fought offensive and defensive wars against one another, while ever on guard against internal threats. Only the coming of the Romans succeeded in finally imposing unity by absorbing Alexander's conquests into an empire spreading west to the Atlantic.

Yet in other respects the Hellenistic Age did create achievements worthy of Alexander's dream. Greek ideas about politics, economics, and the nature of the universe traveled from a small, isolated country to a stage spanning half the known world. In the process they came into contact with the older, more varied cultures of Asia. The two never really "fused": the Greeks, like later imperialists, were far too certain of their own superiority for that to have been possible. Yet the result was an immense enrichment for both sides, with Greek-style city-states within reach of the borders of India, and temples to Asian gods on the islands of Rhodes and Delos.

For the first time in history, an international culture circulated in a multiethnic world. A common language, political system, and currency were shared by a series of independent states each of which preserved its own special characteristics and ethnic mixture. For all the inevitable conflict between the Hellenistic kingdoms—in some ways, in fact, because of their rivalry—scientists and intellectuals continued to make progress, and laid many of the bases of Western civilization. With the rise of Rome, their achievements were to reach an even wider stage.

Questions for Further Study

1. How did Alexander's conquests survive his death? What were the chief differences among the Hellenistic kingdoms?
2. Which aspects of Greek culture were transplanted most successfully to the Hellenistic world? How did they blend with the preexisting cultures of Egypt and western Asia?
3. What are the characteristic features of Hellenistic religious developments?

Suggestions for Further Reading

Barnes, J. et al. *Science and Speculation*. New York, 1982.
Fox, R. L. *The Search for Alexander*. Boston, 1980.
Green, P. *Alexander of Macedon, 356–323 B.C.: A Historical Biography*. Berkeley, 1991.
Jones, H. *The Epicurean Tradition*. London, 1989.
Pollitt, J. J. *Art in the Hellenistic Age*. New York, 1986.
Pomeroy, S. *Women in Hellenistic Egypt: From Alexander to Cleopatra*. New York, 1984.
Walbank, F. W. *The Hellenistic World*. Cambridge, MA, 1982.

II

Topic 7

The Rise of Rome

In the early centuries of Rome's history, a number of distinct peoples were established in Italy, of whom the most important were the Etruscans. Technologically advanced and successful in commerce, the Etruscans spread throughout central Italy, and conquered Rome itself at the end of the 7th century B.C.

The city of Rome had been founded a century and a half earlier as an amalgamation of several villages on the hills around the river Tiber. The period of Etruscan occupation brought the Romans in contact with a new level of culture. The Etruscans carried out important engineering and construction projects, taught the Romans new technologies, and introduced the alphabet.

After a century of Etruscan rule, the Romans were sufficiently advanced to drive out their conquerors and begin their own climb to power. They replaced the system of government by kings, which went back to the foundation of the city, with a republic, based on a careful balance of the two chief social groups, the aristocratic patricians, and the plebs, or people. The process of devising a constitution went hand in hand with the creation of a law code.

By the end of the 5th century B.C., the Romans had become the dominant power in their region as leaders of the Latin League, and were ready to take on the rest of Italy. In a series of campaigns against the Etruscans and other independent peoples in Italy, they gradually assumed control of the peninsula.

In the mid-3rd century B.C., Rome began to move against the leading power in the western Mediterranean, Carthage (the Phoenician colony in North Africa). The first of the wars between the Romans and the Carthaginians, known as the Punic Wars, left Rome in control of Sicily, Corsica, and Sardinia. The Second Punic War began with the invasion of Italy by a Carthaginian army led by Hannibal, but the attack petered out. The end of the war, in 202 B.C., brought Roman victory and the collapse of Carthaginian power. The Romans' domination now extended throughout the western Mediterranean.

The chief powers of the eastern Mediterranean were the three largest of the Hellenistic kingdoms created after the death of Alexander: Syria, Macedon, and Egypt. The first of these to fall victim to Roman expansion was Macedon, which became a Roman province in 148 B.C. Two years later it was the turn of the rest of Greece.

The Roman conquest of the rest of Alexander's former empire was as much by diplomacy as by military force. An alternation of Roman threats and alliances weakened the resistance of the Syrian and Egyptian rulers. Syria fragmented into a series of tiny kingdoms, while Egypt was subservient to Rome long before its "official" conquest in 31 B.C.

By the end of the Republic, the Romans were the masters of the Mediterranean world. At Rome itself, however, the price of success abroad was increasing political turmoil, and the last century of Republican history (133–31 B.C.) brought internal collapse.

THE ETRUSCANS AND THE FOUNDATION OF ROME

Throughout the Bronze Age, Italy remained relatively isolated from events elsewhere in the Mediterranean, cut off to the north by the Alps and reachable from east, west or south only by long sea voyage. By around 900 B.C., at the dawn of the Iron Age, the population consisted of a series of separate ethnic groups, each with its own culture.

Shortly after 800 B.C., three major developments occurred, which were to prove crucial to the history of Western civilization. The first was the arrival of Greek colonists who began to found trading settlements in southern Italy and Sicily and to transplant their culture into the western Mediterranean region (see Part II, Topic 1). Around the same time, herdsmen and farmers living in the valley of the river Tiber pooled their resources to form a new community, the future imperial city of Rome. Meanwhile the Etruscans became the leading power in central Italy.

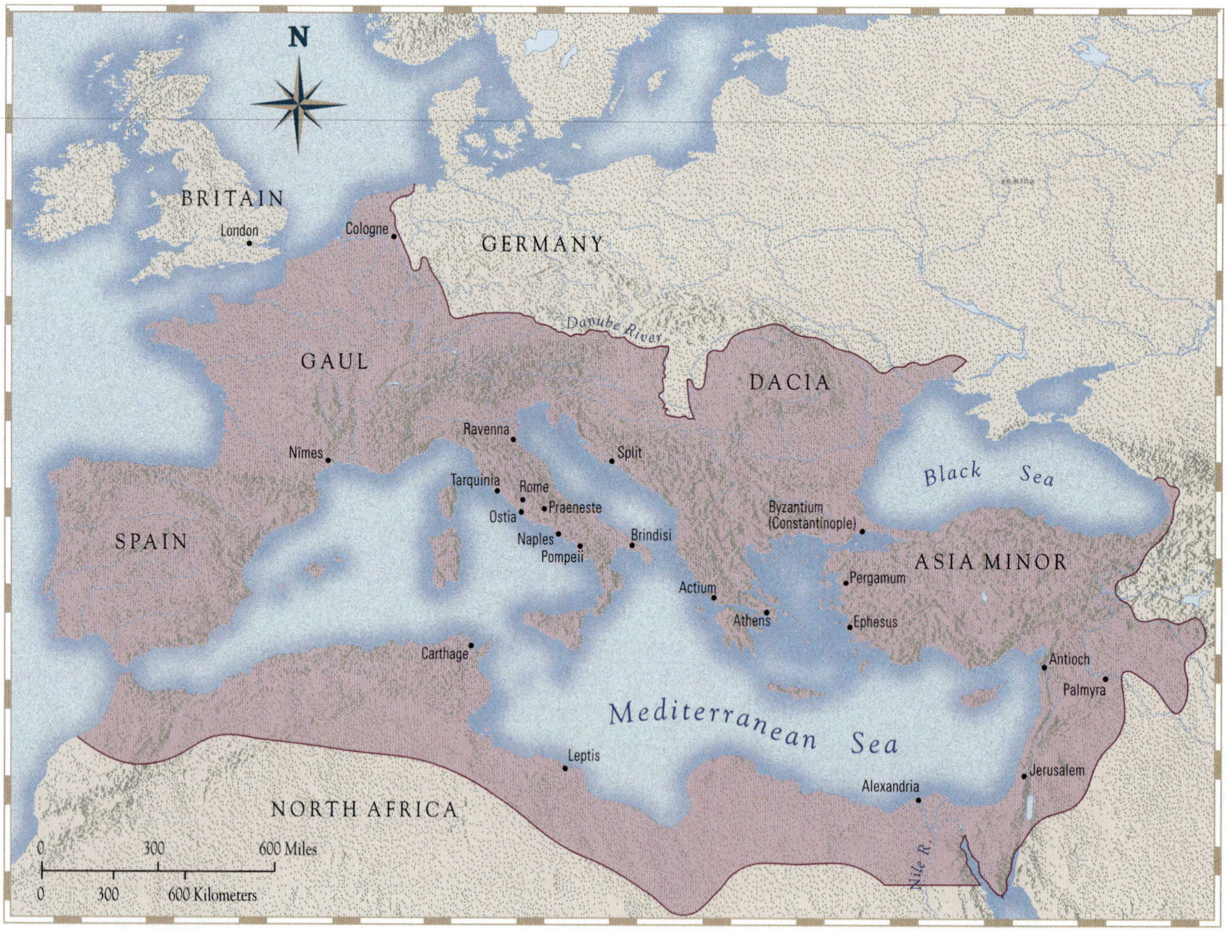

Map 7.1 The Roman World

The Etruscans

Even in ancient times the Etruscans seemed mysterious to their neighbors. The first evidence for their existence dates to the mid-8th century B.C., and by 700 B.C. they were well established in that part of Italy, Tuscany, which still bears their name. The Greeks and Romans believed that the Etruscans were immigrants from the East. According to one story, reported to us by the Greek historian Herodotus, they fled westward from the kingdom of Lydia in Asia Minor at a time of terrible famine.

Both their way of life and art show, in fact, many eastern characteristics. Etruscan art makes frequent use of eastern motifs, including the sphinx and palmette. Like many Asian cults, Etruscan religion placed strong emphasis on foretelling the future and appeasing the gods. The methods used by Etruscan soothsayers to interpret the gods' wishes and intentions—"reading" the entrails of animals and watching the flight of birds and natural phenomena such as lightning flashes—are remarkably similar to Babylonian rituals.

Furthermore, the importance and high social standing of women in Etruscan society had little in common with Greek and Roman custom. Etruscan women could both inherit and pass on possessions, and act as the heads of families, legal rights never enjoyed by their Greek or Roman counterparts. The Greeks even regarded the Etruscan custom of husbands and wives reclining together to eat as immoral.

Yet, for all its eastern characteristics, in other ways Etruscan culture seems a natural development of their predecessors in central Italy. Their patterns of settlement also suggest an indigenous origin. New immigrants from an outside culture would either have founded their own centers (as the Greeks did in southern Italy) or fought with the established population for control of their territory (as the Romans were to do over the following centuries). All the main Etruscan cities developed peacefully where there had been longstanding Iron Age communities before them, and there are no signs of violence in the transition.

Nor does the Etruscan language throw any light on the mystery of their origins, since it is related neither to any Italian language nor to any spoken in the East. Although our understanding of how Etruscan works is still far from complete, many of the thousands of surviving inscriptions can be translated.

Whatever their origins, from their earliest appearance the Etruscans were wealthy and technologically adept. The gold treasures buried in their tombs demonstrate a high level of technical skill, as well as their prosperity. Trading widely in the western Mediterranean, the Etruscans also established commercial links with the Phoenicians and other eastern peoples.

By the 6th century B.C., the chief Etruscan cities were allied with Carthage in a trade war with the western Greeks. A series of painted tombs at Tarquinia, one of the richest of the Etruscan cities, reveals the existence there of an aristocratic society with a high standard of living and extravagant tastes. At the same time, Etruscan forces were in control of most of central Italy, including the city of Rome, founded just over a century earlier.

Husband and wife on the lid of an Etruscan sarcophagus from Cerveteri.

Etruscan Rule in Rome

Later Romans, with typical precision, dated the foundation of their city to April 21, 753 B.C., and celebrated the day each year as Rome's birthday. Their own account of the city's origins was intended to provide a worthy ancestor to the mighty Rome of the Empire. In reality, however, at the time the Etruscans occupied Rome—the traditional date is 616 B.C.—it was still little more than a small country town. The "kings" who ruled there were probably more like tribal chiefs, the descendants of those early farmers who collected together on the seven hills near the river Tiber in the mid-8th century B.C.

Under the Etruscans, Rome began to grow and develop. Etruscan engineers drained and paved a large marshy area at the foot of the Palatine and Capitoline hills, which was to become the site of the future Roman Forum, center of the city and of the Empire. Etruscan builders constructed roads and temples, including the Temple of Capitoline Jupiter, destined to become the most important shrine in the Roman world. Etruscan craftsmen taught the locals how to import and work gold, silver, and ivory.

This terra-cotta statue of Apollo stood on the roof of the Etruscan temple at Veii.

Other Etruscan importations into Rome included the alphabet still used today by all Western languages (and many others)—the Etruscans had probably learned it from the Greeks. Some of the customs which became typically Roman, such as public games, chariot racing, and even the wearing of the toga, the most common form of Roman dress, were probably of Etruscan origin.

The greatest of all Etruscan contributions to the Romans, however, was to give them a new and wider outlook on the world. From being villagers living in a small, isolated community, the Romans found that they had become part of an international power with a highly developed culture and connections throughout Italy and the Mediterranean. Within a century, transformed technologically and psychologically, the Romans were ready to repay their conquerors. In 510 B.C. they drove out the Etruscans and began the unrelenting climb to power that was to bring much of the known world under Roman sway.

THE ROMAN REPUBLIC: CLASS AND THE POLITICS OF COMPROMISE

From the early days of Roman history, the population fell into two classes. The kings and ruling class, known as the patricians, formed a kind of self-perpetuating aristocracy based on a closed group of families which intermarried amongst themselves. The vast majority of Romans were plebeians, with no privileges of birth or rank. In the beginning the patricians controlled the resources of land as well as government, but during the time of Etruscan domination growing numbers of plebeian craftsmen and traders began to acquire money.

With the Etruscans expelled, members of successful and ambitious plebeian families were anxious to play a part in running their city, while poorer plebeians wanted to reduce the economic exploitation under which they lived. The republican political system which patricians and plebeians hammered out over the following centuries involved compromise on both sides. Indeed, it was the Roman ability to negotiate compromises between conflicting interests which made possible long-term political stability.

The Roman Republic

The choice of a republican government was due to the Romans' bitter experience of a century of rule by

Bronze portrait of Brutus (?), one of the leaders of the Roman revolt which drove out the Etruscan kings and established the Roman Republic.

Etruscan kings. In 509 B.C. the new state vowed never again to accept royal rule, and drew up a constitution.

In its first form, the system concentrated power in the hands of the patricians. The principal legislative assembly, the Senate, was made up of members of the aristocracy, and the two chief magistrates—the consuls, who were elected annually—were also patricians. Each consul had his own army, to prevent the other one from seizing power, and in time of national crisis one stepped down to let the other serve as *dictator,* or supreme commander, for a maximum term of six months. The Senate's powers included control of finance, state security, and relations with foreign governments. In the case of a decision for war or peace, however, the people were also involved.

The plebeians had their own popular assembly which elected spokesmen known as tribunes; the office of the tribunate was established in 494 B.C. These representatives guarded the plebeians' interests and protected them against injustice on the part of state magistrates. Among the tactics used by the tribunes to obtain their rights was the threat of military strikes. Both assemblies met in the Roman Forum and functioned in the same way. A speaker could address his fellow members only if invited to do so by the presiding magistrate, who at the end of the debate called on those present to vote for or against a proposal under discussion. Blanket acceptance or rejection were the only possibilities.

During the years that followed, the plebeians managed to win an important series of concessions from the aristocracy. The tribunes acquired the right to veto any action by either a magistrate or the Senate, and their person was sacrosanct: anyone killing a tribune was held guilty of a capital crime. In 343 B.C. a new law made it possible for plebeians to stand for election to the consulship, while the succeeding decades opened up all remaining state offices to plebeian candidates. The final plebeian victory came in 287 B.C. with the passage of the Hortensian Law. This made the decisions of the plebeian assembly binding on the Senate and Roman people.

The gradual, peaceful process whereby the two classes reached political agreement was in strong contrast to the often bloody class struggles of the Greek city-states. Writing toward the end of the Republic, the Greek historian Polybius (c. 203–c. 120 B.C.) praised the virtues of what he called a "mixed constitution." The popular assembly represented the democratic element and the Senate the aristocratic, while the powers of the consuls were equivalent to those of a king—except that they held office for only a year. This mixture of political types, according to Polybius, gave Rome the stability necessary for the winning of an empire (his analysis blurs the distinction between Rome's social stratification and its political organization).

In its final form, the Roman constitution was not the product of philosophical theory but the result of years of tough political experience. In the words of Cato, a distinguished senator of the 2nd century B.C., "Our Republic was not made by the work of one man, but of many, not in a single lifetime, but through many generations and centuries."

The Twelve Tables

If the plebeians' eventual political victory depended on a spirit of compromise, it also required the existence of an impartial code of law. In the first years of the Republic, laws were based on custom, and subject to the interpretation of the aristocrats. The plebeians insisted that the state establish a fixed legal code, and a board of ten commissioners was set up to study the laws of other states. The board visited the chief Greek cities of southern Italy, and may even have gone to Athens. The result of their work was a codification of public, private, criminal, and religious law. The popular assembly, after approving the new code in 451 B.C., had it engraved on twelve bronze tablets known as the Twelve Tables, which were set up in the Forum, in full view of all.

The Roman Forum, seen from the Capitoline Hill.

Although Julius Caesar thoroughly overhauled the Law of the Twelve Tables in 46 B.C., he based his new Civil Law upon it, and some of its provisions survived into Byzantine times. Over the centuries, the Romans built up a body of legal opinion aimed at being comprehensive and valid for all times and places. The principle governing it was "equity"—fairness for all. Even today millions of people live in countries whose legal systems ultimately derive from the Roman tradition of law based on the Twelve Tables. In the words of one eminent British judge, "There is not a problem of jurisprudence which Roman law does not touch; there is scarcely a corner of political science on which its light has not fallen."

DIPLOMACY AND WAR: THE ROMANIZATION OF ITALY

During the first two centuries of the Republic, while the Romans were refining their political system at home, they also gradually extended their influence in Italy: by mid-3rd century B.C. they were the dominating power from the Gulf of Genoa to the Straits of Messina.

The Romans and Their Neighbors

Even before the end of Etruscan rule at Rome, the Romans had formed an alliance with the other Latin cities of the region, known as the Latin League, in which they played the dominant role. The expulsion of the Etruscans was a clear signal of Roman strength, and Rome's fellow members of the League tried to shake off the alliance with so forceful a partner. The Romans had no intention of giving up their regional dominance, however. They defeated a combined Latin army and in 493 B.C. the two sides signed a treaty, the text of which has survived. The terms seem equitable: "Let there be peace between the Romans and all the Latin cities so long as heaven and earth are still in the same place." Yet clearly Rome maintained its primacy, and the Roman technique of conquering a rival and then making peace as if between equals was to prove useful on many future occasions.

With the Latins taken care of, the Romans moved on to subdue other local peoples, including the Volscians to the south, before dealing with their true rivals in Italy, the Etruscans. The Etruscan city closest to Rome was Veii, and in 405 B.C. Roman forces began a siege of Veii that was to last for ten years. When the Etruscans finally capitulated, the Romans razed the city to the ground. All trace of Veii disappeared. Only in 1916 did archeologists finally recover magnificent Etruscan sculptures buried under the devastation of 2300 years earlier.

The Gallic Invasion

Before Rome could follow up this initial success, disaster struck. In 390 B.C. bands of plundering Gauls moved south down the Italian peninsula, in search of booty. A Roman army moved north to check their advance at the river Allia, and—for the first time in Rome's

Roman copy of a statue group from Pergamum showing two Gauls: the husband, having killed his wife, commits suicide.

history—suffered a shattering defeat. For centuries to come, the Romans grimly commemorated "the day of the Allia," July 18, 390 B.C. The victorious Gauls pressed on and took Rome itself. Eight hundred years were to pass before the next enemy occupation of the city. Only the payment of a large, and humiliating, tribute persuaded the Gallic invaders to move back north.

Yet even this setback did little more than postpone Rome's conquest of the chief Etruscan cities of central Italy. Within a few years of the Gallic invasion, the Romans were once again on the offensive. Between 353 and 270 B.C., the Romans attacked and either occupied or destroyed the cities of their former rulers, and consolidated their hold on the territory to their north.

The Samnites

To the south, the Romans faced the Samnites, a fierce mountain people who had moved from their homeland in the rugged country of central Italy to occupy Campania, the area around Naples. In a series of hard-fought wars, Roman legionaries, accustomed to fighting on flat land, learned to defeat their enemies on the Samnites' own hilly terrain.

The Samnites proved tougher to subdue than the Etruscans, and in one never-to-be-forgotten battle at the Caudine Forks in 321 B.C. they forced an entire Roman army to surrender. In the end, Roman persistence brought victory. Samnite resistance effectively ended with the signing of a peace treaty in 304 B.C. which—in spite of its diplomatic wording—signaled the confirmation of Roman supremacy in Italy.

A number of factors contributed to Rome's success in winning control of Italy. One was the speed with which the Romans recovered from the Gallic invasion and were able to take advantage of the havoc the Gauls had wrought. Another was continued political stability at Rome itself, which enabled the city to overcome the few serious defeats the Roman army suffered. A third was that same army's fighting efficiency and flexibility. Most important of all, however, was the Romans' policy of being magnanimous in victory. They generally treated their conquered enemies favorably, immediately designating them as "allies," and extending to them the benefits of Rome's growing prosperity. As a result, the victors inspired loyalty in those who, defeated in battle, were then bound to Rome by treaties of friendship and self-interest. The allies were legally independent, but their room for maneuver in foreign affairs was limited, and the Romans generally favored aristocratic local governments where it was possible. Over time, Rome began to play a greater role in the allies' internal affairs. With the essential security at home that this guaranteed, the Romans could face external threats.

Significant Dates

The Rise of Rome (all dates B.C.)

753	Traditional date of foundation of Rome
616–510	Traditional dates of Etruscan rule at Rome
509	Roman Republic inaugurated
493	Treaty with Latin League
451	Law of the Twelve Tables
405–396	Romans besiege Veii
390	Gallic invasion of Italy
304	Romans sign treaty with Samnites
279	Pyrrhus defeats Romans
264–241	First Punic War
218–202	Second Punic War
146	Destruction of Carthage; Roman conquest of Greece

THE PUNIC WARS

Rome's chief rival in the western Mediterranean was Carthage, but before that deadly struggle began, the Romans had to deal with a challenge from the east. One of the northern Greek kingdoms to splinter off from Alexander's empire was Epirus. Its king, Pyrrhus (ruled 306–302, 297–272 B.C.), took advantage of an appeal for protection by Taranto, a Greek city in southern Italy, to invade Italy in the hope of taking over Rome's growing empire there. He succeeded in defeating the Romans in 279 B.C., but the battle caused such heavy losses in his own army that "a pyrrhic victory" became proverbial for one gained at too great a cost. His rueful departure home signaled Rome's first success against an outside invader, while leaving the Romans in control of all the Greek city-states in southern Italy.

The Carthaginians and the First Punic War (264–241 B.C.)

The next opponent presented a far more serious challenge. As the Roman poet Lucretius put it 200 years later, the Roman conflict with Carthage was the Great War—"the struggle for universal empire by land and sea."

Carthage was the richest city in the western Mediterranean, founded around 800 B.C. by Phoenician colonists (see Part I, Topic 4). The Roman name for the Phoenicians, *Poeni* or *Puni,* came to be used for the wars fought against the Carthaginians. With a superb natural harbor in the Gulf of Tunis, the Carthaginians had control of both the eastern and western Mediterranean. In the east, Carthage's trading partners included Egypt and the cities of Asia Minor, while to the west Carthaginian merchants controlled business in Sardinia and Corsica. Their commercial empire stretched even farther. By 500 B.C., Carthaginian explorers had reached as far south as Sierra Leone, and perhaps to the mouth of the river Congo, and to the north, beyond the Strait of Gibraltar, the Bay of Biscay was within their reach.

If Rome was to continue its economic expansion, a clash between the leading commercial power of the day and the rising force in Italy was inevitable. The immediate cause was a Carthaginian attempt to head off Roman expansion by gaining control of the Strait of Messina. Lying between the tip of Italy and Sicily, the straits were crucial to communication between the eastern and western Mediterranean. In 264 B.C., with the Senate hesitant whether to risk a conflict, the popular assembly at Rome belligerently voted to send a fleet to Sicily to break the Carthaginian grip there. The First Punic War had begun.

An initial success brought the Romans their first major victory at sea, but Carthage fought back, in a series of naval battles which proved to be among the bloodiest ever fought in the ancient world. In 256 B.C. the Romans tried to cut the conflict short by landing an army in North Africa and striking directly at Carthage, but the bold move failed, the army was defeated, and its commander Regulus humiliatingly captured.

In the end, Roman persistence paid off. They besieged the Carthaginians' stronghold in western Sicily, Lilybaeum, by land and sea. The siege lasted eight years, and saw the Carthaginian garrison ingeniously countering the Roman blockade. The Roman admiral Claudius rashly attacked a Carthaginian fleet when even the divine omens counseled caution. Hearing that the sacred chickens refused to eat, he retorted, "Then let them drink," and had them thrown into the sea. A later Roman fleet was wrecked on Sicily's rocky southern coast.

After further violent fighting around western Sicily, with the Romans throwing all their resources into strengthening their fleet, an uneasy peace finally came in 241 B.C. Rome was able to dictate the terms. The Carthaginians had to withdraw from Sicily and pay a heavy indemnity. Western Sicily became the first Roman province (Roman territory outside mainland Italy). Neither side was under any illusion, however, that hostilities were over. The Romans' victory, and their seizure of Corsica and Sardinia after Carthage had surrendered, left the Carthaginians weakened and mortified, but thirsting for revenge.

The Second Punic War (218–202 B.C.)

Sicily had provided the immediate cause for the first round of hostilities. Spain proved the excuse for the second. In the years following their defeat, the Carthaginians strengthened their position in the western Mediterranean by conquering territory in southeastern Spain, gaining access to Spanish copper mines and adding Spanish troops to their already formidable army.

With the Romans on the point of intervening to drive Carthaginian forces out of Spain, Hannibal (247–183/2 B.C.), the brilliant Carthaginian military commander, decided to strike first. The Romans controlled the sea, but they were still vulnerable on land. Furthermore, if the Carthaginians attacked Italy directly, there was a chance that some of Rome's recent Italian "allies" might take the chance to turn on their new masters and throw their support behind Hannibal.

So, in April 218 B.C., Hannibal led his army across to Spain and southern France. Later that summer the Carthaginian forces, which included a herd of elephants—the secret weapons which had so scared Alexander's troops a century earlier—crossed the Alps into northern Italy. The Romans, confident on their

Coin showing one of Hannibal's elephants.

home ground, sent forces to block the Carthaginian advance, but they were unprepared for Hannibal's strategic genius in battle. Three times—at the rivers Ticinus and Trebia in 218 B.C., and at Lake Trasimene early in 217 B.C.—Hannibal's army routed the Romans. The last defeat was the worst of all. In the fighting around Trasimene, two Roman legions fell, together with their commanders, and the lake ran red with Roman blood.

Never before had Rome come so close to disaster as Hannibal moved south, bypassing the capital itself to find fresh supplies in the rich farmland of Campania and hoping to win allies in southern Italy. In the summer of 216 B.C. the two sides faced off again at Cannae in Apulia, and Hannibal scored his greatest triumph yet. At first Hannibal's battle line gave way under Roman pressure, only to close around the Roman attackers, leaving them no room to fight. The Carthaginian cavalry, having put the Roman horses to flight, then attacked the Roman foot soldiers from the rear, completing the rout. Of the 50,000 Roman troops, only 10,000 escaped. Twenty-five thousand died, and the rest were taken prisoner. Centuries later the Romans still remembered the peril of those times, and nursemaids would scare the children in their charge by threatening them that "Hannibal will come and get you."

The Romans could not know it, but the worst was over. Two factors worked in their favor: time and numbers. The longer Hannibal fought so far from home, the weaker his supplies and fewer his men became. In addition, one of Hannibal's gambles failed to pay off, as Rome's allies in central Italy remained loyal. The war ground on for 14 more years, but Rome doggedly resisted the Carthaginians in Italy while fighting their forces in Spain more aggressively. As the end seemed in sight, Scipio (236–184 B.C.), the Romans' brilliant young commander, took the fight back on to Carthaginian territory. In the last, terrible battle at Zama in North Africa in 202 B.C., Hannibal, the old lion, led his Carthaginian army to defeat against Scipio. The war was over.

For Carthage, the peace was scarcely less devastating. Fearful of a repeat, the Romans imposed brutal terms. The Carthaginians had to disband their navy and give up all their foreign possessions, and pay yet another huge indemnity. All that remained of their former greatness was the city of Carthage itself and the land around.

Yet even this proved too much for the Romans to tolerate. The so-called Third Punic War of 149–146 B.C. was nothing more than an extended Roman siege of Carthage, its citizens driven by desperation to hopeless resistance. When the end came in 146 B.C., the Romans burned the city, wrecked what remained standing, plowed up the ground, and sowed salt to prevent anything ever growing there again. They sold into slavery any inhabitants unlucky enough to have survived.

The end of the Second Punic War in 202 B.C. left Rome the dominating power in the west, taking over control in North Africa, Spain, and southern France. By the time of the destruction of Carthage in 146 B.C., the Romans were well on the way to extending their empire to Asia.

THE ANNEXATION OF THE EASTERN MEDITERRANEAN

The three great powers of the eastern Mediterranean were the successor kingdoms formed at the death of Alexander: Syria (all that was left of Seleucus' original Asian kingdom), Egypt, and Macedon. A few smaller states had managed to preserve their independence and even play a role in relations between the leading powers. The two most important of these were the maritime republic of Rhodes, leader in the battle against pirates in the eastern Mediterranean, and the kingdom of Pergamum. With its abundant agricultural production and rich mineral resources, Pergamum, in northeastern Asia Minor, was a leading cultural center in the Hellenistic world.

The Romans Move East

The Romans' first brush with Macedon came in 200 B.C., when they accepted a plea for help from the Greek city-states against the Macedonian king Philip V (ruled 221–179 B.C.). The Roman forces drove Philip out of Greece and then, to everyone's surprise, withdrew back to Italy.

The delay was only temporary. The Macedonians, warned by the example of Carthage, began to strengthen their forces and repair relations with the Greeks, only to be plunged into a full-scale war with Rome in 171 B.C. Roman victory was followed a few years later in 148 B.C. by the conversion of the former kingdom of Macedon into an imperial province under direct rule from Rome.

In 146 B.C.—the same year in which Carthage was destroyed—there occurred a turning point in the history of the ancient world. A Roman army under Lucius Mummius attacked Greece itself, and devastated Corinth, the richest city there. As at Carthage, the Romans killed most of the men and sold into slavery the rest of the population. Mummius, whose name was to become a byword for wanton brutality, carried off or sold shiploads of precious masterpieces of art, and Greece ended up as part of the province of Macedon. The military triumph was slight, but for Greece's city-states the sack of Corinth ended their hundreds of years of independence.

The message was not lost on the rulers of the remaining Hellenistic kingdoms, who were having trouble enough defending themselves against one another. Attalus III of Pergamum (ruled 138–133 B.C.) made the best of a bad job, and bequeathed his kingdom to Rome on his death.

It required no more massive military actions for Rome to become the dominating influence over Syria and Egypt, merely astute diplomacy to keep the two on the defensive. The effect on Syria was to erode its already shaky unity, and by the end of the 2nd century B.C. Seleucus' once formidable kingdom was fragmented into a series of mini-states. The Romans let Egypt retain a nominal independence as a threat to any potential troublemakers, but exploited the abundant Egyptian grain supplies to feed the population back in Rome. Octavian completed Egypt's subjugation in 30 B.C., by officially annexing it as his personal estate.

The she-wolf, symbol of Rome.

The Romans were right to see Carthage as their most formidable enemy. The struggle to defeat the Carthaginians was by far the toughest in their history, and their victory radically changed the political landscape in the ancient world. Even before the Roman successes in the East, the balance of power between East and West was shifting.

By contrast with their ferocious wars with Carthage, Roman supremacy in the East seems to have come about with comparative ease. One reason was that the Romans, tried by defeat and near disaster, had learned the rewards of dogged persistence. Another was that the naked brutality of the destruction of Carthage and Corinth brought horrified condemnation from Rome's contemporaries, but taught a lesson that was all too obvious. It was suicide to resist Roman determination, and after 146 B.C. no one did.

In 241 B.C., at the end of the First Punic War, Rome was still only the leading state in a relatively obscure part of the Mediterranean. Within a century she was the world's first superpower. The following years were to bring battles of a different kind, as forces within Rome itself clashed, and two bitter civil wars brought the Republic crashing down.

Questions for Further Study

1. What were the chief characteristics of Etruscan culture? Which of them—if any—influenced the development of Roman civilization?
2. How did Rome's political system evolve? Which factors helped to make it successful?
3. What were the main stages in Rome's expansion in the western Mediterranean? Which military strategies proved decisive in the defeat of the Carthaginians?

Suggestions for Further Reading

Beard, M., and M. Crawford. *Rome in the Late Republic*. Ithaca, NY, 1985.
Boardman, J., J. Griffin, and O. Murray. *The Roman World*. New York, 1988.
Crawford, M. *The Roman Republic*. Cambridge, MA, 1982.
Grant, M. *The Etruscans*. New York, 1981.
Gruen, E. S. *The Hellenistic World and the Coming of Rome*. Berkeley, 1984.
Keaveny, A. *Rome and the Unification of Italy*. London, 1988.

II

Topic 8

Romans of the Republic

By the mid-2nd century B.C. virtually the entire Mediterranean world was to some degree subject to Roman influence. With the growth of their territory, the Romans devised ways of organizing and administering the subject provinces outside Italy. As in the slow evolution of their own political system, Rome's ruling classes worked out their approaches to provincial governors and their duties—to taxation, and the ever-present problems of bribery and corruption—by trial and error.

Meanwhile, at Rome itself, the years following the Punic Wars saw radical changes in economic patterns as large estates, or *latifundia*, replaced small farms, and industry and commerce began to provide the principal source of wealth. As banking, insurance, and investment programs spread, the rise of a new business class changed old established patterns of social relations.

One of the areas affected by shifting class lines was the family. By the late Republic, as money was no longer concentrated in the hands of the patricians, birth was no longer the prime factor in the choice of a marriage partner. With the general improvement in standards of living, girls from the families of businessmen received a better education, and well-to-do women began to lead relatively independent lives, although their progress aroused criticism and mysogyny. A number were distinguished authors while others were famous for their oratory.

The chief intellectual influence on the late Republic was Greece. Even before the sack of Corinth in 146 B.C., the Romans looked to the Greeks for guidance in art and philosophy. By the 1st century B.C. educated Roman women and men regarded Greek culture as superior to their own. Traditional Roman religion continued to serve the interests of the state, while Hellenistic philosophical systems such as Stoicism and Epicureanism provided more individual enlightenment. Large numbers of the urban masses, impressed neither by philosophy nor by the rituals of power, turned to dramatic and emotional cults introduced from Asia.

The same Greek influences came to dominate Roman literature of the period. Plautus and Terence based their comic plays on Greek originals. The epic poetry of Lucretius set out to expound Epicureanism to a Roman audience. One field in which Roman writers found their own authentic voice was that of intimate, personal love poetry, through which writers like Catullus analyzed the nature of love. At the very end of the Republic, the great orator Cicero, although openly acknowledging the influence of the Greek statesman Demosthenes, composed (and generally delivered) some of the most powerful and eloquent speeches in the Western tradition.

THE TRIALS OF PROVINCIAL ADMINISTRATION

The Romans continued to describe the peoples they conquered in Italy as "allies," whose independence was limited by their obligations (legal and financial) to Rome. Outside Italy, some territories were called "protectorates," or "client states," theoretically self-ruling but in practice bound to Rome by treaties in which they were the inferior partners. Macedon occupied this status for some 20 years, before becoming a province, and Egypt remained a client kingdom until the time of Julius Caesar. The reigning pharaoh was the nominal head of state, but powerless to oppose Roman wishes.

The rest of Rome's overseas territories were provinces, administered directly by a representative of the Senate and Roman people. Roman writers of the Republic regularly described the citizens of the provinces as people who had surrendered to and were therefore at the disposal of the Roman state, with no rights of their own, and with the obligation to pay for the occupying troops who had conquered them. Even as enlightened an observer as Cicero referred to the provinces as "the estates of the Roman people."

The Provincial Governor and His Staff

The head of each province's administration was the governor. Usually a magistrate sent out from Rome, and receiving no pay, the governor was in charge of the day-to-day running of his province, as well as functioning as its military commander and chief justice. He had the right to introduce new laws when he thought it necessary. As commander-in-chief, he was responsible for internal order as well as defense against outside attack. As chief law enforcer, he was required to hear all cases involving Roman citizens, and all other important cases. In order to do this, he traveled on fixed "circuits" within his province, hearing trials in the chief cities.

In theory, governors served for one year, and then returned to their duties in Rome, but—as the number of provinces grew—the Senate tended to renew a magistrate's mandate. The acts and decrees of a governor were valid only for his term of office, but his successors rarely undid or revised a predecessor's decisions. Over time, a body of policies, laws, and edicts from the provinces began to accumulate. The material was kept available in the office of the urban magistrate at Rome, and newly appointed governors would consult the files before taking up their post.

Most governors had a chief assistant, who was also appointed annually in Rome (the governor of Sicily had two chief assistants). Known as the *quaestor*, he was in charge of financial matters, accounting for income and expenditures. The quaestor's ability to limit his superior's tendency to exploit the provincials depended on the relationship the two established. Perhaps as a result, governors encouraged their assistants to regard them "as a son does his father."

The Pont du Gard, a Roman aqueduct near Nîmes in southern France. The bridge was built in the late 1st century B.C., and is still functional.

The Senate chose both the governor and his deputy. The governor himself could select his aides, or *legati*, although the Senate had to ratify his selections. The aides helped in the administration, and could represent the governor in his absence. It was customary for the team also to include some *comites*, "companions," young men from good families in search of experience and adventure, with the added possibility of making some money.

Taxation in the Provinces

The original justification for the taxes imposed on the provincials was to cover the cost to Rome of their conquest, but over time the Romans came to look on the funds raised by taxation as income from property which by now belonged to Rome, and was being "rented" by its inhabitants. Only under the emperors did administrators claim that taxes actually paid for the running and defense of the provinces.

The tax generally took the form of either a fixed annual sum, or a percentage of a province's annual income or agricultural produce. In the case of the former, collection was easy and each community handed over its share to the quaestor. In the latter case, where each year's income fluctuated and therefore had to be assessed to decide how much was due, the state contracted out the collection to tax farmers, or *publicani*. The tax farmers bid against one another for contracts, hoping to bid enough to beat their rivals, but sufficiently little for the sum they actually collected to leave them with a handsome profit.

Over time the system led predictably to abuses. The problem lay not so much in the way the money was collected but in the misuse of office by many of the governors. The internal political structure of Rome depended on a careful series of checks and balances which permitted control of the acts of individual administrators. By contrast, a provincial governor was the equivalent of a king, unchallenged on his territory, and answerable only to the Roman Senate, a long way off and in any case more likely to sympathize with "one of their own" than with complaining provincials.

Over time, the tax farmers tended to work for companies, or *societates*, at Rome, which were mainly interested in getting a good return on their investments. The businessmen running the companies would often use their influence with prominent members of the Roman Senate to put pressure on provincial administrators—either to turn a blind eye to cases of extortion, or even to take a part of the profits for themselves.

Victims sometimes appealed to Rome, and the Senate established standing juries to hear cases of maladministration, but the juries became as corrupt as the businessmen and politicians involved in the tax scandals. One of the few cases to reach trial in court was Cicero's prosecution of the former governor of Sicily, Gaius Verres (115–43 B.C.) in 70 B.C. The charges were extortion, embezzlement, looting of works of art, bribery and corruption, and general misgovernment over three years. Cicero prepared six speeches, but after the first blasting oration, Verres fled to France, taking most of his loot with him.

Portrait bust of Cicero, Roman lawyer and politician, fierce opponent of Caesar and, later, Mark Antony.

On the whole, the justice or injustice of a provincial administration depended on the character of each individual governor. Serving for only a short term, with no adequate control by the central government, irresponsible or corrupt ones could virtually act as they pleased. The abuse was very great, and we hear of several who did.

THE ROMAN ECONOMY: LAND TENURE, TRADE, AND CLASS

Agriculture in Italy during the first three centuries of the Republic was mainly in the hands of farmers living in country villages and working their own small parcels of land. The Punic Wars produced devastating changes to this pattern of rural life. In the first place, many farmers and agricultural laborers ended up in the army, and never came home. The level of casualties in battle was frequently staggering: just in

Hannibal's first three victories of 218–217 B.C., over 100,000 Roman soldiers died. Secondly, those who did live to return to their villages often found them destroyed and abandoned as a result of Hannibal's campaigns in Italy. During the years of travel up and down the peninsula, the Carthaginian army ravaged the communities that refused to collaborate, while Roman troops later took reprisals against those that did provide aid to the invaders.

The Latifundia

By the time peace returned to Italy, large tracts of land lay abandoned. Many of them were confiscated by the state, and sold or rented to those who had made fortunes in trading or selling war supplies, and were looking for a way to invest their new income. The farmers of the prewar years, with their small landholdings, cultivated grain, but this had little appeal for the new "agri-businessmen." The profit margin was slim, and in any case the newly acquired provinces provided an abundant supply of cheap grain.

The landowners who purchased large estates turned instead to cattle ranching, since both meat and dairy products were in great demand at Rome, or to the planting of vines and olive trees: good quality wine and olive oil fetched high prices. Both types of farming required large landholdings and were labor-intensive. The land was already available, and the vast numbers of slaves taken as prisoners in the course of the wars were cheap and expendable. In some cases, the former owners of small landholdings stayed on to work the land as hired help.

Thus, in one generation, the agricultural customs of centuries disappeared, and the working of the latifundia went to enrich wealthy politicians and businessmen who rarely set foot on their properties and whose only concern was profit. Although northern Italy was less affected by the exploitation, many parts of the south were seriously overfarmed, and massive programs of deforestation caused soil erosion and the formation of malarial swamps. The land exploitation left scars throughout Italy, especially in the south, that were to last for centuries.

Meanwhile the peasants, having lost their source of work, drifted to the city, attracted by tales of the fortunes to be made there. By the end of the Second Punic War, Rome was drawing rapidly increasing crowds of immigrants: farmworkers from rural Italy, returning veterans whose campaigning abroad had given them a taste for excitement, tradesmen and craftsmen from other parts of the Empire attracted by the possibilities the market offered. At the same time the numbers of slaves working in the capital rose sharply, many of whom eventually obtained their freedom. The result of all these changes was to produce, for the first time in the ancient world, a huge urban proletariat, destined to play an important role in the collapse of the Republic in the 1st century B.C.

Manufacturing and Trade

Rome's origins were rustic, and even with the city swollen to vast proportions Roman poets and writers looked back nostalgically to the times when their forebears had been farmers and shepherds. Perhaps as a result, manufacturing was never popular in the capital. The Romans preferred to develop regional centers of

Painting of a Roman garden with fruit trees.

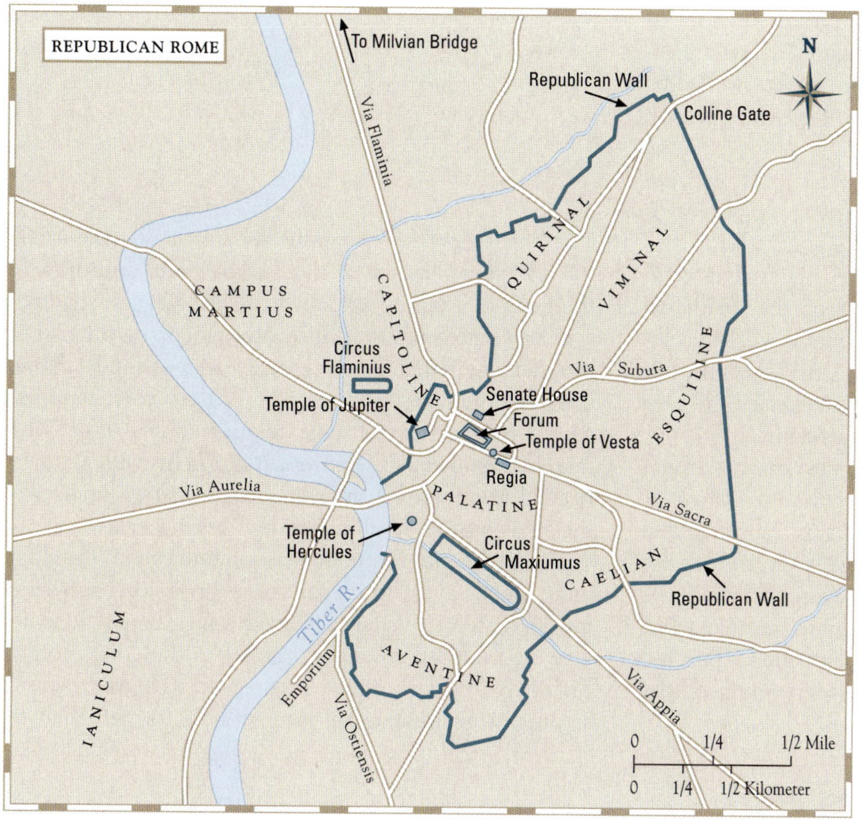

Map 8.1 Republican Rome

production. The former Etruscan lands continued to manufacture bronze and iron objects and cloth. Campania, the center of rich farmland, turned out farm and household implements, and rope. The production of weapons remained based in central Italy, within reach of Rome and the politicians.

If Roman businessmen were unwilling to soil their hands with the actual process of manufacture, they were only too happy to put their money to work. Shareholders invested in companies that then put in bids for public contracts: road building, feeding and transport of troops, construction of new law courts. Other companies imported luxury goods from the provinces, for which there was an insatiable demand at Rome. Still others ran transport firms—by land and sea—to deal with the growth in trade. The result of all these developments was to create jobs for the urban poor: stevedores, storehouse keepers, roadworkers.

As the circulation of money increased, other forms of financial institutions arose to fill the need. Banking became international, as houses established branches in several different countries. Although Roman currency circulated widely, many of the Asian markets preferred to use gold for buying and selling, and some Greek cities chose to keep their own coinage. The result was the appearance of exchange offices to handle currency conversion.

The formation of credit and loan institutions met another need. At first the chief clients were businessmen in need of help with their cash flow, but the lending institutions also provided credit to cities in the provinces which could not pay the annual tribute due to Rome. These loans, made outside Italy at interest rates that were often shockingly high, provided investors with extremely profitable returns.

The Rise of the Business Classes

The effect of all these rapid economic changes was the gradual but inexorable erosion of Rome's system of political and social balance. In the new postwar climate, the old compromise worked out between patricians and plebeians had to take account of an additional political

Roman *denarius* coined during the Second Punic War.

force, the prosperous business class created by the increase in commerce. As many of the middle-class businessmen saw their fortunes grow even larger, swelled by the commercial boom, they began to lobby for political recognition.

Centuries earlier, one of the ways for a plebeian to rise above his humble origins was to volunteer to provide his own horse (an expensive undertaking) and serve in the cavalry. Such men styled themselves *equites*, or horsemen—the equivalent of the Medieval knights. By the 2nd century B.C., many wealthy plebeians could buy and sell horses by the thousands, but the term "equites" remained in use to describe the new class of self-made men and their descendants.

For the old established patrician families, these "new men" at first remained no more than wealthy plebeians, to be excluded from the highest social order. Over time, however, as intermarriage began to blur the lines, the new "equestrian order" played a growing role in factional politics, and both patricians and plebeians vied for their support. Like the urban mob, they too were to play a crucial role in the unraveling of the Republic.

WOMEN AND THE FAMILY IN A PATRIARCHAL SOCIETY

The head of a Roman family was its eldest male—the *pater familias*, "father of the family." The authority of the head of a family extended to all males, of whatever age, and ended only on his death, when the others became emancipated. In the early history of the Republic custody of females, on the death of their pater familias, passed to the nearest male relative, unless the dying man had named a different guardian in his will. Women needed the approval of their guardian when undertaking a business deal, selling land, or freeing a slave.

By the late Republic, as women began to lead far more open lives, many of these provisions were no longer in force. When a woman's guardian refused to give his consent, she could appeal to the courts to get his veto waived or to have him replaced. In many cases, serving as guardian gave more trouble to men than to

Mother Earth with two children, symbol of fertility and abundance. From the *Ara Pacis*, 13–9 B.C.

women, and prosperous women of the late Republic often ran large households without ever consulting an adviser. By the reign of Augustus, the first emperor, the law reflected the reality of women's status: any woman with three children was exempt from the need for a protector.

Marriage and Power

Roman marriage customs differed in significant ways from those of Classical Greece. In the first place, both bride and groom were usually around the same age, around 14, and were generally not close relatives, although among the elite marriage alliances between cousins were fairly common. In early Republican times there were two forms of marriage. The first gave the husband power over his wife. Under the second, which came to be predominant, a wife did not pass under her husband's control at marriage; she remained under the authority of her pater familias. The practical effect of this was to give a woman more freedom, answerable as she was not to the man with whom she lived, but to one residing in a different house and sometimes in a different town or country. Furthermore, a woman who could easily return to her father's household was less likely to put up with ill-treatment.

A marriage could take place only with the consent of both partners, but the woman had to prove that her prospective husband was "morally unfit" in order for her to escape the match. A father generally, but not always, picked his daughter's husband, generally in consultation with her mother. Cicero found his daughter's first two husbands, but she selected her third herself, with her mother's help, while her father was away—Cicero grumbled, and threatened not to pay the dowry, but in the end gave way. A woman whose father lived far off or was dead could also find her own husband.

In the highest ranks of Roman society both marriage and divorce served as means of financial and political alliance. At the end of the Republic, both Julius Caesar and Octavian (the future Emperor Augustus) used marriage to gain the favor of a political opponent. Caesar betrothed his daughter to his rival Pompey, while Octavian broke one engagement to make another with the stepdaughter of Mark Antony (which he also later broke), and Mark Antony married Octavian's sister.

At the other end of the social scale, lower-class men often married slave women, whom they had to free beforehand. In some cases masters freed their slaves and subsequently married them to make children previously born to the couple free and legitimate. Roman women sometimes freed a male slave to marry him, but this was generally frowned upon.

Divorce was common among middle- and upper-class couples, and could be initiated by either partner. No legal reason was necessary, but divorce was generally for political or personal motives. One husband of the late Republic recorded in a funerary inscription at his wife's death that years earlier she had offered to divorce him, because she was unable to bear children, and was willing to live with him as his sister while he took a new wife. Forty-three years later, when she died, he affectionately recalled turning down her offer, and choosing a life shared with her over marrying another woman and having descendants.

Women in Society

The Romans were themselves aware of the differences between the lifestyles of Greek and Roman women. As the late Republican writer Cornelius Nepos (c. 99–c. 24 B.C.) succinctly put it, "Greek women sit secluded in the interior parts of the house, while ours accompany their husbands to dinner parties." Not only did many upper-class Romans regard education as important for both men and women, but successful middle-class families sometimes hired tutors for both sons and daughters, while it was not unusual for the daughters of plebeian fathers to attend elementary school.

For some Romans, education, far from bringing censure, only served to enhance a woman's charms. One writer praises Cornelia, Julius Caesar's wife, because she was well read, could play the lyre, and was well trained in geometry and philosophy, while Quintilian (c. A.D. 30–c. 100), the leading Roman expert on education, recommended that both parents

The baker and his wife at Pompeii.

should be as highly educated as possible, for the good of their children.

By the end of the Republic, some of the more sophisticated women-about-town were becoming famous for their love affairs with writers and public figures. Poets such as Catullus, Ovid, and Propertius address their mistresses in their poetry. Propertius' beloved herself wrote verse, he tells us, the equal of the Archaic Greek poet Corinna, and another woman poet of the day, Sulpicia, wrote an elegy in praise of her lover Cerinthus. Some of the glamorous and intellectual women of the age initiated a custom which proved highly important in women's intellectual history: the literary "salon," where men and women could meet and exchange ideas. On the other hand, the increasing prominence of a handful of upper-class women provoked a backlash of considerable criticism and scorn, including predictable bursts of mysogyny, on the part of many Roman males.

Greek women poets, although rare, were not unknown. The notion of a woman orator would probably have horrified an ancient Athenian, but there were a number of famous and admired Roman women who spoke in public. One of the speeches of Hortensia, the daughter of Cicero's rival Hortensius, which has survived in a Greek translation, was highly praised by Quintilian. The custom also developed at the end of the 2nd century B.C. of men pronouncing a flattering speech, or encomium, at the death of a distinguished woman. In 68 B.C. Julius Caesar won considerable public approval for delivering an encomium on the death of his first wife, Cornelia. These examples, however, were exceptional. In general, those women who rose above an elementary level of education, or distinguished themselves in some area of public life, aroused suspicion and often hostility.

Although there were distinct limits to the freedom of Roman upper-class women, there were a number of ways in which they could influence the society and politics of their times—and frequently did. They could not vote or hold office, but they could endorse candidates, exercise patronage, be public benefactors, and have buildings and statues erected in their honor. The importance of some women of the elite was such that if their private behavior went too far beyond the accepted norm, they might suffer social ostracism or even, in extreme cases, banishment—Augustus himself banished his granddaughter for her involvement in a scandal which he subsequently hushed up, because of the important public status of the female members of his family.

The relative increase in the areas of life open to women by the end of the Republic was almost entirely limited to those from elite families, and met with considerable resistance. Yet at least some Roman women had choices. In general, the lives of upper-class women were conditioned as much by their family, income, social status, and physical and intellectual gifts as by their gender. Dining out with their husbands or lovers, going to parties, attending performances in the theater or stadium, taking part in political gatherings, elite women of the late Republic had greater freedom than most women before their times, and many after.

RELIGION AND PHILOSOPHY: GREEK IDEAS IN ROMAN FORMS

The early Romans shared the religious beliefs of many of their Italian neighbors. Like the Samnites, the Oscans, and other Italic peoples, they worshiped a series of nature spirits, many of whom were connected with agriculture. With the foundation of the Republic, the state began to adapt traditional religious practices to the needs of official ritual, and throughout Roman history the central government used religion and ceremonial to reinforce its authority. As Roman society became increasingly urban, however, the country spirits of its early rural days seemed less and less relevant to the experience and needs of its citizens. As a result, the Romans always remained open to other forms of belief, exploring the cults and philosophical ideas of the peoples with whom they came into contact. At the same time, the official, public forms of religious observance served the political aims of the state, rather than the spiritual needs of its citizens.

Growing awareness of Greek religion led the Romans to identify their own supernatural spirits with the Greek gods and goddesses in human form. The narrative element in Greek mythology appealed to writers and artists, who produced their own versions of the age-old stories of the gods' loves and squabbles. Yet the tales provided entertainment rather than spiritual consolation, and the search for deeper emotional satisfaction led many ordinary Romans to turn to cults imported from Asia.

In 204 B.C., the state officially introduced into Rome the worship of Cybele, a form of the Great Mother Goddess, whose chief shrines had been in Lydia and Phrygia (both now part of modern Turkey). The purpose was to win the help of the goddess in driving Hannibal out of Italy. Once arrived, she stayed. The ecstatic and colorful celebrations in her honor, which often involved orgiastic rites, drew large numbers of enthusiastic devotees among the poorer classes at

Rome, seeking distraction from the social upheaval surrounding them. The cult of Cybele retained its grip on the popular imagination for centuries, in spite of various official attempts to limit its wilder manifestations, including self-castration.

Hellenistic Philosophy at Rome

Many Roman intellectuals found an explanation of the mysteries of life in Greek philosophy, in particular the schools developed during the Hellenistic Age (see Part II, Topic 6). As power in the Mediterranean shifted westwards toward Italy, increasing numbers of Greek philosophers and teachers found their way to Rome in search of patrons and students. By the end of the 2nd century B.C., their ideas circulated widely in Roman society.

The two main schools of Hellenistic thought, Stoicism and Epicureanism, each found enthusiastic followers, although Epicureanism's philosophy of seeking active withdrawal from life's battles never really appealed to the practical Roman temperament. The late Republican poet Lucretius (c. 95–c. 55 B.C.) composed a lengthy work, *On the Nature of Things*, aimed at converting his contemporaries to the Epicurean view of the world. On the whole, however, the majority of Romans continued to think of it as an alien system, mainly of interest to intellectuals, while some Roman aristocrats used Epicureanism as an excuse for wanton self-indulgence.

Stoicism, with its clarion call to duty, made a broader appeal, especially to soldiers and public servants. Furthermore, the Stoics' belief in the force of reason, which animated all living things, fitted more comfortably with ancient Italian nature cults, while the notion of Stoic behavior—virtuous, grave, impervious to obstacles—reinforced the Romans' sense of their own historical role as world leaders. Moral fortitude and trust in Divine Providence fitted in well with the austerity of the founding fathers of the Republic.

The Sceptical philosophers also had their adherents. Their belief that truth was unknowable, and their constant questioning of conventional attitudes, attracted lawyers and jurists who were themselves in search of clarification and interpretation.

Along with philosophy, Greek literature and art also found a new and enthusiastic audience at Rome. For all the barbarity of Mummius' looting of Corinth, the conquest of Greece and the shipping home of its treasures brought the Romans into contact with actual Greek bronzes and marbles on a scale hitherto unknown. The first reaction was uncritical admiration. Only with time did Roman artists feel able to make their own contribution to the Classical tradition (see Part II, Topic 11).

THE LITERATURE OF THE ROMAN REPUBLIC

Even before their conquests in the East, the Romans were well acquainted with Greek literature. As Roman writers began to lay the foundations of their own literary tradition, they turned to Greek models. Later ages regarded Ennius (239–169 B.C.) as the "father of Roman poetry." Most of his works are lost, but it is clear that Ennius borrowed his forms from the Greeks, adapting his tragedies from Greek ones and using Greek meters for his most celebrated work, the *Annals*. This was an epic chronicle of the early history of Rome, aimed at providing his fellow Romans with a Latin equivalent of the heroic tradition of Homer.

For all the awe in which his contemporaries held Ennius, they preferred comedy to tragedy, and the first successful popular writers were the comic dramatists Plautus (c. 254–184 B.C.) and Terence (c. 195–159 B.C.). Of the two, Plautus is the more boisterous, Terence more sophisticated, but both drew on the same

Hallway of one of the large and sumptuously decorated houses at Herculaneum.

sources—urbane Greek comedies of the Hellenistic Age—and adapted them to Roman taste.

Roman Love Poetry of the Late Republic: Catullus

By the 1st century B.C., Roman poets were using the forms of Greek love poetry, many of which went back to the 6th century B.C., to relate to their own contemporary world. In lyrics that are at the same time intimate in their revelations and universal in the emotions they express, Roman poets cast an entirely new light on an age of social turmoil.

The poet Catullus (c. 84–c. 54 B.C.) was born at Verona. When he came to Rome around 62 B.C., he was able to see the hectic life of the capital with an outsider's eyes, and he passes on his impressions to us with delighted eagerness: the dinner guests who rob their hosts, the pretty wives who make fools of their pompous husbands, whispered scandals, the white-toothed smiles of a corrupt politician.

When Catullus arrived in Rome, the most famous woman there was Clodia (1st century B.C.), the central figure in most of the gossip of the day. Her brother (and, it was rumored, lover) Clodius was a notorious gang leader, involved in open warfare with his rival Milo. Meanwhile, with her husband absent on duty in Gaul as governor, Clodia could pursue her own amorous interests with relative freedom. As Catullus began to move in Roman high society, the young provincial's freshness and cynicism were of little defense against her charms—after all, even the staid Cicero was struck by her alluring brown eyes. A series of 25 or so lyrics written by Catullus over the course of the next couple of years charts the course—perhaps based on personal experience—of one of the poet's love affairs.

In addressing his beloved in the poems (perhaps Clodia), Catullus used the name Lesbia, thereby invoking the memory of one of the greatest Greek love poets of the Archaic age, Sappho (who came from Lesbos). At the same time he used verse forms created and popularized at Alexandria in the Hellenistic period, blending the Archaic and Hellenistic traditions to produce his own individual voice.

Catullus' poems describe the various phases of love: blind passion, the dawn of mistrust, disillusion, and final despairing hatred—the moods range from "My darling, let us live and love for ever" to his frantic railing at "Rome's prostitute." Many of the poems of the few years remaining to him after the composition of these earlier works describe the hectic travels in the East in which he sought distraction, but in the end only his secluded villa on Lake Garda, near Verona, brought peace.

In the years following the Punic Wars, the Romans of the Republic lived through external growth and internal upheaval. Social and economic patterns that had lasted for centuries shifted beyond recovery. It took two centuries for Rome to become the dominating power in Italy, a region out of the mainstream of Mediterranean politics and culture. With the passing of only a few more years, the Romans ruled the Mediterranean world, the successors to Alexander the Great.

In developing their system of external rule, Roman administrators had to work out a way of transforming violent conquest into firm and effective rule. In many cases, the Romans' outbursts of arrogant brutality—as at Carthage and Corinth—provoked widespread indignation.

Internally, the acquisition of empire imposed strains on the fabric of life and politics at Rome itself which led to violent change. In 133 B.C., the year in which Attalus, the prudent king of Pergamum, willed his kingdom to the Roman people, the first ominous signals appeared of the impending collapse of the Republic.

Questions for Further Study

1. What were the main characteristics of Roman provincial administration, and how did they evolve? How efficient were they?
2. What part did economic development play in Rome's growth? What was its effect on social patterns?
3. How did the role of upper-class women in the late Republic differ from that of women in Classical Athens? What were its limitations?
4. What contribution did Republican writers make to Latin literature? How original was it?

Suggestions for Further Reading

Alfoldy, G. *The Social History of Rome*. Berlin, 1988.
Bradley, K. R. *Discovering the Roman Family*. New York, 1990.
Dixon, S. *The Roman Mother*. Norman, OK, 1988.
Earl, D. C. *The Moral and Political Tradition of Rome*. Ithaca, NY, 1984.
Gardner, J. F. *Women in Roman Law and Society*. Bloomington, IN, 1986.
Hallett, J. P. *Fathers and Daughters in Roman Society: Women and the Elite Family*. Princeton, NJ, 1984.
Wacher, J., ed. *The Roman World*. London, 1987.

II

Topic 9

The Collapse of the Roman Republic

The first serious attempt to deal with the underlying political and economic problems of late Republican Rome came in the tribunates of the Gracchus brothers. First Tiberius Gracchus, and then Gaius, tried to help the popular cause by introducing land reform measures, while Gaius also moved to establish a political alliance with the middle-class equites. Both brothers died violent deaths at the hands of their political opponents.

By the beginning of the 1st century B.C., wars in Africa and Central Europe, a slave revolt in Sicily, and an uprising in Italy itself brought two rival generals to power at Rome. The first, Marius, claimed to represent the popular interest. His eventually successful rival, the arch-conservative Sulla, reformed the state along archaic lines, before unexpectedly resigning all his powers and retiring to private life.

With the political situation at Rome ever worsening, the stage was set for the disastrous conflict between Pompey, champion of the Senate, and Julius Caesar, backed by the popular party. In 49 B.C., after years of successful campaigning in Gaul, Caesar led his victorious troops in a march on Rome, while Pompey and his supporters fled to Greece. The result was the Civil War, the first in the Republic's 500-year history.

The following year Caesar defeated Pompey's forces in pitched battle. After a brief period in Egypt, where his liaison with Cleopatra produced a son, Caesar returned to Rome and became dictator. The reform program he began to carry out addressed three separate areas: relief of economic decline and debt at Rome, planning for the welfare of the provinces, and reconstruction of effective central government.

When Caesar fell victim to the blows of a band of idealistic republican conspirators in 44 B.C., he had already made important steps in the first two of these fields. Rome's internal political order, however, remained on the point of collapse. Mark Antony, Caesar's deputy, took immediate command of the situation but his supremacy came under almost immediate challenge: Octavian, Caesar's young great-nephew and adopted heir, arrived in Rome to claim his inheritance.

Antony and Octavian formed an uneasy alliance to pursue and defeat the conspirators responsible for Caesar's murder. Thereafter, the last ten years of the Republic saw the return of civil war between the two. Antony's flight to Egypt to seek the help of Cleopatra provided Octavian with a powerful propaganda weapon. In 31 B.C. Octavian's army and navy, fighting for Italy against the "traitor" and his Egyptian queen, decisively overcame their enemies' joint forces at Actium. The Republic was shattered, and the Roman state lay at Octavian's command.

THE GRACCHUS BROTHERS AND THE FAILURE OF REFORM

Throughout the years of the Punic Wars and Rome's successive acquisition of the provinces, the aristocratic Senatorial party retained its supremacy in Roman affairs. Bolstered by the wealth of their great estates, and with their prestige enhanced by Rome's success against Carthage and the defeat of Hannibal, members of the Senate dominated the political scene at Rome and the government of the provinces abroad. By the mid-2nd century B.C., however, demand was growing at a popular level for political reform. When the revolution finally came, its first leaders, the two aristocratic Gracchus brothers, were members of the very social class against which the protest was aimed.

Tiberius Gracchus and Agrarian Reform

Tiberius Gracchus (163–133 B.C.) and his younger brother Gaius (153–121 B.C.) were from one of Rome's most distinguished noble families. Their father was widely admired for his governorship of Spain, and Tiberius himself served in the army there. His experiences on military duty led him to formulate a single overriding reason for Rome's manifold problems. In Tiberius' view, the low morale of the Roman army, urban discontent at Rome, and the constant threat of slave rebellions in the provinces all had the same cause: the excessive growth in power and wealth of the great estate owners.

To remedy this, Tiberius proposed a program of agrarian reform that would redistribute public land, limiting the size of farm holdings and settling them with retired veteran soldiers and the urban poor. The aim was to repopulate the countryside with a flourishing peasant class, while at the same time reducing the need for massive slave labor.

In 133 B.C., running on his reform program, the aristocratic Tiberius won election as tribune of the people. His campaign speeches gave eloquent voice to the injustices felt by many: "Wild beasts have their lairs, but the men who fight and die for Italy can call nothing their own except the air and the sunshine." Once elected, Tiberius and his supporters in the Senate set up a Land Commission, and its three commissioners began to redistribute public farmland.

The wealthy senators and landowners were outraged, but worse was to come. In the same year, King Attalus of Pergamum died, leaving his kingdom to the Roman state (see Part II, Topic 7). Tiberius proposed not only to use the income from Pergamum to underwrite the Commission's work, but to have the

A section of the plastic model of ancient Rome produced in the 1930s.

assembly of the people discuss the organization of the new province. At one blow, Tiberius challenged the Senate's authority in the two areas over which it had always maintained control: finance and foreign affairs.

Time was running out, and Tiberius announced that he was standing for reelection as tribune for 132 B.C. Consecutive terms were unusual, although not unconstitutional, and rumors arose—adroitly spread by Senate representatives—that Tiberius intended to make himself tyrant of Rome. On election day riots broke out, and a band led by a leading Senate conservative surrounded Tiberius and 300 of his supporters and clubbed them to death. In the aftermath of the violence, the consuls investigated Tiberius' "conspiracy," exiling or executing those accused of taking part.

The openness of Tiberius' challenge to the Senate, together with the bloody circumstances of his death, were ominous. His oversimplistic idea of returning to the ways of earlier times, and the speed with which he tried to bring about radical reform, both proved fatal to his cause. Yet they highlighted the existence of grave popular resentment and dissatisfaction. The violence used by Tiberius' enemies to suppress political opposition was the prelude to a century of bitter civil strife.

Gaius, Grain, and the Equites

Warned by the brutal ending to his brother's political career, Gaius lay low in the years immediately following Tiberius' death. He served on the Land Commission, which the Senate stripped of its judicial powers while allowing it to continue in operation. Unlike Tiberius, who concentrated all his attention on a single issue, Gaius used the time to prepare a far more general program of reform. To achieve lasting victory, he set about putting together a coalition of support: the urban poor, Rome's Italian allies, and—crucially—the middle-class equites with their business interests.

In December 124 B.C., he was ready. He stood for election as tribune, Tiberius' old office, and won triumphantly. The following year he ran again, and again he was elected. He used his two years in power to buttress his support. Contracts in a massive program of public works—roads, harbors, public buildings—went to his business supporters. Better still from their point of view, they secured the contracts to collect taxes in the new province of Asia. Furthermore, Gaius changed the law by which governors accused of misconduct were tried by a jury of senators. From now on, any governor unwise enough to resist pressure from businessmen collecting taxes would be tried before a jury made up of equites, the representatives of big business.

Meanwhile Gaius consolidated his backing among the urban poor by introducing a grain law, giving every Roman the right to a fixed monthly allowance of grain at a specially controlled price. At the same time he strengthened the working of the Land Commission by restoring its judicial powers, and planned new colonies where settlers—some from the proletariat, others businessmen of experience—could go to make their fortunes. There was even to be a new colony built on the ruins of Carthage.

For Rome's Italian "allies," Gaius proposed an extension of Roman citizenship to all Latins, and Latin rights (including immunity from punishment at the hands of Roman soldiers) to all Italians from the Alps to Sicily.

Such a varied plan of reform was far more threatening to senatorial interests than Tiberius' mere agrarian program of a decade earlier, and the Senate acted accordingly. A Senate proposal outbidding Gaius offered to quadruple the number of colonies to be founded. Meanwhile, rumors of mysterious horrors at Carthage—where, in defiance of the Roman curse of 20 years earlier, Gaius laid the foundation stone of the new settlement—began to unsettle popular feeling. Even more effectively, Gaius' opponents reminded Roman voters that if they shared their rights with other Italians, they would also have to share their privileges.

As Gaius returned from Carthage to face reelection in December 122 B.C., his coalition fell apart. Amid street riots and frenzied demonstrations by all sides, Gaius lost his bid to be elected for a third term as tribune. Early in the new year, 121 B.C., with the popular leader barely out of office, the senators hastily began repealing Gaius' legislation. In the course of protest rallies one of the consul's attendants was killed, and the senators lost no time in moving against their enemies. Passing the equivalent of martial law, they instructed the consuls "to provide that the State shall receive no harm." A posse hunted down Gaius' supporters and liquidated 3000 of them. Gaius himself fell as he tried to escape from the city: he may have committed suicide to avoid finishing in his enemies' hands.

With unconscious irony, a grateful Senate ordered the construction of a new Temple to Concord, to mark the return of harmony to Rome. Yet the result of the lives—and deaths—of the Gracchus brothers was to put the Senate and the popular party on a collision course that could end only with the supremacy of one side and the destruction of the other. Even more ominously, by legalizing the deaths of the brothers, their enemies legitimized the use of political violence and the abrogation of citizen rights. The urban political strife which marked the Gracchus brothers' attempts at reform led in due course to outright civil war.

POLITICS AND THE GENERALS: THE STRUGGLE FOR POWER

With the upper classes back in control, and without a charismatic leader to rally the popular interests, the Senate ensured itself the support, for the moment at least, of the equites by making important business concessions to them. It took a long drawn-out war in Africa to create the next popular leader capable of challenging the newly forged alliance of aristocracy and businessmen.

Marius the Populist

Gaius Marius (157-86 B.C.) was born at Arpinum, in the hills to the southeast of Rome. A provincial, he first emerged as a spokesman for the popular interests in 119 B.C., when he won election as tribune. He went on to serve in the provincial administration of Spain.

During the years of Marius' rise, Rome became embroiled in a frustrating conflict in North Africa. Their chief opponent there was the Numidian king Jugurtha (ruled 118–105 B.C.), who cleverly involved the Roman Senate in the internal politics of his kingdom. As the hostilities dragged on, a succession of aristocratic generals led the Roman forces in Africa from one setback to another.

Finally, in 107 B.C., Marius ran for the consulship, campaigning on his promise to put an end to the interminable African conflict. The popular faction, sensing a new champion of their cause, backed him. Marius won, and went on to beat Jugurtha by enlisting a fresh, volunteer army from the urban proletariat at Rome and the rural poor, trained by Marius himself—in the past, the Romans had required only citizens with property to undertake military duty, and Marius' recruitment of landless men was, in fact, illegal. All troops carried standardized weapons, and learned to march 40 miles a day with their equipment strapped to their backs. Proud of their arduous training, they called themselves "Marius' mules," and their loyalty to their commander meant that for the first time a general representing the popular side had his own military backing. At the same time, and more dangerous still, Marius' recruitment of a voluntary army was a serious violation of constitutional procedures, since the soldiers' allegiance was not to the Roman state but directly to Marius himself.

By 106 B.C. the African war was over and Marius returned to Italy, having transformed the Roman Army into a professional machine. He organized it in regiments, or "legions," with each legion broken down into ten smaller units called "cohorts." Every legion had its silver eagle, or "standard," with which it marched into battle and to which the men pledged allegiance.

Marius finished his reorganization just in time to fend off a threatened invasion from two northern tribes, the Cimbri and Teutoni. Cutting their way south from Scandinavia to Gaul and Spain, in 102 B.C. they were poised to invade Italy. Marius and his legions were ready for them, however, and routed them in two bloody battles at which, the Romans claimed, 100,000 of the enemy were killed or captured.

Throughout his years of army organization and the subsequent wars with the Cimbri and Teutoni, Marius had repeatedly won election as consul, chiefly as a means of reinforcing his military command. When peace came and he stood for reelection in 100 B.C., he ran as political leader of the popular faction. A brilliant soldier, Marius had poor political judgment, and threw his weight behind the extreme fringe of the democratic interests. Faced with their violent behavior, which virtually ended the long-standing alliance between the popular faction and the equites, Marius found himself forced to arrest his erstwhile supporters. By the end of the year, his political credit exhausted, he left on a tour of Asia rather than risk certain defeat at the polls.

The Social War

One of the aims of Gaius Gracchus' program in 123–122 B.C. had been the extension of rights to Rome's Italian allies, or *socii*. With Gaius' death the scheme made little appeal to politicians at Rome, but the allies themselves continued to press for tax reform and the granting of citizenship. Moderate and liberal Romans recognized the justice of their cause, but both businessmen and the lower classes opposed it. The former feared the competition from Italian manufacturers and traders, while the plebs had no wish to share their power to vote or their supplies of subsidized grain.

Angry and frustrated, the Italians joined forces to throw off Roman rule. The conflict, called the Social War, lasted from 91 to 88 B.C. The combined Italian armies, inspired by their indignation, fought bravely, and only the recall of Marius prevented the rout of the Roman troops in central Italy. In the south, a promising young commander, Lucius Sulla, led the Roman force defending Campania.

In the end, the Romans won not by military action but by making the allies the concessions they were fighting for. The state awarded citizenship first to all those Italian communities prepared to lay down their arms, and then to all individual Italians who withdrew from the fighting. Within weeks the war was over. By 88 B.C. citizenship rights extended from the Alps to Sicily, and Sulla, by now serving as consul, had mopped up resistance from the rebellious Samnites in the south.

Reconstructed model of a Roman catapult, used to attack besieged cities.

The Triumph of Sulla

Lucius Sulla (138–78 B.C.) had first come to prominence under Marius in the war against Jugurtha, and in many ways his career paralleled that of the older man. A successful field commander, worshiped by his men, Sulla, like Marius, nourished political ambitions. The similarities ended there, however, for if Marius' political sympathies lay with the popular cause, Sulla was as thoroughgoing a conservative as any figure in Rome's history.

It was inevitable that the two men would become rivals. In 88 B.C. Sulla, then consul, was awarded the prestigious command of the Roman force in Bithynia for the following year, where Roman control was under challenge. Mithridates, king of Pontus, had earlier occupied Bithynia, a Roman protectorate. When the Romans forced him to withdraw, he overran many of the cities of the Roman province of Asia and ignited the whole Greek east in revolt against Rome.

In a bitterly contested move in the Senate, Sulpicius Rufus, one of the tribunes of 88 B.C., had the command of Asia transferred to Marius in return for his political support. In rage Sulla marched on Rome with his troops—an unprecedented and illegal act which moved Rome one step nearer to military dictatorship—took the city, and had his political enemies declared outlaws. Sulpicius was captured and put to death, Sulla regained his eastern command, and in due course left for Asia.

With Sulla and his troops gone, it was Marius' turn to march on Rome, ordering the murder of the senators and other figures who had opposed him. Within a month Marius was dead, but his supporters—who claimed to be democratic representatives of the popular interest against the Senate—remained in power.

The war against Mithridates finally over, and peace negotiated on terms lenient to the king (Sulla had other matters to settle), the victorious general returned to Italy in 82 B.C. Now his time had come, and the relieved Senate happily agreed to its champion's demand for appointment as "dictator, to take such steps and issue such laws without veto or appeal as were necessary." Armed with these drastic powers, Sulla was ready for revenge on his political opponents.

The first of his "proscription lists" appeared within days of his entry into Rome. Sulla issued a series of these lists, encouraging informers to supply names of leaders of the popular cause and former supporters of Marius. In all, they contained the names of 90 senators, 15 men of consular rank, and some 2600 equites. All of them were to lose their lives, with their property confiscated by the state. Many who provided additional victims did so in pursuit of private feuds, but Sulla did not hesitate to put the names down—later Romans never forgot his cold-blooded casualness.

With (as he thought) the popular faction wiped out for ever, Sulla then turned to reform of the state. His aim was to eliminate democracy and strengthen the power of the Senate by returning to the constitution of the 5th century B.C. He abolished the cheap grain allowance and removed many of the powers of the tribunes of the people. He increased the numbers of the senators to 500, adding an additional 300. (The reform was intended as a conservative move to reinforce the Senate's authority. Ironically, however, since many of the new senators came from the recently enfranchised Italian municipalities, Sulla's move introduced new, destabilizing groups into the struggle for power.) He established seven permanent courts for seven types of crime—extortion, murder, treason, and so on—with juries drawn exclusively from the Senate. This legal reform, which took the control of corruption trials away from the equites, was the only part of the Sullan reform program to have a lasting effect.

With Rome returned to an archaic and outdated system of rule, and his own position guaranteed by fear of further bloodshed, Sulla then bewildered all of his contemporaries by retiring to private life on his country estate in Campania. Within a few months he was dead. His constitutional reform fell into ruins, and the battle for supremacy between the Senate and its opponents, the equites and the popular front, was on again.

The careers of both Marius and Sulla illustrate the danger of successful generals taking up politics, especially in the extreme form that the two of them espoused. Both of them used politics—and were used by the politicians—as a means of achieving personal power. Sulla's epitaph, composed by himself, claimed that no man had ever done more good to his friends or harm to his enemies, and Marius might well have claimed likewise. Both of them caused immense damage to the state.

POMPEY AND CAESAR: RIVALRY AND CIVIL WAR

With Sulla gone, the two groups which had suffered most as a result of his reforms—the poor and the business class—hastened to challenge the Senate and reclaim their lost rights. Even if the senators could have presented a united front against the opposition, and their continued squabbling made this impossible, events in the provinces provided a series of urgent crises that demanded their attention.

In Asia, Mithridates was on the offensive once again, challenging the Roman presence there. To the west, Sertorius, a former governor of Spain, led a revolt by the local Spanish population to break away from Rome. Both Mithridates and Sertorius encouraged the pirates active in the eastern Mediterranean to play havoc with Roman shipping, and in 70 B.C. the pirates were emboldened enough to threaten the port of Rome itself, Ostia. Meanwhile, the runaway slave Spartacus and an increasing number of fellow deserters moved up and down Italy for two years, from 73 to 71 B.C., looting the smaller towns and causing terror among the local population.

Portrait of Pompey the Great.

Pompey Takes Charge

As the Senate tried to handle the worsening situation, it turned increasingly to one of the leading generals of the day, Gnaeus Pompeius (106–48 B.C.)—the self-styled Pompey the Great. It was Sulla who first, in ironic reference to Pompey's arrogance and self-importance, dubbed him with the nickname, and Pompey—not known for his sense of humor—always used it thereafter.

Pompey's first major assignment was in 76 B.C., to Spain, where Sertorius managed to hold his own against the Roman forces until he was assassinated in 72 B.C. by a jealous subordinate. Without his charismatic leadership the revolt collapsed, with Pompey taking credit for its ending. Returning to Italy to celebrate a triumph, he took the time to crush the few rebel slaves still loose (another Roman expedition had already defeated the overwhelming majority of Spartacus' followers), and claimed when he reached Rome that he had put down the entire uprising.

By now Pompey was ready, like Marius and Sulla before him, to aim for the consulship. He ran in 70 B.C., and won election. His fellow consul was Crassus (c. 112–53 B.C.), a highly successful businessman and military leader—he had led the expedition which crushed Spartacus' followers—and a real estate magnate reputed to be the richest man at Rome. Once in power, the two of them finished the job of dismantling the few remaining traces of Sulla's constitution, and Pompey received special command over the entire Mediterranean to eliminate the menace of piracy.

That done, the only serious problem remaining was Mithridates. Between 74 and 67 B.C. the Roman general Lucullus (c. 117–55 B.C.), later to become famous for his extravagant tastes, campaigned against Mithridates with considerable success. The Roman forces drove him out of his kingdom of Pontus and Lucullus reorganized the finances of Rome's Asian subjects, bringing welcome relief from rapacious tax collectors. For Pompey, however, the Roman world was big enough for only one successful general, and in 66 B.C. the Senate passed a special law transferring to him the command of Asia. Lucullus bitterly observed that Pompey was like a vulture, preying on the corpses that others had killed.

The Rise of Julius Caesar

With Pompey away in Asia from 66 to 62 B.C., a new figure began to dominate Roman public life: Gaius Julius Caesar (c. 100–44 B.C.). A patrician by birth, in 84 B.C. Caesar married Cornelia, the daughter of the head of the popular faction at Rome, Lucius Cinna. Identifying himself with the popular cause, he was elected quaestor in 69 B.C., and pontifex maximus (chief priest) in 63 B.C. Later that same year he spoke eloquently in the debate over a conspiracy plotted against the state by Catiline, a violent young revolutionary. From the beginning Caesar backed the populist faction, defending the memory of Marius and laying on lavish public entertainments during the time he served as magistrate. The cost of winning popular favor was debt, and Caesar turned to Crassus for substantial loans.

When Pompey duly returned to Rome, after having completed Lucullus' work in Asia, he disbanded his army, celebrated a triumph, and settled back to enjoy the Senate's grateful thanks for a decade of hard campaigning. Far from flattering him, the jealous senators took the chance to cut him down to size, quibbling over his accounts and refusing to provide land for his veteran troops to settle on. Caesar, ever alert, seized the chance to make political capital. He was running for the consulship of 59 B.C. In return for their support, he proposed to Crassus and Pompey the formation of a secret alliance, which became known as the First Triumvirate. As consul, he would get Crassus favorable terms for the contract to collect taxes in Asia, and settle Pompey's difficulties with the Senate.

Caesar's plan worked. The "Three-Headed Monster," as its enemies called it, achieved all its goals. When the three met secretly at Lucca in 56 B.C., they renewed their alliance. This time they agreed that Pompey and Crassus were to be elected consuls for 55 B.C., while Caesar would receive a special term of five years as commander in Gaul. Caesar left to take up his position, returning to Rome only in 49 B.C.

A portrait of Julius Caesar, carved around the time of his death.

Civil War

Gaul occupied a crucial position on Italy's northern frontiers, and served as a base for driving invading Germans back across the Rhine. It was also rich in fertile farmland. In 55 B.C., under Caesar's command, the Roman troops in Gaul crushed the Germans, and over the next two years put down a series of local Gallic rebellions. The uprisings culminated in 52 B.C. in a great national revolt led by the formidable Gallic chieftain Vercingetorix, which brought Caesar his greatest challenge yet. By 51 B.C., he had conquered a vast area, and gradually brought the entire region under Roman rule.

Caesar was able to create a united administration for the three separate parts of Gaul that made it one of the most peaceful and loyal provinces in the Roman world. More importantly for his political future, he led a magnificently trained army devoted to their commander and willing to follow him anywhere.

At Rome, Pompey was now the dominant figure. In 53 B.C., Crassus—anxious to add yet another military success to his fortune—mounted an expedition against the Parthians on the borders of India (modern Afghanistan). The campaign was a disaster. Crassus was killed in the fighting, and the Parthians captured the standards carried by the Roman soldiers into battle—a fate literally worse than death for a Roman commander.

As the time for Caesar's return approached, it became clear that the headlong collision so long delayed between Pompey and Caesar was looming. In 49 B.C. the Senate ordered Caesar to disband his army and return to Rome. When he refused, they passed a decree naming him an enemy of the state. Caesar continued his march south, crossing the Rubicon (a small river in the Po Valley), and heading for the capital. Pompey, in panic, fled with his supporters to Greece.

There, in sultry summer heat on the plains of central Greece, at Pharsalus, Roman faced Roman in pitched battle. Pompey's men were more numerous, Caesar's far better trained and ready to fight. The conclusion was never really in doubt, and by the end of the day half of Pompey's forces surrendered to their opponents. Pompey himself fled to Egypt, to seek refuge there at the court of Cleopatra and her brother, Ptolemy XIII. Ptolemy's advisers had Pompey stabbed, decapitated his body, and embalmed the head as a present for Caesar.

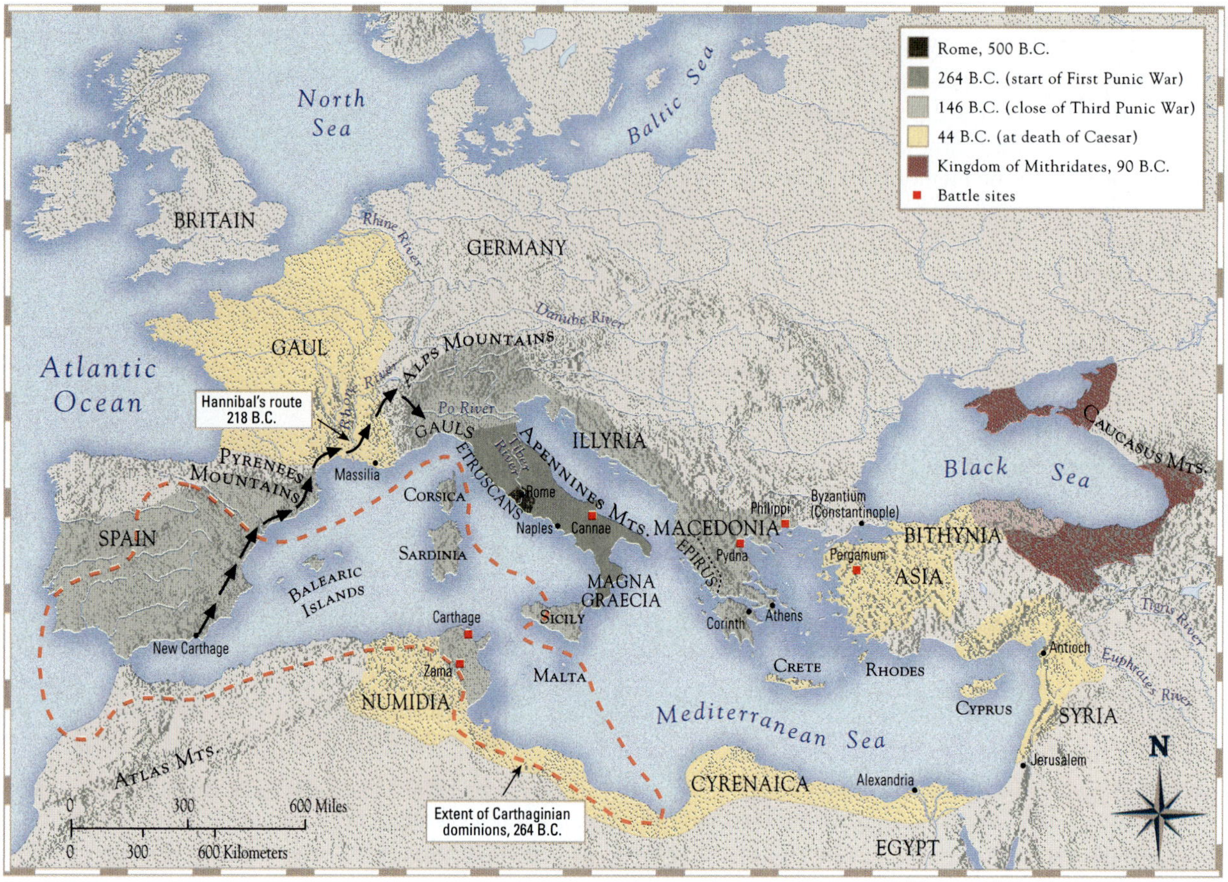

Map 9.1 Growth of the Roman Provinces during the Republic

THE DICTATORSHIP AND ASSASSINATION OF JULIUS CAESAR

Caesar followed Pompey to Egypt, where he found himself in the middle of a quarrel between the joint rulers, Cleopatra and her brother Ptolemy. Caesar put his forces at the disposal of the queen, and—with Ptolemy disposed of—spent the rest of the summer in Cleopatra's company. By the time he was ready to pay a flying visit to Rome, she was pregnant with their son—she named him Caesarion.

By now the Senate had nominated Caesar dictator, but he did not spend long in Rome, putting his lieutenant Mark Antony in control of affairs there. Instead he returned to Africa and Asia, to mop up the remaining pockets of resistance. Even then there were distractions from the task of restoring political order at Rome. Back in the capital briefly in 46 B.C., Caesar left once again the following year to crush a last desperate revolt by supporters of Pompey in Spain.

Caesar's Program of Reform

It was under these unsettled conditions that Caesar began to bring under control a century of growing political and social chaos. The most immediately pressing problem was the ruinous state of the economy. Many of his supporters, particularly among the lower classes, hoped that he would wipe out all their debts. To do so, however, would have alienated the business class on whom he depended for a speedy return to financial order. He did cancel interest accumulated during the war, and introduced regulations overseeing the valuation of property seized in payment of debt.

At Rome, he brought the urban mob under control by taking a rigorous census of those who claimed the right to the corn allowance. The number was reduced, and many of those whose names were struck from the lists were resettled on land elsewhere in Italy. All estate owners had to hire at least one third of their workforce from these newcomers, a measure that provided employment for many who had hitherto formed part of Rome's proletariat, while reducing the need for large slave gangs.

Within Italy, Caesar codified city charters and the duties of local officials. (One minor piece of reorganization at this time was his reform of the calendar which, with the addition of a minor adjustment in the 16th century, still remains in use.) Elsewhere in the provinces he extended Roman citizenship to parts of Gaul and some towns in Spain. To settle his veteran soldiers and

Coin struck by Brutus, one of Caesar's assassins, showing two daggers with the inscription, "Ides of March" (March 15, the day of Caesar's death).

further reduce the numbers of unemployed at Rome, he set up an extensive program of new colonies in Spain, Gaul, Greece, and Africa—including the reoccupation of Carthage, Gaius Gracchus' old dream.

Caesar's plans for constitutional reform are more vague. He certainly permitted none of the settling of old scores typical of Marius' and Sulla's time in power. He strengthened the role of the Senate, increasing its enrollment and including senators from Italy and the provinces. Yet at the same time he concentrated the chief powers of the state in his own hands; he chose the magistrates, controlled the treasury, and commanded all the armies.

In January 44 B.C., he received the title of dictator for life. Perhaps even Caesar himself did not know whether this was a temporary solution to Rome's crisis, or represented the foundation of a system of autocratic rule. Two months later, on March 15, 44 B.C., he was dead, struck down by a band of ideologue conspirators, led by Brutus and Cassius, who saw in his new title and office the death of the Republic.

THE TRIUMPH OF OCTAVIAN AND THE DEATH OF THE REPUBLIC

Even with Caesar gone, his supporters remained, together with the army. In the days of confusion following the assassination, two of Caesar's ablest officers, Mark Antony and Lepidus, took control. The only senior political figure to speak out against them, in favor of the republican cause, was Cicero.

Octavius Becomes Octavian

In his will, Caesar made his nearest male relative, his great-nephew Octavius (ruled as Emperor Augustus 27 B.C.–A.D. 14), his heir, adopting him as his son under the name Gaius Julius Caesar Octavianus—historians conventionally term him Octavian during this period. Caesar may have intended to groom Octavian for a political role. In any case the young man—he was 18 at the time—had the highest of ambitions. Arriving in Rome, he found ready support from those who thought Antony's tactful pardon of Caesar's assassins too lenient. For many, also, the magic of the name "Caesar," which Octavian began immediately to use, remained potent.

By November 43 B.C., Antony and Lepidus on one side, and Octavian on the other, came to a compromise, known as the Second Triumvirate. The First Triumvirate had been a secret agreement. This one was public and sanctioned by law. It gave the three men joint rule of the Roman world. (Lepidus' role soon became subordinate to that of the other two.) The new rulers began by eliminating those whom they considered their political opponents—among the victims was Cicero, whose eloquent opposition Antony had never forgiven. The next task was to follow up and defeat the conspirators, and Antony and Octavian led a joint force to victory over them in 42 B.C. at Philippi in northern Greece.

The End of the Republic

The last ten years of the Republic saw Antony and Octavian locked in a struggle for supreme power, in which the younger man showed an increasingly brilliant command of the power of propaganda. The first move was to create an appearance of unity, and in 40 B.C. Antony married Octavia, Octavian's sister. The two leaders then divided the Roman world between them, Octavian taking Italy and the west, and Antony the far richer, but less stable, eastern provinces.

Within three years Octavia was back in Italy with her brother, and Antony had fallen under the spell of Cleopatra. He settled in Alexandria, which the two intended to make the capital of a new universal kingdom—Cleopatra had long cherished dreams of reviving the glories of Ptolemaic Egypt. When Antony made the fatal error of going through a form of marriage with "that Eastern Queen," Octavian portrayed himself as the defender of noble Roman traditions and the gods of Italy against the corruption of the mysterious east.

Once again, the end came in Greece, as it had for Pompey and for the conspirators. In September 31 B.C., Octavian routed the combined forces of Antony and Cleopatra at Actium. The two fled back to Egypt. Octavian followed and easily defeated their few remaining troops. Antony, returning at the end to the

PUBLIC FIGURES AND PRIVATE LIVES

ANTONY AND FULVIA

The status of upper-class women in the late Republic, and the nature of their relationship with their husbands, is epitomized in contemporary views of the three wives of one of the dominating figures of the age, Mark Antony: the manipulative, "masculine" Fulvia, the politically correct and docile Octavia, and Cleopatra, the dangerously seductive Egyptian beauty.

His second wife, Octavian's sister Octavia, provided a political link with Antony's colleague and rival. Newly widowed, Octavia was available in 40 B.C. when, following their defeat of Caesar's murderers, Octavian and Antony needed to cement their unstable political alliance by a dynastic marriage. Traditionally, ever since the Sabine women—seized by the first Romans shortly after the foundation of Rome—brought peace to the city, women had served as agents of reconciliation in the history of the Republic. During the three years they lived together, Octavia fulfilled this role, bearing Antony two children and mediating between her husband and her brother.

Even when Antony abandoned Octavia for his third wife, Cleopatra, Octavia remained loyal, disregarding Antony's marriage to the Egyptian queen in 37 B.C. since—by Roman law—marriage to a non-Roman citizen was not valid. She continued to live in Antony's Roman residence, leaving it only in 32 B.C., when her brother Octavian used Antony's formal divorce from Octavia as a justification for declaring war on him.

If Octavia represented the traditional role of woman as peacemaker, Cleopatra became symbolic of the other side of the conventional view of the feminine: woman as seducer and destroyer. Cleopatra had already exercised her charms on Julius Caesar, and in 37 B.C. her political ambitions joined with Antony's drive for supremacy in the Roman world to make them a formidable couple. The intensity of Octavian's propaganda campaign against Cleopatra demonstrates the threat he saw in her. When the future emperor declared war in 32 B.C., he did so against Cleopatra alone. After the defeat of Antony's and Cleopatra's forces at Actium in 31 B.C., Octavian reinforced his attacks on the *fatale monstrum*—the "deadly monster"—and drove her to suicide.

Fulvia, Antony's first wife, provides a far less clear-cut example of the late Republican wife as symbol. Neither the conventional "good" influence, nor the equally conventional "foreign seductress," Fulvia came from a noble Roman family. Her mother, Sempronia, had been implicated in the conspiracy of Catiline in 63 B.C. Famous for her beauty, wit, and charm, Sempronia was described even by her enemies as endowed with considerable intellectual strengths. Even the charge that she had often committed "crimes of masculine daring" seems almost an unwilling tribute to her courage.

Fulvia lacked her mother's charm, but not her audacity. Although she had been married twice before she married Antony, and bore children in each of her three marriages, her contemporaries—encouraged by Octavian's propaganda machine—described her as "female in body only," an accusation commonly leveled against politically active women such as her own mother. The stories that circulated about her emphasized her "unwomanly" cruelty. Thus, after the formation of the Second Triumvirate following Caesar's assassination, Octavian's mother and sister gave a sympathetic hearing to the female relatives of those listed for execution by the triumvirs, while Fulvia rudely rejected their pleas.

Later historians, including Plutarch, credited Fulvia with causing Antony's downfall. By dominating him, she taught him to obey a woman, and thus prepared the way for Cleopatra. Fulvia accompanied her husband on his military expeditions, behavior unthinkable for traditional wives. Later, while Antony was away in the east, and beginning his liaison with the Egyptian queen (Cleopatra gave birth to twins fathered by Antony in 41 B.C.), Fulvia instigated a revolt against Octavian in the hope of drawing Antony away from Egypt and her rival. Her death in 40 B.C. conveniently left him free to repair the damage with Octavian and marry Octavia.

Virtually all we know about Fulvia—and about Cleopatra and Octavia, too, for that matter—comes from sources heavily conditioned by Octavian's influence. Cleopatra's power, her Roman enemies believed, was the result of her exotic charm and the "Oriental debauchery" with which she corrupted her Roman lover. Fulvia presented a more difficult case: a woman of impeccable family and inherited wealth, who managed, at least for a while, to play a significant role in the turbulent history of the collapse of the Republic. Faced with such an anomaly, and with the victory of the future Augustus, Roman public opinion reverted to stereotype. Like her mother, Fulvia "took the initiative with men far more often than they did with her." The hatred which her "masculinity" provoked is perhaps in the end a tribute to the ability of some women, at least, to make their mark on late Republican political life.

old Roman ways, committed suicide, but the queen was less hasty, waiting for an interview with Octavian. Whatever her hopes, it became quickly clear that he was keeping her alive only so that she could march in his triumphal procession, and she, too, killed herself.

Thus, at the age of 32, Octavian was the ruler of a world numbed by a century of conflict and three bloody civil wars. The conspirators had been right that the Republic was in its death throes, but fatally wrong in thinking that the removal of Julius Caesar could prevent the inevitable. Those who killed Caesar and those who avenged his death were all members of the Roman elite locked in a struggle for supreme power.

The rise of the business classes, the stubborn refusal of the Senate to recognize that conditions were changed, the growing role of the urban mob, all these were factors in making Rome no longer governable by the alternation of rival aristocratic politicians. Caesar was the only statesman who might have been able to break the cycle of political rivalry and bloodletting, but he died before he could devise a solution. Octavian's task was a formidable one: to create a system of authoritarian rule capable of being faithful to Rome's past while guaranteeing future stability.

Questions for Further Study

1. What basic issues were the reforms of the Gracchus brothers intended to address? What did they actually achieve?
2. How far was self-interest the chief motivation for the political leaders of the last century of the Republic? Was it the only one?

3. What were the decisive stages in Julius Caesar's rise to power? Once in control, how did he set about dealing with the problems Rome faced?
4. What part did civil war play in the collapse of the Republic? What does its role indicate about the nature of Rome's political crisis?

Suggestions for Further Reading

Grant, M. *From Alexander to Cleopatra*. New York, 1982.
Greenhalgh, P. *Pompey: The Roman Alexander*. New York, 1980.
Gruen, E. S. *The Last Generation of the Roman Republic*. Berkeley, CA, 1973.
Keaveny, A. *Sulla: The Last Republican*. London, 1987.
Leach, J. *Pompey the Great*. London, 1987.
Nicolet, C. *The World of the Citizen in Republican Rome*. London, 1980.
Scullard, H. H. *Roman Politics, 220–150* B.C. Westport, CT, 1982.
Seager, R. *Pompey: A Political Biography*. Berkeley, CA, 1980.
Stockton, D. *The Gracchi*. Oxford, 1979.

Topic 10

The Empire: From Augustus to Marcus Aurelius

Having taken control of the state in 31 B.C., Octavian claimed that he was restoring the Republic in 27 B.C., when the Senate granted him the name Augustus. In fact, however, he consolidated his hold on the Roman world and reinforced the rule of one man, governing through his control of the civil service and official appointments.

Augustus' revolution affected virtually all aspects of Roman life: political, economic, social, and cultural. By the time of his death, the Empire was at peace and the authority of its ruler unchallenged. One of the problems which Augustus left unsolved—one that was to cause constantly recurring conflict during the following centuries of imperial rule—was that of the succession. Augustus finally left the government of the Empire to Tiberius, his stepson.

When, after a generally constructive but unpopular reign, Tiberius died in A.D. 37, he left no successor, and the Senate stepped in to appoint Gaius—better known by his nickname Caligula—who was a young relative of Augustus. At the end of Caligula's disastrous rule, it fell to the imperial guard to impose their choice by force: Claudius, Caligula's uncle. In spite of Claudius' extensive achievements, the principle of succession according to membership in Augustus' Julio-Claudian family finally collapsed with the reign of Caligula's nephew, the deservedly notorious Nero.

With Nero's downfall in A.D. 68, the power to create new emperors passed to the strongest force available, in this case the army. In the space of a few months—the Year of the Four Emperors—successive military contingents imposed their candidates. The figure who eventually emerged was Vespasian, whose ten years in office marked a welcome respite from the confusion and violence of the preceding generation. Once again, however, for all the positive achievements of his reign, Vespasian failed to resolve the crucial constitutional problem inherent in the imperial system. If his elder son, Titus, proved the merits of family succession, his younger son, Domitian, confirmed its dangers in a long and turbulent reign.

Domitian had no son, and the Senate chose his successor, Nerva, on merit. Nerva, who was also childless, nominated his own successor and legitimized his choice by adopting him. His four successors, none of whom produced a son, followed the same system. This led to a century of peace and stability in which the Empire reached its maximum size and general prosperity was widespread. The arts, which had enjoyed a Golden Age under Augustus, flourished again in a period known as the Silver Age.

THE AUGUSTAN REVOLUTION: APPEARANCE AND REALITY

Augustus' achievement was to take on an Empire lacking a coherent political system and paralyzed by decades of conflict, and to leave it at his death with a smoothly running political machine, capable of absorbing the wilder excesses of many of his successors. In some ways the total degree of devastation he found helped his task, since by 31 B.C. virtually all Romans of whatever party shared a single overriding desire for peace. Another factor contributing to his success was the sheer length of his reign: 45 years of continuity provided time to lay solid foundations for the transformation of the state. Of his own gifts, perhaps that which helped him most was the one which had served him in the struggle with Antony, his masterly use of propaganda. Time after time, Augustus concealed his real intentions under an outward appearance meant for public consumption.

The New Order

In the immediate aftermath of his victory at Actium, Octavian (the future Augustus) renounced his position as triumvir and ran for election as consul. His long-term aim was to retain an autocratic grip on all aspects of power, while appearing to restore the institutions of the Republic—thus avoiding the tactical error of Julius Caesar, who had accepted the title of dictator for life.

The first step came in 27 B.C., when, as he later claimed in his autobiography, "I handed back the state from my own power to that of the Senate and Roman People." He continued to go through the fiction of running for the consulship, but resigned all other special powers to the republican magistrates of the old constitution. The only honor he would agree to accept was Augustus, "the revered one," the name by which he was thereafter known.

For all the apparent restoration of the old ways, however, the reality was very different. After Augustus' thorough revision of the Senate's list of members, it was made up almost exclusively of his supporters. The magistrates—although going through the appearance of popular election—were first chosen by Augustus himself, who also kept control of the treasury and the army.

This arrangement, known as the First Settlement, was perhaps intended as a trial solution. A second one followed in 23 B.C., when finally, after holding the consulship for an unprecedented eleven times, Augustus gave it up. He took instead the ancient power of a tribune, historically the defender of the people, and a vague *imperium* (power) over all officers of the state. His real source of authority, however, lay in the loyalty of the army and, over time, the immense prestige—the Latin word is *auctoritas*—with which a grateful world came to regard him. From now on, his official title was *Princeps*, or First Citizen of the state.

The *Augustus of Prima Porta,* showing the emperor about to address his people.

The Economics of Peace

The belief that an era of peace had finally dawned was itself one of the prime causes for the immense increase in investment after the Battle of Actium, with interest rates dropping by a third. As a result, there was a boom in trade and industry which created an even wider circulation of capital.

Augustus encouraged small-scale local industry as a counterbalance to the wealthy nobles of Rome. Pottery and glass remained important sectors, with exportation of high-class Arretine ware (pottery produced at Arezzo) throughout the Empire, from Britain to India. The metal industry developed specialized production systems, with iron mined on the island of Elba and transported to foundries on the Bay of Naples for smelting. The flourishing construction industry, repairing the damage of a century of civil wars, needed supplies of building materials such as bricks and tiles, lead pipes and cement. During Augustus' reign, the spread of economic prosperity produced a hard-working industrial middle class, loyal to the central government.

With the Mediterranean once again at peace, commerce became truly international. Raw materials and manufactured goods passed between the provinces and reached the marketplaces of Rome. Trade in fine linen from Egypt, Syrian dates and wine, asphalt from the Dead Sea, Spanish gold and silver, and many other products soared as a result of a stable currency. Other factors in the trade boom included good, safe roads, and the revival of leading centers of international commerce like Corinth, Carthage, and—above all—Alexandria, which soon became the second city of the Empire. Nor was business limited to the Mediterranean world. By the late 1st century B.C., Roman traders were importing ivory, incense, and spices from India and silk from China.

The economic boom which marked Augustus' reign was reinforced by a general improvement in the administration of the provinces. During the last centuries of the Republic, the worst excesses in financial corruption on the part of provincial governors and their staffs had served to pay the bills of political leaders and their supporters at Rome. With power now concentrated in the hands of the emperor, the ruinous expenses typical of the career of Marius or Caesar no longer formed part of the political process.

The Augustan Image

Just as Augustus aimed to restore Rome's ancient political institutions—at least in appearance—so his social legislation, aimed chiefly at the upper classes, was intended to return his subjects to traditional family values. Laws provided tax breaks for large families and penalized childlessness and the unmarried. Adultery became a crime against the state. In a revival of ancient religious practices aimed to provide the new laws with moral support, Augustus carried out an ambitious program of restoration for Rome's temples and encouraged the return to ancient deities and ceremonies.

One important aspect of Rome's traditional image was the central role of agriculture and the land. Farming underwent the same expansion as other economic activities during Augustus' rule, but the imperial economy became far more diversified than that of republican times, while increasing numbers of Romans, both in Italy and the provinces, lived in cities. To remind them of Rome's peasant origins, Augustus encouraged artists and writers to portray the joys of the countryside in works such as Vergil's *Georgics*, a lengthy poem on farming (for art and literature under Augustus, see Part II, Topic 11).

Despite the success of the Augustan political revolution, it is doubtful if his moral reforming zeal met with more than polite attention. His own daughter and granddaughter, both named Julia, were notorious for the scandals they were involved in. To make matters worse, one of his daughter Julia's lovers was a son of Mark Antony, her father's old enemy. Duty forced Augustus to banish Julia to a remote Mediterranean

A relief showing a peasant driving his cow to market.

DOCUMENTS ON HISTORY

Political Propaganda in the Roman Empire

From the earliest days of the reign of Augustus, the state carefully controlled all comments on public policy. Virtually no criticism of Augustus' rule was permitted. Few portraits of his opponents, Antony and Cleopatra, have survived, and Augustus even had coins bearing their images melted down. Any challenge to the imperial policy brought at the least permanent exile. Among those banished were Augustus' daughter and granddaughter, and the distinguished poet Ovid.

Later emperors, without Augustus' moral authority, were less able to repress all criticisms, but as in the extract from Tacitus opponents of the regime had to be indirect, and let their readers deduce for themselves the implicit message of condemnation. Juvenal's savage description of Nero's infamies was written only at the safe distance of 70 years later.

The last two passages date to the reigns of Hadrian and Marcus Aurelius. The first, an inscription which claims to represent popular enthusiasm for the Emperor Hadrian, illustrates how simple "official" statements often conceal more complex issues. The other one is an extract from the meditations of Marcus Aurelius which offers an insider's view of the job of being a Roman emperor.

THE VICTORY OF AUGUSTUS AT THE BATTLE OF ACTIUM

Vergil's Aeneid *provides the "official" description of the naval battle of Actium (31 B.C.) which brought Augustus to power. Augustus and Agrippa are portrayed as the champions of a united Italian Senate and people. Vergil contemptuously lists the "foreigners" fighting for Antony, while he cannot even bring himself to mention Cleopatra by name. As monstrous Oriental deities face off against the divine protectors of Rome, it is easy to forget that the battle formed the last decisive encounter in a bloody civil war, itself the sequel to an earlier civil war in which Augustus and Antony had fought on the same side.*

The Shield of Aeneas

The center (of Aeneas' shield) showed the battle of Actium—
the bronze-clad ships attacking in a line,
Leucata seething, and billows bright with gold.
Augustus led the Italians into battle
with Senate and people, with gods both small and great.
He stood in the sternsheets. Flame poured from his brows
exultant; above him dawned his father's star.
Elsewhere, Agrippa, blessed by gods and winds,
swooped down with his fleet; that proud ensign of war,
the naval crown, shone bright upon his brow.
There Antony, like some savage, gaudy sheik,
hero of Araby and the Sea of Pearls,
led Egypt, the lords of the East, and Bactria;
behind him (God forfend!) his gypsy Queen.
The fleets advance full speed; then oars aback
in a welter of foam, while spiked rams ripped the wave.
Then—out to sea! As were the Isles of Greece
Torn loose and floating, or Alp attacking Alp,
So huge, so tall, were the battling men-o'-war.
Men lobbed the fireball; iron spear-points fell
Like rain; fresh bloodshed reddened Neptune's realm.

Her majesty rang her gong for battle stations,
not yet aware of twin asps at her back.
Weird gods, fantastic shapes, the dog Anubis,
stood in phalanx against Minerva, Neptune,
and Venus.

Vergil, *The Aeneid* (Book 8, lines 675–700), trans. F. O. Copley. Bobbs-Merrill, 1965.

AN AUGUSTAN VIEW OF THE FIRST SETTLEMENT

The year before his death, Augustus approved an official description of his achievements, the Deeds of the Deified Augustus. *In his will he instructed that inscribed copies should be set up in every province of the Empire. The following extract gives his highly misleading account of the First Settlement of 27* B.C. *(see above). Far from handing over power to the Senate and people, he concentrated it further in his own hands.*

The First Settlement

In my sixth and seventh consulships (28 and 27 B.C.) after I had put an end to the civil wars and had acquired, by unanimous vote, supreme control, I transferred the Republic from my power over to the authority of the Senate and the Roman People. In return for this service of mine, I acquired the title of Augustus in accordance with a decree of the Senate, and the doorposts of my house were publicly wreathed with laurel and a civic crown was fastened above the entrance. A golden shield was placed in the Julian Senate house which, as the inscription on it bears witness, the Senate and the Roman People gave to me because of my virtue, clemency, justice, and piety. At this time I exceeded all in prestige, but I had no more power than those who were my colleagues in each magistracy.

From MacKendrick, Paul, and Herbert M. Howe, eds. *Classics in Translation, Volume II: Latin Literature.* Copyright © 1952. Reprinted by permission of The University of Wisconsin Press.

DIFFERENCES BETWEEN THE GERMANS AND THE ROMANS

The great historian Tacitus lived through the reigns of Nero and Domitian, a period notorious for its moral and political corruption. His monograph Germania, *published in* A.D. *98, provides a unique insight into the social customs of the ancient Germans. At the same time, sophisticated readers at Rome would make inevitable—and intended—comparisons between the noble "barbarians" to the north, and the decadent ways of the city. The reference in the last sentence is to the continuing decline in the birthrate in Italy during the 1st century* A.D., *in spite of the passing of laws in favor of large families, and the economic damage this provoked (see below).*

Only a decade later, around A.D. *107, did Tacitus feel able to begin the publication of his unvarnished accounts of the Julio-Claudian and Flavian eras.*

The Superiority of German Morals

The chastity (of German women) is well protected and there are no allurements of shows, no attractions of parties to corrupt them. Secret love notes are unknown to men and women alike. In so populous a nation there are very few cases of adultery and for these the punishment is immediate and left to the husbands. The adulteress' husband cuts off her hair, strips her naked, and in the presence of

continued next page

the kinsmen expels her from his house and drives her with a whip through the entire village. If a woman surrenders her chastity, she can receive no pardon. Not beauty nor youth nor wealth will find her a husband. Vice is no laughing matter there, and seducing or being seduced is not called the modern fashion. Even higher is the moral standard of those states where only virgins get married and so the wife's hopes and expectations are settled once for all. Thus they receive just one husband, as they receive one body and one life, so that they may have no thought beyond, no further desire, and love their husband not so much as an individual but as representing the state of marriage. To practice birth control or destroy any of the later-born offspring is regarded as criminal, and good morals are more effective there than good laws elsewhere.

From MacKendrick, Paul, and Herbert M. Howe, eds. *Classics in Translation, Volume II. Latin Literature.* Copyright © 1952. Reprinted by permission of The University of Wisconsin Press.

NERO ON STAGE

Some 70 years later, the satirical poet Juvenal could describe more openly the horrors of Nero's reign. Juvenal has his own axe to grind, though: a violent hater of "foreigners," especially Greeks, he begins by comparing Nero's murder of his mother with the most famous matricide of Greek myth, and reaches a rather incongruous climax in his catalogue of Nero's sins by describing the emperor's public appearances on stage before Greek audiences.

The Misdeeds of an Emperor

If the people could vote, and were free in their right of election,
How could they fail to choose a Seneca over a Nero?
More than one sack, one asp, one ape, one dog, would be needed
If his parricides earned the punishments due to their number.
Agamemnon's son, Orestes, murdered his mother.
That was a different case, with the gods giving orders for vengeance
Over a father slain while drunk. But even Orestes
Never polluted himself by cutting the throat of his sister,
Never murdered his wife nor poisoned cups for his cousins,
Never sang on the stage, nor attempted original epics!
Nothing in all the reign of this cruel and merciless tyrant,
Nothing he did was more deserving of vengeance.
Hail, our noble prince and his works of art! What a leader,
Happy to pimp for the foreign stage, and with horrible singing
Earn the laurel wreath, or a Grecian garland of parsley!

From Juvenal, *Eighth Satire,* translated by Rolfe Humphries. Copyright © 1958. Reprinted by permission of the Indiana University Press.

island. A few years later he had to find another distant location for the banishment of his granddaughter. He hushed up the details of both of the affairs, but there was much gossip.

Yet for all the gulf that often existed between appearance and reality in his rule, by the end of his life Augustus was the living symbol of Rome's renewed greatness. As early as 42 B.C., the young Octavian decreed divine honors for the late Julius Caesar. Worship of Augustus himself as divine began while he was still alive, not in Italy—where public opinion would not tolerate worship of a living man—but in many parts of the Empire. The veneration and simple gratitude with which his fellow-countrymen regarded him seem to

HADRIAN INAUGURATES HIS REIGN

The issue of how each emperor's successor should be chosen continued to create problems for the Julio-Claudian and Flavian dynasties. In the end, the solution was that of the adoptive emperors. Even this had its problems, however. When Hadrian came to power in A.D. *118, he faced an immediate challenge from the "Conspiracy of the Four Senators." In order to win popular support, Hadrian immediately issued a proclamation announcing the cancellation of 900 million sesterces of back taxes. The following inscription supposedly records the gratitude of Senate and people at Hadrian's generosity, and tactfully makes no reference to the reason for the emperor's openhandedness.*

A relief sculpture showing the public burning of records of tax arrears, in the presence of Hadrian himself, was set up in the Forum (the sculpture is now in the Senate House there). Clearly the emperor intended to make the maximum propaganda use of his gesture.

Rome Expresses Gratitude to Hadrian

To the emperor Hadrian [there follows a catalogue of his titles], who, first and alone of emperors, remitted nine hundred million sesterces owed to the imperial treasury, and who by this generosity freed from anxiety not only the Roman citizens of his own day, but also their posterity, the Senate and People of Rome [dedicated this inscription].

From ILS, 309, trans. Donald R. Dudley in *Urbs Roma.*

AN EMPEROR'S ADVICE TO HIMSELF

Toward the end of the 2nd century A.D. *the philosopher emperor Marcus Aurelius tried to apply Stoic ideals to the administration of a vast state bureaucracy. His* Meditations *form a kind of journal or diary, recording his successes and—more often—failures in living up to his beliefs. The following passage seems a particularly poignant attempt on his part to adjust to the realities of empire.*

The Moral Burden of Power

Say to yourself in the morning: I shall meet people who are interfering, ungracious, insolent, full of guile, deceitful and antisocial; they have all become like that because they have no understanding of good and evil. But I, who have contemplated the essential beauty of good and the essential ugliness of evil, who know that the nature of the wrongdoer is of one kin with mine—not indeed of the same blood or seed but sharing the same mind, the same portion of the divine—I cannot be harmed by any one of them, and no one can involve me in shame. I cannot feel anger against him who is of my kin, nor hate him. We were born to labor together, like the feet, the hands, the eyes, and the rows of upper and lower teeth. To work against one another is therefore contrary to nature, and to be angry against a man or turn one's back on him is to work against him.

From Marcus Aurelius, *The Meditations* (No. 1), Book II, trans. G. M. A. Grube.

have transcended a formal cult, and they deified him soon after his death.

The restoration of order which his reign brought came at a price. In all the fulsome tributes his contemporaries paid to his greatness, scarcely a single dissenting voice is ever heard. Whatever the many virtues and achievements of the Augustan Age, freedom of expression was not among them. In life, Augustus aimed to exemplify by his own personal behavior the ancient Roman virtues of frugality and morality, while retaining the absolute power of an eastern potentate. Perhaps the dying emperor meant to express the complexity of his role when he turned to the attendants surrounding his deathbed and asked: "Tell me, have I played well my

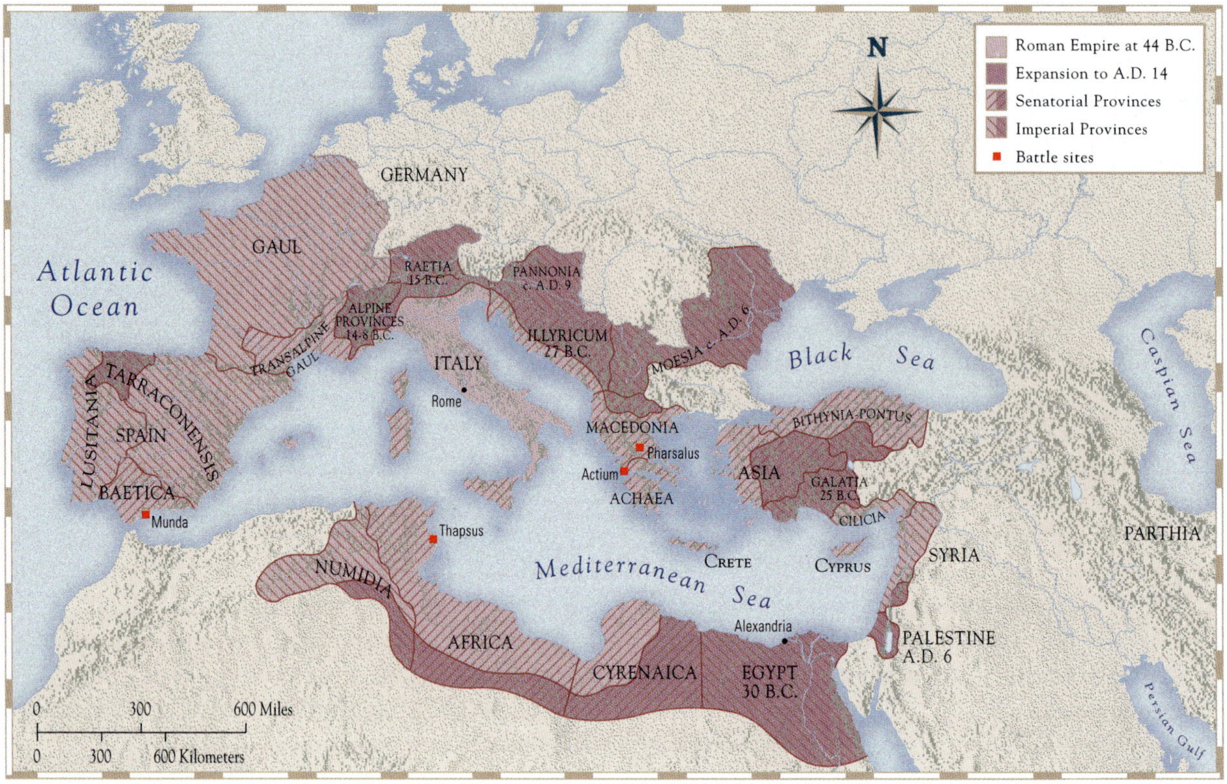

Map 10.1 The Roman Empire in A.D. 14, at the Death of Augustus

part in this comedy of life? If so, applaud me and send me on my way."

PROBLEMS OF IMPERIAL SUCCESSION: THE JULIO-CLAUDIANS

Augustus, the "father of his native land," died leaving no son or other direct male heir. Thus, from the beginning of the history of the Empire, the problem of the succession became crucial. In order to avert the danger of rival ambitions leading to renewed civil war, Augustus' plan was to keep rule of the Empire in his own family, that of the Julio-Claudians, by naming his own successor. To that end, he organized a bewildering series of marriages and divorces involving various branches of the family, but as a result of the length of his reign—and sheer accident—he outlived all the candidates he chose.

Tiberius, Successor to Augustus

In the end Augustus turned to Tiberius (ruled A.D. 14–37), his stepson by his wife Livia's first marriage. The emperor had earlier forced Tiberius to divorce his own wife to marry Julia, Augustus' daughter, but then passed him over for the succession at the time of Julia's disgrace and banishment. When no alternative remained open to Augustus, he recalled the embittered Tiberius from self-imposed exile. To add to Tiberius' resentment, Augustus required him to name as his own successor not his own son, but Augustus' favorite great-nephew, Germanicus.

When Tiberius finally became emperor at the age of 55, he was already disillusioned. A solitary and unpopular figure, he suffered the further disadvantage of having to follow one of the best loved leaders in Roman history. He spent as much time as he could in seclusion at his villa on the island of Capri, and Roman gossips outdid themselves in speculating on the vices he practiced there. His popular reputation, already low, declined further when in A.D. 23 he delegated authority to Sejanus, the wily and sinister captain of the imperial guard. Only eight years later, in A.D. 31, did Tiberius learn of Sejanus' plot to become the next emperor. He ordered Sejanus' immediate execution.

Tiberius' successful administration of the Empire was a result of his careful choice of officials and prompt dismissal of those who proved inefficient or corrupt. Under his watchful control, the bureaucratic machinery of government ran smoothly both at home and in the provinces. His fiscal conservatism made it possible to invest public funds in important road construction projects in Gaul and Spain, and for an urgently needed overhaul of Rome's water system. The public, used to Augustus' lavish displays and games, grumbled at Tiberius' tight-fistedness.

At the time of his death, there was general peace throughout the Empire, the authority of the Senate was even higher than under Augustus, and the treasury contained a surplus. Yet his contemporaries rejoiced at his demise, and later Roman historians painted him as a bloodthirsty tyrant. Lacking the charisma and sense of public relations of his great predecessor, by his positive achievements Tiberius maintained the stability and prosperity of the Augustan years.

Caligula the Divine

In naming a successor, Tiberius was limited by Augustus' choice of his great-nephew Germanicus. When Germanicus died in A.D. 19, Tiberius turned to the dead man's son Gaius (ruled A.D. 37–41). The results were catastrophic.

Gaius spent much of his childhood with his father on the Rhine frontier where Germanicus held command. The troops dressed the child in miniature military costume, and his nickname Caligula (by which he is best-known) means "little boots." Already a favorite of the soldiers, and coming to power after the remote and gloomy old Tiberius, Caligula appeared to offer new promise. The frequent games and festivals he organized at Rome during the early months of his reign aroused wild popular enthusiasm.

Yet nothing had prepared him for the responsibilities of office, and the absolute power he wielded went to his head. He seems to have spent his mercifully brief reign testing the extent of that power—limitless, he claimed, because of his divine descent from Julius Caesar and Augustus. Among his schemes was the construction of a bridge connecting the Palatine Hill (residence of the emperor) with the Temple of Jupiter on the Capitoline Hill, to make it easier for him to visit his brother god. To fund this and other extravagances, he appointed professional informers to accuse wealthy citizens of treason. The emperor would then have them executed and confiscate their estates.

His "marriage" to his sister, the naming of his favorite horse to the consulship, an expedition to conquer Britain which took the army up to the northern coast of France, only to have them collect seashells and return to Rome again—the result of all these actions was that the army, which had idolized him as a child, killed him in response to the widespread hatred he had aroused. The feeling was mutual. Caligula once expressed regret that the Roman people did not have just one neck, so that he could sever it with a single blow.

Claudius the Bureaucrat

Whatever the impact of Caligula's reign at Rome, the administration of the provinces continued to run smoothly—a tribute to Tiberius' organizational skills. With the accession of Claudius (ruled A.D. 41–54) came the restoration of order at Rome itself.

There is no evidence that Caligula ever gave a moment's thought to naming his successor. In the confusion following his assassination, the palace guard picked on the dead ruler's old uncle, Claudius, whose physical disabilities (they included a stammer and a limp) meant that hitherto he had played little part in public life. A professional writer and historian, Claudius brought to his duties a learning and sense of perspective greater than any of his predecessors—and most of his successors.

The soldiers may have chosen Claudius because they considered him weak and therefore easy to manipulate. In the event, Claudius' administration of the state was firm and, above all, efficient. His reorganization of the complex maze of bureaucracy at Rome divided it into a series of departments, whose bureau chiefs reported directly to the emperor. The senators complained that these department heads, often former imperial slaves of Greek origin, had more power and easier access to the emperor than the Senate itself, but Claudius' reforms proved fundamental to stable government over the next two centuries.

Unlike Caligula, Claudius mounted a serious expedition to conquer Britain and add it to the imperial territory. In A.D. 43 Claudius himself, the scholar emperor, led the forces which won control of most of southern England and made it into a Roman province. Like Caesar in Gaul, Claudius treated provincial citizens in Britain and elsewhere with liberality, extending to them Latin rights or citizenship. He also encouraged them to run for political office at Rome.

For his contemporaries and immediate successors, Claudius' significant contributions to the welfare of the Empire were far less interesting than the scandalous behavior of his last two wives (he had a total of four). Gossip had it that when the emperor died suddenly in A.D. 54, apparently from eating poisoned mushrooms, Agrippina, his last wife, was responsible. Whatever the truth of the stories (and there seems little reason to doubt them), Agrippina seized her chance and maneuvered her 16-year-old son by a previous marriage into succeeding Claudius as emperor. His name, Nero (ruled A.D. 54–68), has become a byword for wanton brutality.

Nero the Artist

The first five years of Nero's reign passed relatively uneventfully. Agrippina, his mother, governed on Nero's behalf, together with his tutor Seneca (4 B.C.?–A.D.

65), and Burrus, head of the palace guard. The two men had little patience with Agrippina's autocratic ways, and tried to restore elements of a republican system. All three made the mistake of encouraging Nero to distract himself with his stage performances (he sang and played the lyre), and with a series of violent sexual escapades.

The result was to create a monster. On coming of age in A.D. 59, Nero demonstrated his new independence by having his formidable mother murdered. This was the first in a chain of killings, to be followed by his wife and then his mistress Poppaea, whom Nero himself kicked to death when she was pregnant. In a series of fake treason trials, he adopted Caligula's method of obtaining funds from rich citizens by having them condemned and their fortunes confiscated.

In A.D. 64 a great fire swept Rome. Many suspected Nero of starting it, although the emperor tried to deflect the accusations by blaming the Christians, a sect which had recently appeared at Rome (see Part II, Topic 13). At all events, Nero took advantage of the damage caused to the buildings of central Rome to have a large area cleared for the construction of a new imperial residence, the *Domus Aurea*, or Golden House. Many of its buildings were torn down by angry crowds after Nero's fall, while one part of it—Nero's private lake—was cleared to provide the foundations of the most famous of all Roman structures, the Colosseum.

Growing discontent at Rome led to two conspiracies, in A.D. 65 and 66, put down with predictable ferocity, while misgovernment of the provinces provoked a major uprising in Britain under the leadership of the British queen Boadicea. Some 70,000 Roman soldiers fell in the fighting before order was restored. In A.D. 68 further revolts broke out in Gaul and Spain, which were actually led by the two provinces' Roman governors. As the situation precipitated, the Senate in desperation declared Nero a public enemy. The emperor, by now abandoned by all, lamented that so great an artist as he was should have to die, and then called on a slave to cut his throat. The Julio-Claudian dynasty was over.

At the beginning of Augustus' reign, the founder of the Empire did everything possible to hide the fact that the emperor was all-powerful. By the death of Nero the possible consequences of unlimited power were clear to all. Part of the cause lies in the personal characters of Caligula and Nero, but in part the responsibility also lay with the Senate and—to a lesser extent—the people. Neither class made any real attempt to use the powers which first Augustus and then Tiberius and Claudius tried to share with them. First fawning respect and then simple fear kept the authority of the emperor unchallenged until the situation reached a point of crisis.

Significant Dates

The Julio-Claudian Emperors

31 B.C.	Octavian wins Battle of Actium
27 B.C.	Octavian takes name of Augustus
23 B.C.–A.D. 14	Establishment of Principate and reign of Augustus
A.D. 14–37	Reign of Tiberius
A.D. 37–41	Reign of Caligula
A.D. 41–54	Reign of Claudius
A.D. 54–68	Reign of Nero
A.D. 69	Year of the Four Emperors

The one force which did increase its influence was the army. The last two Julio-Claudian emperors owed their position to military backing or connivance, and, when crisis came under Nero, rival military commanders struggled for control.

THE ARMY AND THE EMPERORS: VESPASIAN AND HIS SONS

From April A.D. 68 to December A.D. 69, four successive generals seized imperial power, in a period known as the "Year of the Four Emperors." The last of them, Vespasian (ruled A.D. 69–79), used Roman troops from his command in Jerusalem to march on Italy and win control of Rome. Once again, the army played the chief role in deciding the succession. As the Roman historian Tacitus put it, the secret of empire was that its control depended on the legions.

Vespasian, Second Founder of the Empire

When Vespasian came to power, the situation he faced was the same as the one Augustus had tried to resolve 100 years earlier: the aftermath of bitter civil conflict combined with financial crisis. Vespasian lacked some of Augustus' advantages. The founder of the Empire came to power young, and benefited from the charisma that came from having Julius Caesar in the family. Even more seriously, by Vespasian's time the Romans' faith in the Augustan system was badly shaken. It was clearly flawed, and could be capable of spectacular failure.

A street in Pompeii. The stepping-stones in the foreground would have kept the passerby's feet dry after a rainstorm.

In one crucial respect, however, Vespasian had an advantage of his own: two sons. From the beginning of his reign he declared them his heirs, and set about training them for their future role (the reigns of father and the two sons formed the Flavian dynasty, their family name). He shared the consulship with Titus, his elder son (ruled A.D. 79–81), on seven occasions, and appointed him to most of the highest offices of state. Domitian (ruled A.D. 81–96) held the title of Prince of the Youth. Some Cynic and Stoic philosophers grumbled that a man's sons were not necessarily the best candidates to succeed him, but on the whole Vespasian's subjects greeted his scheme with relief.

In a deliberate attempt to summon up memories of Augustus, the new emperor opened his reign by adding two new buildings to the heart of Rome, a Temple of Peace and a Forum of Peace. At the same time, in constructing the Colosseum as a place of mass entertainment in the ruins of Nero's Golden House, he underlined the contrast between his concern for the public interest and his predecessor's monstrous megalomania: the private playground of one man became a stadium holding some 50,000.

The combination of Nero's extravagance and civil war had left the treasury in disastrous condition, and Vespasian tried to repair the damage by reforming the tax system. In A.D. 73–74, he ordered a census and reevaluation of all property in the Empire, and raised taxes to correspond to the rise of property values. He granted Latin rights to all Spaniards, a privilege which brought the obligation of having to pay inheritance taxes.

Unlike Augustus, Vespasian made no pretense that the Senate still ran the government, but used it principally to draw on as a pool of administrative talent. By the time of his death, the emperor was firmly established as the head of a vast centralized bureaucracy, which the imperial staff ran on a day-to-day basis, but in which the final decision was the emperor's alone.

A conscientious worker, Vespasian maintained a grueling schedule and led a modest personal life, sharing the sacrifices of his fellow-citizens. During the extensive rebuilding program at Rome, in an adroit public relations gesture, he helped the workmen to cart away baskets full of rubble still remaining from the fire of Nero's reign. His subjects mourned his passing, and after the funeral they made him a god.

Flavian Successors

Had he lived longer, Titus might have been one of Rome's greatest emperors. None came so well prepared to power. Experienced in warfare, a proven administrator, in his brief reign Titus became legendary for his generosity. Posterity credits him with remembering one evening at dinner that he had performed no kindness since morning, and remarking: "Friends, I have wasted a day." When he died suddenly, a grieving Senate and people sent him to join his father in heaven.

The Romans had cause to grieve. Domitian, Vespasian's younger son, made it clear from the first that he intended to rule as an autocrat. He held the office of censor permanently, giving him control of membership of the Senate. His own personal behavior recalled the worst excesses of Caligula and Nero. One of his mistresses was his niece, and he required his aides to address him as "master and god."

On the other hand, unlike the worst of his predecessors, Domitian was an efficient and painstaking administrator. He chose provincial governors who proved honest, maintained the support of the legionaries by raising their pay, and won popularity in Italy by giving farmers who were working public land the right to own it. In the end, Domitian's undoing was his own growing paranoia. Fearing plots against his life, he ordered the arrest of anyone whom he suspected, basing his acts on information received from a band of spies who worked for the state. The more victims he executed, the more he feared reprisals, sleeping with a dagger by his side and having the walls of his living quarters polished, so that he could see the slightest movement behind him. The conspiracy which finally led to his assassination had amongst its members not only many of his palace staff, but even his own wife.

Unlike the reigns of Caligula and Nero, Domitian's rule left most Romans better-off. The Flavian dynasty as a whole provided the longest period of ordered, methodical government since Augustus. Yet the same problem remained: how should the next emperor be chosen? Domitian died without leaving an heir, and in any case his example showed that passing power down in the family was not without its disadvantages. This time, however, the conspirators—with the cooperation of the Senate—addressed the problem of the succession before eliminating Domitian, rather than waiting until he was dead to find a replacement.

THE PAX ROMANA AND THE "FIVE GOOD EMPERORS"

The Senate and conspirators picked on a distinguished elderly senator to provide a period of transition and then Domitian was duly assassinated. The chosen replacement was Nerva (ruled A.D. 96–98). One of the few lasting legislative acts of his brief reign was a scheme to provide food and education for poor Italian children. Known as the "alimentary institution," over the next century it developed into an elaborate welfare system, designed to protect the less well-off. Realizing the possibility of a military challenge from army forces loyal to Domitian, Nerva hastened to choose and adopt a popular general as his successor (he himself was childless, as were his four successors), and then died three months later.

Roman aqueduct in Segovia, Spain, built in the 2nd century A.D.

The Spanish Succession

Trajan (ruled A.D. 98–117), whose family was from Italica in Spain, was the first provincial to achieve imperial power. A successful general, Trajan was governor of Upper Germany at the time of Nerva's death.

Trajan based his administration on meticulous organization and care for detail. The correspondence has survived between the emperor and one of the provincial governors, Pliny the Younger, governor of Bithynia (in modern central Turkey), and it documents the emperor's operating procedures. Pliny's letters contained many queries and requests for instructions on matters ranging from collapsing buildings to the new sect of Christians. A secretarial staff at Rome consulted the imperial archives to see if there had been a similar problem in the past, and passed on any precedent to Pliny. Where a matter broke new ground, Trajan himself provided carefully considered advice that was generally practical and humane.

Trajan's own ambitious building plans at Rome, including roads, a new aqueduct bringing water to the poorer parts of the city, and a grandiose Forum, inspired widespread construction throughout the Empire. The Forum commemorates Trajan's chief foreign success, his conquest of Dacia (modern Romania)—the last piece of new territory in Europe to be added to the Empire. The gold from Dacia's mines helped to fund much of the rebuilding at Rome.

His last foreign adventure was more ambitious: the defeat of Rome's old enemies, the Parthians. Although weary from years of campaigning and weakened by his heavy consumption of alcohol, Trajan personally led the expedition to the East. Initial victories turned to disappointment as the Parthians fought back, and the emperor—who had suffered a stroke—finally decided to make for home. He died on the way, in the middle of Asia, in the blazing heat of August A.D. 117.

Right at the end of his life, Trajan finally made official what had long seemed his intention by adopting

Portrait of the emperor Hadrian.

Significant Dates

The Flavians and Their Successors (all dates A.D.)

69–79	Reign of Vespasian
79–81	Reign of Titus
81–96	Reign of Domitian
96–98	Reign of Nerva
98–117	Reign of Trajan
117–138	Reign of Hadrian
138–161	Reign of Antoninus Pius
161–180	Reign of Marcus Aurelius
180–192	Reign of Commodus

as his son and successor a distant Spanish relative, Hadrian (ruled A.D. 117–138). Most of Hadrian's life in the years before he became emperor was spent in preparation, holding offices and acquiring experience at home and abroad. When he finally achieved power, therefore, he had a definite program. His economic policy was one of generosity. One of his first acts was to cancel the debts of all citizens to the state. During his reign he reduced taxes and established fair maximum prices in years of bad harvests, and extended Nerva's welfare schemes.

In foreign policy, Hadrian reversed Trajan's plans for yet more conquest. The new policy was to maintain and guarantee the peace of the Empire as it was by strengthening its defenses. He had troops stationed on the frontiers, building walls and reinforcing preexisting defense systems. To keep their morale high, Hadrian spent much of his reign traveling to virtually every part of the Empire, inspecting his soldiers' conditions. His peace policy succeeded. The only serious uprising against Rome during his time was a revolt of the Jews in Jerusalem (A.D. 132–134). Hadrian ordered it crushed with the utmost ferocity.

The Antonines

Hadrian's successor, Antoninus Pius (ruled A.D. 138–161), continued the general lines of his policy, but without the personal supervision that was one of the main factors in Hadrian's success—Antoninus spent the whole of his reign in Italy. At his death, wars broke out in many parts of the empire.

Marcus Aurelius (ruled A.D. 161–180), the last of the "five good emperors," had to deal with trouble in Parthia and the invasion of German tribes across the northern frontiers. A Stoic philosopher, Marcus spent most of his reign in incessant military campaigning.

Equestrian statue of Marcus Aurelius.

No sooner did he achieve temporary peace in one region, than he rushed with his troops to the next crisis spot. He died before reestablishing a strong northern frontier.

The first emperor since Vespasian to produce a son, Marcus Aurelius nominated him as his successor. Commodus (ruled A.D. 180–192) was an incompetent coward, devoted to the pursuit of pleasure. The result of his father's bad judgment was to place Rome in the hands of a series of military despots. As early as A.D. 193, the palace guards auctioned off the Empire to the highest bidder, and throughout the following century the army and its warring leaders presided over a state in increasing decline.

The 18th-century English historian Edward Gibbon, in an oft-cited passage, described the years from the death of Domitian to the accession of Commodus as "the period in the history of the world during which the condition of the human race was most happy and prosperous." So sweeping a claim is difficult to justify. For all the welfare legislation and building projects, increasing prosperity and generally efficient provincial government, widespread poverty existed in many parts of the Empire—not least in the urban slums of Rome itself.

Yet on the whole the adoptive emperors did provide an extended period of tranquillity. Their own sense of duty to the state inspired wealthy citizens to spend money on public projects. It is no chance that the 2nd century A.D. saw the construction of libraries in many provincial cities, accompanied by the spread of education. Rome probably remained free of epidemic disease until the end of the 2nd century

A.D., and produced enough food to avoid major famines until the last two decades of the century.

The emperor remained an autocratic ruler. For all the polite gestures which Trajan or Hadrian made toward the Senate, they made their own decisions. Yet by comparison with the repressive regimes of many of the later emperors, they shine as dedicated servants of the state. Gibbon's judgment may exaggerate, but it contains a germ of truth.

Questions for Further Study

1. What were the fundamental reforms whereby Augustus changed the Roman political system from Republic to monarchy? What, if anything, made them necessary, and how successful were they?
2. What were the chief elements in Roman political life in the first two centuries of the Empire? What part did the army play?
3. What were the effects of imperial rule on life in the provinces? How did it vary under Augustus' successors?
4. How did Augustus and his successors use propaganda?

Suggestions for Further Reading

Barrett, A. *Caligula, the Corruption of Power.* New Haven, CT, 1990.

Campbell, J. B. *The Emperor and the Roman Army.* New York, 1984.

Isaac, B. *The Limits of Empire: The Roman Army in the East.* New York, 1990.

Levick, B. *Tiberius the Politician.* London, 1986.

Millar, F. *The Roman Empire and Its Neighbors.* New York, 1981.

Millar, F., and E. Segal, eds. *Caesar Augustus.* Oxford, 1984.

Perowne, S. *Hadrian.* London, 1987.

Topic 11

Politics and the Arts: Roman Imperial Culture

The cultural program of the Augustan age played a central role in conveying the political significance of the emperor's reforms. Through his adviser on cultural affairs, Maecenas, Augustus used the visual arts and literature to spell out his main themes: the return of peace, the importance of Rome's agricultural origins, the Romans' sense of destiny as world rulers.

The historian Livy provided an official account of Rome's early history. The chief poets of the regime, including above all Vergil and Horace, composed works expressing a sense of renewal in keeping with the spirit of the times, while the sculptors of the great Altar of Peace combined myth and historical reality to provide visible proof of the Augustan achievement. The effect of such sustained cultural energy was to produce a Golden Age in the arts.

The art of the portrait bust was first developed in the late Republic, as a means of reflecting the values of the Republican elite. It became an important element in the official art of the Empire. Augustus maintained an iron control over the use of imperial images. Under his successors, sculptors often succeeded in conveying more complex statements about the ruling classes. In the 2nd century A.D., Hadrian used the style of High Classical Greek art to recreate—in stone at least—a return to the idealizing world of Periclean Athens.

Hadrian also made an important impact on Roman architecture, an artistic field in which the Roman genius for adaptation and control found its highest expression. At Rome itself, and throughout the Empire, architects produced buildings to satisfy the needs of large sectors of the population, not just a ruling elite. Theaters, stadiums, public baths, forum complexes—each type of structure took the same basic form throughout the Empire.

In this way urban planning and design reinforced the sense of a supranational Roman identity, which transcended the enormous differences between the Roman provinces of Europe, Asia, and Africa. At the same time, domestic architects provided comfortable houses in styles suitable to local climates. The best preserved dwellings are those at Pompeii.

The literature of the late 1st and the 2nd centuries A.D., a period known as the Silver Age, is less elevated but more varied than that of the Augustan period. Pliny the Elder combined a wide range of topics in his *Natural History*. Growing interest in theories of education finds its reflection in the writings of Quintilian. Many writers turned to satire to express their anger at the confusion of the times.

Above all, the Silver Age produced one of the greatest historians of antiquity, Tacitus. In his own inimitable style, biting, ironic, pessimistic, he provides unforgettable portraits of the figures dominating the tumultuous years he lived through.

THE WORLD ACCORDING TO AUGUSTUS: THE GOLDEN AGE OF ART AND LITERATURE

In the last two centuries of the Republic, the Romans looked to Greece for artistic inspiration. They imported Greek statues and based their works of literature on Greek models (see Part II, Topic 8). The cultural renewal under Augustus thus served two distinct purposes. It spelled out clearly the chief lines of Augustus' political and social reforms, while also giving the Romans an artistic legacy that was specifically their own. Even Augustus could not turn away completely from the influence of the Greeks, but under his guidance writers and artists created Roman equivalents of the masterpieces of Greek art.

Augustus entrusted the day-to-day administration of his cultural program to Maecenas (c. 70–8 B.C.), a diplomat and the emperor's personal friend. Maecenas was famous for his wealth, and used it to provide subsidies for the leading poets of the day, many of whom he personally discovered and encouraged. Enlisting them in the service of the regime, he offered them the support and respect their talents needed—to this day his name is synonymous with enlightened and generous patronage.

The Achievements of Latin Literature

The hectic years of the late Republic left little time for leisurely contemplation and study of the past. When Augustus came to power, one of his first acts was therefore to commission an official history of Rome from legendary times to his own day, the first complete history of Rome ever written. His chosen author was Livy (59 B.C.–A.D. 17), who came to Rome from Padua as a young man and spent the rest of his life on the project.

Livy's *History of Rome* was in 142 books, of which only 35 survive intact. He began with the (mythical) arrival of Aeneas in Italy, and took his narrative up to 9 B.C. Central to his vision of Rome's past—and, of course, to Augustus'—is the belief in Rome's destiny to rule the world. Without ever falsifying evidence or wilfully distorting facts, Livy paints a picture that glorifies Rome's origins and emphasizes the heroism of the Roman conquest of the Mediterranean. The battles of the Punic Wars take on an almost cosmic significance.

Even in his day, some of the literary lions at court criticized Livy for his "provincialism," but in general his contemporaries greeted the *History* with enthusiasm. It was just the type of picture of their past for which many Romans had been waiting, one that stressed the nobility of their climb to power and underplayed the bitterness of the last century of the Republic. His rich style—contemporaries called it "creamy"—and the vividness of his descriptions won him instant popularity as the leading prose writer of the Augustan age.

The greatest poet of the times—and one of the towering figures in Western literature—was Vergil (70–19 B.C.), a far more complex figure than Livy. Vergil's origins made him an ideal candidate for official patronage. His parents were farmers near Mantua who lost their estate in the chaos of the civil wars. A personal intervention by Augustus (or Octavian, as he still was known then) seems to have resulted in the restoration of his land and Vergil, who had come to Rome to appeal to Rome's new ruler, stayed on in gratitude to his benefactor.

The political context of his first two works was Augustus' plan to revive Italian agriculture. The *Eclogues* (or *Bucolics*) are short pastoral poems describing the lives of shepherds and farmers, with their feuds and rival loves, set against a landscape blending northern Italy and Sicily. His second work, the *Georgics*, is more serious. Composed while Vergil was living in a house near Naples lent him by Maecenas, the *Georgics* offers a poetic guide to farming in Italy: how to cultivate vines and olives, the breeding of horses and cattle, beekeeping. The leading character is Italy herself, "mighty mother of crops and men."

So great was the success of the young poet's work that Augustus entrusted to him the most ambitious literary project of the age. At the head of Greek literature stood the epic poems of Homer, the *Iliad* and *Odyssey*, telling of the Greeks' victory over Troy. Now Rome was to have its own epic poem, the *Aeneid*, describing its heroic foundation, and Augustus commissioned Vergil

Part of a page from an illustrated manuscript of Vergil's *Aeneid*.

to write it. The poet spent the last ten years of his life on the *Aeneid*, and when he died the work was still incomplete. In his will, Vergil asked his friends to destroy the manuscript, but Augustus ordered them to disregard his wishes.

The *Aeneid* tells the story of the flight of the Trojan prince Aeneas from the wreckage of burning Troy. In response to a divine command, Aeneas and a small band of Trojan survivors sail westward to build a new Troy in Italy. The first six of the *Aeneid*'s twelve books describe Aeneas' wanderings—a Latin version of the wanderings of Odysseus described in Homer's *Odyssey*. The later half of the *Aeneid* recounts Aeneas' struggles and eventual success in laying the foundations of his Italian kingdom—the ancestor of Rome. This provides a reverse equivalent of the *Iliad*. Homer's epic deals with the Greek siege of Troy leading to the city's destruction, while in the second part of the *Aeneid*, Aeneas constructs the future of Rome.

The entire *Aeneid* is permeated with Augustan echoes. Aeneas himself, loyal, responsible, aware of the burden of destiny, seems an idealized portrait of Augustus, the man engaged in refounding Rome's greatness. The importance of family, the function of leadership, above all Rome's divine mission to govern, are all fundamental aspects of the *Aeneid* and of Augustus' program. There is even an Eastern queen to foreshadow the danger of Cleopatra: Queen Dido of Carthage, whose love affair with Aeneas almost distracts him from fulfilling his destiny.

Yet for all the brazen fanfares with which Vergil foretells the future glory of Rome and the mighty achievements of Augustus himself, the *Aeneid* is not a happy work. Some of its most profound moments deal with loss and sacrifice: "The world has tears, and mortal affairs touch the heart." Aeneas himself, for all his public heroics, is filled with self-doubt and his break with Dido causes them both deep suffering. Vergil seems to be asking if the sacrifices involved in a revolution on the Augustan scale are worth the price paid in human grief. His instructions to destroy the *Aeneid* may indicate his doubts about the emperor's achievement.

The poetry of Horace (65–8 B.C.) provides a more wholehearted appreciation of Augustus' restoration of peace and prosperity. A more personal poet than Vergil, Horace responds to the mood of the moment, to the warmth of friendship and the slow dying down of the fires of love. His acute sense of time passing increases his delight in the present. Some of his *Odes* are openly political, but for the most part they express the return of civilization to Roman life, Augustus' greatest gift to his subjects.

The Augustan Altar of Peace

Augustus claimed in his autobiography: "I found Rome a city of brick, and left it a city of marble." His massive architectural reconstruction at Rome involved the restoration of old temples and the building of new ones, including the Temple of Mars the Avenger which housed the legionary standards recovered from the Parthians.

The most complete artistic statement of the Augustan worldview was the Altar of Peace (Ara Pacis), begun in 13 B.C., on Augustus' return to Rome from a tour of the Empire. The dedication ceremony took place on January 30, 9 B.C., his wife Livia's birthday. The four sides of the screen surrounding the altar itself combine historical and mythological events. The two side panels show the procession making its way to the inauguration in 9 B.C. Preceded by attendants, Augustus leads the priests of Romulus and Remus—legendary founders of Rome—while the imperial family brings up the rear and, on the opposite side, senators and magistrates walk in separate procession.

The front and back panels display myths referring to Rome's past and present greatness. On the front, to left and right of the steps leading to the altar, are scenes referring to Rome's two foundation myths: the birth of Romulus and Remus, and the arrival in Italy of Aeneas. The rear shows on the left Mother Earth, with the bounty of nature which peace makes possible, and on the right the goddess Rome, seated quietly but fully armed—the only way to guarantee a lasting peace is to be prepared to go to war.

Entrance to the Altar of Peace (Ara Pacis), symbol of Augustus' gift of peace to the Empire.

Beneath all, running around the entire altar, is a richly carved band of vegetation, with fruits, flowers, and birds intertwined, to indicate that both history and myth rest symbolically on the secure foundation of the land. Finally, Augustus' deliberate evocation of a Golden Age is reflected in the style of the altar's sculptures, based on that of Periclean Athens, the Golden Age of Greece.

HISTORY AND PERSONALITY IN IMPERIAL SCULPTURE

By the late Republic, sculptors were producing portraits that combined physical realism with psychological insight. For once Roman art was not based on Greek models, since Classical Greek sculpture aimed for idealizing beauty. The Romans derived their interest in realism from the Etruscans, and developed it to express individual character. Late Republican images of anonymous patricians or of leading statesmen like Caesar and Cicero reveal much about their subjects' personalities.

Augustus, seeing the possibilities offered by the medium, commissioned official portraits that presented the emperor in the way he wanted to be seen. The most famous, the *Augustus of Prima Porta,* dates to A.D. 13, when the emperor was in his mid-seventies. The figure, wearing a combination of civic and military dress, retains all the quiet command and ageless vigor of Augustus' portraits of 40 years earlier.

Portraiture under Augustus' Successors

Under later emperors, artists tempered the idealism of Augustan art with realism. Official portraits of both Caligula and Nero leave little doubt as to their inherent brutality. Vespasian emerges as capable and considerate, but his image remains unglamorized, with the scanty hair and lined face revealing the years of hard campaigning.

By the time of Trajan, official art was consciously realistic. The column Trajan set up to commemorate his victories over the Dacians provided scene after scene illustrating the Roman campaign, from the expedition's first moves north across the river Danube to the final enemy surrender. We see troops setting up camp, attacking the walls of a city, marching in formation. Among the more than 2500 figures on the column, Trajan appears some 50 times. Far from idealized, the emperor often seems worried and under strain as he ad-

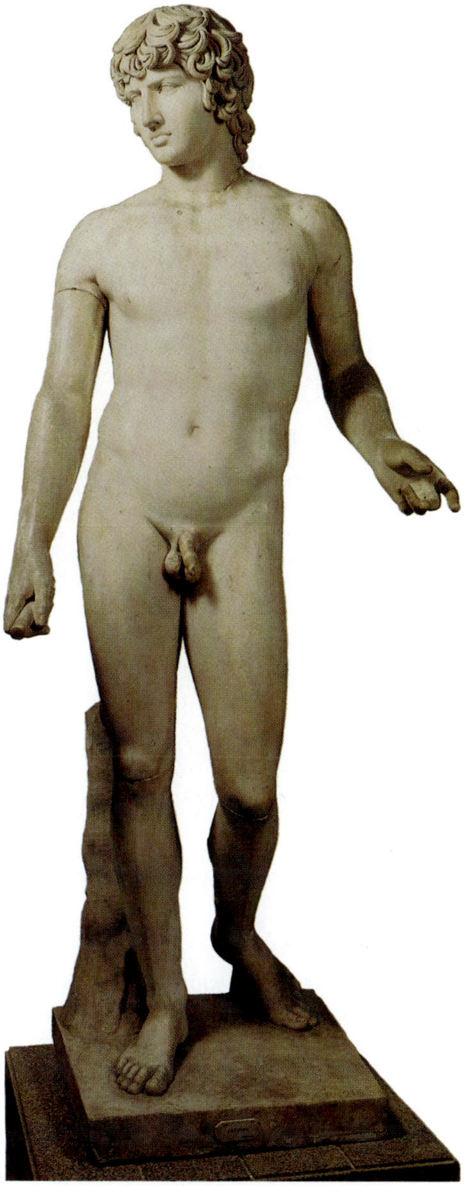

Statue of Antinous (c. 130), showing a return to the style of Classical Athens.

dresses the troops or takes part in war councils with his generals. The overall effect is to downplay the glory and show war as efficient and deadly business.

The ideal beauty of High Classical art returned in the sculpture of the reign of Hadrian. From his youth, Hadrian was infatuated with Greek culture, and one of his first acts as emperor was to visit Athens, where he commissioned the building of a library. Hadrian left Greece in A.D. 121 for the Roman province of Asia (modern Turkey), where he met a young man, Antinous, who was thereafter to be his constant companion and lover. In A.D. 130 Antinous died under mysterious circumstances, and Hadrian, heartbroken at his death, commissioned statue after statue to preserve Antinous' memory. Many of them show Antinous as a Greek god—now Apollo, now Dionysus—and all of them try to recapture the youthful perfection of the art of Classical Athens.

BUILDING THE EMPIRE: ARCHITECTURE IN ROME AND THE PROVINCES

Hadrian himself was an imaginative working architect, whose masterpiece, the Pantheon in Rome, dates to A.D. 125–126, and of all the arts, architecture was the one in which the Romans made their most original and influential contribution to Western culture. The Roman genius excelled at borrowing from other peoples and creating something new from various elements. Thus the Roman form of temple takes aspects of Greek temple architecture and combines them with Etruscan characteristics to produce a new type. Over time, Roman architects produced a series of standard forms of building, ranging from baths to law courts. This standardization of design served a political purpose. The existence of similar types of building in cities throughout the Empire imposed a single, instantly recognizable Roman influence on very different cultures. Wherever Romans went they could find a familiar urban setting.

Roman temples and other building forms first developed as a response to the fact that Roman culture was predominantly urban. Although the vast majority of Roman subjects continued to live in rural areas, Rome itself and the other big cities of the Empire contained millions of citizens whose daily needs became crucial to the survival of the Empire. For the first time in Western history, administrators had to worry about mass water supplies, efficient transport systems, and the manifold problems of city life. They introduced building codes, devised a postal system, and set up police and fire services.

Places of Entertainment

One of the ways in which many of the emperors tried to gain the support of the urban proletariat was by the provision of mass entertainment. The origins of Roman theater and sports and games went back to Etruscan times. Drama was popular by the 2nd century B.C., and theaters built for the performance of Roman plays were a typical Roman adaptation of Greek theater design to an urban Roman setting. Unlike the Greek theaters, with their splendid natural locations offering

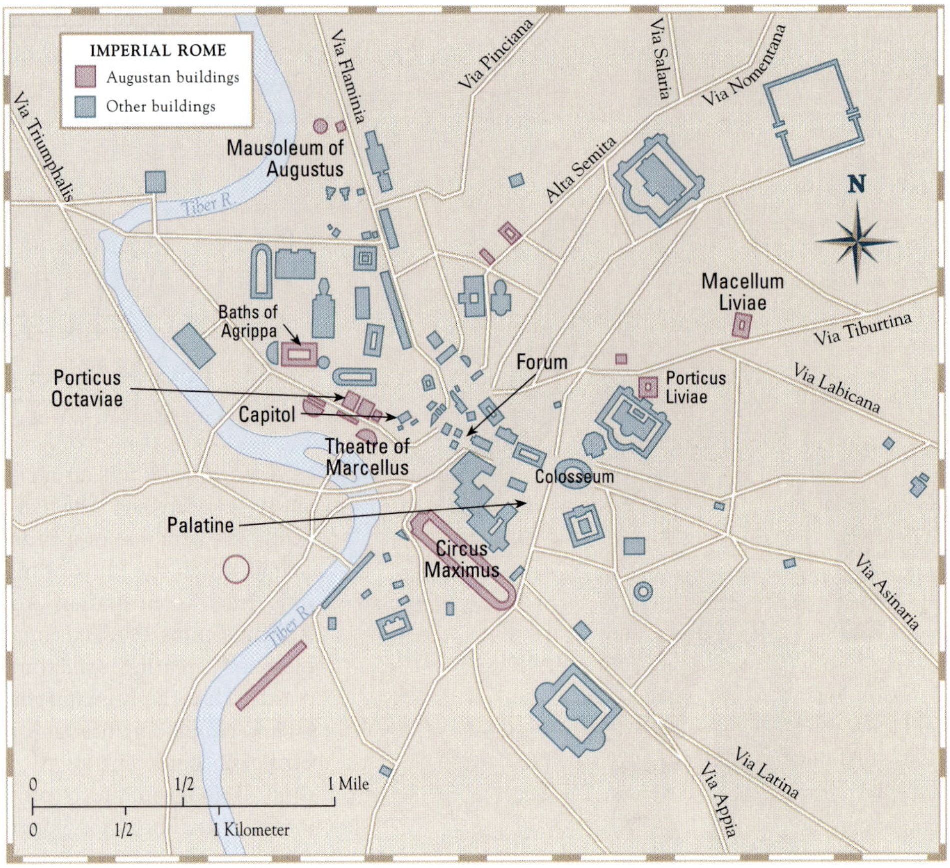

Map 11.1 Imperial Rome

breathtaking views over the surrounding countryside, Roman ones were completely enclosed.

The growing popularity of events such as gladiatorial contests required the invention of a special kind of structure, the amphitheater. The most famous example, Vespasian's Colosseum (see Part II, Topic 10), is only one of hundreds of similar stadiums in every part of the Empire. Nor is its capacity—around 50,000 spectators—exceptional. The most popular of all sports at Rome was chariot racing, and the racetrack where events took place, the Circus Maximus, could contain crowds of a quarter of a million.

Roman amphitheater in Arles, France. Note the electric lights, used for modern performances.

The use of architectural facilities for public activities was not limited to spectator sports. One of the most popular Roman pastimes was attendance at the public baths. Wealthy Romans had their own bath structures at home, but huge public complexes formed an essential part of the urban landscape. The Baths of Caracalla, built at Rome around A.D. 215, could contain 3000 people at one time in its largest hall.

The Use of Concrete

One of the chief factors in the construction of these immense buildings was the Roman invention of concrete and its use in the construction of arches, vaults, and domes—all making it possible to build structures which could contain large numbers of people. Before the Romans, problems of stone cutting and balance meant that architects could build only small-scale arches and domes, and the Greeks never really explored the possibilities of the arch. By the 2nd century B.C., Roman builders had discovered how to dissolve stone fragments in quicklime, and pour the cement over a wooden frame into the shape of vaults and other curved structures. When hardened, the forms were free of any internal stresses and virtually indestructible.

The new method was cheap and tidy, since it used up all the stone fragments left over from other parts of the building. It avoided the need to cut stones of irregular shape, and created huge interiors which were incomparably strong. By the time of Domitian, the use of concrete was widespread in great urban building projects throughout the Empire. Hadrian employed it for the dome of his Pantheon, and experimented with different kinds of arch and vault in his private villa at Tivoli, outside Rome.

The Roman House

Roman building ingenuity was by no means limited to great public constructions. Domestic comfort was also important, and architects adapted their plans to local climates. Most residents of Rome in Augustan times lived in apartment blocks limited to four floors and a total height of 70 Roman feet (68 modern feet). A century later, as crowded conditions at Rome led to hasty and careless construction, Trajan reduced the legal height permitted to 60 Roman feet (58 modern). The apartments were built in rows, with narrow alleys between them, and staircases in the entrances led to the upper floors.

The ground floor almost always contained shops or warehouses. Pipes generally carried water up to the first floor, but residents of the upper-floor apartments had to fetch their own water from public fountains on the street level. Some complexes had an inner courtyard with its own fountain. The most luxurious dwellings were on the lower floors, but rooms in the poorer accommodations above often had elegant mosaic decorations on the floor.

The mild Roman climate meant that houses there could be heated with portable stoves. Residences in northern Italy, France, and Britain often had underfloor central heating. Architects in Roman Syria, where summer brings intense heat, built dwellings with thick stone walls and narrow windows, some of which are still lived in today.

The Evidence of Pompeii

Our most complete picture of urban life in Roman times comes from the excavations at Pompeii and Herculaneum, cities on the Bay of Naples, which were buried by the eruption of the volcano Vesuvius on August 24, A.D. 79. The slow work of exploring the ruins began in the mid-18th century and still goes on. By

Entrance to one of the most elaborate private dwellings at Pompeii.

An aerial view of the excavations at Pompeii.

the end of the 20th century just over three fifths of Pompeii are once more visible.

Pompeii was a small, prosperous market town with a population of around 20,000. The main industry was the production and dying of fabric. There were three sets of baths and three places of public entertainment: a theater seating 5000, a concert hall seating 1000, and an amphitheater with room for 20,000. Other facilities included sidewalk bars and cafés, and a number of brothels.

The private houses were generally open-plan, with rooms grouped around a central hall, or atrium, and with a pleasant enclosed garden in the rear. Some houses had a summer and a winter dining area, to take advantage of the sun, while the largest of all, the House of the Faun, had four dining rooms, one for each season. Frescoes decorated the walls, and the furniture included bronze candlesticks, wooden beds, and iron safes for holding money and family treasures such as silver tableware.

To a modern visitor, familiar with the squalor of late-20th century urban life, a stroll in Pompeii suggests a level of comfort unimaginable for many today. Yet Pompeii and Herculaneum were small, provincial centers, inhabited by hard-working lower-middle-class and lower-class citizens. One of the most elaborate houses was probably that of the baker, Pacuvius Proclus. The streets of Pompeii offer only the most distant glimmer of the quality of life in the elegant quarters of Rome, Alexandria, or many another center of Roman culture.

WRITERS OF THE SILVER AGE: RHETORIC, SATIRE, AND HISTORY

The Silver Age of Latin literature extended from the death of Augustus to the end of Hadrian's reign. Although it produced no single writer of the calibre of Vergil, the Silver Age saw a broader range of literary topics and genres. The very grandeur of Augustan literature, in fact, served to inhibit later writers. Who, after Vergil, would dare to compose an epic, and who, after Livy, could imagine writing a universal history? Furthermore, emperors after Augustus were less concerned to treat writers with tact. The authors of works that offended Caligula, Nero, or Domitian well knew what fate awaited them.

In general, therefore, writers of the Silver Age sought to impress their audience with style rather than content, and rhetoric became an end in itself. Learned references, obscure allusions, and clever epigrams were some of the ways in which authors of the period aimed to make their mark. One of the rare exceptions was the *Natural History* of Pliny the Elder (A.D. 23–79), an extraordinary collection of information which was intended for reference rather than entertainment. The subjects covered include animals, insects, trees and plants, medicines, and metals. Influential in Medieval Europe, Pliny's work has been described by a modern commentator as "a compendium of all the errors of the ancient world."

Rhetoric in the Early Empire

The leading authority on education in the Silver Age was Quintilian (c. A.D. 35–c. 95). In the reign of Vespasian, his preeminence in the field earned him an official position and salary as head of the teaching profession, awarded to him by the emperor himself. Among his pupils were Pliny the Younger—Trajan's correspondent from Bithynia—and Domitian's great-nephews. In addition to teaching, he also practiced as a lawyer.

Quintilian's *Education of an Orator,* published at the end of his life, combined his two main interests: educational theory and rhetoric. Most of the work consists of a rigorous analysis of various kinds of oratorical subject, style, and delivery—"much wormwood and too little honey," as the author disarmingly says of his own dry style. The first part, however, offers a surprisingly enlightened discussion of the education of children. The teacher, he believed, should be the pupil's friend, inspiring by enthusiasm and fundamental human decency and wisdom. Unlike many later theoreticians, Quintilian discouraged the use of corporal punishment, which he felt had only a negative effect.

The Satirists: Petronius and Juvenal

If Pliny and Quintilian represent the serious side of the literature of their age, Petronius (?–A.D. 66) shows us the bizarre and comic aspects of life during Nero's reign. A favorite at Nero's court, Petronius became the "Arbiter of Taste" there, only to fall foul of the commander of the palace guard. In A.D. 66 he committed suicide, but not before smashing a precious vase which he knew the emperor coveted.

His novel, the *Satyricon,* of which only parts survive, describes the adventures of three disreputable young men in the bars and brothels of southern Italy. The climax comes with an account of a dinner party given by a vulgar multi-millionaire social climber, Trimalchio. Petronius makes fun of the host's absurd costume, pretentious behavior, and tasteless menu. Later scenes alternate graphically erotic episodes with an ironic plan to fleece legacy hunters—hanging around rich men in the hope of being left something in their wills was a notorious practice in imperial Rome.

Petronius piles on ridiculous details to comic effect. The greatest of all Roman satirists, Juvenal (A.D. ?60–?130), tries to evoke a very different emotion: outrage at the corruption and decadence of his day. Born in central Italy, he came to Rome to make a career as a magistrate, and fell foul of Domitian. After a period of exile he returned to Rome to live in poverty, before ending his days in modest comfort, apparently thanks to help from Hadrian.

Juvenal's 16 *Satires* purport to deal with the age of Domitian, and attack only the dead, but his rage against his own time remains blazing. In the Third Satire, he takes on Rome, the center of vice and corruption, filled with extremes of poverty and extravagance, where foreigners—Greeks and Easterners—are among the worst offenders. The Sixth Satire is directed against women. Chastity, says Juvenal, left the earth centuries ago, and he describes in vivid detail what

Remains of food preserved at Pompeii.

replaced it. All types of women fall victim to his hatred: quarrelsome and bickering ones, gossips, women who procure abortions and drive their husbands insane with drugs, and—in the same breath—learned women who spout Greek quotations.

Juvenal aims his fire at so many targets, and allows rhetoric to carry him to such extremes, that his anger sometimes seems counterproductive. Yet there is no denying the brilliance of his character-drawing or the power of his flashing epigrams, while the picture he paints of imperial Rome provides a dramatic corrective to official propaganda.

Tacitus the Historian

Tacitus (A.D. c. 56–120), the greatest historian of his age—and many other ages, too—was also, like Juvenal, concerned to set the record straight. Unlike Juvenal, however, Tacitus was an insider. Vespasian made him a senator, he was consul in A.D. 97, and governor of Asia in A.D. 112–113. His two chief works were the *Histories* and the *Annals*. Written in the reigns of Trajan and Hadrian, they tell the story of the period from the death of Augustus to the assassination of Domitian—an age he describes as "rich in catastrophe, fearful in its battles, fertile in mutinies—bloody even in peace."

Tacitus recounts his terrible tale in a style that combines irony and biting scorn, wit and dignified pessimism. The first of his targets is Tiberius, and other unforgettable figures to emerge include Nero and his mother Agrippina. Unlike Juvenal, Tacitus sought to express a serious historical judgment: however bad the Republic was at its worst, it was better than the imperial system at its best. In order to make his point, he is not free from bias, and his belief that those in power determine the course of history would not be shared by all historians. Yet the drama of his narration and the eloquence of his language make him one of the highest masters of Latin literature.

The comedy of Petronius, the savage indignation of Juvenal, and the profundity of Tacitus' moral judgments reveal the darker side of the splendor of empire, one very distant from the self-conscious pride of the art and literature of the Augustan age. Both viewpoints are complementary. As Vergil hints, the peace which Augustus brought came at a price. It was inevitable that the sense of relief that permeates the art of the Golden Age would turn to restlessness as the defects of Augustus' political reforms became increasingly glaring after his death.

Both the official character of Augustan art and the growing hostility of tone in sculpture and Silver Age literature have in common one important factor. From the beginning of the Empire, artists were politically "engaged," using their art either in support of or against the regime. Even in the art of ancient Greece, there were few creative figures who dealt with the events of their own times in so direct and down-to-earth a way. For the dramatists, sculptors, and painters of Classical Athens, art was a means of exploring the universal questions of human existence. With the exception of one or two plays by Aristophanes, their works referred to contemporary events only indirectly.

For better or worse, the links binding art and politics in imperial Rome were unbreakable. With the decline and eventual fall of the Empire, the arts shifted to safer, more solid ground at the service of church and state. Only centuries later, at the end of the 18th century, on the eve of the French Revolution, did artists once again take up an active political and social role.

Questions for Further Study

1. In what ways does the *Aeneid* fulfill its aim to provide the Romans with a national epic? How does it compare in this respect with the Greeks' *Iliad* and *Odyssey*?
2. What was the impact of urban life on Roman architecture and planning? In what ways, if any, were the Romans faced with problems similar to those of modern urban existence, and how did they try to solve them?
3. How did Augustus use the visual arts as a means of propaganda? To what extent did his successors follow his example?

Suggestions for Further Reading

Christ, K. *The Romans: An Introduction to Their History and Civilization*. Berkeley, CA, 1987.

Deiss J. J. *Herculaneum: Italy's Buried Treasure*. New York, 1985.

Ogilvie, R. M. *Roman Literature and Society*. New York, 1980.

Ward-Perkins, J. B. *Roman Imperial Architecture*. New York, 1981.

West, D. A., and A. J. Woodman. *Poetry and Politics in the Age of Augustus*. New York, 1984.

Zanker, P. *The Power of Images in the Age of Augustus*. Ann Arbor, MI, 1988.

II

Topic 12

Daily Life in the Roman World

The aim of the Roman state was to strengthen the sense of Roman unity throughout the Empire by promoting its way of life. A single universal legal system was in operation. The law functioned by the use of past decisions to create precedents in the light of which new cases were tried. The prime source of law was the emperor, who ratified earlier decisions and served as the final court of appeal. Other factors in encouraging trust in the central authority included efficient municipal government and the role of the army.

The day-to-day running of the state was in the hands of the imperial bureaucracy. Under the Julio-Claudians, many of the most powerful administrators were not Roman citizens but freedmen. By the reign of Trajan, as resentment grew at the influence wielded by these freedmen, members of the class of equites began to serve as bureau chiefs, both at Rome and in the provinces. Toward the end of the Empire, the state bureaucracy would be dominated by the military.

The first century of the Empire saw the rise of commerce at the expense of agriculture, especially in Italy, where farming continued to decline. Trade became decentralized, with the great cities of Asia and North Africa offering stiff competition to Italian manufacturers. By the 3rd century A.D., with imperial rule in a state of military anarchy, and Germanic raids on many of the chief trade routes, the economy went into serious decline. The result was a further weakening of state regulation.

The family remained the basis of social life. From the time of Augustus successive emperors tried in vain to produce a rise in the birthrate. In spite of incentives to encourage large families and penalties for the childless, Roman men and women of the upper classes continued to use contraception to avoid pregnancies, and families remained small, especially in Italy.

The chief family of the state was that of the emperor, who was "father of his native land." The women in the imperial family also received honors. Livia, wife of Augustus, was worshiped as divine during her lifetime, and cities in Asia raised temples to her. After Augustus' death she received the title "Augusta." Women continued to enjoy far more personal freedom than in the Republic, although they still played little visible part in politics. The empresses of the Flavian dynasty maintained an influential salon at court, while in the early 3rd century A.D. the women of the Severan family exercised considerable political power.

One of the functions of the state was to protect the interests of citizens, freedmen, and freedwomen. Slaves and gladiators, two underclasses that played an important role in Roman life, received varying treatment. Slaves could win their freedom and then integrate fully into society. Gladiators, who were often condemned criminals, were expendable once they had provided entertainment in the stadium.

LAW, CITIZENSHIP, AND BUREAUCRACY

Augustus believed that one of the responsibilities of imperial rule was to spread Roman civilization throughout the Empire. Under his successors, the Romanization of the provinces imposed order on a wide variety of different cultures. One of the chief tools for the diffusion of Roman ways was education, and both public schools and private endowments became increasingly common. Vespasian endowed chairs in the universities of the great cities, while Hadrian introduced a tax-exempt status for teachers.

Universal Law

The single most effective force for establishing a standard way of life was the law. In the Republic, the source of legal authority was a body of written statutes, which needed regular updating, and was available for public consultation. By the time of the early emperors, the old system was hopelessly out of date, and a new one came into operation.

The law was based on the word of the emperor. Its chief sources were his edicts, his written instructions to officials, and official correspondence. The legal office of the civil service catalogued all this material and used it to provide precedents for future cases in all parts of the Empire. Augustus defended the concentration of legal power in the hands of the emperor by claiming that in nominating him, the Senate and people had delegated him to exercise their power for them. The same principle justified the emperor's functioning as the final court of appeal, a role originally played by an ancient assembly of the people.

By the time of Hadrian, the legal affairs of the Empire were under the control of a board of professional jurists directly under the supervision of the emperor and his staff. The criminal courts, with their juries of ordinary citizens, which Sulla had introduced (see Part II, Topic 9), were replaced by special courts run by the emperor's delegates. In the mid-2nd century A.D., the jurist Gaius (fl. A.D. 130–180) published a textbook, *The Institutes of Roman Law,* which set out the principles of civil law (law affecting private rights). It remained a best-seller for over three centuries, and served as the basis for Justinian's reforms in the 6th century (see Part III, Topic 3).

Citizenship: Civilians and Soldiers

In the late Republic, the Senate used the grant of citizenship rights as a peaceful means of resolving conflicts (as at the end of the Social War in 88 B.C.; see Part II, Topic 9), and to raise the number of people eligible to pay taxes. By the time of the adoptive emperors, citizenship grants provided another means of creating a universal state, all of whose members had the same rights.

The emperors used two other methods to unite the Empire's subjects. The first was the standardization of local government. The administration of towns throughout the provinces continued to follow the lines of Julius Caesar's municipal constitution (see Part II, Topic 9). The free citizens of each town elected the magistrates, who were in charge of financial affairs and

Relief showing tax collectors receiving payments.

public services. The local government had specific responsibility for ensuring a regular supply of oil and flour at fixed prices, and for maintaining reasonable quantities of other provisions, even in times of shortage. The planning of public entertainments was another of the magistrates' duties. Many towns ran municipal shops, baths, and hotels, and used the profits to fund public activities.

The other means of promoting unity, the settlement of Italians in remote parts of the Empire, was less successful. The early emperors encouraged Italians to spread Roman culture and the Latin language and religious tradition by establishing Italian colonies throughout the eastern and western provinces. In many cases the reverse occurred. Italians in Asia or Egypt became converted to local cults and introduced them back into Italy, as in the case of Mithraism and the worship of Isis. A more serious problem was the rapidly declining birthrate in Italy, caused in part by economic deterioration, which severely limited the numbers of Italians who could be sent abroad without depleting the workforce at home.

Tombstone relief of standard-bearer Gnius Musius of the 14th Legion.

The military played a more active role in nation building. All legionaries were Roman citizens, but noncitizens could serve as "auxiliaries," and they and their descendants became citizens on discharge. Since Latin was the official language of the army, the auxiliary troops—Gauls, Cappadocians, and others—who learned it became a means of spreading Roman culture.

The armed forces also had an important influence on the regions in which they were posted. For many provincial citizens, nominally Roman but living hundreds or even thousands of miles from Rome, the army was the only state institution with which they had any regular contact. In some cases, army camps evolved into towns and cities. Since the soldiers built many of the canals, baths, theaters, and other public structures and acted as police force, protecting citizens from robbers and highwaymen, the army often came to represent the positive aspect of state interference in local affairs. It could also, of course, play a more malignant role, as Apuleius' *Golden Ass* makes clear.

The Imperial Bureaucracy

The other arm of state power, the civil service, far from spreading Roman culture, provided non-Romans with a means of winning influence and wealth. The reforms of Claudius strengthened the role of the imperial bureaucracy in the running of government, and many of his former slaves rose to high civil service positions. Unlike the Roman middle-class equites, who despised the notion of office work or bookkeeping, these imperial freedmen were efficient and experienced. Some of the best came from Greek families in Asia, and their level of education was higher than that of many Roman senators.

Standing between the emperor and the reports, petitions, and requests that poured in from all over the Empire, the freedmen prepared answers and submitted them to the emperor for his approval. The mass of paperwork fell into a series of categories, each of which had its own department with an imperial freedman attached as permanent secretary. One office handled correspondence from the provinces, another provincial revenues, another legal cases in which the emperor was interested or involved. A special bureau handled the imperial archives.

Other freedmen occupied positions in the palace that were far below the dignity of Roman citizens, but that brought considerable power with them. None was closer to the emperor himself and his family than the chamberlain, or *cubicularius*. This official controlled access to the emperor, and unscrupulous ones auctioned the chance of an audience to the highest bidder. Some even sold reports on the emperor's mood or state of health—a practice the Romans called "selling smoke."

From the time of Trajan and Hadrian, in response to the resentment felt by many Romans in seeing former slaves running the state, emperors appointed equites as department heads. Hadrian also set up a career service with regular promotions for equestrians, and established generous salary increases.

By the 3rd century A.D., with rule passing chaotically from one military despot to another, the civil service was gradually taken over by the military. Its organization came to resemble the army's, with a chain of command passing from the lowest bureaucrats through the various levels up to the emperor and his chief-of-staff at the top. In the process, the bureaucracy was weighed down with massive increases in the amount of paperwork, while ex-centurions did not always make the most efficient or flexible administrators. Nonetheless, the continued presence of freedmen and imperial slaves as accountants, paymasters, and other office personnel allowed the civil service to continue to function even in time of civil war.

Roman builders using a crane powered by slaves on a treadmill.

THE IMPERIAL ECONOMY: RECOVERY, STABILITY, DECLINE

The reign of Augustus brought an extended period of peace and the conditions for economic recovery. Manufacturing and trade flourished throughout the Empire, with production centers springing up to satisfy local needs. Factories in Gaul made pottery and metal goods for the northern market, while Carthage produced oil lamps for sale in North Africa.

The Spread of Trade

As economic stability spread, so did commerce. The trade with India, which opened up in the time of Augustus, was a lucrative source of profits. Over time, Asian businessmen became the chief traders in the Indian market, as well as increasing their share of profits in the Mediterranean. In northern Europe, by the early 2nd century A.D. Gallic and German traders were the leading commercial force.

One of the factors favoring trade was Roman control of the Mediterranean. The Roman Navy, one of the chief forces in Rome's rise to power, had little fighting to do once the Empire was won. From the reign of Augustus to the late 3rd century A.D. there were no real naval wars. The fleet's main duties were to accompany convoys of goods and keep the seas free of pirates. Ease of shipping brought greater prosperity, leading to improved harbors and canal systems, and extended road networks.

Another factor in the growth of commerce in all parts of the Empire was an international banking system which facilitated currency exchange. Banks accepted deposits, on which they paid interest. Merchants transferred credit from one country to another to pay for goods without having to move cash. The use of Roman currency remained widespread, but in certain periods its value began to fluctuate. Nero was the first ruler to save money by debasing the standard coinage (using less valuable metals), and several of his successors followed his example. As a result, many local mints continued to produce coins that local banks exchanged at rates fixed by the state.

Trade and Agriculture in Italy

There was a price to pay for the spread of stable trading conditions throughout the Empire: recession in Italy. Under Augustus, the factories of central and southern Italy produced goods for sale abroad without much competition. As prosperity spread, the provinces no longer needed to import goods—it was cheaper to make them or to buy them locally. Even the state itself often saved money on transport by feeding and equipping troops on duty in the East with supplies bought on the spot, rather than shipped from Italy.

It was easy for provincial factories to turn out pottery or metal goods of the same quality as those manufactured in Italy at highly competitive prices.

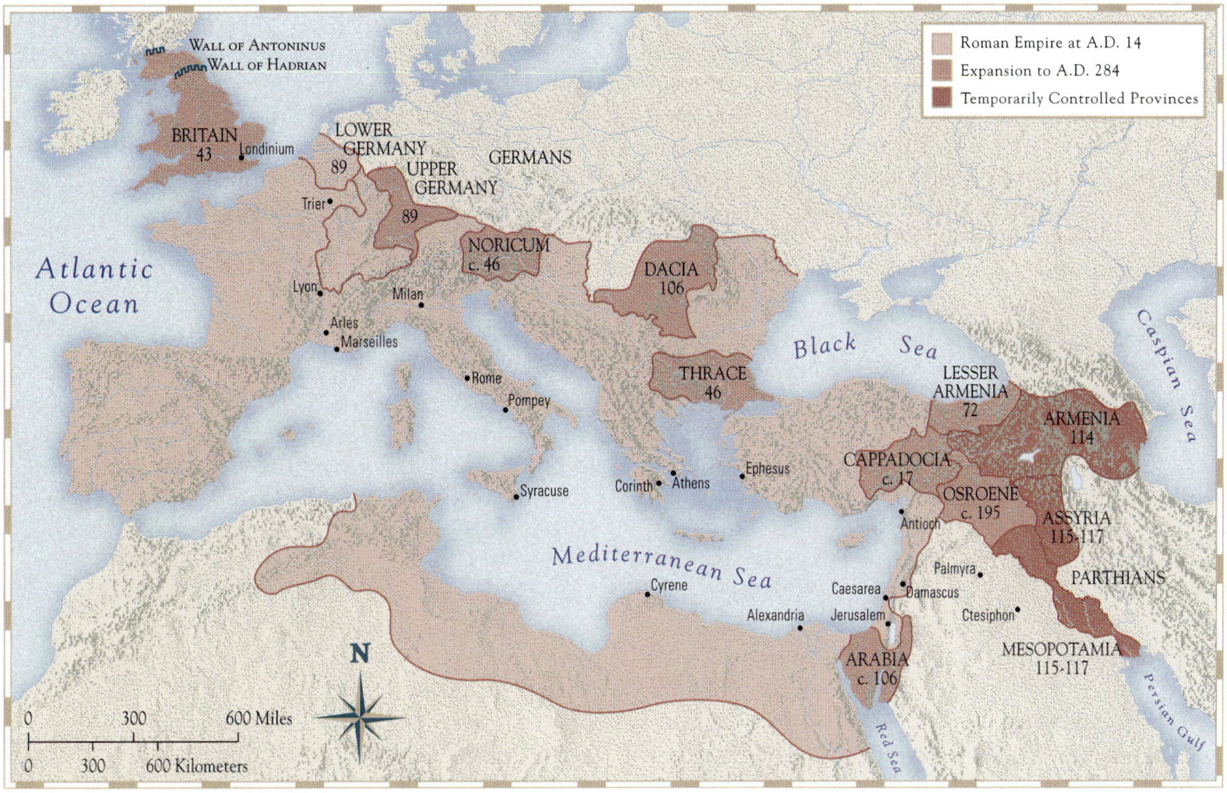

Map 12.1 The Roman Empire in the Time of Diocletian

Fresco from Pompeii showing a busy harbor scene in the Bay of Naples.

Italian factories, however, could not fight back by manufacturing the kinds of goods produced in the provinces because Italy lacked the raw materials. Egypt maintained its monopoly on papyrus, Spain that on steel, and Asia on glass. Thus the richer the Roman Empire grew, the more trade and industry in Italy declined. The gradual shift of economic weight from Italy to the provinces, particularly the wealthy eastern ones, was to have enormous consequences for later imperial history, and continued to affect the West after the Empire's fall.

Nor was Italian agriculture in much better shape. For all Augustus' insistence on the fundamental role of agriculture in Italian life, by the early Empire farming in Italy was in decline. One cause was competition from farmers in Spain and Greece, whose olive oil and wine were often of better quality than those produced in Italy. Furthermore grain producers in the Crimea and Ukraine could supply Roman troops stationed in the East more cheaply than their Italian counterparts.

In the late 1st century A.D. many owners of medium-sized Italian estates gave up trying to make ends meet and sold their land, which was bought up by wealthy absentee landlords. One of the consequences was the decline of country towns, whose income came from the small farmers of their region. Latifundia (large estates) continued to take up most of the arable land in other parts of the Empire as well as in Italy, but the negative effects of the concentration of land in a few hands were most marked in Italian agriculture.

SEXUALITY AND DOMESTIC LIFE

One of the key factors in the increasing economic decline of Italy was the continual fall in the birthrate. Augustus' attempt to restore traditional views of marriage and the family was partly inspired by moral considerations, but it also tried to address a growing economic problem: the reduction in the size of the average Italian family.

Augustan Family Legislation

Under the legislation introduced by Augustus, women who were unmarried and childless at the age of 20 suffered penalties. The equivalent age for men was 25. Couples could divorce, provided that each of them remarried and continued to produce children. The law treated men more favorably than women. Males could marry an underage female and still enjoy the tax benefits of married status, while women could not marry prepubescent males. These legal provisions were applied consistently only to the upper classes.

In spite of the Augustan legislation, which Domitian confirmed, and later emperors in the 2nd and 3rd centuries A.D. reinforced, Italian families—particularly those of the upper classes—continued to remain small. When parents did decide to rear a child, they were more likely to allow a male child to survive than a female. The usual ratio of female to male births is 105 to 100. Census figures for the Roman Empire in the 2nd century A.D., however, show the survival rate in Roman Egypt to be 100 females to 105 males. At Rome the rate was 100 females to 131 males, and in Roman Italy 100 females to 140 males.

An additional cause of this imbalance was the impact of a grain-based diet, short of protein and iron, which was greater for women than for men. From the time of menarche, females require twice as much iron as men of a similar age, while pregnant women need three times the quantity. Lack of iron led to anemia and the possibility of premature death due to complications of respiratory and circulatory diseases—a problem which continued to exist for women of the poorer classes in Europe until the late Middle Ages.

Contraception and Abortion

One important reason for the striking reduction in the size of Italian families, in contrast with those elsewhere in the Empire, was the general knowledge of contraceptive techniques at Rome.

Many of the contraceptive methods commonly used by upper-class Romans were predictably based on superstition. Thus ancient authors recommended the power of magic amulets or talismans to prevent fertility. Among the more bizarre were the liver of a cat, worn in a tube on the left foot, and part of a lioness' womb kept in an ivory container.

Other techniques had a greater chance of working. One was the use of various ointments, both by women and by men, to block the entry to the uterus. The ingredients included oils and honey, and the cream was smeared on the genitals. The Romans also developed a form of condom made of animal bladder and practiced the rhythm method. The most common of all forms of birth control was probably withdrawal.

Opinion on the use of abortion to prevent births was mixed. The rate of death in pregnancy remained high enough for most women to prefer contraception, if they did not intend to carry the pregnancy to term. The Hippocratic Oath forbade the administration of medicines to induce abortion, but not all doctors followed its instructions. The physician Soranus (active 2nd century A.D.), who practiced at Alexandria and later at Rome, wrote an important treatise entitled *On Midwifery and the Diseases of Women* which remained influential for centuries. He does not forbid the use of abortion-inducing drugs, but recommends contraception as a better means of preventing unwanted pregnancies. For Soranus, the welfare of the mother took precedence over that of the child, and he describes various methods of relieving labor pains.

The Alimentary Institution

In spite of successive attempts to slow down the decline in population, by the end of the 1st century A.D. the problem continued to present a threat to the economy of Italy and hindered schemes to spread Roman culture by encouraging Italian colonization in the provinces. Attempts to penalize childlessness were clearly not working, and the introduction of the alimentary institution by Nerva (see Part II, Topic 10) was an attempt to find a different solution.

If well-to-do couples refused to produce large families, the children of poor parents would have to serve as a substitute. Nerva had Italy divided into a series of regions, and appointed a program director in each. These officials had the job of identifying how many children there were in their region who needed financial aid for their support and education. The central government then invested money in local estates—thereby providing much-needed assistance to farmers—and the interest from the loans went to support the needy children. Officials on the spot administered the scheme once it was set up, to avoid involving Rome in unnecessary paperwork.

Government intervention inspired similar programs in the private sector. Businessmen set up funds whose income went to pay for the rearing and education of poor children, and to provide them with a small sum of money when they came of age. Many of the private schools operating in Italy were similarly dependent on grants from private individuals. Pliny the Younger, who himself had no children, wanted his hometown, Como, to have a teacher of literature and rhetoric. He offered to pay one third of the salary of a suitably qualified person, if his fellow-citizens would contribute the remainder.

Eumachia, a wealthy benefactress at Pompeii.

WOMEN IN PUBLIC LIFE

Women in the Empire continued to increase their degree of freedom from restrictions, although some areas remained inaccessible. The chief of these was active participation in politics. Women did engage in business, however. At Pompeii, the moneylender Faustilla signed loan notes, charging 45 percent interest a year, and Julia Felix owned a building in which she rented out rooms and shops.

Some professional fields were open to women. Midwifery was, of course, exclusively a female occupation, and there were also some woman doctors—often the wife or daughter of a medical man. The same applied to woman artists, many of whom studied with their fathers. Those who became adept competed on equal terms in the market. One writer observed of Iaia of Cyzicus, a portrait painter who was active at Rome around 100 B.C., that "her talent was so great that her prices far exceeded those of the most famous painters of the day."

Women of the Imperial Family

Augustus' insistence on the importance of the family led to the inclusion of the female members of the family in the distribution of imperial honors. In 27 B.C., at the beginning of his reign, he named an important building in the center of Rome the Portico of Octavia, in honor of his sister, and over the following years dedicated buildings to his wife Livia. When Octavia died in 11 B.C., the emperor declared public mourning and personally delivered the eulogy in her memory.

Livia herself became the object of a cult. Within her lifetime several cities in Asia declared her divine and raised temples to her. On the death of Augustus, the Senate voted her the title of "Augusta," and Claudius conferred the same honor on his wife Agrippina while he was still alive. Imperial women also often appeared on coinage minted either to mark the birth of a child to them or to commemorate their deaths.

Agrippina, Claudius' wife, was the first imperial woman to wield power openly. For the first five years of her son Nero's reign, she acted as co-regent with his tutor Seneca and Burrus, captain of the palace guard (see Part II, Topic 10). Her portrait appeared on coins next to Nero's and she received visitors on official business—although from behind a curtain. When Nero ordered her assassination in A.D. 59, she is said to have pointed to her womb and told her murderers to "Strike here!"

The Empress Livia, wife of Augustus.

Agrippina's example seems to have taught most subsequent empresses the danger of overt political involvement. Trajan's wife Plotina provided advice to her husband and even went with him on his last military campaign, against the Parthians, but her contemporaries noted her fidelity and praised her piety rather than her contribution to politics.

The most active and independent of all empresses was probably Julia Domna (A.D. ?167–217), wife of Septimius Severus (ruled A.D. 193–211). She took part in her husband's political decisions, and also maintained a high-powered salon which attracted the leading intellectuals of the day. Julia's sister, Julia Maesa (?–A.D. 226), went even further. After the murder of her nephew Caracalla (ruled A.D. 211–217), she managed to get her grandson, the eccentric Elagabalus (ruled A.D. 218–222), proclaimed emperor. While Elagabalus entertained and mystified the crowds at Rome with bizarre religious ceremonies in honor of his god Elagabal (imported from Syria), Julia Maesa ran the Empire.

On her death, her daughter, Julia Soaemias (?–A.D. 235), assumed the same role for Elagabalus' successor, her own son Alexander Severus (ruled A.D. 222–235). Alexander was 14 when Julia installed him as emperor and took control into her own hands. Wielding power openly, the third of these redoubtable Syrian Julias had herself voted the title "Augusta, Mother of Augustus, Mother of the Army and the Senate, Mother of the Fatherland." A Senate and people worn out by the reigns of Caracalla and Elagabalus wearily let her have her way, until mother and son went campaigning against the Germans. Julia persuaded her son to offer the German troops money in exchange for peace, and the disgusted Roman forces under their command killed them both.

SLAVES, CRIMINALS, AND GLADIATORS

Roman society, for all its rules written and unwritten, could be surprisingly flexible, as the attitude toward slaves demonstrates. The example of the gladiators, however, demonstrates that the treatment of the underclasses could be brutal and dehumanizing.

Slavery in the Roman World

By the time of the Empire, the large slave gangs used in Republican days for farm and other labor were far less commonly employed: the security risk was far too high, as Spartacus' revolt demonstrated. Most slaves worked either alongside their owners or in the home, and many achieved social mobility. Any Roman citizen could bestow freedom on a slave, who then

A slave, probably a captured German, 1st century A.D.

became a freedman. Freedmen were barred from certain political positions, but all children born to them after the grant of freedom had the full rights of Roman citizenship.

The majority of slaves at Rome came from the Greek-speaking East, captured as prisoners of war, or bought from slave traders. Some were sold into slavery by their families. In many cases they were better educated than their masters, and were qualified to do skilled professional and commercial work. In a town like Pompeii, most businesses were run by slaves or freedmen. Some of the latter operated as agents of their former masters, while others were independent and worked for themselves.

By the end of the 1st century A.D., in Rome and throughout the rest of Italy, slaves, ex-slaves, or the descendants of slaves held a virtual monopoly of professions such as teaching, medicine, accounting, and architecture as well as providing the majority of barbers, cooks, and office workers. The millionaire Trimalchio in Petronius' *Satyricon* is a freedman, who has made his fortune in trade (see Part II, Topic 11). As election posters at Pompeii and elsewhere demonstrate, freedmen often ran for local political office.

Life in the Amphitheater: The Gladiators

The growth of an urban proletariat in Rome, Alexandria, and the other large cities of the Empire created many of the problems of city life familiar to the late 20th century: urban ghettoes, pollution, violent crime. Those at the lowest end of the social scale could expect no mercy if caught for committing a serious offense for which the penalty was death. The state executioner, always a slave, executed Roman citizens by strangling them with a leather strap in the state jail across from the Roman Forum, the Tullianum, which dated back to the time of the early kings. In order to prevent their burial, the bodies of criminals were thrown through a hole in the basement of the prison into the great drain, which emptied into the river Tiber.

Non-Roman citizens might expect to die more publicly, as a form of spectacle. The most frequent method for common criminals and political agitators was crucifixion. In other cases offenders were sentenced to provide a different type of public entertainment by taking part in the gladiatorial combats of the arena. In Republican times no Roman citizen could fight in the games. Under the Empire, it was not unknown for a citizen to volunteer to fight as a gladiator—sometimes the last refuge for a ruined man.

As the taste for these contests grew, and emperors and magistrates vied for popular favor by staging larger and larger games, specially trained gladiators began to take part. Most of them were slaves or prisoners of war, but there were also some tough professionals. They trained in schools, most of which were under state control—the four gladiatorial schools at Rome dated to the time of Domitian—where they were put on a special muscle-building diet.

Each gladiator had special training in a specific skill. Some fought with heavy arms, others with only helmet, sword, and shield, and still others with a net, a fisherman's trident, and a dagger—the last type was called the *retiarius* or net-thrower. Other forms of contest involved wild animals or gladiators on horseback. One particularly brutal (and popular) type was between two mounted fighters armed with shield and spear, and wearing helmets without eyeholes. The two charged each other blindly on horseback in the dark. Posters for the shows advertised the specialties of the gladiators taking part, the training school from which they came, and their previous record of successes. In this way the spectators would know what to expect and how to lay their bets.

Mosaic showing a "retiarius" gladiator armed with a trident.

The games began with a procession of the contestants, after which the trumpet sounded for the first fight, which might be between two individuals or involve two teams of fighters. A wounded gladiator could beg for mercy, appealing either to the organizer of the occasion or—at Rome—to the emperor when he was present. In most cases a wise organizer would follow the wishes of the audience, giving the sign of "thumbs up" for mercy and "thumbs down" to indicate that the contest should be fought to the death. Condemned criminals had no chance of mercy. Professional fighters who were spared lived to fight another day.

The winner of a contest received a palm branch and sometimes money. A gladiator who, by frequently winning or by showing special courage, won popular favor became free from the obligation to fight again. Some retired to private life. Those who chose to continue in the profession could command high fees.

In the earliest period of its history Rome was a monarchy, ruled by kings, and in the following centuries the great aristocratic families tracing their origins back to those of the city acquired immense prestige. Yet even in the last two centuries of the Republic, self-made men and their descendants were among the leading players in Roman politics and society. The noble birth of the brothers Gracchus was a handicap rather than an advantage in their attempt to promote reform. By the time of the Empire social origins were by no means the only conditioning factor in a Roman's life.

One important factor in this change was the growing importance of personal wealth. The businessmen who made fortunes in Rome's various wars could buy, generally for their sons and daughters, the respectability which their birth denied them. Under the Empire, few cared about having exclusive origins except those who had nothing else to care about. A vulgar nouveau riche like Trimalchio would cause some raised eyebrows and sniggers, but guests would still go to his banquets.

Yet perhaps the most significant of all Roman attitudes to social status and behavior was their sense of practicality. The Romans themselves claimed to be doers rather than thinkers, and the best architects or generals or emperors were not necessarily the highest born. The essentially pragmatic quality of Roman attitudes to birth emerged in the invention of the system of adoptive emperors: the first requirement was talent, then adoption could take care of the family connections. It also determined the status of women and slaves in Roman society. Both categories operated under significant restrictions many of which, in practice, they could work around. For many Romans, ability could often carry its owners far beyond their official standing.

Questions for Further Study

1. How did the status of women evolve during the later Empire? To what extent were changes limited to the upper classes?
2. What was the Roman attitude to slaves? How did it compare with the treatment of slaves in other ancient societies?
3. What were the chief factors that promoted the unity of the Roman Empire?
4. What were the main economic developments in the later history of the Empire? How far were they responsible for the decline of the central authority?

Suggestions for Further Reading

Boren, H. C. *Roman Society: A Social, Economic, and Cultural History*, 2nd ed. Lexington, MA, 1992.
Bradley, K. R. *Discovering the Roman Family*. New York, 1990.
Earl, D. C. *The Moral and Political Tradition of Rome*. Ithaca, NY, 1984.
Gardner, J. F. *Women in Roman Law and Society*. Bloomington, IN, 1986.
Garnsey, P., and R. Saller. *The Roman Empire: Economy, Society, and Culture*. Berkeley, CA, 1987.
Hopkins, K. *Conquerors and Slaves*. Cambridge, England, 1981.
Kebric, R. B. *Roman People*. Mountain View, CA, 1993.
Thompson, L. *Romans and Blacks*. Norman, OK, 1989.
Wiedemann, T. *Greek and Roman Slavery*. London, 1989.

II

Topic 13

Christianity and the Crisis of Empire

With the spread of Christianity in the later centuries of the Roman Empire, the history of the ancient world entered its final stages. Christian teachings originated in Palestine, among the Jews living there under Roman rule. The Romans' contact with the Jews extended back into Republican times: the first Jewish community at Rome dated to the 2nd century B.C. The Roman Republic's benevolent policy toward the Jews in Italy was confirmed by Julius Caesar.

Christianity was born in Jerusalem, capital of a Roman province. The Roman community became the western center of the new religion. The first Christians spoke Aramaic, and many of the early converts were Greek-speaking, the language of the New Testament, but after A.D. 200 the number of Latin converts began to rise. In spite of periods of persecution by the state, the church continued to grow in influence, and in A.D. 313 the emperor Constantine legalized the practice of Christianity.

The period marked by the rise of Christianity saw the Roman world slipping into serious decline as a series of military emperor-despots did little to halt increasing economic collapse. Only the successful military campaigns of Aurelian and the sweeping reforms of Diocletian at the end of the 3rd century A.D., followed by Constantine's own reign in the 4th century A.D., managed to bring temporary relief.

When Constantine founded a new eastern capital for the Empire at Byzantium, thereafter known as Constantinople, he intended it to be a Christian city. He himself accepted baptism only on his deathbed, but by the end of the 4th century A.D., Christianity was the official religion of the state.

With the shift of power to the eastern Mediterranean, western Europe became vulnerable to a century-long wave of invasions by Germanic tribes on the move from the steppe lands of Eurasia. First the Visigoths under Alaric, then the Vandals and Huns overran Italy, Gaul, and Spain. The effect of the Germanic victories was to complete the long process of decline in the West. While the eastern half of the Empire continued to flourish economically and culturally under the unifying rule of the Byzantine emperors, the West fragmented into a series of kingdoms, with continuing economic deterioration and population shrinkage.

The debate on the reasons for the decline and fall of the Roman Empire began with the writings of St. Augustine, active at the beginning of the 5th century A.D. Among the factors cited by his many successors have been climate changes, illness, errors of individual rulers, the triumph of Christianity. Most modern observers would probably hold that no single cause or set of causes can explain a process that took centuries to work to a conclusion. A pattern of civilization that had lasted well over 1000 years slowly broke down.

THE JEWS: A RELIGIOUS MINORITY IN THE ROMAN WORLD

The Jewish community in Rome has a continuous history from the 2nd century B.C. to the present. The first settlers came shortly after 161 B.C., the year in which the Jewish leader Judas Maccabaeus (died 160 B.C.) sent an embassy to the Roman Senate. The ambassadors, Jason (Joshua) ben Eleazar and Eupolemos (Ephraim?) ben Johanan, were the first Jews known to have visited the West. The Senate gave them written assurances of friendship and protection.

In 63 B.C., Pompey the Great conquered Palestine, which under the Empire became the Roman province of Judaea, and a fresh influx of Jewish traders and professionals arrived in Italy. Among the reforms introduced by Julius Caesar in his brief dictatorship of 46–44 B.C. were several involving the Italian Jews. They included exemption from military service and the setting up of special courts where Jews could try cases according to their own law. Augustus and Tiberius renewed these privileges. When St. Paul visited Rome in A.D. 61, he found active Jewish communities both there and in southern Italy.

The Jews under the Empire

In Palestine itself there was constant friction between Roman officials, who found Jewish customs unfamiliar and grotesque, and the Jews for whom Roman rule was intolerable. Among the Jews themselves there were divisions between many of the upper classes, who tended to adopt Greek ways and had come to terms with the Romans, and the Pharisees and other orthodox groups who maintained strict adherence to traditional Jewish law. Rioting broke out in A.D. 66, and spread to many of the cities, including Caesarea and Jerusalem. In A.D. 70, Titus put down a Jewish revolt in Judaea by sacking Jerusalem and destroying the Temple, and took back to Rome large numbers of Jewish slaves. Some were put to work on the Colosseum and other public building projects, while Titus settled others in Bari, Taranto, and Otranto. Jews throughout the Empire, who had contributed money each year for the upkeep of the Temple in Jerusalem, were now ordered to send the same sum to the Roman treasury, a tax known as the "Fiscus Judaicus," or "Jewish Tax."

Arch of Titus in the Roman Forum, commemorating the victory of Titus over the Jews, and the destruction of the Temple at Jerusalem.

Hadrian's brutal suppression of the Jewish revolt of A.D. 132–135 in Palestine led to the introduction of repressive measures elsewhere in the Empire, but apart from this brief period—Hadrian's immediate successor Antoninus Pius revoked the anti-Jewish legislation—the Jews living outside Palestine enjoyed relative freedom. In A.D. 212, Caracalla passed an edict giving Roman citizenship to almost all free residents of the Empire, including the Jews and other minorities.

The Jewish Community at Rome

The size of the Jewish community in Rome during the Empire was around 30,000, although the various revolts in Palestine, which were brutally suppressed, swelled the numbers with prisoners and exiles. Tombstones provide an interesting source of information on Jewish activities at Rome. Among the dead they commemorate are Jewish painters and poets, and a Jewish physician. Other more humble Jews were butchers, tentmakers, and cobblers. Jewish women of the lower classes had a reputation as fortune tellers.

The center of Jewish life was the synagogue, and Rome had twelve, each with its own congregation. The dead were buried in catacombs, underground galleries, the oldest of which dates back to late Republican times. The richer tombs often combine typical Jewish symbols—the palm branch, the seven-branched candelabrum used in the temple services—with pagan images, suggesting a fair degree of assimilation.

Their Roman neighbors seem to have had some notion of Jewish traditions, although often in a garbled form. For the Romans, "wasting" one day in every seven—the Sabbath—seemed inexplicable. The poet Juvenal, no lover of "Orientals" or other foreigners (see Part II, Topic 11), describes with contempt a Roman father who followed Jewish custom and observed the Sabbath. The man's son became a fully fledged Jew who spent all his time in prayer, and someone who meets him in the street scornfully asks "What synagogue can I find you in?" Jewish missionary activity among the Romans was, in fact, common and often successful.

Anti-Semitism was common in the Roman Empire, especially in Egypt, where the Greeks of Alexandria were in constant friction with their Jewish neighbors. Elsewhere, too, popular opinion was hostile to traditional Jewish customs, sometimes violently so. On the whole, however, and certainly in comparison with many later periods, the official state treatment of the Jews' life under the Empire was tolerant. They alone of all Roman citizens were not required to take part in the state religious rituals, or to hold municipal offices, since both activities conflicted with their own faith. A Roman jurist of the 3rd century A.D. described Judaism as "a highly distinguished religion, of indubitable legality."

The Jews and the Coming of Christianity

With Constantine's edict of A.D. 313 legalizing Christianity, the status of Jews under Roman rule changed abruptly. The "highly distinguished religion" of a few years earlier became a "nefarious sect" or a "sacrilegious gathering." In A.D. 315, Constantine threatened to burn any Jew who tried to "persecute" former Jews who had converted to Christianity, "the faith of the True God." Intermarriage between Jews and Christians became a capital offense, unless the Jewish partner became a Christian. Six years later, in A.D. 321, the emperor cancelled the Jewish exemption from public and religious obligations to the state.

From A.D. 339, Jews were forbidden to have slaves, or to employ non-Jews. In practice this meant their exclusion from most professional activities, including industry and agriculture. The first destruction of a synagogue took place in A.D. 350, when Bishop Innocentius of Tortona (near Genoa) destroyed the temple there, replaced it with a chapel, and offered the Jews the choice of exile or baptism. At the end of the 4th century A.D., with Christianity installed as the official state religion, St. Ambrose of Milan observed in a letter that he regretted that through laziness he had failed to burn down his city's synagogue.

Over the next century the Jewish population of Italy shrank drastically. With the formal division of the Empire into east and west, in A.D. 395 (see Part III, Topic 3), the Jews of Palestine and those in Europe were no longer under a single benevolent rule, and the long years of hardship began.

THE RISE OF CHRISTIANITY AND THE EARLY CHURCH

According to the Hebrew prophets, one day their God would send the Messiah (the Hebrew word means "anointed one") to restore Israel and begin a glorious age of peace. In the 1st century B.C., following Pompey's conquest of Palestine, some Jews living there believed that a Messiah would come to bring political liberation. By contrast, the Jewish sect known as the Essenes (active c. 200 B.C.–A.D. 68) withdrew into monastic communities to practice their ascetic lifestyle. Some of their writings are still preserved in the Dead Sea Scrolls, discovered shortly after World War II.

The Origins of Christianity

The historical Jesus (c. 6 B.C.–c. A.D. 30) was born in Palestine in the reign of Augustus. He taught that the Messiah would not be an earthly ruler, but would come as spiritual judge to usher in the Last Judgment. The virtues Jesus extolled were humility, charity, and love of others. His teachings offended both conservative and radical Jewish leaders, while the Romans saw his ideas as potentially subversive to Roman rule. As a result, the Roman governor Pontius Pilate ordered his execution.

After the crucifixion of Jesus, his followers continued to spread his ideas, claiming that he himself was the Messiah and calling him Christ, the Greek word for "the anointed one." Paul of Tarsus (died c. A.D. 65), one of the earliest converts to Christianity, was a Jewish Roman citizen who traveled in Asia Minor after his conversion, setting up small Christian communities.

Eventually Paul, together with Peter (died c. A.D. 64)—one of Jesus' original twelve Apostles—reached Rome, where, according to tradition, they were both martyred. Before he died, Peter probably founded at Rome the church regarded by later Christians as central to Christianity, in fulfillment of Jesus' prophecy:

PERSPECTIVES ON HISTORY

The Dead Sea Scrolls

Frederick M. Lauritsen
Eastern Washington University

When a young Arab teenager squeezed into a cave above the Dead Sea in early 1947, he was looking for treasure. He found, instead, something far more important and valuable—the ancient manuscripts known as the Dead Sea Scrolls. These 2000-year-old manuscripts from the cliffs above the Dead Sea are among the most significant archeological discoveries of the 20th century. This discovery, like another famous find, the tomb of King Tutankhamen, was embroiled in controversy from the start. There were personality rivalries, political intrigue, exaggerated claims, and wild speculation, to say nothing of wishful thinking.

According to the nomads, seven scrolls were found in large pottery jars in cave one. These first scrolls contained both religious and sectarian writings, including a complete book of Isaiah, a *Commentary on Habakkuk*, and a *Manual of Discipline*. Eventually eleven caves yielded hundreds of complete scrolls and fragments of leather, papyrus, and a few of metal. (Scrolls, which preceded the codex or book form we now use, were common until late in the Roman Empire. Perhaps Christianity and the need for cross-referencing scriptures had something to do with the change.) Most of the scrolls were written in Hebrew or Aramaic (a Semitic language close to Hebrew and widely used in the first centuries B.C. and A.D.), and a few in Greek.

Many discoveries were made by the nomads or Bedouins from the Ta'amira tribe before the archeologists had a chance to examine the area. These nomads became quite adept at finding and exploring caves. Some of the caves were either in inaccessible regions or virtually impossible to reach. Understandably the nomads were reluctant to provide complete information. They were able to cross the boundary between Israel and Jordan with a skill that embarrassed the security forces on both sides, and once they found how much the scrolls were worth it was in their self-interest to maximize their value. Fifty years after their discovery, controversy still surrounds many details.

In the 1960s, the Bedouins moved into eastern Galilee, an area north of the Dead Sea. There, using their cave-finding skills, they found papyrus manuscripts belonging to the Samaritan sect and dating from the time of Alexander the Great. The Bedouins also continued their explorations south along the western shores of the Dead Sea and made additional finds. Israeli archeologists also found manuscripts, the most famous from the Cave of Letters, which contained letters from Bar Kosiba, better known as bar Kokhba, who led a revolt against Rome in A.D. 133. These finds lie, however, beyond the scope of our essay, which is restricted to the original eleven caves.

There are many more caves in the vicinity of the first that did not contain manuscripts but did have archeological remains of the same era as the scrolls. Pottery found in these caves matched the jars found in cave one, showing that they were contemporary with each other. There is no certain count of the number of scrolls found but of the original eleven caves it is safe to say they numbered in the hundreds. In one cave fragments of hundreds of documents were found, some of which are still being identified and joined to other pieces. Private collectors may also have bought some of the manuscripts or pieces.

The documents raise questions as to how close to the original is the Bible (Old Testament) we use today as well as about our understanding of early Jewish-Christian relations and Judaism. Other controversies include Jewish religious beliefs around the time of Jesus, the background of Christian belief, and who buried the scrolls.

Though there were challenges at first from some who said the documents came only from the Middle Ages, scientific tests such as carbon 14 dating have placed the scrolls between 200 B.C. and A.D. 60. These scrolls are the earliest known examples of biblical writings, and as with all texts, the closer we can come to the original the better and more complete our understanding will be. It is important to both Jews and Christians to know that the Bible of today has been accurately copied. The scrolls include at least portions of every book in the Old Testament except the book of Esther (perhaps because Esther is the only book that does not mention God). In the case of the Great Isaiah Scroll, it turns out that the copy found in the caves and today's text are virtually the same except that the Great Isaiah Scroll included a verse not in the current version (although this verse is now being restored to modern Bibles). On the other hand, other scrolls are quite different from the current versions, and the scrolls point to the fact that the text of the Old Testament was still fluid until the end of the first century.

Not all of the scrolls are copies of books of the Bible; others contain sectarian writings that are religious in nature, background, or content. They cover a variety of subjects: some are handbooks of rules, others are commentaries on books of the Bible, and there are even astrological texts and calendars and training exercises for would-be scribes. One document, called the War Scroll, deals with a battle (similar to or the same as the New Testament Armageddon) during the last days of the Sons of Light against the Sons of Darkness. Other scrolls mention names and titles of individuals, such as the Man of Falsehood, Man of Scorn, Furious Lion, Interpreter of the Law, and Prince of the Congregation, but the most important names are the Teacher of Righteousness and the Wicked Priest.

Many candidates have been put forward for the Teacher of Righteousness, including John the Baptist and—most sensational of all—Jesus of Nazareth. These extravagant claims are typical of the reaction to the new discoveries. No one sees Jesus in these documents anymore and though the Teacher is believed to be real, he has not been identified. One Spanish scholar tried to prove (on the basis of three words, one of which was "and") that there were New Testament scriptures among the scrolls. While this claim received wide publicity it remains unproved and few scholars have accepted it. Candidates for the Wicked Priest are just as wide-ranging. At one time the name of the Apostle Paul was put forward.

Most of the people making these claims are serious, well respected scholars, trained in ancient languages, history, and theology. Scholars want very much to find some identifiable historical event or person in these fragments. The search continues, though as of now there are still no undisputed historical "facts" in the scrolls.

One of the most unusual scrolls is the Copper Scroll. It was so fragile that after its discovery it had to be delicately sawed apart in strips. The document is a list of "treasures" hidden in various places around Palestine. Many attempts have been made to locate these treasures but so far nothing has been found. An alternative reading is to take this scroll as a kind of science fiction. Recently much publicity has been given to a man who is using the Copper Scroll to search for the Ashes of the Red Heifer, so far without luck.

The Red Heifer is found in Numbers 19. A special animal was sacrificed and then cremated. The ashes were mixed with spring water and the results were called the Water of Purification. This mixture was used by those who had been polluted to become ritually clean. After the destruction of the Temple in Jerusalem in A.D. 70, no more heifers were sacrificed. The claim is that the ashes were hidden along with the treasures mentioned in the Copper Scroll.

Who wrote the scrolls and who buried them? If the scrolls were written over a period of 250 or 300 years, they were of course written by many hands. One name that continues to be repeated is the Essenes. The Essenes were one of several Jewish sects active around the time of Jesus. They had withdrawn from participation in mainstream Judaism and are thought to have established a community at Qumran on the northwest corner of the Dead Sea—the immediate area where the scrolls were found. Though there are other views, a majority of scholars believes that the scrolls represent a library of Essene beliefs and practices. Perhaps some of the caves surrounding Qumran were used by members of the community as living quarters, and when the Roman Army attacked in A.D. 66 the caves were used to hide the manuscripts from the Roman soldiers. This does not account for the condition of

continued next page

some of the manuscripts that were torn, mutilated, and disfigured. Or perhaps the caves are where the library was stored. In this case it seems the Dead Sea Scrolls have raised more questions than answers.

After the scrolls were found, a select committee was set up by the British authorities who governed Palestine at that time. This committee was given complete control over all the manuscripts. When a member of the committee died, resigned, or retired, they chose the replacement. The committee parceled out the documents among its own members. Some members in turn gave a document to their graduate students to use for dissertations or articles. In this way publication was agonizingly slow. Finally, in the late 1980s pressure led by Hershel Shanks, editor of *Biblical Archaeology Review,* began to build against this monopoly. By 1992 all the scrolls, whole and fragments, were released to the public.

The result has been a rapid increase in translations of the manuscripts and research articles. Our knowledge of Judaism in the first centuries B.C. and A.D. is growing. It is now becoming clearer that this is the crucial background from which both modern Judaism and Christianity emerged. We now realize that Christianity and Judaism of this period were much more alike, much closer than had been previously thought. As more documents are translated, studied, and published, we will see profound effects on our understanding of this era and of our own roots.

One of the roots of modern Western civilization lies in religious beliefs and practices and more precisely in those of Judaism and Christianity. It is inescapable: we are the heirs. We cannot comprehend Nathaniel Hawthorne's *The Scarlet Letter* without understanding Puritan religious beliefs based on their interpretation of the Bible. The religious wars of Europe and religious persecution resulting in emigration to America would also have happened even if the Dead Sea Scrolls had been available at the time. The Dead Sea Scrolls can give us a better understanding of our religious roots. When examined beside recent archeological discoveries, we are developing a clearer idea of how Jews and early Christians were understood by the Romans.

"Thou art Peter, and upon this rock I will build my Church." (The name "Peter" is a form of the Greek word for "rock.") This traditional belief served to justify the importance of the Roman Church.

By the early 2nd century A.D., most large cities in the Empire had communities of Christians. They met in private to celebrate the Eucharist, or Holy Communion, a ritual enactment of the Last Supper. Most of the early Christians were Greek speakers, and the New Testament (the account of the life and death of Jesus, and the beginnings of Christianity) was written in Greek. It is made up of the four Gospels, named after their traditional authors—Matthew, Mark, Luke, and John—the Epistles, or letters written by early church leaders to local churches or individuals, and the book of Revelation. The earliest fragments surviving date to the beginning of the 2nd century, and the text was first standardized in the 4th century, by which time there were increasing numbers of Latin converts.

For most pagan Romans the Christians were just one more of the many sects flourishing in various parts of the Empire. Yet in important ways Christianity was different from other cults. In the first place Christians claimed that their way was the only true way. No pagan cult ever laid claim to exclusivity. Only the Jews believed that there was no true God but theirs, and even the Jews did not try to persuade others to follow their example. The Christians not only encouraged conversion to their faith, they actively sought it by missionary work.

Secondly, the early Christians believed in firm organization. Around each church was a community, and the various communities throughout the Empire maintained links that bound them together. Christians could travel to most countries under Roman rule and find fellow Christians who would provide help and comfort to them.

During its first two centuries, Christianity enjoyed the same theoretical tolerance on the part of the state as the Jews, but from the beginning public opinion was generally hostile; popular dislike and suspicion drove early Christians to be discreet in practicing their

Roman statue of Christ as the Good Shepherd.

faith. Two waves of persecutions in the 3rd century A.D., on the grounds that the Christians refused to worship the official state gods, were followed in A.D. 313 by the decision of Constantine and Licinius, promulgated in the Edict of Milan, to allow universal tolerance of all religions in the Empire. Since around a third of the Empire was Christian by the beginning of the 4th century, Constantine's policy was an attempt to reinforce unity in the Roman world.

According to the account of a contemporary writer, Constantine's inspiration was a dream he had had the previous year, on the eve of the crucial Battle of the Milvian Bridge against his rival Maxentius. A voice told him to mark "the sign of God" on the shields of his soldiers, in the form of the Greek letter *Chi* (X) turned and with a loop on top—this would produce the *Chi-Rho* monogram, spelling the first two letters of the word *Christ* in Greek. Constantine won the battle, and with it control of Italy. Whatever the significance of the dream in Constantine's decision, another reason for his sympathy toward Christianity was the influence of his mother Helena (c. A.D. 248–328). A missionary to her native Britain converted her to Christianity in her youth, and she remained active in promoting her faith throughout her life. In A.D. 326, while on a pilgrimage to Jerusalem, she ordered the construction there of the Church of the Holy Sepulchre, and Medieval legend credited her with the discovery of the True Cross.

The Organization of the Early Church

Jerusalem was the birthplace of Christianity, but over time each major city developed its own church. In theory, all of them shared a common creed. In practice, however, beliefs varied widely, as did local forms of organization. The most important Christian communities included those of Antioch, Alexandria, and Carthage.

A general view of the excavated frescoes at Dura on the Europos, c. A.D. 240.

Map 13.1 The Spread of Christianity

Rome occupied a special position, because its church was founded by Peter, but before the Council of Nicaea in 325 the other centers did not treat the Roman Church as entitled to automatic obedience. Even after the Council, the eastern churches never accepted the final authority of Rome, a disagreement that became an important factor in the eventual split between Catholic and Orthodox Christianity.

The head of each local church was known as the bishop. According to the doctrine of Apostolic Succession, the powers which Jesus' disciples received at his hands were passed down from bishop to bishop, giving them the right to ordain new priests and bishops who could conduct the sacraments. These included baptism into the faith and Holy Communion, whereby the wine and wafer of the Communion ceremony became the blood and body of Christ. The bishop also administered, with the help of a board of Deacons, the church property and any bequests left by members of the congregation.

In order to provide a general overall structure for the church, bishops began to meet regularly with their fellow bishops to coordinate belief and policy. The structural system they devised took the Roman Empire,

Significant Dates

The End of the Roman Empire (all dates A.D.)

c. 30	Crucifixion of Jesus
70	Titus sacks Jerusalem
132–135	Jewish Revolt
270–275	Reign of Aurelian
284–305	Reign of Diocletian
306–337	Reign of Constantine
312	Battle of Milvian Bridge
313	Edict of Milan
325	Council of Nicaea
330	Inauguration of Constantinople
410	Sack of Rome by Visigoths
451	Defeat of Attila
476	Last Western emperor deposed

with its carefully ordered hierarchy, as model. In this way the organization of the church was comprehensible to Christian and non-Christian Romans alike. By the early 3rd century A.D., church councils began to assemble in major provincial centers, in order to distinguish between *orthodox* (literally "right-thinking") doctrines and heresies, or wrong opinions. The first Empire-wide church council took place at Nicaea in A.D. 325, under the patronage of Constantine, to discuss definitions of the Trinity (for a discussion of the controversies of the early church, see Part III, Topic 2).

PROBLEMS OF EMPIRE AND THE REFORMS OF DIOCLETIAN

By the time Constantine issued his epoch-making edict, the Roman Empire was emerging from a century of decline. Successive emperors after Alexander Severus (see Part II, Topic 12) came to power with army backing, only to fall at the hands of those who had placed them on the throne. In the 50 years from A.D. 235 to A.D. 284, the Senate recognized 25 legitimate emperors, while more than twice as many failed to establish their "legitimacy." In the reign of Gallienus (ruled A.D. 253–268), there were no less than 18 unsuccessful claimants to the throne.

The effects of such chronic instability were economic collapse and social disorder, as the bankruptcy of many middle-class citizens left Roman society polarized into upper and lower classes. Matters abroad fared little better. On the eastern limits of the Empire, the Sassanians replaced the Romans' old enemies the Parthians, and in A.D. 259 a Sassanian army captured the Roman emperor Valerian (ruled A.D. 253–260). The only Roman emperor ever taken prisoner, Valerian died in captivity. To the north, the Germanic tribes of Franks drove across Gaul to Spain, while the Goths, another Germanic tribe, sacked much of the Balkans and even briefly occupied Athens.

Military relief came with the reign of Aurelian (ruled A.D. 270–275), whose energetic campaigns reversed a century of territorial decline. Although he failed to displace the Goths from Central Europe, Aurelian reestablished Roman authority in Britain, Gaul, Spain, and Syria (for Aurelian in the East, see

Relief showing the victory of the Sassanian king, Shapur I, over the Roman emperor Valerian.

The walls built by Aurelian between 271 and 275 to protect Rome.

Part I, Topic 6). Many parts of the walls he ordered built for the defense of Rome itself, which were over 50 feet high and 11 miles in circumference, are still standing today.

Diocletian and the Late Roman Empire

The restorer of political order in the Roman state was the emperor Diocletian (ruled A.D. 284–305), whose reorganization of government made possible another century of unified Roman rule of the Mediterranean. The main thrust of his reforms was to restore the authority of central rule, abolishing the rights of the provinces to local self-government.

To reinforce his status, Diocletian changed the emperor's title from *Princeps*, or "First Citizen," to *Dominus*—"Lord"—and ruled as a living god. Elaborate court ceremonial underlined the gulf between the figure of the emperor and his mortal subjects, who were not even permitted to set eyes on their divine ruler. A complex bureaucracy stretched downwards from the emperor through various levels to the provincial administrations, which were responsible for collecting taxes, finding recruits for the army, and imposing orders handed down from above.

Diocletian's reforms required a sound economic base, and to achieve this he restored the full value of the currency and reorganized the tax system. One of his edicts sets out the principle by which he operated: "No man shall possess any property that is tax-exempt." Every year the emperor and his advisers established the state's budget, and then calculated the tax rate accordingly. A general review took place every five years. Members of the provincial governments had to collect the revenues, and make up any shortages from their own property.

One of the effects of Diocletian's reform of the coinage was rampant inflation, as people tried to get rid of their old coins. To offset this, in A.D. 301 the emperor introduced an edict setting maximum prices for goods and services. The penalty for overcharging was death. The price list casts interesting light on life in the last century of the Empire. A pound of cheese and a pint of ordinary wine both cost eight denarii. Meat varied from eight denarii a pound for beef and mutton to twenty for ham. A haircut cost two denarii. Farm laborers and camel drivers earned 25 denarii a day, elementary teachers 50 denarii per student per month, and lawyers were paid 1000 denarii for pleading a case.

To help carry out his ambitious program, Diocletian introduced important political changes. In A.D. 286 he nominated a co-emperor, Maximian (ruled A.D. 286–305, 306–308) and in A.D. 293 appointed two deputies, one for himself and one for his co-ruler, to train them as successors. Under this new system, the tetrarchy (rule of four), Diocletian and his deputy Galerius (ruled A.D. 305–311) took charge of the East and Maximian and his deputy Constantius Chlorus (ruled A.D. 305–306) of the West.

In A.D. 304 Diocletian suffered a serious illness, perhaps a stroke, and the following year he abdicated and retired to Spalato (modern Split)—one of the very few reigning monarchs in history to give up power voluntarily. He spent the last ten years of his life working in his garden. In the chaos that followed his resignation, Maximian, the co-emperor—whom Diocletian had also persuaded to retire—begged him to come back to Rome and take up the reins of government again. Calmly but firmly Diocletian refused. If he could only show Maximian the cabbages, he said, which he planted with his own hands in the garden, his former colleague would not try to persuade him to give up the enjoyment of happiness for the pursuit of power.

The Civil Wars of Diocletian's Successors

When the two emperors retired, they promoted their assistants to the rank of emperor, and named two new deputies, passing over Constantine (ruled A.D. 306–337), the son of Constantius, and Maxentius (ruled A.D. 306–312), the son of Maximian. With the sudden death of Constantius in A.D. 306, the Roman world plunged once more into confusion, as the two sons battled for supremacy and Diocletian steadfastly refused to return to the fray. The decisive confrontation came in A.D. 312 at the Milvian Bridge. With, as he believed, the God of the Christians fighting on his side, Constantine defeated Maxentius and took control of the Empire. In spite of the edict of the following year, which legitimized Christianity, Constantine himself refused baptism until he was on the point of death, believing that he could best retain the support of his subjects—most of whom were pagan—by continuing as head of the state religion. He had his sons brought up as Christians, however, and maintained an iron control over church policy and dogma for the rest of his life.

THE FOUNDATION OF CONSTANTINOPLE AND THE DECLINE OF THE WEST

The crowning achievement of Constantine's reign was to be the creation of the Empire's new Christian capital, unsullied by pagan temples. Between A.D. 324 and 330, Constantinople, the city of Constantine, arose on the magnificent harbor of the Bosphorus (see Part III, Topic 3). In his last years Constantine ruled with ever greater pomp, reflecting in his own life as emperor his vision of the Christians' king of heaven—a long way from Christian ideals of charity and love for others. In A.D. 326 he ordered the execution of his wife, eldest son, and nephew, whom he believed to be more popular than he was.

Constantine had held together an Empire on the point of collapse, and it survived for barely 50 years after his death. When Theodosius divided the Empire between his sons in A.D. 395 (see Part III, Topic 3), the split became permanent. The Eastern half continued in the form of the Byzantine Empire, while the West sank into decline.

Colossal head of Constantine, now on the Capitoline Hill in Rome.

The German Invasions

Contact between Roman frontier troops stationed on the Rhine and the Danube and German invaders went back to the time of Julius Caesar, half a millennium before the fall of the Roman Empire. Over the years following, Roman culture left its mark on the nomadic tribesmen to the north, as Roman businessmen traded with them and carried German slaves back to Rome, and German families moved across the borders to live on Roman territory. The Roman acceptance of Christianity quickly spread among the Germanic peoples.

By the mid-4th century A.D., there were larger numbers of Germanic tribespeople massed on the frontiers than ever before. The Franks and Alamanni occupied the lower Rhine region and south Germany, while to the east, in Hungary and southern Russia, were the Vandals, Visigoths, and Ostrogoths. With the Roman Army split by imperial rivalries, and the Empire finally divided into two unequal halves—the East far more prosperous than the West—the eventual movement of Germanic tribes into western and southern Europe was inevitable (see Part III, Topic 1).

The push came at the end of the 4th century A.D., when the Germanic peoples themselves came under pressure. Invaders from the great steppe lands of Eurasia to the east began moving westward into Germanic territory. In A.D. 374, the Huns, a nomadic steppe people, stormed into the land of the Ostrogoths. The Visigoths, neighbors of the Ostrogoths, feared it was their turn next and moved into Roman territory in the Balkans, defeating a Roman army sent to subdue them. When the Romans refused to grant them more land, the Visigothic king Alaric (ruled A.D. 395–410) led his troops to Rome, and in A.D. 410 the Visigoths sacked the city.

The lesson was not lost on the other Germanic peoples. The Vandals took Spain in A.D. 408, and then drove on to North Africa. By the middle of the 5th century A.D. the Franks held most of north and central Gaul. Britain, abandoned by its Roman legions in A.D. 407, fell under Saxons, Angles, and Jutes.

Rome's last stand came in A.D. 451, when Roman and Visigothic troops united against a common enemy and defeated the army of the Huns led by their king, Attila (ruled A.D. 434–453), who had invaded Italy. With Germanic commanders in charge of Roman forces, the Roman government lost its last claim to independence. In A.D. 476 a Germanic general deposed the last emperor of the West, Romulus Augustulus (ruled A.D. 475–476). A century of continual decline reached its symbolic end.

Portrait of a captured Barbarian woman from the 1st or 2nd century.

DECLINE AND FALL: THE DEBATE

The fall of Rome moved even the most devout of Christians. When Alaric's Visigoths sacked the city in A.D. 410, St. Jerome wrote: "The whole world has perished in one city." A few years later, St. Augustine (A.D. 354–430) began to write *The City of God*, in which he contrasted the earthly city, built on pride and home to materialism and imperialism, with the eternal city of God, the realm of faith. For Augustine, the collapse of Rome was one more stage on the journey toward the Last Judgment and salvation in the kingdom of heaven (see Part III, Topic 2).

Over the centuries since Augustine, students of the history of human affairs have often debated the cause of an event which was apparently so cataclysmic. Some have pointed to the fundamental economic difference between the eastern and western provinces. In the East, commerce flourished and prosperity was measured in terms of money and profits. In Italy, the most valuable asset was land, and the old Roman aristocracy never really abandoned its disdain for trade and manufacturing.

Another factor was the continual decline in population in the West. As living standards increased in the period after Augustus, the Italians were unwilling to give up their newly acquired comforts to raise children. The reduction in population had serious effects on agriculture and industry. At the same time, traditional Roman culture and values began to lose their dominating status in the Empire.

Then the imperial system of government, protective and paternalistic, discouraged the kind of personal initiative that had helped to build the Republic. At the same time, the army became increasingly alienated from the welfare of the state, and became embroiled in power struggles among its various leaders. With the drop in civilian population in Italy, more and more soldiers were recruited on the fringes of the Empire, where the austere moral virtues of the ancient Roman Republic were virtually unknown.

Some observers have pointed to external factors. These include a devastating plague in the reign of Marcus Aurelius, the gradual spread of malaria, and possible climate changes which might have produced less fertile farmland. Other scholars isolate specific moments when a wrong decision proved fatal. Marcus Aurelius' choice of his son Commodus as his successor led to the disastrous dynasty of the Severans. Many, particularly in the Middle Ages, would simply have echoed Augustine's judgment that the fall of Rome was another stage in God's plan for human redemption.

Many of these factors played their part to some degree or another, but the process of decline extended over centuries and to look for a single overriding cause is to oversimplify. When it came, the exact moment of collapse was arbitrary, and for many purely symbolic. There is no reason to think that the exile of Romulus Augustulus had the faintest significance in the daily lives of the overwhelming majority of Western Europeans then living.

The most important feature of the last phase of the Roman Empire was the rise of Christianity to the status of a world religion. Yet the victory of the Church Triumphant came at a price for Christians themselves. Freedom from persecution set loose three centuries of theological debate which led to Christian persecution of pagan and heretic alike. Once in power, church leaders used force rather than persuasion to convert the mass of the population. Furthermore, the church adopted a structure based on the authoritarian government of Diocletian, by which its leaders acquired vast worldly power at the expense of the spiritual domain.

The final collapse of Rome left a triple legacy. In the East, for 1000 years the Byzantine Empire continued to operate under Constantine's system. The emperor controlled the secular policy of the state while simultaneously maintaining supreme religious authority. In the West, the former Roman provinces fragmented into a series of king-

doms which still form the basis of the states of modern Europe. In the southern region of the Mediterranean, a century after the fall of Rome, Muhammad was born. The religion he founded, Islam, helped to create an empire stretching by the 8th century A.D. *from Spain to India. The fall of the Roman Empire was a transition, not an end.*

Questions for Further Study

1. What were the most important stages in the rise of Christianity? How did they relate to the later history of the Roman Empire?
2. What role did women play in the early development of Christianity?
3. What methods did Diocletian use to halt the erosion of the Empire? How far was he successful?
4. What were the long-term causes of the end of the Roman Empire in the West? What effect did the foundation of Constantinople have on its decline?

Suggestions for Further Reading

Barnes, T. D. *The New Empire of Diocletian and Constantine*. Cambridge, MA, 1982.

Benko, S. *Pagan Rome and the Early Christians*. Bloomington, IN, 1986.

Fox, R. L. *Pagans and Christians*. New York, 1986.

Jones, A. H. M. *The Later Roman Empire, 284–602: A Social, Economic and Administrative Survey*. Baltimore, 1986.

MacMullen, R. *Christianizing the Roman Empire (100–400)*. New Haven, CT, 1984.

McNamara, J. A. *A New Song: Celibate Women in the First Three Christian Centuries*. New York, 1983.

Morrison, K. E., ed. *The Church in the Roman Empire*. Chicago, 1986.

Wise, M., M. Abegg, and E. Cook. *The Dead Sea Scrolls: A New Translation*. San Francisco, 1996.

Witherington, B., III. *Women in the Earliest Churches*. Cambridge, England, 1988.

Witherington, B., III. *The Jesus Quest: The Third Search for the Jew of Nazareth*. Downers Grove, IL, 1995.

PART III

THE WORLDS OF MEDIEVAL EUROPE

Between the collapse of the Roman Empire around A.D. 400 and the beginning of the Renaissance about 1350 or 1400 lay a thousand years of Western experience. Appropriately enough, historians call this stretch of history the "Middle Ages," or the "Medieval" period.

For many scholars of an earlier generation, the Middle Ages was seen as the "Dark Ages," for in contrasting the political grandeur of Rome and the cultural glory of the Renaissance, they found Medieval civilization lacking. Historians saw in the Medieval period the failure of efforts to recreate political unity, the embroilment of the church in political conflicts and internal dissension, and unoriginal cultural movements that did little more than attempt to revive a world of art and ideas that had long since disappeared.

Yet despite this long-held prejudice against

the Middle Ages, these were centuries of crucial historical development that saw the formation of a unique and vigorous civilization. Today we know that the Middle Ages was a period of great creativity and experimentation, and of growth and expansion, in which many fundamental institutions and practices of the modern world were born. It is important for us to realize that Medieval civilization was not merely a lackluster revival of Roman civilization but something entirely new and original. Based on a melding of elements from Roman and Germanic cultures as well as from Christianity, the Middle Ages was in effect the first European civilization.

The different Germanic migrations that settled in the component regions of the old Roman Empire each gave rise to variations of language, social arrangements, and political institutions. On this basis there eventually emerged distinct "national" cultures and, by the 9th century, a series of embryonic kingdoms. Later still, in the 11th and 12th centuries, feudal monarchies arose in places like England and France, where increasingly stronger royal rule laid the distant foundations of the modern national state.

The expansion of Islam under the Arabs that began in the 7th century disrupted trade and broke the unity of the Mediterranean world, yet it introduced new cultural elements that blended with European civilization, especially in North Africa, Spain, and in islands such as Sicily.

Medieval people thirsted for a sense of community, which some scholars refer to as the Medieval commonwealth. The Christian struggle against Islam in part provided Europeans with a common enemy and a single cause. The desire for unity was supplemented by two ideas and two institutions—the mythology of a universal empire in the form of what came to be called the Holy Roman Empire, and the spirit of Christianity as embodied in the Roman Church and the papacy. While often at odds with each other, the empire and the papacy provided an important degree of leadership in what had otherwise become a system of localized political and legal power known as feudalism and a system of economic self-sufficiency known as manorialism.

It is difficult to exaggerate the importance of Christianity and the church to Medieval civilization, for religious faith permeated all aspects of daily life and all levels of society. Members of the clergy were deeply involved in the feudal system, in land tenure, and in government, and popes fought with kings and emperors to maintain papal authority. Many of the most critical intellectual and artistic achievements of the period were either inspired by Christian faith or executed in the service of the church. Monasteries and cathedral schools, priests and missionaries, preserved knowledge and shared learning. The first great example of European expansion, the series of expeditions to the Near East known as the Crusades, took place under papal sponsorship and in the name of religion.

The Middle Ages was by no means a stagnant era. Instead, while experiencing great political upheaval, destructive warfare, and social stress, the period also saw significant growth—the revival of trade and commerce, the rise of cities and the development of urban middle classes, the emergence of forms of popular piety and spiritual reform, and advances in the arts and philosophy. Medieval civilization was a complex affair, a series of diverse worlds of rich and complex achievement, out of which evolved many of the institutions and ideas that characterized European life for centuries.

III

Topic 1

Politics after Rome: The Germanic Kingdoms

Of the three fundamental elements that comprised the basis of European civilization, the migration and settlement of the Germanic peoples wrought the most dramatic changes. The Germans, like all the "barbarians"—as the Romans had called the peoples living beyond the Empire—had their own social institutions, legal systems, and political cultures. In the West, the barbarians included the Celtic Picts (Scotland), Gaels (Ireland), Britons (England), and Gauls (France), while the Slavic tribes inhabited Russia and eastern Europe. The Germans occupied Scandinavia and the coast of northern Germany. These groups all spoke Indo-European dialects but developed distinct cultures.

During the first centuries of the Roman Empire, the Germans had established communities along its fringes and absorbed some Roman values and ideas through trade and other forms of contact. In the 4th century, however, sudden pressure from the Huns, nomadic tribes of central Asia, drove the barbarians to move forcibly across the frontiers and settle among the Roman populations of the Empire. The Germanic invasions did not destroy the political unity of the Roman Empire so much as take advantage of and perhaps hasten the gradual disintegration that was already under way in the West. In time, the resulting German settlements gave way to a number of "successor states." Foremost among these were the kingdoms of the Visigoths in Spain, the Ostrogoths in Italy, the Anglo-Saxons in England, and the Franks in what is today France, Germany, Belgium, and Holland.

Although they eventually mixed with the Roman populations, the Germanic peoples left their distinctive mark on the emerging civilization of western Europe. The Germanic tribes assimilated much of the Classical tradition handed down from Greece and Rome, while adapting their social and military customs to the evolving societies. Christianity acted as the cohesive element that helped to blend the two traditions and forge a new civilization.

THE GERMANIC MIGRATIONS AND THE WEST

The Germans of North and Central Europe consisted of a number of tribal confederations organized for military purposes, chief among them the Goths, Vandals, Lombards, Alemanni, Burgundians, Angles, and Saxons. In the 4th century A.D., they began to spread out in great migrations westward, south, and southeastward, displacing Celtic and Slavic settlements and coming up against the Rhine and Danube frontiers of the Roman Empire. Their contact with the Romans was first as slaves or prisoners, but later many became peasants under Roman rule. Occasionally the Romans settled a whole tribe as *foederati*, or allies, and assigned them the task of guarding the frontiers against their fellow Germans. Eventually they were able to serve in the imperial military and even gain Roman citizenship. Around 350 they began to absorb the Arian form of Christianity (on Arianism see Part III, Topic 2) as a result of the missionary efforts of Bishop Ulfilas (c. 311–383), who translated the Bible into their language and preached among the Germans.

Germanic Society: Warfare, Kinship, and Family

Long before the process of Romanization, the Germanic peoples had a well established culture that was first called to the attention of the Romans by Julius Caesar and then described by the historian Cornelius Tacitus (c. 55–c. 117) in his treatise *Germania*. Tacitus, bitter and out of favor at the Roman court, presented an admiring picture of a "simple, virtuous, and rugged" German civilization in stark contrast to what he believed was a decadent Roman society. Perhaps less admirable for Tacitus was the male bonding that took the form of rituals during which large quantities of beer

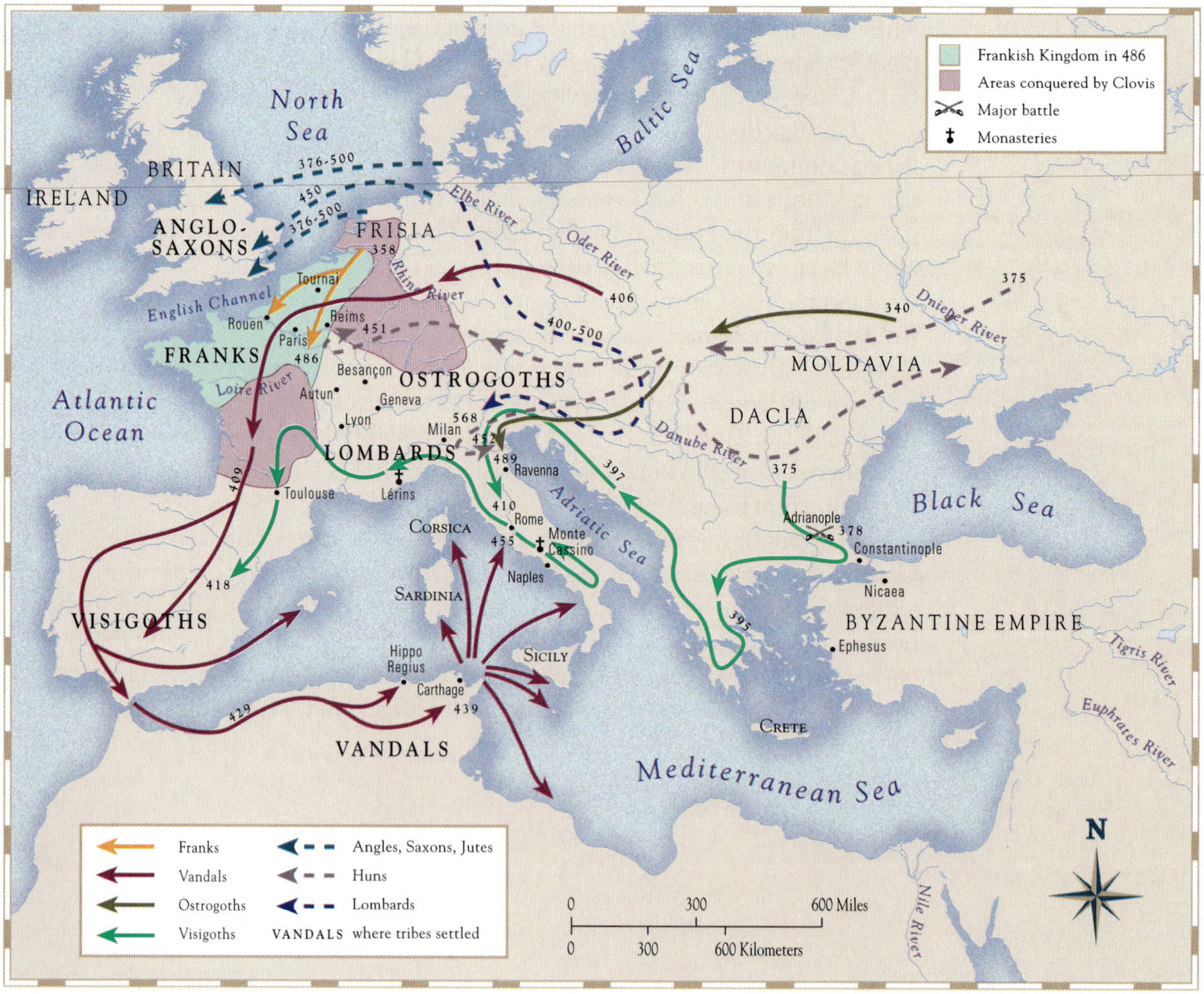

Map 1.1 The Germanic Migrations

were consumed. Such practices did, however, reinforce tribal unity.

Some three centuries following Tacitus, the numerous German tribes—each tribe consisting of clans of related families—had begun to consolidate into a series of large military confederations. The Germanic peoples continued, however, to maintain a social structure centered in villages and around the patriarchal family, a unit consisting of husbands, wives, children, grandparents, and cousins. Clans generally governed themselves, with little interference from the central tribal authorities. Slavery was widely practiced in Germanic society.

In addition to crop farming, the Germans had two other principal occupations: cattle raising and warfare. The women engaged in agriculture and household chores, while the men were the warriors. Their status generally depended on their valor on the battlefield, the size of their herds, and the number of wives they had. Warfare was an important part of a male's social existence and strict rules determined how he should conduct it. One of these traditions was that fighting within a clan was prohibited. Within a given tribe, however, clan often fought against clan. Warfare was also common between tribes, whose reputation and status grew with each conquest.

Because German society emphasized kinship rather than citizenship, German law, as opposed to Roman, dealt with individual rights rather than social structures. Thus, family honor required kinsmen to defend and protect each other and to seek vengeance for crimes committed against a family member. Because the mutual destruction due to kin feuding was so widespread, the tribes developed a system of payments, called the *wergeld,* that took the place of clan vengeance by the spilling of blood.

Warfare sometimes provided a means of creating intertribal connections. Warrior bands, which the Romans called *comitati,* linked brave young fighters to outstanding leaders through personal bonds. In return for their loyalty, the young warriors received a share of booty. Over time, the military basis of society produced large tribal confederations, such as that of the Alemanni and the Franks, which formed around a charismatic warrior leader. The Goths, on the other hand, were consolidated under the leadership of a royal dynasty that passed on military and governing authority within the same family.

Huns and Germans

In the last third of the 4th century, the Germans were assaulted by waves of ferocious warriors known as the Huns, a people of Tartar or Mongolian ancestry from the steppes and deserts of Central Asia and Russia. Because they had inhabited the region between the Ural and the Altai mountains, the languages of the Huns are called Ural-Altaic. The Huns spread terror as they drove into the Black Sea region and eastern Europe, driving the Visigoths (western Goths) and Ostrogoths (eastern Goths) before them. In 375, after suffering defeat by the Huns, the Goths moved west and south across the Danube and into the Empire, where the Eastern emperor Valens allowed them to settle as *foederati.* Three years later, the desperate Visigoths rebelled against the shoddy treatment they received from the Romans, using their strength in cavalry to wipe out the imperial army at Adrianople. Valens himself died in the fighting. The Visigoths were now able to settle within the Empire along the Danube frontier, where they maintained a degree of autonomy.

Encouraged by the Visigothic victory over the Romans, the Germans began settling within the Empire in ever larger numbers. Under their leader Alaric (c. 370–410), the Visigoths then moved across the Balkans and into Italy itself. In 410, in their boldest move yet, Alaric's forces sacked the city of Rome for three days, an event of great symbolic importance that shook the confidence of the Empire. After Alaric's death, the Visigoths abandoned Italy, eventually settling in southern Gaul and in Spain.

In the 430s, the Huns themselves invaded western Europe under their chieftain Attila (c. 406–453), whom terrorized westerners called "the scourge of God." Pushing into Gaul, Attila's forces were defeated in 451 at Châlons by a Germanic army under the command of a Roman general, Flavius Aetius. The Huns then turned back and invaded Italy, reaching Rome that same year. In 452, however, near Mantua in northern Italy, Attila met with Pope Leo I (ruled 440–461), who persuaded the Huns to leave Italy. Leo's intervention greatly enhanced the prestige of the bishops of Rome as the protector of the imperial city and helped to establish the temporal power of the papacy. With Attila's death in 453, the threat of the Huns to western Europe collapsed and his followers returned to Asia.

In addition to the Visigoths and the Huns, the rapidly declining Roman Empire was also overrun by the Vandals, who had penetrated the imperial defenses along the Rhine in 406. After marching through Gaul and Spain, the Vandals crossed over to North Africa and conquered it. Establishing a kingdom there in 429 under Gaiseric, they built a fleet, seized Sardinia and Corsica, and harassed the Empire and its commercial shipping in the Mediterranean. In 455 Vandal troops sailed to the mainland of Italy and reached Rome, which they sacked with great violence, leaving devastation in their wake. The survival of the word *vandal* in the English language reflects the Roman view that the Vandals committed senseless acts of destruction against what had once been a well-ordered society.

Late 5th-, early 6th-century mosaic showing a Vandal lord outside his villa in North Africa.

On the heels of the Vandals came the Burgundians, who also invaded Gaul around 410–411, founding a kingdom known as Burgundy along the reaches of the upper Rhône River. Northeast of Burgundy, along the Rhine River, the Alemanni also established a kingdom of their own, bequeathing to the French language the word *Allemagne*, their name for Germany.

VISIGOTHS, OSTROGOTHS, AND LOMBARDS: GERMAN KINGDOMS IN SOUTHERN EUROPE

The repeated Germanic invasions of the 5th century revealed the degree to which the effective rule of the Roman Empire in the West had deteriorated. It is sometimes said that the Empire "fell" between 476–480, when Germanic leaders replaced the last emperors of the West. The details are somewhat more complicated. In 474, Pope Leo I anointed an emperor in the West, but one of his generals forced him to flee into exile, where he was murdered in 480. In the meantime, the usurping general, Orestes, proclaimed his own son, Romulus Augustulus, as the new emperor. In 476, Romulus was in turn overthrown by the Germanic warrior Odoacer. In this way all Roman claims to rule the western half of the Empire came to a squalid end.

The Kingdom of the Visigoths

In Constantinople, imperial government remained intact, but in the West it disappeared. In place of the political unity of the western empire, the Germans created a series of independent kingdoms that blended their customs and institutions with those of their former Roman rulers. The earliest of these successor states was the Visigothic kingdom in Gaul and Spain, the first autonomous Germanic kingdom in the Empire. Ataulf (d. 415), Alaric's successor, was a typical German leader in his desire to enjoy the benefits of imperial glory rather than destroy it. In 414 he married Galla Placidia (c. 388–c. 450), the daughter of Emperor Theodosius I, and established a government at Bordeaux. Ataulf's successors arranged a treaty with the eastern emperor that recognized the Visigothic state, known as the Kingdom of Toulouse.

The Visigoths tried to unify the peoples of their kingdoms through a combination of military power, law, and religion. Roman law became a model for Visigothic law codes, but the efforts of the new rulers to convert the Gallo-Roman population to Arianism produced local unrest. In 507, the Gallic nobles joined with Clovis, king of the Franks, in conquering the Kingdom of Toulouse. The Visigoths then moved into Spain, where they eventually created another kingdom that endured for more than two centuries. The Spanish state, utilizing Roman administrative practices and the imperial tax system, proved to be a prosperous kingdom. Late in the 6th century, one of its rulers, Recared (ruled 586–601), converted to Roman Catholicism, thus ending the religious conflict that had long divided the Visigoths from the local population and securing the church as an important ally for the Gothic monarchy. At the same time, Recared began a systematic persecution of the large Jewish population of Spain.

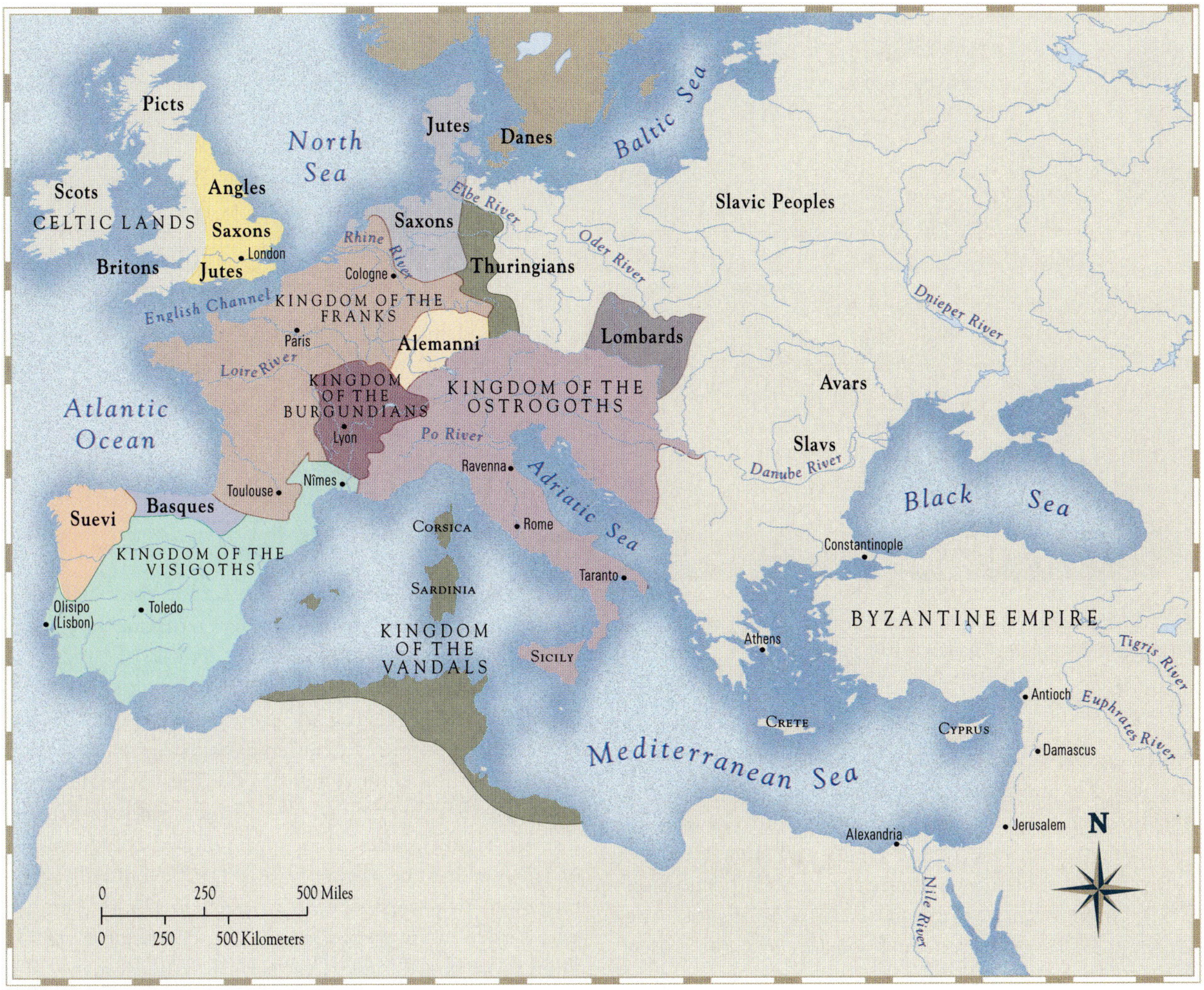

Map 1.2 The Barbarian Kingdoms

Although the Romans did not always observe the principle of hereditary succession, the Visigoths rejected the practice entirely. As a result, rival contenders struggled constantly for the throne, producing political instability. In 711, a Muslim invasion from North Africa conquered the kingdom and ended the Visigothic experiment in government.

The Ostrogoths in Italy and Their Successors

Roman traditions were preserved most fully in the Ostrogothic (eastern Gothic) kingdom of Italy under the rule of Theodoric the Great (493–526). Theodoric had been educated at Constantinople and had an abiding respect for the civic culture of the Romans. In 493, the Emperor Zeno sent Theodoric to Italy to reconquer it for the Empire, but after murdering Odoacer at a banquet he established his own kingdom in the peninsula with its capital at Ravenna. Although the eastern emperors never accepted the legitimacy of Theodoric's reign, they did recognize him as their theoretical representative in the West.

Theodoric, the most powerful of the Germanic kings, sought to create a system in which Romans and Goths could live side by side in peace. While the Ostrogoths were ruled by their own laws and officials, the Italian population was governed according to Roman law by Roman officials. Theodoric maintained the structure of the imperial government and administration, including the consuls and magistrates, although the Goths dominated the army. He repaired the old Roman roads, aqueducts, and public buildings. As in the Visigothic kingdom, religious disputes divided the Ostrogoths from the local population and were the cause of some unrest. Unlike Recared, Theodoric never abandoned his Arian beliefs, although he did not seek to force his subjects to abandon their Roman Catholicism. A ruler of practical outlook, he declared that "no one can be forced to believe against his will."

A gold medallion of the Emperor Justinian, possibly marking the imperial victory over the Vandals in 534.

After Theodoric's death, the Byzantine emperor Justinian (see Part III, Topic 3) reconquered Italy, laying waste to much of the peninsula. In 568, however, the Lombards, a Germanic tribe from the Danube region, took advantage of the chaos and invaded Italy, seizing control of the northern and central portions of Theodoric's former kingdom. Resistance against the Lombards was organized by Pope Gregory the Great (590–604), but the Byzantines were able to keep control only of a strip of territory from Ravenna to Rome and portions of the eastern coast. The Lombards were even more violent than the Ostrogoths and showed little interest in preserving Roman civilization. Establishing the seat of government at Pavia, they divided their realm into military districts governed by dukes, who replaced the old Roman administrators. Despite their lack of interest in the Roman heritage, by the 7th century the Lombards had converted to Catholicism and merged into the basic elements of Roman culture that continued to characterize Italian life, including law and language.

Significant Dates

The Germanic Kingdoms

378	Visigoths defeat Emperor Valens at Adrianople
410	Alaric's Visigothic forces sack Rome
429	Vandals invade North Africa
c. 435–453	Huns under Attila invade Europe
455	Vandals sack Rome
476	Odoacer deposes last Roman emperor
481–511	Clovis rules Franks
493	Ostrogothic kingdom established
550s	Angles and Saxons complete conquest of England
560s	Lombards conquer Italy

THE FRANKS AND CHRISTIANITY

In terms of the long-range impact of their achievement, the most important of the Germanic kingdoms on the Continent was that of the Franks. Founded in the early 5th century, the principal Frankish dynasty, known as the Merovingian, eventually gave rise to the 8th-century empire of Charlemagne, the greatest political and cultural achievement of the Early Middle Ages.

The Franks emerged as a distinct unit sometime in the 4th century, when they appeared as a confederation of tribes along the Rhine. The Franks eventually separated into two main groups—the Salian ("salty") Franks who settled along the coast, and the Ripuarian ("river") Franks on the Rhine. Defeated by the Romans, the Salians resettled in what is today Belgium and the Netherlands, where they coalesced and grew in mili- importance around the leadership of Merovech, probably a powerful tribal chieftain, from whom the Merovingian dynasty took its name.

Clovis, King of the Franks

The first ruler of the Franks to exercise real power was Merovech's grandson, Clovis (ruled 481–511). After becoming sole leader of the Salians through the force of his personality—and by murdering a number of his relatives—Clovis had himself elected king of the Ripuarians. Then began his policy of trying to unite all of Gaul under his rule. This dream came close to reality in 486, when he defeated the Roman legions at Soissons, followed by victories over the Alemanni and the Visigoths. Other Germanic groups had migrated from one region to another, but the Franks expanded, maintaining the core of their homeland.

Important to Clovis' success as ruler was his conversion to orthodox Christianity. Clovis' wife, the Burgundian princess Clotilda, urged his conversion from the Arian heresy and the couple had their children baptized. It was, however, during his battle against

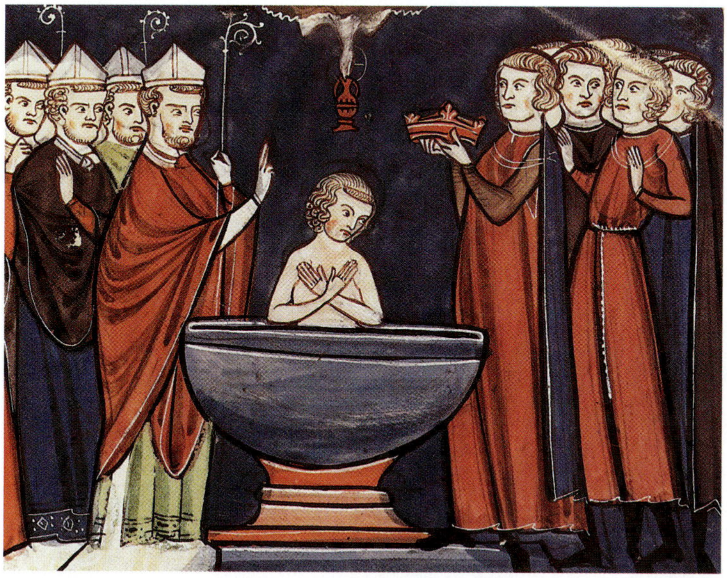

Clovis, king of the Franks, at his baptism. A dove, symbolizing the Holy Spirit, bears oil while nobles and bishops attend the king.

the Alemanni that Clovis vowed to become a Christian if he gained victory. Thereafter he became a champion of Orthodox Christianity against the Arians.

By the time of his death, Clovis had forged the largest kingdom in Europe, ruled from his capital at Paris and reaching from east of the Rhine to the Pyrenees. He ruled this vast domain partly with the cooperation of the Catholic bishops, and partly through Frankish counts stationed in the provincial cities. His role as defender of the western church gained him the support of the Gallo-Roman clergy in his efforts to build a strong royal government. Several factors, however, worked against this trend: a new noble class had begun to develop which steadily increased its power and wealth through the accumulation of land. These nobles exercised extensive rights through the law of custom—as opposed to royal legislation—over the peasants who lived and worked on their estates, and they held a virtual monopoly over the bishoprics of the realm. Royal authority was also diminished by the emergence of a royal official known as the *major domus*, or mayor of the palace, as the principal figure in the royal household. As administrators of the royal estates, these officers often distributed land to the nobles in return for securing pledges of loyalty. After Clovis died, the *major domus* accumulated significant power in his own right, eventually replacing the king in all but name.

The conversion of the Franks to Christianity helped the fusion of the old Gallic population and the Frankish elite into a cohesive society. As Frankish nobles intermarried with Gallo-Roman families, a new ruling class emerged. This successful synthesis was an enduring legacy of the kingdom of the Franks, for while the kingdoms of the Huns and the Ostrogoths quickly faded after the deaths of their leaders, the dynasty founded by Clovis persisted in one form or another for centuries. Frankish society was not a recreated Roman world but the beginning of a new, European civilization.

Upon his death in 511, Clovis' four sons broke up the kingdom. After a long period of disastrous civil wars, the Frankish lands were eventually divided into

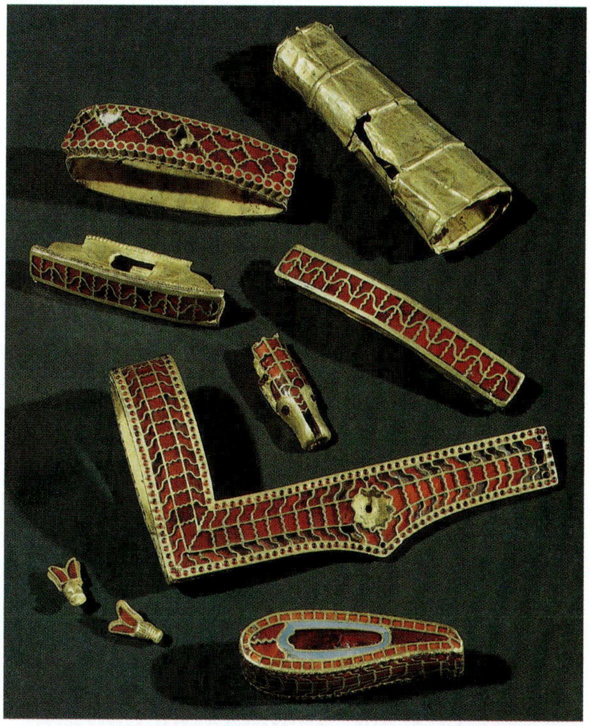

A group of elaborate Merovingian sword hilts and scabbards in cloisonné, gold, and garnets, dating from the 5th century.

three main parts, Neustria (northern Gaul), Austrasia (the southern half of western Germany), and Burgundy, each ruled by a Merovingian. In the 8th century the Merovingians would be replaced by the Carolingian dynasty, which built on the foundations laid by Clovis.

THE MAKING OF ANGLO-SAXON ENGLAND

Britain had come into the Roman Empire in the 1st century A.D., when it was annexed by the Emperor Claudius. During the reign of Hadrian, the Romans built a 50-mile-long defensive wall that separated Scotland from Britain, making the line one of the principal defense borders between Germanic territories and the *Pax Romana*. With the abandonment of Britain in the early 5th century, the island was open to invasion by federated Germanic troops, especially the Angles, Saxons, Jutes, and Frisians. Without Roman legions to protect them, the resistance of the Celtic Britons rapidly collapsed. Later legends developed in Welsh and Irish folklore of a King Arthur whose knights fought the invaders, but by 550 Germans had begun to complete their conquest of Britain.

The impact of these Germans, who had been raiding the coast for years, was far different from that of the Goths on the Continent, for these German invaders did not try to blend with the Roman population. Instead, they either eradicated or enslaved the Britons or pushed them westward into Wales and Cornwall. Some Britons even fled across the Channel to northwestern Gaul, which became known as Brittany, or "little Britain."

Because these Germanic groups, unlike the Goths, had had little direct contact with the Romans, they imported their culture and pagan beliefs to Britain. Most of the Angles and Saxons were farmers rather than warriors, and as they settled on the land they replaced the language and customs of the Britons with their own. Urban life and commerce all but ceased as the Germans developed farming communities according to their own traditions. Nor did the conquerors consolidate their rule into a centralized monarchy. Rather, prominent warriors each established small kingdoms, although they recognized the symbolic authority of the strongest of their kings, known as the "wide ruler," who settled disputes among the others. Gradually, Roman Britain became Anglo-Saxon "England"—the land of the Angles.

Christianity and Anglo-Saxon Culture

Because the Anglo-Saxons were pagans, Christianity came to England as a result of conversion efforts from two places—Ireland and Rome. In Ireland, which had remained outside the Roman Empire, Celtic traditions remained largely unchanged until the 5th century, when missionaries and traders began to spread Christianity. The most important of these early missionaries to Ireland was St. Patrick (c. 390–461). As a young man Patrick was kidnapped by Irish raiders and sent to Ireland as a slave. Later, after his escape, he became a monk and returned to Ireland to convert the population to Christianity. Although the form of Christian doctrine introduced was fully orthodox, it stressed the monastic tradition and its early converts maintained close contact with tribal traditions. As a result, unlike the practice that developed elsewhere in Europe, where bishops became the most important authorities in the church, the Irish church was in the hands of the abbots of monasteries. It was followers of the Irish monk Columba (521–597) who began the conversion of Scotland and northern England.

Irish illuminated manuscript from the *Book of Kells*, possibly made by the monks of Iona. This is the opening page of the Gospel of St. Mark.

In 596, the second effort to convert the Anglo-Saxons began when Pope Gregory the Great sent an Italian missionary, known as Augustine of Canterbury (d. c. 605), to England to head a group of some 40 monks. Augustine was first allowed to preach by the

The Venerable Bede, the "Father of English History," shown here in a manuscript from his *Vita Sancti Cuthberti.*

rulers of Kent, the pagan Ethelbert and his Christian wife Bertha. Ethelbert became the first Christian king of Anglo-Saxon England, and in 601 Augustine became the first bishop of Canterbury. A few years later he established another bishopric in London, then a town of some 30,000 inhabitants.

The Christianity introduced by Augustine followed the Roman pattern in which bishops were the central authority in the church. Tensions developed between Augustine's converts and the more ascetic followers of Columba, who followed the decentralized Celtic model revolving around abbots. Although both were orthodox in their beliefs, they observed different rituals and religious holidays. To resolve these differences, a meeting of bishops, known as a synod, met in 664 at Whitby, after which the "wide ruler," King Oswy (d. 670), settled the controversy by siding with the Roman Church.

Once Roman Catholicism became the dominant religion on the island, greater contact with the Continent diminished the cultural isolation of Anglo-Saxon England. Within a generation of the Synod of Whitby, England produced the most prominent scholar of the age, the Venerable Bede (c. 673–735). Bede, an Anglo-Saxon monk who followed the rule of Benedict (see Part III, Topic 2), wrote about theological, historical, and scientific subjects. His *Ecclesiastical History of the English Nation*, written in Latin, was based on an analysis of many documents and gives the most reliable account of the growth of Anglo-Saxon culture and the political events of the period from 597 to 731. Bede's works not only represent a great achievement in early Medieval scholarship, but reflect the fact that by the 8th century Anglo-Saxon England had become an important center of European culture.

GERMAN CUSTOMS AND ROMAN TRADITIONS: THE FORMATION OF EUROPE

The transformation of the western part of the Roman Empire was virtually complete. During a period that lasted some two centuries, this vast region had been overrun by barbarians. But although the Germanic kingdoms replaced Roman provincial administration everywhere, Roman law, language, and institutions remained sufficiently strong to influence the new conquerors. For one thing, the Germans were relatively few in number compared to the much larger Roman population—perhaps as few as 5 percent of the total—while a millennium of Roman tradition was a lure too powerful for the Germans to resist.

The new societies of the West represented a gradual blending of Roman institutions, Germanic customs, and Christian ideals. In the 6th century, Gregory of Tours (538–594), a Gallo-Roman historian and bishop, wrote *The Histories*. This work, although handed down to us in the form of badly copied versions from later centuries, nevertheless presents an original portrait of Gregory's time. It is important to remember that the Germanic society he described bore only partial resemblance to that recorded by Tacitus five centuries earlier. The customs and experiences of the different German peoples reveal considerable variation in the degree of Romanization. All of them, however, eventually found their societies and cultures transformed by the Roman legacy, especially as later Germanic rulers absorbed a respect for Roman government and law.

Germanic Government and Law

Most of the Germanic states developed monarchies that were elective in theory and adopted the notion of dynastic succession. In imitation of the Roman imperial court, German kings like Clovis and Theodoric wore purple robes on state occasions and maintained courts in which officials with Latin titles advised them. There were important differences as well. The Romans conceived of the state as *res publica*, a public matter, whereas the German kings thought of state territory as private estates and royal authority as a personal prerogative. Hence the royal court was the home of the king, and moved with him as he traveled through his domains. The courts were attended by powerful nobles but were not permanent seats of civil administration. On the local level, Roman bureaucratic machinery continued to operate much as before, for the Germans had developed no permanent administrative system. They did, however, institute a system of trusted representatives called counts who exercised military and judicial powers in the name of the king. Most kings also retained the Roman financial apparatus.

As we have seen, the personal nature of Germanic law differed from the public basis of Roman law. The Roman population continued to live under Roman law, and under German law the *wergeld* was higher for an injured German than for a Roman. Some of the kingdoms eventually adopted the Roman practice of codifying their laws, and the Visigoths, Franks, Saxons, and Lombards drew up their law codes in Latin. The *Lex Salica* (Salic Law), compiled under Clovis, reflected ancient German customs and the values of a more pastoral civilization. The customs of the past, not the will of the king, were regarded as the source of Germanic law.

Germanic law allowed for the determination of guilt or innocence through trial by ordeal. The theory was that divine intervention would prevent the accused from experiencing permanent physical harm during such painful tests as plunging an arm or leg into boiling water or grasping a red-hot iron with bare hands. The Germans also practiced ordeal by battle, believing that God would protect the innocent. Compurgation, on the other hand, was a process that involved obtaining a sufficient number of people who would swear that the accused was either innocent or was telling the truth. Compurgation, which was often used in cases involving nobles, required no real hard evidence.

German law recognized class and gender distinctions. The *wergeld* system of payment carried a higher tariff for nobles than for a commoner. Because German men placed so much status value on cattle, the penalty for injuring a cow was severe, including in some instances death. The *wergeld* was generally higher for men than for women, except when a woman was of child-bearing age; on the other hand, after a woman could no longer bear children, the payment for killing her declined. Provisions in the Salic Law prohibited female succession to property.

In the West, beginning in the 4th century, the Roman Empire effectively came to an end as waves of Germanic migrations moved across Europe. Within a short time, these peoples had established the bases for new governments that replaced the centralized Roman authority with regional kingdoms. Slowly, the new population merged with the old, and by the end of the 7th century many of those elements that had kept the Romans and Germans separated had disappeared. With the decline of Arianism and the conversion of Germans to Catholicism, religious differences faded. In the 5th century the Visigoths abandoned the ban on intermarriage, which was in any case already becoming widespread. In practical terms, the inability of the Byzantine emperors to exercise real influence in the West eventually led the old Roman population to recognize the sovereignty of the Germanic kings and to accept the new situation as permanent. As popular customs and administrative systems changed, the separate legal systems blended. Thus the Visigoths in 654 issued a new law code that applied to Romans and Germans. Language both reflected and influenced the fusion of the two peoples. Among the new German states Latin remained the official language, and the Romance languages of France, Spain, and Italy evolved from the Latin spoken by the inhabitants of those regions, to which some German words were added. By the 8th century a new, original society had begun to emerge in Europe, a society that was deeply changed by the German migrations but still retained much of its Roman character. The process of assimilation was encouraged by the church, which had emerged as the real inheritor of universal authority in the West.

Questions for Further Study

1. How did the Romans view "outsiders"? How did the Germans view the Romans?
2. How would you describe the differing patterns of settlement of the Germanic tribes in the Roman Empire?
3. In what ways did the Germans contribute to the formation of a new "European" civilization?

Suggestions for Further Reading

Burns, Thomas S. *A History of the Ostrogoths*. Bloomington, IN, 1984.

Geary, Patrick J. *Before France and Germany: The Creation and Transformation of the Merovingian World*. Oxford, 1988.

Goffart, Walter. *Barbarians and Romans*, A.D. *418–554*. Princeton, NJ, 1980.

Grant, Michael. *Dawn of the Middle Ages*. New York, 1981.

Heather, Peter J. *Goths and Romans, 322–448*. New York, 1994.

James, Edward. *The Franks*. Oxford, 1988.

Murray, Alexander. *Germanic Kingship Structure*. Toronto, 1983.

Musset, Lucien. *The German Invasions*. University Park, TX, 1975.

Wolfram, Herwig. *History of the Goths*, rev. ed. Trans. T. J. Dunlap. Berkeley, CA, 1988.

III

Topic 2

Early Medieval Christianity

As the political and economic influence of the Roman Empire disintegrated, the Christian Church emerged as the only institution capable of providing continuity and leadership in the West. During the period of relative peace that stretched from 325 to the Germanic invasions a hundred years later, the church spread throughout the Empire, grew in prestige, and strengthened its authority as Christianity became the bedrock of the Medieval civilization that was to emerge.

The early Christian intellectuals reconciled the Classical heritage of the Greco-Roman world with the ideals of Christianity. The synthesis of pagan and Christian culture achieved by these Fathers of the Church contributed to the transition from Roman to European civilization. They also established the moral justification for preserving Classical learning for future generations. At the same time, St. Augustine's *City of God,* the most important work of these early church intellectuals, laid the foundation for the Christian worldview that would eventually prevail throughout most of the Middle Ages.

Christianity developed two institutions—the papacy and the monastic orders—that were to shape much of Medieval life in significant ways. The growth and centralization of papal authority began under Pope Leo I, who established the basis for papal claims to lead the church, at least in the West. The doctrine of papal primacy had a profound impact not only on the theological unity of the church but on relations between the Roman Church and secular authority. Monasticism provided an environment in which Christian men and women could devote themselves to the worship of God while experimenting with a new form of communal living that met the economic needs of the age. Monasteries also served as the chief institutional setting for the preservation and transmission of learning. Christianity deeply influenced life in the Middle Ages, for women as well as men of all social classes.

Significant Dates

Early Medieval Christianity

313	Emperor Constantine decrees freedom of worship for Christians
325	Council of Nicaea
410	Augustine's *City of God* written
440–461	Leo I rules as pope
c. 500	Clovis converts to Christianity
c. 540	Rule of St. Benedict established for monastic life
590–604	Gregory the Great rules as pope
664	Synod of Whitby

CHRISTIANITY AND THE CLASSICAL HERITAGE

The Emperor Constantine had legalized Christianity in 313. Nevertheless, by the beginning of the 5th century most Christians remained removed and alien from what was still a predominantly Classical and pagan world. Indeed, many Christians even expressed an hostility toward Greco-Roman culture that went beyond the memory of the early persecutions. The Christian belief in the end of the world and the second coming of Christ meant that they attributed little importance to secular knowledge and learning. Roman culture was perceived as the embodiment of spiritual sin and material corruption, of sexual desire and excess. "We have no need for speculation after Jesus Christ," proclaimed the Christian writer Tertullian (c. 160–c. 225), "nor any need for inquiry after the Gospel."

The Latin Fathers of the Church

There were some Christian intellectuals, however, who had urged appreciation for and accommodation with the world of Classical learning. Origen (c. 185–c. 254), an early Christian scholar born in Egypt, wrote extensively in an effort to synthesize the fundamental principles of Greek philosophy with Christianity. A stern ascetic, he castrated himself and devoted his life to teaching. The blending of pagan and Christian values that Origen and others helped to achieve was to be a principal ingredient in the emerging new "European" civilization. Among the early Christian thinkers, the most influential were four men known as the Fathers of the Latin Church: Ambrose, Jerome, Augustine, and Gregory. (There are also Four Fathers of the Greek Church: Basil, Gregory Nazianzen, John Chrysostom, and Athanasius). Collectively these eight figures are known as the Doctors of the Church.

The life of St. Ambrose of Milan (c. 339–397) bridged the gulf between the Roman and the Christian

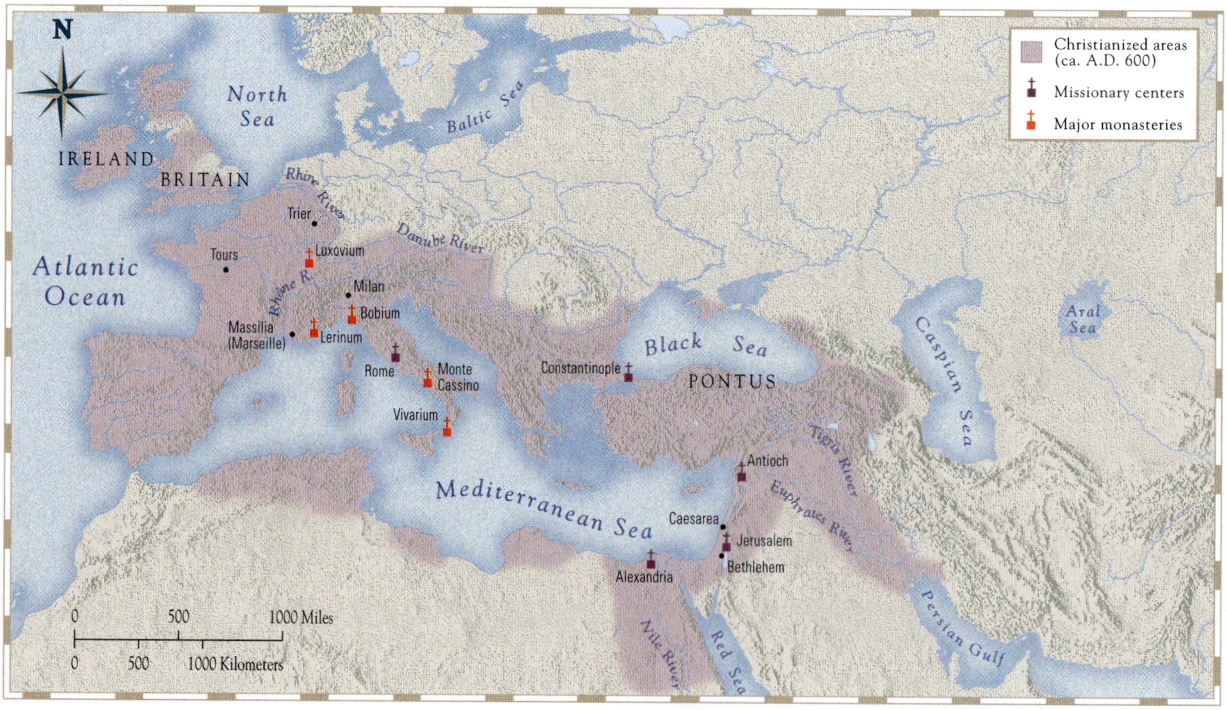

Map 2.1 Christianity, c. 600

A 4th-century Christian carving of Adam and Eve from the sarcophagus of a Roman official.

worlds. The son of an imperial official, Ambrose was educated in the Roman tradition and entered the state administration, eventually becoming governor of Milan. The people of the city then chose him as bishop.

According to Ambrose, the choice for Christians was not between learning and belief but between the church and the state; accordingly, he defined his duty as a bishop as the protection of the church's independence from the authority of the emperor. When the Emperor Theodosius slaughtered civilians in Thessalonica and Ambrose severely criticized him, Theodosius tried to force Ambrose to give up his church seat. The bishop responded, however, by arguing that "It is written, God's to God and Caesar's to Caesar. The palace is the emperor's, the churches are the Bishop's." Ambrose refused to celebrate Mass in the presence of the emperor, and finally forced Theodosius to do public penance. The independence of the church from the state that Ambrose insisted on would become a major ecclesiastical and political doctrine of Medieval civilization. In matters of faith, Ambrose maintained that the bishops should take precedence over the emperors, and that in Christian society at large the church was superior since it cared for the salvation of the soul.

St. Jerome (c. 347–c. 420) was born in the Balkans but received training in Rome as a Latin writer. In Antioch he experienced a vision in which Christ reproved him for his love of pagan culture. He then fled into the desert to live as an ascetic and devote himself to scriptural studies, becoming a distinguished scholar who was often called upon to settle doctrinal disputes. Jerome never gave up his love for the Classical authors, however, arguing that the ancients should be examined in the context of Christian principles. His facility with both Hebrew and Greek equipped him to compile the letters and writings that

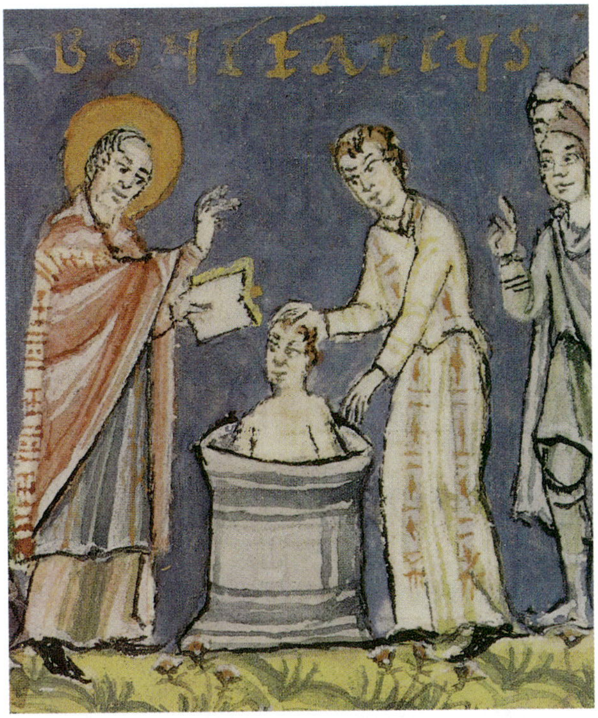

St. Boniface, Apostle to the Germans, baptizing a convert. From a manuscript illumination of the Fulda Abbey.

formed the basis for the Bible. In Bethlehem, where he lived from 386 until his death, Jerome worked on a translation of the Old and New Testaments into vernacular Latin. This so-called Vulgate, or common text, became the standard Catholic version of the Scriptures for more than 1000 years.

THE CITY OF GOD: AUGUSTINE AND HIS VISION

The greatest of the Latin Fathers was St. Augustine (354–430), whose intellect fashioned a blending of Classical and Christian thought that profoundly influenced subsequent generations. Born in North Africa of a pagan father and a Christian mother, he enjoyed an indulgent youth but showed promise as a student and received a limited education in grammar, rhetoric, and law in local schools. At the age of 17, he went to Carthage for further study, where he met a woman with whom he lived for many years and who bore him an illegitimate son.

Augustine underwent a long period of spiritual doubt during which he experimented with alternative Christian doctrines and eastern philosophies. After an unsuccessful teaching stint in Rome, in 384 Augustine went to Milan. Further study and the influence of

Bishop Ambrose, with whom he corresponded for many years, eventually led him to be baptized a Christian. Armed with his newfound faith, Augustine returned to North Africa to establish a monastery. In 396, the population of Hippo made him their bishop.

In later life Augustine's conversion led him to preach strict moral teachings, especially on sexual behavior, which he saw as the triumph of passion over reason. For the unmarried, sex should be banned altogether, and married couples should have sex only to procreate. Arguing, however, that the world's population had grown large enough, he insisted that procreation was no longer necessary and that all Christians should practice celibacy. The argument that celibacy was superior to married life stemmed from Paul of Tarsus, a Hellenized Jew whose writings in the 1st century A.D. helped to define many basic Christian beliefs.

The Confessions of Augustine

Around 400, Augustine began work on an autobiography, *The Confessions*, a literary gem as well as a classic of Christian mysticism. Remarkably frank in the details of his wild youth in Carthage, *The Confessions* offers an explanation of his inner struggle between the spirit and the flesh and his conversion to Christianity.

The Confessions is not only our principal source of information about Augustine's life. Written as an extended prayer in beautifully crafted Latin, the work is a moving chronicle of a classically trained scholar engaged on a spiritual journey to faith. One result of that journey was that Augustine came to reject the Greco-Roman notion that human virtue was an outgrowth of knowledge. His own wayward youth taught him that knowledge of what is right does not by itself lead a person to act in a righteous or rational manner. He concluded, therefore, that human will—even the will of a scholar—is by nature weak and subject to corruption. Augustine hoped that the story of his own experience would guide others.

In addition to his autobiography, Augustine also wrote numerous learned theological works that dealt with heresies and doctrinal disputes. His *On the Trinity* offered a systematic assessment of Christian doctrine, while *On the Work of Monks* was widely used by men and women living in monastic communities. Much of his energy, however, was taken up with efforts to counter an heretical movement known as Donatism, named after Donatus, the bishop of Carthage who promoted the doctrine in the early 4th century. Donatus argued that sacraments were valid only if administered by a priest free of sin. His followers saw themselves as a specially chosen Christian elite that kept their purity in an evil world, and believed that only those living a blameless life belonged in the church. Condemned by a synod and by the Emperor Constantine, Donatism nevertheless spread rapidly, especially in North Africa. Augustine began to write treatises against Donatism, insisting that God's action gave the church its authority, which was the guarantee of the Christian faith, and proclaiming the permanent validity of the sacraments. Instead of remaining apart from society, Augustine said that true Christians should strive for holiness while living in and transforming the world.

The City of God

Augustine's most important work is his monumental *The City of God*, written in 410 in the aftermath of the sack of Rome by the Visigoths that same year. Pagan philosophers attributed the catastrophe to the recognition of Christianity by the Roman state and the Romans' abandonment of the pagan gods. In his attempt to refute this argument, Augustine's *City of God* presents an interpretation of Roman experience in the light of a Christian philosophy of history, in which divine providence affects all earthly events. This philosophy stems in part from Augustine's distinction between God as creator and God as redeemer. He argued that original sin made human beings incapable of their own salvation. Only through God's grace, earned through the sacrifice of Jesus, could salvation be achieved. Even before the creation, however, God had decided which human beings were to receive or to be denied divine grace. Each person, therefore, is predestined to heaven or hell.

There are, said Augustine, two planes of existence, the earthly and the heavenly (the City of God). The earthly city is not the true home of those Christians who, because of the grace of God, will have eternal happiness in the kingdom of heaven. Augustine urged his fellow Christians to focus their energies on the divine rather than on the earthly world. Yet he also taught that the latter was not entirely evil. Because humans are inclined to sin, governments—the cities of earthly society—are needed in order to preserve peace and order. But, Augustine concluded—along with Ambrose—the church is superior even to Christian rulers.

Augustine and the other Fathers of the Church provided guidance and a voice of certitude for many in a troubled age, and although he himself died even as the Vandals were besieging the earthly city in which he lived, his vision held out the promise of a better life to come.

THE PAPACY AND THE PRIMACY OF ROME

The ability of the church to provide spiritual and secular guidance after the collapse of the Empire was due in

Map 2.2 The Early Papacy

large part to the intelligence and will of two men, Pope Leo I (ruled 440–461) and Pope Gregory I (ruled 590–604), who provided vigorous leadership as the early bishops of Rome. They succeeded not only in imposing doctrinal unity and building the administrative structure of the church, but in asserting the powers and independence of the papacy over the secular rulers of Europe.

The Search for Doctrinal Unity

A number of heresies—or conflicting interpretations of doctrine—plagued early Christianity. The Emperor Constantine had attempted to end the problem of heresy by convening a group of bishops and prelates in the Council of Nicaea in A.D. 325. The council was to settle questions regarding the nature of the Trinity raised by Arianism, the principal heresy. Named after Arius, a priest from the Egyptian city of Alexandria, Arianism argued that Jesus Christ was human and therefore of a lower order than God the Father. The Nicene Creed reaffirmed the view that Christ coexisted eternally with and was equal to God. Despite the condemnation of Arianism, however, the heresy persisted and was later adopted by many of the German Goths.

The idea of using ecclesiastical councils to settle doctrinal disputes actually increased the authority of the church, which assumed control over dealing with heresy. Moreover, although held in the East under imperial auspices, two prelates attended the meeting at Nicaea as representatives of the bishop of Rome. In 431, the practice was continued with the Council of Ephesus, convened to deal with the teachings of Nestorius, who argued that the divine and the human natures of Christ were two separate personalities and that the Virgin Mary was the mother of his human persona only. The council upheld the orthodox doctrine against Nestorianism and also described Mary as "Mother of God," thus establishing the basis for the veneration of the Virgin Mary as the most important of the saints.

Twenty years later, the Council of Chalcedon addressed the heresy professed by the Monophysites, who went to the opposite extreme by asserting that Christ possessed a single, combined nature in which his divinity was emphasized over his humanity. When the bishops assembled at Chalcedon failed to agree on this heresy, Leo I settled the argument by issuing a letter condemning the Monophysites. Like Arianism, they continued to attract adherents, especially in eastern regions of the Empire such as Syria, Egypt, and Palestine.

Papal Primacy

Leo I's initiative at Chalcedon strengthened his position as bishop of Rome, whose powers he believed took precedence in ecclesiastical matters over those of all other cities. Leo based these claims on a tradition that was already several centuries old. When the first bishops were originally elected as leaders of the early Christian communities, they set up their sees, or seats, in the more important cities of the imperial dioceses (administrative units). Those in larger cities exercised influence over those in the smaller towns and in the provinces. Leo I turned to Scripture to support the idea of Rome's primacy. The claim of the Roman bishops to supremacy went back to the Scriptures, according to which Christ had given the keys to the kingdom of heaven to St. Peter, his chief apostle. Peter had then founded the Christian Church in Rome and had been its first bishop. Later bishops of Rome therefore thought of themselves as Peter's heirs. At Chalcedon, Leo's declaration was received by the attending bishops with the words, "Peter speaks through Leo."

Once the capital of the Empire was moved to Constantinople, the lack of an emperor in the West allowed the bishops of Rome to assume the prestige identified with the former imperial city for themselves. By the 5th century, the bishops of Rome had adopted the word *pope* (from the ecclesiastical Latin word *papa*, or father) for themselves and referred to other bishops as "sons."

From Leo to Gregory

The pontificate of Leo I firmly established the doctrine of papal primacy, under which the pope became the leader of the Roman Church. Leo, a member of a

An ivory sculpture showing Pope Gregory the Great at his desk.

Roman aristocratic family, was well educated. He deliberately identified himself as the successor of Peter, a claim eventually recognized in the West but not in the East, and assumed the title of *pontifex maximus*, or highest priest. He saw himself as the shepherd of all Christians and the representative (vicar) of Christ on earth. Leo's vision for the church was that of a highly centralized institution with power focused in the hands of the pope at the top and a host of learned, dedicated priests at the bottom.

Early in Leo's pontificate, he reconfirmed his authority as pope over his bishops in a confrontation with Hilary (d. 449), archbishop of Arles and head of the church in Gaul. Hilary deposed two bishops, who thereupon appealed to Rome. Leo, supported by a letter from the emperor, deprived Hilary of his authority over the Gallic bishops and declared the sovereignty of Rome over all bishops. The prestige of the pope was further enhanced when Leo negotiated with the Hun leader Attila in 452 and with the Vandal leader Gaiseric in 455, thus preventing the destruction of Rome. These actions established the pope's temporal leadership, which he joined to his spiritual authority.

Gregory I, like Leo, was also of noble origins. He began his career in local politics and became, at the age of 30, prefect of Rome, the city's highest civil office. Within several years, however, Gregory felt the need for religious seclusion and, giving up his considerable wealth, converted his home into a monastery. In 578, he became archdeacon of Rome, a position of great importance in the papal administration, and for about six years he resided at Constantinople as a papal representative. He was elected pope by acclamation in 590, much against his will.

Gregory followed Leo's program by insisting vigorously on papal supremacy in religious matters, and worked to extend the authority of Rome over the entire western church. He intervened in ecclesiastical disputes in Italy and Gaul, kept in contact with secular rulers, and began the missionary activities that converted England and parts of the Continent to Christianity (see Part III, Topic 1). The pope also insisted that the clergy were exempt from trial in civil courts, a precedent that was to have important repercussions later in the Middle Ages.

Gregory was personally responsible for the production of a series of written works that, while not representing original scholarship, were nevertheless useful in the day-to-day functioning of the church. His *Pastoral Care* gave practical guidance to bishops and priests in carrying out their duties, while his *Dialogues* recorded the lives of saints and the miracles attributed to them. Although tradition holds that his interest in the liturgy led to the adoption of official church music that included the official prayers sung during the Mass (see Part III, Topic 9), this is now recognized as a legend.

Gregory's pontificate was distinguished above all by the establishment of the papacy's temporal position. The emperors in Constantinople refused to act in the face of continued disorders and war in Italy, particularly the invasion of the Lombards. The emperor's representative in the West was the exarch of Ravenna, who claimed secular jurisdiction over the city of Rome. Nevertheless, when Rome was threatened by a Lombard attack in 592, the exarch did nothing and Gregory negotiated his own peace with the Lombards. In this way, he made the papacy independent of the Byzantine emperor in matters concerning the jurisdiction of Rome and the surrounding region, laying the foundation for what would later be called the Papal States. Inside the city, Gregory organized the defense of the city and provided food and water to the population during emergencies.

Because of their contributions to the development of Christianity and the church, Leo I and Gregory I were both styled "the Great." During the course of the 100 years that stretched between their reigns, the foundations of the papacy as an institution and as a moral force in the West were established.

THE MONASTIC IDEAL

Monasticism was just as important as the papacy to the development of Christianity and Medieval civilization. The general concept of the monastic ideal is common to many religions, and the followers of many faiths have sought to withdraw from the ordinary world and the corruption of society in order to devote themselves completely to worship and prayer. In Europe of the Middle Ages the monk (from the Greek word *monos*, meaning alone) became an exceptionally important figure who helped to shape the values and norms of everyday life and exercised enormous social, cultural, and economic influence.

Hermits and the Flight from Worldliness

Monasticism had its origins in the desire of particularly devout men and women to escape from what they perceived as the immorality of the cities. They chose instead to live alone high up on mountains or deep in deserts—the term *hermit* comes from the Greek *eremos*, or desert. Removed from civilization, hermits could practice asceticism, rejecting bodily pleasures and indulging in fasting and self-mortification as they gave themselves totally to God. The ascetics included women—and although nuns, abbesses, and other official members of the church were not yet part of the hierarchy, there were many virgins and widows who subjected themselves to the same deprivations in their efforts to purify their bodies and come closer to God. Such individuals became mythic figures for the common people and were sought out by rulers for advice and counsel. One of the earliest persons to make the transition from the life of the hermit to the life of the monk was Anthony (c. 250–355). Anthony gave up all his worldly possessions and fled into the Egyptian desert, where he engaged in self-mortification and constant prayer. But Anthony's reputation began to attract devout Christians, who regarded him as their spiritual leader and formed a religious community around him as their abbot (from the Semitic *abba*, meaning father). This form of eremitical monasticism, centered around the hermit, was particularly widespread in the East, where local conditions enabled it to persist for many years. In the desert of Syria, for example, the climate was milder and both water and food were more easily available than in the Egyptian desert. The best known of these Syrian hermits was Simeon Stylites (c. 390–459), who for more than 30 years lived in a basket on top of a 60-foot-high pillar.

Figures such as Simeon were less common in the West, where bishops rather than hermits remained the focus of religious and ecclesiastical authority. In Italy, Gaul, and elsewhere, conditions favored cenobitic monasticism, in which monks lived in organized communities according to established rules. Yet the founding of cenobitic monasticism is usually attributed to another eastern figure, Pachomius (c. 290–346), who wrote the first rule for such communal living and emphasized chastity, poverty, physical labor, and obedience to the abbot. Later, Basil (329–379) established a monastic community in Turkey and wrote commentaries for the spiritual advice of his followers.

One of the early monastic communities in the West was founded in Marseilles in the early 5th century by John Cassian (360–435), who rejected the model of the solitary hermit. His *Institutes* had considerable influence on the idea of structured communal living. In the following century, Cassiodorus (c. 485–c. 585), a Roman senator, founded two monasteries in Italy, where he gathered learned monks who devoted themselves to scholarship and the copying of old manuscripts. Monasticism was particularly strong in Ireland, and beginning in the 6th century Irish monks became missionaries, founding monasteries on the Continent.

The Rule of Benedict

The form of monasticism that came to characterize Western Christianity was principally the work of an Italian monk, Benedict of Nursia (c. 480–c. 543).

St. Benedict, shown here holding his famous rule.

Benedict was from a noble family and had enjoyed a first-rate education, but his religious faith drove him to seek the isolation of the eremitic life in southern Italy. Soon, however, he attracted numerous followers and founded a monastic community in Subiaco. In 529, after a local priest forced him out of Subiaco, he built a monastery on the top of the mountain at Monte Cassino, and later wrote the most famous and important rule of monastic life.

The principles behind Benedict's rule contrasted with the extreme intensity of eastern Mediterranean asceticism. Although Benedict envisioned a highly structured world for his monks, including vows of chastity and poverty, the underlying notion was that of balance and moderation. Indeed, damaging acts of self-mortification, as practiced by some Byzantine hermits, were prohibited. The Benedictine rule was a practical document designed to make a community economically self-sufficient and enable a group of people to live and work together in harmony. Monks who entered a Benedictine monastery underwent a trial period of one year to determine whether they were suited to monastic existence. They then took a vow of stability, promising to remain in the monastery of their choice and not wander from one community to another.

Each monastery was ruled by an abbot who was elected for life, and to whom absolute obedience was to be given. In return, the monks expected the abbot to demonstrate wisdom and understanding. After the Council of Chalcedon, abbots became subject to the authority of their local bishops, thus integrating the monasteries into the overall life of the church. The distinction was soon made between the secular clergy, who performed church services in the temporal world *(saeculum)*, and the regular clergy who lived away from the world according to a monastic rule *(regula)*.

Monks were to devote themselves not only to worship but to study or physical labor and were encouraged not to be idle. Every day was carefully divided into hours consisting of designated tasks and duties, from farming, wine making, crafts, and the copying of manuscripts to the celebration of Mass, communal prayer, and the chanting of psalms. Monks ate and worked together and observed a social equality unknown in secular society. The number of monks in the larger monasteries ranged from 70 to 150, although a few more imposing houses counted as many as 300.

Monasteries were important economic units in the early Middle Ages. Self-sufficiency meant that each monastery grew and produced whatever was necessary to sustain the community. Although the individual monks followed a vow of poverty, the monastery itself usually owned considerable land donated to it by devout patrons. The monks knew and practiced the best farming methods of the age, including crop rotation, and managed their estates with great efficiency. They also cleared forests and drained swampy lands, contributing to the agricultural advancement of Europe. Monasteries often provided food and supplies to the local population during periods of shortage or military crisis. In more normal times, products like honey or wine made on the monastic estates were traded to townspeople.

Monasteries sometimes functioned as schools, libraries, and centers of learning, not only for the monks themselves but also for lay children from the local community. Many monasteries maintained writing units, called *scriptoria,* where religious and secular manuscripts were copied, and where the practice of illumination—the painting of illustrations and decorative motifs—became an important art form.

The Benedictine rule had great appeal in western Europe, where within a century of Benedict's death hundreds of monasteries followed its regulations. For many Christians, monasteries were a refuge both from the temptations of material life and from an age characterized by the breakdown of government. The creation of self-sufficient communities based on agricultural estates was a practical response to the broad trends in European civilization, especially the decline of cities and trade and the collapse of centralized authority. The monastic ideal represented another important way in which Christianity profoundly affected Medieval civilization.

WOMEN, CHRISTIANITY, AND THE CHURCH

Christian doctrine acted as a liberating force, for the teachings of Jesus did not make any real distinction between men and women and found flaws in both men's and women's natures. He preached equality and equal access to the kingdom of heaven. Nevertheless, the church had a contradictory impact on the lives of early Medieval women.

Christianity and the Status of Women

The Christian view of women was first presented in detail by Paul the Apostle, who argued the equality of women with regard to salvation but not within the institution of the church. Women helped spread the faith, functioned as deaconesses, and helped the poor through charities. Many of the martyrs to Roman persecution were women, and some early Christian sects permitted women to act as priests. As late as the early 6th century women officiated with priests in churches in Ireland and some areas of Gaul.

On the other hand, Paul also instructed women not to teach or to exercise authority over men. As a result, canon law (the law of the Roman Church) prevented Christian women from taking the priestly sacrament or preaching. Paul also maintained that in marriage women should be clearly subordinate to their husbands. "Let your women keep silence in the churches," he admonished, "for it is not permitted unto them to speak; but they are commanded to be under obedience, as also saith the law. And if they will learn any thing, let them ask their husbands at home" (I Corinthians 14:34–36). In prohibiting women from serving as priests, Paul reflected the Judaic tradition, which barred women from religious service and segregated them in the temple.

The Judeo-Christian tradition provided the rationale for excluding women from the priesthood through the story of the role of Eve in Original Sin. Augustine viewed women as the descendants of Eve, who had seduced Adam when the devil could not. Hence, her subjugation to man is the result of her sin. This view of women as inferior and the mother of all sin came to be widely accepted by the Church Fathers and is repeated throughout Medieval literature. Moreover, the eating of the forbidden fruit in the story of Original Sin became symbolic of women's sexual seduction of men, so that women who led an active sexual life were regarded as unclean. The Church Fathers condemned all women for the lust they inspired in men, and older traditions regarding women's physiology and the reproductive process soon became part of Christian attitudes. As early as the 4th century, women were not permitted to enter the sanctuary because of their menstruation. Virgins were regarded as the only ideal brides for Christ, and Christian writers advocated the exclusive roles of wife and mother for women who rejected celibacy.

The Female Monastic Orders

Although Christianity reinforced the inferior status of women, the church did provide women with an opportunity for a life beyond marriage and the family. The first monks were men but monasteries for women quickly developed in parallel fashion. The communities founded by Pachomius had convents for women, but the laymen who did the physical labor for the convents lived and slept apart. A rule for a female order was written as early as the 5th century in Gaul, but the Benedictine rule proved the most popular among communities for women.

Double monasteries arose almost from the beginning. In these arrangements, monks and nuns lived in separate houses in the same monastery and under a single head. A few were actually headed by an abbess who ruled over both monks and nuns, although many male ecclesiastics opposed this. Hilda (614–680) of Whitby Abbey in England was the most famous abbess of a double monastery. In addition to running Whitby, she supervised two other houses. A princess from

Hilda served as superior of a monastery of men and women in Whitby, England. Here she receives a copy of the treatise *In Praise of Holy Virgins* by Aldhelm.

Northumbria, Hilda became a leading figure in the church and hosted the Synod of Whitby (663) that settled differences between the Roman and Celtic rites (see Part III, Topic 1).

To what degree was Hilda the exception? Double monasteries were certainly not the norm, and like their male counterparts, abbesses were under the jurisdiction of the local bishop. In theory, abbesses could not preach to nuns in public or attend high councils of the order to which they belonged, nor were they supposed to receive the vows of nuns or hear their confessions, as did priests. In some double monasteries males had to pledge obedience to the abbess, although she was forbidden by canon law to exercise judicial authority over them. Moreover, abbesses, like abbots, ruled over the peasants who worked the monastic lands, and managed the order's estates.

Like men, most women entered religious houses out of devotion, but some did so for other reasons. The overwhelming majority were daughters of the nobility or the upper middle class—this because almost all girls wanting to enter a monastery were expected to bring a dowry with them, although the amount was lower than was expected for marriage. Those daughters for whom a family could not provide a sufficiently large bridal dowry often took the veil. In addition, the nunnery was often an alternative to marriage for illegitimate daughters or those who were physically handicapped or learning-impaired. Rulers, husbands, or male relatives sometimes sent girls to nunneries as punishment or in order to gain control over their inheritances. Some women, of course, went into religious orders simply to escape male authority or an unwanted marriage.

Women in monasteries lived according to the rules of their orders, with their days divided between prayer and work. In the wealthier nunneries, servants generally did the physical labor, but nuns engaged in a variety of activities that included sewing and crafts, studying, and copying manuscripts. Abbesses were among the few Medieval women who could act as organizers and administrators, while women had more opportunity for education in the nunneries than in secular society.

From its position as a persecuted religious sect in the late Roman Empire, Christianity had become by the 5th century one of the essential elements of the new civilization developing in western Europe. The early Christian philosophers and theologians laid the basis for orthodox doctrine and reconciled their beliefs with the Classical heritage of the pagan world. During the centuries from 400 to 700—a period of instability and change as Europe adjusted to the Germanic invasions and the collapse of imperial authority in the West—the church also built an institutional structure that proved remarkably enduring. The bishops of Rome evolved into popes who wielded great power and influence, and established the claim to papal supremacy that was to shape much of Medieval political thought. The monastic ideal not only gave expression to the deep religious beliefs of early Christians, but had a considerable impact on secular society. The Medieval period was an age of faith, and the church its most important institution.

Questions for Further Study

1. What were the principal doctrinal concerns of the Fathers of the Latin Church?
2. What factors led to the growth of papal power and prestige in the early Middle Ages?
3. What contributions did monasticism make to Medieval civilization?
4. In what ways were women excluded from the Christian Church? How did they define roles for themselves within the church?

Suggestions for Further Reading

Brown, Peter. *The Body and Society: Men, Women, and Sexual Renunciation in Early Christianity*. New York, 1988.

Chadwick, Henry. *The Early Church*. Baltimore, 1967.

Chadwick, Owen. *The Making of the Benedictine Ideal*. London, 1981.

Dodds, Eric R. *Pagan and Christian in an Age of Anxiety*. New York, 1965.

Lawrence, Clifford H. *Medieval Monasticism*. London, 1984.

MacMullen, Ramsay. *Christianizing the Roman Empire, A.D. 100–400*. New Haven, CT, 1984.

Markus, Robert A. *Christianity in the Roman World*. London, 1974.

McNamara, Jo Ann Kay. *Sisters in Arms*. Cambridge, MA, 1996.

Pelikan, Jaroslav. *The Growth of Medieval Theology*. Chicago, 1978.

Southern, Robert W. *Western Society and the Church in the Middle Ages*. Baltimore, 1970.

Ward, Benedicta, trans. *The Sayings of the Desert Fathers*, rev. ed. Kalamazoo, MI, 1984.

Zarnecki, George. *The Monastic Achievement*. New York, 1972.

III

Topic 3

Byzantium: The Eastern Empire

Constantine intended his city on the Bosphorus to be a second Rome. Constantinople was to serve as the Empire's new capital, where church and state would jointly govern in the name of Christ. At the same time its location, on the site of the ancient Greek city of Byzantium, gave it access to the culture of the Greek world. Thus, from the beginning three forces dominated the Byzantine Empire: Roman imperial tradition, Christianity (in the Orthodox form defined under Constantine), and Greek culture.

Under Constantine's successors, the Eastern Roman Empire became increasingly detached from the West. Religious disputes split the two halves. While the Western Empire began to crumble as waves of Central Asian peoples invaded the Western provinces, Constantinople provided strong centralized government for the increasingly prosperous cities of Asia Minor, Egypt, and Syria.

In the 6th century, the Emperor Justinian tried to restore the unity of the old Roman Empire. Byzantine forces reconquered Italy and southern Spain, and dominated shipping in the Mediterranean. Justinian had the frontiers protected with a vast new system of fortifications and reorganized provincial administration. He also made important contributions in law and architecture.

His successors faced enemies from the east and north. After a triumphant victory over the Persians in 627, Byzantium failed to prevent the Arab conquest of Syria and Egypt. At the same time Asian peoples like the Bulgars combined with Slavic tribes to push south and overrun the Balkans. An unending series of wars with Arab and Bulgar forces dominated the next three centuries of Byzantine foreign policy.

One of the long-term consequences of Byzantine contacts with the Balkans and other peoples of Eastern Europe was to be the spread there of Orthodox Christianity; Byzantine missionaries converted first the Bulgars, and then the Russians. Two of the first missionaries, Cyril and Methodius, invented the Cyrillic alphabet for the writing of Slavic languages.

At Constantinople itself the Iconoclast controversy (726–843) caused bitter religious conflict. This movement, which sought to ban the use of images in religious art, brought a temporary break in the development of Byzantine art. The artistic achievements of Justinian's reign had marked the First Golden Age. After the defeat of the Iconoclasts, the 10th and 11th centuries saw a second wave of artistic creation, marked by the Byzantine love of rich display and magnificent color.

Constantinople's geographical position assured it a central role in international trade; Byzantine merchants bought goods from Russia, India, and Arabia, and sold them to Western buyers. Its business community was active and prosperous. Both economic and social life were regulated by a complex and rigid state bureaucracy. While the tax system was hard on the urban lower classes, farm workers on the large monastic and aristocratic estates were reduced to the status of serfs.

NEW ROME IN THE EAST: THE SUCCESSORS OF CONSTANTINE

The foundation of Constantine's new capital in 330 marked one of the great turning points in the history of the Mediterranean. The emperor transferred many features of Roman civilization to the former site of the Greek city of Byzantium. He established a senate there, and recreated the structure of the Roman bureaucracy. He encouraged aristocratic Roman families to build villas on the Bosphorus, and ordered the construction of a great racetrack to duplicate the chariot races that had provided popular entertainment in his former capital.

More importantly, he intended to renew and revitalize the centuries-old traditions of Roman government by establishing and maintaining religious unity. The Council of Nicaea of 325 had laid down the tenets of Orthodox Christianity by banning Arianism as heresy (see Part III, Topic 2). The Nicene creed, promulgated by the council, declared that God the Father and God the Son were of the same substance.

Now the patriarch of Constantinople and the emperor, representing church and state, were to promote these Orthodox teachings and, in their name, preserve the Empire, freed from its pagan associations. Through all the tumultuous struggles of the following centuries, Byzantine rulers maintained their conviction that the Empire was based on the will of the Christian God, as whose representatives they ruled.

If this renewed Empire drew its inspiration from Christianity, and its political and administrative strength from ancient Rome, its cultural foundation was Greek. In its language, literature, and intellectual tradition, the Byzantine Empire followed the Hellenistic reverence for the Classical Greeks and the Golden Age of Periclean Athens. The task for Constantine and his successors was to fuse these three forces—Classical Greece, Rome, and Christianity—into a single civilization and defend them from barbarian attack.

The Beginnings of the Byzantine State

For all his emphasis on orthodoxy, Constantine had stopped short of making Christianity the official religion of the Roman state. His son and successor, Constantius II (ruled 337–361), maintained his father's caution, while passing edicts against pagan sacrifices and "superstitions."

The Emperor Julian (ruled 361–363) made an attempt to revive the pagan traditions which his predecessor had sought to eliminate. Inspired by the teachings of Neoplatonist philosophers, Julian publicly proclaimed his adherence to paganism and the gods of Homer. He prohibited Christians from teaching literature, but otherwise left them free to practice their religion. The revival did not outlast Julian's reign, and his

Mosaic in the dome of the Orthodox Baptistry, Ravenna.

successors dubbed him Julian the Apostate—he who turns from his own religion.

Toward the end of the century Theodosius the Great (ruled 379–395) proclaimed Orthodox Christianity as established at Nicaea to be the only state religion. His edict banned both paganism and Arianism. Theodosius was the last emperor to rule over a united Empire. Under his two sons, Arcadius and Honorius, the Eastern and Western halves split apart, and within a generation of his death the former Roman territories of Britain, France, Spain, and North Africa had fallen to barbarian conquest.

The break between the two halves was exacerbated by a series of religious controversies that pitted the authority of the pope in Rome against that of the patriarch of Constantinople. The struggle became even more complicated when the Egyptian Church, in the person of the patriarch of Alexandria, made a bid for leadership, although a temporary alliance between Rome and Constantinople defeated the Alexandrian claims.

Any chance for the two parts of the Empire to negotiate on equal terms vanished in the course of the 5th century, as the Western church saw its territories conquered. Waves of Visigoths, Huns, and Ostrogoths poured across the Rhine and Danube into Central Europe. In 476 barbarian generals drove out the last Roman emperor and took over as rulers of Italy. With the collapse of centralized government, the Western Empire fragmented.

The geographical position of Constantinople and the rest of the Eastern Empire provided protection from the worst of these invasions. In 400, and again in 471, the capital successfully resisted attack, while wealthy cities like Alexandria and Damascus remained virtually untouched. Trade and commerce continued to flourish. More importantly, government throughout the Byzantine East remained under central rule. Constantinople continued to control the army, collect taxes, and to govern the provinces by appointing local governors.

JUSTINIAN AND THE IMPERIAL QUEST

The extraordinary reign of Justinian the Great (ruled 527–565), the nephew of a Macedonian peasant, dominated the history of 6th-century Byzantium, and left its mark on many of the following centuries. In his attempt to recreate the Roman Empire in the East, Justinian waged war on two fronts: abroad, he aimed to

Mosaic from San Vitale, Ravenna, showing Justinian and his retinue (c. 547).

recapture imperial territory in the West lost to the barbarians; at home, he used his imperial authority to exert absolute control over church affairs. Both campaigns succeeded in the short term, but produced disastrous long-term effects. His most significant permanent contributions to Byzantine civilization were the codification of Roman law and the building of the Church of Hagia Sophia (Holy Wisdom).

The Wars of Justinian

Our knowledge of Justinian as man and emperor owes much to the writings of a contemporary historian, Procopius (born c. 500). *A History of the Wars of Justinian*—his official account of the campaigns of Belisarius, Justinian's leading general—describes the reconquest of Roman Africa from the Vandals (533–534) and Belisarius' brilliant series of triumphs over the Ostrogoths in Italy (536–540). Procopius served on Belisarius' staff as adviser and clearly admired his master, about whom he writes with affection.

In the descriptions of events back in Constantinople which intersperse the military narrative, Procopius' attitude to Justinian and Theodora, the emperor's powerful wife, is much more ambiguous. His implicit criticism of the imperial couple becomes open hostility in the notorious *Secret History*, which retraces the events covered in the official account, this time in the form of a virulent and sustained attack upon them. The character and early career of Theodora—an actress famous for her beauty—are described in scurrilous detail, while Justinian emerges as vicious and vacillating, responsible for every kind of disaster, from bankruptcy to earthquakes.

Whatever the emperor's personal failings, his policies aimed to reinforce the newly reconquered territories. Byzantine fleets patrolled the Mediterranean, protecting trade routes. In Europe, Asia, and Africa, imposing fortifications guarded the Empire's borders, with their reorganized and strengthened garrisons. The imperial staff tightened up provincial administration.

In the capital, Justinian reorganized the mass of Roman law to simplify the machinery of government. The result, the *Corpus Juris Civilis* (Corpus of Civil Law), still forms the foundation of actual law in most of continental Europe today.

Justinian and the Church

Military and political supremacy was not enough, however: Justinian was determined to establish his spiritual superiority as God's representative on earth. This assertion of complete authority is sometimes called "Caesaropapism." One tangible way to achieve it was to give Constantinople (now Istanbul) the foremost church in Christendom as the center of Orthodoxy. To this

The Church of Hagia Sophia, Istanbul (Constantinople). The minarets were added when the building was turned into a mosque after 1453.

end, the emperor commissioned the building of the Church of Hagia Sophia, the architectural masterpiece of the First Golden Age of Byzantine art. Justinian's words on first entering the completed church at its grand dedication reflect his intentions: "O Solomon, I have surpassed you!"

In other respects, imperial policy on religious matters created lasting problems. Among the seemingly interminable dogmatic disputes in the Orthodox Church was the question of Monophysitism (see Part III, Topic 2). An earlier church council had branded the Monophysite position as heretical, and Justinian set out to eliminate its followers. Wholesale and bloody persecution of those in Syria and Egypt was only lessened by the intervention of Theodora, herself a Monophysite sympathizer. Popular anger and resentment at the imperial interference remained high. Fed by its memory, the local populations welcomed the Persian and Arab invaders of a few decades later.

Nor were the effects of Justinian's Western conquests destined to last. The imperial administration sought to make good the devastating financial drain of expensive military campaigns by raising taxes, in particular those of the newly reacquired Western provinces. As in the East, the embittered locals subsequently did little to resist the invading enemies of Byzantium, in this case the Germanic Lombards. By the end of the century, Justinian's gains were swept away. Furthermore, the long-term results of Justinian's reign were undoubtedly influenced by the plague which struck Constantinople in 542, killing many of its citizens and weakening its resistance.

More disasters followed. By concentrating on winning territory in the West, Justinian had been unable to take any significant action against his chief Eastern rivals, the Persians. Only low-key defensive wars and expensive alliances with local enemies of the Persians held back their advance. As the Western conquests disappeared, the threat of first Persian and then Arab invaders cast foreboding shadows over Justinian's legacy.

BYZANTIUM UNDER STRESS: MILITARY THREAT AND RELIGIOUS CONFLICT

The reign of Heraclius (ruled 610–641), son of the Byzantine governor of Africa, began with a string of disastrous losses to the Persians. The Byzantine-held cities of Antioch, Damascus, Jerusalem, and Alexandria all fell to Persian troops between 611 and 619. To make matters worse, the Avars, another Asian nomadic tribe, moved through Central Europe to threaten the capital itself.

The turning point came in 626. In that year the heroic efforts of Constantinople's united population

Map 3.1 The Byzantine, Islamic, and Carolingian Empires, c. 800

Christ Pantocrater, icon from the Monastery of St. Catherine, Sinai.

defeated an attack on it by the combined forces of Avars, Slavs, and Bulgars. By the end of the century, the latter were to pose a fresh threat, but Heraclius won time to concentrate on defeating the Persians, who in 614 had taken Jerusalem and carried off the wood of the True Cross, Christianity's most sacred relic. In 627 Heraclius moved on to the offensive and invaded Persia. In a lightning series of attacks, his troops recaptured all the lost provinces and forced the Persian king to sue for peace. As Christ's representative on earth, the emperor secured the relic and returned it to Jerusalem. In 629 Heraclius reentered Constantinople in a blaze of glory, the supremacy of his Empire reasserted.

Byzantium and the Rise of Islam

Heraclius' triumph was brief. By the end of his reign a new, far more formidable rival appeared on the scene to challenge Byzantine power. Both the Byzantine and Persian empires were weary from centuries of struggle. The rise of Islam and the spread of Arab forces throughout the Mediterranean brought fresh, energetic warrior bands, inspired by their new religion (see Part III, Topic 4).

The result was to reverse Heraclius' victories. By the last year of his life, Palestine and Syria were in Muslim hands. In 642 the Muslims took Alexandria and began the conquest of North Africa that would in turn lead them to Spain. Between 673 and 677, Arab forces besieged Constantinople itself. A further, even more devastating attack came in 717, and only the use of "Greek Fire," the Byzantine secret weapon, saved it from being taken by an Arab fleet ("Greek Fire" was a liquid of unknown composition—probably petroleum-based—thrown in grenades, which caught on fire when wet and burned under water). Meanwhile, the Arab capture of Cyprus and Rhodes put an end to the supremacy of Byzantine shipping in the Mediterranean.

The Iconoclastic Controversy

No sooner were the Arab forces repulsed than the Byzantine world plunged into a century of religious conflict. The cause was the widespread use of religious images, or icons—both painted and sculpted—as objects of reverence. The Old Testament prohibited the use of "graven images," but over time icons had become central to Orthodox faith. The Western church also encouraged the veneration, though not the worship, of sacred images.

In 726 the Emperor Leo III issued an edict against the use of icons, and declared that those in existence should be destroyed—the word "iconoclasm" literally means the "breaking of images." The Empress Irene ordered their restoration in 787, but her successors banned them again in 813, and icon worship was reintroduced only in 843.

The icon controversy was more than a learned dispute about theological practice. Echoing Justinian's moves of two centuries earlier, it pitted the authority of the emperor against that of the church. The chief centers of icon worship were the monasteries, where

Significant Dates

Byzantine Achievements and Crises

330	Constantinople established
527–565	Reign of Justinian the Great
610–641	Wars of Heraclius against the Persians
642	Muslims take Alexandria
726–787, 813–843	The use of icons banned
811	Bulgars defeat Byzantine army and besiege Constantinople

Byzantine monks jealously guarded sacred images handed down over centuries. Many of these monasteries were the focus of popular religious cults. The iconoclastic emperors were thus challenging church leadership and asserting their own supremacy. At the same time, they also underlined their differences with the Western church, for the pope condemned the iconoclastic decrees.

The final triumph of the icon defenders reinforced the power of the monasteries, which were to play an increasingly important part in the later centuries of Byzantine history. At the same time, it was a victory for popular religion and underlined the importance of tradition.

BYZANTIUM IN THE NORTH: THE SLAVS

The most permanent legacy of Byzantine culture was its influence on the Slavs. The origins of these peoples are obscure. Their original homeland seems to have been deep in the forests of western Russia, from where they spread east into the heart of Russia and south into the Balkan peninsula.

It was here, to the north of Greece, that conflicts developed between the Byzantine Empire and the Slavic Bulgars. As early as the reign of Heraclius, Byzantine forces had used the double weapon of military conquest and enforced conversion to Christianity. By the late 7th century, however, the Bulgars were once again on the offensive, and in 716 the Emperor Theodosius III (ruled 715–717) made peace with them, and was forced to agree to an annual payment of silks and gold in tribute.

Distracted by the threat of Arab invasions and the iconoclast controversy at home, successive emperors failed to take decisive action against the buildup of Slavic power. In 811, in one of the most disastrous defeats in Byzantine history, the Bulgarian king Krum (ruled 802–814) destroyed the entire army and its generals and laid siege to Constantinople. The city survived, but the Bulgars continued to threaten the Empire until their final defeat 200 years later, in 1014, by the troops of Basil II (ruled 976–1025), whose grateful subjects dubbed him Basil the Bulgar Slayer.

The Conversion of Russia

In the mid-9th century, two Byzantine missionaries, Cyril (827–869) and his brother Methodius (825–884), traveled to Moravia (now part of the Czech Republic) to convert the Slavic inhabitants to Orthodox Christianity. As part of their campaign they devised the Glagolitic alphabet, a version of the Greek alphabet, in order to write down the Slavic language. This alphabet, in a modified form known as the Cyrillic, is still used by the Russians and Bulgarians today. Under the counterinfluence of German missionaries, the Moravians eventually rejected Byzantium in favor of Rome, but at the end of the 9th century their Bulgar neighbors and rivals accepted Orthodox Christianity and adopted the new alphabet.

Even more significant in its long-term consequences was the Byzantine impact on Russia. In the course of the 9th century, Scandinavian nomads—they are known as the Rus—overran the steppes of European Russia, to rule over the Slavonic peoples living there. In 862, the Viking Rurik (died c. 879) founded a state at the old Slavonic capital of Novgorod. His dynasty was to rule Russia for the following 700 years. Rurik's successor Oleg (died c. 912) conquered Kiev in 882, and made it the new capital of the state. Oleg went on to defeat Constantinople in 907. The treaty he negotiated was the basis for trade relations between Byzantium and Kievan Rus, which continued under successive grand princes of Kiev.

Byzantine missionaries, armed with the Cyrillic alphabet, were soon at work at the court of Kiev. In 954 they acquired an eminent new convert in the Dowager Grand Duchess Olga (890–969), who traveled to Constantinople for her formal baptism. Olga eventually became the first Russian saint of the Orthodox Church. Her grandson, Vladimir (ruled 980–1015), after consolidating his rule over a kingdom that stretched from the Baltic to the Ukraine, made a pact in 987 with the Byzantine Emperor Basil II. Converting to Christianity, he was baptized and in return received Basil's sister in marriage. Vladimir's

Cathedral of St. Basil, Red Square, Moscow.

subsequent forcible conversion of his subjects to the Orthodox faith did much to reinforce the authority and prestige of Kiev.

The Orthodox Church soon became a major force in the state. Its clergy established land-owning monasteries, on the pattern of those in the Byzantine Empire. Many of the monasteries served as centers of education, where the earliest works of Russian literature were written; most of them were religious in subject. In the visual arts, too, Russian painters and architects followed Byzantine models. The effects on the subsequent development of Russian culture were to last for centuries. It was only in the 19th century that Russian intellectuals and artists began to look to Western Europe for inspiration.

ARTISTIC SPLENDOR IN THE BYZANTINE WORLD

The years following the foundation of Constantinople saw the gradual development of a distinct style of Byzantine art. As successive emperors sought to establish their control over church and state, they used the visual arts as a means of reinforcing their authority. The artistic style that resulted was on the whole static and conservative, emphasizing the glory of God and the splendor of the emperor and his court.

Many of the most important buildings were centrally planned, with the various spaces around the dominating center arranged to reflect the pivotal role of the emperor and the hierarchy of Byzantine society around him. The internal decorations used gold and semiprecious mosaics to present symbolic depictions of their subjects. These were mainly religious: throughout the long history of the Empire, little secular or popular art was produced.

The First Golden Age

By the time of Justinian, in the First Golden Age of Byzantine art, architects and mosaic artists had evolved styles capable of expressing the emperor's combined political and spiritual authority. In the great series of mosaics at Ravenna, Justinian's Italian capital, the emperor and his wife Theodora appear as the equivalents of Christ and the Virgin. Justinian is accompanied

Empress Theodora and her attendants. San Vitale, Ravenna, c. 547.

by twelve companions, corresponding to the twelve apostles, while the embroidery on Theodora's robe shows the three Magi carrying their gifts to Mary and the infant Jesus.

The major monument of Justinian's reign, the Church of Hagia Sophia, combines the basilica plan of Western Christian churches with a vast central dome. Beneath this floating dome—described by one of its first viewers as "like the radiant heavens"—the inside space glitters with gold mosaics illuminated by beams of light from the hundreds of windows. Even today the effect is dramatic. Justinian's contemporaries, overwhelmed by the sweep of heavily embroidered vestments and the pungent smell of incense, might well have believed themselves in the presence of the divine.

The Second Golden Age

The two centuries following Justinian produced nothing to equal his achievement. Constant warfare abroad diverted funds for other, less exalted purposes, while the iconoclast controversy effectively blocked artistic production at home. The Second Golden Age of Byzantine art, which lasted from the late 9th to the 11th centuries, followed the defeat of the iconoclasts.

Many of the greatest achievements of the Second Golden Age show an emotional, suffering quality new to Byzantine art. Artists of the First Golden Age had depicted the wisdom and power of Christ, and either avoided the Crucifixion as a subject or showed the crucified Christ as triumphant. Perhaps as a result of the victory of popular religion over the iconoclasts, Crucifixion scenes in the Second Golden Age depict Christ in more human terms. The dramatic and pathetic figures of the Crucifixion mosaic in the monastery church of Daphni, just outside Athens, leave no doubt as to the agony of Christ or the grief of the bystanders.

The expression of intense emotion reaches its extreme in a cycle of paintings dating from the early 14th century, which decorate a chapel in the former Church of St. Saviour in Chora at Istanbul. The dynamic and energetic figure of Christ who sweeps down to limbo to raise the dead seems a far cry from the static images of earlier Byzantine art.

The Art of Icons

The earliest Christian sacred images, according to a tradition often cited by the defenders of icons, were the portraits of Christ painted by St. Luke. We know little about the development of icon painting before the end of the icon controversy, since the iconoclasts destroyed the existing ones. With the renewal of their production in the 9th century, a standard type began to circulate, with fixed patterns of composition and decoration repeated on countless examples—the Orthodox Church required that these images be only two-dimensional.

The veneration of icons spread to the newly converted state of Kiev, and they remained popular in Russia over the following centuries. The work of one of the first great Russian artists, Andrei Rublev (c. 1370–c. 1430), shows the influence of standard Byzantine models, but adds extra intensity by the use of brighter and more contrasting color effects. Russian

Fresco of the Anastasis, Church of St. Saviour in Chora (Kariye Camli), Istanbul, (c. 1310–20).

painters continued to develop their own styles in the centuries following the fall of Constantinople, thereby continuing the evolution of Byzantine art even after the end of the Byzantine Empire.

ECONOMIC VITALITY AND SOCIAL INEQUALITY

The ability of the Byzantine Empire to survive depended on its financial stability. During the centuries of decline in the West, trade and commerce continued to flourish in the Eastern Empire. City life remained active, not only at Constantinople but also at other centers such as Antioch, Thessalonika, and Trebizond. Production of silk and of gold embroidery, and the maintenance of a stable gold and silver currency, enriched the economy.

With the slow revival of Western Europe which began in the 9th century, Byzantium served as the link for trade between East and West. Constantinople's central position in the Mediterranean made it a natural marketplace, and traders from Italy and farther west came there to buy precious stones and spices from Arabia and India, skins and furs from Russia, and slaves from Africa and the Caucasus.

Although individual merchants and craftsmen profited from their work, trade remained under state control. Official guilds were in charge of manufacturing, and sales took place at state salerooms. The taxes levied on these transactions enriched the imperial treasury, which also collected revenues from state-owned farms, mines, and quarries.

Byzantine Land Tenure

For all the importance of domestic and foreign trade, the chief and continuing economic basis of the Empire's prosperity was agriculture. Both landowners and those who worked it paid taxes. Originally Byzantine farmers were smallholders, working their own plots of land. Over time, however, individual private landowners began to build large estates, on which the peasants became reduced to the level of serfs, bound to the land and unable to alter their status.

The earliest of these estates belonged to the wealthy aristocratic families of the capital, but with the rise of the monasteries much of the richest land passed into the control of the church. Some small private farmers managed to survive, but by the later history of the Empire most of the state's agricultural revenues came from the large tenant farms.

Society and Class

From the beginning Byzantine society was based on a rigid system of class hierarchy, with the emperor at the head of both church and state. His chief rivals for power were the wealthy aristocratic families and, increasingly, the monks of the richer monasteries.

Some rulers made an effort to protect the rights of the poorer citizens, while extending the power of the central government. Basil the Bulgar Slayer, for example, confiscated the estates of owners who had acquired them over the previous 70 years, and forced more established owners to pay the tax arrears of their peasant laborers. On the whole, though, the wealthy landowners continued to expand at the expense of both the central authority and the workers. The same process occurred in the cities, where the urban lower classes bore an increasing share of the tax burden.

Middle-class Byzantine citizens benefited from a higher level of education than their equivalents in the West or in the world of Islam. Literacy was encouraged, and devotion to Christian texts did not mean that Classical Greek literature was neglected. Most of the Classical texts we possess, in fact, owe their survival to the Byzantine scribes who continued to copy them. Byzantine exiles, fleeing from the Turks in the last days of the Empire, brought many Greek manuscripts with them to the West.

Nor was education exclusively a male preserve. Although young women of upper-class families did not attend school, they had private tutors and on occasion developed careers. Some became physicians, while others established themselves as literary figures. The most famous was the princess Anna Comnena (1083–c. 1153), whose history of the reign of her father, the Emperor Alexius (ruled 1081–1118), shows a profound knowledge of ancient literature and philosophy. Violently anti-western—in condemning the First Crusade, she apologizes for sullying her pages with the names of Norman barbarians—she paints a fascinating picture of her childhood and early political career, and at one point she apparently took part in a plot to assassinate her own brother.

The Bureaucracy

The survival of the Byzantine Empire for a millennium in the face of continual external threats and internal feudings was due in large measure to the efficiency of its bureaucracy. The education of the middle and upper classes provided a substantial body of citizens on whom to draw for the government of the state. Whereas in the West only the clergy were literate, lay literacy provided the Byzantine world with an effective civil service.

This bureaucracy, under the supervision of imperial officials, regulated just about all aspects of Byzantine life and society. State bureaucrats controlled prices, issued licenses, regulated wages, and supervised exports and imports. Other offices dealt with education and religion, enforcing such matters as the observance of the

The fortress monastery of St. Catherine, Sinai.

sabbath. The law courts, the army and navy, and the diplomatic service all had their own civil service departments to run and control them. The efficiency of this administrative system allowed the Empire to survive many of its most severe crises.

In many ways the world of Byzantium seems remote and exotic. The obsession with religion and the finer points of theological dogma, the tumultuous nature of Byzantine politics, with its labyrinthine palace intrigues (which give the word "Byzantine" its modern sense), the glittering, fairy-tale qualities of Byzantine art—all these seem more alien to the late 20th century than the workaday world of Byzantium's predecessors, the Romans.

Yet behind the gilded facade lay practical and solid achievements. In political and military terms, Byzantine actions preserved Western Europe for almost 1000 years from a bewildering range of enemies. Constantinople sustained the economy of the eastern Mediterranean region over the centuries that preceded the revival of the West. Culturally, Byzantium provided the link with the world of Classical Antiquity.

The later stages of Byzantine history (see Part III, Topic 8) were clouded by hostility between Eastern and Western Christians. The schism of 1054 and the Crusades fed a mutual hatred which eventually left Constantinople helpless in the face of its Turkish conquerors of 1453. If for the West the Byzantines were "the dregs of the dregs," the Byzantines saw their Western rivals as "the children of darkness." Yet without the stubborn and often heroic survival of civilization in the East, most of the cultural legacy of ancient Greece would have been lost, and the Renaissance, one of the highest points of Western history and culture, would have been unimaginable.

Questions for Further Study

1. What are the main similarities and differences between the former Roman Empire and the Byzantine Empire? How did the function of the emperor differ in the two institutions?
2. What can we learn about Byzantine society and culture from a study of Byzantine art?
3. What lasting effect did Byzantine civilization produce on the development of Western culture?

4. How successful was Justinian in his attempt to recreate the Roman Empire in the East? What were the main problems he faced?

Suggestions for Further Reading

Barker, J. W. *Justinian and the Later Roman Empire*. Madison, WI, 1975.

Hussey, Joan M. *The Orthodox Church in the Byzantine Empire*. New York, 1986.

Kazhdan, Alexander, ed. *The Oxford Dictionary of Byzantium*. Oxford, 1991.

Kitzinger, E. *Byzantine Art in the Making*. Cambridge, MA, 1977.

Loverance, R. *Byzantium*. Cambridge, MA, 1988.

Mango, Cyril. *Byzantium: The Empire of New Rome*. New York, 1980.

Obolensky, D. *The Byzantine Commonwealth: Eastern Europe 500–1453*. Crestwood, NY, 1983.

Talbot Rice, David, and Tamara Talbot Rice. *Icons and Their History*. London, 1974.

Topic 4

Europe and Islam

The history of Islam begins with the birth of Muhammad, around 570. At that time, the Arabian peninsula was inhabited by tribes of Arab nomads, whose way of life had been untouched by the rise and fall of the Roman Empire.

Muhammad's early career as a merchant ended around 610 when he experienced the spiritual revelation which forms the basis of Islam. He regarded the new religion which he founded as the highest and final stage in the spiritual development which had led first to Judaism and then to Christianity. Islam's chief teachings are expounded in the Koran, the sacred text put together by the time of the Prophet's death in 632.

Muhammad regarded Islam as a universal faith, which would serve to unite the world. To this end his immediate successors began a series of military actions against their Arab neighbors. In 636 Arab forces defeated the Byzantine army in Syria, occupying the principal cities of the region, Antioch, Damascus, and Jerusalem. Ten years later they added Egypt to their conquests. At the same time the Persian Empire quickly disintegrated under Arab invasion, falling under their control by 651. Early in the 8th century an Arab army crossed from North Africa to conquer southern Spain.

Both Islam and the Arabic language served as unifying forces to hold together this vast range of territories. Islamic culture flourished in great urban centers linked by long-distance trade routes stretching by the 10th century as far as equatorial Africa and China.

The two regions of Europe to fall under direct Muslim rule were Spain and Sicily. Muslim troops conquered Spain in the early 8th century, establishing Cordova as its capital. A later Muslim kingdom was founded by the Nasrid dynasty at Granada, where science and philosophy flourished under their patronage. The rise of the Christian kingdoms of northern Spain in the 13th century presented a growing challenge to the Muslims, who were finally driven from the Spanish peninsula in 1492. Arab forces made their first important conquests in Sicily in 831, and they retained control over the island until 1060. Their Norman conquerors maintained many aspects of Muslim culture, diffusing them in due course throughout Europe.

The overall Islamic influence on Western culture was vast. It ranged from new systems of irrigation to paper making (the latter learned from the Chinese). Islamic scholars preserved ancient Greek scientific texts, and used them as the basis of their own studies. When Arab discoveries eventually reached the West, they revolutionized fields such as medicine, mathematics, and astronomy. In the arts, Muslim poetry and music inspired the troubadours of Medieval France, while the Western intellectual tradition owes an enormous debt to the Muslim world's preservation of the works of Aristotle, and the commentaries on them by the eminent scholar Averroes.

THE ARABIAN PENINSULA AND ITS PEOPLES

Islam, the religion today of around 600 million Muslims, was born in the Arabian peninsula (the word "Muslim" literally means "one who submits"). The land is mainly desert, with some fertile areas in the south where monsoon rains swell the mountain rivers. To the north only a few oases offer meager vegetation for the nomads and their flocks. As early as the 3rd millennium B.C., people from Arabia fled north from their inhospitable territory. The ancestors of the Babylonians who settled in Mesopotamia and those of the Hebrews who finally arrived in Palestine were all Arabian in origin; their languages belonged to the family known as Semitic (the two principal Semitic languages spoken today are Arabic and Hebrew).

In the 4th century B.C., the kingdom of Nabataea formed a center of the caravan route from Arabia to the Mediterranean. As the Roman Empire expanded southward, the Romans allowed the Nabataeans the status of independent allies. In A.D. 106, however, in the reign of Trajan, Nabataea fell to Roman forces. Around the middle of the 3rd century A.D., the Arab Queen Zenobia (ruled 267–272) ruled over the independent state of Palmyra. Famous for her beauty and ruthlessness—she may have arranged the murder of her husband as the result of which she came to power—she was eventually defeated by a Roman army led by the Emperor Aurelian. Her conqueror brought the formidable Zenobia back to Italy to march in his triumphal procession, and then pensioned her off in a villa outside Rome.

The nomadic tribes of Arabia who maintained their ancient lifestyle over the centuries lived on the meat and milk of their flocks and on the fruit produced in the desert oases. They worshiped the forces of nature and natural objects: trees, caves, springs, and large stones. At the city of Mecca, in the building called the Ka'bah, there still stands a black stone which was the object of pilgrimages long before the time of Muhammad.

MUHAMMAD, THE FOUNDER OF ISLAM

Mecca, the Prophet's birthplace, lies in the stony, barren valley of the Hijaz. The city was subject to the Kuraish tribe. Its prosperity depended on pilgrims to the Ka'bah and on its position on the caravan route between southern Arabia and Syria. The traditional date of Muhammad's birth is 570.

Muhammad's father, a merchant, and his mother both died shortly after his birth, leaving him in the care of relatives. As a young man he worked for a rich merchant's widow, 15 years his senior, whom he subsequently married. He seems to have devoted himself enthusiastically to her business interests, and trade forms a frequent metaphor in his later teachings. In the course of his travels he met both Jews and Christians, and began to feel unsatisfied with the Arabian pagan tradition in which he had grown up.

In 610 Muhammad experienced a spiritual revelation when a voice from heaven told him that there was but one god, Allah. In later visions he received further illuminations, which formed the basis for the new religion of Islam which he began to preach. His fellow citizens were hostile, and so in 622 he and his few followers were forced to move to a nearby city to which they gave the name of Medina ("the City of the Prophet"). This move, known as the "Hegira," became the symbolic inauguration of Islam: 622 is the first year of the Muslim era.

By the time of his triumphant return to Mecca in 630, Muhammad had established the notion of a "jihad," a holy war to convert unbelievers, in which those who die fighting for the cause win salvation. Muhammad's own death in 632 saw the new faith well established in Arabia. Within a century Muslim forces were on the offensive against the Byzantine Empire and in Western Europe, and the teachings of Islam had arrived in India.

The Doctrines of Islam

Muhammad conceived of Islam as the final stage, the spiritual fulfillment, of the Jewish and Christian tradi-

The Sanctuary at Mecca, center of the Muslim celebration of the Festival of Ramadan.

tion. Like the two earlier religions, Islam is monotheistic, emphasizes personal responsibility and morality, and is based on a written, sacred text. Muslims regard the Koran, the collection of teachings written down during the Prophet's life, as the completion of the Old and New Testaments, and think of themselves, like Jews and Christians, as "people of the Book."

At the heart of Islam are the beliefs that Allah is omnipotent, that Muhammad is his last and greatest prophet, and that humans will be judged on the basis of their actions. On Judgment Day, Allah will reward the good with eternal life in paradise and condemn the wicked to everlasting torture.

Islam requires its followers to pray five times a day, facing in the direction of Mecca, to fast during the daylight hours of the sacred month of Ramadan, to give alms to the poor, and if possible to make a pilgrimage—or "haj"—to the holy city of Mecca at least once in their lives. The consumption of alcohol and of certain foods is prohibited. Traditionally men can marry four wives, and can divorce by pronouncing a simple formula.

The Successors of the Prophet

Upon Muhammad's death, his followers named Abu-Bakr, his father-in-law, "caliph." The term, meaning "deputy of the Prophet," was used for the next 300 years for the supreme head of all Muslims. When Abu-Bakr's successor, the caliph Umar, died in 644, the naming of his replacement caused a split in the Muslim world which still exists today. The majority supported Uthman, a member of the powerful Umayyad family of Mecca which had earlier opposed Muhammad; others rallied around Ali, the Prophet's cousin and son-in-law.

When Ali was murdered, the Umayyad family took control of the caliphate, and held it until 750. Ali's followers broke off from their fellow-Muslims to form a minority sect known as Shi'ites: to this day, Shi'ites—who form about one-tenth of the world's Muslim population—believe that only a descendant of Ali has any authority over Muslims. Mainstream Muslim believers are called Sunnites.

Muhammad's immediate successors defeated the Byzantine forces occupying Syria in 636 and occupied their principal cities, Antioch, Damascus, and Jerusalem. The following year it was the turn of the Persians: Ctesiphon, the Persian capital, fell to Arab forces, who were in control of the entire Persian Empire by 651. The conquests continued under the Umayyad Dynasty, with the first Arab moves into Europe. In 711, using North Africa as a base (Egypt had fallen in 646), Muslim troops occupied southern Spain.

The only significant failure in the Arab offensive was its inability to take Constantinople, in spite of a massive attack launched there in 717. The defeat seriously weakened the prestige of the Umayyad Dynasty.

A page from the Koran, the sacred text of Islam; the script here is in a kind known as Kufic.

In 750 a new family, the Abbasids, took over the caliphate and moved the capital from Damascus to Baghdad.

ISLAM AND THE MEDITERRANEAN: CONQUEST, CONVERSION, SETTLEMENT

With their conquest of territory in the Mediterranean and the Middle East, the Arabs spread their religion and culture in regions once governed by the Romans. The Umayyad caliphs followed the example of the Roman and the Byzantine empires in seeking to construct a centralized state. Their capital of Damascus became the seat of a government bureaucracy from which officials administered this new Arab empire. Many of the new bureaucrats were Christian Egyptians and Syrians. The Umayyad caliphate did not particularly encourage conversion to Islam among their Christian or Jewish subjects, whom they accepted as fellow "peoples of the Book." This policy was successful in Syria, where there were many Christians. Further east, particularly in the former Persian Empire, it caused resentment among new converts and pious Muslims. As a result, many of the local population there became Shi'ite Muslims, supporting the cause of Ali, the Umayyads' opponent. The majority of Muslims in modern Iran (the name for Persia since 1935) are still Shi'ites.

Society under Muslim Rule

Islamic society was cosmopolitan and based on trade. The chief cities occupied strategic positions on the major commercial routes between the western Mediterranean and the East. By the 10th century Muslim traders were active south of the Sahara and as far east as China.

Because the Koran claimed that all Muslims were equal, social equality for males was also the norm—by contrast with the far more hierarchic society of the Byzantine Empire. At the Abbasid court of Baghdad, few bureaucratic positions were hereditary and talent rather than birth was the way to a career in public life. Education was encouraged. Estimates place the rate of literacy in the Arab world around 1000 at 20 percent of Muslim males, a level which Western European society was not to achieve for centuries. Furthermore both the Umayyad and Abbasid courts placed a high value on learning and science, commissioning translations into Arabic of important works in Persian and Greek.

Women in the Muslim World

One of the consequences of the mobility of social status was that a man's position could be improved or damaged by his treatment of his possessions. This led to a curious double standard in the treatment of women. On the one hand, a man's wives were sacrosanct; they

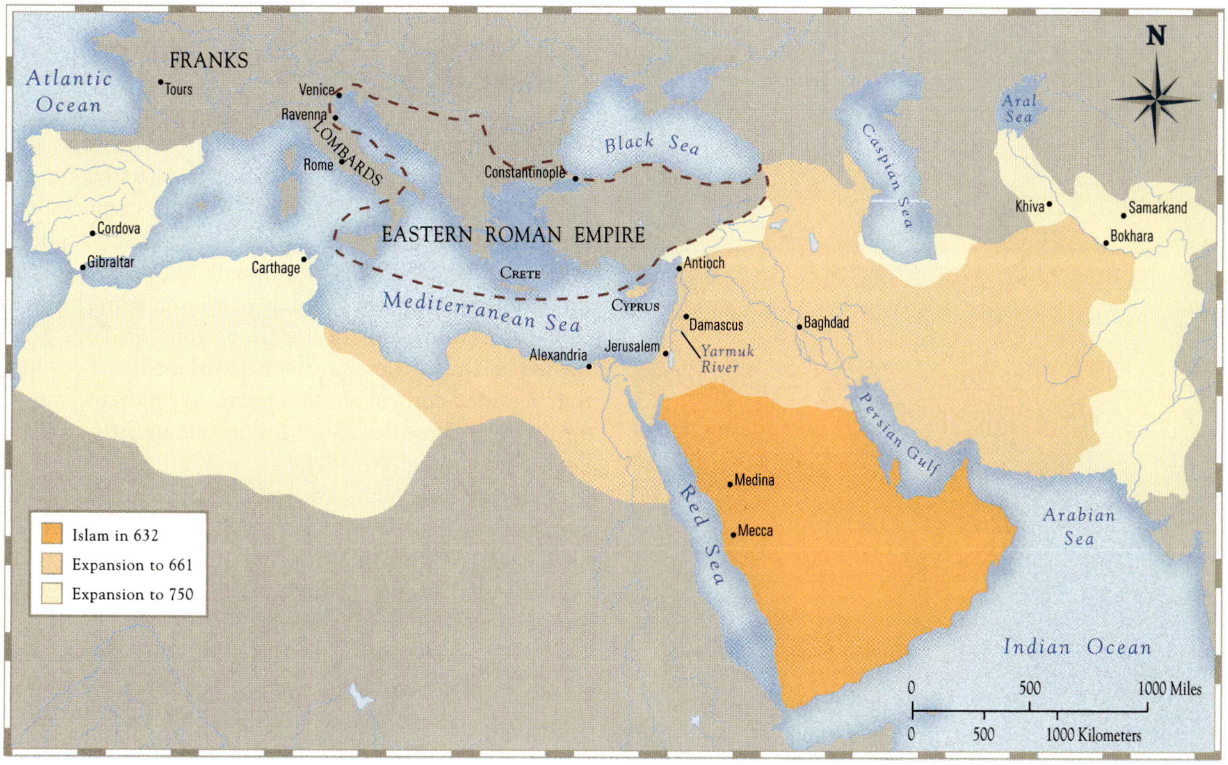

Map 4.1 The Growth of the Islamic Caliphate, 632–750

lived in seclusion, cut off from other males. On the other hand, the possession of large numbers of female servants and concubines was a sign of prosperity. Living in the harem, a private part of the house, and guarded by eunuchs (castrated men), Muslim wives had little to do other than to promote their own interests and those of their children by complex intrigues.

It must be added that the position of Islam with regard to family life was—and is—a complex one. The Koran claims a superior right for both fathers and husbands, legalizes polygamy, and permits both husbands and wives to initiate divorce proceedings, although the process is more complicated for women. At the same time it regulates the terms by which men should behave to women and children under their protection, and forbids the killing of female infants. By comparison with the treatment of women in the pre-Islamic Arab world, these laws seem comparatively humane. Some later interpreters of the Koran, however, took them to harsh extremes, while in many modern Muslim countries there have been moves to liberalize them.

Significant Dates

The Spread of Islam

c. 570	Birth of Muhammad
622	The Hegira: Muhammad flees Mecca
632	Death of Muhammad
636	Syria under Muslim control
646	Muslim conquest of Egypt
651	Persia under Muslim control
661–750	Umayyad caliphate in Damascus
710–711	Muslim invasion of Spain
732	Muslims defeated near Tours
750–1258	Abbasid caliphate in Baghdad

SPAIN AND SICILY: MUSLIM RULE IN EUROPE

The first thrust of Muslim conquest had been north and east, toward Syria and Persia. Then, with Egypt won in 642, the Arabs could turn their attention to the western Mediterranean. The former Roman provinces along the coast of North Africa were at that time under Byzantine rule, reconquered by the Emperor Justinian from the Vandals. Justinian's heavy taxation of the provincials, and the persecution of local Monophysite "heretics" (see Part III, Topic 3), had created a climate of bitter resentment against Constantinople. When the Arabs moved westward from Egypt, the local population of Berbers

Mosque of Mutawakki, Samarra, Iraq, an example of Muslim architecture of the Abbasid period.

(North African tribespeople) resisted as well as they could, but refused to cooperate with their Byzantine rulers.

By 708 the entire region was under Arab control. With the remnants of the Byzantine population dead or in exile, the Berbers put up no more resistance. Many of them converted to Islam (virtually all present-day Berbers are Muslims), and their numbers swelled the ranks of the Arab army, ready now for its final push into Christian Europe.

The Muslims in Spain

On July 25, 711, a Muslim force made up in large measure of Berber soldiers crossed the Straits of Gibraltar and landed on the southern coast of Spain. Gibraltar, the mountain on which the troops assembled, takes its name from their leader Tariq: "Jabal Tariq" means "the hill of Tariq." The expedition was intended as a reconnoitering mission but Tariq pushed on and defeated a Visigothic army the following day. (For the earlier history of the Germanic kingdoms of Southern Europe see Part III, Topic 1.) Roderick, the last Visigothic king, was killed in the fighting.

Quick to follow Tariq and jealous of his success, Tariq's superiors sent reinforcements, mainly Arab soldiers. The combined Muslim forces soon overran the whole of Spain, establishing Cordova as its capital in 725. Flushed by their victories, the Arab commanders drove on north across the Pyrenees, into the Kingdom of the Franks. Here they were finally brought to a halt by a Frankish army led by Charles Martel, who checked the Muslim forces at the Battle of Tours in 732. This was to be the farthest north the Muslims reached, but they retained control of some towns in southern France for the next three decades. Muslim rule in Spain was to last for over three centuries.

By around 850, Cordova had a population of over 1 million, and the Great Mosque there became a center of pilgrimage rivalling Mecca—the building could hold 200,000 people at one time. Cordova's university attracted the finest Islamic and Jewish scholars of the time and its libraries were the most complete in the world. There were twelve royal palaces in Cordova, each with its own name: "the Flower," "the Diadem," "the Joyful." A thousand mosques, hundreds of public baths, and botanical gardens filled with exotic plants adorned the city. Today only the Great Mosque survives, covered over by a later church.

Around 1100 the Christian kingdoms of the north began to drive back the forces of Islam (for an account of the "Reconquista" see Part III, Topic 7). Even when the rest of Spain had been reconquered, the state of Granada remained under the Muslim rule of the Nasrid Dynasty, a center of art and learning, until the expulsion of the Muslims from Spain in 1492. The Royal Palace of the Alhambra, with its gardens and fountains, and forests of slender columns supporting tiled and honeycombed walls, still survives; one visitor described its beauty as "a dream petrified by the wand of a magician."

Sicily and the Muslims

Only one city in Europe rivalled the splendor of Cordova in the Middle Ages: Palermo, in western Sicily. The Arabs first arrived in Sicily in 827; by 831 they were in control of Palermo. Muslim rule brought vast numbers of North African and Spanish settlers, and was marked by a spirit of tolerance.

By 900, Palermo was one of the great centers of art and scholarship. Surpassed in size in the Christian world only by Constantinople itself, its population at the time is estimated at 300,000. The island's agriculture flourished, and cotton, oranges, and sugar cane were cultivated in Europe for the first time.

Muslim influence in Sicily was so strong that when, in 1091, the island fell into the hands of the

One of the last examples of Muslim architecture in Spain: the Court of the Lions in the Alhambra, Granada (1354–1391).

Norman Count Roger de Hautville (1031–1101), its culture remained markedly Muslim. Norman knights took up the flowing robes of Arab dress, and built their own alhambras in which they installed harems. Roger's court was the wealthiest and most brilliant in Europe.

The spirit of tolerance lasted into the reign of Frederick II in the 13th century (for a full discussion of Frederick Hohenstaufen see Part III, Topic 10). Frederick's court, where Islamic, Christian, and Jewish cultures combined, was famous throughout Europe for its luxury and learning. Under Frederick's influence Muslim scientific and intellectual achievements spread throughout Europe and profoundly influenced Western culture.

SCIENCE AND CULTURE: THE ISLAMIC IMPACT ON THE WEST

The impact of the Islamic world upon Europe was threefold. Practically, Islamic science, industry, and technology developed or passed on new ideas and methods which eventually greatly affected European social and economic life. Intellectually, Muslim thinkers and writers preserved and interpreted the tradition of Classical and Hellenistic Greece. In the arts, Muslim poetry and architecture inspired creative movements in the West.

Industrial production of goods for trading provided the basis of Islamic commerce. Individual cities had their specialties, such as woven figured silk—or damask—in Damascus and fine swords in the Spanish city of Toledo. Techniques of manufacture became refined, and the secrets of Muslim craftsmen in due course helped European workers to improve their products. Muslim traders brought back from China the art of papermaking. When the technology finally reached Europe, it provided a whole new industry that revolutionized European cultural life.

Western farmers benefited from improved techniques, devised for the extreme climates of many Arab lands, and first introduced into Europe in Sicily and Spain; they included improved irrigation. Among the new plants cultivated was coffee, which is indigenous to tropical Africa. Arab settlers in Ethiopia first began making a hot drink from pulverized coffee beans around 1000. The new drink caught on and soon enterprising dealers were opening coffee houses in Mecca, Damascus, and Constantinople. The Italians learned how to make marzipan, a mixture of ground almonds and fine sugar, from their Muslim rulers—marzipan candies are still popular in Sicily.

Muslim Science and Medicine

In physics, Arabs invented the science of optics, and used magnifying lenses to perform experiments involving the transmission, speed, and refraction of light. Arab chemists discovered or created new substances and compounds, including carbonate of soda, nitrate of silver, and sulfuric acid.

Perhaps the most overarching Arab contribution to the world of science—and to many other fields—was in mathematics. Borrowing a method of numbering (which became known as "Arabic numerals") from the Hindus, together with the concept of zero, they developed a decimal system and devised plane and spherical trigonometry, besides making progress in algebra.

Advances in medicine were equally remarkable. The greatest physician of the Muslim world was Razi (c. 865–c. 930), known in the West as Rhazes. Head of the hospital of Baghdad, he wrote treatises on smallpox and measles (he was the first to discover the difference between them), as well as a compendium of medical knowledge. Latin translations of his works had an immense influence on the later development of medical science in the West. Other discoveries included the diagnosis of stomach cancer, improved treatment of eye diseases, and an understanding of the nature and spread of infectious diseases.

An illustration from an Arabic medical manuscript translated from the Greek.

Equally impressive was the hospital system, which reached a level attained in most European countries only in the 19th century. Hospitals had separate wards for the various fields of medicine, a dispensary for the preparation of medicine, and a library. Medical students attended lectures and demonstrations by the leading physicians and surgeons, who also conducted the students' examinations and issued licenses to practice.

Muslim Philosophy and the Greeks

The texts of Plato, Aristotle, and the Neoplatonist philosophers, translated into Arabic, formed the basis of much Muslim speculation. The great scientist and philosopher known in the West as Avicenna (980–1037) was one of the leading interpreters of Aristotle, and translations of his works into Latin rekindled knowledge of Aristotle's ideas in the West.

Not all scholars accepted the rational approach of the Greek thinkers. The mystical philosopher al-Ghazali (1059–1111) wrote *The Incoherence of the Philosophers* in order to attack all philosophical systems, including those of Plato and Aristotle. A generation later the doctor and philosopher Averroes (1126–1198) answered him in *The Incoherence of the Incoherence*. Averroes was the leading Aristotelian of his day, seeking to reconcile Greek philosophy and Muslim teachings. Within half a century of his death, Latin translations of his books were influencing Jewish and Christian thinkers in Western Europe.

Islam and the Arts

For most cultured Muslims the highest form of art was poetry. One of the earliest and most attractive of Arab poets, Abu Nuwas (762–815), established the popularity of lyrical love poetry, drinking songs, and satirical verse. A favorite at the court of Harun al-Rashid, he appears as one of the characters in the most famous of all Arabic works of literature, *The Arabian Nights*. This celebrated collection of stories is told by the ingenious Scheherazade night after night to her royal husband, to deter him from having her put to death: the cynical and embittered king, after his experience of his previous wives' infidelity, has decided to take a new wife each night and execute her the next morning. Scheherazade's fascinating and exciting tales, needless to say, save her life.

The best-known Islamic poet for most Western readers is Omar Khayyam (d. ?1122), if only through the "translation"—rewriting, rather—of his work the *Rubaiyat* by the Victorian poet Edward Fitzgerald. Omar's skeptical irony and blend of enjoyment and regret in the poem represent only one side of his output. He also wrote treatises on algebra and physics.

The love songs of the Muslim poets of Spain had a special influence on European literature. The traveling poets, or troubadours, of southwestern France picked up the Muslim approach to "courtly" or idealized love, whereby the submissive lover seeks his reward in devotion to his lady, rather than in the fulfillment of his passion. Thus ideas and conceits devised to entertain the courts of Damascus or Baghdad circulated in the aristocratic world of 12th- and 13th-century France. From there they spread to Germany in the work of the German lyric poets known as the Minnesingers.

Islam's ban on the representation of the human form in painting or sculpture—ignored in the later Islamic art of Persia and Moghul India—meant that Arab artists often worked in fields that Western traditions regard as "minor": carpets, tapestry, bookbinding. The range of design, often making use of the Arabic script, and richness of detail are frequently breathtaking. Even more impressive are the achievements of

The Dome of the Rock, Jerusalem, the second holiest site in Islam.

Muslim architecture. At a time when most Western building projects were limited to churches, palaces, and defensive walls, Muslim architects were designing and building schools, libraries, and hospitals. The level of domestic architecture was also high, as can be seen from some of the Muslim private houses that still survive in southern Spain.

The variety and depth of Western culture's debt to the world of Islam emerge in a simple list of some of the Arabic words—and concepts—adopted by our language. Traffic and tariff; orange, lemon, sugar, saffron, syrup; alcohol; zenith and nadir; and cipher too. The Arabs invented chewing gum and introduced the windmill and the profession of bread making to Europe.

Above all, they demonstrated that it was possible to build a multinational and multiracial society that spanned three continents and a bewildering variety of peoples, united by a common language, religion, and institutions.

Of the three parts into which the Roman Empire split in Late Antiquity, the Muslim world was by far the richest and most cosmopolitan; its trade linked Atlantic Spain and Portugal with India and China. By comparison the Byzantine Empire was conservative and unadventurous, and in its last centuries mainly confined to Constantinople and the surrounding territories. As for Western Europe, poverty-stricken and divided into warring kingdoms, it was to take centuries before life there could approach the stability or level of comfort and culture of the great cities of Islam.

Questions for Further Study

1. What are the main features of Islam? How do they resemble or differ from the Judeo-Christian tradition?
2. What impact have art and culture made in the growth of Islamic life? How have they influenced Western ideas?
3. What role does Islam play in the modern world? How far does this relate to its historical foundation and development?

Suggestions for Further Reading

Armstrong, K. *Muhammed: A Western Attempt to Understand Islam*. San Francisco, 1992.

Donner, F. M. *The Early Islamic Conquests*. Princeton, NJ, 1981.

Endress, G. *Islam: A Historical Introduction*. New York, 1987.

Esposito, J. L. *Women in Muslim Family Law*. Syracuse, NY, 1982.

Kennedy, Hugh. *The Prophet and the Age of the Caliphates*. White Plains, NY, 1986.

Lapidus, I. M. *A History of Islamic Societies*. Cambridge, MA, 1988.

Lewis, B. *The Muslim Discovery of Europe*. New York, 1985.

Mottadeh, R. P. *The Mantle of the Prophet*. New York, 1985.

III

Topic 5

The First Europe: The West in the Age of Charlemagne

The synthesis of Classical, Christian, and Germanic elements making up Medieval civilization first appeared in the early Germanic kingdoms of the Ostrogoths, Visigoths, and Anglo-Saxons, founded between the 5th and the 7th centuries. It was, however, in the Frankish kingdom forged by the Carolingian dynasty in the late 8th century that this fusion resulted for the first time since the Romans in a truly impressive European civilization. The empire created by Charlemagne was the first large governing unit to appear in the West since the collapse of the Roman Empire; after it broke apart following Charlemagne's death, no empire would cover as huge an expanse of territory for another 1000 years.

The age of Charlemagne also saw the revival and preservation of the learning of the Classical world. Although this was an accidental by-product of Charlemagne's drive to reform his society and establish a biblically centered culture, the Carolingian cultural achievement had important implications for the future. The decentralized agricultural economy of the era was less successful, for it was an economic system incapable of sustaining the enormous military and political requirements of a centralized empire. New invasions by Vikings and Magyars in the 9th and 10th centuries hastened the disintegration of the Carolingian empire.

THE CAROLINGIANS

In the years after the death of Clovis in 511, the Frankish kingdom was divided into three major units, Neustria, Austrasia, and Burgundy (see Part III, Topic 1). A series of weak Merovingian kings sat on the thrones of these realms, but real power was wielded by the *major domus*, or mayor of the palace. By the 7th century, Pepin of Landen (died c. 639), the *major domus* of Austrasia, had reunited parts of the kingdom. His great-grandson, Charles Martel (c. 688–741) subdued unruly nobles and began the reconquest of Burgundy. Charles' greatest achievement, however, came at the Battle of Tours in 732, when he crushed the Muslim advance into Gaul. For this victory he earned the name "Martel," or hammer, as well as the status of defender of Christendom.

Pepin the Short and the Carolingian Revolution

It was Charles Martel's son, Pepin III (ruled 751–768), better known as Pepin the Short, who finally ended the fiction of Merovingian rule. Determined to seize power in name as well as in fact, but knowing that his assumption of the throne would not be legitimate, Pepin sent two personal envoys to Rome to seek recognition from Pope Zacharias (ruled 741–752). The pope responded that "he who actually had the power should be called king." In 751 Pepin deposed the last Merovingian, Childeric—who was "shaved and thrust into the cloister"—and made himself king of the Franks.

Pepin's appeal to Pope Zacharias rekindled the relationship of mutual support between the papacy and the Franks. When the Lombards invaded Italy and were poised to descend on Rome, the new pope, Stephen II (ruled 752–757), asked the Byzantine emperor for help. After Constantinople refused the appeal, Stephen turned to the Franks. In 754, he crowned Pepin king of the Franks in the Cathedral of St. Denis, Paris, establishing a tradition for future Frankish rulers. Pepin not only defeated the Lombards in 756 but later ceded to the papacy the Italian territory that he conquered, which technically belonged to the Byzantine emperor. Known as the Donation of Pepin, this grant of territory eventually stretched southwest from Ravenna across the peninsula to Rome, forming the basis for what later became the Papal States. The pope exercised temporal authority over these lands for more than 1000 years.

CHARLEMAGNE: FROM FRANKISH KING TO HOLY ROMAN EMPEROR

The greatest of the Carolingian rulers was Charles (king 771–814; emperor 800–814), Pepin the Short's son. Known to history as Charlemagne (from the Latin *Carolus magnus*, or Charles the Great), we have a great deal of information about his personal life thanks to a biography written by Einhard, a Saxon scholar who served as Charlemagne's secretary. Einhard, who wrote in Latin, described him this way:

> Charles was large and strong, and of lofty stature . . . (his height is well known to have been seven times the length of his foot); the upper part of his head was round, his eyes very large and animated, nose a little long, hair fair, and face laughing and merry. Thus his appearance was always stately and dignified . . . ; although his neck was thick and somewhat short, and his belly rather prominent; but the symmetry of the rest of his body concealed these defects. His gait was firm, his whole carriage manly, and his voice clear. . . .[1]

Charlemagne was an energetic and lusty man, possibly able to read but not to write his own name. For relaxation he enjoyed hunting, horseback riding, swimming, and taking the cure at natural springs—as well as overeating. In addition to marrying four times, he spent much time in the company of concubines and fathered children when well into his sixties. Charlemagne was more complicated than an ordinary Germanic warlord, for he also enjoyed listening to reading, especially Augustine's *City of God*, and debating with scholars. He had a great respect for culture and the arts and knew Latin and some Greek. He was a hardworking and conscientious ruler who wanted to fashion an administrative structure inspired by the traditions of ancient Rome, and was especially interested in the reigns of the Christian emperors Constantine and Theodosius.

Charlemagne depicted in a gold equestrian statue.

Military Conquests

Charlemagne was first and foremost a warrior king. His army, though small by modern standards, was powerful and disciplined, and consisted mainly of foot soldiers. Cavalry were limited in number and effectiveness until the 8th century, when the introduction of the stirrup changed the character of warfare. The stirrup enabled a mounted soldier to strike at the enemy with a lance or sword without falling off his horse. The military cavalry were first used effectively in Western Europe at the Battle of Tours in 732. This innovation not only made cavalry the predominant instrument of warfare, but had social consequences as well. The high cost of horses and arms meant that fighting was increasingly limited to nobles, who became the full-time warriors, whereas ordinary freemen were now limited to farming.

After stabilizing his rule, Charlemagne fought military campaigns that greatly extended the borders

[1] Einhard, *Life of Charlemagne,* trans. Samuel Epes Turner (Ann Arbor: University of Michigan Press, 1960), 50.

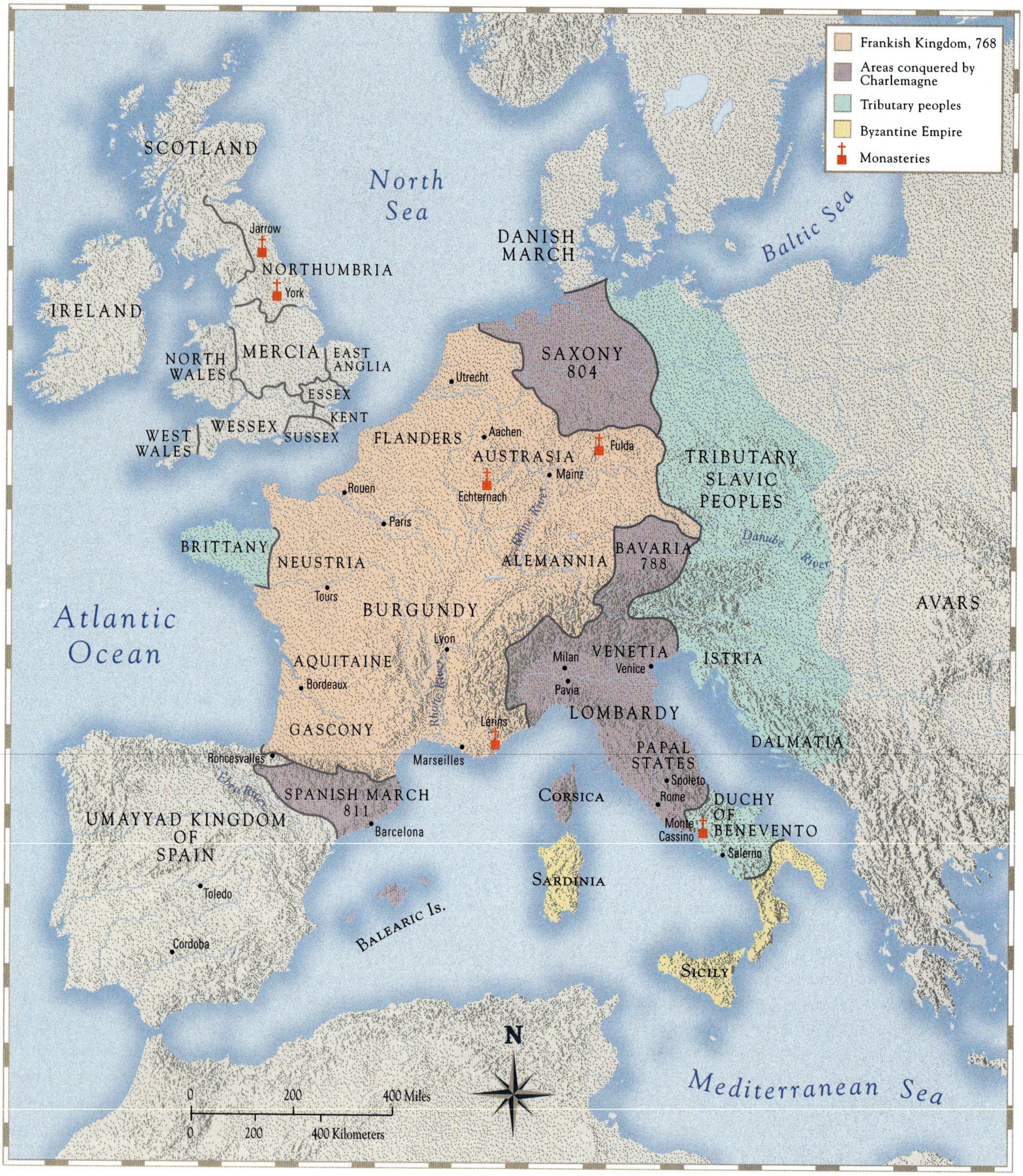

Map 5.1 The Carolingian Empire

of his kingdom. In 774, he, too, answered a call from the papacy and brought his army into northern Italy to deal with the Lombards, who had seized part of the papal lands. Charlemagne defeated the Lombards and made himself their king, and then visited Rome, where he reconfirmed the donation of territory made by his father.

Four years later, taking advantage of the division among Muslim forces, Charlemagne invaded Spain. He had limited success against the Muslims and on his way back across the Pyrenees his forces were attacked from behind by the Basques. One of his commanders, Roland, fell in this assault, an event that gave rise to the first great epic poem of the Middle Ages, *The Song of Roland*. Written in an early form of French sometime about 1100, the epic changed the Basques, who were Christians, into Muslims, and made Charlemagne's soldiers into French knights. *The Song of Roland* portrayed Charlemagne himself as a devout crusader against the Muslims (see Part III, Topic 9). Although he maintained good relations with Muslim rulers in the East, in subsequent campaigns Charlemagne's armies managed to clear the Muslims out of the region south of the Pyrenees, which became a frontier defense area called the Spanish March (or Mark). Later, when French settlers moved into the region, the region became known as Catalonia. Eventually, seven marches would protect the perimeter of the empire.

Another series of military efforts was directed against the last two remaining independent tribes in Germany, the Saxons and the Bavarians. These were long, harsh campaigns made especially fierce by the resistance from the Saxons, who refused to bow to Charlemagne's orders that they convert to Christianity. Once the Saxons were defeated, he forcefully removed much of the population and imposed rigid measures on those who remained in order to stamp out paganism. In 788 he annexed Bavaria, but that victory led to further wars. In the Danube region on Germany's southeastern border were two groups, the Slavs and the Avars, the latter Asiatic nomads. It took a half dozen expeditions to crush the Avars, after which Charlemagne established a military district (similar to the Spanish March) known as the East Mark, later called Austria.

St. Peter invests Pope Leo III (left) with religious authority and Charlemagne with temporal power. This mosaic was commissioned by Leo as a sign of papal greatness.

The Carolingian Bureaucracy

It was during one of his later campaigns that the most famous event in the reign of Charlemagne took place. In 800, he made a trip to Rome at the request of Pope Leo III (795–816), whose papacy was being threatened by supporters of a rival family. On Christmas Day, while Charlemagne was kneeling before the altar of St. Peter, the grateful Leo placed a crown on his head and, according to Einhard, proclaimed him "Emperor and Augustus."

Whether Charlemagne knew ahead of time of Leo's intention is much disputed, as is the meaning of the imperial coronation. The ceremony marked the permanent division of Western Europe from the Byzantine Empire. Moreover, in bestowing the imperial title on Charlemagne, the pope had underscored the reality that power in the West had passed to the Frankish monarchy. Charles' motto, "Revival of the Roman Empire," suggested that he was very much conscious of the historical significance of his new title and wished to see himself in the tradition of the Christian Roman emperors—on important state occasions, he even wore the imperial purple robe. Charlemagne saw his empire as the reestablishment of the political unity that had once been the pride of Rome. It was equally clear that Charlemagne considered himself a Christian ruler, and that Leo had granted him the imperial crown by virtue of the pope's role as the vicar of Christ on earth, thus asserting the superiority of papal authority over temporal rulers. Nevertheless, it is also true that during the coronation ceremony, Leo knelt at Charlemagne's feet and kissed the hem of his garment. These were issues that would resurface over the course of the Middle Ages.

Charlemagne's administration was far less sophisticated than the ancient Roman state that he wanted to emulate. In geographical extent the Frankish empire was smaller than the Roman Empire; in Europe alone it lacked control of southern Italy, most of Spain, and Britain. Nevertheless, its government would be without equal for more than 400 years. On the other hand, the empire consisted largely of sparsely populated stretches of rural areas inhabited by peasants who lived in isolated villages or on landed estates. Disease and famine had combined to reduce the population, and it appears

DOCUMENTS ON HISTORY

Charlemagne and His Government

The "government" Charlemagne designed to administer his far-flung empire should not be thought of in the modern sense—or, for that matter, in the Roman sense—of a centralized state with a permanent and professional bureaucracy. Instead, he saw the question of imperial government very much in the Frankish tradition as a personal matter. He relied heavily on the loyalty of the local nobility and the clergy, who acted as royal officials, and the seat of government shifted constantly as he and his retinue traveled around the realm. That the administration of his empire was effective at all was due largely to the fear that Charlemagne instilled in his subjects and to his determination to govern the West, to the conscientious attitude of his officials, and perhaps to the persistence of the memory of the Roman Empire.

CAPITULARIES

Among the devices used by Charlemagne to ensure control over local affairs and extend royal commands to the provinces were the capitularies, *instructions prepared by clerics working in the royal court. These documents reveal fascinating details about Charlemagne's interest in all aspects of daily life, from church matters and price controls to coinage and crime. The following are representative selections from a* capitulary *of 794:*

Administering the Realm

4. Our most pious lord the king, with the consent of the holy synod, gave instructions that no man, whether cleric or layman, should ever sell corn [grain] in time of abundance or in time of scarcity at a greater price than the public level recently decided upon, that is, a *modius* of oats one penny, a *modius* of barley two pennies, a *modius* of rye three pennies, a *modius* of wheat four pennies. If he should wish to sell it in the form of bread, he should give 12 loaves of wheat bread, each weighing two pounds, for one penny, . . . Anyone who holds a benefice of us should take the greatest possible care that, if God but provide, none of the slaves of the benefice should die of hunger; and anything that remains above what is necessary for the household he may freely sell in the manner laid down.

5. Concerning the pennies [royal coinage], you should be fully aware of our edict, that in every place, in every city and in every market these new pennies must be current and must be accepted by everyone. Provided they bear the imprint of our name and are of pure silver and of full weight, if anyone should refuse to allow them in any place, in any transaction of buying or selling, he shall, if he is a free man, pay 15 shillings to the king, and, if he is of servile status and the transaction is his own, shall lose the transaction or be flogged naked at the stake in the presence of the people. . . .

16. We have heard that certain abbots, led on by greed, require a payment on behalf of those entering their monastery. . . . under no circumstances shall money be required for receiving brothers into a holy order, but that they should be received in accordance with the rule of St Benedict.

18. That whatever sin is committed by the monks, we do not allow the abbots under any circumstances to blind them or inflict the mutilation of members upon them, unless the discipline of the rule provides it.

19. That priests, deacons, monks and clerks should not go into taverns to drink.

24. Concerning clerks and monks, that they should remain steadfast in their chosen way of life.

31. Concerning plots and conspiracies, that they should not occur; and where they are discovered they are to be crushed.

39. If a priest is caught in a criminal act, he should be brought before his bishop and be dealt with according to the ruling of the canons.

41. That no bishop should abandon his proper see by spending his time elsewhere, nor dare to stay on his own property for more than three weeks. . . .

The next capitulary, dating from the late 8th century, reflects a consistent royal concern for agricultural matters and the ecology.

The Royal Demesnes

34. They [royal stewards] are to take particular care that anything which they do or make with their hands—that is, lard, smoked meat, sausage, newly-salted meat, wine, vinegar, mulberry wine, boiled wine, garum, mustard, cheese, butter, malt, beer, mead, honey, wax and flour—that all these are made or prepared with the greatest attention to cleanliness.

36. That our woods and forests shall be well protected; if there is an area to be cleared, the stewards are to have it cleared, and shall not allow fields to become overgrown with woodland. Where woods are supposed to exist they shall not allow them to be excessively cut and damaged. Inside the forests they are to take good care of our game; likewise they shall keep our hawks and falcons in readiness for our use, and shall diligently collect our dues there. . . .

41. That the buildings inside our demesnes, together with the fences around them, shall be well looked-after, and that the stables and kitchens, bakeries and wine-presses, shall be carefully constructed, so that our servants who work in them can carry out their tasks properly and cleanly.

43. They are to supply the women's workshops with materials at the appropriate times, according to their instructions—that is, linen, wool, wood, vermilion, madder, wool-combs, teazles, soap, oil, vessels and other small things that are needed there.

49. That our women's quarters shall be properly arranged—that is, with houses, heated rooms and living rooms; and let them have good fences all around, and strong doors, so that they can do our work well.

54. That every steward shall see to it that our people work well at their tasks, and do not go wasting time at markets.

56. That every steward in his district shall hold frequent hearings and dispense justice, and see to it that our people live a law-abiding life.

60. Mayors [of the palace] are never to be chosen from among powerful men, but from men of more modest station who are likely to be loyal.

62. That each steward shall make an annual statement of all our income . . . [there follows a long list of sources of royal income]. All these things they shall set out in order under separate headings, and shall send the information to us at Christmas time, so that we may know the character and amount of our income from the various sources.

continued next page

THE MISSI DOMINICI

As Charlemagne visited parts of his realm, he took with him his family, servants, and a host of officials, relying on noble hospitality for food and shelter. But travel was slow, and efficient administration required personal visits from royal administrators as well as by the king himself. He therefore appointed officials known as missi dominici, *or envoys of the lord, who traveled in pairs (usually one bishop and one lay aristocrat), inspecting secular and ecclesiastical conditions, investigating local officials, and reporting to the imperial court. The* missi *were given precise instructions and informed of the most recent decrees and laws. Charlemagne transferred them regularly and broke up the teams each year to prevent corruption. The following document, dating from the year 802, describes the* missi.

1. Concerning the commission despatched by our lord the emperor. Our most serene and most Christian lord and emperor, Charles, has selected the most prudent and wise from among his leading men, archbishops and bishops, together with venerable abbots and devout laymen, and has sent them out into all his kingdom, and bestowed through them on all his subjects the right to live in accordance with a right rule of law. Wherever there is any provision in the law that is other than right or just he has ordered them to inquire most diligently into it and bring it to his notice, it being his desire, with God's help, to rectify it. . . . And the *missi* themselves, as they wish to have the favour of Almighty God and to preserve it through the loyalty they have promised, are to make diligent inquiry wherever a man claims that someone has done him an injustice. . . . And if there be anything which they themselves, together with the counts of the provinces, cannot correct or bring to a just settlement, they should refer it without any hesitation to the emperor's judgement along with their reports.

28. The counts and the *centenarii* should, as they are desirous of the favour of our lord the emperor, provide for the *missi* who are sent upon them with all possible attention, that they may go about their duties without any delay. . . .

36. That all men should contribute to the full administration of justice by giving their agreement to our *missi*.

From H. R. Loyn and John Percival, *The Reign of Charlemagne: Documents on Carolingian Government and Administration.*

A SURVEY OF ROYAL ESTATES

Charlemagne was intensely concerned about the condition and upkeep of his royal estates and commissioned detailed surveys of them and their contents. The following passage, from a survey of the early 9th century, is typical.

We found on the crown estate of *Asnapius* a royal house, well built of stone, with three chambers; the

that little more than 10 percent of the arable land was under cultivation. Cities, once the pride of Roman civilization, were now little more than the seats of bishops, and trade had diminished.

Governing this huge empire in a time of frequent violence and extremely poor communications was difficult. No bureaucratic institutions such as those found in Roman government—law courts, a permanent civil service, a finance ministry—existed. Instead, the emperor relied heavily on the loyalty of the local nobility, who lived on fortified estates and commanded strong armies. Clerics working in the royal court prepared instructions known as *capitularies* for local officials. Charlemagne's predecessors had begun the custom of rewarding these aristocrats with grants of land—generally only for use during their lifetime—in return for service to the crown. Gradually, however, these holdings had become hereditary. From the ranks of the whole house surrounded by galleries, with 11 rooms for women; underneath, one cellar; two porches; 17 other houses inside the courtyard, built of wood, with as many rooms and with the other amenities all in good order; one stable, one kitchen, one bakehouse, two barns, three haylofts. . . . Household linen: one set of bedding, one tablecloth, one towel. Equipment: two bronze bowls, two cups, two bronze cauldrons and one of iron, one cooking pan, one pot-hook, one fire-dog, one lamp, two axes, one adze, two augers, one hatchet, one chisel, one scraper, one plane, two scythes, two sickles, two iron-tipped spades. Wooden equipment: a sufficient quantity. Produce: nine baskets of old spelt from the previous year, which will yield 450 measures of flour; 100 *modii* of barley. In the present year there were 110 baskets of spelt; of these 60 baskets have been sown, and we found the rest [in store]; . . . Livestock: 51 head of older horses, five three-year-olds, seven two-year-olds, seven yearlings, 10 two-year-old colts, eight yearlings, three stallions, 16 oxen, two donkeys, 50 cows with calves, 20 bullocks. . . .

From H. R. Loyn and John Percival, *The Reign of Charlemagne: Documents on Carolingian Government and Administration.*

THE ADMINISTRATION OF JUSTICE

The observance of law and procedure in the realm was vital to effective imperial government. Charlemagne exercised his power in administering the law in a number of different ways—he could settle disputes himself directly, through his missi, *or by delegating authority to a noble. The following extract from a* notitia, *or notice of judgment, dated 781, describes how he delegated judicial authority to the Duke of Spoleto and how the case was settled.*

At the time when our lord Charles, most excellent king of the Franks and Lombards, was returning from Rome and from the churches of the blessed apostles St Peter and St Paul, and had come to *Vadum Medianum* in the territory of Florence, and when the lord and most glorious duke Hildebrand was present there with him to do him service, Paul, the son of Pando of Rieti, made a complaint to the lord king concerning the monastery of San Angelo which is situated near the town of Rieti, saying that it had belonged to his parents. 'And yet,' he said, 'our duke has unlawfully taken the monastery from us and has given it to bishop Guigpertus.' . . . The lord king therefore instructed him [the duke] that when he returned to Spoleto he should with his justices inquire carefully into the case and settle it. . . . [After testimony of witnesses who swore that the document giving the monastery to the bishop had been burned, the duke found in favor of the bishop]. . . . Wherefore, to put an end to the dispute, this brief notice of the judgement, on the order of the above-mentioned authority and at the dictation of Dagarinus the *gastaldius*, was written by me Totemannus the notary, in the month of July of the fourth indiction.

From H. R. Loyn and John Percival, *The Reign of Charlemagne: Documents on Carolingian Government and Administration.*

nobility came the counts *(Grafen)*, who administered the 300 units into which the imperial lands were divided. Each of the seven marches was under the jurisdiction of a *markgraf*. The *graf* was appointed for life and wielded extensive judicial, fiscal, and military power.

Charlemagne himself traveled constantly, moving his court and retinue with him, and relying on the noble estates for food and supplies. Such personal visits, on which the emperor was accompanied by the aristocrats who ran his administration, were by themselves not enough. The emperor appointed officials known as *missi dominici*, or envoys of the lord, who traveled in pairs (usually one bishop and one lay aristocrat), inspecting secular and ecclesiastical conditions, investigating local officials, and reporting to the imperial court. The *missi* were transferred regularly and the teams broken up each year to prevent corruption.

THE CAROLINGIAN RENAISSANCE: THE REVIVAL OF LEARNING IN THE WEST

Charlemagne's demand for efficient government led him to seek educated men to serve as officials in the state bureaucracy, while his desire to regenerate the spiritual life of his realm required an educated clergy. Although he was without formal education, Charlemagne had a genuine intellectual curiosity that led him to value knowledge and to encourage a revival of learning in his realm. This development is sometimes described as a cultural "renaissance," or rebirth, and in the narrow sense of that word the description is correct, for the Carolingian period produced few new or original ideas. Instead, a revival of study in Classical works took place and a great effort was made to preserve the intellectual legacy of the ancient world as it

A Bible manuscript from Tours showing Moses and the Ten Commandments, part of the legacy of brilliant manuscripts created during the Carolingian Renaissance.

was then known. It was in the arts that the Carolingian era produced a measure of originality.

The Revival of Learning

The program of educational reform was carried out under the aegis of the Anglo-Saxon scholar Alcuin of York (c. 732–804). Alcuin advised Charlemagne on ecclesiastical matters and also directed the palace school established for the education of ecclesiastical and lay aristocrats. Alcuin emphasized the study of Classical Latin and the ancient texts. Adopting the ideas of Cassiodorus (see Part III, Topic 2), a Roman scholar who worked in Italy under the Emperor Theodoric, Alcuin classified all secular knowledge into two groups of seven "liberal arts": the *trivium* (logic, grammar, and rhetoric) and the *quadrivium* (arithmetic, astronomy, geometry, and music). These categories became the foundations of education for the next 700 years. Alcuin combed Italy, England, Ireland, and Spain for scholars and persuaded Charlemagne to establish schools in many of the monasteries of his realm. Later, royal support was substituted by annual donations, known as the tithe, of one-tenth of all harvests, which would be used to sustain church programs and buildings.

The palace school and the monasteries began the systematic collection of texts by the Classical Latin and early Christian authors. Monks working in special writing rooms, known as *scriptoria,* corrected and copied the old texts and evolved innovative techniques for making books. Working on parchment pages (instead of papyrus rolls), they developed a way of writing called Carolingian minuscule, a style that was easier to read and that became the basis of modern book printing. Manuscript production also led to the development of a new artistic style used for illustrations, or "illuminations." This style combined abstract decorative motifs inherited from Germanic tradition with naturalistic representations of figures adopted from Mediterranean artists. The books were often bound in richly decorated covers encrusted with precious stones. This salvage operation by Carolingian monks was responsible for the preservation of most of the Classical Latin texts that are available today and contributed directly to the revival of Classical learning that took place centuries later in the West.

The palace school as well as the seat of government in later years was located in Charlemagne's palace at Aachen (later known as Aix-la-Chapelle). The palace was built between 792 and 805 upon the site of natural hot springs, where the emperor enjoyed relaxing. His architects and builders gathered ancient marbles, columns, and decorative pieces from Roman sites in Europe and developed an ensemble of rooms that combined the private quarters of the imperial family and court officials with public rooms for state purposes. The Palatine Chapel was built in a three-tiered octagonal form modeled after a church in Ravenna, which had been the capital of Theodoric's empire. Charlemagne's throne sat on the middle level, above the altar, and worshipers below could look up to the emperor's exalted station between heaven and earth.

The palace chapel at Aachen, begun in the 790s. Charlemagne's throne was located on the second floor, above the main altar.

Significant Dates

The Age of Charlemagne

687	Pepin II major domus of Austrasia and Neustria
732	Charles Martel defeats Muslims at Tours
751	Pepin III becomes king of Franks
771–814	Reign of Charlemagne
843	Treaty of Verdun divides Carolingian Empire
c. 850–950	Viking expansion

MANORIALISM AND THE CAROLINGIAN ECONOMY

The fundamentally agrarian economy of early Medieval Europe was centered on the large estates, or manors, which originated in the Roman *latifundia* (see Part II, Topic 12). Many of the old Roman estates had continued to exist during and after the barbarian invasions, although in the Germanic kingdoms much of the land came into the hands of the new German aristocracy and the church. The ecclesiastical or lay lords who owned the estates—and often they owned more than one—provided protection to the dependent peasant class that lived on and worked the land. In an era marked by the breakdown of trade, poor communications, and the devolution of authority from central government to local aristocrats, the manors grew in importance and became increasingly self-sufficient. *Manorialism* is therefore the term used to describe the economic system of the early Middle Ages. By the 9th century, manorialism was well established in northern France, western Germany, the Low Countries, and in northern Italy. Eventually it spread to England, Spain, and Central and Eastern Europe.

A page from the devotional book of the duke of Berry, showing the duke's castle and lands at Saumur in France.

Agriculture and the Manor

The population of Carolingian Europe was relatively small and most people lived in isolated rural centers that were heavily forested. Perhaps as much as 90 percent of the population worked the land. Nevertheless, hunting and fishing remained important sources of food, for farming took place on perhaps as little as 10 percent of the land. Moreover, the crop yield was low because laborers relied on primitive tools and an inefficient "two field" planting system that left half of the farm land fallow every other year. During periods of bad weather and crop failure, starvation was widespread and the death rate high. During the later Carolingian period, farmers devised a three-field system that allowed for planting cereal crops in one field in the fall and another in the spring, leaving only a third of the land fallow. Plowing, sowing, and harvesting were heavy work. They generally required cooperation among the peasants and involved the entire population of the village.

The manors varied enormously in size, anywhere from a 300-acre estate supporting a dozen families to one consisting of 4000–5000 acres inhabited by 50 families. However, each estate was organized roughly in the same way. The peasants lived in cottages in a village, usually located near a stream, while the lord and his family resided in a castle or manor house. Part of the arable land, called the *demesne*, was reserved for the lord's use and was farmed for him by the peasants. The peasants held and cultivated the rest for their own use in the open field system, whereby scattered strips of land of about an acre from different sections of the manor were allotted to each villager. Since not all land was equally fertile, the open field system allowed for the distribution of plots of roughly similar quality to each peasant. The nonarable land, usually pasture, meadow, and woods, was used in common by the peasants.

The use of slaves to work the large estates had declined during the Merovingian era, for landowners found slave labor less economical; moreover, the church had endorsed the freeing of slaves, although it did not prohibit slavery, which continued to operate within wealthy households. Instead, two classes of peasants evolved during the early Middle Ages: freemen and serfs. Freemen were peasants who paid rent for their land, were not required to work in the demesne, and were free to leave the manor by finding other tenants to take their place. The number of free peasants on a

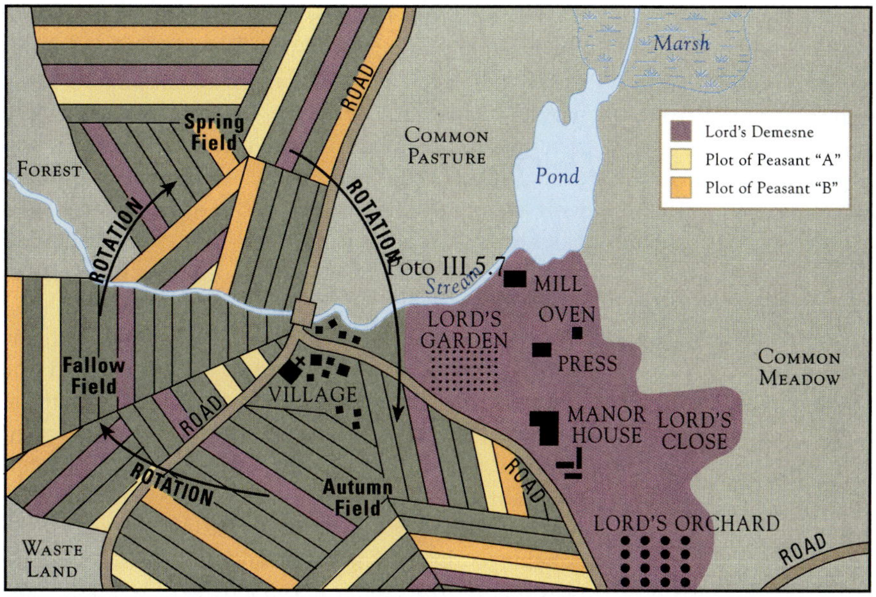

Plan of a typical Medieval manor, showing the village, manor house, and field system.

manor declined as deteriorating conditions forced them to give up their rights in return for protection and food.

More than half the population of Charlemagne's realm consisted of serfs—peasants attached by heredity to the land who could not leave the manor without the lord's permission. Serfs owed certain services and dues to the lord, such as obligatory labor on the demesne for two or three days each week and the payment of a yearly tax known as the *taille*. On the other hand, serfs could not be bought or sold like a slave and could not be evicted from their land. Serfs also had the right to appeal to the manor court for redress against a fellow serf, although they could not do so against a noble or a freeman. The lords obtained additional services or fees from both serfs and freemen by charging for the use of the grinding mills, ovens, and oil and wine presses on their estates.

The manors were administered by a series of officials appointed by the lord. The steward, for example, acted as general supervisor of the manor, including the manorial court, while the bailiff collected rents and fees for the lord and supervised the farming of the demesne. Villagers elected their own foreman, known in Anglo-Saxon communities as the *reeve*, who represented them in dealings with the lord's officials.

The Wider Economy

As a result of the breakdown of central government, the disintegration of the road system, and the capture of Mediterranean routes by the Muslims, trade declined during the early Medieval period. Although scholars debate the degree to which commerce shrank, it did not disappear entirely.

By the start of the Carolingian era, gold coinage had virtually disappeared in the West. The Merovingians had minted gold coins but these were probably part of a gift-giving economy rather than a real exchange economy. Charlemagne struck a new silver coin, called the *denarius*, but in general fewer coins were available and those in existence were often hoarded, so that local trade generally took the form of barter in surplus agricultural and artisan products. Local markets were usually held every eight days in towns and larger villages, while bigger markets usually took place around feast days. In the early 8th century, the emperor issued professional merchants a charter granting them special rights and protections. Aristocrats demanded rare goods not locally available, such as spices, jewelry, and silk, and a luxury trade for these items continued with the Byzantine Empire and the Muslim cities of Western Asia and North Africa. Western and Northern Europe supplied natural products such as furs, timber, and iron, which were moved by river barge or overland by mule and horse caravans. Slaves from Eastern Europe—the modern word *slave* comes from *Slav*—were also in great demand.

In the West, traders were often Jews, but by 900 Venetians and other Italian merchants were establishing port facilities and outfitting ships to trade with the Byzantines and the Muslims. Nevertheless, the Viking and Magyar invaders who struck Europe in the 10th and 11th centuries contributed to the further decline of trade. In the East, Arabs acted as middlemen for items coming from as far away as India and China.

Contrary to what scholars once believed, the early Medieval economy was by no means static. Innovations in planting methods and technology eventually enabled farmers to open new areas to cultivation and to increase the crop yield. While the volume of trade was light, it would begin to revive substantially by the 11th century, at the same time that towns began to grow in size and number. Nevertheless, the Western European economy could not match the vibrancy and strength of the older Roman imperial economy or of the contemporary Byzantine Empire.

THE DISINTEGRATION OF THE CAROLINGIAN EMPIRE

The Carolingian Empire did not long survive the death of Charlemagne in 814. The kind of genuine unity achieved by ancient Rome had never been forged by the Franks. Nor had Christianity prevented the dissension and competition that divided the Frankish nobles. Charlemagne's empire had been held together mainly by the force of his own personality. Moreover, the Franks persisted in the notion of the state as a personal possession and followed the practice of dividing royal lands among the king's sons. Aristocrats followed the same custom, so that estates were constantly subdivided. As Charlemagne's successors found it increasingly necessary to purchase support from one faction of nobles by exchanging grants of land for military service, the royal estates were further diminished.

Map 5.2 The Division of the Carolingian Empire, 843

The Breakup of the Empire

On the emperor's death, his only surviving son, Louis the Pious (ruled 814–840), inherited the empire. Louis proved unable to control the unruly aristocrats or the rivalries that divided his own three sons. After Louis' death, Charles the Bald (ruled 843–877) joined forces with Louis the German (ruled 843–876) against their older brother Lothair (ruled 840–855), who had inherited the imperial crown. In 842, the two brothers cemented their alliance with the "Strasbourg Oaths," written in early forms of French and German, and the next year they defeated Lothair and concluded the Treaty of Verdun with him. One of the most crucial treaties of the Medieval period, the Verdun agreement provided the basis for all future subdivisions of the empire. Three kingdoms were defined: Charles took possession of the area west of a line running from the Scheldt to the Rhône rivers and to the Atlantic, approximating the region of modern France; Louis ruled over most of the territory east of the Rhine that is today Germany; and Lothair was left the imperial title and an unwieldy realm known as the middle kingdom. It stretched from the North Sea, including the Netherlands and the Rhineland, to Rome.

Lothair's middle kingdom remained the source of frequent conflict. In his will, he followed Frankish practice by dividing his realm among his three sons; one of these sons, Lothair II, received a northern portion that came to be called Lotharingia, or Lorraine. Charles and Louis then seized Lorraine and by the treaty of Mersen in 870 divided it among themselves, thus establishing a contiguous border between France and Germany and a constant cause of trouble between the two countries. The southern portion of Lothair's kingdom was divided into Burgundy and the kingdom of Italy. One section of the Carolingian family vied with another over the years for control of the imperial title, and by 887, when Charlemagne's great-grandson was deposed by the nobles, the dynasty had all but come to an end.

Muslims, Bulgars, and Magyars

Ever since the Germanic migrations of the 5th century crossed the frontiers of Rome, Europe had been the target of successive waves of invasions. The most disturbing of these assaults had been the Muslim expansion of the 8th century, which had broken the Christian unity of the Mediterranean world (see Part III, Topic 4). In the 9th and 10th centuries, as the Carolingian empire disintegrated from within, a new series of invasions by non-Christian peoples occurred: Muslims from the south, Bulgars and Magyars from the east, and Vikings from the north.

From their bases on the coasts of North Africa, Gaul, and Spain, the Muslims launched the conquest of Sicily in 827. Raiding the Italian peninsula, they

Map 5.3 The Invasions of the 9th Century

sacked Rome in 846. In response, Pope Leo IV had a wall built to protect St. Peter's and the Vatican palace, defining an area that today approximates Vatican City. The Muslims swept across Sardinia and Corsica, seized the Carolingian defense positions in northern Spain, and menaced the Alpine passes. Muslim navies virtually cleared the western half of the Mediterranean of European trade. Yet, although the Muslims proved themselves to be a civilization capable of rivalling Carolingian Europe in power and vitality, their European conquests did not survive the next century.

While Muslims were threatening the Mediterranean frontier, Slavs from Poland and Bohemia periodically attacked northeastern Germany but were repulsed. Both Germans and Slavs were in turn threatened by two new Asiatic peoples, the Bulgars and the Magyars. The Bulgars, distantly related to the Huns, had driven into the Balkans and laid siege to Constantinople, but they soon adopted the civilized customs they came in contact with. The Bulgar king took the title of tsar (Caesar) and eventually accepted Greek Orthodox Christianity. The Magyars moved from the Black Sea area into Carpathia and Moravia, driving a permanent wedge between the southern, or

Yugo, Slavs of the Balkans and the western Slavs of Bohemia, Moravia, and Poland. The Magyars, who came to be called Hungarians because they were mistakenly thought to resemble the Huns, assaulted eastern Germany and penetrated as far west as Lorraine. Only after their defeat at Lechfeld by the German king Otto I in 955, did the Magyars settle into a stable kingdom in east-central Europe and adopt Christianity.

The Vikings

The most widespread and devastating of the new invasions were those of the Norsemen, or Vikings, a Germanic people from Scandinavia. The Vikings had sporadically raided the coasts of Ireland and England in the 8th century but a growing population, together with the limited resources of the forests of Denmark and the rocky land of Norway and Sweden, drove them to more systematic and powerful invasions in the 9th century.

The Norsemen were consummate shipbuilders and sailors with unparalleled knowledge of winds, currents, and navigation techniques. Their ships were elegant affairs, long and narrow with double ends adorned by tall prows that were often carved in the form of dragonheads. The shallow draft of these ships enabled the Vikings to sail or row up rivers to inland cities of Europe, their sudden appearance and dragon prows striking terror in the inhabitants of European towns.

The Vikings were pagans and fierce fighters. Danish raids on Ireland had destroyed numerous monasteries and had terrorized the coasts of Germany and France. It was in England, however, that they made their most important conquest and eventually accommodated themselves to the Christian civilization they encountered. In 878, after repeated assaults on the east coast of England, the Saxon King Alfred the Great (ruled 871–899) of Wessex ceded a large area of northeastern England to the Danes. Those who settled in Danelaw, as this area was called, became Christians and pledged allegiance to Alfred but remained nominally independent until the region was reconquered in the following century and united with the rest of the kingdom. Another group of Danes settled around the mouth of the Seine River in northern France, where some 40,000 Vikings besieged the city of Paris. In 911 the French king ceded their chieftain Rollo an area that came to be known as Normandy, in return for pledging fealty to the king and becoming Christian.

Further afield, Swedish sailors gained control of the Baltic Sea and moved east into northern Russia. Eventually they sailed down the Russian rivers as far south as Novgorod and Kiev, and from there to the Black Sea, establishing commercial contact with the Byzantine Empire. Because these Norsemen were called Varangians, their trade path from northern Russia to Constantinople was known as the Varangian route. Further east, they encountered Arab traders on the Sea of Azov. Bands of Viking warriors sometimes hired themselves to local Slavic rulers and established their own settlements in Russia. Rurik, the leader of one such group, became the prince of Novgorod in 862 (see Part III, Topic 3).

The Norwegians generally took a western route, crossing the north Atlantic in the second half of the 9th century as far as Iceland. From this outpost they sailed still further west. Erik the Red reached Greenland in 975 and established a settlement there. Erik's son, Leif Erikson, is thought to have reached North America—evidence of Norsemen landings has been found in Newfoundland.

The impact of the Viking invasions was considerable. They extended their influence from the Atlantic to Russia and from the Baltic to the Mediterranean. They encouraged trade and advanced western sailing techniques, and their adoption of Christianity expanded the strength of the Medieval church. But despite the positive features of the Viking expansion, the destruction and chaos of the combined invasions were devastating. Moreover, the failure of royal governments to combat the invaders led Europeans to turn increasingly to local magnates for protection, thus maintaining the trend toward political decentralization that had been in force since the 3rd century. Nevertheless, with the exception of the Muslims, all the invaders of the 9th and 10th centuries were eventually absorbed into European civilization.

The core of Western European civilization evolved around the Frankish settlements in what is today modern France and Germany. There, the Carolingians emerged as the leaders of an important and far-reaching political and cultural revival that reached its most fully developed form during the reign of Charlemagne. The Carolingian period saw the melding of Roman and Germanic cultures into a new and vigorous European civilization. While using early Christian Rome as his model, Charlemagne applied much energy as a warrior to reestablishing an impressive measure of central authority and was responsible for the preservation of much of the written culture of the Roman world. Yet the achievement was limited by the constraints of new economic conditions and was short-lived. Within less than a century, the Carolingian Empire disintegrated and Europe fell prey to a series of powerful invasions. Out of these circumstances, a pattern of evolving social relationships now became predominant and was to characterize the European experience for centuries.

Questions for Further Study

1. Explain the political success of the Franks in building a state.

while honor demanded both faithfulness to the lord and the willingness to accept any challenge. Yet the true knight had to observe a code of uprightness even in dealing with an enemy and in return expected honorable treatment if captured in battle. So completely did military values permeate Medieval society that knights were prone to fight one another as easily as a common enemy, and in 1179 the church felt it necessary to prohibit jousts and tournaments fought for amusement.

Becoming a knight required long and dedicated training. Aristocratic boys were generally "apprenticed" at the court of a friendly lord or relative, where they served as pages and learned the basic skills of horsemanship and fighting. Later, they became "squires" and followed their lord to battle, although they did not actually take part in the fighting and many never became knights. Sometime in their late teens, the boys were knighted in a ceremony during which they received their own sword, thus entering the exclusive ranks of young knights who fought for their lords.

Fighting on horseback was the virtual monopoly of the aristocrats, who generally scorned the commoners who made up the ranks of the infantry. The mounted knight, who dressed in chain mail—later replaced by steel plate armor—and a steel helmet, could be wounded but not often killed in battle. Protection against military assault was afforded by castles, which were more often than not resistant to besiegers. In early days, these consisted of square towers of wood known as *keeps*, commonly built on elevated mounds and surrounded by stockades or moats. The round stone towers that dot much of the European countryside today were a later design, while more sophisticated structures with concentric circles of walls connecting a series of towers were built after Europeans became familiar with Byzantine and Muslim military architecture.

THE REVIVAL OF TRADE AND EMERGENCE OF CITIES

Nowhere was the changing tempo of the Medieval age more evident than in the growth of cities. Commerce was a major factor in the urban development of the 11th and 12th centuries. An increasingly sophisticated aristocratic society demanded luxury goods that could be provided by merchants based in cities, while nobles and kings both required money and credit that only urban moneylenders were able to lend. The stimulation of trade was a major cause of the revival of older towns that had not experienced significant growth since the Roman Empire. Towns also became centers of manufacturing and themselves grew into large markets for trade.

In an important feudal ceremony known as commendation, warriors were endowed with the virtues of strength and loyalty, after which they received their swords.

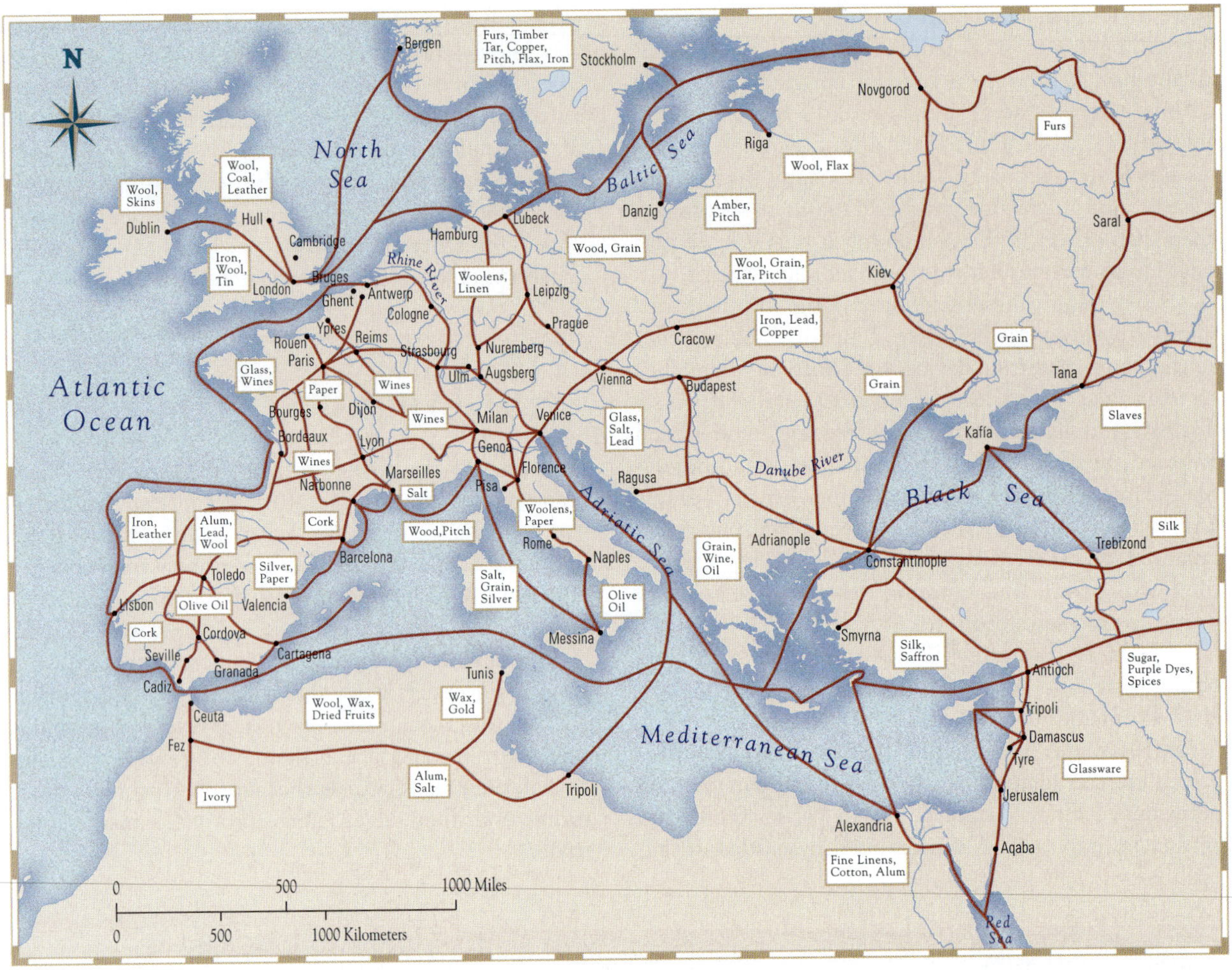

Map 6.1 Trade Routes and Commercial Products of Europe, 800–1300

As the population of Europe grew because of increased food production and the end of the invasions, town populations swelled. To the urban merchant class and accompanying service industries of the expanding cities were added numerous peasants who began moving to the cities to find refuge from the drudgery of their lives in the countryside. Cities increasingly obtained special rights and privileges in the form of charters from kings and lords, and the new air of freedom identified with the towns attracted the feudal underclass.

The Expansion of Trade

In the centuries immediately following the Carolingian era, western European trade—by contrast with that of the Byzantine Empire—was mostly local. A limited number of necessities such as iron, salt, and fish came into the manors from outside together with luxuries like oriental goods, especially silk, ivory, spices, and pepper. Nevertheless, most inland regions of the Continent were relatively isolated, for overland transportation was difficult and dangerous. The exception to this pattern was to be found along the coasts, especially in the Mediterranean and along the North and the Baltic seas.

The more settled conditions achieved by the feudal system in the West eventually encouraged commercial expansion. Merchants in Venice, Pisa, and Genoa, together with the Norman conquests in southern Italy, had destroyed the Muslim hold on Mediterranean trade. As early as the 11th century, Venetian traders grew so wealthy and powerful that they were able to forge an independent republic that emerged as a great sea power. The Crusades (see Part III, Topic 8) not only stimulated trade by making initial contact with Muslims but enhanced the growing power of European merchants, for Western traders who transported and supplied the Christian armies gained control of crucial ports in the eastern Mediterranean. Improvements in ship design, port facilities, and navigation—including the wide use of the magnetized needle (for direction-finding) by the 13th century—further stimulated maritime commerce.

In the North, the Low Countries remained the most important commercial area. Cloth manufacturing using raw wool imported from England thrived in Bruges, Ghent, Lille, and Arras, and Flemish cloth was sold throughout Europe. German and Scandinavian merchants joined with Italian, French, and Spanish shippers in securing and transporting northern finished goods. By 1230, the native cities of the German merchants operating in foreign ports formed a commercial association eventually known as the Hanseatic League, embracing more than 70 cities. Just as Venice and Genoa came to dominate much of the Mediterranean trade, so the Hanseatic League controlled the commerce of northern Europe.

Progress in overland trade came more slowly. Merchants organized to improve roads, bridges, and inland security. As the volume of trade grew, regional markets developed at designated locations into trade fairs (from the Latin *feria,* meaning feast day, because fairs usually opened on a saint's day or a holy day). Fairs usually developed at places along established trade routes and generally in spots convenient to merchants from several countries or regions. Kings or feudal lords granted special protection to merchants in order to promote fairs. Perhaps the most famous were the fairs in Champagne, in northern France, located at the crossroads of inland commerce; these drew merchants principally from France, Flanders, and Germany as well as from Italy and Switzerland. Special courts were instituted to hear commercial lawsuits and money bureaus sprang up to deal with the exchange of currencies. An early form of a letter of credit, known as "fair letters," allowed merchants to obtain goods in exchange for a promise to pay bills at a future date. Fairs were also occasions for popular amusement.

The manufacture of goods for sale to regional rather than exclusively local markets developed apace with the expansion of trade. Florentines and Venetians began to purchase Flemish woolens for "finishing" with special dyes imported from the Middle East, after which they were resold. The manufacturing of glassware grew more sophisticated at Limoges and in Venice, while ore production developed in Bohemia, Sweden, Spain, Lombardy, and England. In the North, trade was mainly in raw products such as furs, lumber, salt, beer, and metals that included iron, tin, and copper.

Commercial expansion necessitated more efficient methods of exchange and business practice. New coins with a more stable value were minted in Venice (the silver groat) in 1192 and in Florence (the gold florin) in 1252, although the Middle Ages produced no monetary system that was universally accepted throughout Europe. But better systems of credit and borrowing of money did evolve despite church strictures against the practice of usury—charging interest on borrowed money. In theory only non-Christians, especially Jews, were able to engage in moneylending for profit, although the practice was spreading among Christians by the 13th century.

The Rise of Cities

Unlike other parts of Europe, cities in Italy had continued to flourish because of the peninsula's strong urban traditions and commercial links to the Mediterranean. Northern Italian cities, especially Venice, Genoa, and Pisa, were at the center of the commercial revival in the Mediterranean region, where they acted as middlemen between Europe and the Middle East. Florence and other manufacturing cities also participated early in the new economic growth based on finished textiles. In the 13th century, merchant firms in Venice, Pisa, and Florence had begun to pioneer new techniques in banking and business, including insurance, double-entry bookkeeping, and limited liability partnerships, and had established branches as far west as the Atlantic coast of Morocco, east as far as the Black Sea and Persia, and north as far as London and Scandinavia. In northern Europe, the towns of Flanders were expanded and prospered in similar fashion.

It was in the Italian towns that the capitalist ethic first developed hand in hand with new class distinctions based on economic status. In place of the old feudal orders, there now arose differences between the "popular" citizens and the elite "magnates," whether merchants or landowning aristocrats. In the cities, feudal values were undermined as Italians abandoned noble prejudices against business activity and experienced a new form of social mobility based on commercial profits. Many of these cities achieved the status of self-governing centers known as *communes* as they either rebelled against their overlords or purchased charters from them. The communes developed distinctive forms of self-government that stimulated patriotism and civic pride and controlled all aspects of economic activity. In addition, serfs who escaped to such towns could gain their freedom if they lived there for a year and one day.

Magnates in these cities banded together and established corporative associations known as guilds, which maintained a monopoly of trade in a region, settled disputes, insisted on quality control, and established fair weights and measures. The merchant guilds also acted as charitable institutions and protected the families of members who fell into hard times.

As early as the 11th century, the skilled artisans of the towns also established their own craft guilds, open only to those engaged in the same craft, to protect and regulate their interests. These guilds functioned much the same as the merchant guilds, regulating production, quality, and prices, and setting standards for artisan training in three stages. Apprentices were youths who lived for about seven years in the master's house while learning the craft. The young man could then become a journeyman who received wages for his work. After reaching the age of 23 or so, the journeyman could apply for membership in the guild and thereby become a master, usually after crafting a "master piece" that met the standards of the guild. Below the artisans on the social scale were the day laborers and unskilled workers, who lived in miserable conditions and occasionally were behind uprisings and protests.

In general, the merchant-artisan inhabitants of these towns, who were neither peasant nor noble, evolved into a new social and economic class of *burghers* (from the German word for *town*), who came to be known as the *bourgeoisie*. These city dwellers, who represented a new culture opposed to the ideals and values of the feudal system, became influential allies of the kings in their struggles to resist the power of the traditional lords. As the manorial system, serfdom, and chivalry declined, the bourgeoisie symbolized the new society evolving under the impetus of Western capitalism.

The bourgeoisie grew more independent and powerful with time, electing their own officials to councils in communal government and participating directly in assemblies and civic life. Executive power was generally placed in the hands of councils, although partisan disputes often made them incapable of managing the cities effectively. In the face of growing factional strife, some towns resorted to importing officials, known as the *podestà*, from other towns. These *podestà* ran the communal governments on salary for specified periods and were supposed to remain aloof from the local partisan disputes. The Italian cities eventually expanded their territorial control into the surrounding countryside, becoming powerful city-states.

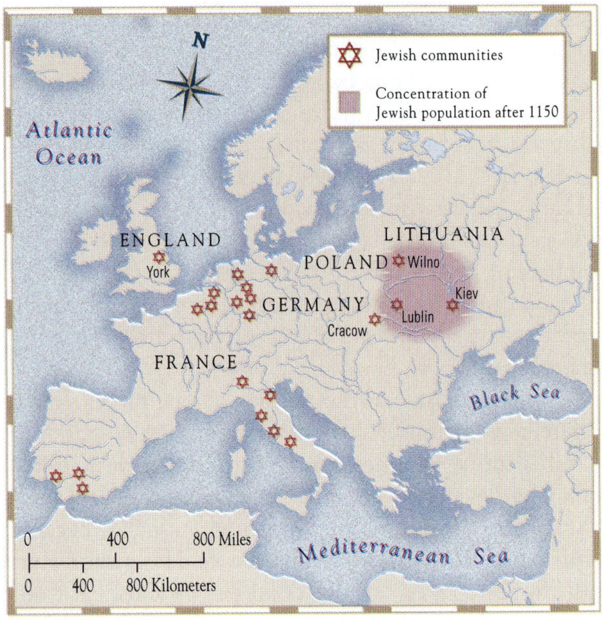

Map 6.2 Jewish Communities of Europe in the Middle Ages

JEWISH LIFE IN THE MIDDLE AGES

Ever since the *Diaspora*—the dispersion of the Jews out of Palestine—Jews lived mainly in cities, both in Muslim and in Christian territories. In the Roman era, they had settled in Ravenna, Pavia, and Rome itself and migrated as far west as Spain and France. After the collapse of the Empire, Jewish communities were to be found in Visigothic towns of Spain such as Burgos and Toledo as well as in French cities such as Arles, Marseilles, Lyon, and Narbonne. Jews of this era were closely integrated into the general communities and stood out neither in language, dress, nor occupation. While some Jews owned land and engaged in agriculture, most tended to live in towns, where they engaged in the entire range of professions and trades. This pattern was reinforced in North Africa, Spain and other regions overrun by the Muslims, whose tolerant policies enabled Jews to thrive economically and culturally.

During Charlemagne's reign, Jews also settled under imperial charters in Aix-la-Chapelle and Soissons, and during the 9th century Jewish migrants moved from Champagne and the south into the Rhine basin, expanding from there further eastward into Germany and northward into Flanders. Cities sometimes even competed to attract Jews, as when in 1084 the bishop of Speyer succeeded in drawing Jews to his community from Mainz. In 1066, immediately after the Norman Conquest, French Jews established a community in England.

Throughout this era, Jews lived under either Christianity or Islam, monotheistic religions that claimed that Jews had misunderstood the concepts of their own religious experience. The Jews condemned the worship of a son of God within a Trinity as idolatry and the Christian rejection of the Commandments as prescribed in the Scriptures. The Christians, on the other hand, charged that the Jews rejected their Jewish Messiah and had crucified the son of God. There was no real dispute with the Muslims about the nature of God, only the argument that the Jews had refused to recognize Muhammad as his prophet. Nevertheless, both faiths called upon Jews to convert and in the face of Jewish resistance often enacted policies of persecution and suppression against the Jews. On the whole, however, the Muslims seem to have treated the Jews with greater tolerance. Medieval Jews therefore developed in circumstances of both conflict and contact with the dominant cultures in whose midst they lived.

Economic Life

Jewish economic life varied widely, with Jews found in practically every trade and profession, from medicine and banking to more lowly occupations that included shopkeeping and skilled craftsmanship. Jewish doctors were particularly prized by Christians for their skill and learning, and many served as physicians at royal courts. In the early Middle Ages, Jews had engaged extensively in long-distance trade, chiefly because Christians had shown little interest in commercial activities and because Jews in Western Europe maintained contact with those in Western Asia and North Africa as well as good relations with the Muslims. Jews therefore became the international merchants of Western Europe, supplying spices and other luxuries. As early as the 6th century, Gregory of Tours mentions the presence of prosperous and respected Jewish traders among the Franks. By the 9th century, Christian accounts record Jewish merchants in the West whose trade networks reached as far as India and China. Much of the trade was based on agreements contained in written documents and private letters.

By the late 10th century, Jewish merchants began to engage increasingly in local trade, including the buying and selling of cattle and other local products, and to conduct financial business on behalf of the feudal lords. Jewish merchants on occasion lent money to local nobles. In the 11th century, Jews were already engaged extensively in credit transactions.

Many of those Jews involved in large-scale trade achieved living standards comparable to the most successful Christians or Muslims. The best Jewish homes even kept slaves, permitted by special charter, and employed Christian domestic help. During periods distinguished by famine and economic dislocation, the Jewish chronicles often make no reference to such hardships. Most Jewish families no doubt lived more modestly but the degree of prosperity recorded among Jewish merchants speaks to the considerable success they had achieved.

The general revival of trade after the 11th century and the high levels of profit to be earned from it attracted more and more Christians to commercial activity. As a result, Jews began to be pushed out of the field. The guilds that came to dominate city life were, after all, Christian associations that excluded nonbelievers from their ranks. The Jews eventually became dependent on moneylending, one of the few fields still open to them. As the church intensified its regulations against usury, Jewish lenders became more plentiful—although the Torah prohibited interest loans, they

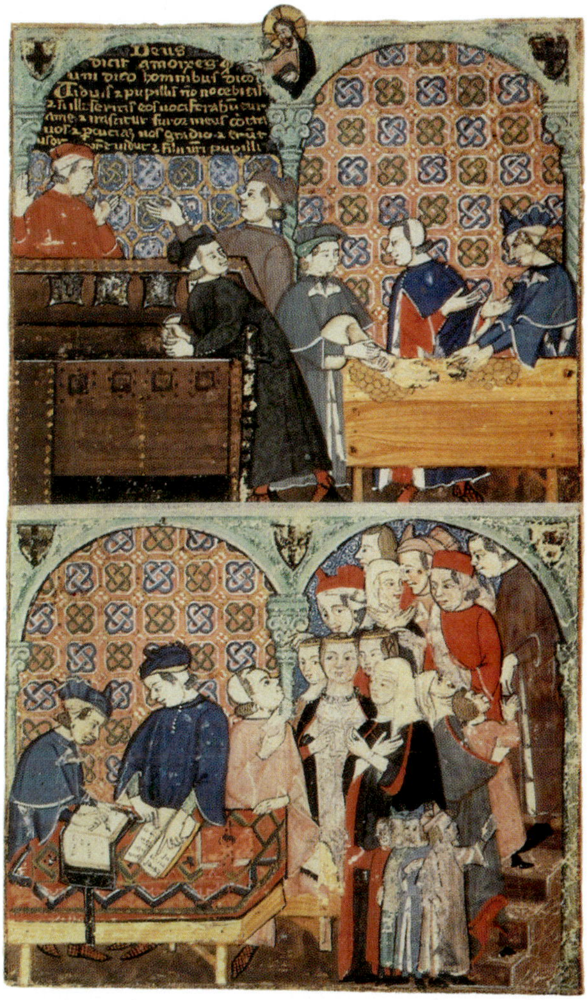

Jewish businessmen acted as moneylenders and merchants in the Middle Ages, occupations that were often frowned upon by Christian society. This illumination is from a 14th-century book of vices.

A 15th-century illuminated manuscript showing a typical country fair. This one, in Lendit, France, was held every June.

believed such rules applied to loans to other Jews, not to Christians. Such transactions were risky but highly profitable, with interest rates sometimes as high as 33 percent.

By the middle of the 12th century, the lending of money for interest became the principal Jewish business activity in the cities of western and central Europe. For purposes of taxation, careful records of Jewish loans were kept by royal governments in England, France, and elsewhere. During the second half of the 12th century, one such lender, Aaron of Lincoln, granted loans in 25 English counties to clients that included monasteries and cathedrals. Nevertheless, after 1230, the church promoted initiatives to limit Jewish moneylending. French laws against Jewish usury were followed in 1275 by similar measures in England and later in Spain. Such measures had a devastating impact on the prosperity of many Jewish businessmen.

The Growth of Intolerance

The prominence of Jews in moneylending, together with Christian charges that they had murdered Christ, made Jews easy targets of social prejudice and religious hatred. Persecutions against them mounted in the 11th century in France and Germany. The First Crusade in 1096 stimulated an intensity of feeling against them. The religious fervor of the times, aroused by fanatical sermons preached against all nonbelievers, provoked devastating massacres of the Jewish population in the Rhineland and elsewhere. The Jews defended themselves as best they could but thousands were killed in cities from Mainz to Prague and as far away as Jerusalem. Although the violence eventually subsided, such incidents recurred with frightening regularity.

Secular and ecclesiastical authorities continued to inflame anti-Semitism. In 1182, King Philip II of France expelled the Jews from his realm, and eight years later, following riots that spread to the countryside from London, Jews were besieged in the town of York and committed mass suicide to avoid death at the hands of Christians. A series of church councils—especially the Third Lateran (1179) and the Fourth Lateran (1215) Councils—adopted increasingly severe regulations that forced Jews to wear identifying symbols on their clothing, to live in segregated sections of cities, and to endure Christian sermons designed to convert them. In 1290, Edward I expelled the Jews from England, forcing thousands to emigrate abroad, and further banishments were enacted in France and the German states. Jews began fleeing to Poland and eastern Europe, creating a growing population there of *Ashkenazi* Jews, as opposed to the *Sephardic* Jews of Spain. The persecutions and expulsions would recur in the 15th and 16th centuries.

MEDIEVAL WOMEN: THE PRIVATE AND PUBLIC SPHERES

The position of women in Medieval society was at best ambiguous. Among peasant families, the typical household was a family consisting of husband, wife, and several children, along with extended relatives such as grandparents and widowed female relations. Harvesting saw men and women working together but the Medieval peasant family generally observed a clear division of labor: men worked in the fields while women held responsibility for household tasks that included baking and cooking, caring for domestic animals and the vegetable garden, and spinning and weaving. In addition to these duties, women were expected to raise the children. The nuclear family, consisting of parents

A 12th-century family portrait for Siboto, count of Falkenstein, shows the new patriarchal model in which his daughters were not represented—only his wife and oldest son.

and children, actually replaced the extended family. Although the husbands continued to dominate their wives, in the smaller family units the wife rather than female elders had greater control over household matters and the raising of children.

Bourgeois women in the towns generally had wider opportunities, and in many cases were active in the guild system and in a wide variety of crafts. A growing number of women took employment as domestic servants in the homes of wealthier merchants and also ran retail shops.

The position of women in the chivalric society of the aristocrats was less restricted. In noble families, the chief function of daughters was to marry the sons (generally 15 years older) of other noble families by prearrangement and to bear children. In the castles, young girls were trained to assume some responsibility over castle and estate management, particularly as the men were often away fighting for long periods of time. Young women generally married at age 16 and, because of the high death rate for babies, were expected to have as many children as possible. In turn, women often died giving birth, although poor nutrition seems to have taken an even greater toll on women and children. In a society in which warfare was the central concern, the status of women suffered.

Women were generally excluded from public functions and often could not inherit property, although some, especially widows, did act as property managers and control estates through their infant sons. The feudal order did allow women to inherit fiefs but generally on condition that the lord would arrange a marriage to a suitable vassal. Gradually, however, the principle of primogeniture took hold, whereby property could be inherited only by the oldest son whenever possible. In the later Middle Ages, women played an important role as hosts in manor houses and castles, while courtly literature and chivalric codes elevated women to an ideal pedestal. Medieval clergy often regarded women as temptresses who used sexuality and cunning to corrupt men.

Beginning in the late 11th century, leadership in the church became exclusively a male domain. The Gregorian reforms (see Part III, Topic 8) weakened the role of women in church affairs by insisting on clerical celibacy. Moreover, the increased prominence of bishops further limited the influence of women, who could not have positions in the church similar to those they occupied as heads of abbeys. The development of cathedral schools and universities created a chasm in the world of learning between men and women, the latter being excluded from the new institutions. Furthermore, when the new Cistercian monastic order was created in the 13th century, women were forced to enter separate and subordinate female orders.

THE CLERGY AND SECULAR SOCIETY

The role of the clergy in the feudal system rested on the land tenure system, as did that of all social groups. Abbots and bishops, who managed properties in the name of the church, supervised the lives of peasants in the same way as did lay landlords and were often both feudal vassals and lords. Moreover, in the face of the decline of civil authority, ecclesiastical figures assumed a wide range of functions and duties outside the church, often acting as advisers to noble lords and as representatives of kings, and fulfilled a myriad of administrative responsibilities.

Corruption and Abuse in the Feudal Church

Apart from its spiritual mission and the monastic thrust of early Medieval Christianity, the Catholic Church became fully enmeshed in secular society. As it became involved in worldly matters, the church experienced a variety of problems that undermined its spiritual functions. High officials frequently conducted themselves more like political leaders than religious figures and engaged in practices that weakened the church's stature. Simony, the sale of church offices, became widespread and many priests ignored the rule against marriage.

One of the most serious problems surrounded the election of bishops. Because success in the feudal system made it essential that secular leaders be able to control their vassals, the king or feudal nobles often selected the candidates, who were then actually elected by canons of cathedral churches. Bishoprics were highly desirable offices, especially for the younger noble sons who did not inherit property. After being rushed through Holy Orders without proper training or religious zeal, these young men entered into their duties with no real interest and continued to lead the lives of feudal knights. An even more explosive issue eventually arose over what came to be known as "lay investiture." In feudalism, investiture was the ceremony whereby a lord transferred a fief to his vassal, whereas in the church it was the ceremony in which the cleric, once elected, received the pastoral ring and staff that were symbols of his spiritual office. The problem arose when laymen began investing bishops not only with symbols of their fiefs but with these spiritual symbols as well. Did this mean that laymen could control ecclesiastical as well as temporal matters? By the end of the 11th century, this controversy would explode in a struggle for power between the papacy and the rulers of Germany.

The investiture problem was an example of how the forces of feudalism threatened the authority of the church, often diluting its hierarchical principle in the far-flung regions of Europe where local feudal power was strongest. Over the next several centuries, the popes struggled to build the mechanisms through which to implement the principle of supreme papal authority, a task made more difficult by the chaotic conditions prevailing in Rome and the surrounding areas of central Italy.

The impact of feudalism on the church was not, however, entirely negative. For example, simony actually strengthened the stature of the church by making the ecclesiastical establishment important to the dukes, counts, and other nobles. Moreover, by enmeshing Christianity into the feudal system, European became Christianized at a fundamental level and began at last to have meaning for large numbers of laypeople.

From the 10th to the 12th centuries, European society generally reflected the values and the socioeconomic conditions of feudalism. The Carolingians deliberately used feudalism as part of a management strategy for their vast empire, consciously encouraging and spreading feudal practices. After the collapse of Charlemagne's empire and the disappearance of central government, feudalism assumed even greater importance. During the height of the feudal age, three social groups, or "estates," comprised the feudal order: the nobility, or first estate, and the clergy, or second estate, were the dominant orders; and the rest of the population, ranging from serfs and rural peasants to servants and wealthy urban merchants, comprised the third estate. Although this arrangement was supposed to be a fixed and permanent one in an unchanging social system ordained by God, Medieval society was in fact a dynamic system that saw significant long-range change. Just as feudalism was inevitably if slowly transformed by the new economic forces of urban capitalism and the burgher class, so too it was undermined by the growth of centralized monarchies throughout Europe.

Questions for Further Study

1. What were the main features of feudalism?
2. What was the relationship between trade and cities?
3. In what ways did women and Jews have similar experiences in Medieval society?
4. How were the clergy involved in secular society?

Suggestions for Further Reading

Bloch, Marc. *Feudal Society*, trans. L. A. Manyon. London, 1961.

Brooke, Christopher N. L. *The Structure of Medieval Society*. New York, 1971.

Cipolla, Carlo M. *The Fontana Economic History of Europe*, vol. I, *The Middle Ages*. London, 1972.

Delort, Robert. *Life in the Middle Ages*, trans. R. Allen. New York, 1972.

Duby, Georges. *The Early Growth of the European Economy: Warriors and Peasants from the Seventh to the Twelfth Century*. Ithaca, NY, 1974.

Fossier, Robert. *Peasant Life in the Medieval West*. New York, 1988.

Ganshof, François L. *Feudalism*, trans. P. Grierson. London, 1952.

Ladurie, Emmanuel L. *Times of Feast, Times of Famine*. New York, 1971.

Lopez, Robert S. *The Commercial Revolution of the Middle Ages, 950–1350*. Englewood Cliffs, NJ, 1971.

Marcus, J. *The Jew in the Medieval World*. New York, 1972.

Miskimin, Harry A., D. Herlihy, and A. L. Udovich, eds. *The Medieval City*. New Haven, CT, 1977.

Pounds, Norman J. G. *An Economic History of Medieval Europe*. New York, 1974.

Reuter, Timothy A., ed. *The Medieval Nobility*. Amsterdam and Oxford, 1978.

Stuard, Susan M., ed. *Women in Medieval Society*. Philadelphia, 1976.

Wemple, Suzanne F. *Women in Frankish Society: Marriage and the Cloister, 500–900*. Philadelphia, 1981.

III

Topic 7

The Feudal Monarchies

After the disintegration of the Carolingian Empire in the 9th century, Western and Central Europe underwent a period of great difficulty. The collapse of political authority was accompanied by the new invasions and the subsequent breakdown of communications, trade, and centralized economy. Yet by the 10th century, patterns of recovery began to appear. Despite the emergence of the great lords of the feudal era, the foundations of a new political system were established by the early kings who stood at the apex of the feudal hierarchy.

In the feudal era, kings were in theory the supreme rulers of their realms, who led all their subjects in war. Nevertheless, the realities of feudalism limited the real power of the kings in a number of ways. Some of the great feudal lords of the age held larger tracts of land and were far wealthier than their kings. As a result, these lords could control more vassal warriors than did the sovereigns. The nature of feudal relationships was such that kings were obliged to respect the privileges of their vassals and any transgressions against the legitimate rights of vassals could and often did result in rebellions against royal authority.

Yet the feudal kings did have some significant advantages over the lords and vassals of their kingdoms. The institution of liege homage clarified the sometimes contradictory feudal relationships that evolved among lords and vassals, giving kings the primary loyalty of some of the nobles. The authority of kings was, moreover, sanctified by divine grace since they were anointed during coronation ceremonies with holy oil. Kings shrewdly extended their realms and their prestige by arranging strategic marriages for their children with powerful noble families. Victory in war often meant that they could distribute to their loyal vassals fiefs taken from vanquished enemies. Finally, monarchs slowly built up the administrative and legal institutions of royal governments in ways that undermined the power of the lords and built a centrifugal momentum that eventually restored centralized authority on a national level.

During the 11th and 12th centuries, the feudal kings so effectively extended their authority that the monarchies formed the basis for the powerful kingdoms that would shape European history for centuries to come. The institution of feudal monarchy flourished in England under the kings who reigned following the Norman Conquest of 1066, and in France under the reign of the Capetian kings from the 10th century. In Germany, the development of monarchy was complicated by the position of the imperial crown but central authority grew there under the Salian kings and then especially during the reign of the great Hohenstaufen emperor Frederick I. In Spain, the small Christian kingdoms began the reconquest of the territory from the Muslims in the 11th century and established the basis of royal power there.

NORMAN AND ANGEVIN ENGLAND: THE DEVELOPMENT OF ROYAL ADMINISTRATION

In the 10th century, the descendants of Alfred the Great (see Part III, Topic 5) had produced a united kingdom and an effective royal government in England. The monarchy became for all practical purposes hereditary as kings were elected from members of Alfred's family. The basic administrative unit of the kingdom became the shire, or county, in which the sheriff *(shire-reeve)* supervised local affairs in the name of the king. The king communicated with his sheriffs through written letters, known as writs, issued by the chancery office. Despite such administrative advances, however, by the late 10th century, the efficiency of the royal government deteriorated and the great earls asserted their power. In 1016, the Danes successfully overran England again, although the victorious King Canute of Denmark (ruled 1016–1035) retained English institutions and accepted the Catholic Church. On Canute's death, the throne passed to Ethelred's son, Edward the Confessor (ruled 1042–1066), a devout but weak ruler whose prerogatives were taken over by the nobles.

The Norman Conquest

Edward died without children and the throne was given to Harold Godwinson, an important English earl. Harold's claim was quickly challenged by Edward's cousin, William, Duke of Normandy (ruled 1066–1087). William claimed that during an earlier visit to England, Edward had promised him the throne. In Normandy, a region of northern France across the English Channel, William had used the feudal system to build a centralized feudal state. Technically, William was a vassal of the king of France, but he achieved more power than his sovereign. After subduing the rebellious nobles of his duchy, William established a network of loyal vassals that provided him with the most powerful army in Western Europe.

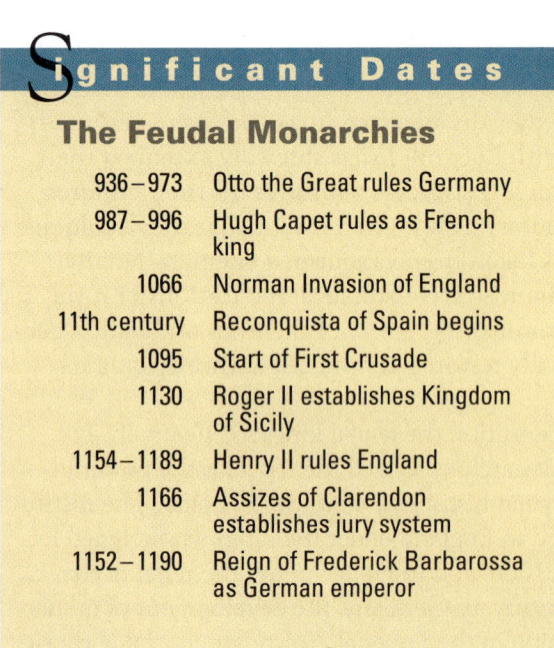

Significant Dates

The Feudal Monarchies

936–973	Otto the Great rules Germany
987–996	Hugh Capet rules as French king
1066	Norman Invasion of England
11th century	Reconquista of Spain begins
1095	Start of First Crusade
1130	Roger II establishes Kingdom of Sicily
1154–1189	Henry II rules England
1166	Assizes of Clarendon establishes jury system
1152–1190	Reign of Frederick Barbarossa as German emperor

Alfred the Great, warrior and early English ruler.

In the fall of 1066, William and an army of some 6000–7000 men, including several thousand mounted knights, crossed the Channel to secure the English throne. On October 14, the Norman knights defeated the English infantry at the Battle of Hastings, where Harold died. Two months later William was crowned king of England, while retaining his position as Duke of Normandy.

The Norman system of feudalism that William had used so successfully in France replaced Anglo-Saxon rule in England, although he needed another five years to pacify the country fully. William claimed all English land by right of conquest. Keeping about one-fifth of national territory for his own royal demesne, he distributed the rest in the form of fiefs to royal vassals (mostly French-speaking Normans), including bishops and abbots. In return, the vassals provided William with specified numbers of soldiers by subdividing their fiefs into smaller units which they granted to their vassals. In order to eliminate warfare between nobles, he prohibited the construction of private castles. In 1086, every fief holder in this system, whether one of William's great vassals or a lesser holder, pledged liege loyalty directly to William by swearing the so-called Salisbury Oath. That same year, William commissioned the Domesday Book, a kind of survey of all property throughout the realm. He used this information as a basis for collecting taxes and feudal aids from landholders. William also continued the tradition of collecting the Danegeld, a tax first raised in the 9th century to buy off raiding Danes.

The Bayeux Tapestry, more than two hundred feet long, describes the events associated with the Norman Conquest of England, and serves as a source for many details of 11th-century life. Here, Halley's Comet passes overhead.

Map 7.1 The Norman Conquest

William built a strong, centralized monarchy that blended Anglo-Saxon and Norman institutions and practices. Gradually, the French-speaking nobles intermarried with the English families, creating a ruling class that spoke a new form of English. He continued to use the former system of local administration through the sheriffs, although he replaced the Anglo-Saxon sheriffs with Normans, and extended the practice of using royal courts and the tax system to increase the wealth and authority of the king. He replaced the former English advisory body known as the *Witan* with the Great Council (later called the *curia regis*, or royal council). The council served as an advisory body to the king and as a court of justice for the barons of the realm. The Great Council is the ancestor of the English Parliament.

Henry II and Common Law

William was succeeded in turn by two of his sons. Thereafter, and for almost 20 years, a civil war disturbed England until the succession of Henry II (ruled 1154–1189), founder of the Plantagenet, or Angevin, dynasty. The new king had an impressive if complicated inheritance. Through his mother, wife of Geoffrey Plantagenet, he inherited the French provinces of Anjou and Normandy. Moreover, through his marriage to Eleanor of Aquitaine (1122?–1204), Henry also became Duke of Aquitaine, a territory that stretched through southwestern France to the Pyrenees.

Henry, a man of great energy, rapidly restored the power of the monarchy in England. In matters of administration, he made the collection and recording of taxes more efficient and regular through the office of the "exchequer," or treasury, so named after the checkered table top on which his officials counted the royal receipts. Perhaps his greatest achievement lay in extending the authority of the royal courts. In 1166,

PUBLIC FIGURES AND PRIVATE LIVES

MATILDA OF FLANDERS AND WILLIAM THE CONQUEROR

William the Conqueror was born illegitimate in 1027, and had to fight repeatedly to secure his rule in Normandy. Unable to shake off the shame of his birth, William seems to have been a temperate man with a deep distaste for sexual promiscuity. Tall and rugged, some 5′ 10″ in height, he was described by contemporary chroniclers as "robust" and "burly." Uneducated and crude, and known for bouts of cruelty and harshness, William was an ambitious man of considerable military and administrative ability.

It is unknown when William and Matilda of Flanders first met, but they began courting when he was in his early twenties and she presumably younger. Matilda was herself descended from Alfred the Great and her father was the count of Flanders, a wealthy principality positioned strategically in the north between France and Germany. The political advantages of a marriage to Matilda could not fail to capture William's attention but he seems also to have become captivated by her personality and intelligence. Although we have no accurate description of her appearance—we do know that she was only 4 feet tall—one historian called her "a completely colorless figure," but that opinion was clearly not shared by William or those who knew her. He seems genuinely to have fallen deeply in love with her.

William proposed marriage in 1049. One story, perhaps apocryphal, recorded that at first Matilda refused William's proposal, declaring that she would never marry a bastard, but that an enraged William rode furiously to Bruges, where he beat and kicked her, after which she took to her bed and declared that she would marry none but William. In any case, Pope Leo IX forbade the marriage, perhaps because Matilda and William were distantly related but possibly for political reasons. Nonetheless, in 1053, while Pope Leo was a prisoner of the Normans in Italy, William and Matilda married. As a result, the pope placed Normandy under an interdict, which prohibited most public church ceremonies, including Christian burial. In 1059, Pope Nicholas II granted the couple a dispensation in return for a pledge that each would build monasteries, Matilda later endowing the Abbey of the Holy Trinity at Caen and making rich gifts to the Cluniac order. They eventually had ten children.

During William's preparations for the invasion of England, Matilda, who had considerable financial resources of her own, presented him with a ship called the *Mora*, which had on its prow a golden boy with his left hand holding an ivory horn to his lips and his right hand pointing toward England. Legend had it that after Hastings, the devoted Matilda dedicated herself to the wifely task of embroidering the famous Bayeux Tapestry, which recorded the Norman victory. In fact, however, the tapestry was commissioned by William's half brother Odo, the bishop of Bayeux. When William departed, he left the affairs of Normandy in the hands of Matilda, who acted as regent for their oldest son, Robert Curthose. She was assisted by a council of nobles and proved herself a capable and vigorous administrator (the custom of wives taking over the management of their husband's estates became commonplace a century later during the Crusades).

William had thought it advisable not to delay his own coronation until Matilda could join him in England, but in 1068 she crossed the Channel and was crowned queen of England in an elaborate ceremony at Westminster Abbey. Parts of the royal demesne were placed in her name. In the following year, after the birth of their fourth son, Henry, Matilda returned to Normandy. There she resumed her regency, together with Robert, her favorite son. In 1074, after William had subdued England, he was faced with a difficult situation when Robert, anxious to assume his own rule over Normandy, joined a rebellion against his father with discontented local nobles. Father and son made up and quarreled again several times, and Robert soon found himself in exile. In 1079, while her destitute son wandered in France and Flanders, Matilda sent him gold and silver without William's knowledge. When William learned of Matilda's gifts to their son, he became furious, proclaiming that "a faithless woman is her husband's bane." Matilda's defense was that of a mother's love for her son, and this event seems to have been the only known quarrel between husband and wife. William eventually forgave Robert and bequeathed him the duchy of Normandy. Matilda died in November 1083. A saddened William mourned for her the rest of his life. When he died four years later, William was buried in St. Stephen's Church in Caen, not far from Matilda's tomb in the Church of the Holy Trinity.

Henry armed his itinerant justices with a series of instructions known as the Assizes of Clarendon, which established a jury in each shire consisting of twelve important men sworn to report all crimes of which they had knowledge. This method, also used to decide civil cases, is the origin of the present-day grand jury. The efficiency of the new system appealed to many of Henry's subjects and the royal courts grew rapidly in jurisdiction and popularity. These legal reforms formed the basis for the development of the English common law. The local courts and the feudal justice system had long administered customary law that differed widely from one county to another. The royal justices, on the other hand, administered law that was common throughout the realm, and their decisions became precedents for future decisions. Common law differed from Roman law in that it reflected not the will of the ruler but the principles established by judges in deciding cases.

The Murder of Thomas Becket

If Henry was able to build the royal judicial administration while undermining the legal authority of baronial courts, he was less successful in dealing with the church, whose system of canon law operated independently of the state. In 1162, Henry appointed Thomas Becket (c. 1118–1170), his former chancellor, archbishop of Canterbury, making him the highest cleric in the English Church. The king mistakenly believed that their friendship would guarantee a smooth relationship with the church, but Becket proved to be fiercely independent. The issue came to a head in 1164 when Henry decreed that clergymen found guilty of serious civil crimes, such as larceny or murder, should be tried in royal rather than in ecclesiastical courts. Becket stubbornly opposed Henry's decree, going into exile in France. Although Becket returned to England, all efforts at compromise failed and Becket excommunicated the English bishops who supported the king.

Eleanor of Aquitaine depicted in an effigy from Fontevrault Abbey in Normandy.

In a moment of exasperation Henry is supposed to have lamented that none of his retainers were courageous enough to "rid me of this troublesome priest." On December 29, 1170, four knights took Henry's reckless words at face value and killed Becket before the altar of Canterbury Cathedral. Public outrage was so intense that Henry had to do public penance for the murder and compromise with the church by permitting the right of appeal from church courts in England to the papal court in Rome, bypassing the royal courts altogether. Becket was instantly a popular hero and became a saint. His tomb at Canterbury was the site of pilgrimages and the symbol of church resistance against royal pride.

FRANCE AND THE CAPETIAN MONARCHY: NOBLES VERSUS THE KING

The descendants of Charlemagne who ruled the West Frankish kingdom—which came to be known as France—were ineffective monarchs who proved unable to defend the realm against invasion. In place of the king, therefore, the great feudal nobles assumed absolute powers on a local level and provided their subjects with military protection and political authority. In 987, when the last Carolingian king, Louis the Sluggard, died, the lords elected Hugh Capet (ruled 987–996), count of Paris, to the throne. Hugh was by no means the strongest of the feudal princes of France, personally controlling only a small area around Paris known as the Île de France, which was surrounded by the lands of other nobles who were wealthier and more powerful. But Hugh was determined to extend his domains and rebuild the royal government.

Building the Capetian Monarchy

No one expected that the Capetian dynasty would rule France for very long. Hugh cleverly arranged to have his son crowned as "associate" ruler during his lifetime, a practice that Hugh's successors followed regularly. Hugh strengthened his hold on the monarchy by securing the support of the church. Furthermore, every Capetian king for several centuries had a male heir, thus securing their hold on the throne. By the 13th century, the principle of hereditary rule had become a fixed tradition.

The beginning of the growth of the Capetian monarchy came with the reign of Louis VI (ruled 1108–1137), called Louis the Fat. Louis broke the resistance of the rebellious nobles in the Île de France, where he destroyed their castles and pacified the countryside. He also capitalized on his alliance with the church, which defended his prerogatives against the claims of the feudal barons. One of Louis' most able advisers was the Abbot Suger (1081–1151), from the

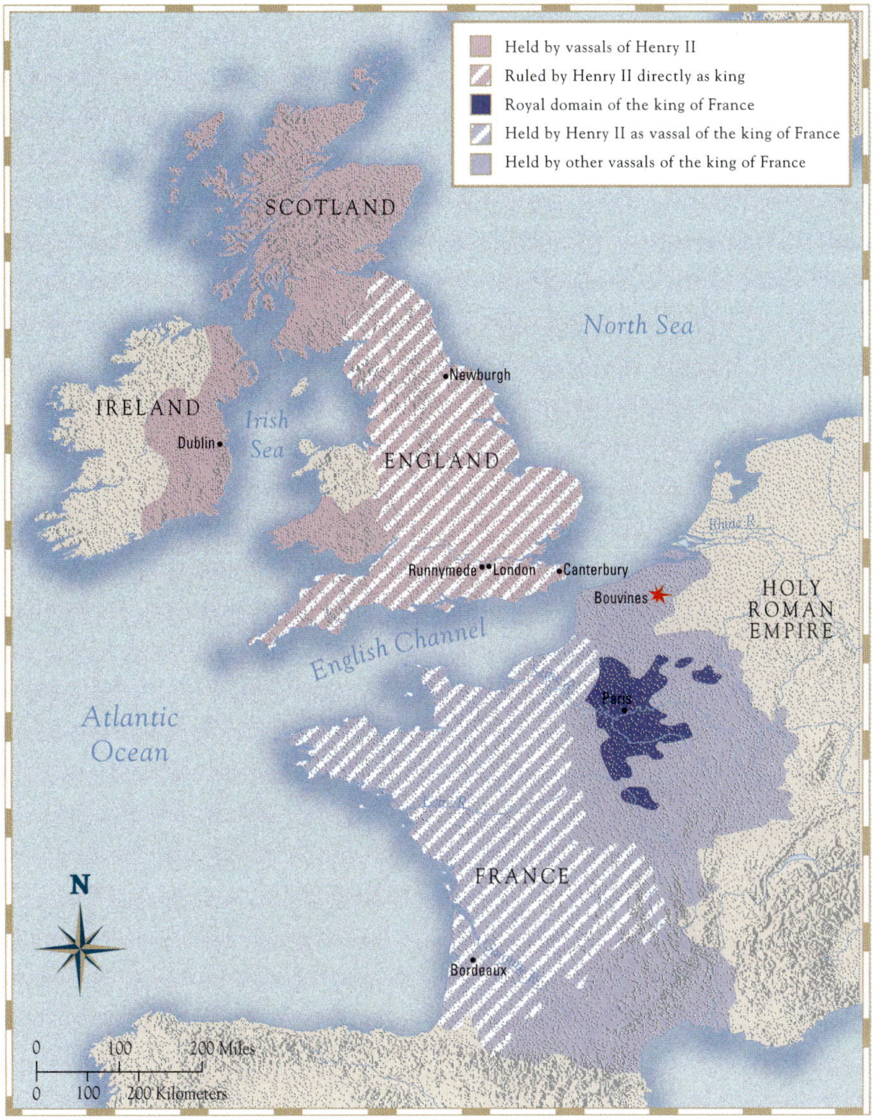

Map 7.2 England and France in the Age of Henry II

monastery of Saint-Denis. Suger was responsible for instituting enlightened economic policies in the royal domain, where he established villages, colonized forests, and supported the growth of towns.

Louis the Fat's success in laying the foundations of royal authority increased the status of the dynasty but his son, Louis VII (1137–1180), was less skillful. It was Suger who arranged for Louis VII to marry Eleanor, the daughter of the duke of Aquitaine and heiress to her father's large holdings, which would have doubled the size of the royal domain. But the hapless Louis and the brilliant Eleanor were ill-matched and when Eleanor failed to produce a son for the king, Louis had the marriage annulled. Two months later, in 1152, Eleanor married Henry II of England. The loss of Aquitaine, which now became an English possession, was a crucial blow to Capetian ambitions and Philip, Louis' son by a second marriage, was determined to regain the lost province.

GERMAN KINGS AND THE LURE OF EMPIRE: FROM OTTO I TO FREDERICK BARBAROSSA

The same pattern of the usurpation of royal authority by ambitious nobles that characterized France was repeated in Germany, the land of the East Franks. On the demise of the last of Charlemagne's successors in 911, the dukes of Bavaria, Saxony, Swabia, and other important states elected as their king Conrad of Franconia, the weakest of their fellow nobles. Conrad ruled only eight years and before his death endorsed the election of Henry the Fowler, duke of Saxony, who took the throne as Henry I (ruled 919–936). Henry proved to be an effective military leader who fought off incursions by the Danes in the north and the Slavs to the east, but he was otherwise unable to build a strong royal government.

Otto the Great and Imperial Authority

Henry's successor, Otto I (ruled 936–973), was the greatest of the Saxon kings. He expanded royal authority by appointing loyal counts to supervise his domains and maneuvering relatives and associates into positions of power in the other duchies. Otto also forged a close alliance with the church, and, as in France, church officials served as royal advisers and administrators. Otto regularly appointed bishops and abbots to their posts and received from their estates monetary gifts and even soldiers. The king's insistence on his right to nominate the high prelates of Germany contained the seeds of future discord.

Otto's prestige grew with his defeat of the pagan Magyars at the Battle of Lechfeld (955), ending the threat they had posed to the West. By the end of the 10th century, they had converted to Christianity. To secure Germany's eastern frontiers, he established military provinces along the eastern borders and supported

Map 7.3 Germany and Central Europe, 12th Century

The crown of Otto I, made for his coronation as Holy Roman emperor.

the Christianization of the Slavs. Otto's ambitions extended beyond his role as German king, for he saw himself in the tradition of the Romans and the Carolingians as the emperor of the West. He already claimed for himself the provinces of Burgundy and Lorraine on the southeastern border of France and Lombardy in northern Italy, all of which had once been part of the middle kingdom ruled by Lothair, Charlemagne's grandson and one of the last Carolingians to hold the title of emperor. In 951, Otto led his army across the Alps in order to preempt a German noble with designs on northern Italy. By making himself king of Italy, Otto established a link between Germany and Italy that would be a distinguishing feature of Medieval politics. Eleven years later, during a second expedition to Italy to protect the papacy, the pope rewarded Otto by crowning him emperor. While he had not added any real powers to his position, Otto had become the most prestigious figure in the West since Charlemagne. At his death, Otto's empire—soon to be known as the Holy Roman Empire—was the largest and most powerful in Europe, and he himself was known as Otto the Great. So powerful had the lure of empire become that one of Otto's successors, Otto III (ruled 983–1002), actually moved his capital to Rome and called himself "emperor of the Romans," although the local population eventually turned against him.

With the death of the last Saxon king in 1024, the Salian dynasty assumed control of German affairs for the next century. The Salian kings continued to follow with varying degrees of success the goal of strengthening the powers of the monarchy in Germany against the feudal lords, while pursuing the Italian policy begun by Otto I. But serious obstacles stood in the way of the royal ambitions and no effective centralized monarchy emerged in Germany as it did in England and France. Most significant was the power of the great German nobles, known as the *electors*, to control the selection of the kings. When in time it became customary for the German kings to seek the imperial title, matters were further complicated because the popes claimed the exclusive right to designate the emperors. The experience of Henry IV (ruled 1056–1106) demonstrated the burdens under which the German kings labored. When Henry attempted to appoint church officials as his predecessors had done, a reformed papacy under Pope Gregory VII opposed him. The German nobles seized the occasion of this "Investiture Controversy" to rebel against royal power and Henry was forced to submit to the pope in a humiliating act of penitence (see Part III, Topic 8).

Italy and the Imperial Dream

In the wake of the Investiture Controversy, which had weakened the prestige of the monarchy, many German nobles began to side with the popes in their struggles against the imperial aspirations of the German kings. Moreover, the unstable conditions prevailing in Italy made the military adventures of the German emperors still more dangerous. In the north of Italy, the city-states that had become wealthy with the revived Mediterranean trade jealously guarded their independence against the encroachments of the German rulers by siding with the papacy. In central Italy, the popes ruled the Papal States as absolute monarchs from their capital at Rome, often playing one city-state off against another.

In the south, where the Byzantines and the Muslims had posed a constant threat to the papacy, a new civilization was taking form. In the 11th century, armies of Norman knights under the sons of Tancred de Hauteville invaded southern Italy, fighting the Byzantines, the Muslims, and the popes. In 1059, Pope Nicholas II invested one of Tancred's sons, Robert Guiscard, with the duchies of Calabria and Apulia, while his brother Roger undertook the conquest of Sicily from the Muslims. Robert's death in 1085 left the Norman possessions in Roger's hands, and in 1130 his son, Roger II (ruled 1130–1154), established the Kingdom of Sicily, which included the island as well as the Norman possessions on the mainland. Roger II also conquered most of the North African coast from Tunis to Tripoli. The Norman kingdom was administered

The imperial court at Palermo kept its records in a variety of languages, including Latin, Greek, and Arabic, that reflected the multifaceted nature of its civilization.

through a strong central government and fused the Muslim, Christian, Norman, and even Jewish influences into a brilliant civilization in which the arts and sciences flourished (see Part III, Topic 4).

No German king was more caught up in the imperial dream and in the desire to extend the empire into Italy than Frederick I (ruled 1152–1190) of the Hohenstaufen family of Swabia. Frederick became king of Germany in 1152, while Roger II still ruled Sicily. Known to the Italians as Barbarossa, or Redbeard, Frederick was a big, handsome man of courage and ambition. Determined to impose his authority over the German nobles, he used diplomacy, military force, and religion to forge the first effective feudal monarchy in Germany. His constant need for financial resources made him turn to Italy, where he hoped to secure revenue by taxing the prosperous cities of the North. Unlike previous kings, who saw Germany as the center of the realm, Frederick focused his attention on Italy, demanding from the German princes only that they acknowledge his overlordship.

Frederick's Italian campaign centered in Lombardy but papal opposition made his efforts difficult and costly. The pope encouraged the Lombard communes to organize themselves into a defensive alliance known as the Lombard League, which defeated Frederick's forces at the Battle of Legnano in 1176. Through the Peace of Constance (1183), Frederick reached a compromise with the Lombard cities: in return for recognizing Frederick's supreme authority and his control over the Italian countryside, he acknowledged the right of the towns to full control over their internal affairs. Eventually he extracted from the cities an annual payment that gave him the financial resources he had wanted. The coming of peace, after more than two decades of fighting, allowed Frederick to return to Germany, where he subdued one of his most recalcitrant vassals, his cousin Henry the Lion, duke of Saxony. Henry, who had refused to come to Frederick's assistance during the Lombard war, was now condemned by an imperial court and his lands confiscated. Frederick emerged as the most powerful ruler in Germany since Charlemagne. The emperor died in Asia Minor in 1190 while on the Third Crusade, but before his death he had cemented the connection between Hohenstaufen ambitions and Italy by marrying his son, Henry VI (ruled 1191–1197), to Constance, the daughter and heiress of Roger II of Sicily. In the next century, Frederick's grandson and namesake, Frederick II, would revive the imperial dream.

THE RECONQUISTA AND THE KINGDOMS OF MEDIEVAL SPAIN

Islamic civilization in Europe had centered in Spain, where the Muslims had established a flourishing economy and culture since the 8th century. Islamic architects erected brilliant monuments such as the mosque at Cordova, one of the largest cities in Europe, while Islamic scholars advanced knowledge and Islamic tolerance also enabled Jewish communities in Spain to prosper (see Part III, Topic 4).

The Great Mosque of Cordova in Spain was built by Abd al-Rahman, who founded the Umayyad Dynasty.

The Christian Offensive

Islamic control began to weaken in the late 10th century as disunity among the Muslims enabled a series of minor Christian states such as Aragon, Castile, León, and Navarre to emerge in northern Spain. By 1100, the Christians, fired by fanatical religious zeal and a growing sense of patriotism, had reconquered most of Portugal and central Spain from the Atlantic to the Mediterranean. Popular enthusiasm for the Reconquista was focused in the late 11th century on the figure of Rodrigo Díaz de Vivar (d. 1099), popularly known as El Cid, a soldier of fortune whose exploits were the basis for the 12th-century epic *Song of the Cid* (see Part III, Topic 9). El Cid fought against the Muslims in Castile before being banished by the king, who distrusted his motives, and then fought for the Moors of Saragossa. In 1094 he conquered the kingdom of Valencia, which he ruled until his death. As the Christians pushed the Muslims farther south, they recruited settlers to occupy the reconquered territories. In 1212, a Christian army defeated a Muslim invasion from North Africa, and this victory was followed by the taking of Cordova and Seville. Only Granada was still in Muslim hands.

During the intervening centuries, the Christian rulers consolidated their hold over their kingdoms, which now included Portugal as well as Aragon and Castile. As the price for popular support of the reconquest, the kings had extended considerable autonomy and local rights to their subjects, whether Christian, Muslim, or Jewish. Many of the noble landowners held their properties outright, not as feudal fiefs, so that the kings were forced to recognize the necessity of ruling with the consent of the great nobles. By the late 12th century, the magnates were often represented in institutions known as *Cortes*, which exercised powerful influence in the kingdoms. Some of the kings followed the example of the English monarchs in attempting to extend their authority by codifying laws and

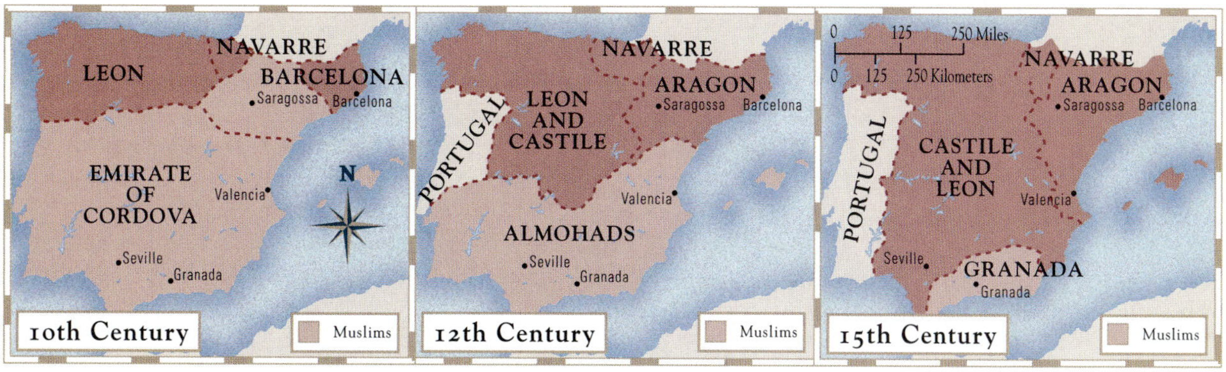

Map 7.4 The Reconquista

developing royal systems of justice. In Castile and León, for example, Alfonso X (ruled 1252–1284), known as "the Wise," issued the Siete Partidas legal code that established royal law as the principal source of justice. Alfonso, whose wife Beatriz was a Swabian princess, vainly sought to become Holy Roman emperor. By the following century, Spanish rulers were extending their sway into the Mediterranean, where they seized the Balearic Islands and Sicily and for a time even occupied Athens. The completion of the reconquest and the unification of the Spanish monarchy into a single state would have to wait until the 15th century, when Spain emerged as one of the most powerful states in Europe.

By the 13th century, an entirely new political configuration had emerged in Europe as the decentralized feudal system was replaced by a series of fledgling monarchies. These new states, although still in their infancy, had established efficient royal administrations which increasingly centralized authority, especially through the extension of royal law. In England, the Normans had led the way in using the principles of feudalism to forge an effective monarchy, while in France the Capetian kings took longer to subdue the feudal nobles by slowly building and extending the royal domain. In Germany, the lure of imperial power both added to the prestige and moral authority of the kings and sapped their resources as they sought to extend their control into Italy. The Spanish kings, faced with a powerful noble opposition, used the moral fervor of the Christian reconquest to strengthen their position. Everywhere, the overall pattern of growing royal authority was similar, and over the following centuries the centralizing efforts of the kings would triumph over the feudal lords.

Questions for Further Study

1. In what ways did feudal kings strengthen their power over the nobility?
2. What does the relationship between Matilda and William tell us about relations between aristocratic men and women in feudal society?
3. What special political conditions existed in feudal Germany that made it different from France and England?

Suggestions for Further Reading

Barlow, Frank. *The Feudal Kingdom of England, 1042–1216*, 3rd ed. New York, 1972.

Brooke, Christopher N. L. *Europe in the Central Middle Ages, 962–1154*, rev. ed. New York, 1988.

Douglas, David C. *William the Conqueror: The Norman Impact upon England*. Berkeley, CA, 1964.

Dunbabin, J. *France in the Making, 843–1180*. Oxford, 1985.

Fuhrmann, Helmut. *Germany in the High Middle Ages, 1050–1250*. Cambridge, MA, 1986.

Hallam, Elizabeth M. *Capetian France, 987–1328*. London, 1980.

III

Topic 8

The Militant Church: Reform and the Papacy

By the 10th century, the Catholic Church and the papacy were both in deep crisis. The problems of the church were largely the result of its involvement in the feudal system and deteriorating political conditions in the Italian peninsula. A major problem was the fact that in the 11th century the Eastern Christian Church broke away from the authority of Rome.

Nevertheless, the church also demonstrated a remarkable capacity for reform and spiritual renewal, especially during the period from the 11th to the 13th century. Reform began on the local level, through the establishment of a number of new monastic orders, especially the Cluniac and the Cistercian orders. From the monastic movement, the reforming impulse spread to the papacy itself in the 11th century under the leadership first of Pope Leo IX and then of Gregory VII. It was under Gregory that the Investiture Controversy with the German emperors culminated in the submission of Henry IV to papal authority at Canossa. The renewed vigor of the church and the spiritual influence of Christianity in secular society were reflected in the militant expansion of Western Christendom as in 1095 the first of a series of Crusades was launched against the Muslims. During the reign of Pope Innocent III in the early 13th century, the papacy successfully asserted its supremacy not only in ecclesiastical matters, but in secular affairs as well. Along with the highly efficient papal administration that evolved with canon law, new religious orders of mendicant friars were formed that brought a fresh measure of spiritual devotion and proselytizing fervor to Medieval civilization.

REFORM AND RENEWAL IN THE CHURCH

The principal cause of the breakdown of discipline within the church in the 9th and 10th centuries was that the land tenure system of feudalism tied religious leaders closely to feudal politics. One result of this was that the clergy came increasingly under lay influence. High ecclesiastical officials, especially bishops and abbots, controlled huge estates that were held as fiefs, thereby making them vassals of secular nobles and kings, who wanted to control the selection and appointment of these important prelates. Bishops and abbots chosen in this manner, generally from noble families, often had little concern for the spiritual well-being of the church or its members. The sale of church offices—the practice known as simony—and the growing number of married priests were signs of the decline in ecclesiastical discipline. Meanwhile, papal leadership was generally lacking in the early Middle Ages as a result of the chaotic political situation in

Italy, where the papacy was often the prize over which the local nobility fought and its lands the target of Byzantine and Muslim forces occupying much of southern Italy.

The Reforming Impulse

The first serious move toward reform came in 910, when Duke William of Aquitaine established the abbey of Cluny in the Burgundy region of France. In the charter granted to the monastery William insisted that the order be entirely independent in running its own affairs and in electing its officials. The monks of Cluny strictly observed the Benedictine rule, which had fallen into widespread disuse. The order also adopted the principle of centralization whereby each branch monastery that was started—and eventually there were more than 1000, spread from Western Europe to Palestine—was headed by a prior who remained under the authority of the abbot at Cluny itself. This tendency was encouraged by a provision in the Cluny charter that any layperson who interfered with the election of the abbot would be excommunicated, a safeguard that prompted other monastic houses to ask to become dependencies of Cluny.

The centralized organization enabled the order to resist the temptations of secular interference on a local level that the feudal system embodied. The abbot of Cluny regularly visited dependent monasteries to ensure spiritual ideals and adherence to the reforming principles of Cluny: the elimination of secular influence and abuses such as simony, the practice of clerical celibacy, and obedience to the supremacy of the pope, who assumed direct authority over the order. Inside the monasteries, monks rededicated themselves to the work ethic and to the spirit of community participation in religious worship.

By the following century, the spirit of reform began to affect both the imperial office and, by extension, the papacy. In 1046, the Emperor Henry III (ruled 1039–1056) faced an embarrassing situation in which three men each claimed to be the legitimate pope. Henry responded by deposing all three rivals and appointing a new pope, Leo IX (ruled 1049–1054). Leo, the last pope to be appointed by an emperor, was dedicated to the reforming ideal and began a series of institutional changes designed to free the church of secular interference. Leo sent papal legates throughout Christendom to inspect and reform local conditions and frequently summoned corrupt bishops to Rome for disciplining. He also relied increasingly on "cardinals," an honorary title he granted to priests and bishops committed to reform, to act as papal administrators. In 1059, a church council issued a decree stipulating that only the cardinals of Rome, who formed the College of Cardinals, had the power to elect popes, a tradition that continues to be followed in modified form to this day. This practice virtually eliminated the interference of aristocratic Roman families in the selection of the popes. Moreover, since the pope selected the cardinals, the church became something of a closed society. Other reforms, including insistence on clerical celibacy and the prohibition of simony, eventually followed.

The Investiture Controversy between Emperor Henry IV and Pope Gregory VII is depicted here in a series of scenes showing (top) Henry replacing Gregory with Bishop Guibert and (bottom) the mourning of Gregory as he lies dead in exile.

THE INVESTITURE CONTROVERSY

The most vigorous of the reforming popes was Gregory VII (ruled 1073–1085), a monk of peasant origin named Hildebrand whom Leo had brought to Rome. Gregory was a true ascetic and a zealous reformer who insisted on the absolute authority of the pope within the church and the spiritual supremacy of the pope over secular rulers, including kings and emperors. While humble in manner, Gregory did not shrink from taking bold action when he believed it was necessary for the welfare of the church.

The Road to Canossa

Gregory furthered the centralization of papal authority, using cardinals armed with full papal authority as legates to impose discipline, and making wide use of ecclesiastical councils, known as synods, to reform institutions and practices. In Rome, a curia, or papal court, was established and a system of canon law elaborated. Most challenging of all, Gregory decided to eliminate the most important cause of corruption, lay investiture. As with many of his predecessors, Henry had continued the practice of investing bishops with the ring and staff, symbols of their spiritual authority, as well as with their fiefs. Gregory's policy now meant direct confrontation with the emperor, who had always insisted on the imperial right to control the church but was uninterested in church reform (see Part III, Topic 7).

The confrontation came to a head in 1075, when a synod held in Rome issued the first direct decree pro-

Henry IV pleads with Abbot Hugh of Cluny and Countess Matilda of Tuscany at Canossa so that they might intercede with Pope Gregory VII.

hibiting lay investiture, a measure that Henry disregarded. Gregory then directly challenged Henry by threatening to excommunicate him (in which case he would be unable to receive the sacraments and would in theory be unable to associate with any good Christians) and depose him as emperor. Henry countered by convening a council of loyal German bishops who voted in turn to depose the pope. In response to such blatant defiance of papal authority, Gregory excommunicated Henry—the first time an emperor had ever been placed under the ban of the church—and declared him deposed. All German bishops who refused to submit to the papal order were also excommunicated. The pope then followed this action by declaring that all of the emperor's subjects were free of their oaths of fealty to him. This action, as expected, resulted in many German nobles using the excommunication as an excuse to rebel against the imperial authority. After meeting with the legates in Germany, the nobles demanded that Henry obtain papal absolution in order to regain their loyalty, and invited Gregory to Germany to hold a synod that would discuss Henry's case.

Henry, realizing that his authority could not survive attack from both his nobles and the papacy, decided to resolve the issue before Gregory could convene the proposed synod. In January 1077, the emperor

Map 8.1 The Investiture Controversy: Germany and Italy

crossed the Alps with a small group of followers and determined to meet Gregory at Canossa, where the pope had stopped en route to Germany. There Henry shrewdly asked Gregory for forgiveness. Although Gregory suspected Henry's motives were political rather than spiritual, he could not as a priest refuse the pleas of a penitent sinner for absolution. This maneuver gave rise to one of the most famous legends of the High Middle Ages: that Henry, barefoot and wearing peasant garb, had stood in the snows before the castle for three days, begging for papal forgiveness.

Henry's supposed act of humiliation was seen as evidence of the supreme authority of the church over secular rulers. The truth is more complex. Henry had successfully restored his position, depriving his unruly nobles of their justification for rebellion. On the other hand, in the long run the emperors may have lost more than they achieved, for imperial prestige was never the same again, and this weakness paved the way for a long period of German decline and disunity.

The Concordat of Worms

Gregory was correct in doubting Henry's motives, for the emperor soon returned to his former habits and in 1080 the pope once again excommunicated him. This time Henry was determined not to give in. He arranged to have an anti-pope elected in Gregory's place and invaded Italy in 1081, occupying Rome itself and besieging Gregory in the Castel Sant' Angelo. Gregory called upon his Norman vassals in southern Italy for assistance, but was forced to flee Rome and died in Salerno in 1085, depressed and broken. Although these events damaged papal prestige, the status of the papacy would be renewed when Gregory's successor, Urban II, launched the First Crusade (see below).

The Investiture Controversy was finally resolved in 1122, when Pope Calixtus II and Emperor Henry V concluded the Concordat of Worms. By this agreement, the emperor was allowed to invest a new bishop only with the temporal symbols of his rule, whereas he could no longer bestow the ring and staff, which symbolized spiritual authority. Election of bishops was to be held by church officials but in the presence of the emperor, who could resolve the election in the event of a tie. The compromise did not grant a full victory to either side but it ensured that thenceforth bishops would have to be acceptable to both church and state. Moreover, although the concordat did not eliminate imperial interference in ecclesiastical matters, it did effectively end the practice of lay investiture.

The reform impulse continued apace in the 12th century as new monastic orders were founded. The most significant effort was the establishment of the Cistercians (named after their first monastery, located at Citeaux in Burgundy) in 1098. The purpose of the Cistercian order was to restore the vigor and purity of the Benedictine and Cluniac monasteries, in which discipline had lapsed. The Cistercians adopted an organizational principle that was more hierarchical than the original Benedictine system but less centralized than the Cluniac order: each monastery was ruled independently by its own abbot but every year a meeting of all the abbots was held to ensure uniformity of discipline and procedures.

St. Bernard of Clairvaux, a 12th-century Cistercian monk who preached a more personal relationship between God and humans.

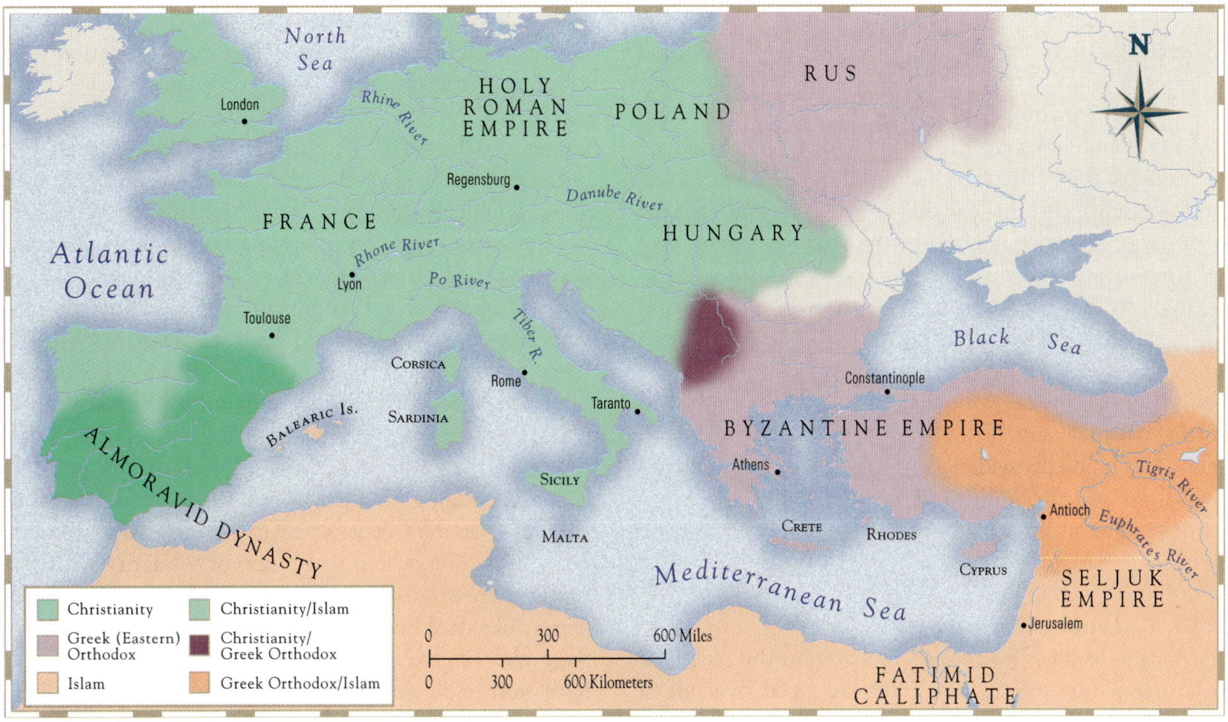

Map 8.2 Major European Religions, c. 1100

The Cistercians were fortunate in having as one of their abbots St. Bernard of Clairvaux (1090–1153), who combined ascetic spiritualism with a practical bent for action. Bernard insisted on a severe and disciplined life within the monasteries, which were generally located in isolated spots. The Cistercian orders cleared forests and contributed to the reclamation of unproductive land. Monks observed a strict regimen of manual labor, fasts, and worship, while the monastic buildings themselves were devoid of stained glass, statues, and other ornamentation. Bernard's preaching inspired thousands of pious Christians and launched a crusade against the Muslims. He advised temporal rulers on ecclesiastical affairs and supported the papacy against its secular enemies.

While monastic reform continued, the papacy strengthened and expanded the jurisdiction of ecclesiastical courts. Canon law now covered all matters involving religion, including disputes over marriage, wills, and heresies, and widows and orphans as well as clerics. A careful compilation of canon law was adopted in 1142 as binding on all church officials.

SCHISM AND THE DECLINE OF BYZANTIUM

The religious policies of the Byzantine Emperor Leo III, who had launched the iconoclastic campaign against the veneration of images by Christians (see Part III, Topic 3), had created tensions between the Eastern and the Western churches. Even though the use of images was eventually restored, the issue served to add another dimension to the divisions between Rome and Constantinople. Indeed, the popes had responded in part by sponsoring the Frankish kings and bestowing the imperial title on Charlemagne in 800.

Toward the Schism

The Eastern emperor was a sacred figure who fulfilled a religious as well as a secular mission. Although he was not a priest, the Eastern emperor exercised considerable influence over the church. This tradition was contrary to the experience in the West, where the popes and bishops had assumed political responsibilities as secular authority disintegrated. None of the ecclesiastical leaders in the Byzantine Empire, including the patriarch of Constantinople, ever developed the authority over the Eastern Church that the pope did over the church in the West. Differences did emerge in religious belief and practice, including the Eastern tradition of allowing married men to become priests and the Western belief in purgatory as a stage between heaven and hell. In liturgical matters, the Western Church insisted on Latin as the language of the church, whereas the Eastern Church permitted the use of vernacular languages, including Greek, Slavonic, and Coptic. The only major doctrinal dispute, however, had to do with the Trinity, for Eastern clerics believed that the Holy Spirit derived from the Father, not, as the Roman Church argued, from both the Father and the Son.

The growing chasm between the Eastern and Western churches came to a head in 1054, when Michael Cerularius, the patriarch of Constantinople, declared the independence of the Byzantine Church from Rome. Cerularius had been angered by the haughty behavior of a Roman cardinal who had come to Constantinople to extract concessions from the patriarch. But the notion of papal supremacy, together with papal support for the universal claims of the Western emperors, were the real causes of the break. Although the schism initially had little popular support, the separation of the two churches gradually widened and the Slavic populations of Russia and the Balkans eventually followed the authority and spiritual leadership of the Byzantine Church.

The Crisis of Byzantium

Byzantine leaders had refused to abandon the idea that there was only one true empire that ruled over all of Christendom. From the 9th to the end of the 11th centuries, the Byzantine emperors managed partially to restore the military position of the empire. They had waged campaigns against the Bulgars who had invaded the Balkans and against the Muslims in southern Italy. In the Middle East, they had recaptured Antioch in 969 and forced the Muslims to retreat into Syria. But as the old military system of *themes*, which supported an army of peasant soldiers, disintegrated in the 11th century, the number of imperial troops declined and the landed aristocracy increased their power. Mercenary armies were hired to make up for the shortage in soldiers. In the place of a once highly centralized imperial government, a feudal system evolved as a series of weak emperors began to give away imperial estates in order to ensure the loyalty of the nobles. Commercial concessions to Venice and other Italian cities led to a decline in badly needed revenues and weakened the economic position of Byzantium.

Military setbacks began to accumulate. During the course of the 11th century, the Normans under Robert Guiscard wrested Sicily and southern Italy from Muslim control. This loss was followed by the expansion of the Seljuk Turks, a nomadic people from Turkestan in Central Asia who invaded Persia, Syria, and Palestine. The Seljuks embraced the Sunni Muslim faith and eventually took over the Abbasid empire. In 1055 they seized Baghdad and in 1071 they defeated the Byzantines at the Battle of Manzikert and began to overrun Asia Minor. Sometime before 1095, a desperate Byzantine Emperor Alexius Comnenus I (ruled 1081–1118) appealed to Pope Urban II (ruled 1088–1099) for help.

The appeal was religious as well as political. One of the most popular forms of religious devotion had long been the practice of visiting shrines sacred to Christians, especially the sites that contained relics of Christ or the saints. The most important of such pilgrimages had been to the Holy Land, where the towns of Jerusalem, Nazareth, and Bethlehem had been particular goals. The Turkish conquests now threatened access to the holiest of Christian shrines.

Urban was a Frenchman and a Cluniac monk who saw the danger posed by the Turks to Western Christendom. In 1095, at the French town of Clermont, Urban preached a remarkable sermon in which he called upon Christians to take arms against the Turks. With the growth of religious zeal in the 11th century, the idea of waging a holy war against the Muslim "infidel"—as had been done in Spain—gained popularity. Urban appealed to a sense of solidarity with the Eastern Christians but also pictured the Holy Land as a region of untold riches. As an added inducement, the pope also offered a plenary indulgence—meaning the remission of all earthly punishment for sins—for those who died in the effort. Out of these circumstances developed the Crusades, military expeditions through which several generations of European leaders attempted to recapture the Holy Land from the Muslims.

Significant Dates

The Militant Church

910	Cluny monastery founded
1054	Schism between Roman and Eastern churches
1059	College of Cardinals begins to elect popes
1077	Henry IV and Gregory VII at Canossa
1096	First Crusade begins
1122	Concordat of Worms
1147	Second Crusade launched
1187	Saladin seizes Jerusalem
1189	Third Crusade begins
1198–1216	Innocent III reigns as pope
1204	Fourth Crusade sacks Constantinople
1212	Children's Crusade
1215	Fourth Lateran Council; Dominican order established
1182–1226	Life of Francis of Assisi

THE ERA OF THE CRUSADES

The Crusades had their origins partly in the reforms within the church, which strengthened the position of the papacy and began to infuse Medieval society with a renewed religious fervor. While the Crusades were a sign of the expanded authority of the church, they were also a sign of the expansion of economic and social life that accompanied the revival of trade and the growth of European cities. In the period from 1095 to 1248, seven official Crusades struck out toward the Middle East, and although in the end they failed to achieve their major objective, they had significant impact on the religious, economic, and political life of the High Middle Ages.

The First Crusade

Urban's appeal in 1095 received a zealous and unexpectedly broad response. He appointed a bishop to organize the expedition and proclaimed the church's protection for the families and property of volunteers. Women were forbidden to join without the permission of their husbands, but many nonprofessional fighters followed the leadership of two fanatical preachers, Peter the Hermit and Walter the Penniless. Both groups were wiped out by the Turks in Asia Minor. The first real soldiers, mostly French, left Western Europe in the summer of 1096 under the separate command of several feudal lords, one of whom was a son of Robert Guiscard and another a son of William the Conqueror. In all, they probably numbered less than 10,000 men, although some sources give larger numbers. When they reached Constantinople, trouble immediately arose, for while the Emperor Alexius had wanted assistance in recovering the Holy Lands, the French warriors were determined to keep for themselves whatever land they conquered. Although they eventually swore an oath of allegiance to the Byzantine emperor, the tensions between the Byzantines and the crusaders were never overcome. The crusading armies also were divided among themselves and often proved less effective as fighters because of their rivalries.

The crusaders fought their way successfully across Asia Minor and in 1098, having been reinforced with equipment and supplies by Italian shippers, they took the city of Antioch in Syria. The Italian merchants became indispensable to the crusaders and reaped huge profits for their assistance, eventually establishing important port facilities in the Middle East. In July 1099, the crusaders captured Jerusalem after a six-week siege and massacred most of the Muslim population of the city.

Having achieved the chief purpose of their expedition, many crusaders remained in the Middle East, where they created a group of four independent Christian states: Edessa, Antioch, Tripoli, and Jerusalem, the latter stretching south from Beirut to Egypt. Each of these states was ruled by a Western crusader in the

The Peasant's Crusade, led by Peter the Hermit, preceded the crusade of noble warriors in response to Pope Urban II's appeal.

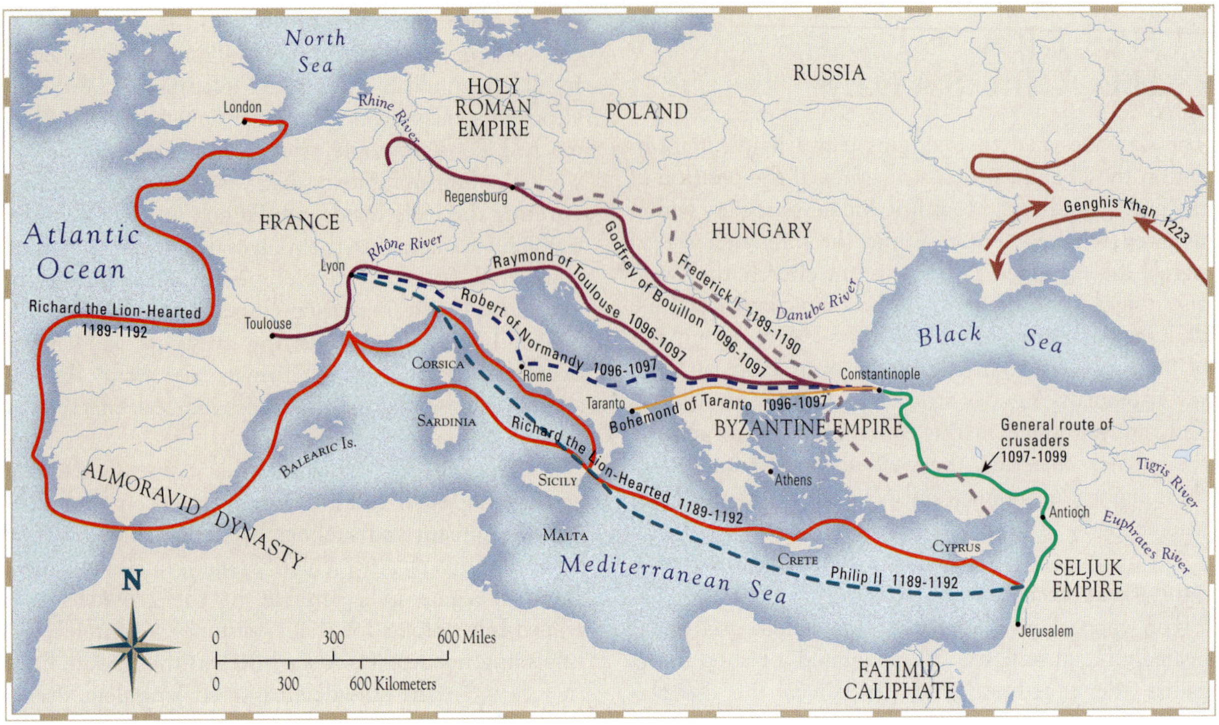

Map 8.3 The Crusader Routes

feudal manner, with vassals and fiefs. The landed estates were taken from their former Muslim owners and divided among the Christian knights, although in other respects Muslims were tolerated and were permitted to carry on business activities in the cities. Although the Christian states were surrounded by Muslim and Turkish territory, they survived for almost 200 years.

The Roman Church quickly reestablished jurisdiction over the hierarchy in the Holy Land and exercised authority principally through the patriarchs of Antioch and Jerusalem. Most of the Western monastic orders established houses in the crusader kingdoms, and a new kind of religious organization made its appearance in the form of orders of military monks. The two most famous and powerful, both headquartered in Jerusalem, were the Knights of the Temple, known as the Templars, and the Knights of St. John of Jerusalem, known as the Hospitalers. Their members were devoted to protecting pilgrims and providing care for the sick, but were also dedicated to keeping up a holy war against the infidel. They eventually received papal recognition and through repeated bequests became the owners of extensive estates in the Middle East as well as in Europe.

The Crusdes and the Decline of Byzantium

The Second Crusade began as a result of the efforts by the Turks to recapture the Holy Land. In 1144, when news arrived in the West that the Turks had taken back Edessa, the northernmost of the Latin kingdoms, St. Bernard of Clairvaux persuaded King Louis VII of France and Emperor Conrad III of Germany to lead another campaign against them. After two years of futile effort (1147–1149), however, their inability to cooperate either with each other or with the Byzantine generals led them to defeat.

The Third Crusade came after a lull of 40 years. Between 1169 and 1187, the Muslim leader Saladin (1137?–1193), a warrior of Kurdish descent, swept across Syria and Egypt, surrounding the Kingdom of Jerusalem on two sides. In 1187, Saladin took Jerusalem. Saladin was an enlightened ruler who rebuilt cities, restored agriculture, and exhibited tolerance toward the Christians he conquered, but his victory sent shock waves through Europe. In response, in 1189 Frederick Barbarossa of Germany, Philip II Augustus of France, and Richard I (the Lion-Hearted) of England all personally led armies toward Palestine after raising money through a tax known as the "Saladin tithe." But disaster also overtook this effort. After moving overland through Asia Minor, Frederick died of a drowning accident. The French and English, who had traveled by sea, encountered repeated defeats once they began fighting on land. After Philip returned to France in frustration, Richard and Saladin, each of whom respected the other's bravery and chivalry, negotiated an agreement that gave free access to Christians wanting to visit Jerusalem.

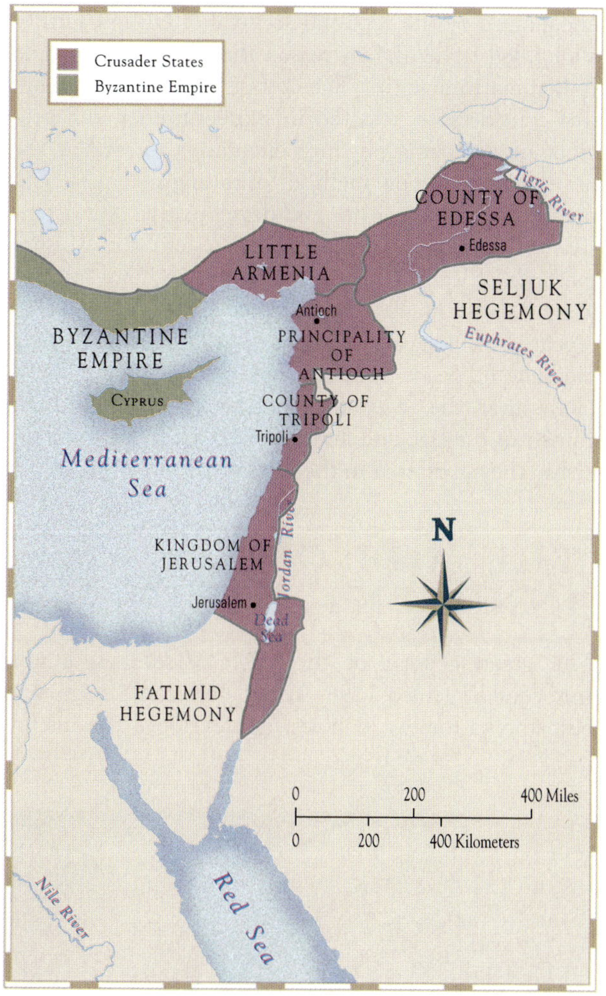

Map 8.4 The Crusader States

If the Second and Third crusades were military failures, the Fourth Crusade (1202–1204) proved to be a failure in quite another way. After Saladin's death in 1193 and the collapse of his empire, Pope Innocent III encouraged Christian leaders to launch still another attack against the Muslims. But in order to pay for their transportation to the Holy Land, the nobles who answered Innocent's call were induced by the Venetian shippers to seize Zara, a Christian port city on the Dalmatian coast across from Italy. This gave Venice complete control of Adriatic commerce but put into doubt the real motivations of the crusaders.

Then, as if to confirm their real reason for their campaign, in 1204 events diverted the crusaders to Constantinople, where a struggle for the succession to the Byzantine throne was under way. One of the claimants had promised the knights a large payment for their help, but when the agreed amount was not forthcoming, the crusaders sacked the Byzantine capital, stealing precious metals and holy relics. While the Venetians imposed a trade monopoly on the eastern Mediterranean, the Latin nobles divided the empire into small states, the principal one being the Latin Empire of Constantinople ruled by a Flemish noble. Pope Innocent, who mildly condemned the attack on Constantinople, attempted to force the reunification of the Eastern and Western churches and appointed a Venetian patriarch to Constantinople.

One of the most intriguing episodes of the era of the Crusades was the so-called Children's Crusade of 1212. Led by a visionary French boy, Stephen of Cloyes, and fired by a belief that the innocence of children

Christian forces fight with Saladin's army at Hattin in 1187. The Christians were defeated in the battle depicted here in a 13th-century illustration.

could achieve what corrupt adults could not, the children embarked at Marseilles but were sold into slavery by unscrupulous ship captains. A group of German children who set out overland made it to Italy before perishing of hunger and disease. However irrational or impractical the Children's Crusade may seem to modern minds, the phenomenon suggests the range of experiences characteristic of Medieval Christian faith.

In the face of constant fighting among themselves, the Latin states in Asia Minor did not survive very long. In 1261, the Byzantine leader Michael VIII Paleologus reconquered Constantinople and Innocent's efforts to reunite the two churches collapsed. Michael's dynasty ruled for another two centuries but the Byzantine Empire had been shattered beyond repair. Moreover, the Fourth Crusade had so embittered relations between East and West that no unity of Christian forces was again possible.

During the 13th century three other Crusades struck out from Europe toward the Middle East. Despite temporary achievements, none resulted in permanent Christian victories. Yet in other ways the impact of the Crusades was considerable. The Crusades, themselves encouraged by the economic revival of Europe, further stimulated trade and increased the prosperity of some Italian maritime cities. The cost of the Crusades, which was considerable, resulted in more currency and precious metals being put into circulation as well as the development of new methods of raising revenues. The need to construct castles and develop siege and defensive techniques influenced both Western and Muslim methods of warfare. The departure of so many warrior knights, who might otherwise have been involved in repeated conflicts at home, may have helped to bring a measure of peace to European society. Finally, it is likely that the Western kings and the popes both gained in prestige and authority as a result of the leadership they exhibited in the Crusades.

THE AGE OF INNOCENT III

The greatest pope of the High Middle Ages was Innocent III (ruled 1198–1216). Innocent's reign was best known for two policies: he developed the instru-

Innocent III in a fresco that shows the powerful pope as a young man.

ments of papal government to their fullest extent, and insisted on the supremacy of the papacy not only within the church but over secular rulers as well.

The Papal Government

Gregory VII and most of the other reforming popes had been priests who came out of the monastic tradition. Innocent and the other popes of the 13th century, on the other hand, were canon lawyers and professional administrators who viewed the church as a secular as well as a spiritual institution. Innocent, who was 38 when he succeeded to the papal throne, was an energetic and ambitious ruler. Although the papal conflicts with secular rulers absorbed much public attention, most of the time and energy of popes like Innocent was devoted to the day-to-day routine of building what was rapidly becoming a highly complex and efficient bureaucracy. The papal *curia*, or court, was staffed by a host of highly trained men. At the top of the hierarchy were the cardinals, whose official number varied from 52 to 70 and almost all of whom lived in and around Rome. The cardinals acted as advisers and heads of important administrative departments. When they met as a full body, known as a *consistory*, they decided important matters, but the routine business of papal government was carried out by the curia. In the age of Innocent III, two departments were paramount in the curia, the *chancery* and the *camera*. The chancery drafted, sent, and received papal correspondence and the more formal bulls. The camera acted as the papal treasury, which was kept busy collecting taxes and other rents and fees from the estates controlled by the church. The curia also functioned as the supreme court of appeal for all matters concerning canon law. Under Innocent, the papal bureaucracy became the best organized institution in the West.

When the pope wanted to deal with important doctrinal or policy issues for the church, he often called special church councils of high prelates. The earlier Third Lateran Council of 1179 was followed by the Fourth Lateran Council in 1215, a gathering of more than 1200 bishops and abbots which issued important decisions that helped to improve standards of priestly behavior. The latter council also concerned itself with clarifying matters of dogma, especially the question of "transubstantiation," the belief that the bread and wine of the Eucharist were changed into the body and blood of Christ. The council declared that although the outer appearance of the bread and wine remained the same, the inner reality of them was transformed.

Papal Supremacy and Church-State Relations

As canon law developed, the authority of the pope in ecclesiastical affairs was defined and broadened. Innocent III was fond of describing the pope as the "vicar of Christ," a divinely sanctioned role derived as the successor of St. Peter. In this capacity, however, Innocent believed that the notion of papal authority included supremacy over temporal rulers. "The Lord Jesus Christ," wrote Innocent, "has set up one ruler over all things as His universal vicar," and some of the most powerful princes of the age were forced to bow to his will. For example, between 1205 and 1213 Innocent fought a particularly relentless campaign against King John of England (see Part III, Topic 10). The dispute arose when Innocent intervened in a contested election for a new archbishop of Canterbury, appointing Stephen Langton as his own candidate. John, who maintained it was his own right to nominate English bishops, refused to recognize Langton. The pope responded by excommunicating John and placing England under an interdict, which banned all public worship in the kingdom and prohibited all sacraments except baptism and extreme unction. When Innocent learned that the barons were plotting against John, he announced that the king had been deposed and released all his subjects from their loyalty to him. As in the case of Henry IV and Pope Gregory VII, John now saw the wisdom of submitting to papal authority. In 1213, John accepted Langton's appointment and, in a move designed to secure papal support in his struggle with the barons, acknowledged his kingdom to be a papal fief.

Innocent secured similar recognition from the rulers of Portugal and the kingdom of Aragon, and applied papal sanctions against King Philip II Augustus of France, who had arranged to have his marriage to Ingeborg of Denmark annulled immediately after receipt of her 10,000-mark dowry. Innocent demanded that Philip take Ingeborg back as his legitimate wife and placed France under an interdict, although the king bowed to papal will only after many years. The pope also intervened in German affairs. After the death of King Henry VI, the German nobles quarreled over a successor. Henry's son, Frederick, was only three at the time but the boy's mother, acting as regent, made Frederick's royal inheritance in Sicily a fief of the papacy. When his mother died in 1198, Frederick automatically became the pope's ward (see Part III, Topic 10 for details of Frederick's reign). While Innocent's policy toward secular rulers was controversial, he did substantially enhance the power of the papacy.

Heresy and the Inquisition

Beginning in the 11th century, the West was increasingly troubled by the appearance of heresies, which may be simply defined as doctrinal beliefs that differed from those officially accepted by the church. The roots of heresy are varied. No doubt many followers of heresies were disturbed by the decline in moral standards

PERSPECTIVES ON HISTORY

Francis of Assisi

Lawrence S. Cunningham
University of Notre Dame

The fact that one can find cast concrete statues of Francis of Assisi with a bird perched on his shoulder in almost every American suburban garden center is testimony to the persistent fame of this son of a 12th-century Umbrian cloth merchant who went on to become one of the most celebrated saints in the Christian church.

In many ways Francis was a revolutionary, although he did not think of himself as one. In a rare autobiographical moment he described himself as "unlettered and subject to every one." He was also a child of his own time in that there were others who wanted to live a poor life as a quiet protest against the wealth of the Medieval church or to be itinerant preachers to serve the swelling urban populations of the day. It was given to Francis, however, to crystallize these impulses and, in the process, to become so famous that he was immortalized less than a century after his death in Dante's *Paradiso* as the exemplar of the Christian gospel.

Francis taught a way of life that was an alternative to the monasteries which had been so crucial in earlier times. He did not want his followers to live in rural settings in a stable environment of prayer and work. He wanted his friars (the word means "brothers") to move from place to place, working with their hands or begging like the other poor when there was no work, while preaching in the city squares. In the wonderful aphorism of the English writer Gilbert Keith Chesterton, "What Benedict [i.e., the founder of Western monasticism] stored, Francis scattered."

This was a contagious idea. Francis began with a handful of followers but before 1220 there were nearly 3000 "little brothers" who were spread all over western Europe and into North Africa. His friendship with Clare Offreduccio (1193–1253) resulted in a "second order" of women who lived a life of poverty in a stable community. This growth inevitably led to a certain institutionalization of his simple ideals but the plain fact is that his friars were active in every major European city before Francis' death in 1226.

Francis emphasized in his life and preaching a fundamental belief in the capacity of the natural world to teach people about the presence of God. He was not a pantheist or, in the modern sense of the term, a "nature lover." He did very much believe and teach in the natural world as a visible sign of the reality of God. Toward the end of his life he wrote a poem called the "Canticle of the Creatures"—it was one of the very first poems written in Italian—expressing this idea. Here is a sample from that poem:

Praised be You, My Lord, for Brother Fire
Through whom You light the night
He is beautiful and playful, robust and strong.
Praised be You, My Lord, for our sister Mother Earth,
Who sustains and governs us,
Who produces varied fruits, colored flowers and herbs. . . .

Some scholars, as early as the last century, have argued that this Franciscan emphasis on love for the natural world and respect for animal life (stories tell of Francis preaching to the birds and taming a wild wolf) had a profound impact on the European artistic imagination of the 14th century and may have influenced the Renaissance turn to the natural world in the visual arts. To say it another way, the shift away from the rather "otherworldly" air of Italian and Byzantine painting to a more naturalistic setting may have been hastened by the Franciscan concern for seeing the divine in the natural world.

Francis introduced a new kind of spirituality into Western Christian religiousness. He had a deep conviction that it was possible in life to imitate Christ in a literal and fundamental fashion. Francis sold his possessions and lived without material goods because Jesus had said in the gospels that this was the perfect way to follow Him. He attempted *literally* to give away everything to the poor. In 1223 he decided to observe Christmas in the town of Greccio in a stable in order to experience the poverty into which Jesus was born. From that event derived the later custom of building a Christmas crèche as a sign of the Christmas season. Francis found the supreme expression of poverty in the passion of Christ on the cross. It is that link between poverty and the cross which most impressed Dante when he speaks of the saint in Canto XI of the *Paradiso*.

Francis' deep meditation on the Passion of Christ in the fall of 1224 triggered a phenomenon called the *stigmata*, i.e. Francis showed signs of the wounds of Christ on his own hands, feet, and side. As far as we know, this was the first time that this phenomenon had been reported in the history of Christianity.

One result of the stigmata was, especially after the death of Francis, an intensified emphasis on the human sufferings of Christ which showed up in everything from more realistic depictions of Christ's wounds in art to new forms of religious devotion which focused on the cross or the crown of thorns or other such incidents in the Passion narratives.

While Francis always remained a popular saint within the Catholic tradition, he faded from popular view after the Reformation in Protestant Christianity and was severely criticized by nonbelievers like Voltaire in the Enlightenment era. It is noteworthy that the German poet Goethe showed no interest in either Francis or the art inspired by him when he visited Assisi in the late 18th century; according to his *Italian Journey* (written in 1816), Goethe observed the Roman temple in Assisi's main square, got back in his carriage, and headed south to Rome. Of Francis, he recorded not a word.

It was the Romantics, late in the 19th century, who rediscovered Francis of Assisi for the world outside of Catholic piety. They admired his feel for beauty, the simplicity of his poverty, the free wandering of his life, and his capacity for love. In religious circles, Francis is now seen as an ecumenical figure and his city of Assisi is often visited by both Christians and non-Christians.

The common tendency is to "read" Francis through the lens of this romantic rediscovery of him. It is important to realize, however, that he was, despite his extraordinary personality, very much a child of his time. He was an orthodox Catholic, interested in conversion from sin, who nonetheless had a capacity for love and forgiveness. Much of his energies was spent in healing civic feuds (his motto was "*Pax et Bonum*"—"Peace and Goodness"), preaching to the poor, and serving those in need (he wrote in his *Testament* that his own conversion came when he learned to embrace lepers instead of avoiding them).

Francis lived at an important moment in Western history. His exact contemporary, Dominic de Guzmán, founded the Friar Preachers (known as the "Dominicans") in the same period. Dominic's followers were to distinguish themselves as intellectuals as did the later Franciscans. Toward the end of the 13th century, both the Franciscans and the Dominicans dominated the intellectual life at the University of Paris. From their modest origins as mendicant brothers, these movements produced two great intellectuals: the Dominican Thomas Aquinas and the Franciscan John Bonaventure (both died in 1274) who were at the apex of what later historians would call the golden age of Gothic Medieval culture.

among the clergy. Heresy was particularly popular in the new towns, where social and economic change created a large population of urban poor who resented ecclesiastical privileges and the wealth of the merchant class. Disenfranchised elements of society, especially young men without careers and women who lacked dowry money to marry or enter convents, were also attracted to heresies.

The sect known as the Waldensians was founded in the 12th century by a pious merchant named Peter Waldo of Lyons. He established a lay order, known as the Poor Men of Lyons, who preached and gave charity to the poor. Although his order received papal approval, his ideas soon ran into trouble, especially the notion that the sacraments were not effective unless given by priests who observed high standards of morality and the belief that laymen could preach the Gospels. The Waldensian heresy, which spread to Spain, Germany, and northern Italy, was officially condemned by the Fourth Vatican Council in 1215 and was virtually wiped out in most places.

The Albigensian movement, which attracted wider support, posed a more serious challenge to the church. Named after the southern French town of Albi, where it had many followers, the movement was also called Catharism, after the Greek for "purity." This heresy seems to have originated in the pre-Christian Manichean movement of the Middle East, from where it spread to the Balkans, Italy, and then to France. The belief hinged on the notion of the struggle between good and evil, and the doctrine that everything associated with the material world was evil. The human soul, the Albigensians argued, was good but was imprisoned in the body, which was evil. The Albigensians preached against marriage and sexual intercourse because these acts furthered procreation of the material world, and denied that Christ had ever assumed flesh and blood. They also rejected the sacraments and the notion of priests, holding that pure believers led lives of asceticism in the service of good.

The church fought the Albigensians in a number of ways. About 1205, a Spanish priest named Dominic de Guzmán (1170–1221) began to preach among the Albigensians in order to reconvert them. Dominic and his followers observed vows of poverty and lived by begging. Ten years later, Pope Innocent III officially approved the Dominican order, formally known as the Order of Preachers. It soon became obvious, however, that reconversion alone was not sufficient to deal with the heresies. The secular ruler of Toulouse refused to work with the church in suppressing the Albigensians, causing Innocent to excommunicate him and call for a crusade against the heresy. The campaign unleashed a wave of terrible violence resulting in the deaths of thousands and the twisting of the holy war into an excuse by leaders from other regions to seize the property of local nobles.

In 1233, one of Innocent's successors, Pope Gregory IX (1227–1241), created a papal tribunal known as the Inquisition to cope with the threat of heresies (not to be confused with the later Spanish Inquisition of the 16th century). The papal Inquisition operated according to established procedures of canon and Roman law, the latter permitting the use of torture to force confessions. Accused heretics who refused to confess and repent could be punished and executed by the secular authorities.

The Albigensian heresy was eventually wiped out but at such a high price that even Innocent was shocked at the violence. Moreover, the atmosphere of fear and hatred aroused by the war against the heretics was often responsible for persecutions against other kinds of minorities, including Jews and Muslims, and spilled over into intolerance and legislation against homosexuality.

THE RISE OF POPULAR DEVOTION

Papal recognition of the Dominican order in 1215 occurred not only as a response to heresy but in recognition of the need for the church to engage more directly in the lives of Christians and the social realities of the day. Rather than closing themselves off from the secular world in isolated monasteries, these new mendicant (begging) orders lived and worked among the people of the cities, preaching and doing good works.

The Franciscan Renewal

The most famous and popular saint of the Middle Ages was Francis of Assisi (1182?–1226), the son of a prosperous Italian family. At first he led an unruly and dissolute life typical of many young men of his class, but at the age of 22 he underwent a profound religious experience that caused him to abandon all worldly comforts and devote himself to God. Rather than adopting the severe asceticism that drove some Christians into religious melancholy, Francis embraced the challenge before him with joyous fervor.

In 1206, with the approval of the bishop of Assisi, Francis went on a pilgrimage to Rome and began preaching the lessons of love and joy that God bestowed upon all creatures of the earth. Soon he had gathered a following of disciples around him who lived in crude huts which they built themselves and went from house to house begging and preaching. In 1208, Francis received approval from Innocent III to found a new religious order of mendicant friars, known as the

Francis of Assisi, shown here in an altarpiece with scenes of his life.

Order of Friars Minor, better known as the Franciscans. Eventually he drew up a simple but persuasive rule based on biblical inspiration.

Francis sent his followers abroad and he himself traveled widely. He visited Spain, France, and Dalmatia, and in 1219 went to Palestine. When he returned he found his growing order riddled with dissension and gave up its leadership to devote himself to preaching. Francis wrote a testament stressing the need to observe simplicity and poverty and was made a saint two years after his death.

Francis inspired many followers and the order grew rapidly throughout Europe. The orders founded by Francis and Clare attracted members because the 13th century was an age of great religious enthusiasm among all classes. The veneration of saints, and especially the Virgin Mary, and the thousands of people who went on pilgrimages to their shrines, attested to the strength of popular devotion.

Religion was a real and significant part of everyday life in Medieval society and the church was undoubtedly the most important institution of the Middle Ages. Despite setbacks, it demonstrated remarkable powers of regeneration. Out of the criticism of its worldliness and corruption, the church renewed itself through a strenuous movement of reform that reached from the ascetic monks of remote monasteries to the popes of Rome. The reforming popes built an elaborate and effective institution that played a critical and ever-expanding role in the spiritual and secular lives of millions of people. Popes such as Gregory VII and Innocent III undermined secular control of the church, successfully challenged the temporal rulers of the day, and launched a series of dramatic Crusades against unbelievers. And although the rise of a number of heresies suggests that not all believers were satisfied with the spiritual standards of the age, the orders of mendicant friars that arose in the 13th century reveal the profound commitment that many felt to the spiritual and moral ideals of the church.

Questions for Further Study

1. What were the sources of spiritual reform in the church?
2. Over what issues did the papacy and the Holy Roman Empire clash?
3. What factors explain the Crusades? What caused their failure?
4. Describe the nature of Franciscan spirituality.

Suggestions for Further Reading

Bolton, Brenda. *The Medieval Reformation*. London, 1983.
Boswell, John. *Christianity, Social Tolerance, and Homosexuality*. Chicago, 1980.
Brooke, Rosalind. *Popular Religion in the Middle Ages*. London, 1984.
Cadra, Herbert E. J. *The Cluniacs and the Gregorian Reform*. Oxford, 1970.
Cunningham, Lawrence S. *Saint Francis of Assisi*. Boston, 1976.
Gurevich, Avon. *Medieval Popular Culture: Problems of Belief and Perception*. Cambridge, MA, 1988.
Kedar, Benjamin Z. *Crusade and Mission: European Approaches Towards the Muslim*. Princeton, NJ, 1984.
Ladner, Gerhart. *The Idea of Reform*. Cambridge, MA, 1959.
Lambert, Malcolm. *Medieval Heresy*. New York, 1977.
Lawrence, Clifford H. *Medieval Monasticism*. London, 1984.
Little, Lyle. *Religious Poverty and the Profit Economy in Medieval Europe*. Ithaca, NY, 1978.
Mayer, Hans E. *The Crusades*. New York, 1972.
Riley-Smith, Jonathan. *The First Crusade and the Idea of Crusading*. London, 1986.
Rosenwein, Barbara. *Rhinoceros Bound: Cluny in the Tenth Century*. Philadelphia, 1982.
Tierney, Brian. *The Crisis of Church and State, 1050–1300*. Englewood Cliffs, NJ, 1964.
Tillmann, Helene. *Innocent III*. Amsterdam, 1980.
Ullmann, Walter. *The Growth of Papal Government in the Middle Ages*, 3rd ed. London, 1970.

III

Topic 9

Scholars, Troubadours, and Builders

In the 11th and 12th centuries, Western European society made a series of cultural advances that were to prove central to its intellectual and artistic growth. The foundation of the first universities marked a crucial development in Western thought. With the revival of town life, in addition to the cathedral schools—training institutions for priests—secular institutions began to appear that took lay pupils. During the 12th century universities evolved first at Paris and Bologna and then in England. For all the differences between the study programs at a Medieval university and a present-day one, the degree system and the organizational structure of a modern university have much in common with the earliest institutions. So do many aspects of student life.

Medieval professors used a systematic approach to teaching called *Scholasticism*. By this method they sought to reconcile the rational views of the Greeks with the requirements of Christian faith. The development of Scholasticism reached its highest point in the two great *Summaries* of St. Thomas Aquinas. In them Aquinas uses philosophical methods to analyze theological questions, while admitting the existence of "mysteries of the faith" which resist rational explanation.

With the rise of lay education, writers began to use their own vernacular languages instead of Latin. Two literary traditions gradually appeared: heroic epics such as the *Song of Roland*, and shorter love lyrics, first composed and sung by the troubadours at the courts of southern France.

The history of music took a giant step forward with the beginnings of the polyphonic style, which, unlike earlier Gregorian plainsong, combined several different melodic lines. The result was the first stage in the foundation of modern harmony and counterpoint. Modern methods of musical notation owe their origins to the work of Guido of Arezzo, who in the 11th century invented a way to record the pitch of notes by means of a "staff" of horizontal lines.

The architectural style of the age of Guido and the *Song of Roland* was the Romanesque. Romanesque churches are massive and robust, and many of them have immense towers. Sculptured figures often appear both inside and on the exterior façade. For the first time since the Romans, sculptors began to explore the expressive possibilities of the human body, producing works of striking emotional power.

The result of all these developments was the formation of a cultural movement common to all of Western Europe. The provincialism of feudal life gave way to a broader-based, more dynamic approach to the arts and the world of the mind. The Romanesque age combined veneration for centuries-old religious beliefs with a search for new secular approaches.

THE FIRST UNIVERSITIES

The idea of places of higher learning, where students could hear lectures and scholars could conduct research, was not a Medieval invention. Organized schools existed in the ancient world. Both Plato and Aristotle gave formal courses of lectures, and the School of Alexandria was famous in Greek and Roman times for its library and other research facilities. The main contributions of the Medieval university system to the history of Western education were three: fixed curricula (courses of study), organized bodies of professors, and the awarding of degrees.

From School to University

With the fall of the Roman Empire, the general level of education in Western Europe collapsed. Even the efforts of Charlemagne to improve the culture of his day by founding primary schools attached to bishoprics and monasteries did little to produce any real change. Several factors combined around 1100 to alter this. The growth of towns, the stabilization of the economy, and the development of effective civic government all created an urban society with a demand for better education. Before then, the few people who could read had learned at monasteries, which mainly operated to teach monks.

By 1100 the cathedrals in the towns began to replace the more remote monastic schools with their own urban centers for education. Over the following century the curriculum, originally designed to train priests, began to broaden. The new civic communities required trained lawyers. Furthermore, as economic improvements brought increased travel and trade, Latin—the language of the Catholic Church—began to serve both legal and commercial needs. With the renewed study of Latin grammar and composition came a revival of interest in the Roman classics.

While the cathedral schools continued to devote themselves primarily to training clerics, alternative institutions began to spring up for the children of upper-class citizens and merchants. Both teachers and pupils in these schools were laymen, while women generally learned to read at home under the instruction of private tutors. As a result, for the first time for centuries the church no longer controlled education.

The rise in literacy was enormous. Around 1100, less than 1 percent of Western Europeans could read, and most of those were clerics. By 1340 perhaps 40 percent of Florentine women and men were literate. The

Illuminated manuscript showing a university lecture.

consequence was the development of a class of educated laypeople, able to question—or even to ignore—the teachings of the church.

The earliest universities came into being to provide more specialized training for those who had received a standard elementary education at a cathedral or secular school. The University of Bologna, the oldest in Italy, specialized in law. The University of Paris actually started as a cathedral school. As it began to attract increasingly eminent teachers, its level of instruction rose, and by shortly after 1200 it had become the intellectual center of Europe.

The University of Paris

The transition from school to university at Paris began when its teachers formed a corporation to control the level of instruction and to supervise student admissions. The Latin word for a guild or corporation is *universitas*. The new institution served to protect its members, since both students and teachers were at first looked upon with suspicion by Medieval society. At the same time the university had a legal status which permitted it to raise money and to issue official documents. When students completed a course of studies and satisfied the examiners, they received a certificate which entitled them in turn to teach. The Latin term for teacher, *magister*, gave its name to the rank, or degree, of Master of Arts. Further training was necessary to earn the degree of Doctor (Latin *doctus* means "learned").

The arts curriculum at Paris increasingly emphasized secular learning rather than theology. In 1210 the tension this caused between arts and theology professors led to a split. The masters and students of arts moved their operations to the Left Bank of the river Seine. To this day that district of Paris, still associated with student and intellectual life, retains a name reminiscent of the first university classes taught there: the Latin Quarter.

Student Life in a Medieval University

By 1250 there were around 7000 students at the University of Paris—an astonishing number for a Medieval city, and higher than the entire population of many a town. At the same period the University of Oxford, founded shortly after Paris, had about 2000 students enrolled.

Students could turn to a range of sources for financial support, including family, civic grants, and charitable individuals. Some generous benefactors paid for the construction of student housing. The most famous of these was Robert de Sorbon, who founded the Sorbonne in 1257. The college became part of the university in the 19th century, and its name now generally serves to refer to the University of Paris as a whole.

Student complaints about their housing included the poor quality of the food and inadequate heating. Books—handwritten on expensive parchment—and writing materials were in short supply. Days were long. Most arts students attended their first lectures at 5 A.M., following it with attendance at Mass and then breakfast. More lectures followed for most of the morning, and the hour before lunch was set aside for formal debates, which provided training in clear thinking and public speaking. In the afternoon, tutorial sessions reworked the material of the morning's lessons. After supper at 6 P.M. students could study until bedtime, 9 P.M.

If this seems an improbably austere description of student life, we receive a far more lively picture of the undergraduates of Medieval days from the student poetry which has survived. One of the most interesting collections, the *Carmina Burana (Songs of Beuren)* turned up in a Bavarian monastery (Benediktbeuren) in the 19th century. The poems, dating to the late 12th and 13th centuries, are in Latin, French, and German.

The subjects of these student verses are the perennial ones of student life: drinking songs, love songs (some romantic, some lamenting lost loves, some simply obscene), satires on pompous professors or lousy housing. The patron saint of college life was the mythical St. Golias, in whose honor students composed Goliardic poems and songs. They illustrate the exhilaration and sense of freedom that the new educational opportunities opened up for increasing numbers of people.

SCHOLASTICISM: FAITH, REALITY, AND REASON

Professors in the expanding universities of the 12th century drew their ideas from three sources. The first, that of traditional church teachings, had remained authoritative for a millennium. The second consisted of the advances of ancient Greek thinkers. Knowledge of these had been lost to the West with the disappearance of an understanding of the Greek language. They reentered the Western tradition by means of the third source, Medieval Arabic philosophy and science. Muslim scholars had translated many of the most important Greek scientific texts and many of the works of Aristotle into Arabic, and used them as the basis of their own inquiries. For Western readers, however, Arabic was as remote as Greek.

The vital key which unlocked the accumulated wisdom of the Greeks and their Muslim commentators for Western culture was the appearance at the end of the 12th century of a flood of Latin translations. Many of these emerged from the Muslim communities in Spain and Sicily (see Part III, Topic 4), where Christians could have contact with Arabic speakers or with Jews who spoke both Arabic and Latin. By around 1260, Western

A mosaic in the Palace of the Normans, Palermo, Sicily, c. 1132.

scholars could read Latin versions of virtually all of Aristotle's surviving works, and writings by major Greek scientists such as Euclid and Ptolemy. At the same time they became acquainted with the ideas of their Muslim contemporaries, including the philosophers Avicenna and Averroes.

The Scholastic System

Scholasticism represented the attempt to reconcile the sacred teachings of the church with the knowledge acquired by human reason and experience. Its practitioners sought to apply Greek philosophical ideas—principally those of Aristotle—to Christian doctrine. They believed that reason, although always subordinate to faith, served to increase the faithful's understanding of their beliefs.

The most important, and certainly the most controversial, forerunner of Scholasticism was the French philosopher Peter Abelard (1079–1142), one of the few figures in the history of Western intellectual development whose lovelife is as well-known as his theology.

A brilliant student under William of Champeaux in Paris, Abelard alienated his fellow students and professors alike by his arrogant superiority in public debates. In 1113, after a nervous breakdown caused by the strain of founding and running a series of schools, he began teaching at the University of Paris. Handsome and eloquent, he soon became the most popular instructor there. His courses at the university drew foreign pupils from many countries, including two future popes and some twenty who later became cardinals.

His most famous student, however, lived within closer reach. Héloise (c. 1098–1164) was the niece of a canon at the Church of Notre Dame, famous for her learning as well as her beauty. Attracted by Héloise's reputation, Abelard took lodgings in the canon's house to act as her tutor. He was 35 at the time and she was 15. Abelard himself in his later autobiography, *The Story of My Calamities*, describes what happened next: "Under the pretext of work we made ourselves entirely free for love, and the pursuit of her studies provided the secrecy which love desired."

To the fury of her uncle, Héloise became pregnant and gave birth to a son. Abelard proposed marriage, but Héloise at first refused: "What could be in common between scholars and cradles? Who is there bent on philosophical reflection who could bear the wailing of babies?" Abelard insisted, and the two were married secretly in Paris. Thereafter events are confused. Héloise's uncle, although present at the marriage, seems to have plotted revenge for the loss of his niece's "honor." A gang of his servants attacked and castrated Abelard, and Héloise sought refuge in a convent.

Abelard retreated to a monastery but soon returned to teaching in Paris, driven by student demand and his own restless intellect. His autobiography reveals nostalgia for his former life as well as remorse: "I ought to groan for the sins I have perpetrated yet I sigh for those which now I am unable to commit." He continued to teach and to write for the rest of his life.

So controversial were Abelard's philosophical writings that in 1141, the year before his death, a church council condemned him for heresy. One of his

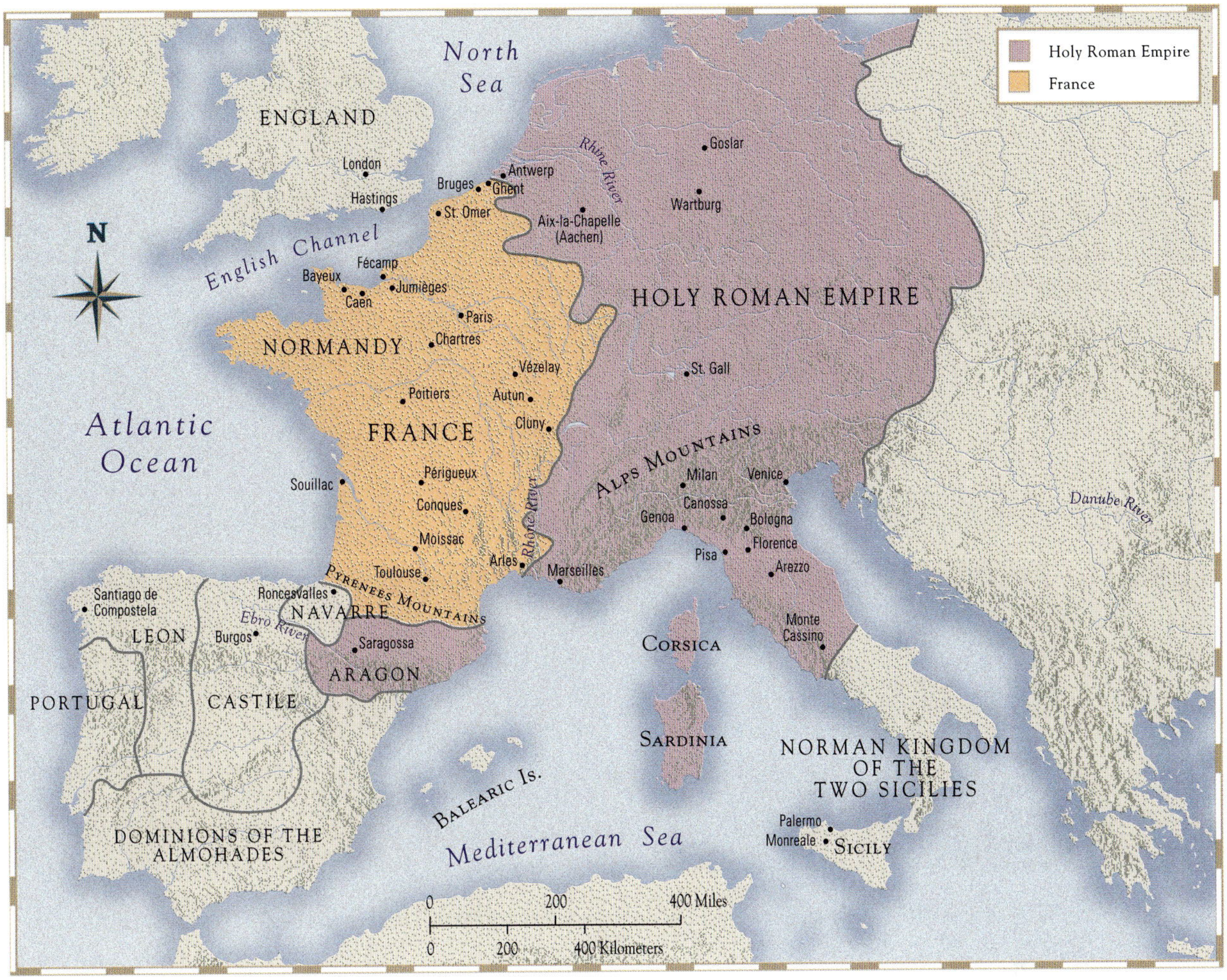

Map 9.1 Europe c. 1140

works which aroused particular anger was *Sic et Non (Yes and No)*, setting out a series of quotations from the Bible and the early Fathers of the Church which apparently take contradictory points of view on various theological points. His contemporaries saw this as an attempt to embarrass and confuse the authority of the church, but Abelard's intention was to apply the tools of logic and reason to theology and to reconcile religion and reason—the very method which Scholastic thinkers were to develop.

Thomas Aquinas

The most famous of all Medieval Scholastic philosophers, and by far the most influential, was St. Thomas Aquinas (c. 1225–1274). Born in southern Italy, he studied in Naples, where he became a Dominican, as well as in Cologne and Paris. He was the leading theologian at the University of Paris, and also taught at the universities of Bologna and Rome—a measure of the international spirit of the age.

The constant theme of Aquinas' writings was the reconciliation of faith and experience: "nature complements grace." Although only trust in the truths of the Bible could reinforce the highest mysteries of religion, human reason and the natural world confirmed these revelations, and thus enabled humans to accomplish their own salvation. The foundation of his teachings was the philosophy of Aristotle, translated from the Arabic and interpreted according to Christian principles.

Aquinas' most important work was the *Summa Theologica (Summary of Theology)*, in which he used Aristotelian logic to demonstrate the existence of God. God is the uncaused cause, the prime reason for order in the universe. Humans are rational social animals, whose morality is based on harmony with others and with God. The emphasis on human experience and reason as a guide to faith came as a revelation to his contemporaries; it was also to become a basic tenet of subsequent Roman Catholic philosophy.

This fresco in the Church of Santa Maria Novella, Florence, shows St. Thomas Aquinas flanked by figures from the Old and New Testaments.

SONGS OF LOVE AND BATTLE: HEROIC EPICS AND TROUBADOUR POETRY

Before the rise of education and the growth in literacy, the composition of works of literature in the *vernacular* (everyday, spoken languages, as opposed to Latin) was unsurprisingly rare. The only outstanding achievement of the early Medieval period was the Anglo-Saxon epic poem *Beowulf*. Although there are elements of Christianity in *Beowulf*, the society it depicts is pagan. The story tells of the triumph of the Scandinavian hero, Beowulf, over the monster Grendel, and is replete with gory feuds and black magic.

The Epic Tradition

In the century between 1050 and 1150, the three chief continental European languages, French, German, and Spanish, acquired their first major works of vernacular literature. Italian took longer to split off from Latin, and thus developed into a modern language a little later. Its first great writer, Dante, wrote in the early 14th century (see Part III, Topic 11). All three are epic poems belonging to the tradition of the "*chanson de gestes*," or "song of deeds" in which a minstrel recounted heroic deeds.

The French *Chanson de Roland (Song of Roland)* was first written down around 1100, probably just before the First Crusade, although it was composed shortly after the event it describes—Charlemagne's invasion of Spain in 778—and passed down by word of mouth. The epic combines two main themes, one public and the other private: Charlemagne's struggle against the Muslim rulers of Spain, to defend the honor of his knights, of France, and of Christendom; and the personal relationships between the hero Roland and his fellow warriors.

Roland's deadly enemy is his stepfather Ganelon, who plots treachery against the hero with the help of the crafty Muslim king. Tempted into rash action and beset by overwhelming enemy forces, Roland manages to summon Charlemagne's troops with a magic ivory horn before falling to his attackers. Ganelon subse-

A performance of minstrels, from a 14th-century German manuscript.

quently suffers trial and execution for his betrayal of Roland.

The hero is rather more fortunate in his relationship with Oliver, his beloved friend. The two together summarize Medieval notions of heroism: Roland is fearless and ambitious for glory, while Oliver, prudent and moderate, tries in vain to restrain his companion from running the risk which eventually proves fatal.

The Spanish *Song of the Cid,* less bloody than the French epic, describes the career of the Spanish knight known as El Cid (his name derives from the Arabic word *Sidi,* "my lord"). The hero appears not only as an exemplary warrior, fighting in the cause of honor, but also as an ideal husband and father, and a devout Christian. If the *Song of the Cid* lacks the energy and concentration of the *Song of Roland,* its characterization is more subtle.

The spirit of the German *Nibelungenlied (Song of the Nibelungs)* is very different from the chivalric world of Roland and the Cid. Set in dark forests, with a plot involving stolen treasure, trickery and assassination, a race of dwarfs and a bloodthirsty dragon, it was to inspire the 19th-century German composer Richard Wagner to create an epic cycle of music-dramas (see Part VII, Topic 21).

The Troubadours

The other literary form of the age, troubadour love poetry, was a far cry from the heroic, often violent world of the chansons de gestes. The troubadour poets first appeared at the courts of southern France around 1100, where their verses reflected a new attitude toward love and lovers. Inspired by Platonic notions in the writings of Muslim and Christian philosophers, and by the works of contemporary Muslim poets in neighboring Spain (see Part III, Topic 4), the troubadours developed a "code" of "Courtly Love."

The quest for true love was, for the troubadours, like a knight's mission. The submissive lover dedicated himself to the service of his lady—the roles were never reversed. He fulfilled his love by the intensity of his devotion, neither hoping for nor achieving any actual consummation. The reward was the reputation for "spiritual valor" he acquired in the eyes of his peers. Modern readers are generally struck by the artificial quality of troubadour love poetry, but for Medieval society it represented an attitude to women in advance of that depicted in the chansons de gestes. In one French heroic epic that reflects traditional misogynist attitudes, a queen, trying to convince her husband to change his mind, receives a blow to the nose which draws blood. For the troubadours and their audience, far from being battered, the beloved was idealized as superior to her devoted servant.

A NEW MUSICAL LANGUAGE: THE POLYPHONIC STYLE

The earliest surviving music of the Medieval world is plainsong. This consists of a single or "monophonic" musical line to which one voice (either a solo or a group in unison) chants the words of a religious text, generally without any form of accompaniment. The tradition of Christian plainsong developed out of Jewish synagogue rituals. By the 4th century, several distinct schools of chant were in use, some in Eastern Church ceremonies, others in the West.

As part of his campaign to unify his empire and its religious practices, Charlemagne allowed the use in the Western liturgy of only one school of plainsong, that of Gregorian chant, and banned the others. Another tradition, that of Ambrosian chant, continued to survive in and around Milan. Scholars used to believe that Gregorian chant originated at Rome in the time of Pope Gregory (590–604): hence its name. It is now thought to have come into being around 800, at the court of Charlemagne himself, created to become the "universal" form of church music.

The Rise of Polyphony

The musical content of plainsong was essentially limited to melody. The elements of harmony and rhythm, fundamental to Western music since the late Medieval period, were not yet present. A move in the direction of harmony—that is, the simultaneous sounding of more than one note—came in the 10th century, with the invention of "organum" or "consonant music," whereby the musical line of the chant was accompanied by another line, or "voice."

Over the next two centuries, musicians began slowly to develop a more complex style of music which consisted of several different strands of melody sounding together and making up a harmonic whole. The first important works to use the new technique, known as polyphonic ("many voices"), date to the Gothic age of the 13th century (see Part III, Topic 11).

Guido of Arezzo

As music grew in complexity, it became necessary to find a form of notation for writing down the pitches of the notes. The composers of plainsong had developed a series of signs which they added to the words to indicate the relative musical patterns to which the text was sung, but these did not convey the actual notes. With the rise of polyphonic music, in which individual performers needed an objective written "part," setting out their musical line and that of the other participants, some form of written musical "score" became necessary.

The essential breakthrough came shortly after 1000. Guido of Arezzo (c. 991–after 1033), while working in the city of Arezzo in central Italy as a trainer of singers for the cathedral, devised a system of notation. It made use of a series of parallel horizontal lines, with the lines themselves and the spaces between them representing precise notes or pitches—the forerunner of the modern musical "staff." Guido also gave names to the notes, based on the melody and text of a hymn to St. John: *Ut* (later changed to *Do*) for the note "c," *Re* for "d," *Mi* for "e," and so on.

In 1028 the pope called Guido to Rome to expound his new system, which was to become the basis for all further musical notation in the West. His treatise *Micrologus* set out the Guidonian method and included a discussion of the new polyphonic musical style. The work was the most copied and read musical handbook of the Middle Ages.

ARCHITECTS AND SCULPTORS: THE ROMANESQUE CATHEDRAL

The uncertainties of the early Medieval period, beset by conflict and political unrest, had discouraged the construction of new buildings. With the gradual return of stability in the 11th century, towns and monasteries began to commission churches. The growing popularity of pilgrimages to holy sites along "pilgrimage routes" throughout Europe provided an additional stimulus to build pilgrimage churches as well as facilities for the thousands of pilgrims on the move each year.

The architects responsible for the first major building programs since Roman times turned to the style of Roman architecture for their inspiration. The new architectural style they created is known as *Romanesque*—"Roman-like." Its characteristics are in part due to the need for large buildings capable of containing crowds of people. Heavy stone walls could support Roman-style stone arches and barrel-vaulted stone roofs, providing a structure that, unlike the early Christian basilicas, was fireproof.

Romanesque churches are massive, with dark, simple interiors, many of them with lofty towers supported by round arches. There was ample space for the movement of large numbers of people, but little light. As a result, the most important decorations were not placed inside the building but on the exterior. Since paintings would have been subject to damage in the open air, artists turned for the first time since the fall of Rome to stone sculpture to portray the human figure. The scenes and figures decorating Romanesque churches represent a revival of the art of sculpture in

The interior of the church of St. Senin, Toulouse, c. 1080–1120.

Tympanum from the abbey church of La Madeleine, Vézelay, c. 1120–1132.

stone that was to lead in time to developments in Renaissance art.

One of the chief areas of a Romanesque church to be filled with sculpture was that around the main doorway, where the pilgrims as they entered would see the biblical stories or figures. The semicircular space above the door itself was especially important; known as the *tympanum*, it often contained an elaborate "program" or message for the devout.

One of the most elaborate is the tympanum above the west door of the Benedictine abbey church of Vézelay in France, dating to around 1120. The central figure of Christ inspires the apostles around him and the assorted peoples of the world below, while healing the lepers and cripples depicted in the scenes above. The whole complex ensemble is surrounded with an abstract decorative pattern perhaps derived from Islamic art of a kind produced by Muslim artists in nearby Spain.

Thus, at the time when contact with the Muslim world was reintroducing the West to Greek and Roman literature, Western artists were rediscovering the most important—and lasting—of Greek and Roman artistic genres, stone statues of the human form. Something of the excitement of Romanesque sculptors is visible in the emotional power of the figures they carved. Elongated, grave, often dramatic, Romanesque statues and relief carvings are an appropriate complement to the massive buildings they decorate.

Architects and builders throughout Western Europe employed the Romanesque style. There are regional variations, of course, but pilgrims traveling, say, from the North through France to the shrine of St. James of Compostela in Spain would see familiar buildings and art works along their route. The more learned ones who visited the monastic libraries could find there manuscripts illustrated in the same style. Some of the sculpted scenes in Romanesque church decorations were probably based on illuminated manuscripts.

The gradual development of a common European culture owed much to the increasing ease of travel. The pilgrims moving from northern Europe to Italy and Spain—and eventually, after the Crusades, to the Holy Land—the troubadours passing from one aristocratic court to another, university professors traveling to lecture in the major centers of learning—all of these led to the circulation of ideas and a shared artistic culture. With its renewed interest in education, and rediscovery of the Greeks and their philosophy, the Romanesque age provided a solid foundation for the international cultural achievements of the succeeding Gothic period.

Questions for Further Study

1. How far do the organization and function of a modern university reflect those of its Medieval ancestors?

2. What are the general principles underlying the philosophy of Thomas Aquinas? To what extent do they reflect the intellectual climate of his age?
3. In what ways did the spread of literacy change Medieval society? Did it have a significant effect upon the status of women?
4. What are the main features of the Romanesque style?

Suggestions for Further Reading

Artz, F. B. *The Mind of the Middle Ages, A.D. 200–1500*. Chicago, 1980.

Bogin, M. *The Women Troubadours*. New York, 1976.

Cobban, A. B. *The Medieval Universities: Their Development and Organization*. London, 1975.

Duby, Georges. *The Knight, the Lady, and the Priest*. New York, 1984.

Ennen, Edith. *The Medieval Town*. New York, 1979.

Keen, M. *Chivalry*. New Haven, CT, 1984.

McInerny, R. *Romanesque*. New York, 1978.

Weisheipl, James. *Friar Thomas D'Aquino: His Life, Thought, and Work*. Garden City, NY, 1974.

III

Topic 10

Monarchy and Its Limits: Government in the High Middle Ages

The territorial and bureaucratic foundations of the European monarchies became established during the 11th and 12th centuries. Decentralized feudal arrangements, in which vassal nobles were generally more powerful than kings, gradually gave way to centralized royal authority, especially in England after the Norman Conquest and in France under the reign of the Capetian kings. On the other hand, in Germany, the development of a strong monarchy was complicated by the imperial aspirations of the German kings. Although central authority grew even in the Holy Roman Empire, especially during the reign of the great Hohenstaufen emperor Frederick I, the claim to universal power began to decline in the wake of the Empire's struggle with the other contender for universal authority, the papacy.

As royal government evolved in practical ways on a day-to-day basis, political theory also reinforced the position of the new monarchs. The Medieval political debate essentially revolved around one crucial question: the nature of the relationship between church and state. Despite the repeated claims of the popes, the overall direction of philosophical opinion pressed for the separation of the two spheres of authority, a trend that had the effect of strengthening the sovereignty of national kings.

In the 13th century, the monarchies continued to grow in power as centralized government was extended in a variety of ways. The development and application of royal law were perhaps the single most important means by which the kings built their authority, a policy they pursued both in England and France. Especially in England, the expansion of the royal judicial system and its merger with common law proved to have important implications for the growth of constitutionalism. The notion of the protection of certain basic rights under the law was the basis for the Magna Carta, through which the English barons forced John in 1215 to recognize the limits of his power.

The elaboration of administrative machinery for royal government enabled kings to exercise real power on a regular basis through established procedures of public policy. This was especially true in the collection of taxes and the expenditure of royal funds. Here, too, however, there were unexpected results, as concern over the king's power to impose taxes was combined with the growth of legal procedure to produce representative institutions, such as the Parliament of England, that served further to limit the power of the king.

Significant Dates

Government in the High Middle Ages

1073	Pope Gregory VII publishes *Dictatus Papae*
1215	Magna Carta
1198–1216	Reign of Innocent III as pope
1199–1216	Reign of John as king of England
1180–1223	Reign of Philip II Augustus as king of France
1212–1250	Reign of Frederick II as Holy Roman emperor
1295	"Model Parliament" meets
1302	Boniface issues *Unam Sanctam*
1324	Marsilio of Padua publishes *Defensor Pacis*
1356	Charles IV issues Golden Bull

POLITICAL THEORY AND CHURCH-STATE RELATIONS IN THE HIGH MIDDLE AGES

In the Middle Ages the two "universal" states, the Holy Roman Empire and the papacy, competed for recognition as the supreme sources of authority in western Christendom. The Empire, which drew Germany and Italy into the same political orbit, claimed a special role as the successor to Charlemagne's vast state. Medieval theorists and millions of people also recognized the temporal government of the popes, which ruled directly over the Papal States of central Italy while simultaneously claiming theoretical supremacy over all secular governments. The origins of this notion went back to the early Middle Ages.

The Nature of Royal Power

Papal power remained strong well into the late Middle Ages, but by the opening of the 13th century England and France, as well as Spain and Hungary, were expanding the power and influence of their national monarchies. The new kings there could look back to an earlier theory that saw secular rulers not as separate from the church but as integral to the universal church and to Western Christendom. When the pope recognized the right of Pepin III in 751 to take the Merovingian throne, St. Boniface anointed the new king with holy oil, thus beginning the tradition of theocratic monarchy, or monarchy with divine sanction. This kind of government characterized the Carolingian state, in which the church blessed and supported the monarchy while the king protected and rewarded the church.

The great reform movement that began to sweep the church in the 11th century complicated the relationship between royal and spiritual authority. In 1073, Pope Gregory VII published *Dictatus Papae*, an essay claiming that papal power was supreme over all authority of this world, including emperors and kings. This was a new and startling challenge to secular government that undermined the idea of theocratic kingship prevalent in the early Middle Ages. Gregory revived

Thomas Aquinas, the theologian who was influenced by both Plato (lower right) and Aristotle (lower left). While a series of Christian thinkers are depicted above him, the Islamic philosopher Averroes appears at his feet in defeat.

the principle of St. Augustine's *City of God*, claiming that the secular state derived moral strength only from its position as a servant of the church. Hence, the only legitimate power resided in the priesthood.

The first serious clash between kings and popes had come over the question of lay investiture, but the concordat of 1122 settled the issue through a compromise in which neither side won a decisive victory. Strong popes, such as Innocent III, would continue to challenge secular rulers, especially in the case of King John of England and Frederick II of the Holy Roman Empire. Yet the struggle with the papacy had the effect of strengthening the monarchs as defenders of national sovereignty and the church's position was slowly eroded, a process that culminated two centuries later in the period of the Reformation. Kings, moreover, were becoming increasingly popular as the benefits of orderly and efficient government were appreciated by all social classes. The exercise of royal power in more dramatic fashion depended on the personality and character of individual kings, as in the case of Frederick Barbarossa or Henry II. By the end of the 13th century, citizens accepted royal authority in such matters as law, finance, and military policy as routine. National governments had become secular bureaucratic states.

The development of legal studies and the rise of universities contributed to this trend not only by training the first cadres of professional administrators for royal government: university professors strengthened the authority of the king by arguing for the separation of church and state. Early Medieval theorists had proclaimed that political power was an expression of divine will, and in the 13th century the philosopher Thomas Aquinas continued to argue that a basic harmony existed between the temporal state and divine will. Later in the century, however, the Italian poet Dante Alighieri (see Part III, Topic 11) maintained in *De Monarchia* that government was a secular institution that should be dominated by kings and independent of spiritual authority.

The most powerful theoretical defense of secular authority was made by another Italian, Marsilio of Padua (d. 1342?), who studied and taught at the University of Paris. In *Defensor Pacis* (1324), Marsilio strongly opposed ecclesiastical claims of supremacy in temporal matters. Reaching back to Aristotle, he argued that the purpose of the state—which was the creation of human will—was to provide peace and security for its citizens. Although he insisted that only the king was the legitimate ruler of the state, Marsilio also held that all secular power is derived from popular will and that the ruler is the servant of the people. It was no wonder that Pope Clement VI (1342–1352) called Marsilio "the greatest heretic of the age."

ENGLAND: MAGNA CARTA AND THE EVOLUTION OF PARLIAMENT

The foundations of royal government in England had been established by Henry II in the 12th century. Henry created the office of the exchequer to collect taxes and manage finances, and enlarged the jurisdiction of royal justice through the jury system, measures which met with popular approval. He established common law, as opposed to the customary law used in feudal courts, as the legal system of the entire realm. By the time of the king's death in 1189, royal authority had increased significantly at the expense of the power of the feudal barons.

The King and the Barons

Henry recognized no limits to his royal power, nor created any institutions through which the barons could participate in public affairs. As royal government evolved, these issues became increasingly more important in English politics. The two sons who succeeded Henry, Richard and John, were unable to increase their power without resistance and eventually were forced to accept limits on their authority.

The talents of Richard I, the Lion-Hearted (ruled 1189–1199), were those of a feudal warrior rather than of a bureaucratic king. Although brave and dashing, he lacked the interest or skill to develop his government. During a decade-long reign, he was actually in England less than a year, spending most of his time attacking Muslims in the Holy Land or fighting the Capetians in France. Nevertheless, despite his long absence, the government developed by his father operated with great efficiency.

Richard's brother, John (ruled 1199–1216), was a man of a much less appealing personality and ability, and the contrast between the two has served to give John a much maligned reputation, in the eyes of his contemporaries and of historians. John's unsuccessful attempts to control the English Church resulted in a conflict with Pope Innocent III over the selection of Stephen Langton as archbishop of Canterbury (see Part III, Topic 8). John's position further deteriorated in 1204 when Philip Augustus, the French king, took Normandy from him. When John tried to reconquer his lost provinces, he was defeated at the Battle of Bouvines (1214). The feudal barons, from whom John had tried to extort monies to help pay for the French wars, seized their chance to resist the king. Innocent encouraged the rebellious barons by imposing an interdict on England and declaring John deposed.

The Great Seal of King John of England was placed on the Magna Carta, the Medieval document that limited the power of the sovereign.

These combined blows finally forced the beleaguered king to accept Langton's appointment. In an effort to secure papal support in his struggle with the barons, John also recognized England as a papal fief.

In June 1215, John faced the defiant barons at Runnymede, where they insisted that he endorse and set his seal to the Magna Carta (Great Charter), a document that may have been drafted in its original form by Stephen Langton. The Magna Carta was not a radical departure from tradition, for as part of their coronation ceremonies English kings had always sworn to uphold the rights of their subjects. But the Magna Carta was so detailed and direct—it contained more than 60 provisions—and the circumstances surrounding its adoption were so unusual, that its influence grew far beyond its immediate implications.

Magna Carta was a feudal document that restated the rights and obligations of king and vassals "for the reform of our realm." It is in this context that some of its clauses concerning John's relations with his vassals should be seen, including those dealing with property rights, feudal dues, inheritance, and the powers of guardians over their wards. Henceforth, John could not force the payment of special levies from the barons to support his wars. Similarly, the English Church was declared "free" with "its rights undiminished and its liberties unimpaired." The king now recognized the clergy's right to select bishops and to appeal under canon law to papal courts. At a time when towns and their burgher class were growing, John also agreed to recognize the freedoms of the cities, to guarantee the right of travel to all merchants, and to adopt uniform weights and measures in order to streamline commercial transactions.

With respect to the development of English constitutionalism, the Magna Carta contained a number of general statements that were especially important. "No free man," it commanded, "shall be arrested or imprisoned or disseised or outlawed or exiled or in any way victimized, neither will we attack him or send anyone to attack him, except by the lawful judgment of his peers or by the law of the land." The last clause stated that the king as well as the barons had taken an oath to the effect that "the men in our kingdom shall have and hold all the aforesaid liberties, rights and concessions well and peacefully, freely and quietly, fully and completely, for themselves and their heirs from us and our heirs, in all matters and in all places for ever."[2]

Later generations see the Magna Carta as a source of English constitutionalism, but the barons merely wanted to protect their own feudal rights against the encroachments of royal government. The barons were not concerned about the great majority of English subjects, who were not free to enjoy the liberties guaranteed in Magna Carta. Only subsequent interpretations extended to the entire English population the notions of due process and trial by jury, and broadened the meaning of the Magna Carta to include the idea that royal power should be limited by law and the consent of the governed.

John's son Henry III (ruled 1216–1272) was also unable to control the barons, who continued to protest royal efforts to tax them and the king's right to appoint officials. These protests came to a head in 1258, when the barons imposed on Henry the Provisions of Oxford, which established a number of councils of barons to assist him in governing the country. When Henry and the barons could not agree on how to put the provisions into practice, they decided in 1264 to accept the arbitration of John's feudal overlord, Louis IX of France, who ruled that Henry should not be forced to accept the provisions. The following year, the steady erosion of royal authority was halted when Henry's son and successor Edward defeated a group of rebellious barons led by Simon de Montfort.

The Evolution of Parliament

Edward I (ruled 1272–1307), one of the most important kings of Medieval England, was responsible for the first effort to unite the entire island. He conquered Wales in 1284, extending English law and administration there and giving his eldest son the title of Prince of Wales. But similar efforts to bring Scotland into the realm failed and in 1314 Scottish nationalists under Robert Bruce defeated the English and reasserted Scottish independence. The two kingdoms were united only in 1603.

[2] Quoted in Harry Rothwell, ed., *English Historical Documents, 1189–1327*, III (London: Eyre & Spottiswoode, 1975).

Edward, known as the "English Justinian," brought a measure of organization to the common law that had been evolving over the centuries. He began publishing new laws in the Statutes of the Realm, which continues to be issued to this day, took special interest in systematizing laws regulating land ownership, and further reduced the jurisdiction of baronial courts.

The most important development during Edward's reign was the emergence of Parliament. The first meeting of this body had already taken place in 1265, when Simon de Montfort called it into session during his revolt against Henry III. In order to obtain the widest possible support, de Montfort increased its membership by adding two knights from each shire and two burghers from every town. The tradition was followed by Edward when he summoned what is known as the "Model Parliament" in 1295.

Sometime in the early years of the 14th century, the knights and burghers began meeting together separately from the barons as the "Commons," thus creating a division between the House of Commons and the House of Lords. In the early days, the king used Parliament mainly to obtain endorsement of royal decisions and to secure additional taxes. Because new taxation demanded popular consent, Edward ordered the shires and towns to elect representatives who would meet in Parliament to discuss and grant the needed taxes. Parliament also functioned as a kind of supreme court to which members would bring petitions or appeals from lower court decisions. Although in these matters Parliament served the interests of the king, it also learned that by withholding taxes it could force the king to redress grievances or endorse laws introduced by members of Parliament in the form of petitions.

Edward I, shown here presiding at a session of Parliament.

While institutions similar to the Parliament developed in other countries, it was in England that it became a body of government that represented the authority of the people over that of the king. Moreover, the king's power was further limited by the observance of uniform laws derived from custom and tradition.

THE CONSOLIDATION OF THE FRENCH MONARCHY

The creation of France, which had long been divided by significant regional differences in culture, language, and history, was the work of the Capetian monarchs of the High Middle Ages. The three kings who ruled between 1180 and 1314—Philip II "Augustus," Louis IX, and Philip IV "the Fair"—strengthened royal government and reinforced national identity on foundations already established in the long reign of Louis VII. The result was that France eventually became the most powerful state in Europe.

Philip Augustus

The essential institutions of the French monarchy had been established in the 12th century. The great lords had each become so powerful that the peaceful resolution of conflicts now became more appealing than the destructive feudal wars that had once brought havoc to the French countryside. The legal developments sponsored by the monarchy offered an alternative to fighting. Like his contemporary Henry II in England, Louis VII had greatly expanded the royal judicial system and by the end of his reign some of the vassals of France were bringing legal disputes before royal courts for impartial settlement. He had also begun the consolidation of the royal domains in the Île de France.

Louis VII's great failure came as a result of the annulment of his marriage to Eleanor of Aquitaine, since her subsequent marriage to Henry II of England transferred her vast lands to the English monarchy. Perhaps to soothe his sensitivity over the loss, Louis had lectured the English envoy to Paris that "Your master, the King of England, wants for nothing. He has experienced soldiers, horses, gold, silks, jewels, choice of fruits, game worth hunting, and everything the heart could wish. . . . In France things are different. We have only our bread, our wine, and our simple pleasures." Yet already a growing sense of national identity was beginning to separate the French outlook from their English neighbors across the Channel.

Map 10.1 Expansion of the French Monarchy

Philip Augustus (ruled 1180–1223) reinforced this tendency in real ways. Philip lacked the kind of personal glamour that made Frederick Barbarossa and Henry II so appealing to contemporaries. He was instead shrewd and calculating and excelled in deviousness. Yet he was determined to restore the territories now held by the English Plantagenets in France—Aquitaine, Anjou, Maine, and Normandy. To achieve this goal, he exploited Henry's quarrels with Eleanor and encouraged his sons, Richard and John, to revolt against their father. Using a dispute between John and a French noble as the excuse, Philip invaded the English lands in France. In 1214, Philip crushed the forces of John and his allies at Bouvines and took Anjou, Maine, and Normandy, greatly increasing the size of the French royal domain and its revenues.

To administer his enlarged territories, Philip perfected an administrative procedure that had been tried on a limited scale by Louis. Each local area of the royal domain had been formerly administered by a *prévôt*, an official similar to the English sheriff, but this system had resulted in corruption and inefficiency. Now Philip divided the royal domain into units called bailiwicks, which were administered by bailiffs. He recruited these new officials from the bourgeoisie. In the southern provinces later acquired by the king, similar officials, but usually of noble rather than bourgeois origin, were called seneschals. The bailiffs were direct representatives of the king, administering justice and collecting taxes. When combined with the king's specialized offices, such as the privy council of advisers and the treasury (usually run by Italians), these administrators began a system of centralized royal government that was to endure for many centuries.

St. Louis

Philip's successor Louis VIII (ruled 1223–1226) reigned for only a few years but his campaigns against the Albigensian heretics in southern France established the basis for the incorporation of that region into the royal domain. He was succeeded in turn by Louis IX (ruled 1226–1270), a devoutly religious man who ministered to the poor and sick and was later made a saint. His religious convictions also caused him to lead two crusades against the Muslims in North Africa, both of which were failures. Nevertheless, Louis was one of the dominant personalities of the age. Despite his asceticism, he embellished the kingship with elaborate ceremonies and symbolic ritual designed to enhance royal prestige.

Louis extended royal authority over the feudal lords of France in a number of ways. He imposed a king's peace on the country by forbidding wars among his vassals and began hearing legal appeals and petitions from nobles and commoners alike. He also established the *Parlement* of Paris (a legal tribunal not to be confused with the English Parliament) as the supreme court of France. The king's legal experts, trained in universities, began to codify French laws and ordinances.

Louis pursued a policy of peace with his neighbors that resulted in better defined borders for France. In 1258, he negotiated a treaty with the king of Aragon that established the frontier between Spain and France along the Pyrenees. The next year, he also signed a treaty with the English monarch Henry III, who agreed to recognize the loss of all the lands taken from John in exchange for accepting the area of Gascony in southwestern France, which he still held, as a fief from Louis.

Philip the Fair

The success of the Capetian kings in building a powerful monarchy capable of molding France into a single state reached its high point in the reign of Philip IV (ruled 1285–1314). Philip IV lacked a strong personality and was not especially popular. He did, however, have the good sense to rely heavily on talented ministers, who sought to increase his authority and strengthen the monarchy in general. Philip's advisers were usually salaried laymen who formed a professional bureaucracy and made the institutions of royal government more efficient. These officials, many of whom were trained in Roman law, separated the offices of the royal household from the king's council, thus initiating a break between the long-established custom of regarding the state as a private possession of the king. Thenceforth, royal authority became more impersonal as a more modern notion of the state developed. As the English kings did in England, Philip began to expand the idea of a royal council by including in it members of the bourgeoisie from the towns. In England, the nobles and clergy first met together in the early years of Parliament, but eventually the clergy withdrew and gathered in their own ecclesiastical assemblies, leaving Parliament an entirely lay affair. In France, the nobles, clergy, and bourgeoisie formed the three principal "estates" of the realm, each meeting in separate halls but as part of a single institution known as the Estates General. This body performed the same function as the Parliament, namely to endorse the king's decisions and approve new taxes. It was not until centuries later, and under extraordinary circumstances, that the Estates General became a real representative institution.

The need for revenue for the royal government became a major theme of Philip's reign. He needed money principally for two reasons, the payment of salaries for a growing bureaucracy, and the defraying of military expenses for the war that he launched to drive the English out of Gascony in 1294. Desperate to raise revenue, Philip resorted to underhanded methods. He extorted payments from foreign merchants in France, whom he threatened with imprisonment, and in 1306 expelled the Jews from the country in order to confiscate their property. He also turned to the Order of the Knights Templars, an organization founded during the Crusades to help pilgrims (see Part III, Topic 8). As a result of the generous donations the order received over the centuries, the Templars had grown so wealthy that in France they had gone into international banking. Philip, hoping to be able to confiscate this wealth, brought the Templars to trial on trumped-up charges of heresy and persuaded the papacy to suppress the order. Philip was subsequently outmaneuvered when the pope ordered the Templars' property to be given to a similar religious order, the Knights Hospitalers.

It was also the need for revenue that drove Philip into open conflict with the papacy, thus breaking with a long tradition of close cooperation between the church and the French monarchy. Philip, like Edward I of England, had taken periodically to asking the clergy for special financial "gifts," which they had generally granted. In 1296, however, Pope Boniface VIII (ruled 1294–1303) prohibited the clergy from making such payments to kings without permission from Rome. In response, Philip called the Estates General into session and had them endorse an order against exporting money to Rome. Boniface, stunned by Philip's rash determination, let the matter drop.

The conflict with the church escalated several years later, when Philip had a bishop who served as a papal legate arrested on charges of treason. Tensions worsened when Boniface reprimanded Philip for his actions and the king responded by defaming Boniface's reputation. In 1302, Boniface rose to the challenge by issuing the papal bull *Unam Sanctam*, which declared that Philip had to submit to papal authority or risk damnation of his soul. Philip retaliated by sending agents to Italy to kidnap Boniface and bring him to France to be tried by a church council. Boniface was taken prisoner at his summer residence at Agnani but then rescued by supporters, and the deeply distressed pope died soon after. Philip's triumph over the papacy seemed to be confirmed when in 1305 a French prelate who took the name of Clement V was elected pope and made the fateful decision to establish his pontificate in France rather than in Rome.

STUPOR MUNDI: FREDERICK OF HOHENSTAUFEN AND THE IMPERIAL DREAM

During the reign of Frederick Barbarossa the Holy Roman Empire had grown to include both Germany and Italy, much as it had after the coronation of Charlemagne in 800. Yet even at the height of Frederick's power, the Empire remained more an idea than a reality. In his effort to secure his hold over northern Italy, Barbarossa had been forced to grant concessions to the feudal nobles of Germany. Thus while France and England moved toward consolidated national states, Germany continued to be held in the grip of feudal vassals.

On his death in 1190, Barbarossa was succeeded by his son, Henry VI (ruled 1191–1197). Henry reigned for only seven years, however, and it was Frederick, his son with Constance of Sicily, who revived the Hohenstaufen dream of creating a Western empire that would once again dazzle the world. Frederick II (ruled 1212–1250), one of the principal figures of the High Middle Ages, was a brilliant ruler called by some "terror of the earth," and by others *stupor mundi*, or "wonder of the world." Unlike his grandfather Barbarossa, who was a German prince captivated by the vision of a grander empire south of the Alps, Frederick was an Italian, born in Sicily and steeped in the multicultural traditions of the Mediterranean. His closest advisers included Muslims and Jews as well as Christians, he spoke and read numerous languages, and he commissioned treatises on falconry as well as on political theory. His capital at Palermo was host to a dazzling court that boasted mosques and cathedrals, monasteries and harems.

Germany and the Kingdom of Sicily

From his mother, heiress of Roger II, Frederick inherited the Norman Kingdom of the Two Sicilies, which included the southern half of the peninsula from Naples to the Straits of Messina as well as the island of Sicily. From his father Frederick inherited a claim to the German throne. This dual legacy threatened the papacy and the Lombard cities of northern Italy

Pope Boniface VIII, presiding over a meeting of cardinals, posed a major challenge to the power of King Philip IV of France.

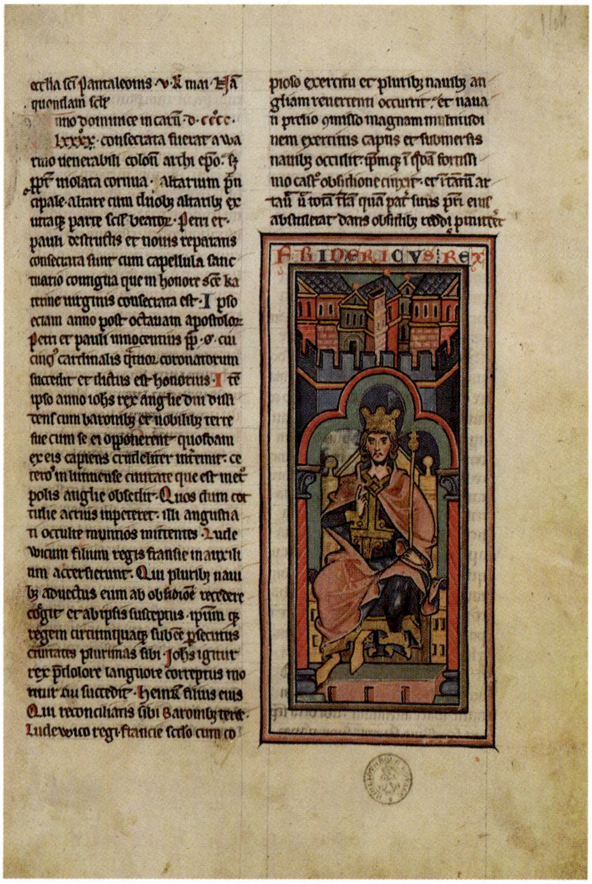

Frederick II, the powerful Hohenstaufen emperor.

more directly than had Barbarossa's military expeditions, both of whom feared encirclement by the Hohenstaufen lands. Frederick was thus faced with powerful enemies from the moment of his birth.

Since he was a child when his father died, a number of German nobles fought over the German kingship while Frederick remained a ward of the papacy. In 1212, when one faction of German princes finally chose the teenage Frederick as their king, Pope Innocent III approved the appointment but extracted from Frederick a promise to remain loyal to the papacy. In 1219 Pope Honorius III (ruled 1216–1227) crowned Frederick emperor on the two conditions that he lead a crusade to the Holy Land and never unite Germany and Italy under one crown. Frederick's unwillingness to meet this second condition so incurred the pope's wrath that he was repeatedly excommunicated. After long delays, Frederick at last pretended to start on his crusade in 1226 but fell ill and abandoned the journey; he started out again the next year without first receiving absolution from the papal ban. In Jerusalem, instead of fighting, Frederick negotiated an arrangement with Muslim leaders that permitted freedom of worship for Christians and Muslims alike, while returning control of the city to the crusaders. Only in 1230 was the excommunication lifted after Frederick promised to respect the church and protect the lands of the papacy.

Despite his promise to the contrary, Frederick's policy was based on the idea of union between Germany and Italy. He traveled to Germany, however, only to deal with pressing questions. He set up an order of religious warriors known as the Teutonic Knights to guard the eastern frontiers, and recognized Bohemia as an hereditary kingdom within the Empire. Like his grandfather before him, he made concessions to the German princes: in return for control over the Empire's foreign and military policies and the right to settle disputes between the nobles, Frederick recognized the complete authority of the princes within their own territories.

The German settlement allowed Frederick to focus on Italy, where he established an efficient and highly centralized government. Frederick portrayed himself as the supreme representative of divine will and justice and the state as the creation of rulers inspired by divine reason. If the church's mission was the salvation of souls, the purpose of the state, which was ordained

Map 10.2 The Hohenstaufen Empire under Frederick II

by God, was to establish a reign of law and order in the temporal world. These ideas he explained in a code of laws known as the Constitutions of Melfi issued in 1231, which Frederick liked to call in more grandiose terms the *Liber Augustalis*. He imposed military conscription for his armies and founded a university at Naples for the purpose of training administrators for his bureaucracy. His economic policies included the vigorous taxation of all his subjects, the abolition of tariff barriers within the realm, and the minting of new coins of uniform value.

In an effort to complete his domination of Italy, Frederick demanded that the Lombard cities of the north submit to his will, but they formed a second Lombard League to resist him. He defeated the League in 1237 at the Battle of Cartenuova and proceeded to conquer all of northern Italy, appointing an imperial official known as the *podestà* in each of the cities that he conquered. Since the pope had encouraged the League, Frederick then invaded the Papal States themselves. In 1245, Pope Innocent IV (ruled 1243–1254) fled to France, where the Council of Lyons excommunicated and deposed Frederick and declared a crusade against him.

Despite the defiant resistance of the church, however, it was only Frederick's death in 1250 that brought an end to the imperial dreams of the Hohenstaufens. Frederick's heirs were unable to regain the momentum and the pope invited Charles of Anjou, the brother of Louis IX of France, to rule the Kingdom of the Two Sicilies and wipe out the Hohenstaufen "viper breed."

Frederick's demise did not mean peace for Italy, for the new Angevin kings were almost as ambitious as the Hohenstaufens and threatened the papacy's control over central Italy. In 1282 a rebellion known as the "Sicilian Vespers" drove the French out of Sicily, which was subsequently taken by the king of Aragon. This

Map 10.3 Europe in the High Middle Ages

disintegration of the former Norman kingdom was clearly a victory for the papacy, which had prevented a unified kingdom from encircling its lands. Nor was the Hohenstaufen dream of binding Italy and Germany together in the Holy Roman Empire ever again seriously revived. German emperors henceforth abandoned Italian affairs and refused even to go to Rome for the imperial coronation. Germany disintegrated further into a conglomeration of independent principalities that prevented the kind of political unity that the rulers of France and England achieved. In 1356, the Emperor Charles IV (1347–1378) issued a document known as the Golden Bull reinforcing the sovereignty of the great princes and regularizing the election of emperors by recognizing seven official electors. The Golden Bull made no mention of any role for the papacy in the selection of the emperor.

The end of real power for the emperors in German affairs confirmed the political trend away from the universalism of the Middle Ages and toward an era of national states ruled by secular monarchs. Medieval theorists argued increasingly for the legitimate power of secular rulers and the separation of church and state. Through the creation of systems of royal justice, regular legal procedures, and professional bureaucracies, kings established centralized governments that removed more and more authority from the old feudal order. At the same time, although the power of the monarchs was limited by the rise of representative institutions, kingship was becoming deeply imbedded in popular imagination and in emerging national identities.

Questions for Further Study

1. What patterns can be discerned in Medieval political theory with regard to church-state relations?
2. Was the Magna Carta a feudal or a democratic document?
3. What methods did the early French kings use to consolidate their power over the feudal nobility? In what ways did these methods differ from those used in England?
4. What were Frederick Hohenstaufen's imperial ambitions? Were they realistic?

Suggestions for Further Reading

Abulafia, David. *Frederick II: A Medieval Emperor*. London, 1988.
Baldwin, John W. *The Government of Philip Augustus*. Berkeley, CA, 1986.
Holt, James C. *Magna Carta*. Cambridge, MA, 1965.
Labarge, Margaret W. *St. Louis: The Life of Louis IX of France*. London, 1968.
Strayer, Joseph R. *The Reign of Philip the Fair*. Princeton, NJ, 1980.
Tillmann, Helene. *Innocent III*. Amsterdam, 1980.
Turner, Ralph V. *The King and His Courts*. Ithaca, NY, 1968.
Van Cleve, T. C. *The Emperor Frederick the Second of Hohenstaufen*. Oxford, 1973.
Warren, William L. *King John*. Berkeley, CA, 1978.

III

Topic 11

Art and Ideas in the Gothic Age

The later part of the Medieval period was marked, intellectually and artistically, by a series of major and lasting developments. Not only are they of intrinsic interest and value in themselves, they also helped to prepare the way for the watershed of the Italian Renaissance.

The leading Scholastic theologian Thomas Aquinas had proclaimed the reconciliation of faith and reason. His immediate successors were less certain of the powers of the human mind. The doubts of thinkers such as Duns Scotus and William of Ockham produced important effects on the course of Western philosophy. Ockham's ideas, in particular, were to influence the study of nature and the rise of science two centuries later.

The literature of the age reflected the same concern with naturalism. Writers rejected Latin in favor of their own languages. New forms included long narrative poems called *romances* and short fables in verse. Dante's *Divine Comedy,* the colossal inauguration of Italian literature, provides a majestic synthesis of Scholastic theology, Classical learning, and personal experience. It stands as one of the supreme achievements of the Medieval Age. Dante's successors—Boccaccio in Italy and Chaucer in England—used the device of the naturalistic story to describe the life and characters of their own day.

The last great achievement in Medieval art, the counterpart in stone of Dante's literary edifice, was the creation of the Gothic style of architecture. The 13th-century architects and stone carvers of Gothic cathedrals adapted the construction principles of Romanesque style to produce light and airy structures decorated with glowing stained-glass windows and naturalistic sculptures. The achievement of an entire community of workers, a Gothic cathedral represented at the same time the summation of centuries of Medieval knowledge and the new spirit of community pride.

Late Medieval painters and sculptors, like their counterparts in the other arts, were attracted by the possibilities of realism. The art of naturalistic portraiture and the careful depiction of plants and animals appear in the repertory of late 14th-century painters and illuminators. While art in northern Europe still remained connected to Medieval traditions, Italian artists used naturalism to move beyond and foreshadow Renaissance humanism. The Pisano family of sculptors and, above all, the painter Giotto revolutionized art in the West.

Thus, against a background of turmoil and human suffering, the thinkers and creative artists of the 13th and 14th centuries continued to explore the concerns of the Medieval world and push them to their limits, while in Italy the link with the next great turning point in Western culture was already being forged.

FAITH VERSUS REASON: THE HEIRS OF AQUINAS

By the mid-13th century, St. Thomas Aquinas had expressed in his *Summa Theologica* complete confidence in the reconciliation of human reason, as understood by the Greeks, and Christian faith (see Part III, Topic 9). Toward the end of the Medieval period, thinkers became less convinced of the certainty of the Scholastic vision. Perhaps they were inevitably influenced by the natural disasters and political strife that beset western Europe in the course of the 14th century. In the face of the apparently arbitrary blows of destiny—war, famine, plague—it was increasingly difficult to believe that human understanding could grasp God's purpose. Faith in God remained constant; reason, however, seemed unable to explain why or how the divine scheme of things operated as it did.

One of the earliest critics of Aquinas' speculative method was the Scottish Franciscan John Duns Scotus (1265?–1308), whose analytical approach to philosophy marked a break with the Medieval synthetic tradition of Aquinas. So dense and difficult was the reasoning of Scotus and his followers that uncomprehending critics labeled them "dunces."

Duns claimed that love and faith were more important than reason and personal experience in understanding God. Indeed, reason was capable of only imagining the existence of God because faith had already accepted it. Thus, instead of trying to deduce the concept of the divine by observing the way in which the natural world worked, as Aquinas had, Scotus held that purely intellectual analysis proved that God necessarily exists. Another version of this argument, which is known as the "ontological proof," lay at the basis of the thinking of the 17th-century philosopher René Descartes (see Part VI, Topic 1).

William of Ockham

At the very end of the Medieval age, William of Ockham (c. 1285–1349) stressed the inability of human reason to understand God's unlimited freedom and power. Surrounded by the uncertainties of the times—Ockham probably died of the plague—it was easier to

Hell, as depicted in a detail of a mosaic in a vault of the Baptistry, Florence.

accept an incomprehensible deity than to count on an ordered, knowable natural world.

In any case, in observing the world around him, Ockham looked for truth in individual things, not in universal principles. It was not possible to know what a table was by simply thinking of the idea, but only by actually seeing one and touching it. Ockham summarized his search for specific concrete examples rather than universal theories in a methodological principle which came to be known as "Ockham's razor." According to this, when there are alternative explanations for the same phenomenon, the simpler is always preferable.

Philosophers following this method were called nominalists. With their distrust for the more abstruse speculations of their predecessors, and their emphasis on method and solid fact—they claimed that knowledge should rest on direct experience and not on abstract reason—they helped to lay the intellectual foundation for the rise of modern scientific method. At the same time, Ockham's belief in God's absolute autonomy and power became one of the chief tenets of the Protestant Reformation in the 16th century.

Botticelli's painting of the great Florentine poet Dante.

THE CLIMAX OF MEDIEVAL LITERATURE: DANTE'S *DIVINE COMEDY*

With the rise of vernacular literature in the Romanesque period, new literary genres appeared that reflected a growing interest in individual human behavior and emotions rather than heroic stereotypes. One of the earliest forms to develop was the *romance;* these were long narrative poems whose interest in plot and character prefigures the modern novel. The first great writer of romances was the French Chrétien de Troyes (c. 1135–1183), many of whose works have an Arthurian setting and describe the quest of his knightly heroes for self-knowledge.

Very different in spirit were the French verse *fabliaux,* short stories written during the 13th and 14th centuries. Satirical, coarse, sometimes obscene, they are often anticlerical, and seem to have been aimed at a new urban public, as much as for literature's traditional aristocratic readership.

Dante Alighieri

At the pinnacle of Medieval literature and culture stands the work of Dante Alighieri (1265–1321), whose *Divine Comedy* ranges over the religion, politics, and intellectual concerns of the Middle Ages to offer a synthesis of Christian and pagan values, the same combination of faith and reason extolled by Aquinas. Furthermore, Dante brings to the intellectual vision of the Scholastic philosopher a richness of poetic language that ranges from gross and violent realism to the heights of spiritual ecstasy.

Dante was born in Florence, the son of a minor noble Guelph family. In his youth, he tells us, he fell in love with a young woman he calls Beatrice, but concealed his devotion. He took an active part in the government of Florence, and served as an ambassador for the city. In 1301, during Dante's absence in Rome on a diplomatic mission, political rivals came to power and pronounced sentence of banishment on him. He never saw Florence again. He died in exile in Ravenna, where—in spite of later Florentine efforts to recover the body—he is still buried.

The *Divine Comedy* traces the poet's passage from Hell to Purgatory to Paradise. The journey takes place on two levels: in one sense it is Dante's own quest, begun on a specific day and time (the dawn of Good Friday, 1300) which occurred at the symbolic midpoint of Dante's life—his 35th year. At the same time the journey takes on universal significance as a comprehensive view of the destiny of all humans, in this world and the next.

His guide to Hell and Purgatory is the Roman poet Vergil, symbol of human reason and the wisdom of antiquity. They begin by descending into Hell and passing through its circles, peopled by those men and women who have rejected the love of God in favor of worldly sins and temptations: riches, power, greed, fraud, treachery. At the lowest point is the monstrous Satan, frozen in a lake of ice. Climbing out through the Antipodes (the opposite side of the world), the two poets ascend the mount of Purgatory.

For the final stage of the journey Vergil, the voice of human reason, can no longer serve as guide. Beatrice herself, symbol of divine grace and revelation, leads Dante through Paradise to the supreme bliss, the contemplation of God.

A number of features characteristic of High Medieval culture permeate the work. One is the way in which Dante combines references to Classical myth and Christian tradition. Thus the ferryman of the dead in Hell is Charon, of Greek and Roman myth. Then, numbers play an important symbolic role. The poem is in 100 sections, or cantos: an introductory one, and then 33 in each of the stages of the journey. The rhyme scheme mirrors the significance of the number three, symbolic of the Trinity, and is called *terza rima;* it consists of verses of three lines with the rhyming pattern *aba, bcb, cdc,* and so on. Hell and Purgatory are both divided into an entrance and nine regions, while Paradise has nine heavens (based on the ancient Ptolemaic system—another reference to the pagan tradition) and the Empyrean, the supreme heaven.

Perhaps the most important symbol in the *Divine Comedy* is light, an important element of much Medieval allegory. Dante begins in the "dark forest" of doubt and despair, and darkness engulfs the regions of Hell. When Dante and Vergil climb out of the last of them, they see the stars above them. Their passage through Purgatory is marked by the daylight of divine light but ends with the sunset of Vergil's exclusion from Christian revelation. At the climax of Paradise, Dante sees God as the "Light Supreme."

If the overall subject of the *Divine Comedy* is the destiny of humanity and the ultimate meaning of history and nature, the poet finds time within his cosmic vision to create a host of memorable characters, some mythological, some historical, some Dante's own acquaintances. Among them are the doomed lovers Paolo and Francesca and the glutton Ciacco the Hog in Hell, and, in Paradise, the young St. Francis, who is presented to Dante by St. Thomas Aquinas himself.

Late Medieval Literature

At the very end of the Medieval period, the growing number of readers inspired writers to produce works aimed at an ever broader public. The *Decameron* of Giovanni Boccaccio (1313–1375) is the first major piece of prose fiction in the Western tradition. A collection of 100 short stories, the *Decameron* seeks neither to elevate nor to enlighten, but simply to entertain.

Boccaccio's slightly later contemporary, Geoffrey Chaucer (1340–1400), created a similar collection of narratives in his *Canterbury Tales*. Both writers are among the first in Western literature to make their women characters as lively, witty, and sexually sophisticated as the men.

THE GOTHIC CATHEDRAL

In the last lines of the *Divine Comedy*, Dante tells us that God's Radiance is the light that moves the sun and the other stars. The architectural style of his age, the Gothic, similarly uses light to illuminate the divine presence. Furthermore, just as Aquinas' theological synthesis and Dante's metaphorical journey reconciled faith and reason to present a unity of vision, so the builders and sculptors responsible for the great Gothic cathedrals sought to represent the unity of human knowledge and the divine.

The practical Romanesque style of a century earlier produced buildings that were sturdy, fireproof, and capable of containing large numbers of people. With their small windows, however, they were so dark inside that most of the sculpture decorating them was on the outside.

Gothic architects took the two most characteristic features of the Romanesque—barrel vaults and stone supporting ribs—and combined them to form high, pointed rib vaults: the ribs provided support for the slender vaults. The results were lofty, light, and airy structures, with the spaces between the vaults cut away and filled with stained-glass windows. To ensure that the buildings were stable, architects added outside supports called "flying buttresses" that shored up the walls. Occasionally the desire to construct buildings that reached to the heavens proved counterproductive, and the structures collapsed before being completed, or shortly after.

The sense of lightness and grace, contrasting with the weightiness of Romanesque architecture, was enhanced by the decorations. The stained-glass windows consisted of multicolored panels placed in a setting of delicate stone framework, or tracery. The shapes of the windows varied. Among the most complex was the great round or "rose" window which often decorated the main façade of a church. By careful use of the

Chartres Cathedral towers over the town around it.

shape, position, and color scheme of the windows, architects could achieve their own control over the light of God.

Outside, the buildings are decorated with a profusion of sculpture combining Christian and pagan stories, fabulous monsters and scientific discoveries, portraits of nobles and merchants, and gutter spouts with grotesque heads, or gargoyles. Other elements include plants and animals as manifestations of the natural world. The total effect has been described as "an encyclopedia of Medieval knowledge for those who cannot read." At the same time, the statues and stained-glass windows provided a permanent record of historical events as well as biblical stories, as in the case of the window at Chartres commemorating Charlemagne.

The earliest Gothic church to be built was that of the Abbey of Saint-Denis near Paris, finished in 1144 under the Abbot Suger. Most of the Gothic churches, however, were built over the following century for cities rather than for monasteries. The Gothic style, in fact, was invented for an urban context. Like the universities, it arose as a consequence of the rise of city life. The immense spires served to signal to travelers through the countryside that they were approaching their destination, and the houses of many a Medieval city clustered around its cathedral.

The primary purpose for the construction of a cathedral was religious, but the building projects of the Gothic Age served a variety of other needs. They helped to provide employment for large numbers of people, from the permanent building staff to the specialized craftsmen responsible for stained glass and other decorations to the traveling sculptors who moved from one building site to another. Because they served so wide a variety of community interests, none of the major Gothic building projects was ever completely finished, but continued to provide work as long as there were funds and workers. Only the devastation of the Black Death brought construction to a halt.

At the same time, the cathedrals gave a sense of pride and identity to the communities responsible for their construction. Nor did they serve only religious purposes. Inside there was space for public occasions

La Sainte Chapelle, Paris, one of the finest surviving examples of Medieval stained glass.

such as town meetings, concerts, or lectures, and outside minstrels and jugglers provided popular entertainment against the background of the façade.

Music in the Gothic Age

It is no coincidence that the most important musical developments of the Gothic Age occurred in Paris, the center of Gothic architecture and of European intellectual life. The musicians of the 12th-century School of Notre Dame in Paris took the earlier Romanesque form of polyphony known as organum and developed it further.

Around 1200 one of the leading composers of the School, Pérotin (d. 1238?), moved from the improvisational style of his predecessors toward a greater sense of musical structure. By simultaneously combining three and even four musical lines in his compositions, Pérotin anticipated developments a century later in harmony, counterpoint, and rhythm.

SCULPTURE AND PAINTING IN THE GOTHIC AGE: ART IN TRANSITION

Throughout the 13th century, the most advanced centers of western European art were in the North, in Paris and the leading cities of England and Germany where major building programs were under way. One of the inspirations for Gothic sculptors working there was ancient Roman art, under the influence of which their statues had increasingly realistic anatomy and drapery.

Yet in Italy itself, once the center of Roman art, artists remained conservative and isolated from developments to the north of the Alps. The style of their frescoes and mosaics, known as Italo-Byzantine, was still rooted in a Medieval tradition of centuries earlier.

Tympanum of the right door of the royal portal of the west façade, Chartres Cathedral.

Early in the 14th century, this situation abruptly reversed. The Italian painter Giotto and his followers revolutionized the history of painting with their new approaches to realism and emotional expression. Renaissance art was a direct consequence of their breakthrough. Meanwhile throughout the rest of Europe artists continued to work in a late Medieval version of the Gothic style called the International Style. By 1400, with the early phases of Renaissance art emerging in central Italy, northern European artists were still producing Gothic works.

Late Gothic Art in the North

The chief feature of the International Style is its choice of realistic subjects and love of naturalistic detail. Its appearance throughout Europe—from which comes its name—was the result of growing cultural contacts between European countries and the increasing spread of ideas among the leading aristocratic courts. Thus, when the future Holy Roman emperor Charles IV (ruled 1355–1378) became king of Bohemia in 1347 he made Prague, the city of his residence, into an art center rivalling even Paris and founded the Charles University there. Similarly in the second half of the 14th century the dukes of Burgundy invited to their court at Dijon the leading European artists of the day.

One of these was the Dutch sculptor Claus Sluter (c. 1350–1406). His carvings for the *Well of Moses* at a monastery near Dijon show typically elongated Gothic figures, but Sluter, working in the International Style, adds a whole series of realistic details: weighty drapery, the soft hair of the beard, the lined faces.

The most attractive and complete picture of life in the late Gothic period emerges from the *Très Riches Heures du Duc de Berry (The Book of Hours of the Duke of Berry)*. This collection of twelve illuminated pages is the work of the three Flemish Limbourg brothers—Pol, Hennequin, and Herman—and dates to 1416. The scenes illustrate the months of the year, and are filled with realistic observation and the depiction of details from nature.

The February page contrasts the farm laborers thawing themselves out in front of the fireplace with the sheep outside in their icy pen huddled together for warmth. In May, behind the verdant spring leaves of forest trees, we can see the spires and turrets of a castle, while in the foreground a procession of Medieval courtiers rides out to the sound of music.

The world of the Limbourg brothers and their Burgundian patrons is that of courtly love and the romances. It comes as something of a shock to realize that by the time they painted their masterpiece some of the greatest artists of the early Renaissance—Ghiberti, Donatello, Fra Angelico—were

Limbourg brothers, the May page from the *Très Riches Heures du Duc de Berry.*

already at work in Florence laying the foundations of Renaissance humanism.

Sculpture in Italy: The Pisano Family

The achievements of Donatello and other great Renaissance sculptors were foreshadowed by the extraordinary art of Nicola Pisano (1220/1225–1284?) and his son Giovanni (1245/1250–1314).

Originally from Apulia in southern Italy, Nicola probably saw work by French and German masters working at the court of Frederick II (see Part III, Topic 10). When Frederick died in 1250, Nicola moved north to Tuscany, and in 1260 carved a marble pulpit for the baptistry in Pisa. Influenced by the Classical style of the pieces produced in the south for Frederick and by a collection of carved Roman sarcophagi in Pisa itself, Nicola combined the realism and vitality of the Roman relief carvings with the expressive qualities of Gothic art.

His son Giovanni worked on the pulpit for the Cathedral of Pisa between 1302 and 1310. The figures are more Gothic, and less obviously Classical, than Nicola's, but his use of space, naturalism, and sense of drama all prefigure the sculpture of the early Italian Renaissance.

Giotto's Predecessors

For all its break with the past, Giotto's revolutionary art has its roots in the style of his immediate predecessors. The most important, Cimabue (1240?–1302?), may even have been Giotto's teacher. Little of Cimabue's work survives, and what there is has been badly damaged—most recently in the disastrous Florence flood of 1966 and the Assisi earthquake of 1997. The crucifix he painted for a church in Arezzo shows an understanding of the anatomy of Christ's body that is new to Italian art. More importantly, the sense of strain and weight conveys an emotional quality lacking in earlier Italo-Byzantine painting.

The same sense of dramatic and emotional involvement emerges in the painting of Cimabue's Sienese contemporary Duccio (1255/1256–1318/9). Many of the scenes from the lives of Christ and the Virgin, painted on his vast altarpiece for the high altar of Siena's cathedral between 1308 and 1311, the *Maestà*, achieve a sense of vividness by their convincing use of architecture. For the first time in the history of painting, an artist had succeeded in showing figures that appear to be inside an architectural setting. Before Duccio, no painter had conveyed so great a sense of space.

The Art of Giotto

The career of the Florentine painter and architect Giotto di Bondone (c. 1266–1337) symbolizes the transition from Medieval to Renaissance art. His contemporaries were quick to recognize his originality and the profound importance of his work for the future

A panel for Duccio's *Maestà* altar (1308–1311) showing the scene of the Annunciation.

development of painting. One of the figures whom Dante meets in Purgatory describes Giotto as the most renowned artist of the age, and a character in Boccaccio's *Decameron* remarks that Giotto "brought back to light the art of painting."

For Renaissance critics, Giotto's most important innovation was his realism. Vasari, the 16th-century painter and writer, summed up reactions when he wrote that Giotto "deserves to be called the pupil of Nature and no other." By the careful use of light and dark, he created a sense of depth and volume which made the figures in his paintings seem as solid as sculptures, as lifelike as real people.

Later ages came to appreciate his genius for using this technique to dramatic and emotional effect, and giving his apparently real figures a convincing emotional life. Time and time again Giotto manages to touch us by conveying the most complete expression of human feelings—and the range of emotions he can summon up is almost inexhaustible.

Rather than confine himself to individual paintings, Giotto preferred to work on a more monumental scale. His greatest surviving work is the cycle of frescoes painted around 1305–1306 in the Arena Chapel in Padua, a building also known as the Scrovegni Chapel, the name of Giotto's patron. The panels illustrate the lives of the Virgin and of Christ.

In *The Meeting of Joachim and Anna*, the parents of the Virgin, Giotto communicates to us the couple's deep affection and mutual dependence by the strength of their embrace and the position of Anna's hands. The arch behind echoes the unity of husband and wife.

In another scene, the *Pietà* (Lament over the dead body of Christ), the mood is of cosmic grief. Angels circle above, howling their sorrow, while Mary stares with disbelief into the face of her dead son and John flings out his arms in despair. Nor does Giotto always use dramatic poses to express extreme emotions. The silent hunched figures in the foreground add their own poignancy. So, too, does the bare tree behind. The painting not only conveys a religious image, the emotions of the living are as important to the viewer as the identity of the dead figure. Humans and their feelings, hopes and fears, have become the subject of art.

Giotto's fresco of the *Pietà*, one of the scenes he painted in the Arena Chapel, Padua, between 1305 and 1306.

Artists and thinkers in the Gothic Age were driven by their urge to find unity in an increasingly complex and threatening universe. Dante's mighty masterpiece and the towering Gothic spires of the cathedrals of Europe looked heavenward for a demonstration of the essential meaning of human life. The Scholastic theologians, led by St. Thomas Aquinas, combined human knowledge with divine law to reinforce the message of religious faith.

Toward the end of the Medieval period, some philosophers began to lose confidence in the capacity of humans to understand such cosmic questions. They chose to concentrate on matters capable of being tested by practical examination. At the same time writers like Boccaccio and Chaucer turned from the great issues of life, death, and eternity to portray the daily lives and emotions of people with whom they and their readers could identify.

Then came the terror of the Black Death. As the 14th century drew to its painful close, waves of the plague continued to wash over much of Europe, and the later stages of the Hundred Years' War added their own grim confusion to the general political and economic chaos. Artists like the Limbourg brothers tried to put back the clock, and recapture the charm and elegance of a courtly era which a century of trouble had virtually destroyed.

Across the Alps in Italy, the process of intellectual and artistic recovery had already begun. The work of Giotto is the first sign of a cultural revolution that was to remake the Western tradition by going back to the beginnings of Western culture: the Greeks. Just as for the Greeks, so, too, for Renaissance artists, at the heart of their vision of the world was neither God nor nature, but humans themselves. In the slow and painful rebuilding of European society during the 15th century, that vision was to pass northward across the Alps, and transform Western life and art.

Questions for Further Study

1. What are the chief features of Dante's style, and to what extent do they reflect the political and intellectual climate of the High Middle Ages?
2. In what ways did the art of Pisano and Giotto break with the past?
3. How does the Gothic style of architecture differ from the Romanesque?
4. What were the reactions of Thomas Aquinas' successors to his ideas, and how did they justify their criticisms?

Suggestions for Further Reading

Bony, J. *French Gothic Architecture of the 12th and 13th Centuries*. Berkeley, CA, 1983.

Freccero, John. *Dante and the Poetics of Conversion*. Cambridge, MA, 1986.

Grodecki, L., and C. Brisac. *Gothic Stained Glass, 1200–1300*. Ithaca, NY, 1985.

Kane, G. *Chaucer*. New York, 1984.

Larner, J. *Italy in the Age of Dante and Petrarch, 1216–1380*. New York, 1980.

Oberman, H. A. *The Harvest of Medieval Theology*. Cambridge, MA, 1963.

III

Topic 12

The Fourteenth Century: Stress and Change in European Society

Between 1312 and 1314, while in political exile from his home in Florence, the Italian poet Dante Alighieri wrote the *Inferno*, the first part of his great epic the *Divine Comedy*. Dante's vision of the horrors of Hell might well serve as a metaphor for the world of violence, fear, and upheaval that characterized the 14th century. The period that opened around 1300 marked the end of what had been a long era of sustained growth for European civilization, a material and spiritual expansion that had begun centuries earlier with the reform of the church and the Crusades, the revival of learning, and the rebirth of towns and commerce. Moreover, the political stability experienced by Europe with the development of royal government was shattered as a result of a long and destructive war between France and England that stretched on into the following century.

By the middle of the 14th century, a difficult era of famine and plague began that decimated Europe's population and caused a more depressed outlook on life. The frenzy of fear that struck millions gave rise to terrible incidents of reprisal against innocent victims blamed for the disasters, including the Jews. The fall in population that resulted from the plague and famine led to a severe labor shortage, which at first stimulated living conditions for workers, but then enabled landowners and manufacturers to reduce wages while governments increased taxes. The subsequent economic pressures began a series of violent peasant and worker revolts throughout Europe. The era ended with a schism that split a papacy already "captured" by a hostile French monarchy and the rise of new forms of religious heresy that challenged the hold of the church over the faithful.

Overpopulation and Its Consequences

By the end of the 13th century, Europe's population had swelled to unprecedented size after a long period of sustained growth. The rising number of inhabitants in cities and countryside had prompted landowners to bring even the most marginal land under cultivation in order to meet the demand for food. The population growth had also increased the labor force, which caused wages—and therefore living standards—to decline.

The Great Famine

By the early decades of the new century, serious food shortages began to appear. The scarcity of food seems to have been due not only to the larger number of people but also to a cycle of crop failures caused by changes in Europe's weather pattern. The continent entered what is known as the "little ice age," in which temperatures dropped and winters lasted longer. These climate

Significant Dates

The Fourteenth Century

1309–1378	Babylonian Captivity of the church
1315–1317	Famine strikes throughout Europe
1337	Hundred Years' War begins
1348–1350	Black Death
1357	Peasant disturbances in France
1378	Ciompi revolt in Florence
1381	Peasant uprising in England

changes reduced the size of harvests, and hoarding in rural areas became common, causing severe hunger in the cities. The incessant wars of the period, especially the Hundred Years' War between England and France (see Part IV, Topic 1), added to the dislocation and made the already difficult transportation of grain and other foodstuffs worse. On top of these setbacks, disastrous floods destroyed crops throughout northwestern Europe.

Conditions were made worse by the fact that on the farms people consumed even the seed that normally was saved for the next season's planting, producing even more devastating shortages the following year. People resorted to eating domestic animals and pets and, when these were gone, even mice and rats. The result was that the most extensive and severe famine in centuries struck, killing hundreds of thousands. Famine had not been unknown in Europe but those of the 14th century were both recurrent and more severe.

The famine, combined with the colder, more humid climate of the period, took its toll on Europe's people, and especially on the poor and working-class population. Medieval sanitation and health conditions were at best poor, especially in the cities, where overcrowding meant that people lived in close proximity to each other and sewage flowed in open gutters in the streets. The result was that a population already suffering from malnutrition became more susceptible than usual to disease.

THE PLAGUE

In 1347–1348, a pandemic of infectious disease known as the Black Death swept across Europe, decimating the population with unparalleled ferocity. This was not the first time that a massive plague had afflicted Europe. In the 5th century B.C. Athens was overcome for several years by a virulent plague that originated in Ethiopia, wiping out large segments of the city's population; in 547, the so-called Plague of Justinian reached Europe from Byzantium and annihilated millions.

The Black Death

The plague reappeared in 1346, this time near the Caspian Sea, having spread from central Asia. In October 1347, a galley of ships from the Crimea carried the plague, presumably through fleas from infected rats, to the port of Messina, Sicily, where it caused an epidemic. It then spread quickly, mainly along trade

The Black Death of the 14th century created economic and demographic havoc in Europe. This illustration shows the mass burial of victims.

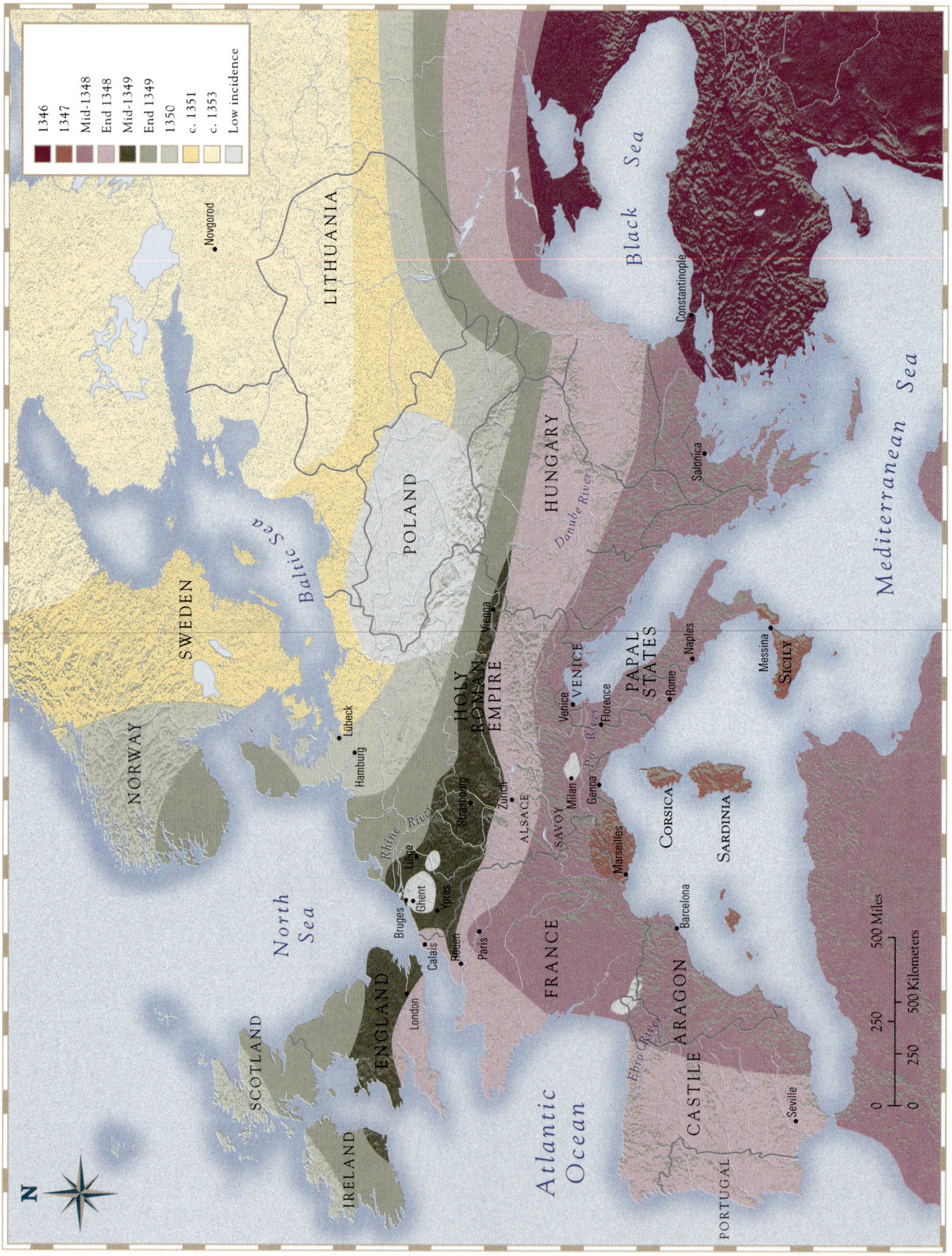

Map 12.1 The Black Death

routes, to Italy, France, Spain, and Portugal. Eventually the disease spread north, reaching Germany, England, Scandinavia, and then moved back east to Russia.

The Black Death seems to have been of two basic kinds, bubonic and pneumonic. Bubonic plague was caused by a bacterium transmitted by the bite of fleas infected from humans or rats; the more virulent pneumonic variety, spread by airborne bacteria that attacked

This painting vividly depicts the impact of the plague. While St. Sebastian begs for mercy in the sky, a man writhing in agony reveals bubo boils on his neck.

DOCUMENTS ON HISTORY

The Black Death

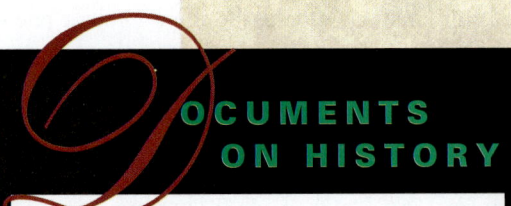

The devastating impact of the Black Death on 14th-century Europe was echoed in numerous chronicles and contemporary accounts, including fictional stories, poems, and religious chants. The Italian writer Petrarch lost his famous lover Laura to the plague in 1348, and Boccaccio made flight from the plague the setting for his stories in the *Decameron.* The contemporary sources tell us not only how people reacted to the plague—the fear, horror, and panic that struck millions. They also provide historians with valuable information about the disease itself, about efforts, both scientific and spiritual, to combat it, and its social consequences. The items that follow are a few of the many sources that document the Black Death and suggest the possibilities and range of material scholars use.

THE PLAGUE IN SICILY: AN EARLY DESCRIPTION

The Black Death arrived in Europe on ships from the Black Sea region that docked in Sicily. In 1361, a Franciscan friar named Michael di Piazza described what happened in the following narrative:

At the beginning of October, in the year of the incarnation of the Son of God 1347, twelve Genoese galleys were fleeing from the vengeance which our Lord was taking on account of their nefarious deeds and entered the harbor of Messina. In their bones they bore so virulent a disease that anyone who only spoke to them was seized by a mortal illness and in no manner could evade death. The infection spread to everyone who had any intercourse with the diseased. Those infected felt themselves penetrated by a pain throughout their whole bodies and, so to say, undermined. Then there developed on their thighs or on their upper arms a boil about the size of a lentil which the people called 'burn boil' *(antrachi)*. This infected the whole body and penetrated it so that the patient violently vomited blood. This vomiting of blood continued without intermission for three days, there being no means of healing it, and then the patient expired. But not only all those who had intercourse with them died, but also those who had touched or used any of their things. When the inhabitants of Messina discovered that this sudden death emanated from the Genoese ships they hurriedly expulsed them from their harbor and town. But the evil remained with them and caused a fearful outbreak of death. Soon men hated each other so much that, if a son was attacked by the disease, his father would not tend him. If, in spite of all, he dared to approach him, he was immediately infected and could by no means escape death, but was bound to expire within three days. Nor was this all: all those belonging to him, dwelling in the same house with him, even the cats and other domestic animals, followed him in death. As the number of deaths increased in Messina many desired to confess their sins to the priests and to draw up their last will and testament. But ecclesiastics, lawyers and attorneys refused to enter the houses of the deceased. . . . Minor friars and Dominicans and members of other orders who heard the confessions of the dying were themselves immediately overcome by death, so that some even remained in the rooms of the dying. Soon corpses were lying forsaken in the houses. . . .

When the catastrophe had reached its climax the Messinians resolved to emigrate. One portion of them settled in the vineyards and fields, but a larger portion sought refuge in the town of Catania, trusting that the holy virgin Agatha of Catania would deliver them from their evil. . . . But the plague raged with greater vehemence than before. Flight was no longer of avail. The disease clung to the fugitives and accompanied them everywhere they turned in search of help. . . . Those who reached Catania breathed their last in the hospitals there. The terrified citizens demanded from the Patriarch prohibition, on pain of ecclesiastical ban, of burying fugitives from Messina within the town, and so they were all thrown into deep trenches outside the walls. . . .

Here [Catania] not only the 'burn blisters' appeared, but there developed in different parts of the body gland boils, in some on the sexual organs, in others on the thighs, in others on the arms, and in others on the neck. At first these were of the size of a hazel-nut and developed accompanied by violent shivering fits, which soon rendered those attacked so weak that they could no longer stand upright but were forced to lie in their beds consumed by violent fever and overcome by great tribulation. Soon the boils grew to the size of a walnut, then to that of a hen's egg or a goose's egg, and they were exceedingly painful, and irritated the body, causing it to vomit blood by vitiating the juices. The blood rose from the affected lungs to the throat, producing on the whole body a putrifying and ultimately decomposing effect.

From Johannes Nohl, *The Black Death: A Chronicle of the Plague,* trans. C. H. Clarke. George Allen & Unwin. Copyright © 1926.

BOCCACCIO'S DESCRIPTION OF THE PLAGUE IN FLORENCE

In the introduction to the Decameron, *the Florentine writer Giovanni Boccaccio gives an eye-witness description of the symptoms and the terrible scenes in the city that parallel those described by Friar Michael.*

It did not act as it had done in the East, where bleeding from the nose was a manifest sign of inevitable death, but it began in both men and women with certain swellings either in the groin or under the armpits, some of which grew to the size of a normal apple and others to the size of an egg (more or less), and the people called them *gavoccioli* [buboes]. And from the two parts of the body already mentioned, within a brief space of time, the said deadly *gavoccioli* began to spread indiscriminately over every part of the body; and after this, the symptoms of the illness changed to black or livid spots appearing on the arms and thighs, and on every part of the body, some large ones and sometimes many little ones scattered all around. . . .

Many ended their lives in the public streets, during the day or at night, while many others who died in their homes were discovered dead by their neighbors only by the smell of their decomposing bodies. The city was full of corpses. . . . they would drag the corpse out of

continued next page

the home and place it in front of the doorstep where, usually in the morning, quantities of dead bodies could be seen by any passerby. . . .

FOURTEENTH-CENTURY MEDICAL ADVICE

The first case of the Black Death in Paris was noted in May or June 1348. In October, the medical faculty of the University of Paris conducted an investigation of the plague on instructions from King Philip VI. The report they issued explained that the conjunction of three planets—Saturn, Jupiter, and Mars—had caused the disaster. Among the measures they recommended for prevention were the following:

No poultry should be eaten, no waterfowl, no sucking pig, no old beef, altogether no fat meat. The meat of animals of a warm, dry constitution should be eaten, but no heating or irritating meat. We recommend broths with ground pepper, cinnamon, and spices, particularly to such people who eat little but choice food. It is injurious to sleep during the daytime. Sleep should not be extended beyond dawn or very little beyond it. Very little should be drunk at breakfast, lunch should be taken at 11 o'clock, and a little more wine may be drunk than at breakfast and the drink should be a clear, light wine mixed with one-sixth water. Dried or fresh fruit is innoxious if eaten together with wine. Without wine it may be dangerous. Beetroot and other fresh or preserved vegetables may prove injurious; spicy herbs such as sage and rosemary are, on the other hand, wholesome. Cold, moist, and watery foods are generally harmful. It is dangerous to go out at night till three in the morning on account of the dew. Fish should not be eaten, too much exercise may be injurious; the clothing should be warm, giving protection from cold, damp and rain, and nothing should be cooked in rain-water. With the meals a little treacle *(theriaca)* should be taken; olive oil with food is mortal. Fat people should expose themselves to the sun. Excess of abstinence, excitement, anger, and drunkenness are dangerous. Diarrhoea is serious. Bathing dangerous. The bowels should be kept open by a clyster. Intercourse with women is mortal; there should be no coition nor should one sleep in any women's bed.

Quarantine Measures

Contemporaries understood at least that close contact could spread the disease, and in one Italian town the authorities issued the following decree (January 17, 1374):

Everyone sick of the plague is to be brought out of the town to the fields, there to die or recover. Those who have nursed plague patients are to remain secluded for ten days before having intercourse with anyone. The clergy are to examine the sick and report to the authorities on pain of being burnt at the stake and confiscation of their possessions. Those who introduce the plague shall forfeit all their goods to the State. Finally, with the exception of those set apart for the purpose, no one shall administer to those sick of the plague on pain of death and forfeiture of their possessions.

THE VISION OF AN ENGLISH POET

William Langland (c. 1332–c. 1400) is generally regarded as the author of "The Vision of William Concerning Piers the Plowman," the greatest Middle English poem before the work of Chaucer. "Piers Plowman" is an allegorical poem in unrhymed alliterative verse. The following lines, written about 1362, are eloquent testimony to the human destruction of the plague:

Hoar Old Age was in the vanguard
And bore the banner before Death, he claimed it as a right.
Nature followed him with many kinds of sores,
Such as pocks and pestilences, and she harmed many people;
So Nature killed many through corruptions.
Death came driving after her and dashed all to dust,
Kings and knights, emperors and popes;
He left no man standing, whether learned or ignorant;
Whatever he hit stirred never afterwards.
Many a lovely lady and their lover-knights
Swooned and died in sorrow of Death's blows.

From "Friar Grimestone's Poems on Death," in Daniel Williman, ed., *The Black Death: The Impact of the Fourteenth-Century Plague.* Center for Medieval & Early Renaissance Studies. Copyright © 1982.

THE IMPACT ON RELIGIOUS LIFE

Among the many problems caused by the Black Death was the toll it took on the clergy, whose ministrations to the sick put them at high risk or who were unwilling to work in villages with high incidence of the disease. In January 1349, when the plague became particularly virulent in England, the bishop of Bath and Wells sent the following appeal to his diocese:

The contagion of pestilence, in these days of ours, spreading everywhere, hath left many parish churches and other livings in our diocese, with their parishioners, desolate and without parson and priest; . . . therefore many folk, as we have heard, die without the sacrament of penance, not knowing what they should do at such a pinch of need, and believing that no other confession of their sins, even in case of necessity, is profitable or meritorious, than that which is made to a priest who hath the keys of the Church. We, therefore, . . . do strictly enjoin and command, in virtue of obedience, that each of you, rectors, vicars, and parish priests in your churches, and rural deans in other places of your deaneries which are destitute of the solace of a priest, should, whether by yourselves or through some other person, publicly and speedily arouse and persuade all men in general . . . that, on the verge of death, if they cannot have a duly ordained priest, they shall in some way make confession to each other, as the Apostle biddeth, even to a layman, or, in default of him, to a woman. . . .

From G. G. Coulton, *The Black Death.* Robert M. McBride & Co., n.d.

THE SOCIAL IMPACT

Matteo Villani (d. c. 1363) was an intelligent and learned citizen of Florence, and the brother of a famed chronicler, Giovanni, who died in the plague. In Matteo's writings on the plague in his city, he described the following social effects in the aftermath of the disaster:

Those few discreet folk who remained alive expected many things, all of which, by reason of the corruption of sin, failed among mankind, whose minds followed marvellously in the contrary direction. They believed that those whom God's grace had saved from death, having beheld the destruction of their neighbors, and having heard the same tidings from all the nations of the world, would become better-conditioned, humble, virtuous, and Catholic; that they would guard themselves from iniquity and sins; and would be full of love and charity one towards another. But no sooner had the plague ceased than we saw the contrary; for, since men were

continued next page

few, and since, by hereditary succession they abounded in earthly goods they forgot the past as though it had never been and gave themselves up to a more shameful and disordered life than they had led before. For, mouldering in ease, they dissolutely abandoned themselves to the sin of gluttony, . . . and again to games of hazard and to unbridled lechery. . . . And the common folk, both men and women, by reason of the abundance and superfluity that they found, would no longer labor at their unaccustomed trades. . . . Men thought that, by reason of the fewness of mankind, there should be abundance of all produce of the land; yet, on the contrary, . . . everything came to unwonted scarcity and remained long thus; nay, in certain countries, as we shall relate, there were grievous and unwonted famines. . . . most commodities were more costly, by twice or more, than before the plague. And the price of labor, and the work of all trades and crafts, rose in disorderly fashion beyond the double. Lawsuits and disputes and quarrels and riots arose everywhere among citizens in every land, by reason of legacies and successions; the law-courts of our own city of Florence were long filled with such pleas, to our great expense and unwonted discomfort.

Quoted in G. G. Coulton, *The Black Death* (New York: Robert M. McBride & Co., n.d.), 97–100.

A UNIVERSAL PLAGUE

The plague had been a recurrent problem since ancient times and in all parts of the world. The Black Death of the mid-14th century had equally disastrous consequences in the Near East as in Europe. In the account that follows, taken from his universal history, the famed 14th-century Muslim historian and geographer Ibn Khaldun summarizes the international significance of the disease.

Civilization both in the East and the West was visited by a destructive plague which devastated nations and caused populations to vanish. It swallowed up many of the good things of civilization and wiped them out. It overtook the dynasties at the time of their senility, when they had reached the limit of their duration. It lessened their power and curtailed their influence. It weakened their authority. Their situation approached the point of annihilation and dissolution. Civilization decreased with the decrease of mankind. Cities and buildings were laid waste, roads and way signs were obliterated, settlements and mansions became empty, dynasties and tribes grew weak. The entire inhabited world changed. The East, it seems, was similarly visited, though in accordance with and in proportion to [the East's more affluent] civilization. It was as if the voice of existence in the world had called out for oblivion and restriction, and the world responded to its call. God inherits the earth and whomever is upon it.

Quoted in Michael W. Dols, *The Black Death in the Middle East* (Princeton: Princeton University Press, 1977), 67.

the lungs, was probably the disease that killed most Europeans in the 14th century.

Medieval physicians did not, of course, know what caused the plague, although they understood that it was spread by infection. In the cities, where the impact was worse, victims fell by the thousands in streets or were left to die in their homes, family members often fleeing in panic. Ships were prevented from entering ports—the word "quarantine" comes from the 40-day period of isolation required of all incoming ships—and rural villages and larger towns tried to keep strangers away. The wealthier classes took refuge in the countryside, a circumstance that provided the setting for the *Decameron* of Giovanni Boccaccio. The fear that the plague engendered sometimes caused desperate and appalling reactions. Boccaccio tells us that while some turned to religious faith in the hope of salvation, others indulged in excesses of drink or physical pleasure. In some cities of Germany, the Low Countries, and Switzerland, the Christian population took out their fears on the Jews, accusing them of poisoning the wells.

There is no way to know how many people the Black Death killed. The Italian city-states, which had the best public health systems of the day, provide an appalling illustration of its impact. The peninsula lost about 2 million people. In the central Italian town of Pistoia some 70 percent of the inhabitants died. Many physicians refused to treat victims, so that the clergy had to attend to the sick, with the result that large numbers of priests and monks were carried off by the disease. In Florence, Boccaccio explains that the cemeteries soon ran out of space:

> Each hour of the day there was such a rush to remove the huge number of bodies that there was not enough sacred burial ground, especially as the custom was to give every body its own spot. When, therefore, the ground was full, they dug large trenches in all the churchyards and stacked hundreds of bodies in them in layers, like cargo in the hold of a ship, covering them with a little dirt until the bodies reached to the top.

Social and Economic Consequences

In all, the plague killed as many as a third of the overall European population—perhaps 35 million people. Like famine, it returned periodically throughout the 14th century and into the next. In the 17th century, plague hit Venice and other Italian towns—between 1630 and 1631, officials in Venice counted more than 50,000 victims—and as late as the late 18th century it killed even more people in Russia. As a result of the combined effect of plague, famine, and war, Europe suffered tremendous demographic losses. Conservative estimates suggest that between 1300 and 1450 the population declined by a half, while others put the figure at two-thirds.

The plague destabilized European society. To many pious Christians the Black Death seemed to spell the coming of the Four Horsemen of the Apocalypse and they responded with both fear and guilt. Fanatical men and women known as flagellants, obsessed by feelings of remorse, traveled together in groups from one village and town to another, chanting and whipping themselves in public to demonstrate their thirst for divine forgiveness. Artists of the period revealed the popular obsession with death by making the Last Judgment a recurrent motif in painting and sculpture. The most impressive treatment of the death theme was in the cemetery building in Pisa, where in 1350 the artist Francesco Traini completed an enormous fresco of the Triumph of Death, in which a group of elegantly clad men and women on horseback encounter three decaying bodies in open coffins. Poetry and folk stories recount the Dance of Death, a bizarre ritual in which corpses danced before stunned observers, and peasants acted out the drama in popular festivals.

In addition to the psychological impact of the disasters, a host of more tangible consequences followed. The drastic decline in population dislocated the economy, interrupting production in craft shops, cloth manufacturing centers, and in the fields. Initially, many of the laborers who survived the plague were neither temperamentally nor physically able to return to work. When they did, the shortage of labor meant that they were generally able to command higher wages, while scarcity also drove up the price of goods. Some governments tried to control the situation by placing limits on wages and prices. Food costs, on the other hand, went down as the demand for cereal crops was no longer fed by population pressures, thus causing a slump in agricultural profits for landowners. In the countryside, bands of mercenary soldiers roamed freely, stealing from peasants and merchants and plundering local villages.

BAD TIMES AND SOCIAL PROTEST: PEASANTS AND WORKERS IN REVOLT

The demographic and economic impact of the years of plague and famine had troublesome social consequences. The period from 1350 to 1450 saw waves of peasant and worker upheavals against the propertied classes. Most of these protests were serious and bloody and beyond anything Europe had ever experienced.

Popular unrest manifested itself both in the countryside and in the towns as tensions rose over the hard times. Faced with lower profit margins due to the rise in wages, rural landowners tried to reimpose tight controls over the serfs and lower wages to earlier levels. Kings and municipal governments, on the other hand, sought to collect higher taxes from the workers who were earning more in order to pay for the wars and increasing costs of government services. The plague had been even more destructive in the towns, where the demand for manufactured goods dropped with the decline in population, resulting in widespread unemployment. Guild members tried to protect their businesses through laws limiting membership and advancement.

Revolts in the Countryside

One of the first and most disturbing peasant revolts took place in 1358 in northern France, an area that

Peasant uprisings, such as the *Jacquerie*, were crushed with great ferocity by the landlords and nobles.

had been devastated by the outbreak of war between England and France. Known as the *Jacquerie*, this insurrection took its name from Jacques Bonnehomme, the nickname which French landlords commonly used for their peasants. After the French defeat in 1356 and the capture of their king, John (1350–1364), the government had tried to make the peasants pay for the king's ransom. Protesting the deprivations and fearing further oppression, the peasants rose against the nobles. With no leaders or specific goals, they murdered landowners and their families with great brutality, and burned manor houses, churches, and local archives containing tax records. The rebels took heart from the fact that the king was in captivity and the government in disarray, and a disheveled band of peasants even tried to march on Paris. But within a month the aristocrats had marshaled their forces, striking back with equal ferocity. They massacred those peasants they caught and hunted down the ones who escaped, drowning some in rivers and burning others alive to set an example for those who managed to survive.

The Jacquerie was followed by similar outbreaks of social violence elsewhere in Europe, including southern France, Spain, Germany, and Sweden. One of the most famous erupted in England in 1381. This Great Rebellion was a protest against government measures to control wages and workers. Peasant anger increased when royal officials levied a poll tax of equal worth on every inhabitant, rather than a proportional tax based on wealth. The landlords made matters worse by trying to restore some of the feudal dues that had been abandoned during good times. After a third poll tax was imposed in 1381, the enraged peasants rebelled under the leadership of a number of men, including one Wat Tyler. The peasants destroyed local records and noble residences and then marched on London, where the 15-year-old Richard II (ruled 1377–1399) persuaded them to disperse with promises to abolish serfdom and lower rents. Tyler was killed and the king, abandoning his promises, wiped out the peasants and their ringleaders.

Disturbances in the Cities

European cities also saw serious social uprisings in the 14th century. Some of these urban revolts were reactions against taxation or the result of struggles between urban political factions. Others were sparked by the frustrations of exploited workers who felt the impact of the economic depression that followed the Black Death. The most important of these worker rebellions was the Ciompi uprising in Florence. The Ciompi were

A manuscript illumination depicting the peasant uprising of 1381 in England. Here Wat Tyler and John Ball lead a peasant army against troops.

clothworkers in the Florentine wool industry, which employed tens of thousands of them as dyers, weavers, and other semiskilled laborers. The wool industry was one of the hardest hit manufacturing sectors in the post-plague slump. As demand fell, the manufacturers created massive unemployment by cutting production to about a third of pre-plague levels. They also passed legislation that controlled wages and shifted the tax burden away from themselves.

In 1378, the Ciompi revolted and forced a number of reforms that included increased production levels, the establishment of their own guild, and representation in Florentine government. Without leaders, however, the Ciompi could not keep control of the situation and the ruling classes soon reestablished their control over the city. Like the other social upheavals of the period, the Ciompi revolt proved to be short-lived. Its significance lies in the fact that it was one of the earliest examples of class conflict in an environment of urban capitalism in which workers suffering from economic hardship seized the initiative.

Other European cities experienced unrest in the 14th century. In London and York, workers supporting the peasants revolted against the royal government, and in Paris a cloth merchant secured the support of the workers in an attempt to reform the royal tax system. These movements of social protest did not have lasting effect but they did serve as a warning to the ruling elites that economic conditions could produce serious social upheaval. Yet the majority of those involved in the revolts were not from the poorest ranks of society. Rather, in the countryside they tended to be relatively prosperous peasants whose condition was threatened by government measures or by the efforts of landlords to increase their profits. The Ciompi, on the other hand, were an exception in that they represented the poorest of the urban workers in Florence. In all cases, it seems clear that the extraordinary circumstances created by the famines, plagues, and war of the period created new social and psychological tensions and further undermined the traditions that had upheld authority in Christian society.

Ironically, by the end of the century the condition of both peasants and workers had improved as Europe began to recover from the disasters and dislocations of the midcentury crisis. Moreover, in western Europe at least, serfdom had practically disappeared and population began to expand once again. Signs of recovery soon obscured the frightening experience of class warfare that had suddenly disrupted the social peace of Medieval Europe.

THE CHURCH IN CAPTIVITY: SCHISM AND THE POPES AT AVIGNON

If economic and social conditions began to improve in the last quarter of the 14th century, the authority and grandeur of the papacy underwent a wrenching experience that seriously weakened the prestige of the Medieval church. Two circumstances, the "capture" of the pope by the French monarchy and a serious division in the leadership of the papacy, paved the way for

Map 12.2 The Schism and Religious Divisions

the later and more serious upheaval that rocked the church in the Reformation of the 16th century.

The Babylonian Captivity

The crisis of the late Medieval church had begun in the struggle for supremacy between Pope Boniface VIII and King Philip IV of France. In 1302 Boniface issued a bull that demanded Philip's submission to papal authority. Although Philip's attempt to abduct Boniface to France to stand trial before a church council failed, the king did manage to secure the election in 1305 of a French pope, Clement V (ruled 1305–1314). Rather than move to the traditional papal palace in Rome, however, the new pope established his court in the city of Avignon in southern France; Avignon was situated within lands belonging to the Holy Roman Empire but in fact lay across the Rhône River from lands of the French monarch. Clement repeatedly said that he planned to go to Rome when local conditions there were more settled, but politics and circumstances kept the papacy at Avignon for three-quarters of a century.

Clement's successors built a huge palace at Avignon which became the official seat of the papacy until 1377. The popes of Avignon lived in great luxury, claiming that it was safer and better located than Rome, but others were scandalized by what the Italian poet Petrarch (1304–1374) called the "Babylonian Captivity." Much to the chagrin of other rulers, the French kings did exercise great influence over papal policies, and all of the popes and most of the cardinals appointed during the 75 years at Avignon were French, a fact that reinforced the popular feeling that the church was being held captive.

Certainly the papacy was weakened as a result of the Avignon experience. An urgent need for revenue led the papacy into a number of practices that contributed to the decline in ecclesiastical standards. The popes at Avignon continued the process of making their government a more efficient and specialized bureaucracy, and this was especially true of fiscal administration. They divided all of Christendom into tax districts and appointed collectors and administrators for

The papal palace at Avignon, where the popes remained under the influence of the French kings for more than a century.

each district. Within each area, the popes used their authority to appoint clergy to benefices in order to raise papal income. *Benefices* were the ecclesiastical equivalent of a secular fief—that is, a church office that provided the person who held the position with an annual income.

The popes at Avignon included in this category the highest, and theoretically elected, positions in the hierarchy, such as bishops and abbots, as well as a variety of less important offices. Under the new fiscal arrangements, the holders of papal benefices had to pay a third of their revenue (above a minimum amount) back to the papacy; under that amount, the benefice holders paid an *annate*, equal to the total revenue for the first year in office. In order to pay the required dues, the holders of benefices pressured the lower clergy under their jurisdiction to increase their contributions, a practice that was especially hard on the poor parish priests. Popes also resorted to the simple sale of benefices for prearranged prices.

In addition to the use of benefices to raise revenue, the Avignonese popes increasingly sold *indulgences*, which granted remission from temporal punishment (such as prayers or fasting) for sins; in addition to purchasing indulgences for themselves, family members could actually buy them for dead relatives, who would then be required to spend less time in purgatory. The papacy also sold *dispensations*, whereby a holder of church office was excused from following certain requirements of church law.

One sign of the weakened power of the popes was to be found in their dealings with the Holy Roman Empire. When Pope John XXII (ruled 1316–1334) tried to stop the election of a Bavarian king as emperor, the German electors simply announced that the emperor did not need papal approval since God had bestowed the position on him. By the end of the 14th century, popes had virtually no real power to intervene in the domestic policies of the European monarchs.

Schism: The Church Divided

It was Pope Gregory XI (ruled 1370–1378) who ended the Babylonian Captivity in 1377 by returning to Rome. His death the following year gave rise to another crisis that only furthered the decline in papal prestige. When the College of Cardinals assembled for the papal election, the people of Rome feared that another French pope would be elected by the French majority of cardinals. The crowds threatened the cardinals unless they chose an Italian pope, and they elected as pope an Italian archbishop, who took the name Urban VI (ruled 1378–1389). Urban announced that he would appoint a large number of new Italian cardinals and embark on a serious reform program.

A crisis arose when the French cardinals reassembled after leaving Rome and declared the election of Urban void. They then elected another pope, this time a Frenchman who called himself Clement VII, and immediately left for Avignon. The existence of two popes, one in Rome and one in Avignon, began what has been called the Great Schism. The division within the church also divided Europe along political lines: France and its allies—the Spanish kingdoms of Aragon and Castile, and Scotland—threw their support behind Clement; most of the rest of Europe, including England and Germany, recognized Urban as the legitimate pope. For almost 40 years, pious Christians watched in horror and confusion as rival claimants to the throne of St. Peter attacked and denounced each other as the false pope and the anti-Christ. Nor did the crisis end with the death of the two popes, for their supporters among the cardinals then elected a new Italian and a new French pope. The credibility and the authority of the papacy were seriously undermined by this steadily deteriorating situation.

The Great Schism reinforced doubts within Christian thought about the nature of ecclesiastical government and the powers of the pope. Marsilio of Padua, whose *Defensor Pacis* had argued for the independence of the church and state, had asserted that the only true source of authority within the church came from the people. He also suggested, as did other theorists, that a general council of the clergy, not the pope, should have the final word in spiritual matters.

This "conciliar" idea took on new urgency in light of the division within the church. Some leaders began to believe that the schism could be resolved by such a council, and in 1409 a group of cardinals from both the Rome and Avignon sides of the controversy organized an assembly in Pisa. Hoping to settle the division, the council deposed both popes and elected a third, John XXIII. When, however, both Clement and Urban refused to step down, the confusion only worsened. Three popes now claimed the leadership of the church. In 1414, however, the Council of Constance met to bring order back to the church. High ecclesiastical officials from every region of Europe gathered together in an assembly organized along national lines. Urban abdicated, but the council had to depose the other two before electing an Italian cardinal from the powerful Colonna family, who took the name Martin V (ruled 1417–1431). The Great Schism was finally over.

Popular Religion

The calamities that beset Europe in the 14th century created a powerful need among many Christians for a new source of spiritual and emotional comfort, a thirst for a more personal and immediate understanding of God's love and grace. The growth in popular devotion that resulted was especially strong in view of the crisis in faith caused by the Babylonian Captivity and the Great Schism. More and more laypeople began to turn away from the formal religious practices of the church and seek comfort in new forms of piety and in mysticism.

The religious practices of the day included numerous forms of devotion designed to elicit divine grace and salvation, especially pilgrimages, processions, and special masses for the dead. Laypeople joined special branches of the mendicant orders founded by St. Dominic and St. Francis, and established religious guilds called *confraternities* that did charity work while enriching their spiritual values. By far the most important expression of the new piety was mysticism. Mystics contended that believers experience God not through formal dogma or sterile institutional rituals but rather through love and emotional availability, by means of establishing a sense of union with God achieved through spiritual exercises and contemplation.

The Rhine Valley of western Germany was an important center of the 14th-century mystics, and it was there that Meister Eckhart (1260–1327) developed a large following through his impassioned preaching. Although a learned scholar and the author of important theological treatises, Eckhart denied the importance of traditional dogma and institutional piety, stressing instead the cultivation of a "divine spark" that would achieve oneness with God. Even more influential was the Dutch mystic Gerhard Groote (1340–1384), whose lay followers founded the Brethren of the Common Life. Groote advocated a new form of piety that came to be known as Modern Devotion *(devotio moderna)*. Groote maintained that communion with God could best be achieved by imitating Christ and devoting oneself to good works. Groote's followers in the Brethren, and in similar female organizations known as the Sisters of the Common Life, established schools and lived according to self-imposed rules of simplicity and humility. One of the most prominent of the Brethren was Thomas à Kempis, who in 1425 wrote a kind of manual entitled *The Imitation of Christ* that stressed ethical behavior and the attainment of internal peace and tranquillity.

Lay piety revealed that popular religious devotion was still very much alive in late Medieval Europe. Moreover, rather than the otherworldliness of an earlier age, it spoke to the desire for more meaningful spiritual experience in everyday life.

The Problem of Heresy

Along with the rise of lay piety, the 14th century also saw the rise of new forms of heresy. That these heresies had widespread appeal was no doubt due to the church's need to adjust to the changed circumstances of European civilization. The church had developed institutions and procedures to deal with heresy but on opposite ends of Europe, in England and in Bohemia, new challenges faced the church and its doctrines.

The most famous heretic of the period was John Wycliffe (c. 1330–1384), an Oxford theologian influenced by the Babylonian Captivity and the new spirit of nationalism generated by the Hundred Years' War. Wycliffe denounced the corruption that he saw in the church and in the papal curia and demanded an end to the payment made every year by England to the papacy. Like others before him, he argued that there was no scriptural justification for papal supremacy in temporal matters, but went further in rejecting the miracle of transubstantiation, according to which during Mass priests change bread and wine into the body and blood of Christ. The Bible, he asserted, was the only true source of authority. He began but never completed an English translation of it in order to make it available to as many ordinary people as possible. In the theological tradition of St. Augustine, he believed that some humans were predestined to salvation, and that these people should live simple lives governed by high ethical standards.

At first Wycliffe had a large number of supporters among the aristocracy but his increasingly radical ideas soon limited his followers to the lower classes. The latter, called Lollards (possibly from the word *lollar*, meaning idler), were attracted to his denunciations of church corruption and property. The popularity of the Lollards diminished after the death penalty for heresy was passed in 1399, and when a Lollard uprising in 1414 was put down the movement went underground. Nevertheless, the Reformation of the 16th century was clearly influenced by Wycliffe's ideas.

In Bohemia, another significant heresy was the work of Jan Hus (1373–1415). A Czech priest who studied at Oxford and was much influenced by Wycliffe's teachings, Hus brought the criticisms of the church and the papacy back to Prague, where they were popular. For a time the king of Bohemia, influenced by the politics of the Babylonian Captivity, protected Hus, and his preachings about social justice gained him a large following. In 1415, however, Hus was summoned to the Council of Constance in order to explain and defend his position on theological matters. Despite the fact that he was granted safe conduct to attend the council, Hus was put on trial for heresy and burned at the stake.

For the immediate future, the impact of Hus' teachings was greater on Bohemia than on Christendom in general. In Bohemia, disagreements among his adherents led to a civil war between 1421 and 1436. At first the movement was headed by lower-class radicals who wanted to realize Hus' preachings about purifying the church, although eventually leadership shifted into the hands of more conservative elements led by aristocrats. Neither faction, however, was willing to return to orthodox Christianity and the supremacy of Rome. As with Wycliffe in England, the Hussite movement generated considerable support among Bohemian nationalists, who opposed the interference of both the papacy and of the Holy Roman emperor in local affairs. Hussite armies led by a Bohemian general defeated several German efforts to wipe out the heresy. By the mid-15th century, the Catholic Church faced the prospect of dealing with serious challenges to its hold on the faithful as well as to its authority within the increasingly hostile boundaries of national states.

The 14th century proved to be an age of unparalleled disaster that shattered the conservative outlook of the Medieval mind and initiated profound changes in the social, economic, religious, and political development of Europe. The disasters that struck the era with such heavy blows—famine, plague, economic dislocation, and social rebellion—were compounded by the crisis that beset the church and the century-long war that broke out between France and England. Yet all these calamities should be regarded not as the tragic end of the spirit and fabric of life as it was known in the High Middle Ages but as the beginning of a complex transition to a new and challenging world.

Questions for Further Study

1. What was the relationship between population growth, agriculture, and the plague?
2. What conditions in European society contributed to the spread and devastation of the plague?
3. What goals did peasant and worker rebels have? What was the outcome of these revolts?
4. What impact did the residence of the popes in Avignon have on the Medieval church?

Suggestions for Further Reading

Barnie, John. *War in Medieval English Society*. Ithaca, NY, 1974.

Gottfried, Robert S. *The Black Death: Natural and Human Disaster in Medieval Europe*. New York, 1983.

Hilton, R. H., and T. H. Aston. *The English Rising of 1381*. New York, 1984.

McNeill, William H. *Plagues and People*. New York, 1976.

Meiss, Millard. *Painting in Florence and Siena After the Black Death*. New York, 1964.

Mollat, Guillaume. *The Popes at Avignon*. New York, 1965.

Mollat, Michael, and P. Wolff. *The Popular Revolutions of the Late Middle Ages*. Winchester, 1973.

Renouard, Yves. *The Avignon Papacy, 1305–1403*. London, 1970.

Ziegler, Philip. *The Black Death*. New York, 1970.

III

Topic 13

The Late Middle Ages

The centuries between 1300 and 1450 saw the transformation of the European economy and social order from the late Medieval world to the era of the Renaissance. After the economic depression associated with the disasters of the mid-14th century, conditions began to improve. Agriculture recovered but changed as new crops and cultivation methods were needed to respond to the decline in agricultural prices. Commerce was not only restored but assumed more modern dimensions as trade zones and cooperative efforts such as the Hanseatic League of northern Germany were developed to deal with increasing competition. Banking became more sophisticated with the growth of accounting procedures, branch-banking concepts, and credit techniques.

Social conditions also underwent transformation. The tempo of urban life accelerated as cities increased their economic and cultural importance. Family structure and the position of women in society reflected these changes. Gender roles were reinforced, marriage patterns altered as people married younger, and parents lavished more energy and resources in rearing children.

The cultural life of the 14th century saw two seemingly contradictory trends in European society. In the North, a late flowering of chivalry and courtly romance reflected preoccupations with an idealized world of the past. The persistence of an exaggerated cult of knightly values has been seen by some historians as the autumn of Medieval culture. South of the Alps, however, a new spirit called humanism was emerging in Italy, a spirit conditioned by a rebirth of interest in Classical culture and its values and a new emphasis on human beings as the center of the world. In the political and social life of Italy, this preoccupation with classical virtues gave rise to civic humanism that encouraged a more active role in public affairs and in the welfare of the community. Out of these sources was born the era of the Renaissance. Above all, then, the 14th and 15th centuries were an era of transition for European civilization.

AGRICULTURE, TRADE, AND FINANCE

After centuries of economic growth and expansion, European agriculture and commerce experienced severe problems of readjustment in the second half of the 14th century. The Black Death had been the most serious aspect of a crisis in the Medieval economy that involved many other causes. In its aftermath, prices, wages, and employment practices changed.

The Agricultural Sector

As population and urbanization moved forward in the late 13th century, agricultural prices had generally gone up while farm wages fell. As a consequence, landlords found it more profitable to use hired help rather than serf labor to cultivate their fields. As a result, most peasants found themselves worse off as this trend accelerated, especially because they were also subjected to higher taxes from royal governments. The Black Death reversed this relationship between prices and wages, for as the decline in urban population reduced the demand for food, agrarian prices fell sharply. At the same time, wages rose as a result of the labor shortage. Employers and landowners tried to reduce wages and reimpose controls over their laborers. The result was rural and urban rebellion.

Despite the failure of most of these revolts, the ruling classes were unable to maintain their social and economic authority over workers. Most peasants in western Europe were not only freed from serfdom—in England such liberated peasants were called *yeomen*—but steadily improved their standard of living, especially through wage-paying jobs. By the 15th century, agricultural workers in England experienced a "golden age" in which real wages reached the highest levels yet known. Many landowners turned to sheep raising, which required a relatively small labor force of shepherds and yielded a variety of products, including wool and skins as well as cheese and lamb. On the Continent, landowners and free peasants turned increasingly to new crops that could command better prices. They moved away from extensive cereal production to more intensive planting of root crops, the cultivation of vines and the production of wine, and the raising of livestock for milk, butter, and cheese. In this way, different areas of Europe began to specialize in those products that they could produce more cheaply and more easily.

A scene of haying in a miniature painting from a French devotional book made for the Duc de Berry.

Conditions in Eastern Europe were different. There a smaller population spread over large areas had meant less urbanization and trade. The Black Death left cities decimated and declining, while most inhabitants lived on a level of subsistence lower than anything known in the West for centuries. Without the effective political leadership of centralized royal government to temper the noble landowners, peasants were forced deeper still into serfdom.

The Rebirth of Trade and Finance

Towns were hard hit by the plague and the recovery was slow. By the start of the 15th century the volume of manufacturing and trade was lower than 100 years earlier. By the 16th century, however, the total had reached new highs. As manufacturing and trade began to expand once again, cities grew in population, although an overall regional shift occurred as northern European cities grew more important and Mediterranean towns steadily lost their formerly unchallenged dominance. Nonetheless, Venice still controlled the spice trade from the East. Its galleys, which linked Italian ports with northern Europe, continued to sail, but at a steadily decreasing rate. The Italians retained a profitable commercial empire until the 16th century, when the development of routes around Africa and across the Atlantic shifted the advantage to European Atlantic states such as Spain and Portugal. For now, however, the real change came as control of trade in the North Sea and the Baltic moved into the hands of German cities.

In 1367, Lübeck, Bremen, and Hamburg organized a number of German trading towns into the Hanseatic League (from the German word *Hansa*, meaning "company") with the aim of keeping foreigners out of northern commerce in favor of their merchants. The League eventually included more than 80 cities and controlled a large fleet and impressive

Map 13.1 Cities of the Hanseatic League

Cloth merchants were an important part of the Medieval economy. Here a tailor measures a client at the Draper's Market in Bologna.

resources, giving it a virtual monopoly over trade in northern Europe. Although the League continued to exist for some 300 years, it began to decline by the end of the 15th century in the face of the growing commercial power of the Dutch.

In manufacturing, textile production remained the dominant industry. By the end of the 14th century, Florence had recovered its former preeminent position in wool making and, along with Milan and Venice, added silk and fine linen manufacturing to its industrial base. In the 15th century new industries developed that were increasingly important in Europe's economy. Metal working, especially armor, became a major industry in Milan, while mining expanded as new technology allowed mine shafts to be sunk hundreds of feet below the surface. The new digging and draining methods opened up rich new mines in central Europe. The discovery of a way to extract silver from lead alloy led to a plentiful supply of silver for making coins, which in turn increased the money supply and economic growth.

The depressed economic climate of the late 14th century drove businesses and banks to become more efficient. The invention of double-entry bookkeeping in the mid-14th century was accompanied by the introduction of insurance and book transfer procedures, and all of these made business practices more sophisticated. In banking the Italians led the way toward new forms of organization, with the Medici of Florence dominating the field (see Part IV, Topic 1). Beginning as textile manufacturers, the Medici expanded into banking and had as their clients the papacy and a number of European monarchs. The Medici bank developed a series of autonomous branches based on partnerships in Rome, Florence, Venice, Bruges, London, and other cities. While central management remained in the hands of Medici family members, each branch functioned as a separate entity, so that the collapse of one branch did not threaten the others. The Medici empire collapsed at the end of the 15th century when a number of major borrowers defaulted on their loans and the French seized the Medici property after invading Italy.

By 1500, Europe had achieved a remarkable recovery from the disasters of the previous century. New agricultural and manufacturing products and better production techniques, combined with rationalized and diversified business organization, all contributed to the building of a reinvigorated and more prosperous economy.

Italian bankers, such as the Bardi and Peruzzi, experienced decline in the aftermath of the Black Death, especially after the English sovereign repudiated his debts.

EUROPEAN SOCIETY BEFORE AND AFTER THE BLACK DEATH

The impact of the Black Death on social conditions was profound and long-lasting. Just as the economy adjusted to changed conditions and new stresses, so urban life, marriage and the family, and the condition of women in late Medieval society all were transformed by the disasters of the age.

Life in the Cities

In the 14th century only a small number of Europeans lived in cities, at the most 10 percent. Some regions had higher concentrations of urban population, especially northern Italy, where perhaps as many as one out of four people lived in towns. By modern standards, however, cities were rather small, with only a handful—among them, London, Paris, Florence, and Venice—boasting around 100,000 people. Yet city life exercised an influence on Europe's cultural and economic life out of all proportion to the size of the urban population.

The plague made the social differences among urban dwellers more stark, so that cities after 1350 tended to have greater contrasts of wealth and poverty. In most Medieval cities land was limited to defined areas within the town walls. As a result, whereas the wealthy occupied ever larger and more luxurious homes, often protected against unruly townspeople by thick walls and high windows, the poor continued to live in even more crowded and unsanitary tenements. In the aftermath of the plague, many cities began to provide medical and health services for their inhabitants. Special boards were established to enforce new health and sanitation laws. Given the lack of medical knowledge, however, such measures had limited value in preventing a recurrence of plague and disease.

The poor and working classes, of course, had suffered extreme deprivations. The plague took a greater toll on them than on the generally healthier upper classes, who also had the opportunity to escape the confines of the city during bad times. Moreover, the post-plague decline in manufacturing created large numbers of urban unemployed. In the face of a mounting social

The Money Exchange in Bruges.

Merchant shops in a Medieval French town, including a grocer, tailor, barber, and furrier.

crisis, officials in many cities throughout Europe developed new methods of social control—in Florence, for example, there was a clear connection between increased poverty and the social unrest that exploded in the revolt of the Ciompi (see Part III, Topic 12).

Public assistance to the poor increasingly took the place of what had once been almost exclusively religious and private charity. Cities created new institutions and used tax revenues to support charity initiatives such as hospitals, food distribution networks, orphanages, and prenatal care centers. Along with aid to the poor, municipal governments sought to curtail the most unpleasant manifestations of poverty and the mounting level of violence that afflicted late Medieval cities. Some towns limited begging to particular neighborhoods and times, while some prohibited it altogether and others allowed the unemployed and homeless to remain within the city walls only for a specified number of days.

As urban crime grew, cities adopted harsher methods of punishment in an effort to repress antisocial activity. The use of torture and execution increasingly replaced the payment of fines, exile, or prison terms even for a crime such as robbery; in places where the death penalty was practiced, hanging was replaced by more horrible methods of execution, including mutilation, breaking on the wheel, and burning at the stake. In an age when violence was common, public executions were often occasions for popular festivities.

Many poor girls and young women from the country who were unable to marry or find employment in the cities resorted to prostitution to survive. As the incidence of prostitution increased after the Black Death, many cities tried to regulate it by issuing licenses, conducting health inspections, and controlling prices. The church, on the other hand, tried to reform prostitutes by providing them with housing and religious instruction.

Craft guilds continued to function as the center of urban professional life for workers, employers, and merchants. In hard times, guilds provided security against economic disaster, and took care of widows and orphans. They also created a sense of community and fellowship. After the Black Death, however, guilds increasingly focused their energies on keeping their monopoly over particular crafts and restricting membership in order to limit competition and preserve a certain standard of living.

By 1450, after a century of decline, the overall population of Europe started to increase again, although the estimated population of 45–50 million people was still only about two-thirds of what it had been before the plague. The Black Death severely impacted mortality rates, lowering life expectancy among the affluent merchant class from a pre-plague level of perhaps 40 years to about 30 years in the 15th century. The infant mortality rate was high, most people died young, and extreme old age was rare.

Marriage and the Family

It is difficult to generalize about marriage and family life for most Europeans in the Middle Ages, principally because written records about poor peasants and the working class are scant. A few sources do exist, such as tax rolls, court records, and folk stories, which tell us something about the lives of better-off peasants and the merchant or noble classes.

We know, for example, that young peasants courted each other actively and often resisted the prearranged marriages that were more common among the nobility. Court records reveal that premarital pregnancy was not uncommon. Fifteenth-century poems called "How the Wise Man Taught His Son" and "How the Good Wife Taught Her Daughter" stress the importance of family tranquillity. Marriages without public ceremonies or the announcements made in church known as *banns*—which the Fourth Lateran Council had required in 1215—were frequent. The dissolution of marriages was extremely rare. Bigamy provided one of the few legitimate reasons, and if the marriage was not consummated it could be annulled after the wife and husband were examined. The wording and dispositions of wills indicate the degree of affection in which most husbands held their wives and children. Among peasant and worker families, training for work came early and the lives of children were austere.

Most of our knowledge about the private lives of Medieval people is limited to the literate men and women of the middle classes and aristocracy. Parental choice and economic factors still tended to determine whom a person married in the upper classes, although emotional affection between spouses and toward children was by no means unusual. Gender relations and functions in these wealthier families more closely resembled modern behavior. Wives, for example, assumed greater responsibility for the management of family finances and estates.

One effect of the plague was to alter the age at which marriages took place. Most young men had generally been forced to put off marriage until after their fathers died in order to have sufficient land or resources to raise a family. As a consequence, husbands were often in their late twenties or thirties before marrying; women, on the other hand, seem to have married younger, while still in their teens. The improved economic conditions after the Black Death led to earlier marriages, especially for men.

The population increase registered in the decades after the Black Death reflected the accelerated pace of marriages and the fact that improved conditions extended the mortality rate. Those children who survived were reared with more parental attention and care than had been the case in earlier centuries. Educational opportunities were increasingly available for middle-class children—principally for sons—in the cities, where municipal governments often provided schools for preteen children. Both parents seem to have regarded their children with more affection. Generally, when a wife died, the husband remarried and had additional children with his new and presumably younger wife. Despite the new concern for children observed by late Medieval parents, the practice of eliminating unwanted infants through exposure was still widespread; because daughters required dowries in order to marry, they were more likely to be killed.

The basic household unit continued to be the nuclear rather than the extended family, with perhaps a widowed mother or aunt living with the husband, wife, and children. Since few people lived to an old age, it was unusual in peasant or worker families for more than two generations to live under one roof. The basic late Medieval family consisted of four to six people, and various birth control methods—*coitus interruptus*, douches and purges, and abortion—were practiced in efforts to limit family size. Wealthier families could afford to maintain extended families as well as servants in the household.

THE LIFE OF WOMEN

Despite the powerful social and economic transformations of the 14th century, the lives of most women in the late Middle Ages remained fundamentally focused on marriage and the family. As young girls, women of all classes were trained to be wives and mothers, to manage households, and to bear and raise children. Yet late Medieval women faced a peculiar situation. The prominent theologians of the age defined an increasingly circumscribed role for women, while the changing economic and social circumstances following the Black Death made more opportunities for women, especially in the towns. Here, too, generalizations are difficult, for the condition and role of women depended greatly on the class to which they belonged.

Women and the Scholars

During the feudal era, women had acquired a significant degree of power that had much to do with the constant warfare that often kept men fighting away from home for long periods of time. In their absence, women not only saw to the raising of the children and the care of the household but took on the additional responsibilities for overseeing the family estates and, if their husbands were monarchs, caring for the interests of the dynasty and the realm. In addition, courtly literature placed women at the center of a society in which they were venerated and protected by their men. Even in the church, women could and did achieve considerable prominence and authority.

But the intellectual developments of the 12th and 13th centuries undermined women's status by using the prestige of earlier authorities to define gender roles in ways that limited female participation in society. Thomas Aquinas, the most influential of the Scholastics, reached back to Aristotle for guidance on the matter of the proper role of men and women. Aquinas argued that it was in the "natural" order for men to be active

Christine de Pisan, a French author, presents her book to Queen Isabella of France, her patron.

PERSPECTIVES ON HISTORY

Gender in Medieval Society

Lisa M. Bitel
University of Kansas

In 585 the bishops of what is now France gathered at Mâcon to discuss policy for the churches under their leadership. Their job was to keep Christian rituals in order, rule on contested points of theology, and set up guidelines for the behavior of priests, deacons, and ordinary believers. One of the council's specific duties was to debate a question with far-reaching effects: were women human? In fact, the clergy at Mâcon were indulging in a grammatical discussion over the wording of the book of Genesis: the Bible said that man (Latin *homo*) was created in God's image, but could the meaning of that word be extended to include women? The bishops decided that the Latin of the Vulgate was flexible enough to include women among the humans.[1]

The Mâcon debate was only one episode in a long Western history of literate men's discussion of women which has lasted since the days of St. Paul. No single view has predominated, now or during the Christian Middle Ages; indeed, Jewish and Muslim scholars in Medieval Europe carried on their own debates about women and gender relations. What is more, never have the ideas of the scholarly elite fully represented the attitudes or behavior of most people in everyday life. Women never held a single status in any given society, nor did men and women interact in the same way in every situation. Yet the writings of scholars have always influenced as well as reflected the acts and thoughts of other men and women. Thus, the Medieval textual debate about women reveals that European Christian societies were deeply divided about whether women were good or bad; whether they were like or unlike men; and whether they were to be loved or shunned by men.

In the Middle Ages this debate had two phases. Until about the year 1000, the argument was left mostly to churchmen. Only priests, monks, and bishops knew how to read and write. If other men and women thought about the nature of women, they rarely had the chance to record their ideas. Even the secular poems, stories, and sagas left to us were usually recorded by churchmen, hence subject to their opinions. In the second phase of the Medieval debate over women, a more diverse group of literate men—and a few women—had a chance to express their views to a wider audience in a greater variety of literary forms, including romances, satires, poetry, and even housekeeping guides. Nonetheless, certain themes and ideas about women pervaded all the texts throughout the European Middle Ages. In particular, questions of women's nature and character—by which writers often meant how women measured up to the free adult male norm—came up time and again.

People's ideas about the other sex were shaped by their social experience and by received tradition. Tradition came from two sources: local secular culture, which people absorbed from family and neighbors and then handed on to their own children in the form of advice, law, and stories; and formal learning, which, during the early Middle Ages, meant church teachings, often informed by Classical Roman ideas. Both of these sources of tradition seem to us extremely sexist. For example, in some barbarian societies, secular laws, which assigned a monetary value to human beings, routinely rated women at a lower price than men. In other areas, only women of childbearing age were worth more than men, because they could bring male babies into the world. But once women ended their childbearing careers and reached menopause, their worth (called *wergeld* in Germanic societies) plunged.[2] Although barbarian sagas occasionally depicted powerful and fiercely sexual heroines, such as the Irish Queen Medb or the Germanic Brynhild, by and large, native tradi-

[1] Gregory of Tours, *Historia francorum*, 8.20.

[2] Katherine Fischer Drew, *The Laws of the Salian Franks* (Philadelphia, 1991), 85, 105–106, 127.

tions treated women as objects to be traded in marriage or, at best, as disenfranchised members of their communities whose status was completely dependent upon that of their male guardians.

Christian theologians and missionaries articulated an ambivalent theory of women derived from gospel and St. Paul, which admitted the equality of all souls but blamed women for sinning and for tempting men to do the same. One 6th-century Irish saint, for instance, fled whenever he heard the bleating of sheep, reasoning that where there were sheep there were shepherdesses, where women sex, where sex sin, and where sin damnation. In the centuries after Paul, Christian writers elaborated on the gospel's ambivalence toward women, although they often weighted their discussions on the negative side. Tertullian, 3rd-century bishop of Carthage, who had called women "the devil's gateway," and St. Jerome, who warned women against marriage and motherhood, influenced almost all later discussions of women. But the most persuasive was St. Augustine who, like many of his Medieval successors, conceived of women as both sinful, like Eve, and saintly, like the Virgin Mary: "through women death," he wrote, "through women life."[3]

At the same time, early Medieval Christian writers admitted that some women could realize the highest forms of Christian life and virtue. Bede, the 8th-century English abbot (d. 735), described heroines such as the Abbess Hilda, who had managed a famous double monastery of monks and nuns at Whitby a century earlier, and chaired an international ecclesiastical conference on the correct date for the Easter holiday.[3] As saints' lives from the period show, male missionaries appreciated the help of nuns who fearlessly accompanied them to the Christian frontiers of Europe in order to convert the natives. Nonetheless, early Medieval theologians believed that only the least woman-like of women could become truly saintly. The ideal Christian woman gave up everything demanded of an ordinary female—husband, children, kin, home, and all feminine decorative trappings—to veil herself literally and socially. Canonists, who wrote church laws, ordered nuns to live as if "dead to the world," for any woman who did not cut herself off from earthly temptations could not be trusted to pursue her Christian vocation and remain sinless.[5]

With all the social, economic, and political changes of the period after 1000, attitudes toward women changed too, but not always for the better. Some of the same old themes continued to appear in theological tracts and other religious literature, and to influence people's behavior. Abelard, the 11th-century philosopher (d. 1142) who initiated a new tradition in logical thought, was enlightened enough to take a brilliant female pupil named Héloise (d. 1163). He also became her lover. But when their affair ended disastrously—a secret marriage, the abandonment of their child to relatives, her forcible claustration, and his castration—he blamed her, or rather, her womanliness. He who had once sung his own love lyrics to Héloise in the streets, complained bitterly that it was Adam's love for Eve that had led all of mankind down the garden path to sin: "from the very beginning of the human race, women had cast down even the noblest men to utter ruin."[6] Despite his personal *calamitas*, Abelard was merely participating in an established tradition when blaming the Fall on women.

Thomas Aquinas (d. 1274), the greatest of all Medieval theologians, discussed the problem of women at length. Although he believed that women could be redeemed along with men, he also quoted Aristotle on the physiological and intellectual deficiencies of the female sex, claiming that the birth of a woman was a mistake of nature caused by a debility or flaw on the part of the parents or an external influence on their coitus, such as a damp south wind.[7] Aquinas also explained at length why, exactly, it was natural for women to

continued next page

[3] J. P. Migne, ed., *Patrologia Latina* (Paris, 1844–1864) 38, col. 1108.
[4] Bede, *History of the English Church and People,* Betram Colgrave and R. A. B. Mynors, ed. and trans. (Oxford, repr. 1991), 298–299, 404–415.
[5] H. Wasserschleben, ed., *Die irische Kanonensammlung* (Leipzig, 1885), 183.
[6] Abelard, *Historia Calamitatum* (St. Paul, 1922), 21.
[7] Thomas Aquinas, *Summa Theologiae,* Ia, 75, 4.

be subservient to their men: their "changeableness of nature" prevented their rational pursuit of virtue, making it necessary for others to govern them.[8]

New voices also entered the debate about women after 1000. The singers of love poetry, male *jongleurs* and *troubadours* and female *trobairitz*, claimed that love (*fine amour*) was a game at which male and female were equally disadvantaged. "Toward you I will never have a treacherous heart or a heart full of deception, even though you treat me badly," lamented one female poet.[9] The theme was taken up by writers who entertained the lords and ladies of the new courts with sophisticated romances. Chrétien de Troyes' *Yvain*, one of the best, described a man forced to choose between his knightly reputation and his promise to remain with his noble wife; when he opted for his reputation, he lost both and was redeemed only after he had been exiled among the beasts of the forest and learned again how to live and love like a proper, civilized, courtly knight. In this tale, women provided the chivalrous example of courage and devotion for men to follow. In other romances, such as the stories of Tristan and Iseult or Lancelot and Guinevere, ladies were duplicitous and adulterous—but so were the men.

The ultimate example of the genre of romance, Jean de Meung's (d. 1305) *Roman de la Rose*, was an allegory of the quest for physical rather than spiritual love, which severely satirized women's character. "All of you are, were, or will be whores by action or intention," proclaimed the author.[10] *Roman de la Rose* sparked a text-to-text quarrel among the intellectuals of Europe around the turn of the 15th century. One of the participants was Christine de Pisan (d. 1434), a poet, historian, and scholar, and the first woman known to have made her living by her pen. Pisan attacked de Meung's romance which, she claimed, "dared to slander and reproach the entire female sex without exception."[11] Her outraged defenses of women, *Livre de la cité des dames* (1404–1405) and *Livre de trois vertus* (1405), rejected traditional misogyny, praised the virtues of women, and set up guidelines for female survival in a patriarchal world.

Other genres of literature treated the problem of women less seriously than Pisan. The *fabliaux* were hilarious and scurrilous tales of would-be knights, peasants, and village priests in which married women constantly had sex with apprentices, traveling salesmen, local clergymen, and sometimes even their own husbands. For instance, in one tale, "La saineresse," a husband boasted that no woman could deceive him, but his wife proceeded to do exactly that by bringing in a lover disguised as a lady-doctor. After her "examination," the wife described—in double entendres only her husband failed to understand—how she took a hundred hard strokes with tools in her loins, was comforted with a soothing salve, and received ointment from a pin-

[8] Thomas Aquinas, *In Octos Libros Policorum Aristotelis*, trans. Diane Gordon (Quebec, 1940), I, 51.

[9] H. Jay Siskin and Julie A. Storme, "Suffering Love: The Reversed Order in the Poetry of Na Castelloza," in William D. Paden, ed., *The Voice of the Trobairitz: Perspectives on the Women Troubadors* (Philadelphia, 1989), 123.

[10] Jean de Meung, *Roman de la Rose* (Paris, 1974), 11. 9155–56; trans. A. Lanly, book 2, vol. 2, 36.

[11] Eric Hicks, *Le débat sur le Roman de la rose* (Paris, 1977), 22.

and women passive, so that while men tended to dominate, women were by nature submissive. The nature of women, he believed, was different from that of men, and it was a difference that Aquinas and other Scholastics believed made women inferior. Theologians often turned to the biblical story of Adam and Eve for proof of this difference, arguing that it was Eve who had tempted and corrupted Adam, so that the influence of women was seen as pernicious and harmful. Even in the songs and tales of the troubadours, women were often portrayed as cunning and crafty, using their allure to trick and defeat men.

Such ideas were widely held and discussed in the cathedral schools and in the universities to which they gave rise. As the educational system trained more and more lawyers, priests, and scholars, these misogynist hole with a stopper.[12] Authors of these tales held up women's ingenuity in deceiving their husbands and other men for laughing admiration, if sometimes also for vilification as the common habit of all women.

Diverse as these texts were, certain themes in them echoed the complaints of earlier Medieval writers. Women were highly sexual beings, according to later Medieval writers, often aiming their desire at the wrong men despite the disruption to social order that their actions might bring. They showed little regard, for instance, for the maintenance of legitimate patrilineages, or the preservation of family reputation, both of which were vitally important to the Medieval nobility. Women were also noisy, impetuous, and emotional; the best women, in fact, idealized by Medieval authors, were quiet, cautious, reasonable, and frigid reminders to their sisters of how to behave. Indeed, one modern scholar has suggested that women and all things female signified, in these texts, violence, noise, and riot—in short, everything feared by the keepers of Medieval social and political order.[13]

The sedate and virtuous lady of 12th-century romance was part of the same world as the careless deceiving wives of *fabliaux*. They were mirror images, as well as descendants of their ambivalent ancestresses of earlier Medieval texts. They sprang from minds who knew what St. Paul, the early Church Fathers, Bede, Aquinas, and all the rest had said about women. Yet these writers also knew the whole variety of real women who surrounded them day by day—the girl next door, the wife, Jeanne d'Arc, famous mystics such as Margery Kempe, queens, servants, good bourgeoises, and a thousand other females encountered briefly or at length. No single text could convey a comprehensive Medieval attitude toward women. Indeed, the ambivalence of the texts suggests the actual diversity of gender relations in Medieval Europe.

Medieval Europeans did not seek systematically to repress women nor to denigrate them. Yet the ambivalence toward women, wrought by native traditions and Christian theologians, persisted throughout the Medieval centuries. It had led the bishops of Mâcon to wonder about the very humanity of women; almost a thousand years later, in 1486, this long tradition of doubt about the female sex caused two Dominican monks to write a tract called *Malleus Maleficarum*, or the *Hammer of Witches*. Women, they claimed, were more prone to desire and lust than men; hence women were more vulnerable to sin and likely to sin sexually with the devil, who would convince them to become witches and attack men. The Dominicans were merely repeating, in exaggerated form, many of the accusations and doubts about women leveled for centuries by respected theologians, philosophers, and poets, as well as joking writers of *fabliaux*. Not many Europeans in the 15th century read the *Malleus Maleficarum*, and surely not everyone agreed with its claim that women were likely to become witches. Yet this vicious little treatise became the justification for the worst persecution of women ever launched in Europe: the witch-hunts of the 16th and 17th centuries, which resulted in the trials and executions of thousands of women and men—but mostly women—from Eastern Europe to the Western Hemisphere.

[12] John DuVal, ed. and trans., *Cuckolds, Clerics, and Countrymen: Medieval French Fabliaux* (Fayetteville, 1982), 105–109.
[13] R. Howard Bloch, *Medieval Misogyny and the Invention of Western Romantic Love* (Chicago, 1991).

ideas gained more currency in the intellectual community. Indeed, women were expressly excluded from the new universities and the renewal of learning—and, by extension, from the new professions that the universities trained men to fill. The intellectual and religious authority of the Scholastics established the theoretical basis on which women were expected to give up any active role in society. Instead, a new and sharper division of roles developed which relegated women to the circumscribed life of household and child rearing.

The economic hardships of the 14th century reinforced these trends by limiting women's opportunities for employment. Even when women worked, a division of labor evolved which dictated that women and men did different kinds of tasks. In the early and high Middle Ages, for example, weaving was a task that women performed regularly, both in the home and in the craft shops. By the late Middle Ages weaving became an almost exclusively male preserve. Instead of weaving, women were increasingly limited to spinning. Moreover, even when women did the same kind of work as men for the same employer, they almost always received lower wages than their male counterparts—women were paid from one-third to one-half the wages paid to men for the same tasks.

Women in Cities and the Church

The economic impact of the Black Death temporarily altered this pattern. The labor shortage that followed the plague increased the need for women workers, both in manufacturing and in the fields, and also had the effect of equalizing wages. Moreover, the growth of towns had a liberating effect on women, as it did on men. Women serfs who escaped their bondage on a master's land could, after one year in a free city, become permanently free. In the cities, working women could marry and find jobs. More than one-half of all working women in towns were employed as domestic servants but other opportunities were abundant. While most guilds, for example, limited their membership to men, some allowed women to become apprentices and masters, especially in the textile crafts. Women could gain and control property in cities and live independent lives—in 15th-century Florence, the tax rolls reveal that more than 15 percent of all households were headed by women. The attraction for women of a freer life in the towns is reflected in the fact that most urban populations revealed a disproportionate ratio of women to men.

In late Medieval times some women continued to make a life outside the family by taking advantage of opportunities in the church. The 12th-century abbess Hildegard of Bingen, who founded the convent at Rupertsberg and wrote a number of learned treatises, wielded considerable power in her day. By the 14th century, the era of the great abbesses was fast fading as the convents came under the authority of male prelates and the papacy limited the powers of women in the church. In 1293, Pope Boniface VIII issued a bull that defined women's roles in the church narrowly and insisted that they be cut off from the outside world: "all and sundry nuns, present and future, to whatever order they belong . . . shall henceforth remain perpetually enclosed . . . ; so that no nun . . . shall henceforth have or be able to have the power of going out of those monasteries for whatever reason or excuse. . . . "[3] Nevertheless, many women found fulfillment in a world of their own choosing in which they could pursue scholarly interests and work as well as religious devotion.

HUMANISM: THE CLASSICAL SOURCES OF A NEW SPIRIT

The Hundred Years' War that raged between England and France in the 14th and 15th centuries (see Part IV, Topic 1) was to be the last gasp of the world of knights and lords and the warrior class that had dominated the feudal order. During the first half of that struggle, a Flemish historian and poet named Jean Froissart (c. 1337–1410?) wrote his elegant and sweeping *Chronicles*, praising the exploits of the brave fighters but arrogantly dismissing the concerns of the common people.

Froissart's aristocratic viewpoint reflected the persistence in northern Europe of interest in courtly life and manners and a preoccupation with an outmoded cult of chivalry. Although feudal warfare was rapidly becoming out of date, the northern aristocracy seemed to want to avoid the reality of changing times by pretending that the virtues of chivalry still determined social and political affairs. Perhaps because of their growing insecurity in the face of rapidly changing conditions—in which a new capitalist merchant class was increasingly dominating society—nobles indulged in deliberately extravagant lives of luxury. They formed exclusive new chivalric orders, such as the Knights of the Golden Fleece and the Knights of the Garter, which they hoped would preserve knightly virtues, and engaged in excesses of courtly ceremony and romantic love. The famous Dutch historian Johan Huizinga speculated in *The Waning of the Middle Ages* (1919) that this aspect of northern civilization reflected a culture in decay.

Italy and the Humanist Spirit

In contrast to the notion of a culture in decline that Huizinga described, the Swiss historian Jacob Burckhardt posited in *The Civilization of the Renaissance in Italy* (1860) that south of the Alps a genuine cultural revolution took place. People there, he claimed, abandoned the otherworldly Medieval outlook and embraced a new, human-centered attitude that emphasized things of this world. The ideas of both Huizinga and Burckhardt continue to be controversial but they underscore the fact that the 14th and 15th centuries represented a period of profound transition.

The values that attracted the Italian "humanists"—a word of much later origin that derived from the Latin term for one who is educated, *humanus*—formed part of the heritage of Greek and Roman civilization. The period

[3] Quoted in Bonnie S. Anderson and Judith P. Zinsser, *A History of Their Own: Women in Europe from Prehistory to the Present,* I (New York, 1988), 193.

saw a marked rebirth of interest in the study of Classical texts of the ancient world. In Italian cities such as Florence and Bologna in the 14th century, numerous scholars turned to Classical authors for inspiration and called for a new kind of education. The conviction grew that humanist learning, as opposed to the Scholastic learning of the 12th and 13th centuries, would perfect and elevate the individual and prepare a new breed of citizens who would lead lives marked by wisdom and civic responsibility.

Petrarch

Fourteenth-century Italy had already seen two major literary geniuses in Dante and Boccaccio, whose works reflected the tension between Medieval and humanist ideals. Another pivotal figure in the emergence of the culture of Italian humanism was Petrarch (1304–1374), a Tuscan writer from the town of Arezzo. After having studied law at the University of Bologna at the insistence of his father, Petrarch embarked on a career as a writer. He lived for a time in Avignon, where his talent attracted the attention of several popes. Petrarch spent most of his life wandering across southern Europe, searching for and copying long-forgotten ancient manuscripts. He corresponded with writers and rulers throughout Europe, and wrote numerous works of poetry and prose. His learning won him the prestigious title of poet laureate of Rome, an award once famous in ancient Rome.

Although he was profoundly religious, Petrarch's vision did not, like Dante, emphasize the afterlife; instead, Petrarch sought to balance his religious convictions with the more earthly goals of fame and success. In a self-revealing book entitled *My Secret* (1343), he confesses his shortcomings and the ambivalence that led him to seek affirmation in this world as well as salvation in the next. In *Letter to Posterity* (1373?), Petrarch gives us the first important example of autobiography since the time of Augustine and reveals the focus on his own life that is an important feature of early Renaissance thought. His interest in individual human personality is also revealed in his letters concerning the great writers of the past such as Cicero and Vergil.

While Petrarch believed his Latin works would be his lasting contribution to learning, it was the work he wrote in Italian that comes down to us today as some of the finest vernacular literature of all time. In the *Canzoniere*, Petrarch collected hundreds of moving and elegant sonnets and songs, which revolve around his love for a woman named Laura, whom he first saw in Avignon in 1327 and to whom he dedicated his poetry. After Laura died in the plague in 1348, Petrarch poured out his mourning in his beautiful sonnets. Although he says that his love for Laura was never consummated, he viewed her as a real flesh and blood woman rather than as an abstraction. Petrarch established a new standard of elegance and grace in Western writing as well as a fresh appreciation for the human-centered concerns of this world. More than any of his contemporaries, Petrarch defined the attitudes and values of the emerging world of the Renaissance.

Between 1300 and 1450, Europe experienced the transformation from the late Medieval world to the early stirrings of the Renaissance. The calamities of the 14th century deeply affected economic and social conditions and altered the character of everyday life, freeing millions from the bonds of serfdom and accelerating the transition from the manorial to the capitalist era. But such profound economic and social shifts were often slow and subtle in manifesting themselves. Life for most Europeans continued to revolve around the family and religion, although with some changes, and a new conservatism among the scholars and prelates of the age conditioned women to increasingly rigid roles in society. The cultural life of Europe was marked by great diversity that in some regions saw the persistence of outmoded values and preoccupations. But in Italy and elsewhere, the humanist spirit was rapidly shaping a new consciousness and a new culture.

Questions for Further Study

1. What were the causes of social and economic change in rural Europe in the 14th and 15th centuries?
2. What impact did the plague have on European society?
3. How did Medieval writers and scholars view women?
4. What were the principal intellectual concerns of the early humanists?

Suggestions for Further Reading

Bois, Guy. *The Crisis of Feudalism: Economy and Society in Eastern Normandy, c. 1300–1550*. New York, 1984.
Cameron, Rondo. *A Concise Economic History of the World*. New York, 1989.
Duby, Georges. *A History of Private Life: II, Revelations of the Medieval World*. Cambridge, MA, 1988.
Huizinga, Johan. *The Waning of the Middle Ages*. New York, 1949.
Larner, John. *Italy in the Age of Dante and Petrarch, 1216–1380*. London, 1980.
Meiss, Millard. *Painting in Florence and Siena After the Black Death*. New York, 1964.
Miskimin, Harry A. *The Economy of Early Renaissance Europe, 1300–1460*. Cambridge, MA, 1975.
Ozment, Steven. *The Age of Reform, 1250–1550*. New Haven, CT, 1980.
Shahar, Shulamith. *The Fourth Estate: A History of Women in the Middle Ages*. New Haven, CT, 1986.

PART IV

THE RENAISSANCE AND REFORMATION

In most histories of Western civilization, the Renaissance and Reformation are usually treated together, for they represent what scholars call a "turning point" in history—that is, a series of developments that together produce fundamental change in the human experience.

In its most immediate sense, the Renaissance was a "rebirth" of interest in Classical civilization and its underlying values that began sometime in the 14th and 15th centuries. In a broader sense, however, it represented a revolution in how human beings thought about themselves and their place in the universe. Renaissance ideas, which first appeared in the sophisticated urban environment of the Italian city-states but soon spread northward, placed people at the center of human concerns, emphasizing both the importance of the human condition and a more secular, worldly ap-

proach to culture and society. Naturalism and harmony became key features in art and architecture, while in literature and philosophy Renaissance writers made an effort to reach wider audiences through the use of the vernacular and the new technology of the printing press.

In politics, the earlier trend toward the growth of royal government at the expense of feudal nobility and the church accelerated. Increasingly efficient, centralized states evolved under the leadership of a number of so-called "new monarchs" in places like England, France, and Spain. The really innovative political development, however, came in Italy, where divisive conditions led to the invention of new methods through which states dealt with each other, methods known collectively as "diplomacy." Moreover, two Italian writers of the period, Machiavelli and Castiglione, evolved theoretical strategies for statecraft that revolutionized political thought.

Closely related to the intellectual and cultural innovations of the Renaissance was the religious upheaval produced by the Protestant and Catholic reformations. The Protestant revolt against the Roman Church and the papacy not only provided people with new ways of thinking about their relationship to God and questions of sin and salvation. In addition, for millions, religious reformers like Luther, Calvin, and Knox helped establish regional and "national" religious identities. The Reformation, then, shattered a millennium of religious unity in the West, while at the same time producing far-reaching impact on the political and social life of Europe. For a variety of reasons that often had little to do with matters of faith, monarchs took sides in the religious struggles of the age, further dividing the Christian commonwealth by making new demands for popular allegiance and state control. On the other hand, the Protestant Reformation was an important step in releasing the Western mind from the constraints of religious and political authority that had been so pervasive in the Middle Ages.

The Renaissance and the Reformation both contributed significantly to the years of intellectual and technical preparation that lay behind the great epoch of exploration and conquest known as the European Reconnaissance. In the space of less than a century, between roughly 1450 and 1550, Europeans broke beyond the isolation of their geographical boundaries and sailed literally around the globe. They claimed dominance over the lands and peoples they encountered, establishing overseas territorial and economic empires while embracing a world of rich cultural diversity, with far-reaching consequences.

Out of the vast upheavals wrought by the Renaissance and Reformation came profound, long-range changes that reshaped Europe and the rest of the globe. The long centuries of transition from the Middle Ages established the foundations for the early modern world.

IV

Topic 1

The Age of the New Monarchs

The great political transformation of the 14th and 15th centuries was the emergence of modern states in Western Europe. At the same time that distinctive national cultures were being consolidated there in the late 15th century, a group of rulers known as the "new monarchs" forged powerful, centralized states that controlled large national territories in England, France, and Spain.

In the case of France and Spain, the new monarchs completed the territorial unity of their nation-states. All of them, however, were characterized by the determination to reinforce their power over the nobility and extend their control over the church within their borders. They also demanded complete loyalty from their subjects and engaged in deliberate efforts to forge a national spirit designed to create popular consensus. To the degree that these monarchs used all the techniques available to increase their power, they were typical princes of the Renaissance and of the age of Machiavelli.

In France, the Valois dynasty fought a long and devastating war with England for mastery of France, and in the aftermath shaped an increasingly powerful national monarchy. The English experienced not only the war with France but also a divisive civil war between two competing noble families, the Yorks and the Lancasters. By the time the domestic conflict was over, Henry Tudor had seized power and became the first of England's "new monarchs," laying the foundation for a powerful new dynasty. In Spain, centralization began to take place in Castile and in Aragon, the two kingdoms that were ruled jointly by Ferdinand and Isabella in the latter part of the 15th century. The process of royal centralization was completed in the next century under the reign of their grandson, Charles V. By then, Spain had become merely one part of a much wider Hapsburg empire.

THE HUNDRED YEARS' WAR AND ITS AFTERMATH

In England and especially in France, the new monarchies emerged against the background of the greatest military conflict of the 14th century, the so-called Hundred Years' War. Rather than a single continuous war, the struggle known as the Hundred Years' War was really a series of conflicts between the two states interspaced by periods of peace.

The Origins of the War

A complicated series of factors lay behind the conflict. The emergence of France as a centralized monarchy

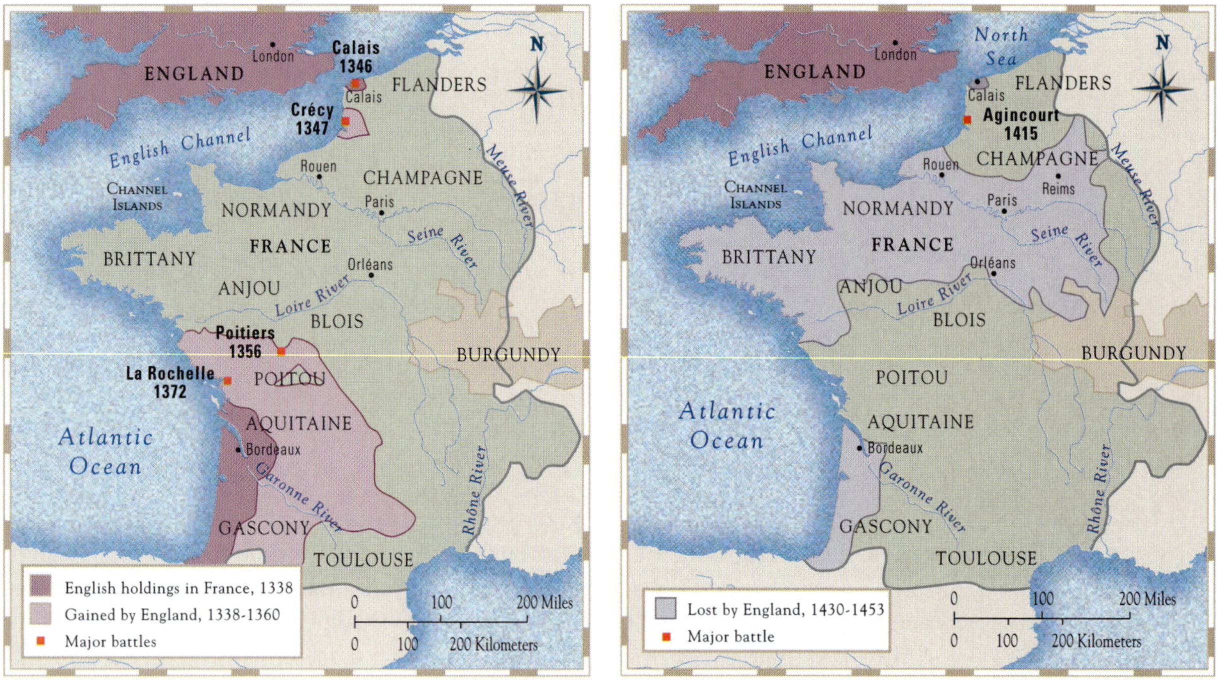

Map 1.1 The Hundred Years' War

was difficult because its territory had long been divided by strong regional differences in culture, language, and history. Complicating the situation was the fact that the English kings were vassals of the French monarch and controlled significant parts of French territory. Henry II (ruled 1154–1189), founder of the Plantagenet, or Angevin, dynasty, had inherited the French provinces of Anjou and Normandy. Moreover, through his marriage to Eleanor of Aquitaine (1122?–1204), Henry also acquired Aquitaine, a territory that stretched through southwestern France to the Pyrenees (see Part III, Topics 7 and 10).

Louis VII had tried to define the borders of France through diplomacy. In 1258, a treaty established the frontier between Spain and France along the Pyrenees. The next year Louis and Henry III of England agreed to accept the return to France of Anjou, Maine, and Normandy, which the French had seized back by force of arms; in exchange, Henry held Gascony in southwestern France as a fief from his feudal lord, Louis. The control of Gascony by the English was the source of continuous trouble, for the increasing interference of the Capetian kings in local areas, including Gascony, inevitably upset the English.

In addition to the territorial problem, economic conflicts disturbed relations between the two monarchies. Flanders, to the northeast of France, was the major market for English wool but serious conflicts between the artisans and the wealthy merchants there threatened to disrupt a lucrative source of revenue for the English kings. Accordingly, when the French monarchy began supporting the merchants, the English gave their support to the artisans.

English and French relations reached another crisis point in 1328, when the Capetian dynasty came to an end with the death of the French king, who had no sons. Because the Salic Law recognized royal inheritance through the male line, a Capetian cousin, Philip of Valois, claimed the throne as Philip VI (ruled 1328–1350). But Edward III (ruled 1327–1377) of

Significant Dates

The New Monarchs

1327–1377	Edward III rules England
1337	Hundred Years' War begins
1346	Battle of Crécy
1412–1431	Life of Joan of Arc
1461–1483	King Louis XI ("the Spider") rules France
1469–1492	Isabella and Ferdinand unite Spain
1485–1509	Henry VII rules England as first Tudor king
1494	Charles VIII invades Italy

England, the son of the dead king's sister, challenged the Valois by claiming the throne for himself. When Philip VI invaded Gascony in 1337, Edward declared war.

The Early Phase of the Conflict

The war changed the nature of warfare and undermined the old feudal system that was based on knightly combat. Both sides still relied on heavily armed aristocratic cavalry to do most of the fighting, and the French knights dismissed the importance of the peasant infantry and crossbow soldiers. The English, on the other hand, already employed large numbers of paid infantry, many of whom carried the much superior longbow, which had greater firing speed and range than the crossbow. This difference would determine the outcome of the early fighting.

In an effort to break the pattern of costly failures that marked the first English campaigns in France, Edward III invaded Normandy in 1346. Here, too, he encountered setbacks. When the French forces cut off the English while they were attempting to retreat into Flanders, a major battle took place at Crécy. There the English longbows decimated the larger French army. Edward then pressed his advantage by seizing the port of Calais, which the English held for 200 years and used for later landings. Despite the victory at Crécy, the war dragged on indecisively, for the English, with less than half the population of France, were unable to muster sufficient troops or resources to achieve total victory. Under the leadership of Edward, the prince of Wales—known as the Black Prince—the English wreaked havoc and destruction on the French countryside. Rather than risking all on head-to-head battles, the Black Prince attacked unfortified towns, burned crops, and spread terror among the peasantry. Finally, at the Battle of Poitiers in 1356, the French forces were again defeated and their king captured. A peace treaty signed three years later at Brétigny increased the size of Gascony (which now ceased to be a fief of the French monarchy) in return for Edward giving up his claim to the French throne.

The peace of Brétigny never went into effect, for the war began again under the leadership of a new French king. Using mercenary soldiers to strengthen their position, the French eventually recovered the territory lost to the English. This time, a truce negotiated in 1396 lasted 20 years.

Joan of Arc and the End of the War

The war erupted again in 1415, when the English invaded France. After a smashing victory at Agincourt in

The Battle of Crécy, where the French suffered a major defeat in the Hundred Years' War, is depicted in a miniature of the era.

A 15th-century portrait of Joan of Arc showing her in a suit of armor.

which some 1500 French knights were killed, the English conquered Normandy and persuaded the duke of Burgundy to join forces with them. The French monarchy, now led by the weak and indecisive dauphin (or royal heir), Charles (ruled 1422–1461 as Charles VII), controlled only the southern two-thirds of the country. When the English pushed south toward the Loire Valley and the heart of France, the moment was unexpectedly saved by a young French peasant girl, Joan of Arc (c. 1412–1431).

The daughter of a comfortable peasant family from the Champagne region, Joan was a devout Catholic who claimed to have experienced divinely inspired visions. In 1429, believing that she was charged by saints to save France from the English, she convinced Charles to allow her to accompany the French army. Inspired by Joan's sincerity and bravery, the French fought with renewed energy and routed the English, driving them from the Loire Valley. Joan's purpose was realized later that year, when the dauphin was crowned as King Charles VII at Rheims, thereby confirming the legitimacy of the Valois line. In 1430, however, the Burgundian allies of the English captured Joan. In a calculated effort to destroy a powerful symbol of a new French patriotism, the English accused her of witchcraft and turned her over to the Inquisition. Although the trial was not conducted by normal Inquisitorial procedures, Joan was condemned as a heretic and burned at the stake in 1431—five centuries later, the Catholic Church made her a saint.

In spite of Joan's lamentable end, the French people rallied around Charles as the war continued for another 20 years. Both sides were exhausted and after a series of English defeats that drove them from Normandy and Aquitaine, the fighting finally stopped in 1453, although no peace treaty was ever signed. England, left only with Calais on the French coast, withdrew from the continent and a devastated France began the slow and difficult process of recovering and solidifying its newly found national unity.

THE VALOIS KINGS AND THE REVIVAL OF FRANCE

The destruction that the Hundred Years' War had caused in France made it difficult for the monarchy to reimpose its authority on the country. Yet the war itself had enabled Charles VII to strengthen royal power, a trend that continued into the following century.

The three principal "estates" of French society—the clergy, the nobles, and the bourgeoisie—composed the institution known as the Estates General (see Part III, Topic 10), a body that endorsed the king's decisions and approved new taxes. During the war crisis, the Estates General had given Charles permission to raise a professional royal army and to pay for it by levying an annual property tax, the *taille*. In 1438, Charles also negotiated with Rome the Pragmatic Sanction of Bourges, which increased the administrative autonomy of the French church. During the last years of the war, Charles drew strength from the advice of his powerful mistress, Agnes Sorel (c. 1422–1450), whose influence so angered the nobility that they are said to have poisoned her to death.

Louis the Spider

The power of the French state was advanced by Charles' successor, King Louis XI (ruled 1461–1483), whose devious and crafty personality earned him the nickname of Louis the Spider. To restore the prosperity of France in the wake of the economic impact of the war, Louis developed new industries, including the manufacture of silk in Lyons, and stimulated trade. Although the *taille* was designed as a temporary war

Louis XI, known as the "Spider," was a shrewd and strong-willed ruler who established the basis of absolute monarchy in France.

measure, Louis continued to impose it as a regular source of royal income.

Louis strengthened the state by keeping in place the standing army of professional soldiers that the *taille* tax had enabled his father to create. Military expenditures absorbed half of all royal revenues, for modern armies were increasingly more expensive and only the royal government could afford them. Once gunpowder was introduced, new weapons required even more revenue. The invention of cannon required costly manufacturing and logistical supplies, while a kind of handgun known as the *arquebus* called for large numbers of additional soldiers carrying pikes to protect those armed with guns. While expensive to maintain, the importance of an army loyal to the monarchy could not be overlooked.

The ambitious Louis increased the royal territory by seizing the powerful Duchy of Burgundy from its ruler, Charles the Bold. He furthered his expansionist policy over the next several years by annexing Anjou, Maine, and Provence, which he had inherited. Until 1469, the monarchy had followed the policy of placing provinces far from the capital in Paris in the hands of relatives. Louis now began to keep these territories directly under his own control, and an increasingly efficient bureaucracy of educated professionals administered them. A treasury department ran the king's finances while a chancery drafted and maintained royal documents.

The royal courts increased their power and the king's use of Roman law gave him the authority to issue edicts and decrees. Nevertheless, the judicial system reflected the fact that the provinces remained important centers of local privilege: while the crown appointed judges of a central court known as the Parlement of Paris, it also granted important provinces their own parlements. Moreover, the Parlement was expected to register all edicts issued by the king. Louis never succeeded in completely destroying the power of the local nobility, but his reign established the monarchy on a solid footing.

The Consolidation of the Monarchy

Charles VIII (ruled 1483–1498), like his father Louis, proved to be an ambitious ruler. His marriage to the heiress of Brittany brought him control of that important province, the last independent region in France. Charles invaded Italy in 1494 at the invitation of Lodovico Sforza of Milan. The Italian campaign eventually went against Charles, who struggled for decades against the Hapsburg rulers of the Holy Roman Empire for hegemony over the Italian peninsula.

The Italian wars had the effect of further expanding the size and powers of the royal government in France. The cost of the campaigns forced the monarchy to increase its revenues but the wealthiest groups, the nobles, the clergy, and the royal towns, were traditionally exempt from taxes. In a desperate effort to raise money, Charles and his successors began the practice of selling government offices in the bureaucracy and the courts to buyers interested in the tax exemptions and titles that generally went with such positions.

King Francis I (ruled 1515–1547) continued the policy of expanding the bureaucracy by selling positions. He also focused on the Catholic Church, which was a major landowner and a source of revenue for the papacy. In 1516, following military successes in Italy, he secured from the papacy the right to appoint all French bishops and abbots, and this new power gave him access to a tremendous patronage system. Francis increased royal authority in a variety of other administrative ways and embarked on a program of overseas exploration (see Part IV, Topic 6). By the death of Francis in the mid-16th century, the power that had been accumulated by the French monarchy was considerable, although the subsequent outbreak of religious unrest was to undermine the royal achievement.

ENGLAND AND THE RISE OF THE TUDORS

Even while England was engaged in the costly and draining experience of the Hundred Years' War, the kingdom was thrown into social and political turmoil. Two branches of the royal family, the House of York, which sported a white rose as its symbol, and the House of Lancaster, whose symbol was a red rose, began a struggle for power. Known as the War of the Roses, this conflict eventually pulled other families and England itself into a 30-year civil war. When it was over, a new dynasty, the House of Tudor, ascended to the throne.

The War of the Roses

Despite the fact that the constant state of warfare between England and France had been the result of intermarriage and disputed inheritances, family links between the two monarchies continued to be forged. In 1420, Henry V of England, head of the House of Lancaster, married Catherine of Valois, the daughter of the French king. The following year, Catherine gave birth to a son, who came to the throne as Henry VI (ruled 1422–1471) when he was still an infant. For some years, an uncle ran the affairs of state for Henry. This hapless monarch was the pawn in the bitter War of the Roses that engulfed his realm.

PUBLIC FIGURES AND PRIVATE LIVES

MARGARET OF ANJOU AND HENRY VI OF ENGLAND

In 1445, a temporary truce in the Hundred Years' War was sealed by Henry's marriage to Margaret of Anjou (1430–1482), the 15-year-old daughter of the count of Anjou. The women in Margaret's own family provided her with important role models, for both her grandmother and her mother ruled their own lands and had frequently acted for the men in the family.

For many years, Henry and Margaret did not have children. By the time the war ended, furthermore, Henry had begun to exhibit clear signs of mental instability. His hold on the crown was further weakened by economic unrest that beset England in the aftermath of the war. The discontent coalesced around the figure of Richard, duke of York, who had gained recognition as Henry's heir; Margaret played a central role in the Lancastrian circle opposed to Richard. In 1453, the situation became suddenly unsettled when Margaret produced a son, who now replaced Richard as heir to the throne. Richard took up arms against Henry and the conflict raged for several years, until in 1460 the Yorkists captured Henry and a compromise was reached by which Henry remained on the throne but Richard was declared his legal heir.

Furious that her son had been disinherited, Margaret formed an army and fought for 16 years in defense of his claim to the throne. She raised money and organized support in her husband's name, acting with courage and determination. The queen's followers defeated the Yorkists and killed Richard on the battlefield. In 1461, Margaret rescued her husband from captivity and together they fled to Scotland, while Richard's son Edward seized the throne, taking the name Edward IV (ruled 1461–1470, 1471–1483). In 1465, Henry was captured a second time by the Yorkists and held in the Tower of London.

Factionalism was so rife that within a few years some of Edward's supporters turned against him and joined forces with Margaret. With help from King Louis XI of France, Margaret invaded England and restored Henry to the throne in 1470, although the Yorkists quickly recovered and captured the entire royal family. Margaret and Henry's son died and Henry himself was murdered in the Tower of London, most likely on Edward's orders.

In 1476, Louis XI secured Margaret's release by paying Edward a ransom, although on condition that Margaret gave up all claims to French territory. The former queen of England returned to France, where she spent her last years in obscurity and poverty.

The First Tudor King

At Edward IV's death in 1483, his eldest son ruled for only three months before the boy's uncle, Richard, duke of Gloucester, sent him and his younger brother to the Tower of London, where they died mysteriously. Richard then assumed the throne as Richard III (ruled 1483–1485). Two years later, Henry Tudor defeated Richard at Bosworth Field and founded the Tudor dynasty.

Henry VII (ruled 1485–1509) was an energetic king who wanted to build an autocratic monarchy that could put an end to domestic discord and govern effectively. To accomplish this purpose, Henry prohibited nobles from maintaining private armies, a practice that

Map 1.2 Europe, c. 1400

had been common because the crown did not yet have a standing army. When recalcitrant nobles refused to comply with the king's demand for internal peace, he had them hauled before a new tribunal, the Court of the Star Chamber, presided over by royal judges.

These methods were balanced, however, by the fact that Henry did not arouse noble resistance by seeking to extract special taxes from them. Instead, he increased revenues from royal estates and made the collection of traditional taxes more efficient. Henry not only paid off the royal debt but also accumulated a vast private fortune. To overcome the economic distress that the disruptions of war had produced, Henry refused to engage in costly military adventures and tried instead to promote trade and manufacturing. He relied increasingly on the landed gentry to staff the administrative offices of his government. After almost 25 years on the throne, Henry—England's first "new monarch"—left a stable and increasingly prosperous kingdom in which the monarchy had once again become a respected institution with much popular support.

SPAIN: FROM ARAGON AND CASTILE TO HAPSBURG MONARCHY

At the time that the new monarchs were forging single nation-states in other parts of Europe, the Iberian peninsula was still divided into a number of separate units. On the western coast, Portugal was a small kingdom with an ambitious monarchy that was leading the way in overseas exploration. On the southern Mediterranean coast lay Granada, the last real stronghold of Muslim power (see Part III, Topic 7). The vast central portion of the peninsula consisted of the kingdom of Castile, whose unruly nobles controlled much of the countryside and still waged the war against the Muslims that had begun centuries earlier. The eastern part of the peninsula was dominated by the kingdom of Aragon, which contained three distinct areas: Valencia, a fishing and farming region on the Mediterranean; Aragon, an interior region of unproductive land; and Catalonia, the commercial center of the kingdom containing the important port of Barcelona.

The Kingdom of Spain

While Portugal remained an independent state, the kingdom of Spain was formed in the late 15th century as a result of the union of Castile and Aragon. In 1469, Isabella (ruled 1474–1504), the heir to the throne of Castile, married Ferdinand (ruled 1479–1516), future ruler of Aragon. Ferdinand was already king of Sicily and his marriage to Isabella promised to create a kingdom of great influence and wealth. After a decade-long civil war against the nobles of Castile, who feared the power of a centralized monarchy, Ferdinand and Isabella were at last able to create the Kingdom of Spain.

Ferdinand and Isabella continued to recognize the deep-rooted local traditions that had long characterized Aragon. The region remained a collection of autonomous provinces, each with a viceroy and a parliamentary assembly known as the *Cortes*. Separate coinage systems, customs, and dialects continued to prevail even after unification. In Castile, however, the unstable conditions produced by the civil war had caused the spread of banditry in the countryside.

In response, the monarchs began to build a more highly centralized administration. Using the Cortes of Castile as a special tribunal to bring criminals to justice, Ferdinand and Isabella pacified the region. They reduced the power of the nobility in the royal government and relied increasingly on the lesser aristocrats known as *hidalgos*, who were more loyal to the crown. The monarchs imposed royal control on the influential military orders to which the nobles belonged as well as on the powerful bishops and abbots of their realms. Indeed, in return for the government's moves to clear Castile and other areas of the Muslims, the papacy recognized the right of the monarchy to appoint important ecclesiastical officials in the reconquered areas. The burghers of the towns were generally loyal to the crown, but royal authority over them was also strengthened, mainly through an official known as the *corregidor*.

The monarchs of Spain used religious policy as a force for cohesion. After the end of the civil war, Ferdinand and Isabella launched a renewed crusade against the Muslims in southern Spain, making themselves the symbols of Catholic unity and popular fervor. In 1478, they obtained permission from the pope to create a Spanish Inquisition, an institution that was used to uncover *Marranos*—Jews who pretended to convert to Christianity—and *Moriscos*—converted Muslims. Headed by the infamous Tomas de Torquemada, the Spanish Inquisitors often abused their authority and were fanatical in their efforts to uncover heretics and other nonconformists, including homosexuals and practitioners of magic. When Granada fell in 1492, Ferdinand and Isabella redirected their attack against the Jews, some 150,000 being expelled that same year. Religious policy, with its emphasis on uniformity and loyalty, became an important weapon in the growing arsenal of royal power.

Unlike the case of England, where Parliament restricted the power of the monarchy, royal authority in Spain was not seriously challenged by the Cortes. The rulers could raise taxes without approval of the Cortes and presided directly over the administration of justice. A royal compendium of law codes made the legal sys-

Albrecht Dürer painted this portrait of the Emperor Maximilian I, who established one of the great dynasties of Europe.

tem uniform for the entire realm. In addition, Ferdinand and Isabella strengthened the state by replacing the old feudal armies, which relied so heavily on the loyalty of nobles, with a professional royal army. The collection of taxes became more efficient, and as royal revenues increased, so did the strength of the central government.

Spain and the Hapsburgs

Ferdinand took an active role in foreign affairs, conquest, and overseas exploration (see Part IV, Topic 6). With both Granada in the south and Navarre in the north now annexed to Spain, Ferdinand began to look beyond the peninsula. In 1495, he sent an army into Italy to prevent Charles VIII of France from bringing all the Italian city-states under his control, and some nine years later he succeeded in conquering Naples. Spain had become a significant power and by the end of the era of Ferdinand and Isabella, they had arranged marriages for their five children into prominent European dynasties. It was through one such marriage alliance with the Hapsburgs of Austria that the fate of Spain became enmeshed with that of the Holy Roman Empire.

Over the centuries, the Hapsburg family had gained control of Austria, a series of possessions along the Danube River in central Europe, and ruled a growing empire from their capital at Vienna. In 1438, the Hapsburgs secured the imperial crown of the Holy Roman Empire, and when Maximilian (ruled 1493–1519) married the daughter of the ruler of Burgundy, he expanded Hapsburg rule over the Low Countries, Luxembourg, and into eastern France. Maximilian continued the Hapsburg policy of carefully arranging marriages to further the family's dynastic interests. The link with Spain came in 1496, when Maximilian's son, Philip of Burgundy, married Joanna, the daughter of Ferdinand and Isabella.

Twenty years later, when Ferdinand died, Aragon and Castile finally came together under the rule of one sovereign, Charles I (ruled 1516–1556), the grandson of both the Hapsburg emperor and the Spanish monarchs. Because Charles had been raised in Flanders, the Spanish nobility resented him. His election as Holy Roman emperor in 1519 (he took the imperial title as Charles V) aroused even further hostility from his Spanish subjects, who felt that Charles' imperial interests had little to do with them. When he left Spain in 1520, a vague sense of Spanish nationalism was already beginning to stir.

Although Charles returned to Spain periodically, his attention was now focused on the immense possessions that he ruled—an empire that, with the exception of France, encompassed virtually all of continental Europe west of Poland and Hungary. Charles V was to be at the center of most of the major political and religious events of the first half of the 16th century (see Part IV, Topic 7).

The development of the modern European nation-state was the work of the new monarchs, ambitious rulers who shaped powerful central governments controlling large national territories. The new Tudor dynasty in England, the Valois kings in France, and the joint reigns of Ferdinand and Isabella in Spain all began the process. The monarchs eliminated or at least reduced the power of the old nobility and extended their control over the church. They also created a bureaucratic structure designed to make the workings of royal government more effective and used a number of instruments of royal power to advance their program, including the extension of royal justice and the efficient collection of taxes.

In the process, they insisted on complete loyalty from their subjects and encouraged a national spirit designed to create popular support for their centralizing policies. The power and influence of the new monarchs and their centralizing states proved to be irresistible. The trends begun in the 15th century accelerated with time and the centralized nation-state provided a model for rulers in other parts of Europe.

Questions for Further Study

1. What were the causes of the Hundred Years' War?
2. What was "new" about the new monarchs?
3. What issues led to the War of the Roses? Why were the Tudors successful in establishing their dynasty?
4. How did Ferdinand and Isabella unite Spain?

Suggestions for Further Reading

Allmand, C. *The Hundred Years' War: England and France, c. 1300–c. 1450*. Cambridge, MA, 1988.

Chrimes, Stanley B. *Henry VII*. Berkeley, CA, 1972.

Gillingham, John. *The War of the Roses: Peace and Conflict in Fifteenth Century England*. London, 1981.

Hay, Denys. *Europe in the Fourteenth and Fifteenth Centuries*, 2nd ed. New York, 1989.

Hillgarth, J. N. *The Spanish Kingdoms, 1250–1516*, vol. II, *Castilian Hegemony*. New York, 1978.

Kendall, Paul M. *Louis XI: The Universal Spider*. New York, 1971.

Major, James R. *Representative Institutions in Renaissance France, 1421–1559*. Madison, WI, 1960.

Shennan, Joseph H. *The Origins of the Modern European State, 1450–1725*. London, 1974.

Warner, Marina. *Joan of Arc: The Image of Female Heroism*. New York, 1981.

Wood, Charles T. *Joan of Arc and Richard III: Sex, Saints, and Government in the Middle Ages*. New York, 1988.

IV

Topic 2

Power and Culture in Renaissance Italy

The period in Western history known as the Renaissance (1300–1550) saw a remarkable flowering of artistic and literary genius. It was accompanied by the rise of a new worldview that placed a concern for the human condition at the center of intellectual life. The Renaissance began in Italy, the product of the peninsula's unique social and economic development. Renaissance culture was urban and increasingly secular and flourished in a land that had largely escaped feudalism. Moreover, the rebirth of Classical values was tied closely to the long tradition of secular learning in Italy as well as to the memory of ancient Roman civilization, the physical remains of which were to be found throughout the peninsula.

Born in Florence and other Italian cities of the 14th century, humanism was a literary movement that stressed the study of Classical texts, new philosophical approaches inspired by Platonic ideas, and the historical sciences. These humanist values gave rise to a new kind of intellectual who participated actively in a political culture inspired by ancient ideals. Humanists regarded themselves as active citizens of their city-states and immersed themselves in the material affairs of their urban settings; they were not ivory tower intellectuals removed from the everyday world. Precisely because they were an educated élite, they believed they had responsibilities to their fellow citizens. This spirit of civic humanism was one of the outstanding characteristics of the Renaissance.

The visual arts played a central role in the public life of the city-states of Renaissance Italy, where political power and culture were inextricably bound together. The princes of Florence and Milan, the aristocratic families of Venice, and the popes of Rome all were active and enthusiastic patrons of painting, sculpture, and architecture. Political leaders recognized the powerful role that the arts could have in forging popular consensus behind authority and instilling civic pride in citizens.

Although Renaissance culture represented a community of shared values, standards, and ideals, the political experience of Italy was far less unified. Because the peninsula was divided among a number of highly competitive and often warring states, it fell prey to more powerful foreign states. In response to their political divisiveness, Italians developed the concept of balance-of-power politics and the new art of diplomacy. By the 16th century, the Florentine writer Machiavelli drew on his Classical training as well as on the bitter political events of his times to fashion a new vision of power removed from the moral codes of Christianity and rooted directly in the gritty realities of everyday experience.

Significant Dates

Renaissance Italy

1311–1447	Viscontis rule Milan
1454	Peace of Lodi
1407–1457	Life of Lorenzo Valla
1450–1494	Sforzas rule Milan
1463–1494	Life of Pico della Mirandola
1494	Charles VIII invades Italy
1433–1499	Life of Marsilio Ficino
1484–1519	Francesco Gonzaga rules Mantua
1434–1494; 1512–1737	Medici rule Florence

POLITICS, CLASS, AND CIVIC IDENTITY: THE ITALIAN CITY-STATES

The political and social development of Italian Renaissance cities followed a similar pattern. The remarkable economic expansion that had occurred in Medieval Italy had caused the rise of northern and central Italian cities such as Venice, Genoa, Milan, and Florence. The merchants and bankers who controlled this commercial revival accumulated great wealth and by the 11th century they allied themselves with the local nobles in the countryside in order to secure independence from the bishops who ruled their cities. The communes came into being as a result of the oaths that the burghers and the nobles took to fight for their common rights. Once independence from the bishops was achieved, the communes took over the municipal governments, often creating new institutions, and soon came to control the hinterland around the cities. On this basis there eventually emerged the city-states of the Renaissance.

From Communes to the Signorie

Political institutions in the cities reflected evolving social arrangements. Many of the rural nobles, attracted to the possibilities of wealth to be gained in trade or by marriage to rich burghers, moved into the cities, forming a new kind of urban nobility connected to the merchants through economic and family ties. This ruling élite strictly limited power and the rights of citizenship in the communes to people like themselves, who owned property and enjoyed high social status. The vast majority of the inhabitants, including males of the middle and lower classes and all women, were excluded from holding office.

The members of the middle class, the so-called *popolo,* particularly resented their second-class status. In the 13th century these alienated groups organized violent seizures of power and replaced communes with republican governments in such important cities as Florence, Siena, and Genoa. Republican institutions were popular both because of their connection to Roman tradition and because they allowed for access to power by new elites. Once in power the popolo sought to exclude the working classes below them—the *popolo minuto,* or little people—from power. As a result, the republican governments never achieved popular consensus and found it difficult to maintain public order. In the early 1300s, republican governments collapsed, replaced by one of two kinds of new regimes: either group rule by wealthy merchants (oligarchies), or individual despotisms *(signorie)*. Oligarchies generally operated behind constitutional façades but continued to limit access to power to a handful of citizens, just as the signori pretended to rule within the law.

The States of Renaissance Italy

By the opening of the 15th century, five major states had so expanded their territorial base that they exercised virtual hegemony over the Italian peninsula: Venice and Milan in the north, Florence in north central Italy, the Papal States in the center, and the Kingdom of Naples in the south. Venice, at the head of the Adriatic Sea, had dominated the commercial revival of the High Middle Ages. Tremendous wealth had poured into the city from its galleys and its overseas outposts. The Venetians had also conquered a mainland empire in Italy in order to have steady access to food and protect themselves from the ambitious Milanese. Behind its long-established republican institutions, some 200 of Venice's merchant nobles ruled one of the most powerful states in Europe.

In Milan, the principal city of the region known as Lombardy, the Visconti family had ruled as tyrants since 1322. In 1395 Gian Galeazzo Visconti (ruled 1395–1402) transformed his rule into an hereditary duchy. By the time of his death his armies had overrun all of Lombardy and were at the gates of Florence. In 1447, when the last of the Visconti died, Francesco Sforza (ruled 1450–1466), a soldier of fortune in the pay of the Milanese, turned against his masters and conquered the city. The Sforza family governed Milan with a strong hand and dominated the lesser cities of northern Italy.

The republic of Florence had long been controlled by representatives of the trade guilds, and from

A painting of Venice, the most powerful seafaring Renaissance city, shows the palace of the Doges (center right). The tall structure at center is the bell tower.

1434 to 1492 the Medici, one of the most powerful and wealthy of the guild families, controlled the city. The Medici, who first made their money in banking, ruled behind the city's republican façade for more than half a century. They turned Florence into a center of international power and cultural brilliance. Cosimo de' Medici (ruled 1434–1464), the great patron of civic humanists and artists, was himself a cultivated man of letters. A

Florence, one of the great city-states of Renaissance Italy, is situated on both banks of the Arno River. This painting, c. 1490, shows the Medieval walls protecting the city and the cathedral in the center.

Map 2.1 Italy, c. 1450

fiercely patriotic Florentine, contemporaries called him *Pater Patriae*, or Father of the Homeland. On Cosimo's death, his son Piero (ruled 1464–1469) assumed the position of de facto ruler of Florence. Piero's era was marked by continuing artistic achievement and much political turmoil. He died after only five years in power and was succeeded in turn by his son Lorenzo de' Medici (ruled 1469–1492). Known as Lorenzo the Magnificent, he was the most distinguished of the Medici rulers of Florence. In his youth he had been tutored by the humanist scholar Marsilio Ficino, who instilled in him a great love for learning and poetry. He continued the family's tradition of patronage for the scholars and artists who worked in Florence during Cosimo's day.

Lorenzo's reign was challenged in 1478 when the so-called Pazzi Conspiracy erupted. This complicated plot was fomented by the prominent Pazzi family, who resented the Medici rule. Lorenzo succeeded in foiling the conspiracy and imposing an even more firm control on the city. The last years of Lorenzo's life were again marked by turmoil, this time surrounding the career of the Dominican preacher Fra Girolamo Savonarola (1452–1498). Savonarola inveighed against what he saw as the degeneration of life and culture in Florence and gathered a large and enthusiastic following, including some of the most talented artists of the city. He wanted a restoration of the Florentine republic based on Christian morality. In 1496 he staged a huge bonfire in the city in which gambling paraphernalia, cosmetics, and other symbols of decadence were burned. Savonarola eventually came into conflict with the papacy, which had him executed for heresy.

The Papal States, stretching across the peninsula from the Adriatic to the Tyrrhenian seas, were ruled by the popes from Rome. During the papal residency at Avignon, however, a number of noble families had grown influential in Rome. Moreover, in the course of the 14th century secular lords had achieved independence in Ferrara, Urbino, and other cities of the Papal States. With the return of the pope to Rome in 1417, the papacy became increasingly more secular and involved in Italian politics. Some of the most famous Renaissance popes illustrated the temporal attitudes of the papacy: Pope Sixtus IV (ruled 1471–1484) became embroiled in the Pazzi Conspiracy; Alexander VI (ruled 1492–1503) and his sinister son Cesare Borgia schemed in the diplomatic intrigues of the day; and Julius II (ruled 1503–1513), the "warrior pope," personally led his armies in battle.

South of the Papal States lay the Kingdom of Naples, including the island of Sicily. After the death of Frederick of Hohenstaufen in the 13th century, the kingdom had fallen prey to the competing ambitions of the rulers of Aragon and France. In 1435, Naples and Sicily came under Aragonese domination and in 1504 were annexed to the Spanish crown.

The Italian cities were able to develop into sovereign territorial states primarily because Italy, like Germany, possessed no powerful central monarchy such as those that emerged in France and England. In this world of small Italian Renaissance states, ruled by despots and oligarchies, the élite learned to derive significant power from the sponsorship of culture. Out of this age of Renaissance humanism, when one neighbor was pitted against another in endless cycles of wars and alliances, a new conception of power politics was born.

THE INTELLECTUAL WORLD OF THE EARLY RENAISSANCE

In the 14th century, Petrarch introduced the notion of the self-conscious artist in search of personal fame (see Part III, Topic 13). The following generation of scholars advanced the notion of humanism further, with the arrival of Byzantine intellectuals who fled westward after the fall of Constantinople in 1453. Under constant external danger from other city-states, especially Milan, Florentine intellectuals turned to the Classical past to find inspiration. Among their models was Marcus Tullius Cicero, the ancient Roman statesman and writer, whose orations, letters, and essays stressed that the educated upper classes should provide leadership for society (see Part II, Topic 8). In 15th-century Florence, the civic humanist Leonardo Bruni (1370–1444) wrote a biography of Cicero that portrayed him as the model of the Renaissance ideal of the scholar-activist. Bruni was part of a circle of scholars around Coluccio Salutati who collected and studied ancient manuscripts; the greatest collector of ancient manuscripts was Poggio Bracciolini (1380–1459), a longtime papal secretary. These and other scholars perceived civic activism not only as a duty but as a stimulant to intellectual creativity.

Petrarch first introduced the idea of the self-conscious artist in search of fame.

Humanists and Neoplatonists

Lorenzo Valla (1407–1457) was the epitome of the civic humanist. Raised and educated in Rome, Valla studied both the Latin and the Greek classics, as Bruni had done. Humanists admired virtually all Latin writers before the 7th century but Valla's studies—especially his *Elegances of the Latin Language*—revealed distinct periods in the development of Latin. He most admired the style of the late Republic and early Empire (1st century B.C.–1st century A.D.). Valla devoted much of his energy to close textual analysis of ancient manuscripts. His discovery that the document known as the Donation of Constantine was a fake, actually written in the 8th century, brought him much attention; the Donation, which claimed that the Emperor Constantine had actually given political authority over the West to the church in 313, had long been used by popes to assert their temporal rule. At the height of his fame, Valla served in the papal secretariat under Pope Nicholas V (ruled 1447–1455).

By the middle of the 15th century, humanism had become widely diffused, its basic tenets and methods were accepted, and many of the key Classical texts were known. Humanists now shifted their attention to philosophy, especially as it was influenced by the Greek philosophers, chief among them Plato. The Florentine humanists flourished under the patronage of the city's de facto ruler, the highly cultivated banker Cosimo de' Medici. Cosimo invested much of his wealth in the search for and copying of Classical manuscripts and in supporting the discussion group that came to be known as the Platonic Academy. Marsilio Ficino (1433–1499), one of the circle's most gifted intellectuals, had been taken under Cosimo's protection as a child. Ficino received a regular income and access to the library at the Medici villa, and it was here that the Neoplatonists gathered for their discussions. Ficino, inspired by Plato's idealism, was especially interested in exploring the nature of the human soul, which he and his fellow philosophers believed was immortal, and in the search for truth

Andrea Mantegna decorated the private rooms of Isabella d'Este in the ducal palace of Mantua.

and beauty. In order to diffuse Plato's ideas, Ficino translated the Platonic dialogues and devoted himself to efforts to reconcile Platonic philosophy with Christianity.

Ficino's numerous translations from Greek into Latin included the *Corpus Hermeticum*, a series of Hermetic essays prepared at Cosimo's request. Among the subjects covered in the *Corpus* were the supposed secrets of the pagan world, including alchemy, astrology, and magic. The Hermeticists held that although human beings had been created as divine creatures, they had elected to be part of the material world. According to this view, humans could reattain their divine state by becoming sages. These magi, as they were known in the Renaissance, were endowed with knowledge of God and of the powers of nature, which they could use to help humans.

Knowledge and Education

Among the best-known of those regarded as magi in the 15th century was Pico della Mirandola (1463–1494), a churchman who had studied with Ficino and was perhaps the most brilliant of the Florentine humanists—he once boasted that he had read every book in Italy. Believing that it was possible to organize human learning so as to reveal basic truth, Pico set out to master all knowledge. He learned Latin, Greek, Hebrew, Aramaic, and Arabic as well as philosophy. When he was 20 years old he claimed to have summed up knowledge in 900 theses, which he described in a treatise called *Oration on the Dignity of Man*. Pico defined the humanist credo when he declared that humanity acts as the link between God and the material world and that human potential was limited only by the will to achieve and through God's grace.

Humanist theories about the perfectibility of human character led to the development of educational programs designed to train the children of the upper classes to function as the ruling élite of society. The most prominent educational theorist of the period was Vittorino da Feltre, who established a well-known school in Mantua (see Part IV, Topic 8). Many humanist scholars themselves achieved status and influence by serving as state chancellors, secretaries to eminent rulers, and advisers at noble courts. Although Vittorino's pupils included some children of poor families on scholarships, humanist education was designed to train the ruling classes.

To the Renaissance mind, education was crucial to the intelligent and proper conduct of public affairs, for humanism placed humans at the center of historical development. The authors of Medieval chronicles had attributed events in human affairs to divine inspiration or direct intervention by God. The humanists, so taken with the search for texts and the analysis of sources, looked to documents rather than miracles for explanations of historical events. Similarly, they saw individual motives behind political developments. The most accomplished of the new secular historians of the Renaissance was Francesco Guicciardini (1483–1540), who had considerable experience as a diplomat and government official. His *History of Italy*, the first work of history since antiquity based on original documents, provided detailed comparative analysis of political affairs in the city-states and decried the lack of unity in Italy. Most of all, Guicciardini saw the need for wise rulers endowed with learning and experience. These and other humanist values remained the core of upper-class education in the West for centuries.

PATRONAGE AND STATECRAFT IN RENAISSANCE ITALY

It was no accident that the cities of the Italian Renaissance were centers of both political power and culture, for art served as a medium of education and as propaganda. The church, of course, had always been a great patron of the arts, using architecture, painting, and sculpture to promote worship and respect for religious institutions. In the Renaissance, just as artistic themes became increasingly secular, so laymen emerged as active and generous patrons of the arts.

The Nature of Renaissance Patronage

Following in the tradition of the Middle Ages, guilds and religious organizations commissioned artists to create works of sculpture and paintings that reflected their wealth and influence. In Florence, the cloth merchants hired Filippo Brunelleschi to design and erect the stunning dome of the city's *duomo* (cathedral).

Individual rulers and nobles also came to recognize the power of culture and patronized art and scholarship in order to show off their wealth and status. Many tried to trace their ancestry back to Roman times and deliberately imitated the lifestyles of the ancient patricians. In their zeal to identify with Classical civilization, princes poured money into excavating archaeological sites and locating lost manuscripts. Wealthy families spent lavishly to build and decorate tombs and chapels in the principal churches of their cities. As families and individual personalities grew in importance, portraits were commissioned to celebrate and remember them.

Princes used the creative talents they supported to strengthen and legitimize their rule. The Medici family, for example, commissioned Sandro Botticelli to paint the *Adoration of the Magi* (1475), in which both Cosimo's and Lorenzo's portraits were represented amid the

PUBLIC FIGURES AND PRIVATE LIVES

ISABELLA D'ESTE AND FRANCESCO GONZAGA

Along with the Medici in Florence and the Sforza in Milan, Italy's smaller city-states were also centers of art and learning. Among the most brilliant of these smaller Renaissance courts was that of Francesco Gonzaga (ruled 1484–1519) of Mantua and his wife, Isabella d'Este (1474–1539).

Like many of his contemporaries, Francesco Gonzaga was first and foremost a warrior-prince. A short, ugly man without serious education, he seems not to have inherited the cultural interests that had long been a tradition at Mantua—while courting his future wife, he sent her poems that he had commissioned but pretended were his own. In 1490, he married Isabella, the 16-year-old daughter of Ercole d'Este, ruler of Ferrara, and Eleonora of Aragon. From that moment, Isabella overshadowed her husband in virtually all matters of domestic state policy and made Mantua a major center of Renaissance culture.

Isabella and her sister Beatrice—"two of the most remarkable women of the Renaissance"[1]—grew up in the rarified atmosphere of the Este court at Ferrara. They were among the best educated women of their time, having been tutored by the humanist scholar Battista Guarini. The sisters were both competitive and different, for while Beatrice enjoyed a luxurious lifestyle, Isabella was more serious and mastered both Greek and Latin. Their arranged marriages resulted in major political alliances: while Isabella went to Mantua, Beatrice married Ludovico Sforza of Milan.

Because Francesco spent much time away from Mantua, the self-assured Isabella, who exhibited considerable skill at diplomacy and matters of state, often assumed the reins of government. Isabella's fame, however, rests on her role as an astute and sophisticated patron of arts and letters. Her cultural tastes were broad, ranging from painting, music, and architecture to philosophy, literature, and astrology. She competed for the talents of some of the greatest artists and writers of the era. Titian and Leonardo da Vinci painted portraits of her,

Mantegna decorated her private rooms in the ducal palace, and Correggio called her "the first lady of the world." She collected works of art with a clear sense of her own taste and a thirst to own the best. The famed Venetian printer Aldus Manutius sent her editions of his books, and the poet Ariosto read to Isabella from the first draft of his epic *Orlando Furioso*. She also encouraged the writer Castiglione, whose famous work *The Courtier* was based on the court of Isabella's sister-in-law Elisabetta Gonzaga at Urbino.

Francesco Gonzaga's fame rests on his victory at the Battle of Fornovo in 1495, where he led the military forces of the Italian League (including Venice, Milan, and the Papal States) against the invading army of Charles VIII of France. Later, however, he continuously switched sides and in 1509 was captured and held prisoner for a year by the Venetians. During that time, Isabella not only made important military decisions and directed the defenses of Mantua but founded the city's lucrative cloth industry. When he was finally liberated, a humiliated Francesco felt resentful of his talented consort's achievements. "We are ashamed," he wrote to her, "that it is our fate to have as a wife a woman who is always ruled by her head."[2] Increasingly estranged from Francesco because of his repeated infidelities, she spent many of her last years at the papal court in Rome. After her husband died in 1519, Isabella acted as regent and adviser to her son Federigo II and was able to have her younger son Ercole made a cardinal. She died a much revered and respected figure, and very much a woman of the Renaissance.

[1] E. M. Jamison, C. M. Ady, K. D. Vernon, and C. Sanford Terry, *Italy, Medieval and Modern: A History* (Oxford, 1919), 223.

[2] Quoted in Maria Bellonci, "Beatrice and Isabella d'Este," in J. H. Plumb, *The Italian Renaissance* (Boston, 1961), 296–297.

Medici court—along with a self-portrait of the artist. They brought poets and essayists to their palaces, hired architects and artists to plan and decorate their public rooms and erect statues and monuments to their achievements. As the social status of the artists themselves grew during the Renaissance, patrons competed to hire the best-known painters and sculptors, for the fame of the artist enhanced the prestige of the patron.

ITALY AND EUROPE: POWER POLITICS AND THE ART OF DIPLOMACY

In 1454, the Italian states established a precarious balance of power through the Peace of Lodi. The agreement between Venice and Milan, which conceded Milan to Francesco Sforza and restored Venetian holdings in northern Italy, brought peace to Italy for many years. The Italian states were exhausted by the continuous warfare and agreed to observe the terms of the peace and to join an Italian League for mutual defense.

The Peace of Lodi collapsed in 1494, when Lodovico Sforza of Milan asked for the military support of Charles VIII of France in the midst of rising tensions with Florence and Naples. The French invasion of Italy began a long series of disastrous wars that revealed the inability of relatively weak city-states to withstand the power of centralized nation-states. Italy became a battleground of larger European dynastic interests as the houses of Hapsburg, Valois, and Aragon jockeyed for hegemony. Charles pushed the Medici out of Florence (they returned in 1512), the Hapsburg Emperor Charles V seized Milan, and Ferdinand of Aragon took Naples. When the wars finally ended in 1559, the Hapsburgs were masters of the peninsula, with only Venice and the Papal States remaining independent. While the memory of Italy's great cultural legacy lingered, its political subservience to foreign powers would not end for three centuries.

Diplomacy and Power Politics

As political life in Europe grew more complex, states began to develop new and more formal ways of relating to each other. The advantages of economic and cultural cooperation, as well as of finding alternatives to war, became increasingly evident to the great powers. Nowhere was the need for organized international relations greater than in Italy, where in the process of creating a balance of power the Italians had invented the art of diplomacy. During the Italian wars that erupted at the end of the 15th century, the Italian style of managing foreign policy was copied by other European states.

The most important novelty devised by Italian diplomats was the use of resident ambassadors. In the

Formal procedures for diplomatic conduct were developed in Renaissance Italy among the city-states. This painting by Carpaccio is entitled *The Departure of the Ambassadors.*

place of roving envoys who traveled to accomplish specific missions, states now maintained permanent ambassadors in foreign capitals. The advantages were obvious—resident ambassadors could not only collect intelligence about conditions and attitudes in their host country, but developed personal relationships that could be used to represent the interests of their sovereign more quickly and efficiently.

Resident ambassadors gave rise to elaborate embassies staffed by military and commercial experts and sophisticated reporting procedures. Diplomatic staffs lived in foreign countries with immunity from local laws, and adopted both fixed procedures and formal styles of protocol to govern diplomatic relations. These procedures evolved under the impact of the Italian wars, for rulers throughout Europe were drawn into the intricate dynastic struggles that marked the struggles for power there. It gradually became clear that the general interests of all states required a balance in which no one power dominated the others.

The collapse of the independence of the Italian city-states, together with the emergence of centralized monarchies elsewhere in Europe, attracted the attention of political analysts, who now began to study diplomacy, politics, and the nature of power itself from a more practical and secular point of view. The Italians, themselves anxious to understand why their independence had disappeared so completely, were in the forefront of this new approach to the study of political power. The historian Guicciardini, for example, had examined the histories of the Italian states comparatively and concluded that the lack of unity in the peninsula had enabled foreign powers to crush them. It was, however, the Florentine Niccolò Machiavelli (1469–1527) who epitomized the new politics of the age (see Part IV, Topic 4).

Machiavelli's *The Prince*, the most original work of political theory to come out of the Renaissance, argued that the prince, or ruler, must exercise power wisely but ruthlessly and amorally, with no thought to any factor other than power aimed at the preservation of the state. The prince is free to use cruelty or hypocrisy but only thoughtfully and with judicious purpose. Fear and respect enable a prince to rule successfully. Machiavelli's point, of course, is that rulers should use power pragmatically for the management of public affairs. Realism rather than morality must be the basis for governance. The purpose of *The Prince* is to demonstrate how power operates, not to inquire philosophically into its origins.

Many contemporaries were shocked by Machiavelli's advocacy of the amoral manipulation of power, and the term "Machiavellian" became a label for unscrupulousness and evil. The 16th century was perhaps not yet ready to accept this new approach to the use of state power but the realities of the day pointed to a different direction in political affairs.

The Renaissance was the product of Europe's cultural and social vitality and it set the tone for the modern age. The humanist concerns with Classical virtues and learning, the strength and beauty of Michelangelo's David, *the raw pragmatism of Machiavelli's advice to the prince, all bespoke a new viewpoint freed from superstition and focused on the human condition. The secular and urban values of Renaissance culture emerged first in Italy, where a combination of history, social development, and economic factors encouraged its flowering. Conditions there first stimulated the growth of humanism, which in turn nurtured the sense of civic virtue and responsibility that marked the public life of the Renaissance city-states.*

As in earlier epochs, rulers of the Renaissance period appreciated and used painting, sculpture, and architecture to enhance their prestige and legitimize their power. Political leaders recognized the powerful role that the arts could have in forging popular consensus behind authority and instilling civic pride in citizens. The experience of numerous city-states vying with each other to control the peninsula had resulted in the invention of important political techniques, although Machiavelli, the most jarringly objective observer of his times, recognized in that lesson that the realities of power were working against the Italians. For all their wisdom and skill in developing effective political systems, Italian rulers were unable to forge unity or to maintain the integrity of their own states against the military power of the newly emerging national monarchies. The Italians, it seemed, had chosen culture over power.

Questions for Further Study

1. What forms did "civic identity" take in Renaissance Italy?
2. With what issues were early Renaissance intellectuals concerned?
3. Why did Italian Renaissance rulers and merchants act as patrons of the arts?
4. What conditions in Italy led to the invention of "diplomacy" in the modern sense?

Suggestions for Further Reading

Brucker, Gene A. *Renaissance Florence,* rev. ed. New York, 1983.

Burke, Peter. *The Italian Renaissance.* Princeton, NJ, 1986.

D'Amico, John F. *Renaissance Humanism in Papal Rome.* Baltimore, 1983.

Hay, Denys, and J. Law. *Italy in the Age of the Renaissance.* London, 1989.

Holmes, George. *Florence, Rome and the Origins of the Renaissance.* Oxford, 1986.

King, Margaret L. *Venetian Humanism in an Age of Patrician Dominance.* Princeton, NJ, 1986.

Marek, George. *The Bed and the Throne.* New York, 1976.

Martines, Lauro. *Power and Imagination: City-States in Renaissance Italy.* New York, 1979.

Mattingly, Garrett. *Renaissance Diplomacy.* Boston, 1955.

Stephens, J. *The Italian Renaissance: The Origins of Intellectual and Artistic Change Before the Reformation.* New York, 1990.

Trinkaus, Charles E. *The Scope of Renaissance Humanism.* Ann Arbor, MI, 1983.

IV

Topic 3

The Visual Arts of the Italian Renaissance

The rise of the Medici in Florence, together with the city's increasing prosperity, culminated in an artistic explosion there. Painters, sculptors, and architects vied to produce works in the "modern style," commissioned by their patrons, which influenced the arts throughout Europe.

Although the Renaissance style was a natural development of the late Medieval interest in the expression of powerful feelings, Renaissance artists felt that in turning back to ancient models they were making a decisive break with their immediate past. The greatest sculptor of the Early Renaissance, Donatello, combined a rediscovery of Classical forms with a strong sense of drama.

Brunelleschi, the leading architect of the period, used techniques learned from his study of ancient Roman buildings to create structures dominated by logic and order. Many of his buildings are centrally planned, and the design of details expresses the Renaissance belief in reason. The paintings of Masaccio show a similar concern with order and proportion, combining them with physical realism.

In the second half of the *Quattrocento* (15th century), the architect Alberti continued Brunelleschi's use of Classical styles in grandiose buildings dominated by precise numerical relationships. Botticelli, one of the leading painters at the Medici court, reflected his patrons' interest in neoplatonic humanism, while in northern Italy the frescoes of Mantegna continued to experiment with perspective.

The three towering figures of the High Renaissance were Leonardo da Vinci, Raphael, and Michelangelo. Leonardo is known as much for the incredible breadth of his ideas and interests as for his few surviving works. Raphael's paintings express the High Renaissance love of ideal beauty based on Classical standards. Michelangelo's vision was more complex. Recognized in his own day as the greatest artist of the Renaissance, he has been regarded ever since as the archetype of the supreme creative genius.

The masterpieces produced in Florence in the Early Renaissance and at Rome in the High Renaissance emphasized order, form, and line. Venetian painters were more interested in color and light, and their works are often mellower and more relaxed than those produced elsewhere in Italy. Bellini and Titian both used Classical themes. Titian was also a master of portraiture, while his reclining female nudes are among the most sensual in Western art. The works of Tintoretto, Titian's successor as leading painter at Venice, are darker and more brooding.

The artistic movement of the late *Cinquecento* (16th century), Mannerism, took the main features of Renaissance style to extremes, with the drama becoming artificial, and technical virtuosity an end in itself. By the end of the 16th century, artists and critics were already looking back with awe at the "old masters" of the High Renaissance.

"THE MODERN STYLE": DONATELLO, BRUNELLESCHI, AND MASACCIO

With the rediscovery of Classical Antiquity, artists began to develop new styles based on ancient models. Turning to Roman sculptures, the remains of ancient Roman buildings, and Classical texts on art, they aimed for a "modern style" that would express Classical ideals of order and balance for their own times. Behind their use of perspective and realism to achieve dramatic effect lay the late Medieval emotionalism seen in the works of Giovanni Pisano (see Part III, Topic 11), but the powerful directness of Early Renaissance art represents a revolutionary break with the past.

Sculpture in the Early Renaissance: Donatello

One of the most profoundly original of all Renaissance artists, the sculptor Donatello (1386?–1466), used Classical principles to achieve startling dramatic effects. His statues of *St. Mark* and *St. George*, carved between 1413 and 1417 to decorate the façade of the Florentine church of Orsanmichele, show a sense of the shifting weight of the bodies. This depiction of movement, which was characteristic of ancient Greek sculpture, disappeared with the end of Classical Antiquity, to be reborn in the Early Renaissance. At the same time Donatello avoids the generalized idealism of Greek art. The two saints emerge as distinct individuals, the venerable St. Mark brooding and intense, St. George youthfully proud and determined.

In his small bronze relief panel of *The Feast of Herod* (c. 1425), which decorates the baptismal font of Siena Cathedral, Donatello's sense of the theatrical makes powerful use of the newly discovered technique of linear perspective. To create the illusion of depth on a flat surface, Early Renaissance artists devised a mathematical system whereby all lines met at a single point on the horizon—an example of the important new relationship in the Early Renaissance between the arts and scholarly learning.

Donatello's panel combines several separate incidents in the story of Salome's dance and the execution of John the Baptist. Herod recoils in terror as the executioner presents the saint's head to him on a dish, and a variety of other figures in the three interconnected rooms express their horror with violent gestures, while Salome continues the sinuous movements of her dance.

Donatello, *St. George*, 1416–1417.

The remarkable sense of depth represents a break with the generally flat backgrounds of most Medieval sculpture. Like ancient Roman artists, Donatello aimed to create the illusion of space, but for the first time in Western art he used the scientific principle of linear perspective to do so.

Brunelleschi and the Classical Tradition of Architecture

The inventor of linear perspective was the architect and sculptor Filippo Brunelleschi (1377–1446). One of his earliest works was a bronze panel of *The Sacrifice of Isaac* (1401–1402), made as an entry in the competition organized in Florence to choose an artist for the north doors of the baptistery there. The winner was the sculptor and goldsmith Lorenzo Ghiberti (c. 1378–1455), whose style blended naturalism and classicism to create realistic figures. In disappointment, Brunelleschi devoted most of his remaining career to architecture, and went on to become the greatest architect of the Early Renaissance.

One of the key events in the formation of Brunelleschi's style was his journey to Rome in 1402, perhaps in the company of his friend Donatello. After several more visits to study the construction principles used by ancient Roman builders there, he returned to Florence, where he managed to solve an engineering problem that baffled his contemporaries: how to construct a dome for the city's huge unfinished cathedral. The vast octagonal-shaped structure, with its inner and outer shells, still dominates the Florence skyline.

Many of Brunelleschi's designs were for centrally planned buildings based on ancient examples such as the Pantheon in Rome. One of the most perfect is the Pazzi Chapel, a small building standing by the Church of Santa Croce in Florence, which served as a meeting room for the monks there. The plan of the chapel incorporated the careful proportions and sober decorations of Classical architecture. A central dome sits over a rectangular space whose length is twice the dome's diameter. On the inside are Classical rosettes and pilasters (relief pillars), while the rounded arches and barrel vaults which Brunelleschi used as decorative elements were to become typical of later Renaissance architectural design.

The Revolutionary Painting of Masaccio

The first painter to adopt Brunelleschi's linear perspective was the young Masaccio (1401–1428), whose brief career—he died at the age of 27, probably of the plague—catapulted painting forward into the "modern style." Breaking completely with the elaborate and crowded style of International Gothic artists (see Part III, Topic 11), Masaccio used principles of mathematical organization to produce startling effects of realism.

His fresco *The Holy Trinity*, painted for the Florentine Church of Santa Maria Novella, creates the illusion of an interior space opening out in front of the viewer. The recessed depths, like those in Donatello's relief panel, are decorated with architectural elements similar to those used by Brunelleschi. At the center stand the monumental figures of the Trinity. The majestic composition rises to a peak with the head of God the Father, while the lowest corners of the pyra-

A view of Florence's Duomo, Giotto's Tower to the left and Brunelleschi's dome to the right.

mid contain two humans in prayer, probably members of the Lenzi family who commissioned the painting.

In the frescoes he painted for the Brancacci Chapel in the Church of Santa Maria del Carmine, Florence, at the very end of his short life, Masaccio added an unforgettable emotional impact to his ability to create the illusion of volume. The figures of Adam and Eve, in *The Expulsion from the Garden of Eden*, stumble out of Eden into an inexorably harsh light—Adam unable to face the future and Eve crying piercingly aloud. The weight of their limbs and their leaden footsteps combine with the hazy background to present one of the most poignant images in Western art.

TRADITION AND EXPERIMENT: THE LATER QUATTROCENTO

The most important of Brunelleschi's successors was the architect and art theorist Leone Battista Alberti (1404–1472), whose writings on architecture and painting profoundly influenced later Renaissance artists. In accordance with the humanist ideas of the period, Alberti believed that beauty—whether of a figure or a building—depended on an ideal balance and order, creating a perfect harmony.

Alberti's unfinished Malatesta Temple at Rimini is named after Sigismondo Malatesta (1417–1468), the ruler of Rimini, who commissioned Alberti to reconstruct a preexisting church dedicated to St. Francis—Malatesta intended the building to house his tomb along with those of his mistress and members of his court. The façade Alberti designed is in the strongest contrast to the rich style of Late Gothic architecture. Simple and symmetrical, with rounded arches and Classical columns, it became a model of Classical restraint and harmony much imitated by subsequent Renaissance architects.

Painting in the Later Quattrocento

Toward the end of the Quattrocento, some painters continued to work within the mainstream of earlier developments, while others broke new ground. Among the traditionalists was Domenico Ghirlandaio (1449–1494), who placed his depictions of scenes drawn from the Bible within the rich Florentine palaces and aristocratic life of his day.

Piero della Francesca's *Resurrection* (c. 1460) shows the risen Christ in the cold light of a Tuscan dawn.

The art of Piero della Francesca (c. 1420–1492) is far more intellectual. Like Alberti, with whom he worked at Rimini, Piero continued to experiment with mathematical and geometrical structures. Many of his paintings use light as one of the elements of composition. *The Resurrection* is based on a triangular arrangement, with the sleeping soldiers forming the base and the head of the risen Christ, set on its strong, column-like body, the apex. The cold light of dawn in the background serves to emphasize Christ's triumphant stance.

If Piero was inspired by the clarity of mathematical proportion, his younger contemporary Sandro Botticelli (1445–1510) began his career under the influence of the neoplatonist ideas circulating at the Medici court. The neoplatonists combined elements of Classical mythology and Christianity in elaborate allegories. Thus the Christian teaching that "God is love" becomes personified in the form of the Roman Venus, goddess of love.

At first sight, Botticelli's *Birth of Venus* seems a purely pagan image, with the nude goddess—one of the earliest female nudes since Classical Antiquity—borne forward by the winds. Yet not only is the beauty of Venus symbolic of Christian love, the idea of the birth of Venus corresponds to Christ's baptism, itself a form of rebirth.

By the end of the 15th century, the overthrow of the Medici and the preaching of Savonarola (see Part IV, Topic 2) reduced the dominant role of Florentine artists, but the main features of Florentine Renaissance art had already spread to other parts of Italy. One of the greatest of northern Italian painters was the Paduan Andrea Mantegna (c. 1431–1506), a learned student of ancient art and literature. His painting of *The Dead Christ* uses the technique of perspective first developed at Florence to produce a harrowing image of a dead body, the emotional effect implicit in the corpse made manifest in two mourning figures on the left. By contrast with the ideal beauty depicted by Botticelli and other Florentine painters, Mantegna's harsh emotionalism seems to embody a last trace of the Gothic religious fervor of northern Europe.

HARMONY AND DESIGN IN THE HIGH RENAISSANCE

For a few brief years, from the French invasion of Italy in 1494 to the death of Raphael in 1520, the Renaissance reached a new peak. Lavish papal patronage made Rome

Botticelli's *The Birth of Venus* (1480) illustrates Renaissance ideas of Christian humanism.

the center of High Renaissance art, although Leonardo da Vinci, one of the three leading figures of the age—the others were Raphael and Michelangelo—mainly worked in Milan and died in France.

Renaissance Man: Leonardo da Vinci

No figure of the Renaissance has evoked greater admiration for the breadth of his mind than Leonardo (1452–1519), the illegitimate son of a notary at Vinci, a small town to the west of Florence. He studied painting in Florence and worked at the court of the Sforza family, rulers of Milan, as architect, military engineer, inventor, scientist, musician, and painter. He set down many of his ideas in thousands of pages of notes and sketches, exploring the human and natural worlds.

Leonardo's fresco of *The Last Supper,* painted for the Milanese Church of Santa Maria delle Grazie, is the first great work of the High Renaissance. In spite of severe damage due to flaking paint, the work remains a powerful illustration of Renaissance ideals of clarity and harmony. The central figure of Jesus, his head outlined against the open window behind, is flanked by six apostles to each side. Jesus himself remains still, while shock waves pass through the others in response to his words to them: "One of you will betray me." The dramatic range of emotions the apostles convey, the careful balance of the composition, and the absence of irrelevant details all combine to produce one of the high points of Western art.

If *The Last Supper* is the most famous of Renaissance religious scenes, Leonardo's portrait of *Mona Lisa,* wife of the merchant Giocondo (the painting is often known as *La Gioconda*—a pun on her husband's name that refers to her smile), is no less celebrated. The sitter's ambiguous smile and the hazy background are made possible by the artist's use of a technique called *sfumato* or "smoky." The rivers and craggy mountains that frame the head illustrate Leonardo's belief that painting should express the laws of light and space, and sciences like botany and geology, as well as purely human nature. The whole forms a blend of ideal beauty and science, the epitome of the High Renaissance.

The Classical Harmony of Raphael

Born in Urbino, the painter Raphael (1483–1520) studied in Florence before moving to Rome in 1508, where he received important papal commissions. His Classical balance and order are visible in the series of frescoes with which he decorated a suite of rooms in the Vatican palace, known as the *Vatican Stanze.* The most famous, *The School of Athens,* depicts the most renowned ancient Greek and Roman philosophers engaged in earnest discussion.

Like Leonardo's *Last Supper,* the scene shows the figures arranged in groups. The two greatest minds of antiquity, Plato and Aristotle, stand at the center under the receding arches. Plato points upward, to indicate abstract thought, while Aristotle gestures to the ground, symbol of practical and down-to-earth experiment. The round arches and coffered ceilings of the background provide a Classical setting.

Leonardo da Vinci's *The Last Supper* (1495–1498).

Raphael, *The School of Athens.*

For his contemporaries, Raphael's most popular works were his many depictions of the Madonna and Child. Among the best-known is the *Madonna with the Goldfinch*, which provides another Renaissance example of pyramidal composition. Unlike Leonardo, with his love of mysterious haze, Raphael bathed his figures in a glowing clarity which emphasizes their High Renaissance blend of Christian devotion and pagan beauty. In the background, the details of the feathery trees are all rendered with loving precision.

The Sublime Michelangelo

Even in an age of giants, Michelangelo Buonarroti (1475–1564) inspired awe mixed with fear in his contemporaries, who spoke of his *terribilità*—a combination of the terrible and the sublime. For posterity he has become the symbol of creative genius, fighting with his patrons and rivals in the pursuit of his titanic visions.

Architect, painter, poet, and engineer, Michelangelo always regarded himself as first and foremost a sculptor, since sculptors possessed the almost divine power to "make man." Wrestling with the stone, he strove to release the image, the Idea, locked within it. The basis for Michelangelo's artistic philosophy was Plato's theory of Forms, or Ideas (see Part II, Topic 4), and he held that by imitating Nature an artist could reveal the highest eternal truths. Unlike other Renaissance artists, he rejected Classical notions of balance and proportion, claiming that only the inspired judgment of the individual artist could create the rules for his art. His stubborn independence, coupled with his irascible and impulsive manner, won him few friends—the popular and worldly Raphael described him as "lonely as the hangman."

One of the early works to win him fame was the *Pietà*, which shows Mary holding the body of the dead Christ. The contrast between the youthful grace of the grieving mother and the leaden weight of the body, legs dangling, already looks forward to the emotional extremes of later versions of the same subject.

Another figure from the same period, the *David*, has become one of the icons of the Florentine Renaissance. After finishing the *Pietà*, Michelangelo returned from Rome to Florence, drawn by the chance to "release" from a gigantic block of stone—on which other sculptors had worked in vain—the "Idea" within

Michelangelo, *David.*

DOCUMENTS ON HISTORY

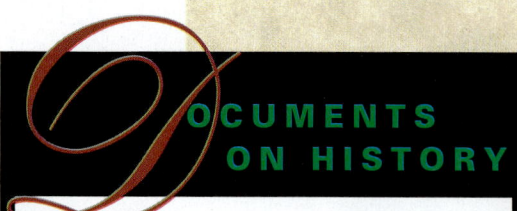

Art and Artists in the Renaissance

Our knowledge of art, artists, and patrons in Renaissance Italy owes much to the *The Lives of the Artists* of Giorgio Vasari (1511–1574), himself a painter and architect. *The Lives* first appeared in 1550, and Vasari published an enlarged version in 1568. His account includes descriptions of over 100 artists working over a period of some three centuries, and combines comments on their works with information about their patrons and the world around them—in the case of the most recent artists, including Michelangelo, based on Vasari's personal observations and inquiries. With regard to the two passages below, the first deals with the greatest sculptor of the Early Renaissance, Donatello, and the second with Michelangelo himself.

Another artist who also wrote was the sculptor Benvenuto Cellini (1500–1571), although his *Autobiography* is devoted to recording, in suitably embroidered form, his own glories rather than the achievements of others. His account of the casting of the *Perseus* describes the artist's triumph in the face of the technical problems of casting a life-size bronze statue, as well as over the knaves, fools, and doubters who surrounded him.

VASARI ON DONATELLO AND MICHELANGELO

Behind Vasari's Lives of the Artists, *there is a not-so-hidden agenda: after the empty years under Byzantine influence, Italian art was brought back to life by Giotto, and proceeded to develop until it reached its highest point in the work of the divinely inspired Michelangelo. The fact that this thesis may seem familiar is a tribute to the enormous influence of Vasari on subsequent art historians.*

One of the heroes of the first part of the Lives *is Donatello (1386–1466). In his comments on Donatello's style, Vasari emphasizes the sculptor's revival of Classical precedents, while his description of Donatello's life underlines the warm friendship between the artist and his patron, Cosimo de' Medici: the notion that an artist's genius placed him on the same level as the aristocracy was characteristic of Renaissance culture.*

Donatello as Man and Artist

Donato, called Donatello by his friends, and who thus signed himself on some of his works, was born in Florence. Devoting himself to the art of design he became not only a most rare sculptor and marvellous statue-maker, but was skillful in stucco, versed in perspective and highly esteemed in architecture, while his works possessed such grace, design and excellence that they were held to resemble the excellent productions of the ancient Greeks and Romans more than those of any other. Thus he is deservedly placed in the front rank of those who first showed the beauty of bas-reliefs, which were executed by him with great facility and mastery, and a more than ordinary beauty showing that he thoroughly understood that work. Indeed no other artist surpassed him in this branch, and even in our own age no one has equaled him. . . .

In short, Donato was so admirable in his every act that in skill, judgement and knowledge he may be said to have been among the first to illustrate the art of sculpture and the good designs of the moderns. He deserves the greater commendation, because in his day antiquities had not yet been dug up, such as columns, sarcophagi and triumphal arches. It was chiefly by his influence that Cosimo de' Medici conceived the desire to introduce to Florence the antiquities which are and were in the Casa Medici, all of which were restored by his hand.

He was free, affectionate and courteous, and more so to his friends than to himself. He thought nothing of money, keeping it in a basket suspended by a rope from the ceiling, so that all his workmen and friends took what they wanted without saying anything to him. He passed his old age very happily, and when he could work no longer he was assisted by Cosimo and other friends. It is said that when Cosimo was on his deathbed he recommended Donato to his son Piero, who diligently executed his father's wish and gave the artist a property which brought in sufficient income to permit him to live in comfort. . . .

Having attained the age of eighty-three, he became so paralytic that he could no longer do the slightest work, and remained in bed in a little house which he had in the Via Del Cocomero, near the nuns of San Niccolò. He died on 13th December, 1466, and was buried in the church of San Lorenzo, near the tomb of Cosimo, as the latter had himself ordained, so that the dead body should be near him in death, as he had always been near him in spirit when alive.

Michelangelo: Cosmic Genius

While the artists who came after Giotto were doing their best to imitate and to understand nature, bending every faculty to increase that high comprehension sometimes called intelligence, the Almighty took pity on their often fruitless labor. He resolved to send to earth a spirit capable of supreme expression in all the arts, one able to give form to painting, perfection to sculpture, and grandeur to architecture. The Almighty Creator also graciously endowed this chosen one with an understanding of philosophy and with the grace of poetry. And because he had observed that in Tuscany men were more zealous in study and more diligent in labor than in the rest of Italy, He decreed that Florence should be the birthplace of this divinely endowed spirit.

In the Casentino, therefore, in 1475, a son was born to Signor Lodovico di Leonardo di Buonarotti Simoni. . . .

[The painting of the Sistine Chapel.] Michelangelo returned to Rome and was asked by Pope Julius II to paint the ceiling of the [Sistine] chapel, a great and difficult labor. Our artist, aware of his own inexperience, excused himself from the undertaking. He proposed that the work be given to Raphael. The more he refused, the more the impetuous Pope insisted. A quarrel threatened. Michelangelo saw that the Pope was determined, so he resolved to accept the task. His Holiness ordered Bramante to prepare the scaffolding. This he did by suspending the ropes through perforations in the ceiling. Michelangelo asked how the holes were going to be filled in when the painting was done. Bramante replied that they could think about it when the time came. Michelangelo saw that the architect was either incapable or unfriendly, and he went straight to the Pope to say that the scaffolding would not do and that Bramante did not know how to construct one. Julius, in the presence of Bramante, replied that Michelangelo might make it his own way. This he did by the use of a method that did not injure the walls, and which has since been pursued by Bramante and others. Michelangelo gave the ropes that were taken from Bramante's scaffolding to a poor carpenter, who sold them for a sum that made up his daughter's dowry.

For this work Michelangelo was paid three thousand crowns by the Pope. He may have spent twenty-five for colors. He worked under great personal inconvenience, constantly

continued next page

looking upward, so that he seriously injured his eyes. For months afterward he could read a letter only when he held it above his head. I can vouch for the pain of this kind of labor. When I painted the ceiling of the palace of Duke Cosimo [Palazzo Vecchio in Florence], I never could have finished the work without a special support for my head. As it is, I still feel the effects of it, and I wonder that Michelangelo endured it so well. But, as the work progressed, his zeal for his art increased daily, and he grudged no labor and was insensible to all fatigue.

Down the center of the ceiling is the *History of the World,* from the Creation to the Deluge. The *Prophets* and the *Sibyls,* five on each side and one at each end, are painted on the corbels. The lunettes portray the genealogy of Christ. Michelangelo used no perspective, nor any one fixed point of sight, but was satisfied to paint each division with perfection of design. Truly this chapel has been, and is, the very light of our art. Everyone capable of judging stands amazed at the excellence of his work, at the grace and flexibility, the beautiful truth of proportion of the exquisite nude forms. These are varied in every way in expression and form. Some of the figures are seated, some are in motion, while others hold up festoons of oak leaves and acorns, the device of Pope Julius. . . .

Michelangelo's powers were so great that his sublime ideas were often inexpressible. He spoiled many works because of this. Shortly before his death he burned a large number of designs, sketches, and cartoons so that none might see the labors he endured in his resolution to achieve perfection. None will marvel that Michelangelo was a lover of solitude, devoted as he was to art, and, therefore, never alone or without food for contemplation. . . . Those who say he would not teach others are wrong. I have been present many times when he assisted his intimates or any who asked his counsels . . . he was an ardent admirer of beauty for art, and knew how to select the most beautiful, but he was not liable to the undue influence of beauty. This his whole life has proved. In all things he was most moderate. He ate frugally at the close of the day's work. Though rich, he lived like a poor man and rarely had a guest at his table. He would accept no gifts for fear of being under an obligation.

This master, as I said at the beginning, was certainly sent by God as an example of what an artist could be. I, who can thank God for unusual happiness, count it among the greatest of my blessings that I was born while Michelangelo still lived, was found worthy to have him for my master, and was accepted as his trusted friend.

From Vasari, G., trans. A. B. Hinds. *Lives of the Painters, Sculptors and Architects.*

CELLINI ON THE CASTING OF THE PERSEUS

By contrast to the unworldly and reclusive Michelangelo, the Florentine goldsmith and sculptor Benvenuto Cellini led a violent and adventurous life. He fought for the pope in Rome and for Francis I in Paris, and spent time in prison on a charge of theft brought by the bastard son of Pope Paul III. Toward the end of his life, he dictated to an apprentice in his workshop his autobiography, from which the following passage comes.

All his stories feature himself as the hero, generally triumphing against the plots of his enemies and overcoming the most insuperable difficulties. The casting of the life-size bronze statue of Perseus with the Head of Medusa, *a work still standing in Florence's Piazza Signoria, presented him with his greatest artistic challenge, and his account of it is justly famous.*

As his workshop prepares the mold and lights the furnace, Cellini himself is overcome with a fever—probably brought on by nervous strain—and takes to his bed in despair: "I feel more ill than I ever did in all my life and verily believe that it will kill me before a few hours are over." When one of his assistants, however, brings him the news that the statue is ruined, he rushes back to take charge.

Casting the Perseus: The Final Stages

When I had got my clothes on, I strode with soul bent on mischief toward the workshop; there I beheld the men, whom I had left erewhile in such high spirits, standing stupefied and downcast. I began at once and spoke: "Up with you! Attend to me! Since you have not been able or willing to obey the directions I gave you, obey me now that I am with you to conduct my work in person. Let no one contradict me, for in cases like this we need the aid of hand and hearing, not advice." When I had uttered these words, a certain Maestro Alessandro Lastricati broke silence and said: "Look you, Benvenuto, you are going to attempt an enterprise which the laws of art do not sanction, and which cannot succeed." I turned on him with such fury and so full of mischief, that he and all the rest of them exclaimed with one voice: "On then! Give orders! We will obey your least commands, so long as life is left in us." I believe they spoke thus feelingly because they thought I must fall shortly dead on the ground. I went immediately to inspect the furnace, and found that the metal was all curdled; an accident which we call "being caked." I told two of the hands to cross the road, and fetch from the house of the butcher Capretta a load of young oak-wood, which had lain dry for above a year; this wood had previously been offered me by Madama Ginevra, wife of the said Capretta. So soon as the first armfuls arrived, I began to fill the grate beneath the furnace. Now oak-wood of that kind heats more powerfully than any other sort of tree; and for this reason, where a slow fire is wanted, as in the case of gun-foundry, alder or pine is preferred. Accordingly, when the logs took fire, oh! how the cake began to stir beneath that awful heat, to glow and sparkle in a blaze! At the same time I kept stirring up the channels, and sent men upon the roof to stop the conflagration, which had gathered force from the increased combustion in the furnace; also, I caused boards, carpets, and other hangings to be set up against the garden, in order to protect us from the violence of the rain of sparks.

All of a sudden an explosion took place, attended by a tremendous flash of flame, as though a thunderbolt had formed and been discharged amongst us. Unwonted and appalling terror astonished every one, and me more even than the rest. When the din was over and the dazzling light extinguished, we began to look each other in the face. Then I discovered that the cap of the furnace had blown up, and the bronze was bubbling up from its source beneath. So I had the mouths of my mold immediately opened, and at the same time drove in the two plugs which kept back the molten metal. But I noticed that it did not flow as rapidly as usual, the reason being probably that the fierce heat of the fire we kindled had consumed its base alloy. Accordingly I sent for all my pewter platters, bowls, and dishes, to the number of some two hundred pieces, and had a portion of them cast one by one into the channels, the rest into the furnace. This expedient succeeded, and every one could now perceive that my bronze was in most perfect liquefaction, and my mold was filling; whereupon they all with heartiness and happy cheer assisted and obeyed my bidding, while I, now here, now there, gave orders, helped with my own hands, and cried aloud: "O God! Thou that by Thy immeasurable power didst rise from the dead, and in Thy glory didst ascend to heaven!" . . . even thus in a moment my mold was filled; and seeing my work finished, I fell upon my knees, and with all my heart gave thanks to God.

From Cellini, B., trans. J. A. Symonds. *The Life of Benvenuto Cellini Written by Himself.* Copyright © 1906.

continued next page

The production of art objects was, of course, a matter of business in Renaissance Italy. The portion from Cellini's *Autobiography* is followed by a rather more prosaic document, a contract drawn up by the Venetian painter Cima da Conegliano (c. 1459–1518) for the payment for one of his altarpieces.

Finally, two of the greatest of all Renaissance artists, Leonardo and Michelangelo, write on the nature of art.

A VENETIAN PAINTER CONTRACTS TO PRODUCE AN ALTARPIECE

Many of the most important Renaissance works of art were made on commission for churches or monasteries. The following document was written in his own hand by the Venetian painter Cima da Conegliano for a work he painted in 1513.

Contract Between Cima da Conegliano and the Fathers of St. Anna

In the name of Jesus Christ and Mary. 18 April 1513, in Venice. Memorandum of agreement between me, Giovanni Battista da Conegliano, painter, living in the parish of San Luca in Venice, and Messer Alvise Grisoni, citizen of Capodistria, and procurator of the reverend fathers of S. Anna, Observants of the order of St. Francis. That I shall make for the said church a painted altarpiece and gild its frame, using good quality colors, all at my own expense, and with the figures represented as they appear in the drawing made by the frame-carver. All this shall be for a fee of seventy ducats, on the condition that when the work is complete, the said Messer Alvise, acting in the name of the aforementioned fathers, shall be at liberty to seek professional advice from experts chosen by him and by myself, Giovanni Battista, regarding the value of the work. And I promise to have the work ready for him by next Christmas. I acknowledge receipt of a first payment of ten ducats now, and I understand that I will receive thirty ducats when the work is complete, and the final thirty when it is delivered. As a sign of my good faith, this agreement is written in my own hand, and it is witnessed by master Vettor da Feltre, woodcarver, and my pupil Marco Luciani, both of whose signatures are appended below.

LEONARDO AND MICHELANGELO ON ART

Like the artists of Classical Antiquity, but unlike the artist craftsmen of the Medieval world, Renaissance artists discussed and wrote on aesthetics and the philosophy of art. One of the

it. The result was the stern, tense image of David, a young man poised between thought and action.

The climax of the first part of Michelangelo's career was the colossal decoration of the ceiling of the Sistine Chapel in the Vatican. Michelangelo painted the entire ceiling, some 5800 square feet in area, in the four years between 1508 and 1512. In glowing, luminous colors (revealed by their recent cleaning), the paintings depict no less a theme than the Creation, Fall, and Redemption of Man. On the sides, Classical and Hebrew figures foretell the coming of Christ, while in the very center Michelangelo shows *The Creation of Adam*. The hand of God reaches out to awaken the first man by endowing him with the divine spark of life.

great Renaissance debates was on whether painting or sculpture was the highest form of art. The two following examples represent the views of the two towering creative figures of the Renaissance, Leonardo and Michelangelo. Both of them worked in an astonishing range of fields, but Leonardo considered himself primarily a painter, and Michelangelo thought his highest achievements were in sculpture. The passage from Leonardo's journals shows that he saw the act of painting as an almost divine act of creation, while Michelangelo's sonnet (addressed to his dear friend Vittoria Colonna) suggests that the virtue of sculpture lies in its capacity to survive.

Leonardo's Journals

If the painter wishes to see beauties that charm him, it lies in his power to create them, and if he wishes to see monstrosities that are frightful, ridiculous, or truly pitiable, he is lord and God thereof; and if he wishes to generate sites and deserts, shady and cool places in hot weather he can do so, and also warm places in cold weather. If he wishes from the high summits of the mountains to uncover great countrysides, and if he wishes after them to see the horizon of the sea, he is lord of it, and if from the low valleys he wishes to see the high mountains, or from the high mountains the low valleys and beaches, and in effect that which is in the universe for essence, presence, or imagination, he has it first in his mind and then in his hands, and these are of such excellence that in equal time they generate a proportionate harmony in a single glance, as does nature. . . .

The deity which invests the science of the painter functions in such a way that the mind of the painter is transformed into a copy of the divine mind, since it operates freely in creating the many kinds of animals, plants, fruits, landscapes, countrysides, ruins, and awe-inspiring places.

From Leonardo's journals cited in Hartt, Frederick. *History of Italian Renaissance Art.* Harry N. Abrams, Copyright © 1979. Reprinted with permission.

A Sonnet by Michelangelo

How can that be, lady, which all men learn
By long experience? Shapes that seem alive,
Wrought in hard mountain marble, will survive
Their maker, whom the years to dust return!
Thus to effect cause yields. Art hath her turn,
And triumphs over Nature. I, who strive
With Sculpture, know this well; her wonders live
In spite of time and death, those tyrants stern.
So I can give long life to both of us
In either way, by color or by stone,
Making the semblance of thy face and mine.
Centuries hence when both are buried, thus
Thy beauty and my sadness shall be shown,
And men shall say, "For her 'twas wise to pine."

From *The Sonnets of Michael Angelo Buonarotti,* trans. J. A. Symonds. Copyright © 1948.

Adam's body represents not only natural beauty but the manifestation of the soul itself.

Toward the end of his long artistic odyssey, Michelangelo's style became increasingly complex and tormented. The terrifying scene of *The Last Judgement*, painted on the end wall of the Sistine Chapel 25 years after the ceiling frescoes, echoes to the blaring of trumpets. All creation seems to cower before the gigantic figure of Christ, as the dead arise and the damned hurtle down to eternal torment. Gone is the idealizing neoplatonic beauty and calm order of the earlier works. The swirling forms and distorted proportions foreshadow the Baroque art of the 17th century which they directly inspired.

Michelangelo, *Creation of Adam,* detail of the Sistine Chapel ceiling, 1508–1512.

HARMONY AND COLOR: THE PAINTING OF THE VENETIAN REPUBLIC

While many of the leading Renaissance artists and their styles moved between Florence, Rome, and the cities of northern Italy, the Republic of Venice maintained its cultural independence. Venetian artists used ideas developed elsewhere in Italy, but in distinct ways. The main interest of Florentine Renaissance artists was design, and drawing was regarded as crucial in achieving a sense of intellectual order. For the Venetians, color was the primary means of expression. The light of the lagoon which surrounds the city, soft and warm in summer, pearly grey with mist in winter, glows in the paintings of the painters of the *Serenissima*—most serene of cities.

Venice's detachment from the mainstream of Renaissance cultural movements in part reflected the strength of earlier Byzantine influence there, but a more important cause was the city's geographical position and economic ties. As gateway to the East, the Venetian Republic found itself increasingly involved in a protracted struggle with the Ottoman Turks in the century following the Turkish conquest of Constantinople (Istanbul) in 1453. The French and Spanish invasions which shook Florence and Rome in the years of the High Renaissance (see Part IV, Topic 2) had no significant effect on Venetian politics. On the only important occasion when the other Italian and European powers did intervene in Venetian affairs, it was to fight at the Battle of Lepanto, in 1571, on the side of the Venetians against the Turks.

Bellini the Colorist

One of the factors which helped Venetian painters to develop their love of color was the arrival in Venice in 1475 of Antonello da Messina (c. 1430–1479), the only major artist of the Quattrocento born south of Rome. Either in Flanders, or, more probably, through contact with a Flemish artist working in northern Italy, Antonello had learned to work with oil paint, and he introduced the new technique to the Venetians. Oil paint permitted a far greater range of colors than the tempera (egg-based paint) or fresco used by artists elsewhere in Italy, and Venetian artists quickly took advantage of its possibilities.

The first great figure in Venetian painting was Giovanni Bellini (c. 1430–1516), whose long career laid the foundations of the Venetian Renaissance style. Trained by his father, and influenced at first by his brother-in-law Mantegna, Bellini's early work was conventional. With his father's death in 1470, and the arrival of Antonello, he began to explore the sensuous possibilities of color.

The most popular subject of the day was known as the *Sacra Conversazione*, or "Sacred Conversation"—the Madonna and Child accompanied by a group of saints—painted on large panels to decorate the altars of Venice's churches. Bellini's *San Zaccaria Altarpiece* shows the figures closely integrated into their setting. The radiant colors and glowing light enhance the mood of calm serenity.

There is little in Venetian art of the intellectual rigor of Leonardo, let alone the *terribilità* of Michelangelo. Instead, Venetian painters concentrated on more gentle, poetic themes. The so-called *Country Celebration* of Giorgione da Castelfranco (1478–1510), a pupil of Bellini, shows a scene of dreamy music-making. Two young men in rich costumes idle in the company of two nude women, whose opulent bodies are bathed in golden shadow. Botticelli's nude Venus illustrates neoplatonic doctrine. The figures in Giorgione's scene give themselves up to the sensuous pleasure of nature, music, and love.

The High Renaissance in Venice: Titian

Titian (c. 1490–1576) was the dominating figure in Venetian art for over 50 years, and one of the supreme masters of Western painting. He was the first to use oil paint on canvas, rather than on wooden panels, the technique followed by most painters ever since. His ability to use color to depict texture—rich satin, glossy skin, thick rich hair—seems limitless. His subjects ranged from frankly sensual nudes to psychologically acute portraits to the deep spirituality of his later religious paintings.

One of his most influential works was *The Venus of Urbino*, painted when Titian was at the height of his powers for the duke of that city. The nude goddess reclines diagonally on crumpled sheets, in a pose imitated countless times by later artists. In the background two servants search in a chest, perhaps for a gown. The warm flesh, the fluffy little dog dozing at the foot of the couch, the deep red tones in the skirt of the standing servant behind, all play their part in building the composition by means of color.

Toward the end of his long life, Titian turned to religious themes, which he depicted with dark, intense emotion. The gleaming light of his earlier work is gone, replaced by deep shadows. His *Martyrdom of St. Lawrence*, still over the altar in the Church of the Jesuits in Venice, the place for which it was painted, shows the saint being roasted over a flickering fire. Only the thin beams of a light from heaven cut through the gloom. The somber, violent mood may reflect Titian's reaction to the religious wars between Catholics and Protestants then raging in Europe (see Part IV, Topic 7), or perhaps the aged artist was turning from worldly pleasures in search of spiritual meaning.

No other Venetian artist after Titian equaled his breadth of vision. In the works of Tintoretto (1518–1594), Titian's mystery becomes theatrical, with twisting figures combined in dynamic compositions. *The Finding of the Body of St. Mark* uses a dramatic setting, its gloomy vault plunging into the rear, while the characters in the foreground act out the story with grandiose gestures.

Tintoretto's emphatic style had much in common with similar developments elsewhere in Italy in the latter part of the Cinquecento. Following the extremes of Michelangelo's *Last Judgment*, artists developed a style

Titian's *Venus of Urbino* (1538) shows the typical Venetian love of rich color and erotic subjects.

called Mannerist, in which the figures were deliberately distorted and exaggerated. Mannerists such as the Florentine Bronzino (1503–1572) replaced the calm, Classical balance of Renaissance art with sophisticated elegance and intricate fantasy. The artificiality of the Mannerist conventions soon proved stilted and repetitive, and by the end of the century Mannerism was a spent force.

The Renaissance in Italy represented the rebirth of Classical culture, and, like the artists of Periclean Athens, the artists of the Renaissance knew that theirs was a unique moment in Western civilization. Like the builders of the Parthenon, Michelangelo intended his work in the Sistine Chapel as a "monument for all time."

In the past, sculptors and painters built on the achievements of their immediate predecessors to create new styles. The artists of the Renaissance, beginning with Brunelleschi and Donatello, deliberately and decisively broke with their traditions, to rediscover truth and beauty by following the aesthetic and philosophical ideals of antiquity. They invented more than they rediscovered, and by looking back they thrust art forward. The rapid speed with which Renaissance artists found new ways of describing human life and the world of nature gives their work a special excitement.

At the same time, Renaissance art represented just one aspect of a more general change of outlook in Western society. The career of a Michelangelo exemplified the growing development of civic identity, coupled with a new awareness of individual possibilities. The new learning, the birth of science, the art of diplomacy, are all other ways in which Renaissance culture and society reflected the sense of a fresh beginning.

The Early Renaissance in Florence was the product of a number of historical forces: the rise of the city-state and the economic developments which made possible the accumulation of personal fortunes such as that of the Medici. Other events also played their part. The precipitous decline of the Byzantine Empire and the fall of Constantinople in 1453 drove Byzantine scholars and intellectuals to take refuge in the West, bringing with them precious manuscripts of Classical works.

The remarkable achievement of Renaissance artists was to forge from these varied historical conditions a "modern style" which changed the way we look at the world. Their works remain relevant still, and central to the Western intellectual tradition.

Questions for Further Study

1. How did Renaissance artists break with traditions? To what extent did they return to Classical styles?
2. What were the main developments in Renaissance architecture?
3. What role did private patronage play in the artistic life of the Renaissance? In what ways did it change the status of the artist?
4. Which characteristics of Michelangelo's art led his contemporaries to regard him as exceptional even by Renaissance standards? How far have later generations echoed their judgment?

Suggestions for Further Reading

D'Amico, J. *Renaissance Humanism in Papal Rome.* Baltimore, MD, 1983.

Goldthwaite, R. A. *The Building of Renaissance Florence.* Baltimore, MD, 1980.

Holmes, G. *Florence, Rome, and the Origins of the Renaissance.* New York, 1987.

Murray, L. *High Renaissance and Mannerism.* London, 1985.

Olson, R. *Italian Renaissance Sculpture.* New York, 1992.

Rosand, D. *Painting in Cinquecento Venice.* New Haven, CT, 1982.

Summers, D. *Michelangelo and the Language of Art.* Princeton, NJ, 1982.

IV

T o p i c 4

Arts and Letters in Renaissance Europe

As the effects of the Italian Renaissance began to diffuse throughout the rest of Europe, they produced vast and rapid cultural changes. The most powerful new force was printing, first invented in the mid-15th century. By 1500, books and pamphlets were circulating in increasing numbers, spreading ideas as the rate of literacy rose. One of the most important long-term consequences was the rise of vernacular literature.

In northern Europe, the humanistic learning developed in Italy took on new forms, as Christian humanists like the Dutch Erasmus combined Classical ideas with traditional Christian attitudes. Both Erasmus and his English friend Thomas More wrote books attacking the religious and social attitudes of their times, in an attempt to define the nature of a truly Christian society. Erasmus' attacks on corruption in the church foreshadowed many of the criticisms of Martin Luther. Although Erasmus himself did not support the Reformation, he did advocate Catholic reform.

In Italy itself, the leading humanists of the High Renaissance continued to develop themes taken from Classical literature and learning. Castiglione's book *The Courtier* discussed the nature of virtue and the ideals of Platonic love. Machiavelli drew on the history of Republican Rome as background for his book *The Prince*, a study of political power.

As the artistic advances made in Italy began to cross the Alps, Northern artists adapted their styles accordingly. Van Eyck and his Flemish school, working in oils, soon established a market throughout Europe—including Italy—for their finely detailed panel paintings. The Flemish painters retained stylistic links with their Late Medieval past. The great German painter Albrecht Dürer, by contrast, drew on the High Renaissance to forge his own personal style.

The art of Renaissance music often transcended national boundaries. The musical traditions of northern Europe influenced composers in both Rome and Venice, where two musicians from the Low Countries, Josquin des Prés and Adrian Willaert, held important posts. Meanwhile, Italian musical forms became popular in the north, including the madrigal. Like painters and sculptors, composers turned increasingly to secular themes.

Toward the middle of the 16th century, the Reformation began to exert a growing influence on the arts in northern Europe. Protestant denunciations of the use of paintings and statues in churches caused a rapid decline in the production of sacred visual art. Literature and music, however, met with the reformers' approval. The results laid the foundations for the flourishing of sacred music and secular painting in 17th-century northern Europe.

THE PRINTING REVOLUTION

The invention of printing with movable type revolutionized Western civilization. The earliest known manufacture of individual characters that could be combined and reused occurred in China as early as the 11th century, but a similar technique developed in Europe only in the mid-15th century. Its introduction is generally credited to the German Johann Gutenberg (c. 1397–1468). The first printed Bible, the so-called Gutenberg Bible, appeared in 1455. Twenty years later, William Caxton (c. 1422–1491) published the first book printed in English, and in 1501 Aldus Manutius (1450–1515) began to sell inexpensive editions of the classics printed by his Aldine Press in Venice.

The Implications of Printing

Probably no technological development before the 19th century created such profound changes in Western culture as the invention of printing. The implications of the communications revolution it inaugurated are still with us at the dawn of the 21st century. Among its consequences were the standardization of texts, the acceleration of science, the spread of education—including, increasingly, that of women—and the rapid diffusion of new ideas. Martin Luther's Protestant Reformation was one of the first movements to benefit from the circulation of books and pamphlets (see Part IV, Topic 7).

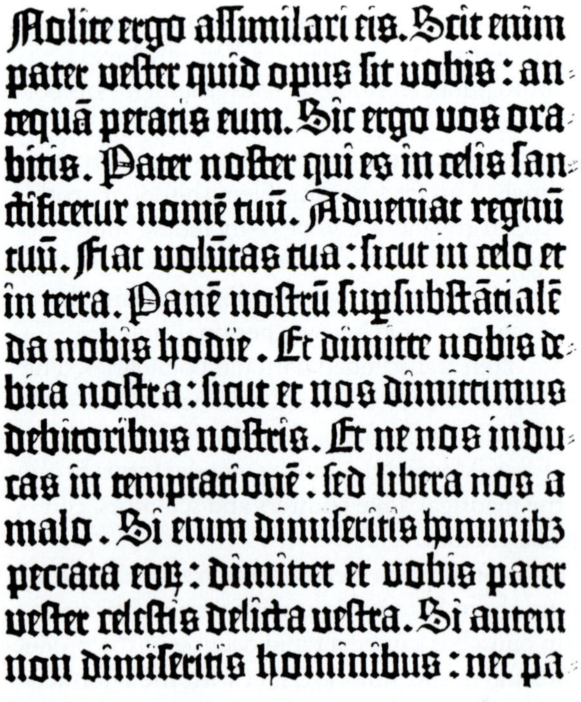
Nolite ergo assimilari eis. Scit enim
pater vester quid opus sit vobis: an-
tequā petatis eum. Sic ergo vos ora-
bitis. Pater noster qui es in celis san-
ctificetur nomē tuū. Adveniat regnū
tuū. Fiat volūtas tua: sicut in celo et
in terra. Panē nostrū supsubstātialē
da nobis hodie. Et dimitte nobis de-
bita nostra: sicut et nos dimittimus
debitoribus nostris. Et ne nos indu-
cas in temptationē: sed libera nos a
malo. Si enim dimiseritis hominib3
peccata eoꝝ: dimittet et vobis pater
vester celestis delicta vestra. Si autem
non dimiseritis hominibus: nec pa-

Portion of a page from the Gutenberg Bible, 1455.

Before the mid-15th century, books were extremely expensive, and the supply never equalled the demand. Handwritten copies were produced by stationers—so-called because they worked in a settled, or stationary, place of business—and sold or rented out by booksellers. Most dealers in books worked for the universities. University officials kept a stringent control on the trade and fixed the prices for the benefit of their students, who often hired a book for use during a university session and then returned it to the bookshop. The only people who received no financial benefit from the circulation of books were the authors.

With the introduction of printing technology, the publishers took over the production and distribution of books. The figures attest to the astonishing growth in the publishing industry. By 1500, European presses had distributed between 6 and 9 million books in 13,000 different editions. One of the most popular works of Erasmus, *In Praise of Folly,* went through 27 editions in his own lifetime. Many of these were pirated, generally from the printers to whom authors customarily sold their rights. Unless authors published their own works, they continued to make little profit from their "intellectual property." The first international copyright agreement was signed only in 1886, and the United States did not subscribe until 1929.

Printing and the Vernacular

Most educated Europeans before the Renaissance used two languages: their own native tongue—the vernacular—and Latin. Some popular literature in the vernacular appeared in France, Germany, and England (see Part III, Topic 9), but in many countries the first literary works in their own languages were printed ones, often translations of the Bible into the vernacular. In Finland, the Finnish language appeared in written form for the first time as late as the 16th century, in the first printed Bible in Finnish.

In preparing their translations, scholars did not restrict themselves to the standard Latin version of the Bible. Erasmus used three separate Greek manuscripts to compile an edition of the New Testament in Greek. Martin Luther used Erasmus' work in making his great translation of the Bible into German, while for the Psalms he turned to the original Hebrew edition, which had been published in 1516.

When, a century later, the so-called King James Version of the Bible appeared in England, its translators claimed to have consulted editions and commentaries in Hebrew, Chaldean, Syriac, Greek, and Latin, as well as modern versions in Spanish, French, Italian, and Dutch. The consequences for the development of literary culture were profound. In England, the wide diffu-

Luther's German psalter has the words of the hymns in German, not Latin.

sion of both the King James Bible and the Anglican *Book of Common Prayer* shaped the future history of the language.

By no means were all printed works in the vernacular religious. Scholars continued to use Latin for learned communications, but authors who wanted to reach the wider, less academic audience made possible by printing, increasingly wrote in their own languages. Castiglione and Machiavelli both published in Italian, and Sir Thomas More in English. Montaigne wrote his essays, inspired by a study of the Classics, in French.

The printing revolution was not limited to literary texts. The publication of music led to the wide circulation of Lutheran hymns and secular Italian madrigals. Dürer and other contemporary artists were quick to exploit the possibilities of the print, first in the form of relatively easily produced woodcuts and then in the more difficult medium of line engravings on copper plates. Book publishers began to include visual material in the form of illustrations or diagrams in their printed volumes. No less important in an era of exploration was the printing and circulation of maps and charts (see Part IV, Topic 6).

The long-term consequence of all these innovations was to undermine the authority of the established institutions of Medieval culture and society. People who could read for themselves had independent access to the ideas of others, and had less need to turn to the church, the monasteries, or the universities for guidance and instruction. The invention of printing was a key factor in the evolution of the secular state.

THE NORTHERN HUMANISTS: EDUCATION FOR A CHRISTIAN SOCIETY

Many of the humanist writers and scholars in Italy adopted wholeheartedly the intellectual values of Classical Antiquity, with its emphasis on the importance of the individual. In his *Oration on the Dignity of Man*, Pico della Mirandola described humans as endowed with free will and in control of their own destinies—a notion that was based on the Classical idea that "Man is the measure of all things."

As humanism began to spread in northern Europe, thinkers there tried to reconcile humanist principles with Christianity. These northern Christian humanists accepted many of the values of Classical Antiquity—idealism, the power of reason, the importance of ancient texts—but used them as a basis for reforming the Christianity of their day, rather than as an end in themselves.

In part, Christian humanism in northern Europe drew its strength from resentment at the corruption of the church in Rome. In Germany, in particular, hostility toward Italian religious leaders combined with nationalism to create a wish to throw off Roman domination and return Christianity to its simple origins. Elsewhere, northern humanists directed their fire against social inequities as well as religious abuses. The English statesman and writer Sir Thomas More (1478–1535) published a satire called *Utopia*

(1516–1517). It describes an ideal state, Utopia (his invented name means "no place" in Greek), on an island in the New World. The citizens of Utopia live in a social and political paradise, and when one of them visits England, he contrasts his own society with the social injustices he finds there. The title of More's book added a new word to the English language.

Erasmus, Prince of Humanists

One of More's closest friends was the man recognized by his contemporaries as the "Prince of Humanists," the Dutch priest and intellectual Desiderius Erasmus (1466–1536). A truly international figure, Erasmus studied and taught in Italy, at Oxford and Cambridge, and at Paris.

The writings of Erasmus were the most comprehensive humanist attempt to reconcile Classical learning and simple Christianity. He revered the Classical emphasis on the personal dignity of the individual, and on the importance of education. He steeped himself in the works of ancient literature available to him. At the same time, as a Christian, he tried to return to the original "philosophy of Christ," as it was expressed in the Sermon on the Mount, claiming that pure faith was more important than formal religious ceremony. He also attacked the complexity of Medieval Catholic theology, claiming that some issues could never be known: he felt that Christians needed to believe only such basic aspects of their faith as the Creed.

Erasmus wrote his most successful book in 1509 while staying in England as a house guest of Sir Thomas More. The original Latin form of its title, *In Praise of Folly*, was a pun in honor of his distinguished host: the Latin words *Encomium Moriae* can mean "praise of folly" or "praise of More." The tone is lighthearted, but Erasmus is unsparing in his denunciations of social and religious corruption. Among his targets are hypocritical priests and cardinals, fraudulent scholars, and venal lawyers.

For all the force of his criticism, Erasmus was a true moderate. Unlike Martin Luther, he believed that it was possible to reform the church from within. When Luther's Reformation split the Christian world, Erasmus remained a Catholic. Both sides denounced him, the Catholics for his criticisms of the church and the Protestants because he would not throw his considerable weight behind the Reform movement. The final break between Erasmus and Luther came in 1524, when Erasmus published a pamphlet asserting that humans had free will. Luther's reply came in a tract published the following year. Human will, he claimed, was fatally flawed, and only the grace of God could rescue an individual from the fires of hell. The two men never spoke again.

Albrecht Dürer, *Erasmus of Rotterdam, 1526.*

THE COURTIER AND THE PRINCE: HANDBOOKS OF RENAISSANCE STRATEGY

While Christian humanists in northern Europe hotly debated the best way to achieve religious reform, humanist writers in Italy occupied themselves with more worldly affairs.

Castiglione the Courtier

Baldassare Castiglione (1478–1529), born into an ancient aristocratic family, received a thorough humanistic education before serving in the diplomatic corps of Milan, Mantua, and eventually Urbino, where he settled for a number of years. The duke of Urbino was one of the leading artistic patrons of the day, and his court was a center for writers and intellectuals.

Early in his stay at Urbino, Castiglione conceived the idea of writing a book about life at an ideal court. The result, *The Courtier*, appeared in an edition published by the Aldine Press in 1528, the year before its author's death. Castiglione's work takes the form of a series of imaginary discussions between members of the court on the qualities of the ideal courtier. Drawing on the works of a host of ancient authors, from Plato to Cicero, Castiglione's characters discuss a wide range of topics: Classical views of virtue, the notion of chivalry, Platonic (that is, ideal) love, and above all the nature of the true courtier.

The most important quality in an ideal courtier—and human being—is versatility. Humanistic learning is important, and a knowledge of Greek and Latin, but so are horsemanship and skills with a sword. The ideal courtier should write both prose and verse, appreciate music and painting, and also hunt, wrestle, and play tennis. Impeccable morals must be combined with exquisite manners and the ability to make fascinating conversation. In love, the true gentleman should worship his beloved's beauty of mind as much as that of her body.

None of these attributes should be so marked that it dominates the others—Castiglione's ideal is the *uomo universale*, the well-rounded person. Equally important is the cultivation of *sprezzatura*, an almost untranslatable Italian word, which suggests an air of casual ease. None of the courtier's accomplishments must seem an effort or draw attention to itself.

The imaginary participants in Castiglione's dialogues also discuss the ideal court lady. With the exception of athletics and warfare, she should cultivate the same skills as men, adding to them charm, grace, and physical attractiveness. She should wear little makeup, and avoid calling attention to herself in dress, conduct, or reputation. Above all, she should be feminine, for women exert a civilizing influence on the rough male world. Castiglione argues that women should be the educated equals of men, since they make an equally important contribution to society. The emphasis on education and the worth of the individual, whether male or female, is the product of Castiglione's humanistic training, and in strong contrast with the Medieval tradition whereby women were excluded from universities.

It is easy to criticize Castiglione for his excessive concern with refinement and the details of courtly decorum, but his description of the ideals of Italian Renaissance court society at the moment of its greatest splendor is deeply felt and elegantly expressed.

Raphael's portrait of Baldassare Castiglione, author of *The Courtier.*

Machiavelli the Realist

Castiglione's essentially optimistic view of human nature is certainly in the strongest contrast with the opinions of Niccolò Machiavelli (1469–1527), whose writings on political theory drew on his practical experience as statesman. In 1498, when the Florentines drove out their Medici rulers and set up a republic, Machiavelli served his city as diplomat. In the course of his missions he met many of the leading figures of the day. Among those to make a mark on the observant ambassador were the ruthless Cesare Borgia (1476–1507) and his notorious sister Lucrezia Borgia (1480–1519).

In 1512, with the fall of the Republic and the return of the Medici, the new rulers dismissed Machiavelli from his post, imprisoned and tortured him, and eventually banished him to his family's country estate just outside Florence. Living in exile there, within a year he had completed his most influential work, *The Prince*, a practical guide to the use of political power. It circulated in manuscript during Machiavelli's lifetime, but was published only in 1532, after his death.

Reactions to its apparently cynical endorsement of tyranny and treachery were predictably mixed. The Catholic Church denounced it, and listed it on the *Index of Prohibited Books*. The very word "Machiavellian" soon came to mean scheming and unscrupulous, and in England "Old Nick" became synonymous with the devil himself. On the other hand many rulers turned to it for practical guidance in running a state. Among Machiavelli's later readers and admirers were Catherine the Great of Russia and Napoleon.

Machiavelli's attitude to political power grew out of the specific historical context of his times. He saw the Italian states of the 16th century as helpless and at the mercy of the rivalries of France and Spain. Italy was "without head, without order, beaten, despoiled, lacerated." When the republic which the Florentines had set up to regain control over their own destiny ended in abject failure, Machiavelli believed that only the creation of a powerful and stable Florentine state could protect Italy against constant foreign intervention. The Medici seemed to offer the promise of strong government, and the Medici pope then ruling in Rome, Leo X, could provide support.

For Florence's new rulers to be effective, however, they needed to set aside moral scruples and take firm charge. Machiavelli's ideal of good government was that of the ancient Roman Republic (509–31 B.C.): he saw its citizens as virtuous, and considered the volunteer citizen legions of ancient Rome infinitely preferable to the mercenary armies of his own day. The first crucial step for a modern ruler, he believed, was to reduce the political power of the church. Christianity's role in government had proved disastrous, and the church should limit itself to purely spiritual matters.

The head of state, the Prince of the book's title, should rule by using power wisely and ruthlessly. No moral consideration should deter the Prince from performing this task. Thus cruelty, sensibly used, consolidates power and discourages revolution. Nor was honesty a factor: "A prince must not keep faith when by doing so it would be against his self-interest." In short, since his subjects lack virtue, the Prince must do whatever is necessary to keep the state intact. Nor should he overestimate his subjects: "They are ungrateful, changeable, runaways in danger, eager for gain; while you do well by them, they are all yours; when you are in need, they turn away."

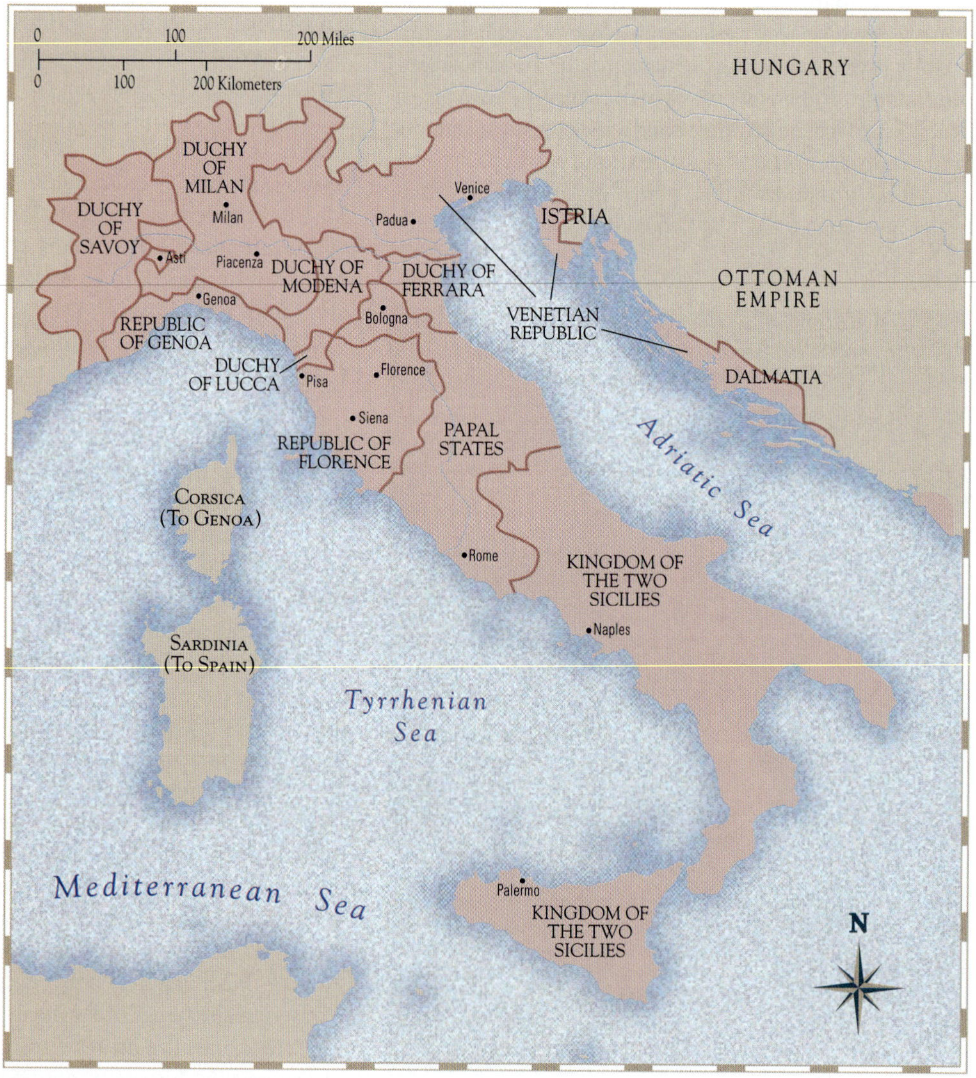

Map 4.1 The States of Renaissance Italy

THE CONQUEST OF REALITY: RENAISSANCE ART IN THE NORTH

As in the other arts, developments in Italian Renaissance painting took a while to circulate north of the Alps. When, in the mid-15th century, Florentine merchants began to expand their trade with Flanders, they found a brilliant school of painters already flourishing there. Some of the earliest exchanges, in fact, saw Flemish works moving south to Italy. Tommaso Portinari, the Medici representative in the Flemish city of Bruges, commissioned a local artist there, Hugo van der Goes (c. 1440–1482), to paint an altarpiece for a church in Florence. His work, the *Portinari Altarpiece*, is now in Florence's Uffizi Gallery.

Jan van Eyck and the Flemish School

Hugo's master was the greatest of all Flemish painters, Jan van Eyck (before 1395–1441), whose art, according to the father of Raphael, "challenges nature itself." His fame was based on his remarkable use of color, his extraordinary ability to render details realistically, and his technical innovations in the use of oil paint. When Antonello da Messina introduced the use of oil paint into Italy in 1475 (see Part IV, Topic 3), he was using methods developed earlier in the century by Jan van Eyck.

One of Van Eyck's most celebrated works is a further illustration of the growing links between Italy and northern Europe. Another of the Medici agents in Flanders, Giovanni Arnolfini, who came from Lucca in Tuscany, was a counsellor of the ruler of Flanders, the duke of Burgundy. The duke was patron of Van Eyck, and it was probably through this connection that Arnolfini commissioned Van Eyck to paint *The Marriage of Giovanni Arnolfini and Giovanna Cenami*. The artist signed the work and dated it, 1434, on the back wall visible in the painting.

Van Eyck's mastery is apparent in his naturalistic depictions of the various textures: fur, wood, metal, cloth. The sense of space is realistically conveyed, with the cool light coming in from the window illuminating bride and groom in the foreground, while the inner recesses of the room are in shadow. On the back wall, below the artist's signature, there hangs a mirror in which two figures (perhaps witnesses to the marriage) are reflected.

The literal, almost photographic, quality of the scene is typical of the finest Flemish art of the period. So is the abundant use of symbolism. The dog at the couple's feet perhaps represents fidelity. The apples by the window symbolize Adam and Eve, and thereby original sin, and the broom leaning on the wall outside stands for domestic care. Giovanna's hand is over her womb, and the tiny carved statue atop the chair in the background is of Margaret, patron saint of childbearing.

Jan van Eyck's *Giovanni Arnolfini and His Bride* (1434) is an important example of early Renaissance oil technique.

Bosch and Brueghel

If many of Van Eyck's contemporaries and immediate successors imitated his style, although without his superlative technique, two other Flemish artists of the period fit into no general category.

The first of them, Hieronymus Bosch (c. 1450–1516), is one of the great originals in the history of painting. His bizarre scenes depict a fantasy world of demons and monsters, in which the human activities seem as inexplicable as the creatures surrounding them. His most elaborate work, *The Garden of Earthly Delights*, illustrates Bosch's belief that the pleasures of the flesh lead to damnation. The journey from the Creation of Adam and Eve in the left-hand panel to the horrors of hell in the right-hand panel involves frantic scenes of erotic activity. Bosch's message seems to be that even if sinners have the possibility of seeking

The Garden of Earthly Delights (c. 1505–1510), one of the most complex and bizarre of the strange works of Hieronymus Bosch.

redemption through Christ, most people are too foolish and depraved to do so.

The other great Flemish painter of the 16th century, Pieter Brueghel (1525–1569), shared Bosch's pessimism, and many of his scenes show the violent consequences of human folly. For Brueghel, however, the transcendent power and beauty of Nature compensate for human sin. In paintings such as *Hunters in the Snow*, the figures shrink to mere specks, dwarfed by the majesty of the mountain landscape—perhaps a memory of the Alps, brought back from a trip the artist made to Italy.

Dürer and the Renaissance in Germany

No northern painter was more influenced by Italian Renaissance ideas than the great German artist Albrecht Dürer (1471–1528). He visited Italy in 1494 and again in 1505–1507, when he spent most of his time in Venice, discussing art with Bellini and other Venetian painters. The splendor of the Venetians' use of color made a deep impression on Dürer, and many of his works at this time imitate Venetian color techniques.

A true student of the Renaissance interest in Classical art, Dürer worked out a careful system of proportion based on his readings of Classical authors. In his engraving of *Adam and Eve*, the anatomy and proportions of the figures are based on Classical sculp-

Dürer's *Adam and Eve* (1504) applies Classical principles of proportion to its Old Testament subject.

tures—an example of Christian humanism in visible form.

Toward the end of his life, Dürer abandoned painting and devoted himself to engraving and the writing of theoretical works on art. At the time of his death he was preparing *Four Books on Human Proportions*, a work which combined two of the basic concerns of the Renaissance: a return to Classical ideals of beauty, and the quest for scientific precision.

MUSIC IN THE HIGH RENAISSANCE

With the invention of printing, and the circulation of printed music, the barriers between musical life in northern and southern Europe became less severe, and by the end of the 15th century musicians were beginning to travel from one to the other. The main musical centers in the High Renaissance were Rome and Venice in Italy; and France, Flanders, and England in the North.

Music at the Papal Court

The leading choir in Italy, that of the Sistine Chapel, was founded by Pope Sixtus IV in 1473. Its members were all male, with adolescent boys, their voices still unbroken, singing the soprano parts. Between 1486 and 1494, the director of music in the Sistine Chapel was the Flemish composer Josquin des Prés (c. 1440–1521), the greatest musician of his day. His works, many of them written especially for the Sistine choir, have a strong sense of formal structure and balance, and show careful attention to the word-setting—all characteristics likely to appeal to the Italian humanists. Many of the 20 settings he wrote of the Mass achieve an almost mystical fervor, but by no means all Josquin's music is serious. His secular songs are often lighthearted and elegant.

Toward the mid-16th century, the dominant musical figure at Rome was Giovanni Pierluigi da Palestrina (1525–1594). After working his way up directing the choirs of various Roman basilicas, in 1571 he took charge of all music at the Vatican.

Palestrina's period at the Vatican coincided with the reforms introduced at the Council of Trent, in response to the Protestant Reformation (see Part V, Topic 1). His music is generally traditional in style, and preserves the roots of church music in Gregorian chant. He apparently wrote his best-known setting of the Mass, *Missa Papae Marcelli*, to demonstrate to the Council of Trent that it was possible to write polyphonic music (i.e. music with several simultaneous voices) without obscuring the text being sung. The work's serene beauty and apparent simplicity do not hide its considerable emotional power.

Venice: Music at St. Mark's

By contrast with the essentially traditional style favored at Rome, Venetian composers were more experimental. In 1527 a Dutchman, Adrian Willaert (c. 1490–1562), became director of music at St. Mark's. Among his pupils were Andrea Gabrieli (c. 1520–1586) and Gabrieli's nephew Giovanni (c. 1556–1612). The latter became the most important Venetian composer of the day, and one of the most remarkable in Europe.

Many of the works written for performance in St. Mark's took advantage of the building's design, with two galleries, one on each side of the church. Giovanni Gabrieli frequently stationed a choir on either side, often reinforced with instruments, generally organ, but sometimes trumpets and even drums. The effect of the sounds coming from left and right—a kind of Renaissance stereophony—is often thrilling, as the massed voices and brass instruments echo and overlap in the interior of the church glittering with mosaics. If Roman composers such as Palestrina sought to find the equivalent of Raphael's ideal Classical beauty, the music of Gabrieli glows with the rich colors of Titian.

Music in Northern Europe

Just as northern composers carried their styles south to Italy, so Italian musical forms worked their way to the North. The Italian madrigal, a setting of secular verse for three or more voices, became especially popular with northern composers. Many of these were written for performance at home, and they played an important part in popularizing nonreligious music. Over time, as the voice parts became increasingly complex, composers added instrumental accompaniments, and the modern accompanied song began to develop.

One of the leading French composers of *chansons*, as madrigals were called in France, was Clément Janequin (c. 1485–c. 1560). Janequin was famous for writing songs that told a story by imitating specific sounds—a form of early "program music." One of his best known pieces was "*La Guerre*"—"The War"—in which the voices reproduce the noises of rattling guns, fanfares, and the shouts of soldiers. These French chansons lack the calm beauty and rich harmonies of the best Italian madrigals, but they have a striking rhythmic vitality and sense of fun to compensate.

The music of the two great Flemish composers of the age, Heinrich Isaac (c. 1450–1517) and Ludwig Senfl (c. 1490–1542), is more serious. Both used a variety of styles in their word-settings, sometimes writing passages in simple block chords, sometimes elaborately interweaving lines. In general, northern European composers, less constrained by official pressures than Palestrina and other Roman contemporaries, were freer to experiment.

The same was true in England, where the leading composer of the 16th century was Thomas Tallis (c. 1505–1585). A master of counterpoint, Tallis developed the art of combining different vocal lines to new heights of complexity. In his great setting of the text, *Spem in Alium*, ("Hope in Another"), he used no less than 40 separate individual voices, each winding independently around the others. The effect is of extraordinary emotional complexity coupled with the highest intellectual control.

While writers and artists in Italy continued in the 16th century to work through many of the implications of the 15th-century Renaissance developments, those in northern Europe had a more complex task. In the first place, the break in the North between Medieval culture and the new Renaissance ideas was less abrupt than in Italy. Painters like Bosch and composers like Tallis retained their links with the long Medieval religious and cultural tradition of their art.

Then, too, Italians had the material remains of ancient culture around them. Raphael could study actual Roman sculptures as they emerged from the excavations he supervised in Rome, while Dürer had to develop his theories of ideal proportion from reading ancient texts.

The greatest difference of all was the religious split caused by the Reformation. There is scarcely a northern creative figure of note whose work was not influenced in one way or another by the upheavals of faith that marked the 16th century. Even Erasmus, who rejected Luther's break with the Catholic Church, reflected the uncertainty of the times in his writings.

Protestant attitudes toward the arts had long-term consequences for future cultural developments in northern Europe. Their rejection of the use of painting and sculpture in sacred buildings meant that, by the end of the 16th century, religious art had virtually died out there, to be replaced by secular themes such as the portrait and still life. Luther's encouragement of music, on the other hand, stimulated a wave of creative energy which was to reach its highest point a century later in the works of Johann Sebastian Bach.

Questions for Further Study

1. How did Renaissance cultural developments differ in Italy and northern Europe? Were the differences consistent in all the arts?
2. What was the effect of printing on Renaissance culture?
3. In what ways did Castiglione and Machiavelli, for all their differences, both express the spirit of their times?

Suggestions for Further Reading

Cameron, E. *The European Reformation*. Oxford, 1991.
Eisenstein, E. *The Printing Revolution in Early Modern Europe*. Cambridge, MA, 1983.
Marius, R. *Thomas More*. New York, 1984.
McGrath, A. E. *The Intellectual Origins of the European Reformation*. Oxford, 1987.
Rabil, A., ed. *Renaissance Humanism*. Philadelphia, 1988.
Skinner, Q. *Machiavelli*. Oxford, 1981.
Snyder, J. *Northern Renaissance Art*. Englewood Cliffs, NJ, 1985.

Topic 5

Upheaval and Transformation in Eastern Europe

During the 15th and 16th centuries, Western Europe underwent important political changes as centralized states emerged in the place of feudal localism. In the East, the same period saw a similar transformation, although often in quite different circumstances. The venerable Byzantine Empire, which had held sway over the eastern half of the Mediterranean world since the 4th century, experienced a severe decline under the impact of the Western crusading armies and the Mongol invasions. The Paleologus restoration in the 13th century tried to halt the decline, but two centuries later the Empire finally collapsed in the face of the rising power of the Ottoman Turks. The Ottomans built their own state on the foundations of Byzantium, extending the rule of Islam throughout the Balkans, Asia Minor, the Middle East, and North Africa.

The process of state formation in eastern Europe was complicated by the fact that portions of the Slavic peoples who inhabited the Balkan region had come under the influence of Eastern Orthodox Christianity, while other Slavs living in areas of central Europe had been converted to Roman Christianity. Despite this religious division, however, centralized monarchies developed in Hungary, Bohemia, and Poland along with distinctive national cultures. Further east, in Russia, which the Mongols dominated for two centuries, a centralized state also emerged, first at Kiev, and then at Moscow.

THE COLLAPSE OF BYZANTIUM

Ever since the 11th century, when the Seljuk Turks began to overrun Asia Minor, the Byzantine Empire had suffered one crippling disaster after another. The Western crusaders who moved east in response to the appeal of the Emperor Alexius Comnenus in 1095 had sacked Constantinople in 1204 and divided the empire into feudal states. When Michael VIII Paleologus managed to retake the throne in 1261, (see Part III, Topic 8), the reestablished Empire was a remnant of its former greatness. Nevertheless, it persisted for almost another two centuries until its final collapse in 1453.

The Paleologus Restoration

The Paleologus dynasty was the last of the Byzantine families to rule the Eastern Empire. Michael and his descendants, under whom the Greeks took back control of the state apparatus as well as of the church, tried to restore the earlier glory of Constantinople. But with their power and wealth reduced, they were increasingly subject to domestic challenges and to the political and military ambitions of their neighbors.

The Byzantine nobles successfully ignored imperial authority and ruled their own estates as independent feudal lords, pressing the peasantry on their lands into archaic forms of serfdom. With the dominance of Venice, Genoa, and other Italian trading empires in the Mediterranean, the Byzantine economy steadily

Significant Dates

Eastern Europe

997–1038	Stephen rules Magyars
c. 1162–1227	Genghis Khan rules Mongols
1253–1278	Ottokar II rules Bohemia
1331–1355	Stephen Dushan rules as king of Serbs
1333–1370	Casimir III "the Great" rules Poland
1374–1415	Life of Jan Hus
1453	Ottoman Turks seize Constantinople
1458–1490	Matthias Corvinus rules as king of Hungary
1462–1505	Ivan III the Great rules Muscovy
1520–1566	Suleiman I "the Magnificent" rules Ottoman Empire
1571	Battle of Lepanto

declined and even its once solid coinage began to be debased as inflation spread. The Eastern Orthodox Church, which had provided the emperors with divine blessing and had played an important role in maintaining imperial authority, was mired in doctrinal disagreements that weakened its hold over the people.

Slavs, Mongols, and Byzantium

Added to these difficulties was the fact that within its own borders, Byzantium experienced growing unrest and resistance from its Slavic populations, while from the outside came a sudden and shocking danger from the Mongols.

In earlier periods, the Byzantines had conquered the Slavs and converted them to Orthodox Christianity. Among the Slavs, the Bulgarians represented the most crucial danger to the Byzantines. The Bulgarians had moved into the Balkans toward the end of the 7th century. In the 8th century, the Byzantine emperor had made peace with the Bulgars, from whom he extracted an annual tribute. The rise of a Bulgar kingdom under Krum, however, posed a real threat to Constantinople, which they besieged, until Basil the Bulgar Slayer crushed them in 1014. During the period

Map 5.1 The Ottoman Empire and Collapse of Byzantium, c. 1450

Byzantine Emperor Basil II, known as "Basil the Bulgar Slayer," crushed the Bulgar threat in 1014. This contemporary illustration shows the Bulgars prostrate before him.

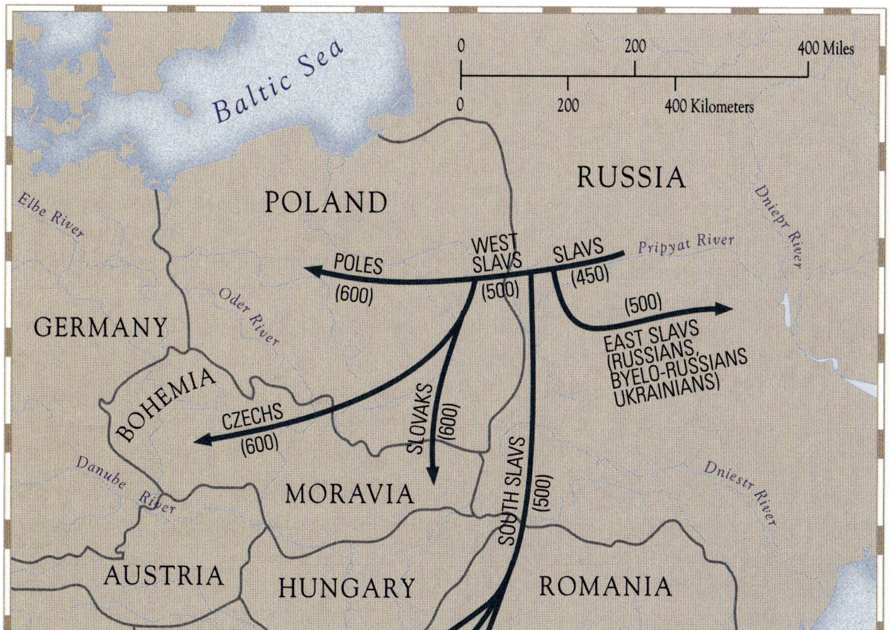

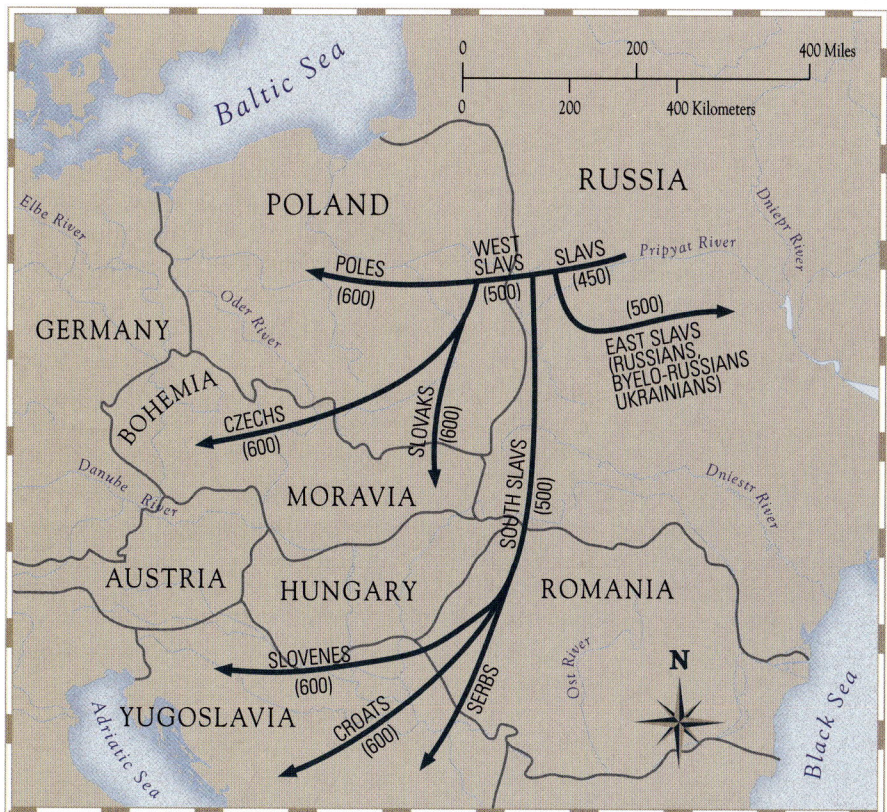

Map 5.2 Expansion of the Slavs

when the crusaders ruled Byzantium, the Bulgarians reorganized their kingdom and pushed south and west into the Balkans, reaching Macedonia and Albania.

The Mongols were nomadic Asiatic tribes from the area of north-central China where Mongolia is located today. Although they were wild and unruly, one of their chieftains, Genghis Khan (c. 1162–1227) succeeded in uniting them and forging a powerful army. From his capital at Karakorum, Genghis Khan's army, known as the Golden Horde, quickly overran large tracts of China before moving westward through Russia and into Persia. The Mongols killed and conquered with great ferocity and struck terror in their enemies.

Under the successors of Genghis Khan, one Mongol force captured Baghdad and destroyed the 500-year-old Abbasid caliphate. Meanwhile, another group moved north into Europe, conquering Russia, invading Poland and Hungary, and subduing the Bulgarians and other Slavic peoples of the region. In 1242, however, as they stood on the plains of Hungary, the Mongols suddenly stopped their westward expansion and began to withdraw, racked by divisions over the question of succession. Although they established their dominance over a vast region that stretched from Russia to the Pacific, the Mongols bequeathed no significant cultural legacy. They did, however, leave the Byzantine Empire seriously weakened and unable to resist the last great external threat that arrived in the form of the Ottoman Turks.

Mehmed II was known as the "Conqueror" because his Ottoman forces seized Constantinople in 1453.

THE OTTOMANS AND THE EUROPEAN RESPONSE

The Ottoman (or Osmanli) Turks had settled in northwestern Asia Minor in the 13th century, where they became vassals of the Seljuks. They began to emerge as an autonomous state as the Seljuk empire disintegrated and subsequently expanded into the Balkans, where they overran the Bulgarians and the Serbs. Like the Bulgarians, the Serbs had converted to Orthodox Christianity and founded their own state under King Stephen Dushan (ruled 1331–1355). The Serbs copied the legal structures and courtly practices of the Byzantines and Stephen laid claim to rule over other peoples in the area, including the Bulgarians, Albanians, and Greeks. The Ottomans crossed the Straits into the Balkans in 1354, defeating the Serbs at the Battle of Kosovo in 1389 and establishing their capital at Adrianople.

The Fall of Constantinople

When the Ottomans proceeded to lay siege to Constantinople, the West gathered a crusade to turn them back. The crusade was poorly organized and at Nicopolis in 1396 the Turks defeated the knights and killed or captured some 10,000 Europeans. Six years later Tamerlane (c. 1336–1405), a Mongol tribal leader who claimed descent from Genghis Khan, defeated the Turks and relieved the siege of Constantinople. But Tamerlane's victory only delayed the inevitable.

In May 1453, some 160,000 Turkish soldiers under Sultan Mehmed (or Muhammad) II (ruled 1451–1481) smashed a tiny force of 9000 Byzantines and Genoese troops led by Constantine XI (ruled 1449–1453). Mehmed personally commanded the attack on the walls of the city, which were breached with specially designed cannon of immense size, and Constantine, the last Byzantine emperor, died defending one of the city's gates. The fall of Constantinople—renamed Istanbul by its conquerors—after only 50 days of fighting came as a great demoralizing shock to the rest of Europe.

Mehmed, known as the Conqueror, must be considered the true founder of the Ottoman Empire, and his policies set the pattern for centuries to come. Moving his capital from Adrianople to Istanbul, he be-

The Church of Hagia Sophia, or "Holy Wisdom," was built under the Emperor Justinian. After the Ottoman conquest, it was converted to a mosque with the mosaics inside painted over and minarets added outside.

gan to restore the city to its former glory, repopulating it with Muslim, Christian, and Jewish immigrants. Mehmed personally embraced the Sunni version of Islam (see Part III, Topic 4), and although he permitted his Christian and Jewish subjects to practice their religion freely, he converted the Church of Hagia Sophia to a mosque. A patron of learning and the arts, he brought skilled craftsmen and the most talented artists to work on his new capital.

The Ottoman Empire

The Ottomans became famous for their excellent military and political organization. Their empire, which reached its peak in the 16th century, extended deep into Persia and Arabia. Selim I "the Grim" (ruled 1512–1520) defeated the Mamelukes of Egypt and Syria, seizing Cairo in 1517. Under the Turks, Egypt became a province ruled by a *pasha*, or viceroy, appointed from Istanbul. The next year, when the Ottomans took Algiers, they created an empire that stretched across North Africa into the Middle East and up into Asia Minor and the Balkans.

In the hinterland of North Africa, known as the Maghreb, the Ottomans ruled a number of separate provinces through the same kind of local administrations as they had established in Egypt. Tripoli, Algiers, and Tunis were quasi-independent of Istanbul and controlled by governors and the famous slave corps of troops known as the Janissaries, originally Christians from the Balkans who were converted to Islam. These cities, especially Algiers, were the headquarters for the Turkish corsairs, or pirates, who raided European shipping off the coast.

Morocco held a unique place in the Ottoman Empire. In the mid-16th century, an Arab family, the Sa'dids—who claimed descent from Muhammad—united Morocco and ruled the region until 1659. The Sa'dids extended their control south, beyond the Sahara, where they conquered the kingdom of Songhay in 1591 and sacked Timbuktu. In the hinterland and the Atlas Mountains, the nomads were sometimes forced to pay tribute but otherwise remained independent.

Ottoman achievements reached their zenith under Selim's son, Suleiman I, "the Magnificent" (ruled 1520–1566). The golden age of Ottoman culture began after the conquest of Istanbul. Poets began writing in original forms rather than copying from the Persians, as they had done in the past, and court writers produced magnificent plays and short stories. Turkish literature,

The Ottomans were defeated by a European fleet in 1571 at the Battle of Lepanto.

architecture, and art also flourished. Mehmed built a great Seraglio Palace, whose formidable walls surrounded courtyards and fountains, while Suleiman achieved even more splendid results in the Suleimanye, a complex containing a mosque and his own mausoleum.

Turks and Europeans

The Ottoman conquest unleashed a struggle between the Turks and the Christian monarchs of Europe. Suleiman's military campaigns won him Rhodes and other Mediterranean islands and the city of Belgrade. In 1526, he won a major victory at Mohacs and took Buda in 1541, absorbing most of Hungary. His armies reached as far west as Vienna, the Hapsburg capital, which he besieged, but logistical problems eventually forced him to withdraw. A shrewd diplomat as well as a warrior, Suleiman forged an alliance with the Valois dynasty of France against the Hapsburgs.

The Ottoman Empire had begun to decline by the time of Suleiman's death. The Ottomans had long vied with European rulers for control of the sea lanes of the western Mediterranean. The important port cities, such as Tangier, Algiers, and Tripoli, changed hands several times as first Christians and then Muslims seized them. In the end, however, the Christians gained mastery of the sea lanes following the seizure of Malta in 1565 and the naval battle of Lepanto, off western Greece, in 1571. The Europeans also reconquered lost territory. The Hapsburgs retook Hungary and by the early 18th century the sultans were forced to surrender Serbia and Dalmatia to the Christians. Moreover, in Istanbul court intrigue and bribery had become rampant and the Janissaries, once the sultan's loyal soldiers, now began to manipulate their former overlords. Over the course of the next two centuries, the once great Turkish empire gradually shrank.

HUNGARY, BOHEMIA, AND POLAND

Although Serbs, Bulgarians, and Bosnians followed Orthodox Christianity, much of Eastern Europe lay in the cultural and religious sphere of the Roman Catholic Church. The Catholic populations, including Hungarians, Czechs, and Poles, achieved a vibrant cultural life during the 13th century through prestigious universities in Prague, Cracow, and elsewhere and scholars from the region took part in the great humanist revival of the Renaissance.

The Kingdom of Hungary

The Hungarians were a group of nomadic tribes from Asia who spoke a language distantly related to Finnish. Under Arpad (d. 907), the Magyars—the largest of the tribes—crossed the Carpathian Mountains into the plains of Hungary along the middle Danube and expanded steadily until 955, when the Holy Roman Emperor Otto the Great defeated them at Augsburg. By then they had established the basis of a state ruled by the king with the help of a royal council consisting of nobles and clergymen. Under King Stephen (ruled 977–1038), Hungary adopted Western Christianity. Stephen acknowledged the supremacy of the papacy in Rome when he received a royal crown sent by Pope Sylvester II for his coronation in the year 1000. Stephen became a zealous Catholic who bestowed land and abbeys on the church and tried to stamp out both Eastern Christianity and heresy in his kingdom. After his death, Stephen was made a saint.

Stephen's reign proved to be the early high point of Hungarian achievement, for over the following century the kingdom was overrun by Germans and Poles and divided by internal strife. In 1046, an uprising of

Map 5.3 Eastern Europe, c. 1450–1500

tribal chieftains, who still professed to follow paganism, resulted in the massacre of Christians and the destruction of many churches. The powerful feudal nobles of the realm, known as magnates, ruled their private lands as virtual sovereign lords, a condition reflected in the autonomy of the provinces and the elective nature of the Hungarian monarchy. The kings relied, instead, on the lesser nobility, who filled positions in the royal administration.

Despite the centrifugal force of feudalism, the state founded by Stephen endured. King Ladislas I (ruled 1077–1095) began to restore royal authority and supported the papacy in its struggles against the Holy Roman Empire. In the 12th century King Bela III (ruled 1173–1196), who had been educated at Constantinople, brought great prestige to the Hungarian crown by marrying the sister of Philip Augustus of France. In 1222, the lesser nobility forced the king to accept a charter of feudal privilege, similar to the Magna Carta, known as the Golden Bull. Unlike the Magna Carta, this document did exempt the clergy and the nobility from taxation, guaranteed them against arbitrary arrest and imprisonment, and established an annual assembly, or diet, in which they could present grievances to the king. The Golden Bull also prohibited foreigners and Jews from receiving offices or land in the realm.

The Mongols invaded Hungary in 1241 and defeated the king's armies. Although the Mongols soon retreated, they left the country in a state of great devastation of which the nobles took advantage to strengthen their own position. In the 14th century, various foreign princes vied with each other for control of the crown and Hungary came under the rule of Charles Robert of Anjou (ruled 1308–1342). Charles established a vibrant dynasty that strengthened royal authority and brought Hungary into closer contact with the West.

The new dynasty expanded Hungarian power south into the northern Balkans and defeated the Ottomans in 1365. Nevertheless, the magnates took back much of their power and the crown eventually came into the hands of a great frontier nobleman, John Hunyadi, whose son Matthias Corvinus (ruled 1458–1490) succeeded him. Matthias was a skilled ruler and soldier who also brought to his court in the city of

Buda famous scholars from France and Italy and was a great patron of Magyar literature and art. With a powerful standing army of mercenaries, Hungary had become the strongest kingdom in eastern Europe at the time of Matthias' death.

Matthias' successors surrendered his conquests in exchange for recognition from the Hapsburgs and also gave up royal power to the magnates. More troubles soon struck the country. In 1514, a great peasant uprising erupted against the exploitation of the magnates, who crushed the revolt with much bloodshed. That same year, the diet passed a constitution, known as the *Tripartitum*, which imposed a permanent system of serfdom on the peasantry. A few years later, the Turks began their invasion of Hungary, which culminated in Suleiman's great victory at Mohacs in 1526 and the occupation of Buda in 1541. The Ottomans occupied the great plain of Hungary and divided it into administrative districts, while the western portion of the country was seized by the Hapsburgs, and Transylvania remained a vassal state of the Turks.

Jan Hus, who brought John Wycliffe's religious reforms to Bohemia, was burned at the stake for heresy in 1415.

Jan Hus and the Czechs

Sandwiched between southeastern Germany, northern Austria, and western Hungary lay the land of the Czechs, the name used for the Moravians and the Bohemians. When the Magyars invaded central Europe in the early 10th century, they destroyed the empire known as Great Moravia, a Bohemian state with its capital at Prague on the Danube. Given their location, the Czechs maintained close economic ties with the Germans and developed a thriving merchant class. Although they had been first converted to Eastern Christianity, the Czechs eventually became Catholics. A native dynasty known as the Přemyslide attempted to restore an effective Czech state and established royal authority over the nobles. In the 12th century, Frederick Barbarossa awarded the Přemyslide a hereditary crown. Under Ottokar II (ruled 1253–1278) the Bohemian state reached the furthest limits of its power in the region. Ottokar was defeated and killed in 1278 by Rudolf of Hapsburg. Early in the next century John of Luxembourg (ruled 1310–1346), son of Emperor Henry VII, who had married the last Přemyslide's daughter, came to the throne. It was John's son, Charles IV (ruled 1347–1378), who made Prague a great European capital with its own university and a rich cultural life. By the Golden Bull of 1356, the king of Bohemia became the principal member of the seven electors of the Holy Roman Empire.

It was at the University of Prague in the 15th century that a professor of philosophy named Jan Hus (1374–1415) unleashed a powerful movement of religious reform that soon swept across Bohemia. Hus was greatly influenced by the works of an English scholar of theology, John Wycliffe (c. 1330–1384), who attacked papal authority and the institutions of the church and looked to the Bible as the only source of doctrine. Hus began to preach sermons in the Czech language calling for church reforms and a simpler religion based on reading the Bible. In 1415, Hus was called under safe conduct before a church council at Constance, which condemned his doctrines and burned him at the stake.

Hus was also the center of a growing nativist movement of Czech patriots who opposed German influence in the kingdom. The condemnation of Hus at Constance led to the outbreak of a revolt in Bohemia, where nobles and burghers joined with peasants in fighting the Hussite Wars against the Germans.

The Polish State

In their migrations across central Europe, the Slavs settled in the region of the Vistula basin in the 7th century. There in the 10th century the Polish state emerged as a result of the unification of six tribes under the Piast dynasty, whose first ruler was Mieszko I (ruled 960–992). The early Poles found themselves constantly at war, whether against the Germans to the east, the Prussians to the north, or the Bohemians and the Hungarians to the south.

Mieszko was converted to Latin Christianity by Bohemian missionaries. Thereafter, Poland became an outpost of crusading Christianity on the northeastern frontiers of Europe. For centuries the church maintained an alliance with the Polish nobles that worked to undermine royal authority. As in Hungary, the Polish nobility remained a powerful and autonomous force in the country.

An early exception to the rule of weak kings, however, was Boleslav I (ruled 992–1025), generally considered the real founder of the Polish state. An ambitious and unscrupulous king, he created an administrative system, endowed the church, and seems to have aimed at bringing all Slavs under his rule. Nevertheless, when the Piast dynasty ended and the Jagiellonian family came to power in 1386, noble power increased even more.

In the 14th century, the history of Poland consisted largely of the struggle by the new dynasty to reestablish royal authority, while the nobility managed to extract numerous privileges and maintain considerable control over the state. Under the reign of Casimir III the Great (ruled 1333–1370), Poland thrived as the king sought to create an efficient administration, encourage trade, and stimulate cultural developments. In 1364, Casimir established a school at Cracow that soon became a full-fledged university. As early as 1474, a printing press operated in Cracow.

Despite his success in domestic and foreign policy, Casimir left a considerably weakened monarchy at his death. Since he had no direct heir, he promised that on his death the crown would pass to Louis of Hungary, but on condition that he respect the rights of the nobles. This gave rise to the practice of electing the king, who generally felt the need to buy off the magnates with concessions. In 1367, the magnates formed the first diet and under Louis they extracted further privileges.

In 1384, Princess Jadwiga (ruled 1384–1399) was elected queen after making significant concessions to the magnates, and this was followed two years later by the granting of still further rights to the nobles. In return, they permitted Jadwiga to marry Jagiello, grand duke of Lithuania. Jagiello, a pagan, converted to Christianity and joined his territory, three times the size of Poland, to the Polish state.

In 1466, after a war against the Teutonic Knights, the Polish monarchy realized the goal of extending its reach to the Baltic Sea by securing a corridor through Prussian territory to the port of Danzig. Members of the Jagiellonian family also ruled in Bohemia and in Hungary. In Poland, however, the power of the nobility had grown so extensive that the monarchy was unable to put together sufficient force to stop the Ottoman invasion of central Europe in the 16th century. Effective centralized government in Poland ceased in fact with the end of the Jagiellonian dynasty.

THE GROWTH OF THE PRINCIPALITY OF MOSCOW

The Russian Empire that straddled the great Eurasian plain in modern times had its origins in two earlier states, the principalities of Kiev and Moscow. The East Slavs who settled this huge region in the early Middle Ages had expanded as far the Volga River, while other Slavic tribes went north almost as far as the Baltic Sea. During the 9th century, Vikings from Scandinavia had pushed into the lands of the East Slavs, where they laid the foundations of the principality of Kiev.

The Greatness and Decline of Kiev

In the late 10th century, Vladimir (ruled 980–1015), who ruled a kingdom that stretched from the Baltic to the Ukraine, converted to Orthodox Christianity (on the early history of Kiev, see Part III, Topic 3). The Principality of Kiev experienced its greatest period during the reign of Vladimir's son, Yaroslav the Wise (ruled 1015–1054).

Yaroslav was both a ruthless military commander and a skilled administrator. After extending his realm to the border of Finland and clearing the area south of Kiev of nomads known as the Pechenegs, he secured religious autonomy for the principality from the patriarch of Constantinople in 1037, establishing an independent "metropolitan" as the head of the East Slavic Church. Yaroslav encouraged cultural development and contact with the West. Known as a great builder, he imported Byzantine architects and artists to construct and decorate important churches, including the great St. Sophia Cathedral in Kiev, inspired by Hagia Sophia in Constantinople. Following Justinian's example in Byzantium, Yaroslav ordered the codification of East Slavic law.

After Yaroslav's death, Kiev was racked by incessant feuds and struggles to secure the succession to the throne. These internal troubles rendered the principality unable to resist the constant incursions of nomadic peoples from the steppes. In the 11th century the Cumans blocked Kiev from the Black Sea, thus breaking a longstanding and profitable trade connection with the Byzantine Empire. Eventually the nomads pushed the southern frontier of Kiev farther and farther north, isolating the Rus, or Russians, around the forests and the city of Moscow. Kiev itself fell to attack from the north in 1169.

The Mongol invasions of the 13th century completed the destruction of Kievan civilization. Because the Mongols were relatively few in number, they could do little more than control southern Russia along the Caspian and Black seas as tributary rulers and asserted

Map 5.4 Growth of Principality of Moscow

even less direct authority over northern regions. In the 1240s, a prince of Novgorod, Alexander Nevsky (c. 1220–1263), began cooperating with the Mongols and defeated invading German forces.

Novgorod was a prosperous commercial city that traded with the Hanseatic League of northern German cities. Unlike their treatment of most of the other Russian cities, the Mongols left Novgorod untouched and for his cooperation the Mongol Khan bestowed on Nevsky the title of Grand Prince. It was from that basis that Nevsky's descendants built a dynasty that would eventually rule most of Russia.

The Origins of Moscow

By the 15th century, the centuries-old traditions of autonomy that the citizens of Novgorod had enjoyed came to an end. Weakened by strife among the citizens of different classes, and with its economy devastated by the decline of Baltic trade, in 1478 Novgorod fell under the aegis of Moscow.

Moscow had been little more than a frontier fortress on the Moskva River protected by surrounding marshes and forests. Its name first appeared in the chronicles only in 1147. Moscow had been established by a son of Nevsky, who skillfully expanded his powers in the service of the Mongols. The princes of Moscow adopted the policy of primogeniture, whereby the lands and possessions of the ruler passed to the oldest son; this ensured the continuation of power from one generation to another.

The city's rulers pursued a policy of steady expansion as they brought more and more Russian cities into its orbit. In 1328 the Mongols gave Ivan I (ruled 1328–1341), like Nevsky, the title of Grand Prince, with the right to collect all Russian tribute for the Khan—a function that brought him the contemporary nickname "money bags." Ivan also made Moscow the center of the Russian Orthodox Church. In 1380, Dmitri (ruled 1359–1389) greatly enhanced the prestige of his family when he won a victory over the Mongols at Kulikovo, on the Don, in 1380, earning him the title "Donskoi."

The greatest of the early princes of Moscow was Ivan III the Great (ruled 1462–1505). It was Ivan the Great who in 1478 acquired control of Novgorod by incorporating its lands into the state of Moscow. Several years later, at the Oka River, he faced down the Mongol armies who finally withdrew from Russia. Under Ivan and his successors, the Muscovite principality continued to expand, almost tripling the size of

Ivan III, the "Great," expanded the size of the Muscovite principality in the 15th century and made himself the first tsar of Russia.

its territory by the mid-16th century. In a deliberate move to enhance his status so as to realize his great ambitions, Ivan married Sophia Paleologus, daughter of the last emperor of Byzantium. Ivan transformed Moscow into the core of a powerful empire and himself into the first tsar of all Russia (see Part VI, Topic 6).

The formation of national monarchies in Hungary, Bohemia, Poland, and Russia, together with the conquests and expansion of the Ottoman Turks, established the pattern of development for the eastern Mediterranean world for the next four centuries. This process was accompanied by equally fundamental social transformations as the system of serfdom that had developed in earlier periods in Western societies now was imposed by deliberate decision in eastern lands. Although separated from the Western European experience by ethnic, cultural, and religious differences, the entire region gradually established links with the dominant states of the West. As a result, as major political and religious upheavals unfolded in the West in the 16th century, Eastern Europe could not remain isolated from their impact.

Questions for Further Study

1. What effect did Ottoman expansion have on Europe?
2. What common social and economic conditions prevailed throughout eastern and central Europe?
3. How would you describe the Mongols and their impact on Russia?
4. What obstacles stood in the way of building a centralized state in Russia?

Suggestions for Further Reading

Crummey, Robert O. *The Formation of Muscovy, 1304–1613.* New York, 1987.

Inalcik, Halil. *The Ottoman Empire: The Classical Age, 1300–1600.* London, 1973.

Knoll, Paul W. *The Rise of the Polish Monarchy.* Chicago, 1972.

Macartney, Carlile A. *Hungary: A Short History.* Edinburgh, 1962.

Runciman, Steven. *The Fall of Constantinople, 1453.* Cambridge, MA, 1965.

Tihany, Leslie C. *A History of Middle Europe.* New Brunswick, NJ, 1976.

IV

Topic 6

The Era of Reconnaissance

While the 16th and 17th centuries were a time of great religious upheaval in Europe, the period also saw serious economic and political crisis compounded by war and revolution. Yet, despite these difficulties, European civilization embarked on an unprecedented era of energetic and often ruthless overseas expansion. This age of "reconnaissance" would dramatically change Europe's relationship with the rest of the world, ushering in another fundamental revolution in modern history. The remarkable experience altered the nature of Europe's economy, had important social and cultural repercussions, and broadened the European imagination.

The age of exploration and expansion actually began in the 15th century with the first forays and technical discoveries of the Portuguese sailors. By the end of the 15th century, a number of Portuguese sailors, especially Bartholomeu Dias and Vasco da Gama, had rounded the Cape of Good Hope and explored the eastern coast of Africa along the Indian Ocean, opening great trade routes to India itself. These early Portuguese adventurers were followed by the Spanish. In 1492, Christopher Columbus reached the Americas and within less than a generation Ferdinand Magellan circumnavigated the entire globe.

The immediate result of these early voyages was the establishment of vast overseas empires ruled by the Portuguese and the Spanish. This early experience in political and economic imperialism had tremendous, and often devastating, consequences for the native populations of the Western Hemisphere. For Europe, it laid the basis for the future commercial—and, eventually, for the industrial—development of the modern age.

EUROPEANS AND THE WORLD: THE EARLY TRAVELERS

The great explorations of the 16th century did not, of course, represent the first expansion beyond Europe's borders. In the 9th and 10th centuries, the Vikings may have crossed the Atlantic and had penetrated into Russia from the north. The waves of successive crusades that invaded the Muslim-controlled Middle East starting in the 11th century had revealed aggressive tendencies in the European psyche that presaged later movements beyond the frontiers of Christian society.

Europe and the Luxury Trade

Europeans had long been fascinated by Africa, India, and East Asia. In the Middle Ages, examples of the fab-

Significant Dates

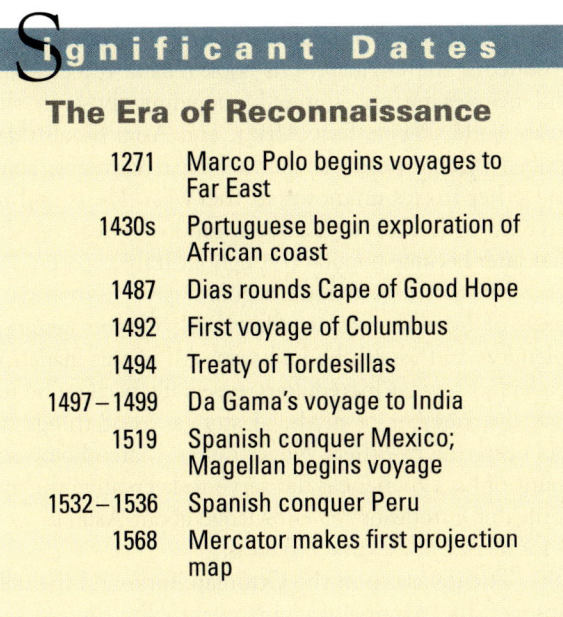

The Era of Reconnaissance

1271	Marco Polo begins voyages to Far East
1430s	Portuguese begin exploration of African coast
1487	Dias rounds Cape of Good Hope
1492	First voyage of Columbus
1494	Treaty of Tordesillas
1497–1499	Da Gama's voyage to India
1519	Spanish conquer Mexico; Magellan begins voyage
1532–1536	Spanish conquer Peru
1568	Mercator makes first projection map

ulous products to be found in these regions had trickled back to Europe. Europe's elite grew thirsty for leopard and zebra skins, ivories, rare silks, and precious gems, to say nothing of the wonderful spices that could transform the bland and boring European diet—indeed, nothing was so coveted by those who could afford it as plain, ordinary black pepper, a product that came principally from India and Indonesia.

Since Roman times, a lucrative trade had supplied Europe with the luxurious products of Africa and Asia. Many silks, spices, and other exotic products had flowed through Constantinople and the Byzantine Empire. After the 7th century, however, when the Arabs began to conquer North Africa and the Middle East, Europeans had to buy such goods mainly from the Muslims, who positioned themselves as middlemen between the European market and the source of most of these items. Muslim traders plied the waters of the Indian Ocean between India and Africa as well as up the Red Sea, and caravans snaked their way into the African and Asian interiors.

The Mongol conquests that began in the 13th century established a broad area of stability in the Asian heartland and also opened a line of communication between Europe and central Asia. It was this situation that prompted the Polo family of Venetian merchants to make the long and hazardous journey to the Mongol court of Kublai Khan (ruled 1259–1294), a grandson of the fierce Genghis Khan. Kublai controlled most of China, which he ruled from his capital at Tatu, the site of present-day Beijing. A man of broad, sophisticated tastes who patronized artists and scholars, Kublai also encouraged contact with outsiders.

A Medieval book of wonders depicts Marco Polo, arriving from India with exotic animals, at Hormuz on the Persian Gulf.

In the 13th century, Pope Innocent IV sent monks to visit the Mongol court, but the Polos were Kublai's most famous Western visitors.

Between 1253 and 1260, Niccolò Polo and his brother Maffeo made a number of trading expeditions to Constantinople. From there, they went eastward into Kublai's kingdom, returning to Venice in 1269. Two years later, the brothers set out once again for Kublai's court, this time with Niccolò's son Marco (c. 1254–c. 1324) and two Catholic missionaries. The group reached the capital in 1275, and the young Marco soon became a favorite of the khan, who sent him on a number of trading missions throughout China, as far south as India and as far west as Japan. He apparently even ruled one Chinese city, Hangchow, for three years in the khan's name, describing his own city of Venice as a poor provincial village when compared to what he called the greatest city in the world. In 1292, the Polos, acting as escort for one of the wives of the khan of Persia, went back to Venice, which they reached in 1295.

Marco Polo is remembered today mainly for his famous account of his travels, which he wrote while a prisoner of the Genoese. His book tells of the customs and peoples he encountered, including those in the Arab world, Persia, East Africa, and Asia; he also described strange products such as paper currency, coal, and other things unknown in the West. He is said to have brought back to Venice a kind of wheat noodle that later became popular throughout Italy as pasta.

Most of all, Marco's account gave Europeans a sense of how he was wonder-struck by the fabulous splendors and wealth he had seen. All of this made his readers somewhat incredulous, especially because he repeated a number of mythical stories about things he had been told by others. Nevertheless, Marco Polo's account of his experiences did serve to keep alive the appetites of Europeans for knowledge about Asia, as well as for its rare and exotic products.

The invasions of the Ottoman Turks and the collapse of the Mongol Empire eventually cut off the routes to Asia for Europeans. Nevertheless, an occasional brave traveler from the West, fed by stories such as Marco's or by religious missionary zeal, continued to

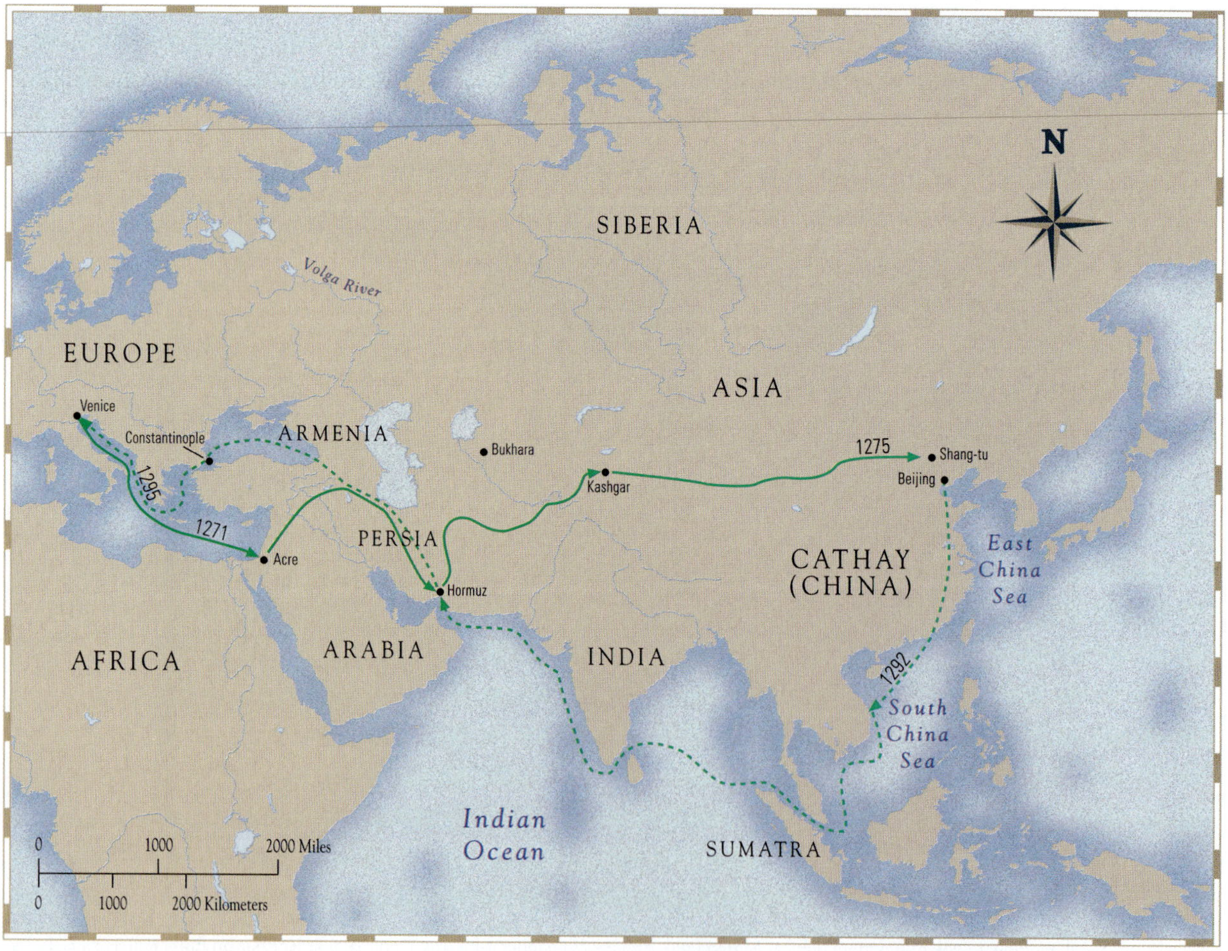

Map 6.1 Travels of Marco Polo

penetrate beyond Europe's now relatively closed borders. The legend of a Christian king known as Prester John beyond the Muslim world prompted the Portuguese to sail along the western African coast as late as the 15th century.

A Thirst for Discovery

The motives that lay behind the growing European interest in the world beyond their borders were complex. Certainly the opportunities for profit in the luxury trade were tremendous, so that the lure of wealth was important. On the other hand, the crusading zeal that European Christians had demonstrated over the centuries also prompted much of the early efforts to reach foreign lands. Nor should we overlook the genuine interest that some of the early explorers and their sponsors had in expanding their knowledge of the world—the first voyages of discovery, it should not be forgotten, took place while Europe was at the height of the Renaissance, when interest in worldly matters was paramount.

The economic motives must surely have been the most powerful and pressing. Some merchants and rulers speculated about the possibility of finding vast deposits of gold and other precious metals. At the time, the Europeans had to pay for most of the luxury goods they imported from Asia with bullion, so that a supply of precious metals was the only real way for the new monarchs of Europe to bring the trade imbalance under control.

But most thought of the incredible riches that could be made if only Europeans could discover direct sea routes to India and East Asia. In this way, they would be able to bypass both the Muslim middlemen and the Venetians, who dominated the trade of the eastern Mediterranean. Moreover, the price of spices was incredibly inflated, not only because of their scarcity but also as a result of the Muslims' marking them up even higher. Spices dominated the trade with Asia and still captured most of the attention of traders. They served to enhance the flavor of foods and preserve them as well as for a variety of other purposes, from the manufacture of perfumes and incense to medicinal potions. In addition to pepper, cinnamon, nutmeg, and cloves were the principal items of the luxury trade. Although the risks of the long-distance spice route were great, the return was enormous.

In the case of Portugal and Spain, the two countries that took the early lead in overseas exploration, the religious factor was also a strong motivation. The popes had sent a number of missionary expeditions to Asia in the Middle Ages. It was, after all, on the Iberian peninsula that the Christians had fought the Muslims for centuries, finally conquering them or driving them out. The Spanish conquerors who overran Mexico and Central America were accompanied by missionaries and spoke constantly of the goal of converting the inhabitants of the New World to Christianity. This was especially true after the Reformation and the launching by Rome of the Counter-Reformation, which the church undertook with a renewed zeal.

One final reason explains why Europeans seemed so taken with the spirit of adventure and the desire to explore new regions of the world. The Muslims and the Chinese had been plying the waters of the Indian Ocean and southeast Asia for centuries, but neither had sailed much beyond the regions with which they were familiar. European society had matured to the point where its people simply could no longer remain prisoners of such restricted regions of the globe; perhaps, too, the development of the nation-states of the era had aroused a spirit of competition that drove the explorers to strike out in new directions. Certainly the centralized monarchies of the age now had the resources and the power to undertake the explorations. In any case, the restless spirit of the Europeans should not be underestimated as an explanation for the remarkable surge in voyaging that began to characterize the West.

GEOGRAPHY AND TECHNOLOGY

The Europeans had been limited by geopolitical factors to fairly well-defined sea basins—the Baltic and North Seas, and the Mediterranean—since the fall of the Roman Empire. As a result, in 1450 their knowledge of the world's geography was still essentially what it had been at the time of the ancient Romans. European travelers acquired the information necessary to make possible the "age of reconnaissance" only in the latter half of the 15th century, but within 100 years they had circled the entire globe. In addition to geographical knowledge, Westerners had to make certain technological advances, especially in ship design and navigational instruments, before they could set out to explore distant seas.

Maps and Geography

Most geographers of the Renaissance were still wedded to the notion put forth by Ptolemy (c. 90–c. 168) that the globe was a large mass of connected land made up of the continents of Europe, Africa, and Asia. Ptolemy also thought the circumference of the globe to be much smaller than it actually is, so that some explorers—like Columbus—thought they could reach Asia easily by sailing westward.

The most up-to-date geographical information available to Europeans came from the so-called *portolani*, which were marine charts drawn on the basis of personal observation by sailors. The portolani mainly showed coastlines along the Mediterranean, the Atlantic coast, and eventually the coast of western Africa. Often drawn by sailors working with mathematicians, they contained detailed practical information needed for sailing, including distances, compass directions, and the depth of channels and ports. Although technically not portolani, 14th-century mapmakers prepared charts based on the information contained in the journals of Marco Polo. In addition, Arab and Indian sailors who came to western ports on European ships provided specific knowledge of distant waterways.

Around 1500, mapmakers began to make important advances. The rediscovery of Ptolemy's *Geographia* at about this time, together with the invention of printing and engraving, made great strides possible. In 1538, by which time the information gathered by the early Portuguese and Spanish sailors was available, Gerardus Mercator (1512–1594), a Flemish cartographer, published his earliest map of the world. In 1568, Mercator made his first projection maps, which became widely used for navigational charts.

Shipbuilding and Navigation

Two developments were necessary in order to establish the practical basis for the age of discovery: a new kind of ship capable of traversing the open seas or the oceans, and new navigational instruments to guide the ships in uncharted regions. In the Mediterranean Sea, ships operated mainly along the coast, which navigators had mapped in great detail over the centuries. These ships were galleys rowed by teams of 50 or more slaves or sailors pressed into service from prisons. Because the oar-propelled ships were difficult to operate in rough, open waters, they traveled away from the coast only when the distance to the next island or land mass was relatively short.

The most famous galleys of the Middle Ages were the Venetian and Genoese fleets that carried commercial goods from the Middle East to European ports. The Venetians also developed an important Flanders Fleet of galleys in the 13th century that sailed regularly into the Atlantic and up through the English Channel into the North Sea.

Ships that hoped to sail in larger bodies of water, such as the Indian Ocean and the Atlantic, had to use sails rather than oars to move them. In addition, instead of the long, narrow shapes of the galleys, which were designed for slicing through calmer waters with the least amount of resistance, oceangoing vessels needed wider hulls that could carry enough provisions to feed crews on long ocean voyages as well as to hold the precious cargoes carried on return trips.

The first ships capable of making the months-long ocean voyages were known as caravels, and were the work of Portuguese shipbuilders. In the 15th century, the Portuguese, whose ports lay on the Atlantic coast, were pushing carefully along the North African coastal waters. The caravel design innovation drew from both European and Muslim sailing experience. Two of its masts carried large square sails which made use of strong winds for moving the ship. A third mast supported a more narrow triangular-shaped lateen sail that the Muslims used on their dhow ships that plied the seas between the East African coast and India; these were used to give the ship more maneuverability. The large hulls solved the problem of carrying provisions and cargo.

The navigational instruments that Medieval European sailors had at their disposal were of limited value. The astrolabe, which may have been available as far back as Roman times, was widely used by the 11th century to determine the height of the sun and stars in order to calculate latitude (measured along imaginary lines around the earth in the form of circles running parallel to the equator). As early as the 13th century, Europeans had developed the compass, which sailors could use to determine direction, especially in bad weather that obscured the stars and the sun. Not until the 18th century, however, were sailors able to calculate longitude (imaginary lines in the form of circles running from pole to pole) with any degree of precision. Once these advances in sailing and navigation had been made, and the national monarchies had developed the resources to fund exploration, the age of reconnaissance could begin in earnest.

THE PORTUGUESE INITIATIVE

Once the Portuguese had pioneered the new caravel ship design, they set out on their first voyages of discovery. These early explorations were the work of the remarkable Prince Henry, who sponsored a navigational school and supplied the funds for the trips. After his death, the voyages continued to ever greater distances around the globe.

Prince Henry the Navigator

Henry (1394–1460) was the younger son of King John I of Portugal (ruled 1385–1433). With little prospect of inheriting the throne, Henry devoted himself to geography and navigation. He built a school and observatory at Sagres, situated on the Atlantic at the southwesternmost point of Portugal. He brought sailors,

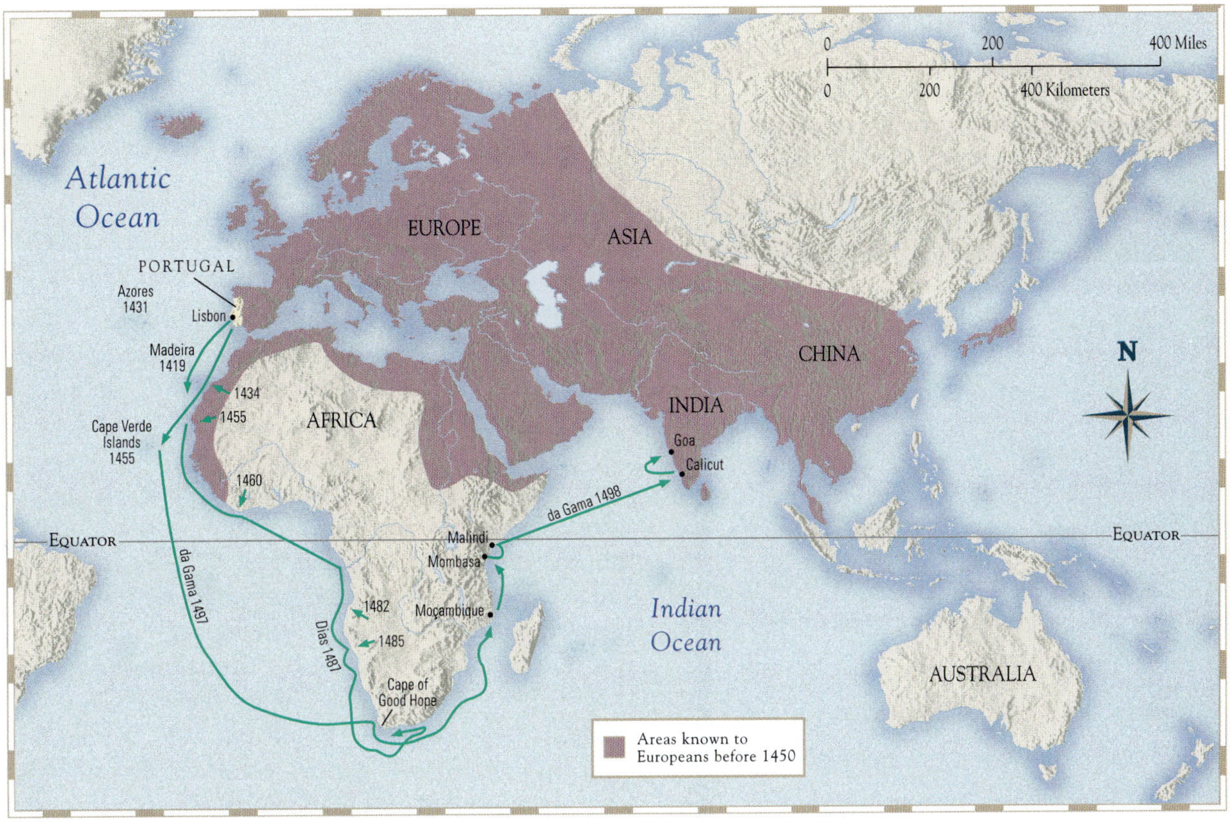

Map 6.2 The Portuguese Voyages

captains, scientists, and mapmakers there and sent out annual expeditions to explore the northwestern coast of Africa.

A stimulus to this interest in Africa came in Henry's youth when the Portuguese captured the Muslim city of Ceuta on the coast of Morocco. Consumed with a passion for knowledge, as well as with the practical ambition of discovering a source of gold that would enrich the kingdom, he eventually sent a fleet as far as Guinea and the Gold Coast (in the vicinity of modern-day Ghana). The hope was that the sea route would circumvent the trans-Saharan caravan routes that the Arabs had used to control the gold supply to the Mediterranean.

The Birth of Portuguese Imperialism

In the years following Henry's death in 1460, the Portuguese expeditions declined for a time, although they did discover the Azores and the Madeiras, two small island groups hundreds of miles out in the Atlantic that would later serve as stopping places for transoceanic voyages. King John II (ruled 1481–1495) eventually organized new expeditions, this time with the specific goal of tracing a sea route to reach the spices of India. John established trading posts on the Guinea coast and was able to send a Portuguese group inland as far as Timbuktu.

In 1487, Bartholomeu Dias discovered and rounded the Cape of Good Hope on the southern tip of Africa, although bad weather, combined with a possible mutiny, made him turn back to Portugal. A decade later, Vasco da Gama retraced the Dias trip and actually crossed the Indian Ocean to the port of Calicut on the coast of India. When da Gama returned to Portugal with a cargo of goods from India, the king sent out a fleet of 13 ships under Pedro Alvares Cabral, who sighted Brazil in April 1500 and claimed it for the king.

From there, Cabral crossed the southern Atlantic, rounded Africa, and arrived in India. Once there, Cabral, assisted by da Gama, set up Portuguese trading posts. Although half his fleet sank before he arrived back in Lisbon, the profit from his cargo of spices was huge. Soon the Portuguese had established regular fleets that sailed to India each year, giving Lisbon a virtual monopoly on the Asian trade with Europe.

To secure their control of that trade, the Portuguese attempted to clear the Indian Ocean of Muslim presence. Under the command of Alfonso de Albuquerque, the Portuguese forces had already taken many of the most strategic ports on the east African coast. Albuquerque, who served as governor of India from 1509 to 1515, now bombarded and seized the Muslim forts along the Indian coast—including Goa and Calicut—and converted them to military and

DOCUMENTS ON HISTORY

The Portuguese in the Wider World

Portugal, a small country that hugged the southernmost corner of Europe's Atlantic coast, had not played a major role in European or in global affairs. Beginning in the 15th century, however, the sailors, explorers, and traders of the kingdom suddenly pushed Portugal to the forefront of overseas expansion. A century later, the Portuguese had circled the globe and brought back to Europe the first accounts of the world beyond the West.

The spirit of enterprise and courage that drove Portugal's global expansion was matched, however, by a cultural arrogance and a thirst for conquest that made them the spearhead of a more general Western colonialism. These conflicting attitudes and values are revealed in the documents that follow.

PRINCE HENRY'S MOTIVES

In the 40 years before his death in 1460, Prince Henry of Portugal sent wave after wave of ships on voyages of exploration into the Atlantic and along the coast of West Africa. Gomes Eannes de Azurara, a Portuguese chronicler of Henry's achievements, gave a succinct explanation of the motives that drove Henry's activities.

And you should note well that the noble spirit of this Prince, by a sort of natural constraint, was ever urging him to begin and to carry out very great deeds. For which reason, after the taking of Ceuta he always kept ships well armed against the Infidel, both for war, and because he had also a wish to know the land that lay beyond the isles of Canary and that Cape called Bojador, for that up to his time . . . was known with any certainty the nature of the land beyond that Cape. Some said indeed that Saint Brandan had passed that way; and there was another tale of two galleys rounding the Cape, which never returned. But this doth not appear at all likely to be true, for it is not to be presumed that if the said galleys went there, some other ships would not have endeavored to learn what voyage they had made. And because the said Lord Infant wished to know the truth of this, . . . and seeing also that no other prince took any pains in this matter, he sent out his own ships against those parts, to have manifest certainty of them all. And to this he was stirred up by his zeal for the service of God and of the King Edward his Lord and brother, who then reigned. And this was the first reason of his action.

The second reason was that if there chanced to be in those lands some population of Christians, or some havens, into which it would be possible to sail without peril, many kinds of merchandise might be brought to this realm, which would find a ready market, and reasonably so, because no other people of these parts traded with them, nor yet people of any other that were known; and also the products of this realm might be taken there, which traffic would bring great profit to our countrymen.

The third reason was that, as it was said that the power of the Moors in that land of Africa was very much greater than was commonly supposed, and that there were no Christians among them, nor any other race of men; and because every wise man is obliged by natural prudence to wish for a knowledge of the power of his enemy; therefore the said Lord Infant exerted himself to cause this to be fully discovered, and to make it known determinately how far the power of those infidels extended.

The fourth reason was because during the one and thirty years that he had warred against the Moors, he had never found a Christian king, nor a lord outside this land, who for the love of our Lord Jesus Christ would aid him in the said war. Therefore he sought to know if there were in those parts any Christian princes, in whom the charity and the love of Christ was so ingrained that they would aid him against those enemies of the faith.

The fifth reason was his great desire to make increase in the faith of our Lord Jesus Christ and to bring to him all the souls that should be saved, understanding that all the mystery of the Incarnation, Death, and Passion of our Lord Jesus Christ was for this sole end—namely the salvation of lost souls—whom the said Lord Infant by his travail and spending would fain bring into the true path. . . .

But over and above these five reasons I have a sixth that would seem to be the root from which all the others proceeded: and this is the inclination of the heavenly wheels. . . .

From Gomes Eannes de Azurara, *The Chronicle of the Discovery and Conquest of Guinea,* trans. C. Beazley and E. Prestage, 2 vols. (The Hakluyt Society.

AN EARLY ACCOUNT OF SLAVERY IN AFRICA

In 1455 and 1456, Alvise da Ca' da Mosto, a Venetian merchant, made two separate voyages to West Africa under a license granted to him by Prince Henry. A hardheaded businessman with a good eye for detail, Cadamosto provides one of the earliest European descriptions of the Guinea coast and the slave trade that had developed there. Along this region of the coast of western Sudan lay Arguim, a small island in the gulf where the Portuguese built a fort in 1448 for the protection of merchants. Arguim was a principal trade site where the Portuguese met caravans coming north from Timbuktu and west from the Sahara.

These Arabs [of the western Sudan] also have many Berber horses, which they trade, and take to the Land of the Blacks, exchanging them with the rulers for slaves. Ten or fifteen slaves are given for one of these horses, according to their quality. The Arabs likewise take articles of Moorish silk, made in Granada and in Tunis for Barbary, silver, and other goods, obtaining in exchange any number of these slaves, and some gold. These slaves are brought to the market and town of Hoden [Wadan, a desert market some 350 miles east of Arguim]; there they are divided: some go to the mountains of Barcha [in Libya], and thence to Sicily, [others to the said town of Tunis and to all the coasts of Barbary], and others again are taken to this place, Argin, and sold to the Portuguese leaseholders. As a result every year the Portuguese carry away from Argin a thousand slaves. Note that before this traffic was organized, the

continued next page

Portuguese caravels, sometimes four, sometimes more, were wont to come armed to the Golfo d'Argin, and descending on the land by night, would assail the fisher villages, and so ravage the land. Thus they took of these Arabs both men and women, and carried them to Portugal for sale; behaving in a like manner along all the rest of the coast, which stretches from Cauo Bianco to the Rio di Senega and even beyond. This is a great river, dividing a race which is called Azanaghi from the first Kingdom of the Blacks. These Azanaghi are brownish, rather dark brown than light, and live in places along this coast beyond Cauo Bianco, and many of them are spread over this desert inland. They are neighbors of the above mentioned Arabs of Hoden.

They live on dates, barley, and camel's milk: but as they are very near the first land of the Blacks, they trade with them, obtaining from this land of the Blacks millet and certain vegetables, such as beans, upon which they support themselves. They are men who require little food and can withstand hunger, so that they sustain themselves throughout the day upon a mess of barley porridge. They are obliged to do this because of the want of victuals they experience. These, as I have said, are taken by the Portuguese as before mentioned and are the best slaves of all the Blacks. But, however, for some time all have been at peace and engaged in trade. The said Lord Infante will not permit further hurt to be done to any, because he hopes that, mixing with Christians, they may without difficulty be converted to our faith, not yet being firmly attached to the tenets of Muhammad, save from what they know by hearsay.

From *The Voyages of Cadamosto,* trans. and ed. G. R. Crone (London: The Hakluyt Society.

VASCO DA GAMA'S VOYAGE TO THE EAST AFRICAN COAST

Toward the end of the 15th century, the intrepid sailor Vasco da Gama rounded the Cape of Good Hope and entered the seaway into the Indian Ocean that had been discovered by Bartholomeu Dias in 1488. Da Gama sailed northward up the coast of East Africa, stopping at Mombasa, a major trading center built by the Muslims. The following is the only surviving account of the Portuguese arrival at the port.

In Saturday we cast anchor off Mombasa, but did not enter the port. No sooner had we been perceived than a *zavra* [a small vessel with a square sail] manned by Moors came out to us; in front of the city there lay numerous vessels all dressed in flags. . . . We anchored here with much pleasure, for we confidently hoped that on the following day we might go on land and hear mass jointly with the Christians reported to live there under their own *alcaide* [judge] in a quarter separate from that of the Moors. . . .

On Palm Sunday the King of Mombasa sent the captain-major a sheep and large quantities of oranges, lemons and sugar-cane, together with a ring, as a pledge of safety, letting him know that in case of his entering the port he would be supplied with all he stood in need of. This present was conveyed to us by two men, almost white, who said they were Christians, which appeared to be the fact. The captain-major sent the king a string of coral beads as a return present, and let him know that he purposed entering the port on the following day. On the same day the captain-major's vessel was visited by four Moors of distinction. . . .

Mombasa is a large city seated upon an eminence washed by the sea. Its port is entered daily by numerous vessels. At its entrance stands a pillar, and by the sea a low-lying fortress. Those who had gone on shore told us that in the town they had seen many men in irons; and it seemed to us that these must be Christians, as the Christians in that country are at war with the Moors.

The Christian merchants in the town are only temporary residents, and are held in much subjection, they not being allowed to do anything except by the order of the Moorish King.

From *A Journal of the First Voyage of Vasco da Gama,* trans. and ed. E. G. Ravenstein.

THE PORTUGUESE IN INDIA

In May 1498, after crossing the Indian Ocean, da Gama sailed into the harbor of Calicut Road on the western coast of India. Other Portuguese sailors followed da Gama's path and explored the cities of the Malabar coast, including Goa and Cochin. In 1510 Alfonso de Albuquerque, who served as governor of India, seized Goa from its Muslim ruler. In Cochin, which Duarte Barbosa described in the following account, the Portuguese found great storehouses of valuable spices.

Further in advance along the coast is the Kingdom of *Cochin,* in which there is much pepper which grows throughout the land on trees like unto ivy, and it climbs on other trees and on palms, also on trellises to a great extent. The pepper grows on these trees in bunches. . . . This Kingdom possesses a very large and excellent river, which here comes forth to the sea by which come in great ships of Moors and Christians, who trade with this Kingdom. On the banks of this river is a city of the Moors natives of the land, wherein also dwell Heathen Chatims, and great merchants. They have many ships and trade with Charamandel, the great Kingdom of Cambaia, Dabul, and Chaul, in *areca*, cocos, pepper, *jagara,* and palm sugar. At the mouth of the river the King our Lord possesses a very fine fortress, which is a large settlement of Portuguese and Christians, natives of the land, who became Christians after the establishment of our fortress. And every day also other Christian Indians who have remained from the teaching of the Blessed Saint Thomas come there also from Coilam and other places. In this fort and settlement of Cochin the King our Lord carries out the repairs of his ships, and other new ships are built, both galleys and caravels in as great perfection as on the Lisbon strand. Great store of pepper is here taken on board, also many other kinds of spices, and drugs which come from Malacca, and are taken hence every year to Portugal. The King of Cochin has a very small country and was not a King before the Portuguese discovered India, for all the Kings who had of late reigned in Calicut had held it for their practice and rule to invade Cochin and drive the King out of his estate, . . . thereafter, according as their pleasure was, they would give it back to him or not. The king of Cochin gave him every year a certain number of elephants, but he might not strike coins, nor roof his palace with tiles under pain of losing his land. Now that the King our Lord has discovered India he has made the King independent and powerful in his own land, so that none can interfere with it, and he strikes whatsoever money he will.

From *The Book of Duarte Barbosa,* trans. and ed. Mansel Longworth Dames, 2 vols.

continued next page

THE FIRST IMPRESSIONS OF CHINA

Since the 1430s, China had been essentially closed to the outside world. The so-called Ming Code had forbidden subjects to travel outside the country, and despite the interest of local merchants in south China in expanding trade, foreign travelers had been discouraged from visiting China. The first Portuguese traders arrived in China in 1514, and three years later Tomé Pires set out as official Portuguese envoy to China. After having been kept in Canton for three years on orders of the emperor, Pires was allowed to proceed to Beijing but never saw the emperor. Instead, in 1521 an imperial decree prohibited trade with foreigners and Pires and his followers were imprisoned in Canton. The letter that follows, written by Cristavao Vieira and smuggled back to Portugal, was the first account of conditions in China to arrive in Europe.

The country of China is divided into fifteen provinces. . . . All these fifteen provinces are under one king. The advantage of this country lies in its rivers all of which descend to the sea. No one sails the sea from north to south; it is prohibited by the king, in order that the country may not become known. Where we went was all rivers. They have boats and ships broad below without number. . . . I must have seen thirty thousand including great and small. . . .

No province in China has trade with strangers except this of Cantao: that which others may have on the borders is a small affair, because foreign folk do not enter the country of China, nor do any go out of China. The sea trade has made this province of great importance, and without trade it would remain dependent on the agriculturalists like the others. . . .

The custom of this country of China is, that every man who administers justice cannot belong to that province; for instance, a person

trading facilities. He also sailed into the Persian Gulf and took the port of Ormuz.

These assaults on the Indian ports gave Portugal control over the spice trade and established Portuguese imperialism in Asia. They reached as far as Macao, situated at the mouth of the Pearl River in China. Despite the early successes of Portugal, however, the country simply did not have the kind of economic or military strength needed to establish a truly global empire or to colonize the regions under their control. Spain eventually took Portugal's place as Europe's leading colonial power.

SPAIN, THE AMERICAS, AND THE EUROPEAN ECONOMY

The Kingdom of Spain, once it had been united under the joint rule of Ferdinand and Isabella and the Muslims had been driven out, proved itself capable of mustering the resources to build a world empire. Moreover, whereas the Portuguese had required a century in order to extend their reach around Africa and across the Indian Ocean, the Spanish sponsored a single expedition that suddenly discovered a vast new continent.

Columbus and the New World

In 1484, even before Dias had rounded the tip of southern Africa, Christopher Columbus (Cristoforo Colombo; 1451–1506), an Italian sailor from Genoa, attempted to convince the Portuguese to fund a voyage westward across the Atlantic. From studying the geography of Ptolemy and the findings of earlier Portuguese expeditions, Columbus was certain that he could reach Japan and China in a much shorter time by sailing due west. When King John II of Portugal turned down his request, Columbus went to Spain, where Queen Isabella agreed to back his voyage. With three ships under his command, Columbus actually reached landfall in the Bahamas in October 1492. Thinking he had reached Asia, Columbus explored Cuba and Haiti before returning to Spain with news of his discovery.

Despite three later expeditions between 1493 and

of Cantao cannot hold an office of justice in Cantao . . . This is vested in the literates; and every literate when he obtains a degree begins in petty posts, and thence goes on rising to higher ones, without their knowing when they are to be moved; . . . These changes are made in Pequim. . . . Hence it comes that no judge in China does equity, because he does not think of the good of the district. . . . they do nothing but rob, kill, whip and put to torture the people. The people are worse treated by these mandarins than is the devil in hell: hence it comes that the people have no love for the king and for the mandarins, and every day they go on rising and becoming robbers. . . .

God grant that these Chinese may be fools enough to lose the country; because up to the present they have had no dominion, but little by little they have gone on taking the land from their neighbors; and for this reason the kingdom is great, because the Chinese are full of much cowardice, and hence they come to be presumptuous, arrogant, cruel; and because up to the present, being a cowardly people, they have managed without arms and without any practice of war, and have always gone on getting the land from their neighbors, and not by force but by stratagems and deceptions; and they imagine that no one can do them harm. They call every foreigner a savage; and their country they call the kingdom of God. Whoever shall come now, let it be a captain with a fleet of ten or fifteen sail. The first thing will be to destroy the fleet if they should have one, which I believe they have not; let it be by fire and blood and cruel fear for this day, without sparing the life of a single person, every junk being burnt, and no one being taken prisoner, in order not to waste the provisions, because at all times a hundred Chinese will be found for one Portuguese. . . .

From "Letters from Portuguese Captives in Canton," trans. and ed. by D. Ferguson, *The Indian Antiquary,* XXXI (January 1902).

1502, during which he sailed the Caribbean as far north as Honduras, Columbus would not abandon his conviction that he had reached Asia—it was for this reason that he called the people inhabiting the islands "Indians."

The explorers who came after Columbus were the first to understand that he had in fact discovered an entirely "New World," a term coined by another Italian, Amerigo Vespucci. A banker who was obsessed by exploration fever, Vespucci sailed on several voyages to the Americas—the name that cartographers gave to the two continents after Vespucci described the regions that he explored. Still a third Italian sailor, John Cabot (Giovanni Caboto), was the first European to reach the North American mainland. Commissioned by the English monarch to find a western route to Asia, Cabot sailed along the coast of Nova Scotia and Newfoundland. His son, Sebastian Cabot, sailed to South America on behalf of the Spanish.

The early Spanish and Portuguese explorers were in open competition with each other and the two states appealed to Pope Alexander VI to divide the world into respective spheres of exploration. In 1493, Alexander, a Spaniard, allocated the New World to Spain and granted Africa and India to Portugal. The Portuguese were not, however, very pleased by this distribution since it removed Brazil, which they had discovered and claimed, from their jurisdiction. In order to avoid war, Spain and Portugal settled the dispute themselves by the Treaty of Tordesillas (1494), which moved the line westward to include Brazil in the Portuguese zone.

By proving that it was possible to sail westward without incident, Columbus had enticed a generation of explorers to try to find the elusive passage to Asia. In 1513, the Spanish explorer Vasco de Balboa crossed Central America, where he became the first European to look on the Pacific Ocean. During the early 16th century, when voyages to the Western Hemisphere became almost commonplace, a Portuguese navigator named Ferdinand Magellan became the first European to circle the globe. Magellan had served in India before joining the service of the Emperor Charles V. In September 1519, he sailed from Spain with five ships, and a year later he discovered the strait now named for him at the southern end of South America. With three

One of the first major steps in Europe's exploration of the globe came with the voyage of Portuguese seaman Vasco da Gama across the Indian Ocean to the western coast of India.

A "portolan" map from the late 16th century of the West Indies. The portolani were based on information supplied by sailors and enabled early explorers to plan their voyages.

Columbus, whose voyages to the Western Hemisphere opened the way for colonization of the Americas, has become the object of controversy for those who see him as the symbol of European imperialism.

of his ships, he sailed north along the coast and then headed west across the Pacific, reaching Guam in March 1521. Magellan himself was killed in a clash with the local inhabitants in the Philippines, but eventually one of his ships made it back to Spain. Magellan's expedition finally put to rest the question as to whether the earth was round, and it demonstrated that Ptolemy had indeed underestimated the size of the earth.

Spanish Empire in the New World

The region that Columbus explored on his four voyages embraced the major islands of the Caribbean. These so-called "West Indies" islands included Cuba, Jamaica, Puerto Rico, Trinidad, San Salvador, and the island the Spanish called Hispaniola (Haiti). For the Spanish, the chief aims of their travels lay in the conversion of the Indians to Christianity and the search for gold and silver. In a short time, the population of the region, estimated to have been about as high as 100,000, had been decimated by the oppressive conditions under which the Indians were forced to work and the impact of

The first European view of Amerindians, printed about 1500, depicts them as cannibals who led carefree lives without government or shame.

European diseases, such as smallpox, to which the Indians had never before been exposed.

The thirst for gold and silver led the Spanish to transfer their attentions from the Caribbean islands to the mainland. Although the American cultures were advanced, their weapons were no match for European military power. In 1519, a *conquistador* named Hernan Cortes' (1485–1547) invaded Mexico with an army of 600 heavily armed soldiers. Cortes' captured the Aztec emperor Montezuma and conquered his wealthy empire. Mexico yielded large quantities of precious metals and provided missionaries with another large population to convert.

In the 1530s, Francisco Pizarro (1470–1541)

The Spanish used Amerindians as slaves to work the sugar plantations in the West Indies.

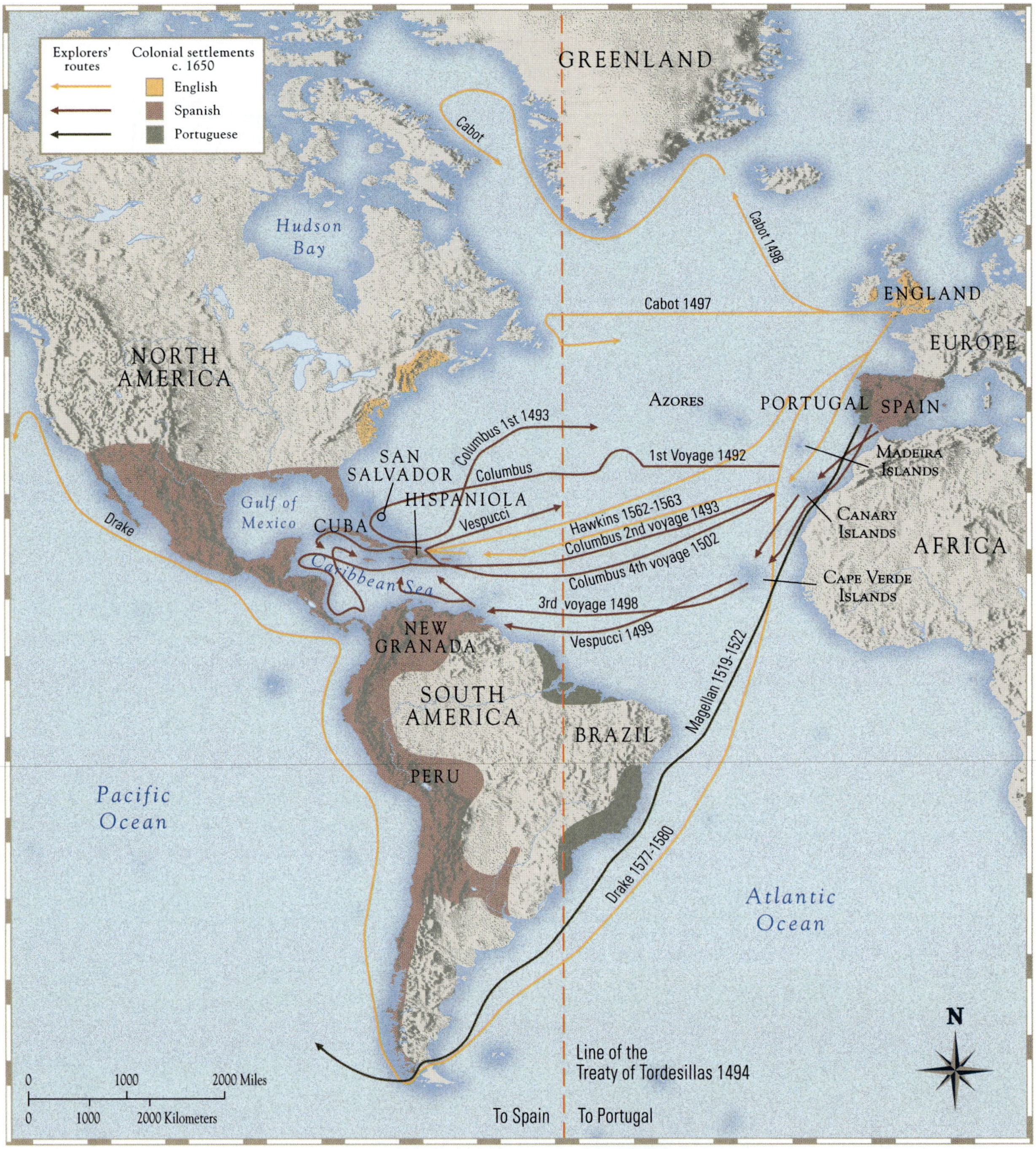

Map 6.3 European Exploration in the Americas

invaded northern South America and destroyed the Inca empire, on whose territory he created the viceroyalty of Peru. Rich silver mines were later discovered both in Mexico and in Peru. In the second half of the 16th century, up to 60 ships a year laden with silver bullion sailed for Spain.

Gold and silver were only part of the return that the Europeans got from their explorations in the New World. Settlers who migrated from Spain to the New World established huge landed estates that they ran with forced labor. When it was found that the Indian population had high mortality rates working the sugar fields, the settlers began to import African slaves to take their place. Smallpox, typhus, and other diseases ravaged those whom forced labor failed to kill.

The European diet, as well as that of much of the rest of the world, was dramatically changed as vegetables and plants indigenous to the region were intro-

This 16th-century manuscript illumination reveals both the mistreatment of Amerindians and the haughty attitude of Europeans toward them.

duced to other cultures: tomatoes, chili peppers, potatoes, and corn, not to speak of tobacco, were some of the important products brought to Europe and Asia. On the other hand, the Spanish introduced goats, sheep, and cattle to the New World, with major ecological results, for as they roamed the ranges they destroyed the roots of plants as well as eating the leaves. The impact of the European invasion was as devastating to South and Central America as it was in the Caribbean. By 1650, the Indian population of Mexico was reduced to about 5 percent of its original size of 25 million. A few Europeans, like the Spanish Dominican friar Bartolomé de Las Casas, tried to secure better treatment for the Indians. Las Casas argued that, once they were converted, the Indians should be thought of as fellow Christians. Spanish scholars and clergy debated the question of whether the Indians were fully human and deserved to be treated as such. As the Spanish administrators applied confused policies wavering between paternal dominance and ruthless enslavement, the toll on both sides was heavy: vast loss of life among the Indian population was accompanied by the moral corruption of the conquerors.

A Widening World Economy

One crucial result of the age of discovery was that Europe placed itself at the center of an ever-widening global economy. On the commercial level, European powers which before 1500 had traded almost entirely along the northern and southern shores of the continent and within Europe itself, now began to establish trade routes that reached out around the world. The implications of this change were felt both in Europe and elsewhere. The first major impact was to be seen in the shifting fortunes of the Italian trading states that had dominated Mediterranean commerce and Europe's supply of spices and other Asian luxury goods for centuries. By 1600, Venice and Genoa were in sharp decline as the nations facing the Atlantic, principally Spain and Portugal, became the new trading powers of Europe. Gradually, the dominant position of the Iberian states was replaced by the Dutch Republic, England, and France.

As in the case of the indigenous American cultures, the spread of Europe's trading network around the globe had equally important consequences for non-European civilizations. In the Indian Ocean, Arab commerce was largely swept away as the Portuguese established their primacy along the East African and Indian coasts. The same was true, although perhaps to a lesser degree, in the trading waters of the Spice Islands and southeast Asia. Profits that had once remained in the hands of Muslim or Chinese merchants now began to flow to Europe, with important results for the decline of prosperity in the regional economy.

The establishment of Portugal's and Spain's overseas empires brought with it both problems and opportunities. The problems of communication and supply made close control from Europe extremely difficult. The principal purpose of these empires had, of course, been to produce revenues for the monarchs, who claimed them as personal property of the crown. At first, the Portuguese kings had allowed for a rather decentralized, almost feudal system of administration in which a series of 15 military governors were granted the right to collect taxes, administer the regions, and make laws in exchange for certain payments to the crown. By 1548, however, this cumbersome system was replaced with a more direct royal control over Brazil and the other colonies, and in 1580 the king established a number of municipal councils which governed in his name. To help administer the Spanish colonies and ensure the steady supply of bullion, Spain's kings established a system of viceroys, who ruled the colonies with the assistance of local governors as well as through advisory councils known as *audiencias*. Because of their obsession with supplying the home country in Europe with revenues, Spain and Portugal strictly limited the commercial opportunities of their colonies. Local trade within the Americas, or between them and other parts of the world, was discouraged. The mining of gold, and eventually of silver alone, was the most important activity as far as the crown was concerned. But settlers and aristocrats who migrated to the Americas to exploit the mining turned to other activities—especially agriculture and herding—as the precious metals ran out. Sugar cane, wheat, coffee, and cotton were the main products of the American agricultural economies, while sheep, cattle, and horses were bred on the extensive plains of the region. Yet the bureaucratic quagmire of the colonial administrations did little to encourage such activity.

Despite such problems, by 1600 the basis for a truly global economy had been established. The effects of this widening system of trade and production would have important implications for Europe (see Part V, Topic 6).

The long-range results of the European "discovery" of the Western Hemisphere were incalculable. The flow of gold and silver bullion to Europe not only enriched the coffers of the national states but seriously affected the economy by impacting prices. Moreover, the increase in trade had a major impact on the development of commercial capitalism and a global economy. The fact, too, that the Europeans assumed an attitude of moral and cultural superiority over the indigenous populations they encountered, and simply "claimed" these vast regions as their own by right of discovery, reflected an attitude of dominance that was to characterize Europe's relationship to the rest of the globe for centuries to come.

Questions for Further Study

1. What conditions in Europe led to the increase in geographic knowledge and overseas discovery?
2. What technical advances were necessary before the age of discovery could take place?
3. What policies characterized Spanish rule in the Americas?

Suggestions for Further Reading

Ball, John N. *Merchants and Merchandise: The Expansion of Trade in Europe, 1500–1630.* London, 1977.

Braudel, Fernand. *Civilization and Capitalism*, trans. S. Reynolds. 3 vols. New York, 1979–1984.

Curtain, Philip D. *Cross-cultural Trade in World History.* Cambridge, MA, 1984.

Davis, Ralph. *The Rise of the Atlantic Economies.* London, 1973.

Diffie, Bailey W., and G. D. Winius. *Foundations of the Portuguese Empire, 1415–1580.* Minneapolis, MN, 1977.

Kriedte, Peter. *Peasants, Landlords and Merchant Capitalists: Europe and the World Economy, 1500–1800.* Leamington, Great Britain, 1983.

McAlister, Lyle N. *Spain and Portugal in the New World, 1492–1700.* Minneapolis, MN, 1984.

Parry, John H. *The Age of Reconnaissance*, 2nd ed. New York, 1966.

Tracy, James E., ed. *The Rise of Merchant Empires.* Cambridge, MA, 1990.

IV

Topic 7

The Reformation

In the early 16th century, the foundations of Western Christianity were severely shaken by the movement of spiritual and institutional reform known as the Reformation. What began as an effort to bring about change and improvement in spiritual life became a genuinely revolutionary wave that broke the 1000-year religious unity of western and central Europe by giving rise to a series of new Protestant churches that rejected the authority of Rome. (The word *Protestant* came from a "protest" which a minority group of German reforming princes issued in 1529 against the Catholic majority at an assembly of the Holy Roman Empire.)

The Reformation, which was the culmination of a long tradition of religious questioning and doubt, first took shape through the ideas and work of a German monk, Martin Luther. Soon, however, Luther's ideas spread beyond the borders of Germany. By the middle of the 16th century, northern Scandinavia, England, Scotland, and a number of cities in Switzerland had all broken from the Roman Catholic Church and embraced new Protestant doctrines. In the next generation after Luther were a number of other religious reformers, including Huldrych Zwingli and John Calvin, who founded new faiths and new churches.

Because European civilization was intimately tied to the spiritual climate of the times, the Reformation had a profound impact on the society and politics of the age. Luther's doctrines attracted broad strata of the population, especially the middle classes and peasantry, and popular response sometimes resulted in widespread unrest. On the political level, Luther appealed directly to the German princes and to the spirit of nationalism in his struggle against the authority of Rome. Monarchs and rulers took sides in the religious controversies of the period, some of them adopting the new faith not only for themselves but for their entire realm. Thus while Emperor Charles V championed the cause of Catholicism, the monarchy in France did not. The long and disastrous wars of religion that disrupted Germany and Europe for decades had complex origins that were sometimes tied to the political ambitions of Catholic and Protestant monarchs.

THE ROOTS OF REFORM: POPULAR DISCONTENT AND THE CRISIS OF THE WESTERN CHURCH

The Reformation had its roots in many of the broad political, social, and economic transformations taking place in Europe in the Early Renaissance. The growing urbanization of Europe's population had given rise to an ever-expanding urban middle class, a social group without traditional close ties to the church and the rural nobility. These middle-class city dwellers were increasingly literate and provided an audience for the circulation of ideas. The very fact that the invention of the printing press made possible the spread of unorthodox teachings to millions of people explains much of the popular success of Protestant thought. By 1520, more than a quarter of a million copies of Luther's works alone were in circulation.

One result of the changing social circumstances was the rise of popular religion and Christian mysticism, which had its most important manifestation in the Modern Devotion movement and its related lay orders known as the Brothers and Sisters of the Common Life. Thomas à Kempis (see Part III, Topic 12), the author of the work *The Imitation of Christ*, had urged Christians to follow the pious example of Christ instead of intellectual discourse and official dogma, although he did stress the importance of the sacrament of communion.

Political change provided another source of support for the Reformation. As the national states emerged and grew stronger in this period, conflict inevitably resulted between the powerful new monarchs, who wanted to control all aspects of national life, and the church, which still owned large amounts of land and demanded complete independence from state control. In eastern Europe, where serfdom and the authority of the feudal princes was still strong, the church held a dominant position. But in western and central Europe, where changing economic and social conditions had undermined noble authority, monarchs had long attempted to free themselves from the control of Rome. In Spain and France, rulers secured autonomy through concordats, or treaties, with the papacy, while others, such as Henry VIII of England, adopted one of the new Protestant faiths as a means of achieving the same end. Charles V, the Hapsburg monarch who ruled over the Holy Roman Empire as well as over Spain, Austria, Bohemia, Hungary, the Netherlands, and other regions, assumed the role of protector of the faith, an alliance that alienated lesser rulers and nobles (on the background of Charles V, see Part IV, Topic 1).

Significant Dates

The Reformation

1517	Luther's ninety-five Theses; Reformation begins
1520	Huldrych Zwingli breaks with Catholic Church
1527	Sack of Rome
1541	John Calvin moves to Geneva
1509–1547	Henry VIII rules England
1555	Peace of Augsburg
1529–1558	Charles V rules Holy Roman Empire
1545–1563	Council of Trent

Institutional and Doctrinal Origins

Ever since the High Middle Ages, the authority of the Catholic Church and its spiritual doctrines had come under mounting criticism both by lay observers and religious reformers. The deepening involvement of the popes in secular affairs reached a low point in the conflict with the German emperors, especially during the reign of Frederick II (see Part III, Topic 10). This experience was compounded in the popular mind by the dismal period of the Babylonian Captivity (1309–1376) and the resulting schism. During this time of crisis for the church, the papacy was divided geographically and there were several competing claimants to the throne of St. Peter (see Part III, Topic 12).

Throughout its history, the church had often followed practices that hurt its prestige and called its leaders into question. During the Renaissance, many popes, for example, had widely practiced *nepotism*—the employment of relatives—and some had even fathered children and kept mistresses in the papal court. High ecclesiastical officials, such as bishops and cardinals, lived luxurious lives that clashed with their spiritual positions.

Moreover, the clergy had long engaged in unseemly practices that had doctrinal as well as practical consequences. For example, *simony*, or the sale of church offices, had been widespread, as had been the profitable traffic in sacred relics, including the bones and body parts of saints. The papacy also sold dispensations, whereby a holder of church office was excused from following certain requirements of church law. Most serious perhaps was the sale of indulgences, which granted pardon from temporal punishment for sins. Indulgences were in effect extra sources of grace accumulated by Christ and the saints, and the penitent who received one had been given credit as if he or she had actually performed a penance. People could purchase indulgences for themselves as well as for dead relatives, who would then be required to spend less time in purgatory. Papal representatives in the indulgences business eventually began touting indulgences as guarantees of entry into heaven, although that was not an accurate description of their function.

Other causes of the Reformation included the spread of humanism out of Italy into northern Europe (Part IV, Topic 4). Christian humanism in the North had been inspired by the possibility that the legacies of morality and ethical behavior inherited from Classical works could influence Christian ethics. Erasmus and other northern humanists had urged the translation of the Bible into vernacular languages and the positive impact of popular education on society. They had, moreover, severely criticized the abuses in the church.

A number of theological issues also attracted the criticism of 16th-century reformers, particularly the influence of rationalist Medieval theologians such as Thomas Aquinas. Their teaching was later used to support the notion that it was the clergy and their institutional functions, rather than faith, that provided the path to salvation. During the 14th and early 15th centuries, John Wycliffe in England and Jan Hus in Bohemia turned to the Bible as the only legitimate source of spiritual truth. Later, the proponents of the Conciliar movement, who argued for the supremacy of church councils in matters of doctrine and ecclesiastical law, questioned papal authority.

Lucas Cranach the Younger depicted "Martin Luther (left) and the Wittenberg Reformers," including Philip Melanchthon (right) and the Elector John Frederick (center).

"HERE I STAND": MARTIN LUTHER AND THE GERMAN REFORMATION

While the Reformation had complicated roots, its immediate source is to be found in the preachings and ideas of Martin Luther (1483–1546) about salvation. As a friar of the Augustinian order, Luther believed that human sinners could be saved only by repentance and faith in divine mercy, not by the good works and indulgences offered by the church. That his ideas were so widely and so quickly accepted reveals the deep sense of spiritual dissatisfaction that prevailed in Christian society. On the other hand, it should be remembered that most Europeans remained Catholic.

The Ninety-Five Theses

Luther was the son of a peasant who had risen into the ranks of the lower middle class by becoming a miner. Luther was raised in a strict Christian household and was extremely well educated according to the standards of the time. In 1502, he earned a bachelor's degree from the University of Erfurt and began to study law. Already, however, he demonstrated signs of deep religious faith, and in 1505 he underwent what he believed was a miraculous experience when he was saved from the effects of a terrible thunderstorm. Vowing to become a monk, he joined an Augustinian monastery in Erfurt, disappointing his father, who had wanted his son to become a lawyer.

Luther, who had always been convinced that he was unworthy of God's grace, became seriously troubled by the issue of salvation. Catholics obtained divine grace principally through the sacraments, with confession as the means of securing forgiveness for sins.

Plagued by disturbing doubts of his own adequacy, he began to study theology, taking a doctorate in 1512 and becoming a professor at the University of Wittenberg. It was there that he found the answer to his dilemma while reading the Epistle of St. Paul to the Romans, which showed him that a believer received the justification of God—and therefore salvation—through faith alone. God, he concluded, freely bestowed his grace on sinners, not because of their good works but as a result of the sacrifice of Christ. The revelation, he said, made him feel reborn. Having discovered the answer to his quest for salvation in the Bible, Luther henceforth argued that it—not the church or the pope—represented the only source of religious authority, although the Church Fathers had to be used to understand Scripture.

It was after having arrived at these conclusions that Luther became embroiled in conflict with the church over the issue of indulgences. In 1517, Pope Leo X commissioned a Dominican monk named John Tetzel to sell a special indulgence which would be used to help finance the completion of St. Peter's Cathedral in Rome. To sell his indulgence, Tetzel chanted to his audiences the catchy refrain, "As soon as the coin in the coffer rings, the soul from purgatory springs." Complicating the matter further was the fact that part of the funds secured from the indulgence would go to pay off a debt that a German archbishop had incurred in order to buy another ecclesiastical office from the pope. Luther was outraged by the crass commercialization of the matter.

In October 1517, he issued the so-called "Ninety-Five Theses," a powerful attack against the abusive sale of indulgences in which he denied the power of the pope to secure salvation. The theses were translated from Latin into German and rapidly disseminated, while Luther was hailed as a champion of popular religious belief. The simplicity and clarity of his position, combined with the resentment that many Germans felt against the church hierarchy in Rome, made them immediately sympathetic to his doctrines.

The Establishment of the Lutheran Church

Although at first Luther moved carefully as a good Catholic who wanted only to reform the church, he was bound to clash with the papacy. Accused of heresy by the Dominicans, he responded by debating a well-known theologian, Johann Eck, in Leipzig in 1519. Challenging the idea of the infallibility of the pope or of church councils, he insisted that the Bible represented the sole authority in matters of religious doctrine. Fired to new enthusiasm as a result of these confrontations, Luther became increasingly convinced of the righteousness of his position.

He followed the debate by issuing several powerful pamphlets that set forth his views on important matters. In *On the Freedom of a Christian Man*, Luther repeated his ideas about salvation, arguing for faith rather than good works as the means to grace. Those who had been saved performed good works out of a spirit of thanks to God. The Christian is at once absolutely free and the servant of humanity. *The Babylonian Captivity of the Church* condemned the idea of sacraments as a means by which the pope had sought to keep from humanity the truth contained in Scripture and to control the process of salvation so as to enhance papal power.

Luther took the occasion also to urge the right of clergy to marry. Indeed, his ideas reflected a belief in the equality of partnership in a Christian marriage and encouraged opportunities for women, although he later drew back from the view that women and men were equal in all things. In a more political vein, Luther's *Address to the Christian Nobility of the German Nation*, written in German, was a frontal assault on the papacy. Attacking the papacy as the persistent source of all resistance to reform, and denying the pope's sole authority to interpret the Scriptures, he appealed to the nobles to found an independent German church free of the authority of Rome.

In December 1520 Luther defiantly burned the papal bull condemning his doctrines. Within a month, he was excommunicated. The Emperor Charles V summoned Luther to appear before the Imperial Diet of the Holy Roman Empire at Worms. Instead of recanting his heretical ideas, however, Luther infuriated the emperor by remaining firm in his convictions. His courageous response, in which he flatly rejected the authority of the pope and of church councils, ended with the ringing words, "I cannot and will not recant anything, for to go against conscience is neither right nor safe. Here I stand, I cannot do otherwise."

In response to Luther's defiance, Charles issued the Edict of Worms that ordered his arrest and the burning of his books. Frederick III, the elector of Saxony, placed Luther under his protection, and the outcast monk took up residence in Wartburg Castle. Luther eventually returned to Wittenberg, where he translated the Bible into German and began teaching at the university, spreading his ideas about the Scriptures to thousands of students. In 1525, he married Katherine von Bora, who remained his lifelong companion and aid.

Luther laid the foundations of a reformed church, which was independent from Rome and based on his teachings but which nevertheless kept many Catholic practices. Stressing the fundamental importance of faith rather than rituals and good works,

Map 7.1 General Religious Divisions in Europe, c. 1560

Luther preserved only baptism and the Eucharist among the sacraments. He replaced the traditional Mass with a communion ceremony in which priests were not necessary to achieve the miracle of transubstantiation, whereby the wine and wafer were transformed into the blood and body of Christ. Instead, Luther spoke of all believers functioning as a new kind of communal priesthood and maintained that Christians were responsible for their own salvation. He also abandoned Latin in favor of German in services and emphasized the importance of music in teaching the Gospel.

Although Luther had inveighed against the hierarchy of the Catholic Church, he felt it necessary to create his own organization, which was based on autonomous congregations. Each congregation was responsible for maintaining church doctrines and the education of its members. Later, Luther approved the creation of central committees that visited each congregation and ensured that the faith was maintained through proper instruction.

THE LUTHERAN MOVEMENT: PEASANT REBELLION AND ARISTOCRATIC STRIFE

Lutheranism spread rapidly throughout the states of northern and central Germany and became especially popular among the middle classes of the free cities. Among Luther's earliest disciples was Philip Melanchthon (1497–1560), a Christian humanist who wrote some of the first rigorous theological statements on the new faith. Erasmus and other humanists, however, eventually rejected Lutheranism both on theological grounds and because they were dismayed at the prospect of a divided Christendom.

Other problems of a political nature also impacted on the early Lutheran movement in Germany. As a former Augustinian, Luther believed in the notion of two spheres of existence, the kingdom of God and the kingdom of the material world. Unlike the popes, who had argued for their supremacy over secular rulers, Luther's ideas gave support and strength to the growing power of secular government, which he saw as the protectors of his church. Luther, whose political and social views were generally quite conservative, supported the position of rulers and state power.

The Peasant Rebellions

If he lent his prestige and that of his new church to the princes of Germany, Luther was, on the other hand, fearful that his appeal for Christian freedom would be used to justify challenges to established authority. This attitude was fully revealed in 1522, when a rebellion broke out among lesser knights who sought to make common cause with the emperor against the more powerful princes, the free cities, and the Catholic Church. Although they declared themselves Lutherans, Luther, who was scandalized by their breach of discipline, gave the rebellious knights no support and the uprising was put down.

More revealing of Luther's conservative social views was the so-called Peasant War that erupted a few years later. The event actually began as a series of revolts among discontented peasants who protested the oppressive treatment that many landowners still meted out to their peasants. Supported by burghers in many cities, and under the leadership of a former follower of Luther, Thomas Muntzer, the peasants presented petitions demanding an end to serfdom and onerous taxes, and claiming religious autonomy.

When violence erupted in 1524, Luther immediately reacted by condemning the peasants in a vicious pamphlet called *Against the Thieving and Murderous Gangs of Peasants*, in which he called upon the princes to wipe out the rebels without mercy. Luther believed it was the responsibility of subjects to obey their rulers, who were divinely chosen, and identified social revolution as a great evil. Luther applauded the massacre of peasants in 1525 by the princes, whom he had identified as the mainstay of his church. His reaction to the rebellions cost him support among the lower classes.

A satirical German print compares the "Papist" sellers of indulgences to the seven-headed beast in the Book of Revelation.

The Hapsburg-Valois Wars

One reason Lutheranism spread with relative ease throughout Germany was because the Emperor Charles V was so preoccupied with holding together his far-flung Hapsburg possessions that he could not focus his attention on stamping out Lutheranism in Germany. The emperor felt that his political aspirations were endangered by the policies of his chief enemy, Francis I (ruled 1515–1547), the Valois king of France. At home, Francis was a vigorous ruler who suppressed the nobles and struck against Protestantism. In the international arena, Francis, whose kingdom was encircled by Hapsburg lands, fought a long and costly series of military engagements—known as the Hapsburg-Valois Wars—against Charles throughout the Continent.

Besides having to contend with Francis, Charles was in frequent disagreement with the papacy. Pope Clement VII (ruled 1523–1534), who saw Hapsburg dominance in Italy as a danger to the Papal States, sided with Francis. In retaliation, in 1527, Charles' army sacked Rome, an event that shocked Catholic opinion in Europe but which strengthened the emperor's position in Italy. It was perhaps a measure of the times that, instead of joining forces with Charles in the struggle against Lutheranism, the papacy had opted to fight its most powerful ally.

Only after the emperor had repelled the Ottoman Turks from the walls of Vienna in 1529, did he try to deal with the German crisis. The next year, Charles convened the Diet of Augsburg, where he presented the Lutherans with an ultimatum that they return to the church by April 1531. Before the deadline, however, a group of Lutheran princes and free cities formed the Schmalkaldic League in order to protect them-

The face of Emperor Charles V, as painted by Titian, reveals the concerns of ruling a far-flung empire.

selves from the emperor. Renewal of war with the Turks and then with Francis diverted Charles' attention once again, and only in 1546, after finally having made peace with both enemies, did he act. That year, with a huge army drawn from his various possessions, Charles launched a war against the Schmalkaldic League. By then, Luther was dead and military victory seemed to presage the end of the Lutheran heresy. In 1552, the League joined forces with Henry II (ruled 1547–1559), the new king of France, and forced Charles to make peace. Dispirited by his efforts and broken in health, Charles abdicated in 1556 and retired to Spain, where he died two years later.

With Charles removed from the scene, in 1555 the religious conflict in Germany ended with the Peace of Augsburg. According to the agreement, Lutheranism was legally recognized and the rulers of the German states were free to choose between Lutheranism and Catholicism, although prince-bishops had to either remain Catholic or resign. The existence of the hundreds of independent territorial states in Germany was thereby accepted as an established principle, while the permanent religious division of Europe had become an unavoidable fact.

THE ADVANCE OF PROTESTANTISM IN CONTINENTAL EUROPE

By the time of the Peace of Augsburg, Scandinavia and part of northern Germany had separated from Roman Catholicism and joined the Protestant Reformation. Not only had Luther shattered more than a millennium of religious unity, but in each area of Europe a different variety of Protestantism evolved. In the countries of Scandinavia—Denmark, Norway, and Sweden—official Lutheran churches were established by the monarchies. Sweden achieved its independence from Denmark in 1520 after a rebellion led by Gustavus Vasa, who became its first king. Under Gustavus' protection, the New Testament was translated and a Lutheran church established. The king of Denmark, Christian III, still controlled Norway, and he founded a Lutheran church in both regions.

John Calvin and the Swiss Reformation

It was in Switzerland rather than in Scandinavia that some of the most important reform developments took place. A former part of the Holy Roman Empire until it won independence in 1499, Switzerland was a prosperous region of hardworking merchants and craftsmen. When the stirrings of reform came, many Swiss reacted favorably to another opportunity of distancing the country from papal Rome.

The first reformer in Switzerland was Huldrych Zwingli (1484–1531), a priest and humanist scholar who lived in Zurich. Zwingli always claimed that he arrived at his ideas about the superiority of biblical over papal authority and about justification by faith alone independently of Luther. He and Luther differed on a number of doctrinal issues, including the meaning of baptism and the Eucharist, which Zwingli thought had only symbolic importance. A practical man with a keen sense of political realities, Zwingli convinced the Zurich town council to authorize an assembly of magistrates and clergymen to oversee religious and secular life in the city. As more cities were influenced by Protestantism, a brief but intense civil war erupted, during which Zwingli was killed. A settlement based on

John Calvin, depicted in a 1574 woodcut that links the Geneva reformer to Luther and Hus.

freedom of religious choice for each canton restored peace to Switzerland.

John Calvin (1509–1564) represented a later generation of Reformation leadership and spearheaded a more radical form of Protestantism. Born in France, he studied law until, in 1533, he underwent a religious awakening that led him to convert to Protestantism. Accused of heresy by the church, he fled to Basel, where he published a treatise entitled *Institutes of the Christian Religion*, in which he tried to make Lutheran principles into a systematic system of belief.

Calvin, like Zwingli, agreed with Luther's insistence on the importance of faith rather than good works, and shared with his German predecessor the notion that Christians were constantly engaged in a struggle between good and evil. Humans, they both believed, were depraved sinners, but Calvin was convinced that God's purpose was beyond any human understanding. Before an omnipotent and supreme God, Calvin believed, humans were weak and lacked necessary free will to bring about their own salvation. Instead, Calvin—like Luther and Zwingli, who were more circumspect in professing the belief—taught the doctrine of predestination, according to which God had decided before the Creation who would be saved and who would be damned. As humans cannot know who has been chosen and rejected, good Christians should focus on doing good works—which Calvin thought were a sign of having been selected for salvation—and leading a moral life. Above all, humans should devote themselves to the worship of God.

Geneva and the Social Vision of Calvinism

A man of strong views and determination, Calvin is often thought of as the organizer of Protestantism. When in 1541 he was invited to come to Geneva he built a Christian society to which reformers of the 16th century looked with pride and where religious refugees found sanctuary. Calvin's most powerful popular attraction was his sermons, and through them he preached his faith and set the tone for the life of morality and seriousness to which he wanted all citizens to aspire. His precepts for living and worshiping were laid out in systematic fashion in his *Catechism*.

Calvin hoped to organize Geneva along religious lines, although a civilian magistracy continued to run the city government. On the other hand, Calvin presided over a Consistory made up of laymen and pastors which established detailed rules by which citizens were to live. Personal conduct, including the manner of dress and the hours during which people could be outside their homes, was strictly controlled. Drunkenness, gambling, and frivolity were prohibited and religious dissent harshly punished.

Calvinism represented the most activist and compelling Protestant faith of the period and his church provided an example that inspired reformers in other countries, from France and Scotland to North America.

The Anabaptists

As we have seen, Zwingli believed that baptism had symbolic rather than real meaning for Christians. Other reformers, known as *Anabaptists* ("baptized again"), made concern over the idea of baptism a central aspect of their doctrine. Rejecting the idea of predestination, the Anabaptists based their doctrine on their belief that adults alone, not children, were able to choose to enter a religious faith. While opposed to baptizing children, they insisted that adults should be baptized.

The Anabaptists were considered radicals who thought that Luther had not gone far enough in his reforms. While the Anabaptists accepted Luther's teachings, they insisted on a literal interpretation of the Scriptures, and engaged in only those practices they believed were followed in the early church. Moreover, they saw the true church as a voluntary community of equal believers, much like the early Christian church as described in the New Testament. This spirit of democracy may have reflected the fact that most of their members were peasants, artisans, and other laborers

The Anabaptists were radical reformers who believed in adult baptism and rejected government authority. This 16th-century illustration shows the torture of an Anabaptist leader.

linked by social and economic dissatisfaction. Indeed, their advocacy of communal property and their prohibition of interest reflected the class base of the movement and in part explains the ferocity of persecution against them. Their radicalism extended to politics as well. Anabaptists, contrary to most other Christians, wanted a total separation of church and state, refusing to serve in government positions or fight in the army.

Anabaptists established groups in Switzerland, Germany, and Austria, and later still in eastern Europe. In Zurich, Zwingli exiled them, and in Germany they were viciously persecuted, for their ideas challenged both religious and secular power. In Münster, Germany, the Anabaptists at first were officially recognized in the early 1530s and the city became a refuge for fellow believers from elsewhere. Here they instituted the practice of polygamy, and women were permitted to become priests. They also expelled nonbelievers and seized their property. When an especially extremist group of Anabaptists took over the town, the Catholic forces waged open warfare against Münster and killed its leaders.

A less radical Anabaptist group under the leadership of Menno Simons (1496–1561) established a movement that came to be known as the Mennonites, who wanted to withdraw from the world so as to live a pure Christian existence. Yet Simons too introduced severe discipline among his followers.

THE BREAK WITH ROME: HENRY VIII AND THE ENGLISH CHURCH

In England, where the monarchy and the papacy had often struggled for supremacy, Protestantism was established for reasons that often had little to do with the desire for religious reform. Here, the Reformation was led—unlike the experiences in Germany or Switzerland—by a monarch rather than a priest: King Henry VIII dominated the religious controversies of his age and lent his weight to the drive to separate the English church from Rome.

King Henry VIII, whose six marriages were designed to produce a legitimate male heir, broke with the Roman Catholic church in order to divorce one of his wives.

The Tudor Succession

The Tudor dynasty had been founded in the 15th century by Henry VII, England's first "new monarch" (see Part IV, Topic 4). His son, Henry VIII (ruled 1509–1547), solidified the Tudor monarchy and proved to be one of the most important kings in English history.

An ambitious, ruthless man of strong appetites, Henry was concerned for the future of the dynasty that accounted for his decision to break with Rome. A long marriage to Catherine of Aragon (1485–1536) failed to produce a male heir to assure the Tudor succession and in 1527 he appealed to the pope for an annulment so that he could take a new queen. Henry had already gone on record in opposition to Luther and under ordinary circumstances his request would no doubt have been approved in Rome. But two factors worked against him. First, Catherine had originally been married to Henry's brother, and only a special papal dispensation had allowed him to marry his dead brother's wife. Henry was now convinced that God's punishment had prevented him from having a son, but an annulment now would have suggested that the first papal dispensation had been a mistake. Perhaps more importantly, Catherine, who refused to accept an annulment, was the aunt of the Emperor Charles V, whose soldiers had already sacked Rome and who had an obvious influence on the pope's decision.

Henry, who had contemplated divorce from Catherine, had already begun an affair with Anne Boleyn (c. 1507–1536), a lady in waiting at the court, who was now pregnant with the king's child. In January 1533, Henry and Anne secretly married. Thomas Cranmer (1489–1556), whom Henry had made archbishop of Canterbury, annulled the marriage to Catherine without waiting for the pope to act and then approved the marriage to Anne. When Anne did give birth, it was to a daughter, whom they named Elizabeth. When the pope finally moved, it was to excommunicate Henry.

The Foundations of the Anglican Church

These actions were taken only after a special act of Parliament had prohibited English ecclesiastical courts from appealing cases to Rome. Moreover, in 1534 Parliament passed the Act of Supremacy, which made Henry the supreme head of the English—or Anglican—church. Thomas Cromwell (1485–1540), the king's secretary, then devised plans that ended payments to the papacy and closed hundreds of monasteries, whose confiscated lands were sold to pay off Henry's debts. Sir Thomas More, the humanist scholar who had served as the king's chancellor, was beheaded when he refused to accept Henry's triumph over the church.

Henry's confrontation with the papacy received wide support in England, where Protestantism was spreading, both from Parliament and from the public. But Henry moved cautiously in matters of doctrine, securing passage in 1539 of the Six Articles Act that endorsed important aspects of Catholic doctrine, including celibacy for priests and the miracle of transubstantiation, and rejected only the idea of papal supremacy. Henry's refusal to make substantial changes in religious doctrine or practice was part of a shrewd policy for gaining popular consensus behind the break with Rome.

The English Reformation

Despite these major transformations made in order to secure Henry's marriage to Anne Boleyn, the irony was that Henry eventually had four other wives, two of whom, Anne Boleyn and Catherine Howard, were accused of adultery and beheaded. The successor he so desperately wanted was produced by his third wife, Jane Seymour, whose son eventually took the throne as Edward VI (ruled 1547–1553). During the minority of Edward's reign, religious reformers such as Cranmer were free to establish Protestantism more firmly in England. Through further acts of Parliament, the clergy were eventually permitted to marry and a new liturgy, contained in the *Book of Common Prayer*, was adopted in 1549.

After Edward's early death, the throne passed to Mary (ruled 1553–1558), Henry's daughter with Catherine. Mary tried to restore Catholicism, a policy that produced widespread hostility and resistance, and the burning of some 300 Protestants earned her the nickname "Bloody Mary." The queen then made herself even more unpopular by marrying Philip II of Spain, the son of Charles V. By the time of her death in 1558, Protestantism had been even more firmly established in England.

In Ireland, which was dominated by the English landlords, the parliament passed measures endorsing the separation from Rome and establishing the Church of Ireland modeled on the Anglican Church, with the king as its head. When the majority of Irish people remained Catholic, no doubt in part to express their opposition to the English, the Catholic monasteries and the churches were ordered closed.

In Scotland, where King James V (ruled 1528–1542) and his daughter, Mary, queen of Scots (ruled 1542–1567) were both strong supporters of the Catholic Church, the state fought the reform movement. The Scottish Reformation was led by John Knox (c. 1505–1572). Knox, a former priest and a fiery preacher, had studied with John Calvin in Geneva. In 1560, he encouraged the parliament in Scotland to pass laws abolishing the Catholic Mass and paving the way for Knox to establish the Presbyterian Church, which took its name from the *presbyters*, or ministers, who controlled it. In 1564, Knox wrote *The Book of Common Order*, which determined the liturgy for the Church of Scotland.

The movement for reform within the Catholic Church started by Martin Luther in the early 16th century destroyed the religious unity that western Europe had enjoyed since the late Roman Empire. The establishment of the Protestant churches and the rapid spread of their doctrines revealed deep popular discontent in spiritual affairs. Its reverberations, however, spilled over from religious issues into the secular realm.

The Reformation profoundly influenced the political and social realities of the day. The broad appeal of many reform doctrines especially touched the lower classes, sometimes unleashing popular unrest. The upper classes responded to the Reformation in different ways. In some regions of Europe, rulers and nobles supported reform as a means of undermining papal authority within their own borders, while others remained attached to Roman Catholicism. In defense, the Church of Rome would soon embark on a vigorous program of internal change and counterreformation that would aim at pushing back the tide of Protestantism. The religious controversies kept Europe in turmoil for centuries to come.

Questions for Further Study

1. What were the origins of the Protestant Reformation?
2. What were Luther's principal ideas and how did they differ from conventional Christianity?
3. In what ways did religious reformation reflect and affect social and political conditions in Germany?
4. How did the ideas of the other major reformers differ from those of Luther?

Suggestions for Further Reading

Bainton, Roland. *Women of the Reformation in Germany and Italy*. Minneapolis, MN, 1971.

Bainton, Roland. *Here I Stand*. New York, 1968.

Bouwsma, William J. *John Calvin: A Sixteenth Century Portrait*. New York, 1987.

Edwards, Mark. *Luther's Last Battles*. Ithaca, NY, 1983.

Elton, Geoffrey R. *Reform and Reformation: England, 1509–1558*. Cambridge, MA, 1977.

Galer, U. *Huldrych Zwingli: His Life and Work*, trans. R. Gritsch. Philadelphia, 1986.

Jensen, De Lamar. *Reformation Europe: Age of Reform and Revolution*. Lexington, KY, 1981.

McGrath, Alister E. *The Intellectual Origins of the European Reformation*. Oxford, 1987.

Oberman, Heiko. *Luther: Man Between God and the Devil*, trans. E. Walliser-Schwarzbart. New Haven, CT, 1989.

Scarisbrick, J. J. *The Reformation and the English People*. Oxford, 1984.

Spitz, Lewis W. *The Protestant Reformation, 1517–1559*. New York, 1985.

IV

Topic 8

The Social Worlds of the Renaissance and Reformation

The sweeping changes that the Renaissance and Reformation produced in cultural and political life in Europe also profoundly affected social patterns. In spite of their long-term significance, however, the immediate repercussions of these developments did not have a consistent impact on all sectors of society. What is clear is that the rate of change was more intense than at any time since the early Middle Ages.

European society was becoming increasingly urbanized, and a new and more complex class structure began to develop in the growing cities. While rural life remained comparatively static, the urban setting allowed for significantly more social mobility. Foremost among the new social groups of the cities to emerge in this period was a rapidly expanding middle class. This category included the wealthier merchants who arose as a result of the commercial revolution, as well as the less affluent burghers who operated shops and small businesses. Other factors in stimulating social change included the spread of education among urban dwellers, and the growing tendency of urban women of the poorer classes to work. This, in turn, affected patterns of marriage and family life.

The broad changes in society had both positive and negative effects on women, depending on their status. Aristocratic women lost some of the authority and equality that they had enjoyed during the High Middle Ages as the values attached to the concept of chivalry were replaced by the more rigid and confining notions associated with formal court life. One of the consequences of the new code of conduct for these women was a double standard of sexual behavior for men and women. For women of the non-noble classes, on the other hand, new employment opportunities, especially in commerce, arose in the walled cities, allowing them the possibility of greater social mobility than ever before.

While Western society remained overwhelmingly Christian and white, urban life contained small but significant minorities, including Jews and Muslims. With the expansion of Europe overseas as a result of the era of reconnaissance, the growth of the slave trade produced a new minority in ever-greater numbers: black slaves, some of whom eventually won their freedom.

The net result of all these developments was to speed up the transformation of European life from its Medieval patterns to a society on the eve of the modern world.

CLASS, MOBILITY, AND CHANGING VALUES

During the 16th century, the three most important long-term forces determining social patterns were demographic change, status, and wealth.

Population Trends

The number of people living in regions of Europe affected political trends, employment and production, the way in which towns and villages evolved, food supply, and often the very question of life and death itself.

During the 16th century, Europe began to recover fully from the destructive effects of the Black Death. Before the 19th century, when governments began to collect the first accurate statistics, all calculations of population can be at best very rough estimates. It seems clear, however, that in the course of the 16th century population increased significantly, perhaps by as much as a third. By 1600, Europe may have had more than 100 million inhabitants. The growth pattern was neither constant in time nor geographically even throughout the continent, and a sometimes wildly fluctuating death rate—determined largely by famine, disease, and war—helped to keep growth in check.

The repercussions of population growth were varied. For one thing, the supply of labor increased significantly. At first, a larger agrarian workforce resulted in an increase in the amount of food available, while rising wages created a demand for manufactured products.

This expansion in turn stimulated economic activity in the towns, which began to attract ever larger numbers of people. By today's standards, towns in the 16th century were quite small. In 1500, Cologne, situated on the Rhine River, was the largest urban center in Germany with a mere 20,000 inhabitants. In that same year, few European cities had populations of more than 100,000. A century later, however, Paris counted a half-million people, Naples 300,000, and London 250,000.

As the urban population of Europe increased, a surplus labor force was created. This had the effect of driving down real wages, a setback accompanied by a startling rise in prices in the later 16th century known as the "price revolution" (see Part V, Topic 6). The inflation in commodity prices, especially for basic necessities such as bread and wheat, was immense—by 1600, prices had risen to four times their level of a century earlier. Wages did not, however, keep up with prices and the standard of living for the poorer classes declined.

This contemporary painting, *Marketplace at Antwerp,* conveys something of the bustling pace of the city's commercial activity in the 16th century.

By the 17th century, therefore, population and economic growth began to slow down and in some cases to reverse themselves. Yet if the rise and decline in population was a volatile aspect of social reality, status remained constant as a determining feature of life for every member of European society. A person's status was fixed in a social hierarchy that determined not only how specific groups related to each other, but how each class lived. The element in 16th-century society that began to undermine social position was wealth.

Old Nobles and New Merchants

The 16th century was a time of great expansion and prosperity for the middle classes, and also saw crisis and readjustment for the traditional noble landowning class. In spite of their declining financial status, they continued to occupy the most important political posts and government offices. With the strengthening of the power of the monarchy, the nobility retained their prestige while losing their old feudal authority over the peasant class.

In France and elsewhere, kings used their ability both to create new categories of nobles and to enlarge the existing ranks of aristocrats in order to enhance royal authority. The French monarchs, for example, limited the power of the old feudal families ("nobles of the sword") by elevating members of the middle class to the status of "nobles of the robe" to serve as bureaucrats in the state system (see Part V, Topic 4). Louis XIV also adopted the strategy of luring the old nobility to his court at Versailles, where they became trapped in a complex and financially draining ritual of court behavior centering around the symbolic figure of the Sun King.

The rise in population and the growth of towns sharply affected the income of those who made their living by manufacturing, creating an ever-rising demand for their products. Moreover, the price revolution redistributed significant wealth to the manufacturing class of the towns by increasing profits. The commercial revolution made possible an equally rapid accumulation of wealth in the hands of a new middle class of merchants and traders. As a result, the definition of status relaxed and position in the social hierarchy became more fluid.

The leading middle-class citizens were those involved in international trade, banking, and industry

This painting, entitled *Bankers,* is by 15th-century Dutch painter Marinus van Reymerswaele.

and who dominated civic affairs. These powerful families established social customs and patronized the arts. Beneath them were the urban shopkeepers and craftsmen, whose prosperity depended on local rather than international markets. Their economic and social status derived from their membership in guilds, the trade and craft organizations that controlled business and professional standards in the cities.

The Poor in Town and Country

For all the increase in prosperity for the upper classes of society, the majority of the urban and rural population remained poor and often lived at the edge of subsistence. In the towns, the bulk of the population consisted of manual laborers who earned their daily wages by working on building sites, at ports, and as carters and carriers. Much of this work was seasonal and in the winter months the laborers who crowded the towns in good weather often found themselves unemployed. Workers with some degree of specialized skill were employed in the small factories that produced textiles, metal and glass goods, and food products such as beer and bread.

Another principal source of employment in the towns was domestic labor. With the rise of middle-class prosperity, the demand for assistance in the home—maids, cooks, and personal servants—continued to grow. Domestic employment sometimes provided greater job security than casual labor, although family servants depended on the good will of their employers. Whatever their occupation, workers in the towns played no part in the political affairs of their community and benefited only marginally from the better standard of living and enlarged horizons of the urban environment.

In the countryside conditions were little better for the peasantry. Nature and the seasons determined the tempo of rural life, where almost all activities focused on farming and the raising of animals. Throughout much of Europe the most widespread and important agricultural product was grain (wheat, rye, barley, and oats), which was baked into bread, the principal item in the peasant diet. In the Mediterranean region, more specialized crops such as grapes and olives provided a more varied source of nutrition while also offering additional products and occupations. In England, the Netherlands, and Germany, the staple drink was beer, while in Italy, France, and Spain farmers used grapes to make wine.

Living conditions for the working classes in both town and country were grim. Urban laborers lived in crowded and unsanitary tenements in slum districts, while peasant housing generally consisted of small and unheated huts in which people dwelled alongside animals. For both groups, fire and disease were constant hazards and starvation a perpetual preoccupation.

EDUCATION, MARRIAGE, AND THE FAMILY

One of the effects of the Renaissance and Reformation was an increase in the importance of education for the nobility and middle classes. The poor and working classes of Europe, who comprised the overwhelming majority of the population, remained excluded from the rise in educational standards until the 19th century. In all classes of society, the family remained the basic

Peasants destroy a German monastery during the Peasant's Revolt of 1524–26.

Pieter Brueghel's *Children's Games* (1560) shows town children at play.

social unit, although the period saw a transition from the traditional extended family to the more modern nuclear family.

Education in Renaissance and Reformation

The humanists of the Renaissance believed that education should prepare citizens to assume their responsibilities to society as well as to shape individual character. Humanist education combined Classical precepts with Christian teaching to create a fully rounded personality.

In the 15th century, Vittorino da Feltre (1378–1446) translated these ideas into an actual curriculum, which he applied to the students who attended his famous secondary school at Mantua. Vittorino provided a core program of Latin, Greek, philosophy, mathematics, and music, as well as physical training. Vittorino's school attracted students from throughout Italy and his model curriculum was adopted widely.

Many of the leading Protestant reformers adapted humanist principles to their religious concerns. Whereas Renaissance schools were designed principally to serve the needs of the upper classes, Reformation educators aimed at reaching a broader range of society. Some leaders, like Martin Luther, even encouraged the state to provide free public education for children of all classes. German Protestants introduced secondary school education, which added religious instruction to the traditional humanist curriculum of the liberal arts. Similarly, the newly founded Jesuit order established colleges whose students were taught the classics along with Catholic doctrine. For women, the Ursuline order, founded by St. Angela Merici, provided girls with training in religion and morals (see Part V, Topic 1).

Marriage and the Family

In all family arrangements, women were subservient to men. Although mothers were responsible for raising children, fathers had ultimate authority over them and arranged their marriages. Husbands also decided matters of family finances and managed their property. Once married, wives generally gave up their independence, including the right to own property in their own name.

Traditionally, European families had consisted of several generations and degrees of kinship living in the same household. A typical family unit might therefore contain father, mother, and children together with grandparents, uncles and aunts, and cousins. With the emphasis on the individual at the heart of both Renaissance and Reformation, this extended family arrangement tended to break up into smaller nuclear units made up of parents and their children. This pattern, typical of Western Europe, foreshadowed the family structure of the 19th and 20th centuries; in eastern Europe, the extended family remained the prevailing model. In spite of the changing living arrangements, however, extended families continued to function as a unit in financial and political matters. This was as true for the old ruling families of the Italian city-states—the Medici and the Visconti, for example—as it was for the newer commercial dynasties of northern Europe, foremost among them the Fugger banking clan of Augsburg.

Given the importance of family connections in business and politics, upper-class parents generally arranged their children's marriages. Such alliances involved the payment of large dowries by the parents of the bride to the husband. Even poor families were expected to provide a dowry for their daughters, making the raising of girls more of an economic strain. In some communities, private charities financed by the wealthy provided subsidies for the payment of dowries among needy families.

Protestants developed new attitudes toward the family. In theory, with the abolition of a celibate clergy the relationship between husband and wife became the focus of family life and marriage partners placed new emphasis on mutual love and respect. In practice, however, husbands continued to be the dominant force in most marriages. Martin Luther's own example demonstrated the contradictions that often characterized Protestant views of marriage. Luther, a conservative in most social matters, encouraged his followers to maintain the authority of the husband: "the wife," he wrote, "is compelled to obey him by God's command." His own private life, however, seemed to reflect a different, more loving relationship. In 1525, Luther, who had been an Augustinian monk, married a former Cistercian nun, Katharine von Bora (1499–1552). She remained for the 21 years of their marriage a constant companion and assistant to Luther, who wrote toward the end of his life, "Next to God's Word there is no more precious treasure than holy matrimony."

THE BURDENS OF GENDER: WOMEN IN A CHANGED WORLD

As European society evolved over the centuries, the status and role of women adapted and responded to new conditions. The changes introduced by the Renaissance and Reformation had a noticeable but uneven impact on women, depending on their social class. In two respects, however, all women shared a common experience: they remained subordinate to men, and most of them were expected to devote their lives to bearing and rearing children.

In the Renaissance period, women generally married while still in their teens, whereas men usually postponed marriage until their late thirties. This discrepancy in age was determined by the need for men to achieve financial independence—while the extended family had offered economic support for young families, nuclear families required that fathers had sufficient financial means to maintain their own wives and children. By the 17th century, as women increasingly entered the workplace, they too tended to marry at a later age.

In both courtship and marriage, women of all classes were expected to conform to different standards from men. Young women were kept under constant supervision in order to preserve their virginity before marriage. Newly wed husbands who found that their wives were not virgins had the right to break the marriage without being obliged to return the dowry. Men, on the other hand, were expected to be sexually experienced. For the many single men in their twenties and thirties, professional prostitutes provided their services, often under state regulation. In reality, of course, both men and women engaged in sexual activity before marriage, and by the 18th century illegitimate births were commonplace.

Education, Culture, and the Economy

The double standard was particularly marked among the aristocracy, who cultivated the courtly way of life. In the Renaissance, children of noble families received a higher level of education than their counterparts in the Medieval period. Whereas the training of boys prepared them to participate in business and public affairs, the education of girls was confined for the most part to the classics, painting, music, and the other fine arts. University students were almost entirely males, whereas women were educated at home by family or private tutors. As a result, women were unable to train for the professions, although printing made it easier for women to study.

Despite these obstacles, we know of several dozen women Renaissance humanists and a number of prominent artists. Christine de Pisan (c. 1364–c. 1434) wrote books of poetry, philosophy, and biography—including a book about Joan of Arc—and challenged the concept of courtly love, while Vittoria Colonna (1492–1547) wrote widely admired love poems and religious sonnets and corresponded with Michelangelo.

Generally, however, women found it extremely difficult to pursue intellectual careers, both because they were expected to marry and bear children and because men regarded intellectual pursuits as unwomanly. Among the well-known artists of the day was Sofonisba Anguissola of Cremona (c. 1535–1625), one of six sisters who painted. Anguissola, whose work was admired by Michelangelo, was court painter for Philip II of Spain and was patronized by rulers and popes.

The Medieval tradition of chivalry had required men to pay homage to and respect women. By contrast, Renaissance experts in life at court, such as Castiglione, expected women primarily to serve a purely decorative function in what was essentially a man's world of power and politics (see Part IV, Topic 4). It was not uncommon for noblewomen in the feudal age to take charge of governments and manage estates in the absence of their husbands. In the leading families of the Renaissance period, however, aristocratic women were limited to performing traditional roles as wives, mothers, and daughters.

Women from the families of wealthy merchants had a greater range of responsibilities. While merchants traveled abroad, their wives ran the family business, and were trained to keep records and balance the books. Contessina de' Medici, the wife of the Florentine banker Cosimo, employed a secretary to assist her with her correspondence, while the English diarist Samuel Pepys (1633–1703) taught his wife mathematics in order to maintain the household accounts.

Sofonisba Anguissola painted this enigmatic self-portrait in 1561, when she was in her mid-thirties.

After the death of her husband, a widow was able to inherit his property and business. Many used the capital thus acquired to enlarge existing businesses or start their own firms. In the 16th century, women in northern Europe engaged in international commerce and became members of overseas trading companies. In Ravensberg, Germany, in the same period, more than 10 percent of the members of the Merchant's Society were women.

For women of lower economic status, opportunities for social mobility and employment were also available in the towns. As early as the 13th century, women in Florence, London, and Paris established their own guilds for silk workers. Most guilds restricted membership to men, but some allowed a widow to inherit her husband's membership and a few even permitted women to be members in their own right. One of the fields open to women was publishing. In Strasbourg in the 16th century and London in the 17th, widows ran publishing houses which they had inherited from their husbands. In the century following 1550, some 10 percent of all publishers in London were women.

In rural areas, women led equally complex but dependent lives. In farming households, wives and daughters were expected to perform multiple roles, including traditional domestic activities, feeding and caring for farm animals, and helping with labor in the fields. The wives of men who worked away from home often ran the farms on their own, including the heavy manual labor of plowing and harvesting. In many cases, women also engaged in cottage industries such as spinning, weaving, and basket making. If she became a widow, a country woman would generally seek to remarry in order to have a man to take charge of work on the farm.

Once they came of age, the daughters of rural families often migrated to the cities. There they looked for employment, generally in domestic work, which remained the chief form of urban women's work until modern times. Domestic labor involved long working hours and low pay, and young girls were frequently subjected to sexual violence by their employers. Women also found jobs in other fields, including manual labor in construction, mining, and retailing. In market towns, women ran most businesses involving the preparation, buying, and selling of food. In all occupations that they shared with men, women were paid significantly less. The overwhelming majority of townswomen were poor, and some of those who did not find employment or a husband supported themselves by prostitution.

The vast transformations that unfolded in the era of the Renaissance and Reformation brought widespread and generally beneficial changes to Europe. For women, however, they had mixed consequences. The overall pattern of European women's lives did not improve substantially until the 18th century, when the industrial revolution wrought a massive restructuring of European society.

Fear of Witches: Superstition and Persecution

Women were also seriously affected by one of the most striking aspects of the fanatical atmosphere that accompanied the religious upheavals of the 16th century—the growing fear of witches that seemed to grip society. When the papacy instituted the Inquisition against the Albigensians in the 13th century (see Part III, Topic 8), it also began to persecute witches as part of that same campaign. On the eve of the Reformation, the church renewed its interest in stamping out witchcraft. The campaign against witchcraft was not, however, limited to Catholic states, and the hysteria over witches appears to have swept Europe, affecting Germany, Switzerland, England and Scotland, and the English colonies in North America.

Witchcraft was an ancient form of worship that had long been widespread in Europe's villages and rural areas. In the Middle Ages, the church identified witches with worship of the devil and made witchcraft a heresy. The Inquisition made witches a target of its activities, and during periods of social and economic crisis witches often became targets of popular wrath. In 1484, the papacy condemned witches as having become instruments of Satan and the cause of a variety of evils. Two Dominican friars investigated witchcraft in Germany on behalf of the papacy and authored a handbook about the practices of witches and methods by which to identify them. Witches were said not only to have participated in nighttime ceremonies and sexual orgies but to have cast spells on others.

At the time of the Reformation, the belief in witches seems to have become the source of popular hysteria, with people accusing each other indiscriminately and tens of thousands being prosecuted for witchcraft. The fear of witches in the 16th and early 17th centuries multiplied and trials of accused persons were a daily occurrence in many parts of Europe. The victims of the witchcraft craze came from all walks of life, although people from the lower classes seem more likely to have been accused.

The frenzy over witchcraft had serious implications for the position of women—three out of four people charged with witchcraft were women, the majority of whom were widows. Most were from the lower classes, including peasants and domestic servants. The identification of women with witches further marginalized them in society, creating identifications in the popular mind with devil worship and sin. Some witch hunters thought women were by nature evil, an attitude supported both by the biblical tale of Eve's corruption of Adam and by Medieval folk tales.

Certainly part of the cause of the witchcraft craze was the aroused passion of religious controversy during a time of heightened sensitivity to charges of heresy. The social turmoil of the period also seems to have contributed to the fear of unrest among the poorer classes. The great witchcraft fear declined in the second half of the 17th century, when the religious conflicts and the wars that accompanied them had come to an end. As conditions began to settle down, the tensions and divisiveness that inspired the trials diminished, and by the early 18th century the superstitions that had fed the fear began to be dispelled.

The great contradiction of the witchcraft craze was, of course, that it occurred at the very time that reformers were seeking spiritual regeneration. Luther, Calvin, and other Protestant leaders condemned witches as savagely as they did the Catholic clergy, and its victims were burned at the stake by both churches.

A 1555 woodcut depicts a witch being abducted by the devil.

PERSPECTIVES ON HISTORY

The First Africans in Europe

Trevor P. Hall
Bethune-Cookman College

The first Africans in Europe fell into three categories: first, élite noblemen, clerics, and ambassadors; second, freemen/women vendors, translators, sailors, artisans, and laborers; and third, slaves. The major questions are, how many Africans lived in ancient Europe, what were they doing in Europe, where did they live, and when did they arrive?

Black Africans have lived in "Europe" since ancient times when North Africa and the Sahara Desert formed the southern frontier of the Roman Empire. Beginning in the 4th century A.D., German invaders sacked Rome and began settling in the Empire, and in the process disrupted long-distance trade with Africa and began the rapid political disintegration of the Empire in the West. Portugal and Spain were removed from Germanic control when Muslims from North Africa conquered the Iberian peninsula in A.D. 711 and linked it to Muslim states in Africa. From A.D. 711 to 1492, a few black Africans who were Muslims lived in Europe's southwest frontiers in Portugal and Spain. During this period, some Africans also lived in Genoa and Venice as Italian ships traded with North Africans from Morocco to Egypt.[1]

From time to time, African clerics from the Coptic Church of Christian Ethiopia visited Rome when benevolent Muslim leaders in Egypt permitted pilgrims to cross Islamic territories. One Portuguese tale has Prince Henry the Navigator of Portugal meeting an Ethiopian cleric in Portugal. The African convinced Prince Henry that the powerful Christian Kingdom of Ethiopia lay south of Muslim Egypt. According to the 15th-century Portuguese royal chronicler, Gomes Eannes de Azurara, one of the five reasons Prince Henry first sent ships to West Africa was to find the Christian king of Ethiopia whom the Portuguese called Prester John.[2] Prince Henry envisioned a military alliance with black Christians of Ethiopia that would destroy Islam by attacking its southern underbelly.

Searching for Ethiopia, Prince Henry the Navigator sent Portuguese mariners past Morocco to West Africa where in 1441, they kidnapped four black Muslim fishermen from the mouth of the Senegal River and brought them back to Europe. The Portuguese became the first to sail from Europe to West Africa. By the 1470s Spain sent ships to West Africa. Over the next four centuries, European ships would transport hundreds of thousands of West Africans to Europe.

The earliest European mariners in 15th-century West Africa were traders, not conquerors. These Portuguese established peaceful diplomatic relationships with a number of African kingdoms, especially states that had strategic Atlantic harbors. In 1488, four years before Christopher Columbus sailed to the Americas, a Muslim nobleman and Portuguese ally named Bemoim visited Portugal from his Wolof kingdom in modern-day Senegal. He sought Portuguese military assistance to regain his lost throne. The mission ended with Bemoim's death at the hands of his Portuguese patrons, but his visit marked the first of a long line of African nobles in Europe.[3]

From the 1480s through the 1700s, African nobles visited Portugal, Spain, and France. Most African nobles in early modern Europe lived in Portugal and came from the Congo. As early as the 1480s, a Congolese ambassador sailed to Portugal where he represented his nation.[4] In the 1490s, Congolese noble children lived in the Portuguese king's castle in Évora, Portugal. According to the modern historian Basil Davidson, 20 young Congolese students were sent to Europe in 1516. A few years later, the son of the Congolese king visited the pope in Rome. One Congolese prince became a bishop in the Catholic Church and was

[1] Jacques Heers, *Escravos E Servidão Doméstica Na Idade Média No Mundo Mediterranico* (Lisbon: Publicacões, 1983).
[2] Gomes Eannes de Azurara, *The Chronicle of the Discovery and Conquest of Guinea*, trans. and eds., Charles Raymond Beazley and Edgar Prestage (London: The Hakluyt Society, 1st wer., no. 100; reprint New York: Burt Franklin, 1899).
[3] José Goncalves and Paul Teyssier, "Textes Portugais sur les Wolofs au XV siècle—Batême du prince Bemoi (1488)" *Bulletin de'IFAN*, t. xxx, ser., B. no. 3 (Paris, 1968), 822–846.
[4] Antonio Brásio, Hortórica Do Reino Do Congo [Ms. 8080 da Biblioteca Nacional de Lisboa] (Lisboa: Centro De Estudos Historicos Ultramarinos, 1969).

then called Dom Henrique.[5] Other African ambassadors in early modern Portugal included representatives from Benin, Angola, and Ethiopia, as well as Serers from Senegal.

After Portuguese ships established direct maritime links with West Africans in 1441, other Africans migrated to Europe where many retained their freedom. A few enslaved Africans in Europe regained their liberty and formed free African communities. In the centuries after 1441, most free Africans in Europe lived in the Portuguese capital Lisbon, or in the Spanish cities Seville and Valencia. However, after the 1520s, small groups of free blacks were found in England, France, and Holland after these nations started trading directly with West Africa.

European historians record isolated cases of Africans who were set free when they arrived in Europe aboard European ships. For example, in 1571 France, "a shipowner placed some blacks on sale in Bordeaux, but they were ordered released by the Parlement."[6] Holland had a similar case, in 1596, when 130 Africans whom Captain Pieter van der Haagen had brought to Middleburg were set free by the town council and ordered to find jobs as free workers.[7] The English romanticize about Africans who regained their freedom upon setting foot on English soil.[8]

Some free Africans discovered innovative ways to maintain their freedom. As early as March 17, 1490, the black man Pedro Alvares secured a letter from the king of England certifying him to be a free man before he migrated to Portugal.[9] One enslaved African regained his freedom from his Portuguese master, Joao de Coimbra, on March 23, 1498, when he jumped ship in East Africa during Vasco da Gama's maiden voyage to India. These cases were the exception; as a rule most free blacks in Europe worked, saved money, and purchased their freedom, or that of their families.

Some free blacks in Portugal worked as mariners and translators aboard European merchant ships that traded in West Africa and the Americas. Portuguese archival records indicate that some blacks who were granted their freedom in a deceased master's will were still kept in bondage. On March 20, 1518, King Manuel of Portugal acted upon the request from a black fraternity in Lisbon to ensure that wills were honored.[10] Free blacks in Seville, Spain, also had a fraternity to protect their interests in the 16th century.[11] Once additional European nations joined Portugal and Spain in trading with Africa, free African communities appeared all over western Europe.

The majority of black Africans in early modern Europe lived in bondage. Most enslaved Africans lived in Lisbon, Portugal's capital city where the 9950 captives formed almost 10 percent of the population in 1551–1553.[12] Thousands of other enslaved Africans lived throughout Portugal, especially in the southern port towns in Algarve province. After Portugal, the greatest number of enslaved blacks lived in the Spanish cities of Seville and Valencia. From 1482 to 1516 some 5000 enslaved Africans arrived in Valencia from Portugal and its colonies.[13]

After the 1530s, France, England, and Holland sent ships to West Africa, and these European merchants transported captive Africans to Europe. By the early 1600s, England and France joined Spain and Portugal in establishing colonies in the West Indies and North America. Once European planters began exploiting enslaved African laborers in the Americas, plantation owners who returned to Europe transported captive Africans to Europe. Despite maritime trade from Africa to Europe, and planters bringing enslaved Africans from their Caribbean plantations, Europe never had more Africans than the 10 percent of 1551–1553 Lisbon.

[5] D. Charles-Martail De Witte, *Henri de Congo, Eveque titulaire d 'Utique* (Roma, 1968).
[6] William B. Cohen, *The French Encounter with Africans, White Response to Blacks, 1530–1880* (Bloomington: Indiana University Press, 1980), 5.
[7] Johannes Menne Posta, *The Dutch in the Atlantic Slave Trade, 1500–1815* (Cambridge: Cambridge University Press, 1990), 10.
[8] Folarin Shyllon, *Black People in Great Britain* (London: Oxford University Press, 1977).
[9] Arquivo Nacional da Torre do Tombo, "Chancelaria De. D. Joao II," livro 16, fol. 61. Printed in Azevedo "Os Escravos" *Archivo Historico Portuquez* 1, no. 9 (1903), 300.
[10] Arquivo Nacional da Torre de Tombo, "Chancelaria de D. Joao III," Liv. 22, fols. 100–100v, and Liv. 17, fol. 44v. Printed in Antonio Brásio, *Monumenta Missionaria Africana, Africa Ocidental,* 2d. ser. (1500–1569) (Lisboa: 1963), vol. 2, 151–152.
[11] Ruth Pike, *Aristocrats and Traders, Sevillian Society in the Sixteenth Century* (Ithaca: Cornell University Press, 1972).
[12] A. Saunders, *A Social History of Black Slaves and Freedmen in Portugal 1441–1555* (London: Cambridge University Press, 1982), 55.
[13] P. E. H. Hair, "Black African Slaves at Valencia, 1482–1516: An Onomastic Inquiry," *History in Africa* 7 (1980).

OUTSIDERS IN CHRISTIAN EUROPE: JEWS, MUSLIMS, AND BLACKS

The 16th and 17th centuries saw much of European life dominated by religious conflict between Catholics and Protestants. On the fringes of European society, a number of non-Christian religious minorities had maintained a precarious existence for centuries. Jews and Muslims lived side by side in Spain and Spanish possessions in Italy until 1492. Yet there were differences in the status of Muslims and Jews in Christian society. Muslims were tolerated partly because strong Muslim states with large Christian populations provided them with some degree of protection. In the Middle Ages, Jews were the only group to whom Christians granted the right of dissent. On the other hand, nowhere were Jews accorded the full rights of active citizenship. The coexistence of Jews and Christians was the result of a complex process, and Christian attitudes were fraught with contradictions. Over the centuries, the Jews encountered periods of expulsion and readmission.

The consolidation of the kingdom of Spain under Ferdinand and Isabella, together with the religious upheavals of the Reformation and Counter-Reformation, had a dramatic effect on the lives of the Jewish minority there. In the early 15th century, the largest concentrations of Jews in Europe were in Iberia, where perhaps 80,000 lived, as well as in Sicily, which had some 35,000. Another 35,000 Jews lived in Italy, while southern France and the German areas of the Holy Roman Empire had smaller numbers. As Jews were forced out of Spain, many moved to eastern Europe and others to the Ottoman Empire. In the 16th century, Jews were expelled from some Italian states, and by the end of that century, there were more than 100,000 Polish Jews (on Jewish life in Europe, see Part V, Topic 1).

This painting by Benozzo Gozzoli shows an African in a procession led by Galeazzo Sforza of Milan (far left, on brown horse) and Sigismondo Malatesta of Rimini (left, on gray horse).

As far back as the age of Classical Greece, artists portrayed blacks on painted vases and in small figurines. The earliest Africans to live in ancient Europe were the slaves brought by traders toward the end of the Roman Republic at the time of the Punic Wars. During the Roman Empire, slave traders imported Africans as both domestic and farm laborers. After the fall of the Empire, Muslim and Christian traders continued to bring black African slaves into the Byzantine Empire and North Africa. Although Medieval artists sometimes portrayed blacks in their works, the number of blacks in Europe remained small.

Blacks began to appear in Europe in larger numbers in the early 16th century, as a result of the Portuguese voyages of exploration. The increasing knowledge about remote regions of the world and their exotic inhabitants stimulated European curiosity about Africans. In addition to serving as domestic servants and manual laborers, blacks were prized as court entertainers and personal attendants for the ruling class. The early interest in Africa and its people would be replaced in later centuries by the horrors of the massive transatlantic slave trade.

Although European society during the Renaissance and Reformation underwent profound change, its effects were uneven.

Among the most significant developments of the period were the growth of urban life and the rise of the merchant classes, which introduced an element of unprecedented social mobility. Other features of social change included the new importance attributed to education among urban dwellers, and the growing number of women of the poorer classes who found work and new lives in the towns. These changes greatly modified existing patterns of marriage and family arrangements. Rural life, on the other hand, retained its essentially Medieval character of isolation and poverty as millions of peasants lived according to the cycle of nature.

Women were affected by the sweeping social changes in both favorable and unfavorable ways, depending on their status. The Renaissance, for example, saw the introduction of a double standard of sexual behavior for men and women. By contrast, poorer women who in earlier times had little opportunity to work outside the home now found new kinds of employment in the towns.

Still another new factor in society was the presence of a largely unknown minority—blacks from Africa—who, together with the Jews and Muslims, formed the only significant non-Christian elements in the population of Europe.

For all the inconsistency of these developments, the general impact was to intensify the slow but irrevocable breakdown of Medieval patterns of European life. The broad structural forces that were transforming Europe—urbanization, the emergence of a global economy, and the development of new modes of production—led in the 18th century to revolutionary change.

Questions for Further Study

1. What were the principal barriers to class mobility? Was movement between classes at all possible?
2. What social and cultural constraints limited the role of women in European society? Does the witchcraft craze reveal anything about attitudes toward women?
3. How did Christian society treat "outsiders"?

Suggestions for Further Reading

Barstow, Anne L. *Witchcraze: A New History of European Witch Hunts*. San Francisco, 1994.
Ben-Sasson, Haim Hillel. *A History of the Jewish People*. Cambridge, MA, 1976.
Davis, Natalie Zemon. *Society and Culture in Early Modern France*. Stanford, CA, 1975.
Hale, John R. *Renaissance Europe: The Individual and Society*. London, 1971.
Herlihy, David. *The Family in Renaissance Italy*. St. Louis, 1974.
Kedar, Benjamin Z. *Crusade and Mission: European Approaches Towards the Muslim*. Princeton, NJ, 1984.
Klapisch-Zuber, Christine. *Women, Family, and Ritual in Renaissance Italy*. Chicago, 1985.
Levack, Brian P. *The Witch-Hunt in Early Modern Europe*. New York, 1987.
Ozment, Steven. *When Fathers Ruled: Family Life in Reformation Europe*. Cambridge, MA, 1983.
Pullan, Brian. *Rich and Poor in Renaissance Venice*. Cambridge, MA, 1971.
Rocke, Michael. *Forbidden Friendships: Homosexuality and Male Culture in Renaissance Florence*. New York, 1996.
Ruggiero, Guido. *The Boundaries of Eros: Sex, Crime and Sexuality in Renaissance Venice*. Oxford, 1985.
Stone, Lawrence. *The Family, Sex and Marriage in England, 1500–1800*. New York, 1979.

PART V

The Early Modern World

The hundred and fifty years following the start of the Protestant Reformation—that is, from 1500 to 1650—were marked by the intensification and culmination of many trends that had begun much earlier. Although the Reformation had caused serious conflicts and left deep divisions, Europe began a period of political consolidation, of growth and expansion, and of cultural innovation, that established its global primacy.

In politics, the early modern period saw the successful concentration of power in the hands of absolutist monarchs in their long struggle with the nobles, and the honing of the bureaucratic power of the state. In England, Henry VIII defied the papacy and established Protestantism in his realm, disciplined the nobility, and bent Parliament to his will. His daughter Elizabeth, avoiding direct confrontation, achieved an uneasy balance in her

relationship with Parliament, but her successors, James I and Charles I, again took up the struggle. The result was a far-reaching civil war that led to the triumph of Parliament and the temporary end of the monarchy. There followed a period of military dictatorship under Oliver Cromwell. Only then, after the English had experimented with alternative forms of government, did they return to the monarchy, but in a form that would share power increasingly with Parliament.

England was the exception to the rule of increasing royal power. In Spain, for example, King Philip II micro-managed almost singlehandedly not only his kingdom but also a vast overseas empire. In France in the 16th and 17th centuries, monarchs laid the foundations of absolutism, building up the royal administration, taming the nobility, and securing state authority over the appointment of bishops and other ecclesiastical officials. The trend reached its apogee with the reign of Louis XIV in the second half of the 17th century.

The age was further characterized by bitter religious conflicts that were in part the legacy of the Protestant Reformation and in part the result of politics. Protestantism gave new urgency to trends toward spiritual and institutional reform that already existed within the Catholic Church. The Council of Trent produced a huge body of revised doctrine and settled a number of important disputes raging within the church. New religious orders such as the Jesuits were founded to work in society at large, and old institutions such as the Inquisition were revived, to take the religious struggle to the people and combat Protestantism.

Religion continued to dominate European politics in the age of the Reformation. In the 16th and 17th centuries, religious wars devastated Germany, shaped much of the domestic history of France, and greatly influenced events in Spain and England. In eastern Europe the offensive launched against Protestantism by the Catholic Church ensured that the region remained largely immune to Protestantism. From 1618 to 1648, most of Europe's great powers were drawn into a terrible religious and secular conflict known as the Thirty Years' War. And while the antagonism between Catholics and Protestants was an important factor in bringing about the war, the conflict also involved an international dynastic struggle between the Bourbon dynasty of France and the Hapsburgs of Spain and the Holy Roman Empire.

Despite the rapid pace of political and religious change, the social patterns of everyday life retained strong links with the Medieval world and changed slowly over the centuries. This gradual evolution influenced the basic aspects of daily experience, including the health and well-being of all classes of Europeans, their diet and housing, and the way in which they dressed. The Western economy was transformed more rapidly. The period was one of economic growth, although not without its difficulties. The principal change after 1500 was the shift in trade patterns from the Mediterranean to the Atlantic and northern European coasts. The resulting commercial revolution was dominated at first by Spain and Portugal, but later by the English and particularly by the emergence of the Dutch Republic.

The cultural life of Europe in the early modern period was characterized by the emergence of a new style known as the Baroque. In the Renaissance, artists had sought ideal principles of beauty and harmony that expressed eternal values. Baroque artists, by contrast, tried to express the emotional states of individuals, whether in words, music, or painting. In doing so, they laid the ground for the arts in the modern era with their search for self-expression and the answers to personal questions. Moreover, Baroque art and architecture were ideally suited to the glorification of the new absolutist monarchs.There was no more striking example of the use of the Baroque in this sense than the immense Palace of Versailles built to glorify the reign of the "Sun King," Louis XIV.

V

Topic 1

Catholic Reform and the Counter-Reformation

The age of the Reformation was also a time of great renewal and change within the Catholic Church. This Catholic reform movement was partly due to the fact that the call for change inspired many devout Catholics to renew their religious faith and restore the purity of their church. After all, there had been Catholic reformers long before Luther and Calvin. On the other hand, the startling spread of Protestantism and the victories scored by the reformers and monarchs alike in breaking with Rome had driven the papacy and the Catholic hierarchy to clean out their own house. As the Catholic Church began to be energized by its own reforms, the papacy struck back at the Protestants, declaring war against them everywhere and creating new institutions to combat the heresies of the day.

The Council of Trent that first met in 1545 began the process of both reaffirming the theological principles of the church and of launching the Counter-Reformation. Moreover, new religious orders dedicated to Catholic revival were founded by Angela Merici and Ignatius Loyola, while the papacy itself established the Inquisition to stamp out heretics. By the late 16th century, the offensive of the Catholic Church had not destroyed Protestantism but had at least halted its spread. Yet in international relations, the religious controversies of the age would continue to be fought out for almost another century.

The Catholic Church and the Spirit of Renewal

Spiritual renewal and institutional reform were not new to the Catholic Church. Throughout the Middle Ages, movements had arisen within the faith to end corruption and rekindle popular belief, and some of these efforts were responses to broader problems in European society. The plague and other problems of the 14th century inspired many Christians to seek new sources of religious comfort and a more immediate communion with God. This new concern for spirituality also evolved in the context of the crisis provoked by the Babylonian Captivity and the Great Schism (see Part III, Topic 12).

The Roots of Catholic Reform

The resulting growth in popular devotion was expressed by turning away from the formal religious practices of the church to mysticism and new forms of piety. Popular religious practices, like the payment of indulgences to escape the consequences of sin, were designed to generate divine grace and achieve salvation; they included pilgrimages, processions, and special masses for the dead. Many devout Christians joined special lay branches of the mendicant orders founded by St. Dominic and St. Francis. They also founded religious "confraternities" that engaged in charity work while reaffirming spirituality.

The most significant expression of the new piety was mysticism. Mystics were convinced that believers experienced God not through theological discourse or institutional rituals but rather through love and emotional availability. Mystics sought to establish a sense of union with God through contemplation and spiritual meditation.

The focus of popular mysticism in the 14th century was the Rhine Valley of western Germany, where Meister Eckhart (1260–1327) developed a large following through his impassioned preaching. Eckhart denied the importance of traditional dogma, stressing instead the cultivation of a "divine spark" that would achieve oneness with God. Lay followers of the Dutch mystic Gerhard Groote (1340–1384) founded the Brethren of the Common Life for men and a similar organization known as the Sisters of the Common Life for women. Groote advocated a new form of piety known as Modern Devotion *(devotio moderna)*.

Groote maintained that communion with God could best be achieved by imitating Christ and devoting oneself to good works. His followers founded schools and lived according to self-imposed rules of simplicity and humility. The best known of the Brethren was Thomas à Kempis, who in 1425 wrote a kind of manual entitled *The Imitation of Christ* that stressed ethical behavior and the attainment of internal peace and tranquillity.

This famous image by Albrecht Dürer, "The Knight, Death, and the Devil," was an illustration for Erasmus' *Handbook of the Militant Christian* and renders a sense of confidence in a world beset by temptation.

A number of localized efforts at church reform had been attempted in the late 15th and early 16th centuries. The Dominican friar Girolamo Savonarola (1452–1498) had tried to bring discipline and moral leadership to the people of Florence, where he held sway for two years before the church ordered his execution for heresy. Working within the church had been Cardinal Francisco Ximines (c. 1437–1517), confessor to Queen Isabella of Spain. He imposed stricter controls over the clergy and infused the Spanish Church with a spirit of discipline and fervor. New religious orders, such as the Capuchins, reached out to the common people in an effort to help improve the lives of the poor and the sick. But leadership from Rome seemed to be needed if the church was to transform itself in a significant way.

Significant Dates

Catholic Reform and Counter-Reform

1425	Thomas à Kempis writes *The Imitation of Christ*
1478	Spanish Inquisition established
1492	Jews expelled from Spain
1452–1498	Life of Savonarola
1542	Papal Inquisition revived
1534–1549	Paul III reigns as pope
1545–1563	Council of Trent
1491–1556	Life of Ignatius Loyola
1515–1582	Life of Teresa of Avila
1600	Giordano Bruno burned at the stake

Pope Paul III

Soon after Luther launched the Protestant revolution against Rome, the Catholic Church had at its head a zealous and learned pope, Paul III (ruled 1534–1549). Paul had been a cardinal from the powerful Roman Farnese family and stood out among his fellow cardinals as an astute diplomat and genuine reformer. Throughout his reign he patronized the great artists of his day, especially Michelangelo, and rebuilt many of the streets and neighborhoods of Rome.

Paul's election to the papacy came at a crucial time, for to many the church appeared on the edge of collapse. Paul gave vigorous leadership to the reforming party within the hierarchy, favoring the calling of a new council that would try to reconcile Protestants and Catholics and reform the church. Attacking the worldliness of the clergy, Paul appointed a special commission of ardent reformers to advise him. The commission recommended curbing the abuses in the sale of indulgences and reported to the pope on the corruption of high officials and cardinals. Paul appointed many new, reform-minded members of the College of Cardinals, and approved the establishment of the Jesuit order.

The Council of Trent

Paul's commission also aided in the detailed preparations for the Council of Trent, the great meeting of church reformers that he had proposed for ten years. The more reactionary-minded clergy had steadily and bitterly opposed the idea of a council, which held its first session in the northern Italian city of Trento in 1545. Just as it began to get down to serious work, however, Paul died, so that the reform initiative was deprived of his leadership.

The council, which met on and off until 1563, devoted its energies to settling theological questions, reinforcing traditions within the church, and to organizing a counterattack against the Protestants. Its sessions were often stormy and rife with dissension and division. Yet in the end, some important decisions were reached. The council condemned the selling of church offices and fake indulgences, limited the secular activities of the clergy, and demanded greater supervision of the clergy by bishops and cardinals. Greater emphasis was placed on quality education for priests, including the opening of many new seminaries. Bishops were now required to live in their dioceses and priests and monks were exhorted to go among the people to preach and act as personal examples of spiritual uprightness. In the war against the Protestants, the council emphasized the importance of church tradition that went back centuries, an approach the Protestants countered with the argument that the church was a human institution.

In the theological sphere, the Council of Trent reaffirmed the basic doctrines that Luther and the Protestant reforms had challenged. These included in particular the seven sacraments, the idea of salvation by good works as well as by faith, and the doctrine of transubstantiation that held that the bread and wine of the communion became by miracle the body and blood of Christ. The Latin translation of the Bible known as the Vulgate was proclaimed as the official version of the Scriptures, the veneration of saints and relics was reasserted, and the clergy were forbidden to marry. These and other changes gave the reform-minded clergy a new sense of energy and provided them with a sense of righteousness in their battle against the Protestants.

The Venetian artist Titian conveyed the solemn nature of the proceedings in the Council of Trent in this painting of 1586.

EDUCATION AND CONVERSION: THE JESUITS AND THE URSULINES

The reforming spirit that Paul had inaugurated resulted in the creation of a number of new religious orders. The Capuchins, a Franciscan brotherhood, devoted themselves to preaching and working among the poor, while the Theatines focused on inspiring faith among the clergy itself. The most famous and important of the new organizations, however, was the Society of Jesus.

Ignatius Loyola and the Jesuits

The Jesuit order, as it is more commonly known, was founded by a Spanish soldier, later priest, named Ignatius Loyola (1491–1556). Loyola, descended from a noble family of the Basque country, had been a soldier in the army of Charles V. While convalescing from wounds he had received in 1521, Loyola began reading the lives of religious figures, including biographies of St. Francis and St. Dominic. As a result, he underwent a conversion and dedicated his life to doing God's work. Loyola engaged in meditation exercises and studied at universities in Spain and France, and in the process developed a small but dedicated following.

Ignatius Loyola, shown here in a 16th-century engraving after a portrait from life.

Loyola founded his society in 1524 at the University of Paris. He wrote *Spiritual Exercises*, a work of powerful Christian inspiration and spiritual discipline, claiming that through critical self-study and the surrender of individual will, each person is able to achieve union with God. His teachings insisted on the importance of obedience and self-discipline rather than the exercise of free choice. Ironically, Loyola himself several times came under suspicion by the Inquisition.

En route to Palestine to convert the Muslims, Loyola and his disciples, chief among them Francis Xavier, found themselves in Italy when they learned that unsettled conditions in the Holy Land made it impossible for them to continue their journey. They decided to remain in Italy and preach their message of devotion there. In 1537, he and his followers were ordained in Rome and two years later he sent a draft of a constitution for a new order to the papacy for approval. In 1540 Pope Paul III endorsed it. The plan called for a centralized order governed along military lines by a "general" who reported directly to the pope. The Jesuits took the same kind of vows of poverty and chastity as members of other orders but were devoted to a militant spirit of defending and advancing the faith.

The Jesuits were trained to push back Protestantism by working among the Catholic masses as well as among their leaders. To the common people they preached the need for confession. They restructured secondary education so as to instill Catholic devotion in the young. In this spirit they launched a program to found a series of schools, later known as colleges, to provide Catholic education and discipline for tens of thousands of boys from among the poor as well as the upper classes. The Jesuit curriculum linked humanist education with Catholic religious teachings. Their schools became the training ground for generations of religious and secular leaders, many of whom found employment in the burgeoning state bureaucracies. In this way, the Jesuit order was able to influence government policies indirectly, while many Jesuits actually became private confessors to important nobles and rulers.

In the spirit of their new militancy, the Jesuits embarked on a worldwide program of missionary work aimed at converting "heathens" in Asia, Africa, and the Americas to the Catholic faith. By the end of the 16th century, Jesuit missions had been established in China, Japan, the Congo, Brazil, Mexico, and many other distant outposts of Catholic activity. Some of their missionaries, such as Francis Xavier and Matteo Ricci, achieved widespread fame as zealous bearers of God's word to non-Christian civilizations around the world.

The Jesuit order was to achieve significant influence in secular as well as religious affairs, especially because of their educational programs and their private influence on individual monarchs. Yet the Jesuit experience was originally conceived as a weapon in the war for religious conviction that had been launched by the Protestant revolt. Loyola's "soldiers of Christ" were sometimes viewed too literally as religious warriors, but certainly he himself was consumed with the passion for discipline and proselytizing. In 1622, the church made Loyola a saint.

The Ursulines and Catholic Women

Societies devoted to religious work by and among women had been founded before Luther's time. The Sisters of the Common Life, for example, had been inspired by the movement for popular religious devotion. St. Teresa of Avila (1515–1582) founded the Carmelite order of nuns who devoted themselves to works of charity.

Most similar to the Jesuits, however, was the Ursuline order, founded by St. Angela Merici (1473–1540). The Ursulines were essentially an order of teaching nuns designed to educate girls in religious and moral affairs. Of Venetian background, the young Merici had been inspired by the good works of local nuns and religious orders and volunteered to work with the Franciscan monks. In 1516, she founded a girl's school for scriptural instruction. While never taking official church vows, Merici devoted herself to helping the sick and the poor. In 1535, she founded the Company of St. Ursula, which was modeled on the Franciscan order. Because her followers—that is, women—chose to work among the people rather than remain in secluded cloisters, it was only some 30 years later that the papacy finally extended formal approval to the company.

THE WAR AGAINST THE HERETICS: THE SACRED CONGREGATION OF THE HOLY OFFICE

The reforms instituted from above by Pope Paul III were complemented by the devotion, discipline, and fervor of countless reformers such as Loyola and Merici. It was through the Inquisition, however, that the church fought its unremitting war against those who had left the Catholic fold. The Inquisition was, of course, only one aspect of the campaign that the church waged against Protestantism. The wider struggle involved the use of military and political influence as well as missionary activity around the world. The harsh and often brutal techniques of the Inquisition, far from advancing the cause, frequently sparked the opposite

St. Teresa of Avila, a devoted visionary, founded the Carmelite order of nuns.

PERSPECTIVES ON HISTORY

The Social Life of European Jewry

Elisheva Carlebach
Queens College, City University of New York

"It passes belief, all the strange things that can happen to us . . . " So wrote Glikl Hameln, a 17th-century Jewish woman, in her remarkable memoir. In it she promised to tell "everything that has happened to me from my youth upward," as a family remembrance and ethical guide for her twelve children. From her colorful descriptions we can glean some of the most important aspects of 17th-century western European Jewish life. Glikl belonged to a class of Jews who were able to prosper during times of turmoil as the Medieval anti-Jewish barriers in western and central Europe began to break down. Her writing provides a marvelous look at the inner rhythms of Jewish life as well as the external forces that shaped it.

Glikl lived in Hamburg, a north German port city which contained two small but separate Jewish communities. The *Ashkenazi* community was comprised of Jews of eastern and central European background; their language of daily discourse was Yiddish. One of Glikl's earliest memories was caring for Jewish refugees who fled westward from Poland's Cossack Rebellion of 1648. The *Sephardi* community, wealthier and more urbane, boasted a splendid synagogue. Its members were descendants of the Jews who had been expelled from Spain and Portugal at the end of the 15th century. Tens of thousands of exiles were left to seek new domiciles; a good number began to settle in western Europe in the 17th century. Many members of the Sephardi community had lived as *marranos*, secret Jews who passed down their Jewish identity for generations until they could escape the coercive pressures of the post–1492 Iberian world.

The Reformation shattered the absolute authority of the Roman Church throughout Europe and paved the way for Jews and members of other religious minorities to be viewed in a more just and realistic way. Although some founders of Protestantism held to malevolent Medieval images of Jews, the prolonged struggle over religious beliefs ultimately led to greater tolerance of different faiths. The chaos caused by the religious wars provided some Jews in central Europe entry into nascent economies. Glikl's family seems to have prospered as a result of the Thirty Years' War (1618–1648) when both sides of the conflict turned to Jewish financiers and suppliers. The new class of European Jews that emerged used their influence to become advocates for Jewish causes, founders of new communities, and patrons of Jewish scholarship.

Events such as the advance of the Ottoman Empire, the rupture in the church, and constant warfare, appeared fearful and momentous to Europeans. These upheavals caused many Europeans, Christian and Jewish, to hope that the end of history was near. Several aspiring redeemers were announced; one 16th-century hopeful, David Reubeni, was greeted by the pope and the emperor. Glikl recalled the excitement of the appearance of Sabbatai Zevi in 1665, leader of a very widespread Jewish messianic movement:

> Throughout the world Thy servants and children rent themselves with repentance, prayer, and charity . . . My good father-in-law left his home in Hameln . . . sent . . . two enormous casks packed with linens and with peas, beans, and dried meats, shredded prunes . . . all manner of food that would keep. For the old man expected to sail any moment from Hamburg to the Holy Land. . . .[1]

While some kings and princes banned Jews from their territories, others pursued more lenient, or sometimes inconsistent policies. The reason for toleration of Jewish communities usually had less to do with the religious or cultural life of Jews than with the economic self-interest of the ruler. Because Jews had been excluded for centuries from land

[1] *The Memoirs of Gluckel of Hameln*, trans. Marvin Lowenthal (New York: Schocken Books, 1977), 45–46.

ownership as well as from crafts guilds, they developed acumen in the areas that were less restricted for them, finance and commerce. The exiled Spanish and Portuguese Jews and the marranos who followed them into Europe acquired a reputation for developing commerce on a grand scale. Retaining or readmitting Jews in western Europe came about as a result of a desire to develop national economies. When an Italian Jew, Simone Luzzatto, presented a plea for toleration to the Venetian authorities in the 17th century, or Menasseh ben Israel petitioned Oliver Cromwell to permit Jews to return to England, their arguments centered on the idea that a flourishing Jewish community aided the commercial and economic development of the cities and nations in which they lived. England and the Netherlands permitted Jews to settle for the purpose of developing their economies. The Jewish resettlement in western Europe reversed a centuries-long Medieval process of expulsion of Jews that had emptied the region of its Jewish communities.

Despite new economic and social opportunities, most European Jews in the 16th through 18th centuries still lived under great restrictions. In many cities, Jews were legally restricted to residing in quarters known as ghettos. The word *ghetto* may have originated from the Italian word for *foundry*, the area of Venice which became the compulsory quarter for Jews in 1516. Jewish quarters existed throughout Europe, in Frankfurt, in Prague, in Rome, in some cases through the 19th century. Surrounded by walls, gates bolted at night, their purpose was to separate Jews from others in every socially significant way. The walled ghetto meant that Jews could not expand their quarters horizontally as their population grew by nature and immigration. Instead, they were forced to extend their living space by building vertically, erecting structures which were higher and closer together than in other areas of European cities. These conditions made the ghettos seem darker, more crowded, and with poorer sanitation than anywhere else in Europe. Ghetto populations were also more vulnerable to plagues and fires than other urban districts. When Christian masses were aroused by anti-Jewish agitation, the same conditions of the ghetto made it more dangerous. When Christian clerics wanted to use coercive measures, from compulsory sermons to burnings of Jewish books, as for example the Talmud in 1553, they knew just where to locate their targets.

Yet a closer look at life inside the ghetto walls, and the many ways these walls were breached, shows a more complex picture. During the Renaissance period, Jews and Christians mingled rather freely during the day. Jews left the ghetto to conduct every sort of business, including serving as physicians and teachers of Hebrew to Christians. Christians found many reasons, curiosity among them, to visit the crowded ghetto.

Nowhere were the paradoxes of a transitional age more evident than in the Italian ghetto, where an indigenous Renaissance culture continued to exert its influence despite the reversals of the Counter-Reformation. The same walls which created harsh restrictions and a sense of inferior difference, also became a place of nurturing values and protection from the dangers that lurked outside. A rich Jewish cultural life flourished within those walls. Universal respect for all forms of learning meant that books and ideas from many cultures quickly found their way inside the ghetto. Prosperous Jewish parents hired private tutors for their children, male and often female as well; the poor were taught in community-funded schools. The Bible and Talmud along with their commentaries formed the basis of every male child's education. The 17th-century rabbi Leon Modena writes that as a youth in the ghetto of Venice, he was taught Latin, music, dance, writing, and drama direction, in addition to his Jewish religious education. In an age when the lines between magic and science were not yet clearly delineated, Jews in early modern Europe participated in many intellectual enterprises. Abraham Zacuto's astronomical tables were used by navigators all over the world, including the crew of Christopher Columbus. The pathbreaking philosophical works of Benedict Spinoza provide a foundation for modern European thought; they contain some of the earliest arguments for complete separation of church and state. Jewish scholars in many countries exchanged manuscripts and letters on

continued next page

the fine points of Jewish law from issues of life and death to the status of a game of tennis on the Sabbath.

Jewish communities maintained a strong and distinctive social organization. Jews educated their own young, cared for their sick and poor, and buried their dead within the framework of an autonomous judicial and cultural structure, known as the *Kehillah*. In addition to serving the traditional functions of worship and study, synagogues also functioned as social centers where news and information circulated together with official announcements.

In addition to the formal communal structures, and essential to the fabric of daily life, were the overlapping networks of voluntary associations. Their goals were religious, educational, or social, such as study of holy texts, dowering poor brides, or occupational association. Rich and poor lived in close proximity, creating a sense of mutual responsibility that expressed itself in every conceivable form of charitable endeavor.

These configurations of Jewish life, which combined Medieval elements with recent European developments, endured through the late 18th century. The ideals of the Enlightenment began to change European thought, so that segregation on the basis of religion no longer remained acceptable policy for European states. When the French Revolution implemented the changes, Jews were granted legal and civic equality.

effect and gave the Counter-Reformation a negative reputation.

The Inquisition

The movement known as the Inquisition had been suggested by Loyola himself with the support of Cardinal Giampietro Caraffa (ruled as Pope Paul IV 1555–1559), who became its head. Nevertheless, there had been precedents, including the formal papal Inquisition established in 1233 by Gregory IX, who had placed the war against the Albigensian heretics in the hands of the Dominicans.

The Dominican friar Savonarola attempted to impose order and morality on Florence and was burned at the stake for heresy.

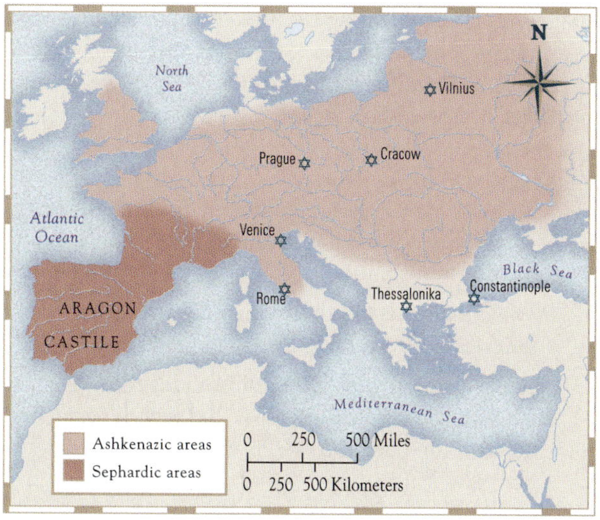

Map 1.1 The Two Major Divisions of European Jewry

The Inquisition, like its Medieval predecessor, was a traveling tribunal that conducted inquiries in various locations. Persons accused of heresy were not given the names of their accusers, although they were often permitted to list their enemies as a way of checking against false accusations. Those who refused to confess were tried, often with the use of torture to extract confessions—and without confession, there could be no conviction. Because heresy was considered a civil as well as a religious crime, those found guilty were punished by the local rulers rather than by the church itself. Penance, fine, and imprisonment were the usual penalties, although burning at the stake was also used. The most notorious manifestation of the Inquisition was the so-called Spanish Inquisition, established in 1478 and headed by the infamous Tomas de Torquemada. Those responsible for the Inquisition in Spain often abused their authority and were fanatical in their efforts to uncover heretics and other nonconformists, including homosexuals and practitioners of magic.

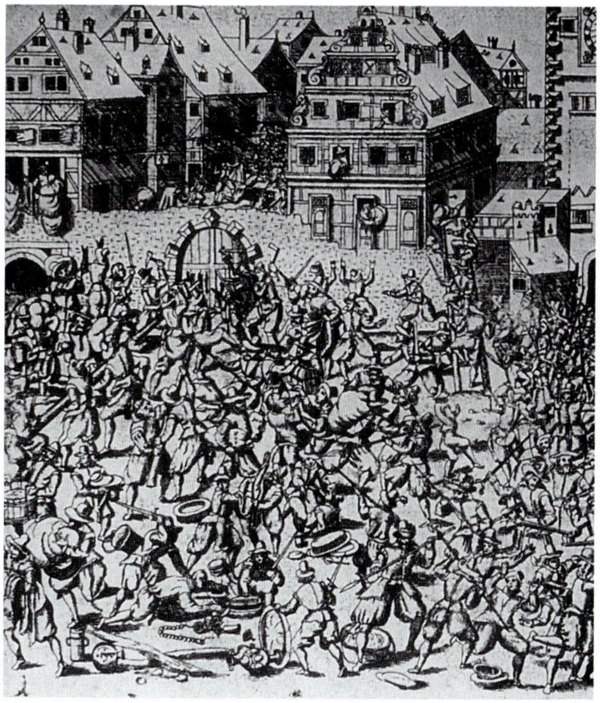

Jews were often the target of prejudice and resentment and, as in the case of the attack against them in Frankfurt (1614) illustrated here, of violence.

In 1542, Pope Paul III revived the Inquisition and assigned it to the Sacred Congregation of the Holy Office under Cardinal Caraffa and six fellow cardinals. Known as the Roman Inquisition, its purpose was to combat Protestantism, but its effects were more widespread. It did succeed in eliminating most vestiges of Protestantism in the Italian states, although pockets of the older Waldensians still remained (see Part III, Topic 8).

The Inquisition demanded religious and intellectual conformity and terrorized university professors as well as students. It was the Roman Inquisition that burned the Dominican philosopher Giordano Bruno (1548–1600) at the stake for his ideas about the nature of the physical universe, just as it was responsible for trying Galileo, the Italian astronomer and mathematician, in 1633 for similar ideas. To prevent the spread of dangerous ideas, the Sacred Congregation instituted an *Index of Prohibited Books*, which established a master list of works that Catholics should not read.

The Jews in the Age of the Counter-Reformation

The era of the Reformation and the Counter-Reformation created an atmosphere of repression and intolerance that also extended to non-Christians throughout society. The Spanish Inquisition had targeted those Jews who had converted to Christianity, known as the *conversos*. Many of these converted Jews continued to practice their own religion in secret. Over the next half century, more than 100,000 Jews emigrated, among them some of the most important merchants, physicians, and bankers.

The Jews were further victimized by the climate of religious zeal in the countries most affected by the Reformation. The German princes who followed Luther's teachings grew increasingly concerned about their Jewish populations when Luther found himself unable to convert them to his doctrines. As a result, many were expelled and their synagogues closed. In Italy, the formerly tolerant policies of the papacy were abandoned under the influence of the Inquisition and in the mid-16th century the first *ghettos*—defined districts within which local Jews were forced to live behind walls and locked gates—were established in Venice and Rome. Nonetheless, Jewish communities throughout Europe managed to maintain a rich and vibrant social and cultural life.

Whether the movement for religious and spiritual renewal is called the Catholic Reformation, as Catholics describe it, or the Counter-Reformation, as Protestants refer to it, there is no doubt that significant change and renewal took place among Catholic believers as well as among leaders of the church. It is also clear that by the end of the 16th century the influence and power of the Roman Catholic Church had been greatly reduced in places where Protestants took over. Almost everywhere secular rulers had taken advantage of the church's weakness to assert their control over the religious lives of their subjects and the ecclesiastical institutions in their realms.

While rulers everywhere assumed greater authority over the church, in countries that remained Catholic, such as Spain, the monarchs sometimes assisted the church in stamping out Protestantism. The centuries-long tradition of alliance between altar and throne had proven a useful tool of governance and was not easily or lightly broken. But despite the vigorous leadership provided to the church by Pope Paul III and the powerful reforming impulse generated by Loyola and others, few Catholic leaders of the late 16th century expected Protestantism to disappear. Moreover, the deep and often bitter religious disputes of the age would continue to affect secular affairs in profound ways. The century and a half following the start of Luther's movement was an age of religious wars. In Europe as a whole, the cultural and spiritual unity that had marked the Middle Ages had been irretrievably shattered.

Questions for Further Study

1. To what extent was the movement for change within the church a Catholic reform or a Catholic counter-reformation?
2. What methods did the Inquisition use against heretics? How did it justify such practices?
3. In the generally hostile environment that was Christian Europe, what forms did Jewish social and cultural life take and under what constraints did it thrive?

Suggestions for Further Reading

Caraman, Philip. *Ignatius Loyola*. San Francisco, 1990.

Evennett, Henry O. *The Spirit of the Counter-Reformation*. Notre Dame, IN, 1970.

Fulop-Miller, Rene. *The Jesuits: A History of the Society of Jesus*. New York, 1963.

Jedin, Hubert. *History of the Council of Trent*, trans. E. Graf, 2 vols. London, 1957–1961.

Jensen, D. Lamar. *Reformation Europe: Age of Reform and Revolution*. Lexington, KY, 1981.

O'Connell, Marvin R. *The Counter Reformation, 1559–1610*. New York, 1974.

Po-Chia Hsia, R. *Society and Reformation in Munster, 1535–1618*. New Haven, CT, 1984.

Williams, George H. *The Radical Reformation*. Philadelphia, 1962.

V

Topic 2

Catholic Spain and the Struggle for Supremacy

For many decades following the beginning of the Protestant Reformation, religion continued to dominate European politics. Religious wars racked Germany until the Peace of Augsburg in 1555, defined much of the domestic history of France, and greatly influenced events in England. In Eastern Europe the offensive launched against Protestantism by the Catholic Church ensured that the region remained largely immune to Protestantism.

Nowhere was the primacy of religion stronger than in the Spain of Philip II. A controversial figure whose historical image has been shaped largely by the religious question, Philip saw himself as the champion of Catholicism. Following in the tradition of his father, the Emperor Charles V, Philip undertook to free Spain of religious differences and remove all traces of dissent, moving in ruthless fashion against the Jews and Muslims of the kingdom. He very much acted the role of the "new monarch," building a highly centralized administration in the tradition of absolutism. He tried, too, to strengthen Spain's hold on its huge colonial possessions in the Americas and to extract from them the maximum profit.

Even under the "most Catholic monarch," the influence of religion on public policy was limited. Moreover, religious controversies prevented Philip from focusing on building and improving the government administration. In the Spanish Netherlands, where first the Anabaptists and then Lutheranism and Calvinism took hold, a bitter religious struggle for power led to a revolt of far-reaching consequences. Nor did Spain's foreign affairs escape the pernicious influence of religious struggle. After the diplomatic settlement with France in 1559, which recognized Spain's predominance in the Netherlands and in Italy, Philip became trapped in a monumental struggle for supremacy with Protestant England that ended in the ignominious defeat of the Spanish Armada.

RELIGION AND MONARCHY: THE REIGN OF PHILIP II

Philip II (ruled 1556–1598) inherited the crown and the burdens of a far-flung empire from his father, the Emperor Charles V, who retired to a monastery in 1556 (see Part IV, Topic 1). Philip's uncle Ferdinand, who became the new Holy Roman emperor, received control of Austria, Bohemia, and Hungary. Philip became ruler of the Hapsburg domains in Italy—Milan, Naples and Sicily—as well as of the Netherlands and Spain, and Spanish colonies outside of Europe.

At the time, Spain was thought to have possessed the greatest military force and was one of the wealthiest states in the West, thanks largely to the silver and gold bullion supplied by the American colonies. Although a relatively large country, it was thinly populated and lacked significant resources of its own. When the king of Portugal died in 1580 without an heir, Philip occupied the country, laying claim to it because his mother was Isabella of Portugal and he himself had married Maria of Portugal (Portugal remained a Spanish possession until a revolt in 1640 secured its independence).

Significant Dates

The Spanish Empire

1566	Revolt in the Netherlands erupts
1571	Ottomans defeated at Battle of Lepanto
1576	Pacification of Ghent
1579	Union of Arras
1588	Defeat of the Armada
1556–1598	Philip II reigns as king of Spain
1618	Thirty Years' War breaks out
1640	Portugal achieves independence
1648	United Provinces achieve independence

The legacy Philip inherited when he became king also included a fierce Catholicism, for the *reconquista* and the Spanish Inquisition had given Spain a reputation as the bastion of the Roman Catholic Church.

Philip II of Spain, the most powerful monarch of his age and Mary Tudor, daughter of Henry VIII, married in 1554. Philip hoped Mary would succeed in restoring Catholicism to England.

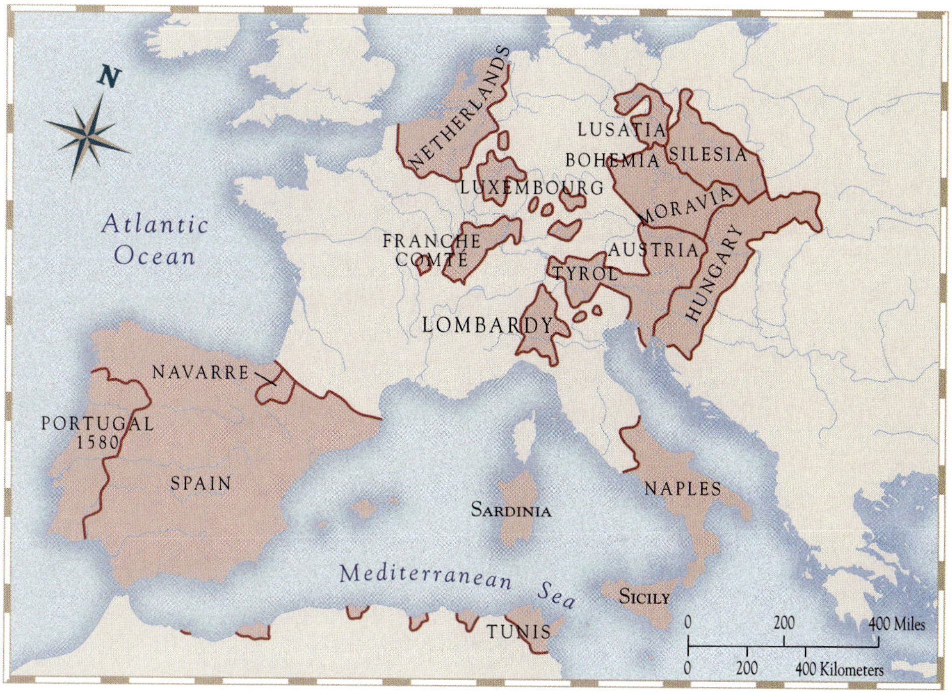

Map 2.1 The European Empire of Philip II

Politics and Religion in Hapsburg Spain

Philip assumed the throne of Spain along with serious burdens, including the task of combating Protestantism in Europe and the Ottoman Turks in the Mediterranean. Moreover, the question of how to keep his widely spread possessions together concerned him deeply. Philip was an intensely serious and deeply religious man who seldom revealed his emotions. He married four times, but always for diplomatic reasons rather than for love, and he seldom spent time with his family. His father had imbued him with a deep distrust of official advisers, and especially of women, so that he tried to keep his own counsel as much as possible.

Despite his religious faith, Philip was a shrewd and calculating ruler who used the church to further his domestic and foreign policies. He was not above employing the Inquisition to destroy resistance to his authority among the nobles and middle class. Philip, like other new monarchs, worked to undermine the power of the church in his country. He insisted on his right to appoint clerical officials in Spain and objected to the pope's control over ecclesiastical courts in his realm. When the influence of the Jesuits grew too powerful, he resisted their policies, and acted in defiance of several popes when they challenged his authority. Philip aided the church when it did not undermine his absolutism but insisted in return that it be a loyal ally of the government. The deep faith of his subjects enabled the king to use religion to arouse popular consensus behind the monarchy.

As a ruler, Philip was a micro-manager who refused to allow his bureaucrats to make most of their decisions without his direct involvement. He spent much of his time in the seclusion of his private office in the Escorial palace outside of Madrid, working on official papers. Heeding his father's advice too well, he was unable to delegate any significant power. Nor did he broach any limitations on his authority. In each of the former kingdoms which constituted the Spanish crown, such as Castile, Aragon, and León, a *Cortes*, or Medieval assembly representing the clergy, nobles, and commoners, often gave Philip considerable trouble. Only in Castile, where he concentrated his attention, was he able to use the *Cortes* to rubber stamp his decisions and legislated personally through the royal decrees. The rest of the kingdom was less effectively managed. In his other European possessions, as well as in the American empire, he used viceroys to represent and implement his will, but he constantly fought the obstructionism of the powerful nobility. Moreover, the slowness of communications in the 16th century made colonial administration all the more difficult.

The administration of Philip's vast empire required tremendous resources, especially as he was almost constantly at war somewhere in the world. Nevertheless, only the more prosperous Castile and the American colonies provided much needed revenue, whereas the bankers and nobles of the Low Countries felt that Spain was a drain on local resources. In Spain,

Philip II's goal was to stamp out all forms of religion except Catholicism in his realm. Here a Spanish relief depicts the baptism of Muslim women.

the church owned half of the landed estates and the nobles owned most of the rest, yet both were essentially tax exempt. The old feudal nobility so ruthlessly impoverished the peasants, and their use of the most productive land for sheep grazing so depleted agricultural productivity, that Spain could not raise enough food for its own needs. Yet in spite of their poverty, the Spanish people were the most heavily taxed in Europe. To operate the government, Philip regularly resorted to borrowing and then just as regularly defaulted on the loans he had contracted.

Religious policies in Spain often hurt economic development, as with the campaigns against the Jews and Muslims. The Spanish Inquisition had been used initially against the so-called *conversos*, the Jews who had converted to Christianity but who continued secretly to practice their own religion. Jews and *conversos* were among the most important merchants, physicians, and bankers and many had achieved significant status in Spanish society. Large numbers of these economic leaders had left Spain to escape the repression and, in 1492, following the conquest of Granada, more than 100,000 Jews emigrated when the crown insisted that all Jews had either to convert or leave.

Similar policies affected the Muslims, who in 1502 were given the same choice as the Jews. Because most Muslims were modest farmers rather than merchants or professionals, and lacked the resources to emigrate, they opted to become Christians. Yet these *Moriscos*, like many of the *conversos*, were Christian in name only. Between 1568 and 1571, Philip brutally suppressed an uprising among the *Moriscos*, and in 1609 they were expelled from Spain. These policies seriously hurt the middle class, on whom most of the tax burden fell, and undermined a valuable source of economic prosperity.

SPAIN AND ITS OVERSEAS EMPIRE

The importance of the empire as a source of much needed revenue explains why the Spanish crown held the colonies so tightly to the authority of Madrid. One result of this policy, however, was that when the supply of bullion from the Americas began to run dry, and other nations competed for a share of colonial trade, Spain began to suffer economic depression.

Economic Policy and the Colonies

After the brutal plundering of the ancient civilizations of the Americas had exhausted the easy supply of wealth, the Spanish introduced European mining techniques to the fabulously rich silver mines of Peru and Mexico. By the end of the 16th century, bullion still made up most of the value of imports from the Spanish possessions in the Americas. Even then, however, although the government directly secured almost half of all the bullion brought to Spain, it made up no more than 25 percent of all revenues. As the mines were gradually exhausted, other products from Asia and the New World began to take their place in Spain's overseas trade. By the end of the 17th century, new kinds of goods—particularly coffee, tea, cocoa, cotton, dyes, and tobacco—began to dominate imports to Europe.

Unlike the Portuguese, the Spanish began from the outset to settle their colonies and develop a local economy that mirrored the techniques and institutions found at home. They introduced European agricultural products into the Americas, including wheat and other grains, a wide variety of vegetables, and citrus fruit, while importing into Europe foodstuffs unknown there, such as the potato, the tomato, and corn.

The cultivation of sugar cane in the Western Hemisphere had a great impact on the economic and demographic patterns of the colonies, especially on the islands of the West Indies, where African slaves were brought in large numbers to work the plantations. Control of labor in the colonies was also managed under the *encomienda* system; this was similar to European manorialism, in which a grant of land gave the landholder the right to use the inhabitants of the land as forced workers. Local landholders and their overseers so widely abused the system, however, that it was eventually abandoned in the second half of the 16th century.

To control all trade, the government had established an agency known as the *Casa de Contrataciòn*, which sought to make commerce a royal monopoly. Since the New World had been discovered by navigators in the employ of Queen Isabella of Castile, Castilian merchants were given a trade monopoly there. Trade with foreigners, including other Spanish merchants, was forbidden. This encouraged smuggling and the subterfuge of foreign merchants hiring Spanish ships to trade with the colonies. Direct commerce between the Americas and the Philippines, Spain's Pacific possession, was virtually prohibited. Within the colonies, manufacturing was discouraged in order to stimulate and support Spanish industries at home.

A crucial shortcoming of Philip's reign was that such a potentially lucrative and important source of wealth as the American colonies was so thoroughly mismanaged. Indeed several times in the course of the 16th century Spain went into bankruptcy. Instead of making Spain a part of a developing and expanding overseas agricultural economy, Philip was content to allow the draining of its resources and the inhuman exploitation of its people. In doing so, he basked in the glow of the Hapsburg empire, little realizing that his policies had planted the seed of future crisis.

REBELLION IN THE NETHERLANDS: RELIGIOUS FREEDOM AND POLITICAL INDEPENDENCE

The Netherlands (sometimes called the Low Countries; their low elevation made them susceptible to flooding)

Map 2.2 The Netherlands

had long been one of the most prosperous and strategically important areas of the Hapsburg domains, supplying Spain with large revenues. Throughout the Middle Ages, the Netherlands was the center of commerce and banking as well as a leading manufacturer of textiles. Amsterdam and Antwerp were important North Sea ports, and the country was densely populated and highly urbanized.

On the other hand, the 17 provinces that comprised the Netherlands had old traditions of self-government and feudal autonomy, and its inhabitants were deeply suspicious of Charles V when he inherited them, despite the fact that he had been raised there. To complicate matters further, the southern provinces were primarily French- and Flemish-speaking, while the northern provinces were populated by people of German origin, whose language was Dutch. Charles annexed the provinces in 1548 and added them to the Hapsburg empire.

Philip II and the Netherlands

To bring the two areas together, Charles had placed them under the regency of Philip, who lived there until he became king in 1556. Thereafter, Philip left the administration of the Netherlands in the hands of his sister, Margaret of Parma (1522–1586), who ruled with a group of Spanish advisers. Estrangement from Philip's absentee overlordship was made worse by the king's Catholic program. By the mid-16th century, Calvinism was spreading rapidly in the Netherlands and, like his father before him, Philip encouraged local officials to use the Inquisition to stamp it and other heresies out. He also instructed his sister to enforce regulations against heresy. These policies enraged the local nobles, many of whom had become Calvinists and were already smarting under Philip's desire to centralize his control at the expense of their privileges.

Philip was forced to drop a hated cardinal from Margaret's government in order to placate popular sen-

William of Orange, "the Silent", painted by Anthony Moro, proved a skillful and popular leader of the Dutch revolt.

HAERLEM.
13
Nachdem sich Harlem ergeben hatt
Ist angericht ein groß bluit batt
Da hangen und kopfen nam khein endt
Die weiber auch wurden geschendt
Vom Hispanigschen gesind dermaßen,
Gehangen seind mitt großer unzucht
Wider alle eher, und Gottes frucht

This print, designed as anti-Spanish propaganda, depicts the atrocities committed by Spain in putting down the revolt in the city of Haarlem.

timent. The concession came too late and in 1566 Calvinists erupted in a fury that desecrated Catholic churches. Philip responded by sending 10,000 Spanish troops to the area under the command of the duke of Alva (1507–1582), who imposed an authoritarian military rule on the inhabitants.

Alva could not have alienated the people more had he deliberately set out to do so. Not only did he levy new taxes but he also established a special tribunal—popularly known as the Council of Blood—to root out heresy and crush the revolt. Alva was a brutal regent, responsible for thousands of deaths, including the execution of prominent Protestant nobles, and the expropriation of property. Tens of thousands of Protestants emigrated in the face of the terror that Alva unleashed. Outraged by his brutality, Margaret of Parma resigned the regency.

Alva's policies eventually provoked full-scale rebellion as merchants and common people joined forces with the Protestant nobles against the Spanish repression. Opposition to Philip centered on William of Nassau, the prince of Orange (ruled 1579–1584). In the north, William organized armed resistance in 1568, and five years later Philip recalled Alva in a futile attempt to calm the population. William was an ideal leader of the rebellion. Although born a Lutheran, he had been raised as a Catholic. An experienced military leader, William had raised a privateer army popularly called the "Sea Beggars." Moreover, William had been an imperial official at the court of Charles V and was not enthusiastic about leading a rebellion against Philip. Nevertheless under the pressures and heat of battle, William eventually became devoted to the Protestant cause.

The Rebellion

For the first six years of the revolt, William and the rebel forces suffered one setback after another. William, who had used his own private wealth to help finance his army, was almost bankrupt and his early military defeats spoiled his reputation. In 1572, however, the tide suddenly changed when his soldiers captured the port of Brill, which inspired a series of uprisings throughout the northern provinces. To stop the advance of the imperial troops, William then opened the dikes and flooded the plains, a tactic that succeeded in cornering Philip's army and prompting the recall of Alva.

The war dragged on and terrible atrocities and brutalities took place on both sides as religious passions inflamed the mutual hatreds. To terrorize the population, Alva had authorized his soldiers to pillage town after town and murder their inhabitants. In 1576, Antwerp was destroyed and thousands massacred. Three years later Spanish troops raped the women of Maestricht, who had helped defend the town against them, and then slaughtered much of the population.

The same year that Maestricht fell, Protestant and Catholic leaders of all 17 provinces joined together against Philip to form an alliance known as the Pacification of Ghent. The Catholic provinces of the South had been goaded into rebellion because of a special tax that Philip had imposed on them in order to fight the Protestants. The agreement at Ghent suggested the possibility that national and political interests could be used in the Netherlands as the basis for forging a new state.

The united citizens of the Netherlands demanded that Philip withdraw his army and allow the provinces to be governed by their traditional assembly, the States General. But the unity that was achieved in adversity soon gave way to religious divisions between the Calvinist nobles of the North and the Catholic nobles of the South.

Philip's new military commander, Alexander Farnese, duke of Parma, skillfully manipulated these divisions by luring the Catholic aristocrats back into the Spanish fold after restoring their confiscated lands. After a series of victories, in 1579 Parma persuaded the southern provinces (which formed a Catholic alliance known as the Union of Arras) to make a separate peace with Philip. In the face of this abandonment, William brought together the Dutch leaders of the northern provinces into the Protestant Union of Utrecht, which announced that they would continue to resist the king.

In 1581, after trying unsuccessfully to become subjects first of the king of France and then of Queen Elizabeth of England, the northern provinces proclaimed their independence. After William was assassinated in 1584, the Dutch continued their struggle for self-government under his 17-year-old son Maurice. Philip never lived to see the end of the revolt of the Netherlands. In 1609, eleven years after his death, a truce was arranged at long last, but not before the Spanish had inflicted much additional brutality and terror on the Protestant population of the region. Spain recognized the Protestant Dutch Republic of the northern provinces in the treaty of Westphalia in 1648, while maintaining control of the southern Catholic provinces.

SPAIN VERSUS ENGLAND: THE ARMADA DISASTER

As if the Netherlands were not sufficient provocation to Philip's Catholic policies, another source of conflict lay in England, where Henry VIII had created and assumed control of the Anglican Church and severed ties with Rome. In 1554, before he assumed the throne, Philip had married the daughter of Henry and Catherine of Aragon, Mary Tudor. Although the marriage was extremely unpopular in England, Mary was hopelessly in love with Philip, who encouraged her efforts to restore Catholicism there (see Part IV, Topic 7).

The Spanish-English Rivalry

A number of factors operated to exacerbate English-Spanish hostility. When Mary died, Philip offered his hand to her sister, Elizabeth (ruled 1558–1603), the new English queen, but Elizabeth spurned the offer. However, the underlying reason for the longstanding hostility between Spain and England was economic rivalry. Elizabeth's ships and English pirates attacked Spanish galleons laden with bullion from the Americas. Moreover, the English, anxious to break into the Spanish monopoly imposed on their colonies, tried to force their way into the lucrative trade. Sir John Hawkins, an ambitious English merchant, violated Spanish policy and sold goods directly to the Spanish colonies. In the late 1570s, Hawkins' cousin Francis Drake seized a fortune in booty from Spanish ships along the Pacific coast of South America.

English and Spanish policy also clashed during the revolt in the Netherlands. Since the Middle Ages, England had close commercial contact with the Flemish cloth manufacturers, who purchased large quantities of English wool. Then, too, the English supported the aspirations of the Dutch Protestants, and English privateers continued to harass Spanish shipping along the coast. For their part, Spanish envoys in England had even been implicated in plots to assassinate Elizabeth.

The Armada and the Eclipse of Spain

In 1587, Francis Drake, who was knighted by Elizabeth, destroyed a large Spanish fleet anchored in the harbor of Cadiz. In reaction to what he regarded as English perfidy and the wounding of his pride, Philip decided to attack England's power directly. He devoted significant resources and energy to the building of a huge fleet, known as the Invincible Armada, which was designed to seize control of the English Channel and permit a Spanish invasion of England. The invasion forces were

A contemporary painting by Nicholas Hilliard depicting the battle against the Spanish Armada.

to be commanded by the duke of Parma. It was an imaginative plan but filled with danger, for much of Philip's war against England rested on this effort.

The Armada consisted of 130 ships carrying some 27,000 men. Arrayed against it was a much weaker flotilla of English ships, which nevertheless were smaller and faster than the cumbersome Spanish vessels. Moreover, some of England's best naval officers, including Hawkins and Drake, were in command of the operations. When running battles between the two fleets drove the Spanish ships to take refuge off Calais, Hawkins sent fire ships into the harbor and caused the Spanish to panic. As the Armada moved north to try to return to Cadiz, the English attacked again, and ferocious storms destroyed more Spanish ships than did the enemy. When the battle was over, less than half of Philip's ships had survived, although the majority of Spain's firepower made it back home.

The outcome of the struggle between England and Spain had immediate significance for Spain and long-range meaning for Europe. Philip's prestige was damaged and Spain's once supreme military power had been compromised. Moreover, the English victory gave encouragement to the Protestant forces struggling against the Counter-Reformation. Had Philip's reign ended with the Battle of Lepanto in 1571, in which his forces defeated the Ottoman Turks, he would no doubt have been regarded as the greatest ruler of his age. Instead, it culminated in the Armada disaster. The moment of Spain's greatness had passed.

The abdication of Charles V in 1556 signaled the fact that even such an ambitious monarch realized the insurmountable challenges and difficulties of ruling the vast Hapsburg empire. Indeed, the division of his empire confirmed that the day of universal empires was over. The ascension of Philip II to the throne of Spain, on the other hand, suggested that greatness might have still been possible on a more limited scale. But Philip was not up to the task, and circumstances seem to have conspired against him.

Philip was an intensely Catholic monarch in an age of religious divisiveness which had shattered a millennium of Catholic unity. Although his inheritance included a huge overseas empire stretching from the Atlantic to the Pacific, shortsighted administrative and economic policies rendered it less useful to Spain than it might have been. Even in Europe, however, Philip's empire was too diverse. Against the centralizing and heavy-handed absolutism of the Hapsburgs, local patriotism and religious faith joined forces to wrest the all-important Dutch provinces from Philip's orbit. The longstanding Hapsburg-Valois conflict had ended with the withdrawal of France, and in the end Spain's nemesis came unexpectedly from England. The Armada symbolized a new era in European history, one that marked the decline of Spain and ushered in the ascendancy of England.

Questions for Further Study

1. What were the chief concerns of Philip's domestic program?
2. What was the nature of the relationship between Spain and its colonies? How did Spain view its American possessions?
3. What were the major aims of Spanish foreign policy under Philip II?

Suggestions for Further Reading

Braudel, Fernand. *The Mediterranean and the Mediterranean World in the Age of Philip II*, trans. S. Reynolds, 2 vols. New York, 1972–1973.

Dunn, Richard S. *The Age of Religious Wars, 1559–1715*, 2nd ed. New York, 1979.

Elliott, John H. *The Revolt of the Catalans: A Study in the Decline of Spain, 1598–1640*. Cambridge, MA, 1963.

Kamen, Henry. *Spain, 1469–1714: A Study of Conflict*. New York, 1991.

Maltby, William S. *Alba*. Berkeley, 1983.

Mattingly, Garrett. *The Armada*. Boston, 1959.

Parker, G. *Philip II*. London, 1978.

Rodriguez-Salgado, Mia. *The Changing Face of Empire: Charles V, Philip II, and Habsburg Authority*. Cambridge, MA, 1988.

Stradling, Robert A. *Europe and the Decline of Spain: A Study of the Spanish System, 1580–1720*. London, 1981.

V

Topic 3

Crown and Parliament in Tudor-Stuart England

The death of Henry VIII in the mid-16th century ended a tumultuous era in English history during which that ambitious monarch had established a powerful royal autocracy. Henry successfully defied the papacy and established Protestantism in his realm, disciplined the nobility, and bent Parliament to his will. The unanswered question was whether Henry's reign had set a precedent for further royal power at the expense of the social and economic elites represented in Parliament. Moreover, the religious controversy stirred up by Henry continued to disturb English life for many years to come.

Contrary to his own expectations, Henry's daughter, Elizabeth I, proved to be one of the most important monarchs of English history. A brilliant and determined queen, she fought back the efforts at mastery of Philip II of Spain and strengthened England's hegemony on the seas, while she presided over an era of significant economic and cultural achievement. Moreover, shrewd tactician that she was, Elizabeth avoided direct confrontation and achieved an uneasy balance in her relationship with Parliament.

It was left to her successors, James I and Charles I, to take up again the struggle between monarch and Parliament. The result was a far-reaching civil war that ended with the triumph of Parliament and the temporary end of the monarchy, with the added complication of renewed religious struggle under the Puritan impulse. In place of the monarchy there followed a difficult period of military dictatorship under Oliver Cromwell. Only then, after the English had experimented with alternative forms of government, did they return to the monarchy, but in a form that would share power increasingly with Parliament.

ELIZABETH I AND THE POLITICS OF COMPROMISE

Following the brief reigns of Edward VI and Mary Tudor, Elizabeth I (ruled 1558–1603) became queen. The daughter of Henry VIII and Ann Boleyn, the young Elizabeth ascended the English throne at a crucial moment in history, when both domestic and foreign affairs were at a crossroads. The Elizabethan era achieved an extraordinary level of power and prosperity, rarely matched in English history. Furthermore, during her reign, English cultural life reached a peak that culminated in the creative genius of William Shakespeare (see Part V, Topic 7).

Elizabeth the Queen

Despite this aspect of real accomplishment, however, Elizabeth was a complex ruler. She believed genuinely

Significant Dates

Tudor–Stuart England

1558–1603	Elizabeth I rules as queen of England
1563	Thirty-nine Articles adopted
1587	Mary Queen of Scots executed
1588	Defeat of Spanish Armada
1603–1625	James I rules as king of England
1611	King James Version of the Bible
1625–1649	Charles I rules as king of England
1628	Petition of Right
1642–1646, 1648	English civil wars
1649–1653	The Commonwealth
1658	Death of Oliver Cromwell
1660	Monarchy restored under Charles II

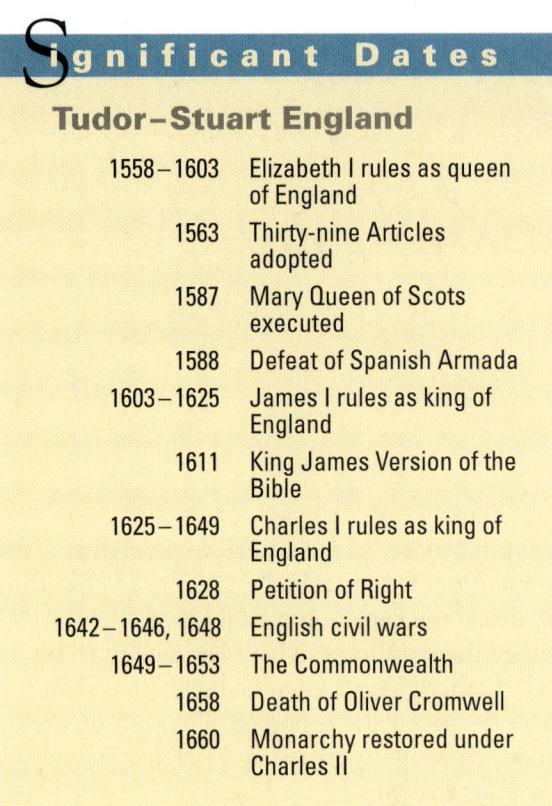

in the advantages and legitimacy of absolute monarchy yet she often compromised these principles for the sake of political expediency. Her personal sympathies in religion were, like those of her father, not predisposed toward Protestantism, although she restored the Protestant Church. Throughout her life she carefully cultivated suitors but never married, suppressing her personal inclinations for the sake of policy. She projected a strong, willful character in public, although in private she was often indecisive. In the end, it can be said that she embraced her country and its people as the inspiration for her life and work.

One of the first serious challenges she faced came from the north, in Scotland, where the Catholic Mary Stuart (ruled 1542–1567) ruled. After the death in 1560 of her husband, Francis II of France, Mary returned to Scotland. When her subjects, converted to Protestantism by John Knox, forced Mary into exile in 1568, she fled to England. Elizabeth treated her coolly and kept her under tight surveillance, for as a direct descendant of Henry VII Mary stood in the line of royal succession. Mary became the focus of a number of plots against Elizabeth hatched by Catholic dissidents. Finally, after Parliament demanded Mary's death and further plots were revealed, in 1587 Elizabeth had Mary executed.

Elizabeth faced other domestic difficulties, including continual uprisings in Ireland fomented by the pope and by Spain, but these problems did not derail her policy of religious reconciliation.

The Return to Protestantism

From the religious point of view, the years from 1547 to 1558 were difficult ones for the average English citizen. Henry's break with the Roman Church had disconcerted many of his subjects, and the support of Edward VI for Protestantism had created further uncertainty. Mary Tudor had then added to the confusion of her subjects by attempting to bring England back into the Catholic faith, at first with moderation and then with brutality and bloodshed. Elizabeth, who had been brought up a Protestant, enjoyed a long reign in which she was able to bring a measure of clarity back to religious life: the secret of her success was pragmatism rather than religious fervor.

Mary Tudor's death had heartened English Protestants, many of whom had left the country for ex-

Elizabeth I, whose regal bearing, elaborate clothing, and heavy makeup made her an icon of English royal authority.

ile abroad and now returned home, relishing the prospect of more radical reform. Elizabeth had Mary's Catholic legislation repealed and restored the major laws setting up the Anglican Church passed by Henry VIII. Under Elizabeth, the Church of England simplified its structure and actually embraced the notion of predestination preached by the Calvinists, whose doctrines the exiles had absorbed abroad.

In 1563, the Thirty-nine Articles adopted a position of compromise on many doctrinal issues but kept a good many long-established Catholic liturgical practices, although now translated into English. The kingdom continued to be home to a large number of dissenters who wanted a purer church, as well as to Jesuits who worked secretly to reestablish Catholicism. The so-called nonconformists, who included Puritans and Presbyterians, kept the religious question unsettled for years to come. The Puritans spearheaded a religious reform movement that wanted to "purify" the Church of England of all remnants of Catholicism. They became noted for their spirit of moral and religious earnestness that drove them to want to reform the entire kingdom.

Elizabeth's reign also saw steady economic progress based on England's widening involvement in overseas trade and the reduction of the debt. Joint stock companies such as the East India Company competed with the Dutch and French counterparts for primacy in global trade (see Part V, Topic 6). Elizabeth positioned England against the expansionist policies of her would-be suitor, Philip II of Spain. In 1588, her sea captains, including Sir Francis Drake, destroyed the Spanish Armada, although Spain continued to be a major power for some time. Lasting peace between Spain and England came only after the death of Philip in 1598 and Elizabeth's death five years later.

TOWARD CONFRONTATION: JAMES I AND PARLIAMENT

During the last years of Elizabeth's reign, tensions with Parliament had risen as a result of the queen's demands for special financial grants to pay for her struggle with Spain. In response, Parliament had raised constitutional issues designed further to weaken the crown. The Stuart kings who followed her turned the relationship of the monarchy with Parliament into a major crisis.

Compromise and Confrontation

Elizabeth was succeeded by James VI of Scotland, the son of Mary Stuart. He ascended the English throne as James I (ruled 1603–1625). Well educated and a fervent believer in the divine right of kings, James disliked the pretensions of Parliament. Before the authority of a monarch, he argued, no other authority could or should prevail. Having been raised in Scotland, he had little direct experience of issues involving English tradition and constitutional history.

Along with the crown, James inherited debt and hard times from the last years of Elizabeth's wars against Spain. He made matters worse by spending lavishly on his court. In addition, the Puritans began pressing James, who had accepted Presbyterianism as the dominant form of Protestantism in Scotland, to move the Reformation forward. In this the radicals were disappointed. James was cautious in matters of faith, and his best remembered contribution to religious life was the English translation of the Bible he commissioned, known as the King James Version, which appeared in 1611.

In politics James was as practical as Elizabeth in his thinking. Only a year after becoming king, he participated in a Protestant conference at Hampton Court, where radicals insisted that the episcopal system be abolished. James turned down their demands and took a hard line against the Calvinists, warning them that they would be banished if they continued waging religious war. On the other hand, after James issued an edict banishing Catholic priests, Protestant sympathies for him increased, especially when the so-called Gunpowder Plot was uncovered in 1605: a Catholic named Guy Fawkes (1578–1606) was caught placing 36 barrels of gunpowder under the houses of Parliament a day before the king was to appear before the assembly. Under torture, Fawkes revealed the names of fellow conspirators, who were tried and executed. November 5—when the explosion was to have occurred—is still celebrated in England as Guy Fawkes Day.

In the years following the plot against him, James experienced growing difficulties with Parliament. Twice—in 1611 and 1614—the king dissolved Parliament after it had turned down his proposed budgets and ruled by decree for a number of years. In 1621, when Parliament threatened to remove some of the king's powers, he went personally to the House of Commons to oppose the challenge. As his popularity began to suffer, James compounded his problems by arranging the marriage of his son Charles to a French princess, whose Catholic faith aroused resentment in England.

Although James angered members of Parliament with his high-handed behavior and his arguments in favor of divine right monarchy, about which he had written a treatise, the skillful monarch ended his reign with restored popularity when he went to war with Spain in 1624.

When Parliament met in the early 17th century, the Lords sat while the Commoners stood at the bar.

Social and Religious Transformations

James' confrontations with Parliament had far-reaching implications, especially because membership in that body had begun to undergo important social change since the mid-16th century. In general, by the early 17th century England had a much larger group of entrepreneurs—virtually all of whom were not nobles—who had made money in trade, manufacturing, and in capitalist farming and sheep raising. The most significant development was the increase in the size of the gentry class—that is, either the younger, landless brothers of nobles or landowners who used their newfound wealth to purchase estates and country residences in order to achieve a higher social status. The rise of the gentry was accompanied by a decline in the importance of the old feudal nobility, whose role as military leaders had all but disappeared as the feudal armies were replaced by a royal army.

Although never a united group, the gentry were forming a majority in the House of Commons, the branch of Parliament that controlled government finances, and were beginning to insist on a larger share of political influence. Indeed, by the time of the death of James I, the gentry formed perhaps three-quarters of the membership of the Commons. Finances were at the heart of the tension between the gentry and the monarchy. The monarchy required ever larger income, and while the gentry bore an increasingly larger share of the tax burden, they demanded a voice in policy making and in how their tax money was to be spent. James I and his successors, however, correctly saw such pursuit of power as undermining royal absolutism.

Compounding these problems was the fact that the period of religious strife was by no means over in England, and religious issues were linked to the country's social transformation. The Calvinists and Puritans, both of which groups were gaining followers, continued to demand a more strenuous program of reform for the Church of England, which they wanted to see shorn of its remaining Catholic influences. The Puritan emphasis on the work ethic and high moral standards in everyday life reflected the values of some of the gentry and the merchant class that had come to dominate the House of Commons. The early settlements in the American colonies in Virginia, Massachusetts, Pennsylvania, and

Rhode Island were organized by Puritans seeking communities of their own.

CHARLES I AND THE CIVIL WAR

The mounting political and religious trouble between Parliament and the monarchy reached the crisis point under Charles I (ruled 1625–1649). His marriage to Henrietta Maria, the sister of King Louis XIII of France, made him unpopular from the start. Matters worsened when Charles' requests for money were met with demands from Parliament for political reforms. He dismissed two Parliaments but in 1628, he was forced to accept the Petition of Right, a constitutional document that asserted the legal rights and protections of the English people as they had evolved since Magna Carta—no taxation without Parliamentary consent, no billeting of troops in civilian homes, freedom from arbitrary arrest and imprisonment, and no martial law in peacetime.

The Civil War

As soon as Charles had his money, however, he dissolved Parliament and refused to call another for more than ten years. The gentry and Puritans of the Commons seethed with revolt, especially as Charles ran the government by imposing special levies that in the eyes of Parliament were improper and represented taxation without consent. The Puritans turned to Parliament for support, finding increasing common cause with sectors of the gentry.

The religious question provoked a crisis that forced Charles to call Parliament back into session. William Laud (1573–1645), archbishop of Canterbury, was a man of moderate persuasion but obstinate mind. Laud attempted to bully the Puritans, prosecuting his Puritan critics in royal law courts. In 1639 Laud attempted to introduce a uniform Anglican Book of Common Prayer in England as well as in Scotland. Riots against Laud's policies erupted in Scotland, where Presbyterianism was dominant, and Charles had to ask Parliament for the money to raise an army to put down the rebellion.

The so-called "Long Parliament," which met from 1640 to 1660, had as its leader a Puritan opponent of the monarchy named John Pym. Under his guidance, the Commons passed a series of measures designed to limit the power of the king, including the abolition of royal courts such as the Star Chamber, which the king had used to try nobles, and an act requiring the king to call Parliament at least every three years. One member of the Commons, Oliver Cromwell (1599–1658), urged Parliament to abolish the Book of Common Prayer and bitterly attacked the institution of bishops in the Anglican Church. Archbishop Laud was impeached, and the following year the House of Commons issued the Grand Remonstrance: a restatement of Parliament's position and the measures it had passed.

An engraving of Charles I and his wife Henrietta Maria, from a painting by Anthony Van Dyck.

Quakers, one of several radical Protestant groups which emerged during the Civil War, allowed women to preach. A contemporary print pokes fun at this Quaker practice.

All the while, Parliament had refused to grant Charles the money he needed for the army, preferring to deal directly with the Scots in the hope of forcing the king to give in to their wishes. Instead, Charles tried unsuccessfully to have the leaders of the Commons arrested. In June 1642, when the Commons put forward its last set of demands, including control of the church and the army and the right to appoint ministers, Charles fled London for the north of England. There he condemned the Parliamentary leaders as traitors and took to the battlefields to reassert royal authority. Civil war had come.

The English Civil War, which lasted from 1642 to 1646, was a struggle in which both sides fought reluctantly. Neither Charles nor the leaders of Parliament had wanted matters to result in violence but the issues were of great importance and fraught with decades of tension. Conflict between the freedoms and laws of England and the power of kings was exacerbated by religious passions that had been brewing since the time of Henry VIII.

Yet the underlying causes of the struggle, long debated by historians, do not appear to be quite so simple. The momentous decision to take up arms against the crown so divided the country, including the Puritans, that half of the members of the House of Commons sided with Charles. Marxist historians have argued that the more prosperous segments of the gentry, anxious to consolidate their power, led the fight for Parliament and the Puritans. On the other hand, another school of thought insists that the most prosperous group supported the king and that it was the less prosperous gentry, living off of declining agricultural incomes, who backed the Puritans and Parliament. Moreover, the southern and eastern areas of England, where merchants and businessmen were concentrated, opposed the king, whereas the more rural northern and western regions supported him. In the end, the Civil War is perhaps best seen as a complicated struggle that was fueled by religious conflict.

While Pym gave the rebels political direction, Cromwell provided military leadership. Cromwell designed what he called the New Model Army, whose soldiers were indoctrinated and impassioned by sermons and religious worship. In June 1645, after almost three years of fighting, the Civil War reached a turning point when the antiroyalists won a major victory at Naseby and took the king.

The End of the Monarchy

During the course of the Civil War, two broad factions emerged in the opposition to Charles: the Independents, whose leader in the Commons was Cromwell, wanted to replace the Anglican Church with a decentralized church in which each congregation chose the kind of worship it wanted; the Presbyterians, on the other hand, wanted a Calvinist church similar to the system in Scotland, where a central authority presided over local congregations. On the religious

Map 3.1 England in the Civil War

issue, Cromwell gave in to the majority, who were Presbyterians, and the victors proceeded to abolish the bishops and establish a Presbyterian church. To Cromwell, however, this was only a temporary compromise, and his determination to break the king's power only served to widen the divisions wrenching apart English society.

Charles' surrender made the struggle even more complicated, for the question of what to do with the king revealed how deeply divided his foes were. When the Independents and the Presbyterians failed to agree on the fate of the king, the Civil War broke out again in 1647. This time, however, the Independents were pitted against the Presbyterians while the Scots now supported the king. The Parliament's army added to the instability, for it had gone unpaid for so long that it was threatening to rebel.

In fact, in June 1647 the army kidnapped Charles and demanded payment in return for his release. When the Presbyterians in London tried to stop the military, the soldiers occupied the capital, gaining the backing of the Independents and other radicals. The next year, Cromwell crushed the royalists completely and his soldiers now insisted on the king's execution. In the House of Commons the Presbyterian majority refused to support the army's demands, but their defiance prompted the army to purge the Parliament of all those who resisted.

The resulting Rump Parliament, consisting of less than 100 members, voted to try the king for crimes against his subjects. Charles was founded guilty and beheaded on January 30, 1649—he went to the block with great dignity, and his execution was by no means universally applauded. Cromwell declared England a republican "commonwealth" without a monarch and without a House of Lords.

Puritan propaganda portrayed Cromwell as a heroic figure who ended social and religious division.

THE PROTECTORATE: THE DICTATORSHIP OF OLIVER CROMWELL

The years from 1649 to 1660 are known in English history as the "Interregnum," or the period between kings. For the first several years of that period, a council of state exercised executive authority, while the Rump Parliament served as the legislature. Unable to decide on a new constitutional system for the country, and increasingly frustrated by the hostility between religious factions, in 1653 Cromwell used the army to close down the Rump institution and replaced it with a new body of his own loyal supporters.

For the next five years, Cromwell ruled England as a military dictator, confusing even further the already debated question of sovereignty, or the source of political power. Under the monarchy, sovereignty had been explained as the divine right of kings; now, in times of upheaval, some claimed that sovereignty rested with the people. But what form of sovereignty did Cromwell exercise?

The Protectorate

Cromwell's hand-picked Parliament proved so destabilizing that a group of army officers took matters into their own hands. They drafted a constitutional document known as the Instrument of Government, which gave Cromwell the title of Lord Protector.

The new ruler of England was a man of the gentry class, a Puritan of the Independent persuasion who believed in parliamentary government. He said repeatedly that he wanted to bring genuine constitutional government and religious freedom to the country, but both goals eluded him. During his rule, he called three different parliaments into session but none was able to arrange a long-term constitutional settlement. Cromwell himself seemed to be inspired by high-minded ideals but he was inflexible and unwilling to make the kind of

Under Charles II, the royal court restored elaborate procedures and elegant dress.

realistic concessions required by the political process. In 1657, one Parliament offered him the crown but he declined it. In the end, he believed the dictatorship to be the only way to bring peace to England.

Cromwell's tenure as Lord Protector of England was made difficult by the bitter factionalism within the Puritan ranks. The most radical group was known as the Diggers, who wanted to abolish private property, while the Levellers made quasi-democratic demands for parliamentary elections based on nearly universal male suffrage. Neither of these views found support among the landed gentry, from whose ranks Cromwell himself had come. A host of other ideologies surfaced during these years, and conspiracies against the Protectorate came from the defeated royalists as well as from the ranks of the Puritans.

The former king's son, the future Charles II, lived in France, where exiled nobles hatched countless plots to restore the monarchy. Caught between opposition to the monarchy and resistance to the Protectorate, Cromwell became reinforced in his conviction that only he had the objective interests of the country at heart.

Cromwell reorganized the country into eleven military and administrative districts, each in the hands of a major general who reported directly to him. The man who claimed to detest power could not, however, abide dissent. To control the opposition and those who would criticize the dictatorship, Cromwell created a system of domestic surveillance and prohibited all newspapers. He crushed a rebellion in Ireland with great brutality, convinced that the Catholicism of the Irish was a form of treason against the state. In religious affairs, Cromwell's record was mixed. Among his Christian subjects, he allowed freedom of worship only for non-Anglican Protestants; on the other hand, he welcomed the return of Jews to England. In social matters, Cromwell tried to influence the tone of public life by banning plays, sports, and popular music, but these policies were never well received.

Cromwell's last days were spent in disillusionment and concern for the future of England. Before his death, he arranged for the Lord Protectorate to be given to his son, Richard (1626–1712), but his unseasoned successor lacked his father's energy and skill and could not maintain control. In truth, the English people were tired of military rule as well as of the drab tenor of life that Cromwell had imposed. In May 1660, General George Monck, who commanded the New Model Army in Scotland, seized control of the government and asked Charles II to return to England. After years of civil war and the execution of a king, of religious strife and a harsh dictatorship, the Stuart monarchy was restored.

In spite of the painful experiences of the mid-17th century, England did derive some positive long-term lessons about the balance of power between Parliament and the crown. The notion that there would be no taxation without the consent of Parliament was now a permanent part of the constitutional arrangement, as was the writ of habeas corpus and the prohibition against quartering soldiers among civilians.

The social transformation of the country that had produced the gentry class also reflected a permanent reality that guided domestic politics for the next two centuries. When, a generation after the restoration of the monarchy, Stuart rule proved unworkable, it was brought to an end peacefully, in what came to be called England's "bloodless revolution."

Questions for Further Study

1. How can Tudor religious policies best be characterized?

2. What were the origins of the civil wars in England?
3. Why was the monarchy restored after the end of the Protectorate?

Suggestions for Further Reading

Ashton, Robert. *The English Civil War: Conservatism and Revolution, 1603–1649*. London, 1978.

Aylmer, Gerald E. *Rebellion or Revolution? England, 1640–1660*. New York, 1986.

Elton, Geoffrey R. *The Parliament of England, 1559–1581*. Cambridge, MA, 1986.

Guy, John, and John Morrill. *The Tudors and the Stuarts*, vol. III of *The Oxford History of Britain*. Oxford, 1992.

Hill, Christopher. *The World Turned Upside Down: Radical Ideas During the English Revolution*. New York, 1972.

MacCaffrey, W. T. *Queen Elizabeth and the Making of Policy, 1572–1588*. Princeton, 1981.

Palliser, David M. *The Age of Elizabeth*. London, 1983.

Russell, Conrad. *The Causes of the English Civil War*. New York, 1990.

Stone, Lawrence. *The Causes of the English Revolution, 1529–1642*. London, 1972.

Zagorin, Perez. *Rebels and Rulers, 1500–1660*, 2 vols. Cambridge, MA, 1982.

V

Topic 4

Religious War and the Ascendancy of the French Monarchy

If in England the 16th and 17th centuries saw the conflict between constitutionalism and monarchy resolve itself in favor of Parliament, in France the same period witnessed the growing power of royal government and the foundations of French absolutism. The French monarchy had developed into a strong and efficient form of government under the Valois dynasty, which came to power in the 14th century (see Part IV, Topic 4). After the conclusion of the Hundred Years' War in 1453, a succession of kings built up the royal administration, tamed the nobility, and secured state authority over the appointment of bishops and other ecclesiastical officials.

As in other states, the Reformation caused deep religious conflicts in France. These erupted into a series of wars of religion that took on the character of civil strife. The religious struggles, primarily those of the monarchy against the Huguenots, or French Calvinists, dominated events in the 16th century, bringing a temporary end to the consolidation of the royal state. Nevertheless, the fact that the end of the strife came as a result of an edict of religious toleration by the king suggested the value that a strong monarchy could have in the country.

In the aftermath of the religious wars, the process of building the national state around the monarchy resumed. With the skillful and energetic leadership of two cardinals, Richelieu and Mazarin, who served as royal ministers, the French monarchs imposed ever greater royal authority over the realm. The government these kings controlled reached into the lives of more of their subjects than ever before.

Religious strife was not, of course, confined to France. In the second decade of the 17th century, while Richelieu still presided as the king's chief minister, most of the great powers of Europe were plunged into a terrible religious and secular conflict known as the Thirty Years' War. The antagonism between Catholics and Protestants was certainly an important factor in bringing about the war, but not the only one: the conflict also involved a broader struggle for mastery between the Bourbon dynasty of France and the imperial aspirations of the Hapsburgs.

RELIGIOUS CONFLICT: FROM THE ST. BARTHOLOMEW'S DAY MASSACRE TO THE EDICT OF NANTES

Nowhere did the spread of Protestantism, and especially of the militant Calvinist variety, inflame religious passions more than in France, where the bitter and bloody French Wars of Religion destroyed social tranquillity and exasperated already existing economic and political tensions.

Catherine de' Medici and the Wars of Religion

The religious turmoil in France endured for a generation, from 1562 to 1598, but its roots went back further, to the reign of Henry II (ruled 1547–1559). Despite his energetic and robust appearance, Henry was a weak and pliable ruler who was influenced by his mistresses and his ambitious advisers. He continued the Valois-Hapsburg war against Emperor Charles V and then against Philip II, siding with the German Protestants in their struggles against the Hapsburg emperor, despite his own Catholic faith.

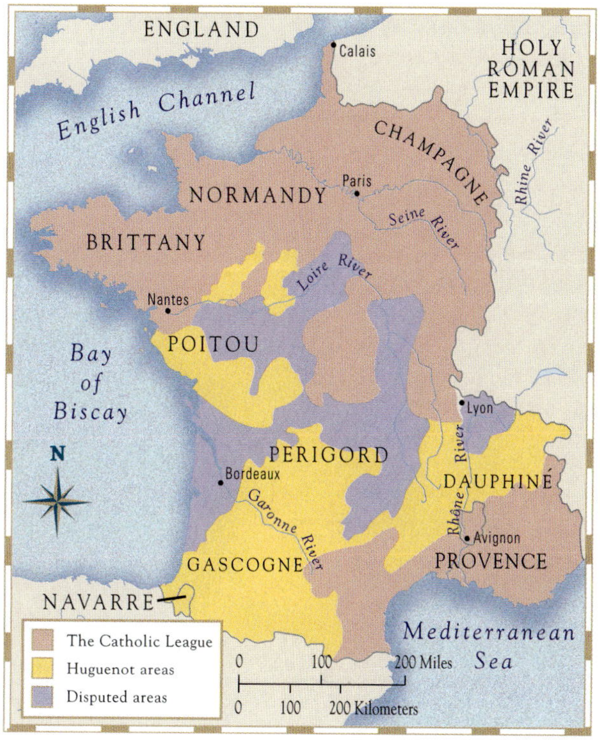

Map 4.1 Religious Conflict in France

When peace came in 1559, Henry reversed himself, instituting severe restrictions against the Protestants in his own country. Later that year, when Henry was accidentally killed in a tournament, his Italian wife, Catherine de' Medici (1519–1589), daughter of Duke Lorenzo de' Medici of Urbino, became regent. Acting for her three sons, who succeeded each other as king over the following years, Catherine's religious policies ranged from toleration to persecution. It was during her regency that the religious question came to a head.

Calvinism had continued to spread despite persecutions by Henry II. During his reign, there were Huguenots among all social classes, from artisans to merchants, and half of the nobility had become Protestant. Because the aristocracy had always challenged the king's efforts to create centralized government, the existence of so large a proportion of Huguenot nobles posed a special danger to the monarchy.

Beyond the nobility, the Huguenots formed a distinct minority of the French population, but they were zealous in their faith and determined to fight for their freedom to worship as they chose. The Huguenot Church was well organized, with a centralized administration that reached down to the provincial and congregational levels. By the time the Wars of Religion began, more than 2000 Huguenot congregations existed throughout the country.

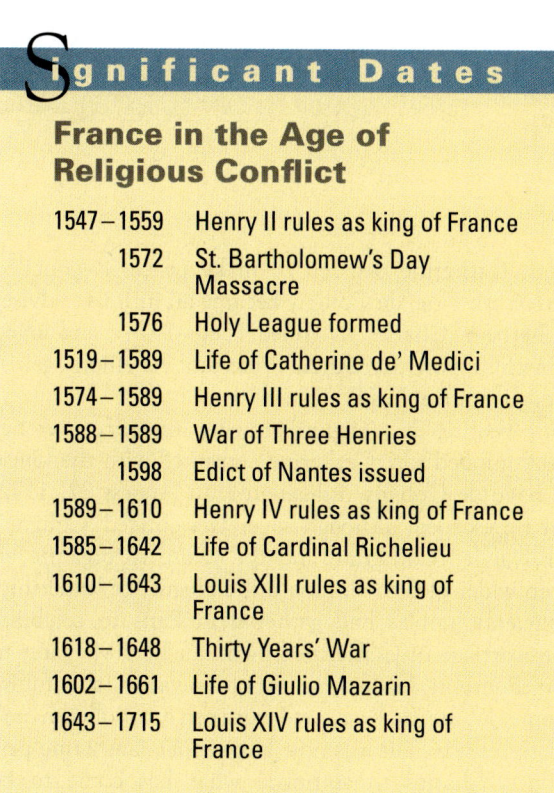

Significant Dates

France in the Age of Religious Conflict

1547–1559	Henry II rules as king of France
1572	St. Bartholomew's Day Massacre
1576	Holy League formed
1519–1589	Life of Catherine de' Medici
1574–1589	Henry III rules as king of France
1588–1589	War of Three Henries
1598	Edict of Nantes issued
1589–1610	Henry IV rules as king of France
1585–1642	Life of Cardinal Richelieu
1610–1643	Louis XIII rules as king of France
1618–1648	Thirty Years' War
1602–1661	Life of Giulio Mazarin
1643–1715	Louis XIV rules as king of France

Map 4.2 Europe, c. 1560

Catherine de' Medici tried unsuccessfully to diffuse the growing tensions by brokering religious compromise and fostering reforms in the French Church. The Catholic extremists, headed by the influential Guise family, demanded unremitting opposition to the Huguenots. The anti-Protestant campaign received support from the papacy and the Jesuits, as well as from Philip II of Spain.

The war broke out in 1562 when the private armies of the Guise slaughtered an entire congregation of Huguenots at the town of Vassy. The fighting spread but both sides found themselves unable to win a clear victory. Catherine, concerned that the crusade against the Protestants might undermine the Valois monarchy, joined forces with the Catholic party led by the Guise family.

In 1570, after the Huguenot military leader Gaspard de Coligny (1519–1572) defeated a royal army, Catherine decided to make peace. Reconciled with Catherine, de Coligny became an intimate adviser to her son, Charles IX (ruled 1560–1574), and urged him to support the Dutch Protestant rebellion against their Spanish rulers.

Fearing de Coligny's growing influence over her weak-minded son, Catherine conspired with the Guise to have de Coligny assassinated on August 22, 1572, but he escaped, although severely wounded. Coligny's survival led Catherine and the Guise to organize an even wider plot to eliminate the Huguenot leadership. Huguenot nobles had gathered in Paris to celebrate the marriage of Catherine's own daughter Margaret to the Bourbon leader Henry of Navarre (the future Henry IV, he had wavered between Catholicism and Protestantism, but was now Huguenot). Catherine persuaded Charles to authorize what has come to be known as the St. Bartholomew's Day Massacre (August

In 1572 thousands of French Protestants—Huguenots—were killed in the St. Bartholomew's Day Massacre.

24, 1572). As the slaughter spread from Paris to the countryside, thousands of Huguenots, including de Coligny, were killed.

Henry IV and the Edict of Nantes

The brutal massacre, which destroyed much popular support for the Valois family, broke the tenuous truce and the religious wars erupted again. In 1576, the Catholic party created the Holy League to wipe out the Protestants and to make Henry of Guise king of France in place of Catherine's son, Henry III (ruled 1574–1589), who had succeeded his brother Charles.

The subsequent War of the Three Henries (1588–1589) first saw Henry of Guise pitted against Henry III. The Catholic king, after having Guise murdered, now joined forces with the Protestant Henry of Navarre in defeating the Holy League. Following the defeat of the extreme Catholics, however, Henry III was himself assassinated, and Henry of Navarre now claimed the throne. As King Henry IV (ruled 1589–1610), he became the first Bourbon ruler of France.

This action immediately drove the extreme Catholics into bitter opposition and provoked the intervention of Philip II of Spain. Henry IV countered this by securing English support and converted again to Catholicism, thus undermining many of his critics.

Henry was determined to bring the devastating Wars of Religion to an end. With this goal in mind, in 1598 he issued the Edict of Nantes, a document that made Catholicism the official religion of the country but gave the Huguenots a number of guaranteed protections. Awarding them the right to control more than 100 fortified towns throughout France, the edict also granted them the right to free worship in certain localities and full political privileges. Henry's willingness to accept religious toleration was a pragmatic political decision based on his recognition that France was exhausted by the destructive wars and required strong, effective government. Henceforth, matters of state became paramount as France's rulers set about rebuilding the country and the monarchy.

Royal Government and Economic Revival

The Wars of Religion had been deeply divisive of French society and had ruined the economy. The most pressing problem facing Henry IV was financial, for the wars had drained the treasury and heaped enormous debt on the government. Only after he had put the economy back on a firm footing could the king turn to rebuilding the power of the monarchy itself.

Henry and his Bourbon successors had the good fortune of being served by a succession of skillful and

PUBLIC FIGURES AND PRIVATE LIVES

MARIE DE' MEDICI AND HENRY IV OF FRANCE

Henry of Navarre's marriage to Catherine de' Medici's daughter, Margaret of Valois (1553–1615), had been arranged for purely political reasons and their relationship was tumultuous. In 1583, her sexual liaisons so scandalized the court that her brother, Henry III, exiled her from Paris. Ever resourceful, Margaret then raised an army of her own and fought against both brother and husband until she was captured and placed under house arrest. When her husband, by now king, wanted an annulment in order to marry one of his mistresses, she refused to give her consent until after the mistress died in 1599.

In 1600, Henry IV married Marie de' Medici (1573–1642), daughter of the grand duke of Tuscany. This alliance solidified Henry's conversion to Catholicism and rekindled the relationship begun by the Valois family with the house of Medici. Marie was a strong-willed, self-possessed woman from one of Italy's most distinguished families. She thought of the French as culturally inferior and set about bringing some of the sophisticated tastes of her own background to the court at Paris. Henry, on the other hand, proved himself a popular sovereign who demonstrated a real concern for the welfare of even his most lowly subjects.

When Henry was assassinated in 1610, Marie became regent for their son, Louis XIII (ruled 1610–1643). She completely dominated her son, and when the nobles began to raise objections to her rule she summoned the Estates General of the Realm in 1614 and declared Louis of age—the Estates General, without real power, was not called again for 175 years, on the eve of the French Revolution.

Despite the fact that in theory the regency was now dissolved, Marie continued to exclude Louis from the affairs of state. Instead, she dismissed Sully and relied on the advice of the Florentine adventurer Concino Concini (d. 1617) and the French cleric, Cardinal Armand du Plessis de Richelieu (1585–1642). Concini set up an elaborate spy system among the nobility and became universally despised for his greed and duplicity. In 1617, the young Louis arranged to have Concini assassinated and forced his mother into exile. She returned, however, five years later and was reconciled with Louis, whom she persuaded to appoint Richelieu secretary of state.

After her husband's death, Marie had built for herself in Paris the Luxembourg Palace, a large and elaborate residence modeled in part on the Pitti Palace in Florence. When Marie returned from exile in 1622, she commissioned the artist Peter Paul Rubens to paint a cycle of huge paintings dedicated to her and her marriage with Henry IV.

Marie's influence on French policy was considerable. She managed to keep the great nobles in check and established close relations with the Hapsburg Catholic powers, Spain and Austria.

Her ambitions finally overstepped her talents when she tried to undermine Richelieu, whose growing influence over the king she began to resent. In 1631, Louis banished her again. She fled to the Netherlands, never returning to France.

dedicated ministers. In reconstructing the economy, Henry had the assistance of a brilliant finance minister, Maximilien, duke of Sully (1560–1641). Like the king, Sully was earlier a Protestant but converted as a matter of policy. Beginning as a member of the king's finance commission, in 1598 he was made superintendent of finances.

Sully set out to increase royal revenues and reduce the debt. He established a new direct tax that was more easily calculated and collected. He raised the *gabelle*, a tax on salt, which virtually all citizens had to use as a preservative for keeping food. He reformed the tax-collecting mechanisms: under earlier kings, the revenue agents took a portion of the revenues they collected for themselves, and Sully now forced them to accept a lower percentage. Sully also raised money by increasing the number of royal offices and, as previous kings had done, continued to sell them for cash to nobles of the robe, a new class of aristocrat created by the monarchy to hold the key bureaucratic positions. Sully induced the older, landowning nobility of feudal origins, the nobles of the sword, to retire to their rural estates with government pensions. At the same time, he required the payment of an annual fee from all those nobles of the robe who occupied government offices.

While royal revenues were being increased, Sully had Henry cancel a portion of the public debt, so that he eventually was able to accumulate a surplus of funds. Sully negotiated trade treaties with the other powers and adopted the mercantilist policies that guided their trade programs. He used the new state income to invest in long-range economic development by building and improving roads, canals, and other infrastructure, a program that also had the immediate effect of putting people to work. Indeed, both Sully and the king were interested in increasing the general prosperity of all classes of French subjects, and Henry is reputed to have said, "There should be a chicken in every peasant's pot every Sunday."

THE CARDINALS AND THE STATE: THE ADMINISTRATIONS OF RICHELIEU AND MAZARIN

Between 1624 and 1661, the government of France was in the hands of two extraordinary ministers, Armand du Richelieu and Giulio Mazarin. Both were cardinals of the Catholic Church and proved to be two of the greatest statesmen in French history. The brilliant and crafty cardinals dedicated all their energies toward making the French monarchy as absolute as possible and keeping themselves in power. They balanced and held in check the various forces working against royal authority: the nobility, the bureaucracy, and the Huguenots.

Toward Royal Absolutism

In light of the destructive force of the Wars of Religion, religious policy was perhaps the most sensitive issue confronting Richelieu. Under Marie de' Medici and her Italian advisers, the Huguenots had worried about renewed persecution. Indeed, incidents of local conflict with royal troops erupted from time to time. In the 1620s, after one Huguenot stronghold had allied itself with the English against the monarchy, the government began to seize the fortified towns the Huguenots had been granted under the terms of the Edict of Nantes. Richelieu then secured the revocation of the edict and replaced it with the Peace of Alais, which granted the Huguenots only religious and political rights.

For years, the constant wars that disturbed French public life had required royal governments to raise monies for their armies, and this had proved to be a major impetus in the drive toward absolutism.

Richelieu, needing revenues to finance his foreign and domestic policies, was no exception. He encouraged the sale of government offices, which continued to grow in number. By the 1630s, almost half of all government income came from this source. As a result, the efficient collection of taxes and control over local affairs assumed increasing importance. Toward this end, Richelieu used special representatives known as *intendants* to enforce royal policy in the provinces and undermine the power of the nobility.

Richelieu was never able to bring royal finances under control and had to resort to increasing taxes on ordinary citizens in order to meet the mounting national debt. The tax burden and the ever-growing power of the royal government sometimes sparked protests and uprisings in the countryside, especially among the peasantry and the nobility. Richelieu was able, however, to put them down with the royal troops.

Cardinal Mazarin and the Fronde

Louis XIII died in 1643. Since his son, Louis XIV (ruled 1643–1715) was only five years old at the time, once again France came under the regency of the queen mother, this time Anne of Austria (1601–1666). Anne turned the government over to Giulio Mazarin (1602–1661), to whom she may have been secretly married (this suspicion has never been confirmed). Mazarin was an Italian-born soldier who had served in the papal diplomatic corps. Although never ordained as a priest, he was Richelieu's protégé and Louis XIII had recommended that he be made a cardinal.

Mazarin continued the two policies of his predecessor: the centralization of power in the hands of the king, and increasing taxation to pay for the costs of royal government. These programs incurred the wrath of both the nobles and the members of the law court

Philippe de Champagne, *Cardinal Richelieu,* depicts the sharp intelligence and authority of Louis XIII's minister.

A portrait of Cardinal Mazarin.

known as the Parlement of Paris, who in any case disliked Mazarin on principle because he was a foreigner. Mazarin further weakened his position by involvement in personal financial corruption. The nobles and the members of the Parlement joined forces against the monarchy when Mazarin tried to squeeze money out of them to meet the mounting costs of the French involvement in the Thirty Years' War (see below). The result was an organized conspiracy against the government, known as the *Fronde*—a word that has come to mean violent political opposition from within the ruling class.

In 1648, the Parlement and nobles of the robe, who held many of the important bureaucratic offices, demanded that the king abolish the *intendants*, accept the idea of habeas corpus, and agree to levy no new taxes without consent. When Mazarin arrested the leaders of the Parlement, a popular revolt in Paris forced him and the royal family to flee the capital. The disturbances spread to other cities, and in a number of locations the protestors took over local governments and random acts of violence erupted. This first episode of the Fronde ended only after Mazarin pledged to give in to the demands of the Parlement.

A second Fronde developed in 1650 around two nobles of the sword who held important military positions. This time, the ringleaders insisted that Mazarin be dismissed and that many of the traditional local powers of the old nobility be restored. The Spanish, with whom the French had continued to fight even after the end of the Thirty Years' War, sent aid to the Fronde. The effort failed, however, when the nobles began fighting among themselves. Mazarin shrewdly played one group off against another and was able to use army elements loyal to the monarchy to crush the conspiracy. In 1652, Mazarin strengthened royal authority by having the minority of Louis XIV declared at an end. Never again would the monarchy be seriously threatened by rebellious nobles. Indeed, the failure of the Fronde had the opposite effect, serving to strengthen the power of the state. After Mazarin's death in 1661, Louis XIV excluded his mother Anne from all participation in the affairs of state and assumed full powers over one of the most powerful forms of absolute monarchy in Western Europe.

A SCANDAL IN BOHEMIA: THE PROTESTANT REVOLT AND THE THIRTY YEARS' WAR

The last of the great wars of religion that shook Europe is known as the Thirty Years' War, a complex struggle that unfolded in four distinct phases between 1618 and 1648: the Bohemian Phase (1618–1625), the Danish Phase (1625–1629), the Swedish Phase (1630–1635), and the French-Swedish Phase (1635–1648). Much of the fighting took place in Germany, but the struggle dragged in most of the great states of Europe and many

Significant Dates

The Thirty Years' War

1608	Protestant Union formed
1609	Catholic League formed
1618	Defenestration of Prague
1618–1625	Bohemian Phase of war
1625–1629	Danish Phase of war
1630–1635	Swedish Phase of war
1635–1648	French-Swedish Phase of war
1648	Peace of Westphalia
1659	Peace of Pyrenees

The death and destruction that befell Germany during the Thirty Years' War were depicted in a series of etchings by Jacques Callot, *The Miseries of War.*

of the lesser powers as well. Three principal participants, Spain, Austria, and France, were at the center of the conflict.

The vast Hapsburg empire had been established when Charles V inherited the throne of Spain and three years later became Holy Roman emperor. Eventually, he ruled over Austria, Bohemia, Hungary, and the Netherlands as well as Spain, the German lands of the Holy Roman Empire, and portions of Italy. When Charles retired in 1556, his holdings were divided. His son Philip II received Spain and its overseas colonies, the Netherlands, and Italy, while his brother Ferdinand took the imperial title along with Austria, Bohemia, and Hungary. From the time of Charles V, the French had felt encircled by the lands and ambitions of the Hapsburgs, and an ongoing struggle between first the Valois and then the Bourbon rulers of France and the Hapsburgs marked European politics for more than a century.

The religious wars that engulfed the German states ended with the Peace of Augsburg in 1555. The two sides, however, continued to fight sporadically and eventually formed opposing military alliances: the Protestant Union, supported by France, England, and the United Provinces of the Netherlands; and the Catholic League, supported by Spain and the Holy Roman Empire. Clearly, then, the war involved political and dynastic issues that had little to do with religious questions.

The war began in Bohemia, however, over religious issues. In 1609, the Holy Roman emperor had pledged himself to a policy of religious toleration for Catholics and Protestants alike. He intended his promise to mollify the Calvinist nobles in Bohemia, where in the early 15th century the reformer Jan Hus had been a popular hero. When, however, Ferdinand II of Hapsburg (ruled as king of Bohemia 1617–1637, and as Holy Roman emperor 1619–1637) became king of Bohemia in 1617, he began an effort to impose Catholicism and a rigid centralizing policy on the country.

The Catholic Triumph

The result was a rebellion in 1618, begun when the nobles threw three imperial officials out of the window of the castle in Prague—the so-called "defenestration of Prague." The Bohemians declared Ferdinand deposed and replaced him with Frederick II of the Palatinate, the leader of the Protestant Union and the most prominent Calvinist prince in the Holy Roman Empire. The war had begun.

The hostilities brought an invading army into Bohemia under Ferdinand, who had now become Holy Roman emperor, and his German ally, Duke Maximilian of Bavaria. In 1620, Catholic forces under the Flemish general Johann von Tilly won a crushing victory against the Calvinists at the Battle of the White Mountain. Ferdinand proceeded to end the autonomy of Bohemia and to declare Catholicism the official religion. The emperor also deprived the Calvinist nobles of their landed estates and forced tens of thousands of Protestants to leave the country.

Moreover, while Frederick was fighting in Bohemia, the Spanish intervened by invading and occupying the Palatinate, which was then divided between them and the Bavarians. The first phase of the Thirty Years' War ended triumphantly with the Catholic forces in possession of Bohemia and the Palatinate and Spanish troops marching once again into the United Provinces in an effort to recapture the northern territories that Spain had lost in the Dutch revolt of the previous century.

In 1625, the Thirty Years' War was widened by intervention from an unexpected source. Christian IV (ruled 1588–1648), king of Denmark and Norway, invaded northern Germany. Ostensibly joining the struggle in order to assist the Protestant forces, Christian was really motivated by his own expansionist drives—he had already fought against Sweden for control of Lapland, and now seemed bent on securing hegemony over the Baltic region around Denmark and Germany.

Christian's ambitions exceeded his abilities. Tilly defeated the Danish army in 1626, and the next year the commander of the imperial forces, Albrecht von Wallenstein, defeated Christian again. Wallenstein, a Bohemian nobleman who had raised an army on the behalf of the emperor, had enriched himself on the lands taken from the Protestants. His troops lived off the lands through which they moved, pillaging and destroying peasant villages and large estates with equal ferocity.

FROM THE SWEDISH VICTORY TO THE FRENCH INTERVENTION

By 1629, Christian was forced to withdraw from the war and the Catholics had occupied Denmark and the principal ports of northern Germany. Following these victories, the Emperor Ferdinand announced the Edict of Restitution, which gave back to the Catholic Church all lands taken from it since 1552. The edict also outlawed Calvinism—which had not been protected by the Peace of Augsburg in 1555—in all imperial territories. Yet the very extent of the Catholic victory proved its undoing. The German princes grew worried by the startling increase in imperial power and began to rebel against Ferdinand. At a meeting of the imperial diet in 1630, they demanded that he relieve Wallenstein of his command or see the end of Hapsburg control of the imperial crown.

Map 4.3 The Expansion of Sweden

Gustavus Adolphus

Ferdinand gave in, and the price was high, for he was deprived of Wallenstein's military talents just as a major new phase of the war began. In 1630, King Gustavus Adolphus of Sweden (ruled 1611–1632) joined the Protestant cause. Gustavus Adolphus had proven to be a vigorous monarch who restructured the Swedish state, disciplined its nobles, and won major victories against the Russians and Poles in the Baltic. Yet he, too, was motivated by political as well as religious questions. Gustavus Adolphus aimed to make Sweden the predominant power in the Baltic and feared the spread of Hapsburg power along the coast of Germany.

Assisted financially by the French, the Swedish king organized a strong military force and moved rapidly and deeply into Germany, pushing the imperial armies before him. Gustavus Adolphus, a brilliant field commander, defeated Tilly at Breitenfield in 1631 and Lech the next year. Recoiling from these blows, Ferdinand recalled Wallenstein to head the imperial forces. At Lutzen in 1632, the Swedes defeated Wallenstein's soldiers but Gustavus Adolphus himself was mortally wounded and died shortly afterwards.

The tide of battle soon turned against the Swedish army still in Germany. In 1634, the imperial armies—although deprived once again of Wallenstein's command when the general was assassinated—won the Battle of Nordlingen and cleared southern Germany of Swedish troops. The following year, Ferdinand signed the Treaty of Prague with the German princes, bringing a settlement of the tensions between them and the Hapsburgs. Ferdinand withdrew the Edict of Restitution in return for their pledge to help in defeating the remaining Swedish forces. Moreover, Ferdinand declared a political amnesty for all German princes who had fought against the empire, except for Frederick of the Palatinate.

Although the war appeared to be over, in 1635 Cardinal Richelieu decided to involve Catholic France in the conflict, but on the side of the Lutheran Swedes against the Catholic Hapsburgs. Thus began the final phase of the war, in which political and dynastic issues

Gustavus Adolphus of Sweden, one of the principal figures in the Thirty Years' War, shown here at the Battle of Breitenfeld.

were paramount. For more than a decade some of the most bitter and destructive fighting took place in Germany and the Netherlands. The international situation had become chaotic and both sides realized that it was in the general interest to stop the carnage. Tentative peace talks started in 1641 but dragged on for seven more years.

The Peace of Westphalia

The French victories over the Spanish in 1643, followed by further victories in southern Germany, reactivated the negotiations. By 1648 all sides were ready to end the fighting (the struggle between Spain and France continued until peace was signed between them in 1659). The Peace of Westphalia was arranged as a result of a large meeting of representatives from all the participants, including France, Spain, Denmark, Sweden, the United Provinces, and the Holy Roman Empire.

France, which dominated the fighting in the last years of the war, gained territories along its northeastern border, notably Alsace and Lorraine. Sweden, France's principal ally, secured control over lands in Germany. In a broad sense, the French finally won their long-standing struggle to tame the Hapsburg empire. The representatives agreed to the independence of the United Provinces and Switzerland, two areas that the Hapsburgs had claimed; at the same time, the German princes of the Holy Roman Empire pledged not to take up arms again against the emperor, who in turn acknowledged their autonomy. This arrangement was confirmed in 1657 when the emperor accepted the German princes' claim that the empire was officially a state of independent principalities.

Westphalia represented a major victory for Protestantism. The religious autonomy of the German princes was confirmed, both for Calvinists and Lutherans, and all Catholic properties seized before 1624 now became possessions of the Protestant states. Most far-reaching was the fact that the treaty ended once and for all the idea that the split between Catholic and Protestant could be healed.

The end of the war signaled the final eclipse of Spain and the rise of France as the dominant power on the Continent. In addition, the religious passions that had been the cause of so much destruction and killing for a century began to subside. Henceforth, economic and political ambitions rather than dynastic and religious issues would determine relations among the states of Europe.

The Westphalia agreements established a peace that remained effective for more than a century. The Thirty

Map 4.4 Europe, 1648

Years' War had caused terrible destruction, including widespread economic havoc and millions of deaths—estimates suggest that the fighting had wiped out almost a third of the people of Germany. Even though these figures may be exaggerated, European leaders recognized the extent of the carnage, and concluded that diplomacy was a better solution than armed conflict.

Questions for Further Study

1. What was the relationship between politics and religion in France?
2. How did Richelieu and Mazarin strengthen the authority of the king?
3. What were the major issues involved in the Thirty Years' War?

Suggestions for Further Reading

Bergin, Joseph. *Cardinal Richelieu: Power and the Pursuit of Wealth*. New Haven, CT, 1985.

Diefendorf, Barbara. *Beneath the Cross: Catholics and Huguenots in Sixteenth-Century Paris*. New York, 1991.

Dunn, Richard S. *The Age of Religious Wars, 1559–1715*, 2nd ed. New York, 1979.
Maltby, William S. *Alba*. Berkeley, CA, 1983.
Parker, Geoffrey. *The Thirty Years War*. London, 1985.
Pennington, Donald H. *Seventeenth-Century Europe*, 2nd ed. London, 1989.
Salmon, John H. M. *Society in Crisis: France in the Sixteenth Century*. New York, 1975.
Salmon, John H. M. *French Government and Society in the Wars of Religion*. St. Louis, MO, 1976.
Steinberg, Sigfrid. *The Thirty Years' War and the Conflict for European Hegemony*. New York, 1966.
Sutherland, Nicola M. *The Massacre of St. Bartholomew and the European Conflict, 1559–1572*. New York, 1973.
Tapie, Victor L. *France in the Age of Louis XIII and Richelieu*, trans. D. Lockie. New York, 1975.

V

Topic 5

Patterns of Life in a Time of Upheaval

The decades following the Reformation saw tumultuous political events and rapid cultural innovation. The social patterns of everyday life, however, still retained links with the Medieval world and changed slowly over many centuries. This gradual evolution influenced the basic aspects of daily experience, including the health and well-being of all classes of Europeans, their diet and housing, and the way in which they dressed.

The two factors that affected health most acutely were the food supply and infectious disease, both of which remained largely beyond the control of humans until the industrial revolution of the 18th century. Life expectancy was low, and repeated cycles of disease continued to take their toll on the population. In spite of advances made in science and medicine, little progress was made in improving conditions of health and sanitation for any level of society.

The rich and poor led vastly different lives in terms of diet and housing. For 200 years following the Black Death, food and nutrition improved for most Europeans. With the religious and political upheavals of the 16th and 17th centuries, however, general standards declined. The consumption of fresh meat went down and was replaced among the poor by salted meat, a substitute made possible by the development of techniques for preserving food. By contrast, wealthy Europeans could now enrich their diet with new and exotic products, many introduced from the overseas colonies.

The same disparity marked the kind of housing available to rich and poor. More durable building materials, such as brick and stone, began to replace wood in public buildings and in the private residences of the wealthy. The houses of the nobility and the rich merchants of the cities made use of elaborate decorations and furnishings, reflecting a new level of domestic comfort and a growing concern for privacy. The urban poor, on the other hand, were increasingly crammed into densely populated and unsanitary tenement buildings, while the rural poor continued to live under much the same conditions as their ancestors had done.

One of the most visible manifestations of the social hierarchy was dress. For the poor and the peasantry, clothing style remained relatively unchanged for hundreds of years after the 14th century. For the rich, however, dress reflected the availability of new raw materials, including cotton and silk, and the development of new manufacturing processes. With the greater variety made possible, fashion became a sign of status and sophistication. One aspect of developing style was the appearance of forms of dress characteristic of particular countries or social classes.

Material aspects of life such as clothing and housing provide a way of understanding broad social and economic transformations. At the same time, they offer insight into the lives of the vast majority of Europeans who played no active part in the great political events of their times but who bring us into contact with the daily realities of human existence.

HEALTH AND MEDICINE

In the two centuries before the French Revolution, Europeans had achieved a rough balance between the rate of births and the rate of deaths. Infant mortality was high, with perhaps as many as a third of all children in the 17th century dying before their first birthday. Among the chief factors keeping the death rate high were disease and starvation, and people lived to an average age of only 25. The wealthy tended to live somewhat longer than the poor, and childbirth made women especially vulnerable to illness and death.

The Cycle of Disease

The great plague of the 14th century, the Black Death, was by no means unique. Throughout European history all segments of society, but especially the poor, were highly susceptible to disease. This was generally because of low resistance to illness caused either by diets lacking in nutritional value or by the famines that periodically struck the population—almost always, in fact, epidemics followed incidences of famine.

The plague recurred time and again from the 15th to the 17th centuries. In a 200-year period, the French town of Besançon experienced it 40 times, while Seville in southern Spain saw outbreaks during eleven of the years from 1507 to 1649. In Western Europe, the plague appeared for the last time in 1720 when it killed perhaps half the inhabitants of the French port city of Marseilles. In Eastern Europe, however, where health and sanitary conditions were even worse, the plague continued to ravage cities into the 19th century—thousands fell victim to it in Moscow in 1770 and in the Balkans as late as 1841.

Plague was merely one among a host of prevalent diseases, and often adverse conditions caused the spread of several different maladies at the same time: smallpox, typhus, cholera, tuberculosis, influenza, grippe, whooping cough, diphtheria, and scarlet fever were some of the diseases that were an ever-present fear. At the time, diseases were often diagnosed incorrectly or confused with the plague, and contemporary descriptions of many illnesses make it difficult to identify them today. Between 1486 and 1551, a strange malady known as the "sweating sickness" struck England five times. It attacked the lungs and heart, bringing on intense rheumatic pains as well as severe bouts of sweat and shivering, and often causing death in a matter of hours.

Epidemics spread from one population group to another, usually following the movement of people along trade routes and other heavily traveled itineraries. The Black Death reached Europe on ships from the Crimea, and in the early 18th century cholera came to the Continent from India. Perhaps the best known example of the movement of disease from one culture to another was the result of the so-called "Columbian Exchange." Spanish explorers and soldiers brought diseases such as smallpox to the Amerindians of the New World, where no resistance had been developed to these unknown illnesses. The result was the devastation of huge numbers of people.

The process also worked in the other direction. Syphilis, which had been rare in Europe, appears to have become widespread after 1492. Indeed, one theory holds that members of Columbus' crew contracted it on their arrival in America following the first voyage. Syphilis became a real epidemic that spread rapidly around Europe and by the end of the 16th century it had affected all classes of society, including many members of royal families.

Medical Care

The measures taken to deal with the plague in the 17th century were the same as those in the 14th. The rich fled the cities for more isolated homes in the country, while the poor remained in the crowded cities, often locked behind the town gates with the roads to and from the cities blocked. The sick were quarantined, dead bodies burned, and neighborhoods sometimes disinfected, although city officials often abandoned their duties until the danger was over. Medical treatment remained generally quite primitive until modern times. In the 16th century, some physicians believed

A gruesome scene of early surgical methods.

they could treat syphilis by cauterizing sores with red-hot irons.

Improved personal hygiene, the replacement of wood with stone or brick as building material for homes, and the elimination of animals from households all reduced fleas and help explain why the plague eventually disappeared. In the 18th century, however, smallpox, which replaced the plague as the most devastating disease, killed perhaps 60 million people. For many years, smallpox had been treated successfully by Muslim physicians, who developed the technique of inoculation. The practice was slowly adopted in the West during the 18th century. Moreover, some scholars suggest that the eventual elimination of particular diseases may be explained not only by such preventative measures, but also by the mutation of the bacteria or virus causing the disease.

A number of important medical techniques—systematic observation and deductive reasoning, the use of dissection to study anatomy, and the discovery of the circulation of blood—led to a better understanding of the human body. Moreover, the number of doctors and their training increased greatly. Yet well into the 18th century, faith healing and peasant folk remedies based largely on superstition continued to be practiced widely. Sometimes herbs and drugs prescribed by apothecaries actually worked to cure a patient. Bloodletting and purging remained common and often harmful treatments. Surgery was performed without the use of anesthetic and under extremely unsanitary conditions, especially on battlefields and in hospital wards for the poor. Until the 19th century saw improvement in treatment of patients, medical knowledge had little practical impact on the health of most Europeans.

Despite the terrible toll on human life taken by the plague and other diseases, the cycle of European marriages and births generally compensated for the demographic losses. In 1451, for example, 21,000 inhabitants of Cologne died of plague, but within a few years 4000 marriages had taken place in the same city. Similarly, after the plague had decimated the inhabitants of Verona, Italy, in 1637, many of the French soldiers occupying the town married the widows. In Germany as a whole, the devastating impact of the Thirty Years' War, which had claimed perhaps a third

In this painting by Madeleine de Boulogne (1646–1710), nuns practice charity by giving medical care to female patients.

of the population, soon eased as the population began to increase again. The overall demographic pattern in the West changed significantly in the course of the 18th century, when births finally began to gain over deaths, with the result that Europe experienced a far-reaching population explosion.

CHANGING TASTES: FOOD AND DIET

Ever since ancient times, the fundamental food source for Europeans was grain, supplemented by vegetables and only very occasionally by other kinds of food. Wealthier people ate meat, fish, and cheese, and were able to improve the taste and variety of their food with spices and sauces. Europe's diet changed significantly as a result of overseas exploration and the discovery of the Americas, and eventually the potato replaced grain as the staple ingredient for many poor people.

Farming and Scarcity

In the Roman Empire and the Middle Ages, Europe's poor—the overwhelming majority of people—consumed the same monotonous, uninspiring diet, consisting largely of grains. Europeans cultivated a variety of them, including millet, spelt, barley, oats, and rye, but the major crop was always wheat. The problem with grain, and especially wheat, was that it required large amounts of land to produce relatively low yields. Wheat could not be grown two years in a row on the same land, for the soil became rapidly depleted. Farmers therefore resorted to the two-field system, and later the three-field system, whereby some portion of the land was allowed to be restored by letting it lie fallow. Although effective, this method of growing made it impossible to use all the land at once. In addition, wheat cultivation also required the use of manure for fertilizer, and this in turn meant that some of the land had to be reserved for the grazing of animals that produced the manure.

The supply of basic foods like grain was always precarious. Crop yields did increase slowly over time, especially between the 16th and the 18th centuries, when the yield was almost twice that in the late Middle Ages. Nevertheless, most of Europe suffered from a condition of chronic scarcity, and devastating famines continued to strike Europe well into the 19th century.

The European Diet

From wheat and other grains, peasants made two kinds of food: bread and gruel. Bread was the staple food item, and it has been estimated that in good times an adult peasant ate more than four pounds of bread a day. Peasant bread was generally made from wheat or rye, and often a combination of the two. Because the grain was ground into flour by rough stone wheels, the wheat germ and outer husk of bran remained as part of the flour. This flour produced a dark, rough-textured bread that was the principal—and often the only—food that peasants consumed. Gruel was a kind of thick porridge, like oatmeal, made by boiling grains in water. It was seldom if ever flavored with spices and rarely contained other ingredients.

Vegetables were also available except in winter and early spring. These most often included peas, beans, lentils, carrots, onions, and cabbages, and less fortunate rural dwellers cooked wild grasses and roots. Vegetables were boiled or mixed with grains to make soups. Only rarely, several times a year, did peasants eat meat or fish, which were usually the preserve of the nobles who owned the land and rivers. More prosperous peasants had a few animals from which they made cheese and butter, but these were eaten sparingly and milk was reserved almost exclusively for the very young and the old.

An old European proverb, "Tell me what you eat and I will tell you who you are," reflects the social reality of how the diet of the poor differed significantly from that of the rich. The upper classes developed a passion for eating meat, whether it was beef, lamb, venison, or pork. For dinner parties, the nobility would often serve several courses of these meats, interspersed with fish and fowl of various kinds. They seldom ate vegetables, which they considered the loathsome diet of the poor. Not only would they prohibit peasants on their lands from hunting and fishing, but they devoted themselves to hunting as a favorite social pastime. Those who "poached" game from their preserves were fined and severely punished.

The meals of the ruling class were certainly more interesting and varied than those of the peasantry. They were the only people who could afford the rare and costly spices that came from Asia, and their cooks used these ingredients and the juices of meats and fish to make sauces to flavor their food. They also could buy fruit, sugar, and honey, which they used to make sweets and pastries. Moreover, the rich avoided the coarse dark bread eaten by the peasants, preferring finer grades of white bread made from sifted flour. Specialty breads contained brewer's yeast, milk, and sometimes eggs and sugar.

It is not surprising that the European diet was determined first and foremost by wealth and social status. The irony, however, is that the poorer classes seem to have consumed a more nutritious diet. Today we know that the common dark bread eaten by peasants was nutritiously balanced, containing a mixture of carbohydrates, proteins, and minerals, and that when they supplemented their diet with vegetables, the vitamin

Jean Michelin's *The Baker's Cart* (1656). Bakeries were originally at the outskirts of towns, and the bread sold on street carts.

and mineral content went up even more. It was during the winter and spring that the diet of the peasantry suffered, for during those months they did not have access to fresh vegetables, with the result that they often suffered from scurvy, brought on by a lack of vitamin C.

The rich, on the other hand, ate a much less healthy diet, heavy in protein but low in vitamins and minerals. This deficiency was compounded by the white bread they preferred, which lacked the minerals and vitamins of the peasant bread. Those with the most balanced, and therefore the healthiest, diets were probably the middle classes, who ate some meat and cheese but also consumed vegetables and often could not afford the white bread of the nobility.

New Foods and Consumption Patterns

The original purpose of the great European explorations that began in the 15th century had been to find a direct sea route to Asia in order to obtain prized spices and luxury products directly from their source. In the process, the explorers accomplished much more than this, for the discovery of the Americas resulted in the importation of a host of new foods to Europe. Among these were the potato, tomatoes, squash, and Indian corn (maize).

These new products changed the kinds of foods eaten in different cultures of the world, including a number of European countries. The chili pepper, which originally developed on the slopes of the Andes in Peru, is not related botanically to the pepper at all. Its piquant flavor led the early explorers to misname it, however, and it soon acquired worldwide popularity, transforming the cuisine of China and much of Asia as well as of Africa. In a similar fashion, the tomato became the rage in much of southern Italy, where it was first introduced into Naples by the Spanish in the 16th century. From there, its use spread to southern France, where Provençal cooking still uses it in great quantity. Sugar, which probably was native to India, had been known in the West since ancient times and was as costly as any of the spices. In the 16th century, however, a Spanish merchant transported cane to

DOCUMENTS ON HISTORY

Food and the Columbian Exchange

When Columbus set foot on the island of Hispaniola in October 1492, he began a complex process of interaction between the Old World and the New known as the "Columbian Exchange." This process had a profound impact—both positive and negative—on both civilizations.

Among the many aspects of European and Amerindian life that each encountered was food. The Spanish introduced such vegetation as wheat, bananas, oranges and lemons, grapes, and sugar cane to the Western Hemisphere. The early European visitors also brought goats, sheep, horses, pigs, chickens, and cattle to the New World, with adverse ecological results, for as these animals roamed the ranges they destroyed the roots of plants and ate the leaves. On the other hand, as we have seen, the diet of much of the rest of the world was dramatically changed as vegetables and plants indigenous to the Americas were introduced to Europe, Africa, and Asia.

FIRST ENCOUNTERS

The earliest Europeans in the Western Hemisphere marveled at the foods the Amerindians grew, manufactured, and ate but noted the absence of familiar items. From Columbus to Cortés, they recorded their findings in great detail.

During this time I walked among the trees, which are the most beautiful I have ever seen. I saw as much greenery, in such density, as I would have seen in Andalusia in May. And all of the trees are as different from ours as day is from night, and so are the fruits, the herbage, the rocks, and everything. . . .

This morning I took the small boat and went up the river until I reached fresh water, which might be about six miles. I beached the boat and went ashore, climbing a slight elevation in order to learn something about this country, but I could not see anything because of the thick forest, which was very fresh and fragrant. I have no doubt that there are many aromatic herbs here. Everything is so beautiful that the eyes never weary of seeing such a sight, nor could one ever tire of the songs of the birds, both large and small. . . .

There are trees . . . that give a fruit like the apricot, which is full of small seeds like the seeds of a fig, red as scarlet which the inhabitants eat, but to us it is none too good. . . . There are also some like the artichoke plant but four times as tall, which give a fruit in the shape of a pine cone, twice as big, which fruit is excellent, and it can be cut with a knife like a turnip and it seems to be very wholesome. . . .

All the land around the village is cultivated, and a river flows through the middle of the valley. It is very large and wide and could irrigate all the lands around. All the trees are green and full of fruit, and the plants are in flower and very tall. The roads are wide and good, and the breezes are like those in Castile in the month of April. The nightingales and other small birds sing as they do in Spain in the same month, and it is the greatest pleasure in the world. Small birds sing sweetly during the night, and one can hear many crickets and frogs. The fish are the same as in Spain. There are many mastic trees and aloes and cotton trees.

From *The Log of Christopher Columbus,* trans. Robert H. Fuson International Marine Publishers, Copyright © Reprinted with permission,1992.

MANIOC: A NEW WORLD STAPLE

Several weeks after arriving in the Bahamas, Columbus tasted a local bread made from manioc *(known to the Spanish as* yuca *and to the English as* cassava*). Manioc had been under cultivation in the Western Hemisphere for thousands of years and to this day remains a staple for millions of people in the tropics. A fast-growing shrub, the manioc plant produces large tubular roots that provide starch energy on a subsistence level. It is generally made into a paste or a porridge eaten with a sauce or made into a flour. Columbus discusses manioc in his journal.*

They [the Amerindians] brought the bread of niamas [manioc], which are tubers and look like large radishes. These are planted in all their fields and are their staff of life. They make bread from them and boil and roast them, and they taste like chestnuts. . . .

These fields are planted mostly with *ajes*. The Indians sow little shoots from which small roots grow that look like carrots. They serve this as bread by grating and kneading it, then baking it in the fire. They plant a small shoot from the same root again in another place, and once more it produces four or five of these roots. They are very palatable and taste exactly like chestnuts. The ones grown here are the largest and best I have seen anywhere. I have also seen them in Guinea, but those that grow there are as thick as your leg.

From *The Log of Christopher Columbus,* trans. Robert H. Fuson International Marine Publishers, Copyright © Reprinted with permission, 1992.

From Poison to Food

Some forms of manioc, however, are poisonous and must be processed to be safe to consume. Roger Barlow, a 16th-century English writer, described the process in his A Brief Summe of Geographie.

[The Amerindians rub the manioc root] on a stone and so it turneth to curdes, which thei take and put in a long, narowe bagge made of ryndes of trees, and so press out the liquor and gather it in a vessell, and when the iuce is out ther resteth in the bagge the floure as fyne and white as the snowe, wherof thei make cakys and bake them upon the fier in a panne, and after this be bakyn it is a very good brede, holsome and medecinable, and will endure a yere without corruptyng. And likewise thei take the licour and seethe it over the fyre and after that it is a good drynke and of grete sustenaunce and strength, but and if one shuld drinke of it before it were boiled over the fire, and litle quantite as wold into a nuttys shelle, thei suld die incontynent.

From Alfred W. Crosby, Jr., *The Columbian Exchange: Biological and Cultural Consequences of 1492,* Greenwood Press, Copyright © 1971.

FOOD OF THE AMERINDIANS

As the Spanish conquistadors *ravaged Mexican and South American cultures, they were generally forced to live off the land and to become accustomed to eating local foods.*

Hernan Cortés

The food they [the inhabitants of islands off the Yucatan] eat is maize and some chili peppers, as on the other islands, and *patata yuca*, just the same as is eaten in Cuba, and they eat it roast, for they do not make bread of it; and they both hunt and fish and breed many chickens [probably

continued next page

turkeys] such as those found on *Tierra Firme*, which are as big as peacocks.

From Hernan Cortés, *Letters from Mexico,* trans. and ed. A. R. Pagden Yale University Press, Copyright © 1971.

Bernal Díaz del Castillo

When we got on shore we found three Caciques, one of them the governor appointed by Montezuma, who had many of the Indians of his household with him. They brought many of the fowls of the country and maize bread such as they always eat, and fruits such as pineapples and zapotes, which in other parts are called mameies, and they were seated under the shade of the trees, and had spread mats on the ground, and they invited us to be seated, all by signs, for Julianillo the man from Cape Catoche, did not understand their language, which is Mexican. Then they brought pottery braziers with live coals, and fumigated us with a sort of resin.

From Bernal Díaz del Castillo, *The Discovery and Conquest of Mexico, 1517–1521,* ed. Genaro Garcia and trans. A. P. Maudslay Farrar, Straus and Giroux, Copyright © 1956.

ON WINE AND OTHER SPIRITS

The Spanish enjoyed wine made from grapes, which Europeans had produced since ancient times. As early as his second voyage in 1493, Columbus brought with him seeds and cuttings from numerous plants, including vines, but Europeans soon discovered that the climate was right only in Peru, Chile, and what is now Argentina. By 1614, one vineyard in Chile produced some 200,000 jugs of wine. The conquistadors found that the Amerindians had their own version of wine made from the maguey *plant, a member of the aloe family. When drunk fresh from the plant, the sap is known as* aguamiel, *or "honey water." When fermented, however, the resulting syrupy liquor becomes* pulque, *a beverage still consumed in the region today. When the Europeans distilled* pulque, *they produced a higher-proof alcohol liquor known today as Tequila.*

In his description of the large market at Temixtitan, Cortés lists the "syrup."

This city has many squares where trading is done and markets are held continuously. There is also one square twice as big as that of Salamanca, with arcades all around, where more than sixty thousand people come each day to buy and sell, and where every kind of merchandise produced in these lands is found; provisions as well as ornaments of gold and silver, lead, brass, copper, tin, stones, shells, bones, and feathers. They also sell lime, hewn and unhewn stone, adobe bricks, tiles, and cut and uncut woods of various kinds. There is a street where they sell game and birds of every species found in this land: chickens, partridges and quails, wild ducks, fly-catchers, widgeons, turtledoves, pigeons, cane birds, parrots, eagles and eagle owls, falcons, sparrow hawks and kestrels, and they sell the skins of some of these birds of prey with their feathers, heads and claws. They sell rabbits and hares, and stags and small gelded dogs which they breed for eating.

There are streets of herbalists where all the medicinal herbs and roots found in the land are sold. There are shops like apothecaries', where they sell ready-made medicines as well as liquid ointments and plasters. There are shops like barbers' where they have their hair washed and shaved, and shops where they sell food and drink. There are also men like porters to carry loads. There is much firewood and charcoal, earthenware braziers and mats of various kinds like mattresses for beds, and other, finer ones, for seats and for covering rooms and hallways. There is every sort of vegetable, especially onions, leeks, garlic, common cress and watercress, borage, sorrel, teasels and artichokes; and there are many sorts of fruit, among which are cherries and plums like those in Spain.

They sell honey, wax, and a syrup made from maize canes, which is as sweet and syrupy as that made from the sugar cane. They also make syrup from a plant which in the islands is called *maguey*, which is much better than most syrups, and from this plant they also make sugar and wine, which they likewise sell. There are many sorts of spun cotton, in hanks of every color, and it seems like the silk market at Granada, except here there is a much greater quantity. They sell as many colors for painters as may be found in Spain and all of excellent hues. They sell deerskins, with and without the hair, and some are dyed white or in various colors. They sell much earthenware, which for the most part is very good; there are both large and small pitchers, jugs, pots, tiles, and many other sorts of vessel, all of good clay and most of them glazed and painted. They sell maize both as grain and as bread and it is better both in appearance and in taste than any found in the islands or on the mainland. They sell chicken and fish pies, and much fresh and salted fish, as well as raw and cooked fish. They sell hen and goose eggs, and eggs of all the other birds I have mentioned, in great number, and they sell *tortillas* made from eggs.

From Hernan Cortés, *Letters from Mexico,* trans. and ed. A. R. Pagden Yale University Press, Copyright © 1971.

FOOD AT THE ROYAL PALACE

The Amerindians ate a number of foods that the Europeans found strange and sometimes disquieting, including dogs and worms from the maguey plant. Columbus records that on first landing in the Americas he encountered "a serpent" about six feet long, no doubt an iguana, which his men killed—"The people here eat them and the meat is white and tastes like chicken." Díaz del Castillo tells that when his party met the Caciques, "they wished to kill us and eat our flesh, and had already prepared the pots with salt and peppers and tomatoes." Cortés wrote briefly of the kind of foods eaten in Montezuma's palace.

When they brought food to Montezuma they also provided for all those chiefs to each according to his rank; and their servants and followers were also given to eat. The pantry and the wine stores were left open each day for those who wished to eat and drink. Three or four hundred boys came bringing the dishes, which were without number, for each time he lunched or dined, he was brought every kind of food: meat, fish, fruit and vegetables.

From Hernan Cortés, *Letters from Mexico,* trans. and ed. A. R. Pagden Yale University Press, Copyright © 1971.

Montezuma's Banquet

Díaz del Castillo gives a detailed description of a great banquet.

For each meal, over thirty different dishes were prepared by his cooks according to their ways and usage, and they placed small pottery braziers beneath the dishes so that they should not get cold. They prepared more than three hundred plates of the food that Montezuma was going to eat, and more than a thousand for the guard. When he was going to eat, Montezuma would sometimes go out with his chiefs and stewards, and they would point out to him which dish was best, and of what birds and other things it was composed, and as they advised him, so he would eat, but it was not often that he would go out to see the food, and then merely as a pastime.

I have heard it said that they were wont to cook for him the flesh of young boys, but as he had such a variety of dishes, made of so many things, we could not succeed in seeing if they were of human flesh or of other things, for they daily cooked fowls, turkeys, pheasants, native partridges, quail, tame and wild ducks, venison, wild boar, reed birds, pigeons, hares and rabbits, and many sorts of birds and other things which are bred in this country, and they are so numerous that I cannot finish naming them in a hurry; so we had no insight into it, but I know for certan that after our Captain censured the sacrifice

continued next page

of human beings, and the eating of their flesh, he ordered that such food should not be prepared for him thenceforth.

Let us cease speaking of this and return to the way things were served to him at meal times. It was in this way: if it was cold they made up a large fire of live coals of a firewood made from the bark of trees which did not give off any smoke, and the scent of the bark from which the fire was made was very fragrant, and so that it should not give off more heat than he required, they placed in front of it a sort of screen adorned with figures of idols worked in gold. He was seated on a low stool, soft and richly worked, and the table, which was also low, was made in the same style as the seats, and on it they placed the table cloths of white cloth and some rather long napkins of the same material. Four very beautiful cleanly women brought water for his hands in a sort of deep basin which they call *xicales* [gourds], and they held others like plates below to catch the water, and they brought him towels. And two other women brought him tortilla bread, and as soon as he began to eat they placed before him a sort of wooden screen painted over with gold, so that no one should watch him eating. Then the four women stood aside, and four great chieftains who were old men came and stood beside them, and with these Montezuma now and then conversed, and asked them questions, and as a great favor he would give to each of these elders a dish of what to him tasted best. . . .

They brought him fruit of all the different kinds that the land produced, but he ate very little of it. From time to time they brought him, in cup-shaped vessels of pure gold, a certain drink made from cacao, and the women served this drink to him with great reverence.

Sometimes at meal-times there were present some very ugly humpbacks, very small of stature and their bodies almost broken in half, who are their jesters, and other Indians, who must have been buffoons, who told him witty sayings, and others who sang and danced, for Montezuma was fond of pleasure and song, and to these he ordered to be given what was left of the food and the jugs of cacao. . . .

As soon as the Great Montezuma had dined, all the men of the Guard had their meal and as many more of the other house servants, and it seems to me that they brought out over a thousand dishes of the food of which I have spoken, and then over two thousand jugs of cacao all frothed up, as they make it in Mexico, and a limitless quantity of fruit, so that with his women and female servants and break makers and cacao makers his expenses must have been very great. . . .

[W]hile Montezuma was at table eating, as I have described, there were waiting on him two other graceful women to bring him tortillas, kneaded with eggs and other sustaining ingredients, and these tortillas were very white, and they were brought on plates covered with clean napkins, and they also brought him another kind of bread, like long balls kneaded with other kinds of sustaining food, and *pan pachol*, for so they call it in this country, which is a sort of wafer. There were also placed on the table three tubes much painted and gilded, which held *liquidambar* mixed with certain herbs which they call *tabaco*, and when he had finished eating, after they had danced before him and sung and the table was removed, he inhaled the smoke from one of those tubes, but he took very little of it and with that he fell asleep.

From Bernal Díaz del Castillo, *The Discovery and Conquest of Mexico, 1517–1521*, ed. Genaro Garcia and trans. A. P. Maudslay Farrar, Straus and Giroux, Copyright © 1956.

AZTEC MARKETS

The Aztecs had a highly sophisticated system of trade and barter, much of which was conducted in the central markets of large towns. Díaz del Castillo was much impressed by the market in Mexico at the Tlaltelolco square.

When we arrived at the great market place, called Tlaltelolco, we were astounded at the number of people and the quantity of merchandise that it contained, and at the good order and control that was maintained, for we had never seen such a thing before. The chieftains who accompanied us acted as guides. Each kind of merchandise was kept by itself and had its fixed place marked out. Let us begin with the dealers in gold, silver, and precious stones, feathers, mantles, and embroidered goods. Then there were other wares consisting of Indian slaves both men and women; and I say that they bring as many of them to that great market for sale as the Portuguese bring negroes from Guinea; and they brought them along tied to long poles, with collars round their necks so that they could not escape, and others they left free. Next there were other traders who sold great pieces of cloth and cotton, and articles of twisted thread, and there were *cacahuateros* who sold cacao. In this way one could see every sort of merchandise that is to be found in the whole of New Spain. There were those who sold cloths of henequen and ropes and the sandals with which they are shod, which are made from the same plant, and sweet cooked roots, and other tubers which they get from this plant, all were kept in one part of the market in the place assigned to them. In another part there were skins of tigers and lions, of otters and jackals, deer and other animals and badgers and mountain cats, some tanned and others untanned, and other classes of merchandise.

Let us go on and speak of those who sold beans and sage and other vegetables and herbs in another part, and to those who sold fowls, cocks with wattles, rabbits, hares, deer, mallards, young dogs and other things of that sort in their part of the market, and let us also mention the fruiterers, and the women who sold cooked food, dough and tripe in their own part of the market; then every sort of pottery made in a thousand different forms from great water jars to little jugs, these also had a place to themselves; then those who sold honey and honey paste and other dainties like nut paste, and those who sold lumber, boards, cradles, beams, blocks and benches, each article by itself, and the vendors of *ocote*[1] firewood, and other things of a similar nature. But why do I waste so many words in recounting what they sell in that great market?—for I shall never finish if I tell it all in detail. Paper, which in this country is called *amal*, and reeds scented with *liquidambar*, and full of tobacco, and yellow ointments and things of that sort are sold by themselves, and much cochineal is sold under the arcades which are in that great market place, and there are many vendors of herbs and other sorts of trades. There are also buildings where three magistrates sit in judgment, and there are executive officers like *Alguacils* who inspect the merchandise. I am forgetting those who sell salt, and those who make the stone knives, and how they split them off the stone itself; and the fisherwomen and others who sell some small cakes made from a sort of ooze which they get out of the great lake, which curdles, and from this they make a bread having a flavor something like cheese. There are for sale axes of brass and copper and tin, and gourds and gaily painted jars made of wood. I could wish that I had finished telling of all the things which are sold there, but they are so numerous and of such different quality and the great market place with its surrounding arcades was so crowded with people, that one would not have been able to see and inquire about it all in two days.

[1] Pitch-pine for torches.

The introduction of coffee into European taste led to the opening of coffeehouses, the popularity of which is suggested by this late 17th-century print.

Hispaniola, where it began to grow profusely and became the crop of a number of plantations.

The potato, which was native to South America, had a major impact on the European diet. Although it could not be used like wheat to make bread, it was rich in vitamins as well as in carbohydrates. It provided a solution to the lack of vitamins and minerals for the peasant diet during those months when vegetables were not available. Moreover, potatoes yield more caloric value than wheat per parcel of land, and thus were especially valuable as a basic food source in places where land was limited.

At first, most Europeans ridiculed the potato and felt it was unworthy of being consumed, but famines in the 18th century proved its importance. Soon, potatoes were being grown extensively in Ireland, Germany, and Eastern Europe, where they joined, and eventually replaced, wheat as the staple item in the peasant diet.

In the 15th and 16th centuries, the growing availability of once extremely rare foodstuffs enabled the wealthy of Europe to develop increasingly more sophisticated and luxurious eating habits. Elaborate formal dinners for the royal courts and official state occasions called for the training of expert chefs. Sauces, creams, and jellies were invented, and special dishes named after monarchs. In Italy and France, multicourse meals were accompanied by rich table decorations, fanciful pastries, and eating rituals. Moreover, from Italy there spread to France and other countries the use of differently shaped plates, the fork, and serving utensils, often made from the gold and silver pouring into Europe from the Americas.

Once the price of pepper and chilies fell as their quantity grew, they ceased to be prestige items for the very wealthy. In their place, coffee, chocolate (or cocoa), tea, sugar, and tobacco rose in popularity among the privileged. In 1664 the British writer Samuel Pepys records in his diary that he went to a coffee house, still a novel establishment, "to drink jocolatte"; by the 18th century the use of habit-forming stimulants like coffee and tobacco became a virtual mania, and the popularity of coffee houses among the middle classes had mushroomed.

THE SOCIAL PATTERN OF HOUSING

In the centuries before 1500, the housing of both the rich and the poor in Europe changed little and continued to use traditional materials, including straw thatching for roofs and wood. By the 16th century, however, urban housing began to make use of stone and brick. Moreover, the increasingly crowded cities made space a premium and building sites became smaller, so that houses took on a more vertical design.

Building the Cities

Over time, the ever-present risk of fire, a constant preoccupation for Medieval city dwellers, lessened because of the new construction materials. In Paris, large numbers of stone masons, plasterers, and tool makers began to transform public buildings and private houses by setting them on stone foundations. During the same period, builders in London abandoned wood and straw. After the great fire of London in 1666, which destroyed three out of every four buildings, most of the new housing was made of brick. This transformation was visible as far east as Moscow, where a Western traveler observed the same change in the mid-17th century. On the Continent, municipal authorities now often prohibited the use of straw roofing and sometimes provided subsidies to encourage builders to make their roofs of tile or slate.

The wealthy nobility and merchants of the cities lived in massive and elaborately decorated palaces, generally designed by major architects. Bramante and Michelangelo were among those who worked on the Palazzo Farnese in Rome, now the French Embassy there. The Carracci brothers from Bologna painted the frescoes in the principal reception hall of the same palace. Many of the residences of the wealthy built after 1500 still stand today, most now used for public purposes. In Paris, for example, the National Archives of France was once the private house of the Guise family, while the Parisian site of the National Library is now located in a palace where Cardinal Mazarin lived. The palace of the Strozzi family in Florence today contains a library and is used for public exhibitions.

Middle-class housing was much less grand than the palaces of the nobility. Plans for a number of houses of the middle class in 16th-century Paris have survived. A typical residence was on three floors, with the rooms arranged around an open courtyard. A spiral staircase connected the levels. On the ground floor was the main reception room, together with the kitchen and larder, while the bedrooms were on the upper floors. Starting in Italy during the 17th century, ceilings—once only the underside of the flooring of the room above—began to be plastered, encased in wood, and painted. Wallpaper was first used in the 18th century. In the homes of artisans, the shop occupied the front ground floor of a building and the masters lived, along with their apprentices, in the back or the upper floors.

Today we know much about housing through the painting of the period. In Amsterdam, the most common form of housing for the lower middle class was made up of two rooms, one at the front and one at the back. These houses, with their narrow façades, were later enlarged by the addition of rooms above and below connected by a series of dangerously steep staircases or ladders. Even today, the house fronts along the canals of the city of Delft preserve the original appearance of the buildings in Vermeer's famous paintings of the period, which also illustrate the new vogue for glass window panes. Vermeer and other Dutch artists depicted the interiors of merchant houses, with their

Pieter de Hooch, *The Linen Cupboard* (1663), depicts the ordered interior of an upper-middle-class Dutch home.

Pieter Brueghel's *Summer* depicts peasants working on the outskirts of a town.

comfortable and up-to-date furnishings and thick carpets, often used as table coverings.

Poor city dwellers generally lived in rented lodgings in the least desirable quarters of the city. The cheapest and most wretched apartments were either in basements or attics. The poor lived alongside prostitutes and criminals in flea-ridden and unsanitary squalor, often subject to unannounced police searches. In the absence of running water and toilet facilities, chamber pots—emptied out of the window—were often kept side by side with cooking utensils.

Country Living

Peasant housing in Europe is much more difficult to document because of the perishability of the materials used in the countryside. Most houses were small huts built of wood, straw, and mud. Farming people generally lived under the same roof as their animals, often sharing a single primitive room. These dwellings were generally unheated except for a small cooking stove, in front of which the inhabitants slept in cold weather.

One source of information about rural housing, although indirect, is the existence of documents from village authorities and local landowners granting permission to use quarries or cut lumber. Thus, a document granting the right to cut down five trees and dig a certain amount of stone in order to build a house can reveal much about the size and construction of the dwelling, even though the house no longer stands.

Recent archeological excavations provide further data about how peasants lived. The sites of deserted villages throughout Europe reveal both the kinds of houses and other facilities—churches, cemeteries, wells, and streets—and the changing layout of the community itself. Nor were conditions always uniform. Some villages were more prosperous than others. In Burgundy, France, for example, one typical village consisted of around 25 dwellings on stone foundations, in which the living rooms had beaten earth floors and small slanting windows.

Many wealthy landowners lived in old and uncomfortable family manor houses dating back to the late Medieval period. By the 16th century, it became fashionable for the new urban rich to invest their money in country residences. They commissioned elaborate stone villas containing works of art and surrounded by formal gardens. Most of the famous and elegant chateaux that dot the French countryside date from the period after 1600, when the French monarchy had created stable political and social conditions. Some of these were built as homes for the royal mistresses. The Medici, by contrast, used their country villas around Florence as centers for intellectual and social gatherings.

CLOTHING, FASHION, AND CLASS

Social distinctions were nowhere more marked than in the kind of clothing people wore. Among the peasants and the urban poor, the form of dress changed little over the centuries from about 1350 to 1600. The wealthy, on the other hand, were quick to adopt new styles and new materials for their clothing.

Dress and Style

As in the case of housing, paintings and engravings are also important sources of information about clothing styles. Even at a quick glance, the viewer can distinguish between peasants and the middle classes from the kind of costume they wear. Some occupations involved their own uniforms or typical forms of dress. Soldiers, fishermen, shepherds, and blacksmiths each wore specific garments. Sometimes the color and design of clothing indicate a particular condition of life—widows, for example, traditionally dressed in plain black clothes, while butchers often wore red smocks.

Peasants owned simple garments of coarse, homespun fabric made of a mixture of hemp and wool and generally dyed black or some other dark color. The paintings of the 16th-century Flemish artist Pieter Bruegel the Elder and his sons Pieter the Younger and Jan record numerous scenes of peasants and tradesmen in villages and market towns, showing the details of their clothing. Until the industrial revolution of the 18th century, cotton was too expensive for all but the wealthiest people. Much of the cotton available in Europe was brought by Venetian galleys from Syria, sometimes in the form of raw cotton and sometimes already worked into cloth.

Jean-Baptiste Chardin's *The Food Supplier* (1739) portrays the dress of a working-class woman.

Poor peasants spent relatively little of their resources on clothing, which had to be practical, both for durability and for protection against the cold weather. When peasants acquired wealth, however, they generally spent lavishly on dress in order to demonstrate their new status and distance themselves from their origins. The standard form of dress for peasants was a loose shirt and tight-fitting pants that hugged the body. Most went barefoot and the wearing of underwear became common only after 1300. The absence of undergarments caused the spread of ringworm, scabies, and other skin diseases. Both rich and poor generally did not wear night clothes to bed.

For the nobility and the wealthy merchant class, clothing was an essential symbol of social status. At the beginning of the 17th century, the Venetian ambassador to the court of France observed that a man was considered rich only if he possessed some 30 suits of different kinds and styles, and changed them daily.

Men's style of dress changed significantly around 1350, when they began to wear short and close-fitting tunics. In the West, men never returned to wearing the long robes that were common in the Middle Ages. Women's costumes also became more clinging and revealed more of their figure.

As style developed into fashion, clothing became associated with national origin. In the 15th century, the most common forms of dress were French, Italian, and English. At royal courts, the ladies of the nobility wore expensive dresses of cotton, silk, and velvet, embroidered and decorated with gold thread and jewels. By the 16th century, with the spread of the Hapsburg empire, the ruling classes of Europe adopted Spanish court dress, which was generally dark and severe, with padded stockings, high collars, and short capes. With the decline of Spain in the 17th century, however, the bright colors of French clothing became fashionable again.

Unlike today's world, in which styles change every season, in early modern Europe fashions remained in vogue for a century or so. The idea of constantly changing styles was introduced to the upper and middle classes of Europe only in the 18th century. The industrial revolution made inexpensive cotton readily available to most of the middle class, while the elaborate court etiquette of France established among the nobility a fetish for the new designs and the latest styles.

Along with the variations in clothing style, hygiene and other aspects of personal appearance also evolved. The ancient Romans had used soap for washing, and bathing was an important social activity for them, and in pre–Black Death Europe public bath houses were common. As late as the 18th century, however, hardly anyone in Paris or London bathed, and those who did took only one or two baths a year. Instead, both men and women used perfumes to cover their body odor. While men grew facial hair, women decorated their faces with makeup. By the early 1600s, both sexes began to wear artificial hairpieces as a form of social distinction. Changes in dress and personal hygiene, among the most intimate aspects of social custom, have always been important because they reflect the way in which people want the world to see them.

The aspects of everyday life discussed in this topic—health, food, housing, and dress—are vital indicators of the condition of a society at a given moment in history. Differences in these factors among the various levels of European society underscore one constant point—the vast gulf separating the lifestyles of most ordinary people from those of the comfortable middle class and the wealthy nobility. Moreover, the fact that for hundreds of years, the lifespan of Europeans remained short while the infant mortality rate stayed high, suggests a great deal about how people might have viewed issues of life, death, and faith. Similarly, the monotonous diet of most Europeans explains much about the sense of excitement and the hunger for the strange and exotic generated by the overseas explorations of the 15th and 16th centuries.

Social behavior and custom also provide considerable insight about the workings of historical change. The relatively stable nature of these "ordinary" but fundamental aspects of life for centuries at a time reveals just how powerful the weight of tradition was and how gradually the lives of most people were altered. Daily life as well as politics moved at a far slower pace and popular attitudes toward change were much more cautious.

How people dressed and the kind of homes they lived in are important indices of social, and even psychological, attitudes. Fashion, as opposed to practical, everyday costume, is not only a sign of social distinction but of the desire of wealthier classes to distance themselves from those below them and to ape those above. Standards of personal hygiene prevalent as late as the 18th century differed markedly from the generally accepted habits of the late 20th century in the West. That fact underscores the degree to which society has become more sophisticated, but it also tells us a great deal about the abysmally low level of material comfort to which millions of Europeans were accustomed.

The history of wars, religion, economics, and politics is of course fundamental to our ability to understand the past. It is often difficult, however, for us to grasp in an immediate sense how these "events" affected human lives. Social history, understood as the way in which real people lived, allows us to identify with people of earlier historical eras because we can compare our immediate daily experiences with theirs.

Questions for Further Study

1. What factors affected the health of Europeans? How would you judge the medical practices of the period?
2. In what ways were food and diet affected by the age of discovery?
3. How did class and social position affect such practices as housing and clothing?
4. Based on what you know about the lifespan of Europeans and infant mortality rates, what would you conclude were people's attitudes toward life, death, and faith?

Suggestions for Further Reading

Braudel, Fernand. *The Structures of Everyday Life*. London, 1981.

Foucault, Michel. *The History of Sexuality*, trans. R. Hurley. New York, 1977.

Fraser, Antonia. *The Weaker Vessel: Woman's Lot in Seventeenth-Century England*. London, 1984.

Goubert, Pierre. *The French Peasantry in the Seventeenth Century*, trans. I. Patterson. Cambridge, MA, 1986.

Hanawalt, Barbara A., ed. *Women and Work in Preindustrial Europe*. Bloomington, IN, 1986.

Houston, Robert A. *Literacy in Early Modern Europe: Culture and Education, 1500–1800*. New York, 1988.

Hunt, David. *Parents and Children in History: The Psychology of Family Life in Early Modern Europe*. New York, 1970.

Kamen, Henry. *European Society, 1500–1700*. London, 1984.

Ladurie, Le Roy. *The French Peasantry, 1450–1660*. Berkeley, CA, 1986.

Macfarlane, Alan. *Marriage and Love in England: Modes of Reproduction, 1300–1840*. New York, 1986.

Maynes, Mary J. *Schooling in Western Europe: A Social History*. New York, 1985.

Ozment, Steven. *When Fathers Ruled: Family Life in Reformation Europe*. Cambridge, MA, 1983.

Schama, Simon. *An Embarrassment of Riches: An Interpretation of Dutch Culture in the Golden Age*. New York, 1987.

Shorter, Edward. *The Making of the Modern Family*. New York, 1977.

Stone, Lawrence. *The Family, Sex, and Marriage in England, 1500–1800*. New York, 1977.

V

T o p i c 6

The European Economy and Overseas Empire

From 1300 to 1650, while Europe underwent the cultural changes associated with the Renaissance as well as the religious upheavals of the Reformation, the Western economy was also transformed. But although the period was one of economic growth, it was not without its difficulties. The profits earned by the rising Medieval merchant class in trade had been reinvested in banking and industry as well as in commerce, producing a long era of expansion. The turmoil and disasters of the 14th century, however, brought the expansion to a halt, and only in the 15th century did the volume of trade and manufacturing begin to rise again.

The principal change after 1500 was the shift in trade patterns from the Mediterranean to the Atlantic and northern European coasts. The commercial revolution was dominated at first by Spain and Portugal, but the decline of their empires was accompanied by the emergence of new economic powers, especially the Dutch Republic. The establishment of colonial and commercial empires and a global economy impacted on conditions in Europe, especially in the area of prices and in the rise of merchant capitalism.

A number of other new features appeared in the economic expansion of the 16th and 17th centuries. For one thing, a new era emerged in banking and international finance as Italian banking firms like the Medici were overshadowed by the new international firm of the Fuggers of Germany. These bankers created networks of credit across the borders of the European states and engaged in high-level loans to monarchs and popes as well as to private business owners.

The new banking firms were themselves overshadowed by the appearance of stock companies that attracted investors in growing numbers. Besides the expansion of international finance, new industries and technologies evolved in this period, including growth in the printing business, luxury industries, and mining. A series of mechanical devices, such as mills and clocks, not to speak of weapons like cannons, also made their appearance and stimulated manufacturing.

By the late 17th century, even the thriving Dutch commercial empire was beginning to decline as the English and French monarchies expanded their colonial holdings around the globe. Britain and France followed a rigidly conceived and highly centralized economic policy known as mercantilism, and the two powers increasingly competed for control of overseas markets and products. By the 18th century, the system of merchant capitalism that drove the commercial revolution was poised to provide the investment necessary to begin the new, industrial phase of capitalism.

TRADE, FINANCE, AND PRICES

The three centuries following the discovery of the New World saw the development of an important economic phenomenon called commercial capitalism, in which merchants sought profits through the buying, selling, and shipping of goods. The profits derived from commerce were tremendous, and the unfolding of global trade patterns made life in Europe infinitely more interesting and colorful. Agriculture, however, remained the primary economic activity of most Europeans. In Eastern Europe, where the commercial revolution was less important, perhaps as much as 95 percent of the population lived off the land; even in Western Europe, where commerce was most intense, 60 or 70 percent of the inhabitants still farmed.

The volume of European manufacturing and trade in 1400 had fallen far below that prevailing a century earlier, but it picked up and reached new heights by the 16th century. As the industrial and commercial sectors began to expand once again, northern European cities grew more important and Mediterranean towns began to lose their predominance.

Significant Dates

The European Economy

1367	Hanseatic League founded
Late 15th century	Collapse of Medici bank
1492	First voyage of Columbus
1459–1525	Life of Jacob Fugger II
c. 1575	Price revolution begins
1601	English East India Company founded
1602	Dutch East India Company founded
1609	Bank of Amsterdam founded
1620	Plymouth Colony founded
1621	Dutch West India Company founded
1651	Navigation Acts passed
1776	Adam Smith publishes *Wealth of Nations*

The Atlantic and Northern Commerce

In the early 15th century, control of trade in the North Sea and the Baltic had moved into the hands of German cities. The formation of the Hanseatic League in 1367 (see Part III, Topic 13) by German trading cities aimed to keep Italians and other foreigners out of northern commerce. The league eventually included more than 80 cities and controlled a large fleet and impressive resources, giving it a virtual monopoly over trade in northern Europe. Although the league continued to exist for some 300 years, it began to decline by the end of the 15th century in the face of the growing commercial power of the Dutch.

Throughout the first half of the 16th century, Venice managed to keep control of the trade in spices

A European sugar mill worked by slave labor in the West Indies.

that came through Muslim hands from the eastern Mediterranean. Yet signs of change were clear as the Venetian galleys, which linked Italian ports with northern Europe, sailed at an alarmingly decreasing rate. As the Atlantic powers like Spain and Portugal developed direct sea routes around Africa to Asia and across the Atlantic to their new colonies in the Americas, the Italian commercial empires fell into serious decline.

By 1600, even the Iberian trading powers were being bypassed by the spectacular rise of Dutch, English, and French traders as commercial patterns shifted once again. The new and exotic products from overseas were flooding Europe's markets in ever greater quantity and creating business opportunities that bypassed the rigid Spanish economic system. Moreover, in the waters off Newfoundland, a seemingly inexhaustible supply of codfish had been discovered that became the basis for a salted cod industry of major proportions, and the French and English eventually seized most of this business. Joint stock companies were formed to pool resources in order to take advantage of the increasing volume of trade.

The Growth of Manufacturing

The rising commercial activities were accompanied by the growth of manufacturing as new industries developed that became increasingly important in Europe's economy. Shipbuilding became a major and highly profitable industry. Metalworking, especially armor and cannon making, also grew enormously, while mining expanded as new technology allowed mine shafts to be sunk hundreds of feet below the surface. The new digging and draining methods opened up rich new mines in central Europe. The discovery of a way to extract silver from lead alloy led to a plentiful supply of silver for making coins, which in turn increased the money supply and economic growth.

One result of the rise in commerce was that merchants involved in the textile business turned increasingly to the domestic, or "putting out" system. Instead of supplying raw wool exclusively to the guild artisans, whose costs were relatively high, the merchants began to deliver the wool to individual workers in the villages. There they spun, wove, and dyed the cloth in their own homes, where they operated as family units and at a lower cost. The domestic system increased merchant profits and remained the basic method of finishing wool until the industrial revolution shifted production to factories.

From the Medici to the Fuggers

The depressed economic climate of the 14th century drove businesses to become more efficient. The invention of double-entry bookkeeping in the mid-14th century was accompanied by the introduction of insurance and book transfer procedures, and all of these made business practices more sophisticated.

New banking and credit operations had evolved in the late Middle Ages. Italians led the way toward new forms of organization, with the Medici of Florence dominating the field. The Medici, who had begun in cloth manufacturing, expanded into banking and had as their clients the papacy and a number of European monarchs. The Medici bank adopted the technique of autonomous branches based on partnerships in Italy and throughout Europe. Keeping central management in the family, each branch operated separately on the principle of limited liability, so that the collapse of one branch did not hurt the others. The Medici empire collapsed at the end of the 15th century when a number of major borrowers defaulted on their loans and the French seized the Medici property after invading Italy.

Merchants from other regions of Europe learned most of the Italian techniques in business organization and began to establish their own firms. The most successful of these were the Fuggers, whose business centered in Augsburg in southern Germany. The earliest Fugger merchants had been weavers and small manufacturers of woolen textiles. Expanding the range of their commercial activity, they opened a branch in Venice, where they ran a wholesale warehouse in spices and silks, and by the 15th century were engaging in banking.

The Fugger dynasty made its first major success when it began lending money to the Holy Roman emperors. Jacob Fugger II (1459–1525) was the dominant figure in the rise of the dynasty. Jacob oversaw branches in major European cities such as Antwerp, Lisbon, and London. In addition to continuing operations in the spice trade, the Fuggers began to engage in a variety of banking operations, such as issuing credit, bills of exchange, and paying interest on deposits. They became major bankers to the kings of Spain and Portugal as well as to the popes.

As a result of extending major loans to Emperor Charles V, Jacob eventually came to control the silver and copper mines of Austria and Hungary, enterprises that gave him a tremendous return on his investment. The house of Fugger collapsed in the late 16th century as the result of the defaulting of the Hapsburgs on their loans.

Eventually, the private family banking firms that had dominated European finance for centuries gave way to large, stock-based banking companies regulated by the state. In the 17th century, England, France, and the Netherlands granted monopolies to companies engaged in overseas trade or for the purpose of settling colonial areas. These establishments were better suited to the new era of commercial capitalism that was unfolding.

Jacob Fugger (right), the greatest banker of his age, dictating to a clerk.

The Price Revolution

Throughout the 16th century, as Europe recovered from the devastating impact of the Black Death, population increased, perhaps by as much as a third. By 1600, Europe may have had more than 100 million inhabitants, although the growth pattern was unevenly spread throughout the continent. The larger workforce meant an increase in the amount of food and in the demand for manufactured products; this expansion in turn stimulated economic activity in the towns as well as in the countryside.

One result of these demographic changes was that as the urban population of Europe increased significantly, a surplus labor force was created, driving down real wages. This setback was accompanied by a startling rise in prices in the later 16th century that had widespread repercussions. The causes and impact of this so-called "price revolution" have been seriously debated by historians, but a few factors seem obvious. The flow of gold and silver into Spain and Portugal in the early 16th century seems to have been the major cause of the inflationary cycle. The supply of bullion in Europe more than tripled, with some 16,000 tons of American silver flowing through the Spanish port of Seville alone by 1650.

Although Spain tried to regulate the bullion it collected by prohibiting its export, the wars it fought and the administrative costs of operating its far-flung government inevitably meant the circulation of silver throughout Europe. Other factors contributed to the inflation besides American bullion. The productivity of European silver mines increased as a result of the application of new mining techniques, and some monarchs sparked price increases by debasing their coinage. The increase in population may also have driven prices up. In any case, the inflation in commodity prices was immense—by the close of the 16th century, prices had risen to four times their level at the start of the century. Prices went up higher and faster in Western Europe than elsewhere on the continent, and the greatest impact was seen in basic necessities such as grains and bread.

Overall, the inflationary pattern increased prices no more than 3 percent a year, which by modern standards is not a significant jump. In the 16th century, however, the price revolution had the effect of redistributing income among social groups. Wages did not, however, rise accordingly, so that the standard of living for the poorer classes declined. Those living on fixed incomes, especially pensioners, were also hurt by the inflation. Similarly, people who rented out property at long-term rates suffered. On the other hand, merchants, farmers, and manufacturers benefited from the rise in prices, especially as the costs of production did not rise as quickly as prices.

The inflationary cycle, which was irregular but of long duration, had a negative impact on governments, whose expenses and deficits rose along with the prices. Cities felt the impact severely, since they depended on the purchase of food, the cost of which rose steadily. The dislocation and social tensions created by the price revolution were felt for decades to come.

MERCHANT CAPITALISTS AND THE STATE

The changes that were transforming the commercial revolution in the 16th and 17th centuries gave rise to a form of economic organization and activity known as *merchant capitalism*. Under this system, merchants with investment resources—venture capital—continued to invest in overseas trade or in necessary support operations such as banking, insurance, and stock companies. The private ownership of shipping firms and banks en-

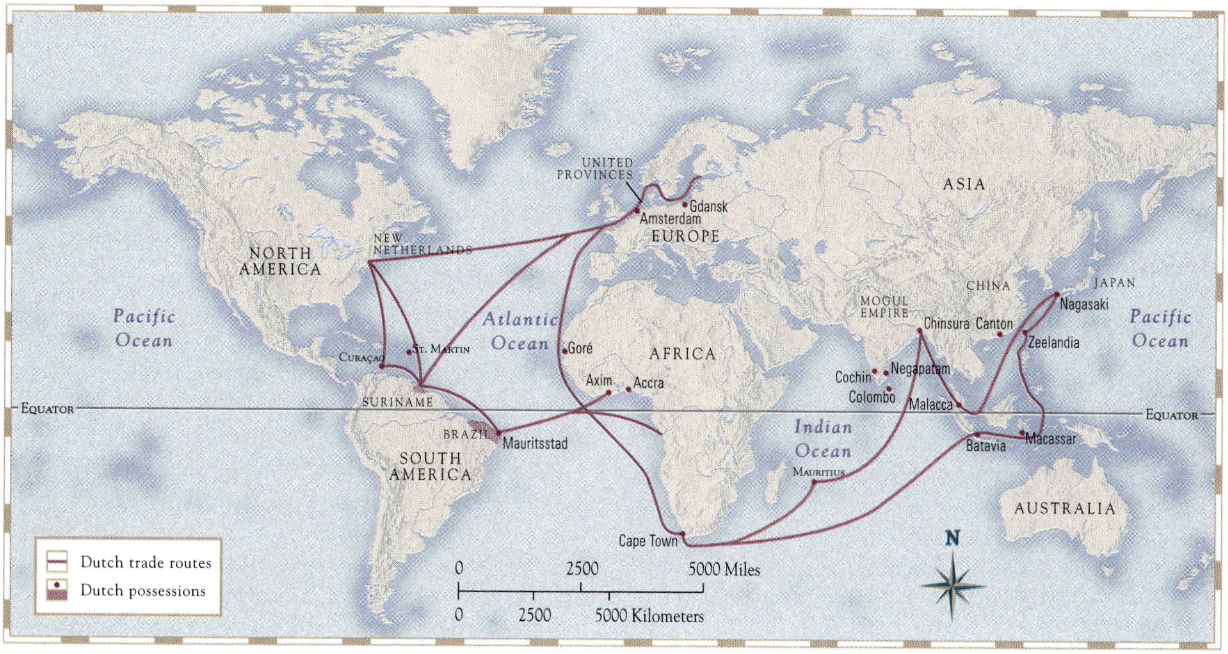

Map 6.1 The Dutch Sea Trade, c. 1650

tailed huge profits, although the risks in commercial activity were also high, and the general rise in prices made the profit potential even greater.

Other developments encouraged commercial capitalism. Not all successful merchants had the cash to invest in risky ventures, but once the church had abandoned its prohibition against *usury*—the charging of interest on loans—credit was more readily available. The state was a major stimulus to capitalist development. In the increasingly competitive arena of a global economy, governments used their military power to protect national trade, while military contracts provided an incentive for investment in manufacturing.

The Mercantilist System

From the onset of the age of exploration, the state had undertaken to regulate the economic activity of its citizens through policies known as mercantilism. These policies were designed to increase national revenue and economic power at the expense of other states, as well as to enhance private business. Hence, at the very time that merchant capitalism was evolving, economic affairs were subjected to increasing state regulation. Mercantilism denied the right of businessmen to operate in a free market in order to ensure the primacy of the state's interests. Under the mercantilist system, the government imposed rigid controls on trade and manufacturing, including import tariffs and monopolies.

International trade was a particular object of mercantilist regulation, for governments believed that a favorable trade balance was the only way to keep a sufficient quantity of bullion at home. Spain was the most vigorous advocate of this theory, for precious metals were necessary to pay for its massive military expenditures. On the other hand, the Dutch, whose wealth came from the fees its ships charged to carry the goods of other countries, sought instead to increase the overall volume of trade in which they were involved.

Tariffs were designed to protect domestic industries, while monopolies gave to a particular individual or company the sole right to trade, manufacture, or sell certain kinds of goods. Sometimes, as in the case of the Spanish empire, the purpose of controls was to block foreign competition or to prevent the all-important precious metals from going anywhere except to the home country.

In the later 18th century, the Scottish economist and philosopher Adam Smith (1723–1790), who advocated an unfettered free market system, attacked mercantilism because it obstructed the natural operation of economic laws. Smith insisted that the only real source of the "wealth of nations" was the flowering of rational self-interest. Depending on the circumstances, mercantilist policies helped or hurt national economies. In the Spanish case, controls hindered the development of domestic industries and retarded the economic welfare of the American colonies, while the monarchy's profligate spending made it impossible for the government to maintain bullion supplies at home. On the other hand, in the 17th century French mercantilist controls under Louis XIV enabled the state to develop manufacturing, attract foreign artisans, and establish a solid economic base.

In all these ways, mercantilist regulations were part of the broader strategy through which the state attempted to centralize and impose its authority on all aspects of national—and in this case, international—life.

THE HEYDAY OF THE DUTCH REPUBLIC

Perhaps the European state with the most intelligent economic policy was the United Provinces of the Netherlands, which was ruled not by a king but by a class of wealthy urban merchants. The rise of the Dutch commercial empire is one of the most spectacular success stories of the age of the commercial revolution. More than any other nation, the Dutch Republic depended on international trade for its economic livelihood.

The Rise of the Netherlands

The foreign affairs of the seven northern provinces that comprised the Dutch Republic were governed by the legislative body known as the States General. Domestic issues, including economic policy, were determined by the provincial town councils, composed of oligarchies of merchants and landlords known as "regents."

The Dutch economy had a number of important strengths. Even during the long and bitter war of independence against Spain, the Dutch prospered on the seas, especially by attacking Spanish bullion ships. In addition, they wisely welcomed the Protestant immigrants who flocked to the northern provinces, a migration that included skilled artisans, bankers, and merchants. The regents managed to maintain a degree of religious freedom in the Netherlands that was unmatched anywhere, and this despite the Calvinist extremists who sometimes tried to work against the Catholics and Jews who lived there.

Because of excellent drainage and irrigation techniques and intensive farming methods, Dutch agriculture was the most productive in Europe. The herring fisheries were also important to the Dutch, who dried, salted, and smoked the catch and sold it throughout Europe. Finally, as their prosperity grew to depend more and more on commerce, the Dutch became master shipbuilders who designed and constructed the best ships of the day, many of which they sold to foreign merchants.

The Dutch were the Venetians of the North, skilled at living and working on the water and at carry-

Rembrandt's famous painting *Syndics of the Cloth Guild* depicts the serious demeanor of leading Dutch merchants studying their accounts.

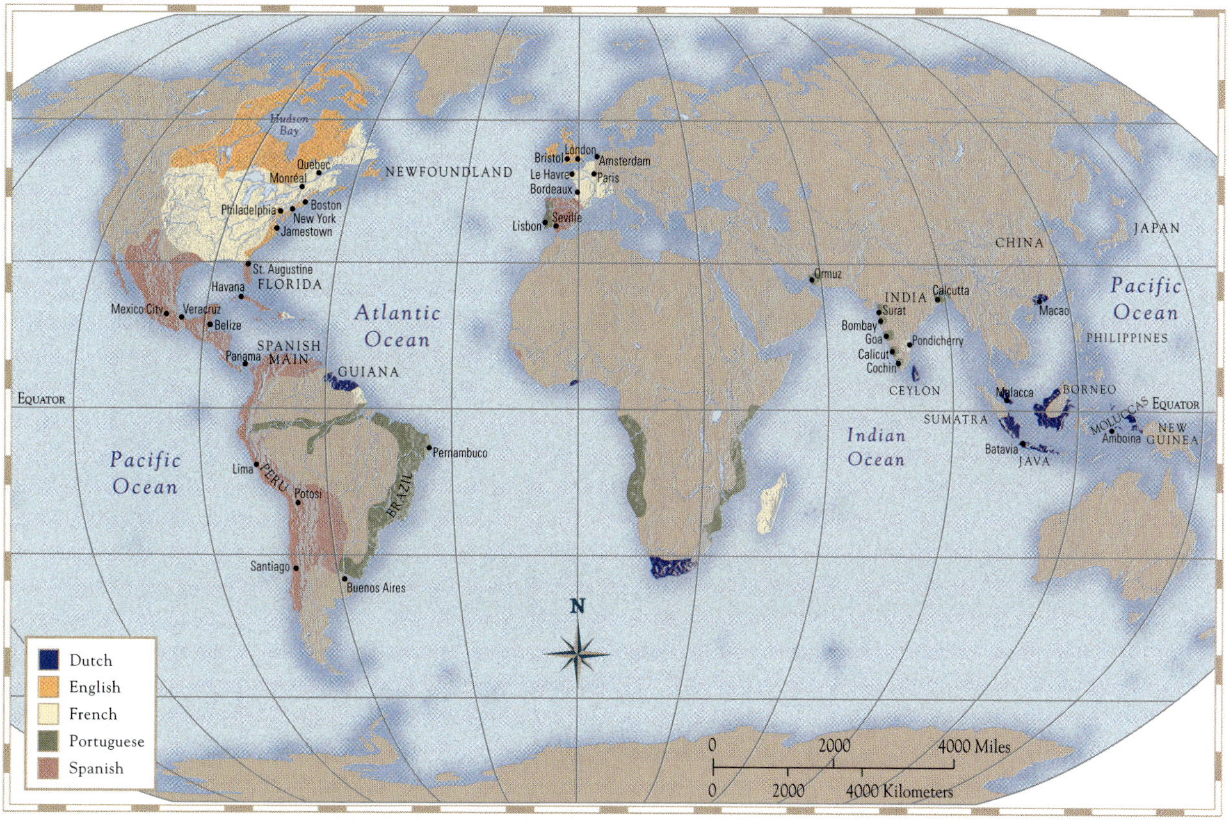

Map 6.2 European Possessions Overseas at the End of the 17th Century

ing their own products and those of other nations in their fleets. Their two chief cities, Antwerp (now in the modern state of Belgium) and Amsterdam, were at the trading crossroads of Europe and became two of the world's greatest commercial and business centers. These well-ordered and teeming cities were well positioned to take advantage of trade from the Mediterranean and the North Atlantic as well as from the Baltic and the North Sea. Antwerp, with 100,000 inhabitants in 1650, ranked second in size to Amsterdam but was a vital commercial hub. English wool and the spice trade of the 15th century came through its port, while the Fuggers and other firms made it an important banking center.

When the Spanish seized Antwerp during the revolt of the Netherlands, Amsterdam easily took its place as the principal Dutch port. Between 1600 and 1650, Amsterdam's population had grown from about 65,000 to 175,000, and its intricate network of docks and warehouses made it one of the most important entrepots in Europe. By building a series of canals, the Dutch were able to enlarge the size of the city to accommodate its growing population. Moreover, the Exchange Bank of Amsterdam, founded in 1609, soon became one of the principal banking institutions in Europe.

The Dutch ensured their economic prosperity by enlightened policies that deviated from the mercantilist norms of most other states. For example, they erected no tariffs either on imports or exports, and all their chief cities observed free trade policies. Because the trade in bullion was also free in the Netherlands, in contrast to policies in Spain and other states, Amsterdam became the chief center of the gold and silver trade.

The essence of Dutch prosperity was the "carrying trade." In 1600, Spanish and Portuguese ships carried a major portion of overseas trade, but by the mid-17th century, half of Europe's merchant ships were Dutch. Their chief strength lay in European commerce, where Dutch shipping made up perhaps three-quarters of all trade in the region. The Dutch Republic was the most prosperous example of merchant capitalism to emerge from the commercial revolution.

GLOBAL COMPETITION: THE INDIA COMPANIES

If the Dutch dominated the carrying trade in Europe, elsewhere in the world the English and French competed with them more effectively. It was there that, in

This painting of the *Head Office of the Dutch East India Company of Hugly in Bengal* (1665), by H. V. Schulylenburgh, shows the extensive facilities constructed to house its administrators.

contrast to their policies of European free trade, the Dutch followed a more conventional mercantilist agenda. The overseas trade soon became a battleground of competing national companies struggling for dominance.

Private Trading Companies

In 1601, the English government of Queen Elizabeth I granted a charter for the establishment of the English East India Company, which monopolized trade with India and operated until 1858. The English also attempted to develop a colonial enterprise along the Atlantic coast of North America and in 1606 the crown extended charters to the Virginia Company, which tried unsuccessfully to establish a permanent settlement there. Farther north, the Plymouth Company was given the right to colonize anywhere from Virginia to Maine. In 1620, it founded the Plymouth Colony, which later merged with the Massachusetts Bay Colony. Nevertheless, these early experiments with permanent settlements did not generate large profits.

The States General of the Netherlands empowered private joint stock companies with almost complete economic and administrative authority to control its trade beyond Europe. In 1602, private merchants and investors of the Netherlands joined forces with the city government of Amsterdam to found the Dutch East India Company. The aim of the new company was to establish commercial primacy in the Indian Ocean and the Southeast Asia seas.

Unlike the Spanish and Portuguese, who made trade a state monopoly, the Dutch East India Company—controlled by the same class of wealthy business interests that dominated the town councils—was given extraordinary power to govern the entire Asian region. Company officials could conduct war on foreign shipping, appoint administrators for the colonies, and operate trading bases.

Although these and other firms assumed differing legal forms, most were joint stock companies in which individual investors pooled resources. This approach was especially useful in long-distance commerce, where the risks were considerable and required large investments. Although originally each voyage was considered a separate undertaking, later the companies established a permanent form of organization in which investors bought shares. In order to leave the company, they had to sell their shares.

Commercial Rivalry on the Seas

The English and the Dutch were rivals in Asia, but both regarded the Portuguese as their principal enemy there. The Dutch East India Company succeeded in pushing the Portuguese out of East Asia and established direct commercial links with Japan and China. In the 18th century, the English company exercised administrative control of most of India, keeping that power until the English government took it from them.

The Dutch West India Company, set up in 1621, was given similar authority along the African coast and in the Americas. In North America, the company actually founded the Dutch settlement of New Netherlands along the Hudson River valley of the future New York. Regardless of how aggressive the Dutch traders were,

Dutch traders are depicted in this 17th-century printed cloth from Golconda, a Muslim stronghold in what is now Hyderabad state, India.

however, they ultimately proved unable to seize and hold control of the Caribbean and the Atlantic seaboard, where the French and the English were operating. In the second half of the 17th century, the English took the New Netherlands from them, renaming it New York. Before long, the Dutch West India Company closed down. The French, who established their own East India companies in Asia, were less successful than the English and Dutch in the region. In North America, where they had greater success, they turned to a different system, governing Canada directly as a possession of the crown, rather than through a private company.

Most countries in the 17th century passed navigation laws designed to give their merchant marines monopolies over their international trade. In 1651, the English Parliament passed the Navigation Acts, which were designed to end the Dutch control over shipping and fishing in English waters. In response, the Netherlands declared war against England. In 1660, another law required that all commodities imported into England had to be carried on English ships (or on ships from the country of origin); moreover, in order to circumvent Amsterdam's primacy, the English government required all foreign goods to be brought directly from the country of origin. Trade along Britain's coast and from its colonies in North America could be carried only on British ships.

These techniques of economic nationalism were applied in the spirit of mercantilism, but they had the effect of stimulating smuggling and were an important factor in driving the American colonies to break with England. In the 18th century, the competition among the commercial powers of Europe unfolded on a global scale and resulted in a continuing series of costly wars for dominance (see Part VI, Topic 9).

By 1500, Europe had achieved a remarkable recovery from the disasters of the previous century. New products and better production techniques, combined with rationalized and diversified business organization, all contributed to the building of a reinvigorated and more prosperous economy. Finance and credit operations were already becoming international in scope when the age of exploration opened. The truly new aspect of the European economy was the commercial revolution that accompanied the encounter with the Western Hemisphere. The voyages of the Portuguese and Spanish seamen opened up an entirely new, unimagined world for the Europeans and set in motion economic forces that transformed the Old World. Moreover, out of the commercial concerns that developed among the great powers in the 17th and 18th centuries, there emerged a global economy and imperial interests that were to provide the basis for the Western dominance of the globe in the modern era.

Questions for Further Study

1. What was the price revolution and what were its causes?
2. In what ways did the state compete with merchants and how did it support their interests?
3. What explains the economic prosperity of the Netherlands?

Suggestions for Further Reading

Ball, John N. *Merchants and Merchandise: The Expansion of Trade in Europe, 1500–1630*. London, 1977.

Boxer, Charles R. *The Dutch Seaborne Empire, 1600–1800*. London, 1965.

Boxer, Charles R. *The Portuguese Seaborne Empire, 1415–1825*. New York, 1969.

Braudel, Fernand. *Civilization and Capitalism*, trans. S. Reynolds. 3 vols. New York, 1979–1984.

Cameron, Rondo. *A Concise Economic History of the World*. New York, 1989.

Davis, Ralph. *The Rise of the Atlantic Economies*. London, 1973.

De Vries, Jan. *The Economy of Europe in an Age of Crisis, 1600–1750*. Cambridge, MA, 1976.

Elliott, John H. *The Old World and the New, 1492–1650*. Cambridge, MA, 1970.

Israel, Jonathan I., ed. *Dutch Primacy in World Trade, 1585–1740*. Oxford, 1989.

Kriedte, Peter. *Peasants, Landlords and Merchant Capitalists: Europe and the World Economy, 1500–1800*. Leamington, England, 1983.

McAlister, Lyle N. *Spain and Portugal in the New World, 1492–1700*. Minneapolis, 1984.

Schama, Simon. *The Embarrassment of Riches: An Interpretation of Dutch Culture in the Golden Age*. New York, 1987.

Tracy, James E., ed. *The Rise of Merchant Empires*. Cambridge, MA, 1990.

V

Topic 7

The Baroque Era

By the early 17th century, in response to the enormous political and economic changes occurring throughout Europe, a new artistic style had developed: the Baroque. One of its features was the appearance of new forms and subjects, ranging from still life painting to the design of private town houses to opera.

In spite of the enormous range of the arts in the Baroque period, they shared certain characteristics in common. The expression of strong emotions, an interest in psychological states of mind, and the invention of elaborate technical display are all typical of 17th-century art.

In the fields of painting, sculpture, and architecture, the first major developments occurred in Rome. Caravaggio's dark, emotional style influenced countless painters in Italy and northern Europe. Bernini's contribution was a double one. As sculptor, he brought his extraordinary technique to subjects as different as religious ecstasy and portraits of his contemporaries. As architect and town planner, he left his mark on the most grandiose project of the times: St. Peter's, Rome.

In the North, the most important architectural project of the age was the Palace of Versailles. Many of the leading painters worked on secular themes: landscape, portraits, scenes from life. The only major northern religious painter was Rembrandt.

While Italy remained the center of religious painting, the years around 1600 saw the birth there of opera, a frankly popular form of entertainment aimed at a broad general public. In the North the situation was reversed. Few painters devoted their careers to sacred subjects, but in Germany Bach composed some of the greatest religious music of all time.

The roots of the supreme writer in the English language, Shakespeare, were in the Renaissance. He wrote many of his masterpieces, however, in the first decade of the 17th century, and their extraordinary richness owes much to the new spirit of the age. The same is true of the greatest novel of the century, Cervantes' *Don Quixote*. In poetry, the works of Donne and others of the Metaphysical poets illustrate the Baroque interest in virtuosity and heightened states of emotion, with their special blend of the spiritual and the erotic.

In the Renaissance, artists sought ideal principles of beauty that would be of eternal value. Baroque artists, by contrast, tried to express the emotional states of individuals, whether in words, music, or painting. In doing so, they laid the ground for the arts in the modern era with their search for self-expression and the answers to personal questions.

EMOTION AND ILLUSIONISM: THE AFFIRMATION OF BAROQUE ART

In the Renaissance, artistic developments began in Italy and gradually spread throughout the rest of Europe. By 1600, Italy was no longer at the center of European culture, and the chief powers in the North—England, France, the Netherlands—began to develop their own independent schools of art. One factor in this shift was the Reformation, and the challenge to a single Universal Church. Another was the rise in northern Europe of the merchant class, which created a new public for the arts. A third was the spread of European culture in other parts of the world, as earlier exploration by the European powers became transformed into colonization, and England, France, the Netherlands, Spain, and Portugal established overseas territories in Africa, Asia, and the Americas.

One of the consequences of this diversification was the growth of new subjects for art. Instead of continuing to paint the same repertory of religious subjects, artists turned to genres like the portrait or scenes from daily life. Architects designed private houses or urban complexes as well as churches. New musical forms developed, including opera and purely instrumental works such as the *concerto grosso*. Writers aimed for a deeper sense of psychological understanding of human behavior.

The Baroque Spirit

Yet behind these different manifestations, certain common principles were in operation. The most striking was the expression of strong emotions. Far from seeking ideal statements of universal truth, as Renaissance artists had done, Baroque artists aimed to portray individual states of mind. The paintings of Rembrandt or the dramas of Shakespeare create specific characters with their own personal dramas. In doing so, the artists turned inward rather than outward to explore the depths of human feeling and not the calm heights of Classical perfection.

In order to express their new insights, artists forged a whole range of fresh techniques. Both painters and sculptors invented ways to convey complex illusions of light and shade. Musicians devised styles of increased virtuosity, which led to the growth of instrumental music, while the birth of opera added new dramatic possibilities. In literature, elaborate imagery and complicated grammatical structure made possible heightened emotional effects—the supreme example of the mid-17th century was Milton's *Paradise Lost*.

The subject of Milton's masterpiece is a reminder that attitudes to religion continued to dominate European culture. Most artists working in northern Europe chose to work under the influence of Reformation ideas, while the leading figures in Italy dedicated themselves to the Counter-Reformation mission to restore the Catholic Church to its triumphant preeminence. At the same time, the 17th century saw the continued rise of science, which challenged both religious camps, and laid the basis for the skepticism of the 18th-century Age of Reason.

THE MAKING OF BAROQUE ROME: CARAVAGGIO AND BERNINI

The spirit of the Counter-Reformation dominating Italian art in the 17th century aimed for effects of power and splendor to exalt the Catholic Church's triumphant resurgence. The most influential painter working there, however, Michelangelo Merisi (1573–1610), better known as Caravaggio, developed a personal style that had little to do with official propaganda.

The Chiaroscuro of Caravaggio

The dark drama of many of Caravaggio's paintings echoes the violence of his own life. Notorious for his stormy temper, the rebellious artist spent his last years in exile, after killing an opponent in a tennis match. His love of strong contrasts between light and dark—the Italian term is *chiaroscuro*—often serves to dramatize his scenes. In *The Calling of St. Matthew,* Caravaggio's first important Roman commission, a beam of light follows the gesture of Jesus, who stands in the shadows and calls the future apostle. Matthew himself leans back into the darkness, as if trying to avoid the summons.

Caravaggio's employers were especially enraged by his emphasis on the poverty of the characters in his paintings. In his painting of the *Madonna of Loreto,* he shows two humble pilgrims who have come to honor the mother and child. They kneel before her, turning their worn and dirty bare feet toward the viewer, while the Madonna stands at her grimy back door, balancing the infant Jesus on her hip like any Roman working mother.

The church may have disapproved of Caravaggio's directness, but both the public and his fellow artists fell under the spell of his dramatic realism and psychological perception. Among the painters to follow his lead was Artemisia Gentileschi (1593–1652/1653), one of the major woman artists of the day. Her *Judith and Holofernes* used Caravaggio's

Caravaggio's painting of *The Calling of St. Matthew* (1597–1598).

strong contrasts to depict the Jewish heroine's beheading of the Assyrian general. In her youth, Gentileschi was the victim of rape, and the calm determination of Judith's blow seems to represent the artist's retaliation. The virtuosity of the foreshortening of Holofernes' body and the realistic painting of the silken sheets are typical of the Baroque style.

The Psychological Realism of Bernini

The most important of all Italian artists of the Baroque was Gian Lorenzo Bernini (1598–1680). Throughout his long career he produced a bewilderingly varied range of sculptures, while his buildings and urban planning changed the face of Rome.

The characteristic uniting his sculptural output was psychological understanding, conveyed by means of his extraordinary technical bravura. His *Cardinal Scipione Borghese* shows the cardinal's quizzical expression and air of alertness, while the rendering of details—the hair and beard, the rumpled collar—helps to give the head its sense of life.

By contrast with the subtlety of the portrait, the marble and gilt bronze *St. Teresa in Ecstasy* is a masterpiece of dramatic expression. The saint, in the midst of her ecstatic vision, awaits the blow to the heart which a smiling angel is poised to deliver. St. Teresa's billowing dress, the cloud on which she floats, and the golden beams of light pouring down on the scene are all

Judith and Holofernes (c. 1620) was painted by Artemisia Gentileschi, daughter of a follower of Caravaggio.

brought to life with theatrical realism—an effect heightened by the figures to the sides of the chapel, who seem to be watching the action from stage boxes. The combination of heightened emotion, religious passion, and the sense of drama make for one of the supreme monuments of the Baroque style.

Bernini poured his seemingly inexhaustible powers of invention into designing palaces, churches, and fountains. His most ambitious project was the piazza (square) in front of St. Peter's Basilica, where he created a huge space surrounded by an oval colonnade, with fountains and a central obelisk, which continues to provide the majestic setting for hundreds of thousands of pilgrims to the Vatican.

REMBRANDT AND HIS CONTEMPORARIES IN NORTHERN EUROPE

If the main architectural achievement of the Roman Baroque was religious in inspiration, the largest construction in northern Europe was Louis XIV's Royal Palace at Versailles (see Part VI, Topic 3). The king intended the building to symbolize his secular power as Grand Monarch, the self-styled Sun King. On rising each morning, Louis made his way through the Hall of Mirrors, surrounded by his courtiers, and entered the main path of the garden, which ran on an east-west axis, following the path of the sun.

Painting in France and Flanders

For all the conscious splendor of Versailles, in general French and Flemish artists avoided the lavishness of the Italian Baroque. Nicholas Poussin (c. 1593–1665) claimed to detest the work of Caravaggio, and intended his own lucid, restrained paintings as a deliberate criticism of the Italian painter's emotionalism. His famous *Et in Arcadia Ego (I Too Am in Arcadia;* the words of Death, present even in the tranquil countryside) conveys a still hush, its figures rapt in solemn thought.

The note of pastoral calm recurs in many of the works of Claude Lorrain (1600–1682), the leading landscape artist of the day. In the Renaissance, artists had painted landscapes as settings for the scenes, generally religious, taking place in the foreground. Baroque painters were the first since ancient Rome to make depictions of landscape or seascape the sole subject of their paintings. Lorrain often placed tiny human figures in his works, but their real subjects are the fields, rivers, and mountains.

Much of the art produced in northern Europe was specifically aimed at the new middle-class public. The most prolific of all northern artists, however, Peter Paul Rubens (1577–1640), produced works of just about every conceivable kind: portraits, landscapes, religious subjects, mythological tales. In addition to his art, Rubens traveled widely as a diplomat, speaking six modern languages and reading Latin fluently.

Something of the restless energy of the man emerges in his scene of *The Rape of the Daughters of Leucippus*. The figures seem to spin before our eyes, as the sensuous, amply proportioned nudes are brought tumbling down. Yet Rubens could also touch quieter, more intimate feelings. At the age of 53, after the death of his first wife, he married the 16-year-old Helene Fourment. His painting of Helene with two of their young children is a rare depiction of the quiet joys of married love, in contrast to the intensity of most Baroque art.

Painting in the Netherlands: Rembrandt

Unlike their colleagues elsewhere in Europe, artists in the Netherlands lacked the two chief sources of patronage: the church and the aristocracy. The Dutch Calvinist Church forbade the use of religious images, and the Netherlands never had the kind of wealthy and powerful nobility that existed in France or England. Dutch painters needed therefore to find middle-class customers to commission works.

Bernini's image of *St. Teresa in Ecstasy* expresses the powerful religious emotion of Baroque art.

One handy source of income was the group portrait. Former soldiers often formed "militia companies," groups of veterans who met from time to time to reminisce, and eat and drink. They sometimes commissioned a painter to make an "official" portrait of the members of a company, to hang in their meeting premises. One of the most successful painters of these group portraits was Frans Hals (1580–1666), whose quick brush strokes and lively sense of composition convey the convivial spirits of the reunions.

The greatest painter of the age, Rembrandt van Rijn (1606–1669), began his career as a successful painter of similar middle-class patrons. One of his early masterpieces is a group portrait of the kind popularized by Hals. The painting is generally known as *The Night Watch*, although recent cleaning has revealed that the chief figures were originally bathed in light.

Yet the complexity of the composition of *The Night Watch* illustrates the far greater subtlety of

Et in Arcadia Ego by the great French Baroque painter Nicholas Poussin.

Rembrandt's genius. As he began to produce more introspective and somber works, his clients gradually stopped commissioning him. They wanted cheerful portraits and colorful still lifes to decorate their houses, not deep spiritual meditations. By the end of his career, he was producing religious paintings inspired by his lifelong meditation on the Scriptures. *Jacob Blessing the Sons of Joseph* conveys all the painful tenderness of the family's three generations, united lovingly at the old man's deathbed. The strong contrasts of light and darkness show the continuing influence of Caravaggio, but the sense of spiritual concentration is a far cry from the drama of Caravaggio and his followers.

MUSIC FOR A NEW PUBLIC: THE BIRTH OF OPERA AND THE WORKS OF BACH

As in the case of the visual arts, musical developments in Italy and northern Europe differed in their attitude to religion, but in opposite ways. Italy saw the birth of musical forms that could satisfy the demand for popular entertainment, while in the North, Bach, Handel, and other composers produced some of the greatest sacred music ever written.

The Birth of Opera

The inventors of opera, a group of Florentine intellectuals known as the "Camerata," intended it as a revival of ancient Greek tragedy. The first play set to music, *Dafne*, by Jacopo Peri (1561–1633), was staged in Florence in 1594. Within a few years the new entertainment had spread throughout Europe. Opera houses sprang up in Austria and Germany and then in England, where by the late 17th century Italian singers could command astronomical fees. Under the encouragement of Louis XIV, French composers developed their own kind of operas, involving long sections of ballet.

Opera made a special appeal to Baroque tastes. In the first place, the combination of words and music could explore psychological states of mind more vividly and dramatically than either on its own. Even in later times, many operas contained a "mad scene" for one of the protagonists. Secondly, an operatic performance was a chance for virtuosity, both in the brilliance and flexibility of the singing and in the sumptuous stage settings and effects. Audiences loved to see magical transformation scenes or blazing fires that seemed to engulf the stage. Thirdly, the design of the opera house, with its tiers of boxes and upper gallery, made it possible for all social classes to attend performances while maintaining them physically separate.

Claudio Monteverdi (1567–1643), the first great genius in the history of opera, proved as early as his first

Peter Paul Rubens' *Helene Fourment and Her Children,* 1636–1637.

stage work, *Orfeo,* the dramatic power of the medium. By skillful use of instrumentation and a vocal line that mirrored the character's emotions, Monteverdi breathed dramatic life into the familiar story. The composer spent the last 30 years of his life at Venice, where 16 opera houses were built in the second half of the 17th century—an astonishing demonstration of the breadth of appeal of the new entertainment.

Music in Germany: Bach

Baroque composers in northern Europe generally did not write operas. The only important exception was Georg Frideric Handel (1685–1759), who composed a string of operatic masterpieces when he moved to England and became a naturalized citizen. London was one of the operatic centers of Europe, and Handel's operas written for performance there depict a wide range of characters and states of mind.

The greatest figure in Baroque music, Johann Sebastian Bach (1685–1750) wrote no operas, and spent his life far from the glamour of London or the other musical capitals of Europe. His music was little known during his lifetime, and virtually forgotten after his death. Rediscovered in the 19th century, Bach's music is now regarded as one of the supreme achievements of Western culture. His work draws together the styles and techniques of the musical tradition from which he came, and builds on its foundations to create new perspectives.

A devout Lutheran, Bach used music to glorify God and explore the deeper mysteries of the Christian faith. He composed masses, organ works, cantatas, and

Rembrandt's *Jacob Blessing the Sons of Joseph* (1656) conveys the melancholy and quiet pathos of the artist's late style.

settings of sections of the Bible. His *Saint Matthew Passion* is a setting of the trial and Crucifixion of Jesus as recorded in the Gospel of St. Matthew. Bach proclaimed his Lutheranism by setting the text in a German translation, rather than Latin, and he included a number of Lutheran *chorales*—a kind of hymn which Luther himself had popularized.

THE GOLDEN AGE OF LITERATURE: SHAKESPEARE AND CERVANTES

The leading writers of the early 17th century owe their formation to the Renaissance. The works of both Shakespeare and Cervantes represent the culmination of a tradition—in drama and the picaresque novel—which goes back to their predecessors of the preceding century. Yet both figures drew on the greater range of expressivity typical of Baroque art to create works that combined profundity with popular appeal. In the case of Shakespeare, moreover, the judgment of his contemporary and rival Ben Jonson (1572–1637) still holds true: "He was not of an age, but for all time!"

Drama in England: William Shakespeare

William Shakespeare (1564–1616) is universally acknowledged as the greatest writer in the English language. Little definite is known of his life. Born at Stratford-upon-Avon, by 1592 he was active as an actor and playwright in London. His early plays, including *The Comedy of Errors,* imitated ancient Roman comedies with their complicated plots involving mistaken identities.

By 1595, with *Romeo and Juliet,* Shakespeare was deepening and enriching both the language and psychological understanding of his characters. In the four tragedies he wrote between 1600 and 1605 (the years in which Caravaggio was at work in Rome)—*Hamlet* (1600), *Othello* (1604), *King Lear* (1604), and *Macbeth* (1605)—he explored the great questions of human existence with a profundity and power of expression which have few if any equals. In emotional depth and virtuosity of language, the plays remain among the peaks of Western culture, and a constant challenge to performers and directors.

Toward the end of his career, Shakespeare explored the frontiers between tragedy and comedy in works written for the court of King James I. *The Tempest* (1611), his last play, creates a world of fantasy in which romantic love and low comedy combine to magical effect.

PUBLIC FIGURES AND PRIVATE LIVES

ANNA MAGDALENA AND JOHANN SEBASTIAN BACH

Bach came from a large family of musicians, and family life was important to him. His first wife died in 1720, after having given birth to seven children, of whom four died in infancy. Within a year the composer remarried a young singer, Anna Magdalena Wülken (1701–1760). He was 36 at the time, she 20. The prince of Cöthen, for whom Bach was then working, allowed the couple to save money by marrying in Bach's lodgings, and the composer used the money to buy Rhine wine at the city cellars.

Early in their marriage, Bach gave his wife a book of blank music paper, on which she wrote the title *"Clavier-Büchlein"* (Little Keyboard Book). He copied into it a series of short keyboard pieces, intended to help Anna Magdalena improve her playing. In 1725, he gave her a new book, in which he continued to write pieces. One of them is a song (perhaps by Bach, perhaps by G. H. Stölzel, a contemporary), *"Bist du bei mir."* The words are: "As long as you are with me, I could face my death and eternal rest with joy. How peaceful would my end be if your beautiful hands could close my faithful eyes." The illustration above shows an excerpt from one of her notebooks—no portrait survives.

Throughout their life together, Anna Magdalena took part in performances of her husband's works and helped him to copy them out, as well as bearing him 13 children. Bach suffered from deteriorating eyesight, and in 1749 he underwent two disastrous operations which left him totally blind. A few months later he was dead. His modest estate was divided between his nine surviving children and his widow. His sons and daughters sold their share of his manuscripts, but Anna Magdalena kept hers, leaving them to the Music School of the Church of St. Thomas, Leipzig. She died in abject poverty ten years after her husband.

The lives of both Johann Sebastian and Anna Magdalena were spent far from the tumultuous events of their times. The sheer amount of music Bach wrote and the couple copied out suggests that most of their time was dedicated to music and its performance. The products of their years together can now be seen as one of the summits of the Western musical tradition, and countless beginning pianists have learned to play with the aid of the pieces Bach wrote in the "Little Keyboard Book for Anna Magdalena."

MR. WILLIAM
SHAKESPEARES
COMEDIES,
HISTORIES, &
TRAGEDIES.
Publiſhed according to the True Originall Copies.
LONDON
Printed by Iſaac Iaggard, and Ed. Blount. 1623.

This portrait of William Shakespeare comes from the first folio edition of his works, published in 1623.

The Novel: Cervantes

Something of the same blend of farce and pathos characterizes the greatest novel of the 17th century, *Don Quixote* (1605–1615). Its author, Miguel de Cervantes (1547–1616), received a humanist education and served as a soldier at the Battle of Lepanto. His most famous work was intended to poke fun at Medieval tales of romance and chivalry. The book's principal character, Don Quixote, is an elderly and rather unworldly gentleman searching for the gallant world of the past in his own troubled times.

The conflict between Don Quixote's idealism and the brutal realities of the world forms Cervantes' main theme, as the novel wanders through an apparently random series of events. The hero is accompanied in his travels by his faithful squire Sancho Panza, who provides a measure of practical common sense to leaven his master's dreams. By the end of his journey, Don Quixote realizes that he cannot reconcile his ideal visions with the real world, and he dies with his illusions finally shattered.

Cervantes' hero has achieved the same archetypal fame in Western culture as Shakespeare's Hamlet or Lear. With its constant exploration of the interplay between illusion and reality, *Don Quixote* touches on many of the chief concerns of 17th-century art, while the Don himself has a depth of character and psychological truth worthy of the brush of a Rembrandt.

Poetry and Religion

The English writers known as the "Metaphysical Poets" combine religion and the erotic in a way typical of the age—Bernini's *St. Teresa in Ecstasy* is a counterpart in the visual arts to the poems of Richard Crashaw (1613–1649), with their blend of pain and religious fervor.

The leading poet of the group was John Donne (1572–1631), whose range and force of expression come close to rivalling those of Shakespeare. Donne's search to understand and expose the conflicting nature of human experience leads him to range from an analysis of sexual love to meditations on human mortality and the soul. The two chief themes of his writing are physical and religious passion, and the counterpoint he weaves between them leads to daring and memorable results.

The greatest of all 17th-century English poets was John Milton (1608–1674), whose artistic life became embroiled with the events of the English Civil War (see Part V, Topic 3). His active support for Cromwell and the Puritans brought him disgrace at the Restoration of Charles II in 1660. He spent the years of his enforced retirement in the composition of his major work, *Paradise Lost* (1667), the only successful epic poem in the English language.

The aim of *Paradise Lost* was to "justify the ways of God to men" by describing the fall of Adam and Eve. The poem's 12 books, written in blank verse, use imagery from the two great streams of Western culture—Classical Antiquity and Christianity—to reconcile humanist philosophical ideas with Christian doctrine. With the sure sense of drama of Bernini, Bach's spiritual convictions, and Rembrandt's understanding of the human heart, Milton's epic epitomizes the Age of the Baroque.

The arts served in the 17th century as weapons in the battle between Reformation and Counter-Reformation. In the process, they acquired new powers of expression and explored fresh areas of human experience. For all the apparent moral conflict between the Catholic Bernini and Puritan Milton, both drew on the advances of the Renaissance to produce works of dazzling insight.

There were times when the Baroque love of display and virtuosity crossed the line between extravagance and tastelessness, and for many at the end of the 20th century Baroque art is less accessible than the more austere products of the Renaissance—the very word "Baroque" has come to mean "grotesque" or "exaggerated." The typical Baroque quest for illusionism can seem artificial and forced.

Yet many of the works created in the Baroque style retain much of the passion which their makers poured into them. Furthermore, in their struggle to represent the emotions and mental states of individuals, the greatest figures of the age—Bach, Rembrandt, Shakespeare—created statements of universal truth.

Questions for Further Study

1. What common characteristics do all the arts share in the Baroque period? How do they vary in different parts of Europe?
2. How did Baroque artists deal with religious subjects? Did their approach differ from that of Renaissance artists?
3. What qualities have made Shakespeare's plays so widely admired and performed? Do the works still seem relevant, and, if so, why?

Suggestions for Further Reading

Boyd, M. *Bach*. London, 1983.

Haskell, F. *Patrons and Painters*. New Haven, CT, 1980.

Hatton, R. H. *Europe in the Age of Louis XIV*. New York, 1979.

Krautheimer, R. *The Rome of Alexander VII, 1655–1667*. Princeton, NJ, 1985.

Lavin, I. *Bernini and the Unity of the Visual Arts*. New York, 1980.

Paliska, C. V. *Baroque Music*. Englewood Cliffs, NJ, 1981.

Wittkower, R. *Art and Architecture in Italy, 1600–1700*. London, 1980.

PART VI

The Old Regime

The term "Old Regime" describes the period of transition in European history that led up to the French Revolution of 1789. On the surface, life in Europe continued to follow patterns established in the Middle Ages. Agriculture remained the chief occupation and economic activity. Most Europeans lived in farming communities, and while peasants in Western Europe were free, many still owed feudal obligations to land owners; in Eastern Europe the majority were still serfs.

Political and economic power remained in the hands of a hereditary aristocracy, and, to a lesser extent, of the religious authorities. Whether in the Dutch republic, in England—a constitutional monarchy—or absolute monarchies such as France or Prussia, participation in government was limited to a tiny section of the population, who used their influence to protect their own interests. Moreover, in

France as well as in Central and Eastern Europe government evolved in the direction of royal absolutism.

Throughout Europe a legally recognized social hierarchy concentrated privilege and status among traditional élites, while the bulk of society—the peasantry, urban workers, and the middle classes—remained excluded from government but bore the brunt of taxation. The trade in African slaves, and the institution of slavery itself, continued to be condoned and advanced by European states.

Yet behind the apparently permanent façade, there were signs of instability. The scientific revolution of the 17th century and the intellectual movement known as the Enlightenment of the 18th century led slowly but inevitably to dissatisfaction with old ways and beliefs. Out of the English political experiment of the 17th century and the ideas of the Enlightenment there emerged theories of political sovereignty that recognized the right of ordinary citizens to resist oppression and overthrow despots. As traditional political patterns came under question, an economic system that had lasted for centuries began to erode. Sectors of the middle class, especially the educated professional groups, became increasingly interested in the issue of political representation. With the growth of cities, an increasing proportion of the population was within reach of education, and ideas began to spread far more rapidly. One of the major factors in the development of urban life was the industrial revolution that began in the late 18th century.

In international affairs, the traditional rivalry between the two great powers of Europe, England and France, continued to dominate politics, while in the 18th century two new continental contenders began to emerge: the German state of Brandenburg-Prussia and Russia. Furthermore, with Europeans busily colonizing in Asia and the Americas, competition among the great powers resulted in military clashes on a global scale.

The buildup of a century and a half of pressure for change exploded in 1789 in the French Revolution. It was a sign of the new world which the revolutionary leaders hoped to create that they took inspiration from a revolution halfway across the globe: that of the Americans against their British colonial rulers.

VI

Topic 1

The Scientific Revolution and Western Thought

During the Renaissance, as ancient scientific theories resurfaced, scholars throughout Europe began to speculate about issues that had been taken for granted in the Medieval period: the nature of the physical universe, the relationship of the earth to the sun, the laws of mathematics. In order to put to the test beliefs based on tradition and Christian dogma, they started to try out theoretical ideas by means of practical experiments.

In the 17th century, growing use of this "scientific method" produced a revolution in European intellectual attitudes, as scientists and thinkers such as Galileo, Descartes, and Newton laid the foundations of modern science. From then on, theologians and philosophers alike were faced with a new authority—scientific truth, objectively demonstrated.

Official church teaching, supported by the Bible, held that the earth formed the center of the universe, around which the sun, moon, and planets moved. The first to question this was the Polish astronomer Nicolaus Copernicus, who published his description of a universe centered around the sun in 1543. The German Johannes Kepler followed up the mathematical implications of Copernicus' revolutionary model, and formulated three laws, describing the motions of the planets, which paved the way for Isaac Newton, the most prestigious mathematician and natural philosopher of early modern times, who produced a wide range of achievements. Among the most important were the theory of universal gravitation and his theories of light and motion. The astronomical observations of the Italian Galileo Galilei, using the newly invented telescope, further undermined official teaching.

The great Swiss physician Paracelsus also emphasized the importance of practical experiment. He based many of his theories on Medieval alchemy, but his insistence on careful clinical observation and his use of a wide range of drugs helped to lay the foundations of modern medicine. Other medical advances included the discovery of the circulation of the blood by the Englishman William Harvey.

The leading philosophical representative of the "new scientists" was the Englishman Francis Bacon, who urged the superiority of objective evidence over untested belief. Two French philosophers, René Descartes and Blaise Pascal, examined the implications of the rational method for theology and mathematics.

Thus, by the beginning of the 18th century there existed a scientific worldview that challenged—implicitly, at least—centuries of accepted belief. The emphasis that scientists placed on reason, and their faith in the ability of the human mind to penetrate the mysteries of the universe, led in turn to the chief intellectual movement of the 18th century: the Enlightenment.

THE WEIGHT OF TRADITION: GOD, NATURE, AND THE WORLD

Throughout the thousand or so years that separated the fall of the Roman Empire from the Renaissance, scholars and theologians in Europe accepted a standard explanation of the nature of the physical universe. It was mainly derived from the writings of three ancient Greeks: Aristotle (384–322 B.C.) for physics, Galen (130–c. A.D. 200) for medicine, and Ptolemy (2nd century A.D.) for astronomy.

According to traditional Christian teaching, based on these authorities, the universe was finite. The earth, the most corrupt and degenerate—and therefore heaviest—part of the cosmos, was located at its center, and was stationary. It was heavy, material, and subject to constant change. Around it there circled the planets, sun, stars, and heavens, moving outward from the earth in a widening series of spheres. The heavenly bodies were light, luminous disks, and in their superlunar realm nothing ever changed. In the Renaissance, most scholars continued to accept these assumptions, and tried to find complicated explanations for apparent inconsistencies rather than question the traditional explanations. When Galileo demonstrated that this distinction between earth and the heavenly bodies was false, he created a storm of protest and bewilderment.

The Dawn of the Scientific Revolution

Yet at the same time, the 15th and 16th centuries saw the first serious doubts about the accepted view of the nature of the universe. The Renaissance humanists discovered other Classical writers whose theories differed from those of Aristotle and Ptolemy. Among the most important was the physicist Archimedes (c. 287–212 B.C.), whose writings on dynamics proved highly influential.

Another reason for rethinking traditional views was a growing interest in various forms of magic, many of which were based on ancient precedents. Students of alchemy (a kind of Medieval chemistry whose chief aim was to turn base metals into gold) believed that they could understand the nature of matter by using secret formulae to combine various ingredients. Others turned to the heavens, and used astrology to interpret the movements of the planets. They hoped to read in them the meaning of the universe.

Various mystical schools of philosophy also flourished in the 16th century. The Hermetics were philosophers who believed that humans already possessed the key to an understanding of nature, locked up somewhere in existing texts (the term *hermetic*, taken from alchemy, refers to an airtight seal). They searched obscure writings, looking for hidden clues which would reveal the structure of the universe. Other thinkers turned to the Jewish mystical teachings of the *Kabbalah*, a Hebrew word, used to describe a body of esoteric Jewish mystical doctrines, that literally means "tradition." These thinkers used magical combinations of numbers to try to understand the world. The chief work recording Kabbalistic teachings was the *Book of Creation*, compiled between the 3rd and 6th centuries, and a later *Book of Splendor* appeared in the 13th century.

More firmly based on Classical tradition were the neoplatonists. The original school of neoplatonist philosophy flourished from the 3rd to the 6th century A.D. It derived from the teachings of the 4th-century B.C. Greek philosopher Plato, and described the universe as consisting of a systematized order, containing all levels and states of existence. Renaissance neoplatonists revived the idea of humans seeking to escape from the bonds of earthly existence in order to rise upward toward union with God, or the One, from whose Divine Mind the World Soul proceeds. Neoplatonist teachings made a profound impact upon Michelangelo, whose statue *The Bound Captive* shows a figure striving to escape from his material bondage.

Most of these scholars may now seem unlikely forerunners of the scientific revolution, but by rejecting traditional solutions to age-old problems, and by using chemical experiments and mathematical formulae, they created an increasingly open spirit of intellectual inquiry.

With the surge of technological expertise that developed in the Renaissance, practical engineers, navigators, and doctors began to apply the experimental approach to their own fields. The result was to create a new way of looking at the world. When writing of motion—and with an eye on Aristotle—the great Medieval thinker St. Thomas Aquinas (1225–1274) provided the baffling explanation that "motion exists because things which are in a state of potentiality seek

An old-fashioned astrologer with all the paraphernalia of his profession.

to actualize themselves." Aquinas seems to have theorized about how things move, rather than actually watching them in motion. At the end of the 16th century, Galileo watched workmen in the Arsenal at Venice moving great weights; he went on to form a theory of motion which disproved Aristotle, and demonstrated it by dropping weights from the top of the Leaning Tower of Pisa. The age of objective scientific proof had dawned.

REDEFINING THE UNIVERSE: FROM COPERNICUS TO GALILEO

In the early 17th century, Galileo's astronomical experiments produced a revolutionary break with church teaching. Half a century earlier, however, the cleric Nicolaus Copernicus (1473–1543) had already challenged traditional opinion.

The Copernican Revolution

Born in Poland of a wealthy German family, Copernicus studied in Italy, at the University of Padua. He learned there of recently rediscovered Greek scientific texts and pursued his mathematical interests. Under the influence of Platonic thought, he sought to replace the highly complex astronomical system of Ptolemy with a simpler formulation. Convinced that the sun, and not the earth, lay at the center of the universe, he devised a system whereby the earth and planets orbit the sun in a series of perfect divine circles.

Unlike his successor Galileo, Copernicus never really tested his ideas by practical experiment. He remained a theoretical philosopher. Nor did his work, based as it was on ancient teachings, represent a real break with the past. He did not even publish his ideas until 1543, the year of his death. Yet in two crucial ways Copernicus foreshadowed the "new science." In the first place his challenge to Christian teachings based on the Bible was so serious that it drew the condemnation of first Protestant and then Catholic theologians.

Secondly, Copernicus' work revealed a new attitude. Before his time, scholars had always assumed that appearances were to be trusted. If the sun appeared to revolve around the earth, then it must be doing so. Questioning this assumption, Copernicus claimed that a system whereby the earth revolved around the sun was equally plausible. Scientific truth alone could be the basis of intellectual advance, even if it ran contrary to superficial observation. Indeed the secrets of nature were often well concealed; in order to discover them it was often necessary to "twist the lion's tail," as Francis Bacon later observed.

The leading astronomer of the late 16th century, the Danish Tycho Brahe (1546–1601), collected important information about the planets and stars. In 1572 he discovered a new star, and three years later a comet, both of which disproved Aristotle's notions of fixed, unmoving heavenly bodies. Brahe himself refused to abandon his belief in the Ptolemaic system, but his remarkably accurate observations helped his successors to demonstrate that the earth revolved around the sun.

Kepler and His Laws

Among Brahe's most brilliant pupils was the German astronomer Johannes Kepler (1571–1630). Kepler was convinced by Brahe's observations that the sun was the center of the universe. In trying to demonstrate this, he formulated three laws, published in 1609 and 1619, to describe the motions of the planets in the solar system. According to the first, each planet, including the earth, orbits the sun in an ellipse, of which the sun is at one focus. The second claims that planets move faster when closer to the sun than when farther away. The third describes the mathematical relationships between the planets' movements.

All these laws completely rejected Aristotelian and Ptolemaic notions of the universe, yet they were based on and confirmed by the practical observation of celestial movements. The Copernican theory of a cosmos centered around the sun was supported by the evidence.

Galileo Galilei

The career of the Italian astronomer and physicist Galileo Galilei (1564–1642) demonstrated both the triumphs and the dangers of the scientific method. His experiments laid the foundations of modern physics, and he used the telescope he built to disprove Aristotle once and for all. He insisted that the Bible and the Aristotelian world it apparently supported should give way to modern science. As a result, he was tried and condemned by the Inquisition.

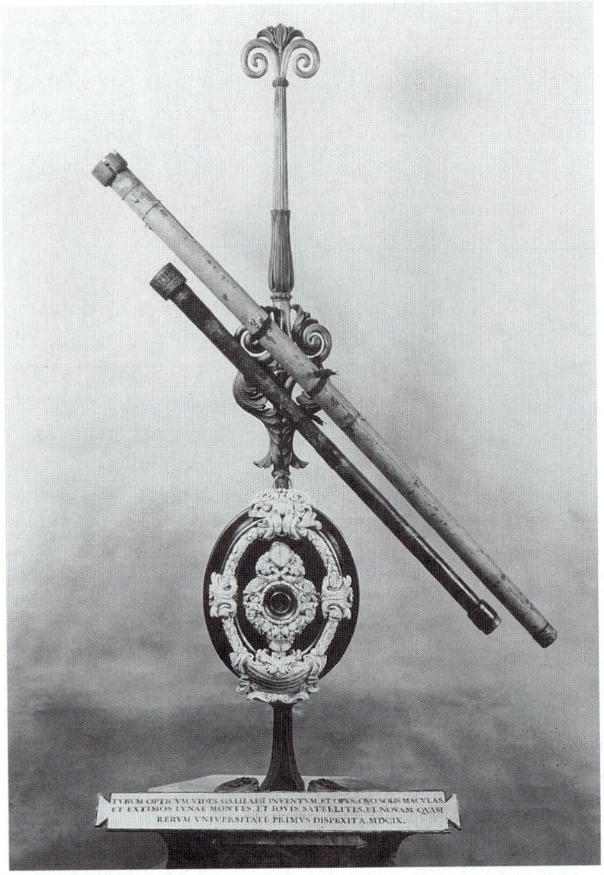

After his death near Florence in 1642, many of Galileo's instruments, including these telescopes, were collected and preserved.

Galileo was born in Pisa in Italy to a talented aristocratic family. After beginning to study medicine at the University of Padua, Galileo changed to mathematics, and stayed on in Padua to teach there. The northern Italian city was already famous throughout Europe for its university, founded in 1222—the central building of the University of Padua today was begun in 1493, and is still in use. Research conducted by scholars at the university in the 16th century played a central role in the development of early modern science. In addition to the Italians, foreign students such as John Harvey (see below) studied there.

The telescope, a new astronomical tool, had been produced in Holland (its invention is generally credited to Hans Lippershey, a spectacle maker), and was used mainly for sighting ships. Driven by the curiosity that helped to inspire the scientific revolution, Galileo designed and built his own model. Then he turned it toward the heavens to show a new vision: the mountains and craters of the moon, the phases of Venus, and sunspots. These observations proved that the universe is in a constant state of change. As early as 1597 he was convinced that the earth was in motion, and in 1610 he published his discovery of the satellites of Jupiter.

Galileo's formidable attacks on traditional ideas, and his claims that he could demonstrate beyond doubt the essential truth of Copernicus' theories, created widespread controversy. One of his outraged colleagues, a Jesuit professor of philosophy at Padua, refused to look through a telescope for fear his traditional views might be shaken. More ominously, Galileo's Jesuit and Dominican opponents began to draw the attention of the Inquisition to his "heretical" ideas.

In 1616, after Galileo had defended his position in the presence of the pope, Paul V, the Inquisition censured him and prohibited him from spreading the doctrine that the earth moves, either by teaching or publication; the harsh reaction was in part due to the aggressive spirit of the Counter-Reformation, which sought to combat all traces of opposition to official views. After a period of tactful silence, Galileo returned to the attack when a former friend was elected pope as Urban VIII. In 1632 he published a *Dialogue Concerning the Two Chief World Systems*, in which he used imaginary characters to express his theories. The strategy failed to protect him. The Inquisition summoned him to Rome, imprisoned him, and in 1633 tried him for heresy. In spite of his poor health and powerful friends, the tribunal forced him to undergo the humiliation of a public recantation, and sentenced him to house arrest for the remainder of his life. The case against him was reopened only in 1980, when Pope John Paul II—like Copernicus, a Pole—ordered that belated justice be done: in 1992, the church formally proclaimed its error.

Galileo spent the rest of his life under house arrest at his villa outside Florence, working on problems in physics. His last work, *Dialogues Concerning Two New Sciences* (1638), made use of observation and experiment to study a variety of phenomena, including motion. In trying to understand the practical character of natural events, rather than seeking to probe their cosmic purpose, he laid the bases of modern physics.

MEDICINE AND THE HUMAN BODY

The growth of scientific medicine in the West began with the Greeks, and throughout Medieval Europe doctors remained largely dependent on more or less corrupted versions of the works of the Greek physician Galen of Pergamum (c. 130–c. 200). Galen catalogued illnesses, distinguished between anatomy and physiology, and described the course of various diseases. By contrast with the West, in the Medieval Muslim world, significant medical and scientific research led to important medical discoveries, some of which gradually circulated in Europe. The *Canon of Medicine* by the great Muslim scientist who was known in the West as Avicenna (980–1037) became a standard European medical text, in use up to the Renaissance.

Paracelsus

The Renaissance, with its revival of interest in ancient texts, and its growing spirit of practical research, brought a wave of new interest. The figure who did most to change and improve methods of medical treatment was a Swiss alchemist and doctor called Theophrastus Bombast von Hohenheim; he proclaimed his superiority to ancient doctors by adopting the name by which he is best known, Paracelsus (1493–1541)—the name means "better than Celsus," who was an eminent Roman surgeon of the 1st century A.D.

Rejecting the authority of Aristotle and Galen, Paracelsus turned to other ancient sources and, above all, to his own careful observation in treating disease. After studying medicine at Ferrara in northern Italy, he taught at the University of Basle, Switzerland. He was one of the earliest university teachers anywhere to lecture in German, his own language, rather than in Latin, and this in itself was a challenge to tradition. His unconventional approach, coupled with a legendary short temper, brought him into constant conflict with his colleagues, and he spent the last years of his life as a traveling physician. Constantly recording the various symptoms of illnesses, and their reaction to different drugs, Paracelsus was the first physician to emphasize the close relationship between chemistry and medicine.

The Circulation of the Blood

The first to make a breakthrough in understanding the system whereby blood circulates in the body was the Spanish theologian and physician Michael Servetus (1511–1553). In a theological treatise, *Christianity Restored* (1553), written while he was teaching in France, he described how blood is carried from the heart to the lungs to be purified, and then returns to the heart to be passed from there to the other parts of the body.

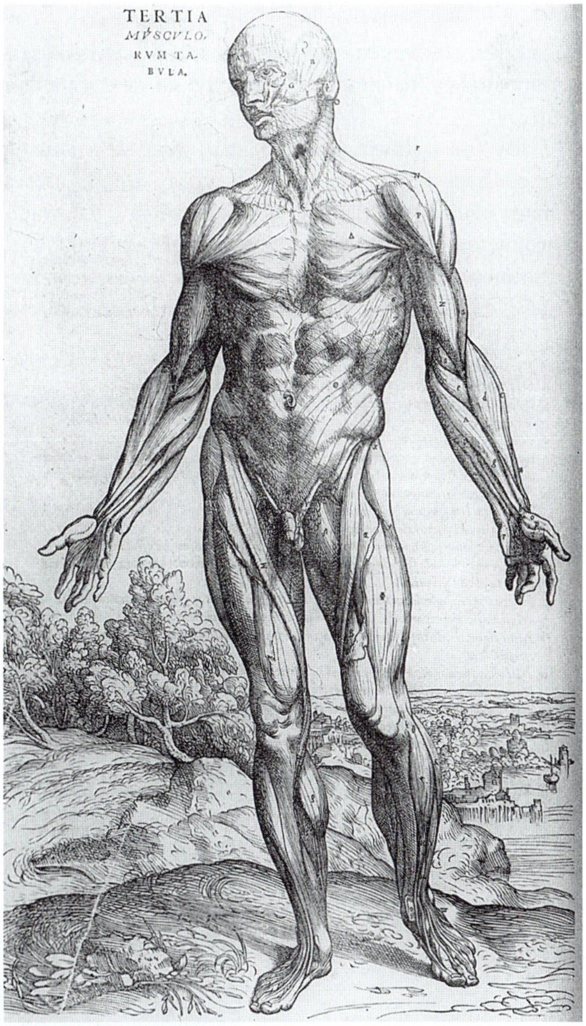

One of the earliest scientific studies of human musculature, by Andreas Vesalius (1543).

For all the importance of his work, Servetus failed to realize that the blood returns to the heart, circulating endlessly by means of the veins. This discovery was made by the English doctor William Harvey (1578–1657). As a young man, Harvey studied under Galileo at Padua and subsequently became personal physician to James I and Charles I. In a publication of 1628, Harvey described the blood circulation system, and explained the function of heart valves and arterial pulse.

The increasing use of dissection improved knowledge of the human body and its organs. Surgeons thus became able to operate more effectively. Over half a century earlier, in 1543—the year in which Copernicus' revolutionary theory appeared—the Flemish biologist Andreas Vesalius (1514–1564) had published *On the Structure of the Human Body*. Vesalius based his anatomical treatise on the observations he made while dissecting corpses. Church leaders who believed in the physical resurrection of the body on the Day of Judgment protested at his use of cadavers, however, and Vesalius abandoned his scientific studies to practice medicine at the Spanish court.

By the following century, the wave of scientific progress had swept away such objections to the use of human cadavers. Medical schools began to teach anatomy, and public dissections provided popular entertainment: Rembrandt's *The Anatomy Lesson of Dr. Nicolaas Tulp* (1632) shows the famous surgeon explaining the anatomy of the corpse he is working on to a crowd of admirers.

The Royal Society of London

The spectacular discoveries in anatomy, like those in astronomy and physics, inevitably aroused widespread interest. This led in turn to the establishment of organizations of scientists, to share research discoveries and promote their spread. The first such institution, the Lincean Academy, was founded in Rome in 1602. By far the most important, however, was the Royal Society of London for Improving Knowledge. The group began to meet informally at Oxford in the 1640s, during the Civil War. In 1660 12 members formed an official organization, which received a royal charter two years later.

The declared aim of the Royal Society was to gather all knowledge about nature, and encourage its use for the public good. The sheer quantity of information with which it was deluged soon forced the Society to function as a central clearinghouse for the circulation of ideas. In 1665 it began to publish on a regular basis *Philosophical Transactions*, the earliest scientific journal.

Similar organizations appeared in other parts of Europe. In France, Louis XIV encouraged the foundation of the Royal Academy of Sciences in 1666, and by the end of the century other academies existed in Berlin and Naples. The "new science," which had aroused so much official hostility a hundred years ear-

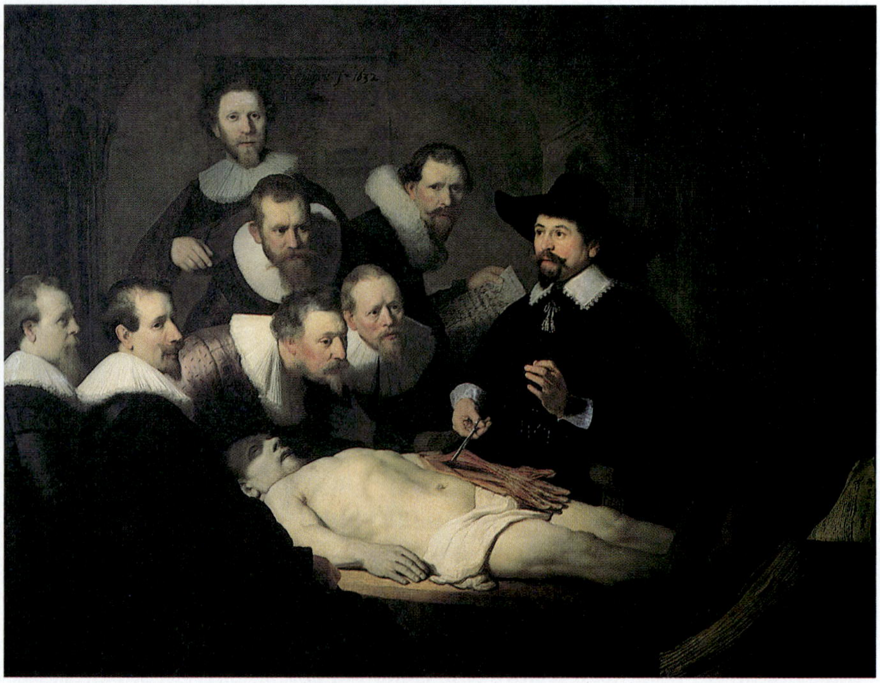

Rembrandt's painting, *The Anatomy Lesson of Dr. Nicolaas Tulp*, depicts a scientific dissection (1632).

lier, was now patronized by royalty and followed enthusiastically by an ever-widening group of nobles and educated middle-class men and women.

THE SCIENTIFIC METHOD: BACON, DESCARTES, AND PASCAL

Many founding members of the Royal Society believed in acquiring and evaluating information by the scientific method. They acknowledged Francis Bacon (1561–1626) as their inspiration. Bacon himself was a philosopher rather than a scientist, but his writings on the importance of science for human development led the way in stimulating scientific research.

A gifted and precocious young man, Bacon was a student at Cambridge by the age of 16. He distinguished himself there by attacking the works of Aristotle, which were regarded as the basis of all philosophical instruction. The character of Bacon's philosophy emerged as early as 1605, in *The Advancement of Learning*. He believed that the myths and fables of primitive peoples expressed true wisdom; Plato, Aristotle, and the other ancient philosophers had strayed from the truth by the arrogance which led them to invent their own intellectual systems. To find truth, it was necessary to study the world around us. Experiment was far more important than theorizing.

He returned to this conviction throughout his life. In *New Atlantis* he described an ideal society in which scientists would work for the state in gathering knowledge. In due course this would lead to the establishing of universal laws creating continuous improvements in human existence. Toward the end of his life he tried to replace Aristotelianism with a new system of philosophy, described in *Novum Organum*. This appeared in Latin in 1620, but two years later Bacon broke with tradition and published an edition in English, The *New Organon*. This meant that a far wider audience read and thought about his challenge to Aristotle's views.

In his last works, he poured his energies into what he believed to be his great mission: the exaltation of science as the savior of humanity. In the *New Atlantis* (1626), he even foreshadowed the formation of associations such as the Royal Society.

The French philosopher René Descartes.

The Methodology of Descartes

If Bacon provided the philosophical underpinning to scientific research, the Frenchman René Descartes (1596–1650) set out the importance of the power of reasoning. After a period of travel, Descartes settled in Holland, where he created the branch of mathematics known as analytic geometry. His interest in mathematics led in turn to his most widely read book, *Discourse on Method* (1637).

In this work he aimed to unify all knowledge as the product of clear reasoning from verifiable evidence. The ideal of objective certitude that could be reached in mathematics should also exist, he claimed, in scientific and philosophical thought. To discover what kind of evidence could have such complete certitude, he adopted the method of universal doubt. Everything was open to question, even his own existence. In the famous phrase "*cogito, ergo sum*" ("I think, therefore I am"), he established his first certitude, his existence, and following from there worked out his philosophical system.

Although the system, which became known as Cartesianism, is firmly based on reason, Descartes included in it a supreme being. His God, not necessarily to be identified with the God of the Old and New Testaments, created a world imbued with perfect mathematical principles.

As a practical scientist and physicist, Descartes produced mixed results. In his theoretical writings on physics, he was the first to make the important distinction between mass and weight. On the other hand, his attempt to locate that part of the human anatomy which contains the soul was a predictable failure. Descartes' profound influence on his contemporaries came less from the details of his theories than from his general intellectual stance. In particular, he taught the immense importance of never accepting a belief without thoroughly questioning it. After Descartes, it was never again safe to argue from tradition.

Pascal and Faith

For all their temperamental differences, Bacon and Descartes shared an essential belief in the positive power of science. The all-too-brief career of the French mathematician and philosopher Blaise Pascal (1623–1662) shows a far more complex attitude to scientific discovery.

As a child, Pascal was a mathematical prodigy. At the age of 16 he completed an original treatise on conic sections, which helped to lay the basis for integral calculus. He also made pioneering discoveries in fluid mechanics and hydrodynamics, and along with his countryman Pierre Fermat (1601–1665), originated the mathematical theory of probabilities.

Pascal's sister was a nun, and through her he came into contact with a new Catholic movement, Jansenism; the name was taken from that of a Dutch theologian, Cornelius Jansen (1585–1638). In opposition to the Jesuits' belief in free will, the Jansenists claimed that human destiny was in the hands of God, so that salvation could come only from unquestioning faith. The ultimate source of these teachings was St. Augustine. The hostility between Jansenists and Jesuits led in the 17th century to Louis XIV's persecution of the French Jansenists (on Louis XIV's efforts to stamp out Jansen's beliefs in France, see Part VI, Topic 3).

The asceticism and piety of the Jansenists he met profoundly shook Pascal's confidence in the value of his scientific work. Late in 1654, at the age of 30, he underwent a mystical experience that led him to abandon science in favor of seeking salvation. In the *Reflections* (1670), the writings of his few remaining years, collected and published after his early death, Pascal urged the importance of spiritual values over dry logic and intellect. He claimed that "the heart has its reasons that the mind cannot know." A lone voice in the growing enthusiasm for scientific progress, he lamented the gulf between the material and the spiritual. Indeed, the passion of his protests is an indication of the degree to which science had come to dominate 17th-century European intellectual life.

NEWTON AND THE LAWS OF THE NATURAL UNIVERSE

Kepler's astronomy, Galileo's physics, and Descartes' idea of universal science reached a majestic synthesis in the work of the Englishman Isaac Newton (1642–1726), the most eminent mathematician and natural philosopher of early modern times. After attending Cambridge as a student, Newton later taught there. He became a fellow of the Royal Society and served as president from 1703 until his death. His whole life was devoted to ceaseless research—alchemy, optics, mathematics, chronology, chemistry, mechanics, theology, and the secrets of the Bible were only some of the fields to which he made significant contributions.

At the heart of Newton's work lay his belief that logic and reason were unsatisfactory tools for a scientist. It was necessary, he maintained, to prove everything by experiment or mathematics. Thus, his most widely read book, *The Mathematical Principles of Natural Philosophy* (1687), deliberately set out to refute Descartes' exaltation of rationalism. One of the last major scholarly works to be written in Latin, the book is generally referred to as the *Principia*, the first word of its Latin title.

The English physicist and mathematician Sir Isaac Newton.

The most influential of his discoveries related to the problem of motion, which he defined in three laws. In formulating these laws, he arrived at concepts of mass, inertia, and force (a term in physics referring to the measurable influence which produces motion) in relation to velocity and acceleration which dominated science down to the early 20th century and are still valid today. He extended his system to the entire universe, applying the same principles to the movements of the moon and planets. In order to explain the consistent nature of motion, he conceived the idea of the law of gravitation, whereby there exists a reciprocal force of attraction between every body in the universe.

The Newtonian Universe

Even if the lay public could not always follow the details of Newton's reasoning, the implications of his discoveries had a growing effect on how people thought about the universe. If all motion, random though it might seem, was really the result of precise and unchanging forces, then the world was like a huge machine that functioned according to laws that could be mathematically expressed. God was like a watchmaker who put the machinery in motion. For Newton, in fact, the creation of the force of gravity was an act of God, since he believed that bodies do not necessarily possess that quality. Like most of his fellow scientists in the 17th century, Newton remained profoundly religious and devoted much time in his later years to theology.

Yet many people increasingly saw the mechanistic view of the universe proposed by Newton as a welcome replacement for traditional theological disputes. After more than a century of bitter religious wars, the sheer levelheadedness and impartiality of scientific debate seemed a happy relief. Science was peaceful, verifiable and, above all, useful. This is one reason why Newton received honors never before awarded to a scholar. He became a member of Parliament, served as director of the Royal Mint, and was the first scientist to be knighted for his work.

For a few thinkers, the Newtonian universe replaced the personal God of traditional belief with a natural order. The Dutch Jewish philosopher Baruch Spinoza (1632–1677) held that nature is a fixed and unchangeable order, which serves no particular purpose. God is neither Creator nor Redeemer, but simply natural law. Humans, as part of the universe, conform to the same laws. In his book, *Ethics* (1677), Spinoza writes: "I shall consider human activities and desires in exactly the same manner as if I were concerned with lines, planes, and solids." Few of his contemporaries, however, were as willing as Spinoza to break with tradition, and he was expelled from the Amsterdam Jewish community for his radical views.

For most thinkers in the 18th century, Isaac Newton's contribution stripped away the ignorance of the past and presented a new view of science and the universe. The newly optimistic spirit was neatly caught in Alexander Pope's ironic couplet, written in the early 1700s:

> Nature and nature's law lay hid in night.
> God said, "Let Newton be!" and all was light.

During the 17th century, Western thought underwent wrenching change, and the foundations of the modern intellectual world were laid. The Aristotelian and Medieval views of the world ended their 1000-year-old monopoly, to be replaced by the Newtonian universe. Modern science had a generally accepted methodology, and physics, chemistry, mathematics, anatomy, and astronomy were already producing startling results.

Early researchers had been persecuted, imprisoned, even executed, but by the early 18th century scientists were honored members of society, supported by governments. The Counter-Reformation Catholic Church remained hostile to much of the new science, but its power was on the wane, at least in western Europe. Since leading figures such as Descartes and Newton saw no difficulty in reconciling their conclusions with a continuing religious faith, most Protestant communities accepted their work. During the Civil War in England, the Puritans had actually encouraged scientific research.

The scientific revolution did more than illuminate problems of astronomy or anatomy. By challenging centuries of tradition and ignorance, and by revealing the importance of questioning received wisdom, it paved the way for a vast rethinking of many of the basic assumptions underlying Western culture. The discovery of universal laws in nature led to a new belief in a "verifiable universe," in which it was possible to know and discover everything through the application of human logic. From the 17th-century scientific revolution was born the chief intellectual movement of the 18th century, the Enlightenment (see Part VII, Topic 1). Furthermore, the demonstrated existence of "natural laws" in the universe inspired 18th-century thinkers and politicians to search for similar universal principles in government and devise new political constitutions. The eventual consequence at the end of the century was revolutionary social and political upheaval.

Questions for Further Study

1. What are the chief features of the scientific method? What new light did it shed on astronomy and medicine?
2. How did Descartes and Newton differ in their research methods? How did this affect their conclusions?

3. What were the long-term political consequences of the 17th-century scientific revolution?

Suggestions for Further Reading

Debus, A. *Man and Nature in the Renaissance*. Cambridge, MA, 1978.

Drake, Stillman. *Galileo*. New York, 1980.

Hall, A. Rupert. *The Revolution in Science 1500–1750*. London, 1983.

Jacob, Margaret C. *The Cultural Meaning of the Scientific Revolution*. New York, 1988.

Webster, C. *The Great Instauration: Science, Medicine, and Reform*. London, 1975.

Westfall, R. S. *Never at Rest: A Biography of Isaac Newton*. Cambridge, MA, 1980.

Willey, B. *The Seventeenth Century Background*. New York, 1982.

Wilson, M. D. *Descartes*. Boston, 1978.

VI

Topic 2

Southern Europe: Spain, Italy, and the Mediterranean

For thousands of years the Mediterranean Sea had played a unique and vital role in the growth of civilization. Around its shores had developed a variety of peoples and states, from the Egyptians and Phoenicians and the Greeks and Romans of the ancient world to the Muslim Arabs and the Christian states of Medieval and Renaissance Italy. During those many centuries, the Mediterranean served as the meeting place of diverse and often hostile cultures and religions, and as the most important trade route of the entire region. From the later Middle Ages to the great age of overseas expansion, countless commercial galleys criss-crossed its trade routes, laden with valuable cargoes of spices and other luxury goods from the East as well as the furs, lumber, and woolen cloth from the North. Yet the 16th century saw the beginning of economic decline for the region, as the newly discovered sailing routes across the Atlantic and around Africa shifted the focus of trade from the Mediterranean to the Atlantic states.

What the Mediterranean lost in economic importance Spain gained. As one of the major beneficiaries of the age of discovery, the Hapsburg kings of Spain grew rich and powerful on the gold and silver bullion and agricultural products of the New World. In the mid-16th century, the resources of the vast Spanish empire enabled its monarchs to extend their political hegemony throughout Europe. Charles V had become king of Spain in 1516 as Charles I and Holy Roman emperor—that is, of the Germanic states—in 1519. In 1556 he divided his possessions, relinquishing the crown of Spain to his son Philip II and the imperial crown to his brother Ferdinand I. Philip ruled an empire that included not only Spain and huge tracts of the Americas, but Milan, Naples, Sicily, Sardinia, and the Netherlands.

Within little more than a century after Philip's death, Spain—seething with domestic unrest and its economy devastated by a combination of virtually continuous warfare, agricultural deterioration, unchecked royal spending, and overtaxation—had lost most of its European possessions. In the diplomatic balance of power, Spain's predominance had been overshadowed by France.

Ever since the rise and expansion of Rome, Italy had played a central role in Mediterranean life, although its political importance after the collapse of the Roman Empire had been eclipsed in the early Middle Ages by the Barbarian invasions, the ambitions of the Holy Roman emperors, and the rise of the Byzantine Empire in the East. By the 15th century, however, the Italian city-states held sway again, but now as centers of a vibrant economic revival and a brilliant cultural Renaissance.

Despite Italy's achievements as the center of Western artistic and intellectual revival, the invasion of the peninsula by the French king Charles VIII in 1494 began a long period of foreign domination. In 1559, the destinies of Spain and Italy met when Philip II confirmed his hold over his Italian lands and ended a protracted struggle for mastery in Italy between Spain and France. Thereafter, Spain influenced Italian affairs until the early 18th century, when the Austrians became the predominant power in Italy.

THE ECLIPSE OF THE MEDITERRANEAN

In the 200 years between 1500 and 1700, the economic and political importance of the Mediterranean Sea diminished as the focus of power shifted to the Atlantic and northwestern Europe. One of the major reasons for this change was the new commercial sea route charted around Africa. Yet other factors, including the expansion of the Ottoman Empire, made the Mediterranean region the object of continuing European concern.

The Changing Dimensions of Trade

As the focus of European commerce, the Mediterranean had become something of an Italian lake by the 14th century, for the carrying trade that sailed its waters was almost exclusively controlled by the Italian maritime states, especially Genoa and Venice. Muslim merchants acted as middlemen, obtaining spices, gold, ivory, and slaves from Africa, India, and the Far East, and selling these goods to the Venetians, who had a monopoly on the spice trade, and other European merchants. In turn, the Venetians either sent the goods overland to Germany or—and this was the bulk of their commerce—by ship through the western Mediterranean, around Spain and up to the northern countries. A series of seven galley fleets made regular voyages to such areas as Alexandria, Beirut, and Barbary (the western coast of North Africa), but the most famous was the so-called Flanders galley. This important run brought sugar or other commodities in Venetian ships to England and exchanged it for wool, which was woven into cloth in Flanders and then brought back to the eastern Mediterranean. In 1423, a Venetian leader boasted that his city commanded some 3345 ships, which employed a total of some 35,000 men.

By the 16th century, this profitable arrangement disappeared as Dutch and English ships began to take over the carrying trade, and the Portuguese began to use the new route around southern Africa, thereby cutting out the Muslim and Venetian middlemen. In 1521, the Venetian Republic, anxious to restore its declining trade position, offered to buy all the spices brought to Europe by Portugal, but the offer was refused. The last Flanders galley sailed from Venice in 1532, that to Alexandria in 1564, and the Beirut galley in 1570.

Mediterranean commerce did not, of course, come to an abrupt end. Rather, setbacks in the luxury trade were interspersed with sudden increases as it moved along its overall downward trajectory. A variety of circumstances accounted for this up and down movement, including interruptions of Portuguese and Dutch shipping due to war in Europe and on the seas. In 1565, for example, as much pepper from India was passing through the Red Sea as arrived by the African route in Lisbon. The spice routes of the Levant remained active until well past the end of the century. In the 1600s, British trade with Italy increased greatly, and by the end of the century Italian goods accounted for some 10 percent of all British imports. There is, in fact, some

Significant Dates

Spain

1492	Columbus' first voyage; beginning of shift in sea trade from Mediterranean to Atlantic
1532	Last Flanders galley
1453–1571	Mediterranean wars with the Turks
1571	First Holy League; Battle of Lepanto
1598–1621	Philip III rules as king of Spain
1621–1665	Philip IV rules as king of Spain
1683	Second Holy League
1700–1746	Philip V rules as first Bourbon king of Spain
1738–1746	War of Jenkins' Ear

Map 2.1 Southern Europe, c. 1700

evidence that by the 18th century the volume of trade had begun to increase.

Nevertheless, the pattern and nature of the sea trade changed, and the Mediterranean became the location for a series of smaller, regional commercial economies, such as the Adriatic area, the eastern Mediterranean, and the Spanish-French coast. Locally produced items, such as finished woolens made in Florence, blown glass in Venice, and steel armor in Milan, were still sold throughout Europe, although by the 17th century the French were offering serious competition in the manufacture of luxury goods. Greek, Italian, and French wines and olive oil were widely enjoyed, while lemons, oranges, figs, dates, and other items grown in the milder climates of the Mediterranean were in demand. Even the fishing industry changed as a result of the new sea routes. Codfish and herring, preserved with salt, became major staples in the diets of Catholic Spain and Italy, for use on Fridays and during Lent, and were used to feed the growing number of slaves in the Americas. In fact, however, the transport of food, especially cereal crops, remained a major aspect of Mediterranean commerce. Not only was wheat, still produced in Sicily, North Africa, and Greece, transported to Spain, France, and Italy, but a more localized traffic, which developed along coastal stretches continued to be quicker and less costly than overland routes.

The Mediterranean War

In addition to the overseas discoveries of the great age of exploration, the Mediterranean economy experienced another change in the 15th century as a result of the capture of Constantinople by the Ottoman Turks in 1453 and the subsequent conquest of Syria and Egypt by 1517 (see Part IV, Topic 5). Thereafter, as the Ottomans attempted to bring the eastern Mediterranean into their sphere, naval warfare between the Turkish Muslims and the European Christians characterized much of the history of the region.

In 1565, the Turks unsuccessfully besieged the island fortress of Malta, ruled by the Knights of Saint John. By 1570, however, the Ottomans controlled some three-quarters of the Mediterranean coastline, a zone stretching east from the Istrian peninsula in the northern Adriatic, around Greece and the Balkans, across to Asia Minor and the Middle East, and thence westward across North Africa almost as far as Gibraltar. The Turkish expansion, coming on top of the new trade routes, seriously affected the economic well-being of the trading states, especially Venice. The Turkish seizure of Cyprus in 1571 greatly alarmed European rulers, who feared the beginning of an effort to sweep the Mediterranean of all Christian shipping.

In response to the Turkish threat, Venice, Spain, and the papacy joined forces in forming the Holy League in 1571, which marshaled a vast fleet of some 300 ships and 80,000 men. In October, this fleet met an equally strong Turkish force off the coast of Greece at Lepanto, an engagement that resulted in a major victory for the League. The Battle of Lepanto did not, however, profoundly alter the course of events. After Lepanto, in the western Mediterranean the Turks confined themselves mainly to the North African coast, although in the east they continued to secure strategic islands, including Crete in 1669. The Venetians, whose already declining economic position would be further reduced by Turkish hegemony, bore the brunt of fighting, especially along the Dalmatian coast and in Greek waters, and even blockaded the Dardanelles. In 1683, when the

Turks were at the gates of Vienna, Venice joined a second holy league, now sponsored by the Austrians, during which they besieged Athens and reconquered the Morea, which they held for the next 30 years.

Despite the frequent state of war between the Turks and the European powers, the economic unity of the Mediterranean did not end. The Ottomans were deeply interested in international trade. Muslim traders maintained representatives and branch offices in Venice and other western cities, while Turkish tax policy favored foreign merchants. The entire range of western commercial products, from coin, cloth, glass, and other manufactures to furs, lumber, and raw materials, found their way to the East, while eastern commodities, including pepper, spices, oils, dyes, ivory, and slaves, continued to be supplied to Europeans. In this commercial sense, the Mediterranean Sea remained neutral in the European-Turkish wars.

On the other hand, if the Turkish military challenge did not stop Mediterranean commerce, merchants faced constant danger from the many pirates who roamed its waters, especially along the western shores of North Africa, where a series of "Barbary" states—named after the Berber tribes who inhabited the regions—had been established under Turkish rule. The Spanish and the Venetians led the struggle against these Muslim corsairs during the 17th century. After the Treaty of Utrecht in 1713–1714 (see Part VI, Topic 3), the British controlled Gibraltar and Minorca, and became the predominant naval force in the Mediterranean. Nevertheless, piracy persisted and in the late 18th century the United States even had to pay tribute to protect its shipping. In 1801, however, the United States declared war against the pasha of Tripoli, and in 1815 against Algiers, thereby curtailing piracy.

FROM HAPSBURG TO BOURBON SPAIN

The first serious efforts to forge a Spanish state had been the work of Ferdinand II of Aragon and Isabella I of Castile, whose marriage in 1469 joined the two kingdoms (see Part IV, Topic 4). Together the Catholic monarchs laid the institutional basis for a unified state,

The Escorial, the massive palace built on the outskirts of Madrid by Philip II.

completing the reconquest of Granada from the Moors and imposing religious unity through the Inquisition and the expulsion of the Jews. Nevertheless, local loyalties and the special rights of the regions remained strong, and neither was fully accepted in the other's realm. The *cortes*, as the representative institutions of the towns were called, proved to be bastions of local independence.

The Twilight of Spanish Power

When the grandson of Ferdinand and Isabella came to the throne in 1516 as King Charles I (later Emperor Charles V), the reaction to a foreign monarch, born and raised in the Low Countries, was deeply hostile. During the long reigns of Charles and his son Philip II, the institutions of the royal government were slowly built. Centralization assumed a new dimension as Philip devoted unprecedented attention to the daily business of government. Under his careful guidance, Spain became the greatest power in Europe, although the long and bitter revolt in the Netherlands (1566–1609) and the humiliating defeat of the Spanish Armada against England (1588) proved costly setbacks which caused bankruptcy and a weakening of royal prestige.

Unlike his father, Philip III (ruled 1598–1621) took little interest in government. Devoting himself to religious ceremonies and the social life of the court, he left the direction of royal affairs to his favorite, the corrupt duke of Lerma (1552–1625). At home, he encouraged a new era of extravagant spending by his personal behavior, while abroad he was continually drawn into disputes that further drained the treasury. The economic plight of the realm worsened as population declined as a result of wars and emigration, a situation aggravated in 1609–1610 when Lerma expelled the *Moriscos*, as the Muslims who had been forcibly converted to Christianity were called. The loss of the Moriscos, whose industry and business skills had enabled them to prosper, was a serious blow to the economy. Nor was Lerma's foreign policy any more successful, and in 1609 Spain was forced to end the revolt of the Netherlands by signing a truce that recognized the independence of the Protestant Dutch Republic, known as the United Provinces. Lerma was finally driven from power in 1618 by a conspiracy of young noblemen that included the count of Olivares (1587–1645).

Philip IV (ruled 1621–1665), only 16 when he became king, proved an even weaker ruler than his father, but had in Olivares a tough and skillful minister. As the youngest son, Olivares had attended university and had prepared for a career in the church, but he succeeded unexpectedly to his father's title and wealth. Before Philip became king, Olivares had joined the prince's retinue and became a favorite courtier. Made a member of the highest noble rank, Olivares became Philip's chief minister in 1621. Although no less corrupt than Lerma, he quickly won the respect of the Spanish cortes by declaring an end to excessive spending at the court.

Velázquez's portrait of the Count-Duke of Olivares, chief minister of Philip II of Spain.

Olivares wanted to preserve Spain's status as a great power and to impose a rigidly centralized government on the nation. In foreign affairs, Olivares was determined to continue the war in Flanders, which soon became merely a minor aspect of two larger conflicts, the Thirty Years' War and the struggle between the Hapsburgs and the Bourbons. Under Richelieu's leadership, France became the chief rival of Spain, which generally remained on the defensive both in Europe and the West Indies and steadily lost ground. The far-flung fighting required considerable money and large armies, and in order to meet both needs Olivares announced plans for a Union of Arms, according to which all parts of the empire would contribute men to a force of 140,000. The actual size of the army proved to be smaller, and some provinces refused to provide either men or money.

The crisis point was reached in 1640, when the French captured Arras and invaded Flanders, and separatist revolts broke out in Catalonia and Portugal.

Catalonia represented a serious problem for Spanish unity, for the fiercely independent Catalans had resisted all efforts by Olivares to undermine local privileges or to wrest increased taxes from the region. In 1640, as the war with France grew more precarious, Olivares sent troops to Catalonia, a move that sparked peasant uprisings against the soldiers and royal officials and resulted in the killing of the provincial viceroy. The revolts became a coordinated rebellion when political leaders in Barcelona, a prosperous port on the Mediterranean, decided to support the outbreaks. Declaring that Philip IV had violated the laws of Catalonia, the rebels invited Louis XIII of France to send troops to support them. Only after 12 years of savage fighting, during which Catalonia was overrun by Spanish and French armies, did Philip IV take Barcelona and end the uprising.

Portugal, which had been seized by Philip II in 1580 but never formally incorporated into the Spanish realm, had been the object of Olivares' centralizing policies, including special taxation and a proposal to unite the cortes of Portugal and Castile. Governed by Philip's aunt, the viceroy Margaret of Savoy, Portugal seethed with discontent. After the outbreak of the Catalan revolt, the Portuguese rallied around the duke of Braganza, who led the break from Spain and was proclaimed King John IV (ruled 1640–1656) of an independent state.

In the wake of repeated setbacks, Olivares fell from power in 1643. Olivares, who objected to women "interfering" in political affairs, had alienated Philip IV's wife, Elizabeth (1602–1644), and it was the queen who now insisted that Olivares be retired.

Las Meninas (the Maids of Honor), by Velázquez (1656), was originally entitled *The Family of Philip IV.* The child in the center is the Infanta Margarita, daughter of Philip IV and his second wife; the royal couple are seen reflected in the mirror on the wall.

The Bourbons and the Spanish Succession

The Peace of the Pyrenees finally ended the fighting between Spain and France in 1659. The next year, the daughter of Elizabeth and Philip IV, Maria Therese, married Louis XIV of France, although the treaty had forced her to renounce any claim to the Spanish succession.

On the death of Philip IV in 1665, Charles II (ruled 1665–1700) became king. Because he was only four at the time, the government was in the hands of his mother, Philip IV's second wife, Mariana of Austria (1634–1696). Moreover, Charles was not only mentally retarded but handicapped by the famous "Hapsburg jaw," a physical deformity that afflicted family members in a more pronounced manner with each generation. The problem kept Charles from speaking or eating properly. After the end of the War of the League of Augsburg in 1697 (see Part VI, Topic 3), a number of treaties were arranged among the great powers to partition the Spanish empire upon the death of Charles, but Charles named Philip of Anjou, Louis XIV's grandson, as his heir. Less than a month later, the unfortunate Charles died.

Philip of Anjou ascended the throne of Spain as Philip V (ruled 1700–1746), the first Bourbon king of Spain. Philip's reign was thought by some to be the start of a new era of peace, but it began with the outbreak of the War of the Spanish Succession (see Part VI, Topic 3) as the other powers feared the possible union of Spain and France. Philip was finally recognized as king of Spain by the Treaty of Utrecht (1713), in which he agreed that the crowns of the two nations would never be united. The next year, Philip had to put down a revolt in Catalonia, which had risen against Madrid during the war.

From the outset, Philip had been influenced by Anne Marie, Princess Orsini (1635–1722), a handsome and intelligent woman who served as lady-in-waiting to the king's wife, Queen Maria Luisa (1688–1714), who ruled as regent while Philip was away during the war. Orsini supported French interests in Spain, and through her Louis XIV influenced Spanish policy. In 1708, however, Louis plotted with the British and Dutch to dismember the Spanish empire, and Orsini threw her support to Philip. When Maria Luisa died, Orsini's influence over Philip grew, together with that of the Italian Cardinal Giulio Alberoni (1664–1752), who served as prime minister of Spain from 1715 to 1719. Together, Orsini and Alberoni persuaded Philip to marry Elizabeth Farnese (1692–1766), daughter of the duke of Parma. Elizabeth, a strong-willed and ambitious woman, immediately dismissed Orsini and became the real ruler of Spain.

Alberoni was determined to restore Spanish influence in Italy, where the Austrians had become dominant, and managed to get Spain involved in a disastrous war with Britain and France. As a price for peace, the allies insisted that Philip dismiss Alberoni and cede Sardinia to Piedmont. Philip once again abandoned his claim to the French crown, while the Hapsburgs surrendered theirs to the Spanish throne. In return, the succession of Elizabeth Farnese's children to the duchies of Parma and Tuscany was recognized. In 1724, Philip abdicated in favor of his son Luis, but he continued to rule because of the bad health of Luis, who died later that year. Philip once again became king.

Charles III ruled Naples from 1734 to 1759 and then succeeded to the Spanish throne on the death of his father, Philip V.

For the remainder of Philip's reign, Spain was constantly embroiled in wars, in large part as a result of Elizabeth Farnese's scheming for her children. In 1733, France and Spain concluded the Treaty of the Escorial, whereby the two states agreed to support each other in wars against the interests of Britain and Austria. In the War of the Polish Succession (1733–1735), in which each alliance supported a different claimant to the Polish throne, Spain occupied Naples and Sicily, and in 1734 Elizabeth Farnese's son Charles was crowned King of the Two Sicilies. Four years later, Spain and Britain began a prolonged trade war, known as the War of Jenkins' Ear, and this struggle was merged into the larger War of the Austrian Succession that erupted in 1740 (see Part VI, Topic 9). Philip V died in 1746, before this conflict ended, leaving a Spain weakened in power and reduced in status.

The successors of Philip II had neither the vision nor the resources with which to continue to rule Spain as a great power. The wealth that had once poured into the Spanish treasury from the Americas caused serious inflation and drove up government spending. Now the supply dwindled with the depletion of the gold and silver mines while the expenses of the crown rose steadily, especially in the face of continual European warfare. All this drained national resources and pressured local authorities for more taxes. In the first half of the 17th century, efforts to increase centralization and to extract men and money from the provinces resulted in a series of revolts that threatened the stability of the kingdom. By the time of the death of Philip V, the once powerful empire had been seriously reduced in territory and prestige, and overshadowed in international affairs by Britain and France.

Significant Dates

Italy

1454	Peace of Lodi
1494	French invasion of Italy
1527	Sack of Rome
1559	Treaty of Cateau-Cambrésis
1559–1700	Spanish preponderance in Italy
1713	Treaty of Utrecht grants Milan, Naples, and Sardinia to Austrians
1720	Duke of Piedmont becomes king of Sardinia
1734–1759	Charles III rules as first Bourbon king of Naples
1741–1790	Joseph II rules Austrian possessions

EUROPE AND THE ITALIAN STATES

During the Renaissance and early modern period, while powerful, centralized monarchies emerged in France, England, and Spain, Italy flourished as the land of culture but had no political identity. By the height of the Renaissance in the 15th century, the Italian peninsula consisted of about a dozen independent city-states, whose relations with each other were marked by economic competition and constant warfare. In response to the political anarchy of the period, Italy fell prey to foreign invasion and the larger struggle for power that consumed the great powers of Europe. For a century and a half, between 1559 and 1700, Italy came under the sway of the Spanish, whose policies greatly influenced social and economic conditions in the peninsula. After the War of the Spanish Succession, Spain's hegemony gave way to the influence of Austria, which dominated Italian affairs until national unification in the 19th century.

The Italian State System

Five states dominated Italian affairs. In the north, the Visconti family had ruled the duchy of Milan, including the surrounding region of Lombardy, for two centuries. Straddling the Po Valley, with the duchy of Savoy to its west, Venice to its east, and Genoa and Modena to the south, Milan was vulnerable to invasion. Because it lacked access to the sea, its economic life was more closely connected to Germany and Austria than to the rest of Italy. The Visconti despots pursued belligerent and aggressive policies toward their neighbors. As we have seen above, Venice, a republican oligarchy ruled by an elected doge and an hereditary senate, managed to maintain its maritime supremacy in the Mediterranean until the 16th century. Thereafter, its interest in the Venetian hinterland grew as its commercial empire shrunk. South of Milan and Venice lay the city of Florence, which ruled the large region of Tuscany and had access to the Tyrrhenian Sea through the port of Leghorn (Livorno). As the chief center of the Renaissance, Florence enjoyed enormous cultural prestige. The city was ruled firmly by the talented Medici, a family that had accumulated enormous wealth in banking, and although they exercised princely power, the Medici rulers maintained the veneer of republican government.

South and east of Florence lay the Papal States, governed from Rome by the pope as an absolute monarch. Its territories spanned the peninsula from the Tyrrhenian to the Adriatic, and included the virtually autonomous cities of Bologna and Ferrara. The papacy had lost much of its temporal authority over this area as a result of the "Babylonian Captivity" (1309–1377), during which the popes resided at Avignon in southern France, and the subsequent Great Schism (1378–1417), when several rival popes claimed the papal

Canaletto (Antonio Canale) painted innumerable scenes of Venice in the early 18th century, when the maritime republic was in economic decline.

throne. In the 15th century, however, the papacy reasserted its control and became active in Italian politics.

South of Rome and covering the remainder of the peninsula was the large Kingdom of Naples, over which the French, Hungarians, and Spanish had fought since the 14th century. In 1443, King Alfonso I of Aragon (1396–1458) took Naples and reunited it with Sicily, which he had ruled since 1416. The cities of Naples and Palermo were major commercial ports, while the large landed estates of southern Italy and Sicily still provided much of the wheat for the Mediterranean world.

The rival interests of these five states brought them repeatedly into conflict, and during the 15th century they began to show signs of developing many of the features of a miniature international system. First, the commercial and political interactions among them and with foreign powers led to the creation of the techniques and instruments of diplomacy. Foreign offices staffed by experts collected information and kept records, while the states stationed ambassadors in foreign capitals to represent their interests and negotiate for them. The development of standards for diplomacy and international relations that began in Italy eventually became the model for Europe. Second, as the major Italian states alternately fought, changed sides, and regrouped in new alliances, they seemed to anticipate the modern principle of the balance of power, whereby the military and diplomatic strength of several states was combined in order to prevent any one state from becoming too powerful.

In 1454, the five Italian states arranged the treaty of Lodi, which maintained peace in the peninsula for the next 40 years. The seizure of power in Milan by the despot Francesco Sforza (1401–1466) was recognized, and a new equilibrium emerged that aligned Milan and Florence against Venice and Naples, with the papacy acting as a balancing force. In 1494, however, Sforza's successor Ludovico il Moro (ruled 1481–1499) found Florence, Naples, and the Papal States allied against him and took the disastrous step of calling upon the French king, Charles VIII, for help. With a mixed army of French soldiers and Swiss mercenaries, Charles pushed deep into Italy, taking Florence, Rome, and Naples. When the pope joined forces with Venice and asked Ferdinand of Aragon and the Holy Roman Empire for assistance, Italy became the "cockpit" of Europe as a larger three-way European struggle for mastery unfolded. A generation of war in the Italian peninsula left the independence and prosperity of the Italian states in ruins. The final blow to Italian pride came, at least symbolically, when German and Spanish mercenaries of the Emperor Charles V sacked the city of Rome in 1527. Peace came at last in 1559 with the Treaty of Cateau-Cambrésis, which left Milan, Naples, Sicily, and Sardinia directly in the hands of the Spanish Hapsburgs, and Genoa and Florence under their protection. Italy's political collapse was all the more shocking to contemporaries because it coincided with the height of Italian cultural influence throughout Europe.

The Era of Spanish Preponderance

The century and a half of Spanish domination that followed Cateau-Cambrésis had an important impact on Italy. The period coincided with general economic difficulties for the peninsula, caused both by the changing sea routes and the fact that the position of the Italian bankers deteriorated as merchant and commercial capital began to develop in western and central Europe.

Spain attempted to centralize its administration in Italy, ruling its possessions through viceroys. In 1558, Philip II set up in Madrid a Council of Italy, whose members included two counselors from Milan and two from Sicily. One result of Spanish rule was that the political influence of the old aristocratic élites was seriously weakened, although they retained their legal and fiscal privileges on their huge estates. At the royal courts, however, a lavish and ornate social life developed among the aristocracy, and Spanish influence accelerated the aristocratic restructuring of Italian life. Campaigns were undertaken to counter periodic uprisings of the pro-French barons. The number of titles of nobility increased significantly and Spanish nobles engaged in massive purchases of land. In addition, the close coordination between state and church that had marked Spanish history was now repeated in Spain's Italian possessions.

Noble landowners lived increasingly in large cities such as Palermo and Naples, leaving their estates in the hands of managers who exploited the agricultural workers. The condition of the peasantry deteriorated and poverty became endemic in the south. It has been estimated that as much as 30 percent of the urban populations of Italy depended on charity.

In Naples, parliament, consisting of landowning nobles and members appointed by the crown, authorized the government to collect taxes, but after 1642 it was no longer summoned. Instead, the municipal government of the city of Naples became in effect the government for the entire realm. As Spain's need for money increased in the 17th century, the crown was forced to sell more of its land in the countryside, which was purchased by the feudal nobility. By the end of the century, some two-thirds of the kingdom's land consisted of feudal estates. The middle class was small and without influence, so that the society of Spanish Italy proved to be inert and inflexible. Occasional popular outbreaks, most sparked by food shortages, plagued Spanish officials. In the spring of 1647, Palermo, a city of some 130,000 people, erupted in the wake of a disastrous harvest that raised food prices. The municipal government subsidized food prices for a time, but when it could no longer do so it reduced the size of the bread loaves, a subterfuge that enraged the housewives of the town. The Palermo action, which temporarily brought an end to food taxes, was copied in Naples, where a young fisherman led the uprising. The viceroy granted concessions but the uprising assumed the character of an anti-Spanish movement that spread into the countryside. A Spanish expedition eventually crushed the rebellion.

In Sicily, events took another course as a result of the island's different historical experience. The desire for independence remained strong in Sicily, especially after the revolution known as the Sicilian Vespers (1282) against the Angevin French kings. Nevertheless, Sicilians remained generally loyal to Spain. The island's society was rigidly feudal, with its agricultural land held by powerful barons in the form of massive estates that grew wheat and other cereals. In Sicily, however, the barons were pillars of the established order. The parliament reflected a version of the hierarchical ordering of Old Regime society—three branches represented the barons, the church, and the crown.

Milan was attached to Spain in 1540. Political power there was exercised by a royal governor, who ruled with a senate. Overall directives, of course, came from Madrid. In Milan, as in Naples, the aristocracy aped Spanish fashions and customs, especially in an ostentatious pomp called "spagnolismo" ("Spanishism").

With the other states of Italy, Spain's relations fell into two categories. Some states, such as the Duchy of Savoy, Genoa, and the Duchy of Tuscany, were satellite clients of Madrid, while the Papal States and Venice continued to operate as independent states.

The Austrian Hegemony

Spanish preponderance in Italy came to an end at the close of the 17th century. With the death of Charles II, Philip IV's son, in 1700 Italy became once again the object of European attention. When Louis XIV's grandson secured the throne of Spain as Philip V, he laid claim to all the former Hapsburg possessions. But the peace treaties that ended the War of the Spanish Succession stripped Spain of its Italian possessions: the Treaty of Utrecht (1713) granted Milan, Naples, and Sardinia to the Austrian Hapsburgs, while Sicily was given to the dukes of Savoy, whose realm was now elevated to a kingdom. The Treaty of Rastatt (1714) confirmed these arrangements.

Austrian dominance brought Italy out of the political and social backwater of the Spanish period. Rule from Vienna not only proved more beneficial to the Italians, but by the middle of the 18th century brought to the peninsula the widespread reforms of enlightened despotism (see Part VII, Topic 1).

Austrian efforts at reform in Milan were made more difficult by the outbreak of a severe economic depression in the 1730s. During the wars of the Polish and Austrian succession, Lombardy was repeatedly overrun. After peace in 1747, the Austrians made plans for sweeping administrative and economic changes. Empress Maria Theresa enacted reforms in tax collection, labor contracts, and legal procedures. In 1765, a Supreme Economic Council was created, and the Inquisition was abolished. In all cases, central power was increased at the expense of local authority. Under Joseph II (1741–1790), who became Holy Roman emperor in 1765, Lombardy and the other Austrian possessions underwent even more far-reaching reforms (on Joseph's reign, see Part VII, Topic 1).

In Naples, too, changes were significant. The nobility and urban upper classes demanded greater local autonomy, and were governed by a number of effective administrators, including Wierich Lorenz, Count von Daun, who served as viceroy from 1713 to 1719. Lorenz not only improved the economy but countered church influence in Naples, and instituted university reforms. These improvements were set back when international wars led Vienna to raise taxes in order to meet a growing demand for money. Although in the 1720s efforts at reform were renewed, famine and economic crisis combined with crushing financial burdens imposed by Vienna. In 1720, international complications caused the powers to take Sicily from the duke of Savoy and give it to the Austrians, in compensation for which the Savoyan rulers were now made kings of Sardinia. Like Naples, the island proved to be a difficult region to rule.

In 1734, Elizabeth Farnese, wife of Philip V of Spain, succeeded in recapturing Sicily and Naples for her son, Don Carlos, who took the throne as Charles III (ruled Naples 1734–1759 and Spain 1759–1788), the first of the Neapolitan Bourbons. When Charles succeeded to the Spanish throne in 1759, he left the Kingdom of Naples to his son, Ferdinand (1751–1825) and an exceptionally able minister, Bernardo Tanucci (1698–1783), who ruled the realm until the young king came of age. Tanucci implemented reforms in the spirit of Enlightenment ideals, attempting to modernize the state administration. Ferdinand proved to have little intelligence and even less interest in matters of state. His wife, Maria Carolina (1752–1814), daughter of the Austrian Empress Maria Theresa, secured Tanucci's dismissal in 1776, thereafter acting as the actual ruler of the kingdom.

Another key change in the Italian state system took place in 1737, when the last of the Medici rulers of Florence died. An international conference awarded the duchy to Francis of Lorraine (ruled 1738–1765), Maria Theresa's husband. Austrian authority in Italy was therefore extended further. Marked improvements in administration came along with a more liberal trade policy, and some efforts were made to rescind feudal legislation. After the death of Francis in 1765, dramatic reforms were introduced by his son Leopold.

The one important counterpoint to Austrian hegemony in Italy was offered by the Savoyan rulers of the Kingdom of Sardinia. Savoy, the original homeland of the ambitious dynasty founded in 1026, lay at the strategically important location along the French Alps. In the 16th century, the Duchy of Savoy was occupied by the French, but the treaty of Cateau-Cambrésis restored its ruler, Emanuele Filiberto (ruled 1553–1580) to his realm. By skillful diplomacy he regained most of the territory that had been lost to the great powers and restored the capital at Turin.

It was Emanuele Filiberto's son Carlo Emanuele (ruled 1580–1630) who made the crucial decision to give portions of western Savoy to France in exchange for the tiny area of Saluzzo in 1601. The exchange marked the determination of the Savoyans to become an Italian power. In the years that followed, the dukes of Savoy gradually expanded their territory to include most of the northwestern region known as Piedmont, a program of expansion based on the skillful switching of sides in international disputes. The Savoyans developed a powerful military establishment to support their ambitions.

In 1713, Vittorio Amedeo II (ruled as duke 1675–1730, king of Sardinia 1713–1720, and king of Sardinia-Piedmont 1720–1730), who had played an important role in the War of the Spanish Succession along with his cousin Prince Eugene of Savoy (see Part VI, Topic 3), was rewarded by his allies with the title of king of Sicily, which he then agreed to exchange for Sardinia in 1720. Thenceforth, the Kingdom of Piedmont-Sardinia was the only independent Italian state to play a vital role in international affairs. In the 19th century, its rulers would position themselves against the Austrian hegemony as they aspired to lead the movement to unite all of Italy under their rule.

In 1500, the Mediterranean world was at the center of European civilization. While Italy represented the spectacular cultural achievements of the Renaissance, the empire of Charles V was the most powerful political and economic unit of the age. By the year 1600, the importance of the entire region had been eclipsed by the rise of the states of northern and central Europe. A century later, Italy and Spain were minor players in the international arena. Spain, no longer the center of a transcontinental empire, had been reduced in territory and was economically depressed. Italy, occupied by foreign powers, underwent a long period of exploitation, only to reemerge again in the mid-18th century under the reforming impulse of the Austrian Hapsburgs.

Questions for Further Study

1. What changing conditions contributed to the decline of Spain and Italy?
2. Why did its American colonies not prevent the economic decline of Spain?
3. Why was Italy unable to achieve political centralization in the same way that France and England did?

Suggestions for Further Reading

Braudel, Fernand. *The Mediterranean and the Mediterranean World in the Age of Philip II*, 2 vols. New York, 1972–1973.

Carpanetto, Dino, and G. Ricuperati. *Italy in the Age of Reason, 1685–1789*, trans. C. Higgitt. London and New York, 1987.

Cochrane, Eric. *Italy 1539–1630*, ed. J. Kirshner. London and New York, 1988.

Cochrane, Eric. *Florence in the Forgotten Centuries, 1527–1800*. Chicago, 1973.

Elliott, John H. *The Count-Duke of Olivares: The Statesman in an Age of Decline*. New Haven, CT, 1986.

Frey, Linda, and M. Frey. *Societies in Upheaval: Insurrections in France, Hungary, and Spain in the Early Eighteenth Century*. New York, 1987.

Lynch, John. *Spain Under the Habsburgs*, 2 vols. New York, 1964.

Parry, John H. *Trade and Dominion: The European Overseas Empires in the Eighteenth Century*. New York, 1971.

Pullan, Brian, ed. *Crisis and Chance in the Venetian Economy in the Sixteenth and Seventeenth Centuries*. London, 1968.

Sella, Domenico. *Crisis and Continuity: The Economy of Spanish Lombardy in the Seventeenth Century*. Cambridge, MA, 1979.

Vives, Jaime V. *An Economic History of Spain*. Princeton, NJ, 1969.

VI

Topic 3

Absolute Monarchy: Louis XIV and the Divine Right of Kings

In the 100 years after the mid-17th century, France stood at the center of European power. The sources of its strength included a population perhaps as large as 20 million by 1700, rich agricultural lands, and a strategic geographical location in western Europe, with its shores edging the English Channel and the North Sea, the Atlantic, and the Mediterranean. French preeminence was also due to an efficient, centralized government, a powerful army, and a growing sense of national identity—all of which were characteristics of the new absolute monarchies then emerging. Much of the credit for these and other French achievements, both domestic and international, was due to the policies of its ruler, King Louis XIV (ruled 1643–1715).

Louis advanced the centralization of the government and the building of a strong state bureaucracy, both of which had begun in the 16th century, by focusing supreme authority on his own person. The consolidation of royal power was achieved in part by further reducing the independence of an already weakened nobility and integrating its members into the structure of government. His long reign was also marked by a degree of prosperity in commerce and agriculture that was the work of his finance minister Jean-Baptiste Colbert, a prosperity unmatched by any other country with the possible exception of the United Provinces.

Louis would brook no domestic dissent and aimed to destroy any internal factors that threatened to weaken national unity, including religious differences. To a greater degree than any other king, he discovered the power of symbolism to mold opinion and create consensus among his subjects. His immense palace at Versailles was not only the most pronounced symbol of his grandeur, but an important tool in bringing the nobility into the absolutist system. The reign of Louis XIV also proved to be so rich in cultural achievement that French painting, letters, and decorative arts became the standard against which all other countries measured their success. The resulting "absolute monarchy" that he forged became the model for many other European states and left a legacy of royal power that was destroyed only in the upheavals of the revolution of 1789.

Louis XIV espoused the beguiling ideology of power that identified reverence and obedience to his person with loyalty to and pride in France. With a thirst for military glory, he lavished huge sums on his army and undertook a series of foreign military campaigns that he hoped would round out the kingdom's borders and make it a powerful player in the international arena, but that cost France dearly in resources and lives.

"I AM THE STATE": THE ABSOLUTIST GOVERNMENT

Contemporaries attributed to Louis XIV the phrase "I am the state." Whether he actually made this remark is unknown, but he certainly believed it. Louis did not, however, create centralized government or royal supremacy—these had been the achievements of King Henry IV, and then of Louis XIII's chief minister, Cardinal Richelieu and his successor, Cardinal Mazarin (on the reign of Henry IV and the administrations of Richelieu and Mazarin, see Part V, Topic 4). Rather, Louis XIV reinforced the process and imbued absolutism with a theoretical framework and a brilliant practical example.

Louis was only a child of five when his father, Louis XIII, died in 1643. His Hapsburg mother, Anne of Austria, took up the reigns of power as regent and delegated extensive authority to Cardinal Mazarin, who ran the day-to-day affairs of state. Between 1648 and 1653, noble opponents led a series of uprisings against the crown, known as the Fronde, which Mazarin crushed. On the death of Mazarin in 1661, Louis announced that he would be his own chief minister. The period from 1661 until his death in 1715 is known, therefore, as the "Age of Louis XIV," during which he ruled in his own right. His reign was the longest in European history.

Hyacinthe Rigaud's portrait of Louis XIV conveys the glamour and stately power of the Sun King.

Significant Dates

The Age of Louis XIV

1648	Peace of Westphalia
1648–1653	Revolt of the Fronde against royal government
1602–1661	Life of Giulio Mazarin
1661	Plans for Palace of Versailles begin
1667–1668	War of Devolution
1672–1679	Dutch war
1619–1683	Life of Jean-Baptiste Colbert
1685	Edict of Nantes revoked
1689–1697	The War of the League of Augsburg
1701–1714	War of the Spanish Succession
1643–1715	Louis XIV rules as king of France

Although he did not have a superior education, Louis XIV's appearance and personality were well suited to the role of king. His well built body and heavy-featured face presented an impressive image. By today's standards he was short (about 5 feet 8 inches), but for his time he was of more than average height. Nevertheless, he wore platform shoes because he felt that the king should stand above his subjects. In public he dressed in the finest robes and furs and sported a long wig, cutting an elegant, if precious, figure. Serious by nature, he cultivated an imperious and dignified manner, yet he was always pleasant and courteous to his guests.

In 1660, Louis sought to solidify the Bourbon claim to the throne of Spain by marrying Princess Maria Theresa (1638–1683), daughter of the Spanish ruler Philip IV. Although they had six children—all of whom died before their father—Louis XIV had little romantic attachment to his wife and kept a number of influential mistresses. He legitimized the six children he had with the Marquise de Montespan (1641–1707), but when he tired of her, she left the court. Her successor, Madame de Maintenon (1635–1719), actually

Map 3.1 The France of Louis XIV

married Louis on the death of Maria Theresa, but when Louis died she too left Versailles.

Divine Right Monarchy and the State

Louis XIV sought unquestioned obedience from his subjects, regardless of their status or rank. He considered the royal will supreme over all political institutions. That he should wield such absolute authority was a claim based both on a political idea that had its roots in the Middle Ages and on a more recent concept. Medieval kings had been blessed with holy oil before assuming their thrones, thus, in effect, having been anointed by God. The concept of divine right implied that the monarch was God's earthly representative, and that to oppose his will was a religious offense as well as political treason. This theory was elaborated by the court philosopher, Bishop Jacques Bossuet (1627–1704), who presented arguments about the biblical sources of royal power.

While Louis XIV used such theories to justify his demand for far-reaching powers, he said that he used that authority for the benefit of France. He wanted his subjects to think of the king as the embodiment of France, and to see themselves as having a common destiny as subjects of a prosperous, well-ordered state. In order to generate a national consciousness, Louis tried to insert the state into more and more aspects of daily life, including the economy, religious affairs, and culture. In a kingdom in which regional loyalties were still strong and where the bulk of the inhabitants lacked a standard education or even a uniform language, the symbolism of the king was a powerful force around which to rally the masses.

Despite the theory of divine right, in actual practice age-old traditions of special rights and privileges enabled the nobility, the cities, the provinces, and the Catholic Church to limit royal authority. Louis XIV devoted considerable energy to undermining these limitations on his power, as his predecessors had done before him. Yet in another sense, Louis was attempting to bring about a social revolution by destroying the corporate structure of society. His goal was for all individuals

Madame de Maintenon, mistress of Louis XIV, who later married the king after the death of Maria Theresa.

to owe loyalty to him rather than to corporations such as guilds, the church, or social class. Moreover, Louis took his duties as king seriously. Although he indulged in too many rich foods, his physical stamina and mental concentration were such that he could spend long hours studying official documents, greeting ambassadors, and attending committee meetings, after which he presided with grace and aplomb over the many social events that were part of the regular life of the court. His talents as ruler included the ability to choose intelligent and able ministers. Together with them, he reshaped the French government and its bureaucracy, reorganizing old and creating new administrative offices, and widening the powers of royal officials. Such bodies as the Council of Finance and the Council of Commerce, which exercised wide-ranging executive, judicial, and legislative powers, were staffed with technical experts drawn mainly from the ranks of the upper middle classes. As a reward for loyal service to the crown, the king sometimes gave high-ranking civil servants titles of nobility. Such "nobles of the pen" had little in common with the hereditary "nobles of the sword," whose estates and privileges were often of feudal origin and who worked incessantly to stave off royal encroachments on their rights.

Agents of the crown, from ministers to clerks, held office at the will of the monarch, and his ability to appoint and remove them made for a bureaucracy dependent on the king but free of other influences. The foundation of royal administration was the intendants, the king's chief representatives in the 30 provincial districts known as "generalities." As developed by Richelieu, the original duty of the intendants had been to collect taxes, but their responsibilities soon included conscripting soldiers, reporting on local economic conditions, taking part in lawsuits, and enforcing royal edicts. As the intendants intervened in more and more aspects of local affairs, they became the target of noble resentment, whose rights and privileges they deliberately undermined. Intendants, almost all of whom were trained in the law, were carefully chosen and began their careers in the smaller provinces, but if they succeeded, they were promoted to more important areas. These royal representatives took the place of nobles who had previously exercised the powers of local magistrates.

Two long-established administrative bodies, the estates and the parlements, continued to exercise independent authority, although their rights were also weakened. The estates were local legislative assemblies, composed of representatives of the clergy, the nobility, and the remaining population. Increasingly, however, their only purpose was to vote special sums of money to the king. In the 15th century, the monarch had gained the right to impose the *taille*, a direct land tax, on his subjects, although the nobles and the clergy were exempt. The Estates General, France's national assembly, was last called in 1614, and would not meet again until 1789. The parlements, on the other hand, were provincial supreme courts of appeal that had the power to register the king's edicts. If they found just cause to do so, they could in effect veto royal action. In such instances, however, Louis XIV resorted to a royal prerogative that had been practiced by his predecessors in the 16th century: by invoking the *lit de justice*, he could appear personally before the parlement and declare his edict registered. The parlement of Paris, with jurisdiction over a vast area of central and northern France, was the only institution that presented serious resistance to Louis XIV's policies, but even here he usually had his way. The magistrates who served in these bodies were composed mainly of nobles of the robe, and held their posts independently of the king.

Colbert and the Prosperity of France

An important aspect of Louis' domestic policy was stimulation of trade and production so as to promote prosperity. As a result, government regulation of commerce and manufacturing increased under the policy known as mercantilism, which sought to make the kingdom as self-sufficient as possible in a government-regulated economy (on mercantilism, see Part VI, Topic 8).

All economic affairs came under the direction of the Controller General Jean Colbert (1619–1683), a financial genius who had trained under Mazarin. Colbert's aims included full employment at home, a vigorous program of trade for a large French merchant marine, and lucrative overseas colonies. He negotiated favorable commercial agreements with other nations and built a powerful navy to protect the French merchant fleet. To promote colonial expansion, Colbert used government funds to found a number of overseas trading companies, including the East India Company and the West India Company. To stimulate domestic industry, in 1667 he sponsored a reformed tariff act that protected domestic industries by raising the import duties on goods made in England, the Dutch Republic, and Italy, while simultaneously reducing export duties on goods manufactured in France.

Colbert did much to improve agricultural productivity and French forestry, although at first he increased the tax burden on the peasantry by raising the *taille*. Nevertheless, industry remained his major interest. He extended government loans to private manufacturers, organized companies, used tax policies to stimulate investment, and encouraged the immigration of skilled workers and artisans from abroad. Government regulations and inspectors ensured the high quality of French textiles, while Colbert fostered entirely new industries tied to colonization, such as sugar and tobacco refining. Roads were reconstructed and maintained, and a network of canals was built, including one that connected the Atlantic to the Mediterranean. Finally, Colbert restructured the French finances and reformed the tax policy so as to make the system more equitable: he lowered the *taille*, from which nobles were exempt, and raised taxes that were shared more equitably by all French subjects.

Colbert's policies were successful and French industry and trade became preeminent in Europe. Nevertheless, the almost endless wars of Louis XIV set back prosperity and worsened living conditions at home for most of the population. Furthermore, while the economic programs sponsored by Colbert worked in the 17th century, by the mid-18th century France began to fall behind England, where new factory methods and machinery stimulated the industrial revolution.

Jean-Baptiste Colbert, the finance minister of Louis XIV, who put France on a sound financial footing.

NOBLES, JANSENISTS, AND HUGUENOTS: THE DOMESTIC OPPOSITION

In his desire to bring all elements in French society under the authority of his absolute government, Louis XIV sought to impose obedience and uniformity on the nobility and religious minorities. His methods in dealing with each were different, but the aim was the same.

Versailles: The Building of a Royal Court

Many aristocrats eventually accommodated themselves to Louis XIV's absolutism, realizing that government offices and royal favors represented a new avenue to status and influence. As the nobles were increasingly integrated into the state, they eschewed revolt and opposition—especially after the harsh repression following the Fronde—in favor of cooperation and service to the king. Louis XIV intentionally made the royal court the center of social and political life for his "domesticated" nobility. The court, located originally in Paris, but eventually moved to Versailles, acted as a magnet

The great Palace of Versailles, with its landscaping and formal gardens.

for the entire range of nobles, from the wealthiest to the poorest, from dukes to bishops and monsignors. The location of the palace at Versailles kept the nobles out of Paris, where the bureaucracy was, and away from their own estates, making it difficult for them to amass regional power.

Louis XIV wanted to use the court as an instrument for molding the nobility into docile servants. In 1668, he ordered his architects to design a royal palace at Versailles, outside Paris, where his father had a hunting lodge. This 40-year project resulted in the most sumptuous royal residence in Europe, a tremendous complex consisting of an original central section designed by Louis Le Vau (1612–1670) and two later wings on each side. The northern wing was the work of the brilliant architect Jules Hardouin-Mansart (1646–1708), whose uncle François had introduced the sloping "mansard" roof. The palace was at the center of huge formal gardens, fountains, and walkways.

The great palace of Versailles, with its impressive façade and a luxurious interior resplendent with rich marbles, the golden glimmer of gilt, and mirrored hallways, proved to be an ideal stage for the court of the Sun King. To decorate the palace, Louis XIV hired a vast army of artists and craftsmen. Charles Le Brun (1619–1690), director of the famous Gobelins tapestry factories, labored for 18 years on paintings and murals showing the glories of the king. Cabinetmakers produced the finest examples of furniture in rare woods and gilt mountings, while glassworkers made glittering chandeliers and embroiderers decorated cushions, bedspreads, and linens. Overall, the architecture of Versailles and its interiors reflect the "grand style" of the Age of Louis XIV, an elegant, Classically inspired backdrop for the daily rituals of court life.

For Louis XIV, Versailles was a system of government and social control as well as a residence. He deliberately encouraged practices in which courtiers competed with each other to carry out minor acts of service that symbolized their status, from awakening the king to lighting his way at night by bearing candles. Maintaining the kind of lifestyle required at Versailles strained the financial resources of many nobles, which in turn made them increasingly dependent on royal patronage. Perhaps as many as 10,000 people, including a vast retinue of cooks and servants, crowded into Versailles, where unheated rooms and a lack of toilet facilities created as much stench as glamour. Because anyone who served at Versailles was exempt from taxes, many of the service personnel were stand-ins for middle-class Parisians who had purchased their positions at court.

Religious Dissent and Its Suppression

Ever since the 15th century, French kings had enjoyed a high degree of control over the French Catholic Church. In 1516 the pope had granted Francis I the right to appoint French bishops, and although the clergy were not subject to taxation, every five years an assembly of the Gallican Church voted a "free gift" to the crown (on the reign of Francis I, see Part V, Topic 4). (The French Church was called the Gallican Church, from "Gaul," the ancient Roman name for France.) Henry IV, who converted to Catholicism, allowed the Jesuits and other orders back into France in 1603, although with restrictions. The Jesuits controlled education for most of the nobility and served as confessors to the 17th-century kings, including Louis XIV. Over the years, a working alliance between the crown and the French clergy evolved, and in 1682, a French ecclesiastical assembly adopted the Declaration of Gallican Liberties, which proclaimed a degree of independence from papal authority.

Yet two religious groups—the Huguenots (Calvinists) and the Catholic Jansenists—disturbed the religious uniformity that was expressed in the formula adopted by Louis, "One king, one law, one faith." During the civil-religious wars of the 16th century, many of the old nobles of the sword had converted to Protestantism largely as an act of defiance against the monarchy, and by the reign of Louis XIV there were still some 1.5 million Huguenots.

From the start of his personal rule, Louis worked systematically to undermine the Edict of Nantes (1598), which had granted the Huguenots a measure of toleration and civil liberties and had made France an anomaly among continental monarchies. He drove them out of public office and certain professions, taxed them heavily, and quartered troops in their towns. Richelieu had suspended the nonreligious aspects of the edict, but in 1685 Louis XIV revoked it entirely, leaving French Protestants little choice but conversion to Catholicism. Some went underground or did convert, but perhaps as many as 200,000 left for the Dutch Republic, Prussia, England, and the New World, depriving France of valuable skills and experience.

Although the Jansenists were smaller in number than the Huguenots, they had many prominent followers, including the philosopher Blaise Pascal (see Part VI, Topic 1) and many of the magistrates in the Paris parlement. The Jansenists formed a closely knit group whose theological beliefs about predestination were close to those of Calvinism. They asserted the central importance of God's grace in achieving salvation, questioned the authority of all human beings, including kings and popes, and openly opposed the Jesuits. In 1660, Louis XIV persuaded the papacy to ban Jansenism and then destroyed its headquarters at Port-Royal. In the years immediately before his death, Louis renewed the campaign against the Jansenists, using the Jesuits to lead the attack.

The attacks against the Huguenots and the Jansenists earned Louis a reputation as a religious bigot and persecutor, but Louis saw both issues as a matter of religious unity and in terms of the maintenance of his authority as an absolute ruler.

The Salon de la Guerre in Versailles showing a stucco relief of Louis XIV on horseback.

PERSPECTIVES ON HISTORY

Louis XIV: A Bureaucratic King

John C. Rule
Ohio State University

Born on September 5, 1638, the infant prince Louis was dubbed "the God-given" by his delighted parents, Louis XIII and Anne of Austria, and by an ecstatic French people. The future Louis XIV's pedigree was impeccable. His mother's forebears were Hapsburgs of Spain, Burgundy, and Austria; his father sprang from a long line of Bourbon-Valois-Capetian kings of France; and his paternal grandmother descended from the Medici princes of Florence. Fortunately for France and for the Bourbon dynasty, Louis lived 77 years and ruled personally for 54.

In 1648 the kingdom was plunged into a bloody civil war, ironically named after a Parisian slingshot, the Fronde. Led by a band of prominent magistrates, great nobles, and princes of the blood, the revolt spread devastation to northern and eastern France. Ultimately the Frondeurs failed to wrest power from either Cardinal Mazarin or Queen Anne herself. Much credit for the preservation of the royal prerogative, and indeed for Louis XIV's own political and personal survival, was due to the dogged determination of his mother, the astute diplomacy of Cardinal Mazarin, and the dedicated service of a faithful group of secretaries of state and their clerks. The Fronde offered the young king practical lessons in statecraft: a fear of overmighty subjects and ambitious princes, like his cousin, the Prince of Condé; and a trust of an inner group of "new men" in politics, career diplomats and enterprising provincial magistrates.

The symbol of Louis XIV as the "Sun King."

Cardinal Mazarin, Louis' faithful guide and tutor, died early in 1661. His enemies accused the cardinal of ruling through fear, favor, and fraud. But whatever his faults, Mazarin instilled in his tutee the desire and courage to rule by himself, without a principal minister. When his courtiers asked him to whom they would now address their petitions, Louis replied: "To me." Even his mother was heard to chuckle but the last laugh was on the king's foes from the Fronde era. Louis excluded from the High Council relatives, churchmen, great nobles, and feudal functionaries like the chancellor of France. This realignment of the High Council and subsequent growth of government departments is termed the Ministerial Revolution of the 1660s.

One of the most significant accomplishments of Louis XIV's reign, of which the Ministerial Revolution represented but a part, was the king's choice to rule his kingdom through a patrimonial bureaucratic government. That is a government of civilian ministers, who through councils and bureaus, formally governed France by executive decrees drafted in the king's name. Informally, these ministers governed through factions of cousins, clients, and "creatures" of the crown, experts and clerks in the various ministries.

Louis XIV promoted two families of Mazarin's "faithful" secretaries to lead the patrimonial bureaucratic government: the Colberts and the Le Telliers. Both families had risen from the financial-legal élite; both had recently been ennobled. These new ministers drew their support in large measure from the urban élites clustered in the provincial capitals, port cities, industrial towns, army strongholds, and from Paris itself. Both families, and their allies among the administrators, sought to influence local politics by extending to urban élites and factions at court, among other rewards, offices in the government, clerical preferment, careers in the armed forces, inexpensive leases of royal lands, long-term loans, contracts for public works, advantageous marriages for their children, noble titles, and even the "honor" of being presented at court. It was government by faction, patronage, and gesture.

The rise of royal patrimonial government witnessed the rapid centralization and increase in bureaucracy. The department of finances, headed by Controller General Colbert, quintupled in size, as did the ministries of the marine, headed by Colbert's son, and war, headed by the Le Telliers. The ministry of foreign affairs followed a similar pattern of expansion under the guidance of Colbert's brother, Croissy, and his nephew, Torcy, two of France's ablest diplomats.

Colbert and Michel-François Le Tellier vied with one another to satisfy the king's passion for the arts and architecture, and, above all, for collecting. Perhaps the king felt deprived as a young man of what he considered to be a regal prerogative: the privilege of surrounding himself with objects of beauty and magnificence. Cardinal Mazarin had amassed a far greater collection of such objects than had Louis XIV. Thus Colbert and the Le Telliers dispatched agents across Europe to purchase paintings, prints, drawings, sculpture, jewels, precious plate, furniture, and rare books. These treasures were housed in the Louvre palace, rebuilt as an art gallery, a library and home for scholars and artists. These privileged artists and men of letters trumpeted Louis as an Apollo of the Arts, a Mars in War, a New Alexander, Louis the Great.

And it was as Louis the Great that the king sought to satisfy his *gloire*, or desire for reputation, by building one of the greatest royal residences and sets of government in the West—the palace of Versailles. Versailles represented the king's vision of a new capital, a city of marble, set in a garden spot, built entirely at his orders; and though only 12 miles from Paris, it was a world apart, remote from overmighty magistrates, street mobs, and the stink of Seine River refuse.

In the mid-1660s Louis instructed Colbert to find money for the construction of his new capital at the site of his father's hunting lodge at Versailles. Completing the work far outstretched Colbert's life and that of the marquis of Louvois. Satellite palaces at the Trianon and Marly were added, as were the extensions of the gardens. "Such wonders rival ancient Rome," exclaimed a visiting noble. "The palace," said an official, "spreads and sustains the glory of His Majesty." Other observers were not so kind. The gossipy duke of Saint-Simon thought of Versailles as a "cold, dark, damp and malodorous pile." And the English poet Matthew Prior remarked that Louis XIV's "house is . . . the foolishest in the world; he is strutting in every panel and galloping over one's head in every ceiling, and if he turns to spit he must see himself in person or his Viceregent the Sun."[1] By the end of the century Versailles had, however, become not only a shrine to kingship and the seat of government but one of the greatest tourist attractions in all Europe.

In the excitement of reorganizing his government, conducting wars, and building Versailles, Louis did not neglect his family. His only legitimate son, Louis, was married to a Bavarian princess, who presented her father-in-law with three healthy grandsons in the decade of the 1680s, thus securing the succession of the senior Bourbon line. One of these grandsons was to become Philip V of Spain and the son of another became Louis XV of France. With the death of his wife Maria Theresa, Louis married privately an old friend, the Marquise de Maintenon. This able woman remained to the end of the king's life an indispensable confidante, a shrewd counselor in political and religious affairs, and an arbiter of family quarrels.

It was during the years of residence at Versailles, from the early 1680s to his death, that the king regulated his life as if he were a player in one of Racine's plays. The routine of Louis' day

[1] John C. Rule, ed., *Louis XIV and the Craft of Kingship* (Columbus, Ohio: Ohio State University Press, 1970), 42.

continued next page

could be told, as one courtier remarked, by looking at the court almanac and one's watch. The king rose at eight in the morning, dressed in public while receiving visits from his family and court officials in a ceremony know as the *lever*. Promptly at nine he attended Mass, then returned to his chamber to set an agenda for his council meetings, whose sessions lasted until noon. He then ate a hearty meal in public, where he sat at table while his courtiers stood around the room watching him. In the afternoon there were more council meetings, followed by hunting in the forests of Marly and a retreat to Madame de Maintenon's rooms, where he received visits from his children and grandchildren. It was on these occasions, when alone with his wife, that he sometimes wept from sheer exhaustion or frustration. In the evening, the king returned to work with his ministers separately or in pairs, again in Madame de Maintenon's chambers. He ate a late supper, attended an *appartement*, entertainments organized for the courtiers in which a dance or a play or cards were offered his guests. The king retired near midnight and was awakened only at the peril of a cross word or a withering glance.

Louis was a man of enormous pride of family and dynasty. His quest for *gloire*—or reputation—in the field of military conquest and religious conformity has been bitterly criticized by Frenchmen and foreigners alike. But his actions at the time were popular, especially among the new urban élite, the financiers, and men of commerce, the solid Catholic middle class, patriotic churchmen, the "new men" in politics, the army and navy, and the arts. After the disturbances of the Fronde and the earlier religious wars, these groups sought a prince who would bring a measure of domestic order and external security to the kingdom. Both of these goals were to a certain extent realized: militarily, with the addition of provinces in the northeast of France and domestically with the extension of royal government, public works, town planning, and encouragement of the arts.

Louis XIV died in September 1715, fearing that he had loved war too much but certain that, though "I am dying the State lives on."

WAR, DIPLOMACY, AND THE QUEST FOR FRENCH HEGEMONY

Louis XIV was a man obsessed by the quest for glory, for France, certainly, but above all for himself. He believed that his achievements would reflect on the French people, and to that end he embarked on a succession of foreign wars that some authorities believe was aimed at achieving what he called France's "natural boundaries"—the Rhine, the Pyrenees, the Alps, and the sea. In the process, Louis created the image of an aggressive, warlike France, and made himself an object of hatred throughout Europe.

Military Reform

In planning and executing his wars, as in pursuing his other policies, Louis XIV had the help of able advisers. From his vantage point as head of economic planning, Colbert had become an advocate of French sea power, having expended huge sums on building a strong navy and a merchant marine. Colbert believed that the chief obstacle to French commercial predominance was the Dutch Republic, the most prosperous trading state, in whose ships much of Europe's trade goods were carried.

In contrast to Colbert's naval strategy, the argument for a powerful land army was made by François Le Tellier, the marquis de Louvois (1641–1691). Louvois, who succeeded his father as war minister in 1666, encouraged Louis XIV in his search for military glory. He completely reorganized the army, introducing the idea of promotion on the basis of merit, providing his troops with standard uniforms, and regularizing enlistment and drafting procedures. Colonel Jean Martinet (?–1672) introduced such vigorous drill regulations that his name became a synonym for a strict disciplinarian. Gradually, Louvois increased the size of the army from about 20,000 to 400,000. He also created the first real "standing army," a permanent military force always ready for deployment, which took the place of both the mercenary private armies and the old fighting groups raised for specific purposes and commanded by feudal nobles. Such a regular army created the need for much greater government revenue. Furthermore, Louvois set up an elaborate supply system, replete with supply depots, and greatly increasing the production of munitions and gunpowder. Working alongside Louvois was Marshal Sébastien de Vauban (1633–1707), the greatest military engineer of the age. He designed and built a ring of fortresses and fortified towns to protect the frontiers, an approach to defense that the French followed for the next 300 years. He also planned brilliant siege operations against enemy installations.

The War of Devolution and the Dutch Campaign

Louis' first foreign adventure was the War of Devolution (1667–1668), waged against Spain on the basis of a claim to the Spanish Netherlands through his wife, who was, it will be remembered, the daughter of Philip IV's first marriage. The immediate point of the claim was that Louis had never received the large dowry that Philip had promised to pay. When the Spanish king died and left all his property to a son by a second marriage, Louis protested and called upon an old Flemish tradition whereby property devolved to the children of a first marriage.

Louis launched an attack against the fortified cities of Flanders and Franche-Comté (Burgundy). Victory seemed in his grasp, but England, Sweden, and the United Provinces, concerned lest Louis XIV tip the balance of power toward France, joined in an alliance and forced Louis to the peace table. By the treaty of Aix-la-Chapelle (1668), Spain ceded to France strategic sections of the Belgian Netherlands, including fortified cities. The first of his wars ended, therefore, with a minor victory for Louis, intensifying his thirst for glory.

Louis blamed the Dutch for having organized the alliance against him. The fact that the United Provinces were also France's chief trade competitor served to whet his appetite further. Louis first broke up the alliance by buying off the Swedes and King Charles II of England. Louis believed that the Dutch would make an easy target, for their country was on the edge of civil war. The republican, middle-class government there, which Louis despised, was led by Jan De Witt (1625–1672), whose party was supported by middle-class town dwellers, the wealthiest business leaders, aristocrats, and religious liberals. The head of the opposition was the prince of Orange, William III (*stadholder* of the United Provinces 1672–1702, king of England 1689–1702), whose family had held the title of *stadholder* for generations and had the backing of the Calvinist clergy and nobles.

Louis declared war against the Dutch Republic in 1672, and De Witt assumed command of the Dutch forces. The French marched rapidly into Lorraine, and from there down the Rhine into the Dutch Republic itself. The Dutch murdered De Witt and his brother, whom they blamed for their setbacks, and William III took command. Acting boldly, William organized a determined Dutch resistance and ordered the dikes opened, thereby flooding the northern areas of the Dutch Republic and halting the French advance. But when Louis refused the generous peace terms offered by William, he aroused the fears of Prussia, the Holy Roman Empire, and Spain into joining a coalition against him. France, now allied to Sweden, defeated each of its enemies, and only when Parliament forced Charles II of England to join the anti-French alliance did Louis agree to make peace. The Dutch, who promised henceforth to remain neutral, lost nothing. Instead, in the treaties of Nijmegen (1678 and 1679), Spain agreed to surrender to France the province of Franche-Comté and several fortified sections of Flanders, the latter areas being contiguous to those obtained in the War of Devolution.

The War of the League of Augsburg

The prestige of Louis XIV and the international stature of France were at a new high, although this had been achieved at a great cost. Louis had succeeded in extending French frontiers, but he nevertheless aspired to win greater glory on the battlefield. The precise extent of his ambitions remains unclear, but to his foreign contemporaries his goal appeared to be nothing less that the establishment of French hegemony over the West. Within a few years after the last Nijmegen treaty in 1679, Louis began pushing along his northern and eastern borders, where a medley of tiny estates, towns, and fiefs coexisted without clear jurisdiction. To establish "legal" claim to these areas, he set up special courts, called "chambers of reunion," which invariably found in his favor. His most important gain in this process was Strasbourg, the principal city of Alsace, which he absorbed in 1681. Alarmed by this thrust into Germany, Emperor Leopold I (ruled 1658–1705) of the Holy Roman Empire formed the League of Augsburg in 1686, eventually bringing German states such as Saxony, Bavaria, and the Palatinate together with England, Spain, Sweden, and the United Provinces. It was this League against which the ever-bolder Louis XIV fought his third war.

The conflict had its immediate origins in the fall of 1688, when Louis sent an army into the Palatinate, a territory located west of the Rhine. This War of the League of Augsburg assumed an international character as a result of the fighting between France and England in North America, the West Indies, and India, where it was known as "King William's War." In the two earlier wars, Louis had enjoyed the neutrality of England, but the Glorious Revolution that unseated the English monarch now put William III of Orange, Louis' staunch enemy, on the English throne (see Part VI,

Topic 4). William set as his goal the defeat of France. The war began in 1689 and lasted almost a decade. For the first several years, the French armies won one important victory after another in Europe, while the war at sea went in favor of the allies. A French attempt to take Ireland and put it under the rule of the deposed Catholic king of England, James II, failed. The Peace of Ryswick (1697) followed a long and ruinous struggle that drained French economic strength and manpower. By its terms, Louis was forced to give back all the territories that his "chambers of reunion" had declared to be his, with the exception of Strasbourg. In addition, the borders of the Spanish Netherlands were henceforth to be protected by Dutch soldiers, and Louis promised to reduce the high import tariffs against Dutch goods that Colbert had introduced. Perhaps most humiliating of all, Louis had to recognize William III as the legitimate king of England.

The War of the Spanish Succession

The fourth and last war of Louis XIV brought the Sun King full circle. Louis had been induced to conclude a peace agreement in 1697 because he saw a grand opportunity to achieve Bourbon dominance over Spain. Although greatly weakened, the Spanish crown still controlled a vast empire in America as well as a portion of the Netherlands and the southern half of Italy. The hapless King Charles II (ruled 1665–1700), the son born from Philip IV's second marriage, proved to be the last Hapsburg king of Spain. Because Charles had no direct heirs, Louis hoped to gain the Spanish throne for one of his own children, since the dowry of his Spanish wife had never been paid. The major stumbling block was the fact that the Emperor Leopold I, a Hapsburg, was the nearest male relative of Charles II and therefore claimed the Spanish throne for himself.

Louis played a double game. He encouraged efforts to resolve the issue of the "Spanish succession" peacefully, and actually negotiated treaties with Leopold I and William III that would have divided the Spanish possessions between Hapsburgs and Bourbons. Charles himself was not consulted about the matter. Yet throughout the period of negotiations, Louis had worked hard to ingratiate himself and the French people with the Spanish ruler, so that shortly before his death in 1700, Charles made a will leaving his undivided inheritance to Philip of Anjou (ruled Spain 1700–1746), the grandson of Louis XIV. After some hesitation, the Sun King accepted in the name of his grandson, satisfied, as Voltaire later claimed, that "The Pyrenees no longer exist," by which he meant that the two realms had been joined. But the result, if allowed to stand, would have been to make the Bourbon dynasty supreme in Europe. This the other great powers would not permit.

An engraving showing Louis XIV as *Pater familias.*

The War of the Spanish Succession (1701–1714) brought together the Grand Alliance of England, the Holy Roman Empire, the United Provinces, Hanover, and a number of German princes, all determined that Louis XIV would not get his way. For his part, Louis had joined forces with Savoy and Bavaria, although England later persuaded the duke of Savoy to change sides in return for the title of king. The brilliant John Churchill, duke of Marlborough (1650–1722), drove the French from Germany at the Battle of Blenheim in 1704, while Prince Eugene of Savoy (1663–1736) pushed them out of Italy. A bloody engagement at Malplaquet in 1709 secured the Spanish Netherlands for the allies at the cost of an unprecedented 40,000 casualties. As one defeat followed another for the French, Louis XIV rallied his subjects with a patriotic appeal and called up his last recruits, melting gold ornaments from the palace at Versailles to raise the necessary funds to fight the war.

By 1712, an exhausted France and a weakened Grand Alliance agreed to a negotiated settlement. William III had died at the beginning of the war, but his successor, Queen Anne (ruled 1702–1714), pursued the conflict relentlessly in the colonies and on the seas, where it was known as "Queen Anne's War." When the Tories came to power, however, they pushed for peace. Moreover, Leopold's son became emperor as Charles VI (ruled 1711–1740), raising the specter of a Hapsburg ruling Spain, Austria, and the Holy Roman Empire. The Treaty of Utrecht (1713) recognized Louis' grandson as King Philip V (ruled 1713–1746) of Spain, with the stipulation that the thrones of Spain and France would never be united. As compensation, the Hapsburgs of Austria obtained the Spanish Netherlands, Naples, Milan, and Sardinia. In 1720 Austria traded Sardinia to Savoy in exchange for Sicily, and the Savoyan possessions were henceforth known as the Kingdom of Piedmont-Sardinia. Britain's reward was in the form of overseas possessions, gaining Newfoundland, Nova Scotia, and Hudson's Bay from France, and Gibraltar, along with the *Asiento* (a monopoly of the slave trade going to Spanish America) from Spain. The Dutch got back their frontier fortifications, while the Hohenzollern ruler of Brandenburg was recognized as king of Prussia.

As a result of the War of the Spanish Succession, France lost colonies but none of its European territory, and had the satisfaction of seeing a Bourbon on the throne of Spain. Louis' daring bid for hegemony had failed, although it had taken the combined weight of Europe's great powers to defeat him. France was burdened with a devastated economy, marked by inflation, a huge debt, ever-higher taxes, and a serious decline in its overseas trade. Crop failures and famine made the conditions caused by war even worse.

The long reign of Louis XIV was fraught with contradictions: Versailles stands not only as the timeless symbol of royal grandeur, but also as an expression of the ambition of one man. As a result of the succession of costly wars that he fought, Louis succeeded in acquiring more territory than any French monarch since the Middle Ages, but the wars also weakened the absolutist state that he had worked so tirelessly to create. He did not succeed in stamping out Protestantism in France, and the prosperity built by Colbert dissipated. Even the immense authority that he accumulated could not be passed on intact to his successors. In the end, the historical memory of glittering mirrors and elegant palaces remains as the vivid legacy of Louis XIV. Yet perhaps only a grand monarch of his stature could have acknowledged his own limitations—on his deathbed in 1715, the Sun King lectured his heir, the Dauphin Louis, to avoid the excesses of state spending and war that he had pursued so relentlessly.

Questions for Further Study

1. How would you describe the goals and methods of the absolutist state?
2. What was the nature of the relationship between Louis XIV and the French nobility? What role did Versailles play in that relationship?
3. Were Louis XIV's foreign policies a failure or success?

Suggestions for Further Reading

Beik, William. *Absolutism and Society in Seventeenth-Century France*. New York, 1985.

Briggs, Robin. *Early Modern France, 1560–1715*. New York, 1977.

Burke, Peter. *The Fabrication of Louis XIV*. New Haven, CT, 1992.

Goubert, Pierre. *Louis XIV and Twenty Million Frenchmen*. New York, 1972.

Hattan, R. M., ed. *Louis XIV and Absolutism*. Columbus, OH, 1977.

Mettam, Roger. *Power and Faction in Louis XIV's France*. Oxford, 1988.

Rule, John, ed. *Louis XIV and the Craft of Kingship*. Columbus, OH, 1970.

VI

Topic 4

England and the Rise of Constitutional Monarchy

The general trend toward absolute monarchy in the 17th century, exemplified by the reign of Louis XIV in France, revealed several exceptions: Poland, the United Provinces, and principally England. In the latter nation, despite the centralizing efforts of the Tudor rulers, especially Elizabeth I (ruled 1558–1603), a different tradition of government developed. A special set of religious, economic, and social conditions, combined with the peculiar personalities of Elizabeth's successors, led to the taming of royal authority.

Restrictions on royal power had been evolving in England since the Middle Ages. Feudal nobles, resisting encroachments on their rights by the kings, had enacted a series of charters, especially the Magna Carta of 1215, which sought to protect basic liberties against royal tyranny. Parliament, consisting of the House of Lords and the House of Commons, had acquired increasing control over legislation and taxation. Finally, much of English common law, made up of legal customs and precedents compiled by judges over the centuries, had the effect of reinforcing individual rights. So strong had the force of common law become that some legal scholars argued that even the king was bound by it.

In the first half of the 17th century the English had directly assaulted the principle of absolute monarchy. The confrontation between Parliament and the Stuart kings who succeeded Elizabeth had resulted in the curtailment of royal authority by documents such as the Petition of Right (1628) and in outright rebellion, a process that culminated in the execution of King Charles I (ruled 1625–1647) in 1649 and the dictatorial rule of Oliver Cromwell. Yet Cromwell's Protectorate rested on a narrow base, for his strength lay largely in his control of the New Model Army.

Cromwell's death created a general sense of relief but left the country without an effective government. The restoration of the Stuart family to the throne in 1660 was therefore a widely popular move. Nevertheless, it seemed that the Stuarts were incapable of learning any lessons from the bloody fate of their predecessor, Charles I. In 1688, three years after the accession of James II, England experienced the "Glorious" Revolution, in which William III of the United Provinces and his wife Mary, daughter of James II, were put on the throne. In accepting the partnership of Parliament, the new monarchs eliminated any further danger of absolute monarchy in England.

Parliamentary rule continued to evolve during the course of the 18th century, as a new form of government began to develop in which day-to-day executive power was exercised by a cabinet of ministers that was responsible to the House of Commons. The members of the elected house came increasingly from two political parties, the Whigs and the Tories.

THE STUART RESTORATION

Cromwell's experiment with republicanism convinced a majority of the English people that monarchy—albeit a chastised monarchy with severely limited powers—was a better system of government. The tumultuous experiences of the past 50 years had made it clear not only that Parliament must share power with the monarch, but that moderate Protestantism was firmly entrenched in England. Surprisingly, neither Charles II nor James II proved capable of absorbing these lessons.

Charles II

Known as the "Merry Monarch," Charles II (ruled 1660–1685) was a man who combined refined taste and polished manners with lustful appetites. The Puritans, scandalized by his private life, accused him of indulging in "fornication, drunkenness, and adultery."

Portrait of Charles II, the "Merry Monarch."

He was an avid patron of the theater, and among his numerous mistresses was the actress Nell Gwyn (1650–1687), who bore him two sons. Cromwell's rigid Calvinist policies, including the banning of plays, sports, and popular music, had never been well received, and Charles now presided over a reinvigorated court life and a new moral laxity among the nobility. Gambling was the rage, and the king led the way in hunting, dancing, and riding. Restoration drama was particularly known for bawdy scenes and dialogue that Puritans found shocking. A monarch without principles, Charles was a shrewd tactician, always willing to compromise or retreat. With the memory of his father's beheading always vivid, he trusted no one—the king, wrote one of his advisers, "lived with his ministers as he did with his mistresses; he used them but he was not in love with them."

Before his return to England from exile in France, Charles had issued the Declaration of Breda, in which he promised to respect Parliament and observe the principles of Magna Carta and the Petition of Right.

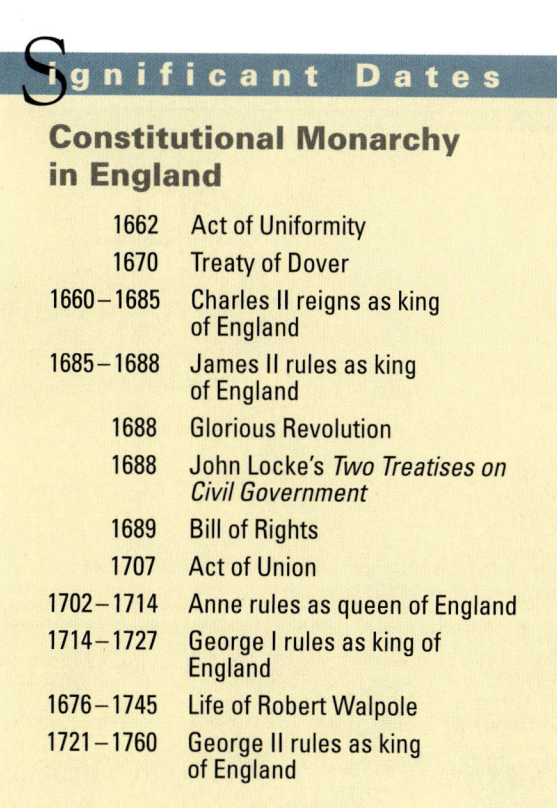

Significant Dates

Constitutional Monarchy in England

1662	Act of Uniformity
1670	Treaty of Dover
1660–1685	Charles II reigns as king of England
1685–1688	James II rules as king of England
1688	Glorious Revolution
1688	John Locke's *Two Treatises on Civil Government*
1689	Bill of Rights
1707	Act of Union
1702–1714	Anne rules as queen of England
1714–1727	George I rules as king of England
1676–1745	Life of Robert Walpole
1721–1760	George II rules as king of England

Map 4.1 England and the Low Countries, c. 1688

He also swore not to levy illegal taxes or to interfere in religious matters. These were all concessions extracted from the king by the so-called Convention Parliament of 1660, made up principally of landowners and nobles. At first, there was little evidence to suggest that a strong monarchy would be restored with the Stuarts, and the notion of "divine right" did not resurface. No effort was made to reestablish either the special law courts used against the enemies of the crown or the king's old feudal privileges.

The return of the Stuarts brought with it the restoration of Anglicanism as the state church in England and Ireland. In Scotland, where it had never been established, Charles would encounter serious opposition in his efforts to impose Anglicanism. Those Protestants who refused to accept the Church of England were called "dissenters," groups that were especially numerous among artisans and merchants. Legal restrictions were imposed on dissenters, including the Corporation Act (1661), which excluded them from town offices. The next year, Charles issued the Declaration of Indulgence, designed to grant tolerance to Catholics and dissenters. In response, the strongly Anglican Parliament passed the Act of Uniformity (1662), which required clergymen to accept the Anglican Book of Common Prayer and deprived well over 1000 Calvinist ministers of their parishes.

Charles II remained uncomfortable with the Church of England, for at heart he and his brother James were Catholics—both had been influenced by their mother and the strongly Catholic atmosphere of the French court, where they had spent their exile. It was this problem that ultimately caused the final undo-

The great fire of London in 1666.

ing of the Stuarts. In 1670, Charles concluded the secret Treaty of Dover with Louis XIV, whereby he secured a financial subsidy in return for supporting the French war against the United Provinces and swearing to convert to Catholicism. But in view of the strong anti-Catholic sentiment in the realm, Charles was careful to keep his sentiments to himself. Indeed, in 1673 he was forced to withdraw the Declaration of Indulgence in place of the Test Act, which drove Catholics from office. Anti-Catholic sentiment reached a new pitch in 1678, when rumors of a "Popish Plot," deliberately manufactured by a rogue named Titus Oates (1649–1705), caused people to believe that Catholics intended to assassinate the king, burn London, and massacre Protestants. In Oxford, a crowd surrounded the royal coach in the mistaken belief that it contained the king's Catholic mistress. Nell Gwyn, who was in fact inside, pleaded with the mob, "Pray good people, be civil; I am the *Protestant* whore." Only when near death in 1685, did Charles formally convert to Catholicism.

James II and the Crisis of the Restoration

Because Charles II had no legitimate children, the crown was due to pass to his brother James, the duke of York (ruled as king, 1685–1688). Less tactful than Charles, James had declared his conversion in 1672. In the aftermath of the Popish Plot, however, Parliament tried several times to enact an Exclusion Bill that would have kept James or any other Catholic from the royal succession. The issue of whether Parliament had the right to change the succession to the crown was of great importance. The bill failed to pass, but from the debates that it engendered there eventually emerged two distinct factions, or "parties." The Whig party, which supported the bill, gained the backing of a variety of people, from liberal Anglicans and landowners who wanted to strengthen Parliament against the king to dissenters and the business class. The Tory group, which opposed the Exclusion Bill, favored a strong hereditary monarchy and sought to avoid another destructive civil war. (The words *Whig* and *Tory* were originally labels used by one side to slander the other: *Whig* was the term for a Scottish horse thief, while *Tory* was the term for an Irish cattle rustler.) Because the Whigs were divided among themselves, however, Charles had been able to fend off their efforts. Nor were the Whigs the only opponents of the king, for a widespread radical underground had opposed royal authority since the start of the Restoration.

When James succeeded to the throne in 1685, he took the place of a king who had actually succeeded in strengthening the monarchy and in ruling for the last four years without Parliament. But James lacked his brother's political skills, and within several years dramatic changes took place in England's political order. His Catholic beliefs, together with his increasing emphasis on royal authority, aroused widespread fear and opposition. Trouble erupted from the moment James became king, for uprisings in Scotland and England greeted his accession, although he put them down easily.

Like Charles, James promised to uphold the constitutional system and the Anglican Church, but he soon gave evidence to the contrary. He created a professional standing army run by Catholic officers, which he stationed near London, a move that shocked even his Tory supporters. In open violation of the Test Act of 1673, he used a "Declaration of Indulgence" to appoint Catholics and others to posts in local and royal government, as well as in Oxford and Cambridge Universities, arguing in self-defense that he was not subject to previous parliamentary acts. In 1688, he issued a second "Declaration of Indulgence," and when seven Anglican bishops—including the archbishop of Canterbury—refused to read it from their pulpits, he had them arrested, although they were later acquitted.

James II pushed royal authority to the limits, but the event that brought his reign to the crisis point was the birth of a son. Until then, his heirs had been two daughters by a first marriage—Mary (1662–1694), who had married her cousin William III of the United Provinces (see Part VI, Topic 3), and Anne (1665–1714), who married a Danish prince. These daughters and their husbands were all Protestants, so that the prospect of one of them inheriting the throne had not caused alarm among the English. But in June 1688, a son was born to James and his second wife, the Catholic Mary Beatrice (1658–1718). Because this son took precedence over his half-sisters in the royal succession, this meant that England would one day have a Catholic king, a prospect that the nobles and gentry found intolerable.

THE GLORIOUS REVOLUTION

The events in England that followed the birth of James II's son in 1688 have been dubbed the "Glorious" Revolution—an upheaval that forced James from the throne and inaugurated the era of constitutional monarchy with the reign of William and Mary.

William and Mary

English leaders, both Whig and Tory alike, quickly joined forces to oust James. They made proposals to William III of Orange, *stadholder* of the Dutch Republic, to assume the crown with his English wife Mary, James II's daughter. William was interested in the idea principally because it would enable him to align

A contemporary engraving showing William and Mary being presented with the crown of England.

England with the United Provinces in the war against Louis XIV (see Part VI, Topic 3). Risking his fleet and the independence of his own country, William landed an invasion force of 14,000 men at Torbay on the southwest coast of England in early November. James quickly discovered that most of his soldiers had deserted him. In December, after having been once captured, he escaped and fled to France, where he joined his young son, who was known as the "Old Pretender," and recognized by Louis XIV as the legitimate English sovereign. Although the fighting in England was minor, in Ireland a popular Catholic uprising in support of James erupted. William crushed the Irish revolt only in July 1690 at the Battle of the Boyne, in which his 35,000 troops defeated some 21,000 Catholic soldiers. In the process, William executed priests and political leaders and devastated much of the land.

The Triumph of Parliament

This unspectacular but tradition-breaking revolution was a decisive turning point in the development of representative government. Early in 1689, Parliament drafted the Declaration of Rights, the fundamental document upon which the "Revolutionary Settlement" of 1689 rested. This Bill of Rights (as it became known once enacted into law) stipulated that all sovereigns were to be Anglican. More important, it provided that the sovereign could not suspend laws, or interfere with free speech, elections, or parliamentary discussion. Furthermore, Parliament was to meet regularly, and the monarch could neither maintain an army nor levy taxes without its consent, whereas the people had the right to petition the ruler. The bill also safeguarded individual rights, making it illegal for an English citizen to be arrested without a warrant or denied just bail. In addition, Parliament approved the Toleration Act, which barred non-Anglicans from public office and imposed severe restrictions on Catholics, but which granted all Protestants full freedom of worship. The triumph of Parliament as set forth in these reforms fundamentally altered the nature of government in England.

William and Mary were asked to accept the Declaration of Rights before being offered the crown. They agreed to rule jointly, for William would not tolerate serving merely as Queen Mary's consort, and Mary refused to rule by herself. Only 15 when they had married, Mary made herself subservient to her husband and was constantly humiliated by William's mistress, who lived in the royal palace. Nevertheless, because William was frequently out of the country conducting military campaigns, Mary ruled alone for much of the time, a task she carried out with intelligence and vigor. Outwardly, William treated her with bad-tempered indifference, but when she died of smallpox in 1694, he grieved deeply.

The forces that controlled Parliament and had brought about these settlements were by no means democratic. The House of Lords, whose members were appointed by the monarch, was composed of landed nobility and could veto legislation passed by the Commons. The system of election for the House of Commons enabled the nobles and landed gentry to control the countryside, but the wealthy members of the middle class who exercised influence in the cities were hardly represented in the House. For a century and a half after the Glorious Revolution, England was ruled by an essentially aristocratic Parliament that chiefly represented the interests of the landlords.

After the Glorious Revolution, the temporary alliance that had bound Tories and Whigs together in common opposition to James II fell apart. Real social-economic differences separated the Whig and the Tory parties: the Tories, who had supported the revolution reluctantly, were landed gentry whose interests centered on rural life and who wanted England to keep aloof from continental affairs; the Whigs, by contrast, were active in commerce and overseas trade and had seen the revolution as a chance to secure the supremacy of Parliament over the king.

The intervention of England in the wars of Louis XIV (see Part VI, Topic 3) was one manifestation of this outlook. But warfare cost money, and taxation was now under the control of Parliament. On the other hand, with state finances on a stable footing as a result of parliamentary supervision, private bankers were more willing to lend money to the government. Unable to raise taxes, William therefore borrowed more than one million pounds for the purpose of fighting the War of the League of Augsburg. In this way, the concept of a permanent national debt, as opposed to private royal debts, came into being. In 1694, with the approval of Parliament, he took the extraordinary step of granting a royal charter to the Bank of England, a private institution which managed the national debt by holding government deposits, sending funds abroad, and advancing credits. England also reformed its monetary system and issued new coinage in consultation with Sir Isaac Newton, master of the Mint. In addition, regular procedures were established for issuing insurance and trading stocks, thus creating an environment in which commerce and manufacturing could prosper.

The Legitimacy of Revolution

Together with the mid-century Civil War, the Glorious Revolution of 1688–1689 broke the pattern of absolutist government that had entrenched itself elsewhere in Europe. The English revolutions of the 17th century had, however, taken place in a broader theoretical context. In the previous century, the Protestant leaders Martin Luther and John Calvin had both preached that magistrates should resist their superiors whenever divine law was violated. From this proposition evolved the view that since God would not impose tyranny on human beings, monarchs who oppressed their subjects stood in violation of divine law. In 1579, the French writer Philippe Duplessis-Mornay (1549–1623) asserted, by extension, that such monarchs could be resisted. Seventy years later, in the midst of the English Civil War, the poet John Milton (1608–1674) published a treatise entitled *The Tenure of Kings and Magistrates* (1649), in which he insisted that society rested upon a contract, or covenant, between a ruler and his subjects. According to the terms of the contract, the subjects agreed to obey their monarch, in return for which the monarch pledged to uphold the law. When a king ceased to represent justice, his right to rule collapsed.

The principal theorist of the Glorious Revolution was John Locke (1632–1704), whose ideas had circulated before 1688, especially among the Whigs. In *Two Treatises on Civil Government* (1690), he sought to justify the events of 1688 (on Locke as an Enlightenment figure, see Part VI, Topic 11). Locke believed that in

John Locke, the principal theorist of the Glorious Revolution.

DOCUMENTS ON HISTORY

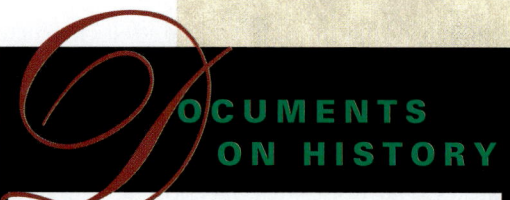

Resistance and Revolution

As the power and authority of centralized states expanded in the 15th and 16th centuries, some political philosophers and active opponents of the absolute monarchs developed theoretical arguments sustaining the right of resistance. Religious reformers like Luther and Calvin, no matter how conservative their political and social views, contributed to the theory of resistance by allowing that magistrates could oppose superior authority in order to uphold divine law. During the wars of religion in France, Huguenots claimed that royal tyrants were not ruling with God's will and that since the king's role was to defend justice, magistrates could legitimately oppose those who failed to do so. This was the theme of an influential work by Philippe Duplessis-Mornay, *A Defense of Liberty Against Tyrants* (1579). The argument was broadened significantly some years later by the Catholic philosopher Juan de Mariana, whose essay on *The King and the Education of the King* (1598) extended the right of resistance to ordinary citizens in cases where kings deliberately violated their own laws and the well-being of their subjects. During the 17th century, other writers expanded on the theory of resistance, especially under the influence of Enlightenment thought.

THE LEVELLERS, ENGLISH RADICALS

During the English Civil War, the Protestant sect known as the Levellers (see Part V, Topic 3) demanded constitutional reform, the abolition of the monarchy, and complete equality. In the following document, issued in 1649 after the civil war, they once again made their radical demands.

We the free People of England . . . agree to ascertain our Government, to abolish all arbitrary Power, and to set bounds and limits both to our Supreme, and all Subordinate Authority. . . .

I. That the Supreme Authority of England and the Territories therewith incorporate, shall be and reside henceforward in a Representative of the People consisting of four hundred persons, but no more; in the choice of whom (according to naturall right) all men of the age of one and twenty years and upwards (not being servants, or receiving alms, or having served the late King in Arms or voluntary Contributions) shall have their voices; and be capable of being elected to that Supreme Trust. . . .

VIII. . . . That the next and all future Representatives, shall continue in full power for the space of one whole year: and that the people shall of course, chuse a Parliament once every year. . . .

X. That we do not impower or entrust our said representatives to continue in force, or to make any Lawes, Oaths, or Covenants, whereby to compell by penalties or otherwise any person to any thing in or about matters of faith, Religion or Gods worship or to restrain any person from the profession of his faith, or exercise of Religion according to his Conscience, nothing having caused more distractions, and heart burnings in all ages, than persecution and molestation for matters of Conscience in and about Religion.

From *The Leveller Tracts, 1647–1653,* William Haller and Godfrey Davies, eds., Columbia University Press, Copyright © 1954.

THE ENGLISH BILL OF RIGHTS

In 1689, after the Glorious Revolution, Parliament passed the Bill of Rights, which guaranteed basic civil rights and consolidated the gains of the revolution.

Whereas the said late King James II having abdicated the government, and the throne being thereby vacant, his Highness the prince of Orange (whom it hath pleased Almighty God to make the glorious instrument of delivering this kingdom from popery and arbitrary power) did (by the device of the lords spiritual and temporal, and diverse principal persons of the Commons) cause letters to be written to the lords spiritual and temporal, being Protestants, and other letters to the several counties, cities, universities, boroughs, and Cinque Ports [five port towns on the English Channel, having special privileges], for the choosing of such persons to represent them, as were of right to be sent to parliament, to meet and sit at Westminster upon the two and twentieth day of January, in this year 1689, in order to such an establishment as that their religion, laws, and liberties might not again be in danger of being subverted; upon which letters elections have been accordingly made.

And thereupon the said lords spiritual and temporal and Commons, pursuant to their respective letters and elections, being now assembled in a full and free representation of this nation, taking into their most serious consideration the best means for attaining the ends aforesaid, do in the first place (as their ancestors in like case have usually done), for the vindication and assertion of their ancient rights and liberties, declare:

1. That the pretended power of suspending laws, or the execution of laws, by regal authority, without consent of parliament is illegal.
2. That the pretended power of dispensing with the laws, or the execution of law by regal authority, as it hath been assumed and exercised of late, is illegal.
3. That the commission for erecting the late court of commissioners for ecclesiastical causes, and all other commissions and courts of like nature, are illegal and pernicious.
4. That levying money for or to the use of the crown by pretense of prerogative, without grant of parliament, for longer time or in other manner than the same is or shall be granted, is illegal.
5. That it is the right of the subjects to petition the king, and all commitments and prosecutions for such petitioning are illegal.
6. That the raising or keeping a standing army within the kingdom in time of peace, unless it be with consent of parliament, is against law.
7. That the subjects which are Protestants may have arms for their defense suitable to their conditions, and as allowed by law.
8. That election of members of parliament ought to be free.
9. That the freedom of speech, and debates or proceedings in parliament, ought not to be impeached or questioned in any court or place out of parliament.
10. That excessive bail ought not to be required, nor excessive fines imposed, nor cruel and unusual punishments inflicted.
11. That jurors ought to be duly impaneled and returned, and jurors which pass upon men in trials for high treason ought to be freeholders.
12. That all grants and promises of fines and forfeitures of particular persons before conviction are illegal and void.
13. And that for redress of all grievances, and for the amending, strengthening, and preserving of the laws, parliament ought to be held frequently.

LOCKE'S SECOND TREATISE ON GOVERNMENT

John Locke, one of the most influential thinkers of the Enlightenment, wrote the Second Treatise *between 1681 and 1683, before the Glorious Revolution. The essay proposed government as the guarantor of life, liberty, and property, the three essential points of Enlightenment political ideals,*

continued next page

and influenced colonial leaders during the American Revolution.

When any one, or more, shall take upon them to make laws, whom the people have not appointed so to do, they make laws without authority, which the people are not therefore bound to obey; by which means they come again to be out of subjection, and may constitute to themselves a new legislative, as they think best, being in full liberty to resist the force of those, who without authority would impose any thing upon them. Every one is at the disposure of his own will, when those who had, by the delegation of the society, the declaring of the public will, are excluded from it, and others usurp the place, who have no such authority or delegation. . . .

In these and the like cases, *when the government is dissolved,* the people are at liberty to provide for themselves, by erecting a new legislative, differing from the other, by the change of persons, or form, or both, as they shall find it most for their safety and good. For the *society* can never, by the fault of another, lose the native and original right it has to preserve itself; which can only be done by a settled legislative, and a fair and impartial execution of the laws made by it. But the state of mankind is not so miserable that they are not capable of using this remedy, till it be too late to look for any. To tell *people* they *may provide for themselves*, by erecting a new legislative, when by oppression, artifice, or being delivered over to a foreign power, their old one is gone, is only to tell them, they may expect relief when it is too late, and the evil is past cure. This is in effect no more, than to bid them first be slaves, and then to take care of their liberty; and when their chains are on, tell them, they may act like freemen. This, if barely so, is rather mockery than relief; and men can never be secure from tyranny, if there be no means to escape it, till they are perfectly under it: And therefore it is, that they have not only a right to get out of it, but to prevent it. . . .

Thirdly, I answer, that *this doctrine* of a power in the people of providing for their safety anew, by a new legislative, when their legislators have acted contrary to their trust, by invading their property, is the *best fence against rebellion*, and the probablest means to hinder it. For *rebellion* being an opposition, not to persons, but authority, which is founded only in the constitutions and laws of the government; those, whoever they be, who by force break through, and by force justify their violation of them, are truly and properly *rebels*. For when men, by entering into society and civil government, have excluded force, and introduced laws for the preservation of property, peace, and unity amongst themselves; those who set up force again in opposition to the laws, do *rebellare*, that is, bring back again the state of war, and are properly rebels: Which they who are in power (by the pretence they have to authority, the temptation of force they have in their hands, and the flattery of those about them) being likeliest to do; the properest way to prevent the evil, is to shew them the danger and injustice of it, who are under the greatest temptation to run into it. . . .

To conclude, the *power that every individual gave the society*, when he entered into it, can never revert to the individuals gain, as long as the society lasts, but will always remain in the community; because without this there can be no community, no commonwealth, which is contrary to the original agreement; so also when the society hath placed the legislative in any assembly of men, to continue in them and their successors, with direction and authority for providing such successors, the *legislative can never revert to the people* whilst that government lasts: Because, having provided a legislative with power to continue for ever, they have given up their political power to the legislative, and cannot resume it. But if they have set limits to the duration of their legislative, and made this supreme power in any person, or assembly, only temporary; or else, when by the miscarriages of those in authority, it is forfeited; upon the forfeiture, or at the determination of the time set, *it reverts to the society*, and the people have a right to act as supreme, and continue the legislative in themselves; or erect a new form, or under the old form place it in new hands, as they think good.

ROUSSEAU ON THE SOCIAL CONTRACT

In 1771 Rousseau wrote An Inquiry into the Nature of the Social Contract *in which he added to theories of the social contract the notion of the General Will, a universal moral law through which humans recognized their interdependence and advocated the idea that the people have the right to dissolve the contract.*

If then we set aside what is not of the essence of the social contract, we shall find that it is reducible to the following terms: "Each of us puts in common his person and his whole power under the supreme direction of the general will, and in return we receive every member as an indivisible part of the whole." [Book I, Chapter 6.]

But the body politic or sovereign, deriving its existence only from the contract, can never bind itself, even to others, in anything that derogates from the original act, such as alienation of some portion of itself, or submission to another sovereign. To violate the act by which it exists would be to annihilate itself, and what is nothing produces nothing. [Book I, Chapter 7.]

It follows from what precedes, that the general will is always right and always tends to the public advantage; but it does not follow that the resolutions of the people have always the same rectitude. Men always desire their own good, but do not always discern it; the people are never corrupted, though often deceived, and it is only then that they seem to will what is evil. [Book II, Chapter 3.]

The public force, then, requires a suitable agent to concentrate it and put it in action according to the directions of the general will, to serve as a means of communication between the state and the sovereign, to effect in some manner in the public person what the union of soul and body effects in a man. This is, in the State, the function of government, improperly confounded with the sovereign of which it is only the minister.

What, then, is the government? An intermediate body established between the subjects and the sovereign for their mutual correspondence, charged with the execution of the laws and with the maintenance of liberty both civil and political. [Book III, Chapter 1.]

So soon as the people are lawfully assembled as a sovereign body, the whole jurisdiction of the government ceases, the executive power is suspended, and the person of the meanest citizen is as sacred and inviolable as that of the first magistrate, because where the represented are, there is no longer any representative. [Book III, Chapter 14.]

These assemblies, which have as their object the maintenance of the social treaty, ought always to be opened with two propositions, which no one should be able to suppress, and which should pass separately by vote. The first: "Whether it pleases the sovereign to maintain the present form of government." The second: "Whether it pleases the people to leave the administration to those at present entrusted with it."

I presuppose here what I believe I have proved, viz., that there is in the State no fundamental law which cannot be revoked, not even this social compact; for if all the citizens assembled in order to break the compact by a solemn agreement, no one can doubt that it could be quite legitimately broken. [Book III, Chapter 18.]

continued next page

THE DECLARATION OF INDEPENDENCE

When Thomas Jefferson drafted the Declaration of Independence in 1776, he had in mind the writings of Locke and other European philosophes.

When in the course of human events, it becomes necessary for one people to dissolve the political bands which have connected them with another, and to assume among the powers of the earth, the separate and equal station to which the laws of nature and of nature's God entitle them, a decent respect to the opinions of mankind requires that they should declare the causes which impel them to the separation.—We hold these truths to be self-evident, that all men are created equal, that they are endowed by their Creator with certain unalienable rights, that among these are life, liberty, and the pursuit of happiness—That to secure these rights, governments are instituted among men, deriving their just powers from the consent of the governed,—That whenever any form of government becomes destructive of

order to escape the brutalities of their original "state of nature," people established government and set up rulers, whose principal role was to defend the natural rights of individuals in society. In establishing a "social contract" with their ruler, subjects gave up part of their natural rights, but they retained the fundamental rights to life, liberty, and the pursuit of property. If the sovereign interfered with these rights, or failed to protect them, then the people were free to remove him. Other revolutionaries, in America and in France, would later make use of Locke's "right to revolution."

THE CABINET SYSTEM AND THE HOUSE OF COMMONS

In the years following the Glorious Revolution, England not only developed the fundamental institutions of constitutional monarchy, but evolved the principles and practice of ministerial government. As a result, by the mid-18th century Parliament had extended its reach beyond its legislative functions and into the executive branch of government.

With the backing of the Whig party, William III spent much of his energy and considerable resources on war and diplomacy, for the Glorious Revolution had taken place in the midst of the wars of Louis XIV. Because of his interest in foreign affairs, William tended to leave the administration of domestic matters to his ministers. It was by day-to-day practice rather than by design that the king soon discovered that the government ran more smoothly, and policy matters were settled more easily, if all his ministers were from the same party that controlled the House of Commons. Thus, he began to appoint Whig ministers when the Whigs held a majority in the Commons, and Tories when they were in the preponderance. In this way, the ability of a cabinet—as the body of ministers came to be called—to remain in office depended increasingly on its ability to command the confidence of a majority in Parliament. To this day, this principle of "ministerial responsibility" prevails, and government ministers must appear before the House of Commons to answer the questions of its members.

Because the Glorious Revolution was, in an immediate sense, a struggle to determine the royal succession, Parliament continued to assert its authority in this vital area. When Queen Mary died, William ruled by himself, but thereafter the succession was in doubt since William and Mary were childless. In 1701, Parliament passed the Act of Settlement, which excluded the son of James II and all other Catholics. Instead, the crown was to pass to Mary's sister, Anne. Should Anne have no children, the crown would then go at her death to Sophia (1630–1714), the granddaughter of James I and the wife of the elector of the German state of Hanover.

Since the Act of Settlement looked toward the eventual succession of "foreign" rulers, it also stipulated these ends, it is the right of the people to alter or to abolish it, and to institute new government, laying its foundation on such principles and organizing its powers in such form, as to them shall seem most likely to effect their safety and happiness. Prudence, indeed, will dictate that governments long established should not be changed for light and transient causes; and accordingly all experience hath shewn, that mankind are more disposed to suffer, while evils are sufferable, than to right themselves by abolishing the forms to which they are accustomed. But when a long train of abuses and usurpations, pursuing invariably the same object evinces a design to reduce them under absolute despotism, it is their right, it is their duty, to throw off such government, and to provide new guards for their future security.—Such has been the patient sufferance of these colonies; and such is now the necessity which constrains them to alter their former systems of government. The history of the present king of Great Britain is a history of repeated injuries and usurpations, all having in direct object the establishment of an absolute tyranny over these states. To prove this, let facts be submitted to a candid world.

that England would not be required to wage war in the interests of the sovereign's foreign possessions without the consent of Parliament. Furthermore, it placed a number of additional restrictions on royal power, the most important of which asserted that judges would hold office "during good behavior," not at the "king's pleasure." Only the houses of Parliament could remove judges who proved unsuitable. Parliament's grip on the reins of government was extending to the judiciary as well as to the executive branch. The removal of arbitrary royal control over the judiciary in England contrasted sharply with the encroachment of royal authority over similar institutions in France.

Queen Anne, whose full figure is suggested in this contemporary medallion.

Good Queen Anne

On William's death in 1702, Anne (ruled 1702–1714) became queen of England. A rather dull woman, she was fat and so crippled with gout that she had to be carried in a chair during her coronation. But she drew a deliberate contrast between William, who was Dutch by birth and sentiment, and her own "English heart," and won the sympathy of the British people, who called her "Good Queen Anne." In a less worshipful mood, a popular ballad of the day alluded to "Brandy-faced Nan," in view of the fact that she was a heavy drinker.

Unlike her predecessor, Anne's reign was marked by tensions between royal authority and Parliament. She disagreed often with Parliament, and was one of the last English rulers to veto its acts and to preside regularly over cabinet meetings. Near the end of her life, she also broke with what was fast becoming established tradition when she appointed a Tory cabinet despite a Whig majority in the House of Commons. Yet Anne was careful to avoid any real crisis, for she realized that her half-brother—the son of James II—still had many supporters.

In order to make sure that the thrones of both England and Scotland would pass to the Protestant descendants of Sophia of Hanover, in 1707 the parliaments of the two realms enacted the Act of Union, which created a single state known as the United

Kingdom of Great Britain. The English Parliament was transformed into the Parliament of the United Kingdom, which now included Scottish lords and commoners. The union was achieved in part by force and pressure, but many Scots saw the advantages of dissolving the trade barriers between the two territories. The Scots kept their own court system but lost their own parliament and their capital. In Ireland, on the other hand, where William had returned to a harsh policy of restrictions against the Catholics, peace still proved elusive.

As a sovereign Anne was surrounded constantly with male politicians, but in private she preferred the company and the advice of Sarah Churchill (1660–1744), the wife of the brilliant military commander John Churchill. Sarah Churchill had become Anne's trusted friend before the Glorious Revolution, and had helped the princess escape during the upheaval in 1688. When Anne ascended the throne, she appointed her friend lady of the queen's bedchamber, a position in which Sarah gained significant political influence. A Whig in politics, she dispensed patronage, controlled the cabinet, and helped herself to a large pension. When John Churchill won the Battle of Blenheim in 1704, Anne made him duke of Marlborough. Sarah's position was partially undermined by the Tories, who planted one of their own supporters among the ladies-in-waiting to counter Sarah's influence. Eventually, Sarah's increasingly haughty attitude alienated Anne and she fell from royal favor.

George I of Great Britain, who began the Hanoverian line of rulers when he succeeded to the throne in 1714.

The British Constitution in the Age of Walpole

Queen Anne, who died in 1714, was the last Stuart monarch. Although she had 17 pregnancies, only five babies were born alive and none of her children lived past the age of eleven. She was succeeded by the first Hanoverian king, George I (ruled 1714–1727). George, a German who never learned English and had little interest in British affairs, was not terribly popular with his new subjects. He was not interested in the details of government and at first he even tried to conduct cabinet meetings in broken Latin, but quickly gave that up and stopped attending them. Instead, the king left politics and the administration of the kingdom in the hands of his ministers.

It was during this period that the office of prime minister became increasingly important. By 1722, Sir Robert Walpole (1676–1745) had emerged as Great Britain's most prominent political leader. Walpole, the third son of a well-to-do member of the gentry, rose to power in Whig politics. He served for more than half his life in Parliament. A skillful administrator, Walpole was made secretary of war in 1708, during the reign of Queen Anne. In 1712, his enemies impeached him on charges of corruption and expelled him from Parliament, but he was restored to favor by George I, whose confidence he had won. Walpole was especially intent on guarding against efforts by supporters of the Stuart pretender, known as Jacobites (from the Latin for James), to unseat the Hanoverians. Indeed, in 1715, "James III," the Old Pretender, supported by some Tories, actually landed in Scotland but was easily defeated and forced to flee once again.

In 1721 Walpole became chancellor of the exchequer, and eventually emerged as the king's "prime," or chief, minister. In that position, he nominated the other ministers who served in his cabinet, and wielded enormous patronage in the form of jobs, pensions, contracts, and honors, which he used to remain in power for more than 20 years. Although George II (ruled 1727–1760) did not share his father's enthusiasm for Walpole, Queen Caroline (1683–1737) helped to keep him in office. Walpole kept the support of Parliament through bribery, eloquence, and political skill.

Despite Walpole's extraordinary power, his immediate successors did not imbue the position of prime minister with the authority that he had wielded. The monarch remained the head of state and the ruler of the kingdom, in whose name all laws were enacted and treaties negotiated. In addition, the British monarch still commanded enormous prestige and exercised considerable informal authority. Nevertheless, by the mid-18th century, the sovereign needed Parliament to make laws, levy taxes, control the judiciary, or maintain an army. He had delegated most of his executive functions to the prime minister and his cabinet, where the real affairs of state were conducted.

Among the great powers of Europe, Great Britain could boast a unique form of government by the mid-18th century. The country was governed by an "unwritten constitution" consisting of traditions, laws, and charters that stretched back to the Middle Ages. As it evolved between 1688 and the death of Walpole in 1745, that system was one in which the aristocracy and a landowning élite divided political power between them in cooperation with the monarchy. In this arrangement, the role of Parliament was crucial, for it was the body that made laws, imposed taxes, and appropriated the revenues needed for the government to function. After the 1707 Act of Union, the House of Commons in the combined British Parliament contained 558 seats, most of which were filled by local interests and patronage. Walpole himself had "inherited" his father's seat in the Commons. Most members—perhaps as many as nine out of ten—came from the ranks of the gentry. The peers in the House of Lords formed a distinct élite from the gentry in the Commons, but the differences between the two groups were not always very great. Indeed, while the oldest sons of nobles sat in the Lords, their younger brothers or cousins often held seats in the lower house.

The fact that the English revolutions took place while Louis XIV sat on the throne of France reflects the range of political systems that unfolded in 17th-century Europe: at one extreme stood the Grand Monarque, *who perfected the instruments of absolutist power at Versailles, while at the other extreme Cromwell experimented with a republican dictatorship built on the ruins of a decapitated monarchy. The governments of most European states were closer to the French than to the English model.*

The English had not been entirely spared from experience with absolute monarchy: the Tudor sovereigns came close to realizing such status in the 16th century, but the Civil War and the Puritan Revolution had stopped the growth of royal power. The restored Stuart kings tried to see how far they could go in reviving royal authority, but when they pushed too far the forces that controlled Parliament staged the Glorious Revolution. Parliament won the struggle for power, and over the next half-century it extended its authority indirectly as a result of the evolution of the cabinet system of government. Limited, constitutional monarchy became the counterpoint to absolute monarchy based on the divine right of kings.

In retrospect, of course, the British system proved more stable and long-lived than the French form of government. England had its revolution in the 17th century, while France experienced a more serious turmoil 100 years later. The events that took place in England between 1640 and 1688 constituted a political rather than a social revolution, but it served to confirm an important social fact, namely, that the landed gentry and merchant class had emerged as the country's uncontested ruling élite. Moreover, unlike the aristocracy on the Continent, in England nobles were not exempt from taxation, and therefore had a greater stake in the success of Parliament. If Great Britain avoided having its own Sun King, it owed its good fortune to a combination of factors, especially the existence of this élite and the strong tradition of individual rights embedded in the common law. Yet, regardless of the differences between the French and British experiences, one essential pattern remained common to both nations: the increasing centralization of power in the modern state.

Questions for Further Study

1. In what ways were the issues that led to the Glorious Revolution different from those behind the earlier civil wars?
2. What general principles of popular sovereignty emerged from the revolution?
3. What are the origins of the cabinet system of government?

Suggestions for Further Reading

Black, Jeremy, ed. *Britain in the Age of Walpole*. New York, 1984.

Clark, G. N. *The Later Stuarts, 1660–1714*, 2nd ed. Oxford, 1958.

Earle, Peter. *The Making of the English Middle Class*. London, 1989.

Harris, Tim. *Politics Under the Later Stuarts*. London and New York, 1993.

Hill, Christopher. *The World Turned Upside Down: Radical Ideas During the English Revolution*. New York, 1972.

Hutton, Richard. *Charles the Second*. Oxford, 1990.

Jones, J. R. *The Revolution of 1688 in England*. London, 1972.

Plumb, John H. *The Growth of Political Stability in England, 1675–1725*. London, 1967.

Topic 5

Central Europe and the Shifting Balance of Power

By the 17th century, most Western European countries had a strong central government. The nobility had been tamed or incorporated into the state, the urban merchant classes were growing in prominence, and most agricultural populations had been largely freed from the restrictions of feudalism. In Central and Eastern Europe, by contrast, the growth of absolute monarchy left the nobility with considerable power and status, the middle classes were weak, and the peasants continued to live as serfs.

The chief political organization of central Europe was the Holy Roman Empire, nominally ruled by the Hapsburgs. In practice, however, the Empire consisted of a welter of separate states, each with its own ruler and political system. Many of these states used war or marriage to increase their power. Austria under the Hapsburgs and Brandenburg-Prussia under the Hohenzollerns were the most successful, although the rulers of Hanover eventually succeeded to the British throne (see Part VI, Topic 4).

In the early 17th century, Hapsburg attempts to revive the Empire led to their defeat in the Thirty Years' War. In mid-century, the Emperor Leopold I tried a different approach by seeking to unify Austria, Bohemia, and Hungary under centralized rule. Since much of Hungary was controlled by the Ottoman Empire, Austrian forces had to confront the Turks. After a Turkish army unsuccessfully besieged Vienna in 1683, Austrian troops under Eugene of Savoy defeated the Ottoman forces in 1697 and Austria obtained complete control of Hungary two years later.

The Hohenzollerns, who had become the rulers of Brandenburg in 1415, emerged as the monarchs of a major new power during the 17th century. Early in the century, the Hohenzollerns added to their holdings by inheriting the territory of Prussia to the northeast, and some scattered lands on the Rhine. Poor and undefended by natural frontiers, Brandenburg-Prussia suffered badly in the Thirty Years' War. In the midst of the destruction of many villages and a fall in population, in 1653 the young Elector Friedrich Wilhelm was able to increase his power at the expense of the regional assemblies.

Friedrich Wilhelm, later known as the Great Elector, welded together his scattered principalities into a single state. He created a powerful standing army second only to the military force of Austria. In order to pay for his army, he forcibly introduced permanent taxation over the protests of the Estates. The Prussian landowning nobles, known as Junkers, tried unsuccessfully to resist, but in return he allowed them to retain control over the serfs on their estates. By the time of the Great Elector's death in 1688, his tough programs at home and shrewd foreign policy had produced a powerful unified state with formidable military forces. In 1701, the electors were elevated to the status of kings.

THE FICTION OF THE HOLY ROMAN EMPIRE

By contrast with the growing prosperity of Western Europe in the 16th and 17th centuries, economic conditions in Central and Eastern Europe were poor. Most of the wealth was concentrated in the hands of the landowning nobility, the middle classes remained small and politically weak, and most peasants were forced to work as unpaid serfs. The establishment of absolute monarchies in Austria, Prussia, and Russia did little to relieve these conditions (for a discussion of Russia and Poland, see Part VI, Topic 6).

One of the most important factors making it possible for rulers to assert their domination was the climate of uncertainty created by decades of wars. As the states of Central and Eastern Europe fought against one another and against outside invaders, even the most independent nobles realized the necessity for a strong central authority. By seizing their opportunity, rulers such as Prussia's Friedrich Wilhelm (ruled 1640–1688) were able to take control of three vital sources of power: the imposition of taxes, control of a standing army, and conduct of foreign affairs. In return, they allowed their nobles to continue to maintain their estates and legal rights over their peasants.

The largest political confederation in central Europe was the Holy Roman Empire. Founded by Charlemagne, it was effectively established in 962 as an organization of some 300 German states, and included the Low Countries, eastern France, northern and central Italy, and western Bohemia. According to procedures set up in 1356 (see Part III, Topic 10), its emperor, usually the dominant German sovereign, was elected by the seven "elector" princes and, until the end of the 15th century, crowned by the pope. The Hapsburg dynasty, which had ruled Austria since 1278, became rulers of the Holy Roman Empire in 1436, and they continued to serve as emperors, at least in theory, until Napoleon finally dismantled the Empire in 1806.

The Holy Roman Empire after the Thirty Years' War

The tendency for the individual member-states of the Holy Roman Empire to go their separate ways, already notable in the 15th century, increased during the Reformation, which set the Catholic Hapsburg emperor against the Protestant princes, most of whom held sway in the northern states. One of the reasons the emperor Ferdinand II (ruled 1619–1637) became embroiled in the disastrous Thirty Years' War was to enforce the Counter-Reformation, and impose Catholicism on Protestants in Bohemia and Hungary. Educated at a Jesuit college, Ferdinand was a fervent supporter of the propagation of Catholic dogma by authoritarian means (on the Thirty Years' War, see Part V, Topic 4).

Far from strengthening the Empire, the negotiations which finally brought the war to an end effectively destroyed any chance of the emperor's reestablishing central authority. The Peace of Westphalia (1648) established the separation of politics and religion, and ended the emperor's attempt to turn Germany into an absolute monarchy. The treaty made it instead into a collection of absolute monarchies, and confirmed the sovereignty of each member-state. In addition, it further reduced Hapsburg power over the Empire by allowing outsiders, France and Sweden, to participate in the deliberations of the Imperial Diet, the Holy Roman Empire's assembly to which the various member-states sent representatives.

By the mid-17th century the ancient organization existed in name only. The Diet continued to meet, but for all practical purposes the Empire was a political fiction. The "rulers" of its various member-states included some 2000 imperial knights, 80 princes (50 ecclesiastical and 30 secular), over 100 counts, around 70 prelates, and 66 city governments. Their territories ranged in size from three or four acres to the entire kingdom of Bohemia. All of the individual rulers were theoretically subordinate to the emperor, but in practice remained politically independent. The Empire had no central administration or taxation system, no common law or customs union, not even a common calendar.

THE HAPSBURGS TURN EAST: THE TURKISH DEFEAT

Traditional Hapsburg territory in Central Europe consisted of three distinct regions: the hereditary lands of Austria, the Kingdom of Bohemia, and the Kingdom of

Swearing the oaths at the Peace of Westphalia, 1648.

Hungary. The Thirty Years' War put an end to Hapsburg expansion westward by legitimizing the independence of the other German states. In consequence, the emperor Leopold I (ruled 1658–1705) decided to create a larger and more powerful centralized state, the equal of those in Western Europe, by unifying these three regions, and making Bohemia and Hungary subordinate to Austria.

Control over Austria was assured by the emperor's traditional ascendancy over the local feudal nobility. The Kingdom of Bohemia was still suffering the effects of the Thirty Years' War. In 1620, Ferdinand II had crushed a revolt led by Bohemia's Protestant Czech nobility, killed his opponents, and confiscated their estates. He replaced them with a new upper class. For the most part, these newcomers were aristocratic mercenaries from all over Europe. Having no allegiance to Bohemia, they owed their position, and thus their loyalty, to the emperor.

With the help of this new ruling class, the Hapsburgs established direct control over Bohemia. The Bohemian peasants were required to work a minimum of three days a week without pay for their new masters, and about a quarter of them worked every day except Sundays and religious holidays. These serfs were also responsible for paying taxes, thereby lifting the burden from the aristocracy.

Hungary and the Ottoman Empire

The real difficulty in Leopold's scheme lay farther east, in Hungary. The Hapsburgs were the elected rulers of the kingdom. In practice, however, since the early 16th century most of Hungary was in Turkish hands, as part of the Ottoman Empire.

The Ottoman Turks came originally from the steppes of central Asia, and had settled in Anatolia, in the heart of what is now modern Turkey. By the end of the 16th century, Ottoman territory extended from central Europe to western Persia, and included holdings in North Africa. Under their greatest ruler, Suleiman the Magnificent (ruled as emperor 1520–1566), Turkish forces dominated the

Mediterranean and controlled the Balkans, part of southern Russia, and most of Hungary. Many central and eastern European peasants, accustomed to exploitation at the hands of their Christian masters, found Turkish rule less oppressive than that of the Hapsburgs, especially since the Turks did not require them to become Muslims. In Hungary, moreover, the Protestant nobility tended to side with the Turks against the hated Catholic Austrians.

The climax of Suleiman's spread westward came in 1529, when his army laid siege to Vienna. When he failed to take the city, he reinforced his hold on Hungary, forcing the Hapsburgs to pay an annual tribute for the small strip of Hungarian territory remaining under their control.

In the late 16th century, Ottoman power began to erode. Suleiman's son and successor, Selim the Sot (ruled 1566–1574), was the first of a series of weak sultans under whom the Turks lost ground. In 1571 combined Spanish, Venetian, and papal forces crushed the Ottoman fleet at Lepanto, off the coast of Greece. Their defeat ended Turkish dominance in the eastern Mediterranean, and initiated the long decline of the Ottoman Empire.

A century later, however, in the reign of Mehmed IV (ruled 1648–1687), Turkish power temporarily revived—the restoration of strong central government was due in large measure to energetic and effective grand viziers. The Turks once again moved westward against Austria, encouraged by Louis XIV of France, who wanted to use the Turks against his old enemies the Hapsburgs. After two unsuccessful campaigns in 1663 and 1664, an Ottoman army of more than 100,000 poured up the Danube Valley and besieged Vienna in July 1683. The Austrian forces were too weak to resist, and the emperor Leopold fled up the river to Passau, to try to put together a coalition of troops to oppose the Turks.

For the next two months, as the rest of Europe waited with horrified fascination to see if the easternmost bastion of Catholicism would fall, the Turkish encampment outside Vienna provided a vision of luxury never before seen in the West. The Turks had brought with them supplies for a long wait: oxen, camels, and mules; a flock of 10,000 sheep; corn, coffee, sugar, honey. The quarters of the commander, Kara Mustapha, included bathrooms with perfumed waters, opulent beds, priceless carpets, and glittering chandeliers. Elsewhere were gardens with fountains and a menagerie with rare birds and animals.

After a tense summer of negotiating, Leopold succeeded in putting together an international relief force. In September, combined troops including Poles, Bavarians, and Saxons, with the blessing of Pope Innocent XI (ruled 1676–1689), came to the rescue. French troops were conspicuous by their absence from the coalition of Christians against Muslims. Louis XIV placed national political interests above religion, and in any case he was also involved in a bitter quarrel with the pope.

Among the heroes of the relief of Vienna was the Polish king, John Sobieski (ruled 1674–1696), who personally led the charge of his country's cavalry. The combined armies came crashing down on the Turks from the heights of the Kahlenberg, overlooking the city, and drove them into a hurried retreat toward Hungary. The Turkish commander stayed only long enough to prevent his two favorite possessions from falling alive into Christian hands: he decapitated a particularly beautiful wife and his ostrich.

The mosque of Suleiman the Magnificent in Istanbul. Suleiman led the Turkish assault on Vienna in 1529.

Eugene of Savoy

Over the following decade, Leopold's forces pursued the Turks down the Danube and drove them out of Hungary. Among the emperor's potent weapons was the most brilliant general of the age, Eugene, prince of Savoy (1663–1736). French by birth, Eugene had clashed with the domineering Louis XIV, and renounced his country. In 1706, he was to have the satisfaction of driving French troops from Italy (see Part VI, Topic 3). Renowned for his qualities of leadership and strategic insights, Eugene was also a notable patron of the arts, and for his Viennese home he commissioned the superb palace and park known as the Belvedere.

In a series of campaigns, the Austrians conquered all of Hungary and added Transylvania (now part of Romania). The final decisive battle took place at Zenta in 1697, where forces under Eugene wiped out a Turkish army triple their size. By the Peace of Carlowitz, of January 1699, the Turks recognized Hapsburg rule over Hungary.

Once in possession, Leopold was quick to impose Catholicism and clamp on Hungary the fetters of Austrian rule. The country became an Austrian colony. Many Hungarian Protestants were executed for treason. The remaining landowning nobles kept their holdings along with the serfs who worked on them, in return for their recognition of the ultimate authority of Vienna.

Significant Dates

Central Europe in the 17th Century

1618	Brandenburg and Prussia joined
1620	Ferdinand II of Austria crushes Protestant Czech uprising
1640–1688	Reign of Friedrich Wilhelm, the Great Elector
1648	Peace of Westphalia
1660	Friedrich founds Prussian Army
1683	Ottoman siege of Vienna
1697	Eugene of Savoy defeats Ottoman forces at Zenta
1701	Friedrich I crowned king of Prussia
1703	Rákóczy leads Hungarian uprising

The Uprising of Rákóczy

Yet Hapsburg attempts to integrate Hungary into a single state, along with Austria and Bohemia, were immediately challenged by a series of uprisings. Hungarian resistance to Austria proved stronger than that of the Bohemians. The Hungarian nobles, though weakened, had not been completely eliminated, as had the Protestant nobility of Bohemia. In addition, both aristocracy and peasants were beginning to develop a shared sense of national identity that was to reach its fulfillment in the 19th century.

In 1703, the young Francis Rákóczy (ruled 1704–1711), a member of a noble Hungarian and Transylvanian family, led a patriotic uprising against the Hapsburg empire. Because the Austrians were at the time involved in the War of the Spanish Succession (see Part VI, Topic 9), Rákóczy's forces were unexpectedly successful, and in 1704 the nobles elected him prince.

Hungarian independence lasted only a few years. The Austrians rallied to inflict a series of crushing defeats, and in 1711 Rákóczy fled into exile. Nevertheless, the Hapsburg emperor was forced to accept the traditional status of the Hungarian aristocracy, in return for their acceptance of Austrian rule. Leopold's aim of creating a single powerful state was thus only partly fulfilled. Austria, Bohemia, and Hungary shared a centralized administration, but the framework under which it operated was a loose one. The consequences of Leopold's actions would emerge a century and a half later.

THE RISE OF THE HOHENZOLLERNS

One of the chief landowning families of northeastern Germany in the 16th century was the Hohenzollerns. The decline of the traditional aristocracy had permitted wealthy landowners like the Hohenzollerns to rise to political power. The senior branch of the family became electors of Brandenburg, a small territory around Berlin, and the junior line acquired the rule of Prussia, a province on the Baltic Sea that technically formed part of the Kingdom of Poland. The two possessions joined together in 1618, when in the absence of a direct heir Prussia passed to Brandenburg by inheritance. Another small collection of scattered territories had been acquired by similar means in 1614.

The three provinces had few advantages. They shared no common interests or loyalties and lacked natural frontiers. They were poor, thinly populated, and unproductive, and Brandenburg's bleak and arid lands had won it the nickname of "the sandbox of Europe." Furthermore, centralized administration of the three territories was made difficult by their individual governments. The overall power of the elector was limited

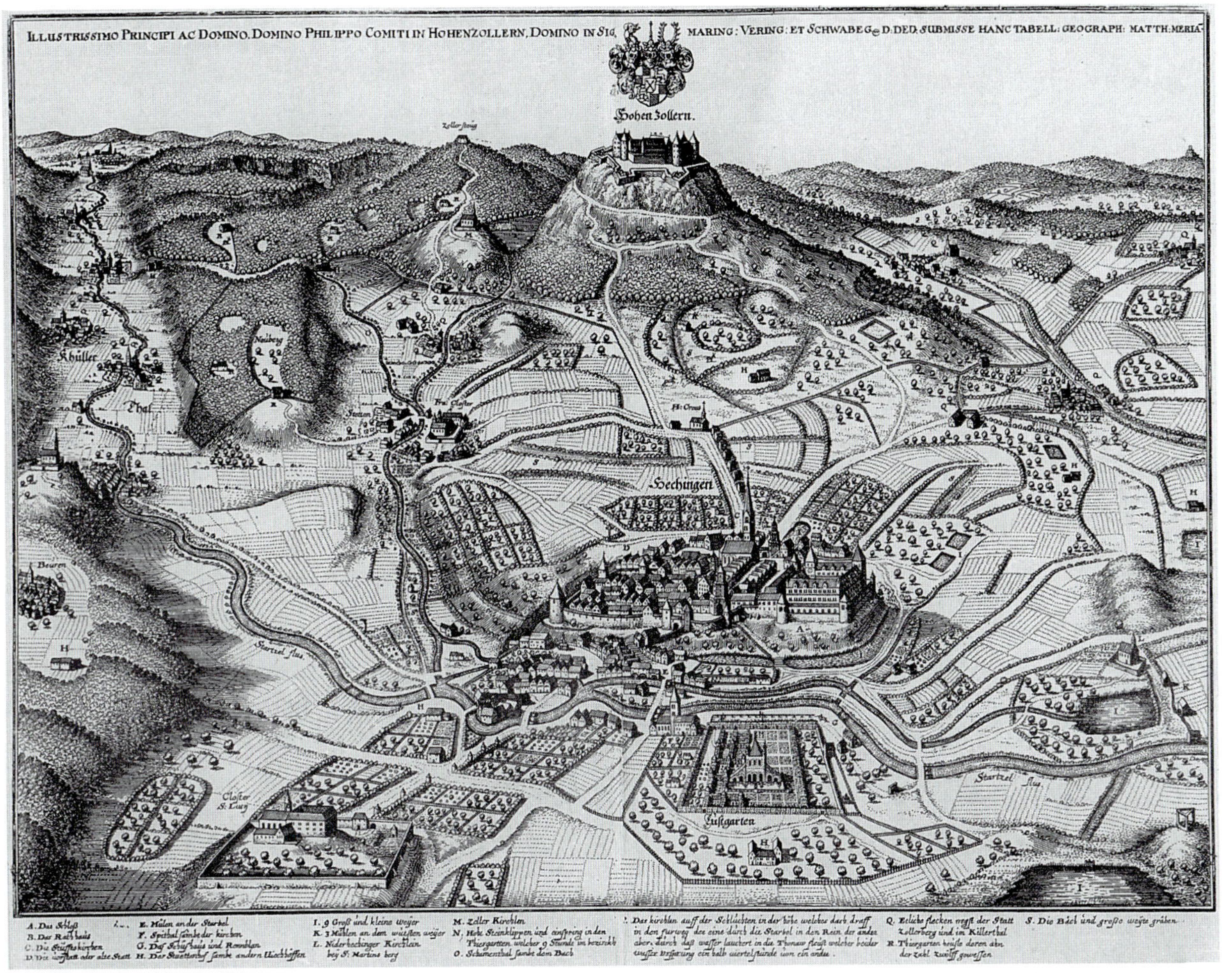

The castle of the Hohenzollerns.

by the existence of provincial assemblies known as Estates. Controlled by the great noble landowners called Junkers, these Estates passed laws, authorized, collected, and spent taxes, and raised troops. The Junker-dominated provincial administrations ran their provinces on a day-to-day basis, reserving the elector as the court of final appeal.

The lack of defendable borders meant that Brandenburg-Prussia lay vulnerable to the ravages of the Thirty Years' War. Brandenburg, in particular, became the battleground for the rival armies of Sweden and the Hapsburgs. By 1648, the population had actually declined and, in the course of the war, Berlin lost half its inhabitants and many villages were abandoned.

Paradoxically, by the end of the 17th century the state of Prussia (the name by which the joint territories became known) was on its way to becoming one of the leading political and military powers in Europe. In part this was made possible because the state of almost total collapse underlined the need for wholesale reconstruction. In large measure, however, Prussia's rise to greatness was the result of the policies of its remarkable ruler, Friedrich Wilhelm, whose achievements won him the title of the Great Elector.

THE GREAT ELECTOR: JUNKERS AND ARMY IN PRUSSIA

The elector of Brandenburg for most of the Thirty Years' War was Friedrich Wilhelm's father, Georg Wilhelm (ruled 1619–1640). Weak and vacillating, Georg Wilhelm was described by one of his descendants as "utterly unfit to rule." Famous for his piety and for his gluttony, he spent most of the war switching from one side to the other. By 1638, with his revenues fallen by seven-eighths, he retired to East Prussia, and died there.

At the age of 14, in the middle of the war, Friedrich Wilhelm had been packed off to the

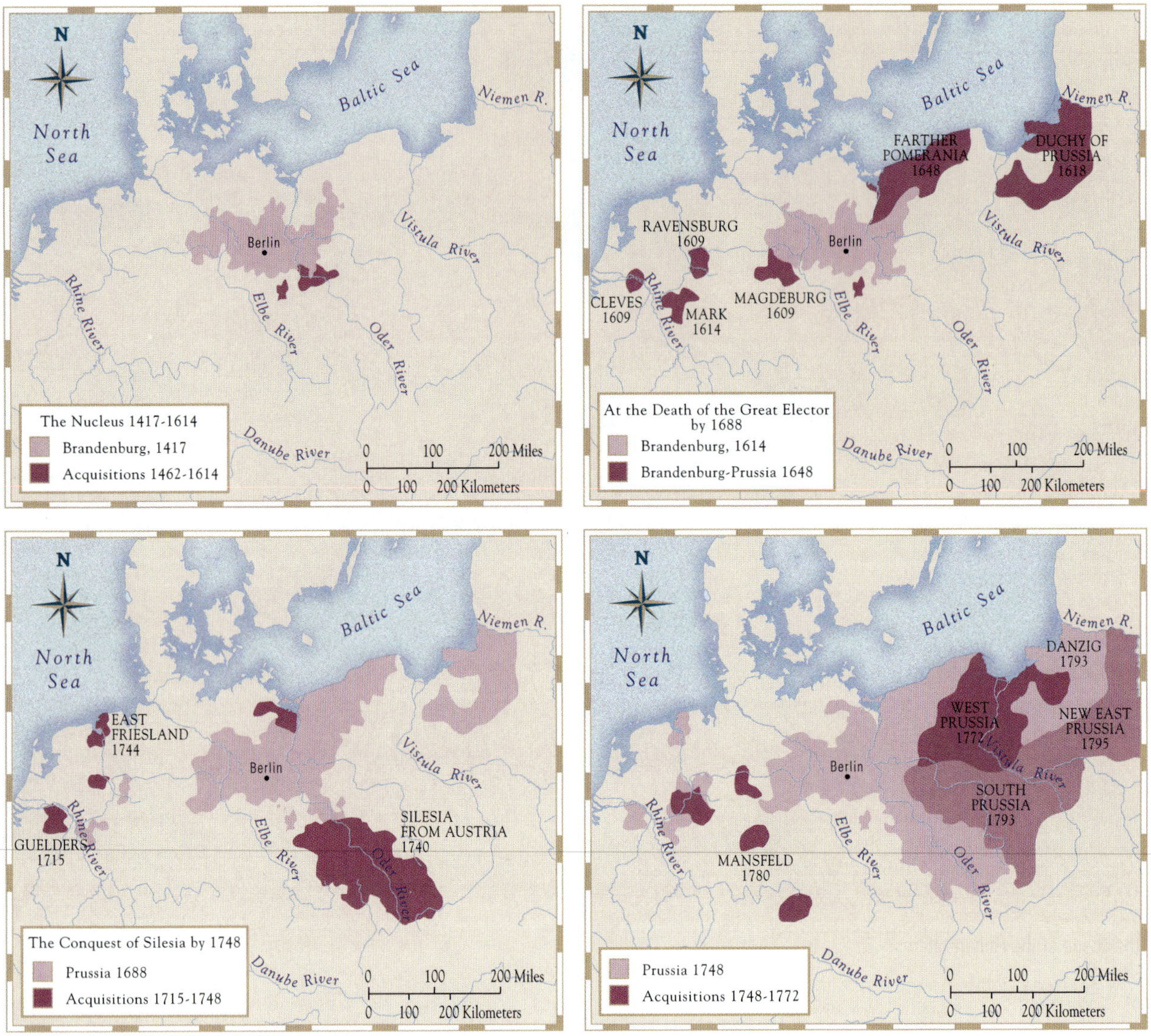

Map 5.1 The Growth of Prussia, 1417–1807

Netherlands. He studied at the University of Leiden, becoming acquainted with new developments in science and technology, while in his spare time he caught up with the latest techniques of warfare and politics. He also became a dedicated Calvinist. By the time he succeeded his father in 1640, at the age of 20, his subjects were exhausted and terrorized by the horrors of a war in which they were only marginally involved.

Tall and powerfully built, with piercing blue eyes, Friedrich Wilhelm used cunning diplomacy allied with ruthless force to achieve his objectives. His first aim was to extricate himself from the fighting and clear his territory of foreign soldiers. The Peace of Westphalia in 1648, which finally brought the war to an inconclusive end, awarded Brandenburg-Prussia some new territory. More importantly, Friedrich Wilhelm successfully defended the Calvinists in the negotiations, winning acknowledgement as the leader of German Protestant interests.

Conflict with the Estates

The bitter events of the previous generation made it clear that a state without an effective standing army was at the mercy of foreign invaders. Thus the creation of a military force became the new elector's priority. Yet building a single army to defend all of the provinces was an expensive proposition, requiring a considerable increase in tax revenues. Since each of the provincial Estates insisted on maintaining control over the collection and spending of taxes, and refused to grant funds except for its own province, Friedrich Wilhelm spent the next few years in a series of political struggles for financial control.

The first breakthrough came in Brandenburg, where in 1653 the elector and the Estates reached an apparent compromise. The agreement guaranteed the Junkers' social and economic privileges, and allowed them to turn more peasants into serfs. Furthermore Friedrich Wilhelm promised to consult the Estates over future policy and appointments. In return the Junkers voted the elector a large sum of money, to be paid over the next six years.

The Prussian Army

In 1660 Friedrich Wilhelm founded his permanent standing army. Once in command of his force, he used it to collect more taxes, without the consent of the Estates. In East Prussia the Estates struggled to preserve their rights, even enlisting the support of Poland. Friedrich Wilhelm used the army to occupy the province, and eliminated those Junkers who continued to defy him by imprisoning and hanging them. By the 1670s, Prussia was an absolute monarchy, in which the elector controlled the finances and the army.

The elector's troops not only served as a fighting force; they helped to shape and even direct the growth of the state, thereby making Prussia unique among European nations. Soldiers functioned as tax collectors and policemen, developing thereby into a rapidly expanding state bureaucracy. Other divisions in the army also worked on public building projects, digging canals and settling underpopulated areas. As prosperity grew, Friedrich Wilhelm became increasingly successful in persuading his former Junker opponents to head his government departments and above all to become army officers.

By 1688, the Prussian army stood at 30,000, and could be expanded in wartime to 40,000. Well trained and well equipped, it was the second strongest military power in the Germanies, after that of Austria. So professional a force was the envy of Europe, and the European powers vied with one another to hire it. Friedrich Wilhelm adroitly used his army to earn ever-increasing foreign subsidies by timely changes of side, as war continued to rack both Eastern and Western Europe. When the Swedes invaded Poland in 1656 (see Part VI, Topic 6), he fought first for Sweden and then for Poland. In the Dutch War of 1672–1679, he supported first the Netherlands, then France, and then the Netherlands again. This was no reflection of the weak indecisiveness of his father. Between 1660 and 1688 he collected handsome payments from a wide range of European powers, without having to do much fighting.

By the time of Friedrich Wilhelm's death in 1688, Prussia was a formidable centralized state, with absolute rule imposed from above. The elector had won the grudging support of the nobles by allowing them to exploit the peasants; social reform was not part of Friedrich Wilhelm's program. The Prussian economy prospered, thanks to improved agriculture and a revival of commerce—both made possible by a generation of peace. The state became a haven for immigrants who could be of use to the state and religious refugees: Lutherans, Calvinists, Jews, and, after the revocation of the Edict of Nantes in 1685 (see Part VI, Topic 3), French Huguenots. The only religious minority to whom Friedrich Wilhelm would not grant entry was the Jesuits, whom he thought too intolerant. Many of the newcomers brought skills that helped in the development of agriculture and industry. A large number of the Huguenots joined the army.

Friedrich Wilhelm I, king of Prussia.

The First Kings of Prussia

It says much for Friedrich Wilhelm's creation that Prussia survived his less dynamic immediate successor, and the eccentricity of the state's next ruler, to increase its international prestige. The Great Elector's son, Friedrich III (ruled 1688–1713 as Elector of Brandenburg and 1701–1713 as king of Prussia), was distinguished more for his ostentatious cultural programs than for his attention to the affairs of state. His principal achievement was to persuade the Hapsburg Holy Roman emperor to grant him the title of king of Prussia. At the end of 1700, on the eve of the War of

Contemporary print showing the recruiting drive to build up the Prussian Army.

the Spanish Succession (see Part VI, Topic 9), Friedrich promised the Hapsburg ruler diplomatic support and a contingent of soldiers in any eventual conflict. In return, Leopold I allowed the elector to crown himself king; after his coronation in January 1701, Friedrich became the only German king, ruling as Friedrich I.

Friedrich's son and successor, Friedrich Wilhelm I (ruled 1713–1740), was known to his enemies, as well as to his few friends, as the Sergeant Major. Tightfisted and prudish, he was notorious for bouts of uncontrollable temper, in which he would attack generals and bureaucrats alike with his stick. Crude and violent in his tastes, he was tormented by boils, gout and colic, and religious anxieties. His obsessive concern for punctuality, obedience, and hard work, all of which he ruthlessly imposed on his hapless subjects, had much to do with creating the image of Prussian character.

His top priority was the army, which had doubled to 80,000 by the time of his death to become the third or fourth strongest in Europe. He formed a special battalion of grenadiers, all of gigantic height, whom his agents recruited throughout Europe. The force became known as the "Battalion of Giants." He is said to have told the French ambassador: "I am utterly indifferent to the most beautiful girl or woman on earth; tall soldiers are my weakness."

In spite of his personal oddities, Prussia prospered under his rule. Rigorous state planning and centralized industrial development doubled revenues by 1740. For all Friedrich Wilhelm's obsessive militarism, his army did little actual fighting. His two reasons for avoiding military action were his belief that "God forbids unjust wars," and his reluctance to risk the lives of his precious troops. On the other hand social rigidity increased, and the peasants and serfs continued to bear the brunt of the entire state system.

The Great Elector had inherited three small provinces, disunited, impoverished, and torn by war. By the time Friedrich Wilhelm I died, Prussia was on the verge of becoming one of the great powers of Europe.

Beginning in the mid-17th century, the states of Austria and Prussia began to dominate central Europe. The Hapsburg rulers of the combined territory of Austria, Bohemia, and Hungary were from one of the oldest of Europe's aristocratic families, and titular monarchs of the Holy Roman

Empire. The Hohenzollerns rose from governing insignificant provinces to presiding over an awesome military machine. Both dynasties established absolutist rule, with the monarch in complete control of financial, military, and foreign policy. The power of the local legislative assemblies was broken.

The relapse into authoritarian government was accompanied by a reinforcement of the social order. The Hungarian nobles extracted some concessions from a reluctant emperor, and the Prussian Junkers obtained a share of the growing prosperity by accepting state and military positions. In both countries, however, the middle classes never had a chance to expand: in Friedrich Wilhelm I's Prussia, private enterprise was rigorously discouraged. As for the peasants and serfs, they continued to work for the nobles, pay taxes to the state, and serve in the armies.

Of the two powers, the unity of the larger and more diverse Hapsburg empire was less secure, and the centralized administration less effective. The Great Elector started with the advantage of building his state virtually from scratch, while Leopold and his successors had to weld together peoples with established national and religious differences. In future struggles for power in central Europe, Prussia was victorious—it went on in the 19th century to unify the German states and create the German empire.

Questions for Further Study

1. How did the rulers of Brandenburg-Prussia create one of the most powerful European states?
2. What role did the Ottoman Turks play in European affairs in the century from the Battle of Lepanto to the siege of Vienna?
3. How did the Hapsburgs prevent the growth of Czech and Hungarian independence? What were the later consequences of their repression?
4. What were the chief differences between the lives of Central European peasant farmers and those in Western Europe?

Suggestions for Further Reading

Carsten, F. L. *The Origins of Prussia*. Westport, CT, 1982.
Evans, R. J. W. *The Making of the Hapsburg Monarchy, 1550–1700*. Oxford, 1979.
Fay, S. B. *The Rise of Brandenburg-Prussia*. New York, 1964.
Koch, H. W. *A History of Prussia*. London, 1978.
Macartney, Carlile A. *The Hapsburg and Hohenzollern Dynasties in the Seventeenth and Eighteenth Centuries*. New York, 1970.
McKay, D., and H. M. Scott. *The Rise of the Great Powers*. London, 1983.
Wangermann, E. *The Austrian Achievement*. New York, 1973.

VI

Topic 6

The Baltic and Eastern Europe in Transition

By the early 16th century, virtually all the lands of the Eastern Slavs were subject to the ruler of the Principality of Moscow, the "Tsar of all the Russias." In mid-century, Ivan the Terrible (Ivan IV) drove out the few remaining Mongols from Russian territory, and concentrated yet more power in his hands by purging the old Muscovite nobles. The 20 years of chaos and violence that followed his turbulent reign were justifiably named the Time of Troubles.

With the election of Michael Romanov as hereditary tsar in 1613, some degree of temporary order was restored. But while the monarch regained autocratic rule and the nobles received concessions, peasant hardships, already considerable, increased. The resulting popular unrest, coupled with the religious controversy of the Old Believers, produced more uprisings.

The reign of Peter the Great came as a turning point in Russian history. Following a policy of westernization, he introduced sweeping reforms in civil administration and the military. The tsar retained absolute power, but the creation of a bureaucracy along Western lines and the modernization of the army led eventually to Russia taking its place alongside the great powers of Western Europe.

After victory in a long conflict with Sweden known as the Great Northern War (1700–1721), Peter founded the city of St. Petersburg on the Baltic as his new capital. A further part of the tsar's program of westernization (he intended it to provide a "window on Europe"), St. Petersburg rapidly became a major commercial and cultural center.

In the second half of the 17th century, Sweden had conquered most of the territory around the Baltic Sea, but rule of this new Swedish empire dangerously overextended the home country's resources. Despite the efforts of Charles XII, Sweden's king and military hero, the Great Northern War brought a series of defeats. Peace negotiations between 1719 and 1721 saw the Swedish conquests on the Baltic divided up between Denmark, Hanover, Prussia, and Russia.

By contrast with the autocratic monarchies of Russia and Sweden, the nobles in Poland retained considerable power, including the right to elect their king. By the late 17th century Poland was virtually governed by the Diet, an aristocratic national assembly. Notoriously argumentative and inefficient, the Diet could not even enforce its decisions on the rare occasions it succeeded in making them. In consequence, internal weakness combined with the scheming of Poland's neighbors to create the conditions for complete collapse: in 1794 Poland ceased to exist as an independent country, and was partitioned among Austria, Prussia, and Russia.

THE EMERGENCE OF RUSSIA

The transformation of the Principality of Moscow into the capital of the territory of all the Eastern Slavs was finally accomplished in the reign of Ivan III (ruled 1462–1505), called Ivan the Great. (The Slavs are peoples of Central and Eastern Europe allied in race and language to the Russians; the chief Eastern Slavonic groups are the Russians themselves, the Belorussians, and the Ukrainians.) With the Turkish capture of Constantinople, capital of the old Byzantine Empire, in 1453, Ivan claimed the title of "tsar"—the Russian equivalent of "Caesar," or "emperor"— and proclaimed himself the heir of the Roman and Byzantine empires, adopting the double-headed eagle of Byzantium as the imperial crest. There had long been close cultural links between the Slavs and the Byzantine Empire, which included the conversion of the Slavs to Christianity. (See Part III, Topic 3.) In the eyes of the Orthodox Church, Moscow was now the "Third Rome," the center of Christendom. Subduing the Mongols of central Asia who had invaded in the 12th century, and conquering the great mercantile republic of Novgorod, Ivan ruled virtually all of Greater Russia by the end of his reign.

Ivan the Terrible, the first Russian ruler formally to use the title of "tsar."

The Byzantine double eagle used as the Russian royal coat of arms.

Ivan the Terrible

The Russian state became even more autocratic in the reign of Ivan IV (ruled 1533–1584)—known as Ivan the Terrible, although his nickname in Russian, Ivan Groznyi, is really better translated Ivan the Awe Inspiring.

Ivan became grand prince of Moscow at the age of three. His youth was warped by fear and neglect, and blighted by the sudden death of his mother, perhaps as the result of poisoning. After a period of bloody misrule by the *boyars* (the Russian nobles) during his early years, Ivan was crowned tsar and grand prince of all Russia in 1547, the first to bear this title officially. Married seven times, Ivan oscillated between states of tender affection and savage cruelty, combining drunken abandon and religious obsession.

On assuming full power, the tsar continued the policy of his predecessors in strengthening the position of the monarchy by reducing the influence of the traditionally independent princes and boyars. Under Ivan, these perpetually feuding nobles lost power to a new rising nobility, the *dvoranye*, who were granted land directly by the tsar in return for their services to him, and thus were bound in allegiance to him.

Ivan revised the legal code, strengthening the hold of masters over peasants. A special army unit, the *streltsy* (shooters), was formed and garrisoned in towns throughout Russia to enforce state policy. Agriculture and industrial production improved, and the Russian economy became increasingly internationalized, as foreign exports (mainly raw materials) and imports increased.

The tsar continued the "gathering of Russia" by driving out the remaining Mongols and gaining control of most of southeastern Russia. He initiated a long and eventually unsuccessful attempt to win territory on the Baltic, losing in the end to an alliance of Poland and Lithuania. Later in his reign, Russian forces had greater success in the east, where they began the conquest of Siberia that was completed half a century later.

The last 20 years of Ivan's rule were marked by a growing reign of terror. In 1565 he assumed despotic powers, surrounding himself with a special élite guard known as the *oprichniky*. Its 6000 members dressed in black and rode black horses. In order to provide them with estates—the land they ruled occupied half the kingdom—Ivan uprooted some 12,000 boyars and confiscated their holdings. When Philip, the saintly metropolitan archbishop of Moscow, reproached the oprichniky for their terrorist behavior, Ivan had him strangled.

The climax of his violence came in 1570. Suspicious that the city of Novgorod was planning to join his enemies the Lithuanians, Ivan razed it and had some 60,000 of its inhabitants killed. A few years later he began to disband the oprichniky, merging them by 1575 with the army.

In 1581, in a sudden fit of anger with his son, Ivan struck him in the face with his spearlike staff. Within four days, his heir was dead. When Ivan himself died three years later, leaving no adequate successor, his country was on the brink of anarchy.

The Time of Troubles

The years following Ivan's death are generally called the Time of Troubles (1584–1613), during which life in Russia was marked by civil war, economic crisis, and foreign invasions. The discontent of the peasants led to a series of uprisings, encouraged by the wandering armies of cossacks, who were originally bands of outlawed warrior peasants. Even the powerful boyar Boris Godunov (ruled 1598–1605), who ruled first as regent and then as tsar, failed to maintain control. Best known as the protagonist of Pushkin's drama (1831) and Mussorgsky's powerful opera (1874), Boris was overthrown by the pretender False Dimitri I, a former monk.

Only a Polish invasion in 1610, during which Polish forces briefly occupied Moscow, finally persuaded the rival boyars of the necessity of restoring some semblance of order. The invasion was sparked by long-standing rivalry between Catholic Poland and Orthodox Russia, intensified by their competition for control of the Ukraine. In 1613 they elected as tsar Michael Romanov (ruled 1613–1645), a distant relative of Ivan the Terrible's first wife. The young ruler was in poor health and thus the least threatening of the various candidates. All subsequent Russian tsars, down to 1917, came from the Romanov family.

The reigns of Michael and his successor, Alexis (ruled 1645–1676), however, saw the restoration of imperial power and the simultaneous granting of concessions to the nobles, including the reduction of their military service. Once again the peasants paid the price, for in 1649 Alexis introduced a law code which legalized serfdom.

The Old Believers

The peasants' resentment at their ever-worsening conditions deepened as the result of a bitter religious controversy in the latter part of the 17th century. Nikon (1605–1681; his real name was Nikita Minin), the powerful and formidable patriarch of Russia from 1652 to 1666, introduced a long list of changes to traditional services and rituals. His innovations, based on the liturgy of the Greek rather than the Russian Orthodox Church, deeply shocked the mass of old-fashioned believers. The peasants, in particular, crushed by financial and military obligations, reacted with bitterness to the loss of the traditional liturgy, their one remaining comfort.

The changes were in many cases symbolic rather than substantial—three fingers were to be used instead of two for making the sign of the cross, for example—but the result was a schism that split the Russian Church. A similar symbolic gesture had contributed to the break between the Roman Catholic and Orthodox churches in 1054. The traditionalists, who called themselves the Old Believers, resisted the changes by political and social protests. When government forces tried to impose reform, groups of Old Believers gathered inside the wooden churches they had constructed and committed suicide by setting fire to the buildings. The religious controversy underlined the degree to which the church was really a state agency, and the resulting disillusionment of the lower classes with ecclesiastical authority lasted down into the 20th century.

As chaos in Russia mounted, the cossacks once again seized their opportunity. Along with a great band of runaway serfs, religious dissidents, and other malcontents, a cossack army led by Stenka Razin (died 1671) swarmed up the Volga in 1670–1671, killing landlords and tsarist officials, and proclaiming freedom. Government troops easily defeated the disorderly force. Razin,

A cossack warrior from the team forming part of Russia's formidable fighting units.

who was captured and executed in Red Square, torn limb from limb, later became one of Russian folklore's great heroes.

The revolt led to increased repression. Frightened by the violence of the rebels, the nobles redoubled the bonds of serfdom, while rallying round the autocratic rule of the tsar. Finally, with the restoration of central authority, the Romanovs began to improve the imperial administration and rebuild the economy. To achieve this, they encouraged contact with Western traders and manufacturers, thus preparing the way for the reforming, if autocratic, rule of Peter the Great.

PETER THE GREAT AND THE ALLURE OF THE WEST

Under Peter the Great (ruled 1682–1725), Russia became transformed into a modern and aggressive European state. Without relaxing his autocratic rule, Peter improved government at both the central and provincial levels. He encouraged expansion in industry and commerce, rebuilt the army, and created a navy, using Western models for many of these reforms. Peter's chief purpose was to increase Russian military power. By raising Russia's fighting power, he aimed to make his country the equal of the other great European nations. Many of his successors, both Russian and later Soviet, followed the same policy. By the end of his reign, Russia had replaced Sweden as the leading state in northern Europe, with a permanent place in European power politics.

Peter's early life was overshadowed by violence, and marked by a series of palace coups and Moscow riots. He ascended to the throne in 1682 at the age of ten and seven years later overthrew the regency of his sister Sofia, making himself sole ruler. Nearly seven feet tall, he was a figure of almost demoniacal energy, ruthless and impetuous. He staggered his contemporaries by his massive consumption of food and drink, and by his incessant activity; he moved without stopping from carpentry to drilling troops to personally decapitating his opponents.

The Army and the Church

The central task in Peter's reform program was to increase Russia's military might. In place of the old amateur militias and various professional bands (such as the streltsy), he created a single standing army. From 1699 onwards, all its members were recruited, dressed, trained, and armed alike. He introduced conscription of nobles and serfs for lifelong service. At the same time he built a navy whose vessels were manned by foreign officers and Russian conscripts. By the end of his

Peter the Great, founder of Russia's new capital, St. Petersburg.

reign the army contained around 130,000 men, and the fleet was made up of 48 ships and almost 800 galleys.

Building the armed forces and paying for their wars consumed some 85 percent of the royal exchequer's revenues. New taxes were necessary to pay for these extraordinary expenses, and Peter replaced the old tax on households with a "soul" tax levied on all individual males, with the important exceptions of nobles and clergy. The Old Believers had to pay double and the neighbors of any man who fled to avoid the tax were required to pay for him. This latter provision was meant to deter peasants from escaping from their villages, and thus reinforced serfdom. Peter and his advisers also introduced indirect taxes, levied on items as varied as beehives and horse collars, and established state monopolies on tobacco, salt, dice and rhubarb.

The church, with its vast wealth and estates, lost its independence and became subordinated to the state. When the old patriarch died in 1700 he was not replaced, and a government department took over control of church property and received monastic revenues. The state paid monks and clergy a salary and laid down detailed regulations for their daily lives. The aim was to discipline them along military lines and make them submit to the government.

The Influence of the West

A further blow to ecclesiastical authority was the establishment of secular institutes of education along Western lines. As a young man, Peter had made friends in the Foreign Quarter of Moscow. Early in his reign he took a trip to Western Europe—his journey is known as the "Great Embassy" of 1697–1698—to see for himself the conditions there. On his return he set up a number of schools. The School of Navigation and Mathematics was founded in 1701, run initially by English and Scottish teachers. Other institutes included those for languages (1701), medicine (1707), and engineering (1712). As a further contribution to general education, Peter began Russia's first newspaper in 1703.

After his inspection of Western manufacturing methods and economic systems, the tsar tried to apply Western mercantilism to Russian agriculture and industry. The aim was to improve the Russian economy, and thus increase the taxable income of its citizens. Although the economy did begin a long period of growth, the overwhelming predominance of the state prevented the development of a middle class; private enterprise had little scope in a system dominated by government controls. Without the incentive of profits, few manufacturers introduced expensive new equipment, and agricultural methods remained generally Medieval.

Not content with changing public policies, Peter also tried to westernize the private lives and attitudes of his subjects. He introduced decrees ordering Russian men to shave off their beards (those who refused had to pay a special tax), wear Western clothes, and bring

Members of the Muscovite cavalry.

Map 6.1 Russian Expansion in Europe, 1689–1796

Contemporary caricature showing Peter the Great cutting off the beard of a boyar (nobleman).

Russian women out of seclusion. In this last respect he set an example. After a brief early marriage, he took as his mistress and drinking companion Catherine Skovorotsky (ruled 1725–1727), a tough, illiterate peasant from Lithuania. Peter married Catherine in 1712, and she ruled as empress on his death.

THE GREAT NORTHERN WAR AND THE FOUNDING OF ST. PETERSBURG

Like his predecessors, Peter devoted most of his energies to enlarging and securing Russia's territories. Among his conquests were parts of Persia, including

Licenses carried by those who paid a tax and kept their beards.

coastal regions of the Caspian Sea, and further holdings in Siberia. In addition, he was determined to obtain easier access to Europe by sea, either through the Baltic, then under Swedish control, or the Black Sea, which was held by the Ottoman Turks. His campaigns against the Turks were inconclusive, and in 1700 he signed the Treaty of Constantinople with them, winning a few concessions, in order to concentrate on the struggle with Sweden.

The Great Northern War (1700–1721)

The war against Sweden occupied most of the rest of Peter's reign. His principal opponent was the Swedish king, Charles XII (see below), whose prowess as a military commander led to a series of early defeats for the Russian forces. As Peter's domestic reforms began to produce results, however, his troops recovered. At the decisive Battle of Poltava in 1709 he destroyed the Swedish army, and advanced into Finland. By 1714, the new Russian fleet was able to defeat the Swedes and threaten the mainland of Sweden itself. By the Treaty of Nystad (1721), which ended the war, Russia kept Lithuania, Poland, and Estonia, all former Swedish conquests, and gave Finland back to Sweden.

Significant Dates

Russia from Ivan the Great to Peter the Great

1462–1505	Reign of Ivan the Great
1547–1584	Reign of Ivan the Terrible
1584–1613	Time of Troubles
1610	Polish invasion of Moscow
1649	Alexis legalizes serfdom
1671	Uprising led by Stenka Razin
1689–1725	Reign of Peter the Great
1700–1721	Great Northern War
1709	Work begins on building St. Petersburg

The Growth of St. Petersburg

Russia's new openness toward the West was symbolized by the creation of the city of St. Petersburg (Petrograd), built to replace Moscow as capital. In 1702, in the early skirmishes of the Great Northern War, Peter's forces seized a small Swedish fortress which stood where the River Neva flows into the Baltic Sea. The land, gloomy and unprepossessing, marshy and largely uninhabited, was nonetheless to provide the setting for Peter's new city.

Serious building began in 1709, after the Russian victory at Poltava. The city's organizers laid down a strict plan. The streets were to be broad and straight, with buildings set uniformly along them. The chief architects were Western, many of them Dutch, since Peter intended his new capital to resemble a Dutch port city. Separate parts of the city were set aside for each social class: a district for the nobility, another one for the artisans, and so on. The plan included provisions for public welfare, including street lighting, drainage canals, and parks.

To carry out this highly organized scheme, Peter made full use of his autocratic powers. He ordered the nobles and merchants to build elaborate palaces and villas, and to move to the new city from Moscow when the buildings were complete. Once again, however, it was the peasants who paid the heaviest price. Each summer peasant workers were drafted to labor on the construction sites, while their families had to cover the costs of their upkeep. Most villages preferred to keep the stronger men at home on their farms, and sent young boys or the elderly. In consequence, many workers died from the heat of summer or from accidents, and the swampy nature of the ground created a constant danger of collapse.

For all of the difficulties, the grandiose project began to take shape. At Peter's death, over 6000 government buildings and private residences stood on the former marshy river mouth. Less than 60 years later, in 1782, the population of St. Petersburg was almost 300,000, one of the largest in the world. During the reign of Peter's youngest daughter, Elizabeth (ruled 1741–1761), the Italian architect Bartolomeo Rastrelli (1700–1771) Europeanized Russian architecture with his Baroque and rococo palaces. One of them, the Winter Palace (Hermitage), housed the royal court and now contains the Hermitage Museum, today among the world's great art collections.

For all the undoubted achievements of Peter's reign, the price was high and the results mixed. Government remained inefficient and corrupt. Moreover, the tsar could issue orders on high, but day-to-day administration was in the hands of local bureaucrats, who maintained their arbitrary tyranny over the helpless lower classes. The condition of the serfs became even more hopeless than under Ivan the Terrible. Religious opposition to the process of westernization came from Old Believers and reformed Orthodox Christians alike. Many conservative nobles, opposed to the tsar's reforms, looked to Peter's son Alexis to restore former conditions. Peter, knowing his son to be pious and old-fashioned, had him and his followers eliminated in a purge in 1718. He claimed the right to nominate his own successor, but died before doing so, thus leaving the way open for the palace revolutions that marked 18th-century Russian political life.

Yet if Peter's reforms of government and the economy were only partially successful, his creation of a formidable military machine and aggressive foreign policy changed the course of European history. By winning the Baltic provinces, Russia replaced Sweden as the leading power in northern Europe. Newly westernized in outlook, it was now ready to assume its role as a major actor on the stage of European power politics.

THE COLLAPSE OF THE SWEDISH EMPIRE

The years of Russia's increasing influence saw the decline of the two other leading northern European powers, Sweden and Poland. Poland's deterioration had been in course for more than a century, but Sweden had only recently acquired an empire. In the early 17th century the charismatic Swedish king, Gustavus Adolphus (ruled 1611–1632), raised his country from a condition of insecurity and weakness to dominance over the Baltic region. By the time of his death in one of the battles of the Thirty Years' War, Sweden was one of the leading military powers in Europe.

Charles XI and the Struggle with the Nobles

Charles XI (ruled 1660–1697) was less concerned with foreign affairs than with weakening the hold of Sweden's high nobility. Charles came to the throne at the age of five, and during the early years of his reign a group of nobles led by his uncle took control of government. Incompetent and rapacious, they plundered crown lands and oscillated in their foreign policy between support of Louis XIV and his enemies. At home they emulated Louis' opulent Versailles lifestyle.

When Charles finally assumed full control, he set about concentrating power in his own hands. Shy and pious, he conscientiously constructed an absolute monarchy whereby the ruler took full control. With the support of the lower nobility, the middle classes, clergy, and peasants, he compelled the high nobility to hand back the royal properties they had taken. By the end of his reign, the crown's holdings of land had risen from 1 percent of the total country to 30 percent.

With the increase in state income, Charles was free to avoid foreign campaigns, with their highly uncertain rewards, and concentrate on domestic matters. He reformed the army by recruiting conscript citizens and paid them for their service by giving them farms, or the income from farms, regained from the nobles. The army's excellent training, and the speed with which it could mobilize, were of great help to Charles' successor. His reform of the bureaucracy saw merit rather than birth rewarded by promotion. Administrative officials were regularly paid and closely supervised. As a result, the machinery of government functioned smoothly.

The king's own power remained supreme. In 1693, Sweden's Diet—its name had been changed from Council of State to King's Council—declared the monarch to be "by God, Nature, and the Crown's high, hereditary right . . . an absolute sovereign king." So disciplined and orderly and popular an absolute ruler offered the promise of great possibilities for his country, but Charles died of stomach cancer at the early age of 41.

Charles XII and the Great Northern War

Charles XII (ruled 1697–1718), the son and successor of Charles XI, was trained from childhood to serve as king. He was well educated in science, philosophy, and the arts, especially music and theater, and accompanied his father on official business. He was tall and fair and so drawn by dreams of military glory that he remained a bachelor, claiming that he was "married to the army." He used hard exercise and self-denial to toughen himself, and made a point of personally leading his troops into battle.

A century earlier, a favorable combination of circumstances enabled Sweden to acquire a Baltic empire. Defending these holdings, however, became increasingly difficult for a country with a small population and modest resources. When Peter the Great became ruler of Russia, Sweden's chief rival, the days of the Swedish empire were numbered. The brief life of Charles XII was dedicated to an increasingly hopeless attempt to hold on to Sweden's empire, in the face of Russian, Polish, Prussian, and Danish opposition. Ironically enough, Sweden's warrior king, one of the military geniuses of the age, presided over the end of Sweden as an imperial power.

The Great Northern War began with a series of Swedish successes, including an invasion of Denmark and a victory over the Russians at Narva (1700). The momentum seemed irresistible, and Charles led his forces deep into Russian territory. Like Napoleon a century later, however, he badly underestimated the difficulties of ensuring supplies and communications.

In the winter of 1708–1709, one of the harshest on record, the Swedish Army traveled into the interior of Russia. By the time Charles made an assault on the Russian camp at Poltava the following June, his troops were demoralized and underequipped. To make matters worse, Charles himself was confined to a stretcher, shot in the foot in an earlier fight. The result was a disaster for the invaders. Most of the Swedish Army surrendered to the Russians, Charles fled to the Ottoman court in Turkey, and Peter the Great emerged as the leader of a new major European power.

For the next few years Charles remained in Turkey. In 1714 he galloped home in a mere 14 days and nights to rebuild his forces and reconquer territory lost to Danes, Prussians, and Russians. By 1718 he had put together an army of 60,000. Late in the year he invaded Norway, only to be killed by a stray bullet at the siege of Fredricksheld, a shot perhaps fired by one of his own soldiers.

During Charles' long absences abroad, his father's efficient bureaucracy governed Sweden. On his death, it introduced parliamentary government, inaugurating Sweden's Age of Liberty. At the same time, it made peace with all Sweden's enemies. The empire was divided up among Hanover, Denmark, Prussia, and Russia, with the last of these receiving the Baltic provinces. Sweden's imperial age was over.

POLAND: THE TRIUMPH OF THE NOBILITY

In the late Middle Ages, the union of Poland and Lithuania (1386) produced one of Europe's leading powers, second in size only to Russia. Many of the commercial routes for trade between the Black Sea and the Baltic passed through Poland, bringing prosperity with them. By the 16th century, however, commerce had shifted westward. The Renaissance and Counter-Reformation brought some renewal to Catholic Poland, but on the whole the country began a period of growing decline which led inexorably to its extinction in the late 18th century.

The King and the Magnates

In complete contrast to the absolutist Sweden of Charles XI, 17th-century Poland was dominated by the nobility, known as the *magnates*. These powerful aristocrats retained the power to elect the king, and saw to it that the ruler they chose was too weak to have any control over them. As a result, the Polish throne offered little more than the prestige of a royal title, appealing mainly to petty German princes.

The Polish magnates governed their country through the Diet, or parliament. The Diet, fearful of a rising bourgeoisie, had actually introduced legislation to restrict trade, and with the decline of commerce the middle class all but disappeared. As for the peasants, the great majority of the population, they were enserfed under conditions as grim as any in Europe.

The Deluge

By the reign of John II (ruled 1648–1668), Poland was so beset by problems that the period is known in Polish tradition as the Deluge. The magnates were sending the grain, timber, and other raw materials produced on their estates for sale in Western Europe, thereby lining their own pockets but impoverishing Poland. The population was falling, the currency was debased, what little city life existed was in decline, and serfdom was spreading.

At a time when only strong centralized government could have counteracted these tendencies, the Diet introduced a device which further restricted the possibility of concerted action. In 1652 the *liberum veto* (free veto) was used for the first time. This meant that a single member of the Diet could veto a decision by his negative vote. Even more dangerously, every member could use the liberum veto to dissolve the Diet and annul previous decisions.

Already notorious for its indecisiveness and inefficiency, the Diet now became paralyzed. In the century following the introduction of the liberum veto, no less than 57 Diets were convened. Administration, already disorganized, degenerated into chaos. The king could only watch helplessly, as the magnates took charge, with their vast labor force of serfs, their private armies, and their control over provincial assemblies.

Poland's neighbors seized their opportunity. First the Russians and then the Swedes invaded; pious Polish Catholics saw the devastating Swedish invasion of 1655–1660 as God's punishment on their country for having harbored Protestants. In 1655 the Swedes captured Warsaw, the Polish capital, and many of the magnates hastened to declare allegiance to the Swedish monarch as a means of saving their own skins. Only the death of the Swedish king five years later brought the war to an end.

After further losses to Russia, and with the threat of a massive Turkish onslaught, John could take no more. In 1668 he abdicated and went to France, where he became the titular abbot of Saint-Germain-des-Prés.

His successors fared little better. John III Sobieski (ruled 1674–1696) helped to restore Polish prestige by his heroic actions at the relief of the Turkish siege of Vienna in 1683 (on the Polish participation in the relief of Vienna, see Part VI, Topic 5). The last years of his reign, however, saw a return to conspiracies and rebellions. A string of powerless puppet kings followed him, as the country degenerated into a collection of feudal territories ruled over by local magnates.

Only in 1772, when Russia, Prussia, and Austria began to plot the carving up of Poland among themselves, was the country driven to act. The government enacted reforms, strengthening the power of the king, and improving the conditions of the peasants. The Polish patriot Thaddeus Kosciusko (1746–1817) returned from America, where he was in the American Revolutionary army and had been in charge of construction at West Point, to serve as major general in the Polish Army.

The changes were too late, and in any case the ill-equipped Polish troops were no match for Europe's three most formidable professional armies. In 1793, Prussian and Russian forces occupied parts of the country. Kosciusko led a rebellion against them, but was captured by the Russians, later returning to America and then to France, from where he continued to campaign for Polish liberty. By 1795 the dismemberment of Poland was complete.

The most important political development in Eastern Europe in the 17th century was the emergence of Russia as a leading European power. Sweden's brief period as the ruler of an empire was never likely to last for long. The willful destruction of Poland by its own nobility continued and Poland ceased for some time to have significant political or economic influence. Russia's appearance in international affairs, however, marked a significant break with the past.

Unlike Western Europe, the countries of Eastern Europe showed no sign of introducing social reform. In Russia, successive tsars maintained authoritarian rule, while Poland's magnates continued their domination. In Sweden, bureaucratic absolutism was replaced for a while in the early 18th century by parliamentary government, but by the end of the century absolute rule was back. In both Poland and Russia peasant conditions remained dismal.

Russia's success was due above all to its military prowess. Even Peter the Great had failed to do much to improve his country's administrative system, and the Russian economy remained backward, inhibited by the massive state bureaucracy. The deficiencies of central state planning were to hamper Russia's economic progress for centuries. As for Peter's attempts at westernization, they led in the 19th century to a bitter polarization of Russian intellectuals into pro-westerners and pro-Slavs (for a discussion of the controversy see Part VII, Topic 10).

Yet once awakened, the mighty country was quick to assume its new position. Throughout the 18th century its chief rivals, Prussia and Austria, had little choice but to acknowledge as an equal a state that only 100 years earlier had seemed far from the mainstream of European life.

Questions for Further Study

1. What role did the Orthodox Church play in Russian affairs? How did this differ from the function of organized religion in the West?
2. What means did Peter the Great use to westernize Russia? What was the effect of his reforms on Russian society?
3. Which were the chief factors leading to the dismemberment of Poland?
4. How did the Great Northern War affect political developments in northern Europe?

Suggestions for Further Reading

Anderson, M. S. *Peter the Great.* London, 1978.

Duffey, C. *Russia's Military Way to the West.* London, 1982.

Dukes, P. *The Making of Russian Absolutism 1613–1801.* London, 1982.

Klyuchevsky, V. O. *A Course in Russian History: The Seventeenth Century.* Chicago, 1968.

Nellie, R. *Enserfment and Military Change in Muscovy.* Chicago, 1971.

Raeff, Marc, ed. *Peter the Great Changes Russia.* Lexington, MA, 1972.

Wandycz, P. S. *The Lands of Partitioned Poland.* Seattle, WA, 1974.

VI

Topic 7

The Culture of the Old Regime

The 18th century marks a period of transition in the arts. When it dawned, Louis XIV still ruled as absolute monarch, and the works produced for his court were intended to satisfy the royal taste. By the end of the century, artists throughout Europe were creating for a much wider audience.

One of the highest achievements of art in the Old Regime was reached in drama at the French court. In the latter part of the 17th century, the three greatest names in the history of the French theater were all active at the same time, working under the patronage of Louis XIV. Pierre Corneille and Jean Racine wrote tragedies generally based on Classical themes, while Molière virtually created the form of French comedy.

In the decades following the death of Louis XIV, the audience for arts and ideas began to broaden. New institutions appeared that satisfied the growing demand for cultural and intellectual exchange. Among them were learned academies, both scientific and literary, and salons, informal gatherings for discussion. The relative openness of the academies and salons provided a forum for middle-class intellectuals, and also permitted women to play an increasingly important cultural role.

With the number of readers rapidly increasing, and writers less dependent on aristocratic patronage, literary ideas were spread in new forms. By the mid-18th century, the popular press was firmly established, and newspapers and periodicals circulated widely. The publications dispensed facts, literature, and opinion. The same period saw the rise of the popular novel, which reflected a middle-class rather than aristocratic morality.

In the visual arts, the heavy magnificence of the Baroque Era gave way to the more delicate charm of the rococo. Painters like the French Jean-Antoine Watteau depicted elegant picnics and romantic encounters. The Venetian Rosalba Carriera used the rococo style in her informal portraits, while her fellow countryman Giovanni Battista Tiepolo applied it to religious art.

Eighteenth-century musicians also tried to develop increased expressivity. Within a few years a new musical style appeared, the Classical, which made possible greater emotional variety. The first great master of the Classical style was the Austrian Franz Joseph Haydn, whose symphonies virtually created a new musical form. Even more versatile was the Austrian Wolfgang Amadeus Mozart, whose music combined beauty with learning. At the same time, in his opera *The Marriage of Figaro,* Mozart reflected the spirit of his age: the transition from an aristocratic society to a more egalitarian one.

By the end of the Old Regime, artists, writers, and intellectuals were already foreshadowing the coming revolutionary changes and the Romantic movement of the 19th century.

THE ARTS IN TRANSITION

The 18th century produced a remarkably varied range of artistic styles. The elevated grandeur of Corneille's and Racine's tragedies, the charmingly erotic scenes depicted in Watteau's canvasses, the social intrigues of Mozart's operas: all these seem to have little in common. Yet they, and the visions of other artists of the same period, share the characteristic of being addressed to an increasingly widening public.

Hitherto, most artists had served a patron, generally the church, the monarchy, or the aristocracy. Works of art, whether for the public domain or for private entertainment, conformed to the requirements of their commissioners. Ever since the 16th century, sections of the European aristocracy had cultivated the arts, playing music, patronizing artists, and engaging in amateur artistic pursuits. Toward the end of the 17th century, however, economic expansion, urbanization, and the spread of literacy produced a new public, as the middle classes began to develop an interest in the arts. Corneille's plays represent, in fact, one of the earliest attempts to address a middle-class audience. By the middle of the next century, drama, novels, and other forms of literature circulated widely, many of them dealing with the concerns of this new public.

With the change in audience came a change in the status of the artist. Although still heavily dependent on some form of patronage—the artist as fiery, freethinking creator did not appear until the 19th century—writers, painters, and musicians acquired a new social status. Friedrich II of Prussia entertained at his court the leading composers of the day, himself wrote music and played the flute and boasted of his intimate friendship with the great French writer Voltaire. The relationship was a fiery one. When Friedrich had "squeezed all the juice from the rind," he dropped Voltaire, who in turn made sure that his own version of the break circulated as widely as possible.

When in his later years the Austrian composer Haydn traveled throughout Europe, he was feted and honored as one of the most famous figures of his times. Haydn's own career, in fact, was symbolic of the new status of the creative artist. He spent his early years as an employee at the court of one of the leading aristocratic families, the Esterhazys, as director of the prince's music; when he wanted to write music for another patron, he was obliged to ask permission. With the growth of his fame, he was able to negotiate a revised contract under which the Esterhazys no longer had exclusive rights to his work. By the time he reached his sixties, he was free to live in Vienna and travel abroad, although he still continued to compose for the Esterhazys.

The new social position that artists occupied, together with the broad changes in society that made it possible, was inevitably reflected in their works. Although the artistic styles of the 18th century were far more varied than those of the Baroque Era, many of the age's most important achievements reflect a new preoccupation: a conscious engagement with social issues. Racine, Watteau, and Mozart, along with Richardson, Hogarth, and many others, used their art to explore ways of advancing and reforming society. By the mid-18th century, the intellectual movement known as the Enlightenment (see Part VI, Topic 11) provided an underpinning for these concerns and helped to focus artistic interests.

TRAGEDY AND COMEDY AT THE COURT OF LOUIS XIV

For Louis XIV, the arts served as a means of projecting his vision of himself as Grand Monarch. The architectural plan of the Palace of Versailles, built in the last decades of the 17th century, provided a setting for the Sun King in keeping with his political ideology. Official court portraits of the king emphasized his outward splendor, although toward the end of Louis' reign the court painter Hyacinthe Rigaud (1649–1753) produced a depiction combining grandeur with more than a hint of physical decadence.

The court at Versailles provided an appreciative audience for the theater, and in the latter part of the 17th century three great playwrights dominated French drama. All of them concentrated on depicting universal human types and emotions, rather than reflecting the world of the court. Not surprisingly, therefore, their works made an immediate appeal.

The Comedies of Molière

Molière was the stage name of Jean-Baptiste Poquelin (1622–1673). He was the son of a court furnisher, but rather than follow his father's profession, at the age of 21 he joined a group of actors to form a theatrical company. The actors soon went bankrupt, and Molière spent some time in prison for debt. Undeterred, he left Paris for the provinces to learn the craft of acting and playwrighting.

When he returned to the capital 13 years later with his own troupe, he performed before the king. In 1665 Louis became patron of his company, and Molière wrote romances and comedies for the royal courts at Saint-Germain and Versailles. He also poured out a stream of plays for a wider public, often acting in them. He died on stage in the middle of a performance of his last play, *Le Malade imaginaire (The Hypochondriac)*—of overwork, it was said.

Ironically for one favored by Louis XIV, Molière's source of comedy was the deflation of pomposity and arrogance. Taking a human weakness or delusion, such as hypochondria, miserliness, or misanthropy, he carries it to an absurd and often explosive conclusion. Yet revelation comes through laughter, not ridicule, and the characters remain believable. Tartuffe, the oily hypocrite in the play of the same name (1664–1669), or Jourdain, the amiable social climber of *Le Bourgeois gentilhomme* (1670), are not merely symbols but living personalities.

Only in one play, *L'Avare (The Miser;* 1668), does a human foible seem cruel and deluded. The miserliness of its chief character, Harpagon, is revealed as a perverse mania, reducing its victim to a childishness that provides the comic element. On the whole the message of Molière's works is to underline the humanity of even the most absurd of his characters, and to advocate reason and balance—the Classical middle way.

The Classical Tragedies of Corneille and Racine

The two leading tragedians of the age were Pierre Corneille (1606–1684) and Jean Racine (1639–1699). Both used as their starting point themes from Classical mythology or history but their approaches were very different.

Corneille was already writing when Louis XIV came to the throne, creating a new kind of play—the Classical verse tragedy—for a middle-class audience. His dramas are serious in tone, often dealing with conflicts of principles that call into question established morality. They thus appealed to a middle-class public that was itself questioning traditional ideas. *Horace* (1640) is based on incidents recorded by the ancient Roman historian Livy, and tells of a patriot who saves the state, but at the cost of the life of his pacifist sister. *Polyeucte* (1643) presents the dilemma of a martyr, whose wish for a glorious death is tempered by duty to his faithful wife.

Corneille's plays are self-consciously artificial. They make no attempt to represent literal time, place, or action. Instead, they provide abstract intellectual conflict in the cut and thrust of rhetorical debate. The characters represent the clash of ideals rather than real personalities. Corneille's elevated style was perhaps the reason for his falling from favor toward the latter part of his career, although his play *Le Cid* may have contributed by offending the king: the drama asserts the claim of its hero to independence from the monarchy. Another factor in Corneille's declining fortunes was the rising popularity of his rival, Racine.

Racine's first tragedy was produced by Molière's company in 1664, and he went on to write works for the leading Paris theaters. Using the Classical verse tragedy form perfected by Corneille, he brought to it a new understanding of human emotions. In plays such as *Phèdre* (1677), he explored the psychological state of mind of his characters.

His dominating theme is the human tendency toward self-destruction through ambition, jealousy, passion, and other forms of what his contemporary La Rochfoucauld (1613–1680) called self-love. His characters realize the tragedy of the human condition, while their understanding of their own helplessness reinforces their suffering and our pity for them. In his last play, *Athalie* (1691), the queen whose name gives the play its title expresses this sense of abandonment in a hostile world: "Pitiless God, Thou hast willed it all!"

ACADEMIES AND SALONS IN THE REPUBLIC OF LETTERS

The growing popularity of science in the 17th century led to the formation of learned societies, or academies, for the discussion and spread of new ideas and discoveries. Among the most famous was the Royal Society of London, which received its royal charter in 1660. By the 18th century, the taste for semi-public discussion of ideas of all sorts spurred the creation of a large number of more or less formal groups. Many of these sprang up in provincial cities in various parts of Europe, often in relatively small centers. As a result, knowledge of new ideas and values became more widespread than before.

In some cases these organizations sponsored the arts. London's Royal Academy of Arts was founded in

A neoclassical painting by Sir Joshua Reynolds: *Three Ladies Adorning a Term of Hymen* (a *term* is a pillar topped with a bust, as in this case of Hymen, god of marriage).

1768 by George III to encourage painting and still maintains an art school and holds open exhibitions annually. The Royal Academy's first president, Sir Joshua Reynolds (1723–1792), also sponsored the Literary Club for the discussion of literary topics. Among its members were Samuel Johnson (1709–1784), perhaps the most brilliant if idiosyncratic writer and critic of his time, the statesman and philosopher Edmund Burke (1729–1797), and the writer Oliver Goldsmith (c. 1730–1774).

Some organizations had specific goals. Catherine the Great entrusted the Imperial Russian Academy with preparing a standard Russian grammar and the first Russian dictionary, in addition to giving it the general task of providing translations of scientific and philosophical works into Russian.

By mid-century the creation of academies swelled to a flood. In Florence alone, there flourished the Accademia delle Belle Arti for painting and drawing, the Accademia della Crusca (*crusca* literally means bran; the academy was formed to preserve the purity of the Italian language by "separating the wheat from the chaff"), the Accademia dei Georgofili (literally "farming-lovers"; its members discussed scientific and economic aspects of farming), the Accademia del Cimento (Academy for Scientific Testing), and the portentously named Accademia Toscana di Scienze e Lettere "La Colombaria" (Tuscan Academy for Science and Letters "The Dovecote," so-called because of the small size of the room in which its members met).

Although some of the academies encouraged women to become members, the majority retained quotas. One of Italy's most admired 18th-century poets was Maria Maddalena Morelli (1727–1800), better known as Corilla. In 1776, the Roman Academy crowned her on the steps of the capitol for her abilities in declamation and improvisation. But most educated, serious women interested in participating in the literary and intellectual debates of the day had to do so informally. As a result of this constraint, women developed a new kind of cultural institution known as the salon: gatherings in private homes for the purpose of intellectual discussion (the term *salon* comes from the French word for sitting room).

The young Mozart entertains at a Paris salon, 1766.

PUBLIC FIGURES AND PRIVATE LIVES

ELIZABETH ROBINSON MONTAGU AND EDWARD MONTAGU

The first salon may have been established by a French noblewoman, the Marquise de Rambouillet (1588–1665). Suffering from an illness that required her to remain in bed wrapped in blankets and furs, she entertained guests from a bedroom alcove in her Parisian home. The marquise soon made the room into a tasteful, genteel environment in which artistic and literary matters were discussed by a mixed group of men and women. The salon eventually became an established institution in Paris, where women brought the talented and the powerful into their homes. By the middle of the following century, when the influence of the salon was at its height, the practice had spread to other European cities.

In Great Britain, the salon was the creation of Elizabeth Montagu (1720–1800). Her parents, Matthew Robinson and Elizabeth Drake, were both wealthy and well connected, and her eldest brother became the Baron Rokeby. Elizabeth developed a serious interest in literature at an early age and read widely. High-spirited and outgoing, she married Edward Montagu (d. 1775), grandson of the first earl of Sandwich, in 1742. Edward was a wealthy and serious-minded man who owned coal mines and estates, liked agriculture and mathematics, and served in Parliament for more than 30 years.

The couple lived in the country, where Elizabeth earned a reputation as an accomplished hostess. Their one child, a son, died after only a year and thereafter the couple led increasingly separate lives. Soon she moved the household to London, where the social season offered more distractions, and she made the Montagu home in Mayfair a gathering place for the most important intellectuals of the city—to a friend she explained, "I never invite idiots to my house."

At first Elizabeth entertained at literary breakfasts but soon added more elaborate evening assemblies which became known as "conversation parties." She refused to allow card playing, encouraging her guests instead to discuss literary subjects. On occasion, a well-known actor would recite. For 50 years, Elizabeth presided over the intellectual society of London, and writers, artists, and politicians vied with one another for invitations to the Montagu salon, where wit counted more than high birth. In addition to the lexicographer and conversationalist Samuel Johnson, the writer Horace Walpole and the painter Joshua Reynolds attended frequently. Among her women friends were Elizabeth Carter (1717–1806), who translated Greek philosophy, Fanny Burney (1752–1840), who wrote popular novels that won a European reputation, and Hannah More (1745–1833), a writer of plays and poems and social reformer. Elizabeth herself wrote letters and essays that were widely admired.

The term "Bluestockings" was first applied to the women intellectuals who attended Montagu's salon. The origin of the name is disputed, but one version of the story recounts that since Elizabeth allowed her guests to dress casually, one of her poorer friends always wore blue wool stockings instead of those made of more elegant black silk. Soon the word became a collective term for the women who attended and hosted such receptions, although it later came to be used derogatively to mean a woman who was pedantic, plain, and "unfeminine."

In 1775, Edward Montagu died and left Elizabeth a large income and many estates. She went to Paris the next year, where she became familiar with the works of Voltaire. She also built a large and sumptuous house in London which became the new center for her salon. To demonstrate her social consciousness, each May she invited the chimney sweeps of London to eat roast beef and plum pudding on the lawn of her home. By 1798, when she was almost blind and very feeble, her entertaining had all but ceased. She died two years later.

The salon not only permitted women to lead and take an active part in cultural debate alongside men; it also provided a forum that brought together aristocrats and middle-class intellectuals, helping both groups to get to know one another's ways. Furthermore the salons of Berlin and Vienna, by their inclusion of Jews, encouraged a greater official tolerance toward Jewish minorities; many of Berlin's leading salons, in fact, were run by Jewish women.

The most successful *salonières*, or hostesses, achieved considerable power behind the scenes, promoting their pet writers' work, or advancing the political careers of their favorites. As one of them boasted, "It is possible to obtain through women what one wants from men." There were, however, limits to their status. The middle-class Madame Marie-Therèse Geoffrin (1699–1777) married money at the age of 14, and turned her salon into the "Kingdom of Rue Saint-Honore," the most brilliant literary and social center of her time. Among her friends were Catherine the Great and King Gustavus III of Sweden. Yet because she was not of noble birth, she could not be presented at court.

THE POPULAR PRESS, NOVELS, AND THE CIRCULATION OF IDEAS

With the rapid growth of a middle-class reading public, literary culture began to spread in new ways. Just as conversation became the chief activity of the salons, so reading aloud came to occupy many middle-class families in their own homes. Since women were on their own territory in front of the family hearth, their tastes in literature became increasingly important. Thus the writers of newspaper articles, pamphlets, or novels looked for readers to this new domestic audience, rather than to aristocratic patrons.

The Growth of the Press

The appearance of the popular press provided a potential challenge to governments, accustomed as they were to controlling the spread of information. In 1662, the British Parliament passed the Licensing Act, limiting the number of licensed printers to 20, "to prevent abuses in printing seditious, treasonable, and unlicensed books and pamphlets." Yet the pressure for new sources of information was too great to resist: in 1695, Parliament decided not to renew the Licensing Act and the next two decades saw the birth of scores of journals.

The first London daily paper, the *Courant*, appeared in 1702, to be followed by a string of competitors. By 1730, 24 provincial papers were in circulation. In 1704, the English novelist Daniel Defoe (1660–1731), author of *Robinson Crusoe* (1719), founded the *Weekly Review*. A few years later two other weekly journals appeared, the *Tatler* (1709) and the *Spectator* (1711)—the latter still published. Even the imposition of state taxes on publications and their advertisements failed to discourage their proliferation.

Much of the contents of the dailies was practical: news of markets and shipping, prices of stocks and exchange rates, and "Names and Descriptions of Persons becoming Bankrupt." Details of births, marriages, deaths, and inquests began to appear. The largest number of pages was devoted to small commercial advertisements. The weekly magazines tended to include articles on more general topics, including politics, reviews of books and plays, and fashion.

In addition, the leading periodicals exercised a more general cultural impact. Addison's *Spectator* helped to form the taste of the age and shaped the values and behavior of its educated middle-class subscribers. Addison's impact was acknowledged by influential London figures, such as Dr. Johnson, but it also had a wider effect as his publication reached provincial and foreign readers. Among many others, David Hume in Edinburgh and Benjamin Franklin in Philadelphia both admired Addison's style, and used it as a model.

The rise in circulation of both daily and weekly publications was rapid and consistent. The total annual sale in Great Britain rose from 2,250,000 in 1711 to 7,000,000 in 1753 and to 12,230,000 in 1776 (the figures are available because of the tax paid on each copy sold). Since many papers were bought by clubs and coffeehouses, the total readership was far larger than the number of copies in circulation. With its growth, the popular press acquired considerable power. The opponents of the British prime minister Sir Robert Walpole accused him of paying out more than £50,000 in bribes to newspapers in the last ten years of his administration, and the freedom of the press became a major political issue.

Women's Magazines

Many of the new publications were specifically addressed to women, who comprised an important and growing class of readership. In the Netherlands and Germany, women themselves contributed many of the articles, and one of the leading Dutch papers, *The Quintessence of News*, was founded by a woman, Madame du Noyer. The most important French periodical for women, the *Journal des Dames*, first appeared in 1759, when its male publishers announced it as a "delicious nothing" for society ladies. Its women editors soon changed its character, however, publishing articles and reviews dealing with the question of women's rights, and making thinly veiled attacks on the government.

In 1703, Peter the Great had founded Russia's first newspaper in the campaign to westernize his country. By the latter part of the 18th century, middle-class families throughout Europe were exposed to a bewildering range of dailies, weeklies, and periodicals, many of which circulated outside their country of origin. One enterprising publisher even found a way to help readers spoiled for choice. The *Grand Magazine of Magazines, or Universal Register* contained "all that is curious, useful, or entertaining in the magazines, reviews, or chronicles, at home or abroad."

The Rise of the Popular Novel

Popular novels had appeared in France as early as the reign of Louis XIV, many of them written by women. From the early 18th century on, popular writers in Europe made a deliberate appeal to middle-class ideals and values. The social background and accepted attitudes of the books reflected a world dominated by class consciousness and economic status. The rise or fall of individuals, often due to marriage, is paralleled by critical developments in fortune and character.

The first significant popular writer in English was Samuel Richardson (1689–1761). His novel *Pamela* (1740), written in the form of a series of letters, describes the triumph of a servant girl, who marries her master after successfully fighting off his attempts at seduction. Produced in only two months, *Pamela* proved a best-seller throughout Europe, especially in France. A later novel, *Clarissa* (1748), also deals with seduction but its moral vision is more complex. Its two chief characters, the virtuous Clarissa and the cunning and immoral (and aristocratic) Lovelace, are both victims of a sexuality that is at the same time obsessive and destructive. After drugging Clarissa, Lovelace rapes her. Although he then offers to marry her, Clarissa proudly chooses to maintain her independence. Her family, not knowing how Clarissa was violently seduced, nor that she prefers solitude to marriage with the destructive Lovelace, consider her a woman ruined by her own choice. They abandon her, and learn the truth only after her death. The novel thus explores the wider implications of sexuality, and at the same time shows a remarkable grasp of the effect of social and economic forces on human character and feelings.

THE ART OF THE ROCOCO: WATTEAU AND HIS WORLD

With the death of Louis XIV in 1715, the French aristocracy abandoned the Baroque extravagance of Versailles for the elegant domestic comfort of Paris, and a new artistic style developed to provide an appropriate setting. The *rococo*—the word derives from the French *rocaille*, or grotto decoration—was intended as a contrast to the Baroque. Rarely weighty or serious, it aims for charm and lightness and replaces Baroque drama with grace and harmony. The interior decoration of buildings such as the Hotel de Soubise in Paris was appropriate for an age that put a new emphasis on civilized conversation. Rococo art, with its frank desire to please, also appealed to middle-class clients, in search of works that were appropriate to an intimate domestic setting, rather than intended for grandiose palaces.

Watteau and His Successors

The first great master of rococo painting was the French Jean-Antoine Watteau (1684–1721). His pictures of *fêtes galantes*, elegant outdoors festivities, show fashionable ladies with their refined suitors engaged in the pleasures of romance. Yet for all their superficial charm, his scenes have an air of wistfulness, even melancholy, that points to the impermanence of the world they depict.

Pilgrimage to Cythera (1717) shows the return home of a group of young lovers from Cythera (the traditional name of the painting is incorrect), the island of Venus, goddess of love. As they leave the sacred spot, some of them glance back longingly toward the statue of Venus; the mood is not so much one of sensuality as of farewell and departure. The glowing autumnal colors emphasize the sense of the loss that the passage of time brings.

Fragonard's *Love Letters* (1773), with its characteristic rococo depiction of an erotic scene.

A typical rococo interior: Germain Boffrand's Salon de la Princesse, Hôtel de Soubise, Paris. Begun 1732.

Many rococo artists who followed Watteau continued to explore the theme of romantic dalliance, but in a more erotic vein. François Boucher (1703–1770) was famous for highly sensual depictions of his scantily clad subjects. Generally set against a rustic background, the abundant pink flesh of his goddesses and shepherdesses is clearly intended to induce a particular kind of pleasure in the viewer.

The last great French rococo painter, Jean-Honoré Fragonard (1732–1806), achieved no less an erotic effect with greater subtlety. His superb lightness of touch and sense of color often emerge in the scenery surrounding his figures. The sense of warmth in the air in paintings such as *Love Letters* (1773) adds a touch of danger to the apparently innocent couple in the foreground.

Not all artists used the rococo style to create romantic fantasies. The Venetian Rosalba Carriera (1675–1757) was one of the leading portrait painters

The rococo decoration of the nave of Vierzehnheiligen Pilgrim Church in southern Germany.

of her day, and was elected to the academies of Bologna, Florence, and Rome. She traveled widely to produce portraits of leading society figures. On a trip to Paris in 1720, one of her first sitters was the young Louis XV. Working in the unusual medium of pastel (dry sticks of color that leave a fine powder when applied to paper), she drew frankly flattering portraits of her subjects, many of them showing the same pale elegance. Far more varied are the society portraits of the English Thomas Gainsborough (1727–1788), in which the background landscapes often play an important part.

The paintings and prints of the English William Hogarth (1697–1764) show a very different side of the fashionable world. Hogarth's intention was to attack hypocrisy and corruption, using the weapon of satire. In two cycles of paintings, *The Harlot's Progress* (1732) and *The Rake's Progress* (1735), he depicted the destruction of his heroine and hero by the decadent, venal, and corrupt forces of society.

Religious Art and the Rococo

The lightness of the rococo style did not lend itself naturally to religious subjects, but the Venetian Giovanni Battista Tiepolo (1696–1770) decorated a large number of church ceilings with saints and angels fully as elegant as Carriera's or Gainsborough's society ladies.

Some of the finest of all rococo architecture can be seen in southern Germany and Austria, where the bitter wars of the 17th century had discouraged the building of new churches. With the more stable conditions of the first part of the 18th century, construction started again, producing a series of rococo masterpieces.

The German architect Balthasar Neumann (1687–1753), an engineer by profession, designed a number of churches and episcopal palaces. Perhaps his most elaborate and intricate work is the interior of the Vierzehnheiligen (Fourteen Saints) Pilgrimage Church (1743–1772) near Bamberg, in southern Germany. The decoration flows down from the ceiling, encrusting walls and columns, in a deliberate rejection of Renaissance notions of balance and symmetry. For those accustomed to the austerity of much religious architecture, the sheer lightness and exuberance of Neumann's creation may seem out of place, but it succeeds in producing a sense of joy that is not inappropriate.

THE CLASSICAL STYLE IN MUSIC: MOZART AND HAYDN

As music, like literature, began to find an ever-widening audience, composers tried to express more complex and varied emotions. One of the more popular styles in the 18th century was the *empfindsamer Stil* (expressive style), which was designed to draw "tears of gentle melancholy." Its leading exponent was Carl Philipp Emanuel Bach (1714–1788), the second son of Johann Sebastian Bach (see Part V, Topic 7). He was engaged as harpsichordist to the Prussian crown prince in 1738; when his employer became King Friedrich II two years later, Bach stayed on as accompanist to the royal chamber music, with the special duty of playing flute sonatas with the king.

Baroque composers had used each individual piece or movement to explore a single emotion, joyful, tragic, energetic, or meditative. Now composers like C. P. E. Bach wanted to achieve expressive variety by putting different emotions side by side. His works use rich harmonies and contrasts in mood to express a considerable emotional range. His orchestral works are fiery and energetic, with dramatic breaks and changes of texture. In searching for a musical form to organize varied emotions, he wrote a number of keyboard pieces that convey a sense of intense and fantastic improvisation.

By the mid-18th century, composers had developed a style to meet the requirement of unity through variety: the Classical style. Its first great master was the Austrian Franz Joseph Haydn (1732–1809), whose more than 100 symphonies won him the name of "Father of the Symphony."

Wolfgang Amadeus Mozart

The life of the Austrian Wolfgang Amadeus Mozart (1756–1791) illustrates that not all artists were as fortunate as Haydn. When Haydn met the young Mozart in 1781, he observed to the young man's father, "Before God and as an honest man, your son is the greatest composer known to me either in person or by name." Posterity has seen no reason to doubt Haydn's judgment, yet Mozart's career was dogged by a constant alternation of successes and setbacks. A child prodigy, he traveled throughout Europe with his father, composing and performing to the acclaim of his aristocratic audiences.

Mozart was less fortunate in his patron than Haydn. After serving the archbishop of Salzburg, where he was born, Mozart tried to follow his great contemporary's example and obtain some measure of independence. When he asked for his freedom, the reigning archbishop, Hieronymous Colloredo, had him literally kicked out of the palace. Haydn managed to win his independence through the cooperation of his employer, and remained tied to some degree to noble patronage. Mozart's break was complete and violent.

Mozart spent the last ten years of his life in Vienna, struggling to find a permanent position and pouring out works to earn a living—symphonies and

A contemporary portrait of Mozart at the piano.

concertos for orchestral concerts, piano sonatas and string quartets, religious music for church performance, even music for Masonic ceremonies (Mozart himself was a Freemason). The Viennese public acclaimed many of his works. With no fixed income, however, Mozart lived on the brink of financial disaster, in part because of his own habit of spending money on gambling and entertainment as fast as he earned it. In 1791, he died at the age of 35 and was buried in a pauper's grave.

Mozart's music reflects little of the outward turbulence of his daily life. Perhaps more than any other musician, in his finest works he combined pure grace with profound learning to create an ideal beauty. Yet his music does not lack in drama or seriousness. His opera, *Don Giovanni* (first performed in Prague in 1787), describes the eventual downfall of its leading character, the restless and driven woman chaser, in powerful and dramatic music. Mozart's operas provide perhaps the easiest, and most enjoyable, access to his work. *The Marriage of Figaro* (1786) was based on a play of the same name by the French dramatist Pierre-Augustin Beaumarchais (1732–1799), which attacked the immorality of the aristocracy. It showed its hero, Figaro, outwitting the attempts of his noble employer to seduce Figaro's wife-to-be. Mozart's opera adds to the social protest of the original a sense of humanity, rather than

The Marriage of Figaro, scene from Act II.

personal resentment. Figaro expresses the frustration of centuries of men and women who had suffered from the injustices of class discrimination.

The plots and subplots eventually resolve themselves happily, but at times toward the end there hovers an air of wistful sadness, as if the future will bring only a return of conflict. A similar ambiguity runs through the opera *Così Fan Tutte* (*That's How All Women Behave*, 1790), which explores the nature of relationships between men and women. Faithfulness in love, it seems to say, is an illusion—or perhaps a self-delusion. Like Watteau, Mozart sees the impermanence of happiness.

By the end of Mozart's life, the French Revolution had broken out and the Old Regime was swept away. Some of the art of the 18th century may have served to distract its aristocratic public from the changing times and attitudes. Certainly Boucher's rosy Venuses or Carriera's haughty princesses represent a fantasy far distant from the growing pressure for reform. Yet the elegant world of rococo art was to be cut short by the guillotine as the result of a revolution due at least in part to other cultural developments in the 18th century.

The social criticisms of Hogarth's paintings, Mozart's operas, or Richardson's novels were directed at the injustice and immorality of the ruling classes. Discussion of the issues of social and political reform began to circulate increasingly widely through popular literary forms. Academies and salons made it possible for the upper and middle classes actually to meet on equal social terms, and raised the question of whether high birth was really superior to inherent ability.

The lowering of social and cultural barriers was limited. The vast majority of Europeans—the lower classes—continued to live as they had for centuries. An 18th-century Italian peasant, Russian serf, or Welsh shepherd was equally deprived educationally and economically dependent. It would take the industrial revolution, with its cities and factories, to draw attention to the hardships of the working classes and the poor, and give them the chance to fight to improve their lot.

Yet with the spread of culture in the 18th century the foundation was laid for future struggles. The forerunners of artists and writers of more recent times who campaigned for political causes were those who in the 18th century used their newly gained freedom to deal with the problems of their societies.

Questions for Further Study

1. What role did social criticism play in the arts in the 18th century?
2. What are the main features of the rococo style? How do they differ from the style of Baroque art?
3. What changes, if any, were there in the status of women in middle-class 18th-century society?
4. In what ways was the public for the arts a broader one than in the Renaissance or the 17th century? What were the causes?

Suggestions for Further Reading

Conisbee, P. *Painting in Eighteenth-Century France*. Ithaca, NY, 1981.

Darnton, R. *The Literary Underground of the Old Regime*. Cambridge, MA, 1982.

Ferguson, M., ed. *First Feminists: British Women Writers 1578–1799*. Bloomington, IN, 1984.

Kalnein, W., and M. Levey. *Art and Architecture of the 18th Century in France*. Baltimore, MD, 1972.

Robbins Landon, H. C. *Essays on the Viennese Classical Style*. New York, 1970.

Sewter, A. C. *Baroque and Rococo*. New York, 1972.

VI

Topic 8

Europe and the World Economy

The overseas discoveries made during the age of exploration in the 16th century had important repercussions for Europe and its economic life. The most dramatic impact came from the flow of huge amounts of gold and silver bullion to Europe from the New World, which produced an inflationary cycle that drove prices upward and created economic hardships for many millions. In addition, new patterns of trade emerged, particularly the shift of the center of gravity from the Mediterranean to the Atlantic (see Part IV, Topic 6, and Part VI, Topic 2), and new sources of wealth developed. The resulting "commercial revolution" saw a sharp rise in trade, both within Europe and on an international scale, and involved important new products from abroad and the increasing exportation of European-made goods. By the 18th century, a world market had come into being with Western Europe at its center.

One feature that both reflected and affected Western values was the growth and spread of the slave trade, as well as efforts to combat it. Similarly, the allure of large and quickly made profits sparked by the prosperity often resulted in risky schemes for financial speculation that caused serious setbacks for European investors. As the profits and opportunities in commerce grew, the centralization and strict state regulation that marked the old economic doctrine of mercantilism began to give way. By the 18th century, private commercial and financial interests had become closely linked with state policy. Finally, the colonial expansion beyond Europe's borders that was a prelude to or came along with the growth in trade had adverse consequences not only on non-European peoples and their cultures, but on the very peace and prosperity of the West (see Part VI, Topic 9).

TOWARD A WORLD ECONOMY

In the aftermath of the great age of discovery, the nature of international trade, and of Europe's position in it, underwent a major transformation, as what had been essentially a series of regional economies blended and merged into an integrated world marketplace. As a by-product of these changes, the new trade patterns proved to have a profound impact on the material and social life of Europe.

Changing Trade Patterns

Before the commercial revolution, a series of rather distinct regional trade patterns and more or less isolated markets had characterized world commerce. Trade within Europe, consisting of long-established local complexes such as those in the eastern Mediterranean, along the southern coast of France, or between Great Britain and Flanders, represented by far the bulk of European trade. Moreover, as central governments consolidated their control over national territories in Great Britain and France, domestic markets loomed increasingly more important. Europe's commercial relations with the rest of the world were also limited largely to two distinct but crucial patterns: the shipment of bullion from colonies in the Americas to mother countries in Europe, and the importation of spices from Asia.

By the 18th century, all continents were linked in an integrated, worldwide marketplace. New markets, such as that in the Baltic region, had expanded the volume of trade within Europe itself, while the old mercantilist monopolies that had once restricted trade between colonies and their mother country had been dissolved. Colonial items, in the form of raw materials and finished products, were increasingly being processed in Europe and then reexported to other parts of the world—the English, for example, reexported Virginia tobacco and the French sugar from the West Indies. One of the most successful innovations of the commercial revolution had been the development of triangular trade. In the typical example, English manufactured goods, such as printed fabrics, were traded to Africa for slaves. The slaves were in turn exchanged in the West Indies for sugar, which was then sold and consumed in Great Britain. Triangular trade flourished in the 18th century, when the British obtained the *asiento*, or the exclusive right to trade slaves in the Spanish colonies, a right that gave them access to Spanish-American markets for illegal goods.

As the volume of domestic and international trade increased, European merchants adjusted and refined their business practices, including marine insurance, credit banking facilities, stock exchanges, and uniform weights and measures. Tremendous fortunes were made in trade among the merchant class in the 18th century, especially in Great Britain and France, which had overtaken not only Spain and Portugal but also the Dutch Republic in the carrying trade. Commercial profits, along with the rising demand for European manufactured goods, acted as a stimulus to the industrial revolution (see Part VII, Topic 2).

One result of Europe's central role in the growth of global trade was that the West became infinitely more wealthy than any other region of the world. Europe's prosperity was, of course, the product of many factors, not the least of which were the natural resources of the Americas and the forced labor of millions of African slaves. Profits led to the accumulation of significant amounts of capital by European merchants. In addition, the general standard of living throughout western Europe increased, especially among the intermediate levels of society. The majority of Europeans, consisting of manual laborers and peasants, still lived close to the margin of subsistence, but Europeans lived better and had more material possessions than any other people in the world.

New World Commodities and Old World Tastes

In the mid-1600s, however, trade patterns began to undergo important changes. Eastern spices and Western bullion were probably still the most important commodities from overseas, but new products were beginning to increase in significance. The imports of bullion began to fall off steadily after 1620, while the European spice market became saturated. Large amounts of New World bullion—including as much as one-third of all silver—were sent to Asia, while spices and a variety of other luxury goods came back. In the years after 1640, such products as sugar, coffee, tea, tobacco, raw cotton and cotton fabrics, dyes, and furs assumed an increasingly larger role in world trade. These new goods had a dual impact: they accounted for the continual expansion of the volume of trade, and altered patterns of consumption and diet in Europe. The 18th century saw a tremendous increase in the new kind of trade—between 1698 and 1775, Great Britain experienced a growth of some 500 percent in exports and almost as much in imports, most of the increase in colonial trade. French trade also expanded significantly in the 18th century.

Spices had made dramatic changes in the European diet by the mid-16th century. Pepper, cloves, nutmeg, cinnamon, and mace were the most popular spices, with pepper by far the most desired. Perhaps as much as 10 million pounds a year of these items were consumed by Europeans bent on improving the taste of their otherwise bland foodstuffs.

Trade in these new items was by no means one-sided. As commercial links among the continents were established, a variety of fruit trees, vegetables, and domestic animals were exchanged. Columbus himself brought back hot and sweet pepper plants on his first voyage. Other products included the tomato, which was introduced to Europe in the early 16th century, and the potato, as well as corn, string beans, and cocoa. Among the animals from the Americas were the turkey and a variety each of duck and geese. On his second voyage in 1493, Columbus carried lemon and orange trees to Cuba, and eventually the Old World also contributed to the Americas sugar cane, wheat, barley, rye, onions, cabbages, carrots, turnips, beets, and radishes, as well as fruit such as apples, pears, peaches, and cherries. European animals sent to the New World included chickens, sheep, goats, horses, and cattle.

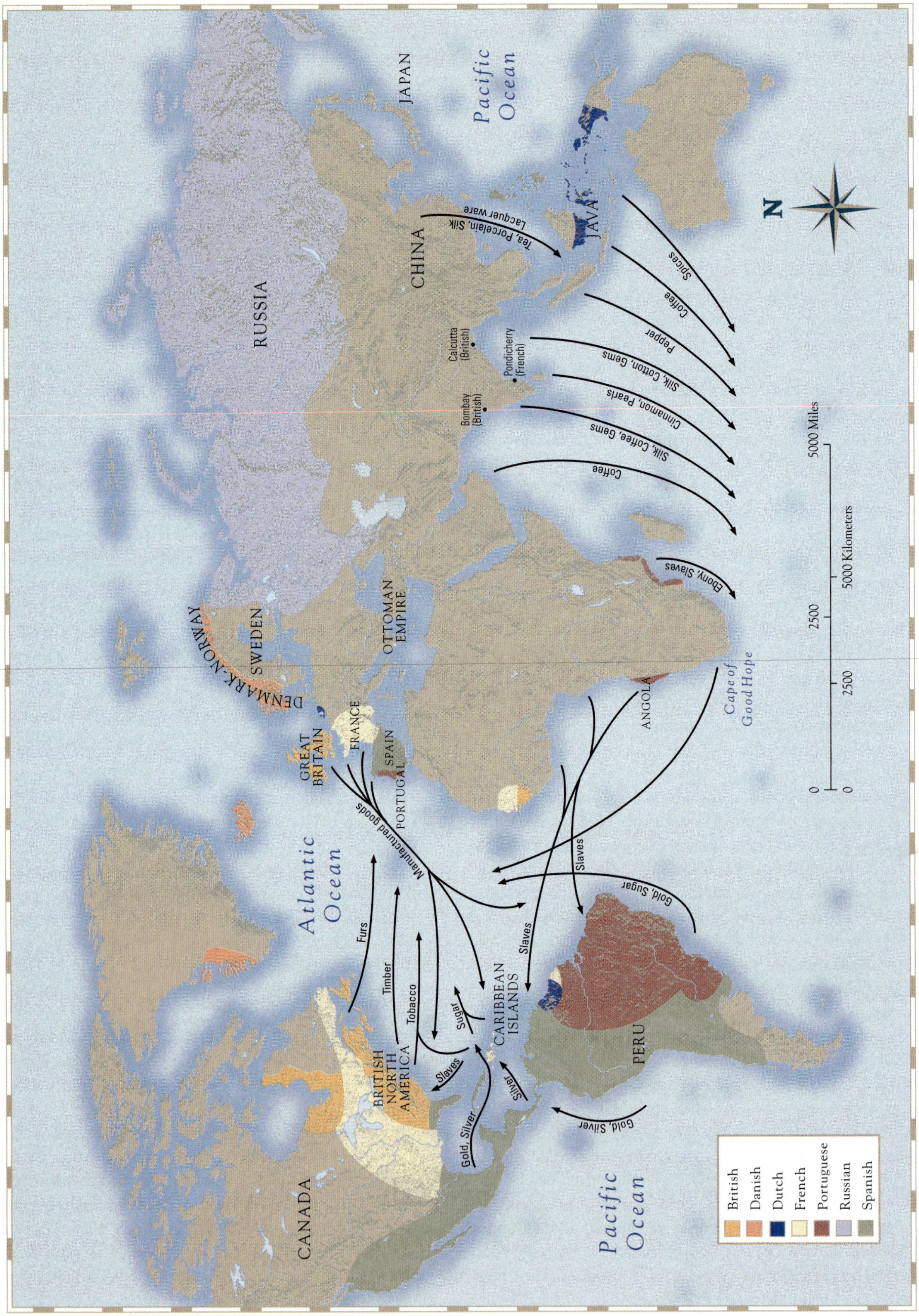

Map 8.1 European Sea Trade, c. 1750

Tobacco was the first new product from the Americas to be used widely by Europeans. Most of the American tobacco was grown in Virginia and Maryland and then shipped to Europe, where it was blended and sold for smoking, chewing, or to be used as snuff. As tobacco became immensely popular, governments throughout Europe imposed import duties and excise taxes on the product to raise revenues. In many nations, including France, Austria, Spain, and the Italian and German states, tobacco became a profitable state monopoly.

Of increasing importance was the importation of textiles, and especially of cotton fabrics. Cotton had been known in Europe for centuries, but had not been widely used. In the 17th century, however, imports of raw cotton from India and America began to increase substantially. Moreover, one of the most popular goods imported from abroad was the brightly colored Indian cotton of exceptionally light weight known as calico (so-called after the Indian city of Calicut). These printed fabrics were of fine quality and the large-scale Indian textile industry produced inexpensive products, for they were made by low cost hand labor. The demand for calicoes grew rapidly, for they could be used for a variety of purposes, including dresses, underclothing, stockings, and upholstery. By 1680, the English East India Company's textile imports were more important than its spice imports.

So much in demand were calicoes by the early 18th century that Great Britain and France both imposed limitations on their importation in order to protect domestic clothing makers. In 1700, the British Parliament passed an act forbidding the importation of all printed calicoes, although it allowed white calicoes to be brought in so as to encourage the English dye and printer factories (printed calicoes could, however, be imported for reexport). The Calico Act of 1720 prohibited the use or wearing of calico prints in Great Britain. But such restrictions only increased the demand for the fabric and stimulated the growth of the domestic cotton industry. The act was repealed in 1774, by which time the English textile industry had so developed that it could supply the home market with enough cotton fabrics.

Three beverages—coffee, tea, and cocoa—had far-reaching effect on European tastes. The trade in coffee, which had been introduced into Europe from the Middle East and Asia in the early 17th century, was largely in the hands of the English and the Dutch, the latter eventually growing their own supply in Java. By the end of the century, coffee had become a popular drink in Great Britain, often replacing beer. Coffeehouses and cafés became meeting places for social and intellectual discourse.

Even more popular was tea, long a staple drink in China and India. In 1664, the English East India Company, which enjoyed a monopoly on the China tea trade, presented King Charles II with the rare gift of two pounds of tea; by 1790, the company was selling millions of pounds of tea a year to the home market. Throughout the century, coffee remained the drink of the privileged classes, while tea became a staple used by all social classes in Great Britain.

Together with tea, sugar imported from the West Indies had an important impact on nutrition and worked both a commercial and a social revolution in Europe. Grown originally in southern Spain and Sicily, it was taken to the Canaries shortly after 1500 and then to Brazil and to the British and French West Indies, where the sugar cane thrived in the heat and humidity. By 1650, it had become another staple item in the European diet, its demand fueled by the growing use of tea, coffee, and cocoa. Sugar refineries in France numbered 18 by 1683 and processed some 18 million pounds of raw sugar each year. As the quantity of sugar produced increased steadily in the 18th century, its price fell and it ceased to be a luxury item as more people could afford it. At this point, American trade, based largely on sugar, became more valuable than Asian trade. Sugar also gave rise to two subsidiary products, molasses and rum. Molasses became a cheap and sweet addition to the European diet, and was the raw material from which rum was produced.

THE SLAVE TRADE

One essential aspect of the craze for American products such as cotton, tobacco, and sugar was their relationship to the slave trade. These and other products, but principally sugar, were grown in the New World on large "plantation" economies by slave labor. The slave trade had flourished since ancient times, when whites and Africans had been taken into captivity by the Roman Empire and Muslim traders. The Ottoman seizure of Constantinople in 1453, however, cut off Europe's supply of white slaves, who had been taken principally from the Black Sea region and the Balkans. In the second half of the 15th century, increasingly larger numbers of African slaves were imported into Europe.

With the discovery of the New World, Europeans began to ship African slaves across the Atlantic to the sugar plantations of Brazil and the West Indies. The massive African slave trade, fueled by the wholesale deaths of Amerindians, began in 1518, when the Emperor Charles V ended Indian slavery and agreed to substitute Africans as the source of plantation labor. By the end of the 18th century, perhaps 9 million African slaves had been brought to the Americas, half of whom

African slaves were employed extensively in the economies of the Western Hemisphere. This 18th-century French engraving shows slaves picking and processing cotton in the West Indies.

This 1823 print depicts slaves harvesting sugar cane on a plantation in Antigua.

A watercolor of a transatlantic slave ship suggests the cruel way in which captives were packed together for transport.

The slave uprising aboard the *Amistad* in 1839 brought the nightmarish plight of African captives to public attention in the U.S. and abroad.

A slave auction in the American South.

PERSPECTIVES ON HISTORY

The Slave Trade and the European Economy

Charles L. Killinger
Valencia Community College

European trade in African slaves and the commercial products they produced and consumed impacted in important ways the economic development of modern Europe. However, economic historians have questioned the scale of the profits from the slave trade and the nature of their impact on European industrialization. They have also studied the influence of the slave trade on the African and American colonial economies. In the context of the European economy, the primary questions facing students of the slave trade are these: how profitable was the slave trade? And in what ways did the slave trade contribute to the growth of the European economy?

Although Europeans had been trading in African slaves since the middle of the 15th century, it was not until 300 years later that the trade increased most dramatically and its profits peaked. By 1700, Portuguese and Spanish slave trade had dwindled with the decline of their imperial power and the British had surpassed the Dutch through a series of maritime victories. In the Treaty of Utrecht of 1713 (see Part VI, Topic 3), the British gained the treasured asiento *(el pacto del asiento de negros),* the exclusive contract for supplying slaves to Spanish America; and although vessels of many nations continued to participate, the British now dominated the shipping of African slaves to the New World. During the 18th century, slavers transported nearly 6 million Africans to the Americas, almost two-thirds of those imported over the entire duration of the trade.

As a result of the massive importation of free labor into the Western Hemisphere, the plantation economy expanded greatly. Plantations in the Americas produced agricultural commodities for export, including tobacco, ginger, indigo, cotton, and sugar. Since all were extremely labor-intensive, the use of free labor guaranteed low production costs. The primary beneficiaries were the British and French, and the most lucrative part of that "triangular" trade was the importation of slave-grown sugar from Caribbean islands.

In the 18th century, primarily on the strength of sugar production, the British West Indies surpassed India, China, and North America as sources of imported British goods, and the French colony of St. Domingue (Haiti) outstripped every British possession in annual sugar production. By the end of the century, 200,000 slaves in the British colony of Jamaica were producing 50,000 tons of sugar annually; a half-million slaves on St. Domingue were producing 100,000 tons each year. By 1700, Brazil was still importing huge numbers of slaves in spite of the decline of the sugar industry there, while in the second half of the century Spanish imports increased as sugar production in Cuba grew.

The success of the West Indian plantations satisfied the demands of mercantilism (see Part V, Topic 6), the dominant European economic practice of the day. The major European nations competed for markets and sources of raw materials for industrial production in order to achieve a favorable balance of trade and thereby gain an advantage over their adversaries. Slave labor assured a competitive advantage to the West Indian plantation colonies; in turn, the colonies not only enriched their owners, but contributed to the national strength, especially of the British and French empires.

In an effort to impose mercantilist regulation of the trade, European nations competed for exclusive rights to slave markets and granted national monopolies to slave trading companies. In 1672, for example, Britain granted such a monopoly to the Royal African Company, a joint-stock company, to compete with the Dutch for general control of international commerce. Soon it was exporting £100,000 worth of goods annually to Africa in order to meet the West Indian demand for slaves. London and Bristol merchants and shippers, envious of the trade, succeeded in breaking the company's monopoly in 1698. Thus both government and private merchants of the day clearly regarded the slave trade as profitable and potentially quite lucrative. However, Parliament dissolved the company a half-century later because of continuing financial difficulties.

The complexity of the triangular trade and the versatility of European merchants illustrate one problem in measuring slave profits with any accuracy: they are extremely difficult to isolate from general commercial profits. For example, in the early 18th century, the London financial house of Perry, Lane and Company shipped slaves to Virginia in exchange for tobacco and other commodities. Because of this overlap in its activities, its records do not clearly discriminate between profits from slaves and profits from tobacco, only partly grown by slave labor.

Frequent maritime warfare, raiding, and smuggling present another serious problem in calculating profits. The Royal African Company, for example, reported losses of £300,000–£400,000 during the War of the League of Augsburg (1689–1697) alone; and yet the slave cargoes, stolen by French privateers, obviously produced sizable—but untraceable—profits for some enterprising traders. Problems such as these illustrate the difficulty of answering the first question: how profitable was the slave trade?

The more significant and controversial question involves broader considerations that tie together the history of the Old and New Worlds. While there is no consensus as to the specific relationship between international trade and the industrialization of Europe, there is strong evidence to link the two in some fundamental way. In particular, the role of the Caribbean islands as both sources of raw materials and as markets has led historians to consider the slave trade a contributing factor to the development of European industry.

Controversy has focused on several issues. Some have argued that the Caribbean and African colonies provided only weak markets with a minimal capacity to consume European exports. And since the major Caribbean product, sugar, was simply consumed by Europeans and not converted into an industrial product, some have argued that the impact of such imports was also insignificant. These historians contend that profits from the slave trade and related European exports comprised such a small percentage of gross domestic product as to be negligible.

Other economic historians, analyzing the same statistics, have disagreed. They have shown, for example, that gross revenues of Jamaican sugar planters increased proportionally to imported slaves and that the Caribbean share of total imports into Britain rose substantially in the second half of the 18th century. Although variables other than the slave trade—such as population growth—may have contributed, the table below demonstrates that gross revenues from sugar shipped to Britain increased significantly over the 18th century.

Table VI.8.1
Caribbean Sugar Imports to Britain in Pounds Sterling

YEAR	AVERAGE GROSS VALUE
1713–1716	£ 959,100
1746–1750	1,479,900
1771–1775	3,234,800

It appears to these historians that such profits, although they may represent only a portion of national economic growth, are significant. They contend that exports such as those stimulated by the slave trade have historically contributed to cycles of growth and did contribute to the late-18th-century growth of Britain in particular. European investors, aware of new growth opportunity, moved money from less profitable investments such as domestic agriculture to the more profitable commerce and industry of Atlantic exports. Therefore, the profits earned by various countries from such activities as the slave trade accelerated the rate of European economic growth.

However, such a debate, regardless of its outcome, tends to ignore the broader economic impact of the slave trade. It is more useful to study the slave trade not as an isolated issue, but as an integral part of Atlantic commercial expansion. The development of the British economy after 1750 provides a good context. English iron foundries produced tools for colonial plantations and chains for the slave trade. Manufacturers produced pottery, furniture, firearms, and ammunition for sale to the slave-worked plantations. English mills produced

continued next page

cotton fabrics exclusively for export to Caribbean and African markets. In fact, the expansion of the British textile industry (see Part VII, Topic 2), often considered the essence of the industrial revolution, was intricately joined to the expansion of the slave trade. Accordingly, the cumulative impact of these new markets appears substantial.

There is another point to consider. Enormous quantities of sugar and other slave-grown commodities provided significant profits that produced a "multiplier effect" on the economy. The most convincing example is the mid-18th-century growth in British demand for colonial staples such as sugar. Increased demand for colonial imports created an opportunity for British exports to Africa and the Caribbean. British industries increased production to supply the thriving colonial markets, expanding employment and spinning off profits. These profits generally enriched the middle class, spurring consumer spending and creating in the process great individual fortunes. Profits also stimulated the related sugar-refining and shipbuilding industries, generated activity in banking and insurance, provided capital for developing factories, mines, and railroads, and led governments to expand their navies in order to protect their growing merchant fleets.

An important by-product of the slave trade was its impact on European cities. Population and economic activity exploded in such slave ports as Liverpool and Bristol in Great Britain and Bordeaux in France. And the development of Liverpool greatly increased the demand for exports that fueled the further development of the fabric mills and factories of Manchester. Consequently it may be argued that the slave trade contributed to another modern trend, the urbanization of the continent.

Despite the inability of historians to agree either on the level of profits of the slave trade or its precise impact on Europe, the weight of evidence suggests that profits were high and that they contributed significantly to European economic development. When considered in the broadest sense, the economic consequences of the slave trade were momentous.

went to the West Indies. Despite a 20 percent fatality rate on the transatlantic voyage, profits in slavery were high. At first, the Portuguese were the most active slavers, but by the 16th century the Dutch and French had begun to participate. In 1562, Sir John Hawkins (1532–1595) captained the first English slaving voyage, breaking the Spanish West Indies monopoly. The English eventually dominated the slave trade, both as a carrying trade and in order to supply its colonies in Jamaica and Barbados as well as the tobacco regions of Virginia and Maryland. Once in the New World, however, disease, forced labor under appalling conditions, and unspeakable living conditions continually decimated the slave population, so that new waves of slaves had to be imported regularly.

THE SPECULATION CRAZE: STOCK BOOMS AND CRASHES

The expansion of commercial capitalism in the 17th and 18th centuries was made difficult by a persistent shortage of money, which in turn was due to the decline in the supply of gold and silver bullion. The money shortage affected governments as well as private investors, for after the costly wars of Louis XIV ended with the peace treaties of 1713–1714, France and Great Britain found themselves deeply in debt. To meet the need for capital, Western states developed modern financial institutions such as stock companies, stock exchanges, and state-run banks, all of which expanded credit.

These developments, together with the return of peace after 1714, encouraged renewed economic confidence and led to unprecedented investment in commercial undertakings. This atmosphere of unrestrained financial speculation, fueled by the fiscal plight of Britain and France, led to the first stock crashes in modern times, which people at the time called "bubbles"—schemes designed to cheat or swindle the public.

John Law and the Mississippi Bubble

Britain and France found it increasingly difficult to deal with the huge debts accumulated during the wars, and both countries faced the possibility of bankruptcy if

Amsterdam boasted the first stock exchange, seen here in a 17th-century painting.

they could not pay the annual interest on their obligations. In each case, the government believed it could solve the problem by allowing private stock companies to manage the public debt for them. The idea was that trading and financial concessions given to these companies would create profits large enough to pay off the interest owed by government and still give investors a huge return.

In France, the experiment was organized by a strange character named John Law (1671–1729), a Scottish financier with a bent for mathematics. Law had led a wild life as a youth, having been imprisoned for killing a man in a duel. Later, while traveling on the Continent, he learned much about gambling as well as the banking business. In Paris after the death of Louis XIV in 1715, Law became a friend of the regent, the duke of Orleans, and devised a plan for solving the problem of French finances. Law believed that paper money, backed by the government's wealth in trade and land, could take the place of gold and silver coin. He therefore set up a bank in 1716 as a private joint-stock company, authorized by government charter. The bank issued notes, accepted deposits, and dealt in bills of exchange and promissory notes. In itself, the idea, modeled after the Bank of Amsterdam, was sound and proved so successful that in 1718 the regent bought out the bank's stockholders and made it a royal institution. Branches were established in principal cities and many of its notes, made legal tender in 1719, were used to pay off the government debt.

The problem with Law's scheme was that he was too ambitious and extended his operations to unchecked financial speculation. In 1717, he organized the Mississippi Company (officially known as the Company of the West), which received a monopoly of the trade with the French colony of Louisiana. The company took over the government debt and also purchased the government's tobacco monopoly. Within another year, the company—now called the Company of the Indies—bought out the East India Company and a number of other trading firms, and then took over the collection of taxes. Law therefore came to control government finances through his bank as well as most of the country's overseas trade.

Each expansion that Law undertook was financed by the issuance of more and more stock, the purchase of which was made easy by the fact that the bank rapidly increased the quantity of its notes. By the spring of 1720 the face value of notes in circulation had gone from about 150 million to almost 2.7 billion livres. The result was an inflation that pushed prices up by 88 percent. In addition, Law's bank actually lent money for the purchase of company stock. This crazed speculation and expansion were sustained by the fact that the shares in Law's enterprise were constantly increasing in value, to the point where the price bore no relation to actual earnings. So amazing seemed the prosperity engineered by Law that in January 1720 the king made him finance minister. The next month, the bank and the company were joined together.

The bubble in Mississippi shares finally burst that spring, when the price of shares rose so high that some speculators decided to sell their holdings in order to protect their investments. As the selling turned into a panic, Law's empire collapsed—for the banknotes that investors received for their stocks were then turned in for gold and silver, and the bank's reserves of specie was exhausted. In December, Law fled into exile.

The South Sea Bubble

The Mississippi Bubble had a serious impact. It undermined French public confidence in stock companies as well as in banks and paper money, yet the inflation had enabled the government to pay off part of the public debt. Moreover, Law's fiasco had international reverberations, for at almost the same time another bubble—the South Sea Bubble—burst in London.

The Bank of England, organized in 1694 by William of Orange, managed the public debt for the government and, like Law's bank, issued notes. In 1710, however, a charter was issued for a joint-stock company known popularly as the South Seas Company (officially the "Governor and Company of Merchants of Great Britain Trading to the South Seas and Other Parts of America and for the Encouragement of Fishing") which took over part of the government's debt. Under the terms of a special agreement, holders of government bonds were to turn them in to the company in exchange for company stock. The interest paid by the government on its bonds would be passed on as dividends to the stockholders. In addition, the company was granted a monopoly on all British trade with Spanish America. The South Sea Company was further strengthened when England obtained the *asiento*, which permitted it to send some 4800 slaves and one merchant ship a year to South America.

As company profits grew, speculative fever mounted, especially as news of Law's operations reached English investors in 1719. The company eventually offered to take over the entire government debt and pay the government a bonus for the privilege. By

The South Sea Bubble of the 18th century was in fact a stock market "crash," depicted here in a contemporary engraving.

June 1720, the price for South Sea Company stock had increased ten times to more than £1000 a share. The thirst for speculation became a craze as innumerable companies—almost 200 in a single year—were created, many of dubious legitimacy, and sold stock to the public with only a minimum down payment. The South Sea Company, concerned over the increased competition, persuaded Parliament to pass the Bubble Act, which prevented any company from selling stock without a royal charter. With the crash in Paris already under way, prices began to tumble on the London exchange and by December the South Sea stock had collapsed to £120.

The British crash exposed a widespread scandal of government corruption as it was discovered that ministers and parliamentary officials had taken bribes from some of the companies. In an effort to clean up this scandal, Sir Robert Walpole was appointed as the king's chief minister (see Part VI, Topic 4). The South Sea Company actually survived on a much reduced scale as a holding company for government securities, and the Bank of England reemerged as the principal financial institution of the nation.

The effects of the bubbles on both sides of the channel were eventually overcome as governments and private investors learned caution from the dangers of speculation. These episodes were, however, symptomatic both of the end of the old mercantilist principle—which held that government protection and monopolies were needed to protect national economic prosperity—and the rise of the new capitalist doctrine, developed first by Adam Smith and then by the later Manchester School (see Part VI, Topic 11), that accompanied the commercial expansion and the industrial revolution.

A global economy had begun to emerge in the 18th century as a result of the expansion of trade. At the center of that commercial economy was an increasingly prosperous Europe, which reaped huge profits from the growing interdependence in production and markets that characterized the world of commerce. European states took tremendous resources from the Americas, first in the form of gold and silver bullion and then in agricultural products.

This economic transformation drastically altered the lives of millions of Europeans, whose hunger for the new products—coffee, tea, sugar, tobacco, and others—resulted in important changes in diet, nutrition, and customs. As the market in such goods as sugar, tobacco, and cotton grew, Europeans began to raid the African continent to obtain the manpower its New World enterprises required, giving rise to a slave trade that persisted with unrelenting horror for three and a half centuries. The European exploitation of the rest of the world that began with the overseas discoveries came to a head as a result of the commercial revolution, to be superseded only in the next century as Western imperialism carved up the continents. As the 18th century opened, the expansion of commerce was closely tied to the evolution of banking systems and public finance, a relationship that led to a series of financial schemes that ended in crisis. By the end of the century, however, these scandals had been set behind as Europe moved into the age of industrial capitalism.

Questions for Further Study

1. What were the principal elements in the emerging world economy?
2. In what ways was the slave trade tied to the European economy? Was it profitable?
3. What were the new forms of investment that emerged? What were the principal causes of the speculation crashes?

Suggestions for Further Reading

Boxer, Charles R. *The Dutch Seaborne Empire, 1600–1800.* London, 1965.

Braudel, Fernand. *Civilization and Capitalism,* trans. S. Reynolds. 3 vols. New York, 1979–1984.

Cameron, Rondo. *A Concise Economic History of the World.* New York, 1989.

Curtin, Philip. *The Atlantic Slave Trade: A Census.* Madison, WI, 1969.

Davis, David B. *The Problem of Slavery in the Age of Revolution.* Ithaca, NY, 1966.

De Vries, Jan. *The Economy of Europe in an Age of Crisis, 1600–1750.* Cambridge, MA, 1976.

Dickson, P. G. M. *The Financial Revolution in England: A Study in the Development of Public Credit, 1688–1756.* London, 1967.

Frank, A. G. *World Accumulation, 1492–1789.* New York, 1978.

Kriedte, Peter. *Peasants, Landlords and Merchant Capitalists: Europe and the World Economy, 1500–1800.* Leamington, England, 1983.

VI

Topic 9

The Global Conflict: Wars for Empire

With the spread of European colonization in the Americas, Asia, and Africa, wars among the leading European powers tended to extend to their colonial possessions. Virtually every major European conflict in the 18th century involved the colonies, and ended with the redistribution of territory outside Europe.

At the end of the War of the Spanish Succession in 1713, Spain was forced to make important concessions to British traders in the Spanish-American colonies. Ill feeling between Spain and Britain continued to smolder, and the War of Jenkins' Ear broke out in 1739—the first important confrontation to involve two European countries fighting over a colonial dispute.

There followed the War of the Austrian Succession (1740–1748), a complex series of interlocking power struggles, which brought France and Spain together to contend with Britain for supremacy in America. In 1744 France declared war on Britain, and in return the British seized the French settlement of Louisbourg in Canada. Both countries, however, were too committed to European campaigns to do more than skirmish overseas, and the peace treaty which brought the war to an inconclusive end returned Louisbourg to France.

It was clear to many contemporaries that a definitive struggle for control of North America was at hand. In the meantime, the French continued to build a chain of forts down the Ohio River, to block British expansion west of the Appalachians and keep them restricted to the Atlantic seaboard. The British prepared for war by despatching two regiments to America—the first British regular soldiers to serve there.

In 1755, in fighting near the French stronghold of Fort Duquesne, the British forces were routed and their general killed. The following year saw a fresh outbreak of general hostilities in the Seven Years' War (1756–1763), which set Britain and Prussia together against France, Austria, and Russia. The alliance was formed to defeat Prussia in reprisal for its conquest of Silesia in the War of the Austrian Succession. The British provided financial subsidies to the Prussians and attacked the French fleet and coast to reduce France's pressure on Prussia. In return, the Prussians pinned down French troops and thereby restricted French efforts in North America.

After early setbacks, Britain increased its American war effort at the insistence of the prime minister, William Pitt. Massive forces crossed the Atlantic, defeated the French at Louisbourg, and then took Quebec (1759) and Montreal (1760). With New France fallen, the British moved on to the Caribbean, where they conquered important French and Spanish islands. By the end of the war, Britain had acquired its first empire.

Meanwhile, in Europe, Friedrich II's Prussian forces were engaged in a tenacious but increasingly desperate attempt to keep their enemies at bay. In 1762, however, the unexpected withdrawal of Russia broke up the quadruple alliance. Prussia kept Silesia, and emerged from the war firmly established as one of Europe's leading military powers.

BRITAIN VERSUS SPAIN IN THE WEST INDIES

As the leading European colonial powers continued to expand their holdings in Asia, Africa, and the Americas, rivalries hitherto fought out on European soil began to spread to the colonies abroad. In the context of the commercial expansion of the 18th century, the domestic economic benefits of overseas territories—access to raw materials, new markets for the sale of manufactured goods—encouraged the colonizers to defend and add to them.

At the same time, the three strongest colonial powers, Britain, France, and Spain, tried equally hard to prevent the growth of each other's overseas holdings. As a result, the incessant wars fought out by the major European nations throughout the 18th century almost invariably involved them in conflicts both in Europe and elsewhere. Even the European powers with no colonies, such as Prussia, became involved in colonial rivalries: most of the conflicts of the 18th century in Europe involved colonial powers like Britain and Spain that were also simultaneously fighting outside Europe. In addition, the peace negotiations that ended the European wars served to pursue colonial competition outside Europe, since treaties generally reassigned colonial holdings, and thus inextricably linked them with European power politics.

The first major redistribution of colonies occurred at the end of the War of the Spanish Succession (see Part VI, Topic 3), from which the British emerged the principal victors. By the Treaty of Utrecht (1713), the French gave up Newfoundland, Nova Scotia, and the Hudson Bay territory to the British, retaining New France (Quebec). Spain held on to its American possessions, but was forced in return to award Britain trading privileges there.

The War of Jenkins' Ear

British expansion only exacerbated the ill feelings between the rising imperial power and a declining Spain,

George III reviews the British fleet.

An anti-Spanish cartoon in 1738. Captain Jenkins shows his ear to Sir Robert Walpole, seated to the left.

embittered by the concessions it had been forced to grant. The focus of tension was the Caribbean, where British undercover traders and Spanish coast guards—often private operators hired by the government—were in constant friction. Most of the illicit ships operated out of Jamaica, a British possession in the middle of Spanish territory. When British vessels fell into the hands of the Spanish *guardacostas*, who were patrolling in search of booty as much as enforcing the law, their crews generally received rough handling.

As reports of the Spanish ill-treatment spread back to Great Britain, public indignation over the behavior of their traditional enemies began to rise. In 1738, an English sailor, Robert Jenkins (active 1731–1738), brought to the House of Commons a jar containing his ear; he claimed it had been ripped off by a Spanish coastguard. The prime minister, Sir Robert Walpole (see Part VI, Topic 4), already under pressure, was accused by his opponents of weak-kneed indifference to Spanish aggression. After trying unsuccessfully to cool tempers, Walpole gave way and declared war on Spain—the War of Jenkins' Ear—in 1739.

The immediate cause of hostilities was allegedly national honor, but deeper considerations prompted the clash. In the first place, Spain, one of the first great imperialist powers, was beginning to decline just at the moment that British fortunes were rising. Furthermore, the real issue at stake was not the theoretical right of smugglers to ply their trade in peace, but the practical ability of one colonial power to deny access to a rival. The War of Jenkins' Ear was in itself trivial enough, and in any case the hostilities between Britain and Spain soon became subsumed in the far more involved War of the Austrian Succession, but it set an important precedent. For the first time two European powers went to war over questions of trade outside Europe.

DYNASTY AND POWER POLITICS: THE WAR OF THE AUSTRIAN SUCCESSION

In the years from 1740 to 1763, the chief European nations fought out a complex series of interrelated power struggles. The War of the Austrian Succession (1740–1748) was followed by a brief period of uneasy peace dominated by feverish diplomatic activity. In 1756 hostilities broke out again, in the form of the Seven Years' War (1756–1763). By its close, there were two main victors: Britain, which had won its first empire, and Prussia, which had confirmed its status as a great power.

The initial cause of the War of the Austrian Succession was the death of the Emperor Charles VI (ruled 1711–1740). In 1713, Charles had devised the so-called Pragmatic Sanction, a document that asserted that the Hapsburg empire would be regarded as indivisible and would recognize Charles' young and inexperienced daughter, Maria Theresa (ruled 1740–1780), as his successor. Most of the powers of Europe, including Prussia, agreed to abide by its provisions. The Prussian king Friedrich II (ruled 1740–1786) subsequently contested her right to inherit her father's possessions and invaded the resource-rich province of Silesia (on Friedrich's career see Part VII, Topic 1). In spite of her youth and inexperience, however, Maria Theresa ultimately proved to be one of the most capable rulers in the long line of Hapsburg monarchs. Years later, Friedrich admiringly described the tenacious young empress as "the only man among my opponents." Meanwhile, French and Bavarian forces attacked Bohemia, while the Spanish took the opportunity to threaten Austrian holdings in central and northern Italy.

Britain came to Maria Theresa's aid, as much to oppose France as to help the Austrians. The British foreign secretary, Sir John Carteret (1690–1763), was an enthusiastic player of diplomatic games who claimed that his favorite pastime was "knocking the heads of the kings of Europe together, and jumbling something out of it that may be of service to this country." In 1743, Carteret put together an alliance of Austria, Britain, and Piedmont-Sardinia, but his achievement had the effect only of driving the former rivals France and Spain to form a counteralliance.

King George's War

Meanwhile, the hostilities between Britain and Spain, the latter now joined by France, continued in America, where the struggle was generally known as King George's War, after the reigning King George II (ruled 1727–1760). George was the last British king personally to command in battle, fighting in the European phase of the War of the Austrian Succession.

Events in Europe were fluctuating too violently for any country to risk committing substantial forces to the American front. The British made disorganized raids on Spanish territories on the mainland and in the Caribbean, but were beaten back, as much by tropical disease as by the Spanish. The only notable reversal in King George's War occurred in 1745, when New England colonial forces captured the French-held Cape Breton Isle and its fortress of Louisbourg, which commanded the St. Lawrence estuary.

British and French troops continued to skirmish elsewhere. In India, the French took the British town of Madras in 1746. The next year, the British Navy defeated two French fleets off the Atlantic coast, and thereby prevented them from carrying reinforcements to overseas French territories.

By 1748, amid general frustration and exhaustion, peace negotiations at Aix-la-Chapelle (Aachen) brought about an end to the war, and a restoration of conquered territory. Britain handed back Louisbourg and regained Madras in return. The only real winners were Prussia, which held on to Silesia, and Maria Theresa, whose right to succeed her father was generally recognized. Eight years of conflict had revealed that British superiority at sea was counterbalanced by French supremacy on land. The resulting stalemate left virtually all the disputes between the European powers unresolved, not the least of them the battle for control of North America.

The Diplomatic Revolution

The period from 1749 to 1756 saw intense negotiation and counternegotiation, as the leading participants prepared for the inevitability of renewed conflict. By the time war broke out again in 1756, the alliances of the War of the Austrian Succession were reversed in a series of changes known as the "Diplomatic Revolution." When the Seven Years' War broke out, the chief enemies were the same: Prussia versus Austria, and Britain versus France. Britain, however, now supported Prussia instead of Austria, and France was allied with Austria rather than Prussia.

The break between Britain and Austria was caused by Britain's refusal to support Maria Theresa's demands for the return of Silesia. The British had backed the Austrians in the earlier war mainly because they were the enemies of France, but they had no interest in becoming embroiled in Austria's territorial disputes. Austria turned to France for support, but Louis XV, the French king (see Part VI, Topic 2), did not immediately respond. Early in 1756, however, Britain and Prussia signed the Convention of Westminster, and the French—furious with Friedrich for allying Prussia with the hated British—hastened to negotiate a defensive alliance with Austria.

At this point, a new player appeared on the scene. The empress of Russia, Elizabeth (ruled 1741–1762), was deeply mistrustful of the British and Prussian agreement. She tried to persuade the French and Austrians to join Russia in an offensive triple alliance to crush Prussia's growing power. With hostilities between the British and French in North America becoming increasingly serious, Louis hesitated, unwilling to encourage a European war that would overstretch French resources.

While the French tried to decide, Friedrich of Prussia suspected that a coalition of powers was planning to attack him. With characteristic boldness he struck first, taking military action on the principle that "negotiations without arms produce as little impression as musical scores without instruments." In August 1756 the Prussians invaded Saxony, thereby provoking the French into action, and bringing into being the alliance that Friedrich wrongly suspected already existed. The Seven Years' War was under way.

Like the earlier War of the Austrian Succession, the Seven Years' War involved action both in Europe and America. On the European front, the Prussians battled their various enemies and struggled to hold on to Silesia. Across the Atlantic, the British and French fought the decisive struggle for control of North America. Both Prussia and Britain emerged victors.

The two wars were interdependent. Britain provided Prussia with an annual subsidy, maintained the so-called Army of Observation in Germany to protect Prussia against a French attack, and made periodic assaults on the French fleet and coast. The purpose of these moves was to reduce French pressure on Prussia. In return, the Prussians' military activities pinned down French troops in Europe and prevented them from throwing all their effort into the North American campaign.

THE STRUGGLE FOR NORTH AMERICA: THE ASCENDANCY OF BRITAIN

Although the British and French were officially at peace until the declaration of war in 1756, fighting between them had continued ever since the end of the War of the Austrian Succession. In India, the British and French East India companies struggled for commercial dominance, as the Moghul empire (the Muslim empire ruling most of north and central India in the 16th and 17th centuries) continued to break up. The British soldier and administrator, Robert Clive (1725–1774), defeated the French in 1751 and captured a string of French strongholds; he subsequently overcame the local ruler of Bengal at the Battle of Plassey (1757), to establish the British East India Company's control over all Bengal and neighboring provinces. The British victory at Plassey thus played a key role in establishing British control in India, and laid the foundation for their eventual empire. In Africa, Britain tried to drive the French out of Senegal, a center for the lucrative slave trade.

This miniature painting depicts an employee of the British East India Company.

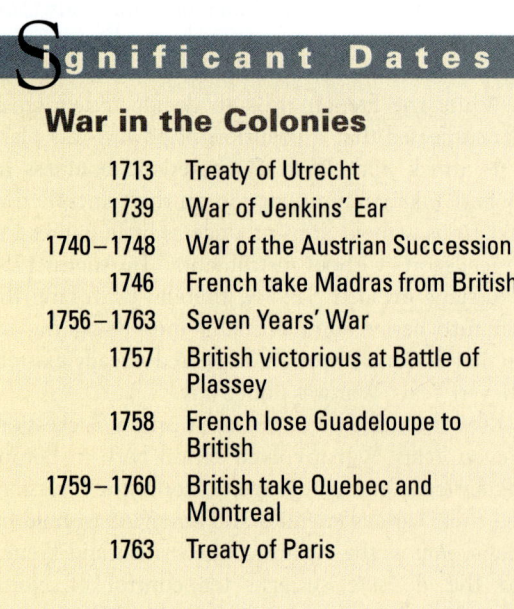

Significant Dates

War in the Colonies

1713	Treaty of Utrecht
1739	War of Jenkins' Ear
1740–1748	War of the Austrian Succession
1746	French take Madras from British
1756–1763	Seven Years' War
1757	British victorious at Battle of Plassey
1758	French lose Guadeloupe to British
1759–1760	British take Quebec and Montreal
1763	Treaty of Paris

British and French Colonists in North America

The most important stage for Anglo-French rivalries, however, was North America, where the culminating struggle—the American side of the Seven Years' War—is often called the French and Indian War.

The attitude of the two nations to their American colonies was very different. The thirteen British colonies in North America grew rapidly, as immigrants from the home country arrived in increasing numbers. By the time war officially broke out, the colonial population numbered around a million and a half. Some of the communities were already the size of a small European city. In 1760, for example, Philadelphia had some 23,000 inhabitants and a well developed commercial life; by 1776, it was the third or fourth largest city in the British Empire.

By contrast, the French were much less enthusiastic about emigrating to Canada or Louisiana, areas that presented formidable environmental challenges to 18th-century immigrants. Unlike the bustling British settlements, the French colonies consisted of large empty spaces with only a scattering of inhabitants. Although smaller, the French communities were efficiently run and on occasion more profitable than the British. Without the distractions of urban life, the new settlers concentrated on sugar planting, fur trading, and other commercial operations.

These differences significantly affected French and British relations with the Native American populations. In order to establish settlements and encourage further immigration from the homeland, the British set up large land investment schemes, making land available by driving native residents from their traditional hunting grounds. The French, by contrast, were interested in trading rather than building settlements. As a result, they were more likely to find native residents cooperative.

The French and Indian War

This cooperation became of considerable importance when French forces began to seal off the Ohio Valley, to block the British on the Atlantic seaboard and prevent them from moving westward. In the years before the official outbreak of war, the French built a north-south chain of forts along the Ohio and Mississippi valleys, hoping to connect up their settlements in Louisiana with those in Canada. The Iroquois and other local tribes supported the French attempts to keep out the British.

In 1754, in an encounter near Fort Duquesne (site of the future city of Pittsburgh), French and Indian fighters combined to defeat a force of Virginian levies under the command of the young George Washington (see Part VII, Topic 1). The colonial troops had been despatched by the Ohio Company of Virginia, a land investment company. The following year, the British government sent regular British soldiers to America for the first time. Once again the French and Indian combined forces proved more effective. Ambushing the British troops nine miles from Fort Duquesne, they killed the expedition's general and captured his men.

The French maintained the initiative in 1756. With war officially declared, the distinguished French commander, Louis Joseph de Montcalm (1712–1759), captured Fort Oswego on Lake Ontario, along with 1400 men. In 1757 he took Fort William Henry, and a year later defeated a British expedition at Ticonderoga.

Yet by the time of the British defeat at Ticonderoga, the French were losing their superiority. The autocratic British politician William Pitt (1708–1778), in spite of George II's implacable hostility to him, took charge as secretary of state in 1756. The king dismissed him in 1757, but the disastrous news from America forced his reappointment, and Pitt took full and determined control over foreign and military affairs.

The Battle for Canada

When Pitt came to power, his strategy was to concentrate on driving the French from Canada. British forces attacked from three different directions: up the St. Lawrence via Louisbourg, into the Ohio Valley against Fort Duquesne, and from the Hudson Valley via Ticonderoga. The last of these was frustrated by Montcalm's victory, but the other two succeeded. By 1758, the British were in control of Louisbourg and Fort Duquesne; the latter was renamed Fort Pitt, in honor of the prime minister.

The British continued to advance. In 1759, the young general James Wolfe (1727–1759) led his troops up the St. Lawrence to Quebec, which was defended by a force under Montcalm. On the night of September 12, advancing soldiers silently climbed the cliffs west of the city, to the Plains of Abraham. After a short,

The siege of Quebec.

bloody battle, in which Montcalm and Wolfe were both fatally wounded, the French fled. The following year, the British besieged Montreal, while back in Europe the British fleet decimated that of France. With France unable to send reinforcements, Montreal fell, and with it all of Canada.

War in the Caribbean

With the accession of George III (ruled 1760–1820) in 1760, a triumphant but war-weary Britain began to move toward peace negotiations with France. Peace talks actually began, but in 1761 the new Spanish king, Charles III (ruled 1759–1788) talked the French into renewing their old alliance and opposing British colonial expansion in the Caribbean. Early the following year, Britain declared war on Spain, and the colonial war entered its final phase.

The French had already lost Guadeloupe to Britain in 1758. Now the British added the important French islands of Martinique and Grenada, and the neutral St. Lucia and St. Vincent, to their Caribbean holdings. Spain lost Havana, Cuba, while the Spanish position in the Pacific was badly shaken by the capture of Manila in the Philippines by a British expedition sent from India.

The Treaty of Paris

Between February and August of 1763, the negotiations of the Treaty of Paris between Britain, France, and Spain formalized the new distribution of territory. In America, France ceded to Britain Canada, Cape Breton Island, and all of Louisiana east of the Mississippi (except for New Orleans). The two countries agreed to share fishing rights off Newfoundland and in the St. Lawrence, and France received two small islands, St. Pierre and Miquelon, which are still French territory and became an overseas department in 1976.

The Spanish regained Havana, but agreed to cede Florida to Britain. In compensation, they received from the French the part of Louisiana lying west of the Mississippi. Elsewhere in the Caribbean, the British held on to Grenada and St. Vincent, but handed over Martinique and St. Lucia to the French.

In Asia, Spain regained Manila. As for India, both Britain and France agreed to restore their mutual conquests, returning to the positions they had occupied in 1749. French influence in India was effectively ended, however, since the terms of the treaty prohibited them from rebuilding their fortifications. In Africa, France lost the colony of Senegal to Britain.

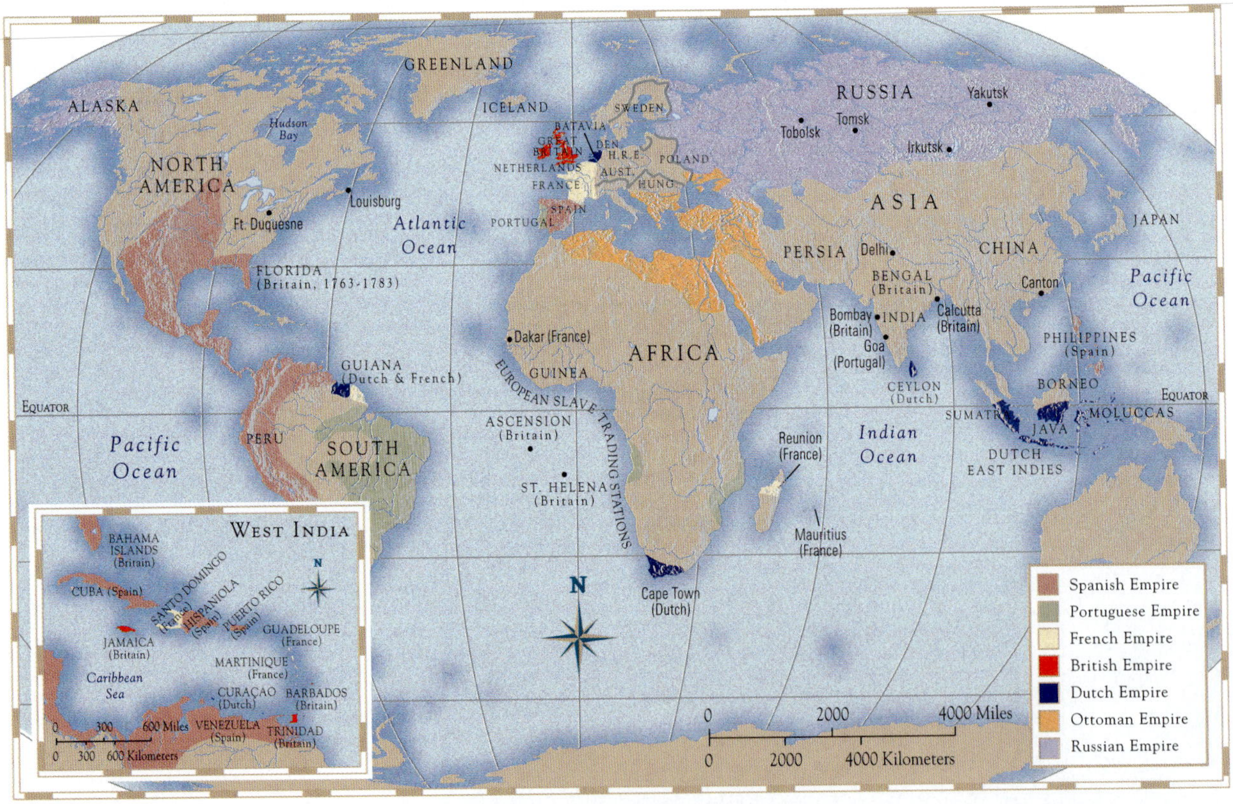

Map 9.1 European Possessions Overseas, c. 1760

British government offices in Calcutta, late 18th century.

In 1759, with the war at its height and with news pouring in of British victories, Pitt observed that "peace will be as hard to make as war." His successor as prime minister, the Earl of Bute (served 1762–1763), feared that if Britain assumed too dominant a position, the rest of Europe would band together against her in resentment. The terms of the Treaty of Paris reflected the British concern to provide at least some satisfaction to France and Spain.

The greatest loss of all to France had been Canada—perhaps French authorities took some comfort in Voltaire's description of the former French possession as a "wretched country, covered with snow and ice eight months out of twelve, and inhabited by savages, bears, and beavers." France had lost its North American empire, but French commercial power remained formidable.

THE SEVEN YEARS' WAR AND THE SUCCESS OF PRUSSIA

Friedrich's gamble in invading Saxony in 1756 and launching a preventative war seemed at first to pay off. He followed one of his favorite maxims, "If you must go to war, fall on your enemy like thunder and lightning." After capturing Dresden, he advanced on the Hapsburg territory of Bohemia. By bringing about the very alliance of Austria, France, and Russia that he had moved to prevent, however, he undid the benefits of his surprise attack. In 1757 an Austrian army drove the Prussians out of Bohemia. Thereafter the fighting followed the same pattern. Friedrich kept his troops moving, beating back repeated attacks by the allies, and winning impressive tactical victories, but he never managed to break the strategic stalemate.

Prussia's long-term prospects seemed doomed. Either the fighting would continue indecisively, with the Prussians gradually losing territory, or the allies would make a breakthrough and crush their enemy. Friedrich was helped to some extent by ill feeling between his opponents. In August 1759 a combined Russian and Austrian force invaded Brandenburg, inflicting on the Prussians their worst defeat of the war, but through mutual distrust they failed to follow it up. A year later the Russians and Austrians actually occupied Berlin, the Prussian capital, but after making a ceremonial entry they left only four days later.

The End of the Seven Years' War

At the beginning of 1762, with Prussian resources stretched to the breaking point and on the verge of collapse, rescue arrived from the most unexpected of directions. Friedrich's old enemy, the Russian Empress Elizabeth, whose suspicion of Prussia had helped to create the anti-Prussian alliance, died at St. Petersburg. Her nephew and liberal successor, Peter III (ruled December 1761–June 1762), had long admired Friedrich's enlightened domestic policies. On his accession he ordered the immediate suspension of Russian attacks on the Prussians, and in May 1762 the Prussians and Russians signed a peace treaty whereby all conquests were returned. Friedrich's luck was all the greater in that six weeks after signing the treaty Peter was deposed by his ambitious wife, Catherine II (see Part VII, Topic 1)—while under arrest, he was assassinated by a group of guardsmen under mysterious circumstances.

With Russia out of the action and France fully occupied in dealing with Britain, the alliance collapsed, leaving Maria Theresa no choice but to accept the loss of Silesia. The Treaty of Hubertusburg (1763) between Prussia, Austria, and Saxony restored the prewar situation, with the Austrians recognizing Prussian possession of Silesia. Saxony regained its independence, but Friedrich paid no compensation for the damage Prussia had inflicted.

Unlike the War of the Austrian Succession, the Seven Years' War significantly changed the balance of power in Europe by reinforcing Prussia's status; at the same time, it underlined the growing importance of colonial strength. Even though the Treaty of Paris sealed Britain's victory on terms that were not excessively vindictive, Britain clearly emerged from the colonial wars as the indisputable imperial leader in Europe.

The triumph did not last long. Within ten years of the Peace of Paris, Britain's thirteen North American colonies were beginning their successful attempt to break away. Their loyalty to Britain had been assured by the threatening presence of France on American soil. With the French driven out and the British asserting their control with ever more unpopular taxes, conditions were right for the Revolutionary War—in which, ironically enough, the colonists received assistance from France (on the American Revolution, see Part VII, Topic 1).

Prussia was the other main victor, but its emergence as a major power was bought at considerable cost. Friedrich spent the first half of his reign (23 years) in virtually continuous war, devoting much energy during the second half to keeping the peace by skillful, if ruthless, diplomacy. Furthermore, the Prussian Army's invincibility did not long survive Friedrich's death. It fell behind in training and equipment, and was decisively crushed by Napoleon's French troops at Jena (1806). Yet the Prussian successes of the mid-18th century proved its right to be taken seriously as an important power, and foreshadowed events a century later, when Prussia, against the will of a declining Hapsburg Austria, succeeded in uniting Germany.

George Washington, commander-in-chief of the Revolutionary War.

At a casual glance, the history of the 18th century seems as filled with conflict as the bloody 16th century. There are important differences, however, between the destructive wars of the earlier period, often fueled by religious hatreds, and the 18th century's careful search for a stable balance of power. European countries fought one another for specific political and economic goals, and not to wipe out whole groups or classes.

When it became clear that the war aims would—or, as the case might be, would not—be achieved, the combatants stopped fighting and made peace. The various treaties of the century sought not so much to reward the winners and punish the losers, as to recreate and maintain the balance. The prudence of 18th-century European statesmen was, of course, dictated by realism rather than charity. In so fluctuating a world, yesterday's enemy might well become tomorrow's most important ally.

The 18th century's other distinction was that of spreading both war and diplomacy beyond the boundaries of Europe to a global context. Battles fought in the Philippines or along the Mississippi affected the political and economic developments of countless European citizens. The wider horizons required new resources: Britain's success in the conflicts outside Europe was due in large measure to the strength and efficiency of its navy, an indispensable force in empire building.

The careful diplomatic balance achieved at Paris and Hubertusburg was destined to be of short duration. Along with the growth of international trade and revolutionary developments in industry, the revolutionary political movements of the late 18th century wrought vast changes in European political life. One factor remained constant, however. Starting with the 18th-century wars for empire, European political and economic life was permanently linked to that of the rest of the world.

Questions for Further Study

1. How did the European powers use the wars in the colonies to continue their struggle for domination in Europe?
2. What role did the British Navy play in Britain's success in the colonial wars?
3. What have been the lasting effects of the 18th-century colonial wars in Africa, Asia, and the Americas?
4. How did war and diplomacy interconnect in settling the colonial disputes of the 18th century? Was the process different from the relationship between war and diplomacy in earlier periods?

Suggestions for Further Reading

Bearce, George D. *British Attitudes Toward India*. Westport, CT, 1982.

Boxer, C. R. *The Dutch Seaborne Empire*. New York, 1965.

Brewer, John. *The Sinews of Power*. New York, 1989.

Christie, I., and B. W. Labaree. *Empire or Independence 1760–1777*. New York, 1977.

Davis, L., and R. Hittenback. *Mammon and the Pursuit of Empire: The Political Economy of British Imperialism*. Cambridge, MA, 1987.

Davis, R. *English Overseas Trade, 1500–1700*. London, 1973.

Mommsen, W. *Theories of Imperialism*, trans. P. S. Falla. Chicago, 1982.

VI

Topic 10

European Society in the Eighteenth Century

In 1789, European society was struck by the great upheaval known as the French Revolution (see Part VII, Topic 3). The leaders of that tumultuous event, who used language as an essential aspect of politics, believed that they were building a new, radically different social order. For this reason, they called the world that had existed before the revolution the Ancien Régime—the "Old Regime." Historians still use the term to describe the way of life and the institutions that characterized Europe before 1789.

It is important to understand that although the society of the Old Regime was based on traditional notions of hierarchy and privilege, what appeared on the surface to be a stable social order was being undermined by powerful forces. European economic life and population were both expanding rapidly. Major innovations were introduced in agriculture and manufacturing that would bring revolutionary transformations. The social structure, which for centuries had seemed to be ordained by God, adjusted to new conditions, especially as the nobility was forced to make concessions to a middle class that was growing in wealth and insisted on sharing power and status. These social realities were rationalized and justified by the intellectual climate of the times, which questioned the principles on which the social structure of the Old Regime rested.

Royal absolutism, itself premised on the idea of a stable society, also underwent change. Many of the rulers cloaked their power in the trappings of "enlightened" monarchy while seeking to increase government efficiency and control. To sustain the increasing centralization of government and pay for the frequent colonial and European wars of the period, rulers constantly squeezed more and more taxes from their subjects, taxes that eventually sparked rebellion in the New World against Britain and threw the Old Regime in France into crisis. The great revolutionary upheaval that erupted in 1789 was the climax of a process that had been underway for decades.

Society and the Old Regime

The Old Regime was an intricate network of political, economic, and social relationships. The political character of the Old Regime was defined by the system of absolute monarchy, with its divine right theory and increasingly centralized state bureaucracy. The economic life of Europe was overwhelmingly rural and agrarian, burdened by isolation and chronic food shortages, and while evolving financial practices often produced instability, restrictive mercantilist policies still constrained commerce. The social patterns of the 18th century had their roots in the Middle Ages.

The Nature of the Old Regime

Unlike modern society, in which status is defined in great part by wealth and economic function, in most countries during the Old Regime a person's position was fixed by birth and heredity within one of three "estates": the clergy, either of the Roman Catholic or the Protestant churches, the upper levels of which were often linked by family ties to the nobility; the noble élites, who possessed an array of legal powers and privileges; and the overwhelming bulk of society, consisting of the rural peasantry and several groups which lived in the towns—the artisans who were members of highly restrictive guilds, manual laborers, and a small but growing commercial middle class whose ranks would be swelled in the course of the industrial revolution. Christian doctrine offered divine sanction for this social order, while in the absolutist system of 18th-century France, it was reflected in an elected national body known as the Estates General, whose powers were vague and its convocation subject to royal will.

The social system of the Old Regime was deliberately based on the notion of inequality and difference, and during the 18th century the hierarchical structure of society actually grew more rigid. In some parts of Europe, so-called sumptuary laws, which regulated extravagance in food or dress, were designed to make social distinctions visible by prohibiting people in one order from wearing clothes worn by those in a higher order. In other countries, members of the middle class were forbidden to marry into noble families, while nobles generally could not be members of guilds or engage in commerce.

Such laws were, however, largely unnecessary, for the social hierarchy was maintained by the constraints of the community of which one was a member. Most 18th-century Europeans did not expect to exercise the "natural rights" of which Locke and the *philosophes* spoke. Rather, citizens had access to special privileges and bore certain responsibilities only in so far as they were members of a given group or community—the nobility or the clergy, a town, a village, or a guild. The nobles, for example, were exempt from direct taxation and could expect certain services from the peasants who worked their land, while the church collected an annual offering known as the *tithe*. In a similar fashion, members of artisan guilds enjoyed the exclusive right to engage in their craft, while inhabitants of a particular village might have access to certain grazing lands or forests. Law books published during the period testify to the fact that these distinctions were imbedded in the legal systems of individual states.

Tradition was the moral basis of 18th-century society. Most people, guided by a belief in a divinely sanctioned order and the experience of their ancestors, did not want or expect change. If people—whether nobles or peasants—expressed grievances against the existing order, more often than not it was because their traditional rights had been undermined by the ever-expanding power of the central government.

Despite these rigid patterns of thought and behavior, the society of the Old Regime was neither uniform nor static. Indeed, it was distinguished by the startling contrast—sharper perhaps than in modern industrial societies—between the lives of people in each of the social orders. The highest ranks of society displayed refined tastes and manners, lived on magnificent estates, and enjoyed a luxurious standard of living; the less fortunate peasants and the urban destitute lived in extreme poverty. Sharp differences also existed within the orders as well as from region to region. While some nobles were very wealthy, others were hardly distinguishable from the wealthier peasants in their communities. Within the church, the economic and social differences between a bishop and a village priest were sharp. Similarly, while most peasants in Western Europe lived well above the subsistence level and enjoyed some legal status, those in Eastern Europe generally tended to be serfs or existed in dire economic straits. In countries with strong commercial economies, such as Britain and the Netherlands, the middle classes were growing rapidly in wealth and status, whereas they hardly existed in the Holy Roman Empire or Russia.

The Growth in Population

One of the most powerful sources of change in the 18th century stemmed from shifting demographic patterns. Europe's population had experienced periods of growth throughout its history, although disease or warfare had at times depopulated parts of the Continent. About mid-century, however, the population began to increase at a startling rate. Population figures for this period can only be estimates rather than exact numbers, for most countries did not conduct census surveys until the 19th century and accurate figures were available only much later. Nevertheless, it is clear that between 1700 and 1800, the number of inhabitants in Europe almost doubled, from slightly more than 100 million to about 190 million, and by 1850 the population had increased to over 265 million. The demographic growth pattern, which continued well into the 19th century at rates varying from 40 to 60 percent, was more rapid in Western and Central Europe but occurred almost everywhere, in rural as well as urban areas.

In England (including Wales), the population increased from 5.5 million to more than 9 million in the century after 1700, and reached 14 million by 1831. France, the most populous western European country at the beginning of the 18th century, grew from 16–17 million to more than 24 million by the time of the Revolution of 1789. Even in 18th-century Russia the demographic pattern repeated itself, with the population growing from 18 to 30 million.

The causes of this dramatic explosion in population are much debated. One theory holds that in traditional agricultural societies the birthrate tends to remain relatively high, so that declining mortality rates explain population growth. Yet while it is true that the annual death rate generally declined from the 18th century onward, in many areas of Southern and Eastern Europe, as well as in large cities, the rate of deaths did not fall below that of births until after 1850. Similarly, strong population growth occurred before the most important advances in medicine could have affected infant mortality and adult health. Nor can it be argued that the industrial revolution itself caused the demographic explosion, for the upward movement of population began before industrialization.

Food supply appears to have been the most significant factor in the growth of population. Scholars have found that up to the 18th century, English demographic growth reflected a relationship between marriage patterns and the availability of food. In periods of population growth, when the demand for food was greater, prices for basic staples rose. Since even in good times the poorer classes lived close to the edge of subsistence, higher food prices—which meant, in effect, a reduction in real wages—tended to discourage marriage in order to avoid the financial burden of maintaining a family. On the other hand, population decline lowered the demand for food and deflated prices, which in turn made marriage—and children—more feasible.

Ireland proved a tragic case in point. Despite the extreme poverty of its peasants, Ireland's population spiraled upward from 2.5 million in the early 1700s to more than 5 million by 1800, a growth rate sustained into the 1840s. A major impetus to the tradition of early marriage and the high birth rates that characterized the Irish was the introduction of the potato from the New World in the late 16th century. Over the following centuries, the widespread planting of the easily cultivated potato increased food supply substantially, for a peasant family could subsist on a potato harvest grown on a third to a fourth less land than that required for grain. But when a blight struck the potato crop repeatedly between 1845 and 1851, the resulting famines were devastating—more than a million people died, and 2 million left Ireland for England and the United States. By the end of the 19th century, the population was halved and the pattern of early marriages reversed.

Over the course of the 18th century, fundamental changes transformed the society of the Old Regime. The depressed economic conditions prevalent in the

Map 10.1 Growth of European Population, c. 1800–1850

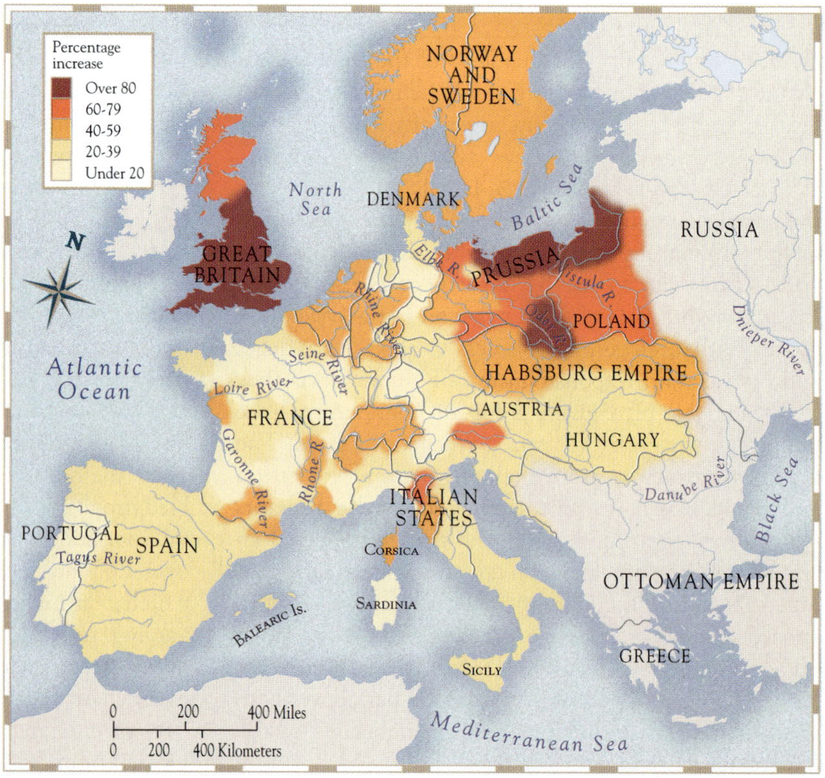

The Village School by Jan Steen (c. 1665), showing a teacher about to discipline a child.

17th century slowly improved. Along with the demographic growth, rapid commercial and financial expansion took place. Most significant of all, Europe was about to experience two far-reaching revolutions, one in agriculture and one in industry (see Part VII, Topic 2).

Marriage and the Family

The family remained the basic unit of European social life. The traditional family was a patriarchy, with the husband wielding authority over wife and children. In upper- and middle-class families, the interests of the family as a whole were generally regarded as taking precedence over those of its individual members, and marriages were usually arranged according to considerations of finance and status.

Throughout Europe, the nuclear family, consisting of parents and children, had been the rule among the upper classes since the 16th century. When finances permitted, married couples set up independent households separate from parents, but young people generally delayed marriage until at least their mid-twenties in order to accumulate sufficient savings. Among noble families, the first-born son usually married at a younger age because his inheritance rights imposed the responsibility to father future heirs.

In Western Europe, where most lower-class couples married in their mid-twenties, the illegitimacy rate was surprisingly low. In mid-century, however, the number of illegitimate children began to increase. In Central Europe, for example, the illegitimacy rate appears to have increased fivefold between 1700 and 1800. The increase in illegitimacy may have been the result of the breakdown of village communities and the weakening role of churches in everyday life.

In any case, the average married couple had five children, and more of them survived infancy and childhood. Several factors, however, acted as a break on the birthrate—about half of all women between the ages of 15 and 44 remained unmarried. Moreover, birth control—achieved by such devices as sheepskin condoms, the vinegar douche, and sponges, and by the application of herbal potions—was being increasingly practiced by the upper classes. Members of noble families generally married younger, but after 1650 declining revenues and the need to keep estates intact contributed to a decline in the average number of children from six to two.

Along with the other developments that began to transform Western society, attitudes toward children began to change. Rousseau, for example, believed that childhood was a stage in human development, and that childhood experiences often proved crucial to adult behavior. And although parental kindness and love did not begin in the Old Regime, a new spirit of humanism and compassion increasingly led parents to treat their offspring as children rather than as small adults, both in their dress, in matters of discipline, and in recreation.

Economically, children were viewed both as a burden and as an opportunity, especially among the lower classes. In peasant families, they were expected to work in the fields or in cottage industries at an early age, and in the towns teenage males were apprenticed in shops. Nevertheless, large numbers of children represented an expense, and in hard times could be a serious burden in poor families. As a result, many parents resorted to infanticide or placed unwanted children in foundling homes, which were supported by private charities. In some large cities, perhaps 30 percent or more of all children were given up by their parents or by unwed mothers. If such unfortunate children survived—mortality rates were shockingly high in these institutions—they were usually sent to workhouses or otherwise exploited.

AGRICULTURE AND THE WORLD OF THE PEASANTRY

European society in the 18th century was still overwhelmingly rural, and the peasantry represented the largest portion of the population—between 80 and 85 percent. Peasant life was harsh and often unrewarding.

Portrait of a peasant family eating black bread and soup, by Louis Le Nain.

Few rural dwellers, except those in military service or on religious pilgrimage, ever traveled much beyond the village where they were born. They ate more or less the same kind of foods that their ancestors had eaten hundreds of years earlier. The staple item in peasant diets was black bread, which provided considerable nourishment. This was supplemented by soups made of grains and vegetables, especially beans, peas, and turnips, and by rice and pastas. By the 18th century, potatoes and tomatoes introduced from the Americas had become important ingredients in the peasant diet. Meat and fish were rarities, especially on the Continent.

Peasants and tenant farmers were constantly dependent on nature, for the productivity of the grain harvest was the crucial fact of life. If the harvest failed, the result could be severe hardship if not starvation.

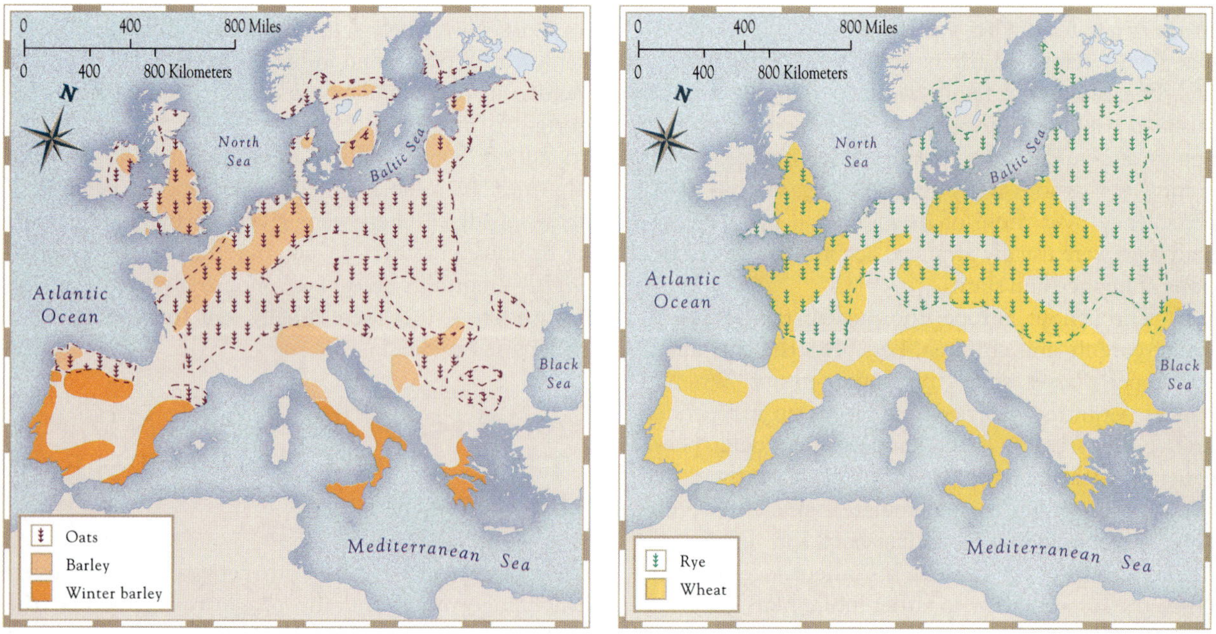

Map 10.2 Grain Production in the 18th Century

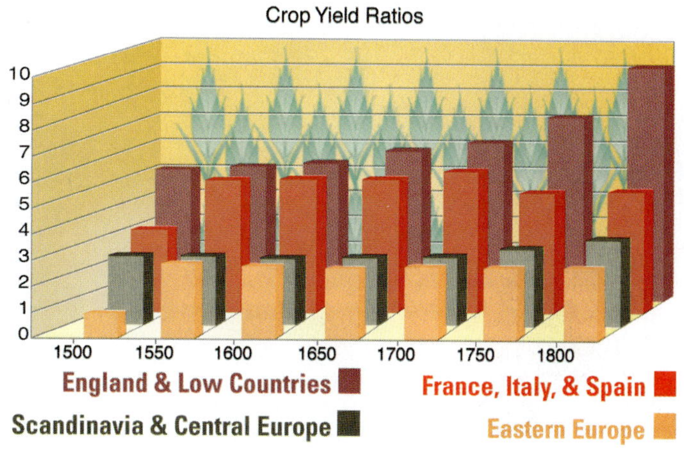

Ironically, in such circumstances rural dwellers found it more difficult to obtain food than did people in towns, where municipalities generally kept reserve supplies. The yield ratio—that is, the relationship between the quantity of seed planted and the quantity of the crop harvested—generally went up in Europe in the 18th century, although with some fluctuations. Market factors also affected peasant existence in a profound way, since bad harvests drove bread prices up. Higher food costs made daily life precarious for peasants, who felt helpless to change their circumstances.

The villages and the immediate countryside around it represented the universe within which the peasants lived and died. Sons learned their father's trade, families intermarried, and loyalty was concentrated in the extended family. The church was the center of civic and religious life, and the priest was often the only local person who had a minimum of literacy. For the peasant, the village community functioned as the real government, for it was responsible for public order, charities, maintaining roads, and enforcing access to common pasture lands and forests. In Western Europe, where rural society was organized around the villages, the owners of small plots would often decide communally what crops to plant. In Eastern Europe, where the land was held in the form of huge estates, the noble landowners made such decisions.

Free Peasants and Serfs

Conditions among the peasantry varied widely from one part of Europe to another. In Western and Central Europe—Britain, France, the Low Countries, Spain, northern Italy, and portions of Germany—most rural dwellers were legally free peasants, although they still faced severe burdens. In places such as Portugal, southern Italy, Sardinia, and Sicily, their lives were overshadowed by stark poverty and the exactions of absentee landowners. In France, slightly more than half the free peasants owned their own land, and these were generally small and inefficient plots. The rest were tenant farmers or day laborers. On the eve of the French Revolution, free peasants still owed nobles tithes as well as special fees—known as *banalités*—for the use of the lord's mill, wine press, and baking oven. In addition to these fees, inherited from the Middle Ages, the peasants also were required to give their lord a number of days of free labor (the *corvée*) each year. Such obligations were bitterly resented. Moreover, in addition to these feudal obligations, the peasantry also bore the burden of taxation, since nobles and the church were normally tax exempt.

The farther east they lived, the greater the degree of authority exercised by landowners over peasants. In Eastern Europe, serfs rather than free peasants predominated. These legally unfree peasants lived and worked on huge estates owned by powerful nobles. At a time when serfdom was being eliminated in most western regions of the Continent, in the 16th and 17th centuries, it became the widespread practice in Eastern Europe. As in the Middle Ages, peasants in Eastern Germany were bound to their lord's estates and could neither marry nor move without their master's consent. By contrast, Russian serfs were bound personally to the landlord, much as slaves, and could be transferred from one estate to another. As we have seen, the Russian monarchs had much to do with the plight of the serfs. Rulers, from Peter the Great to Alexander I, rewarded loyal nobles with huge tracts of state land and the serfs who lived on them. Throughout Eastern Europe the oppressed peasantry and serfs often rose in rebellion against their landlords. In Russia, dozens of revolts in mid-century reached a crisis point in the terrors of the Pugachev Rebellion (1771–1775), brutally crushed by Catherine the Great (see Part VII, Topic 1).

Thomas Gainsborough painted many portraits of the English upper classes enjoying their leisure time, such as this husband and wife.

ARISTOCRATS, URBAN CLASSES, AND THE POOR

Approximately 10 to 15 percent of Europe's population under the Old Regime consisted of the nobility and two urban groups, the middle class and the poor. In sharp contrast to the precarious and harsh existence of the peasantry stood the aristocracy, the social elite that controlled most of the wealth and status in society. The nobles, by far the smallest class in terms of numbers, were long-established in their legally sanctioned privileges and their estates. The middle class, on the other hand, while larger than the nobility, was not yet socially pervasive or powerful. In the larger cities of Europe, such as Paris or Rome, the vast majority of the population was poor, a social fact that presented unexpected challenges to governments and represented a new political element as the Old Regime drew to a close.

The Aristocracy

Aristocrats were by birth at the top of the social hierarchy. Although they represented only a small portion of the overall population—ranging from less than 2 percent to perhaps as much as 5 percent, depending on the country—the nobles dominated society. Among the legal privileges they enjoyed were immunity from certain forms of punishment, exemption from direct taxation, and judgment by their peers. Nobles had the exclusive right to carry swords, to be addressed by special titles, and to hunt on certain properties. Their authority over peasants and serfs, especially in central and eastern Europe, was extensive.

The food the nobility ate was also special, for their meals were elaborate affairs prepared by cooks and presented by servants, consisting of relatively large quantities of meat and fish. Unlike the peasants, they had butter, eggs, cheese, and other dairy products as well as nuts, fruit, and sweets. In addition, while the peasants drank mainly water, or homemade beer and wine, by the mid-18th century the nobles consumed not only the finer wines but coffee and tea.

Since the Middle Ages, the European aristocracy had performed vital military and governmental functions. Feudal lords had, in fact, first received their estates from the king in return for serving as military officers and providing a specified number of soldiers. As the power of the monarchs grew and centralized states developed, nobles continued to hold a virtual monopoly on the highest ranks of the officer caste in most countries. The military represented a dignified career for the younger sons of noble families, most of whom did not inherit the principal estates, and was infused with such aristocratic values as dignity, honor, and hierarchy. Similarly, nobles had once served as advisers to Medieval kings, and in the modern state system they controlled the upper levels of the royal administration. In the late 17th and early 18th centuries, some sovereigns, such as Louis XIV of France and Friedrich Wilhelm I of Prussia, flooded their bureaucracies with commoners in a deliberate effort to weaken the hold of the nobility on the state, although the policy was reversed after 1750. On the provincial level, noble landowners usually had great influence in local affairs, performing duties as magistrates and engaging in poor relief activities.

The major source of noble wealth was revenue derived from their landed estates. Sometimes they obtained money, always in short supply, through inheritance, marriage, or a royal pension. Most nobles turned their noses up at the thought of earning income from such business activities as trade or finance, and in some countries were prohibited from doing so. But as some segments of the nobility found their revenues from agriculture diminishing by the end of the century, they were more willing to take advantage of the nonagricultural resources available on their lands, and set up mining operations, foundries, and other commercial activities.

Like the peasantry, the aristocracy was not a compact or uniform social group. In England, many

The Oyster Luncheon (1731), in which French aristocrats are shown overindulging in food and drink.

"First Reading of Voltaire's *L'orphelin de Chine*" illustrates a salon discussion in 1725, presided over by a wealthy woman (pictured here in blue dress and black bonnet at right).

landowners rented their land to tenant farmers. In Prussia, on the other hand, the Junkers managed their estates directly with a labor force still comprised of serfs, as was the case in Russia. Yet because the number of noble landowners was declining in Prussia—by 1789 some two-thirds of the Junkers no longer possessed estates—the legal code of 1794 prohibited nonnobles from owning land; in Russia, on the other hand, increasing numbers of nobles were being given large estates by the monarchy. In both countries, they served in government positions, while in Spain and the Italian states they did so only at the highest levels.

Differences in wealth, education, and political power also led to differences within countries as well. In France, where there were somewhere between 110,000 and 350,000 nobles out of a total population of 20 million, there was a sharp distinction between the older families and those of more recent origin. For example, only families with ancestries going back before the year 1400—and these numbered a mere 942—enjoyed "Honors of the Court," which permitted them to be presented to the king and hunt with the royal party. Moreover, while some nobles were immensely wealthy, others were quite poor. In France, 250 aristocratic families had incomes of more than 50,000 livres a year, and more than half the nobles had incomes of only 4000 livres. More to the point, 20 percent of all nobles earned less than 1000 livres, a sum equivalent to the income of many peasants. In Eastern Europe, the nobility made up a larger proportion of the overall population, but many—perhaps the majority—were landless and grew progressively poorer. In Venice, where the nobility had derived its wealth from commercial activity, the decline of Mediterranean trade reduced the number of nobles significantly in the 18th century, and in Europe as a whole, the ranks of the aristocracy declined by perhaps as much as one-third.

The nobility, especially those of ancient lineage, jealously guarded their privileges and status, but financial difficulties or state policy often led to new blood entering the ranks. Some noble titles, for instance, were inseparable from the ownership of particular estates, so that commoners who were able to buy that property were also buying noble status. In France, there were about 3700 offices held by royal appointment which automatically gave noble status to their holders. During the course of the 18th century, the king ennobled between 6500 and 10,000 people.

For the most prestigious noble families, the center of life was at the royal court, where proximity to the sovereign was an exclusive privilege. Those nobles who lived at Louis XIV's palace at Versailles enjoyed special honors, although their lives were constantly guided by the will, and sometimes the whim, of the king. Most nobles, however, lived on their country estates, away from the center of power and the largely ceremonial society of the court. Their large houses were symbols of their status and dominance in rural districts. In England, landed aristocrats might own houses in London, and many French nobles built a *hôtel* (townhouse) for visits to the capital, but most spent their time in the country.

In country houses, where an extended noble family could live in relative privacy, the interior layout was designed for a number of particular purposes. Hosts would greet their guests in a grand entrance hall on the ground floor, while common spaces—a drawing room, a dining room, a library or study, and perhaps a conservatory—were designed for entertaining. A large staircase off the entrance led to the upstairs quarters, including the bedrooms and rooms reserved for family activities and other private circumstances. Servants were housed in their own wing of rooms, while gardeners usually lived in separate cottages on the estate.

Cities and the Middle Class

In the 18th century, urban dwellers were a minority of the population in most countries, with the exception of states with long-standing commercial experience such as England and the Dutch Republic. London was the largest European city, with a population of about 1 million, while Paris was only half that size. Some 20 cities, including Rome, Amsterdam, St. Petersburg, and Vienna, had more than 100,000 inhabitants. The rapid growth of Europe's cities would come in the 19th century, when industrialization drew large numbers of rural dwellers to urban centers.

The social and economic differences between Eastern and Western Europe also affected the role and importance of cities in each region. In Eastern Europe, cities tended to be smaller in size, less cosmopolitan, and subject to more direct government control. In the West, they had larger populations and more diverse ones and often enjoyed a greater degree of municipal self-government. In commercial cities, such as Amsterdam, Venice, and Frankfurt, élite oligarchies of nobles and merchants still dominated city councils. In the states in southern Italy and Spain, landed nobles were often absentee landlords who left their estates to the management of overseers and preferred to live in the cities, where they could be close to the royal courts and more sophisticated urban amenities.

Despite the fact that rural dwellers greatly outnumbered those who lived in cities, urban centers exerted considerable influence on European society. In addition to serving as the seats of national and regional governments, large cities were centers of education and culture, of foreign ideas and influences, and of economic activity. Peasants in the hinterland often resented the towns, which they saw as parasites exploiting the countryside by draining food and other resources while serving as dangerous sources of immorality for village youth.

Urban populations were composites of the evolving social structures of 18th-century Europe. At the top stood the nobles and patrician families, virtually a noble class who, although they often controlled city governments, constituted a small fraction of the population. Below these élite groups were the wealthiest layers of the middle classes, who were bankers, merchants, officeholders, and those who lived off rents from the countryside. Some of these urban businessmen were wealthier than many nobles, but they were outranked in social prestige and status. At the lower rungs of middle-class society were the professionals, such as lawyers, physicians, and lower-level bureaucrats, men of education and talent for whom the ideas of equality had a particularly vivid meaning. It was from this professional group that the French Revolution of 1789 would draw many of its leaders.

The lower middle class, larger still, consisted mainly of shopkeepers and artisans. The latter category, however, was divided between the masters, who owned the guild workshops, and those who worked in them. Once they became sufficiently skilled, apprentices could become journeymen, and eventually masters. However, the guilds that regulated the workshops and trades increasingly dealt with growing competition by restricting membership to family connection, so that skilled artisans often had to take lower-paying jobs. At the bottom of the urban social hierarchy were the unskilled working classes, who served as manual laborers and household servants and generally lived at the edge of poverty.

The Urban Poor

Poverty was a serious problem in 18th-century society. It was endemic to the countryside, where increasingly efficient farming required less labor, and where fluctuations in the price of grain had a devastating impact on peasant families. Poverty was especially visible in the cities, where streets were sometimes lined with beggars. For the poor, living conditions were often worse in the cities, where the death rate remained high throughout the 18th century. This was particularly true of children, who were more susceptible to disease caused by overcrowding, bad water, and the almost universal lack of sewers. By the end of the century, perhaps 10 percent of the entire populations of Britain and France lived on

William Hogarth's engravings of life in London were often biting social commentary. In "Gin Lane" (1750) he attacked the evils of alcoholism.

charity or begging. An English Poor Law passed in 1601 made begging illegal, but provided employment on public projects. Some cities, such as Venice, where as much as 20 percent of the city's population was without employment, granted municipal licenses to the poor to beg and live off of the largesse of the many well-to-do tourists who flocked to the city each year. In spite of a tradition of Christian teaching that the poor were God's blessed children, changing social mores made the attitude among the middle classes more harsh. Some political economists, for example, insisted that charity only induced the poor to lead useless lives and encouraged crime. The role of the state in dealing with the problem was still affected by such prejudice, as witnessed by the fact that in the mid-1700s in France beggars and vagrants were still subject to arrest and imprisonment, although their only crime was unemployment. On the eve of the French Revolution, the French adopted policies similar to those in England and Holland, where public works projects provided some jobs. Private charitable groups, particularly religious orders, provided much needed assistance, but the growing problem of poverty overwhelmed such efforts. Poverty remained an ugly and pervasive reality of life in 18th-century Europe.

WOMEN AND THE OLD REGIME

Women were subordinate to men in every society of the Old Regime. Throughout Europe, women had few legal rights of their own. In many societies, women could not own property directly or sue on their own in courts of law. In such cases, fathers, husbands, or other male relatives would manage estates or represent women. In Britain, a husband exercised total control over his wife's property, unless marriage contracts stipulated otherwise. In most cases husbands could file for separation but wives could not, although courts in France and England began to offer some measure of protection for women whose spouses mismanaged their estates. Some women, of course, exercised power as rulers, while the authority of others varied within a particular family setting. But for the overwhelming majority of women, their role was limited to family responsibilities, reproduction, and the rearing of children, along with work that could be performed in the home. By the end of the 18th century, however, some aspects of the lives of women had begun to change. In aristocratic and upper-middle-class circles, women played an increasingly important role in intellectual life, while among the working classes the industrial revolution would begin to bring many women out of the home and into the factory.

Childbirth and its attendant risks remained a constant issue for most young women of all classes. Because the church maintained the view that sexual activity between husband and wife was legitimate only for the purpose of having children, it condemned all forms of contraception except abstinence. Nevertheless, the increasing use of birth control, especially among the upper classes, enabled some women to limit or escape the burdens of childrearing. While abortion was similarly prohibited by the church, it too was widely practiced.

Women and Work

In every historical epoch, women have worked and made important economic contributions, whether in peasant societies or in cities. In the countryside, wives and daughters generally worked in the fields alongside male family members, particularly to harvest crops, and were central to the so-called cottage industry, where families worked in the home to produce textiles and some finished goods (see Part VII, Topic 2). Often, while husbands planted and tended cereal crops, women raised vegetables for family consumption, made cheese and butter, cared for livestock, and sold excess eggs and milk in village markets.

In cities, women from the laboring class worked as household servants for the wealthy—40 percent of all British working women fell into this category—or worked as seamstresses and laundresses. Some women also sold vegetables, fish, and other foodstuffs in city markets, where such women were important elements in the urban economy. Among the lower rungs of the middle classes, wives and daughters served as salesclerks in family shops or helped their artisan husbands informally in craft workshops. It should be noted, however, that much female work of this kind was undertaken as part of a family business, usually within or near the home, and that women's labor was seen by society as a nonessential contribution to the labor of males. In reality, however, among the poor and laboring classes, women's labor often made the difference between survival and destitution.

The coming of the industrial revolution toward the end of the century altered the way women worked. In the new textile factories, women actually represented a significant portion of the workforce—indeed, in cotton mills women and children often made up a large majority. Managers believed that women, like children, could be disciplined more easily than adult men. As late as the mid-19th century, however, almost half of all British and French working women still worked, respectively, as domestic servants or in farming.

Traditional attitudes toward women provided a number of rationalizations for the division of labor along gender lines, a condition that existed both in agriculture and in cottage industry and that persisted in the new factory system. Factory owners assigned men and women workers different tasks. Men were virtually always managers and supervisors. Sometimes differences were a result of women not having had the opportunity to learn certain skills, and sometimes because particular jobs required greater physical strength than others. On the other hand, it was also believed that men and women could not work together without leading to social fraternization and sexual liaisons, both of which would adversely affect productivity. Wherever women worked in the factories, they were almost always supervised by men.

Upper-Class Women

Among the upper-middle and nobles classes, the role of women was far different. In both groups, family wealth freed them from having to earn an income. In middle-class and gentry families, women managed household establishments, while aristocratic women, who had large retinues of staff, enjoyed considerable leisure, which was used either for personal improvement such as music and reading or for social visits.

Wealthy women played an increasingly large role in the organization and functioning of their homes in the late 18th century. Interior decor became more comfortable and "feminine" in appearance, while wives would often entertain female friends in the afternoons over tea or cards. In the evenings, after formal dinner parties, the men usually remained in the dining room or retired to the library for tobacco and brandy, while the women retired to the drawing room for conversation and sweets. During the 18th century, however, some aristocratic women presided over a mixed company of men and women in their own salons, where intellectual discussions took place (on the salon see Part VI, Topic 7).

In the royal courts of Europe, women played still other roles and encountered different opportunities. There, in the extravagant world of luxury, high politics, and intrigue, wives of noblemen were expected to be accomplished in the social graces, not only in order to preside at elaborate dinners and balls, but to flatter and influence men of influence. Some served in official capacities as ladies-in-waiting to the queen, a position from which they could acquire considerable influence of their own.

Despite the privilege that aristocratic women enjoyed, they shared with their lower-class sisters a series of proscriptions and burdens that were mapped out by convention, by their parents, and by the cultural constructs of gender. Not least of the difficulties they faced

PUBLIC FIGURES AND PRIVATE LIVES

JEANNE BÉCU DU BARRY AND LOUIS XV

One of the most successful courtesans in 18th-century Europe was Marie Jeanne Bécu, the Comtesse du Barry (1743–1793), mistress to the French sovereign, Louis XV. Her life was a case study in the limits and constraints of women in the Old Regime.

She was born Jeanne Bécu, the illegitimate daughter of a young woman from the village of Vaucouleurs. In 1748, her family moved to Paris, where the mother worked as a cook in the home of a wealthy businessman. Jeanne was taken into a convent at the age of seven, where she learned the rudiments of reading and writing, and left when she was 16.

The beautiful and quick-witted Jeanne found employment as a clerk in a millinery shop and had a number of affairs with married men. In 1763, she met in a gambling house the Count Jean du Barry (the title actually belonged to a brother), an adventurer who moved in the Paris underworld as well as in aristocratic circles. Du Barry ran a profitable business as a procurer of young women for his noble friends. She served as hostess in his home, where she befriended many important aristocrats.

In 1768 she married Jean's brother, the real Count du Barry, in order to appear at the court, and that summer she met the 58-year-old king privately at Versailles. Louis was particularly lonely at the time, for his wife had died a month earlier and he was without a *maîtresse-en-titre*, or official mistress. Jeanne-Antoinette Poisson, better known as Madame de Pompadour (1721–1764), the immensely influential royal mistress for 20 years, had died some years earlier. Louis was captivated.

Jeanne could not become the new *maîtresse-en-titre* until she was officially "presented" at court, a move that was blocked by a conspiracy between the foreign minister the Duke de Choiseul—who hoped his own sister would become the royal mistress—and the ambassador from Vienna, who wanted nothing to interfere with his attempt to persuade Louis to marry an Austrian princess. The anti–du Barry party at court did everything it could to prevent the presentation, but to no avail—in April 1769, she entered the royal chamber, resplendent in formal dress and diamonds. She was given her own apartment in the palace and a retinue of servants, and over the years Louis bestowed sumptuous gifts on her, including a chateau. The Duke de Choiseul was dismissed the next year.

Jeanne du Barry's success was short-lived. She chose not to exercise her influence in political matters, preferring instead to be a patron of the arts. Nevertheless, she remained immensely unpopular at a court that was increasingly bent on extravagance and intrigue, a fact that contributed to the decline of the monarchy's prestige in the decades before the revolution. On the death of Louis in 1774, she was banished to a nunnery, where she remained for two years, and then was allowed to move to her private estate. She lived there with a lover, the Duke de Brissac, until the outbreak of revolution in 1789, traveling to London in order to aid the noble émigrés living in exile. By the time she had returned to France, she had lost much of her famed beauty. In December 1793, during the Reign of Terror, she was condemned as a counterrevolutionary and guillotined.

were the repeated dangers of pregnancy and childbirth.

It was the position of courtesan that held particular fascination and offered opportunities for those women, regardless of the status into which they were born, who were willing to bear the degradation of having sex with their patrons. Prostitutes had, of course, always existed in European society, and like them courtesans obtained rewards by their physical attraction. An enterprising young woman could become the lover and companion of a wealthy aristocrat or a royal patron, perhaps even of the king himself. Yet courtesans had to cultivate many other talents, including the art of flirtation, literary, musical, and conversational skills, and highly polished social charms.

Regardless of religious proscriptions or secular laws against illicit sex, courtesans had been institutionalized by the 18th century in the courts and in society at large. Sexual infidelity had become more commonplace in aristocratic circles, and married couples—men and women alike—felt free to have affairs. In some cities, courtesans were highly paid professionals who had agents and paid special taxes. In the royal courts, talented young women were actually taken under wing and trained by aristocratic male mentors, who would then present their ward to a royal patron in return for any future influence that she might have.

As the 18th century opened, the Old Regime appeared to be safely and permanently entrenched, much as it had been for centuries, a world of privilege, tradition, and hierarchy. Yet before the century was out, that well-ordered society and many of its values had been turned upside down by a revolutionary upheaval that shook all of Europe.

In retrospect, the period was rent with the forces of change. The commercial and financial life of Europe was expanding rapidly, while the population was growing at an unprecedented rate. Both in agriculture and manufacturing, revolutionary transformations were taking place that would have far-reaching repercussions. Even the social structure, which had appeared fixed by divine sanction, was undergoing important adjustments as the old aristocracy was forced to make room for an increasingly aggressive middle class that wanted a share of power and privilege. And throughout Europe, a new intellectual ferment was questioning many of the fundamental premises that underlay the social structure of the Old Regime.

Absolutist government, which rested on the notion of secure social foundations, was itself undergoing change. Some rulers sought to justify their authority by appearing to be "enlightened" and disinterested sovereigns, and all of them struggled to improve the efficiency of their bureaucracies and the power of their arms. To support the growth of central government and the luxury of the royal court, to fight the all-too-frequent wars that marked the century, rulers made more incessant demands for taxes, demands that ultimately produced a rebellion in the New World against the Old, and the political crisis of the Old Regime in France.

Questions for Further Study

1. In what ways was privilege built into the social system of the Old Regime?
2. How was society changing in the 18th century?
3. What differences existed between the aristocrats and the upper reaches of the middle classes?
4. What does the life of Jeanne Bécu du Barry reveal about the lives of women in the Old Regime?

Suggestions for Further Reading

De Vries, Jan. *European Urbanization, 1500–1800.* Cambridge, MA, 1984.

Earle, Peter. *The Making of the English Middle Class: Business, Society, and the Family in London, 1660–1730*. Berkeley, CA, 1989.

Houston, Robert A. *Literacy in Early Modern Europe: Culture and Education, 1500–1800*. New York, 1988.

Jones, R. E. *The Emancipation of the Russian Nobility, 1762–1785*. Princeton, NJ, 1973.

Macfarlane, Alan. *Marriage and Love in England: Modes of Reproduction, 1300–1840*. New York, 1986.

Pollock, Linda A. *Forgotten Children: Parent-Child Relations from 1500 to 1900*. Cambridge, MA, 1984.

Roche, Daniel. *The People of Paris: An Essay in Popular Culture in the Eighteenth Century*, trans. M. Evans. Berkeley, CA, 1987.

Rogers, Katherine. *Feminism in Eighteenth-Century England*. Urbana, IL, 1982.

Stone, Lawrence. *The Family, Sex and Marriage in England, 1500–1800*. New York, 1977.

Traer, James F. *Marriage and the Family in Eighteenth-Century France*. Ithaca, NY, 1980.

VI

Topic 11

The Age of Reason

Toward the end of the 17th century, scientists and intellectuals began to circulate to a wider public the ideas and principles behind 17th-century science. During the 18th century, philosophers applied the same scientific attitudes to broader questions of human behavior. The school of thought that developed was called the Enlightenment, and the period during which it flourished—1740–1790—is often known as the Age of Reason.

The origins of Enlightenment thought lay in the emphasis placed on reason and order by 17th-century thinkers such as Isaac Newton and John Locke. The latter, in particular, advocated the virtues of political and religious freedom, and claimed that human beings were essentially good.

The center of Enlightenment thinking was France, where a group of intellectuals known as the *philosophes* developed a consistent view of the world. The highest power, they believed, was reason used critically, since only by its means could true knowledge be gained. Reason, in turn, reflected the rational essence of Nature, which is ordered, and operates according to logical and unchanging laws. If humans would only follow reason, and abandon the superstitions of traditional religion, with its emphasis on original sin and divine prescription, they could create personal and social progress.

At the same time, Enlightenment thinkers were believers in practical information and experiment. The chief expression of this conviction was the *Encyclopédie*, a vast multi-authored work describing the contemporary state of science, technology, and philosophy. The project's editors were Denis Diderot and Jean Le Rond d'Alembert. In spite of government interference, Diderot managed to bring out 17 volumes of the *Encyclopédie* between 1747 and 1771, and its sales throughout Europe helped to spread the ideas behind the Enlightenment.

The leader in the Enlightenment battle against organized religion was Voltaire. Poet, novelist, historian, Voltaire also wrote on science and philosophy. The most famous intellectual of his time, in the last 25 years of his life Voltaire constantly attacked organized religion—he called it "the infamous thing"—which he believed caused so much bigotry and fanaticism.

Other thinkers dealt with scientific and social issues. Georges Buffon was the first modern classifier of the animal world, while Marie-Jean Condorcet used his work as a mathematician to reinforce his belief that the human race was capable of systematic progress. In Italy, Cesare Beccaria studied new approaches to criminals and their punishment. The Scottish economist Adam Smith, in writing *The Wealth of Nations* (1776), founded economics as a social science.

Although he was one of the contributors to the *Encyclopédie*, Jean-Jacques Rousseau strongly contested the philosophes' notion that civilization would lead to an improved society. On the contrary, he held that humans were good but civilization evil. The way to happiness, therefore, lay in a return to a simple, natural life. An advocate of free love and unrestrained emotion, Rousseau devised a social contract which proposed a new kind of relationship between individuals and their government.

THE SEEDS OF THE ENLIGHTENMENT

The intellectual movement known as the Enlightenment, which reached its peak in the latter part of the 18th century, represented the fusion of several currents of thought from the late 17th century. The scientific revolution had led the way in seeking to understand how the world works, revealing in the process that many of the teachings of traditional Christianity about natural science and astronomy were simply wrong (on the scientific revolution and Isaac Newton, see Part VI, Topic 1). In particular, the works of the great physicist Sir Isaac Newton demonstrated that the universe operated along orderly lines, which the power of human reason was capable of perceiving.

The Philosophy of John Locke

One of the heroic fathers of the Enlightenment was the English philosopher John Locke (1632–1704). In *An Essay Concerning Human Understanding* (1690), Locke discussed the origin and nature of knowledge. At birth, he argued, the human mind was a blank tablet—a *tabula rasa*—that was filled up by sense impressions gained through direct experience. As a result, all human beings were born as equals, whereas status and privilege usually determined the kind of experiences that each person underwent. Education was, therefore, of prime importance in creating a just and equitable society. Locke's empiricism was clearly inspired by the scientific method of Galileo and others.

In a truly revolutionary move, Locke rejected the traditional Christian teaching of original sin, and the traditional political system of monarchy. Instead, he believed in the essential goodness of humanity, and argued that political power should have a broad popular base. In his *Two Treatises on Civil Government* (1690), written in the wake of the English Revolution, Locke posited the contract theory of government, according to which individuals living in a state of nature entered freely into a political compact in order to protect the essential individual rights of life, liberty, and property. Citizens would act loyally toward government, but if government broke its part of the contract by undermining these liberties, then the people had the right to change it (for a selection from Locke's *Second Treatise* see Part VI, Topic 4).

As the scientific revolution had demonstrated, by the use of reason it was possible for humans to make progress in understanding the workings of nature. Similar beneficial change could be created in society by following the same positive course. Although many of the rationalists who followed him abandoned all belief in God, Locke himself was not an atheist and strongly advocated a degree of religious freedom—although not for Catholics, Jews, or atheists.

By the early part of the 18th century, these ideas had begun to crystallize. Thinkers increasingly rejected the past, and looked forward to social and political reform. Custom and tradition, far from being valuable, were the shackles that bound the human race and prevented progress. Hope for humanity lay not in contemplating the rewards of the next life—the existence of which in any case could not be objectively demonstrated—but in concentrating on improvements in the real world. With this optimistic attitude, civilization could reach new heights, and redress many of the existing injustices.

THE *PHILOSOPHES*: THE BATTLE AGAINST SUPERSTITION

The center of Enlightenment thought was France, where its representatives fought a constant battle against the weakening absolutism of Louis XV and the power of the Catholic Church. Important Enlightenment movements developed in Germany and Italy, and Enlightenment ideas also circulated in North America, especially toward the end of the century, where they influenced the first pronouncements of the founding fathers. Eastern Europe was relatively little affected, its rulers being fully aware of the subversive character of Enlightenment doctrines.

In France, the movement's leaders were the *philosophes* (the word means "philosophers" in French). The philosophes were not so much original thinkers as popularizers and propagandizers, who circulated the ideas of others in the form of pamphlets, plays, novels, or works of history.

Few Enlightenment thinkers completely ruled out the possibility of the existence of a divine force in the universe; even the highly skeptical Edinburgh philosopher David Hume (1711–1776) argued only against the provability of such a power. Most of them, however, attacked the power of the clergy and all traditional religious superstition.

In place of the Christian God stood nature—or Nature—whose natural laws benevolently governed the universe. The same order that existed in astronomy and physics could be found in morality, or politics, or even economics. Only by seeking to understand these natural laws and following them could humans achieve happiness. By emphasizing happiness, rather than salvation, the philosophes rejected the traditional Christian view that misery in this life would receive compensation in the next; the Jeffersonian belief in the right of all humans to "the pursuit of happiness," as well as life and liberty, was a typical Enlightenment concept derived from Locke.

Denis Diderot, editor of the *Encyclopédie.*

The concern with general well-being led to protests at the ill-treatment of prisoners and the insane, and condemnation of slavery. Most Enlightenment thinkers were pacifists and internationalists, who saw patriotism—along with religion—as the cause of most wars. Above all, they believed in freedom. The France of Louis XV, although less repressive than that of his predecessor, still maintained restrictions on freedom of speech, religion, trade, and work.

For all their fervor, however, the philosophes were not revolutionaries. They advocated not immediate democracy, but a gradual transition by means of rulers who were "enlightened despots" such as Friedrich II of Prussia (on the Enlightened Despots, see Part VII, Topic 1). They did not aim at radical change, even though many of their ideas inspired the leaders of the French Revolution. Furthermore, Enlightenment thought circulated chiefly among the urban aristocracy and educated middle classes.

In addition, few of the philosophes had much time for women's rights, even though a number of them reached their audience by means of the salons of the more advanced women of the day. By contrast with centuries of earlier thinkers, they acknowledged women's ability to reason, and encouraged female education, but on the whole they accepted the conventional notion of women as inferior to men. The only real attempt to argue for fundamental change, Mary Wollstonecraft's *Vindication of the Rights of Women* (1792), found few sympathizers.

Diderot and the *Encyclopédie*

One of the leading French philosophes, Denis Diderot (1713–1784), sought to provide an organized basis for Enlightenment thought by preparing an immense encyclopedia. He intended the work to describe the contemporary state of science, technology, and philosophy, and at the same time to establish a classification system for human knowledge.

Working with the physicist and mathematician Jean Le Rond d'Alembert (1717–1783) as his co-editor, Diderot began work on the project in 1747; the last of its 17 volumes of text and 11 of engravings appeared in 1771. The *Encyclopédie*, with its articles by various contributors, provided a wealth of information on a

The *philosophes* at supper. They include Voltaire (with left hand raised), Diderot, and Condorcet.

bewildering range of subjects, from metallurgy to political economy to the raising of asparagus.

Implicit in this philosophy was the idea that no political or religious system should try to limit or control the minds of individuals. The authors of the *Encyclopédie* opposed all corporate privilege, in fact, and believed that no group—the guilds, for example—had exclusive rights to any area of knowledge. As the leading German philosopher of the Enlightenment, Immanuel Kant (1724–1804), pointed out, the very essence of the Enlightenment was to "dare to know." If this meant rejecting established wisdom or resisting authority, then the philosophes were prepared to do so. Voltaire had to leave France, Hume was threatened with excommunication (and thus ostracism), and Diderot spent time in jail. Church and government authorities both tried to stop publication of the *Encyclopédie*, or at least censor it, but Diderot succeeded in bringing his project to completion.

An illustration of a laboratory from the *Encyclopédie* of Diderot.

The *Encyclopédie* sold not only in Europe's great cities, but in small provincial towns. It helped an entire generation to see their lives in an entirely fresh way, and led them to challenge hitherto unquestioned assumptions. Its tone of optimism, and its conviction that humans had their destiny in their own hands, powerfully influenced the Declaration of Independence of the new American nation.

Charles-Louis Montesquieu

A more specific influence on the political growth of America was the political philosophy of one of the contributors to the *Encyclopédie*, Charles-Louis Montesquieu (1689–1755). Aristocratic by birth, Montesquieu argued against the abolition of monarchy. His ideal system of government was based upon a division of powers between king, lords, and commons. This separation of powers would, he believed, create a series of "checks and balances" capable of safeguarding personal liberty. The framers of the American Constitution adapted the principle, transforming Montesquieu's three divisions into the executive, judicial, and legislative branches of government.

Montesquieu's other important contribution to the study of politics was his book *The Spirit of the Laws* (1748). In it he claimed that different forms of government were appropriate to different geographical conditions. Small states such as Venice or 5th-century B.C. Athens were best suited by a republican government, whereas vast countries like Russia required an absolute monarchy. Pioneering in its aims, Montesquieu's work was the first serious attempt to examine the relationship between politics and environment.

"THE INFAMOUS THING": VOLTAIRE AND NATURAL MORALITY

Perhaps the most versatile genius produced by the Enlightenment—if less original than Diderot—was François-Marie Arouet (1694–1778), best known to us as Voltaire, his pen name. As a writer, Voltaire moved with ease from drama to satire to history. His studies included science and politics. He was an honored guest at the courts of Louis XV and Friedrich II, but also spent time in prison. Above all, Voltaire was fully committed to the great issues and battles of his times. An enemy of all forms of tyranny, he spent most of his life in exile.

His early satirical writings pilloried French aristocratic society, and won him a jail sentence in the Bastille (1717–1718). Undeterred, he continued with an epic poem on Henry IV of France, which he published in 1723. After he spent another few months in prison in 1726, the authorities released him on the condition that he left France.

Voltaire chose to spend his exile in England, where the system of government seemed to him far more just and liberal than that of France. Returning home in 1729, he wrote his *Letters on the English* (first published in English in 1733; in French in 1734), extolling English social and political liberalism and religious toleration, and praising the ideas of Newton and Locke. In advocating the experimental approach to science, he held that doubt is the beginning of wisdom and the basis of tolerance. Humans should limit themselves to observing and measuring, and to trying to improve the lot of their fellow mortals, a theme to which he constantly returned.

His contemporaries were enraged by the book's attack on French society and political institutions, and the uproar it created drove him out of Paris into the

The French writer and philosopher Voltaire, perhaps the leading figure of the Enlightenment.

DOCUMENTS ON HISTORY

The Age of Reason

The Enlightenment was known as the Age of Reason because the philosophes argued that superstition, faith, and tradition should be replaced by logic, scientific inquiry, and a secular spirit of the quest for knowledge of the natural laws that governed the universe. These principles informed the works of all the major writers of the era.

THE NATURE OF ENLIGHTENMENT

The German thinker Immanuel Kant, whose complex philosophical system rejected a simpleminded mechanistic understanding of truth and skepticism, explained the meaning of "enlightenment" in an essay of 1784, in which he stressed the fundamental importance of freedom of discussion.

Enlightenment is man's release from his self-incurred tutelage. Tutelage is man's inability to make use of his understanding without direction from another. Self-incurred is this tutelage when its cause lies not in lack of reason but in lack of resolution and courage to use it without direction from another. *Sapere aude!*[1] "Have courage to use your own reason!"—that is the motto of enlightenment.

Laziness and cowardice are the reasons why so great a portion of mankind, after nature has long since discharged them from external direction . . . , nevertheless remains under lifelong tutelage, and why it is so easy for others to set themselves up as their guardians. It is so easy not to be of age. If I have a book which understands for me, a pastor who has a conscience for me, a physician who decides my diet, and so forth, I need not trouble myself. I need not think, if I can only pay—others will readily undertake the irksome work for me.

That the step in competence is held to be very dangerous by the far greater portion of mankind (and by the entire fair sex)—quite apart from its being arduous—is seen to by those guardians who have so kindly assumed superintendence over them. After the guardians have first made their domestic cattle dumb and have made sure that these placid creatures will not dare take a single step without the harness of the cart to which they are tethered, the guardians then show them the danger which threatens if they try to go alone. Actually, however, this danger is not so great, for by falling a few times they would finally

[1] "Dare to know!", the motto of the Society of the Friends of Truth.

learn to walk alone. But an example of this failure makes them timid and ordinarily frightens them away from all further trials.

For any single individual to work himself out of the life under tutelage which has become almost his nature is very difficult. He has come to be fond of this state, and he is for the present really incapable of making use of his reason, for no one has ever let him try it out. Statutes and formulas, those mechanical tools of the rational employment or rather misemployment of his natural gifts, are the fetters of an everlasting tutelage. Whoever throws them off makes only an uncertain leap over the narrowest ditch because he is not accustomed to that kind of free motion. Therefore, there are few who have succeeded by their own exercise of mind both in freeing themselves from incompetence and in achieving a steady pace. . . .

From Immanuel Kant, "What Is Enlightenment?" in L. W. Beck, ed. and trans., *Immanuel Kant on History.* Macmillan, Copyright © 1963.

ON METHOD

René Descartes (1596–1650) was one of the leading figures of the scientific revolution. Perhaps his greatest contribution to the Enlightenment is the set of principles he enunciated in 1637 on the proper method to be followed in pursuing "scientific" truth.

I believed that the four [principles] following would prove perfectly sufficient for me, provided I took the firm and unwavering resolution never in a single instance to fail in observing them.

The *first* was never to accept anything for true which I did not clearly know to be such; that is to say, carefully to avoid precipitancy and prejudice, and to comprise nothing more in my judgment than what was presented to my mind so clearly and distinctly as to exclude all ground of doubt.

The *second,* to divide each of the difficulties under examination into as many parts as possible, and as might be necessary for its adequate solution.

The *third,* to conduct my thoughts in such order that, by commencing with objects the simplest and easiest to know, I might ascend by little and little, and, as it were, step by step, to the knowledge of the more complex; assigning in thought a certain order even to those objects which in their own nature do not stand in a relation of antecedence and sequence.

And the *last,* in every case to make enumerations so complete, and reviews so general, that I might be assured that nothing was omitted.

The long chains of simple and easy reasonings by means of which geometers are accustomed to reach the conclusions of their most difficult demonstrations, had led me to imagine that all things, to the knowledge of which man is competent, are mutually connected in the same way, and that there is nothing so far removed from us as to be beyond our reach, or so hidden that we cannot discover it, provided only we abstain from accepting the false for the true, and always preserve in our thoughts the order necessary for the deduction of one truth from another. . . .

From Brian Tierney, Donald Kagan, and L. Pearce Williams, eds., *Great Issues in Western Civilization,* 4th ed., Vol. II. McGraw-Hill, Copyright © 1992.

NATURAL LAW

Most of the philosophes believed that the universe and the human condition were based on natural law, and that a discovery of truth could be achieved by understanding those laws. The following extract is from an article by Denis Diderot written for his Encyclopédie.

continued next page

In its broadest sense the term [natural law] is taken to designate certain principles which nature alone inspires and which all animals as well as all men have in common. On this law are based the union of male and female, the begetting of children as well as their education, love of liberty, self-preservation, concern for self-defense.

It is improper to call the behavior of animals natural law, for, not being endowed with reason, they can know neither law nor justice.

More commonly we understand by natural law certain laws of justice and equity which only natural reason has established among men, or better, which God has engraved in our hearts.

The fundamental principles of law and all justice are: to live honestly, not to give offense to anyone, and to render unto each whatever is his. From these general principles derive a great many particular rules which nature alone, that is, reason and equity, suggest to mankind. . . .

It would not be proper for men to live without rules; rules presuppose a final goal; that of man is to aspire to happiness; this is the system of Providence; it is the essential desire of man, inseparable from reason which is man's basic guide. Since true happiness cannot be incompatible with the nature and condition of man, rules of conduct consist in a distinction between good and evil, in a comparison of past and present, in not seeking a good that may give rise to greater evil, in accepting a small evil if it is followed by a great good, in giving preference to the greatest good, in certain cases in being persuaded only by probability or verisimilitude and finally in acquiring the inclination toward the truly good.

In order really to know natural law, one has to understand what is meant by obligation in general. Law taken as power produces obligations; rights and obligations are several: some are natural, others are acquired; some are such that they cannot be rigidly fulfilled, others cannot be renounced. These obligations are also distinguished by their object. For instance, there is the right we have over ourselves, which is called liberty; the right of property or estate over things that belong to us; the right one has over the person or actions of another, which is called sovereignty or authority; finally the right one can have over things belonging to someone else, which is also of several kinds.

Man, by nature a dependent being, must take law as the rule of his action, for law is nothing other than a rule set down by the sovereign. The true foundations of sovereignty are power, wisdom, and goodness combined. The goal of laws is not to impede liberty but to direct properly all man's actions.

From *Encyclopedia:* Selections by Denis Diderot, D'Alembert.

THE PRINCIPLES OF MORALS

David Hume (1711–1776), perhaps the most important English philosopher of the 18th century, sought to understand the world beyond the senses. In this essay from 1751 on the nature of morals, he revealed his belief that morality was capable of scientific, rational analysis.

There has been a controversy started of late, much better worth examination, concerning the general foundation of MORALS; whether they be derived from REASON or from SENTIMENT; whether we attain the knowledge of them by a chain of argument and induction, or by an immediate feeling and finer internal sense; whether, like all sound judgment of truth and falsehood, they should be the same to every rational intelligent being; or whether, like the perception of beauty and deformity, they be founded entirely on the particular fabric and constitution of the human species. . . .

It must be acknowledged, that both sides of the question are susceptible of specious arguments. Moral distinctions, it may be said, are discernible by pure *reason:* else, whence the many disputes that reign in common life, as well as in philosophy, with regard to this subject; the long chain of proofs often produced on both sides, the example cited, the authorities appealed to, the analogies employed, the fallacies detected, the inferences drawn, and the several conclusions adjusted to their proper principles? Truth is disputable; not taste: what exists in the nature of things is the standard of our judgment: what each man feels within himself is the standard of sentiment. Propositions in geometry may be proved, systems in physics may be controverted; but the harmony of verse, the tenderness of passion, the brilliancy of wit, must give immediate pleasure. No man reasons concerning another's beauty; but frequently concerning the justice or injustice of his actions. . . .

The end of all moral speculations is to teach us our duty; and, by proper representations of the deformity of vice and beauty of virtue, beget correspondent habits, and engage us to avoid the one, and embrace the other. But is this ever to be expected from inferences and conclusions of the understanding, which of themselves have no hold of the affections, or set in motion the active powers of men? They discover truths: but where the truths which they discover are indifferent, and beget no desire or aversion, they can have no influence on conduct and behaviour. What is honourable, what is fair, what is becoming, what is noble, what is generous, takes possession of the heart, and animates us to embrace and maintain it. What is intelligible, what is evident, what is probable, what is true, procures only the cool assent of the understanding; and gratifying a speculative curiosity, puts an end to our researches.

Extinguish all the warm feeling and prepossessions in favour of virtue, and all disgust or aversion to vice; render men totally indifferent towards these distinctions; and morality is no longer a practical study, nor has any tendency to regulate our lives and actions.

These arguments on each side (and many more might be produced) are so plausible, that I am apt to suspect they may, the one as well as the other, be solid and satisfactory, and that *reason* and *sentiment* concur in almost all moral determinations and conclusions. The final sentence, it is probable, which pronounces characters and actions amiable, or odious, praiseworthy or blameable; that which stamps on them the mark of honour or infamy, approbation or censure; that which renders morality an active principle, and constitutes virtue our happiness, and vice our misery: it is probable, I say, that this final sentence depends on some internal sense or feeling, which nature has made universal in the whole species. For what else can have an influence of this nature? But in order to pave the way for such a sentiment, and give a proper discernment of its object, it is often necessary, we find, that much reasoning should precede, that nice distinctions be made, just conclusions drawn, distant comparisons formed, complicated relations examined, and general facts fixed and ascertained. Some species of beauty, especially the natural kinds, on their first appearance, command our affection and approbation; and where they fail of this effect, it is impossible for any reasoning to redress their influence, or adapt them better to our taste and sentiment. But in many orders of beauty, particularly those of the finer arts, it is requisite to employ much reasoning, in order to feel the proper sentiment; and a false relish may frequently be corrected by argument and reflection. There are just grounds to conclude that moral beauty partakes much of this latter species, and demands the assistance of our intellectual faculties, in order to give it a suitable influence on the human mind.

David Hume, *An Inquiry Concerning the Principles of Morals,* Section I.

THE IDEA OF PROGRESS

Marie-Jean Caritat, the marquis de Condorcet, was one of the leading French philosophes. In the essay that follows, he explains the idea of progress, a fundamental principle of Enlightenment thought that explained history and the future of humankind.

continued next page

The aim of the book that I have undertaken to write, and what it will prove, is that man by using reason and facts will attain perfection. Nature has set no limits to the perfection of the human faculties. The perfectibility of mankind is truly indefinite; and the progress of this perfectibility, henceforth to be free of all hindrances, will last as long as the globe on which nature has placed us. Doubtless his progress will be more or less rapid, but it will never be retrograde, at least as long as the globe occupies its present place in the system of the universe; and unless the general laws that govern this system bring to pass a universal cataclysm, or such changes as will prevent man from maintaining his existence, from using his faculties, and from finding his needed resources. . . .

Since the period when alphabetical writing flourished in Greece the history of mankind has been linked to the condition of men of our time in the most enlightened countries of Europe by an unbroken chain of facts and observations. The picture of the march and progress of the human mind is now revealed as being truly historical. Philosophy no longer has to guess, no longer has to advance hypothetical theories. It now suffices to assemble and to arrange the facts, and to show the truths that arise from their connection and from their totality. . . .

If man can predict with almost complete certainty those phenomena whose laws he knows; and if, when he does not know these laws, he can, on the basis of his experience in the past, predict future events with assurance why then should it be regarded as chimerical to trace with a fair degree of accuracy the picture of man's future on the basis of his history? The sole foundation for belief in the natural sciences is the principle that universal laws, known or unknown, which regulate the universe are necessary and constant. Why then should this principle be less true for the development of the intellectual and moral faculties of man than it is for the other operations of nature? Finally, since beliefs, based on past experience under like conditions, constitute the only rule according to which the wisest men act, why then forbid the philosopher to support his beliefs on the same foundations, as long as he does not attribute to

country. He spent most of the next 15 years living in isolation with his mistress, Madame du Châtelet (1706–1749). A woman of considerable learning, and a prolific writer on scientific subjects—among her works was a translation of Newton's *Principia*—she exercised an important intellectual influence on Voltaire. The two of them returned briefly to Versailles in 1744, but life at the court of Louis XV was sterile and frustrating, and they soon withdrew.

The death of Madame du Châtelet in 1749 came as a bitter blow, and the following year Voltaire accepted an invitation to visit the court of Friedrich II at Potsdam. At first he established a close friendship with the king and worked on a history of the age of Louis XIV, his most important historical work. Two such powerful temperaments were probably bound to clash before long, however. The king made it clear that royal friendship had its limits: when Voltaire dared to criticize his patron's verse, the king abruptly dismissed him. In 1753, Voltaire left Prussia in disillusionment, and circulated throughout Europe his own version of the falling-out.

The last 20 years of his life were spent in the village of Ferney, near Geneva, where he set up his own court. A procession of the leading figures in European political and intellectual life came to visit him, to discuss, and above all to listen to the sage of Ferney. Voltaire returned to Paris only in 1778, but the hero's welcome he received proved too much for his poor health and the excitement probably hastened his death.

"The Infamous Thing"

Voltaire's writings touched on all the great questions raised by Enlightenment thinkers, but the most frequently recurring theme is the importance of freedom them a certainty not warranted by the number, the constancy, and the accuracy of his observations. . . .

From J. Salwyn Schapiro, ed., *Liberalism: Its Meaning and History.* D. Van Nostrand, Copyright © 1958.

A CALL FOR TOLERATION

Voltaire used his brilliant style and sense of irony to debunk many aspects of the Old Regime and its dependence on superstition. In the following essay, he tried to point out that a major step toward toleration was often just a matter of putting oneself in the other person's place.

One does not need great art and skilful eloquence to prove that Christians ought to tolerate each other—nay, even to regard all men as brothers. Why, you say, is the Turk, the Chinese, or the Jew my brother? Assuredly; are we not all children of the same father, creatures of the same God?

But these people despise us and treat us as idolaters. Very well; I will tell them that they are quite wrong. It seems to me that I might astonish, at least, the stubborn pride of a Mohammedan or a Buddhist priest if I spoke to them somewhat as follows:

This little globe, which is but a point, travels in space like many other globes; we are lost in the immensity. Man, about five feet high, is certainly a small thing in the universe. One of these imperceptible beings says to some of his neighbours, in Arabia or South Africa: "Listen to me, for the God of all these worlds has enlightened me. There are nine hundred million little ants like us on the earth, but my ant-hole alone is dear to God. All the others are eternally reprobated by him. Mine alone will be happy."

They would then interrupt me, and ask who was the fool that talked all this nonsense. I should be obliged to tell them that it was themselves. I would then try to appease them, which would be difficult. . . .

From Lynn Hunt, Thomas R. Martin, Barbara H. Rosenwein, R. Po-chia Hsia, Bonnie G. Smith, eds., *Connecting with the Past,* Vol. I. D.C. Heath, Copyright © 1995.

of thought. From the beginning of his career he castigated bigotry and intolerance, and to the end of his life he poured out a stream of pamphlets condemning prejudice and fanaticism: "The superstitious man is ruled by fanatics and he becomes one himself." Many of the letters in his vast correspondence ended with the phrase he made famous: "Crush the infamous thing!" The "thing" in question is organized religion, together with the intolerance bred of superstition.

The chief agents of prejudice, he believed, were the Christians, both Catholic and Protestant. Voltaire ridiculed the notion of the Bible as the inspired word of God. Rather, he saw it as a collection of anecdotes and contradictions that had no relevance to the modern world. Furthermore, it had provided the basis for centuries of disputes and persecutions that were as violent as they were pointless. The results, he said, were self-interested priests and false traditions.

Voltaire's attacks on organized religion were particularly bitter. His book *Candide* contains a famous scene based on an actual historical event—after the earthquake that destroyed most of Lisbon in 1755, killing over 30,000 people, some of the victims who managed to survive the devastation were solemnly burned alive by the "wise men," the priests and monks, in a superstitious attempt to avert further disaster. Yet his position was fully in line with the Enlightenment's chief aims and goals, and most Enlightenment thinkers actively campaigned against the outward manifestations of organized religion.

Yet Voltaire was no atheist. The God in whom he believed created the world, but could not be tied down to any single religion. Like many of the philosophes, the sage of Ferney held that only natural morality—the true religion common to all humans—could cure the ignorance and arrogance that plagued the world: "The only book that needs to be read is the great book of Nature."

Candide

Voltaire's most famous work, the tale *Candide* (1759), presents a rather darker vision of human life. The constant barrage of disasters and suffering to which the good-natured Candide, the story's hero, is subjected make a mockery of the optimism of philosophers such as Gottfried Leibnitz (1646–1716). Leibnitz preached philosophical optimism (the belief in an inherently just world) and wrote of the "pre-established harmony of the universe." Voltaire reduces this to the trite belief that "everything is for the best in the best of all possible worlds," and illustrates its absurdity with bleak humor.

As the innocent Candide travels from Germany to Portugal to the New World and back again to Europe, he finds nothing but evil and ignorance. Candide has to learn the hard way that experience is a better teacher than philosophy, even if its lesson is that pain and disillusionment are unavoidable.

By the book's end, Candide manages to temper the complete despair induced by this message with a note of comfort. The hero's last words of advice to his friends are that "we must cultivate our gardens." Even this suggestion is ambiguous. Many readers have concluded that Voltaire sees the world as cruel and indifferent to our suffering, but advises us not to give way to hopelessness. We should try to find some small, constructive activity we can perform in seclusion, and make an island of sanity and peace in a hostile universe. Others, however, interpreting Voltaire's message as far more positive, believe that the "garden" stands for Europe, or even the world. The instruction to cultivate it is thus a call for a life of political and social activism.

SCIENCE AND SOCIETY: SOCIAL AND ECONOMIC THOUGHT

Many of the philosophes, including Voltaire, took an active interest in science and mathematics. Marie-Jean Condorcet (1743–1794), who helped in the preparation of the *Encyclopédie*, was a mathematician with a special interest in probability theory. Believing as he did in the inevitability of human progress, Condorcet looked forward to a time when even human biology might improve. Like Candide, Condorcet found his optimism tested by his experience. He played an important role in the French Revolution, but incurred the hostility of the extremists for his moderate opinions. After two years in hiding, he was arrested and thrown into prison, where he committed suicide.

The naturalist Georges-Louis Buffon (1707–1788) also believed in the possibility of physical progress. He ran a series of experiments to try to extend the human life span to 120 years or more. Buffon is best known for his work on the classification of the animal kingdom, and he also directed the royal gardens in Paris (the present Jardin des Plantes). The 44-volume *Natural History* (1749–1804) whose production he led was one of the major scientific achievements of the 18th century.

Cesare Beccaria and Prison Reform

The center of the Enlightenment in Italy was Milan, where the brothers Alessandro (1741–1816) and Pietro (1728–1797) Verri headed a group of liberal intellectuals and published the influential journal *Il Caffè* (*The Cafe*). Among the younger members of the group was the economist and criminologist Cesare Beccaria (1738–1794), who derived an interest in political and social issues from his reading of Montesquieu.

In 1764, at the age of 26, Beccaria published *On Crimes and Punishments*, the first systematic treatment of rational criminal punishment. The work was an instant success, and was translated into a variety of languages. Eventually its ideas led the way to criminal reform in many European countries, including Russia, and helped in the shaping of the United States' system of criminal justice. Beccaria's main thesis was that his contemporaries' attitude to criminals was unreasonable and inefficient. The harsh system of punishments, with long prison terms or death sentences for relatively minor crimes, was based on the belief that criminals were hopelessly evil. Since they were believed incapable of repentance, they deserved no mercy. Furthermore, the penalties were applied inconsistently.

As a child of the Enlightenment, Beccaria believed that all humans were capable of improvement. Prisons should thus be places for rehabilitation, whose occupants were adequately housed and fed and given the chance to work, rather than centers of futile and vindictive punishment. His book argued passionately against the death penalty and torture, pointing out that such savage penalties do not stop crime; in any case, torture was uncivilized, and capital punishment was an abuse of the natural rights of humans.

Adam Smith and Free Trade

In his economic lectures, Beccaria anticipated the ideas of the leading economist of the 18th century, the Scot, Adam Smith (1723–1790). While traveling in Europe,

Smith met and was influenced by members of a French school of economists known as the *physiocrats*. Their most famous principle was *"laissez faire"*—"let it be": the natural laws of economics require only noninterference to be successful. Smith also visited Voltaire at Ferney.

On returning home, Smith retired to his native town of Kirkcaldy, near Edinburgh. He spent the next ten years working on his most famous publication, *The Wealth of Nations* (1776), while involving himself on an almost daily basis in Edinburgh's intellectual and cultural life. In *The Wealth of Nations* he worked out his theory of the division of labor, money, prices, wages, and distribution; the classic system of economics he described laid the foundations of the science of political economy. The book had a worldwide influence on politics as well as economics, and inspired the 19th-century Free Trade movement.

Like the physiocrats, Smith argued that if market forces were allowed to operate without state intervention, an "invisible hand" would guide self-interest for the benefit of all. This was another example of Enlightenment optimism. He was in favor of open competition and strongly opposed to price rings (the predecessors of the modern cartels), observing: "People of the same trade seldom meet together even for merriment or diversion, but that the conversation ends in some conspiracy against the public, or in some contrivance to raise prices." Smith thus rejected the government regulations, monopolies, and protective tariffs that characterized the policy of mercantilism. Like the other philosophes, he urged that "natural laws"—in this case, those affecting production and exchange—be allowed to unfold freely.

Later political economists, including Thomas Malthus (1766–1834) and David Ricardo (1772–1823), constituted the so-called "Manchester School" of economic theory, which significantly differed from the ideas of Smith. While their enemies labeled their ideas "laissez faire," they also form the basis of what is known as classical economics. The essential point of this doctrine is that economic relationships are separate and autonomous from government and politics. Instead, the free market regulates itself by laws of supply and demand. Extended beyond the economic realm, they held that all individuals should follow their own self-interest, whereas government should do only those things that are absolutely necessary, such as protecting life and property. Private initiative, not government assistance, should take care of social, cultural, and economic matters. A generation earlier, Adam Smith had advocated the increase of state education, and had deplored the effects on individuals of repetitive industrial work. The severe doctrines of the Manchester School reflected the grim realities of life in 19th-century industrial Europe.

THE OUTSIDER: ROUSSEAU AND THE SOCIAL CONTRACT

Enlightenment belief in the blessings of civilization found one eloquent dissenter: Jean-Jacques Rousseau (1712–1778). Tormented and quarrelsome, Rousseau's unstable temperament shaped most of his life. He lost his mother at birth and was separated from his father at the age of ten. After a brief period as an engraver's apprentice, he met and fell in love with a French noblewoman, Madame de Warens (1700–1762). The two settled down in the country for almost ten years (1732–1741), a period Rousseau later recalled in his autobiographical *Confessions* (1765–1770) as idyllic.

In 1741 he set out for Paris, where he devoted himself to music. In the 1750s, Diderot commissioned him to produce some articles on music for the *Encyclopédie*, and his short opera *The Village Soothsayer* (1752) was an instant success. In 1745 he began an affair with an illiterate servant girl, Thérèse Levasseur.

The first of his major philosophical works, *Discourse on the Sciences and the Arts*, appeared in 1750. It

Jean-Jacques Rousseau, writer, composer, and philosopher.

laid out one of his basic principles: the savage, "natural" condition is superior to civilization. Rousseau was convinced that the growth of society had corrupted the natural goodness of the human race and destroyed the freedom of the individual. Humans, in short, were good; society was bad.

The Social Contract

Rousseau soon became identified with the notion of the "noble savage," but he never advocated a return to some form of primitive existence. Instead he urged the creation of a new social order. In 1762 he published *The Social Contract*, one of the most radical political works of the 18th century, and one which proved immensely influential on modern political theory.

The issue at the heart of *The Social Contract* is how to reconcile individual freedom and the government of society: "The problem is to find a form of association in which each, while uniting himself with all, may still obey himself alone, and remain as free as before." Rousseau's solution was vague and unsatisfactory: a state governed by the "general will" of its citizens, who would delegate power to their rulers when necessary.

Rousseau's ideal was a society in which there was no hereditary, privileged aristocracy. All members should have joined freely, surrendering their individual rights to the group. The "rulers" would be the servants of the community, answerable to the people's will, and instantly removable if the people so decided. Unlike his contemporaries, Rousseau claimed that if the people really governed themselves, there would be no need for checks and balances, separation of powers, or protection of rights.

Clearly such a system could operate only in a small society. In any case Rousseau did not intend *The Social Contract* to be taken as a practical program, although in the bloodiest days of the French Revolution, the extremist Robespierre claimed to be following Rousseau's recommendations in unleashing the Reign of Terror. Its purpose was to set out the basic theory of democratic government. For conservatives, Rousseau was a dangerous emotionalist and an anarchist, while for liberals and democrats, a forerunner of totalitarian dictatorship. Few political thinkers have inspired more controversy.

Rousseau and the Role of Women

For all the importance of *The Social Contract*, most of Rousseau's readers were more interested in the social ideas expressed in his novels than in his political philosophy. His two most popular books, *The New Heloise* (1761) and *Émile* (1762), were best-sellers throughout Europe. These works reveal Rousseau's ideas about education, society, and the role of women. The first of them owed much of its popularity to its praise of the open display of emotion, while the other dealt with education, recommending that children be protected from the harmful effects of civilization, and exposed instead to the moral influence of nature.

In both books, women are assigned specific social roles as nurturers and educators. Julie, the heroine of *The New Heloise*, inspires her children with a sense of right and wrong—law enforcer rather than law maker. In *Émile*, the two children who are the tale's principal characters are both given unconventional educations, but their training is not the same. Émile, the boy, learns knowledge and self-control so that he can become confident and in charge of his own destiny in the wider world. Sophie, his future partner, is educated for the domestic sphere, where she will serve as Émile's faithful and obedient companion. For all Rousseau's revolutionary political thinking, he was quite prepared to institutionalize the traditional "separate spheres" for women and men. Women, he believed, far from receiving a natural education, should be kept away from nature lest they became disruptive.

For many Enlightenment thinkers, their movement marked humanity's coming of age. The power of pragmatism and critical reason had replaced the childish superstitions of the Middle Ages. Their strenuous opposition to the Old Regime and all its works was to help to bring it crashing down, and by undermining respect for established authority they laid the foundations for the increasing intellectual freedom of the 19th century. Some of their ideas, such as Rousseau's praise of open emotional expression, were taken up by the romantics.

On the other hand, most of the philosophes fully realized that further human progress would be neither smooth nor painless. Many of them were concerned at the desperate state in which the vast majority of Europe's population lived. Smith and Hume both wrote about the conditions of the rural and urban poor, and the French physiocrat Jacques Turgot tried to redistribute taxes more fairly and abolish compulsory labor. Hume even argued on his deathbed that "man will never be enlightened." Most Enlightenment thinkers, in fact, aimed to bring about progress on a limited scale, through their local societies and academies, in the hope that someday the total accumulation of their efforts might produce significant change.

The upheavals of the French Revolution and the subsequent Napoleonic era seemed to bear out Hume's skeptical conclusion. Yet in the long run the Enlightenment proved decisive in changing basic attitudes in Western culture. Never again did traditional religion occupy the position it held before the 18th century. From the end of the 18th century, democracy became an increasingly admired political ideal, even if it could not be attained in practice. Science and technology maintained their role as catalysts of social change, while the Encyclopédie *illustrated the immense value of knowledge and practical information.*

Condorcet once described the intellectuals of his time as a "class of men less concerned with discovering the truth than with propagating it." For all the immensity of the task, the leaders of the Enlightenment led the way to the social and political revolutions of the 19th century.

Questions for Further Study

1. What were the main goals of the Enlightenment? How did its philosophers set about achieving their aims, and how successful were they?
2. What effect did Enlightenment thinking have on European economic development?
3. How did the ideas of Voltaire and Rousseau differ? Which of the two was closer to the ideals of the Enlightenment?
4. How far did Beccaria's attitude to prison reform anticipate or inspire modern approaches?

Suggestions for Further Reading

Behrens, C. *Society, Government, and the Enlightenment: The Experiences of Eighteenth-Century France and Prussia.* New York, 1986.

Besterman, T. *Voltaire.* Chicago, 1976.

Hampson, N. *The Enlightenment.* London, 1982.

Rendall, J. *The Origins of Modern Feminism: Women in Britain, France and the United States.* New York, 1984.

Sklar, J. *Montesquieu.* Oxford, 1987.

Scott, H. M. *Enlightened Absolutism.* Ann Arbor, MI, 1990.

Spencer, S. *French Women and the Age of Enlightenment.* Bloomington, IN, 1984.

Wilson, A. M. *Diderot.* Oxford, 1972.

PART VII

THE MODERN AGE

The 18th century produced two revolutionary transformations with profound historical consequences—the industrial revolution and the French Revolution of 1789. Each in its own way led to fundamental structural and ideological changes in European and world civilization and gave birth to the modern age. From these and other events—including startling population growth and major advances in agricultural production—flowed much of the developments in the Western experience for the next two centuries.

In its simplest form, the industrial revolution saw machines and steam power assume functions that had always been the exclusive province of human and animal labor. As a result, the West entered a long period of unprecedented economic growth in which living standards for the vast majority of people improved. The social structure

that came to characterize modern Europe was no longer determined solely by birth and inherited privilege, although these factors continued to be important. Instead, under the dual impact of industrialization and the French Revolution, economic class, defined by the relationship of individuals to labor and capital, now became an increasingly important social determinant. By the opening of the 20th century, Western European civilization had become a predominantly urban, industrial, and secular culture that was able to seize world power as a result of its mastery of science and technology.

Europe's transition from tradition to modernity was accelerated at the end of the 18th century by the French Revolution. Historians often mark the beginning of "modern" history with the start of the French Revolution, for it radically altered centuries of political and social tradition. The revolution swept away the remnants of feudalism in France and the social system of the Old Regime that had rested on the hereditary privilege of the nobility. The events that took place in France from the late 1780s to the mid-1790s ushered in the age of "mass politics," in which social elements that had never been active in politics, such as the peasantry, workers, women, and the urban poor, now became participants in the making of history. The famous rallying cry of those who made the Revolution—

"liberty, equality, fraternity"—entered the Western political consciousness as the ideal slogan of liberal political systems.

In the aftermath of the revolution, three sets of ideas vied with each other in Europe: nationalism, liberalism, and socialism. Nationalism eventually took hold throughout the West, culminating in the process of nation building and, in our own times, in the struggle for decolonization. Liberalism became the political and social doctrine of the emerging middle classes which would dominate the modern era and become the chief form of political system for most of Europe. Socialism, on the other hand, would offer the new urban working classes both a philosophy of emancipation from economic exploitation and a political strategy for seizing power.

At the end of the 19th century, two events of global importance were rapidly making themselves felt in Europe: the last stage of Western imperialism, which resulted in the European conquest of most of Asia and Africa; and the emergence of the United States as an economic and political world power.

By the opening of the 20th century, European civilization was moving rapidly toward a critical phase in its history. Increasing nationalist tensions and imperial competition had divided its great powers into competition with alliance systems, while social tensions and extremist political programs—anarchist, syndicalist, and Marxist—raised serious questions about future stability. Responding to the doubts and uncertainties of the age, artists and intellectuals forged a modernist culture that was at once revolutionary, experimental, and often irrational in its appeal. The outbreak of World War I in 1914 signaled the end of the era of European dominance in world history.

VII

Topic 1

The Politics of Enlightenment: Europe and America

The Enlightenment had a far-reaching impact that extended beyond Western Europe—the ideas of the Enlightenment spread as far west as the New World and as far east as the steppes of Russia. Nor was the Age of Reason only an intellectual revolution. In the course of the 18th century, the thought of the *philosophes* also affected political developments and lay behind a variety of reform impulses in states as diverse as Russia, Prussia, and Austria.

The philosophes were practical people who wanted to see improvement in the condition of human society through meaningful reforms. Despite the legacy of Rousseau, however, few philosophes were democrats who trusted the common people to rule themselves. Some philosophes, who evolved the principles of what was once known as "enlightened despotism" (historians now prefer the term "enlightened absolutism"), were convinced that strong—although not absolute—rulers were needed to maintain order, protect the "natural rights" of individuals, and implement reforms. In this sense, the ideal ruler was one who exercised authority fairly and impartially, permitted domestic tolerance for religious beliefs and free expression, and created conditions in which science and the arts would flourish. Other philosophes looked to the educated, reasonable members of the mercantile classes, who gathered in the academies and literary societies. For most reformers of the period, whether supporters of monarchs or the enlightened middle class, change should come from above, not from below.

To what degree did the monarchs of the 18th century fulfill such expectations and qualify as "enlightened despots"? The question has been often debated by scholars, who have examined the policies of the leading monarchs of the age in order to test the theory. Were Josef II of Austria, Friedrich the Great of Prussia, and Catherine the Great of Russia genuinely inspired by the philosophes and did they actually apply the principles of the Enlightenment in ruling their states?

THE POLITICAL THOUGHT OF THE *PHILOSOPHES*

Political ideas stemmed from the same set of intellectual assumptions that inspired other aspects of the Enlightenment. Whereas scientists such as Sir Isaac Newton and economists such as Adam Smith emphasized adherence to natural laws, in politics the equivalent concept was natural rights. In the 17th century, John Locke had identified these rights broadly as life, liberty, and property—rights which no legitimate ruler should abridge or deny. Should a monarch cease to

Significant Dates

The Politics of Enlightenment

1748	Montesquieu's *The Spirit of the Laws*
1762	Rousseau's *The Social Contract*
1774	First Continental Congress meets in Philadelphia
1775	Cossack rebellion in Russia under Pugachev
1776	American War of Independence begins
1781	Josef II issues the Edict of Toleration
1783	Treaty of Paris
1740–1786	Friedrich II rules as king of Prussia
1789	U.S. Constitution adopted
1765–1790	Josef II rules as Austrian emperor
1765–1790	Leopold II rules as grand duke of Tuscany, and as emperor 1790–1792
1762–1796	Catherine II rules as empress of Russia
1743–1826	Life of Thomas Jefferson

protect such inalienable rights, the people had a further right to change their government, for the monarch had violated the compact formed between ruler and ruled.

Political Ideas in the Age of Reason

Those philosophes who thought most consistently about political reform stressed not only toleration but the practical fact that no one system of government was best for all countries. In *The Spirit of the Laws* (1748), Montesquieu insisted that tradition and environment helped to determine the form of government best suited for a particular society. He argued that the larger the political unit, the more power had to be exercised by the monarch. In Britain, a state of moderate size, the hereditary nobility in the House of Lords was balanced by the elected representatives in the House of Commons. Like most other enlightened thinkers of his age, Montesquieu believed that by themselves the common people were "extremely unfit" to govern a nation. In the case of his own country, he suggested that France might have been better off if the Bourbon monarchs had kept the political power of the aristocracy intact. In Britain, Montesquieu also saw the principles of the separation of powers and checks and balances at work: Parliament checked the powers of the monarch, while within Parliament the House of Lords and the House of Commons checked each other. In the government as a whole, the balance was maintained by means of the separation of powers. Montesquieu could not have known, of course, that over the next century and a half the principle of separation of powers would decline in Britain as the House of Commons gathered more power unto itself, including control over the cabinet, which was becoming an instrument of legislative authority.

More radical in nature were the theories of Jean-Jacques Rousseau, which had a great influence on Enlightenment political ideas. Nature, he believed, dignified people, whereas civilization corrupted them. Hence, social and political institutions should adhere more closely to nature. In *The Social Contract* (1762), Rousseau sought to establish a new version of government by contract by reconciling individual liberty with government. Whereas Locke and other contract theorists had stressed agreement between a ruler and the people's willingness to be governed, Rousseau emphasized the agreement of society as a whole to be ruled by its "general will," to which every person submits. "In our corporate capacity," he argued, "we receive each member as an indivisible part of the whole." When an

The political ideas of the French philosopher Montesquieu were the basis of Enlightenment thought about government.

individual puts selfish interests before the needs of the community, that individual is forced to obey the general will—"forced," in Rousseau's words, "to be free."

Rousseau insisted that determining the general will was the responsibility of all the people and should not be left to an elected body, while the power to implement the general will could be delegated to a smaller group. He did not believe that any society could be governed by a genuine democracy, in which the people themselves both made and carried out the laws. Yet Rousseau's ideas were idealistic, and he maintained a deep personal dislike for royal absolutism. Holders of executive power, he argued, were the officers of the people, not their masters, and could be removed. Placed in the perspective of later history, however, his notion of the general will may appear to offer a justification for totalitarian government. He seems, for example, to be insisting that the whole of the general will is more precious and moral than its individual parts. Some later critics have argued that for Rousseau the welfare of the nation was greater than that of its citizens—an argument used, for example, by 20th-century dictators who claimed that they had a superior understanding of the general will and could set it above individual interests. In any case, this concept of the general will provided a rationale for some rulers who wanted to implement reforms.

Many of the English and Scottish intellectual colleagues of Montesquieu and Rousseau shared their concern for the nature of legislative authority. Those who did not agree believed that the only real responsibility of government was to administer the laws of nature instituted by God and that such authority was too often in the hands of individuals whose personal interests conflicted with the general welfare of society. Only hereditary monarchs, argued some philosophes, could reconcile their personal interests with those of the nation. Legitimacy—the right to rule—was maintained as long as royal policies were both reasonable and natural, and many monarchs of the period saw in the concept of enlightened despotism a useful justification for their powers, a more modern justification than divine right theory.

JOSEF II AND THE FAILURE OF THE AUSTRIAN ENLIGHTENMENT

The victory of Friedrich the Great in the War of the Austrian Succession exposed the weaknesses of the Hapsburg empire (see Part VI, Topic 9). The young and

Map 1.1 The Austrian Empire, 1521–1772

The Empress Maria Theresa and Her Family by Martin van Maytens. Maria Theresa (right, seated) and her husband Francis I (left, seated) had 16 children. Their oldest son (the tall boy on his mother's right) became Josef II, and their youngest daughter, Marie Antoinette (center), married Louis XVI of France.

inexperienced Empress Maria Theresa proved, however, to be a practical champion of reforms designed to strengthen imperial government. Advised by talented ministers, the empress increased the taxes on the nobility and reduced the power of their local assemblies. The central bureaucracy was modernized and staffed with experts, and the non-German populations of the empire were forced to accept both German administrators and language. Most important, however, Maria Theresa took measures to improve conditions among the peasantry, most of whom still lived and worked as serfs. The taxes peasants paid and the amount of labor they owed to their landlords were now limited, in contrast to the trends elsewhere in Europe.

Although the empress was a devout Catholic—Catherine the Great of Russia scornfully called her "Lady Prayerful"—she imposed heavier taxes on the church, confiscated monastic property, and expelled the Jesuits. Despite these reforms, all of which were intended to increase the power of imperial government, Maria Theresa was not sympathetic to many of the critical ideas of the Enlightenment. She prohibited the publication or circulation of the works of Voltaire and Rousseau and suppressed all books that she deemed dangerous to the established order.

Josef II and the Austrian Empire

Not Maria Theresa but her eldest son, Josef II, was the Austrian monarch most responsible for bringing "enlightened absolutism" to the Hapsburg realm. Josef (ruled 1765–1790) ruled as coregent with Maria Theresa but was constantly held back and dominated by his mother until her death in 1780. Stricken with grief when his wife died, Josef became a compulsive worker, impatient with bureaucratic delay and entrenched interests. A serious-minded man, he declared that he would make philosophy the guide for all imperial laws. During the decade that he ruled alone, he promulgated some 17,000 measures. Although his policies were more often than not similar to his mother's, Josef ruled with less caution or concern for the established order.

In 1781, Josef II issued the Edict of Toleration, which gave Lutherans, Calvinists, and Orthodox Christians freedom to worship for the first time in Austrian history. He also improved the condition of his Jewish subjects, lifting the requirement that they live within the ghetto and wear the yellow star that had once branded them as inferior, and allowing them to enter universities—these reforms he regarded not as just and moral but as practical, for he hoped to make the Jews useful to the empire.

Josef reinforced his mother's policy of making the Catholic Church subservient to the authority of the empire. The emperor insisted that he, not the pope, was the final ecclesiastical authority within Hapsburg lands. He reduced the number of religious holidays and the number of nuns and monks, calling the latter "useless." He suppressed a third of all monasteries and convents, selling or renting these lands for the support of hospitals in Vienna, but encouraged those orders dedicated to education and charity.

In dealing with the plight of the peasantry, Josef took the policy of reform initiated by his mother to its logical conclusion. He emancipated the serfs and abolished most of their feudal obligations to the landowners, and also removed the traditional noble right to administer justice among the peasants. Following the suggestion of the physiocrats, he tried collecting a single tax on agricultural land, a revolutionary step because the large noble estates were to be taxed on the same basis as the small peasant holdings.

Like the philosophes, Josef II believed in the leveling effect of popular education, and provided teachers and textbooks for all primary schools. By the end of the century, more children attended school in Austria—about one out of four—than in any other European state. The emperor also accepted, at least in symbolic fashion, the concept of social equality, and opened a large public park in Vienna, known as the Prater, to citizens of every social status. A new legal code reflected the ideas of the Italian reformer Cesare Beccaria (see Part VI, Topic 11) about equality before the law, and abolished both capital punishment and the use of torture. Noblemen found guilty of crimes, like commoners, were often sentenced to sweep the streets of the capital.

The Limits of Austrian Reform

Other aspects of Josef's policies often reflected an unenlightened absolutism. He rejected the economic theories of the physiocrats in favor of old mercantilist policies such as high protective tariffs on imports. In other ways, he continued many of his mother's programs—weakening the influence of the nobility by appointing commoners to important positions and furthering the Germanization of the empire by speaking German and patronizing German writers. Josef also tried to reduce the administrative and cultural autonomy of non-German areas of the empire such as Hungary and Bohemia.

Josef's enlightened reforms and centralizing policies sparked domestic opposition from all directions. The nobility spoke out bitterly against laws enforcing equality and forced him to revoke the single-tax decree. The religious faith of the peasants, who remained oblivious to most of his other reforms, led them to resent his suppression of the Catholic Church. The Hungarians and Bohemians resorted to rebellion to protect their local rights against encroachments from Vienna. Josef was both an absolutist and a realist. More often than not, he dealt with his opponents simply by insisting on having his way.

Josef II died of exhaustion and overwork, believing that his policies had been right but that he had failed to accomplish great things. The judgment of one contemporary was that he had "governed too much and reigned too little." Certainly not all of Josef's reforms succeeded—some of them, such as the abolition of serfdom, were repealed after he died—but many others remained intact.

Josef's lasting reforms were reinforced by the policies of his younger brother, Leopold II (ruled 1790–1792), Grand Duke of Tuscany, who succeeded

One of several paintings and prints intended to show Josef II of Austria as promoter of agricultural reform.

to the imperial throne and proved to be an enlightened absolutist in much the same tradition. In the 25 years that he served as ruler of Tuscany, he had made considerable reforms in the government of the Italian duchy, including economic reforms advocated by the physiocrats and legal reforms suggested by Cesare Beccaria. Leopold sought to bring his subjects into public affairs and, unlike the other enlightened monarchs of the day, was interested in representative government as it was unfolding in the newly created United States of America.

"FIRST SERVANT OF THE STATE": FRIEDRICH THE GREAT OF PRUSSIA

In many ways, Prussian King Friedrich II (ruled 1740–1786), known as "the Great," appeared to be the best example of an enlightened despot. In his youth he had tried to escape from the harsh discipline of his father, Friedrich Wilhelm I (see Part VI, Topic 5), who tried his son as a deserter and executed his son's companion and probable lover. A young man of sensibility and studious habits, he devoted the next ten years of his life to literary pursuits and music. His flute, which he carried with him everywhere, remained one of his favorite pastimes. He studied the writings of the philosophes and corresponded with many of them, favored French writers, and in 1750 invited Voltaire to live for three years at Potsdam Palace, outside Berlin.

Friedrich the Great of Prussia as shown in an 18th-century engraving.

Like Josef II of Austria, Friedrich worked hard at being king and drove his ministers and servants relentlessly. He avoided luxury and overindulgence, often wore dirty, ill-fitting clothing, and appeared obsessed with achieving success. In the conduct of foreign affairs and warfare he proved to be a man of genius and cunning. Friedrich was one of the most efficient and successful monarchs of the 18th century, but there is no doubt that he practiced the art of despotism as much as he believed in the ideas of the Enlightenment.

The Contradictions of Enlightened Absolutism

In economic affairs, Friedrich's policies were marked by deep-seated contradictions. He improved Prussian agriculture by importing from Western Europe crop rotation and the iron plow as well as new crops such as the potato and clover. He reclaimed land from swamps and after the conquest of Silesia established farms there and settled the region with immigrants from other German states. In the aftermath of the Seven Years' War, Friedrich worked to restore ruined forests and supplied the peasants with tools, seed, and animals. Also, like his Austrian counterpart, Friedrich did not accept the physiocratic doctrine of a laissez-faire (free market) economy and resorted to mercantilist protectionism to stimulate Prussian industry, especially for such items as metals and textiles needed by the army. In Prussia, as elsewhere in Europe, the consumption of coffee grew rapidly in the 18th century. When it became apparent, however, that this new consumer fad required the export of Prussian currency, he put a heavy import duty on coffee beans and set up a corps of special agents to stop coffee smuggling. Moreover, Friedrich considered coffee and tea signs of the degeneration of modern society and insisted that his soldiers drink beer instead. Friedrich's military ambitions imposed a heavy tax burden on his subjects.

Despite his adherence to Enlightenment notions of equality, Friedrich believed in the maintenance of social hierarchy. At the same time, he was convinced that the same patriotic duties were expected of both

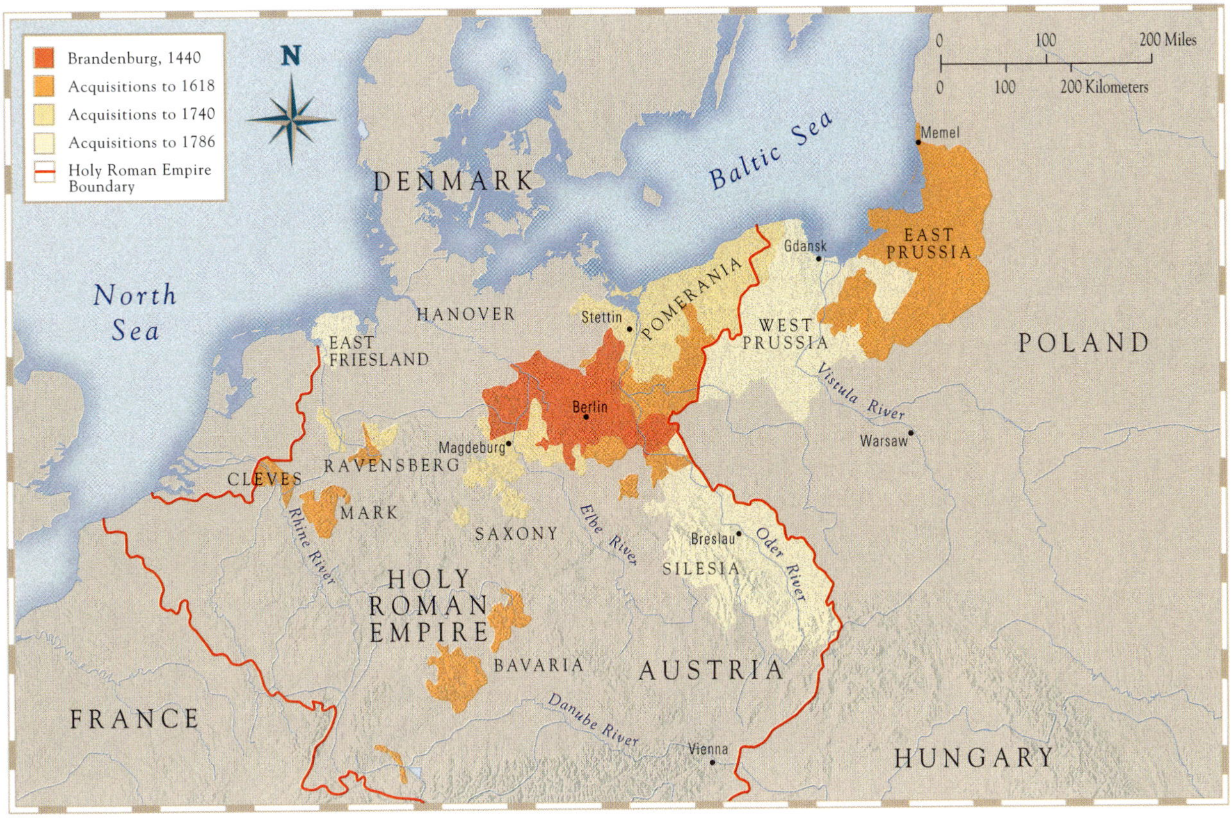

Map 1.2 Prussia, 1440–1786

monarch and subjects—the king, he said, was merely "the first servant of the state." The elite *Junker* class of landowners exercised a monopoly of social prestige in Prussia but Friedrich did not spare them from the consequences of his absolutism. Only Junkers received appointments as army officers, but he discouraged marriage among them in order to avoid having to pay their widows military pensions. He abolished serfdom on the royal estates but not elsewhere in his realm, although in 1773 he did prohibit the sale of landless serfs in East Prussia. For practical reasons, he supported a minimum rural literacy and gave the peasants considerable economic assistance. The middle class he generally held in contempt, although he recognized their usefulness as tax payers. After the Seven Years' War, middle-class officers were forced out of the army and made exempt from military service.

Friedrich was a deist who took pride in his religious tolerance, yet his religious policies were also riddled with contradictions. When the Jesuits were expelled from other states, he invited them to his own Lutheran country. Throughout his realm, the king granted his Catholic subjects almost full equality, and even built an impressive Catholic church in Berlin. On the other hand, in 1779, when the writer Gotthold Lessing (1729–1781) made a Jew the hero of his play *Nathan the Wise*, Friedrich kept him out of the royal academy. Whereas Josef considered his Jewish citizens useful, Friedrich pronounced Prussia's Jews to be useless and levied special taxes on them, and discouraged them from entering the professions and the civil service.

Friedrich made sweeping reforms in the Prussian legal system, freeing the courts from political pressures and reducing the use of torture. He also created a system of appellate courts to replace the strange tradition of allowing university faculties to hear appeals from the courts. Finally, he tried to eliminate the widespread practice of bribery by setting up a special gratuities fund for the purpose of supplementing judicial salaries.

Was Friedrich's enlightened absolutism little more than a clever deception to hide his will to dominance behind the fashionable intellectual discourse of the day? In his last testament, Friedrich insisted that he be buried beside his pet dogs. Some historians, like a number of Friedrich's contemporaries, have seen this gesture as a symbol of his contempt for his fellow human beings. Perhaps that scorn was a result of the difficulties of Friedrich's own life, torn as he was between the severe military traditions of his own Hohenzollern dynasty and the gentler doctrines of the Age of Reason.

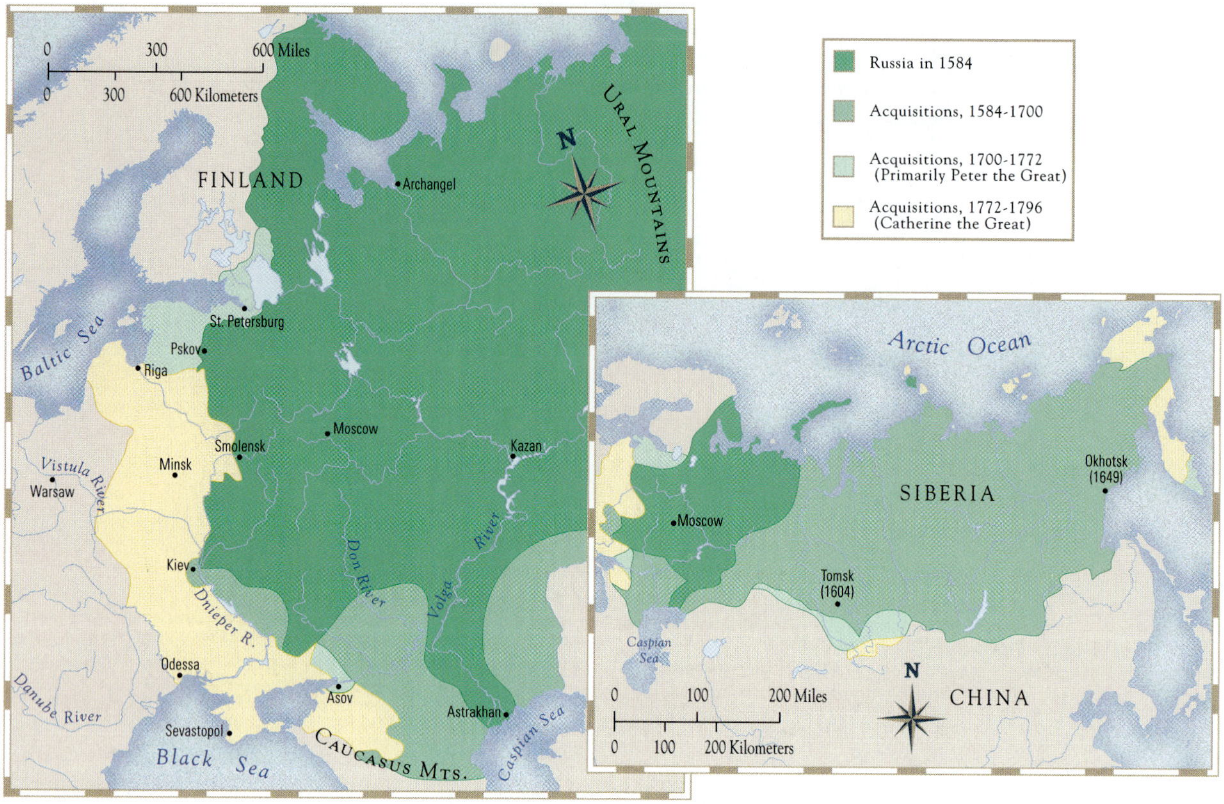

Map 1.3 Russian Expansion, 1584–1796

ENLIGHTENMENT IN THE EAST: RUSSIA FROM CATHERINE TO ALEXANDER

Like the Austrian Empire, Russia had two monarchs whose policies conformed to the general pattern of enlightened absolutism: Catherine II (ruled 1762–1796) and her grandson Alexander I (ruled 1801–1825). The empire that they ruled was a vast country in which feudal traditions were still very strong. In the decades following the death of Peter the Great in 1725, the monarchy suffered from a series of weak and ineffective leaders and the nobility reemerged as a dominant force.

Having chafed under the harsh reign of Peter the Great, the deeply dissatisfied nobles sought to regain their former status and privileges. In 1730 the gentry began to extricate themselves from servitude to the tsar, and by 1762 the nobles gave military service to the tsar only by choice. At the same time, the noble landowners extended their power over the serfs, serving as agents for collecting the poll tax. Masters could still exile their serfs to Siberia and mete out physical punishment at will. Serfs lost the right to gain their freedom by joining the army, and could neither buy land nor engage in commercial activities without permission from their masters.

Catherine the Great

Brought up in a German court, Catherine was married at the age of 15 to the Russian Grand Duke Peter. In St. Petersburg, she ingratiated herself quickly with the Russians, learning their language and embracing the Orthodox religion. She soon came to detest her husband, took on a succession of lovers, and conspired to become empress in her own right. In 1762, a palace coup dethroned and assassinated Peter in a plot that probably involved Catherine, who was proclaimed Empress Catherine II, known as "the Great." The new ruler was a devoted student of the Enlightenment, who wrote plays, edited a journal, and read the works of the philosophes with great eagerness. Catherine wanted a good press in Western Europe both for herself and for the country she ruled, and used the philosophes for that purpose. She invited Diderot, whose library she purchased, to visit St. Petersburg and granted him a pension. Catherine also corresponded with Voltaire, who did not visit Russia but did accept her financial support, praising her in return as "the north star."

Reform and Its Constraints

The empress was no doubt inclined to institute sweeping reforms in Russia, but a combination of personal liabilities—principally the fact that she was both a woman and a foreigner—made it difficult for her to move swiftly or decisively. Because she relied heavily on the support of the nobility, she felt she could not work to eliminate serfdom. On the contrary, in granting huge estates to her supporters, she converted many thousands of state peasants to privately owned serfs.

Like Montesquieu, Catherine believed that a country as large as Russia had to be ruled by an autocrat. Once on the throne, however, Catherine appointed a Legislative Commission to codify the complex laws implemented over the previous century. Catherine personally helped to write the Commission's guidelines, which were replete with theories taken from Montesquieu's *Spirit of the Laws* and Beccaria's *Crimes and Punishments*. In addition, the more than 500 members of the Commission were elected by all social classes except the serfs and had to compile written statements of grievances from their districts. After a year and a half of inconclusive debate, Catherine closed down the Commission without having codified the laws. This was the last attempt by the Russian monarchy to consult its subjects until the 20th century.

Catherine the Great of Russia in a painting depicting the empress as a warrior (1762).

Rebellion and Repression

In 1775, Catherine faced a great Cossack rebellion under the leadership of Yemelyan Pugachev (1726–1775). With a coalition of soldiers and peasants, Pugachev led a revolt against Catherine. The Cossack leader claimed to be Peter III, the murdered husband of the empress, and promised freedom and land to the serfs. Pugachev moved across southeastern Russia toward Moscow, burning and killing, and slaughtering landlords and priests. The outbreak of famine along the Volga River and betrayal by some of his followers brought an end to the rebellion. Pugachev was taken in an iron cage to Moscow in 1775, where he was tried and executed. Like similar revolts in the 17th century, Pugachev's rebellion—which Catherine brutally crushed—reflected the depth of discontent felt for the monarchy as well as for landowners and government officials.

Catherine moved immediately to increase imperial centralization and further repress the serfs. In a major restructuring of local government, she increased the number of provinces from 20 to 50, hoping that the smaller provinces would prove easier to govern. She appointed nobles to most of the new provincial offices while imposing close government supervision on their activities. In 1785, Catherine issued two imperial charters. One charter granted the nobles exemption from taxation and military service and gave them complete control over their serfs. The other charter, which permitted self-government for cities, revealed Catherine's support for the small but growing middle class.

When the empress died in 1796, her son succeeded her as Paul I (ruled 1796–1801). Catherine had always feared that her son might lead a conspiracy against her, so that when Paul became tsar many thought he would eliminate his mother's reforms. Paul proved, however, to be unpredictable. In his more reactionary moments, he placed the population of St. Petersburg under a strict curfew and prohibited Western sheet music, fearing that it would spread revolutionary sentiments among his subjects. He also continued the practice of giving state lands to his supporters, thereby transforming hundreds of thousands of peasants into private serfs. In 1797 he prohibited serfs from working on Sunday but permitted landlords to increase the amount of their labor.

Paul's policy toward the nobles proved to be his undoing. Attempting to reverse the developments of decades, he made the aristocrats once again subject to imperial service and limited their local powers. He also forced them to subsidize the construction of public buildings and to pay new land taxes. In a different area of reform, Paul wanted to modernize his army along Prussian lines, instilling in the officers a sense of responsibility for ordinary soldiers. The élite guards'

PERSPECTIVES ON HISTORY

How Enlightened Were the Enlightened Despots?

John G. Gagliardo
Boston University

A vigorous debate on this question has occurred since the term "enlightened despotism" (now, more commonly "enlightened absolutism") first came into historical usage in the 19th century. The debate has revolved mostly around the motivation and purposes of the domestic policies and programs of those European monarchs of roughly the last half of the 18th century to whom the term has been applied. Over the years, many historians have argued that the reform programs of the so-called "enlightened despots" were neither chiefly called forth by nor primarily intended to serve the higher humanitarian ideals usually associated with the Enlightenment. Such policies were instead not much more than updated versions of periodic earlier efforts to strengthen the political power of absolute monarchy and to improve the economic and military position of their states in the dangerous climate of the 18th-century international system.

These historians hold that the cultivation of power rather than service to the spiritual and material welfare of their peoples was the prime motivator of the "enlightened despots." Their frequent appeal to Enlightenment ideals and principles is seen as rhetorical camouflage designed to justify in the name of philanthropic necessity what was in fact a self-interested campaign to regiment and control their societies more tightly in the service of goals that had little to do with social welfare. At the risk of some simplification, the evidence produced for this interpretation points to the fact that nearly all reforms launched by these princes, including those that did bring some humanitarian benefit, also strengthened the fiscal or governmental apparatus of the monarchical state. Moreover, the programs with the strongest "purely" humanitarian content—popular education, charitable enterprises, reform of the brutal criminal justice system and of prisons, and so on—were persistently underfunded and always the first to be abandoned when money got tight. Some rulers did successfully move to abolish serfdom, and many more to alleviate its burdens, but the record is a very mixed one; and while noble privilege was invaded and curtailed in some respects, no ruler undertook to overthrow the traditional "society of orders" to which the concepts of privilege and legal inequality were fundamental. Even the two reforms most universally demanded by the enlightened community—religious toleration and freedom of the press—were not everywhere realized or well enforced, and some degree of censorship continued to exist in even the most "enlightened" states. This negative interpretation does not deny the achievement of some practical benefits for these monarchs' peoples; it simply asserts that the humanitarian ideas of the Enlightenment were not an important source of their policies, that any popular benefits resulting from those policies were more incidental than purposeful, and that an "enlightened absolutism" therefore did not really exist at all.

Even without disputing the historical facts of this interpretation, however, it is possible to approach the question from a different perspective—one which puts far more weight on the judgment of those contemporaries who first termed these monarchs "enlightened," and who persisted in doing so through all of the failures, partial successes, and supposedly hypocritical rhetoric of their undertakings. Unless we assume stupidity or willful naiveté in a very large part of the enlightened community, we have to believe on their own testimony that they perceived the "enlightened despots" as actual executors of many of their hopes for mankind, and applauded them for the overall direction of their regimes (without necessarily keeping detailed lists of every success or failure). Most enlightened thinkers and publicists, after all, were not dreamers or utopians, but informed and intelligent people living in a real world of real problems they wanted corrected. Almost none of them developed schemes for anything resembling a completely new political or social system; and in spite of much grumbling about the pace or depth of reform, or about the foreign and military policies of even those states they regarded as most enlightened, they also recognized the difficulties of reform. Consequently, they were not uncomfortable with incrementalist approaches to reform as long as they were persistent and real in terms of identifiable progress, however partial. They were, in general terms, "possibilists" rather than revolutionaries, who judged rulers and regimes by their *tendencies* rather than by comparison to some finished blueprint of a perfect society.

The fact that various reform projects corresponding to their own desires also served the self-interest of monarchs by bringing new power and efficiency to their governmental apparatus was not uniformly worrisome to the philosophes of Europe, and indeed had positive aspects: it not only illustrated a favorite truth discovered by the Enlightenment—the cunningly beneficial relationship between self-interest and public utility—but also improved the power of rulers to do good; we should not forget, after all, that most enlightened thinkers supported a powerful absolute monarchy as the form of government best able to reform a stubbornly traditional society, *when animated by enlightened rulership*.

What the philosophes sought, in broadest terms, was a society more tolerant of diversity (especially in matters of religious faith, with all their secondary social consequences); more humane (in caring for the disadvantaged of all sorts, including accused and convicted criminals); and more efficient and less wasteful (quicker and less expensive justice, rationalized civil codes, and elimination of arbitrary and capricious administrative practices through the greater regularity of a government operating under known and comprehensive laws). Even a brief review of the history of the "enlightened despotisms" will reveal much dedicated attention to this agenda—an attention more persistent and successful in some places than in others, but real nonetheless. By the standards employed by the philosophes themselves, therefore, the record of reform achievement in these areas, while not of revolutionary proportions, is undeniable, and suggests that their positive view of these princes was based on observed fact, not on wishful thinking or on such enlightened rhetoric as the latter employed. (A strong case can be made for the personal adherence of many of the "enlightened despots" to the basic premises of the Enlightenment—natural law doctrine, for example—which they knew well through some combination of both formal education and their own reading, and personal contacts with leading literary exponents of Enlightenment. This personal culture cannot be ignored in approaching the question of motivation.)

Another and extremely important objective of the Enlightenment as a whole was a *fairer* society. The abundant social criticism arising from this demand was directed chiefly at the privileges and immunities of both clergy and nobility, but especially the latter, that were built into the Old Regime's "society of orders." Moreover, no government moved to abolish this class-based system. Some historians, seeing in this the *decisive* criterion of monarchs' entitlement to true enlightenment, have denied it to them almost on these grounds alone. But this position ignores the real objection of contemporaries, which was not to the *existence* of privilege but to the current standards of *access* to it. What most of them wanted was certainly not abolition of the traditional social order, but a reformulation of it in which privilege would be accessible to all men on the basis of meritorious achievement, not just by birth or money alone. Nobility (and privilege, and the whole "society of orders" along with it) was perfectly acceptable, in other words, as long as it was justified by merit or, to the extent that merit was not present in already existing aristocracies, would be modified by removal or reduction of privileges and immunities. The "enlightened despots" concurred with the philosophes in this desire. From that arose not only a strengthening of the public service ethic of the "service nobilities" already in place in some countries, as well as new taxes on the nobility, but also a new insistence on performance as the criterion for appointment and promotion in the civil and military bureaucracies. The fact that these developments did not in fact or by intention move in the direction of 20th-century social

continued next page

egalitarianism is irrelevant, since no one at the time either expected or wanted them to. And again, that these reforms were slow, sporadic, and partial, or that the monarchs derived advantage as rulers from them, rendered them no less attractive to the enlightened community, which recognized the great value of the *tendency*—public recognition of the larger principle of social advancement for merit.

In the final analysis, to be sure, it is necessary to recognize several facts that may qualify the degree of enlightenment of the "enlightened despots." Motive, to begin with, is always a murky and perhaps in the end impenetrable question; some of the reforms of the period clearly were continuations of earlier policies more than wholly new initiatives; there was often a considerable gap between announced intentions and results achieved, and what did not get done was at least as impressive as what did; and, finally, there is little evidence that the monarchs of the time had any vision of a breakthrough to an entirely new kind of society that might be made possible by their own efforts. The removal of all these reservations might be necessary to qualify these rulers as "enlightened" by today's standards. Nonetheless, shrewd and critical observers in their own time clearly believed not only that their intellectual receptivity, openness to experimentation, and intentions conformed to the enlightened spirit of the age, but also that their regimes represented a sufficiently progressive chapter in the history of monarchy itself as to justify dubbing them "enlightened."

In the end, then, if one can accept the reality of mixed motives—a genuine degree of humanitarian concern, combined with the imperative to keep the state both solvent and militarily strong—and if one can recognize the numerous and severe obstacles to all reform in societies that were economically marginal and stubbornly traditionalistic, with much ability to resist change, then a reasonable case for a genuine "enlightened despotism" can be made. In all essentials, it is the case made by the Enlightenment itself, and it remains a compelling one today.

regiments resented these changes and hatched a conspiracy that murdered Paul in 1801.

The Liberal Tsar

Alexander I (ruled 1801–1825) was educated by a liberal Swiss tutor who instilled in him a respect for the teachings of the Enlightenment. Despite his liberal leanings, however, Alexander made such extensive compromises that his accomplishments were limited. Perhaps one of his most ambitious reforms was a law that created a class of landowning farmers from former serfs freed by their masters. This measure had only limited success, however, since emancipation by landlords was voluntary—less than 40,000 serfs were freed out of many millions.

The liberal but hesitant Alexander had the benefit of an exceptionally talented adviser, Michael Speransky (1772–1839), the intelligent and well educated son of a priest. Inspired by Montesquieu's doctrine of the separation of powers, Speransky presented Alexander with a plan for constitutional government. It provided for a number of elected provincial assemblies and a Duma, or national parliament, which would approve all laws presented by the tsar. These bodies would be elected by the nobility and the middle classes, with the exclusion of the serfs.

Had it been implemented, Speransky's far-reaching plan would have ended absolutism in Russia, but Alexander refused to put it into effect. Speransky had made powerful enemies in his effort to reform the civil service by requiring examinations and promotion based on merit, a system opposed by the many nobles and illiterates who held government office. He had also proposed an income tax for the nobility. Speransky's enemies found an opportunity to undermine him in 1812, when Napoleon invaded Russia—Speransky, who had arranged an alliance with the French ruler, was exiled. The constitutional scheme was abandoned, but two provisions that did not weaken the tsar's power were implemented. Alexander established a purely advisory council of state, whose members he appointed and dismissed, a measure that increased imperial efficiency. By reorganizing the government ministries and defining their responsibilities, Alexander eliminated overlapping jurisdictions.

During his last years, Alexander was influenced by Count Alexis Arakcheev (1769–1834), a conservative landowner and military officer who was given free reign over most domestic affairs. He instituted a series of "military colonies" in farming communities that it was hoped would pay for the army. When not fighting or training, the soldiers could live with their families and work the farms, although in practice these were staffed by drafting local populations and run by brutal officers. By the end of Alexander's reign, some 400,000 soldiers—about a third of the army—were living in these camps.

Ironically, Alexander proved to be a more liberal tsar in the territories he ruled beyond Russia's borders. In 1809, after he had annexed Finland from Sweden, the tsar allowed the Finns to keep their law codes and a degree of local government. Similarly, when he became king of Poland in 1815, he granted the Poles a constitution and permitted them to have their own army and government officials, as well as to use their own language. It was in Russia itself that tsarist absolutism failed to temper the repressive regime with the political doctrines of the Enlightenment.

THE GREAT EXPERIMENT: THE ENLIGHTENMENT AND THE AMERICAN REVOLUTION

In the context of the Age of Reason, the American Revolution was an important event in European history. Its immediate causes lay in specific fiscal problems between Great Britain and its North American colonies, but the political ideals that undergirded the American revolt were part of the Enlightenment tradition. Inspired by the thought of John Locke, Rousseau, and

Map 1.4 The United States, 1776–1867

other political theorists, colonial leaders such as Benjamin Franklin and Thomas Jefferson posed basic questions about the advantages of monarchy versus constitutional government and about the sources of political authority.

The Roots of Revolution

After the end of the Seven Years' War in 1763, a victorious Great Britain had to deal with several pressing problems in America. London quickly discovered that its much enlarged empire required considerable financial expenditures, and insisted that these be shared with the American colonists, who had benefited most from the war. The problem lay, however, in the fact that the colonists opposed all efforts to tax them, mainly because their economy was no longer suited to Britain's mercantilist policies.

In 1764 Parliament passed the Sugar Act, which aimed to raise revenue through import duties, followed in 1765 by the Stamp Act, which put a tax on such items as legal documents and newspapers. The American response was that since they were not represented in Parliament, they should not be taxed by that body—"no taxation," they insisted, "without representation." That October, the so-called Stamp Act Congress agreed not to import British goods and issued a protest to the king. In the face of this resistance, Parliament repealed the Stamp Act, while asserting its right to legislate for the colonies.

Over the next decade, a familiar pattern repeated itself: whenever Parliament passed a revenue measure or an administrative act affecting the colonies, the Americans resisted it, often with violence, and the British would then back down. Relations between colonies and mother country deteriorated steadily. When the colonies resisted a set of four import duties sponsored by Chancellor of the Exchequer Charles Townshend (1725–1767), the British sent special customs agents and soldiers to Boston in 1768 to enforce the laws. Tensions rose and in March 1770 British troops killed five civilians in what came to be called the Boston Massacre. Parliament repealed all but one—that on tea—of the Townshend duties.

In May 1773 Parliament permitted the East India Company to sell tea directly to American distributors, thereby avoiding American wholesalers. Although the measure lowered the price of tea, colonial merchants viewed it as an oppressive act against American merchants. Some American cities refused to permit the unloading of tea in their ports, and in Boston a cargo of tea was dumped into the harbor. In 1774, British Prime Minister Lord North (1732–1792), determined to assert British authority over the colonies, passed the so-called Intolerable Acts. These laws closed the port of Boston, suspended many rights, and permitted soldiers to be quartered and fed in private homes.

Crisis was at hand. Incensed by what they considered high-handed and unjust treatment, colonists critical of Britain formed committees to discuss their common problems. In September 1774 the First Continental Congress met in Philadelphia, where the 56 delegates demanded redress as British citizens, denounced taxation without representation, and agreed to boycott trade until their rights were restored. The result, however, was war rather than negotiation. By May 1775, when the second Congress met, battles had already been fought at Lexington and Concord. Although the colonists met defeat at Bunker Hill in June, the assemblies of each colony began to meet as sovereign bodies instead of under the king's authority. The revolution had begun.

Thomas Jefferson was perhaps the most important philosophe of the American Enlightenment.

Franklin, Jefferson, and the American Enlightenment

When the Second Continental Congress met that spring, it could boast among its members two of the most illustrious intellects in the American colonies: Benjamin Franklin (1706–1790) and Thomas Jefferson (1743–1826). Both men epitomized the American Enlightenment, and their ideas made important contributions to the course of the revolution and to the political development of the future United States.

Franklin was born in Boston of modest background, the son of a soap and candle maker, and learned the printing trade as a young man. In Philadelphia, he ran his own print shop and published the *Pennsylvania Gazette* as well as *Poor Richard's Almanac*. At the age of 42, he retired from business with enough money to devote his energies to the sciences and public affairs. He had already helped to set up a library, an academy that eventually became the University of Pennsylvania, and a discussion group that gave rise to the American Philosophical Society. He published the influential book *Experiments and Observations on Electricity* in 1751 and was a prolific inventor. The embodiment of a trained observer of natural phenomena in the Age of Reason, Franklin's scientific knowledge included astronomy, medicine, geology, and physics. Serving as Pennsylvania's agent in London from 1764 to 1775, he had been an important voice for conciliation with Britain before becoming a member of the Second Continental Congress.

In contrast to Franklin's humble origins, Jefferson was the son of a Virginia planter and educated as a lawyer. The breadth of his interests and learning was even greater than that of Franklin, who had little interest in aesthetics. Jefferson read widely in the arts and humanities as well as in the sciences, played the violin, and read or spoke seven languages. He was an accomplished architect, and knowledgeable in mathematics and engineering. His book *Notes on Virginia* (1785) showed him to be familiar with botany, zoology, geography, and archeology. Later in his life, one of the contributions of which he was most proud was the founding of the University of Virginia. Jefferson first entered politics in 1769 as a member of the Virginia House of Burgesses. In 1774, in response to the Intolerable Acts, Jefferson wrote *A Summary View of the Rights of British America,* in which he rejected Britain's right to govern in America.

Although the Second Continental Congress sought conciliation with Britain, events led the body to plan for self-government, for King George III had declared the colonies to be in rebellion. In the winter of 1775, an impassioned and immensely influential pamphlet by Thomas Paine (1737–1809) entitled *Common Sense* influenced many Americans toward independence. A colonial army was created under the command of George Washington (1732–1799).

In June 1776, the Continental Congress appointed a five-man committee, including Franklin and Jefferson, to write a Declaration of Independence. Jefferson drafted the document, to which Franklin contributed much discussion and some changes of language. The final version was a moving statement of the essential principles of Enlightenment political thought. Both Franklin and Jefferson were familiar with the works of Locke and the French philosophes, and the emphasis on natural rights embodied in it could not have been more clear: "We hold these truths to be self-evident, that all men are created equal; that they are endowed by their creator with certain inalienable rights; that among these are life, liberty and the pursuit of happiness." The colonies had invoked the notion of contract theory, in which subjects were free to overthrow an unjust monarch. On July 2, the Continental Congress declared the independence of the colonies and on July 4 adopted the Declaration of Independence.

The War of Independence raged on, widening in 1778 into a European conflict when Franklin, then serving as rebel minister to France, persuaded the government of Louis XVI to support the Americans. In 1779–1780 Spain and the Dutch Republic also joined the war on the side of the colonies. In 1781, after Washington's army decisively defeated British forces at Yorktown, the British agreed to sue for peace. Franklin led the negotiations, which culminated in the Treaty of Paris (1783). The thirteen American colonies had won their independence.

The Early United States

Perhaps the most successful application of Enlightenment principles to the world of politics in the 18th century took place not in Europe but in the United States. Between 1781 and 1789, the Americans governed themselves through the Articles of Confederation, which provided for a weak central authority in recognition of the difficulties they had experienced at the hands of the British monarchy. In 1787, however, a convention meeting in Philadelphia drafted an entirely new constitution for the United States. A national government was created with powers that transcended those of the individual states, such as the authority to tax, conduct foreign policy, and raise an army. Montesquieu's dual principles of separation of powers and checks and balances inspired the creation of an executive (an elected president), a legislature (a two-chamber Congress, consisting of a Senate elected by the states and a House of Representatives chosen directly by popular vote), and a Supreme Court.

During the early decades of their republic, Americans were as divided over political ideology as their European counterparts. In the United States, political leaders split between Federalists and Democrats, much as Europeans chose conservatism or liberalism. The

Federalist party, founded by Alexander Hamilton (1755?–1804), was the first true American political party. Hamilton's support came mainly from prosperous business groups and landowners from the northern states; they wanted a strong central government run by the educated and wealthy élite. They were the strongest supporters of the new constitution and pushed for the addition of the Bill of Rights to the document, which were ratified as ten amendments in 1790. These guaranteed such basic rights for citizens as freedom of speech, press, assembly, and worship, and trial by jury. The Democratic Republican party, on the other hand, represented small independent farmers, largely from the south. The titular leader of the Democratic Republicans was Jefferson (president from 1801 to 1809), who preached popular control of government.

Enlightened absolutism had many weaknesses, not the least of which was the fact that a good monarch ruled as an accident of birth, not by the choice of the people. Nor were there any devices built into the system in the event that these monarchs acted as despots without the benefit of enlightened sensibilities. Josef II of Austria proved to be too rigid and wedded to centralized control of an empire that incorporated too many diverse ethnic groups. The Prussian king, Friedrich the Great, was determined to increase the power of the monarchy and reinforced the status and power of the Junkers, who generally opposed the Enlightenment. In Russia, Catherine the Great compromised her reformist principles to satisfy the power of the nobility. Only in the United States, where the political principles of the Enlightenment were applied without a monarch, did democracy thrive.

Questions for Further Study

1. To what degree did the monarchs of the 18th century qualify as "enlightened despots"?
2. What were the political goals of monarchs in Prussia, Austria, and Russia? How did enlightened reforms help them to achieve those goals?
3. What cultural and intellectual connections existed between 18th-century Europe and the American colonies?

Suggestions for Further Study

Beales, Derek. *Joseph II*. Vol. I. Cambridge, MA, 1987.

Blanning, T. C. W. *Joseph II and Enlightened Despotism*. New York, 1970.

Gagliardo, John. *Enlightened Despotism*. Arlington Heights, IL, 1967.

Krieger, Leonard. *An Essay on the Theory of Enlightened Despotism*. Chicago, 1975.

Madariaga, Isabel de. *Russia in the Age of Catherine the Great*. London, 1981.

Palmer, R. R. *The Age of Democratic Revolution: A Political History of Europe and America, 1760–1800*. 2 vols. Princeton, NJ, 1964.

Ritter, Gerhard. *Frederick the Great: A Historical Profile*. Berkeley, CA, 1968.

Scott, Hamish M. *Enlightened Absolutism*. Ann Arbor, MI, 1990.

VII

Topic 2

The Industrial Revolution

Beginning in the 18th century, life in the West underwent a gradual transformation so far-reaching that the term "revolution" has been employed to describe it. The new era, in which machines and steam power took over functions previously the exclusive province of human and animal labor, produced unprecedented and continuing economic growth. Living standards for the vast majority of Europeans improved, while much smaller numbers of entrepreneurs accumulated huge fortunes. The social structure that came to characterize modern Europe was no longer determined by birth and inherited privilege but by economic class, defined by the relationship of individuals to labor and capital. This "revolution" gave rise by the 20th century to the western European civilization with which we are familiar today—a predominantly urban, industrial, and secular culture that was able to seize world power as a result of its mastery of science and technology.

Europe's transition from tradition to modernity was accelerated at the end of the century by the French Revolution (see Part VII, Topic 3). That political upheaval was, however, largely independent of this wider transformation. Three other sweeping changes had been at work in Europe before 1789: revolutions in population growth, in agriculture, and in the means of production. While the industrial revolution—a process rather than an event—unfolded more slowly across a longer period of time than the French Revolution, its consequences were even more crucial to the way in which most Europeans lived.

The Origins of the Industrial Revolution

Industrialization required certain preconditions: a labor supply, markets, investment capital, raw material, and technological innovation. The rate of industrial development also depended on the political, social, and economic circumstances that prevailed in a given country. The industrial revolution began in the 1760s in England, where the prerequisites were present at more or less the same time, and spread to the Continent after 1815.

The Agricultural Revolution

The great population explosion that began to unfold in the 18th century provided one essential element in the complex of factors behind the industrial revolution. This development was, in turn, closely linked to the improvement in farming and stock breeding that constituted an "agricultural revolution" in the 18th century.

Significant Dates

The Industrial Revolution

Jethro Tull (1674–1741) and Charles Townshend (1674–1738) contribute to the agricultural revolution

1705	Pumping machine
1733	Flying shuttle
1768	Water frame
1769	Steam engine
1770	Spinning jenny
1779	Spinning mule
1780s	Proto-power loom
1784	Puddling process developed
1811–1813	Height of Luddite movement
1815	Corn Laws
1825	First steam railroad in England

The tremendous increase in Europe's population had the effect of pushing the price of food higher, and this in turn made life difficult for the poorer peasants. The larger landowners who marketed their crops, however, earned more. As profits grew, so too did the inclination to increase income even further by improving cultivation methods. In the crowded Netherlands, where farmable land was in short supply, the Dutch had pioneered in planting new money crops, particularly turnips, and in reclaiming land through drainage and the construction of dikes.

In the 18th century, English landlords began copying these methods for consumption crops and became enthusiastic proponents of agricultural innovation. There, as on much of the Continent, two Medieval practices mitigated against the widespread adoption of new methods and crops: the three-field and the open field systems. The first consisted of the planting of crops on a rotating basis in which one field was planted with a winter crop, followed by a spring crop, and then allowed to lie fallow for a year in order to restore fertility (the three-field system was used in northern Europe; in the dryer regions of the south, where rainfall was limited in the summer, a two-field system was used). Under that system, a third of the land was unproductive each year. Although manure could alleviate the need for fallow land, the large number of animals needed for the purpose made this method prohibitively expensive.

In England, a number of landowners sought to overcome these problems by diversifying crops, trying other kinds of fertilizer, and developing new techniques and equipment. Jethro Tull (1674–1741), an agricultural inventor, developed a mechanical wheat seeder and used iron plows to dig deeper furrows. Tull's work in agricultural experimentation encouraged others. Charles "Turnip" Townshend (1674–1738) successfully used turnips and other crops on a rotating system—this was a crucial contribution, for by rotating crops that required different nutritional properties from the soil, the fallow field could be eliminated. His innovations were interconnected, for the new methods increased the quantity of animal feed produced per acre, and the resulting larger livestock herds were a source of manure for wheat and barley planting.

Such ideas were disseminated on the Continent through the writings of the French physiocrats. In England, where King George III (ruled 1760–1820) took a personal interest in agricultural improvements, special journals such as the *Farmers' Magazine* and the *Annals of Agriculture* were published. Similar magazines, filled with reports of experiments and practical advice, appeared later on in Italy, France, and other places on the Continent. The influence of British agricultural innovation on the rest of Europe is shown by the publication between 1798 and 1800 of a book by a German professor named Albrecht Thaer, *Introduction to the Knowledge of English Agriculture*.

The "open field" system of landholding was the other impediment to the modernization of agriculture. Traditionally, farmers owned property in the form of small, narrow strips of unconnected land. These strips were not fenced in, but rather open to those of other landowners. In addition, villages usually shared common lands on which animals grazed, while the entire community decided what crops to plant as well as the rotation plan. This splintered pattern of landholding, together with the communal decision-making process, made it virtually impossible for innovative cultivators to apply the new methods on a large scale.

The Enclosure of the Land

In order to create more productive, successful farms that could be effectively managed, some British landowners sought to put together large tracts made up of many contiguous fields that could be enclosed with hedges or fences. This tendency had begun in the 16th century, when farms were converted to sheep pastures and enclosed, in response to the growing wool trade. To achieve this purpose, lands formerly rented to peasants were taken back and consolidated with other small parcels to make larger units. Sometimes common lands and entire villages were enclosed. When poor farmers, who had benefited from the open field system, objected, the landowners secured the legalization of enclosures through the passage of special acts of Parliament. In the

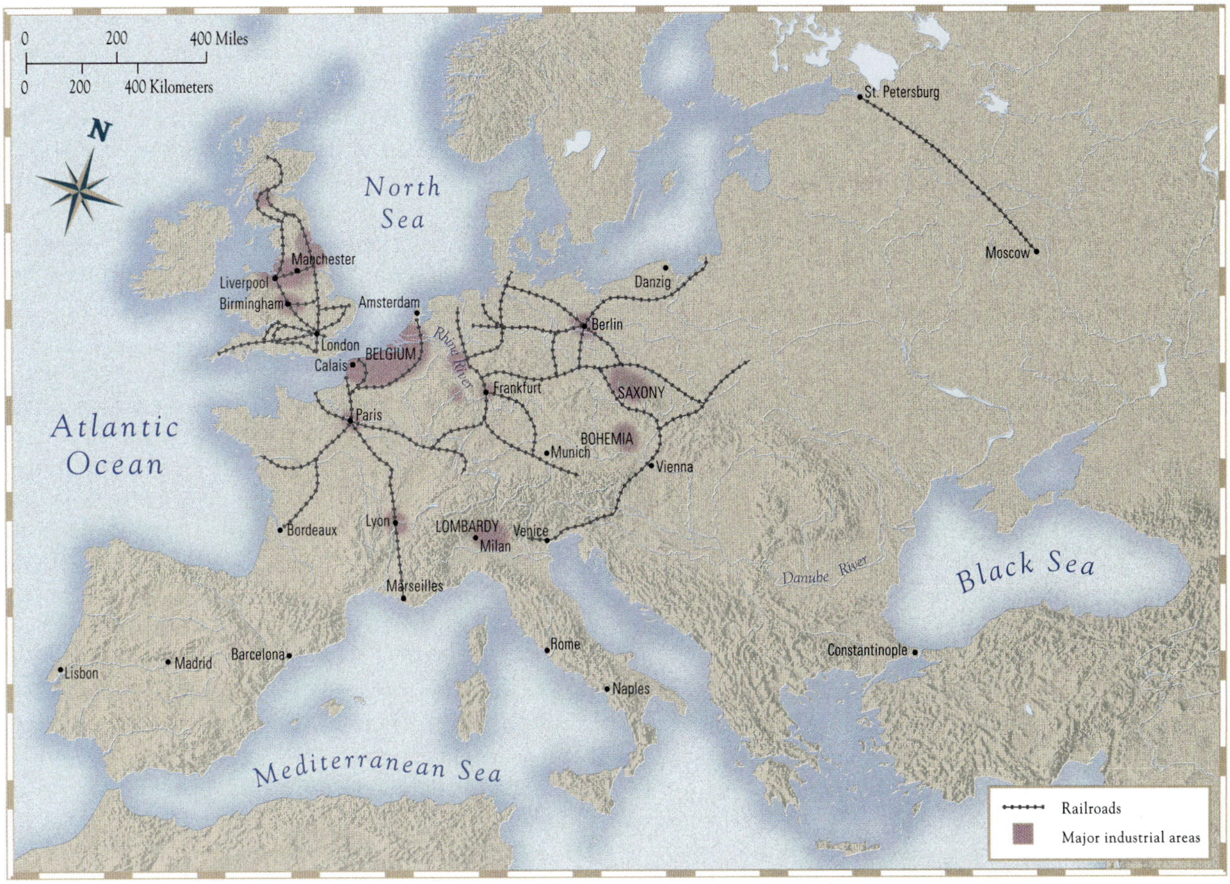

Map 2.1 Industrialization, c. 1850

second half of the 18th century alone, more than half a million acres of English farm land were enclosed in this manner.

The enclosure movement eliminated the open field system and altered English rural life. The small farmer was not only barred from the common fields but often relegated to unproductive pieces of land. Many lost the use of their plots and become workers without property, so that the English yeoman, or independent free landowner, became practically a thing of the past. At the beginning of the 18th century, most people in Great Britain had made their livelihoods in agriculture, but by 1800 less than half did so. And while some displaced peasants did move to the cities to seek employment, it is important to stress that the enclosure movement did not result in the widespread emigration of people from the countryside.

If the enclosure movement did not provide the workforce for the industrial revolution, it did have an impact on industrialization. Profits made from commercial agriculture increased the supply of capital available in England, and the example of rational farming managed by entrepreneurial criteria was increasingly followed in much of Western Europe in the 19th century. Moreover, the agricultural revolution, of which enclosure was a feature, increased productivity so significantly that for the first time food could be produced in sufficient quantity to feed both the countryside and the cities—at lower cost, with less labor, and on a consistent basis.

TECHNOLOGY AND INVENTION IN THE AGE OF STEAM

In its initial stages, the industrial revolution primarily affected three critical industries, textiles, mining, and metals, and was specifically concerned with the most important products of each: cotton, coal, and iron. At the heart of the transformation in these industries were two essential developments: the invention of machines that could make products or exploit raw materials faster, more efficiently, and in greater quantity; and the harnessing of forms of energy other than muscle power to drive the machinery. Together, these two features of industrialization resulted in the transfer of production from homes and small shops, chiefly in the countryside, to urban factories. The factory system, both a new means of production and a social factor of great significance, radically transformed the daily lives and the quality of existence for millions of people. The factory remains to our own day the primary unit of industrial production.

The Textile Industry

The English had been manufacturing wool for centuries. Next to agriculture, wool production employed more people and accounted for a greater volume of trade than any other industry. Wool, made in virtually every county in England and Wales, provided secondary work and income for farmers and agricultural workers. Yet the first significant technological innovations occurred in the manufacturing of cotton rather than wool. The demand for cotton had increased as a result of the India trade, which supplied most of the muslin and calico used in England. It was not only cheaper than wool, but was lightweight and could be cleaned by washing. Moreover, unlike wool, cotton could be dyed or printed by machine in bright, appealing colors. English spinners were unable, however, to make a cotton thread of sufficient strength or quantity, so that production was limited.

Encouragement for the development of new methods of cotton manufacturing came in 1700 when wool merchants, alarmed at the popularity of the competing fabric, secured the passage of import restrictions on printed cottons from India. In 1733, a clock maker from Lancashire named John Kay made an important improvement in the loom called the "flying shuttle," by which one worker could move the shuttle with wooden arms controlled by strings, instead of by hand. This speeded up the weaving and resulted in a much wider fabric at lower cost, although it was slow to be adopted.

Kay's shuttle improved the weaving process but the problem of spinning still remained. In 1738 Lewis Paul of Birmingham developed a device intended to do for spinning what Kay tried for weaving. Technical defects in both Kay's and Paul's inventions, as well as opposition from the spinners and weavers, created difficulties, and it was only in the 1760s that improved versions of these machines came into widespread use.

In 1770 James Hargreaves (?–1778), a weaver and carpenter, patented the *spinning jenny,* which he had developed several years earlier. With this simple machine, a worker could spin up to eight—and, with further improvements, many more—threads at once. The jenny spread rapidly, and by 1788 there were an estimated 20,000 machines in use in England. In 1768, Richard Arkwright (1732–1792), a barber by trade, invented the *water frame*, a device similar to Paul's early spinning machine. The frame required less skill than the jenny but more power than human hands could provide, so that a large installation with water power was needed. In 1771, therefore, Arkwright built a factory that eventually employed some 600 workers, mostly children. The water frame provided a major impetus to the creation of the factory system, its rollers and weights automatically spinning out the yarn at proper tension.

Two additional inventions made it possible for English entrepreneurs to produce cotton fabric on a massive commercial basis. In 1779 Samuel Crompton (1753–1827) invented the *spinning mule*, a steam-powered hybrid of the jenny and the frame that was able to produce high-quality thread. Crompton, a poor weaver, sold his patent rights for a mere £60, although many years later Parliament awarded him a settlement. In the 1780s, when the demand for cotton increased tremendously, Edmund Cartwright (1743–1822), a clergyman, developed a proto-power loom, which could be driven

Spinning mules in an English factory, 1834.

by horse, water, or steam, although it was not widely used until the 1820s.

As cotton factories and the new technology spread, centers that had once been sparsely populated burgeoned into urban communities. The city of Manchester, located in the county of Lancashire, became the first important center of urban industry, having the advantage of water supply, coal deposits, and the nearby port of Liverpool for shipping goods to customers abroad. By the late 1830s, cotton fabric accounted for half of all British exports. Moreover, in order to capture the Indian market entirely, the British made it illegal for Indians to produce cotton textiles, and between 1820 and 1840 exports to India rose from 11 million yards to 145 million yards.

The Industrial Matrix: Coal, Steam, and Iron

The British textile industry did not grow in a technological vacuum, for advances in factory production were dependent on metal processing to build the machines and on the availability of inexpensive energy to power them. This interdependency can be clearly seen in the development of the coal and iron industries, and the steam engine.

For many centuries the fuel for such tasks as heating, brewing, and firing furnaces had been wood or coal, but by the start of the 18th century English forests were depleted. Yet water power, on which the early industrial revolution had been based, also had its limitations, for the supply of water—and therefore its force—varied with the seasons. Moreover, factories had to be located at particular water sources, which were often far from markets, raw materials, and ports.

Coal, of which Britain had immensely rich deposits, provided a solution to the fuel problem. As the demand for coal increased, however, technical obstacles arose. Deep mining required shafts as deep as 200 feet below the surface, and the extensive networks of underground tunnels needed pumps for removing water and for ventilation. In 1698 Thomas Savery invented his "fire engine," a steam pump consisting of a boiler and a condenser. When the steam condensed, it created a vacuum that collected the water; more steam then forced the water up a pipe to the surface. Although it was a successful if primitive prototype of a steam engine, Savery's pumping device wasted energy. The first effective pumping machine was invented in 1705 by a blacksmith named Thomas Newcomen. Here steam was condensed inside a cylinder housing a piston, which was connected to a cross beam. When the steam condensed, producing a vacuum, the piston was driven down by atmospheric pressure and moved the beam, thus pulling up the pump player attached to the other end. Newcomen's engine was only slightly more efficient, but some 100 of them were in use by 1765 in coal mining, where fuel was cheap.

Newcomen's steam pump increased coal production, but it could be used only for pumping, not for turning wheels, so that it had little application in factories. It was James Watt (1736–1819), a mechanical engineer from Scotland, who succeeded in designing the first steam engine capable of operating factory machinery. He came to his discovery by accident when he was asked to repair one of Newcomen's machines for the University of Glasgow. Realizing the great waste of energy in heating and cooling the cylinder for every stroke, Watt made a simple but important design change: he installed a separate condenser in order to save heat. Watt received a patent for his steam engine in 1769, but continued to improve it. In 1782 he developed an even more effective engine that used the pressure of steam itself, rather than atmospheric pressure.

In perfecting the steam engine, Watt, a mechanical genius, would not have succeeded without the entrepreneurial daring and business sense of Matthew Boulton (1728–1809) of Birmingham. Watt moved to that city—the center of Britain's metal crafts and iron manufacture industry—and developed his invention with Boulton's capital. John Wilkinson, a local weapons maker, and other skilled technicians helped Watt to design further improvements, including a gear mechanism that turned the back and forth motion of the piston into the rotating motion of machine shafts.

Watt's new prime mover, twice as efficient as Newcomen's, was the great breakthrough in the industrial revolution, and intensified the interdependency of the various industrial sectors. The rotation device enabled the steam engine to power new iron industrial machinery as well as coal mining pumps. Its first widespread application was in the cotton factories, the rapid growth of which required both ever larger quantities of coal and more machines. In turn, the increased demand for steam engines and the machinery they powered provided the impetus behind the takeoff of the British iron industry and machine tools.

The manufacture of iron, however, faced technological problems of a different sort. The steam engine enabled the blast furnaces used in iron smelting to achieve higher temperatures—an important factor in determining the kind of fuel that could be used and, as a result, the purity of the iron. In smelting, the fuel was burned together with the iron ore. Coal could not be used for this purpose because its impurities mixed with and contaminated the iron. Consequently, charcoal, with less impurities, had always been used to smelt iron ore. This presented another problem, however, because charcoal was made from wood, which was becoming scarce and expensive. The first breakthrough was achieved by Abraham Darby (1678?–1717), who founded the Bristol Iron Company in 1708 and the next year succeeded in using coke—coal from which most of the gases have been removed—to smelt iron ore. In 1784, Henry Cort (1740–1800) took the process another major step forward with his "puddling process." As fuel for this method of melting and mixing the ore Cort used coke. In addition, iron made by the puddling process had a greater purity.

Once England's plentiful supply of coal could be used as a source of fuel for smelting, the iron industry began to expand. Other innovations followed quickly. Cort himself designed the rolling mill, which eliminated the need for ironmasters to beat the semi-molten iron into industrial shapes and thereby dramatically increased productivity while lowering costs. In 1815, James Neilson overcame the last obstacle to the unfettered use of coal with his "hot blast" process, which eventually enabled coal instead of coke to be used in smelting. This, in turn, produced a critical need for cheap transportation, a problem solved between 1770 and 1800 by the extensive network of canals built by the British.

FROM COTTAGE TO FACTORY: THE GROWTH OF INDUSTRIAL CAPITALISM

Until the industrial revolution introduced the factory system, textile manufacturing had been largely a rural affair, an important offshoot of the peasant economy. The rise of the factory toward the end of the 18th century transformed not only the system of production and the pattern of daily life for millions of workers, but the size and appearance of Europe's cities. Moreover, the large amounts of investment capital required to build the industrial system created a new form of capitalist enterprise and altered the relationship between business, finance, and government. It also expanded the distance between worker and management.

The Cottage System

Traditionally, poor farmers added to their incomes by processing, spinning, and weaving linen, wool, and later cotton cloth in their homes. All members of the peasant family—husbands, wives, children, and grandparents—participated in the various stages of the work. The cloth thus produced was not intended for domestic consumption, but for commercial markets. This so-called "cottage industry" spread widely in the 18th century, especially as unemployment increased as a result of population growth in the countryside.

The link between the peasant workers and the marketplace was provided by the merchant middlemen, who operated the "putting out" system as primitive capitalists. The merchants provided (or "put out") the raw wool to the peasant families, who worked it in their cottages with simple hand tools that included combing brushes, washing and dyeing vats, spinning wheels, and looms. The labor itself was generally divided along gender lines, with women and children processing the raw wool and spinning the thread and the men weaving the cloth. The workers received payment by the piece from the merchant, who traveled from village to village to put out the raw material and collected the finished product, which he then sold at regional marketplaces.

The cottage industry of the preindustrial age was a complete production unit. Here an Irish family works flax into cloth.

An illustration from Gustav Doré and Blanchard Jerrold's *London* (1872) showing crowded conditions in a working-class neighborhood.

Enterprising peasants occasionally altered the merchant-worker relationship. Some would buy their own raw wool and then sell the finished cloth to the merchants for a higher profit than the wages would bring, while others in effect acted as subcontractors, putting out the wool or thread to other peasant families. Because the slower spinning process could not keep up with the weaving, unmarried aunts, female cousins, and widows—"spinsters"—were often hired to work additional spinning wheels.

Cottage industry became a vital part of the British rural economy, but was not without its problems. Merchant-worker relations varied according to local practice and custom, and the distribution of the process across the countryside prevented the adoption of standardized procedures or quality control, so that the final product varied greatly. Since cloth making was a secondary occupation for most peasants, who worked long, hard hours tilling the soil, they were not inclined to keep to production quotas. Quantity remained low and, especially after cotton came into vogue, could not keep up with the rising demand.

The Rise of the Factory

The textile industry was the first sector to be affected by the factory system in a major way, but in all industries conversion to factory production was slow, both because of the enormous capital required and worker resistance to the machines and the work environment outside the home. It was also impossible before the age of Watt, cheap iron, and machine tools.

At first, most factories remained modest in size and number. In 1782, Manchester had only two cotton mills, while 20 years later the city boasted 52. In the late 1830s, by which time there were 100,000 power looms operating in England, Manchester had the largest cotton factories, which employed an average of 300 workers each. Between 1800 and 1850, the city's population rose from some 75,000 to more than 300,000.

The growth in population had reduced the scarcity of labor by the end of the 18th century. Nevertheless, though rural laborers were attracted by the higher pay, they moved to the urban factories with some reluctance, and only during periods of unemployment. Indeed, most factory equipment required little or no skill or muscle to operate, and many of the early factory workers seem to have been drawn from the unskilled urban classes. Only later, in the first decades of the next century, did large-scale migration from the countryside to the cities take place.

The concentration of labor under one roof and the new machinery not only increased productivity, but brought an entirely different mode of work and labor organization. "Factory discipline" was imposed on the independent-minded workers who, especially in the countryside, had controlled their own work pace, schedules, and leisure time. Time, once measured by the rising and setting of the sun for rural laborers, was now determined by precise rules laid down by employers. Most factories had bell towers, and later clocks, over their entrances to control the rhythm of life for industrial workers. Starting before sunrise, often at 5:30 A.M., factory employees usually worked for twelve to fourteen hours, and sometimes more, until British factory legislation in the 1840s lowered the workday to ten hours. Workers who arrived late were either locked out or fined.

Women and children were widely employed in coal mines because they were cheaper and less troublesome.

Factory conditions were inflexible, grueling, and dangerous. The long hours and monotony of tasks often led workers to fall asleep or collapse, and the incidence of industrial accidents was high, especially among children. Extremes of temperature from summer to winter, together with high humidity, filth, and polluted air, made the factories unhealthy places for workers. Foremen controlled the discipline inside the factories, imposing fines and layoffs on unruly or slack workers and sometimes meting out physical punishment. During the 19th century, such harsh working conditions were exposed and criticized by social reformers and government investigators, but improvements came slowly (see Part VII, Topic 13).

In the factories, as in the cottage, work was divided according to gender and age. Men did not only the heavier tasks, but were usually assigned the more skilled technical work. Women and children, on the other hand, were relegated to the simpler, repetitive work. In the early stages of the industrial revolution the majority of factory workers were women and children—indeed, even in the late 19th century, women continued to represent some 30 to 40 percent of the industrial workforce. Employers paid women and children less than men, and preferred them because of the assumption that they would conform more easily to discipline. Often workers secured employment for their entire family in the same factory. The division of labor into specialized tasks speeded up productivity and required less worker training. Artisans and skilled craftsmen who were drawn to the factories in hard times resented this simplification of the production process, but when they protested they were usually replaced with women and children (see Part VII, Topic 6).

INDUSTRIALIZATION AND THE EUROPEAN ECONOMY

Although industrialization proceeded slowly, it changed the means of production, the lives of workers, and the general European economy so radically that it has been called a "revolution." In those industries that it affected, productivity increased at an ever-accelerating pace, and in the first half of the 19th century industrialization spread from England to parts of continental Europe.

Industrialization proved to be particularly sensitive to political developments. Periods of war and peace, as well as government tariff regulation, affected markets and prices. Such fundamental transformation destabilized long-established social arrangements and intensified the impact of business and financial cycles on the immediate lives of ordinary people.

The Pace of Industrialization in Great Britain

At the end of the Napoleonic Wars, three-fourths of the population of Europe continued to earn their living from agriculture, and some 90 percent of the world's energy was still generated by human or animal muscle. Even in England, where industrialization was most advanced, two-thirds of the people lived and worked in rural areas. There, as late as 1815, more spinning was being done by hand than by machinery, and half the cotton mills were still powered by water. It was not until the 1820s that England developed a full-fledged industrial system.

Production figures for major industrial sectors reveal the pace of British industrialization. The output of pig iron, for example, jumped from a mere 17,000 tons in 1740 to 127,000 in 1786, and then rose to 248,000 in 1806. Thereafter, iron production generally registered steady increases, so that by 1835 it had reached more than 1 million tons, and by 1850 more than doubled to 2.285 million tons. Between 1815 and 1840, the mining of coal doubled, from 16 to 34 million tons a year, and in 1850 had increased to over 50 million. Similarly, the amount of raw cotton consumed by England's textile mills almost doubled every ten years between 1820 and 1850. In 1852, when the cotton consumption figure stood at 336,000 tons, cotton factories contained more than 20 million spindles and employed 500,000 people. By 1840, half of British workers were industrial.

Technological innovations also continued to multiply. The number of patents issued by the British government rose from less than a dozen a year before 1760 to 250 in 1825 alone. Technological innovations, originally developed for particular purposes, were quickly applied to other tasks—the high-pressure steam engine made it possible to power ships and railways, while the cheap iron was used to make bridges, weapons, buildings, and railway tracks.

In 1825 the British built the earliest steam railway that carried passengers; France followed in 1828, Belgium in 1835, and the German Confederation in 1839. The railroads provided a major stimulus to industrial and financial expansion. Private investors made huge fortunes by speculating in railroads, which also stimulated the demand for machinery, engines, and iron. Together with improved roads, canals, and bridges, the railroads created national—and international—markets, speeding up the movement of raw materials and finished goods as well as increasing worker mobility. Railroads made the industrial process itself more efficient, for they linked factories with mines and ports and the countryside with urban centers. British rail construction reached almost 10,000 kilometers by 1850.

By midcentury, Britain had become the wealthiest nation in the West—not only the "workshop of the world," but also its shipper, for it carried a third of the world's trade on its ships. Its output of coal, iron, and textiles exceeded the total production of all other European countries combined. Britain's role as the world's leading industrial power was maintained until late in the 19th century.

The Expansion of Industrialism

The industrial revolution spread to a number of other European states during the early part of the century. On the whole, industrialization moved more slowly on the Continent than it had in Britain, and it varied widely from country to country because of differences in social mobility, political cohesiveness, and resources. Moreover, most continental societies faced greater resistance to industrialism from traditional values. Nevertheless, industrial development began to transform Europe in the 1830s.

Belgium, which had won its independence from the Netherlands in 1830, led the way. The small country had coal and iron deposits of its own as well as a long tradition of textile manufacturing and trade with Britain. Moreover, its entrepreneurs readily received English technological innovations. The British machine firm of Cockerill, which had a factory branch in Belgium early in the industrial revolution, sold machinery and steam engines to neighboring countries. France, the German Confederation, Russia, and even Sweden outproduced Belgium in charcoal pig iron, but between 1815 and 1850 Belgium mined more coal than they did. The new nation-state planned and built its railroads with lines linking it to France, the German Confederation, and the Netherlands. In 1840,

The Stockton-Darlington Railway opened in England in 1825.

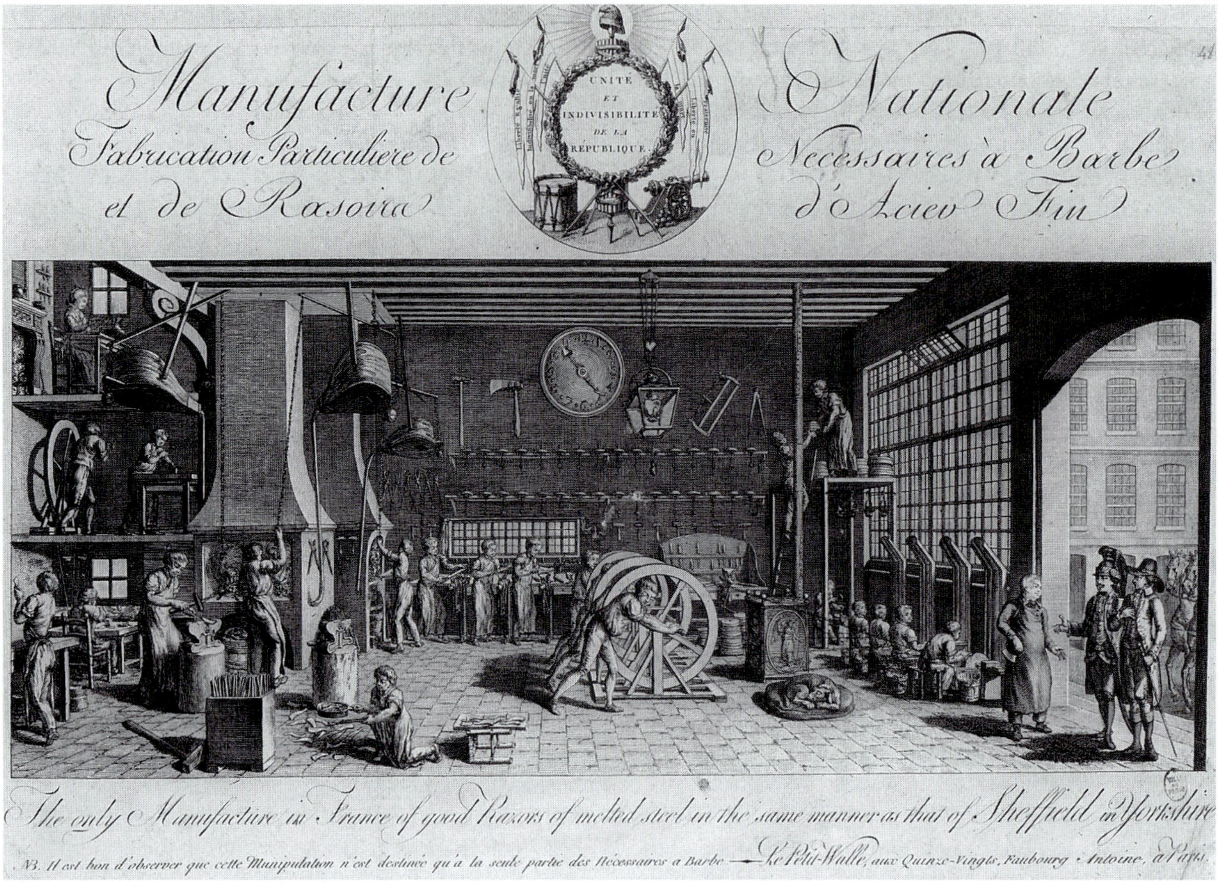

Engraving of a steelworks in Paris in 1800.

10 percent of its population of 4 million were industrial workers, making Belgium the first industrialized country on the Continent.

France ranked as the major industrial power on the Continent throughout the first half of the 19th century, second only to Britain in iron and textile production. Its familiarity with technology dated to the late 18th century, when drawings and entries on traditional machines and industrial processes were published in Diderot's *Encyclopedie*. Napoleon had encouraged scientific inquiry and technological experimentation, and by 1810 the Creusot works were using coke for iron smelting. Lille in northeastern France contained rich coal and iron deposits, and it was there that much of the country's industry developed.

Under the liberal monarchy of Louis Philippe after 1830, private business received some encouragement and support. Railways, roads, and canals were built and improved with capital from private banks. Along with cotton mills in Normandy and Alsace, France also had an important silk manufacturing center at Lyon, and almost doubled its cotton and iron production between 1830 and 1850. Moreover, by midcentury the country had more steam engines than the rest of continental Europe combined. Despite such gains, however, the Prussians were already generating more horsepower, and although more than a million French workers were employed in large-scale industries, half of all Parisian workers—where a total of 400,000 were employed by midcentury—were still in small preindustrial shops.

The German states, which after unification became Europe's new industrial giant in the late 19th century, were hampered by political division. The Prussians took the lead in trying to overcome this disability by eliminating all internal tariffs within their borders in 1818. More important for long-range development, Prussia advanced the 1834 tariff union, which included most of the important German states and did much to increase trade and industry. The coming of the railroads in the mid-1830s was the major factor in sparking industrialization, for a common market was of little use without cheap transportation. The Prussian industrialist August Borsig manufactured locomotives outside Berlin with the support of the future King Friedrich Wilhelm IV, and, between 1835 and 1850, German railway lines grew from 6 to almost 6000 kilometers—half of which were in Prussia alone. The German states had laid the foundations for becoming a center of the continental network of transport and distribution.

The German Confederation was rich in mineral resources, but its early industries imported much of their iron from the French region of Lorraine. German coal and iron mines in the Ruhr, the Saar, and in Silesia were first developed in the 1830s. In the Ruhr a coal merchant named Franz Haniel had pioneered deep shaft mining and then expanded into manufacturing. The firm of Friedrich Krupp (1787–1826), founded in 1810, developed iron and machine factories in Essen in the same period, although at the time the company first used steam engines in the 1840s, it employed less than 200 people. The Krupp Works later went into armaments manufacturing. Nevertheless, during the first half of the 19th century the German states lagged behind France and Russia in pig iron production and were only slightly ahead of Belgium in coal mining. Despite such limited beginnings, before the achievement of national unification in 1870–1871 the Germans had begun to challenge Britain's industrial supremacy.

Instability and Crises in the European Economy

During the first years of the industrial revolution, the profit margin was extremely high in Britain for those enterprises that did not fail, for although wages rose steadily, prices for food and manufactured goods had kept ahead of them. The Napoleonic Wars had helped to create an artificial demand for arms and other industrial goods, but this situation collapsed in 1815 with the coming of peace. Prices dropped, reducing profit and investment. The results were especially harsh for the working class. Some 300,000 veteran soldiers were suddenly added to the labor market. To make matters worse, in 1815 the powerful landowners had secured passage of restrictionist tariffs on grain, known as the Corn Laws. This legislation increased the cost of food and kept it high, thereby reducing spending power for manufactured goods. Across the English Channel, where the economy had been artificially sustained by Napoleon's Continental System, the end of hostilities brought similar distress, with conditions in southern Italy possibly the worst in Europe.

The European economy recovered temporarily in 1820. Britain established its currency on the gold standard and good harvests drove down the price of food. But the rapid expansion of industry in the early 1820s led to uncontrolled speculation and a bust. For the next several decades, economic depressions and bad harvests followed each other in succession in 1825–1826, 1838–1839, and 1846–1847.

The response from manufacturers was to keep profits up by cutting costs. Despite the periods of economic crisis, real wages for British workers had risen during most of the first half of the 19th century, and it was in the area of wages that the savings came. The lowering of wages, the extension of factory work hours and discipline, and cyclical unemployment constituted a general trend in labor-management relations. Factory owners also redoubled their efforts to introduce labor-saving devices, expecting that increased mechanization would reduce production costs.

WORKERS, MACHINES, AND LABOR PROTEST

As machines found their way into more and more factories and industrial sectors, their impact on the lives of workers became more evident. To the workers themselves it was clear that technology and factory production represented elements of a new economic system that would deeply alter their daily lives. The response came in the form of a radical worker movement that sought to destroy the machine and hold back the tide of what they regarded as the increasing repression of the industrialists.

The Machine and the Worker

The factory system was a social institution of major significance as well as a unit of production. As we have seen, workers who took employment in factories during the industrial revolution experienced a degree of regimentation unknown in agrarian society.

As the major component in the factory system, machines were central to the work process. Their introduction caused a serious psychological impact on those operating them. Machine technology created a routine of monotonous dehumanization, in which the workers were removed from what had once been a creative process over which they had exercised control. Now, for the sake of greater productivity and cheap consumer goods, laborers would lose control over their own labor.

Nor were workers themselves alone in seeing the problem of technology in these terms. In 1819, a report issued by inspectors of the Prussian government observed that:

> Factory owners . . . have become accustomed to consider the productive workers and their subordinates and children to be incidental appendages to the machines, and that it is sufficient for them . . . that their bodies go through the appropriate motions.[1]

In 1832 Charles Babbage (1792–1871), who invented a primitive form of the computer, argued in *On*

[1] Quoted from John R. Gillis, *The Development of European Society, 1770–1870* (Boston: Houghton Mifflin Company, 1977), 163.

Economy of Machines and Manufactures that the principles of mathematical precision and the calculating machine could be applied to the factory system.

Some workers of the early 19th century saw the machine as a means of restructuring social relations between the working class and the property-owning middle class to their disadvantage. They realized that layoffs and lower wages were the result of machine-based industry. As one historian has observed, "people at the point of production were the first to comprehend the full significance of the first Industrial Revolution."[2]

The Luddites and Labor Resistance

Workers were no mere passive observers of the process of mechanization. Indeed, as early as the Middle Ages there had been examples of workers who took action to oppose the introduction of new machinery. In 1753, the home of John Kay was destroyed by spinners protesting his flying shuttle. Similarly, Hargreaves' spinning jennies and Arkwright's water frame had also been subject to industrial sabotage by workers.

The most celebrated incident in the movement to smash machines took place in 1811, when stocking knitters in Nottingham began protesting wage cuts. Calling themselves followers of the mythical Ned Ludd, the "Luddites" organized themselves into groups of 50 or so men and wrecked knitting frames with heavy hammers and metal pikes. In January 1812, after the passage of a law making machine breaking an offense punishable by hanging, the Luddites issued a statement from "Ned Ludd's Office, Sherwood Forest," declaring their intention to continue their operations. That year the movement spread to the woolen trade and cotton towns, where William Cartwright's factory was attacked. In all, perhaps as many as 1000 mills were destroyed in the Nottingham area, and some factory owners killed.

The British authorities saw the Luddite movement as a plot against the government and an "insurrection of poor against the rich." A parliamentary committee investigating the uprisings agreed to the use of troops, despite the eloquent appeal of the English poet Lord Byron (1788–1824) in the House of Lords that the machine breakings "have arisen from circumstances of the most unparalleled distress." In January 1813, 17 Luddites were hanged in York. Although the machine breaking continued sporadically over the next several years, including a major incident near Manchester as late as 1829, the movement was eventually crushed.

Later, the Luddites were viewed as irrational primitives intent on holding back progress. More recently, however, some historians have concluded that these workers were not against technology as such, but rather against the social changes that the new technology reinforced. Along with their violent assaults on the factories and machines, the Luddites issued rational statements about wages, market conditions, and other technical issues that affected their livelihoods. In a period when trade unions were outlawed as conspiracies by association, the Luddite movement constituted a form of organized protest against employers and their efforts to replace labor with machines in order to lower costs of production. Against this desperate but deliberate campaign, in which machine breaking was not just a tactic but the central purpose, later critics devised what has been called "an ideology of technological progress" which regarded machines as both inevitable and essential to human welfare.

The Luddites in England were not an isolated case. Throughout the 19th century, similar worker movements incorporated machine breaking in their labor tactics in other countries, including those of the silk weavers in Lyon in 1831 and linen weavers in Silesia in 1844. Yet the labor movement was to take quite another direction, especially after the rise of socialist parties and trade unions in the second half of the century. In the plight and the protests of the Luddites, however, there came together the central issue: the human consequences of the industrial revolution.

On one level, the term "industrial revolution" refers to a series of technological innovations between the mid-18th and the early 19th centuries that enabled human beings to produce food and manufactured goods faster, in greater quantity, and more cheaply. The revolution in production was possible because the new machines were made of cheap iron and run by a new form of energy—the use of coal to produce steam power. In industry proper, these advances were applied first to the making of textiles and iron.

In another sense, however, the industrial revolution is associated with a complex set of social and economic changes that transformed European civilization. These changes involved not only population growth, but the way in which millions of ordinary men and women led their daily lives. The shift from the cottage industry to the factory system altered the relationship between worker and work as well as between worker and entrepreneur. The formation of an industrial labor force affected how society was structured and had important implications for gender relations, family structure, and sexuality. The revolution in industry also brought a radical change in how and where people lived, drawing people from country to city, and affecting housing, health, and general living conditions.

For two centuries after the start of the industrial revolution, the West—Europe and the United States—exercised unchallenged economic and political hegemony over

[2] David F. Noble, "Present Tense Technology," in *Democracy*, vol. 13 (1983), 10.

the rest of the world. This unique position was due above all to technological achievements and industrialization.

Questions for Further Study

1. What did population growth and agriculture have to do with the industrial revolution?
2. Which were the most important inventions of the industrial revolution? How did one invention stimulate a demand for still more inventions?
3. How did the factory system change labor and social life?
4. By what process did industrialization spread from England to the Continent?

Suggestions for Further Reading

Ashton, Thomas S. *The Industrial Revolution, 1760–1830.* London, 1961.

Chambers, Jonathan D., and G. E. Mingay. *The Agricultural Revolution, 1750–1850.* New York, 1966.

Cipolla, Carlo M., ed. *The Industrial Revolution, 1700–1914.* London, 1973.

Crafts, N. F. R. *British Economic Growth During the Industrial Revolution.* New York, 1986.

Dennis, Richard. *English Industrial Cities of the Nineteenth Century.* Cambridge, MA, 1984.

Henderson, William O. *The Industrial Revolution in Europe.* Chicago, 1961.

Hobsbawm, Eric J. *Industry and Empire.* Harmondsworth, England, 1970.

Landes, David. *The Unbound Prometheus: Technological Change and Industrial Development in Western Europe.* Cambridge, MA, 1969.

Mathias, Peter. *The First Industrial Nation: An Economic History of Britain, 1700–1914.* New York, 1969.

Mokyr, Joel, ed. *The Economies of the Industrial Revolution.* London, 1985.

Perkin, Harold. *The Origin of Modern English Society, 1780–1860.* London, 1969.

Thompson, Edward P. *The Making of the English Working Class.* Harmondsworth, England, 1964.

VII

Topic 3

Revolution in France: Liberty, Terror, Reaction

Before 1789, no one had foreseen anything like the French Revolution, a political and social upheaval so vast in its repercussions as to be judged the most important event in Western history in the modern era.

The Revolution swept away the social system of the Old Regime that had rested on noble privilege (on the Old Regime, see Part VI, Topic 10). Thereafter, feudalism ceased to exist in France while power and influence were opened to those with wealth and ability. The events that took place in France from the late 1780s to the mid-1790s gave shape, through trial and error, to the very concept of "revolution" as a means of solving fundamental political and social problems. It ushered in the age of "mass politics," in which once politically passive social groups, such as the peasantry, workers, women, and the urban poor, now became active participants in the making of history. The revolutionary slogan, "liberty, equality, fraternity," became a permanent part of the Western political vocabulary as the ideal expression of political liberalism.

In France itself, the Revolution gave birth to the nation-state, whose sovereignty was seen not as the will of a divine right king, but as the expression, first, of the nation and then of the people. The new state mobilized and claimed the allegiance of all citizens. Beginning in 1793, citizen soldiers extended these revolutionary ideals, together with French conquest and occupation, beyond the borders of France. The Napoleonic Wars provoked staunch resistance that helped to stimulate nationalism throughout the Continent. In less than a generation, the Revolution profoundly and permanently changed the face of Europe.

The Third Estate and the "Rights of Man"

The Revolution had its distant roots in the underlying social trends that had characterized the Old Regime. In a more immediate sense, however, it came as a result of a fiscal crisis that was mishandled by an inept king and his ministers.

The Calling of the Estates General

By the end of the 18th century, the Seven Years' War and intervention in the American Revolution, together with the high costs of the royal court, had brought the French government to the edge of bankruptcy. When he came to the throne in 1774, King Louis XVI (ruled 1774–1792) had appointed the physiocrat Jacques Turgot (1727–1781) as his finance minister. But Turgot's plan to extract revenue from the nobility, together with the opposition of Queen Marie

Significant Dates

The French Revolution

1774–1793	Louis XVI rules as king of France
May 5, 1789	Estates General meets
June 17, 1789	National Assembly formed
July 14, 1789	Bastille stormed
August 4, 1789	Feudalism abolished
August 26, 1789	Declaration of Rights of Man and Citizen
October 5, 1789	March to Versailles
1790	Civil Constitution of the Clergy
June 1791	Flight to Varennes
April 20, 1792	War against Austria
August 10, 1792	Attack on Tuileries Palace
September 1792	"Massacres" in Paris
January 21, 1793	Louis XVI executed
March 1793	Vendeé uprising begins
June 1793–July 1794	Reign of Terror
October 1793	Marie Antoinette executed
February 4, 1794	Slavery abolished
March 1794	Widespread arrests and executions, including Danton
July 27, 1794	Thermidor
November 1799	Coup by Napoleon Bonaparte

Antoinette (1755–1793), led to his downfall. Most of Turgot's replacements followed the same approach and, as a result, fared no better. Jacques Necker (1732–1804) pushed the government further into debt by borrowing heavily at high interest rates and in 1783 he, too, was dismissed. Charles Alexandre de Calonne (1734–1802), Necker's eventual successor, revived Turgot's plan by proposing a single land tax on the First Estate (the clergy) and the Second Estate (the nobility). Both estates had been largely exempt from direct taxation but together controlled perhaps a third of all French agricultural land and a comparable portion of French income.

In February 1787, Louis XVI called a special Assembly of Notables, consisting mainly of great lords and prelates, to endorse Calonne's measures. The assembly insisted on preserving the basic distinctions between the three social orders. Louis then replaced Calonne with the former archbishop of Toulouse, Loménie de Brienne (1727–1794), hoping that he would be able to convince the stubborn nobility and his fellow clergymen to accept the taxation. Brienne took the tax reform to the Parlement of Paris, the judicial body empowered to approve new laws, but he, too, failed to win the backing of the notables. Instead, Parlement demanded the convocation of the Estates General.

Exasperated by the intransigence of the privileged orders, Louis then declared that royal prerogative alone made the new taxes legal, and ordered the closing of the Parlement. Nobles protested and some of the lawyers from the Parlement stirred up provincial riots. It was, however, the middle-class bankers who forced Louis to capitulate by refusing to lend the government any more money. Finally, in 1788 the king recalled Necker and that August agreed to the demand of the nobles and clergy to call the Estates General.

The Estates General represented the three traditional principal social orders of clergy, nobles, and the Third Estate of peasants, workers, and bourgeoisie. The principles of absolutism had led Louis XVI's predecessors to rule without consulting the Estates General, which had not met since 1614. The convening of the assembly was decisive in the coming of the French Revolution, for it brought the less privileged middle classes into the political process.

Delegates were elected in the winter and spring of 1789. The elections provided an opportunity for a public analysis of national problems, for the delegates circulated lists of ills that reflected regional concerns. Most of these documents, called *cahiers de doléances* (grievance reports), were not statements of revolutionary principle. Rather, they were specific complaints concerning provincial abuses, corruption, and administrative waste. Only in Paris and other principal cities did some of the cahiers reflect such Enlightenment ideas as social justice and legal equality.

As the Estates General prepared to meet, Louis XVI reacted ineptly, attempting unsuccessfully to maneuver between the interests of two increasingly competing social groups, the nobility and the bourgeoisie. The nobles, intent on regaining a role in government and preserving their privileges against the monarchy's encroachments, fully expected to dominate the proceedings. The middle classes, aspiring to share power and status as they grew in wealth and numbers, sought to end the monopoly of special privileges enjoyed by the other two orders; more specifically, the bourgeoisie wanted to be certain that the national debt was not repudiated so that their investments would be safeguarded.

The opening of the Estates General in May 1789.

The Tennis Court Oath and the National Assembly

Each estate had roughly the same number of representatives, but the Third Estate, led by lawyers and business groups, represented 98 percent of the population of France, including workers and peasants. It asked, therefore, for double the number of representatives and to vote by head—this would have enabled the Third Estate to control the outcome, since some clergy and liberal nobles wished to support reforms. The aristocrats, on the other hand, had demanded that each estate have one vote, which would have given the First and Second Estates the ability to determine all decisions. Persuaded by Necker to make concessions to the Third Estate, the king agreed to double the number of representatives, but did not give in on the issue of voting by head rather than by order. In January 1789 the Abbé Emmanuel Sieyès (1748–1836) published a pamphlet entitled *What Is the Third Estate?*, proclaiming the political agenda of the middle classes in this way: "What is the Third Estate? *Everything*. What has it been in the political order up to the present? *Nothing*. What does it ask? *To become something*."

When the approximately 1700 deputies (including alternates) gathered at Versailles in May, the hostility of the court was made clear to the delegates of the Third Estate. After the opening ceremonies, each order was assigned its own chamber. Louis' refusal to bend on the voting issue provoked the first major act of revolutionary defiance on the part of the Third Estate, which found another spokesman in the skillful and persuasive politician Honoré Gabriel de Mirabeau (1749–1791), a renegade noble who had won election as a deputy for the Third Estate. On June 17, with Sieyès and Mirabeau to guide it, the Third Estate, along with some clergy, constituted itself as the National Assembly and called upon the other two orders to meet with it as a single body. This prompted the king to act, and the delegates of the Third Estate found themselves locked out of their meeting hall. The outraged deputies gathered instead in a tennis court and swore not to disband until they had written a constitution for France.

The so-called "Tennis Court Oath," taken on June 20, forced the weak-willed monarch to back down again, especially after many of the clergy and liberal nobles joined the middle class. Louis remained indecisive, but at a special session of the Estates General on June 23, he declared that the deputies could discuss constitutional matters only in separate chambers, and warned them not to tamper with the army or property rights. Threatening to dismiss the Estates General if he were not obeyed, he commanded the deputies to separate immediately into the three traditional orders. To the king's aide, who repeated the royal command at the end of the session, Mirabeau is said to have responded for the National Assembly, "Go and tell those who sent you that we are here by the will of the people, and that we will go only if we are driven at the point of the bayonet." On the 27th, the ever-hesitant Louis announced that the three estates would meet together as the National Assembly in order to draft a constitution (the National Assembly later renamed itself the National Constituent Assembly). The king had sanctioned the demise of absolute monarchy in France.

The People and the Revolution

The creation of the National Assembly was the first real revolutionary event, for the inclusion of the middle classes constituted the end of government controlled exclusively by the nobility and the monarchy. Despite the domination of the Third Estate, the National Assembly was a rather conservative body. Its members, drawn from a minority of the French people, were wedded to the protection of property, the maintenance of social order, and the preservation of the monarchy, but they also wanted a role in government decisions that they had lost under absolutism. The summer of 1789, however, saw the entrance of two genuinely revolutionary forces into the already complex political situation—the peasantry of the countryside and the lower classes of the cities. These forces, perceived as a common threat by most of the delegates to the National Assembly, would push the Revolution in a more radical direction.

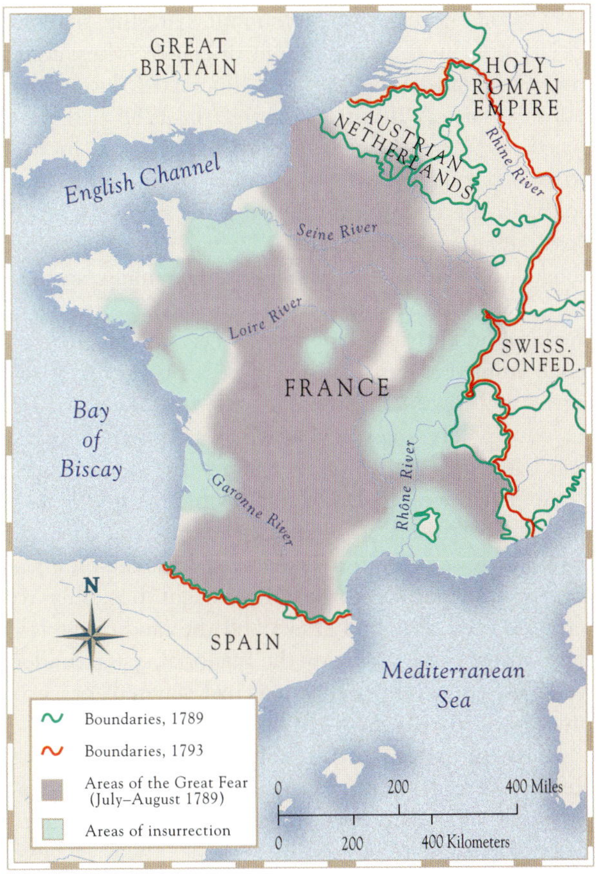

Map 3.1 France in Revolution

The Tennis Court Oath. An oil sketch attributed to Jacques-Louis David depicts the Tennis Court Oath, June 20, 1789.

Food shortages and economic hardship sparked social unrest in the rural regions of France, where farm prices had fallen and taxes had increased during the last 20 years. A disastrous harvest in 1788 had produced severe grain losses and a spiraling rise in the price of bread, the basic staple of most French households. In the countryside the peasants stopped paying taxes and the "seignorial dues" which they had been obliged to render to their landlords, the church, and local nobles since Medieval times. The peasants regarded the local nobility as their enemy. Acts of organized violence erupted as early as May as peasants burned local castles and town halls in order to destroy tax and dues records. In July, these revolts merged with the "Great Fear," a series of panics that swept the countryside. These panics were fueled by rumors that the nobles and their hired brigands were killing peasants and destroying the new crop about to be harvested. As the rural social order deteriorated, peasants sought not only to seize the food they had grown and the land on which they worked, but to destroy the manorial system under which they and their ancestors had suffered for centuries.

In the cities, where food shortages and the increase in bread prices coincided with growing unemployment, demonstrations and riots broke out. In Paris, a city of more than half a million people, the royal government had 5000 troops and police to maintain public order, but as unrest grew, Louis XVI gathered another 20,000 soldiers outside the city. Groups of citizens, consisting mainly of artisans, small shopkeepers, housewives, and wage earners, had been organizing themselves on the ward level ever since the elections to the Estates General. Now, fired by signs that the king was turning against the Revolution, they formed a citizen militia and attacked barracks in search of weapons. Later the militia became the National Guard, commanded by the Marquis de Lafayette (1757–1834), a liberal and respected hero of the American Revolution. Lafayette designed a flag that combined the red and blue of Paris with the white of the royal family, thus producing the "tricolor."

On July 11, Louis suddenly dismissed Necker, the only nonnoble minister in the government and a man who had been regarded as protector of the people. Parisian crowds, intoxicated by alcoholic beverages and revolutionary oratory, erupted in anger. This insurrection, which was also a food riot, climaxed on July 14 with the storming of the Bastille. Rumor spread that arms were stored in the Bastille, an old fortress used to house special prisoners and defended only by 80 retired soldiers and 30 Swiss guards. When the crowd broke into the courtyard of the Bastille, about 100 citizens were shot and killed. With help from renegade government troops who joined the insurgents with cannon, the fortress surrendered. The enraged mob massacred the commander and several guards, cutting off their heads and parading them through the city on pikes. The fall of the Bastille became a powerful symbol of the unfolding revolution.

The peasant violence and the fall of the Bastille were dramatic evidence of the revolutionary spirit of the common people. Radical delegates in the National Constituent Assembly, heeding the temper of the people, seized the initiative. Late on August 4, an exceptionally hot and humid night, a liberal aristocrat who himself owned no land called upon the nobles and clergy to renounce all their feudal rights and dues. Frightened by the growing disorder in the country, and caught up in the passionate scene, the delegates of the

Map 3.2 Revolutionary Paris

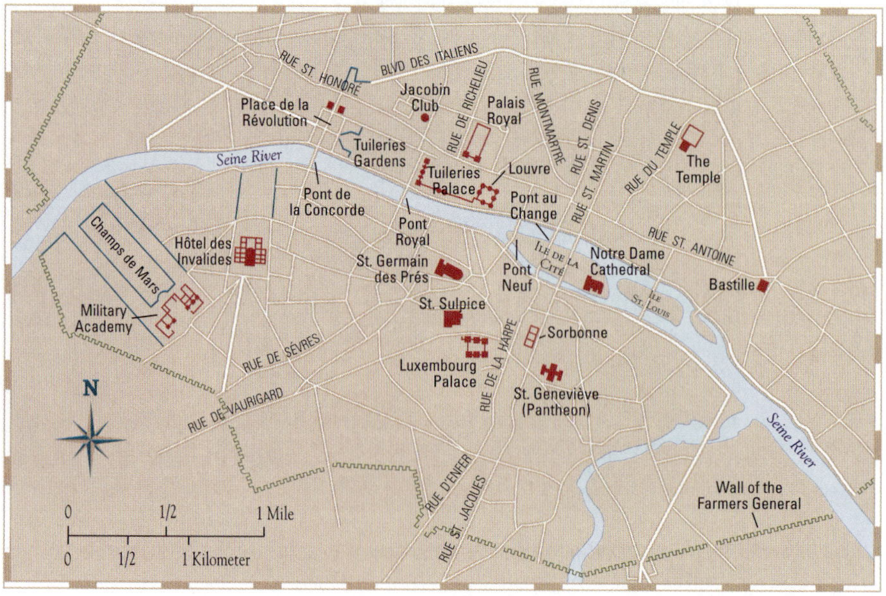

Depart des Heroines de Paris pour Versailles le 5 Octobre 1789.

A sketch of the armed women of Paris marching on Versailles, October 5, 1789.

First and Second Estates rose one by one to surrender their ancient privileges. Later, the assembly thought more carefully about what it had done and tempered its action by declaring forms of compensation for lost rents. By the next morning, however, feudalism had been all but eliminated in France.

Later that month, the National Assembly issued a set of general principles on which to base the constitution that it was drafting. The "Declaration of the Rights of Man and of the Citizen," issued on August 27, reflected Enlightenment thought as well as the ideas that had inspired the leaders of the American struggle for independence. Proclaiming that all people were born "free and equal in rights," the document identified "liberty, property, security, and resistance to oppression" as the most important of these rights. Citizens were to enjoy freedom of worship, equal access to public office, and equality before the law, while government was to protect these rights and tax its citizens only according to their income.

The framers of the Declaration assumed that laws and government were the expression of popular will—that is, that "sovereignty" resided in the nation. This assertion was to have important European consequences. In defining political sovereignty in national terms, the Declaration elevated nationalism to a sacred doctrine that, in its extreme form, claimed blind devotion and loyalty. Under the threat of foreign invasion, the doctrine of revolutionary nationalism would succeed in mobilizing millions of Frenchmen.

Popular unrest continued unabated through the fall, despite the Declaration and reform decrees issued by the National Assembly. In Paris the supply of grain from the bad harvest of the previous year had all but run out. Hunger, together with encouragement from radicals and suspicions against Louis XVI and the unpopular Marie Antoinette, aroused the people to action. On the morning of October 5, a large group of housewives demanding bread caused a disturbance at a baker's shop. After being joined by more women from the market, they moved on to the municipal hall, which they ransacked. Eventually a force of several thousand women began marching to Versailles, their ranks swelled along the way. Lafayette followed them with the National Guard. The next day, after a violent skirmish with palace guards, the mob forced Louis, Marie Antoinette, and their son to follow them back to Paris, where they took up residence in the Tuileries. The crowd chanted, "we have the baker, the baker's wife, and the baker's child." A few days later, the National Assembly also moved to Paris. The king had become a virtual prisoner of the Revolution, and the mob could now keep a watchful eye on both the royal family and the National Assembly.

THE ASCENDANCY OF THE MODERATES

In the two years between the Declaration of the Rights of Man and the adoption of the constitution in 1791, the National Assembly governed the nation. Its policies changed France in a number of fundamental ways that reflected the interests and values of the middle classes that dominated the assembly.

Property and the Church

Economic issues were at the center of the assembly's actions. The Declaration of the Rights of Man had stressed that "Property being a sacred and inviolable right, no one can be deprived of it unless a legally established public necessity evidently demands it, under the condition of a just and prior indemnity." Having made private property secure, however, the assembly still had to deal with the huge debt that had brought the royal government into crisis in the first place. Rather than repudiate the debt—which was owed to the middle-class bankers and merchants—the bishop of Autun, Charles Maurice de Talleyrand (1754–1838), proposed another solution. In November 1789 the assembly endorsed his proposal to confiscate and sell off all lands belonging to the Catholic Church.

With the anticipated revenue from the sale of church property as backing, the assembly issued bonds, called *assignats,* to finance the debt, despite urgent warnings from Necker. The assignats were so popular that they were soon used as currency, and the assembly issued even more, thus fueling inflation. Nevertheless, the sale of church land had a long-range stabilizing effect, for it enlarged the number of property owners in France. Buyers of the land, mainly the middle class and the wealthier peasants, were thereby tied more closely to the successful outcome of the Revolution. Petitions from the landless peasantry for the division of the large estates were ignored.

The church found further reason for declaring itself an enemy of the Revolution. The abolition of ecclesiastical tithes and the confiscation of the land made the Catholic Church in France financially dependent on the government. The following July, therefore, the assembly passed the "Civil Constitution of the Clergy," a measure that placed the church under the jurisdiction of the state. The act reduced the 139 bishoprics in France to 83, and parishes and dioceses were redivided into simpler, more uniform units, the latter conforming in territory to the new administrative *départements* into which the assembly had already divided France itself (see below). Priests and bishops were henceforth popularly elected—even by Protestants and Jews—and paid government salaries.

The Civil Constitution, which undermined the independence of the church and the authority of the pope in the most fundamental ways, generated considerable controversy. When it became clear that some bishops and priests would resist, the assembly went even further by requiring the clergy to swear an oath to abide by and support the constitution. Half of all French priests—the more affluent—and most bishops refused to take the oath, earning them the designation of "nonjuring" or "refractory" clergy. The papacy naturally supported the protests of the clergy. With these and other measures the Revolution had created a rift between the state and the church in France that continued into the next century.

Economic liberalism, together with the interests of the middle classes, influenced the assembly's policies. A number of direct taxes—on land, on income from commerce and manufacturing, and on rents—were voted, but they proved difficult to collect. In order to stimulate trade and business, the assembly abolished internal tariffs and monopolies granted by the crown, and standardized weights and measures by the introduction of the metric system. The old guilds were abolished so as to lift restrictions on professions and crafts, but the assembly passed the so-called Le Chapelier Law (June 14, 1791), which outlawed worker unions and the right to strike in accordance with the principles of 18th-century economic liberalism.

The Constitution of 1791

It was not until September 1791 that the assembly completed the constitution under which France was to be governed. While it did not address all the ills of the Old Regime, the constitution did reflect the theories of Enlightenment reformers who wanted government to be rational, efficient, and just. Local administration was standardized and a simplified judicial system with elected judges and prosecutors introduced. The former patchwork of provincial subdivisions was replaced by 83 départements of roughly equal size, each further subdivided into smaller administrative units in which local assemblies were elected.

The Constitution of 1791 transformed the French government into a limited, rather than an absolute, hereditary monarchy. The king still appointed and dismissed his ministers at will, but the power to legislate was invested in a body called the Legislative Assembly, chosen by indirect election. The king could temporarily veto its measures, although the Legislative Assembly could override the royal veto by approving a bill in three successive assemblies. No one who had served in the National Assembly was permitted to participate in the new body, with the result that its members were more radical and less experienced.

The Constitution was by no means a radical democratic document. The Declaration of the Rights of Man had proclaimed that all citizens were free and equal, but the right to vote was limited in a number of important ways. The population was divided into two categories, "active" and "passive," a distinction based on wealth. Only French males who were 25 years of age or older, and who paid taxes equivalent to three days' wages, had the franchise. A voluntary tax also enabled a passive citizen to become an active one. These men voted for electors, who in turn chose the deputies.

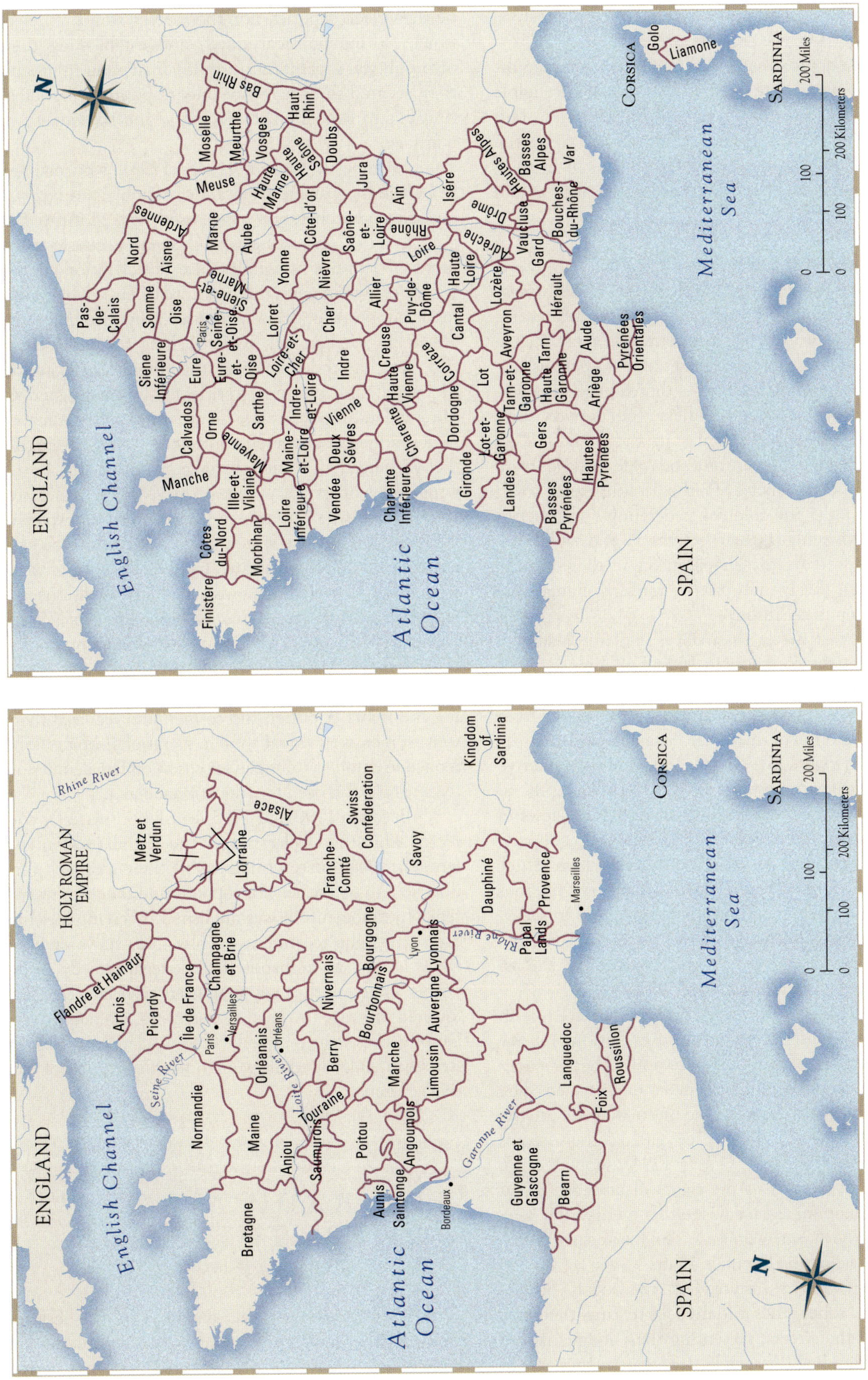

Map 3.3 Administrative Changes in France

Higher income qualifications were required of electors, and deputies had to be property owners.

Of the approximately 26 million French people, 4.25 million could vote, only 50 thousand were eligible to serve as electors, and even fewer as deputies. This formula of limited male suffrage, which was to be the pattern of European constitutions throughout most of the 19th century, essentially placed political power in the hands of men of property.

Women and Minorities

The status of women and minorities in revolutionary France provides further evidence of the moderate outlook of the National Constituent Assembly. Some deputies had, for example, argued in favor of abolishing slavery, but economic interests—those of the shipowners, merchants, and sugar refiners who derived their profits from the sugar colonies in the French West Indies—prevailed. Slavery and the trade in slaves were preserved. In September 1791, the deputies voted to allow assemblies in the colonies to determine whether to give political rights to their free blacks and mulattoes. The results were deeply disappointing to these groups, and in Haiti, the French part of Santo Domingo, the blacks rose up in rebellion.

Jews fared better than slaves and free blacks at the hands of the Revolution. Most Enlightened monarchs had taken steps to integrate Jews into the state in the 18th century, but in France their status varied from region to region. The National Assembly had first debated Jewish rights as part of efforts to define "active citizenship" for voting purposes, but without result. In January 1790, an exception was made for the Jews of Bordeaux, Bayonne, and Provence, whose economic status and social contacts enabled them to claim "élite" status among their people. Some Parisian Jews, rigorous supporters of the Revolution, then succeeded in securing the endorsement of voters for emancipation from most of the city's districts. In September 1791 the assembly passed a law enfranchising all Jews.

As we have seen, women played an active role in some of the leading events of the Revolution. Yet the Declaration of the Rights of Man was just that—a document that proclaimed civil equality among men. The Enlightenment philosophes had been divided on the question of women's rights. A few, such as the Marquis Marie Jean de Condorcet (1743–1794), supported the "admission of women to the rights of citizenship" on the basis of natural rights; most either ignored the issue or, like Rousseau, saw women as childbearers and incapable of participating in public affairs.

Frenchwomen, inspired by the ideals of the Revolution, seized the initiative by taking their demands into the streets, presenting their arguments before the National Assembly (to which they could neither elect deputies nor themselves stand for election), writing political tracts, and establishing their own political organizations. Individually and in groups, they asserted their right not only to political participation but to education, to property, and to equality in marriage.

Olympe de Gouges (1748–1793), who claimed to be the illegitimate daughter of a nobleman but was raised by a butcher, was a successful writer for the theater. In 1791, she wrote what became a classic statement of feminist principles, the "Declaration of the Rights of Woman and the French Citizen," deliberately modeled on the document issued by the National Assembly (see Part VII, Topic 6). In it, she underscored the fact that the framers of the original Declaration had violated revolutionary principles by creating a double standard in politics. De Gouges argued that equality between men and women conformed to the natural order, and urged all women to take an active part in the struggle for liberty. She appealed to Marie Antoinette, "mother and wife," to assume leadership in the women's movement, a mistake which later caused her to be executed as a royalist sympathizer. In 1792, de Gouges' views were echoed by an Englishwoman, Mary Wollstonecraft (1759–1797), in her *Vindication of the Rights of Women* (see Part VII, Topic 6). Basing her argument on the Enlightenment belief in reason, Wollstonecraft chastised the framers of the Constitution of 1791 for limiting the rights of citizenship to men and lectured them that women were equal to men as rational beings. She replied in detail to Rousseau's position on female inferiority, stressing the need for educational equality.

Between 1790 and 1793, legislation partially corrected what the Declaration of the Rights of Man had ignored. Illegitimate children and their mothers were now able to sue fathers for support, and the ancient system of primogeniture was abolished by giving all children the right to inherit equally. New laws enabled wives as well as husbands to seek legal remedy in divorce, while another law permitted civil marriage and lowered the age of legal consent for women to 21. Despite these gains, the Jacobin leaders, inspired by Rousseau, did not admit women to the category of "active" citizens.

THE RADICALS IN POWER: THE REIGN OF TERROR

Within two years of the meeting of the Estates General, the social order and political structure of France had been radically changed. Yet this period represented only the first, more moderate phase of an ongoing revolutionary process. The upheaval grew more extreme over the next several years as conservative opponents, whose world of privilege, monarchy, and tradition had collapsed, and radical patriots, who felt that change had not gone far enough, pressed the Revolution from both sides. Meanwhile, the Revolution also aroused active opposition from the conservative powers of Europe, especially Austria and Prussia.

Revolution Within a Revolution

The crisis of the Revolution had actually begun as a result of a failed effort by Louis XVI to leave the country. Escape plans had been under way ever since October 1789, when the royal family had been forced to leave Versailles and move to Paris. In June 1791, Louis XVI, encouraged by French emigrés, attempted to flee with his family to Belgium but was caught at Varennes and brought back to the capital. Louis, who had maintained secret contacts with monarchist supporters in the National Assembly as well as with emigré nobles and the Austrian government, had thus proven himself an enemy of the Revolution.

The constitution that was then being drafted rested on the premise of a monarch committed to the constitution. Louis' actions had the effect, therefore, of undermining the document even before it was adopted. The king's capture, together with radical threats against the monarch, drew a sharp reaction from abroad. On August 27, 1791, Emperor Leopold II (ruled 1790–1792) of Austria (Marie Antoinette's brother) and King Friedrich Wilhelm II (ruled 1786–1797) of Prussia issued the Declaration of Pillnitz, in which they threatened to intervene in France if the royal family or the monarchy were in danger. Both radicals and moderates began clamoring for war against these external enemies of the Revolution.

The flight to Varennes aroused the ire of the Parisian radicals, who condemned the king as a traitor to the Revolution. The moderates in the assembly, on the other hand, had been weakened by the death of Mirabeau. They spread the story that the king, whom they regarded as a force for stability, had been kidnapped. Indeed, the split between radicals (the "left") and moderates (the "right")—the terms *left* and *right* derived from the seating arrangements in the assembly—had grown sharper ever since 1789. For some time the radicals had been organizing political clubs through which to discuss and spread their ideas. The most influential of them, the Jacobin Club (which took its name from its meeting place, the former St. Jacques monastery of Dominican friars, who were known as Jacobins), consisted chiefly of educated members of the Third Estate such as the physician-turned-journalist Jean Paul Marat (1743–1793) and the lawyer Georges-Jacques Danton (1759–1794). The views of the Jacobins, who corresponded with branches in the provinces, grew increasingly radical. The political clubs provided opportunities for leadership, maintained contact with the deputies, and explained the actions of the assembly to the people. The Jacobins gained control of the municipal government of Paris and began to forge an alliance with the common people of the city. Now, in the face of Louis' attempt to flee, they insisted that France needed a republic instead of a monarchy. An influential radical press controlled by members of these clubs, chief of which was Marat's *L'Ami du Peuple* (*Friend of the People*), incited the Parisians.

The more radical Legislative Assembly elected in 1791 pushed through laws against the noble emigrés and the refractory clergy and spearheaded the call for a declaration of war against Austria, which was passed on April 20, 1792. Soon France was at war with Prussia as well. Over the king's veto, the Legislative Assembly voted to create a force of 20,000 national guardsmen to defend Paris.

The war, depicted at home as a crusade against the enemies of the Revolution, started out poorly. A Prussian army repelled the French troops and pushed their way across the border. Proclaiming the nation to be in mortal danger, the assembly pleaded for citizen volunteers. From abroad, the duke of Brunswick, the Prussian commander, announced on July 15 that he would take any action, including the destruction of Paris itself, in order to prevent harm from befalling the royal family.

Brunswick's threat both energized the spirit of resistance and emboldened the radicals. On August 10, the communal leaders of the capital staged an uprising that changed the course of the Revolution. A large crowd, angry at the king's attempt to escape, broke into the Tuileries. While the Parisians fought a bloody battle with the king's Swiss guard, Louis and Marie Antoinette fled to the Legislative Assembly for safety. The wrath of the people frightened the deputies, and after suspending the king's powers, many of them left the city. Parisian militants forced those deputies who stayed behind to schedule elections to a new body, known as the National Convention, and to dissolve the Legislative Assembly.

Jacobins, Sans-culottes, and the National Convention

In the aftermath of the dethroning of Louis XVI, the Revolution faced three serious problems: a dangerous and expanding war, deepening economic crisis, and the growing anxieties of the Parisian masses. To these dangers were soon added a royalist uprising and a widening factional division within the ranks of the Jacobins.

Under these combined pressures, the temper of the Revolution accelerated and reached its most extreme form in the "Reign of Terror" that engulfed France.

The majority of deputies elected to the Legislative Assembly had originally called themselves royalists or constitutionalists, but leadership soon passed into the hands of two radical groups that emerged out of the Jacobin Club—the Girondists and the Mountain. A group of deputies around Jacques Brissot (1754–1793) and the philosophe Condorcet, known as Girondists, after the region of France from which many had come, formed a fiery cadre of brilliant orators. The Girondists had supported the war and extreme measures against the nobles and the clergy, but they began to draw back from popular violence and feared that the radicalization of the Parisian masses would result in anarchy. The Girondists were soon forced out of the Jacobin Club by more extremist radicals.

In early September 1792, as Paris was rife with rumors of counterrevolutionary plots, common citizens unleashed a startling massacre. Crowds of workers, shopkeepers, and artisans stormed the prisons, from which it was believed that thousands of royalists would break out in the event of foreign invasion. Popular courts were improvised and in ritual fashion they condemned and brutally ordered the executions of more than 1000 prisoners, many of whom were common criminals and prostitutes. These "September Massacres," for which no rational explanation can be adduced, set the tone for the next two years of the Revolution.

News of a French victory at Valmy on September 20 helped to calm the atmosphere of tension in Paris. The National Convention, elected on the basis of universal male suffrage, met for the first time the following day. Among its deputies was a group of extremist Jacobins elected from Paris that included Danton, who had helped to incite the storming of the Tuileries; Marat, who had cheered on the September Massacres; and Maximilien de Robespierre (1758–1794), who became the principal architect of the terror that was to come.

These men formed a nucleus of radical Parisian Jacobins known as the "Mountain," so-called because its members sat high up in the chamber of the convention. The Mountain believed the war would consolidate support at home for radical domestic measures against the counterrevolution. The Girondists outnumbered the Mountain, but Robespierre and his colleagues quickly learned to outmaneuver opponents with help from the crowds of Paris. The Mountain and the Girondists, who attacked each other with increasing bitterness, were soon locked in a deadly battle for control of the convention and the support of the several hundred deputies in the center, known as the Plain. Neither group, however, represented an organized party with consistent ideas.

The fate of Louis XVI was the first major issue over which the Mountain and the Girondists fought their struggle for mastery of the Revolution. As one of its first acts, the convention abolished the monarchy and declared France a republic. But what was to be done with the deposed king? While the Girondists sought to spare Louis, the Mountain demanded his execution. In the trial that took place in December, the Mountain prevailed. Louis XVI was found guilty by an overwhelming margin, although he was then condemned to death by a vote of 361 to 360. He was beheaded by guillotine on January 21, 1793. Marie Antoinette's turn followed in October, after a trial in which her allegedly promiscuous sexual conduct formed part of the charges against her.

The leaders of the Mountain, men skilled in oratory and the manipulation of popular sentiment, had understood from the beginning that the radicalization of the Revolution was the result of direct action by the common people of Paris—the *sans-culottes*, or people "without breeches," so-called because, unlike the aristocrats who wore knee breeches, the working populace wore long trousers. In the sans-culottes the Mountain recognized a unique political force that, if properly guided and manipulated, could be used as an avenue to power. Since the fall of 1789, men like Danton and

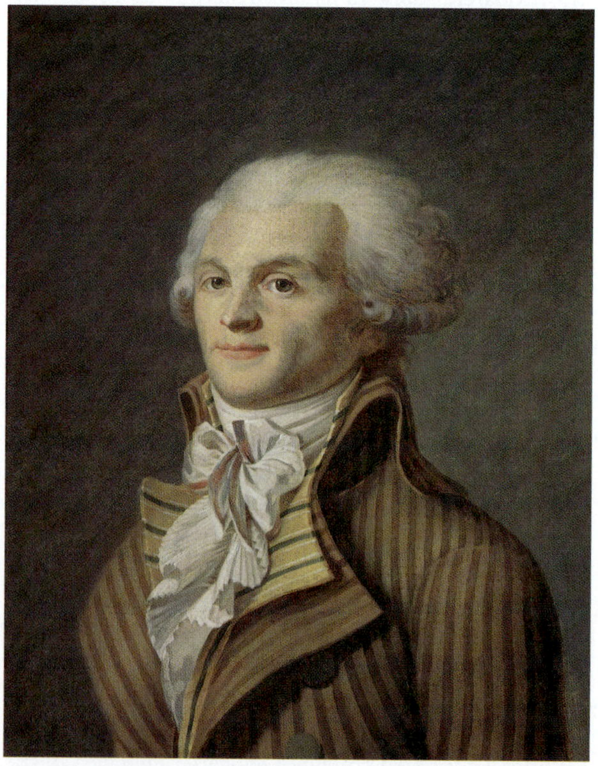

An anonymous portrait of Robespierre.

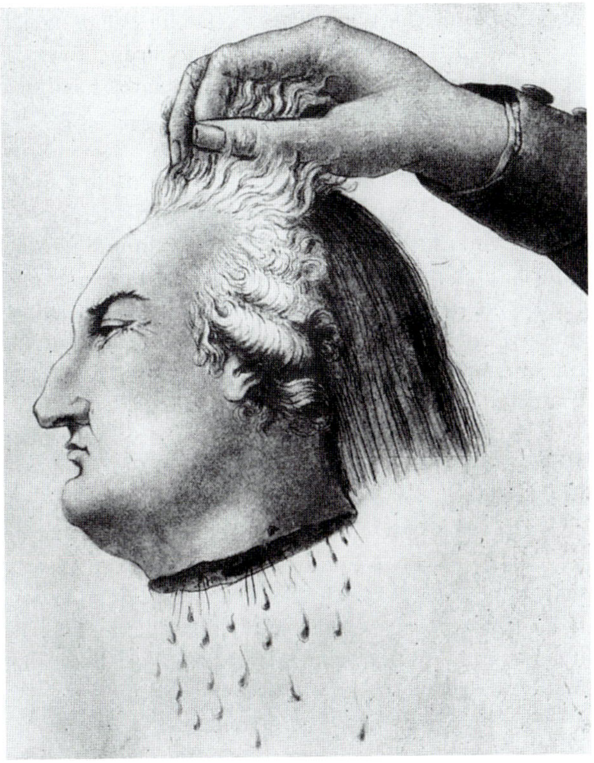

The head of Louis XVI shown to the monarchs of Europe.

Robespierre had been encouraging the Parisian masses with their democratic rhetoric. In the National Constituent Assembly and the Legislative Assembly, they had railed against the moderates for their proroyalist position and the economic problems that beset the nation; now, in the National Convention, they continued to play to the crowds, charging the Girondists with responsibility for the continuing economic hardships and chronic food shortages. Over the next year and half, the Mountain regarded the sansculottes as its constituency, implementing extremist policies in their name and, in turn, being goaded on by them to impel the Revolution further.

The Jacobins in Power

The National Convention came into being as the fate of the Revolution hung in the balance. A week after the execution of the king, the convention declared war on Great Britain. By April, revolutionary France was also at war with Austria, Prussia, the Netherlands, Spain, and Piedmont-Sardinia. At stake, however, were not the traditional issues of power politics. In December 1792 the convention had proclaimed its intention of helping the other peoples of Europe to free themselves from the tyranny of kings and the oppression of the Old Regime. The monarchs of Europe responded, therefore, not only to French military aggression, but to the dangerous ideology of revolution that its armies promised to export. The conflict, with frequent changes in alliances and brief periods of peace, dragged on for the next 20 years.

In the offensive launched by Austria and Prussia in 1793, French troops suffered serious reverses after initial victories. In March their commander, General Charles Dumouriez, defected to the enemy. Unrest at home worsened the crisis. The convention voted to impose a military draft, just as food riots erupted once again in Paris. That same month the peasants of the Vendée, in western France, rose in revolt against the Parisian leaders of the anticlerical Revolution. In the spring and summer, Lyon, Marseilles, and Bordeaux followed suit. In all cases, royalist agitators channeled local discontent into counterrevolutionary insurrections.

The Mountain and the sans-culottes drove the convention into action to deal with these challenges. In March "surveillance" committees were set up in towns and villages to crush counterrevolutionaries. The following month saw the establishment of the twelve-member Committee of Public Safety, which functioned as the executive branch of government. The committee was quickly dominated by Robespierre and his fellow

Marie Antoinette on the way to the guillotine as sketched by David.

radicals, and for the next year or so they acted as the real government of France. In late May, the leaders of the Mountain prepared to assume all power. They charged the Girondists with treason and complicity with the enemy, while the sans-culottes staged a massive demonstration before the convention. On June 2, under the combined pressures of the Mountain and the crowd, the convention voted to expel and arrest some two dozen Girondists. The extremists were now in control of both the convention and the Committee of Public Safety.

With domestic power secured, the committee turned its attention to the war, which was going against the French. The military effort was now placed under the direction of Lazare-Nicolas Carnot (1753–1823), a military engineer who had served in the Legislative Assembly and was now appointed to the Committee of Public Safety. In August, Carnot proclaimed the mobilization of the entire nation—a *levée en masse* that drafted all single males, from every social class, between 18 and 25. Since most high-ranking officers had been nobles, the Revolution produced a critical shortage of military leaders. To solve this problem, as well as to instill patriotic spirit among the conscripted soldiers, noncommissioned officers were elected, while higher ranks were to be appointed on the basis of talent. Within six months, more than 800,000 soldiers were raised and France seized the military initiative once again.

On the home front, civilians were mobilized by propaganda to support the war effort and to produce war materiel. The levée en masse also called upon women, children, and the aged to contribute their skills, from farming to cooking, to the victory. On September 5, following another large demonstration of the sans-culottes, the committee imposed stringent economic policies, including price controls and measures to prevent the hoarding of food. In this unprecedented manner, the entire French nation went to war.

The 1793–1794 period, during which the "Reign of Terror" triumphed, has gone down in history as the most infamous phase of the French Revolution. Under the rule of the Mountain, the government was rigidly centralized and all internal dissent silenced. Along with the economic controls imposed that September, the committee passed the "law of suspects," whereby the local surveillance committees were given authority to arrest citizens suspected of disloyalty and, in turn, try them by revolutionary tribunals. Local branches of the Jacobin Club, reporting back to the central club in Paris, acted as watchdogs of the Revolution in the provinces. Over the following months, domestic revolutionary armies were created to crush the peasant uprisings in the Vendée and put down the rebellion of the southern cities. All local committees were made directly responsible to the Committee of Public Safety, which demanded total unity and obedience to its directives.

In July 1793, a young woman named Charlotte Corday (1768–1793), inspired by Girondist rhetoric, assassinated Marat in his bath, convinced that she had rid France of an evil influence. For her deed, Corday was guillotined. With Marat dead, Robespierre came to be regarded as the leader of the Mountain and now assumed direction of the Committee of Public Safety. Under his command, the committee not only orchestrated a campaign of systematic terror aimed at purging the enemies of the Revolution but also undertook to transform the everyday life of all citizens.

Robespierre and the Republic of Virtue

Robespierre was a complex man, selfless in his absolute commitment to preserve the republic, single-minded in his determination to protect the Revolution. A self-righteous, ascetic young bachelor, a lawyer by profession, he had earned a reputation among his colleagues as "the Incorruptible." Yet despite his radicalism, Robespierre refused to alter his elegant prerevolutionary dress. An admirer of Rousseau's *Social Contract,* he claimed to speak for oppressed humanity and made himself the spokesman of the sans-culottes. Robespierre asserted that revolutionary times required two qualities—virtue and terror. The republic created by the Revolution would, he believed, engender civic virtue in all citizens, who should devote themselves to the service of the nation and their fellow citizens. He took from Rousseau the vision of an ideal republic—a "Republic of Virtue"—in which both poverty and excessive wealth would be eliminated, and in which reason, trust, and justice would reign.

For all his idealism, Robespierre was cold-blooded in ordering the execution of the Revolution's enemies—or his own. His fanaticism led him to believe that terror was another name for revolutionary justice. The purpose of the Terror was to purify the nation and impose obedience on it by impressing citizens with the severity of republican discipline. The justification for the Terror was that immediate liberties had to be sacrificed to the future of a free republic.

The Terror was used against a wide variety of people, many of whom simply disagreed with the policies of the Committee of Public Safety. The victims of the guillotine included former nobles and priests, peasants and workers, members of the convention and some of Robespierre's own colleagues in the government. By the winter of 1794 the Terror was turned against republican politicians, both on the right and the left. In March, extreme radicals in Paris known as the *enragés* (the "wild men"), led by Jacques Hébert, were beheaded for plotting to destroy the republic. The next month came executions of conservative republicans,

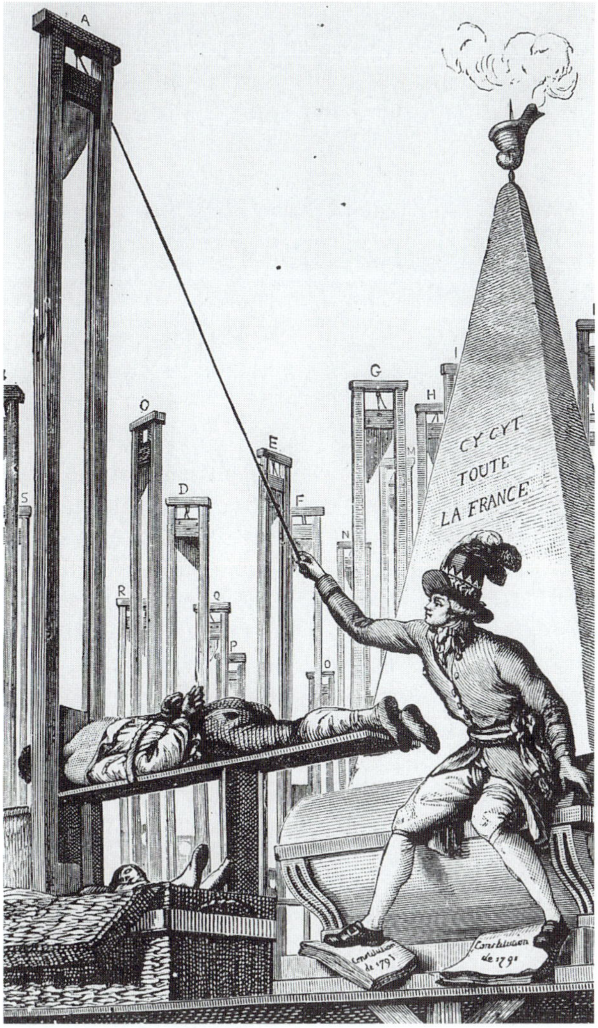

A contemporary print satirizing the Reign of Terror—Robespierre executing the executioner.

including Danton himself. In June, Robespierre had a law approved that allowed for the conviction of suspects without evidence. In all, nearly 30,000 people were executed before the Terror was over.

Along with the Terror came deliberate efforts to demonstrate in tangible ways that the Revolution had remade history and created an entirely new world. Beginning in September 1792, government documents were dated from "Year I of the French Republic." In October 1793, a new calendar was put into effect (used until 1806), based on "reason" and "nature." The new dating system began with the first day of the republic. There were ten days in a week, three weeks in a month, and twelve months in a year. The remaining five days were declared republican holidays. The months were named after seasons and the weather, such as Brumaire (fog) and Thermidor (heat).

Not only did the calendar symbolize a new era in human history, but it was also part of a larger effort to dechristianize the nation. In place of established religions the Revolution now proclaimed the worship of Reason. Churches were systematically closed and the clergy persecuted, and the Cathedral of Notre Dame in Paris was turned into a "Temple of Reason." In May 1794, Robespierre abandoned the worship of Reason because he believed it too difficult for common people to understand. In its place he substituted the deistic Cult of the Supreme Being, which he hoped would promote civic morality.

The transformation of everyday life went further. New forms of public discourse were adopted—"citizen" became the proper term of address for all French people—and streets, buildings, and even cities were renamed according to the revolutionary vocabulary. In dress, trousers of the sans-culottes were adopted by men, while more severe dresses with high necklines and flattened skirts became the style of female attire. Prostitution and gambling, identified by revolutionary propagandists as typically aristocratic vices, were repressed, and a cult of veneration for the virtuous mother became the order of the day. Even chess pieces and playing cards were changed in order to eliminate references to such vestiges of the past as kings, queens, and knights.

If the Revolution had proclaimed the general will as the basis for French politics, the Terror and the changes in social custom and mentality were part of a program to create a particular kind of public will, not to allow for free expression. As expressed through the Jacobin Clubs of the cities, these policies represented the high point of the influence of the sans-culottes and those who claimed to speak for them. When the inevitable reaction to these policies came, the Revolution shifted course once again.

RETURN FROM THE BRINK: FROM THERMIDOR TO THE DIRECTORY

The dictatorial rule of Robespierre and the Committee of Public Safety was sustained by the need for strong government in the midst of the war and domestic instability. In 1793–1794, following the levée en masse, the French armies once again went on the offensive and won a series of important victories. In June 1794, French troops occupied the Austrian Netherlands, as they had done once before, and annexed the territory. Similar successes on the Rhine frontier and the Pyrenees led to the negotiation of peace terms with Prussia, Spain, Piedmont-Sardinia, and Austria. Having also crushed provincial rebellions against the republic, by

PERSPECTIVES ON HISTORY

The Historians' French Revolution

Jack R. Censer
George Mason University

The tumultuous political storms of the French Revolution as well as the complexity of the event itself have made agreement among historians extremely elusive. To understand the current controversies requires a survey of how earlier scholars interpreted its causes and development. Early in this century the most visible battle was the struggle between two French historians, Alphonse Aulard (1849–1928) and Albert Mathiez (1874–1932). Like many other scholars of his day, Aulard ignored social and economic factors and focused on ideas and politics. In his best-known book, *The French Revolution: A Political History* (1901), he approvingly chronicled the rise of republicanism. But what is most notable about Aulard's work was his overwhelming commitment to the moderate Georges Danton rather than to the Jacobin Maximilien Robespierre as the representative man of the Revolution. Aulard and his followers were especially concerned about rescuing Danton's reputation from charges of corruption. By cheering on revolutionary republicanism and embodying it in Danton, Aulard could praise a government vaguely similar to the moderate reformist Third Republic—the regime of his own day to which he wished to lend support (on the Third Republic, see Part VII, Topic 15).

Mathiez, who had been Aulard's student, broke with the older man in nearly every way. Interested more in social and economic than political factors, Mathiez also glorified Robespierre and the Jacobin dictatorship. Mathiez's politics—sometimes socialist, occasionally communist—doubtless influenced this perspective, so contrary to his mentor's. In particular, in Robespierre's speeches about equality Mathiez could find forerunners of his own 20th-century positions.

Although Aulard and Mathiez both demonstrated extraordinary knowledge of the historical sources, the tendency of each to praise his personal hero often made their work unconvincing. Such history seemed to approach propaganda and encouraged the emergence of an entirely new focus. It was mainly the avowedly Marxist Georges Lefebvre (1874–1959) who supplied a fresh perspective in the 1930s. This historical vision, whose later champions would include Albert Soboul (1914–1982), generally maintained—like other Marxists—that antagonisms among different social classes led to the founding of a new order. But even earlier during the Old Regime, argued Lefebvre, a political competition between the monarchy and nobility had demolished the solidarity of the elite. Social tensions then intervened. Peasants, workers, and particularly the middle class, or bourgeoisie, went into the Revolution hoping to redress their long-term grievances against the aristocracy. Class conflict likewise explained revolutionary developments. Once in charge, the bourgeoisie forgot its alliance with the other two classes and pursued its own interests until the summer of 1793, when middle-class radicals came to power assisted by the Parisian working class. From this point on, revolutionary governments mainly reflected how power-hungry bourgeois politicians capitalized upon the lower classes' social and economic problems. Politics moved leftward as leaders increasingly sought the support of urban workers; and it reversed direction after the summer and fall of 1794 when politicians, stunned by growing working-class independence, drew back from the demands of the poor. The middle class found the only sure protection against both the working class and nobility to be an agreement with the military in general and Napoleon in particular. Finally, this class conflict interpretation used the dominance of the bourgeoisie to explain the consequences of the Revolution.

But by the beginning of the 1980s new findings of North American and English historians had largely undermined this widely accepted view. First, it seems that prior to 1789 there may have been little social conflict between aristocracy and bourgeoisie. Furthermore, under the Old Regime, nobles proved as likely as commoners to support Enlightenment notions that challenged, at least in theory, both the absolute monarchy and the social organization of the Old Regime. Such positions suggested that an independent revolutionary middle class, vital to Lefebvre's position, did not exist. And historians also found problems in the Marxist interpretation of the revolutionary decade itself.

In the last 20 years new general interpretations have come along to replace Lefebvre and Soboul's. Of all these overviews of the French Revolution, François Furet's remains the most influential. To Furet, ideas possessed the power that Lefebvre attributed to social class. Thus he presented a story of competing ideologies. Ways of thinking—not class interests—played the determining role. Furet began by describing (and defending) the ideology that undergirded the French Old Regime. Although revolutionaries criticized this philosophy for protecting a system of special privileges, Furet argued that they did not understand the benefits of such privileges. Under the Old Regime, he claimed, residency in a city or participation in a craft guild, just like the rank of nobility, served to guarantee individuals' freedom (here defined as lack of oppression). But such traditional privileges came under attack, ironically, from the monarchy, and French society became particularly interested in the appeals of new political ideologies. In this changeable situation, Rousseauian notions of equality, best explained in *The Social Contract*, emerged as the strongest competitor to tradition according to Furet, and gradually upstaged defenders of the system of privileges.

According to Furet, the events of the Revolution settled this ideological conflict. First, the financial crisis in 1787 had undermined royal authority, but it took two years for the people to appreciate fully what had happened. Then, in the midst of the Revolution, with the exercise of power believed to be responsible for the ills of society, "language was substituted for power, for it was the sole guarantee that power would belong only to the people, that is, to nobody." With politics reduced to a struggle over language, Rousseauian thinking, already ascendant, emerged dominant. In these circumstances, politicians could no longer wield power in the traditional sense. Although some resisted, in the end they were forced to compete in the arena of ideas and language. The most influential revolutionary leaders clearly understood that if they were to play the game of politics, they had no choice about its rules. Leadership passed to those who promised the greatest subservience to the people and the greatest equality. Once extreme notions of equality that denied individual differences dominated political debate, the coming of the Terror seemed inevitable. Fortunately, Furet went on, the Thermidorians broke the tyranny of language and returned politics to competition among classes and political groups.

Like Furet, Lynn Hunt is interested in language and owes much to him, but she tends to focus on subtle shifts in word usage and grammar rather than on the clash of ideas. For Hunt, language and image serve as barometers of revolutionary sentiment. In her pathbreaking work *Politics, Culture, and Class in the French Revolution* (1984), Hunt scrutinized the everyday language used to express the ideology of "democratic republicanism," which she found at the core of the revolutionary spirit. Her concern was first to uncover and then to explain its underlying structure, which she calls grammar. To do so, she turned to a range of theoretical writings, particularly those regarding theatricality. She also borrowed insights from the works of literary critics, anthropologists, and linguists. She used their theories to help her arrange and rearrange the content of revolutionaries' language, to uncover their basic values, the deeply imbedded categories of revolutionary thinking. Revolutionaries' intentions, she argued, could be inferred especially well from their symbolic usages. Hunt's interest in discourse analysis strongly shaped her overview of the French Revolution. Within revolutionary thought, she argued, there was no past, only a "mythic present," composed of belief in the nation and the Revolution. Revolutionaries, ever fearful of conspiracies, spoke and wrote first as if actors in a comedy, cheering their successes; then as if in a romance, struggling with good and evil; and finally as if in a tragedy,

continued next page

watching things fall apart. In all three stages, Hunt believes their thought to be transparent, that is, hostile to artificiality. It was also ever vigilant and always subservient to the people. Through the revolutionaries' use of symbols, they developed this litany of new beliefs.

Another important tendency emerges collectively in the works of four recent historians: William Doyle, D. M. G. Sutherland, Simon Schama, and John Bosher. Although they do not constitute a formal school, these historians share common concerns, including similar strategies to describe and explain the Revolution. Politics take center stage, and extensive political chronologies fill their works. Yet they also consider social, intellectual, and economic factors, a commonsense approach typical of historians for whom political and literary theories are relatively unimportant. In particular, they make no attempt to deal with current debates about the relation of discourse to reality. They simply accept that these factors coexist, one alongside the other. Although these authors differ about some specific aspects of the Revolution, their views accord on some important issues. They all find redeeming value in the Old Regime and also believe that overall the Revolution failed to advance the good of humanity. This simultaneous praise for the Old Regime and attack on the new provides an especially strong blast against the claims of many participants and later historians. Such considerable concurrence of opinion should not obscure considerable disagreements over the Revolution. For example, Schama and Bosher argue that France experienced its problems in large part because of the machinations of ruthless and unscrupulous Jacobins. To the contrary, Sutherland and Doyle tend not to blame the revolutionaries but to point to outside problems, especially those of the war and counterrevolution.

To some degree the variations in these four interpretations matter less because of their distance from Furet's and Hunt's emphasis on ideas. But the interpretations mentioned here hardly exhaust the list of new approaches that continue to tumble forward. Fertile as the Revolution was for contemporaries, it also shows no sign of withering for historians.

the late summer of 1794 the government of the radical Jacobins had achieved its most important success.

Thermidor: The Revolution in Reverse

Ironically, the end of the military crisis proved to be the undoing of the rule of the radicals. Once relieved of its foreign enemies, many leaders of the Revolution began calling for relief from the stringent domestic policies of the Committee of Public Safety. Moreover, Robespierre and his colleagues had alienated far too many political forces and social groups on the right and the left, and by mid-1794 found themselves isolated. Even the sans-culottes, whose power base in Paris had been curbed, were alienated from the Jacobins. The moderates in the National Convention, who once cowed before the Terror, now reasserted themselves.

It was Robespierre himself who pushed the growing discontent to the breaking point and provoked his enemies into the "Thermidorian Reaction" that at last ended the Terror. On July 26 he went before the convention to denounce unnamed conspirators in the government who were plotting against him and against the Revolution. Robespierre had followed the tactic in the past in preparation for purging opponents. This time, however, members of the convention organized against him. The next day, the ninth of Thermidor, as Robespierre rose to speak again, he was shouted down and a special decree ordering the arrest of the Robespierrists was pushed through. On the tenth of Thermidor, Robespierre and 60 of his colleagues were guillotined. The Revolution had devoured its most fanatical children.

The Thermidorian Reaction was much more than a political coup against a group of leaders—it reversed many of the trends and policies that had marked the Revolution since the purge of the Girondists. The Committee of Public Safety was stripped of much of its authority and the instruments of the Terror, such as the revolutionary committees and their tribunals, were eliminated. A general amnesty for political prisoners was declared and even the Jacobin Club of Paris closed down.

The social policies of Thermidor also altered the general atmosphere of the nation. The emphasis on civic morality, with its attendant campaigns against gambling, pornography, and prostitution, disappeared, while the middle classes reverted to their former styles of dress and speech. Many Catholic priests returned to France as freedom of worship was restored.

Even Thermidor, however, was not without its own violence, for a "white terror" in the form of street fighting and massacres now struck the Jacobins and their supporters as well as the sans-culottes. Along with the reaction came an extremely poor harvest in 1795 that resulted in food shortages worse than those of 1789. The Thermidorians were, however, unwilling to intervene in the economy despite widespread misery and the result was an abortive uprising followed by a bloody repression.

The Directory

Following the fall of Robespierre, the convention issued a third constitution, which operated from 1795 to 1799. The system of universal male suffrage adopted in 1793 was now abandoned and the country returned to a franchise similar to that incorporated in the 1791 Constitution, based on property and wealth—an exception was made for soldiers, who were entitled to vote regardless of whether they owned property. A two-chamber legislature was established, consisting of a Council of Elders and a Council of Five Hundred. The new document created a five-person directory to function as a plural executive branch of government.

On October 5, a royalist-supported insurrection rose against the government, which had only 4000 soldiers available, but a young artillery officer, General Napoleon Bonaparte (1769–1821), put down the rebellion by ordering his troops to fire cannon point-blank into the crowd. Thermidor effectively ended the active role of the crowd in the Revolution (see Part VII, Topic 4).

The Directory sought to reestablish political consensus by assuming a moderate position that eschewed extremists on both sides. Thus, while it eliminated the popular democracy of the radical phase of the Revolution, it also opposed a complete resurgence of either royalism or Jacobinism. With stability as the goal, the directors refused to tolerate any organized political opposition that could threaten their rule, although their efforts to repress the extremists did not include a return to wholesale terror. In the spring of 1796, François "Gracchus" Babeuf (1760–1797) led the last real effort at mobilizing the crowds of Paris. Babeuf, who espoused a society based on agrarian communism, attempted to stage a "Conspiracy of Equals," but it failed miserably and he was executed.

Despite its aim of restoring stability to the French body politic, the Directory's rule proved to be unstable. Coups and plots continued to challenge the new government, and a wide range of political ideologies flourished just below the level of organized political opposition. The renewal of war with the monarchs of Europe once again brought reliance on the army. When elections in the spring of 1799 went against the candidates sponsored by the Directory, the legislature replaced four of the Directory's five members with a group led by the Abbé Sieyès, who had championed the middle classes in 1789. In turning to the ambitious and brilliant General Bonaparte for support, Sieyès introduced a new factor into the ever-changing course of the French Revolution.

The importance of the Revolution transcended France, for its repercussions would be felt for many decades to come throughout Europe and, indeed, on a worldwide scale. In its aftermath, the society of the Old Regime was increasingly undermined and eventually replaced in most of Western and Central Europe. The social changes that the Revolution had introduced with such drama and violence were reinforced by the long-range repercussions of industrialization. In the 1790s, France had joined Great Britain as the second major European state to apply the ideas of resistance and to depose—indeed, behead—its ruler. Coming on the heels of the recent American Revolution, the revolution in France had forever altered politics in the West. By the late 19th century, the liberal ideas of the French moderates characterized most European governments, while the radical experiment with mass politics would become the predominant pattern of political discourse as the 20th century opened. Perhaps more than anything, however, the French Revolution had given vivid and tangible proof of the Enlightenment belief in the possibilities of change for the human condition.

Questions for Further Study

1. What were the causes of the French Revolution?
2. What role did the bourgeoisie play in the Revolution? Why was the concept of property important to the revolutionary leaders?
3. How did the sans-culottes affect the course of the Revolution? What was their relationship to the Jacobins?
4. What caused the reaction against the Reign of Terror?

Suggestions for Further Reading

Blanning, T. C. W. *The French Revolution: Aristocrats Versus Bourgeois?* Atlantic Highlands, NJ, 1987.

Cobban, Alfred. *The Social Interpretation of the French Revolution*. Cambridge, MA, 1964.

Furet, François. *Interpreting the French Revolution*, trans. E. Forster. New York, 1981.

Hunt, Lynn. *Politics, Culture, and Class in the French Revolution*. Berkeley, CA, 1984.

Jones, P. M. *The Peasantry in the French Revolution*. Cambridge, MA, 1988.

Jordan, David. P. *The King's Trial: The French Revolution Versus Louis XVI*. Berkeley, CA, 1979.

Landes, Joan. *Women and the Public Sphere in the Age of the French Revolution*. Ithaca, NY, 1988.

Lefebvre, Georges. *The Coming of the French Revolution*, trans. R. R. Palmer. Princeton, NJ, 1947.

Palmer, R. R. *Twelve Who Ruled: The Year of the Terror in the French Revolution*. Princeton, NJ, 1970.

Schama, Simon. *Citizens: A Chronicle of the French Revolution*. New York, 1989.

Soboul, Albert. *The Sans-Culottes: The Popular Movement and Revolutionary Government, 1793–1794*, trans. R. Hall. Princeton, NJ, 1980.

Sutherland, Donald M. G. *France, 1789–1815: Revolution and Counterrevolution*. Oxford, 1986.

VII

Topic 4

Europe in the Napoleonic Era

The Directory brought welcome relief from the excesses of the Revolution, but it did little to solve France's underlying political problems, or the dependence of the economy on war booty and government military contracts. In turning to the young general, Napoleon Bonaparte, to overturn the results of the elections of 1799, its moderate leaders launched the final stage of revolutionary transformation.

Napoleon's rapid ascent to power, based like much of his career on a potent combination of military virtuosity and personal charisma, saw him assume the title of first consul in 1799. His Consulate brought about widespread domestic reform in France. He reorganized the institutions of law, religion, education, and the economy. Peace at home was generally restored, together with public self-esteem.

With his coronation as emperor in 1804, Napoleon moved to the wider stage of continental Europe. Britain was protected by its superior naval power, but virtually the whole of the rest of Europe fell more or less under Napoleonic rule. Even Russia had to negotiate an alliance that reduced the tsar to the status of a junior partner.

The Napoleonic empire was short-lived. The attempt to blockade all trade with Britain was a predictable failure, and French domination of Spain proved costly in men and resources. In 1812, while still embroiled with the Spanish rebels, Napoleon launched an expedition to the other end of Europe, against Russia, where massive losses, combined with the blizzards of the harsh winter, devastated the French Army. Other European nations were emboldened to unite with Russia in a war of liberation.

The end came quickly. In 1813, after the inconclusive Battle of Leipzig, Napoleon retreated back to France. The following year the European allies invaded Paris, forced the emperor to abdicate, and shipped him off to the island of Elba. His last attempt to return to power lasted no more than 100 days. He escaped back to France in March 1815 and gathered an army, but was finally defeated at the Battle of Waterloo that June.

With the triumph of the European powers and a Bourbon monarch once more on the throne of France, the forces of the Revolution seemed exhausted. Yet by the end of the Napoleonic period, Europe had been transformed. Revolutionary political and social concepts permeated all levels of society throughout the Continent. Furthermore, the desire for national independence, born out of resistance to Napoleon, was to become a dominating theme in the history of the 19th century.

THE RISE OF BONAPARTE: FROM CONSUL TO EMPEROR

Napoleon (ruled as first consul 1799–1804 and as emperor 1804–1814) was unquestionably a figure whose decisions and actions irrevocably changed the lives of countless people. He was known to many of his contemporaries, both admirers and enemies, simply as "The Man"; decades after his death in exile, English children were scared into obedience by the mere mention of his name—"Old Boney."

Many believed that they had reason to be grateful to him. In Italy and the Rhineland his troops threw down the walls of the ghettoes and allowed the Jews to emerge into freedom for the first time since the Counter-Reformation. In other cases his social and political policies undermined some of the achievements of the Revolution: the civil liberties of women, to which revolutionary legislators had been more sympathetic, were removed by the Napoleonic Code of Law. Nor did his many opponents, from Spain to Russia, hesitate to characterize him as a bloodthirsty dictator.

Napoleon the Administrator

It is misleading to look for a broad, consistent philosophy behind the details of Napoleon's actions. Indeed, some of the contradictions that marked his rise and fall were present in his childhood and early career. He was born in 1769 in Corsica, an island ruled by France but predominantly Italian-speaking; the Genoese sold it to France in 1768, and Napoleon himself never managed to speak French without an accent. In his youth, moreover, the first political ambitions of the future emperor of France were to free Corsica from French control.

At the military academies he attended in France (he was sent to his first at the age of nine), he set out to shock his aristocratic fellow students by spectacular displays of bad behavior, which were intended to show his contempt for their genteel world. His own family was noble but impoverished, and throughout his life he was proud of the fact that he had achieved success by his own merits rather than by family influence. Yet his career was one of contradictions: once in power, he introduced reforms that helped others of ability to overcome the disadvantage of their nonaristocratic birth and rise to positions of influence, yet he also created a new aristocracy and made family members the rulers of states throughout Europe.

For all his love of the unconventional, Napoleon's intellectual interests marked him as a child of the Enlightenment. Like many of his contemporaries, he was an enthusiastic reader of history and a keen student of mathematics. His distinction lay in the imagination and speed with which he was able to transform theoretical ideas into practice: even Napoleon's enemies recognized his outstanding administrative gifts.

His talent for organization and demand for efficiency were formidable, and he was famous for his ability to dictate three letters on different topics to three secretaries simultaneously, without losing concentration or creating confusion. When he applied these skills to major issues, he produced rapid and significant results. Thus his interest in law culminated in the Napoleonic Code, a massive program of legal reform that was destined to have wide-reaching effects—both for better and for worse—far beyond the borders of France.

Napoleon's Early Career

His rise in the army was helped by the need for talented officers, since many former commanders, drawn from aristocratic families, had either fled or had been demoted during the Revolution. Nonetheless his astonishing ability to make a rapid decision and then act on it soon drew attention.

Among those impressed was General Paul Barras, one of the five leaders of the Directory. In 1795, at the National Convention to set up the Directory's constitution, monarchist leaders mounted a huge public demonstration against the convention. When called upon to deal with the emergency, Barras summoned Napoleon, whom he had seen in action at the siege of Toulon in 1793, and the crowds were scattered by cannon fired by troops under Napoleon's orders.

In return for his help, Napoleon asked for command of the French forces in northern Italy, which offered the chance of winning military glory in more conventional style. With a dazzling series of moves he defeated the Austrians and occupied Milan. Exceeding his orders, he pushed into north-central Italy and in October 1797 he personally negotiated the Treaty of Campo Formio, whereby Austria recognized the new state of the Cisalpine Republic, made up of Lombardy, Genoa, and several smaller duchies, in return for control over Venice.

Within the next two years, as French armies moved through Italy, French-controlled republics also sprang up in the Papal States, Naples, and Tuscany. The strategically important Kingdom of Piedmont was occupied and eventually annexed to France. By the end of his command, Napoleon had demonstrated his abilities as statesman, as well as military leader.

Napoleon's sense of drama and love of excitement had a great appeal for the Italians, whose own dreams of independence he astutely encouraged. The leaders of the Directory back in Paris were less enthusi-

Jacques-Louis David, *Napoleon in His Study,* 1812.

astic at the growing popularity of the young hero (to say nothing of the prospect of a liberated and united Italy), and Napoleon's next move was cunningly designed to enhance his domestic standing. France's greatest enemy was Britain. Even Napoleon was not yet prepared to undertake an armed invasion of the British Isles, but why not attack British interests elsewhere?

The Egyptian Campaign

The expedition he led to Egypt in the spring of 1798 was aimed at interfering with British colonial trade and striking a symbolic blow at the British Empire. Furthermore he hoped to find in North Africa an appropriate setting for sensational new heroic exploits, while avoiding the full might of the British Navy.

In the end, the expedition proved disastrous. The French fleet was destroyed by British forces under Admiral Nelson (1758–1805) at the Battle of the Nile on August 1, 1798, and the French army was left stranded. Napoleon hastily abandoned his troops in order to return to France as quickly as possible, and try to limit the damage to his reputation. He and his supporters concealed the military catastrophe as best they could by adroit manipulation of the news from Egypt, and by circulating information about the expedition's various scientific exploits. Among the most valuable of these was the discovery of the Rosetta Stone, a carved stone inscription, which made it possible in 1822 to decode the ancient Egyptian hieroglyphic script.

The ease with which he succeeded in reinstating himself was due in large measure to the chaotic political situation he found in Paris on his return. During his absence, further French moves in Italy had provoked Britain, Austria, and Russia into forming a coalition against France. The subsequent military crisis, which led to a series of French setbacks in Italy, undermined the credibility of the Directory and led to violent conflict between conservatives and democrats. Napoleon's reappearance on the scene provided the conservatives with a popular hero to lead a political coup.

The Brumaire Coup

On November 9, 1799, Napoleon seized power and appointed himself first consul, with virtually dictatorial powers; two other consuls were named, but they were never given any real authority. This act is generally known as the "Brumaire Coup," since its date, according to the revolutionary calendar, was 18 Brumaire VIII. Among the coup's supporters was the Abbé Sieyès (see Part VII, Topic 3), the former revolutionary and advocate of national sovereignty, who now called for "Confidence from below, authority from above."

The conservatives had intended the takeover to institute a republican oligarchy, but the first consul had other ideas. He maintained control of the armed forces, and thereby of both internal security and foreign affairs. A carefully picked Council of State was put in charge of all national legislation. Regional governments, corresponding to the departments established by the revolutionary government, became subject to strict surveillance by the appointment of prefects, officials sent from Paris to act as agents of the central government, and report back to Napoleon.

Like many another dictator, Napoleon did what he could to obtain the appearance of popular support, using censorship where necessary to block the circulation of opposing views: for all the rhetoric of his public statements, Napoleon was, in his own way, as repressive as the Old Regime. The constitution he and his advisers drafted included two national legislative bodies with vague general powers, for which all French adult males could vote (women lost the rights which they had gained under the Revolution). In reality these two councils had no power to introduce new laws, but when Napoleon's proposed reforms were submitted to a popular referendum, approval was overwhelming.

The Consulate

The years of the Consulate—1799–1804—saw a return to stability in France. The authority of the central government was restored and citizens could count on the protection of the law. The achievement of a balanced budget and the efficient collecting of a more justly assessed tax burden (there were no more exemptions for the aristocracy and the clergy) reestablished the economy on a sound footing. By 1802, the average Frenchman paid less taxes than in 1789, and received more and better services. The Bank of France, an institution founded by Napoleon, was privately owned but state controlled; it took charge of government funds and the distribution of paper currency and proved a strong centralizing force.

Napoleon put an end to the Revolution's battle with the Catholic Church by negotiating a concordat, signed by the first consul and Pope Pius VII in 1801. This agreement proclaimed Catholicism the "preferred" religion in France, but maintained the freedom of religion established during the Revolution. Among its provisions, it held that the church would renounce its claims to the land and other church property confiscated by the National Assembly. Napoleon's own attitude to religion was practical, to say the least: he is said to have claimed that "God is always on the side of those with the most cannon." The concordat was intended to reassure traditional Catholics in France, who had been shocked by the atheism of many of the revolutionary leaders. On the whole, however, it strengthened the power of the state and was never popular with the Catholic clergy. The pope later renounced it.

The Code Napoleon

Amid this whirl of reform, the foundations were laid for radical changes in law and education, two areas which had been of particular interest to Napoleon in his youth. With his customary genius for bureaucratic efficiency, he supervised the drawing up of a systematic and consistent body of laws, the Code Napoleon. Among the code's aims was the creation of a rational system for the buying, selling, and holding of property, which established sound general principles and yet did not interfere with individual rights.

On the other hand, in dealing with family questions, the code was far less egalitarian: it awarded husbands complete control over their wives, children, and possessions. Furthermore, women's occupations were to be limited as far as possible to the marital, maternal, and domestic spheres, with men in complete charge of public matters. Those women who worked were required to give their wages to their husbands; any woman operating a business—selling in a market, for example—could do so only with the permission of her husband, who had a legal right to all her profits.

The code's bias did not go unnoticed: as one woman wrote in the early 19th century, "From the way the Code treats women, you can tell it was written by men." Its effects spread far beyond France. Many new nations, both in the Old and New Worlds, which came into being in the 19th century adopted the Code Napoleon as the basis of their own legal systems. In the process its attitude to gender roles became widely diffused and enforced.

In education as elsewhere, Napoleon was concerned to strengthen the power of the central authority. The University of France was founded to supervise educational institutions throughout the country, and new categories of schools were introduced: professional and technical academies, and a nationwide high school (or *lycée*) system. As in the case of financial and legal reform, the chief beneficiaries of these new schools were the middle classes and their families; they had begun to win a new status for themselves before the Revolution, and now their progress was confirmed.

The return of law, order, and prosperity ensured Napoleon's popularity, and in 1802 he was acclaimed "consul for life"; the popular vote gave him over 95 percent support. So far his achievements had been principally limited to France, but early in his Consulate he had staged a highly successful campaign against Hapsburg forces in northern Italy and Germany. The Treaty of Luneville, signed in 1801 as a result of his victories, returned to French control the territory lost in 1799, and, more importantly, France's self-esteem.

The only real failure of the Consulate occurred far enough away from France to make little impact. Although Napoleon won back the North American territory of Louisiana from Spain, he was unable to occupy and develop it and eventually sold the territory to the United States for $15 million.

With security and stability ensured at home, wider horizons beckoned again: the dream of European conquest. For this enterprise, however, a more grandiose title was in order. In 1804, in the cathedral of Notre Dame, he crowned himself emperor with a laurel wreath, symbol of ancient Rome, before crowning his wife, Josephine, in more opulent style. His goal was to recreate the Roman Empire and unite Europe under his rule. The artistic legacy of the Napoleonic period, produced in a style known as *Empire*, provided an

Jacques-Louis David, *The Coronation of Napoleon in the presence of Pope Pius VII in 1804.*

appropriate background for these conquests, with its triumphal arches, columns, and "antique" dresses.

EUROPE AND THE FRENCH IMPERIUM

Within a few months of Napoleon's coronation, France was faced for a third time by a hostile coalition of Britain, Austria, and Russia, an alliance formed the previous year to combat the spread of French influence. The most potentially threatening of these three were the British, who joined the coalition even though Napoleon had, in fact, signed a peace treaty with them in 1801. This treaty, the Peace of Amiens, had been negotiated unenthusiastically on both sides. Both Britain and France refused essential concessions—a British withdrawal from Gibraltar and Malta in return for a French evacuation of the Low Countries—and the treaty soon collapsed.

Napoleon's first strategy for undermining his opponents was to eliminate their strongest member by direct attack. The invasion he launched against England, however, was soon discouraged by the presence of the massed forces of the British Navy in the English Channel. Furthermore, in October 1805 any future threat of a French naval offensive was eliminated by British victory over the combined French and Spanish fleets at the Battle of Trafalgar. Under the command once again of Admiral Nelson, a tactician as brilliantly unorthodox at sea as Napoleon was on land, the British Navy devastated the French and Spanish forces. The battle cost Nelson his life, but effectively guaranteed the security of the British Isles from invasion, and limited Napoleon's enterprises to continental Europe.

The Conquest of Continental Europe

With characteristic boldness, Napoleon was quick to regain the offensive. French troops moved across Europe at astonishing speed. After occupying Vienna, they took on the combined Austrian and Russian armies at Austerlitz and crushed them; in the battle the French pretended to retreat, only to trap their enemies into taking up an overexposed position, and Napoleon won one of his most famous victories. The Austrians had little choice but to negotiate a peace settlement, the terms of which were distinctly unfavorable to them, while favoring the French position in central Europe. The Russians, badly shaken, retreated back east in the hope of better luck in the future.

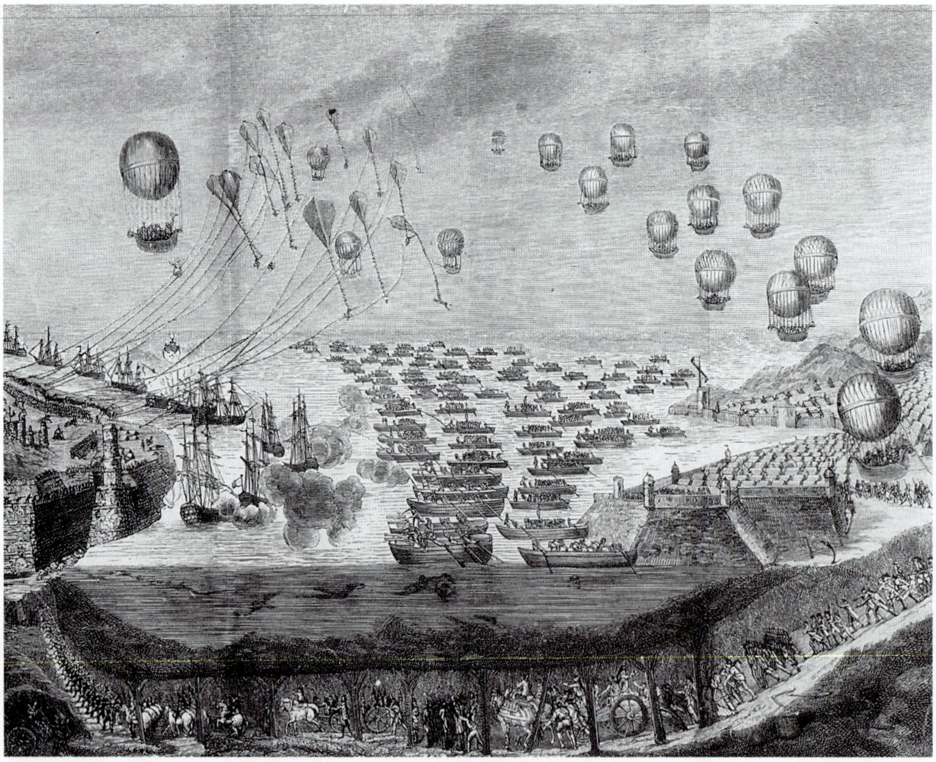

Engraving of a supposed plan by Napoleon to invade England by a combination of ships, balloons, and an underground tunnel.

Napoleon's imperial seal.

Throughout the hostilities the Prussians had remained neutral, unwilling to come to the aid of their Austrian neighbors and unable to see that their turn was next. With Austria disposed of, Napoleon could turn his attention north and by the time the Prussians finally declared war it was too late for them to put up much resistance. The legendary Prussian army, a mere shadow of its former glory, was soundly whipped in October 1806, at the Battle of Jena. Napoleon was master of central Europe.

Formally declaring the end of the Holy Roman Empire, he reorganized its many kingdoms and principalities into a series of new states. Some of these were placed under the rule of family members: his youngest brother, Jerome, was given Westphalia, while Marshal Joachim Murat, the husband of his sister Caroline Bonaparte, became ruler of the Grand Duchy of Berg. Napoleon's purpose in dividing up his conquests among the family was partly to establish dynasties, while at the same time it enabled him to retain control in his own hands. His brother Louis became king of Holland, but when he began to show too much interest in the welfare of his Dutch subjects, Napoleon deposed him and made Holland French territory.

The French in Eastern Europe

Among the newly created states was the Grand Duchy of Warsaw, made up of that part of Poland which had been carved out by the Prussians. By appearing to favor the cause of Polish independence, Napoleon could claim to be the champion of national aspirations, as he had in his earlier days in Italy.

More to the point, he provided himself with a base from which to move against his last unconquered enemy, Russia. After an indecisive battle at Eylau, which was fought in a raging blizzard and produced terrible casualties on both sides, the Russians were finally defeated at Friedland in June 1807. Within weeks Tsar Alexander I and Emperor Napoleon I met at Tilsit to sign an agreement which divided Europe into two halves. In return for a relatively free hand in extending Russian influence into the Ottoman-controlled Balkans, Alexander accepted Napoleon's annexation and reorganization of Western Europe, and agreed to restrict trade and other contacts with Britain. The terms were in France's favor, but the tsar had little choice.

Italy and Spain

With eastern and central Europe reshaped, it was then the turn of the Mediterranean region to provide thrones for the Bonaparte family. Parts of Italy, including Piedmont, Tuscany, the Papal States, and several smaller duchies, had already become French territory. Napoleon merged the former Cisalpine Republic, together with a recaptured Venice and the remaining central parts of the peninsula, into the Kingdom of Italy, governing himself as king through his stepson. In southern Italy, his brother Joseph became king of the Kingdom of Naples in 1806.

In 1808, Napoleon sent Murat to Naples and transferred Joseph to Spain in an attempt to secure power in Iberia. Since 1795 the Spanish had been only fitful allies of the French in their joint attempt to undermine British influence in Europe and the colonies. The destruction of a considerable portion of the Spanish Navy at Trafalgar further reduced Spain's enthusiasm for the French cause. To complicate matters even more, the Spanish royal house was racked by bitter in-fighting and scandal. Napoleon's solution to dealing with his supposed allies was, as might be expected, radical and direct. In 1808 the Spanish king and his son were paid off, and Joseph led French troops to Madrid to oversee the introduction of the new regime.

For once, Napoleon's political instincts had deserted him. By this blatant takeover the former supporter of nationalist causes provoked a nationalist uprising that was to last for several years. The popular riots of early May 1808 were soon put down by bloody and brutal troop action on the part of the French, but the very memory of the repression served to galvanize the forces of rebellion. Regular Spanish troops combined with local civilian forces to challenge French occupation of their country, and bitter fighting dragged on until the French were finally driven out of Spain in 1814.

Francisco Goya's dramatic depiction of *The Executions of May 3, 1808,* when Spanish resistance fighters were gunned down by Napoleonic troops.

Significant Dates

The Career of Napoleon

1793	Siege of Toulon
1795	Protest ended with a "whiff of grapeshot"
1797	Treaty of Campo Formio
1799	"Brumaire Coup"; Napoleon becomes first consul
1801	Concordat with Pius VII
1802	Napoleon becomes "consul for life"
1804	Napoleon crowned emperor
1805	British victory at Trafalgar
1806	Napoleon victorious at Battle of Jena
1807	Napoleon victorious at Battle of Friedland
1808	Campaign in Spain
1812	Campaign against Russia
1813	Napoleon defeated at Battle of Leipzig
1814	Napoleon abdicates, exiled to Elba
1815	Battle of Waterloo; Napoleon exiled to St. Helena

Napoleon's move backfired in a number of ways. He had provoked genuine popular resistance among the Spanish. This in turn encouraged nations elsewhere in Europe to resist French strongarm tactics; while the conflict in Spain itself provided a golden opportunity to Napoleon's greatest enemies, the British, who despatched a force to drive the French out of the Iberian peninsula, in a campaign known as the Peninsular War.

The war trapped a large part of the French Army in a hopeless struggle against a mixture of British troops, the local anti-French forces, and several thousand Spanish guerrilla fighters, these latter inspired by memory of the horrors of the May brutalities. The term *guerrilla* is the Spanish word for "little war"; the development in the Peninsular War of "guerrilla tactics"—hit-and-run, ambush, sabotage, surprise attack—against larger and better-equipped forces proved highly influential in many subsequent conflicts around the globe.

In 1808, with all western and central Europe at Napoleon's command, the problem of Spain must have seemed relatively unimportant; in the end it proved one of the chief causes of his downfall, since over 200,000 troops embroiled in the fighting there were urgently needed elsewhere.

THE GRAND EXPERIMENT: OCCUPATION AND REFORM

The Napoleonic empire lasted for a shorter time than just about any empire of comparable size in Western history. In 1808 the French controlled, in one way or another, much of Central and Western Europe (with the exception of the British Isles). By 1813 Napoleon's domination was over. Yet for all the brevity of its duration, French imperial rule had a profound and lasting effect on European life.

The Imperial Administration

In order to administer these vast territories, Napoleon introduced throughout Europe many of the reforms that had succeeded so well in France. The old ranks and privileges were abolished, and family status no longer assured a successful career: the Napoleonic bureaucracy offered the possibility of advancement in public life to those of talent and ability, regardless of their origins. Many of the special powers of the church were curtailed, or—as in the case of church courts—abolished. Under the Code Napoleon, which was valid in the conquered territories, all were equal in the eyes of the law.

Financial reorganization and the implementation of a coherent tax system helped improve local

Map 4.1 Europe at the Height of the Napoleonic Empire

economies. In the process, those involved in trade and commerce were more able to pursue their business and advance their interests. In one area, however, even the emperor failed to remove old barriers. In spite of his attempts to abolish customs tariffs for the importation of goods across national boundaries, the various European economic groups maintained their rival tariff systems. With the end of Napoleonic rule, the concept of European free trade disappeared, until it was revived almost 150 years later in the years of rebuilding after World War II.

All these various reforms were, of course, principally intended to strengthen French rule over her empire. The local populations were free to pursue their own careers, protect their property rights, work as they pleased. They were not free to govern themselves. The efficient working of the system was intended to maintain control by a centralized government in Paris that, in turn, was responsible to the emperor. A prosperous Europe, in addition, would pay taxes to pay for the French armies of occupation and finance future military adventures.

Napoleonic Rule in Practice: The Case of Pauline Borghese

The internal contradictions of Napoleon's occupation policies, with all of their much-needed reforms and blatant exploitation, and their cultural and social brilliance and personal intrigues, can be seen in microcosm in the life of his sister Pauline.

Pauline Bonaparte (1780–1825), whom Napoleon once called "the most beautiful woman of her time," grew up spoiled, rebellious, and strong-willed. Although she constantly fought his efforts to control her life, she was devoted to her brother. After an early marriage to one of his favorites, General Charles Leclerc, she reluctantly accompanied her husband to Santo Domingo when he was sent there to assert French control over the island's black population. When Leclerc died in 1802 of yellow fever, Pauline returned with relief to Paris.

The role of a general's widow ill-suited Pauline's vivacious temperament. In 1803, in order to avoid the scandal her illicit affairs were causing, Napoleon allowed her to marry Camillo Borghese (1775–1832), the handsome, outgoing heir to one of Rome's oldest and most distinguished noble families. Pauline, together with a sumptuous wardrobe, valuable jewels, and her new husband, moved to the Villa Borghese in Rome. Pauline soon tired of Rome's staid, monotonous social life, however, and began a series of liaisons with writers, actors, and intellectuals. Between 1804 and 1805, the neoclassical sculptor Antonio Canova (1757–1822) executed a sensuously lifelike statue of Pauline depicting her as a semi-nude Venus lounging alluringly on a bed while holding an apple of temptation. When Borghese saw the statue, he was so scandalized that he banished it to the basement.

In 1808 Napoleon appointed Borghese governor general of the French-annexed territories of northern Italy, and the couple moved to Turin, the capital of Piedmont. Borghese's work as administrator was efficient if unspectacular, but he did implement Napoleon's reforms. Pauline, bored with politics, was

A sculpture by Canova of Napoleon's sister Pauline as Venus.

soon ready for a change. Leaving Borghese, she returned to Paris, bringing glamour to the social life of the court and, in an age noted for its amorous liaisons, outdoing most women of the empire.

After Napoleon's defeat and abdication in 1814, the last years of Pauline's life were filled with sadness and depression. Borghese rapidly divested himself of his association with the former emperor. He attempted to have his marriage annulled, but Pauline managed to obtain a legal separation and a generous annual stipend. She visited her brother in exile on the island of Elba and later tried without success to join him at St. Helena.

Her beauty and her health rapidly fading, Pauline returned to Italy in 1816 and, after a last affair with the young composer Giovanni Pacini (1796–1867), asked for a reconciliation with Borghese. Wounded by her past infidelities, however, the prince spurned her. Only in 1824, after she had fallen gravely ill and had written countless letters of entreaty, did Borghese agree to be reunited. She died a few months later and was buried in the Borghese chapel in Rome.

In retrospect, Pauline Bonaparte and Camillo Borghese were each victims of the lure of the Grand Empire—Borghese, an opportunist who rose to fame and influence by siding with the French against both the ruler of Italy and the pope, and who then just as astutely abandoned his fallen protector; Pauline, a spirited woman who, while living in the shadow of her egoistic brother, used his power for her own ends while seeking personal freedom from the men who had wanted to possess her.

Napoleon and Liberty

While the reasons for the Napoleonic reorganization of Europe were practical, they were underpinned by broader philosophical principles. Napoleon had, after all, come to power with the claim that he would implement some of the ideals of the Revolution, with its doctrines of liberty and equality. Many of his reforms, both in France and throughout the empire, did produce a more free and just society.

In many cases, even after his fall, the old vested interests of the aristocracy were unable to impose themselves again. Furthermore the spirit of national independence and self-determination, which both the Revolution and Napoleon claimed to support, was an intoxicating one; in Germany, in particular, resistance to Napoleon played an important role in stimulating nationalism. The very peoples who finally united to overthrow the empire did so following the vision of freedom which the Revolution seemed to offer, and which the Napoleonic reforms made at least partly real. After Napoleon, Europe could never return to the old social and political ways.

The Jews Under Napoleon

In the case of one people, however—the Jews—progress did not survive the end of the Napoleonic era. As early as 1791 the National Assembly had decreed that French Jews possessed the rights of full citizens. Napoleon, with his enlightened attitude to religious tolerance, continued to work for the integration of the Jews into society. The constitution of the Cisalpine Republic that he founded in 1797 in northern Italy provided for their freedom of worship, and the concordat signed with the Catholic Church in 1801 contained nothing to undermine the Jews' new civic status in France.

In the years of conquest, as French armies moved through Europe, they freed Jews from their ghettoes and extended full rights to them, although the Jews were often required to pay heavy taxes in return. Jewish candidates were able to stand as candidates for election to public office, and Jewish intellectuals were nominated as members of learned societies such as the Italian Academy of Sciences.

With a characteristic care for detail, Napoleon tried to regularize the position of the Jews, a people who transcended national boundaries, by convening an international congress. In 1806 Jewish representatives were summoned to Paris from all parts of the empire to discuss such questions as divorce and mixed marriages, and Jewish difficulties in entering the professions. A Napoleonic decree emerged two years later; it established local administrative councils in Jewish communities throughout the empire, which were answerable to a central council in Paris.

With the defeat of Napoleon, however, the entire system collapsed. In France the Jews retained their rights, but elsewhere in Europe they were repressed even more ferociously, precisely because they had been set free by the hated French conquerors, and in gratitude had exchanged their yellow stars for the French *tricouleurs*. The walls of the ghetto at Rome were thrown up again and the Jews confined there as soon as Napoleon's downfall seemed assured. The Jews of Italy finally won their freedom in the mid-19th century, following the Italian struggle for independence, but many of those in central and eastern Europe could only hope to find theirs by emigrating to the New World at the end of the century.

THE EUROPEAN COALITION AND THE COLLAPSE OF FRANCE

Napoleon was finally overthrown by a third coalition of the European powers, although their success was due as much to the emperor's miscalculations as to their own military prowess. Both in economic and foreign policy, the French undermined their own strength.

The Continental System

In the aftermath of the disastrous defeat at Trafalgar, with the British unshaken in their naval power, Napoleon tried to find a way to undermine Britain economically. His device was the Continental System, introduced for the first time in 1806; among its other policies, it prohibited the importation of British goods into continental Europe. The aim was to destroy the commercial life of a country which Napoleon himself referred to as "a nation of shopkeepers." When the British in turn imposed their own countermeasures, the ensuing naval blockade and counterblockade involved virtually all trading nations, including neutral powers such as the United States. Indeed, American irritation at being drawn into the conflict contributed to the brief and inconclusive War of 1812 with Britain.

Although the barriers created by the Continental System stimulated the British to exploit alternative markets, including a number in South America, they undoubtedly proved disruptive to business. The riots and popular demonstrations that racked England in 1811 were a direct result of the unemployment caused by the trade war. In the end, however, the consequences for the economies of continental Europe were much more disastrous. It became increasingly difficult to obtain the raw materials essential for manufacturing. The economic life of great ports and business centers such as Amsterdam was paralyzed. Production declined and unemployment rose. The Continent—including France—lost more than Britain by the boycott, and the general resentment at French interference did much to fuel the European powers' final military resistance to Napoleon.

The Russian Campaign

It was against a background of developing restlessness that the emperor made his fatal mistake—he launched a campaign against the Russians. The most obvious pretext for his invasion was revenge for Alexander's flouting of the Continental System. The Russian economy was heavily dependent on the export of agricultural produce in exchange for manufactured goods, and one of Russia's most important trading partners was Britain. The French demand that the Baltic ports remain closed to British ships caused a serious economic crisis in Russia, and Alexander gradually began to break the embargo.

Napoleon's response was to muster the "*Grande Armée*," the largest army the world had seen—over 600,000 in number; many of the troops were conscripts from countries under French rule and thus neither professional soldiers nor enthusiastic supporters of the French cause.

In the spring of 1812, the emperor and his army set out to conquer Russia. After the long march to the Russian border, the French force advanced into the heart of the country. The Russians avoided battle and retreated toward Moscow, destroying their own spring crops as they went. The French lines of communication

A contemporary depiction of Napoleon's retreat from Moscow, 1812.

became ever longer and more tenuous, and supplies increasingly difficult to obtain.

The Russians finally took a stand at Borodino, some 70 miles southwest of Moscow. In the battle that followed, both sides suffered terrible losses. Although Napoleon pushed on to Moscow, the Russian army maintained its discipline. The tsar refused to sue for peace, and retreated to positions east and south of Moscow. On the evening after the French entered the ancient Russian capital, a mysterious fire broke out, destroying many of its buildings, and leaving the French soldiers with little in the way of shelter. The city's population had fled, taking with them all available supplies.

For once Napoleon's decisiveness deserted him. Weeks passed as he waited in vain for signs that Russian resistance was crumbling. Only toward the end of October did he finally order the retreat of the Grande Armée, and the delay proved fatal. Loaded down with plunder, his troops trudged into the depths of the Russian winter. As rivers overflowed, swollen by the seasonal rains, the French army was engulfed in mud and battered by blizzards. Disease and hunger ran rampant, while the weary soldiers were harried by bands of mounted Russian Cossacks, who rode out of the storms to wreak yet more havoc.

Six weeks later the survivors staggered back across the border into Germany, the pitiful remnants of the mighty expedition—of the original force of over 600,000, only 100,000 were left. Napoleon hastened back to Paris to build a new army, apparently neither discouraged by the horrors of the retreat nor deterred by the human misery his campaign had inflicted on so many. The Prussian conscripts deserted.

The End of the Empire

At last the spell was broken, and European statesmen began to plan a war of liberation that would see the end of French domination; one of their leaders was Prince Klemens von Metternich of Austria, a figure to play a crucial role in the post-Napoleonic era. In March 1813 a treaty was signed between Russia and Prussia, and Europe waited in suspense to see whether Austria would join the allied coalition against France or remain neutral. The news that the Austrian emperor had finally declared war on France was accompanied by tidings of further French losses in Spain, where the Peninsular War still dragged on.

Faced with the collapse of his empire, Napoleon succeeded in mounting an army, but only by recruiting conscripted troops who were underage. In October 1813 at Leipzig, in central Germany, his forces were defeated, and he was driven back to France. As the European powers began to close in, the British joined the coalition. Terms were offered to Napoleon which allowed him to remain emperor, but required France's return to her "normal borders"—the term was deliberately vague. When the conditions were rejected, the allies invaded France.

In March 1814 Paris was taken and Napoleon forced to abdicate. A brother of Louis XVI was recognized as king of France, and took the title of Louis XVIII (ruled 1814–1824). Meanwhile the allied powers summoned a congress to meet in Vienna a few months later, to negotiate a settlement for the rest of Europe. Somewhat at a loss as to what to do with the former emperor, they exiled him to Elba, a tiny island off the coast of Italy.

He was set up as ruler of the island in a modest villa, and permitted to organize a miniature court, for which he designed the uniforms and prescribed the ceremonials. Among those who attended receptions there was his redoubtable sister Pauline. The rooms of the villa were decorated with paintings showing scenes from his campaigns; on the wall of one of them visitors can still see an inscription, in the former emperor's handwriting, which says: "Napoleon can be happy everywhere."

His happiness seems to have lasted no more than ten months. As the allies gathered at Vienna and bickered amongst themselves about the reshaping of Europe, "The Man" escaped and returned to France, where in the famous "Hundred Days" he reawakened popular enthusiasm and raised an army. Only on June 18, 1815, was he finally defeated at the Battle of Waterloo, in Belgium. At one stage in the fighting Napoleon's army came within sight of victory, and afterwards he bitterly blamed his marshals for the loss.

This time the allies were taking no chances. He was shipped out to the remote island of St. Helena far off in the south Atlantic, where he lived out the last six years of his life in seclusion.

During the Napoleonic period Europe underwent a transformation. In France, the confused and often brutal measures of the Revolution and its aftermath gave way to the relative order of the Consulate. Even before the Revolution the middle classes had demonstrated their special role in French society, and the effect of Napoleonic reform was to strengthen their position. Preservation of the land settlement, reform of secondary and higher education, and the establishment of a civil service all played a crucial role in middle-class achievements later in the 19th century.

As Napoleon's power spread throughout continental Europe, it brought to an end the rule of the Old Regime. A system of states that was the product of centuries of development became irrevocably dismantled. The period immediately following his overthrow saw a strongly conservative reaction, but the ideas of individual and national freedom released into the mainstream of European thought remained a powerful force in 19th-century politics. Even some of the most reactionary rulers were forced to compromise with the advocates of liberty.

Britain, Napoleon's bitterest enemy, was the only country in Europe to have no firsthand experience of his reforms. Nonetheless the Napoleonic Wars produced major changes in British life. During the years of war the country's economy suffered the strains imposed by the Continental System, but industrial production was high, and on the whole hatred and fear of Old Boney kept internal divisions within bounds. With the coming of peace, Britain plunged into a period of economic depression. As a consequence of the trade blockade, manufactured goods had piled up unsold. The return home of soldiers from the Peninsular War and other campaigns flooded the market with workers for whom there were no jobs. The social unrest that followed introduced elements of revolutionary struggle into British life and politics.

As for the Russians, the Napoleonic Wars succeeded in introducing them into the mainstream of European events, and they played a decisive role in liberating the Continent. Yet the spirit of revolution had little immediate effect on Russian society. Even Tsar Alexander I, who flirted briefly with liberal notions, soon returned to conservative orthodoxy. The chief memory left by Napoleon's invasion was that of the heroic Russian resistance. Whether in Tolstoy's epic narrative of War and Peace, *or in the clashing national anthems of Tchaikovsky's* 1812 Overture, *future Russians commemorated the victory against Napoleon as one of their country's proudest achievements.*

Questions for Further Discussion

1. What were the main features of Napoleon's administrative and legal reorganization in Europe? How many of them had a permanent effect?
2. What were the chief economic consequences of the Napoleonic Wars? Which European countries were most affected by them?
3. To what extent did Napoleon undermine his own achievements by his miscalculations? What were his principal mistakes?

Suggestions for Further Reading

Applewhite, H. B., and D. G. Levy. *Women and Politics in the Age of the Democratic Revolution*. Ann Arbor, MI, 1990.

Bergeron, L. *France under Napoleon*. Princeton, NJ, 1981.

Chandler, David G. *The Campaigns of Napoleon*. New York, 1973.

Connelly, O. *Napoleon's Satellite Kingdoms*. New York, 1970.

Godechot, J., B. Hyslop, and D. Dowd. *The Napoleonic Era in Europe*. New York, 1971.

Hesse, Carla. *Publishing and Cultural Politics in Revolutionary Paris, 1789–1810*. Berkeley, CA, 1991.

Holtman, R. *The Napoleonic Revolution*. Baton Rouge, LA, 1979.

Woloch, Isser. *The French Veteran from the Revolution to the Restoration*. Chapel Hill, NC, 1979.

VII

Topic 5

Restoration and Resistance in the Age of Metternich

The years following Napoleon's defeat saw conflicting attempts to remodel European politics and society. Conservative statesmen aimed to construct a balance of power which left no single state in a dominant position. At the same time, they tried to restore the social patterns of prerevolutionary life and stamp out the vestiges of revolutionary ideology.

Set against this were two important new forces in European political thought: liberalism and nationalism. For liberals, successful government required that an increased portion of those being governed play some part in the process of political decision making. The liberal state, the ideal form of which was a constitutional monarchy, should protect the rights of the individual, encourage the development of business and industry, and establish friendly relations with other nations. Those who most eagerly took up the liberal cause were those most likely to benefit from it: the middle classes.

Many liberals, especially in central Europe and Italy, believed that their goals could best be obtained by the creation of self-ruling nation-states to replace the tangled network of principalities, monarchies, and empires typical of pre-Napoleonic Europe. Nationalism thus served the liberal interest; indeed many saw a nationalist revolution as the essential prelude to the formation of a liberal government.

At the Congress of Vienna, the five chief European powers—Austria, Britain, France, Prussia, and Russia—agreed to redistribute territory while paying little heed to the interests of those whose frontiers were being redrawn. The results came under almost immediate fire from reformers and revolutionaries. Yet however high-handed the settlement, its provisions helped to keep widespread international conflict at bay up to World War I.

The conservative statesmen at Vienna believed that society could be successfully governed only by maintaining the distinctions and privileges that had evolved over time. The country where this ideology was most rigidly enforced was Russia, where the still absolutist tsar exercised virtually complete control over social and political life.

Elsewhere, conservative rulers struggled to maintain their positions intact. The ethnically complex Hapsburg empire tried to protect itself against nationalist revolts by the formation of a police state, and in the German states student demonstrations were suppressed. Only intervention by foreign powers reestablished reactionary governments in Spain and Italy, where military uprisings against Bourbon rulers had introduced liberal reforms.

The purpose of these interventions was to enforce the agreements reached at the Congress of Vienna, where Britain, Prussia, and Russia had joined with Austria in acting as guarantors of the new map of Europe. France was admitted to the alliance in 1818. The concept of united action against the forces of revolution is known as the Concert of Europe. Far from strengthening the unity of the allies, however, the Concert of Europe soon proved discordant, with the British opposed to the idea of "superintending" the Continent. When the concept was extended by Russian intervention on behalf of Spain in the New World colonies, the president of the United States issued the Monroe Declaration (which established the policy known as the Monroe Doctrine), warning the Europeans not to interfere in the Western Hemisphere. The political scene in France after Napoleon was shaped by conflict between Louis XVIII's cautiously reforming conservatism and the ultra-right wing. Although the restoration of the Bourbons began with a return to relative peace and prosperity, tension between the two extremes soon began to wreck the compromise which Louis XVIII sought. Louis was succeeded by his arrogant younger brother, who reigned as Charles X until his ultra-royalist policies and political maneuverings forced him into exile in 1830. His replacement, Louis Philippe, avoided making the same mistake. Increasing the power of the middle class, he was generally successful in rebuilding order and prosperity.

In Britain there was no need to restore the old order, because it had never been seriously challenged. The number of those eligible to vote was severely limited and tied to property. Both houses of Parliament were predominantly aristocratic, as were members of the two political parties, the ruling conservative Tories and the slightly more liberal Whigs, who thus came essentially from the same class. Popular unrest provoked by the economic depression following the Napoleonic Wars led to demands for parliamentary reform. From 1829 to 1835, Parliament passed a series of reform bills that, while far from radical, marked a significant change.

THE CONGRESS OF VIENNA AND THE SEARCH FOR STABILITY

Against a background of pomp and ceremony, the leaders of the great powers of Europe gathered in Vienna to restore the Continent to what they conceived to be its rightful order.

Leaders at the Congress of Vienna

The central figure in the deliberations was Prince Klemens von Metternich (1773–1859), Austrian foreign minister from 1809 to 1848. An urbane aristocrat whose name has become synonymous with cunning intrigue and the manipulation of power, Metternich's aim at the Congress was to return Europe as far as possible to its pre-Napoleonic state, and do whatever possible to prevent any future outbreaks of "the virus of revolution." For decades Metternich's political and social views made him the chief spokesman of European conservatism, while some of his policies justifiably earned him the label of reactionary.

His only equal as a diplomat was the French representative, Prince Talleyrand, whose years of service to a bewildering variety of masters—the church under the Old Regime, then the various revolutionary governments, and most recently Napoleon—had made him a wily negotiator. Talleyrand was sent to Vienna to secure a deal for France that would not only involve the fewest possible penalties for his former master's misdeeds, but would restore French influence on the European political scene.

The participants in the Congress of Vienna, 1815.

The British spokesman, Lord Castlereagh (1769–1822), was, like the other two, his country's foreign minister. Less occupied with the finer details than his colleagues, Castlereagh's chief concern was to see that the final agreement posed no threat to Britain's position as the leading European power. Although a less dominating figure than Metternich, Castlereagh was probably the most influential in framing the final decisions of the Congress.

In such professional company the Prussian king, Friedrich Wilhelm III (ruled 1797–1840), played a lesser role. The remaining great power, Russia, was represented by its ruler, Tsar Alexander I. In the early part of his reign, the tsar demonstrated some interest in the ideas of the Enlightenment, but after the defeat of Napoleon he turned to mystical visions of converting his fellow rulers to Christian virtue. By the time of the Congress he was as staunchly conservative as Metternich, but the Austrian, more interested in balancing self-interest and expediency, and violently anti-Russian, had little patience with Alexander's grandiose and incoherent notions.

The Reshaping of Europe

The guiding principle at Vienna was "legitimacy." This referred to the idea that the status of rulers and their borders should revert to that of 1789, before the Revolution. The concept was actually suggested by Talleyrand and accepted by Metternich and Alexander for two reasons: it legitimized the return of a Bourbon monarch to France, and it avoided the loss of any French territory as punishment for Napoleon's aggression. Metternich adopted the idea of legitimacy as a means of justifying his reactionary policies, but it was applied selectively. In the case of France, Talleyrand obtained what he wanted, together with the restoration of Bourbon monarchies in Spain and Naples and the kingdom of Piedmont-Sardinia.

Even though France retained its territory, the other participants were concerned with other issues than the simple one of legitimacy. The redrawing of frontiers aimed to compensate France's conquerors, while providing a secure balance of power. Furthermore, Metternich and his colleagues were determined to block any future French attempt at expansion. To that end the Dutch Republic was combined with the Austrian Netherlands (Belgium), to form the Kingdom of the Netherlands. This arrangement also satisfied the British concern that the vital North Sea ports remain in neutral hands.

In return for their giving up the Netherlands, the Austrians received two provinces in northern Italy, Lombardy and Venetia. Through dynastic connections, Austria played a decisive role in the policies of the restored Grand Duchy of Tuscany and the Kingdom of the Two Sicilies. The strong Austrian presence just to the south of the Alps served as another barrier against French expansion. As for Italy itself, dominated by the Austrians and divided for the rest into a series of small kingdoms and duchies and the Papal States, it

Prince Metternich, the leading diplomat at the Congress of Vienna.

remained, as Metternich put it, "only a geographical expression."

To block France on the Rhine frontier, Prussia received a chunk of German territory on the river's left bank. Prussia's claim to all of Saxony, however, caused serious disagreement. The tsar agreed to back the Prussians on Saxony if they in turn would support his taking the lion's share of Poland. Both Castlereagh and Metternich objected to the enlargement and strengthening of two of their chief rivals. In consequence, Metternich, Castlereagh, and Talleyrand formed a secret pact, whereby the three powers would go to war rather than see the deal struck. In the end a compromise was worked out: Prussia took about half of Saxony, and Russia was given most of Poland.

Nowhere was the principle of legitimacy less observed than in Germany and central Europe. Napoleon's organization of the numerous states and kingdoms into 39 (37 states, Austria, and Prussia) was retained, and they were brought together into a larger unit called the German Confederation, which thus replaced the Holy Roman Empire. Although an appearance of German political unity was obtained, the confederation had little power, and in any case it was dominated by Austria.

The final agreement, as Metternich had intended, left no one the clear winner, and everyone with something. Britain, more interested in trade outside Europe, received territories in South Africa, South America, and the island of Ceylon. The mere description of the decisions of the Congress, which never once met in formal session, emphasizes the element of game playing. In the elegant drawing rooms of the Hapsburg capital, the fates of millions were decided by a handful of aristocratic diplomats. These men were profoundly unsympathetic to the dawning hopes of liberals and nationalists.

Yet the achievements of Metternich and his colleagues have more positive aspects. In the first place they negotiated rather than fought, itself a notable improvement after a generation of bloodshed. Secondly, the temptation to punish France for the excesses of Napoleon was avoided. Finally, the balance worked out at Vienna, for all its defects, provided a relative degree of stability in Europe for the next 100 years. This stability made possible precisely the revolutionary changes that Metternich so feared.

THE RESTORATION AND THE CONSERVATIVE ORDER

Metternich and his fellow conservatives were not merely trying to preserve the past for its own sake: their views reflected a coherent philosophical position, most cogently expressed in the writings of Edmund Burke (1729–1797). His *Reflections on the Revolution in France*

The British statesman, orator, and philosopher, Edmund Burke.

(1790), which appeared as early as the Revolution's second year, came to have a significant influence on conservative thought throughout Europe.

An outspoken opponent of the doctrines of the French Revolution, Burke believed that society should evolve slowly, in accordance with existing varieties of rank and status. Radical change, by its very unpredictability, was seen as dangerous. The intellectual movement from which the Revolution had sprung, the Enlightenment, emphasized the power of reason. Conservative thinkers argued just the opposite. Society was far too complex, and susceptible to human emotions and weaknesses, to be organized by any kind of rational scheme—a point of view that had much in common with the Romantic movement in the arts (see Part VII, Topic 7).

The conservative rulers of the restoration believed in preserving the existing institutions at all cost. If that required censorship, limits to free speech, the execution of dissenters, those were necessary prices. So rigid an attitude inevitably proved self-defeating. Even in Metternich's Austria, with its spies and police, its border controls and censorship of books and even music, the forces of change were irresistible. In 1848, a few weeks after the outbreak of revolution in France, public protests spread to Austria, and Metternich was forced to flee for his life.

Russia Under Alexander and Nicholas

The country whose rulers most thoroughly repressed attempts at reform was Russia. By comparison with western Europe Russia was still overwhelmingly an agricultural nation, made up of peasants and their aristocratic masters. There were few cities of any size, and thus no urban middle class had developed. The Orthodox church, far from defending the rights of its adherents, reinforced the policies of the tsar.

Once Alexander had recovered from his early bout of liberalism, he proved a formidable conservative, both at home and abroad. Censorship was strict, and the universities were carefully watched to crush the growth of any dangerous new ideas. Alexander ruled the Kingdom of Poland, given to Russia at the Congress of Vienna, with the same iron hand, even though in theory it had its own constitution with the tsar acting as king.

The only real challenge to authority came when Alexander died in 1825. A group of army officers inspired by Western ideas staged a revolt; they are known as the *Decembrists,* after the month of their attempt. The young liberals had little chance of success. Their uprising was poorly organized and soon crushed, but they gave Alexander's successor, Nicholas I (ruled 1825–1855), an excuse to tighten his grip even further; the 1820s and 1830s saw the introduction of many conspicuously reactionary measures. Nicholas put down a Polish revolt in 1831 with equal ruthlessness, and for the rest of his reign he maintained his rule unchallenged. He strengthened the army and police, and increased the power of the state bureaucracy. Little was done to improve the living and working conditions of Russia's vast peasant population, and all their attempts at rebellions were suppressed.

In spite of the lack of progress, however, with the slow spread of literacy Russians began to ask questions about their country's future. In the rarified intellectual circles of Moscow and St. Petersburg a debate developed between the westernizers and the Slavophiles. The former wanted their country to adopt Western European models, while the latter claimed that Russia's unique character should be preserved untouched by Western ideas and institutions, since it gave her a special destiny. The dispute was to play an important part in Russian cultural life later in the century.

The German Confederation and the Hapsburgs

The two rival major powers in central Europe, Austria and Prussia, shared a common fear: the rise of German nationalism. Charlemagne's original attempt to unite Germany, the Holy Roman Empire, had long since broken up into over 300 separate states. As a result, the idea of a united Germany had been impossible for centuries. With Napoleon, however, the separate states were consolidated under French rule in the Confederation of the Rhine, one of the consequences of which was a burst of German nationalism in protest.

Even the archconservative Metternich could hardly propose a return to the multitude of separate states. The creation in its place of the German Confederation was intended to prevent Germany from achieving any real political union by giving Austria, the confederation's permanent president, an edge over Prussia.

The Burschenschaften

Signs of nationalist and antiforeign stirrings began to occur in Germany during the war against Napoleon. Shortly after 1815, the nationalist mood intensified with the appearance of groups of student activists known as *Burschenschaften* (Brotherhoods) in university circles. In 1817, the 300th anniversary of Luther's publication of his 95 theses was celebrated by the Burschenschaften at the Wartburg Festival. The occasion was supposed to be a religious one, but the heady effects of speeches, song, and beer began to take over. To cheers from the crowd, a French officer's staff and a Prussian military text were symbolically burnt.

The Austrian and Prussian authorities anxiously waited for further confirmation of their fears. Two years

German students demonstrating for a liberal constitution at the Wartburg Festival, 1817.

later, when a fanatical student murdered a reactionary writer, Metternich seized his opportunity and summoned the rulers of the leading German states to a meeting at Carlsbad. The Carlsbad Decrees of 1819 abolished the Burschenschaften, tightened censorship, and had students and professors suspected of liberal tendencies put under careful watch. These measures revealed Metternich at his most reactionary.

Prussia and the Customs Union

The ruling family of Prussia, the Hohenzollern, shared Metternich's contempt for liberalism. The chief instrument of their power in Prussia was still the army which, together with the bureaucracy, was in the hands of the landed nobility, the Junkers. Any gesture toward nationalism would have been regarded by these warlords as a betrayal of Prussian virtue, yet ironically it was the Prussians who began to advance German economic unity.

Their motive was commercial self-interest. With the acquisition at the Congress of Vienna of the German territory on the left bank of the Rhine, Prussia consisted of two separate and unconnected parts. In 1819, to help facilitate the movement of trade, Prussia began to negotiate treaties with the neighboring German states, and encouraged them to adopt the Prussian system of unified tariffs. The leading advocate of removing tariff barriers was the German economist Georg Friedrich List (1789–1846), who later became a naturalized U.S. citizen and wrote on the American economy.

By 1834 almost all German governments were members of the Prussian *Zollverein* (customs union); the notable—and predictable—exception was Austria. The formation of the Zollverein proved to be a major step in the building of a united German nation, and helped Prussia emerge as its eventual leader.

Repression in the Hapsburg Empire

Prussia and the other German states were at least linked by a common language. The fear of nationalism which obsessed Metternich and his Hapsburg masters was based on the multilingual and multicultural nature of the Hapsburg state. With the acquisition in 1815 of Lombardy and Venetia, Italians were added to the Hungarians, Serbs, Croatians, Slovenians, Czechs, Slovaks, and others who chafed under Austrian rule.

The danger of a nationalist uprising took precedence over all other political considerations. Plans for internal reforms included the establishment of local councils of landholders and a decentralization of the bureaucracy, but they foundered on the necessity of maintaining a police state, albeit an extremely inefficient one. Censorship, surveillance by both police and spies, and the close supervision of universities and libraries combined to produce a regime second only to Russia for severity of repression.

THE CONCERT OF EUROPE

Not content with reinforcing their convictions in their own countries, Europe's conservative leaders felt the duty to go to the help of one another whenever a reactionary regime was challenged: the French Revolution had taught them that an uprising in one state could threaten another. Two of those present at the Congress of Vienna proposed schemes to present a united front against the forces of revolution. Tsar Alexander asked for support for his Holy Alliance, whose members would use Christian principles to govern their states and defend their interests in Christian brotherhood. Most European governments joined, although with little enthusiasm. The two states that refused to sign were Britain, unwilling to become involved in a continental enterprise, and the Papal States: the pope had no intention of surrendering his moral lead to an Eastern Orthodox ruler.

Metternich's Concert of Europe was a far more formidable affair: a military alliance among Austria, Britain, Prussia, and Russia, which guaranteed to maintain the Vienna agreement for 20 years. This international "force for order" was to meet at regular intervals to survey the situation and strengthen its resolve, as well as intervene to crush revolutions wherever they should occur. Metternich had called the tsar's Holy Alliance a "sonorous nothing"; for all its initial success, in the long run the Concert of Europe had little more lasting influence than Alexander's scheme.

Francisco Goya's horrific vision of *Saturn Devouring One of His Sons* (c. 1821).

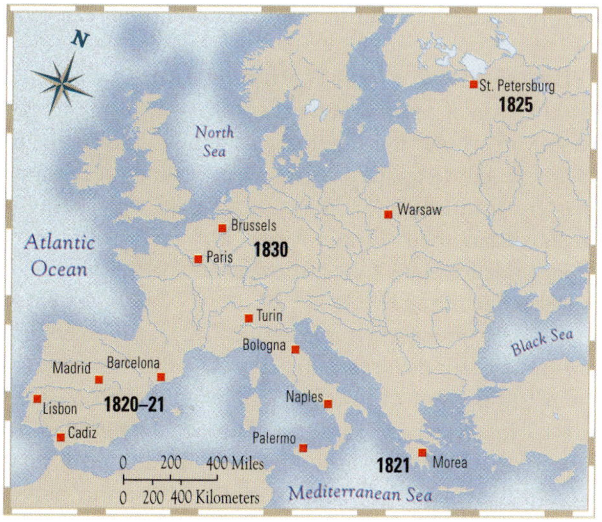

Map 5.1 European Revolutionary Movements, 1820–1830

The allies' first congress, which took place at Aix-la-Chapelle in 1818 with Britain present as an observer, witnessed the successful resolution of postwar problems: foreign occupation troops were removed from French soil, and France, where Bourbon rule had been peacefully restored, was admitted to the alliance. The next meetings, however—at Troppau in 1820 and at Laibach in 1821—came in response to serious unrest in Italy and Spain.

The Conservative Order Challenged: Spain and Italy

The first signs of trouble appeared in Spain. With the expulsion of the French in 1814, the restoration of Ferdinand VII (ruled 1808, 1814–1833) seemed cause for celebration. It did not take him long, in true Bourbon style, to abandon the constitution and set up all the apparatus of state repression. Liberal leaders were arrested, the universities were closed down, censorship was revived, and even the Inquisition was restored.

Popular resentment came to a head in 1820, when an army which was formed to put down uprisings in the Spanish colonies in America turned on Madrid instead, and forced the king to accept a return to the Spanish Constitution of 1812, a liberal document adopted during the Napoleonic occupation and modeled after the French Constitution of 1791. The reforms did not last long, but news of the successful Spanish revolt had a galvanizing effect on revolutionaries in Italy.

For the Italian states, Napoleonic rule had meant more enlightened rule and fairer taxes. With virtually the whole of Italy now under the Bourbons, the Hapsburgs, or their supporters, the various states slid again into absolutism. Ruthless government repression put down all traces of public protest. In response, Italian nationalists soon began to form secret societies; their members, known as the *Carbonari* (the name means "charcoal burners," and may have been intended to emphasize support for the underprivileged), differed as to the degree of violence necessary to produce political change, but advocated free and independent Italian states governed by constitutional monarchies.

When word reached Naples of the events in Spain, a group of young army officers led a revolt against the hated Neapolitan Bourbon king, Ferdinand I (ruled 1759–1806, 1815–1825). As in the case of their Spanish military counterparts, at first the move succeeded, and the king of Naples was forced to introduce a liberal constitution based on the Spanish Constitution of 1812. Here was exactly the kind of situation that Metternich had envisaged. With the agreement of Prussia and Russia, an Austrian army was dispatched to Naples, and to Piedmont where a liberal revolt had also broken out in 1821. The young prince Charles Albert also adopted the Spanish Constitution. The rebels were crushed; those who did not manage to escape were either executed or thrown into prison. The Spanish liberals' turn was next. In 1822, the allies of the Concert of Europe met at Verona; this time it fell to the French to send troops, stamp out the revolt, suppress the constitution, and restore the Bourbon monarchy.

The interventions in Italy and Spain successfully fulfilled Metternich's scheme to oppose the forces of change, but they were the last effective antirevolutionary action taken by the great powers. The British observers at the Troppau congress in 1820, who had protested against interfering in other nations' affairs, objected to the dispatch of French forces. The Spanish king's violent and bloodthirsty treatment of his liberal opponents had a powerful impact on the horrified French soldiers, and France ceased to play an active part in the alliance. Austria's only remaining dependable allies were Russia and Prussia, and the Concert's next test was too severe even for them.

The Monroe Doctrine

The troops who started the Spanish uprising had been on their way to the Spanish New World colonies to put down rebellions led by, among others, Simón Bolívar (1783–1830). Replacing Ferdinand on his tottering throne did nothing to end the unrest in America, and Metternich decided that the principle of suppressing revolts in Europe should be extended to European possessions abroad. With his encouragement, therefore, Alexander prepared to launch a great fleet to bring the colonies to their senses, and return them to Spanish rule.

The British, quite apart from their opposition to interference in another nation's business, had every reason to wish the rebels well: they were causing trouble to Spain, Britain's chief trade rival in America, while at the same time providing new markets for the sale of British goods, the production of which had vastly increased since the industrial revolution. George Canning (1770–1827), who became foreign minister in 1822, therefore proposed to the United States that a joint British–United States declaration should condemn the involvement of the Holy Alliance—a name in itself offensive to American susceptibilities—in the affairs of the Western Hemisphere.

The Monroe Doctrine, announced by President James Monroe (served 1817–1825) to Congress in December 1823, consisted of a unilateral U.S. statement: any attempt by European nations to interfere in the Americas would be regarded by the United States as an "unfriendly act." With Britain, still Europe's supreme naval power, supporting the United States' position, Alexander chose to abandon any thought of sailing to restore Spanish rule in the colonies.

The Greek War of Independence

In the case of Spain's western colonies, at least the tsar was sympathetic to Metternich's urgings, if powerless to act. In a contemporary nationalist uprising on Europe's eastern frontiers, the Greeks' struggle to win independence from their Turkish rulers and found their own state, the Russians found themselves for the first time on the side of the rebels.

The Greeks' revolt began in 1821, only to be met by brutal Turkish reprisals. In 1824 the massacre of some 90 percent of the Greek population of the island of Chios shocked much of Europe, accustomed to thinking of Greece as the birthplace of European civilization; in addition, leaders of the Romantic movement such as Lord Byron did much to foster sympathy for the Greek cause. The Russians, furthermore, shared the Greeks' Christian Orthodox religion; indeed, Russia had been converted to Christianity by two Greek missionaries. To add a practical consideration to the demands of religious brotherhood, if Russia managed to defeat Turkey on behalf of the Greeks, her own position in the Mediterranean would be reinforced by winning control of the straits of the Bosphorus, an aim dating back to the reign of Peter the Great.

In such circumstances the founder of the Holy Alliance could hardly stand by idle. Britain, unwilling to see Russia use the Greeks' cause to gain a power base at the Turks' expense, surrendered its objections to involvement in other people's business; by joining the Russian forces, the British were able to keep a careful eye on their "allies." Against the agonized protests of Metternich, in 1827 Britain, Russia, and France intervened on the side of the Greeks. By 1829 the defeated Turks had no choice but to concede independence to a small mainland Greece, along with a measure of self-government to those Romanians and Serbs who lived in the Ottoman Empire.

Thus, by supreme irony one of the most reactionary members of the Concert of Europe joined with the two powers who had left the original alliance, in support of the very cause the allies had come together to combat in the first place: nationalism. Furthermore, the victory of the Greeks and their supporters violated the principle of legitimacy established at the Congress of Vienna. If the Greek War of Independence did not kill off Metternich's cherished notion entirely, it certainly dealt it a death blow. The concept of a united reactionary Europe, ready to crush the specter of revolution wherever it appeared, had no longer any relevance to a political and social world on the brink of revolutionary changes.

Significant Dates

The Congress of Vienna and Its Aftermath

1814–1815	The Congress of Vienna meets
1818	First meeting of the Concert of Europe at Aix-la-Chapelle
1819	Peterloo Massacre
1820	Spanish Army revolts against Bourbons
1821	Revolt in Piedmont; Greeks begin struggle for independence
1823	Monroe Doctrine proclaimed
1824	Massacre of Chios; coronation of Charles X of France
1829	Greece becomes independent
1830	Revolution in France and Italy; Belgium becomes independent
1832	Reform Bill passed in Britain

Eugène Delacroix's painting *The Massacre at Chios* (1824) helped rouse support for the Greeks in their struggle for independence.

FRANCE AND THE POLITICS OF COMPROMISE

Louis XVIII, the Bourbon king restored to the throne of France, was by temperament a political moderate. His brother, Louis XVI, had died on the guillotine, and the so-called Louis XVII, Louis XVI's son and heir, died in prison without ever reigning. Any notion that his return to France might be the signal for popular demonstrations in favor of the Bourbons was soon scotched by the enthusiasm with which Napoleon's escape from Elba was greeted. In any case Louis himself, almost 60 and too fat and gouty to walk without help, had no wish to be deposed from what he called "the most comfortable of armchairs."

Shortly after occupying that chair, he issued a charter, which laid out the principles by which he intended to rule. Napoleon's legal system and centralized bureaucracy were to remain in force, along with the

Napoleonic tax structure. The country was to be governed by a parliament consisting of two chambers: the Chamber of Peers, made up of the aristocracy, and the Chamber of Deputies, elected by the votes of a tiny wealthy minority. The king could dissolve the Chamber of Deputies, appoint and dismiss his own ministers, and deal directly with foreign countries. Since he was also head of the army, the authority of either chamber of Parliament was, to say the least, limited.

The Ultraroyalists

Far from using his own concentration of power in the interests of the nobility, Louis fought to oppose the often reactionary demands of the "ultraroyalist" aristocrats who had trickled back into France. Eager to avenge the injuries inflicted on them by the Revolution, they returned to reclaim their lands and privileges.

If the aristocrats expected to see their property automatically restored to them by Louis' charter, they were bitterly disappointed. Peasants and middle-class citizens who had bought land from nobles or from the church were confirmed in possession of their holdings. Furthermore, the retention of Napoleon's legal and bureaucratic systems meant that all citizens were equal in the eyes of the law, and that all had the chance of professional advancement.

While the aristocracy was enraged by the charter, middle-class liberal reformers were far from completely satisfied. It gave the middle classes little actual political power, for since political representation was based on land, rather than business wealth, most of them could neither vote for, nor take part in, the two chambers of Parliament. Nonetheless the presence of Louis himself, steering a moderate course between the "ultras" and the reformers, maintained a precarious peace.

Among the more autocratic leaders of the rebellious nobles was the king's younger brother and eventual successor, the count of Artois (ruled 1824–1830). While alive, Louis managed to keep his brother under control, and tried to persuade him of the need for moderation if the Bourbon family was to remain in power. In 1824 Louis died, and the new king, Charles X, did not take long to demonstrate the truth of the saying that "the Bourbons learnt nothing and forgot nothing" from the years following 1789. Charles' coronation at Rheims

Revolution breaks out at the Pont Neuf in Paris in 1830.

became the excuse for an ornate ceremony in Medieval style, to symbolize his intention to return to past glories.

Aristocratic landowners were given compensation for the loss of their estates; the money was raised from the interest on government bonds chiefly held by middle-class investors. A series of measures concerned with inheritance threatened to undermine the principle of equality before the law, alarming both middle classes and peasants. The church regained a strong role, with increased control of education, and the Jesuits were allowed to return to France and to their earlier influential position in the country's educational policies and political life.

The Revolution of 1830

Within a few years Charles had so alienated vast sections of public opinion that in the spring of 1830 even the chamber turned against him. The king dismissed it and called new elections. In spite of press censorship and official pressures, another liberal majority was returned. In July 1830 Charles again dissolved the chamber and produced an electoral system that would guarantee him a majority: only some 25,000 people—the richest men in France—could vote. All freedom of the press was suspended.

The result was revolution. In the July uprisings the workers and students of Paris blocked the streets with barricades. Among the first groups were workers in the printing trade. With the army unwilling to fire on the crowds, and in the absence of any firm political support, the last Bourbon king of France abdicated and took himself off to England, where he died, unmourned, in exile.

The revolutionaries had fought to bring back a republic, but France's political and business leaders were more cautious. Remembering the excesses of the Revolution of 1789, they decided to avoid the extremes of absolute monarchy and popular republic by creating a constitutional monarchy. In this way they hoped to achieve stability and at the same time maintain their own influence.

The same sense of compromise governed their choice for the new king. The duke of Orleans was an aristocrat, the descendant of a cousin of Louis XVI who had served on the convention and voted for Louis' execution in 1793. The duke thus had both noble and appropriately revolutionary family credentials, and had lived an unexceptionable middle-class life. After promising to honor the Constitution of 1814, he was duly crowned as Louis Philippe (ruled 1830–1848).

The Revolution of 1830, fought by workers, students, and artisans, served to abolish the absolute power of the king, but its chief beneficiaries were the middle-class property owners, who now controlled the legislature.

CONSERVATISM CHALLENGED: POLITICAL UNREST AND CONSTITUTIONALISM IN BRITAIN

The tumultuous events that swept continental Europe in the early 19th century reinforced the innate conservatism of British politicians. The Tory party, Britain's conservatives, had held virtually uninterrupted power since the 1780s, and guided their country to victory over Napoleon. Their parliamentary opponents, the Whigs, shared the Tories' aristocratic background. Whatever differences there might be on niceties of policy, neither party had any interest in a wider sharing of power or in a more equitable distribution of property.

The country was governed by two houses of Parliament, the Lords and the Commons. Members of both houses, virtually always landed aristocrats, were elected by a tiny minority of around 5 percent of the adult male population, themselves property owners. The counties and boroughs that these members represented were traditional aristocratic strongholds; the growing industrial centers of central and northern England sent no members to Parliament.

The Peterloo Massacre

In the aftermath of Waterloo and the economic depression that beset Britain, popular unrest began to mount. The misery of living and working conditions in northern cities such as Manchester, together with the fear of unemployment, inspired radical leaders to press for wider parliamentary representation, despite the economic character of their grievances. The very violence of government reaction proved its own undoing. In 1819 a crowd of some 60,000 gathered in St. Peter's Fields, in the center of Manchester, to attend a political demonstration in favor of reform. Troops of the Manchester and Cheshire Cavalry fired on the assembly, killing eleven people and wounding over 400. Radical leaders and critics in the press, in reference to the decisive Battle of Waterloo, dubbed the event the "Peterloo Massacre," and its victims became the first martyrs of the struggle for reform.

The Peterloo Massacre proved significant in another respect: over a quarter of those injured were women, demonstrating alongside men for political change. By the second decade of the 19th century, the development of industry had begun to change the part that gender played in the division of labor. Machines provided their own energy and required no special strength on the part of their users; they could be operated by women or men. The growing cities provided a greater range of employment for women, which often led to their exploitation by factory owners. At the same time women became increasingly aware of the domestic problems created by urban growth.

If the victims of Peterloo had chosen politics as a field for activism, other women turned to popular religion as a means of redressing injustices. A series of woman preachers began to address meetings of workers on the need for social justice. These preachers included Elizabeth Gorse Gaunt (b. 1777) and Ann Cutler (b. 1759), who was known as "Praying Nanny."

Pressure for Reform

In Parliament, however, the demand for social and political reform fell on deaf ears. Indeed, the Six Acts of 1819 passed in the same year as Peterloo—and the same year as the Carlsbad decrees—limited the right of public assembly, censored literature, and imposed a tax on newspapers.

So extreme a response alarmed many moderate Tories, whose general inclination was to aim for compromise. Some feared that government stubbornness could lead to revolution, while others were attracted by the new ideas of utilitarianism and genuinely interested in social reform. Under pressure from George Canning, Robert Peel, and other moderates, the criminal code was reformed, and workers were allowed to form unions, although not to strike. The tariffs on cheap imported grain, controlled by the Corn Laws—which had raised the tax after the Napoleonic Wars—were reduced; these taxes, which protected English landowners while keeping the price of bread high, had long been a source of popular resentment.

Reform of Parliament was a different matter. No Tory majority backed by the Anglican Church and the aristocracy would agree to revising the conditions of parliamentary representation. Many members of Parliament were either directly appointed by wealthy landowners or were elected by "rotten" or "pocket" boroughs—districts where electors were bullied and bribed to vote for the candidate of their landlord's choice; thus the election was in the "pocket" of the landowner. In the case of the "rotten" boroughs, members represented districts that were virtually unpopulated or had actually been abandoned.

It fell to the Whigs, with the support of the rising manufacturing and trading classes, to lead the cause of reform. They were inspired not by democratic principles but by the pragmatic belief that change would be "in the interests of the realm"; this characteristically British formula was bolstered in many cases by the ideas of utilitarian thinkers such as Jeremy Bentham (on the utilitarians, see Part VII, Topic 8). Furthermore, they hoped that middle-class members of Parliament would represent both middle- and working-class interests. In this way the workers would be satisfied and make no further protests, and a revolution could be avoided.

In 1830 an alliance of the Whigs and reform-minded liberals succeeded in defeating the Tories and forming a government. (Toward the end of the 19th century, the Whig party would change its name to the Liberal party.) The Whig prime minister, Earl Charles Grey (1764–1845), hastily drew up and forced through Parliament the Reform Bill of 1832.

Although the bill was to have momentous importance for British democratic life, it was intended to preserve the existing situation as far as possible. The vote was extended, but only on the basis of property; about 400,000 new electors were added to the voting rolls. Electoral districts were redistributed: the "rotten" boroughs were abolished and their seats given to the industrial cities of the north. No attempt was made, however, to create an equal balance between population size and political representation. As in France under Louis Philippe, the chief victors in 1830s Britain were the industrial middle classes, and their accession to a share in power served to promote a whole series of social reforms. Liberal legislation reorganized the church, reformed the divorce laws, and introduced the Poor Law of 1834. In 1833, on behalf of a reform society, a private member of Parliament successfully introduced a bill abolishing slavery throughout the British Empire.

In the years between then and 1847 the criminal code was further reformed, reducing the number of capital offenses to three; 20 years earlier there had been hundreds of crimes for which those found guilty had been executed. Working conditions for women and children were improved. Government grants were awarded to schools. In 1846, a Tory administration finally repealed the hated Corn Laws. The British had achieved the beginnings of revolutionary change without a revolution.

The years following Waterloo saw the apparent triumph of conservatism throughout most of Europe. The decisions of the Congress of Vienna and the subsequent formation of the Concert of Europe seemed to doom the liberal and nationalist causes to defeat right from the start. Effective power either remained in aristocratic hands, as in Prussia and Austria, or was returned there, as in France, Spain, and the kingdoms of Italy.

Yet, with the single exception of Russia, liberalism and nationalism were to have a profound effect on virtually every country in Europe, including Britain. Even where its manifestations were repressed, as in the Hapsburg empire, the demand for reform built to an irrepressible force. Further attempts to produce changes a generation after the Congress of Vienna led to violent action. In Britain, by contrast, political compromise led to a gradual process of reform that proved a continuous one.

In many cases one of the chief factors was economic. The growing demands of the rising industrial class in France proved fatal to the rule of Charles X, although his own misjudgments helped to hasten his fall. Prussia's plans for economic expansion led to the formation of a customs union that in turn prepared the way for a united Germany.

In some countries the very repression of nationalist uprisings served to inspire the forces of protest. The struggle to form a united Italy, know as the Risorgimento, had its roots in the Carbonari movement, born in opposition to Bourbon rule. The Greeks actually managed to achieve their freedom from the Turks, in large measure because the great powers—for selfish reasons of their own—decided to intervene.

Thus a battle that seemed definitively won in 1815 continued to rage at one level or another over the following decades. It says much for the persistence of the liberals and nationalists that so much progress was made so quickly. On the other hand the conservatives were determined and stubborn opponents: when the next round of protests came, in 1848, it led to violent revolution.

Questions for Further Discussion

1. How successful was the Concert of Europe in maintaining conservative policies in European affairs?
2. What role did Russia play in European politics following the Congress of Vienna? To what extent was this influenced by internal Russian developments?
3. What were the main stages of the Greek struggle for independence, and why was it successful?

Suggestions for Further Reading

Carr, R. *Spain, 1808–1939*. Oxford, 1982.

Church, C. *Europe in 1830: Revolution and Political Change*. London, 1983.

Dakin, D. *The Greek Struggle for Independence, 1821–1833*. Berkeley, CA, 1973.

Gildea, Robert. *Barricades and Borders, Europe 1800–1914*. Oxford, 1987.

Nicolson, Harold. *The Congress of Vienna: A Study in Allied Unity, 1812–1822*. New York, 1965.

Rude, G. *Debate on Europe*. New York, 1972.

de Sauvigny, G. *Metternich and His Times*. Atlantic Highlands, NJ, 1962.

Talmon, J. L. *Romanticism and Revolt*. New York, 1979.

VII

Topic 6

The New Social Order: Workers, Women, and the Middle Class

In the mid-18th century, Europe was still an overwhelmingly rural, agrarian society. Life for most people centered around traditional values associated with labor in the fields, family, and the church. The authority of the nobility on their lands and over the people who lived on them was largely unquestioned. The extended family, with several generations of relatives living and working together, prevailed. In agrarian families, women remained subservient to males, their roles limited to childbearing and rearing, to household duties, and to occasional participation in fieldwork and home-based textile making. Peasants, nobles, and clergy comprised the major social categories, while the merchant-capitalist class and those who lived in towns represented a small percentage of the population.

A hundred years later, much of that traditional way of life had changed. The development of technology and factory-based manufacturing pushed Europe increasingly toward an urban, industrial civilization. The structure of society grew more complex as two new groups—industrial workers and the middle class—joined the social order in ever larger numbers, giving rise to the modern class structure. As rural dwellers migrated to the cities in search of work, traditional values and family bonds began to break down, replaced by the urban nuclear family of parents and children. The status and role of women in this emerging industrial society also assumed new dimensions as tens of thousands of them left home for work in the factories.

By the middle of the 19th century, the general contours of European society as we know it today were formed. The years from 1789 to 1850 represented, then, a period of social transition, marked by great mobility and flux, and accompanied by growing political instability.

European Society in Transition

While advanced industrialization brought many changes to Europe, it also intensified some earlier social and demographic trends. The lure of the city for people living in the countryside, manifest even in the Middle Ages, accelerated, as did the growth pattern in Europe's population. The nascent industrial economy opened new opportunities for merchants and other longtime urban dwellers, while for others, such as artisans, it created problems and challenges. Moreover, as the French Revolution had shown, the political aspirations of different social groups could result in violence. Now, however, the new emerging social classes began to struggle over competing economic interests. The political struggles of the period after 1789 were to a great extent the result of growing class consciousness among both industrial workers and the middle class. Finally, while urban life had always presented governments with special challenges in public policy, the dramatic growth in the size and number of cities in the 19th century raised new dilemmas of planning and infrastructure and presented problems of enormous dimension in areas such as health, housing, transportation, and social control.

Population Patterns in the Age of Industrialization

As we have seen (see Part VII, Topic 2), in the first half of the 18th century Europe began to experience a tremendous growth in population. As industrialization spread, the numbers continued to increase, although not at a uniform or regular rate. The population of Europe grew by 40 percent between 1800 and 1850, from about 190 million to some 265 million. On the Continent (excluding Russia) the sharpest population rise occurred in the periods 1800–1820 (14 percent) and 1820–1830 (11 percent).

The agricultural revolution had enlarged the food supply in England, and during the 1820s and 1830s improved farming methods, including new machines and the cultivation of the potato, were gradually adopted on the Continent. Crop failures were less frequent but when they did occur, as in the Irish potato famine of the 1840s, they still caused widespread distress. A lower incidence of disease and improvements in diet slowly helped to raise the average life expectancy. Nevertheless, the basic staple of most diets, which for the majority of people were extremely limited and unbalanced, consisted of bread, grains, or potato. Milk, cheese, and green vegetables sometimes supplemented the staple foods, and meat or fish more rarely. In the town of Ghent, for example, an average of 2435 calories a day were consumed by each citizen, but 80 percent of that total—1479 from cereals and potatoes and 428 from beer—came from cereal carbohydrates.

Higher income levels also encouraged people to marry at a younger age and to have more children. The expanding cottage industry had the effect of improving the rural standard of living, while the relatively high factory wages increased the urban incomes.

Earlier marriage patterns and lower annual death rates slowly altered the general demographic profile of 19th-century Europe. Initially, younger age groups increased at a faster rate than the rest of the population, but during the second half of the century medical advances allowed older people to live longer. Moreover, the peasantry and working class tended to have more children than those higher up in the social hierarchy.

Population growth and higher living standards expanded the market for manufactured goods and provided a labor supply for the factories. Indeed, the combination of economic factors and political conditions in the 19th century produced massive shifts in Europe's population. Initially, factories in cities drew much of their labor from the urban poor, but increasingly after 1815 the cities attracted rural workers, especially the young. The volume of migration from villages to cities intensified as people flocked to the factories to take advantage of higher salaries and new opportunities. Typically the migrant was a male between the ages of 15 and 30, although women also moved. Many young girls left the countryside to take positions as domestic servants in the homes of the rising middle class, often returning to their villages to marry, while others sought employment in the textile mills after the decline of cottage spinning.

The numbers of people moving from country to city during the 19th century ran into the tens of millions. In addition to the permanent migration to urban areas, seasonal migration in agriculture was also common in many European countries, and it has been estimated that there were some 900,000 seasonal migrants in France alone in 1852. Migration between countries was more difficult, although in 19th-century Europe only Turkey and Russia had passport regulations. Nearly 400,000 foreign workers were employed in France at midcentury. Poverty and political repression also drove an estimated 50 million Europeans abroad during the 19th century, many of them emigrating to the United States and Latin America.

The Rise of the City

The most far-reaching population change in 19th-century Europe was the dramatic rise in the number and size of its cities. By 1850, many rural districts in England and the Continent were sparsely populated as millions moved to industrial towns and cities. Industrialization, together with the expansion of financial enterprises and government, spawned an urban revolution of unprecedented dimensions.

At the opening of the 19th century, London alone among European cities had a population over a million. Paris, the second largest, had half that number, while only five other cities could boast 200,000 or more. Within half a century, however, London had reached 2.6 million, Paris more than 1 million, and some 30 additional cities had in excess of 200,000 inhabitants. Most urban centers had at least doubled—and many trebled—in population. Glasgow, Leeds, Liverpool, and other British manufacturing cities experienced massive growth, while on the Continent Berlin, Brussels, Budapest, and Munich saw increases almost as startling.

Despite the rapid urbanization pattern, however, Europe remained a predominantly rural or small-town society throughout the 19th century. One estimate

Table 6.1
The Growth of European Cities, 1800–1850 (in 1000s)

	1800	1850
Barcelona	115	175
Belfast	37	103
Berlin	172	419
Birmingham	74	233
Bordeaux	91	131
Bristol	64	137
Brussels	66	251
Budapest	54	178
Cologne	50	97
Cracow	24	50
Dresden	60	97
Edinburgh	83	202
Glasgow	77	357
Kiev	23	50
Leeds	53	721
Leipzig	30	63
Liverpool	80	376
London	1,117	2,685
Lyon	110	177
Madrid	160	281
Manchester	90	303
Marseilles	111	194
Milan	135	242
Moscow	250	365
Munich	40	110
Naples	427	449
Paris	547	1,053
Rotterdam	53	90
Sheffield	31	135
St. Petersburg	220	485
Stuttgart	18	47
Vienna	247	444

classified 14.5 percent of Europe's population as urban in 1800 (counting cities of 5000 or more), a figure that rose to only 22.3 percent by 1850. England, Europe's industrial leader, had the most highly urbanized population: in 1850, 35 percent of its people lived in cities, whereas in that same year only 10 percent of the French and 7 percent of the German population fell into the urban category (counting cities of 20,000 or more). Even as late as 1910, only 43 percent of Europe's population was urban.

As Europeans increasingly lived in cities during the 19th century, a corresponding pattern of change took place, although at a slower pace, within the workforce. The percentage of the overall population earning its livelihood from agriculture dropped, while the percentage of those in industry and the service sector of the economy grew. England passed the halfway mark by 1850, when 51 percent of its working population were engaged in industry and only 22 percent in agriculture. The French were a distant second, after England, with 27 percent of their working population in industry and fully half still in farming.

Nevertheless, the industrial cities defined the flavor and character of European civilization and its new social hierarchy. The huge concentration of people in these burgeoning centers created unprecedented dilemmas for their inhabitants. Some of the new industrial cities had mushroomed rapidly and without planning from hardly more than small towns, while others had grown from already sizable foundations. In all cases, neither local nor national administrations were prepared to deal with the seemingly insurmountable array of problems that they now confronted. Public transportation was nonexistent during the first half of the century, so that workers had to live close to the factories. In older towns, workers crowded into inadequate housing in conditions of extreme congestion—in Paris, for instance, the number of people living in an average house rose from 21.9 in 1800 to 35.2 in 1851. Entire families lived in one or two tiny rooms, often in cellars or attics, most without heat, toilet facilities, or water. New working-class housing, thrown up in the form of cheaply constructed, densely packed tenements, was little better.

Sulfurous fumes from the burning of cheap coal and factories hung over the narrow alleys, while soot, garbage, and human excrement often filled the streets. Public water supplies were limited and generally unsafe. In the 1850s, only one out of five houses in Paris had its own water and most people in Berlin still used public fountains. Sewers, when they existed at all, were often merely open drains that emptied into the nearest river. In Britain, the first Public Health Act was passed only in 1875, while in France it was not until 1894 that sewage systems were required in all towns. The failure to separate the water supply from the sewage disposal was the cause for periodic outbreaks of epidemic. Ancient Rome of the 1st century A.D. had a cleaner water supply than most European cities in the 19th century.

Such conditions presented serious health hazards in the form of infectious diseases, especially for the urban poor. Cholera and typhoid, carried by polluted

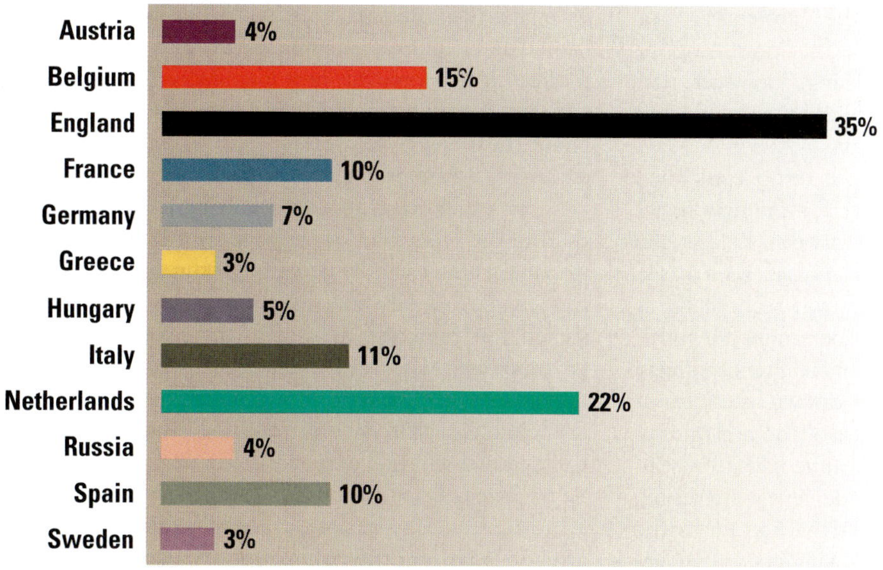

Graph 6.1 **The Urban Population of Europe in 1850**
(Percentage living in cities of 20,000 or more)

water, and typhus, spread by lice, were common. In Western Europe alone, tens of thousands of people were killed by a cholera epidemic in 1831–1832, and recurrences in 1846, 1848–1849, and 1866 continued to claim many lives. For the poor—the bulk of the population—the quality of urban life was generally worse than in the countryside during the first half of the century. The mortality rate was higher and the birthrate lower in the cities, and within large cities such as Paris or London death rates were higher in working-class areas than in fashionable districts. Reform movements to deal with issues such as health and urban welfare began in England in the 1830s (see Part VII, Topic 13), and efforts to improve the infrastructure of the cities spread through the Continent in the 1840s and 1850s. Not until the end of the 19th century, however, did conditions in most of Europe's cities begin to approach modern standards.

The Emergence of Class Structure

In 1844, the young German Friedrich Engels (1820–1895)—who later became a close friend and collaborator of Karl Marx—wrote a now classic book, *The Condition of the Working Class in England*. In this study of the laboring people, Engels explained how the industrial revolution had created both a "middle class" and

Mid-19th-century Manchester revealed the worst aspects of industrial pollution.

"an integral, permanent class," the "proletariat," or working class. The first he defined as the "possessing" or property-owning class (distinguishing, however, between them and the old landowning aristocracy) and the second as the "propertyless" class.

At the time Engels wrote, the term "class" had only recently come into use to describe the new social categories produced by industrialization. Before the Revolution of 1789, European society had been based on legally defined status groups known technically as "orders," membership in which was determined by birth and legal privilege. In prerevolutionary France society had been divided into three orders known as estates—the clergy, the nobility, and the rest of the population. The social hierarchy of the Old Regime had been seen as a pyramid, with a series of wide levels stretching from the poor and the peasantry at the bottom to the apex of princes and king at the top. Members of this social system were linked by relationships of authority and obligation.

By the beginning of the 19th century social classes were increasingly identified by income and occupation. Less tangible indicators, such as aspirations and values, were also important factors in determining one's class, but wealth or property, and how a person earned a living, became the chief measure of status.

Class identification along these lines was, however, neither absolute nor clear-cut, and the transition from the old hierarchy to the new structure evolved throughout the century. The distinctive male clothing of the privileged orders of the Old Regime—with its breeches, lace cuffs, and wigs—eventually disappeared for all except ceremonial occasions. Trousers and jackets which we associate today with "business" dress became the order of the day for both aristocrats and the middle class. Moreover, new manufacturing techniques reduced costs and enabled the working class to purchase inexpensive leisure clothing that was similar in appearance to middle-class dress.

In other ways, too, class distinctions were looser than in the prerevolutionary period. As liberal constitutional systems came to be adopted throughout most of Europe, the nobility and the middle classes increasingly shared the franchise as well as appointment to high government office. The richer segments of the upper middle class also bought or built luxurious residences in fashionable neighborhoods furnished in ways that made them indistinguishable from aristocratic palaces.

Titles of nobility, access to the royal court, and a sense of solidarity at first kept the old aristocracy at arm's length from the rising business magnates. Yet social relationships between the nobles and the upper middle class were not totally rigid. By the end of the 18th century, impoverished nobles and the wealthiest industrialists began to see mutual advantages in arranging marriages between their families, a trend that accelerated in the next century. Monarchs frequently bestowed titles on businessmen and received them at court, while some more enterprising nobles made the transition from living off land rents to capitalist agriculture and investment in industry. In the same way, successful artisans and skilled laborers began to accumulate sufficient resources and property, and move up into the ranks of the middle classes.

The new class structure revealed an unprecedented degree of mobility in which individuals often

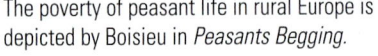

The poverty of peasant life in rural Europe is depicted by Boisieu in *Peasants Begging*.

Robert Adam's design for the Marble Hall at Kedleston Hall, Derbyshire, suggests the opulence of life for the English aristocracy in the late 18th century.

moved from one level to another. This was especially true of Britain. Yet, although the pyramid of the Old Regime was no longer a valid representation of social structure, a different urban social hierarchy emerged in which the new distinctions of income and wealth between categories were at least as sharp.

THE CONDITION OF THE WORKING CLASS

As Engels himself recognized, the European working population was comprised not only of factory employees. Workers represented a much broader category that included artisans, domestic servants, cottage industry workers, and agricultural laborers. The complexities of social change brought on by the industrial revolution increased or further defined differences in status, income, and attitude within the worker hierarchy itself.

All working-class persons were linked by the factor of dependency—that is, they depended on others for employment, for the kind of work they did, and for the conditions under which they labored. Beyond this common denominator, the differences among them reflected the degree and nature of their skills. Industrialization not only created the new social category of the urban factory worker, but also affected existing categories. It had the effect of greatly extending the number of domestic servants by enlarging the middle classes; it also reduced the number of cottage workers, and it affected the status and income of artisans.

The Working-Class Hierarchy

As a whole, the working class comprised some 80 percent of Europe's urban population at midcentury (more than 90 percent if we include rural laborers and peasants). Industrial workers accounted for a small portion of that number, and only after 1850 did factory workers begin to dominate the production system. In France, at that point much less industrialized than England, 27 percent of the labor force was in industry, but factory workers were less than 5 percent. Moreover, industrial workers were unevenly distributed—they formed most

The Peterloo Massacre of 1819 revealed the class antagonisms of industrial England.

of the population of new industrial towns such as Manchester or Birmingham, but represented only a small portion of the inhabitants of older, large cities like London.

While the number of factory workers was relatively small in the first half of the 19th century, they were the fastest growing urban class. "The mightiest result," wrote Engels of the industrial revolution, "is the English proletariat."[1] In the early stages of industrialization, the majority of factory laborers came from rural areas. Most peasants went to the factories with great reluctance and kept their ties to the countryside. Among the first generation of industrial workers, as many as 25 percent went back to their rural areas in the summer for the harvesting of crops. Subsequent generations of workers, however, broke their ties with the countryside as they developed urban roots.

Skilled factory labor was generally scarce in the first half of the century, so that industrial pay was higher than rural wages. Even among industrial workers, however, differences were clearly delineated, most often according to the level of skill commanded. Unskilled workers, by far the largest group, earned too little to maintain the average working-class family of father, mother, and three children. This accounts for the presence of large numbers of women and children in the labor force, both in the factories and as servants. Indeed, domestic servants made up an increasingly large portion of the working population. Among the unskilled were manual laborers such as ditch diggers and construction helpers, teamsters, dock workers, and factory employees who were assigned the simplest tasks.

Women and children were a strong presence in the lower ranks of the workforce, especially in the textile industry. Women constituted between 40 and 50 percent of all workers in cotton mills and children from 15 to 25 percent. In production requiring heavy operations, such as metal manufacturing, women and children were less seldom used, whereas in mechanical weaving they held virtually a monopoly of jobs. Perhaps as many as one-third of all teenage girls in England were domestic servants. Because employers knew that most—although by no means all—women and children worked to supplement family income, they were paid the lowest wages in the workforce. Women earned half as much as men in the same jobs, and children half as much as women.

Higher up in the social hierarchy were semiskilled workers, who earned an average of one and a half times the lowest rates. These included tradesmen such as carpenters (as opposed to cabinetmakers), plumbers, and brick masons. Moreover, as machinery came into wider use in the factories, the number of semiskilled industrial workers increased.

Skilled workers were the élite, representing only some 15 percent of the labor force. The pay of most skilled workers was at least twice that of the unskilled category, and some—such as expert machinists and

[1] Friedrich Engels, *The Condition of the Working Class in England,* ed. and trans. Victor Kiernan (Harmondsworth: Penguin, 1987), 61. First published in Germany in 1845.

iron puddlers—earned as much as five times the lowest rates. A few skilled workers eventually made their way into the lowest rung of management as foremen. Technological developments expanded the number of skilled workers as the need grew for machine toolmakers, railroad engineers, and other specialists.

Artisans Under Stress

The artisans engaged in highly skilled crafts—jewelers and goldsmiths, glassblowers, cabinet and instrument makers, bookbinders and printers—were the "aristocracy" of the skilled workers. Strong traditions of group identity and quality craftsmanship bound them together. Through their self-regulating guilds, hundreds of years old, artisans had established work standards, pay scales, and conditions of employment in small workshops. Under the guild system, years of experience were required for workers to pass from apprentice to journeyman, and only a few achieved the rank of master.

Industrialization adversely affected artisans, who outnumbered factory workers in the first half of the 19th century, even in countries such as Great Britain, France, and Prussia. They were, however, widely distributed in large European cities such as London, Paris, and Vienna, where the demand for high-quality luxury goods actually grew as middle-class wealth expanded.

Olaudah Equiano, a former slave from West Africa, gained his freedom in England and campaigned vigorously for abolition, while writing books and lecturing.

At first, factory production hurt specialty textile manufacturing, such as the finishing of wool cloth or lace making, and artisans in the cottage industry were most severely displaced by the new mechanical inventions in weaving. By midcentury mechanization and the factory system threatened to make the skills of artisans obsolete on a massive level. As a result, the guilds attempted to tighten their control over the craft trades and to make advancement more difficult, but new laws and capitalist economic policy often made this impossible. The revolutionary government in France had abolished the guilds in 1791, and in Britain the guilds disappeared gradually in the 1830s. By 1850, they had been eliminated in many of the German and Italian states as well as in the Low Countries and Spain.

As a group, artisans felt distinct from factory workers and the middle class. Industrial laborers increased three or four times as rapidly as artisans, but direct contact between the two categories was limited. Artisans inhabited long-established residential sections in cities, and their sense of dignity and higher status led them to regard ordinary workers as beneath them. Clinging resolutely to their traditional ways of life and work methods as the factory system spread, they tried to maintain tight family unity—artisan wives, for example, did not generally work in factories—and to limit the number of children they had in order to sustain their living standards. In addition, artisans tended to take great interest in education and self-improvement, and had disciplined savings habits.

Artisans clearly saw themselves under attack by the new forces of production. In the early stages of industrialization the artisans reacted to the introduction of new technology by smashing machines. As the crisis of the artisan class continued to unfold over the course of the 19th century, they became an element of increasing political instability in European society.

The Standard of Living

When he visited the English manufacturing towns in the 1840s, Engels came away with a devastating impression of the condition of the working class:

> Thus the working class of the great cities offers a graduated scale of conditions of life, in the best cases a temporarily endurable existence for hard work and good wages, good and endurable, that is, from the worker's standpoint; in the worst cases, bitter want, reaching even homelessness and death by starvation.[2]

Engels was not alone in calling attention to the miserable living conditions of the industrial workers, for some of the English Romantic poets (see Part VII, Topic 7) had also done so. These protests began an

[2] Engels, *The Condition of the Working Class.*

important and continuing debate over the impact of industrialization on working-class lives which centers on whether workers shared in the wealth created by the industrial revolution, or whether the new prosperity benefited only the middle class.

Throughout the 19th century, wages stayed ahead of the rise in the cost of living, except during periods of economic slump. This was especially true in England, where per capita real income doubled. Wages also rose on the Continent as industrialization spread after 1850. By comparison with the countryside, real wages in the cities were higher. Even Engels, who believed that working-class conditions would steadily deteriorate, admitted that the situation was complex and that his examples stressed the worst cases.

On the other hand, unskilled workers outside the factory system and cottage industry laborers suffered seriously from the dislocations. The housing conditions for factory workers that Engels described in the British cities were indeed miserable and the mortality rate rose among urban workers. Food consumption was hardly above subsistence for most urban workers, although they had better diets than peasants. The high consumption of alcohol among workers, regarded as a serious problem by contemporary social observers, reflected the stress of daily life and the limited opportunities for leisure time activities. In working-class families, wives and children worked more often than not in order to buy basic necessities rather than luxuries. Indeed, the poorest segment of Europe's population—a third of the whole, including the families of rural and urban workers—earned only about 10 percent of all income. Moreover, the uncertainty of employment was an ever-present source of demoralization, and a large percentage of male laborers were regularly without work in industrial towns. Chronic poverty remained widespread, affecting as much as 10 percent of the population of Great Britain, although it was, of course, by no means unknown before the industrial period.

Living standards among artisans were equally complex. Those with skills in demand earned high wages and increased their real income, while many less fortunate craftsmen who faced factory competition experienced declining pay and rising work hours. Wages for most artisans were higher than for most workers, and they generally enjoyed more material comfort. Yet the position of artisans was especially vulnerable in times of economic hardship, when the demand for their high quality products collapsed more quickly than for basic necessities.

On the whole, industrialization eventually raised the living standards of millions of Europeans, although the transformation was slow and took place against a backdrop of privation, dependency, and widespread suffering.

THE COMFORTABLE BOURGEOISIE

The middle class was as complex and varied as the other social groups, perhaps more so, and during the first half of the 19th century it underwent considerable growth and change. The category was so broad as to include at the top those whose wealth rivaled that of the old nobility, and at the bottom those whose income was scarcely higher than that of the best paid skilled worker. In fact, the wide range of economic status found within this social category suggests a range of middle classes rather than just one.

Certain general characteristics, however, help to define the middle classes as a social unit. By midcentury, they comprised perhaps 20 percent of the urban population of Europe, although the figure was lower in eastern and southern Europe, where industry and commerce were less advanced. Their numbers grew steadily along with industrial and economic development, as did their wealth. Elements of the middle classes were both the driving force behind industrialization and business expansion and its principal beneficiaries. Most, although not all, members of the middle classes owned some form of property. Their income afforded them a degree of comfort that was unattainable by the working classes.

The middle classes were the most mobile sector within the new urban social hierarchy. By midcentury, most members of the group had risen above their origins, and they regarded themselves as distinct from both the working classes and the titled nobility. Wealth and new status led the middle classes to demand participation in government alongside the aristocracy—indeed, the leaders of most political revolutions in Europe between 1789 and 1848 were from the middle classes. By 1870, the middle classes not only achieved a measure of political power almost everywhere, but also set the tone and values for most of society.

The Structure of the Middle Classes

During the first phase of the industrial revolution, most entrepreneurs came from relatively modest backgrounds: small businessmen, engineers, and artisans with their own shops. Three distinct segments are discernible among the middle classes. The upper level, consisting of large-scale industrialists, bankers, and merchants, was the smallest but wealthiest sector, making up less than 5 percent of the middle class. Together with the aristocracy, this group earned one-third of all income. As a result, the upper middle class was able to enjoy a sumptuous existence, with private mansions in exclusive areas of the city and villas in the country, a retinue of servants, and luxuries that imitated the lifestyle of the aristocracy.

The middle range of the bourgeoisie consisted of small manufacturers, moderate-sized merchants, and businessmen, as well as professionals. This group usually lived either in rented apartments in genteel urban neighborhoods, or owned their own homes in newer sections of the cities. The professionals included lawyers, physicians, and university professors, and a rapidly growing number of accountants, engineers, and chemists. While most lawyers and physicians had adequate but not spectacular incomes and little property, they had more advanced education than other middle-class groups. The professionals also stood apart from the business elements because they tended to be active in political and social reform. From this same segment also came most of Europe's intellectuals and creative artists, who often rebelled against the social conventions and material values of their class.

The largest and fastest growing element within the bourgeoisie was the lower middle class, consisting mainly of small shopkeepers and the relatively new white-collar workers, especially civil servants such as teachers, postal clerks, and secretaries. This group accounted for approximately half of the entire middle-class population. Their income was considerably less than the two higher bourgeois strata, and they owned little or no property. Nevertheless, they lived modestly but comfortably in decent apartments, managed to save money, and gave their children elementary educations.

As a whole, much of the wealth generated by industrial and economic growth—actually, almost one-half of all income—went to the middle classes. That wealth was unevenly distributed among the three levels of the bourgeois class. In England, for example, the savings of taxpayers in the highest income bracket increased fourfold between 1800 and 1850, while those of the lower middle class grew much more slowly. For manufacturers, the need for capital investment and rising pay scales for workers were offset by steadily falling production costs. For the shopkeepers, cheaper goods and the expanding purchasing power of all classes meant more customers. In the complex social environment of the cities, the lives of the middle classes contrasted vividly with those of the working class.

How the Middle Classes Lived

The bourgeoisie lived comfortably. The homes of the lower and middle classes, whether owned or rented, were furnished with solid, sensible furniture that conveyed a cozy, respectable well-being. In Austria and Germany before 1850, the popular style of middle-class furniture was known as *Biedermeier*, constructed of sturdy, light-colored woods with simple, clean lines. In England darker, carved pieces of what was later called "Victorian" furniture were to be found in bourgeois homes, while in France after midcentury the so-called "Empire" style—a heavier, less elegant variation of the neoclassical style favored during Napoleon's reign—prevailed. Success was partially measured by the number of servants a family had and by the elaborate, multicourse dinner parties that were provided for guests. The middle classes ate well, and in fact virtually half of all their income was spent on food and servants.

A French middle-class family at home.

The lower ranks of the middle classes generally prized education, not as an end in itself but as a means of preparing children for adult responsibilities. Two standards of education, determined by gender, prevailed. Boys were taught practical subjects such as mathematics and accounting or technical skills, while training for girls was usually limited to music, poetry, sewing, and household management. This educational hierarchy, in turn, reflected the bourgeois separation of the outside male world of work from the protected sphere of domestic life that was thought to be the proper sphere of women. For most of the century, classical education in universities was largely the preserve of the sons of the wealthiest families and the aristocracy.

The middle classes centered their lives principally around work and the family. Hard work was thought to be the moral responsibility of every person, regardless of rank or status. The middle-class ethic held that those with the requisite energy and drive could succeed and prosper, while the poor had only themselves to blame for their plight. This attitude was in part a product of Enlightenment thought and the French Revolution, both of which had encouraged the notion that advancement depended on talent and ability rather than on birth or privilege. Habits of self-discipline and work were instilled in children from an early age because it was believed that these traits built character and would help to develop strong and responsible adults. Political economists and social theorists of the liberal persuasion incorporated this view into their analyses, which often offered contradictory approaches to the growing problem of urban poverty. While some argued that charity and aid to the poor would only serve to encourage laziness and dependency, others saw humanitarian assistance and charitable work as the responsibility of the more fortunate groups in society.

The work ethic reinforced the middle-class belief in *laissez-faire* economics and the spirit of free competition. Thrift, together with the importance and sanctity of private property, which all classes were encouraged to accumulate, were also central to the bourgeois worldview. Such attitudes contributed to the cult of material and spiritual progress that became a hallmark of middle-class thinking. Self-improvement would inevitably mean a better society for all, and modern technology and science would enable society to achieve unprecedented material advances and harness nature for human security and comfort.

In their efforts not only to order and control their own lives, but to imbue society at large with their values, the middle classes developed a moralizing ideology of respectability. This set of ideas particularly affected the way in which women could lead their lives and the structure of family life.

WOMEN IN A REVOLUTIONARY AGE

During the first half of the 19th century, the two major developments of the period—the French Revolution and the industrial revolution—deeply affected the status and role of women in European society. The Revolution of 1789 provoked the first serious public consideration of women's rights and gender relationships in a political and legal context, and stimulated women themselves to take up their own struggle for equality. Women entered the new industrial job market in a significant way, and the results changed not only how they worked and the nature of their dependency, but also their roles within the family.

Women, Law, and Government

The early revolutionary governments of France had legislated some basic legal rights for women in such matters as marriage, consensual age, divorce, and inheritance. These advances did not, however, survive the republican experience, for the Napoleonic Code of 1804 reestablished a patriarchal society, giving power to males in family matters. In this reversal of earlier reforms, a married woman had to assume her husband's nationality, could not take part in court proceedings or sue for paternity rights or support, and—unlike the husband—could be punished for adultery. These measures had the effect of removing women from a direct civil relationship with government. Women were denied not only legal identity as independent human beings but also those very "rights" of citizenship that the Revolution of 1789 had proclaimed so loudly.

Property laws further marginalized women in ways that were important to the new middle-class ideology of wealth. The Napoleonic Code allowed women to have virtually no control over their property, even when prenuptial contracts required that dowries be kept separate from other family resources. Wages earned by married working women passed to the husband, as did profits made by women who owned tiny shops or market stalls. Because the pattern of government in the 19th century was moving toward liberal institutions in which political rights hinged on property ownership, such measures were crucial to the status of women. As a consequence, nowhere in the Western world did women have equal civil status or political rights in the first half of the 19th century, although women soon began to organize themselves to achieve them (see Part VII, Topic 13).

The Napoleonic Code provided the basis for legal reform and precedent throughout much of Europe and the Americas. Implicit in its provisions regarding women were certain assumptions about gender differences—that women were "weaker" than men both

Mary Wollstonecraft, the prominent English writer and feminist.

physically and in character, and therefore required their protection. According to the jurists who wrote the code, women's place should remain within the one "natural" sphere of their competency, the home.

Women and the Industrial Revolution

The industrial transformation of Europe brought contradictory results for women as it affected patterns of work and home life. On the one hand, it widened the scope of activities for some women, and on the other it reinforced the separation of men's and women's roles endorsed by the Napoleonic Code. Women had, of course, always worked. In preindustrial Europe, rural wives often shared agricultural labor with their husbands, especially during harvesting, and were an important element in cottage industry. In urban centers, women had worked chiefly as domestic servants for the aristocracy or as sales clerks in family-run shops. Some women also sold food products in city markets and occasionally helped their husbands in artisan workshops. In almost all cases, however, these occupations were carried out as part of a family production unit, usually within the home, and their labor was viewed as a supplement to male labor rather than having any intrinsic value.

Industrialization changed female work patterns significantly. In the new textile factories women constituted a major portion of the labor force, and many also worked in tobacco and food processing. Women and children were often the largest number of workers in cotton mills. On the other hand, while an important element in the industrial working class, factory labor was not the typical work experience for women. At midcentury, for example, 40 percent of all British working women were servants and 20 percent textile workers, while 40 percent of Frenchwomen still worked in agriculture and only 10 percent in textiles.

Division of labor based on gender had existed in cottage industry and agriculture, and it continued in the factories, as men and women were separated by task and by area in the workplace. This was done not only because of differences in skill or physical strength, but because factory owners assumed that males and females working in close proximity to each other, often dressed in scanty clothing, would lead to immorality and thereby hamper productivity. Wherever women worked in the factories, they were almost always supervised by men.

Contrary to a once commonly held view, industrialization did not tear working families apart. In the early stages of the factory system, entire families—husbands, wives, and children—frequently worked together. Moreover, throughout the century most women in the factories were young and single. Some factory owners provided dormitories or boardinghouses where single women employees were able to live and eat at low cost, and in England the Factory Acts of 1842 and 1844 limited the number of hours a day women could work. Some married working-class women earned extra income by sewing or doing laundry, but the growth of mass-produced consumer goods formerly made at home, such as ready-to-wear clothing, soap, and candles, limited domestic work in the cities.

For some women, a less respectable but profitable source of income was prostitution. Prostitutes in European cities numbered in the tens of thousands, and brothels were to be found in many neighborhoods. It has been estimated that by 1850 there were perhaps 80,000 prostitutes in London alone and 50,000 in Paris. Some women engaged in prostitution, which paid much better than most jobs open to them, only when they were unemployed or when their regular employment hit a slow season. Migrants from the countryside also turned to prostitution to support themselves when they first arrived in the city, as did women abandoned by their husbands or lovers. Most prostitutes, though, were single young women in desperate straits rather than women from very poor families.

Once working in this occupation, women often found that their income could be measurably improved over the meager factory wages they could earn. Some worked independently as streetwalkers, while others operated on a fee basis out of brothels. Beginning with the Napoleonic Code, many European governments regulated the prostitution business, requiring that prostitutes register with the police and submit to medical examinations. Despite periodic roundups and police raids, the 19th-century middle classes seem to have regarded prostitution as a "necessary evil"—the double standard of the period held that while women had no sexual drive, the "natural" sexual energy of men needed release.

Increasingly, married urban women, whether of the working or the middle classes, found themselves relegated to the role of homemaker, giving birth to and raising children, cooking, and caring for the family, while the new work discipline of the factories gave husbands little time to share in domestic duties. The growing distinction between the "paid" labor of males and the "unpaid" labor of females marginalized women further and contributed to the development of "separate spheres" defined according to gender.

MARRIAGE, FAMILY, AND SEX

The family remained the focus of life for the vast majority of women, including not only wives but also servants and unmarried female relatives. Nevertheless, the ways

DOCUMENTS ON HISTORY

The Rights of Women

Throughout most of the 18th century, the majority of women in middle-class and working families remained subservient to males, their roles limited to childbearing and rearing, to household duties, and to occasional participation in fieldwork and home-based textile making. But under the impact of industrialization, the status and role of women in the emerging industrial society began to assume new dimensions as tens of thousands of them left home for work in the factories. Moreover, as a result of the Enlightenment and the French Revolution, women increasingly struggled to achieve political and social rights, and in the half-century after 1789 developed theoretical and political arguments for those rights.

THE PETITION OF RIGHTS, 1790

Just as French citizens had petitioned the king with their grievances in preparation for the meeting of the Estates General, a group of working women appealed directly to Louis XVI for the opportunity for work and a better education.

Sire,

At a time when the different orders of the state are occupied with their interests; when everyone seeks to make the most of his titles and rights; when some anxiously recall the centuries of servitude and anarchy, while others make every effort to shake off the last links that still bind them to the imperious remains of feudalism; women—continual objects of the admiration and scorn of men—could they not also make their voices heard midst this general agitation?

Excluded from the national assemblies by laws so well consolidated that they allow no hope of infringement, they do not ask, Sire, for your permission to send their deputies to the Estates General; they know too well how much favor will play a part in the election, and how easy it would be for those elected to impede the freedom of voting.

We prefer, Sire, to place our cause at your feet; not wishing to obtain anything except from your heart, it is to it that we address our complaints and confide our miseries.

The women of the Third Estate are almost all born without wealth; their education is very neglected or very defective: it consists in their being sent to school with a teacher who himself does not know the first word of the language [Latin] he teaches. They continue to go there until they can read the service of the Mass in French and Vespers in Latin. Having fulfilled the first duties of religion, they are taught to work; having reached the age of fifteen or sixteen, they can earn five or six sous a day. If nature has refused them beauty they get married, without a dowry, to unfortunate artisans; lead aimless, difficult lives stuck in the provinces; and give birth to children they are incapable of raising. If, on the contrary, they are born pretty, without breeding, without principles, with no idea of morals, they become the prey of the first seducer, commit a first sin, come to Paris to bury their shame, end by losing it altogether, and die victims of dissolute ways. . . .

From *The French Revolution and Human Rights: A Brief Documentary History*, ed. and trans. Lynn Hunt (Boston and New York: Bedford Books of St. Martin's Press, 1996), 60–62.

THE DECLARATION OF THE RIGHTS OF WOMAN

Although self-educated, Olympe de Gouges (1748–1793) was a successful writer for the theater. In 1791, she wrote the "Declaration of the Rights of Woman and the French Citizen," modeled on the document issued by the National Assembly in 1789. In it, she argued that the framers of the original Declaration had ignored women and that equality between men and women conformed to the natural order. She urged women to take part in the struggle for liberty and sent her appeal to Marie Antoinette, "mother and wife."

In consequence, the sex that is superior in beauty as in courage, needed in maternal sufferings, recognizes and declares, in the presence and under the auspices of the Supreme Being, the following rights of woman and the citizens.

1. Woman is born free and remains equal to man in rights. Social distinctions may be based only on common utility.
2. The purpose of all political association is the preservation of the natural and imprescriptible rights of woman and man. These rights are liberty, property, security, and especially resistance to oppression.
3. The principle of all sovereignty rests essentially in the nation, which is but the reuniting of woman and man. No body and no individual may exercise authority which does not emanate expressly from the nation.
4. Liberty and justice consist in restoring all that belongs to another; hence the exercise of the natural rights of woman has no other limits than those that the perpetual tyranny of man opposes to them; these limits must be reformed according to the laws of nature and reason.
5. The laws of nature and reason prohibit all actions which are injurious to society. No hindrance should be put in the way of anything not prohibited by these wise and divine laws, nor may anyone be forced to do what they do not require.
6. The law should be the expression of the general will. All citizenesses and citizens should take part, in person or by their representatives, in its formation. It must be the same for everyone. All citizenesses and citizens, being equal in its eyes, should be equally admissible to all public dignities, offices, and employments, according to their ability, and with no other distinction than that of their virtues and talents.
7. No woman is exempted; she is indicted, arrested, and detained in the cases determined by the law. Women like men obey this rigorous law.
8. Only strictly and obviously necessary punishments should be established by the law, and no one may be punished except by virtue of a law established and promulgated

continued next page

before the time of the offense, and legally applied to women.

9. Any woman being declared guilty, all rigor is exercised by the law.
10. No one should be disturbed for his fundamental opinions; woman has the right to mount the scaffold, so she should have the right equally to mount the tribune, provided that these manifestations do not trouble public order as established by law.
11. The free communication of thoughts and opinions is one of the most precious of the rights of woman, since this liberty assures the recognition of children by their fathers. Every citizeness may therefore say freely, I am the mother of your child; a barbarous prejudice [against unmarried women having children] should not force her to hide the truth, so long as responsibility is accepted for any abuse of this liberty in cases determined by the law [women are not allowed to lie about the paternity of their children].
12. The safeguard of the rights of woman and citizeness requires public powers. These powers are instituted for the advantage of all and not for the private benefit of those to whom they are entrusted.
13. For maintenance of public authority and for expenses of administration, taxation of women and men is equal; she takes part in all forced labor service, in all painful tasks; she must therefore have the same proportion in the distribution of places, employments, offices, dignities, and in industry.
14. The citizenesses and citizens have the right, by themselves or through their representatives, to have demonstrated to them the necessity of public taxes. The citizenesses can only agree to them upon admission of an equal division, not only in wealth, but also in the public administration, and to determine the means of apportionment, assessment, and collection, and the duration of the taxes.
15. The mass of women, joining with men in paying taxes, have the right to hold accountable every public agent of the administration.
16. Any society in which the guarantee of rights is not assured or the separation of powers not settled has no constitution. The constitution is null and void if the majority of individuals composing the nation has not cooperated in its drafting.
17. Property belongs to both sexes whether united or separated; it is for each of them an inviolable and sacred right, and no one may be deprived of it as a true patrimony of nature, except when public necessity, certified by law, obviously requires it, and then on condition of a just compensation in advance.

From *The French Revolution and Human Rights: A Brief Documentary History*, ed. and trans. Lynn Hunt (Boston and New York: Bedford Books of St. Martin's Press, 1996), 125–126.

WOLLSTONECRAFT'S *VINDICATION OF THE RIGHTS OF WOMEN*

Mary Wollstonecraft (1759–1797), an English writer and the wife of anarchist philosopher William Godwin (see Part VII, Topic 7), was a woman of the Enlightenment. In her Vindication of the Rights of Women *(1792), she based her argument on the belief in reason. Wollstonecraft chastised the framers of the French Constitution of 1791 for limiting the rights of citizenship to men and lectured them that women were equal to men as rational beings. She also replied in detail to Rousseau's position on female inferiority, stressing the need for educational equality.*

Consider—I address you as a legislator—whether, when men contend for their freedom, and to be allowed to judge for themselves respecting their own happiness, it be not inconsistent and unjust to subjugate women, even though you firmly believe that you are acting in the manner best calculated to promote their happiness? Who made man the exclusive judge, if woman partake with him the gift of reason.

In this style, argue tyrants of every denomination, from the weak king to the weak father of a family; they are all eager to crush reason; yet always assert that they usurp its throne only to be useful. Do you not act a similar part, when you *force* all women, by denying them civil and political rights, to remain immured in their families groping in the dark? For surely, sir, you will not assert that a duty can be binding which is not founded on reason? If, indeed, this be their destination, arguments may be drawn from reason; and thus augustly supported, the more understanding women acquire, the more they will be attached to their duty—comprehending it—for unless they comprehend it, unless their morals be fixed on the same immutable principle as those of man, no authority can make them discharge it in a virtuous manner. They may be convenient slaves, but slavery will have its constant effect, degrading the master and the abject dependent.

But, if women are to be excluded, without having a voice, from a participation of the natural rights of mankind, prove first, to ward off the charge of injustice and inconsistency, that they want reason—else this flaw in your NEW CONSTITUTION will ever show that man must, in some shape, act like a tyrant; and tyranny, in whatever part of society it rears its brazen front, will ever undermine morality.

I have repeatedly asserted, and produced what appeared to me irrefragable arguments drawn from matters of fact, to prove my assertion, that women cannot, by force, be confined to domestic concerns; for they will, however ignorant, intermeddle with more weighty affairs, neglecting private duties only to disturb, by cunning tricks, the orderly plans of reason which rise above their comprehension. . . .

From Mary Wollstonecraft, *Vindication of the Rights of Women.*

WOMEN AND POVERTY

By the mid-19th century, the struggle for women's rights had extended well beyond Enlightenment ideals to more concrete economic issues. In 1841, the Belgian utopian socialist Zoe Gatti de Gamond argued that the abolition of poverty among women would be a major step toward social justice.

The most direct cause of women's misfortune is poverty; demanding their freedom means above all demanding reform in the economy of society which will eradicate poverty and give everyone education, a minimum standard of living, and the right to work. It is not only that class called "women of the people" for whom the major source of all their misfortunes is poverty, but rather women of all classes.

From that comes the subjection of women, their narrow dependence on men, and their reduction to a negative influence. Men have thus materialized love, perverted the angelic nature of women, and created a being who submits to their caprices, their desires—a domesticated animal shaped to their pleasures and to their needs. Using their powers, they have split women into the appearance of two classes; for the privileged group, marriage, the care of the household, and maternal love; for the other, the sad role of seduced woman and of the misfortunate one reduced to the last degree of misery and degradation. Everywhere oppression and nowhere liberty.

The question is not to decide whether it is fitting to give women political rights or to put

continued next page

them on an equal footing with men when it comes to admission to employment. Rather the question exists above all in the question of poverty; and to make women ready to fill political roles, it is poverty above all that must be effaced. Nor can the independence of women be reconciled with the isolation of households, which prevents even the working woman from being independent.

The system of Fourier, imperceptibly and smoothly introducing associations within society, resolves all the difficulties in the position of women; without changing legislation or proclaiming new rights, it will regenerate them, silence the sources of corruption and reform with one blow education and morals with the single fact that results naturally from the associational principles of his system: a common education and the independence of women assured by the right to work; independence rendered possible by the association of households, attractive and harmonious work, and the multiplication of wealth.

From Bonnie G. Smith, *Changing Lives: Women in European History Since 1700.* D.C. Heath and Company.

NATIONALISM AND FEMINISM

The Italian feminist and socialist Anna Maria Mozzoni (1837–1920) worked to secure basic rights for women in the context of the movement for Italian unification. In 1864, three years after the creation of the Kingdom of Italy, she wrote about the contributions that free women could make to national life and argued that the new national laws did not recognize women's rights.

The revision of the Civil Code by the Italian Parliament has placed in my mind the following argument: woman, excluded by worn out customs from the councils of state, has always submitted to the law without participating in the making of it, has always contributed her resources and work to the public good and always without any reward.

For her, taxes but not an education; for her, sacrifices but not employment; for her, strict virtue but not honor; for her, the struggle to maintain the family but not even control of her own person; for her, the capacity to be punished but not the right to be independent; strong enough to be laden with an array of painful duties, but sufficiently weak not to be allowed to govern herself.

I begin with the principles that all rights and all duties have as their foundation and rationale to serve as the force which gives the conscience its ostensible legitimacy. This principle holds for each human being of whatever sex and I do not see for what reason this faculty should be in one case exercised freely and sometimes with force and in the other case buried and entirely suffocated. This occurs so much that in the miserable conditions in which society has cast her, woman, deprived of half her wealth, weakened because of the degrading work actually given her, finds herself dragged down to the fatal necessity to destroy herself through trade in her unhappy body.

Humanity and the nation, civilization and morality, need women on their side.

From Bonnie G. Smith, *Changing Lives: Women in European History Since 1700.* D.C. Heath and Company.

WOMEN AND WORK

In the 19th century many feminists began to address the question of work and women's relationship to it from a practical and a theoretical point of view. For some work was increasingly seen as both a right and a necessity for women who would be fulfilled and happy, while for others it was seen as a means toward liberation. In 1866 Jenny Heynrichs, a middle-class German woman and the coeditor of a journal entitled Neue Bahnen *(New Paths), addressed the question in an article entitled "What is Work?"*

Work, liberating and liberated work, is the slogan of our association, the banner around which we gather. It may seem superfluous, therefore, to raise once more the question "What is work?" in the pages of our magazine; one should assume that no one could have any further doubt about the importance of our association with this word. . . .

Work, be it intellectual or physical, is always the lively and vigorous union of our intellectual and physical powers for a definite, clearly articulated purpose. Work is creativity accompanied by the comforting realization that one is bringing forth something really good and necessary, with the conviction that a sudden, arbitrary cessation would cause a sensitive void, produce a loss. The worker, wherever he may be employed, feels himself to be a link in a chain that holds society together, a link which, should it drop out, would have to be replaced at once by another. He knows that such a replacement could be found at once, that no man is irreplaceable. Yet there is something very inspiring in the knowledge that through his dropping out a replacement is required; that one does not disappear without vacating a place, as if one never had it. This knowledge makes one feel content, fit, strong; it ennobles the lowest kind of work. This knowledge is given to all men and if they lack it, they have only themselves to blame, not society. But thousands of women are lacking that knowledge because they are brought up for only one vocation—marriage. . . .

Most of our young women, not only those from the well-to-do and aristocratic families, but also those from families of modest and limited means, are taught a variety of things. They embroider and crochet, sing and play the piano, draw, read French and English, possibly lend a hand in the household while attending balls and going promenading, all this with the expectation of a suitor who is to provide them with a home and their own domain. But the years go by, the hoped-for savior does not arrive, and the home, the parental house that has sheltered them falls into ruin with the death of the father. They are left behind, uncared for as the sad saying goes. Thrown back on their own resources and taking stock of the many things they have learned, they discover with dismay that while keeping occupied they have whiled away their lives and are unable to do any kind of work.

Work is the practical application of that which one thoroughly understands, for which one has prepared oneself and has chosen as the business of one's life. And this kind of work is only open in a very few fields to our women and many among them have not grasped yet that this alone is what is meant by work. The goal of our endeavors is to open to women the blessings of the world. We do not want a break up of the social order, no political conquests, only a breakthrough for work. In this manner, we think we can deliver the world from the insufferable old maids, at odds with themselves and others, from the women who through poverty and misery have fallen victim to vice, from luxury which like a cancer erodes the happiness of family life. We think we can restore to marriage meaning and sanctity and the right to noble love. May God help us in this task.

in which women conducted their lives and defined their roles changed. The increasingly complex urban environment and the factory system also affected marriage patterns, sexual behavior, and family structures.

Marriage and the Family

Industrialization was one cause of a growing conflict for women between the private sphere and the workplace. The low pay scale for female workers meant that single women without family support experienced severe difficulties in maintaining themselves. Moreover, the spreading social ideology of the middle classes established norms of expected behavior for women that proscribed activity beyond that of wife and mother. For most women, marriage continued to be the only avenue for economic security.

European marriage patterns varied according to region and economic status. Among the urban working classes, poverty often prevented or delayed marriage. On average, working-class women married in their mid-twenties and men somewhat older, although the age for both began to reduce as living standards improved among low-income groups. Working couples usually married out of mutual attraction and love, so that when circumstances mitigated against a formal marriage, couples often lived together in common-law unions. City dwellers generally abandoned the tradition of long courtship common in the countryside, and parental consent ceased to be as important.

Middle-class customs differed from those of the working class in several ways. Among bourgeois families, marriages were to a large extent viewed as serious financial undertakings. Although arranged marriages were rapidly disappearing, parents were concerned about the economic prospects of possible sons-in-law or the dowries of daughters-in-law. The correct social environment, in which daughters could meet eligible men, was therefore vitally important. Longer courtships were also the rule for the middle classes and marriage plans frequently included prenuptial contracts and inheritance agreements. Because the middle classes valued financial security so much, their sons tended to wait until their incomes were sufficient to support a family. As a result, men were almost always older than their wives. Before marriage, parents carefully guarded the virginity of their daughters, while sons usually had considerable sexual experience by the time they became husbands.

Although ties among family members loosened as a result of the urban-industrial environment, family relationships remained vital, especially among the poor. In an age when government assistance was limited or nonexistent, family members were needed for financial help during periods of unemployment and for support during illness. Relatives also generally took in indigent widows and orphans.

Except among the wealthiest groups, the size of families began to shrink by midcentury. The marked decline in the birthrate in most Western European countries was due to a combination of factors. Efforts to sustain or improve an acceptable standard of living limited family size, especially among the middle classes, for whom educational expenses were a growing priority. Parents also restricted the number of children they had because declining infant mortality meant that more children survived into adulthood. Moreover, technological and medical advances in the 1840s made possible new and inexpensive birth control devices, although they were not yet widely available. Until then, *coitus interruptus* (withdrawal) and vinegar solutions had been the only widely practiced birth control methods, but thereafter condoms, vaginal sponges, and diaphragms were increasingly available as a result of the vulcanization of rubber. As early as the 1820s, birth control information was being distributed in England, although its proponents risked fines and imprisonment.

The typical early 19th-century family was a "patriarchal" unit in that the husband had legal authority over the wife and children. In actual practice, however, the influence of the wife within the family grew stronger as her role was confined to the home. Wives kept the family's budget and determined how a large portion of its income would be expended. Mothers controlled the rearing of children on a daily basis, including such matters as education and religious training. Affection between spouses and the nurturing care of children were the guideposts of the ideal bourgeois family, while the home was to be a tranquil haven from the harsh realities of the world outside. For wives, however, running a household was full-time work, often complicated and hectic.

Sex and the New Society

Sexuality is a difficult subject for social historians to write about because of the scarcity of accurate information about the intimate lives of past generations. Moreover, 19th-century middle-class morality made any discussion of sex a taboo. Nevertheless, government and church statistics on marriages, births, and family sizes, as well as private sources such as diaries and letters, provide some basis for generalizations.

The most basic statement we can make is that while men and women have always had sex, the circumstances in which it took place, attitudes toward it, and how people dealt with its consequences have changed over time. We know, for example, that premarital sex was widespread among working-class couples, for illegitimacy rates rose significantly in the early 19th century—in Austria, for example, as many as one in three peasant children was born out of wedlock. The migration of young men and women to the cities, away from the restraints of family and village community, made for freer sexual behavior. In the first decades of the 19th century, almost 40 percent of all births in Paris were illegitimate, while in Vienna illegitimate births outnumbered legitimate ones. By 1840, perhaps as many as one out of every three European babies was born out of wedlock.

Before 1850, celibacy among unmarried men and women seems to have been more prevalent in the middle than in the working classes, due in part to the greater bourgeois concern for financial security and moral conduct. Nevertheless, after midcentury the illegitimacy rate reversed itself. This was not, however, because premarital sex declined: it has been estimated that in the years after 1850, one out of every three working-class women was pregnant at the time of marriage. Rather, marriage itself had grown more popular among the working classes as their income grew and they absorbed notions of respectability.

Gender influenced attitudes about sex as well as sexual behavior. The middle class professed to adhere to a strict code of morality, particularly for women, who were conditioned to remain chaste and virtuous. Sex was supposed to be a distasteful obligation for women, necessary for purposes of procreation. The flavor of this 19th-century bourgeois convention is reflected in the premarital advice that Queen Victoria—the British sovereign who herself had nine children—is supposed to have given her daughter: during sexual intercourse, the royal mother suggested, "Close your eyes and think of England."

The anecdote about Victoria underscores the nature of the double standard that developed during this period. Not only were women not supposed to enjoy sex, but medical opinion of the time held that they did not have orgasms; men, on the other hand, were virile creatures who had to expend their natural urges in the sexual act. While fidelity in marriage was publicly expected of both men and women, law and custom imposed it only on wives. There are, of course, numerous contemporary accounts testifying to the fulfilling sexual relationships that many wives had with their husbands, but the prevailing ethos of conduct made it impossible for women to express their needs openly. The double standard served largely to reinforce the increasingly exclusive roles of mother and wife to which women were limited.

The transformations that took place in the half century following the French Revolution, with their attendant stresses and upheavals, shaped the character of European society. High-density population, large, rapidly growing cities, and a complex and changing social structure were the outward manifestations of this great transformation. The large and expanding working class received only a small portion of national wealth, while dependency and discipline in the workplace, together with widespread urban poverty, marked the material lives of much of the new industrial labor force. For the new middle classes, however, increasing comfort and influence were the order of the day. Although women participated in both the political and the industrial revolutions of the period, their role in society was steadily circumscribed by an ideology that stressed family and home above all else. From these and related developments of the period from 1789 to 1850 came the political and social struggles of late-19th-century Europe.

Questions for Further Study

1. What was the impact of the industrial revolution on European society?
2. How would you describe the way in which most workers lived? How did life change for most people in the period under discussion?
3. In what ways was middle-class life different from working-class life?
4. Was the role of women in society different after the French Revolution? If so, in what ways? If not, why not?

Suggestions for Further Reading

Applewhite, Harriet B., and D. G. Levy, eds. *Women and Politics in the Age of the Democratic Revolution*. Ann Arbor, MI, 1990.

Coleman, William. *Death Is a Social Disease: Public Health and Political Economy in Early Industrial France*. Madison, WI, 1982.

Corbin, Alain. *The Lure of the Sea: The Discovery of the Seaside in the Western World, 1750–1840*, trans. J. Phelps. Berkeley, CA, 1994.

Davidoff, Leonore, and C. Hall. *Family Fortunes: Men and Women of the English Middle Class, 1780–1850*. Chicago, 1987.

Harrison, F. *The Dark Angel: Aspects of Victorian Sexuality*. New York, 1977.

Himmelfarb, Gertrude. *The Idea of Poverty: England in the Early Industrial Age*. New York, 1984.

Landes, Joan. *Women and the Public Sphere in the Age of the French Revolution*. Ithaca, NY, 1988.

Lynch, Katherine A. *Family, Class, and Ideology in Early Industrial France: Social Policy and the Working Class Family, 1825–1848*. Madison, WI, 1988.

Marsden, G., ed. *Victorian Values: Personalities and Perspectives in 19th-Century Society*. New York, 1990.

O'Grada, Cormac. *The Great Irish Famine*. Houndmills, Ireland, 1989.

Sewell, William H. *Work and Revolution in France: The Language of Labor from the Old Regime to 1848*. New York, 1980.

Shapiro, Ann-Louise. *Housing the Poor of Paris, 1850–1902*. Madison, WI, 1985.

Sutcliffe, Anthony. *Towards the Planned City: Germany, Britain, and the United States, 1789–1914*. New York, 1981.

VII

Topic 7

The Romantic Vision: Art and Culture in a Revolutionary World

The comfortable and elegant world of the Rococo represented an essentially aristocratic artistic style. As the shadow of revolution began to loom over European political life, artists turned to new forms of expression.

In the latter part of the 18th century, the chief source of inspiration was the world of Classical Antiquity, in particular that of Republican Rome, with its emphasis on virtue and patriotism; painting and sculpture in this style are known as "neoclassical." Architects also followed Classical models, while writers turned to ancient sources for the plots of their plays and librettos or for historical accounts of the ancient world.

With the revolutionary changes which had swept over most of Europe by the early 19th century, a new artistic vision was thrust forward: Romanticism. Although Romantic artists produced works of a bewildering variety of types, they shared certain characteristics. Instead of exalting the power of reason, they explored the irrational, probing the world of emotion. In contrast to earlier artists, the Romantics were openly subjective, even autobiographical. Two aspects of life made a special appeal: nature, with its mysterious unpredictability; and the exotic, in the form of remote times and faraway places.

One of the early centers of Romanticism was Germany, where the philosophy of Immanuel Kant sought to describe the nature of artistic experience. The literary giant of the age was Goethe. Although many of his works were Classical, they provided inspiration to the Romantic writers who followed him.

In England the Romantic poets gave expression to many of the concerns of their times. William Wordsworth, often regarded as the founder of the English Romantic movement, used a simple and direct style to explore the relationship between humans and the natural world around them. George Gordon Byron, who became the very symbol of Romantic melancholy, supported the liberal causes of his day, including the Greek struggle for independence.

Romantic painters often used their art to protest against the violence of the times. The Spanish painter Francisco José de Goya depicted the cruelty of the French troops occupying Madrid. The leading French Romantic artist was Eugène Delacroix, whose subjects ranged from political support for Greek independence to fantastic depictions of ancient Assyria.

Perhaps the supreme expression of Romanticism can be found in music, the most intuitive and emotional of the arts. The towering figure of Ludwig van Beethoven dominated the age. Firmly grounded in the Classical tradition, he extended the range of his music to include the detailed depiction of emotion, the evocation of nature, and the striving for universal human peace.

By the mid-19th century Romanticism took a new turn, reflecting the preoccupations of the age; among its concerns were nationalism and a variety of social issues. The works produced in the century's first half, under the direct impact of revolution, are among the freshest and most vital in the Western artistic tradition.

NEOCLASSICISM AND THE REDISCOVERY OF ANTIQUITY

The art of the early 18th century reflected the lives of its aristocratic patrons. In reaction against the rhetoric and magnificence of the Baroque style, Rococo artists created a world of comfort and leisure to entertain the enlightened despots and their courts.

By the latter part of the century, with the growing interest in rational humanism, as evidenced in the work of the French Encyclopedists, and the increasing challenge to centuries-old social patterns, a new artistic style began to develop: *neoclassicism*, a revival of the art of ancient Greece and Rome. To some degree its inspiration was intellectual, even philosophical. The history of ancient Rome, in particular, contained many tales of stern patriotic virtue, and Greek and Roman Stoic philosophers put much emphasis on the notions of duty and lack of self-interest.

The Discovery of Herculaneum and Pompeii

An even more direct stimulus to the development of the neoclassical style, however, came from the chance discovery of the ancient cities of Campania, which lay just to the south of Naples. Buried by an eruption of the volcano Vesuvius in A.D. 79, they had virtually disappeared from history. A series of random events led to the discovery first of Herculaneum, in 1711, and then, in 1748, to that of Pompeii, the better preserved.

David's *The Oath of the Horatii* evokes the heroic spirit of Republican Rome.

The houses and villas of Pompeii, with their frescoes and fountains, public baths, theaters and shops, all provided an incomparably vivid picture of life almost two millennia earlier. Visitors from all over Europe traveled to the excavations, sketching the paintings and taking back copies of ancient objects. Among those most impressed was the greatest German writer of the age, Johann Wolfgang von Goethe, who commented that "There have been many disasters in this world, but few which have given so much delight to posterity."

Thus, at just the time that artists were searching for a language to express their new—if age-old—ideals, the discoveries at Pompeii and the other sites provided exactly what they were looking for. *The Oath of the Horatii,* painted by the French artist Jacques-Louis David (1748–1825) in 1784–1785, was a call to patriotic action. The subject, drawn from the early history of Rome, uses weapons, costumes, and even poses based on those in Pompeian frescoes. In 1791, Wolfgang Amadeus Mozart (1756–1791) composed his opera *The Clemency of Titus,* in which the Roman emperor Titus behaves with reason and moderation; the libretto was by the Italian poet Metastasio (1698–1782). One of the greatest literary achievements of the times, the vast and learned *Decline and Fall of the Roman Empire,* written by Edward Gibbon (1738–1794), provided a more general setting for this revival of interest in ancient Rome; the first volume was published in 1776.

A portrait of Beethoven by his contemporary, Waldmüller.

Along with the writings of the *philosophes,* works such as these provided the intellectual background to the French Revolution. Gibbon believed that the decline of Rome was in large measure due to the rise of Christianity. His negative attitude to Christianity—and, indeed, to religion in general—was shared by the greatest philosophe of the day, Voltaire. In due course the Revolution's National Constituent Assembly secularized the church (see Part VII, Topic 3) and subordinated it to the state.

The neoclassical style forecast and underpinned the revolutionary changes which shook Europe at the end of the 18th century, but it could not express the immensely varied consequences of those events. In order to do justice to the new world they themselves were helping to construct, artists forged a new means of expressing themselves: Romanticism.

ROMANTICISM AND THE DISCOVERY OF SELF

The 18th century had exalted the power of human reason. The successes and, more significantly, the failures of the Revolution demonstrated the limits of human ability to construct a better world, and the uncertainties of history were reflected in the arts. Beethoven, one of the towering musical figures of the period, was inspired by Napoleon's early career to compose a symphony subtitled *Eroica*—"The Heroic"—dedicated to the Frenchman; Beethoven's own democratic convictions led him to see Napoleon as the champion of liberty. When his hero had himself crowned emperor in 1804, Beethoven in disgust struck out the dedication on the title page.

The Concerns of Romanticism

One of Beethoven's most quoted remarks provides us with a valuable insight into the perceptions of Romantic artists: "There will always be thousands of princes, but there is only one Beethoven." The chief concern of the Romantics was themselves: their emotions, their reactions to the world around them, their own individuality—all viewed in a context where freedom and social equality were the highest good. Artists used painting, music, and literature not to satisfy their patrons or to set forth generally accepted truths, but to express themselves.

In the quest for subjective emotional revelation, practitioners of all the arts turned to the irrational. Rejecting their 18th-century predecessors' emphasis on reason, they explored the power of dreams and the subconscious. This led in turn to a new vision of nature. The natural universe was no longer seen merely as a background for human activities, but as a mysterious world of its own, whose unpredictable workings corresponded to the fluctuations of human emotion. The desire to escape the constraints of their own objective situation produced another rich source for Romantic artists: remoteness of time or place. The Druids of ancient Britain and the Medieval world of knights in armor inspired operas and paintings. Writers and artists depicted the mysterious East and the wilderness of America.

The political enthusiasms of most Romantic artists were democratic and libertarian, and figures such as Byron and Delacroix publicly supported liberal causes. But the Romantic movement also had much in common with the other political philosophy of the day, conservatism. Both Romantics and conservatives distrusted the ability of human reason to create a better world. The conservative solution was to reconstruct the old political and social order, while Romantic artists tried to escape all confinements in the search for self-expression. Neither group had much sympathy for the chief proponents of liberalism, the middle classes.

THE ROMANTIC MOVEMENT IN GERMANY

Romanticism flourished throughout Europe, but nowhere did it affect as many aspects of culture as in Germany. Moral philosophy and theology, sociology and education, the natural sciences and chemistry were all influenced by the Romantic movement.

In addition to its cultural and intellectual interest, Romanticism presented an escape from the realities of German political life, together with the prospect of reform. At the time of the French Revolution, Germany was made up of hundreds of separate states, with no real chance of unification. Both the Revolution and the rise of Napoleon offered the possibility of decisive changes. Indeed, Napoleon's abolition of the Holy Roman Empire and merging of the smaller states into larger units seemed to presage the formation of a German nation-state.

The defeat and occupation of Prussia by the French armies served only to intensify the spirit of German patriotic fervor that had been created by the hectic course of events. In 1813 a coalition of German states, under Prussian leadership, defeated Napoleon at Leipzig.

Then came the realities of the Congress of Vienna, the Carlsbad Decrees of 1819 (see Part VII, Topic 5), and the return to conservative censorship. In an age when the promise of political freedom had withered, thinkers and artists turned to the interior world of their own emotions in search of free expression. If hope had disappeared in the external universe, it could perhaps be regained in contemplating the ideal and the infinite.

The philosophical foundation of the German Romantic movement was provided by the writings of Immanuel Kant (1724–1804), who questioned the very nature of the real world. According to Kant, our impressions of external events are derived from our internal mental processes. Thus, what appears to be objective is, in fact, subjective. Kant's liberal religious views brought him into conflict with the Prussian government. A generation later, the German philosopher Friedrich Schleiermacher (1768–1834) laid the bases of modern Protestant theology (for a discussion of biblical higher criticism later in the 19th century, see Part VII, Topic 14). Kant himself was a rationalist, but his ideas, together with the high value he put on aesthetic pleasure, inspired a host of Romantic artists. In some cases his doctrines were pushed to extremes; the German dramatist Heinrich von Kleist (1777–1811) used Kant's theories on the limits of objective knowledge to prove that all knowledge is an illusion, and that the true will always be mistaken for the false. A stormy, even unstable personality, Kleist wrote both comedies and tragedies in which appearance and reality are constantly confused; only unqualified love and trust provide the hope of escape from disaster.

The Work of Goethe

Kleist's unrelieved pessimism is in strong contrast to the ethical and aesthetic worldview of the leading literary figure of the age, Johann Wolfgang von Goethe (1749–1832). Poet, critic, dramatist, novelist, Goethe also wrote on botany and zoology, and played an active role in politics. Many of his plays and poems are Classical in style, and throughout his long life he followed Classical principles of balance and order. Yet his works are touched by many of the characteristics of Romanticism; his early writings belong to a movement known as "Storm and Stress."

His first great success, the novel *The Sorrows of Young Werther*, is a largely autobiographical account of an unhappy love affair. Many of his lyric poems express emotional reactions to human experience and to the world of nature; and among the enormous range of influences he absorbed were the writings of Hafiz (?1326–1390), the Persian poet of love and wine. He was profoundly influenced by his travels in Italy, which he described in the *Italian Journey*; the journal provides an engrossing guide to the rich variety of his intellectual interests.

Etching of a dramatic scene in Goethe's novel, *The Sorrows of Young Werther.*

Goethe's most famous work, *Faust,* was published in two parts. The first, which appeared in 1808, deals with the nature of human experience and responsibility as seen in the relationship between Faust and Gretchen. In Part Two, published in 1832, at the end of his life, Goethe meditated on no less a subject than the nature and future of civilization. In spite of all the sufferings and faults that beset humanity, the divine spark which drives us in quest of knowledge—a search symbolized by Faust's pact with the devil—will guarantee our salvation.

The leading German Romantic painter was Caspar David Friedrich (1774–1840). Friedrich's mysterious landscapes seem to express the vastness and uncertainty of the world around us, in which isolated figures contemplate a dizzying emptiness or a remote seashore. In a sense Friedrich seems to deny the Romantic premise of the importance of the individual, yet in portraying the irrationality of human existence he illustrates one of the most important ways in which the Romantics broke with their predecessors.

"SPIRIT OF THE AGE": THE ENGLISH ROMANTIC POETS

Many of the chief poets of the early 19th century in England embodied an aspect of Romanticism in their

One of the key works of German Romanticism: Caspar David Friedrich's *Cloister Graveyard in the Snow.*

works. William Wordsworth (1770–1850), often held to be the founder of the English Romantic movement, personally witnessed the confusion of revolutionary France. He visited there in 1790, the year after the fall of the Bastille, and was inspired by the political idealism of the times—"Bliss was it," he wrote, "in that dawn to be alive." The later course of the Revolution, however, together with the ensuing war between England and France, undermined much of his enthusiasm for politics. He withdrew to the quiet of the English countryside, and by 1799 had settled in the Lake District in northwest England which his poetry was to make so famous.

The theme of his best works was the natural world and its relation to human experience. In language of deliberate simplicity, he aimed to express the calm remembrance of powerful emotions, and to draw from this contrast an understanding of human nature. He was strongly influenced by his sister Dorothy (1771–1855), whom he called "sister of my soul"; her *Grasmere Journal* contains vividly evocative descriptions of cloud and light, and of the local wildflowers.

Very different from Wordsworth's "emotion recollected in tranquility" were the stormy romances of George Gordon, Lord Byron (1788–1824). His mysterious and gloomy heroes and his own unconventional life provided the Romantic movement with one of its archetypal characters: the Byronic hero. Works like *Childe Harold's Pilgrimage*, set against exotic backgrounds, fed the public appetite for Romantic melodrama, while in *Don Juan* Byron struck a note of sophisticated irony. One of the most famous figures of his times, he shocked English public opinion by his relationship with his half-sister Augusta, and left London to resettle in Italy.

With his move to the Continent, Byron's fame and influence spread throughout Europe, where the writers inspired by his tormented heroes included the Russian Alexander Pushkin (1799–1837). The character who gives his name to Pushkin's novel *Eugene Onegin* is truly Byronic. Byron's support for libertarian causes led him to identify with the Greek fight for independence, and he died in 1824 while training soldiers in Greece.

By contrast with Byron's tempestuous career, the short life of John Keats (1795–1821) was outwardly uneventful. The influence of Romanticism on his work is superficially evident in *The Eve of Saint Agnes*, with its Medieval setting. A more profoundly Romantic vision of life and death infuses the *Ode to a Nightingale*, in which the poet's longing for extinction is set against the superhuman beauty of the song of a bird. The *Ode to Autumn* is also inspired by an identification with the splendors of nature, although in less tragic terms. Within a year of its composition Keats was dead, a victim of tuberculosis.

"THE HORRORS OF WAR": FROM GOYA TO DELACROIX

Neoclassical paintings such as David's *Oath of the Horatii* had set the stage for the heroics of the Revolution. Reality proved far less picturesque, and the early Romantic painters chronicled the brutality and suffering of war and violence.

The Art of Goya

In 1808 French troops imposed Napoleonic rule on Spain (see Part VII, Topic 4). When the French were finally driven out in 1814, the Spanish government commissioned the painter Francisco Goya (1746–1828) to commemorate the citizens of Madrid who had been executed for demonstrating against French occupation. The artist was also responsible for a series of etchings entitled *The Disasters of War*, begun a few years earlier. Goya's work achieves its terrible effect by throwing into relief the agonized emotions of the terror-struck victims, unforgettably illuminated by the light of torches, while their executioners, in shadow, turn towards us their hunched shoulders.

Goya had begun his career by painting Rococo scenes of aristocratic life, but his true interest lay in themes dear to the Romantic movement: dreams, the unconscious, the demonic. Toward the end of his life, cut off by deafness from the world around him, he decorated his own house with frescoes depicting an interior vision more hopeless than that of even the most melancholy Byronic hero.

Romantic Painting in France

Goya's despair drove him into seclusion. Other Romantic artists responded to cruelty and injustice in a more public manner. In 1816 the newly restored government of Louis XVIII was shaken by scandal. *The Medusa*, a French government ship, was wrecked off the coast of Africa. The vessel was ill-equipped with safety boats, and the captain and ship's officers were incompetent to deal with the emergency—it was later learned that they owed their appointments to political influence. A raft was thrown together, and passengers and crew spent days drifting under the tropical sun before the raft was spotted. Of the original 149 who were evacuated from the abandoned ship, 15 survived.

In *The Raft of the Medusa*, Théodore Géricault (1791–1824), a young French liberal, produced a dramatic rendering of the conditions of the last survivors at the moment of their sighting. The painting was put on public exhibition in 1819, and produced a sensation. Like Goya, Géricault used violent lighting

Théodore Géricault's *The Raft of the Medusa* (1818) illustrated one of the major scandals of the day.

contrasts to enhance the emotional effect of the scene. Other works of Géricault explore the Romantic obsession with madness and death, many of them painted directly from observation in mental institutions.

The greatest of all French Romantic artists, Eugène Delacroix (1798–1863), combined a virtuoso use of color with elaborate composition to create another masterpiece of Romantic political protest in *The Massacre at Chios*. The painting, which illustrates the Turkish slaughter of 20,000 of the Greek inhabitants of the island of Chios in 1824, was intended to rally support for the cause of Greek independence. Delacroix drew his inspiration from the writings of his distinguished English contemporary: "To set fire to yourself, remember certain passages from Byron," he recorded in his journal.

A work by Byron also inspired *The Death of Sardanapalus*. In this orgy of violence, the Assyrian king is seen seated atop his own funeral pyre. The Medes are at the gates of his capital, and he has chosen to destroy his possessions (including his wives) rather than let them fall into enemy hands. For all the brutality of the scene, the painting has a dreamlike quality, echoed in the brooding figure of Sardanapalus himself. Delacroix's own sense of detachment is suggested by his nickname for the work: *Massacre No. 2*.

Although the Romantic style dominated French art in the early 19th century, one eminent painter of the period claimed to be a defender of Classicism. Jean-Auguste-Dominique Ingres (1780–1867) described the art of Delacroix as "the complete expression of an incomplete intelligence." Yet Ingres himself, brilliant academician that he was, did not remain untouched by the Romantic movement. Even in painting Classical themes, his treatment is often dreamy and sensual, and in his Turkish bath scenes the eroticism becomes explicit.

In any case, when in the mid-19th century Romanticism began to lose its appeal, it was replaced not by a return to Classicism but by a new movement called realism (see Part VII, Topic 14).

BEETHOVEN AND THE HEROIC IDEAL

The composer Ludwig van Beethoven (1770–1827) is the supreme example of an artist whose works passionately advocate liberty and universal peace. Deeply stirred by the lofty principles of the French Revolution, he was equally appalled by its degeneration into dictatorship. His one opera, *Fidelio*, is subtitled *Conjugal Love*: it describes how a devoted wife rescues her husband, a political prisoner, and sees just punishment meted out to his oppressor.

With his detailed depiction of nature in the *Pastoral* Symphony, daring use of harmony in the last string quartets, and introduction of words into the hitherto instrumental form of the symphony (Ninth Symphony), Beethoven served as the inspiration for generations of Romantic musicians. His own musical roots, however, were firmly imbedded in the Classical tradition.

Born in Bonn, Germany, he spent most of his creative life in Vienna, winning his first successes there as a virtuoso pianist. It was in writing for this instrument that he began to explore a freedom of form and a range of emotional content that were truly revolutionary. He himself subtitled the *Moonlight* Sonata "almost a fantasy."

The age of 32 marked a turning point in Beethoven's life: he realized that his increasing deafness was incurable. Driven to despair, he contemplated suicide. With the emotional crisis past, and determination renewed, his works took on a new heroic tone. One of the first fruits of this middle period was the Third Symphony, the *Eroica* (The Heroic), originally dedicated to Napoleon. In the Fifth Symphony the ominous sounds of "Fate knocking at the door," which open the work, give way to a triumphant conclusion in the final movement.

The music of his last years is in a deeper, more complex style, marked by emotional intensity and abrupt contrasts. At one end of the scale, the *Missa Solemnis* (Solemn Mass) and the Ninth Symphony, with its setting of Schiller's *Ode to Joy*, express the search for universal unity and peace. At the other extreme, the last string quartets lay bare the most intimate

Delacroix's *The Death of Sardanapalus* (1826): a typically Romantic blend of violence and eroticism.

PUBLIC FIGURES AND PRIVATE LIVES

MARY WOLLSTONECRAFT AND PERCY BYSSHE SHELLEY

It is hardly surprising that Mary Wollstonecraft's life (1797–1851) should have been an unconventional one, given the independent spirits of her parents. Her father was William Godwin (1756–1836), the political philosopher. Her mother, also named Mary, maintained herself by keeping a school and by writing and translating; her best-known work is *Vindication of the Rights of Women,* which appeared in 1792 during a crucial phase of the French Revolution (see Part VII, Topic 2). The following year she visited France and had an unhappy love affair there. On returning to England she attempted suicide.

Even before her trip to France she had formed part of a circle of radical thinkers, which included Thomas Paine, the Romantic painter John Henry Fuseli, and the anarchist philosopher William Godwin. Godwin now set up house with Mary. Four years later, in 1797, they married in order to protect the rights of the unborn child that she was by then carrying. A daughter was born to them that year, and named after her mother, who died shortly thereafter of puerperal fever.

The young Mary Wollstonecraft's early life was clouded by her mother's reputation. Her father had proudly published his late wife's posthumous works, which included *Maria, or The Rights and Wrongs of Women,* a novel which made a powerful case for sexual rights for women. He followed this up by writing her full and frank biography. Given the climate of the times, an outburst of public outrage was inevitable.

Brought up by her father and his second wife, Mary Wollstonecraft first met Percy Shelley when she was 16 and he 22—and already married for three years. Of all the English Romantics, none was more politically committed than Shelley (1792–1822). The son of a landed aristocrat, he was expelled from Oxford because of his publication of atheist beliefs. He had established something of a reputation for his unconventional ideas and behavior. This was reinforced when in 1814 Shelley and Wollstonecraft ran off together

continued next page

to Italy, and invited his wife to join them and live together.

A few months later Shelley's wife committed suicide, and shortly thereafter he and Wollstonecraft married. From 1818 to 1822 they were at the center of a group of English poets living in Italy that included Byron and Keats. Indeed, one of Shelley's greatest works, *Adonais*, was dedicated to Keats' memory. Shelley never developed a consistent and practical approach to social and political issues. He preferred instead to express large-scale visions of the human condition, and of ways of improving it. In the verse drama *Prometheus Unbound*, Shelley describes love as the only means of moral salvation. Elsewhere, particularly in lyric poems such as *Ode to the West Wind* and *The Cloud*, he uses ecstatic language to capture moments of high emotion.

While Shelley developed a series of warm if idealized relationships with women in his circle, he encouraged his wife to write fiction. Her first book was *Frankenstein*, one of the best of all horror stories.

This remarkable novel describes a character, Dr. Frankenstein, so arrogant and certain of himself that he circumvents the normal processes of procreation and makes a monster in his laboratory. A creature so abnormally produced is bound to act without love, and the monster—which at one point has been reading *The Sorrows of Young Werther*—ends by destroying its maker and mournfully seeking to obliterate its own vital spark. If the negative message of this is that a world without women is doomed to violence, the positive aspect is that maternal love is the key to happiness. The overriding theme of this complex work is the relationship between nature and science, especially when science is out of control—a growing issue for the 19th century.

Shelley himself was drowned in 1822 off the west coast of Italy, under circumstances that still remain mysterious. The following year Wollstonecraft returned to England, where she continued to write novels, two of which (*Lodore* and *Falkner*) include sympathetic portraits of Shelley.

Surviving her husband by almost 30 years, she wrote other romances; among them is *The Last Man*, set in the 21st century, in which humanity is destroyed by a plague which leaves only a single survivor.

and profound personal emotions; a section of one of them is explicitly described as a "song of thanksgiving for recovery from an illness."

Beethoven's visionary final works were far beyond the comprehension of his contemporaries, yet he was widely acclaimed as the greatest composer of his time. When he died in 1827, 10,000 people are said to have attended his funeral. The first musician to become a public figure, Beethoven played a vital part in creating the image of the artist as hero, voicing the feelings of all humans, not just a privileged few.

The Romantics After Beethoven

Beethoven's symphonies and sonatas, large-scale instrumental works, served as one model for Romantic musicians: the French composer Hector Berlioz (1803–1869) wrote a *Fantastic Symphony*, which uses the orchestra to portray his own drug-induced hallucinations, and other major writers of symphonies included Felix Mendelssohn (1809–1847) and Robert Schumann (1810–1856).

Another form that appealed to Romantic composers was the small, intimate song or piano piece. The first great writer of *Lieder* (the German word for "songs") was Beethoven's younger contemporary Franz Schubert (1797–1828), who composed more than 600 songs to a wide variety of verse—some of it by Goethe. Schubert's lyric gifts also emerge in his chamber music, written for performance in the home. Like Schubert, Robert Schumann wrote songs on Romantic texts. Both composers produced superb piano miniatures, in Schumann's case often linked together into sets and inspired by literary characters and themes.

Beethoven had begun his career as a virtuoso performer, and the Romantic love of the spectacular encouraged the development of brilliant displays of instrumental skill. The most famous pianist-composers of the first half of the 19th century were Frédéric Chopin (1810–1849) and Franz Liszt (1811–1886), both of whom came to Paris from eastern Europe to make their careers. Chopin's music alternates between dreamy, often brooding, melancholy and fiery liveliness. Essentially retiring and introverted by temperament, his performances were generally given in the upper-class drawing rooms of Louis Philippe's Paris. Liszt was more robust, his music more rhetorical.

Portrait of the Romantic composer Chopin by the arch-Romantic Delacroix.

Among the sources of inspiration for this arch-Romantic were Dante's *Divine Comedy*, the Faust story, and poems by Byron.

The cult of the virtuoso reached its peak in the figure of Niccolò Paganini (1782–1840), perhaps the most astonishing violinist of all time. So impressive was his technical prowess that audiences whispered that, like Faust, he had sold his soul to the devil—a rumor that Paganini, enterprising showman that he was, did nothing to discourage. In his compositions he exploited every conceivable violin technique, producing solo pieces and concertos that, in his own time at least, only he had the skill to perform.

The French Revolution and the Napoleonic conquests opened up possibilities for social and political change that threatened the survival of the old aristocratic order throughout Europe. The process came to a halt at the Congress of Vienna, where Metternich and the other conservative statesmen endeavored to reconstruct the Old Regime and combat the cause of liberalism. The artistic and intellectual revolution of the period could not be so easily checked. Many of those Romantic artists who had been inspired by the Revolution's original aims were disillusioned at its consequences, but that did not mean that painters, poets, and composers could go back to creating in prerevolutionary styles.

The Romantic movement was born of a desire for freedom, both personal and political. With liberty came a sense of a new status: Beethoven, Goethe, and Byron were among the most famous figures of their times, and the public exhibition of an important new painting was a major event. On occasions artists reacted against their privileges and responsibilities, for having to please a middle-class public could be just as frustrating as working for an aristocratic patron.

In response there began to develop a process of artistic alienation—the artist as rebel rather than as hero. Furthermore, creators who felt that they no longer needed to satisfy a specific audience were free to develop as they pleased. The notion of an "avant garde," whose ideas were always ahead of the public, grew throughout the 19th century, and with the rise and diffusion of popular culture, "high" art began to follow a course of its own.

But in the early decades of the 19th century this had not yet occurred. Artists were at the forefront of the campaign for reform, and their voices were still heard when political reformers could be—and were—silenced.

Questions for Further Study

1. Which characteristics of Romanticism are common to all the arts? What form do they take in the various artistic media?
2. What factors—cultural, social, historical—favored the development of the novel in the 19th century?
3. What role did nationalism play in the Romantic movement?

Suggestions for Further Reading

Canaday, J. *Mainstreams of Modern Art*. New York, 1981.
Chissell, J. *Clara Schumann: A Dedicated Spirit*. London, 1983.
Cooper, M. *Beethoven: The Last Decade*. New York, 1985.
Gage, J., ed. and trans. *Goethe on Art*. Berkeley, CA, 1980.
Paulson, R. *Literary Landscape: Turner and Constable*. New Haven, CT, 1982.
Talmon, J. L. *Romanticism and Revolt, 1815–1848*. New York, 1979.
Wolf, B. *Romantic Re-vision: Culture and Consciousness in Nineteenth-Century Painting and Literature*. Chicago, 1982.

Topic 8

Thought and Action: The Revolutions of 1848

In the 30 years following Waterloo, a number of important factors changed European life. The growth of industrialism revolutionized social and economic patterns. The old aristocratic order began to face an increasing challenge to its monopoly on political power from the middle classes, the champions of liberalism. The pressure of nationalism, generally with liberal support, offered the prospect of radical change in many parts of Europe, most notably in Italy, Germany, and Eastern Europe.

So widespread a reshaping of values and priorities depended on a series of intellectual and philosophical positions. In Britain the new industrial middle class found justification for their social and economic overturning of the old order in the writings of Thomas Malthus and Jeremy Bentham, both of whom advocated the primacy of the individual over society as a whole.

The most important systematic political philosophy to develop was socialism. Its general aims were an equitable distribution of wealth and social and political equality. Methods to achieve this, however, varied widely. "Utopian" socialists such as François Charles Fourier and Robert Owen put their faith in natural human goodness. By contrast, the more militant "scientific" socialists Marx and Engels advocated revolution: their *Communist Manifesto* appeared during the revolutions of 1848.

The 1830 revolution in France and the British electoral reforms of the 1830s (see Part VII, Topic 5) raised hopeful expectations for many elsewhere in Europe, but on the whole they were disappointed. The chief beneficiaries were the industrial middle class. The workers, who had erected the barricades in Paris, and demonstrated in the streets of Britain, won nothing. This lack of substantial change led to frustration not only in Britain and France, but throughout continental Europe. The growing discontent at the suppression of national freedom, and at the lack of representative government, led to a wave of revolutionary uprisings which swept over most of Europe in 1848.

As in 1830, France led the way. The frustrations of the industrial poor provoked savage street fighting in Paris. Within days Louis Philippe abdicated, and the Second French Republic was proclaimed. Others were quickly fired by the success of the French revolutionaries. Student liberals in Vienna, and nationalists in Hungary, Czechoslovakia, and Italy rebelled against Hapsburg rule and local monarchs. Metternich fled for his life, followed by his emperor, Ferdinand I. Tuscany, Naples, and Sicily all staged revolts against their rulers. Street riots in Berlin scared the Prussian king, Friedrich Wilhelm IV, into appointing a liberal government. The only countries not affected were Britain, where hasty compromise averted revolution, and Russia, still firmly under repressive tsarist rule.

Judged in terms of immediate success, the 1848 revolutions were a failure. Conservative forces returned to power throughout Europe. In France the middle and peasant classes, nervous at the rise of socialism, elected Louis Napoleon Bonaparte as president. Austrian troops restored Hapsburg rule to virtually all of the empire. Their success prompted the Prussian king to withdraw his liberal concessions, and the Prussian Army put down all protests. Only in Piedmont did a liberal constitution survive.

Yet the causes for which the rebels of 1830 had fought and lost the struggle—nationalism, liberalism, and socialism—were by no means doomed. A new realism replaced the idealism of much pre-1848 political thought. For the rest of the century both socialist and nationalist issues dominated the European political scene, with increasing success.

LIBERALS, NATIONALISTS, AND SOCIALISTS: REVOLUTIONARIES AND THEIR IDEALS

The conflicts that shook European society throughout the 19th century were in large part the result of a growing challenge to the conservative order. The three ideologies inspiring this opposition were liberalism, nationalism, and socialism. The first two played a part in the struggles immediately following the Congress of Vienna; the early development of modern socialism dates to the 1830s, and is best understood as a result of the gradual rise of the working classes.

Liberalism

Liberals could trace their ideas back to the Enlightenment and the moderate stages of the French Revolution, and both Romanticism and nationalism helped to shape their views of government. Political liberalism held that a representative system, generally in the form of constitutional monarchy, was the wisest form of government, for it allowed for stability, the participation of the middle classes, and the protection of basic freedoms such as equality before the law and freedom of speech. Liberalism itself was neither a systematic nor a static political philosophy. Rather, liberalism represented a set of attitudes that combined notions of social and political justice with a commitment to economic progress.

Liberalism varied greatly from country to country in the 19th century, but nowhere was it intended to be a democratic doctrine. As a political system of the middle classes, liberalism was based on a belief in the importance of private property, education, and the wisdom of the leisured classes. Liberals believed in change, but change that was the result of balanced, orderly growth as society in general underwent moral and material progress.

Liberal economic theory lay at the core of political liberalism. In the *Wealth of Nations* (1776) and other writings, the 18th-century thinker Adam Smith (1723–1790) had argued that prosperity would result from economic forces that were allowed to operate freely without government intervention. David Ricardo (1772–1823) expanded on Smith's theory, especially in his *Principles of Political Economy and Taxation* (1817). He expounded the "iron law of wages," which held that the price of labor, like commodities, depended on supply and demand. When the number of available workers is high, their pay will be low—around a mere subsistence level. Ricardo believed that labor, like land, is a commodity that should not be regulated but allowed to fluctuate with the marketplace.

Malthus and the Malthusians

The economic inequities of the industrial revolution that Ricardo found inevitable were reinforced by the pessimistic predictions of Thomas Robert Malthus (1766–1834). Malthus held that human suffering and poverty were unavoidable, a natural result of overpopulation; this in turn was due to the fact that people increased in number faster than food could be produced to feed them. Unless there was some conscious check on population growth, only famine or plague could restore the natural equilibrium. Even an increase in agricultural production would lead only to a rise in population and a repetition of the whole cycle.

In spite of his gloomy predictions, Malthus viewed himself as a humanitarian, believing that if society would only listen to his conclusions and take action to reduce population growth, it could reduce the quantity of human suffering. Nonetheless, in general he remained pessimistic, opposing any attempt by government or employers to alleviate the poverty and misery of the workers or the unemployed: charity, he believed, would make the situation worse by allowing more people to survive. Some economic liberals, however, tended to adopt a more positive attitude toward the Malthusian predictions. If human suffering was inevitable, middle-class manufacturers should not be surprised if their workers starved while they themselves grew rich, and liberals could reconcile themselves to manifest social injustice because it was unavoidable. Revolutionary concepts of equality were replaced by the realities of the marketplace, and the field of political economy became known as the "dismal science."

Although the harsh views of this "classical economics" were systematized into social theories later in the 19th century, other liberals rejected them. Original liberal notions of general freedom of thought and action crystallized into the concept of the "greatest good for the greatest number." The "utilitarianism" of political reform—its practical benefits as opposed to its theoretical desirability—was first clearly expounded in the writings of Jeremy Bentham (1748–1832).

According to Bentham, the criterion for judging a policy was not its natural appropriateness, but its utility. That which is good avoids pain and gives pleasure. Individuals can make their own estimates of what is to their advantage, while governments should aim for the same end result for their societies. The correct calculation of pleasure and pain would lead to a just society. Democratic government is useful because it satisfies the largest number of people, an argument that steps back from the doctrine of universal liberty. The broader implications of Bentham's ideas were explored in mid-century by John Stuart Mill (see Part VII, Topic 9).

The more immediate implications of Bentham's utilitarianism inspired a group of liberals known as the philosophic radicals. In their pursuit of "the greatest good for the greatest number," they pressed for widespread social reform. By 1832, the year of Bentham's death and passage of the Reform Bill, the philosophic radicals were leading campaigns to reform the legal system, education, prisons, and welfare.

Nationalism

The concerns of nationalism were of a different order. In its simplest form, nationalism is an awareness of cultural and territorial identity—the identity, that is, of people who share a common language, history, and traditions in a given region. The French Revolution and Napoleon's conquests were both major stimuli to the emergence of nationalism. Not only did the Revolution identify popular will with national sovereignty, but it also succeeded in mobilizing French citizens in defense of the revolutionary nation-state.

National consciousness in Germany, Italy, and eastern Europe was generated by French conquests in those regions. Under the impact of French invasion, two intellectuals, Johann Gottfried von Herder (1744–1803) and Johann Gottlieb Fichte (1762–1814) appealed to fellow Germans to seek for the common roots and culture of their *Volk* (people). With the growth of national awareness came a call for national self-determination, as peoples living under foreign rule began to demand political independence and unity.

Cultural campaigns were often as useful as political ones in instilling national consciousness. In Germany, Jakob and Wilhelm Grimm compiled Germanic folktales as well as German dictionaries and grammar books. In Hungary, Lajos Kossuth (1802–1894), future revolutionary leader, promoted the cause in articles appearing in the daily newspaper he edited from 1841 to 1844. He wrote these articles in Magyar, which had become the official government language in Hungary only in 1826. Frantisek Palacky (1798–1876), a Czech historian, fanned national consciousness with his five-volume *History of Bohemia,* which he began publishing in the 1830s.

The Polish poet Adam Mickiewicz (1798–1855) was deported to Russia for his political activities. On his release he settled in Paris, where in 1834 he published *Pan Tadeusz,* an epic poem set in the Polish Lithuanian villages where he grew up.

Giuseppe Mazzini

Like Mickiewicz, the Italian patriot Giuseppe Mazzini (1805–1872) spent most of his life in exile. The most important proponent of nationalism in the 19th century, Mazzini was a leading figure in the struggle to unify Italy, but his nationalist philosophy became a European as well as an Italian doctrine of liberty. A passionate, idealistic revolutionary, he believed in national self-determination as in a religion—indeed, he was sometimes called the "high priest" of Italian nationalism.

A member of the *Carbonari* in his youth, Mazzini took part in its conspiracies during the late 1820s. After a time in jail, he rallied the cause of Italian unity first from Switzerland and, when the Swiss government banished him, from France and later from London. In 1831 he created a revolutionary group of his own called *Giovine Italia* (Young Italy) with a tight organization and a specific program: popular insurrection led by youthful enthusiasts, Italian unity and independence, and—most subversive of all, from the point of view of the authorities—a republican government based on popular will and democratic principles. Mazzini, determined foe of the papacy as well as of kings, was a Romantic who hoped that a united Italy would establish its capital at Rome. From there, Italy would inspire a new "Europe of the Peoples," based on universal brotherhood, a sense of duty, and social justice.

Mazzini's very breadth of vision made him impatient with the necessities of practical politics, and his relations with other Italian leaders were generally stormy. In the 1830s and 1840s, Young Italy fomented countless ill-conceived conspiracies and uprisings, each of which failed, but in the process Mazzini had given a generation of idealistic Italians a strong sense of their common destiny. Throughout Europe, too, his example was followed as nationalist organizations modeled after Young Italy sprang up among other subject peoples. By the middle of the century, nationalism became a major force in European affairs, but after the achievement of national unity in Italy and Germany, nationalist idealism would be converted into a doctrine of national conflict and dominance: a state of mind rather than the fulfillment of national need.

The Rise of Socialism

At the same time as the industrial revolution was permanently changing European society, the first critics of industrialism began to appear. Their fundamental objection was that the growth of manufacturing did nothing to produce a more equitable distribution of wealth and, indeed, contributed to the exploitation of millions of workers.

The idea of a community in which the products of common labor are divided among all, according to their needs, was not a new one, although it had in general been limited to relatively simple societies. In modern Europe, this notion was first applied to industrial society in the 1820s, under the general name of "socialism." Socialists further advocated that economic equality should be accompanied by similar political and social reform.

The earliest socialist thinkers were derided by their more militant successors as "utopians," because their ideas were regarded as naive and impractical; later socialists tried to argue from objective, "scientific" principles, or, like Marx, from the notion of historical inevitability. Like many of the Utopians, Count Henri de Saint-Simon (1760–1825) was noble by birth. For all the oversimplification of his beliefs—he proposed a massive plan of social reorganization based on the rule of technical experts and scientists—Saint-Simon coined what was to become one of the central teachings of the socialist creed: "From each according to his capacity, to each according to his work."

In Saint-Simon's ideal society, work had the highest value, and industrialists and technicians would replace theologians or philosophers as leaders. In the coming industrial age, he believed, the government of humans would give way to the administration of things. Religion also had a part to play, for it "should direct society toward the great aim of the most rapid amelioration of the lot of the poorest class."

After his death a cooperative farming and manufacturing community was organized in his name in Paris. In theory, women and men had equal status, and the community had a male and female leader. Before a suitable woman could be chosen, however, the community was closed down by the authorities, for it had extended equal rights to sexual as well as working relations. Women followers of Saint-Simon continued to meet, forming the most sophisticated women's movement of the times. They organized a women's newspaper and discussed the formation of a women's association, which would not imitate male organizations but take its own explicitly female form.

Another form of ideal community was proposed by Charles Fourier (1772–1837). Fourier believed that most of the ills of society were the result of the unsuitable physical and social conditions under which the vast majority of people lived. Thus the way to create a better society was to produce a more favorable environment. Fourier proposed to provide this in the shape of self-sufficient agricultural communities called "phalanxes," each with a limited population and economically self-sufficient, on pieces of land set aside for the purpose. Members of the community would receive wages according to their abilities and contributions.

Among Fourier's followers was Flora Tristan (1801–1844). In her speeches, letters, and diaries, Tristan proclaimed that at the root of industrial misery was the competition between women and men workers. The working class, she urged, should unite in the cause of women, and thereby help all workers.

In Britain, the chief proponent of utopian community life was Robert Owen (1771–1858). A prominent cotton manufacturer, in his own factories he cut the normal workday nearly in half, provided child care for working parents, and increased both productivity and profit. Owen believed that the price of manufactured products should be based on three factors: the cost of the raw material, the cost of labor, and an added amount to provide capital for future supplies.

Significant Dates

Between the Revolutions of 1830 and 1848

1830	Belgium achieves independence; revolution in France makes Louis Philippe king
1831	Mazzini forms Giovine Italia
1834	Mickiewicz publishes *Pan Tadeusz*
1838	The Chartists circulate their "People's Charter"
1844	Marx and Engels found the Communist League
1846	Repeal of the Corn Laws
1848	*The Communist Manifesto* published

Owen actually created a model community, to demonstrate that by minimizing profits and improving working conditions, he could still increase productivity; the community had its own housing and clubs, and a system of workers' benefits. Inspired by Owen, a number of crafts—weavers, glove makers, and others—set up unions and cooperative workshops, and working-class newspapers were founded. An industrial dispute put an end to the practical side of "Owenism," when tailors struck to protest at the hiring of women to work part-time in their own homes. Their successful action destroyed the ideal of solidarity which later socialists developed.

By the time of the 1848 revolutions, socialism had taken a new turn. In France and Germany, societies were formed calling for the abolition of all private property: communism. In 1844 two young Germans, Karl Marx (1818–1883) and Friedrich Engels (1820–1895), helped to found the Communist League, whose purpose was to overthrow the middle class (their term was the "bourgeoisie"); Marx used the term "Communist" to avoid confusion with the utopian socialists who, he believed, failed to see the historical laws that made revolution inevitable.

Engels, the son of a wealthy cotton manufacturer, met Marx in Paris, where they worked together on an analysis of the state of contemporary society, and a radical prescription for its reform. Their conclusions were outlined in *The Communist Manifesto*, published in 1848 for the gathering of Communists held in that year, in the midst of the revolutions. In the years after 1850, their ideas spread throughout Europe (see Part VII, Topic 13).

A TIME FOR CHANGE: THE ROOTS OF DISCONTENT

The revolutions of 1830 had signaled the advance of the liberal cause, but over the following years political reformers began to realize that the conservative order remained entrenched. Furthermore, those liberal concessions which had been won by popular demonstrations ended by benefiting the industrial middle class. The workers who erected the barricades in Paris or risked their lives at Peterloo gained little, if anything, from their actions.

The decade began with a nationalist victory. At the Congress of Vienna, Belgium (the former Austrian Netherlands) had been made part of the kingdom of Holland. Inspired by the French success in deposing the Bourbons, in August 1830 the Flemish citizens of Brussels staged a revolt in favor of Belgian independence. The Dutch held back, while Britain and France discouraged the threatened intervention of Russia and

Engraving of 1832 showing Whig leaders united with the king to pass the Reform Bill.

Chartists at a protest meeting in London, April 1848.

Austria, and Belgium became an independent state guaranteed by international treaty.

Elsewhere, however, there were less encouraging signs of progress. A revolt in Poland was crushed by the Russians, and Mazzinian-inspired revolts in Italy were put down by Austrian troops. In a few German states minor upheavals did result in the granting of liberal constitutions, but Metternich was determined to prevent the rise of a nationalist movement which could benefit Prussia, and encouraged states to repress any uprisings. The Diet of the German Confederation duly followed Metternich's instructions.

As for the Hapsburg possessions in eastern Europe, the failure of revolt there is explained by the strength of the Austrians' control, and the ferocity of their reprisals at the first sign of rebellion. In addition, unlike Britain and France, and even Belgium, southern and eastern Europe had no industrialized middle class to organize and lead a revolution.

Britain: The Repeal of the Corn Laws

The first signs of popular discontent arose, ironically enough, in the one Western European nation which managed to avoid open revolutionary conflict: Britain. The Reform Bill of 1832 (see Part VII, Topic 5) had gone some way toward satisfying popular demands for increased parliamentary representation, but many were disappointed by it. In 1838 a group of radical reformers drew up a "People's Charter," which called for wholesale parliamentary reform; among the provisions were universal adult male suffrage, a secret ballot, and the abolition of property qualifications for members of Parliament. The Chartists, as supporters of the proposals were called, also campaigned against the revised Poor Laws (in theory, laws to protect the needy) which had been passed in 1834. As one of them wrote, "The new poor law is a law to punish poverty; making working men dislike the country of their birth, brood over their wrongs, and hate the rich of the land." The Chartists twice presented their Charter to Parliament, which rejected it out of hand both times.

The repeal of the hated Corn Laws in 1846 went some way to redressing the general sense of grievance, and its effects help to explain the sudden collapse of the Chartist movement. In 1848 a final petition demanding reform, accompanied by some 6 million signatures (many bogus), was carried to London by a mob so threatening that the government prepared to disperse it by force. In the end the crowd broke up peacefully, and so did the Chartist movement. Subsequent campaigns for reform were conducted by more orthodox means. Thereafter Britain remained untouched by events on the Continent, except for its function as refuge for political exiles. Among those who could have met one

Honoré Daumier, *Louis Philippe, the Last King of France.*

another in London in the 1850s were Marx and Metternich. There is no evidence that they did.

Revolution in France

By the early spring of 1848 the general frustration symbolized in Britain by the Chartist movement was spreading throughout Europe. Growing unemployment, and bad harvests in 1846 and 1847, increased tensions. As in 1830, the explosion originated in France, where on the surface the political scene seemed relatively calm. Both Louis Philippe and his chief minister, François Guizot (who served as premier of France 1847–1848), followed a policy of order and prosperity at home and peace abroad.

Guizot, a self-proclaimed liberal, believed that the Constitution of 1830, which extended political power to the property-owning classes, provided a proper balance between liberty and order. Cautious and rigid, he opposed any further broadening of the franchise, hoping to combine industrial growth with political stability by preserving the status quo.

As elsewhere in Europe, however, industrialization had brought with it the rise of a large and underprivileged urban proletariat. The slum dwellers of Paris and France's northeastern industrial cities began to demand the right to form labor unions and to vote. When they received neither, workers protested at their living conditions and demanded reform; socialist ideas were increasingly circulated at political banquets.

A mass protest, in the form of a banquet, announced for February 22, 1848, was banned the day before by government decree. When a crowd in Paris gathered to protest against the restriction, street brawling broke out and workers began to build barricades. Louis Philippe tried to pacify the mob by dismissing Guizot,

Map 8.1 The Revolutions of 1848–1849

but in the rioting around the prime minister's residence a shot rang out. The troops guarding the house lost their nerve and fired on the crowd, killing a number of the demonstrators. The reverberations of their bullets echoed throughout Europe.

EUROPE AT THE BARRICADES: THE PATTERN OF REVOLT

For two days Paris was racked by street fighting. Workers erected some 1500 barricades. The troops of the National Guard either disappeared or joined the rioters. Louis Philippe had been brought to power by the 1830 revolution, and on February 25, 1848, he left it by the same route, abdicating like his predecessor and leaving for England. Always a moderate, he prevented a bloodbath by refusing to call out the army and by leaving so quickly.

The Second Republic

A provisional government assumed power and, to appease the demonstrators, proclaimed the Second Republic, its leaders chosen by acclamation from the crowds outside the Hotel de Ville (city hall). The poet Alphonse de Lamartine, an overnight convert to the republican cause, led the government, with a cabinet that included the socialist Louis Blanc, a token worker named Albert Martin, and a radical republican, Alexandre Ledru-Rollin. The provisional government announced April elections for a new National Constituent Assembly.

The overthrow of the monarchy had temporarily united the competing political factions. Once the king was gone, the politicians took over and rival forces openly waged a struggle for power. The liberals favored a moderate extension of the vote. The republicans advocated permanent abolition of the monarchy and radical reform. Blanc, the only real socialist in the government, proposed a system of "national workshops" to pay the unemployed a small stipend and put them to work. The government set up a version of the scheme, but organized it so badly that the plan proved disastrous. Thousands of workers flocked to Paris to join the workshops, at immense cost to the taxpayers, while Blanc complained that the scheme had been deliberately set up in such a way as to guarantee its failure.

In spite of the political battles, the provisional government managed to make some positive steps. The new republic adopted universal male suffrage, abolished the death penalty, and rejected participation in any for-

A contemporary caricature by Andre Gill satirizing Louis Blanc.

Barricades at the Charles Bridge, in Prague, in June 1848.

eign wars. It also improved relations with the Catholic Church. The elections in April took place in relative calm, with around 85 percent of those eligible to vote actually doing so. The result was a triumph for the moderate and conservative republicans. Even the monarchists did better than the socialists, who won only a handful of seats.

Revolution in the Hapsburg Empire

While France began to rebuild some form of order, news of the cataclysmic events there reached Vienna. On March 12, workers and students finally threw off years of repression and rampaged through the city. The imperial palace was invaded. Under pressure from the emperor, Ferdinand I, Metternich resigned. The architect of conservative Europe hastily disguised himself and fled into exile in England, never returning to Austria. The emperor followed him, although only as far as Innsbruck, and a hastily convened liberal National Assembly drafted a constitution. Among other measures, peasant feudalism was abolished.

Elsewhere in the Hapsburg empire, Austrian rule faltered. Before the end of March, Milan and Venice rose up against their foreign rulers, while disturbances in Piedmont, Tuscany, Naples, and the Papal States forced the granting of constitutions. Taking advantage of these developments, Charles Albert (ruled 1831–1849), king of Piedmont-Sardinia, declared war on the Austrians with the aim of removing them from the affairs of the peninsula.

Charles Albert was an enigmatic and unstable man who, during the abortive Piedmontese revolt of 1821, had led an unsuccessful campaign against Austria. Now he planned to redeem himself and, once having driven out the hated foreigners, unite northern Italy under his rule. The constitution which he issued in February 1848 was a slightly modified version of the Spanish Constitution of 1812. Although it provided for representative government based on limited male suffrage, it also gave the monarch considerable powers and left the question of parliamentary authority vague. Thirteen years later, it would provide the basis for the constitution of a united Italy.

Units arrived from other Italian states, along with volunteers led by the dashing guerrilla fighter Giuseppe Garibaldi. Nevertheless, not all Italian patriots supported Charles Albert. Mazzini, from his exile in London, inveighed against the king of Piedmont and advocated a republic.

The election of Pope Pius IX (ruled 1846–1878) two years earlier had inspired liberal hopes and encouraged the Piedmontese moderate Vincenzo Gioberti (1801–1852), who had earlier proposed a "Neo-Guelph" program consisting of a federation of Italian princes under papal leadership (the Guelphs were the pro-papal forces in Medieval Italy who opposed the encroachments of the Holy Roman emperor). Pius had even sent a small detachment to assist Charles Albert, but by April he had concluded that he could not declare war against Austria. When Pius fled Rome in November, Mazzini rushed to the city with his followers, and in February 1849 became head of the Roman Republic. "The war of the kings is over," declared Mazzini, "the war of the people begins." Ideological

German troops storm a barricade in Frankfurt, September 18, 1848.

Significant Dates

The Revolutions of 1848

France:	
February 22–24, 1848	Louis Philippe abdicates; Provisional Government formed
February 26	National Workshops begin
April	Constituent Assembly
June	Workers Revolt in Paris
November	Second Republic founded
December	Louis Napoleon elected president
Germany:	
March 1848	Riots in Berlin; King Friedrich Wilhelm IV promises reforms
May	Frankfurt Assembly meets
December	Prussian constitution issued
March 1849	Friedrich Wilhelm refuses crown of Germany
June	Frankfurt Assembly dispersed
Italy:	
January 1848	Uprising in Sicily
January–March	Constitutions issued in Naples, Piedmont, Tuscany, and Rome
July	Austrians defeat Charles Albert
November 1848–February 1849	Uprising in Rome, republic proclaimed
March	Charles Albert defeated and abdicates
March–August	Revolutions crushed in Italy
Austria:	
March 1848	Revolt in Vienna, Metternich dismissed; Milan revolts
June	Revolt in Prague put down
October	Movement in Vienna crushed
April–August 1849	Hungarian independence proclaimed; crushed by Russians

divisions, together with considerations of religion, prevented a united front among the proindependence forces in Italy.

In Hungary, where Kossuth led the Magyar nationalist party, the Austrians agreed to the March Laws, guaranteeing a large measure of Hungarian self-rule. One of the new government's first acts, the reaffirmation of Magyar as the country's official language, alienated Hungary's ethnic minorities, in particular the Croats.

Such divisiveness did not augur well for the revolution's success. In Bohemia too there were ominous signs of the national rivalries that were to prove fatal to the cause of reform. The Czech majority and the German minority feuded over rival national conferences, a pan-Slavic one to be convened in Prague, and a pan-German one meeting in Frankfurt. By mid-1848, the Hapsburg empire may have seemed on the brink of collapse, but the revolutionary gains were precarious.

Riots in Berlin

In Berlin, the Prussian capital, Friedrich Wilhelm IV (ruled 1840–1861), the Hohenzollern king, had come to power supporting liberal reforms but had never carried them out. Now, in March, when he heard that Metternich had fled Vienna, the king issued a manifesto promising a constitution. Events took an unexpected turn, however. Crowds of demonstrators celebrating the news from abroad were provoked into bloody violence when government troops fired shots at them. Barricades went up in Berlin and the king eventually relented, appointing a liberal government and announcing a national assembly. This left both conservatives and radicals angry, the former because they wanted to see the demonstrations crushed, and the latter because they had already been fired on.

By May, liberals throughout the German states had sent delegates to an assembly at Frankfurt, where the Diet of the German Confederation had its seat. The Frankfurt Assembly was a well-meaning gathering of middle-class professionals—lawyers, professors, bureaucrats—convened to create a united German nation. The absence of any working-class representation, however, was a dangerous indication of the narrow base of the German revolutionary movement.

HOPES CRUSHED: THE REACTIONARIES TRIUMPHANT

Within less than a year the fires of revolution were spent. The revolutionaries were dead or in exile, and the reactionaries back in power. In France the return to order was self-imposed: in the April elections for the National Assembly, the middle class and the peasants, fearful of "socialist excesses," had voted for moderate candidates.

One of the new government's first acts was to abolish the national workshops, and to order the workers, who had collected in Paris, either to join the army or to go and look for jobs in the provinces. Rioting broke out in Paris, as desperate workers took once again to the barricades, with the slogan "better a death from bullets than from starvation." During four bloody "June Days," rebels fought troops in the streets until government forces under General Louis Cavaignac (1802–1857) brutally crushed the uprising at the cost of perhaps 5000 lives. The government victory, and the subsequent execution and deportation to the French colonies of rebel leaders, restored domestic peace. It also left wounds in French society that remained open for generations.

The assembly proceeded to draw up a constitution establishing the Second French Republic. Rule was divided between a one-chamber parliament, which retained legislative control, and a president, who had executive and administrative powers. Both instruments of government were to be elected by universal male suffrage; a bill for women's suffrage was defeated by 899 votes to 1.

The Election of Louis Napoleon

In December 1848 elections were held for president. Among the candidates to present themselves were Lamartine, Ledru-Rollin, Cavaignac, the conservative hero of the June Days, and Louis Napoleon Bonaparte (1808–1873), the late emperor's nephew, who claimed that he could restore the glory of France's imperial days.

A complex and eccentric figure, Louis Napoleon had acquired liberal ideas during his youth and something of a revolutionary pedigree. After living in exile in Germany and Switzerland with his mother, he had taken part in uprisings in Italy in 1830–1831. In 1840 he had been arrested for plotting a seizure of power in France, but escaped from prison and fled to England. A wily politician with a skillful instinct for creating popular poses, while in prison he had published a pamphlet entitled *The Extinction of Pauperism*, which won him support among the workers.

Amid utter confusion, the country prepared to vote. To the great surprise of many, Louis Napoleon swept the elections with 70 percent of the vote, becoming the republic's first president. A clever manipulator of opinion, he had played on the glamour of his name, promising to repeat his uncle's achievements—or at least some of them—and restore France to greatness. Moreover, he appealed to workers and revolutionaries as easily as he did to conservative peasants and monarchists. Less than four years later, in 1852, he overthrew the constitution, seized power, and crowned himself Napoleon III (the so-called Napoleon II, the dictator's son, died in 1832 without ever ruling). Thus France returned from the heady days of February 1848 to 20 years of authoritarian rule.

Revolution Crushed in Central and Southern Europe

The reassertion of Hapsburg rule was made possible by two factors: the innate strength of the Austrian Army and the continued destructive feuding amongst various ethnic groups. In Bohemia, divided by rivalry between the Czech majority and the German minority, the anti-German Czechs summoned a confederation of Slavs to gather in Prague, and refused to send a delegation to participate in the pan-German assembly meeting in Frankfurt. The German minority resented their government's refusal to allow them to participate in the Frankfurt discussions. Austrian forces took advantage of the mutual hostility between Slavs and Germans to reassert control in Prague. The troops were ordered in, moreover, not by the emperor, but by the new Austrian government, which, for all its liberalism had no intention of presiding over the breakup of the empire.

In northern Italy the excitement of freedom soon gave way to the only-too-familiar inability of the Italian states to cooperate. The troops of Piedmont, left to fight alone, were no match for General Radetzky and the Austrian forces, and in July concluded an armistice. In March 1849, under the urging of the Piedmontese radicals and his own desire for vindication, Charles Albert denounced the armistice and declared war on Austria for a second time.

Within a week the struggle ended in defeat. Abdicating in favor of his son, Victor Emmanuel II (ruled as king of Piedmont 1849–1861; and as king of Italy 1861–1878), from whom he had extracted a promise never to abrogate the constitution, he went into exile and died a few months later. To the south, the Roman Republic was soon surrounded and, although gallantly defended by Garibaldi, was finally defeated in 1849 by a force sent by none other than Louis Napoleon, the new president of France, anxious to impress his Catholic subjects by a show of support for the papacy.

Even before then, Hapsburg rule had been restored in Vienna. At the end of October 1848 forces loyal to the emperor occupied the city, and the government resigned. The new Austrian chief minister, Prince Felix von Schwarzenberg (1800–1852), proceeded to dissolve the National Assembly and impose his own authoritarian constitution throughout the empire.

Only Hungary remained independent for a short while longer. Early in 1849 the new emperor—

Ferdinand I had abdicated at Schwarzenberg's bidding—Franz Josef (ruled 1848–1916), accepted the assistance of Nicholas I of Russia in regaining Austrian control there. The tsar's motives were hardly altruistic. Quite apart from any loyalty to a fellow monarch, he feared the spread of revolt to Poland and Russia's western provinces. To make matters easier for the Austrians, they were joined by Hungary's own Croat population, who resented and feared the Magyars' success.

As for Prussia, where a middle-class National Assembly had been elected and was drafting a liberal constitution, as soon as Friedrich Wilhelm realized that the Hapsburgs were back in power, he dissolved the assembly and reasserted his authority. In the face of the Prussian Army, street demonstrations by radical workers were soon put down. The riots also confirmed middle-class distaste for the socialists, and scared them into accepting the king's rule. Later in 1849, the king surprised conservatives, however, by granting a constitution of his own (revised in 1850) that provided for a two-chamber *Landtag*, or legislature. The lower house of the Prussian *Landtag* was elected by a complicated voting system that gave control to the upper middle class.

The one continuing sign of liberal activity was the assembly in session at Frankfurt to discuss the future of a united Germany. One of the chief issues to divide the delegates was whether Austria should be included in the future German state. Those in favor comprised the *Grossdeutsch* ("Great Germany") faction; the others were called the *Kleindeutsch* ("Little Germany") party. After months of lofty debate, the matter was resolved in the end by the reactionaries' return to full control in Vienna: Hapsburg Austria could have no place in a liberal Germany.

In March 1849 the victorious "Little Germany" delegates offered the leadership of the German world to Friedrich Wilhelm. The Prussian king contemptuously refused it, proclaiming disdainfully that he had no need of a "crown from the gutter." The delegates despondently returned home. Just over a year after the first riots in Paris, the last sparks of reform were extinguished.

THE REVOLUTIONARY EXPERIENCE AND ITS MEANING

By midcentury even the most ardent revolutionaries had to admit that their prospects were not promising. For a few months the whole of Europe seemed on the

Satirical depiction by Daumier of the French Chamber of Deputies.

brink of irreversible change, only to slide back into reactionary hands. The reformers' failure was, of course, partly due to their opponents' superior strength. In the long run the Austrian Army and the Prussian Junkers had an advantage that not even the most fiery rebel could withstand.

Yet with hindsight it was clear that the revolutionaries themselves were in large measure responsible for the abruptness of their failure. In virtually all cases, leadership was indecisive and divided. Much of the actual fighting, with its consequent loss of life, involved the workers. With the battles over, and the time come for debating future moves, the middle class took over. The two factions never really shared a common interest, for the workers wanted to overturn existing society, while the others—who had not wanted a revolution in the first place—were concerned to reassert earlier gains. In addition the more extreme forms of socialism were used by conservatives to scare middle-class revolutionaries back into obedience. As a result of their experience in 1848, both parties learned to mistrust the other.

One of the principal goals of the revolutions, the promoting of national identity, turned out to be a two-edged sword. Divisions among ethnic minorities, which had often existed for centuries, allowed the Austrians to divide and rule. Broader national rivalries prevented the coordination of revolutionary movements across frontiers. Where, as in Germany or Italy, there was no actual difference of nationality, political disagreements and local rivalries stood in the way of united opposition to conservative regimes. Yet the experience of 1848 was not entirely in vain. At least some German and Italian nationalists drew the obvious conclusion that only united opposition could cause the collapse of a hated regime, and applied them with varying degrees of success in their struggles for unification later in the century.

Quite apart from political, social, or national differences, the events of 1848 demonstrated another gulf: the one between city dwellers and rural populations. For the most part the grievances that the revolutionaries sought most urgently to redress were those of city life—overcrowding, bad working conditions, unemployment. Issues such as these were of little interest to peasants and farmers, the wealthier of whom actually stood to lose by a wholesale restructuring of society. In France and Prussia self-interest, bolstered by a mortal fear of the "red peril" of socialism, led peasants to join the middle classes in putting down the revolution.

In the second half of the 19th century, as urban populations came to dominate most European countries, the balance of power shifted decisively to the cities; the working classes consolidated their power, and peasant farmers ceased to play a significant political role.

The 1848 revolutions were not totally without positive results for the liberal cause. A few measures enacted by liberal assemblies—the abolition of serfdom in Austria and Hungary, for example—remained in force. Some former conservative leaders remained in exile; Metternich was one who never returned to power. More intangibly, those who continued to press for reform learned to value realism, rather than idealism. Political theories and notions of human rights, or the rights of nations, could be put into practice only by organized and efficient leadership. The events of 1848 had demonstrated to even the most idealistic that utopianism was not enough.

The French Revolution anticipated the beginning of the modern world, but the revolutions of 1848 seemed to reinstate the old order. Yet although the conservatives were back in power, the society over which they ruled was undergoing a period of profound upheaval. Vast numbers of people were bitterly unhappy with the systems under which they lived. The causes of their dissatisfaction were only too clear. Most of them lived crowded together in cities, which increasingly became Europe's dominant social and economic units. Each country's wealth and political power remained in the hands of a tiny minority. The citizens of many parts of Europe remained under foreign domination.

For many of those who felt themselves oppressed, socialism offered the hope of escape. The rewards of liberalism seemed limited to one segment of society, while the triumph of nationalism still appeared distant. Under the influence of socialist ideas, working-class people began to take practical steps to organize themselves. Trade union and cooperative leaders forced industrialists to take them seriously. Many socialist theorists encouraged the feminist movement, which first developed in the 1850s in Britain.

Thus out of the ashes of 1848 arose the industrial world of the late 19th century. The conflicts which permeated it involved in increasing measure citizens who had hitherto played little part in shaping history: the industrial working class.

Questions for Further Study

1. What were the principal aims of liberalism and socialism, and how did they differ?
2. How did the political developments of the 1830s and 1840s in Britain differ from those in continental Europe?
3. What caused the rise of nationalism in the 19th century? How successful were its early leaders, and what were their methods?

Suggestions for Further Reading

Beecher, J. *Charles Fourier: The Visionary and His World*. Berkeley, CA, 1986.

Calhoun, C. *The Question of Class Struggle: Social Foundations of Popular Radicalism During the Industrial Revolution*. Chicago, 1982.

Church, C. *Europe in 1830: Revolution and Political Change*. London, 1983.

Droz, J. *Europe Between Revolutions, 1815–1848*. Ithaca, NY, 1980.

Seidman, S. *Liberalism and the Origins of European Social Theory*. Berkeley, CA, 1983.

Stearns, P. *1848: The Revolutionary Tide in Europe*. New York, 1974.

Thompson, D. *The Chartists: Popular Politics in the Industrial Revolution*. New York, 1984.

VII

Topic 9

The Liberal State: Domestic Politics in Britain and France

Events in Britain and France in the years from 1850 to 1870 offer a contrast in the application of liberal doctrines at home and abroad. In both countries economic liberalism produced increasing domestic prosperity. Britain maintained its political liberalism, while avoiding involvement in European affairs. In the first part of his reign, Napoleon III restricted political freedom at home, and in foreign policy set aside the basic liberal ideal of international peace. During the 1860s, however, the French governmental system underwent a liberal transformation.

By mid-19th century, Britain embarked on a period of prosperity greater than at any earlier time in its history. Under a system of two-party parliamentary government, public opinion could play a part in producing peaceful political change. A policy of nonintervention in Europe (apart from the Crimean War) brought two decades of peace, further industrial growth, and a boom in free trade.

The chief political issue was parliamentary reform. The 1832 Reform Bill extended the franchise. In the 1850s and 1860s the Liberals (formerly the Whigs) sought to increase the number of eligible voters still further. The government of William Gladstone, the Liberal leader of the day, was defeated on the issue in 1866, but the following year his political rival Benjamin Disraeli, leader of the Conservatives (formerly the Tories), succeeded in passing a bill which doubled the number of eligible voters. He was subsequently defeated in the election of 1868.

In France in 1848 a cautious electorate chose, as the first president of the Second Republic, Prince Louis Napoleon, who had campaigned on a platform of "law and order" after the violence of the "June Days." During the Second Republic, Louis Napoleon did everything possible to enlarge his power base and popularity. In 1851 he became a virtual dictator, and the following year he assumed the title of Napoleon III, emperor of the French.

For a country long torn by political bloodshed, the Second Empire held out hopes of stability and peace. Napoleon's constitution, like that of his uncle a half-century earlier, offered the appearance of democracy while leaving all effective power in the emperor's hands. Political opposition was suppressed, newspapers censored, the universities strictly controlled. In economic terms, however, Napoleon encouraged private investment and free trade; he used social legislation to retain the support of the working class.

The merits of Napoleon's domestic program were undermined by his international involvements. In his quest for a French empire, he completed the colonization of Algeria. French troops were sent as far afield as Indochina; a century later, the struggle for independence of the French colonies both in Indochina and Algeria proved disastrous. Napoleon's most grandiose scheme, the conquest of Mexico, was equally doomed.

Apart from the joint Franco-British force sent to the Crimea in 1854, the French were no more successful closer at hand. In 1859 the emperor first joined the Piedmontese and then abandoned them. His government's final miscalculation, the war with Prussia of 1870, proved his downfall.

SIR ROBERT PEEL AND THE RISE OF THE POLITICAL PARTY SYSTEM

British success in avoiding the outbreak of widespread public violence in 1848 was due in large part to the country's method of parliamentary government. Popular revolt had been forestalled in 1832, when a Whig majority, convinced that without some reform open class war would become inevitable, passed the Reform Bill (see Part VII, Topic 5). The British parliamentary system, with its two large parties, made possible the discussion of a change of policy and its carrying out, without the elimination of those upholding the minority position. Furthermore the parliamentary debates which led to the bill's passage inevitably reflected public opinion of the times.

Sir Robert Peel (1788–1850), the son of a wealthy manufacturer, was a major reformer in this tradition of realistic politicians. A member of Parliament from the age of 21 and a frequent cabinet minister, Peel evolved into an advocate for Catholic and Jewish rights, an equitable income tax, and penal reform. His best known innovation was his organization of a force of professional policemen for London, known popularly as "Peelers," or "Bobbies."

Repeal of the Corn Laws

Peel served briefly as prime minister in 1834–1835, and after resigning he set about forming a new coalition that would later become the Conservative party. During his second term as prime minister from 1841 to 1846, the repeal of the Corn Laws became the dominant issue in British politics. The Corn Laws, passed in 1815 to protect landowners by imposing a tariff on imported grains, not only caused hardship among the poor but offended liberal free traders. Furthermore, the rise in bread prices which they caused forced employers to pay higher wages to their workers.

Peel supported repeal in response to popular protest and the agitation of the Anti–Corn Law League established in 1839 by Richard Cobden (1804–1865). Peel hoped that increased trade and an income tax would offset the impact of repeal, and the misery caused by the potato famine in Ireland in 1845 convinced him to oppose the agricultural interests in his own party: in 1845, and again in 1846, a blight caused the potato crops in Ireland to fail. In the subsequent famine nearly a million Irish died and over a million emigrated, particularly to the United States. The repeal of the Corn Laws was passed in 1846 after bitter debates in the House of Commons.

The move split Peel's own Tory party and ended his political career. He can have had little doubt of his action's unpopularity with the Tories, many of them landowners with a vested interest in maintaining an artificially high price for domestic grain. He openly acknowledged, however, that his chief motive apart from his belief in free trade was to avoid a class war. The collapse of the Chartist movement two years later underlines the success of his achievement (see Part VII, Topic 8).

By 1850 there existed general public confidence in the ability of the parliamentary system to work out solutions to political problems based on compromises and practical considerations, rather than on theoretical dogmas. The controversy surrounding the Corn Laws contributed to the emergence of new political alignments and parties, but the ensuing battle over further reform was waged, for the most part, in the Houses of Parliament and not in the streets.

BRITAIN IN THE AGE OF VICTORIA AND ALBERT

The nominal head of that Parliament was, of course, the monarch, whose powers were limited but constitutionally significant. Queen Victoria (ruled 1837–1901)

Map 9.1 The Railway System in Britain, Mid-19th Century

brought a welcome stability to her role, both by the sheer length of her reign and by virtue of her public image. In place of the traditions of sovereigns who indulged their own selfish interests, taking lovers and squandering national resources, Victoria deliberately set an example of virtuous behavior.

The Victorian Example

Her own marriage—much of which was lived in the public eye—to Albert of Saxe-Coburg-Gotha (1819–1861), a minor German aristocrat, was tranquil and loving. Indeed, Albert's death in 1861 so devastated Victoria that for some time she hid herself from public life in Windsor Castle, earning the popular title of "the widow of Windsor." For years afterward she continued to have Albert's shaving kit put out each morning. Among the monuments to her late husband which she commissioned are the Albert Memorial in London's Hyde Park, and the nearby Royal Albert Hall.

As wife, mother, and widow, Victoria provided her subjects with an exemplary model for their behavior. She was clearly conscious of her public responsibilities. On ceremonial occasions she was always accompanied by one or two of her numerous children to emphasize the importance of the family (on "Victorian" values, see Part VII, Topic 13). In private, though, she confessed to disliking infants, their constantly waving arms and legs reminding her of frogs.

John Stuart Mill and the Feminist Cause

The placid, confident image that Victoria presented was only one aspect of her age. The rapid development of urban society and the political and economic issues it raised continued to perplex many liberal thinkers. In 1848 the greatest liberal philosopher of his times, John Stuart Mill (1806–1873), published *Principles of Political Economy,* in which he studied the effects of the growth in size and importance of the working class. Mill was also concerned with the theoretical principles of liberalism: *On Liberty,* published in 1859, is the most complete statement of his belief in the inherent value of individuals and their actions, while it also warns against the "tyranny of the majority." Mill took this conviction to its logical consequence both in his own lifestyle and in supporting the cause of women's suffrage.

The young Mill's interest in political philosophy had been first stimulated by his father, who subjected the child to a grueling training in the principles of Jeremy Bentham. After a period in which he became interested in the Romantic ideas of Coleridge, Saint-Simon, and other thinkers, Mill turned to politics, liberalism, and the philosophical thinking behind the French Revolution.

One of his least happy achievements was, in fact, the destruction of his friend Thomas Carlyle's book, *The French Revolution* (1837). Mill had borrowed the book in manuscript form to review and an overzealous maid found the untidy pages lying around in his house and burned them. Carlyle heroically rewrote the entire

Commemorative plate issued for Queen Victoria's Jubilee in 1887.

The British philosopher and economist, John Stuart Mill.

text, later grumbling that he had devoted so much effort to comforting the guilt-torn Mill that he was unable to think much about himself.

Among Mill's closest and most intimate friends was Harriet Taylor (1807–1858), whom he first met in 1829, and to whose influence and help he attributed many of his most important works. They labored together for the cause of women's rights, a movement which became organized in London in the mid-1850s. In contrast to Victorian attitudes toward gender, their partnership and subsequent marriage represented an early example of the feminist ideal of equality of status.

Mill's relationship with the smart and cultivated Taylor had the reluctant sanction of her husband, but caused much public gossip. Combined with his open support of the feminist movement, it made them favorite figures of fun for newspaper cartoonists. In 1833 Taylor and her husband separated, but neither she nor Mill would take the daring step of living together. Only in 1852, two years after her husband's death, did Taylor and Mill marry. Mill conceived of marriage as a voluntary business partnership between equals, one that was dissolvable, and he tried, perhaps excessively, to avoid the conventional relationship between husband and wife in which the power of the male predominated. Before their marriage, he even gave Taylor a kind of contract in which he renounced his rights, financially and sexually, as a husband.

After Taylor's death, Mill devoted considerable energy to the cause of women's rights. In *On the Subjection of Women* (1869), which incorporated many of Taylor's ideas, he stated many of the key doctrines of feminism: injustices in society were the result of the inequality of the sexes; if men were no longer tyrants and women slaves, happiness would increase both at home and in society. Two years before the book's publication, at the time of the great reform debate, Mill was one of the 73 members of Parliament who voted for a provision to introduce female suffrage; 193 voted against, and the measure failed to pass.

With the defeat of the bill, the feminist movement split over whether men should be allowed to continue to serve on its committees. Mill remained an active member of the campaign, however. *On the Subjection of Women* became one of feminism's classic texts, and his death in 1873 was seen as a major setback for the cause.

LIBERALS, CONSERVATIVES, AND THE POLITICS OF REFORM

The campaign for female suffrage waged by Mill and Taylor was part of a larger battle for electoral reform that dominated British political life for almost two decades. The issue of electoral reform brought together on the same side two groups: traditional middle-class liberals and workers. Many of those employed in the textile and manufacturing industries had achieved a measure of economic independence; now they felt unjustly excluded from the political system. The middle-class liberals, for their part, resented the hold that the landed gentry maintained on many institutions. The Anglican Church, for example, was dominated by the younger sons of aristocratic families and was supported by public taxes paid by all citizens, even those who were not members of the Church of England.

The Reform Bill of 1867

In general the Whigs were sympathetic to the cause of reform, but Lord Palmerston (1784–1865), the Whig prime minister for most of the period between 1855 and 1865, was more interested in rousing patriotic fervor at home and supporting nationalist movements abroad. The two rising politicians of the age, the Whig William E. Gladstone (1809–1898) and the Tory Benjamin Disraeli (1804–1881), were more responsive to public demands. In 1866, together with the Whig Prime Minister Lord John Russell, Gladstone introduced a reform bill to widen the suffrage. The measure was defeated and the government fell. The following year, however, a Tory government led by Disraeli introduced its own, more radical reform bill. Disraeli, a consummate politician, realized reform was inevitable and stepped in to claim the credit for it.

The Second Reform Bill of 1867 effectively doubled the number of the electors. All adult males paying ten pounds rent a year in the cities, or twelve pounds a year in the country, could now vote; in effect the measure enfranchised the upper working classes—the "skilled workers"—and the lower middle classes. Parliamentary seats were redistributed, with an increased number going to the populated and industrial north. The results of Disraeli's bill were a long way from universal suffrage: in addition to the poor, half of Britain's citizens—women—remained unenfranchised. The measure was sufficient, though, to satisfy most of the reformers.

Gladstone and Disraeli continued to lead their parties, by now known respectively as the Liberals and Conservatives, in a series of governments that promoted the liberal causes of representative government and free trade. Apart from joining other western European countries in the Crimean War against Russia (see Part VII, Topic 16), Britain avoided involvement in European affairs. Closer to home, the question of whether to grant home rule to Ireland became increasingly controversial. The Irish nationalist leader Charles Stewart Parnell (1846–1891) led the battle from within Parliament in the years following 1877, finally convincing Gladstone to adopt a home rule policy (on the Irish question, see Part VII, Topic 15).

Significant Dates

Britain and France from 1846 to 1871

1846	Repeal of Corn Laws
1848	Louis Napoleon elected president
1852	Louis Napoleon becomes emperor
1856	Paris Peace Conference on Crimean War
1860	Chevalier-Cobden Treaty
1862–1867	French campaign in Mexico
1866	Gladstone's unsuccessful First Reform Bill
1867	Disraeli passes Second Reform Bill
1869	Mill publishes *On the Subjection of Women*
1870–1871	Franco-Prussian War

A trade union membership certificate, 1851.

LOUIS NAPOLEON AND THE SECOND FRENCH REPUBLIC

With the election of Louis Napoleon as president in 1848, after decades of political in-fighting, ideological debate, and upheaval, the French were ready to unite behind a figure who seemed to promise peace, and provide conditions for the growth of prosperity. If their new leader was also able to become an international figure of consequence and place France back on the world stage, so much the better. Napoleon I had, after all, come close to conquering all of Europe. Who could tell what his nephew might accomplish?

Louis Napoleon and Public Opinion

Hopes like these, which Louis Napoleon adroitly fanned, persuaded the electors to trust him when, in the early months of his presidency, he imposed a series of repressive measures. Socialists were expelled from the assembly, press censorship was introduced, and public meetings were restricted. To distract attention, and to win the support of the majority, he appealed to the interests of large sections of the population. Thus the Catholics were pleased when the schools were returned to church control, and when a French military expedition overthrew Mazzini's Roman Republic to restore the pope to power (see Part VII, Topic 8). Other French patriots were also encouraged to see their country reasserting a role in international affairs.

For all his aristocratic origins, Louis Napoleon fully realized the need to establish a broad power base, and he set out to win over the middle class and the workers. The middle class was distracted from its loss of liberties by the enactment of laws encouraging business and trade. The introduction of state-supported old age insurance won him support among the poor. In 1851 he felt sufficiently sure of himself to dissolve the assembly and proclaim a temporary dictatorship; the alleged excuse was that of protecting the rights of the "masses."

Louis Napoleon's confidence was justified. In a plebiscite held in December 1851, an overwhelming majority awarded him unlimited power to create a new constitution. A year later another popular vote approved his assumption of the title Napoleon III, emperor of the French; more than 90 percent of the electors voted in favor. The Second Republic became the Second Empire.

A few lone voices of protest were heard, the most notable that of Victor Hugo (1802–1885), the leading writer of the day. Hugo at first supported Louis Napoleon, but when he realized the authoritarian direction in which the president was moving he changed his mind. In July 1851 he publicly denounced the intentions of the "Little Napoleon." After trying unsuccessfully to organize opposition, Hugo went into exile in the Channel Islands, from where he published works which bitterly attacked the emperor. He returned to France only on the fall of the empire.

Photograph of French Emperor Napoleon III and his wife, the Empress Eugénie.

NAPOLEON III AND THE SECOND EMPIRE

It is worth underlining the implacable hatred of Hugo and other French intellectuals for Napoleon III because it was far from generally shared. For the first half of his reign, the emperor maintained an iron grip on the state while remaining popular and admired. In the 1860s he permitted the transformation of his authoritarian regime into a more liberal rule, in a series of moves which served to pave the way for the Third Republic. With the relaxation of control, opposition to the emperor began to grow in Parliament, in part because it was safer to oppose him and in part to urge him toward more liberal government, but he retained his general popularity. The empire was finally swept away only by the calamitous Franco-Prussian War, in which France was utterly routed.

Louis Napoleon himself remains a complex character. His rise to power shows him as devious. Fully aware of the havoc that his uncle had wreaked on most of Europe, he had no hesitation in playing on French thirst for glory and their highly selective memories. In personal dealings he impressed most of his contemporaries as gentle and charming, albeit a womanizer. Others found him a sensualist, sinister and insincere. Like Napoleon, he claimed to rule as tribune, rising above factions, and expressing the popular will. Yet he lacked his uncle's administrative brilliance, and his attempts to win an empire proved disastrous. Above all, it is difficult to see a consistent vision behind his rule—except that of retaining power by a constant series of manipulations. He was helped by the fact that a weary country seemed willing to be manipulated.

Politics in the Second Empire

The element of deception was present from the beginning of his reign, in the new constitution introduced in January 1852. Like Napoleon's constitution of 1799, it provided for a legislative body to be elected by universal male suffrage. This body had no real power or influence and could approve only measures which were drawn up by a Council of State, itself appointed by the emperor. In any case, elections were controlled, and candidates carefully selected. The emperor kept charge of the army, and of foreign and economic policy. When he desired to "consult" his subjects he could call a referendum, the result of which would be a foregone conclusion.

It is difficult to imagine a more complete rejection of liberal politics, yet this authoritarian regime was combined with a liberal economic policy that explains much of the widespread middle-class support for Napoleon III's rule. A number of successful credit institutions (see Part VII, Topic 12) were created to collect money available for investment; the funds were then used to increase the rate of industrial development and improve services such as the railroads. Private citizens were encouraged to invest by a law that limited their liability, if the company in which they had bought stock ran into debt. The fundamental liberal doctrine of free trade was honored in the signing of a pact with Britain in 1860—the Chevalier-Cobden Treaty—which reduced tariffs on both sides.

All these measures were intended to stimulate the economy and win the backing of the business classes. Meanwhile, other means were used to discourage any possible protests at government high-handedness. For the first decade of the Second Empire, no political opposition was tolerated, the press was censored, and the universities, traditional centers of rebellion, were kept under careful observation. In the years after 1860 there was a steady process of relaxation of these restrictions in an effort to cut off popular resentment before it had a chance to become dangerous. Open debate in the assembly was permitted, and the proceedings were made public.

While the middle classes were happily making money, and the intellectuals effectively silenced, the urban proletariat was provided with new social benefits. Medical facilities, public housing, and homes for the old were built, and in the process many jobs were created. A workers' insurance scheme offered security against loss of earnings in case of injury or ill-health, while a new law recognized workers' rights to certain limited strike action. As for the rural population, whose votes had helped to put Louis Napoleon in power in the first place, they were delighted with the general national prosperity and political stability.

The "Empire" Style

Napoleon III, like many another authoritarian ruler, set out to provide an appropriate setting for his reign. His most lasting legacy, the rebuilding of Paris, served a double purpose, in fact. The broad boulevards, elegant squares, and public parks, designed by Baron Georges Haussmann (1809–1891), give the city its special, personal character. At the same time the streets were intended to be too wide for any future revolutionaries to construct barricades, while the broad, direct routes facilitated the coordinated movement of troops if the need ever arose to put down demonstrations.

The plan was controversial at the time, and remains so still. The shady gardens continue to provide rest and refreshment in warm weather, but the formal squares, crossed by roads leading in several different directions, are apt to become jammed with traffic. The great monumental vistas—Place de la Concorde, Place de l'Étoile, with its Arch of Triumph—were conceived as ceremonial backdrops for imperial ceremonies, rather than as parts of a living city. Haussmann's ideas, which included such practical innovations as clean water supply and sewage systems, influenced designers of other 19th-century urban renewal projects such as those in Rome, Washington, and Mexico City.

Among the new buildings commissioned by the emperor was the Opéra, the Salle Garnier, named after its architect, Charles Garnier (1825–1898), a temple to the middle-class enthusiasm for public entertainment on a grand scale. The elaborate ornamentation visible on the façade of the Opéra is typical of the "Empire" style, with its blend of sober Classical elements and massive, swirling statues. The French use of the theater as political symbol was not limited to Napoleon III. The Bicentennial of the French Revolution in 1989 was marked by the inauguration of a new opera house on the site of the Bastille.

From clothes to furniture, clocks to table settings, the richly elaborate "Empire" style appeared in just about every aspect of daily life. One of its prime promoters was the emperor's Spanish wife, Eugénie (1826–1920). Her ornate silk gowns became famous—and much imitated—throughout Europe, and confirmed France's reputation as the center of high fashion. In contrast to Victoria and Albert, pillars of bourgeois respectability across the Channel, Napoleon and Eugénie set out to create an image of glamour and luxury, a picture which was only slightly marred in the

Boulevard de Sebastopol, Paris, in 1859.

public eye by Napoleon's philanderings. Eugénie's dignified behavior in the face of her husband's conduct won her the approval of many feminists, who applauded her encouragement of improved education for women. On the other hand, the empress was inclined to be narrow-minded, leading the unsuccessful fight to ban Gustave Flaubert's novel *Madame Bovary* (see Part VII, Topic 14).

The excitement generated by the Second Empire and its prosperity subdued early attempts at criticism, but over the long term Napoleon III had to deal with his liberal opponents. Throughout the 1860s, he continued to make concessions to them, which only fed the demands for more reforms. By 1869, opposition had crystallized in the form of a renewed republican party, which at one point actually named a premier. The government introduced an amended constitution, entrusting virtually complete power to Parliament, which was approved by a great margin—even including the opposition leaders, who supported the government. The sudden collapse overnight of the Second Empire was due not to Napoleon III's political difficulties at home but to his failure to win success in France's overseas ventures.

FRANCE AND THE POLITICS OF EMPIRE

Louis Napoleon came to power with the claim that he could renew France's imperial glory. For all his domestic achievements, his mismanagement of foreign policy fatally undermined his popularity. He used the magic name "Bonaparte" to evoke memories of a French empire, but a string of French military losses was more likely to bring Waterloo to mind, and his disappointed subjects did not forgive him.

Matters began promisingly enough. The overthrow of the Roman Republic in 1849 was an early, if easy, victory. It was followed by France's leading role in the Crimean War, in which Russia was defeated. The ensuing peace conference met in Paris in 1856, expansively hosted by the emperor, who used it to demonstrate to his subjects his growing international prestige.

The French in Italy

Among the other European powers represented at the Paris Peace Conference was the small Italian state of Piedmont-Sardinia (see Part VII, Topic 11). Its prime minister, Camillo di Cavour, was trying to rally support in freeing the northern Italian provinces of Lombardy and Venetia from Austrian rule. In 1858, Napoleon III promised Cavour French aid in a war against Austria, in return for which France was to gain Nice and Savoy. More than territorial expansion, the emperor seems to have been motivated by a desire to enhance French prestige. When the war broke out the following year, Napoleon sent troops, and the combined French and Piedmontese forces did drive the Austrians out of Lombardy. At this point, to the general disgust of the supporters of Italian independence, Napoleon III suddenly signed an armistice with the Austrians, and withdrew his troops (see Part VII, Topic 11).

Whatever the consequences of French interventionism were for the Italians, its effect on morale in France was predictable. By opposing Catholic Austria, the emperor had offended Catholics back home. By deserting the Italian cause he confirmed the liberals' mistrust of him. Furthermore, the fighting, though brief, had been ferocious and the losses heavy. The only gains were Savoy and Nice, which France obtained from Piedmont in 1859–1860.

The expansion of French power outside Europe offered easier prospects. Charles X had begun the occupation of Algeria and Napoleon III completed it. French settlements were founded in West Africa and Indochina, although control of Indochina was not completed until the Third Republic. In the Pacific region, New Caledonia was occupied. The prestige that these conquests generated was not matched by any tangible benefits and Napoleon showed little interest in matching the commercial success of the British Empire. Indeed in the long run, the French colonies in Africa and Asia proved disastrous for many nations other than the French. The bloody history of Southeast Asia in the years following World War II, and the violence which ravaged New Caledonia in the late 1980s, are legacies of Napoleon III's attempts to build an empire.

The French in Mexico

His attempt to conquer Mexico was even more disastrous. Mexico had recently won its independence from Spain, and its government was ruled by the revolutionary leader, Benito Juárez. French forces were originally sent in 1862 as part of a joint expedition which also included British and Spanish troops; the motive was to compel the new regime to pay debts it allegedly owed to the countries involved. When it became clear that the French intended to annex the country, the British and Spanish troops returned home. Mexico City was captured; Juárez and his government retreated into the countryside, and the French installed as emperor a

A scene from the Franco-Prussian War: Leon Gambetta escaped by balloon from German-besieged Paris in October 1870.

Hapsburg prince, Maximilian (1832–1867), archduke of Austria and brother of the reigning Hapsburg emperor.

The United States invoked the Monroe Doctrine of 40 years earlier, prohibiting the Europeans from interfering in the affairs of their former colonies in the Western Hemisphere. In 1865, Union troops lately victorious in the American Civil War were despatched toward Mexico, and once again Napoleon III threw in his hand. In 1867 the last French soldiers set off back to France. The hapless Maximilian refused to leave, and remained in the hands of Juárez' men. They shot him. His young wife Carlota (1840–1927) had returned to Europe at her husband's request in a vain attempt to secure aid from Napoleon III and the pope. The news of Maximilian's failure and impending execution drove her hopelessly insane, and she spent the remaining 60 years of her life in seclusion near Brussels.

Napoleon III's final defeat was at the hands of Prussia, the culminating act in the German drive for national unification (see Part VII, Topic 11). From the French viewpoint, the Franco-Prussian War of 1870 was an unmitigated disaster. It ended France's role as the leading power of continental Europe. More immediately, France was invaded by the Prussian Army, Napoleon III was taken prisoner, and Paris was besieged for four terrible months in the winter of 1870. When news of the emperor's surrender of the army at Sedan reached Paris in September 1870, the Second Empire was declared dead, and liberal republicans formed a provisional government. Its first needs were to survive the starvation of the Prussian siege, and to begin the painful process of rebuilding the state.

Britain and France experienced the radical transformations of the years from 1850 to 1870 in very different ways. In one a constitutional monarchy and a parliamentary government presided over the peaceful extension of political power. In the other a charismatic leader offered high hopes but eventual calamity. Britain saw the victory of traditional liberalism and the triumph of compromise. In France, Napoleon III offered something to everyone, with a liberal economy and an authoritarian, aggressive state.

To judge with hindsight is notoriously easy, and the early years of the Second Empire seem to have had a genuine sense of exhilaration, especially when contrasted with the more stolid virtues of the Victorian age in Britain. The French desire for renewed self-esteem, fueled by the domestic successes of Napoleon III's early reign, led to their emperor's attempts to satisfy them abroad. Nor was he responsible for the tragedy of the Franco-Prussian War, which formed part of Bismarck's schemes for the birth of the new German nation. In any case, by 1870 the political balance of power in Europe was radically changed.

Yet the long-term consequences of Britain's success and France's defeat were to prove dire. The blow to French self-esteem left wounds which were reopened in 1914 and again in 1940, in the opening phases of the two world wars, when Anglo-French cooperation was vital. At the same time, pride in the achievements of Victorian Britain was easily converted into a belief in the divine right of the British Empire. The result was an aggressive, arrogant world power. A weakened France left Germany as Britain's chief rival on the European, and eventually world, scene. The German challenge to British superiority became increasingly strident. Eventual conflict between the two seemed inevitable, and in response militarism continued to grow during the last quarter of the 19th century.

Questions for Further Study

1. What are the main factors accounting for the differences in the political life of Britain and France from 1850 to 1870? How much were they the result of differing styles of leadership?
2. How did the Second Empire affect the social and cultural climate in France? What permanent changes, if any, did it leave?
3. What was Louis Napoleon's foreign policy, and what consequences did it have?
4. Why was Disraeli more successful than Gladstone in passing a reform bill, and what did his measure accomplish?

Suggestions for Further Reading

Guerard, A. *Napoleon III*. Westport, CT, 1979.

Joyce, P. *Visions of the People: Industrial England and the Question of Class, c. 1848–1914*. New York, 1991.

Mokyr, J. *Why Ireland Starved: A Quantitative and Analytical History of the Irish Economy, 1800–1850*. London, 1983.

Plessis, Alain. *The Rise and Fall of the Second Empire, 1852–1871*. Cambridge, MA, 1985.

Price, R. *A Social History of Nineteenth-Century France*. New York, 1988.

Seidman, S. *Liberalism and the Origins of European Social Theory*. Berkeley, CA, 1983.

Thompson, F. M. L. *The Rise of Respectable Society: A Social History of Victorian Britain, 1830–1900*. Cambridge, MA, 1988.

VII

Topic 10

Austria and Russia: Conservatism Entrenched

In the decades after 1848, most of Western Europe felt the growing effects of liberalism and nationalism. In Eastern Europe, however, the Hapsburg monarchy fought to limit the consequences of the revolutionary uprisings of 1848 by centralizing the empire. In Russia, virtually untouched by the ferment into which the rest of Europe was plunged, the first signs of a relaxation of autocratic rule appeared. Yet in spite of early reforms, political repression reemerged by the 1880s.

With the overthrow of Metternich in March 1848 and the abdication of Ferdinand I, the new emperor, Franz Josef, hoped that strong central government would provide the empire with greater authority. He believed that a single administration, with uniform laws and a consistent tax structure, would counterbalance the empire's ethnic and linguistic diversity.

Yet ethnic divisions ran too deep for bureaucratic solutions. The non-German-speaking peoples, including Magyars, Czechs, Slovaks, Croats, and Poles, were united in only one respect: their resistance to the German-speaking rulers who governed them from Vienna. In everything else, from territorial borders to school systems, they struggled for independence both from Hapsburg rule and from each other.

The chief opponents of Vienna's supremacy were the Magyars of Hungary. In order to meet some of their demands and still preserve the empire, in 1867 the Austrians—weakened by their defeat in the Austro-Prussian War of 1866 and plagued by economic problems—devised the *Ausgleich* ("Compromise"), which created the Dual Monarchy. Austria and Hungary became two separate nations. Franz Josef, while remaining emperor of Austria, was also king of Hungary.

The Dual Monarchy of the Austro-Hungarian empire was an uneasy attempt to provide an artificial bureaucratic solution to an impossibly complex dilemma. Predictably it provoked demands for similar treatment among other minorities, and required a careful balancing between large ethnic groups such as the Hungarians and smaller ones such as the Slovaks. The Austro-Hungarian empire survived for almost half a century, but its suppression of Slavic minorities fueled continuing resentments.

The Russians found themselves increasingly at odds with the Western European powers. The tough, authoritarian Nicholas I died during the Crimean War of 1853–1856. His successor, Alexander II, at first favored the liberalization of Russian society—if only to prevent spread of the "contagion" of revolution to

Russia. An additional strong motivation was the military ineptness of his army. In 1861 the land-bound serfs were emancipated, but the success of this long-awaited reform was limited. In the absence of a rigorous reshaping of the Russian economy, it merely transferred control over the serfs from their former noble masters to the village communities, or *mirs*, for which they now worked. At the same time, the Emancipation Edict created unrealistic hopes for real change that were further aroused by Alexander's reforms in education and local self-government.

A surge of socialist and intellectual enthusiasm produced by the mood of progress led to open advocacy of extreme radicalism and nihilism, aimed at the dismantling of the state. The official backlash was inevitable. When Alexander II was killed by a terrorist bomb in 1881, his son and successor Alexander III used harsh, autocratic methods to eradicate all liberalism in Russia.

THE AUSTRIAN EMPIRE: A MULTIETHNIC STATE IN THE AGE OF NATIONALISM

In the generation after 1848, in Western Europe, the spirit of nationalism inspired and brought to birth the new nations of Germany and Italy. During the same period, the unity of the Austrian empire was increasingly threatened by the ethnic minorities. They resented the rule of their German-speaking masters, who made up a minority of 23 percent of the population. Austrian domination was chiefly maintained by a careful manipulation of the divisions between the various nationalities. The national and cultural diversity of the territories under Hapsburg rule was, of course, one of the leading factors in the outbreak of revolt there in 1848. Even within each of the three principal geographical areas, Austria itself, Hungary, and Bohemia, there were ethnic tensions that the reassertion of Austrian control only exacerbated.

Pan-Slavism

The broadest of nationalist causes in Eastern Europe was Pan-Slavism, which involved peoples beyond the borders of the Austrian empire itself. Those who considered themselves Slavs included Czechs, Slovaks, Slovenes, Serbs, Croats, and Ruthenians, all of whom were under Austrian rule. The Poles, also Slavs, were divided. Some lived in territories governed by the Hapsburgs, while others were in that part of Poland which remained under Russian control (there were also Poles resident in Prussia). To complicate the situation still further, a growing number of Russian intellectuals began to identify with the cause of Pan-Slavism, and to consider themselves not Russian but Slav.

All of these peoples spoke related languages, and could thereby distinguish themselves from the other groups in Eastern Europe and, more specifically, in the Hapsburg empire. These were the Magyars (Hungarian speakers whose ancestors had settled there in the 9th century), the Italians, and—above all—the German-

Conflict at the University of Vienna during the Revolution of 1848.

Map 10.1 Nationalities in Central and Eastern Europe, c. 1900

speaking ruling class. Yet for all their numbers and nationalist fervor, the various Slavic peoples never managed to forget their own differences and cooperate to throw off Hapsburg rule.

The Austrians, for their part, adroitly exploited national rivalries. Not the least of these was the traditional hostility between the Magyars and the Slavic peoples living in Hungary. In Hapsburg Poland, where Polish nationalist feeling was strong among the aristocracy, the authorities used tensions between the nobles and their serfs to create a class war and keep the country divided.

Yet the events of 1848 provided a warning: even conservative Austria could not maintain a monolithic indifference to the dissatisfactions of its subjects. The sense of a turn of direction was symbolized by the departure from the scene of the two figures who represented the old regime: the emperor Ferdinand I and his chief minister, the orchestrator of the Concert of Europe, Prince Metternich. The crown was assumed by Franz Josef (ruled 1848–1916), then barely 18 years old, while the government of the empire passed into the hands of the archconservative Prince Felix Schwarzenberg (1800–1852). Even Franz Josef's most fervent supporters could hardly have imagined that he would remain Austrian emperor for the better part of 70 years: he died in 1916, in the middle of World War I.

Schwarzenberg intended to forge the basis of unity throughout the empire in two ways: a single system of laws and taxes, and the administration of that system by an absolutist, centralized bureaucracy. His new constitution imposed political uniformity even on regions like Bohemia and Hungary that had won a measure of independence. The railway, which had already begun to revolutionize communications in western Europe, connected many of the chief urban centers under Hapsburg rule. Roads across the Alps, into the Austrian provinces of northern Italy, were improved.

Schwarzenberg died in 1852, before he was able to see his schemes fully implemented. In any case, any thoroughgoing change of government of the kind he contemplated would have required massive bureaucratic reorganization, together with the cooperation of the local officials whose job it was to carry out the reforms. In the end things reverted to their former state: German-speaking regional administrators, who were only nominally responsible to Vienna, continued to run the affairs of peoples whose cultures they looked down on, and whose languages they chose not to speak. Bureaucratic inefficiency, coupled with insensitivity to minority feelings, produced resentment and frustration among Austria's subject peoples.

Franz Josef and Constitutional Reform

In 1859 events in northern Italy brought about a crisis. French forces, with the help of Piedmont-Sardinia, defeated the Austrians and drove them out of Lombardy (see Part VII, Topic 11). Franz Josef, by now old enough to be his own master, and realizing the risk of further rebellions elsewhere in his empire, sought to forestall them by introducing a revised constitution. This document decentralized the government and gave considerable powers to regional assemblies. The reform drew a united burst of hostility from all sides. In the various regions, the nationalists could not agree on who should represent whom; the liberals in Vienna were appalled by the monarch's high-handedness; and bureaucrats throughout the empire protested at the confusion.

In the face of such opposition, within a few months the emperor reversed himself. In February 1861 yet another new constitution was introduced, which created a two-chamber parliament in Vienna: the *Reichsrat*. Having held up the promise of local independence, Franz Josef was now withdrawing it. To make matters worse, his electoral system guaranteed the German speakers a majority in the parliament's lower chamber. Anger among the ethnic minorities ran high, and Hungary's Magyars refused to send representatives. By the fall of 1865 the emperor was forced to admit failure and suspend the constitution.

In the midst of political crisis, troubles abroad once again distracted attention. In his struggle to create a united German nation, Bismarck's plans required the elimination of the only other serious candidate for German leadership, Austria; he therefore sought a military confrontation, since Prussian supremacy was most easily established on the battlefield. By the end of the Austro-Prussian War of 1866 (see Part VII, Topic 11), Austria's defeat left its prestige in the German-speaking world considerably undermined. In addition, the new Kingdom of Italy, which supported Prussia in the war, was rewarded with Venetia, Austria's remaining province in northern Italy. If the emperor was to hold on to the rest of his possessions, a compromise was required.

THE *AUSGLEICH:* ILLUSION OF THE DUAL MONARCHY

The fiercest and most persistent opposition to Austrian rule was in Hungary, where the temporary successes of 1848 fueled an active Magyar independence movement. In 1867, Hungarian nationalist leaders seized on Austria's weakness and forced through a political compromise; the German word for "compromise," *Ausgleich,* is used to refer to the Austro-Hungarian agreement. Franz Josef's wife, Elizabeth, who had actively sympathized with the cause of Italian freedom, was a strong advocate of an independent Hungary.

Hungary and Compromise

In 1867, after Austria's defeat by Prussia, under the Ausgleich Hungary became an autonomous state with its own parliament, with Franz Josef as its king. This inaugurated the Dual Monarchy, whereby the emperor of Austria ruled simultaneously as king of Hungary. Theoretically, joint ministries of the two states, known as the "Delegations," decided questions of finance, foreign policy, and war. In practice, however, most of Hungary's domestic policies were now established internally. The Magyar business class and landowning nobility took control of the Hungarian economy. Foreign policy and defense remained under the control of the Delegations.

As part of the agreement the Romanian, Serbian, and Croatian minorities in Hungary were left to Magyar rule. Most of the other Slavic minorities in the empire, including the Slovenes, Slovaks, and Ruthenians, remained under the Austrians. The Czechs and Poles were given some privileges as a means of buying their collabo-

Significant Dates

Austria and Russia from 1848 to 1867

1848	Overthrow of Metternich and abdication of Ferdinand I
1853–1856	Crimean War
1859	French and Piedmontese drive Austrians out of Lombardy
1861	Emancipation of land-bound serfs in Russia
1864	Alexander establishes local regional councils
1865	Franz Josef suspends constitution; Russia suppresses uprising in Poland
1866	Austro-Prussian War
1867	*Ausgleich* creates Dual Monarchy

ration. In this way the Austrians hoped to eliminate the risk of a Pan-Slavic union. The Hungarians were not a Slavic people, and their treatment of their Slavic minorities was notable for its harshness. A few years later, when the idea of a triple monarchy was voiced, in which the Slavs would have been represented, German speakers and Hungarians alike opposed it.

In Vienna the emperor played liberals and nationalists off against one another. The result was an impotent Austrian parliament, riven by ethnic divisions. Sessions were notorious for violent fighting, not always only verbal, between the delegates, and often paralyzed by noise makers. Effective power was held by the ethnic German bureaucrats, who continued to implement conservative policies. In combined numbers the minorities actually formed a majority in each half of the Dual Monarchy, but they remained as far as ever from self-government.

The Ausgleich was an attempt to buy off the Magyars at the expense of the other ethnic groups. In the long term so precarious a compromise was doomed to failure. The crisis finally came with World War I, when the collapse of the Austro-Hungarian empire, with its labyrinthine interweaving of alliances, brought with it conflict throughout Europe. Yet viewed as a desperate expedient, the Dual Monarchy achieved its limited objectives. For all their mutual mistrust, Austrians and Magyars shared a common interest in making the compromise work. The political stalemate in Austria and the dominance of the upper classes in Hungary reinforced and prolonged the strength of the empire, while at the same time bringing some economic advantages.

Nonetheless, the price of survival was a heavy one, and it was mainly paid by the nationalist minorities. The legacy of hatred and rivalry lasted late into the 20th century. Furthermore, the climate of growing frustration and resentment proved all too fertile for the growth of anti-Semitism. Peoples divided by so much shared in common their irrational discrimination against the Jews. Franz Josef's Vienna became at the same time a center for Jewish cultural life, and a breeding ground of anti-Semitism.

RUSSIA UNDER THE TSARS: THE EMANCIPATION OF THE SERFS

The only two major powers in Europe untouched by revolution in 1848 were Britain and Russia. Britain's way of dealing with the demand for political change was a policy of compromise. Russia's method was the precise reverse: repression. From the time of the Congress of Vienna in 1815, Tsar Alexander I maintained strict authoritarian control at home while generally assuming the role of defender of the conservative cause in Europe. His only significant departures from this, his initial support for Poland and for the Greeks in

A cartoon showing the hierarchical structure of the Russian state.

their war of independence, were sufficiently striking to worry Metternich. All domestic attempts at protest, such as the Decembrists' revolt in 1825, the Polish uprising of 1831, and periodic peasant rebellions, were ruthlessly repressed and served only to reinforce the hostility of Tsar Nicholas I (ruled 1825–1855) to any form of liberalism. Russia's only contributions to the events of 1848–1849 were to help the Austrians regain control in Hungary and to put pressure on Prussia to end the Frankfurt Assembly.

One consequence of so rigid a political stance was economic stagnation. While the rest of Europe underwent the transformation of industrialization, Russia remained primarily an agricultural country, dependent on the labor of the serfs, virtual slaves tied to the land of the great estate owners. A few factories were opened, but the technological progress that was reshaping western Europe made little impact in Russia.

The first impetus for change came as the result of Russia's defeat in a relatively limited conflict, the Crimean War, fought on the Crimean peninsula, which projects into the Black Sea. Formerly part of the crumbling Ottoman Empire, it had been conquered by Russia in 1783. In 1853, Nicholas I decided to use it as the base for further seizure of Ottoman territory in order to gain access to the Mediterranean and establish a presence in the Middle East. This drew the opposition of most of the Western European powers, and when the Turks declared war on Russia, Britain and France joined them in a triple alliance against Nicholas. Superior equipment and more efficient transport gave the Western allies an advantage that allowed them to cut short Russian ambitions. At the Paris Peace Conference of 1856, the terms negotiated underlined Russia's loss of military prestige.

Alexander II and the Serfs

A year before the conference, Nicholas I died, and was succeeded by the more moderate Alexander II (ruled 1855–1881). One of the first acts of the new tsar was to issue a manifesto promising reforms in working conditions, education, and the legal system. His motives were practical as much as humanitarian. Limited but controlled changes imposed from above were better than revolutionary uprisings from below. In any case, although a few aristocratic intellectuals already opposed serfdom on liberal grounds, most Russian nobles reluctantly accepted reform because they were con-

The allied fleet anchored at Balaclava in the Crimea, 1855.

vinced that the old system was making their country uncompetitive. Russia needed to develop urban manufacturing centers; even in farming the easy availability of serf labor had stood in the way of technological progress.

In a climate of hesitation and uncertainty, the tsar emancipated most of the serfs in 1861, a year before Lincoln's Emancipation Proclamation that freed slaves in areas in rebellion in the United States. (Alexander's emancipation of the serfs affected some 52 million, while the number of slaves freed by Lincoln was around 3 million.) Domestic serfs had to continue their service for two more years, and were then freed without any land. The others received most of the land they worked, but they had to redeem it by paying with interest for it over a long period of time, often at inflated prices. The most productive pastures, furthermore, generally remained in the hands of the aristocrats. Control of the land and farming was entrusted to the *mir*, or village commune, whose representatives assigned and redistributed holdings and decided what should be grown. The former serfs paid the landowners for their land, and paid taxes to the government; these "redemption dues" were collected by the mir and handed over to the state.

Far from satisfying liberal hopes, the Emancipation Decree's limited provisions increased resentment. The serfs had no economic independence and no political rights. Instead of working for an aristocratic landowner, they were now tied to their village commune, and spent most of their lives working to pay off their debts. (Freed serfs, on the other hand, could leave to go elsewhere, thus providing a potential labor force for the coming industrial revolution in Russia.) Peasant opposition continued to take the form of open rebellion, which was put down by official intervention.

REFORM AND REACTION UNDER ALEXANDER II

Alexander II's other reforms were more successful in addressing class grievances. In 1864 the *zemstvos* were introduced. These were local regional administrative councils, whose elected members were responsible for the roads, primary schools, and welfare institutions of their districts. Although the zemstvos had no influence on issues outside their immediate sphere of influence, and never led to the formation of a national assembly, they provided a forum for public debate and permitted middle-class professionals such as doctors and lawyers to take part in civic life. All effective power, however, remained in the hands of the tsar and his ministers.

The Russian mathematician, Sofia Kofalevskaya.

Educational reorganization ranged from a notable increase in the number of primary schools to the relaxation of controls in the universities. Alexander himself initiated secondary-level education for girls, and special university courses for women were introduced. Even though some of the changes were short-lasting, they broke down centuries of custom. In 1861, the Medical Surgical Academy in St. Petersburg admitted women for the first time, only to ban them again three years later. Thereafter, women who wanted a medical career left Russia to study in Western Europe. Zurich, one of their most popular refuges, developed a small Russian community which later became a center for political dissidents—among them Lenin.

Alexander II's reforms affected other aspects of Russian life. The legal code was revised. The new system introduced some Western liberal ideas by relaxing punishments for some crimes, although it never challenged the authority of the state. Modernization of the army led to greater efficiency. Most of the recruits were peasants, and the education they received while enrolled helped to increase the general spread of literacy. Beginning in the 1870s, planning and construction began on a vast railroad system, including the vital trans-Siberian line, intended to consolidate links within the vast spaces of Russia itself and to help in the delivery of exports to the West.

The results of Alexander II's reforms were to strengthen both extremes of the political spectrum. In response, police repression was used to control any protests that the apparent relaxation might encourage. A rebellion in the Polish territory under Russian rule was ferociously repressed in 1865. Ten years later the zemstvos were prohibited from even debating national political issues, and censorship was strengthened both in the press and in the universities.

The Radical Movement

The hopes encouraged by the new measures led at the same time to the growth of a radical socialist movement. The intellectual father of Russian socialism was Alexander Herzen (1812–1870), who became an early advocate of the "Westernization" of Russian society. Herzen spent 1848 in revolutionary Paris, and saw the failure there of socialism at the barricades. From exile in London, he wrote and published works in which he hailed the peasant commune as the best basis for socialism in Russia. By building on the communes, the Russians could avoid capitalism which, he believed, disfigured Western society, and move directly from an agricultural to a socialist society.

Herzen's writings and his journal, *The Bell*, inspired a number of intellectuals to live in peasant communities and try to sow the seeds of revolution. Those participating in this "back to the people" movement were called *Narodniki*. The innate conservatism of both the peasants and the authorities stood in the way of any success, however, and Herzen's followers were further inhibited by his strict advocacy of nonviolence.

By the 1870s Herzen's ideas were regarded as old-fashioned, and there developed in reaction a new radical socialism. Younger intellectuals called themselves "nihilists," or believers in nothing. Under the influence of the anarchist philosopher Michail Bakunin (1814–1876), they proposed to use violent means to overthrow the state and revolutionize society (on Bakunin and the anarchists, see Part VII, Topic 19). Although most limited themselves to talking about action, in 1877 Vera Zasulich (1849–1919), a young radical, killed the governor of St. Petersburg for mistreating prisoners. Two years later, some formed a secret society called "The Will of the People." The organization included a large number of young female activists—indeed, a third of its executive committee consisted of women. Its aim was to bring down the government by assassinating the state's leading figures. As socialist extremists moved further from their popular roots, the Pan-Slavic movement encouraged contempt for Western liberalism. The result was an increasing sense of isolation among Russia's intellectuals.

Alexander II's response to the restlessness and threats was at first to return to a policy of repression. By the end of his reign, however, he had reached the conclusion that he needed to give way to liberal sentiment.

The assassination of Alexander II, March 13, 1881.

The change came too late. In March 1881, the Will of the People assassinated the tsar in a bombing plot coordinated by Sophia Perovskaia (1853–1881) and others. Most of those involved in the plot were captured and hanged, and Perovskaia was the first woman executed in Russia for terrorism. On the dead tsar's desk was found legislation for providing Russia with a constitution, awaiting his signature.

The tsar's son and successor, Alexander III (ruled 1881–1894), blamed his father's death on excessive political reform. He had no intention of making the same mistake, and initiated a period of harsh, autocratic rule. Using the police, the army, and the Orthodox Church, he kept a careful watch on all levels of society. Most local control was taken away from the zemstvos, and given back to the landowning aristocrats. Local governors were appointed with wide powers. The persecution of Russia's Jewish population was encouraged. Almost a generation was to pass before socialist and liberal reformers had regained the strength to renew their protests.

At a time of widespread economic growth and rapid social change throughout Western Europe, Austria and Russia succeeded in maintaining conservative and authoritarian rule. In both cases liberal causes met with little success; even the emancipation of Russia's serfs created as many problems as it solved. In both countries nationalism, far from leading to reform, served the purposes of state repression. The Austrians, with Hungarian help, used nationalist divisiveness to keep the regime's opponents divided. In Russia, the strength of pan-Slavic sentiment presented a barrier to the introduction of Western-style reforms.

A number of common factors help to explain the ability of the conservatives to retain power. Russia and the Austro-Hungarian empire were, at least in comparison with the rest of Europe, economically underdeveloped. In conse-

quence, they lacked the great urban centers where a large working class was built up, and reform movements traditionally developed.

In vast countries, covering huge geographical areas, communications were poor. Intellectual life was limited to a handful of cities. Vienna was really the only Austro-Hungarian cultural center on the level of the capitals of western Europe, and Prague was the empire's other artistic center. In Russia, artists and thinkers were divided between Moscow and St. Petersburg. Many creative artists from Eastern Europe left their homelands to make their reputation abroad: the Hungarian Franz Liszt, the Pole Frédéric Chopin, the Russian Ivan Turgenev, all won their fame in Paris. Even as nationalist an author as Feodor Dostoevsky wrote most of his greatest works while living in Western Europe.

The result was an isolationism in political thinking as well as in culture that affected both the countries involved and also those parts of Europe from which they were isolated. To most observers in London, Brussels, or Rome, Russia was a remote and mysterious land, with its own version of Christianity, and a unique set of political institutions. As for the Austro-Hungarian empire, few in the West were likely to fight for the liberation of the Serbs or the Slovaks. The only genuine support for the independence of a people in Eastern Europe, the Greeks, was inspired by a kind of historical Romanticism. Vienna, it is true, played a key role in the formation of late 19th-century culture, but the Hapsburg capital always had an air of exoticism, and in any case showed the empire's multiethnic character at its best.

Yet, ironically enough, when these two conservative giants collapsed, they did so along with much of the rest of the world. It took World War I and its aftermath to depose the Austro-Hungarian emperor and tsar of Holy Mother Russia. The process and its consequences were cataclysmic.

Questions for Further Study

1. What political and economic factors created the differences between the speed of reform in Western Europe and in Austria and Russia?
2. What part did intellectual developments in Russia play in changing Russian society?
3. What was the impact of ethnic differences and the Pan-Slavic movement on the Hapsburg empire? What lasting effects, if any, was it to have in the 20th century?
4. In what ways did the Crimean War influence international European affairs in the mid-19th century?

Suggestions for Further Reading

Cahm, C. *Peter Kropotkin and the Rise of Revolutionary Anarchism*. New York, 1989.

Riasanovsky, N. V. *Russia and the West in the Teaching of the Slavophiles*. Boston, 1980.

Seton-Watson, H. *The Russian Empire, 1801–1917*. Oxford, 1967.

Schorske, Carl E. *Fin-de-Siècle Vienna: Politics and Culture*. New York, 1981.

Stites, R. *The Women's Liberation Movement in Russia: Feminism, Nihilism, and Bolshevism, 1860–1930*. Princeton, NJ, 1978.

Taylor, A. J. P. *The Habsburg Monarchy, 1809–1918*. Baltimore, MD, 1990.

VII

Topic 11

Diplomacy and War: The Age of Nation Building

In the period from 1815 to 1849, those revolutions which had been influenced by a combination of Romanticism and nationalism produced little in the way of concrete political change. After midcentury, however, nationalism shed its Romantic idealism in favor of power politics and emerged as the most effective political ideology in Europe. The new nationalist movements achieved a measure of success denied to the previous generation only because they adopted the ideas and techniques of power politics. The ability of post-1850 leaders to forge national unity depended more on diplomacy and war than on cultural awareness or insurrection.

The amalgam of power politics and nationalism resulted in the creation of national states in Italy and Germany between 1850 and 1871. This was largely the work of two men—the Piedmontese prime minister Camillo Cavour and the Prussian minister-president Otto von Bismarck. Cavour and Bismarck were realists who wanted to achieve results and cared little about the morality of their means.

Cavour, the architect of Italian unification, enhanced Piedmont's prestige among the great powers by strengthening his country's economy and joining Britain and France in the Crimean War. In 1858–1859, Cavour and Napoleon III forged a military alliance and waged a successful war against Austria that allowed Piedmont to annex Lombardy and the smaller states of central Italy. In the following two years, Cavour seized the initiative again in the wake of Giuseppe Garibaldi's conquest of southern Italy and, using the Piedmontese army and the benevolent support of Great Britain, forged the Kingdom of Italy.

The territorial completion of the Italian state took place against the backdrop of German unification. Bismarck, who became minister-president of Prussia in 1862, strengthened the Prussian Army and the power of its king at the expense of constitutional liberalism. In 1866, he waged a brilliant war against Austria that excluded Austrian influence from German affairs and created a Prussian-dominated North German Confederation; the new Italian state, which had joined Prussia in the war, received Venetia as its prize. Finally, in 1870–1871, Bismarck eliminated French opposition to a unified Germany by defeating Napoleon III in another war and bringing all the states of Germany together in a single German empire; Italy, taking advantage of Napoleon's withdrawal of French troops from Rome, seized the Papal States and made Rome the new Italian capital.

While the peoples of Germany and Italy struggled to create new nation-states, the American people fought over the issue of national unity. In the Civil War of 1861–1865, regional loyalties combined with economic interests and moral issues to divide the young republic. As in Europe, the victory of the industrialized North under the leadership of Abraham Lincoln over the agrarian South reflected the triumph of power politics.

ITALY, GERMANY, AND THE UNITED STATES: PATHS TO UNIFICATION

At the opening of the 19th century, Europeans had begun to think increasingly about Italian and German unification. Nevertheless, Metternich's definition of Italy as a "geographical expression" accurately reflected the views of most delegates at the Congress of Vienna. A half-dozen sovereign states occupied the Italian peninsula, while the word "Germany" merely referred to a large area in central Europe made up of 38 independent kingdoms and smaller states. History had given each region a distinctive role which nationalists would later claim as the basis for national self-identity: for Italy, the heritage of the Roman Empire and the Renaissance, for Germany, the memory of the Holy Roman Empire. However, regional divisions and great power intrigue worked to prevent the development of centralized national states such as had emerged in England or France.

The wars of the French Revolution had first sparked nationalist sentiment in Italy and Germany. Napoleon Bonaparte reduced the number of states in the two territories and encouraged Italians and Germans to hope for unification, while the harsher aspects of his occupation elicited a nationalist reaction against French domination. The Congress of Vienna crushed these early nationalist aspirations by reestablishing most of the "legitimate" monarchies of the pre-Napoleonic period and sanctioning the principle of Austrian domination in both regions. Yet the failure of revolutionary movements to prevent the reactionary policies of the restoration of 1815 (see Part VII, Topic 5) did not hinder the growth of nationalist sentiment.

The revolutions of 1848–1849 represented the first major efforts to create national states in Italy and Germany, but the armies of Austria (and, in the case of Mazzini's Roman Republic, of France) proved triumphant. Yet the setbacks of 1849 were not without result. The ill-fated military campaigns of Charles Albert (see Part VII, Topic 8) had at least positioned the Kingdom of Piedmont-Sardinia as the one Italian state committed to fighting for national independence. Similarly, Prussia emerged as the unquestioned leader of the German unification movement, especially because of its role in forging economic unity through the *Zollverein*, or customs union. Together and separately, Piedmont and Prussia would challenge the dominance of the Austrian empire in central Europe.

Significant Dates

Italian Unification

1820–1821	Revolutions in Naples and Piedmont
1831	Young Italy formed by Mazzini
1831–1848	Charles Albert reigns as king of Piedmont-Sardinia
1848–1849	Revolutions in Italy; Piedmontese *Statuto* decreed
1854–1856	Crimean War; 1856 Paris Peace Conference
1858	Treaty of Plombières
1859	Austro-Piedmontese War
1860	Garibaldi's expedition to Sicily
1849–1861	Victor Emmanuel II rules as king of Piedmont-Sardinia
1852–1861	Cavour prime minister of Piedmont-Sardinia
1861	Kingdom of Italy created
1861–1865	American Civil War; Lincoln serves as president
1866	Austro-Prussian War; Italians seize Venice
1870–1871	Franco-Prussian War; Italians seize Rome
1846–1878	Pius IX rules as pope
1861–1878	Victor Emmanuel II rules as king of Italy

Although Cavour and Bismarck revolutionized the European state system, their methods reflected the most conservative aspects of 19th-century liberal philosophy. They preferred monarchy to republicanism, had little faith in democratic principles, and manipulated both popular opinion and constitutional process to achieve their goals. Each believed that history was made from above, by political and economic élites, rather than from below, by "the people."

In the midst of this process of unification in Italy and Germany, the United States also faced its own serious crisis of national unity—the Civil War (1861–1865). In the 1840s and 1850s, American nationalism under the guise of "Manifest Destiny" expanded the boundaries of the United States west to the Pacific coast and south to Mexico. Like Cavour and Bismarck, the American president Abraham Lincoln struggled to impose centralized authority over regional and particularist forces that challenged the unity of this far-flung national state. Yet, although Lincoln also resorted to war and enhanced his executive power in order to preserve the American republic, his political faith derived from democratic principles.

PIEDMONT AND THE ITALIAN QUESTION

The regimes restored to power in Italy in 1815 fell into three geographical-historical categories. The first was northern Italy, which consisted of the provinces of Lombardy-Venetia, given to Austria by the Congress of Vienna, and the Kingdom of Piedmont-Sardinia. The Hapsburgs administered Lombardy-Venetia through a viceroy, and, because of the relative prosperity of the region, its citizens deeply resented Austrian domination. Piedmont, ruled by the House of Savoy, lay in the militarily vital northwest corner of the peninsula, along the French border. The Savoy kings, descended from an old and distinguished dynasty, had for centuries sought to extend their domain across northern Italy.

Map 11.1 The Risorgimento

The second, all of southern Italy, known as the Kingdom of the Two Sicilies, was ruled by the Bourbons of Naples. The kingdom stretched from Naples to Sicily, a vast region of poor peasantry who toiled on the estates of noble absentee landlords. Here, too, the Hapsburgs had considerable influence, as a result of dynastic connections. The Bourbon king, Ferdinand II (ruled 1830–1859), was scornfully dubbed "King Bomba" because he had ruthlessly bombed Sicilian cities in order to crush the 1848 insurrections.

The third, central Italy, included the Papal States and a group of small principalities, the most important of which was the Grand Duchy of Tuscany, also under the influence of Austria. The Papal States were territories of the Catholic Church. Their subjects experienced considerable political repression and widespread poverty, but the rule of the pope was supported by French troops stationed in Rome and the ever-vigilant Austrian Army of Italy.

Giuseppe Mazzini, Italian patriot and a leading theorist of European nationalism.

The Debate over Unification

In addition to the opposition of the monarchs themselves, the movement for Italian unification—known as the *Risorgimento* ("resurgence")—was hampered by strong sectional loyalties. Moreover, Italian patriots were deeply divided over how to achieve the common goal of Italian unity and independence. Three major currents of thought proposed different solutions. The Young Italy organization founded by the nationalist leader Giuseppe Mazzini (see Part VII, Topic 8), called for a popular revolution and the establishment of a republic based on democratic principles and universal suffrage. Mazzini's radical ideas, which served to gain wide acceptance for unification among middle-class Italians, frightened many Italian nationalists who were more conservative in their politics. Mazzini's determination to make Rome the capital of a free Italy also pitted him against supporters of the papacy.

For those who saw the Catholic Church and monarchy as the twin pillars of a united Italy, the liberal priest Vincenzo Gioberti (see Part VII, Topic 8) organized a "Neo-Guelph" movement (during the Middle Ages, the popes and their allies called themselves Guelphs in the struggle with the Holy Roman emperors). Gioberti, a Piedmontese by birth, wanted a confederation of Italian states with the pope as its political head and the king of Piedmont-Sardinia as its military defender. Gioberti based the right of the Italian people to independence on their historical and cultural legacy, which he described in a book entitled *On the Civil and Moral Primacy of the Italians* (1842–1843). The Neo-Guelph movement received momentary encouragement with the election of Pius IX—born Giovanni Mastai-Ferretti (ruled 1846–1878)—as pope in 1846. Although at first Pius seemed to harbor nationalist sentiments, his abandonment of Charles Albert in the war of 1848 doomed Gioberti's hopes. Moreover, most contemporaries believed it impossible to preserve the territories of the Catholic Church in the context of a united Italy, for not only did they cut the peninsula in half, but an ecclesiastical state could not easily coexist within a temporal state.

The third, and ultimately successful, solution for Italian unification was known simply as the "moderate" program. Led by Count Cesare Balbo (1789–1853) and other liberal aristocrats from Piedmont, the moderates rejected both the radical strategies of the Mazzinians and the pro-papal ideas of the Neo-Guelphs. Most of the moderates were Piedmontese patriots who had supported the reforms that Napoleon Bonaparte had brought to Italy. In 1843, Balbo published *The Hopes of Italy*, in which he argued that Piedmont's armies would drive out the Austrians and establish a constitutional monarchy ruled by the Savoy dynasty. Viewed from the perspective of these competing programs for unification, the Risorgimento was a struggle between conflicting political and social philosophies. The more practical and realistic approach was to succeed.

Cavour and the Triumph of the Moderates

The Austro-Piedmontese war of 1848–1849 greatly strengthened the position of the moderates. Although Charles Albert had been soundly defeated in 1849, Piedmont was the only Italian state to preserve its constitution in the wake of the revolutions. The new Piedmontese king, Victor Emmanuel II (ruled as king of Piedmont 1849–1861, as king of Italy 1861–1878), successfully maintained his father's constitution in the face of Austrian threats. It was, however, Camillo Cavour rather than the king who brought the moderate program to fruition.

Count Camillo Benso di Cavour (1810–1861) was born into the Piedmontese nobility, but like many liberal statesmen of his day he was more bourgeois than aristocratic in his values. Cavour was distinctly unimpressive in appearance—he was round in girth and short in stature, and wore sober frock coats and wire-rim spectacles—and an uninspired public speaker. Moreover, he thought of himself first as a Piedmontese and only latterly as an Italian—in fact, he wrote more often in French than in Italian. Cavour possessed a razor-sharp intellect and proved to be one of the 19th century's most adept practitioners of the art of diplomacy. Calculating and single-minded, he never allowed moral principles to interfere with practical considerations. In his youth he had traveled widely, and in England had spent days on end watching the House of Commons from the visitors' gallery. His experience in industry, banking, and farming made him an advocate of economic liberalism.

Camillo di Cavour, the Piedmontese statesman whose skillful diplomacy and manipulation of European opinion laid the basis for Italian unity.

Cavour won election to the Piedmontese Chamber of Deputies in 1848. Two years later Victor Emmanuel II appointed him minister of agriculture and trade, and his efficiency and experience gained him the prime ministership in 1852. In order to carry out an ambitious program of reform aimed at improving the country's economy, he forged an alliance of moderate forces in the Chamber of Deputies that served his purposes for the next decade. Cavour's domestic policies were tied to his Italian strategy, for he used them to enhance Piedmont's prestige in Italy and abroad. Realizing that by itself Piedmont was unable to oust the Austrians, he sought to gain the backing of Europe's great powers for Italian unification under Piedmontese leadership. Although he eventually created the Kingdom of Italy, Cavour had a more limited conception of unification than either Mazzini or Gioberti. At first, his goal was merely to expand Piedmontese territory throughout northern Italy, without involving either the Papal States or the Kingdom of the Two Sicilies.

In order to gain the favor of Britain and France, Cavour brought Piedmont into the Crimean War in 1854. Piedmont had no political stake in Near Eastern affairs, but its military alliance with the Western powers enabled Cavour to take part in the peace conference that convened in Paris in 1856. There Cavour convinced the British to condemn Austrian interference in Italian affairs, and established a friendship with the French emperor. As a young man Napoleon III had taken part in revolutionary uprisings in Italy. Cavour now convinced him to become an advocate of Italian independence.

In July 1858 the two ambitious politicians secretly concluded the Treaty of Plombières, which secured French assistance in fighting a war against Austria. They agreed that if the Franco-Piedmontese alliance proved victorious, Piedmont would annex Lombardy and Venetia and create a kingdom of northern Italy. The new kingdom would then join with the other Italian states in a federation under papal leadership. The Plombières agreement combined aspects of the moderate and the Neo-Guelph programs, the latter a concession to Napoleon's concern for Catholic opinion at home. Napoleon's reward would be the French annexation of Savoy and Nice, both Piedmontese territory. Because Napoleon was sensitive to European opinion, however, he insisted that Austria be made to appear the aggressor, and Cavour agreed to stage an incident designed for that purpose.

In April 1859, Cavour goaded the Austrians into making unacceptable demands against Piedmont. Napoleon immediately went to war against Austria and sent a large army to Italy to fight alongside the Piedmontese. The allies drove quickly through Lombardy, but before the invasion of Venetia could begin Napoleon—horrified at French losses, under pressure from domestic opponents, and nervous about Prussian military movements on the Rhine—unexpectedly concluded a separate armistice with the Austrians. The armistice of Villafranca, signed by Napoleon and the Austrian Emperor Franz Josef in July without Cavour's consent, violated the Plombières agreement—Austria agreed to cede Lombardy but not Venetia. Cavour, outraged at Napoleon's perfidy and Victor Emmanuel's acquiescence, submitted his resignation as prime minister.

Cavour himself had secretly made plans to go beyond the terms of the Plombières agreement. Even before Lombardy had been liberated, he had arranged uprisings to overthrow the monarchs of the central Italian duchies. After Villafranca, Cavour's agents aroused the inhabitants of the duchies to demand to be incorporated in the Kingdom of Piedmont. In January, Cavour—now back in office—put aside his grievance against Napoleon and secured French agreement to allow the Piedmontese annexation of the duchies. Cavour then manipulated local plebiscites to give the appearance of overwhelming public endorsement for his action.

CAVOUR V. GARIBALDI: UNIFICATION ACHIEVED

Cavour's machinations had largely determined the first phase of the Risorgimento. In 1860, however, he began to respond to events as leadership of the unification movement was unexpectedly grasped by Giuseppe Garibaldi (1807–1882). Unlike the unscrupulous and

Giuseppe Garibaldi conquered southern Italy and forced Cavour to include it in the united kingdom. This photo shows him wearing his South American poncho.

plotting Cavour, Garibaldi was an uncomplicated idealist—he had, noted the British poet Alfred Tennyson, "the divine stupidity of a hero." The son of a sea captain, from whom he inherited a love of adventure, Garibaldi had already become a popular figure who fought on behalf of Italy's common people. A populist in the Mazzinian mold, Garibaldi wanted a democratic republic, but his first goal was to secure Italian unification.

In the 1830s, after the failure of an uprising in which he participated, Garibaldi fled to South America, where he and his Brazilian wife Anita took part in a number of revolutions. While fighting in the jungles of Brazil and Uruguay, Garibaldi developed the tactics of guerrilla insurrection. With the outbreak of the 1848 revolutions he came back to Italy and raised a volunteer army in support of Charles Albert's war against Austria. When that campaign collapsed, he joined Mazzini in Rome and coordinated the defense of the republic. In 1859 Garibaldi led another volunteer force in the Austro-Piedmontese war.

The meeting of Garibaldi and Victor Emmanuel II in 1860, represented here in a contemporary engraving, was the culminating moment of Italian unification.

Garibaldi and the Red Shirts

Garibaldi was able to seize the initiative from Cavour because he conceived of Italian unity as embracing all existing regions, including the south. He planned an invasion of the Bourbon kingdom, starting from the island of Sicily and working his way northward. Cavour, who learned of the plans in the spring of 1860, worried about two things: Garibaldi's Mazzinian beliefs, and the possibility that Garibaldi would try to take Rome—a move that would certainly bring intervention by Napoleon III. Cavour decided, therefore, to make his own plans. While supplying weapons to Garibaldi and supporting his efforts to recruit an army of about 1000 "Red Shirts," he also secretly ordered the Piedmontese Navy to sink Garibaldi's ships if they turned toward Rome. (The term "Red Shirts" was derived from the fact that while in South America the only uniforms Garibaldi could afford to provide for his men were butcher's shirts, which were red in color; he dressed his men the same way.)

In May 1860, Garibaldi's expedition reached Sicily. The Bourbons had a considerable garrison stationed there, far outnumbering the Red Shirt forces, but Garibaldi managed to outflank them. With additional troop strength recruited from the local population, he conquered all of Sicily. He then landed on the mainland in September and seized the city of Naples, where he established a temporary government for the former Kingdom of the Two Sicilies.

As Garibaldi moved up the mainland, Cavour sent a Piedmontese army down into the Papal States—but while claiming that he wanted to secure the papacy against a possible attack from Garibaldi, he quickly occupied the Papal States, leaving Pope Pius IX only Rome itself and the territory immediately around the city.

The most dramatic moment in the Risorgimento took place in October, when the armies of Garibaldi and King Victor Emmanuel II met at Teano, north of Naples. The meeting between the leader of the radical movement and the king, the symbolic head of the moderates, could have resulted in a disastrous civil war. The day was saved, however, because Garibaldi, who placed the unity of Italy above all else, surrendered the lands he had conquered to Victor Emmanuel. Garibaldi himself remained a controversial figure in the Risorgimento, finally retiring to self-imposed exile on the island of Caprera. The Kingdom of Italy was established in March 1861, with Victor Emmanuel II as its sovereign and Cavour as its first prime minister. Charles Albert's *statuto* of 1848 became, with minor modifications, the Italian constitution.

As soon as the new nation had been proclaimed, it found itself overwhelmed with an array of serious domestic challenges. Italy lost its most adept political leader when Cavour died that May. Deeply rooted regional loyalties delayed the development of a sense of national identity, a fact poignantly underscored by the comment of one Piedmontese nobleman in 1861: "We have made Italy—now we must make Italians." Although a national economy had been created on paper, the differences between the northern and southern regions grew even sharper. In the North, capitalist farming was already widespread and a nascent industrial base emerging, while in the South agrarian poverty was chronic and disease and illiteracy were widespread. Suspicion and resentment of government compounded the fact that most Italians had no real political experience with parliamentary systems. Indeed, the bulk of the citizens were denied the right to vote, and the new parliament proved excruciatingly slow in coming to grips with such staggering problems. The challenges of nationhood would sorely test the new Italian leadership over the next half-century.

BISMARCK AND THE STRUGGLE FOR POWER IN PRUSSIA

The Vienna settlement of 1815 did not completely restore the prerevolutionary situation in Germany. The Holy Roman Empire, which Napoleon had dissolved, was too unwieldy to resurrect. Instead, a new German Confederation comprising 39 independent states was established. The members of the confederation varied greatly in status, from tiny states ruled by the Thuringian princes to the much larger and powerful kingdoms of Prussia and Bavaria. All members were represented in a parliament, known as the "Diet," which assembled periodically at Frankfurt to discuss common issues. Austria, technically a part of the confederation, dominated German affairs and its ambassador served as the confederation's permanent president. Religious differences reinforced Austrian control: since Prussia and the surrounding northern states were Protestant, Austria could present itself as the protector of the southern Catholic states. Austrian domination of the German Confederation was even more complete than its control of Italian affairs.

Prussian Ambitions and the German Confederation

On the surface, the parallels between the German and the Italian situations seemed obvious. Prussia's role was similar to that of Piedmont in Italy: Prussia was the only state capable of challenging Austrian preponderance in the German Confederation. The House of Hohenzollern, Prussia's autocratic dynasty, had greatly expanded its domains over the centuries, and King Friedrich Wilhelm IV (ruled 1840–1861) thought in terms of extending Hohenzollern authority through most of Germany. The major difference between the two ambitious states was one of scale and power, for while Piedmont had not been strong enough to best Austria by itself, Prussian industrial and military resources made it a formidable antagonist.

Dynastic ambition rather than the ideals of German nationalism put Prussia in the forefront of the German unification movement. The core of the kingdom's nobility, the conservative landowning *Junkers* from East Prussia, were narrowly insular in their outlook and hardly thought of themselves as "Germans." The middle classes, on the other hand, were vigorous advocates of both political liberalism and nationalism, as they were elsewhere in Europe. As far back as 1818, Prussian merchants had actively sponsored a free trade movement that was gradually extended into the *Zollverein,* or customs union, among neighboring states. The middle classes quickly came to see the economic possibilities of political unity. In deliberately keeping Austria out of the customs union, the Zollverein implemented on the economic level what political nationalists called the *Kleindeutsch,* or "Small Germany," approach to German unification (see Part VII, Topic 8).

During the revolutions of 1848–1849, the nobility and the military had blocked middle-class efforts to give Prussia a constitutional government and unify Germany. The reactionaries persuaded Friedrich Wilhelm to withdraw his support for a liberal constitution.

Later in 1849, with the revolution behind him, Friedrich Wilhelm issued a conservative constitution. This document established a parliament with two chambers, similar to that of the Piedmontese constitution of 1848: an upper house, the *Herrenhaus*, appointed by the king and an elected lower house known as the *Landtag*. Elections were in theory on the basis of universal male suffrage, but a complicated method of indirect voting kept poorer citizens greatly underrepresented and gave the advantage to the upper classes. Royal power remained far-reaching, and even in budget appropriations—a function that liberal constitutions generally reserved for the lower houses of parliament—the powers of the Landtag were unclear. Prussian liberals, resentful of the conservative nature of the constitution, worked to clarify budget procedures in order to assert parliamentary control over government spending.

Friedrich Wilhelm had turned down the Frankfurt Assembly's offer of the German crown in March 1849 (see Part VII, Topic 8) because he refused to accept the principle of popular sovereignty. He did not, however, reject the notion of German unification under Prussian

Significant Dates

German Unification

1834	Zollverein created
1840–1861	Friedrich Wilhelm IV rules as king of Prussia
1848–1849	Revolutions in Germany; 1849 Prussian constitution issued
1861–1888	Wilhelm I rules as king of Prussia
1866	Austro-Prussian War; North German Confederation created
1862–1870	Bismarck serves as minister of Prussia
1870–1871	Franco-Prussian War; German empire created

DOCUMENTS ON HISTORY

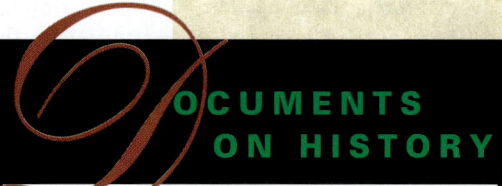

The Risorgimento

The Italian movement for liberation and unification was in one sense an ideological struggle among a series of competing philosophies of government and society. From the time of the Congress of Vienna in 1815, Italian patriots argued about the methods that should be employed to achieve their goals and the kind of state that should govern a unified nation.

THE REVOLUTIONARY VISION

Santorre di Santarosa (1783–1825) was a young army officer in Piedmont-Sardinia and a liberal patriot. In 1821 he joined in a conspiracy that sought to force a constitution on his country and drive Austria from Italy. Here are his views on the Italian question after the failed revolution.

Italians must examine their country's situation and the weaknesses exposed by the revolt. Ours was the first revolution for centuries which was attempted in Italy without foreign help; it was the first in which two Italian peoples worked together at the two extremities of our peninsula. Its result, I know too well, has been to subject Italy entirely to Austria; but let the Austrians beware; Italy is conquered, but not subdued. Besides, what was Italy before July 1820? Had it not already been enslaved to the Austrian Emperor by the courts of Naples and Turin when they promised him to refuse to their people any beneficial political institutions? Our late misfortunes have only rendered our position clearer, our servitude more direct, our chains more obvious. . . .

The emancipation of Italy will occur in this present century; the signal has already been given. Our enemies may prepare at leisure their proscription lists, and docile Italian princes may continue to serve Austria, for they would sooner reign by her strength than by law. The Austrians may leave them to do so and thus begin to reap the fruits of their blindness. But all are deceived, because our passion for national independence feeds on the sacrifices which it imposes on us. Austria may retard the moment, but that will serve only to make the explosion more terrible. Our ancestors have given us great examples which will not be wasted; and when another European war shall arrive, when Austria then demands our children and money to support her cause, Italians will perhaps know better how to employ their resources.

Arbitrary royal rule is now confusing the great issue which confronts Europe. Italy is more involved in this than other nations. We have to conquer our national identity and win internal liberties, both at the same time.

From Denis Mack Smith, ed., *The Making of Italy 1796–1870.* Harper & Row.

YOUNG ITALY

The nationalist leader Giuseppe Mazzini founded the Young Italy society in 1831 as a vehicle for coordinating patriotic revolution throughout Italy. His goal was the creation of a unified republic.

It was during these months of imprisonment that I conceived the plan of the association of Young Italy *(La Giovine Italia)*. I meditated deeply upon the principles upon which to base the organization of the party, the aim and purpose of its labors—which I intended should be publicly declared—the method of its formation, the individuals to be selected to aid me in its creation, and the possibility of linking its operations with those of the existing revolutionary elements of Europe.

We were few in number, young in years, and of limited means and influence; but I believed the whole problem to consist in appealing to the true instincts and tendencies of the Italian heart, mute at that time, but revealed to us both by history and our own previsions of the future. Our strength must lie in our right appreciation of what those instincts and tendencies really were.

All great national enterprises have ever been originated by men of the people, whose sole strength lay in that power of *faith* and of *will*, which neither counts obstacles nor measures time. Men of means and influence follow after, either to support and carry on the movement created by the first, or, as too often happens, to divert it from its original aim. . . .

At that time even the immature conception inspired me with a mighty hope that flashed before my spirit like a star. I saw regenerate Italy becoming at one bound the missionary of a religion of progress and fraternity, far grander and vaster than that she gave to humanity in the past. . . .

Why should not a new Rome, the Rome of the Italian people—portents of whose coming I deemed I saw—arise to create a third and still vaster Unity; to link together and harmonize earth and heaven, right [law] and duty; and utter, not to individuals but to peoples, the great word Association—to make known to free men and equal their mission here below?

From Denis Mack Smith, ed., *The Making of Italy 1796–1870.* Harper & Row.

GIOBERTI'S NEO-GUELPH IDEA

Vincenzo Gioberti's notion that only the pope could act as symbolic leader of a federated Italy of autonomous princes was widely accepted by Catholics and monarchists but its credibility collapsed in the wake of the 1848 revolution, when Pius IX abandoned the patriotic cause.

I propose to prove that Italy contains within herself, above all through religion, all the conditions required for her national and political resurrection or risorgimento, and that to bring this about she has no need of revolutions within and still less of foreign invasions or foreign exemplars. And to begin with I say that Italy must first and foremost regain her life as a nation; and that her life as a nation cannot come into being without some degree of union between her various members. This union can be interpreted and

continued next page

established in various ways, but, however it is achieved, it is a necessity, and if it fails our nation will be weakened and enfeebled beyond repair. . . .

Supposing we succeeded in putting an end to the present division in Italy by revolutionary means? Far from achieving the union we desire, we would be opening the door to fresh disorders. For political union cannot bring happiness to a people if it is confused and vacillating instead of tranquil and stable. The principle of public peace and security must be sought in the sovereign power, whatever form it may take; because without sovereignty there is no order, and without order there is neither peace nor security nor free living nor any other civil good. The sovereign power is based partly on moral force, that is to say on law, and partly on material force, that is to say on the army; and although, given human wickedness, arms are needed to protect public opinion, they cannot replace it, for it is impossible to restrain a few malcontents unless there is a general consensus among many men of good will. Only moral authority can justify a sovereign power, it being inconsistent that others should be expected to obey a system of rule that they think it morally legitimate to offend or annihilate. . . .

That the Pope is naturally, and should be effectively, the civil head of Italy is a truth forecast in the nature of things, confirmed by many centuries of history, recognized on past occasions by the peoples and princes of our land, and only thrown into doubt by those commentators who drank at foreign springs and diverted their poison to the motherland. Nor, to achieve this confederation, is there any need for the Pope to receive or take over any new power, but only to revive an ancient and inalienable right that has merely been interrupted. This selfsame right has been exercised in many ways, but always directed to one end, namely that of bringing the Italian states together in union. Thus, if Leo III provided for Italy's salvation by reviving the Empire and crowning Charlemagne (in which we should admire the intention rather than the outcome), at a later date Alexander III championed freedom by opposing that Emperor's degenerate successors. Alexander precisely obtained his intention by forming the Lombard cities into a League of which he was supreme head and military chief; and if this League was transitory and embraced only a part of Italy, the fault was certainly not that of the Pope.

The benefits Italy would gain from a political confederation under the moderating authority of the pontiff are beyond enumeration.

CAVOUR'S REALISM

Count Camillo di Cavour, prime minister of Piedmont and architect of Italian unity, was above all a realist with a practical sense of the possible. In this famous article, dealing ostensibly with railroads, he explained the idea of a gradual program of moderate development for unification under the leadership of the Piedmontese monarch.

If the future holds a happy fortune for Italy, if this fair country, so one may hope, is destined to regain her nationality, it can only be the consequence of a remodeling of Europe, or as a result of one of those great providential explosions in which the mere ability to move troops quickly by rail will be unimportant. The time of conspiracies has passed; the emancipation of peoples cannot result from mere plots or from a surprise attack. It has become the necessary consequence of the progress of Christian civilization and the spread of enlightenment. Once the hour of deliverance sounds, the material forces which governments possess will be powerless to keep conquered nations in bondage. Moral forces are growing daily which sooner or later, with the aid of providence, must cause a political upheaval in Europe; and governments will then have to yield. . . .

All history proves that no people can attain a high degree of intelligence and morality unless the feeling of its nationality is strongly developed. This remarkable fact is a necessary consequence of the laws which govern human nature. The intellectual life of the masses moves within a very limited range of ideas. Among the ideas which they are capable of acquiring, the noblest and most elevated are first those of religion, then those of country and nationality. . . .

[I]t seems likely that the precious triumph of our nationality cannot be realized except by the combined action of all the live forces in the country, that is to say, of the national rulers openly supported by every party. The history of the last thirty years, as well as an analysis of the various elements in Italian society, will prove that military or democratic revolutions can have little success in Italy. All true friends of the country must therefore reject such means as useless. They must recognize that they cannot truly help their fatherland except by gathering in support of legitimate monarchs who have their roots deep in the national soil. . . .

But more than by any other administrative reform, as much perhaps as by liberal political concessions, the building of the railways will help to consolidate the mutual confidence between governments and people, and this is the basis of our hopes for the future. These governments have the destiny of their peoples in trust, and railway building is therefore a powerful instrument of progress which testifies to the benevolent intentions of each government and the security they feel. On their side the people will be grateful for this and will come to hold their sovereigns in complete trust; docile, but full of enthusiasm, they will let themselves be guided by their rulers in the acquisition of national independence.

GARIBALDI AND VICTOR EMMANUEL

Giuseppe Garibaldi, the heroic guerrilla leader, had begun his career as a follower of Mazzini. After Garibaldi's troops wrested Sicily and southern Italy from the Bourbons in 1860, he made the fateful decision to turn his conquests over to King Victor Emmanuel of Piedmont in order to secure the unification of the country. The two men met at Teano on the Volturno River on October 26, 1860, as described here by British historian George Macaulay Trevelyan:

So the early morning wore on, while regiment after regiment of the Royal army marched past the Liberator. It was a damp autumn air, and Garibaldi was not only wearing his *poncho*, but had in homely fashion bound a coloured handkerchief over his head. His staff, in their war-stained red shirts, presented a curious contrast to the brilliant uniforms that were filing by them hour by hour. Suddenly the strains of the Royal march were heard, and the cry arose, "The King! The King is coming!" Garibaldi and his staff mounted their horses and rode forward to the edge of the road. Victor Emmanuel, on a prancing Arab, dashed up to meet them. The Dictator, sweeping his hat off his kerchiefed head, cried aloud—"*Saluto il primo Re d'Italia*"—"I hail the first King of Italy." The King stretched out his hand and the two men clasped and held hands for more than a minute.

"*Come state, caro Garibaldi?*" [How are you, dear Garibaldi?]

"*Bene, Maestà, e Lei?*" [Well, your Majesty, and yourself?]

"*Benone.*" [Very well.]

Then they rode on together, and the two staffs behind them, red shirts side by side with resplendent uniforms, crosses, and cordons of honour. It was an epitome of the union of

continued next page

conservative and revolutionary forces that had crushed the obscurantists and expelled the foreigners. The constrained conversation between the two groups betrayed the heart-burnings on either side and the grudging sacrifices that each was making to the other. But although there was cold politeness where there should have been enthusiasm, none the less that ride together was the making of Italy, and seen down history's lengthening vista, remains evermore a goodly sight.

After a while Garibaldi and his men turned off the road to the left and made their way back by country lanes to Calvi, while the King held on to Teano. "Garibaldi's countenance," writes Mario, "was full of melancholy sweetness. Never did I feel drawn to him with such tenderness." He said little that evening to his friends. Next morning they met Jessie Mario, who had crossed the Volturno to provide hospital arrangements north of the river. "My wounded," said Garibaldi to her somewhat sternly, "are all on the south of the Volturno." And then, relapsing into his gentlest mood, he added, "Jessie, they have sent us to the rear" (*"ci hanno messi alla coda"*). During their ride together Victor Emmanuel had told him in soft words the hard decree that the Royal army would take over all the operations of war and that the Garibaldini were no longer required.

From George Macaulay Trevelyan, *Garibaldi and the Making of Italy* (London: Longmans, Green and Co., 1911), 271–272.

leadership from above, although he preferred to achieve the goal in cooperation with Austria. In 1849, the Prussian chief minister, Josef von Radowitz (1797–1853), presented the king with a unification plan that called for the creation of a single German government based on the federal system, headed by Prussia but in permanent union with Austria. Foreign relations and military affairs would be conducted jointly by representatives of each state. Many of the smaller German states joined the union, but some of the larger ones, such as Bavaria, refused to adopt the plan. Austria rejected the Prussian proposal outright, and Friedrich Wilhelm backed down. In November he dismissed Radowitz and, in the face of an Austrian threat to go to war, humiliated himself by agreeing to a series of terms dictated at a meeting in Olmütz.

Bismarck: The Iron Chancellor

The "humiliation of Olmütz" weakened Prussia's self-appointed role as the leader of German unification. Not only did Friedrich Wilhelm's foreign policy fail to inspire confidence, but the unhappy monarch was afflicted with periodic bouts of insanity. In 1858 his brother Wilhelm was made regent, and in 1861 he succeeded his brother as king.

Wilhelm I (ruled 1861–1888 as king of Prussia, 1871–1888 as emperor of Germany), a soldier by training, was no less conservative and autocratic than his brother. In February 1860, he sent a controversial military reform bill to the Landtag. With the shadow of Olmütz still looming, he proposed a new budget meant to double the size of the Prussian Army and raise the terms of required military duty from two to three years. He also wanted to abolish the reserve militia, for he regarded its unprofessional civilian soldiers with disdain.

For the middle-class liberals who represented a majority in the Landtag, the reorganization bill presented a unique opportunity to assert the budgetary authority of parliament over the king, as well as to strike a blow against the influence of the military. Liberal opposition succeeded in forcing Friedrich Wilhelm to withdraw the measure, and in 1862 a similar measure was also defeated. Wilhelm dissolved the Landtag and called for new elections, but he was further embittered when an even larger liberal majority was returned. So frustrated was the king that he came close to renouncing the throne. Finally he decided to appoint Count Otto von Bismarck (1815–1898) as his new minister-president in an effort to resolve what had become a major constitutional crisis. Bismarck's own views on unification and his political philosophy seemed well suited to the moment. He envisioned a Prussian-dominated Germany from which Austria would have to be ejected by force, and he detested the liberals.

Bismarck's influence on the course of modern German history cannot be exaggerated. In appearance he was the exact opposite of Cavour: a towering and vigorous man, he seemed the embodiment of the patriarchal landowning class of Junkers from which he came. Yet, while more conservative than Cavour in his

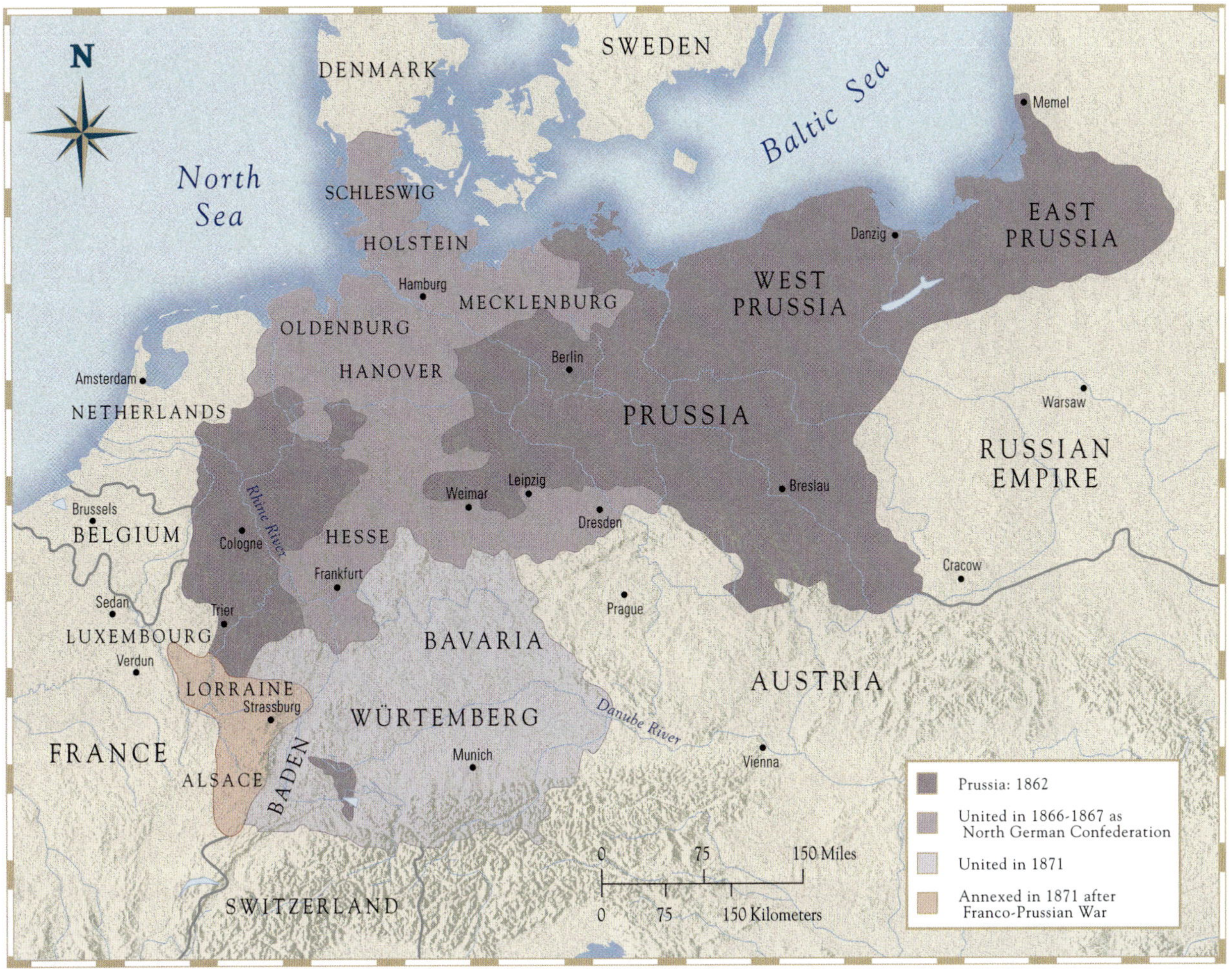

Map 11.2 Unification of Germany

politics, he had none of the narrowness of vision of the Prussian élite—his service in the Frankfurt Diet had given him a deep awareness of German affairs, while his experience as Prussian ambassador first to Russia and then to France had broadened his knowledge of European diplomacy. Flexible rather than rigid, he could nevertheless be unbending in the face of opposition. He cared little for constitutions and disdained liberals as impractical idealists. Like Cavour, Bismarck thrived on the intricacies and maneuverings of power politics.

Prussian liberals proved to be his bitterest enemies. He understood, however, that the industrial and financial expertise of the middle classes was essential to a strong Prussia, and that they themselves were the major advocates of national unification. At first Bismarck saw unification only in terms of Prussian dominance over the Protestant states of the north, and only gradually did his perspective widen to embrace all of Germany. He understood, too, that unification required the elimination of Austria from German affairs.

Bismarck saw the king's army reorganization bill as essential to the extension of Prussian power, for he was determined to give Prussia a military force capable of defeating the Austrian empire. Bismarck sidestepped the Landtag altogether not only by continuing to collect taxes but by raising funds for the army through the sale of bonds in government railroads and the sale of mines and iron works. The liberals attacked Bismarck's subversion of the constitutional process, but both he and the king ignored them. More difficult to ignore were the liberal views of Victoria, the princess of Hohenzollern (1840–1901), the English-born wife of Crown Prince Friedrich (1831–1888), the heir apparent, who ruled for only three months as German emperor before his death in 1888. This daughter of Britain's Queen Victoria was highly cultured and knowledgeable about politics and encouraged her husband to favor a unified German state free from military influence.

Bismarck viewed the liberal opposition as shortsighted obstructionists who failed to understand power

The proclamation of King Wilhelm I of Prussia as emperor of Germany in the Palace of Versailles.

Otto von Bismarck, minister-president of Prussia whose policies of diplomacy and war united Germany.

politics. He proclaimed unabashedly that only "iron and blood," not parliamentary speeches, would unify Germany. Constitutional theory, he told the Landtag, must give way to the necessities of military strength. Bismarck was certain that victory on the battlefield would convince the liberals that his budget manipulations were irrelevant.

The Seven Weeks' War

The war with Austria that Bismarck wanted began to take shape in the 1860s, and had its roots in the so-called "Schleswig-Holstein question." Years later, the British prime minister of the day, Lord Palmerston, remarked that the Schleswig-Holstein affair was so complicated that only three people had ever fully understood it: one of them was dead, a second had become insane, and the third—Palmerston himself—had forgotten the details.

The international status of these two duchies, both administered by the Danish king, was uncertain. Holstein, predominantly German-speaking, was a member of the German Confederation, but Schleswig, inhabited by Danes as well as Germans, was not. A crisis broke out in 1863, when Denmark annexed Schleswig. On Bismarck's suggestion, Prussia and Austria fought a joint war to reclaim the two provinces. After peace had been made, Austria and Prussia agreed to a joint administration of Schleswig-Holstein.

As Bismarck anticipated, disagreement over the future status of the provinces increased tensions between the two powers. Indeed, the Austrians soon demanded the union of Schleswig and Holstein as an independent state under a German monarch; Bismarck, however, wanted special economic privileges designed to integrate the region into the Prussian sphere. In 1865, the Convention of Gastein placed Holstein under Austrian administration and Schleswig under Prussian authority. Disputes between Austria and Prussia followed, and Bismarck soon found a suitable pretext for war with Austria.

Bismarck first cleared the way by ensuring that none of the other powers would intervene on Austria's side. Tsar Alexander II was likely to stay neutral, since Bismarck had assisted the Russians in crushing a revolt in their area of Poland in 1863. He was uncertain, however, of Napoleon III, and in 1865 he met secretly with Napoleon at Biarritz to discuss the situation. Napoleon assured Bismarck that he would remain neutral in a war between Prussia and Austria, and was made to believe that France would get land along the Rhine in return—a promise Bismarck had no intention of keeping. Napoleon expected, in any case, to secure Belgium no matter who won, for the Austrians had also promised the territory to France. In 1866 Bismarck, encouraged by Napoleon, offered Italy the province of Venetia in return for Italian help in the war he was preparing against Austria.

On June 1, 1866, Bismarck ordered the Prussian Army into Holstein after alleging that Austria had violated the Convention of Gastein. The Austrians responded by pushing the German Confederation into war against Prussia. Elated, Bismarck announced the end of the confederation and declared war against Austria.

Bismarck couched Prussian aggression in nationalist rhetoric, asserting that the future of Germany hung in the balance. Moving troops by rail, and employing the new breech-loading "needle" gun—Prussia was the first nation to do so—Count Helmuth von Moltke (1800–1891), chief of the Prussian general staff, stunned all of Europe by swiftly reducing one of the most powerful empires in Europe to total defeat. The effect of the Austro-Prussian War—known as the "Seven Weeks' War"—on subsequent European history cannot be overestimated, for it shifted the balance of power in central Europe.

Bismarck chose to deal reasonably with vanquished Austria. The Treaty of Prague, signed in August 1866, did not require Austria to pay reparations, and no part of its territory other than Venetia—ceded as promised to the Italians—was lost. On the other hand, Vienna had to agree to the dissolution of the German Confederation and to renounce its interest in Germany. Prussia annexed Schleswig-Holstein and some of the other states in northern Germany. The Catholic states in the south, which had supported Austria, were forced to enter into military alliances with Prussia.

Bismarck then forced all German states north of the river Main into a new North German Confederation, with the king of Prussia as its president and Bismarck as its chancellor. While its member states still controlled local affairs, military and foreign policy was in the hands of the central government. The confederation's parliament had two chambers, an upper house known as the *Bundesrat*, representing the states, and a lower house, the *Reichstag*, elected by universal male suffrage. The constitution granted extensive powers to the king of Prussia.

THE BIRTH OF THE SECOND REICH

Bismarck no doubt saw the North German Confederation as a temporary expedient, but he had not counted on the reaction of Napoleon III. The French emperor, who had not expected such a complete Prussian victory, was stunned by the rapid Austrian defeat, which left him no time to intervene. Moreover, Bismarck did not reward Napoleon for his neutrality with the territories hinted at in the Biarritz talks.

The Franco-Prussian War, 1870–1871

Coming on the heels of the failure of Napoleon's intervention in Mexico (see Part VII, Topic 9), the emperor's domestic opponents attacked him where he was most vulnerable—on the issue of French prestige. Napoleon saw belatedly that he would have to oppose the creation of a unified Germany on France's borders. Bismarck, on the other hand, believed that he could use a war with France to arouse nationalism and rally the other German states around Prussia's leadership in order to complete the unification process.

Relations between France and Prussia deteriorated as both sides fanned popular sentiment through press campaigns and formal protests. As in the case of the war with Austria, an obscure diplomatic issue provided the excuse for war—the question of whether a member of the Hohenzollern family would be made king of Spain. Much to Bismarck's dismay, Wilhelm I backed down in the face of French pressure. But the French, pressing their diplomatic victory too far, then demanded a formal guarantee that no Hohenzollern would ever again become a candidate for the Spanish throne. Wilhelm I met with the French ambassador at the resort town of Ems in July 1870, but politely refused the French demand for such a guarantee, and sent

Map 11.3 Europe in 1871

Bismarck a telegram recounting the details of the meeting. Bismarck, unwilling to see an excellent pretext for war disappear, carefully abbreviated the wording of the so-called "Ems Dispatch" so as to make it appear that the king had abruptly rejected the French proposal. Bismarck then made the telegram public. With the enthusiastic help of the popular press in both countries, the doctored telegram enraged public opinion and gave Napoleon III little choice—he announced hostilities on July 19, 1870. The Franco-Prussian War had begun.

Once again the devastating precision of Prussia's armies stunned Europe. Despite its defeat in 1866, Austria remained neutral, principally because Bismarck had imposed such moderate peace terms on Vienna. Bismarck could also claim that the war was a "German," rather than a Prussian, struggle, since the other German states were bound to Prussia by military alliances.

The war was over in six months. On September 1, 1870, the Prussians struck a devastating blow against France at Sedan, capturing 100,000 French troops and taking Napoleon himself prisoner. In Paris, Napoleon was dethroned and a republic proclaimed on September 4. Although the outcome of the war was certain, for five months Republican France refused to give in and the Prussians laid siege to Paris. The French surrendered in January, and two months later Parisian radicals led the desperate population in a rebellion against the republican government and proclaimed the Commune (see Part VII, Topic 19).

Against the backdrop of the terrible siege of Paris, Bismarck staged the last act in the unification of Germany. On January 18, 1871, Wilhelm I was crowned German emperor in a ceremony held in the symbolic heart of former French glory—the Hall of Mirrors of the Palace of Versailles. The "Second Reich"—German nationalists counted the Holy Roman Empire as the "First" Reich—had been created.

Adolphe Thiers (1797–1877), the provisional head of the French government, negotiated with the German empire. The Treaty of Frankfurt was far different in spirit and intent from the generous terms Bismarck had given Austria five years earlier. Germany annexed most of the strategically vital province of Alsace and a large portion of Lorraine—areas in eastern France that held rich iron mines and flourishing textile mills. Although the inhabitants were mainly German-speaking, most preferred French rule. For the next five decades the loss of Alsace and Lorraine rankled deeply in the French psyche. The Prussians marched triumphantly through Paris and, to make matters worse, France was required to bear the humiliation of German occupation until it had paid a huge indemnity of 5 billion francs, a sum that amounted to more than twice the cost of the war for Prussia.

The Franco-Prussian War was one of the most far-reaching events of the 19th century. Bismarck had succeeded in unifying Germany under Prussian control, not through the spirit of liberal nationalism that had wanted it in 1848–1849 but in alliance with the conservative élites who had made Prussia into an autocratic, military state. The new Kingdom of Italy also took advantage of the Franco-Prussian War to complete its territorial unity: when Napoleon III was forced to recall the soldiers he had kept in Rome to protect the pope, the Italians marched into the city and made it their new capital. Bismarck's armies had defeated the two most powerful states on the Continent, and the German empire had emerged as the most powerful state in Europe. The European balance of power was irrevocably altered.

NATIONALISM, REGIONALISM, AND THE AMERICAN CIVIL WAR

The struggle for political unification that transformed Europe in the 19th century was also played out in the New World, where the recently created United States underwent a process of expansion and crisis (see Part VII, Topic 1).

European radicals, struggling against the Vienna settlement of 1815, were encouraged by the triumph of democratic principles in the United States, in particular by the adoption of the Bill of Rights. In 1828, while the Restoration was still firmly entrenched in Europe, Americans gave their democratic system a still broader popular base by sending Andrew Jackson (president 1828–1835) to the White House. In Italy, nationalists considered the American Revolution a model for the Risorgimento, and both Mazzini and Garibaldi identified with its struggle for independence.

Nationalism and the Civil War

American nationalism grew steadily in the first half of the 19th century, especially after the War of 1812 with Great Britain. Moreover, Americans not only believed that their national interests conflicted with those of Europe's great powers, but also thought of their political culture as fundamentally different from that of the Old World. A thirst for expansion further fueled nationalist sentiment as Americans pushed west and south from the original thirteen states, bringing enormous areas such as the Louisiana Purchase and the Northwest Territory under the control of the United States. America's "Manifest Destiny," claimed imperialists, was "to overspread the continent allotted by Providence for the free development of our multiplying millions." In this aggressive spirit, President James Polk (served 1845–1849) fought the Mexican War in 1846–1848 and, with the seizure of Texas and California, extended the boundaries of the United States to the Rio Grande and the Pacific coast.

This rapid expansion deeply divided Americans, for it raised the issue of the extension of slavery to the new territories. Tensions mounted between the southern states, where slavery was a key element in the plantation-based agriculture of the region, and those in the North, where industrialization was taking hold. Although slavery was only one element in a complex web of sectional disputes, it became the chief focus of the Civil War (1861–1865).

European nationalist leaders, particularly those in Italy, watched the Civil War closely. Because Abraham Lincoln (president 1861–1865) led the federal government in the struggle to maintain the American union, Italians regarded him as one of the most important statesmen of the century. Cavour and Garibaldi had been longtime admirers of the American political system, although for quite different reasons. Garibaldi had lived in New York in the early 1850s, and on several occasions Cavour seriously contemplated emigrating to the United States. While Cavour expressed dismay that the Civil War might set back the cause of national

A famous photograph of President Lincoln and the Union commanders during the American Civil War.

unification, Garibaldi was more interested in the moral urgency of suppressing slavery. In 1861 Lincoln actually offered Garibaldi command of an army corps, but the offer was never formalized: the American president was not prepared to accept Garibaldi's demands that he be given supreme command of the Union army and that slavery be abolished immediately. Cavour did not live to see the northern victory over the Confederacy, which eliminated slavery in the United States and successfully preserved the union. A half-century later, the amateur American historian William R. Thayer drew a deliberate comparison between the U.S. president and the Piedmontese prime minister.

In the two decades after the revolutions of 1848–1849, nationalism achieved its greatest successes. National unity in the United States was preserved, Italy and Germany were created, the Hungarians had forced the Hapsburgs to grant them a measure of autonomy within the Austrian state, and the inhabitants of the Balkans were beginning to stir against Turkish domination.

By the end of the 19th century, however, nationalism had taken on a new and significantly different meaning. The idealistic vision of Mazzini, who had seen nationalism as a liberating force that would give rise to an era of international cooperation among free nations, all but disappeared as a new brand of chauvinist patriotism gained sway. Cavour and Bismarck, who applied the methods of power politics to the task of national liberation, had forged domestic alliances with conservative élites—army officers, businessmen, and aristocrats—in order to achieve their goals. These conservative forces now controlled the destinies of the newly unified states and ushered in a period of intense national rivalry. After 1871, competition between nations for prestige and dominance increasingly shaped international relations.

Questions for Further Study

1. What were the principal programs for Italian unification? How did they differ?
2. What methods did Bismarck employ in his efforts to unify Germany? With which Italian leader would he be most readily compared?
3. What were the consequences of the way in which Italy and Germany were unified?
4. In what ways was the unification experience of the United States different from that of Italy and Germany?

Suggestions for Further Reading

Crankshaw, Edward. *Bismarck*. New York, 1981.
Di Scala, Spencer. *Italy from Revolution to Republic*. 2nd ed. Boulder, CO, 1998.
Hamerow, Theodore S. *The Social Foundations of German Unification, 1858–1871*. 2 vols. Princeton, NJ, 1969.
Kohn, Hans. *The Idea of Nationalism*. New York, 1944.
Mack Smith, Denis. *Cavour*. New York, 1985.
Mack Smith, Denis. *Garibaldi*. Englewood Cliffs, NJ, 1969.
Mack Smith, Denis. *Mazzini*. New Haven, CT, 1994.
Pflanze. Otto. *Bismarck and the Development of Germany*. 3 vols. Princeton, NJ, 1990.
Taylor, A. J. P. *Bismarck, the Man and the Statesman*. New York, 1955.
Woolf, Stuart. *A History of Italy, 1700–1860*. New York, 1986.

Topic 12

Technology and the European Economy

By 1850 Britain, long in the vanguard of the industrial revolution, had established its superiority over the rest of Europe in virtually all facets of economic life—technology, the factory system, energy production, commerce and trade. At mid-century a proud and self-satisfied Great Britain determined to show off its achievements to the rest of the world in the Great Exhibition of 1851.

The exhibition at the Crystal Palace was not, however, an exclusively British affair, but rather the first world's fair. Other European countries and the United States also displayed their machines and products. The international nature of the event underscored the fact that industrialization was spreading. The British economy maintained its lead until overtaken by Germany and the United States in the 1890s, but between 1850 and 1873, the rapid pace of its early growth slowed as continental Europe and the United States began to close the gap.

The two decades after 1850 were years of rapid industrialization on the Continent. Production levels in key sectors such as coal, iron, and textiles increased enormously. On the Continent, development took place as France, Germany, and other countries adopted—and sometimes improved—the new machines and factory organization already in place in Britain.

The railroad came into its own in this period. Indeed, Europe and America experienced something of a "railroad revolution," as country after country built dense networks of rail lines, creating national markets for the first time. The railroad boom became a major sphere of investment and banking activity and stimulated the further expansion of heavy industry.

Agriculture, having improved significantly since the late 18th century, also entered a phase of increased productivity. New farming regions were opened up in Eastern Europe, and increased mechanization went hand in hand with land reclamation and new fertilizers. The growth of urban centers also provided larger agricultural markets.

The accelerating growth of the continental economy in this period required significant change in the way in which Europeans conducted business. Old laws hampered modern financial operations, while huge amounts of capital were needed to buy machinery and to build factories and railroads. Industrial expansion encouraged the development of the modern corporation and banking systems, and contributed to the decline of trade barriers. Finance, business organization, and the nature of private property had been revolutionized.

By the 1870s, the industrial and financial world looked quite different from that of 1850. Europe was poised on the edge of the era of modern capitalism and global economy.

THE GREAT EXHIBITION OF 1851: THE PROMISE OF TECHNOLOGY

While visiting the Paris Exposition of 1849, Henry Cole (1808–1882), an English civil servant, conceived the idea of organizing an event in London that would reveal Britain's industrial superiority. With a population half the size of France, Britain produced two-thirds of the world's coal and more than half its iron and cotton cloth; its manufactured goods flooded markets everywhere and its ships carried the bulk of the world's trade. British per capita income was 50 percent higher than French and more than twice that of Germany.

The Crystal Palace

Prince Albert, Queen Victoria's husband, sponsored the exhibition through the Society of Arts, of which he was president. A competition was announced for the design for the exhibit pavilion, to be located in Hyde Park. After considering and rejecting some 245 projects, the organizers turned to Joseph Paxton (1803–1865). Paxton was a horticulturalist and self-trained landscape architect. He had achieved fame for the gardens and landscaping he supervised for the duke of Devonshire, including the construction of a glass-roofed conservatory supported by cast-iron columns.

Significant Dates

Technology and the Economy

1830	First successful steam railway opened in England
1843	End of British ban on exporting machinery
1844	Bank Charter Act in England; 1846, Bank of Prussia
1851	The Crystal Palace Exhibition
1852	Crédit Mobilier
1856	Incorporation with limited liability
1840–1860	Railroad boom
1865	Belgium, France, Italy, and Switzerland form the Latin Monetary Union
1871	Gold standard begins
1850–1900	Second industrial revolution

Paxton came up with an imaginative concept: a long, three-story building consisting of numerous round-headed bays in the neo-Gothic style then popular, each story stepped in from the one below. The roof was in the form of an enormous arc. In the interior, galleries for individual exhibits lined either side of the huge central space. Most daring of all, the pavilion would be built entirely of glass (a material never before used for major construction) and held together by wrought-iron framing supports—in effect, a "crystal palace."

The genius of Paxton's idea derived in part from the requirement that the entire building had to be erected in nine months. His design made it possible to accomplish this because the building could be put together from prefabricated, interchangeable parts assembled in modules. A triumph of civil engineering in the age of iron, the Crystal Palace covered an area of almost 20 acres and utilized 2224 wrought-iron girders, 3300 cast-iron columns, and 300,000 panes of glass—some being, at the time, the largest ever made. Sixteen huge semicircular arches of wood, reaching more than 100 feet high, provided additional support.

Londoners marveled as the structure went up, and Victoria and Albert made numerous visits to the construction site. Despite dire predictions of disaster from skeptics, the Crystal Palace did not collapse. The queen officially opened the exhibition on May 1, 1851, with some 500,000 people crowding Hyde Park for the occasion. "The sight," Victoria recorded in her diary, "was magical—so vast, so glorious, so touching."

Industrial Civilization on Display

Within Paxton's palace were displayed more than 100,000 industrial products from around the world, submitted by 7351 exhibitors from the British Empire and 6556 from other countries. The items were grouped into categories such as raw materials, machinery, textiles, metal and ceramic products, and the fine arts.

Not unexpectedly, the machine displays most interested the public. Visitors could see the full range of 19th-century industrial items, including many that were already dated, from railroad locomotives and steamship engines to machine tools of all sorts, from power looms to printing presses and envelope-making machines, from hydraulic turbines to fireplaces. The American exhibit attracted particular attention, for it was the most forward-looking and included such practical items as ice-making machines, a Cyrus McCormick reaper, a sewing machine, and Colt revolvers made from standardized parts. From California came a device for winnowing gold, and from Canada a hand-operated fire pump.

Engineering and architectural firms exhibited a variety of construction schemes, including lighthouses,

Exterior view of the Crystal Palace, Hyde Park, London, 1851.

iron bridges, and a model for a canal across the Suez isthmus. Amid the products and inventions were also coal and iron ores, and the German firm of Krupp—described as "a manufacturer of Essen"—startled the public with a two-ton block of cast steel, the largest steel ingot ever seen. Weapons and scientific objects intermingled with telegraph machines, cameras, and cooking utensils. For the mid-19th-century consumer, the exhibition presented a feast of incredible items that delighted and awed spectators.

The Crystal Palace show was a major success. The queen came several times a week. The duke of Wellington was a frequent visitor, and was called upon for advice when a peculiar problem developed. The Palace had trees inside it, and the sparrows that nested in them constantly bespattered the visitors. Wellington's recommendation was "sparrow hawks"—trained birds that would kill the sparrows and then fly out of the building.

More than 6 million people, including streams of English schoolchildren, saw the exhibition (the Crystal Palace was dismantled after the exhibition and moved to another location, where it remained until a fire destroyed it in 1936). German princes and other dignitaries headed a long list of foreign notables and thousands of other pilgrims, all intent on seeing the wonders of the industrial age. Europeans had enjoyed a singular glimpse of the promise of technology.

CONTINENTAL INDUSTRY COMES OF AGE

Historians often speak of a "second industrial revolution" as having occurred between 1850 and 1900. Whereas the most important advances of the first industrial revolution were in textiles, iron, and the steam engine, this second phase of industrial and economic development focused on new industries—especially chemicals, steel, electricity, and, later, oil (on the latter phase of the second industrial revolution, see Part VII, Topic 17). Some scholars of technology have argued, however, that the years from 1850 to 1870 represented a distinct, preliminary stage of this second industrial revolution. In this period, an important convergence between technological adaptation and economic structure took place—that is, continental industry adopted British technology while also developing its economic institutions. Together, the two developments accounted for much of the growth experienced by the European economy.

The pace of industrialization in continental Europe between 1850 and 1873 was unprecedented. This expansion, best measured by production figures in coal, iron, textiles, and steam power, sometimes increased as much as 10 percent each year in the so-called industrial "inner zone" of France, Belgium, and Germany. Resources, government policies, political instability, and capital availability all affected the rate of growth.

Economic Growth: Wages, Prices, and Demand

The second industrial revolution took place in the context of a marked demographic change. The rapid and sustained growth in Europe's population that had accompanied the first industrial revolution slowed down considerably after 1850. The decline in births, especially in France, seems to have been due to a large degree to a conscious decision on the part of parents to limit the size of families in order to enjoy a better standard of living, as well as to a general effort to police the fertility of unmarried women more intensely. Population did continue to grow, since more and more children lived to maturity, but now at a reduced rate. Significantly, the lower birthrate did not have an adverse impact on the demand for consumer goods. On the contrary, the number of potential consumers had become less important than the volume of consumption, which rose on a per capita basis. Two factors account for this rising demand. As Europe's population aged, more emphasis was placed on industrial products than on food, and the general increase in prosperity produced rising sales. The opening of new markets overseas, especially in the United States, India, and East Asia, also stimulated demand.

Prices for both industrial goods and food generally went up between 1848 and 1873, when a long depression brought an end to this growth. Contributing to this pattern were the discovery of gold in California and Australia, which increased the money supply and investment; inflationary cycles during the Crimean War, the U.S. Civil War, and the wars of German unification; the high costs of capital investment required for

Table VII.12.1
Real Wages, 1848–1872 (1850 = 100)

YEAR	BRITAIN	FRANCE	UNITED STATES
1848	90	92	100
1850	100	100	100
1852	102	95	90
1854	96	84	88
1856	96	76	85
1858	102	100	83
1860	103	97	97
1862	105	103	86
1864	117	111	76
1866	116	111	83
1868	110	103	93
1870	118	113	120
1872	122	108	132

Adapted from Walt W. Rostow, *The World Economy: History & Prospect* (Austin and London: University of Texas Press, 1978), 157.

technological improvement and for the developing of new farmlands; and the overall rise in wages.

Despite the steady increase in prices, real wages—that is, actual purchasing power—grew in the more advanced countries. This increase in prosperity and wealth was an important spur to industrial development.

The Textile Industry

Industrialization affected the production of textiles after 1850 on the Continent as fully as it had in Britain at the opening of the century. Although heavy industry experienced more significant developments, the manufacture of textiles continued to be important because of the great demand and the huge number of workers employed in making them. Improved machinery was introduced into regions where preindustrial methods had prevailed, steam power became more widespread, and advances in chemistry were applied to the finishing of cloth, both cotton and wool.

By midcentury, Great Britain had completed its transformation to a fully mechanized textile industry. The self-acting mule—a steam-powered, fully mechanized spinning machine—had all but replaced hand-operated spinning jennies. Cotton remained the predominant fabric in terms of demand and quantity, a position enhanced by the expanded supply of cheap raw material from the United States. The wool industry was mechanized later than cotton making, but in the 1850s it, too, changed as wool combing became a mechanical process. In the following decade improved power looms, capable of turning out a high quality fabric, had begun to be introduced almost everywhere, with the result that productivity rose sharply.

In 1843 Britain lifted the ban on the exporting of machinery. As a result, spinning machines were widely introduced in Alsace, the center of the French cotton industry, as well as in Switzerland, Germany, and even Russia. Those factories producing higher quality fabrics adopted the most technically advanced equipment. By 1870, France and Germany had made great progress in mechanization, although Britain still remained ahead: whereas the hand loom had virtually disappeared in Britain, France had only 80,000 power looms as opposed to 200,000 hand-operated looms, while Germany had 57,000 of the former type and 125,000 of the latter.

One of the most important aspects of textile manufacturing was the increase in output and the resulting decrease in production costs. Here again, Britain maintained its lead over continental regions. Compared to the best French and German factories, English mills used fewer workers—from a third to half

Women workers with a male overseer in an English mill—an idealized version of industrial labor far different from the harsher reality.

the number—to produce the same amount of spun yarn. By the 1860s, however, even on the Continent the hourly output per worker increased and the labor cost for each pound of yarn was drastically cut. One of the new wool-combing machines could turn out more than 45,000 pounds of combed wool a year, while even a good hand worker could produce less than 800 pounds.

The Expansion of Coal Production and Steam Power

Because coal was the major fuel source for 19th-century industries, the quantity produced helps to reveal the rate of industrial expansion. Between 1850 and 1870, the world's volume of coal increased almost threefold, from some 81 million tons to 213 million. Until the 1890s, when the United States began to take the lead, Britain remained the greatest coal-producing nation in the world.

Because many of France's coal deposits were of an inferior quality, one-third of its supply was imported. Many German states, however, possessed rich mineral resources, and after 1840 coal production rose rapidly. By the time of unification in 1871, Germany turned out two and a half times the amount of coal as France, and its output had reached almost a third of Britain's. The British consumption pattern, fairly typical of the period, revealed that iron makers and steam-driven factories used more than half of all British coal, while the rest went for heating, export, and as fuel in railroad engines and steamships.

For most countries, a critical problem in coal production was transportation. Many British coalfields were near the coast, so that the coal could be brought directly to ships, but in France transport costs increased the cost of coal tenfold. The exploitation of inland deposits required cheap transportation which canals and inland waterways only partially provided. It was the railroad that created a national market—that is, the condition which prevails when the price of a particular item is generally similar in all regions of a country. Once markets were easily accessible, new mines were developed in areas such as Pennsylvania, the Donets Basin, northern Britain, and the Ruhr. In the 1840s, French mining engineers discovered a major extension of their northern coalfields, which brought production up from less than 5000 tons in 1851 to more than 2 million in 1870. In addition, a method for sinking shafts was developed in order to extract coal from deeper beds, and improvements were made in mine ventilation, water removal, and lighting.

The increase in coal supplies went hand in hand with the development of more efficient steam engines, which drove the new machinery. Great increases in horsepower were achieved by the introduction of high-pressure steam engines fitted with elaborate valve systems. The amount of steam energy generated in Europe followed the established pattern: Britain was in first place, with Germany second and France third. A French tariff on imported steam engines curtailed their adoption and French mills continued to rely on water-power years after British and German manufacturers had converted to steam. Even in Germany, only 62,000 horsepower was generated by 1855, although within 20 years it increased tenfold. World production of steam shot upward between 1850 and 1870, from some 4 million horsepower to more than 18 million.

Iron and Its Limitations

British breakthroughs in cheap iron making also moved across the channel in full force by midcentury. The Belgians were the first on the Continent to adopt British methods: instead of costly charcoal, coke was used in the blast furnace to smelt ore into cast iron. The "puddling" process, whereby the molten cast iron was constantly stirred in order to remove impurities, produced a cheap but tough wrought iron that would bend without breaking under tension (see Part VII, Topic 2). In addition, in the mid-1840s rolling mills had been designed that permitted large-scale production of iron "I" beams, which could be used in making rails for railroads.

In 1845, 90 percent of Belgian cast iron was made in coke blast furnaces. By contrast, in France, Germany, and the United States, where wood for charcoal was cheaper, the transition to coke took place much more slowly, primarily because of the shortage of good coal and the distance between the coal and iron deposits. In the 1850s, when railroads brought the two

Table VII.12.2
Coal Production (in millions of tons), 1850–1870

	BRITAIN	FRANCE	GERMANY	UNITED STATES
1850	50	4.4	6.9	2.5
1860	81	8.3	16.6	15.2
1870	112	13.3	34	42.5

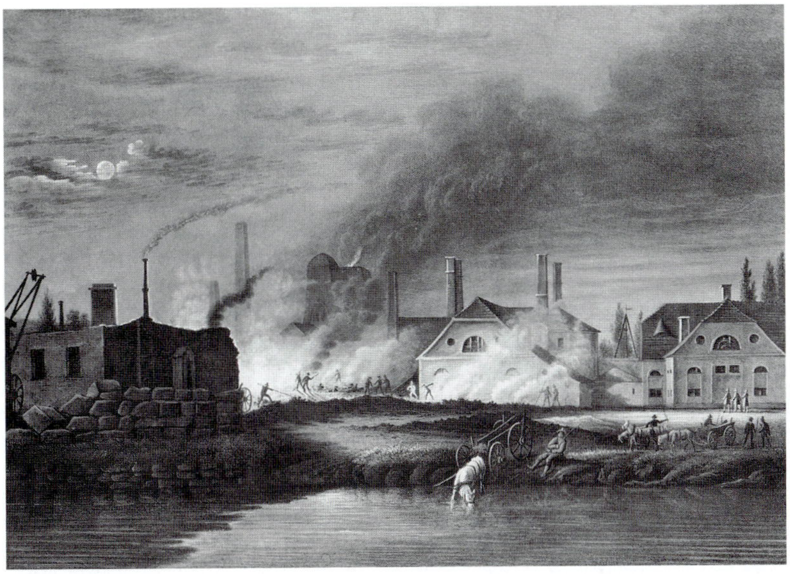

A coke smelting operation in Upper Silesia in the 1840s.

materials together, France tripled its iron output within two decades. Coke smelting was introduced into Germany only in the 1840s, but the new technique took hold rapidly, and by 1862 Prussia—which accounted for most of the iron produced in the Zollverein states—was making almost 90 percent of its iron with coke.

The production of pig iron in major western areas between 1850 and 1870 increased about 70 percent each decade, with worldwide volume increasing threefold as the United States became a major producer.

Because cast iron made in coke blast furnaces was so brittle, it could be used only under compression for such items as columns, as in those of Paxton's Crystal Palace. Wrought iron was used for all purposes where tension bending was involved, such as the construction of suspension bridges. The demand for a stronger metal became intense after midcentury with the tremendous expansion of railroads throughout the Continent. The answer was steel, provided it could be made cheaply. Steel had been manufactured in limited quantities since the 18th century, but further technological breakthroughs were needed before the age of steel could be realized (see Part VII, Topic 17).

THE RAILROAD ERA

The world's first commercially successful steam railway opened in Great Britain in 1830, from Liverpool to Manchester. By 1835 the commercial benefits of the railroad had been proven, for in three hours goods could now travel the same distance that once required 36 hours on a canal. Within 20 years Britain had more than 8000 miles of rail lines that crisscrossed the country in all directions. Fifteen years later, the figure had almost doubled. Because of its small size and intense commercial activity, Britain had a traffic density on its rails greater than that of any other country.

The Railroad Boom

Britain had undergone its industrial revolution before the coming of the railroad, using waterways for moving coal and iron—the only country to have done so. On the Continent and in the United States, industrialization took place along with the development of railroads. Indeed, the two decades after 1850 saw the expansion of railroads on such a massive scale that one can speak of the "railroadization" of Western Europe.

Table VII.12.3
Pig Iron Production (in thousands of tons), 1850–1870

	BRITAIN	FRANCE	GERMANY	UNITED STATES
1850	2,285	406	210	560
1860	3,890	898	529	821
1870	6,059	1,180	1,260	1,690

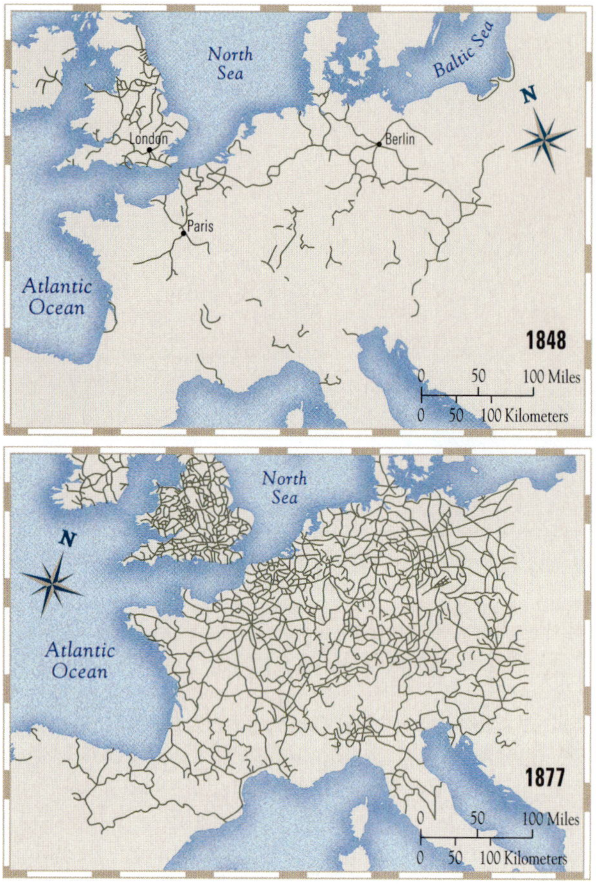

Map 12.1 The Railroad Explosion

By 1840, Belgium had essentially completed its main rail lines of more than 200 miles, whereas the much larger territories of France and Germany each had less than 400. By the end of the century, Belgium actually surpassed Britain in traffic density on its rails, in part because the Belgians built trunk lines to the German and French borders in order to attract freight headed for export to its port cities. The boom hit in the decades between 1840 and 1860, when a combination of political leadership and commercial factors pushed railroad building to the extreme. In France, an 1842 law called for close cooperation between government and private capital in realizing a national plan of trunk lines radiating from Paris. Napoleon III, a railroad enthusiast, encouraged rail construction with state support, and the Crédit Mobilier made large-scale financing possible. By 1870, France had almost 10,000 miles of rails. In Germany, after initial reluctance Prussia eventually took the lead in railroad building, and Berlin became the kingdom's rail hub. The Prussians, who paid particular attention to the military uses of the railroad, quickly outstripped France in total mileage—in 1850, German lines were already twice as long, while the main French line was completed only in 1860. On the other hand, on a per capita and area basis, the French railroad network was denser.

The Impact of the Railroad

Railroad lines were built and operated according to varying national policies. The British railroads were built with private capital, just as their turnpikes and canals had been private enterprises. Other governments either built the rail lines themselves, subsidized private enterprise, or combined these approaches. Belgium and Austria both decided on public ownership, whereas the French solution was a compromise. The state provided the land, planned the layout and prepared the roadbed, and then granted long-term leases to private companies that would run the lines.

Regardless of the particular national strategy, the impact of the railroad on economic and industrial development was enormous. It substantially lowered transportation costs and regional, national, and international markets. Railroads also stimulated the adoption of new technologies in the iron, coal, and machine engineering industries, and created a huge demand for these and other products. The need for more durable rails would act as a major inducement for the birth of the modern steel industry.

The enormous amounts of capital required to build railroads deeply affected systems of finance and business cycles in the second half of the 19th century. Railroads opened up vast new tracts of farmland, especially in the United States, where much European capital was invested. Investments in railroads, along with

Table VII.12.4
The Railroad Revolution (in miles), 1840–1870

	BRITAIN	FRANCE	GERMANY	UNITED STATES
1840	838	360	341	2,820
1850	6,620	1,890	3,640	9,020
1860	10,430	5,880	6,980	30,630
1870	15,540	9,770	11,730	53,400

This painting by Claude Monet, *Gare Saint-Lazare* (1877), was one of several treatments by the artist of the French railway station and the modern steam engine.

similar speculation in real estate, became a veritable craze at times, and widespread speculation was both the source of huge profits as well as the cause of financial panics. Investment banks were often started in order to raise capital, international loans were granted, and trading in rail bonds and stocks contributed to the rise of modern exchanges. Not less important was the fact that in many instances the capital accumulated in railroad speculation was then available for reinvestment in other industries.

The political and social consequences of railroad construction were equally far-reaching. Lines linking regions once isolated from one another contributed to the rise of national spirit and helped the process of domestic consolidation after unification. Generals rethought modern military strategy in the light of the rapid transportation of troops and war materiel now possible. Railroads encouraged the growth of cities, and changed their appearance as rail lines and stations dotted the urban landscape. Moreover, people—ordinary, working-class citizens—now had for the first time the possibility of traveling long distances at relatively modest cost, both for leisure and for work, and the railroads offered an opportunity for some to escape the inner cities and live in healthier, more pleasant suburbs.

MODERNIZING THE EUROPEAN ECONOMY: TRADE, FINANCE, AND THE CORPORATION

Two facts dominated the changing character of the European industrial economy in the period 1850–1873: technological modernization and the expansion of markets. These developments required money on a

The Great Eastern laying the transatlantic cable in 1866.

scale hitherto unknown—money to make the capital improvements dictated by the new technology, and money to operate the burgeoning industries in order to meet the production requirements of an increasingly international demand.

Barriers to European trade were generally lowered after midcentury. The formation of the Prussian-dominated Zollverein in the 1830s stimulated commercial relations in central Europe, and Great Britain moved toward free trade by the repeal of the Corn Laws in

The opening-day procession of ships through the Suez Canal, November 17, 1869.

1846. In the 1850s, international waterways such as the Danube, the Rhine, the Elbe, and the Baltic and North Seas were opened to free commerce by the elimination of levies and restrictions. But the most important move in this direction came in the following decade as a result of a series of commercial treaties between the leading industrial nations. The gradual adoption of the gold standard (see below) made international trade still easier in the latter part of the century, although the trend toward free trade was reversed after 1870.

The Rise of the Corporation

The pressures of expanding markets and industrialization meant that after 1850 business units had to be much larger than the old firms and partnerships. Joint-stock or corporate forms of business organization provided clear advantages. In joint-stock firms, a number of people pooled their capital in a common enterprise, usually with transferable shares. If incorporated, such enterprises are recognized by law as single units, or bodies *(corpora)*, which can sue and be sued independently of their members. Thus, shareholders could have "limited liability" that protected their individual property.

Because unbridled speculation had resulted in a major financial crash in the early 18th century, Britain had passed the Bubble Act of 1720, which required special acts of Parliament to grant a joint-stock charter. This restriction was repealed in 1825, and further changes made it much easier to form such companies. In 1856, incorporation with limited liability became a simple matter of registration, and in the next decades France and Germany followed suit, while in the United States individual state governments chartered companies. The corporation soon became widely utilized by railroad companies in Europe and America, and by the end of the 19th century corporations took over most industries.

The Gold Standard and Banks

The rise of large corporations controlling huge assets and doing business across national boundaries created a need for new sources of money and a variety of banking institutions. In addition, the worldwide movement of capital was intensified and facilitated by the development of a new international monetary system based on gold.

As in the case of industrialization, Great Britain moved toward the gold standard before the rest of Europe. In 1821, the Bank of England made its notes convertible into gold, and the British pound sterling was guaranteed at a specific gold weight. In 1865, Belgium, France, Italy, and Switzerland formed the Latin Monetary Union, which sought to encourage a world currency system by adopting the franc as a common unit and minting coins of uniform weight in each country. Greece was the only other nation, however, to join the group, and in the 1870s the union gave up its efforts in favor of the gold standard, which the German empire had adopted in 1871. By the eve of World War I, all the other major powers had followed suit.

Despite the fact that most currencies eventually based their standard on gold, it was not the actual medium of exchange. Rather, gold became a form of reserve money, housed in banks, which in turn issued notes and bank certificates for circulation. Three kinds of banks evolved in the second half of the 19th century: central, commercial, and investment banks. Central banking came into being in Britain with the Bank Charter Act of 1844, which required that the Bank of England increase the quantity of its banknotes only if it increased its bullion reserves by the same amount. A new Issue Department received a monopoly on the printing of all future banknotes in England, while a Banking Department established a commercial checking system, which was also tied to reserves of cash and notes. Because the Banking Department maintained its reserves at from 30 to 50 percent, while smaller banks kept much smaller reserves, the Bank of England became the lender of last resort in times of emergency—in effect, a kind of bankers' bank.

The Bank of France, founded by Napoleon Bonaparte in 1800, received a monopoly on the issue of banknotes in 1848. Although the bank was privately owned, the government maintained close supervision of its activities, and it, too, kept high levels of reserves to support its notes. In Germany, central banking began when the Bank of Prussia, established in 1846, was converted into the Reichsbank in 1875. Both the Bank of France and the Reichsbank served an important business function by discounting bills of exchange (that is, exchanging them for cash), and established numerous branch banks for that purpose.

Unlike central banks, the chief function of commercial banks is to serve commerce and industry directly by providing short-term loans to businesses. Commercial banks became joint-stock companies in the 19th century, and tended toward a high degree of monopoly: the so-called "Big Five" (Barclays, Lloyds, Midland, National Provincial, and Westminister) dominated British commercial banking, while four firms—including Crédit Lyonnais and Société Générale—monopolized most of French commercial banking, and the Big Four "D" banks—such as the Deutsche Bank and the Dresdner Bank—controlled such operations in Germany.

Investment banks, on the other hand, were concerned principally with extending long-term credit in the form of stocks and bonds. Investment banks arose in order to provide capital for plants and equipment for railroads and large industrial firms. In the early 19th century the principal "investment" bank of Europe was really the House of Rothschild, which engaged mainly in financing government loans. Five brothers operated the firm, one in each of five major cities—Frankfurt, London, Paris, Vienna, and Naples. These and other international bankers facilitated the financing of railroads by marketing stocks and bonds.

Yet such investment banks tended to be cautious in underwriting new industries, and by the mid-19th century other avenues were needed. Napoleon III, unhappy over his dealings with the Rothschilds, promoted one of the most interesting experiments in investment banking—the Crédit Mobilier. Founded by the Pereire Brothers in 1852, it accumulated capital by selling its own stocks and bonds, and then lending the capital to make long-term loans to start new businesses; once the firms were established, the Crédit Mobilier would also sell the securities of the new enterprises to investors. It was highly successful for a time in promoting railroads, utilities, and industrial firms. Given the nature of its operations, the Crédit Mobilier was vulnerable in financial crises because it had little liquid assets. The company went bankrupt in 1867 and was liquidated in 1871. Similar institutions were established in Germany in the 1850s and in Britain in the following decade. Even the Rothschilds joined the trend, establishing the Credit-Anstalt in Austria. Later the American investment banks of J. P. Morgan and Kuhn, Loeb and Co. were to become giants on the international banking scene.

The national and international money markets established between 1850 and 1873 played a critical role in the industrialization of the Continent. The capital raised, invested, and circulated by these new banking institutions provided the financial basis for the remarkable growth of the European industrial economy, particularly in the decades after 1870, and in the creation of a global capitalist system.

The 20 years after 1850 represented an important phase of maturation for the European economy. The essentials of the industrialization process had reached the Continent. The growth rate maintained generally high levels as production in textiles, coal, and iron rose steadily—and sometimes dramatically.

The revolution in transportation, caused chiefly by the railroad, deeply affected every aspect of European civilization, from industrial and financial growth and market expansion to the shape of cities and the way in which millions of people led their daily lives. Along with the equally far-reaching revolution in banking and business organization, the railroads pointed the way toward an age of capitalist enterprise in which the links between technology, heavy industry, and the world of finance grew increasingly close.

As industrial and agricultural profits reached new heights in this era, the wealth of Europe was reflected in the improvement of real wages and living standards. Rather than a sign of crisis, the declining birthrate meant the emergence of new patterns of consumption and higher levels of comfort for many Europeans. The Great Exhibition of 1851, with which the period opened, symbolized the beginning of an age of enthusiastic and self-conscious materialism for European civilization.

Questions for Further Study

1. How did technology transform the European economy in the 19th century?
2. How did the development of railroads influence industrial and economic policy?
3. To what conditions did the rise of the corporations respond?

Suggestions for Further Reading

Ashworth, William. *An Economic History of England, 1870–1939*. London, 1960.

Cameron, Rondo. *A Concise Economic History of the World*. New York, 1989.

Carter, E. C., et al., eds. *Enterprise and Entrepreneurs in Nineteenth and Twentieth Century France*. Baltimore, MD, 1976.

Henderson, William O. *The Rise of German Industrial Power, 1834–1914*. Berkeley, CA, 1975.

Hobsbawm, Eric J. *The Age of Capital, 1848–1875*. New York, 1979.

Landes, David. *The Unbound Prometheus: Technological Change and Industrial Development in Western Europe from 1750 to the Present*. Cambridge, MA, 1969.

Milward, Alan S., and S. B. Saul. *The Development of the Economies of Continental Europe, 1850–1914*. Cambridge, MA, 1977.

Trebilcock, Clive. *The Industrialization of the Continent*. New York, 1981.

VII

Topic 13

Middle-Class Values and Working-Class Realities

By the mid-19th century, the focus of European life had decisively shifted from the country to industrial cities. In this urban context the aristocracy slowly lost some of its traditional authority, while the middle classes, involved in trade and industry, grew in wealth and power. Bourgeois attitudes toward work and private life established a norm for all levels of society.

At the bottom of the social scale, the condition of the workers and urban poor seemed, if anything, even worse than that of agricultural laborers. Yet the sheer concentration of their numbers, and the manifest unfairness of their grim living conditions, led to pressure for reform. In some cases governments spontaneously tried to correct social and economic injustices; in others, public protest was needed to produce results. At any event, all classes of society were compelled to adjust to the new problems and pleasures offered by city life.

The moral tone of the midcentury was set by those who had gained most from the confrontations of earlier years: the middle classes. From the security of their financial independence, manufacturers, merchants, and professionals praised the virtues of hard work, honesty, and self-reliance. Material success, they claimed, could be achieved by combining these merits with a healthy dose of personal ambition. The high self-image sustained by the bourgeoisie was accompanied by a rigid code of behavior, laying out the duties of public and private conduct.

At the heart of the middle-class worldview lay the family. The house itself, with its furniture and decorations, provided the setting for domestic life and was defined as women's narrowly circumscribed sphere of influence. By contrast all other activities were largely restricted to men. Thus bourgeois women were enshrined at the center of a cult whose effects on all aspects of their lives were claustrophobic.

Such an idealizing vision did not, of course, apply to the whole range of 19th-century society. Even within the middle classes, there were rebels. The mid-1850s saw the formation of some of the earliest feminist groups. For many of the working-class poor, living in urban squalor, the bourgeois prescription for domestic happiness was meaningless. By the middle of the century, charity workers and social reformers had begun to attack some of the more basic problems. Public health, working conditions, education, and housing were all the subject of increasing government action. Progress was slow, in part because the continued rapid growth of the cities compounded the difficulties.

Pressure for reform began to come not only from middle-class humanitarians but also from the working classes themselves. Earlier worker protests had lacked a coherent sense of direction. In the mid-19th century the cause of the rights of the working class was given a philosophical basis and powerful expression in the writings of Karl Marx. His aggressive socialist vision of a newly ordered society, first published on the eve of the 1848 revolutions, prepared the way for the working-class parties which played a growing role in late-19th-century politics.

THE URBANIZATION OF EUROPE

The rapid transformation of European life from an agricultural to an urban society had begun in the early 19th century, spurred by industrialization and a quickly rising population (on urbanization between 1800 and 1850, see Part VII, Topic 6). In the two decades after 1850, the trend continued, but with some differences. Earlier the most dramatic urban growth had occurred in British towns, where industrial development had been concentrated. Although urban growth continued in Great Britain, after midcentury the pace of development there slowed down. It was on the Continent, and especially in German cities, that the most startling increase in urban populations took place along with the spread of industrialization. In Berlin, for example, the number of inhabitants doubled between 1850 and 1870 from some 400,000 to more than 800,000. In London during the same period, however, the population grew by little more than 40 percent, from 2,685,000 to 3,890,000.

The Social Impact of Cities

Despite its uneven character, urban growth, especially in western Europe, continued to produce revolutionary changes in social customs and patterns. By the 1870s, almost a third of all Europeans, regardless of class, gender, or income, lived in cities. Some of these were capitals that combined manufacturing and government offices, as in the cases of London and Berlin, while others were major industrial centers, such as Glasgow and Düsseldorf. In most cases the problems of urban life were the same.

The consequences of so vast and rapid a change in the lifestyles of millions of people were naturally complex and far-reaching. Viewed from the perspective of the late 20th century, with its fears of urban chaos and collapse, it is tempting to accentuate the drawbacks of city life at the expense of its very real benefits. Widespread application of new technologies and improved medical methods benefited increasing numbers of people. The continual growth of national prosperity helped to underwrite public welfare programs. Furthermore, the rise in the general level of education created a wider

Map 13.1 European Urbanization, 1860

Table VII.13.1
The Growth of European Cities (in thousands), 1850–1870

CITY	1850	1870
Berlin	419	826
Glasgow	345	522
Hamburg	132	240
London	2,685	3,890
Moscow	365	612
Paris	1,053	1,852
Rome	175	244
Sheffield	135	240
Vienna	444	834

audience for intellectual debate and cultural entertainment.

At a more mundane level, great cities like London, Paris, or Vienna provided public gardens, fireworks, and dance halls, pleasures that were easily accessible to the working class. The infinite variety of daily experience, street entertainments ranging from Moroccan dancers to mechanical men, the "busy idleness" of the throngs of people, all offered novelty to those who flocked from the provinces to enjoy the excitement of metropolitan existence. One visitor to Paris called it "a glass beehive, a treat to the student of humanity"—the essence of existence there was "the consciousness of being observed."

Yet inevitably behind the passing scene there lay the other side of city life: grinding poverty, overcrowding, squalor. Nor were such conditions limited to the northern industrial cities. When the novelist Charles Dickens (see Part VII, Topic 14) first arrived in the Italian city of Genoa in 1844, he was horrified at "the unusual smells, the unaccountable filth, the disorderly jumbling of dirty houses, one upon the roofs of another. I never, in my life, was so dismayed!" Conditions had little changed 20 years later. Many agricultural workers drawn from declining rural centers by the hope of making their fortunes in the cities found themselves drifting into marginal jobs: rag picking, scissor grinding, collecting human excrement. Others took to crime. More fortunate were those who found employment in domestic service, thanks to the growing demand of prosperous middle-class householders for servants. Nor did urban existence always prove fulfilling in social terms. One migrant to London described it as "a wilderness of human beings."

Dealing with the problems of expanding communities was complicated by a number of factors. Many provincial towns had drawn their prosperity from travelers on the old coaching routes, which had been busy for

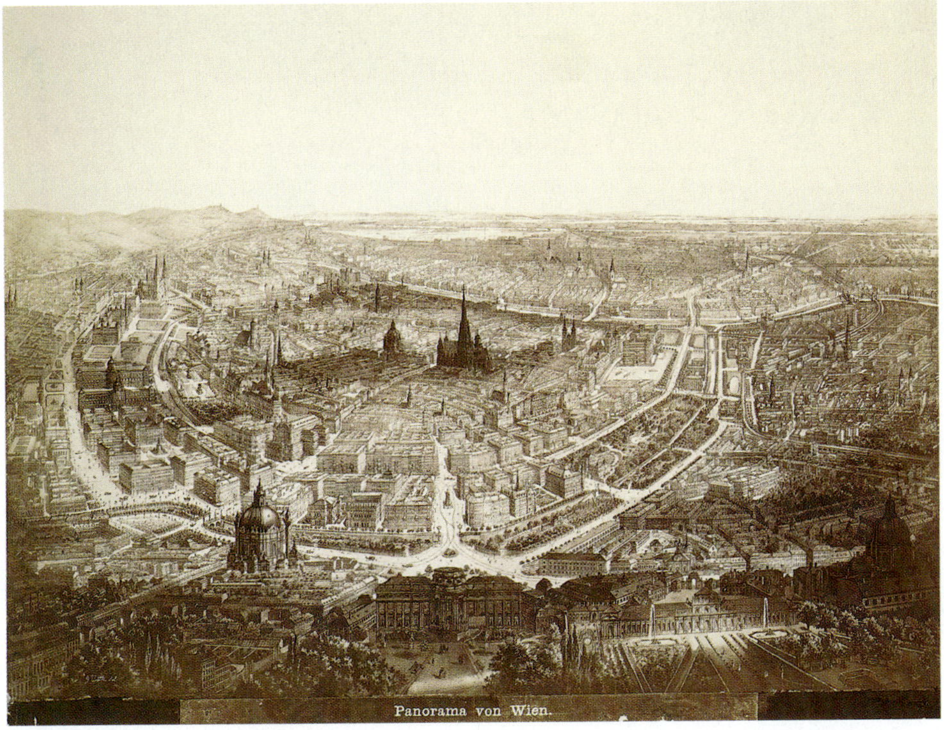

The expanding cities of late 19th-century Europe encompassed large areas beyond the historical core. Here is a bird's-eye view of Vienna.

a century or more. With the coming of the railroads, the economies of these centers collapsed overnight. Their populations abandoned them and poured into the big cities, providing yet another wave of homeless migrants.

The faster people crowded into the cities, the worse their conditions became. At the same time increasing industrial production created ever greater pollution, especially in the great mining and textile cities. "Muck means money," one Manchester cotton manufacturer is said to have observed. For his employees it also meant blackened windows, clothes, and lungs. The general replacement of wood by coal as a means of heating increased pollution further; it also meant that those who could not afford to buy coal lived in cold, damp conditions, with inevitable consequences for their health. In rural communities, on the other hand, firewood was collected routinely and at no expense as a natural resource.

Further difficulties were presented by the urgent need for urban planning. Some big industrial and commercial cities began to grow only in the late 18th century; they included the manufacturing centers of the Midlands and northern England, the Ruhr district of northern Germany, and Madrid. In these, at least, coherent planning was theoretically possible. Athens, one of the oldest cities in Europe, is the only European capital whose present center was laid out in the 19th century. After centuries of neglect under the Turks, the city was completely rebuilt by the German architects whom Otto (ruled 1832–1862), the first king of independent Greece, brought with him from Bavaria.

Most of the chief 19th-century cities, however, had been centers of population for centuries. Those of Medieval foundation frequently still had their city walls intact, adding to the complexity of organized expansion. Baron Haussmann's rebuilding of Paris during

Map 13.2 European Nationalities

In the countryside, poverty and primitive conditions still prevailed widely in many parts of Europe—here in a Russian village.

the Second Empire (see Part VII, Topic 9) had involved the demolition of Medieval quarters. Similarly, in 1865, in trying to adapt Florence to its new, although temporary, role as capital of united Italy, the architect Giuseppe Poggi chose the drastic solution of demolishing virtually the whole of the city's circuit of Medieval walls, and replacing them with broad avenues. Later generations severely criticized Poggi's decision, but its radical nature illustrates the seriousness of the problem he and other town planners faced. Haussmann's work in Paris inspired a similar project in Vienna, where walls were torn down to make way for the famous *Ringstrasse* in the 1870s.

Further difficulties lay in anticipating and providing for the new needs of urban life. The arrival of the railways required that cities be organized around station terminals and the various branch lines. Increased street traffic made it necessary to build wide avenues and to separate pedestrians and vehicles by constructing sidewalks. By the end of the 19th century, when it was clear that still more transport facilities were needed, subway systems were begun in London and Paris. Underground sewers and waterpipes had to be laid—the ancient Romans had both almost 2000 years earlier, but their use died out with the decline of the Roman Empire. Streets needed lighting, and garbage collection had to be organized.

With the increase in crime, city police forces were vastly expanded. Until the 19th century, order was generally maintained by the military. The police served principally as government spies, on the lookout for those regarded as opponents of the regime. As property holders came to demand protection, and the anonymous crowds of the big cities needed controlling, the police began to serve as maintainers of civic order. Sir Robert Peel, it will be recalled, established the first British police force in London in 1820 (see Part VII, Topic 9).

The teeming cities of 19th-century Europe provided the stage on which the political and social battles of the remainder of the century were fought: the struggle for the suffrage, women's rights, and social justice.

VICTORIAN VIRTUES: THE THEORY AND PRACTICE OF THE BOURGEOISIE

The attitudes to life developed by the prosperous middle classes in western Europe are often summed up under the general term "Victorian." "Victorian morality" is practically synonymous with a rigidly puritan lifestyle, involving pure women and upright men, whose duty was to produce children to serve the public good. Living in respectable homes, gathering daily for family prayers, spending their Sundays in decorous inactivity, Victorian families often seem to have lived in numbing respectability. The outward impression is of stern and decisive husbands and fathers, and women trapped as tightly in their domestic role as they were in the whalebone and steel corsets they wore.

Victorian Religion

The age was marked by a revival in religious observance, especially among women, who attended church services more regularly than men. What little opportunity middle-class wives, in particular, had for lives outside the home was often found in prayer societies and charitable organizations. In Catholic countries, including France and Italy, women who seemed unlikely to marry often entered convents; indeed, in the eyes of many, a cloistered life was the only respectable alternative to marriage. One of the most important aspects of child raising was religious education: the catechism, prayer, and regular church attendance.

The virtues which the devout hoped to encourage in their families were those that would maintain a tranquil home life. Children were taught to accept their destiny, forgive their enemies, and help those less fortunate than themselves. A home strengthened

Queen Victoria, Prince Albert, and their children (1846)—the idealized "Victorian" family.

by these would, in turn, serve as protection against the snares of the world outside: impiety, greed, and, most dangerous of all, sexual immorality. As for the poor, who clearly had little chance of enjoying the benefits of domestic bliss, they could best be helped by the distribution of hot soup and improving religious tracts.

So determined a program of self-denial and gloom did not make for an agreeable existence. Florence Nightingale (1820–1910), the "Lady with the Lamp" who revolutionized the care of the sick, wrote that "Life is a hard fight, a struggle, a wrestling with the Principle of Evil."

Yet the conventional version of bourgeois life provides a very one-sided impression of 19th-century society. The battle to maintain such exalted standards of virtue was probably won by only a few. Even at the time, the traditional picture of Victorian morality was recognized for what it was: a decorous façade behind which life remained as varied as it had always been. The young Queen Victoria grew up at a time when London's social life was dominated by luxurious whores and dissolute dandies, yet in the same years, Thomas Bowdler produced an edition of Shakespeare censored for family reading (the term *bowdlerized* derives from his name), and the Society for the Suppression of Vice was founded; the English wit Sydney Smith (1771–1845) suggested that this latter should have been called the Society for Suppressing the Vices of Persons Whose Income Does Not Exceed Five Hundred Pounds per Annum.

The "Necessary Evil"

Loose living and zealous puritanism continued to coexist throughout Victoria's reign. The spread of bourgeois propriety did nothing to decrease prostitution in the period after 1850. An English clergyman remarked in 1858 that England was "the most religious in pretension but in reality the most immoral and licentious under the sun." One source in 1857 claimed that the number of prostitutes in London was around 80,000, an estimate generally accepted by contemporary observers. If each prostitute received only 25 customers a week, the number of weekly male visits to a prostitute amounted to some 2 million—in a city whose total male population was about 1,300,000. Along with the British Museum and Buckingham Palace, the city's elegantly dressed courtesans were among its principal tourist attractions.

A phenomenon so widespread could hardly be ignored or concealed, and bourgeois society debated at length both prostitution and other social problems, including child abuse, alcoholism, infanticide, wife beating, and a thriving subculture of pornography. In the case of prostitution, some governments intervened. In 1860 Cavour introduced to the new nation of Italy a system of state control which he had worked out in Sardinia. Based on the assumption that prostitution was a "necessary evil," it regulated dress, living conditions, and the scale of payments. Cavour's system became popular with its clients, and by 1880 almost two-thirds of Italian prostitutes worked in officially regulated "closed houses," with the women having regular health controls. Legalized prostitution in Italy was abolished only in the 1950s.

Throughout the 1860s and 1870s, social reformers in France and Germany tried to construct brothels along the same humanitarian lines as hospitals or factories. The overwhelming majority of those employed in them were working-class women. Their purpose and justification were twofold: to free middle-class (and other) men from excessive passion, so that they could return purged to a tranquil domestic life, and to guarantee the virtue of pure women.

High society had its own share of courtesans. One of the most famous and admired was the French Marie Duplessis (1824–1847). Fragile and melancholy in appearance, she was described by one admirer as "a young woman of exquisite distinction, a pure and delicate type of beauty." Among her first conquests was the Prince de Bidache, who was to become Napoleon III's foreign minister. Her affair with the dramatist Alexandre Dumas *fils* (1824–1895), and her subsequent premature death of tuberculosis at the age of 23, inspired his play *The Lady of the Camellias*, which in turn formed the basis of the opera *La Traviata* by Giuseppe Verdi (see Part VII, Topic 14). In both play and opera, the heroine dies in poverty. The real-life character earned enough in her short career to leave quantities of jewelry, silver and porcelain, furniture, works of art, a horse and carriage, and a pony. The sale of her estate after her death took four days, and realized almost 100,000 francs.

The Bourgeoisie at Table

If state control and the laws of the marketplace took care of one basic human appetite, middle-class households became increasingly adept at satisfying another one. During the period from 1830 to 1865, the midday meal developed into the major social occasion of daily life, with children and governess taking their place at the parents' table. Preceded by a lavish breakfast and a glass of wine with a biscuit in the middle of the morning, lunch became a hot meal—it had previously consisted of a cold collation. Working-class men frequently could not return home at midday, and a hot supper was generally kept for them.

Outside the house, the middle classes sought to maintain the same practice of formal meals. Honoré de Balzac, the realistic novelist of French life (see Part VII, Topic 14), describes the menu of two young men of fortune in a Paris restaurant: six dozen oysters, six veal cutlets, a chicken, a lobster mayonnaise, peas, and a mushroom patty, washed down with three bottles of Bordeaux and three of Champagne. Even boarding schools provided lavish spreads. In September 1853, the French Ministry of Public Education circulated a list of standard meals to be served in state institutions, organized by days of the week. On Tuesdays, lunch consisted of meat soup, boiled beef, veal or mutton stew, poultry or game in pastry, and cold pâtés, while at dinner—a lighter meal, as was customary by midcentury—roast mutton and stewed fruit were served.

Thus behind the theoretical austerity and self-sacrifice of the bourgeois ideal, the middle classes used their growing prosperity to live in as much comfort as possible. As the century progressed, furthermore, new discoveries made it possible to extend life's pleasures and conveniences to the less prosperous. Mechanized manufacturing processes made cheap shoes and clothing widely available. The wealthy had their clothes made for them, but their income was often based on the mass production and sale of ready-made garments, known as "reach-me-downs," stacked on the shelves of clothing stores. In the 1870s new processes of food preservation were developed, including canning and bottling. In 1870 margarine was invented and became a substitute for those who could not afford butter—twice the price—or fat drippings. A decade earlier, in 1860, the invention of the earth closet provided a more healthy sanitary system. The absence of drains meant that water closets did not become widespread, even in middle-class homes, until the turn of the century. The first water closets in Manchester appeared in 1898.

While preaching resignation and simplicity, the middle classes schemed and planned to lead lives of ever-increasing complexity. Yet the façade of Victorian virtue certainly had its effects, and claimed its victims. Its central tenet, the sanctity of the home and family, left women trapped in performing an increasingly burdensome role.

WOMEN AND THE CULT OF DOMESTICITY

Middle-class morality revolved around a basic principle. In the midst of social ferment and political revolution, the privacy of domestic family life, presided over by women, offered protection and tranquillity. Raising their children and looking after their homes, wives and mothers would fulfill their natural function. This simple belief served in practice to reinforce a whole series of prejudices, and to bolster the high self-esteem of the new bourgeoisie.

In the first place, the cult of domesticity drew immediate attention to the greatest strength of the middle classes: their strong financial position. The working class and the poor were automatically excluded from being home owners, while many of the aristocracy were forced to reduce their expenditures, in part because of

A photograph, around 1860, depicting women's place in the cult of domesticity.

their unwillingness to engage in commercial ventures. In any case, those great lords or princes who still maintained estates or palaces lived in splendor and opulence, but hardly in comfort. A middle-class home was intended to impress not by its frescoes or the grandeur of its salons, but by the convenience and ease of its appointments. Far more important than the possession of ancient treasures was the latest plumbing device or heating system. By comparison with the gilded elegance of the 18th century, 19th-century furniture was solid, and the chairs and couches stuffed—even overstuffed.

If their homes provided one way of defining their position, the difference between the lifestyles of middle-class and working-class women offered a second. The latter were compelled by necessity to seek labor, whether in factories or in the kitchens of bourgeois families, or in the brothels that served, paradoxically, to maintain middle-class respectability. They spent considerable time away from their own families, in the case of those in domestic service actually living in the houses of strangers. Working women often exchanged their freedom from the repression they had left behind at home for other forms of tyranny at the hands of their employers.

Bourgeois women, by contrast, were virtually forbidden to work, or to spend significant amounts of time away from home. Indeed, the more their status came to depend on their inactivity, the more the idea of an actively employed woman became discouraged. Thus the financial progress of the middle classes left bourgeois women theoretically superior, but in practice even less free than ever.

The exaltation of domesticity reinforced the controlling role of bourgeois husbands and fathers, for whose benefit the whole system operated. By entrusting the care of the home, although not the physical labor there, to their womenfolk, Victorian males assured themselves a monopoly on all other forms of activity: business, finance, higher education, politics, and public life. The only appropriate interests for women in public life, such as philanthropy and moral reform, evoked their maternal role. The cult of domesticity consisted of a means to occupy the time, or at least some of it, of urban middle-class women, and keep them safely trapped at home.

If women's sphere—or, as one writer described it, "kingdom"—was the home, they needed guidance in administering it. Handbooks on the new "domestic science" began to circulate widely. One of the most successful was the *Book of Household Management* (1861), by Isabella Beaton (1836–1865). Her advice on hiring and managing the servants, supervising the household accounts, and a host of bewildering social customs (the use of finger bowls, for example) was read, if not always followed, by more than one generation of Victorian housewives. She also provided information on hygiene and health, and on legal issues. Most important of all, she helped her readers to keep their husbands at home by maintaining an agreeable atmosphere and pleasing them with tasty, nourishing meals. The world of restaurants and clubs, a specifically male preserve, was seen as a potential threat to domestic peace.

The Feminist Movement

Not all 19th-century women accepted the role assigned to them. In some cases, however, the form their protest took was a tacit acknowledgement of the advantages in being a man. The French novelist George Sand (Aurore Dudevant) dressed as a man, and smoked cigars and a pipe. George Eliot (Mary Ann Evans), one of the leading literary figures of Victorian England, refused to marry the man with whom she lived, while her French contemporary, Daniel Stern (Marie d'Agoult), gave birth to several illegitimate children (whose father was the composer Franz Liszt). All three of these unconventional women wrote novels, which they published under male pseudonyms (on these authors and the novels they wrote, see Part VII, Topic 14).

A far greater threat to male supremacy was posed by the emergence, in midcentury England and America, of an organized feminist movement. In a general sense, feminism arose as a result of the social changes produced by industrialization, which had pushed countless women into the workforce. In a more immediate sense, however, middle-class women rebelled against the repressive limitations of the cult of domesticity. This was the theme of *A Doll's House* (1879), by the Norwegian playwright Henrik Ibsen (1828–1906): its heroine, a repressed housewife who leaves her husband for the challenges of the larger world outside marriage, shocked middle-class audiences of the day.

Like Ibsen's character, many bourgeois women resisted their exclusion from the world beyond the home, although in less dramatic ways. Women tried, for example, to find more meaningful lives by putting their time and energies into religious and charitable activities. Both American and British women joined the abolitionist cause, and after 1850 volunteered in ever-larger numbers to work in hospitals and working-class slums. By the end of the century, women were gravitating toward careers in nursing, teaching, and social work.

Participation in campaigns against slavery increased female consciousness of their own oppression. An important step in this direction came in 1840, when delegates to an international antislavery congress gathered in London. The American abolitionist Elizabeth Cady Stanton (1815–1902) and the other women present were outraged when they were required to observe the proceedings from an upstairs gallery, separated off from the male delegates. In 1848, Mrs. Lucretia Mott (1793–1880) joined Stanton in spearheading the first women's rights convention, which met in Seneca Falls, New York. The participants announced a "Declaration of Sentiments" that demanded equal rights to divorce, to own property, and to hold jobs, as well as to vote.

These demands were echoed by early British feminists, particularly Barbara Smith Bodichon (1827–1891), whose London address gave their organization its name: the Langdon Place Group. The *English Women's Journal*, which she helped to found, led to the creation of an employment agency in order to help women find jobs. By the 1860s, feminist groups had begun the long battle for the vote. Among their supporters was John Stuart Mill (see Part VII, Topic 9), who published his famous essay, *On the Subjection of Women*, in 1869, two years after Parliament had rejected a motion to extend the suffrage to women. Ironically, many of the leading opponents of the female franchise were Liberals, who feared that women would mainly vote for the Conservatives.

On the Continent, the cause of feminism advanced much more slowly. In France, Napoleon III was hostile to feminism, which he regarded as another form of revolution. The prominent working-class leader Pierre-Joseph Proudhon (see Part VII, Topic 19) actually opposed women's rights, asserting that women's physical, mental, and moral inferiority justified their being restricted to the home. Nor did the Society to Claim the Rights of Women, founded in France in the 1860s, advocate radical change, but rather continued in the broadly utopian traditions of Saint-Simon. Nevertheless, a real feminist movement under the leadership of Juliette Lamber and Jenny d'Hercourt did operate as a kind of underground political opposition to the repressive policies of the Second Empire. In the German states, Louise Otto-Peters (1819–1895) headed the All German Women's Union, formed in 1865, and founded the feminist newspaper *Neue Bahnen* (New Roads), which proclaimed that "Work, liberating and liberated work, is the motto of our organization."

Italian feminists were among many whose high hopes in unification were disappointed by subsequent events. Indeed, with the introduction of the Napoleonic Code, women lost many of the rights they had possessed under the previous Austrian administration. Nor was Cavour's official regulation of prostitution greeted with any enthusiasm by feminists who had fought in Garibaldi's army to liberate their people. Anna Maria Mozzoni (1837–1920), the best-known feminist in Italy, criticized the laws that regulated women's rights and family relations and attacked the Catholic Church. She also translated Mill's *On the Subjection of Women*. In 1868, Italian feminists began publishing *La Donna* (Woman), a newspaper that advocated Mazzini's notion of women as citizen-mothers.

Progress during the years from 1850 to 1870 was slow, yet the early feminists succeeded in establishing their cause as of fundamental importance in social and political reform. Together with that of universal suffrage, it became one of the central issues of public life in the late 19th and early 20th century (on feminism after 1870, see Part VII, Topic 19).

THE URBAN POOR AND SOCIAL REFORM

Unlike the middle classes, the working-class urban population seemed to have gained little from the industrial revolution. Many had given up the bare livelihood of a rural existence for the even grimmer task of scraping a living in overcrowded and polluted cities. Those engaged in work in middle-class homes were able to contrast their lot with that of their employers. Others could see the shops filled with luxury goods, and the

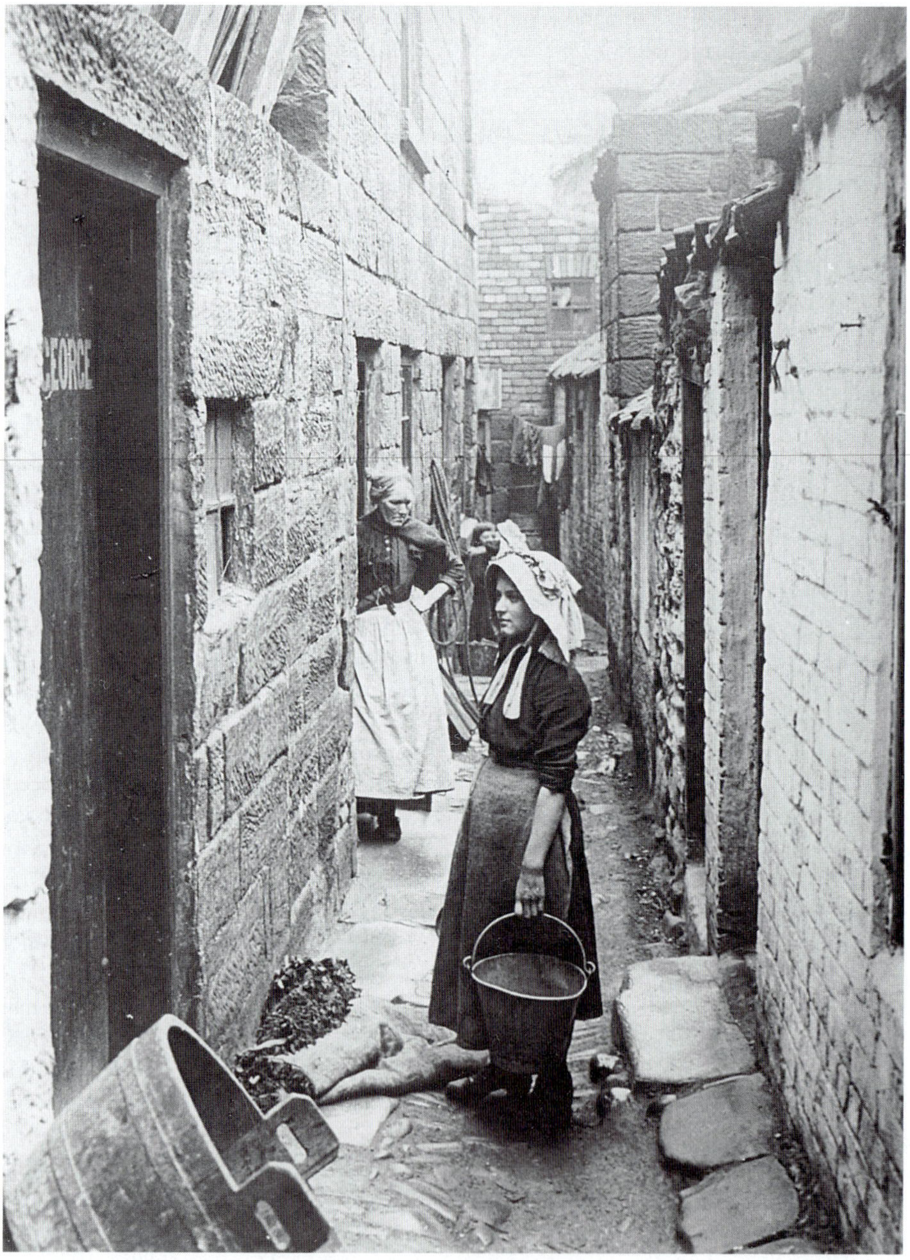

An urban working-class slum in Yorkshire, England.

An English classroom in the mid-19th century with working-class children of both sexes.

streets crowded with carriages. City life made class differences only too visible.

The struggle to improve the conditions of the poor was a long one, fraught with setbacks. In Great Britain, a system of poor relief administered by local counties added to wages that were below subsistence. The Poor Law of 1834, passed after much controversy, took a different approach. In order to make public assistance unappealing, paupers and unemployed were required to live in workhouses, where conditions were minimal and treatment harsh. As late as 1900 in Britain, then the most prosperous country in the world, one out of every five people received a pauper's funeral.

The problem lay partly, as we have seen, in the speed and complexity of urban growth. Another factor was the lack of sympathy on the part of artisans and the more successful workers, who saw the urban poor as a threat to their own upward mobility. Those who could see their way to social advancement eagerly accepted middle-class notions of property as the only real indication of status. As a result, they had little time for those with no hope of escape from the squalor of poverty, with its slums and chronic alcoholism. Middle-class attitudes blamed poverty on the poor themselves.

By the end of the century, working-class support for social reform at the bottom of the scale began to grow, in part due to the politicization of workers' movements. In the 1850s and 1860s, however, the poor were mainly dependent on government actions and the charity of middle-class benefactors.

Living Standards in Second Empire Paris

Even among the urban masses, there were wide divergences of income and lifestyles. In the Paris of Napoleon III, the average worker earned two francs 50 centimes a day, and a meal in a cheap, working-class tavern cost just over a franc. Those employed in the lower ranks of domestic service, such as footmen or maids, were paid 60 to 70 francs a month in addition to their board and lodging. A master chef or the chief butler could receive up to 200 francs a month.

Lower down in the scale were those who barely got by. Bernard D. was a laborer who had migrated to Paris from rural Lorraine. In 1859 he was supporting himself, his wife, and six of his fifteen children; two other children lived at home but worked, contributing part of their earnings to the family; the remaining seven children were independent. The family's total income for that year, including the earnings of the two working dependents, was 1612 francs, of which 200 went for rent. That left about 115 francs a month to support ten people. Their annual expenditure on meat was 70 francs, most of which was spent on two kilos of ox head a week; cooked in water, it provided soup and boiled meat.

At least the family was self-supporting. Many Parisian residents depended for their survival on charitable contributions. In December 1856 an appeal was circulated in the 1st *arrondissement* (district) of Paris: "More urgently than ever before, we solicit charitable offerings for the relief of many poor folk." The number of the destitute in this single district in danger of dying of starvation was listed as 4839.

Private Charity

The appeal described above was made by the city administration, but the most common form of relief was that provided by private organizations, whose numbers multiplied rapidly by midcentury. By the 1850s, over 450 charitable groups were operating in London. Many charities were inspired by religious motives. The Society of St. Vincent de Paul, founded in Paris in 1835, was active throughout France, Italy, Spain, and the Catholic parts of the Austrian empire. Its members, successful, educated men, were required to visit the poor and improve their lot both by financial help and by teaching them thrift. In addition to benefiting the needy, organizations such as this did much to inform the better-off of the terrible conditions of many of their fellow citizens.

The Society of St. Vincent de Paul was unusual in that its membership was restricted to men. The overwhelming majority of those engaged in practical charitable work were middle- and upper-class women. Often inspired by religious motives, they tried to establish direct personal contact with those from whom they were isolated both psychologically and physically—middle-class residential areas were kept at a distance from the poorer parts of cities. In addition to fulfilling Christian teachings of charity towards all, their work also became an extension of their domestic role, expressing "the flow of maternal love," applied to a broader notion of family.

In some cases the contribution was financial. The English philanthropist Angela Burdett-Coutts (1814–1906) donated over 3 million pounds for charitable purposes. In others the founding of an organization led to wide-ranging consequences. The Bible and Domestic Female Mission Society, created in London by Ellen Ranyard (1814–1879), sold Bibles and other religious works, and used the profits to help the needy. The Society grew rapidly, and became an important relief force. A similar organization was founded in Hamburg, the Female Association for the Care of the Poor and the Sick.

Others had more specific goals. In France, maternal societies provided help to mothers in need; during the Second Empire, the Empress Eugénie became actively involved in their work. Around 1850 the Italian reformer Laura Mantegazza established day care centers for the children of working mothers, and a few years later set up schools for the illiterate. In Spain, Concepción Arenal (1820–1893) campaigned for prison reform, and also wrote a guide for those engaged in charitable work, *The Visitor of the Poor* (1860).

The active participation of so many women in relief work made an enormous contribution to public welfare at a time when government aid was limited. It also caused many to question the bourgeois assumptions that lay behind the cult of domesticity. After seeing the conditions under which the poor lived, it was difficult to return unchanged to their material comforts, often enjoyed at the expense of others. Furthermore, women came to realize that, far from being helpless and best confined to the home, they could play a vital part in producing social reform. The growing sense of their own powers helped to inspire the movement for female suffrage later in the century.

KARL MARX AND THE VISION OF A NEW SOCIAL ORDER

One of the chief aims of 19th-century reformers was to redress social injustice. Those who had most to gain from reform—the workers and the needy—were in no doubt about their own plight, but for the first half of the century they were unable to articulate their case. When working-class protests were heard, they were often misdirected or unsustained. The Luddites' destruction of machinery (see Part VII, Topic 2) did nothing to hold back the industrial revolution. The Chartists mounted a more organized campaign but failed to carry it through.

What was lacking was an overarching vision of the radical social reordering needed to change the entrenched system. The middle class was too satisfied with its victories to theorize about the rights of others, and the establishment certainly had no interest in overturning an order of which they were the chief beneficiaries. When serious and sustained workers' protests did finally make themselves heard, toward the end of the century, they were based on a worldview derived in large measure from the writings of Karl Marx and his collaborator, Friedrich Engels (see Part VII, Topic 8).

Both men came from prosperous middle-class families, although Marx's financial position deteriorated with the death of his father. After studying at the universities of Bonn and Berlin, and obtaining a doctorate from the University of Jena, Marx—already a radical in his ideas—took up journalism. Hoping to be able to influence contemporary society, in 1842 he be-

Karl Marx and one of his three daughters. Note the cross hanging from her neck.

came editor of *The Rhineland Gazette*, a well-known liberal newspaper. Within a year his articles had won him the enmity of the Prussian government and of his own publishers, and he moved to Paris, the center in continental Europe of political exiles and radical debate.

There he renewed an earlier friendship with Engels, who had firsthand experience of the appalling conditions under which industrial workers lived. The Engels family owned a cotton mill near Manchester, and Engels wrote a searing account of his observations there, *The Condition of the Working Class in England* (see Part VII, Topic 6). Marx and Engels joined forces to diagnose the cause of society's ills, and to provide a prescription for their cure. On the eve of the revolutions of 1848 they published the *Communist Manifesto*. At the time the work made little impression, and with the end of the revolution in Paris, Marx made his way to London. He lived there in exile for the rest of his life, continuing his collaboration with Engels, who also provided him with financial support. The first volume of *Das Kapital* appeared in 1867; Engels edited the other two volumes (1885, 1894) after Marx's death.

The *Communist Manifesto*

Marx and Engels intended their work to accomplish two ends: to explain the nature of contemporary society by looking back to the pattern of European history, and to provide a practical means for correcting its faults. Thus the *Manifesto* is at the same time a broad philosophical statement and a handbook to revolution.

The Marxist theory of history takes its departure from the ideas of the German philosopher Georg Hegel (see Part VII, Topic 7). Hegel believed that "dialectic"—the clash of ideas in thesis and antithesis—would lead to a "synthesis," and that this resolution of conflict would mark a new stage in historical evolution. The clashing ideas were purely intellectual, however, and the resolution would always be a positive one. Rejecting Hegel's abstraction, Marx claimed that history was propelled forward by conflict not over ideas, but over economic interests, and that all aspects of society were determined by materialist factors, in particular by the means of production.

This "dialectical materialism" was responsible for changes in the past. The economy of the Middle Ages had been dependent upon the feudal system, whereby large numbers of serfs worked for a small, landowning, hereditary aristocracy. With the rise of commerce and trade, a new middle class began to develop. The "dialectic," or struggle, between aristocracy and middle class was resolved in the triumph of the bourgeoisie, first in England and the Netherlands in the 18th century, then in the American War of Independence and the French Revolution, and finally and decisively in the middle-class victories of the 19th century.

This Marxist analysis reveals his belief that historical change depends not only on economic factors, but also on an inherent and inevitable class struggle. Just as the middle class overcame the aristocracy, so in the next stage the workers—the proletariat—would overcome the middle class. In order to accomplish this and throw off their oppressors, the workers of the world needed to organize and unite, under the inspiration of their newly developed class consciousness. In the new order, the "dictatorship of the proletariat" would abolish existing political systems, make all production public, and bring about a classless society in which the state would "wither away."

The struggle would be made easier by the inherent defects in the middle-class economic system of capitalism. Since, Marx argued, capitalism by its nature required competition, those capitalists who succeeded would do so at the expense of others. Those who went out of business would join the proletariat. Since successful employers would be forced to cut wages and expenditures to remain competitive, the poor would continue to get poorer and the rich richer. In the end the capitalist system would collapse.

Marx and Marxism

The accuracy of Marx's historical and economic analyses has frequently been challenged. Furthemore, never did he or Engels really describe the precise nature of the society to be brought about under the dictatorship of the proletariat. Many developments that Marx did not live to see, such as mass communications, the spread of popular democracy, and expanding technologies, outdated some of his conclusions. The poor have not all continued to get poorer, and the capitalist system has not collapsed. Nor did Marx's rigorously economic determinism leave any place for the part played in history by individual human characteristics, or even pure random chance.

Yet after its early neglect, the *Manifesto*, along with Marx's other writings, went on to influence, directly or indirectly, countless millions of lives, and served as the inspiration for revolutionary movements throughout the world. The degree to which Marxist ideas have ever been applied in practice can be debated, as can the relationship between Marx's communism and the Communist party which came to power in Russia following the Bolshevik Revolution of 1917. Nevertheless, generations of political, social, and economic reformers turned to his writings.

Much of the appeal of Marxism lay in its positive view of the social role of workers and other underprivileged citizens, who had been accustomed to think of themselves as the dregs of society, beyond hope. Marx had less enthusiasm for them intellectually, believing them basically unable to discern their own interests, and thus in need of a "vanguard of intellectuals" to lead them. The socialist parties that were formed in the late 19th century drew much of their pride and energy from Marx's essentially optimistic view of their role in history and the inevitability of their eventual success, although by no means all of them were Marxists. Nor, like some other thinkers, did Marx seek to reverse the industrial revolution and return to a problem-free (and nonexistent) rural past. Indeed it was by means of greater productivity that the lot of most human beings was to be improved: Marx was the prophet of modernism, not its enemy. In addition, although he overstressed the role played by economics, his assertion of the need for radical economic change drove many to challenge the status quo. Finally, he made two claims for his analysis that were bound to appeal to many. It was, he said, scientific, and therefore intellectually sound. Furthermore, given his determinist view of history, sooner or later his long-term predictions were bound to come true; any setbacks or defeats would be only temporary.

Neither Marx nor Engels claimed that the dictatorship of the proletariat would be achieved quickly, but they and their followers believed that history was on their side. By the end of the 19th century, with the spread of socialism and the rise of the trade unions, many who were not Marxists began to share their conviction.

By 1870, the certainties of bourgeois existence were coming under increasing challenge. Just as Marx was undermining economic attitudes, so Darwin's work questioned the entire basis of traditional morality (see Part VII, Topic 14). Increasing numbers of middle-class women were becoming restless with the position assigned them in society. These developments took place at a time when governments in Western Europe were beginning to come under pressure to extend the franchise beyond the aristocracy and the prosperous middle class.

In Britain, Victoria continued her apparently everlasting reign, but the social situation was in a state of growing ferment. Elsewhere in Europe instabilities began to develop. The French Second Empire came abruptly to an end. Germany and Italy were faced with the new uncertainties of nationhood. The Austro-Hungarian empire lived on the brink of perpetual crisis. The only country where social conditions seemed likely to remain unchanged for centuries, as they had for centuries past, was Russia. By one of the ironies of history, amid the cataclysm of World War I Russian society was overturned and remade by self-proclaimed followers of the obscure German philosopher of the mid-19th century.

Questions for Further Study

1. What factors influenced the urbanization of Europe? How did urbanization affect social patterns?
2. Describe the principal values of the middle classes. How did they affect daily life?
3. What roles did "Victorian" values assign to women?
4. How did Marx explain the inevitability of the proletarian revolution? What would happen after the revolution?

Suggestions for Further Reading

Accampo, Elinor. *Industrialization, Family Life, and Class Relations: Saint Chamond, 1815–1914*. Berkeley, CA, 1989.

Berlanstein, Lenard R. *The Working People of Paris, 1871–1914*. Baltimore, MD, 1984.

Girouard, Mark. *Cities and People: A Social and Architectural History*. New Haven, CT, 1985.

Himmelfarb, Gertrude. *The Idea of Poverty: England in the Early Industrial Age*. New York, 1984.

Joyce, P. *Visions of the People: Industrial England and the Question of Class, c. 1848–1914*. New York, 1991.

Jones, Gareth. *Outcast London*. Oxford, 1984.

Marsden, G., ed. *Victorian Values: Personalities and Perspectives in 19th-Century Society*. New York, 1990.

Miller, Michael. *The Bon Marché: Bourgeois Culture and the Department Store, 1869–1920*. Princeton, NJ, 1981.

Pilbeam, Pamela M. *The Middle Classes in Europe, 1789–1914*. Chicago, 1990.

Ross, Ellen. *Love and Toil: Motherhood in Outcast London, 1870–1918*. New York, 1993.

Shapiro, Ann-Louise. *Housing the Poor of Paris, 1850–1902*. Madison, WI, 1985.

Stearns, Peter N. *European Society in Upheaval: Social History Since 1800*. New York, 1967.

Sutcliffe, Anthony. *Towards the Planned City: Germany, Britain, and the United States, 1789–1914*. New York, 1981.

Vicinus, Martha, ed. *Suffer and Be Still: Women in the Victorian Age*. Bloomington, IN, 1972.

Walkowitz, Judith. *City of Dreadful Delight*. Chicago, 1993.

VII

Topic 14

Arts, Ideas, and Social Consciousness

By mid-19th century, European artists and thinkers were already beginning to take a critical look at the society produced by industrialization and political reform. The enormous speed with which the world was changing, not only politically but also as the result of developments in science and technology, encouraged analysis of the present and speculation about the future. At the same time, the rapidly rising literacy rate made new ideas circulate with ever-increasing speed.

The scientific study of human society—sociology—was enthusiastically advocated by Auguste Comte, whose optimistic belief in the power of human achievement inspired the rise of new fields of research: psychology, anthropology, and the social sciences in general. Charles Darwin's work on evolution presented a more serious challenge to conventional notions of the world. Plants and animals (humans included), he claimed, had not been created in their present form by divine plan, but had evolved over millions of years. Some of his successors sought to reconcile the principle of natural selection with Christian traditions, but the initial impact of his work produced widespread controversy.

The diffusion of worldviews which seriously questioned the teachings of Christianity increased debate by instilling tension between religion and scientific discovery. Furthermore, with the rise of the secular nation-state, Christian churches had to work out new ways of coexisting with civil powers.

In literature the most popular form of the day was the novel. No longer seeking merely to entertain, writers aimed to make public the chief issues of the times—social injustice, religious intolerance, evolving political patterns. Many of the leading novelists attracted a mass readership and succeeded in influencing substantial bodies of opinion.

Musicians also saw themselves as promoters of political causes, in particular that of nationalism. In Russia and among the peoples of Eastern Europe, traditional folk music was used as the basis for works that set out to reinforce ideas of national consciousness. The leading musician in Italy, Giuseppe Verdi, became the symbol of the unification of Italy under the House of Savoy. Many of his operas made indirect reference to political events, and served to ignite popular support for the *Risorgimento*.

In the visual arts, Romanticism gave way to a new movement, realism. Some painters produced realistic, unglamorized depictions of peasant and working-class life, while for others art was a means for revealing social injustice. Interest in realism was stimulated around midcentury by the invention and spread of photography.

In the arts, as in intellectual developments, the age was marked by an ever-widening popular audience for culture. Increasing ease of transport, the spread of literacy, and improvements in education meant that the ideas of Darwin and the novels of Dickens were widely distributed throughout Europe. They also made their way with increasing speed across the Atlantic, where American artists and thinkers were already forming their own rich tradition.

AUGUSTE COMTE AND THE PHILOSOPHY OF POSITIVISM

The chief artistic and intellectual movements of the early 19th century, Romanticism and utopian socialism, were inspired by the ferment of change that the revolutionary spirit of the times seemed to open up. Released from the bondage of traditional patterns of society, artists and thinkers explored possibilities for a new future. Even where, as in Germany, the old ways soon reestablished themselves, Romanticism continued to offer an escape from the realities of political power. Amid the hopes and delusions of postrevolutionary France, the utopian socialists tried to prescribe for a future ideal society (see Part VII, Topic 8).

By midcentury, Romanticism was giving way to realism, while new currents of thought examined humanity's place in the universe. Auguste Comte (1798–1857) arrived at an overarching view of civilization, which sought to rationalize the development of human understanding. Comte had spent many years as private secretary to the utopian Saint-Simon and inherited his predecessor's optimistic confidence in the progress of society. At the same time he constructed a philosophical system to explain the nature of historical change.

The Philosophy of Positivism

By the time of his death in 1857, Comte's philosophy of positivism was established as an international movement. His basic belief was that knowledge must be derived from experience or observation, and not from speculation. It was impossible to know why things happen, let alone what would happen in the future; the only certainties could be found by learning how things actually occur in the world. Study of this "positive" knowledge would eventually lead to an improved, "positive" society, based not on beliefs but on scientific facts.

Comte divided the history of civilization into a series of "progressive" stages. In the first, the "theological," people had tried to explain the world in terms of nature deities. This was followed by the "metaphysical" stage, in which religion was used to find hidden causes and understand abstract principles. By his day a new age was dawning, the "positive," in which society would achieve its highest form. Traditional religions such as Christianity played an important role in the development of civilization, but would in due course be replaced by a new "religion of humanity."

Reduced to its essence, Comte's positivism seems no more convincing than other optimistic philosophies—that of the 17th-century German Gottfried von Leibnitz, for example, parodied by Voltaire in *Candide*. Its appeal to his contemporaries lay in two factors. In the first place he warned that the progress from the "metaphysical" stage to "positivism" would involve struggle. The outward sign of this struggle was the upheaval of industrialization, with its social injustices and human misery. Thus his followers could accept the troubles of their times as the inevitable price to be paid for progress. The message was especially welcome to those members of the prosperous middle classes who felt pangs of guilt at the ignoble foundations on which their wealth seemed to rest.

Second, Comte's insistence on the scientific observation of human society created a new and intriguing way of looking at the world: sociology (Comte himself coined the term). During the second half of the 19th century, the scientific study of different forms taken by various societies led to widespread interest in the social sciences. Economics, psychology, anthropology, political science, sociology, history, all are ways of trying to satisfy Comte's requirement and provide objective, "positive" knowledge about society.

CHARLES DARWIN AND THE CASE FOR NATURAL SELECTION

Comte's positivism saw traditional religion as benign, although in the end to be superseded by humanism. The publication in 1859 of Charles Darwin's *On the Origin of Species* presented a far more severe challenge

Charles Darwin

to established Christian beliefs; its implications still remain controversial.

As a young man, Darwin (1809–1882) began by studying medicine, his father's profession. He soon changed his mind, and decided to become a minister of religion, although without abandoning his interest in natural history. In 1831 the offer of an unpaid position as naturalist aboard H.M.S. *Beagle,* which was about to sail on an expedition to South America, tempted him away from his theological studies at Cambridge. The voyage lasted five years, and Darwin's work on South American fossils and bird and animal life gave him the basis for his theory of natural selection.

Like many important intellectual ideas, natural selection did not suddenly appear in a vacuum. Other scholars and scientists had begun to look for natural rather than divine explanations for the order of creation. The Scottish geologist James Hutton (1726–1797) published *Theory of the Earth* in 1795, which claimed that a continual process of geological evolution was responsible for the earth's natural features; his theory was called uniformitarianism. In 1809 the French biologist Jean Lamarck (1744–1829) proposed a hypothesis whereby animals that changed their characteristics due to the environment, or the acquisition of new habits, could transmit these changes to their offspring. The theory was unsound. A man who develops strong muscles as a result of hauling sacks of flour will not pass on his physique to his sons and daughters. Nevertheless Lamarck's notion began to question the traditional religious teaching that life had been created according to a divine and unchanging scheme.

In his geological studies, Darwin was inspired by his contemporary Charles Lyell (1797–1875), whose *Principles of Geology* (1830) argued that all geological phenomena could be explained by natural causes. A general philosophical rationale was provided by the writings of Malthus (see Part VII, Topic 8), and the struggle for existence they describe. This struggle became, for Darwin, the basis of the process of natural selection.

Although all members of a species are generally similar, no two living creatures are identical. The random differences between individual members are transmitted to their offspring in a process that is, as we now know, genetic. Some variations are apparently irrelevant, while others—strength, speed, natural markings—are likely to improve the chances of survival. According to Darwin's theory of the survival of the fittest, the characteristics that are most likely to help in the struggle for life will, over millennia, be strengthened by the simple fact that the members of the species possessing them have a better chance of surviving.

When Darwin published his conclusions in 1859, encouraged by the independent formation of a similar theory by Alfred Wallace, he did not intend them as an open challenge to religion. He avoided speculation about the origins of life, or on why so many species have characteristics that cannot apparently be explained by this process. Nor did he emphasize natural selection as the most important of his ideas. Instead, the avowed tone of his publication was one of optimism at the notion of the "rising swell of the Great Chorus of Being."

The Impact of Darwinism

Inevitably, however, Darwin's work was seen as inextricably opposed to Christian teaching. The fittest survive, by implication, only because the overwhelming majority of living organisms are destroyed, a principle which Darwin clearly extended to the human species. This was impossible to reconcile with belief in an all-loving God—and one, at that, who created the world according to His own scheme and humans in His own image. Church leaders were horrified, and controversy raged. Darwin's publication of *The Descent of Man* (1871), which claimed that humans and anthropoid apes were both descended from a common apelike ancestor, was hardly likely to still the debate.

The theological implications of Darwinism remain unresolved. Many Christians, and others, managed to reconcile the idea of natural selection with the Bible's account of creation by taking the biblical description as poetic rather than literal. There continue to be those whose understanding of the Bible leads them to reject Darwin's theory of evolution by natural selection.

Darwinism also had widespread influence in social thinking and the arts, often in ways that went far beyond the intentions of its originator. For Darwin, survival was a fact that of itself was morally neutral. A species was neither "better" nor "worse" for having won the struggle. Self-styled "Social Darwinists," however, began to use the notion of the survival of the fittest to imply the survival of the best (see Part VII, Topic 20).

For contemporary poets and novelists, Darwin suggested new insights into the human condition. Romanticism drew attention to the uniqueness of the individual, but Darwin's work put existence into a very different perspective. The vision was not always a comforting one. In his famous poem, "In Memoriam," the eminent Victorian poet Alfred, Lord Tennyson (1809–1892) gloomily accepted the notion of a "Nature, red in tooth and claw," which proclaims: "A thousand types are gone; I care for nothing, all shall go." Under such conditions, life was "as futile, then, as frail!"

Writers began to emphasize the development of character and the external events that molded it. To do justice to their material, and the concept of change over time, they wrote novels that were longer and contained more naturalistic descriptions than those of their predecessors. Among the major writers influenced by the Darwinian worldview were Thomas Hardy and Émile Zola (see Part VII, Topic 21). Some students of literature collected information about conditions among the working class: the German essayist Bettina von Arnim (1785–1857), an important figure in the early-19th-century Romantic movement, now began to compile notebooks in which she documented working conditions in Berlin.

The immediate impact of Darwin gradually abated, and by the end of the century the new disciplines of psychology and sociology probably had a greater influence on European intellectual life than the religious implications of natural selection. Yet the theory of evolution remains an important and controversial topic, and not only for theologians. Modern scientists, using methods of genetic research and the study of the physico-chemical composition of DNA, are rapidly revising Darwin's conclusions. Darwin himself would surely not have been surprised: he himself predicted that future scientists would modify his theories as they explored the many unanswered questions concerning natural selection.

SCIENCE AND RELIGION IN A CHANGING WORLD

The theory of evolution was not the only idea to present problems for 19th-century organized religion. With the advance of science and the growth of the secular state, Christian leaders found themselves facing serious challenges. For centuries the various branches of Christianity had at least agreed on a central body of teaching, and they regarded themselves as uniquely qualified to expound it. Lutherans and Catholics alike agreed on the importance of the Scriptures. Biblical accounts had, it is true, been attacked since the 17th century by scientists like Galileo and philosophers such as Voltaire. Now, however, increasing numbers of laypeople exposed to the new ideas began to question truths that had been held immutable since the Middle Ages.

Some of the doubts came from biblical historians, who were trying, as they thought, to save Christianity from being too closely tied to the teachings of the Bible. The French scholar Ernest Renan (1832–1892) pointed out historical inconsistencies in the Scriptures, emphasizing that the human fallibility of its authors did not invalidate its general message. His most widely read book was *The Life of Jesus*, which appeared in 1863. It perfectly expresses the intellectual spirit of the times by substituting a heightened appreciation of the poetry and human achievements described in the Bible for blind faith. Renan's purpose was to emphasize the continuing relevance of the Christian story to modern life, and he described Jesus as "an incomparable man." However, the authorities of the Collège de France, under the influence of the Catholic party, forbade him to teach his version of Christianity.

A far more hostile opponent of Christianity was the English philosopher Thomas Henry Huxley (1825–1895). An energetic defender of Darwin, Huxley invented the term "agnosticism" to describe the belief that the existence and nature of God are unknowable. He was a pioneer in the field of popular scientific education, and a champion of free speech and investigation. Among the opponents of Darwin whom he lambasted in his newspaper articles was the British prime minister, William Gladstone, a deeply religious man who ranked among Darwin's most vocal opponents.

The German philosopher Ludwig Andreas Feuerbach (1804–1872) took an even more extreme position. The most fiery and uncompromising prophet of philosophical materialism, Feuerbach attacked belief in an afterlife and declared that all deities are merely personifications of human fears. Religion, he claimed, prevented the full understanding and enjoyment of physical and moral reality. Expressing one of

Louis Pasteur conducting an experiment.

the 19th century's most typical ideas, he wrote that "the characteristic of the modern age is that man sees himself as divine and infinite, and that the individual feels these qualities within himself in his individuality."

Meanwhile, science and technology did not so much challenge traditional religion as ignore it. Furthermore, by visibly improving the lives of countless people, advances in these areas were seen as a source of "progress" and material well-being. The work of Louis Pasteur (1822–1895) on bacteria revolutionized standards of public health and nutrition. Joseph Lister's (1827–1912) discovery of the value of carbolic acid as a disinfectant vastly improved surgical techniques. The development of the telegraph and the subsequent laying of a transatlantic cable from Europe to America between 1858 and 1866 produced miraculous changes in communication.

None of these innovations was hostile to Christianity, but to some puzzled believers they seemed to make religion increasingly irrelevant to modern life. The Catholic Church responded by taking the offensive, motivated by reasons of dogma, and also by its loss of temporal power in Italy as a consequence of Italian unification. In 1864 Pope Pius IX issued the *Syllabus of Errors*, in which he castigated materialism, freedom of thought, and the belief that all religions are equally valid. Five years later, in 1869, he summoned the first church council since the Counter-Reformation, and proclaimed the doctrine of papal infallibility. According to this teaching, when the pope speaks "ex cathedra," from his position as head of the church, on any issue of faith or morals, he is infallible. Pius was speaking precisely from this position in condemning what he saw as dangerous modern tendencies.

The pope's assertion of authority met with a mixed reception, not least in Italy where tensions already existed between church and state. Protestants, lacking a central authority or a body of established dogma, were left with their consciences to guide them to an accommodation with new ways of thinking. Some turned to social commitment, and tried to contribute to progress by active work among the poor. They emphasized the ethical teachings of Jesus rather than faith in miracles and belief in original sin.

Christianity and the State

At the same time as the Catholic Church was fighting its moral battles, it was involved in a more temporal struggle. The papacy had never been sympathetic to the cause of Italian unification, which had sought to incorporate the Papal States into the new Italian nation. In 1871, the year after the seizure of Rome, the Italian parliament passed a law designed to define and guarantee the pope's status. Pius IX, who never accepted the loss of the Papal States, refused to accept the Italian government's stand. Instead, he withdrew into the Vatican, causing serious liabilities for the Italian government (see Part VII, Topic 15).

Elsewhere in Europe, political leaders and religious authorities found themselves in conflict. The governments of France and Spain, both predominantly Catholic countries, denounced the dogma of papal infallibility as proclaimed by the Vatican Council in 1870. In Germany, Bismarck's *Kulturkampf* (battle over culture) saw the introduction of a number of anti-Catholic laws between 1872 and 1875 which expelled the Jesuits and gave the state control over seminaries and the appointment of priests and bishops. Bismarck was concerned about a possible alliance of Catholic powers, and wanted to limit outside influence in Germany (see Part VII, Topic 15). The strength of the Catholic Center party forced the eventual repeal of the measures. Even the Church of England, whose official head was the monarch, found itself increasingly stripped by Parliament of the special privileges it had accumulated over the centuries.

By the end of the century the decades of controversy succeeded in producing a renewal of religious influence, as Christians of all denominations struggled to address theological and social problems with increasing flexibility. Yet in the end the real threat to organized religion came not from scientists or liberal governments, but from the rise of socialism.

THE WRITER AS CRITIC: SOCIAL REALISM AND THE NOVEL

With the spread of education and an increase in literacy throughout most of Europe, public demand for literature increased. The most popular form was the novel, and the most successful writers of the 19th century were those who managed both to entertain and to instruct their readers.

As industrialization and the growth of urban life intensified social discontent, authors turned from the self-centered images of Romanticism to deal with the practical problems of the day in a realistic style. Not content merely to describe society's injustices, in many cases they fought to correct them. In the process they criticized many of the mid-19th century's conventional beliefs.

The realities of social existence were memorably expressed by a number of women writers, many of whom took male names to reassure some readers who might not have otherwise taken them seriously. In England, George Eliot (1819–1880; her real name was Mary Ann Evans) dealt with questions of morality and philosophy, as well as creating, in *Middlemarch* (1871–1872), an unforgettable picture of provincial life. The French writer George Sand (1804–1876; in real life Aurore Dudevant) tackled just about every issue of the day, including women's rights. Her contemporary, the English poet Elizabeth Barrett Browning, called Sand "true genius but true woman."

Perhaps the most devastating attack on middle-class values and society is that found in *Madame Bovary*, the masterpiece of Sand's friend Gustave Flaubert (1821–1880). When the work first appeared in print in 1856–1857, its reception did much to confirm Flaubert's low opinion of his times: he was prosecuted for offenses against public morals, although in the end he was acquitted. The story's main character, Emma Bovary, has been brought up on a diet of romantic novels, which leave her unsatisfied by the dull reality of her respectable life in the provinces. Married to a boorish country doctor, she embarks on a shoddy affair and ends up fatally in debt. Flaubert's understated, impersonal recounting of the banal tragedy is filled with carefully observed details.

The most successful English novelist of the period was Charles Dickens (1812–1870), whose rich, many-layered books are filled with characters both realistic and bizarre—a far cry from the restraint of Flaubert or the measured tone of Eliot. Dickens' style is poetic, with an endlessly imaginative use of language.

An illustration for Dickens' *Oliver Twist:* "Please sir, May I have some more. . ."

His finest works combine insights into human behavior with searing indictments of the flaws and social inequities of his times. *Bleak House* (1853) attacked the British legal system, which was notorious for its interminable, inhumane delays and incomprehensible proceedings. The book played a part in the movement which led to legal reform in the 1860s. In *Hard Times* (1854), Dickens analyzed the ills of industrialized society, and powerfully underlined the fact that education without humanity can destroy those whom it seeks to help. Often unpopular with the establishment, Dickens won a huge and affectionate audience both in Europe and in America. The arrival in New York of a ship carrying the latest episode of one of his works attracted crowds to the docks.

Not all authors met with so appreciative a reception. The Russian novelist Nikolai Gogol (1809–1852) spent many years abroad, most of them in Rome, where he wrote his satirical masterpiece, *Dead Souls* (1842). Gogol's readers saw his satires of bureaucracy and serfdom as blows in the struggle for progress. He was, however, more concerned to castigate moral evil than social or political error.

Ivan Turgenev and Pauline Viardot

Gogol's contemporary, Ivan Turgenev (1818–1883), was a liberal and an advocate of the importation of Western ideas into his country. Among his early writings was a series of depictions of peasant life. His novels dealt with the great issues facing Russian society: the emancipation of the serfs in *On the Eve* (1860—a year before the emancipation became law); nihilism in *Fathers and Children* (1862); populist revolution in *Virgin Soil* (1877). The last of these was written in Paris, for discouraged by the lack of sympathy on the part of Russian readers and critics, Turgenev spent the last 21 years of his life in Germany and France. While in Paris he maintained a close relationship with Pauline Viardot, one of the most prominent opera singers of the 19th century.

Viardot and Turgenev provided a rare 19th-century example of two creative people who maintained a long relationship while preserving their personal and professional independence. Unlike traditional gender patterns of the period, the character of their interaction was one of equality. Each provided the other with a source of artistic inspiration. Furthermore, quite apart from their private lives, Turgenev and Viardot played an important role in introducing Russian artistic achievements to Western audiences. Viardot performed a great deal of Russian music written by Turgenev's friends, while her acquaintances, who numbered Flaubert and the young Henry James, acquired from their meetings with Turgenev a love of Russian literature.

Viardot and Turgenev met in Berlin in 1845, where he heard her sing, and they remained on close terms for the next 40 years. When Turgenev left Russia in 1862 to settle in Western Europe, he and the Viardots developed what their contemporaries thought was a "menage à trois." The three spent the first decade in Germany, since Louis Viardot was a vehement opponent of Napoleon III. When the Second Empire fell, all three moved back to Paris.

Many speculated on the exact nature of their relationship. Pauline Viardot no doubt avoided a breach with her husband in order to preserve her career. She saw advantages in maintaining her rapport with both men rather than choosing between them. While openly remaining her husband's wife, she and Turgenev—like John Stuart Mill and Harriet Taylor—traveled and visited friends as a couple. During a stay with George Sand, Viardot sang some of her songs and Turgenev told stories. "Last day of musical bliss," Sand noted in her diary as they prepared to leave: "Pauline sings bits of her operettas and Turgenev explains them. It's charming."

Viardot's attachment to Turgenev was a close one. Although she never had any children of her own, she brought up in her own household Turgenev's illegitimate daughter, born of a casual encounter between the writer and his mother's seamstress. Something of Turgenev's own ambiguous feelings about marriage can be gleaned from his play, *A Month in the Country*. Their relationship, certainly outside the gender norms prescribed by society, reflected the unorthodox values of many European artists of the period, whose works and lives shocked the virtuous bourgeoisie.

MUSIC AND THE RISE OF NATIONAL CONSCIOUSNESS

Around the middle of the 19th century, composers in many parts of Europe became eager to write music that openly proclaimed their nationality. Some, such as the Czechs Bedřich Smetana and Antonin Dvořák, and the Italian Giuseppe Verdi, were inspired by their country's struggles to achieve nationhood. In other cases musicians of long-established countries began to turn from traditional musical forms and material, and incorporate folk tunes and popular melodies into their works.

In Bohemia, Bedřich Smetana (1824–1884) gave the Czech people a new sense of identity and self-confidence by the musical style he developed, and by his choice of nationalistic subjects for his operas and symphonic poems. In addition to *The Bartered Bride* (1866), his best-loved work, with its sparkling dances and lyrical songs, he wrote a set of six orchestral pieces called *Ma Vlast* (My Fatherland). The most popular, "Vltava," paints a musical picture of the river Vltava, flowing from its bubbling source through the Czech landscape, and finally rolling majestically into Prague.

His younger contemporary, Antonin Dvořák (1841–1904), became famous for his Slavonic dances and rhapsodies. Much of his music, including the symphonies and string quartets, uses traditional Czech folk rhythms like the polka. The famous *New World* Symphony (Ninth Symphony; 1893), composed during Dvořák's stay in America to commemorate the 500th anniversary of Christopher Columbus' landing in the Americas, is far more Czech in character than American, although his interest in folk music of all kinds led him to collect American spirituals and incorporate them in his later works.

The greatest Italian composer of the century, Giuseppe Verdi (1813–1901), became a symbol of his country's Risorgimento. He began his career at a time when Milan, the center of Italian operatic life, was under Austrian rule. Although forbidden by the Austrian censor from depicting politically suggestive subjects on stage, he found ways to allude to the nationalist cause. His opera *Nabucco* (1842) shows the captivity of the Jews under the Babylonians in the 6th century B.C. His Italian audience, under Austrian captivity, had no difficulty in identifying themselves with the plight of the suffering Jews, and the work was greeted with wild enthusiasm at its first performances.

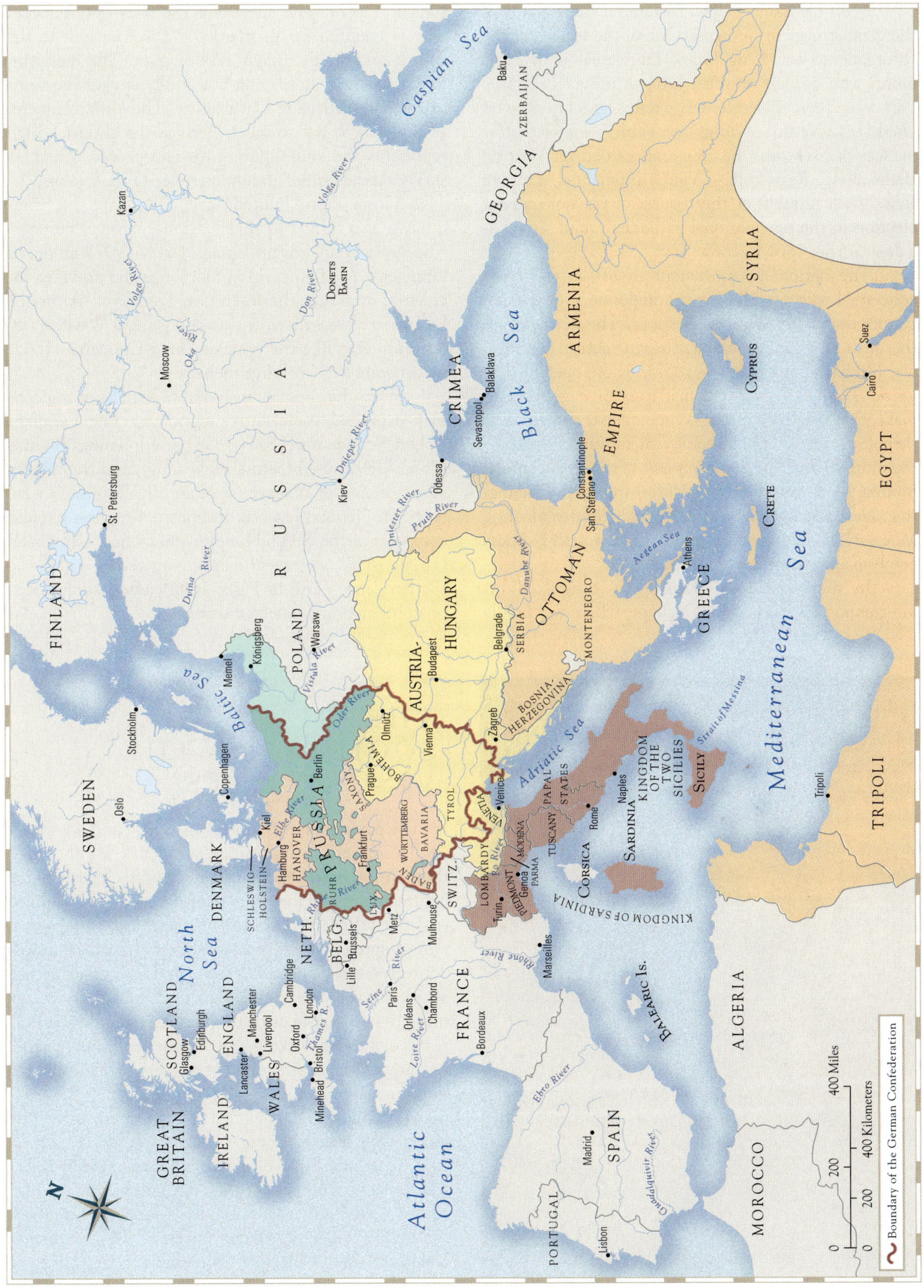

Map 14.1 Europe, Mid-19th Century

Even his name helped to remind the Italians of the great struggle in progress. One of the leaders of the Risorgimento was King Victor Emmanuel II of Piedmont, who became the first king of united Italy (see Part VII, Topic 11). For the excited spectators, who cried "Viva Verdi!"—"long live Verdi!"—after performances of his works, his name also stood for Vittorio Emmanuele, Re d'Italia—Victor Emmanuel, king of Italy. Verdi himself, at the request of Cavour, ran for election to the new national parliament, and served as a deputy from 1861 to 1865.

The nationalist movement in Russia was more concerned with establishing the importance of Russian culture than with political questions. The key figure in the birth of an independent Russian musical tradition was Mikhail Glinka (1804–1857), whose opera *A Life for the Tsar* (1836) was the first Russian stage work to make widespread use of folklike melodies. From an artistic point of view, Glinka's achievement was surpassed by the most original Russian composer of the 19th century, Modest Moussorgsky (1839–1881). Intensely imaginative, but tormented by a lifelong addiction to alcohol, Moussorgsky combined his musical career with political activism and family responsibilities.

In the late 1860s Moussorgsky completed his most important work, *Boris Godunov*, which was finally staged in 1874. The opera tells the story of Tsar Boris, who is haunted by his murder of the true heir to the throne and finally driven mad by guilt. The music incorporates folk motifs and powerfully evokes the spirit of Russian Orthodox Christianity. The chief character of the work is not so much Boris as the chorus, which represents the long-suffering Russian people, somehow surviving the crimes and indifference of their rulers.

On a more limited scale, musicians in Scandinavia also turned to their national musical heritage. The Norwegian Edvard Grieg (1843–1907) produced arrangements of Norwegian folk songs and provided incidental music for the Ibsen play *Peer Gynt*. Although his works were written within the general Western tradition, pieces like the popular Piano Concerto (1868) incorporate fresh, folklike melodies.

Even the most mainstream musicians of midcentury exploited their native resources. The Germans Robert Schumann (1810–1856) and Johannes Brahms (1833–1897) used German folk songs, and the mighty music dramas of Wagner (see Part VII, Topic 21) were based on German legends. In France, the most popular composer of the Second Empire was Jacques Offenbach (1819–1880), whose exhilarating operettas, such as *La Vie Parisienne* (Life in Paris; 1866), often commented on contemporary society and politics.

A scene from Act II of Verdi's opera, *La Traviata*.

THE IMAGE OF SOCIETY IN THE VISUAL ARTS

French painters and sculptors of the period showed a similar interest in the political and social world around them. Just as Offenbach made fun of the excesses of his contemporaries, Honoré Daumier (1808–1879) pilloried the follies of the times in paintings, lithographs, and sculpted statuettes. More bitter than his musical contemporary, Daumier often expressed anger at the abuse of power. He shared with Dickens a deep resentment of the injustices of the legal system and the corruption of those working in it. In a series of lithographs, he showed the indifference of lawyers to their clients' sufferings. Many of his small sculptures depict the leading politicians of Napoleon III's Paris, characterized by greed and self-satisfaction.

The paintings of Rosa Bonheur (1822–1899) and Gustave Courbet (1819–1877) also show realistic scenes, although they are less explicitly political in tone. Both of them rejected the full-blown Romanticism of Delacroix for naturalistic depictions of the world around them. Courbet preferred to paint peasants and workers, while Bonheur specialized in ani-

Honoré Daumier, *Third-Class Carriage* (c. 1862): the working class on public transportation.

Courbet's depiction of manual laborers, *The Stone Breakers.*

Thomas Eakins' *The Swimming Hole* shows the influence of photography.

mals. Her huge painting *The Horse Fair* was much admired by Napoleon III in 1853, and two years later she became the first woman to receive the Grand Cross of the Legion of Honor, France's highest official honor.

Courbet, who was a socialist, produced plain and unromantic scenes of village life. In *The Stone Breakers* (1849) his avoidance of the sentimental and underlining of realistic details are a visual parallel to the literary realism of his contemporary Flaubert.

The increasing tendency of artists to approach their subjects naturalistically was further stimulated by one of the most important inventions of the century: photography. In 1839, Louis Daguerre (1787–1851) gave the first public demonstration of a type of photographic process in Paris. The new technique was soon improved and hailed with excited enthusiasm by artists as different as Delacroix and Ingres, in part because, as Ingres observed, photographs provided "an exactitude that I shall like to achieve." The impact of photography on art and culture in general was vast and far-reaching. As the American painter Thomas Eakins perceptively realized, it represented no less a convention than traditional art. By stimulating painters to examine the actual process of literal observation, it inspired one of the most important artistic movements of the late 19th century, Impressionism (see Part VII, Topic 21).

In the early 19th century, artists and thinkers often saw themselves as leaders in the battle for social and political change. As time wore on they became commentators on the process, rather than participants. A number of factors were responsible for this gradual alienation from politics. In the first place, philosophical and intellectual developments such as the evolution controversy and the growing interest in psychology created a barrier between "advanced" intellectuals and the general public. The level of popular education was increasing, but not sufficiently to deal with these basic challenges to widespread beliefs.

Second, the increasing complexity of the industrialized world ruled out the broad, simple solutions of the early revolutionaries. Whatever the defects of urban life—and Dickens, Daumier, and others did not hesitate to point them out—nobody could seriously advocate that the process of modernization be suspended or reversed. Thus artists, whose ability to influence economic or technological developments was inevitably limited, began to describe rather than prescribe.

Furthermore, at least some of the goals of the early years of the century had been achieved. By the 1870s the new nations of Germany and Italy had been created, Hungary had obtained a measure of independence, political compromise had been relatively peacefully achieved in Britain, and even in Russia, bastion of conservatism, the serfs had been emancipated. All these developments brought their own problems with them. The rise of Germany entailed the humiliating defeat of France, and both the Austrians and their subjects were unhappy with the compromise of the Dual Monarchy. Yet many liberal aims had been fulfilled, few wept for Napoleon III, and the rapid rate of industrial transformation held out hope of further progress. Artists needed to absorb and reflect on the significance of their world, and reveal its true essence in their works, before they could move on.

Thus, in all the arts midcentury was a time for reacting to contemporary society and its problems, and relating it to an ever-wider public. The thirst for novels, opera performances, more easily affordable art objects in the form of prints and lithographs, and the immediate popularity of photography, were all signs that public enthusiasm for culture, far from diminishing, was in rapid increase. In part, the demand was due to the greater spread of affluence in western Europe. The middle classes of Victoria's Britain or the Second Empire in France were among the first worshipers at the shrine of conspicuous consumption, that cult which came to dominate Western society a century later. Yet in turning to the arts to seek explanations for their own lives and times, the public expressed a need that many artists fulfilled.

The spread of culture was not limited to Europe. In America the importation of European culture provided a stimulus to the growth of an indigenous artistic legacy. Paradoxically, the more the United States became exposed to European ideas and works of art, the more distinct was the voice with which American artists and intellectuals spoke. In response to the crisis of faith produced by Darwin, American thinkers developed the philosophy of Pragmatism: truth was whatever "worked." Painters like Winslow Homer and Thomas Eakins used the new realistic style to illustrate their own landscape and people. Walt Whitman sang of himself and his country.

As the century neared its end, and the first ominous signs of future conflict began to appear, the arts themselves increasingly reflected contemporary uncertainties. In the generation after Turgenev, Verdi, and Daumier, the very language and structure of art were to be questioned and, in many cases rejected. The mood of growing political concern is perceptible in artistic developments between 1880 and 1914. In the 1870s, however, artists could still touch large numbers of people by revealing to them the nature of the world in which they lived.

Questions for Further Study

1. How did the role of artists change in the course of the 19th century? What effects did this have on the subjects and style of their works?
2. What were the philosophical and moral implications of Darwin's theories? How has reaction to them evolved since his time?
3. What was the impact of nationalism on the arts? Did it have a stronger influence on some art forms than on others?

Suggestions for Further Reading

Barzun, J. *Darwin, Marx and Wagner*. Chicago, 1981.
Bowler, P. J. *Evolution: The History of an Idea*. Berkeley, CA, 1989.
Chadwick, O. *The Secularization of the European Mind in the Nineteenth Century*. Cambridge, MA, 1977.
Dale, P. A. *In Pursuit of a Scientific Culture: Science, Art, and Society in the Victorian Age*. Madison, WI, 1990.
Kaplan, F. *Dickens: A Biography*. New York, 1989.
Longford, E. *Eminent Victorian Women*. New York, 1981.

VII

Topic 15

Politics and National Development in Europe, 1870–1914

In the last decades of the 19th century a widening gulf separated the apparent condition of Western European society from its real state. For many liberal politicians, increased domestic prosperity and improved social conditions created a mood of optimism and encouraged a belief in uninterrupted progress. In fact, however, several factors combined to undermine stability, both in individual nations and in international relations.

In spite of a century's battles for broad-based political participation, huge numbers of Western Europeans still had no vote. The liberal reforms of midcentury gave political power to those with money or property, but left the majority of citizens disenfranchised. In another respect, political discrimination even transcended class, for no women could vote in national elections anywhere in Europe. Behind the apparent diffusion of political power, élite interests remained entrenched. A resurgent aristocracy continued to resist the spread of democracy, the rise of the workers, the women's movement, and ethnic nationalism, and thereby preserved domestic divisions within each country.

The successful struggle to build new nations left its own tensions and potential conflicts. In relations between countries, national pride encouraged rivalry and competition. Internally, it led to suspicion of minority groups and radicals, perceived as threatening to social stability and national interests.

With the rise of organized labor matched by the growing power of big business, widespread and at times violent industrial conflict developed, especially where workers failed to obtain from the state adequate social welfare legislation. All these factors gradually undermined confidence in liberal systems.

Instability in domestic politics was less manifest in Britain than elsewhere in Europe. Between 1867 and 1914, the extension of the suffrage was accompanied by social reform. Yet in the years immediately preceding World War I, British political life began to show signs of the turmoil already visible on the Continent. Strikes and industrial agitation led to clashes between workers and police. The suffragist campaign to obtain the vote for women became increasingly militant. In Ireland, the demand for national independence met with a combination of repression and reform.

Nowhere in Europe was there a greater contrast to the stability of Victorian England than in France. The bloodshed of the Paris Commune was followed by bitter political conflict between republicans and monarchists as the Third Republic was founded in 1875. For most of the rest of the century French politics were dominated by the moderate wing of the republicans. Periodic crises challenged government authority—first anarchists, then the threat of a coup led by the glamorous General Boulanger, labor unrest, and finally the Dreyfus affair.

The new national governments of Germany and Italy were both intent on crushing perceived internal enemies. In Germany, Bismarck first waged a campaign against the Catholics and then against the socialists. Bismarck undercut the socialists by introducing his own social welfare legislation. Kaiser Wilhelm II, who dismissed Bismarck in 1890, was determined to reassert the power of the monarchy. Nevertheless in 1912 the German Socialist party became the largest single party in Parliament.

In Italy, a very limited number of citizens could vote. Moreover, the similarity of the two chief parliamentary groupings reflected the dominance of upper-class élites. Under both parties, anarchists and socialists were crushed with equal severity. The lack of any significant difference between the two major political forces led to the phenomenon of *trasformismo,* whereby deputies elected from one group served in governments of the other and voted across party lines. The system did little to increase confidence in parliamentary government. After 1900, Prime Minister Giovanni Giolitti eased social and political tensions by the enactment of social welfare measures, increasing tolerance of the socialists, and a generally improving economy. Yet in 1914 Italy was still racked by political divisions.

Similar social conflicts unfolded in other parts of Europe. In the poorer regions of southern and eastern Europe, rural and working-class resentments led to revolts. Governments were brought down in Greece and Portugal, and mass protests erupted in Bulgaria and Spain. In the wealthier north, dissatisfaction focused on the demand for political and social reform. Sweden, Belgium, and the Netherlands all experienced strikes and demonstrations. Even the monolithic governments of Russia and the Austro-Hungarian empire were subject to serious challenges. In a climate of such massive disaffection, some political leaders welcomed the outbreak of war in 1914 as a distraction from domestic unrest.

POLITICAL REPRESSION AND PARLIAMENTARY RULE

By the 1870s many liberals in Western Europe looked with satisfaction at the world they had created. Revolutions earlier in the century had accomplished many of their goals: the property-owning middle classes had the right to vote; social welfare legislation was introduced by many governments; the nationalist cause triumphed in Germany and Italy; industrial development, together with scientific and technological advances, was almost daily improving the lives of thousands of people.

Yet only a few decades later, in the early years of the 20th century, the general mood of optimism was replaced with the fear that government and society were on the brink of collapse throughout Europe. When the Great War came in 1914, most of the participants were facing internal crises which seemed impossible to resolve without serious and wrenching changes. The issues varied from country to country, but the results were the same: mass demonstrations put down by police violence, the resurgence of deep class divisions, and economic dislocation.

The earlier optimism had been ill-founded. For all the achievements of the 19th century, serious problems remained in European society, many inherent in the very advances made. Thus nationalism led to dangerous rivalry for national superiority. The social welfare measures that had been passed were generally inadequate and only drew attention to the widespread poverty and misery still existing. Scientific and

Map 15.1 The Industrialization of Europe, c. 1860

technological progress created new problems and aggravated old ones, even as it solved others. By reducing infant mortality and prolonging life expectancy, and by constructing huge new cities with the means to travel around them, the advances led to overcrowded urban squalor.

The Right to Vote

For all the revolutions and reforms, effective political power remained in the hands of a restricted few. Most countries of Western and Central Europe were governed by constitutional monarchies, in which royal power was limited through a combination of constitutional guarantees and parliaments. These political systems had been the result of the triumph of bourgeois liberals in the revolutionary upheavals of the first half of the 19th century.

Parliaments consisted of two chambers, an upper and a lower. In Britain, members of the House of Lords either inherited their titles or were appointed by the monarch. The French Senate was elected by regional bodies. The German Bundesrat represented the constituent states of the empire, while the Italian Senate was appointed by the king. The lower houses were generally elected through limited male suffrage, although France and Germany had universal male suffrage for their lower houses. The guiding principle of parliamentary liberalism was that through national elections the citizens of a country would choose representatives to formulate and enact national policies.

Parliamentary government distinguished countries such as Britain and Italy from autocratic monarchies such as Russia. Yet by 1900 only in France did more than a quarter of the citizens have the right to vote. In Britain, about one person in six was enfranchised, whereas of the Italians, new citizens of a new country, about one in fourteen could vote.

The right to vote depended on three criteria: gender, financial worth, and literacy. At the beginning of the 20th century, women had no vote in the election of any national assembly in any European country. The suffragist campaign (see Part VII, Topic 19) became increasingly active in the years before World War I, especially in Britain, but only in Finland (1906) and

Norway (1907) did women actually win the right to vote before World War I.

The other criteria, money and literacy, were deliberately applied in order to restrict the vote to the middle classes and the aristocracy, and to exclude the peasants and working classes from the political process. Even "enlightened" liberals did not advocate universal suffrage. Around midcentury the British historian and parliamentarian Thomas Macaulay (1800–1859) called it "utterly incompatible with the existence of civilization," and declared that if the people at large were given the vote, they would "plunder every man in the kingdom who had a good coat on his back and a good roof over his head." Restricting the suffrage to the wealthy was a way of protecting established interests.

Liberals and conservatives alike justified this limitation in several ways. In the first place, it was claimed that wealth was in itself a sign of intelligence, and that poverty indicated both stupidity and moral laxity. The rich saw themselves as being more involved in society, and thus having more at risk. Finally, in clear contradiction to this last argument, they asserted that their wealth provided them with the security to be able to make political decisions without consulting their own self-interest.

Throughout Europe complex electoral systems were devised that not only limited the vote to the prosperous, but gave additional votes according to the degree of prosperity. As late as 1911, British citizens who met property requirements in more than one constituency could vote in each of them—some cast as many as 20 votes. In other cases education was a criterion. In 1893 Belgium introduced a system whereby all males 25 or older received one vote, wealthy ones a second vote, and those with a higher education a third. By this means the effectiveness of universal male suffrage was virtually annulled, since the wealthy and educated could always outvote the rest.

Striking matchworkers in England, 1888. They won this case and went on to organize a union.

So determined a grasp on power led in the end to widespread resentment on the part of the disenfranchised masses. Many who had fought for reform, or who had battled in the nationalist cause, found themselves still shut out from any political rights. The sense of frustration found release in the bitter and often bloody industrial disputes that shook most of western Europe in the years before World War I, and in the increasing militancy of the suffragist movement.

One other effect of frustrated nationalism was to drive some political extremists to terrorism and assassination as a means of undermining existing regimes. Indeed, the anarchists, generally associated in the public mind with political violence, advocated the overthrow of all governments (see Part VII, Topic 19). A rash of assassinations around the turn of the century, including the Empress Elizabeth of Austria (1898), King Umberto I of Italy (1900), and U.S. President William McKinley (1901), coincided with alleged terrorist activities in Spain, Ireland, and elsewhere.

GREAT BRITAIN: FROM VICTORIA TO EDWARD

In general, British political life remained relatively tranquil until around 1910, at least in part due to the sense of continuity and security provided by the monarchy. When Victoria died in 1901, the vast majority of her mourning citizens could not remember a time when she had not been queen. Although her son and successor, Edward VII (ruled 1901–1910), lacked his mother's immense prestige, his famous (for some, infamous) appetite for pleasure and self-indulgence gave its own character to his reign. Later, the Edwardian Era came to be looked on nostalgically as a last time of comfort and sunny confidence, before the darkness of war.

In 1867 the Conservative Prime Minister Benjamin Disraeli, with Liberal support, had passed the Second Reform Bill, widening the suffrage. William Gladstone, the Liberal leader, returned to power in

Prime Ministers Benjamin Disraeli (left) and William Gladstone (right) alternated in introducing political reforms in Great Britain.

1880, and during the 1870s and 1880s both parties collaborated in approving a number of liberalizing measures (see Part VII, Topic 9). Secret balloting in elections was instituted, trade unions were legally recognized, elementary education was provided for virtually all children, and slum clearance projects were initiated.

In 1884, under Liberal leadership, Parliament accepted the principle of universal male suffrage. Yet once again theory and reality did not coincide, since only those males with an independent place of residence were qualified to vote. Given the living conditions of the time, around one out of five adult males was excluded. In another issue that arose at the same time, one group of voters managed for once to impose their wishes on Parliament. Charles Bradlaugh (1833–1891) was elected by the constituency of Northampton. On taking his seat in the House of Commons, he refused to swear the oath required of members on the grounds that he was an atheist. Bradlaugh was barred and reelected six times before finally being seated in 1886, and atheists were thereafter permitted to enter Parliament.

Ireland and Home Rule

For most of the period between 1870 and 1914, the most divisive issue in Britain was the Irish question. Irish farmers and laborers had long resented the fact that about half the island belonged to absentee landlords, most of them Anglo-Protestants. Bad harvests in the late 1870s, and the subsequent eviction of many of the tenant farmers, led in 1879 to the formation of the Irish National Land League under the leadership of the fiery Irish parliamentarian, Charles Parnell (1846–1891). The League's slogan was: "The land of Ireland for the people of Ireland."

Gladstone tried to compromise. Those deemed agitators were arrested—Parnell himself was jailed in 1881—while tenant farmers were offered some measure of protection from eviction and excessive rent increases. An already tense situation became complicated the following year when the government's representative in Dublin was murdered by members of a secret society, although the group was not connected to the League. Public outrage forced Gladstone to impose three years of virtual martial law in Ireland.

In 1886, Gladstone's Liberals finally adopted Home Rule as party policy. The First Home Rule Bill, however, which was introduced in the same year, went down to defeat, precipitating a general election and a Conservative victory. The Conservatives subsequently maintained power almost uninterruptedly until 1906. The same tactics of combined repression and reform were adopted by the Conservative leader, Lord Salisbury (1830–1903). The government improved the terms of low-interest loans available to Irish tenant farmers for buying their own farms, instituted various public works, and introduced industrial and agricultural improvements. At the same time, however, harsh new laws clamped down on Irish nationalist activities. Salisbury's measures bought a brief period of calm, but resentment at the inequities remained. The issue flared up again in 1911, and a relatively long-lasting if uneasy compromise was not agreed on until 1922 (see Part VIII, Topic 5).

The Struggle for Reform

Successive Conservative governments introduced a number of moderate reforms in the structure of local government, the civil service, and education. Yet Conservative hostility to the trade unions led to a wave of strike protests, and in 1900 to the formation of a new political party, the Labour party. In the general elections of 1906, 29 Labour members were elected (see Part VII, Topic 19).

In that same election the Conservatives were overwhelmingly defeated, and the Liberals who swept back to power set out to redress working-class grievances by wholesale social reform. In 1909 the Liberal chancellor of the exchequer, David Lloyd George (1863–1945), prepared a budget that required extra revenue for social programs and for increased military spending. He proposed to raise the funds with a system of progressive taxes according to which the more wealthy would pay a higher rate. His bill passed the House of Commons, but was rejected by an outraged House of Lords.

Seizing his opportunity, the Liberal prime minister, Herbert Henry Asquith (1852–1928), dissolved Parliament and fought an election on the two issues of the budget and the power of the House of Lords to block the government. In a famous speech during the election campaign, Lloyd George derided the noble members of the upper chamber, who inherited their seats from their fathers: "They need not be sound, either in body or in mind. They only require a certificate of birth, just to prove they are the first of the litter. You would not choose a spaniel on these principles."

Returned victorious to office, the Liberals carried their budget in both chambers. A bill to reform the House of Lords was passed by the Commons, but predictably rejected by the Lords themselves. At the end of 1910 Asquith repeated his move: he dissolved Parliament again, was voted back into office, and in August 1911 drove through a bill which effectively removed the Lords' power of veto.

The Liberal actions, far from satisfying the desire for thorough-going political reform, initiated a period

David Lloyd George in a photograph taken about 1904.

of widespread unrest. Between 1911 and 1914, strikes and demonstrations brought workers and troops into violent conflict. Labor leaders were jailed and strikers killed. During the same period the British suffragist movement pursued the cause of votes for women by increasingly militant means. Its members interrupted meetings, cut telephone wires, and smashed and burned public buildings. With violence erupting again in Ireland, Britain was plunged into a state of national disorder. The outbreak of war postponed the resolution of a crisis whose roots lay far back in the self-confidence of the Victorian Era.

FRANCE AND THE DILEMMAS OF THE THIRD REPUBLIC

If Britain's journey from the 1870s to the eve of war began in peace and prosperity, France began with a decade of social and political turbulence. After the Prussian victory over France at the Battle of Sedan in September 1870, the French republic had been proclaimed (see Part VII, Topic 11). The National Assembly chose as provisional president Adolphe Thiers (1797–1877), a liberal with monarchist sympathies.

In March 1871, the National Assembly angered the Parisians by moving the seat of government to Versailles, from where the monarchy had once ruled. This unpopular action was compounded by a cancellation of the moratorium on debts and a refusal to continue paying the National Guard, measures that had provided financial survival for many civilians during the siege of Paris. The final insult came when Thiers ordered the confiscation of some 200 cannon which the people of Paris had financed to fight the Prussians. In an outburst of popular fury, crowds rescued the cannon and killed two generals.

In the bloody civil war that ensued, Parisian radicals, inspired by the example of the 1792 revolutionary regime, proclaimed a Commune. The initial demands of its leaders were relatively moderate, but in May the republican government sent troops to crush the rebellion. The "Communards" defended the capital in bitter street fighting that lasted a week. The army shot hundreds of civilians. After the government had recaptured the city, some 20,000 Communards were executed and tens of thousands of others were sent to penal colonies. The brutal suppression of the Commune claimed more lives than any single event in the French Revolution.

In the aftermath of the Paris Commune, the Government of National Defense saw continued military rule in Paris and other large cities (see Part VII, Topic 19). The press and public meetings remained under strict control, the International was banned, and suspected political agitators were arrested and transported to penal colonies in distant French Pacific territories.

The Third Republic

Meanwhile the politicians fought over the kind of political system that should govern France. Once again, as in 1849, the chief opponents were monarchists and republicans. In the elections of 1871 the voters returned a clear monarchist majority to the National Assembly. The main issue was that of war or peace, and the conservatives' support for the latter brought them victory.

Had it not been for a bitter split within the monarchist ranks into three factions—the two leading ones were the Bourbons who sought to establish a monarchy and the Orleanists who wanted a return to the empire—France would have seen the reestablishment of conservative rule. In any event, a prolonged standoff between the two royal clans led to an impasse and the creation of the Third Republic. The decision was passed in January 1875 by a majority of one vote, 353 to 352.

A two-chamber parliament was established, consisting of a Senate indirectly elected by local officials and a Chamber of Deputies chosen by universal male suffrage. Parliament was assigned the responsibility of electing a president to serve for seven years, who would appoint ministers, but much of whose power became ceremonial. Marshal Marie MacMahon (1808–1893), a monarchist, served as president until 1879. The stability of the Third Republic, which lasted until 1940, lay, paradoxically enough, in the lack of strong party rivalries and interests. Although ministries changed almost annually, most of them consisted of a reshuffling of the same politicians.

The only significant change of direction came in 1900, when the moderate republicans, the "Opportunists," were turned out of office by the repercussions of the Dreyfus affair, and were replaced by the so-called Radical republicans. In truth, the new government introduced few changes. One Radical faction fought for reform, but socialism was hardly influential in France until after World War I. For most of the period between the formation of the Third Republic and 1914, the government in office responded with varying success to the crisis of the day, while the ongoing task of running the country was left to an increasingly powerful civil service.

The Opportunists and the Dreyfus Affair

By 1879 both chambers of Parliament had a moderate republican majority. The Opportunists were so called because they believed in introducing reforms only when it was "opportune." Their leader, Leon Gambetta (1838–1882), once remarked, "There is no social question." Instead of social legislation, they concentrated on limiting the power of forces they thought dangerous: the church, the monarchists, and working-class radicals. The last of these, in the absence of serious government attempts at reform, began to develop an increasingly strong independent socialist party.

In the early 1880s a series of bomb attacks and attempted assassinations were attributed to anarchist plotters, and the authorities rounded up a number of well-known anarchists, including the Russian political theoretician Prince Peter Kropotkin (1842–1921). None of them could be linked to any of the incidents, but several, including Kropotkin, were sent to jail. The arrests aroused widespread protests in France and elsewhere in western Europe. When demonstrators took to the streets of Paris, the police made more arrests. Among those sentenced to jail was a woman named Louise Michel (1830–1905), known popularly as the "red virgin," one of the leading popular activists, who had played an important part in the Commune. By 1886 public opinion forced the release of all the jailed anarchists.

The anarchist scare was followed by a more serious potential threat to the government, in the shape of General Georges Boulanger (1837–1891). A dashing army officer, Boulanger appealed to the French weakness for glamorous authority figures, who promised to restore real or imagined past glories, and seemed to offer war and revenge against Germany. His danger lay in the fact that he managed to put together an informal coalition that included not only monarchists and nationalists, but also disgruntled urban poor. By the beginning of 1889, Boulanger-led forces seemed on the verge of power. At the news that the government was preparing to press false charges against him, however, the general suddenly took fright and fled to Belgium and the arms of his mistress. He subsequently committed suicide at her grave. His support abruptly melted away, but the very fact that such disparate elements backed him was a clear sign of serious discontent in French society.

At the turn of the century, French public life was rocked by the Dreyfus affair, a scandal which deeply divided the country and attracted attention throughout Europe. In 1894 Alfred Dreyfus (1859–1935), a Jewish member of the Army General Staff, was tried for espionage on behalf of the Germans; he was convicted, and transported to Devil's Island, France's notorious prison camp off the coast of South America. His brother Mathieu protested his innocence, avowing that his accusers, a group of monarchist army officers, were inspired by anti-Semitism. Both monarchists and nationalists became increasingly openly anti-Semitic in the late 19th century. Another cause of discrimination was that Dreyfus came originally from Alsace, an eastern province annexed by Germany in the Franco-Prussian War; Alsatians who moved to central France after the war were never really regarded as fully French.

In 1897 evidence came to light which demonstrated conclusively that Dreyfus' conviction had been obtained by the use of forged documents. The government was asked to reopen the case. It refused, claiming that his supporters were trying to attack the honor of France in general, and the army in particular. With that, the entire country lined up as either pro-Dreyfus or anti-Dreyfus. On his side were liberals, socialists, and Radical republicans—the most famous of Dreyfus' defenders was the novelist Émile Zola (see Part VII, Topic 21). The distinguished general Georges Picquart also defended his military colleague, for which he was forcibly retired from the army and imprisoned. Arrayed against him were monarchists, nationalists, and reactionary Catholics, and also a substantial body of conservative working-class opinion.

Captain Alfred Dreyfus watches the breaking of his sword after his conviction for treason.

When one of the officers accused of forgery committed suicide, the government was forced to act. In 1899 a new court martial reached the absurd verdict that Dreyfus was guilty of espionage, but under "extenuating circumstances." In the face of widespread public protests, Dreyfus received a presidential pardon, and a further hearing in 1906 cleared him completely. His defender, General Picquart, was restored to active service, and served as minister of war from 1906 to 1909. Throughout the whole affair, in which strong opinions were often violently expressed and demonstrators frequently came to blows, the person who seemed least moved was Dreyfus himself. Unemotional, tight-lipped, as patriotic as the most fanatical of his accusers, he formed the still center of a storm that wrecked the Opportunists' grip on power.

The controversy left no doubt as to the continued strength of antirepublican sentiment in France, and Dreyfus' acquittal did nothing to lessen anti-Semitism. On the other hand justice was finally, if belatedly, done, and extended public debate ended with the monarchist forces largely discredited.

The Radicals in Power

The Opportunists' Radical successors did little to improve on the Opportunists' unimpressive record of social reform. French living and working conditions remained inferior to those in many other parts of western Europe. Government legislation concentrated on curbing the power of the church with sweeping anticlerical measures, provoked at least in part by the Catholic stand on the Dreyfus affair. Unauthorized schools and religious orders were prohibited, and in 1905 the union of church and state was dissolved. For the first time since Napoleon's reforms of 1801, all religions had equal status.

The industrial reforms of the 1870s, which included protective legislation for youths, women, and miners, went some way to reduce industrial unrest, and over the following decade, France had fewer strikes than most other western European countries. Around the turn of the century, however, the climate rapidly deteriorated. On several occasions between 1906 and 1910, militant strikers were ruthlessly beaten back, with deaths and injuries. Other demonstrators were arrested and jailed. France's prime minister, Georges Clemenceau (served 1906–1909, 1917–1920), openly described himself as his country's "number one policeman."

In 1910 and 1911 housewives across France staged massive protests at the steep rise in the price of basic commodities such as eggs and milk. In general French trade unions did not encourage women members. Now, however, in a mood of growing frustration, and impressed by the energy of the women's lobby, union leaders organized them into consumer associations or enlisted them in the unions. Yet labor's struggle was an uphill one. When the railway strike of 1910 was crushed, most French socialists and political radicals came to believe that it was useless to look to the government to produce any serious reform in living and working conditions. Only direct action, they claimed, could bring about change. The fragile political stalemate between workers and management was barely maintained up to the outbreak of war in 1914.

GERMANY AND ITALY: THE PROBLEMS OF NATIONHOOD

For all the obstacles overcome, Europe's two new nations had yet more problems to solve in the task of achieving stable government and social justice. Political parties needed to be developed that could balance the existing social and economic forces against the requirements of nationhood—and this at a time of growing international tension. Both German and Italian leaders first tried to deal with groups they con-

Kaiser Wilhelm II put Germany on a collision course with France and England after the forced retirement of Bismarck.

sidered hostile to their regimes before addressing social and political reform, often failing to recognize the connection between the two issues. By 1914, neither country had reached a satisfactory resolution for its institutional problems.

The new German empire, created in January 1871, was in theory democratically based. Of the two chambers of Parliament, the lower house, or *Reichstag*, was elected by universal male suffrage, and the upper house, or *Bundesrat*, was made up of appointed representatives of the 25 states comprising the empire. In practice, however, Germany was among the least democratic nations in Western Europe. Prussia dominated all the other German states by means of its power of veto over constitutional changes, and by the authority of the Prussian king, who was also German emperor. He served as head of the army, and thus controlled foreign policy and the waging of war. Furthermore, German chancellors invariably came from Prussia. Bismarck served as minister-president of Prussia as well as chancellor of the Reich. Had there been a strong tradition of political parties represented in the Reichstag, the emperor's position might have been challenged. The failure of Prussian liberals to oppose Bismarck's manipulations of the constitutional system in the 1860s had sorely weakened German liberalism. As it was, even the most influential of his ministers served only at the monarch's pleasure, as Bismarck himself was to discover. Since the Prussian king continued to favor the interests of the Junker and business classes, the creation of Germany brought no real change in political policies. The consequence of reactionary government was the rise of an increasingly aggressive socialist movement.

Catholics and Socialists in Bismarck's Germany

Bismarck, who served as German chancellor from 1871 to 1890, was well aware of the threat posed to traditional interests by socialism. His first target, though, was the Catholic Church, and in particular the Jesuits, whom he believed to be the natural enemies of a Protestant Germany. In the early 1870s he began to wage the *Kulturkampf* (the "struggle for civilization") against the Catholic Church. His motives were by no means only religious. He was anxious to cement the new Germany, and resented the outside influence of the church; in addition, he feared a possible alliance of Catholic powers—Austria, France, Italy—against Germany.

The Jesuits were expelled from Germany, members of religious orders were not allowed to teach in Prussian schools, and political statements by members of the clergy were censored. Bismarck's reforms introduced civil marriage and divorce. The same program was extended to Prussian Poland, which was predominantly Catholic. There, in addition to religious legislation, the elementary schools were required to teach their classes in German rather than Polish.

Discrimination against Poles continued, but in Prussia the German Catholics fought back. By 1878 Bismarck was forced by public support for the Catholic Center party to incorporate them in his alliance, and to withdraw most of the *Kulturkampf* legislation. Thereafter the church occupied the same position as elsewhere in continental Europe, one of support for conservative interests and opposition to socialism. In addition, Bismarck's questioning of Catholics' patriotism made them especially anxious to appear nationalistic.

Bismarck's battle with the socialists was a far more bitter and long-drawn-out affair. Indeed, government persecution of individual socialist workers' groups backfired. The separate organizations banded together in self-defense, and in 1875 laid the foundations of what was to become the Social Democratic party (SPD), Europe's first real socialist party. To Bismarck's horror, the new party soon had thousands of members, was publishing widely circulating newspapers, and won almost 10 percent of the votes in the elections of 1877.

The following year two unsuccessful attempts to assassinate the emperor gave Bismarck his chance to strike back. Even though the SPD had no connection with the attacks, in October 1878 the *Reichstag* passed an antisocialist law, banning any activity aimed at "the overthrow of the existing political or social order." The law remained in force until 1890. During the interim, thousands were arrested or driven into exile, and almost 1300 books, periodicals, and newspapers were banned.

The antisocialist law represented the negative side of Bismarck's campaign. His more positive effort consisted of a series of reforms that he hoped would eliminate working-class support for socialism. Beginning in 1883–1884, he introduced measures that made Germany a model of progressive social welfare. Workers were insured against incapacity due to illness, accidents, or old age. Maximum working hours were fixed for men, and limits were established for the employment of women and children. Official inspection of working conditions became mandatory. The aim of all this legislation was to wean workers from socialism.

Germany Under the Emperor

Whether the bizarre combination of repression and social benevolence would have enabled Bismarck to keep the socialists under control is impossible to say: in 1890 he was dismissed by the new emperor, Wilhelm II (ruled 1888–1918). Although Wilhelm's immediate pretext was his opposition to the renewal of Bismarck's antisocialist law, which lapsed in 1890, his real reason was that he was determined to rule in his own right. Wilhelm asserted Germany's role as a great power and would unravel Bismarck's cautious international policies.

Although the SPD could once again function openly, Wilhelm was a strong believer in the principle of divine right. After an initial period of tolerance in the "new course" of 1890 to 1894 that followed Bismarck's dismissal, he showed no greater sympathy with working-class problems than his Hohenzollern ancestors.

The emperor's chancellor from 1900 to 1909 was Bernhard Heinrich Martin von Bülow, who had previously held a wide variety of diplomatic posts. Bülow was anxious to achieve imperial glory for Germany, but his manipulation of foreign affairs led to the formation of an anti-German alliance of Britain, France, and Russia, and eventually to World War I. In 1909, in an argument over the budget, he lost the emperor's confidence and resigned.

Over the previous two decades an increasingly threatening gap had begun to appear between a rapidly swelling socialist party and a ruling class bent on preserving the privileges of the wealthy, the landowners, and the military. In the elections of 1912, the SPD became the largest party in the *Reichstag* and the strongest socialist party in Europe. When war came in 1914, the class divisions that had been endemic to German life throughout the 19th century were no nearer resolution.

Political Inequity in Italy

When, with the annexation of Rome in 1870, the patriots of the Italian Risorgimento finally achieved their goal, the high expectations aroused in the struggle for unity were far from matched by reality. The political system under which the new nation was governed between 1870 and 1922—the period of the so-called "Liberal State"—left much to be desired. As in Germany, the Italian constitution left significant powers to the king. The two-chamber parliament consisted of a Senate, appointed by the monarch, and an elected Chamber of Deputies. Formal political parties were not yet in existence, but in theory the two chief parliamentary groups stood for two opposing positions: the *Destra* (the Right), representing the conservative tradition inherited from Cavour, and the *Sinistra* (the Left), the forces that had opposed Cavour. Although the Sinistra began by championing the poor, especially those of southern Italy, in practice any real difference between the groups soon disappeared. Both proved to be equally repressive of those they saw as challenging their own élite interests. Before the end of the century, they had merged into a single "liberal" party.

In any case, the number of those qualified to vote was so limited that few Italians felt seriously involved in the political process. From 1870 to 1882, only about 2 percent of the population could vote; from 1882 to 1911 the average was around 8 percent. Virtually all voters were drawn from the traditional power bases: the upper and upper-middle classes. In consequence, the Destra and the Sinistra soon came to reflect the interests of the élite. As for the average Italian, frustration at being excluded from political life became expressed in the wry observation that "Things were better off when they were worse off."

Popular Protests and the Italian Socialist Movement

The Destra governments of 1869–1876 and the Sinistra administrations of the following decades followed the same policy of repressing radical movements. In 1877, the Italian branch of the International was banned outright, its leaders were arrested, and socialist newspapers were destroyed. Both were equally anticlerical and antirepublican. Repression reached its height during the premierships of Francesco Crispi (served as prime minister 1887–1891, 1893–1896), especially after the formation of the Italian Socialist party in 1892. In 1894 Crispi passed a series of harsh laws against those guilty of "incitement to class hatred." Crispi, once a radical hero of the Risorgimento, emerged as an ambitious prime minister with a bent for dictatorship.

Serious peasant uprisings in Sicily were followed in the fall of 1897 by a wave of strikes and demonstrations that swept through the country and was met with brutal government reaction; in some regions martial law was imposed. The worst violence was in Milan in 1898, where troops fired indiscriminately on unarmed demonstrators. General Fiorenzo Bava-Beccaris, who was decorated by the king for ordering the shootings, became popularly dubbed "the butcher of Milan." Even a Capuchin monastery was raided, and its monks charged with being revolutionaries in disguise. The government insisted that the various spontaneous riots formed a single socialist conspiracy to overthrow the regime. With the disorders under control, the government proceeded to round up thousands of "dissidents," ranging from Catholic priests to trade union leaders.

Trasformismo

The antigovernment riots were provoked by a variety of causes—rent increases, land seizures, rises in the price of bread. Beneath them all, however, lay deep popular resentment at the failure of Italy's parliamentary system to resolve the widespread poverty that afflicted the peasantry and the slowly developing working class. By the 1880s a phenomenon known as *trasformismo* developed, which lasted up to 1914. Under trasformismo, a politician of the left could hold office under the right by becoming "transformed." In practice this meant that the two chief parties divided up between themselves the advantages of power and handed them out to their respective members. This arrangement recognized that the labels left and right, used during the Risorgimento to describe differences of approach to the unification question, were no longer applicable. Patronage, coupled with the manipulation of election results, meant that the only politicians who had any chance of success were those who cooperated and joined the system.

Faced with such cynicism on the part of their rulers, many Italians lost any remaining faith in the possibility of serious social or political reform. The benefits of the few social welfare measures that were introduced, which included penal, educational, and public health reform, were outweighed by the bitter hostility between workers and government. By the end of the century the only major country in Europe with a more repressive regime was Russia.

Even the extension of the suffrage in 1882 had little effect, since on the urging of the pope, large numbers of Catholic voters abstained in protest at the government's anticlericalism. The Italian seizure of Rome in 1870 had driven a wedge between the new kingdom and the papacy that persisted for more than half a century. Pope Pius IX protested the Italian action by declaring himself a "prisoner of the Vatican," and refused to recognize the existence of the Italian state. In 1874 he issued the encyclical *Non Expedit*, by which he discouraged Italian Catholics from taking part in the political life of the kingdom, thereby preventing the formation of a Catholic-oriented political party.

Prime Minister Giovanni Giolitti dominated Italian politics from the turn of the century until World War I.

Giolitti and the Politics of Compromise

In 1900, King Umberto I (ruled 1878–1900) was assassinated by an emigrant anarchist named Gaetano Bresci, who had returned to Italy from Paterson, New Jersey, to exact retribution for the bloodshed of 1898. The new king, Victor Emmanuel III (ruled 1900–1946), proved more sensitive to the need for a relaxation of social tensions. Under the leading Italian politician of the early 20th century, Giovanni Giolitti (1842–1928), a measure of confidence was restored. Far from abolishing trasformismo, Giolitti extended it to include those opposition elements that had previously been excluded: the Catholics, and, more crucially, the socialists. Thus the responsibility of power was shared over a wider political base as Giolitti attempted to coopt these new elements into the parliamentary system. Giolitti's motives were practical. He saw that the continual exclusion of Catholic and working-class interests from participation in government could lead only to crisis.

The result of his policies was a notable lessening of social tension, although the compromise was often an uncomfortable one. Just as Giolitti accepted the necessity of collaborating with the socialists, so he also relied on the support of a substantial group of corrupt right-wing southern Italian and Sicilian politicians who were notorious for their manipulation of elections. To those reproaching him with double dealing, he replied that, "A tailor who has to cut a suit for a hunchback has no choice but to make a hunchback suit."

With the help of a major improvement in the Italian economy, and the reduction of class conflict, Giolitti's government introduced a program of social legislation. Life insurance and the railways were nationalized, with lower prices and better services made available on a broader basis, and the public health system was reformed. In 1911, to consolidate his support on the left, he passed a bill that introduced universal male suffrage; the Italian Socialist party did not yet officially endorse giving women the vote, although left-wing parties elsewhere in western Europe supported the suffragist cause (see Part VII, Topic 19). Not until after

World War I, however, did the full impact of the new suffrage law make itself felt.

In characteristically Giolittian style, at the same time he sought to mollify Italian nationalists by giving them what they wanted: a colonial war in Libya. Italy's desire to emulate her European neighbors and acquire an empire had already led to trouble at the end of the previous century, when Crispi had been forced to resign in 1896 by the disastrous failure of a colonial expedition he sent to Abyssinia (Ethiopia). In the Battle of Adowra, troops led by Menelik II (ruled 1889–1913) crushed the badly outnumbered Italian expedition, the first African army to defeat a European colonizing force. In the period of increasing international tension that preceded World War I, Giolitti saw a chance to move into North Africa. Libya officially belonged to the Ottoman Empire, but the Turks were in no condition in 1911 to defend their property. Italian forces occupied Tripoli, together with the group of Greek islands known as the Dodecanese (the largest is Rhodes), and the sultan conceded Libya and the islands to Italy. The general rejoicing this victory inspired underlined the Italian thirst for imperial status.

Significant Dates

Western Europe 1870–1914

1875	France inaugurates Third Republic
1878	Bismarck withdraws *Kulturkampf* reform
1879	Parnell forms Irish National party
1880	Gladstone returns to power
1883–1884	Bismarck introduces social welfare legislation
1886	Gladstone's Home Rule Bill defeated
1892	Italian Socialist party formed
1894	Dreyfus convicted of treason
1900	Umberto I assassinated
1900	British Labour Party formed
1901	Death of Queen Victoria
1905	Finland first European country in which women can vote
1910–1911	Strikes across France
1912	German SPD becomes strongest socialist party in Europe
1901–1914	Giolittian era in Italy

Yet, in the long run Giolitti's policy of trying to please all sides led to the return of political polarization. The nationalist right, fearing the consequences of the extension of the suffrage, created the Italian Nationalist Association and formed armed bands "for the defense of order." Radical socialists, opposed to the seizure of Libya, moved their party into a position of extreme opposition to the government. An economic decline in 1913 led to a resurgence of widespread strikes and industrial protests. In June 1914 a general strike led to violent demonstrations in many parts of the country. During "Red Week," rioters in central Italy cut telegraph lines and blocked train tracks, and managed to unfurl a red flag over the town hall of Bologna. By the late summer of 1914, with war being openly declared elsewhere in Europe, Italy was bitterly divided.

THE PACE OF DEVELOPMENT: NORTH AND SOUTH

Protest and repression were not limited to the major European powers. Industrialization and the gradual diffusion of socialist ideas affected the political climate throughout the continent. Even the absolutist regimes of Austria-Hungary and Russia were shaken by the spirit of the times (see Part VII, Topic 16). In general, protestors in the poorer countries of southern Europe continued to fight for political and economic reform right up to World War I. In northern Europe, where a measure of political and economic progress had been won by the 1890s, the remaining goals were social reforms: improvement of working and living conditions, the provision of insurance schemes, health care.

Political Oppression in Southern Europe

Spain, Portugal, and the Balkans remained the poorest, least developed parts of Europe right up to World War I. In 1868, Spain had been racked by a revolution that unseated its unpopular ruler, Queen Isabella II (ruled 1833–1868). A later revolt in 1873 forced the king to abdicate and created a short-lived republic. Thereafter, alternating conservative and liberal governments protected the interests of the ruling classes and exploited the advantages of power, while ruthlessly putting down workers' protests. The system of alternation was called *turno pacifico* ("taking turns peacefully"). In the 1880s the Spanish police used the alleged formation of a terrorist organization called the Black Hand to arrest and imprison thousands, although there is considerable doubt as to whether the Black Hand ever really existed. Worker response included massive demonstrations. In 1892–1893 some 20,000 Spaniards were jailed on the accusation of having been involved in a series of violent incidents. In 1897 an anarchist assassinated Prime Minister Antonio Canovas del Castillo.

During the first decade of the 20th century, terrorist bombings and police reprisals continued to wreak havoc in Spain's public life. The coming of age of King Alfonso XIII (ruled 1886–1931) in 1902 did little to resolve national problems. A climax of sorts came in 1909, when in the *Semana Tragica* (Tragic Week), 30,000 demonstrators took over the city of Barcelona for several days. The police regained control by firing on the crowds. Among those arrested and executed afterwards was Francisco Ferrar, one of Spain's leading anarchist theoreticians. The day of Ferrar's execution was marked by massive demonstrations throughout Europe. The situation continued to degenerate, and by 1914 both political parties were torn by internal disputes. In the elections of that year the government failed to win a majority.

Portuguese public life was also controlled by two parties who protected one another's interests, the cynically named Regenerators and Progressives. The system that was devised to make sure they retained power, and thereby access to public funds—the equivalent of the Spanish turno pacifico—was called "rotavism." It led to widespread popular disgust at political corruption. In addition to worker protests, an increasingly strong middle-class republican movement began to form, which attributed Portugal's problems to its king, Carlos I (ruled 1889–1908).

In 1908 Carlos and the heir to the throne were both assassinated in Lisbon, and two years later, in October 1910, a republican uprising overthrew the regime and abolished the monarchy. The republicans were joined in the coup by left-wing forces, who shared their hatred of the Catholic Church and the crown, but the republicans soon alienated their allies. Republican Prime Minister Alfonso Costa (served 1913) enforced the violent repression of demonstrators. He also won the dubious distinction of being the only European government leader to secure passage of a bill actually reducing the suffrage. The electoral law of 1913 cut the number of voters in half.

At the other side of southern Europe, in the Balkans, economic conditions were even more wretched, and liberal government proved elusive. In the absence of an hereditary aristocracy, two forces, the ruling princes and kings, and professional city politicians, battled for power. The instruments used in the struggle were the army and the police, which were kept strong by the conscription and heavy taxes imposed on the peasants.

Bulgaria had been part of the Ottoman Empire from 1396 to 1878, when Turkish rule there was restricted by the Congress of Berlin. In 1894, the Bulgarian state spent less money on the combination of education, agriculture, justice, administration, and other public services than went to support the army. Thus living conditions which had been grim under the Turks deteriorated still further.

At the end of the century a series of disastrous harvests drove the Bulgarian peasants into open revolt. In 1900 thousands of demonstrators were dispersed only by wildly firing troops. In January 1907, a national railway strike led to widespread rioting. Among the leaders of the protests were students and professors from Sofia University. In retaliation the government closed the university and jailed many of the students. A few weeks later the prime minister was assassinated. By 1914 opposition to the regime was so strong that in the elections of that year only massive rigging, including the kidnapping of antigovernment candidates, kept the government in power.

Greece was the only country in southeastern Europe where some degree of liberal reform was introduced. In 1875 the young liberal politician Charilaos Tricoupis persuaded the king to call the first fair elections in his nation's history. In the absence of any democratic party tradition, the results were predictably confused. Between 1875 and 1882 Greece was governed by thirteen different ministries. Tricoupis managed to create somewhat more settled conditions for a few years, during which he encouraged economic development and tried to build a stable civil service.

On the death of Tricoupis in 1896, Greece's political life once again fragmented, with eight elections over the next twelve years. Finally, in 1909, army demands for reform were supported by mass popular demonstrations in Athens. The government fell, to be replaced by military rule. When that, too, proved unpopular, the Cretan politician Eleutherios Venizelos was chosen to lead a new national assembly, charged with rewriting the constitution. Venizelos' reforms were generally progressive, but they did little to change the basic character of Greek politics.

Social Protest in the North

In Scandinavia, political affairs were complicated at the turn of the century by hostility between Norway and Sweden, for Norway was ruled by the Swedish king, although it had its own parliament. After much diplomatic skirmishing, Norway was finally declared independent in 1905.

In all three of the principal Scandinavian countries—Norway, Sweden, and Denmark—the early years of the 20th century were marked by significant extensions of the suffrage. Socialist groups in Denmark and Sweden continued to lead protests, even though the International was banned in Denmark and socialists were harassed in Sweden during the 1880s. In 1893 and 1896 Swedish socialists organized two "People's Parliaments" in Stockholm to agitate for electoral reform. A reform bill was finally passed by the Swedish Parliament in 1907–1909, and followed by a flurry of social legislation. Old age pensions were introduced, the penal code was brought up to date, and working hours and conditions were made subject to control.

A similar process occurred in the Netherlands and Belgium: conservative governments unwillingly introduced electoral reform in response to widespread popular uprisings. The first serious riots broke out in 1886 in Belgium. Although they were violently quashed, they succeeded in making politicians aware of the degree of working-class discontent. Minor reforms were introduced, including restrictions on the employment of women and children. Demonstrations continued to rock Belgium almost annually, until in 1893 a form of universal male suffrage was introduced. Demands for the introduction of a more equitable system continued up to the war, including a socialist-led general strike in 1913, but universal and equal male suffrage became law only in 1919.

Although protests in the Netherlands were less violent, they proved in the long run more effective. A liberal government, in office from 1897 to 1901, passed a large number of social measures: it was dubbed the "Cabinet of Social Justice." Electoral reform proved more elusive. Large-scale demonstrations were held in 1910, 1911, and 1912, and hundreds of thousands of people signed petitions in favor of extending the suffrage. As elsewhere in Europe, however, it took World War I to effect the change: universal male suffrage was finally adopted in 1917.

By the outbreak of World War I, the optimistic confidence of the mid-19th century was long gone. Those countries which had tried to reconcile the interests of rulers and ruled had discovered it to be an agonizing process. Furthermore, there were still many areas on the fringes of Europe where conditions remained untouched by liberal reforms. However noble the ideal of a constitutional monarchy and parliamentary democracy might be, it proved almost impossible to implement to general satisfaction. The greater the pressure for change, the stiffer the resistance of those in power became. Since the rulers controlled the instruments of their rule—the police and the army—violent conflict was inevitable. When war came in 1914, the established order in most European countries was faced with serious challenges. Within the ruling classes, not a few regarded the war as an escape from the mounting threat to their authority. Events were to prove them wrong.

Questions for Further Study

1. What were the chief differences between the pace of political reform in Britain, France, Germany, and Italy?
2. What part did the development of socialist parties and trade unions play in the political crises of the early 20th century?
3. Why did the "Dreyfus affair" become so important at the turn of the century? What light does it throw on the nature of French society at the time?
4. To what extent were countries in northern and southern Europe faced with the same political problems as those in western Europe? To what extent—if at all—did they resolve them?

Suggestions for Further Reading

Avrich, P. *Anarchist Portraits*. Princeton, NJ, 1988.

Burns, M. *Rural Society and French Politics: Boulangism and the Dreyfus Affair*. Princeton, NJ, 1984.

Hause, S. C., and A. R. Kenney. *Women's Suffrage and Social Politics in the French Third Republic*. Princeton, NJ, 1984.

Lovett, Clara M. *The Democratic Movement in Italy*. Cambridge, MA, 1982.

Mommsen, W. J., and H.-G. Husung, eds. *The Development of Trade Unionism in Great Britain and Germany, 1880–1914*. Boston, 1985.

Sheehan, J. J. *German Liberalism in the Nineteenth Century*. Chicago, 1978.

Wehler, Hans-Ulrich. *The German Empire, 1871–1918*. Leamington Spa, England, 1985.

VII

T o p i c   1 6

The Crisis of Empire in Eastern Europe

The trend toward increased democracy in Western Europe was slow, but in most countries reformers made progress. In Eastern Europe, by contrast, liberal and worker demands were ever more rigorously and consistently repressed, with the result that opposition forces never managed to organize themselves. Where parliaments existed, they had little or no real power. In the absence of adequate social welfare legislation in countries that were inherently poor, living standards were far inferior to those in the West. Health care and education remained primitive, and the lack of widespread industrialization limited the development of organized labor. The one serious challenge to a regime, the Russian Revolution of 1905, was led by the only relatively industrialized working class in eastern Europe.

In the Austro-Hungarian empire, the Dual Monarchy became increasingly paralyzed by conflict between the empire's various nationalities. Power remained firmly in the hands of Emperor Franz Josef. Between 1870 and 1890 a socialist movement began to develop, but the government arrested its members and crushed any sign of rebellion. Civil liberties were repeatedly suspended. On the other hand, like Bismarck in Germany, the emperor tried to placate the workers with welfare legislation, to the disgust of conservatives. The years after 1890 saw the gradual extension of the vote, leading to universal male suffrage in 1906.

The Hungarians, like the Germans within the empire—a minority but a far more independent one—maintained their control by a blend of nationalist fervor and bureaucratic corruption in favor of the aristocratic landowners. Other ethnic minorities in Hungary were forcibly repressed. When the Magyars threatened to assert themselves even further by nationalizing their army regiments, Franz Josef suspended the constitution.

In Russia, Alexander III intensified the persecution of opponents and minorities. From 1881 until 1891, the government ruled with virtually unlimited powers of repression. Nonetheless, the gradual spread of education and the rise of an urban working class, coupled with a series of disastrous famines and cholera epidemics, produced growing public resentment. Under Alexander's successor, Nicholas II, agitation led to demonstrations and the revolution of 1905. Nicholas made concessions, but within a year he had withdrawn most of these reforms.

By the 1870s, the Ottoman Empire was in the last stages of disintegration. Turkish territories in the Balkans revolted continuously, and by 1878 the Turks had lost most of their European possessions. Within Turkey itself contempt for the sultan's corrupt and inefficient rule was compounded by the dawning of a new national pride. In 1908 a group known as the "Young Turks," supporting Western ideas, forced the sultan to introduce an elected parliament. A year later, they deposed him.

The effects of the Balkan conflicts went far beyond the Ottoman Empire, for they brought the European great powers into increasing tension. The period from 1870 to 1890 was dominated by Bismarck's elaborate but cautious diplomatic maneuverings. After 1890, however, international relations were marked by shifting alliances that ended with Europe split into two camps: Britain, France, and Russia versus Germany, Austria, and Italy. Repeated diplomatic crises after 1905 raised international tensions to a fever pitch. On July 28, 1914, a Serbian nationalist assassinated the Austrian Archduke Franz Ferdinand at Sarajevo, and the world was plunged into war.

THE SUNSET OF THE AUSTRO-HUNGARIAN EMPIRE

The formation of the Dual Monarchy (see Part VII, Topic 10) went some way to relieving tensions between Austria and Hungary, but the basic problem underlying the Hapsburg empire—the conflict between its numerous ethnic groups—remained unresolved. The few gestures in the direction of liberalization made things only worse, since as soon as minorities received a measure of political power they used it to protest their grievances. The only public figure in Austria who seemed to support liberal reform was Crown Prince Rudolf (1858–1889), who was found shot in the royal hunting lodge at Meyerling, together with the 17-year-old Baroness Mary Vetsera. The exact circumstances of their deaths have never been clarified, but it appears that the two may have taken part in a suicide pact.

The sheer number of parties and interest groups ensured that the Emperor Franz Josef remained firmly in control. Both the national parliament, the *Reichsrat*, and the regional parliaments served as little more than debating chambers, and were all dissolved by the time of the outbreak of war in 1914. The emperor and his governments ruled by decree. To maintain a sort of balance, Franz Josef shifted between liberal and conservative prime ministers, but the repression of left-wing opposition remained constant. The press was kept under strict control, and the authorities maintained a careful surveillance over the socialist and trade union movements that began to develop in Austria after 1870. By contrast to Vienna's reactionary political condition, cultural life there was astonishingly rich, varied, and creative (see Part VII, Topic 21).

The conservative Count Eduard von Taaffe (1833–1895) served as prime minister from 1879 to 1893. Following an outbreak of anarchist terrorism in the early 1880s, his government suspended civil rights in Vienna, broke up political associations, and made numerous arrests. Taking his example from Bismarck in Germany, Taaffe tried to head off workers' support for the socialists by offering a program of welfare legislation. One of the measures, the spread of education, exacerbated ethnic tensions, since the issue of which language should be used in the empire's various school districts became a major fighting point. His social reforms had already won him the opposition of his fellow conservatives, and the renewed bout of nationalist feuding brought down his ministry; the immediate cause was his attempt to introduce universal male suffrage.

Taaffe's successors drew the moral that to introduce even minor reform was dangerous, and later governments tried to maintain as inactive a position as possible. Public demonstrations compelled some degree of liberalization in 1896, when a form of suffrage was extended to virtually all adult males. In theory, some 20 percent of the population was thenceforth entitled to vote, but a complex class electoral system ensured that control over elections remained in the hands of the richest 2 percent. The Russian Revolution of 1905 encouraged a fresh outburst of popular resentment: in November of that year a quarter of a million people joined demonstrations in Vienna, and protests were also organized in other cities of the empire, including Prague and Trieste. In consequence, universal and equal male suffrage was introduced in 1906. Since parliament had such limited powers, however, this concession did little to change the political realities.

Emperor Franz Josef (center left) with dignitaries at a court ball in the Imperial Palace, Vienna, in 1913.

Ethnic Conflicts

Even if the Reichsrat had been given far more authority—and it was in any case disastrously divided into warring factions—there would have been scant possibility of its resolving the multiplying nationalist crises that bedeviled the last years of the empire. In Bohemia, Czechs and Germans remained locked in conflict, and Franz Josef's policy of favoring first one and then the other only compounded the mutual hostility. In the summer of 1893 the German-speaking authorities in Prague took advantage of a wave of violence directed against German and imperial signs and emblems to declare a state of emergency. Trials by jury and public meetings were suspended, stiff press censorship was renewed, and members of left-wing organizations were jailed. Schools were forbidden to fly Czech flags; when teachers protested, Count Franz Thun, the governor, told them: "If you do not do as you are told, I shall break your necks."

Several years later, in a characteristic attempt to balance both sides, the central government sought to win over the Czechs by requiring that all civil servants should speak both Czech and German. This time it was the turn of the German speakers to riot, both in Bohemia and Vienna. The dismissal of the prime minister responsible for the pro-Czech legislation led inevitably to another round of Czech protests and to the imposition of martial law.

The same pattern of worsening ethnic clashes occurred throughout the empire. In those parts of northern Italy still under Austrian rule, fighting broke out in 1904 between Italian and German speakers. In the former territory of Poland, now under Austrian rule, where there were very few resident Germans, the Austrians encouraged the Polish upper classes in their repression of the Polish and Ruthenian peasants, who lived as virtual serfs. Revolts against aristocratic landowners occurred in 1899 and 1902, and in 1908 a Ruthenian student assassinated the governor.

Nationalism in Hungary

The case of Hungary was rather different, at least in theory. Hungarian nationalists had already won many of the concessions for which other minorities in the empire were fighting: the Magyar language was used in schools, the courts, and public services, and the Hungarians, by the provisions of the *Ausgleich* (see Part VII, Topic 10), had their own government. These powers were used systematically to defend the interests of the landed aristocracy and to repress the other minorities resident in Hungary, in particular the Romanians. The result was further ethnic hostility. In one of the most notorious episodes, in 1892 a group of Romanians was jailed for having sent a petition of complaint to Franz Josef, who refused to read it and reported it to the local authorities.

In spite of the rights they had won, many Hungarians continued to demand further concessions from Vienna. In 1903 nationalist politicians began to agitate for the reorganization of the army, with the use of the Magyar language for Hungarian regiments. The scheme inevitably met with a blunt veto from Franz Josef, but the nationalists insisted, and parliamentary proceedings degenerated into uproar, with members overturning benches and tearing down paneling from the walls. In the political confusion that followed, socialist and trade union organizations, hitherto tightly controlled, staged strikes and protests.

Early in 1906, Franz Josef stepped in. Parliament was dissolved with the use of military force. The emperor appointed the new prime minister, and guaranteed him the grudging support of the Hungarians by threatening to introduce universal male suffrage if they did not cooperate: the extension of the vote to the lower classes and the other minorities would have meant the end of Hungarian aristocratic supremacy. The reality of the emperor's threat was brought home by repeated mass protests in favor of electoral reform in the years from 1906 to 1913. When parliament finally passed a reform bill, in March 1913, it raised the percentage of those eligible to vote from 6 to 8 percent of the population; on the eve of war, Hungary's electorate was the most restricted of any European country, including Russia.

By 1914 the Austro-Hungarian empire was irretrievably damaged by decades of bitter interethnic strife. Taaffe, the prime minister of the 1880s, had described his method of government as *fortwursteln*—"muddling through." Much the same could have been said of Franz Josef (who died in 1916), but with the coming of war the confusion was too great to resolve even by more systematic methods. To the astonishment and bewilderment of many of its citizens, who believed it, for better or worse, indestructible, in 1917, after three years of fighting, the Hapsburg empire simply collapsed in defeat.

THE RUSSIAN EMPIRE: INDUSTRIALIZATION AND POLITICAL CRISIS

When Tsar Alexander III (ruled 1881–1894) was brought to power in 1881 by the assassination of his father, Alexander II, one of his first acts was to order the public execution of those implicated in the attack. A crowd of over 100,000 attended. It set the tone for a reign marked by unrelieved reactionary repression. In August of the same year, a "provisional decree" gave the government almost unlimited powers of censorship, arrest, and deportation; the decree was regularly renewed, and remained in effect until the last tsar was deposed in 1917. The press and universities were placed under rigid control, and all student organizations were abolished.

By the time of Alexander's death in 1894, his policies had effectively suppressed all organized opposition throughout the Russian empire. His son and successor, Nicholas II (ruled 1894–1917), continued Alexander's methods. All minority groups, especially Poles, Finns, and Jews, were subject to the process of "Russification." The Poles were forced to use the Russian language in their schools. In 1899 the Finnish Parliament was stripped of its powers and replaced by direct rule by the tsar. Protesting Finnish nationalists were roused by Jean Sibelius' stirring musical tone poem *Finlandia*.

Yet in 1905 massive public protests forced Nicholas to make major concessions. Several factors contributed to so remarkable a reversal. Nicholas himself, deceptively mild-mannered in appearance, was as committed to maintaining his autocratic rule as his father had been, but less aggressively single-minded in enforcing it. In addition, a series of terrible famines and epidemics of cholera in the 1890s led to widespread poverty and distress in the rural districts, and fueled anger among the peasants.

Perhaps even more significant was the rise of a working-class population, as industrialization began to concentrate large numbers of urban poor in the big centers of production. Although the pace of Russian industrial development lagged behind that in the West, by the end of the 19th century manufacturing and heavy industry plants existed in Moscow, St. Petersburg, Rostov-on-Don, and throughout southern Russia. In the 1890s, the tsar's minister of finances, Count Sergei Witte (1849–1915), adopted the gold standard in order to make the Russian currency easily convertible and instituted other fiscal reforms. Capital from France was used to finance Russian railway and telegraph construction, and the Franco-Russian understanding became ratified into a formal alliance in 1894. With the spread of the railways raw materials were transported to these new industrial centers, and the finished products distributed both in Russia and elsewhere in Europe.

The growth of manufacturing and trade, and improvements in transport, produced radical changes in Russian society, which had been stagnant for so long. At the bottom end of the ladder, the peasants were now joined by urban workers, who were congregated in the big cities. Unlike the rural poor, they could make their presence felt both by mass strike action and by demonstrations in the most important cities of the empire. At the same time a middle, business class began to appear, eager to speed the process of westernization in Russia, if necessary by the introduction of liberal principles of government.

The new classes sought to change Russia's monolithic regime by the formation of political parties. The Constitutional Democratic party represented the middle class and progressive landowners, while the Social Revolutionary and Social Democratic parties were led by radicals. The latter two had to operate for the most part underground, and many of their leaders either fled to exile in Western Europe, or had to face imprisonment, often in Siberia. The Social Democratic party was to play a crucial role in the later Russian Revolution of 1917. In 1903 it split into two groups, the more moderate Mensheviks, and the firmly revolutionary Bolsheviks, whose leader was Vladimir Ulianov (1870–1924), better known as Lenin.

The general mood of change also encouraged Russian feminists. The regime made considerable effort to prevent the Russian women's movement from forming links with international groups, and discouraged even the most harmless of feminist activities. Nicholas' wife, Alexandra, forbade the reproduction of her portrait on diplomas awarded for women's courses. Under the leadership of Anna Nikitichna Shabanova (1848–1932), however, Russian women began to combine philanthropic activities—the provision of housing and day care centers—with the demand for political rights. The Women's Progressive party was founded in the early years of the 20th century.

The Revolution of 1905

The time was ripe for major political protest, and would-be revolutionaries were unexpectedly given their opportunity by the outcome of the brief but bitter Russo-Japanese War of 1904, which occurred when the two countries tried to expand at the expense of the decaying Chinese empire. The Russians occupied Manchuria during the Boxer Rebellion (see Part VII, Topic 18), and seemed ready to take Korea. In February 1904, the Japanese attacked the Russian naval base of Port Arthur (now Lu-shun), and in May 1905 destroyed the Russian Baltic fleet in the Battle of Tsushima.

The humiliating defeat and the food shortages resulting from an inadequate transport system overworked by the war underlined the Russian government's failings, and protestors were quick to mount demonstrations. Their leader was a 35-year-old Russian Orthodox priest, Georgi Apollonovich Gapon, who persuaded them that their best hope lay in presenting a petition to the tsar in person, humbly begging him to set right the terrible injustices afflicting them.

On January 9, 1905 a crowd of some 200,000 people moved toward the Winter Palace in St. Petersburg. A few days earlier Gapon had written to Nicholas, telling him of the demonstration's peaceful intentions, and imploring him to accept the petition. The tsar's response was to depart at once for the country, leaving behind ranks of armed police and mounted Cossack soldiers. As the crowd collected in front of the palace, many holding up crosses and pictures of Nicholas and singing "God Save the Tsar," it was generally believed that their ruler would appear on the balcony and hear their pleas.

The palace guards ordered them to disband. As the throng stood in bewilderment, Cossacks and police

Theodore Roosevelt with the Russian and Japanese delegations to the peace conference ending the Russo-Japanese War.

Tsarist troops gun down protesters on "Bloody Sunday," Moscow, January 1905.

opened fire. They shot into the dense mass of people until the snow was stained red by the over 100 dead and hundreds of others wounded. Gapon escaped the massacre of what came to be called "Bloody Sunday" (according to some because as a police informer he was intentionally spared), and fled to Finland. In a letter to the tsar he wrote: "The blood of innocent workers, women, and children forever separates you and the people of Russia. May all the blood still to be shed, executioner, fall on thee and thine own kin!"

For once the regime had gone too far. The wave of strikes and agitations that followed forced even Nicholas to propose a compromise. First in March 1905, and then in August, he offered concessions. His limited reforms, which included the establishment of a *Duma*, or parliament, elected by a restricted franchise and with limited powers, were greeted with further riots. By the end of October, public anger was so widespread that Russia's economic life had ground to a halt. Finally, on October 30, 1905, the tsar gave way and issued his October Manifesto. It guaranteed individual freedoms, broadened the electoral basis for the Duma, and gave it legislative power. Crowds danced in the streets.

Then the revolution petered out. In part the October Manifesto split the demonstrators. The moderates, who became known as the Octobrists, were satisfied, while the Social Revolutionaries and Social Democrats saw it as a trick. In part the mass of the population was simply exhausted by almost a year of chaos. A major factor, however, was the regime's use of massive repression to crush any remaining signs of protest. In the Baltic provinces alone over 2000 were executed. A last attempt at rebellion in Moscow in December, led by the Bolshevik wing of the Social Democrats, was ferociously put down by three days of heavy bombardment which left parts of the city in ruins.

Meanwhile Nicholas issued a series of decrees that withdrew almost all his concessions. An upper house was added to the Duma, with half its members appointed by the tsar, who also retained his power of veto and of appointing ministers; subsequently a new set of electoral laws gave the Duma itself a guaranteed conservative majority. At least Russia now had a parliament, and the aristocracy no longer possessed unlimited powers, but the tsar still controlled the army and Russia's foreign policy, and could dissolve the Duma.

The prime minister from 1906 to 1911, Peter Stolypin (1863–1911), sought to modernize the economy by introducing a land reform program. This redistributed the holdings of the communes and encouraged private ownership. At the same time increased foreign investment speeded the process of industrialization. Any chance that labor might organize itself sufficiently to challenge the regime once again was eliminated by Stolypin's ruthless repression of any sign of protest. By the time of his assassination in 1911 by a revolutionary who was also a police agent, all radical organizations had been crushed; their leaders were dead, in jail, or in exile abroad.

Yet the 1905 Revolution proved not entirely in vain, although its long-term effects were psychological as much as practical. The mystical awe with which the tsar was regarded by his subjects was irretrievably damaged. Nicholas' public image was that of a shy, kindly man, most at ease with his family (on the influence of Nicholas' wife, Alexandra, and the role of Rasputin, see Part VIII, Topic 2). After Bloody Sunday and the subsequent extended campaigns of reprisal, even the most loyal of his citizens knew that behind the façade Nicholas was willing to unleash violence. Furthermore the growing pace of industrialization made further clashes inevitable, as a country in the course of rapid modernization remained ruled by an archaic and inflexible autocrat.

The first indications of new unrest began to appear in 1912, when half a million workers in Moscow and St. Petersburg went on strike. By the early part of 1914, three times that number struck. In July of that year, with war looming, a demonstration of St. Petersburg metal workers was fired on by the police. In their anger, fellow workers took to the streets and built barricades. The city was plunged into chaos.

Significant Dates

Central and Eastern Europe 1870–1914

1873	Bismarck negotiates League of Three Emperors
1878	Berlin Congress on the Balkans
1881	Alexander III encourages *pogroms*
1882	Triple alliance of Austria, Germany, and Italy
1893	State of emergency in Prague
1894	Franco-Russian Alliance
1896	Herzl publishes *The Jewish State*
1897	Lueger becomes mayor of Vienna
1903	Nationalist agitation in Hungary
1904	Russo-Japanese War; Entente Cordiale between Britain and France
1905	Revolution in Russia
1906	Franz Josef dissolves Hungarian Parliament
1907	Settlement of dispute between Britain and Russia
1908	Young Turks introduce liberal constitution; Bosnian crisis
1912–1913	Balkan wars

EUROPEAN JEWS AND ANTI-SEMITISM

In 1903 the Russian secret police faked and published a pamphlet entitled *The Protocols of the Elders of Zion*. The document, they claimed, proved the existence of a Jewish plot to take over the world. This notorious forgery represented a deliberate move to rekindle a long tradition of anti-Semitism in Russia. Nor was prejudice against the Jews limited to Russia, for in the late 19th century anti-Semitism became a factor in the national politics of many European countries.

Russian Jews and the Pogroms

Millions of Jews had become Russian subjects with the partition of Poland in the late 18th century. In 1791 Jews were confined to towns within a limited area in Russian-occupied Poland known as the Pale of Settlement. The repressive measures introduced by successive tsars in the course of the 19th century culminated in violent anti-Semitic outbreaks against Russia's approximately 5 million Jews.

Beginning in 1881, Alexander III encouraged "pogroms" (the Russian word for "devastation"), in which thousands of Jews were beaten or massacred and their property destroyed. In May 1882, the gov-

Map 16.1 The Jewish Population of Europe

ernment required all Jews living in the Pale to leave rural centers and move to already overcrowded cities. The pogrom of April 1903 was so savage that it shocked even enlightened public opinion in Russia as well as elsewhere in Europe. During the reigns of Alexander III and Nicholas II, countless Jews escaped the horrors of persecution by fleeing abroad. Some 2 million of them reached the United States.

During the 19th century, anti-Semitism flourished throughout Europe. Some extremists, largely from the radical right, began to develop theoretical justifications for age-old prejudices. Their pseudo-scientific theories of racial superiority inflamed extreme nationalist sentiments. The French diplomat Count Joseph de Gobineau (1816–1882) published *The Inequality of the Human Races* (1853–1855), which propounded the theory that the Nordic races were superior. Such notions reached an even more extreme expression in the works of the Anglo-German writer Houston Stewart Chamberlain (1855–1927), the son-in-law of Richard Wagner. His *Foundations of the Nineteenth Century* (1899) offered a racialist glorification of the Germanic past which depicted history as a struggle between "heroic" Aryans and the "destructive" Semitic peoples. Kaiser Wilhelm II himself read the book aloud to his children and urged its adoption by officer-training schools. A generation later, Adolf Hitler drew many of his Nazi ideas from Chamberlain's book (see Part VIII, Topic 2).

Since the time of Napoleon, many Jews in central and western Europe had undergone a gradual process of assimilation into the societies in which they lived. Nonetheless, considerable social prejudice and religious discrimination continued to flourish. During the same period, discrimination began to take the form of political anti-Semitism. German Jews in the latter part of the 19th century had received increasing legal rights. In reaction, Adolf Stoecker (1835–1909), Protestant minister at the imperial court, founded the Christian Social Workers' party, which developed a comprehensive anti-Semitic program. In Austria-Hungary, Karl Lueger (1844–1910) took control of the anti-Semitic Christian Social Union in 1890 and became mayor of Vienna in 1897, having been triumphantly elected two years earlier but vetoed by Emperor Franz Josef. With his election, Vienna became the first major city in Europe to support a political party that included in its platform hatred for the Jews. Lueger was famous for his declaration: "I'll decide who is a Jew"—an attitude typical of his opportunistic anti-Semitism. As a student living in Vienna on the eve of World War I, Hitler admired Lueger but thought him too moderate.

In France, where Jews were prominent in politics and culture, public attitudes toward them became polarized by the notorious Dreyfus case. Catholic leaders, conservatives, and monarchists supported the government's treatment of the Jewish officer, while liberals, socialists, and intellectuals rallied to his support. In the process, anti-Semitism rather than the innocence or guilt of Dreyfus emerged as the real issue. Despite the victory of the Dreyfusards, anti-Semitism remained a potent force in French right-wing politics. Elsewhere in Europe, the path to Jewish emancipation was smoother. In Britain, the last restrictions against Jewish participation in public life were removed in 1858 when Jewish members of the House of Commons were able to take their seats. In Italy, Jews had taken their place as full citizens following the Risorgimento, and many played a prominent part in public and intellectual affairs. One Italian Jew became war minister—at a time when Jews in Germany could not even hold an army commission—and in 1910 Luigi Luzzatti (1841–1927) was appointed prime minister.

The Zionist Movement

By the late 19th century, many Jews felt themselves threatened from two separate directions: the continuing persecutions in eastern Europe and weakening of Jewish tradition through assimilation in the West. To meet these challenges, Jewish leaders organized the Zionist movement, the ultimate goal of which was the

The Zionist leader Theodor Herzl.

creation of a separate Jewish state in Palestine, the home of their ancestors. Zionists believed that only in this way could Jews live in freedom.

The leading exponent of Zionism was Theodor Herzl (1860–1904). Herzl was born in Hungary and studied law in Vienna. While serving as foreign correspondent for an Austrian newspaper in Paris, Herzl covered the Dreyfus affair. The anti-Semitism associated with the case brought home to him his own sense of Jewishness (he had earlier advocated the mass conversion of Austrian Jews to Catholicism). In 1896, he published an influential pamphlet, *Der Judenstaat—The Jewish State: An Attempt at a Modern Solution of the Jewish Question*.

Herzl urged the formation of an international Jewish movement to secure a homeland in Palestine. In 1897, he presided over the first meeting of the World Zionist Organization, a movement which rapidly spread throughout the world. Encouraged by the enthusiasm of many Jews, Herzl sought the backing of government officials for the Zionist cause. Britain supported the idea with caution, and in 1903 he met with British officials to discuss plans for a Jewish settlement. After Herzl's death, these aims were advanced further by Chaim Weizmann (1874–1952), who succeeded him as head of the Zionist movement. Weizmann secured the cooperation of Arthur Balfour (1848–1930), British prime minister and later foreign secretary, in the creation of a Jewish state in Palestine. The return to Palestine after 2000 years was, however, to prove fraught with problems.

THE DISINTEGRATION OF THE OTTOMAN EMPIRE

To the southeast of Russia lay its long-term enemy, the Ottoman Empire. The sultan ruled some 40 million subjects, but his authority was seriously weakened by corruption and the pressures of nationalism. In Egypt, the sultan's strong-willed viceroy, Mohammed Ali (1769–1849), made the territory virtually independent, while elsewhere in North Africa the French seized Algiers. The first major loss of Ottoman territory in Europe occurred in 1829, when the Turks were forced to grant independence to Greece and autonomy to Serbia (see Part VII, Topic 5).

The Crimean War of 1853–1856, in which the Turks lost additional Balkan territory, was part of a larger international issue known as the "Eastern Question." The war stemmed in part from increasing competition between Austria and Russia over the Balkans, and in part from the longstanding Russian desire to gain control over the Dardanelles Straits so as to secure naval access to the Mediterranean. The latter issue especially concerned the British, who regarded the Middle East as a vital link to their empire in India, while the French vied with the Russians for the role of protector of the Christian holy places, an issue that masked more mundane political ambitions in the region.

The conflict, the first major breakdown of the Concert of Europe, broke out in 1853, when the Turks declared war following the Russian occupation of the provinces of Moldavia and Walachia. The following March, Britain and France allied with Turkey against Russia. Piedmont soon joined the allies as an active participant, and Austria became an allied nonbelligerent. At the peace conference that met in Paris in 1856, the powers stipulated the neutrality of the Black Sea and forced Russia to withdraw from Moldavia and Walachia (several years later the provinces were merged into the new Kingdom of Romania). The protection of the Christian holy places was left in the hands of the sultan.

The Paris conference preserved the Ottoman Empire only temporarily. By the 1870s Bosnia, Herzegovina, and Bulgaria were struggling against their Turkish rulers. The uprisings met with ferocious reprisals, and the Russians again took the opportunity to intervene. In the Russo-Turkish War of 1877–1878, the Russians proved so successful that they drove the Turks out of most of their European possessions. The Treaty of San Stefano would have made Russia the dominant force in the Balkans, but the other European powers had no intention of letting that happen. At the urging

Map 16.2 Europe in 1878, after the Congress of Berlin

of Britain and Austria, Bismarck convened a congress in 1878 in Berlin, at which the captured land was divided. Russia, who felt cheated out of what it regarded as its just deserts, managed to hold on only to Bessarabia, while Greece was given Thessaly, Bulgaria became autonomous (a few years later it became an independent kingdom), and Bosnia and Herzegovina were placed under Austrian administration; this last decision proved to have ominous consequences 30 years later.

Internal Reform in Turkey

For many Turks the loss of their European empire was the final proof of the inefficiency and corruption of their rulers. Nationalist politicians began to claim that Turkey could make progress and enter the modern world only by adopting Western approaches to government and society. The movement for reform was led by a group of army officers and students calling themselves the Young Turks, who succeeded in 1908 in compelling the sultan, Abdul-Hamid II (ruled 1876–1909), to implement a liberal constitution; it had been drafted some 30 years earlier but completely ignored. The following year the sultan, who was known to his subjects as "Abdul the Damned," tried to reverse himself. The Young Turks seized their chance and deposed him.

Turkey's new nationalist rulers were liberal in their domestic politics, but continued to deal harshly with the ethnic and religious minorities living in the remnants of the empire. In 1908 Bulgaria was quick to assert itself as an independent kingdom. Crete, after suffering considerably under Turkish rule, became part of Greece, and the following year Albania finally won its freedom. Nor were Turkish losses limited to the eastern Mediterranean. In 1911 the Italians moved to fulfill a long-cherished ambition of founding their own North African empire by annexing Tripoli. By 1912 the Turks were forced to concede them Libya and the Greek islands of the Dodecanese.

Abdul-Hamid II, "Abdul the Damned."

GREAT POWER RIVALRY AND THE BALKANS

The political uncertainties hanging over all three of the empires described here produced an ominous instability in eastern Europe. The various national crises, furthermore, were compounded by increasing tensions between the great powers, whose relations were complicated by a series of fluctuating alliances. Rivalry between the leading European nations led eventually to global conflict, but the first skirmishes took place on the fringes of the Continent, in the Balkans.

The Bismarckian Alliance System

After the unification of Germany, Bismarck had determined to consolidate and develop the empire domestically. In his view, this effort required peace and security for Germany. Over the next 20 years, therefore, he devised a diplomatic system aimed chiefly at isolating France, Germany's acknowledged enemy. He sought to achieve this purpose by binding most of the great powers to Germany in a series of intricate, and sometimes conflicting, alliances.

The first step in building his system was to create a modern version of the old "Holy Alliance" (see Part VII, Topic 5). In 1873 Bismarck concluded the *Dreikaiserbund*, or League of the Three Emperors, with Austria and Russia, which bound the three conservative powers to consult with each other in the event of international crisis, but the league collapsed as a result of Russia's anger over the outcome of the Congress of Berlin. In 1879, Bismarck, faced with choosing between Austria-Hungary or Russia as principal ally, chose the former; he sought to bolster German security through the Dual Alliance with Austria, which provided that each partner would assist the other in the event of a Russian attack. Bismarck then succeeded in resurrecting the Three Emperors' League in 1881, but now strengthened by a provision that, should one of the three partners go to war with a fourth nation, the others would stay neutral. The next year, Bismarck added still further to this web of agreements by negotiating the Triple Alliance, which pulled Italy—disgruntled over the French seizure of Tunis—into a defensive treaty with Germany and Austria.

Because of Russian suspicions concerning the Triple Alliance, Bismarck conceived the cornerstone of his diplomatic system, the Reinsurance Treaty of 1887 with Russia. This agreement provided for friendly neutrality should either partner be involved in a war with another power (a specific proviso, however, released the partners from this obligation should Russia attack Austria, or Germany attack France). Germany was therefore freed from what Bismarck called the "nightmare" possibility of a two-front war with France and Russia, while Russia was assured that Germany would not combine with Austria against her.

The relationship among these various alliances was dubious at best. There was even direct conflict between the Dual Alliance and the Reinsurance Treaty, since Bismarck promised both Austria and Russia that he would support them in the Balkans. Yet, despite the Iron Chancellor's having overstepped the thin line of diplomatic ethics, he had established German security. Moreover, while the delicate balance of his system depended largely on his own diplomatic skills, European peace was maintained for two decades.

Realignments and New Alliances

Bismarck's dismissal as German chancellor in 1890 brought about a diplomatic revolution. Kaiser Wilhelm II proceeded to reverse or cast overboard the basic tenets of Bismarck's foreign policy. In the first place, the emperor refused a Russian request to renew the Reinsurance Treaty, for he believed that Germany's proper ally was Austria and that a German-Russian alliance was counter to the spirit of Germany's obligations to the Austro-Hungarian empire. Naturally alarmed, the Russians approached France, which seized the opportunity to end its forced diplomatic isolation. The two nations concluded a defensive alliance in 1894, which was reinforced in 1904.

Although Britain was not tied to Germany by formal treaty, Bismarck had carefully avoided threatening British interests; he undertook no overseas ventures that might antagonize them, and refused to build up the German Navy. Wilhelm, however, was bent on achieving a "place in the sun" for Germany equal to England's empire. In addition to launching German expansion in Africa, he also began a massive naval buildup. The British saw both policies as serious threats to their world interests. Furthermore, Germany sought to play an important role in the Near East by proposing the construction of a railway from Berlin to Baghdad. The German threat to Britain eventually led to the conclusion in 1904 of the "friendly understanding," or *Entente Cordiale*, between Britain and France, resolving among other issues their longstanding colonial conflicts in North Africa.

The Entente Cordiale may have been informal, but it hardened in the face of Germany's new aggressive course. In 1905–1906, when Kaiser Wilhelm threatened French interests in Morocco, the British backed their new ally at an international conference at Algeciras, much to German chagrin. A second attempt to force a German presence in Morocco in 1911 was similarly prevented by Anglo-French cooperation.

The last step in the reshaping of European alliances occurred in 1907, when Britain settled its colonial differences with France's ally Russia (the British and Russians agreed to neutralize Tibet, to recognize British predominance in Afghanistan, and to divide Persia—modern Iran—into spheres of influence). The so-called *Triple Entente*, a loose series of agreements among the three powers, came into being. To the Germans' alarm their Triple Alliance was now matched by this potentially more dangerous alignment.

The Bosnian Crisis

The Russians, now able to rely on British and French backing, were in a far better position to interfere in the Balkans. When they did so, conflict with Austria was inevitable. In the past, Germany had tried to discourage Austrian aggressiveness in Eastern Europe, but now Austria was Germany's only important ally. As a result, Germany had little choice but to support Austria under all conditions. Any crisis breaking out in the Balkans was thus all too likely to lead to major international trouble.

The Austrians moved first. In 1908 they annexed Bosnia and Herzegovina, which had been placed under their administration at the Congress of Berlin 30 years earlier. Russia protested, and threatened action, encouraged to do so by the Serbians. Serbia, which had plans of its own to carve a great Slavic kingdom out of the southern parts of the Hapsburg empire, had wanted to include Bosnia in its territory. The Serbs looked to the Russians, fellow Slavs, for support. Russia, however, weakened by its defeat by Japan, racked by internal troubles, and pressured by the British, was in no condition to fight a war. When Germany announced its support for Austria, the Russians were forced to back down and to persuade the Serbians to reconcile themselves to the Austrian action.

Both Russia and Serbia were humiliated. As a consequence, the Russians stepped up their preparations

Bulgarian artillery during the First Balkan War, 1912.

for a war that seemed increasingly inevitable, while the Serbians continued to incite Austria's Slavic minorities to revolt against their imperial masters. The only comfort for Russia was that the Italians, feeling offended that their allies the Austrians had not even consulted them about annexing Bosnia and Herzegovina, signed a secret Italo-Russian pact promising mutual help: Russia would back Italy in North Africa in return for Italian support in the Balkans.

The Balkan Wars

In September 1911, Italy declared war on Turkey and seized Libya, which it annexed the following year. Encouraged by the weakening of the Ottoman Empire and goaded on by Russia, in 1912 an alliance of four Balkan states—Serbia, Bulgaria, Montenegro, and Greece—invaded the last Ottoman possession on European soil, the province of Macedonia. The Turks were in no condition to resist, beset as they were by an uprising in Albania. The revolt was just coming to an end when the First Balkan War began.

Austria then entered the struggle, however, in order to keep the Serbs from expanding to the Adriatic. Russian protests led in May 1913 to an international conference in London to settle the matter. As a result, the independent state of Albania was created on the Adriatic; Serbia received other land in compensation but remained deeply frustrated. That June, another war broke out in the Balkans. Serbia, together with Greece, Romania, and Turkey, relieved Bulgaria of much of Macedonia. In the process, Serbia doubled its territory.

The Balkan wars failed to resolve either Serbian ambitions or the growing tensions. In 1913, the Serbs had attempted to retake portions of Albania, but when Vienna demanded that they withdraw, Russia refused once again to support them. Moreover, the struggle for hegemony in the Balkans unsettled both Russia and Austria-Hungary, which began to question the loyalty of their own allies. The Austro-Hungarians harbored resentments over Germany's failure to support them more vigorously, blaming Serbia's aggressiveness on Berlin's timidity. For their part, the Russians were highly critical of their British allies, who had endorsed the creation of an independent Albania and thereby checked Serbia's access to the Adriatic. Within the Triple Entente and the Triple Alliance, the mood seemed grim.

The battle over the disintegrating Ottoman Empire thus intensified hostility between Austria on the one side and Russia and Serbia on the other, and served as an indicator of the climate of international tension. The rapid extension of regional conflict in the Balkans to the international level in 1914 would reveal clearly enough the desperate state of relations between the European powers. Torn by rivalry in Europe, Asia, and Africa, beset by domestic crises which in the case of the ruling classes of the Hapsburg and Russian empires proved fatal, the nations of Europe plunged from the disaster of uncertainty to the all-too-certain catastrophe of world war.

Questions for Further Study

1. What caused the breakdown of the Hapsburg empire? What part did its collapse play in precipitating World War I?
2. How did resistance to authoritarian rule begin to develop in Russia? How did Russian rulers try to deal with their opponents, and how successful were they?
3. What were the main factors in the spread of anti-Semitism in Europe? What were the long-term consequences?
4. What were the main stages in the crisis in the Balkans of the decade before World War I?

Suggestions for Further Reading

Ascher, A. *The Revolution of 1905: Russia in Disarray.* Stanford, CA, 1988.

Evans, R. J. W., and H. P. von Strandmann, eds. *The Coming of the First World War.* New York, 1989.

Jelavich, C., and B. Jelavich. *The Establishment of the Balkan States, 1804–1920.* Seattle, WA, 1977.

Kennan, G. *The Decline of Bismarck's European Order: Franco-Russian Relations, 1875–1890.* Princeton, NJ, 1979.

McKean, R. B. *St. Petersburg Between the Revolutions: Workers and Revolutionaries, June 1907–February 1917.* New Haven, CT, 1990.

Sked, Alan. *The Decline and Fall of the Habsburg Empire, 1815–1918.* London, 1989.

VII

Topic 17

Europe, the United States, and the World Economy

In the half-century after 1871, European social and economic conditions suggested contradictory trends. Most indices of social development, such as nutrition and health, education, mortality rates, housing and transportation, revealed a previously unknown degree of physical comfort. This achievement was due in large measure to the advances in science and technology. The economy, on the other hand, showed signs of considerable instability. After two decades of virtually uninterrupted growth and prosperity, in which industrial production, profits, and real wages rose to new levels, Europe entered a phase marked by recurrent cycles of alternating recession—in some sectors, of serious depression—and renewed economic vitality.

These economic setbacks were a result of the particular stage of Europe's industrial development and the structural nature of its economy. First of all, after 1870 Europe entered the later phase of the so-called "second industrial revolution" (on the two phases of the "second industrial revolution," see Part VII, Topic 12). Since midcentury, the Continent had been industrializing rapidly and the industrial zone was spreading. Moreover, new technologies—first in steel, then chemicals and electricity, and finally the internal combustion engine—began to give industrialization the main features that would distinguish it well into the 20th century. Germany, the United States, and even Japan eventually outstripped Great Britain both in the rate of growth as well as in the quantity of these and other goods produced. Even Russia experienced tremendous growth in this period. On the other hand, Britain remained unsurpassed in trade, banking, and insurance.

This was also the period in which business organization assumed the characteristics of what has been called "monopoly capitalism." The corporation had already emerged in preceding decades as the basic form of industrial and commercial structure (see Part VII, Topic 12). By the end of the 19th century, a few giant corporations dominated many industries. With huge resources at its disposal, "big business" formed monopolies within each industrial sector by gaining control of raw materials, transportation, production, and marketing, while consolidating many smaller concerns or driving them out of the field.

The emergence of the United States as a major industrial power not only had important economic repercussions in Europe, but reflected the development of a true global economy. Europe increasingly had to compete for worldwide customers as well as in its own domestic markets, and the international flow of investment capital linked the transatlantic economy. One of the first indicators of this growing interdependence was the so-called "Long Depression" that stretched off and on from 1873 to 1896, with effects in both America and Europe.

THE SECOND INDUSTRIAL REVOLUTION

The 18th-century industrial revolution had introduced machines and steam power as a substitute for human muscle and water power, principally in the making of textiles and iron. In the second industrial revolution, electricity and the internal combustion engine began to offer new sources and ways of producing energy, while two new industries—steel and chemicals—were born. Nonetheless, at the end of the 19th century, coal still provided some 90 percent of the world's energy.

The Age of Steel

Iron technology had made significant advances since the first industrial revolution, but the metal, whether wrought or cast, had basic disadvantages. Pig iron, which is hard and brittle, contains between 2.5 and 4 percent carbon. When cast, it cracked or snapped under tension. Wrought iron, on the other hand, which has a carbon content of less than 0.1 percent, is malleable, so that it wears easily and gives under pressure. Machines were made of both kinds of iron: cast iron for parts working under compression, and wrought iron for members working under tension. The early railroads had relied mainly on wrought iron for making rails, but the boom in railroad construction in midcentury, with heavier locomotives and increased traffic, created a serious financial problem: the iron rails wore out quickly and the expense of replacing them grew prohibitive.

Steel combines the characteristics of both forms of iron: with a carbon content within the range of 0.1 to 2.0 percent, it is simultaneously hard and elastic. It resists wear and abrasion and is exceedingly strong in relation to its weight and volume. For rail construction, and many other uses, steel appeared to be the answer, but in the mid-19th century it was not yet commercially available on a large-scale basis.

In the 18th century, a method had been developed whereby steel, far stronger than iron, could be made by melting iron in small crucibles (less than 12 inches high), skimming off the slag, and pouring it. It was an expensive, time-consuming process in which large pieces could be made only by the simultaneous pouring of many hundreds of crucibles.

The first technical breakthrough that made possible cheap steel was the work of the British technician Henry Bessemer (1813–1898), whose converter—patented in 1856—reduced the carbon content of pig iron cheaply and quickly. Bessemer's process forced air through molten pig iron in a converter (a brick-lined crucible housed in a wrought-iron casing) in order to reduce the carbon and produce steel, which could be made at about one-seventh of its former cost. This technique took about ten minutes instead of 24 hours to produce several tons of steel. The speed with which the operation took place, however, made it difficult to control the carbon content with any great precision. Moreover, because Bessemer's technique did not burn off phosphorus or sulfur, small quantities of which made the steel unworkable, only nonphosphoric iron ores could be used.

Significant Dates

The World Economy

1856	Bessemer process for steel making
1866	Underwater telegraph cables laid
1870s	German chemical industry develops
1873–1896	Long Depression
1876	Bell's telephone
1876	Internal combustion engine
1879–1892	European tariffs imposed
1881	Siemens electric power plant
1884	Steam turbine
1885	Daimler's automobile
1895	Marconi's wireless
1895	Principles of "Taylorism" developed
1909	Bakelite, the first synthetic resin

Improvements in the Bessemer method were made by several technicians. In the 1850s, the Siemens brothers in Germany developed a heat exchanger for blast furnaces that used waste gases from cheap grade coal to heat the air, thus achieving extremely high temperatures for melting and reducing the carbon content of the pig iron to make steel at a much lower cost. They then designed an open hearth version which was subsequently modified for steel making. In the 1860s, the Martins, a family of French metallurgists, succeeded in making steel by using the Siemens heat exchanger to fuse a mixture of scrap and pig iron. This "Siemens-Martin" process was slower than Bessemer's method, but allowed for careful control of the quality of steel by stopping the carbon reduction process at the desired point. In 1878, two British cousins, Sidney Thomas and Percy Gilchrist, made the final innovations by adding limestone into the molten iron and devising a crucible liner made of lime and magnesium, techniques which eliminated the phosphorus from iron ores and allowed for the use of more abundant, cheaper ores.

The production of inexpensive steel on a large-scale basis made possible by the combination of these technical advances did not really begin until the 1880s. When it occurred, however, it revolutionized industry and commerce. By 1885, the steel rail had taken the place of iron in railroads, and in the early 20th century steel became the fundamental material of industry, replacing iron not only in railroads but in ships, buildings, machines, engines, tools, armaments, and tens of thousands of consumer products.

Table VII.17.1
Steel Production (thousands of tons), 1870–1913

	1870	1890	1913
Britain	240	3636	8500
Germany	126	2135	20,500
USA	69	4277	31,300
France	84	683	5100

An 1876 print of steel manufacturing using the Bessemer process.

The Chemical Industry

Before the age of steel, chemicals had already proven important to the development of the textile industry. Dyestuffs had long been obtained from vegetable and animal substances, but in midcentury British and French chemists had begun producing dyes from organic sources such as coal tar. Beginning in the 1870s, the Germans made significant advances in applying chemistry to industrial uses by developing synthetics.

In Germany, where the government placed a major emphasis on technical and scientific education, universities developed close ties with industry. Large sums of public money were made available for chemical research, and in 1872 British visitors in Germany discovered that the University of Munich alone had more chemistry students than all the English universities combined. By 1900, German firms produced 90 percent of the world's synthetic dyes.

The scientific principles on which the synthetic dye industry was based were also applied to a wide range of other products. From cellulose, for example, were derived explosives, lacquers, film, celluloid plastic, and artificial fibers. "Artificial silk," or rayon, was patented as early as 1889; bakelite, the first synthetic resin, in 1909; and cellophane was produced in 1912. Building on the research of Justus von Liebig (1803–1873) in the 1840s, German firms also pioneered in artificial fertilizers. Among the new products were pharmaceuticals such as aspirin and, much later, sulphur-based antiseptics and antibiotics.

The Energy Revolution

The turn of the century also saw a profound transformation in the forms of energy. Along with important

The gun shop at the Krupp factories in Essen, which provided Germany with much of its military hardware.

advances in steam power and steam-driven motors came the harnessing of electricity and the invention of the internal combustion engine—developments that would not only drive modern industry cheaply and more efficiently, but would eventually also transform the daily lives of millions of people.

The expansive working of steam at ever-higher pressures dramatically increased the efficiency and power of steam engines. By the 1890s, for example, big steamships had 30,000-horsepower engines as compared to the 60 horsepower of the first paddle wheel steamers. The steam turbine after 1884 made possible a breakthrough in power and economy. With the engine, the force of steam was first turned into reciprocating motion, and then converted into rotary motion; the turbine eliminated the middle step by receiving steam directly on to vanes mounted on a turning axis, much like a pinwheel, which could then turn a generator at much higher speeds.

The internal combustion engine dates to midcentury, when Étienne Lenoir devised the prototype of a motor fired by a mixture of air and coal gas. In 1876, Nikolaus A. Otto (1832–1891), making use of subsequent improvements, built the first practical engine. Otto's motor had marginal application in small industries. Within a few years some 35,000 were in use, but his system proved a dead end. Steam was finally replaced by electric motors. Labor costs were reduced and inexpensive gas was obtainable as a by-product of other industrial processes. Once liquid fuels were developed from petroleum, the internal combustion engine became even more practical because it could be moved from place to place without being tied to the source of the gas supply.

The cost of oil dropped significantly as new sources were exploited at the end of the century in Borneo, Mexico, Texas, and Persia. Ocean liners subsequently adopted oil in place of coal, followed soon after by naval ships. Although Gottlieb Daimler (1834–1900) built the earliest automobile in 1885, it was not until after World War I that gasoline-fueled automobiles gained significant ground. Eventually, France led in auto production in Europe, while the United States was the world's leading producer of cars. Airplanes, first flown successfully in 1903, were driven by internal combustion engines during World War I.

The telephone exchange in Paris, 1884.

Electrification

Electricity has two crucial characteristics—it can move energy across long distances without great power loss, and it can be easily converted into other forms of energy, such as light, heat, or motion. Electrification depended upon the development of the electric motor and generator. During the course of the 19th century, electrical experiments demonstrated its commercial potential, first applied in communications. The electromagnetic telegraph, using very little current, was first demonstrated in the 1830s in Britain and the United States, and by 1866 underwater telegraph cables had been laid across the English Channel and the Atlantic. Alexander Graham Bell's telephone (1876) and Guglielmo Marconi's wireless (1895) followed, both of which used feeble current.

By the end of the century, electric lighting, which had an important economic impact, came into use. Thomas A. Edison (1847–1931) perfected a high-resistance incandescent lamp, or lightbulb, which made electricity useful for the private home as well as for industry and commerce. Edison also understood that the illumination of hundreds of thousands of homes, as well as city streets, required a central power system. The generation and distribution of power in this broad sense were made possible by theoretical and practical advances achieved during the century.

The first public power station in Europe was built in England in 1881 by the German firm founded by Werner Siemens (1816–1892), who invented the dynamo and built the first electric railroad. By the mid-1890s a series of local stations had appeared throughout western and central Europe, but with no uniform equipment or standards. Here, too, the Germans took the lead, and in the years immediately before the war firms such as the General Electric Company *(Allgemeine Elektrizitäts-Gesellschaft)* had begun to adopt the principle of power distribution grids servicing commercial and home customers over large regions. By 1914, Germany led the world in the production of electrical equipment and products. The war itself created a tremendous demand for even more electrical energy, and after 1919 army engineers had plans for the building of huge centralized power grids crisscrossing entire countries.

In the less than 50 years between the Franco-Prussian War and the outbreak of World War I, the second industrial revolution transformed the material basis of much of European civilization. The practical applications of science and technology radically altered the relationship between human beings and their environment. The advent of steel not only made possible new, more precise and durable machines, but also enabled architects and builders to shift the growth of cities from a horizontal direction to a vertical profile—the Eiffel

Tower in Paris, built between 1887 and 1889, was the best-known symbol of this development. The chemical industry, for good or ill, reduced human reliance on the products of nature, and electrical power offered a seemingly unlimited source of energy and brightened the world for millions of ordinary people. Advances in transportation and communications "shortened" physical distances and changed the very conception of time itself.

THE AMERICAN CHALLENGE AND THE LONG DEPRESSION

By 1871, important shifts were beginning to take place in the industrial and economic development of Europe. For the long term, the two most crucial changes were Germany's steady encroachment on Britain's position as the prime industrial power, and the rise of the United States as a great industrial nation, soon to eclipse Europe's economic position.

The United States eventually surpassed Europe not only in the production of industrial products and manufactured goods, but in agriculture as well. The "invasion" of Europe by American—and Russian—wheat imports had serious repercussions on European agriculture and rural life.

American competition, both in industry and agriculture, contributed to economic setbacks in Europe. The transatlantic economy had become so closely intertwined that events on one continent directly affected conditions in the other. Uncontrolled speculation and bank panics, along with agricultural and industrial overproduction, combined to create a serious slump in the Western economy between 1873 and 1896.

The Growth of American Industry

The Civil War (1861–1865) stimulated American industry by sharply increasing demand for manufactured goods. Over the next several decades, the United States experienced unparalleled economic expansion as a variety of factors came together. Rich natural resources provided a basis for the technological applications in agriculture and industry that characterized the second industrial revolution. The railroad boom and westward expansion, together with a steady increase in population as a result of the flood of immigration from Europe, provided both employment and labor.

The increase in productivity was even more impressive than in Europe. The timber from America's forests provided an abundant supply of charcoal for making iron, but this advantage served to delay the transition to coke as fuel for iron smelting. America's localized and scattered iron industries were inadequate to meet its needs, and as late as 1850 some 60 percent of its iron for railroad tracks was imported from Great Britain. Once the British methods of iron production were adopted, however, the iron industry expanded rapidly. Production was concentrated near the coal mines of Pennsylvania. As in Europe, railroad construction provided a stimulus for iron manufacturing. Production of coal and iron rose in spectacular increments.

American coal and iron production virtually doubled every decade after 1860. By 1890, the United States was producing twice as much iron and coal as Germany. The most revealing figures, however, showed that by that date the United States had actually pulled ahead of Great Britain in iron, and at the turn of the century was producing twice as much iron and coal as the former leading industrial nation in the world. Moreover, American factories turned the world's steel production figures completely around. In 1870, both Britain and Germany each exceeded America's steel production, whereas in 1913 the United States made one-third of the world's steel, more than both European powers together. By World War I, the United States had become the world's leading industrial nation.

Table VII.17.2
Pig Iron and Coal Production (thousands of tons), 1870–1910

	PIG IRON			COAL		
	GB	USA	GERMANY	GB	USA	GERMANY
1870	5960	1690	1400	117,000	42,000	29,000
1880	7749	3835	2429	147,000	65,000	47,000
1890	7900	9200	4000	181,000	143,000	70,000
1900	8960	13,800	7429	225,000	244,000	109,000
1910	10,000	27,300	12,905	292,000	571,000	190,100

American Wheat and European Agriculture

The opening of the Great Plains to agricultural settlement in the years after 1865 coincided with two technological advances of great significance: the mechanization of farming and the westward expansion of the railroad. Among the important agricultural innovations were the polished steel plow, which enabled farmers to break the tough soil of the prairie; the mechanical, horse-drawn reaper designed by Cyrus McCormick; and the threshing machine. All three inventions had been first patented in the 1830s, but after the Civil War they came into wide use.

Once railroads had penetrated beyond the Ohio Valley and across the plains in the 1860s, the productivity of farms was linked to the rapidly increasing urban consumers of the east and American agriculture became market-based. During the decade before the Civil War, the United States had grown an average of some 137 million bushels of wheat a year. In the 1870s American farmers produced an average annual yield of 338 million bushels, and in the 1890s more than 1.3 billion bushels a year.

The abundance of wheat represented a huge surplus beyond the needs of the domestic market. Improvements in transatlantic transportation—the speed and cargo capacity of steamships and a significant drop in shipping rates—enabled American merchants to flood Europe with the surplus wheat at considerably reduced prices. Nor were American wheat exporters alone. In the 1880s, Canada, Australia, Argentina, and even India also began to send wheat to Europe, and at the turn of the century Russian wheat production surpassed that of the United States.

In the meantime, European agriculture had undergone its own transformations. There, too, railroads had linked urban markets to rural areas. In addition to higher productivity derived from mechanization and fertilization processes, new areas came under cultivation, especially in Russia (which tripled its wheat production between 1871 and 1914) and the Russian part of Poland, Hungary, and Romania. Markets that western European farmers once had almost completely to themselves suddenly closed with the influx of new wheat. The result was a severe drop in agricultural prices—by 1894, wheat could be bought in Britain for one-third of its price in 1867.

Individual countries weathered the crisis in different ways. In Britain, free trade policies had eliminated agricultural tariffs in the 1840s, and public opinion demanded continuing low food prices. The depression in agriculture caused by massive food imports hurt British landowners seriously. Many gave up farming and the total arable land under cultivation dropped by one-half in the two decades after 1875. France, on the other hand, protected its farmers by raising tariff walls against foreign grains starting in 1885. Although French wheat growers did not suffer like their British counterparts, wine makers in France experienced a serious depression because their vines were attacked by an insect pest, phylloxera. The Meline Tariff of 1892 placed almost all French agricultural products under tariff protection. In Germany, where a combination of Junker landowners, small farmers, and industrialists pushed for protection against foreign imports, Bismarck imposed a moderate tariff in 1879.

The crisis in agriculture had contradictory results. The lower wheat prices meant that basic food staples cost less, so that the urban working class did not suffer as it had during the famines of the 1840s; on the other hand, the drop in farming income created widespread hardship in the countryside, where peasants had generally experienced considerable prosperity in the preceding decades. In Britain, the hardest-hit country, the number of people involved in farm labor fell by 40 percent.

The Long Depression

The agricultural crisis caused by the flood of American wheat into Europe was one aspect of the overall slump that hit the transatlantic economy between 1873 and 1896. Although generally known as the "Long Depression," the period actually saw a series of separate economic setbacks and business cycle troughs punctuated by intermittent phases of recovery. The collective downturn of the economy appeared worse than it really was, because it came after two decades of sustained growth between 1850 and 1873.

The Long Depression encompassed three interrelated elements: agricultural depression, financial retrenchment, and industrial overproduction and contraction. The beginning of the agricultural depression coincided with a banking panic precipitated in 1873. The financial collapse occurred as a result of rampant speculation, especially in railroads, because the banks had made excessive loans based on securities issued by these firms. The first major bank failure occurred in Vienna, and panic spread from there to Berlin, Rome, London, and other European cities, and then to the United States, where Europeans had also invested heavily in railroads. One of the most catastrophic panics hit after the failure of Jay Cooke & Company, one of the leading American brokerage firms. Jay Cooke (1821–1905) had underwritten massive amounts of railroad stock, which he then resold. As banks failed and credit dried up, manufacturing slowed down. British iron production fell by almost 1 million tons in the 1870s and the wholesale price index dropped from 130 to 107. Unemployment soared from less than 1 percent to an all-time high of almost 12 percent, before declining again to around 2 percent.

Further recessions, less severe than the previous one, occurred in the 1880s. In 1890, however, another serious depression began with the failure (largely as a result of a revolution in Argentina) of the London banking house of Baring Brothers. Partly because of the gold standard, the financial panic spread to the United States. As British banks called in gold, the gold supply in the U.S. treasury began to move off to London and the stock market crashed in 1893. The gold drain became so severe that the investment banker John Pierpont Morgan (1837–1913) formed a private consortium which lent gold to the government, much to the anger of the public and Morgan's immense profit.

Prices, which had fallen irregularly since 1873, collapsed still further. Industrial overproduction was one factor that caused the deflation. The gold standard also contributed to lower prices because a shortage in the quantity of world gold had the effect of reducing the money supply, which in turn drove prices down. European industry experienced the same problem that had plagued agriculture—excessive supply in relation to demand. Indeed, the two factors were intertwined, since the decline in farming income as a result of the agricultural crisis meant that the rural population—some 60 percent of Europe's total—had less money to spend on consumer goods. Moreover, the techniques of mass production were so successful that the supply of manufactured items pushed ahead of the market. In an era when unregulated capitalism still held sway, overproduction led to cutthroat competition and destructive price wars.

The wholesale price index in most European countries reached its lowest level since midcentury—in Britain, it dropped from the 1873 high of 130 to 76 in 1896. International trade also declined. Industries cut back production and laid off workers. In 1892, Britain produced almost 2 million tons less of pig iron than it had a decade earlier, and unemployment jumped from 2.1 percent in 1890 to almost 7.5 percent in 1893.

Despite the recurrent cycles of economic slump, the Long Depression did not prove to be seriously destructive, and full-scale recovery began in late 1896. Although wages declined slightly during the worst years of the depression, they experienced an overall rise between 1873 and 1900. Moreover, low food and commodity prices offset some of the impact. By the end of the century, demand for consumer goods had risen again, especially in urban centers. Producers began to cultivate buyers and develop marketing strategies, including advertising, sale in large department stores, and mail-order firms such as Sears, Roebuck & Co. Prices recovered as a result of higher demand and protective tariffs. Governments also adopted new regulations to prevent speculative busts of the kind that had set off the panics of 1873 and 1890.

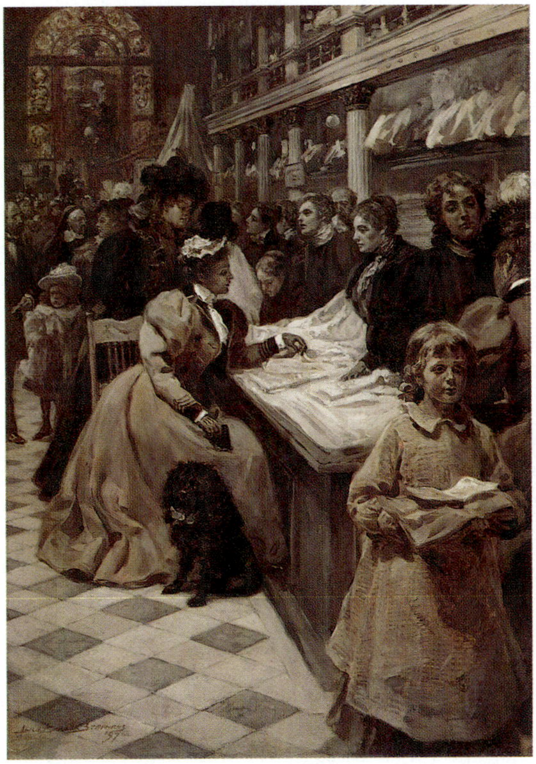

Alice Barber Stephens' painting *The Woman in Business* (1897), created as an illustration for *The Ladies Home Journal*, depicts women working as clerks in a large department store.

The followers of Karl Marx had predicted that in its final stage of development, capitalism would produce the seeds of its own destruction. The Long Depression, however, proved not to be the crisis of capitalism but rather a series of phases of readjustment that came after decades of extraordinary expansion. Moreover, the precarious nature of laissez-faire capitalism taught business leaders important lessons about the advantages of cooperation over unrestrained competition. Marx had also argued that wealth would tend to concentrate increasingly in the hands of fewer people as business moved toward the "monopoly" stage of its evolution. From the setbacks of the post-1873 period, industrial capitalism emerged altered but stronger than ever.

BIG BUSINESS IN THE AGE OF MASS PRODUCTION

The Long Depression encouraged the development of "big business" and the trend toward monopolies, thus bringing to an end the era of "heroic" capitalism that had prevailed since the first industrial revolution. By the turn of the century, a few huge companies dominated the field in most major industrial and commercial sectors, reversing the pattern of the early industrial period in which many small factories and firms had sprung up. The corporation, with its limited liability and large resources, made monopolistic-type agreements possible. Although business combinations took many forms, they all sought either to reduce costs or raise prices in order to accumulate capital to offset the huge capital costs of steel as opposed to iron production.

Cartels, Trusts, and Mergers

Business combinations generally fall into one of three types: (1) agreements known as *cartels,* in which firms remain separate and autonomous; (2) *trusts* or holding companies, in which financial control is exercised over several firms through a company created for that purpose; and (3) *mergers* or consolidations, in which individual firms are dissolved and their assets are put together into one new company.

Some of these business combinations were formed in order to achieve "horizontal" integration among firms within the same industry or stage of production, such as railroad companies or makers of steel girders. Other combinations sought to integrate companies "vertically," at separate stages of production or in different industries—such a combination, for example, might include coal mines, railroads, blast furnaces, and steel producers all in the same cartel or trust. Whatever the form, business combinations set prices and production quotas, reduced costs, delineated markets, and controlled or eliminated competition.

The legal traditions and economic attitudes of individual countries affected the way in which such combinations were formed. In Britain, Adam Smith's laissez-faire theories, together with business failures in the 18th century, reinforced hostility to monopolies and agreements that restrained trade. In Germany, however, where no such traditions existed, combinations were seen as desirable and even necessary. One of the earliest and strongest German combinations was the cartel of potash companies established in the 1870s. German coal producers also created loose agreements in the 1870s, and during the serious depression of 1893 they formed a famous cartel, the Rhenish–Westphalian Coal Syndicate, which fixed prices by limiting the output of coal for all its members. Steel manufacturers similarly created a number of cartels, and in 1904 these joined together in the German Steelwork Association, a huge combination that not only set prices by limiting production but also lobbied successfully for protective tariffs. By the turn of the century, two firms, Siemens and the AEG, dominated Germany's electrical industry and made agreements between them that fixed prices, defined areas of influence, and divided product specialization. By 1914, German industry boasted more than 600 cartels.

In Great Britain, the tendency toward monopoly manifested itself less intensely and by means of mergers (which the British called amalgamations) instead of cartels. British soap firms, for example, formed a cartel in 1906, but it was quickly replaced by the merging of almost a dozen companies into a giant amalgamation, Lever Brothers. The British-controlled Royal Dutch Shell Company, resulting from the merger of several petroleum firms, became one of the world's largest business combinations.

American businesses followed the European pattern. In the 1870s, the owners of the New York Central and the Erie Railroad created a "pool," or informal combination, to end a rate war that was wiping out profits. The pool divided rail traffic among them at fixed rates. One of the largest and most controversial combinations in the United States was the Standard Oil Trust, formed by John D. Rockefeller (1839–1937) in 1882. Even before the trust, however, Rockefeller had engineered a huge conspiracy to drive competitors out of business by controlling railroad transportation rates. He brought together more than 40 firms engaged in all phases of the oil business. The government saw such trends as a threat to consumer interests, however, and passed the Sherman Antitrust Act in 1890, which outlawed all trusts in restraint of trade, although the measure did not halt the trend toward monopoly. Between 1898 and 1900, monopoly combinations were established among makers of steel products. In 1900, Andrew Carnegie (1835–1919), owner of the largest steel company in America, sold out to John Pierpont Morgan for 500 million dollars. Morgan then formed a giant holding company known as the United States Steel Corporation, the world's first billion-dollar corporation, controlling three-fifths of the steel business in America.

At the turn of the century, big business came to be identified with the careers of business tycoons who amassed fabulous fortunes through ruthless business practices and preached a philosophy of "rugged individualism." Yet these "captains of industry"—Americans such as Rockefeller, Germans such as Alfred Krupp (1812–1887), or Britons such as William Armstrong (1810–1900)—were really products of a business system that had abandoned unrestrained free market capitalism under competitive pressure.

Mass Production and Scientific Management

Railroads and the rise in real wages created huge national markets, and the second industrial revolution met the consumer demand with a tremendous growth in productivity.

J. P. Morgan, American finance banker and "captain of industry."

Mass production resulted from a combination of two interrelated factors—technology and business management. The generation of electric power with the steam turbine permitted machines to run faster and more efficiently, while cheap steel and new machine tools made possible both standardized parts and more accurate machines. Machine tools—machines for precision cutting and finishing metals, such as planers, boring instruments, grinders, and lathes and other precision instruments—were a prerequisite for the making of interchangeable parts.

The American inventors Eli Whitney (1765–1825) and Samuel Colt (1814–1862) had used crude interchangeable parts to make small arms in what came to be called "the American system of manufacture," but neither adopted the principle of the moving assembly line, which began to come into use at about the time of the Civil War. It was Henry Ford (1863–1947) who combined interchangeable parts with moving assembly lines in his automobile plant in order to take advantage of economies of scale. By using several thousand standardized parts, with workers specializing in particular tasks, Ford was able to turn out a thousand Model "T" cars a day prior to World War I.

Along with the assembly line process, principles of management were devised in an effort to increase the rate of production and to raise the cost-effectiveness of labor in connection with the new factory equipment. Frederick Winslow Taylor (1856–1915), an American mechanical engineer, first proposed "scientific management." After developing high-speed machine tools, Taylor turned to a study of shop management. In 1895 he proposed two revolutionary principles: the establishment of performance standards and the creation of a permanent staff of "planners" who were not shop foremen. Basing his calculations on how long a job took, Taylor urged that workers be paid incentives for producing more than the minimum within the allotted time.

Taylor's theories were developed more fully in *The Principles of Scientific Management* (1911). His idea of task design was based on the notion that workers should be told "not only what is to be done but how to do it and the exact time allowed for doing it." He also advocated a total approach that included plant layout

The assembly line at the Ford Motor Company, 1913, which produced a thousand automobiles a day.

and tool design to maximize efficiency. By 1914, "Taylorism" had spread to Europe and Japan.

The consequences of the new "American" system of manufacture were many. Large-scale production met the growing demand of millions of working-class and middle-class buyers for inexpensive consumer goods. On the other hand, the quality and aesthetic appeal of industrial products generally declined. Corporate profit margins increased dramatically, but mass production eventually led to overproduction and business downturns. For those on the assembly lines, the new productivity standards and work pace depersonalized labor. The results were psychological as well as physical exhaustion, and increased worker hostility toward foremen and employers. The "management revolution" had an important social impact, for the growth of corporate organizations greatly expanded the white-collar group within the lower middle class.

EUROPE AND THE GLOBAL ECONOMY

Between 1870 and 1913, western Europe and the United States emerged as the focus of the modern industrial-capitalist world. Science, technology, and economic organization all combined to focus extraordinary wealth and power in the grasp of a half-dozen nations. Yet as the circle of industrializing nations slowly widened, important shifts in the international balance of power took place.

The World Dimensions of Competition

The most apparent change resulted from the fact that by the 1890s Britain had lost its industrial primacy as Germany and the United States raced ahead in the production of essential commodities, such as coal, iron, and steel, and seized greater shares of world trade and finance.

In the European context, Germany, united into a single state only in 1871, provided the most dramatic evidence of this transformation as it quickly became the new industrial colossus. By 1913, Germany produced more than twice the amount of steel as Britain, and also led all other countries in the chemical and electrical industries. Between 1870 and World War I, Britain's rate of growth slowed to 2.2 percent, while Germany achieved a 2.9 percent annual growth and the United States 4.3 percent. Although Britain

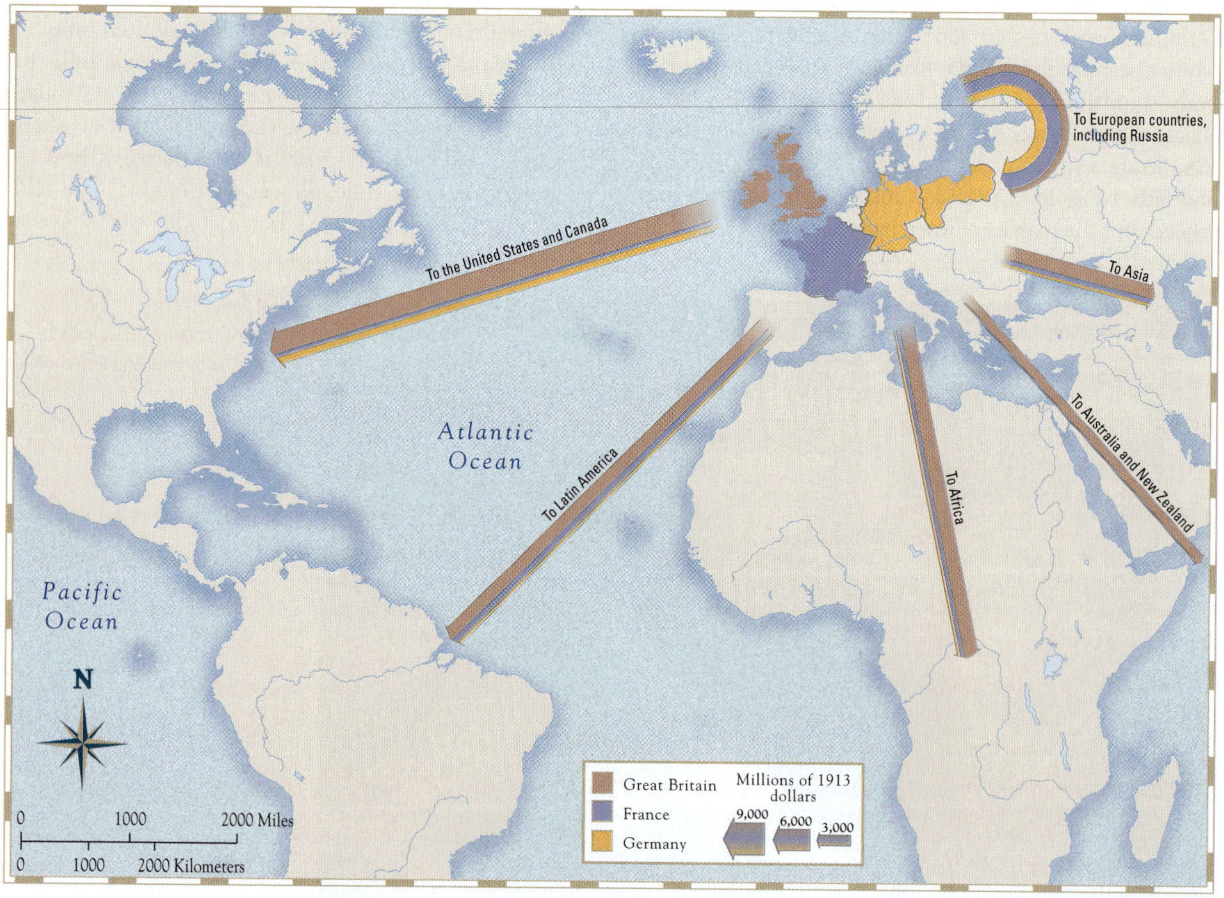

Map 17.1 European Foreign Investment, 1850–1914

remained immensely strong in trade, finance, and industry, statistically it had fallen to the world's third-ranking power.

Moreover, as Belgium and France slipped in terms of their share of industrial manufacturing, Russia, Italy, and Sweden entered the industrial ranks. Russia's industrial growth came late in the century, but it possessed more resources. Between 1860 and 1900, the number of cotton mills rose from less than 40 to more than 700, principally around St. Petersburg and Moscow. Private companies built railroads with government subsidies and foreign investment—by 1900 Russia had more than 35,000 miles of track and a Trans-Siberian line that connected Moscow to the Pacific coast at Vladivostok.

Russian coal production jumped from 1 million tons a year in 1873 to more than 36 million tons by 1913, yet it remained a small fraction of Germany's or Britain's output. Russia did produce iron, but by using fuels and methods long since abandoned in western Europe. By 1913, however, it boasted a steel output equal to two-thirds that of Britain. Russia stood out, furthermore, in the petroleum industry, for its rich fields near Baku and Grozny made it the world's leading oil producer until overtaken by the United States at the turn of the century. Moreover, damage to the Baku wells in the war with Japan in 1905 restricted production for years.

Although poor in natural resources, Italy began a phase of rapid industrialization in the 1890s, with heavy industry consuming enormous amounts of imported coal, which jumped from 300,000 tons a year in 1880 to 12 million by 1914. The silk industry had a world market, and railroads and shipping made considerable progress by the turn of the century, when the development of hydroelectricity enabled Italian industry to accelerate. On the other hand, Italian industrial development was concentrated within the northwestern triangle defined by Turin, Milan, and Genoa; most of southern Italy and Sicily remained untouched by industrialization. Sweden also began to industrialize, expanding its metalworking and silk industries and increasing exports in wood pulp, dressed lumber, paper, iron ore, and special varieties of coal.

The following table suggests the changing picture of world industrial production between 1870 and 1913.

International Trade and Investment

In the years after 1850, railroads had created not only national but international markets. Railroads, along with technical advances in steamship construction—steel hulls and fast, powerful steam engines—pushed the volume of world trade steadily upward. Although the British position in industrial production had slipped, it maintained an impressive lead in mercantile shipping. By 1914, Britain could claim 39 percent of the world's commercial tonnage, while Germany and the United States together possessed only 22 percent.

In the half-century after 1870, the volume of world imports and exports increased threefold, despite the slumps occasioned by the Long Depression. Overall trends revealed that Europe's share of this trade declined in that same period, while that of the United States and Japan grew accordingly. U.S. imports and exports were tied closely to Europe in the decades before 1914—60 percent of exports went to Europe, while half of American imports came from Europe. The position of Britain, which retained the largest single percentage of international commerce in 1913—61 percent—had fallen by more than 10 percent since 1870. Trade among European countries represented about two-fifths of all world commerce, although as the century drew to a close, European and American trade with Asia, Africa, and Latin America increased.

Europe's trade with the rest of the world consisted largely of an exchange of manufactured goods for raw materials. Most major countries imported more than they exported. With the exception of Britain, the industrializing nations ran up heavy balance of payments deficits with the suppliers of raw materials. The British, and other countries to a lesser extent, offset the payments imbalance with "invisible earnings," such as shipping and insurance charges and earnings on foreign investments.

International trade grew despite a general move toward protectionism after 1870, both on the part of the United States and of European nations. Trade treaties between individual nations helped to overcome tariff barriers, although, as we have seen, the exportation of American and Russian wheat to Europe in the 1870s led Germany, France, and other countries to

Table VII.17.3
Manufacturing (percent of total) by Nation

	GB	USA	GERMANY	FRANCE	RUSSIA	BELGIUM	ITALY	SWEDEN
1870	31.8	23.3	13.2	10.3	3.7	2.9	2.4	.4
1913	14.0	35.8	15.7	6.4	5.5	2.1	2.7	1.0

impose tariffs on agricultural goods. Some nations, such as Italy and France, engaged in tariff wars with one another. Industrialists joined the clamor for tariffs as the business slumps took hold, and nationalist rhetoric added to the impulse toward protectionism. Besides Britain, only Denmark, Finland, and the Netherlands retained free trade systems between 1880 and 1913. In addition to the tariff barriers, the existence of some 100 international cartels—in such industries as shipping, armaments, and aluminum—also restricted commercial competition. Nevertheless, neither tariffs nor cartels appear to have seriously hindered the growth of international trade.

During the second half of the 19th century, Europe "exported" huge portions of the capital that had been accumulated in industry and trade. Britain, France, and Germany took the lead in overseas investment, chiefly by buying foreign stocks and bonds or by extending loans to foreign banks and governments.

Britain remained the single most important source of foreign funds between 1870 and 1914, exporting between 4 percent and 9 percent of its national income each year. In 1914, British overseas investments accounted for 43 percent of all exported capital, with France coming in a distant second (20%) and Germany third (13%). Most revealing, perhaps, is the fact that almost half of these funds went to Latin America, Asia, and Africa.

On the eve of World War I, industrialization had ceased to be the preserve either of Great Britain or western Europe. Competition among nations, rather than the primacy of a single one, had become a principal feature of economic development. Moreover, patterns of trade, investments, and monetary policies revealed the formation of a global economy—one in which Europe played an important but no longer exclusive role.

The last three decades of the 19th century and the years immediately before World War I witnessed significant advancements in industrial technology and economic growth, both in Europe and the United States. The second industrial revolution, founded on steel, energy, and large-scale manufacturing, drew the two continents into a tightly knit transatlantic economy that became increasingly interdependent. The abundance of American wheat caused a sharp depression in European agriculture in the 1870s, and financial panic in Europe's capitals resounded in New York and Washington.

Changes of far-reaching consequence emerged from the economic slumps that beset Europe and America between 1873 and 1896. Corporations and industries adopted new forms of business organization designed to control economic fluctuations, limit price competition, and stimulate consumer demand. From an era of overproduction—one cause of the Long Depression—came an age of mass production.

The transatlantic economy grew more complex as nations changed their industrial position in an absolute sense as well as their status vis-à-vis each other. The degree of economic competition intensified within Europe, while the industrializing countries expanded the parameters of their operations to Africa, Asia, and Latin America, creating a truly global economy.

It should be remembered, however, that the process by which Europe had achieved its economic ascendancy had not been entirely peaceful. Armed with scientific knowledge, technological skill, and great wealth, Europeans inaugurated an era of imperial expansion after 1870 that enabled them to subjugate and exploit vast portions of the globe (see Part VII, Topic 18).

From their position at the center of the world economy, Europeans—the great majority of whom enjoyed more physical comforts and a higher standard of living than any people in history—regarded the rest of the world with a sense of superiority. The exploitation of Asia and Africa, which accompanied the second industrial revolution, was intended to promote further European economic expansion. Some imperialists claimed that it also provided a means for extending the "advantages" of Western civilization to less developed regions of the globe.

Questions for Further Study

1. What was the second industrial revolution, and how was it different from the first?
2. How did the development of the American economy affect Europe?
3. To what extent is it accurate to use the term "Long Depression" to describe the European economy between 1870 and 1914?
4. What were the principles of "Taylorism," and why were they important to the modern world economy?

Suggestions for Further Reading

Ashworth, William. *A Short History of the International Economy Since 1850*, 4th ed. London, 1987.
Ashworth, William. *An Economic History of England, 1870–1939*. London, 1960.
Cameron, Rondo. *A Concise Economic History of the World*. New York, 1989.
Carter, E. C. et al., eds. *Enterprise and Entrepreneurs in Nineteenth and Twentieth Century France*. Baltimore, MD, 1976.
Davis, Lance E. et al. *American Economic Growth: An Economist's History of the United States*. New York, 1972.
Henderson, William O. *The Rise of German Industrial Power, 1834–1914*. Berkeley, CA, 1975.

Kenwood, A. G., and A. L. Lougheed, *The Growth of the International Economy, 1820–1960*. London, 1971.

Landes, David. *The Unbound Prometheus: Technological Change and Industrial Development in Western Europe from 1750 to the Present*. Cambridge, MA, 1969.

Milward, Alan S., and S. B. Saul. *The Development of the Economies of Continental Europe, 1850–1914*. Cambridge, MA, 1977.

Saul, S. B. *The Myth of the Great Depression, 1873–1896*. London, 1969.

Trebilcock, Clive. *The Industrialization of the Continent*. New York, 1981.

VII

Topic 18

The Drive for Empire: European Imperialism in Asia and Africa

The latter half of the 19th century saw an increasingly frenzied drive on the part of many European powers for territorial conquest beyond Europe. Known as the "New Imperialism," to distinguish it from the earlier phase of European expansion beginning in the 15th century, this sudden surge of aggression resulted in the domination of virtually all of Asia and Africa by a handful of Western powers.

The most direct motivating force was economic, but other factors also encouraged the pursuit of empire. Pressure groups of business, military, and conservative interests promoted colonial expansion as a means of enhancing national prestige in the context of European power rivalries. The various Christian churches saw imperialist conquest as a means of spreading their faith, while some Europeans were genuinely interested in improving conditions in other parts of the world. Many Westerners believed that the exportation of their culture abroad fulfilled a mission to spread a superior culture and "civilize" the world.

The unification of India under British rule represented the crowning achievement of the age of imperialism. Nonetheless, as early as 1857 the "Indian Mutiny," as the British styled it, revealed Indian determination to resist foreign domination. After the unsuccessful rebellion, the British introduced limited political representation, educated Indians of the upper classes in schools under their supervision, and encouraged them to enter government service. This process of "westernization" speeded the development of national consciousness.

The Western powers had little need for direct rule over China, for they found it relatively easy to impose demands on the declining Chinese empire. Racked by internal disorder, China was forced to make continual concessions to Western nations. By 1900, the Chinese emperor allowed a combined European and American military expedition to restore order.

China's problems were compounded by Japan's highly successful adaptation to Western ways. In 1867 the Japanese, who had maintained their isolation from the outside world until as late as 1853, began a wholesale replacement of their feudal system of government and introduced Western-style reforms. They also emulated the Europeans by seeking their own imperialist conquests.

In Africa, the last quarter of the 19th century saw virtually all the western European nations fighting to win territory. In North Africa, the British and French took control of the tangled finances of Egypt, anxious as joint owners of the Suez Canal to protect their investment. In 1882, the British occupied the country, leading the French to find compensation in the Sudan, where the two powers came close to war at the end of the century.

With the fear growing that hostilities in Africa could lead to war in Europe as Belgium, Germany, and other states began to seize holdings in central Africa, a conference met in Berlin in 1885 to establish some rules for the dismemberment of Africa.

In South Africa, conflict was unavoidable. The British Cape Colony became increasingly at odds with two neighboring states settled by the Boers, colonial farmers of Dutch origin who had subdued or pushed out the Bantu. The Boer War broke out in 1899. It took over three years for the British to defeat their stubborn and determined opponents.

By the eve of World War I, Western nations—including the United States—dominated the economy and the political life of much of the globe. Yet competition outside Europe, far from resolving the tensions between the European states, only added to them. The result—global war—ended the age of European world influence with a speed that would have seemed inconceivable to the enthusiastic imperialists of the late 19th century.

THE IMPERIALISTS: EXPLORATION, COMMERCE, AND COMPETITION

Europeans had been in contact with other parts of the world for centuries, but with the new methods of transport, communication, and warfare available by midcentury, conquest and occupation of distant lands became a serious possibility for the first time.

The New Imperialism and Its Causes

The New Imperialism differed from earlier European expansion in a variety of ways. The first was the sheer speed—a mere 30 years—with which a handful of nations assumed control of vast portions of the globe. Britain took 4 million square miles, France 3.5 million, Russia 3 million, and Germany, Belgium, and Italy 1 million each. Second, instead of limiting contact to commercial exploitation, the European powers assumed direct administrative control over conquered territories. In the process, they made enormous capital investments which they sought to maintain by setting up colonial bureaucracies and military forces.

The advocates of imperialism claimed a variety of motives as their inspiration, including converting the "heathen," spreading Western civilization, advancing national glory, and exploration for its own sake—as in the daring exploits of Henry M. Stanley (1841–1904) or Sir Richard Burton (1821–1890), who charted much of the African interior. Moreover, the aggressive spirit of capitalism, buoyed by the advances of science and technology, favored an outward drive for expansion.

Yet the deeper causes powering that drive were more prosaic. The pace of industrial growth had been so hectic that European economic interests needed a wider stage. With the vast increase in production and intense competition in European domestic markets, manufacturers had to find new customers. As businesses became more and more profitable, wealthy industrialists looked for ways to invest the capital they had accumulated. By 1870, with industrialization well under way throughout most of Europe, they were turning to other parts of the world where investment often brought quicker and higher profits than at home. Furthermore, mining and processing a country's natural resources—vital supplies for the investing nation—were in themselves forms of imperialism, as the Germans demonstrated by winning control of Chilean nitrates. Thus imperialism represented the domination of nonindustrialized areas of the world by industrialized or industrializing nations.

European prosperity also contributed to the imperialist impulse. With the transformation from an agricultural to an urban society, and the general rise in prosperity, the European demand was increasing not only for staple commodities such as beef and grain, but specialty goods not produced in Europe, such as coffee and sugar, as well as luxury items such as ivory and animal skins. Furthermore, manufacturers came to depend on a ready supply of materials not available in the West, including cocoa, rubber, and copper.

The ceremony, or *durbar,* investing Queen Victoria (in her absence) as empress of India, which took place at Delhi.

By the last third of the 19th century, a global economy had come into being that inextricably linked Western and non-Western interests (see Part VII, Topic 17). The two sides were not, however, equal partners, for modern technology gave the West an enormous power advantage. Moreover, the non-Western nations traded raw materials and food, while the West produced sophisticated and expensive manufactured goods, and transported the bulk of the world's trade. As European economic prosperity became increasingly dependent on maintaining its dominance, the European powers looked for ways to control those regions that were necessary for their prosperity. Given their military and technological superiority, the most direct means was outright conquest. The superiority of European weapons reinforced the notion of racial superiority. In Nigeria in 1897, 32 Europeans and 500 African mercenaries defeated an army of 31,000 with the use of machine guns; the following year the British killed some 10,000 Muslims with machine guns at Omdurman in the Sudan.

Yet a generation that had seen the abolition of the European slave trade (it ended in 1834), and upheld the importance of "morality," could hardly acknowledge so calculating a motive for acquiring foreign territory. The notion that it was "the white man's burden" to civilize the world—that is, to westernize it—provided a moral justification for taking over and governing other people. Other important factors could be adduced. From the time of the Crusades, there had been a strong belief in the superiority and eventual triumph of Christianity. With the growth of Western power throughout the world, European missionaries, both Protestant and Catholic, could spread their faith, while improving local health care and bringing Western education to local populations. Some religious leaders saw imperial conquest as not only justifiable but as an obligation, particularly at a time of growing religious doubt at home.

For many European governments, imperialistic projects helped to distract attention from domestic dissatisfactions. A successful campaign or a heroic victory, appropriately celebrated by the press, could serve to deflect, at least temporarily, demands for broader political participation and for increased social justice. Some classes and individuals for whom urban, industrial life had little appeal were naturally drawn to colonial existence. Aristocrats, by becoming imperial administrators, could take up positions of authority and superiority. Those for whom the cities of 19th-century Europe were anonymous, and for whom industrial employment represented monotonous drudgery, had the prospect of excitement, and maybe financial profit, in the colonies. In Germany, colonial expansion was a safe outlet for German nationalism.

Imperialism and National Rivalries

One motive for imperialism that no government ever tried to conceal was *patriotism*—the enhancement of national interests, especially when in conflict with those of a rival nation. France's imperial ambitions increased after 1871 in order to compensate abroad for her defeat by Germany at home. Britain sought to maintain a dominant position in Egypt after 1882 in order to protect the Suez Canal and offset the risk of the crumbling Ottoman Empire falling under Russian control. Even those smaller countries without the public resources to launch a campaign entered the race. In 1876, the king of Belgium, Leopold II (ruled 1865–

1909) joined with a group of financiers to found the International Association for the Exploration and Civilization of Central Africa. Intended in theory to underwrite the explorations of Henry M. Stanley, the association helped Leopold to claim "trusteeship" of large tracts of the Congo as possessions of the crown.

With tension between nations rising in Europe, and the pace of imperialism increasing, particularly in Africa, the danger of outright war was clear. In 1884–1885, a conference met in Berlin to lay some ground rules for the acquisition of empire, and thereby avoid clashing interests. The participants agreed that possession of coastal territory brought with it the right to the interior, provided, however, that the claimant was actually occupying the land with military or administrative forces. This arbitrary drawing of borders, with no regard for indigenous African cultures, produced a set of artificial "countries" that satisfied the colonizers, but proved disastrous in the years of decolonization after World War II (see Part VIII, Topic 10).

By the early years of the 20th century, India and virtually the whole of Africa were under European rule, China was at the mercy of Western demands, and Japan had adapted itself to Western political ideas, including that of territorial conquest. For many Europeans, it seemed that imperialism had triumphed and that Western civilization was destined to become the dominant world culture. Yet the European grip on the world was soon shaken by three factors. Growing hostility among the European powers themselves reached its peak in World War I, while the United States played an increasingly prominent role in international affairs. Within the colonial territories, the rise of national consciousness eventually combined with the weakening position of the Western powers to bring an end to imperialism.

THE BRITISH IN INDIA: FROM MUTINY TO NATIONAL CONSCIOUSNESS

Through the East India Company, the British had maintained commercial links with India since the 18th century, and by the middle of the 19th century, with virtually the whole subcontinent informally "ruled" by the Company, British domination was producing considerable resentment.

The Sepoy Rebellion

The first signs of trouble developed in May 1857, among *Sepoys* (the Hindi word for "troops") in the Company's Bengal Army, stationed near Delhi. A new type of rifle, lately introduced, employed greased bullets. A false rumor spread that the fat used for the cartridges came from cows and pigs—the former sacred to Hindus, the latter regarded by Muslims as unclean. In the ensuing revolt, which the British contemptuously

Lord Curzon, viceroy of India, and his wife with the raja of Chamba and staff.

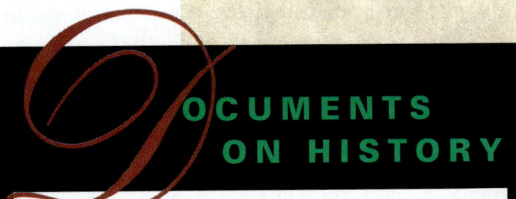

Documents on History

The Drive for Empire

Even at the time, imperialism was the subject of great debate in Europe and the United States among social critics, political and business leaders, and writers. Arguments for and against imperialism disagreed not only about its causes but about its impact and its future.

THE ARROGANCE OF EUROPEAN IMPERIALISTS

The British journalist and explorer Henry M. Stanley (1841–1904) embodied the arrogant attitudes toward non-Westerners that typified many of his generation. In his memoirs, he explained the "necessity" of his harsh manner in dealing with Africans.

The natives rapidly learned that though everything was to be gained by friendship with me, wars brought nothing but ruin.

When a young white officer quits England for the first time, to lead blacks, he has got to learn to unlearn a great deal. We *must* have white men in Africa; but the raw white is a great nuisance there during the first year. In the second year, he begins to mend; during the third year, if his nature permits it, he has developed into a superior man, whose intelligence may be of transcendent utility for directing masses of inferior men.

My officers were possessed with the notion that my manner was "hard," because I had not many compliments for them. That is the kind of pap which we may offer women and boys. Besides, I thought they were superior natures, and required none of that encouragement, which the more childish blacks almost daily received.

From Henry M. Stanley, *Autobiography,* ed. Dorothy Stanley. Houghton Mifflin. Copyright © 1909.

THE ECONOMIC IMPULSE

In 1898 the American financial expert Charles A. Conant wrote an important article on the economic necessity for American participation in imperial expansion.

This new movement [imperialism] is not a matter of sentiment. It is the result of a natural law of economic and race development. The great civilized peoples have to-day at their command the means of developing the decadent nations of the world. What this means, in its material aspects, is the great excess of saved capital which is the result of machine production. . . . There must always be savings in a progressive industrial society to repair the wear of existing equipment and to meet new demands, but under the present social order it is becoming impossible to find at home in the great capitalistic countries employment for all the capital saved which is at once safe and remunerative. . . .

For the means of finding new productive employments for capital, it is necessary that the great industrial countries should turn to countries which have not felt the pulse of modern progress. Such countries have yet to be equipped with the mechanism of production and of luxury, which has been created in the progressive countries by the savings of recent generations. They have not only to obtain buildings and machinery—the necessary elements in producing machine-made goods—but they have to build their roads, drain their marshes, dam their rivers, build aqueducts for their water supplies and sewers for their towns and cities. Asia and Africa are the most promising of these countries. Japan has already made her entry, almost like Athene full-armed from the brain of Zeus, into the modern industrial world. . . .

The United States cannot afford to adhere to a policy of isolation while other nations are reaching out for the command of these new markets. The United States are still large users of foreign capital, but American investors are not willing to see the return upon their investments reduced to the European level. Interest rates have already declined here within the last five years. New markets and new opportunities for investment must be found if surplus capital is to be profitably employed. . . .

From Charles A. Conant, "The Economic Basis of 'Imperialism'," *North American Review* (September 1898).

IMPERIALISM AS SOCIAL ATAVISM

Austrian economist Joseph Schumpeter (1883–1950) rejected the view that imperialism was driven by capital economics. Instead, in 1919 he argued that imperialism was actually a precapitalist phenomenon, a social throwback to an earlier stage of human development in which expansionism was undertaken for its own sake.

Wherever capitalism penetrated, peace parties of such strength arose that virtually every war meant a political struggle in the domestic scene. The exceptions are rare—Germany in the Franco-Prussian war of 1870–1871, both belligerents in the Russo-Turkish war of 1877–1878. That is why every war is carefully justified as a defensive war by the governments involved, and by all the political parties, in their official utterances—indicating a realization that a war of a different nature would scarcely be tenable in a political sense. . . . In the distant past, imperialism had needed no disguise whatever, and in the absolute autocracies only a very transparent one; but today imperialism is carefully hidden from public view—even though there may still be an unofficial appeal to warlike instincts. . . . Every expansionist urge must be carefully related to a concrete goal. All this is primarily a matter of political phraseology, to be sure. But the necessity of this phraseology is a symptom of the popular attitude. And that

continued next page

attitude makes a policy of imperialism more and more difficult—indeed, the very word imperialism is applied only to the enemy, in a reproachful sense, being carefully avoided with reference to the speaker's own policies. . . .

Among all capitalist economies, that of the United States is least burdened with precapitalist elements, survivals, reminiscences, and power factors. Certainly we cannot expect to find imperialist tendencies altogether lacking even in the United States, for the immigrants came from Europe with their convictions fully formed, and the environment certainly favored the revival of instincts of pugnacity. But we can conjecture that among all countries the United States is likely to exhibit the weakest imperialist trend. This turns out to be the truth. . . . The United States was the first advocate of disarmament and arbitration. . . . Even in the United States, of course, politicians need slogans—especially slogans calculated to divert attention from domestic issues. Theodore Roosevelt and certain magnates of the press actually resorted to imperialism—and the result, in that world of high capitalism, was utter defeat, a defeat that would have been even more abject, if other slogans, notably those appealing to anti-trust sentiment, had not met with better success. . . .

These facts are scarcely in dispute. . . .

It follows that *it is a basic fallacy to describe imperialism as a necessary phase of capitalism, or even to speak of the development of capitalism into imperialism*.

From Joseph A. Schumpeter, *Imperialism and Social Classes,* trans. Heinz Norden.

A CRITIQUE OF IMPERIALISM

One of the most important analyses of imperialism was the critique of British economist John A. Hobson (1850–1940), who in 1902 argued that the scramble for colonies served the interests of unregulated capitalism. Hobson asserted that colonization impeded social reform at home and maintained the gap between rich and poor.

In view of the part which the non-economic factors of patriotism, adventure, military enterprise, political ambition, and philanthropy play in imperial expansion, it may appear that to impute to financiers so much power is to take a too narrow view of history. And it is true that the motor-power of Imperialism is not chiefly financial: finance is rather the governor of the imperial engine, directing the energy and determining its work: it does not constitute the fuel of the engine, nor does it directly generate the power. Finance manipulates the patriotic forces which politicians, soldiers, philanthropists, and traders generate; the enthusiasm for expansion which issues from these sources, though strong and genuine, is irregular and blind; the financial interest has those qualities of concentration and clear-sighted calculation which are needed to set Imperialism to work. An ambitious statesman, a frontier soldier, an overzealous missionary, a pushing trader, may suggest or even initiate a step of imperial expansion, may assist in educating public opinion to the urgent need for some fresh advance, but the final determination rests with the financial power. The direct influence exercised by great financial houses in "high politics" is supported by the control which they exercise over the body of public opinion through the Press, which, in every "civilised" country, is becoming more and more their obedient instrument. . . . Add to this the natural sympathy with a sensational policy which a cheap Press always manifests, and it becomes evident that the Press has been strongly biased towards Imperialism, and has lent itself with great facility to the suggestion of financial or political Imperialists who have desired to work up patriotism for some new piece of expansion.

Such is the array of distinctively economic forces making for Imperialism, a large loose group of trades and professions seeking profitable business and lucrative employment from the expansion of military and civil services, and from the expenditure on military operations, the opening up of new tracts of territory and trade with the same, and the provision of new capital which these operations require, all these finding their central guiding and directing force in the power of the general financier.

From John A. Hobson, *Imperialism: A Study*. Copyright © 1938.

THE MARXIST INTERPRETATION

Russian radical activist V. I. Ulianov (1870–1924), better known by his pseudonym Lenin, was leader of the Bolshevik (Communist) party. He wrote the most sophisticated early Marxist interpretation of imperialism. Influenced by the ideas of Hobson, Lenin claimed that imperialist economic competition abroad represented the last phase of a dying capitalism.

If it were necessary to give the briefest possible definition of imperialism, it would be defined as the monopoly stage of capitalism. Such a definition would include the essential feature; for, on the one hand, finance-capital is the banking capital of the few biggest monopolist banks, fused with the capital of the monopolist groups of manufacturers; and, on the other, the division of the world is a transition from a colonial policy, ceaselessly extended without encountering opposition in regions not as yet appropriated by any capitalist power, to a colonial policy of monopolized territorial possession—the sharing out of the world being completed. . . .

Imperialism is capitalism in that phase of its development in which the domination of monopolies and finance-capital has established itself; in which the export of capital has acquired very great importance; in which the division of the world among the big, international trusts has begun; in which the partition of all the territories of the earth amongst the great capitalist powers has been completed. . . .

Monopoly has grown out of colonial policy. To the numerous "old" motives of colonial policy the capitalist financier has added the struggle for the sources of raw materials, for the exportation of capital, for "spheres of influence," *i.e.*, for spheres of good business, concessions, monopolist profits, and so on; in fine, for economic territory in general. When the European powers did not as yet occupy with their colonies a tenth part of Africa (as was the case in 1876), colonial policy was able to develop otherwise than by the methods of monopoly—by "free grabbing" of territories, so to speak. But when nine-tenths of Africa had been seized (towards 1900), when the whole world had been shared out, the period of colonial monopoly opened and as a result the period of bitterest struggle for the partition and the repartition of the world. . . .

From all that has been said on the economic nature of imperialism, it follows that we must define it as capitalism in transition, or, more precisely, as dying capitalism. It is very instructive in this respect to note that the bourgeois economists, describing modern capitalism, employ with great fluency such terms as "interlacing," "absence of isolation," etc.; the banks are "enterprises which by their objective and their course of development have a character not purely economic, but are departing more and more from the sphere of private economic management." And the same Reisser, to whom these last words belong, declares with the greatest seriousness that the "prophecy" of the Marxists concerning "socialization" has not been realized!

From V. I. Lenin, *Imperialism: The Highest Stage of Capitalism*. Vanguard Press. Copyright © 1926.

continued next page

THE HUBRIS OF WORLD POWER

British Nobel prize–winning poet Rudyard Kipling (1865–1936) was thought of as the official poet of the empire. His famous poem "The White Man's Burden," which appeared in 1899, was an appeal to the United States to help the British and other powers in assuming the "burden" of imperial rule. But in this poem, written two years earlier on the occasion of Queen Victoria's diamond jubilee, he pointed out that all things pass, including world empire.

God of our fathers, known of old—
Lord of our far-flung battle line—
Beneath whose awful hand we hold
Dominion over palm and pine—
Lord God of Hosts, be with us yet,
Lest we forget—lest we forget!

The tumult and the shouting die—
The Captains and the Kings depart—
Still stands thine ancient sacrifice,
An humble and a contrite heart. . . .

Far-called, our navies melt away—
On dune and headland sinks the fire—
Lo, all our pomp of yesterday
Is one with Nineveh and Tyre!
Judge of the Nations, spare us yet,
Lest we forget . . .

If, drunk with sight of power, we loose
Wild tongues that have not Thee in awe—
Such boasting as the Gentiles use
Or lesser breeds without the Law—. . . .

For heathen heart that puts her trust
In reeking tube and iron shard—
All valiant dust that builds on dust,
And guarding calls not Thee to guard,
For frantic boast and foolish word,
Thy Mercy on Thy People, Lord!

From Rudyard Kipling, "Recessional," *Barrack Room Ballads: Recessional and Other Verses.* Robert McBride. Copyright © 1910.

labeled the "Indian Mutiny," the rebels seized Delhi, where they killed many of the British inhabitants, together with large sections of north-central India.

In March 1858, with the aid of considerable reinforcements, British troops finally broke the rebellion, and the British government took over direct control of India, ruled by a viceroy. In 1876, Queen Victoria was crowned empress of India. It was clear that, whatever the immediate cause, the "Mutiny" had reflected widespread discontent, and a few measures were taken to redress grievances. Indians received limited political representation at a local government level. Social reforms included the abolition of slavery.

The British made a thoroughgoing attempt to replace traditional cultural patterns with Western values. The government discouraged the rigid barriers of the caste system, whereby members of different castes could not mix in public places or on trains, and put limitations on child marriages. Hindus who became Christians were eligible for government jobs. Although regional variation was unavoidable in so vast a country, a British-type legal system operated nationally, and taxes were collected by the government, rather than by regional princes.

Schools and universities were run along British lines. Instruction was generally in English, which thus became the common language of the educated, who in due course were to lead the battle for Indian independence. Science and technology replaced traditional Hindu and Muslim learning. The products of this educational system were eligible for posts in the Indian Civil Service. After 1864, Indians in theory could be appointed to the highest ranks; in practice, appointees (generally Hindus) were restricted to lower positions, where many became familiar with Western notions of bureaucracy.

Improved communications assured effective control of the colony. The authorities constructed a telegraph system during the 1850s, and laid thousands of miles of rail tracks. By 1900, the Indian rail network

Sir Chamrajendra Wadiyar, maharaja of Mysore, and his children, 1890.

extended for over 26,000 miles. These modernizations, together with the introduction of Western agricultural methods, also served to increase prosperity for colonial entrepreneurs and the limited but growing number of local business interests.

For the majority of Indians, illiterate and living at a bare subsistence level as their ancestors had for centuries, the effects of British rule were mixed. Among those better off, there continued to be considerable resentment. Upper-caste Hindus disliked seeing the caste system challenged. Muslims, who had been accustomed to forming the ruling class, now found themselves discriminated against. Both groups resented the Christian missionary work that often formed part of the school program.

Another challenge to the British came from a number of educated Indians who combined a sense of national identity with a belief in Western ideals of freedom. The Indian National Congress party first met in 1885 to advocate greater Indian participation in the Civil Service. Over the next few decades, it campaigned with increasing vigor for Indian independence, both political and economic. Yet, ironically, the very fact that Congress party leaders represented progressive ideas cut them off from most of their fellow Indians, traditionalists who saw no essential difference between British governors and upper-caste intellectuals. India did not achieve independence until 1947.

THE OPENING OF CHINA AND THE BOXER REBELLION

For the first centuries of European exploration in Asia, the Chinese empire succeeded in maintaining its isolation from Western culture. By the early decades of the 19th century, however, internal administrative and financial problems hampered Chinese resistance to the presence of foreign merchants and traders. As the imperial government found itself under increasing challenge from peasant rebels, it turned to outside help in the struggle to retain control.

Chinese helplessness in the face of European military force became manifest in the Opium War of 1839–1842. British merchants in India had developed the custom of exchanging opium for Chinese tea, porcelain, and other goods. The Chinese wanted silver and gold in return, but the British feared problems with their balance of payments, and traded opium instead. Use of the drug, the harmful effects of which were well-known, was not traditional in China, and the government attempted to prevent its importation. The Chinese emperor even addressed a personal appeal to Queen Victoria, but she turned a deaf ear, feeling that it would be inopportune to give up such a major source of revenue.

The result of the Chinese attempts to ban opium was open war and a British blockade of the Chinese coast. China, with no real sea power, was forced to give way and accept humiliating terms of settlement. Several ports, including Shanghai and Canton, were opened to the British, who also received the island of Hong Kong. Hong Kong's mainland territory was added in 1898, when China gave the British a 99-year lease, which expired in 1997. British merchants continued to trade in ever-increasing quantities of opium: 6,000 cases were shipped to China in 1820, 100,000 in 1880.

Chinese suspicion of Western influences received further reinforcement when peasants led by Christian converts staged a major uprising to demand tax and land reform. The Tai Ping Rebellion lasted from 1851 to 1864, and was finally crushed only with the help of Western forces, including a British contingent led by General Charles "Chinese" Gordon (1833–1885). During its course, a number of other nations, including France and the United States, took advantage of the government's weakness to force further trade and territorial concessions. In 1860 a Franco-British force occupied Peking (now spelled Beijing), drove out the emperor, and burned the Summer Palace.

Whereas in India a colonial power had taken the responsibility of direct rule, in China competition among Western imperialists led European powers to seek financial control without taking the country over. As long as a weak central government was dependent on European troops and advisers, the Chinese were at the mercy of Western demands. Nor, given the Chinese reverence for tradition, was there any move to modernize. With the Tai Ping Rebellion crushed, the government tried to revive traditional principles of Confucianism. Among its tenets was the saying, "Acknowledgement of limits leads to happiness," a dangerous attitude with which to face driving capitalist Europeans.

Before the century was over, China lost territory to its neighbor Japan. The Japanese had followed the opposite tactic of adopting Western ways wholesale, and used them to wrest control of Korea from China in 1894–1895. The shock of defeat by its much smaller rival finally induced the Chinese emperor to initiate a campaign of reforms.

The Boxer Rebellion

The attempt at domestic reform came too late. In 1898, Tz'u-Hsi (1835–1908), the previous emperor's formidable widow who had earlier ruled as regent, seized power. Bitterly anti-Western, she maintained control through a small clique of conservative ministers. To reinforce her rejection of outside influences, she also encouraged the activities of a secret society,

Dead bodies of Boxer rebels executed by Chinese officials.

the "Harmonious Fists," called by Europeans the "Boxers." In the Boxer Rebellion of 1900–1901, members of the society killed missionaries and Chinese converts to Christianity, murdered the German minister in Peking, and besieged the foreign embassies there.

The uprising was suppressed by a joint European and United States military force, which in turn demanded yet further concessions. By the terms of the Boxer Protocol, China paid a huge indemnity to the United States and the European powers involved. New treaties gave Britain, France, Germany, and Russia long-term leases on ports, from which they could expand inland. With effective power and no responsibility, the European nations constructed railroads and developed river transport to open up the interior. The dowager empress grimly held on to what authority she could, finally westernizing the army and imperial bureaucracy, but by now the internal pressure for change was too great. Within three years of her death in 1908, open revolution ended imperial rule and replaced it with the Chinese Republic.

JAPAN AND THE WEST

Like China, Japan came under heavy pressure from Americans and Europeans to end its isolation and open itself to international trade. In contrast to their neighbors, however, the Japanese quickly reformed their country along Western lines and adopted Western technologies. So swift was the transformation that by the end of the century Japan, too, had become an imperialist power.

Japan's exposure to international pressure was both later and more violent than that of China. In 1853, the American Commodore Matthew Perry (1794–1858) sailed four vessels into Tokyo Harbor, threatening bombardment and refusing to leave until a Japanese envoy agreed to accept a United States demand for a diplomatic and trade treaty. The next year he returned to conclude the agreement. Britain, the Netherlands, and Russia were quick to follow, claiming their rights to fish in Japanese waters and to trade. With little in the way of naval power, the Japanese had little choice but to concede.

Both progressives and conservatives in Japan began to urge reform, the former inspired by Western models, the latter in the belief that their nation's independence could be assured only by radical change. In 1867 they found a leader in the new young emperor, Meiji (ruled 1867–1912)—a word meaning "the enlightened one," chosen in place of his real name, Mutsuhito. In place of the old feudal system of regional lords known as shoguns, the emperor himself assumed

Japanese portrait of Commodore Matthew Perry.

symbolic leadership, and the country was governed by his advisers, a small group of elder statesmen. Responsible to the emperor rather than to the Diet (parliament), they provided the authoritarian leadership that made possible rapid change.

In looking for a model for their institutions, the Japanese turned to Europe and the United States. Western experts were brought in to help build up a navy, while the new Japanese army adopted German systems of conscription and training. A new constitution, introduced in 1890, was also based on that of Germany. State investment and the rise of a business class encouraged industrialization along Western lines. On the other hand a new system of universal education, while it included scientific and technical subjects, also laid strong emphasis on patriotism and loyalty to the emperor.

During the last three decades of the 19th century, Japan adopted a variety of aspects of Western culture, including the metric system and the calendar. Christianity made little impact, however. Nor did the Japanese have any interest in taking up the cause of feminism, which was beginning to advance in western Europe, and Japanese women retained their traditionally inferior status, confined to the home.

Japan's first major adventure abroad, the war with China over Korea (1894–1895), was almost too successful. By its end, the Japanese had taken not only Korea itself, but the island of Taiwan (Formosa) and a piece of the Chinese mainland. This was too much for Russia, which found support in France and Germany. The European powers had no intention of sharing China with another Asian nation and insisted that the Japanese withdraw from the mainland. Yet the acceptance of Japan as an imperialist country was underscored in 1902, when Britain, the leading colonial power, and Japan signed an alliance. Further success came in the Russo-Japanese War of 1904–1905, when superior Japanese naval power helped them to victory.

By the early 20th century, Japan had achieved many of the goals of Western society, including industrialization, prosperity, and imperial conquest, without the upheaval or revolution that marked the modernization of most European countries. The methods—the encouragement of obedience and unquestioning patriotism, and firm repression of any dissent—helped to shape the character of modern Japan.

NORTH AFRICA: THE BRITISH AND FRENCH IN CONFLICT

The fiercest competition of all for imperialist conquest occurred in the "scramble for Africa." In 1870, a European presence in Africa was limited to the northern regions above the Sahara and a few coastal ports. By the end of the century virtually the entire continent was under European rule.

In the north, a new era began with the completion of the Suez Canal in 1869. The construction of the canal was jointly financed by the khedive (viceroy) of Egypt, ruling on behalf of the Ottoman Empire, and French investors. The original inventor of the scheme,

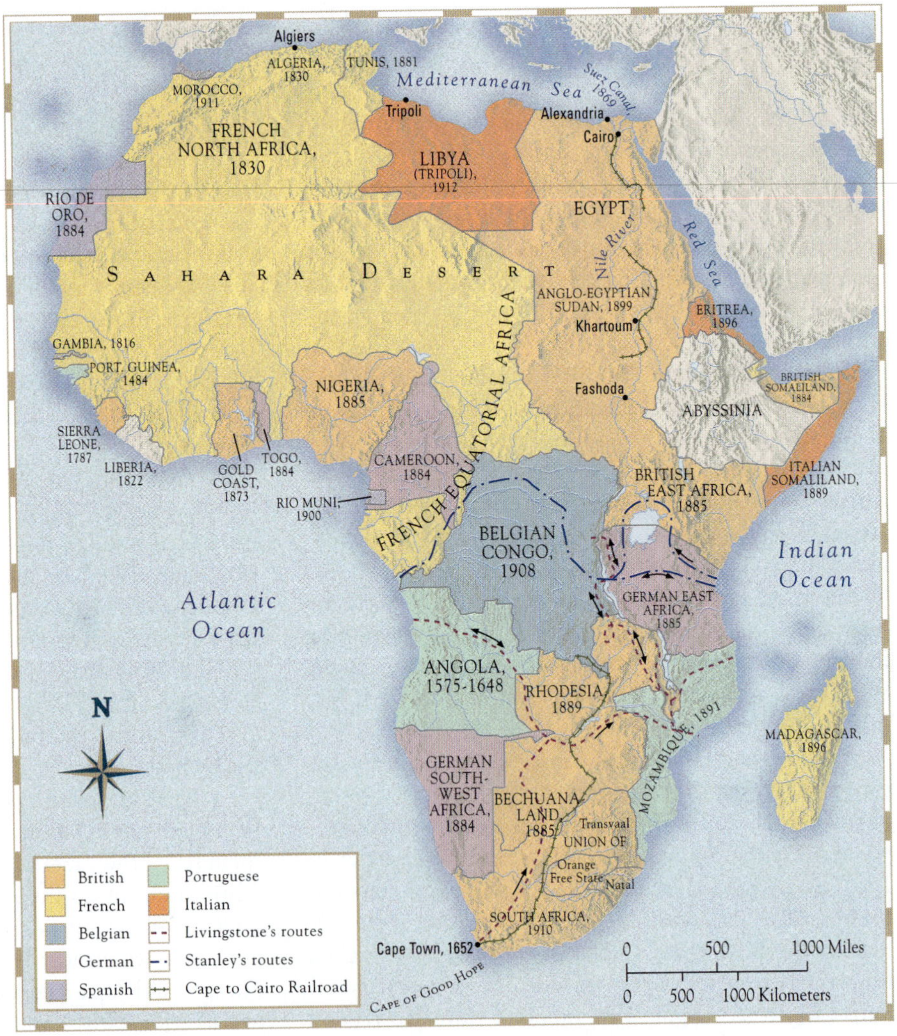

Map 18.1 Africa on the Eve of World War I.

Scottish troops relaxing in front of the Sphinx.

and the director of the company involved in the canal's construction between 1859 and 1869, was Ferdinand-Marie de Lesseps (1805–1894), who later worked on the Panama Canal project. The immense engineering project was intended to facilitate French commercial expansion to the east, since ships bound for India and East Asia would be able to sail directly from the Mediterranean to the Indian Ocean, without having to circumnavigate Africa.

Egypt's participation had resulted in heavy debts to British banks, and by as early as 1875 its financial state was so calamitous that the khedive was forced to sell his shares. The British prime minister, Benjamin Disraeli, jumped at the chance to buy into France's engineering achievement and challenge French influence in North Africa. The two great rivals thus found themselves in joint control of Egypt.

When in 1882 a nationalist revolt by the Egyptian Army tried to drive out the foreigners, the French and British planned a joint intervention. The French cabinet fell and France backed off, whereupon the British went ahead on their own, taking the opportunity to reinforce their position. Ships of the Royal Navy bombarded Alexandria, and British troops moved in to take control of the country, leaving the khedive as a mere figurehead. The British protectorate over Egypt lasted until well after World War II.

With the British established in Egypt, the French were anxious to strengthen their bases elsewhere in North Africa. They had begun their conquest of Algeria, also Ottoman territory, in 1830. In 1881 they took Tunisia, another possession of the crumbling Ottoman Empire. Shortly after 1900, a French military force also entered Morocco, where their control was unsuccessfully challenged by Germany in the years leading up to World War I (see Part VII, Topic 16). A subsequent Franco-British agreement of 1904 recognized French control of Morocco in return for British rule in Egypt. With the Italian capture of Libya in 1912, by the eve of World War I the whole of Muslim North Africa was in European hands.

The direct confrontation between two imperialist powers, which the British and French avoided in Egypt, reached a crisis point in the Sudan. In 1898, a French

Significant Dates

The Drive for Imperialism

1839–1842	The Opium War
1851–1864	The Tai Ping Rebellion
1853	Admiral Perry arrives in Tokyo Harbor
1869	Construction of Suez Canal completed
1876	Leopold forms International Association for the Exploration and Civilization of Central Africa
1881	French take Tunisia
1882	British establish protectorate over Egypt
1884	Germans in South-West Africa
1885	Indian National Congress party first meets
1895	Jameson Raid
1896	Italians defeated at Adowra
1898	Kitchener defeats Mahdi's forces at Omdurman
1899–1902	Boer War
1902	Alliance between Britain and Japan
1910	Union of South Africa formed
1911–1912	Italy seizes Libya

military expedition under commander Jean-Baptiste Marchand (1863–1934) making its way toward the Red Sea from West Africa arrived at the Nile settlement of Fashoda, just as British troops led by General Herbert Kitchener (1850–1916) were occupying the southern Sudan. In the steamy swamplands, two grand imperialist schemes came face to face: the French plan for a territory stretching across the continent from the Atlantic to the Indian Ocean, and the British idea of an equally vast empire running north to south, from Cairo to the Cape of Good Hope. After several weeks of tension, the French troops withdrew on government orders. The French government realized the error of risking war with Britain when their real enemy was Germany; as the radical republican leader, Georges Clemenceau (1841–1929), said, "war with Britain is not worth a few marshes on the upper Nile."

The British had begun the subjugation of the Sudan in the 1880s but they were opposed by Sunni Muslim forces led by Muhammad Ahmad (1844–1885), the self-styled *Mahdi* (the Mahdi were a series of self-proclaimed saviors in the Sunni Muslim tradition). In 1885, the Mahdi's army attacked a British garrison in the city of Khartoum, killing General Gordon and massacring its inhabitants. The death of Gordon, who had won popularity in Britain for his role in the suppression of the Tai Ping Rebellion in China and for ending the slave trade in the Sudan, provoked British anger and the collapse of William Gladstone's government. Ten years later, in 1898, Kitchener decisively defeated the Mahdi forces at Omdurman, where British soldiers mowed the Muslims down with machine guns.

THE DISMEMBERMENT OF CENTRAL AFRICA

European involvement in the affairs of North Africa went back to the days of ancient Rome. Africa south of the Sahara, however, was little known to Europeans before the mid-19th century. Coastal cities such as Lagos and Dakar served as trading centers, principally for slaves, but the interior remained unvisited except by Arab traders and the most intrepid explorers. With the decline and eventual end of the slave trade, two states on the West African coast were settled by freed slaves. Liberia, the oldest black African republic, became independent in 1847, although it remained under informal American influence. Sierra Leone, which became a British colony in 1808, combined an indigenous population with freed slaves from the West Indies and prisoners liberated from slave ships intercepted by the British Navy.

With the burst of imperialism after 1870, the Europeans forced their way into the African interior, drawing artificial boundaries, and inventing new countries. By 1900, the British controlled Nigeria in West Africa and a string of territories running south from Egypt, consisting of Kenya, Uganda, and Rhodesia (the territory comprising Rhodesia now forms the two countries of Zambia and Zimbabwe). The French held most of the rest of West Africa, with Dakar, the largest city in Senegal, as their administrative center. They constructed roads, railways, and harbor facilities there, and opened a university. Senegal had sent a deputy to the French parliament as early as 1848, although the first black deputy was elected only in 1914.

The heart of the continent fell to the Belgians, whose ruthless exploitation of the Belgian Congo soon became notorious. In the Horn of Africa on the Red Sea and the Indian Ocean, the Italians seized part of Somaliland (modern Somalia), other portions of which were occupied by the British and French, and Eritrea (now part of Ethiopia). They tried to conquer Ethiopia itself in 1896 but were driven back by the Ethiopian army at the Battle of Adowra, the first European colonizers to be defeated by indigenous African forces.

Leaders of the German forces in East Africa (1889) with local officers.

Portugal increased its hold on Angola and Mozambique, both of which it had used as trading bases for slaves as early as the 16th century. Unlike other colonizing powers, Portugal was not rich enough to invest in building infrastructure for its colonies (Belgium was in the same position). Work was done by a system of forced labor—virtually a form of slavery—and contracts were farmed out to foreign companies, which had even less interest than the government in the welfare of the indigenous populations.

The Germans were slow in developing a serious colonial drive. Bismarck was one of the few statesmen of the times who remained doubtful of the benefits of imperialism, and realized that the quest for German colonies would serve only to antagonize Britain. Nevertheless he began the German colonization of South-West Africa and the Cameroons in 1884, more as an outlet for German nationalism than for economic motives. After Bismarck's dismissal by Kaiser Wilhelm II in 1890 (see Part VII, Topic 15), Germany embarked on a vigorous imperialist policy. Its only possessions of any size were South-West Africa (now Namibia), a barren area of little economic value, German East Africa (now Tanzania), gained in 1891, and some important Pacific islands.

THE BOER WAR AND THE UNION OF SOUTH AFRICA

Although the southern part of Africa is farthest from Europe, the history of European involvement there goes back to the end of the 15th century, when Portuguese mariners sailed past the Cape of Good Hope into the Indian Ocean. In 1652, the Dutch East India Company founded a settlement at the Cape, to serve as a supply base for ships, and to search the interior for slaves and precious metals. Over the next century and a half the Dutch expanded eastward, taking land from the indigenous Bantu, Bush people, and Hottentots, who were either killed off, enslaved, or pushed out of the region. Other slaves were imported from West Africa and Mozambique. The present "colored" people of South Africa are the descendants of children born to unions between Dutch settlers and indigenous people, and Dutch and imported slaves. South Africa's "Indians" are descended from Indian and Malayan workers and merchants imported during the 19th century.

The Dutch colonists, who called themselves the *Boers* (the Dutch word for "farmers"), spoke a Dutch dialect which came to be known as Afrikaans. As they continued to take over good farming land wherever they found it, the only native people to put up any serious resistance were the Bantu. The first Bantu War of the 1770s was only the beginning of a series of bitter conflicts in which the Europeans gradually gained possession of Bantu lands. In the process, the Boers developed their notion of "apartheid," which claimed that the two cultures were separate and irreconcilable. Opposition to any form of multi-racialism was thus embedded in Boer political life from the beginning of their destruction of indigenous culture.

The Cape of Good Hope was annexed by the British in 1815. Relations between newly arrived British settlers and the Boers, unfriendly at best, were exacerbated further when in 1834 the British authorities banned slavery. From 1835 to 1845, in a migration known as the Great Trek, Boer farmers moved northeastward out of the British Cape Colony in search of new land. They founded two independent republics, the Orange Free State and the Transvaal. The indigenous Zulu warriors who opposed them, armed with shields and spears, were shot down in large numbers, and in the 1870s the British crushed the remaining Zulu forces in spite of fierce resistance.

Cecil Rhodes, colonial administrator and financier.

A few years later, first diamonds (in 1867) and then gold (in 1886) were discovered in the Transvaal. The conquered peoples provided cheap labor for the mines, but the Boers urgently needed capital to exploit their resources. The British were only too willing to step in. The Cape Colony's aggressive prime minister, Cecil Rhodes (1853–1902), went further. He had first come to Africa as a sickly young man, and quickly made a fabulous fortune in diamonds. Driven by ambition to unite Africa from the Cape to Cairo under British rule, Rhodes set out to subvert the Boer republics. In 1895, having first encouraged a rebellion among white, non-Boer mineworkers, he sent a force of volunteers to raid the Transvaal. The illegal and disastrous Jameson Raid, named after its leader, Leander Starr Jameson (1853–1917), was supposed to spark an uprising of foreigners in the Transvaal and provoke the Boers into outright war. The Boers located the arms caches the British had hidden, and the scheme failed. International outrage at the unprovoked attack on fellow westerners drove Rhodes from office.

Boer resentment at growing British interference was bound to lead to conflict sooner or later. The Boer War broke out in 1899, and bitter fighting went on until 1902. After taking the offensive, well equipped with arms by Germany, the Boers soon began to give way as British reinforcements were poured into South Africa. For the last two years Boer efforts were confined to guerrilla fighting, in a struggle that was grim and determined on both sides. The British, for their part, spared no means to discourage the guerrilla combatants, burning their farms and imprisoning their families in detention centers—the first modern concentration camps.

The British finally prevailed, and in 1910 the various territories were incorporated into the Union of South Africa. The legacy of resentment continued to influence relations between the British and the Afrikaaners for decades, while the true losers in the "white man's war" were the native populations. At the same time, the spectacle of two European, "civilized" peoples fighting over land and natural resources to which neither had any right underlined the true nature of imperialism, and the lengths to which Europeans were prepared to go to achieve conquest.

By the first decade of the 20th century, the history of Africa had been irrevocably changed. A few regional kingdoms remained, and Ethiopia retained its independence; the rest of the continent was divided up into a series of colonies, which often fragmented single tribal groups or combined rival peoples.

The impact of westernization varied according to the policies of the colonizing power. The British tried to introduce educational and health systems on a fairly broad scale, but did not encourage local peoples to become involved in administrative positions. The French, by contrast, aimed to produce an African élite, versed in Western culture; it is no coincidence that many of the leading African writers of the first half of the 20th century came from French colonies. Other imperialist powers, notably Belgium and Portugal, were almost exclusively concerned with making profits from their colonies.

The overall phenomenon of Western imperialism in Africa and Asia was so vast, affecting so many millions of lives, that generalization about its effects is difficult. For many of the conquering powers the benefits of empire were dubious. With the exception of the British Empire, most of the colonies cost vast sums of money to maintain, and few Europeans actually wanted to live in them. Yet one recurring pattern can be seen: the growth of nationalism. The pursuit of national identity, one of the most powerful forces in the late 20th century, first developed in many parts of the world as a way of resisting the imperialists of the late 19th century and their successors.

Questions for Further Study

1. How did motives for colonization vary among the European powers? How did these differences affect their approach to establishing and governing their colonies?
2. To what extent were economic interests significant in the drive for colonization? How far were economic expectations fulfilled?
3. What effect did European colonization have on the creation of nationalist identities in the colonized territories? What were the long-term effects?

Suggestions for Further Reading

Baumgart, W. *Imperialism: The Idea of British and French Colonial Expansion, 1880–1914.* New York, 1982.
Christopher, A. J. *Colonial Africa.* Totowa, NJ, 1984.
Doyle, M. W. *Empires.* Ithaca, NY, 1986.
Hobshawm, E. J. *The Age of Empire, 1875–1914.* New York, 1987.
Lewis, D. L. *The Race to Fashoda: European Colonialism and African Resistance in the Scramble for Africa.* London, 1988.
Moon, P. *The British Conquest and Domination of India.* Bloomington, IN, 1989.
Pakenham, T. *The Scramble for Africa.* New York, 1991.

VII

Topic 19

The Social Order Challenged

The triumph of modern capitalism in the half-century before World War I did not go unchallenged. Opponents of laissez-faire economics attacked big business for exploiting the working class in the quest for ever-increasing profits. Social critics insisted that while prosperity enhanced the already privileged existence of the bourgeoisie, grinding poverty oppressed the daily lives of millions. Radical political leaders charged that parliamentary liberalism served the interests of the upper classes through repressive domestic policies designed to maintain the status quo.

Critics of the established order claimed to speak for two distinct but overlapping groups that represented most of Europe's population: the working classes and women. Governments everywhere saw the demands of these groups as dangerous to political stability and social peace, and used the coercive apparatus of the state—the police and the armed forces—against the forces of change. Neither working-class nor women's organizations, however, were united in their leadership, methods, or aims, and often there was little cooperation between them.

The divisions within the working-class and women's movements centered on a fundamental disagreement over long-range goals. Moderates wanted to improve conditions by reforming the existing political and social systems. This was essentially the aim of reformist socialists, trade unionists, and middle-class feminists, all of whom sought to extend the suffrage, elect representatives to parliaments or achieve other forms of representation, and pressure governments or business into granting concessions. Radicals, on the other hand, wanted to destroy the existing order completely and replace it with a new society in which the underlying causes of inequality and exploitation would be eliminated—this was the intention of anarchists, revolutionary socialists, and socialist feminists.

By 1914, moderates and radicals found themselves no closer to resolving their differences. Some significant reforms had been achieved, including the right to strike and to unionize, and the adoption of universal male suffrage in almost all countries. Yet capitalism was still fully entrenched, and almost nowhere did women even gain the vote, let alone more deeply rooted personal and legal rights. It took the trauma of the Great War and the subsequent Russian Revolution to shake the liberal-capitalist order to its foundations.

Significant Dates

Socialism, Anarchism, and Workers

1840	Proudhon's *What Is Property?*
1848	*The Communist Manifesto*
1869	Social Democratic Labor party in Germany
1871	Paris Commune
1875	"Gotha Program" adopted
1864–1876	First International
1884	Fabian Society
1889–1914	Second International
1892	Italian Socialist party
1895	Confédération Générale du Travail
1899	Bernstein's *Evolutionary Socialism*
1894–1900	Anarchist assassinations
1905	French Socialist party; Russian Revolution
1908	Sorel's *Reflections on Violence*

THE FIRST INTERNATIONAL: ANARCHISTS V. SOCIALISTS

In the mid-19th century, the working-class movement found two major theories—among a host of other possibilities—on which to base its revolutionary struggle against industrial capitalism: anarchism and Marxism. Among the early anarchists were the "Mutualists," who followed the ideas of the Frenchman Pierre Proudhon (1809–1865). In *What Is Property?* (1840), Proudhon declared that "Property is Theft!" and asserted that small-scale private ownership of property in a federation of communes was the best guarantee of individual freedom.

The Russian exile Mikhail Bakunin (1814–1876) advocated a different direction: the elimination of the state and all private property, to be achieved by revolutionary violence. By the 1860s, anarchism emerged as the principal rival to Marxism. The worker movement itself began to divide between anarchist principles and the "scientific" socialism advocated by Karl Marx and Friedrich Engels (see Part VII, Topic 13). Anarchists and Marxist socialists agreed, at least theoretically, that revolutionary violence was the only means of destroying capitalism. Marxists and most anarchists also accepted the idea that private property was the root cause of inequality and exploitation and had to be eliminated.

Where anarchists and Marxists clashed was in their view of the nature and the purpose of the state. Marx declared that the immediate aim of the revolution was for the workers to wrest power from the bourgeoisie by conquering the state and creating a working-class government—the "dictatorship of the proletariat." The anarchists, on the other hand, saw the state as the principal source of oppression, regardless of its nature, and insisted on eliminating it completely, along with other forms of authority. "All exercise of power perverts," wrote Bakunin, "and all submission to authority humiliates."

Mikhail Bakunin, Russian revolutionary exile and leader of the anarchist opposition to Marx in the First International.

Cover of the original edition of *The Communist Manifesto* (1848), by Karl Marx and Friedrich Engels. The slogan "Workers of the world, unite" appears on the page.

Another theoretical point of disagreement lay in identifying the revolutionary class that would lead the struggle. Marx pinned his hopes on the modern industrial proletariat of advanced nations such as Britain and Germany, which he identified as the only true revolutionary class. Bakunin, on the other hand, argued that the industrial proletariat was already in the process of being indoctrinated by bourgeois values and had lost its revolutionary potential. Instead, Bakunin focused on what he called the "proletariat in rags," those desperately poor elements at the bottom of society—workers in small shops and landless peasants—in preindustrial countries such as Spain, Italy, and Russia.

These and other ideological currents derived inspiration from the uprising of the Paris Commune, a crucial moment in the development of European radicalism (see Part VII, Topic 15).

European radicals saw the Commune as a class war between workers and the bourgeoisie. In his analysis of the Commune, *The Civil War in France* (1871), Marx described it as the first example of the dictatorship of the proletariat. But although communists, socialists, and anarchists had fought against the government, many more thousands of French citizens with no ideological agenda sustained the Commune, which could not be described as a Marxist phenomenon. Nevertheless, the uprising struck terror among European governments, most of which clamped down on their own radicals and workers.

Marx, Bakunin, and the First International

The International Workingmen's Association—commonly known as the First International—was founded in London in 1864 by a disparate group of radicals that included German Marxists, anarchists, British and Belgian trade unionists, French supporters of Proudhon, and Italian followers of Mazzini. The International sought to act as a clearing house for radicalism and to focus revolutionary strategy. Instead, it became the stage for an ongoing debate between Marx and Bakunin, whose personalities and ideas represented the extreme alternatives of revolutionary leadership.

From the outset, Marx tried to run the International, but Bakunin opposed him. In September 1871, after the repression of the Commune, its representatives met at a congress in London, where Marx pushed for the adoption of a platform calling for the seizure of political power by the workers through the creation of socialist parties in all countries. Moreover, he insisted that the International's executive committee be given the power to impose centralized control and ideological uniformity over the International's local sections and federations. Bakunin's anarchist followers and other "antiauthoritarian" radicals lined up against Marx, whose rigid program was supported chiefly by German communists. A year later, at the Hague Congress, the struggle between Marxists and antiauthoritarians further polarized the International, but Marx triumphed by securing the expulsion of Bakunin and the anarchists.

Regrouping after the Hague meeting, Bakunin and the antiauthoritarians held their own meeting at Saint-Imier, Switzerland, where they rejected the principle that central committees or congresses could dictate policy to members. Instead of the seizure of political power that Marx demanded, the Saint-Imier delegates called for the destruction of power.

The First International, by then consisting only of Marxists, was officially dissolved in 1876. Over the next 20 years, while the Marxists forged ahead with the creation of socialist parties, militant action remained largely in the hands of the anarchists. Bakunin and a

The Paris Commune, a radical republican government in opposition to the National Assembly. This photograph is a portrayal, probably used as anti-Communard propaganda, of the killing of 62 hostages. The massacre actually occurred at night at the hands of a mob the Commune leaders could not control.

new generation of libertarian leaders worked to arouse the masses. Peter Kropotkin, a Russian prince living in London, called for working-class solidarity, while the Italian Errico Malatesta (1850–1932) shifted his anarchist doctrine away from the collectivist formula of "from each according to his abilities to each according to his labor" to that of anarchist communism, which replaced the word "labor" with "need."

Most anarchists maintained the antiauthoritarian tradition, while some individuals, not all of whom were anarchists, adopted terrorist tactics. In the 1870s German anarchists made two attempts to kill Kaiser Wilhelm I, and in the 1890s a cycle of retaliation against state repression induced a few practitioners of "propaganda of the deed" to assassinate political leaders and monarchs—among them, French President François Sadi-Carnot in 1894, Prime Minister Antonio Canovas del Castillo of Spain in 1897, the Empress Elizabeth of Austria-Hungary in 1898, and King Umberto I of Italy in 1900. Most anarchist theorists did not believe that such terrorist acts would bring the revolution into being, but saw them as the inevitable result of government oppression. Governments reacted sharply to the assassinations, convening an antianarchist conference in Rome in 1898 to coordinate police efforts on an international level.

THE SECOND INTERNATIONAL: IDEOLOGY AND SOCIALIST POLITICS

Socialism emerged as a major force in Europe between 1870 and 1914. Mass-based political parties inspired by Marxist principles grew rapidly, and by the 1890s one existed in almost every country, together with a vast network of subsidiary organizations, unions, newspapers, and clubs. Their leaders were optimistic that they were on the verge of attaining a socialist society.

The Rise of Socialist Parties

The first and most important socialist party in Europe developed in Germany. From the beginning, however, German socialists were divided into two camps—Marxists and those who followed the ideas of Ferdinand Lassalle (1825–1864). Flamboyant and brilliant, Lassalle had taken part in the 1848 revolutions before studying political philosophy and socialist theory. Unlike Marx, who wanted to "smash" the bourgeois state, Lassalle sought to democratize it for the working class. Lassalle had taken from the British economist David Ricardo (see Part VI, Topic 11) the notion of the "iron law of wages." According to this theory, wage increases resulted in the growth in the number of workers, which in turn created labor competition that drove down wages to the subsistence level. To overcome this tendency, Lassalle urged the formation of worker cooperatives, in which the workers would be the owners and thus control their own earnings. In his view, strikes and unions were futile. In 1863, a year before his death in a duel, he established the General Association of German Workers, which advocated universal suffrage and a program of peaceful, legal means to achieve socialism.

In opposition to Lassalle, Wilhelm Liebknecht (1826–1900) and August Bebel (1840–1913) founded the Social Democratic Labor party in 1869. Although not officially a Marxist party, the group was closer to the ideas of Marx and Engels than those of Lassalle. In 1875, they agreed to issue a joint platform, the "Gotha Program," in alliance with Lassalle's moderate supporters. This policy, which merged aspects of Marxist dogma with the reform strategy of Lassalle, formed the basis of the German Social Democratic party (SPD). Three years later, Bismarck passed the Anti-Socialist Laws designed to stamp out socialism, but the repression actually served to give a focus to the party's identity and it struggled underground for years before Kaiser Wilhelm II repealed the laws (see Part VII, Topic 15).

Marx criticized such blending of his revolutionary ideas with the reformist approach of the Lassallians, but the latter seemed appropriate to the many German socialists who felt that working-class power could be attained peacefully. This was the view of Eduard Bernstein (1850–1932), whose book *Evolutionary Socialism* (1899) was the first major work to "revise" Marxist theory in the light of changing circumstances. Bernstein, an old friend of Engels who had absorbed the views of British moderates known as the Fabians, argued on the basis of the German experience that Marx was wrong in predicting that the status of the working class would inevitably deteriorate. Marxist socialists, he contended, should eschew revolutionary violence and work through the political process to achieve bread-and-butter benefits for workers. He therefore believed that socialist deputies in the Reichstag should collaborate with bourgeois political parties to reform German society. Orthodox Marxists in the SPD attacked Bernstein's revisionism and virtually drummed him out of the party.

The success of German "social democracy" and the trade unions in winning worker support acted as a model for socialists throughout continental Europe. Despite efforts to create a Marxist party in Great Britain, socialism there was generally moderate and a socialist party developed after the trade unions. The most important socialist group was the Fabian Society (1884), named after Quintus Fabius Maximus, a Roman general of the 2nd century B.C. who used evasive tactics instead of direct battles in the Punic Wars. Its founders were middle-class intellectuals such as the writer H. G. Wells (1866–1946) and the dramatist George Bernard Shaw (1856–1950), and among its most important members were Sidney and Beatrice Webb (see Part VIII, Topic 5). In 1900 the Fabians, who favored peaceful political change rather than revolution, combined with the growing trade union movement and other socialist organizations to found the Labour party, in which Marxist elements were a distinct minority.

Belgians, Russians, Austrians, and Italians established their own parties in the two decades after 1870. The first Marxist party in France was formed by Jules Guesde (1845–1922), but several other groups vied for the loyalty of French workers, including the "Possibilists," so-called because they rejected Marx's all-or-nothing doctrines, and a group of "Independent" socialist intellectuals. Only in 1905 did French socialists unite under the leadership of Jean Jaures (1859–1914) with a largely Marxist party program.

The Second International

In 1889, on the centenary of the French Revolution, a large assembly of socialist societies gathered in Paris and founded the Second International. Unlike the First International, whose members were a disparate group of individuals, the Second—known as the "Socialist International"—was based on party affiliation. Marxist revolutionary as well as reformist parties were included, but from the beginning the anarchists were kept out. Through propaganda activities such as "May Day" parades and periodic congresses, the International coordinated socialist activity on a worldwide level in order to raise the consciousness of workers. International congresses were held in 1891, 1893, 1896, 1900, 1904, 1907, 1910, and 1912.

Just as Marx had dominated the First International, the SPD was able to exercise considerable hegemony over the Second, largely because of its more than 1 million members and the large number of deputies it had in the *Reichstag*. Yet the ideological divisions between Marxist orthodoxy and reformism continued to mark the International's deliberations.

Within the International, the German socialist August Bebel and his French rival Jean Jaures epitomized the cleavage between revolutionaries and reformists. The main controversy that divided them revolved around whether socialists should accept ministerial positions in nonsocialist governments. Bebel and Jaures debated these questions constantly at International congresses.

Bebel led the German Social Democrats with an iron hand for almost 50 years, and achieved a series of electoral gains that by 1912 made the SPD the largest party in the *Reichstag*. His orthodox Marxism maintained that socialist parties should be formed to seize power, not to work within parliamentary systems or cooperate with bourgeois parties. As a result, he bitterly criticized his French comrades when one of them agreed to serve in a republican cabinet in 1899. Yet, despite its revolutionary rhetoric, in practice the SPD's parliamentary behavior was moderate.

Jaures, an energetic and courageous politician, had helped to galvanize the coalition that defended Captain Dreyfus in the wrenching scandal dividing turn-of-the-century France. He advocated collaboration between socialists and bourgeois parties in order to obtain reforms. In his polemics with Bebel, Jaures argued that the strength of French parliamentary democracy made it possible for socialists to transform capitalist society peacefully, whereas in Germany that was not possible because the *Reichstag* had no real power. He attacked the SPD for seeking to impose its doctrines on the socialists of all other countries. Later, after the Second International came out in opposition to what it called the "opportunism" of the reformists, Jaures agreed to adhere to a truer Marxist position in the interests of socialist solidarity.

A trade union and socialist protest in London.

LABOR ON THE OFFENSIVE: TRADE UNIONS, STRIKES, AND REVOLUTIONARY SYNDICALISM

As Bernstein pointed out, events eventually demonstrated the inaccuracy of Marx's conclusion that the material lives of workers would deteriorate. In the decades after 1850, working-class living standards tended to rise as prosperity spread throughout European society. Better conditions, together with the widening of the franchise, in turn made labor leaders less radical and inhibited the appeal of unions for many workers. Labor unionists agreed to operate within the context of capitalist society—hence, the role of unions was not to foment revolution but rather to improve working conditions, raise wages, and secure benefits for their members.

The Rise of Trade Unions

In many European countries restrictions on trade unions predated the French Revolution. In 1791, the revolutionary government of France passed the Le Chapelier Law, which prohibited labor gatherings as detrimental to "the free exercise of industry and work." In 1810 Napoleon's penal code outlawed strikes for changes in salaries and contracts. In Britain similar measures had been enacted, and although unions were given partial recognition in 1824, they were too weak to sustain lengthy strikes. The utopian reformer Robert Owen tried to create a single Grand National Union in 1834, but it too collapsed in the face of opposition from the Whig government. Unions and strikes were similarly banned at midcentury in Prussia, Russia, Austria, Spain, and most of the Italian states. Only later in the 19th century did unions win the legal right to exist and to strike, although many countries retained limitations on union activity and prohibited strikes until well toward the end of the century.

After 1870, the development of large-scale unions coincided with economic expansion and the rise of big business. In 1871, when William Gladstone's Liberal government granted full recognition to unions and legalized strikes, British trade unionists demonstrated their moderation by disassociating themselves from the violence of the Paris Commune. On the Continent, effective trade unions emerged in the years between the economic depression of the 1870s and the end of the century. Napoleon III, who had once used the army to put down strikes, allowed the formation of French unions in 1864. The French republican government curtailed union activity after the Commune, but the Third Republic finally extended legal status to them in 1884. Although unions were theoretically legal in the Second Reich, Bismarck used the antisocialist laws to suppress them between 1878 and 1890. In 1891 the German Imperial Industrial Code did legalize strikes, but imposed severe penalties on worker violence.

The end to the prohibition of strikes led to a large increase in the number of industrial work stoppages. Between 1880 and 1914, strikes—especially during periods of economic crisis—were a common aspect of industrial life, with hundreds of thousands of workers participating every year. By the late 1880s a "new unionism," different in character and dimension, was emerging. The early efforts at labor organization had involved craft unions, embracing only skilled workers and artisans. Now, however, industrial unions of unskilled workers began to form as a result of long and often bitter strike activity, involving many thousands of workers: they included the strike of Belgian miners and glass workers in 1886, the British match girl strike of 1888, and those of London dock workers and Ruhr coal miners in 1889.

As mass-based unions were established, labor leaders sought to create unified national organizations embracing workers in different industries. French unions formed a national federation in 1895, the *Confédération Générale du Travail* (CGT), while in England the British Trades Union Congress, established in 1868, merged with socialist groups and created the Labour Representation Committee. In 1906 Italian socialist unions set up the *Confederazione Generale del Lavoro* (CGL). By the eve of World War I European labor unions had a total membership of more than 9 million, including 4 million in Britain, 3 million in Germany, 1 million in France, some 700,000 in Italy, and 250,000 in Russia.

Revolutionary Syndicalism

In the 1870s, elements of the anarchist tradition merged with an aspect of trade union strategy to produce a unique current of radical thought known as *revolutionary syndicalism* (the term is derived from the French word for "union," *syndicat*). Fernand Pelloutier (1867–1901), its principal theorist, propounded the view that the seed of the future stateless society lay in the concept of the union. Syndicalists proposed direct action by the working class to bring about the revolution, with the general strike as their principal weapon. Pelloutier rejected all forms of the state. Instead, he advocated a social organization "limited exclusively to the needs of production and consumption."

Many syndicalists were influenced by the theories of the French intellectual Georges Sorel (1847–1922). A civil engineer by profession, Sorel argued that it was through the union rather than through political parties that socialism would be achieved. He believed that governments would repress general strikes with violence, and that the workers would respond with revolution. Sorel's major theoretical work was *Reflections on Violence* (1908), in which he posited the "myth of violence" as a force in history. Such all-encompassing strikes were attempted on a number of occasions—in 1893 in Belgium, in 1902 in Belgium, Sweden, and Spain, in 1903 in the Netherlands, in 1904 in Italy, and in 1909 in France and Sweden—but had little success. Nevertheless, socialist and syndicalist theorists continued to believe in the efficacy of the strike.

Significant Dates

The Suffrage Movement

- **1868** British women given the right to vote in local elections
- **1869** National American Women's Suffrage Association
- **1879** Bebel's *Women in the Past, Present and Future*
- **1884** Engels' *The Origins of the Family, Private Property, and the State*
- **1903** Emmeline Pankhurst founds Women's Social and Political Union
- **1904** International Women's Suffrage Alliance
- **1906** Finland gives women right to vote

WOMEN AND THE VOTE

The rise of socialism after midcentury coincided with the development of feminism, a term just then coming into use. By the 1870s European women interested in liberation strategies had the option of joining a variety of organizations. Women not inclined to direct political activism had worked in an array of reform movements, from the older temperance societies and private charities to settlement houses and educational groups. For those more urgently committed to improving women's rights and gender relations through political action, the choices were challenging. They could opt for Marxist-based movements associated with political parties striving to create socialist societies, or "bourgeois" movements that sought rights for women within the framework of capitalist society.

Politics and the Women's Movement

Like their male counterparts in liberal or socialist politics, feminist leaders debated aims and strategies. What united them was a commitment to break down the institutional and cultural legacies of a patriarchal society in which women's identities and rights had been long submerged under a system of male dominance. Laws in every country still limited the equality of women in such basic social institutions as marriage and divorce, or property ownership and inheritance. Yet the issue around which women of all social classes and nationalities rallied in the last decades of the 19th century was suffrage.

The right to vote was central to the privileges and responsibilities of citizenship in parliamentary systems of government. Some women viewed the right to vote as their reward for having served as coparticipants with men in the development of modern society, while others saw the vote as a means to improve conditions for themselves as well as for the working classes. By the eve of World War I, the suffrage issue had become the foundation for the first mass-based women's political movement, in the United States as well as in Europe. Hundreds of thousands of women joined suffrage groups in France, Britain, Italy, Russia, and other countries.

British women were given the right to vote in local elections in 1868. The following year American activists Susan B. Anthony (1820–1906) and Elizabeth Cady Stanton (see Part VII, Topic 13) founded an organization that later became the larger National American Women's Suffrage Association, with a membership of over 2 million. By the 1870s, local governments in Finland and Sweden granted some women the vote, as did some American states in the 1890s, but in these cases suffrage was limited to single women who owned property. In no European country—Finland was the exception—did women have the franchise in national elections before World War I.

Most nonsocialist women's movements included suffrage in their platforms. French women had a popular if controversial hero in Louise Michel, a former schoolteacher turned political activist who had suffered years in prison at hard labor for her role in the Paris Commune (see Part VII, Topic 15). Under the Third Republic, the French feminists Maria Deraismes (1828–1894) and Hubertine Auclert (1848–1914) began to organize French women around the suffrage issue, despite strong resistance from republican leaders.

When Emmeline Pankhurst (second from left) issued a manifesto urging people to storm the House of Parliament in 1908, she was arrested. Here an officer reads the arrest warrant.

PUBLIC FIGURES AND PRIVATE LIVES

ANNA KULISCIOFF AND FILIPPO TURATI

The lives of Anna Kuliscioff (1854–1925) and Filippo Turati (1857–1932) exemplified the trials and achievements of the many European men and women who challenged the established order at the turn of the century. Turati and Kuliscioff combined a lifelong commitment to the welfare of both the working class and women. Their own relationship was one of mutual respect, but the conventional gender patterns of the day compelled them to adopt distinct roles: Turati was able to build an active career both in socialist politics and as a member of the Italian Parliament. Kuliscioff, on the other hand, exerted her indirect influence chiefly through the intellectual discourse of her salon, one of the few ways in which women could traditionally affect politics.

Kuliscioff was born Anna Rosenstein in Simferopol, a small town in the Crimea. At 17, the precocious and strong-willed Kuliscioff went to Zurich to study medicine, since Russian women were not permitted advanced technical educations at home. In Switzerland, the center of radical exiles from all over Europe, she joined a group of Russian revolutionaries, and in 1872 married a young anarchist, Peter Makarevic. A year later the couple returned to Russia to work in the underground with a terrorist group. Makarevic was arrested in 1877 and renounced anarchism while in prison. Kuliscioff fled Russia, never to see her husband again.

In Paris, she impressed the radicals who met her by her commitment to revolution as well as by her beauty. The blonde, blue-eyed Kuliscioff had a brilliant intellect. One of the men attracted to her was Andrea Costa, a handsome young Italian anarchist. They fell in love, and collaborated in the anarchist cause. It was then that she took the alias of Kuliscioff: many exiled radicals lived under false names as a security measure. Both she and Costa were arrested. Kuliscioff was freed after the Russian novelist Ivan Turgenev intervened on her behalf, and she was expelled from France. When she attended a radical meeting in Florence in 1878, the Italian authorities arrested her and sent her to jail for two years.

The harsh prison experiences, together with the inability of the anarchist movement to achieve results, prompted Kuliscioff and Costa to move toward socialism and the creation of a working-class political party. They helped to establish *Avanti!*, which became the official newspaper of Italian socialists, and Costa soon became the first socialist elected to the Italian parliament.

In 1881 Kuliscioff gave birth to a daughter, named Andreina, but the relationship with Costa had cooled. Kuliscioff spent several unhappy years alone in Naples, where she went for her health—her long stays in cold prison cells had brought on a pulmonary disorder and severe arthritis.

In 1885, while resuming her medical studies in Naples, Kuliscioff met Filippo Turati. A young man of middle-class background ridden with psychological neuroses, Turati studied law but was drawn to literary and social issues. His interest in politics and in socialism was recent, but Kuliscioff sensed in him a quiet courage and deep humanitarian instincts.

Turati went to Milan to help organize the socialists. After completing her medical degree despite great prejudice against her in the Italian universities, she joined him there. They spent the next 35 years together. Their Milan apartment became the headquarters for *Critica Sociale*, an important journal of socialist theory which they edited. As their fame and stature grew, their home also became a well-known political salon. Young and idealistic socialists, as well as more seasoned radicals of European fame, called on them and debated the issues of the day.

Turati is generally considered the principal strategist of the Italian Socialist party (PSI), which he and Kuliscioff helped to found in 1892. Yet Turati evolved his political ideology under Kuliscioff's influence and, after his election as a deputy in 1896, was guided in much of his political dealings by her advice. Kuliscioff no doubt had the superior intellect. She was more decisive and, as outsider to parliamentary politics, less plagued by doubts, whereas he often agonized over decisions and lived in a world of political compromise. One frequent visitor to their salon perceived the gender distinction that marked the couple's relationship when she described Kuliscioff as "the grey eminence behind the red cardinal."

Kuliscioff introduced Turati to the study of Marxism, and under her influence his socialist philosophy acquired a "scientific" basis—the belief that in order to understand society, it was necessary to understand the nature and causes of economic change. As a "positivist" who emphasized factual data, he came to the conclusion that day-to-day changes in the material condition of society should guide political strategy, as Bernstein's revisionist ideas had suggested.

Kuliscioff's interest in women's issues was long-standing and committed. Her lecture on "The Monopoly of Men" (1890) was a point of departure for Italian women—like Zetkin in Germany, Kuliscioff argued that women were oppressed both as workers and as women. At the PSI congress in 1897 she proposed a law regulating female labor, and Turati pushed for such legislation in Parliament. In 1912 she and other Italian women started a newspaper for women, *La difesa delle lavoratrici* (Defense of Women Workers).

The same divisions between reformists and revolutionaries that disturbed party unity elsewhere in Europe also caused a major rift in the PSI, and the Turati–Kuliscioff reformist wing of the party was alternately in and out of power. At the congress of 1912, however, the revolutionaries seized control of the party, and Turati never again exercised an equal degree of influence.

Their last years were clouded by the trauma of World War I and the rise of Fascism. Kuliscioff's death in December 1925 devastated Turati. He escaped from the Fascists the following year and fled to Paris, where he died in 1932. Together, they had inspired and led the left-wing struggle for freedom for more than a generation.

Auclert gained notoriety for her symbolic acts of protest, which included refusing to pay taxes and overturning voting urns. In 1909 a French Union for Women's Suffrage was founded.

As early as the 1880s American leaders had proposed the creation of an international organization to advance women's suffrage, but only in 1904 did an organizing conference meet. It gave rise to the International Women's Suffrage Alliance (IWSA). Like the Second International of socialist parties, the IWSA sponsored several world congresses in the years before World War I.

The Suffrage War in Britain

British women created a number of suffrage organizations in the late 19th century. The first group of prominence was the National Union of Women's Suffrage Societies (NUWSS), led by Millicent Garrett Fawcett (1847–1929). Working-class women in the textile mills set up associations of their own that underscored the middle-class interests of the NUWSS. The best-known suffrage movement, however, was the Women's Social and Political Union (WSPU), founded by Emmeline Pankhurst (1858–1928) in 1903.

Pankhurst's uncompromising militancy made the suffrage issue a cause célèbre in the early years of the 20th century. While a student in Paris she had been impressed by French feminists. Later she and her husband campaigned in England on behalf of women's rights to control their own property.

Pankhurst, who had joined women in the London match girl strike, believed that Fawcett's NUWSS was too timid. She concluded that only direct, violent action would secure women the vote. The WSPU campaigned against political candidates who refused to endorse female suffrage. With the help of her daughters Sylvia and Cristabel, Pankhurst declared war on the British government, organizing suffragist marches against Parliament and rallies before the royal palace.

When Prime Minister Herbert Asquith (served 1908–1916) refused to endorse women's suffrage in 1911, Pankhurst led a systematic assault on London's most exclusive shops, breaking windows to draw attention to the suffrage cause. Yet, despite a nine-month prison sentence, her activities became still more dramatic. One of her followers slashed a famous painting that feminists found offensive, while another assaulted Winston Churchill (1875–1965), then a young antifeminist politician serving as home secretary. A WSPU member chained herself to the gate outside the official home of the prime minister, shouting at passersby, and a few militants even started fires. As a result of a bomb plot against David Lloyd George, chancellor of the exchequer in Asquith's cabinet, Pankhurst was given a three-year prison term. Even prison, however, did not dampen her enthusiasm for the cause—to the dismay of government authorities, she and her daughters repeatedly declared hunger strikes.

Enemies of women's rights criticized such tactics, but the suffragists succeeded in making the vote for women a public issue that would not go away. The final victory in the suffragist war was not won until after World War I, but Pankhurst's struggles symbolized the determination of countless other women in all countries to secure their rights.

THE SOCIALIST PATH TO FEMINISM

Most socialist parties and labor unions recognized the importance of gaining the adherence of women, who in some countries accounted for almost half the industrial workforce. In Germany, Eleanor Marx, the daughter of Karl Marx, was among those who recruited women into separate organizations affiliated with the SPD. By 1914, the party had some 175,000 women involved in its activities.

Socialism and Feminism

Socialist parties generally supported women's suffrage, along with civil—as opposed to religious—marriage and the right to divorce. Birth control was a more problematic issue, since socialists long viewed birth control as associated with the ideas of Thomas Malthus and the notion that workers were to blame for their own poverty. Nevertheless, many socialists did not see gender issues as separate or distinct from working-class concerns and notions of masculinity often excluded women from socialist or union activism. While some women won positions of prominence within labor or socialist movements, few actually held important executive posts—exceptions to the rule were the Russian exile Angelica Balabanoff (1869–1965), who served on the executive committee of the Italian Socialist party and later was secretary of the Third (Communist) International, and Ottilie Baader (1847–1925), a longtime member of the SPD's executive committee.

The SPD produced two important theoretical works on the women's question: Bebel's *Women in the Past, Present and Future* (1879) and Engels' *The Origins of the Family, Private Property, and the State* (1884). Each traced the suppression of women to the development of the principle of private property—men, they argued, oppressed women so as to guarantee the legitimacy of children, which they deemed necessary in order to transfer property to their sons. Bebel saw in the relationship of wives to their husbands a parallel with the worker's relationship to employers, concluding that women were oppressed both as workers and as women.

The most important proponent of feminism within the SPD was Clara Zetkin (1857–1933), an incisive thinker and the editor of *Die Gleichheit* (Equality), a women's paper. A committed revolutionary socialist, Zetkin strongly disliked revisionism and denounced reformists as bitterly as Bebel and others did. She decried collaboration between the socialist women's movement and bourgeois feminism as loudly as they condemned cooperation between socialist and bourgeois parties.

Zetkin had two related concerns: to keep working-class men and women united in the socialist movement, and to prevent bourgeois feminists from drawing working women into their movement. She paid close attention to the economic status of women, stressing that they were not paid for their work as homemakers and mothers. She agreed with the arguments of Engels and Bebel that under capitalism women had become simply a form of male property. She was convinced, therefore, that the liberation of women could be achieved only within the larger socialist effort to eliminate private property. On the other hand, Zetkin joined other socialists in aiming to avoid a division of the working class along gender lines, and stressed the need to focus on women as workers rather than as wives.

In the half-century between 1870 and 1914, Europe witnessed the emergence of two major but unequal forces—socialism and feminism. Each stood in stark opposition to the prevailing values and power structure of the age. Anarchism and socialism posited drastic solutions to the problems of capitalist society, and the alternatives appealed to an increasing number of Europeans. The Marxists eventually gained command of the socialist movement, but their ranks were also split as revisionists challenged the assumptions of Marx's strategies. The creation of huge political parties and labor unions nevertheless gained the adherence of millions of workers, while syndicalists proposed to bring down the capitalist system with the general strike.

To the élites governing society, the women's movement appeared to be almost as dangerous. Many women rallied around the issue of the suffrage, creating national groups and an international organization devoted to gaining the vote. Other, more radical feminists emphasized broader questions of gender relations and political revolution. Some women combined feminism and socialism in their militancy, creating further disputes over strategy and theory within their ranks.

While there was little unity of position within either movement, both fought with great determination to eliminate economic and social injustice in European society, providing a rich legacy that was inherited by later generations of men and women.

Questions for Further Study

1. What theoretical and practical differences separated anarchism from socialism?
2. What issues were of most importance to socialist parties?
3. Why did the idea of the strike assume political importance?
4. Why were many women drawn to radical movements? What was the difference between the goals of suffragettes and those of women socialists?

Suggestions for Further Reading

Adams, Carole. *Women Clerks in Wilhelmine Germany: Issues of Class and Gender.* New York, 1988.

Berlanstein, Lenard R. *The Working People of Paris, 1871–1914.* Baltimore, MD, 1984.

Cahm, Caroline. *Peter Kropotkin and the Rise of Revolutionary Anarchism.* New York, 1989.

Franzoi, Barbara. *At the Very Least She Pays the Rent: Women and German Industrialization.* Westport, CT, 1985.

Joll, James. *The Second International, 1889–1914.* New York, 1966.

McClellan, David. *Karl Marx: His Life and Thought.* New York, 1978.

Ross, Ellen. *Love and Toil: Motherhood in Outcast London, 1870–1918.* New York, 1993.

Taylor, Barbara. *Eve and the New Jerusalem: Socialism and Feminism in the Nineteenth Century.* New York, 1983.

Thoennessen, W. *The Emancipation of Women: The Rise and Decline of the Women's Movement in German Social Democracy.* London, 1973.

Tickner, Lisa. *The Spectacle of Women: Imagery of the Suffrage Campaign, 1907–1914.* Chicago, 1988.

VII

Topic 20

Society in Transition: The Modernization of Europe

With the coming of the second industrial revolution, European society underwent major changes, developing a structure that in the course of the 20th century spread throughout much of the world. The concentration of large numbers of people in ever-growing cities, many of them living at an adequate economic level and possessing the right to vote, produced a new element—the proletarian masses.

The rise of an urban proletariat had an important effect on the role of the middle classes. For much of the 19th century, middle-class liberalism was the chief spur to political and social change. By the end of the century, however, many businessmen saw working-class advancement as a threat to their own interests. As a result, the wealthiest and best educated—the upper middle class—developed alliances with the old aristocracy. The formation of this upper-class élite left the remaining members of the middle classes with considerably reduced influence. Society became increasingly polarized into élites and the masses.

The continued growth of big business underlined the division by enlarging the gulf between the vast incomes of the new industrial barons and the modest wages of the workers. Earlier industrialists, many of them traditional liberals, had at least made some attempt to use their prosperity to enhance the lot of their employees. The upper classes of the turn of the century proudly and ostentatiously flaunted their wealth as a sign of their superior power and status.

Behind the changes in social structure and within classes lay vast changes in population patterns. Improved medical care reduced the rate of infant mortality and extended life expectancy. At the same time, all over Western Europe birthrates were dropping by the end of the 19th century. This was due in part to the introduction of contraceptive methods, which helped parents to plan their families. On the whole, there seemed to be a general resolve to limit the size of families. In Eastern Europe, where social change was slower, the population continued to increase, and by 1910, population growth was higher there than in Western Europe. This represented a reversal of the situation 50 years earlier.

The political and social battles of the 19th century, along with the general rise of prosperity, had enlarged the numbers of people able to vote. Both liberals and the new conservative élite concurred in the need for the education of these new electors, in order to prepare them for the duties of citizenship. As a result, state-run systems of mass education were introduced, with important political consequences. Increasing popular literacy played some part in strengthening trade union activities and protest movements. The principal thrust of school curricula, however, was to encourage nationalism, in order to encourage loyalty to the state and its ruling classes. The spread of mass peacetime military conscription also increased the sense of national consciousness. The growing mood of strident nationalism in Europe provided an appropriately belligerent setting for the events leading to World War I.

THE CHANGING SOCIAL STRUCTURE

As in earlier periods of the 19th century, industrialization continued to affect social patterns in important ways in the decades after 1871. By the eve of World War I, factories had swelled cities with many more workers and middle-class inhabitants, so that much of Europe reached the halfway mark in the transition from a rural to an urban society.

Population Growth and Urbanization

Between 1870 and 1910, Europe's population (excluding Russia) rose by 44 percent, from approximately 230 million to 330 million. This growth was not, however, constant everywhere, since the size of families in western Europe tended to diminish. Throughout the latter part of the 19th century, in fact, the birthrate declined rapidly, and only a reduction in the mortality rate allowed for population increase.

The pace of urbanization intensified toward the end of the 19th century because of three factors: the continuing shift of people away from the countryside, the increase in the number and size of cities, and their growing population density. In Britain, the most highly urbanized nation, city dwellers in 1914 comprised almost 80 percent of the population, as compared to about 60 percent 50 years earlier, while France similarly increased its urban population from 33 to almost 45 percent. Because Germany underwent a dramatic rate of industrialization in this period, the proportion of people living in cities there virtually doubled to 55 percent, while 90 percent of the country's overall population increase was in urban areas.

Table VII.20.1
Population (in thousands) of Selected European Countries

COUNTRY	1870	1900	1910
Britain	22,712	32,528	36,070
France	36,103	38,451	39,192
Germany	41,059	56,367	64,926
Hungary	15,512	19,255	20,886
Spain	16,622	18,594	19,927
Sweden	4169	5137	5522

Table VII.20.2
Population Growth (in thousands) for Major European Cities

CITY	1870	1900	1910
Amsterdam	264	511	574
Belfast	174	349	387
Berlin	826	1889	2071
St. Petersburg	667	1267	1962
London	3890	6586	7256
Milan	262	493	579
Paris	1852	2714	2888
Rome	244	463	542
Stockholm	136	301	342
Vienna	834	1675	2031

In the years between 1870 and 1900, most large European cities, including the older capitals, doubled their populations and continued to increase sharply over the following decade.

The railroad contributed greatly to urbanization. Many large cities, especially capitals, formed concentrations of rail systems. Urban facilities such as water supply, sidewalks, and sewers, or fire and police forces, expanded by the end of the 19th century, and the physical appearance of cities began to change as the construction industry was revolutionized by developments in civil engineering and building materials. The use of steel and reinforced concrete made it possible for architects to design skyscrapers: the first of these tall buildings, New York's 130-foot-high Equitable Life Assurance Society Building, was built in 1870. By combining steel and wrought iron with glass, European city planners created new forms of public space, such as the enclosed galleries built in London, Paris, Milan, and Naples.

The Growth of the Urban Proletariat

Most of the political and social progress made in the first part of the 19th century was due to the informal alliance of middle-class liberalism and working-class protest. The combination of the two forces succeeded in challenging established values and reducing the power of the old aristocracy. By the end of the century, however, conditions were changing. The cooperation between the two classes had depended upon the tacit understanding that middle-class reformers would decide what was in the best interests of the workers. With the gradual improvement in conditions of urban life and the extension of the franchise, the urban masses were becoming a political force in themselves.

The emergence of an urban proletariat in western European society profoundly affected old alliances. Trade unions and socialist parties were no longer dependent on the good will of the middle class for reforms, for an increasingly active membership provided them with new bargaining power. The wealthier members of the middle class, in turn, began to see the various protest movements as a challenge to their business interests. In their search for allies, they turned to their former opponents, the aristocracy. The combination of rich industrialists and aristocrats who were prepared to compromise formed a new upper-class élite.

Although the influence of the aristocratic ruling classes had declined, they still retained considerable prestige. Marriages between the daughters of wealthy businessmen and impoverished heirs to noble titles provided both sides with gains. Although money was beginning to replace birth as the ultimate social status symbol, the combination of both was the most desirable aim of all. In some cases European aristocrats turned to America in search of rich brides. In 1874, Lord Randolph Churchill (1849–1895) married Jennie Jerome, a member of a prosperous New York family. Their elder son was Winston S. Churchill.

Contact between the two classes was not limited to family affairs. Aristocrats who became involved in public life, whether in politics, government bureaucracy, or the army, often found themselves working with colleagues of business origins. Relations became even more closely cemented as the richest industrialists began to send their sons to schools hitherto attended only by the nobility.

With an increasingly militant working class at one end of the social spectrum, and a new alliance of upper-class élites at the other, the median segment of the middle classes lost influence. Growing religious skepticism undermined bourgeois Victorian morality. Social élites developed ever more elaborate and glamorized forms of traditional "high" culture such as opera houses and art galleries. New York's Metropolitan

Map 20.1 Europe's Population, c. 1890

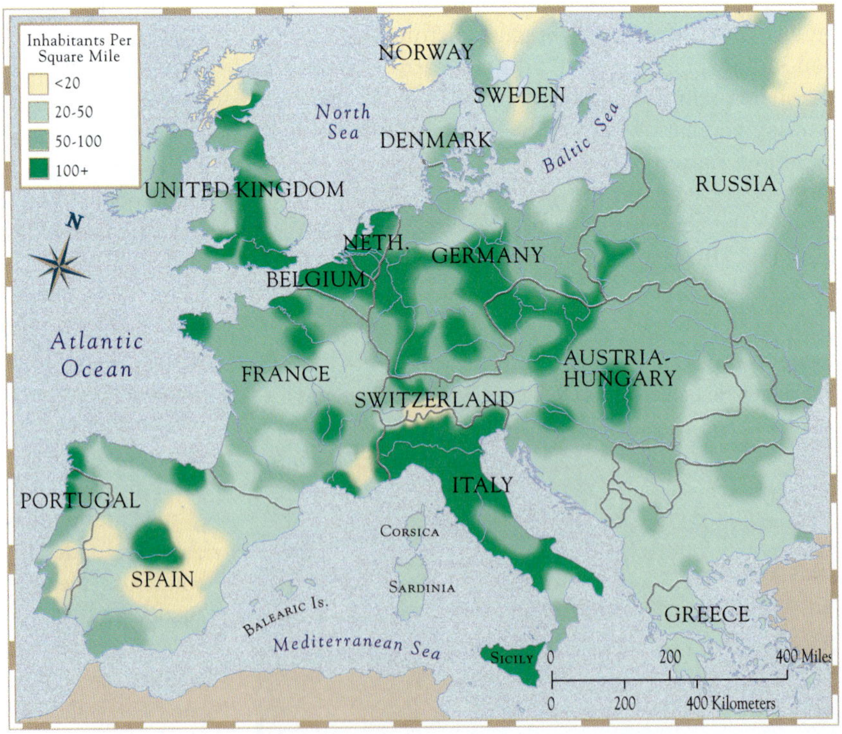

Paul-Emile Chabas, *A Corner of the Table* (1907) captures a moment in the rarified lives of the wealthy classes.

Museum of Art was founded in 1870, and the Paris Opera opened in 1875. At the same time, the working classes began to enjoy their own forms of popular culture. London's first music hall, a place for popular shows, was built in 1849, and held 100 people. By 1890 London had some 500 music halls; the largest offered continuous performances to a changing audience of as many as 45,000 in a single evening.

The class structure of European society became increasingly polarized between two extremes. The rise of the masses created vast new commercial possibilities that business entrepreneurs were quick to exploit. At the same time it posed a potential threat to governments, which they sought to defuse by developing ways to manipulate and control mass responses. Meanwhile, as conditions for most citizens continued slowly but perceptibly to improve, the very rich became even richer.

WEALTH, POVERTY, AND SOCIAL DARWINISM

For those living in Europe at the turn of the century, the age seemed, and for the privileged few was, one of unprecedented luxury and extravagance. In Paris, the *Belle Époque* (Beautiful Age) brought lavish banquets and balls. The city's cabarets and night life, vividly depicted in the art of Impressionist painters such as Auguste Renoir (1841–1919), were as famous as its parade of elegant courtesans, described by Parisian wits as *"les grandes horizontales"* (the great recliners). No less a figure than the eldest son of Queen Victoria, the future Edward VII, entertained his mistress at Maxim's, a glamorous Parisian restaurant.

When Edward became king in 1901, his reign introduced a similar mood of opulence to Britain. The Edwardian Era was marked by extravagant "house parties," weekends in the country at which the nobility and eminent industrialists ate, drank, and shot together. On December 18, 1913, at Hall Barn in Buckinghamshire, seven marksmen killed 3937 pheasants, still a record for a single shoot. The Austrian Archduke Franz Ferdinand, whose assassination in 1914 finally precipitated the outbreak of war, was also an enthusiastic shot. Shortly before his death he expressed satisfaction at having killed his 3000th stag.

The English well-to-do, like American travelers of later days, were famous in continental Europe for their demand for hygiene and efficient plumbing. Individual water closets with flushing toilets, rare in England before 1900, became increasingly common in the larger towns, although only the largest establishments were equipped with more than one. Even a big upper-class English house, scene of weekend parties, generally had only one bathroom, which was usually reserved for the family. Fixed baths were first made of porcelain, but by 1910 cast-iron tubs were becoming popular. Bathroom fixtures included showers, either in the bath itself or independent, and heated towel rails. As overnight guests took their morning tea and biscuits, a maid would draw the curtains, light the fire, and set out a portable bath in front of the hearth, to be filled from a hot water can. The comfort of the upper

A street scene of working-class children in London's East End.

classes required the existence of a household of servants, although the growing introduction of inventions such as vacuum cleaners and washing machines began to reduce the size of domestic staffs.

The Urban Poor

The lives of most of the population were in stark contrast to those of the rich. In the London district of Bermondsey at the turn of the century, an observer noted that one water pipe served for 25 houses, with the water turned on for only two hours a day and not at all on Sundays. The same 25 families had one water closet between them, outside which queues of people lined up every morning before going to work.

Despite the material progress of the 19th century, large sectors of the populations of all European countries continued to live in poverty. A survey conducted around the turn of the century in London, the capital of the richest country in the world, found the proportion of paupers to be 30.7 percent. In eastern and southern Europe, conditions were even worse. In 1900, the average life expectancy in Spain or the Balkans was under 35 years.

Even those whose earnings allowed them to live above the level of bare subsistence were subject to the constant threat of insecurity. The loss of a job through illness or age brought inevitable ruin to a family. The first country to introduce health insurance and pensions was Germany, where Bismarck enacted legislation in 1883 to combat the appeal of socialism among workers. In Britain, early voluntary insurance programs had been run by some of the trade unions, and the government introduced national policies only in 1911. Even these measures, however, did not cover large categories of workers, including the domestic servants, upon whom the upper classes depended, and the self-employed. The uncertainties of illness, accident, or premature death hung over most working homes.

Yet the lives of urban workers did undergo some improvements. Between 1880 and 1914, wages rose considerably, and purchasing power almost doubled in England, Germany, and France. Mass production and marketing, combined with fast transport, reduced the price of many goods. The production and sale of food continued to increase and its price to decline (see Part VII, Topic 17). By 1891, nearly 600,000 in England were employed in the food trades. At the same time, there were 40 percent more grocers and fishmongers than ten years earlier, and 82 percent more jam and preserve makers. Most workers' families ate vegetables and some form of meat (often a poor one) on a regular basis. One student of working-class conditions noted that "puddings and tarts are not uncommon, and bread ceases to be the staff of life. In this class no-one goes short of food."

One of the results of the gradual improvement in material conditions was increased leisure time. The increased pace of production meant that most factory workers no longer needed to put in 12- or 14-hour days to maintain output. Workers and trade unions themselves fought for less hours, to devote more time to their families and leisure activities. In the earlier years of the industrial revolution, factory employees had time for little but working and sleeping. By 1900, many urban workers still put in ten-hour days or more, with Sunday free. In Britain some had Saturday afternoon free as well, in what became called the "English weekend."

Leisure pursuits increased as fast as people had the chance to enjoy them. Technical advances in paper making and printing made possible mass circulation newspapers and magazines, which higher literacy made available to a growing readership. They stirred patriotic fervor and popular enthusiasm for imperialism by running dramatic stories of adventure and conquest in exotic places. Popular writers of the day reached mass audiences with science fiction tales and detective stories. The Frenchman Jules Verne (1828–1905) incorporated the latest scientific developments in fantasies such as *Twenty Thousand Leagues Under the Sea* (1870), while the British writer Sir Arthur Conan Doyle (1859–1930) created Sherlock Holmes, the most memorable fictional detective in Western literature. Amusement parks and dance halls offered the chance for relaxed entertainment. Cycling led to a new exercise craze and had a special appeal to middle-class women. Competitive team sports became popular. In Britain in the 1880s, associations were founded to organize athletics, boxing, lawn tennis, rowing, swimming, hockey, and football events. In 1896, the first modern Olympiad took place in Athens, reviving the Olympic Games of ancient Greece.

The increased use of leisure time for simple relaxation and fun was accompanied by a decline in religious observance. Sunday became a day to spend in the country or at the seaside, rather than at church. Virtually the only country in Europe where church attendance actually increased was Ireland, where the Catholic Church symbolized opposition to the hated Protestant British rulers. During the reign of Pope Leo XIII (ruled 1878–1903), official Catholic teaching sought to reconcile church dogma with science and liberalism. Leo's famous encyclical, *Rerum Novarum* (1891), on the condition of the working classes, tried to counter anticlericalism by linking the church to the working class. Churches began to organize their own leisure activities, including youth groups, for the urban masses. On the whole, however, the trend away from organized religion continued.

Social Darwinism

Those who were struck by the increasing gulf between the modest improvements in the living conditions of the workers and the extravagance of the wealthy found a handy explanation in the philosophy of Social Darwinism. Charles Darwin's *Origin of Species* (1859) (see Part VII, Topic 14) taught that life is a fierce and constant struggle, in which only the fittest survive. Darwin had been concerned with the natural process of evolution, but a rising business class was all too ready to apply his arguments to commercial progress. The bitter strife of competitive industry, they claimed, would lead slowly but inevitably to the upward movement of civilization. Thus, Social Darwinists asserted that those who were emerging at the top were evidently the fittest and thus qualified to survive and continue the process.

The philosophical underpinning of this worldview was to be found in the writings of the British philosopher Herbert Spencer (1820–1903). His version of evolution argued that species develop from simple to complex forms, in a process of automatic improvement, and that any attempt to interfere with change (including economic change) would stand in the way of progress. Spencer's most enthusiastic followers were to be found in the United States, where a Rockefeller remarked that "the growth of a large business is merely the survival of the fittest."

In contrast to the Social Darwinists, increasing numbers of people found new ways of alleviating the plight of the urban poor. Beatrice Potter Webb (1858–1943), a British social reformer, investigated conditions in London's slums to demonstrate their misery. Social workers, both government employees and private individuals, developed organizations to provide practical assistance and training to the needy. The most famous such institution was the Salvation Army, which was formed in 1878 by William Booth (1829–1912). The organization grew out of a mission he founded in 1865.

PATTERNS OF GENDER AND SEXUALITY

As society as a whole underwent profound change, many women and some men began to question traditional attitudes to family and gender roles. In the late 19th century, increasing numbers of women had jobs outside the home. Most women worked in textile and clothing factories, or in domestic service, the most common field of female employment. The number of

By the beginning of the 20th century, women were entering the workforce in even larger numbers in areas once filled by men, including secretarial work in corporations.

single female employees rose steadily. By the eve of World War I, more than 90 percent of working women were unmarried.

Traditional attitudes toward the division of labor within the family, however, remained unchanged. Working-class men played no role in domestic life, apart from providing their wives at intervals with a sum of money to cover expenses. Some men even left their wives to pay for household needs, requiring them to earn money by working themselves or by taking in boarders. Working women remained wholly responsible for all domestic duties.

Domestic violence was common, frequently the result of heavy drinking. The center of working-class life was generally the café or pub, where friends could meet. Alcohol offered an escape from grinding poverty and the rigors of overwork and a temporary warmth for those whose houses were unheated. Returning drunk to a cold home, many men took out their frustrations on their family, beating their wives and children.

In other cases, the violence was sexual. Within the confines of her home, a woman ran the risk of assault by relatives or boarders. With increased numbers of women at work, the phenomenon of sexual harassment on the job developed, whereby a woman was threatened with the loss of her work if she did not submit to sexual advances. Some women gave in under pressure, but as more acquired their working independence, women employees sometimes stood up and defended their rights. Single women living and working in large cities were subject to rape and other forms of sexual violence.

Violence against women in late 19th-century cities riveted the lurid fascination of a mass public. In London, poor working-class women were the victims of a notorious killer nicknamed Jack the Ripper, a man

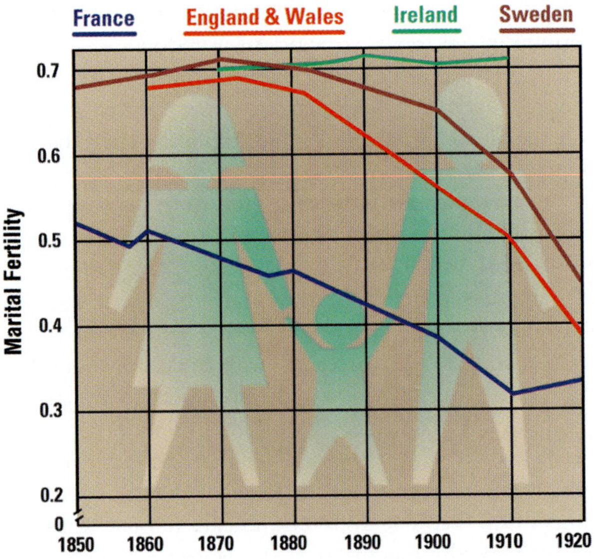

Graph 20.1

whose real identity has still not been definitively established. In the months from August to November of 1888, he perpetrated a series of gruesome murders, all of them involving single women. Similar, if less spectacular, killings, occurred in Paris and the main German cities. For many contemporary observers, the moral to be drawn from the violence was not that single women needed better protection, but that women who did not follow traditional patterns of behavior were likely to suffer for their daring.

Sexual Rights and the Middle Classes

The work of the Austrian psychoanalyst Sigmund Freud (see Part VIII, Topic 7) made sexual behavior a subject for explicit discussion among the educated. In the flood of investigation and imaginative writing that followed, some longstanding attitudes came into question. Homosexuality and lesbianism were studied more sympathetically. The German psychiatrist Magnus Hirschfeld (1868–1935) wrote of homosexuality as a "third sex," and under his influence the Scientific Humanitarian Committee was formed in Berlin for the study of homosexual culture. In Paris, the salon of Natalie Barney (1876–1972) became a center for women whose rebellion against conventions took the form of lesbianism.

Oscar Wilde (left) and Lord Alfred Douglas, c. 1893. Their affair was the cause of great scandal in the 1890s.

Nevertheless, society as a whole still condemned sexual minorities, and laws were passed that made sexual relations between men illegal. In 1885 the British Parliament enacted the Criminal Law Amendment Act, which for the first time prohibited "indecent" sexual relations between adult consenting males and prescribed a sentence of up to two years in prison with hard labor. One of the most prominent public figures to be punished under this law was the Irish writer Oscar Wilde (1854–1900), who was prosecuted for his relationship with Lord Alfred Douglas (1870–1945). The middle-class refusal to see women as sexual beings was reflected in the fact that the law was restricted to men. When this omission was pointed out to Queen Victoria, she is reported to have replied, "No women would do that."

Freud's theories promoted a new openness toward sexual behavior. This led in turn to new attitudes to the relationship between the sexes. No longer regarded as either untouchably pure or mere reproductive machines, women began to change their self-perceptions. Many played an increasingly aggressive role in the feminist movement (see Part VII, Topic 19). Among those campaigning for a change of attitudes was the German Helene Stocker (1869–1943), who believed that a new way of talking and thinking about sex would make sexual relations more ennobling. Other women took the opposite extreme, claiming that traditional relations between the sexes were the curse of civilization and should be completely overthrown. In her book *The Great Scourge* (1913), Cristabel Pankhurst (1880–1958) described marriage as a dangerous institution, and men as the scourge of society.

Birth Control

The growing use of methods of contraception in the late 19th century was another vital factor in changing society and the nature of family life. With the reduced rate of infant mortality, parents no longer needed to produce more children than they could support, under the assumption that some would die early. Furthermore, with the spread of education and the ability of more families to accumulate savings, parents preferred to have fewer children, better educated, to whom to leave their property.

Methods of contraception varied, and knowledge of them spread both by word of mouth and by active campaigning. British laws forbade the publication of birth control material, but in 1878 the Fabian reformer Annie Besant (1847–1933) joined Charles Bradlaugh (1833–1891) in challenging the law. After 1880 they circulated tens of thousands of birth control leaflets. On the Continent, one of the early promoters of birth control was Arletta Jacobs (1851?–1929), the first woman awarded a medical degree in the Netherlands. In her work among the poor in Amsterdam, she encouraged the use of the "Dutch cap," a form of individual cervical covering first invented in Germany. One of the most common methods for dealing with unwanted pregnancies was abortion.

Inspired by the writings of the early-19th-century economic philosopher Thomas Malthus (see Part VII, Topic 2), Neo-Malthusian leagues were formed in many countries. They advocated population control as a means to improving marital relations and promoting social harmony. Although the Neo-Malthusians encouraged working-class support, the movement was basically a middle-class one.

The effect of contraception on population growth was dramatic. Around 1870, the average English family contained 6.6 children; 50 years later, the number had fallen to just over two. The most extreme declines occurred in the countries of western Europe, where by 1910 the birthrate had fallen by 30 percent or more; the only exception was Ireland, where it actually rose slightly. In southern and eastern Europe, birthrates did not begin to decline until after World War I, with the result that on the eve of war Western Europe was actually surpassed in population growth.

Although contraception was used by working-class couples, the predominantly middle-class advocacy and adoption of birth control were reflected in birth patterns. In the period from 1879 to 1893, the number of children born to families in Rotterdam varied according to social class: for every three children whose parents were professionals, there were six whose fathers were laborers or artisans. In London at the turn of the century, the birthrate in the working-class East End was a third higher than in more fashionable districts.

Yet as the use of contraception spread, it had far-reaching consequences for all levels of society. Free of the necessity of continual childbearing, growing numbers of women strove to take their place alongside men in the workplace and in public life.

THE INTEGRATION OF SOCIETY: LITERACY AND MILITARY SERVICE

Between 1870 and 1914, most European governments deliberately indoctrinated large groups of citizens with a sense of national consciousness, especially the work-

Compulsory elementary education was being adopted by most Western nations in the last quarter of the 19th century. Jennie Brownscombe's *The New Scholar* (1878) reveals growing consciousness among women of the importance of education.

Universal military service was a major element in forging national identity. Here this is seen in a photograph of British recruiting in 1915.

ers and peasants who had traditionally been marginalized. Universal elementary education and compulsory military service provided two important instruments for national integration.

Public Education

Beginning after 1880, most Western governments took the first steps to introduce mass education. In France, the government of Jules-François-Camille Ferry (served as prime minister 1880–1881, 1883–1885) established free compulsory secular education as part of anticlerical legislation. By 1890, primary education for males and females up to the age of twelve was compulsory in many countries. In Austria, for example, the number of children attending primary schools rose from 1.9 million in 1870 to 4.2 million in 1914, while in Britain during the same period enrollment increased from 1.4 million to 6.2 million. The possibilities of secondary education for women began to increase, but universities were still mainly reserved for men. At the first lecture of the Greek scientist Angeliki Panajiotatou (1875–1954), students shouted at her: "Back to the kitchen!" In 1881, Spain's first female medical students were stoned.

Although both liberals and conservatives agreed on the need for the spread of education, their motives differed. For those who encouraged upward social mobility, education—in particular the basic ability to read, write, and perform simple calculations—was an essential key to advancement. In some countries, notably France and Italy, secular leaders also encouraged state-run education as a means of offsetting the influence of the Catholic Church.

Conservative governments, on the other hand, saw public education as a way of maintaining control over the masses. As growing numbers of citizens acquired the right to vote, they needed to be directed toward using their powers in a way acceptable to the authorities. General literacy played some part, it is true, in helping protest groups to circulate written campaign material and win new members. On the whole, however, compulsory education served to promote carefully devised state programs.

The chief goal of these was to instill strong feelings of national pride. Official textbooks presented the view of national history and development that favored each state's image, often by denigrating other nations. On many occasions the very language used, or not used, for lessons became a nationalist issue, as in parts of the Austro-Hungarian empire. After leaving school, former students would read similar nationalistic messages in popular newspapers, which celebrated their country's achievements and vigorously bemoaned any perceived slight to national honor.

Military Service

Although obligatory military service dates back to the ancient world, it first began to evolve in modern

Albert Morrow's poster (c. 1896), *The New Woman*, depicted the modern woman who flouted convention and assumed new roles in society.

Europe in the late 18th century; it was introduced by the radicals in France in the fall of 1792, and took the form of mass conscription. Prussia's successes in the 1860s were due in large measure to its custom of maintaining a large body of trained soldiers, even in peacetime. After the Prussian victory over the French in 1870, France took a lesson from its enemy and introduced the military draft. Austria followed suit, as did many other continental nations. Britain did not introduce peacetime conscription until just before World War II, although military service was required during World War I.

The effects of conscription reinforced those of compulsory education. Recruits were generally sent away from their home district in order to break their local loyalties. In their place, military training encouraged recruits to develop a broader sense of identification with the military itself, and, ultimately, with the nation-state.

The increasing appetite for nationalist victories, nourished by imperialist conquests, distracted attention from discontent at home. It also succeeded in uniting large masses of each country's population in a common enthusiasm. Socialist leaders opposed nationalism and called for class solidarity to transcend frontiers, but in general members of the urban proletariat showed no less fervor for national interests than their rulers. As a result, there developed a popular demand for diplomatic and military victories that played a significant part in the buildup to war. When World War I came, furthermore, even the socialist parties which had condemned nationalism rallied to the national cause.

By 1914, European society was beginning to shed some of its traditional characteristics. Class patterns created by 19th-century reforms were shifting, as social groups changed alliances. Rich tradesmen and impecunious aristocrats, former enemies, joined forces. The ranks of the lower middle class swelled with the growth of government and corporate bureaucracies. With the coming of universal male suffrage, the working classes, whose condition slowly improved, began to emerge as a potentially powerful political force.

Radical changes in birthrates modified ways of family life that had been constant for centuries. The hitherto universally accepted notion of male dominance was under increasing attack. The taboo on open discussion of sexual matters had begun to be challenged. Traditional habits of religious observance were yielding to secular pressures. Popular literacy made it possible for large numbers of people to follow debate on the great issues of the times.

Questions for Further Study

1. How was the condition of the aristocracy and the middle class changing after 1870?
2. In what ways was science applied to social analysis?
3. To what degree did sexual practices conform to social expectations?
4. What is meant by the "modernization" of society? What factors were most important to that process?

Suggestions for Further Reading

Accampo, Elinor. *Industrialization, Family Life, and Class Relations: Saint Chamond, 1815–1914*. Berkeley, CA, 1989.

Duberman, Martin, M. Vicinus, and G. Chauncey. *Hidden from History: Reclaiming the Gay and Lesbian Past*. New York, 1989.

Girouard, Mark. *Cities and People: A Social and Architectural History*. New Haven, CT, 1985.

Hayes, Carlton J. H. *The Generation of Materialism, 1871–1900*. New York, 1941.

Joyce, P. *Visions of the People: Industrial England and the Question of Class, c. 1848–1914*. New York, 1991.

McLaren, Angus. *Birth Control in Nineteenth-Century England*. New York, 1978.

Miller, Michael. *The Bon Marché: Bourgeois Culture and the Department Store, 1869–1920*. Princeton, NJ, 1981.

Moch, Leslie P. *Moving Europeans: Migration in Western Europe Since 1650*. Bloomington, IN, 1993.

Pilbeam, Pamela M. *The Middle Classes in Europe, 1789–1914*. Chicago, 1990.

Shapiro, Ann-Louise. *Housing the Poor of Paris, 1850–1902*. Madison, WI, 1985.

Stearns, Peter N. *European Society in Upheaval: Social History Since 1800*. New York, 1967.

Sutcliffe, Anthony. *Towards the Planned City: Germany, Britain, and the United States, 1789–1914*. New York, 1981.

Wiener, Joel H., ed. *Papers for the Millions: The New Journalism in Britain, 1850s to 1914*. New York, 1988.

Topic 21

Art and Science: The Modernist Revolution

The decisive break with the past which World War I was to produce was foreshadowed in the artistic and intellectual developments of the preceding decades. Beginning in the last quarter of the 19th century, changes began to occur that revolutionized Western culture, although to some extent these had their roots in earlier artistic movements: Richard Wagner, the prophet of the "art work of the future," was also the high priest of Romanticism. In many cases the new ideas made return to former ways impossible. The philosophy of Henri Bergson, and the psychoanalytical theories of Sigmund Freud conditioned vast areas of 20th-century behavior, while the writings of Friedrich Nietzsche anticipated the darker aspects of 20th-century political life.

In literature, Freud's ideas stimulated writers to explore the human subconscious, probing neuroses and repressions. Sympathy for the growing tide of political protest in western Europe led some writers, including Émile Zola, to adopt an increasingly realistic style. By contrast, others sought refuge from the harsh realities of the times in devising complex, symbolic language. By the early 20th century, in the works of Marcel Proust and James Joyce, the very use of language itself represented a revolutionary break with the past.

Painters, too, explored new attitudes to their art, increasingly rejecting traditional pictorial values in favor of abstract qualities. The Impressionists emphasized how things appeared to their eyes rather than how they really were. Their abstract treatment of form reached a point of no return around the turn of the century in the works of Paul Cézanne. It was only a step from here to the total breakdown of formal realism that Cubism and Futurism represented.

Just as Cubism opened a new chapter in painting by rejecting centuries of traditions, so the revolutionary musical style of atonality broke with 400 years of Western musical history. Devised by Arnold Schoenberg, it abandoned traditional harmony (or "tonality") in search of a new musical language. Not all composers accepted Schoenberg's method, but many agreed that the times required a break with the past. Igor Stravinsky, in his revolutionary masterpiece *The Rite of Spring,* experimented with new approaches to rhythm.

At the same time as artists were forging the ideas of Modernism, science was making its own contribution to the changing world. Einstein's "special theory" of relativity, first formulated in 1905, not only conditioned developments in modern physics but also opened the way to the nuclear age.

Thus the intellectual and cultural life of the generation before World War I reflected forces of disruption that were also operating on a much larger scale. At a time when traditional philosophies or religious belief seemed inadequate for the restless spirit of the age, artists sought refuge for their own disturbed visions in reshaping the world of their art.

TOWARD A NEW CULTURE: THE ART OF RICHARD WAGNER

The revolutionary artistic and intellectual movements of the late 19th century abruptly thrust Western culture into the Modernist era. Even so, they did not represent a complete novelty which appeared overnight. Few, if any, developments in the history of human thought occur without a process of transition. In the case of Modernism, the transformation of Western culture was symbolized to a remarkable degree by the life and art of Richard Wagner (1813–1883).

Wagner is best known today for his huge music dramas, the name he coined for his operatic works. In his time, he was also involved in many of the political issues that shook the second half of the 19th century, from the revolutions of 1848—he fought on the barricades in Dresden, later fleeing to Switzerland—to Prussia's nationalist war against France in 1870. A tireless campaigner on behalf of a bewildering array of causes from vicious anti-Semitism to wholehearted vegetarianism, he also wrote extensively on the arts. Among his early writings of significance was *The Artwork of the Future*, which appeared in 1849.

Many features of his operas are firmly within the German Romantic tradition. He often based them on his own versions of traditional Teutonic myths, or used them to recreate an ideal world of Medieval chivalry. Like many Romantic artists, Wagner incorporated elements of the natural world in his works, such as the surge of a great river or the radiant beauty of spring sunshine. Furthermore, his music often

Painting by Wilhelm Beckmann of Wagner at home in Bayreuth (1880).

reflects the characteristic Romantic preoccupation with death.

Yet this supremely Romantic creator was, at the same time, the most revolutionary artistic figure of his day, in many ways a true Modern. His musical style pushed the harmonic language of the mid-19th century to its limits, paving the way for the atonality of the early 20th century. His use of a short theme *(Leitmotiv)* to represent an individual, object, or concept allowed him to explore depths of psychological penetration. The use of these often reveals a character's subconscious thoughts or motivations. In the opera *Tristan und Isolde* (1865), he depicted virtually every shade of sexual love with a frankness generally unknown in works for public performance until our own time. His last stage work, *Parsifal* (1882), portrays the renunciation of sex with insights that can only be called Freudian. His advocacy of the *Gesamtkunstwerk* (Total Work of Art), a creative work that connects music, the visual arts, words, and movement into one experience, foreshadowed the achievement of Sergei Eisenstein (1898–1948) and other important filmmakers.

The Cycle of *The Ring*

Most remarkably of all, his most complex work, *Der Ring des Nibelungen* (The Ring of the Nibelung, 1851–1874), can be seen as a diagnosis of the flaw at the heart of industrial society: the corrupting influence of power and money. This tetralogy (made up of four separate operas) is in many respects the climax of Romanticism, with its gods, giants, and magic dragon. Yet, as productions in the late 20th century continue to reveal, by drawing on the world of myth supplemented by acute psychological insight, it also makes a powerful commentary on the development, and eventual crisis in 1914, of European civilization.

Even in his own lifetime, Wagner aroused enormous controversy. Today his music continues to divide opinion between those for whom a performance of his greatest works provides a supreme aesthetic experience, and those who find them long and bombastic. Yet there can be little debate over his influence on Western culture, for better or worse. Many subsequent composers followed him, many reacted against him, but few ignored him. His work was an inspiration to the French poet Charles Baudelaire (1821–1867) and the Symbolist poetic movement which arose from Baudelaire's writings at the turn of the century. More generally, by raising the importance of the arts to a level where they acquired an almost "sacred" function, he revolutionized aesthetic attitudes. The theater he had built at Bayreuth, in Germany, for the staging of his works soon became known to friends and foes alike as the "Temple on the Green Hill." Finally, in showing the power of mythic symbols to express universals, he anticipated much important 20th-century thought.

PHILOSOPHERS OF INSTINCT AND LIFE: NIETZSCHE, BERGSON, AND FREUD

Among Wagner's most passionate admirers in the 1860s was the German philosopher Friedrich Nietzsche (1844–1900). A brilliant Classical scholar, he heralded the Wagnerian works as the first since the time of the Greeks to develop a philosophy of culture based on tragedy. Beginning in 1876, however, he abruptly reversed his opinion and rejected Wagner and the idea of aesthetic redemption. The romantic illusions of art, Wagner's in particular, were contributing to a mood of human weakness and self-deception, which would lead to a crisis in European civilization. Only strong, free

Edvard Munch, who also painted *The Scream* (see p. 996), executed this portrait of Friedrich Nietzsche in 1906–1907.

spirits would survive the inevitable collapse, with its basic message that "God is dead."

Nietzsche expanded on his vision of a new world order in the remaining years of his active life. Civilization, he claimed, is nothing more than a collective fantasy. Religion, morality, the arts, even science, are all ways of distracting attention from reality, which lies in the "will to power." Only those who reject all moral restraints, and use their unbridled energy in their "will to power," can win independence. An individual who rejects all illusions in a free assertion of the will is capable of establishing a new order of nobility and goodness. Such a person would be an *Übermensch* (Superman). The most poetic description of these new humans appears in *Also sprach Zarathustra* (Thus Spoke Zarathustra, 1883–1892). In the process of the emergence of a new race of Supermen, all the weak and helpless should be cast aside, together with Judaism and Christianity, which traditionally protected the downtrodden.

Nietzsche's profound and original analysis of the crisis in Western culture proved increasingly influential as his ominous predictions seemed to be coming true. Indeed, the rise of Fascism and Nazism in the 1920s was explained by some as the realization of his ideas. It is true that Nietzsche despised militarism and nationalism as much as he did democracy or equality. In any case, his concept of the new world in which his Supermen would live seems poetic at best, and often shadowy. Yet the anger he expressed toward contemporary society, and the ruthlessness with which he contemplated the tearing down of all barriers, provided a dangerously heady brew. Nietzsche may be more prophet than instigator of 20th-century dictatorships and racial persecution, but a distorted version of his concepts served to fuel them.

Henri Bergson

No less original are the writings of Henri Bergson (1859–1941), one of the most influential intellectual forces in the early 20th century. Bergson urged a move from reason and abstraction to the subjective, and to a kind of inner reflection he called "intuition." This attitude required, in turn, a new attitude to time, which was not merely quantifiable in terms of physics, but became "experienced duration." Unlike Nietzsche, Bergson esteemed the creative process highly. In *Creative Evolution* (1907), he describes it as the expression of an *élan vital* (vital impulse). Nor did he reject the value of religion and morality, although he distinguished between "closed," or formal, elements and "open," or spiritual, ones.

Bergson's overall contribution to the intellectual life of his time was to free it of an excessive dependence on intellectualism and rationalism. Furthermore, the Existentialist philosophers of the later 20th century (see Part VII, Topic 13) built their notions of the self providing its own sense (and justification) on Bergson's emphasis of the dynamic power of the subconscious. Contemporary authors were also quick to exploit the literary device of recording the stream-of-consciousness thought processes of their characters. Among the most successful were Marcel Proust (1871–1922), James Joyce (1882–1941), and Virginia Woolf (1882–1941).

Freud and Psychoanalysis

Nietzsche addressed himself to the political ills of European culture, and Bergson was concerned with providing the means of intellectual renewal. The Viennese physician Sigmund Freud (1856–1939) sought to understand nothing less than the human subconscious and unconscious. In the process he developed ideas that have revolutionized the way humans see themselves and their relationships with others. His theories remain controversial, and some of his successors challenged specific points of interpretation while accepting the general direction of his research. Nonetheless, Freud probably played a larger part in the formation of the characteristically 20th-century Western view of human existence than any other single individual.

Regardless of the accuracy of his analyses, Freud was one of the first figures to write frankly and explicitly about human sexual behavior, discussing it in clinical and not moral terms. At a time when society in general preferred to ignore open discussion of sex, Freud openly claimed that all individuals were born with a strong sexual identity, with genital, anal, and oral drives. These components, however, had no inherent gender identity. The quality of masculinity or femininity was acquired during childhood, as a result of specific experiences, in particular those involving the relationship with parents. Freud described the most powerful of these in terms of the Greek myth of Oedipus. Children are aware of parental power to block their sexual functioning; in the act of rejecting this, they achieve a "normal" gender identity.

In a society where the family was conventionally regarded as a bastion against worldly vice, Freud taught that family relationships based on incest were at the root of the human psyche and were often the cause of emotional disturbance. Nor was sex simply an anatomical function, for it was strongly affected by psychological and cultural factors. The challenge to traditional middle-class attitudes could hardly have been stronger.

Yet even more shocking for many of his contemporaries was Freud's claim that society's repression of women's sexual drives was responsible for many cases of female "hysteria." Far from being a sign of weakness or sickness, the symptoms of women prone to fits or fainting attacks were due to abnormal sexual development. Whatever the accuracy of his diagnosis, in making this claim Freud broke new ground. He demonstrated that women's sexual drive is equally as powerful—and potentially as fulfilling or destructive—as that of men.

Freud himself was cautious in exploring some of the implications of his insights. Although he portrayed women as trapped by the conventions of society, he approved of their maintaining a passive domestic role to offset the more aggressive male function. As for homosexuality, he believed that although all children pass through a homoerotic phase, "normal" children emerge from it. His contemporary, Havelock Ellis (1859–1939), by contrast saw homosexuality as merely another form of human sexual behavior. Freud's subsequent work continued his research into the nature of the human subconscious by studying various forms of neurosis, and the significance of dreams. In doing so, he established methods of psychoanalysis that subsequently led to the foundation of a variety of analytical techniques. At the end of his career he wrote *The Future of an Illusion* (1927) and *Civilization and Its Discontents* (1930), two magisterial works which offered a broad analysis of modern culture.

The achievement of founding the new and important discipline of psychoanalysis was in itself outstanding enough, but Freud's contribution to the modern world goes much further. Ever since his time, it has been impossible to ignore those aspects of human behavior which cannot be explained by reason. Furthermore, his demonstration of the existence of deeply buried forces in the human personality, capable of both dynamic and destructive acts, was confirmed by the carnage of two world wars.

Sigmund Freud.

VARIETIES OF LITERARY EXPERIENCE: REALISM AND SYMBOLISM

Writers throughout Europe continued to produce realistic novels in the tradition firmly established earlier in the 19th century by Flaubert and Dickens (see Part VII, Topic 14). With increasing social and political tensions, however, the treatment of the issues of the day became more polemical.

The French writer Émile Zola (1840–1902) set out to dissect society in order to understand its workings, comparing the novelist's "enquiries" with the experiments of a scientist. Zola believed that individual lives were principally shaped by heredity and environment. As a result, many of his characters are destroyed by forces of nature that they are seemingly powerless to control, and Zola's work is often called, in fact, naturalistic rather than realistic.

His best novels deal with specific social ills: alcoholism in *The Dram Shop* (1877), prostitution in *Nana* (1880), and industrial exploitation in *Germinal* (1885). The brutal, often lurid evocation of life at its grimmest horrified many of his readers, and led to accusations of distortion and pornography. Zola made his own accusations when, in 1898, he became one of the antigovernment forces in the Dreyfus affair, wading into the fray at considerable risk to himself (see Part VII, Topic 15). In a short but powerfully worded pamphlet, *J'accuse!* (I Accuse, 1898), he attacked the army's handling of the case and rallied liberal and intellectual support on Dreyfus's side.

Whereas Zola's bleak world contains shafts of hope, the novels of Thomas Hardy (1840–1928) offer a picture of unrelieved despair, in which one character after another is broken on the wheel of an unrelenting fate. The background of most of his stories is English country life. He actually invented a county, "Wessex," (bearing a close resemblance to the English West Country county of Dorset) to provide their realistic setting.

Hardy wrote at a time when industrial progress had wrecked traditional agricultural life, and he saw modern efficiency as a profoundly destructive force. Yet for all his nostalgia at the passing of a way of life, he showed the confining conventions of rural existence to be no less devastating. The heroine of *Tess of the D'Urbervilles* (1891) is destroyed by a rigid code of social behavior that ends with her execution (by hanging) at the hands of a self-righteous society. In his last novel, *Jude the Obscure* (1896), the chief character sees every one of his attempts to emerge from obscurity relentlessly frustrated by the workings of destiny. Hardy has sometimes been criticized for his uncompromising pessimism, an angry man shaking his fist at an indifferent Creator. Yet the hopeless tone of his works is tempered by their passionate and sensitive concern for the sufferings of humanity.

The novels of Mrs. Humphry Ward (1851–1920; her real name was Mary Augusta Arnold) present a much more optimistic view of contemporary society, albeit one that reflected her own comfortable background. Coming from a well-to-do family, she actively campaigned against the feminist movement. Like Hardy's, her books contain realistic and well drawn accounts of agricultural life, as well as urban settings. One of their recurring themes is the nature of religion, reflecting contemporary doubts about the meaning of Christianity. In *Robert Elsmere* (1888), a young clergyman loses his faith in the divinity of Jesus, leaves the church, and devotes himself to helping the poor in the slums of London's East End. In addition to producing a stream of highly successful books, Mrs. Ward devoted considerable time to her own charitable activities.

The primitive, brooding world of Grazia Deledda (1871–1936) is a far cry from the intellectual doubts of cultivated Londoners. Deledda was born and grew up in Sardinia, and most of her books and stories are set in the island's wild landscape. They describe the struggles of inarticulate peasant folk to surmount the obstacles provided by nature and by destiny. In her best books, which include *Ceneri* (Ashes, 1904), she offers a lyrical picture of the gaunt beauty of her island, while at the same time conveying the harsh lives of its inhabitants.

The Symbolists

At the opposite extreme from these realistic writers, the Symbolists aimed to use poetry as a means of escaping from reality. In often difficult and obscure verse, they endowed words with a rich, magic quality that transcends their mundane significance.

The Symbolist movement was born in France in the early 1870s. Among the small group of writers groping for new forms of expression was Arthur Rimbaud (1854–1891), who claimed that a poet should sharpen his perceptions by undergoing every kind of experience, and then transmit what he perceived without any conscious control. In poetic terms this meant abandoning traditional notions of rhyme and meter. Rimbaud called his collection of passages entitled *Les Illuminations* (Illuminations; written 1872–1873, published 1886) "prose poems."

Rimbaud's own life was equally unconventional. Rebellious and violently anti-Christian, he set out to shock the bourgeois world of the Third Republic. At the time of writing *Les Illuminations*, he was in a relationship with a fellow poet, Paul Verlaine (1844–1896). After a bitter quarrel, in the course of which Verlaine shot Rimbaud in the wrist, the younger poet abandoned writing altogether. At the age of 19 he set off on a series of wanderings through Europe and the East, exploring, trading, and gunrunning.

The leading German Symbolist poet, Stefan George (1868–1933), was associated for a while with Baudelaire, Verlaine, and other writers in Paris, and with the Pre-Raphaelite group in London. In 1890, claiming to despise the decadence of his age, he withdrew to Munich, where he lived among a circle of admiring disciples, self-consciously dedicated to a life of the spirit. His attacks on materialism and naturalism dominated German intellectual debate, while in his lyric poems he sought to revitalize German poetry by the use of classicism.

The Belgian Maurice Maeterlinck (1862–1949) was one of the few dramatists to write successful Symbolist plays. They involve legend, allegory, and fairy tale to create a sense of mystery and brooding; their characters are passive victims of nameless, unseen forces. The best known, *Pelleas et Melisande* (1892), which was turned into an opera by Debussy, takes place in a kind of dreamworld, filled with mysterious silences and symbolic events, in which even the characters themselves do not know what is real. In one scene, a flock of sheep being led unknowingly to the slaughter symbolizes the helplessness of the human condition in the face of fate.

IMPRESSIONISM, POSTIMPRESSIONISM, AND EXPRESSIONISM

The restless search for new forms of expression in the visual arts produced a flurry of styles in rapid succession: Impressionism, Postimpressionism, Fauvism, and Expressionism. The burst of "isms" culminated in the birth of Cubism and Futurism just before World War I, and the complete overturning of traditional ways of looking at the world. All these styles rejected realism, and emphasized abstract qualities of color, shape, and line. In doing so, they broke with an approach to art that was initiated by Giotto at the dawn of the Renaissance.

Mother and Child (c. 1899) by the American painter Mary Cassatt, one of her many works on this subject.

Just as Rimbaud tried to communicate experience directly, without shaping it, the Impressionists (the name was derisively applied to them by an unenthusiastic critic) sought to give a literal impression of light and color. Avoiding any kind of organized form, and hoping to paint without interpreting their subject, they tried to reproduce the overall visual impact of what they saw. Thus, when Claude Monet (1840–1926) painted a pool with water lilies, he was concerned to record glowing colors and reflecting lights, rather than an actual pond with real flowers.

A number of the leading Impressionist painters were women. Berthe Morisot (1841–1895) gave up a career as a successful society painter to join the radical new movement. Her landscapes and scenes of Paris show a fascination with light, conveyed by free brush strokes and subtle colors. The American Mary Cassatt (1844–1926) settled in Paris to study with the Impressionists. Like her close friend Edgar Degas (1834–1917), she preferred to paint spontaneous scenes from daily life. Her unsentimental depictions of mothers and children, like Degas' scenes of women bathing, show their subjects caught unawares, in a moment of intimacy.

Postimpressionism

Although many artists continued to work in the Impressionist style—Monet used it right up to his death—the restless spirit of the times drove other painters to find new approaches. The Postimpressionists are so called because they all rejected Impressionism, but have little else in common. Georges Seurat (1859–1891) used thousands of tiny dots of color to build up simple geometrical forms. By contrast, the exotic scenes of Paul Gauguin (1848–1903) consist of broad washes of paint.

The range of Postimpressionist artists emerges most vividly in the work of the two greatest, Paul Cézanne (1839–1906) and Vincent van Gogh (1853–1890). Cézanne's monumental landscapes and ordered still lifes achieve an abstract sense of balance that derives from their use of geometric forms. He advised his fellow-painters to "treat Nature in terms of its geometrical shapes, the sphere, the cylinder, and the cone." At the opposite emotional extreme, van Gogh depicted the "terrible passions of humanity," in works filled with swirling lines and violent color contrasts.

Fauvism and Expressionism

Although the emotional intensity typical of van Gogh's work was partly due to his own tragic life, it also reflected the uneasy climate of the times. Two other schools of painting developed in the first decade of the 20th century which pushed the sense of explosiveness even further. In France the *Fauves*—the word

The Scream (1893), a painting by the Norwegian Expressionist artist Edvard Munch.

Vincent van Gogh's ecstatic painting, *The Starry Night* (1899).

means "wild beasts"—painted canvasses that broke with all traditions of form and color. The movement was so destructive, in fact, that it soon fell apart. One of its members, however, went on to become a major influence in 20th-century art. Henri Matisse (1869–1954), unlike most of his contemporaries, painted luminous, festive scenes and glowing still lifes. One of his first important works was actually called *The Joy of Life*.

The Expressionists, who were mainly German, used their art to express strong emotions. The tone of the Expressionist movement had been set at the end of the 19th century by the Norwegian Edvard Munch (1863–1944). Munch said of his famous and horrifying painting *The Scream*, "I hear the scream in nature." His German successors used similarly bold images to capture the expression of extreme states of mind, frequently those of loneliness and alienation. The alarming, even hysterical mood of their paintings reflects all too clearly the mood of the age.

THE MODERNIST REVOLT: CUBISM, FUTURISM, AND ATONALITY

During the years from 1908 to 1914, the hectic speed of cultural change reached a breakneck pace. A mere catalogue of some of the main events conveys the sense of upheaval. In 1908, the Cubist paintings of Pablo Picasso and Georges Braque challenged centuries of pictorial conventions, and Schoenberg was the first composer for 300 years to write music with no tonal center. In 1910, the Futurist works of Umberto Boccioni attempted to combine time and space, and Wassily Kandinsky produced the first purely abstract work of art. In 1913, the first volume of Marcel Proust's stream-of-consciousness novel appeared, and a year later Joyce, who revolutionized the use of language in his later books, published his first prose work.

Cubism

If Cézanne had laid the foundations for a new way of painting, two young artists working in Paris between 1908 and 1914 built on them to create Cubism. The French Georges Braque (1882–1963) and his Spanish fellow-artist Pablo Picasso (1881–1973) challenged the idea, universal since the Renaissance, that works painted on a two-dimensional surface should try to show three dimensions. They abandoned traditional perspective, and in a series of experimental canvasses tried to find new ways of seeing their subjects geometrically. In some of Picasso's early Cubist works, he used the entire surface of the painting as a geometric grid. The image to be depicted was then broken up into separate squares and located in various places. Braque developed the technique of showing simultaneously aspects of an object that could in reality be perceived only separately. In one well-known picture, he showed the front, back, and sides of a violin on a single plane.

Violin and Palette (1909–1910), an early Cubist painting by Georges Braque.

In the years following World War I, Picasso, Braque, and a host of other artists moved from a strictly analytical style to develop a wide range of variations on Cubism. Guillaume Apollinaire (1880–1918), a leading writer in Modernist circles in Paris, was one of the first champions of the new style. The important contribution of the early works was to release painters definitively from the bonds of realism, and encourage them to produce abstract art, in which the most important ingredients were color, line, and geometrical composition.

Braque and Picasso had at least based their early Cubist works on real subjects, such as portraits or violins. At exactly the time of analytical Cubism, another artist was producing purely abstract art. Wassily Kandinsky (1866–1944) began his career as an Expressionist painter. His interest in expressing mystical emotions through color led him to increasing abstraction, however. In 1910 he painted the first pure abstraction in the Western tradition, *First Abstract Watercolor*. In the period between the wars, Kandinsky continued to produce works inspired by his belief in the infinite nature of the cosmos. He also wrote a pioneering treatise on the theory of abstract art, *Concerning the Spiritual in Art* (1922).

The Futurist Movement

In Italy, the Modernist revolt in the arts took a dramatic form with the appearance of the Futurist movement. In their first manifesto (1909), the Futurists boldly rejected all traditional forms of culture. They turned instead to the cult of the machine and the technological future. Filippo T. Marinetti (1876–1944), its founder, proclaimed that "a roaring automobile, which runs like a machine-gun, is more beautiful than the Winged Victory of Samothrace. . . . We wish to glorify war."

Umberto Boccioni (1882–1916), the greatest of Futurist artists, developed an aesthetic theory called Dynamism that sought to express energy in terms of motion and light. His *Unique Forms of Continuity in Space* (1913) seeks to convey a sense of accelerating movement in sculpture. Boccioni and his fellow Futurists glorified violence and war as means of overthrowing established values, and they greeted the coming of World War I with great nationalist enthusiasm.

The most original phase of Futurism ended with the death of many of its leading exponents in the course of fighting.

Atonality in Music

Many composers of the turn of the century followed Wagner's example in their increasingly free attitude to conventional rules of harmony. The Frenchman Claude Debussy (1862–1918) wrote music that drifts from key to key, with frequent dissonances. His abandonment of traditional forms for shifting sound pictures led his contemporaries to compare his works to Impressionist paintings, while his opera *Pelleas et Melisande* (1902), based on Maeterlinck's play, allied him for a while with the Symbolists.

Yet even Debussy's shimmering, evanescent works do not represent a dramatic break with the past. The decisive move came in 1908, when the Austrian Arnold Schoenberg (1874–1951) wrote his *Three Piano Pieces*, Op. 11. Schoenberg was convinced that the traditional system of harmony, which had been used in Western music for 300 years, had lost its value. Pursuing Wagner's experiments to their ultimate conclusion, he wrote piano pieces that were "atonal"—that avoided any sense of a fixed tonal center, or key.

In the period immediately preceding World War I, Schoenberg's free atonal works eerily echo the instability and morbidity of the times. His musical composition, *Pierrot Lunaire* (1912), employing texts of symbolist poems, uses a cross between song and speech to create an Expressionist mood of macabre fantasy. Schoenberg also produced a number of Expressionist paintings. In the 1920s, Schoenberg and his followers developed new ways of organizing their musical material to replace those that they had rejected. The most important was the famous twelve-tone system, or serialism.

Critics reviled Schoenberg's atonality as a "perversion." His great contemporary Igor Stravinsky (1882–1971) met with even less sympathy. When in 1913 Stravinsky's ballet *Le Sacre du Printemps* (The Rite of Spring) was first performed in Paris, the composer was accused of "the destruction of music as an art." Throughout his long career, Stravinsky continued to write in an astonishing variety of styles, many of which used a version of traditional harmony; years later he finally adopted serialism. His revolutionary contribution to music lay in his new approach to rhythm. In *Le Sacre*, Stravinsky replaced the more or less regular beat of conventional music with a combination of constantly fluctuating rhythmical patterns. The sense of barbaric energy, whipped up by a vast orchestra, drove its first hearers, sophisticated Parisians though many of them were, to unprecedented scenes of shouting and stamping.

Developments in Literature

The Modernist movement in literature was to emerge at the end of World War I, but its character was already established. In 1913, the French novelist Marcel Proust (1871–1922) published the first volume of his seven-part work *À la recherche du temps perdu* (Remembrance of Things Past; the work was written between 1907 and 1919, and published between 1913 and 1927). Semiautobiographical, Proust's work explores the nature of time and memory, and the role of the subconscious. Its narrator sets out to recreate his past life. In the process, he realizes that all past experiences remain within us but can be called up again either by the perceptions of our senses or by the agency of art. Thus, for all the futility of individual human effort, art can recreate the past and transcend death.

The Irish writer James Joyce (1882–1941) took the stream-of-consciousness style used by Proust's narrator to even greater lengths. His first work of fiction, *Dubliners*, appeared in 1914. It sets out many of the themes that were to dominate his later books: the need to escape one's environment (in this case Dublin), the loss of illusions, or the acknowledgement of failure. Although *Dubliners* includes realistic treatments of the lower-middle-class setting, it also foreshadows the subtlety of Joyce's later work. In *Ulysses*, begun at the beginning of the war and finished in 1922, he used a stream-of-consciousness technique to describe a single day in the lives of two Dublin men. The resultant blend of fantasy, surrealism, and pastiche, filled with complex wordplay, proved to be one of the 20th century's most influential novels.

SCIENCE FROM CERTAINTY TO RELATIVITY

The astonishing technological advances of the late 19th century were accompanied by new discoveries in all branches of science, especially in physics. These developments, which profoundly altered human perceptions of the nature of the physical world, may have seemed theoretical and of little relevance to everyday life. Yet discoveries made shortly after 1900 eventually ushered in the atomic age.

Virtually all scientists working at the end of the 19th century accepted the view that matter consisted of indivisible atoms that responded to fixed natural laws observed by Sir Isaac Newton (1642–1727) in the 17th century. According to Newton, absolute time passed uniformly, and absolute space was immovable—both "were unrelated to any outward circumstances."

Yet classical physics failed to account for certain observations. In 1895 the German physicist Wilhelm

Albert Einstein outside his laboratory in Berlin, 1920.

Roentgen (1845–1923) discovered X-rays when he observed the highly energetic, invisible electromagnetic radiation emitted by certain wavelengths. These rays produced a form of energy capable of penetrating opaque materials. Other scientists discovered similar rays produced by uranium. The British physicist Ernest Rutherford (1871–1937) built on this work to develop a theory of radioactivity. He argued that radiation was caused when atoms of radioactive substances disintegrated. In 1911, Rutherford proposed his nuclear theory of the atom and the potential energy within it.

To explain the phenomenon of radioactivity, the German physicist Max Planck (1858–1947) developed in the early years of the 20th century his quantum theory. According to this, energy is not infinitely subdivisible, but exists as a series of discrete bundles, or quanta. In light of this, Newton's laws of motion as graduated and continuous could not be correct.

Einstein and Relativity

The most shattering theoretical advances in physics were made by the German physicist Albert Einstein (1879–1955). His theory of relativity, which was first formulated in 1905, was to have far more general consequences and represented an even more decisive break with past ideas of stability. Since everything in our universe is in motion, any observation will be affected by the observer's relative position. Thus space and time, far from being uniform, are relative. The change of relative position governs the measurement of space; the duration of movement, in the space crossed in that spatial change, governs the measurement of time. All energy and matter are related in this space-time continuum.

The notion that it is not possible to distinguish between space and time, or between matter and energy, was startling enough. Einstein's famous equation, $E = mc^2$, went on to prove the relationship between mass (m), energy (E), and the speed of light (c). This played a vital part in the development of nuclear physics, since it explained the nature of nuclear energy.

Einstein's demonstration of the relativity of forces that had always been regarded as unchanging was a major blow to the idea of a stable universe. Intensifying challenge to the established political order, struggles for wide-ranging social reform, the shattering of centuries of artistic traditions—all these were now joined by a view of the material world based on perpetual change. By 1914, European society and culture were on the brink of the most complete and wrenching shift of all.

Questions for Further Study

1. In what ways did art and literature at the turn of the century reflect the changing role of women?
2. How did the ideas of Freud and Einstein revolutionize Western culture?
3. What similarities are there in developments in music, painting, and literature in the early years of the 20th century? How are they linked with parallel historical events?

Suggestions for Further Reading

Calder, N. *Einstein's Universe*. New York, 1980.
Clark, T. J. *The Painting of Modern Life: Paris in the Art of Manet and His Followers*. New York, 1984.

Gay, P. *Freud: A Life for Our Times*. New York, 1988.
Golding, J. *Cubism: A History and an Analysis*. Cambridge, MA, 1988.
Herbert, R. L. *Impressionism: Art, Leisure, and Parisian Society*. New Haven, CT, 1988.
Kern, S. *The Culture of Time and Space*. Cambridge, MA, 1983.
Lipton, E. *Looking into Degas: Uneasy Images of Women and Modern Life*. Berkeley, CA, 1986.
Watson, D. *Richard Wagner: A Biography*. New York, 1981.

PART VIII

The Contemporary Era

Conflict, doubt, and pessimism have dominated the mood of much of the 20th century. The century began with the basic values of European civilization under attack by cultural and intellectual revolution. From the philosophical "revolt against positivism" to the iconoclastic Postimpressionist artists and the belligerent Futurists of the years before the Great War, the assumptions of rationality and order were steadily undermined. Einstein's theories of the universe and Freud's revelations about the subconscious reinforced the sense that humans were unable to grasp, let alone control their destinies.

The political and diplomatic crises of the early 20th century reinforced the collapse of the old moral order—the first half of the 20th century was dominated by two gigantic military conflicts. The Great War of 1914–1918 wreaked unimag-

ined destruction and death on the European world, shattering permanently the notion of Western superiority and dominance. In its wake, as Europeans experimented with new forms of social and cultural energy, they also invented new forms of political control that in their worst manifestations produced totalitarian regimes in the Soviet Union as well as in Fascist Italy and Nazi Germany. The economic chaos of the Great Depression not only helped to bring the new totalitarian movements to power, but threw Western society in general into deep crisis.

The ultimate consequence of the totalitarian nightmare was World War II (1939–1945), in which the struggle for mastery assumed more horrific proportions than in the Great War, reaching its nadir in the racial policies of the Nazi dictatorship and the Holocaust. This second conflict was a truly global one, and its implications for the future were enormous.

The last half of the 20th century in Europe has seen the passage from the grim certainties of the Cold War to the increasing unpredictability of its final decade. The fall of the Berlin Wall in 1989 brought to an end a period in which Europe was firmly divided into two blocs. Western Europe, much of which emerged shattered from World War II, rebuilt its cities and the institutions of its sovereign states with help from the Marshall Plan organized by the United

States. The western European nations based their transatlantic alliances on NATO. At the same time, they sought a closer form of unity among themselves by forming the European Economic Community (EEC), intended to provide an economic union which might eventually lead to forms of political cooperation.

Meanwhile, in eastern Europe, the Soviet Union led the postwar recovery, in the process imposing client regimes. The defensive organization uniting the Soviet Union and the countries of eastern Europe was the Warsaw Pact. Yugoslavia, the only significant East European country to defy Stalin and leave the Soviet bloc, subsequently became one of the leading members of a third bloc—that of the "nonaligned" nations, many of which were Asian.

Relations between East and West were ultimately conditioned by each side's capability to wreak destruction on the other by use of atomic weapons. A series of crises, beginning with the Berlin Blockade of 1948, and continuing with Soviet invasions of Hungary and Czechoslovakia, saw the two blocs develop the art of "brinkmanship," with neither side finally willing to push the dispute to outright confrontation. Meanwhile, the United States was embroiled in a series of conflicts outside Europe. They included the Korean and Vietnam wars, and—in a clash that seemed to bring the world to the edge of nuclear war—the Cuban missile crisis.

By the end of the 20th century, in a world where technology and culture were ever more global, European history was inextricably linked with that of the rest of the globe. The original EEC membership of six had grown to fifteen by 1997, with the possibility of adding eastern European members by 2000. Its founders' hopes that a European Union might some day provide the basis of a United States of Europe still seemed optimistic, however. Individual nations preferred to find their own solutions to the problems dominating the end of the century: unemployment, increasingly aging populations, terrorism, and the threat of ecological disasters, among others. The collapse of the Soviet Union, and the future of its former members—most importantly Russia itself—raised new questions about the role Europe will play in the next century.

VIII

Topic 1

The Great War

Today, historians refer to the events of 1914–1918 as "World War I," but those who experienced the conflagration called it "the Great War."

At the time, there was nothing to compare with the Great War. The last conflict that had engulfed all of Europe—the wars of Napoleon—had ended a century earlier. Thereafter, wars were localized or of short duration. In the Great War, the European battles were fought as far west as France, as far east as Russia, and as far south as Italy and the Balkans. Fighting also took place in Africa, the Middle East, and East Asia.

Few generals or political leaders expected the war to last more than a few months. Nevertheless, in all the belligerent countries many idealistic young men enlisted with enthusiasm. "It's all great fun," the English poet Rupert Brooke (1885–1915) wrote to his family in the first winter of the war.

As the realities of the catastrophe into which Europe stumbled were driven home, participants came to regard it with a bitter sense of irony. "Great" hardly described the horrors of the battlefield, the destruction of life and property, and the social and political upheavals caused by the fighting. The war burned itself deep into the human psyche, with consequences that made themselves felt for much of the rest of the 20th century.

The immediate cause of the Great War was a murder in a province of the Austro-Hungarian empire in June 1914. Monarchs and their ministers mismanaged the resulting diplomatic crisis, and in August the guns began firing. In another sense, however, the war was the culmination of historical developments, including nationalism, militarism, and imperialism. Decades of international tensions, aggressive national policies, and diplomatic suspicions had fed the roots of the 1914 crisis.

Europe's great powers aligned themselves into two military blocs: Britain, France, and Russia—the "Allies"—on one side, Germany and Austria-Hungary—the "Central Powers"—on the other. As the war unfolded, each side drew other states into its camp. Because of their geographical position, the Central Powers fought a two-front war. On the Eastern front, they effectively cut Russia off from vital supplies, and under the pressure of great losses and internal opposition, the tsarist autocracy finally collapsed in 1917. On the Western front, where the military character of the war was defined almost immediately, both sides became locked in the terrible stalemate of trench warfare. The entrance of the United States on the side of the Allies in 1917, coupled with the exhaustion of Germany, brought about the collapse of the Central Powers and the end of the war.

The signing of the armistice in November 1918 ended the fighting, but the impact of the war continued to reverberate throughout the rest of the 20th century. Tens of millions of human beings had died. The effects on society of "total war," in which civilians played as vital a role as soldiers in the outcome, were first seen on the home front. Governments mobilized entire populations—men, women, and children—behind the war effort, reorganized national economies, and bolstered civilian morale as a vital military operation. Gender and class lines were blurred, family life reshaped, social values altered, and liberal ideals suspended.

THE ORIGINS OF THE FIRST WORLD WAR

Since the mid-19th century, technological developments had changed the way in which modern wars were fought, while the likelihood of war was enhanced by the growing political influence of military officers. Arms manufacturers, who derived economic benefits from hostilities, also influenced government policy.

Modern Weapons and Military Competition

During the last third of the 19th century, several factors contributed to a huge increase in armaments: the intense competition among the great powers for colonial territories, the rise of nationalist tensions in the Balkans, the hardening alliance systems, and repeated diplomatic crises. The major powers were engaged in a dangerous race to strengthen their military postures.

Each major country had its own armaments manufacturers, most of which also sold weapons on the international market to all parties. Krupp, the German firm, and Armstrong-Whitworth, the British company, poured large sums into research and development and made large profits. Other industries often combined with armaments makers to influence defense programs. They backed nationalist and imperialist organizations that supported the arms race and, together with anti-foreign propaganda and the popular press, pressured politicians to vote for larger military budgets. By 1914, per capita military expenditures had increased to six times their 1871 level in Germany and had more than doubled in France.

Military strategy continued to be based on the infantry soldier. By the 1870s, Britain was the only great power that had not enacted a peacetime draft. When war broke out in August 1914, Russia's 1 million-man army was the largest, followed by Germany with about 850,000, France with 700,000, and Austria-Hungary with 450,000; Britain, which relied on its naval superiority for defense, had only 250,000 men under arms. Strategists believed that reserve training would allow each of the great powers to mobilize a force more than five times the size of its standing army. During the war itself, the number of men actually brought under arms more than doubled these estimates—Russia eventually mobilized 12 million, Germany 11 million, France 8 million, and Britain and the British Dominions 9.5 million.

Sheer numbers themselves were not decisive, for the quality of training and weaponry, military planning, transportation facilities, and industrial productivity all affected a country's ability to wage war. Most governments adopted the German practice of maintaining a permanent general staff, which was responsible for military strategy, training, and weapons development.

Hand-held infantry weapons were greatly improved during the 19th century. By the 1870s most armies had substituted the breech-loading rifle for the muzzle-loading musket. In the 1880s, the introduction of the magazine rifle permitted more rapid firing. But the most significant change came with the development of the machine gun, which fired several hundred rounds a minute. Its considerable weight—about 100 pounds—made it effective only when fixed in position, but the machine gun greatly enhanced defensive operations and, during World War I, caused enormous casualties.

Special alloys of hardened steel and the use of ferroconcrete enabled countries to build huge fortresses as protection against invasion, and even the most sophisticated technological advances in heavy weapons systems failed to undermine the effectiveness of such defenses. Siege howitzers could pound enemy positions and reduce cities to rubble from long distances, but after months of the heaviest artillery bombardment in history, fortresses such as Verdun did not fall to the enemy.

Other developments took place at sea, where Britain and Germany engaged in a feverish "naval race"

Map 1.1 The European Alliances, 1914

that heightened tensions between them. With the passage of the Naval Defense Act in 1889, Britain aimed to make its fleet twice as large as the combined size of the two next biggest navies. The competition began when Admiral Alfred von Tirpitz (1849–1930) became German naval secretary in 1897. Tirpitz was an Anglophobe and under his direction Germany passed a series of naval bills between 1898 and 1912 designed to build a battle fleet two-thirds the size of Britain's. Tirpitz's "risk theory" held that such a fleet would be so powerful that in the event of war Britain would not risk attempts to destroy it.

Britain responded to Germany with a massive naval buildup and the creation of a North Sea Fleet. In 1906, the British revolutionized naval warfare with the *Dreadnought*, a large, heavily armored, and highly maneuverable battleship. Driven by powerful oil-fueled turbine engines, it carried 12-inch guns that could strike targets many miles away. Despite these advantages, *Dreadnought*-class ships were by no means invincible—other countries copied the technology, and both torpedo boats and destroyers could sink even the *Dreadnought*. By 1914, heavy-oil engines and storage batteries made possible the building of submarine fleets that would challenge conventional naval warfare.

The Germans did copy the *Dreadnought* idea, and by the eve of World War I had 18 such ships to Britain's 29. Germany's naval strength rose from seventh to second place. Berlin brushed aside proposals to limit naval construction, and British fears of German ambitions grew accordingly. Secretary of War Richard Haldane (1856–1928) went to Berlin in 1912 to seek an accommodation with Germany, but the mission proved unsuccessful. As a result, Britain and France then reached an important agreement: Britain concentrated its naval forces in the North Sea, France in the Mediterranean. Although no formal alliance was made, self-interest now bound the two nations as never before.

Military Strategy and the Schlieffen Plan

Despite the new weapons, military planners continued to employ strategies inspired by the theories of the Prussian General Karl von Clausewitz (1780–1831), who advocated offensive operations designed to achieve victory with speed, mobility, and surprise. Moreover, most general staffs worked out military plans for fighting wars with anticipated enemies.

Based on accurate maps, railroad transportation, and precise timetables, such plans aimed at moving huge numbers of troops rapidly over large areas. The so-called Schlieffen Plan, developed by General Alfred von Schlieffen (1833–1913), chief of the German General Staff, was the most famous. Although his strategy anticipated that Germany would be at war with both Russia and France at the same time, Schlieffen thought principally in terms of how to defeat the French in the West. He devised his plan in 1905, while Russia was still reeling from its defeat by the Japanese and from domestic uprisings. He argued that since Russia, weak and disorganized, would require at least a month to mobilize its armies, Germany should concentrate on a quick victory against France, after which it could deal easily with Russia.

Schlieffen held that because French fortifications such as those at Verdun were too formidable, Germany's only alternative was to launch a surprise attack against France through the level terrain of the Low Countries. Keeping the Russians at bay in the East, two separate German armies would form a large pincer in the West, with one larger arm closing around the French from behind. Schlieffen planned for a powerful right wing to drive through the Netherlands, Luxembourg, and Belgium while a much weaker left wing would move toward Alsace-Lorraine. When the French counterattacked in the South, as he believed they would, two German army corps would be shifted from there in order to reinforce the right flank—the weakened left wing would then retreat on to German soil in order to draw the enemy away from the real arena of decision in the North.

Schlieffen's plan held several strategic risks—he had banked on the assumption that Russia would not attack until its mobilization had been completed, that the Belgians would offer no serious resistance, and that the timing would go according to schedule. Furthermore, the German authorities believed that military needs would outweigh the political repercussions of violating Belgian neutrality. In 1906, von Schlieffen was succeeded by Count Helmuth Johannes von Moltke (1848–1916), the plodding and insecure nephew of the brilliant strategist who had executed Prussia's victories during the struggle for German unification. The younger Moltke so changed Schlieffen's original plan as to enhance the risks of disaster. He increased the strength of the left wing significantly, partly by weakening the Russian Front, and thereby changed the fundamental thrust of the assault.

The French, who had gained a sense of the Schlieffen Plan, developed their own "Plan XVII," which called for a holding action against the German armies in Belgium while attacking Germany with a superior force through Lorraine. The logic of "military necessity" made both the German and French generals overconfident. Strategies such as the Schlieffen Plan increased the chances of war, for their success hinged on the ability of the general staffs to deploy millions of soldiers and a huge quantity of equipment on a war footing *before* the outbreak of hostilities—hence, while civilian authorities attempted to resolve diplomatic crises through negotiation, the military demanded immediate mobilization so as to be able to strike first.

FROM CONFRONTATION TO CRISIS: THE COMING OF WAR

Between 1882 and 1914, countries chose membership in one of the two great alliance systems in order to gain a measure of security against their enemies. Thus Great Britain, France, and Russia were aligned in the Triple Entente, and Germany, Austria-Hungary, and Italy were grouped in the Triple Alliance. Yet the increasingly tense character of diplomatic relations, especially after 1905, produced the opposite effect. Based on the assumption that powerful alliances supported them, countries tended to be less cautious during international disputes. Such disputes restricted the maneuverability of the blocs as allies strove to demonstrate their support for each other. Thus, the alternatives available to the great powers narrowed dangerously during international confrontations.

Assassination at Sarajevo

Relations between the Triple Alliance and the Entente deteriorated as one international face-off followed another. The Balkans, the scene of considerable turmoil as a result of the Bosnian crisis of 1908 and the wars of 1912–1913, proved to be the seedbed of the Great

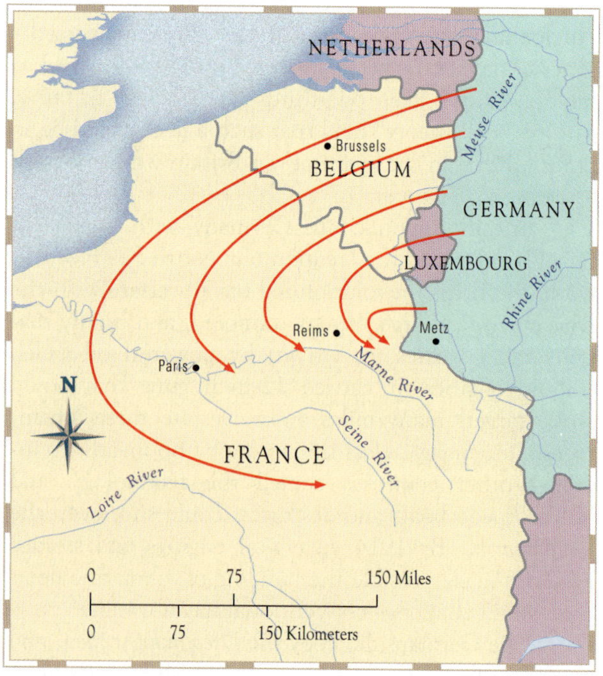

Map 1.2 The Schlieffen Plan

Map 1.3 The Balkans, c. 1914

War, for the clashes between Russia and Austria-Hungary destabilized the region (see Part VII, Topic 16). Serbian nationalists, who wanted their country to form the core of a large Slavic empire, expected Russia to back them. Austria-Hungary was intent on blocking Serb ambitions, which could undermine the multiethnic Dual Monarchy.

These forces clashed head-on at Sarajevo, the capital of the Austrian possession of Bosnia, in the summer of 1914. On the morning of June 28, the Archduke Franz Ferdinand (1863–1914), heir to the Austro-Hungarian throne and nephew of Emperor Franz Josef, was shot and killed while riding through the streets of Sarajevo in an open car. His wife, the former Countess Sophie Chotek (1868–1914), was also killed. The royal couple was on an official tour of Bosnia and at the moment of their death had been returning from a reception at the town hall.

Seven young men—five teenagers and two in their twenties—took part in the assassination conspiracy. A student named Gavrilo Princip (1895–1918) fired the fatal shots. All were members of a nationalist organization called "Young Bosnia." They had made Franz Ferdinand their target because he was known to favor autonomy for the Slavs of the empire, much as the Magyars enjoyed. Were Franz Ferdinand to come to the throne and implement this policy, Serbian ambitions would be crushed.

Serbia bore indirect responsibility for the murder. Officers in the Serbian Army had provided the assassins with rudimentary training and weapons. Princip and his friends had been in contact with a Serbian terrorist group known as the "Black Hand," which had been supported by the Ministry of War. Perhaps most damning, although members of the Serb cabinet had known

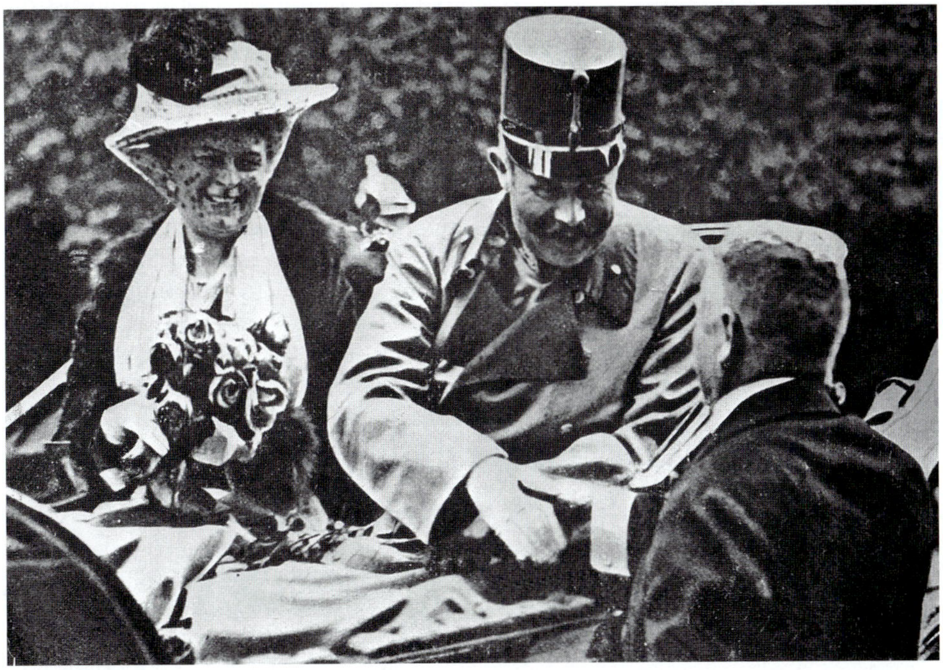

Archduke Franz Ferdinand and his wife Sophie in Sarajevo, the fateful day, June 28, 1914.

Gavrilo Princip, the gunman responsible for the assassination of Franz Ferdinand and his wife Sophie.

that an attempt on Ferdinand's life would be made, they did almost nothing to stop it.

Austrian officials were not unduly upset at the murder, for many thought Ferdinand's political ideas dangerous. Moreover, his marriage to a minor aristocrat had angered the emperor and the royal court, who felt that the archduke had married beneath his station. Despite these private misgivings, Austria-Hungary decided to use the event as a pretext for extracting retribution from Serbia. Count Leopold von Berchtold (1863–1942), the wealthy aristocrat who served as Austrian foreign minister, advocated a march on Belgrade. But the army chief of staff urged caution, for an attack against Serbia could mean war with Russia. Berchtold then turned to Berlin, hoping to secure assurances that Germany would back Austria-Hungary if war broke out.

How Europe Stumbled into War

On July 5, Wilhelm II gave Count Berchtold what he wanted: the infamous "blank check," by which Germany pledged military assistance in the event of war between Austria-Hungary and Russia. The German chancellor, Theobald von Bethmann-Hollweg (served 1909 to 1917), confidently predicted that Russia would not intervene if Austria acted quickly. Unknown to him, however, on July 21 French President Raymond Poincaré, who was visiting St. Petersburg, encouraged Russia to be firm. On both sides, the inevitable logic of the alliance systems took hold.

Over the weeks that followed the German assurance of support, Berchtold deliberately kept Berlin ill-informed of Austrian plans. Finally, on July 23, Vienna issued an ultimatum that clearly threatened to violate Serbian sovereignty. The Austrians insisted that the Serb government suppress all anti-Austrian activities and that Austrian officials be permitted to investigate the assassination in Serbia. At 5:55 P.M. on July 25, Belgrade—which had already ordered mobilization—responded with some concessions, but refused to accept all of Vienna's demands. At 9:23 P.M., the Emperor Franz Josef ordered Austro-Hungarian mobilization.

The two mobilizations shocked Europe's diplomats into action. The German ambassador in St. Petersburg persuaded the Russians to suggest talks with Berchtold to end the crisis. British Foreign Secretary Sir Edward Grey (1862–1933) appealed to the kaiser to hold the Austrians in check and called for mediation talks. Bethmann-Hollweg, who misunderstood the gravity of events because of Berchtold's deceptions, failed to forward Grey's proposals to Vienna, and when Wilhelm returned from a cruise on July 27, he angrily asked his chancellor, "How did it all happen?"

That night, the chastened German minister wired Berchtold that Austria must agree to discuss the Serbian concessions. But in Vienna, a declaration of war had been drafted and Berchtold got the aged Emperor Franz Josef to sign it by falsely claiming that the Serbians had already begun to attack. On the morning of July 28, Austria delivered its declaration of war to Serbia, while in Berlin the kaiser decided that he would attempt to mediate the dispute between Austria-Hungary and Serbia. The next day, Bethmann-Hollweg telegraphed sternly to Berchtold that "We [Germany] must refuse to let ourselves be drawn . . . by Vienna into any general conflagration because she has ignored our advice." Had such a message been delivered on July 5 instead of the "blank check," events might have taken a different course.

On July 28, the French ambassador assured the Russians that France would stand by its ally. Tsar Nicholas II, who had been persuaded to order partial mobilization, telegraphed to Kaiser Wilhelm: "Very soon I shall be forced to take extreme measures that will lead to war." The royal cousins exchanged telegrams, signed "Willy" and "Nicky," which were so friendly that Nicholas countermanded the mobilization order. But when Wilhelm learned that Russian mobilization had been under way, he exploded in anger and ended the discussions. The tsar signed a full mobilization decree on July 29.

Although Germany had not been a direct party to the events in the Balkans, General Helmuth von Moltke, bearing in mind the time constraints of the Schlieffen Plan, now urged immediate mobilization.

Events rushed forward. On July 31, Austria-Hungary mobilized against Russia; Germany issued two ultimatums—one demanding that Russia call off its mobilization, the other giving France 18 hours to decide whether it would remain neutral if Germany and Russia fought; France ordered mobilization. On August 1, Sir Edward Grey promised that Britain would keep France neutral if Germany would not act, but the German ambassador misinterpreted the comment. The kaiser concluded that he would be free to attack Russia if he left France alone, although von Moltke insisted that the Schlieffen Plan could not be changed. Nevertheless, Wilhelm ordered German troops already moving toward Luxembourg to stop, but von Moltke deliberately held the order back. The same day, the German ambassador in St. Petersburg asked the Russian foreign minister whether his country would cancel the mobilization. Having received a negative answer, the ambassador then presented a declaration of war.

Throughout the crisis, France had pressed Britain for a clear statement of support, but without result. Instead, Sir Edward Grey had asked for assurances from both France and Germany that the international treaty guaranteeing Belgian neutrality would not be violated. France agreed but the Germans avoided a clear answer. On August 2, Germany demanded free passage for its troops through Belgium, but King Albert I (reigned 1909–1934) refused, declaring that "Belgium is a country and not a road." The next day, Grey got an endorsement from the House of Commons to defend Belgian neutrality if it were violated. In the meantime, Germany had declared war on France and its armies were marching. Using an unhappy choice of words to describe the treaty on Belgian neutrality, on August 4 Bethmann-Hollweg expressed his chagrin that Britain would go to war over "a scrap of paper." War between Britain and Germany began at midnight.

For two tension-ridden months, Europe's statesmen had stumbled their way through a mounting crisis. With the failure of the diplomats, the generals now took command. In a mood of deep despondency, Grey gazed out of the window of his London office at the street lights. "The lamps are going out all over Europe," an aide heard him say; "we shall not see them lit again in our lifetime." It is a measure of the bitter irony surrounding these events that Grey did not remember having made that remark.

FIGHTING THE WAR

From the first, the Schlieffen Plan broke down. Belgian resistance slowed the German advance, a British force of 100,000 quickly joined the French Army, and the Russians moved against East Prussia sooner than expected. Surprised by these developments, von Moltke made further changes—instead of retreating on the left flank so as to draw the French away from the real battle zone, German reinforcements were sent to Lorraine. More crucial still, von Moltke weakened the assault against France by withdrawing troops from the West to halt the Russian attack.

As the Germans advanced to within 30 miles of Paris, General Joseph Joffre (1852–1931), the French commander-in-chief, retreated in orderly fashion. In September, Joffre counterattacked along the Marne River, pushing the Germans back. Once the Germans halted, however, the front line stabilized. Following the Battle of the Marne, each side tried unsuccessfully to outflank the other by moving northward around the enemy in what has been called the "race to the sea"—when that tactic failed, the combatants moved southward, so that the front soon consisted of a 400-mile line stretching from the North Sea to Switzerland. For

Significant Dates

The Great War

August 1914	Outbreak of war
September 1914	Failure of Schlieffen Plan
November 1914	Turkey joins Central Powers
April 1915	Chlorine gas used at Ypres
May 1915	Italy joins Allies; *Lusitania* sunk
1916	Battles of Verdun and the Somme
March 1917	Russian Revolution; November, Bolshevik coup
1917–1918	Offenses on Western front
April 1917	U.S. joins Allies
November 11, 1918	Armistice
January 1919	Paris Peace Conference opens
June 28, 1919	Treaty of Versailles

DOCUMENTS ON HISTORY

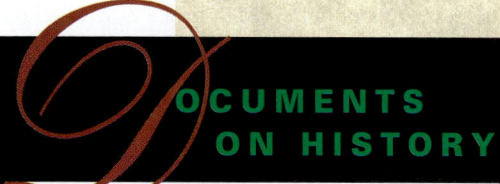

World War I: Who Was Responsible?

Ever since the outbreak of World War I in August 1914, diplomats, politicians, and scholars have debated the question of responsibility: did the blame for the war rest on one country, as the Allies claimed for Germany, or did some or all of the European powers share responsibility collectively? Were the causes of the war systemic—that is, was it the result of the kind of diplomatic system that prevailed in Europe, with its secret military alliances? Did the clash of imperial interests globally contribute to the war, or did the arms race and the influence of military industrialists bring about the disaster? At the time, each of the major states involved in the war issued its own diplomatic documents, and later statesmen and generals published their memoirs, all in an effort to explain the causes of the war in a way that would be advantageous to their own nations or to their personal interests. The selection of documents that follows may shed some light on the vexing question and on the difficulties of sifting historical truth out of official records.

WAR GUILT AND THE VERSAILLES TREATY

Although diplomats were aware of the importance of responsibility while the events were unfolding, it was with the formulation of Article 231 of the Treaty of Versailles—the famous "war guilt" clause—that the entire blame for the war was forced on Germany and its wartime allies:

The Allied and Associated Governments affirm and Germany accepts the responsibility of Germany and her allies for causing all the loss and damage to which the Allied and Associated Governments and their nationals have been subjected as a consequence of the war imposed upon them by the aggression of Germany and her allies.

From Alexander Baltzly and A. William Salomone, eds., *Readings in Twentieth-Century European History,* Appleton-Century-Crofts, Copyright © 1950.

After the outbreak of the war, the major powers published collections of official documents designed to prove their innocence in bringing about the conflict. The following selection of documents is designed to suggest the complexity of the "war guilt" question.

THE GERMAN RESPONSE

On July 5, 1914, Count A. Hoyos of the Austrian Foreign Ministry and Ambassador Count L. de Szogyény saw Kaiser Wilhelm in Berlin, where they asked whether they could count on German support if Austria took strong action against Serbia. The next day, Theobald von Bethmann-Hollweg, German foreign minister, described the kaiser's response to his ambassador, Heinrich von Tschirschky, in Vienna:

Finally, as regards Serbia, His Majesty, of course, cannot take any position in regard to the questions pending between that country and Austria-Hungary, as they are outside his authority. But Emperor Francis Joseph can rely on His Majesty's taking his stand loyally at the side of Austria-Hungary in accordance with his duties as an ally and his old friendship.

Quoted in Luigi Albertini, *The Origins of the War of 1914*, trans. I. M. Massey, II. Oxford University Press. Copyright © 1952.

AUSTRIA-HUNGARY'S ULTIMATUM TO SERBIA

During conversations in Vienna as to the nature of the Austro-Hungarian response to Serbia, Austrian Foreign Minister Count Leopold Berchtold told German Ambassador Heinrich von Tschirschky that he would advise Emperor Franz Josef "so to formulate these demands that their acceptance appears impossible." When Russian Foreign Minister Sergei Sazonov heard the text of the ultimatum (technically the Austrians called it a "timed note" rather than an ultimatum), he exclaimed, "This means a European war." The following terms were presented to Serbia on July 23:

The Royal Servian Government further undertakes:

1. To suppress any publication which incites to hatred and contempt of the Austro-Hungarian Monarchy and the general tendency of which is directed against its territorial integrity;
2. To dissolve immediately the society called Narodna Odbrana [The People's Defense], to confiscate all its means of propaganda, and to proceed in the same manner against all other secret societies and their branches in Servia which engage in propaganda against the Austro-Hungarian Monarchy. . . .
3. To eliminate without delay from public instruction in Servia, both as regards the teaching body and the methods of instruction, everything that serves, or might serve, to foment the propaganda against Austria-Hungary;
4. To remove from the military service, and from the administration in general, all officers and functionaries guilty of propaganda against the Austro-Hungarian Monarchy whose names and deeds the Austro-Hungarian Government reserves the right of communicating to the Royal Government;
5. To accept the cooperation in Servia of representatives of the Austro-Hungarian Government in the suppression of the subversive movement directed against the territorial integrity of the Monarchy;
6. To take judicial proceedings against accomplices in the plot of the 28th of June who are on Servian territory. Delegates of the Austro-Hungarian Government will take part in the investigation relating thereto;
7. To proceed without delay to the arrest of Major Voja Tankositch and of the individual named Milan Ciganovitch, a Servian State employee, who have been compromised by the results of the preliminary investigation at Sarajevo;
8. To prevent by effective measures the participation of the Servian authorities in the illicit traffic in arms and explosives across the frontier; to dismiss and punish severely the officials of the frontier service at Schabatz and Loznica who have been guilty of having assisted the perpetrators of the Sarajevo

continued next page

crime by facilitating their passage across the frontier;

9. To furnish the Imperial and Royal Government with explanations regarding the unjustifiable utterances of high Servian officials, both in Servia and abroad, who, notwithstanding their official positions, did not hesitate after the crime of the 28th of June to give utterance, in published interviews, to expressions of hostility to the Austro-Hungarian Government; and finally
10. To notify the Imperial and Royal Government without delay of the execution of the measures comprised under the preceding heads.

The Austro-Hungarian Government awaits the reply of the Royal Government at the latest by 6 o'clock on Saturday evening, the 25th of July.

James Brown Scott, ed., *Diplomatic Documents Relating to the Outbreak of the European War,* Part I. Oxford University Press. Copyright © 1916.

THE FRENCH RESPONSE

French President Raymond Poincaré and Foreign Minister René Viviani had been in St. Petersburg on an official visit in late July, and the Austrians had deliberately waited until after their departure before submitting the ultimatum to Serbia. On July 24, Maurice Paléologue, French ambassador in St. Petersburg, gave a luncheon for the English ambassador and Sazonov, and later wrote in his memoirs that he had said the following to his guests:

. . . I had no hesitation in advocating a policy of firmness.

'But suppose that policy is bound to lead to war?' said Sazonov.

'It will only lead to war if the Germanic powers have already made up their minds to resort to force to secure the hegemony of the East. Firmness does not exclude conciliation. But it is essential for the other side to be prepared to negotiate and compromise. You know my own views as to Germany's designs. The Austrian ultimatum seems to me to provoke the dangerous crisis I have anticipated for a long time. Henceforth we must recognize that war may break out at any moment. That prospect must govern all our diplomatic action.'

The English ambassador, Sir George Buchanan, reported to London the following:

The French Ambassador gave me to understand that France would not only give Russia strong diplomatic support but would, if necessary, fulfil all the obligations imposed on her by the alliance.

Paléologue, *An Ambassador's Memoirs,* 3 vols.

BRITISH RESPONSE TO THE CRISIS

Sir Edward Grey, British foreign secretary, consistently took a rather detached and almost fatalistic attitude toward the unfolding diplomatic crisis. On July 24—a day on which the cabinet spent almost all its time discussing the Irish problem rather than the diplomatic crisis—he told German Ambassador Lichnowsky that Britain was in no position to rein in its Russian ally following the Austro-Hungarian ultimatum:

I said that if the Austrian ultimatum to Servia did not lead to trouble between Austria and Russia I had no concern with it; . . . I was very apprehensive of the view Russia would take of the situation. I reminded the German Ambassador that some days ago he had expressed a personal hope that if need arose I would endeavor to exercise moderating influence at St. Petersburg, but now I said that, in view of the extraordinarily stiff character of the

Austrian note, the shortness of the time allowed, and the wide scope of the demands upon Servia, I felt quite helpless as far as Russia was concerned, and I did not believe any Power could exercise influence alone.

The only chance I could see of mediating or moderating influence being effective, was that the four Powers, Germany, Italy, France and ourselves, should work together simultaneously at Vienna and St. Petersburg. . . .

The immediate danger was that in a few hours Austria might march into Servia and Russian Slav opinion demand that Russia should march to help Servia; it would be very desirable to get Austria not to precipitate military action and so to gain more time. But none of us could influence Austria in this direction unless Germany would propose and participate in such action at Vienna.

From *British Documents on the Origins of the World War, 1898-1914,* ed. by G.P. Gooch and Harold Temperly, Vol. II. Copyright © 1938.

The Serbs rejected outright only the sixth clause of the ultimatum, and the kaiser thought that their carefully worded response made war avoidable—"every reason for war drops away. . . . On the strength of this, I should never have ordered mobilization." Nevertheless, on July 26 General Helmuth von Moltke, chief of the German General Staff, drafted for his files an ultimatum demanding free passage for German troops through Belgian territory. When Austria-Hungary declared war against Serbia on July 28, Moltke wrote a memorandum to the German chancellor on the military necessity for swift action, and the next day he sent the Belgian ultimatum, sealed inside two envelopes, to the German Embassy in Brussels with orders to be opened only upon instructions from Berlin. Here is Moltke's memorandum:

Austria, if she enters Serbia, will be faced not only with the Serbian Army but with strong Russian superiority; she will thus not be able to wage war with Serbia without making Russian intervention certain. That means she will be forced to mobilize the other half of her army, for she cannot possibly put herself at the mercy of a Russia ready for war. The instant Austria mobilizes her whole army, the clash between her and Russia will become inevitable. Now that is for Germany the *causus foederis*. Unless Germany means to break her word and allow her ally to succumb to Russian superior strength, she must also mobilize. That will lead to the mobilization of the remaining Russian military districts. Russia will then be able to say, "I am being attacked by Germany" and that will make her sure of the support of France who is bound by treaty to go to war if her ally Russia is attacked. The Franco-Russian agreement, so often praised as a purely defensive alliance brought about only to meet German plans of aggression, comes thereby into operation and the civilized states of Europe will begin to tear one another to pieces. . . .

From Helmuth von Moltke, *Essays, Speeches, and Memoirs of Field Marshal Helmuth von Moltke,* J. R. Osgood McLlvane and Company. Copyright © 1893.

THE RUSSIAN DECISION TO MOBILIZE

The Russians, who responded to the Austrian declaration of war with alarm, had two military contingencies. They could declare partial mobilization for operations along the Austro-Hungarian frontier, or general mobilization along both the Austro-Hungarian and the German borders. Tsar Nicholas II signed both edicts and on July 29–30 shifted back and forth twice between ordering general and then partial mobilization. But Russian military commanders put increasing pressure on Foreign Minister Sazonov and the tsar, pointing out that partial mobilization would jeopardize Russia's ability to carry out general mobilization in the event of an enemy declaration of war. The following account of the fateful meeting with

continued next page

Nicholas on July 30 is from the memoirs of Baron von Schilling, head of the Chancery of the Russian Ministry of Foreign Affairs:

During the course of nearly an hour the Minister [Sazonov] proceeded to show that war was becoming inevitable, as it was clear to everybody that Germany had decided to bring about a collision, as otherwise she would not have rejected all the pacificatory proposals that had been made. . . . Therefore it was necessary to put away any fears that our warlike preparations would bring about a war and to continue these preparations carefully, rather than by reason of such fears to be taken unawares by war.

The firm desire of the Tsar to avoid war at all costs, the horrors of which filled him with repulsion, led His Majesty . . . to explore every possible means for averting the approaching danger. Consequently he refused during a long time to agree to the adoption of measures which, however indispensable from a military point of view, were calculated, as he clearly saw, to hasten a decision in an undesirable sense. . . .

Finally the Tsar agreed that in the existing circumstances it would be very dangerous not to make timely preparations for what was apparently an inevitable war, and therefore gave his decision in favour of an immediate general mobilization.

On Friday, July 31, Germany presented two ultimatums: one to Russia that it would mobilize unless the tsar suspended all military operations within twelve hours; and one to France asking whether Paris would remain neutral in the event of a German-Russian war and, if so, to permit German occupation of French frontier fortresses. At five P.M. *on Saturday, having received no answer from either the Russians or the French, the Germans began mobilization. An hour later, the German ambassador in St. Petersburg handed the Russians the text of their declaration of war.*

the remainder of the war, the Western front hardly moved more than a few miles in either direction.

Stalemate in the West

The Battle of the Marne shattered German hopes for a quick victory. General Erich von Falkenhayn (1861–1922) replaced von Moltke as chief of staff. For the next four years, each side slaughtered the other repeatedly in futile attempts to wear the enemy down and achieve a breakthrough. Despite some differences in military and industrial capability, the Allies and the Central Powers were each sufficiently strong to prevent victory or defeat.

The assumptions behind modern military strategy collapsed as armies constructed a web of trenches that eventually measured a combined length of 25,000 miles. These trench systems were cordoned by miles of barbed wire, with a fearful "no man's land" dividing them. Behind the trenches, a vast transportation network moved millions of soldiers and hundreds of millions of tons of equipment in preparation for assaults. To all except the generals who commanded the front, the principal tactic adopted by both sides was horrific in its simplicity: long-range artillery pounded the enemy for days. Then, at a prearranged moment, officers led the infantry soldiers out of the trenches to attack. Machine guns cut them down as they scrambled through exploding shells that blasted craters in the earth and filled the air with dirt and smoke. Eighty percent of all casualties were caused in this manner—between August and November 1914 alone, more than 1,640,000.

The Great War produced few "heroes" in the traditional sense of the word. Each assault caused tens of thousands to die anonymously on the battlefields, while millions more huddled in the trenches amid mud, slime, and the stench of rotting corpses. New weapons, such as poison gas and tanks, were employed—the

British soldiers leaving the trenches for a night attack.

Germans first used chlorine gas at Ypres in April 1915, and the Allies responded in kind—but it failed to prove decisive and only introduced a fiendish element into the conflict. Yet the generals refused to see the futility of their tactics, instead waging a war of attrition.

This war attained grotesque dimensions in 1916. The Germans deliberately sought to bleed the French into defeat by unleashing a major assault on Verdun. They correctly expected the French to defend the fortress at any price. More than 1 million German artillery shells fell on Verdun on February 21, the opening day of the attack. In August, daily German casualties began to exceed French losses and the kaiser replaced von Falkenhayn with General Paul von Hindenburg (1847–1934), who had been called out of retirement to command the Eastern front. When the siege was finally lifted in December, 700,000 had died—600,000 French soldiers and 100,000 Germans.

The most fearsome battle of the Great War, which began while Verdun was still under siege, took place along the Somme River. General Douglas Haig (1861–1928), the British commander, had for some

A French soldier shot while advancing from the trenches.

Map 1.4 The Great War, 1914–1918

time planned a "big push" at the Somme, and the bloodletting at Verdun failed to dissuade him. The British first pounded the Germans with an immense artillery attack that began on June 24, sublimely confident that the three-quarters of a million soldiers they had amassed would then be able to occupy the enemy trenches. But when the offensive opened on July 1, the damage to German installations proved to be superficial: 20,000 British were killed and 40,000 wounded.

Haig refused to call off the battle, which raged on throughout the summer. In September, for the first time, he used tanks, which the British had been developing, but they proved unreliable. A snowstorm ended the Somme offensive in November, but not before the blood of more than 1 million had soaked the battlefields: Haig's "big push" had cost the British and French 600,000 casualties, and the Germans 500,000. When David Lloyd George (1863–1945) became prime minister in 1916, he tried to end these costly offenses but gave in when Sir William Robertson (1860–1933), chief of the Imperial General Staff and a man with powerful political and newspaper connections, insisted that they continue.

Crisis in the East

In the East, the imbalance between the combatants and the huge space over which supplies and armies had to move prevented the kind of stalemate that had bogged down the fighting on the Western front. When the war broke out, the Russians had moved against Germany before completing mobilization and achieved a surprise advantage in East Prussia. It was at that point that von Moltke had shifted four divisions from the Western theater to stop the Russians.

Rather than fighting the numerically larger Russian forces along all points, Hindenburg, who had taken command of the Eastern front with General Erich Ludendorff (1865–1937) as his deputy, chose to take on sections of the Russian armies individually. In this way, they won an important engagement at the Battle of Tannenberg, where the Germans took over 100,000 prisoners, and another at the Masurian Lakes. By the time the Battle of the Marne had been determined in the West, the Russian "steam roller" had been stopped. Farther to the south, along the Austro-Hungarian front, Germany's principal ally was less successful, for the Russians drove through Galicia and invaded Hungary. In the Balkans, the Austrians also experienced reverses as the Serbs repulsed their armies and retook Belgrade. By the end of 1914, the results of the fighting on the Eastern front were therefore equally inconclusive.

Turkey's declaration of war against the Allies in November 1914 seriously weakened Russia's position. Tensions between the two countries, already sharp, were exacerbated by the presence of the Armenians, a Christian people living on both sides of the Russo-Turkish border. The Armenians had suffered centuries of persecution by both the Russians and the Turks. In 1915, after failing to secure their support against Russia in the war effort, the Turks forcibly relocated the Armenians in the Anatolian interior. In the process, more than a million Armenians died of disease, starvation, and slaughter.

Upon entering the war, the Turks closed the Dardanelles Straits in order to stop vital supplies from reaching Russia. In March 1915, British and French naval forces attempted to open the straits, but the plan failed. In April, the Allies landed along the Gallipoli peninsula, which juts out from the southern coast of European Turkey and guards the straits, but the Turks were able to trap the invading forces below from their higher ground. After suffering great losses, the expedition was recalled.

In the spring of 1915, von Falkenhayn launched a major offensive against the Russians. The Germans pierced the Russian line and moved forward, taking Warsaw and pushing east from the foothills of the Carpathian Mountains. Because the Russians lacked machine guns and heavy artillery, the offensive cost them some 2,500,000 men killed, wounded, or taken prisoner.

The Allied position was strengthened in May 1915 by Italy's declaration of war against Austria-Hungary. The previous month, Italy had concluded a secret agreement with the Allies that ended months of bitter domestic debate over the war. In return for its intervention, the Treaty of London pledged to give Italy the Trentino, the southern Tyrol, Istria, and the city of Trieste, as well as territory along the Dalmatian coast—all territories under Austrian rule. The new front thus opened along the Italian-Austrian border relieved some German pressure against Russia. That October, Bulgaria threw in its lot with the Central Powers, and the following August Romania joined the Allies.

The year 1917 brought major crises to the Allies. In March, revolution broke out in the Russian capital and forced the abdication of Tsar Nicholas (see Part

French troops pass through the ruins of Verdun, 1916.

VIII, Topic 2). A provisional government dominated by Alexander Kerensky (1881–1970) proclaimed a continuation of the war, but the Russian people demanded peace. Convinced that the imminent collapse of Russia would soon end the two-front war, the Germans erected a fortified defense system on the Western front known as the Hindenburg Line. While the German armies waited, the French flung themselves at the Hindenburg Line in April in a wasted effort that cost 250,000 casualties. Between July and November, Haig led another huge assault at Ypres, but the fighting in the muddy fields of Flanders resulted in an additional 300,000 British casualties.

THE HOME FRONT

The Great War placed tremendous stress on society. Europeans found it difficult to absorb the psychological impact of the carnage. As each side suffered millions of casualties, the excitement that had greeted the outbreak of war in 1914 turned to horror. At home, morale began to waver under the joint pressures of the fighting and the demands increasingly placed on civilian populations.

Domestic Opposition

The war aroused opposition from pacifists, women's groups, churches, and the left. Almost all the socialist parties, however, had voted for war credits in 1914—only in Italy did they adopt the neutral position of "neither sabotage nor support"—and leaders of churches in belligerent countries rallied to national interests. Governments of national unity brought all major parties into coalitions, including socialists. In August 1917 Pope Benedict XV (ruled 1914–1922) issued an appeal for peace.

As the terrible toll of dead and wounded mounted, opposition took more direct forms. In May 1917, after the failure of a bloody offensive, some French regiments that had suffered heavy casualties ignored orders to attack and revolts broke out in other units. A total of between 30,000 and 40,000 soldiers may have been involved in such incidents, and the French command issued some 400 death sentences against mutineers. One British camp in France experienced a riot, and even the Germans had to deal with individual cases of desertion. During the summer, the crew of one German ship staged a hunger strike to protest the better food rations of their officers. In the Russian Army, chronically short of weapons, uniforms, and food, mutiny and desertion were widespread.

Incidents of civilian revolt were deeply troubling to wartime governments. The British faced a critical problem in Ireland, where support for the war effort clashed with anti-British sentiment. During Easter of 1916, Irish nationalists tried to capitalize on the war to stage a rebellion against British rule. The Irish politician Sir Roger Casement (1864–1918) arranged for the Germans to supply arms to the rebels from a U-boat, but British destroyers intercepted the vessel and Casement was captured. After a week of street fighting, the rebellion was crushed and 15 nationalist leaders, including Casement, were hanged.

The March 1917 revolution in Russia, provoked in part by conditions at the front, sent shock waves throughout Europe. In July, Matthias Erzberger (1875–1921) of the German Center party introduced a peace resolution in the Reichstag. The resolution, which called for a peace based on understanding, and rejected territorial acquisitions achieved by force, passed by a margin of almost two to one. The following month, revolutionary socialists staged an antiwar uprising in the Italian industrial city of Turin. Some 50 workers were killed and 200 wounded when the government used army units to restore order.

Morale on the home front was as vital to victory as the willingness of soldiers to fight. The war made tremendous demands on national economies and the workforce. In order to deal with continued shortages of food and clothing, most nations imposed rationing as well as limited wages and prices, and most labor unions adopted voluntary restraints. Industrial commissions, composed of business and labor leaders, government officials, and experts, directed national production. Every country was caught off guard by the "technical surprise" of the war—that is, the insatiable demand for raw materials and weapons that increased beyond all expectations every day of the fighting. Stock piles of artillery shells, for example, that prewar estimates assumed would last for six months were consumed in a single day at the front.

Women and the War

The wartime economy created an artificial prosperity that greatly affected women. At first, many female workers found themselves unemployed because the demand for consumer goods traditionally made by women, such as dresses and textiles, declined. But the drafting of millions of young men created a labor shortage. By the second year of the war, women were working in heavy industry and munitions plants, and by 1918, perhaps one out of three industrial workers was a woman. Women appeared on streetcars and subways as drivers, ticket takers, and conductors. In addition to the home front, they served in combat zones as ambulance drivers and military nurses, and were active in assisting civilian refugees.

Governments proclaimed female labor essential to the war effort, although they were not always wel-

German women working in a shell factory.

comed by male workers and were paid lower wages. Nor were women taught technical skills beyond those required for their immediate work, for industry and labor unions considered female labor a temporary measure. Many munitions factories provided day care centers for working mothers, but after ten- or twelve-hour shifts, they still had to care for their families.

Yet the war made a great difference in the lives of many women and on how men perceived them. Not only did a great number earn wages for the first time, but they often experienced a degree of social independence that they were unwilling to give up when peace came. Single women appeared in public, attended theaters and ate in restaurants alone, dated more freely, and dressed with fewer constraints. The criticism and ridicule that some working women experienced resulted in part from sexual tensions that accompanied changing female roles. The unprecedented requirements of "total war" made it impossible to maintain a traditional gender separation between the male warrior and the female wife or mother. "Girls are doing things," wrote the poet Nina Macdonald, "They've never done before . . . All the world is topsy-turvey/Since the War began."

Official propaganda attempted to mitigate the impact of the war on gender roles, as in the case of the British nurse Edith Cavell (1865–1915). Volunteer nurses were in high demand because of the terrible casualty rate of trench warfare. These women faced daily the searing psychological experience of dealing with bloodshed, mutilation, and death. Working near the front lines, they, like the soldiers they assisted, confronted serious physical dangers. Although a professional nurse, Cavell was a British patriot who used her position at a Red Cross facility in Belgium to aid captured Allied soldiers. The Germans tried Cavell for espionage and executed her. In Britain, France, and Italy, she provided a powerful symbol of the virtuous, brave woman murdered by an uncivilized enemy. In the wake of Cavell's death, posters were printed portraying monstrous German soldiers raping women and mutilating children. Such propaganda themes played on patriarchal notions of gender roles—by portraying themselves as fighting for the honor of women, the Allies not only presented the enemy in the worst possible light, but reconfirmed the manhood of soldiers at the front. A famous Red Cross poster of 1918, entitled "The Greatest Mother in the World," portrayed a huge nurse, holding a wounded soldier on a stretcher, in the pose of a *pietà*.

Vera Brittain (1893–1970), on the other hand, demonstrated how the wartime experience actually helped her to achieve personal independence. Brittain, who had been studying at Oxford, became a volunteer nurse in London and then in France. Devastated when both her brother and her fiancé were killed at the front, she found herself at first "without confidence or security." Eventually, however, she came to realize that, contrary to what women had been brought up to believe, a man was not essential to personal fulfillment. Instead, she resumed her studies at Oxford after the war, where she developed a deep friendship with Winifred Holtby (1898–1935). Brittain and Holtby inspired each other and both eventually became noted writers.

A propaganda cartoon portraying the German execution of English nurse Edith Cavell.

Civilian Populations and Total War

Inevitably, society became regimented under the pressures of the war. Governments demanded complete loyalty and dedication from all citizens in order to wage total war. Civilians were subjected to military requirements, which took precedence over matters not essential to the war effort. Fundamental legal rights, such as freedom of the press and habeas corpus, were set aside. Generals wielded more authority than civilians in government deliberations. In Germany, General Ludendorff practically dictated domestic policy until 1918. Political leaders asked their populations for more and more sacrifices, and to justify the steadily mounting cost in lives and money, governments developed war aims that stressed lofty ideals such as democracy, justice, and permanent peace.

Domestic propaganda created the impression that class differences diminished as all social groups pulled together for the general good. Working-class women rolled bandages together with duchesses; businessmen and labor leaders served together on production committees; and in the trenches peasants died along with intellectuals and shopkeepers. Peasants comprised the majority of all draftees, whereas officers came from the upper classes. Because lieutenants and captains were the first out of the trenchees in assaults against the enemy, the casualty rate among social élites was disproportionately high. In most armies, lower-rank officers and drafted soldiers tended to work together in the face of common peril.

In the war of attrition, great stress was put on efforts to undermine enemy civilian resistance. Cities of no military significance were bombed by long-range artillery and Zeppelins, and blockades attempted to keep food, medicines, and other vital supplies from reaching the enemy. Turkey's control of the Dardanelles Straits severely restricted Russia's access to Allied supplies, and Britain's dominance of the sea was effective in cutting off Germany and Austria-Hungary from much maritime trade. France and Britain, on the other hand, had access to American and other overseas sources of food and matériel, even during the height of submarine warfare. Germany was the first to adopt a ration system, and most of the other belligerents followed suit. In the so-called "Turnip Winter" of 1916–1917, when frigid temperatures and the naval blockade created extreme food shortages, many Germans lived at the edge of starvation.

THE WORLD CONFLICT

The conflict widened steadily as more nations intervened and, alongside the main theater of operations in Europe, a peripheral war was fought in the Middle East, Africa, and the Pacific. In 1917, the balance of power among the belligerents finally shifted as the United States abandoned its neutrality and joined the Allied cause.

The Global Dimensions of War

The military outcome of the Great War was to be determined in Europe, but both sides were concerned about global strategic issues. Britain was especially interested in the Middle East because of the importance of the Suez Canal to its Indian realm, and tried to wrest control of the region from the Turks.

After their failure to seize Baghdad in November 1915, the British sought to foment a revolt against the Turks by openly encouraging Arab independence. They supported Hussein ibn-Ali (1856–1931), of the Holy City of Mecca, who declared himself ruler of an Arab kingdom embracing the region between the Red Sea and the Persian Gulf. Hussein raised an army in 1916 and declared a holy war against the Ottoman Empire. At the same time, however, the French and the British planned to divide the Middle East between themselves. The Sykes-Picot Agreement, named after British diplomat Mark Sykes and French diplomat Georges Picot, stipulated that Lebanon and Syria would come under French authority, and that Palestine and Iraq would fall within the British sphere. In 1917, the archeologist T. E. Lawrence (1888–1935), then a British officer, worked with Hussein's son, Prince Faisal (1885–1933), in organizing an Arab Army. Together, Hussein and "Lawrence of Arabia" succeeded in taking Jerusalem and Damascus. Despite Britain's pro-Arab stance, however, in November 1917 Foreign Secretary Arthur Balfour angered Arab leaders when he announced support for the Zionist goal of establishing a Jewish state in Palestine.

The British also occupied the German colonies of South-West Africa (Namibia) and Togoland (Togo). The Germans managed, however, to keep the Allies busy in German East Africa (Tanzania) until 1918, using local African recruits to wage a guerrilla campaign. In Asia, the British believed their interests were endangered by their Japanese allies, who immediately occupied the German islands in the north Pacific. To prevent further Japanese expansion, troops from New Zealand and Australia seized Samoa and New Guinea. In 1917 the Chinese government also joined the Allied cause, yet when Japan ousted the Germans from the port of Tsingtao, it refused to return the stronghold to China.

The United States and the European War

Public opinion in the United States was divided over the war, but President Woodrow Wilson's (served 1913–1921) own sentiments leaned toward Britain, although publicly he argued for strict neutrality. In the end, it was Germany's reliance on the submarine that acted as the catalyst for American intervention.

International law proscribed attacking neutral ships not carrying war contraband. In 1915, however, each side attempted illegally to keep all goods from reaching the other, although only the British blockade proved to be effective. Germany's U-boat fleet was a powerful weapon in this campaign, but submarines sank enemy ships by underwater torpedo, not by surface battle, and could not lose the advantage of surprise in order to determine whether a vessel's cargo contained war matériel. As a result, unarmed merchant ships as well as citizens of neutral countries fell victim to U-boat attacks, which caused significant shipping losses.

The United States reacted sharply against the U-boat campaign, especially after more than a hundred Americans were among the almost 1200 passengers killed when the Germans sank the British passenger liner *Lusitania* in May 1915. The crisis caused a debate inside the German government, with Chancellor Bethmann-Hollweg arguing for a cessation of submarine warfare and Admiral von Tirpitz insisting that it was Germany's only chance for victory.

In September 1915, the kaiser limited submarine operations, but he was finally convinced that the military advantage of submarine warfare outweighed the danger of antagonizing American opinion. In late January 1917, Wilhelm therefore ordered unrestricted U-boat attacks to be resumed. During February, the U-boats destroyed 781,500 tons of Allied shipping.

In protest, President Wilson severed formal ties with Germany on February 3, 1917. Toward the end of that month, the British passed on to American authorities an intercepted coded telegram from a German Foreign Ministry official, Arthur Zimmermann (1864–1940), to the German minister in Mexico. The Zimmermann telegram proposed an alliance between Mexico and Germany in the event of American belligerency, with Mexico receiving Texas, New Mexico, and Arizona as its compensation. Wilson's outrage reached the breaking point in March 1917, when the Germans torpedoed two American ships. By the end of the month, an additional 500,000 tons of Allied shipping had been lost. On April 2, he asked for a declaration of war against Germany, which Congress passed overwhelmingly four days later.

General John J. Pershing (1860–1948), commanding the American Expeditionary Force (AEF), brought the first U.S. troops to France in July. The contribution of the United States to the Allied cause came in the form of industrial supplies as well as soldiers. American intervention also struck an important blow for morale at a critical moment. In March, Russia had been shaken by revolution; that October, Italy was almost overrun by the Central Powers during the disastrous rout of Caporetto, and lost a half-million soldiers in their efforts to halt the enemy at the Piave River; in November, the Bolshevik coup augured the eventual withdrawal of Russia from the war.

At the beginning of 1918, President Wilson declared the famous "Fourteen Points," which he believed would provide the basis for a permanent peace—hence, the slogan, "the war to end all wars." Wilson's goals included elimination of the arms race and secret diplomacy, adherence to the principle of self-determination for all peoples, and freedom of the seas. One legacy he left to the future would be the idea of a world organization, known later as the League of Nations, designed to preserve peace.

PEACE AND ITS CONSEQUENCES

While Wilson issued the Fourteen Points, Germany still planned for a decisive breakthrough on the battlefield. Teenagers were being called up as its manpower was depleted, and the supply of food and equipment

Map 1.5 The Peace Settlements

grew critically short. Moreover, on January 28, 400,000 Berlin workers stopped working to demand peace and democracy, and the strike spread to other industrial cities. On the other hand, Russia finally withdrew from the war in March 1918 after Germany and the Bolshevik regime concluded the Treaty of Brest-Litovsk (see Part VIII, Topic 2).

Germany Sues for Peace

The end of the fighting on the Eastern front allowed General Ludendorff to strengthen German forces in the West and to attempt a large offensive against the Allies. The last-ditch attack, initiated on March 21, succeeded at first in pushing the enemy back to the Marne. By June, however, the Allies, now reinforced by large numbers of American soldiers, broke the advance and shattered all hopes for a German victory. In mid-July, the Allies counterattacked.

In September 1918, General Ludendorff reluctantly told the Crown Council that German forces had to go on the defensive, and by the end of the following month they were in retreat along most of the Western front.

A new, more liberal German government was formed in late September under Prince Max of Baden (served as chancellor October–November 1918), who then asked Wilson for armistice terms derived from the Fourteen Points. The American president, however, insisted that Kaiser Wilhelm abdicate before an armistice was concluded. During the weeks that followed, Germany's allies withdrew from the war and a full-scale mutiny among German sailors at Kiel sparked revolutions in Berlin and elsewhere. Still the kaiser vacillated, until on November 9, Prince Max forced the issue by publicly announcing the abdication. Wilhelm II left secretly the next day for the Netherlands, where he spent the rest of his days in exile. In Berlin, a republic was declared and Social Democratic leader Friedrich Ebert (1871–1925) took the reins of government (see Part VIII, Topic 2). The armistice agreement, concluded in a railway car at Compiègne, went into effect at 11 A.M. on November 11, 1918. The Great War was over.

The Politics of Peace Making

The armistice ended the fighting, but technically the great powers still remained at war until peace treaties were signed. The making of peace proved to be difficult because the price of war had been so high. Almost three dozen nations had fought in the Great War. Some 11 million people—soldiers and civilians—had been killed as a direct result of the fighting, and 20 million were wounded or disabled; countless others died of disease, starvation, and forced relocation. The monetary costs of the conflict forced Europe to reverse its former position as a capital exporter: henceforth, the United States was Europe's creditor. The economic transition to peace was made more difficult by the fact that widespread physical destruction had weakened Europe's capacity to produce food and industrial goods.

Wartime propaganda raised public expectations that both domestic governments and the peacemakers were unable to fulfill. National interests and broad Wilsonian principles clashed at the conference table, despite the fact that both sides had agreed to make peace on the basis of the Fourteen Points. Moreover, the generally conservative mood of the victorious nations stood in sharp contrast to the radical revolution unfolding in Russia.

The international conference called to make peace gathered in Paris in January 1919. It included delegates from some three dozen states as well as leaders hoping to gain recognition from the great powers, such as Prince Faisal and his Arab delegation. The immediate purpose of the Paris Peace Conference was, of course, to arrange peace treaties with the defeated Central Powers and their allies.

Not since the Congress of Vienna of 1814–1815 had so many heads of state and their ministers assembled in one place to discuss common problems. In a dramatic departure from America's isolationist past, Woodrow Wilson crossed the Atlantic to argue for the ideals he had publicly declared. His erstwhile colleagues were experienced and shrewd statesmen—French Premier Georges Clemenceau (1841–1929), British Prime Minister David Lloyd George (1863–1945), and Italian Prime Minister Vittorio E. Orlando (1860–1952). Each leader was accompanied by a staff of advisers and experts in matters ranging from economics and international law to linguistics and cartography.

Despite the rhetoric of democracy that marked Allied propaganda, decision making at the Paris Peace Conference operated according to traditional

The Big Four at the Paris Peace Conference—V. E. Orlando, Lloyd George, Georges Clemenceau, and Woodrow Wilson.

principles of power politics. An informal executive group of the "Big Five"—the United States, Britain, France, Italy, and Japan—was supposed to settle basic positions, but in reality both Italy and Japan were excluded from the inner core of the "Big Three," consisting of Clemenceau, Lloyd George, and Wilson. Their ideological antipathy to Communism led them to exclude the new Bolshevik regime in Russia from the conference, and public opinion among their political constituencies at home demanded that the Germans not be accorded equal status with the other participants. The new German republican government was invited, therefore, merely to send observers. Peace would be dictated to the defeated enemy, not negotiated.

The Peace Treaties and the League of Nations

Discussions surrounding the German question divided the Allies from the outset, and the final settlement with Germany—the Treaty of Versailles—represented an unhappy compromise. The French, painfully aware of the experiences of both 1870 and 1914, wanted to carve an independent state out of German territory in the Rhineland that would protect France's eastern border against attack. Clemenceau and Wilson clashed head-on over this issue, the American president insisting that the French proposal ran counter to the spirit of self-determination. They finally reached a compromise, one that the French accepted reluctantly and that proved in the long run to be unworkable. In return for an American commitment to sign a military alliance with France, Clemenceau agreed that Germany would be forbidden to keep a military force in the Rhineland and in an area 50 kilometers east of the Rhine River. The Allies would occupy this "demilitarized" region for a period of 15 years. The coal mines and factories of the Rhineland's Saar district formed part of the arrangement, for Britain and France wanted to use these economic resources to offset the huge debt they had incurred to the United States. The Allies agreed that during their occupation, the newly founded League of Nations would administer the Saarland in order to ensure the delivery of fixed amounts of goods and raw materials to them.

Although Germany did not permanently lose the Rhineland, it did lose other territories. In the west, France received the provinces of Alsace and part of Lorraine, which Germany had taken from it in 1871, and Belgium obtained several strategic towns and fortresses. In eastern Europe, where the Allies created a series of new independent states, Germany lost additional territory: Poland received portions of East Prussia and Upper Silesia, and the port city of Danzig (now Gdansk, Poland) was made a free city under League of Nations authority. From territory formerly in the Austro-Hungarian empire, Czechoslovakia was given the German-speaking area of Bohemia known as the Sudetenland. Because the new state of Austria consisted chiefly of the German-speaking portion of the old Hapsburg empire, there was considerable sentiment both in Germany and Austria for a union (known in German as *Anschluss*) between the two countries. In November, the provisional Austrian assembly declared itself to be a part of Germany, but the Allies expressly prohibited *Anschluss*.

These territorial losses clearly implied that the Allies held Germany responsible for the war, as did the economic provisions of the settlement, which required Germany to pay reparations for costs inflicted on Allied

The signing of the Treaty of Versailles.

civilians. The concept of responsibility was directly incorporated into the peace treaty with Germany in the form of Article 231. This "war guilt" clause made Germany liable for all financial losses suffered by the Allies "as a consequence of the war imposed upon them by the aggression of Germany and her allies." Reparations were eventually set at 35 billion dollars.

The Versailles Treaty also imposed rigid military restrictions on Germany. The army was limited to 100,000 volunteer officers and soldiers, and the General Staff and all officer-training schools were eliminated. The navy was permitted a few ships under 10,000 tons and no submarines. Offensive weapons, such as tanks, long-range artillery, military airplanes, and chemical weapons, were similarly forbidden.

The Treaty of Versailles was both unconventional and unusually harsh. Contrary to any precedent in international affairs, the Allies charged Kaiser Wilhelm with war crimes and demanded a trial, although the Dutch government granted him political asylum. Then, too, the unstated purpose of the peace settlement was clearly to destroy Germany's status as a first-rank world power, but the statesmen at Paris failed to consider the human suffering it would cause or its long-range political impact. In 1919 one prominent British expert at the conference, John Maynard Keynes (1883–1946), denounced the Versailles Treaty in a book entitled *The Economic Consequences of the Peace*. Keynes warned that the economic provisions of the treaty would make Germany unstable and endanger the peace, arguing that the reparations payments were unreasonable because of the loss of coal and iron deposits as well as other vital assets that Germany was forced to sustain (on Keynesian economic theory see Part VIII, Topic 3).

The text of the Versailles Treaty was made known just as the infant German republic was struggling to establish itself against serious odds. When the Germans balked at the terms, the Allies said they would continue to fight. On June 28, 1919, two German political leaders, Hermann Muller of the Majority Socialists and Johannes Bell of the Center party, signed the document in the Hall of Mirrors of the Versailles Palace.

The Paris Peace Conference completely recast Eastern Europe, including the Balkan region where the Great War had begun. The Dual Monarchy was dismantled in conformity with the notion of self-determination (see Part VIII, Topic 5). In addition to Poland, created from former German, Austro-Hungarian, and Russian territory, Austria and Hungary—both considerably reduced in size—became separate states, as did Czechoslovakia. The new nation of Yugoslavia was created out of the former states of Serbia and Montenegro and the provinces of Bosnia, Herzegovina, Slovenia, and Croatia. Greece was enlarged at the expense of Bulgaria and Turkey, the latter retaining a small area around Istanbul and Asia Minor itself. Although Turkey kept control of the Dardanelles, they were henceforth open to the peacetime commerce of all nations.

When Woodrow Wilson first suggested the idea for a League of Nations, the other Allied statesmen had not given it an enthusiastic reception. Wilson persisted, however, and the League's charter (known as the Covenant) was included as an integral part of the individual treaties. The League sought to preserve peace through collective security, largely by providing a forum for discussion and arbitration. The League had limited authority in administering international agreements, as in the case of the free city of Danzig and the Saarland. Through the mandate system, it also supervised the administration of Germany's former colonies by France and Britain, which were to prepare the mandates for independence.

Serious weaknesses doomed the League from the start. It could fight aggression only with the moral force of its decisions, for it could not enforce even its economic sanctions against sovereign nations. Germany and Russia were not invited to join the international body, and despite Wilson's key role in its conception, the U.S. Congress rejected the Treaty of Versailles and membership in the League.

The Great War vastly changed the nature and focus of international power. Europe's economy never fully recovered from the physical destruction to farmland and factories, the dislocation of trade, and the draining of its resources. Nor did the European psyche, deeply wounded by the trauma of a war of attrition, regain its equilibrium. In politics, the impact of the war was equally devastating. Even before peace was restored, three historic empires—Russia, Austria-Hungary, and Germany—had collapsed. Within a few years, the world's first socialist government had been established by Lenin in Russia and the first fascist state in Italy by Mussolini. Britain and France, once the dominant Western powers, never regained their former positions of world influence, for their hold on their imperial domains steadily weakened and the United States began to emerge as the arbiter of world affairs. The Great War was truly the great divide in European history.

Questions for Further Study

1. Is the question of "responsibility" for the war a useful one for historians?
2. How would you describe the causes of the war?
3. In what ways was the fighting in World War I different from that of previous wars?

4. How did the war affect social conditions behind the lines?
5. Was the Paris Peace Conference a success or a failure?

Suggestions for Further Reading

Evans, R. J. W., and H. P. von Strandmann, eds. *The Coming of the First World War*. New York, 1989.

Fussell, Paul. *The Great War and Modern Memory*. New York, 1975.

Higgonet, Margaret R., J. Jenson, S. Michel, and M. C. Weitz, eds. *Behind the Lines: Gender and the Two World Wars*. New Haven, CT, 1987.

Hynes, Samuel. *A War Imagined: The First World War and English Culture*. New York, 1991.

Joll, James. *The Origins of the First World War*. London, 1984.

Kocka, Jurgen. *Facing Total War: German Society, 1914–1918*. Cambridge, MA, 1984.

Leed, Eric J. *No Man's Land: Combat and Identity in World War I*. New York, 1979.

Schmitt, Bernadotte E., and H. C. Vederler. *The World in the Crucible, 1914–1919*. New York, 1984.

Travers, Tim. *The Killing Ground: The British Army, the Western Front, and the Emergence of Modern Warfare, 1900–1918*. Boston, 1978.

Williams, John. *The Other Battleground: The Home Fronts*. Chicago, 1972.

Winter, J. M., and R. M. Wall. *The Upheaval of War: Family, Work, and Welfare in Europe, 1914–1918*. New York, 1988.

Wohl, Robert. *The Generation of 1914*. Cambridge, MA, 1979.

VIII

Topic 2

Radical Extremes: The Russian Revolution and the Rise of Fascism

Between 1917 and 1919, Europe experienced a series of events that would shape the course of the 20th century. To the east, imperial Russia was struck by two successive revolutionary upheavals in the spring and fall of 1917 that toppled the centuries-old tsarist autocracy and set in its place the first self-proclaimed socialist state in history. Two years later, in central and southern Europe, events took place that would eventually bear no less far-reaching significance: Italy gave birth to Europe's first Fascist movement, while Germany followed six months later with the founding of the Nazi party.

Russia had been ill-prepared to fight the Great War. After three years of social and economic strain that brought the Russian war effort near to collapse, riots and demonstrations at home forced Tsar Nicholas II to abdicate in March. A provisional government led by liberals took power, first under Prince Georgi Lvov and then under the moderate Alexander Kerensky. Their refusal to take Russia out of the war proved their undoing. In November, V. I. Lenin led his radical Marxists, known as Bolsheviks, in a successful coup against the provisional government.

Lenin proclaimed the founding of the Communist state, eventually called the Union of Soviet Socialist Republics (U.S.S.R.). Over the next three years, after withdrawing Russia from the war, the Bolsheviks struggled to secure their power through a bloody civil war with political opponents and a military campaign against foreign intervention. Upon Lenin's death in 1924, a power struggle ended with the victory of Joseph Stalin, who ruled the Soviet Union as a dictator for 25 years.

In Italy in March 1919, a former socialist and war veteran named Benito Mussolini, once hailed as "Italy's Lenin," created a radical movement of another kind, known as Fascism. Its program combined left-wing and right-wing elements, and it took advantage of the postwar atmosphere of nationalist frustration and the fear of Bolshevik revolution that pervaded Italian political life. Mussolini came to power in 1922 on a wave of systematic violence carried out by his paramilitary "Black Shirt" squads. Three years later, after a major political crisis, Mussolini proclaimed a dictatorship.

In Germany, the fascist seizure of power took longer. There, in September 1919, Adolf Hitler, would-be artist and himself a war veteran, joined and soon dominated the National Socialist German Workers' party. The Nazis, as its members came to be called, capitalized on the political weakness of the new

German state, known as the Weimar Republic, as well as on the economic and social dislocation following Germany's defeat in World War I.

Hitler's propaganda stressed a combination of extreme nationalism, working-class rhetoric, and middle-class values, but the core of his new ideology was a rabid racism that took the form of virulent anti-Semitism. Hitler, too, created a paramilitary organization of "Brown Shirts," which he used against his political enemies. After a failed coup in 1923, it took another decade of political maneuvering, violence, and propaganda, combined with the disaster of the Great Depression, before Hitler came to power in 1933.

REVOLUTION, LEFT AND RIGHT

The upheaval in Russia in 1917 was a revolution on the extreme left, inspired by the theories of Karl Marx and Lenin's Bolshevik political strategies. The fascist revolutions in Italy and Germany began with a blend of socialist and nationalist principles, but by the 1920s, fascism became symbolic of extreme right-wing political values.

Both Bolshevism and fascism entailed revolutionary change. The existing governments fell in a context of social upheaval and civil war. In the aftermath of the revolutionary seizure of power in the countries involved, new political and economic structures were created. Lenin, Mussolini, and Hitler were revolutionary leaders who came from segments of society with hitherto little influence, and who rose to power on a wave of mass support. Each, whether of the left or the right, was a masterful manipulator of public opinion who sought to evoke blind obedience and ideological fervor from his followers. These men represented a new kind of political power, claiming authority from popular will or historical inevitability and maintaining it in part by modern technology and new systems of mass communications. The political movements they brought to power established a new form of government known as totalitarianism. It was characterized by the use of terror and repression to stamp out political opposition and minorities, backed up by educational programs and massive propaganda campaigns designed to impose conformity of thought.

Although inspired by opposite political ideologies, both left-wing and right-wing revolutionaries wanted to create economic systems dominated by state planning and control. Under the Bolsheviks, private property rights were abolished and the state dictated production levels in accordance with socialist principles. In the fascist regimes of Italy and Germany, however, capitalism and private property continued to exist, although they were subject to government regulation.

Between the two world wars, European political life was dominated in large part by the struggle between the ideologies of communism and fascism. Supporters of both camps battled one another in bloody confrontations while simultaneously threatening estab-

Significant Dates

The Russian Revolution

March 8, 1917	Women's march in Petrograd
March 10, 1917	General Strike
March 12, 1917	Provisional government
March 15, 1917	Nicholas II abdicates
March 1917	Petrograd Soviet formed
April 20, 1917	Lenin's "April Theses"
May 16, 1917	Kerensky heads provisional government
July 1917	Coup against provisional government fails
November 6–7, 1917	Bolshevik coup
January 1918	Lenin closes Constituent Assembly and establishes dictatorship
March 15, 1918	Treaty of Brest-Litovsk
1918–1922	Russian civil war
March 1921	New Economic Policy introduced
December 1922	Union of Soviet Socialist Republics established
1924	Lenin dies
1929	Trotsky exiled

lished governments almost everywhere in Europe. By the early 1930s, traditional liberal democratic notions were under siege from both right and left.

THE MARCH REVOLUTION AND THE BOLSHEVIK SEIZURE OF POWER

The Russian Revolution of 1917 consisted of two separate upheavals—the first in March, the second in November—which occurred against the background of the enormous strains caused by World War I. The first stage saw the overthrow of the centuries-old monarchy of the tsars, and the establishment of a provisional government. In November, the Bolsheviks staged a coup d'état and seized power in their own right, laying the basis for a communist state. In their determination to demonstrate the irreversible break with the past, Bolshevik leaders ordered the execution of Tsar Nicholas II and his family.

The Crisis of Tsarist Russia

The first serious threat to the autocratic rule of the tsars had come in 1905, when working-class protestors managed to extract limited political concessions from Nicholas (see Part VII, Topic 16). The tsar had permitted the formation of the Duma, or parliament, and promised a measure of individual freedom. Two years later, however, the electoral law had been changed and the tsar resumed autocratic rule. The result was growing alienation among wider segments of Russian society.

The problems of the imperial government were compounded by the character and personality of the tsar and his wife, Alexandra (1872–1918). Nicholas lacked sufficient strength of will or keenness of intellect to be an effective ruler. He believed in absolutism and divine guidance, but was too easily influenced by those around him. Nor was Nicholas comfortable with change. The Tsarina Alexandra, a German princess by birth, was even more of an absolutist than her husband, and she counseled Nicholas not to give in to pressures for reform. Deeply religious, to the point of superstition, Alexandra's views were reinforced by Gregori Yefimovich Rasputin (1871?–1916), a bizarre holy man of peasant origins. As a young man he gained such an unsavory reputation that he was given the nickname of "Rasputin," meaning a debauchee. When he arrived in St. Petersburg in 1905, he came to the attention of the tsarina for his mystical powers and his supposed ability to improve the hemophiliac condition of her young son. Soon he exerted enormous influence over the royal family and in political affairs. Rumors of corruption and sexual license within the court helped to erode public confidence in the imperial government.

Although Nicholas had no military experience, he assumed personal charge of Russia's armies in 1915. He also changed the name of the capital from its German form, St. Petersburg, to the Russian Petrograd, so as to stress Russian nationalism. These efforts had

The Bolsheviks storm the Winter Palace in Petrograd (formerly St. Petersburg), November 6, 1917.

little impact, for when military defeats took place he then had to bear personal responsibility for them. Russian soldiers lacked food and equipment, and were often sent into the field without even a rifle. With each military defeat, the troops grew more discontented.

The Tsarina Alexandra actually ran the day-to-day operations of the government while her husband was at the front. Food shortages and the lack of basic necessities aroused civilian restlessness in the cities, and advisers and court officials urged reforms in order to bolster morale. But at Rasputin's insistence, Alexandra refused any concessions and temporarily closed the Duma (legislative assembly). In a desperate effort to end his pernicious control of government policy, three noblemen killed Rasputin in December 1916. His death was as strange as his life. At a private party arranged for the purpose, he was fed a cake containing an enormous amount of poison, but he remained alive; in the end, the assassins had finally to shoot him and fling his body into a river. When the corpse was recovered, the authorities determined that he had died of drowning.

Such desperate actions came too late to prevent the revolution. When the Duma reopened, the conservative deputies joined the radicals in calling for the end of the monarchy.

The First Revolution

By 1917, some 7 million soldiers were dead, wounded, or missing. In early March, workers joined housewives in protests against the lack of food. When the socialists staged a massive Woman's Day demonstration, thousands of workers moved into the city avenues and squares. Nicholas demanded that the demonstrations be crushed, and on March 11 soldiers fired at the demonstrators. Soon, however, the troops went over to the side of the rioters. As the tsar became the target of popular outrage, the Duma formed a provisional government led by Prince Georgi Lvov (1861–1925). Nicholas was persuaded to abdicate when it became clear that the army's loyalty could not be guaranteed.

Lvov announced plans to hold elections for a constituent assembly and for the introduction of universal suffrage for males, and enacted basic civil liberties. To gain popular support, the provisional government promised to distribute land to the peasants, mandated an eight-hour day for workers, freed the tsar's political prisoners, and proclaimed that Jews would no longer be persecuted.

Although the provisional government gained the support of a wide stratum of Russians, its leadership was undermined by the Soviet (Council) of Workers' and Soldiers' Deputies, a radical organization consisting of worker representatives. The Petrograd Soviet quickly came to direct the activities of hundreds of similar councils that were created in industrial factories, the armed forces, and in rural villages across Russia.

The Soviets were formed mainly by socialists, who were divided amongst themselves, however, into Social Revolutionaries and members of the Marxist-inspired Social Democratic Workers party. The Social Revolutionaries were agrarian radicals who believed that Russian society could best be changed by the peasants through established village councils. Members of the Social Democratic Workers party had split into two groups, the Mensheviks and the Bolsheviks. *Menshevik* means "minority" and *Bolshevik* "majority." The terms had nothing to do, however, with their size but rather were derived from a vote that had been taken in 1903 on matters of party organization, in which the Mensheviks had gotten a minority of the vote. Both shared an adherence to Marxist principles, but they disagreed over fundamental questions of strategy. The reformist Mensheviks wanted to create a mass-based party in the way that socialists had done in Western Europe. The Mensheviks expected to bring about a socialist society by peaceful reform, but not until industrial capitalism had spread more fully and had created a large urban working class.

The Bolsheviks disagreed with both principles. Their leader, Vladimir Ilyich Lenin (born Vladimir Ilyich Ulianov, 1870–1924), fought against the reformist ideas of the Mensheviks. He believed that such peaceful tactics were not possible under tsarist absolutism and insisted that revolutionary violence alone could achieve socialism. Lenin also disagreed with Marx's notion that revolution was not feasible in an agrarian society like Russia's that had only an infant industrial working class. Moreover, Lenin saw the party not as a mass movement but as a small élite of professional revolutionaries. Such a vanguard would not only provide the party with discipline and leadership, but would be able to seize power when circumstances were favorable. Although the Soviets lacked a uniform ideological position, they competed with the provisional government by backing the demands of the urban workers and rural peasants. The Duma, on the other hand, which supported the government, was dominated by liberal elements who favored a constitutional monarchy. Because the Bolsheviks were not in the government, they could distance themselves from the Lvov regime.

The provisional government and the Duma stubbornly refused to make a separate peace with the Germans, declaring it their duty to fight alongside the Allies. In May, after the government announced once again its determination to pursue the war effort, popular pressure persuaded some members of the government to resign. This crisis was compounded by the government's inability to meet the demands of the workers or the peasants' cry for land.

The Bolshevik Seizure of Power

Under the skillful leadership of Lenin, the Bolsheviks took full advantage of the government's failure to secure popular support. Despite his unassuming appearance, Lenin had an immense appeal, not only to party militants but to workers. Possessed of a brilliant mind, he had become an opponent of the tsarist regime at the age of 17, when his brother was executed for attempting to kill Tsar Alexander III. He later became a militant in the Social Democratic Workers party and spent years in prison and in Siberian exile because of his antigovernment activism. In 1900 he escaped to Western Europe, from where he directed the Bolshevik faction of the party and led the split with the Mensheviks over tactics for achieving a socialist state.

Lenin was in Switzerland at the time of the March revolution, but the Germans, hoping that the Bolsheviks would disrupt the Russian war effort, allowed him to cross their country by railway to reach Russia. Not until April did Lenin arrive in Petrograd, but he immediately went on the offensive. Instead of supporting the provisional government, he ordered his fellow Bolsheviks to plan for another revolution. The seizure of power in Russia, he said, would be the first step toward upheaval in the industrialized societies of Western Europe.

The collapse of the government's offensive against the Central Powers in July 1917 sparked a large-scale military insurrection in Petrograd. Lvov, who quelled the mutiny, accused the Bolsheviks of treachery and arrested some of their leaders. Lenin escaped in disguise to Finland. Yet the uprising suggested the need for the provisional government to broaden its support. Alexander Kerensky (1881–1970), a moderate Social Revolutionary, therefore became head of government. Like Lvov, however, Kerensky quickly lost credibility by refusing to make immediate peace with the Germans. In September, Kerensky followed this mistake with another—permitting a reactionary officer, Lavr Kornilov, to strike at the Soviets. Kerensky panicked, however, when he thought that Kornilov intended to seize the government and he provided arms for the Soviet's Red Guards. Kornilov's attempt was forestalled.

By now, Kerensky's ability to govern rested on the Soviets, which Lenin sought to take over. Bolshevik support grew rapidly as he launched a campaign for "peace, land, and bread" that contrasted sharply with the government's inability to achieve any of the three. Lenin then demanded "all power to the Soviets." When the Bolsheviks won control of the Soviets of both Petrograd and Moscow, Lenin made his way back to Russia in October.

Lenin prepared to take power with the help of Leon Trotsky (real name Lev Bronstein, 1879–1940), whose keen mind and organizational genius made him the mastermind of the Bolshevik victory. Trotsky, who headed the Petrograd Soviet, first gained crucial advantage by securing appointment as the council's military commander of the capital. He then persuaded government soldiers to join with the Soviets. Together, on the night of November 6, Trotsky's forces quickly took control of the railroads, power stations, telephone building, bridges, and important government departments. At the same time, Soviet sailors moved the ship *Aurora* along the Neva River and trained its guns on the Winter Palace, Kerensky's headquarters. Kerensky fled. While these events transpired, the Bolsheviks announced that the Soviets had taken power and had made Lenin the new head of government. In one sudden blow, the Bolsheviks had won.

THE SOVIET UNION IN THE MAKING

A stable Bolshevik government would not emerge for more than three years, during which the country was racked by civil war, famine, and foreign invasion.

The Leninist Dictatorship

The first goal of Lenin's regime was to satisfy the people's demands for an end to war and hunger. Lenin nationalized the land, and the Soviets were to convert the large estates into collective farms. In fact, however, many peasants had already taken plots of land and were allowed to keep them. These measures did not, however, address the burning problem of hunger, since the small landowners refused to send their crops to the cities. The civil war, combined with successive harvest failures, exacerbated the problem and contributed to mass starvation.

Lenin also found the restoration of peace difficult. Germany demanded severe terms from the Soviets, and some Bolsheviks even suggested continuing the war as a revolutionary struggle against the West. But Lenin was determined to make peace. The Treaty of Brest-Litovsk, negotiated by Trotsky and concluded on March 15, 1918, gave to Germany all the land it had conquered from Russia during the war, including the Baltic regions of Finland, Estonia, Latvia, and Lithuania, as well as the Ukraine and eastern Poland. Despite the heavy price, the return of peace was greeted with deep satisfaction by millions of Russians.

Russia had no experience with democracy, either on the national level or among the local peasant councils. Only the Soviets practiced a form of democracy,

Map 2.1 Russia, 1918–1919

and in factories and army units workers and soldiers elected officials and exercised some authority. The lack of democratic tradition conformed to Lenin's purposes, for his idea of a centralized, highly disciplined party would prevail in the aftermath of the November revolution. The Bolsheviks never claimed to admire Western-style democracy. Lenin's dictatorial views were made clear when elections for a constituent assembly were held in November: the Social Revolutionaries won nearly twice as many delegates as the Bolsheviks, and Lenin closed the assembly down after only one meeting. In its place he created a "dictatorship of the proletariat." The Communist party—the new name assumed by the Bolsheviks—now ruled Russia.

The Bolsheviks began to put their political and economic policies into practice in 1918. The capital of the country was moved from Petrograd to Moscow, deep in the interior. There, a centralized state bureaucracy controlled by the Communist party was established. All peasants were now forced to surrender their crops to urban markets. When it was clear that the factory committees were failing to meet the government's demand for higher industrial production, party trade unions replaced the worker committees. Every branch of industry was nationalized and placed under centralized state control. Dozens of state trusts were created within several years, and each was placed under the authority of a Supreme Council of National Economy that coordinated economic planning and production.

The Civil War

Lenin argued that these measures—he called them "war communism"—were needed because the new Communist government had to fight for its existence against foreign and internal opponents. Reactionaries, moderates, and Social Revolutionaries formed legions known as the "White Army" to bring down the regime. Then, too, a host of ethnic minorities and nationalities sought independence from Russia. In 1918, some 100,000 soldiers from the United States, France, Great Britain, Japan, and other nations invaded Russia in an effort to topple the Communists from power. Finally, peasants launched a counterrevolutionary war against the Red Army that was confiscating their crops.

The Treaty of Brest-Litovsk hurt the Allied military position, for the Germans were now able to move their troops from the Eastern to the Western front. The German Army pierced Allied lines and advanced against Paris. Although the Germans were turned back, Allied governments worried that Communist revolution might affect their own war-torn societies. On July 16, 1918, after the British and French sent some 20,000 troops to Archangel and Murmansk on the Arctic Sea, the Bolsheviks killed the imperial family lest the White Army or the Czechs try to rescue them.

The United States intervened ostensibly in response to the plight of thousands of Czech prisoners of war in Siberia who broke out of their prison camps and seized the railroad in order to get home, where they hoped to fight for Czech independence. To support the Czechs, the United States agreed to a combined landing of American and Japanese soldiers at Vladivostok, on the Pacific coast. That winter British troops captured the railroads between the Caspian and the Black seas, and a French-Greek operation seized Odessa.

After the armistice was concluded in November, Allied troops stayed in Russia. Yet Lenin's immense prestige, together with the Communist party's internal discipline, kept the Red Army intact, while the White Army was deeply divided by ideological differences. The Bolsheviks dominated the center of Russia and fought along interior lines, while the enemy forces were stretched out along an immense border.

Trotsky, who had been the architect of the Bolshevik coup in 1917, now directed the government's military operations with masterful efficiency. He raised, equipped, and trained the Red Army, traveling incessantly across the huge theater of operations in a railroad headquarters. Special political commissars attached to each army unit were responsible for soldier morale.

By late 1920, the Red Army victory was so complete that the Allies withdrew their forces from Russia. The Bolsheviks succeeded in recovering much of the territory they had lost to the Germans. The Soviet state now began to take shape. Some ethnic minorities and border nationalities had achieved a measure of self-determination during the civil war, but the Soviets now reestablished command of Russian Armenia, Azerbaijan, and Georgia. In December 1922, Lenin created a centralized Russian-dominated federal system of "autonomous" states united into the Union of Soviet Socialist Republics.

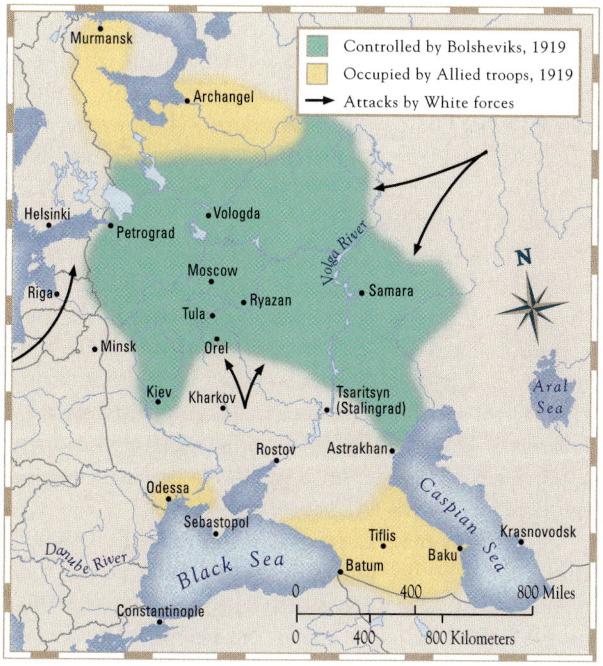

Map 2.2 The Russian Civil War

The New Economic Policy

The civil war, together with disease and starvation, killed millions of Russians. Farms and urban centers had been destroyed and the transportation network was in shambles. Engineers, doctors, and other professionals were desperately needed, and the shortage of raw materials was critical. Industrial production fell to less than a fifth of its pre-1914 level. Crop failures and hoarding contributed to persistent starvation. The Bolsheviks, who now had responsibility for government policies, lost more popular backing.

In the wake of worker and peasant unrest, a military uprising at Kronstadt broke out in March 1921. Lenin moved to regain control of the situation. He introduced a "New Economic Policy" (NEP), which represented a compromise with socialist theory. The NEP allowed a measure of private ownership in retail shops and small industries. In the countryside, it stopped crop confiscation and permitted peasants to sell their goods competitively. Communists debated the NEP hotly, for it created a new category of middle-class peasants

Lenin (left) and Stalin: Stalin had his own image added to this photograph of Lenin to show how closely they had worked together.

known as *kulaks* ("big peasants"), in contradiction to the socialist ideal of a society with no class distinctions. Viewed as a temporary expedient, the NEP did not end state ownership and management of banking, large industries, and transportation. The program had limited success, and only by 1928 did industry and farming return to prewar production levels.

The Soviet constitution provided for an All-Union Congress of Soviets, a representative body that in theory wielded supreme authority. The Congress elected a Council of People's Commissars, an Executive Committee, and a Presidium that presided when the Congress was not in session. In 1936 the name of the Congress was changed to the Supreme Soviet, and that of the People's Commissars was altered in 1946 to the Council of Ministers. It was the party, however, that actually governed the Soviet Union. The party's Central Committee, with some 50 members, gathered only occasionally and chose a ten-member Politburo. Executive power rested in a Secretariat of from one to three members, selected by the Politburo.

The Rise of Stalin

Lenin had two strokes in 1922 that prevented him from exercising leadership on a regular basis. Many thought that Trotsky, his closest collaborator, would be his successor, but Trotsky's ambitions led important party officials to oppose him. Late that year the party leaders created a *troika*—a three-person executive—that included the general secretary of the party, Joseph Stalin (real name Joseph Djugashvili, 1879–1953).

While most of the Old Bolsheviks—those who had led the 1917 Revolution—were from the middle class, Stalin was a man of the people, born in the region of Georgia. Stalin's father had been a shoemaker and his grandfather a serf. He became a Bolshevik when he was about 20, when he adopted the underground name of Stalin ("man of steel"). Like Lenin, he spent years in prison and in Siberia, but Stalin never lived abroad. As a result, he was more provincial in outlook and lacked perspective. His thirst for power was limitless, and he was shrewd and ruthless. He used his position as general secretary of the party to create a cadre of bureaucrats who owed allegiance to him.

In December 1922, after his second stroke, Lenin began to think about his successor, but was anxious about Stalin just as others were becoming concerned about Trotsky. He dictated to his wife and confidant, Nadezhda Krupskaya (1869–1939), a political testament in which he analyzed the strengths and weaknesses of Stalin and Trotsky as possible successors. He was uncertain as to whether Stalin was capable of exercising power prudently and when he learned that Stalin had used brutal methods in subduing the anticommunist opposition in Georgia, Lenin added a codicil to his testament rejecting Stalin and advising his comrades to select another leader.

After Lenin's death in 1924, Krupskaya tried unsuccessfully to have his testament and the codicil read to a party congress. Instead, Stalin presented to the congress his theory of "Socialism in One Country." He wanted the Soviet Union to build an industrial economy that would preserve socialism inside the country and eschew the export of revolution elsewhere. Trotsky countered Stalin's position with the more orthodox Marxist idea of "Permanent Revolution," in which the Soviets would struggle continuously to destroy capitalism in every country. Stalin understood, however, that the Russian people were tired of struggle and crisis, and that the country did not have the strength for armed conflict with the Western powers.

In his power struggle with Trotsky, Stalin outmaneuvered the hero of the civil war, and in 1925 won the backing of party members in removing him as war commissar. In 1929, Trotsky was forced into exile. One by one, Stalin then disposed of the Old Bolsheviks, including those who had supported him against Trotsky. For years Trotsky stood as a symbol of opposition to Stalin's brutal regime, until in 1940 a Stalinist assassin murdered him with an axe in Mexico City.

For the next 20 years, Stalin was the absolute ruler of the Soviet Union, wielding more power than the tsars. Krupskaya lived through the terror of Stalin's purges and held a position on the party's Central Committee until her death in 1939, but the fact that Lenin had rejected Stalin remained secret. Under

Stalin, Lenin's goal of creating a workers' democracy disappeared, replaced by a program of forced modernization aimed at making Russia a world power. For that goal, the Russian people paid a heavy price.

"MUTILATED VICTORY": ITALY FROM WAR TO FASCISM

Italy entered World War I a year later than the other European powers. From the summer of 1914 to May 1915—the period known as the "interventionist crisis"—the country remained neutral while negotiating with both sides the highest price for its support. By the Treaty of London, which promised her extensive territorial gains in the event of an Allied victory, Italy joined the war in 1915 alongside Britain, France, and Russia (see Part VIII, Topic 1).

At war's end, however, Italy found itself in a difficult position. Politicians and intellectuals had agonized over the question of intervention. Millions of men, mainly peasants, had been drafted, and many of them had been killed or wounded. The fighting had drained the national treasury, and the government had made generous promises to the lower classes in order to maintain morale. By late 1919, inflation had struck, and angry veterans wanted jobs at a time when some 2 million Italians were out of work.

At the Paris Peace Conference, the Italians were denied most of the territory that had been promised them—the south Tyrol and the Trentino, the Istrian peninsula and the city of Trieste, the Dodecanese Islands, and the entire Dalmatian coast. Instead, Dalmatia was given to the new nation of Yugoslavia. When Italy demanded the port of Fiume (now Rijeka) as compensation, the Allies refused. This blow to Italian national prestige was especially hard for the veterans. Irate nationalists fanned the flames of patriotism, blaming government for having accepted a "mutilated victory."

Significant Dates

The Rise of Fascism

1883–1945	Life of Benito Mussolini
1902–1904	Mussolini in Switzerland
1912	Mussolini becomes editor of *Avanti!*
November–August 1914	Mussolini breaks with PSI; founds *Popolo d'Italia*
April–May 1915	Pact of London; Italy's entrance into war
1916	Mussolini serves at front and is wounded
November 1918	Armistice
March 1919	*Fascio di Combattimento* formed
September 1919	D'Annunzio invades Fiume
1920–1922	Fascist violence
October 29, 1922	Mussolini becomes prime minister
1924	Fascist electoral victory; Matteotti crisis
1924–1926	Fascist dictatorship created

Mussolini the Revolutionary

One of the most outspoken critics of the government was Benito Mussolini (1883–1945), who had become an ardent interventionist during the war. Mussolini was a native of the Romagna region in northeastern Italy, where his father had been a blacksmith and a socialist agitator. Prone to violence even as a child, he had been expelled from several schools before becoming a schoolteacher. By 1901, he too had joined the Socialist party. He spent the years 1902–1904 in Switzerland as a draft dodger, and it was there that he completed his political education. Neutral Switzerland was refuge for hundreds of revolutionary exiles from all over Europe, especially Russian radicals such as Lenin who had escaped the tsar's police. There Mussolini helped organize workers and gave speeches on behalf of the Italian Socialist party (PSI).

Back in Italy again in 1904, Mussolini began to make a name for himself among revolutionary socialists. He proved to be a powerful orator and writer. When Italy and Turkey fought over Libya in 1911–1912 (see Part VII, Topic 16), he joined other pacifist socialists in condemning imperialism, spending several months in prison for his antiwar activities. In 1912 he took part in a revolutionary socialist coup against the reformist leaders of the PSI, and became editor of *Avanti!*, the official Socialist party newspaper.

During the interventionist crisis, Mussolini did an about-face. Arguing that the war would spark revolution, he pressed for Italian intervention on the Allied side, for which the PSI expelled him. He then began publishing an interventionist newspaper, *Il Popolo d'Italia*, and volunteered for military service, serving at the front and being promoted to sergeant. In 1916 he was wounded and mustered out of the army, returning to politics. During the last years of the war, Mussolini's

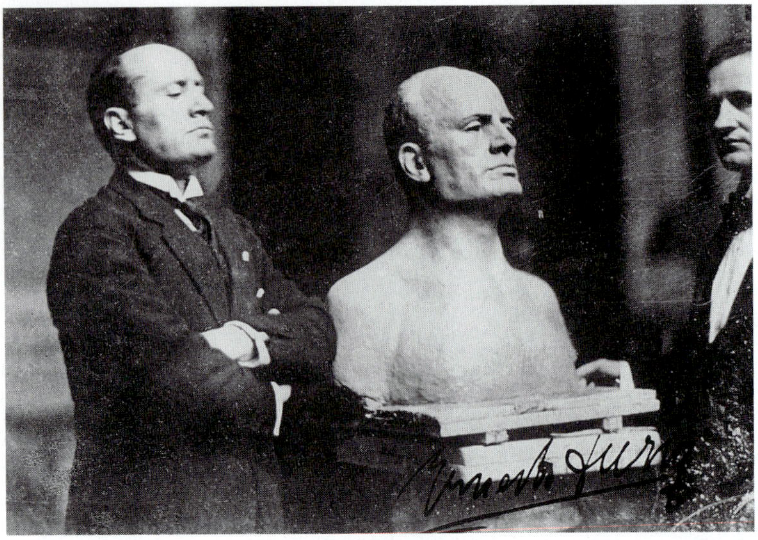

The day after becoming prime minister, Mussolini posed for a sculptor.

thinking underwent a further evolution as he replaced the Marxist doctrine of class struggle with the principle of nationalism.

The Birth of Fascism

Mussolini soon emerged as spokesman for the war veterans, repeatedly condemning Italy's lost peace. Some of his thunder was stolen in September 1919 by the flamboyant nationalist poet Gabriele D'Annunzio (1863–1938), who led war veterans in the seizure of Fiume. When the Italian government refused to accept Fiume from his hands, D'Annunzio proclaimed it an independent state. Italy expelled him from the city a year later, but the expedition had inflamed nationalist feeling and suggested the ease of staging a military takeover. From D'Annunzio, Mussolini learned something about the choreography of political propaganda, and eventually took as his own D'Annunzio's Roman salute, with its outstretched arm and cry of *"Viva il Duce!"—Duce*, from the Latin *dux*, is the Italian word meaning "leader."

Meanwhile, the liberal government had become the target of popular resentment. In November 1919, national elections based on universal manhood suffrage were held, and the liberals lost the majority they had held in Parliament since 1861. Instead, the PSI and a new Catholic party became, respectively, the two largest parties. But with the socialists and Catholics refusing to form a coalition government, King Victor Emmanuel III felt free to choose liberal prime ministers.

This political crisis unfolded in a context of massive social unrest—almost 2000 industrial and agrarian strikes took place in 1919. Poor peasants seized land in the South, and others organized huge associations in the northern Po Valley, while in September 1920 some 500,000 workers, supported by socialist leaders such as Antonio Gramsci (1891–1937), occupied factories in the major industrial cities of the North. Such labor tensions, together with the electoral success of the PSI, frightened many middle-class Italians into thinking that Bolshevik revolution was imminent.

Fascism was born in these unstable conditions. Mussolini founded the movement in Milan on March 23, 1919, at an unimpressive rally of little more than 100 followers who were later called the "Fascists of the

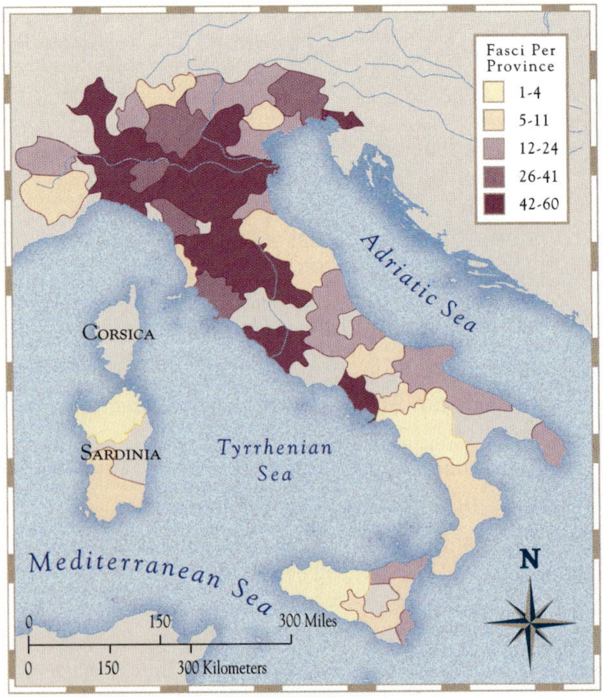

Map 2.3 Fascism in Italy (May 1922)

first hour." The members of this *Fascio di Combattimento* ("combat group") were war veterans, nationalist intellectuals, Futurists (see Part VII, Topic 21), and former interventionist socialists and syndicalists like Mussolini. He took the movement's name from the Latin *fasces* (sticks bound around an axe handle and used in ancient Rome as a symbol of unity), a common term for left-wing radical movements at the time.

A program issued later that year combined left-wing ingredients such as the eight-hour workday, worker participation in management, a republican constitution, and the vote for women and 18-year-olds, with right-wing demands for an aggressive foreign policy and strong secular, nationalist education. Later, under pressure from conservative supporters, the program underwent a pronounced shift to the right.

The Struggle for Power

Most active members of the Fascist movement were from the lower middle class, especially young veterans inspired by the spirit of bravery and comradeship they had experienced in the war, and bound by loyalty and discipline. These men generally stood against the established order, resentful of privilege and wealth, and committed to avenging the "mutilated victory" of 1919. They made up the rank and file of the armed Fascist squads, whose bludgeons and daggers, blackshirted uniforms, and skull and crossbones insignia represented a new, dangerous element in European politics.

Organized in military fashion and led by powerful regional chieftains, these so-called *squadristi*, many of whom were simply brutish thugs, plunged Italy into a bloody nightmare of violence aimed not only against Fascism's political enemies, but against those perceived as defeatists and pacifists. Armed with military weapons, they went on "punitive expeditions" against socialists and labor union activists, terrorized peasant groups, and broke up strikes.

THE FASCIST VICTORY AND MUSSOLINI'S DICTATORSHIP

Because of the "Red Scare" that swept over Italy in 1920–1921, the war against the socialists enabled Mussolini to secure financial support from landowners and industrialists. The liberal government, secretly anxious to see the weakening of the PSI, failed to stop the Black Shirt violence. In 1921, the Fascists began attacking the state, raiding municipal halls, provincial councils, and railroad and telegraph stations. Soon they threatened to take over the central government itself. Fascism had grown rapidly—the number of recruits, which had numbered not quite 1000 in the summer of 1919, jumped to 250,000 by 1922. Fascist violence, combined with official inaction, gave the appearance that the movement was the only viable force capable of governing the nation.

From Duce to Prime Minister

Mussolini himself played a shrewd game, preserving the public fiction that he was an ordinary, respectable political leader while goading on his Black Shirt followers. In 1921 he changed the Fascist movement into the Fascist National party (PNF). In the elections that year Mussolini and 34 other Fascists won seats in the Chamber of Deputies. Giovanni Giolitti, the liberal prime minister (see Part VII, Topic 15), failed, however, to understand that Fascism was no ordinary political party. He tried unsuccessfully to entice Mussolini into the government as part of a moderate-conservative front called the National Bloc. But the Fascists would not be drawn into traditional establishment politics—they wanted nothing less than full power.

In late 1922, Mussolini's hardline Fascists convinced him to attempt the seizure of power. They planned a "March on Rome" to force King Victor Emmanuel III into appointing a Fascist government. At the end of October, while Mussolini remained in his office in Milan, the Black Shirt chieftains launched a three-pronged drive toward Rome with some 50,000 men. The regular army could have mustered much stronger forces to protect the capital, but the king, afraid that the country would be thrown into civil war or that the military would go over to the Fascists, failed to declare a state of emergency. The prime minister, Luigi Facta (served February to October 1922), resigned, and the king then collapsed in the face of the Fascist threat. On October 29, Victor Emmanuel offered Mussolini the prime ministership. Traveling to Rome by train, Mussolini, having discarded his Fascist uniform, took the oath of office as the youngest prime minister in Italian history.

The March on Rome never really happened. Mussolini became prime minister in accordance with the provisions of the Italian constitution. Nor was he yet a dictator, for only half of his cabinet members were Fascists, and of the more than 500 deputies in Parliament, the party could still count only 35. As a result, Mussolini worked to solidify his position.

Mussolini asked for and received special powers to rule by decree and to censor the press, and in 1923 convinced the liberals to enact legislation aimed at giving the Fascist party control of Parliament. The so-called "Acerbo Law" provided that the party that made the strongest showing in a national election would, provided it received at least 25 percent of all votes cast,

After the March on Rome, October 1922, Mussolini and his Black Shirts celebrate the Fascist victory.

receive two-thirds of all seats in the Chamber of Deputies. In the 1924 elections, the Fascists won the required number of votes by renewed violence and poll fixing. With the party now dominant in Parliament, Mussolini felt more secure, but relations with the Italian Army remained unresolved. He secured the backing of the military only after agreeing to turn the Black Shirt squads into a Fascist militia, controlled by the regular army.

Still, Mussolini hesitated to move toward full dictatorship. An unexpected political crisis later in 1924 changed the situation. Giacomo Matteotti (1885–1924), a bold and popular Socialist deputy, began to expose the illegal manner in which the Fascists had stolen the recent election. That summer Fascist agents murdered him, possibly on orders from Mussolini. A wave of public indignation exploded, and the non-Fascist press turned against the prime minister. Even the king wavered in his support of Mussolini, and some liberal statesmen urged that he be dismissed. Leaders of the anti-Fascist opposition withdrew en masse from Parliament and called themselves the

After he moved his office to Palazzo Venezia, Mussolini used the piazza under his balcony for mass demonstrations.

"Aventine Secession," in memory of the secession of the Roman people in the years of the ancient Roman Republic, some two and a half millennia earlier. While Mussolini wavered, the more intransigent Fascist chieftains confronted him and forced him to abandon all pretense of democratic rule. Going before a special session of Parliament on January 3, 1925, Mussolini delivered the most important speech of his life, in which he took total responsibility for everything that had happened and announced that he would restore order to Italy. In the following weeks, the "second wave" of Black Shirt terror was unleashed against the anti-Fascists. In this way, Mussolini silenced the opposition and either arrested or forced into exile its most prominent leaders. Between 1925 and 1929, he began to build the Fascist state.

THE GERMAN REVOLUTION AND THE WEIMAR REPUBLIC

Nazism is the German variety of generic fascism—indeed, scholars refer to Italian Fascism with a capital "F," and to the generic phenomenon with a lowercase "f."

Significant Dates

The Rise of Nazism

1889–1945	Life of Adolf Hitler
1909–1913	Hitler in Vienna
1914–1918	Hitler serves in army and is wounded
November 9, 1918	Kaiser Wilhelm II abdicates; German Republic established under provisional government
November 11, 1918	Armistice
January 6–15, 1919	Spartacist Week
June 1919	Treaty of Versailles
September 1919	Hitler joins the DAP
1920	DAP becomes the NSDAP, or Nazi party
March 1920	Kapp Putsch
1923	French occupation of Ruhr
November 1923	Munich Putsch

To contemporaries, the two seemed virtually the same. Each was, after all, a radical movement with utopian ideologies that mixed nationalism with socialist and syndicalist ideas, each worshiped an all-powerful *Duce* or *Führer*, and in both instances the average militant was a lower-middle-class veteran. Moreover, Fascism and Nazism boasted paramilitary armed squads and both exalted violence, which they used against Marxists and their other political enemies, including liberal democracy.

There were, however, differences. Nazism was based on a theory of racism, whereas a more conventional form of extreme nationalism lay at the heart of Fascist philosophy—a fact that has something to do with the more pervasive and systematic violence that marked the Nazi regime. Hitler's Nazi government is also considered a more efficient example of totalitarianism than Mussolini's Fascist state, and this difference may be partially explained by Germany's more advanced levels of technical education and industrialization.

The Weimar Republic

At the end of 1918, Germany seemed poised at the edge of a revolution as far-reaching as that in Russia. Defeated on the battlefield, Germany's society and economy were exhausted. Moreover, its political system—based on the old Prussian constitution and an all but absolute emperor—had lost its credibility. As a result, left-wing agitation erupted and soldiers and workers set up groups that resembled the Russian Soviets. Sailors at the northern ports, inspired by revolutionary ideas, staged mutinies in late October. The most dramatic event took place on November 8, when the Independent Socialist Kurt Eisner (1867–1919) formed a Bavarian Republic in Munich. Eisner himself was assassinated and the radical experiment crushed in the wake of bitter street fighting with right-wing reactionaries.

In Berlin, events took a similar turn. Kaiser Wilhelm II abdicated on November 9, 1918, following pressure from the Allies, and Prince Max, the imperial chancellor, resigned. Philipp Scheidemann (1865–1939) and Friedrich Ebert (1871–1925), leaders of the Social Democratic party, formed a provisional government. Then, in order to forestall the more radical Revolutionary Marxists, otherwise known as Spartacists (from Spartacus, a gladiator who led a rebellion of slaves against Rome in the first century B.C.), Scheidemann announced the birth of the German Republic. Scheidemann became president and Ebert his chancellor.

The republic quickly became the target of Marxist and right-wing radicals, each of which tried to take power from it. In order to protect the republic, Ebert struck a deal with the German officer corps: in return

Karl Liebknecht and Rosa Luxemburg, leaders of the radical German socialists known as the Spartacists, were both killed while in government custody.

for protecting the republic against its enemies, the government would pledge to maintain the army intact. The agreement worked only too well. Between January 6 and 15, 1919, the Spartacists, led by Rosa Luxemburg (1870–1919) and Karl Liebknecht (1871–1919), attempted a coup in Berlin known as "Spartacist Week." Government troops, assisted by illegal paramilitary organizations known as the *Freikorps*, put down the revolution with considerable bloodshed. Luxemburg and Liebknecht were arrested, but they were both mysteriously killed on the way to jail. The Freikorps, composed of veterans, were to provide Nazism with some of its first members.

In the midst of this instability, delegates to a National Assembly gathered in the city of Weimar to create a permanent government for Germany. The delegates represented a large number of political parties, including the Social Democrats, the Catholic Center party, and the liberal Democratic party—together these three parties constituted the moderate "Weimar Coalition" that was to govern the nation throughout the 1920s. In July 1919 they approved a constitution that created the German Republic, one of the most progressive European governments in interwar Europe. Because of its association with the liberal city of Weimar, the republic came to be known as the Weimar Republic.

The constitution, inspired in part by the example of the United States, embodied modern notions of social justice and popular democracy. "Political authority," read its first article, "derives from the people." The head of state was a president, elected for a seven-year term by universal suffrage, and a British-style cabinet government over which a chancellor, appointed by the president, presided. Legislative power resided in a parliament, consisting of a lower house called the *Reichstag*, and an upper chamber, the *Reichrat*, that represented the various German states. A bill of rights protected civil liberties. As a safeguard, Article 48 permitted the president to enact special powers in the event of national emergency.

In retrospect, it seems as if the Weimar Republic was a compromise that no one wanted. It attracted enemies on the left and the right. A series of coups tried to overthrow the government, the most serious of which was the March 1920 *Putsch*, or coup, led by Wolfgang Kapp (1858–1922), who wanted to restore the monarchy. A general strike organized by the socialists put an end to Kapp's revolt.

In the summer of 1920, elections for the *Reichstag* were held. Ominously, the Weimar Coalition lost significant popular support, its share of the vote falling in subsequent elections from more than 75 to less than 50 percent. Instead, the smaller, extremist parties gained considerable strength. Because the centrist parties were unable to secure a majority thereafter, the republic experienced 20 governments between 1920 and 1933.

At best, most Germans regarded the Weimar Republic with skepticism. The very circumstances of its birth were the cause of considerable concern. The kaiser had, after all, abdicated because the Allies wanted him to, not because the German people had expressed their will. The Allies had also pronounced Germany "guilty" of having caused war, but many Germans did not believe that their weakness had really lost it. Reactionary elements, especially monarchists and the military, invented the "stab in the back" myth, according to which internal traitors had destroyed Germany's war effort. Hitler would tell the people that these traitors were Jews and Marxists. Finally, of course, the Allies had forced Germany to accept the Treaty of Versailles.

The army pledged its support to the government, but senior officers never fully accepted the republic, and senior civil servants, such as judges and police officials, favored the right. When extremists murdered two cabinet ministers—Matthias Erzberger (1875–1921) and Walther Rathenau (1867–1922)—the courts gave those responsible light sentences.

The serious economic difficulties that plagued Germany after 1919 further undermined public confidence in the republic. The economic provisions of the Versailles Treaty had deprived Germany of vital resources and income, and unemployment was widespread. Lacking the resources to deal effectively with the crisis, the government printed millions of dollars worth of paper money, which made the *mark* worthless and sparked rampant inflation. When the French occupied the Ruhr Valley in 1923 in order to extract late reparations payments from Germany, the economy declined further. The cost-of-living index rose on a daily basis, wiping out the value of salaries and pensions. Millions of working- and middle-class Germans were ruined by the inflation, and life in the Weimar Republic took on a real sense of desperation.

HITLER AND NATIONAL SOCIALISM

Like Fascism in Italy, Nazism was a product of the postwar crisis. Yet to an even greater degree than was the case with Mussolini and his movement, Adolf Hitler shaped and dominated the Nazi party.

Adolf Hitler

The most infamous man in German history actually began life as a subject of the Austro-Hungarian empire. Hitler (1889–1945) was born in Braunau, Austria, the son of an unimportant customs bureaucrat. As a youth, Hitler was estranged from his father, who tried to discourage him from studying art. The boy was bright but was not a good student. He failed to graduate from high school, and remained intent on becoming an artist.

Hitler moved to Vienna in 1909, and remained there until the eve of World War I. It was there that he first sought to develop his aesthetic inclinations by study at the Vienna School of Architecture. Despite limited talent as an architectural draftsman, however, Hitler was twice disappointed when his application to school was rejected. Thereafter, he led a squalid, frustrated life trying to earn a living by painting street scenes and working at menial jobs.

Vienna served for Hitler the same purpose that Switzerland had for Mussolini: it provided an opportunity for study and practical experience, during which he

An enthusiastic crowd in Munich welcomes news of the war, August 1, 1914, among them a young Adolf Hitler.

PERSPECTIVES ON HISTORY

The Nature of Fascism

Stanley G. Payne
University of Wisconsin–Madison

Fascism was the only completely new force among the major radical movements active in European affairs after World War I. Though ingredients that made up fascism were not themselves new, they had never coalesced into a specific form prior to 1919. Moreover, fascism was also difficult to understand or to categorize. Though fascists strongly opposed the movements of the left, such as communism and socialism, they denied that fascists themselves were of the right. Fascists claimed to represent a synthesis of both the left and right, and some fascist movements even called themselves "national socialists," as distinct from Marxist or international socialists. Communists, in turn, usually denounced fascism as the instrument of the "most reactionary and violent" sector of the bourgeoisie, but fascists always claimed to be a popular force that united people of diverse social and class backgrounds in the service of the nation.

Fascism was even more confusing because fascist leaders boasted of being activists and pragmatists, relatively indifferent to doctrines or ideology. Later, after World War II, the understanding of fascism even sparked controversy among professional historians. Some would complain that the term "fascist" was applied too loosely and vaguely as a mere political epithet, or used to encompass a wide variety of political movements that were mutually contradictory. Others sought to explain the nature or historical meaning of fascism according to social, economic, philosophical, or even psychological factors.

The term "fascism" was derived from the Italian *fascio*, meaning a union or league, and commonly adopted by new Italian political forces in the later 19th and early 20th centuries. Thus a new group of radical Italian nationalists led by Benito Mussolini found it natural to call themselves the "Fasci Italiani" in 1919 and later transformed the term into an adjective when they organized the "Italian National Fascist Party" two years later, giving rise to "fascist" and "fascism." The movement soon developed a mass membership, enabling its leader to become prime minister in October 1922 and to convert Italy's government into a one-party dictatorship in January 1925.

Its nearest major counterpart, the National Socialist German Workers' party (known to their enemies as "Nazis") sprang from a small group organized in Munich in 1917, then reorganized under Adolf Hitler three years later. Whereas Mussolini came to power relatively rapidly, the same process took Hitler much longer, though he built an even larger and more potent political movement along the way. By the time that Hitler took power in 1933, other new radical nationalist parties had appeared in most other European countries. They became strong mass movements, in one form or another, in only four other countries: Hungary (the Arrow Cross), Romania (the Iron Guard), Austria (the Austrian Nazis), and Spain (Spanish Phalanx).

Though these individual fascist-type movements sometimes differed a good deal among themselves, they also shared certain fundamental characteristics and goals which as a whole tended to set them off from other kinds of political forces. The fascists were first of all unique because they were opposed to nearly all the existing political sectors. They were antiliberal, anticommunist (as well as antisocialist in the social democratic sense), and also anticonservative, though sometimes willing to undertake temporary alliances with rightist groups.

Fascist movements represented the most intense and radical form of nationalism known to modern Europe. They intended to create new nationalist authoritarian states not based on traditional models. They all planned to develop some new kind of regulated, multiclass national economic structure, diversely called national corporatist, national socialist, or national syndicalist. In foreign affairs, all the fascist movements aimed at national imperial expansion or at least at a radical change in the nation's relationship with other powers to enhance its strength and prestige. Though fascist movements did not have a formalized ideology such as Marxism, they had distinctive mentalities, based on a philosophical orientation of idealism as opposed to materialism, and voluntarism or willpower as opposed to rationalism.

Fascist uniqueness was expressed through style and organization. Fascist leaders placed great emphasis on the aesthetic structure of meetings, symbols, and political "choreography," relying especially on romantic and mystical aspects. The fascist movements all attempted to achieve a mass mobilization, with the specific intent of militarizing political relations and creating a mass party militia. Fascists not merely practiced violence (like some other radical groups) but also espoused violence philosophically as a desired end in itself, as a positive value that made nations stronger, more serious, and more unified. They strongly stressed the masculine principle and male dominance, while championing a new élitism and exalting youth over other phases of life. They also cherished the cult of the authoritarian leader—a special figure endowed with charismatic powers, which German Nazis called the *Führerprinzip*, or "leadership principle."

What differentiated fascists from the right was their rejection of philosophical as well as economic conservatism, and their determination to replace the established social élites of the right. They differed profoundly from the left in their rejection of internationalism and egalitarianism or equal rights, as well as in their antipathy to socialized materialism. They sought to remake Europe in the form of a nationalist/imperialist "New Order," profoundly different from the liberal 19th century or the new Marxist-Leninist system of the Soviet Union.

Fascist movements drew support from highly diverse social sectors. In their earliest phase, followers came from former military personnel and small sectors of the radical intelligentsia, sometimes university students. Though some fascist movements enjoyed a degree of backing from the upper bourgeoisie, the broadest sector of support was often provided by the lower middle class. In Germany and Hungary, considerable support also came from workers, while university students were especially important in Italy, Germany, Spain, and Romania, and poor farmers were often recruited in Romania.

A bewildering variety of theories and interpretations have been advanced since 1923 to explain fascism. Among them are (1) theories of socioeconomic causation, primarily of Marxist inspiration; (2) the application of modernization theory, which posits fascism as a phase in modern development; and (3) the theory of totalitarianism, which interprets fascism as one aspect of the broader phenomenon of 20th-century totalitarianism. None of these theories is entirely convincing. The diversity of the basis of social recruitment and political backing makes any simple theory of social determinism implausible, while the fact that numerous societies have undergone modernization without succumbing to fascism seriously weakens any theory drawn primarily from modernization. The theory of "totalitarianism" is of little help because it tends to ignore the differences between fascism and communism, as well as the differences in historical milieu between the countries in which these two diverse movements triumphed.

Probably the only way to account for fascism is by a "historic" approach that isolates the five key variables in the historical situation of countries in which the main fascist movements emerged. The main *national* variable was one of military defeat, frustration, disunity, and status deprivation. The main *political* variable had to do with countries that were just beginning, or had only recently begun, the transition to direct political democracy. (Conversely, stable and satisfied countries, and those in which political democracy had already existed for a generation or more, were not susceptible.) The key *cultural* variable was the influence of currents of new philosophical idealism and vitalism (propitious to fascism) in a nation's cultural life, as contrasted with materialism and rationalism. The key *economic* variable was either depression or underdevelopment in a context where problems seemed both national in scope and to some

continued next page

extent international in origin. The key *social* variable involved widespread discontent not merely among the young and sectors of the lower classes, but among the lower middle class as well. No one or two or even three of these variables by themselves sufficed to produce a significant fascist movement. Only in those few countries where all five variables were present at approximately the same time were conditions propitious for the emergence of major fascist movements.

Even comparatively large fascist movements were rarely successful. The only independent regimes established by fascist leaders were those of Mussolini in Italy (1922–1943) and Hitler in Germany (1933–1945), and only in the German case did the movement's leader achieve complete power over the state. In nearly all countries antifascists were much more numerous than fascists and profascists. The fascists' own calls to violence and extremism tended to limit their appeal, as did the nonrationalist, voluntarist character of their doctrines. The broader influence of fascism during the decade 1935–1945 was due above all to the great expansion of military power of Nazi Germany, not to the individual political victories of the various national fascist movements, which were in fact few. Similarly, the complete military defeat of Italy and Germany shattered the hopes of all the fascist movements, and in the great majority of cases resulted in their physical obliteration as well.

Does fascism have a future? Worried foes sometimes fear so, but it is doubtful that the specific forms of early 20th-century European fascism can be revived. Broad cultural, psychological, edu-

developed his political ideas and his notions about race. Reading widely but without purpose, he was exposed to the kinds of extremist, irrational prejudices that proved to be the foundation of his Nazi philosophy.

Vienna was a microcosm of the ethnic diversity of the Austro-Hungarian empire, and it was in that environment that Hitler discovered racism. At the turn of the century, Vienna bred a number of political leaders who tried to capitalize on racial fears and on Austrian anti-Semitism. Such men were among Hitler's first political heroes. Karl Lueger (1844–1910), the leader of the reactionary Christian Social party, won election as mayor of Vienna—"the greatest German mayor of all times," Hitler wrote of him years later—on an anti-Semitic platform. Lueger's example taught Hitler how a radical movement could achieve power by making a campaign against the Jews the basis of mass-based urban politics. Another contemporary, Georg von Schoenerer, was a parliamentary deputy who preached Pan-Germanism and described the Germans as a higher race who deserved to dominate the other peoples of Europe. From such views he derived his belief that all Germans everywhere had to be united into a "greater Germany." Racial theories soon dominated Hitler's mind, and by the time he left Vienna, he had become convinced that Jews and Marxists were the cause of Western cultural and political corruption and the cause of Europe's degeneracy.

At the start of World War I, Hitler immediately joined the German Army. He saw frontline combat, for which he earned a corporal's rank, and was injured in a poison gas attack at the end of the war. It was while undergoing recovery that he was approached by Captain Ernst Roehm (1887–1934), later a major Nazi leader, and recruited to work for the army in Munich as a civilian investigator.

The Nazi Party

In September 1919, while engaged in gathering information on extremist politics for Roehm, Hitler joined the German Worker's party (DAP). The tiny organization was founded by an anti-Marxist, anti-Semitic worker who wanted the working classes to become fervid nationalists.

Hitler soon dominated the party and emerged as a brilliant public speaker and a powerfully inspiring leader, despite a somewhat comical appearance. He was able to conjure up a unique intensity of emotion in his audiences that eventually captured the loyalty of millions of Germans. In 1920 the party was rebaptized as the National Socialist German Workers' party (NSDAP), soon known popularly as the "Nazi" party—"Nazi" is derived from the German pronunciation of the first two syllables of the German word for "National." He gave talks at rallies all over Munich, increasing the party's membership and shouting his political and racial ideas to all who would listen. His appeal cational, and economic changes have made the reemergence of something so murderous as Nazism in a modern industrial nation almost impossible, just as international interdependence seems to rule out war among the major European and industrial countries. The prevailing culture of materialism and consumerism militates against extreme positions, and any appeal to mass vitalist and irrationalist politics.

Movements and regimes most similar to fascism during the second half of the century have been more important in certain "Third World" countries than in the West. There, nationalist one-party dictatorships have not been uncommon. More than a few governments in Africa, Asia, and the Middle East have preached their own versions of national socialism (for example, "Arab socialism") and have propagated doctrines based on violence, and grounded in mysticism, idealism, and willpower. There too the "cult of personality" and charismatic dictatorship have sometimes been popular. Nonetheless, it is not possible to refer to more than specific features and tendencies. The nationalist movements and dictatorships of the Third World have also developed unique identities and profiles of their own, and in no instance have literally copied or revived European fascist movements. The exact characteristics of interwar Europe, like those of any particular historical epoch, cannot be precisely repeated or reproduced. New authoritarian movements of the 1990s would have to develop qualities appropriate to their own times to achieve support, for a literal revival of the past—particularly of a past so discredited as that of fascism—is doomed to sterility.

grew as he made the "stab in the back" legend and the Treaty of Versailles the cornerstones of his platform. His devoted followers called him the *Führer* (leader), and within five years his tiny party had become a large and vocal force in Weimar politics.

The Nazi party soon had a daily newspaper, the *Völkischer Beobachter* (The People's Observer). Its official platform contained 25 points, chief among them being the creation of a "Greater Germany," an end to the hated *Diktat*—the Treaty of Versailles—and the creation of a prosperous and loyal working and middle class. The platform also aimed to remove the rights of citizenship from Jews. Hitler never believed in the importance of the socialist rhetoric in which the Nazis couched their appeals to the workers. "Left-wing" Nazis like Gregor Strasser (1892–1934) were important in spreading Nazism among the industrial workers of the North, but once they had served their purposes Hitler purged them from the party.

In 1921, Roehm created and took charge of the SA *(Sturmabteilung)*, a paramilitary unit that wore brown-shirted uniforms with the swastika as its symbol. The swastika symbol was used in a variety of ancient cultures, from Egypt to China, and it appeared later in Estonia, where the Freikorps saw it during the fighting in 1918–1919. The Ehrhardt Brigade used it on their steel helmets in Berlin during the Kapp Putsch, and Hitler no doubt saw it when the brigade came to Munich in 1920. Soon the swastika appeared on arm bands, flag, and uniforms, for Hitler saw it as the symbol of "the mission of the struggle for the victory of the Aryan man."

The SA's rank and file came from the lower middle class, especially war veterans and Freikorps members, many of whom were little more than hooligans. Roehm told his followers that only through violence would the Nazis achieve power. Later, in 1925, Heinrich Himmler (1900–1945) organized the elite guard unit called the SS *(Schutzstaffel)*, whose black uniforms and lightning bolt symbols became dreaded symbols of Nazi brutality. Like Mussolini, Hitler used torch-lit parades, impressive ceremonies, and other techniques that Joseph Goebbels (1897–1945) eventually made into the most effective propaganda machine in history.

In 1923, a year after Mussolini's March on Rome, Hitler tried to take power, but only on a local level. The French occupation of the Ruhr and the severe inflationary cycle that erupted that year had been psychologically and economically devastating to most Germans (see Part VIII, Topic 3). In Munich Hitler sought to exploit these conditions by plotting a Putsch that he thought would be supported by municipal authorities. He also enlisted the retired General Erich von Ludendorff to bring a measure of national prestige to the attempt. The abortive coup took place on November 8, but it ended less than 24 hours later when the police intervened. Hitler and several others were

Adolf Hitler in a characteristic pose while speaking.

arrested, and although he was sentenced to five years in prison, he spent only nine months in jail. While serving his time, Hitler dictated *Mein Kampf* (My Struggle), a long and discursive book in which he laid out his political and racial theories and explained how he intended to conquer. The Munich fiasco also taught him that he had to adopt a legal strategy for achieving power that would go hand in hand with Nazi violence.

In 1924, Hitler and Roehm vied with each other for control of the Nazi party, whose membership now reached some 25,000. Roehm tried to make the SA the focus of the party's power, whereas Hitler sought to make the SA the party's tool. Hitler proved the more skillful of the two, driving Roehm into exile and restoring his own authority over the party.

Hitler's new strategy had only limited success, electing some twelve deputies in 1928. Economic conditions in Germany improved after 1924 and the political unrest that had weakened the Weimar Republic quietened down. Although Hitler succeeded in raising Nazi membership to more than 175,000, his prospects for obtaining power legally seemed dim. It would require another five years and the impact of the Great Depression before Hitler came to power (see Part VIII, Topic 4).

Between 1917 and 1933, three new political regimes came to power in Europe—the Soviets in Russia, the Fascists in Italy, and the Nazis in Germany. Together they posed a major challenge to the Western notion of parliamentary democracy. Indeed, in all three cases absolute dictators now controlled the destinies of their countries. Each proclaimed that he would completely reorganize society according to a utopian ideology that stressed community, discipline, and sacrifice for the general good. While the communists in Russia rejected capitalism, the fascists claimed to represent an alternative to both capitalism and communism. As the Great Depression imposed suffering and misery on millions of Europeans, many lost hope with traditional governments and turned in desperation to these radical extremes.

Questions for Further Study

1. What is meant by "Leninism"? How does it differ from conventional socialism?
2. Why did revolution come to Russia instead of to England or France?
3. What were the origins of fascism? How did fascism differ from Bolshevism? How did Italian Fascism differ from German Nazism?
4. Is it useful to speak of a generic "fascism" that combines the Italian and the German varieties?

Suggestions for Further Reading

Bullock, Alan. *Hitler, A Study in Tyranny*. New York, 1964.
Carr, Edward H. *The Russian Revolution: From Lenin to Stalin*. New York, 1979.
Daniels, Roger V. *Red October: The Bolshevik Revolution of 1917*. New York, 1967.
De Felice, Renzo. *Interpretations of Fascism*. Cambridge, MA, 1977.
De Grand, Alexander. *Italian Fascism: Origins and Development*, 2nd ed. Lincoln, NE, 1989.
Fest, Joachim. *Hitler*. New York, 1974.
Fitzpatrick, Sheila. *The Russian Revolution*. New York, 1982.
Lyttelton, Adrian. *The Seizure of Power: Fascism in Italy, 1919–1929*. London, 1973.
Mack Smith, Denis. *Mussolini*. New York, 1982.
Payne, Stanley. *A History of Fascism*. Madison, WI, 1995.
Ulam, Adam. *The Bolsheviks*. New York, 1965.

VIII

Topic 3

The European Economy: Boom and Bust

The impact of the Great War was felt for decades to come, not only within Europe but on its position in world affairs. As we have seen in the preceding two topics, the political upheavals wrought as a consequence of the war changed Europe's map, altered relationships among the great powers, and gave rise to new kinds of political systems. No less dramatic, however, were the effects of the war on Europe's—and the world's—economy.

Wartime government controls, together with the demands made by the military, had created an essentially artificial economic situation in every belligerent country. Once peace came, the domestic and international economies had to readjust suddenly to peacetime production as well as to free market conditions. The European economy responded with a brief but intense postwar boom, followed in turn by collapse. Thereafter, despite periodic adjustments in economic conditions, the 1920s saw considerable prosperity and growth. The new prosperity greatly affected social developments as millions took part in the unprecedented economic expansion and the spread of mass-produced consumer products (on the social conditions of the interwar period, see Part VIII, Topic 6).

Not that the 1920s were without economic difficulties. Two long-range financial legacies of the war, reparations and war debts, made recovery more difficult and fueled international tensions. A series of agreements—the Dawes Plan in 1924 and the Young Plan in 1929—attempted unsuccessfully to settle these touchy questions, but only the Great Depression put an end to both issues in any real sense. Moreover, the wartime economic dislocations, together with the peace settlements and inflationary cycles, destabilized Europe's major currencies, causing them to drop in value in international exchange. Governments attempted with varying degrees of success to deal with this problem by instituting deflationary policies and balanced budgets at home. This was combined with a return to the gold standard.

In the 1920s, the United States and Great Britain made extensive foreign loans, generally to countries with weak economies, thus adding an element of instability to the world financial markets, while at the same time the unchecked speculative boom in the American stock market only added to the stresses on the economic system. Nor was the boom of the 1920s universal: chronic agricultural depression marked most regions, while some countries, such as Germany, Great Britain, Italy, and Japan, hardly shared in the prosperity of the period.

When the New York stock market crashed in October 1929, the first major crack in the world economic system appeared. By 1930, the Great Depression had begun, shattering industrial productivity and making conditions in the already depressed agricultural sector worse. The following year, the financial markets collapsed in Europe. The Great Depression proved to be the most serious, deep-seated economic crisis in modern history, causing enormous human misery and putting huge pressures on political and social stability. Lasting well into the decade, governments—both democratic and authoritarian, both of the left and the right—adopted strategies of public spending and public works projects to cope with the massive unemployment. In addition, the widespread suffering attendant on the Depression led governments to expand public assistance programs and the passage of legislation that gave rise to the modern welfare state.

THE ECONOMIC CONSEQUENCES OF THE WAR

The economic impact of the war took a variety of forms, from the direct physical destruction of factories, railroads, and farms to the disruption of trade and the financial drain on national budgets. The peace settlements, responsive as they were to nationalist pressures, made the economic terms of the peace treaties political issues of great importance that were to hound international relations throughout the decade.

Significant Dates

The European Economy

1919	Keynes' *The Economic Consequences of the Peace*
April 1921	Reparations Commission announces $33 billion debt for Germany
1923	French occupation of the Ruhr
1924	Inflation in Germany
January 1925	Gold Standard Act in England
1929	Young Plan
October 1929	Wall Street crash; onset of Great Depression
May 1931	*Creditanstalt* fails
June 1931	Moratorium on war debts
1933	Franklin D. Roosevelt elected U.S. president

Readjustment and Boom

In 1919, Europeans found it necessary to deal with two industrial issues: the need to change over from the production of war matériel to peacetime consumer goods, and the task of raising production back up to prewar levels. In the period from 1914 to 1920, industrial output had declined by 39 percent in Germany, 34 percent in France, 26 percent in Italy, and 12 percent in Britain. These production drops were the result of a combination of circumstances, especially lower demand caused by the closing of foreign markets and the lack of raw materials. In countries overrun by armies, the physical destruction was an equally important factor. Belgium, for example, lost half of its steel mills and the bulk of its railroad lines.

Four years of fighting had undermined Europe's industrial supremacy. The productive capacities of the United States, Canada, and Japan expanded as each country took a larger share of the world's exports, and new home industries had begun to spring up in Latin America, India, and most of the British Dominions.

Table VIII.3.1
Share of Selected Countries in World Exports (in percent)

	1913	1925
Great Britain	13.9	12.4
Germany	13.1	7.0
France	7.2	7.2
Italy	2.6	2.4
Russia	4.2	1.0
USA	13.3	16.0
Canada	2.4	4.4
Japan	1.7	3.0

The resulting change in the pattern of world trade reflected the fact that Europe's economic status had been significantly altered.

The wartime naval blockades, the shortage of commercial carriers, and the loss by European nations of overseas markets all contributed to this changed trade pattern, although in the case of Russia the Bolshevik Revolution, the civil war, and the loss of territory to newly created nations explained the drastic drop of that country's exports.

Another important change in Europe's economic posture was in its role in international finance. The belligerent nations had borrowed huge amounts of money to finance the war. As a consequence, Germany's national debt rose from roughly 5 billion to more than 100 billion marks. In Germany's case, this money had been raised entirely by floating domestic war bonds. Although the British and French were equally burdened (the British and French debts, when measured in real purchasing power, were about the same size), about 25 percent of their increased debts came from American loans—by doing so, the two Western powers, once the world's greatest creditor states, had become debtor nations, even though they continued to lend money to the other Allies during the war. Countries on both sides had also resorted to the increased printing of paper money, thus fueling inflation.

Despite these problems, the years 1919–1920 saw an economic boom in Europe and the United States, characterized by high profits and low unemployment. The sudden prosperity was due to the fact that because the stock of consumer goods had been depleted during the war, with peace the demand for these goods rose sharply. As a result, prices—and profits—grew, and producers borrowed heavily at increasing rates of interest to expand their operations. A speculative boom followed as businesses recapitalized and expanded. Official British figures put unemployment at only 2.4 percent, or about half the prewar levels. The boom was short, for by the summer of 1920 the supply of consumer goods caught up to the demand, especially as prices rose so high as to discourage some buying. To encourage sales, prices were lowered. This did not work. As the price index fell precipitously, production slackened off, unemployment increased, and numerous bankruptcies were declared. By the end of 1921, British unemployment stood at 17 percent.

The postwar depression was temporary, and was followed in a few years by a longer period of increasing prosperity. For Europe, however, the significant fact was that although the world's productive capacity grew in the 1920s, a greater proportion of that capacity lay elsewhere.

REPARATIONS, INFLATION, AND WAR DEBTS

In the century before the Great War, Europe had created and maintained perhaps the highest standard of living in history. In a sense, this material well-being had been achieved in large measure because it had been able to import more than it exported. The difference had been paid for by two sources of income: interest earned from loans and investments made abroad, and profits from shipping charges. All this changed, however, once European nations became debtor states, a condition made worse by the huge costs of reconstruction, which required even more foreign loans.

The Allies hoped to meet their war debt obligations by reparations from Germany, which had been forced by the Treaty of Versailles to make such payments. Yet the onerous economic terms imposed on Germany by the peace treaty made it virtually impossible for Germany to make its reparations payments.

Problems of German Recovery

The payment of reparations was a political issue as well as an economic problem. Public opinion in the Allied countries demanded a punitive peace with Germany. To complicate matters, the French regarded reparations as a means of keeping Germany in a weakened state. Article 231 of the Treaty of Versailles had stipulated that Germany would pay reparations because it was responsible for having caused the war, a position that the German people strongly resented. Moreover, the Allies could not agree on a specific sum in 1919, and created a Reparations Commission that would eventually determine the amount and collect the payments. At the time they signed the treaty, therefore, the Germans did not know how much they would be required to pay.

In April 1921, the Reparations Commission settled on a figure equivalent to $33 billion, a staggering sum in view of the fact that Germany had lost some 15 percent of its total productive capacity, 36 percent of its coal supply, 72 percent of its iron ore, more than 90 percent of its merchant shipping, and almost all of its foreign investments. In a brilliant book entitled *The Economic Consequences of the Peace*, the British economist John Maynard Keynes (1883–1946) argued that the harsh economic terms of the Versailles settlement would make it impossible for Germany to meet its obligations and would have an adverse effect on the European economy as a whole.

Germany paid its first installment late, and only after a loan from British bankers. By 1923, the Germans had made additional payments only in kind

Inflation in Germany was so severe that it was cheaper to light stoves with currency than to buy kindling wood with it.

and then announced that they could not continue payments at all. It was then that the French and Belgians occupied the Ruhr Valley, sparking passive resistance in the mines and factories of the region and prompting the German government to begin printing paper currency recklessly. The mark, 100,000 to the dollar in June, reached a low of 6.30 trillion by November. Wages could not keep up with prices, and every day saw a stampede to convert the almost worthless currency into real goods. The most serious result of this hyperinflation was to ruin the entire German middle class, whose savings and pensions were wiped out, thus making the soil in which the Nazi party grew more fertile—indeed, it was in the midst of the inflation crisis that Hitler attempted his Munich *Putsch* (see Part VIII, Topic 2).

Reparations and War Debt Settlements

The German economy was stabilized beginning in late 1923, when the government issued new currency tied to the gold standard in the context of an international settlement of the reparations problem. A committee of financial experts headed by the American Charles G. Dawes (1865–1951) agreed to a two-year moratorium on reparations, the return of the Ruhr to Germany, and a $200 million loan to the beleaguered Germans. Germany committed itself to making regular payments on an increasing scale.

A large part of the international loan was sold in the United States, where it was underwritten by the House of Morgan. The success of this loan stimulated a frenzy of foreign loans, not only to European countries but to South America as well. Moreover, as confidence was restored in the economy, the Germans borrowed lavishly from abroad for public works projects and to rebuild their industrial base.

In 1929, another committee, also chaired by an American, Owen D. Young (1874–1962), devised a revised reparations arrangement. The Young Plan also involved an international loan, this time for $300 million, and the creation of a Bank for International Settlements, through which Germany would pay its reparations over a period of 59 years.

War debts similarly plagued international relations. By 1919, European nations owed the United

France sent troops, including these colonial soldiers, to occupy Germany's Ruhr district in 1923 to force reparation payments.

States almost $10 billion in war debts, including some $4.7 billion from France, $4.2 billion from Great Britain, and $1.6 billion from Italy. In addition, however, significant debts existed among the smaller Allies—France and Italy, for example, were in debt to Britain, and Belgium and Yugoslavia to France. Russia owed $2.5 billion to Britain and $900 million to France, but these loans were repudiated by the new Soviet government.

Some economists had suggested that all war debts be canceled, and British leaders repeated the idea formally to the United States in the early 1920s. American authorities, however, refused, insisting that they were willing to negotiate the debts owed to them, but with each individual nation. The European Allies had hoped that the combination of war debts and reparations would create a three-tiered financial relationship: German reparations payments would be made to countries such as Belgium and France, which would use that income to pay their war debts to Great Britain, which would in turn repay the wartime American loans. The United States insisted on keeping the reparations and war debt issues separate. Beginning in 1923, the United States began to settle the debt question with some 13 countries, beginning with Great Britain, which agreed to pay its obligation with interest over a period of 62 years.

RECOVERY AND PROSPERITY

After the collapse of 1921–1922, the European economy underwent a period of recovery, centered principally around the stabilization of Europe's major currencies. The end of runaway inflation and the issuance of the new currency in Germany, capped by the settlement of reparations in the Dawes Plan, marked the beginning of this process.

Currency Stabilization

The 19th century had been a period of relative monetary stability, with major paper currencies retaining their relative values and readily convertible into silver or gold. The war changed all this, lowering the buying power of Europe's major currencies, and doing so unequally. Wartime inflation had struck every belligerent country, and in the first postwar boom of 1919–1920, price inflation rose higher, although nowhere so drastically as in Germany. Moreover, the gold standard, adopted in the late 19th century (see Part VII, Topic 17), collapsed during the war and currencies fell still further in value. By the end of the war, the monetary systems of Germany, Austria, Hungary, and Russia were virtually destroyed. International monetary conferences attempted to restore some stability in the 1920s, and the German rescue operation was the most dramatic of these efforts.

In Britain, where the commitment to restoring the prewar parity of the pound to the dollar—$4.86—was a moral as well as a financial question, recovery was slow in coming and never fully realized. The British had lost important markets to the Americans and Japanese, and by 1921 were exporting half the value of goods traded in 1913. To get its huge national debt under control, Britain imposed heavy taxation at home and reduced government expenditures. Although the pound fluctuated, in the second half of 1923 it recovered to about $4.30, and when it almost reached parity in January 1925, the government passed the Gold Standard Act that pegged the pound at $4.79. In retrospect, it is clear that the pound was overvalued, and this had the effect of making British exports even more difficult to sell abroad. By then, unemployment was down to around 11 percent, where it hovered for most of the decade after its high point of 17 percent in 1921. Britain never fully regained its prewar prosperity.

In 1919, the French franc stood at only half its prewar value of 19¢, and by 1926 depreciated to 2¢. French leaders insisted on the importance of reconstruction, even at the price of ever larger deficits and more foreign loans, especially after the fiasco of the Ruhr occupation. In less than two years, ten finance ministers tried unsuccessfully to resolve the chaos of French finances. When Premier Raymond Poincaré (see Part VIII, Topic 5) came to office in July 1926, he finally took stern measures to stabilize the franc at 25 to the dollar, or one-quarter of its prewar value. This cheap franc helped to sell French goods abroad. That same year France also settled its debt with the United States.

The Era of Prosperity

After the stabilization of inflated currencies and the settlement of war debts, the pace of economic development picked up. New industries developed or expanded, with industrial growth taking place mainly in the production of consumer goods that were designed to make life easier or more enjoyable. A host of new appliances invaded the middle-class home, from vacuum cleaners and electric mixers to refrigerators and radios. In Britain alone, there were perhaps 36,000 radio sets in 1922, but by the end of 1929 that number had jumped to almost 3 million. The output in rayon, plastics, chemicals, and aluminum also rose substantially—in the case of aluminum, for example, from 64,000 tons in 1913 to more than 580,000 in 1938. The production of electrical energy doubled in the 1920s, and by the end of the next decade had doubled again in the major industrial countries.

Map 3.1 Industrialized Zones of Europe, c. 1930

The automobile was by far the most important product of the period, both from the economic viewpoint as well as in terms of its social impact. Automobiles had been appearing on European roads since the early 20th century—France alone produced some 16,500 in 1902—but they had not come into mass use before the Great War. The war itself, however, greatly increased the demand for automobiles and trucks. Henry Ford's ability to produce the Model T inexpensively and in great quantity made the automobile the biggest selling wholesale product in the United States by 1928. European manufacturers copied Ford's methods, lowering production costs by using standardized parts on the assembly line and concentrating production in fewer companies. High protective tariffs shielded European producers from American cars in the 1920s. The table below shows the remarkable expansion in the ownership of automobiles.

Table VIII.3.2
Registered Motor Vehicles, 1913–1938 (in 1000s)

	BRITAIN	GERMANY	FRANCE	U.S.
1913	208	93	125	1258
1921	464	91	236	10,494
1926	1042	319	891	22,053
1930	1524	67	1460	26,532
1938	2422	1816	2251	29,443

The automobile industry acted as an important stimulus to other industries and raw materials, including metals, rubber, gasoline, and lubricants—the world's production of crude petroleum increased from 400 million barrels in 1914 to 1.5 billion in 1938. Road construction came into its own in the 1920s as a result of the spreading use of the automobile.

In the late 1920s, industrialization began to spread to less developed nations, especially to the Soviet Union and the countries of Eastern Europe. In addition, industry everywhere underwent a process of rationalization, whereby less economical plants with older equipment and production methods were closed down and production either shifted to new factories or concentrated in more efficient ones. Rationalization was further enhanced by the introduction of new labor-saving machinery, the standardization of parts, and the adoption of mass production assembly line techniques. In the postwar period, this process was easier in those countries, such as France and Belgium, where physical destruction required that new factories be built, or in planned economies such as the Soviet Union and Fascist Italy.

Britain did not participate fully in the era of prosperity. Unemployment never fell below 1 million and the British share in world trade never returned to prewar levels. Moreover, while the United States outproduced Britain in the new industries, the former "workshop of the world" faced serious handicaps in traditional industries such as coal mining, steel, and textiles. Production declines were registered in all three industries during the two decades following the war. That British industries could no longer compete as they had once done was fully revealed by the steady abandonment of the free trade that had been followed since the 19th century.

France was troubled less by trade patterns than by the need for industrial reconstruction. Reparations, together with the recovery of Alsace-Lorraine and the new, modernized factories that were built in the north-

Unemployed British workers march on London, 1930.

ern portions of the country, stimulated French industrialization. As a result, France emerged in the interwar era with a greatly expanded industrial sector. Germany relied on massive foreign loans to rebuild and modernize its industry. The Germans also experienced a boom in construction, especially by public funds, after 1924. On the other hand, in the entire period from 1923 to 1936 unemployment fell below 7 percent only once, in 1925, when it registered 6.9 percent, and it actually soared to 18 percent in the following year. In 1929, with the boom in full swing, some 2 million German workers were without jobs. For Europe as a whole, figures show that the number of unemployed rose from a low estimate of 3.5 million in the first half of the decade to perhaps as high as 5.5 million during the era of prosperity.

Hence, although the second postwar economic boom stretched across the second half of the 1920s, it was by no means general and all-pervasive. European production as a whole regained the 1913 level only in 1925, whereas in the same period it had increased by 25 percent in North America and 20 percent in Asia. Textiles, once the most important product of Europe's industrial revolution, stagnated in the face of cheaper Japanese production. Moreover, Europe's share of world industrial production shrunk steadily, from 57.6 percent in 1913 to 47.1 percent in 1928, while that of the United States rose from 32 to 39.3 percent. In the same period, Europe's share of world trade declined from 54.5 to about 49.2 percent. From 1913 to 1939, per capita real income actually grew in Western Europe, but the growth was slower than it had been during the Long Depression of the late 19th century (see Part VII, Topic 17).

THE CRASH: WALL STREET AND THE FINANCIAL COLLAPSE

There is no agreement among economists or economic historians as to the underlying causes of the Great Depression, nor is there consensus as to where it began or why it was so widespread. On several other points, however, experts do agree. In view of the crucial role played by the United States in world affairs after 1917, its economic policies, both internally and externally, had much to do with the coming of the Depression as well as its longevity. Unlike the pre-1914 era, the new international financial system had shown itself to be unstable, and the United States would not play the role that Britain had once played as watchdog of the system. Then, too, postwar recovery had proved to be less than universal, and much of the newly generated wealth was poorly distributed. Moreover, there were signs that the economy was far from in perfect order well before the stock market crash of 1929.

America in the Twenties

In the United States the age of postwar prosperity was known as the "Roaring Twenties," a term that captured the sense of modern, fast-paced life in a society marked by uncontrolled speculative investment, soaring profits, and the thirst for material well-being. Two Republican presidents, Warren G. Harding (served 1921–1923) and Calvin Coolidge (served 1923–1929), identified the nation's welfare with that of private business and followed a policy of noninterference in the workings of the economy. "This is a business country," proclaimed Coolidge, "and wants a business government." Federal spending was slashed, as were taxes for the highest income levels. Laws regulating business monopoly were eased, and the stock market was permitted to soar upward virtually without regulation.

The United States was not immune from the kind of flaws that marred European prosperity. A boom in Florida land speculation had burst in 1925, and in 1927 the industrial production index fell as a result of Ford's decision to close down his automobile plants in order to change over from the Model T to the Model A. Nevertheless, between 1923 and 1929, corporate profits increased by 62 percent, while real income for the average worker rose only 11 percent. One-third of all personal income went to the richest 5 percent of the population, and workers were unable to share adequately in the prosperity or to buy the huge quantity of industrial goods being produced. Overexpansion and large inventories of unsold goods led to job layoffs and business slowdowns even before the crash.

The economic growth of the 1920s had been financed largely by credit—business, personal, and international. Those who extended credit for business expansion assumed that borrowers could repay their loans with their profits while continuing to purchase capital goods. Similarly, stock investors bought heavily on a credit system known as "margin trading," which permitted them to pay out only a small part of the cost of their securities by borrowing most of the price from the brokers, who were themselves operating on bank credit. These practices fueled the unchecked financial speculation that led to the 1929 crash. Consumer credit was widely available in the form of installment plans. The ease of obtaining credit encouraged overspending for major purchases such as automobiles, appliances, and even houses. High sales expectations induced retailers and wholesalers to pay their suppliers with borrowed money. The danger, of course, lay in the fact that a call for repayment by any creditor would require everyone in the system to pay their debts in cash. Because most investors borrowed more than they could repay, the system was fraught with potential disaster.

America, Europe, and the Crash

On the international level, the credit system of the 1920s was equally precarious. Lavish loans were extended to many small nations, especially in Latin America and eastern Europe, despite their inability to repay the obligations. The decision of one creditor state to withdraw funds from a foreign bank or call in its loans threatened at any moment to upset international finances.

In the six years from 1924, the United States loaned 6.4 billion dollars abroad, mainly in short-term loans liable to sudden recall. Then, starting in June 1928, the American loans suddenly began to dry up. This shift in foreign lending was due primarily to the fact that as profits soared on the stock market, investors removed their resources from loans and put them into securities. (High interest rates in the United States also attracted foreign capital.) The problem, of course, was that the market value of securities was being inflated far beyond their actual worth. In 1928–1929, the average price of stocks on the New York Stock Exchange rose by 60 percent. The halt to U.S. lending placed a severe financial strain on a number of debtor countries, where economic activity began to decline.

The crash itself was precipitated when the Bank of England raised its interest rates at the end of September 1929, largely in order to attract capital back to London—the same day that the New York Stock Exchange reached its peak. Prices began to slip on October 3, and gave way to panic on October 24, known as "Black Thursday," as orders to sell exceeded orders to buy. A frenzy of selling swept the floor of the exchange, and panicked brokers demanded payment of margin payments that triggered bankruptcies among thousands of small investors. Confidence was partially restored when a group of powerful bankers pooled resources to buy securities. The next week, on "Black Tuesday," October 29, the market fell even more precipitously. Many who had bought cheaply the previous week were now forced to sell at great losses. As the collapse continued into November, increasingly larger investors went under. The spiral of ever-rising prices reversed itself as the market collapsed.

Given the fragile nature of the international financial system, the impact of the crash was bound to be felt abroad. American creditors called in their overseas loans. In May 1931 the *Creditanstalt*, which held two-thirds of all Austrian assets, failed, despite a loan from the Bank of England. The panic spread across Europe. Investors withdrew their capital from Germany, the largest recipient of foreign loans, and banks also began to fail there. In June 1931, U.S. President Herbert Hoover (served 1929–1933) declared a moratorium on all international debt payments. By July, British banks began to suffer, and in

October 1929 outside the New York Stock Exchange.

September the government there took the country off the gold standard.

THE GREAT DEPRESSION

The stock market crash did not cause the Great Depression, for the economy was already in deep trouble, but the panic brought a sudden halt to the years of economic optimism and led to a scramble for liquidity. Banks that had themselves invested heavily in securities failed, businesses cut back as sales and orders declined, both at home and abroad. Unemployment figures shot up throughout the world as the financial panic gave way to general economic depression.

Industry and Agriculture

As the financial crisis spread to business, large corporations slowed down or stopped production, for markets for industrial goods and raw materials soon disappeared. Compared to 1929, world industrial production dropped by 38 percent and global trade by two-thirds. The human impact of the Great Depression was devastating, giving rise to unprecedented misery. The ranks of the unemployed had grown so large that the very fabric of society was on the verge of being torn apart. As early as 1931, one-third of the entire German labor force—more than 6 million people—was jobless. The next year, when the Depression was at its worst, the number of unemployed in the United States reached 13 million. The following table gives an idea of the dimensions of the problem.

Table VIII.3.3
Percentage of the Labor Force Unemployed
(selected countries, 1929–1936)

	BRITAIN	GERMANY	SWEDEN	U.S.
1929	10.4	13.1	10.7	3.2
1930	16.1	22.2	12.2	8.7
1931	21.3	33.7	17.2	15.8
1932	22.1	43.7	22.8	23.6
1933	19.9	26.3	23.7	24.9
1934	16.7	14.9	18.9	26.7
1935	15.5	11.6	16.1	20.1
1936	13.1	8.3	13.6	16.9

The Depression caused widespread demoralization, both on the individual level and throughout society in general. In many instances, desperation grew into anger against existing governments and often expressed itself in radical political movements.

Throughout the 1920s, agriculture had been suffering from a chronic state of depression. One-fifth of Europe's wheat fields had been taken out of cultivation by the war, and the resulting rise in prices had encouraged farmers in North America to increase their output and to buy more land at relatively high prices. European output increased substantially for a variety of reasons. Improvements in mechanization now permitted a farmer to reap and bind five times more grain than was possible before the war. Political changes also

Parisians stood in long lines to collect free food during the Depression.

affected agriculture. In the new countries of Eastern Europe, the bulk of the population was still agrarian: three-quarters of the population of Yugoslavia, Romania, and Bulgaria, and two-thirds of all Poles, lived by farming. Between 1913 and 1939, cultivated areas increased by more than 17 million acres. Many of the large landed estates that had once dominated the economic life of the region were broken up and small plots distributed to peasants.

Despite these reforms, however, the fall in agricultural prices—some 30 percent between 1925 and 1929—resulting from overproduction and competition from abroad hurt farmers everywhere. European governments tried to protect their farmers by raising agri-

Graph 3.1 Industrial Production in the Great Depression

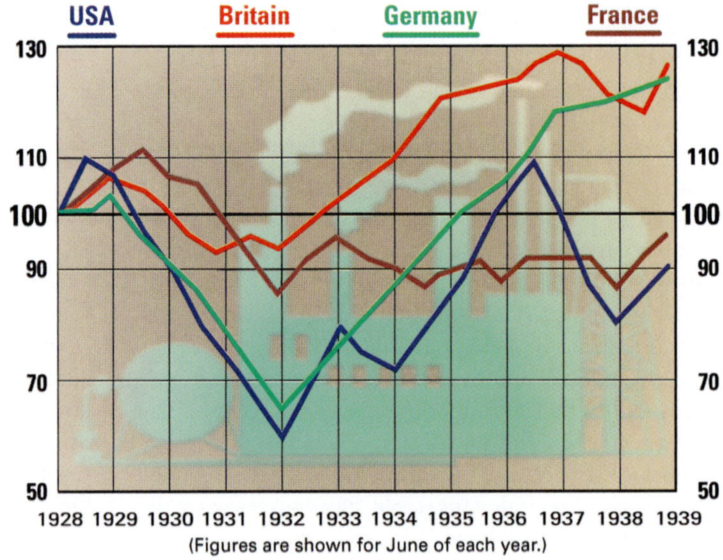

cultural tariffs, a move that damaged producers elsewhere. With the coming of the Great Depression, prices fell even more sharply, making a bad situation worse. In general, agricultural interests suffered heavier losses than industrial interests during the Depression.

The New Economics and the New Deal

For many contemporaries, the Great Depression represented a crisis that confirmed long-held beliefs about the evils and weaknesses of capitalism. Karl Marx had asserted the inevitability of class conflict, and during World War I, Lenin had foreseen the collapse of capitalism as Western nations competed with each other over colonies and markets. Now, Marxists and others seemed about to be proven correct. Prime Minister Ramsay MacDonald of Great Britain (see Part VIII, Topic 5), himself a socialist, announced in 1930 that capitalism had to be blamed for the Depression: "We are not on trial," he said, "it is the system under which we live. It has broken down . . . everywhere, as it was bound to break down."

Government reaction to the Great Depression differed from country to country. In would-be totalitarian regimes such as Fascist Italy and the Soviet Union, governments created jobs for the unemployed and already provided a range of social services, including health care and other benefits (see Part VIII, Topic 4). In democratic states, however, where the principles of laissez-faire economics and limited government intervention prevailed, the policy adjustments caused by the economic collapse were more wrenching to tradition (see Part VIII, Topic 5).

First reactions, even under MacDonald's Labour government, included government spending cuts and tight fiscal policies, but when it was clear that such deflationary approaches only worsened conditions, the democracies turned increasingly to methods already in place elsewhere, including public works projects and extensive social insurance programs. Public officials took a more active role in shaping the economic and social affairs as the Depression forced governments to deal with the devastating impact of the collapse on millions of their citizens.

Even before the Depression had struck, the British economist John Maynard Keynes had begun to evolve theories about the economic responsibilities of government. A brilliant and eclectic thinker, Keynes was a member of the Bloomsbury Circle of intellectuals and artists (see Part VIII, Topic 7), a high-ranking civil servant, and taught at Cambridge University. He served as chief economist with the British delegation to the Paris Peace Conference in 1919.

As Keynes observed the already depressed conditions under which the British working class suffered in the second half of the 1920s, he began to rethink the entire basis of prevailing economic principles, and in the process offered a powerful critique of both laissez-faire capitalism and socialism. Keynes published his ideas in a variety of articles and books, including *The End of Laissez-Faire* (1926), and brought his arguments together in *The General Theory of Employment, Interest and Money* (1936). The classical theory of capitalist economic policy had long been that the laws of supply and demand would, if left to operate without interference, establish a healthy equilibrium of prices, wages, and production. But the chronic state of unemployment that dogged the British economy, together with his analysis of the Depression, led Keynes to conclude that the economics of free enterprise was imperfect and misguided. Instead, he argued that government should intervene actively in the economy, manipulating such controls as the interest rate, monetary expansion, and public works programs, to correct the weaknesses of capitalism. According to his theory, in times of economic dislocation governments could stimulate demand by priming the economic pump through public spending, which would in turn spark production and create jobs. Whether consciously or not, as bad times dragged on, most governments eventually adopted Keynesian principles in dealing with the Depression, and his ideas came to dominate economic thinking for generations to come.

It was in the United States, rather than in Europe, that Keynesian theories found their first widespread application among the democratic states of the West. As we have seen, nowhere had the principles of the free enterprise market economy been more freely or completely practiced than in the American economy of the 1920s, and nowhere was the collapse more extreme. The Hoover administration had initiated a number of programs to deal with the financial crisis as well as with the effects of the Depression. It was, however, with the election of Franklin D. Roosevelt (served 1933–1945) as president that American society underwent a major transformation.

Roosevelt's "New Deal" policies were aimed at bringing America out of the Depression by reforming the capitalist system so as to save it from destruction. His economic advisers, familiar with Keynesian ideas, pushed for massive government intervention in the economy. Roosevelt introduced far-reaching laws to regulate banking and investment, and created a host of government programs to stimulate business recovery, help the devastated farmers, strengthen labor organization, and create jobs. He also introduced several basic social welfare programs into American national life, including Social Security and unemployment compensation. The New Deal programs did stimulate recovery and cushioned the impact of the Depression for millions of citizens, although by the eve of World War II employment had not returned to pre-1929 levels. Nevertheless, the improvement in economic conditions was so successful that American voters eventually endorsed the New Deal reforms by reelecting Roosevelt to an unprecedented third term.

As soon as he was elected, Roosevelt had sent a special envoy to Fascist Italy to study how Mussolini's corporate state was coping with the Depression. The president's political opponents on the right charged that he was replacing capitalism with socialism, while those on the left accused him of fascism. It was, however, the ideas of Keynes that provided both the inspiration and the theoretical justification for the most radical transformation in modern Western economic thought. Reformers in Great Britain, France, and other democratic states eventually adopted similar programs, although not always with such enthusiasm as the New Dealers in the United States.

Despite the optimism that had greeted the end of the First World War, and the flashes of fast living and prosperity that marked the postwar era, the economic life of the interwar years was also characterized by partial recovery, instability, and uneven development. The momentary boom of 1919–1920 was followed by a longer period of recession and readjustment, after which some countries enjoyed a wave of prosperity while others went through a variety of economic experiences that ranged from the doldrums to real crisis. The legacies of reparations and war debts were in themselves partially responsible for the difficulties of recovery and for making the international financial system uncertain. The crisis of the Great Depression, when it came in 1929, should not have been totally unexpected.

The Depression was responsible in many instances for major change: in politics, for a radicalization of popular opinion that resulted in the rise of extremist movements and, in the case of Germany, contributed to the Nazi seizure of power; in social and economic policy, for an abandonment of the principles of laissez-faire economics by most Western nations and the inauguration of an era of government activism. The economic crisis weakened democracy and made other, totalitarian alternatives attractive to many millions of people who experienced the trauma of a world turned upside down.

Questions for Further Study

1. What effect did World War I have on the European economy?
2. What caused the Great Depression?
3. How did governments respond to the Great Depression?

Suggestions for Further Reading

Cameron, Rondo. *A Concise Economic History of the World.* New York, 1989.

Evans, Richard J., and D. Geary. *The German Unemployed: Experiences and Consequences of Mass Unemployment from the Weimar Republic to the Third Reich.* New York, 1987.

Galbraith, John K. *The Great Crash, 1929*, rev. ed. Boston, 1962.

Holtfrerich, Carl-Ludwig. *The German Inflation, 1914–1923.* Berlin, 1986.

Jackson, Julian. *The Politics of Depression in France, 1932–1936.* New York, 1985.

James, Harold. *The German Slump: Politics and Economics, 1924–1936.* Oxford, 1986.

Keynes, John M. *The Economic Consequences of the Peace.* London, 1919.

Kindleberger, Charles P. *The World in Depression, 1929–1939.* Berkeley, 1973.

Kuromiya, Hiroaki. *Stalin's Industrial Revolution: Politics and Workers, 1928–1932.* New York, 1988.

Maier, Charles S. *Recasting Bourgeois Europe: Stabilization in France, Germany, and Italy.* Princeton, NJ, 1975.

VIII

Topic 4

Mussolini, Hitler, Stalin: The Totalitarian Nightmare

The years between the two world wars saw the development of a new kind of antidemocratic political system known as totalitarianism. Europe had, of course, known powerful, centralized government in past centuries, and many of its monarchs had wanted to incorporate all power in their own hands, invoking the notion of divine right to legitimize their authority. The totalitarian state was a unique development in political theory, although in practice it is doubtful that a true totalitarian society was achieved in any of the three nations—Fascist Italy, Nazi Germany, and the Soviet Union—in which leaders aspired to create one.

Mussolini had become a dictator of Italy by 1925, and over the next 20 years he sought to make his government the first totalitarian regime in history, although it fell short of such expectations. Alongside the preexisting constitutional structure that had governed the country since unification, he created new Fascist institutions which he empowered with theoretically supreme authority.

After coming to terms with the Catholic Church, which exercised a powerful influence over Italian loyalties, he set about regimenting Italian society in an unparalleled fashion: revamping the educational system and dragooning all Italian youth into special organizations designed to indoctrinate and train them according to Fascist ideology. Mussolini's bureaucrats brought all aspects of intellectual and cultural life under government authority.

In order to mold popular consensus and extract obedience, the Fascist state combined positive image making with an atmosphere of terror. Mussolini did this by twin policies: by building a vast propaganda machine that shaped the values, ideas, and information received by the entire population; and by creating an elaborate police state that rounded up anti-Fascists and employed paid informants, torture, and internment programs.

Hitler built his totalitarian state in much the same manner. In Germany, where official theory was more clearly articulated, the degree of control exercised by the government was more effective and the party permeated the government bureaucracy and daily life more completely. Moreover, whereas Mussolini was largely uninterested in art and viewed it as propaganda, Hitler had clear and definite views about the kind of style and image he wanted German art to project.

There had been no real tradition of anti-Semitism in Italian Fascism, and Fascist racial policies were not as drastic as Nazi programs, nor were they implemented with any degree of enthusiasm. Most Italians greeted them with revulsion. Hitler's anti-Semitic policies, on the other hand, were at the core of Nazi belief. They began by stripping Jews of their rights as citizens, and ended with the horrors of the Holocaust. The Nazis' racism, together with the efficiency they were able to achieve in German society, made the regime there infinitely more brutal than that of Italy.

The totalitarian state in Stalin's Russia also reflected differences that derived from ideology and national circumstances. In his obsession to modernize Russia's economy, Stalin pushed his country into a vast experiment in social regimentation that aimed at maximizing agricultural and industrial productivity. Stalin was so driven to accumulate all power in his own hands, that he destroyed an entire generation of Soviet leaders to safeguard it. To combat the resistance against his development plans, and in a blind effort to wipe out his enemies, Stalin resorted to mass exterminations, labor camps, and purges that were unparalleled in their scope.

THE NATURE OF TOTALITARIANISM

The historical examples of Fascist Italy and Nazi Germany on the one hand and of the Soviet Union on the other suggest that totalitarianism is a politically neutral concept, linked neither to the left nor the right. Totalitarianism is a type of government that seeks to exercise total control over the citizens of a given country, and to put into practice a set of beliefs designed to alter human society radically.

A set of common characteristics is usually found in all totalitarian regimes. Totalitarian states are dictatorships in which the ruler claims to exercise authority in the name of a political ideology. Mussolini, Hitler, and Stalin were radicals, each bent on forcing millions of citizens to conform to his values and each with a vision of an ideal future society. In the name of ideology, the most extreme crimes and horrors were committed and rationalized. In each case, the dictator was made the object of secular worship in order to justify his unlimited power.

Totalitarian governments are dominated by one political party and by the suspension of the most basic civil liberties. So intertwined are the dominant political party and the state bureaucracy that lines of authority are blurred. Totalitarian regimes are police states, in which force, violence, and terror are used against their own citizens. Such governments normally control the educational systems and mass media, and create an array of social institutions to indoctrinate and mobilize the population. Regardless of whether a particular regime rests on a socialist or capitalist footing, all totalitarian governments aim to centralize and shape economic policy.

Significant Dates

Fascist Italy and Nazi Germany

October 1922	Mussolini becomes prime minister of Italy
1926	Ministry of Corporations created
1929	Lateran Pacts
1930s	Fascistization of Italian society and culture
1930	Nazi electoral victories
January 1933	Hitler becomes chancellor
1930s	Regimentation of German life
1933	Mussolini sets up Institute for Industrial Reconstruction
June 30, 1934	Night of the Long Knives
1935	Nuremberg Laws
1938	Night of the Broken Glass
1938	Mussolini creates Chamber of Fasci and Corporations
October–November 1938	Anti-Semitic laws passed in Italy

ITALY UNDER MUSSOLINI: REGIMENTATION IN THE FASCIST STATE

Mussolini's totalitarian state continued to evolve over the entire two decades that he was in power. Yet within less than three years he had established the basic struc-

Map 4.1 Interwar Europe

ture of the regime: the one-party state, a secret police to arrest and a military tribunal to try anti-Fascists, press censorship, and loyalty oaths for government employees.

The Fascist State

Mussolini's regime grafted Fascist institutions on to already established government. Technically, the Italian constitution was the fundamental legal document of the realm and King Victor Emmanuel III still ruled, with the right to appoint and dismiss the prime minister (see Part VII, Topic 15). Mussolini allowed traditional forms to persist alongside his own, partially in order to preserve the fiction of legitimacy. He created, however, a Fascist Grand Council that included party and state officials and was to be the supreme organ of state. Mussolini personally selected the members of the Grand Council as well as candidates for Chamber of Deputies elections. The Grand Council was to abolish Parliament altogether in 1938 and put in its place the Chamber of Fasci and Corporations, whose members were elected not from political parties but job categories.

Ever since Italy had seized Rome from the papacy in 1870, the Vatican had refused to recognize the existence of the Italian state. One of Mussolini's most popular decisions was to make peace with the Catholic Church. There were two chief reasons for this. Millions of Italians were devout Catholics and were loath to divide their loyalties between church and state; and the church was perceived as acting as a stable, conservative influence in modern society. In 1929, therefore, he and Pope Pius XI (ruled 1922–1939) concluded the Lateran Pacts, according to which the Vatican City became an independent state ruled by the pope inside the confines of Rome. The government also repealed the anticlerical legislation passed since 1870. Mussolini further agreed to pay the Vatican a large sum of money in compensation for the lost papal territory around Rome. Perhaps more important, however, the church's popular

Official "Fascist" architecture under Mussolini evolved into a modernized classicism, as in this "Palace of Civilization" built for the 1942 world's fair in Rome.

youth organizations were now permitted to operate without harassment, and the Vatican was to have its own newspaper and radio station. Mussolini also implemented compulsory religious instruction in public schools. This "concordat" was an important success for Mussolini, who not only guaranteed himself the public support of the church, but instantly won the admiration of Catholics everywhere.

The Making of Consensus

Mussolini enjoyed considerable popular support, at least until his foreign adventures in the mid-1930s. Such consensus was the result of a dual policy of coercion and socialization. The Fascist police system was a complicated affair, consisting of several traditional Italian police units as well as a special division of "political police" and a network of paid informants operated by an agency known as OVRA. In addition, tens of thousands of anti-Fascists were rounded up and placed under surveillance or sent to domestic exile in remote and barren parts of Italy. As effective as this structure was, it proved less gruesome than the mass killings in Hitler's or Stalin's police states.

The Fascists devised numerous methods for forging consensus among intellectuals and artists. Some were appointed to a new Royal Academy, others were given secret government subsidies or government employment, and others were simply ignored as long as they did not openly oppose the regime. In the 1930s Mussolini created a Ministry of Popular Culture that controlled newspapers, radio, theater, film production, and book publishing. Mussolini's longtime mistress and confidant, the art critic Margherita Sarfatti (1880–1961), presided over a famous salon and attracted many talented artists and writers to the regime. She even started an art movement of her favorite painters that stressed a return to classical values couched in a modern style. While the regime did not officially endorse this or any other artistic movement, it also did not condemn artists for their style or theories. Within limits, intellectuals and artists were allowed a surprisingly wide margin of freedom.

The Fascist party played a crucial role in regimentation. A host of organizations provided Italian youth with political indoctrination and physical training. Although many parents refused to send their children to party groups, by the mid-1930s they had enrolled more than 3 million boys and girls. Popular

Regimentation programs in Fascist Italy included Fascist party organizations that trained and indoctrinated children and youths from the age of six. Here "Sons of the Wolf" are on parade in Rome.

leisure time programs, including cultural events, vacations, and light entertainment, were provided by the "after work" organization, known as the *Dopolavoro*. Millions of Italians joined the party in the 1930s, for job opportunities if not out of conviction.

Under the fanatical direction of party secretary Achille Starace (1889–1945), the regime even tried to change the way in which Italians behaved in their daily lives. Starace, who became something of a joke among many Italians, ordered civilians not to use words of foreign origin, to salute each other instead of shaking hands, and to wear black shirts instead of dresses and business suits.

The party propaganda machine exalted Mussolini as the *Duce* of Fascism, the wise, strong, and all-powerful leader who would make Italy great again. Absurd slogans, plastered on public buildings and taught to schoolchildren, were intended as secular chants to the myth of the Duce: "Better one day as a lion than a hundred years as a sheep," or "Believe! Obey! Fight!" Partly under Sarfatti's influence, the regime merged Fascist themes with ancient Roman images, and Mussolini—portrayed in official sculpture and painting as the new Caesar—promised to restore the glories of the imperial age.

The other side of life in Mussolini's Italy was represented by the many ordinary Italians who opposed Fascism. When Mussolini declared his dictatorship, many anti-Fascists were beaten or arrested, but a remarkable number of prominent political leaders managed to escape abroad, where they regrouped and established resistance organizations. Inside the country, many others engaged in minor acts of opposition or were involved in underground networks. Not all such people were active anti-Fascists, but during World War II, hundreds of thousands of Italians participated in the armed resistance.

HITLER'S GERMANY: RACE AND REPRESSION IN THE NAZI REGIME

The coming of the Great Depression in 1930 gave the Nazis the huge popular following that Hitler needed. In 1925, Field Marshal Paul von Hindenburg, the hero of World War I, was elected president of the Republic. Hindenburg, already in his late seventies, was an upright, stolid patriarchal figure who gave Germany an aura of stability. Yet not even Hindenburg's prestige could stave off the terrible economic plight that struck Germany, which experienced a more severe setback than any other European state in 1930. With industrial production at 39 percent of its former level and some 6 million out of work, the economic crisis devastated the German working class and wiped out the incomes and savings of much of the middle class.

The National Socialist Victory

Such extreme conditions undermined popular consensus for the centrist parties that had stabilized the Weimar Republic since its birth, and created the conditions under which the Nazis could come to power. In their desperation, the German electorate turned to extremist forces on the right and the left. The Nazis increased their seats in the Reichstag dramatically, first to 107 in September 1930 and then to a startling 230 in July 1932, making it the largest single party in Parliament. The Communists jumped from 54 to 89. Hitler stood at the edge of power.

In 1932 Germany experienced a three-way race for the office of president. The aged Hindenburg was persuaded to run again, and against him were arrayed the Communist candidate Ernst Thaelmann and Hitler. Hitler won enough votes to enter a runoff election with Hindenburg, who won. Nevertheless, Hitler had attracted some 13 million voters, many of them from the working class. In the November parliamentary elections that same year, the Nazis dropped down to 196 seats while the Communists increased their strength to 100. In Germany, as in postwar Italy, the specter of the radical left frightened many middle-class citizens into the arms of the right. Conservative forces grew more comfortable with the notion of a Hitler-led government and began to provide the Nazis with money and support, thinking that once in office Hitler would become tame. Hindenburg was finally persuaded to ask Hitler to form a cabinet.

Hitler took office as chancellor on January 30, 1933. He immediately dissolved Parliament and prepared for elections. At that moment, the Reichstag building itself burned down in a mysterious fire, and Hitler accused the Communists of responsibility. The German people went to the polls in an angry mood, while the Nazis unleashed another round of violence on their enemies. The Nazis won 44 percent of the seats in the Reichstag, enabling them to form a coalition with the Nationalists, who held 8 percent.

Armed with a majority, Hitler then invoked Article 48 of the constitution and proclaimed a state of emergency. He ejected the Communists from Parliament and had the rump Reichstag grant him extraordinary powers. All political parties except the Nazis were outlawed, and when Hindenburg died in August 1934, Hitler merged the offices of president and chancellor into his own hands. Adolf Hitler had become dictator of Germany.

Hitler's totalitarian state took shape more rapidly than Mussolini's. Within a year of coming to power in 1933, he had established most of the institutions that would characterize Nazi Germany. The Nazi restructuring of German life was in many respects more radical, and the impact on Europe more profound. Hitler, who liked to think in sweeping historical clichés, called his creation the "Third Reich" (the first *Reich* was the Holy Roman Empire, from 800 to 1806, and the second was imperial Germany, from 1871 to 1918) and predicted that it would remain for a thousand years.

The Third Reich

Hitler made himself the supreme leader *(Führer)* of the German state. So powerful was he that the very concept of sovereignty—the legitimate right to rule—emanated not from the people or a deity, but from himself. The German legal system was completely Nazified. Thenceforth, the higher interests of the state provided the basis for all laws. Nazi "justice" was meted out by People's Courts in the name of the Führer.

The German Republic, like the Second Reich before it, had been a federal arrangement composed of a variety of state governments, such as Prussia and Bavaria. Hitler did away with these states, substituting in their place a highly centralized government. In keeping with the Nazi theory of the "conquest of the state," appropriate party leaders assumed command of equivalent positions in the government administration. Hitler retained the Reichstag, but removed all real authority from it.

Hitler could neither remain in power very long nor carry out his strategy for world hegemony without the support of the German Army. But most of the German officer corps, with a long tradition of status and aristocratic privilege behind it, considered Hitler and his Nazi entourage low-class thugs. From their perspective, the generals saw Hitler as a temporary expedient who would serve a useful purpose in destroying the Republic and restoring the army to its former position of strength. Like Mussolini, Hitler had to compromise with the generals, and like Mussolini he did so by sacrificing his own storm troops, the SA.

Ernst Roehm, the deposed leader of the SA, had come back to Germany on Hitler's urging in 1930 and had been instrumental in the seizure of power (see Part VIII, Topic 2). But Roehm had always resented the power and pretensions of the generals, and after 1933 he demanded that Hitler replace the German Army with the SA. For Hitler, the choice between the SA and the army was clear, and he secured a pledge of loyalty from the generals in return for the destruction of Roehm's forces. The agreement was executed on the night of June 30 in a series of surprise raids of SA camps throughout Germany. The purge, known as the "Night of the Long Knives," ended with the cold-blooded murder of Roehm and his followers.

The Nazi police state was as complex as Mussolini's structure. The secret police *(Gestapo)* sought out anti-Nazis and other internal political enemies. Information and confessions were extracted by torture and blackmail, but the victims of Nazi terror were often summarily executed or incarcerated without

Nazi propagandists organized carefully choreographed public ceremonies and party rallies. Here Hitler addresses a huge 1936 event.

SA commander Ernst Roehm (right) and SS leader Heinrich Himmler (center) confer with police officer Kurt Daluege, 1933.

formal charges. As early as 1933, Hitler opened the first concentration camp at Dachau, where political prisoners were kept. Almost a dozen more were subsequently constructed. Heinrich Himmler, who served both as head of the Gestapo and the SS, ran the camps, where prisoners were either used as slave labor, were allowed to die of hunger, or were otherwise brutalized. During World War II, the death camps became the most horrible manifestation of Nazism.

Hitler, Mussolini, and Racial Policy

Hitler's own twisted contempt for Jews, Slavs, gypsies, and other ethnic groups that he considered "inferior" became the basis of Nazi ideology. Yet, in making racism a part of his political program, he called upon an extensive European tradition of prejudice and hatred. The Nazis mixed these traditions with 19th-century Pan-German sentiment, believing with Hitler that the German "Master Race" would inevitably rule the world. Hitler's obsessive hatred for the Jews was the focus of a huge and systematic effort by the Nazi state of unparalleled evil—their mass extermination.

Anti-Semitism became official policy almost immediately. Jews were purged from government employment in April 1933. Two years later, in 1935, the so-called Nuremberg Laws stripped Jews of their rights as citizens, and made it a crime for them to marry "pure" Germans. Jews were forbidden to practice medicine or law and could no longer attend or teach in universities (see Part VIII, Topic 9). The regime then launched a moral and physical assault against the Jewish communities of Germany.

In November 1938, Goebbels orchestrated an assault on Jewish businesses and synagogues known as *Kristallnacht*.

Those Jews who recognized the danger tried to leave Germany, but too many found it impossible. In 1938, a Polish Jew killed a German diplomat in Paris, and the crime became the excuse for the unleashing of a premeditated attack against German Jewish synagogues, homes, and businesses. Many Jews lost their lives in the carnage, and the government then levied heavy taxes on the victims. After this destruction—known as *Kristallnacht* (Night of the Broken Glass)—it was increasingly difficult for Jews to flee the country, and those who managed to get away found in many cases that the Western powers were not disposed to take them in. While some Western leaders criticized German policy, their warnings fell on deaf ears.

In November 1938, Mussolini reversed himself on the question of the Jews. Before that, he had claimed repeatedly that Fascism was not anti-Semitic. Indeed, his mistress, Margherita Sarfatti, was Jewish. The decision to introduce anti-Semitic legislation was a purely political one—his desire to align Italy in a united front with Germany. The measures that Mussolini enacted, although thoroughly reprehensible, were not nearly as severe as those in Germany. Italy's 50,000 Jews had to abandon most professions and universities, but Italian-born Jews retained their citizenship. Mixed marriages were forbidden and Jews were not allowed to own land. On the other hand, unlike Nazism's immutable "scientific" racism, Fascist laws enabled some Jews—such as early members of the Fascist movement, war veterans, and children of mixed marriages who did not profess Judaism—to escape their provisions.

The Regimentation of German Life

To Nazi ideologues, the German churches, whether Catholic or Protestant, competed with the state for control over the minds of the German people. Parents were pressured not to send their children to religious schools and the authorities deliberately encouraged anti-Christian cults based on old Teutonic deities. Hitler, therefore, persecuted the churches, confiscated their newspapers, and even arrested their priests and bishops. The state tried without success to impose a "German Christian" church on Protestants. A group of clergy under the leadership of Pastor Martin Niemoeller (1892–1984) and others was the center of Protestant resistance. Niemoeller himself was an outspoken critic of Hitler and was interned in a concentration camp in 1937. Many Catholic priests were similarly engaged in anti-Nazi activities and offered refuge to Jews and other victims of Nazi persecution. In 1937, Pope Pius XI issued the encyclical *Mit Brennender Sorge* (With Burning Sorrow) to reject Nazi racism.

Nazism presented itself as a revolutionary force in German society, promising prosperity and equality. Its propaganda was most successful among the middle classes, who saw the regime as having saved them from the despair of the Great Depression. The Nazi party instituted the same array of social and leisure organizations as Mussolini had created in Italy, including "Strength Through Joy," similar to Mussolini's *Dopolavoro*. The *Hitler Jugend* (Hitler Youth) indoctrinated young Germans with Nazi ideas and the virtues of discipline and obedience. The educational system, from elementary schools to universities, was reorganized and the faculties purged. Hitler did actually break down some of the social distinctions that had existed, especially for middle-class German men, and both the government and the party bureaucracies offered opportunities to many for rapid advancement.

Joseph Goebbels (1897–1945), one of Hitler's closest associates, a brilliant manipulator of public opinion, was minister of Propaganda and Enlightenment. Goebbels imposed rigid controls on all aspects of intellectual and artistic life, including the mass media, literature, publishing, music, and art. Books that were banned by the government were burned in dramatic public bonfires.

Hitler was, for obvious reasons, especially concerned with art and architecture. Modernism and abstraction were anathema to him, examples of what he called "decadence." He purged the art academies and the museum staffs and in 1937 opened an "Exhibition of Degenerate Art," in which were displayed the works of the Cubists, Expressionists, and other modern movements. He insisted that art inspire German values. Official painting presented versions of Nazi mythology: Germanic knights, idealized peasant families, nudes in classical poses, and beautiful youths enraptured by the Nazi ideal. In architecture, Hitler closed down the Bauhaus, which had been the center of Europe's functional international style (see Part VIII, Topic 7), and worked closely with Albert Speer (1905–1981), the government's official architect, in designing monumental structures in the neo-Greek revival style.

THE DICTATORS AND THE DEPRESSION: LABOR, BUSINESS, AND ECONOMIC POLICY

Mussolini and Hitler pursued similar economic policies, designed to make their countries self-sufficient and capable of waging modern war. Although neither dictator wanted to end private property, both imposed state intervention in the economy that went far beyond the measures taken by the Western powers during the Great Depression. The fascist regimes devised new methods for government control and participation in private industry, and set production goals for key sectors vital to national security. Public works programs and rearmament did much to alleviate unemployment caused by the Depression, and public monies funded state welfare agencies and unemployment insurance, and pensions. Each pursued strong currency policies and inflation control.

Mussolini's Corporate State

The Fascists, who came to power in part because they opposed Marxism, appeased the business interests by outlawing strikes and traditional labor unions. They also permitted manufacturing associations to bargain with Fascist unions and the government.

Such measures did not sit well with Fascist syndicalists, and in 1926 Mussolini created the Ministry of Corporations. Corporativism was to be a system of institutional arrangements in which capital and labor were integrated into units. In this arrangement, each unit, or corporation, was supposed to regulate a particular sector of industry or the economy, supervised by the disinterested power of the state. The theory behind this unique concept was that class conflict, which Marx had said was inevitable, would be overcome.

Between 1929 and 1932, the minister of Corporations was the Fascist intellectual Giuseppe Bottai (1895–1959), who tried unsuccessfully to use state authority to dictate to both management and labor. Mussolini insisted the "corporate state" remain a fiction, for the private sector had grown too powerful. The corporate system, which was advertised to the world as a "third way" between capitalism and communism, served only as a propaganda device.

The effects of the Depression were not as severe in Italy as they were in Germany. Nevertheless, it did wipe out many of the gains that the boom of the 1920s had created. Unemployment stood at 1 million in 1933, stock prices fell by 39 percent, and the previously balanced budget went into deficit. The policy of "autarchy," designed to make Italy self-sufficient in agriculture and some industries, tended to force workers into unprofitable areas of production and to drive up prices. Although wheat production went up, other kinds of crops went down. Higher tariffs, used to protect Italian manufacturers, pushed the cost of living up and created shortages.

Another novel aspect of Fascist economic policy was the Institute for Industrial Reconstruction (IRI), established in 1933. The IRI bought up the large stock holdings of big banks and companies on the edge of bankruptcy, thus making the government a major stockholder. By 1939, the government owned 70 percent of pig iron production and 45 percent of steel manufacturing, and could control both.

Spending on public works projects, used by most governments in Europe and America to alleviate effects of the Depression in the 1930s, doubled. Mussolini drained swamps and marshes to produce more farmland, roads and rail lines were constructed, and thousands of government buildings and subsidized housing projects sprang up the length of the peninsula. Nevertheless, the Depression, combined with Mussolini's economic policies, meant a decline in the standard of living for most Italians.

The Nazi Economy

Hitler's efforts to fight the Great Depression with public works projects were even more extensive. Here, too, swamps were drained and forests replanted, public housing was built and highways extended across the country. Agriculture was important to the Nazis, not only because of their back to the soil movement, but to make Germany self-reliant in the event of war. Government subsidies were extended to farmers along with long-term loans. The regime also encouraged scientists working in private industry to develop synthetic products such as plastics and alternative food stuffs.

As in Italy, German workers lost most of their economic rights, although unemployment virtually disappeared and the standard of living improved. In 1936 Hitler launched a Four-Year Plan that regulated all sectors of the economy, from prices to wages and from factory regulations to production levels. A National Labor Front took the place of labor unions and strikes were forbidden, while industrial associations were recognized as part of the state structure. Private industry remained intact, although government regulations were more stringent. Although most workers had more stable jobs, they generally worked longer hours and earned lower wages.

In the case of both fascist regimes, economic policies were not based on long-term development, and whatever stability existed was achieved at the price of the destruction of working-class freedoms.

STALINIST RUSSIA: STATE PLANNING, COLLECTIVIZATION, AND THE POLICE STATE

Stalin's totalitarian dictatorship differed in several respects from those in the West. In the first place, according to Marxist theory, the state itself was supposed to be temporary. Then, too, instead of having to create a new revolutionary regime, when Stalin came to power in the late 1920s the communist state was already in place. Politically, his aim was simple—to consolidate

Significant Dates

The Soviet Union Under Stalin

1924	Stalin begins to emerge as Soviet dictator
1928–1932	First Five-Year Plan
1928–1933	Collectivization of Soviet agriculture
1934	Kirov murder
1936–1938	"Great Purges"

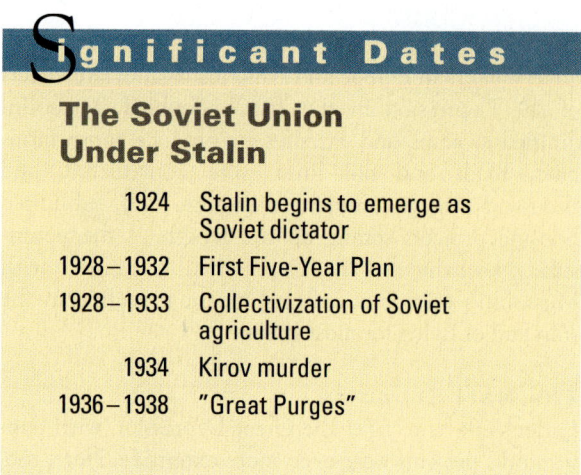

and strengthen his personal power (on Stalin's rise to power, see Part VIII, Topic 2).

Stalin was, of course, committed to Communism, and had always considered Lenin's NEP program a temporary makeshift. His ambition was to make the Soviet Union a great industrial giant and to socialize agriculture as well as industry. To achieve these goals, Stalin would remake the country's society.

The fundamental techniques employed by Stalin in his drive to industrialize and modernize the Soviet economy were similar to those employed in Italy and Germany: state intervention and centralized planning. Here, however, the degree of regimentation and coercion of the working class was even greater.

The Planned Economy

Stalin devised the idea of a Five-Year Plan, the first of which unfolded between 1928 and 1932. Under this plan, every national resource was to be mobilized in order to achieve a fundamental transformation. Stalin eliminated all vestiges of private property and instituted industrial quotas that were determined by an agency of the Communist party. The emphasis was placed on heavy industry and transportation, which received the greatest resources, so that the production and availability of consumer goods suffered and rationing was imposed.

The quotas established for every individual worker and production unit were almost always too high. Stalin's plan anticipated more than doubling industrial manufacturing and tripling steel making. While workers and plant managers who reached their goals were rewarded, those who failed to meet the quotas were penalized. Most Russian workers were unskilled and not accustomed to the pace and discipline imposed by the Five-Year Plan, and managers had to learn on the job.

The first Plan achieved only part of its goals, largely because of the unreasonably high quotas. Equipment was overused and often of poor quality, so that mechanical breakdowns were not unusual, and parts were difficult to obtain. The same could be said for the products themselves, since quantity was stressed at the expense of quality. Much of the machinery and many technical advisers were brought to the Soviet Union from Western countries.

Despite these setbacks, Stalin, who had learned some lessons, announced the second Five-Year Plan in 1932, which moved at a more reasonable rate (the Second Plan covered the years 1933–1937, and the Third 1938–1942). By 1938, iron and steel production had increased four times and coal three and one-half times. On the eve of World War II, the Soviet Union was the third nation in the world in industrial output, being surpassed only by the United States and Germany, and was ahead of Great Britain in steel and iron.

In the agricultural sector, Stalin sought to place the entire Soviet harvest under government control. Surpluses could be sold abroad to buy the sophisticated machinery needed at home. To achieve these goals, Stalin decided on the destruction of the entire class of landowning peasants known as the *kulaks,* who had prospered under the NEP. The kulaks—a term of derision used to describe greedy money lenders—were sufficiently prosperous to hire farm laborers and to extend loans to the local villagers. The elimination of the kulaks would enable the government to consolidate the numerous small farms into huge agricultural collectives, where modern equipment and farming techniques could be used efficiently.

Collectivization and the Peasantry

The collectivization program required that all peasants turn their land and livestock over to the state, keeping only their houses and personal property. As in industry, every collective received production quotas. Peasants shared the work as well as the profits or losses the cooperative earned.

The peasants staunchly resisted collectivization, and fought back against the state by hiding or burning their crops and killing their animals. The resulting shortages of food caused deep concern in Moscow. In the Russian countryside, a massive rebellion soon consumed an untold number of lives—Stalin himself admitted later to 10 million.

Collectivization wreaked havoc on Soviet agriculture. The kulaks, generally the best farmers, were either killed or deported to Siberia, and half of all farm animals destroyed. Grain production hardly increased in the decade after 1928. Collectivization also produced a terrible famine in 1932–1933, and it killed an estimated 3 million persons. The heavy price paid by Russian peasants brought Stalin a political success, for he could now claim that socialism had reached the

In the 1930s, Stalin sought to collectivize Soviet agriculture. Here farm workers engage in a meeting to discuss production.

countryside. By 1933, more than half of all farming families had joined collectives, and five years later the figure had passed 90 percent.

Soviet Society Under Stalin

The ambitious plans that Stalin set transformed the Soviet Union. Thousands of factories were built in the 1930s, and the industrial expansion swelled the size of older cities and gave rise to new urban centers in isolated regions of Siberia and Asiatic Russia. Millions of people were moved en masse from rural regions to the new cities to supply the workforce.

Life everywhere was difficult for the average Soviet citizen. Housing was primitive and in short supply and the steady rise in prices produced a serious drop in the standard of living. In the decade following the start of the Five-Year Plans, for example, the purchasing power of an industrial worker declined by some 40 percent. The constraints of political indoctrination were oppressive. Adults and children alike became captive audiences for party lecturers, and the government-operated mass media were filled with official information. Mass organizations for the young, women, and workers assisted in the indoctrination process. In addition to selling the virtues of Communism, Soviet propaganda stressed a theme that was crucial to the dictatorship: the creation of the cult of Stalin. Stalin's face became familiar to all Russians as his photograph and portrait appeared everywhere.

Some important positive advances were made in Soviet life during Stalin's dictatorship. Nearly every able-bodied citizen found a job, although most involved unskilled heavy labor. The government provided free education and medical care, cheap housing, and pensions. In education the progress was more impressive. Stalin sought to wipe out illiteracy and brought free elementary schooling to the far reaches of the country. For those with superior skills, higher education was available. Education, especially of a technical nature, could lead to higher salaries, privileges, and status. A managerial class eventually joined the political and intellectual élites, giving the lie to the notion of a "classless society."

The Stalinist Terror

Although the police state was a pervasive feature of life in the fascist dictatorships, neither Hitler nor Mussolini used it in quite the same way as Stalin, who unleashed a reign of terror on a vast scale against the Soviet population at large.

The suppression of the peasants during the collectivization and the Five-Year Plans had caused considerable unrest, not only among ordinary Soviet citizens but in the inner circles of the Communist party and the state administration as well. Stalin decided in the mid-1930s to use his domestic security forces to crush any signs of discontent and eliminate possible opposition to his rule. The so-called "Great Purges" were so indiscriminate that even high-ranking military officers suffered the fate of dissidents. For two years, between 1936 and 1938, millions of Soviets suffered imprisonment, forced labor, and death at the hands of a ruthless dictator.

Stalin first struck in late 1934, when one of his most trusted followers, Sergei Kirov (1888–1934), was murdered. Stalin himself no doubt had Kirov killed, and then used the murder as a pretext for wide-scale purges. Announcing a plot against him by Trotsky's followers, he held a number of infamous show trials in Moscow. In 1936, the court accused 16 prominent Old Bolsheviks of conspiracy and ordered their execution. The next year, a number of less important party leaders were similarly eliminated, followed by the court martial of General Mikhail Tukhachevsky (1893–1937) and other high-ranking officers. Soon, vast numbers of innocent people, including government and party bureaucrats and intellectuals, workers and factory foremen, fell victim to the ever-expanding purge. In the end, Stalin completed the process by having officials of the NKVD—the internal security unit—themselves eliminated. The statistics of Stalin's terror can only be estimated, but perhaps as many as 8 million people were held in prisons or work camps, 90 percent of whom eventually died, and the total number of deaths may have exceeded 10 million.

When the Great Purges were over, Stalin had succeeded in clearing out entire categories of the Soviet leadership. The officials whom he appointed to the vacant positions represented a new breed of bureaucrat, not tied to the Old Bolsheviks or to the Revolution of 1917, but bound only by loyalty and fear to Stalin himself. Stalin's power was now virtually without limits.

WOMEN AND TOTALITARIANISM

The interwar totalitarian dictatorships were the first national governments to implement clear policies regarding the position of women. These programs responded in part to the ideologies of each movement, and in part to the economic and social priorities of the regimes. Fascism was a philosophy of conquest, in which women were to be subsumed to men's desires, whereas the earliest Soviet laws had accepted the notion of women's equality. Yet both forms of totalitarianism allowed only limited scope for women to develop their potential in society or to share in the exercise of power.

Fascism and Women

Among the "Fascists of the First Hour" in 1919 were to be found a number of Italian women, including the female Black Shirt leader Regina Teruzzi and Mussolini's lover, Sarfatti. Nevertheless, Fascists in general held most women in contempt, regarding them primarily as wives, mistresses, and mothers. Mussolini himself was never loyal to the many women in his life, and yet his public reputation as a womanizer inflated his popular image.

Fascists considered it the natural duty of men to possess women sexually. In official lore, Fascists were by definition young and virile warriors, and all Italian males were to be "new men," ruthless, hard, and heroic. Women, on the other hand, were to be pure and subservient keepers of the hearth. The regime's propaganda machine reinforced a stable and traditional patriarchal social order of the kind that was familiar to most Italians. The Fascist party ran separate youth organizations for all males and females ages six through seventeen.

Because Mussolini wanted to increase Italy's population, the regime encouraged large families. Adolescent females were given instruction in caring for a home and children, and the state gave mothers free birthing and medical assistance, hygiene care, and prizes to the families with the largest number of children.

For a brief period before coming to power, Mussolini had demanded women's suffrage, but he later changed his mind. During the 1920s and 1930s, fewer and fewer women were active in the industrial workforce, a trend accelerated by the large unemployment figures of the Great Depression. Some specialized fields, such as nursing and teaching, were regarded as suitable for women, but by and large females were discouraged from entering the professions. By law, husbands retained superior rights over children and property, and divorce went unrecognized.

Women and the Nazi State

Like Mussolini, Hitler found little room for women in his Nazi movement or in his government. He did not marry until just before his suicide in 1945, and although for a number of years he had maintained a liaison with Eva Braun, the relationship may have been purely platonic. The Führer demanded that women provide Germany with children who would become workers and soldiers. Government policies and party programs encouraged larger families and modern medical care for mothers and children.

The Nazi party deliberately recruited women, and in the early 1920s about one in five members of the NSDAP was women. After the seizure of power, women never achieved important positions in the regime. Nazi women, on the other hand, supported Hitler's goal of restoring family values, and were active in community work designed to foster such attitudes. At first, women were not encouraged to work in factories or agriculture, but when Hitler began to rearm Germany, they moved into the labor force in larger numbers.

Women were an important part of the Soviet workforce in industry as well as agriculture.

There was in Nazi aesthetics an element of repressed sexuality, whether in painting, sculpture, or film. Hitler had always railed against cultural decadence and pornography, but prized the nude in art. Women were portrayed as the embodiment of the ideal German female, virtuous and pure, while male bodies were presented as athletes and warriors. In the propaganda films of the great director Leni Riefenstahl (see Part VIII, Topic 7), there is, among the thousands of semi-clothed young Germans whom she idolized, an underlying if unacknowledged sexual tension. Riefenstahl subsumed that tension in images of perfect beauty, choreographing them in dances of dominance and power.

Soviet Women

Marx and Engels had both seen the repression of women as a function of the suppression of the working class, arguing that in capitalist societies women were a form of property. Lenin agreed, and as early as 1918, the party had set up a special Women's Bureau to mobilize women into the party. Alexandra Kollontai (1872–1952), an early Bolshevik leader, pushed for sexual freedom and laws that would make her feminist ideals a reality. The Soviet constitution embodied full rights and equality for women, yet although Russian women did gain the right to divorce and abortion in the 1920s, reality never matched the official rhetoric.

Under Stalin, the position of Soviet women changed. He played down talk of gender equality, but his drive to industrialize and increase production brought women into the workforce in large numbers, just as the collectivization of agriculture did for rural women. Low salaries encouraged women to seek employment in even the heaviest kind of work. The acute shortage of trained professionals and technicians also led Stalin to make education available to Soviet women. Although women had greater access to employment and education in the Soviet Union than in the West, they did not receive equal pay for equal work. Nor were they relieved of the burdens of child rearing and housekeeping.

The totalitarian experience in interwar Europe had profound repercussions. In their effort to control the minds and the values as well as the loyalties of their subjects, these regimes succeeded in mobilizing millions of people in an unprecedented fashion. Programs of indoctrination and socialization drew formerly isolated sectors of Europe's population into the mainstream of national life, and politicized them for the first time. Never before were the lives and deaths of such vast numbers of citizens so directly affected by government actions.

Mussolini, Hitler, and Stalin were major figures of the period, whose personalities and policies dominated public events for years. Their revolutions were designed to destroy ordinary politics of the kind familiar to most westerners, and each of their regimes was built with the intention of implementing a particular worldview and a philosophy of life. That philosophy preached the attainment of utopia through dominance, power, and control. The human suffering that resulted has perhaps never been equaled in modern history.

Questions for Further Study

1. Is the concept of "totalitarianism" useful for historians? Why? Why not?
2. What similarities and differences existed between the Fascist state and the Nazi state?
3. What was the nature of totalitarian economic policy? How did the fascist dictators respond to the Great Depression?
4. What factors explain Stalinist terror?
5. What role did women have in totalitarian societies? Was it different from their role in democratic societies?

Suggestions for Further Reading

Bracher, Karl D. *The German Dictatorship*. New York, 1970.

Cannistraro, Philip V., and B. R. Sullivan. *Il Duce's Other Woman*. New York, 1993.

Conquest, Robert. *The Great Terror: A Reassessment*. New York, 1989.

De Grand, Alexander. *Fascist Italy and Nazi Germany: The Fascist Style of Rule*. London, 1995.

Kerhsaw, Ian. *The Hitler Myth: Image and Reality in the Third Reich*. New York, 1987.

Koonz, Claudia. *Mothers in the Fatherland: Women, the Family, and Nazi Politics*. New York, 1987.

Mack Smith, Denis. *Mussolini*. New York, 1982.

Peukert, Detlev J. K. *Inside Nazi Germany*. New Haven, CT, 1987.

Tannenbaum, Edward R. *The Fascist Experience: Italian Society and Culture, 1922–1945*. New York, 1972.

Tucker, Robert C. *Stalin in Power*. New York, 1990.

Ulam, Adam. *Stalin: The Man and His Era*. New York, 1973.

Topic 5

The Western Democracies and Eastern Europe

In the 20 years between the two world wars, the viability of European democracy was put to the test by a variety of destructive forces. The rise of fascism, and particularly the success of the movements in Italy and Germany, combined with the triumph of communism in Russia, appeared to forecast the wave of the future. With the 1929 crash and the resultant Great Depression, the social and economic systems of the two great Western democracies, Britain and France, came under tremendous stress.

In the 1920s, the prevalent trend in domestic politics was the search for stability, a goal that proved impossible in the context of postwar conditions. Readjustment to peacetime economies had been difficult, and alternating cycles of unemployment, inflation, and depression jarred Britain and France. Working-class discontent grew markedly, and even the formation of Britain's first socialist government—that of Ramsay MacDonald in 1924—failed to quell the unrest or its causes. The Conservatives returned quickly to power in an atmosphere of fear over communism, and despite their unsympathetic handling of the 1926 general strike, they remained in power until 1929. MacDonald formed another government that year but quickly abandoned full responsibility for dealing with the Depression by forming a coalition cabinet that persisted for five years. Nevertheless, drift rather than decisive action remained the order of the day.

In France, where the Depression hit later than elsewhere, the right and the left also alternated in power and produced equally unimpressive results. As in Britain, the first postwar elections returned a conservative majority, but its strident nationalism over the Ruhr invasion in 1923 frightened many Frenchmen into voting for the left. The Socialists formed a coalition with the Radicals, but the financial irresponsibility of Édouard Herriot's ministry saw serious inflation and the collapse of the franc. Confidence was restored for a time by the temperate administration of Raymond Poincaré. When the Depression finally did arrive in France in 1932, retrenchment and the lack of clear policies made matters worse. The outbreak of serious riots in 1934 and the growing polarization of French politics created a crisis of confidence unequaled since the Dreyfus affair (see Part VII, Topic 15).

Despite the unimpressive record of government in responding to the Depression, the economic collapse did cause liberal democratic governments to readjust their thinking about the obligations of the state to its citizens. As a result, they inaugurated an era of social intervention and economic activism that has marked Western society ever since. The United States, with the election of

Franklin D. Roosevelt and the implementation of his vigorous New Deal programs, went further than either Britain or France in restructuring the government-citizen relationship. By the end of the 1930s, the institutional basis of the modern welfare state had been built.

In Eastern Europe, the prospects for democracy were equally uncertain. There, upon the ruins of the old Austro-Hungarian, German, and Russian empires, a series of newly created, independent states arose after World War I. From the start, these new countries were burdened with serious, sometimes insurmountable, problems: illiteracy and the lack of social modernization, and economies that rested primarily on agriculture and that suffered from a small and underdeveloped middle class. Moreover, the myriad of nationalities that comprised the region meant that every nation had ethnic minorities within its borders to cause unrest and tension, as well as constant friction with neighbors over borders and nationality issues. Finally, the lack of liberal parliamentary traditions in Eastern Europe put the new democratic regimes on shaky ground, and the area experienced a decisive trend toward authoritarian and fascist regimes.

GREAT BRITAIN AND THE IRISH QUESTION

It is difficult to speak of a British "recovery" from the trauma of World War I, for in the domestic arena the country experienced the next 20 years as one long, continual series of trials and failures. If government—whether of the left or the right—was unable to cope adequately with the economic dislocations of the postwar period and the accompanying labor unrest, it could hardly have been expected to deal successfully with the Great Depression. And while the British did succeed, at long last, in coming to terms with Ireland's future as an independent state, the agonizing ordeal of the Irish people continued in a devastating civil war.

The Postwar Drift

The British electorate, like that in France, was in a decidedly conservative mood as World War I drew to an end. Wanting a harsh settlement with defeated Germany, the 1918 "khaki election"—so-called because of the large number of veterans who participated—returned a strong Conservative majority to the House of Commons. The Conservatives permitted Liberal Prime Minister David Lloyd George to continue in office at the head of a coalition government, but they held the real power. In the autumn of 1922, however, the Conservatives pushed Lloyd George out, chiefly over his Irish policies, and formed a cabinet under the elderly Scotsman, Andrew Bonar Law (served 1922–1923).

Significant Dates

European Democracy

1916	Easter Rebellion in Ireland
1918	"Khaki election" in England
1921	Irish Free State (Catholic) and Northern Ireland (Protestant) created
1923–1930	Dictatorship of Primo de Rivera in Spain
1923	Labour government in England
1924–1926	Cartel of the Left in France
1925–1929	Conservatives return to power in England
1926	Dictatorship of Pilsudski in Poland
1926–1929	Poincaré premier of France
1926	General strike in England
1929	Royal dictatorship under Alexander I in Yugoslavia
1929–1931	Labour government in England
1931	Spanish Republic founded
1932	Gombos prime minister of Hungary
1936	Dictatorship under Metaxas in Greece
1936	Popular Front in France

In the elections of 1922, the working class was in an especially aggressive mood, for the Labour party doubled its strength, making it the second party in Parliament. Nevertheless, the Conservatives gained even more ground and elected Stanley Baldwin (served 1923–1924, 1924–1929, 1935–1937). The following year, further elections increased the strength of the Liberals, now in a position to form a coalition with the Conservatives or Labour. Instead, Herbert Asquith (1852–1928), the Liberal leader, declared that Labour should have an opportunity to form a government. The decision was an important one for two reasons: the liberals would never again head the government, and Ramsay MacDonald, who led the new Labour ministry, became the first socialist prime minister in Western Europe.

Ramsay MacDonald (served 1924, 1929–1931, 1931–1935), the man who held that distinction, was a Scotsman of working-class origin. Although good-looking and eloquent, MacDonald possessed little leadership ability or firmness of character. Not only did he prove indecisive, but once in office he felt it necessary to convince everyone that the country had little to fear from the Labour party. His recognition of the Soviet Union did not, however, endear him to those on the political right.

MacDonald fell as a result of scare tactics. The opposition accused the government of not prosecuting a communist editor who advocated sedition, and during the election itself a letter was circulated, allegedly from Grigori Zinoviev, head of the Comintern (the communist international organization), suggesting connections with the Labour party. The letter was a fake, but it was sufficient to give the Conservatives a huge majority.

Baldwin came back to 10 Downing Street, heading the British government for the next five years. During that time, he offered the country what he described as "sane, commonsense government," and his manner inspired public confidence. In reality, however, this meant an almost total failure to come to grips with the problems of inflation, industrial slump, and unemployment that were plaguing British society. The most progressive steps taken between 1924 and 1929 were the measures instituted by Baldwin's health minister, Neville Chamberlain (1869–1940), who established pensions for widows and retired people and reformed local government.

The low point of Baldwin's second ministry was the general strike of 1926, during which he succeeded in exasperating class tensions and antagonizing the workers. In 1925 a royal commission was appointed to investigate conditions in the coal industry, which had been suffering badly as a result of the general economic slump. Neither the miners nor the owners were satisfied by the commission's report, and in the face of a

London in the 1926 General Strike—machine-gun-armed vehicles patrol the city.

threatened general strike, the mine owners shut down operations. For nine days in May 1926, some 2,500,000 workers in all fields of endeavor struck, while the government organized middle-class volunteers to run basic services. Some local violence and considerable anger marked the strike, and when negotiations collapsed, Baldwin forced the unions into a settlement that virtually gave up the miners' demands. When the general strike ended, the miners stayed out on their own for another six months, embittered at the government for having engineered their defeat. To make matters worse, in 1927, the government passed the Trade Disputes Act, which prohibited sympathy strikes and otherwise weakened labor's position.

The National Government

In the wake of the 1926 strike, working-class sentiment against Baldwin intensified, and when he called elections in 1929, he was swept out of office. Labourites campaigned on the unemployment issue and blamed the Conservatives for Britain's economic troubles. Although Labour won more seats than the Tories, it lacked a majority and had to form a coalition government with the Liberals. In addition, Labour was still burdened with Ramsay MacDonald as its leader.

The second MacDonald government faced a deteriorating economic situation. During 1930 alone, unemployment jumped from 1 million to 2.5 million. The government's response was simply to increase government financial support for the unemployed (known as the "dole"). This caused a huge increase in the deficit. The next year, experts advised MacDonald that only a cut in expenditures—that is, a reduction in the dole—would prevent bankruptcy. An atmosphere of crisis spread, causing heavy withdrawals from banks and the virtual depletion of the country's gold reserves. American financiers refused to extend further credits to Britain without cutbacks. In August 1931, MacDonald told his cabinet that unemployment benefits would have to be cut; when they balked, he asked them to resign.

Instead of submitting his own resignation, however, King George V (ruled 1910–1936) persuaded him to form a new, broad-based coalition with himself as prime minister and Stanley Baldwin as second in command. In fact, the Conservatives dominated this so-called National Government and MacDonald was their pawn. Labour, stunned by what they considered MacDonald's betrayal, expelled him from the party.

From 1931 to 1935, MacDonald and Baldwin ran the government. Together, they added Britain to the growing number of countries that were abandoning the gold standard. The international value of the pound did drop from $4.86, but held at $3.40, thus defying the warnings of conventional economists. Parliament also approved a 10 percent reduction in unemployment benefits. The financial crisis began to ease, and the government called for new elections for a vote of confidence. Despite a coalition effort, the Conservatives took the lion's share of votes—out of 556 seats in Parliament, they won 472 while Labour lost some 85 percent of its seats.

MacDonald continued to serve as prime minister until 1935. With the National Government ratified, it pushed through Parliament a program of tariff protection, thus ending Britain's long-standing tradition of free trade. When failing health led to MacDonald's retirement, Baldwin moved to Downing Street, where he remained until 1937.

Britain came through the Depression with minimal damage to its political traditions, despite the rather lame policies of the Labour and Conservative ministries. Conditions in some parts of England, as well as those in Wales and Scotland, remained depressed, but something of an economic revival began to take hold by the end of the decade. The coming of World War II interrupted that process, and in its aftermath Britain seemed to pick up where it had left off.

Britain, Europe's most advanced industrial society, was the perfect microcosm for studying the shortcomings of industrial capitalism. In the 19th century, social and economic conditions there had attracted incisive critics, from the German Friedrich Engels to England's own John Stuart Mill. No one, however, was more knowledgeable about or more committed to the improvement of the working class than Beatrice and Sidney Webb, Britain's greatest social reformers.

Beatrice Potter (1858–1943) was born into a well-to-do provincial family. She educated herself, principally by reading extensively and by discussions with the numerous visitors whom her father entertained. In London she immersed herself in social work among the poor. She now questioned the assumptions of her father's world and found charitable organizations ill-equipped to deal with the overwhelming poverty she saw. In *The Cooperative Movement in Great Britain* (1891), she examined working-class organizations. One of the people she had been advised to consult while doing her research was Sidney Webb (1859–1947).

Webb was a native of London, born into a lower-middle-class family. He left school at 16 and obtained a civil service job by studying at night, and eventually passed the bar examinations. In 1885, Webb was persuaded by his close friend George Bernard Shaw (1856–1950) to join a newly founded socialist organization called the Fabian Society (see Part VII, Topic 19).

Potter and Webb met in 1890, and he immediately fell in love with the good-looking and intellectual young woman. For her part, Potter had been greatly impressed by Webb's socialist ideas, although she was not immediately attracted to this unkempt, rather ugly little man. They were married in 1892 and set up house in London. For the next 50 years, the couple devoted themselves to pioneering social research and political reform, turning out important books such as *The History of Trade Unionism* (1894) and *Industrial Democracy* (1897).

Webb and Potter also collaborated in bringing about significant social reforms and the creation of important new institutions. Webb, who served on the London County Council, introduced the basis for the system of public secondary education and helped to establish technical schools. Together, they founded the London School of Economics, which became part of the University of London. The Webbs believed that the government must provide a minimum education for all citizens, just as it had to provide minimum standards of health and sanitation. Webb also provided the basic content for the Education Acts of 1902 and 1903, which became the basis for English public education for generations.

Like their fellow Fabians, Beatrice and Sidney Webb combined a belief in socialism and scientific principles with a moral "righteousness." In 1905 Potter, as a member of the Royal Commission on the Poor Laws, produced her important *Minority Report*, which advocated social security and provided a detailed outline for what later became the welfare state.

In 1913 they founded the left-wing journal *The New Statesman*, and the next year, after the ranks of the Fabian Society split, the Webbs joined the Labour party. In 1918 Webb drafted the party's policy statement on "Labour and the New Social Order," and was chosen by the miners' union to serve as their representative on a commission to investigate mining conditions. He so won the loyalty of the miners that in 1922 they elected him to Parliament. In 1924, Prime Minister Ramsay MacDonald appointed him to the Labour cabinet as president of the Board of Trade.

When MacDonald formed the National Government in 1931, the Webbs became disheartened with Labour's prospects and left England for the Soviet Union. They "fell in love" with what they saw in Stalin's Russia and seem to have lost their confidence in the idea of gradual social reform.

The Quest for Irish Independence

The Irish question remained one of the most vexing and agonizing issues in modern British history. Since the 17th century, Ireland had been virtually a British colony, ruled by a small Protestant gentry which insisted on maintaining ties with England. The Protestant minority comprised the six counties of Ulster in the northeastern portion of Ireland. The

Map 5.1 Ireland

larger section of the island, in the south and west, was comprised of Catholics who increasingly demanded Home Rule—that is, Irish control over domestic affairs. The Liberal party under William Gladstone had incorporated Home Rule in its platform, but the Conservatives opposed it.

In the late 19th century, two efforts to get Home Rule approved in Parliament failed. The extension of the suffrage to Irish males, however, resulted in the election of a growing Irish Catholic delegation to Parliament. A third Home Rule bill passed in 1914 but was then postponed because of the war. Among Irish nationalists, extremists grew impatient and sparked the 1916 Easter Rebellion (see Part VIII, Topic 1), which intensified feeling on both sides.

In the 1918 elections, Irish nationalist sentiment triumphed when some 70 candidates were sent to Parliament by a new party, Sinn Fein (Gaelic for "We Ourselves"). Its members abandoned Home Rule in favor of complete freedom and, instead of taking their seats in Parliament, proclaimed themselves an Irish Parliament called Dail Eireann. That January, they declared Ireland independent.

The government of Lloyd George responded slowly to the Sinn Fein's actions, but by the end of the year was lending the "Black and Tans," a special army of volunteers in Ireland that distinguished itself by its exceptional brutality, official support. As this cruel war escalated and casualties grew, public opinion in Britain began to turn against the repression. Finally, in the summer of 1921 Lloyd George agreed to meet with Irish leaders, and the result was the signing of a formal treaty in December that created the Irish Free State out of the Catholic regions as a self-governing nation with

The ruins of Dublin following the British bombardment during the Easter Rising, 1916.

Dominion status. Protestant Ulster became an autonomous region within the United Kingdom, under the name of Northern Ireland.

The Irish Free State did not satisfy a radical minority of Irish nationalists who united under the leadership of Eamon De Valera (1882–1975). Born in New York City, De Valera was raised in Ireland and became an ardent republican who played an active role in the Easter Rebellion. Refusing to recognize the treaty, his followers organized the clandestine Irish Republican Army (IRA) and carried on a terrorist civil war to prevent the separation of Northern Ireland. The bombings, raids, and deaths escalated on both sides of the border. In 1923, De Valera's forces were overwhelmed and he was imprisoned. The next year, however, he started a new party, Fianna Fáil, continued the struggle, and won power in 1932. De Valera was elected prime minister five years later, and declared the country independent, renaming it Eire. During World War II, Eire remained neutral, and in 1949 it left the British Commonwealth and became the Republic of Ireland. The 1921 Irish settlement remains unchanged and the tragic civil war goes on, as does the agony of the Irish people.

FRANCE: THE QUEST FOR STABILITY

The somber mood of British public life in the 1920s contrasted sharply with the more exuberant tone of life in France. In the aftermath of World War I, Paris regained its position as the capital of the European avant-garde (see Part VIII, Topic 6). But if France led the way in cultural life, its politics left much to be desired. The relative stability of Britain's governmental experience contrasted sharply with the tense, unstable French political arena. One reason for this difference was the extensive damage the country suffered in the war, and the considerable resources needed to rebuild. The French had not managed their war financing well, and between 1914 and 1919 the circulation of banknotes had increased sixfold. War debts to Britain and the United States added to the pressure, and politicians wavered in their determination to raise taxes both to meet the deficit and to reconstruct the economy. Once the Depression hit in 1932, the strain on financial resources increased still further.

The Era of Stability

Because the electoral system was based on proportional representation, a myriad of political parties competed for power. Pressure on the republic was particularly strong from the right, which formed a coalition known as the Bloc National to compete in the postwar elections. In 1919, the French people chose a solidly conservative, highly nationalist Chamber of Deputies—the "Blue Horizon Chamber," so named after the large number of veterans in blue uniforms represented in it.

In 1923, however, Premier Raymond Poincaré (served 1912, 1922–1924, 1926–1929) occupied the Ruhr Valley in order to force payment of German reparations. The resulting war scare, combined with high inflation, led voters to turn to the left. The radical socialist Édouard Herriot (served 1924–1925, 1932), supported by the *Cartel des Gauches* (Cartel of the Left), succeeded Poincaré but lasted only one year. Herriot, ignorant of financial matters, did nothing to deal with the country's enormous war debts, nor could he control the rising inflation that seriously hurt the working and middle classes. The ineffective Herriot stepped down, but his two immediate successors did not improve the situation. By 1926 the French franc, once among the most stable currencies in the world, had lost 90 percent of its value on the international market. More serious still was the fact that the middle classes lost three-quarters of their savings.

Poincaré came back into office in 1926 and established a "National Union" ministry that included six former premiers. Aloof, sober, and unimaginative, yet with a strict sense of duty, he was the right man for the moment. Poincaré did nothing dramatic to deal with the economic crisis. Rather, he moved carefully and precisely to improve specific aspects of the larger problem, collecting taxes more effectively, making administrative savings, ending overspending in government programs, and generally presenting an air of confidence and stability that had been lacking in the body politic. Gradually, the franc was stabilized and the sense of relief that resulted helped to soothe national tensions. Poincaré remained in office for three years, longer than any other interwar premier, and retired in 1929.

Depression Politics

Between 1929 and 1932, a large number of premiers held office, but none of them had Poincaré's stature or his commitment to the republican tradition. When the Depression struck France in 1932, unemployment in France was not as severe as in other countries, but it did have a destabilizing effect on political life. Herriot returned to the premiership for six months, and was quickly followed by four others. Once again the government failed to deal effectively with the crisis, and when the restored prosperity of the late 1920s dissolved, social tensions reemerged.

The most dramatic proof of the instability of French political life was the upheaval following the mysterious Stavisky scandal. Serge Stavisky (1886?–1934) was a master financial swindler who had sold millions of worthless bonds. His trial in December 1933 and his subsequent suicide caused a sensation. The radical right exploited the scandal, spreading accusations that high government officials had been implicated with him in the affair and that the government had then covered up their involvement. The findings of the official investigation supported these charges. On February 6, 1934, huge crowds organized by right-wing forces filled the streets of Paris demanding the ouster of Premier Édouard Daladier (served 1933, 1934, 1938–1940). When they attempted to break into the Chamber of Deputies, police fired on the crowd, killing eleven people. The Daladier government collapsed in a storm of indignation.

Not since the Dreyfus affair at the turn of the century (see Part VII, Topic 15) had the people of France been so violently divided, nor the republic so completely called into question. Nor did subsequent governments have any more success than their predecessors in dealing with the effects of the Depression. France was the only country to remain stubbornly on the gold standard. Moreover, social unrest increased as a result of the government retrenchment and the lowering of salary levels.

The danger from the right grew so threatening that the French communists—taking their cue from the Comintern, which the year before had endorsed alliances with other leftist parties—formed a "Popular Front" with the socialists and Radicals, and presented a

Socialist Léon Blum (left with glasses) and communist Maurice Thorez with other members of the French Popular Front, July 1937.

joint platform in the 1936 elections. The Front won a huge victory, and formed a government under socialist Léon Blum (served 1936–1937). A cultured and sensitive man, Blum brought union officials and employers together and produced an agreement that laid the basis for the welfare state, including minimum wages, the 40-hour week, and collective bargaining.

Blum's reforms reduced social stress, but he was the target of attack from enemies to his right and his left. Bigots pointed to the fact that he was Jewish as evidence of the decline of France, while conservatives gathered strength from business interests and eventually slowed down his programs. Meanwhile, the communists attacked him for not going far enough. The Blum government resigned in June 1937. By the eve of World War II, the French people were deeply divided over the future of the republic. For many, the widening appeal of the radical right, and especially the coming to power of Adolf Hitler in Germany, was deeply troublesome.

THE SPREAD OF FASCISM

Blum's dilemma was repeated elsewhere in Europe. By the mid-1930s, European political life was polarized between the extremes of communism and fascism. Every country experienced, to one degree or another, an increasingly bitter ideological war, and the danger was especially fierce from the right. From the British Isles to the shores of the Black Sea, fascism—which had already come to power in Italy and Germany—appeared to be on the ascendancy.

Great Britain and France spawned their own native varieties of fascism, although they neither created a mass following nor seriously challenged the power base of those democratic societies. In Great Britain, a number of small groups inspired by Mussolini's Black Shirts were started in the 1920s, but never amounted to very much. In the early 1930s the rich and well-educated Sir Oswald Mosley (1896–1980) founded the British Union of Fascists. A great fan of Mussolini, Mosley based his organization on the Italian model. Like Mussolini, he had been a prominent member of the British socialist movement, having served as a Labour minister. Mosley became increasingly interested in Hitler's regime after 1933. He spoke of a "Greater Britain" in which all citizens were regimented to achieve broad national goals. The British Union attracted many disreputable thugs, and Mosley himself extolled the use of violence, a fact that led the government to try to limit the movement by placing a ban on the wearing of political uniforms. It did not, however, represent a serious threat to British political stability.

In France, conservative and reactionary movements drawing inspiration from the country's monarchist past were established as early as the turn of the century. In 1898, the poet and journalist Charles Maurras (1868–1952) started the *Action Française* (French Action), a group that stressed extreme nationalism and advocated anti-Semitism. Maurras wanted a restoration of the monarchy and a return to a corporative society based on hierarchy and aristocracy. The government banned the movement in 1936.

In the interwar period, an array of proto-fascist political groups, some directly modeled on Mussolini's

Oswald Mosley, leader of the British Union of Fascists, marches in a rally.

Fascism or Hitler's Nazism, appeared in France. The most notorious of these were the *Jeunesses Patriotes* (Young Patriots) and the infamous *Capoulards* (Hooded Men). At the height of the Depression the *Parti Populaire Française* (French Popular Party) attracted some 500,000 followers. The sheer number of such radical movements, each with its own ideology and platform, mitigated against the creation of a united right.

The Spanish monarchy, incapable of guiding the country's transformation into the 20th century, proved no barrier to the formation of a fascist movement. By the early 1920s, a dictatorship was created by General Miguel Primo de Rivera (1870–1930). The dictator's son, José Antonio Primo de Rivera, organized a real fascist movement, the *Falange*, in 1931. When the Spanish Civil War erupted, the movement was taken over by General Francisco Franco (1892–1975) and eventually merged into his own party (see Part VIII, Topic 8).

The Austrian case is a good example of how fascist movements competed against each other. The situation there was complicated by the fact that two paramilitary groups, the Social Democratic *Schutzbund* (Alliance for Defense) and the Christian Socialist *Heimwehr* (Home Guard), not only espoused conflicting ideologies, but opposed the Austrian Nazis. The Heimwehr, headed by Prince Ernst Rudiger von Starhemberg (1899–1956), fought to undermine the country's republican government but wanted to preserve Austrian independence. Chancellor Engelbert Dollfuss (1892–1934) tried to play the Heimwehr off against the Nazis and the Social Democrats, inviting it to join the "Fatherland Front" that worked against the *Anschluss* (union) of Austria and Germany.

As fascist movements spread across Europe in the 1930s, the prospects for democracy looked grim indeed.

THE NEW SHAPE OF EASTERN EUROPE

At the Paris Peace Conference, the Allied statesmen had made a deliberate decision to create a group of new states in Eastern Europe from the ruins of four empires—Austria-Hungary, Germany, Russia, and Ottoman Turkey. Eastern Europe provided a test case for the principle of self-determination that President Wilson advocated so strenuously. Yet there were other reasons that had to do more with power politics than justice which compelled the creation of these new nations: they would serve a useful purpose for the Allies in acting as a buffer along the western border of the Bolshevik Russia, and along the eastern frontiers of Germany.

These newly created nations—Austria, Hungary, Poland, Czechoslovakia, Yugoslavia, and the Baltic republics of Latvia, Estonia, and Lithuania—are known as "successor states," because they took the place of the older empires. With the inclusion of Greece, Romania, Bulgaria, and Albania, Eastern Europe consisted of a dozen independent states.

The States of Eastern Europe

The governments of the successor states began as models of the parliamentary system. Each was either a Western-style republic or a constitutional monarchy. Yet, by the eve of World War II, most of these nations had yielded to authoritarianism. They found that the combination of domestic and foreign policy problems

Map 5.2 Ethnic Groups in Central and Eastern Europe

was so demanding that parliamentary government was not adequate to their needs.

Because of history and geography, the new states of Eastern Europe had remarkably mixed populations. Along with the dominant ethnic and religious group in each country, one or more minority nationalities coexisted in uneasy rapport. In Czechoslovakia, Poland, Hungary, Yugoslavia, and Romania, these minorities were themselves large groups. The minorities posed serious problems for the governments, most of which wanted to forge cohesive social and political units out of their populations. The minorities, on the other hand, sought to maintain their distinctiveness and to protect their separate identities. In some instances, such as the case of Nazi Germany and the German minority in Czechoslovakia, a foreign power deliberately appealed to these minorities over the heads of their governments. On the whole, most states in the area treated their minority populations unfairly. The exception was Finland, where the Swedish minority enjoyed constitutionally assured rights. The result was continuing tension that kept domestic tranquillity off balance.

After the euphoria of independence had subsided, the successor states found themselves burdened with the legacy of the past. For one thing, their efforts to develop their economies were blocked by a wide range of liabilities. Before World War I, Eastern Europe had been by and large a semicolonial region in which the great powers made investments and sold manufactured goods, while the area itself supplied raw materials and agricultural goods. With the coming of independence, however, these new states lost what had been guaranteed markets for their products. Hence, while they lacked sufficient revenue, the resources they now needed in order to undertake industrialization were expensive. The entire infrastructure and financial structure of the region mitigated against rapid development: local capital was virtually nonexistent; trading and business practices were antiquated; and roads, railways, and communication systems required building from the ground up. Moreover, in an area that was overwhelmingly agricultural, farming techniques and mechanization were outdated.

In Austria and Czechoslovakia, a small but thriving middle class, mainly of German and Jewish origin, had existed for some time, but the other states lacked managers and experts. Wealth and status were concentrated in the hands of a relatively small but powerful landowning aristocracy, as well as in the ranks of the church hierarchy. The workforce in such traditional agricultural societies—that is, the bulk of the population—consisted of millions of poor peasants whose lives were not much better than their serf ancestors. As a result, poor health care and nutrition, high birth and death rates, and illiteracy made the task of national development still more difficult and in the long run weakened the strength of the new parliamentary governments.

The Failure of Democracy

Under these circumstances, the prospects for democratic government in Eastern Europe were bleak. The fact that most of these societies lacked formal experience with parliamentary government undermined the opportunities for stable political progress. To make matters worse, while authoritarian traditions were strong in many states, the new parliamentary systems generally spawned numerous political parties, a fact that made for instability and a poor legislative record.

Nationalism represented by far the most serious political problem facing the East European states. Nationalist sentiment in the region was fierce, especially in Poland, Bohemia, and Hungary, each of which had an old nationalist heritage. World War I had intensified the nationalist animosities between the states of the region. Austria, Hungary, and Bulgaria were "revisionist" states which were unhappy with the peace settlements and wanted to regain lost territories. The older independent nations of Greece, Albania, and Romania, on the other hand, wanted to keep what they had gained from the war. Finally, the new countries of Poland, Czechoslovakia, Estonia, Latvia, and Lithuania indoctrinated their citizens with patriotic fervor in an

Marshal Pilsudski, authoritarian leader of the new Poland.

effort to create a loyal population willing to fight to preserve independence. The result was an intricately intense web of national fears and animosities that made regional cooperation difficult and kept international relations tense.

Liberal democracy did not fare well in these circumstances, and in virtually all cases eventually collapsed in the face of authoritarianism. The Hungarian case was one of the saddest. In 1919, the communists set up a socialist dictatorship in Hungary under Béla Kun (1885–1937), which was put down by a Romanian army sanctioned by the Allies. Admiral Miklós Horthy (1858–1957) was made regent of the country, remaining as a figurehead until the Nazis deposed him in 1944. Horthy appointed Count Stephen Bethlen prime minister (served 1921–1931), and he ran the government with only a pretense of parliamentary responsibility for a decade. Then followed General Julius Gombos (prime minister 1932–1936), the head of the anti-Semitic Race Defense party who made a farce of Hungary's representative system and worked closely with Mussolini and Hitler in foreign affairs.

In the 1920s, dictators or authoritarian leaders took power in Albania, Lithuania, Yugoslavia, and Poland. In the latter country, Marshal Jozef Pilsudski served as president from 1918 to 1922. When internal divisions paralyzed the state, Pilsudski staged a "march on Warsaw" in 1926 and seized the government, making himself dictator. In the following decade, a combined leadership emerged under army officers and a fascist-like organization.

In Eastern Europe, unlike Britain and France, parliamentary government could not withstand the strains of the Depression. In 1930 the controversial Romanian monarch, King Carol II (1893–1953) returned to his country after having deserted his throne and family to live in Paris with a mistress. Carol deposed his son Michael and ruled as a dictator, being deposed by Hitler in 1940. Over the next several years, dictators also took power in Austria, Estonia, Latvia, Bulgaria, and Greece.

The one successor state in central Europe able to prevent its democratic system from succumbing to dictatorship was Czechoslovakia. The Czech state was relatively prosperous, and the government had implemented important reforms, including the breakup of the large estates. Its founder and first president was Thomas Masaryk (1850–1937), a former professor of philosophy and a humane man of principle. He served as president for 17 years. His successor, Edouard Benes (1884–1948), was a close associate of Masaryk. Together, such upright leaders might have resolved the country's serious domestic problems had it not become the target of Hitler's aggression.

The record of European democracy in the interwar period was mixed. In Western Europe, Great Britain and France, along with most of the smaller states, maintained their political systems intact. After World War I, most of them had instituted universal suffrage and had begun to develop social programs designed to integrate their citizens into a uniform national experience. During the Great Depression, this trend accelerated as the governments created the basic institutions of the welfare state, designed to insulate their citizens from the worst aspects of the crisis.

The Western democracies successfully resisted the lure of fascism, although such movements appeared in virtually every country. Only in Italy and Germany did fascism seize power before World War II, although in Spain a right-wing dictator came to power in the 1930s after a tragic civil war. The experiment with democracy in Eastern Europe, however, proved a dismal failure, as the enthusiastic hopes of the Allied statesmen of 1919 were dashed by the rise of authoritarian dictatorship.

Questions for Further Study

1. What were the chief political concerns in postwar England and France?
2. What were the origins of the Irish question?
3. To what conditions did fascism appeal?
4. Why was democracy so tenuous in postwar eastern Europe?

Suggestions for Further Reading

Cassels, Alan. *Fascism*. New York, 1975.

Greene, Nathanael. *From Versailles to Vichy*. New York, 1970.

Hughes, Judith M. *To the Maginot Line: The Politics of French Military Preparations in the 1920s*. Cambridge, MA, 1971.

Jackson, Julian. *The Popular Front in France: Defending Democracy, 1934–1938*. New York, 1988.

Jelavich, Barbara. *History of the Balkans: Twentieth Century*. New York, 1983.

Kitchen, Martin. *Europe Between the Wars: A Political History*. London, 1988.

Roberts, Mary L. *Civilization Without Sexes: Reconstructing Gender in Postwar France*. Chicago, 1994.

Seton-Watson, Hugh. *Eastern Europe Between the Wars, 1918–1941*. Cambridge, MA, 1962.

Taylor, A. J. P. *English History, 1914–1945*. New York, 1965.

VIII

Topic 6

Social Values and the Lost Generation

In 1914, European social conditions still reflected the manners and mores of the Victorian Age. Life both within and beyond the family was bound by tradition, patriarchy, and class, and the prevailing sexual code insisted on virtuous behavior but in reality condoned dual standards for men and women. Moreover, European civilization was still predominantly rural and the majority of people lived by farming.

The Great War began a process of social transformation that profoundly changed the way in which most Europeans lived. Daily life became more open to change and more democratic, social and sexual codes relaxed, and people felt less tied to tradition. The new yearning for personal freedom and modern life was reflected in the public behavior of the so-called "Jazz Age," in which fast-paced, expressive dancing and music became the rage as high society flocked in large numbers to the new nightclubs. The postwar era also saw the rise of a new mass culture in which millions of citizens with greater leisure time enjoyed the automobile, radio, motion pictures, and sports as part of everyday experience.

The new social values reflected the shift to an urban-based, industrial, nonagrarian society. In the 1920s and 1930s, the most important social factor was the expansion of the white-collar class, a social category composed of people who worked for a living and did not own significant property, but who thought and behaved like the middle class. At the same time, the upper ranks of the bourgeoisie and the old aristocracy increasingly joined together in support of social stability and authoritarian government in the face of the new political and organizational power of the industrial working classes, whose cause was now championed by the Soviet Union and the growing strength of socialist parties.

The year 1929 marked a phase in social development that was different in tone and spirit from the 1920s. Social stress increased markedly in the 1930s, as the effects of the Great Depression made themselves felt. The spirit of class conflict, already noticeable in the previous decade, became more intense, especially among the middle classes, whose security and savings were decimated by the economic collapse, and among the working classes, who experienced widespread misery. As optimism and opportunity gave way to fear and insecurity, Europe underwent a loss of social momentum. The birthrate declined because young people delayed marriage and the rearing of families. Along with the economic difficulties of the decade, Europe's political future seemed dark as totalitarian dictatorships held millions in their grip and the threat of war loomed.

MOBILITY AND STATUS: SOCIAL CLASS UNDER STRESS

Since the first industrial revolution in the 18th century, two broad trends had characterized European development: the rise of cities in what had been a predominantly rural society, and the diversification of a once overwhelmingly agrarian economy with the growth of the industrial and service sectors. In the 20th century, these trends matured. As a result, class structure became more complicated as wealth and status shifted and tensions among the classes increased.

Trends in European Society

Industrialization had drawn millions of Europeans from the countryside to the cities. During the 19th century urban dwellers steadily increased in proportion to the total population, and this process of urbanization transformed society. By 1910, Great Britain was the most urban European nation, with some 65 percent of its population living in cities, while Belgium, Germany, and the Netherlands each counted slightly less than half their populations in the urban category. France was still only around 38 percent urban, and in Italy, Denmark, Austria, and Hungary about a third of the people lived in cities with 20,000 or more inhabitants. In the agrarian countries of southern and eastern Europe, much smaller proportions of the populations were urban—Bulgaria, for example, was only 9 percent urban.

On the Continent, only the Netherlands reached the 50 percent mark before World War II, but everywhere the trend was apparent. The position of cities with more than 100,000 inhabitants was strengthened in some countries: between 1910 and 1930, the proportion of Germans living in such large cities rose from 21 to 37 percent, while for Italians the increase was from 11 to 17 percent. In 1910 there were seven European cities with populations over 1 million, while in 1940 the number had more than doubled. The table (at top right) shows the population growth of some of Europe's largest cities in the interwar period.

Another indicator of a society's development is the distribution of the working population among the three "sectors" of agriculture, industry, and services (the latter including such work categories as trade, banking, public administration, and education). All European countries have followed the same general pattern, although at different rates of development. The percentage of people employed in agriculture has fallen steadily, that of industry first rose and then fell, while the service sector has increased constantly. In 1910, 41 percent of the European workforce was in agriculture, 34 percent in industry, and 25 percent in the service sector. By 1930, agriculture remained at 41 percent, but industry had declined to 30 percent, and services had grown to 29 percent. This trend continued through the rest of the century; by 1950 the services represented 31 percent of the workforce and in the 1980s Europe entered the "postindustrial" era when the service sector reached 50 percent.

As in the case of urbanization, this pattern differed widely, depending on the region of Europe and the country. In Eastern Europe, for example, the agricultural sector stood at 75 percent in 1910 and by 1930 had fallen only to 64 percent. The following table illustrates the developmental variation among countries:

Table VIII.6.1
Major Cities of Interwar Europe (in 1000s)

	1920	1940
Berlin	3801	4332
Brussels	685	913
Budapest	1185	1163
Glasgow	1052	1132
Hamburg	986	1682
London	7488	8700
Madrid	751	1089
Milan	836	1116
Moscow	1050	4137
Paris	2907	2830
Prague	677	928
Rome	692	1156
Vienna	1866	1918
Warsaw	931	1266

Table VIII.6.2
The Working Population of Selected Countries by Sector, 1910/1930 (in percent)

	1910			1930		
	A	I	S	A	I	S
Britain	9	51	40	6	46	48
Germany	37	41	22	29	40	31
France	41	33	26	36	33	31
Italy	55	27	18	47	31	22
Hungary	58	20	22	53	24	23
Poland	77	9	14	66	17	17

Source: Adapted from Gerold Ambrosius and William H. Hubbard, *A Social and Economic History of Twentieth-Century Europe* (Cambridge, MA: Harvard University Press, 1989), 58. A, I, and S stand for agricultural, industrial, and service.

The same general pattern could also be discerned for a variety of other social indicators, including rates of literacy, mortality, industrial production, and income. In the case of literacy, important gains had been made since the last decade of the 19th century, when systems of universal primary education were widely introduced. By 1900, 95 percent of the British and French people could read and write, whereas in Italy almost half the population could not. After 1918, a wave of democratization swept school systems in many countries. Between 1920 and 1940, the proportion of secondary school students doubled in countries such as Britain, Germany, Italy, Sweden, and Austria. By 1921, the number of illiterates in Italy had been almost halved, and a decade later the illiteracy rate there had fallen to 21 percent. By the 1930s one-third of all secondary school students in western Europe were girls. With the exception of the Soviet Union, however, higher education remained a class prerogative, and in the more developed nations of Europe only 2 percent of the college-age population attended university. In the 1930s, women comprised 25 percent of university students in Britain, but the percentage was much less in other countries.

Class Boundaries, Wealth, and Status

Class distinctions are determined by a variety of factors, ranging from legal differences in the case of the aristocracy to manner of dress, and they generally involve lifestyles and attitudes. Income and wealth are, however, among the most crucial factors, not only of class but of the broader question of social equality. Measured by gains in per capita national product and real wages, a process of leveling has characterized European development during the 20th century, although the greatest gains in a more equal income distribution have been made since World War II.

One important change was that the economic significance of the very wealthy declined. In 1913, British society was still marked by an immense gulf between rich and poor: the richest 1 percent of the population controlled 70 percent of all personal wealth. By 1930, that proportion had declined to about 60 percent, and by 1945 to some 50 percent. In France, similar changes took place. Real wages followed the broad economic trends of the postwar period (see Part VIII, Topic 3). In Western Europe they dropped sharply after the bust of 1921, rose until the Great Depression, and then rose again beginning in the mid to late 1930s, depending on the particular country. After 1950, they jumped significantly. Nevertheless, living standards continued to differ considerably between classes. For workers and the lower middle classes, the bulk of all income—as much as 80 percent—still went for basic necessities such as food, clothing, and shelter, as well as taxes. Moreover, poverty grew significantly during the Great Depression, when mass unemployment affected millions in all but the highest social classes.

Contrary to the trend begun in the 19th century, the post-1919 period did not see the continuing growth of the working class. Instead, the fastest growing group was the white-collar worker, whose ranks swelled with the expansion of government and private sector bureaucracies. Self-defining attitudes put most of these employees in the lowest levels of the middle classes, but in fact many earned salaries that were the same or even lower than factory workers. In Germany, one out of four white-collar workers had come from a working-class family. In this respect, the Depression stimulated considerable social instability, for unemployment forced many white-collar workers to go back to the factories.

Generally, upward mobility within the middle classes declined in the interwar period. A few speculators made huge fortunes, but most of the bourgeoisie experienced slow gains, if any, in income and status, and for many living standards actually declined as inflation and then depression wiped out their savings. In Germany, where they were hardest hit, inflation destroyed more than half of the capital of the lower middle class. The professional classes were in oversupply in some countries, and many college graduates were unemployable.

Because the condition of the middle classes declined in the 1930s, the gap between them and the upper classes widened. Despite the decline in the position of the wealthiest portion of the population, most of this group weathered the Depression relatively unscathed. The aristocracy, which maintained its status and power most fully in eastern and southern Europe, experienced some difficulties. This was especially true of those who derived their income from landed estates, for the agricultural depression and land reform both weakened the landed nobility. Political reforms, particularly in the new nations of Eastern Europe, also weakened aristocratic power. Only in the Soviet Union, however, was the aristocracy actually wiped out, and in countries such as Britain and France it retained significant influence.

In those countries in which the nobility was weakened, the status of the peasantry generally improved. In agrarian countries where parliamentary democracy was introduced, peasant political parties developed and reforms gave many peasants their first opportunity to own their own land. In Czechoslovakia, slightly more than 10 percent of the land was divided, and in Romania significant progress was made, whereas much less land distribution took place in Poland and Hungary. Such changes did not always mean a real improvement in peasant lives, for they tended to use antiquated farming methods and generally were forced into debt to meet the costs of their own production. By the late 1920s, peasants everywhere faced increasing economic hardships.

Millions of workers were without jobs for most of the Depression years, having to subsist on limited public assistance. For them, the 1930s were demoralizing and without hope. Most countries saw considerable labor agitation. A minority of workers supported the communists, but most gravitated either to socialist parties or trade unions, using the strike as their principal instrument of protest. Radical political movements such as Italian Fascism were in part a response to worker demands and in part a reaction against them. As the Great Depression descended, the middle and upper classes grew more agitated and insecure, not only about their own condition but about working-class demands. The result everywhere was heightened social tension and class conflict. The Depression, like the Great War, proved to be a profoundly unsettling experience for European society.

NEW YORK, PARIS, AND BERLIN: THE AGE OF CABARET

The postwar years were filled with contradictions. While government leaders spoke of a return to "normalcy" after the deprivations and sacrifices of wartime, popular opinion clamored for a new era of expressive freedom and self-indulgence unlike anything known before the war. In the United States, the era of Prohibition was simultaneously the era of the "speakeasy." Indeed, one reflection of the relaxed social conditions that prevailed in the postwar period was the popularity of the nightclub. Although not an entirely new social institution, the modern nightclub offered an ideal backdrop for the culture of the "Jazz Age."

Prohibition and the Jazz Age

In the United States, where a sense of Protestant moralism remained strong, the Eighteenth Amendment, passed in January 1919, prohibited the consumption or sale of "intoxicating beverages," and later that year the Volstead Act made traffic in such beverages illegal. The

Photographer Lewis Hine captured the soaring spirit of New York City in this image, entitled *Skyboy,* of a young worker during the construction of the Empire State Building (1931).

Actress Louise Brooks embodied the modern Jazz-Age look of postwar American women.

anti-alcohol campaign reflected the more conservative values of rural America, but in the big cities life assumed a frenetic and modern pace despite—and in part because of—Prohibition.

The Eighteenth Amendment was widely ignored by average Americans, and some used the demand for whisky and beer to reap huge profits from bootlegging. Illegal clubs, known as "speakeasies," served these beverages to private customers—in New York City alone there were some 5000 of them by 1922. Gangsters such as Al "Scarface" Capone (1899–1947) in Chicago and Arthur "Dutch Schultz" Flegenheimer (1902–1935) in New York built powerful criminal organizations on the profits from bootlegging. With their machine guns, big automobiles, and flashy lives, these hoodlums became folk heroes to some Americans, especially when Hollywood immortalized them in the new talking films. In the literary imagination, the hero of "Roaring Twenties" America was the protagonist of the novel *The Great Gatsby* (1925), by F. Scott Fitzgerald (1896–1940). A wealthy young man of mysterious origins who made a fortune in bootlegging, Jay Gatsby grew famous by giving fabulous parties at his elaborate Long Island estate. Fitzgerald himself lived a dissolute life not dissimilar to Gatsby, and his female characters were "flappers," young women with men's hair styles and short, slinky dresses who used lipstick and smoked and drank in public.

The nightclub became the quintessential entertainment spot of the era, and New York City was the nightclub capital. The first nightclub opened in New York in 1921, and they spread rapidly. High society frequented the clubs, especially those in Harlem, then the scene of a major black cultural movement known as the Harlem Renaissance.

One of the most famous of Harlem's nightclubs was the Cotton Club, owned by a mobster. Duke Ellington and Fats Waller (1904–1943) performed there, as well as singers such as Ethel Waters (1896–1977) and the dancer Josephine Baker (1906–1975).

The Cotton Club, the Harlem nightclub that was all the rage in the 1920s.

But although the best black entertainers could be seen at the Cotton Club, black patrons were prohibited. "Everyone rushed up to Harlem at night," remembered one socialite, "to sit around places thick with smoke and the smell of bad gin, where Negroes danced about with each other until the small hours of the morning." While wealthy white audiences packed the Harlem clubs night after night, the black writer Langston Hughes (1902–1967) underscored the exploitation and racism involved in this experience with his cynical comment, "the Negro was in vogue."

The 1929 crash brought the flashy era of the Harlem night spots to an end, for the clubs there had been driven largely by white money. The end to Prohibition in 1933 destroyed the speakeasies, which had attracted many of their high-society customers by the very allure of illegality. As the grim realities of the Depression set in, the "Gatsby" set's fascination with Harlem dissipated and blacks there were left to the miseries of ghetto impoverishment.

Europe and the Image of America

In the 1920s, America and its popular culture became the rage in Europe. European travelers to the United States brought back images of a super-modern society of skyscrapers and machines that looked to the future. In Fascist Italy, young Italians of anti-Fascist sentiment gravitated toward American culture as an escape from the conformity of the reactionary regime, and Mussolini eventually prohibited jazz as a "corrupting" influence.

Europeans became especially fascinated with black American culture. Foremost among the cultural imports was jazz (see Part VIII, Topic 7), whose chief admirers were the French. Indeed, in this respect, Europe's counterpart to New York was Paris, the city that since the second half of the 19th century had been the premier European center of the cultural avant-garde.

In the 1920s, many Americans made Paris their home, attracted by the Bohemian atmosphere and liberal attitudes that the city extended to even the most unconventional behavior. Paris drew a large number of expatriate American intellectuals. The writer Gertrude Stein (1874–1946) had been there since 1904 and, together with her lover Alice B. Toklas (1877–1967), held court at one of the most famous cultural salons of the century. Stein was one of the first to appreciate the genius of the painter Pablo Picasso and other artists, and her apartment became a mecca for young American writers—Stein called them the "lost generation"—searching for their own cultural identity. F. Scott Fitzgerald lived in Paris much of the time, as did the writer Ernest Hemingway (1899–1961). Black American entertainers flocked to Paris, where they performed in a host of cabarets famous since the 1880s, foremost among them the Moulin Rouge, immortalized by the artist Toulouse-Lautrec. Parisians found black Americans, especially women, exotically sensuous. In 1925, an all-black musical called *La Revue Nègre*, which ran first in New York, was booked to play in Paris at the Théâtre des Champs-Elysées. When Josephine Baker arrived in Paris as the lead in the review, she joined a group of black musicians who played the blues in the bohemian quarters of the city. The singer Bricktop was already there, and owned a popular night spot. Baker became an overnight hit and remained in Paris for the next 50 years, opening her own cabaret, the Chez Joséphine, and marrying an Italian count. Duke Ellington made his first European tour in the late 1920s and was wildly acclaimed.

Pablo Picasso painted this portrait of American writer Gertrude Stein in 1905–1906, when they both were relatively unknown émigrés in Paris.

If Paris had long been a major cultural center of Europe, Berlin had no such heritage. Rather, the city of almost 4 million inhabitants had been the capital of the former German empire and its economic life. Yet in the 1920s, Berlin transformed itself into the center of an extraordinary flowering of modern culture, and also earned a reputation as one of Europe's most notorious fleshpots. "Sex," said the actress Louise Brooks, "was the business of the town."

The atmosphere in postwar Berlin was iconoclastic and innovative, and the city drew creative young

African-American entertainer Josephine Baker was a sensation at the Folies-Bergère in Paris.

Germans attracted by the counterculture of modernity. Bars, restaurants, prostitution houses, and music halls sprang up, offering free-wheeling entertainment. The city became especially known for its hundreds of bars frequented by lesbians and gays, whose experiences were chronicled in a series of short stories by British-born author Christopher Isherwood (1904–1986). American jazz became the rage here, too, and cabarets, originally imported from France, flourished. In Berlin, however, the cabarets assumed an original aspect, for in many of them light music and comedy were used to convey serious political and social satire. The cabarets also inspired the artist George Grosz (1893–1959), a communist supporter. His brilliant talent created political drawings that savagely assaulted reactionary forces, especially the Nazis, whom he passionately hated.

As in America, in Europe, too, conditions in the 1930s altered the social atmosphere. The Great Depression, the rise of Hitler, and the looming threat of war combined to bring an end to the era of rampant pleasure seeking and the spirit of the age of cabaret.

GENDER, SEXUALITY, AND THE FAMILY

The great popularity of the nightclub among the middle and upper classes reflected the greatly changed attitudes about women, gender, and sexuality. Women not only attended the cabarets, but acted in public places generally much as men did, for they drank, smoked, danced, and enjoyed themselves, often without male companions. Women's fashions, revealing portions of the body that had been kept hidden during the Victorian era, paralleled the emergence of a "new woman"—independent, accomplished, and interested in self-fulfillment. Such attitudes and behavior would have been inconceivable for most women 20 years earlier. The changing status of women in society was part of a broader social transformation that included major shifts in sexual standards and behavior, in marriage and birth patterns, and in the way in which the household was organized.

The New Woman: Opportunities and Limitations

World War I had begun the process of altering gender roles, for hundreds of thousands of women had moved into the factories to replace the men who served in the armies (see Part VIII, Topic 1). In the aftermath, women gained new freedoms and privileges. The contribution of women to the war effort was in part responsible for the passage of female suffrage laws in the immediate postwar period. Denmark and Iceland, both neutral during the war, actually gave women the vote in 1915, and the Netherlands followed in 1917. In 1918, Britain was the first major European state to enact female suffrage, although it was limited to women over 30. The first women candidates who ran in the elections that year were all defeated. The Weimar Republic gave German women the vote in 1919, while Belgium did so for war widows only. In the new states of Eastern Europe, women also achieved the vote, while in France and Italy voting remained a male preserve until after World War II.

Despite the politically conservative mood of most Western European countries in the postwar era, women's attitudes and their social position changed significantly, creating a clash of opinion between those who wanted to restore prewar social values and those who demanded the modernization of society. Women

Otto Dix's "Metropolis" (1927–28) ironically depicts a Berlin nightclub with its "new morality."

seemed more ubiquitous in postwar society, both because millions of men had been killed in the war and because women increasingly did things once reserved only for men—women became journalists, took part in professional sports, flew airplanes, and entered mainstream politics. Women's public conduct became more relaxed, and many now demanded careers of their own. The role of women in the professions and the arts assumed greater importance, and the modern middle-class housewife emerged in the 1920s.

Women changed their physical appearance in a number of ways. In dress, they began to reveal their arms, legs, and shoulders. The length of their skirts was shortened by about twelve inches and sleeves, once wrist-length even in summer, disappeared. Women who thought of themselves as modern adopted varying degrees of male appearance—short, bobbed hair, flattened breasts, and a slim figure, and wore slacks and trench coats. Scanty bathing suits were fashionable, and the ideal of a suntanned body replaced the Victorian preference for pale skin. The cosmetic business grew to a mass industry as millions of women began to use lipstick, rouge, and mascara, items once identified only with prostitutes.

In the 1920s, the gains in employment made by women during the war were generally pushed back. With the coming of peace, many governments encouraged women to return to the home and allow men to take their place in the workforce, a policy that unions and even reform-minded socialists supported. The percentage of women working declined almost everywhere. Some of the women who lost their jobs went back to low-paying work as domestics or in agriculture, occupations in which they could not qualify for unemployment insurance. In Britain, unemployment insurance payments were lower for women than for men and not enough for a woman to live on. The expansion of bureaucracies and the growth of department stores did give many women new job opportunities as office workers or salesclerks, and the spread of the telephone led many women to become operators. In factories, where men sometimes outnumbered women nine to one, women were relegated to the most menial jobs. Only in the Soviet Union, where the desire to industrialize took precedence over everything else, did women constitute a major portion—as high as 45 percent—of the workforce.

In those countries where unemployment was high in the 1920s, women workers suffered more than men. The Great Depression made the plight of working women even worse. As conditions deteriorated, increasing numbers of women were forced out of jobs, in both democratic and authoritarian countries. In 1931, British Labour Minister Margaret Bondfield (1873–1953) excluded most women from unemployment insurance. In Fascist Italy and Nazi Germany, women were encouraged as a matter of ideology to be wives and mothers, not workers (see Part VIII, Topic 4).

Varieties of Sexuality

If women demanded the development of a modern outlook, much of the new mentality focused on sexuality.

In the Victorian era, the prevailing middle-class attitude had been the exercise of sexual restraint for men, virtue for women, and the general repression of overt sexual references in daily life (see Part VII, Topic 13). These conventions began to change with the war, when men and women mingled more freely in an atmosphere of "living for today." Modern medicine and postwar psychology both undermined the earlier emphasis on restraint by stressing the benefits of release and self-expression. Finally, the rise of consumerism led to the discovery of the power of sex as an advertising device, while mass culture, especially the movies, promoted sex symbols on the silver screen.

The struggle against gender tradition inevitably contributed to a more open discussion of sex, but the issue often aroused bitter debate. One of the most controversial figures in the postwar encounter with sexuality was Marie Stopes (1880–1938), a British paleobotanist and birth control advocate. A university lecturer and author, in 1921 Stopes founded the Mothers' Clinic for Constructive Birth Control. She argued that sexual pleasure was an important part of marriage and life in general, and should not be limited to procreation—indeed, the search for physical pleasure, she said, was a woman's right. In 1918 she published *Married Love*, vividly describing the sexual joy that could be attained in marriage. In 1926, she also wrote *Sex and the Young*, which countered Victorian assumptions about the innocence of youth.

The year 1926 also saw the appearance of *Ideal Marriage: Its Physiology and Technique*, by the Dutch physician Theodor von de Velde. The book was one of the most authoritative sex manuals, and became an international bestseller. Its popularity, like that of Stopes' books, was due to the fact that it provided women with detailed practical information.

Europeans not only read such works, but increasingly practiced birth control and abortion. Between 1850 and 1914, Europe's population increased steadily. After the war, however, marriage and birthrates changed in a manner that suggests deliberate efforts to control fertility. The bloody battles of the war, together with disease and undernourishment, killed some 11 million people, or about 3 percent of Europe's population. The war also disrupted the pattern of marriages and births. In the interwar period, mortality rates fell and life expectancy grew, yet the birthrate declined everywhere. A number of factors explain the change: economic hardships and unemployment, especially after the Depression, the diffusion of birth control information, and the changing role of women. In many countries, politicians expressed concern about the population decline, and France, Italy, and Germany passed laws restricting birth control information and abortions. Nevertheless, it has been estimated that perhaps as many as 1 million German women had abortions each year in the 1920s. On the other hand, nations as diverse as France and Sweden, Fascist Italy and Nazi Germany instituted programs to encourage large families.

Sexual minorities also encountered a freer atmosphere in the postwar era. Gays and lesbians came out of the closet in increasingly larger numbers, and many prominent intellectuals and artists made their orientation known publicly. The German psychiatrist Magnus Hirschfeld (1868–1935) founded his famous Institute for Sexual Science, where homosexuals had access to counseling and psychological support in coping with a society that still retained deep hostility toward them. The problem of lesbian identity was directly discussed in the novel *The Well of Loneliness* (1928), by the British writer Radclyffe Hall (1880–1943). Although the book was banned by the government, it appeared in many languages throughout the world.

The Life of the Family

The family as it had developed over the 19th century had also begun to undergo profound changes after World War I, and many of the trends continue to this day. Men and women both postponed marriage longer than ever before, and when they did marry they had fewer children. The average size of the family declined steadily as the number of offspring dropped by almost half.

Within the family, the dynamics of gender moved slowly away from the patriarchal model of the Victorian bourgeoisie. Husbands increasingly shared household responsibilities and became more directly involved in child rearing. Nevertheless, most working-class and middle-class women continued to have major responsibility for managing the household. Technology and consumerism did, however, change the role of the housewife. The 1920s saw the beginnings of modernization in the middle-class home, primarily through the introduction of new machines and the application of technology to household tasks. Electric washing machines and irons transformed those tasks, while the vacuum cleaner came into general use. Such machines made strenuous work less demanding for the average housewife, although some experts have argued that they also raised the standards to which women had to aspire.

The most dramatic change came in the kitchen. During World War I, working women, often without the responsibility of feeding husbands, sons, or brothers, adopted lighter meals that were quick and easy to prepare, and the widespread availability of preservatives and canning after the war encouraged a continuation of such practices. A host of new cookbooks catered to the modern diet, with a new emphasis on nutrition and health. Electric mixers and juicers were introduced, and gas or electric stoves and ovens replaced wood-burning stoves, while electric refrigerators eliminated the need for hauling ice and for daily shopping.

In the mid-1920s, industrial design altered the way in which both home appliances and the home itself looked. The International Exposition of Modern Decorative and Industrial Arts, held in Paris in 1925, presented the first views of streamlined everyday objects and furniture, while the so-called International Style of architecture, developed in Europe by Walter Gropius and Le Corbusier and in the United States by Frank Lloyd Wright, stressed simplicity, modern building materials such as steel, reinforced concrete, and glass, and functionalism (see Part VIII, Topic 7). By the 1930s, a "streamlined modern" style had shaped the design of everything from vacuum cleaners to airplanes to railroad engines and refrigerators, while kitchens became laboratory-like in their cleanliness, organization, and functionalism. The modern household, like the modern family, assumed a new, more progressive aspect.

The social transformations that took place in the 20 years between 1919 and 1939 explain much about how Europeans and others live today. As the West began to emerge out of the industrial revolution and toward the postindustrial world, the composition and status of social classes also changed. The middle classes grew increasingly complex, especially with the growth of the white-collar group, and while the condition of the working classes improved, that of the upper classes deteriorated. The result was a general leveling of society, at least in terms of a more equal distribution of income and standard of living. The social impact of the Great Depression, by threatening the well-being and security of the middle and the working classes, increased class tensions and encouraged the radicalization of domestic politics.

Despite the grim aspects of life between the wars, the era was one of self-conscious modernity, in which many of the repressive features of Victorian society were replaced by values that stressed nonconformity, free expression, and individualism. Women enhanced their social equality, advanced sexual freedom, and won the vote in most democratic countries; in the totalitarian dictatorships, however, the status of women regressed under the impact of a self-consciously male-dominated ideology. Everywhere, working women experienced a mixture of new opportunities and exclusion from the workforce.

The 1920s especially were an age of hedonism marked by a desire for fast-paced, unconventional public behavior. Behind the glitter of the jazz clubs and cabarets lay evidence of a society bent on excess and overindulgence after the shattering experience of a war that had upset tradition more than any single event since the French Revolution. By the 1930s, a more sober, solemn mood set in as society grappled with the ravages of the Great Depression.

Questions for Further Study

1. What was the impact of World War I on European society? How did that impact manifest itself in the 1920s?
2. What were the chief characteristics of popular culture and leisure time activities in the postwar period?
3. In what ways did postwar society reflect the changing role of women?

Suggestions for Further Reading

Bridenthal, Renate, A. Grossmann, and M. Kaplan, eds. *When Biology Became Destiny: Women in Weimar and Nazi Germany*. New York, 1984.

Cantor, Norman. *The History of Popular Culture Since 1815*. New York, 1968.

Gay, Peter. *Weimar Culture*. New York, 1968.

Grossmann, Atina. *Reforming Sex: The German Movement for Birth Control and Abortion Reform, 1920–1950*. New York, 1995.

Gruber, Helmut. *Red Vienna: Experiment in Working-Class Culture, 1919–1943*. New York, 1991.

Kent, Susan. *Making Peace: The Reconstruction of Gender in Postwar Britain*. Princeton, NJ, 1994.

Maier, Charles S. *Recasting Bourgeois Europe: Stabilization in France, Germany, and Italy*. Princeton, NJ, 1975.

Roberts, Mary L. *Civilization Without Sexes: Reconstructing Gender in Postwar France, 1917–1927*. Chicago, 1994.

Stearns, Peter N. *European Society in Upheaval: Social History Since 1800*. New York, 1967.

Winter, J. M., and R. M. Wall, eds. *The Upheaval of War: Family, Work and Welfare in Europe, 1914–1918*. Cambridge, MA, 1988.

VIII

Topic 7

Civilization and Its Discontents: Psychoanalysis and the Arts

World War I led many Europeans to question the basic values of their society and culture. Concepts such as patriotism, the glory of war, aristocracy, rationalism and technology, and the notion of progress itself were tarnished by the carnage of the trenches. Profound doubts arose about the ability of Western civilization to survive. Some artists reacted by seeking refuge in frivolity, often combined with a spirit of cynicism. Others sought to understand human motives by exploring ideas that had been developed before the war, in particular psychoanalysis.

Freud's emphasis on irrationality and the nature of the unconscious proved especially fruitful. The French critic André Breton ushered in a movement called Surrealism which affected literature and the visual arts, while the English writer Virginia Woolf used her novels to explore the "stream of consciousness" of her characters. In drama, the American Eugene O'Neill made explicit the Freudian theme of the relations between parents and children.

Woolf was one of the leading members of an intellectual circle known as the Bloomsbury Group, whose members were responsible for many important cultural developments between the wars. In his poem "The Waste Land," T. S. Eliot analyzed the failure of modern civilization. The philosopher Bertrand Russell and the economist John Maynard Keynes also had contacts with the world of Bloomsbury. In painting, the two leading movements represented opposite attitudes. The Dadaists fought against the idea of any kind of meaning, while the Surrealists explored the intellectual implications of the subconscious and the meaning of dreams. Meanwhile, other painters continued to explore the possibilities of Cubism, the style invented just before World War I. The work of one of them, the Dutch painter Piet Mondrian, influenced much modern design.

With the spread of modern urban culture some artists and designers tried consciously to create a style which would be valid in a wide variety of settings. At the *Bauhaus* in Germany, Walter Gropius and his colleagues devised the International Style, which had a great influence on the urban landscape of the 20th century. Bauhaus artists also sought to provide a modernist idiom for all aspects of everyday life.

Artists were profoundly affected by the growing popularity of photography and the movies, and the diffusion of the radio and recorded sound. Among the most widespread influences of the day was jazz, originally a form of music indigenous to America. Jazz became popular among all those with access to a radio or a phonograph. The leading composers of the day, including Igor Stravinsky and Paul Hindemith, incorporated jazz elements in their music.

The interwar years were overshadowed not only by the horrors of World War I, but by the growing realization that further conflict seemed ahead. The Spanish Civil War drove many artists and writers to protest the brutality of fascism. The German novelist Thomas Mann warned against the direction the Nazi regime was taking, before joining other intellectuals in exile. Yet if art could warn, it could not prevent. With the outbreak of World War II, Freud's insistence on the power of the irrational seemed frighteningly justified.

STREAM OF CONSCIOUSNESS: LITERATURE AND PSYCHOANALYSIS

World War I brought into question many of Europe's most cherished values. Some, such as a belief in the inherent superiority and leadership qualities of noble birth, were already being challenged in the 19th century. Others, most notably the importance of patriotism and national pride, retained their potency and their potential destructiveness. Technological progress, the proud achievement of the late 19th century, was now revealed as morally neutral. Its ability to cause good or ill was vast, and depended on how it was used: tanks, planes, and poison gas were responsible for the slaughter of millions of troops.

For some the shock to civilization marked the beginning of the end. The Irish poet William Butler Yeats (1865–1939) spoke for many who were fearful of the future when he wrote: "Things fall apart: the center cannot hold; Mere anarchy is loosed upon the world." The sense that Western civilization was deteriorating permeated *The Decline of the West* (1918–1922), a massive historical study by the German philosopher Oswald Spengler (1880–1936). According to Spengler, history moved in cycles. Western culture, he believed, had passed its high point and was on the way down.

Those of less apocalyptic temperament sought escape from recent memories in the lighthearted, even trivial. The English novelist Evelyn Waugh (1903–1966) caricatured the dizzy world of London's "bright young things" with a mixture of attraction and repulsion. In Paris, Picasso designed sets for a ballet, *Parade*, with music by Erik Satie (1866–1925), which included sound effects such as whistles, automobile horns, and typewriters to evoke everyday life.

The 1920s was the age of the "flappers" (see Part VIII, Topic 6). Elegant young women with broad hats and tight-fitting short skirts, smoking cigarettes in long holders (a sign of their emancipation), spent their afternoons at tea dances, or listening to the latest jazz records from America. For their generation, or so it seemed, nationalism and the wars it provoked were unthinkable. Students at Oxford University debated the notion of fighting for king and country, and voted overwhelmingly against it.

Literature and the Unconscious

Among those to look deeply at the problems of the modern age was Sigmund Freud, who published *Civilization and its Discontents* in 1930 (see Part VII, Topic 21). Freud's work earlier in the century proved an increasing source of inspiration to artists searching to understand the motives for human behavior. By stressing the importance of the unconscious and the inner meaning of dreams, he underlined the power of the irrational to affect apparently rational thought processes.

Exploration of the unconscious was the chief goal of Surrealism, an artistic movement which influenced both writers and painters. The high priest of Surrealism was the French poet André Breton (1896–1966), who published his *Manifesto of Surrealism* in 1924. In his poems he intermingled the everyday and the fantastic, probing the connections between dream and reality, the subjective and the objective. The finest poet of the Surrealist movement, Paul Éluard (1895–1952; real name Eugène Grindel), even turned to various forms of mental alienation as a means of shedding light on hidden mental processes. By the use of mysterious images and fragmentary language, his love poems tried to recreate the dreamlike disorder of the subconscious.

The novels of Virginia Woolf (1882–1941) use the "stream of consciousness" technique to deal with themes of time, change, and human personality. Instead of providing a chronological account of her characters' lives, she moved back and forth in time, describing the effect of the past on present consciousness. In *To the Lighthouse* (1927), the central section of the three parts into which the novel is divided is called "Time Passes." It provides an impressionistic rendering of the effects of the passage of time on people and things. In further

A curtain designed by Picasso for the performance of the ballet *Parade*, with music by Erik Satie, given in Paris in 1917 by Diaghilev's Ballets Russes company.

refining on the techniques of Joyce and Proust (see Part VII, Topic 21), Woolf paid special attention to the experiences of women. Her book *Mrs. Dalloway* (1925) described a single day in the life of the novel's heroine. Woolf's own frustration at the exclusion of women from intellectual life found expression in *A Room of One's Own* (1929), in which she argued that only financial independence and freedom from the demands of family could give women the same possibilities as men. A later polemical work, *Three Guineas* (1938), described a fascist-like world dominated by men, in which individual rights, freedom, and justice were suppressed.

The great American dramatist Eugene O'Neill (1888–1953) used psychology and symbolism to illuminate another of Freud's revelations: the complexity of the relationship between parents and children, and the fundamental importance of early family experience in creating human personalities. In *Mourning Becomes Electra* (1931), ancient Greek tragedy became reenacted in Civil War New England, with Aeschylus' idea of the unavoidability of fate given modern form as psychological destiny.

THE WORLD OF BLOOMSBURY

Amid the confusion of the interwar years, a group of writers and intellectuals in England sought to maintain a coherence of thought and action. They were called after the area of London in which many of them lived and worked, Bloomsbury. The name acquired further cultural resonance from the fact that the Bloomsbury district also contained the British Museum. Virginia Woolf and her husband, Leonard Woolf (1880–1969), were at the center of the Bloomsbury Group. From the basement of their house they operated a publishing company, the Hogarth Press, which circulated works by many of the most influential writers of the time. Among the offerings in Hogarth Press editions were the first complete English translations of the works of Freud, and the first English translations of the German poet Rainer Maria Rilke (1875–1926) and the Italian novelist Italo Svevo (1861–1928; real name Ettore Schmitz).

Eliot and "The Waste Land"

Although an American, and on the periphery of the Bloomsbury circle, the poet T[homas] S[tearns] Eliot (1888–1965) was among the writers the Woolfs published. His most famous work, "The Waste Land," appeared on their list in 1922, and over the following years Eliot acted as informal adviser to them.

After studying at Harvard, Eliot moved to London, where he eked out a living by teaching and writing reviews, and working in a bank. "The Waste Land" placed him immediately at the center of the modernist movement. Its theme was the spiritual and moral chaos of postwar Europe. Abandoning traditional forms, the style of the poem conveys the bleakness of its theme in broken lines and fragmented images. The overwhelming mood of the work is one of alienation and exile, expressing the disillusionment of an entire generation.

In subsequent works, Eliot moved from the despair of "The Waste Land" to an affirmation of traditional culture. The foundation of his growing optimism was Christianity. The most fully worked-out meditation on his Christian faith appeared in the *Four Quartets* (1944). Not only the most widely read poet of his generation, Eliot was also an enormously influential literary critic.

The Influence of Bloomsbury

Bloomsbury's cultural influence extended far beyond poetry. Lytton Strachey (1880–1932) brought new life to the writing of biography by taking an irreverent look at pillars of the Victorian establishment. His *Eminent Victorians* (1918) caught the postwar mood of cynicism by depicting Florence Nightingale as an interfering busybody, and General Charles George "Chinese" Gordon as an alcoholic. In a slightly later work he took on even Queen Victoria herself.

The art critic and painter Roger Fry (1866–1934) was one of the leading champions of Cézanne and the other Postimpressionist painters; the exhibitions he organized of their works helped to inspire public interest and enthusiasm for them. The historical writings and translations of Arthur Waley (1889–1966) introduced Chinese and Japanese culture to a wide audience. Although many of them are now superseded, his versions of Chinese poetry and the great Japanese novel *The Tale of Genji* (written around 1000 by Lady Murasaki) opened up new cultural horizons for many readers.

Other influential figures who maintained links with Bloomsbury included John Maynard Keynes (See Part VIII, Topic 3), a major pioneer in the development of modern economics. The leading philosopher of the day, Bertrand Russell (1872–1970), although not an inner member of the group, was in contact with many who were. Far more closely involved—she had a love affair with Virginia Woolf—was Victoria Sackville-West (1892–1962), whose unconventional marriage to the critic and diplomat Harold Nicolson (1886–1968) illustrated the iconoclastic spirit of the world of Bloomsbury.

MOVEMENTS IN MODERN ART: DADA, SURREALISM, ABSTRACTION

The years before World War I saw a succession of "isms," including Fauvism, Cubism, and Futurism, as artists tried to build on the innovations of their prede-

Marcel Duchamp's famous "defacement" of Leonardo da Vinci's *Mona Lisa*, with an obscene reference beneath (1919).

PUBLIC FIGURES AND PRIVATE LIVES

VITA SACKVILLE-WEST AND HAROLD NICOLSON

Daughter of an eccentric English aristocrat, Vita Sackville-West became one of the most flamboyant and well-known figures of her era. Passionately attached to her family and its ancestral home, Knole, her two absorbing interests were literature and gardening. After meeting her for the first time around Christmas 1922, Virginia Woolf wrote of her: "Not much to my severer taste—florid, mustached, parakeet-colored, with all the supple ease of the aristocracy, but not the wit of the artist." Two years later, under the spell of her infatuation, Virginia described Vita's legs: "Oh they are exquisite—running like slender pillars up into her trunk, which is that of a breastless cuirassier."

In 1913 Vita married Harold Nicolson, an eligible young man in the diplomatic service, whose early emotional relationships included a number of lighthearted homosexual affairs. When they first met in 1910, Vita herself was involved in a romantic crush on another young girl. While maintaining their own independent lifestyles, they brought up two sons and wrote. Nicolson published literary criticism, including an influential monograph on Tennyson. From 1935 to 1945 he served in Parliament.

Vita's first work, a collection of poems, was inspired by the time she spent in Teheran, where her diplomat husband had been posted. A later long poem, "The Land," won an important literary prize in 1927. She followed this with novels, works on family history, and innumerable articles on gardening. Many of these latter were based on her restoration of the garden at Sissinghurst Castle, which is still visited annually by thousands.

Throughout their marriage, Sackville-West and Nicolson kept diaries, and exchanged a flood of correspondence with one another during their frequent separations. Their relationship has been described, in fact, as one of the best-documented marriages in history. They constantly brooded on their own lives, and on the question of relations between men and women, as well as on the issue of feminism. In 1934, Nicolson recorded in his diary a discussion about women's lives and their approach to freedom: "V says that in every revolution there is a transitional stage. That women have for centuries been suppressed and that one cannot expect them to slide quite naturally into freedom. This saddens me."

Twenty years later, Vita summed up her feelings about her marriage in a letter to a friend: "We have gone our own ways for about 30 years; never asked questions; never been in the least curious about that side of our respective lives, though deeply devoted and sharing our interests. I love him deeply, and he loves me. . . ."

To some extent, the openness of their marriage was facilitated by the well-to-do British social world in which they moved and by Sackville-West's utter indifference to convention. Both of them drew considerable strength and satisfaction from their independent literary work. Nicolson's early pleasure in his political career gave way to a growing sense of not being taken seriously enough, but his diary reveals a keen if somewhat detached interest in diplomatic affairs. Certainly they both took their duties as parents seriously. In a letter to her elder son, in fact, Vita spelled out the oddness and success of an unlikely union: "Two of the happiest married people I know, whose names I must conceal for reasons of discretion, are both homosexual." Their son had little doubt about whom his mother meant.

cessors. The movement of the immediate postwar period, Dada, rejected the past and sought to begin again.

The Dadaists

The Dadaist movement was born out of anger, frustration, and despair. In 1915, as war raged, a group of artists met around a café table in Zurich, Switzerland, to protest the madness of their times. Their response was to reject the past and all its works, and to create meaningless nonsense. The very word "Dada" seems to have been chosen for its similarity to childlike babble. The leading Dada poet, the Romanian-born Tristan Tzara (1896–1963), wrote a manifesto in 1918 calling for the destruction of memory, the end of good manners, and the practice of the spontaneous.

Dada's most original, and iconoclastic, figure was the French Marcel Duchamp (1887–1968). An early proponent of Cubism, he created a sensation in New York in 1913 with his *Nude Descending a Staircase*. Duchamp invented the Dada form of sculpture, the "ready-made," by taking ordinary objects—a snow shovel, a urinal—and putting them on display. ("Ready-made" sculptures enjoyed a revival after World War II; among those producing them was Picasso.) No masterpiece of high culture was safe from his scorn, as his notorious defacement of a copy of Leonardo's *Mona Lisa* vividly illustrated. For all the anger, however, the sheer energy of the Dada movement soon worked itself out. Duchamp abandoned art for chess in 1923, and many Dada artists went on to produce Surrealist paintings.

Surrealist Art

Unlike the Dada pursuit of the meaningless, Surrealism set out to discover the deeper meanings that lay beneath the surface of the conscious mind. According to Breton's Surrealist manifesto of 1924, artists should set out to express "the real functioning of thought without any control by reason." One of the leading exponents of Surrealism, the Spanish painter Salvador Dalí (1904–1989), described his works as "hand-painted dream photographs." Like many others of the period, Dalí was obsessed with the nature of time. His best-known work, *The Persistence of Memory* (1931), has become virtually an icon of Surrealism. The work combines precisely painted detail with melting watches to create a sense of quiet alarm.

Dalí's paintings are often foreboding, even threatening. His Belgian contemporary René Magritte (1898–1967) used absurdity to call into question the nature of reality. His haunting images show familiar subjects, but play tricks with the viewer's expectations; the title of the painting often plays a part in the surprise effect. Thus, his *Man with a Newspaper* (1928) is divided into four identical quadrants, in which the man seen in the upper left quadrant disappears thereafter.

The form of Magritte's painting, with its four separate "frames," reveals one of the sources of inspiration for Surrealist art: the cinema and photography. Dalí worked on a number of film projects, as did the French Surrealist author and artist Jean Cocteau (1889–1963).

Other Surrealist artists adopted a less literal approach. The Swiss painter Paul Klee (1879–1940) once said: "I want to be as though new-born, knowing nothing." His small, beautifully executed works depict a world of pure imagination, avoiding any trace of the realism of Magritte or Dalí. Klee experimented with "psychic automatism," a technique by which the artist set down lines at random, without rational control.

The finished drawings and watercolors (he rarely used other mediums) are subtle and delicate in line and color. The element of humor in Klee's work—an unusual quality in modern art—also appears in that of the Spanish artist Joan Miró (1893–1983).

Cubism After World War I

Both Pablo Picasso and Georges Braque, the coinventors of Cubism, continued to explore the possibilities of the style, while generally moving away from the highly analytical character of their prewar work (see Part VII, Topic 21). In works such as the *Three Musicians* (1921), Picasso still used flat planes, but the figures have a liveliness and color—even humor—absent in earlier Cubist work. One of the chief exponents of this freer, "Synthetic Cubism" was Picasso's fellow-Spaniard Juan Gris (1887–1927), who applied the technique to still life subjects.

By contrast, the Dutch artist Piet Mondrian (1872–1944) moved toward ever greater abstraction. Art, he believed, should have "balance, unity, and stability." Using pure colors and clean lines, he constructed rectangles of varying dimensions that seem almost to be street plans—Mondrian wrote, in fact, that "the new style will spring from the metropolis." The spare, abstract repose of his works had a considerable influence on many aspects of modern design, from fashion to advertising.

BAUHAUS: THE INTERNATIONAL STYLE IN BUILDING AND DESIGN

Mondrian was one of a group of Dutch artists who joined forces in a movement known as *De Stijl* (Dutch for "The Style"). At the end of World War I, De Stijl architects constructed buildings according to Mondrian's principles of geometrical balance. The Schroder House in Utrecht, designed in 1924 by Gerrit Rietveld (1888–1964), has a façade whose severely geometrical lines form the three-dimensional equivalent of a Mondrian canvas. In addition to buildings, Rietveld also designed furniture, using a similar spare geometrical style.

Gropius and the Bauhaus

The most comprehensive attempt to devise an all-embracing design style for modern living developed in Germany in the 1920s. In 1919, the German architect Walter Gropius (1883–1969) was commissioned to organize a German art school. The result, the Bauhaus (Building Institute), became the 20th century's most influential school of architecture and design.

The innovations of Gropius and his colleagues derived from a new attitude to the nature and function

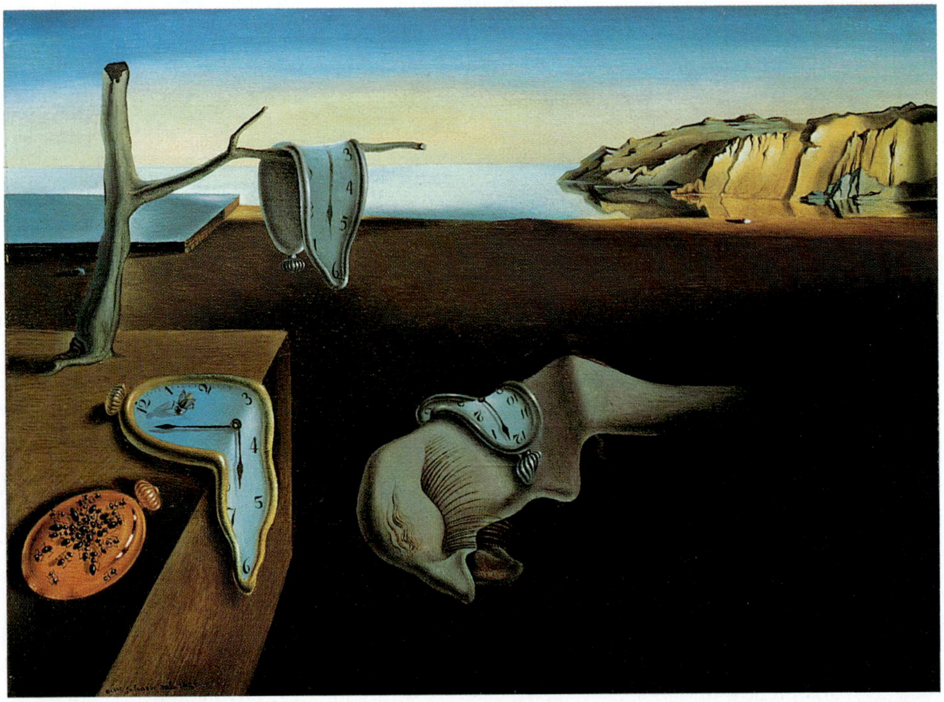

Salvador Dalí's *The Persistence of Memory* (1931), with its distortion of time, is one of the key works of the Surrealist movement.

Three Musicians (1921), a colorful, lighthearted work in Picasso's later Cubist style.

of a building, based on the possibilities of advanced construction techniques. The three principal ingredients were a reinforced concrete base, a structural framework made of steel, and glass panels for walls. By using the principle of cantilevering (projecting beams to support balconies) Bauhaus architects were able to construct upper stories which overhung their supporting bases.

The most visually daring of these elements was the use of glass for walls. Since glass reflects light, as well as transmitting it, changing weather patterns outside a building, along with illumination inside, affect its appearance. At times both inside and outside are visible simultaneously, creating the equivalent of the Cubist effect whereby two different views can be seen at the same time. At other times the glass walls produce a mirror-like effect, reflecting the buildings around. In Bauhaus architecture, in fact, the wall became a decorative rather than structural element, acting as a curtain against the outside environment.

The inventors of the Bauhaus style intended it to serve for constructions in any urban setting. Their "International Style" became widely diffused throughout Europe, and was carried to the United States when Gropius and his colleague Mies van der Rohe fled there in the late 1930s.

One of the first important Modernist buildings, Mies van der Rohe and Philip Johnson's Seagram Building in New York City.

The Bauhaus philosophy of design affected far more than architecture. Its governing principle, that of unadorned utility, characterized the forms of a wide variety of objects and processes. Printmaking and metalwork techniques laid emphasis on clarity of line and ease of production. Mass-produced tubular chairs combined simple comfort and convenient storage capacity. Household appliances were streamlined, and easy to use and to clean.

The characteristically "modern" look of most post–World War II industrial production owed much of its inspiration to the Bauhaus group. Followers of the school praised the clean lines, efficiency, and practical advantages. Others, less convinced, lamented the uniformity and lack of character of the International Style. In architecture, at least, a reaction against Bauhaus simplicity began to develop in the 1980s, when the Postmodernist movement reintroduced elements of decoration (see Part VIII, Topic 14). Yet in the late 20th century the urban landscape of most large cities throughout the world remained firmly conditioned by Bauhaus ideas, and modern design continued to pay homage to the Bauhaus principle: "Less is more."

THE JAZZ AGE: MUSIC, RADIO, AND THE MOVIES

The years after World War I saw the rapid spread of mass communications. Radio, first invented by Guglielmo Marconi (1874–1937) at the turn of the century, became an increasingly popular source of information, culture, and simple entertainment. It linked city and country dwellers, it crossed over national boundaries, it spanned the Atlantic. By the outbreak of World War II, more than 300 million people had access to radio sets. In most European countries, radio networks were state-controlled. Transmissions throughout the 1930s served to reinforce government attitudes, especially in Fascist Italy, Nazi Germany, and Soviet Russia. During World War II, radio broadcasts were used for psychological warfare.

The effect of radio on popular culture, especially music, was to produce a growing standardization of "consumer product," whereby listeners in remote regions or countries could hear the latest Berlin cabaret song or Broadway hit almost as soon as their first local audiences. At the same time, radio also won new listeners for symphonies and operas. In the United States, nationwide transmissions of Metropolitan Opera broadcasts began in 1931. That same year, when Arturo Toscanini (1867–1957), one of the towering figures in European musical life, fled Fascism and went to America, he became the chief conductor of a radio orchestra, the NBC Symphony.

The Movies

Scarcely less revolutionary was the impact of the movies. Like radio, the movies had been around before World War I, but their great age was the 1920s and, with the coming of sound, the 1930s. In the decade before World War II, giant picture palaces sprang up in the big cities, and few rural communities did not have access to a movie theater in a provincial center nearby. Between 1933 and 1942, annual cinema attendance in Germany rose from a quarter of a billion to 1 billion. Over the same period in Britain it remained constant at around 1 billion.

As in the case of radio, movies could and did serve propaganda purposes. Weekly newsreels, feature films, and documentaries poured out of government propaganda ministries. The most notorious examples of film at the service of the state are the works of the German Leni Riefenstahl (1902–1987). Her *Triumph of the Will* (1936) set out to glorify the Nazi party and its doctrines of mass ritual and racial superiority, using highly controlled and sexually charged images of young athletes and physical beauty.

Still shot from the diving sequence of Riefenstahl's film of the 1936 Berlin Olympics, *Olympia.*

The Russian filmmaker Sergei Eisenstein (1898–1948) was more equivocal. His works illustrated Lenin's belief in the high importance of the cinema in winning proletarian support for the Revolution. Most of his films, including his last masterpieces *Ivan the Terrible, Parts I and II* (1944–1946), showed the sufferings of the working class and the inevitability of the class struggle. Yet Eisenstein maintained control over his works; they aimed to teach historical lessons by reference to past events, rather than documenting contemporary politics.

In spite of the politicians' efforts, most people went to the movies for entertainment. With the rise of Hollywood in the 1930s, and the cult of the superstar, the cinema reached new heights of popularity. One of the most successful types of film, the musical, became possible with the improvement of sound techniques and the introduction of color processing.

The first sound film, *The Jazz Singer* (1927), had seemed to many to mark a setback in movie history. The first sound cameras were immobile, and permitted only very limited flexibility. Many of the stars of the silent screen, furthermore, feared the effect of the sound of their voice on their adoring public: adroit publicists cleverly managed to capitalize on this, and turned the first sound appearance of Greta Garbo (1905–1990) into an international event. By the 1930s, however, the movie industry had developed improved methods, and musicals such as *Showboat* (1936; original stage version 1927) played to audiences of millions.

Jazz

It is no coincidence that the movie chosen to inaugurate the new age of sound was *The Jazz Singer*. Not only did it provide even wider circulation for jazz music itself; by casting a white actor, Al Jolson (1886–1950), as a black jazz musician, it illustrated the degree to which a black musical idiom had been appropriated by white America (see Part VIII, Topic 6).

Jazz grew out of the black culture of the southern United States. Complex in rhythm, making frequent use of syncopation (the stress of normally unstressed beats), jazz was at first improvised. It took its mood from the work songs, laments, and spirituals (religious folk songs) of the slaves and black communities of the Deep South; its distant origins were derived from the folk music of Africa. The first organized performances were given by street bands of black musicians in New Orleans and other southern cities around 1900.

In the 1920s, as the black populations of the northern cities began to grow, jazz found a wider audience. Listeners in Chicago, New York, and other centers developed a taste for the blues singing of Bessie Smith (c. 1898–1937), and the trumpet playing of Louis Armstrong (1900–1971). White musicians took up the idiom, often forming big bands that developed a commercialized form of jazz known as "swing." The popularity of bandleaders such as Benny Goodman (1909–1986) or "Count" Basie (1904–1984) would be further spread by radio and phonograph records.

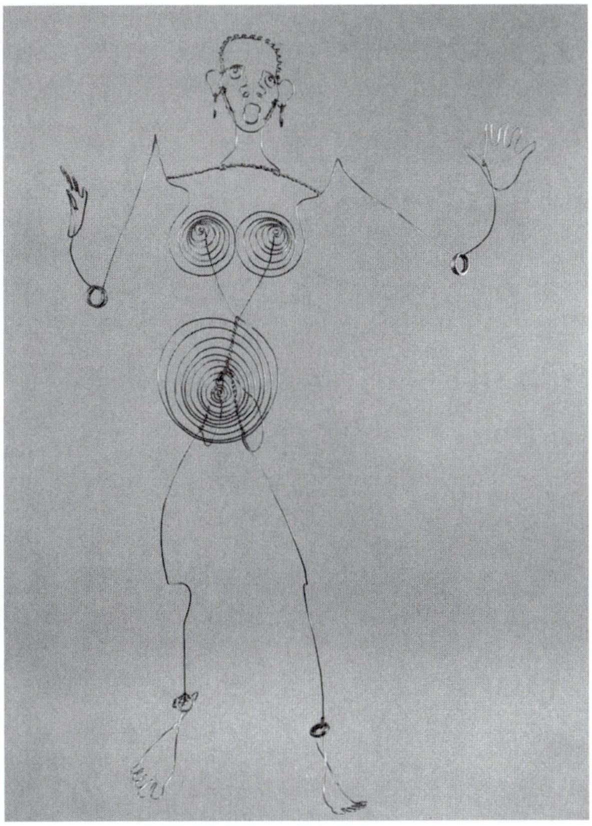

Alexander Calder, *Josephine Baker.* 1927–1929.

In a short time the new music spread to Europe. In Paris there grew up a cult following for *"le jazz hot,"* and one of the jazz world's most celebrated figures, the singer and dancer Josephine Baker, settled there permanently (See Part VIII, Topic 6). She was later to play a part in the French Resistance movement during World War II. Cabaret artists in Berlin included jazz numbers in their acts, and in 1933 recordings by Benny Goodman and his band created a sensation in Britain. So pervasive was the influence of jazz that some spoke of "the Jazz Age," a phrase derived from the title of a collection of short stories by F. Scott Fitzgerald, himself one of the chroniclers of the expatriate American community in Paris.

European composers soon began to explore the possibilities of jazz in their own music. Igor Stravinsky incorporated elements of "ragtime" (one of the early stages in the development of jazz) in his work *The Soldier's Tale* (1918). In the slow movement of his Violin Concerto of 1931, he made use of a blues-like theme. In Germany, Kurt Weill (1900–1950) developed a sophisticated blend of jazz and popular music to create works filled with powerful social criticism. The best-known is *The Threepenny Opera* (1928), the most ambitious *The Rise and Fall of the City of Mahagonny* (1929). (In Weill's later works, written after his move to the United States in 1935, he drew on the Broadway musical tradition.) The French composer Darius Milhaud (1892–1974) traveled to Harlem, New York, to hear the latest jazz for himself. He then incorporated his discoveries in the score for a ballet, *The Creation of the World* (1923).

The most consistent attempt to combine jazz and traditional musical forms occurred in the work of the American composer George Gershwin (1898–1937). His *Rhapsody in Blue* (1924), a piano concerto in all but name, was written for the jazz band of Paul Whiteman (1890–1967); Gershwin himself played the solo part at the sensationally successful first performance in New York. His full-length "American folk opera," *Porgy and Bess* (1935), incorporated jazz and spiritual music. Received with only limited enthusiasm at first, the work enjoyed increasing success at its revivals in the 1970s. By the 1990s it had entered the repertory of such traditional companies as the Metropolitan Opera, New York, and Glyndebourne, England.

COMING SHADOWS

Over the restless energy of the Jazz Age there began to fall the shadow of war. The sense of trouble ahead emerged in the work of a number of European artists and writers. The German satirical artist George Grosz savagely chronicled the corruption and militarism of post–World War I Germany, before fleeing to the United States in 1933. The brutalities of the Spanish Civil War (1936–1939) provoked widespread protests. Among the most eloquent were those of the English poet W. H. Auden (1907–1973) and Picasso—his painting *Guernica* (1937) commemorated the bombing of the small Basque town by German planes fighting for Franco's fascist forces (See Part VIII, Topic 8).

One of the first to warn of the dangers of Nazism was the eminent German writer Thomas Mann (1875–1955). Mann's reverence for the conservative, philosophical, and musical traditions of German culture permeated his first successful novel *Buddenbrooks* (1901), a sensitive and moving picture of German provincial family life. In the 1920s he began to diagnose the sick state of contemporary society; his novel *The Magic Mountain* (1924) used the metaphorical background of a tuberculosis sanatorium to describe the intellectual and moral uncertainties of the postwar years. In 1933, while Mann was abroad, the Nazi regime denounced him and confiscated his property.

Mann settled in Switzerland, from where he continued to issue warnings, some of them in the form of broadcasts to Germany itself. In 1939, on the eve of war, he took up a visiting professorship at Princeton University. Many other leading German and Austrian intellectuals and artists sought refuge in the years preceding and during the war in the United States; they included Albert Einstein and Arnold Schoenberg, both of them Jewish. Mann was one of the few major non-Jewish European figures—Toscanini was another notable example—to protest their country's regime and go into exile.

With the benefit of hindsight, it is clear that the sense of instability that permeated the culture of the interwar years—Dada, Eliot's alienation, the Surrealists' rejection of reality—represented not only a reaction against the values of life before World War I; they reflected a greater sense of doubt. If old political and social realities were dead, there was nothing firm with which to replace them. An understanding of the unconscious proved a difficult foundation on which to rebuild civilization. Nor did Freud's insistence on the power of the irrational provide much comfort for those who had already seen its capacity for destruction.

Thus the arts of the years between the wars reflected the agitated mood of the times. The new freedom from traditional restraints opened up exciting possibilities in painting, music, and fiction. New means of communication created a vast public for art at all levels. Yet for all the vitality and variety of the Jazz Age, its spirited energy failed to hide completely a sense of foreboding. The Great War had shown one terrible direction civilization could take, and a repeat of the "war to end all wars" seemed increasingly likely.

In 1918, a week before the armistice ending World War I was signed, a young Englishman, Wilfred Owen (1893–1918), was killed in action. A year earlier, he had been invalided out of the fighting in France, and spent some time in a military hospital. While there he wrote poems, describing the horror and human sacrifice of war. One of them contains the line: "All a poet can do today is to warn."

Questions for Further Study

1. How did both poets and painters use symbolism and surrealism? What other styles influenced more than one art medium?
2. How did the ideas of Freud influence the arts between the world wars?
3. Is Owen's observation, "All a poet can do today is to warn," a true reflection of the role of the arts in the 20th century? How far is it still true today?

Suggestions for Further Reading

Ackroyd, P. *T. S. Eliot*. London, 1984.
Berman, M. *All That Is Solid Melts into Air: The Experience of Modernity*. New York, 1981.
Cantor, N. F. *Twentieth Century Culture: Modernism to Deconstruction*. New York, 1988.
Hayman, R. *Kafka: A Biography*. New York, 1981.
Hughes, R. *The Shock of the New*. New York, 1981.
Richardson, J. *Pablo Picasso*. New York, 1991.

VIII

Topic 8

The Road to War

International relations in the interwar period fell into two broad phases. In the first, from 1919 to 1931, the major Western powers put their hopes for peace on the League of Nations and a general spirit of reconciliation; in the second, from 1931 to 1939, Japan and the two fascist powers of Europe—Italy and Germany—unleashed one act of aggression after another, demonstrating the helplessness of the League and testing to the limits the policy of appeasement adopted by Britain and France. The Nazi invasion of Poland in September 1939, coming in the wake of Adolf Hitler's violation of earlier agreements, pushed the West to the wall and triggered war.

In the 1920s, many Western statesmen believed that they could create a condition of permanent peace by simply willing it into existence. International efforts at disarmament and the abandonment of war as an instrument of national policy were well-intentioned, but belied the fact that the 1919 peace settlements had created an imbalance of power in the world. Germany and Italy demanded a revision of the settlements, while France recognized the danger to its own interests but could not convince Britain that alliances rather than the League of Nations were needed.

Appeasement had begun in 1931, even before Hitler came to power, when the West protested Japan's aggression against China but did nothing. Mussolini's invasion of Ethiopia in 1935 was the crucial test case for the efficacy of the League. On the other hand, wars in East Asia and in Africa were not perceived as immediate dangers to Europe. The intervention of the fascist powers in the Spanish Civil War should have been a clearer lesson as to the direction of German and Italian policy, but the ideological nature of the conflict there made Britain and France prefer not to intervene.

When Hitler moved against Austria and the Czech Sudetenland in 1938, the Western powers rationalized his demands as legitimate goals based on the argument of self-determination. Only in 1939, when it became clear that the appetites of the dictators would not be quenched by appeasement, did Britain and France conclude that war was necessary.

THE ILLUSION OF PEACE

The League of Nations (see Part VIII, Topic 1), with which President Woodrow Wilson hoped peace would be permanently preserved, rested on the concept of "collective security," which meant that its members guaranteed each other's security. But the European powers did not find this arrangement sufficient for their purposes, and during the 1920s a variety of separate treaties created the illusion of stability. When the U.S. Senate refused to ratify the Treaty of Versailles and Wilson's commitment to offer the French an assistance pact, France arranged a military alliance with Poland in 1921 and with the so-called "Little Entente" of Czechoslovakia, Yugoslavia, and Romania. In doing so, France had attempted to link the preservation of the peace settlement in the West with that in the East.

Significant Dates

The Road to War

October 1925	Treaty of Locarno
1928	"Kellogg-Briand" Pact
1931	Japanese invade Manchuria
October 1933	Hitler withdraws from League
March 1935	German Air Force announced
1935	Mussolini proposes Stresa Front
October 1935	Ethiopian War
March 1936	Hitler occupies Rhineland
1936	Mussolini and Hitler support Franco in Spain
October 1936	Rome-Berlin Axis
November 1936	Anti-Comintern Pact between Germany and Japan
1937	Japanese invasion of China
March 1938	German annexation of Austria
September 1938	Munich conference
March 1939	Germany occupies all of Czechoslovakia
August 1939	Nazi-Soviet Non-Aggression Pact
September 1, 1939	Germany invades Poland

The Spirit of Locarno

In the 1920s, Europe entered a period of relative stability and sought alternative ways of guaranteeing security. In 1923, the Draft Treaty of Mutual Assistance came before the Assembly of the League. It stipulated that in the event of hostilities, the League Council should determine the aggressor, and that members were then obliged to offer military assistance. This treaty would have made military sanctions by the League automatic instead of optional. France, worried about future German aggression, was enthusiastic, but Britain opposed it. In the autumn of 1924, Premier Herriot of France and Prime Minister MacDonald of Great Britain met in Geneva and proposed compulsory arbitration of disputes, but MacDonald's fall from power wrecked the initiative.

Unable to strengthen the League, France turned to efforts aimed at securing a guarantee of her border with Germany. This aim succeeded, in part, due to the policies of German Foreign Minister Gustav Stresemann (1878–1929), who sought reconciliation with the great powers. In 1922, Germany had already proposed a mutual pledge with France not to resort to war and had signed the Treaty of Rapallo with the Soviet Union in which each side had agreed to stay neutral in the event of an attack. The Rapallo agreement made the international community uneasy, for it ended the diplomatic isolation of both Germany and the Soviet Union.

In October 1925, Britain, France, Germany, Poland, and Czechoslovakia met at Locarno, Switzerland, and signed a number of agreements. The Treaty of Locarno stipulated that any changes in the French-German and the Belgian-German borders would come as a result of negotiations; meanwhile, France concluded a treaty with Poland and Czechoslovakia that guaranteed the eastern borders. Germany further agreed to submit all frontier disputes to arbitration. The next year, Germany became a member of the League of Nations.

The mood of international cooperation was expanded further with the Pact of Paris. In 1927, French Foreign Minister Aristide Briand (1862–1932) proposed to U.S. Secretary of State Frank B. Kellogg (1856–1937) that each country renounce war as an instrument of national policy. This "Kellogg-Briand" Pact, signed in 1928, was eventually endorsed by all the great powers (except the Soviet Union) and a total of 65 nations. Making war "illegal" did much to foster an illusion of international peace, but did little for its reality.

By the end of the decade, a more self-confident Germany had rejoined the community of nations, and many of the conditions imposed on her by the peace settlement had been removed. In June 1930, Allied troops left the Rhineland. By then, France had begun the construction of the Maginot line of fortifications along the frontier with Germany, and in September the Nazis had 107 deputies in the Reichstag.

Map 8.1 Japanese Expansion

EUROPE, JAPAN, AND THE LEAGUE OF NATIONS

In the 1920s, few observers anticipated the first real challenge to the League of Nations would come from East Asia. But in 1931, Japan embarked upon a program of deliberate expansion that tested the willingness of the Western powers to stand behind treaty obligations, even when the participants in the dispute were Asian nations.

Japan as a World Power

Japan had burst upon the international scene during the Sino-Japanese War of 1894–1895, when it defeated China in a struggle over Korea. To Europeans, even more startling had been Japan's smashing victory over Russia in the 1904–1905 war. The Japanese eyed China and adjoining territories as a natural sphere of interest. During World War I and the Civil War in Russia, Japan had moved on to the Chinese mainland and captured markets once controlled by the Western powers.

Crown Prince Hirohito of Japan toured Europe in 1921, visiting King George V in London.

In the 1920s, Japanese factories supplied most of Asia with a host of consumer products, but the foundations of its economy were fragile. Japan had created modern industrial and financial institutions, mainly by large family-owned trusts, but it lacked raw materials. Political economists argued that Japanese power would depend on securing both raw materials and markets.

Japan's government was modeled on the European example. In 1889, a constitution had been adopted and, in 1925, universal male suffrage went into effect. Nevertheless, Parliament's authority was limited, and ministers served at the pleasure of the emperor, whose powers were supreme. Militarism had a strong influence in society and high army officers wielded significant influence in government circles. As in 19th-century Germany, many officers came from the landed nobility, where the code of the Samurai warrior still prevailed.

In the postwar period, Japanese imperialist expansion was widely discussed in military circles. Not only was expansion for economic gain proposed, but some insisted that the future of Asia itself was in the hands of Japan, the only local power capable of freeing it from European influence.

The Manchurian Crisis

The Japanese first turned their attention to Manchuria. Manchuria had been wrested from Russian control in the Russo-Japanese War of 1904–1905. On paper,

The Japanese broke the peace in Asia when they invaded China in 1934. Here Japanese soldiers man a position in the streets of Shanghai, a city they first bombed.

Japan allowed Manchuria to revert to China, but in reality the region became a Japanese protectorate. Border tensions between the Soviet Union and Japan occurred over the years. They culminated in September 1931 in a bomb explosion on the south Manchurian railroad, a few miles from the Japanese garrison at Mukden. The Japanese used the incident as a pretext for occupying strategic points in southern Manchuria. The Chinese government appealed to the League of Nations, and also to the United States under the terms of the Kellogg-Briand Pact. Secretary of State Henry L. Stimson insisted that the matter be settled peacefully, but took no real action. In January 1932, by which time Japan had conquered all of Manchuria, Stimson announced that the United States would not recognize the Japanese gains.

China, otherwise powerless, announced an economic boycott, but Japan responded with a temporary occupation of Shanghai. In March, Japan proclaimed the territory an independent nation called Manchukuo ("Land of the Manchus"), and eventually installed Henry Pu Yi (1906–1967), the last emperor of China, as its ruler.

The League of Nations sent a commission to Manchuria headed by Lord Victor Lytton (1871–1947). The commission's report, in October, condemned the Japanese invasion and exposed the pretense of Manchukuo. Japan, a member of the League, withdrew from that international body and invaded the Chinese mainland southwest of Manchuria. By mid-1935, Japanese had penetrated deep into China. Neither the League nor the United States took any action beyond verbal protests. The League of Nations had been dealt a deadly blow.

In July 1937, after a two-year hiatus, the war between Japan and China was renewed. The Japanese took the cities of Shanghai, Nanking, and Canton and drove Chinese forces under General Chiang Kai-shek (1887–1975) deep into western China. In Nanking, the Japanese troops killed perhaps 300,000 civilians in reprisal for their resistance. The invasion finally came to a halt when the Japanese reached the mountains of western China, while in the north a guerrilla resistance was led by the communists. The Japanese occupation of China proved to be a brutal experience.

AUSTRIA, ETHIOPIA, AND THE AXIS

The failure of the League to stop Japan's aggression in China lent encouragement to European dictators. In 1934, Hitler attempted to seize Austria, but Mussolini prevented him from doing so. The following year,

The coffin of Austrian Chancellor Engelbert Dollfuss passing Vienna's city hall, July 28, 1934.

however, Mussolini himself tested the mood of the powers in the West by his invasion of Ethiopia in October 1935. Before that conflict was over, Hitler had violated the Versailles Treaty by remilitarizing the Rhineland. Again, neither the League nor the Western powers acted. The era of appeasement had begun.

The Austrian Coup and the Stresa Front

Upon coming to power, Hitler began immediately to strengthen Germany's military position. That March, Mussolini had proposed a joint agreement among Britain, France, Germany, and Italy designed both to keep Hitler in check and to prevent a war between Germany and France. In October 1933, however, Hitler withdrew Germany from the League and allowed Mussolini's pact to lapse without signing it. The following year he made his first move toward the creation of his "Greater Germany." In July, the Austrian Nazis, some 100,000 strong, attempted to seize power in a coup supported by Hitler. Chancellor Engelbert Dollfuss (1892–1934), who had befriended Mussolini in an effort to keep Austria independent of Germany, was assassinated, but martial law was proclaimed in Vienna and the coup failed. Kurt von Schuschnigg (1897–1977), one of Dollfuss' collaborators, became the new chancellor and Mussolini sent Italian troops to the Brenner Pass to dissuade Hitler from invading Austria.

Mussolini later reminded the European powers that he could not always be the one to "march to the Brenner," by which he meant that they too would have to take responsibility for controlling Hitler's expansionist ambitions. In March 1935, Hitler demonstrated his complete contempt for international agreements by announcing that Germany would no longer abide by the disarmament clauses of the Treaty of Versailles. Secret German rearmament had been going on ever since 1933, but now Hitler reintroduced peacetime conscription. Taking their cue from Mussolini, Britain and France met with Italian representatives at Stresa, in northern Italy, and agreed to Mussolini's proposal for common action against Germany. But British and French unwillingness to take the idea of the "Stresa Front" beyond mere words made it useless. Instead, in June, Britain signed a naval pact with Hitler that permitted Germany to build a fleet equal to one-third of British strength. The French felt betrayed.

The Italian Invasion of Ethiopia

In the meantime, Mussolini had been laying his plans for colonial conquest. For this he had been preaching to Italians that Fascism would restore the grandeur of

Ethiopian soldiers, including young boys, fought Italians armed with modern weapons in 1935–1936, when Mussolini invaded the African country.

the Roman Empire and give Italy its rightful position in international affairs. Since the summer of 1934 he had been preparing for the military conquest of Ethiopia (then known as Abyssinia). The country was one of two independent states in Africa. The Italians had tried unsuccessfully to conquer it in the 1890s, but were disastrously defeated by Ethiopian troops at the Battle of Adowra. Mussolini now promised to "wipe clean the stain of Adowra."

In January 1935 Mussolini persuaded French Foreign Minister Pierre Laval (1883–1945) to give Italy a free hand in Ethiopia, but the British balked. In September British Foreign Minister Sir Samuel Hoare (1880–1959) assured the League that Britain would resist Italian aggression. On October 3, Mussolini launched his attack. Ethiopian Emperor Haile Selassie (1892–1975) went before the League and warned that Europe would be next if Mussolini was not stopped. Less than a week later, the League voted to condemn Italy and imposed economic sanctions. The sanctions, however, omitted petroleum from its list of proscribed materials. Moreover, Germany, the United States, and Japan did not participate in the sanctions. Toward the end of the year, Laval and Hoare met in Paris, where they agreed to offer Mussolini a compromise—he could have two-thirds of Ethiopia. When news of the Hoare-Laval Agreement became public, a storm of public indignation broke.

Mussolini, gambling everything on a military victory, proclaimed that Italy would stand alone against the world. In truth, much-needed oil was still flowing to her ports. Hitler, hoping to make Mussolini grateful for his friendship, shipped Italy essential supplies, while at the same time secretly sending arms to the Ethiopians. On May 5, Italian troops marched into Addis Ababa, the capital.

During the Ethiopian War, Hitler had been active. On March 7, 1936, he remilitarized the Rhineland

Map 8.2 The Ethiopian War

After Mussolini's visit to Germany in 1937, the *Duce* and the *Führer* were inseparably linked—they signed the military Pact of Steel the next year.

in direct violation of Versailles, and denounced the Treaty of Locarno. In October, Mussolini, who felt at once betrayed by the Western powers and grateful to Hitler, sent his foreign minister, Count Galeazzo Ciano (1903–1944), to Berlin to arrange a treaty with Germany. The result was the signing of an agreement to collaborate on anticommunist propaganda in their foreign policies. Proclaiming this the beginning of a "Rome-Berlin Axis," Mussolini moved increasingly closer to Germany over the next two years.

THE MARCH OF FASCISM: THE SPANISH CIVIL WAR

Ever since Lenin had created the Communist International (Comintern) in 1919, European communist parties had been instructed by Moscow not to participate in political coalitions with bourgeois parties. The spread of fascism, however, gave Stalin pause. In September 1934, the Soviet Union joined the League of Nations. When the Comintern held its 1935 world congress, Italian and French communists suggested that the policy be reversed in order to fight fascism. The result was that communist parties now joined with socialists and democrats in what came to be known as "Popular Fronts." The most prominent Popular Front government was that of Léon Blum in France (see Part VIII, Topic 5). Over the next four years, the Popular Front concept would be sorely tested in the tragedy of the Spanish Civil War.

The Spanish Labyrinth

The civil war in Spain was a struggle fought on several levels at once: an ideological war between fascism on one side and an international alliance of democratic, socialist, communist, and anarchist forces on the other; an internecine struggle among these antifascist forces; an internal Spanish political struggle for power; finally, as a test of wills between the Axis powers and the Western democracies it represented the real prelude to World War II.

The war broke out in July 1936 and raged on until March 1939. Its origins lay in the political culture of modern Spain. In September 1923, General Primo de Rivera staged a coup d'état and created a military dictatorship, although King Alfonso XIII (ruled 1902–1931) continued to rule in name. In 1930, Alfonso dismissed the unpopular general and in 1931 restored the constitution. In the elections that followed, the repub-

This photograph of a Loyalist fighter carrying a wounded friend to safety, was one of the best known images of the Spanish Civil War.

lican forces won a landslide in the cities and the king, interpreting the vote to be against him, left the country, although he never abdicated. The Spanish Republic was proclaimed on April 14, 1931.

The Constituent Assembly was divided over the policies of the government, from those on the left who wanted social revolution to Catholics on the right who hated the Republic. The new democratic government began to initiate major social and economic reforms, including civilian control of the army, land reform, and regional autonomy. By late 1933, when the first *Cortes*, or parliament, met, the conservative majority under the leadership of the clerical José Gil Robles (1898–1980) began to undo the reforms and move Spain toward fascist dictatorship.

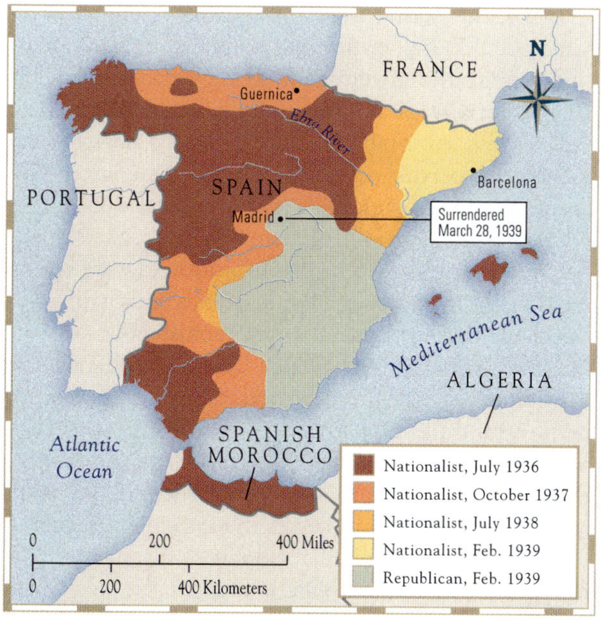

Map 8.3 The Civil War in Spain

In 1936 the Republicans, syndicalists, anarchists, and communists joined together in a Popular Front to halt the reaction and succeeded in winning power. They immediately began to push for radical change, seizing landed estates and staging revolutionary strikes. Then, after a well-known reactionary deputy was assassinated, the forces of counterrevolution responded. On July 17, a military garrison in Spanish Morocco revolted under the leadership of General Francisco Franco (1892–1975). Other generals on the mainland joined in support. At the end of July, the rebels set up their headquarters in Burgos, in the north, and proclaimed a Junta of National Defense. Franco was named its *caudillo*, or chief.

Franco was a shrewd, calculating man, wedded to tradition and authority but with no precise ideology of his own. He gathered under his leadership nationalists, monarchists, and members of the fascist *Falange*. He also had the support of landowners, business interests, and Catholics. The Popular Front forces were as disparate a group as Franco's, although the left—composed of socialists, communists, a Trotskyite group, and the Anarcho-Syndicalists—dominated.

With the backing of most of the regular army, Franco's forces—known as the Nationalists—quickly hemmed the Republicans into four areas: Madrid, Valencia (where the government had fled), Barcelona, and the Basque provinces. For the next two and half years, Spain was racked by a cruel and bloody civil war that was complicated by foreign intervention.

Intervention and Ideology

Foreign nations quickly took sides in the Spanish conflict. Blum's French government supported the Popular

Pablo Picasso's powerful painting *Guernica* was conceived in response to the German bombing of civilians in the Basque city by that name in northern Spain, April 1937.

Front, while Mussolini and Hitler made common cause with the Nationalists. In November the two dictators officially recognized Franco's government, while the first antifascist volunteers organized by the Comintern began to arrive in the form of the International Brigades. The French Popular Front sent equipment and the Soviet Union fighter planes, equipment, and advisers. Hitler supplied Franco with tanks, planes, and military advisers, while Mussolini sent troops. In March 1937 the antifascist forces won a major moral victory when the International Brigades repulsed the Nationalists at Guadalajara. By the end of 1937, the war had reached a stalemate.

With the Spanish participants more or less evenly matched and deadlocked, foreign intervention became decisive. Portuguese dictator António Salazar (1889–1970) sympathized with Franco, British Prime Minister Stanley Baldwin expected the Nationalists to become the future government, and even Blum was careful not to antagonize the right wing in France by openly supporting the Republicans. As a result, when Blum suggested the formation of a Non-Intervention Committee, Britain readily agreed. The purpose of the committee was to prevent foreign powers from intervening and to withhold military assistance from both sides. The committee, composed of representatives from 27 states, met in September 1936. The League of Nations backed its position.

Despite such appeals for neutrality, volunteers continued to arrive from abroad while the fascist powers poured in men and supplies. In effect, nonintervention meant that the legitimate government of Spain was prevented from purchasing supplies from abroad, while the Nationalists received significant illegal help. Morally, the Axis intervention aided the Republicans, especially after German planes bombed the town of Guernica in April 1937, inspiring Pablo Picasso's famous painting by that name. In September, unidentified submarines—now known to have been mostly Italian—attacked ships carrying goods to the Republicans. When Britain and France called a conference at Lyon to prevent such actions, Germany and Italy boycotted the meeting, whereupon the Western powers jointly patrolled the Spanish waters and the piracy stopped.

By the spring of 1938, Franco—supported by some 100,000 Italian troops—launched a major offensive against the government. Franco had the advantage, especially as the Republican forces had become bitterly divided. Stalin had decided on a policy of no support for socialist revolutions in Spain, in order to reassure Western opinion. It was a cynical policy that persuaded no one and undermined the Spanish left. Before the war was over, communist forces were killing Anarcho-Syndicalists by the thousands and Stalin's advisers had taken command of communist groups.

In mid-1938 the Soviet Union abandoned the Republic, convinced that Britain and France would not help. With the end of Soviet support, Franco succeeded in cutting government holdings in half. In the months that followed, the Nationalists proceeded to take more and more territory and began the systematic bombing of civilian populations. Barcelona fell in January 1939, followed by Madrid in March. The struggle was a particularly bitter one on both sides. The Republicans had killed priests and nuns, and now tens of thousands of

Spaniards met the fate of brutal reprisals from Franco's victorious forces. Many thousands more fled Spain, and Franco imprisoned hundreds of thousands of opponents. When it was over, the civil war had bled the country of perhaps 1 million lives.

The civil war was a devastating blow for the democratic forces of Europe. The defeat of the Republicans became a symbol of fascist victory, and the war deeply divided opinion abroad. Mussolini and Hitler had shown that they could defy international opinion and the Western powers with impunity.

THE PRICE OF APPEASEMENT: AUSTRIA AND CZECHOSLOVAKIA

The year 1938 proved to be crucial. Hitler had been planning for some time to strike at Austria, determined to bring about *Anschluss* (union) with Germany. No sooner was that goal accomplished, than Hitler began working against Czechoslovakia, whose German minority provided the pretext for aggression there. In the case of the Czech crisis, however, the Western powers did not merely stand by—they actively participated in the dismemberment of an independent country.

Even before Hitler moved against Austria, political conditions in Britain and France mitigated against Western opposition. In Britain, the government of Neville Chamberlain (served as prime minister 1937–1940) was doggedly determined to do whatever it could to prevent war. Chamberlain embarked, therefore, on a policy that came to be known as "appeasement," by which the British were willing to make major concessions to Hitler for the sake of peace. The foreign minister, Anthony Eden (1897–1977), was a staunch opponent of the fascist dictators and in 1938 he resigned in protest against appeasement. Thereafter, Chamberlain really conducted his own foreign policy. In France, the resignation of Blum's Popular Front in 1937 eventually brought to the premiership Edouard Daladier (served 1933, 1934, 1938–1940). Claiming that he would prepare France for war, he assumed the defense ministry himself. Yet French resolve, already softened by the fear of war, hinged to a great degree on Britain.

Anschluss

In February 1938, Hitler began to pressure Austria, using the Nazi radio and press to agitate for union with Germany. The Führer insisted that Chancellor Schuschnigg come to Berchtesgaden, his retreat in the Bavarian mountains, where Hitler proceeded to harangue the hapless Austrian leader for hours. After Hitler's bullying, Schuschnigg consented to concessions—he would appoint a Nazi as minister of the interior (who controlled the police) and issue an amnesty for imprisoned Austrian Nazis.

Once back in Vienna, however, Schuschnigg's resolve returned and he began to mobilize public opinion against Germany. The chancellor decided to hold a plebiscite to secure public endorsement of his anti-German position. Hitler exploded and sent an ultimatum to Vienna demanding that the plebiscite be canceled. When Schuschnigg refused, Hitler moved German troops to the border. Faced with the prospect of invasion, Schuschnigg resigned. The Germans began marching against Austria even before Schuschnigg's successor, the Nazi Arthur Seyss-Inquart (1892–1946), had invited the Germans into his country, which Hitler then annexed to Germany. In April, a rigged plebiscite registered 99.75 percent public approval.

In Britain, Chamberlain had already written Austria off to appease Hitler, and France was caught between governments. The most interesting reaction came from Italy. In 1934, Mussolini had sent troops to the Brenner to prevent what he now congratulated Hitler for accomplishing. Hitler had not bothered to inform the Duce of his plans, but Mussolini pretended to ignore the slight. In any case, by then Mussolini's Italy was in no position to stand up to the Third Reich. Hitler rejoiced that he had added this strategically important nation to his realm, and no doubt remembered the difficulties of his youthful days spent in Vienna.

Czechoslovakia and the Sudetenland

When the Paris Peace Conference of 1919 decided on the creation of Czechoslovakia as an independent state, it burdened the new republic with a serious problem: the mountainous rim of territory known as the Sudetenland, where some 3 million German-speaking people lived. In truth, Thomas Masaryk, the founder of the Czech state, had insisted on having the area, arguing that Bohemia and Moravia were an historical and economic unit and should not be broken up. Moreover, a border drawn strictly along linguistic lines would have been impossible.

The Sudeten Germans received better treatment at the hands of the Prague government than most ethnic minorities in Eastern Europe. After 1933, however, Nazi agents, led by Konrad Henlein (1898–1945), worked feverishly to arouse German sentiment and to push for an autonomous Sudetenland independent of Czechoslovakia. Nevertheless, most Czechs, including President Eduard Benes, knew that the real intention behind Hitler's rhetoric was annexation.

A week after the annexation of Austria, Henlein's followers inflamed the Sudetenland question. Consultations between Britain and France followed. The French,

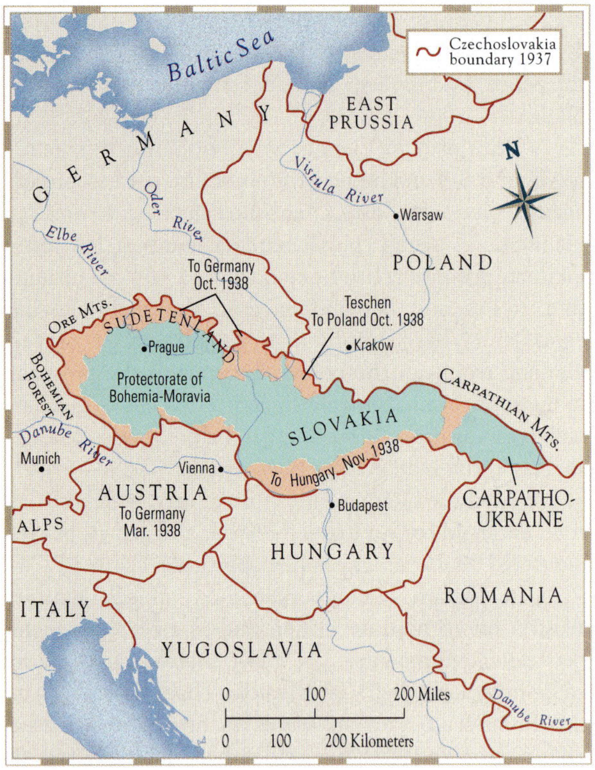

Map 8.4 The Dismemberment of Czechoslovakia

who were bound to Czechoslovakia by a defensive treaty, were prepared to come to Czechoslovakia's aid, but Chamberlain announced in the House of Commons that Britain would not commit itself to supporting France in such an event. Chamberlain was convinced that any effort to coerce Hitler would result in war. With support for this position within the French cabinet, Premier Daladier agreed to follow Britain's lead.

In April, Henlein increased his demands for autonomy. When Benes refused, the Nazis erupted in open violence, hoping no doubt to provoke German intervention. Czechoslovakia partially mobilized. When Chamberlain actually warned that Britain might have to get involved, Hitler backed off publicly but ordered plans for a military attack on Czechoslovakia. In the meantime, Chamberlain sent a mediator to Prague to arrange a compromise. When the Czechs agreed to Henlein's demands, the Nazi leader broke off the talks. On September 15, a distraught Chamberlain boarded a plane—the first time in his life—and flew to Berchtesgaden to make a personal appeal to Hitler. In a three-hour meeting, Hitler insisted that he would now settle only for outright German annexation of the Sudetenland, and convinced the prime minister to join with France in trying to extract this concession from Prague. Chamberlain was undaunted, not understanding that he was about to be a party to the dismemberment of a sovereign state. He wrote at the time that Hitler "was a man who could be relied upon when he had given his word."

The Munich Tragedy

On September 19, the French and British governments told Benes that he had to concede the Sudetenland, warning that they would not be responsible for the consequences if the Czechs refused. Without the support of the Western powers, Benes had no choice but to give in. Chamberlain flew to Germany again, this time to Godesberg on the Rhine, where Hitler now raised his demands still further, presenting the prime minister with a strongly worded memorandum insisting on immediate occupation of the territories in question. Chamberlain was wounded and disillusioned. On September 24, the Czechs mobilized and the French called up reservists. Four days later, the British Navy was mobilized. Chamberlain wrote to Mussolini and Hitler asking for a four-power conference to resolve the crisis.

Munich, September 1938—Chamberlain (left), Daladier, Hitler, Mussolini, and Ciano.

Mussolini convinced Hitler to attend, and the four statesmen—Hitler, Mussolini, Chamberlain, and Daladier—met in Munich on September 29. The Soviet Union was not invited.

The Munich conference was brief. The participants agreed to the terms of the Godesberg Memorandum, but now also to guarantee Czechoslovakia's borders. On September 30, Chamberlain and Daladier presented the terms of the agreement to the Czechs, who had no choice but to accept. Benes resigned as president.

When Chamberlain arrived in England that day, he held aloft a piece of paper on which he and Hitler had indicated that henceforth they renounced war. "This," he declared in one of the most haunting phrases of the age, "means peace in our time."

Chamberlain may have believed his own words, but he nevertheless embarked upon a massive rearmament program for Great Britain. The end came with a kind of numbed disbelief. On March 14, the new Czech president, Emil Hacha (1872–1945), was summoned to Berlin, where he was subjected to six hours of continuous verbal abuse from Hitler and his entourage. When Hermann Goering, one of Hitler's associates, threatened to reduce Prague to rubble, Hacha agreed to surrender his country, and Hitler's troops carved up the remainder of Czechoslovakia. Chamberlain was stunned, and British opinion suddenly hardened against the man who could so callously violate a solemn agreement.

The Czech fiasco created a mood of fatalism in Europe, for both sides now began to prepare for war. Hitler clearly did not believe that the Western powers would act, and by the end of March 1939 he was already making it clear that Poland was his next target. A much sobered Chamberlain assured the Poles that Britain and France would protect them, and the next month gave similar guarantees to Romania, Greece, and Turkey. On April 3, Hitler secretly told his generals to be ready for an assault against Poland in September. Mussolini, who had remained an observer of Hitler's triumphs, invaded Albania on April 8. Britain introduced peacetime compulsory military service for the first time in its history. On May 22, Mussolini and Hitler concluded a military alliance that Mussolini dubbed the "Pact of Steel." The pact bound each partner to render assistance to the other in the event of war.

Map 8.5 The Expansion of Nazi Germany

The Nazi-Soviet Pact

One more shock awaited the Western powers. The Soviet Union now controlled the balance of power in Europe. In planning for the attack against Poland, Hitler wanted to prevent interference from Stalin and thereby avoid the danger of a two-front war. Since the Spanish Civil War, the Soviet Union had suspected that the Western powers would not stand against the fascist dictators. Yet, while talking secretly with Hitler, Stalin also carried on secret negotiations with the West. He insisted that any mutual defense pact include guarantees for the Baltic states, but these nations feared the Soviet Union as much as they did Germany and would have nothing of it.

On May 3, Stalin appointed a new foreign minister, Vyacheslav Molotov (1890–1986), a man with a much narrower sense of Russian national interests than his predecessor, Maxim Litvinov. Because Litvinov was Jewish, Molotov's appointment was a clear signal to Hitler that accommodation was possible. In Molotov's view, an alliance with Britain and France would most certainly lead to war against Germany, but with little advantage for the Soviet Union. Stalin was interested, on the other hand, in reaching an agreement with Hitler to divide Poland, thus providing a buffer between the two countries. In talks with Molotov, the Nazis suggested not only that the Soviets remain neutral in the event of a German war with the West, but that the Soviet Union and Germany divide Eastern Europe between them.

On August 23 Germany and the Soviet Union signed a trade agreement, a ten-year Non-Aggression Pact, and a secret protocol. The news took almost everyone, including Mussolini, by surprise, since communism andNazism had been such deep ideological enemies for so long. The real import of the pact, however, lay in the "Secret Additional Protocol" added to the treaty. The protocol created spheres of influence in eastern Europe. Western Poland and Lithuania were to fall to Germany, while eastern Poland, Finland, Estonia, Latvia, and the Romanian province of Bessarabia would go to the Soviet Union.

If Hitler hoped that news of the pact would frighten Britain and France into abandoning support for Poland, he miscalculated. On August 25, Britain signed a mutual assistance pact with Poland. When German troops invaded Poland at the beginning of September, the Western powers declared war.

From 1931 to 1939, the Western powers remained on the defensive against policies of aggression and expansion by Japan, Italy, and Germany. The repeated violation of the League of Nations charter made a shambles of the spirit of internationalism that had spread in the 1920s and meant, inevitably, a return to power politics. In this circumstance, however, Britain and France were unwilling to see the outbreak of another world war, and adopted appeasement as the way to avoid it.

That Britain and France were militarily unprepared for war as late as 1938 added an element of sober logic to the policy of appeasement. In retrospect, that policy appears more foolish and morally reprehensible than it did at the time. Yet in the atmosphere of reconciliation that began with Locarno, European statesmen had begun to accept German and Italian arguments that the 1919 settlements had been unfair. In negotiating with Hitler, Chamberlain tacitly admitted the justice of Germany's demands for union with Austria and the Sudetenland.

Yet Mussolini and Hitler were no ordinary statesmen. They did not believe in the sanctity of treaties or conventional notions of balance of power. In dealing with such men, Chamberlain and Daladier were at a supreme disadvantage in not understanding the ideological imperatives that drove them. After appeasement had given up too much and the dictators were still not satisfied, the realization dawned on the West that war was inevitable.

Questions for Further Study

1. To what extent were the origins of World War II to be found in World War I? In the peace conference?
2. What was the policy of "appeasement"? Was it a logical and credible policy in the 1930s?
3. To what degree was the Rome-Berlin Axis inevitable?
4. Did fascist ideology affect foreign policy? How do you explain the Nazi-Soviet Non-Aggression Pact in light of the ideological clash between fascism and communism?

Suggestions for Further Reading

Burgwyn, H. James. *Italian Foreign Policy, 1919–1940*. New York, 1996.
Divine, Robert. *The Reluctant Belligerent: American Entry into World War II*. New York, 1979.
Hildebrandt, K. *The Foreign Policy of the Third Reich*, trans. A. Fothergill. London, 1973.
Iriye, Akira. *The Origins of the Second World War in Asia and the Pacific*. London, 1987.
Kitchen, Martin. *Europe Between the Wars: A Political History*. London, 1988.
Marks, Sally. *The Illusion of Peace: Europe's International Relations, 1918–1933*. New York, 1976.
Preston, Paul. *Franco*. New York, 1994.
Robertson, E. M. *Mussolini as Empire Builder*. London, 1977.
Sontag, Raymond J. *A Broken World, 1919–1939*. New York, 1971.
Taylor, A. J. P. *The Origins of the Second World War*. New York, 1972.
Thomas, Hugh. *The Spanish Civil War*. New York, 1987.
Ulam, Adam. *Expansion and Coexistence: The History of Soviet Foreign Policy, 1917–1943*, 2nd ed. New York, 1974.
Watt, D. C. *How War Came: The Immediate Origins of the Second World War, 1938–1939*. New York, 1989.

VIII

Topic 9

The Second World War

The Munich agreements of September 1938 created a sense of relief in British and French opinion that peace had been preserved. A year later the general feeling in those countries had shifted decisively, most citizens now sensing that war was inevitable. The change was due to the dismemberment of Czechoslovakia, which made it clear that Nazi ambitions would not be satisfied by appeasement. By the time Adolf Hitler targeted Poland for his aggression, Britain and France were no longer in a mood to compromise.

The outbreak of World War II in September 1939 brought almost six years of unparalleled death and destruction. Hitler's armies rolled quickly across Poland, which he and Joseph Stalin proceeded to divide between them. Soviet forces then occupied the Baltic states and attacked Finland. Until the spring of 1940, however, no real fighting between Germany and the West occurred. The Nazi *Blitzkrieg* began in April, when the Germans smashed Norway and Denmark, and the following month attacked Belgium, the Netherlands, and France. By mid-June, France had fallen. When months of aerial bombardment could not induce the British to surrender to Hitler, the Axis (the alliance of Germany and Italy) turned toward North Africa and the Balkans and occupied both regions. The high tide of Axis power came in 1941, when Hitler began his assault against the Soviet Union and the Japanese attack at Pearl Harbor brought the United States into the war.

The year 1942 saw a crucial shift in the fortunes of war, as Soviet troops stopped the German advance and American forces struck back at the Japanese in the Pacific. But even while the Allies won some headway, the most horrible of tragedies unfolded: in Germany and the occupied regions of Eastern Europe, the Nazi extermination of the Jews began to take shape. In the course of the war, more than 6 million victims of Nazi hatred were claimed by the Holocaust. By the end of 1942, the Allies had invaded the Axis stronghold in North Africa, and Hitler's armies had been defeated at Stalingrad. In 1943, Mussolini was overthrown by an internal coup and the Allies launched the invasion of Italy. The principal Allied heads of state—Winston Churchill, Franklin D. Roosevelt, and Stalin—met for the first of a series of wartime conferences that determined not only military strategies but the shape of the postwar peace settlements. In June 1944, the Western powers finally opened a second front in Europe by invading France. By the spring of 1945, Mussolini and Hitler were dead and the war in Europe was over.

The war in Asia came to an end several months later. The Allies began to advance in the Pacific in the second half of 1942. American and Australian forces slowly reclaimed the captured islands of the Pacific, and by 1944 U.S. aircraft were bombing mainland Japan. In August 1945, Japan surrendered after the United States dropped two atomic weapons on its cities.

World War II proved to be the most costly conflict in history, both in human lives and in material terms. In response to the tremendous suffering that the Axis powers had caused, the Allies held a series of tribunals in which Axis leaders were tried for "war crimes," and a new international organization—the United Nations—was created in an effort to maintain the peace so dearly won.

FROM BLITZKRIEG TO THE BATTLE OF BRITAIN

By late 1939, the city of Danzig and the Polish Corridor contained the only important German populations still living beyond the frontiers of the Third Reich, and these territories Hitler wanted to add to the Reich. Yet by then no amount of appeasement could have prevented war. On August 11, the Germans informed their Italian allies that Hitler was determined to resolve the Polish question at any cost. Mussolini sought to temper German demands in order to prevent the outbreak of a general European conflict, but German Foreign Minister Ribbentrop declared unabashedly that the *Führer* wanted war, not compromise.

Blitzkrieg in Poland

With the signing of the Nazi-Soviet Non-Aggression Pact on August 23 (see Part VIII, Topic 8), Hitler positioned himself for the assault on Poland: the Soviets had been neutralized and the Poles isolated. The Germans wanted to strike a quick knockout blow before the fall rains limited the effectiveness of their tanks. At dawn on September 1, without a formal declaration of war, the Germans struck against Poland. Britain and France went to war on September 3.

The Polish campaign was the first demonstration of the new German strategy known as *Blitzkrieg,* or "lightning war." Blitzkrieg was the brainchild of Heinz Guderian (1886–1954), a German officer who had experienced the senseless war of attrition on the Western front during World War I. In 1933, Guderian—whose ideas were derived in part from British strategic thinkers—won Hitler over to the idea that the outcome of the next European war would be determined by a combination of rapid-moving, heavily armed armored tanks, supported by aircraft and motorized infantry units. Blitzkrieg involved the close coordination of these three kinds of forces. The armored tank *(Panzer)* divisions would drive wedges into the enemy's territory and rapidly cut off its troops from behind. The *Luftwaffe* (air force) would simultaneously destroy the enemy's air force before turning against its communications system and infantry troops. The German motorized infantry, moving behind the Panzers, would then secure the overrun territory while the tanks continued to press forward. When the regular infantry had moved up, the motorized troops would rejoin the Panzers.

Panzer divisions under the command of Guderian pushed through Poland ahead of the mobilized units and foot infantry. German dive bombers, called *Stukas*, assaulted civilians not only with bombs and machine guns, but with shrill sirens that struck terror in their victims. Polish military forces lacked modern military equipment, especially tanks, heavy artillery, and transportation units. Hitler's Luftwaffe had ten times more operational planes than the Polish Air Force, and Poland's 39 divisions were no match for Germany's 60 divisions. After a few days, the Germans broke through Polish lines. On September 17, the Soviet Union invaded Poland from the east in conformity with the intent of the Nazi-Soviet Pact and overran the rest of the country.

Warsaw was surrounded by German armies and on September 25 Hitler ordered his bombers to reduce the city to ruins. The capital surrendered on September 27. The next day Ribbentrop and Soviet Foreign Minister Molotov met to partition Polish territory. The Soviet Union occupied a little more than half the country, including a third of the population, while Germany took the bulk of the population and the core of the industrial and farming regions. The western half of the German area was annexed into the Reich along with Danzig, thus pushing the frontiers beyond Germany's 1914 borders. The rest was placed under Nazi occupation as the "Government General" of Poland. Poland ceased to exist as an independent nation. General Wladyslaw Sikorski (1881–1943) formed a new Polish government, first in France and then in London, the first of many such governments in exile.

Significant Dates

World War II

September 3, 1939	World War II breaks out; Blitzkrieg against Poland
April–May 1940	Blitzkrieg in West
May 10, 1940	Churchill becomes prime minister
June 10, 1940	Italy declares war on France
June 22, 1940	Surrender of France
April 1941	Germany occupies Yugoslavia and Greece
June 22, 1941	Germany invades Soviet Union
December 7, 1941	Japanese attack Pearl Harbor
June 4, 1942	Battle of Midway
November 1942	Allied invasion of North Africa
February 2, 1943	German surrender at Stalingrad
May 1943	Axis surrender in North Africa
June 1943	Allied invasion of Sicily
July 5–12, 1943	Battle of Kursk
July 25, 1943	Coup against Mussolini
September 1943	Allied invasion of Italy; Italian armistice with Allies
June 6, 1944	Normandy invasion
February 1945	Yalta conference
April 28–30, 1945	Mussolini shot and Hitler commits suicide
May 7, 1945	Surrender of Germany
July–August 1945	Potsdam conference
August 6, 1945	Atomic bomb destroys Hiroshima
August 14, 1945	Japan surrenders

The Fall of Western Europe

While the Blitzkrieg ravaged Poland in the East, a strange, tension-filled peace known as the "Phony War" prevailed in the West. Hitler, planning to attack Western Europe in the fall of 1939, had moved his troops from Poland to the Western frontiers in October but did not order them into battle. Leading German generals believed that an all-out war with the West at that moment was premature. When Hitler overruled them, a conspiracy to overthrow him evolved in military circles but came to nothing. Bad weather and the capture of German military plans by Belgian authorities in January 1940 caused a delay in the attack until the spring.

French military leaders expected that their defense system would suffice to ward off any German attack. This Maginot Line consisted of an intricate system of fixed fortifications, built in the 1930s, that ran from the Swiss border northward to where Luxembourg and Belgium joined. Its weakness lay in the fact that it gave the French a false sense of security that retarded military modernization. In any case, it was through Belgium that a German attack was likely to come. British Prime Minister Chamberlain, still hoping for a negotiated settlement, doubted that Hitler would attack in the West. Instead, he believed that the German economy would collapse under the stress of a major war and instituted, together with the French, a naval blockade. Unlike the blockade imposed during World War I, this one did not prove effective because of a far-reaching economic agreement between Berlin and Moscow that provided Germany with essential resources such as oil, grain, and rubber. The British used the respite provided by the Phony War to build up their air force.

Stunned by Hitler's overwhelming victory in Poland, Stalin had begun to worry about Soviet security and tried to create a buffer zone between his own country and Germany. By the middle of October 1939, he had forced Latvia and Estonia to accept Soviet bases and soldiers on their territories. When the Finnish government refused to grant similar concessions to the USSR, the Soviets attacked Finland in late November. This so-called "Winter War" lasted longer than Stalin had anticipated, requiring the use of some 45 divisions to crush the stubborn Finnish resistance, which was led by Field Marshal Carl Mannerheim (1867–1951). Only in March 1940 did the Soviets finally force an armistice, according to which Finland conceded extensive territories and military bases.

The Allies had seriously considered sending help to the Finns, largely because they suddenly grew worried that the mines and strategic location of Scandinavia might make the region a target of German operations. At the beginning of April, Hitler's armies quickly invaded and overran Denmark, whose 15,000-man army collapsed after a day of fighting. Geography made Norway more difficult to take, and the Allies landed troops there to assist the Norwegians. After several weeks, however, Norway fell and Hitler set up a collaborationist regime under the leadership of Vidkun Quisling (1887–1945), a name that became identified with treason.

With Scandinavia secured, Hitler turned next to the Low Countries. The long-awaited war against the West began on May 10 with the invasion of Belgium,

Map 9.1 The Second World War, Europe and North Africa

the Netherlands, and Luxembourg. In terms of troop numbers, the Allies actually enjoyed some superiority. Germany had 136 divisions (42 of which were held in reserve), while the Allies counted 144 divisions—101 French (36 involved in the Maginot Line defense), 11 British, 22 Belgian, and 10 Dutch. The Allies also had more tanks, although the Germans concentrated theirs in armored divisions while the French dispersed them. Similarly, the French actually possessed 4360 aircraft to Germany's 3270, but French air strategy had been so inadequate that when Hitler attacked they could put only a fourth of their planes in the air.

The French proved indecisive against Hitler's Blitzkrieg, but the country's premier, Paul Reynaud (1878–1966), was a strong-willed leader who had warned repeatedly that France needed to adopt modern military strategies.

The capture of secret German documents in 1939 was partially responsible for Hitler's decision to adopt an entirely new plan for the assault against Western Europe. The original plan provided for a heavy concentration of strength in a northern spearhead that was to push through the Netherlands, Belgium, and northern France, while a support group was to move through southern Belgium and Luxembourg. The revised plan, designed to overcome the possibility of stalemate similar to that of World War I, called for making the southern force the armored spearhead of the assault. Once the southern army group had broken into France, it could push on to Paris, swing behind the Maginot Line, or—and this in the end was the decision—rush to the English Channel in order to cut off Allied forces. Some generals thought this plan too risky, but Hitler overruled them.

Only in recent years has it become known that by the outbreak of the war the Allies possessed the ability to break the German codes. Before Hitler came to power, German engineers had developed an incredibly sophisticated coding machine known as Enigma, capable of creating literally billions of different coding patterns. When the Germans attempted to deliver an Enigma machine to their embassy in Warsaw, Polish intelligence agents intercepted it and, unknown to the Germans, had it reproduced. The Poles then discovered how the machines operated and in July 1939 turned copies of Enigma over to the French and British. Tragically, the French failed to exploit Enigma—although it provided numerous deciphered German messages concerning the new invasion strategy, the generals remained convinced by the documents captured in 1939 that the original attack plan was still operative. The British, on the other hand, created a top-secret intelligence network, known as Ultra, that monitored and decoded Enigma messages throughout the war.

The recast invasion plan worked brilliantly. When British and French forces entered Belgium, they were quickly outflanked and the Germans broke through the French lines at Sedan on May 13. "We are beaten," a tearful Reynaud telephoned to British Prime Minister Winston S. Churchill (1874–1965), who had replaced Chamberlain the very day the German attack began. A week later, Guderian's swiftly moving armored divisions reached the English Channel in order to encircle the Allies between the two converging German armies. The British Expeditionary Force retreated quickly to the French Channel ports of Boulogne, Calais, and Dunkirk, from where they hoped to evacuate. Guderian drove toward the same destination, but just as he reached the outskirts of Dunkirk he was ordered to halt. Despite the German conviction that such a massive escape was not possible, on May 26, 338,000 Allied soldiers began leaving France. Although Dunkirk proved an amazing success as an evacuation operation, it symbolized an unprecedented military defeat for the British.

Reynaud reorganized his government, appointing General Maxim Weygand (1867–1965) as military commander and the venerable Marshal Henri Pétain (1856–1951) as vice premier. Neither man, however, believed that France could be saved, although Weygand was at least determined to fight to the last. After Dunkirk, the Germans made rapid headway. On June 5, they sent 95 divisions across northern France, with one spearhead driving into Normandy and the other toward Paris.

When Mussolini joined Hitler in the Pact of Steel in May 1938, the dictators bound themselves to provide each other with total assistance in the event of war. But Mussolini had informed the Germans that Italy would not be prepared for full-scale war until 1943. Mussolini had, therefore, remained neutral in 1939, but the dazzling success of Hitler's Blitzkrieg shocked the *Duce* into acting, lest the war end before Italy could claim a part in the victory. Mussolini declared war on France on June 10, 1940, although he did not send Italian troops into battle until a week later. In the meantime, Paris fell to the Germans on June 14 and the government, which fled south, grew deeply divided over whether to continue to resist. Reynaud

A jubilant Hitler hears news of the French capitulation in 1940.

proposed fighting from French possessions in North Africa, but Weygand and Pétain secured the cabinet's support to sue for an armistice. Pétain took Reynaud's place as premier on July 16, and while he awaited Hitler's response to his request for peace terms, the Germans pushed deeper into France and Mussolini's armies attacked in the southeast.

Hitler demanded severe terms for an armistice, which he insisted be signed on the same site in Compiègne, northeast of Paris, where the Allies had forced terms on Germany in 1918. The document, executed on June 22, 1940, provided for German occupation of two-thirds of France, comprising the north and central portions of the country and the city of Paris. Alsace-Lorraine was given to Germany for the second time in less than a century. The remaining southern third of French territory, together with the colonial empire, continued to be headed by Pétain, whose government ruled from Vichy in collaboration with the German authorities. The Third Republic, founded in the wake of the Prussian victory of 1871, now came to an ignominious end.

While Pétain headed a rump state in the name of the humiliated French, national honor was kept alive by General Charles de Gaulle (1890–1970), the undersecretary of war who opposed both the armistice and the Vichy government. De Gaulle had taught military history at the Saint-Cyr military academy, where he himself had been educated. An advocate of tank warfare from whose books the Germans had learned some of their tactics, the strong-willed general had never been popular among his more traditional fellow officers. Refusing to recognize the armistice, he flew to Britain and appealed to the French people to continue the fight under his leadership. In London, he set up a government in exile, the Free French National Committee, and recruited an army of volunteers.

The Battle of Britain

Germany's Blitzkrieg gave Hitler control over as much of Europe as Napoleon had once ruled. Victory was, however, not yet his, for Great Britain remained still at war, although Hitler believed that the British had no choice but to make peace. The British rejected all offers of a settlement. Churchill, the new prime minister, was a pugnacious leader in the face of adversity, a brilliant speaker, and a tireless proponent of British national interests. Out of office for much of the 1930s, he had been a staunch advocate of rearmament and a bitter critic of appeasement.

Hitler saw no alternative other than to force Britain into submission, but he recognized that an invasion would be virtually impossible as long as British air and naval power remained intact. Nevertheless, in July Hitler ordered his strategists to develop an invasion plan, called Operation Sea Lion, which was to begin on September 15. Before the invasion could start, however, German leaders agreed that the Luftwaffe

St. Paul's Cathedral seen through the smoke of the German *Blitz* on London, January 1941.

would have to destroy the Royal Air Force (RAF) fighter planes, after which bombers could destroy British ships, coastal defenses, and ground troops. Reichsmarshal Hermann Goering was supremely confident that his Luftwaffe could not only destroy the RAF but also bomb the British people into surrendering without an invasion. Preparations for Operation Sea Lion were known to the British through Ultra reports.

Goering failed to appreciate the British spirit of resistance and overestimated the strength of the Luftwaffe. The two chief German air fleets consisted of 1200 bombers, which lacked sufficient range and bomb capacity, and 280 Stukas. The latter, which had proved so effective elsewhere, were decimated by British fighters and withdrawn. For daytime missions, the German bombers had to be escorted by Messerschmitt fighters, whose range was equally limited. In all, the two German air fleets had 980 Messerschmitts of various kinds. Because the RAF boasted only 650 Hurricane and Spitfire fighters, its commanders insisted on keeping large numbers of their planes in reserve. Aircraft production soon increased significantly, however, and the British also developed a radar system.

After a month of preliminary bombing of British shipping, the Germans began to attack airfields in mid-August in an effort to destroy the RAF. During the Battle of Britain, RAF pilots engaged in intense aerial combat with the Luftwaffe, losing more than 800 fighters while destroying 668 German fighters and 500 bombers during the first two months. On September 7, Goering began raids on London, but it was soon clear that the Germans could not destroy the RAF. Hitler canceled Operation Sea Lion in mid-September, although the bombing of civilian targets in Britain continued through the spring of 1941. The Battle of Britain cost the RAF some 1265 planes and the Luftwaffe 1882 aircraft.

THE PARALLEL WAR AND BARBAROSSA

When it was clear that the Battle of Britain had proved to be a standoff, Hitler undertook operations against British forces in the Mediterranean Sea. It was Mussolini, however, who forced Hitler's hand in campaigns designed as his own "parallel" war, but that the German leader considered merely a sideshow to a much larger goal: the invasion of Russia.

North Africa and the Balkans

In September 1940, Italian forces in Libya invaded Egypt. The Italian thrust came quickly to a halt at Sidi Barrani, 50 miles across the border, where they wanted to build a supply base. In early December, British General Archibald Wavell (1883–1950), commanding half the number of troops but with double the tank strength, counterattacked. The British pushed the Italians out of Egypt and across the North African desert, taking huge numbers of prisoners.

The Italian defeat was so sweeping that it forced Hitler to intervene. He sent General Erwin Rommel (1891–1944) to North Africa with meager forces consisting of one light motorized and one Panzer division, information that came to Wavell through Ultra. In March, Rommel attacked, driving the British back into Egypt, but because his supply lines were stretched thin he could not move further. The war in North Africa had turned into a stalemate. In East Africa, however, the British won a clear victory, overrunning Italian possessions in Eritrea, Ethiopia, and Somaliland.

In October, while the North African campaign was under way, Mussolini ordered an attack against Greece—an ill-advised move taken against the opinions of his generals. The attack deeply angered Hitler because it threatened German domination of the Balkans. The Italian invasion met with torrential rains, and the tough if small Greek army fought back fiercely. Italian forces suffered huge casualties as they overextended themselves into the mountains. Churchill also sent some 58,000 troops to help the Greeks. That April, Hitler moved to rescue Mussolini from disaster in Greece, while simultaneously invading Yugoslavia, and by the end of the month had conquered both countries. In late May, these successes were followed by a remarkable airborne conquest of Crete.

Operation Barbarossa

Even as the Battle of Britain began, Hitler had turned his mind eastward to the Soviet Union. He had long regarded Eastern Europe and Russia as providing the necessary *Lebensraum* ("living space") that Germany would require if the Reich was to dominate Europe. For Hitler, the Nazi-Soviet Pact of 1939 had been a temporary expedient. His long-range plans called for the destruction of Bolshevism and the seizure of Soviet oil and food resources. Once he had defeated the Soviet Union, he believed, Britain would be forced to capitulate. The invasion of Russia proved, however, to be a fatal error that would eventually cost Hitler victory.

Convinced that Britain was near collapse and that the USSR was too weak to stop him, Hitler told his generals in July 1940 to plan for "Operation Barbarossa," an attack on the Soviet Union. In this instance, the generals shared with Hitler a gross misconception of the difficulties ahead and sorely underestimated Soviet military strength. The Germans assembled some 145 divisions along the long Russian front, while the Soviets had more than 230 divisions. Hitler disagreed, however, with the generals over strategy: the latter wanted to focus on taking Moscow, not only the Soviet capital but an important industrial and rail center, while Hitler wanted to aim both at Leningrad in the north and the Ukraine in the south. In the end, Hitler approved an ambitious plan that consisted of three army groups, each aimed at one of the targets.

The invasion, which began a month later than scheduled on June 22, 1941, caught the Soviets completely off guard. German planes took off before the start of hostilities and within hours had destroyed some 1200 Soviet aircraft. The northern army group got to within 80 miles of Leningrad in five days, while the center army group captured almost 500,000 prisoners and were 200 miles from Moscow within a month. Only in the south, where the Soviets fought strenuously, was progress slower than expected. In mid-July, however, Hitler overruled his generals and weakened the center army group by shifting armored divisions to Leningrad and the Ukraine. In September, Hitler ordered the siege of Leningrad, which he intended to starve into surrender. The population suffered gruesome deprivations and enormous casualties as it fought with the Soviet army to defend the city. Only in 1944 was the siege finally lifted. In the south, the Germans succeeded in encircling Soviet forces near Kiev and took 600,000 prisoners. At the end of the month, Hitler changed strategy again, this time ordering an all-out drive toward Moscow and a simultaneous push deep into the industrial regions of the Ukraine. Hundreds of thousands of additional Russian soldiers were captured along with vast amounts of material. As the Germans moved forward, Stalin had more than 1500 Soviet factories dismantled and moved to the east of Moscow along with some 2 million workers.

The coming of heavy rains toward the end of October halted the advance of Hitler's armies, which had come as close as 40 miles to Moscow. German supply lines were in serious jeopardy when the winter set in, but, on November 15, Hitler and his generals began what they believed would be the final assault on Moscow. However, extreme temperatures, as low as minus-40, and heavy snows forced the Germans to stop. On November 28, the Nazi armies sustained their first setback when a Soviet counteroffensive in the south forced them to abandon positions. On December 5, Marshal Georgi Zhukov (1896–1974) attacked the German flanks north and south of Moscow, but instead of making a tactical withdrawal Hitler ordered his forces to fight on. It was Stalin's turn now to make a serious error. He overruled Zhukov, who wanted to make an all-out offensive at the Moscow front, and dispersed the Red Army along all sectors, a decision that helped make it possible for the Germans to resist the counteroffensive.

Both sides suffered enormous losses and the war on the Eastern front, like the war in North Africa, ground temporarily to a stalemate. The failure of the German attack against the Soviet Union resulted in a major shake-up of the German high command, and Hitler himself now assumed the role of commander-in-chief of the army. By the beginning of 1942, victory over both Britain and the Soviet Union had eluded Hitler's grasp.

THE JEWS AND HITLER'S "NEW ORDER"

Hitler's dream of creating a Greater Germany went far beyond any traditional thirst for territory. His aims were determined by the racial concepts that were the basis of Nazi ideology. It is difficult to say precisely what form Hitler's empire would have taken had he won the war, but Nazi policies in conquered territories suggest the fiendish nature of the "New Order" he hoped to create.

Hitler's "New Order"

By the end of 1941, Hitler held sway over as much European territory as any ruler in modern history. In addition to an expanded Germany that included Austria, portions of Czechoslovakia, and half of Poland, his troops occupied northern France, Belgium, the Netherlands, Luxembourg, Denmark, Norway, Greece, part of Yugoslavia, and a vast segment of the Soviet Union. At the height of the war, Vichy France, Italy, Hungary, Romania, Albania, Bulgaria, Slovakia, Croatia, and Finland were allied with Germany. Moreover, much of North African territory was in Axis hands. Spain, Portugal, the Irish Republic, Sweden, and Switzerland remained neutral.

According to Nazi plans, the Germans of the Third Reich were to be the rulers of the new Europe, and Germany its core. The so-called Aryans whom the Nazis extolled as the superior race also included Germanic peoples such as the English, the Scandinavians, and the Dutch, and Hitler hoped one day to incorporate most of them in Greater Germany. At first, Hitler allowed those Germanic states which he conquered to administer themselves, but resistance to Nazi occupation led to direct German control. In any case, the status assigned to each conquered area was only temporary, until victory enabled Hitler the leisure to impose a final settlement on Europe.

Hitler's attitude toward the Latin peoples of Europe, including the Italians, the French, and the

Spanish, was mixed. Although the Latins were not in the élite Germanic category, Nazi ideologues argued that they had some Aryan blood. His admiration and friendship for Mussolini led him to treat Italy with special regard, and after Mussolini adopted anti-Semitic policies in 1938, Fascist theorists there claimed that Italians were an Aryan race.

Despite such gradations, the Nazis generally considered all non-Germans to be inferior, and some—such as the Slavs of eastern Europe, who were low in the Nazi racial hierarchy—were thought useful only as a source of manual labor. The Third Reich regarded the populations and resources of other European nations as German resources. In occupied areas, inhabitants were conscripted into forced labor squads—over 2.5 million Poles and Russians, for example, were brought to Germany as forced workers and industrial equipment and agricultural produce were confiscated on a grand scale. By 1944, some 7 million foreign workers were eventually conscripted to Germany, where they were overworked and treated poorly.

Hermann Goering, who supervised economic policies in occupied areas, announced blatantly, "I intend to plunder, and plunder copiously." Occupation was generally more severe in the East than in Western Europe, where local populations were assessed for the cost of occupation troops but most private property was not actually confiscated. Policies were often confused, for Nazi authorities such as the army, the SS, and the Gestapo often vied with each other for control. Regardless of which Nazi officials ruled, however, their policies were harsh and brutal.

Nazi cruelty engendered resistance almost everywhere. In occupied territories active underground movements sprang up in opposition to German authority. Sometimes resisters engaged in symbolic acts of defiance, but more often they were involved in intelligence gathering, sabotage, and other meaningful acts that helped the Allied war effort. The attack against the Soviet Union pulled hundreds of thousands of communists into the underground, and after 1943 resistance forces became mass movements, increasingly armed by the Allies.

In France, where the resistance forces were generally called the *Maquis* (meaning "underbrush"), a number of groups fought against both Vichy and the Nazis. In 1943, French resistance leaders unified them into a single National Resistance Council and a Military Action Committee, and by the time of the Allied invasion some 200,000 armed resisters were in the field. Yugoslav and Russian partisans achieved significant military successes, and hundreds of thousands of German soldiers were bogged down in antiresistance operations. After Mussolini was overthrown by a coup in the summer of 1943, the anti-Fascist armed resistance played an equally significant role in northern Italy, where perhaps 250,000 partisans fought.

Nazi victims did not all go to their slaughter passively. In Warsaw, the Nazis had herded some 400,000 Jews together into the overcrowded ghetto, where SS-Chief Heinrich Himmler planned to starve and work them to death. In the spring of 1943, however, Himmler tired of the slow process and ordered the ghetto and its inhabitants destroyed. A group of Jewish survivors, led by the youth of the ghetto, fought heroically against the Nazis for 42 days.

The Nazis tried to keep their crimes secret, but word began to leak out as early as late 1941, and by the following year the U.S. government knew about the death camps. Nevertheless, Churchill and Roosevelt decided that the Jewish problem would have to await the opening of a second front. Only when the Allies liberated the camps in 1945 did the full horror of what had happened become public knowledge. What made the horror even more difficult to comprehend was the fact that so many millions of human beings were destroyed with careful deliberation and according to scientific principles by a state whose people had otherwise made such significant contributions to the civilization of Europe.

Map 9.2 The Holocaust

DOCUMENTS ON HISTORY

The Destruction of the European Jews

The most horrendous aspect of Hitler's New Order was its policies toward the Jews—policies that resulted in the planned extermination of millions of innocent people. This Holocaust, as the destruction of the European Jews is known, made an already gruesome and inhumane war even more terrible.

HITLER'S PLANS FOR THE JEWS

Hitler's anti-Semitism had been one of the principal forces in his early development (see Part VIII, Topic 2). During his rise to power he made the "Jewish question" a central issue of the Nazi platform. Although he did not explain the exact nature of his plans for the Jews, he did talk of creating a Germany free of Jews. In an interview as early as 1922, he was outspoken about what he would do once he took full power.

His eyes no longer saw me but instead bore past me and off into empty space; his explanations grew increasingly voluble until he fell into a kind of paroxysm that ended with his shouting, as if to a whole public gathering: "Once I really am in power, my first and foremost task will be the annihilation of the Jews. As soon as I have the power to do so, I will have gallows built in rows—at the Marienplatz in Munich, for example—as many as traffic allows. Then the Jews will be hanged indiscriminately, and they will remain hanging until they stink; they will hang there as long as the principles of hygiene permit. As soon as they have been untied, the next batch will be strung up, and so on down the line, until the last Jew in Munich has been exterminated. Other cities will follow suit, precisely in this fashion, until all Germany has been completely cleansed of Jews."

Quoted in Gerald Fleming, *Hitler and the Final Solution.* University of California Press. Copyright © 1984.

THE NUREMBERG LAWS

Once in power, the Nazis made life difficult for German Jews. Acting on a direct order from Hitler, the Reichstag passed two measures on September 15, 1935, which, together with the Reich citizenship law of November 14, constituted the so-called Nuremberg laws. The laws, selected portions of which follow, stripped Jews of their rights as citizens.

The Reich citizenship law of September 15:

1. (1) A subject is anyone who enjoys the protection of the German Reich and for this reason is specifically obligated to it.
   (2) Nationality is acquired according to the provisions of the Reich and state nationality law.
2. (1) A Reich citizen is only that subject of German or kindred blood who proves by his conduct that he is willing and suited loyally to serve the German people and the Reich.
   (2) Reich citizenship is acquired through the conferment of a certificate of Reich citizenship.
   (3) The Reich citizen is the sole bearer of full political rights as provided by the laws.

The Law for the Protection of German Blood and German Honor:

Imbued with the insight that the purity of German blood is a prerequisite for the continued existence of the German people and inspired by the inflexible will to ensure the existence of the German nation for all times, the Reichstag has unanimously adopted the following law, which is hereby promulgated:

1. (1) Marriages between Jews and subjects of German or kindred blood are forbidden. Marriages nevertheless concluded are invalid, even if concluded abroad to circumvent this law.
   (2) Only the State Attorney may initiate the annulment suit.
2. Extramarital intercourse between Jews and subjects of German or kindred blood is forbidden.
3. Jews must not employ in their households female subjects of German or kindred blood who are under 45 years old.
4. (1) Jews are forbidden to fly the Reich or national flag and to display the Reich colors.
   (2) They are, on the other hand, allowed to display the Jewish colors. The exercise of this right enjoys the protection of the state.

Quoted in Yehuda Bauer, *A History of the Holocaust.* Franklin Watts. Copyright © 1982.

THE KILLING FIELDS

The systematic destruction of Europe's Jews began to be implemented in the wake of the attack against the Soviet Union. As the German armies moved eastward and some 2 million Polish Jews fell under their rule, Nazi policy makers began thinking about the "Jewish question" on a more far-reaching basis. At first they debated forced emigration to the east. Reinhard Heydrich (1904–1942), head of the SS security service (the SD), organized SS Einsatzgruppen ("special-duty groups"), squads that followed the armies into Poland and later into the Soviet Union. The squads rounded up Polish workers and Russian prisoners for shipment to German slave labor camps and herded Jews into ghettos.

As Operation Barbarossa unfolded and the number of Jews under their control increased, the concentration strategy was replaced by what came to be known as the "Final Solution." Sometime in the spring or summer of 1941, Hitler made mass murder official policy and in July ordered Heydrich to draw up plans for this gruesome purpose. The Einsatzgruppen began to round up and shoot Jews and bury them in mass graves. In all, some 1 million men, women, and children may have been killed in this way. Here an SS colonel reports on the activities of his "Strike Commando" unit in Kovno, which covered parts of Lithuania and Latvia.

Lithuania could be freed of Jews only because a specially selected raiding party was set up under SS-1st Lieutenant Hamann who shared my aims in full and who knew how to cooperate with

continued next page

Lithuanian [anti-communist] partisans and the appropriate civil offices.

The implementation of such actions is in the first instance an organizational problem. The decision to free each district of Jews necessitated thorough preparation of each action as well as acquisition of information about local conditions. The Jews had to be collected in one or more towns and a ditch had to be dug at the right site for the right number. The marching distance from collecting points to the ditches averaged about 3 miles. The Jews were brought in groups of 500, separated by at least 1.2 miles, to the place of execution.

Vehicles are seldom available. Escapes, which were attempted here and there, were frustrated solely by my men at the risk of their lives. For example, 3 men of the Commando at Mariampole shot 38 escaping Jews and communist functionaries on a path in the woods, so that no one got away. Distances to and from actions were never less than 90–120 miles. Only careful planning enabled the Commando to carry out up to 5 actions a week and at the same time continue the work in Kovno without interruption.

Kovno itself, where trained Lithuanian partisans are available in sufficient numbers, was comparatively speaking a shooting paradise.

All officers and men of the Commando in Kovno participated in the major actions in the city. Only one intelligence official was excused because of illness.

I regard the Jewish actions of Strike Commando 3 as virtually completed. The remaining work Jews and Jewesses are urgently needed, and I can imagine that they will still be needed after the winter. I am of the opinion that the male work Jews should be sterilized immediately to prevent any procreation. A Jewess who nevertheless becomes pregnant is to be liquidated. . . .

From photostats of documents in the Institut für Zeitgeschichte, Munich, report of December 1, 1941, as reproduced in Raul Hilberg, ed., *Documents of Destruction: Germany and Jewry 1933–1945.* Copyright © 1971, Raul Hilberg.

AN EYEWITNESS ACCOUNT

Here is the terrible testimony of Mrs. Rivka Yosselevscka, who as a young girl survived one of the innumerable episodes of killings in Russia.

When it came to our turn, our father was beaten. We prayed, we begged with my father to undress, but he would not undress, he wanted to keep his underclothes. . . .

Then they tore the clothing off the old man and he was shot. I saw it with my own eyes. And then they took my mother, and she said, let us go before her; but they caught mother and shot her too; and then there was my grandmother, my father's mother, standing there; she was eighty years old and she had two children in her arms. And then there was my father's sister. She also had children in her arms and she was shot on the spot with the babies in her arms. . . .

And finally my turn came. There was my younger sister, and she wanted to leave; she prayed with the Germans; she asked to run, naked; she went up to the Germans with one of her friends; they were embracing each other; and she asked to be spared, standing there naked. He looked into her eyes and shot the two of them. . . . Then my second sister was shot and then my turn did come. . . .

We were already facing the grave. The German asked "Who do you want me to shoot first?" I did not answer. I felt him take the child from my arms. The child cried out and was shot immediately. And then he aimed at me. First he held on to my hair and turned my head around; I stayed standing; I heard a shot, but I continued to stand and then he turned my head again and he aimed the revolver at me and ordered me to watch and then turned my head around and shot at me. Then I fell to the ground into the pit amongst the bodies; but I felt nothing. The moment I did feel I felt a sort of heaviness. . . . Then I felt that I was choking; people falling over me. I tried to move and felt that I was alive and that I could rise. I was strangling. I heard the shots and I was praying for another bullet to put an end to my suffering, but I continued to move about. I felt that I was choking, strangling, but I tried to save myself, to find some air to breathe, and then I felt that I was climbing towards the top of the grave above the bodies. I rose, and I felt bodies pulling at me with their hands, biting at my legs, pulling me down, down. And yet with my last strength I came up on top of the grave, and when I did I did not know the place, so many bodies were lying all over, dead people; I wanted to see the end of this stretch of dead bodies but I could not. It was impossible. They were lying, all dying; suffering; not all of them dead, but in their last sufferings; naked; shot, but not dead. Children crying "Mother," "Father". . . .

From the English transcript of the Eichmann trial, May 8, 1961, as reproduced in Raul Hilberg, ed., *Documents of Destruction: Germany and Jewry 1933–1945.* Copyright © 1971, Raul Hilberg.

THE FINAL SOLUTION

At the end of July 1941, Hermann Goering sent the following order to Heydrich:

Complementing the task already assigned to you in the decree of January 24, 1939, to undertake, by emigration or evacuation, a solution of the Jewish question as advantageous as possible under the conditions at the time, I hereby charge you with making all necessary organizational, functional, and material preparations for a complete solution of the Jewish question in the German sphere of influence in Europe.

In so far as the jurisdiction of other central agencies may be touched thereby, they are to be involved.

I charge you furthermore with submitting to me in the near future an overall plan of the organizational, functional, and material measures to be taken in preparing for the implementation of the aspired final solution of the Jewish question.

Quoted in Raul Hilberg, ed., *Documents of Destruction: Germany and Jewry 1933–1945.* Copyright © 1971, Raul Hilberg.

The Nazis established death camps in order to murder Jews in large numbers by rational, systematic methods. Camps were built in Auschwitz, Chełmno, Bełzec, Treblinka, and at numerous other sites. These policies were discussed and approved at the Wannsee Conference of high German officials in January 1942. The text of the discussion was carefully sanitized by SS officer Adolf Eichmann (1906–1962), who took the minutes.

Chief of Security Policy and Security Service, SS-Lieutenant General Heydrich, opened the meeting by informing everyone that the Reich Marshal [Göring] had placed him in charge of preparations for the final solution of the Jewish question, and that the invitations to this conference had been issued to obtain clarity in fundamental questions. The Reich Marshal's wish to have a draft submitted to him on the organizational, functional, and material considerations aimed at a final solution of the European Jewish question requires that all of the central agencies, which are directly concerned with these problems, first join together with a view to paralleling their lines of action.

The implementation of the final solution of the Jewish question is to be guided centrally without regard to geographic boundaries from the office of the Reichsführer-SS and Chief of the German Police (Chief of Security Police and Security Service).

The Chief of Security Police and Security Service then reviewed briefly the battle fought thus far against these opponents. The principal stages constituted

a) Forcing the Jews out of individual sectors of life *[Lebensgebiete]* of the German people

continued next page

b) Forcing the Jews out of the living space *[Lebensraum]* of the German people

In pursuance of this endeavor, a systematic and concentrated effort was made to accelerate Jewish emigration from Reich territory as the only temporary solution possibility. . . .

The disadvantages brought forth by such forcing of emigration were clear to every agency. In the meantime, however, they had to be accepted for the lack of any other solution possibility. . . .

In lieu of emigration, the evacuation of the Jews to the east has emerged, after an appropriate prior authorization by the Führer [Hitler], as a further solution possibility.

While these actions are to be regarded solely as temporary measures, practical experiences are already being gathered here which will be of great importance during the coming final solution of the Jewish question. . . .

In the course of the final solution, the Jews should be brought under appropriate direction in a suitable manner to the east for labor utilization. Separated by sex, the Jews capable of work will be led into these areas in large labor columns to build roads, whereby doubtless a large part will fall away through natural reduction.

The inevitable final remainder which doubtless constitutes the toughest element will have to be dealt with appropriately, since it represents a natural selection which upon liberation is to be regarded as a germ cell of a new Jewish development. (See the lesson of history.)

In the course of the practical implementation of the final solution, Europe will be combed from west to east. If only because of the apartment shortage and other socio-political necessities, the Reich area—including the Protectorate of Bohemia and Moravia—will have to be placed ahead of the line. . . .

Quoted in Raul Hilberg, ed., *Documents of Destruction: Germany and Jewry 1933–1945.*

Eichmann rounded up his victims and used railroads to ship them to death camps in Poland, the largest at Auschwitz. After Jews were killed in the gas chambers, the Nazis processed all usable items, including clothing, gold teeth, eyeglasses, and even human hair, and burned the bodies in ovens. Here is a description of the first testing of gas on Russian prisoners by Rudolf F. Hess, commandant of Auschwitz:

While I was away on duty, my deputy, Fritzsch, the commander of the protective custody camp, first tried gas for these killings. It was a preparation of prussic acid, called cyclon B, which was used in the camp as an insecticide and of which there was always a stock on hand. On my return, Fritzsch reported this to me, and the gas was used again for the next transport. . . .
Protected by a gas-mask, I watched the killing myself. In the crowded cells death came instantaneously the moment the cyclon B was thrown in. A short, almost smothered cry, and it was all over. . . . I have a clearer recollection of the gassing of nine hundred Russians. . . . While the transport was detraining, holes were pierced in the earth and concrete ceiling of the mortuary. The Russians were ordered to undress in an

AMERICAN INTERVENTION AND THE WAR IN ASIA

While the war raged for two years in Europe, the United States maintained a guarded neutrality. Isolationism remained deeply rooted in American public opinion. In 1935 Congress had passed a law that ensured U.S. neutrality during Mussolini's invasion of Ethiopia, and in 1937 an even stronger measure prevented the government and U.S. manufacturers from shipping armaments and vital war materiel to belligerents on any side of a conflict. On the other hand, President Franklin D. Roosevelt was deeply concerned over the dangers of Nazianteroom; they then quietly entered the mortuary, for they had been told they were to be deloused. The whole transport exactly filled the mortuary to capacity. The doors were then sealed and the gas shaken down through the holes in the roof. I do not know how long this killing took. For a little while a humming sound could be heard. When the powder was thrown in, there were cries of "Gas!", then a great bellowing, and the trapped prisoners hurled themselves against both doors. . . . The mass extermination of the Jews was to start soon and at that time neither Eichmann nor I was certain how these mass killings were to be carried out. . . . Now we had the gas, and we had established a procedure.

Quoted in Yehuda Bauer, *A History of the Holocaust.* Franklin Watts. Copyright © 1982.

At his trial for crimes against humanity in Jerusalem in 1957, Eichmann gave this chilling explanation of his "moral" universe:

I did not take on the job as a senseless exercise. It gave me uncommon joy, I found it fascinating to have to deal with these matters. . . . My job was to catch these enemies and transport them to their destination. . . . I lived in this stuff, otherwise I would have remained only an assistant, a cog, something soulless. . . .

I thought it over, and I realized the necessity for it, I carried it through with all the fanaticism that an old Nazi would expect of himself and that my superiors undoubtedly expected from me. They found me, according to their experience, to be the right man in the right place. . . . This I say today, in 1957, to my own disadvantage. I could make it easy for myself. I could now claim it was an order I had to carry out because of my oath of allegiance. But that would be just a cheap excuse, which I am not prepared to give. . . .

To be frank with you, had we killed all of them, the 10.3 million, I would be happy and say, Alright, we managed to destroy an enemy. . . .

I suggested these words ["Final Solution"]. At that time I meant by this the elimination of the Jews, their marching out of the German Nation. Later. . . . these harmless words were used as a camouflage for the killing.

Quoted in Gideon Hausner, *Justice in Jerusalem.* Herzl Press. Copyright © 1966.

By the end of the war, as many as 6 million Jews—three-fourths of all Jews in Europe—may have been murdered. The Holocaust consumed others as well, including political enemies and resisters, some 200,000 gypsies, and 60,000 homosexuals. Hitler regarded most Slavs, particularly the Poles, with utter contempt, and during the Nazi occupation millions perished as prisoners of war or in labor camps. History as well as aspects of the social and economic structures of modern Germany had contributed to the Holocaust, and Nazi policy had evolved over the years. There is no doubt, however, that by 1942, the Nazis intended to destroy the Jews of the whole of Europe.

Fascist aggression in Europe and Japanese ambitions in East Asia.

The Crisis of American Neutrality

A move away from neutrality first appeared in connection with the Japanese invasion of China in 1937, when the Roosevelt administration came out openly against Japan. The president, in his famous "Quarantine Speech" delivered in October, asked that the world community oppose violations of international law. There was, he declared ominously, no escaping responsibility through "mere isolation or neutrality."

When war erupted in Europe, most Americans supported the Western democracies but still opposed intervention. Nevertheless, Roosevelt moved to strengthen U.S. defenses and to make America what

Jews from the Warsaw ghetto are rounded up by German troops—and headed toward death.

When the Nazi death and concentration camps were liberated, Allied troops discovered unbelievable horrors—here, piles of corpses at Belsen concentration camp.

he called the "arsenal of democracy." In November 1939, he persuaded Congress to repeal the arms embargo and permit the sale of war supplies to Britain through a "cash and carry" program—the measure did, however, prohibit U.S. ships from transporting the arms so as to avoid German submarine attacks. Congress also approved a huge defense budget and in September 1940 instituted the draft. After he had won reelection that year, the president introduced the Lend-Lease Bill into Congress—Britain was about to exhaust its financial resources, and the law, passed in March 1941, allowed the president to lend or lease arms, with payment to be made after the war. That summer, lend-lease was extended to the Soviet Union.

Under Roosevelt's leadership, the United States inched its way closer to active intervention on the side of the Allies. In January 1941, British and American military officials met in Washington, DC, to develop plans in the event the United States entered the war. In April and July, U.S. military forces took possession respectively of Greenland and Iceland, two Danish possessions in the North Atlantic. In August, Roosevelt met Churchill on a British battleship off the coast of Newfoundland. Despite Roosevelt's suspicions that Churchill was intent on maintaining the British Empire, the two leaders issued an important statement known as the Atlantic Charter. The document described a joint postwar policy that affirmed the right of all peoples to self-government, rejected any territorial acquisition as a result of the war, and called for the destruction of Nazism. For the United States, still a neutral nation, the Atlantic Charter represented a virtual announcement of war goals.

War in Asia

It was Japan, rather than Germany, that actually provoked American intervention (see Part VIII, Topic 8). In September 1940, Japan joined Germany and Italy in a Tripartite Pact, a defensive alliance aimed indirectly at the United States that gave Japanese expansionism the endorsement of the Axis. Japanese leaders now took advantage of the war in Europe to build their own empire in Asia—one that they hoped would reach from Manchuria in the North to embrace all of Southeast Asia, including Indochina, Indonesia (the Dutch East Indies), Singapore, and the Philippines. Japanese strategists, claiming that they would free Asia from Western control, conceived of this empire as the "Greater East Asia Co-Prosperity Sphere," a far-flung economic zone in which Japan's industrial and technological superiority would be combined with the vast resources and labor supply of East Asia.

In 1940, Japan pressed the Dutch government to grant trade concessions and forced the French to cut off supply lines to China through their colony in Indochina. The American reaction was to impose an embargo in July on the export of such items as steel and aviation fuel to Japan. Working against pressure from Japanese military leaders, Premier Fumimaro Konoye (1891–1945), a moderate aristocrat, began talks with the United States in 1941 in an effort to reach a peaceful agreement. When the German attack against the Soviet Union removed the danger of Soviet action in East Asia, Japan overran Indochina. Roosevelt responded by freezing Japanese assets in the United States and announcing a severe trade embargo, including the shipment of oil.

Konoye resigned in October and was replaced by Tojo Hideki (1885–1948), an army general who favored war with America. His colleague, Admiral Isoroku Yamamoto (1884–1943), commander of the Japanese Fleet, believed that such a war could be successful only if Japan destroyed the U.S. Pacific Fleet in a surprise attack. Emperor Hirohito (ruled 1926–1989) insisted that negotiations continue, while Tojo's cabinet decided on war should this second diplomatic effort fail. In November 1941, Washington insisted that Japan withdraw completely from China and Indochina before it would lift economic sanctions. The Japanese considered this an ultimatum and at the end of the month secretly decided on war. The Americans, who had broken the Japanese diplomatic code, knew that war seemed likely but did not anticipate that an assault would come where it did, although debate on the background to the Pearl Harbor attack continues.

The Japanese launched their surprise attack on the morning of December 7. The target was the U.S. naval base at Pearl Harbor, in the Hawaiian Islands. Hundreds of planes from Japanese aircraft carriers caught the Americans by surprise, sinking four out of eight U.S. battleships, three destroyers, and four smaller ships, and destroying 160 planes. The United States, its military strength in the Pacific severely damaged, was at war.

Immediately after Pearl Harbor, the Japanese also struck against the British fleet near Singapore and the U.S. Air Force base in the Philippines. Japan overran Malaya, Burma, the Dutch East Indies, and the Philippines, campaigns made possible by its control of Indochina. Thailand was forced to let Japan use its military bases, and by 1942, Japan had seized most of the islands in the western Pacific. Japanese occupation policies were no less brutal than those of the Nazis in Europe, for the Japanese regarded other Asians with their own attitude of racial superiority. By the beginning of 1942, Japan controlled most of East Asia, and its newly created empire appeared to be invincible.

The Japanese attack on Pearl Harbor, December 7, 1941 brought the United States into the war. Here U.S. battleships are shown shortly after the raid.

TURNING THE TIDE: THE RUSSIAN ADVANCE AND THE ECLIPSE OF JAPAN

With America's entrance into the war in December 1941, the Axis powers now faced an informal alliance consisting of Great Britain, the United States, and the Soviet Union (the three powers were allies only in the European theater, since the USSR and Japan were not at war). From December 22 to January 14, Churchill and his chiefs of staff met in Washington with Roosevelt and American officials to develop a grand strategy. The two nations agreed that the defeat of Germany and victory in Europe would be the first goal, to be followed by the defeat of Japan. The Allies accepted two other essential points: that a second front had to be opened in the West to relieve the Russian war effort, and that a cross-channel invasion of the European continent would have to come. The Anglo-American conference ended with the issuance of a "United Nations Declaration" in which the 26 countries fighting against the Axis endorsed the principles of the Atlantic Charter, accepted the premises of the Anglo-American conference, and agreed to postpone political questions until after military victory.

The Allies disagreed over both strategy and broader political issues. The Americans believed that victory could be achieved only by a direct frontal assault on Hitler's "Fortress Europe" through an invasion of France. The British, however, feared that a premature landing there would spell disaster, and Churchill pushed for an attack against what he called the "soft underbelly" of Europe—either in the Balkans or in Italy. A compromise was reached, whereby the Allies would first seize North Africa and use it as a base for a campaign against the "underbelly," followed then by an invasion of France.

Strategic disagreements combined with political mistrust, for each of the three leaders came from a totally different political background. Stalin, a lifelong communist, worried that the two Western statesmen were intent on keeping the Soviet Union from sharing in the postwar settlement and from expanding into Eastern Europe. Even Roosevelt and Churchill had doubts about each other—Roosevelt, a Wilsonian internationalist, believed that Churchill was driven by the desire to extend Britain's empire into the Mediterranean basin, while Churchill thought the

U.S. president naive about international politics. Nevertheless, the three men forged an alliance of convenience around the immediate goal of defeating the Axis.

The Soviets Push West

The fortunes of war began to turn against the Axis in 1942, in North Africa, Europe, and the Pacific. That fall, British General Bernard Montgomery (1887–1976) won a decisive victory over Rommel's desert forces at El-Alamein. In November, while the fighting was still raging at El-Alamein, a joint Anglo-American army commanded by U.S. General Dwight D. Eisenhower (1890–1969) landed in Morocco and Algeria, and by May 1943 had captured all of North Africa.

It was in the Soviet Union, however, that Hitler suffered his greatest setbacks, the accumulated weight of which proved decisive. The Führer's decision not to pull back his forces in the winter of 1941–1942 proved crucial in draining his eastern armies. The Germans were fighting the Red Army on a front line that stretched almost 2000 miles. Hitler then decided to abandon the Moscow campaign and concentrate his strength in a huge offensive in the south. The aim of this strategy was to seize the vital oil fields in the Caucasus. The drive began in late June 1942 by attempting to encircle the Soviet forces in the region where the Don and the Volga rivers flowed close to each other, near the industrial city of Stalingrad. The Soviets withdrew toward Stalingrad under the impact of the German attack, leaving Hitler to believe that the Soviet war effort was on the verge of collapse. Yet the strategic withdrawal induced the Germans into dividing their strength in pursuit of several different objectives.

As one German force made its way toward Stalingrad in late August, Marshal Zhukov prepared to defend the city. Stalingrad itself was important primarily as a symbol—Stalin was determined that the city named after him would not fall to the Germans, and Hitler became obsessed with the goal. After the Germans reduced most of the city to rubble, they and the Soviets fought desperately in street-to-street fighting that took a terrible toll on both sides. By November, the Germans held almost the entire city, a success won at the price of having exposed themselves along a dangerously overextended line. The Soviets, who had been steadily building up their forces, counterattacked, and on November 23 they surrounded the city and trapped the entire German Sixth Army as well as a Panzer corps. Hitler refused irrationally to permit a withdrawal—as the situation worsened and the cruel Russian winter set in, he ordered his troops to fight to the last man. Nevertheless, the remaining soldiers of the Sixth Army surrendered on February 2, 1943, the Germans having lost more than 300,000 men. Thereafter, the Germans would be on the defensive in the East. A major turning point in the war had been reached at Stalingrad.

Faced with a significant inferiority in manpower, the Germans were now forced to adopt a defensive posture that involved carefully planned withdrawals at key points along the Russian front. In July, Hitler approved an attempt to eliminate a Russian bulge that extended into the German line at Kursk. Marshal Zhukov, whose intelligence agents learned of the German plans, prepared a defensive position. In the Battle of the Kursk

Stalingrad during the raging battle, November 1942.

Salient, July 5–12, the Russians outnumbered the Germans in all areas: 1,300,000 to 900,000 men, 3300 tanks to 2700, and 20,000 artillery pieces to 10,000. After a week of exceptionally heavy German losses, Hitler ordered an end to the attack. The Germans reeled under heavy counterattacks that fall, and the Soviets began pushing the enemy westward.

Japan on the Defensive

The Japanese position in the Pacific began to weaken in the summer of 1942, when American forces struck two major blows. On May 4–8, U.S. carriers stopped the Japanese advance toward New Guinea in the Battle of the Coral Sea, an engagement fought by aircraft from ships that never made visual contact with each other. Then, in June 1942, the U.S. Navy attacked a Japanese force approaching the American base at Midway, northwest of the Hawaiian Islands, winning a decisive victory that passed the initiative to the Allies in the Pacific.

The war in the Pacific became the primary responsibility of the Americans, assisted by Australia and New Zealand. Roosevelt divided military command between General Douglas MacArthur (1880–1964), the commander-in-chief of Allied forces in the Southwest Pacific, and Admiral Chester Nimitz (1885–1966), who commanded the rest of the Pacific theater. Together they began a costly strategy of "island-hopping," in which they retook the Pacific islands in a continual series of bloody invasions. Beginning in 1943 with battles in New Guinea, the Solomon Islands, and the Bismarck Archipelago, in 1944 they pushed northward, taking Saipan in June. In October, the Americans won a major victory at the Battle of Leyte Gulf in the Philippines, which struck a death blow to Japanese naval power.

In 1945, Americans retook the Philippines, and in February Nimitz launched an invasion of Iwo Jima, a small but heavily defended volcanic island some 660 miles from Tokyo. Iwo Jima was taken after five terrible

Map 9.3 The War in Asia

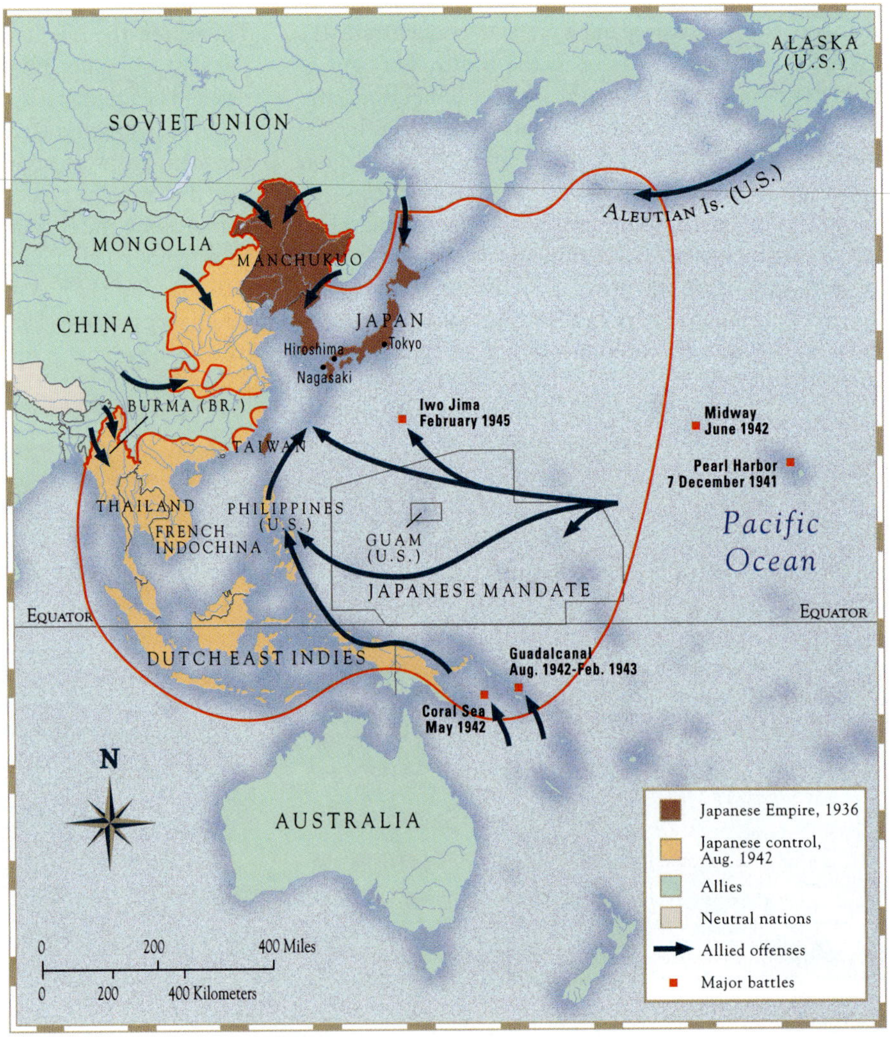

weeks of battle, followed in June by the seizure of Okinawa, which cost 12,000 U.S. lives. In these and other confrontations, the Japanese fought almost to the last man. During the Battle of Leyte Gulf, the Japanese also introduced a new weapon known as *kamikaze,* or "divine wind" ("Kamikaze" was the name for the typhoon that destroyed the Mongol fleet that hoped to invade Japan in the 13th century)—suicide missions in which pilots deliberately smashed their planes into enemy ships. Despite the determination of its military commanders to hold out, Japan's naval power had practically disappeared, its cities had been bombed and gutted by U.S. planes, and its population was on the edge of starvation. By the spring of 1945, Japanese authorities were beginning to probe the Allies for peace terms. The collapse of Japan was imminent.

YALTA, POTSDAM, AND THE DIVISION OF EUROPE

In January 1943, while the campaign in North Africa was still under way, Roosevelt and Churchill held a meeting in Casablanca, Morocco. The two leaders agreed to a cross-channel invasion of France in 1944, and chose Italy as the target for the "soft underbelly" assault in the Mediterranean.

The Fall of Mussolini and the Invasion of Normandy

In June, Eisenhower commanded an Allied invasion of Sicily, and its success led to widespread dissatisfaction among Fascist leaders over Mussolini's conduct of the war. On the evening of July 25, at a meeting of the Fascist Grand Council, a group of dissidents—including Count Ciano, Mussolini's son-in-law—voted no confidence in the Duce. During an audience with King Victor Emmanuel III the next morning, Mussolini was arrested. Marshal Pietro Badoglio (1871–1956) was named prime minister, a position Mussolini had held for more than 20 years. Badoglio opened secret talks with the Allies for an armistice. Hitler immediately sent German troops into Italy and around Rome in anticipation of an Allied assault against the mainland. In September, as the Allies made their first landings on the mainland, Badoglio signed an armistice according to which Italy abandoned the Axis and now fought on the side of the Allies.

Shortly before the armistice, the Führer sent a special mission to rescue Mussolini, who then set up a new Fascist government in northern Italy known as the Italian Social Republic (RSI). The Duce had little autonomy, however, as German military authorities made most important decisions. Over the next year and a half, Italy was cut in two—Mussolini ruled in the region north of Rome, while Badoglio and the king governed the southern portion of the peninsula. In the RSI, hundreds of thousands of armed partisans fought the Germans as well as a bloody civil war with Fascists.

In November, while the Allies pushed their way up the Italian mainland, the foreign ministers of the chief Allied powers gathered in Moscow. They again insisted on the unconditional surrender of Germany and Japan as well as the postwar occupation of Germany. The Moscow meeting was prelude to the conference in Teheran, where Stalin met for the first time with Roosevelt and Churchill. The three leaders agreed on basic aspects of "Operation Overlord," the assault against France planned for the spring of 1944, and Roosevelt announced the appointment of Eisenhower as supreme commander of the Allied forces.

The landings on the Normandy coast on June 6, 1944, were part of the largest sea-to-land operation ever undertaken. Within a week of D-Day, some 300,000 soldiers—three-fourths of them American—and endless supplies had landed and began spreading out through Fortress Europe. On July 20, an unsuccessful attempt on Hitler's life was made by army officers who wanted to make peace. Field Marshal Rommel, implicated in the plot, was forced to commit suicide. Paris was liberated on August 25, and by mid-September, Eisenhower's forces had advanced steadily, pushing the Germans to the borders of France. In December, Hitler ordered a powerful counterattack that struck hard at Allied positions in the Ardennes forest, but at the cost of seriously weakening the Eastern front. This Battle of the Bulge was his last important military offensive.

In January 1945, the millions of Soviet soldiers who were pushing westward overran Hungary, Poland, and Czechoslovakia and entered German territory. American and British forces crossed the Rhine in March, and over the next two months the noose tightened around the Third Reich.

The End of the Second World War

With victory in Europe in sight at last, in February 1945 the three Allied leaders gathered once again, this time at the Black Sea resort of Yalta in the Soviet Union. In a show of unity, they repeated what had now become fundamental Allied policy: unconditional surrender; the occupation, disarmament, and denazification of Germany; and the establishment of the United Nations.

The three great powers were already engaged in a struggle among themselves to win the peace and create spheres of influence in Europe. In this context, the

U.S. soldiers wading toward the beach of Normandy on D-Day, June 6,1944.

controversial Yalta meeting has been viewed by some as a shortsighted capitulation to Soviet demands, but Roosevelt and Churchill had little choice. For one thing, the Red Army had reached eastern Europe, Germany, and the Balkans at the time of the conference. Furthermore, the United States and Britain had already approved a democratic, capitalist government for postwar Italy without consulting the Soviets, and

The Yalta conference, February 1945—Churchill, Roosevelt, and Stalin.

Stalin felt free to act with the same independence in Eastern Europe. Finally, Roosevelt felt he had to make concessions in order to induce the Soviet Union to declare war on Japan. Roosevelt and Churchill therefore agreed in principle to Stalin's demands that portions of eastern Poland be given to Russia and German territory be transferred to the new Polish state. For his part, Stalin agreed to the "Declaration on a Liberated Europe," a purposefully vague statement about free elections and self-determination.

Within two months of the Yalta conference, the war in Europe ended. On April 25, U.S. and Soviet forces linked arms on the Elbe River. Mussolini was captured by Italian partisans and executed on April 28, two days before Hitler committed suicide. Admiral Karl Doenitz (1891–1980) became head of state and officially surrendered to the Allies. Berlin, the capital of the thousand-year Reich, lay in ruins, and Germany surrendered unconditionally on May 7, 1945. Roosevelt, who died on April 12 of a cerebral hemorrhage, did not live to see V-E Day—Victory in Europe.

The war in the Pacific ended after the Big Three had held still one more conference, this time at Potsdam, Germany, in July–August 1945. Of the original leaders, only Stalin remained, for the United States was represented by its new president, Harry S. Truman (1884–1972), and Britain by Clement Attlee (1883–1967), who had replaced Churchill as prime minister. It was at Potsdam that the political divisions between the Soviet Union and its Allies surfaced openly for the first

Map 9.4 Postwar Europe

time, and some scholars have seen in this meeting the origins of the Cold War (see Part VIII, Topic 12). Truman accused Stalin of having gone back on the promises made at Yalta by setting up communist-dominated regimes in eastern Europe.

It was at Potsdam that Truman revealed to the other powers that the United States possessed a powerful new weapon, the atomic bomb. Scientists had been working feverishly on the top secret Manhattan Project since 1942, and the bomb was tested in the New Mexico desert on July 16. That same month, although the Japanese agreed to all the Allied terms of surrender except the deposition of the emperor, Truman approved the use of the atomic bomb against Japan, a much-debated decision. The president himself explained that he and his military advisers believed that the bomb was the only way to avoid massive American casualties during an invasion of Japan. Yet Truman may well have wanted to impress the Soviets with America's new power. At the same time, he could bring the Pacific war to an end before the Russians declared war on Tokyo and claimed the right to take part in a Pacific peace settlement.

On August 6, the *Enola Gay*, an American B-29 bomber, dropped a five-ton atomic weapon on Hiroshima, reducing the city to rubble and killing a fourth of its inhabitants—almost 80,000 people. Truman warned the Japanese that another nuclear explosion would come if they did not surrender. The Soviets officially entered the war against Japan two days later, and on August 9, the Americans dropped an atomic bomb on Nagasaki. On August 10, Emperor Hirohito ordered his government to prepare to surrender, and declared to his people that they must now endure "the unendurable" pain of defeat. Americans celebrated August 14 as "V-J Day," although the Japanese signed the surrender document officially on September 2 aboard the U.S.S. *Missouri* in Tokyo Bay.

The controversy surrounding the decision to use atomic weapons on civilian populations should be seen in the wider context of the saturation bombing of German and Japanese cities. The Germans had begun bombing London and other British cities in 1940, and by 1942 the British began to respond in kind—that May, hundreds of bombers struck against Cologne, leaving the city in ruins; the next year some 50,000 inhabitants of Hamburg were killed as a result of massive incendiary bomb raids, while as late as February 1945—six months before the dropping of the atomic bombs—British planes killed more than 100,000 civilians in Dresden. In Asia, American B-29 bombers began the large-scale bombing of Japanese cities in late 1944. The atomic bombing of Japan was the last, terrifying, consequence of modern warfare.

Since the Atlantic Charter in 1941, the Allies had demanded unconditional surrender from the Axis powers and the elimination of fascism. In order to ensure that history would not repeat itself, they forced a series of social and political reforms on the defeated enemy states, drafting democratic constitutions and implementing far-reaching changes in the educational systems. They also insisted on purging fascists and militarists from government bureaucracies. As the horrors of the Holocaust became widely known in 1945, the Allies decided that the chief enemy war leaders should be tried and punished for their "crimes against humanity." The Nuremberg Military Tribunal was the most famous of these trials. Among the most prominent fascist leaders, some committed suicide, while others were executed or given long prison terms. Hitler and Mussolini escaped the judgment of the victors, if not of history.

World War II was the most terrible conflict in history. Before it was over, perhaps as many as 50 million people had perished, nations had vanished, and the battles had destroyed property and economic life around the globe.

The great powers fought World War II as a "total war," mobilizing their societies and economies toward the single goal of victory. The war became the focus not only of private industry and farmers, but of ethnic groups, writers, the scientific establishment, the entertainment industry and filmmakers, universities, and every other resource that could be useful to the military effort. As in the First World War, traditional social arrangements were altered and some trends accelerated. Millions of men from all walks of life were drafted or volunteered to serve in the armed forces, while women joined in noncombatant positions or moved to fill assembly line jobs in factories making munitions, tanks, planes, and ships. Rationing, wage and price controls, and government production quotas became the norm. The vast intervention of government in the daily lives of citizens required by this huge effort established the foundations for the welfare state that was to evolve in the postwar period.

Once again, as they had done at the end of the First World War, the winners put their hopes in the idea of an international organization to preserve the peace won with such difficulty. At the Moscow foreign ministers' meeting in October 1943, the Allies had agreed to create a United Nations when the fighting was over. The new body, formally endorsed by 50 sovereign states in July 1945, took the place of Woodrow Wilson's old League of Nations, which had proven unable to prevent aggression in the years between the wars. But although the nuclear superpowers, not the United Nations, would dominate world affairs over the next half-century, Europe was to remember the harsh lessons of the past as it reshaped its future.

Questions for Further Study

1. What were the principles of modern warfare embodied in Blitzkrieg?
2. Can the Holocaust be explained historically? What in your opinion is the explanation?
3. What were the principal contributions of the United States to the outcome of the war? Of the Soviet Union?
4. What factors were behind the expansionist policies of the Japanese?
5. Was the use of the atomic bomb necessary and/or justified?

Suggestions for Further Reading

Ambrose, Stephen. *Eisenhower: The Soldier*. London, 1984.
Boyle, John H. *China and Japan at War, 1937–1945*. Stanford, CA, 1972.
Calvocoressi, Peter, and G. Wint. *Total War*. Harmondsworth, England, 1972.
Costello, John. *Love, Sex and War: Changing Values, 1939–1945*. London, 1985.
Dower, John. *War Without Mercy: Race and Power in the Pacific War*. New York, 1986.
Dziewanowski, Michael K. *War at Any Price: World War II in Europe*. Englewood Cliffs, NJ, 1987.
Erickson, John. *Stalin's War with Germany*, 2 vols. London, 1973–1985.
Gilbert, Martin. *The Holocaust: The History of the Jews of Europe During the Second World War*. New York, 1985.
Harrison, Tom. *Living Through the Blitz*. London, 1985.
Hilberg, Raul. *The Destruction of the European Jews*, rev. ed. New York, 1985.
Lewin, Ronald. *Hitler's Mistakes*. New York, 1986.
Loth, Wilfred. *The Division of the World, 1941–1955*. New York, 1988.
Marrus, Michael. *The Holocaust in History*. New York, 1987.
Milward, Alan S. *War, Economy and Society, 1939–1945*. London, 1977.
Rupp, Leila J. *Mobilizing Women for War: German and American Propaganda, 1939–1945*. Princeton, NJ, 1978.
Weinberg, Gerhard. *A World at Arms: A Global History of World War II*. New York 1994.

VIII

Topic 10

The End of Empire: Decolonization and the Third World

World War II wrought major transformations around the globe, especially in regions that had been held in the grip of European domination. Nationalist movements for independence had begun to develop in some of the European colonies of Africa and Asia as early as the beginning of the 20th century. With the disruption of the war, and the resulting military and financial weakness of the great powers, the European grip over their colonial possessions was loosened. Political independence for colonial peoples was the result not only of external forces, but of struggles for freedom. World War II had been waged in the cause of freedom from oppression and by 1945 Britain's new Labour government saw imperial domination as neither acceptable nor feasible. Involved in repairing the ravages of war and building a welfare state at home, it was not eager to invest resources in maintaining colonial possessions. India and Pakistan, the chief British colonies in Asia, became independent in 1947. Subsequent Conservative governments continued the process of decolonization, and most of Britain's West African territories were self-governing by 1960. In East Africa, however, resistance by white residents led to protracted negotiations. African rule was not achieved there until the mid-1970s. The major exception was the white minority government of South Africa, which declared its own independence and resisted both internal and international efforts to liberalize rule there.

Postwar French leaders were less willing to give up their empire. Bitter fighting between French troops and nationalist guerrillas continued in Indochina until 1954, and in Algeria, France's principal North African colony, until 1962. In both cases the French finally negotiated a withdrawal. The struggle over Algeria deeply split public opinion in France itself and produced considerable political upheaval.

The withdrawal of the European powers from the Middle East was accompanied by the founding of a new nation there, Israel. In 1947, the United Nations voted to divide Palestine (at the time a British mandate) into an Arab and a Jewish state. The subsequent history of the region has been dominated by fighting between Israel and its Arab neighbors, together with feuding among the Arab states themselves. The volatile situation was further complicated by the conflicting interests of the two superpowers—the United States and the Soviet Union—concerned to preserve their access to a region that contains about half of the world's oil supplies.

Elsewhere in Asia and Africa, former rulers struggled to maintain control. After several years of bloody fighting, the Dutch finally recognized Indonesia's independence in 1949. Alarmed by a series of riots in 1959, Belgium suddenly withdrew from the Congo, leaving a vacuum that plunged the region into a state of confusion threatening Western economic interests there. In spite of substantial guerrilla campaigning, the Portuguese colonies of southern Africa won their independence only in the mid-1970s, when Portugal's authoritarian rule at home was replaced by democratic government.

By the late 20th century, European colonial holdings were reduced to a handful of small territories. One of the first indicators of autonomous politics among developing countries came when a group of nations describing themselves as "nonaligned"—uncommitted, that is, to alliance with either the United States or the Soviet Union—joined together in a loose association. Their aim was to establish a basis for economic assistance on the part of the superpowers and other rich Western countries for the poorer countries of the world, many of which were former colonies.

The problems in providing European and U.S. aid to developing countries were formidable, and the results were mixed. Furthermore, the collapse of Communist regimes in Eastern Europe in the winter of 1989–1990, and the subsequent Western efforts to help economic reconstruction there, threatened to divert resources from other regions of the globe. Nevertheless, by the 1990s it was clearly in the interests of both the affluent and the poorer countries throughout the world to work together in raising living standards and creating stable economies.

THE LEGACY OF EMPIRE: COLONIES IN A CHANGING WORLD

The dismantlement of the European colonial empires in Asia and Africa was hastened by World War II, but long before the war, effective nationalist movements were developing in a number of countries.

Gandhi and Indian Nationalism

The Indian National Congress party, founded in the late 19th century (see Part VII, Topic 18), was led by Mohandas Gandhi (1869–1948), whose policy of nonviolent civil disobedience became an inspiration to liberation movements throughout the world. Born into a wealthy Hindu family, Gandhi studied law in London. He went to South Africa to practice, and discovered brutal discrimination there against Indian laborers who had been imported by the British. In seeking to devise a strategy that would enable weak victims to overcome their oppressors, he organized peaceful protest marches, and nonviolent resistance to police actions.

In 1915 Gandhi returned to India, where his emphasis on the spiritual values of nonviolence exerted a profound influence on sophisticated nationalist leaders and, more importantly, on the Hindu rural masses. His own austere lifestyle (he was known as the *Mahatma*, or saintly one) was combined with the organization of mass demonstrations, at which thousands of peaceful protestors surrounded government offices, or lay down on railway lines. Gandhi himself was frequently arrested, but time after time public indignation, exacerbated by the Mahatma's hunger strikes, forced the authorities to release him.

In 1935, as a result of the demonstrations, the British introduced a new constitution which extended the right to vote to 35 million people, and which provided a limited measure of Indian participation in government. Although Gandhi favored trying out the new system of government, more radical leaders, anxious to obtain complete independence, pressed for continued opposition to Britain. With the onset of World War II, and the refusal of the nationalists to support the British cause, Gandhi and others were arrested. In 1939, India found itself under British military rule and at war with the Axis through no choice of its own.

Although lacking a charismatic leader of the stature of Gandhi, nationalist movements elsewhere in Asia began to agitate for independence. In Indochina one of the chief organizers of the struggle against the French was Nguyen That Thanh (1890–1969), better known as "Ho Chi Minh," the name (meaning "He who enlightens") which he took in 1940. Like Gandhi,

Gandhi leading a protest march in 1930.

he was to play a crucial role in his country's liberation after the war. In response to popular demonstrations and rioting, the French introduced some reform measures, but made it clear that they intended to retain power. The Dutch authorities in their colony of Indonesia similarly tried to discourage nationalist uprisings, but their arrest of popular leaders only led to increased agitation.

The Vietnamese nationalist leader, Ho Chi Minh.

Africa Between the Wars

By contrast with their limited concessions to nationalist movements in Asia, the colonial powers in Africa showed few signs of relinquishing their grip. At the same time, however the capital investment that had marked the early years of the 20th century, most of which went to regions north of the Sahara, had almost completely faded. Europeans seeking prosperity abroad after World War I continued to make for North America rather than the African colonies.

In the face of increasing political neglect and economic decline, Africans in many parts of the continent began to form nationalist organizations to achieve independence. One of the first leaders to emerge in North Africa was Habib Bourguiba, one of the founders in 1934 of a liberation party seeking independence for the French Protectorate of Tunisia. Although the authorities imprisoned Bourguiba and banned his organization, his campaigning led to Tunisia's independence after World War II.

In the European colonies of West Africa, increasing numbers of Africans were frustrated by their continued exclusion from political participation in spite of their Western-style educations. In 1918, the West African National Congress was formed to fight for the creation of national parliaments in the British-held territories. These new bodies would replace the existing legislative councils, which generally consisted of British civil servants with a handful of African "advisers."

African leaders in the French colonies strove to advance the cause of black African nationalism by demonstrating the richness of the African cultural tradition. Leopold Senghor (1906–1989), who was to become Senegal's first president in 1960, used both poetry and prose to expound the idea of *negritude*, a version of socialism which incorporates black African values.

The efforts of Senghor and other African intellectuals to promote the intrinsic importance of black African culture were reinforced by the development of similar ideas in the United States and the West Indies. The American William E. B. Du Bois (1868–1963) helped to create the National Association for the Advancement of Colored People (NAACP) (1909). His advocacy of Pan-Africanism stressed the common destiny of American and African black people. Marcus Moziah Garvey (1887–1940), born in the British West Indies, founded the Universal Negro Improvement Association (UNIA) in 1914. Two years later, he went to the United States, where he started UNIA branches in Harlem (New York City) and other northern ghettos. Like Du Bois, he preached pride of race and black self-sufficiency, and planned a "Back to Africa" movement to establish a black-governed country in Africa.

Only in South Africa was there no overt sign of a developing nationalist movement. With the discovery of diamonds and gold in the 1870s and 1880s and the growth of mining operations (see Part VII, Topic 18), unskilled African laborers began to live in "shantytowns" on the outskirts of the large industrial centers. By comparison with white workers, the black laborers, ununionized and underpaid, endured unspeakable conditions. Nonetheless, dependent as they were on employment by white mine owners, they were able to accumulate enough money to buy the consumer goods manufactured and sold to them by white South Africans. Thus the industrial development of South Africa created a black urban proletariat politically and economically under the control of the white bourgeoisie.

The white inhabitants, made up of the descendants of British and Dutch settlers (the latter known as Boers), retained complete political control and economic power. By the policy called *apartheid* ("separateness"), legally enacted in 1948, this minority maintained strict racial segregation, with separate and inferior housing, education, and public services for nonwhites. The apparatus of a repressive police state enforced the dominance of the whites. Although those of Asian descent received limited political rights, the black majority remained disenfranchised.

In both Asia and Africa, the end of World War II in 1945 brought renewed demands for national independence. After the years of fighting, most European powers were in no condition to resist for long. Given the importance of reconstruction at home, taxpayers were unwilling to see large amounts of money diverted to support colonial empires. In any case, public opinion, convinced that the war had been fought in the name of freedom and liberation, was less sympathetic to the notion of imperialism. Nor, after the experience of two world wars, could Europeans seriously claim a right to rule on the grounds of moral superiority.

Both of the superpowers encouraged the process of decolonization. The United States favored the granting of self-determination to European colonies, while the Soviet Union (and, after 1948, the People's Republic of China) provided help to revolutionary nationalists in Africa and Asia. Once begun, the drive for independence gained rapid speed: in less than 20 years from the end of the war, almost all the European empires were gone.

THE DISSOLUTION OF THE BRITISH EMPIRE

The Labour government of postwar Britain, faced with the problems of reconstruction, and committed to implementing a massive program of domestic social welfare, was only too eager to avoid further conflict in India. One of the most divisive issues on the subcontinent was the rivalry between Hindus and Muslims, which led to violent rioting. The creation in 1947 of two independent states, a mainly Hindu India and a predominantly Muslim Pakistan, served only to exacerbate tensions. The following year, Gandhi's attempts to conciliate the two sides led to his assassination by a Hindu fanatic who resented his tolerance of Muslims.

British Decolonization in Africa

By 1945, most British politicians realized the necessity of preparing the populations of their colonies for independence. In introducing advances in health care, housing, and sanitation, colonial administrators aimed at social as well as economic improvements. Educational opportunities were also enlarged. As early as 1943, Britain had formulated a scheme to set up universities in the colonies. By contrast, other colonial powers showed less concern for their subjects. Belgian fears that educational advances could be destabilizing led them to invest only in primary and vocational schooling.

The first British colony in Africa to win independence was Ghana, formerly known as the Gold Coast, because of the early coastal trade in gold. In 1945, its American-educated nationalist leader, Kwame Nkrumah (1901–1972), formed a mass political movement with the slogan "Self-Government Now." After a decade of strikes and riots, the British yielded to the inevitable, and Ghana became independent in 1957.

The decolonization of other British West African possessions followed swiftly. Like many former colonies, Nigeria, which achieved independence in 1960, was subsequently beset by rivalries among its many tribal

Map 10.1 Contemporary Asia

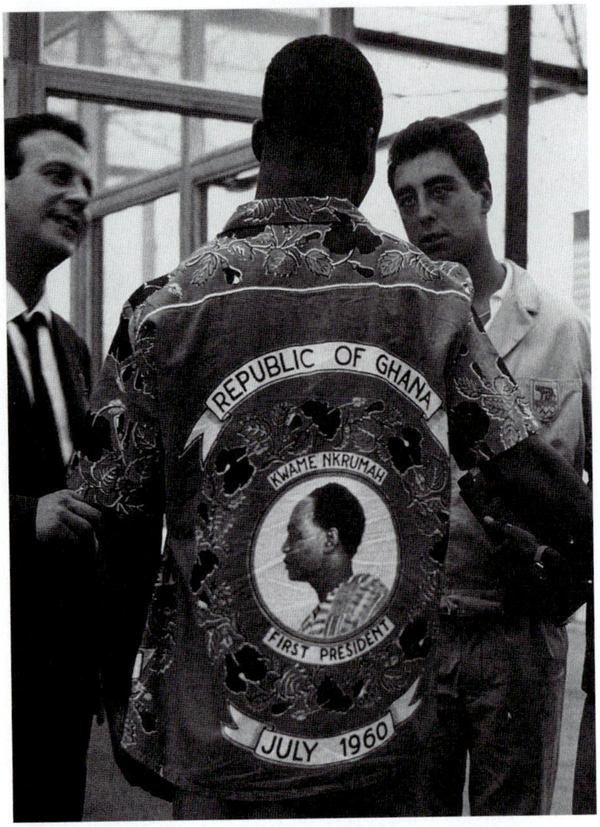

Ghanaian wearing a shirt printed with a portrait of Nkrumah, Ghana's president.

groups. Different cultures had evolved in the northern and southern regions of the country. The cultural disparity was compounded by both colonial rule and religious missionaries. In the north the Hausa had been converted to Islam by Mali traders in the 14th century, while the southern and coastal Ibos—Christians and animists—were affected by the fact that their territory contained Nigeria's colonial capital, Lagos. More involved with the British colonial administration, the Ibos were in general better educated and more active in their new country's government. In 1967, tribal hostilities led the Ibos east of the Niger River to secede as the Republic of Biafra. Only in 1970, after bitter fighting, did the central government manage to reincorporate the rebel province into the Nigerian state.

In the British colonies of East Africa, resistance by white settlers complicated the granting of independence. In 1965, as the tide of nationalism swept through Africa, the white government of Southern Rhodesia refused to grant black majority rule, and illegally issued a "unilateral declaration of independence" from British control. Only in 1980, after years of conflict, international pressure, and eventually negotiation, did the country become legally independent, under the name Zimbabwe.

In Kenya, the final years of British rule were marked by the rise of the Mau Mau, a secret society made up of members of the dominant Kikuyu tribe. The aim of the Mau Mau was to drive out the British and all other white settlers, and set up an independent Kenya. After more than a decade of terrorist activity, the movement's aims were undermined by peaceful acquisition of independence. In 1960 Kenya became self-governing, under the leadership of Jomo Kenyatta (1893?–1978).

The Commonwealth

As Britain's possessions obtained their independence, the vast majority chose to retain a link with their former rulers by joining the Commonwealth of Nations. This free association operates without any constitution or specific treaty. Members are linked by common economic and cultural interests and, more broadly, by a shared heritage that includes the English language; they all recognize the British sovereign as symbolic head of the Commonwealth. Nations involved range in size from India (population 800 million) to the tiny Pacific kingdom of Tonga (population 95,000). Commonwealth prime ministers and leaders meet at regular intervals. Their conferences discuss issues of mutual concern, and sometimes succeed in bringing moral pressure to bear as a means of settling differences.

The most intractable problem facing the Commonwealth was political repression in South Africa. Black resistance to *apartheid* was led by the

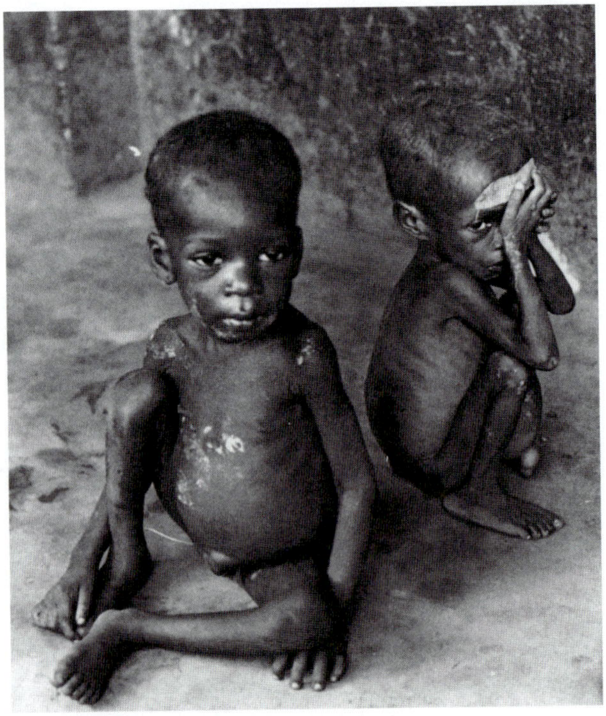

Starving children in Biafra, 1970.

African National Congress (ANC), which was formed in 1912. Throughout the 1950s, the ANC embraced both moderates and radicals, including Marxists, and pursued both political and terrorist tactics, organizing strikes and demonstrations against the government that culminated in the massacres by the police at Sharpeville in 1960. The authorities continued to refuse any form of negotiation with the ANC. They outlawed it and arrested its leader, Nelson Mandela (born 1918).

South Africa withdrew from the Commonwealth in 1961 over criticism of its apartheid policies. Over the years, various commissions of Commonwealth statesmen and resolutions passed at conferences tried to induce the South African government to dismantle its police state and introduce a democratic system of government. A program of economic sanctions was introduced, backed by the European Economic Community and the United States.

Bowing to continual international pressures, the South African government began a fitful dismantling of apartheid. Prime Minister F. W. de Klerk (born 1936), who came to power in 1989, began a new policy of tentative negotiation with the ANC and released Nelson Mandela, leader of the African National Congress, from prison. Economic sanctions by the Commonwealth, the European Community, and the United States seemed to play some part in encouraging the South African government to open the subsequent talks with black leaders. Tribal and racial violence persisted, however, allowing the authorities to maintain their authoritarian controls. Nevertheless, by 1991 most of the laws sustaining apartheid had been repealed, and in April 1994 Mandela was elected president of South Africa.

Last Vestiges of Empire

By the early 1980s, little remained of the British Empire except a few scattered possessions, and nostalgic memories. In 1982, one of these last British holdings, the Falkland Islands in the South Atlantic, served to demonstrate the continuing allure of British imperial power. At the same time the Falkland crisis illustrated the use by the Argentine regime of nationalism and expansionism as a means of bolstering its unpopular dictatorship—a practice not uncommon in the Third World.

When Argentina's military government invaded and conquered the territory (it lies about 500 miles off the Argentine coast), renaming the islands the Malvinas, Conservative Prime Minister Margaret Thatcher sent British troops to drive out the Argentine forces and retake them. Her success in reasserting British rule over the barren, sparsely populated islands won her government massive popular approval. Her opponents claimed that the Falklands War was a cynical diversion, to distract public opinion from problems at home. At all events, the mood of patriotism the war stirred up, enthusiastically endorsed by the press, was in the best—or worst—19th-century tradition.

By the early 1990s, the last British holding of any importance was Hong Kong, a Crown Colony on the South China coast. Hong Kong had been acquired during the 19th century, on terms which foresaw its return to Chinese rule in 1997. A major financial center, and one of the world's busiest ports, Hong Kong is a free trade area, while relying heavily on China for water and food supplies. In 1984 Britain agreed to honor the original agreement and hand the territory over to China in 1997, on condition that it would remain capitalist for 50 years and have a high degree of autonomy. In 1988, the first draft of the Chinese Basic Law for Hong Kong was made public; it suggested that China felt free to interpret "autonomy" as it saw fit. The early 1990s saw increasing waves of business and professional people leaving the colony for Australia, Canada, and the United States. Meanwhile the British government wrestled with the problems, moral as well as practical, involved in denying subjects of Hong Kong (who were technically British) admission to Britain. At midnight on June 30, 1997, Hong Kong returned to China and HMS *Britannia* sailed out of its harbor carrying on board its last British governor, Chris Patten.

THE FRENCH IN INDOCHINA AND AFRICA: THE AGONY OF WITHDRAWAL

Like the British government, postwar French leaders were forced to adjust their imperial ambitions in the light of the calamitous state of the economy. In the hope of maintaining some measure of control over their colonies, in 1946 France created a federation known as the French Union. Some of its members, however, successfully demanded their independence: Syria in 1946, Morocco and Tunisia in 1956. By 1958 the Union had become the French Community, a loose alliance of France itself, its few remaining possessions, and those African nations which formed French Equatorial and West Africa.

Yet in two places—Indochina and Algeria—French pride in imperial rule, coupled with a desire to efface memories of their disastrous defeat by the Germans in 1940, led to prolonged and bitter conflict. Both former colonies obtained their independence only after struggles that were fought not just on the field but in French public opinion.

Significant Dates

Decolonization After World War II

1946	France creates French Union
1947	Partition of India and Pakistan
1948	UN votes to divide Palestine into Jewish and Arab states
1949	Indonesia becomes independent
1954	French withdraw from Vietnam
1955	First conference of nonaligned nations at Bandung
1956	Tunisia becomes independent
1957	Ghana first West African state to become independent
1960	Nigeria and Kenya become independent
1961	South Africa withdraws from Commonwealth
1965	Rhodesia declares unilateral independence
1967	Secession of Biafra
1975	United States withdraws from Vietnam
1978	Camp David accords
1982	Falklands War
1987	Palestinian Intifada begins
1991	Gulf War
1994	Mandela elected president of South Africa
1997	Hong Kong returned to China

The Battle for Indochina

French suppression of independence movements in Vietnam, Laos, and Cambodia was encouraged by the United States, fearful of the spread of communist regimes in Southeast Asia. During World War II, Ho Chi Minh, the founder of the Vietnamese Communist party, had led the resistance to Japanese occupying forces. In 1945 he declared his country a republic, only to see it reclaimed by the French the following year. From 1946 to 1954 the French waged an increasingly bloody and hopeless war against Ho Chi Minh's Vietminh guerrilla forces whose activities were aided by the support they received from the peasantry. The increasing casualties provoked growing protests at home. At the Battle of Dien Bien Phu in 1954, the French Army, besieged for 55 days, lost 15,000 troops to the Vietminh.

Later the same year, at an international conference convened in Geneva, the French formally withdrew from Vietnam. It was agreed to divide Vietnam on a temporary basis: the Vietminh were to take the north, while Vietnamese supporters of the French were to move to the south. Within two years free elections would be held, and the country reunited. The United States refused to sign the Geneva accords, and over the next few years discouraged any attempt at reunification, creating a South Vietnamese state with its own government. The claim that this "independent" state was under attack by equally "independent" North Vietnam served to justify increasing American intervention, leading to the Vietnam War. Only in 1975 did the last U.S. troops leave Saigon, and the following year a unified republic was proclaimed.

Khrushchev, Mao Tse-Tung, and Ho Chi Minh, 1959.

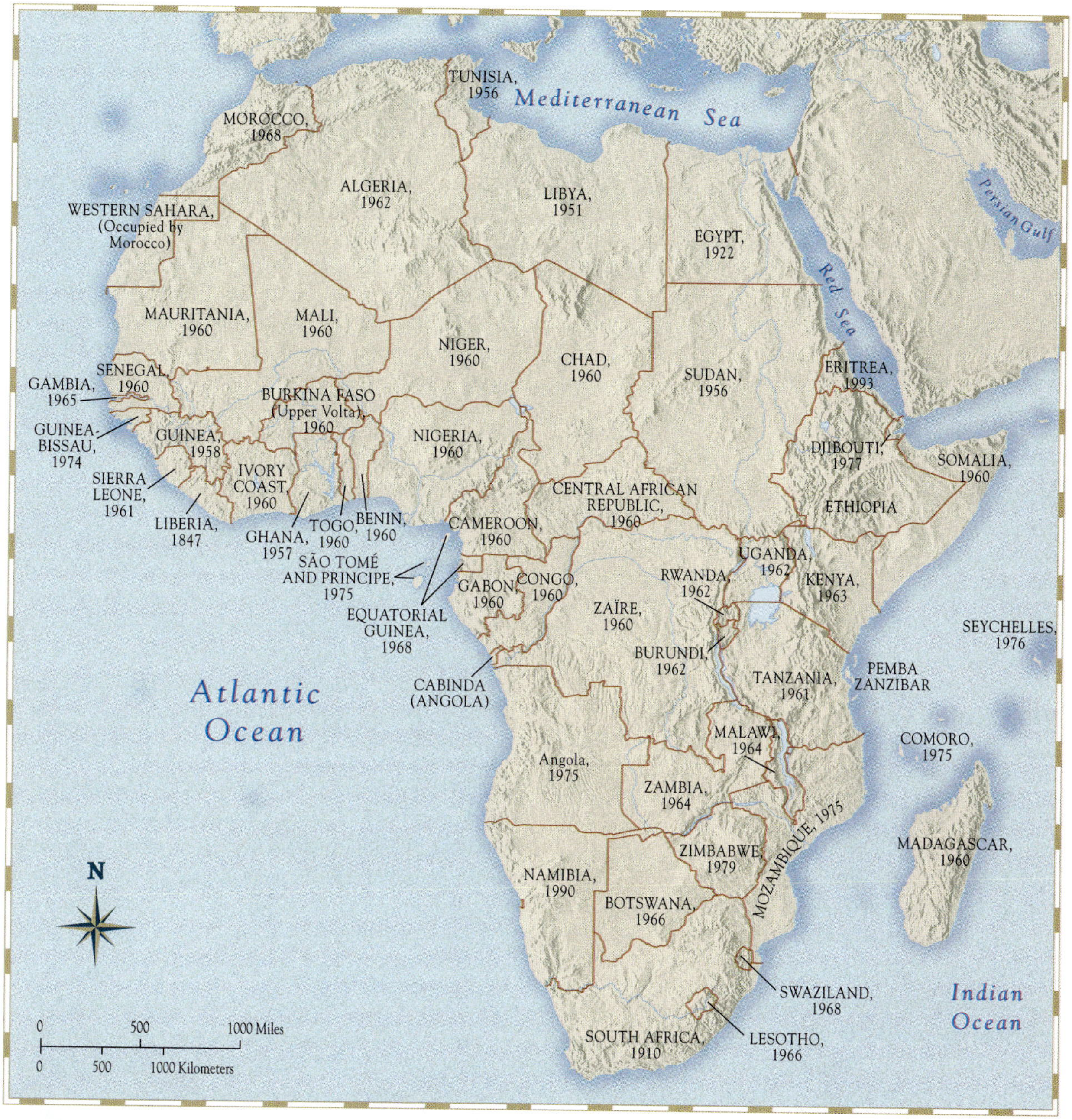

Map 10.2 Independent Africa

The French Settlers and Algeria

With the rest of their former empire melting away, the French determination to hold on to their most important North African colony, Algeria, became increasingly grim. Nor was the issue only one of French national pride. The longstanding community of French residents in Algeria, faced with the possibility of losing their rights and property, became more vocal in urging the government to maintain French rule. Meanwhile, under the impact of growing terrorist and guerrilla attacks, French troops and their commanders resorted to violent countermeasures.

Back home in France, as governments fell over the "Algerian question," intellectuals and socialists furiously protested army brutalities, and called for France to leave Algeria to the Algerians. By 1958, tension between army officers and the indecisive authorities was so high that a group of soldiers staged an insurgency and seized control of Algeria. Both government and rebels turned in desperation to Charles de Gaulle (see Part VIII, Topics 9 and 11). The French National Assembly invested him with extraordinary powers as president for a period of six months (in fact he remained France's leader for ten years).

Although the insurgents believed that the former general would be sympathetic to their revolt, de Gaulle moved quietly to dissolve the rebellion, and began to promote the cause of Algerian self-determination. In January 1961, a referendum in its favor was approved by some 75 percent of French voters. Those army elements most implacably opposed to Algerian independence went undercover in the Secret Army Organization (OAS), and staged a series of terrorist attacks both in Algeria and in France itself. By 1962, however, de Gaulle's firmness put an end to the OAS, and Algeria was declared independent.

ISRAEL AND THE MIDDLE EAST

The Arab states of North Africa and the Middle East, many of which achieved independence after World War II, demonstrated a wide range of political perspectives and systems of government. Yet one characteristic united virtually all of them: implacable opposition to the founding and continued existence of the state of Israel.

The Founding of Israel

The Zionist movement was founded in the 19th century (see Part VII, Topic 16), and grew rapidly after World War I. In the 1930s, increasing numbers of European Jews sought to escape the horrors of persecution by emigrating to Palestine, where they swelled the population of the *Yishuv,* as the Jewish community was called, to almost half a million—a third of the overall population of Palestine. The British, under whose rule the League of Nations had placed Palestine, resisted the settlement of Jewish immigrants there, as did the surrounding Arab nations. After World War II, mounting violence, and terrorist attacks by both Arabs and Jewish settlers, led in 1947 to a United Nations decision to divide Palestine into separate Jewish and Arab states of roughly the same size. Later that year, the British withdrew. Against a mounting swell of Arab hostility, in May 1948 the Jewish settlers proclaimed the existence of the State of Israel. The new nation's first task was to beat off an attack mounted by the surrounding Arab countries—Egypt, Iraq, Jordan, Lebanon, and Syria—which had refused to accept the United Nations decision. The Israelis' successful campaign, which left them in control of most of Palestine, ensured the survival of their state. At the same time, however, it created the problem which embittered future Arab-Israeli relations and lay at the heart of the unrest in the Middle East: the fate of the Arab refugees displaced by Israel's victory.

Refugee settlements were established, under United Nations administration, in southern Lebanon, on the West Bank of the river Jordan, and in the Gaza Strip. Over the following decades these camps continued to pose political and social problems, while also proving to be the breeding ground for Palestinian guerrilla and terrorist groups. Tension rose further when, in the Six-Day War of 1967, Israel won control of the West Bank and Gaza Strip territories, and thus assumed direct administration of the refugee settlements. In December 1987, frustrated by the lack of progress on the issue of Palestinian independence, and angered by Israeli plans for development on the West Bank territory, Palestinian Arabs launched an uprising, known as the *Intifada,* which won their case considerable attention in Europe and the United States.

Israeli soldiers in the Negev Desert, 1948.

The Camp David peace accord: Israeli Prime Minister Menachem Begin, Egyptian President Anwar Sadat, and U.S. President Jimmy Carter.

Israel and Her Neighbors

The general pattern of unremitting hostility toward Israel on the part of her Arab neighbors, exemplified by another Arab-Israeli war in 1972, was broken in 1977, when the Egyptian president, Anwar Sadat (1918–1981), traveled to Israel and subsequently succeeded, with the help of U.S. President Jimmy Carter, in negotiating an Egyptian-Israeli peace treaty; the agreement, signed in 1978, became known as the Camp David Accords. Apart from a brief reduction of tension, and the return to Egypt of some of the territory captured in 1967, the agreement did little to produce any lasting improvement in Middle East affairs.

Relations with Lebanon, Israel's neighbor to the north, were further complicated by the fact that Palestinian guerrilla groups, notably the Palestinian Liberation Organization (PLO), were using the country as a base. In 1982, Israeli forces invaded southern Lebanon and succeeded in driving the guerrillas out. The result, however, was to produce even greater conflict in Lebanon, a country already racked by religious and political civil war. Multinational attempts at peace-keeping operations, including the sending of French, Italian, and Syrian troops, as well as U.S. Marines, proved fruitless; the international forces withdrew in 1984, and most of the Israeli troops were gone by 1985.

With almost 50 years behind it, Israel's future remained overshadowed by two apparently irresolvable issues: the refusal of most Arabs to recognize the country's right to exist, and Israel's own refusal, on security grounds, to surrender territory won in 1967. In 1988, Yasir Arafat (born 1929), the leader of the PLO, declared that his organization accepted the United Nations resolutions recognizing the legitimacy of Israel; no other Arab leaders followed, and the Israelis dismissed the declaration as a propaganda move. As for territorial concessions, in the late 1980s Israel began moving in the reverse direction, by extending settlements into the West Bank area. With the liberalization of the Soviet Union in the late 1980s, and the revolutions of 1989 in Eastern Europe, Arab spokesmen began to voice fears that waves of Russian and other Jewish immigrants would prove permanent occupants for these new settlements.

Israel's problems were compounded by domestic political divisions. In the elections of 1988, support for the two chief political parties, Labour and Likud, was almost equally divided. The right-wing Likud party managed to put together a government which included support from conservative religious forces, making the prospects of compromise even more remote.

The upheaval of the Gulf War of early 1991, fought under UN auspices to free Kuwait after Iraq had occupied it in August 1990, produced some significant shifts in a situation that had seemed deadlocked for a generation. Hard-line Arab states such as Saudi Arabia and Syria seemed on the verge of following Egypt's earlier lead and recognizing Israel, while Israeli restraint in not responding to Iraq's missile attacks won general approval. Furthermore, American influence in the Middle East was sufficiently strong to allow the United States to play a significant role in working toward a settlement of the Palestinian question. Yet the problem of who would represent the Palestinians in any negotiations leading to such a settlement remained crucial. The PLO had backed Iraq in the conflict, and as a result it lost many of its supporters, not least among the Arab countries that had supported the mission to free Kuwait. In the confusion that followed the Gulf War, however, the Palestinians seemed bereft of any other spokesmen. Secret negotiations in Oslo led to a public reconciliation in 1993 between Labour Prime Minister Yitzhak Rabin and Yasir Arafat, but Rabin's subsequent assassination and the return of the Likud party to power seemed bound to set back progress toward peace.

BELGIUM, THE NETHERLANDS, AND PORTUGAL: END OF EMPIRE

The dismantling of the British and French empires presented a multitude of problems, but most political leaders recognized the irresistible force of nationalism. Other imperial powers were less willing to relinquish their possessions. The Dutch colony of Indonesia was occupied by the Japanese during World War II. At the end of the war, the Indonesian nationalist leader Sukarno (1901–1970) declared his country a republic. When the Dutch tried to reconquer it, they encountered bitter resistance. By 1949, they were forced to withdraw and recognize Indonesia's independence.

Belgium's departure from the Congo was equally violent and even more precipitate. In 1959, demonstrations there in favor of independence developed into violent riots. Within a year the Belgians were gone. The result was chaos. Whereas elsewhere in Africa the British and French had tried to prepare their colonies for independence, the Belgians had limited the education of their subjects, and prevented any African participation in political affairs. The elections held in May 1960, a month before the Belgian withdrawal, were the first ever held in the country. There were no Congolese doctors or army officers, and the only teachers were at the primary school level. The number of African university graduates living in the country totaled 16.

Belgian financial interests assumed that, in the light of such complete inexperience, the citizens of the new Republic of the Congo would leave their old colonial masters in control. Instead the army mutinied; in the growing confusion the mineral-rich province of Katanga broke away from the rest of the country, encouraged to do so by Belgian investors. The Katangese rebellion ended in 1962, but the country returned to stability only in 1965, when Joseph Mobutu (1930–1997; later took the name Mobutu Sese Seko) led an army coup.

Mobutu's rule led to hopes for reform, which were at first fulfilled. The mining production of minerals increased, and the educational system improved. In 1971 Mobutu changed the country's name to Zaire, one of the names for the Congo River, as a symbol of the new spirit of "Africanness." Yet general poverty remained widespread; in 1988, the per capita annual income was $180, 10 percent of that in 1960, and the eighth lowest in the world—in spite of Zaire's considerable natural resources. Meanwhile, the ruling class became notorious for its corruption, and Mobutu himself amassed a fortune estimated at between $3 and $5 billion. The country's economic survival was assured only by massive support from Europe, the United States, and international financial agencies, anxious not to lose access to valuable mineral resources. Only in 1997 was Mobutu finally driven from power by an army led by one of his longtime opponents, Laurent Kabila. Mobutu himself, abandoned by his former Western protectors, died shortly after in exile.

No European country held on to its colonies longer than Portugal. Like the Belgians, the Portuguese exploited their natural assets, while doing nothing to provide lasting political or economic stability. Only a political revolution at home, which ended 40 years of dictatorship, finally brought independence to Portugal's African colonies—Guinea-Bissau in 1974, and Angola and Mozambique in 1975. The lack of any preparation for nationhood led to bitter civil war in the latter two, exacerbated by interference by South Africa.

EUROPE AND THE THIRD WORLD

With the end of European colonial power, many of the new nations in the Third World (the poorer, developing countries of Africa and Asia) faced the task of building politically viable systems against a background of economic instability and social injustice. In response to this need for assistance, Western governments created a number of international agencies whose task was to help developing nations. The International Monetary Fund (IMF), an organization affiliated with the United Nations, began operations in 1947. Led by the "Group of Ten" (Britain, France, West Germany, Italy, Belgium, the Netherlands, Sweden, Japan, Canada, and the United States), its purpose was to provide international credit and stabilize exchange rates. The World Bank, a specialized agency of the United Nations, was established to perform similar functions.

The results of massive loans by richer, industrialized Western nations to the Third World were mixed. The steep rise in oil prices after 1973 prompted heavy borrowing. By the early 1980s, Third World debts amounted to over $400 billion. When rising interest rates combined with inflation to produce a general worldwide recession, many countries found themselves unable to repay even the interest on their loans, let alone the principal. The first government temporarily to suspend payments was Mexico, and others soon followed. Banks and international agencies were forced to renegotiate loans, and impose tough (and often highly unpopular) conditions before extending further credit. The economic hardship these measures created proved dangerously destabilizing in many Third World coun-

Leaders of the nonaligned movement: Egyptian President Gamal Abdel Nasser, Indian Prime Minister Jawaharlal Nehru, and Yugoslav President Josip Broz Tito (1956).

tries. Their difficulties increased in the late 1980s and early 1990s, when the newly democratic countries of Eastern Europe attracted Western capital and investment away from Africa, Asia, and Latin America.

Under the threat of serious global economic crisis, a number of international movements developed. The major Western nations began in the 1970s to hold regular meetings on financial and trade problems. The intention was to coordinate policy on issues such as interest rates and export regulations. Differences between the group's members prevented the agreement on a common policy of economic assistance to developing countries, however, and international development remained largely controlled by banks and private corporations.

The Nonaligned Movement

In the 1950s and 1960s, in response to what they regarded as the inadequate response of Western governments, Third World nations created their own organizations. In 1955, at a conference in Bandung, Indonesia, leaders of countries claiming to belong neither to the Western nor the Soviet bloc met to proclaim their independence. Among the governments represented were those of Egypt, Yugoslavia (Tito had broken with Moscow), and India. The group met intermittently over the following years. In 1960, the Organization of Petroleum Exporting Countries (OPEC) was formed. A more formal alliance, the "Group of 77," was born in 1964, as the result of the United Nations Conference on Trade and Development (UNCTAD), held at Geneva. The organization, which eventually acquired over 100 members, represented the interests of nonaligned countries. When oil prices rose steeply in 1973 as a result of an OPEC agreement, a special session of the United Nations General Assembly was held at which Third World countries, coordinated by the Group of 77, succeeded in passing two resolutions. The first called for a New International Economic Order (NIEO), whereby all nations would be equal; the second called for the transfer of Western technology to poorer countries, and the end of Western exploitation.

In further meetings held in the 1970s and 1980s, the economic imbalance between the prosperous Northern Hemisphere and poorer Southern countries became the subject of intense discussion. A few actual decisions were made: by the Lome Convention of 1975, 46 former European colonies could export their products to the European Community free of tariffs. On the whole, however, prosperous Western nations were unwilling to surrender the advantages of cheap labor and natural resources provided by Third World countries, or to share their own wealth.

At the end of World War II, European domination of world affairs seemed over. Quite apart from the moral responsibility for two global conflicts, the European nations had lost the economic capacity to maintain their prewar power. Many of them—Germany, Italy, France—were faced with rebuilding workable political systems. All, even the most stubborn, eventually withdrew from their imperial possessions.

For most of the new nations born in Africa, the Middle East, and Asia, the euphoria of independence was followed by the grinding problems of political and economic reality. Many of them had been deliberately left unprepared for self-government. For all the talk, furthermore, there was little concerted economic assistance from their former rulers. Relations between the richer countries and the Third World were further complicated by the growing power of the big multinational corporations, which often moved into developing countries as Western governments moved out. The multinationals frequently operated on financial assets greater than the national budgets of the countries in which they set up factories; they exploited natural and labor resources, while being concerned almost exclusively with profit. Not surprisingly their activities drew considerable resentment.

For the Europeans themselves, however, the loss of empire provided the chance to concentrate on rebuilding at home. The economic chaos of the immediate postwar years gave way to an economic rebirth that was slowed only by the oil crisis of the 1970s. By the 1990s, political tensions were lowered by the collapse of Communist regimes in Eastern Europe, and economic expectations raised by the prospect of vast new markets developing there. With its emergence as an economic power potentially as great as the United States or Japan, Europe was in a position to provide vitally needed aid to its former colonies.

Questions for Further Study

1. What part did the United States and the Soviet Union play in the process of decolonization?
2. How did the European powers differ in their handling of independence movements? How far were they motivated by political factors, and how far by economic ones?
3. To what extent have international organizations—the UN, the World Bank, OPEC, the Nonaligned Movement—been able to provide help to developing nations? What are the future prospects?

Suggestions for Further Reading

Adu Boahen, A. *African Perspectives on Colonialism.* Baltimore, MD, 1989.

Davidson, B. *Modern Africa.* London, 1984.

Herring, G. C. *America's Longest War: The United States and Vietnam, 1950–1975.* New York, 1986.

Lockman, Z., and J. Beinin, eds. *Intifada.* Boston, 1989.

Richards, A., and J. Waterbury. *A Political Economy of the Middle East.* Boulder, CO, 1989.

Sampson, A. *Black and Gold.* New York, 1987.

Wolpert, S. *Roots of Confrontation in South Asia.* New York, 1982.

VIII

Topic 11

The Politics of Stability in Western Europe

Faced with the devastation created by World War II, the nations of Western Europe strove to reconstruct political and economic institutions, and—literally—to rebuild cities and industries. With the old guard of European statesmen discredited by the failures of the 1930s, many of the political and financial leaders who rose to power represented a new generation.

The task of reconstruction was complicated in many countries by the need to reject the past as decisively as possible. In Germany, Italy, and Vichy France, an entire ruling class had to be replaced and, in some cases, tried for its complicity in Fascist and Nazi crimes. New, or in some cases renewed, political parties found themselves in unlikely coalitions: in Belgium, France, and Italy the first postwar governments included Communists, Socialists, and liberal Christian Democrats. In Britain, despite the personal popularity of Winston Churchill, his Conservatives lost decisively to the Labour party.

On the international scene, growing tensions between the Soviet Union and the United States polarized European loyalties, and the Cold War came to dominate political life. After the Berlin crisis of 1948–1949, Western Europe and the United States formalized their alliance in the North Atlantic Treaty Organization (NATO), signed in 1949. Among the provisions was the stationing of U.S. troops both in West Germany and elsewhere in Western Europe.

In part to build Western Europe's ability to withstand Communist pressures, and in part to make possible its economic recovery, the United States launched the European Recovery Program, generally known as the "Marshall Plan," which operated between 1947 and 1952. This provided massive financial aid to 17 Western European countries.

In Britain, the postwar Labour government established a welfare state (assistance for the needy), expanding social services and nationalizing key industries. Subsequent Conservative governments continued Labour's social policies, and took Britain into the Common Market. After an economic boom in the early 1960s, chronic inflation and strained labor relations undermined British industrial competitiveness, and brought down successive Conservative and Labour governments. When the Conservative leader Margaret Thatcher became prime minister in 1979, she began to dismantle aspects of the welfare state, to check the power of the unions, and to create a free market economy.

The French Fourth Republic, which lasted from 1946 to 1958, was marked by political instability. It was replaced by the strongly presidential Fifth Republic, created by Charles de Gaulle; the former general left retirement to lead his country for the following decade. Conservative in domestic policies, De Gaulle encouraged an independent French line in foreign affairs, which involved loosening ties with the United States; he also negotiated the French withdrawal from Algeria. De Gaulle resigned in 1969. After another decade of conservative government, in 1981 François Mitterand, a Socialist, was elected president. Apart from the period between 1986 and 1988, the Socialists maintained a majority in Parliament throughout the 1980s.

At the end of the war, the Allies divided Germany into four zones of occupation. In 1949 three of these became the German Federal Republic, and the fourth the German Democratic Republic. Berlin, the former capital of Germany, lay in the Soviet zone but was divided between the Soviets and the other Allies. West Germany's postwar boom, the so-called "Economic Miracle," created under the leadership of the Christian Democrat Konrad Adenauer, saw the country become Europe's leading economic and industrial power. Eventual reunification of the two Germanies remained a long-term West German goal. With the collapse of the East German communist regime in 1989, the dream became a reality. Economic union in the summer of 1990 was the first stage in the creation of a newly united Germany, formally proclaimed in October 1990.

Given its lack of natural resources, Italy's postwar reconstruction was as impressive as Germany's. Under a new republican constitution, introduced in 1948, a series of coalition governments (virtually all of them dominated by the Christian Democrats) sought political stability, while private management developed Italian industry along modern lines. Apart from the deep south, living standards vastly improved. As a founding member of the Common Market, Italy benefited from European economic initiatives.

THE NEW GENERATION IN POWER

The reconstruction of postwar Europe began under the most daunting of conditions. Through a continent whose chief cities were scarred by bomb devastation, there streamed millions of refugees: the former occupants of the Nazi concentration camps, people displaced by wartime action, increasing numbers fleeing from Soviet-occupied eastern Europe. Food supplies were woefully inadequate. The destruction of war had created havoc in rail and road transport. Inflation and economic chaos made cigarettes the most stable currency for buying necessities—when goods were available.

Behind the difficulties of day-to-day survival lay other, more general fears. Already by the last year of the war the Grand Alliance was under a strain, and as the Soviet Union moved toward taking over Eastern Europe, the shadows of the coming Cold War began to close in. To make matters worse, the possibility of renewed conflict threatened horrors even greater than those of the recent past. In the new age of the atom bomb a third world war, played out once again on the battlefields of Europe, might well be the end of the Continent.

A decade or so later, much of Western Europe's industry was more productive than ever. In West Germany and Italy, democratic governments replaced the dictatorships of the years between the wars. British, French, and Belgian transport systems were reconstructed. In most West European countries, more people led more prosperous and comfortable lives than ever before.

One of the paths to solving Europe's problems proved to be treating them, in fact, as broad European issues rather than simply national concerns. Beginning in the early 1950s, national leaders began to work toward European collaboration and cooperation, at least in economic matters (see Part VIII, Topic 15). Here we are concerned with the internal affairs of individual European countries.

New Leaders

Each country faced its own particular set of issues, but many shared certain broad trends. Among the most significant of these was a major change of leadership, both in politics and in other aspects of public life—business, the law, education. For most of continental Europe, politicians, judges, administrators were irrevocably tainted by their wartime actions and collaboration. There were practical limitations to the extent to which it was possible totally to remake society. The Nuremberg Trials of 1945–1949 tried to establish as a principle of international law the fact that individuals are responsible for their actions, but the ordinary business of daily life had to continue. Many card-carrying Nazis and Fascists lost their positions, or even their lives, but many others quietly transferred their allegiances. At the same time, inconvenient aspects of recent history were buried or forgotten. Until 1983, French school textbooks made no mention of the Vichy collaborationist government.

With the coming of peace, those who had been active in Resistance movements, or in fighting against the Axis, came forward to play a part in shaping the freedom they had fought to save. Many of this new generation of leaders came from the parties of the left. Communists served in the immediate postwar governments of France, Belgium, and Italy. Socialists reinforced their position in the Scandinavian countries. In Britain, the election of 1945 brought a socialist government to office. Britain's wartime government had been a coalition one, and the Conservative leader, Winston Churchill, was a national hero. Nonetheless prewar Conservative leaders were seen as responsible for not having prevented the outbreak of war, and for having left the country so unprepared.

The result of the perceptible shift to the left was a new emphasis on technical and leadership skills. The last traces of aristocratic power disappeared from political life and the business world. Noble birth did not prevent a career in public life, but it certainly ceased to guarantee one. At least one British politician gave up his hereditary title rather than abandon his seat in the House of Commons. The doings of Europe's aristocracy—marriages in Monaco or Westminster Abbey—retained their glamour and fascination for many, but almost exclusively as a kind of branch of the entertainment industry.

Efforts to remove the old business families proved less successful. After the war, the head of the leading German armaments producer, Alfred Krupp (1907–1967), spent three years in jail for war crimes, but although the company was reorganized, it still retained most of its original holdings. Nonetheless, in the business world as in politics, expertise in engineering or economics became more important than family connections.

Konrad Adenauer and Charles de Gaulle, 1963.

Thus, as Europe faced the difficult problems involved in reconstruction, leadership passed to an increasingly broad-based and highly qualified "meritocracy." Most of the new generation accepted a more limited role for their own country and for Europe in international affairs. The only European leader who continued to sound the note of national pride was De Gaulle, one of the few survivors of an earlier generation.

THE POLITICS OF RECONSTRUCTION

The immediate task of postwar governments was a double one: to restore democratic institutions and to reconstruct shattered economies. Following Britain's lead, many countries introduced welfare state programs, which aimed at improving the lives of their less affluent citizens.

The Welfare State

Although a few social welfare programs had been launched in the late 19th century, and then expanded

Prefabricated housing under construction in Bedforshire, 1965.

during the Great Depression, the notion of a complete welfare state did not become common until after World War II. In Britain, the Labour government of 1945 to 1951, led by Clement Attlee (1883–1967), passed legislation to provide virtually free medical care to all, and to expand unemployment insurance and educational opportunities. In an attempt to put basic facilities under the control of all citizens, Labour nationalized the steel and mining industries, and the railways.

By the 1950s, most other Western European nations had introduced similar schemes. Subsidies for housing, financial support for child raising, the provision of education beyond the primary level, all improved the opportunities for poorer citizens. Measures such as these, together with increasing government control of industry, enlarged the power of the state. To offset this, many countries set up "worker councils," groups of workers elected to discuss with management various aspects of working conditions.

Political Parties

European political life after the war was characterized by the development of democratic multiparty systems, in which government generally alternated between two main parties. The chief exceptions were Spain and Portugal, where dictatorships established well before World War II remained in place. Most politicians avoided extremes. The horrors of Fascism and Nazism had completely discredited the radical right. A small neo-Fascist party remained active in Italy, although it was regarded as "outside the constitutional arc" (not constitutionally legitimate) by the other political forces. Otherwise, apart from a few fanatical terrorist groups, extreme right-wing politics was unrepresented in the decades immediately following the war. By the 1980s, an extremist party began to collect some support in France, campaigning principally on the issue of immigration restrictions. All official conservative parties were fully committed to maintaining democratic government, and rarely dismantled welfare legislation introduced by socialist predecessors. The most notable exception to the latter characteristic was Thatcher's government in Britain in the 1980s.

On the left, no respectable communist or socialist movement in Western Europe publicly advocated extreme views in theory, or tried to put them into practice when in power. Communists never achieved control of national governments, but where they won administration of a city or region they proved no more doctrinaire—and no more or less efficient—than their opponents. The socialists who came to power showed the same concern for individual liberties and the democratic process as their conservative rivals. Extreme differences of ideology and opinion still existed, but no political leader posed a radical challenge to the prevailing system, as Hitler, Mussolini, or Stalin had done.

THE UNITED STATES IN EUROPE

The international background against which the process of European renewal began to unfold was dominated by growing tension between the world's two superpowers and former allies—the United States and the Soviet Union. In the last year of the war, while the Allies began to make plans for the future of Europe, Stalin took advantage of the reigning confusion to move Soviet troops into the chief Eastern European countries. By 1947, pro-Soviet regimes were firmly installed in Bulgaria, Czechoslovakia, Hungary, Poland, and Romania. The Baltic states of Estonia, Latvia, and Lithuania remained under Soviet rule, incorporated into the Soviet Union. In 1945, when the Allies had divided Germany into four zones, the most eastern zone came under Russian occupation. Berlin, the former capital of Germany, lay in the Soviet zone but was divided between them and the other Allies.

If Stalin were planning further aggressive expansion, the "Eastern Bloc" he had created would provide an effective base. At the same time he built a psychological division between two Europes, one free and democratic, the other repressed. The "Iron Curtain," a memorable phrase of Winston Churchill's, left both sides in mutual fear and incomprehension. The nations most likely to be affected by Soviet aggression were those of Western Europe, in particular the western zones of Germany. Yet the Allies had disarmed the Germans at the end of the war, and in any case no European state was in a condition to confront Stalin.

The Marshall Plan

This vacuum was filled by the United States. Regimes that seemed under threat from the Soviets received American backing. In some cases U.S. intervention helped to prevent communist takeovers. In 1947, President Harry S. Truman (served 1945–1952) sent a massive amount of American military assistance to Greece, thereby securing the defeat of communist guerrillas and the installation of a parliamentary system. Elsewhere, as in Iran, American support for regimes that were strongly anticommunist but also strongly repressive embarrassed some Western observers, and led the Soviets to accuse the United States of doing its own empire building. The American efforts to "contain" communism in those areas the United States already controlled came to be known as the "Truman Doctrine."

In a similar vein, the United States introduced its European Recovery Program, which operated from 1947 to 1952; the scheme is better known as the Marshall Plan, after its originator, U.S. Secretary of State George C. Marshall (1880–1959). Seventeen European countries, which formed the Organization for European Economic Cooperation, received some

The Brandenburg Gate, dividing East and West Berlin.

Map 11.1 Europe During the Cold War

$13 billion in money and materials, to help their economic recovery.

The plan was clearly intended to combine humanitarian concerns with a strong dose of self-interest. Its provisions undoubtedly gave vital and much-needed aid to war-ravaged Europe, and brought about improvements in the daily lives of countless ordinary citizens. For the Soviets, however, the help represented yet another case of American economic imperialism. It also created the possibility of U.S. control over its allies' politics. In countries such as France and Italy, where communist parties made a strong showing immediately after the war, governments receiving aid were also under American pressure to "control the spread of communism" in their internal politics. In any case, strong economic growth certainly reinforced the capitalist system, and undercut support for the left among voters. On balance, the Marshall Plan not only provided much-needed financial assistance but became an important element in America's politics of stabilization in Western Europe.

The Berlin Crisis

The confrontation between the two superpowers—the "Cold War"—was most direct at the heart of Europe, in Germany. The three allied zones there soon began to function as a single unit, with local and national elections and a unified economy. The Soviet response to the revival of German strength was to blockade access by rail, river, or road to West Berlin, which was completely surrounded by Soviet-controlled territory. The Berlin blockade lasted from late June 1948 to mid-May 1949. During that period, the United States and Britain mounted a massive airlift to provide the West Berliners with food, water, and other essential supplies. The total number of flights amounted to around a quarter of a million, carrying two million tons of goods, at a cost of $224 million.

By the end of the blockade, the Americans had made their point. They would defend the interests of their allies, at whatever price, but would seek to do so without open conflict whenever possible. In May 1949, a separate West German nation, known as the Federal Republic of

One of the flights of the Berlin airlift.

Germany, was established at Bonn, which became its capital. In response the Soviets formalized the existence of their zone of Germany as a separate country, called the German Democratic Republic, with its capital in East Berlin. East Germany hailed the division of the country as irreversible, while West Germany's leaders at first refused even to recognize the existence of East Germany, and maintained the goal of eventual reunification.

The Creation of NATO

Even before the blockade was over, the Western allies had formed an organization specifically directed at the "threat of armed communist attack in Europe or the North Atlantic or Mediterranean area." The nations that joined the North Atlantic Treaty Organization (NATO) in April 1949 were Belgium, Britain, Canada, Denmark, France, the Netherlands, Iceland, Italy, Luxembourg, Norway, Portugal, and the United States. Greece and Turkey became members two years later, West Germany in 1955, and Spain in 1982. The terms of the treaty affirmed that an attack on any one member would be regarded as an attack on all.

Among the provisions of NATO was that American forces would remain in Europe, both in Germany and elsewhere. The popularity of the American presence rose and fell on both sides of the Atlantic as the intensity of the Cold War fluctuated. In the decade following the end of World War II, the United States' "umbrella" protection, by now nuclear, was widely regarded as essential to the continued security of Western Europe. In the 1960s, as new trouble spots developed outside Europe—the Middle East, Vietnam—complaints began to be heard in the United States about the high cost of European security to American taxpayers. At the same time, some European political movements started to agitate for the closing of U.S. military facilities in their countries. In 1966, De Gaulle actually expelled NATO forces from French territory. Throughout the 1980s, the Greek government threatened to close American bases in Greece. With the apparent collapse of the "Soviet Bloc" in the revolutions of 1989, heated debate began to rage about the future role of NATO and of its Soviet equivalent, the Warsaw Pact (see Part VIII, Topic 12).

GREAT BRITAIN: BEYOND THE WELFARE STATE

British politics following World War II was dominated by alternating Labour and Conservative governments. Other forces included a small Liberal party, and a Social Democratic party (founded in 1981). In the early 1980s, these two groups formed an alliance which seemed at first able to challenge Labour and Conservatives, but by the end of the decade, with the Conservatives in power, the Labour party remained the only real alternative.

The first postwar Labour government, following both its socialist principles and the spirit of the times, began the dismantlement of Britain's former imperial possessions and laid the foundations of the welfare state. Conservative governments followed from 1951 to 1964, continued the granting of independence to colonies, and led the country into a period of economic prosperity. Prime Minister Harold Macmillan (served 1957–1963) used the slogan "You've never had it so good" to win the election of 1959.

Macmillan had become prime minister two years earlier, in 1957, following the resignation of his predecessor, Sir Anthony Eden (served 1955–1957). Eden's departure was the result of the Suez crisis of 1956, which clearly illustrated the limits on postwar Britain's freedom to follow an independent course in foreign affairs. When Egypt's President Gamal Abdel Nasser (1918–1970) nationalized the Suez Canal, hitherto under joint Franco-British ownership, Britain and France invaded Egypt to regain possession. Under strong U.S. pressure, and with UN intervention, the occupying forces withdrew, and the canal reopened under Egyptian control. Eden, who had served earlier as Churchill's foreign secretary, was professionally and physically wrecked by the crisis; at its height, his wife later observed, it felt as if the canal itself were flowing through their living room.

By 1964, Britain's economy was facing serious problems. The government's failure to enable industry to compete in international markets, coupled with rising unemployment and chronic inflation, persuaded the electors to turn to Labour. For the next fifteen years each party in turn failed to solve the country's economic difficulties. In 1971, after years of heated controversy and debate, Britain became a member of the Common Market.

The Trade Unions in Britain

Britain's labor unions played a central role in the existence of the Labour party. Their delegates helped in the selection of parliamentary candidates, while their annual meetings were influential in the shaping of party policy, and their money kept the party going. The issue of relations between labor and management was thus far more complicated a matter than simple negotiation. When a Conservative government undertook to resolve an industrial dispute, it was in effect negotiating with its political opponents. A Labour government was equally, if differently, hampered: the unions expected their own party automatically to support their position.

Much of Britain's industrial and social life was paralyzed by more than a decade of union conflicts. In 1972, with factories opening only three days a week, and London in nightly darkness, a Conservative government introduced a bill to limit the unions' powers. The attempt broke down, creating yet further mutual mistrust, and the bill was repealed by a subsequent Labour government.

Once back in office again in 1979, the Conservatives introduced further legislation to make strike action more difficult. By now the public was generally in favor of greater control of the unions. A coal miners' strike in 1984–1985, which openly aimed to defy the legislation, was marked by violence. It was finally broken by a combination of government firmness and public disapproval of the miners' actions.

The Conservatives Under Thatcher

The Conservative leader from 1975 was Margaret Thatcher (born 1925), who served continuously as prime minister from 1979 to the end of 1990. From the beginning she announced an abrupt change of direction: no concessions. In her first year in office, steel, railway, and national health service workers all struck. All their strikes collapsed. The price was massive unemployment and social unrest.

Thatcher's own personal popularity, dimmed by the disastrous state of the economy, received a sudden boost from the Falklands War of 1982 (see Part VIII, Topic 16). In the following year's election, the Conservatives won the largest number of seats any party had gained since 1935. In part, this was due to the extreme program on which Labour had fought the election. Among other pledges, Labour promised to withdraw from the Common Market, abandon Britain's nuclear weapons (a long-standing cause of furious debate in the party), nationalize more industries, and suppress foxhunting. In large measure, however, the Conservatives' success was helped by the intervention of candidates representing the alliance between Liberals and Social Democrats, than at the height of its popularity.

With her huge parliamentary majority, Thatcher pushed forward to rein in the welfare state and develop a free market economy. The unsuccessful coal miners' strike of 1984–1985 served to reinforce her reputation for getting her way. (The letters of one of her nicknames, "Tina," stood for "There Is No Alternative.") Her admirers praised her firmness; her critics pointed to the increasing gulf between the prosperous and the poor, and to the growing violence on the part of the jobless and hopeless in Britain's big cities.

Reelected in 1987, her government began to run into increasing trouble as the economy went into decline again. Thatcher herself, once the Conservatives' biggest asset, came under increasing fire for her uncaring, confrontational attitude. When in 1990 she insisted on pushing through an unpopular reorganization of the local taxation system—the new method became known as the "Poll Tax"—rioting broke out not only in London but in hitherto firmly Conservative provincial regions of the country.

With her leadership of the party increasingly open to challenge, the annual election by Conservative Members of Parliament (MPs) of their leader was held in December 1990. These contests were generally a formality, and Thatcher herself was out of the country at the time of the first ballot, representing Britain at a Paris summit conference. Amid general surprise, she failed to gain the necessary percentage of votes for outright victory, and after a day or so of uncharacteristic hesitation withdrew her candidacy. John Major (born 1943) became the new prime minister and leader of the Conservative party. Thus a handful of Tory Members of Parliament, voting in secret, brought to an end the Thatcher years.

Postwar Britain, in spite of victory, had to face adjustment to a world position far below that of the preceding centuries. Firmly overshadowed by U.S. policy on the international scene, surpassed as a European economic power by Germany and France, and in the mid-1980s by Italy, Britain's own commitment to a European identity remained less than wholehearted. The left wing of the Labour party continued to fight, unsuccessfully after the 1983 debacle, for a promise that Labour would negotiate Britain's withdrawal from the Common Market. Thatcher for her part had remained deeply suspicious of growing European economic interdependence, and firmly opposed to any form of political union. With her replacement by Major, Britain seemed likely to reverse its anti-European stance and move toward a policy of cooperation rather than isolation, although the Conservative party remained deeply divided. With the victory of Tony Blair's New Labour party in 1997, British official attitudes to European unity became far more positive.

FRANCE IN THE FOURTH AND FIFTH REPUBLICS

By contrast with Britain, France's modern political history has been marked by discontinuity. The 19th century saw a constant alternation of republican and monarchical rule. As a result, by the 20th century, French politics became conditioned by the average citizen's distrust of the state and its agencies. Unlike the British, the French tended to defend themselves against collective action, rather than turning to the state for help. At the same time French political culture held abstract ideology in high esteem, seeking logical and rational solutions, rather than the kind of pragmatic compromises favored by the British.

The Fourth Republic

In comparison with its European competitors, by the beginning of World War II French industry was relatively stagnant. Between 1870 and 1940 German gross national income had increased five times, and British three and a half; that of France rose only 80 percent. Reconstruction thus involved not only repairing war damage, but also strengthening the economy as a whole. The architect of the plan to modernize France, Jean Monnet (1888–1979), began a series of five-year schemes to rebuild basic industries and develop exports. The first Monnet Plan covered the period from 1947 to 1952. Even before it went into effect, the government had nationalized key industries, including electricity, gas, rail transportation, and the Renault automobile plants (their former owner was accused of collaboration with the Germans). Economic reform was accompanied by an extensive program of social legislation, including accident and unemployment compensation, medical care, maternity benefits, and family allowances.

The constitutional framework which governed France from 1946 to 1958 was that of the Fourth Republic, already sharply criticized on its introduction in October 1946. Parliament exercised supreme power, and the conflicting interests of various parties and political groups threw up and then destroyed a continual series of prime ministers and cabinets. Unlike Italy, where the apparently endless series of governments concealed a genuine stability, the 20 different cabinets of the Fourth Republic's twelve years were a sign of serious political uncertainty. In Britain the chief political parties represented, in theory at least, clearly distinct points of view, and electors had some idea of what they were voting for. The French political parties often supported different policies in different parts of the country, and even after an election it was not clear which groups would support—and eventually abandon—which leaders.

De Gaulle and the Fifth Republic

By 1958, the combination of political instability and public agitation over the Algerian crisis clearly indicated the need for major reform. Charles de Gaulle, leader of the Free French movement in exile during World War II, had served as president during the transition to the Fourth Republic and retired from active political life in 1953. Yet because he stood as a powerful symbol of French national determination, in June 1958, at the height of the Algerian crisis, he returned as prime minister, with authorization to prepare a new constitution. De Gaulle remained France's leader until 1969, when he resigned on the failure of a referendum to give him further powers for constitutional reform.

By contrast with the Fourth Republic, the Fifth Republic vested strong powers in the president, who became not only the symbol but the instrument of executive authority. The original constitution of the Fifth Republic called for the president to be chosen by an electoral college, but in 1962 De Gaulle successfully campaigned for presidential election by a direct popular vote. Independent of any political party, presidents have exercised a wide range of powers, including the designation of prime ministers, the dissolution of Parliament, and control of French foreign policy. De Gaulle himself claimed, in fact, that "the President elected by the nation is the source and holder of the power of the state."

Already in the early years of the Fifth Republic the multiple parties of the postwar period began to coalesce into two main groups: on the left, communists, socialists, and radicals; on the center-right, Gaullists and various centrist parties, including the UDF (Union for French Democracy) and RPR (Rally for the Republic). In the early 1980s, the FN (National Front) began to attract increasing attention as a party of the extreme right, campaigning mainly on the issue of immigrant workers.

Under De Gaulle, France pursued generally conservative policies at home, while seeking to maintain an independent line in foreign affairs. Growing resentment of U.S. domination led to France's withdrawal from NATO in 1966. Deeper signs of unrest at the president's paternalistic style of government became manifest in the student and worker uprisings of two years later; 1968 was marked, in fact, by student protests throughout much of Europe.

The following year, when De Gaulle resigned, his former prime minister, Georges Pompidou (served 1969–1974, died in office), won election as president. Both Pompidou and his successor Valéry Giscard-D'Estaing (served 1974–1981) continued De Gaulle's conservative financial policies, while failing to prevent rising inflation and unemployment.

Mitterand and the Socialists

In 1981, for the first time the voters turned to a socialist to head the Fifth Republic. With the Communist party in decline, and the parties of the right divided, François Mitterand (served 1981–1995) won election in May 1981 as president. A month later he called a general election in which the Socialist party won a clear majority and the Communists lost half their members of Parliament.

For many in Europe, Mitterand's victory signaled the beginning of a new era for European socialism. His government began, indeed, by introducing generous new social legislation that increased minimum wages, family allowances, and housing subsidies. After a year, however, it was clear that the program had backfired. The French were spending more and more money on imported goods, imports were increasing while exports lagged. As a result, unemployment remained high.

At the end of 1982, despite union and communist protests, the government changed direction. State spending became lowered, wages were frozen, and state and industrial employees dismissed. The austerity program succeeded in lowering inflation and balancing the budget, but it disappointed, and actually hurt, many who had voted socialist.

The general election of 1986, fought two years before Mitterand's term expired, saw the Socialist party hold most of its strength—it lost 5 percent of the support it had won in 1981. On the right, however, the two major parties, the RPR and the UDF, put together a temporary agreement which gave them jointly a majority of seats in Parliament. The RPR leader, Jacques Chirac (born 1932), became prime minister, facing Mitterand with two years of "Cohabitation" with a premier who was a political opponent. The Socialist president maintained his right to control French foreign policy, while the conservative Chirac began to privatize the economy, selling off state-owned enterprises to private investors.

In 1988 Mitterand's term was up. In the presidential election of that year Mitterand stood again, with

Significant Dates

Western Europe After 1945

1947-1952	The Marshall Plan
1948-1949	The Berlin Blockade
1949	Creation of NATO
1951	European Coal and Steel Community formed
1956	The Suez crisis
1958	De Gaulle returns to power
1961	Construction of Berlin Wall
1968	Strikes and student demonstrations
1971	Britain enters Common Market
1979	Thatcher becomes British prime minister
1981	Mitterand elected first Socialist French president
1982	Kohl becomes West German chancellor
1983-1986	Craxi serves as Italian prime minister
1989	Fall of Berlin Wall

Chirac running as his principal opponent. This time the socialist represented stability and the conservative change. The voters chose the former. Chirac lost and resigned as prime minister. As in 1981, Mitterand called a general election, gambling on the electors returning a socialist majority. In the event the socialists won enough seats to be able to form a government, although by no means by as wide a margin as that giving Mitterand the presidency. While political pundits had a field day interpreting the public mood, Mitterand appointed Michel Rocard, a moderate socialist, as prime minister. On both left and right, candidates began to look toward the presidential election of 1995. The two leading candidates were Jacques Chirac and the Socialist Lionel Jospin. On the final ballot, Chirac emerged as the winner, although—to the surprise of many observers—Jospin won more votes in the first round than any other candidate (although not an absolute majority). Two years later, when President Chirac called a snap general election, the socialists astonished most observers by winning, and formed a government with the support of Communist and Green deputies.

WEST GERMANY: REBUILDING THE INDUSTRIAL GIANT

In 1945 Germany lay in ruins, split among its conquerors. Ten years later, the Federal Republic of Germany joined NATO and attained full sovereignty. At the end of 1989, the communist regime in the German Democratic Republic collapsed; a government installed after free elections in March 1990 began negotiations to prepare for reunification in late 1990.

German Economic Recovery

This astonishing reconstruction of a nation that seemed shattered beyond repair was made possible in part by West Germany's rapid financial recovery. By 1960, West German national income had surpassed that of France; in 1964 it overtook that of Britain; by 1973, German and American workers were paid the same. By the late 1980s the only country in the world to exceed West Germany (population 61 million) in total exports was the United States. At the same time as rebuilding industry, creating jobs, and providing housing, the postwar German government found shelter and employment for over 14 million Germans fleeing from or expelled from eastern Europe. All of these achievements were accomplished against a background of relative social peace, broken only by recurrent bursts of extremist terrorism.

The political scene in West Germany provided a firm and generally tranquil foundation for this rebirth. The two main parties, the conservative Christian Democrats and the left-wing Social Democrats, alternated in power, each on occasion forming a coalition with the much smaller liberal Free Democratic party. Politicians resigned or were removed from office generally as the result of personal scandal rather than for political reasons.

Konrad Adenauer

The tone of German public life, serious and responsible, was set by West Germany's first chancellor, Konrad Adenauer (served 1949–1963). No newcomer to political office, Adenauer had served as mayor of Cologne during the Weimar Republic. Having avoided involvement with the Nazis, he was an appropriate choice to provide his country with authoritative leadership. A venerable figure of lofty dignity, he was 73 when he became chancellor. Adenauer did much to repair Franco-German relations by the cooperative relationship he established with De Gaulle.

American aid in the form of the Marshall Plan certainly contributed to the German economic revival, but other important factors were also involved. Management was efficient and the labor force hardworking. Trade unions concentrated on increasing production rather than seeking to improve conditions for their members. The influx of refugees from Eastern Europe provided cheap and plentiful labor, with a strong incentive to improve their conditions by hard work. German Economic Minister Ludwig Erhard (served as West German chancellor 1963–1966) skillfully balanced a free market economy with welfare programs for the workers and government incentives for management. Unlike Britain, France, and Italy, the government nationalized no important services or industries.

In foreign policy, Adenauer maintained close relations with the United States, while beginning to work toward European cooperation. In 1951 the foundations of the Common Market were laid with the establishment of the European Coal and Steel Community (see Part VIII, Topic 15), of which Germany was a member. In the same year Adenauer addressed the painful issue of German responsibility for the Holocaust. Germany signed an agreement with Israel, pledging to make financial reparation over the following twelve years. As for East Germany, and the "German Question," at first Adenauer's government recognized neither East Germany nor the Soviet Union.

By the mid-1950s, West Germany was ready to assume the status of a fully sovereign state. In 1955 it joined NATO, and the following year the Western

Allies declared the occupation formally over. Later in 1955, Adenauer traveled to Moscow to establish diplomatic relations with the Kremlin. In March 1957 West Germany became one of the founding members of the Common Market. Toward the end of Adenauer's chancellorship, in 1961, relations with the Soviet Union grew tense with the construction of the Berlin Wall—built by the East Germans to cut off their citizens from access to the West.

"Ostpolitik"

Under Adenauer's successors West Germany began to try to improve relations with the governments of eastern Europe. The policy of "Ostpolitik"—politics looking east—was the special creation of the socialist Willy Brandt (1913–1992), who served first as foreign minister and then, from 1969 to 1974, as chancellor. Brandt was especially qualified to open up relations with eastern Europe, for as mayor of West Berlin from 1957 to 1966, he had dealt directly with the problems of isolation. In 1972 a treaty was finally signed between the two German states, which established mutual recognition. Brandt's "Ostpolitik" marked a major step in easing East-West relations, and paving the way for eventual reunification. Brandt himself resigned in 1974 as the result of a spy scandal in his administration.

Under the leadership of Helmut Schmidt (born 1918), Brandt's successor as head of the Social Democrats and chancellor from 1974 to 1982, the German economy remained strong. Beginning in the late 1970s, however, the general calm of German life became increasingly shattered by terrorist outbreaks. The revolutionary Red Army Faction claimed responsibility for a rash of bombings of NATO installations and the murder of prominent industrialists. The other social problem that helped to bring down Schmidt's Socialist government and return the Christian Democrats to power in 1982 was that of the *Gastarbeiter* ("guest workers")—the large and increasing number of foreign workers living in West Germany.

Helmut Kohl (born 1930), chancellor since 1982, favored a move to a free market economy. Under continued opposition from employers and unions, both unwilling to change the status quo, most of his initiatives failed, and by the end of the 1980s the German economy had begun to falter. Growth was slow and unemployment relatively high.

Kohl's most visible initiative was his immediate espousing of the cause of German reunification after the events of November 1989. Leading the East German Christian Democrats' campaign in the elections of March 1990, and appearing at packed rallies where he was hailed as a second Bismarck, Kohl helped his East German counterparts to achieve an overwhelming victory. The effects of this on his popularity in his own country were more difficult to assess, depending as they did on the economic consequences of eventual reunification (see Part VIII, Topic 16).

The booming center of West Berlin (1965), a stark contrast with the poverty of East Berlin.

By the early 1990s, then, after nearly half a century of rehabilitation, West Germany moved toward leading a renewed and reunited Germany. While the United States and West Germany's European allies underlined the need for safeguards, the Soviet Union expressed fears of future aggression. Yet the general realization that the choice of reunification was and should be essentially a German one underlined the degree to which 50 years of responsible leadership had changed the defeated country of 1945. For many years it was said that the key to German reunification lay in Moscow. Now, for the first time, it lay in Bonn.

ITALY'S ECONOMIC MIRACLE

With the collapse of Fascism in 1943, Italy faced the choice of either restoring the monarchy or introducing a republican form of government. In June 1946 a referendum decided by a narrow margin to abolish the monarchy, which had collaborated with Mussolini. The republican constitution which went into effect on January 1, 1948, was based on those of other Western democracies, with two chambers of parliament and universal suffrage. Unlike France of the Fifth Republic or the United States, the president had few powers; the prime minister became head of the government.

Party Politics in Italy

Unlike Britain or Germany, Italian political life was made up of a host of parties, most of which were represented in Parliament as a result of a system of proportional representation. Governments depended on the formation of coalitions, which either made up a parliamentary majority, however precarious, or which could count on opposing parties not voting against them. Since virtually all parties, even the small ones, had internal divisions, the making and unmaking of coalition cabinets became an apparently endless process. Between 1950 and 1980, 35 governments held office, some lasting no more than a few weeks.

Yet, by contrast with the confusion of the French Fourth Republic, the Italian economy was strengthened, major social changes such as divorce and abortion were introduced, and the scourge of terrorism was brought under control. By the 1980s Italy was one of the "Club of Seven," one of the seven most wealthy and industrialized nations in the world. Italian automobile manufacturers controlled the largest share of the European market, and Italian fashion and leather goods were popular throughout the world. A founding member of the Common Market, Italy was one of the countries that pressed most enthusiastically for greater European union.

One important reason for this apparent contradiction was that changes of government did not necessarily produce a change of party. By far the most powerful force in postwar Italian political life was the Christian Democratic party, whose members led virtually every Italian government from 1945 to 1981, with various assortments of coalition partners. A loose association of factions representing shades of opinion from center left to fairly far right, the Christian Democrats confirmed the Italian propensity for individualism, negotiation, and compromise. Although the party was promoted and supported by the Catholic Church, Christian Democratic governments introduced the referenda that legalized divorce and abortion—both vigorously opposed by church leaders.

Italy's second largest party, the Communists, continued throughout the postwar period to attract the votes of almost a third of the country's electors. Although never admitted to any of the national coalitions, they held seats on the important parliamentary committees that administered much of the day-to-day running of the country. They also won control of many city and regional governments. In the mid-1970s the Communist party began a period of rapprochement with center-right forces. The Communist leader Enrico Berlinguer (1922–1984) and the Christian Democrat leader Aldo Moro (1916–1978) began to talk cautiously of the "historic compromise," and in 1977–1978 the Communists supported (i.e., did not oppose)

Alcide de Gasperi, Christian Democratic leader and Italy's first postwar prime minister.

a Christian Democrat government. Then Moro was captured and murdered by extreme left-wing terrorists known as the "Red Brigades," in one of the grimmest periods of Italy's "*anni di piombo*" (years of lead). Talk of cooperation faded. Support for the party began to diminish in the late 1980s.

The Socialist party, the third largest in Italy, began to increase its share of the vote in the late 1970s and 1980s. Its leader, Bettino Craxi (born 1934), was strong enough to head Italy's longest-lasting government since World War II, from 1983 to 1986.

Thus, for all of its political fragmentation, the Italian system permitted a surprising degree of political stability. At the same time it also achieved the intentions of its creators, by never allowing a single individual to attain significant power—the success of Mussolini had taught a grim lesson. It was no accident that Italian politics never produced an Adenauer or De Gaulle, a Mitterand or a Thatcher. Significantly enough, Craxi's fall from popular favor in the late 1980s was due to his being perceived as too strong.

By 1990, Western Europe had enjoyed four and a half decades of peace and prosperity, broken only by the steep rise in oil prices in the mid-1970s. Democratic government was introduced in Spain and Portugal, and Greece's brief period of dictatorship in the late 1960s was over. The success of the Common Market was demonstrated by the number of nations seeking to join it. The challenge of the next decade was to achieve economic unity as painlessly as possible, and, as some believed, to look toward Western European political unity in the future.

Then, in a few weeks at the end of 1989, the division between Eastern and Western Europe, which had seemed permanent, fell apart. The road to a Europe united from the Atlantic to the Urals was infinitely long, and filled with wrong turnings. Many did not want to make the journey. Yet even the remote possibility of accomplishing a small part of it was an indication of the degree of European recovery after two disastrous world wars.

Questions for Further Study

1. How did the major Western European nations emerge from World War II? How did their populations see the role of the state?
2. What part did social protest and mass demonstrations play in postwar political life in western Europe?
3. What were the immediate effects of the fall of the Berlin Wall? What are its long-term consequences likely to be?

Suggestions for Further Reading

Bark, D. L., and D. R. Gress. *A History of West Germany: Vol. II. Democracy and Its Discontents, 1963–1988*. Oxford, 1989.

Bashevkin, S., ed. *Women and Politics in Western Europe*. London, 1985.

Hughes, H. S. *Sophisticated Rebels: The Political Culture of European Dissent, 1968–1987*. Cambridge, MA, 1988.

Mazey, S., and M. Newman, eds. *Mitterand's France*. New York, 1987.

Lewis, R. *Margaret Thatcher: A Personal and Political Biography*. London, 1984.

Spotts, F., and T. Wieser. *Italy, A Difficult Democracy*. New York, 1986.

VIII

Topic 12

The Soviet Union and Eastern Europe

With the end of World War II, the Soviet Union faced the daunting task of domestic reconstruction. In accordance with Stalin's policies, priority was given to heavy industry and weapons production. Governmental bureaucratic decisions controlled centralized state industrial development. In foreign affairs, relations between East and West grew tense and confrontational, as the Cold War dominated international relations.

In the period immediately following the war, most of the governments in Eastern Europe were taken over by Soviet-backed Communists. By 1948, these "Eastern bloc" countries were under firm Soviet control. Only Yugoslavia succeeded in breaking away from Soviet influence. The countries of Eastern Europe were bound to the Soviet Union economically by the COMECON organization, and militarily by the Warsaw Pact, although individual countries developed along different paths.

After Stalin's death in 1953, his eventual successor, Nikita Khrushchev, denounced the crimes of "Stalinism" and assumed sole power in 1958. Khrushchev encouraged the beginnings of East-West détente. Partly as a result, Soviet relations with China became strained and were eventually broken. In 1964, the failure of Soviet agriculture, coupled with the diplomatic consequences of the Cuban missile crisis of 1962, brought about Khrushchev's downfall.

The Soviet Union was ruled from 1964 to 1982 by Leonid Brezhnev. Brezhnev's policies were cautious. Amid intermittent signs of détente, the massive Soviet arms buildup continued. The power of the bureaucracy was intensified, and agricultural and industrial production remained backward.

Both Khrushchev and Brezhnev maintained a repressive policy in Eastern Europe. Soviet troops put down the Hungarian Revolt of 1956 and Warsaw Pact forces intervened to end the attempts at liberalization in Czechoslovakia in 1968. When in the late 1970s, unrest in Poland led in 1980 to the formation of an independent trade union, Solidarity, a Soviet-backed government imposed martial law and arrested Solidarity's organizers.

With the coming to power of Mikhail Gorbachev in 1985, Soviet policy underwent a dramatic change of direction. In an attempt to revitalize the Soviet economy, Gorbachev turned to more open, reformist policies. By decentralizing and privatizing sectors of the economy, democratizing party rule, and encouraging individual creativity, he aimed at raising productivity and improving the lives of Soviet citizens. This program required a reduction in weapons spending, and as a result the Soviet Union proved increasingly flexible in negotiating arms control treaties.

The degree of change in Soviet policy was demonstrated by the freedom with which the countries of Eastern Europe were able to overthrow their governments in the revolutions of 1989. The long-term effects of these revolutions remained uncertain. In the spring of 1990, free elections were held in Czechoslovakia, East Germany, and Hungary, all of which led to center-right, pro-Western governments. Later in the 1990s, many Eastern European countries returned former communist leaders to power. Internal affairs and relations between Eastern European nations, however, remained afflicted by ethnic rivalries, survivals from the Hapsburg empire. Yet it was a sign of the degree of change that throughout the upheavals the Soviet Union, preoccupied with its own ethnic minorities, made no move to interfere.

THE SOVIET UNION FACES RECONSTRUCTION

World War II left havoc throughout Europe, but the problems that faced the Soviet Union were especially daunting. Estimates of the number killed are impossible to confirm, but the figure generally given of 22 million does not seem exaggerated. Innumerable towns and villages were in ruins. Leningrad suffered massive damage during its long siege by the Germans, and many industrial plants elsewhere in the Soviet Union had been obliterated. Living conditions were grim: around 25 million Soviets were homeless, and many of those who did have shelter had to share kitchen and bathroom facilities with other families for decades.

Soviet victory in the war had been due in large measure to the industrialization of the Soviet Union in the 1930s. Furthermore, the German invasion had reinforced Russian fears of foreign interference. Thus, Stalin's top priority in 1945 was to rebuild the heavy steel and iron industries and to step up armaments production: "In industry lies power." The relatively little attention paid to the manufacture of consumer goods meant that the standard of living of most Soviet citizens remained low.

Control of planning and production was kept firmly in the hands of the Communist party, itself subject to Stalin. The system was that of a "command" economy in which all decisions were centralized and carried out by the state bureaucracy. Capital investment, production levels, and pricing, matters that in a free market economy are decided by private industries or even individual factories, remained subject to state control. Multi-year plans, and more detailed annual and even monthly production quotas, were imposed on all industrial enterprises and state collective farms. In practice, however, plans and deadlines were rarely met. The weight of bureaucratic obstructionism and inactivity led to growing inefficiency, and the stifling of initiative and creativity.

Stalinism

By the end of the war, Stalin was able to use the Soviet Union's victory to enhance his image as his country's savior. The purges of the 1930s had removed any chance of serious opposition, but the paraphernalia of a secret police state remained firmly entrenched. Spies and police terror ensured that even his immediate subordinates feared their master, whose bursts of suspicion and sudden changes of mood were notorious. Prisons and labor camps remained the fate for political and intellectual dissidents. Both in the Soviet Union and in the Eastern bloc countries, art, music, and literature served to glorify Stalin's "genius."

In 1949, when the dictator celebrated his 70th birthday, the gifts he received were sufficient to fill a warehouse. Yet, to the end of his life, he remained insecure and untrusting, capable of turning on his closest supporters.

STALIN AND THE SOVIET BLOC

World War II had resulted in German invasion and occupation of Eastern Europe. Bulgaria, Hungary, and Romania became allies of Germany; Poland was divided between the Soviet Union and Germany at the outset of war and subsequently occupied by the Germans. At the end of the war, Bulgaria, Hungary,

Poland, and Romania, together with the Soviet zone of Germany (the future East Germany), all fell under the control of the Red Army. In Stalin's mind, Soviet control of Eastern Europe would guarantee protection against future threats. The governments which were formed there, known as "national fronts," originally consisted of coalitions between local politicians and Moscow-backed Communists. In 1947, however, local communist parties seized power and created one-party regimes.

The postwar Government of National Unity in Czechoslovakia had been made up of both Communist and noncommunist parties, and enjoyed broad popular support. Its program of economic reform included land redistribution. In 1948, however, the Czech Communist party engineered a coup that placed their country also under Soviet domination. The only Eastern European nation to retain its independence was Yugoslavia, where Josip Broz Tito (1892–1980) had led Communist partisan resistance to the brutal German occupation. After the war, Tito suppressed all noncommunist opposition to establish a one-party Communist state, but managed to avoid becoming part of Stalin's empire.

© WALT KELLY

Cartoon showing the two sides in the Cold War as children.

The Stalinization of Eastern Europe

In all of the Soviet Union's Eastern "satellites," the Stalinist totalitarian system of government imposed the Communist party as sole political force, and the Kremlin as leader: all policy decisions and choices were made or at least approved by Moscow. Eastern bloc countries introduced constitutions based on Stalin's Soviet Constitution of 1936, developed élite leaderships, severely restricted individual liberties, including religious worship, established central planning, and imposed Soviet-approved culture. Industries in each of the states were nationalized.

Methods used in the Soviet Union in the 1930s served to suppress all traces of indigenous opposition in Eastern Europe. In the late 1940s and early 1950s, local Communist leaders in Hungary and Bulgaria were purged, tried for "treason," and executed. Other show trials took place in Romania and East Germany. In Czechoslovakia in 1952, fourteen party leaders, eleven of whom were Jewish, were tried; all but three were subsequently executed. By such means Moscow crushed any possibility of autonomous development, and maintained an iron grip on events.

Stalinist control became further reinforced by the creation of a number of organizations. The formation of the Council for Mutual Economic Assistance (COMECON) in 1949 provided a means of subordinating the economies of Eastern Europe to that of the Soviet Union. Since Soviet industry was geared to the production of armaments, iron, and steel, the Soviet Union came to rely on eastern Europe for consumer and other manufactured goods. These became increasingly traded for Soviet raw materials and energy supplies. In the 1970s, COMECON helped eastern European countries to invest capital in developing technology and equipment for the processing of Soviet natural resources. In its initial stages, however, the organization was chiefly a means for ensuring the dependence of the Eastern bloc on the Soviets.

Soviet military domination of the region was formalized in the Warsaw Pact treaty, signed in 1955, which represented the East European equivalent of NATO. The original members were the Soviet Union and Albania, Bulgaria, Czechoslovakia, East Germany, Hungary, Poland, and Romania. Albania's idiosyncratic Communist regime, led by Enver Hoxha (1908–1985), broke with Moscow in 1961 to form a temporary alliance with Communist China, the Soviet Union's ideological and political rival. The Albanians formally withdrew from the Warsaw Pact alliance in 1968, claiming as their reason the invasion of Czechoslovakia in that year by Warsaw Pact forces.

Yugoslavia: Stalin Versus Tito

In 1945, no East European political leadership more enthusiastically espoused communism than Yugoslavia, where the Communist party's heading of the resistance to the Germans had won it considerable popular support. Tito, the former resistance leader, nationalized the economy and introduced centralized planning, and collectivized agriculture. As Stalin increased his control of the rest of eastern Europe, the Yugoslavian leadership began to emphasize nationalism, and to resist Soviet pressures to conform to Moscow's directives. Stalin is said to have told Nikita Khrushchev in anger: "I will shake my little finger and there will be no more Tito. He will fall."

In 1948, when Yugoslavia was expelled from the Communist Information Bureau (COMINFORM), Tito held firm to an independent line, and began to establish contacts with nations describing themselves as "nonaligned." Strict party control was maintained within Yugoslavia, but communist policy became increasingly modified. By the time of Stalin's death in 1953, the Yugoslavs had introduced "self-management" in factories. In foreign affairs, they firmly rejected Soviet domination in favor of neutrality toward the West.

Tito's success in creating the first nationalist Communist state received official acknowledgment after Khrushchev's denunciation of Stalin in 1956, when Khrushchev admitted that "the ways of socialist development vary in different countries and conditions." Future Soviet actions made clear, however, that the rest of Eastern Europe was to be denied the possibility of trying out variations of their own.

Nikita Khrushchev, Stalin's successor, harangues the delegates at the United Nations.

THE SOVIET UNION FROM KHRUSHCHEV TO BREZHNEV

The death of the "Wisest of the Wise" was followed by a power struggle in the Soviet Presidium from which Nikita Khrushchev (served 1958–1964) emerged victorious. The Ukrainian-born Khrushchev was groomed by Stalin to succeed him, and in 1953 became party secretary.

De-Stalinization

At the Party Congress of 1956, Khrushchev began his campaign of "de-Stalinization." For the first time a Soviet leader attacked some of the Soviet Union's most sacred myths. In a fiery speech he denounced Stalin's excesses and "cult of personality," accusing him of crimes against his political opponents. As Khrushchev subsequently moved to take over the premiership, he abandoned two of Stalin's chief doctrines: the notion that the closer the Soviet Union moved to true Communism, the more intense the class struggle would become; and the labeling of political opponents as "enemies of the people." Both of these had been important in Stalin's reign of terror. Khrushchev's own rivals, rather than being purged, were dismissed or demoted as "antiparty."

Khrushchev's policies were generally conservative, but the release from Stalinist oppression triggered a period of economic growth. By the 1960s only the United States surpassed the Soviet Union in overall wealth and production. His rule also saw a number of technological breakthroughs. In 1957 the Russians launched *Sputnik I*, the first artificial satellite, and in 1961 they put the first man in space.

Khrushchev's foreign policy, at the same time argumentative and conciliatory, seemed to take its character from his own brash personality. He traveled to Western Europe and the United States, where his much-publicized encounters with government leaders and ordinary citizens served to humanize the Soviet Union's image. The increasing rapprochement with the West was accompanied in 1960 by a diplomatic break with China. The direct cause of the split was a long-standing border dispute between the two nations, but a deeper reason lay in Chinese resentment of Soviet approaches to the West; a Chinese newspaper article of

The Soviet space capsule *Sputnik,* on display at the Brussels World Fair, 1958.

the time referred to the "filthy Soviet revisionist swine." With accusations such as these hurled by both sides, the idea of a united world Communist movement seemed increasingly improbable.

The Cuban Missile Crisis

Amid the general relaxation of tension between East and West, the Cuban missile crisis of 1962 came as a fearful warning of the precariousness of peace in the nuclear age. In 1959, Cuba's revolutionary leader Fidel Castro (born 1926) seized power and set up a Communist state less than 100 miles off the U.S. mainland. The following year, when Castro accepted Soviet military aid, America broke off relations with Cuba and supported an unsuccessful invasion of the island by a band of Cuban exiles.

In October 1962, American intelligence sources reported that Soviet forces in Cuba were constructing nuclear missile sites, from which nuclear warheads could be launched well into the heart of the continental United States. The American president, John F. Kennedy (1917–1963), promised reprisal against the Soviets for any missile dispatched from Cuba against the United States, and blockaded the seas around the island to prevent the delivery of the warheads themselves.

For the week of October 22 to 28, 1962, amid frantic diplomatic activity, the world faced the most serious crisis of the Cold War. While Khrushchev and Kennedy established direct communication by telephone, Soviet actions gave contradictory signals: Soviet ships sailing toward Cuba turned back, but work continued on the missile sites. Finally, the Soviet Union agreed to dismantle the missile launchers in return for an American promise not to invade Cuba. Khrushchev's face-saving proposal that the Americans should also dismantle some missiles of their own in Turkey led eventually to their removal, but as part of an existing United States–Turkish policy.

The appearance of Soviet weakness that the Cuban adventure created did much to undermine Khrushchev's power. Together with the Sino-Soviet split and growing restlessness in Eastern Europe, it reflected an uneasy instability in Soviet foreign policy. Khrushchev's opponents drew further ammunition from the continuing poor performance of Soviet agriculture, where new technologies he had introduced failed to produce significant improvements. The Central Committee and the Presidium voted him out of office in October 1964. His retreat into quiet retirement represented another stage in the Soviet Union's development of an orderly system of transition.

The Brezhnev Era

The years in power of Leonid Brezhnev (served as first secretary of the Communist party 1964–1982; chief of state 1977–1982) were generally a period of stagnation. The Soviet bureaucracy assumed ever-greater powers, and the state continued to throw its most massive efforts into armaments manufacture. By 1981, the Soviet Union was probably the most fully armed power in history. Yet poor agricultural yields continued to create food shortages. In 1972 and 1975, the Soviet Union had no choice but to purchase large supplies of grain from the United States.

In spite of firm attempts to muzzle it, the issue of human rights in the Soviet Union began to create some attention. Soviet Jews, some 3 million in number, were subject to discrimination at home. At times, Jews were permitted to emigrate, although at other times the government arbitrarily removed the right of emigration. One of the most vocal Soviet dissenters was the writer Alexander Solzhenitsyn (born 1918), who was denied permission to leave the Soviet Union to accept the Nobel Prize awarded him in 1970. (An earlier Nobel Prize winner, Boris Pasternak, received similar

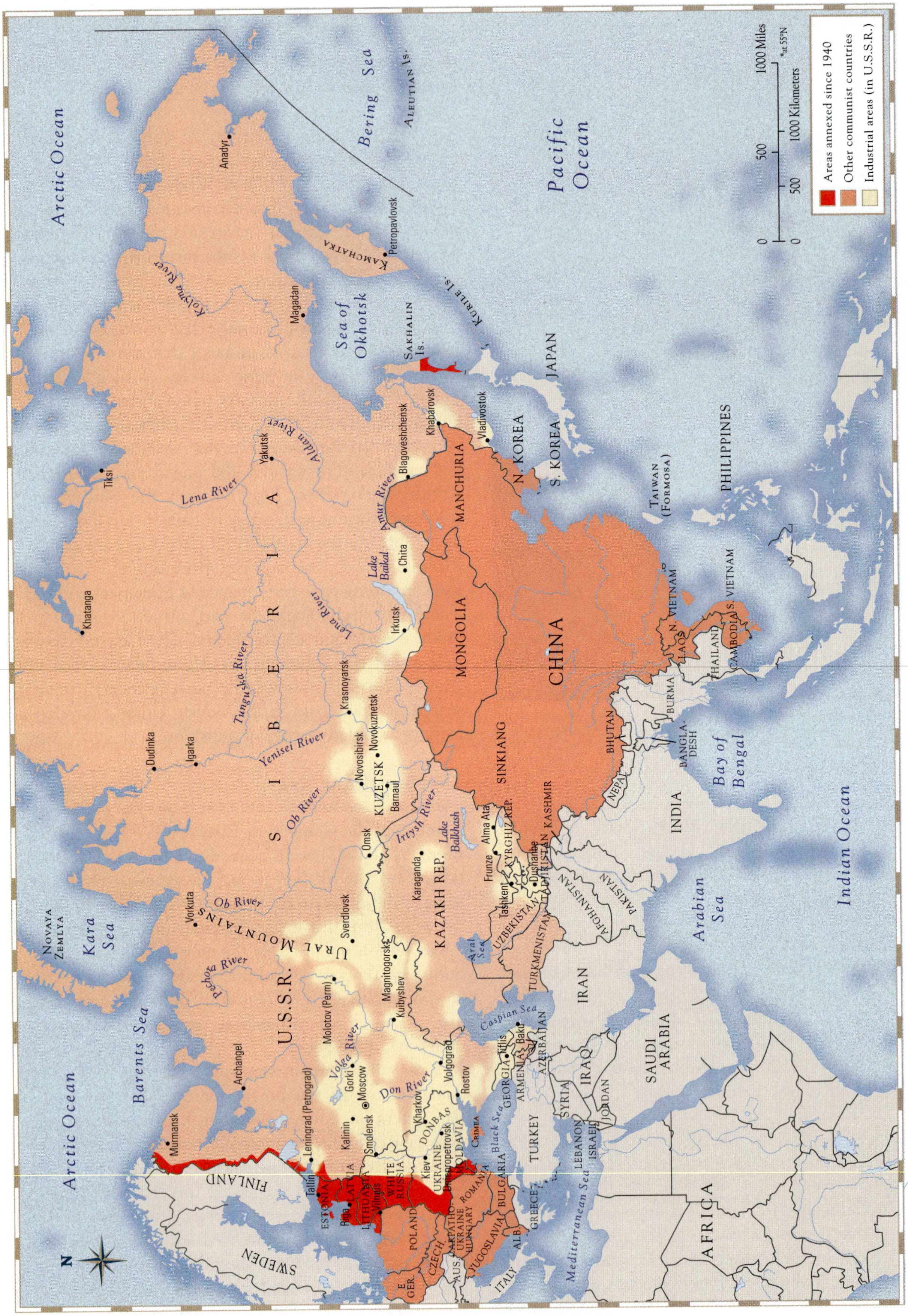

Map 12.1 The Soviet Union in 1988, on the Eve of its Collapse

Significant Dates

The Soviet Union and Eastern Europe After 1945

1948	Communist party coup in Czechoslovakia
1949	Formation of COMECON
1953	Death of Stalin; Khrushchev in office
1955	Creation of Warsaw Pact
1956	Hungarian uprising
1957	*Sputnik* satellite launched
1960	Soviet break with China
1961	Soviets put first man in space
1962	Cuban missile crisis
1968	Prague spring
1974	Deportation of Solzhenitsyn
1979	Soviet invasion of Afghanistan
1980	Solidarity labor union formed in Poland
1985	Gorbachev general secretary of Soviet Communist party
1989	Fall of Berlin Wall

treatment in 1958.) His *Gulag Archipelago* exposed the brutality of Stalin's labor camps. In 1974, Solzhenitsyn was arrested and deported, and he continued his denunciation of the Soviet regime from his exile in the West.

In foreign policy outside Europe, the Brezhnev years saw the extension of Soviet influence in Africa and Asia. Cuban troops with Soviet arms and support helped to set up a Marxist regime in Angola. Similar forces assisted the revolutionary government of Ethiopia to put down rebellions. The biggest, and most disastrous, Soviet adventure was the invasion in 1979 of Afghanistan, to support a Marxist regime Moscow had installed there. In 1988, after years of fruitless fighting between the Soviet troops and United States–backed guerrillas, the Soviet forces began to withdraw.

REPRESSION AND RESISTANCE IN EASTERN EUROPE

For all the signs of growing détente between the superpowers that intermittently marked the years after Stalin, the Soviet grip on Eastern Europe remained tight. Both Khrushchev and Brezhnev left no doubt that they were prepared to use brute force to remove any government not fully under Soviet control.

The Hungarian Uprising of 1956

Khrushchev's speech to the Moscow Party Congress of 1956 acknowledged that the Yugoslav-Soviet break had been avoidable, and hinted that different forms of socialist development were legitimate. Events later that same year proved the emptiness of his words.

Late in October 1956, mass demonstrations in favor of political change—including withdrawal from the Warsaw Pact alliance—broke out in Poland. The situation was resolved peacefully, when a faction of the official party threw its support behind the reformist leader Władysław Gomułka (served 1956–1970). Gomułka managed to convince the Soviet leadership that the central institutions of party government remained intact, and that Poland intended to keep unchanged its close ties with the Soviet Union and membership in the Warsaw Pact. Throughout the 1960s, Gomułka continued a policy of cautious social and economic reform.

The Hungarians were encouraged by the Polish success. Within days, crowds gathered in Budapest and in Hungary's other big cities, demanding similar changes—withdrawal from the Warsaw Pact among them. The Central Committee of the Hungarian Communist party turned to Imre Nagy (1896–1958). During an earlier period as premier, from 1953 to 1955, Nagy had been openly critical of the Soviets, and was ousted by the Stalinist party secretary. Now he was restored to office. In an atmosphere of considerable nervousness, Soviet troops entered Budapest to keep the situation under control, only to be withdrawn four days later. Nagy and the new party secretary, Janos Kadar (1912–1989), were given the chance to set up a regime acceptable to Moscow, as Gomułka had done a few days earlier in Poland. On October 30, the Soviet government issued a statement affirming the principle of noninterference.

The same day Nagy, perhaps under the influence of his more extreme supporters, declared that a multiparty system would be introduced, and moved to make the Hungarian army independent of the Soviets. A day later, he announced Hungary's intention of withdrawing from the Warsaw Pact. On November 1, he proclaimed Hungary neutral. On November 4, Soviet tanks again entered Budapest. They were met with mass uprisings, which they crushed. With the revolt under control, the troops arrested thousands of Hungarians. Many were executed, others deported to Siberia. As for Nagy himself, the Soviets seized him from the Hungarians and executed him. (In 1989, Nagy was officially rehabilitated, and his remains received a solemn state funeral.)

Soviet tanks invade Budapest, Hungary, in 1956 to crush the Hungarian Revolution.

Kadar, Nagy's former associate, became premier and helped the Soviets eliminate the remaining rebel leaders. He served as prime minister from 1956 to 1958, and again from 1961 to 1965, and remained party secretary until 1988. Although Kadar permitted a certain flexibility—the so-called "goulash communism"—he remained close to Moscow. His death in 1989 came at exactly the same time as the collapse of the Communist regime in Hungary.

World reaction to the brutal extinction of the 1956 uprising was one of shock, but became confused by the fact that the events occurred in the middle of another international crisis, that involving the Suez Canal (see Part VIII, Topic 11). In the course of a few days in the fall of 1956, the two superpowers asserted themselves, albeit by very different means. The United States reined in its allies by opposing the British and French takeover of the Canal; the Soviet Union made it only too clear that it would tolerate no true independence in Eastern Europe.

The Prague Spring of 1968

Unlike Hungary and Poland, Czechoslovakia remained under continuous Stalinist rule. Its president from 1957 to 1968 was Antonín Novotny (1904–1975), a hard-line supporter of Moscow. By the late 1960s, however, with the centrally planned economy performing increasingly poorly, dissent began to grow. The Slovaks, in particular, claimed that Czech regions were receiving preferential treatment. Matters came to a head at the beginning of 1968, when reformers within the official Communist party ousted Novotny, and replaced him with Alexander Dubcek.

As spring approached, Dubcek and his supporters carried out an ever-increasing process of democratization. They allowed independent political movements to develop, reduced censorship, promised to guarantee individual freedoms, and proposed to create a federation giving equal rights to Czechs and Slovaks. A special congress was scheduled for September, to reform the party along democratic lines.

Soviet reaction began with press criticism and escalated in July with Soviet troop movements in bordering countries. In the same month, all the Warsaw Pact members except Czechoslovakia (and Albania, which had broken with Moscow earlier) met to discuss the conditions that would legitimize intervention. These conditions were made public a few months later and constituted the "Brezhnev Doctrine." They stated that "when internal and external forces hostile to socialism seek to reverse the development of any socialist country whatsoever in the direction of the restoration of the capitalist order . . . this becomes a common problem and concern of all socialist countries."

In August 1968, Warsaw Pact forces moved into Czechoslovakia. Dubcek and the others who had tried to introduce "socialism with a human face" were purged, and the staunchly pro-Soviet Gustav Husak was put in charge. Husak enforced rigidly Stalinist policies of state planning which, together with inept management, undermined the economy. By the late 1980s, with Gorbachev's reforms in effect in the Soviet Union, Czechoslovakia remained the only bastion of orthodox Stalinism in Eastern Europe. In 1989, in the regime's last weeks, Dubcek emerged from retirement to play a part in leading the revolution.

Poland and the Birth of Solidarity

In Poland, Gomułka's program of cautious reform failed to prevent food shortages, and a steep rise in the prices of the available supplies. In 1970, Gomułka resigned, and was replaced by Edward Gierek (born 1913). The problem of the scarcity of food remained unsolved, however, and in the late 1970s public unrest led to the creation in 1980 of an independent trade union movement, "Solidarity." Solidarity led a series of strikes to demand lower prices; toward the end of the 1970s, the staggering size of the national debt had forced the government to raise the price of basic supplies to more realistic levels.

After beginning as a protest against the rising cost of living, the Solidarity movement began to press for political reform, including the establishment of independent trade unions. In 1981, Gierek was driven out of office and at the end of the year, under Soviet pressure, Poland's new leader, General Wojciech Jaruzelski (born 1923), imposed martial law and arrested Solidarity's leaders. In the year of their release, 1983, Solidarity's head, Lech Wałesa (born 1943), received the Nobel Peace Prize for his contribution "to ensure workers' rights to establish their own organizations."

Solidarity maintained a low profile for the next five years. With the beginnings of reform in the Soviet Union, however, the trade union returned to the fray. In 1987, with the economy still in poor shape, the government announced reforms that included a reduction in central planning and wage incentives. For the first time a popular referendum was held to approve the plan. Massive public rejection of the government's proposals, the result of general lack of confidence, led to further rises in food prices. In a mood of widespread hostility, a wave of strikes broke out throughout the country.

In 1988, Solidarity was revived. The movement's leaders sat down with government representatives and other political forces, and negotiated an end to the strikes. Subsequent talks led to the establishment of a noncommunist prime minister—ending the Communist party's monopoly on power—and the holding of free elections. Thus, Poland set the lead in breaking Soviet control of eastern Europe.

THE GORBACHEV ERA: GLASNOST AND PERESTROIKA

The liberalization of Eastern Europe would have been inconceivable in the Brezhnev era. With the death of Brezhnev and his two elderly successors, however,

Demonstrators in Prague, August 1968, rally round the name of their leader, Dubcek.

Lech Wałesa speaking to Polish workers, December 1981.

power passed to a new generation of Soviet leadership. The changes inaugurated by Mikhail Gorbachev (born 1931), general secretary of the Soviet Communist party from 1985 to 1992, produced radical and far-reaching reforms in the Soviet Union, freed Eastern Europe from dependence on Moscow, and began to end the Cold War.

Gorbachev was born in the Stavropol region of southern Russia, and began his political career as party first secretary there in 1970. In 1978, he was called to Moscow to take over the controversial task of running Soviet agriculture. Within two years he was promoted to the Politburo, becoming its youngest member.

Gorbachev's election as party leader in 1985 signaled a dramatic change in direction. The conservatives in the Kremlin, led by Yegor Ligachev (born 1921), continued to oppose the Gorbachev reform program, but most of the Brezhnev generation of political leaders were forced into retirement. The leading figures in Soviet government during Gorbachev's first five years in office—Nicolai Ryzhkov (born 1929), the prime minister, Eduard Shevardnadze (born 1928), the foreign minister—were all supporters of reform. Indeed, Gorbachev's most vocal opponents in the early 1990s were those who felt that the pace of change was too slow; their leader was Boris Yeltsin (born 1931).

The Reforms of Gorbachev

By the mid-1980s the Soviet economy was still stubbornly resisting all attempts at improvement. Sluggish and backward, it was responsible for keeping the quality of life of most Soviet citizens well below that of capitalist countries, and even inferior to that of some East European nations. In the 1950s, the Soviet annual growth rate was around 6 percent; by the 1980s it had fallen to 1.5 percent. Gorbachev's economic reforms were intended to free industry from the stifling hand of centralized state planning by encouraging decentralization, reducing bureaucratic inefficiency, and using market incentives to encourage increased output. At the same time he aimed to modernize Soviet industry by eliminating unproductive labor and introducing the latest technology.

Ronald Reagan and Mikhail Gorbachev in New York, 1988.

He symbolized these goals in two words: *glasnost* (openness) and *perestroika* (restructuring). The first signified an opening up of Soviet society, so that individuals could use their initiative to break through the heavy weight of bureaucracy and general apathy. Glasnost also signaled an openness to comment and criticism. With perestroika, the institutions of the state were to be restudied and, if necessary, restructured.

The Soviet economy was in so desperate a state, and its habits so deeply ingrained, that little progress was visible. Food supplies and consumer goods remained in short supply, and living conditions showed no real sign of improvement. Yet the more general effects of glasnost and perestroika transformed Soviet society and wrought important change in international relations.

Within the Soviet Union, the Gorbachev era brought a degree of genuine freedom for political dissent, and open discussion of problems past and present. Political dissidents, including the distinguished physicist Andrei Sakharov (1921–1989), were released. Artists, musicians, and writers had a new freedom of expression. Heated parliamentary debate accompanied the passage of reform measures. Yet the new democratic spirit had its limitations. By 1990, Gorbachev had assumed virtually supreme power, ruling as the Soviet Union's first president to be "elected" by Parliament. It seemed that, in order to deal with his opponents on left and right, extraordinary powers were still necessary.

In international relations, the need to reduce Soviet spending on armaments produced a new flexibility in negotiations to reduce weapons. A series of summit meetings between Gorbachev and American President Ronald Reagan (born 1911) produced the signing of a treaty to reduce intermediate-range nuclear weapons in 1987. Further arms talks on both conventional and nuclear weapons seemed likely to produce more agreements. Soviet involvement in Africa, Asia, and the Caribbean was reduced, economic aid to Cuba was cut, and in 1988 Soviet troops began to withdraw from Afghanistan.

THE REVOLUTIONS OF 1989

In the last three months of 1989, almost half a century of Soviet and Communist domination in Eastern Europe collapsed. Inspired by the sight of free elections in Poland, increasing crowds of peaceful demonstrators drove their governments from power.

Latvians watch as a colossal statue of Lenin is torn down, 1991.

The Fall of 1989

The long process of negotiating a means of shared rule in Poland ended in August 1989, when Tadeusz Mazowiecki, a Solidarity member, became prime minister; his cabinet included both Solidarity representatives and Communists. Over the late summer months, thousands of East Germans, "voting with their feet," began to pour westward. Many had sought visas at the West German Embassy in Budapest, but needed to find a way out of Hungary to travel through Austria to West Germany. In September, the Hungarians opened their border with Austria to allow them to leave. October, ironically, saw the celebration of the 40th anniversary of the founding of East Germany. As parades marched through East Berlin, at a ceremony attended by an impassively smiling Gorbachev, the stream of refugees became a flood. By the end of the month, East Germany's leader, Erich Honecker (1912–1997), who had had a series of anxious meetings with Gorbachev during the latter's visit, quit as party chief. Meanwhile in Hungary, liberalization was being effected within the party. Already in the previous June the government had signaled its change of attitude by staging the imposing ceremonies that accompanied the hero's reburial accorded to Imre Nagy. Their facilitating the exit of East German refugees was another sign of yielding. Now, as the crisis intensified in East Germany, the Hungarian Communist party changed its name, and announced free multi-party elections for the following year.

In November, the already hectic pace intensified. In a last desperate attempt to deter its people from abandoning their country, the East German authorities began to tear down the Berlin Wall—hated symbol of oppression. As the world watched in disbelief, East and West Berliners danced and drank champagne on the spot where armed guards had patrolled hours earlier. Far from quieting the excitement, the removal of the wall increased the upheaval, as evidence of massive corruption at the highest level of the party began to circulate. Within weeks the Communists abandoned their positions, and a coalition of political representatives began to prepare for free elections early in the following year.

Inspired by success elsewhere, the people of Czechoslovakia began their own mass demonstrations. At first, the government responded with tough police action, but once again the sheer force of events drove the Communist party from power. The weary but jubilant Dubcek addressed the crowds, and the playwright Václav Havel (born 1936) began to emerge as the dominant figure in his country's political rebirth. Again, elections were promised for the following year.

Even Bulgaria, a country with virtually no experience of democratic politics, deposed its aging Stalinist dictator, Todor Zhivkov (born 1911); he was subsequently accused of corruption.

Revolution in Romania

The only remaining Soviet bloc country hitherto unaffected by the ferment was Romania, where Nicolae Ceausescu (1918–1990) and his wife Elena presided over a bizarre form of Communist dictatorship. Ceausescu's relations with Moscow had been strained for years. In the 1980s, as his country lurched from one economic crisis to another, and against a background of serious food and energy shortages, he poured resources into grandiose construction projects. Much of Bucharest was bulldozed to make space for a new "imperial" capital, with a vast palace, in which Nicolae and Elena were each to have two immense office suites. In the countryside, villages were destroyed, and their inhabitants forcibly gathered together in "collectives." Overseeing all of this was the dreaded secret police, infamous for their cruelty.

At first, the apparatus of repression seemed sufficient to deter protest demonstrations. In mid-December 1989, when protestors began to gather, police fired on the crowd; around 200 people were killed. The violence provoked an immediate reaction. Angry demonstrators stormed through Bucharest. Gun battles broke out between army units sympathetic to the crowds and the secret police force. Ceausescu and his wife fled. Captured by army forces, within hours they received a military trial, were sentenced to death, and summarily executed.

The path toward democratic government in Romania remained fraught with obstacles. Many of those remaining in power were compromised by their complicity with the Ceausescus. The holding of genuine free elections seemed problematic. Yet at least a start had been made on dismantling a regime that—even for Eastern Europe—had found new extremes of repression.

The end of World War II found the Soviet Union and the United States facing one another as opposing powers, anxious to demonstrate their own supremacy, and fearing one another's military capacity. With its political stability and economic dynamism, the United States was able, in a gesture of enlightened self-interest, to help western European reconstruction of economies and democratic institutions. While Stalin consolidated his dominion over Eastern Europe, his natural paranoia was reinforced by the American success.

Khrushchev aimed at achieving recognition of his country's superpower status by a combination of promises and threats. During his rule, the Soviet Union extended its activities to the Third World, which Stalin had largely ignored. Thus, the struggle of former colonies in Africa,

Asia, and Central America for national independence became the battleground for confrontation between the two superpowers.

The same policy was continued under Brezhnev. No less than fourteen Soviet-backed revolutionary movements around the world achieved power in the second half of the 1970s. At the same time, the Soviet Union claimed military parity by building huge numbers of nuclear missiles, while investing unprecedented sums in its naval forces. In Eastern Europe, the Brezhnev Doctrine maintained rigid control until the upheavals of 1989.

Fundamental to Gorbachev's attempt to modernize the Soviet state was the realization that it could not afford massive spending abroad to support friendly regimes, and equally vast sums at home on an armaments buildup. The maintenance of revolutionary movements and governments drained national resources and brought in return little power or prestige. To cut the military budget required better relations with the United States—an end to the Cold War—and a stable and independent Eastern Europe.

To move on so many fronts at the same time inevitably presented enormous risks. In the first place, domestic opposition to the Gorbachev reform plan from both right and left remained an unpredictable factor. Secondly, the very existence of the Soviet Union came under threat, not from outside, but from the growing demands of individual republics for independence (see Part VIII, Topic 16). Thirdly, old rivalries and hostilities between the various eastern European nations and ethnic groups, stifled under the grey weight of Stalinism, soon began to emerge. Yet another complication was the reunification of Germany, with its effect on the balance of power in Europe, and on plans for European unity.

Yet by the early 1990s, many Europeans, both West and East, were more hopeful about the future of the old Continent than at any time in the century. The arms buildup to World War I, the tensions and failures of the interwar years, the grim confrontations of the Cold War, were replaced by talk of the common house of Europe (see Part VIII, Topic 16). It was at least possible that at some future time NATO and the Warsaw Pact would no longer be needed—or at least would no longer serve their original purpose. The Western European union of 1992 began to appear not as the final stage in European unification, but as a beginning.

Questions for Further Study

1. What were the main stages in the "de-Stalinization" of the Soviet Union? How far was the process reversed under Brezhnev?
2. How did the Communist regimes of Eastern Europe differ in their relationship to the Soviet Union?
3. What factors helped to prepare the countries of Eastern Europe for the collapse of Soviet influence? Were they chiefly political, economic, or social?
4. To what extent were Gorbachev's reforms in the Soviet Union a reaction to a process that could not be halted?

Suggestions for Further Reading

Banac, Ivo. *With Stalin Against Tito: Conformist Splits in Yugoslav Communism.* Ithaca, NY, 1989.
Cohen, S. E., and K. vanden Heuvel. *Voices of Glasnost. Interviews with Gorbachev's Reformers.* New York, 1989.
Davies, R. W. *Soviet History in the Gorbachev Revolution.* Bloomington, IN, 1989.
Garton Ash, T. *We the People: The Revolutions of 1989.* London, 1990.
Hosking, G. *The Awakening of the Soviet Union.* Cambridge, MA, 1990.
Rothschild, J. *Return to Diversity: A Political History of East Central Europe.* New York, 1989.
Selbourne, D. *Death of the Dark Hero: Eastern Europe 1987–1990.* London, 1990.
Wolchnik, S. L., and A. G. Meyer. *Women, State, and Party in Eastern Europe.* Durham, NC, 1985.

Topic 13

Mobility and Social Change: Toward the Consumer Society

Throughout most of Europe, the postwar years saw the restructuring of society by increasing state support for the lives of large numbers of citizens. Social welfare legislation proved so popular that even when, in the 1970s, national economies began to decline, governments avoided cutbacks as much as possible.

Several groups played a special role in the formation of postwar society. Many intellectuals, who had seen left-wing movements as the only real defense against fascism and capitalist dictatorship, grew increasingly disillusioned with the political alternatives facing them. Some, like the Frenchman André Malraux, chose to play an active role in political life. Others, including the German Heinrich Böll and the Englishman John Osborne, used their novels and plays to comment on contemporary problems. A third category, led by the French existentialist philosopher Jean-Paul Sartre, maintained a broader theoretical concern.

Other groups preferred action to words. Growing dissatisfaction with the direction in which capitalist society was moving led to widespread protests, which reached a head in 1968 with violent student and worker demonstrations. On the whole, the "Spirit of '68" consisted of a release of accumulated tensions without producing any major change of direction. The 1970s and 1980s brought a general relaxation in the polarization between left and right. The only major exception in Western Europe was Britain, where confrontation between government and trade unions continued to influence political life. In Eastern Europe, and in particular in Poland, the trade union movement played a vital role in the transition to more democratic government.

Perhaps the most significant changes in late-20th-century society were produced by the women's movement. As women became an increasingly important part of the workforce, and began to play a part in running industry and government, their traditional role became increasingly questioned and rethought. The battle for equal rights was fought at a variety of levels and few elements of society remained untouched, from campaigns for national office to individual families.

The whole structure of family life in Western society entered a period of considerable turmoil. Greater sexual freedom, coupled with vastly improved methods of contraception, caused many to rethink the institution of marriage. The birthrate declined. Perhaps more significantly, divorce became widespread and by 1980 had more than doubled.

The increase in prosperity created new attitudes and expectations. Urban-industrial society became virtually the only form of life, as traditional food production was taken over by "agribusiness." Within the cities, young workers and professionals—without family responsibilities, and therefore with more money to spend—were barraged by publicity, as advertising assumed ever greater importance for most corporation budgets. Many workers from the Third World, attracted by Western prosperity, settled in Western European countries. Their arrival provided a source of cheap labor for unpopular jobs but also led to an increase in racism and the resurgence of the far right.

By the early 1990s, society in Western Europe was moving into a postindustrial phase. As machines, in particular the computer, revolutionized the processes of industrial production, more and more people were working in service industries rather than in factories. This "new industrial revolution" seemed bound to lead to radical changes in the lifestyles and social roles of both individuals and institutions.

LIFE IN THE WELFARE STATE

The spread of the welfare state ushered in profound changes in the lives of ordinary citizens. Social policy was no longer only a means of improving the lives of the workers, for the expanded concept of welfare aimed to achieve a broad social balance. An all-party agreement in France in 1946 looked to the extension of social security to "promote the solidarity and renewal of French society." The Basic Law of West Germany, formulated in 1948, declared that the state was a "social state" with a "social market economy." Not all these egalitarian aims were achieved in practice. In West Germany, different classes received different treatment: blue-collar workers and white-collar salaried employees had separate insurance funds.

Welfare systems spread rapidly in the 1950s and 1960s. In 1950, the only Western European countries where more than 70 percent of the population were covered by welfare legislation were Britain, Denmark, Norway, and Sweden. By 1975, the only countries where coverage was still below 70 percent were Greece, Portugal, and Spain. Although Eastern Europe dismissed the notion of welfare as a "bourgeois capitalist concept," these governments tended to introduce legislation providing insurance and pensions. These were initially reserved for state employees, leaving peasants and the self-employed uncovered. Retirement age was low—in Czechoslovakia and Hungary 60 for men and 55 for women—but so were the pensions.

The Welfare State and the Family

The welfare state affected life from birth to death. In Sweden in the 1970s, public doctors treated 99.7 percent of all newborn babies, and all parents were required by law to submit their children to a medical checkup when they reached the age of four. Children throughout Western and Eastern Europe went to state-subsidized schools, and then on to public universities. Unlike the United States, there were very few private European universities.

A young couple could generally count on some form of subsidized housing, and help in bringing up their children. Welfare legislation introduced in France in 1946 gave women benefits and maternity leave before and after pregnancy, and provided day care centers and after-school programs. Most European countries followed suit. At work, employees were covered by national insurance schemes, which would allow them treatment by a national health service. On retirement, they spent the last years of their lives drawing a state pension.

Nor did the welfare state cover only basic expenses such as these. The state ran, and therefore controlled the cost of, services such as energy, communications, and transport. Culture and the arts were also subsidized, and most postwar governments in Europe had a Ministry of Culture. One of France's most distinguished literary figures, André Malraux (see below), served in such a post, and ministers of culture played important if controversial roles in East European politics. The notion of state support for the arts continued into the 1980s. In the opera season of 1987–1988, La Scala (Milan) received public funds to cover 74 percent of its expenses; similar grants were 78 percent for the Munich opera, 76 percent for Vienna, and 82 percent for Paris. In the same period, the Metropolitan Opera House in New York could count on 2 percent.

The Welfare Crisis

In 1950 the average proportion of the gross national product devoted by Western European countries to social welfare was 9.4 percent. By 1977 this figure had risen to 22.4 percent. The expense of health care alone more than doubled. At the same time, the average age of the European population continued to rise. Improved medical techniques, which were more widely available, enabled increasing numbers of people to survive to retirement age; on retirement, they began drawing pensions and continued to need state medical care.

The vast rise in costs coincided with the economic recessions of the 1970s. The enormous growth of the 1950s and 1960s turned stagnant, and most western European countries were badly hit by the 1970s oil crises. The welfare state, which had seemed a permanent feature of postwar European life, became subject to agonized debate. Conservatives argued that social welfare was too expensive and too inefficient, and should be dismantled, while private enterprise and individual initiative should be encouraged. On the other side, radical critics claimed that social legislation emphasized material welfare without creating a sense of community.

Throughout the 1980s, both conservative and socialist governments in Western Europe cut back benefit levels. Nonetheless welfare was so integral a part of the lives of millions that most countries continued to devote large proportions of their annual budget to it, hoping to cover the costs with higher taxes and increased production. Only in Thatcher's Britain was there a sustained attempt to shift back the cost of welfare to the private sector. The results produced furious public debate about the consequences for Britain's educational and medical systems, and about the general issue of social justice.

THE INTELLECTUALS' DILEMMA: EXISTENTIALISM OR COMMITMENT

In the euphoria of victory in 1945, the intellectual map seemed easy enough to interpret. Of the two chief movements of the 1930s, the radical right was discredited beyond repair. The left was triumphant, for Communists and Socialists had been among the leaders in resistance struggles throughout Europe, both West and East. Furthermore, the Soviet Union, the supreme Communist power, had been one of the principal architects of military victory.

Yet as the Soviets moved to occupy eastern Europe and set up their puppet governments there, doubts began to arise. Even before the war, some intellectuals had seen the darker side of the Russian Revolution and its consequences. In 1940, Arthur Koestler (1905–1983) published *Darkness at Noon*, a novel which drew on the Moscow purges of the 1930s to indict the excesses of Stalinism.

The Intellectual and Society

As many began to face disillusionment with all forms of social organization, some artists and thinkers turned with increased despair to the search for meaning in a hostile world. The works of the Irish playwright Samuel Beckett (1906–1989) presented an enigmatic vision of a world beyond logic. In his best-known play, *Waiting for Godot*, two bizarre characters wait for an event that never takes place: the arrival of Godot. Is Godot God? Does his nonarrival illustrate the hopelessness of life? At least the two continue their vigil. In other works, Beckett presented a bleaker vision of the possibilities of human communication, and of the significance of existence.

Other intellectuals sought to illuminate aspects of the modern dilemma. The Swedish filmmaker Ingmar Bergman used his films to explore the disappearance of religious faith and the demands of contemporary despair. As knowledge of the atrocities of the Nazi death camps began to come to light, some writers tried to give voice to the experience. In some cases they were actual survivors. The Italian Primo Levi (1919–1985), and the Romanian-born Elie Wiesel (born 1928) both wrote works meditating on their experiences in the camps.

Not all thinkers took so hopeless a view of the possibilities for change. Among the first postwar writers to take an active role in government was André Malraux (1901–1976), one of the most distinguished figures in French 20th-century culture. Although never a Marxist, Malraux had impeccable left-wing credentials. He fought for the Republicans in the Spanish Civil War, was one of France's leading antifascists before World War II, and was active in the Resistance. He served as minister of information from 1945 to 1946, and as minister of culture from 1959 to 1969.

Many on the left accused Malraux of betraying their cause by taking the Gaullist (that is, right-wing) side in the Cold War. Malraux himself insisted that he was defending society against Stalinism. In perhaps his most profound literary work, *The Voices of Silence* (1951), he claimed that art—"the essential, eternal assertion of human freedom over destiny"—transcended history.

In some cases intellectuals used their work to fight for social and political change without actually playing an active role. Few voices spoke out more powerfully or authoritatively about the evils of Stalinism than Alexander Solzhenitsyn (born 1918), who based his descriptions of Stalin's labor camps on his own experiences there. At first suppressed, then expelled, Solzhenitsyn moved from epic denunciations of Stalinism to broader criticism of the nature of modern society.

In Germany, Heinrich Böll (1917–1985) used bitter satire to expose what he saw as the moral vacuum behind the West German "economic miracle." His books saw love as the only mitigator of despair in postwar Europe. Another critic of German society was Günter Grass (born 1927). A committed socialist, Grass explored the nature of human identity, and the moral fragmentation of modern (in particular, German) European society.

In Britain, social criticism became symbolized in the figure of the "angry young man"—classless, disillusioned, rebellious. The archetypal example appeared in *Look Back in Anger*, a play by John Osborne (born 1929), first performed in 1956. Osborne and others bitterly questioned the comfortable assurances of the welfare state and of middle-class society. A more specific issue which a number of writers addressed was that of feminism (discussed below). Sylvia Plath (1932–1963) and Doris Lessing (born 1919) both moved to England—Plath from the United States and Lessing from southern Africa. Their works explore feminine consciousness from a variety of angles.

STUDENTS, WORKERS, AND POWER: 1968 AND ITS AFTERMATH

By the mid-1960s, the driving force of European renewal had begun to run out of steam. After the initial excitement of reconstruction, society began to show deep signs of protest and grievance. The two chief groups to lead demonstrations against the state were students and workers.

The Student Uprisings of 1968

The wave of student demonstrations that peaked in the spring of 1968 was by no means limited to Western Europe. Similar protest rallies took place in Eastern Europe, in Africa, and in the United States; in the latter, there were passionate demonstrations against American participation in the Vietnam War.

The war in Vietnam also figured in the European protests, but there were also more local causes. By the late 1960s, the baby boom of the war years had led to overcrowded classrooms and teaching facilities. Furthermore the increased number of students qualifying meant that job opportunities were becoming scarcer. To some extent the problem became seen in terms of class warfare: few university professors and not enough students were from the working classes.

The disorders in Germany lasted from 1967 to 1971 and their eventual suppression led to the formation of secret left-wing terrorist groups. Similar "revolutionary cells" were created in Italy, where left-wing agitation produced neofascist counterdemonstrations and a revival of the far right. Those killed on both sides were hailed as martyrs to their cause; the chain of reprisal lasted well into the 1980s.

The most spectacular demonstrations occurred in Paris in May 1968. When clumsy police actions tried to prevent student sit-ins and classroom occupations, the situation erupted. Students occupied the main university quarter, and set up street barricades—in the spirit of 1848—to prevent police access. The general goals of the demonstrators remained vague. They felt that society should be changed, but were inspired by no coherent ideology. "Be realistic: demand the impossible!" was one of the popular slogans.

This lack of an overall strategy diminished the long-term effect of the protests. When order was restored, most governments reformed university structures and increased the influence in academic affairs of students and younger faculty members. On the whole, though, the student demonstrations gave voice to a general sense of uncertainty about contemporary society without producing a real change of direction. When, 30 years later, former participants gathered throughout Europe to remember and commemorate the events of their youth, the mood was generally more of nostalgia than of political protest. Many of those involved admitted that they themselves had become as "bourgeois" as those against whom they had protested.

Labor Protests

One direct effect of the student demonstrations, however, was to galvanize workers into protest action. In the inflation-ridden 1960s, wages often failed to keep up with prices. Factory work, with its unending assembly line monotony, provided little work satisfaction. In many countries, trade unions seemed less concerned with the welfare of their members than with waging their own political battles.

The problems came to a head in France in 1968, as workers followed the example of the students and took to the streets; at the height of the protests, some 10 million were involved. A frightened government increased wages. A month later it consolidated its power when De Gaulle and his party swept to victory in a

PUBLIC FIGURES AND PRIVATE LIVES

SIMONE DE BEAUVOIR AND JEAN-PAUL SARTRE

The most overarching attempt to find a path forward for modern society was that of the existentialists. More an attitude than a coherent system of philosophy, existentialism began in the 19th century with the ideas of the Danish theologian Søren Kierkegaard (1813–1855). According to Kierkegaard, individual humans are more important than collective abstractions—"The crowd is untruth."

The most important exponent of the existentialist view after World War II was the Frenchman Jean-Paul Sartre (1905–1980). Sartre's intellectual position was reinforced by his experiences; after being a prisoner of war, he lived through the German occupation of France, and played a part in the Resistance. After the war, his writings served as inspiration to a generation of intellectuals.

In politics, Sartre tried to reconcile two opposed convictions: his belief in freedom and individualism, and his attraction to the ideas of brotherhood and community represented by an ideal Communism. Sartre's own relationship with the Communist party remained ambiguous. While generally approving many of the aims of Marxism, he wrestled throughout his life with the degree to which they justified the means used to achieve them.

His existentialist works tried to come to terms with the problems of living in a world without God, where there is no ultimate significance to existence. People are alone, forced to decide who they are, "condemned to be free." In such a world, it was necessary to come to terms with freedom, and try to devise a system of behavior.

It was typical of Sartre's commitment to intellectual enquiry that he both wrote about and explored in his actual life the issue of feminism. His inspiration in this was Simone de Beauvoir (1908–1986). Together, they became the most celebrated intellectual couple in the postwar period.

De Beauvoir grew up conventionally enough in a Parisian middle-class family. After World War I, when she needed to find some means of supporting herself, against her family's wishes she decided to become an academic. De Beauvoir and Sartre met at the Sorbonne and fell in love. For the rest of Sartre's life, they maintained an intense emotional and intellectual union. Refusing to marry, they also remained independent, often living separately and having other love affairs.

De Beauvoir's most widely read book, *The Second Sex* (1949), dealt with the nature of womanhood, and analyzed the way in which women are locked into gender definitions. For many women, the traditional feminine role had its attractions. The "independent woman," by contrast, preferred the harder but more rewarding life of work, self-definition, and significant interaction with the male "Other."

The Second Sex was widely read, at least in part because of De Beauvoir's relationship with Sartre. Some readers were shocked (or claimed to be) by her frank discussion of issues such as misogyny and lesbianism. Others accused Sartre of having written the book. His influence on her thought emerged far more consistently, however, in her four volumes of memoirs. Following the existential principles advocated by Sartre, she described her own self-creation by means of her relationships with Sartre and others.

De Beauvoir and Sartre illustrated by the example of their own public lives the possibilities opened up by collaboration between individual men and women on equal terms. (In private, De Beauvoir seems to have been rather more conventionally bourgeois, often abandoning her feminism to cater to Sartre's wishes.) Both of them inspired countless individuals to question the basic premises that underpinned society, and to search for new and more satisfying ways to face the uncertainties of the modern world. De Beauvoir, although criticized by early feminists for underestimating the need for radical change, became in the late 1960s one of the women's movement's most important leaders.

Students rioting at the Sorbonne, Paris, 1968.

general election. Many of those who voted for him, including Communists, were also voting against the radical student protestors who had challenged the values of postwar society.

WOMEN IN A CHANGING SOCIETY: THE CHALLENGE OF FEMINISM

Since the days of the French Revolution of 1789, European women have been active participants in shaping their own lives. Women's movements inspired by a variety of ideologies sought equality for women throughout the 19th and 20th centuries.

After World War II, women gained the right to vote in every European nation except Switzerland and the principality of Liechtenstein. Women have been particularly active in Socialist and Communist political parties, where a long tradition of support for women's rights attracted them. In the 1950s and 1960s, politically active women tended to involve themselves in the great international issues of the day: the dangers of nuclear testing, oppression in Eastern Europe, the Vietnam War.

Beginning in the late 1960s, new feminist groups began to form to deal specifically with the treatment of women. The first international meeting of the new women's movement was held at Oxford, Great Britain, in 1970. By the end of the decade, hundreds of groups throughout Europe debated women's issues from widely different and sometimes conflicting positions. Some of these distinctions were due to the specific situation of women in individual countries.

European Women, East and West

The Soviet Union was the first government in history to include female emancipation in its constitution. Liberal divorce laws, state child care facilities, and legalized abortion also existed. Yet the reality of gender relations there was far from ideal. As late as the 1980s, Soviet women earned only two-thirds of male income for the same work. Almost half of the women in the labor force held unskilled manual jobs. While women held almost a third of all membership cards in the Communist party, they represented only a tiny minority in party or government posts. At home, conditions also remained unequal, for Soviet men generally refused to assume household responsibilities.

In Western Europe, conditions for women were mixed. In 1970, women in most European countries earned little more than half the wages earned by men in equivalent positions. In technical professions, such as medicine and engineering, Soviet women held a significantly higher percentage of positions than American women. Yet legislation favoring equality and women's rights had been passed in virtually every Western nation. Even in southern countries such as Italy, where the influence of the Catholic Church was still pervasive, divorce laws were enacted.

Feminism in West Germany

Women in West Germany faced two problems in organizing themselves as a separate and distinct category. In the first place, postwar German society encouraged conformity, and the avoidance of anything that could be construed as extreme. Secondly, in the very shadow of the Berlin Wall, the Marxist and Socialist origins of 19th-century feminism created instant suspicion.

The first major feminist initiative in West Germany proved, in fact, a failure. In 1971, a national conference of women began a drive to legalize abortion. Not only was the law's antiabortion stance intensified, but proabortion groups became subject to police harassment and those suspected of political activism found themselves without jobs.

One of the consequences of official opposition to the feminist movement was that the most extreme of its leaders took to terrorist activities to fight their battles. Ulrike Meinhof (1934–1976) was one of the leading journalists to promote the feminist cause. In 1970, she helped to found the Red Army Faction, which was responsible for a burst of murder and arson over the next decade. Meinhof herself was captured in 1972, and died in her cell four years later under mysterious circumstances.

Other women found a more congenial setting in the Green Movement, which aimed at defending the environment. Claiming that the destruction of nature represented a negative aspect of male supremacy, they helped the Green party to become a significant force in West German political life. Some women expected the Greens to respond by promoting feminist causes in return. On the whole, however, the predominantly male leadership resisted attempts to become involved in women's issues.

Italian Feminism

The Italian feminist movement had greater success in spearheading reform. In 1945, Italian women were among those least-well-off in Western Europe. They were a source of cheap labor, and had little legal protection. In the 1950s, married women could not apply for a passport or travel abroad without their husband's permission.

The first victory of the Union of Italian Women was the successful campaign to introduce divorce; a popular referendum legalized it in 1970. If West

Women political leaders: Sirimaro Bandaranaike of Sri Lanka, 1971; Golda Meir of Israel, 1973; Indira Gandhi of India, 1977; Margaret Thatcher of Great Britain, 1979; Vigdis Finnbogadottir of Iceland, 1980.

Women demonstrating in Rome against outdated laws, 1974.

German women had to contend with conservatism and fear of communism, Italian feminists were faced with the opposition of the Catholic Church in many of their battles. Only after mass demonstrations, which included women chaining themselves to the gates of the Vatican, did the Christian Democrat government make the distribution of contraceptive information legal. Even more impressive was the success in 1978 of the campaign to legalize abortion.

Women activists were also in the lead in seeking reform of other aspects of society. Throughout the 1980s, feminist groups sponsored demonstrations against the Mafia and other organized crime, pointing to them as extreme forms of *machismo*.

By the late 1980s, the European women's movement was facing conservative reaction. Pope John Paul II reaffirmed the Catholic Church's traditional view of women. In Britain, Margaret Thatcher, the country's first woman prime minister, began to cut social benefits that had given women the possibility of self-support. The scourge of AIDS, a sexually transmittable disease, encouraged monogamous relationships. Originally believed to affect only homosexual males, AIDS also spread by means of heterosexual contact and by the exchange of hypodermic needles used in drug abuse.

Yet the feminist challenge had changed perceptions about gender differences and their effects throughout large sections of Western society. No politician could afford to ignore the "woman's question," or fail to pursue the women's vote. At the humblest level,

American feminist leader Betty Friedan with Indian, Kenyan, and Egyptian delegates, 1984.

few families were unaware that new ways of viewing old stereotypes were in the air. As so often is the case, revolution sometimes brought reaction, but in the last decade of the 20th century the issue of feminism showed no sign of disappearing.

SEX, MARRIAGE, AND THE FAMILY: NEW DIRECTIONS

The postwar period saw a loosening of centuries-old sexual attitudes. Women's fashions emphasized breasts and legs, rather than concealing them. In the 1960s women sunbathers of all ages wore bikinis, and a decade later "topless" sunbathing became increasingly common in Europe. Even Spain, for long under Franco a bastion of conservative social attitudes, permitted the new fashion after the dictator's death. Books, magazines, and films encouraged women to take pleasure in sex and provided them with detailed instructions on how to do so.

In the mid-1950s the appearance of *Playboy* magazine and other similar publications heralded a change in the male sexual image. Instead of emphasizing the man's role as husband and father, they glamorized the attractions of personal gratification and sexual freedom. Partial or even total female nudity became acceptable in publicity posters and images, and sex shops opened up in many northern European capitals.

Attitudes toward "alternative" sexual patterns remained mixed. Sweden decriminalized homosexuality between consenting adults in 1944, as did Britain in the early 1960s. Most Western European countries had never had specific legislation, in fact, that treated homosexuality as a crime. In the 1960s, gay and lesbian activists joined women, blacks, and other groups struggling for civil rights and organized vocal protest movements. Yet in general, although awareness and tolerance increased, homosexuality remained frowned on and a barrier to public office. The appearance and rapid spread of AIDS, at first mistakenly associated exclusively with homosexuality, served to increase prejudice against gays and lesbians.

Contraception and the Birthrate

For both men and women, especially young ones, the appearance of the birth control "pill," and the wide diffusion of other contraceptive methods, meant that more-or-less casual sexual contacts no longer ran the risk of producing unwanted pregnancies. As a result, many began to have sexual relations at an early age. In Scandinavia in the 1980s, the average for a girl was fifteen years, two months; for a boy fifteen years, five months.

The new ease of contraception meant that married couples had even greater freedom in planning their families. Increased numbers of women, freed from the burdens of repeated pregnancies, joined the workforce. The birthrate, which soared during the "baby boom" of the war and the postwar period of the "economic miracle," declined steeply after 1964. In France, the rate of births per 1000 population fell from 22 in 1950 to 14 in 1980; in Czechoslovakia for the same period, the fall was from 18 per 1000 to 12. Even Italy, with its traditionalist family attitudes, and Spain (after Franco's death) followed suit. More permissive legislation on abortion, introduced in most of eastern Europe (1956–1957), Britain (1967), and France (1975–1979), further reduced the rate of population increase.

By the 1980s, the rate became stabilized in most European countries at "zero population growth": the annual number of births equaled that of deaths. The average in Western Europe was 1.7 children per woman, that in Eastern Europe 1.9 to 2.2. One of the chief effects of this was the disappearance of large families. Except for Ireland and Albania, the relative number of third births fell from 15 to 20 percent in 1950 to 9 to 12 in 1980. The two-child family became more than ever the most common family unit.

Patterns of Marriage and Divorce

In the years of renewed prosperity after the war, the rate of marriage rose steeply. In 1950, the proportion of unmarried women in their late 40s was 20.5 percent in Norway and 16.6 percent in England. By 1975 the number had fallen to, respectively, 5.9 and 7. Ireland again proved the exception: in the 1980s, 25 percent of Irish women never married.

Along with the increase in marriage rates went a corresponding rise in divorce. The factors involved were many and complex. With marriages often contracted at an early age, and a higher life expectancy, couples were faced with longer periods of living together, with the increased possibility of friction. In the early 20th century, the average marriage lasted 20 years, before being terminated by the death of one of the partners. By 1980 the average duration of marriages unbroken by divorce was 35 years.

The drastic fall in the birthrate enabled increasing numbers of women to develop their own careers, or at least to contribute to the family income. The consequent rethinking of traditional family roles, encouraged by the women's movement, inevitably changed conventional attitudes. As a result, legal discouragement of divorce, together with cultural disapproval, greatly lessened.

On average in the 1980s, in both Eastern and Western Europe, the rate of marriages ending in divorce was around 25 percent. The highest rate was in

Denmark and Sweden—almost 50 percent—and the lowest in Poland—around 11 percent. Divorce remained difficult in Portugal, and impossible in Ireland and Spain; Italy legalized divorce in 1971.

Thus the phenomena of a high rate of marriage and an increasing number of divorces coexisted in European society. Many of those who ended one marriage contracted another. Others chose to return to a single life, and the number of those living alone rose dramatically. In 1980 over half the households in Paris, Vienna, and West Berlin consisted of only one person; 25 percent of the cities' populations lived alone. In this as in other respects the late 20th century was marked by a strong break with past social habits.

THE AGE OF CONSUMERISM: AFFLUENCE AND ITS CONSEQUENCES

The general increase in prosperity of the postwar years transformed the lives of most of Western Europe's citizens. Some of this, at least, made its way across the Iron Curtain into Eastern Europe: by the 1980s, East Germans and Czechs could buy McDonald's hamburgers and Italian Benetton sweaters. The spread of technology made for more leisure time. Among the ways of passing it was travel, facilitated by postwar developments in air transport and packaged vacations. In the late 1980s, an average summer saw some 400 million Europeans on the move, taking holidays that ranged from a day at the beach to a cruise halfway round the world.

The concentration of society in great cities and their suburbs forced traditional agricultural life patterns into further decline. In part this was due to continued migration from country to city, a tendency especially strong in Greece and southern Italy. An additional cause was the inability of traditional farming methods to provide food for increasing populations. As a result, governments encouraged the development of "agribusinesses"—large corporations that mass produced and marketed food products such as milk, eggs, and poultry.

As goods began to circulate within the Common Market, they crossed national lines. A shopper in a small-town West German supermarket could expect to find olive oil from Spain, Greece, and Italy; chocolates from Belgium; flowers from the Netherlands; tea from Britain; cheese from France; and smoked salmon from Ireland. In some cases the free flow of goods caused resentment. In the "wine wars" of the 1970s and 1980s, French protestors overturned and emptied trucks containing inexpensive Italian wine. The same diffusion of products occurred in Eastern Europe, although at a much lower consumer level. Food shortages became unknown in Western Europe, and increasingly resented in the Soviet bloc countries; they helped in bringing down several governments in the fall of 1989, and remained one of the Soviet Union's severest problems in the early 1990s.

As wages and the number of wage earners rose, young workers and professionals began to attract the attention of marketing organizations. Many young people continued to live at home until they married—far more than in the United States—and thus had considerable disposable incomes. Companies began to direct their products and advertising at this new "youth market," rather than toward the traditional family one.

A resort condominium complex on the French Riviera.

Throughout the 1970s and 1980s, attendance at "family films" declined, while discotheques mushroomed even in small provincial centers.

The "youth cult" led to a new emphasis on physical fitness, and changing eating patterns. In traditionally meat-eating countries such as Germany and Britain, the consumption of red meat fell, and in France the "Nouvelle Cuisine" (New Cooking) provided a lighter approach to the preparation of elaborate dishes. Vegetarian and macrobiotic restaurants became more common. At home, as more family members worked, meals ceased to be an important and extended period for family life and exchange. They shrank in size, and working women turned increasingly to pre-prepared or frozen food for their families, which microwave ovens—now an essential tool in many kitchens—heated up in a few minutes.

Immigration

As standards of living rose in Western Europe, immigrants began to arrive from Third World countries. Earlier immigration had seen waves of movement from the poorer parts of Europe itself—principally the Mediterranean region—to the richer northern countries. In the late 1940s and 1950s, large numbers of Italians from the rural south migrated to Belgium, where they worked in the mines. By the 1980s, as one of the four most industrialized European nations, Italy attracted immigrants from North and Sub-Saharan Africa, and from the Philippines.

In many cases, immigrants took menial and unpopular jobs as hospital orderlies, road workers, garbage collectors. Many worked illegally, and received less than official minimum wages. On some occasions, local authorities made efforts to allow ethnic groups to maintain some form of identity, while encouraging community participation. The Turkish *"Gastarbeiter"* ("guest workers" in German) were an example of relatively peaceful integration.

Elsewhere racial tension proved pervasive. Britain, as head of the multiracial Commonwealth, attracted widespread immigration, both black and white. Whereas Australians and Canadians were easily absorbed, Caribbean and Pakistani immigrants often had difficulty in finding acceptance. A generation of immigrants' children born in Britain grew up, regarding themselves as British but often resented by their neighbors. Successive governments introduced legislation to combat various forms of racism. Nonetheless, during the 1970s and 1980s race riots broke out at intervals. In some cases they were provoked by the National Front, an extreme right-wing organization which rose to prominence in the general election campaign of 1979. At other times, ethnic minorities held their own demonstrations, to protest discrimination.

Computer skills are taught to children in a predominantly immigrant neighborhood.

Similar problems developed elsewhere in Europe. A French version of the National Front campaigned in favor of "France for the French." In the 1986 general election, there seemed a possibility, although it remained unfulfilled, that center-right candidates would seek its support. In 1990 Italy, one of the European countries most open to Third World immigrants, was the scene of growing racial tension, as African street vendors were banned from the streets of Florence. Government officials and social workers in most countries remained only too aware of the possibility of increased tensions, but the best that seemed possible was an uneasy truce.

Europe in the Postindustrial Era

By the early 1990s, it seemed that European life, like that of North America, was entering a new phase. The computer technology developed over the preceding decade now controlled most heavy industrial production. Following the example of Japan, industries from automobile manufacturing to printing used machines, appropriately programmed, to make their products. In countries where the trade unions were traditionally powerful, including Britain and Italy, automation led to bitter strike action. Modern day Luddites, however, had no more success than their predecessors in halting technological progress.

In this new postindustrial era, more and more people were working in "service industries." Banking, insurance, communications, entertainment—these and others replaced traditional manufacturing jobs, whether at labor or management level. With the rise of the personal computer, many ordinary tasks—depositing a check, buying a pair of shoes or a plane ticket, registering for school—could be done without leaving home.

Wilder imaginations pictured the 20th-century city as redundant in the postindustrial world. People would live in the suburbs, linked to one another and to the outside world by telecommunications and their computer screens. The office would be at home. Social patterns would be revolutionized. The gap between the late 20th century and the late 21st would become as great as that between the end of the 19th century and the 20th.

Some of the effects of these broad changes were already visible. The ability to work at even the most complex jobs from their own homes enabled growing numbers of women to combine family and career. Yet on the whole the postindustrial revolution had a considerable way to go. As it spread and intensified, it seemed bound to lead to radical changes in social and political life.

In the second half of the 20th century, many long-cherished social institutions came under attack. In public life, authoritarian leadership gave way to a search for consensus. Most European nations made a determined attempt to achieve a consistent standard of social welfare. Women continued to battle for equal rights. At home, traditional roles and gender relationships gave way to a period of uncertainty about the rules and function of family life.

By the late 20th century, two competing tendencies drove society. On the one hand the forces of mass communication, ease of transport, and sheer economic necessity produced a "global village." The search for some form of political and economic unity, or at least community of interests, was accompanied by the spread of social and cultural uniformity. Yet, at the same time, there developed growing pressure toward the assertion of national and ethnic identity, real or imagined. From Wales to Lithuania to Lombardy, Corsica to Croatia, minorities campaigned, often violently, for some form of independence. The long-term effects on society of the inevitable conflicts between the two forces at play remained difficult to predict.

Questions for Further Study

1. What have been the main changes accomplished by the feminist movement since World War II? What has their effect been on Western society?
2. What role has nationalism played in the evolution of postwar European life? How far—if at all—has it been linked with racism?
3. In what ways do western European and American attitudes to politics, society, and culture differ? How do people in former Soviet bloc countries compare with either?

Suggestions for Further Reading

Caute, D. *The Year of the Barricades: A Journey Through 1968.* New York, 1988.

Gillis, J. R. *Youth and History: Tradition and Change in European Age Relations, 1770–Present.* New York, 1981.

Hellman, J. A. *Journeys Among Women: Feminism in Five Italian Cities.* New York, 1987.

Hughes, H. S. *Sophisticated Rebels: The Political Culture of European Dissent.* Cambridge, MA, 1988.

Mead, M. *Culture and Commitment: The New Relationship Between the Generations in the 1970s.* New York, 1978.

Schlesinger, J. R. *America at Century's End.* New York, 1989.

Topic 14

Culture in the Age of Uncertainty

In the immediate postwar period, with Europe in ruins, American culture assumed a dominating role in Western civilization. Just as the United States, as the Western superpower, led in the reconstruction of the Western European economies, so American ideas, styles, and themes became widely diffused throughout all levels of European life.

The area to be most radically affected was popular culture. The rapid spread of American popular music, movies, and television programs, of Coca-Cola and blue jeans, made an impact that extended from the smallest Irish hamlet to the Greek islands. Over the following decades they even penetrated behind the Iron Curtain, where enthusiasm for American ways and products provided a way of rebelling against conformist regimes.

In the world of painting, American artists led the way in the move toward abstraction of the 1940s and the return to realism in the early 1960s. Painters like Jasper Johns and Andy Warhol invented a vision of "the American scene," and then diffused it. American emphasis on technology encouraged sculptors to use metals such as stainless steel welded into shapes combining weightiness with grace. By contrast, the Englishman Henry Moore—perhaps the best-known sculptor of the 1950s and 1960s—evoked primordial forms in stone figures on a Renaissance scale.

A number of influential European architects had fled to the United States in the late 1930s. The most important of these, Mies van der Rohe, set the style for much urban architecture in the late 20th century. The clean lines and repetitive forms of city skyscrapers spread in both western and eastern Europe, often with deadening aesthetic and human consequences. The Frenchman Le Corbusier opposed the "inhumanity" of such buildings by creating structures with greater variety.

In music, a vast gulf opened up between average music lovers and the avant-garde. Most performers limited themselves to the basic repertory of the Classical, Romantic, and early 20th-century eras. Advanced contemporary composers found their public increasingly shrinking. In the 1980s, minimalist composers began to close the gap, and the works of Philip Glass appealed to wider numbers. In the field of pop music, commercial interests combined with social statement (on occasion, at least) to achieve global circulation. The distribution of music videos, and worldwide telecasts of concerts such as the Live Aid concert of 1987, or the Mandela concert of 1990, reached a public of proportions inconceivable before the late 20th century.

The leading literary movement of the latter part of the century was postmodernism, a term more easily used than explained. The postmodernists generally rejected the modernist preoccupation with alienation and self-analysis. Using unconventional literary forms, they created works containing meanings to be teased out by the reader—the text itself, not the author, was the point.

By the 1990s Europe had withdrawn from the cultural shadow of the United States. Yet popular culture, and in particular pop music, remained under strong American domination. In the arts, however, the age of mass communications not surprisingly produced a constant exchange of cultural influences, which tended to extend increasingly to non-Western culture.

THE AMERICANIZATION OF EUROPE

In the early part of the 20th century, Americans turned to Europe as cultural arbiter. European artists and intellectuals set the pace and style of cultural development, headed American publishing companies and symphony orchestras, and helped American art collectors to build their holdings. French fashions, British automobiles, Italian aristocrats—all represented old world elegance and charm. Even in Hollywood, most quintessential of American settings, many of the most glamorous stars and directors were European: Greta Garbo, Rudolph Valentino, Fritz Lang, Alfred Hitchcock.

By the end of the war, with Europe's leading cultural nations either vanquished and in ruins, or exhausted from the conflict, roles became reversed. A weary Europe looked to America for spiritual recharging. The wide open spaces, the sense of unflagging optimism, the illusion of innocence, attracted a continent war-torn and deeply insecure.

Other, more practical factors helped to reinforce the Americanization of Europe. From Scotland to Hungary, many families had relatives in the United States, and so thought of it as a possible future home. The affluence and plenty of American life, represented by the cigarettes and nylons so freely dispensed by American servicemen, made a special appeal in the bare postwar years. Most importantly of all, American intervention had been decisive in helping the Europeans to put their own house in order; American troops seemed likely to stay around for the foreseeable future to help maintain that order.

As the Marshall Plan helped the western European nations to rebuild their economies, Europe's debt to the United States continued to be cultural as well as financial. With the diffusion of television, American programs and personalities became as familiar to audiences in Manchester, Munich, or Milan as on their home territory. The art-buying market moved from Paris to Manhattan. Success for an opera singer required an engagement at the Metropolitan Opera. American universities attracted the leading scholars in fields as diverse as nuclear physics and art history, while European universities began to offer courses in a new area: American Studies.

The process had, in fact, begun before the war. Many European artists and intellectuals fled to the United States in the 1930s to escape persecution or war. W. H. Auden, Arnold Schoenberg, Thomas Mann, Mies van der Rohe, Albert Einstein—all major influences in modern culture—spent the war in America.

POPULAR CULTURE: THE UNIVERSAL LANGUAGE

The aspect of life most overwhelmingly influenced by American ways was popular culture. In the 19th century, each country sought to develop its own national characteristics in the arts, and nationalism was a powerful force in art and politics alike. In the second half of the 20th century, the lifestyles of Europeans came to follow American models. As prosperity returned to western Europe, blue jeans, T-bone steaks, and supermarkets became the symbols of progress, followed in turn by fast food and disco nightclubs. In Eastern Europe, political and economic realities precluded such open Americanization. American pop music, however, provided at least temporary refuge from the bleakness of life under Stalin and Brezhnev.

The most singular feature of this popular culture was its universality. Never before had personalities, products, and fashions had so wide a diffusion. One

A German McDonald's, 1988. Note the inclusion of beer on the menu, and the punk teenagers.

obvious explanation was the phenomenon of mass communication, in particular television. Although introduced on a limited scale before World War II, television became generally available only in the 1950s. By 1980, one out of every five Poles owned a television set, while in France, Italy, and West Germany the figure was one in three. Its impact was instant. When a few years later space satellites made international telecasting possible, the "global village" became even smaller. The daily lives of countless millions of people, many of them in remote parts of the globe, could suddenly share common experiences. In some cases these were great public events: the Kennedy funeral, royal weddings, the dismantling of the Berlin Wall, the death of Princess Diana. In other cases television coverage contributed, for better or worse, in forming public opinion: the Vietnam War, the Tienanmen massacres of 1989, the Palestinian Intifada. More important, however, was the general sense of a shared culture, operating on the most basic day-to-day level.

The spread of American-style popular culture was not without its critics. Some charged the sheer act of watching television with causing physical damage. In 1964, surveys showed that television-watching habits in the United States, Britain, and Japan were much the same. A report to the American Academy of Pediatrics released in the same year accused television of causing fatigue, headache, loss of appetite, and vomiting, all of which could be cured only by abstinence. Others claimed that exposure to violence would adversely affect children and adults alike.

More serious critics feared that the relentless Americanization of everything from fast foods to buildings would lead to monotonous conformity, and the loss of individual character. Furthermore, giant United States–based conglomerate corporations came to wield enormous power, especially in developing countries. As the Cold War dragged on, and the United States became embroiled in Vietnam, European critics of America became more vocal. With political disillusionment came cultural doubts, and talk of urban wastelands and "Coca-Cola-ization."

By the 1990s it seemed as if "the American Century," proudly proclaimed in 1945, was drawing to its political conclusion. In the arts, global communications led to a growing internationalization of styles and movements. Yet, in popular culture, American models, promoted by American salesmanship, continued to appeal. The opening of a McDonald's in Moscow at the end of 1989 served as clearly as any summit meeting to proclaim the end of the Cold War.

THE VISUAL ARTS: FROM ABSTRACT EXPRESSIONISM TO CONCEPTUAL ART

Just as Paris dominated the art world at the beginning of the 20th century, so did New York in the years after World War II. Among the factors was the flight to the United States of a number of leading European avant-garde artists, including Hans Hoffmann (1880–1966), Josef Albers (1888–1976), and George Grosz (1893–1959). An important role was played by the American patron and collector Peggy Guggenheim (1898–1979), whose Art of This Century Gallery in New York became an important center for modern art.

Abstract Expressionism

Jackson Pollock (1912–1956), one of the leading members of the New York School, held his first one-man show at this gallery in 1943. The works he exhibited there were in a style that came to be known as "abstract expressionist." The paintings made no reference to recognizable subjects—they were abstract—and sought to express interior states of feeling—as the early 20th-century German Expressionists had.

Pollock's paintings used elements of random dripping, splashing, and pouring to produce intricate webs of color, filled with energy and movement.

Other abstract expressionists devised complex systems of color and image symbolism. Mark Rothko (1903–1970) experimented in using floating blocks of color to capture a sense of mystical transcendence; among his most ambitious works are those he painted for a chapel at Rice University, Houston. By the 1960s, artists were expanding the possibilities of pure color, with no reference to a specific state of mind. Helen Frankenthaler (born 1928) contrasted the liquid quality of her paint with stretches of bare, unpainted canvas.

Pop Art

In the mid-1950s, a new generation of painters was moving in exactly the opposite direction, toward the literal representation of mundane objects. Paintings of the American flag, beer cans, and toothbrushes by Jasper Johns (born 1930) were intended to reject the emotional and intellectual portentousness of abstract expressionism in favor of the symbols of popular culture.

The high priest of the cult of pop art was Andy Warhol (1930–1987), whose depictions of soap boxes and Coca-Cola bottles helped to reinforce the image of American conspicuous consumption. Some claimed that Warhol's apparent high seriousness, especially in his notorious icons of Marilyn Monroe and other celebrities, masked a severe social critic. Whatever Warhol's attitude to his subjects, his deliberately banal paintings and silk screen prints perfectly captured the spirit of an era which they contributed to create.

Faced with the explosion of American talent and interest in contemporary art, a number of important European artists were drawn to the United States. The English David Hockney (born 1937) moved to California, where he produced sunny, colorful works that owed something to the pop art "tradition." Francis Bacon (1909–1989) was an English artist in a very different tradition. His tormented figures and distorted images convey isolation and horror. Both in composition and in actual subject, Bacon's work often made reference to the old masters of the past, especially Velázquez.

Conceptual Art

By the 1970s, some artists were trying to break away entirely from what they saw as the straitjacket of any tradition, old or new. Conceptual artists aimed to cre-

November 1, 1948 by Jackson Pollack, one of the leading Abstract Impressionist artists.

Andy Warhol, *Mick Jagger.*

ate "objects" or experiences that were not intended to be bought or sold, or put in a museum. Their works, often consisting of unlikely materials such as corn flakes or ice, were installed and then dismantled.

The most spectacular environmental artists, Christo and Jeanne-Claude (both born 1935), devised projects involving hundreds of people and vast quantities of material. Their *Valley Curtain* stretched 1 million square feet of orange fabric across Rifle Gap in Colorado. Their major project was the *Running Fence*, 18 feet high and 24½ miles long, which ran through the farmland north of San Francisco in Marin and Sonoma Counties for two weeks in 1976; it had taken four years to bring the project to fulfillment.

Contemporary Sculpture

The sculptural equivalent of abstract expressionism was to be found in the work of David Smith (1906–1965). Instead of carving his pieces in stone or casting them in bronze, Smith constructed them by welding together sections of steel. He claimed that the metal expressed the spirit of the age: "power, structure, movement, progress, suspension, destruction, brutality." Some of Smith's works include objects found in junkyards, given new significance by the artistic context in which he placed them.

Pop art's use of the everyday and mundane reached a new degree of realism in the uncannily lifelike figures of Duane Hanson (born 1925). Common-place, dull, ordinary people, pushing a handcart, shopping at a supermarket, became transmuted into powerful criticism of the social forces that had produced them. Painstakingly built of polyester resin and fiberglass, the statues often wear real wigs, jewelry, and clothes. They alarmingly evoke precisely that banality and weariness of the age of affluence which critics of the "American dream" often castigate.

Henry Moore (1898–1986), the grand old man of 20th-century sculpture, drew his inspiration not from the present, but from the remote past. The art of ancient Egypt, pre-Columbian America, Africa, and natural objects—bones, caves, stones—all provided sources for his work. His creation of monumental sculptures for specific locations, often out-of-doors, put him in line with the sculptors of the Renaissance. His themes included the basic stuff of humanity: mother and child, sexuality, death. Moore's own attitude to sculpture—his own and others'—saw the art form as

Christo's work, like this *Valley Curtain* in Rifle, Colorado, uses forms of sculpture to decorate buildings or, as here, natural sites.

still vital in the late 20th century: "The best sculptures are static and strong and vital, giving out something of the energy and power of great mountains."

ARCHITECTURE AND THE ENVIRONMENT

By the nature of their profession, architects are as much concerned with the practical use of their buildings as with aesthetic considerations. In general, the architecture of the second half of the 20th century tried to balance the two not necessarily opposing elements of form and function.

The foundations of much modern architecture were laid in the 1920s by Ludwig Mies van der Rohe (1896–1969) and his fellow members of the Bauhaus, an influential school of design and architecture, founded in Germany in 1919 (see Part VIII, Topic 7). The Bauhaus taught that "less is more," and when Mies fled Germany for the United States in the late 1930s, he brought this approach with him. The austere lines, absence of fussy decorative details, and use of reinforced concrete in works such as the Seagram Building, New York, influenced innumerable skyscraper structures throughout Europe and the United States.

Not all buildings in this "International Style" achieved the elegance and practicality of Mies' best work. Many of his followers' steel, concrete, and glass public and office buildings filled the urban landscape with the same forms endlessly repeated. Nor did they always wear well; as metal discolored and concrete cracked, indifferently built International Style constructions brought their own touch of desolation to eastern European and Third World capitals.

The Swiss-born, French-trained Le Corbusier (1887–1965; his real name was Charles-Edouard Jeanneret) brought a rather different approach to the International Style. Emphasizing function, he claimed that a house was "a machine to live in." Among his most important constructions was a housing complex built in Marseilles between 1947 and 1952. The complex includes both living space and areas for shopping, recreation, and walking. Unlike Mies and his followers, Le Corbusier aimed to place his constructions in green park settings, with the natural world as a background. Colored panels and rough concrete walls provided decorative touches. Like Mies, Le Corbusier was unlucky in his imitators. Much grim public housing copied the general lines of his work, without matching the care for detail and aesthetic effect.

By the 1970s, both architects and public were beginning to be weary of stark concrete piles. The Pompidou Center for Arts and Culture, which opened in Paris in 1977, made a complete break with the idea of less as more. Its architects, Renzo Piano and Richard Rogers, covered the surface of the building with decoration that was also functional—heating ducts, elevators, escalators.

Few architects were prepared to go as far as this in decorating their buildings, but in the 1980s decorative design came back into fashion with the postmodern style (the name is little more than a convenient label). Postmodernist architects continued to build large structures with simple, basic lines, but added decorative elements derived from Classical architecture: arches, columns, pediments.

Thus the late 20th century witnessed a modernist form of neoclassical revival, and a return to greater variety in architecture. Public interest in the effects of construction and reconstruction upon the environment became increasingly vocal. The vast new building plan for Paris, which reached its first stage of completion in time for the Bicentennial of the French Revolution in 1989, was greeted with furious debate. In Britain, Prince Charles became embroiled with the country's leading architects, as he lambasted many of London's new buildings. Not surprisingly, of all the contemporary arts, architecture aroused the most enthusiasm and condemnation.

CONTEMPORARY COMPOSERS IN SEARCH OF AN AUDIENCE

By contrast with architecture, advanced developments in contemporary music left many music lovers and performers bewildered or indifferent. First the long-playing record, then stereo sound, and then digital recording on tape and compact disc made music increasingly available to an ever-wider public. Concert audiences grew, and regional opera companies sprang up throughout Europe and the United States. Yet the music that audiences wanted to hear, and performers to play and sing, was overwhelmingly drawn from the standard repertory of Baroque, Classical, Romantic, and early 20th-century works. A leading contemporary composer accused the opera houses of being only museums, endlessly repeating the same dead works. Certainly few operas written and performed since World War II succeeded in winning themselves a permanent place in the

Renzo Piano and Richard Rogers' *Georges Pompidou Cultural Center* in Paris (1977) broke new ground by using the building's functional tubes and pipes as decorative elements.

repertory. Significantly enough, one exception, *Amahl and the Night Visitors*, by Gian-Carlo Menotti (born 1911), was written for television performance.

In a way that has no parallel with the other arts, the musical world of the second half of the 20th century was characterized by a growing tendency to look back to earlier times, in a series of revivals. In the 1950s, listeners discovered Baroque music, especially that of Vivaldi, and, under the inspiration of the operatic soprano Maria Callas (1923–1977), the world of 19th-century Italian bel canto opera. The 1960s saw the growing popularity of the music of Gustav Mahler, up until then virtually unknown. By the 1990s, the early music and original instrument movement was in full swing, as musicians tried to reconstruct the original performing conditions of works ranging from Bach to Verdi by using authentic instruments.

The Musical Avant-Garde

Viewed from the end of the 20th century, the break between audiences and contemporary music seems to go back to the early 1900s, when Arnold Schoenberg rejected tonality in favor of other systems of musical organization (see Part VII, Topic 21). One of the postwar period's leading composers, the Frenchman Pierre Boulez (born 1925), extended Schoenberg's ordering of pitch to other musical elements: length of notes, volume, method of performance. This total control eliminated any traditional sense of melody, harmony, or counterpoint. The purely abstract structures that resulted deliberately avoided any kind of subjective emotional expression.

In the 1950s and 1960s, as technology came to dominate modern life, composers turned to machines to generate their works. In *concrete music*, everyday sounds were taped and then combined and manipulated in the recording studio. Composers of *electronic music* produced artificial sounds by means of an electronic oscillator; the invention of the Moog synthesizer provided an easy means of combining and changing these sounds. Few of the experiments produced lasting results. The leading composer of electronic music, the German Karlheinz Stockhausen (born 1928), tended increasingly to combine electronic sounds with these produced by conventional instruments. In his massive "seven-day" opera, *Licht* (Light), parts of which were performed in the 1990s, he used singers, dancers, and instrumentalists, as well as electronic equipment.

Faced with the dilemmas of the contemporary musical scene, the American John Cage (1912–1992) produced pieces that seemed to question the very nature of music. Many of his works, in reaction against the rigid ordering of Boulez and Stockhausen (or Bach and Brahms, for that matter), used elements of chance. The performers tossed coins or shuffled the pages of the work to determine in what order the sections should be played.

A page from Karlheinz Stockhausen's *Nr. 11 Refrain.*

The Minimalists

In the 1980s, several young American composers found a very different solution to the search for a new musical style. One of the first was Steve Reich (born 1936), who built substantial pieces out of the extended repetition of simple chords and rhythms; the use of these basic elements earned the music the stylistic label of "minimalist."

The most successful minimalist composer was Philip Glass (born 1937). Glass was influenced by Indian and West African music, and some of the repeated rhythmical structures in his pieces derive from classical Indian pieces. The seemingly endless repetitions produce either a mood of hypnotic concentration or growing irritation, depending on the individual listener. Glass' best-known works were three large-scale stage pieces—*Einstein on the Beach*, *Satyagraha*, and *Akhnaten*—performed between 1975 and 1985. His collaborator, the American dramatist Robert Wilson, described their "apparent motionlessness and endless durations during which dreams are dreamed and significant matters are understood." Although enthusiasm for Glass and the whole minimalist school remained

The Beatles.

mixed, performances of his works drew large and generally enthusiastic audiences, a rare phenomenon in the field of contemporary music.

Popular Music

The worldwide appeal and circulation of pop music continued unabated in the decades after World War II. Between 1965 and 1973, "Yesterday"—a John Lennon and Paul McCartney song originally recorded by the immensely popular British group, the Beatles—appeared in some 1200 other versions. By the late 1970s, the Beatles had sold over 100 million record albums and an equal number of singles.

Throughout the 1980s and 1990s, rock music took changing forms, mirroring the mood of the times. Acid rock tried to reproduce musically the experience of hallucinogenic drugs, using advanced electronic sound effects. Performers of glitter rock aimed to challenge all the social conventions by their outrageous costumes and makeup. The bitter violence of punk rock grew out of the hopelessness of the working-class youth in postindustrial Britain.

Other popular musicians used their songs for open political protest. Bob Dylan (born 1941; real name Robert Zimmerman) combined American folk idioms and the blues style. Protest singers were among the first to incorporate non-Western music; by the late 1980s, pop music had absorbed elements from the Caribbean, West Africa, and Latin America.

The internationalization of pop music itself was matched by its ever-wider circulation. With the coming of the video cassette and world television broadcasting,

Punk culture in London.

concerts of pop music became global events. In many cases these were inspired by political, or at least humanitarian, motives. The first was the Live Aid concert of 1987, which was intended to raise money for aid to Third World countries. Among its successors was the Mandela concert, held in London in 1990 to greet and acclaim the recently released South African black leader, Nelson Mandela.

Music has provided the best evidence for the formation of a global culture. The same pop music echoed from continent to continent, while audiences in Europe, America, India, and Japan filled concert halls to hear the great masterpieces of European music. Ironically, at a time when the demand for music had never been greater, avant-garde composers seemed searching for the right direction in which to advance their art.

POSTMODERNISM

By the 1980s, a number of writers had moved beyond the modernist preoccupation with alienation and self-analysis. Critics tended to collect them under the name of postmodernists, although it was not always clear what specific characteristics they had in common. Nor was the term itself exactly helpful in defining the nature of their work, although it served to indicate a change of direction. The postmodernists did not break with their modern past; they built on it.

As far as it is possible to obtain a perspective on their work, the postmodernists seemed less concerned with traditional plot and character lines, and less interested in rational organization. Their visions were more private, and their works created isolated worlds with their own meanings and significance. They often used language in an elaborate, even virtuoso way.

Among the leading writers to be labeled postmodernist was the Italian Italo Calvino (1923–1985), whose works draw heavily on fantasy. He produced science fiction and historical allegory, explored the genre of the folk tale (*Italian Folktales;* 1956, revised 1980), and toward the end of his life wrote experimental fiction (*If on a Winter's Night a Traveler;* 1979).

Other postmodernists reveal a wide variety of influences. The complexity and ingenious wordplay of the American Thomas Pynchon (born 1937) recalls the style of James Joyce. The short stories and novels of Donald Barthelme (1931–1989) evoke a mood of surrealism. The grand old man of postmodernism, the Argentinean Jorge Luis Borges (1899–1986), created his own unique blend of essay and short story.

Although in the 1990s traditional fiction was far from dead, postmodernist writers seemed to be exploring a variety of different directions. Without breaking with the past—an impossible aim, in any case—their work suggested rich new possibilities for future literature.

Western culture in the second half of the 20th century was shaped by two contrasting forces: unity and diversity. Instant communication and ever-advancing technology made possible a global culture, whereby events and ideas could span the world in minutes. People on every continent could watch the same television programs, admire the same sports stars, share the same fashions and food—and they did. Yet the very speed of communication meant that styles and ideas became outdated and were replaced with dizzying speed. The appetite for variety grew as it was fed, and the 200 or so television channels of postindustrial society offered a choice so bewildering as to be no choice at all.

Faced with this homogenized culture, people in many parts of the world found a renewed sense of national or ethnic identity. For many European countries, the 1970s and 1980s were a period of nationalist sentiment and active nationalist movements. Belgium, Britain, Italy, and Spain all saw separatist demonstrations. By 1990, it was clear that the fall of communism in Eastern Europe would lead to renewed tensions between rival ethnic groups.

The battle to promote national identity was often fought with cultural weapons. Welsh nationalists won a notable victory in establishing their right to a fixed number of hours a week of television programs in the Welsh language. The language issue remained a sensitive one in countries as different as Canada and Yugoslavia; it even arose in the United States, as Spanish became increasingly widespread. Virtually nowhere on earth seemed untouched by nationalist sentiments. When in 1990 even remote Mongolia began to liberalize, one of the state's first moves was to reintroduce the Mongolian alphabet, which had been replaced by a form of the Russian one.

Thus by the 1990s Western culture, by now part of global civilization, enjoyed both the advantages and disadvantages of postmodern times: the freedom and constraints of pluralism.

Questions for Further Study

1. In what ways have technological developments—the communications revolution, computers, etc.—changed the nature of Western culture? What are the effects of the speed of these developments?
2. What are the main characteristics of pop culture? What forms do they take in music, the visual arts, and popular entertainment?
3. How does culture reflect the historical experiences of the world after World War II? In comparison with earlier periods, have the role and function of the artist changed?

Suggestions for Further Reading

Burgess, A. *Ninety-Nine Novels*. London, 1984.

Connor, S. *Postmodernist Culture: An Introduction to Theories of the Contemporary*. Cambridge, MA, 1989.

Gianetti, L., and S. Eyman. *Flashback: A Brief History of Film*. Englewood Cliffs, NJ, 1991.

Glass, P., and R. T. Jones. *Music by Philip Glass*. New York, 1987.

Hampton, W. *Guerrilla Minstrels: John Lennon, Joe Hill, Woodie Guthrie, Bob Dylan*. New York, 1986.

Maltby, R. *Passing Parade: A History of Popular Culture in the 20th Century*. Oxford, 1989.

VIII

Topic 15

The Path Toward European Integration

In the aftermath of World War II, some European political leaders began to see cooperation, and not competition, as essential to survival. In 1952, the first stage of European integration saw the combining of the coal and steel industries of all the major Western European nations except Britain—France, West Germany, Italy, Belgium, the Netherlands, and Luxembourg.

In 1957, the same nations signed two agreements in Rome: the first was to share nuclear energy research, the second to create an economic unit by eliminating tariffs and trade barriers between member states. This European Economic Community (EEC), founded by the Treaty of Rome, proved so successful that it led to an economic boom in Western Europe. In consequence, more optimistic politicians began to see economic union as the prelude to some future time when Europe could achieve political union.

The only major Western European industrialized power that refused to join the EEC was Britain, in large measure because of doubts about surrendering its sovereignty in a future united Europe. As the EEC continued to prosper, however, Britain's Conservative government opened prolonged and difficult negotiations to become a member. In 1973, Britain and Denmark left EFTA to join the EEC, and Ireland was also admitted.

The EEC soon developed a complex—some said too complex—institutional apparatus, including a dual executive: a Council of Ministers, and the European Commission. A European Parliament whose members are elected directly in their home countries is seen by enthusiastic European federalists as a step toward future political unity. The remaining EEC institutions are the European Court of Justice, and the European Council, which provides a forum for the heads of governments and their foreign ministers to meet at regular intervals.

In 1981, Greece joined the EEC, and in 1986 Spain and Portugal became members. In the same year, the Single European Act was ratified, which listed a series of future goals. The most immediate was the creation by the end of 1992 of a European community with no frontiers or trade barriers.

Relations with Switzerland and Austria were complex. Both, as neutral nations, had avoided participation because of its eventual political implications. In the early 1990s, however, Austria became a member together with Finland. With the revolutions of 1989, the notion of European unity suddenly took on far vaster dimensions.

Thus by the early 1990s, Europe already provided a market and economic force to compete with the United States and Japan. The chances of any form of political union that would be acceptable to all its members still seemed distant, but the divisive and destructive national rivalries that had riven the first half of the 20th century had been replaced by constructive cooperation. As the millennium approached, plans advanced for a single European currency.

THE FIRST STEPS TOWARD EUROPEAN UNITY

For the first four centuries of the Christian era, most of Europe was united under the strong political and legal rule of the Roman Empire. With the decline and fall of the Roman Empire, individual rulers fought over territory, religion, and dynastic questions. The empire of Charlemagne (742–814) imposed unity on a part of Europe, but the authority of his successors in the Holy Roman Empire as leaders of Europe was challenged by the papacy.

Over the centuries, plans for European integration occasionally emerged. The Duc de Sully (1560–1641), finance minister to the French king Henry IV, produced a "Grand Design" for a council of Europe, backed by a European peace-keeping army. A hundred years later, the French political reformer the Abbé de Saint Pierre (1658–1743; real name Charles-Irénée Castel) advocated the creation of a "European Republic," with a European senate; another of his visionary ideas was the establishment of a peace-keeping international organization. All these proposals foundered on the realities of dynastic and colonial rivalries.

Toward European Integration

The modern notion of a Europe united both politically and economically dated back to the troubled years between the two world wars, when some politicians saw a federal United States of Europe as a means of preventing renewed hostilities. Moves were made toward introducing some degree of economic cooperation, but in 1930 the French politician Aristide Briand argued that a limited customs union would not work. Economic union was possible only if each member's security was guaranteed, but security depended on political decisions. Thus, an economic partnership required the setting up of political institutions and structures. With these in place, a "common market" (the term was Briand's own) could be established. The growing nationalism of the 1930s swept away all such notions of cooperation.

During the war, many of those fighting to free Europe from Hitler's "New Order" began to look to the idea of federalism as a hope for the future. "*Libérer et fédérer*" ("Liberate and federate") was one of the slogans of the French Resistance movement, and freedom fighters in the Netherlands, Italy, Czechoslovakia, and Poland developed similar goals. In July 1944, resistance leaders from various countries, meeting in Geneva, called for the creation of a European Federal Union.

After the war had proved yet again the futility and destructiveness of national rivalries, politicians began to talk seriously about the idea of a European federation. One of the leading promoters of the cause of European integration was the French economist Jean Monnet (1888–1979), who became known as the "father of Europe." Another important figure was the Belgian politician Paul-Henri Spaak (1899–1972), author of the report which eventually established the European Economic Community (EEC). The Belgians, in fact, helped to lead the way in demonstrating the possibilities of European cooperation. In 1947, Belgium, the Netherlands, and Luxembourg—the so-called Benelux countries—agreed to form a customs union. From 1948 all tariffs between the three partners were abolished, and a standard tariff became imposed on outside imports.

The chief spokesmen for European cooperation were fervent believers in the ideal of a united Europe, but even Winston Churchill and Charles de Gaulle, strong defenders of national sovereignty, spoke approvingly of federation. During the war, Churchill had proposed a postwar European state, governed by a joint

European Community headquarters under construction in Brussels. With the need to use a bilingual sign within one small country (the top line is in French, the one below in Flemish), Belgium, illustrates the challenge of European unity.

council and with its own armed forces. In 1945, De Gaulle called for some form of all-European association "between Slavs, Germans, Gauls, and Latins."

The supporters of European unification saw that the only way to achieve progress was to advance slowly and cautiously, with the goal of maintaining peace. The industries most vital to a war effort were those of coal and steel production. If countries would surrender control of these to a supranational authority, an important step would have been taken toward making future conflict less likely. In 1951 an agreement was signed to form the European Coal and Steel Community (ECSC); the agreement went into effect the following year. The member states were France, West Germany, Italy, and the Benelux countries. Thus six nations, which only a few years earlier had been locked in bloody conflict, agreed to share their goods rather than fight over them.

Encouraged by the success of the ECSC, the same nations tried to establish a European Defense Community (EDC), for the purpose of creating a European army and establishing a common European foreign policy. In the end, however, neither France nor Italy was prepared to give up control of its defense forces or independent policies. In 1954, the attempt was abandoned.

THE TREATY OF ROME

By 1957, confidence and growing experience led to the next step. On March 25 of that year the Treaty of Rome, signed by the same members, created two new bodies: the European Atomic Energy Community (Euratom), and the European Economic Community (EEC). (The ECSC subsequently became absorbed into the EEC, which in turn became the European Union.) The ceremonies took place on Rome's Capitoline hill, ancient center of the first and only power to unite most of Europe under a single rule, the Roman Empire.

Euratom was set up to encourage cooperation in research and development of nuclear energy. It proved to have only limited success, mainly because each country had its own attitude to the use of nuclear energy. France soon came to rely on it for a significant proportion of its energy needs; Italy, after an initial investment in nuclear plants, responded to public uneasiness about nuclear energy by drastically reducing its dependence on nuclear power.

The European Economic Community

From the beginning, the EEC proved a success. The long-term goal of the Treaty of Rome was to achieve some sort of political union. Its terms claimed that its purpose was "to establish the foundation of an ever-closer union among the people of Europe." The aims of the EEC, however, were strictly practical, and limited to what could be actually accomplished. It sought to create one large economic market—the Common Market—for its members, by eliminating tariffs and customs barriers between them. Common tariffs and trade restrictions were erected toward nonmembers. Within the EEC, labor and capital could in theory circulate freely (in practice, some countries maintained restrictions), and a Common Agricultural Program (CAP) established equal price levels for agricultural products. Agricultural prices were to become a much-fought-over issue in the future, bringing the farming-intensive countries of southern Europe into conflict with the northern industrial

Many European tariff and customs barriers fell in January 1993, making German beer available to British shoppers in a French supermarket near the Calais ferry docks.

members, which were unwilling to pay huge farming subsidies.

The treaty laid down a timetable for bringing these policies into effect. The first steps to bring the national customs tariffs of the EEC's six members together took place at the beginning of 1961; EEC countries then had until July 1, 1968, to eliminate all customs duties between one another, and establish common tariffs toward outsiders.

Map 15.1 The European Common Market and the Soviet-Led COMECON, c. 1970

BRITAIN AND THE COMMON MARKET

The most obvious absentee from the negotiations that led to the signing of the Treaty of Rome was Britain. For all the British approval of the general idea of a European federation, politicians there were unwilling to embark on a journey whose ultimate destination—however distantly—was political union. Even Churchill had no doubt that Britain was in some important way different from the continental nations. His attitude summed up the position of many of his fellow citizens: "We are with Europe, but not of it. We are interested and associated, but not absorbed."

The possible loss of national sovereignty became a hotly discussed public issue. The nations of continental Europe accused the British of insularity and lack of commitment to the European ideal. The British counterattacked by pointing out that their insularity had saved them from invasion and occupation for hundreds of years. When the foreign ministers of the future EEC met in 1955 to formulate a common policy, they officially invited Britain to take part. The British government refused.

The European Free Trade Association

As the success of the EEC became apparent, Britain and other European nations began to look toward forming a similar organization that could both liberalize trade among themselves and act as a bargaining force with the EEC. In 1959, a group of seven countries created the European Free Trade Association (EFTA); it came into force the following year. The founding members of EFTA were Austria, Britain, Denmark, Norway, Portugal, Sweden, and Switzerland. Finland became an associate member in 1961, and a full member in 1985; Iceland joined in 1970.

EFTA's goals were avowedly completely nonpolitical, and none of its members had any intention of forming a supranational union. This factor was important not only to Britain but also to the neutral nations of Austria and Switzerland. Even in economic terms, EFTA was less binding than the EEC: although tariffs on industrial goods were eliminated between its members, they remained in place on agricultural and fishing products. The provision on fishing was especially important for the Scandinavian members and the British, who often found themselves in fierce competition for the catch and sale of fish.

Barely had EFTA come into being than opinion in Britain began to swing in favor of joining the EEC. The trade barriers that the EEC had erected against outsiders left British trade in a dangerously uncompetitive position. Then, as wartime memories receded, the idea of peaceful cooperation took precedence over defensiveness. No less important a consideration was the fact that France and Germany—under the leadership of the two senior statesmen, Konrad Adenauer and De Gaulle—were tending to dominate the decision making. Both Britain and the other EEC members could see the potential advantage of a British counterbalance in the community.

In 1961, Britain formally applied for application; it was followed by Denmark, Ireland, and Norway. Negotiations began later the same year. The bargaining was hard. As head of the Commonwealth, Britain was concerned to safeguard the reciprocal trading rights existing between itself and the various Commonwealth nations. Nor had the earlier British refusal, followed by the abrupt reversal that led to its application, created a sympathetic atmosphere for negotiating. France, in particular, resented what it saw as the British attempt to obtain "special treatment."

After a period of increasing tension, the French blocked Britain's entry; in January 1963, De Gaulle announced at a press conference that Britain was not yet ready to join the Common Market. Among his reasons was the fear that British membership would undermine the ability of continental nations to control their own affairs. As he put it, with Britain in the EEC, "in the end there would appear a colossal Atlantic Community under American dependence and leadership which would soon swallow up the European Community."

It took ten more years before Britain was finally admitted. In 1969, the year in which De Gaulle stepped down as head of state, the EEC members agreed to reopen negotiations. One of the leading British representatives at earlier sessions had been the Conservative Edward Heath (born 1916). In 1970, he became prime minister, and two years later his government signed the treaty which was to admit Britain. On January 1, 1973, the EEC received three new members: Britain, Denmark, and Ireland. The first two withdrew from EFTA. Norway, which was also offered membership, rejected it in a popular referendum. By 1990, three more states had joined: Greece in 1981, and Spain and Portugal in 1986.

The French statesman, Charles de Gaulle.

Significant Dates

The Formation of the European Union

1947	Benelux countries form customs union
1951	Creation of European Coal and Steel Community
1957	Treaty of Rome establishes ECC
1959	Creation of EFTA
1963	Britain's application to EEC blocked
1973	Britain, Denmark, and Ireland join EEC
1981	Greece becomes member of EEC
1986	Spain and Portugal join EEC; Single European Act passed

THE ORGANIZATION OF THE EUROPEAN UNION

The devisers of the EU's institutions tried to take into consideration the fact that members would often find their own interests in conflict with those of the EU as a whole. They therefore created an organization that would balance national interests against intergovernmental cooperation. The vast bureaucracy that developed (in 1989 there were 18,000 civil servants—or "Eurocrats"—working for the EU) is a frequent cause of criticism. Jobs and subsequent promotions are assigned on the basis of nationality rather than merit, and Eurocrats can be moved to other positions or dismissed only under exceptional circumstances.

The Executive of the EU

The EU has a dual executive. The European Commission, which meets in Brussels, represents the supranational component. According to the Treaty of Rome, it acts in the general interest of the European Community. Its commissioners, appointed for four years by the member states, must judge for themselves what the interests of the Community are; they cannot receive instructions from the governments that nominate them. The commission can initiate policy and make recommendations; it cannot make policy.

That task is performed by the Council of Ministers, the second half of the executive, which guards national interests. It consists of the foreign ministers of the member states, who are at times represented by other ministers when specific problem areas are under discussion—energy, transport, health, agriculture, and so on. The council meets several times a month; every six months the presidency passes in rotation among the member nations. It discusses measures proposed by the commissioners, and votes either to accept or to reject them.

The voting system whereby decisions are made is a "weighted" one. The larger states have more votes. (In 1990 Britain, France, West Germany, and Italy had ten votes each; Spain eight; Belgium, Greece, the Netherlands, and Portugal five; Denmark and Ireland three; Luxembourg two. Proposals are considered passed if they obtain 54 votes.) If, however, a state feels that its vital national interests are at stake, it has the right to block a decision by vetoing it, even if every other government votes in favor.

The existence of the power of veto remains controversial. In 1984, French President Mitterand pointed out the absurdity of running as complex an organization as the EU "by the rules of the Diet of the old kingdom of Poland, where every member could block the decisions." By the 1990s, there was strong support for a reform to eliminate it, but members failed to reach overall agreement—the countries in favor of retaining the veto were Britain, Denmark, and Greece.

The EU Institutions

The notion of a European Parliament was established by the Treaty of Rome. Enlarged along with the EU, and elected by popular vote since 1979, its powers are limited. It cannot legislate and has no right to control or replace the executive organs. It oversees and expresses opinions on the commission's proposals, and has control over part of the EU budget; the greater part of the funds—71 percent—is under the supervision of the Council of Ministers.

The members of the European Parliament are directly elected in their home countries, by the electoral system in force in each. In 1989, there were 81 members from each of the four largest nations, 60 from Spain, 25 from the Netherlands, 24 each from Belgium, Greece, and Portugal, sixteen from Denmark, fifteen from Ireland, and six from Luxembourg. They take their seats in the assembly not as national delegations, but according to their party—Christian Democrats, Liberals, Socialists, Communists, and so on. A Rainbow Group brings together Greens and other ecologists, as well as a number of smaller parties—one of which is the Danish anti-EU party, the People's Movement against the community.

The Parliament originally met in both Strasbourg and Luxembourg, and Eurocrats spent considerable time and energy in transporting files and records back and forth each month. In 1981, it voted to hold all its sessions in Strasbourg, where it meets about eight times a year for one-week sessions.

The EU's legal arm is the European Court of Justice, composed of thirteen members, which meets in Luxembourg. It oversees compliance with the Treaty of Rome, and makes sure that all executive decisions are in accordance with the treaty's provisions. It hears cases at all levels, from member nations to individual persons.

More broadly, the European Court sought to develop a body of "community law." This chiefly concerns economic, trade, and social issues. Community law applies throughout the member states, and supersedes national law. It thus represents the principal instance to date of the surrendering of national sovereignty to a supranational institution.

Both the Parliament and court were created by the Treaty of Rome. A new institution, the European Council, came into being in 1974. Made up of the

PERSPECTIVES ON HISTORY

Sovereignty, Law, and Unity

Mary Volcansek
Florida International University

The treaties establishing the European Community followed the standard model of modern democratic governments by instituting three separate powers—executive, legislative, and judicial. An underlying assumption was that the judicial arm, the European Court of Justice, would be the more passive, because judges typically, by virtue of age and training, are expected to respect tradition more often than boldly to break new ground. The Court of Justice, hidden away in the Duchy of Luxembourg, has often shattered conventional assumptions about the behavior of courts as its judges defined the limits of national sovereignty and pushed for greater unity through its interpretation of the treaties. The Court, which now hears more than 500 cases each year, has significantly contributed to European integration, particularly in its decisions announcing the supremacy of European law over that of individual member states, the legal rights of individuals, human rights protected by the treaties, and rules that foster economic integration.

The relevance of community law for individual nations was firmly fixed by the Court of Justice in 1964 by its decision in *Costa v. ENEL*. That case stands as the source from which the authority of the court and of community law flows. Flaminio Costa was a lawyer and also a small stockholder in Italy's electric company ENEL, an operation that was nationalized by the Italian government in 1962. He refused to pay his electric bill of less than three dollars and filed a lawsuit charging that the Italian government had violated the article in the Treaty of Rome relating to national monopolies. The Italian judge hearing the case followed Costa's recommendation that he seek an interpretation of that specific treaty article from the European Court of Justice. The European Court declared that community law was superior to the laws in any member state and was absorbed into the legal systems of each nation. Community law was declared to supersede any existing national law or constitution. That stark assertion of supremacy provided a legal basis giving force to all laws passed by the Community and transforming the founding treaties into the "constitution" of the Community.

If the treaties are a constitution and regulations passed by other institutions of the Community are lawful in any nation, how can an individual secure the protections offered by them? The Court of Justice's answer was to create the doctrine of "legal rights of individuals." This concept was first announced in the 1958 case of *Van Gend en Loos* that dealt with duties on imports from Germany into the Netherlands that interfered with free movement of goods. The case involved not only the validity of the customs taxes, but also the recourse of individuals who felt that the guarantees of the treaties were being ignored by a national government. The Court of Justice announced that the European Community constituted a "new legal order," that signatories to the treaties had limited their sovereign rights, and that the treaties conferred legal rights, as well as obligations, on individual citizens. The doctrine of legal rights for individuals was given a more human face in the 1975 decision of the Court of Justice in *Van Duyn v. Home Office*. Ms. Van Duyn, a Dutch citizen, was denied entrance into Great Britain because she would be employed by the Church of Scientology. The court in Luxembourg acknowledged that a citizen of another EC country can be barred from immigrating to a different member state on grounds of public policy, but provided that such an exclusion must be based solely on the behavior of the specific individual. Britain could not, therefore, prohibit Ms. Van Duyn from coming to the United Kingdom simply because the British government disapproved of her employer.

The treaties of the Community include no "bill of rights," though certain economic rights are specifically mentioned. The Court of Justice has, nonetheless, moved far in the creation of a set of rights, both economic and social. The Treaty of Rome, for example, specifically dictates comparable pay for men and women, inclusive of indirect compensation. Gabrielle DeFrenne, a flight attendant on Sabena, the Belgian national airline, challenged a Belgian law that made retirement for cabin crews mandatory at age 40 for women, but not for men. Though Ms. DeFrenne lost her argument that pension schemes are a form of indirect compensation, she did, in her second suit, obtain the satisfaction that back pay could be ordered because gender discrimination was barred by the treaties. The *DeFrenne* cases address economic rights, but the Court of Justice has also recognized other human rights. That there existed "fundamental rights" for citizens under Community law was first recognized in 1974 in the case of *Nold v. Commission*. In the years following that decision, the court has found due process rights, guarantees of respect for private lives, protections against ex post facto laws, and rights against self-incrimination and illegal search and seizure as being fundamental rights of citizens of all EC countries. None of these is specifically mentioned or necessarily implied in any of the treaties.

The European Court of Justice has also been active in removing trade barriers among nations that interfered with the Community's stated goal of a common market. The landmark *Cassis de Dijon* decision in 1979 emerged when Germany tried to halt the sale of a French beverage in Germany because it had an insufficient alcoholic content. The court concluded, as it would again later when Italy refused the sale of German pasta, that "if it's good enough for a Frenchman, it is good enough for a German." The equation is the same for any two or more nationalities within the Community. That single legal principle was able to sweep away thousands of restrictions that had been erected to halt imports among the member states. Imports from sister countries could, thereafter, be barred only on grounds of public health or safety.

Proponents of greater economic and political integration in Europe have applauded the bold initiatives of the European Court of Justice. The judges in Luxembourg have been hailed for assuring integration of the markets of western Europe and for "democratizing" the Community through their handling of human rights. The court has, in fact, been in the forefront of integration.

Some commentators on both sides of the Atlantic have criticized the court's extreme activism or its willingness to exceed the legal tradition's norms of simply applying the law objectively and impartially. These critics note the court's tendency to create law that comports with the judges' personal notions of how things *ought* to be and accuse the court of usurping legislative powers. They argue that when judges exceed their mandate of interpreting law and make forays into lawmaking, the legitimacy and efficacy of the judiciary may be jeopardized. This line of argument says less about the outcomes of specific court decisions or their policy implications and more directly focuses on the traditional role of courts and judges in Western democracies. Another criticism addresses the policies that the court has pursued. That analysis targets the political agenda of the judges, who, as the argument goes, have allowed their enthusiasm for the European experiment, not the treaties or other relevant laws, to guide their decisions. The European Court of Justice, like other Western courts, is undoubtedly politicized, but whether that should be viewed as positive or negative is likely dependent on the political persuasion of the observer.

The European Community entered a new era with the passage of the Single European Act with its goals for the end of 1992. Before that deadline arrived, the leaders of the member states had already made a commitment to amend the founding treaties to achieve monetary union and

continued next page

to explore closer political union. A reconsideration of the division of powers of the Parliament also received implicit agreement. These developments may well transform the role of the European Court, as may the sheer size of the Community, as the number of countries seems likely to swell beyond fifteen to eighteen or even more. What will not change, however, is the significant contribution that the European Court made in defining sovereignty and forging unity in the first 35 years of community history.

heads and foreign ministers of the member governments, it generally meets three times a year at highly publicized "European Summts," held in appropriately picturesque settings. The Council is the only EU body that has some jurisdiction in all fields. Since its meetings permit direct confrontation of government leaders, they are often stormy. At the same time, they sometimes manage to resolve thorny problems by hard bargaining.

THE FUTURE OF THE EUROPEAN UNION

Throughout the 1970s and 1980s, public opinion in Europe varied widely on whether membership of the EU was a good thing. In a poll taken in 1985, 72 percent of Italians polled were in favor of EU membership, and only 4 percent against. At the other extreme, only 29 percent of Danes, and 37 percent of Britons favored the organization, and 31 and 30 percent respectively were against it.

The Single European Act

Meanwhile in 1986 the EU moved another stage forward with the passage of the Single European Act. The most immediate new goal the act set out was the completion by the end of 1992 of a unified European internal market. By that date there were to be no more trade barriers between members. All frontier and border formalities would disappear for European Community citizens. Labor and capital could circulate freely. There

The Parliament Building for the European Community, Strasbourg, France.

The Euro, intended to be valid in all countries of the European Union.

would be further progress toward economic and monetary union. More generally, members would work together to improve the environment, and to establish a common plan of social legislation. These last two aims met with less than unanimous approval; some states, most vocally Britain, felt that the ecological and social plans were unrealizable, and represented interference in domestic affairs.

The late 1980s were marked by bursts of frantic activity as the various nations began to prepare themselves for the end of 1992. With no forms of restriction in effect, each individual firm and company would be in direct competition with the whole of Europe. This had increasingly been the case for manufacturers and traders since the EU's early days. After 1992, however, it applied to a host of service industries, such as banking and insurance, that in many cases had been protected by government regulations. Portuguese or Irish investors looking for the best interest rates could send their money to Germany. Car owners in Italy, where insurance rates are high, could insure their vehicles with French or Belgian companies. Many insurance and other service firms began to open branches in countries other than their own. American and Japanese firms, hitherto discouraged by protectionist legislation in individual European countries, also began to eye the vast new market with interest.

On the other hand, for all the difficulties it presented, European economic unity could create a bloc strong enough and independent enough to stand up to the United States and Japan. Already by 1987, in fact, western Europe was the world's largest trading power, although not, of course, a unified power in the political sense; it handled 37 percent of global trade, more than that of the United States and the Soviet Union combined. The Western European nations also held a third of the world's monetary reserves, and contributed 36 percent of the world's development aid—all this with only 6 percent of the world's population.

New Members for the European Union

As the EU prepared to face 1992, it had to grapple with a new problem: whether to admit new members. Switzerland, a member of EFTA, signed an agreement in 1977 to abolish tariffs on industrial products for EU partners. Its neutral status, and its unwillingness to allow free movement of labor, meant that it would not seek membership in the foreseeable future.

Austria and Finland, however, presented different issues. Neutral since the end of World War II, they theoretically served as bridges between East and West. Even so, by 1987 around half of Austria's exports went to EU countries, principally West Germany, and only about 12 percent to the Soviet Union and eastern Europe. Finland's position was similar. With the collapse of the Soviet bloc's communist regimes in 1989, and the imminent end of the Cold War, the status of these two countries inevitably changed. The interests of European economic unity, as well as their own interests, led both Austria and Finland to become full members in 1995.

The application of Turkey presented more formidable problems. Although only a small part of Turkey lies on the European continent, the Turkish government contended that the country's economy was basically linked with that of Mediterranean Europe. Morocco, in informal approaches to the EU, made a similar argument. In addition, as a leading partner in NATO, Turkey plays an important role in European defense.

Several factors combined to make it unlikely that the Turkish application would be accepted in the near future. In the first place, government rule in Turkey did not correspond to the broadly based democratic systems and traditions that operated in most of the EU member countries most of the time. Secondly, political instability in Turkey would make negotiations difficult. Thirdly, years of implacable animosity between Greece and Turkey—intensified by the Turkish invasion and annexation of northern Cyprus in 1974—made a Greek veto likely. Finally, the admission of Turkey would create a precedent with far-reaching consequences. The European Community began as an association of partners sharing a common history and culture; divergence from that principle could prejudice the chances of a later political union. When Turkey renewed its application in 1997, members' reactions

An anti-fundamentalist demonstration in Istanbul, 1993.

continued to be negative. On the other hand, Cyprus—providing that it achieved unification—was encouraged to apply.

The EU and Eastern Europe

It was precisely the idea of a shared history and culture, however, which made the liberalization of eastern Europe a potential milestone in the EU's history. Countries such as Czechoslovakia, Hungary, and Poland had played a key role in European history, and produced some of the leading figures in European intellectual life, literature, and music. Furthermore, access to the EU's rich markets would help them rebuild economies worn down by years of Stalinism. As a final touch of enlightened self-interest, if the EU members helped to reconstruct the eastern European economies, they would be creating a future market for their own products.

One Eastern bloc country—East Germany—was assured entry by the unification of East and West Germany. Most of the others began negotiations as soon as new governments had been installed. After the spring elections of 1990, Hungary and Czechoslovakia made their initial approaches. Czechoslovakia signed an agreement of economic cooperation with the EU, and began the process of adaptation that membership would require. Hungary, whose economy was in a healthier state, looked to joining the EU at an earlier date. Poland seemed another future applicant, and Bulgaria also signed a treaty of economic cooperation in 1990. At the 1997 meeting which rejected Turkey's renewed application, the slow process of admitting Hungary, Poland, and the Czech Republic (the richer half of the now divided former Czechoslovakia) began. All these should become full members by 2002.

By the early 1990s, the cause of European economic unity had done much to heal the scars of half a century earlier. The countries of Western Europe weathered the economic slumps and political uncertainties of the 1970s, to emerge as a leading world economic force. By committing themselves to the 1992 deadline, they hastened the further process of unification. Few claimed that 1992 would be less than traumatic; it was clear that the pressures of competition would strain each country's resources and run the risk of adversely affecting the lives of countless ordinary citizens. Yet the process was by now irreversible.

Many factors remained vague. Monetary union, the next stage if any form of political union was to be achieved, fiercely divided the EU membership, with Britain resisting anything that could be construed as a loss of national sovereignty. By the spring of 1998, it was decided that most of the members would proceed to monetary union beginning January 1, 1999. The economies of Greece and Portugal were judged too weak to participate, and Britain and Denmark chose not to join the single European currency, the Euro. The plan was for participating members to phase out their national currencies over three years, leaving only the Euro in circulation by 2002.

The landscape of European history seemed permanently changed. As a tumultuous and often cataclysmic century drew toward its close, the Old Continent, whose economic strength and moral standing had been shattered in 1945, once again began to emerge as a leading world power.

Questions for Further Study

1. How successfully does the political and administrative structure of the European Union compensate for national differences among the various members?
2. Which are the most likely candidates for new members by the early 21st century? What effect would their joining have on the EU?
3. What are the arguments for and against monetary union?

Suggestions for Further Reading

Daltrop, A. *Politics and the European Community*. New York, 1987.

Frey-Wouters, E. *The EC and the Third World*. New York, 1980.

Kerr, A. *The Common Market and How It Works*. Oxford, 1983.

Mayne, R. *Postwar: The Dawn of Today's Europe*. New York, 1983.

Padoa-Schioppa, T. *Efficiency, Stability and Equity: A Strategy for the Evolution of the Economic System of the European Community*. Oxford, 1988.

Wallace, H., W. Wallace, and C. Webb. *Policy-making in the European Community*. London, 1983.

VIII

Topic 16

Epilogue: Facing the 21st Century

By the 1990s, with the prospect of economic union in sight, Europe had regained an independent position in world political and economic affairs. With the end of Soviet control in Eastern Europe, and the relaxation of the tensions of the Cold War, European nations began to look toward a status that did not lock them into an unconditional alliance with either the United States or the Soviet Union.

The generation of political leaders of the late 1980s saw a series of European figures attain international standing. The conservatives Margaret Thatcher and Helmut Kohl, and the socialists François Mitterand and Felipe Gonzalez, all represented around a decade of continuity in their respective countries—Britain, West Germany, France, and Spain. In Italy the Socialists, under the leadership of Bettino Craxi, became key members of the ruling government coalition. The Greek Socialist leader Andreas Papandreou finally lost power in 1989, when a series of scandals brought down his government.

In Eastern Europe, the Czech Václav Havel became one of the most articulate spokesmen of the "new politics." Above all, the rise of Mikhail Gorbachev in the Soviet Union produced a thaw in East-West relations, and made possible the abrupt dismantlement of the Soviet-supported regimes in eastern Europe.

A number of new problems began to excite public attention. The oil crisis of the 1970s had led many countries to explore the alternative of nuclear energy. The Three Mile Island accident in the United States of 1979, followed by the much more serious accident at Chernobyl in the Soviet Union in 1986, raised widespread doubts about dependence on nuclear power. General concern about damage to the environment became focused in the growing strength of the "Green" movement. In several countries, most notably West Germany and Italy, the Greens became a political force of some significance.

The general mood of political stability continued to be overshadowed by terrorist activities on both right and left. In some cases, such as Northern Ireland and Spain, terrorism was related to specific local issues, often nationalist in origin. In West Germany and Italy, terrorists tried to bring down political and social systems on ideological grounds. A third category of terrorist attacks was related to issues outside Europe, most notably the Palestinian problem.

As the nations of Eastern Europe began to rebuild their governments, and Western Europe prepared for European monetary union by 2002, some visionary politicians began to talk of Europe's "common house," a single continent stretching from the Atlantic to the Urals, which would combine differing social and political systems in a single family. Yet, at the same time, the divisive issue of nationalism continued to create frictions in both East and West. Conflict between the two opposing tendencies dominated the last decade of the 20th century.

BETWEEN EAST AND WEST: THE SEARCH FOR EUROPEAN INDEPENDENCE

The two world wars brought to an end centuries of European dominance in international affairs, and left most European countries unable to rebuild their economies without aid from one of the two superpowers: the United States and the Soviet Union. In the case of Western Europe, U.S. assistance was offered and accepted; in Eastern Europe, the Soviet Union imposed Stalinism. The result in both cases was to create alliances that left Europe divided, and locked into virtually unconditional support for their respective patrons.

Europe and Nuclear Weapons

After 1945, a few strong European leaders asserted their right to independence, including Tito in Yugoslavia and De Gaulle in France. For the most part, however, Western Europe welcomed the "Atlantic Alliance," seeing the American military presence as essential to European security. European leaders, most notably West German Social Democratic leader Helmut Schmidt, supported the installation of medium-range American nuclear missiles on NATO bases in West Germany, Britain, Italy, Belgium, and the Netherlands. The "Two-Track Decision"—to continue arming and negotiating at the same time—was taken late in 1979; it provoked widespread demonstrations and protests in the countries involved.

The missiles were installed in response to the Soviet deployment of nuclear weapons on eastern European soil, in particular in East Germany. Thus, by the mid-1980s each superpower possessed the ability to wage nuclear war in Europe without using weapons located in its own territory.

In 1985 the growing economic crisis in the Soviet Union, and the arrival on the scene of Mikhail Gorbachev, led to the renewal of détente. As Gorbachev sought ways to reduce the burden on the Soviet economy of defense spending, he proved increasingly willing to negotiate significant arms reductions. The American position under Ronald Reagan—that negotiation required a further armsbuildup—became moderated. In 1987 the two superpowers signed a treaty to reduce medium-range nuclear weapons. Thus, at the end of the 1980s both sides began to dismantle their European armaments.

Although the medium-range arms were under American control, they formed part of the NATO forces. Two countries, Britain and France, maintained their own independent nuclear forces. The French continued a program of nuclear testing in the Pacific. In 1985, when the Greenpeace environmental movement threatened to send its boat, *Rainbow Warrior*, to interfere in the tests, the French Defense Ministry had the vessel sunk; one person was killed. Public protests in France forced the resignation of the defense minister and the head of foreign intelligence operations. Nonetheless, France continued to maintain its nuclear capacity, and in 1987 embarked on an expensive and ambitious five-year rearmament plan. In 1996, to a barrage of international protest, the French carried out a series of underground nuclear tests in the Pacific. Similar outrage greeted the nuclear tests of three non-European powers—those of China in 1996 and of India and Pakistan in 1998.

Britain's aging nuclear force became the focus of fierce public debate in the late 1980s. The Thatcher government announced its intention of replacing the old Polaris submarines with updated craft, capable of firing American-made Trident missiles. Thatcher's opponents argued that, in addition to the vast expense of the change, the easing of tension between East and West made an independent British nuclear deterrent increasingly irrelevant.

The process of détente continued through the end of the 1980s, and was rapidly accelerated by the liberalization in eastern Europe of 1989. As politicians and generals alike began to rethink the future role of NATO and the Warsaw Pact alliance, it seemed possible that by the 21st century European security would be in predominantly European hands. The role of the independent British and French nuclear forces in a European defense plan would depend on government decisions and on public reactions. In 1983 an opinion poll in Britain showed eight out of ten people in favor of an independent British deterrent, but this broad support began to shrink.

Nuclear disarmament demonstrators gather in the rain, England, 1981.

By 1997, as NATO prepared to consider applications from a number of former Soviet allies, including the Czech Republic, Poland, and Hungary, NATO leaders signed an agreement with the Soviet Union: the "Partnership for Peace." The occasion signaled reluctant Soviet acceptance of the enlargement eastward of NATO.

POLITICAL LEADERSHIP IN THE LATE 20TH CENTURY

Although the progress in disarmament of the 1980s was due principally to the improved relations between the United States and the Soviet Union, European nations and their leaders continued to play a part on the international scene. French and Italian troops joined the U.S. Marines in an unsuccessful attempt to stabilize conditions in Lebanon between 1982 and 1984. In 1987, with Iraq and Iran locked in violent conflict, British and American ships swept the waters of the Persian Gulf to protect neutral ships from underwater missiles.

New Leaders in Britain and West Germany

The chief political leaders of the 1980s remained in power for most of the decade, although by 1990 several seemed to be losing popular support (see Part VIII, Topic 11). In Britain and West Germany, conservative parties governed. The British prime minister for the entire decade was Margaret Thatcher—Britain's first woman premier—who was elected in 1979. A firm advocate of transatlantic cooperation, she helped U.S. forces to make an air attack on Libya in 1986 by providing the use of British landing and refueling facilities.

By 1990, with Britain's fundamental economic problems still unsolved, there was a growing feeling that a new leader should take the Conservatives into the next election. In the routine leadership election of December 1990, Thatcher failed to win the necessary percentage of votes on the first ballot and withdrew. John Major subsequently was elected Conservative leader and became prime minister. After narrowly winning the general election of 1992, the Conservatives were finally swept from power by a Labour landslide in 1997. In the intervening years, Labour's popular new leader, Tony Blair (born 1954), succeeded in replacing his party's old working-class image with one of efficient modernity.

Helmut Kohl became chancellor of West Germany in 1982. Like Thatcher's, his chief support came from the prosperous middle classes. Less divisive than his British equivalent, he used his exuberance and glowing optimism to promote party unity and present the most favorable image possible of West Germany's international standing. He strengthened ties with eastern Europe and the Soviet Union, while remaining a strong ally of the United States. Indeed, by the end of the decade the American–West German relationship seemed about to supersede the American–British as the cornerstone of the United States' ties to Western Europe.

Domestic problems—unemployment, immigration, pollution—were beginning to erode the Christian

Democrats' popularity, when German politics were suddenly shaken up by the fall of East Germany's communist regime. From the very start, Kohl led the drive for a reunited Germany. In the East German elections he campaigned widely and visibly for the East German Christian Democratic party, promising that West Germany would guarantee the value of the East German mark as equal with that of the West German currency. The West German mark was, in fact, worth around ten times the value of its East German equivalent. His promise, which cost West Germany an enormous amount of money and led to inflation and unemployment there, was implemented a few months later with certain provisos.

Kohl's wholehearted support helped the East German Christian Democrats to win the election and become the country's leading political force. Back in West Germany, however, the economic strain of reunification began to create doubts about the wisdom of Kohl's speed. The Social Democrats, while endorsing the goal of eventual German unity, advocated a slower pace. In regional elections in May 1990, the Social Democrats made significant gains, and the Christian Democrats lost control of one of the houses of Parliament. As both parties prepared for national elections in December 1990, it seemed that West Germans were as concerned with their pocketbooks as with the notion of a reunited Germany, yet the speed of events was irresistible: on October 3, 1990, Germany became reunited. With the approaching end of the century, optimism at the end of 45 years of division became tempered, however, with preoccupation at the financial price of reunification. Voters' worries about the German economy—in particular the replacement of the German mark with the proposed standard European currency, the euro—threatened Kohl's bid for reelection in 1998.

Socialist Leaders in France and Spain

The socialist leaders of France and Spain, François Mitterand and Felipe Gonzalez, came to power respectively in 1981 and 1982. By 1990, both were undergoing a fall in popularity, in part because of their jettisoning of socialist principles in an attempt to solve economic problems.

By the early 1990s, with the political parties preparing for the presidential elections of 1995, the Socialists began to divide up in support of various potential candidates. In consequence, Mitterand's legendary skill at political maneuvering was tested to its limits. Nonetheless, Mitterand's own standing as a senior European statesman allowed him, together with Kohl, to coordinate a European response to the issue of German reunification. His lofty dignity and air of sibylline wisdom also served to resolve differences at fractious European summits. The 1995 election saw the victory of Mitterand's old rival Jacques Chirac, with a strong showing by the socialist candidate, Lionel Jospin. Two years later, in May 1997, Jospin led his socialists to victory in a surprise general election, thus inaugurating five years of "cohabitation" with a right-wing president.

For most of the 1980s, the moderate and pragmatic Gonzalez presided over Europe's most popular socialist government. Before his election in 1982 he opposed Spanish membership in NATO. By 1986, the year in which Spain entered the EU, he had changed his mind; he was sufficiently convinced of the importance of continued membership to call a popular referendum. To the general surprise, he won victory by a wide margin. An avowed internationalist, Gonzalez did much to facilitate Spain's return to European affairs after the Franco years of isolation.

Like his colleagues elsewhere in Europe, Gonzalez proved less successful in solving domestic economic problems. His mildly conservative policies of wage restraint and monetary caution failed to halt rising inflation, while angering the unions and his left-wing support. Widespread demonstrations led to a decline in Socialist power. By 1990 the Socialists were still in control, and Gonzalez a popular figure, but neither party nor party leader could afford to ignore their supporters; the honeymoon had been a long one, but it was over. In the spring of 1996, a conservative government came to power, although only with the support of smaller regional parties.

Government Crises in Italy and Greece

In Italy the usual creation and collapse of coalition governments dominated by the Christian Democrats was briefly interrupted in 1981–1982, when the Republican leader Giovanni Spadolini (1925–1994) formed two center-left governments of short duration. The Socialists provided a more consistent interlude, when Bettino Craxi led a left-center government which lasted from 1983 to 1986—three and a half years, a record in postwar Italian politics.

Craxi's rise to prominence in Italian political life began with his election as Socialist leader in 1976. Over the following decade the Socialists slowly increased their share of the votes, rising from 9.6 percent in 1976 to 16.8 percent in the regional elections of 1990. (The same period saw the Italian Communist party in precipitous decline, falling from 34.4 to 24.4 percent.) Craxi's own combative and aggressive personality proved a mixed blessing. There was a general feeling that his government was efficient and "got things done." On the other hand his histrionic oratory and tough political style, coupled with an unfortunate resemblance to

Mussolini—both leaders bald and portly—led to doubts. In cartoons and television satirical programs, Craxi became regularly portrayed as Italy's late and unlamented *Duce*.

The fall of the Craxi government was followed by another long-drawn-out period of instability, during which the country's economy continued to boom. Carlo de Benedetti, a leading industrialist, was heard to remark that, with all the confusion in Rome, he and his colleagues could get on with running Italian business successfully and uninterruptedly. By 1988, however, government was firmly back in the hands of the Christian Democrats, under the leadership of Giuliano Andreotti (born 1919). The coalition's chief partners, Christian Democrats and Socialists, continued to bicker as Craxi alternately threatened and cajoled. As Italy entered the 1990s, its eccentric political system seemed likely to continue relatively unchanged.

Yet in the spring of 1993, a series of investigations began to unfold that implicated a high proportion of Italy's ruling class in massive bribery and corruption. The scandal came to be known as "*Mani Pulite*," or "Clean Hands." The base of operations was Milan, and one of the chief investigating magistrates, Antonio di Pietro, rapidly became a popular hero. In a matter of months, many of Italy's leading politicians, most notably Craxi himself, were driven from office. After a period of caretaker governments, and seven months during which Silvio Berlusconi, one of the leading business men in Italy, served as prime minister, elections in April 1996 brought a center-left alliance, the Olive Branch, to power for the first time in Italian history. The largest single party, the Democratic Party of the Left (PDS), consisted of the majority of the former Italian Communist party, but the alliance also included former Christian Democrats: its leader, Romano Prodi, had served as a state bureaucrat under Christian Democratic rule.

Greece spent the 1980s under socialist government. In 1981 the Panhellenic Socialist Movement (PASOK) won an electoral victory whose size was unparalleled anywhere else in Europe. Their leader, the charismatic if controversial Andreas Papandreou (born 1919), instituted a wide-ranging program of reform. His government liberalized the divorce laws, restructured agriculture, and began to move from a pro-Western position in foreign affairs to an independent nationalism: among the recurrent causes of tension between Greece and the United States was the presence of American forces on Greek territory.

The Greek economy remained in bad shape. The Socialists did little to modernize industry or introduce new technologies, and the country remained dependent on foreign aid. In 1988, a personal scandal involving Papandreou—he announced plans to divorce his wife and marry his mistress—shook his party. Subsequent revelations of widespread corruption in government circles, which also involved Papandreou directly, led to his fall from power. A period of inconclusive elections finally ended in May 1990, when a conservative government was returned to office with the narrowest of margins—one seat. By the late 1990s, with the Socialists once again in power, the economic problems facing Greece's new rulers were formidable: rampant inflation, growing unemployment, and increasing foreign debt.

THE DISSOLUTION OF THE SOVIET UNION

The two years from 1989 to 1991 dramatically transformed the entire situation in Eastern Europe as well as the nature of global politics. The revolution of 1989 (see Part VIII, Topic 12) had brought an end to Soviet hegemony over the nations behind what was once called the "Iron Curtain." Then, in 1990–1991, the Soviet Union itself collapsed under the stress of the fundamental changes that had been wrought by Gorbachev.

New Leadership in Eastern Europe

With the revolutions of 1989, virtually all countries in Eastern Europe underwent a change of leadership. In some cases this was more apparent than real. The new regime in Romania, under the leadership of Ion Iliescu (born 1930), retained a suspicious number of those politicians who had served under Ceausescu. Bulgaria, too, moved slowly in replacing the old guard. Hungary, East Germany, and Czechoslovakia, however, all elected new noncommunist leaders, who in turn nominated new heads of state.

One of these, the Czech Václav Havel (born 1936), began to emerge as one of the leading representatives of the new order in Eastern Europe. A playwright and intellectual, Havel became president of Czechoslovakia in 1990. Traveling widely in Eastern and Western Europe, and to the United States, he spoke eloquently and feelingly of the needs of the new democratic nations, and of the urgency of reconciling old hatreds. Even his influence, however, could not prevent the country from splitting into two independent nations, the Czech Republic and Slovakia.

In Poland, the beginning of 1990 saw the beginnings of a split in the hitherto united Solidarity leadership. As Polish Prime Minister Tadeusz Mazowiecki (born 1927) introduced unpopular economic reforms along generally liberal lines, Lech Wałesa, Solidarity's most prominent leader, began to press for more conservative policies. Wałesa had been prepared earlier to hand over the business of government to his colleagues and occupy a symbolic leadership position, but there were signs of coming conflict. Wałesa and Mazowiecki both ran for election as Poland's president. Wałesa won. By the time of Poland's next presidential election in 1995, however, disillusioned voters rejected Wałesa and turned to a former Communist politician.

The End of Soviet History

By 1990, the greatest of all changes in post–world war history had been wrought by the leader whose own position seemed least secure: Mikhail Gorbachev (see Part VIII, Topic 12). Almost as striking as the actual achievements themselves was the change in the character of Soviet leadership, symbolized by the prominent role played in Soviet public life and visits abroad by Gorbachev's wife, Raisa.

Among the qualities brought by Mikhail Gorbachev to his position was an awareness of the importance of "image" in a world of global communications. His predecessors had done nothing to relieve the monolithic uniformity of Soviet leadership or its secrecy. Gorbachev took part in much-publicized "walk-arounds," on which he met people in the street. Outside the Soviet Union these mainly consisted of opportunities for passersby to shake hands with the famous man; the public relations sessions blocked traffic in most of the cities Gorbachev visited. On home ground, the "walk-arounds" often led to lively debate, with Gorbachev listening to complaints and arguing back. Early in 1990, when the possibility of Lithuania breaking away from the Soviet Union seemed increasingly likely, Gorbachev made an unsuccessful attempt to prevent the move by going there and presenting his case against independence.

Soviet leaders after Stalin severely discouraged the "cult of personality." Little was known about their private lives or families—Yuri Andropov's wife made her first public appearance at her late husband's funeral in 1984. Furthermore, although women were officially equal to men in Soviet society, very few played any part in public life.

From his first visits abroad, Gorbachev was accompanied by his wife Raisa (born 1932). Like an American president's wife, the Soviet first lady played an important role in humanizing the lofty affairs of state. Indeed, Raisa's role seemed modeled on the American system. While her husband held meetings with President Reagan on his visit to the United States in 1987, she visited the White House; a less than friendly encounter there with Nancy Reagan led to a distinctly cool relationship between the two wives.

Gorbachev's power clearly remained dependent on the success of his economic reforms, and not on his public image. In the winter of 1990–1991, as food supplies grew increasingly short in the Soviet Union's principal cities, Boris Yeltsin, elected president of the Russian Republic in 1989, stepped up his hostile criticism of Gorbachev's program. The issue of whether individual republics could break away from the Soviet Union became the cause of widespread demonstrations and protests.

Early in 1991, Soviet troops used tanks to block demonstrators in Lithuania who were threatening to take over a radio station. Worldwide disapproval of the bloodshed focused on the timing of the move, which came as the crisis in the Persian Gulf turned into open war (see below), and many feared that events in the Middle East would distract international attention from the Baltic, as the Suez crisis of 1956 had from Hungary (see Part VIII, Topic 12). Gorbachev himself condemned the use of force, and claimed that he had not been consulted in advance. In any event, the political future of the Soviet Union remained shrouded in uncertainty. A referendum held in the spring of 1991—which was boycotted by a number of the republics—gave Gorbachev a majority in favor of maintaining Soviet unity. Nevertheless, although the central government in Moscow continued to direct defense, foreign policy, and currency matters, the individual republics assumed considerable power over internal regional affairs. Gorbachev then stunned party followers by dropping Marxism-Leninism as the nation's official doctrine. Other changes followed rapidly. By 1991, Moscow had begun to abandon the state-directed economy in favor of a market-driven system. Russian voters also backed Yeltsin's proposal of popular election for the Soviet president.

Yeltsin's standing became further enhanced when he led the opposition to an abortive coup by a group of conservative hardliners in the fall of 1991. As huge crowds filled Moscow's streets in protest against the coup, Yeltsin's public defiance made him the hero of the moment. In the ensuing confusion, a discredited Gorbachev stepped down and Yeltsin was elected president. In spite of recurrent bouts of ill health, he ran for reelection in 1997 and won. It was thus under his leadership that the Soviet Union dissolved into Russia and a series of independent republics, and the complex process of negotiating the terms of new relationships began. The new loosely linked confederation became known as the Commonwealth of Independent States.

The Gulf War

Events in the Middle East clearly demonstrated the collapse of Soviet power. On August 2, 1990, Iraqi troops

Map 16.1 The Middle East, Mid-1980s

invaded the neighboring oil-rich state of Kuwait. Over the following weeks, a consensus gradually emerged at the United Nations to impose economic sanctions on Iraq, while 29 nations began to send troops and supplies to the Persian Gulf to form an alliance under UN auspices. By far the largest contingent—almost half a million participants—came from the United States, but other members of the alliance included Britain, France, and Italy. Egypt and Syria were among the Arab states to participate.

As the months passed, with no sign of concessions from Iraq's increasingly belligerent dictator, Saddam Hussein (born 1937), at the urging of the United States the United Nations issued an ultimatum: if Iraq failed to withdraw from Kuwait by January 15, 1991, the coalition forces would take military action. The Soviet Union sent no forces to the Persian Gulf, and launched a number of independent peace initiatives, but in the end supported UN action.

The deadlock was broken when the allied forces duly began massive aerial bombardments of Baghdad and other Iraqi cities and military installations. Among Iraq's responses was the shelling of Israel—itself not a member of the UN coalition—in the hope of provoking Israeli forces into action, and thereby detaching from the coalition states such as Syria, traditionally hostile to Israel. For the first time in its history Israel did not respond to provocation, and the allied forces remained intact (see Part VIII, Topic 10).

After a month of bombing had crushed Iraqi powers of resistance and morale, allied victory in the ground campaign took only a few days. Iraq and the allies signed a cease-fire agreement which restored Kuwait's sovereignty. Iraqi forces withdrew, leaving Kuwait devastated with many of its oil wells in flames. Iraq itself plunged into civil war, with the remaining forces of Saddam Hussein battling with Kurdish and Shiite rebels.

Among the terms of the cease-fire was a proviso that Iraq would dismantle and destroy its stockpile of chemical weapons, and UN inspectors were given the task of overseeing the process. Seven years later, in the winter of 1997–1998, tensions again flared when the Iraqis refused to open certain "Presidential Palace Compounds" to inspection.

THE ENERGY CRISIS AND THE NUCLEAR DILEMMA

Europe's industrial rebirth after World War II was heavily dependent on imported oil supplies. Unlike the United States, there are only scanty oil deposits on European territory. In 1960, the Organization of Petroleum Exporting Countries (OPEC) was founded by the world's main oil producers: Iran, Iraq, Kuwait, Libya, Saudi Arabia, and Venezuela. Membership subsequently extended to Qatar, Indonesia, United Arab Emirates, Algeria, Nigeria, Ecuador, and Gabon. As the industries of many countries came to rely on oil supplies, the power of OPEC increased dramatically.

In 1973, OPEC quadrupled world oil prices, and in the years between 1974 and 1980 the price of oil tripled again. In the 1980s, OPEC's ability to control the market began to decline, as its members failed to agree on production limits, and non-OPEC members started to produce oil and natural gas. Nevertheless, the industrial world had received a severe shock. The booming years of the 1960s gave way to a period of economic crisis, as energy costs began to absorb production profits.

Nuclear Energy

One solution to steeply rising energy costs was to introduce conservation measures. A more attractive, and less stringent, answer seemed to lie in the development of nuclear energy programs. The heat generated by the process of nuclear fission within a reactor can be used to produce electricity. The disposal of radioactive waste from the process presented problems; at first, it was stored in concrete vaults lined with stainless steel.

For many European countries, lacking their own natural energy supplies, the production of artificial energy seemed an ideal solution to the problem of outside suppliers and their demands. In France, government sponsorship encouraged the construction of a network of nuclear plants that was to provide more than 60 percent of the country's energy needs. By 1985, West Germany was producing a third of its energy by nuclear processes.

The potential dangers of this new energy source were the difficulty of storing increasing quantities of waste, and the possibility of a major accident at a nuclear energy plant. The cost of such a disaster, it was clear, would be immense in both human and financial terms. As early as 1957, the U.S. Congress passed the Price-Anderson Act, limiting insurance company liability for nuclear disasters to a small fraction of any projected claims. Yet the construction of nuclear plants continued throughout the industrialized world, as businesses sought to cut their dependence on imported energy, and governments saw an easy way to meet their needs.

The first serious nuclear failure occurred in 1979, at the Three Mile Island site, near Middletown, Pennsylvania. As a result of a failure of the reactor's cooling system, it began to emit "puffs" of radiation. Hasty action prevented the meltdown of the reactor's core and the explosion of a hydrogen bubble that had formed inside.

Far more disastrous was the accident at Chernobyl, near Kiev, in the Soviet Union. On April 26, 1986, one of the reactors there exploded, scattering radioactive debris over thousands of miles. One hundred thirty-five thousand people living in the region were evacuated, and food products throughout Europe

A meeting of OPEC.

Atomic power station at Calder Hall, England.

were contaminated—from Welsh lamb to Parmesan cheese. The burning reactor was eventually buried in concrete.

The Environmental Movement

The dangers of nuclear pollution would be added to the list of causes that environmental movements were waging throughout western Europe and the United States. The effects of nuclear fallout had, of course, been all too clear at the end of World War II, with the bombing of Hiroshima and Nagasaki. During the 1950s public preoccupation about human interference with nature continued to mount. In 1962, an American biologist, Rachel Carson (1907–1964), published *Silent Spring*, a dramatic account of the dangers of other forms of pollution, in particular pesticides.

Pollution from oil shale ash, Estonia.

By the late 1960s, environmental groups—the "Greens"—were drawing attention to crisis situations in many parts of Europe. In the heart of the continent, industrial plants in Austria, Switzerland, West Germany, France, and Holland were discharging ever-greater quantities of industrial waste into the river Rhine. The Mediterranean was so polluted in places that swimming in it was dangerous. In many cities exhaust fumes and traffic vibrations were damaging historic buildings and monuments; they included the Gothic cathedrals of northern Europe and the Parthenon in Athens. Industrial cities, both in Europe and in North America, were plagued with smog, a form of air pollution produced by factory and automobile fumes.

The Greens roused considerable public support. Britain set up a Department of the Environment in 1970, and France followed a year later. In 1972 a conference meeting in Stockholm established a United Nations Environment Program to deal with issues on an international basis.

The Environmentalists and Nuclear Energy

In West Germany, the Greens developed into a significant political force. Part of their success was due to the grave problem presented by the condition of the country's forests: between a third and a half of them were at risk of dying of pollution, much of it caused by acid rain (the result of air moisture combining with chemicals emitted by factories and automobiles). The Chernobyl disaster galvanized the Greens into action, and increased their public support. In the election of 1987 they won 8.3 percent of the votes, a notable improvement over their 5.6 percent in 1983.

The protests led by the Greens forced the West German government to cut back its nuclear energy program. The building of plants and waste disposal facilities was halted, often blocked by angry crowds of demonstrators. As a result, West Germany was forced to import increasing quantities from abroad. In 1988 it was the highest per capita importer of energy of any major industrialized country.

In Italy, also, public protests led to the suspension of a nuclear energy program. As a country particularly poor in natural energy resources, Italy had welcomed the chance to produce its own nuclear resources. Three plants were constructed, and plans were made to increase the number. With growing concern, however, fueled by the Chernobyl disaster, the Socialists and other parties sponsored a referendum that allowed the public to express its opinion: no more nuclear energy. Work at the existing plants was phased out, and new construction suspended. The Italians turned for energy supplies to natural gas, to be supplied by two pipelines, one from the Soviet Union and one from Algeria and Libya. Both projects were inaugurated in 1982, and work was stepped up in the late 1980s.

France was too dependent on nuclear energy to be able to eliminate it. Although Mitterand's Socialist government briefly suspended new plant construction in the early 1980s, by 1986 two-thirds of the country's electricity was generated by nuclear plants. Britain's coal supplies, together with natural gas from under the North Sea, made the provision of nuclear energy less vital. Nonetheless, by the 1990s nuclear power provided 13 percent of electricity there.

The European country most dependent on nuclear energy was Sweden, in spite of strenuous efforts on the part of environmentalists to block the building of new plants. In 1980, a referendum produced a compromise. The government would complete twelve plants, to be functioning by 1985, but all of them would be shut down by 2010. No Swedish political party opposed a nuclear phase-out, although it presented huge problems, and the future of the country's energy supplies remained in doubt.

Demonstration poster of the West German ecological party, the Greens.

In Search of Safe Nuclear Power

The dilemma presented by the dangers of nuclear energy dominated the planning of individual governments, but also crossed national boundaries. As Chernobyl showed, radioactive fallout could spread over thousands of miles. One solution was the construction of safer reactors. In the late 1980s, the Swedes started to pioneer the latest nuclear technology in their Process Inherent Ultimately Safe Reactor (PIUS).

The invention of a process to manufacture energy by nuclear fusion, rather than by fission, offered the hope of a more long-term solution. Fusion would require only small amounts of fuel, and none of the byproducts would be radioactive. Research into methods of generating energy by fusion led to the construction of particle accelerators in Western Europe and the United States. In 1988, the U.S. Energy Department announced the building of a "Supercollider" near Dallas, at a cost of $6 billion.

By the last decade of the 20th century efforts were stepped up to find an alternative solution to the problem that faced countries in all parts of the world: the advantages of nuclear energy—clean, capable of being produced in quantity—were overshadowed by its dangers.

TERRORISM AND THE POLITICS OF VIOLENCE

One of the problems that continued to plague the world in the latter part of the 20th century was terrorism. In a reaction to the general political stability of the major Western democracies, groups supporting a variety of causes used violence—or the threat of violence—for political ends.

Terrorism and Nationalism

In a number of Western European countries, nationalist groups or regions claimed the right to independence. The Basques, a people of unknown origins, inhabit the Pyrenees area of southwestern France and northern Spain; there are around 100,000 in France and 600,000 in Spain. In the Spanish Civil War, many Basques fought against Franco's Falangists, and the region was subsequently subdued. In 1952, a Basque nationalist movement was formed, which soon split into a militant and a moderate wing. The moderates stood for election; the militants turned to the gun. Both wings demanded local autonomy.

The 1970s and 1980s were marked by a string of assassinations, for which ETA (the militant Basque organization) claimed credit. The moderates, condemning the use of violence, became an increasing force in local politics. In the 1986 regional elections, Basque nationalist parties won two-thirds of the seats. The government made concessions, giving the Basques the right to raise their own taxes, and to replace the national police and the Civil Guard with an all-Basque police force. The moves reduced support for the terrorists, and cooperation between French and Spanish antiterrorist forces produced a higher level of arrests. Nonetheless, the assassinations continued sporadically, and discouraged foreign investors in the region, one of Spain's most industrialized areas.

Similar separatist violence scarred Corsica and the German-speaking region of northern Italy. Europe's most bitter terrorist campaign, however, was that waged by the Irish Republican Army (IRA) for control of Northern Ireland. In 1922, the island had been divided, with the lower 26 counties forming the independent, predominantly Catholic Republic of Ireland. The northern, mainly Protestant part rejected "Home Rule" (independence), and remained part of Britain, although with its own parliament, Stormont.

British soldiers with 1,000 pounds of homemade fertilizer explosives which were found in an abandoned van on the grounds of Belfast Castle, 1997.

Relations between Protestants and the Catholic minority in Northern Ireland were soured by centuries of mutual mistrust and hate. In 1969, peaceful street demonstrations led to open violence. By 1972, the British government felt obliged to disband Stormont and govern the region directly, seeking to satisfy the Protestant majority while protecting Catholic interests. Over the following decades the IRA battled against a string of illegal paramilitary Protestant groups in their campaign to drive out the British and assume control. Between 1969 and 1998, some 3000 people were killed in bombings and street fighting.

The British tried a series of ways to reduce the bloodletting and restore local government. After the death of ten IRA hunger strikers in prison in 1981, a new Northern Ireland Assembly was elected in 1982, but dissolved four years later. In 1983 a law was passed granting pardon (or at least lenience) to "informers" in either the Protestant organizations or the IRA; it led to a dramatic increase in the number of arrests. Yet at the end of the same year, IRA terrorists exploded a bomb outside London's Harrod's department store in the middle of Christmas shopping crowds, and in 1984 blew up a hotel in Brighton at which a Conservative party conference was taking place. Further IRA and paramilitary Protestant bombings continued throughout the late 1980s, some of them aimed at British troops outside Northern Ireland, on bases in England and West Germany. An IRA cease-fire, announced in 1994, lasted only a little more than a year. With the exclusion from all-party talks of the Sinn Fein movement, widely seen as the political wing of the IRA, there seemed little hope of progress, although the arrival in power of Tony Blair's "New Labour" party offered the possibility of a fresh start to negotiations. They resumed in the winter of 1997–1998, with both Sinn Fein and the leading Protestant groups represented at the conference table. Discussions were overshadowed by a series of acts of violence by extremists on both sides. Nonetheless, agreement was reached in April 1998, and its terms were approved by a large majority a month later in a referendum held in both Northern Ireland and the Republic of Ireland. As preparations began for the selection of a Cross-border Council later that year, the mood seemed cautiously optimistic.

International Terrorism

Terrorist activities elsewhere in Europe were inspired by ideological rather than nationalistic issues. In West Germany and Italy, extreme left-wing groups tried to destabilize the established social and economic order, as a prelude to political revolution (see Part VIII, Topic 11). Italy was further plagued by extreme right-wing violence. The worst single incident was the bomb explosion in Bologna's railway station in August 1980, at the height of the holiday season; more than 80 people were killed. Although those responsible were never caught, they seem to have been part of a far-right terrorist group.

As investigators throughout Europe and the Middle East began pooling information and working more closely in collaboration, a picture began to emerge of links between the various terrorist groups. The IRA, the Italian

Aftermath of a terrorist car bomb explosion in Paris.

Documents on History

Analyzing Terrorism

Two of the leading terrorist organizations operating in Europe after World War II were the Irish Republican Army (IRA) in Northern Ireland and the Red Army Fraction (RAF) in Germany, both of which accompanied their campaigns of violence with barrages of propaganda. The first two selections below consist of an objective description of the RAF and an example of their propaganda. Then follow a statement of intentions of the IRA and a counterstatement from an opposing Protestant extremist group. Perhaps the most notorious terrorist operating in the last 20 years has been Abu Nidal, whose career is described in a "portrait" first published in the *Washington Post.* Finally, Walter Laqueur, one of the world's leading authorities on terrorism, places the phenomenon in perspective.

TERRORISM IN GERMANY: THE RAF

The description of the RAF reprinted below comes from a longer article by Hans Josef Horchem on terrorism in Europe. It is followed by a section from one of the RAF's propaganda statements, which sets out the organization's notion of the "urban guerilla."

The RAF is the oldest and most dangerous German terrorist organization. In June 1980 the RAF took over the remaining cadre of the second German terrorist group, the "Movement of 2nd of June."

The RAF retained its structure and its system of organization after the unification with the "Movement of 2nd of June." Hierarchical order does not exist and decisions are made collectively. In an attack every member has to fight unto death.

The commando unit includes only 20 people. The attack against Hanns Martin Schleyer was made with only 20 members of the RAF, in spite of the fact that extensive logistic preparations were necessary.

The commando unit is living underground and depends on the "legal environment," which includes approximately 200 people. In the seventies the legal units were organized in "Anti-Fascist Groups" or in "Committees against Isolation-Torture." These names don't exist anymore. But the supporters of these groups compose a reservoir for illegal activities in the future.

Enough money is available. The "war booty" of the "Movement of 2nd of June" after the kidnaping of the Austrian industrialist Palmers in November 1977 is now in the hands of the RAF. Of the original 4 million Deutschmark the RAF has spent about 2 million Deutschmark.

The RAF propagates only one thing, that is armed conflict, and tries to win comrades-in-arms for this. "The armed campaign is the highest form of class struggle." The leading force and the avant-garde of the class-struggle is not the working class but the "revolutionary intelligence."

Already in 1971 the RAF said in its publication "Close the Loop-holes of the Revolutionary Theory—

Build up the Red Army": "It is not the organizations of the industrial working class, but the revolutionary sections of the student bodies that are today the bearers of the contemporary conscience." The industrial proletarians inside the developed capitalist countries have changed into an "aristocracy of workers." Therefore a true revolutionary cannot rely on them anymore.

The long-range strategy of the RAF was then and is today aimed at "U.S. imperialism" and its chief ally in Europe, the Federal Republic of Germany.

From Horchem, H. J. "European Terrorism: A German Perspective." *Terrorism: An International Journal,* Vol. 6, no.1. Copyright © 1982.

If we are correct in saying that American imperialism is a paper tiger, i.e., that it can ultimately be defeated, and if the Chinese Communists are correct in their thesis that victory over American imperialism has become possible because the struggle against it is now being waged in all four corners of the earth, with the result that the forces of imperialism are now fragmented, a fragmentation which makes them possible to defeat—if this is correct, then there is no reason to exclude or disqualify any particular country or any particular region from taking part in the anti-imperialist struggle because the forces of revolution are especially weak there and the forces of reaction especially strong.

As it is wrong to discourage the forces of revolution by underestimating their power, so it is wrong to suggest that they should seek confrontations in which these forces cannot but be squandered or annihilated. The contradictions between the sincere comrades in the organizations—let's forget about the prattlers—and the Red Army Fraction, is that we charge them with discouraging the forces of revolution, and they suspect us of squandering the forces of revolution. Certainly, this analysis does indicate the directions in which the fraction of those comrades working in the factories and at local level and the Red Army Fraction are overdoing things, if they are overdoing things. Dogmatism and adventurism have since time immemorial been characteristic deviations in periods of revolutionary weakness in all countries. Anarchists having since time immemorial been the sharpest critics of opportunism, anyone criticizing the opportunists exposes himself to the charge of anarchism. This is something of an old chestnut.

The concept of the "urban guerilla" originated in Latin America. Here, the urban guerilla can only be what he is there: the only revolutionary method available to what are on the whole weak revolutionary forces.

The urban guerilla starts by recognizing that there will be no Prussian order of march of the kind in which so many so-called revolutionaries would like to lead the people into battle. He starts by recognizing that by the time the moment for armed struggle arrives, it will already be too late to start preparing for it; that in a country whose potential for violence is as great and whose revolutionary traditions are as broken and feeble as the Federal Republic's, there will not—without revolutionary initiative—even be a revolutionary orientation when conditions for revolutionary struggle are better than they are at present—which will happen as an inevitable consequence of the development of late capitalism itself.

To this extent, the "urban guerilla" is the logical consequence of the negation of parliamentary democracy long since perpetrated by its very own representatives; the only and inevitable response to emergency laws and the rule of the hand grenade; the readiness to fight with those same means the system has chosen

continued next page

to use in trying to eliminate its opponents. The "urban guerilla" is based on a recognition of the facts instead of an apologia of the facts.

From Rote Armee Fraktion (RAF). *The Concept of the Urban Guerilla,* April, 1971.

THE IRA AND THEIR PROTESTANT EXTREMIST OPPONENTS

Both the IRA and the extremist Protestant groups in Northern Ireland who oppose them have used propaganda as well as violence in their campaign for public support. For all the extreme divergences in their positions, they perceive a common enemy in the British government, as the following two excerpts from their declarations make clear.

The effect of the IRA bombing campaign can be gauged in many different ways. Firstly, they have struck at the very root of enemy morale, confining and tying down large numbers of troops and armored vehicles in center city areas, thus relieving much of the pressure on the much-oppressed nationalist areas. In terms of direct financial loss (structural damage, goods, machinery), also in the crippling of industrial output and perhaps worst of all in the scaring-off of foreign capital investments, IRA bombs have hit Britain where she feels it most—in her pocket.

England always found unfortunate soldiers quite dispensable and to a certain extent replaceable, but she always counted in terms of cost to the Treasury. Any peace through the granting of freedom emanating to rebellious colonies from London came by means of calculation—the cost of occupation. Since 1969 a bill of warfare running to at least a conservative 500,000,000 pounds has not gone unnoticed back home in Britain where recent opinion polls showed that over 54% of the ordinary people wanted the troops withdrawn forthwith.

Already some 1,500 troops have left Northern Ireland never to return. In many cases death certificates have been issued as for fatal road accident victims to the unsuspecting next-of-kin of soldiers killed in action in a heartless attempt at cooking records and hiding telling manpower losses. Suddenly Northern Ireland has become England's Vietnam. In the knowledge that the will to overcome of a risen people can never be defeated by brute force or even overwhelming odds more enlightened politicians have seen the light and are themselves thinking along Tone's famous dictum: "Break the connection!"

Great Britain too, of course, has suffered losses other than bomb damage and loss of personnel. Her prestige and credibility in terms of world opinion and world finance have been severely shaken; her duplicity and selective sense of justice have been seriously exposed; her puerile hankering after "holding the last vestige of the Empire" has marked her as a recidivist nation, psychologically vulnerable, unstable, and mentally immature.

From *Freedom Struggle by the Provisional IRA.*

We are not good at propaganda and not good at extolling our Virtues or admitting our faults. We just stick to our points of view, bow our heads, and pray for it all to die down for another fifty years or so.

Gradually, however, we have come to realize that this time other factors have come into the age-old conflict of the Scots-Irish versus the Irish-Irish, or if you prefer it that way, the Protestants versus the Catholics in Ireland.

Traditionally the English politicians let us down—betrayal we call it. The Catholics try to overwhelm us so we are caught in between two lines of fire. Second-class Englishmen, half-caste Irishmen, this we can live with, and even defeat, but how can we be expected to beat the world revolutionary movement which supplies arms and training, not to mention most sophisticated advice on publicity, promotion, and expertise to the IRA?

The British army in Ulster has good soldiers who are being set up like dummy targets. The orders of the politicians are tying both hands behind their backs. The British public says: "Send the soldiers home." We say: "Send the politicians and the officers home and leave us the men and the weapons—or, why not send the soldiers home and leave us the weapons and we will send you the IRA wrapped up in little boxes and little tins like cans of baked beans."

The politicians who rule our lives from England do not understand us. They stop the army from defending us properly and stop us from defending ourselves. We do not like these flabby-faced men with pop eyes and fancy accents. . . .

From statement of Protestant Extremist Group, Dublin *Sunday World,* June 9, 1973.

ABU NIDAL: A PORTRAIT

One of the features of terrorism over the past 20 years has been the link between terrorist campaigns in various parts of the world. The Palestinian Abu Nidal, who has operated in Europe and throughout the Middle East, is a powerful and frightening symbol of international terrorism.

Abu Nidal left a calling card last fall in an interview with the German magazine *Der Spiegel.* "I can assure you of one thing," he said. "If we have the chance to inflict the slightest harm to Americans, we will not hesitate to do it. In the months and years to come, the Americans will think of us."

Americans may indeed be thinking of Abu Nidal following recent events. His real name is Sabri Khalil al-Banna, and he is one of those on whom Libyan leader Muammar Khadafy will most likely depend to carry out his campaign to attack American interests. It is clear that the Libyans are supporting Abu Nidal, and he is linked to last December's bloody attacks at the Rome and Vienna airports, only the most recent example of the mayhem that he has made his life's work.

Here is a snapshot of the man who describes himself as America's enemy: His politics are those of revenge and revolution on a grand scale. He seeks through terror a retributive and perfect justice that can never be achieved. He moves through a shadowy inter-connected world of international and Arab terrorist networks that have given him a mystique larger than life. And yet through all of this there is something very ordinary, small and marginal about him—something that seems to reinforce the fact that terror, no matter how brutal, is only a symptom of a failed cause and of the frustrations of a desperate man.

Perhaps even more frightening than the man himself is his relationship to those Arab regimes willing to tolerate his excesses. In a world where assassinations and violence have become legitimate tools of political struggle, Abu Nidal and those like him provide important services in the never-ending fight for influence and power. He is not simply a product of the Arab-Israeli conflict but of an intra-Arab struggle in which ideology is subordinated to regime survival and personal vendetta. How else can we explain that a man who in 1976 tried to kill the Syrian foreign minister could be operating out of Damascus seven years later?

Who is this elusive figure and what is the nature of the environment in which he operates? Is he simply the hired gun of state-sponsored terrorism, or is he the genuine revolutionary he claims to be?

One of the most frustrating aspects of dealing with Abu Nidal is that so little is known about him. Even in the murky subterranean world of international terrorism, he is a mystery.

continued next page

Despite two recent interviews, rumors still abound that he is dead or incapacitated and that his operations are run by committee. In a recent interview, Abu Nidal claimed that he had undergone plastic surgery. His interviewers usually ask him for some proof of his identity and wonder themselves whether he is who he claims to be. During one interview, Abu Nidal reportedly ripped open his shirt to show an inquisitive journalist scars from a much rumored heart operation.

His method of operation only enhances his reputation as a secretive shadowy force likely to appear anywhere at any time. The entire Abu Nidal organization is tightly compartmentalized and may not number more than a few hundred. The structure of the organization further obscures the links between operations and the master command. Capitalizing on the shadowy terrorist network in Europe and the Middle East, Abu Nidal further covers his tracks. Thus, in the Rome and Vienna operations, the terrorists could have been trained in Lebanon, acquired Libyan confiscated Tunisian passports, and obtained weapons in Europe. . . .

The lessons drawn from studying Abu Nidal and his world are not heartening ones. Indeed the consistency and effectiveness of his operations lead to the conclusion that his brand of terrorism is likely to remain a permanent feature of the Middle East's political landscape. Even more sobering is the recognition that Abu Nidal's terror has become very much a permanent fixture of shifting rivalries between Arab regimes. He remains effective because he is willing and able to provide services for a variety of patrons.

Nonetheless, in the end there are limits to what Abu Nidal can hope to achieve. He represents no constituency with any real power, he can never achieve anything positive for Palestinians. He can only destroy and intimidate until he himself is destroyed. More like him may follow, but their legacy will not be any more enduring.

From Miller, Aaron. "Portrait of Abu Nidal," *Washington Post,* March 30, 1986. Reprinted with permission of Aaron Miller.

REFLECTIONS ON TERRORISM

The following extracts come from an article by Walter Laqueur, chairman of the International Research Council of the Center for Strategic and International Studies in Washington, DC, one of the leading experts on terrorism in all its forms.

Fifty years hence, puzzled historians will try to make sense of the behavior of Western governments and media in the 1980s vis-a-vis terrorism. Presidents and other leaders have frequently referred to terrorism as one of the greatest dangers facing mankind. For days and weeks on end, television networks devoted most of their prime-time news to terrorist operations. Publicists referred to terrorism as the cancer of the modern world, growing inexorably until it poisoned and engulfed the society on which it fed, dragging it down to destruction.

Naturally, our future historian will expect that a danger of such magnitude must have figured very highly on the agenda of our period—equal, say, to the danger of war, starvation, overpopulation, deadly diseases, debts, and so on. He will assume that determined action was taken and major resources allocated to the fight against this threat. And he will be no little surprised to learn that, when the Swedish Prime Minister was killed in 1986, the Swedish government promised a reward for information leading to the apprehension of his killer that amounted to less than 10% of the annual income of an investment banker or a popular entertainer—not necessarily of the front rank; that the French government offered even less for its terrorists; that West Germany was willing to pay only up to $50,000 "for the most dangerous." The United States, always a great believer in the effectiveness of money, offered up to $500,000, again not an overwhelming sum considering the frequency of the speeches about terrorism and the intensity of the rhetoric. . . .

On the basis of these and other facts, our historian will lean towards revisionism. He may well reach the conclusion that there was no terrorism, only a case of mass delusion—or that hysteria was deliberately fanned by certain vested interests, such as producers of anti-terrorist equipment perhaps or the television networks which had established a symbiotic relationship with the terrorists, providing them with free (or almost free) entertainment for long periods.

These are, of course, the wrong conclusions. The impact of terrorism is measured not only in the number of victims. Terrorism is an attempt to destabilize democratic societies and to show that their governments are impotent. And if this can be achieved with a minimum effort, if so much publicity can be achieved on the basis of a few attacks, there is no need to make greater exertions. It is also true that there have been ominous new developments such as the emergence of narco-terrorism and of state-sponsored terrorism on a broader level than before. If terrorism was never a serious threat as far as America was concerned, let alone other major powers such as Russia, China or Japan, it is also true that in certain Latin American countries, but also in places like Turkey and Italy, it was for a while a real danger.

In short, there has been (and is) a terrorist menace in our time. But the historian of the future will still be right in pointing to the wide discrepancy between the strong speeches and the weak actions of those who felt threatened. And he must be forgiven if he should draw the conclusion that the "age of terrorism" perhaps never understood the exact nature of the threat. . . .

How to eradicate terrorism? Moralists believe that terrorism is the natural response to injustice, oppression, and persecution. Hence the seemingly obvious conclusion: Remove the underlying causes which cause terrorism and it will wither away! This sounds plausible enough, for happy and content people are unlikely to commit savage acts of violence. But while this may be true as an abstract general proposition, it seldom applies to the real world, which is never quite free of conflicts. The historical record shows that while, in the nineteenth century, terrorism frequently developed in response to repression, the correlation between grievance and terrorism in our day and age is far less obvious. The historical record shows that the more severe the repression, the less terrorism tends to occur. This is an uncomfortable, shocking fact, and has, therefore, encountered much resistance. But it is still true that terrorism in Spain only gathered speed after Franco died, that the terrorist upsurge in West Germany, France, and Turkey took place under social democratic or left-of-center governments, that the same is true with regard to Peru and Colombia, and that more such examples could easily be adduced.

Terrorism has never had a chance in an effective dictatorship, but hardly a major democratic country has escaped it. There is a limit to the perfection of political institutions, and however just and humane the social order, there will always be a few people deeply convinced that it ought to be radically changed and that it can be changed only through violent action. . . .

From Laqueur, Walter. "Reflections on Terrorism," *Foreign Affairs,* October 1986.

Red Brigade, and the West German Red Army Fraction all used similar weapons, often Soviet made. Libya provided training camps for would-be terrorists. There were even connections between groups in Europe and Japanese terrorists.

The threat of terrorism was intensified by the activities of groups from outside Europe. The Palestine Liberation Organization (PLO) and its various splinter factions were all active throughout the 1970s and 1980s; their operations provoked Israeli reprisals and counterattacks (see Part VIII, Topic 10). Iran, Iraq, and Syria were accused of harboring, if not encouraging, terrorists. A string of airplane hijackings and bombings culminated in the explosion over Lockerbie, Scotland, of a crowded Pan American flight bound for the United States a few days before Christmas, 1988. Suspicion fell on Iran or Syria as the base from which the bomb planting was organized; experts later discovered that the plastic explosive responsible was manufactured in Czechoslovakia, a claim subsequently confirmed by Václav Havel, Czechoslovakia's new president.

By the 1990s most governments were resigned to the fact that only a drastic and unacceptable curtailment of their citizens' liberties could lead to a serious curtailment of terrorist activities. They turned instead to increased security measures, international police collaboration, and diplomatic pressure to limit the damage. The last years of the 20th century continued to be marked by outbursts of terrorist violence.

A space photograph of Earth—humanity's "common house."

FROM THE ATLANTIC TO THE URALS: EUROPE'S "COMMON HOUSE"

As national governments and international bodies wrestled with the day-to-day problems of environmental pollution and political violence, more visionary leaders began to look to a distant time when the geographical unit of Europe would achieve some form of union. Mikhail Gorbachev wrote of a "common house," in which members of the family might live at peace, all in their own ways.

Gorbachev's image implied a continuing political and social diversity, but economic developments and the communications revolution increased the speed with which conformity spread. The revolutions of 1989, furthermore, were waged by people anxious to share in the benefits—as they perceived them—of capitalism. Hungarians, Czechs, and Poles of the last decade of the 20th century tried to build societies modeled on those of Western European nations.

Perhaps in reaction against the tendency toward broad supranational groupings, nationalism continued to create friction in both East and West. In Western Europe, the various separatist movements continued to agitate. Attempts to establish order in the new Eastern European democracies were challenged by ethnic divisions going back to the Hapsburg and Ottoman empires. The country most dramatically affected was the region of the former Yugoslavia known as Bosnia, where conflict raged between Serb, Croat, and Muslim groups. An international peace-keeping force, led by U.S. troops, tried to impose the settlement terms negotiated in the "Dayton Accord," a peace plan negotiated in 1995. The peace-keepers were originally scheduled to withdraw by the summer of 1998, but by the beginning of that year it became clear that they would need to remain in place to prevent further conflict.

Europe faced the 21st century with new hopes and old fears. The burying of old national rivalries, the end of the Cold War, the search for increased cooperation and eventual union—all these held out possibilities of peace, and an improvement in the material conditions of millions.

Yet many problems remained unsolved, and are probably incapable of solution. The consequences of a transition to a postindustrial society in the West and the breakup of the Soviet Empire in the East were unpredictable. The nuclear energy issue demonstrated all too clearly that technological progress was a two-edged sword. Most importantly, the ability of the European family members to live peaceably with one another in their respective parts of the "common house" was going to be sorely tested.

Questions for Further Study

1. How have events since 1989 changed the global political landscape? What are their consequences likely to be for the early 21st century?
2. On the basis of the experience of the past half-century, how successful is terrorism as a means of producing radical change?
3. What are the major environmental issues of our times, and how great is their threat? Is uncontrolled population growth more or less dangerous to the quality of human life?

Suggestions for Further Reading

Alexander, Y., and C. K. Ebinger, eds. *Nuclear Terrorism: Defining the Threat*. New York, 1986.
Kidder, R. M. *Reinventing the Future: Global Goals for the 21st Century*. Cambridge, MA, 1989.
Lovenduski, J. *Women and European Politics: Contemporary Feminism and Public Policy*. Amherst, MA, 1986.
Maier, C. S., ed. *In Search of Stability: Explorations in Historical Political Economy*. Cambridge, MA, 1987.
Schlesinger, J. R. *America at Century's End*. New York, 1989.
Spretnak, C., and F. Capra. *Green Politics*. Toronto, 1986.

Credits

Abbreviations: Ancient Art & Architecture Collection (Pinner, U.K.): AA&A. AP/Wide World Photos (NY): AP/WW. Archiv fur Kunst und Geschichte (London and Berlin): AKG. Art Resource (NY): AR. Bibliotheque Nationale (Paris): BN. Bildarchiv Preussischer Kulturbesitz (Berlin): BPK. Bridgeman Art Library (London & NY): BAL Corbis-Bettmann (NY): C-B. The Granger Collection (NY): GC. Hirmer Fotoarchiv (Munich): HF. Hulton Getty Collection/Tony Stone Images (Chicago): HGC. Mary Evans Picture Library (London): MEPL. Réunion des Musées Nationaux/Cliché © RMN (Paris): RMN.

<u>**Page**</u> <u>**Credit**</u>

Part Opener I, p. 1 Zev Radovan, Jerusalem
Part Opener II, p. 73 Scala/AR
Part Opener III, p. 225 Cameraphoto/AR
Part Opener IV, p. 387 By courtesy of the Trustees of the National Gallery, London
Part Opener V, p. 489 Scala/AR
Part Opener VI, p. 571 Tate Gallery, London/AR
Part Opener VII, p. 707 Museo del Prado, Madrid.
Part Opener VIII, p. 1003 Copyright © 1998 Artists Rights Society (ARS), New York/Demart Pro Arte, Paris. Photo copyright © 1998 The Museum of Modern Art, New York.
5 Culver Pictures
6 C. M. Dixon
7 From Brian M. Fagan, IN THE BEGINNING: AN INTRODUCTION TO ARCHAEOLOGY, 4/e. © 1981 Brian M. Fagan. Published by Little, Brown & Co. Reprinted by permission of Orion Publishing Group Ltd.
8 top From Brian M. Fagan, IN THE BEGINNING: AN INTRODUCTION TO ARCHAEOLOGY, 4/e. © 1981 Brian M. Fagan. Published by Little, Brown & Co. Reprinted by permission of Orion Publishing Group Ltd.
8 bottom Colorphoto Hans Hinz, Allschwil/Basel
9 Naturhistorisches Museum, Vienna/HF
10 AA&A
16 top SuperStock
16 bottom The University of Pennsylvania Museum, Philadelphia
17 top HF
17 center HF
17 bottom HF
19 Metropolitan Museum of Art, New York (Harris Brisbane Dick Fund, 1959/59.2), photo copyright © 1985 Metropolitan Museum of Art.
20 RMN
21 British Museum, London (reproduced by courtesy of the Trustees)
25 HF
26 Robert Harding Picture Library, London
28 Katherine Young, NYC/AP/Wide World Photos
29L C-B
29R GC
30 Werner Forman Archive/AR
31 Agyptishes Museum, Staatliche Museen/Bildarchiv Preussischer Kulturbesitz, Berlin
32 John P. Stevens/AA&A
36 HF
37 From Donald Benjamin Harden, THE PHOENICIANS. © Donald Harden 1962. Reprinted by permission of the publishers, Thames & Hudson.
38 H. Lewandowski/Musee du Louvre/RMN
39 AA&A
41 Lee C. Ellenberger for The American Schools of Oriental Research, Boston
42 Alinari/AR
45 Werner Forman Archive/AR
46 HF
47 C. M. Dixon
52 HF
53 The Oriental Institute, University of Chicago
54 British Museum (reproduced by courtesy of the Trustees)
56 Zev Radovan, Jerusalem
59 Chuzeville/Musee du Louvre/RMN
60 HF
61 Margarete Busing/Bildarchiv Preussischer Kulturbesitz, Berlin
65 Metropolitan Museum of Art (Fletcher Fund, 57.80.10)
65 Canali Photobank, Italy
66 Werner Forman Archive/AR
69L Neg. No. 319376, Photo Edward Bailey. Courtesy Dept. of Library Services, American Museum of Natural History
69R Neg. No. 319377, Photo Edward Bailey. Courtesy Dept. of Library Services, American Museum of Natural History
70 AA&A
76 British Museum, London (reproduced by courtesy of the Trustees)
77 Robert Harding Picture Library, London
78 top Leonard Von Matt
78 bottom HF
81 Paul Warhol/AR
83 HF
84 © Tony Gervis/F. R. P. S./Robert Harding Picture Library
85 top Colorphoto Hans Hinz, Allschwil/Basel
85 bottom Deutsches Archaeologisches Institut, Athens (Hege 1100)
86 Metropolitan Museum of Art, New York (Fletcher Fund, 1932), copyright © 1985 The Metropolitan Museum of Art
88 AA&A
90 British Museum (reproduced by courtesy of the Trustees)
91 Metropolitan Museum of Art (bequest of Joseph H. Durkee, gift of Darlus Ogden Mills and gift of C. Ruxton Love, by exchange, 1972/1972.11.10), copyright © 1993 by the Metropolitan Museum of Art
93 HF
96 top Alinari/AR
96 bottom HF
97 Alison Frantz/copyright © Agora Excavations 1998, American School of Classical Studies at Athens, all rights reserved
100 From Chester G. Starr, THE ANCIENT GREEKS. Copyright © 1971 by Oxford University Press, Inc. Used by permission.
101 HF
102L AA&A
102R Vatican Museum
105 HF
106 Giraudon/AR
107 E.T. Archive
108 Courtesy Professor Manolis Andronikos
111 Rhoda Sidney/PhotoEdit
112 Courtesy, Museum of Fine Arts, Boston (William Francis Warden Fund)
113 top Scala/AR
113 bottom British Museum/HF
114 Capitoline Museums, Rome/Barbara Malter
115 D. Lada/H. Armstrong Roberts
121 C. M. Dixon
122 Metropolitan Museum of Art (Catharine Lorillard Wolfe Collection, Wolfe Fund/ 31.45), photograph © 1995 The Metropolitan Museum of Art
125L Margot Granitsas/Photo Researchers, Inc.
125R Erich Lessing/AR
127 British Museum (reproduced by courtesy of the Trustees)
129 Staatliches Museen zu Berlin/Preussischer Kulturbesitz Antikensammlung/BPK
131 Staatliche Museen zu Berlin/Gian Berto Vanni/AR
132 C. M. Dixon
133 E.T. Archive
136 Scala/AR
137 HF
138 Ronald Sheridan/AA&A
140 Staatliche Museen zu Berlin/Preussischer Kulturbesitz Antikensammlung/BPK
141 E.T. Archive
142 Scala/AR
143 From Hermann Thiersch, Pharos Antike, Islam und Occident (Leipzig: B. G. Teubner, 1909), opp. title page/New York Public Library, Astor, Lenox & Tilden Foundations
147 Scala/AR
149 Scala/AR
150 © 1994 Richard T. Nowitz/Photo Researchers, Inc.
151 Scala/AR
153 British Museum (reproduced by courtesy of the Trustees)
154 German Archaeological Institute, Rome
156 © M. Thonig/H. Armstrong Roberts
157 Alinari/AR
158 Scala/AR
159 GC
160 Nimatallah/AR
161 Scala/AR
163 Scala/AR
166 C. M. Dixon
169 AA&A
170 E.T. Archive
171 Scala/AR
173 British Museum (reproduced by courtesy of the Trustees)
174L GC
174R BAL
178 Hirmer Fotorarchiv, Munich
178 Scala/AR
179 Marburg/AR
187 K. Harrison/The Image Works
188 top Miwako Ikeda/International Stock
188 bottom British Museum/Werner Forman Archive/AR
189 C. M. Dixon
193 Biblioteca apostolica vaticana/Pizzi/ INDEX, Florence
194 Scala/AR
195 Scala/AR
196 L. Snider/The Image Works
197 Scala/AR
198 SuperStock
199 Alinari/AR
202 R. Sheridan/AA&A
203 C. M. Dixon
204 C. M. Dixon
205 Scala/AR
207 Alinari/AR
208 Alinari/AR
209 top AA&A
209 bottom AA&A
212 Allinari/AR

217 top Scala/AR
217 bottom © Zev Radovan, Jerusalem
219 Courtesy Herzfeld Archives, Freer Gallery of Art
220 Domenico Ruzza/Envision
221 Scala/AR
222 AA&A
230 Michael Holford
232 GC
233L BN
233R Erich Lessing/AR
234 Board of Trinity College, Dublin
235 Master of the Vienna Gregorian reliefs/Kunsthistorisches Museum, Vienna
239L Alinari/AR
239R Staatsbibliothek, Bamberg
242 The British Library (reproduced by courtesy of the Trustees)
243 Biblioteca del Seminario Arcivescovile/ INDEX, Florence
245 His Grace the Archbishop of Canterbury and the Trustees of Lambeth Palace Library
248 Scala/AR
249 Canali Photobank
250 Alan Oddie/PhotoEdit, Long Beach, CA
252 AA&A
253 John Lamb/Tony Stone Images
254 Canali Photobank, Italy
255 Ara Guler, Istanbul
257 © 1991 Laura Zito/Photo Researchers, Inc.
261 Mehmet Biber/Photo Researchers, Inc.
262 Bildarchiv Preussischer Kulturbesitz, Berlin
264 The Hutchison Library
265 Institut Amatller d'Art Hispanic
266 C-B
267 Yoram Lehmann, Jerusalem
269 Musee du Louvre/RMN
271 Alinari/AR
276 BN
277 AKG
278 Giraudon/AR
279 From Jackson J. Spielvogel, WESTERN CIVILIZATION. Copyright West Publishing Company 1991. Reprinted by permission of Wadsworth Publishing Co.
286 BN
287 Trinity College Library, Cambridge
288 Oesterreichische Nationalbibliothek, Vienna
289 British Library/E.T. Archive
293L BN
293R E.T. Archive
294 Codex Falkensteinensis/Bayerisches Hauptstaatsarchiv, Munich
298 The British Library (reproduced by courtesy of the Trustees)
299 GC
300L Roger-Viollet
300R Roger-Viollet
302 Giraudon/AR
305 Kunsthistorisches Museum, Vienna
306 Burgerbibliothek, Bern
307 Scala/AR
310 Ullstein Bilderdienst
311 AKG/SuperStock
312 Musee Conde, Chantilly/Giraudon/AR
315 BN
317 The Master and Fellows of Corpus Christi College, Cambridge
318 Scala/AR
321 Alinari/AR
326 Bildarchiv Preussischer Kulturbesitz, Berlin
328 G. Dagli Orti, Paris
330 Scala/AR
331 E.T. Archive
333 Scala/AR
334 J. E. Bulloz Editions, Paris
337 Scala/AR
339 British Museum (reproduced by courtesy of the Trustees)
340 Windsor Castle, Royal Library, © 1992 H. M. Queen Elizabeth II
343 British Library/BAL
344 Bibliotheque Royale Albert 1er/INDEX, Florence
348 Scala/AR
349 Colorphoto Hans Hinz/Artothek
351 Hunting Aerofilms Ltd.
352 © Sonia Halliday & Laura Lushington, Weston Turville, England
353 Giraudon/AR
354 Giraudon
355 Scala/AR
356 Cameraphoto/AR
359 Ms. 13076-77, f. 12v, Bibliotheque Royale Albert 1er, Brussels
361 Walters Art Gallery, Baltimore
368 BN
369 Jean Froissart CHRONIQUES/BAL
370 Giraudon/AR
375 Musee Conde, Chantilly/Giraudon/AR
376 Museo Civico, Bologna/Scala/AR
377 top The British Library (reproduced by courtesy of the Trustees)
377 bottom Roger-Viollet
378 BN
379 British Library/BAL
391L BN
391R Archives Nationales, Paris/Giraudon/AR
392 Private Collection/Giraudon/AR
394L By Courtesy of the National Portrait Gallery, London
394R HGC
397 Kunsthistorisches Museum, Vienna
401 top © Christie's Images
401 bottom Museo di Firenze Com'era/Scala/AR
403 © Christie's Images
404 Scala/AR
406L Kunsthistorisches Museum, Vienna/Erich Lessing/AR
406R Gallerie degli Uffizi/Tosi/INDEX, Florence
408 Scala/AR
411 Summerfield Press, Ltd.
412 Scala/AR
413 Pinacoteca, Palazzo Communale, Borgo San Sepolcro/Tosi/INDEX, Florence
414 Summerfield Press, Ltd.
415 Scala/AR
416 Erich Lessing/AR
417 Erich Lessing/AR
424 Erich Lessing/AR
425 Canali Photobank, Italy
428 Rare Books and Manuscript Division, New York Public Library, Astor, Lenox and Tilden Foundations
429 Lutherhalle (History of the Reformation Museum), Wittenberg, Germany
430 Metropolitan Museum of Art (Fletcher Fund, 1919/19. 73. 120), all rights reserved
431 RMN
433 By courtesy of the Trustees of the National Gallery, London
434 top Museo del Prado, Madrid
434 bottom Courtesy Museum of Fine Arts, Boston (Centennial gift of Landon T. Clay)
439 Biblioteca apostolica vaticana/INDEX, Florence
440 Ara Guler, Istanbul
441 Giraudon/AR
442 © National Maritime Museum Picture Library
444 GC
447 Sovfoto/Eastfoto
449 BN/BAL
460 top L BN
460 bottom L Sebastiano del Piombo, *Portrait of a Man Called Christopher Columbus*, 1519. Metropolitan Museum of Art (J. P. Morgan gift, 00.18.2).
460R Edward E. Ayer Collection, Newberry Library, Chicago/SuperStock
461 top GC
461 bottom GC
463 AA&A
467 The Toledo Museum of Art, Toledo, Ohio (Purchased with funds from the Libbey Endowment, Gift of Edward Drummond Libbey)
470 MEPL
471 Alte Pinakothek/Giraudon/AR
472 BN/Snark/AR
473L AA&A
473R By Courtesy of the National Portrait Gallery, London
477 Musees royaux des Beaux-Arts de Belgique/ A. C. L.
478 National Gallery, London
479 Collection Furstlich Waldburg-Zeil'sches Gesamtarchiv Leutkirch/Artothek
480 Kunsthistorisches Museum, Vienna/Artothek
482 Collection The Right Honorable Earl Spencer, Althorp House
483 Olaus Magnus, Historia de Gentibus Septentrionalibus/AKG
486 BAL
492 © 1998 Museum of Fine Arts, Boston. All rights reserved. Bequest of Mrs. Horatio G. Curtis.
493 Giraudon/AR
494 AKG
495 Institut Amatller d'Art Hispanic, Barcelona
498 Scala/AR
499 Marburg/AR
502 MEPL
504 © G. Dagli Orti
506 Mauritshuis, The Hague/Erich Lessing/AR
507 C-B
509 BAL
512 By Courtesy of the National Portrait Gallery, London
514 Stock Montage, Inc.
515 Alinari/AR
516 MEPL
517 Mansell/Time Inc.
518 Mansell/Time Inc.
523 AKG
524L Musee du Louvre, Paris/Photo R. M. N.
524R SuperStock
526 The National Gallery, London
527 BAL
528 C-B
530 AKG
535 top Mansell/Time Inc.
535 bottom GC
537 Metropolitan Museum of Art, New York (Fletcher Fund, 27.59)
544 British Museum/BAL
545 Rijksmuseum, Amsterdam
546 © Elke Walford/Hamburger Kunsthalle, Hamburg
547 Giraudon/AR
550 British Library
552 Herzog Anton Ulrich Museum, Braunschweig
554 Rijksmuseum, Amsterdam
556 Rijksmuseum, Amsterdam
557 Victoria & Albert Museum, London/AR
561 Scala/AR
562 Scala/AR
563 Canali Photobank, Italy
564 Hervé Lewandowski/RMN
565 RMN
566 Staatliche Kunstsammlungen Kassel, Galerie Alte Meister, GK 249
567L Johann Sebastian Bach, "Klavierbuchlein fur Anna Magdalena Bach," 1725. Courtesy of Riemenschneider Bach Institute, Baldwin-Wallace College, Berea, OH.
567R AKG
568 Rare Books and Manuscript Division, New York Public Library, Astor, Lenox and Tilden Foundations
575 British Museum, London (reproduced by courtesy of the Trustees)
576 Scala/AR
577 National Library of Medicine, Bethesda, Maryland

578 Mauritshuis, The Hague
579 Hans Peterson, Copenhagen
580 By courtesy of the National Portrait Gallery, London
586 Museo Nacional del Prado. Photo Copyright, Patrimonio Nacional, Madrid
587 Scala/AR
588 Museo Nacional del Prado. Photo Copyright, Patrimonio Nacional, Madrid
589 C-B
591 Christie's Images
596 Musee du Louvre, Paris/Photo R. M. N./ Hervé Lewandowski
598 AR
599 Metropolitan Museum of Art (gift of the Wildenstein Foundation, 1951—51.34)
600 Peter Willi/BAL
601 Giraudon/AR
602 BN
606 MEPL
609 By Courtesy of the National Portrait Gallery, London
610 Museum of London
612 C-B
613 By Courtesy of the National Portrait Gallery, London
619 Courtesy of the Trustees of the British Museum
620 By Courtesy of the National Portrait Gallery, London
624 Artothek
625 Travel Photo International
627 AKG
629 AKG
630 Marburg/AR
633L AKG
633R GC
635L GC
635R Bildarchiv Preussischer Kulturbesitz
636 Bildarchiv Preussischer Kulturbesitz
637 top AKG
637 bottom Sovfoto/Eastfoto
645 top Tate Gallery, London/AR
645 bottom GC
646L Picture Library, National Portrait Gallery, London
646R Picture Library, National Portrait Gallery, London
649L Scala/AR
649R Copyright © Frick Collection, New York
650 A. F. Kersting. London
652 top Mozart Museum, Salzburg
652 bottom © 1993 Beth Bergman
658 top GC
658 bottom British Library/BAL
659 top © National Maritime Museum Picture Library, Greenwich, England
659 center GC
659 bottom GC
663 Museum Boymans van Beuningen, Rotterdam
664 Copyright Guildhall Library Corporation of London
667 MEPL
668 C-B
670 Victoria & Albert Museum, London/AR
671 GC
673 C-B
674 National Portrait Gallery, Smithsonian Institution
679 National Gallery of Ireland
680 Louvre, Paris/photo RMN - G. Blot/J. Schor
682 The National Gallery, London
683 Giraudon/AR
684 Giraudon/AR
686 Metropolitan Museum of Art (Harris Brisbane Dick Fund, 1932)
688L Giraudon/AR
688R SuperStock
693 Hervé Lewandowski/RMN
694 top GC
694 bottom C-B
695 Giraudon/AR
703 SuperStock
710 Giraudon/AR
712 Giraudon/AR
713 Oesterreische Nationalbibliothek, Vienna
714 Giraudon/AR
717 Novosti/Sovfoto/Eastfoto
722 GC
728 GC
730 GC
731 J. Freeman/Barnaby's Picture Library
732 Mansell/Time Inc.
733 Mansell/Time Inc.
734 Musee Carnavalet/photo J. E. Bulloz, Paris
740 J. E. Bulloz, Paris
741 GC
743 BN/photo J. E. Bulloz, Paris
748 Giraudon/AR
749 top C-B
749 bottom J. E. Bulloz, Paris
751 C-B
759 National Gallery of Art, Washington (Samuel H. Kress Collection)
761 Louvre/BAL
762 C-B
763 C-B
764 Museo del Prado, Madrid
766 Scala/AR
768 HGC
773 GC
774L Brown Brothers
774R GC
776 C-B
777 Museo del Prado, Madrid
779 © Hervé Lewandowski/RMN
780 HGC
787 HGC
788 BN
789 Andrew Haslam/National Trust Photographic Library
790 Mansell/Time Inc.
791 GC
793 Collection J. Kugel/Lauros/Giraudon
794 GC
805 G. Blot/C. Jean/RMN
806 AKG
808 top By permission of the Houghton Library, Harvard University
808 bottom Staatliche Museen zu Berlin
810 RMN
811 Giraudon/AR
812L GC
812R GC
814 RMN
819 MEPL
820 C-B
821 Photographie Bulloz
822L C-B
822R MEPL
823 GC
826 Harlingue-Viollet
831 MEPL
832 HGC
833 HGC
834 HGC
836 HGC
837 GC
840 GC
843 David King Collection, London
844 GC
845 Sovfoto
846 C-B
851 HGC
852 MEPL
853 Culver Pictures
854 HGC
862 bottom GC
862 top GC
866 Brown Brothers
869 Culver Pictures
871 Mansell/Time Inc.
873 Deutsches Museum, Munich
875 Fogg Art Museum, © President and Fellows, Harvard College, Harvard University Art Museums
876 top HGC
876 bottom GC
881 GC
883 Keystone Mast Collection/California Museum Photography/University of California, Riverside
884 GC
886 James Helme/Royal Photographic Society
888 MEPL
889 Culver Pictures
891 Culver Pictures
896 GC
898 Culver Pictures
899 Print Collection, Miriam and Ira D. Wallach Division of Art, Prints and Photographs, The New York Public Library, Astor, Lenox and Tilden Foundations.
902 © 1993 Beth Bergman, New York
903 top Bequest of Mrs. H. O. Havemeyer, 1929. Photo © 1985 The Metropolitan Museum of Art
903 bottom BAL
904 Presented to the Amon Carter Museum, 1990, from the Modern Art Museum of Fort Worth through grants and donations from the Amon G. Carter Foundation, the Sid W. Richardson Foundation, the Anne Burnett and Charles Tandy Foundation, Capital Cities/ABC Foundation, *Fort Worth Star-Telegram*, the R. D. and Joan Dale Hubbard Foundation, and the people of Fort Worth.
909 GC
910L GC
910R GC
911 HGC
913 MEPL
914 HGC
917 UPI/C-B
923 Wilhelm Gause/Historisches Museum der Stadt Wien/Erich Lessing/AR
925 C-B
926 Sovfoto
929 Culver Pictures
931 MEPL
932 GC
936 GC
937 UPI/C-B
938 Culver Pictures
941 Collection, Brandywine River Museum (acquisition made possible by Beverly and Ray Sacks)
943 top National Portrait Gallery, Smithsonian Institution/AR
943 bottom Brown Brothers
950 India Office Library
951 India Office Library
957 Bowring Collection/India Office Library
958 MEPL
959 SuperStock
961 HGC
963 C-B
964 GC
968 Culver Pictures
967 Sovfoto
969 HGC
971 C-B
973 Culver Pictures
974L INDEX/Pizzi
974R Culver Pictures
981 MEPL
982 HGC
984 C-B
985 GC
986 Thomas Gilcrease Institute of American History & Art, Tulsa, OK
987 ILN Picture Library
988 MEPL
991 Richard Wagner Museum, Triebschen-Luzern, Switzerland

992 GC
994 GC
996 bottom Copyright © 1992 Munch Museum, Oslo
996 top Cincinnati Art Museum (John J. Emery Endowment, 1928)
997 Museum of Modern Art, New York (acquired through the Lillie P. Bliss bequest). Copyright © 1998 The Museum of Modern Art, New York.
998 Copyright © 1998 Artists Rights Society (ARS), New York/ADAGP, Paris. Photo by David Heald/ © The Solomon R. Guggenheim Foundation, New York (PN 54.1412)
1000 Brown Brothers
1009 Robert Hunt Library
1010 Robert Hunt Library
1017 top MEPL
1017 bottom Bilderdienst Suddeutscher Verlag, Munich
1019 UPI/C-B
1021 AKG
1022 Topham Picture Source
1025 GC
1026 UPI/C-B
1031 UPI/C-B
1036 MEPL
1038 C-B
1040 top UPI/C-B
1040 bottom UPI/C-B
1042 Ullstein Bilderdienst
1043 Robert Hunt Library
1048 C-B
1052 top UPI/C-B
1052 bottom Bilderdienst Suddeutscher Verlag
1055 Barnaby's Picture Library
1057 Robert Hunt Library
1058 Harlingue/Viollet
1064 top R. Bettini/Grazia Neri
1064 bottom AP/WW
1066 UPI/C-B
1067 top Suddeutscher Verlag
1067 bottom UPI/C-B
1071 AP/WW
1073 Sovfoto
1077 AP/WW
1080 C-B
1081 AKG
1082 UPI/C-B
1084 C-B
1089 Lewis Hine Collection, Div. of Drawings & Archives, Avery Library, Columbia University
1090 top Frank Driggs/Archive Photos
1090 bottom Frank Driggs/Archive Photos
1091 Copyright © 1998 by the Estate of Pablo Picasso/Artists Rights Society (ARS), New York. Metropolitan Museum of Art, New York (Bequest of Gertrude Stein, 1946). Photo © 1996 The Metropolitan Museum of Art.
1092 GC
1093 AKG
1098 Copyright © 1998 by the Estate of Pablo Picasso/Artists Rights Society (ARS), New York. Photo courtesy of Musée National d'Art Moderne, Centre Georges Pompidou, Paris.
1099 Copyright © 1998 Artists Rights Society (ARS), New York/ADAGP, Paris/Estate of Marcel Duchamp. Photo by Alain Tarica.
1100L Courtesy of Nigel Nicolson
1100R Courtesy of Nigel Nicolson
1102 Copyright © 1998 Artists Rights Society (ARS), New York/Demart Pro Arte, Paris. Photo copyright © 1998 The Museum of Modern Art, New York.
1103 Copyright © 1998 by the Estate of Pablo Picasso/Artists Rights Society (ARS), New York. Photo copyright © 1995 ARS, NY/ SPADEM, Paris
1104 Ezra Stoller © ESTO. All rights reserved.
1105L Phoenix Films, Richard Sabol/Promotions
1105R Collection, Museum of Modern Art, New York (gift of the artist). Photo copyright © 1998 The Museum of Modern Art, New York.
1110 HGC
1111 AP/WW
1112 AP/WW
1113 UPI/C-B
1114 AKG
1115 Robert Capa/Magnum
1116 Museo Nacional Centro de Arte Reina Sofia/ARS, NY/SPADEM
1118 AP/WW
1125 AP/WW
1126 UPI/Bettmann
1136 top C-B
1136 bottom AKG
1138 GC
1139 RIA/Novosti/Sovfoto
1142 top C-B
1142 bottom Imperial War Museum/E.T. Archive, London
1147 top UPI/C-B
1147 bottom AKG
1150L UPI/C-B
1150R HGC
1152 AP/WW
1154 Robert Hunt Library
1155 AP/WW
1157 UPI/C-B
1161 AP/WW
1162 Topham Picturepoint
1163 AKG
1165 AKG
1170 Robert Hunt Library
1171 AP/WW
1175 © Walt Kelly
1176 UPI/C-B
1177 Suddeutsch
1180 AKG
1181 Robert Hunt Library
1182L Keystone/HGC
1182R Markel/Liaison
1183 Reuters/Stinger/Archive Photos
1190L Robert Hunt Library
1190R Robert Hunt Library
1191 UPI/C-B
1193 top L AP/WW
1193 top R Michael Peto/HGC
1193 center Archive Photos
1193 bottom L Keystone/HGC
1193 bottom R AP/WW
1194 top AP/WW
1194 bottom AP/WW
1196 Tim Gibson/Envision
1197 Robert Deyrail/Gamma-Liaison
1201 Suddeutscher Verlag
1202 Copyright © 1998 Pollock-Krasner Foundation/Artists Rights Society (ARS), New York. Museum of Modern Art, New York. Photo copyright © 1998 The Museum of Modern Art, New York.
1203 Copyright © 1998 The Andy Warhol Foundation for the Visual Arts/Artists Rights Society (ARS), New York. Photo copyright © AR
1204 Harry Shunk/ © Christo and Jeanne-Claude 1972
1205 Patrick Ingrad/Tony Stone Images
1206 Stockhausen. nr. 11 Refrain, © Universal Editions (London) Ltd., 1961. Copyright renewed. All rights reserved. Used by permission of European American Music Distributors Corporation, sole U.S. and Canadian Agent for Universal Editions London.
1207 top Robert Hunt Library
1207 bottom Gamma-Liaison
1212 Photo News/Gamma-Liaison
1214 AKG
1218 Suddeutscher Verlag
1219 Ulrich Baumgarten/Suddeutscher Verlag
1220 Reuters/Fatih Saribas/Archive Photos
1223 AP/WW
1224 Earl Young/Archive Photos
1229 Alain Morvan/Gamma-Liaison
1230 top Keystone/HGC
1230 bottom Bob Stern/The Image Works
1231 Meike Scholz/Suddeutscher Verlag
1232 Brian Little/Topham Picturepoint
1233 Sola-Maous-Gaillarde/Gamma-Liaison
1240 European Space Agency/Science Photo Library/Photo Researchers

Page numbers in italics refer to illustrations and maps.